HOLT **TEACHER'S EDITION**

American Anthem

Edward L. Ayers

Robert D. Schulzinger

Jesús F. de la Teja

Deborah Gray White

Senior Program Consultant

Sam Wineburg

HOLT, RINEHART AND WINSTON

A Harcourt Education Company

Orlando • **Austin** • New York • San Diego • London

Explanation of Correlation

The following document is a correlation of **Holt Social Studies: American Anthem** to the North Carolina Course of Study, Social Studies Standards, 2003. The first correlation reflects standard coverage by Student Edition chapter. The format for the second correlation follows the same basic format established by the Social Studies Standards, modified to accommodate the addition of page references. The correlation provides a cross-reference between the skills in the Social Studies Standards and representative page numbers where those skills are taught or assessed.

The references contained in this correlation reflect Holt, Rinehart and Winston's interpretation of the Social Science objectives outlined in the North Carolina state curriculum.

KEY TO REFERENCES	
SE	*Student's Edition*

ISBN-13: 9-78-0-03-096309-4
ISBN-10: 0-03-096309-5
23 048 09 08

Chapter correlation of
Holt Social Studies: American Anthem to the
North Carolina Course of Study, Grade 11

Chapter	North Carolina Course of Study, Grade 11 U.S. History
Chapter 1 The World Before 1600	
Chapter 2 European Colonies in America	**1.02** Analyze the political freedoms available to the following groups prior to 1820: women, wage earners, landless farmers, American Indians, African Americans, and other ethnic groups.
Chapter 3 Colonial Life	**1.03** Assess commercial and diplomatic relationships with Britain, France, and other nations.
Chapter 4 The Revolutionary Era	**1.01** Identify the major domestic issues and conflicts experienced by the nation during the Federalist Period.
Chapter 5 Creating a New Government	**1.01** Identify the major domestic issues and conflicts experienced by the nation during the Federalist Period| **12.02** Evaluate the impact of recent constitutional amendments, court rulings, and federal legislation on United States' citizens.

North Carolina
The Tar Heel State

Chapter 6 Forging the New Republic	**1.01** Identify the major domestic issues and conflicts experienced by the nation during the Federalist Period| **1.03** Assess commercial and diplomatic relationships with Britain, France, and other nations.
Chapter 7 From Nationalism to Sectionalism	**2.02** Describe how the growth of nationalism and sectionalism were reflected in art, literature, and language| **2.03** Distinguish between the economic and social issues that led to sectionalism and nationalism| **2.04** Assess political events, issues, and personalities that contributed to sectionalism and nationalism.
Chapter 8 A Push for Reform	**2.05** Identify the major reform movements and evaluate their effectiveness| **2.06** Evaluate the role of religion in the debate over slavery and other social movements and issues.
Chapter 9 Expansion Leads to Conflict	**2.01** Analyze the effects of territorial expansion and the admission of new states to the Union| **3.01** Trace the economic, social, and political events from the Mexican War to the outbreak of the Civil War.
Chapter 10 The Nation Splits Apart	**3.01** Trace the economic, social, and political events from the Mexican War to the outbreak of the Civil War| **3.02** Analyze and assess the causes of the Civil War.
Chapter 11 The Civil War	**3.03** Identify political and military turning points of the Civil War and assess their significance to the outcome of the conflict.
Chapter 12 Reconstruction	**3.04** Analyze the political, economic, and social impact of Reconstruction on the nation and identify the reasons why Reconstruction came to an end| **3.05** Evaluate the degree to which the Civil War and Reconstruction proved to be a test of the supremacy of the national government.

Chapter 13 The American West	**4.01** Compare and contrast the different groups of people who migrated to the West and describe the problems they experienced| **4.02** Evaluate the impact that settlement in the West had upon different groups of people and the environment| **4.04** Describe innovations in agricultural technology and business practices and assess their impact on the West.
Chapter 14 The Second Industrial Revolution	**5.02** Explain how business and industrial leaders accumulated wealth and wielded political and economic power| **5.03** Assess the impact of labor unions on industry and the lives of workers.
Chapter 15 Life at the Turn of the 20th Century	**4.03** Describe the causes and effects of the financial difficulties that plagued the American farmer and trace the rise and decline of Populism| **5.01** Evaluate the influence of immigration and rapid industrialization on urban life| **5.04** Describe the changing role of government in economic and political affairs| **7.03** Evaluate the effects of racial segregation on different regions and segments of the United States' society.
Chapter 16 The Progressives	**7.01** Explain the conditions that led to the rise of Progressivism| **7.02** Analyze how different groups of Americans made economic and political gains in the Progressive Period| **7.04** Examine the impact of technological changes on economic, social, and cultural life in the United States.
Chapter 17 Entering the World Stage	**6.01** Examine the factors that led to the United States taking an increasingly active role in world affairs| **6.02** Identify the areas of United States military, economic, and political involvement and influence| **6.03** Describe how the policies and actions of the United States government impacted the affairs of other countries.

Chapter 24 The United States in World War II	**10.02** Identify military, political, and diplomatic turning points of the war and determine their significance to the outcome and aftermath of the conflict| **10.03** Describe and analyze the effects of the war on American economic, social, political, and cultural life.
Chapter 25 The Cold War Begins	**10.04** Elaborate on changes in the direction of foreign policy related to the beginnings of the Cold War| **10.05** Assess the role of organizations established to maintain peace and examine their continuing effectiveness.
Chapter 26 Postwar America	**11.01** Describe the effects of the Cold War on economic, political, and social life in America| **11.05** Examine the impact of technological innovations that have impacted American life.
Chapter 27 The New Frontier and the Great Society	**11.01** Describe the effects of the Cold War on economic, political, and social life in America| **11.05** Examine the impact of technological innovations that have impacted American life.
Chapter 28 The Civil Rights Movement	**11.02** Trace major events of the Civil Rights Movement and evaluate its impact.
Chapter 29 The Vietnam War	**11.04** Identify the causes of United States' involvement in Vietnam and examine how this involvement affected society.
Chapter 30 A Time of Social Change	**11.01** Identify major social movements including, but not limited to, those involving women, young people, and the environment, and evaluate the impact of these movements on the United States' society.

Chapter 31 A Search for Order	**11.02** Examine the impact of technological innovations that have impacted American life| **11.06** Identify political events and the actions and reactions of the government officials and citizens, and assess the social and political consequences| **12.01** Summarize significant events in foreign policy since the Vietnam War| **12.02** Evaluate the impact of recent constitutional amendments, court rulings, and federal legislation on United States' citizens| **12.04** Identify and assess the impact of social, political, and cultural changes in the United States.
Chapter 32 A Conservative Era	**12.01** Summarize significant events in foreign policy since the Vietnam War| **12.02** Evaluate the impact of recent constitutional amendments, court rulings, and federal legislation on United States' citizens| **12.03** Identify and assess the impact of economic, technological, and environmental changes in the United States| **12.04** Identify and assess the impact of social, political, and cultural changes in the United States.
Chapter 33 Into the Twenty-First Century	**12.01** Summarize significant events in foreign policy since the Vietnam War| **12.02** Evaluate the impact of recent constitutional amendments, court rulings, and federal legislation on United States' citizens| **12.03** Identify and assess the impact of economic, technological, and environmental changes in the United States| **12.05** Assess the impact of growing racial and ethnic diversity in American society| **12.06** Assess the impact of twenty-first century terrorist activity on American society.

Detailed correlation of
Holt Social Studies: American Anthem to the

North Carolina Course of Study, Grade 11

Student Edition page number references also apply to the Teacher's Edition.

COMPETENCY GOAL 1: The New Nation (1789-1820) - The learner will identify, investigate, and assess the effectiveness of the institutions of the emerging republic.

1.01	Identify the major domestic issues and conflicts experienced by the nation during the Federalist Period.	SE	104-105, 106-108, 109-113, 114-120, 125-130, 132-137, 142-143, 144-149, 150-156, 157-163, 168-187, 200-201, 202-208, 209-214, 215-220, 221, 222-223, 224-227, 232
1.02	Analyze the political freedoms available to the following groups prior to 1820: women, wage earners, landless farmers, American Indians, African Americans, and other ethnic groups.	SE	47, 48, 49, 50, 51, 54, 55, 56, 65
1.03	Assess commercial and diplomatic relationships with Britain, France, and other nations.	SE	70-71, 73, 74-75, 76, 77-81, 85, 87-88, 91-93, 200-201, 209, 210, 211, 217-218, 224-225, 226-227

COMPETENCY GOAL 2: Expansion and Reform (1801-1850) - The learner will assess the competing forces of expansionism, nationalism, and sectionalism.

2.01	Analyze the effects of territorial expansion and the admission of new states to the Union.	SE	297, 300-301, 303-307, 308-311
2.02	Describe how the growth of nationalism and sectionalism were reflected in art, literature, and language.	SE	236-237, 238, 239-240, 249

2.03	Distinguish between the economic and social issues that led to sectionalism and nationalism.	SE	238, 239, 243, 248-250, 252-255, 257-259
2.04	Assess political events, issues, and personalities that contributed to sectionalism and nationalism.	SE	236-237, 240-243, 245, 246, 249-250
2.05	Identify the major reform movements and evaluate their effectiveness.	SE	264-265, 266-269, 275-277, 280-283
2.06	Evaluate the role of religion in the debate over slavery and other social movements and issues.	SE	267-268, 285-289

COMPETENCY Goal 3: Crisis, Civil War, and Reconstruction (1848-1877) - The learner will analyze the issues that led to the Civil War, the effects of the war, and the impact of Reconstruction on the nation.

3.01	Trace the economic, social, and political events from the Mexican War to the outbreak of the Civil War.	SE	310, 311, 320-321, 322-328, 329, 330-335, 336, 338-343, 344-349
3.02	Analyze and assess the causes of the Civil War.	SE	320-321, 322-328, 329, 330-335, 336, 338-343, 344-349
3.03	Identify political and military turning points of the Civil War and assess their significance to the outcome of the conflict.	SE	354-355, 357-362, 363, 364-370, 371, 372-378, 381-387, 388-389, 391-395
3.04	Analyze the political, economic, and social impact of Reconstruction on the nation and identify the reasons why Reconstruction came to an end.	SE	403-408, 409, 410-415, 416-422, 423-427
3.05	Evaluate the degree to which the Civil War and Reconstruction proved to be a test of the supremacy of the national government.	SE	404-408, 409, 410-413, 414-415, 416-418

COMPETENCY GOAL 4: The Great West and the Rise of the Debtor (1860s-1896) - The learner will evaluate the great westward movement and assess the impact of the agricultural revolution on the nation.

4.01	Compare and contrast the different groups of people who migrated to the West and describe the problems they experienced.	SE	438-439, 440-443, 445-446, 447-448, 449, 450-453
4.02	Evaluate the impact that settlement in the West had upon different groups of people and the environment.	SE	439, 440-441, 446, 448, 450-451, 453
4.03	Describe the causes and effects of the financial difficulties that plagued the American farmer and trace the rise and decline of Populism.	SE	502-506
4.04	Describe innovations in agricultural technology and business practices and assess their impact on the West.	SE	446, 448, 453

COMPETENCY GOAL 5: Becoming an Industrial Society (1877-1900) - The learner will describe innovations in technology and business practices and assess their impact on economic, political, and social life in America.

5.01	Evaluate the influence of immigration and rapid industrialization on urban life.	SE	488, 489, 490, 491, 492, 493, 494
5.02	Explain how business and industrial leaders accumulated wealth and wielded political and economic power.	SE	460-465, 466-471
5.03	Assess the impact of labor unions on industry and the lives of workers.	SE	473-476, 482-483
5.04	Describe the changing role of government in economic and political affairs.	SE	500-501, 502

North Carolina
The Tar Heel State

COMPETENCY GOAL 6: The emergence of the United States in World Affairs (1890-1914) - The learner will analyze causes and effects of the United States emergence as a world power.

6.01	Examine the factors that led to the United States taking an increasingly active role in world affairs	SE	550-551, 553-555, 556-557, 559-564, 566-569, 573-575
6.02	Identify the areas of United States military, economic, and political involvement and influence.	SE	556, 557, 559-564, 573-575, 578
6.03	Describe how the policies and actions of the United States government impacted the affairs of other countries.	SE	556, 557, 559, 560, 561-564, 565, 566-568

COMPETENCY GOAL 7: The Progressive Movement in the United States (1890-1914) - The learner will analyze the economic, political, and social reforms of the Progressive Period.

7.01	Explain the conditions that led to the rise of Progressivism.	SE	523-527
7.02	Analyze how different groups of Americans made economic and political gains in the Progressive Period.	SE	529, 530-534, 544, 545
7.03	Evaluate the effects of racial segregation on different regions and segments of the United States' society.	SE	507, 508, 509, 510
7.04	Examine the impact of technological changes on economic, social, and cultural life in the United States	SE	522, 523, 524, 525, 526, 527

COMPETENCY GOAL 8: The Great War and Its Aftermath (1914-1930) - The learner will analyze United States involvement in World War I and the war's influence on international affairs during the 1920's.

8.01	Examine the reasons why the United States remained neutral at the beginning of World War I but later became involved.	SE	591, 592, 593, 594, 595, 596
8.02	Identify political and military turning points of the war and determine their significance to the outcome of the conflict.	SE	580, 581, 584-587, 592-595, 614
8.03	Assess the political, economic, social, and cultural effects of the war on the United States and other nations.	SE	607, 608, 609, 610, 611, 622, 623, 624, 625, 626, 627

COMPETENCY GOAL 9: Prosperity and Depression (1919-1939) - The learner will appraise the economic, social, and political changes of the decades of "The Twenties" and "The Thirties."

9.01	Elaborate on the cycle of economic boom and bust in the 1920's and 1930's.	SE	629-633, 635-639, 673-677, 681-685, 701-703, 704-705, 709-716, 717-722, 724-727
9.02	Analyze the extent of prosperity for different segments of society during this period.	SE	631, 632, 633, 673-677, 678, 679, 680, 681-685, 701-702, 709, 711-713, 714, 717, 718, 719, 723, 726, 729
9.03	Analyze the significance of social, intellectual, and technological changes of lifestyles in the United States.	SE	647, 648, 649, 650, 651, 652, 653, 654, 655-659, 661-665, 668
9.04	Describe challenges to traditional practices in religion, race, and gender.	SE	647, 648, 649, 650, 651, 655, 656, 657, 659
9.05	Assess the impact of New Deal reforms in enlarging the role of the federal government in American life.	SE	702, 703, 704, 705, 710-713

COMPETENCY GOAL 10: World War II and the Beginning of the Cold War (1930s-1963) - The learner will analyze United States involvement in World War II and the war's influence on international affairs in following decades.

10.01	Elaborate on the causes of World War II and reasons for United States entry into the war.	SE	739, 740-745, 747-750, 751-757
10.02	Identify military, political, and diplomatic turning points of the war and determine their significance to the outcome and aftermath of the conflict.	SE	736-737, 739-745, 747-750, 752-757, 759-760, 766, 768-769, 770-777, 778-783, 785-792, 801, 802-807, 812
10.03	Describe and analyze the effects of the war on American economic, social, political, and cultural life.	SE	759, 760, 761, 762-763, 793, 794, 795, 797-799
10.04	Elaborate on changes in the direction of foreign policy related to the beginnings of the Cold War.	SE	817, 818, 819, 820, 821, 822
10.05	Assess the role of organizations established to maintain peace and examine their continuing effectiveness.	SE	815, 822, 827-828

COMPETENCY GOAL 11: Recovery, Prosperity, and Turmoil (1945-1980) - The learner will trace economic, political, and social developments and assess their significance for the lives of Americans during this time period.

11.01	Describe the effects of the Cold War on economic, political, and social life in America.	SE	849, 850, 851, 852, 853, 854, 855-860, 880-881, 882-884, 884-885849, 850, 851, 852, 853, 854, 855-860, 880-881, 882-884, 884-885
11.02	Trace major events of the Civil Rights Movement and evaluate its impact.	SE	906-907, 909-915, 916, 917-923, 926-930, 931, 933-937, 939-941
11.03	Identify major social movements including, but not limited to, those involving women, young people, and the environment, and evaluate the impact of these movements on the United States' society.	SE	984-985, 987-993, 995-1001, 1003-1007, 1008-1009
11.04	Identify the causes of United States' involvement in Vietnam and examine how this involvement affected society.	SE	949-955, 957-963, 966-967, 974-975
11.05	Examine the impact of technological innovations that have impacted American life.	SE	855, 856, 857, 858, 862-865, 866-867, 889-890, 1024
11.06	Identify political events and the actions and reactions of the government officials and citizens, and assess the social and political consequences.	SE	1016-1017, 1019-1025, 1027, 1028-1032, 1033, 1034-1038, 1040-1041

COMPETENCY GOAL 12: The United States since the Vietnam War (1973-present) - The learner will identify and analyze trends in domestic and foreign affairs of the United States during this time period.

12.01	Summarize significant events in foreign policy since the Vietnam War.	SE	1016-1017, 1020, 1021, 1022, 1023, 1036, 1037, 1038, 1053, 1054-1055, 1056-1058, 1060-1065, 1081-1083, 1089-1090
12.02	Evaluate the impact of recent constitutional amendments, court rulings, and federal legislation on United States' citizens.	SE	197, 1026, 1039, 1052, 1070-1071, 1084, 1087
12.03	Identify and assess the impact of economic, technological, and environmental changes in the United States.	SE	1047-1048, 1050-1051, 1066-1069, 1079-1080, 1088, 1101-1102, 1103-1104
12.04	Identify and assess the impact of social, political, and cultural changes in the United States.	SE	1026, 1027, 1029, 1031, 1034-1035, 1039, 1040-1041, 1069-1071
12.05	Assess the impact of growing racial and ethnic diversity in American society.	SE	1099, 1100, 1101, 1105, 1106-1107
12.06	Assess the impact of twenty-first century terrorist activity on American society.	SE	1091, 1092, 1093, 1094, 1095, 1096, 1097, 1098

HOLT

TEACHER'S EDITION

American **Anthem**

Edward L. Ayers

Robert D. Schulzinger

Jesús F. de la Teja

Deborah Gray White

Senior Program Consultant

Sam Wineburg

HOLT, RINEHART AND WINSTON

A Harcourt Education Company

Orlando • **Austin** • New York • San Diego • London

Authors

Edward L. Ayers

Edward L. Ayers is Dean of the College and Graduate School of Arts & Sciences at the University of Virginia. He was named National Professor of the Year in 2003 and his book *In the Presence of Mine Enemies: The Civil War in the Heart of America, 1859–1863* won the Bancroft Prize and the Beveridge Prize in 2004. *The Promise of the New South: Life After Reconstruction* was a finalist for the Pulitzer Prize and the National Book Award. Ayers is also the creator of the acclaimed Web project, "Valley of the Shadow: Two Communities in the American Civil War," a comprehensive examination of everyday life before and during the Civil War in two small communities on either side of the Mason-Dixon Line.

Jesús F. de la Teja

Jesús F. de la Teja is chair of the history department at Texas State University at San Marcos, Texas. Prof. de la Teja has a number of books either in progress or recently published on colonial history of Mexico and Spanish borderlands including *Texas: Crossroads of North America* and *San Antonio de Béxar: A Community on New Spain's Northern Frontier,* which was the 1996 winner of the Presidio La Bahia Award. A Fellow of the Texas State Historical Association, Prof. de la Teja has received Texas State's Excellence Award for teaching. He earned under-graduate and Master's degrees from Seton Hall and a Ph.D. from the University of Texas, Austin. Prof. de la Teja has received a MacArthur Foundation grant for scholarly work on Texas colonization and independence.

Printed in the United States of America

ISBN-13: 978-0-03-096309-4

ISBN 0-03-096309-5

2 3 4 5 6 7 8 048 09 08

Deborah Gray White

Deborah Gray White is Distinguished Professor of History at Rutgers University. She received her undergraduate degree from SUNY Binghamton, her Master's from Columbia University, and a Ph.D. from the University of Illinois at Chicago. A specialist in American history and the history of African Americans, she is the author of several books including: *Ar'n't I a Woman?: Female Slaves in the Antebellum South; Too Heavy A Load: Black Women in Defense of Themselves, 1894–1994;* and *Let My People Go: African Americans 1804–1860.* From 1997–1999 she was the co-director of the Rutgers Center for Historical Analysis, which sponsored the very successful "Black Atlantic: Race, Nation and Gender" project.

Robert Schulzinger

Robert Schulzinger is Director of the International Affairs Program and Professor of History at the University of Colorado, Boulder. Dr. Schulzinger, a member of the U.S. State Department's Historical Advisory Committee, received his undergraduate degree from Columbia University, and a Master's and Ph.D. from Yale. He has written extensively on post-World War II history; his books include *A Time for War: The United States & Vietnam, 1941–1975.*

Senior Program Consultant

Sam Wineburg

Sam Wineburg is Professor of Education at Stanford University, where he directs the only Ph.D. program in History Education in the nation. Educated at Brown and Berkeley, he has spent several years teaching history at the middle and high school level before completing a doctorate in Psychological Studies in Education at Stanford. His book *Historical Thinking and Other Unnatural Acts: Charting the Future of Teaching the Past* won the Frederic W. Ness Award from the Association of American Colleges and Universities. His work with the teacher community won the 2002 "Exemplary Research on Teaching and Teacher Education Award" from the American Educational Research Association. He was a member of the blue-ribbon commission of the National Research Council that wrote the widely circulated report, *How People Learn: Brain, Mind, Experience, and School.*

Consultants

Program Consultant

Kylene Beers, Ed.D
Senior Reading Researcher
School Development Program
Yale University
New Haven, Connecticut

Academic Consultants

John Ferguson
Senior Religion Consultant
Assistant Professor
Political Science/Criminal
 Justice
Howard Payne University
Brownwood, Texas

Gregory Massing
*Constitutional Law
 Consultant; author,
 Holt's Civics in Practice*
Adjunct Professor
Boston College Law School
Chestnut Hill, Massachusetts

Walter Schroeder
Geography Consultant
Assistant Professor Emeritus
Department of Geography
University of Missouri
Columbia, Missouri

North Carolina Program Advisors

Rebecca N. Finger
K-12 Social Studies Curriculum
 Specialist
Charlotte-Mecklenburg Schools,
 North Carolina

Susan Hirsch
Social Studies Chair
East Wake High School
Wendell, North Carolina

Melissa Hockaday
Grade 7 Team Leader
East Garner Middle School
Garner, North Carolina

Jerri Jeffries
Grade 8 Team Leader
Lufkin Road Middle School
Apex, North Carolina

Karen Kimrey
Grade 8 Team Leader
Social Studies Chair
Heritage Middle School
Wake Forest, North Carolina

Scott King-Owen
Instructional Specialist
New Hanover Public Schools
Wilmington, North Carolina

Channing Kirkpatrick
Social Studies Chair
Independence High School
Charlotte, North Carolina

Marion O'Quinn
Social Studies Chair
Cary High School
Cary, North Carolina

Mary Propes
Social Studies Chair
Leesville Road High School
Raleigh, North Carolina

Wyndy Rorie
Social Studies Chair
Providence High School
Charlotte, North Carolina

David W. Wiggs
Social Studies Chair
Myers Park High School
Charlotte, North Carolina

Program Advisors

Academic Reviewers

Raymond Hyser, Ph. D.
James Madison University
Harrisonburg, Virginia

Michael S. Mayer, Ph.D.
Department of History
University of Montana
Missoula, Montana

Silvana Siddali, Ph.D
Department of History
St. Louis University
St. Louis, Missouri

Rebecca Tannenbaum, Ph.D
Department of History
Yale University
New Haven, Connecticut

Senior Consulting Writer

Peter Lacey
Sunderland, Massachusetts

Educational Reviewers

Gina Capelli
Liberty High School
Brentwood, California

Brent Duggins
Glenwood High School
Chatham, Illinois

Conrad Graf
Wayne High School
Fort Wayne, Indiana

Traci S. Lipscomb
Rustburg High School
Rustburg, Virginia

Nancy A. Llombart
Lakeview High School
St. Clair Shores, Michigan

Dean Melson
Niagara Falls High School
Niagara Falls, New York

Kris Oliveira
Clovis West High School
Fresno, California

Robert M. Rodrigues
Chartiers Valley High School
Bridgeville, Pennsylvania

Avon Ruffin
Winston-Salem Forsyth County
 Schools
Winston-Salem,
 North Carolina

Glenda Watanabe
Banning High School
Wilmington, California

Field Test Teachers

Melanie Adamek
Niagara Wheatfield
 Senior High School
Sandborn, New York

David Breen
Fels High School
Philadelphia, Pennsylvania

Jackie Burris
Asheville High School
Asheville, North Carolina

Patrick Eviston
Colonel White High School
Dayton, Ohio

Dena Grevis
Libbey High School
Toledo, Ohio

Ernesto Quiroz
Fillmore High School
Fillmore, California

Judith L. Spurlock
Meadowdale High School
Dayton, Ohio

James Toby
Everett High School
Lansing, Michigan

Robyn Webb
Elsik High School
Houston, Texas

Teacher's Edition
Contents

CRISS® Strategies

Log on to the **go.hrw.com** Web site and enter the keyword
NC Teacher for information about how your History program
addresses CRISS strategies.

go.hrw.com
CRISS Strategies
KEYWORD: NC TEACHER

Contents

THE GRANGER COLLECTION, NEW YORK

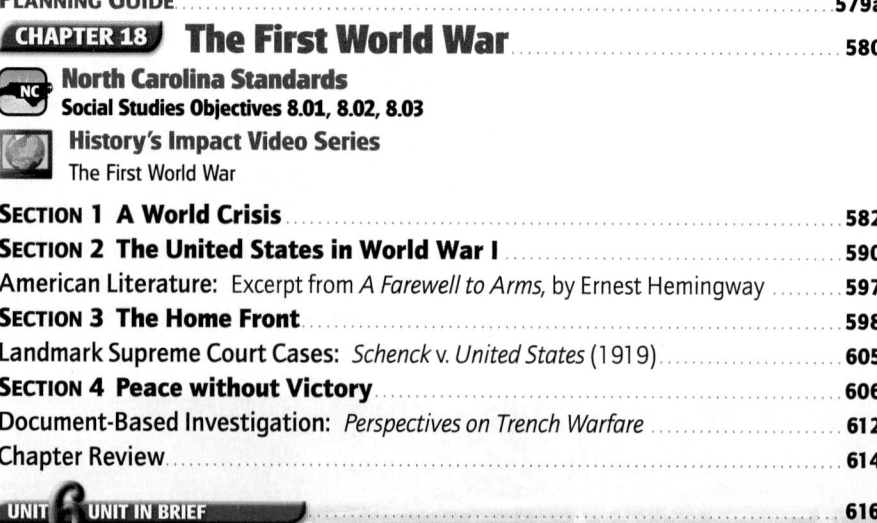

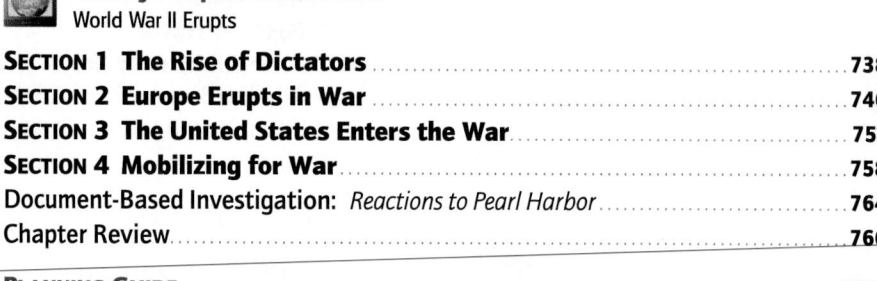

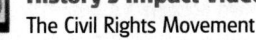

UNIT 10

1968–Present
Looking Toward the Future 1013

Reference Section R1

Features

Linking to Today

Link people and events from the past to the world you live in today.

LANDMARK SUPREME COURT CASES

Study the impact of Supreme Court decisions on American history.

TRACING HISTORY

Study historical themes through key dates and moments in American history.

HISTORY & Geography

Explore the relationships between history and geography.

✳ Interactive

American Liberty

Learn about important civil and religious liberties established by the Constitution.

Maps

Interpret maps to see where important events happened and analyze how geography has influenced history.

*Interactive Maps

Go online to extend your learning with interactive maps.

Charts and Graphs

Charts, Graphs, and Time Lines

Analyze information presented visually to learn more about history. To examine key facts and concepts, look for this special logo:

CHARTS

BATTLE OF THE SOMME

Duration of battle: July 1-Nov. 18, 1916

Total Allied casualties: about 630,000

British casualties on day 1: about 57,000

Total German casualties: about 650,000

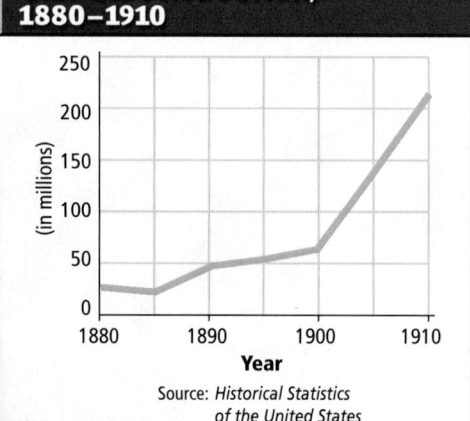

U.S. OIL PRODUCTION, 1880–1910

Source: *Historical Statistics of the United States*

Primary Sources

Relive history through eyewitness accounts, literature, and documents.

HOLT brings history to life with an **engaging narrative** and **instructional visuals**

THE INSIDE STORY

Why was it so hard to capture a tiny island? Iwo Jima lies deep in the Pacific Ocean. It is a small island of barely eight square miles of rocks and beaches. Yet during World War II over 100,000 soldiers fought for a month to capture this tiny scrap of land. It was some of the bloodiest fighting of the war.

On February 19, 1945, the U.S. Marines stormed the beaches of Iwo Jima. They made easy targets for the Japanese guns mounted high above on the extinct volcano of Mount Suribachi, which forms the southern tip of the island. The marines suffered terrible losses. They knew that they must capture Suribachi.

The fighting for Iwo Jima was exceptionally bloody. This was largely because the Japanese had dug miles of tunnels and caves through the island. From these hiding places they could pick off American troops without being exposed.

On the morning of February 23, a group of marines finally made it to the top of Mount Suribachi and raised the American flag as thousands of soldiers below watched and cheered. A few hours later a larger flag was raised. This second flag raising is shown in the famous photograph on this page.

Raising the Flag at Iwo Jima

The American flag now flew over Iwo Jima, but fierce fighting lasted for another month before the Americans finally captured the island. Two out of every three American soldiers were killed or wounded.

Of the six men in this photograph, only three lived through the battle. The other three are buried on Iwo Jima. ∎

◀ **U.S. Marines claim Mount Suribachi with a proud display of the Stars and Stripes.**

The Inside Story introduces each section with a "story behind the story" that examines key historical events and defines them in compelling human terms.

Dynamic Maps and **Quick Facts Charts** offer a way to engage students and help them review key content. **Online Interactive Maps** provide activities that develop map skills.

THE HOLOCAUST, 1939–1945

NETHERLANDS · EAST PRUSSIA · POLAND · Amsterdam · Bergen-Belsen · Berlin · Chelmno · Treblinka · BELGIUM · GERMANY · Warsaw · Sobibor · LUX. · Buchenwald · Auschwitz · Majdanek · Paris · Dachau · CZECHOSLOVAKIA · FRANCE · SWITZ. · Vienna · AUSTRIA · HUNGARY · ROMANIA · ITALY · YUGOSLAVIA

- ● Major concentration camp
- ● Concentration camp
- ▢ Extent of German control

0   150   300 Miles
0   150   300 Kilometers
Albers equal-area projection

GEOGRAPHY SKILLS | INTERPRETING MAPS

The Nazis expanded the number of camps as their conquests brought more Jews under their control.

1. **Place** Which country had the greatest number of camps?
2. **Location** Why do you think the Nazis built so many camps there?

See Skills Handbook, p. H20

the establishment of six new camps. These were to be extermination camps for the widespread murder of Jews. Unlike the concentration camps you read about earlier, nearly all inmates at the extermination camps were murdered upon their arrival. The method of killing was by exposure to poison gas in specially built gas chambers. Inmates might also be selected for cruel medical experiments, which often ended in death. Some were also forced to perform labor.

Some 3 million Jews died in Nazi extermination camps. Another 3 million died at Nazi hands by other means. Nazis murdered men, women, and children alike. Wrote Nazi leader Heinrich Himmler, "I did not feel justified in exterminating the men... while allowing the avengers, in the form of their children, to grow up."

In addition to the Jews, the Nazi death machine killed about 5 million others. Among these victims were prisoners of war, disabled people, and the Romany, an ethnic group also known as Gypsies.

READING CHECK **Identifying the Main Idea**
What was the purpose of the Final Solution?

JEWISH LOSSES IN THE HOLOCAUST

	c. 1933	c. 1950	Percent Decrease
Europe	9,500,000	3,500,000	63
Selected Countries			
Poland	3,000,000	45,000	98.5
Romania	980,000	28,000	97
Germany	565,000	37,000	93.5
Hungary	445,000	155,000	65
Czechoslovakia	357,000	17,000	95
Austria	250,000	18,000	93
Greece	100,000	7,000	93
Yugoslavia	70,000	3,500	95
Bulgaria	50,000	6,500	87

Source: United States Holocaust Memorial Museum

THE UNITED STATES IN WORLD WAR II **781**

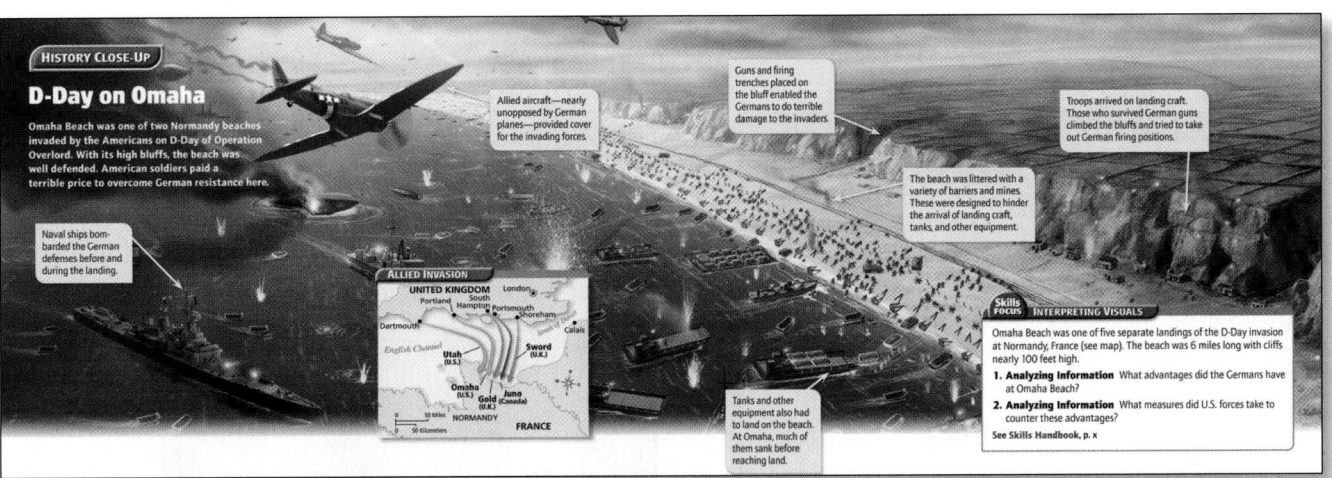

HISTORY CLOSE-UP

D-Day on Omaha

Omaha Beach was one of two Normandy beaches invaded by the Americans on D-Day of Operation Overlord. With its high bluffs, the beach was well defended. American soldiers paid a terrible price to overcome German resistance here.

Allied aircraft—nearly unopposed by German planes—provided cover for the invading forces.

Guns and firing trenches placed on the bluff enabled the Germans to do terrible damage to the invaders.

Troops arrived on landing craft. Those who survived German guns climbed the bluffs and tried to take out German firing positions.

Naval ships bombarded the German defenses before and during the landing.

The beach was littered with a variety of barriers and mines. These were designed to hinder the arrival of landing craft, tanks, and other equipment.

ALLIED INVASION

Tanks and other equipment also had to land on the beach. At Omaha, much of them sank before reaching land.

Skills Focus   INTERPRETING VISUALS

Omaha Beach was one of five separate landings of the D-Day invasion at Normandy, France (see map). The beach was 6 miles long with cliffs nearly 100 feet high.

1. **Analyzing Information** What advantages did the Germans have at Omaha Beach?

2. **Analyzing Information** What measures did U.S. forces take to counter these advantages?

See Skills Handbook, p. x

Dramatic visuals put students into the context of the time period, bringing to life the people, places, and concepts that they will learn.

Video Program
on DVD

HOLT
SOCIAL
STUDIES

History's Impact:
American History

Also Available
on VHS

History's Impact video program
Watch the video to understand the impact of World War II.

History's Impact Video Program helps students make connections between the impact of historical events in America and the world they live in today.

HOLT integrates reading strategies and fosters comprehensive skill development

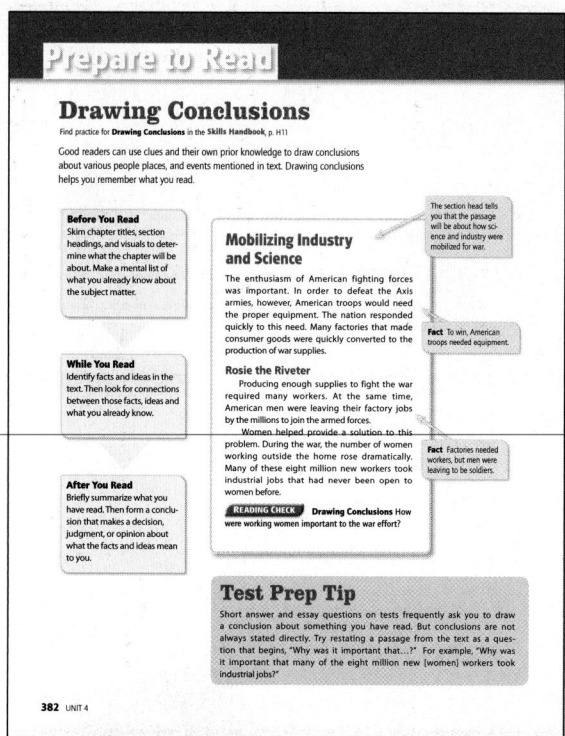

The **North Carolina Teacher Support System** offers standards practice for all objectives and includes teaching suggestions, student activities, a transparency for each competency goal, and all answer keys for related North Carolina resources.

Prepare to Read lessons focus on reading skills to help students learn how to access the information that they will learn.

History and Geography features incorporate visual images and special-purpose map activities that help students see the connections between geography and history.

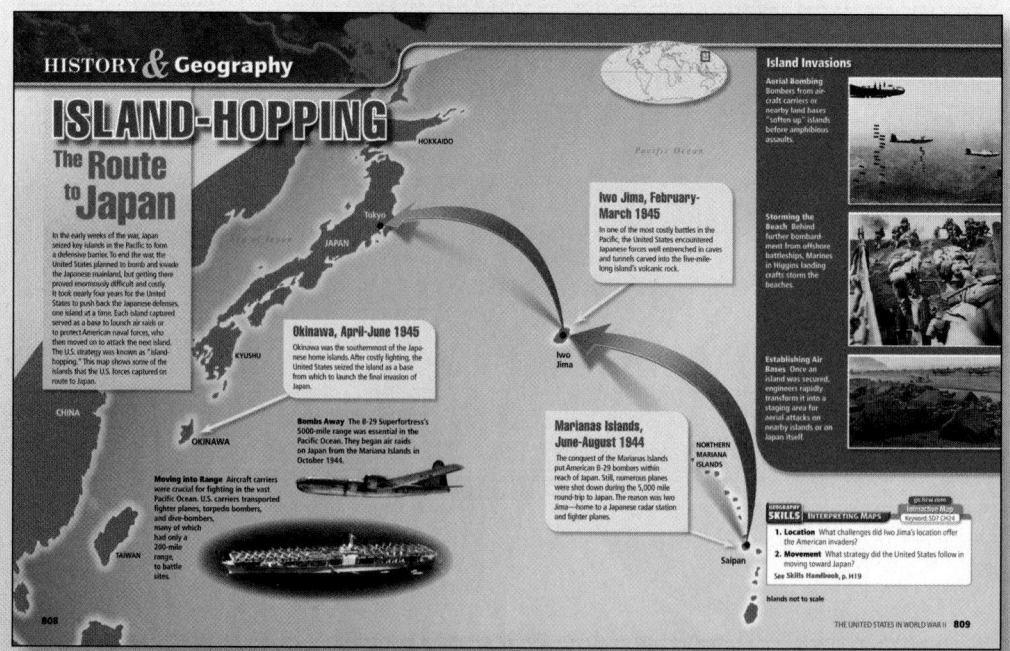

The **Interactive Reader and Study Guide** helps **all** students understand and master the content using:
- visual summary and critical thinking questions to organize chapter content
- section-by-section interactive note-taking to master main ideas
- challenge activities to extend concept learning

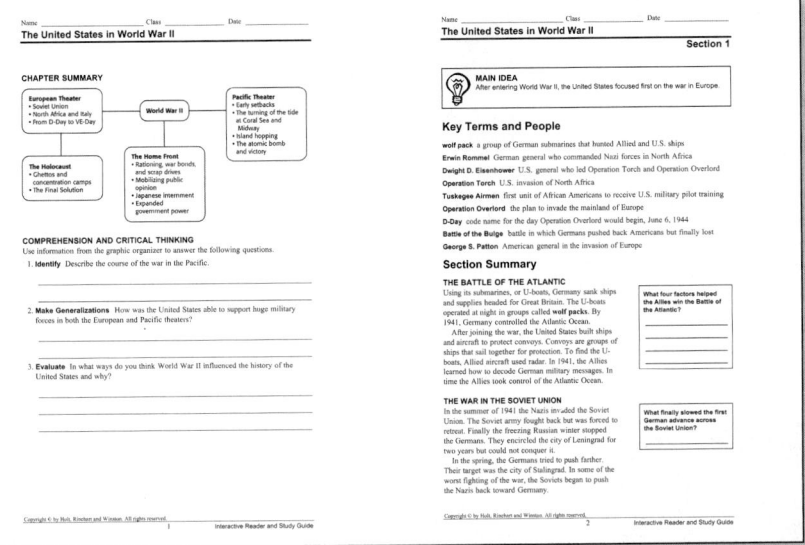

Political Cartoons Activities encourage students to analyze and evaluate cartoons for their historical context.

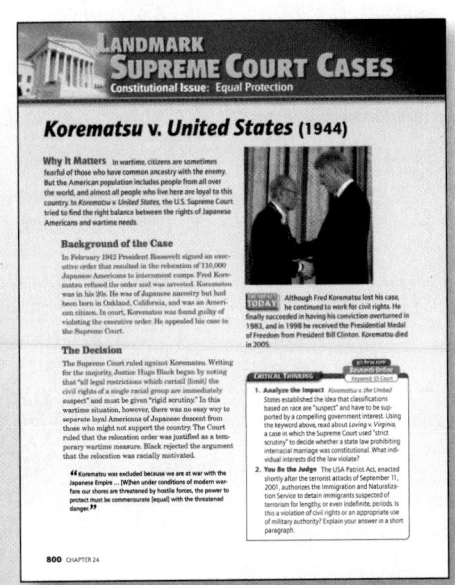

Landmark Supreme Court Case features present the background of the case, explain the impact of the decision on today, and foster students' critical thinking skills.

HOLT encourages the investigation of history and prepares students to succeed on tests through **document-based instruction**

Reading like a Historian

A note from Sam Wineburg

When I asked Kevin, a 16-year-old high school junior, what he needed most to do well in history class, he had little doubt: "A good memory."

"Anything else?"

"Nope. Just memorize facts and stuff, know 'em cold, and when you get the test, give it all back to the teacher."

"What about thinking—does thinking have anything to do with history?"

"Not really. It's all pretty simple. Random stuff happened a long time ago. People wrote it down. Others copied it and put it in a book. Poof—history."

I was saddened but not surprised by Kevin's answers. I've spent nearly twenty years studying how high school kids learn history. Over the years I've met many Kevins, students who knew history as nothing but a grim list of names and dates—one random fact after another.

In *American Anthem*, we have created a textbook that I hope will change the way students such as Kevin learn history. To explore the past and feel its excitement, you must learn to read like a historian.

Senior Program Consultant

Be a History Detective

Names, facts, and dates: this is what history has become for a lot of you. But the funny thing is that when you ask historians what they do, an entirely different picture emerges. They see themselves as detectives searching for clues to a puzzle that can never be entirely solved.

Asking questions Traced back to its earliest meaning, the word *history* (in Greek, *istor*) is about *inquiry*. To engage in inquiry means trying to figure things out, asking questions open to debate. Inquiry is about as far from mindless memorization as you can get.

Artist Gilbert Stuart's portrait of George Washington was painted in 1796, while Washington was president. It is a primary source.

xxvi READING LIKE A HISTORIAN

Reading Like a Historian, integrated throughout the text, teaches students to analyze written and visual documents.

CHAPTER

24 DOCUMENT-BASED INVESTIGATION

Perspectives on Life in Uniform

Historical Context The documents below provide different information on the hardships and sacrifices of American military personnel during World War II.

Task Examine the documents and answer the questions that follow. Then write an essay about the hardships U.S. soldiers faced. Use facts from the documents and from Chapter 24 to support the position you take in your thesis statement.

DOCUMENT 1

Cartoonist Bill Mauldin chronicled the sufferings of the everyday soldier in *Stars and Stripes*, a newspaper published by the U.S. Army. His gritty cartoons featured the characters Willie and Joe, who stood for all ordinary soldiers. Mauldin served during the entire war and was wounded in battle in Sicily.

"Joe, yestiddy ya saved my life an' I swore I'd pay ya back. Here's my last pair of dry socks."

DOCUMENT 2

Army nurses saw much of the worst suffering of the war up close. June Wandrey served as a combat nurse during some of the bloodiest battles in North Africa and western Europe. She helped save many lives and was awarded eight battle stars for her service under fire. She wrote this letter to her family in Wautoma, Wisconsin, in January 1944.

"We now have a mix of wounded, medical patients, and battle-fatigued soldiers ... The wounded were happy to be missing only one arm or leg ... I have a terrible ear ache but as usual I have to work. The patients need me."

DOCUMENT 3

For many Americans, the war was draining both physically and spiritually. Paul Curtis was from a small town in Tennessee. Fighting in the Italian campaign was unlike anything he had ever experienced. In this letter home from May 1944, he tried to explain his reactions to his brother. Curtis was killed in action shortly after writing this letter.

"Take a combination of fear, anger, hunger, thirst, exhaustion, disgust, loneliness, homesickness, and wrap that all up in one reaction and you might approach the feelings a fellow has. It makes you feel mighty small, helpless, and alone ... Without faith, I don't see how anyone could stand this."

DOCUMENT 4

Many African American soldiers faced an extra hardship during the war. In addition to the dangers and shortages experienced by all soldiers, African Americans also encountered racial discrimination. Corporal Rupert Trimmingham wrote the following letter to *Yank*, a weekly magazine published by the U.S. Army. In the letter, Trimmingham refers to "Old Man Jim Crow," a name for the discriminatory laws then in force across much of the United States.

"Myself and eight other Negro soldiers were on our way from Camp Claiborne, La., to the hospital here at Fort Huachuca, Arizona ... We could not purchase a cup of coffee at any of the lunchrooms around there ... As you know, Old Man Jim Crow rules. But that's not all; 11:30 A.M. about two dozen German prisoners of war, with two American guards, came to the station. They entered the lunchroom, sat at the tables, had their meals served, talked, smoked, in fact had quite a swell time. I stood on the outside looking on ... Are we not American soldiers, sworn to fight for and die if need be for this our country?"

DOCUMENT 5

Popular comedian Bob Hope never served in the armed forces, but he traveled throughout the war zones entertaining the troops for the United Service Organizations (USO). In 1944 he wrote *I Never Left Home*, a memoir of his experiences during the war. In the preface he told the public about the soldiers he encountered. President Lyndon Johnson awarded Hope the Presidential Medal of Freedom in 1969. Hope was still entertaining American troops far from home at the age of 90, when he took his act to the Persian Gulf on the eve of the Gulf War.

"I saw your sons and your husbands, your soldiers and your sweethearts. I saw how they worked, fought, and lived. I saw some of them die. I saw more courage, more good humor in the face of discomfort, more love in an era of hate, and more devotion to duty than could ever exist under tyranny.

I saw American minds, American skill, and American strength breaking the backbone of evil ... And I came back to find people exulting over the thousand plane-raids over Germany ... and saying how wonderful they are! Those people never watched the face of a pilot as he read a bulletin board and saw his buddy marked up missing ...

Dying is sometimes easier than living through it ..."

Skills Focus   READING LIKE A HISTORIAN

1. **a. Identify** Refer to Document 1. What does the character of Willie offer to Joe in exchange for saving his life?
   b. Interpret What does this cartoon say about the living conditions and supplies for soldiers?

2. **a. Identify** Refer to Document 2. What was Wandrey's job?
   b. Analyze Why were the wounded soldiers happy to be missing an arm or a leg?

3. **a. Identify** Refer to Document 3. What is the overall impression that Curtis gives of his experience?
   b. Elaborate How do you think Curtis's faith helped him during the war?

4. **a. Identify** Refer to Document 4. Why could the African American soldiers not buy coffee at the southern bases?

   b. Analyze How might seeing the German soldiers being treated better than African American soldiers have affected Trimmingham's views of the war?

5. **a. Identify** Refer to Document 5. What was Bob Hope's role in the war?
   b. Explain What did Hope mean when he wrote, "Dying is sometimes easier than living through it"?

6. **Document-Based Essay Question** Consider the question below and form a thesis statement. Using examples from Documents 1, 2, 3, 4, and 5, create an outline and write a short essay supporting your position.
   What kinds of hardships and suffering did American soldiers face during World War II?
   See Skills Handbook, p. <xx>.

810 CHAPTER 24

THE UNITED STATES IN WORLD WAR II **811**

Document-Based Investigation features have students examine multiple documents, reach conclusions based on the investigation, answer critical thinking questions, and write DBQ essays.

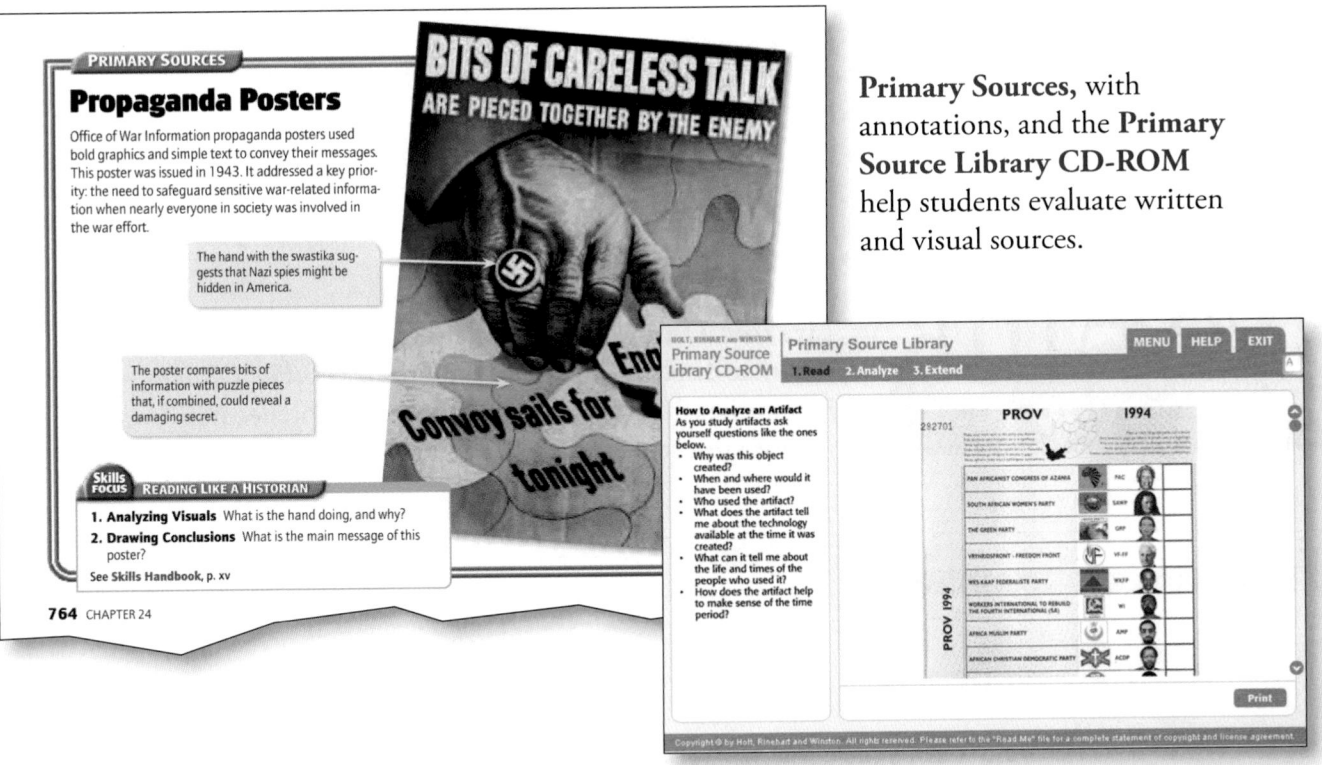

Primary Sources, with annotations, and the **Primary Source Library CD-ROM** help students evaluate written and visual sources.

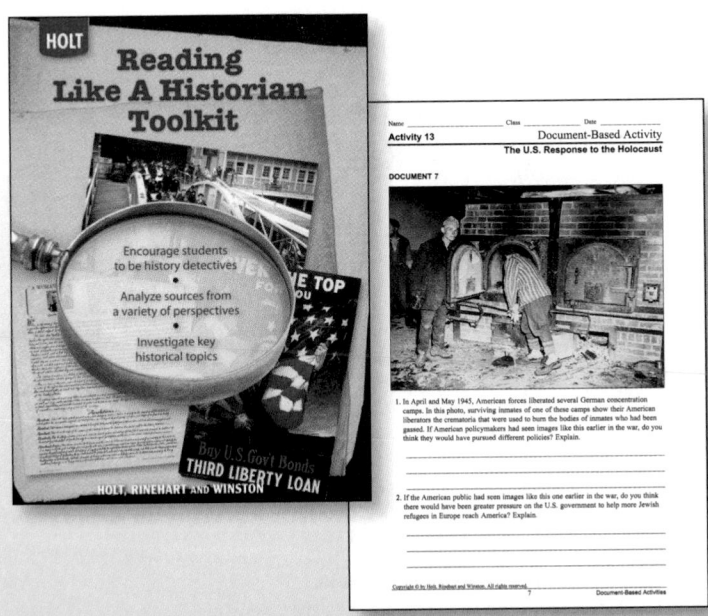

Reading Like a Historian Toolkit—developed with Dr. Sam Wineburg—encourages students to be historical detectives. The Toolkit includes teaching strategies, document-based activities from varied perspectives, transparencies, rubrics, and online presentation resources.

Document-Based Activities offer students opportunities to make intelligent, informed opinions based on analysis of primary sources.

HOLT ensures you can **differentiate instruction** for all students

Live Ink® Online Reading Help is an innovative online tool that displays the text of the *Premier Online Editions* in a format that is proven to improve comprehension and increase test scores.

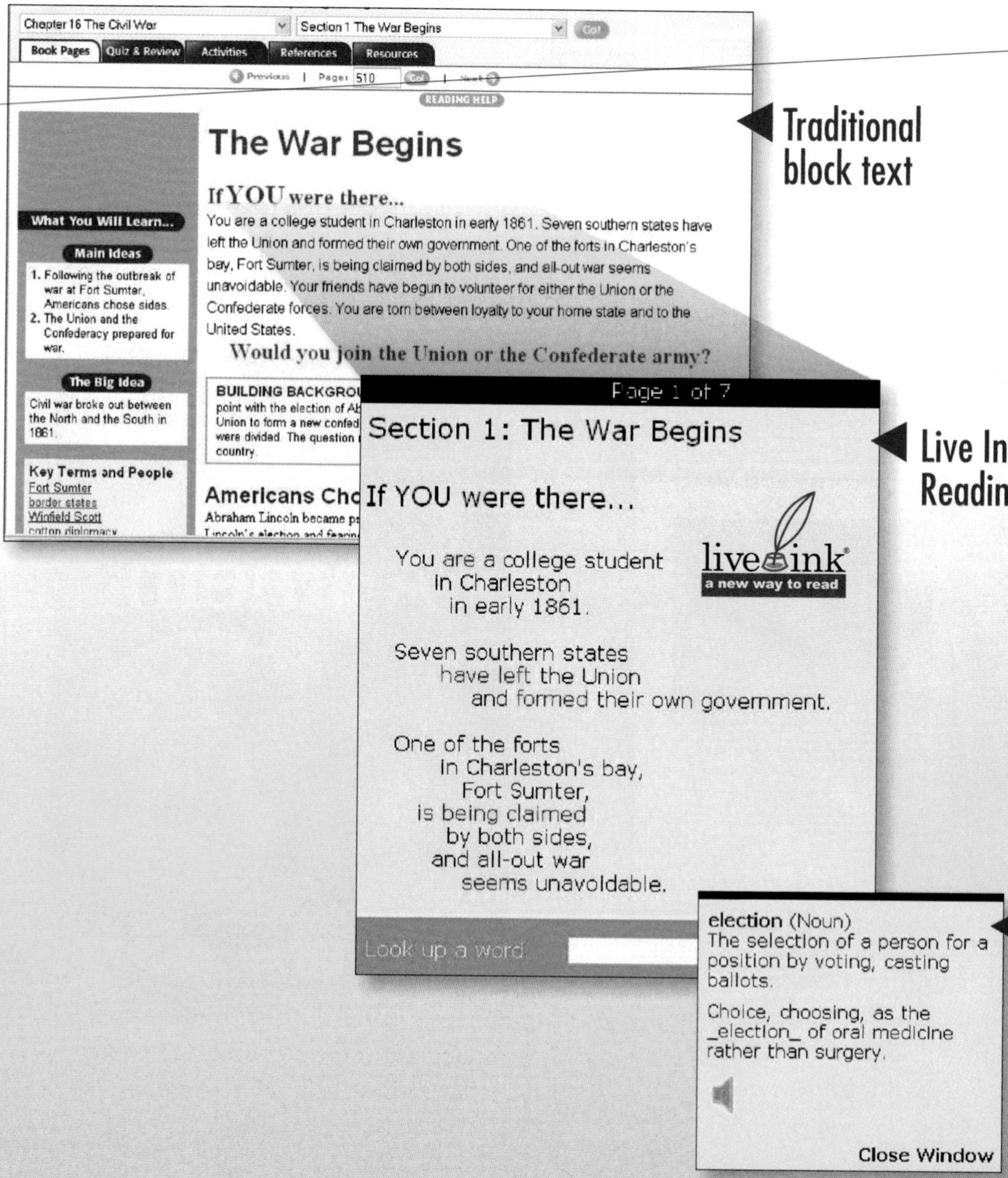

Chapter 16 The Civil War | Section 1 The War Begins | Go!

Book Pages | Quiz & Review | Activities | References | Resources

← Previous | Page: 510 | Go! | Next →

READING HELP

The War Begins

What You Will Learn...

Main Ideas

1. Following the outbreak of war at Fort Sumter, Americans chose sides.
2. The Union and the Confederacy prepared for war.

The Big Idea

Civil war broke out between the North and the South in 1861.

Key Terms and People

Fort Sumter
border states
Winfield Scott
cotton diplomacy

If **YOU** were there...

You are a college student in Charleston in early 1861. Seven southern states have left the Union and formed their own government. One of the forts in Charleston's bay, Fort Sumter, is being claimed by both sides, and all-out war seems unavoidable. Your friends have begun to volunteer for either the Union or the Confederate forces. You are torn between loyalty to your home state and to the United States.

Would you join the Union or the Confederate army?

BUILDING BACKGROU...
point with the election of A[braham]...
Union to form a new confed[eracy]...
were divided. The question [was]...
country.

Americans Cho[ose]...

Abraham Lincoln became p[resident]...
Lincoln's election and fear[ing]...

◄ Traditional block text

Page 1 of 7

Section 1: The War Begins

If YOU were there...

You are a college student
    In Charleston
        in early 1861.

Seven southern states
    have left the Union
        and formed their own government.

One of the forts
    In Charleston's bay,
        Fort Sumter,
    is being claimed
        by both sides,
    and all-out war
        seems unavoidable.

Look up a word

◄ Live Ink® Online Reading Help text

election (Noun)
The selection of a person for a position by voting, casting ballots.

Choice, choosing, as the _election_ of oral medicine rather than surgery.

Close Window

◄ Includes a built-in dictionary for vocabulary development

Differentiated Instruction Teacher Management System

HOLT
American Anthem

INCLUDES:
- Benchmarking Guides
- Section Lesson Plans
- Lesson Plans for Differentiated Instruction
- Interactive Reader and Study Guide Teacher's Guide and Answer Key
- Test Preparation Workbook Answer Key

HOLT, RINEHART AND WINSTON

Differentiated Instruction Teacher Management System provides Benchmarking Guides, Section Lesson Plans, Lesson Plans for Differentiated Instruction, Teacher's Guide, and Answer Keys to meet the needs of **all** students.

Differentiated Instruction Modified Worksheets and Tests on CD-ROM

HOLT
American Anthem

Differentiated Instruction Modified Worksheets and Tests CD-ROM provides all the key resources for the program, modified to meet the specifications for students' Individualized Education Plans (IEPs.)

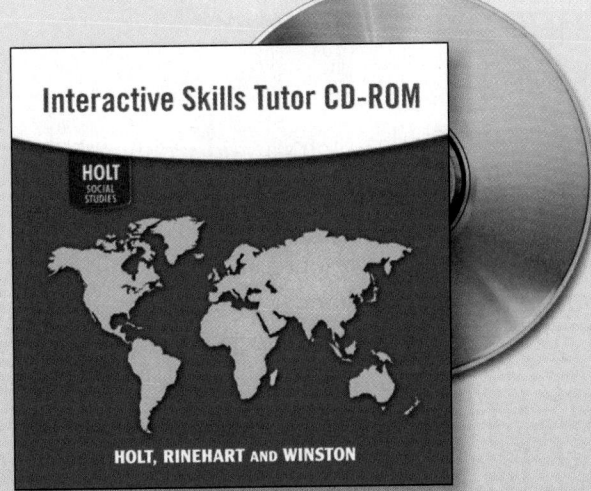

Interactive Skills Tutor CD-ROM

HOLT
SOCIAL STUDIES

HOLT, RINEHART AND WINSTON

Interactive Skills Tutor CD-ROM helps students learn the social studies skills presented in the program. Each skill is introduced, practiced through interactive activities, and then assessed for student mastery.

HOLT includes a range of **assessment options** to effectively monitor students' progress

Progress Assessment Support System (PASS) includes assessment for every chapter and unit to help you monitor students' progress.

PASS includes:
- Test-Taking Tips
- Diagnostic Test
- Section Quizzes
- Chapter Tests
- Unit Tests
- End-of-the-Year Test
- Answer Keys

North Carolina U.S. History EOC Test Preparation Workbook prepares students to succeed on the end-of-course exam.

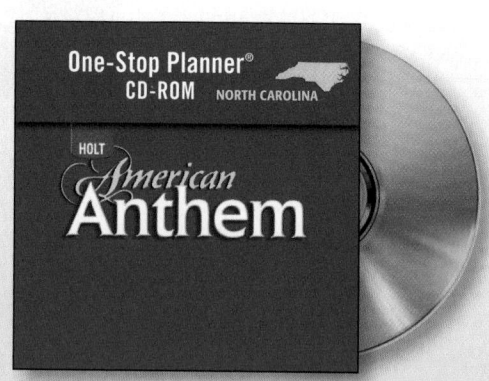

Holt's award-winning *North Carolina One-Stop Planner® CD-ROM* provides easy-to-use print and technology resources, correlated to North Carolina standards, that allow teachers to maximize their effectiveness and save time in planning, teaching, and assessing students' understanding of each lesson. Includes the powerful ExamView® Version 5 Assessment Suite.

Located on the *North Carolina One-Stop Planner*®, MindPoint® Quiz Show is an interactive multimedia game that assesses student understanding, makes learning fun, and tracks student performance. Also available on the *Quiz Game CD-ROM*.

Holt Online Assessment helps you assess students' mastery of the content.

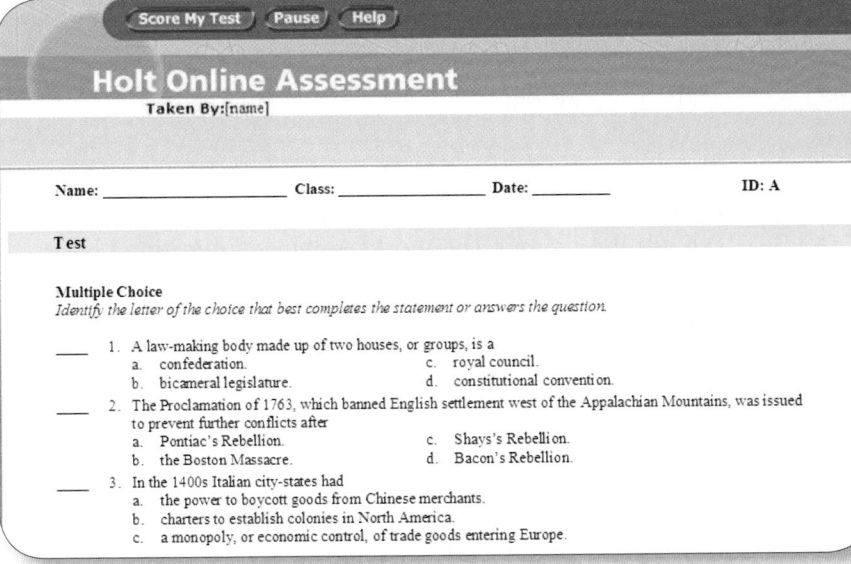

◄ Step 1
Create a test

Step 2 ►
Assign a test

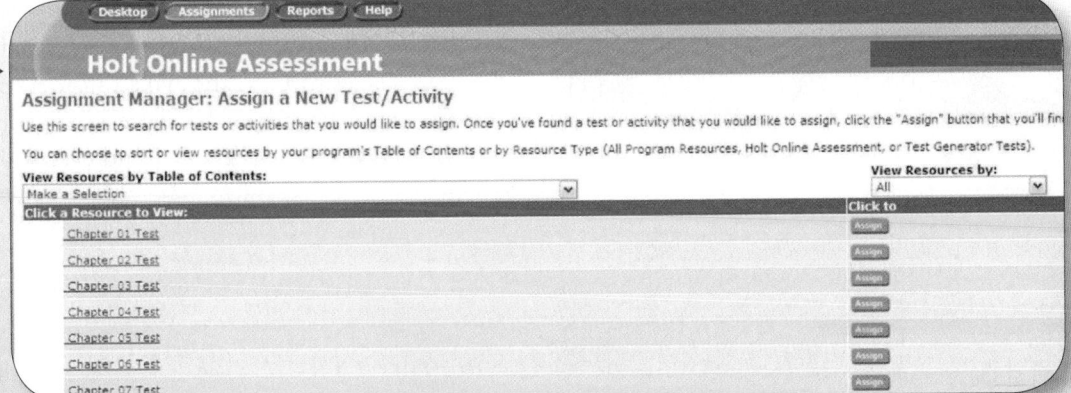

Step 3 ►
View and Print Reports

THE WORLD ALMANAC EDUCATION GROUP

Teaching Readers About Our World Since 1868

#1 New York Times Bestseller

THE WORLD ALMANAC AND BOOK OF FACTS

80 MILLION COPIES SOLD

The World Almanac and Book of Facts has been delivering information about the world since the presidency of Johnson—Andrew Johnson! First published in 1868, The World Almanac and Book of Facts is America's all-time, best-selling reference book, with more than 80 million copies sold.

Today, The World Almanac's experience and expertise at compiling, authenticating, and distributing information extends throughout The World Almanac Education Group. We specialize in helping illuminate American Government, American History, Economics, Civic Education, and the other social studies for students.

World Almanac **Key Events** in American History is a brief summary of important turning points in the history of the nation. It provides a capsule description of an event or movement along with brief accounts of its significance. Use this section to review the content in *American Anthem.*

The World Almanac and Book of Facts itself devotes more than 200 pages to U.S. and world history, providing quick answers about presidents, Congress, the Supreme Court, states, elections, world leaders, and events of the most recent year.

For information on all of these products,
please contact
The World Almanac Education Group at

1-800-321-1147

or visit
www.worldalmanacbooks.com

Social Studies Books, Kits, and Databases for Your Classroom and Library

The World Almanac Education Group comprises *World Almanac Books, Facts On File News Services, World Almanac Education Library Services,* and *Gareth Stevens Inc.* These companies all offer valuable resources for American history, and the other social studies. From engaging worksheet activities to supplemental classroom books that delve deeply into key curriculum areas to on-line database subscriptions, these materials can help you inspire your students to inquire about the world around them.

Social Studies Books

Gareth Stevens publishes acclaimed books series (with Teacher's Guides) in U.S. and World Geography, American and World History, and American Government. Popular series include: *World Almanac Library of American Government, A Primary Source History of the United States, Landmark Events in American History, Native Tribes of North America,* and the *World Almanac Library of the States.*

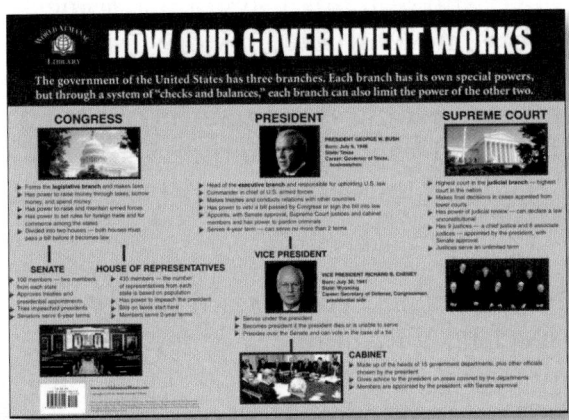

Teaching Kits

World Almanac Education Library Services offers skills kits that combine class sets of authoritative reference works with worksheets, videos, and posters to teach students valuable map and research skills. With a set of almanacs or atlases at hand, students quickly learn how to find and use information, while discovering the world around the corner and around the globe.

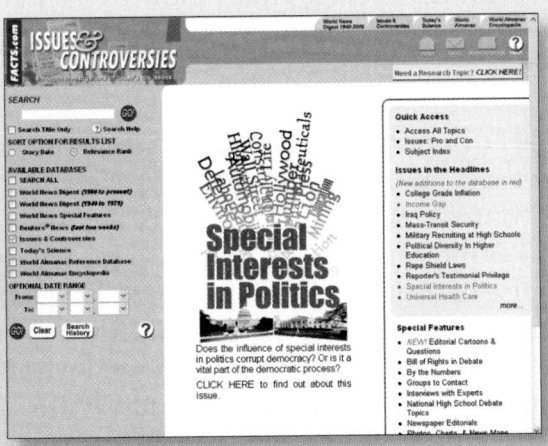

Online Databases

Facts On File News Services delivers award-winning online subscription databases at FACTS.com. These easy-to-use, accessible-from-anywhere databases teach kids about current events, topical issues, and science news. For a free trial visit: **www.facts.com/anthem** . Teachers also love the *Issues & Controversies Yearbooks,* which give students a quick understanding of more than 60 of the year's most talked-about topics.

The World Almanac & World Almanac Book of Records

Of course the World Almanac Education Group is founded on the reputation of *The World Almanac and Book of Facts,* the perennial number-one bestseller. Also look for the brand new *World Almanac Book of Records,* which includes fun and extensive coverage of American and World History.

Making Social Studies Accessible to English Learners

by Dr. Julie M.T. Chan

Dr. Julie M.T. Chan, Ed.D., is Director of Literacy Instruction in the Newport-Mesa Unified School District, located in Costa Mesa, California. She is a member of the California Reading and Literature Project, UCI/Orange County region, and serves on the state level CRLP Secondary Academic Language Tools development team. In addition, Dr. Chan teaches graduate courses on "The Sociocultural Contexts of Literacy and Learning" in the Masters of Reading program at California State University, Fullerton, and "Linguistics in Action in the Multicultural Classroom" at Concordia University in Irvine, California.

As increasing numbers of English-Language Learners (ELLs) enter the nation's secondary schools each year, it is incumbent upon all of us to help each student fully access the Social Studies curriculum.

Social Studies instruction relies heavily on language—oral language (listening/speaking) and written language (reading/writing). Because of their limited—but developing—proficiency in the English language, ELLs have a difficult time grasping the information presented orally by the teacher. In addition, they struggle when reading the printed text in Social Studies textbooks.

Chamot and O'Malley (1994) identified six areas where teachers can support ELLs: (1) Conceptual understanding, (2) Vocabulary, (3) Language functions and discourse, (4) Structures, (5) Academic language skills, and (6) Study skills and learning strategies. Here are some ways that teachers can make Social Studies accessible to English-Language Learners.

Conceptual Understanding While all students need to develop the concepts of time, chronology, distance, and differing ways of life, some ELLs may have never studied history or geography. Teachers could approach unfamiliar concepts and content by reading aloud trade books to build background knowledge and/or to provide a mental model at the beginning of a unit of study.

Vocabulary Students need to learn the content-specific, specialized terminology of Social Studies in order to discuss and report on the ideas studied. As students move up through the grades, the academic vocabulary of Social Studies becomes increasingly difficult because of the complexity of the concepts it represents. Thus, knowing which words to introduce and how and when to introduce them is critical.

Language Functions and Discourse In most school districts, students are expected to analyze, compare, contrast, and make judgments about Social Studies information. In contrast to the narrative discourse of texts designed for English language development, Social Studies materials feature expository patterns across various text structures. By using graphic organizers or mind maps that match the different text structures, teachers can make abstract ideas, concepts, and content visible and concrete for English Learners.

Differentiating Instruction

At Level

English-Language Learners

1. Have students give the names and dates of the early turning points of the war in the Pacific. Write student responses for the class to see.

2. Display a current map of the Pacific Ocean. Ask volunteers to indicate the location of each of the battles.

3. Organize the class into six groups, two groups for each battle. Assign one of the battles to each group. Have three groups develop a radio news report of its battle. Have the other three groups create an illustrated newspaper account of its battle. Each report or account should include the five "Ws" of the battle: Who, What, When, Where, and Why it was significant.

4. Have volunteers present their radio reports and newspaper accounts to the class. Then guide the class in a discussion of the three battles. **LS Interpersonal, Verbal/Linguistic**

Alternative Assessment Handbook, Rubric 14: Group Activity

Lessons designed to support instructions for English-Language Learners can be found throughout the Teacher's Edition.

Structures Oral and written language structures present special challenges to English-Language Learners. When teachers use research-based effective strategies to support oral and written language as well as published text structures, they can nudge their ELLs toward thinking, talking, reading, and writing like historians.

Academic Language Skills Students typically learn Social Studies through the receptive modes of listening and reading. In contrast, they "show what they know" through the productive modes of class discussions, oral presentations, and written products such as projects, reports, and expository/analytical essays. When the academic vocabulary of the content/concept to be studied is explicitly taught, ELLs can be more productive and therefore more successful at showing what they know.

Study Skills and Learning Strategies Chamot and O'Malley (1994) note that study skills, thinking skills, and social skills are also important components of the Social Studies curriculum. ELLs may not have, as yet, developed the learning strategies essential to these three skill areas. Thus teachers should help ELLs develop these skills so they can be better prepared to cope with the growing demands of new and abstract information found in grade-level Social Studies classrooms, textbooks, print materials, and primary source documents.

Teachers who are aware of the difficulties that ELLs encounter in their Social Studies classes will use this as an opportunity to explicitly teach those skills and strategies needed to be successful learners. Whether a teacher instructs regular Social Studies classes or a sheltered section, the result will be ELLs who have greater access to the Social Studies curriculum and who experience greater success as students moving toward the mainstream.

Billmeyer, Rachel (1996). *Teaching Reading in the Content Areas: If Not Me, Then Who?* Aurora, CO: McREL.

Buehl, Doug (2001). *Classroom Strategies for Interactive Learning*. Newark, DE: International Reading Association.

Chamot, Anna Uhl and J. Michael O'Malley (1994). *The CALLA Handbook: Implementing the Cognitive Academic Language Learning Approach*. Reading, MA: Addison-Wesley Publishing Company.

Roe, Betty, et al (1991). *Secondary School Reading Instruction: The Content Areas*. Boston, MA: Houghton Mifflin.

Tompkins, Gail E. (1997). *Literacy for the Twenty-First Century: A Balanced Approach*. Upper Saddle River, N.J.: Merrill.

ELL Instructional Support Services

- Use graphic organizers to teach abstract ideas.
- Teach specialized Social Studies vocabulary and usage.
- Promote development of study skills, thinking skills, and social skills.
- Read aloud content-related materials to help students build background knowledge.

Literacy and the Social Studies Teacher

by Carol Jago

Carol Jago teaches English at Santa Monica High School and directs the California Reading and Literature Project at UCLA. She is the author of *Cohesive Writing: Why Concept Is Not Enough* and *Papers, Papers, Papers: A Teacher's Survival Guide* (Heinemann 2005).

Q: Why should a Social Studies teacher have to teach reading and writing?

A: With a full curriculum of their own, many Social Studies teachers wonder why they should be expected to provide instruction in reading and writing. Isn't there enough to do just teaching history? There certainly is, but without strong literacy skills, students' ability to learn history is impaired. The idea is not that Social Studies teachers should become reading and writing teachers but rather that they should emphasize the classroom practices that are specific to learning history. For example, by helping students learn how to determine the gist of a textbook passage, Social Studies teachers reinforce what students need to know about distinguishing between important concepts and supporting details. By encouraging students to write like a historian, Social Studies teachers help students see how writing can be a powerful tool for thinking about controversial issues. By guiding students as they examine conflicting historical sources, Social Studies teachers help their students become critical readers with an eye for detail and point of view. The more students read and write, the more likely they are to retain what has been taught. Reading and writing help students learn history.

Q: What does research say about writing in Social Studies curriculum?

A: The National Commission on Writing in America's Schools and Colleges issued a report titled "The Neglected 'R'" calling for a writing revolution. NAEP research shows that only 50 percent of students meet "basic" levels of performance in writing and only one in five can be called "proficient." One student in five produces completely unsatisfactory prose. The 2003 report recommends that writing be incorporated into all state standards and that writing be required in every curriculum at all grade levels. "Very few things are more important to improving student achievement that restoring writing to its proper place in the classroom," said Commission Vice-Chair Arlene Ackerman, San Francisco superintendent of schools. "Writing is how we can teach students complex skills of synthesis, analysis, and problem solving." Given the controversial nature of so many topics in their curriculum, Social Studies teachers are uniquely positioned to help students develop these skills through persuasive writing.

Q: But how am I supposed to grade all those papers?

A: It isn't possible for teachers to work any harder. We need to work smarter. One method for assessing student writing effectively is to use rubrics. When the features of each numerical rubric score are laid out alongside a writing task, it is possible to assign a number to each student paper with confidence and, if not ease, efficiency. Social Studies teachers needn't feel that they must teach the mechanics of correctness. Language arts teachers recognize that this as

Sample Scoring Rubric: Persuasive Essays

4 The Writing

- Clearly addresses all parts of the writing task
- Authoritatively defends a position with precise and relevant evidence
- Demonstrates a clear understanding of purpose and audience
- Maintains a consistent point of view, focus, and organizational structure, including the effective use of transitions
- Includes a clearly presented central idea with relevant facts, details, and/or explanations
- Includes a variety of sentence types
- Contains few, if any, errors in the conventions of the English language

2 The Writing

- Addresses only parts of the writing task
- Defends a position with little, if any, evidence and may address the reader's concerns, biases, and expectations
- Demonstrates little understanding of purpose and audience
- Maintains an inconsistent point of view, focus, and organizational structure, which may include ineffective or awkward transitions that do not unify important ideas
- Suggests a central idea with relevant facts, details, and/or explanations
- Includes little variety of sentence types
- Contains several errors in the conventions of the English language

3 The Writing

- Addresses all parts of the writing task
- Generally defends a position with relevant evidence and addresses the reader's concerns, biases, and expectations
- Demonstrates a general understanding of purpose and audience
- Maintains a mostly consistent point of view, focus, and organizational structure, including the effective use of some transitions
- Includes a central idea with relevant facts, details, and/or explanations
- Includes a variety of sentence types
- Contains some errors in the conventions of the English language

1 The Writing

- Addresses only one part of the writing task
- Fails to defend a position with any evidence and fails to address the reader's concerns, biases, and expectations
- Demonstrates no understanding of purpose and audience
- Lacks a point of view, focus, organizational structure, and transitions that unify important ideas
- Lacks a central idea but may contain marginally relevant facts, details, and/or explanations
- Includes no sentence variety
- Contains serious errors in the conventions of the English language

Scoring rubrics help Social Studies teachers assess student writing efficiently and effectively.

their primary responsibility. By assigning writing, Social Studies teachers reinforce the lessons learned in English.

Q: With so much history to read, why are we asking students to read literature?

A: Literature helps bring history to life, animating historical events and allowing students to walk in the shoes of those who have lived long ago in places distant from their own experience. Good literature is also disturbing. It forces readers to examine the lives of others from the inside out, exposing young people to the complexity of the world they live in. Literature doesn't offer simple solutions. While reading fiction is not a vaccine for small-mindedness, it does make it difficult to think only of one's self. If one purpose of public education is to prepare students for the complex responsibilities of citizenship, I can think of no better preparation for these responsibilities than reading the work of Stephen Crane, Jack London, Frank Norris, Theodore Dreiser, and Upton Sinclair. Literature creates empathy and without empathy there can be little hope of a civilized society.

Standard English Learners
Language Acquisition as a Scaffold to Social Studies Curricula
by Dr. Noma LeMoine

Dr. Noma LeMoine, Ph.D., is a nationally recognized expert on issues of language variation and learning in African American and other students for whom Standard English is not native. She is Director of Academic English Mastery and Closing the Achievement Gap Branch for the Los Angeles Unified School District. She is a member of the National Citizen's Commission on African American Education, an arm of the Congressional Black Caucus Education Brain Trust. Dr. LeMoine is also the author of *English for Your Success: A Language Development Program for African American Students.*

Standard English Learners arrive at school in kindergarten as competent users of the language of their home but demonstrating limited proficiency in the language of school, that is, Standard American English. They are generally classified as English Only on school language surveys even though many of the rules that govern their home language are based in languages other than English. Because of their designation as English Only, these students' need for structured programs that support their acquisition of standard and academic English is often overlooked.

Who are Standard English Learners?

Standard English Learners (SELs) are students for whom standard English is not native or whose home language—the language acquired between infancy and five years of age—structurally does not match the language of school. Standard English Learners include African American, Hawaiian American, Mexican American, and Native American students who have in common a linguistic history grounded in languages other than English. Prior to coming in contact with English their ancestors spoke African languages, Hawaiian languages, Latin American Spanish, or Native American languages. In each case these "involuntary minorities"—people who were enslaved, colonized, conquered, or otherwise subordinated in the context of America—combined English vocabulary with their native language and fashioned new ways of communicating in their new environments. These language forms, African American Language (often referred to as Black English); Hawaiian American Language (referred

SEL Administrative Support Strategies

- Provide ongoing, comprehensive professional development for teachers and paraeducators including "literature circles" centered around the literature on the culturally and linguistically responsive instruction.

- Support the development of cooperative learning communities at the school site that engage teachers in review of the research, lesson study, peer coaching, and analysis of student work as a condition necessary for effectively educating SELs.

- Infuse information on the origin and historical development of standard and non-standard languages into the instructional curriculum.

to as Hawaiian Pidgin English); Mexican American Language (referred to as Chicano English); and Native American Language (sometimes referred to as Red English) incorporate English vocabulary, but differ in structure and form from standard American English.

Language Variation and Learning in SELs

In order for culturally and linguistically diverse Standard English Learners to succeed academically they must acquire the language, culture, and literacies of school. They must become literate in the forms of English that appear in newspapers, magazines, textbooks, voting materials, and consumer contracts. How best to facilitate this learning in Standard English Learners has proven elusive for most American public educational institutions and minimal emphasis has been placed on identifying instructional methodologies that scaffold SELs' access to core curricula. Learning is viewed as a social phenomenon and knowledge is recognized as a social construction that is influenced by the cultural and linguistic experiences, perspectives, and frames of references both students and teachers bring to the learning environment. For Standard English Learners this suggests that an instructional model which validates and builds on prior knowledge, experiences, language and culture while supporting the acquisition of school language through content learning is an appropriate pedagogy.

The Social Studies curriculum is perhaps the best vehicle for creating learning opportunities in both content and language acquisition areas. Opportunities to engage in critical thinking and participate in knowledge building abound in the Social Studies curriculum. As teachers help students develop skills as historians who re-create and share knowledge, students can also be provided opportunities to develop skills as speakers, readers, and writers.

SELs must be provided opportunities to add school language and literacy to their repertoire

SEL Instructional Support Strategies

- Incorporate contrastive analysis strategies (linguistic, contextual, situational, and elicited) into the daily instruction of SELs to facilitate mastery of academic language.

- Incorporate applicable SDAIE (Specially Designed Academic Instruction in English) strategies into instruction including utilization of visuals, manipulatives, graphic organizers, media and other tools to explain concepts.

- Provide continuous and varied opportunities for students to use language to interact with each other and the content through instructional conversations.

- Provide 30 to 45 minutes per day of Mainstream English Language Development (MELD) instruction that promotes the development of listening, speaking, reading, and writing skills in standard and academic English.

- Establish classroom libraries that include culturally relevant books and provide opportunities for SELs to be read to and to engage in free voluntary reading (FVR) on a daily basis.

- Encourage student/classroom development of a personal thesaurus of conceptually coded words to support the acquisition of academic vocabulary.

- Convey knowledge on ancient Africa, Mexico, Hawaii, and North America; their cultures and history.

- Convey knowledge of the impact of diverse cultures on the modern world with an emphasis on historical and contemporary achievers.

- Make connections to students' prior knowledge, experiences, and cultural funds of knowledge to support learning and retention of learned concepts.

of skills using instructional approaches that build on the culture and language they bring to the classroom. In order for SELs to experience greater success in accessing core curricula, teachers will need to construct learning environments that are authentic, culturally responsive, support language acquisition, and build upon the experiences, learning styles, and strengths of SELs.

Teaching Vocabulary and Comprehension

by Dr. Kylene Beers

Dr. Kylene Beers, Ed.D., is a Senior Reading Researcher in the School Development Program of the Child Study Center at Yale University. A former middle school teacher, Dr. Beers is a respected authority on struggling readers. She is the current editor of *Voices from the Middle,* the journal of the National Council of Teachers of English; co-editor of *Into Focus: Understanding and Creating Middle School Readers;* and the author of *When Kids Can't Read—What Teachers Can Do.* Dr. Beers was the 2001 recipient of the Richard W. Halle Award given by NCTE for outstanding contributions to middle school education.

Effective Vocabulary Instruction

"Preteaching vocabulary . . . requires that the words to be taught must be key words . . . be taught in semantically and topically related sets, . . . and that only a few words be taught per lesson."

—Tierney and Cunningham

The Right Words and the Right Number

The more vocabulary words we give students to learn weekly, the less chance students have of learning a word to the level needed to move it from short-term to long-term memory. Keeping the number between 5 and 10 means students have a better chance of retaining that word beyond the end of the week (Beers, 2002).

Consequently, choose wisely the words to be taught. Avid readers benefit by studying rare words—those highly unusual ones—because these students already have a solid vocabulary of the more common words. Struggling readers, however, benefit by focusing on high-utility words—those more common words that they are likely to see in other contexts. So, in the sentence, "The boys banked the canoe to the lee side of the rock," the inclination might be to teach the word *lee,* a rare word. However, if students don't know what *banked* means in this context or don't know the word *canoe,* it matters little what *lee* means. For struggling readers, a focus on high-utility words is more beneficial than a focus on rare words.

The Right Instructional Approach

Tierney and Cunningham (1984) explain that offering students a list of vocabulary words with their definitions is not as effective as placing each word within a semantic context. Students learn how to use words as they read or hear them used correctly. This textbook lists the key terms and people for each section at the beginning of that section. Defining these terms and using them in a sentence provides students with the semantic placement that most helps them learn words. Choosing the right number of the right words and presenting words in a semantic context helps students build their vocabulary and, as a consequence, improve their comprehension.

Improving Comprehension

"Comprehension is both a product and a process, something that requires purposeful, strategic effort on the reader's part as he or she predicts, visualizes, clarifies, questions, connects, summarizes, and infers."
—Kylene Beers

When the Text is Tough

"Comprehension is only tough when you can't do it," explained the eleventh-grader. I almost dismissed his words until I realized what truth they offered. We aren't aware of all the thinking we do to comprehend a text until faced with a difficult text. Then all too clearly, we're aware of what words we don't understand, what syntax seems convoluted, and what ideas are beyond our immediate grasp. As skilled readers, we know what to do—we slow our pace, reread, ask questions, connect whatever we do understand to what we don't understand, summarize what we've read thus far, and make inferences about what the author is saying. In short, we make that invisible act of comprehension visible as we consciously push our way through the difficult text. At those times, we realize that, indeed, comprehension is tough.

Reading Strategies for Struggling Readers

It's even tougher if you lack strategies that would help you through the difficult text. Many struggling readers believe they aren't successful readers because that's just the way things are (Beers, 2002). They believe successful readers know some secret that they haven't been told (Duffy, 2002). While we don't mean to keep comprehension a secret, at times that is what we do. For example, though we tell students to "reread," we haven't shown them how to alter their reading. We tell them to "make inferences," or "make predictions," but we haven't taught them how to do such things. In other words, we tell them what to do, but don't show them how to do it, in spite of several decades of research showing the benefit of direct instruction in reading strategies to struggling readers (Baumann, 1984; Pearson, P. D., 1984; Dole, et al., 1996; Beers, 2002).

Direct Instruction Direct instruction means telling students what you are going to teach them, modeling it for them, providing assistance as they practice it, then letting them practice it on their own. It's not saying, "visualize while you read," but, instead, explaining, "today, I'm going to read this part aloud to you. I'm going to focus on seeing some of the action in my mind as I read. I'm going to stop occasionally and tell you what I'm seeing and what in the text helped me see that." When we directly teach comprehension strategies to students by means of modeling and repeated practice, we show students that good readers don't just get it. They work hard to get it. Direct instruction takes the secret out of comprehension as it provides teachers the support they need to reach struggling readers.

Baumann, J. 1984.
"Effectiveness of a Direct Instruction Paradigm for Teaching Main Idea Comprehension." *Reading Research Quarterly,* 20: 93–108.

Beers, K. 2002.
When Kids Can't Read—What Teachers Can Do. Portsmouth: Heinemann.

Dole, J., Brown, K., and Trathen, W. 1996.
"The Effects of Strategy Instruction on the Comprehension Performance of At-Risk Students." *Reading Research Quarterly,* 31: 62–89.

Duffy, G. 2002.
"The Case for Direct Explanation of Strategies." *Comprehension Instruction: Research-Based Best Practices.* Eds. C. Block and M. Pressley. New York: Guilford Press. 28–41.

Pearson, P. D. 1984.
"Direct Explicit Teaching of Reading Comprehension." *Comprehension Instruction: Perspectives and Suggestions.* Eds. G. Duffy, L. Roehler, and J. Mason. New York: Longman. 222–233.

Tierney, R. J., and Cunningham, J. W. 1984.
"Research on Teaching Reading Comprehension." *Handbook of Reading Research.* Eds. P. D. Pearson, R. Barr, M. Kamil, P. Mosenthal. New York: Longman. 609–656.

North Carolina's Thinking Skills

by Scott King-Owen, Instructional Specialist
New Hanover County Schools, North Carolina

Robert Marzano's *Dimensions of Learning* (1992) provides the framework by which the North Carolina Standard Course of Study as well as all end–of–course and end–of–grade tests are designed. The North Carolina Department of Public Instruction adapted Marzano's model, hybridizing it with the one developed by Benjamin Bloom over a half–century ago. The resulting "levels of thinking" have continued to be used through standard course–of–study revisions to ensure that goals and objectives have measurable cognitive levels which can be correlated to the cognitive demands of test questions.

Levels of Thinking

In the hybrid model, there are nine levels of thinking: knowing, organizing, applying, analyzing, generating, integrating, and evaluating. Anyone familiar with Bloom's Taxonomy will recognize knowing, applying, analyzing, and evaluating, but may be less familiar with organizing, generating, and integrating. Organizing, according to Marzano, refers to arranging information in a way that make it useful; this can be done through comparing, classifying, sequencing, or changing the representation of information. Generating involves producing new information or meaning through inference, prediction, or elaboration of already learned material. Integrating is the opposite of analyzing: it refers to putting information back together through summarizing or restructuring existing categories.

Using North Carolina's Model

Teachers can use these levels of thinking in the classroom in a variety of ways. First, by knowing what each level means, teachers can dissect what a standard course-of-study objective really demands of students. For example, when an objective calls for assessing, teachers will know that students should be setting criteria and evaluating information. Second, teachers will understand how end-of-course and end-of-grade test questions are written, and they will therefore be able to make their own

tests match the cognitive demands of the state testing program. They can also design formative and summative assessments that will truly match the thinking skills required in the goals and objectives.

Helping Students Succeed

Although North Carolina did not incorporate Marzano's entire framework into designs for testing and curriculum, teachers can benefit from knowing and using the rest of Marzano's framework from *Dimensions of Learning*. The framework consists of five dimensions: attitudes and perceptions, acquisition and utilization of knowledge, refinement and extension of knowledge, application of knowledge, and productive habits of mind. The first and last dimensions were not explicitly written into North Carolina's model but are of vital importance in the classroom. In them, Marzano emphasizes the importance of metacognition, or being in control of one's own thinking processes, as well as the central role that emotion and belief play in inhibiting or enhancing learning. Using Marzano's ideas, along with North Carolina thinking-skills levels, can have a profound impact on how we teach and how our students learn.

Holt Skill Labels and North Carolina Thinking Skills

To help students become competent and critical thinkers and learners, Holt Social Studies has developed a scaffolding system for its assessment items. Each of Holt's leveled questions bears a skill label that correlates easily to the North Carolina Thinking Skills.

Correlating Skill Labels to Thinking Skills

Holt Skill Labels	North Carolina Thinking Skill
Define, Describe, Identify, Recall, Explain	**Knowing** Focusing, gathering, and remembering information
Compare and/or Contrast, Sequence, Categorize, Identify Cause and Effect	**Organizing** Arranging information so it can be used effectively
Solve Problems, Identify Bias	**Applying** Demonstrating prior knowledge within a new situation; using appropriate information to solve a problem
Analyze, Find Main Ideas, Identify Cause and Effect, Identify Point of View	**Analyzing** Clarifying existing information by examining parts and relationships
Make Inferences, Draw Conclusions, Make Generalizations, Develop, Elaborate, Predict, Generalize	**Generating** Producing new information, meaning, or ideas
Summarize, Develop, Design, Solve Problems, Make Decisions, Support a Point of View	**Integrating** Connecting and combining information
Rank, Rate, Evaluate	**Evaluating** Assessing the reasonableness and quality of ideas

Leveled Assessments in Your Book

Holt's section and chapter reviews include question sets that test student knowledge and ability at three levels. Each review question also bears a skill label. Understanding how Holt levels and labels questions will help you determine which North Carolina Thinking Skill each question supports.

Assessment Level 1:
Knowledge and Comprehension

Holt's question sets always begin with Level 1 "**a**" questions that test for knowledge or comprehension.

Assessment Level 2:
Inference and Analysis

The "**b**" review questions require inference and analysis.

Assessment Level 3:
Synthesize and Evaluate

Level 3 questions, or "**c**" questions, have students synthesize and evaluate information.

3. a. Recall What two cultures are known as Mound Builders, and why?
b. Make Generalizations What were the typical characteristics of the early cultures of the Southwest?
c. Evaluate What achievements marked the Mississippians as having an advanced culture?

The Anasazi built some of their pueblos on flat mesas and on steep cliffs. Major pueblos, some with hundreds of rooms, were located in Chaco Canyon. Miles of roads linked them with distant Anasazi settlements. Traders carried food and luxuries such as turquoise.

By about 1300, the Anasazi culture was beginning to decline. So were other ancient societies of the Southwest. One reason may have been a great drought in the late 1200s. Wars or invasions may also have contributed. Dispersing eastward, some Anasazi groups settled in present-day New Mexico, becoming the ancestors of today's Pueblo Indians.

By about 100 BC, Adena culture had been absorbed by the Hopewell culture. Hopewell people were skillful artists who carved realistic human statues and ceremonial pipes depicting animals. They also worked with copper, shells, mica, and other materials from as far away as the Great Lakes and the Gulf of Mexico.

By about AD 400 or 500, the trade network that linked Hopewell settlements was falling apart. Mound-building traditions, however, continued for hundreds of years.

Mississippian culture The last major mound-building culture in North America was the Mississippian. Theirs was the most society north of Mexico. The grew maize and beans, and new farming tool—the hoe. outheast and southern Mid-sippians built towns. These eremonial temple-mounds plazas. The homes of rulers pyramids around the cen- reatest Mississippian cities r present-day St. Louis, and bama.

Cahokia was a great pop- erhaps as large as London. 0s, its central pyramid was re in the United States.

from distant places. They obtained copper and pearls, for example, to adorn the rings and ornaments that were buried with important people.

READING CHECK Drawing Conclusions How did the landscape and climate of the Southwest affect early peoples there?

SECTION 1 ASSESSMENT

go.hrw.com
Online Quiz
Keyword SD7 HP1

Reviewing Ideas, Terms, and People
1. a. Recall Where did the original settlers in the Americas come from?
b. Analyze What changes in the environment led to the agricultural revolution?
2. a. Identify What is Mesoamerica?
b. Sequence Trace, in order, the development of different cultures in Central and South America.
3. a. Recall What two cultures are known as Mound Builders, and why?
b. Make Generalizations What were the typical characteristics of the early cultures of the Southwest?
c. Evaluate What achievements marked the Mississippians as having an advanced culture?

Critical Thinking
4. Sequencing Copy the chart below and fill it in to show the differences before and after the agricultural revolution.

Before	After

FOCUS ON SPEAKING

5. Persuasive As a member of a hunter-gatherer band long ago, write a speech explaining why a particular location will be a good place for your group to settle.

10 CHAPTER 1

Teaching for Understanding

by Scott King-Owen, Instructional Specialist
New Hanover County Schools, North Carolina

Grant Wiggins and Jay McTighe published *Understanding by Design* (UbD) in 1998. Along with H. Lynn Erickson's *Concept-Based Curriculum and Instruction*, UbD has become an important framework in promoting rigor in many states' development of curricular materials. Both works use the same language, though UbD offers a more robust view of how to design curricula, units, and lessons with what is known as the "backwards" approach. By "backwards," Wiggins and McTighe refer to beginning with the end in mind: what should students know, understand, and be able to do as a result of learning? Though this approach works for any level, the language of the North Carolina Honors Course Standards is illuminated by the terminology of UbD. *Understanding by Design* proposes three stages of instructional design:

1. identifying desired results
2. determining acceptable evidence
3. planning learning experiences

Teachers should, therefore, plan activities, assessments, and assignments only after they have carefully delineated what students should know, understand, and be able to do.

Stage 1
Identifying Desired Results

UbD helps students get to deep levels of understanding by asking essential questions and identifying understandings. An essential question provokes deep inquiry into a subject and because it has no right or wrong answer, it raises other questions and brings attention to the very core of a discipline. An understanding is a generalization derived from studying essential questions; as a generalization, it is arguable and prone to misunderstanding. By creating essential questions and generalizations, teachers can do more than merely cover the content and march through the textbook.

In Your Book
Each chapter begins with a two-page **Chapter Preview** designed to help you focus on desired results and teach for understanding. As you begin each chapter, take time to post the **North Carolina Social Studies Competency Goals**, **The Big Idea**, and **Essential Questions** in your classroom. Reviewing these materials in class will help you lead your students towards standards mastery and a meaningful understanding of chapter content.

Standards Focus
This information tells exactly which North Carolina Competency Goals each chapter has been designed to meet. Remind students that these goals outline what they should know, understand, and be able to do to master content and succeed on tests.

The Big Idea and Essential Questions

The Big Idea The Big Idea provides a focal point for instruction and a foundation for student understanding. Each chapter's Big Idea expresses a core concept or a key process that students can use to meaningfully organize information.

Essential Questions The Essential Questions go to the heart of chapter content. Use these questions to frame your teaching and student learning. One topical essential question has been written for each section of every chapter.

• Chapter Preview •

Standards Focus
Social Studies Competency Goals
Goal 4 The learner will evaluate the great westward movement and assess the impact of the agricultural revolution on the nation.
4.01, 4.02, 4.04

The Big Idea and Essential Questions
To foster student understanding of this chapter's big idea, design your lesson to address each section's essential question.

Big Idea As the federal government forcibly relocated Native Americans to reservations, Americans and immigrants settled on the new frontier as miners, ranchers, and farmers.

Essential Questions

1. In what ways did Native Americans respond to the efforts of American settlers to move westward?

2. How did the mining industry and cattle ranching develop in the West?

3. How did agriculture develop in the West?

Stage 2
Determining Acceptable Evidence

The second stage of UbD asks teachers to consider what evidence would prove that a student really understands the material. Wiggins and McTighe define understanding as the ability to use knowledge in new situations; this ability is known as transfer. Additionally, they propose to look at understanding through the lens of six facets: explanation, interpretation, application, perspective, empathy, and self-knowledge. UbD recommends developing performance assessments—complex tasks that require students to do real-world applications of knowledge—in order to measure these six facets. A student who truly understands not only can explain the material but can tell why it is important, how to use it, what others have thought about it, how it looks from a single perspective, and why he or she makes use of it.

In Your Book

Throughout **Holt's Student Edition** varied assessment opportunities—including **Reading Check Questions**, **Section Reviews**, **Chapter Reviews**, and **chapter-level Standardized Test Practice**—let students demonstrate their understanding in multiple ways.

Six Facets of Student Understanding

	Assessment Options in Holt's Student Edition			
	Reading Check Questions	Section Assessment	Chapter Review	Chapter-Level Standardized Test Practice
Explanation	✔	✔	✔	✔
Interpretation	✔	✔	✔	✔
Application	✔	✔	✔	✔
Perspective	✔	✔	✔	✔
Empathy	✔	✔	✔	✔
Self-knowledge	✔	✔	✔	✔

Stage 3
Planning Learning Experiences

The third stage of UbD asks teachers to design instructional activities based on the planning in stages one and two. When teachers carefully narrow the content down to big ideas and essential understandings, they can then create assessments that will test that understanding and design lessons that help students truly understand the material. A focus of the third stage is to help students engage the material in a way that respects the learning needs of all students and to make sure that the material is relevant as well as rigorous. By using all three stages in designing curriculum materials, units, and lessons, teachers can help students learn for a lifetime.

In Your Book

To ensure that all students have access to effective learning experiences that leads to understanding, **Holt's Teacher Edition** provides a variety of **differentiated lesson activities**. These activities help teachers reach out to students with different interests and learning styles, English language learners, as well as those students learning below level, at level, and above level.

Professional Resources and Bibliography

Professional References

This section provides information about resources that can enrich your Social Studies class. Included is information about guest speakers, museum visits, electronic field trips, nonprofit organizations, and many others. Since addresses change frequently, you may want to verify them before you send your requests. You may also want to refer to the HRW Web site at http://www.hrw.com for current information.

Project CRISS

Project CRISS (**CR**eating **I**ndependence through **S**tudent-owned **S**trategies) is an instructional method in which students learn how to learn. The program helps students identify teaching strategies that work for them, integrate new information with their prior knowledge, and secure their learning by organizing, discussing, and writing about what they have learned.
Log on to the go.hrw.com Web site (http://go.hrw.com) and enter the keyword **NC Teacher** for information about how your *American Anthem* program addresses CRISS strategies.

www.projectcriss.com

GUEST SPEAKERS
National Council for History Education
26915 Westwood Rd., Suite B-2
Westlake, Ohio 44145
440-835-1776
www.nche.net

MUSEUM VISITS
American Association of Museums
1575 Eye Street NW, Suite 400
Washington, DC 20005
202-289-1818
www.aam-us.org

ELECTRONIC FIELD TRIPS
Library of Congress/Congressional Server
www.loc.gov

E3 Electronic Field Trips
Teachers College (TC 1008)
Ball State University
Muncie IN 47306
866-279-8716
www.bsu.edu/eft

eFieldTrips.org
2960 W. Player Dr.
Snowflake, Arizona 85937
928-536-4954

NONPROFIT ORGANIZATIONS
Constitutional Rights Foundation
601 South Kingsley Drive
Los Angeles, CA 90005
213-487-5590
www.crf-usa.org

Center for Civic Education
5145 Douglas Fir Road
Calabasas, CA 91302-1440
Tel: 818-591-9321
www.civiced.org

National Council for the Social Studies
8555 Sixteenth Street, Suite 500
Silver Spring, MD 20910
301-588-1800
www.socialstudies.org

National Trust for Historic Preservation
1785 Massachusetts Ave. NW
Washington, DC 20036
202-588-6000
www.nationaltrust.org

National History Day
University of Maryland
at College Park
0119 Cecil Hall
College Park, MD 20742
301-314-9739
www.nationalhistoryday.org

American Association for State and Local History
1717 Church Street
Nashville, TN 37203
615-320-3203
www.aaslh.org

American Bar Association
Division for Public Education
321 North Clark Street
Chicago, IL 60610
312-988-5000
www.abanet.org

PERIODICALS
American Spirit Magazine
DAR Magazine Office
1776 D Street NW
Washington, DC 20006-5303
866-327-6242
www.dar.org/natsociety/magazine.cfm

American History
Primedia History Group
6405 Flank Drive
Harrisburg, PA 17112
800-829-3340
www.thehistorynet.com/ah

OAH Magazine of History
Organization of American Historians
P.O. Box 5457
Bloomington, IN 47408-5457
812-855-7311
www.oah.org

GOVERNMENT RESOURCES

National Park Service
Office of Public Inquiries
Washington, DC 20013-7127
www.nps.gov

National Register of Historic Places
National Park Service
1201 Eye Street, NW MS 2280
Washington, DC 20005
202-354-2213
www.cr.nps.gov/nr

U.S. Department of Education
400 Maryland Ave., SW
Washington, D.C. 20202-0498
800-USA-LEARN
www.ed.gov

Smithsonian Institution
Smithsonian Information
P.O. Box 37012
SI Building, Room 153, MRC 010
Washington, DC 20013-7012
202-357-2700
www.si.edu

The Library of Congress
101 Independence Ave, SE
Washington, DC 20540
202-707-5000
www.loc.gov

SUBSCRIPTION SERVICES

Magazines.com Inc.
P.O. Box 682108
Franklin, TN 37068
800-929-2691
www.magazines.com

MISCELLANEOUS

Educational Resources Information Center (ERIC)
ERIC Project
c/o Computer Sciences Corporation
4483-A Forbes Blvd.
Lanham, MD 20705
800-538-3742
www.eric.ed.gov

Busy Teachers' WebSite K-12
http://www.ceismc.gatech.edu/busyt

A Bibliography for the Social Studies Teacher

This bibliography is a select compilation of resources available for professional enrichment.

SELECTED AND ANNOTATED LIST OF READINGS

Social Studies and Language Arts

Burke, Jim. *Writing Reminders: Tools, Tips, and Techniques*
Portsmouth, NH: Heinemann, 2003
Burke offers a collection of strategies for teaching writing, complete with the instructional tools for implementing the strategies.

Jago, Carol. *Cohesive Writing: Why Concept Is Not Enough*
Portsmouth, NH: Heinemann, 2002
This book provides a coherent roadmap for teaching students how to write in each of the writing types required for the STAR assessment: summary, narrative, response to literature, and persuasion.

Social Studies and Standard English Mastery

LeMoine, N. and Los Angeles Unified School District. *English for Your Success: A Language Development Program for African American Students. Handbook of Successful Strategies for Educators.*
New Jersey: The Peoples Publishing Group, 1999
English for Your Success provides lessons using proven strategies for facilitating language acquisition and learning in African American Standard English Learners.

Ornstein-Galicia, J. *Form and Function in Chicano English*
Malabar, FL: Krieger Publishing Co., 1988
This text address issues of language and learning in Mexican American Standard English Learners (SELs) who speak mainly Chicano English.

Social Studies and English Learners

Billmeyer, Rachel and Mary Lee Barton. *Teaching Reading in the Content Areas: If Not Me, Then Who?* Second Edition
Aurora, CO: Mid-Continent Regional Educational Laboratory (McREL), 1998
These 40 strategies help students of all ages expand their vocabularies, understand different types of texts, and discuss what they have read.

Buehl, Doug. *Classroom Strategies for Interactive Learning,* Second Edition
Newark, DE: International Reading Assoc., 2001
More than 40 literacy strategies for middle school and high school educators outside the reading field.

Readance, John, Thomas W. Bean and R. Scott Baldwin. *Content Area Literacy: An Integrated Approach.* Eighth Edition
Dubuque, IA: Kendall/Hunt Publishing Company, 2000
The authors provide strategies for helping students read, understand, and enjoy nonfiction. A CD accompanies this widely used text.

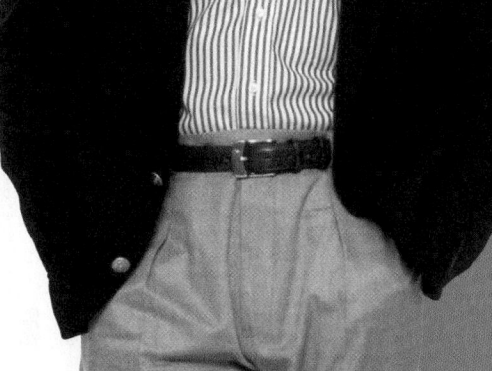

Reading like a Historian

When I asked Kevin, a 16-year-old high school junior, what he needed most to do well in history class, he had little doubt: "A good memory."

"Anything else?"

"Nope. Just memorize facts and stuff, know 'em cold, and when you get the test, give it all back to the teacher."

"What about thinking—does thinking have anything to do with history?"

"Not really. It's all pretty simple. Random stuff happened a long time ago. People wrote it down. Others copied it and put it in a book. Poof—history."

I was saddened but not surprised by Kevin's answers. I've spent nearly twenty years studying how high school kids learn history. Over the years I've met many Kevins, students who knew history as nothing but a grim list of names and dates—one random fact after another.

In *American Anthem,* we have created a textbook that I hope will change the way students such as Kevin learn history. To explore the past and feel its excitement , you must learn to read like a historian.

Senior Program Consultant

Gilbert Stuart painted this portrait of George Washington in 1796, while Washington was president. Historians consider this painting a primary source because it was created during Washington's lifetime.

Be a History Detective

Names, facts, and dates: this is what history has become for a lot of you. But the funny thing is that when you ask historians what they do, an entirely different picture emerges. They see themselves as detectives searching for clues to a puzzle that can never be entirely solved.

Asking questions Traced back to its earliest meaning, the word *history* (in Greek, *istor*) is about *inquiry*. To engage in inquiry means trying to figure things out, asking questions open to debate. Inquiry is about as far from mindless memorization as you can get.

Even when historians are able to piece together the basic story of what happened in the past, rarely do they all line up in agreement about what an event means or what caused it. Historians argue amongst themselves about the past's meaning and what it has to tell us in the present. The past may be over, but history is a moving target.

Facts and Their Meaning

Where do facts fit into this picture? Facts are important but hardly the whole story. To historians, history is an argument about what facts *mean*.

If history already happened, you might ask, what's there to argue about? It turns out, a lot. Was the American Revolution a fight against tyranny or an attempt by the well bred to preserve their social position? Was the Civil War fought over the issue of slavery or was it a conflict over states' rights? Was the "Progressive Era" really so progressive? Could the Vietnam War have been prevented?

Reviewing sources Take, for example, a story you probably know—or think you do. Pocahontas, a beautiful Native American woman, falls in love with the handsome English captain John Smith, and later saves his life just as her dad, Powhatan, is ready to club him to death.

Do you believe it?

The facts are these: John Smith wrote two different accounts of his time in Jamestown, one in 1608, the other in 1624. In his first book, he talks about meeting Chief Powhatan, but there is no mention of any threat. In fact he says the opposite: Powhatan "kindly welcomed me with such good wordes, and great Platters...assuring me his friendship." Nor is there any mention of being saved by a young Indian girl—anyway, Pocahontas was only 11 or 12, hardly the gorgeous teenager of cartoon fame—and no hint of any love affair anywhere. Only when Smith published a second book in 1624, well after Pocahontas had already married another colonist, John Rolfe, had a son, became ill, and died in 1617, do we hear of Smith's dramatic rescue by the Indian princess. So which account should we believe, the one Smith wrote in 1608 or 1624?

Weighing opinions Different opinions swirl around this question, and there are actually good reasons for believing a number of them. But while everyone is entitled to an opinion, not every opinion is entitled to being believed. In history, a persuasive opinion is backed up by evidence. It is evidence that distinguishes a solid interpretation from a wild guess. *American Anthem* offers you numerous opportunities to develop the critical reading skills you'll need to analyze evidence like a historian.

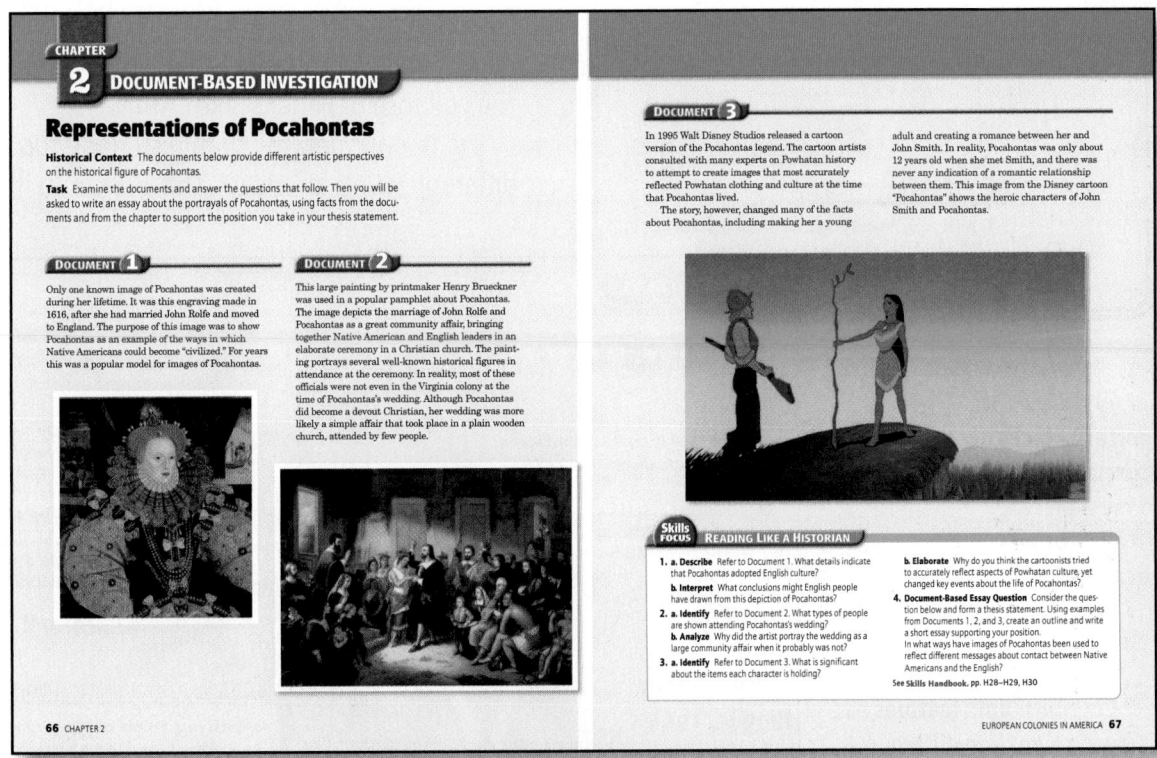

Document-Based Investigations give you opportunities to inquire like a historian. You will study a series of documents and then draw your own conclusions about what they mean.

Evidence in History

To find evidence in history we can't talk to the dead. What we can do is examine what they left behind—their diaries, letters, telegrams, secret memos, and in the modern era, their tape recordings and computer records. This is what historians mean when they talk about reading *primary* sources. These sources are considered to be primary—*most important, appearing in the first position, essential*—because they are written by the people we are trying to understand. Their words come to us directly, without being filtered by someone else.

How Historians Read

Learning to read like a historian is different from the other kind of reading you do, like reading your driver's ed manual or your math book. In practically every country, a red road sign means stop. In math 2 + 2 = 4 no matter where you live—in Dallas, San Francisco, or Paris. But because history is always written from a particular perspective, its meanings change from place to place and from one era to the next. Even the book you're holding, while trying to balance different perspectives, makes choices that reflect its perspective: where to begin its story, where to end it, which events to narrate and which to leave out.

Points of view In our chapter covering the Revolutionary War, the rebellious American colonists are referred to as "patriots." Would you expect them to be so described in a British textbook? When you come to the chapters on World War II, D-Day is a large part of the story on the war in Europe. In Russian textbooks, D-Day—referred to as the "opening of the second front"—barely gets mentioned. There, the big story is the siege of Stalingrad, in which the Red Army held off the Nazis for six months, and in the process lost a million of its own citizens—but not before causing the collapse of Hitler's Sixth Army.

It is only natural that historians today have different points of view. The people at the time

---

PRIMARY SOURCES

Speech

In what became known as the Checkers speech, Richard M. Nixon admitted having a secret political fund but denied using it improperly. He detailed his personal finances—and admitted to having accepted one special gift in 1952. The speech was well received, and it saved his political career.

"We did get something, a gift, after the election. A man down in Texas heard [my wife] Pat on the radio mention the fact that our two youngsters would like to have a dog, and . . . the day before we left on this campaign trip we got a message from Union Station down in Baltimore, saying they had a package for us. We went down to get it. You know what it was? It was a little cocker spaniel dog, in a crate that he had sent all the way from Texas, black and white, spotted, and our little girl, Tricia, the six-year-old, named it Checkers. And, you know, the kids, like all kids, loved the dog, and I just want to say this, right now, that regardless of what they say about it, we're going to keep it."

Nixon used the image of his daughter and her puppy to build sympathy.

Skills FOCUS READING LIKE A HISTORIAN

1. **Analyzing Primary Sources** What was the gift that Nixon admitted to having received?

2. **Drawing Conclusions** W[...] speech was effective at end[...]

See **Skills Handbook**, pp. H12, [...]

Primary sources are important pieces of historical evidence—and must be read with a historian's critical eye.

Counterpoints features ask you to analyze different points of view about key historical issues.

COUNTERPOINTS

Tactics of Change

Martin Luther King's commitment to nonviolence never wavered.

❝ [V]iolence . . . seeks to annihilate rather than convert . . . Nonviolence is a powerful and just weapon . . . which cuts without wounding and ennobles the man who wields it. ❞

Martin Luther King Jr., 1964

Malcolm X was blunt and uncompromising. He inspired hatred from some and respect from others.

❝ [N]ow you're facing a situation where the young Negro's coming up. They don't want to hear that 'turn-the-other-cheek' stuff, no. . . . There's new thinking coming in. There's new strategy coming in . . . It'll be ballots, or it'll be bullets. It'll be liberty, or it will be death. ❞

Malcolm X, 1964

Skills FOCUS READING LIKE A HISTORIAN

Identifying Points of View What does King mean when he says that nonviolence "cuts without wounding"? To what is Malcolm X referring when he speaks of "ballots" or "bullets"?

See **Skills Handbook**, pp. H28–H29

---

did too. The Counterpoints features found in this book show that as history was being made, people disagreed about what was happening and what to do.

Reading for perspective Perspective means a place to stand, and each one of us has to stand somewhere. Where the authors of this book stand is revealed in the words they choose—just think about the difference between calling this book "American Anthem," versus, say, "American Dilemma" or "American Crisis." But determining perspective means paying more attention to words than you're probably used to.

Attention to detail Consider two facts: first, Harry Truman became the 32nd president; and second, he never went to college. The moment we try to combine them, we no longer have two neutral bits of information. We have a historical interpretation. Think about the sentence, "Harry Truman became the 32nd president *but* he never went to college." Change one little word—substitute *because* for *but*—and see what happens. The first sentence suggests that the lack of a college education was something Truman had to overcome. The second seems to say that Truman's humble education *caused*, or at least partially caused, his success. Two completely different ideas rest on one word. Without paying attention, you'd miss it.

The Role of Thinking

The book you are holding offers an interpretation of history, but not the final word. It does its best to combine perspectives, but like any book, it can never escape the fact that it was written by human beings living in a particular time and place. As such, it

records the unrecognized assumptions, biases, and blind spots of our time. In reading like a historian, one of your goals is to treat this book like any other account of the past. You should analyze it, evaluate the evidence it offers for its assertions, and read it carefully—more carefully than you've ever read a history textbook before. The thread connecting all of these goals is the very thing that escaped Kevin: the role of thinking.

Kevin's right. Without thinking, history *is* meaningless. But when you add thinking—an ingredient only you can provide—the past springs to life. That is what reading like a historian is all about.

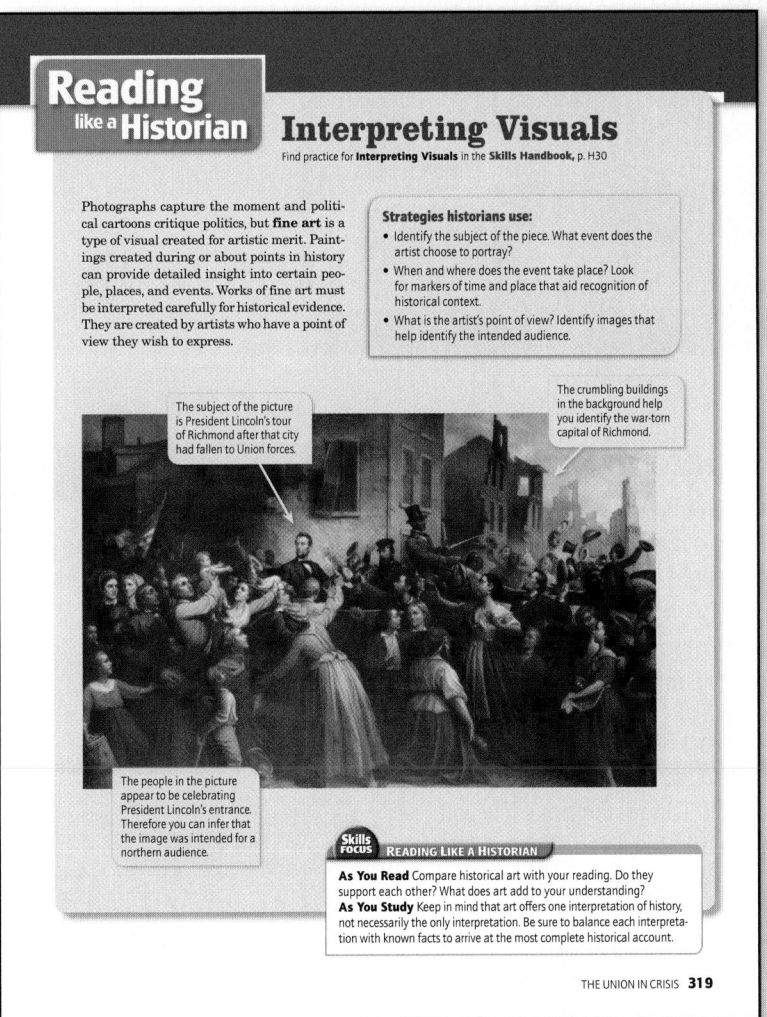

A historian looks at all evidence critically. Valuable information comes not only from text-based documents, but also from paintings, photographs, political cartoons, and other visual media.

How to Use Your Textbook

American Anthem was created to make your study of American history an enjoyable, meaningful experience. Take a few minutes to become familiar with the book's easy-to-use structure and special features.

Unit

Each unit of study focuses on a particular time period. Unit openers list the chapter titles and the years the chapters cover. They also provide an overview of the main themes covered in the unit. A historic photograph or illustration previews the material you are about to explore.

Prepare to Read

Each unit begins with an opportunity to reinforce important skills first taught in the Skills Handbook. Taking the time to review these skills will help you as you read the unit.

Reading Skills Call-outs give practical how-to instruction about the skill. Test-taking tips show you how reading skills can help you when taking exams.

Reading Like a Historian This book provides strategies to help you think like a historian. Each call-out applies one of the strategies to the passage or visual being analyzed.

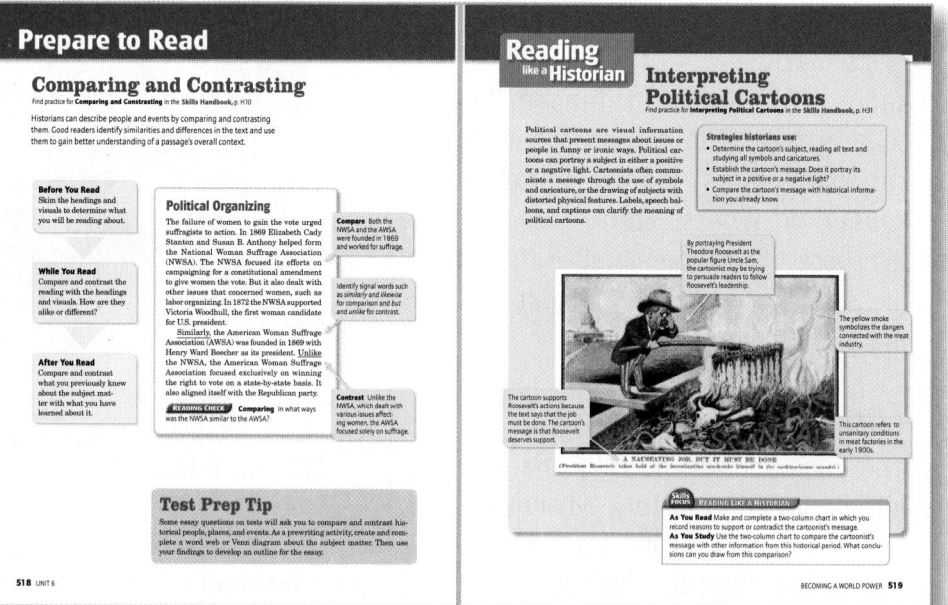

Chapter

Chapter Openers include an introduction called The Big Picture, a timeline for the years covered in the chapter, and photos and illustrations.

Chapter Review pages provide a full array of assessments.

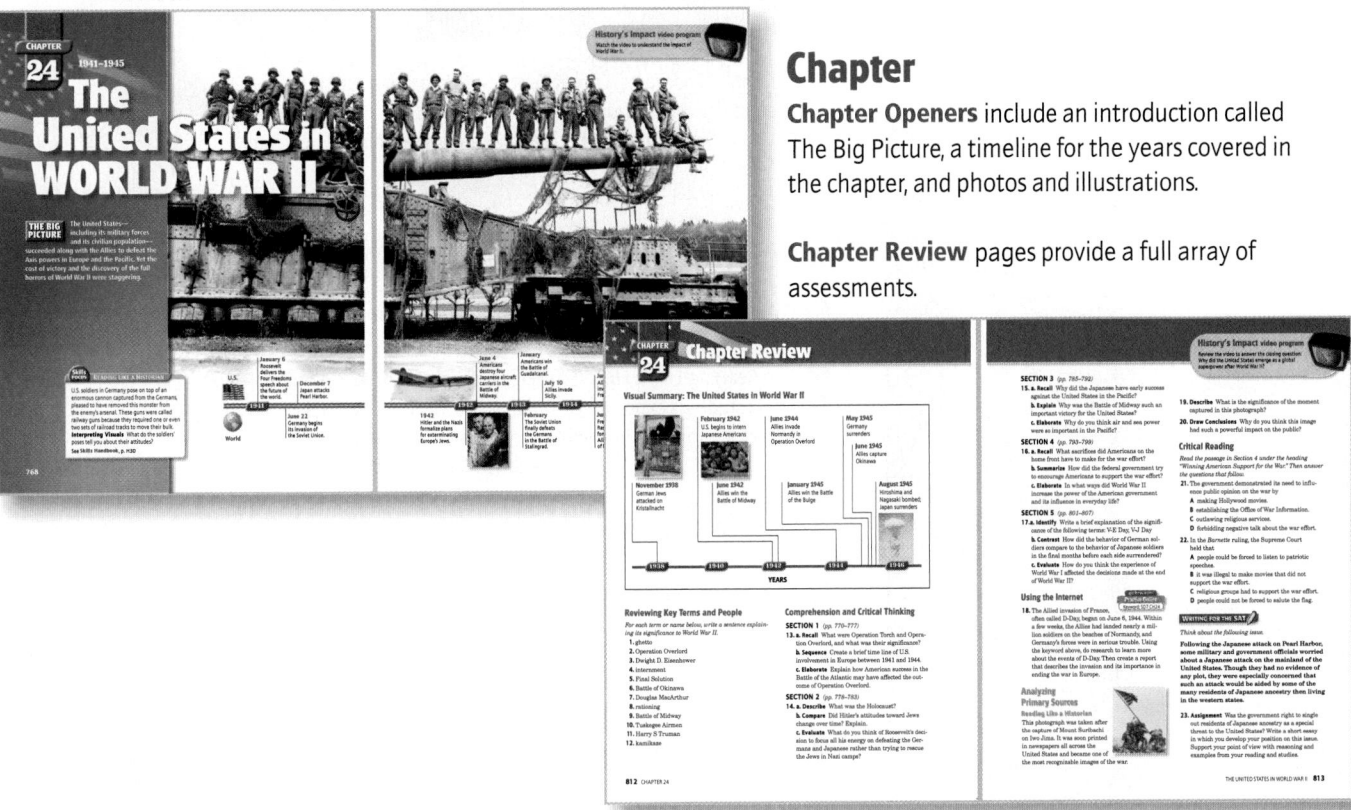

Section

Section opener pages include a Main Idea statement, Focus Questions, and Key Terms and People. In addition, each section includes the following special features:

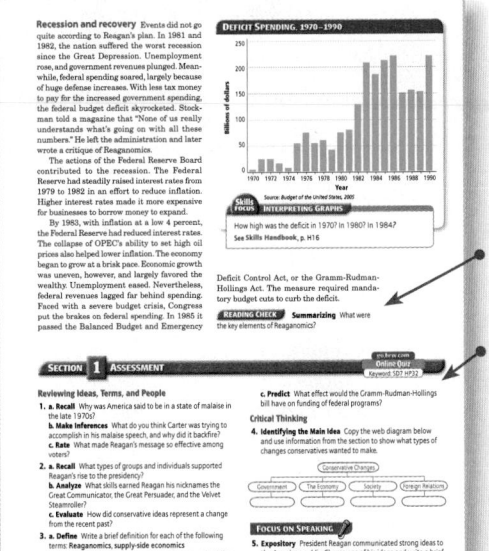

Taking Notes graphic organizers help you record key ideas as you read.

Reading Check Questions provide opportunities to review and assess your understanding.

Section Assessment boxes offer a quick way to check your understanding of a section's main ideas. There is also assessment practice online.

The Inside Story introduces each section with a compelling story from history.

Scavenger Hunt

American Anthem contains a great deal of information about U.S. history. Before you begin your journey into the past, take a minute to familiarize yourself with this book and its contents. This will help make your journey easier.

1 How many units and chapters are in the book? How do you know?

2 Where in *American Anthem* do you find the atlas?

3 The Reading Like a Historian Skills section of the Skills handbook offers students exposure to and practice in various skills, such as analyzing primary sources. Where in the book do you find additional Reading Like a Historian skill practice?

4 Where and how do you find key terms and people for Chapter 11, Section 2?

5 Where in *American Anthem* do you find strategies for various kinds of test questions?

6 Where do you find important academic vocabulary words defined?

7 Where do you find review questions to help you study?

8 Where do you look to find information about interactive maps and other map essentials?

9 Where do you look to find a list of all of the primary sources used?

10 Where can you find reading support for each unit?

Answers

1. *10 units and 33 chapters; by checking the table of contents;* **2.** *in the end matter;* **3.** *Reading Like a Historian questions accompany Primary Sources, Counterpoints, and American Literature features.* **4.** *beneath the heading "Key Terms and People" at the top of page 363;* **5.** *the Test Taking Strategies section of the front matter;* **6.** *throughout each section in the margins;* **7.** *throughout each section in the Reading Check questions and at the end of each section and chapter in the Section Assessments and Chapter Reviews;* **8.** *the Geography and Map Skills Handbook, which begins on page R62;* **9.** *in the table of contents;* **10.** *on the Prepare to Read pages at the beginning of each unit*

North Carolina Standard Course of Study:
Social Studies:
Eleventh Grade United States History

What is the North Carolina Standard Course of Study?

The North Carolina State Board of Education and Department of Public Instruction have organized the teaching of social studies, including eleventh grade United States History, by creating **Competency Goals** with distinct **Objectives**, or "standards," that every student should master. The goals and objectives focus on political, social, economic, and cultural issues and how these issues have affected American society. These goals describe what you are expected to know, understand, and be able to do as a result of your education.

In this section you will find the Competency Goals that have been approved by the State Board of Education. No matter where you are in North Carolina, these standards will tell you what you are expected to learn. You might notice that some of the subjects are familiar to you. This course is meant to build on the skills and knowledge you already have.

How can the North Carolina Competency Goals and Objectives help me?

These goals are helpful because they give you a clear picture of what you are expected to learn. This can help you to focus on key material as you work through the school year. You can think of the goals and objectives as a kind of checklist—and you can even check off important subjects and skills as you master them. Another advantage of becoming familiar with the goals is that teachers often base lesson plans and tests on these goals. That means that the standards can give you a preview of what to expect in this course.

Eleventh Grade: United States History

The study of United States History in the eleventh grade is a survey course that continues the North Carolina Civics and Economics curriculum. Throughout the competency goals, there will be some overlap of time periods to allow for teacher flexibility and to address the complexity of the issues and events. The overall curriculum continues to current times.

The focus of this course provides students with a framework for studying political, social, economic, and cultural issues and for analyzing the impact these issues have had on American society. This course goes beyond memorization of isolated facts to the development of higher level thinking skills, encouraging students to make historical assessments and evaluations.

COMPETENCY GOAL 1 The New Nation (1789–1820) The learner will identify, investigate, and assess the effectiveness of the institutions of the emerging republic.

OBJECTIVES

1.01 Identify the major domestic issues and conflicts experienced by the nation during the Federalist Period.

1.02 Analyze the political freedoms available to the following groups prior to 1820: women, wage earners, landless farmers, American Indians, African Americans, and other ethnic groups.

1.03 Assess commercial and diplomatic relationships with Britain, France, and other nations.

COMPETENCY GOAL 2 Expansion and Reform (1801–1850) The learner will assess the competing forces of expansionism, nationalism, and sectionalism.

OBJECTIVES

2.01 Analyze the effects of territorial expansion and the admission of new states to the Union.

2.02 Describe how the growth of nationalism and sectionalism were reflected in art, literature, and language.

2.03 Distinguish between the economic and social issues that led to sectionalism and nationalism.

2.04 Assess political events, issues, and personalities that contributed to sectionalism and nationalism.

2.05 Identify the major reform movements and evaluate their effectiveness.

2.06 Evaluate the role of religion in the debate over slavery and other social movements and issues.

COMPETENCY GOAL 3 Crisis, Civil War, and Reconstruction (1848–1877) The learner will analyze the issues that led to the Civil War, the effects of the war, and the impact of Reconstruction on the nation.

OBJECTIVES

3.01 Trace the economic, social, and political events from the Mexican War to the outbreak of the Civil War.

3.02 Analyze and assess the causes of the Civil War.

3.03 Identify political and military turning points of the Civil War and assess their significance to the outcome of the conflict.

3.04 Analyze the political, economic, and social impact of Reconstruction on the nation and identify the reasons why Reconstruction came to an end.

3.05 Evaluate the degree to which the Civil War and Reconstruction proved to be a test of the supremacy of the national government.

NORTH CAROLINA STATE STANDARDS

COMPETENCY GOAL 4 The Great West and the Rise of the Debtor (1860s–1896) The learner will evaluate the great westward movement and assess the impact of the agricultural revolution on the nation.

OBJECTIVES

4.01 Compare and contrast the different groups of people who migrated to the West and describe the problems they experienced.

4.02 Evaluate the impact that settlement in the West had upon different groups of people and the environment.

4.03 Describe the causes and effects of the financial difficulties that plagued the American farmer and trace the rise and decline of Populism.

4.04 Describe innovations in agricultural technology and business practices and assess their impact on the West.

COMPETENCY GOAL 5 Becoming an Industrial Society (1877–1900) The learner will describe innovations in technology and business practices and assess their impact on economic, political, and social life in America.

OBJECTIVES

5.01 Evaluate the influence of immigration and rapid industrialization on urban life.

5.02 Explain how business and industrial leaders accumulated wealth and wielded political and economic power.

5.03 Assess the impact of labor unions on industry and the lives of workers.

5.04 Describe the changing role of government in economic and political affairs.

COMPETENCY GOAL 6 The Emergence of the United States in World Affairs (1890–1914) The learner will analyze causes and effects of the United States emergence as a world power.

OBJECTIVES

6.01 Examine the factors that led to the United States taking an increasingly active role in world affairs.

6.02 Identify the areas of United States military, economic, and political involvement and influence.

6.03 Describe how the policies and actions of the United States government impacted the affairs of other countries.

COMPETENCY GOAL 7 The Progressive Movement in the United States (1890–1914) The learner will analyze the economic, political, and social reforms of the Progressive Period.

OBJECTIVES

7.01 Explain the conditions that led to the rise of Progressivism.

7.02 Analyze how different groups of Americans made economic and political gains in the Progressive Period.

7.03 Evaluate the effects of racial segregation on different regions and segments of the United States' society.

7.04 Examine the impact of technological changes on economic, social, and cultural life in the United States.

COMPETENCY GOAL 8 The Great War and Its Aftermath (1914–1930) The learner will analyze United States involvement in World War I and the war's influence on international affairs during the 1920's.

OBJECTIVES

8.01 Examine the reasons why the United States remained neutral at the beginning of World War I but later became involved.

8.02 Identify political and military turning points of the war and determine their significance to the outcome of the conflict.

8.03 Assess the political, economic, social, and cultural effects of the war on the United States and other nations.

COMPETENCY GOAL 9 **Prosperity and Depression (1919–1939)** The learner will appraise the economic, social, and political changes of the decades of "The Twenties" and "The Thirties."

OBJECTIVES

9.01 Elaborate on the cycle of economic boom and bust in the 1920's and 1930's.

9.02 Analyze the extent of prosperity for different segments of society during this period.

9.03 Analyze the significance of social, intellectual, and technological changes of lifestyles in the United States.

9.04 Describe challenges to traditional practices in religion, race, and gender.

9.05 Assess the impact of New Deal reforms in enlarging the role of the federal government in American life.

 COMPETENCY GOAL 10 **World War II and the Beginning of the Cold War (1930s–1963)** The learner will analyze United States involvement in World War II and the war's influence on international affairs in following decades.

OBJECTIVES

10.01 Elaborate on the causes of World War II and reasons for United States entry into the war.

10.02 Identify military, political, and diplomatic turning points of the war and determine their significance to the outcome and aftermath of the conflict.

10.03 Describe and analyze the effects of the war on American economic, social, political, and cultural life.

10.04 Elaborate on changes in the direction of foreign policy related to the beginnings of the Cold War.

10.05 Assess the role of organizations established to maintain peace and examine their continuing effectiveness.

COMPETENCY GOAL 11 Recovery, Prosperity, and Turmoil (1945–1980)
The learner will trace economic, political, and social developments and assess their significance for the lives of Americans during this time period.

OBJECTIVES

11.01 Describe the effects of the Cold War on economic, political, and social life in America.

11.02 Trace major events of the Civil Rights Movement and evaluate its impact.

11.03 Identify major social movements including, but not limited to, those involving women, young people, and the environment, and evaluate the impact of these movements on the United States' society.

11.04 Identify the causes of United States' involvement in Vietnam and examine how this involvement affected society.

11.05 Examine the impact of technological innovations that have impacted American life.

11.06 Identify political events and the actions and reactions of the government officials and citizens, and assess the social and political consequences.

COMPETENCY GOAL 12 The United States since the Vietnam War (1973–present)
The learner will identify and analyze trends in domestic and foreign affairs of the United States during this time period.

OBJECTIVES

12.01 Summarize significant events in foreign policy since the Vietnam War.

12.02 Evaluate the impact of recent constitutional amendments, court rulings, and federal legislation on United States' citizens.

12.03 Identify and assess the impact of economic, technological, and environmental changes in the United States.

12.04 Identify and assess the impact of social, political, and cultural changes in the United States.

12.05 Assess the impact of growing racial and ethnic diversity in American society.

12.06 Assess the impact of twenty-first century terrorist activity on American society.

Countdown to Testing

How does Holt *American Anthem, North Carolina Edition,* help me practice the state goals and objectives?

Holt *American Anthem, North Carolina Edition,* provides complete coverage of the North Carolina Goals and Objectives for Eleventh Grade United States History. To learn and practice the standards, use your textbook's at-home practice tests for each week.

How can I use the Countdown to Testing tests?

- Each week has a practice test. You will see that each week's test focuses on one of the Competency Goals from the North Carolina Standard Course of Study.

- As you study the book with your class, ask yourself the questions on the practice test.

> There are 24 weeks of practice questions. Each week has one question for each weekday.

- There is one question for each day of the week. Each of these questions addresses one of the Objectives under that week's Competency Goal. By the time you finish the week, you will have answered questions related to all Objectives.

- If you have trouble answering the question, refer to the chapter and section listed at the end of each question to find the information.

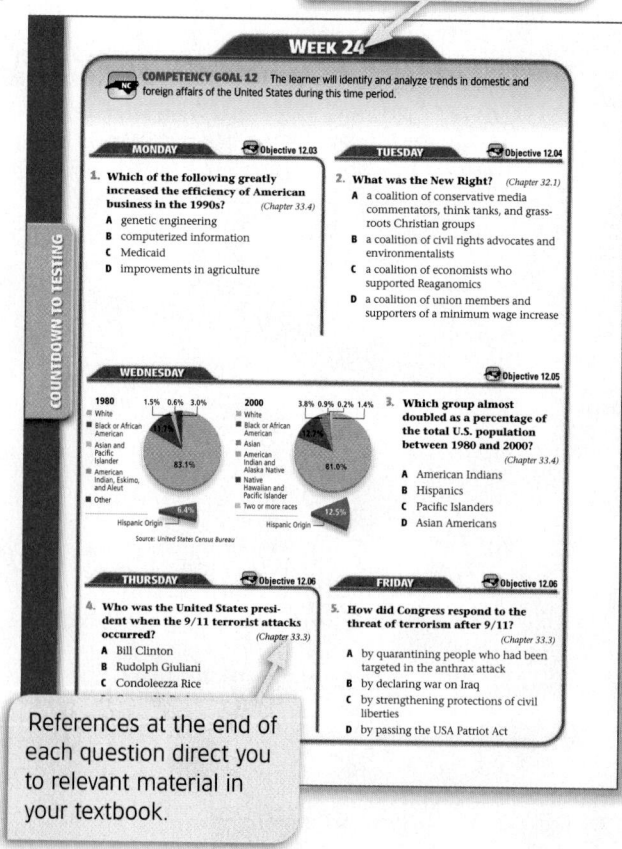

> References at the end of each question direct you to relevant material in your textbook.

WEEK 1

 COMPETENCY GOAL 1 The learner will identify, investigate, and assess the effectiveness of the institutions of the emerging republic.

1. **Which of the following best describes the type of government envisioned by the Federalists?** *(Chapter 5.3)*

   A a smaller central government with a good deal of power left to the states

   B a smaller central government, more urban than rural

   Ⓒ a strong central government with broad powers

   D a strong centralized government based on prospering farms

2. **Which of the following actions was *not* part of Alexander Hamilton's economic plan?** *(Chapter 6.1)*

   A create a national bank

   Ⓑ make individual states pay for their Revolutionary War debt

   C pass the Tariff of 1789 to raise money to pay the national debt

   D create a national mint

3. **What was the significance of President Washington's actions during the Whiskey Rebellion?** *(Chapter 6.1)*

   Ⓐ He showed that armed rebellion against the national government would not be tolerated.

   B He showed his support for rebel farmers who opposed the excise tax on whiskey.

   C He signed the bill to charter the first Bank of the United States.

   D He asked Congress to repeal the excise tax on whiskey.

4. **What was the significance of *Marbury v. Madison*?** *(Chapter 6.3)*

   A It upheld the president's power to appoint judges.

   B It led to the formation of new positions in the judiciary branch.

   Ⓒ It established the Supreme Court's right to declare a law unconstitutional.

   D It established the Supreme Court's right to refuse presidential appointments.

5. **Which statement best describes the political status of Native Americans prior to 1820?** *(Chapter 6.2)*

   A Native Americans did not believe they were affected by U.S. government decisions.

   B Native Americans supported the U.S. expansion west of the Mississippi River.

   C Native Americans refused to sign treaties because of different views on land ownership.

   Ⓓ Native Americans were denied U.S. citizenship.

COMPETENCY GOAL 1 The learner will identify, investigate, and assess the effectiveness of the institutions of the emerging republic.

MONDAY  Objective 1.02

1. The large-scale production of cotton made possible by the cotton gin led to which of the following? *(Chapter 7.4)*

A greater political freedoms for enslaved African Americans

B increased cotton production in the South

C an increase in demand for slave labor

D greater use of labor-saving devices in the South

TUESDAY  Objective 1.03

2. The XYZ Affair nearly led to war between the United States and what other country? *(Chapter 6.2)*

A France

B Great Britain

C Spain

D Canada

WEDNESDAY  Objective 1.03

3. Which of the following was a cause of the War of 1812? *(Chapter 6.4)*

A British impressments of American sailors

B the Battle of New Orleans

C French military aid to Native Americans in the Northwest Territory

D the British invasion of Washington, D.C.

THURSDAY  Objective 1.03

4. Which of the following settled border disputes between the United States and Spain? *(Chapter 6.2)*

A Jay's Treaty

B Pinckney's Treaty

C Neutrality Proclamation

D President Washington's Farewell Address

FRIDAY  Objective 1.03

5. What country or region did the United States make several unsuccessful attempts to invade during the War of 1812? *(Chapter 6.4)*

A Spanish Florida

B Great Britain

C Canada

D France

WEEK 3

 COMPETENCY GOAL 2 The learner will assess the competing forces of expansionism, nationalism, and sectionalism.

MONDAY  Objective 2.01

1. **What was a result of Andrew Jackson's Native American policy in the 1830s?** *(Chapter 7.2)*

   A Creation of an independent Cherokee state.

   (B) Forced removal of thousands of Native Americans.

   C A war that destroyed most of the Native American population east of the Mississippi.

   D New treaties guaranteeing mutual respect and cooperation between Native Americans and the United States.

TUESDAY  Objective 2.02

2. **What name was given to a group of painters whose work reflected pride in the grandeur of the American landscape?** *(Chapter 7.1)*

   A the Thames River school

   B the American Wilderness school

   C the Nationalistic school

   (D) the Hudson River school

WEDNESDAY  Objective 2.03

3. **Which of the following best describes the Industrial Revolution?** *(Chapter 7.3)*

   (A) It began in Great Britain and spread to the United States, where its impact was greatest in the North.

   B It began in Great Britain and spread to the United States, where its impact was greatest in the South.

   C It began in the United States and spread to Great Britain.

   D It began in Great Britain and was limited to the textile industry.

THURSDAY  Objective 2.03

4. **Which of the following led to sectionalism?** *(Chapter 7.3 and Chapter 7.4)*

   A the Monroe Doctrine

   B the invention of the telegraph

   (C) the economic differences between the primarily industrial North and the primarily agricultural South

   D the switch from long-staple cotton to short-staple cotton

FRIDAY  Objective 2.04

5. **In what Andrew Jackson and his supporters called a "corrupt bargain," John Quincy Adams became president and Henry Clay took what office?** *(Chapter 7.2)*

   A vice president

   (B) secretary of state

   C chief justice of the United States

   D secretary of the treasury

WEEK 4

 COMPETENCY GOAL 2 The learner will assess the competing forces of expansionism, nationalism, and sectionalism.

MONDAY
 Objective 2.04

1. How was South Carolina's nullification crisis finally resolved? *(Chapter 7.2)*

A Andrew Jackson used military force to collect the tariff in South Carolina.

B South Carolina seceded, and the tariff was not collected in that state.

C Henry Clay worked out a compromise in which tariffs would be reduced over a period of 10 years.

D Congress repealed the tariff.

TUESDAY
 Objective 2.05

2. What was one accomplishment of the women's rights movement during the Reform Era? *(Chapter 8.3)*

A Dorothea Dix convinced states to create institutions to house and treat people with mental illnesses.

B Horace Mann improved the nation's system of education.

C Henry David Thoreau wrote "Civil Disobedience."

D Elizabeth Cady Stanton and Lucretia Mott organized the Seneca Falls Convention.

WEDNESDAY
 Objective 2.05

3. Which reform movement in the United States in the mid-1800s helped to inspire the women's rights movement? *(Chapter 8.4)*

A the abolitionist movement

B the education reform movement

C the temperance movement

D the transcendentalist movement

THURSDAY
 Objective 2.06

4. How did William Lloyd Garrison spread his message calling for an immediate abolition of slavery? *(Chapter 8.4)*

A He published his autobiography.

B He published an abolitionist newspaper called *The Liberator.*

C He published an abolitionist newspaper called the *North Star.*

D He published an abolitionist newspaper called *The Emancipator.*

FRIDAY
 Objective 2.06

5. What reform movement was most aided by the religious movement known as the Second Great Awakening? *(Chapter 8.1)*

A the women's rights movement

B the abolitionist movement

C the common-school movement

D the anti-immigration movement

WEEK 5

COMPETENCY GOAL 3 The learner will analyze the issues that led to the Civil War, the effects of the war, and the impact of Reconstruction on the nation.

MONDAY  Objective 3.01

1. **What significant social effect did the Kansas-Nebraska Act have on settlement in those territories?** *(Chapter 10.1)*

   A It caused a rapid decline in settlement.

   B It contributed to a rapid growth in urbanization.

   C It established a precedent for deciding the slavery issue peaceably by ballot.

   (D) It led to violence between competing waves of pro-slavery and Free-Soil settlers.

TUESDAY  Objective 3.01

2. **Which of the following people led a raid on the U.S. arsenal at Harpers Ferry with the intention of starting a slave revolt?** *(Chapter 10.2)*

   A Dred Scott

   (B) John Brown

   C Preston Brooks

   D Stephen Douglas

WEDNESDAY

Objective 3.02

3. **The national split caused by Abraham Lincoln's election led to which of the following?** *(Chapter 10.3)*

   A Fugitive Slave Law

   B call for a new election

   C formation of the Republican Party

   (D) secession of southern states

Candidate	Political Affiliation	Electoral Votes	Popular Votes
Abraham Lincoln	Republican	180	1,866,452
Stephen A. Douglas	Northern Democratic	12	1,375,157
John C. Breckinridge	Southern Democratic	72	847,953
John Bell	Constitutional Union	39	590,631

THURSDAY  Objective 3.02

4. **Which of these events marked the beginning of the Civil War?** *(Chapter 11.1)*

   A the inauguration of Abraham Lincoln

   B the secession of South Carolina

   (C) the firing of Confederate guns on Fort Sumter in Charleston Harbor

   D the announcement of the Supreme Court's ruling in *Scott* v. *Sandford*

FRIDAY  Objective 3.03

5. **Why was the surrender of Vicksburg a turning point in the Civil War?** *(Chapter 11.4)*

   (A) It gave the Union control of the Mississippi River and split the Confederacy from east to west.

   B It marked the surrender of the Confederate capital to Union forces.

   C It was the largest battle ever fought in North America.

   D It gave the Union control of Atlanta.

WEEK 6

COMPETENCY GOAL 3 The learner will analyze the issues that led to the Civil War, the effects of the war, and the impact of Reconstruction on the nation.

1. What was the purpose of Lincoln's Gettysburg Address? *(Chapter 11.4)*

(A) to remind Americans of the reasons that the Civil War was being fought

B to congratulate the Union forces for their victory at Gettysburg

C to free slaves in all areas that were in rebellion against the United States

D to announce the passage of the Thirteenth Amendment

2. Why did southern states pass Black Codes? *(Chapter 12.2)*

(A) to segregate black people from white people

B to give freedmen basic rights

C to force freedmen to work as cheap labor on plantations

D to restore slavery

3. Hiram Revels was the first African American to hold which post? *(Chapter 12.3)*

A secretary of state

(B) U.S. senator

C U.S. House representative

D Supreme Court justice

4. What happened after the presidential election of 1876? *(Chapter 12.4)*

A Democrats threatened war if Hayes did not win the disputed votes.

(B) The Compromise of 1877 helped settle the dispute.

C Republicans were found guilty of voter fraud.

D A new era of Reconstruction began.

Amendment	Function
Thirteenth	banned slavery
Fourteenth	granted "equal protection"
Fifteenth	extended voting rights

5. According to the table, which amendment granted suffrage rights to African American males? *(Chapter 12.2)*

A the Thirteenth Amendment

B the Fourteenth Amendment

(C) the Fifteenth Amendment

D a combination of all three

COUNTDOWN TO TESTING

WEEK 7

MONDAY  Objective 4.01

1. **What region of the United States did most white settlers of the West come from?** *(Chapter 13.3)*

   A New England

   B states along the East Coast

   Ⓒ the Mississippi Valley

   D lands bordering Mexico

TUESDAY  Objective 4.01

2. **Which group of settlers faced discriminatory laws regarding land ownership?** *(Chapter 13.3)*

   A white settlers

   Ⓑ Chinese immigrants

   C African Americans

   D Scandinavians

WEDNESDAY  Objective 4.01

3. **Which of the following was a problem that settlers in the West faced?**

   (Chapter 13.3)

   Ⓐ lack of wood for construction

   B desert climate

   C plentiful land for farming

   D competition from Native Americans

THURSDAY  Objective 4.02

4. **Which of the following best defines the term *Americanization*?** *(Chapter 13.1)*

   A making Native American practices understandable to white people

   Ⓑ requiring Native Americans to adopt the culture of white people

   C creating conflicts that led to passage of the Dawes Act

   D persuading Native Americans to be U.S. citizens

FRIDAY  Objective 4.02

5. **Which of the following best completes the graphic organizer?** *(Chapter 13.1)*

   Ⓐ disease

   B drought

   C prairie fires

   D blizzards

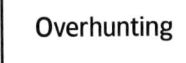

Overhunting → As few as 25 buffalo survive.

? → As few as 25 buffalo survive.

COMPETENCY GOAL 4 The learner will evaluate the great westward movement and assess the impact of the agricultural revolution on the nation.

MONDAY  Objective 4.03

1. **Why were many farmers in debt in the late 1800s?** *(Chapter 15.3)*

   A They had to pay very high taxes.

   (B) They borrowed money to purchase new machinery.

   C They spent too much money on luxury items they did not need.

   D They did not produce enough goods to meet demand and make high profits.

TUESDAY  Objective 4.03

2. **Which of the following Populist Party demands was adopted by the Democratic Party in 1896?** *(Chapter 15.3)*

   A an income tax

   B the eight-hour workday

   (C) unlimited coinage of silver

   D government ownership of railroads

WEDNESDAY  Objective 4.03

3. **Which of the following best describes the influence of the Populist Party on American politics?** *(Chapter 15.3)*

   A proving that a third-party presidential candidate can win office

   B uniting people of different races

   C requiring political candidates to be members of a political machine

   (D) crafting political messages that appealed to ordinary people

THURSDAY  Objective 4.04

4. **How did the combine harvester change farming?** *(Chapter 13.3)*

   (A) It made harvesting wheat more efficient.

   B It reduced farmers' debts.

   C It reduced the time needed to harvest corn.

   D It increased the size of the harvest.

FRIDAY  Objective 4.04

5. **What effect did new technologies have on small farmers?** *(Chapter 15.3)*

   A New technologies always increased farmers' profits.

   (B) New technologies often increased farmers' debt.

   C New technologies were too difficult to use.

   D New technologies did little to change farming practices.

WEEK 9

MONDAY  Objective 5.01

1. **What social function did settlement houses serve?** *(Chapter 15.2)*

   A They were centers for nativist organizations.

   B They collected dues every month from members.

   C They helped immigrants assimilate.

   D They were immigration inspection stations.

TUESDAY  Objective 5.01

2. **Changes in urban life in the late 1800s led to the development of which of the following?** *(Chapter 15.2)*

   A the field of urban planning

   B laws that limited building occupancy

   C bans on buildings over a certain height

   D new restrictions on immigration

WEDNESDAY  Objective 5.02

3. **How did Cornelius Vanderbilt make his vast fortune?** *(Chapter 14.2)*

   A in the steel industry

   B in the oil industry

   C in the railroad industry

   D in politics

THURSDAY  Objective 5.02

4. **How did Andrew Carnegie make U.S. Steel the dominant company in the steel industry?** *(Chapter 14.2)*

   A He practiced horizontal integration.

   B He gave millions to charity.

   C He increased his workers' wages.

   D He practiced vertical integration.

FRIDAY  Objective 5.03

5. **Which of the following statements about the National Labor Union is true?** *(Chapter 14.3)*

   A It called for higher wages.

   B It worked closely with industry leaders.

   C It achieved all its goals.

   D It pushed for an eight-hour workday but was not successful.

COMPETENCY GOAL 5 The learner will describe innovations in technology and business practices and assess their impact on economic, political, and social life in America.

MONDAY  Objective 5.03

1. **What strategy did the Knights of Labor use in pursuing its goals?**
(Chapter 14.3)

   A partnerships with government

   B frequent use of strikes

   (C) negotiations with employers

   D threats of violence

TUESDAY  Objective 5.03

2. **How was the Knights of Labor different from other labor unions?**
(Chapter 14.3)

   A The Knights accepted men only.

   B The Knights limited membership to the workers in the steel industry.

   (C) The Knights accepted unskilled laborers.

   D The Knights denied membership to African Americans.

WEDNESDAY  Objective 5.04

3. **What was the goal of the Sherman Antitrust Act?** *(Chapter 14.3)*

   A to help businesses grow in size

   (B) to stop trusts from unfairly limiting competition

   C to prevent competitors from challenging monopolies

   D to provide politicians with new sources of campaign contributions

THURSDAY  Objective 5.04

4. **In what way was the Sherman Antitrust Act flawed?** *(Chapter 14.3)*

   A It required federal officials to pay court costs if the trusts won their lawsuits.

   B It required monopolies to voluntarily end unfair competition.

   (C) It was vaguely written.

   D Congress never approved the act.

FRIDAY  Objective 5.04

5. **What did the Interstate Commerce Act allow the federal government to do?** *(Chapter 15.3)*

   (A) regulate interstate railroads

   B purchase and own railroads

   C build new transportation networks with taxpayer dollars

   D end regulation of commerce

COMPETENCY GOAL 6 The learner will analyze causes and effects of the United States emergence as a world power.

MONDAY  Objective 6.01

1. **What motivated industrial nations to claim territories abroad in the 1800s?**
(Chapter 17.1)

A an interest in learning about other nations' economic theories

B curiosity about other religions

C desire for new markets and naval bases

D a need for unpolluted vacation areas

TUESDAY  Objective 6.01

2. **What military justification was used to promote territorial expansion?**
(Chapter 17.1)

A the need for raw materials to produce gunpowder

B a shortage of people willing to serve as soldiers

C the need for workers able to construct large ships

D a desire for naval bases

WEDNESDAY  Objective 6.01

3. **What popular ideology contributed to imperialism?** *(Chapter 17.1)*

A a spirit of international cooperation

B a belief in transcendentalism

C a commitment to the rights of organized labor

D a feeling of cultural superiority

THURSDAY  Objective 6.02

4. **How did the United States exert influence on Japan?** *(Chapter 17.1)*

A by holding the Edo Bay summit

B by siding with Russia in the Russo-Japanese War

C by agreeing not to expand into the Pacific

D by carrying out impressive displays of naval power

FRIDAY  Objective 6.02

5. **Theodore Roosevelt wanted to build the Panama Canal to shorten travel time between what two points?**
(Chapter 17.3)

A Panama and Colombia

B the Atlantic Ocean and the Gulf of Mexico

C the Atlantic and Pacific oceans

D the Atlantic Ocean and the West Indies

COMPETENCY GOAL 6   The learner will analyze causes and effects of the United States emergence as a world power.

MONDAY  Objective 6.02

1. After the Spanish-American War, controversy arose over U.S. annexation of which of the following territories?

(Chapter 17.2)

A Cuba

B Puerto Rico

C Samoa

Ⓓ the Philippines

TUESDAY  Objective 6.03

2. Which of the following was granted to Puerto Ricans as the result of a 1917 law?   *(Chapter 17.3)*

A self-rule

Ⓑ U.S. citizenship

C control over interstate trade

D the power to regulate immigration

WEDNESDAY  Objective 6.03

3. What term describes the U.S. practice of using economic power to achieve foreign policy goals?   *(Chapter 17.3)*

A the Open Door Policy

B the Roosevelt Corollary

C laissez-faire

Ⓓ dollar diplomacy

THURSDAY Objective 6.03

4. What is one reason that the Platt Amendment was significant?

(Chapter 17.3)

Ⓐ It led to the establishment of a U.S. naval base at Guantánamo Bay.

B It achieved annexation of Cuba.

C It revoked the right of the United States to intervene in Cuban affairs.

D It allowed for the eradication of yellow fever in Cuba.

FRIDAY  Objective 6.03

5. How did the United States respond to the Boxer Rebellion?   *(Chapter 17.1)*

A It removed its troops from China.

B It abandoned the Open Door Policy.

Ⓒ It sent troops to suppress the rebellion.

D It sent troops to support the rebellion.

COMPETENCY GOAL 7 The learner will analyze the economic, political, and social reforms of the Progressive Period.

MONDAY  Objective 7.01

1. **Which of the following groups laid the foundation of the Progressive movement?** *(Chapter 16.1)*

   A politicians

   (B) muckrakers

   C Civil War veterans

   D Redeemers

TUESDAY  Objective 7.01

2. **The novel *The Jungle* revealed unsafe working conditions in which of the following industries?** *(Chapter 16.1)*

   A railroad industry

   (B) meatpacking industry

   C mining industry

   D housing industry

WEDNESDAY  Objective 7.02

3. **Women suffragists achieved a final victory with the ratification of which of the following?** *(Chapter 16.4)*

   A the NAWSA

   (B) the Nineteenth Amendment

   C the Constitution

   D the Suffrage Act

THURSDAY  Objective 7.02

4. **Soon after he took office as president, Theodore Roosevelt intervened in which of the following movements?** *(Chapter 16.3)*

   A prohibition

   B suffrage

   C nativist

   (D) labor

FRIDAY  Objective 7.02

5. **For what did the Sixteenth Amendment provide?** *(Chapter 16.4)*

   (A) an income tax

   B women's suffrage

   C direct election of senators

   D prohibition of alcohol

COMPETENCY GOAL 7 The learner will analyze the economic, political, and social reforms of the Progressive Period.

MONDAY  Objective 7.03

1. What did Jim Crow laws require?
(Chapter 15.4)

(A) racial segregation
B equal treatment of African Americans
C equal access to education for all citizens
D payment of a fee before voting

TUESDAY  Objective 7.03

2. What effect did the poll tax have on African American voting? *(Chapter 15.4)*

A It increased the number of African American voters.
(B) It prevented many African Americans from voting.
C It had no effect on voting.
D It allowed poor African Americans to vote in larger numbers.

WEDNESDAY  Objective 7.03

3. Which of the following best completes the graphic organizer? *(Chapter 15.4)*

A organize protest marches
B migrate to Africa
(C) focus on practical skills for self-sufficiency
D organize voter registration drives

African American Activism
W. E. B. Du Bois: protest against discrimination
National Association of Colored Women: struggle against lynching and segregation
Booker T. Washington: ?

THURSDAY  Objective 7.04

4. What impact did automobiles have in the late 19th century? *(Chapter 14.4)*

(A) They had little effect because they were seen as toys for the wealthy.
B They changed the shape of the city.
C They reduced traffic on city roads.
D They reduced the cost of mass transit.

FRIDAY  Objective 7.04

5. What group benefited from the use of the typewriter in the workplace? *(Chapter 14.4)*

(A) women
B immigrants from eastern Europe
C unskilled laborers
D migrants who moved to the North from the South

COMPETENCY GOAL 8 The learner will analyze United States involvement in World War I and the war's influence on international affairs during the 1920s.

MONDAY  Objective 8.01

1. **What was the official position of the United States when war broke out in Europe in 1914?** *(Chapter 18.2)*

   A The United States supported the Allied Powers.

   (B) The United States declared its neutrality.

   C The United States abandoned its policy of isolationism.

   D The United States supported the Central Powers.

TUESDAY  Objective 8.01

2. **What was the name of the German pledge not to sink merchant ships without warning?** *(Chapter 18.2)*

   A the *Lusitania* promise

   B the Zimmermann Note

   C the U-boat pledge

   (D) the *Sussex* pledge

WEDNESDAY  Objective 8.01

3. **Which of the following events prompted the United States to enter World War I against Germany?** *(Chapter 18.2)*

   A Germany forced the Russian czar to give up his throne.

   (B) Germany violated U.S. neutrality by sinking three U.S. merchant ships.

   C Germany invaded the neutral country of Belgium.

   D Germany attacked and sank the British luxury ship *Lusitania*.

THURSDAY  Objective 8.02

4. **What slogan captures Wilson's position in the 1916 election?** *(Chapter 18.2)*

   A "Defeat the Germans"

   B "Fight for Freedom"

   (C) "Peace without Victory"

   D "War Is Evil"

FRIDAY 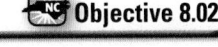 Objective 8.02

5. **How did the Russian Revolution affect events in World War I?** *(Chapter 18.2)*

   A Russia's declaration of war on capitalism prolonged the conflict.

   (B) Russia's peace treaty with Germany allowed the Germans to concentrate on the Western Front.

   C Fearful of a German victory, the new Russian government doubled the number of troops in combat.

   D Russia allied with Germany, which made an Allied victory more difficult to achieve.

WEEK 16

 COMPETENCY GOAL 8 The learner will analyze United States involvement in World War I and the war's influence on international affairs during the 1920s.

MONDAY  **Objective 8.02**

1. **Which of the following best describes the modernization of warfare during World War I?** *(Chapter 18.1)*
   - **A** the use of swords and bayonets
   - **B** the use of bright red uniforms and brass helmets
   - **(C)** the use of machine guns, poisonous gas, and airplanes
   - **D** the introduction of trench warfare

TUESDAY  **Objective 8.02**

2. **What battle cost the French 250,000 lives but was successful in stopping the German advance into France?** *(Chapter 18.1)*
   - **(A)** the First Battle of the Marne
   - **B** the Battle of the Somme
   - **C** the Battle at Belleau Wood
   - **D** Chateau-Thierry

WEDNESDAY  **Objective 8.03**

3. **What was an important political outcome of World War I?** *(Chapter 18.4)*
   - **A** The Bolsheviks were overthrown in Russia.
   - **B** The war resolved territorial disputes and restored pre-war boundaries in Europe.
   - **(C)** The war led to the overthrow of monarchies across Europe.
   - **D** The war resolved tensions over colonialism in the Middle East and Southeast Asia.

THURSDAY  **Objective 8.03**

4. **Which nation emerged as the world's leading economic power at the war's end?** *(Chapter 18.4)*
   - **A** France
   - **B** Great Britain
   - **(C)** the United States
   - **D** Russia

FRIDAY  **Objective 8.03**

5. **What activity did the Sedition Act prohibit?** *(Chapter 18.3)*
   - **A** giving aid or comfort to the enemy
   - **B** refusing military duty
   - **C** questioning the loyalty of German Americans
   - **(D)** criticizing the government or the military

COUNTDOWN TO TESTING

WEEK 17

 COMPETENCY GOAL 9 The learner will appraise the economic, social, and political changes of the decades of "The Twenties" and "The Thirties."

MONDAY — Objective 9.01

1. **Who revolutionized manufacturing in the United States?** *(Chapter 19.2)*
   A Warren G. Harding
   B Henry Ford
   C Carl Sandburg
   D A. Mitchell Palmer

TUESDAY — Objective 9.01

2. **What is the practice of buying stocks with loans called?** *(Chapter 21.1)*
   A installment plans
   B tariff purchases
   C buying on margin
   D bank runs

WEDNESDAY — Objective 9.02

3. **What business practice helped Americans purchase consumer goods in the 1920s?** *(Chapter 19.2)*
   A the barter system
   B name-brand recognition
   C installment buying
   D delayed gratification

THURSDAY — Objective 9.02

4. **How did the foreclosures of the 1930s change American life?** *(Chapter 21.2)*
   A Americans built shanty neighborhoods in many areas.
   B Americans hunkered down and stayed in one place.
   C Americans took jobs with the railroads.
   D More Americans became farmers.

FRIDAY — Objective 9.03

5. **What was one way the radio helped create a common culture in the United States?** *(Chapter 20.3)*
   A The radio moved from being a novelty to a luxury item only the wealthy could afford.
   B Good programming could be taken for granted across the country.
   C Mass production of radios created a market for vacuum tubes.
   D Radio broke down barriers that separated rural and urban populations.

WEEK 18

 COMPETENCY GOAL 9 The learner will appraise the economic, social, and political changes of the decades of "The Twenties" and "The Thirties."

MONDAY
 **Objective 9.03**

1. **What development occurred as a consequence of Prohibition?** *(Chapter 20.1)*

   A the Great Migration

   B American entry into World War I

   C fundamentalism

   (D) the rise of organized crime

TUESDAY
 **Objective 9.04**

2. **What are beliefs based on a literal interpretation of the Bible called?**
   (Chapter 20.1)

   (A) fundamentalism

   B evolution

   C urbanization

   D values

WEDNESDAY
 **Objective 9.04**

3. **What was the movement of African Americans from the South to the North called?** *(Chapter 20.2)*

   A the Harlem Renaissance

   B the Black Star Line

   (C) the Great Migration

   D the Underground Railroad

THURSDAY
 **Objective 9.05**

4. **What was one effect of the New Deal?**
   (Chapter 22.4)

   A The New Deal established a passive role for government.

   (B) The New Deal established a more active role for government.

   C The New Deal promoted dependence on the government.

   D The New Deal destroyed the system of checks and balances.

FRIDAY
 **Objective 9.05**

5. **Which agency restored public confidence in the banking system?**
   (Chapter 22.1)

   A Social Security Administration

   B Works Progress Administration

   (C) Federal Deposit Insurance Corporation

   D Civilian Conservation Corps

COMPETENCY GOAL 10 The learner will analyze United States involvement in World War II and the war's influence on international affairs in following decades.

MONDAY  Objective 10.01

1. **What country did Germany invade in September 1939?** *(Chapter 23.2)*

   A Belgium

   B Poland

   C the Soviet Union

   D France

TUESDAY  Objective 10.01

2. **How did the United States respond to the attack on Pearl Harbor?** *(Chapter 23.3)*

   A It declared war on Japan.

   B It asked Japan to pay for the costs of damage to Pearl Harbor.

   C It asked for negotiations with Japan.

   D It attacked Germany.

WEDNESDAY  Objective 10.02

3. **Why was the Battle of Midway a turning point in the war in the Pacific?** *(Chapter 24.3)*

   A It led to victory at D-Day.

   B It devastated American morale.

   C It changed the balance of power in the Pacific.

   D It was the first Allied victory in World War II.

THURSDAY  Objective 10.02

4. **Which Allied victory in the Pacific cost 12,000 American lives?** *(Chapter 24.3)*

   A Battle of Okinawa

   B Battle of the Bulge

   C Battle of Iwo Jima

   D Guadalcanal

FRIDAY  Objective 10.03

5. **What effect did World War II have on the American economy?** *(Chapter 23.4)*

   A The war had no direct effect on the American economy.

   B The war worsened the Great Depression because resources were diverted that could have been used to raise the standard of living.

   C The war created millions of jobs by sparking economic growth and ending the Great Depression.

   D World War II led to some economic growth but did not solve the problem of unemployment.

COMPETENCY GOAL 10 The learner will analyze United States involvement in World War II and the war's influence on international affairs in following decades.

MONDAY  Objective 10.03

1. What factor determined if a person was relocated to an internment camp? *(Chapter 24.4)*

A the individual's citizenship status

B the person's criminal record

C evidence of sabotage or espionage

(D) a person's racial background

TUESDAY  Objective 10.04

2. What was the policy of preventing the spread of communism called? *(Chapter 25.1)*

A Iron Curtain

(B) containment

C International Monetary Fund

D General Agreement on Tariffs and Trade

WEDNESDAY  Objective 10.04

3. Why did the United States and Britain begin the Berlin airlift? *(Chapter 25.1)*

A to prevent Germany from becoming Communist

B to rescue Allied troops trapped in Berlin

(C) to prevent all of Berlin from becoming Communist

D to implement the Marshall Plan

THURSDAY  Objective 10.05

4. What is one goal of the United Nations? *(Chapter 25.2)*

A to promote the U.S. policy of containing communism

B to provide a minimum income to people around the globe

(C) to preserve peace and provide security

D to help its members acquire territory

FRIDAY  Objective 10.05

5. Which of the following was one of the UN's first efforts to fulfill its mission? *(Chapter 25.2)*

A creation of the Peace Corps

B founding of the World Bank

(C) adoption of the Universal Declaration of Human Rights

D intervention in Greece

WEEK 21

COMPETENCY GOAL 11 The learner will trace economic, political, and social developments and assess their significance for the lives of Americans during this period.

MONDAY  Objective 11.01

1. **What did HUAC investigate in the 1950s?** *(Chapter 25.3)*

   (A) domestic Communist threats

   B the possibility of creating a worldwide currency

   C Chiang Kai-shek's government

   D President Truman's firing of General Douglas MacArthur

TUESDAY  Objective 11.02

2. **What did the U.S. Supreme Court rule in the case of *Brown v. Board of Education of Topeka, Kansas?*** *(Chapter 28.1)*

   A All racial segregation was unconstitutional.

   B Racial segregation was constitutional.

   (C) Racial segregation in public schools was unconstitutional.

   D Segregation was an issue for the state courts.

WEDNESDAY  Objective 11.02

"I have a dream that one day this nation will rise up and live out the true meaning of its creed: 'We hold these truths to be self-evident; that all men are created equal.' . . . I have a dream that my four little children will one day live in a nation where they will not be judged by the color of their skin, but by the content of their character. I have a dream today!"
—Martin Luther King Jr., August 28, 1963

3. **During what event in 1963 did Martin Luther King Jr. give this speech?** *(Chapter 28.2)*

   A Selma march

   B Freedom Rides

   (C) March on Washington

   D Birmingham campaign

THURSDAY  Objective 11.03

4. **The American Indian Movement called for which of the following?** *(Chapter 30.1)*

   A financial aid for Indian children

   (B) better education for Indian children

   C giving white foster parents preference over Native American foster parents

   D passage of the Equal Rights Amendment

FRIDAY 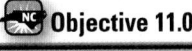 Objective 11.03

5. **Who wrote *The Feminine Mystique?*** *(Chapter 30.1)*

   A Phyllis Schlafly

   B Shirley Chisholm

   C Gloria Steinem

   (D) Betty Friedan

COMPETENCY GOAL 11 The learner will trace economic, political, and social developments and assess their significance for the lives of Americans during this period.

MONDAY  Objective 11.04

1. **What did President Eisenhower call the belief that if one nation fell to communism, its neighbors would also fall to communism?** *(Chapter 29.1)*

   A containment

   Ⓑ the domino theory

   C pacification

   D the Geneva Accords

TUESDAY  Objective 11.04

2. **Which of the following was most influential in changing U.S. public opinion on the Vietnam War?** *(Chapter 29.2)*

   A student protests

   B military defeats

   C police response to antiwar protests

   Ⓓ media coverage of the war

WEDNESDAY  Objective 11.05

3. **Which statement best completes the graphic organizer?** *(Chapter 26.2)*

   Ⓐ NASA is established.

   B The United States abandons its efforts to put a human on the moon.

   C The United States tests the first hydrogen bomb.

   D The United States calls for a ban on the development of satellites.

Responding to *Sputnik*

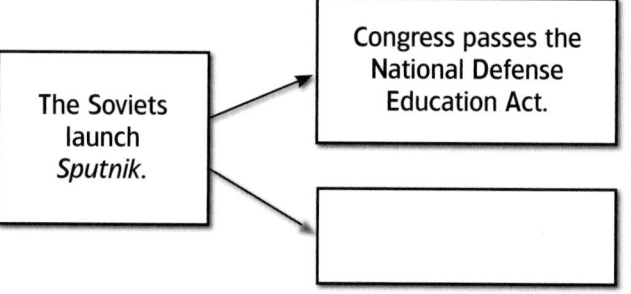

The Soviets launch *Sputnik*.

→ Congress passes the National Defense Education Act.

THURSDAY  Objective 11.05

4. **Why were computers not marketed for home use in the 1950s?** *(Chapter 26.2)*

   A They had yet to be invented.

   Ⓑ They were too big and expensive for home use.

   C They were too dangerous to use at home.

   D Advertisers did not realize ordinary people would want a computer.

FRIDAY  Objective 11.06

5. **Who pardoned Richard Nixon for his role in Watergate?** *(Chapter 31.2)*

   A President Jimmy Carter

   B the U.S. Congress

   Ⓒ President Gerald R. Ford

   D the U.S. Supreme Court

WEEK 23

 **MONDAY**  **Objective 12.01**

1. **Who controlled Iran after the overthrow of the shah?** *(Chapter 31.3)*

   (A) Ayatollah Ruhollah Khomeini
   B the United States
   C the Soviet Union
   D Zbigniew Brzezinski

TUESDAY **Objective 12.01**

2. **Why did a U.S.-led coalition attack Iraq in 1991?** *(Chapter 32.3)*

   A to defend Kuwait's democratically elected government from aggression
   B to defend Operation Desert Storm
   C to remove Iraq's ruthless dictator from power
   (D) to protect petroleum supplies and to respond to reports of atrocities in Iraqi-occupied Kuwait

 **WEDNESDAY**  **Objective 12.02**

3. **What did the U.S. Supreme Court rule in the case of *Bush* v. *Gore*?** *(Chapter 33.2)*

   A Because Al Gore had won the popular vote, he would become the next president.
   B George Bush should become president because it was the Republican Party's turn to control the White House.
   C George Bush should be president because his father had once held that office.
   (D) A recount of votes in Florida was unconstitutional because there were no clear standards in place for a recount.

THURSDAY **Objective 12.02**

4. **What issue was addressed in the Supreme Court case of *Vernonia School District* v. *Acton*?** *(Chapter 33.1)*

   (A) drug testing for student athletes in public schools
   B the right of children to vote
   C searching student belongings
   D equal rights for women

FRIDAY  **Objective 12.03**

Reaganomics

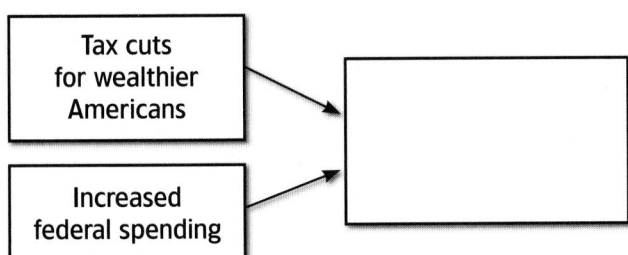

5. **As a result of tax cuts during President Reagan's first six years in office, the federal budget deficit** *(Chapter 32.1)*

   (A) grew.
   B decreased.
   C did not increase or decrease.
   D was eliminated.

COMPETENCY GOAL 12 The learner will identify and analyze trends in domestic and foreign affairs of the United States during this time period.

MONDAY  Objective 12.03

1. Which of the following greatly increased the efficiency of American business in the 1990s? *(Chapter 33.4)*

A genetic engineering

(B) computerized information

C Medicaid

D improvements in agriculture

TUESDAY  Objective 12.04

2. What was the New Right? *(Chapter 32.1)*

(A) a coalition of conservative media commentators, think tanks, and grass-roots Christian groups

B a coalition of civil rights advocates and environmentalists

C a coalition of economists who supported Reaganomics

D a coalition of union members and supporters of a minimum wage increase

WEDNESDAY Objective 12.05

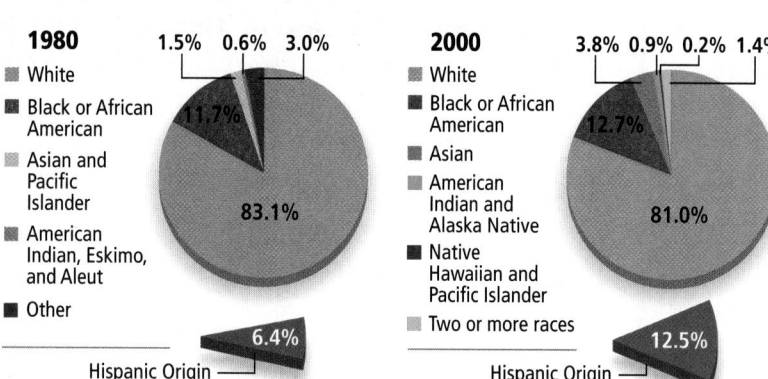

1980
- White
- Black or African American
- Asian and Pacific Islander
- American Indian, Eskimo, and Aleut
- Other

1.5% 0.6% 3.0%
11.7%
83.1%
6.4%
Hispanic Origin

2000
- White
- Black or African American
- Asian
- American Indian and Alaska Native
- Native Hawaiian and Pacific Islander
- Two or more races

3.8% 0.9% 0.2% 1.4%
12.7%
81.0%
12.5%
Hispanic Origin

Source: *United States Census Bureau*

3. Which group almost doubled as a percentage of the total U.S. population between 1980 and 2000? *(Chapter 33.4)*

A American Indians

(B) Hispanics

C Pacific Islanders

D Asian Americans

THURSDAY  Objective 12.06

4. Who was the United States president when the 9/11 terrorist attacks occurred? *(Chapter 33.3)*

A Bill Clinton

B Rudolph Giuliani

C Condoleezza Rice

(D) George W. Bush

FRIDAY Objective 12.06

5. How did Congress respond to the threat of terrorism after 9/11? *(Chapter 33.3)*

A by quarantining people who had been targeted in the anthrax attack

B by declaring war on Iraq

C by strengthening protections of civil liberties

(D) by passing the USA Patriot Act

Skills Handbook

To maximize your study and enjoyment of U.S. history, use the Skills Handbook to review and practice a variety of Reading, Social Studies, and Reading Like a Historian skills.

Reading Skills

Social Studies Skills

Reading Like a Historian

A mural showing the construction of a dam

Becoming an Active Reader

by Dr. Kylene Beers

Words surround us. In fact, it's unlikely that you can escape written words during a typical day. Each day, you see printed words in books, magazines, and newspapers; on television and the Internet; at home and in shops and restaurants; and along roads and interstates. Just as you are doing now, every day and in almost every place, you are reading. But just as words can be found in different places, so too can words be used for different purposes. Some words are used to educate, others to inform, and still others to entertain. You will read a textbook such as this one differently from how you would read an advertisement for a new video game or a letter from a friend.

Because you read material differently depending on your purpose for reading, it is important to learn and use various skills and strategies to improve your recognition and comprehension of material. In this Handbook, there are opportunities to learn reading skills that you can master and use throughout *American Anthem* to gain greater understanding of your reading.

① Key Terms and People At the beginning of each section you will find a list of terms, people, and events that you will need to know. Watch for these words as you read.

② Reading Focus and Reading Check The Reading Focus questions act as a type of outline for each section, and the Reading Check questions offer opportunities to assess what you have learned as you go.

③ Academic Vocabulary When we use a word that is important in all classes, not just in social studies, we define it in the margin under the heading Academic Vocabulary. Because you will see these academic words in other texts, you will benefit by learning what the words mean while reading this book.

Read Like a Skilled Reader

How can you become a more skilled reader? For starters, you first need to *think* about how to become a better reader. You also can use the following ideas and strategies.

Skilled readers . . .

- Preview what they are supposed to read before they begin reading. They look for titles of chapters and sections, listings of main ideas and focus questions, key terms and information in the margin such as Academic Vocabulary, and visuals such as charts, graphs, maps, and photographs.
- Construct tables or K-W-L charts into which they organize ideas from the reading. They write notes in the tables or charts as they read.

- Use clues from the text, such as the signal words shown below, to help determine or cement understanding.

Sequencing words: *first, second, third, before, after, sooner, later, next, then, following that, earlier, finally*

Cause and effect words: *because, so, since, due to, as a result of, the reason for, therefore, brought about, led to, thus, consequently*

Comparison and contrast words: *likewise, similarly, also, as well as, unlike, however, on the other hand*

Read Like an Active Reader

Active readers know that it is up to them to figure out what the text means. Here are some steps you can take to become an active and successful reader.

Predict what will happen next on the basis of what already has happened in the text. When your predictions do not match what happens in the text, reread to clarify meaning.

Question what is happening as you read. Constantly ask yourself why events happen, what certain ideas mean, and what causes events to occur.

Summarize smaller parts of a chapter. Do not try to summarize an entire chapter! Instead, read some of the text and summarize. Then move on.

Connect events in the text to what you already know or have read.

Clarify your understanding by pausing occasionally to ask questions and check for meaning. You may need to reread to clarify or read further to collect more information to gain understanding.

Visualize people, places, and events in the text. Envision events or places by drawing maps, making charts, or taking notes about what you are reading.

Building Your Vocabulary

As you know, skilled readers implement various strategies and use the text itself to answer questions and clarify meaning. Becoming a skilled reader means that you understand not only how ideas relate but also the words that shape the ideas.

Within this textbook, there are two main types of words. The first, academic words, are words that are important in all classes, not just in social studies. Academic words are found in the margin of most sections under the heading Academic Vocabulary. A second type includes words used primarily in social studies. A sampling of both types appears in the chart below.

By understanding the prefixes, suffixes, roots, and **etymologies,** or origins, of words, you can gain greater understanding of words and how they are related to one another. You can see such relationships by grouping previously unfamiliar words in a notebook, on note cards, or on a word wall.

A **word wall** is just what it sounds like it is—a wall of words. Each day, students add words to a wall, grouping them alphabetically or in categories. Over the course of a school year, a word wall becomes like a large dictionary, with words attached to a wall, to a whiteboard, or to a bulletin board.

Academic Word/Definition	Etymology
authority—firm self-assurance	from the Latin *auctoritas,* meaning "opinion, decision, power"
federal—national	from the Latin *foedus,* meaning "compact" or "league"
hypothesis—an idea that is based on facts and is used as a basis for reasoning	from the Greek *hypotithenai,* meaning "to put under, suppose"
interpret—to understand in light of circumstances	from Latin *interpretari* and *interpres,* meaning "agent, negotiator, interpreter"
revolution—a drastic and far-reaching change	from the Latin *revolvere,* meaning "to revolve or roll back"
technique—method	from the Greek *technikos,* meaning "technical"

Social Studies Word/Definition	Prefix/Suffix
civilization—the culture of a particular time or place	Suffix *–ation,* meaning "action" or "resulting state"
century—a period of 100 years	Prefix *cent,* meaning "hundred"
democracy—governmental rule by the people, usually through majority rule	Prefix *demo,* meaning "people"
geography—the study of Earth's physical and cultural features	Prefix *geo,* meaning "Earth"; suffix *graph,* meaning "to write, draw"
independence—the state of being free from rule	Prefix *in,* meaning "not"; root *depend,* meaning "to need"; suffix *–ence,* meaning "action," "state," or "process"
society—a group of people who share common traditions	Prefix *soci,* meaning "to join," "companions"

Identifying Main Idea and Details

North Carolina Skills
1.02 Summarize to select main ideas.

Define the Skill

The **main idea** is the central thought in a passage. It is general and conveys the key concept that the author wants you to know. The main idea can come at the beginning, middle, or end of a passage, though you usually find it near the beginning. The main idea can be one or two sentences and can be implied or directly stated.

Details are facts that support or explain the main idea. Details are specific and provide additional information, such as the *who, what, when, where, why,* and *how.* These include facts, statistics, examples, explanations, and descriptions.

Learn the Skill

Use the following strategies to identify main ideas and details in the reading.

1 Identify the topic by examining the title or other headings.
A section heading usually describes the topic.

2 Find the topic sentence that summarizes the passage's main idea.
Then restate the main idea in your own words.

Life in Colonial America

Early British settlers and newcomers from many countries were creating a new American culture. As Crèvecoeur had noticed, it was not British or European, but something new.

Colonial cities Colonial cities were lively, exciting places. Some had paved streets and sidewalks lit by oil lamps. Ships from foreign ports were anchored in the harbors. People waited eagerly for letters from relatives and the latest British newspapers and magazines, with gossip and drawings of new fashions.

Many colonial cities had libraries, bookshops, and impressive public buildings. City dwellers could go to plays or concerts. They shopped in markets for country produce and luxury goods from Europe. Schools taught music, dancing, drawing, and painting.

3 Look for details that support the main idea.
Supporting details usually follow the main idea and provide more information about it.

Apply the Skill

1. Identify the main idea of the passage and restate it in your own words.
2. What details support the main idea?
3. How do the details add to the main idea?

SKILLS HANDBOOK

Answers

Apply the Skill 1. *Settlers from Britain and other places built lively cities in the colonies.* **2.** *The details of various features and buildings support the main idea that settlers built lively cities.*
3. *The details follow the main idea and provide more information to support it.*

READING SKILL

Summarizing

Define the Skill

Summarizing is the process of condensing what you read into a briefer, easier-to-understand format. A good summary should include only a passage's main ideas and its most important supporting details. When summarizing, remember to use your own words. Knowing how to summarize can help you understand and recall the main ideas of what you read.

Learn the Skill

Use the following strategies to summarize the reading.

1 Identify main ideas in the passage.
Often, a main idea is located at the beginning of a passage or a paragraph.

2 Look for key supporting details.
Include only the most important details in the summary.

Different worlds The economic differences between the primarily industrial North and the primarily agricultural South led to even greater differences between the two regions. Trade and industry encouraged urbanization, and so cities grew in the North much more than in the South. Moreover, the Industrial Revolution and the revolutions in transportation and communication had the greatest impact on the North, where new technology was seized by businesses in pursuit of efficiency and growth.

By contrast, in the South, after the widespread use of the cotton gin, there was relatively little in the way of technological development. Many Southerners saw little use in labor-saving devices, for example, when they had an ample supply of enslaved people to do their bidding.

3 Ask questions and look up unfamiliar words.
Then restate the passage's main idea and most important details in your own words.

Apply the Skill

1. What is the main idea of the second paragraph? How do you know?
2. What details support the main idea in the second paragraph?
3. Write a brief summary of the above passage, including only the main ideas and most important details.

Answers

Apply the Skill 1. *The South had little in the way of technological development. That is the main idea of the passage because all subsequent details support it.* **2.** *Southerners did not need to develop machinery since they had enslaved people that they could use for labor.* **3.** *The North's economy was primarily industrial, which encouraged urbanization and the development of technological advances there. The South's economy was primarily agricultural, which encouraged the continued use of enslaved people as labor and discouraged technological development there.*

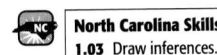
READING SKILL

Making Inferences

North Carolina Skills
1.03 Draw inferences.

Define the Skill

Inferences are implied, or unstated, ideas drawn from details in the reading. Making inferences means using clues in the text to connect implied ideas with stated facts and your own prior knowledge and common sense. Learning how to make inferences will help you gain greater understanding about particular historical people, places, and events from the reading.

Learn the Skill

Use the following strategies to make inferences about the reading.

1 Identify main ideas and details.
Note stated facts and information in the reading.

> The vote in November 1860 was almost completely along sectional lines. Lincoln won every northern state—although he and Douglas split the electoral vote in New Jersey. In the South, Breckinridge and Bell split the vote, with the Lower South going entirely to Breckinridge. What was troubling, however, was that the split in the Democratic Party allowed Lincoln to be elected president with less than 40 percent of the popular vote. Even more worrisome was the fact that of the nearly 2 million votes Lincoln received, only 26,000 came from slave states.
>
> Many Northerners celebrated Lincoln's victory. "The great revolution has finally taken place," one free-soiler wrote. "The country has once and for all thrown off the domination of the slaveholders." Many Southerners looked at the results with concern. "A party founded on the ... hatred of African slavery is now the controlling power," the *New Orleans Delta* warned the slaveholding South.

2 Identify implied ideas in the text.
What ideas are suggested but not directly stated in the reading? Statistics and opinionated language can lead to implied understanding.

3 Compare stated and unstated ideas with your prior knowledge.
Use facts from the reading, your common sense, and what you already know about a topic or an event to make a valid inference about it.

Apply the Skill

1. From a national perspective, what was troubling about Lincoln's election in 1860?
2. What can you infer about the effect of Lincoln's election on the future of the South?
3. Using the reading and your prior knowledge, explain the effect that multiple candidates can have on a general election.

SKILLS HANDBOOK **H7**

Answers

Apply the Skill 1. *elected president with less than 40 percent of the popular vote; only 26,000 of more than 2 million total votes cast for Lincoln came from slave states;* **2.** *Lincoln was an antislavery candidate who many Southerners believed would push for the end of slavery throughout the United States. That led many in the South to evaluate whether they wanted to remain as part of the United States.* **3.** *When voters choose from multiple candidates, the vote can be split several ways and a given candidate can win with less than a majority of the total votes cast.*

READING SKILL

Sequencing

North Carolina Skills
1.08 Use context clues and appropriate sources such as glossaries, texts, and dictionaries to gain meaning.

Define the Skill

By **sequencing** events in chronological, or time order, you can gain greater and more accurate understanding of them. Learning to sequence also can help you understand relationships among events, including how a past event may influence a pending one and eventually lead to a future outcome.

Learn the Skill

Use the following strategies to sequence the reading.

1 Examine all text and visuals for specific dates. Times of the day, seasons of the year, and people's ages are helpful in determining the specific sequence of events, which is known as absolute chronology.

2 Look for words signal. Clue words such as *by, in, after, first, last, before, next, then, soon,* and *finally* help indicate the general sequence of events, which is known as relative chronology.

3 Identify events that occurred at the same time. Words such as *while, meanwhile,* and *during* signal the occurrence of simultaneous events.

Carnegie and Steel **Andrew Carnegie** lived a true rags-to-riches story. Born in 1835 in Scotland to poor parents, Carnegie immigrated to the United States when he was 12. At age 17, he took a job with the Pennsylvania Railroad. He advanced quickly and began investing in the iron, oil, railroad, and telegraph industries. He soon founded his own company and rose to the top of the steel business.

Carnegie held down costs by using vertical integration, buying supplies in bulk, and producing items in large quantities. By 1899 the Carnegie Steel Company dominated the American steel industry. In 1901 Carnegie sold the company to banker J.P. Morgan for $480 million. After retiring, Carnegie began to devote his time to philanthropy, or charity.

Apply the Skill

1. In what year did Carnegie take a job with the Pennsylvania Railroad? How long after that did he build Carnegie Steel Company into the nation's dominant steel business?
2. To what cause did Carnegie devote himself after his retirement?
3. Use information from the reading to produce a time line of significant events from Carnegie's life.

Answers

Apply the Skill 1. *1852; became dominant 47 years later, in 1899;* **2.** *philanthropy;* **3.** *1835—Carnegie is born; 1852—Carnegie begins working for the Pennsylvania Railroad; 1899—Carnegie Steel dominates American steel industry; 1901—Carnegie sells Carnegie Steel and becomes a philanthropist*

Identifying Cause and Effect

Define the Skill

By using **cause and effect,** you can determine why certain events occurred and whether events are related and, if so, how they are related.

A cause is an action that makes another event happen. Often, a cause will be directly stated in the text, but sometimes it will be implied. An effect is something that happens as a result of a cause. One cause may have more than one effect. Similarly, one effect may have more than one cause. Identifying causes and effects can help you better understand what you read.

Learn the Skill

Use the following strategies to identify cause and effect in the reading.

1 Identify the causes of events. Look for a reason or reasons that prompted a given event to occur. Words such as *since, because, so, therefore,* and *due to* can signal a causal relationship among events.

2 Identify the effects of events. Look for phrases and clue words that indicate consequences, such as *thus, brought about, led to, consequently,* and *as a result.*

War Breaks Out

Since Russia had promised to protect Serbian Slavs, the Russian army quickly began to mobilize, or prepare for war. Germany viewed Russia's mobilization as an act of aggression against its ally Austria-Hungary and thus declared war on Russia. Then Germany declared war on France, Russia's ally. All-out war was about to begin.

The Germans take Belgium Germany made the first move in the war, following the Schlieffen Plan. On August 14, 1914, German troops crossed the German border into the neutral country of Belgium. Kaiser Wilhelm II believed that he had to catch Belgium and France by surprise. Germany's invasion of Belgium drew a new, powerful nation into the conflict. Because the British had planned to defend Belgium, Great Britain declared war on Germany.

3 Connect causes and effects. Consider why certain causes led to an event, and why the event turned out as it did. Remember that an event can be both a cause and an effect.

Apply the Skill

1. Why did the Russian army begin to mobilize for war?
2. What was the effect of Russia's mobilization? Explain.
3. List an effect of Germany's decision to invade the neutral nation of Belgium.

Answers

Apply the Skill 1. *They had promised to protect Serbian Slavs.* **2.** *Germany viewed Russia's mobilization as an act of aggression against its ally, Austria-Hungary, and declared war first on Russia and then on France, Russia's ally.* **3.** *Effect: Germany's invasion of Belgium prompted Britain, which had planned to protect Belgium, to declare war against Germany.*

READING SKILL

Comparing and Contrasting

North Carolina Skills
1.08 Use context clues and appropriate sources such as glossaries, texts, and dictionaries to gain meaning.

Define the Skill

You usually can find the greater meaning of certain time periods, people, places, and events by **comparing and contrasting** information and details from them. Comparing involves looking at both the similarities and differences between two or more people, places, or events. Contrasting means examining only the differences between them. Learning to compare and contrast effectively can give you a deeper contextual understanding of the reading.

Learn the Skill

Use the following strategies in comparing and contrasting parts of the reading.

1 Identify similarities in the reading.
Words such as *also, both, all, like, likewise, similar,* and *as* can signal comparison between people, places, and events.

2 Identify differences in the reading.
Words such as *unlike, different, but, however, not, though, only,* and *while* can indicate differences between people, places, and events.

The Effects of the Crash

In the aftermath of the crash, American business and political leaders rushed to calm the panic and reassure the nation. One business leader wrote optimistically in the days following Black Tuesday, "The recent collapse of stock market prices has no significance as regards the real wealth of the American people as a whole." President Hoover <u>also</u> downplayed the effects of the crash. He and many others firmly believed that the economy would soon recover from the shock and return to prosperity.

The impact on individuals No one denied, <u>however</u>, that the stock market collapse had ruined countless individual investors. Some had lost years of gains. Many saw huge fortunes disappear before their eyes.

Margin buyers were particularly hard hit. When stock prices began to fall, brokers demanded that they pay back the borrowed money. To "make" these margin calls, investors were forced to sell their shares for far less than they had paid for them. Some lost their savings trying to make up the difference.

3 Analyze the information.
Identify relationships between similarities and differences in the text. What do they tell you about a topic in a big-picture sense?

Apply the Skill

1. How did President Hoover's initial reaction to the stock market crash compare to the reactions of other business and political leaders?
2. What did all parties agree was an effect of the stock market collapse?
3. Which group of investors was hit hardest by the stock market collapse? Explain.

Answers

Apply the Skill 1. *Business and political leaders as well as President Hoover tried to downplay the crash and reassure Americans that the stock market would soon return to prosperity.*
2. *The stock market collapse ruined many individual investors.*
3. *margin buyers, because in order to "make" margin calls they had to sell their shares for far less than they had paid*

Identifying Problem and Solution

North Carolina Skills
4.01 Use hypothetical reasoning processes.

Define the Skill

By **identifying problem and solution,** you can better understand the challenges that people have faced over time and the means by which they have resolved such difficulties. Learning to effectively identify problems and solutions is a valuable skill that you can apply to your understanding of history.

Learn the Skill

Use the following strategies to identify problems and solutions in the reading.

1 Identify the problem. Note the problem to be solved. Some problems are directly stated, while others are not.

2 List all possible solutions to it. Because there is usually more than one way to solve a problem, identify and weigh all of the alternatives. Then consider the advantages and disadvantages of each.

Trade and economic development

World War II had raised a number of concerns about the financial relationships between countries. These problems had helped bring about the Great Depression. Now they threatened to limit trade and create conflict between nations. Many leaders hoped that solving these problems would lead to greater prosperity around the world. This, in turn, would promote peace.

Even before the war was over, representatives of many of the world's great powers met at a conference in Bretton Woods, New Hampshire. Out of this conference came an agreement to create two organizations—the **World Bank** and the **International Monetary Fund** (IMF). Both began operating in 1947.

The World Bank aimed to help poor countries build their economies. It provided grants of money and loans to help with projects that could provide jobs and wealth.

Economic policy was the focus of the IMF. The IMF was designed to encourage economic policies that promoted international trade.

3 Evaluate the chosen solution. Later, use what you know about the topic and your own common sense to evaluate a solution's effectiveness.

Apply the Skill

1. What problems did world leaders identify after World War II?
2. What solution did world leaders offer to these problems?
3. What did world leaders hope to accomplish by solving the problem?

Answers

Apply the Skill 1. *Financial relationships between countries threatened to limit trade and create international conflicts.*
2. *World powers created the World Bank and the International Monetary Fund.* **3.** *By creating the World Bank and International Monetary Fund, world leaders hoped to increase prosperity and promote peace.*

READING SKILL

Drawing Conclusions

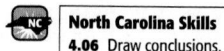 **North Carolina Skills**
4.06 Draw conclusions.

Define the Skill

Historical writing often features cause-and-effect relationships between and among events. In some cases, however, outcomes in the text are implied. In such instances, you can use facts and your own knowledge and experience to **draw conclusions** about the reading. In drawing conclusions, you analyze the reading and form opinions or make judgments about its meaning.

Learn the Skill

Use the following strategies to draw conclusions from the reading.

1 Identify the main idea and supporting details. Read the passage carefully to find clue words and establish meaning.

2 Connect the reading and your prior knowledge. Look for connections between stated facts, implied ideas, and what you already know about the topic.

Creating the Great Society Now that he was an elected president, Johnson pushed even harder for his plans. On inauguration day, he told aides at an inaugural ball, "Don't stay up late. There's work to be done. We're on our way to the Great Society."

Johnson had a personal interest in providing education for the children of the poor. In 1965 Congress passed the Elementary and Secondary School Act, the first large-scale program of government aid to public schools. The Higher Education Act created the first federal scholarships for college students. In February 1965 the Office of Economic Opportunity launched Head Start, an education program for the preschool children of low-income parents.

The president also persuaded Congress to pass the Omnibus Housing Act in 1965. To oversee this and other federal housing programs, Congress created the Department of Housing and Urban Development (HUD). Johnson appointed Robert Weaver to head this new department, making him the first African American to be part of a president's cabinet.

3 Summarize the reading. Summarize the reading in your own words. Then draw a conclusion that states an opinion or makes a judgment about what the reading means to you.

Apply the Skill

1. What can you conclude about Johnson's interest in education?
2. What led Johnson to push even harder for his plans after he became an elected president?
3. What did Johnson mean when he said, "Don't stay up late. There's work to be done. We're on our way to the Great Society"?

H12 SKILLS HANDBOOK

Answers

Apply the Skill **1.** *Johnson thought education was a critical part of creating a Great Society.* **2.** *Johnson knew that, as an elected president and not one serving out another's term, he had a mandate from voters to enact his policies.* **3.** *Johnson meant that they were working to create a better future. He knew there was a lot to do and he wanted to begin working as soon as possible.*

Making Generalizations

North Carolina Skills
1.08 Use context clues and appropriate sources such as glossaries, texts, and dictionaries to gain meaning.

Define the Skill

A generalization is made by combining details from a passage with a reader's prior knowledge. People **make generalizations** by looking for people, events, or ideas that share something in common and identifying their connection. As a reader, look for a generalization if an author suggests that a series of facts are connected. Look for clue words, including *all, none, every,* and *never*. Other clue words that sometimes show a generalization are *most, many, few, some, usually,* and *sometimes*.

Learn the Skill

Use the following strategies to make generalizations from the reading.

1 Look for the main idea of the passage. Find similarities between paragraphs that link main ideas together.

> **John Lewis** took part in some of the first sit-ins in 1960. He was also a Freedom Rider in 1961 and participated in the ill-fated Selma march in 1965. The leader of the Student Non-violent Coordinating Committee in the early 1960s, Lewis was later elected to many terms representing the people of Atlanta, Georgia, in Congress.
>
> As a staff member of Southern Christian Leadership Conference, **Andrew Young** played major roles in the 1963 Birmingham campaign and the Selma march. In 1972, he became Georgia's first black member of Congress since Reconstruction. Young later served as U.S. ambassador to the United Nations and as mayor of Atlanta.
>
> **Jesse Jackson** was a close adviser to Martin Luther King, Jr. and was with him at the motel in Memphis on the day King was assassinated. Jackson later founded his own civil rights organization, Operation PUSH, and became an international figure for his work on behalf of poor and oppressed peoples around the world. His strong campaigns for the Democratic presidential nomination in the 1980s raised the real possibility that the nation might one day have a black president.

2 Locate supporting details. Listing facts will help you determine what people, places, or events are being grouped together.

3 Identify a common thread and relate it to your prior knowledge. Determine which words (*most, few,* etc.) will be most useful for a generalization. Then compare the generalization against what you already know about the subject.

Apply the Skill

1. What is the main idea of the passage?
2. Make a generalization based on the passage above.
3. What facts support that generalization?

Answers

Apply the Skill 1. *Several people involved in the civil rights movement later became involved in politics.* **2.** *possible answer— Many political figures today were influenced by the civil rights movement of the 1960s.* **3.** *Answers will vary, but students should use facts from the passage to support their answers to the previous question.*

Interpreting Time Lines

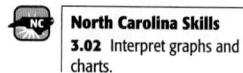

North Carolina Skills
3.02 Interpret graphs and charts.

Define the Skill

A **time line** chronologically organizes events that occurred during a specific period of time. It has a beginning date and an ending date. The **time span** is the years between the beginning date and the ending date. **Time intervals** mark shorter increments of time within the time span. They appear at regular intervals, such as every 10 or 20 years. Two time lines can be used to list events that happened within a certain time span but at different places. These are called **parallel time lines**.

By organizing events chronologically, time lines can help you see how events are related. Seeing how events are related can help you find cause and effect relationships among the events and remember them. Time lines also allow you to compare, contrast, and draw conclusions about historical events.

Learn the Skill

Use the following strategies to read the time line.

1 Identify the time span of the time line. Look at the beginning date and the ending date to determine the time period.

TIME LINE

The English in North America

1607 Captain John Smith and more than 100 colonists settle Jamestown.

1639 Connecticut settlers adopt the Fundamental Orders of Connecticut, which allowed men who were not church members to vote.

1619 Virginia's House of Burgesses becomes the first legislature in America.

1620 The Pilgrims sign the Mayflower Compact.

2 Determine the time intervals of the time line. Check to see whether the years are evenly spaced. Determine whether the time is divided by decades, by centuries, or by another division.

3 Analyze the events on the time line. Recognize the types of events that the time line describes and determine how they are related.

Apply the Skill

1. What is the time span of the time line?
2. What are the time intervals of the time line?
3. How are the events on the time line related?

Answers

Apply the Skill 1. *1607 to 1639;* **2.** *one year* **3.** *The time line shows events that occurred in North America when the English were beginning to settle the East Coast.*

Interpreting Charts

North Carolina Skills
3.02 Interpret graphs and charts.

Define the Skill

Charts, including simple charts, tables, and diagrams, are visual representations of information, such as facts and statistics. Historians use charts to organize, condense, simplify, and summarize information. **Simple charts** combine or compare information.

Tables classify information by groups. Numbers, percentages, dates, and other data can be classified in the columns and rows of a table for easy reference and comparison. **Diagrams** illustrate processes or steps so that they are easier to understand. Knowing how to read and use charts allows you to interpret, compare, analyze, and evaluate historical information.

Learn the Skill

Use the following strategies to interpret the chart.

1 **Identify the type of information presented in the chart.**
Read the title and any column headings to understand what the chart is about. The title of this chart is "The English Colonies in America."

2 **Look at the way information is organized.**
Charts can be organized alphabetically, chronologically, or in other ways.

3 **Analyze the information found in the chart.**
Interpret, compare, and contrast the information in the chart to draw conclusions and make inferences or predictions.

THE ENGLISH COLONIES IN AMERICA

Joint-stock colonies were established by groups of investors who pooled their money hoping to make a profit.	Virginia* (1607) Massachusetts* (1620)
Royal colonies were under the direct control of the king of England, who appointed a governor.	Delaware (1664)
Proprietary colonies were established by private individuals, or Lord Proprietors, who had power to make and execute laws.	New Hampshire* (1623) New Jersey* (1630) Pennsylvania* (1634) Maryland* (1632) North Carolina* (1655) South Carolina* (1670) Georgia* (1732)
Self-governing colonies were independent of the king or a joint-stock company.	Connecticut (1634) Rhode Island (1636)

* Later became a royal colony

Apply the Skill

1. How is the information in the chart organized?
2. According to the chart, what is one difference and one similarity between the colonies of Virginia and Pennsylvania?

Answers

Apply the Skill **1.** *This chart gives definitions in the left column and examples in the right column.* **2.** *One difference is that Virginia was a joint-stock colony and Pennsylvania was a proprietary colony. One similarity is that Virginia and Pennsylvania later became royal colonies.*

SOCIAL STUDIES SKILL

Interpreting Pie and Bar Graphs

North Carolina Skills
3.02 Interpret graphs and charts.

Define the Skill

Graphs are diagrams that present statistical or numeric data. They can display amounts, trends, ratios, and changes over time. A **pie graph** is a circular chart that shows how individual parts relate to the whole. The circle of the pie symbolizes the whole amount. The slices of the pie represent the individual parts of the whole. A **bar graph** compares quantities. A single bar graph compares one set of data. A double bar graph compares two sets of data. Knowing how to interpret graphs will allow you to better understand and evaluate historical data as well as recognize historical trends.

Learn the Skill

Use the following strategies to interpret the pie graph.

1 Identify the subject of the pie graphs.
Read the title and the legend to determine the subject of the pie graphs.

Use the following strategies to interpret the bar graph.

1 Read the title and the legend.
This will allow you to determine the subject of the graph.

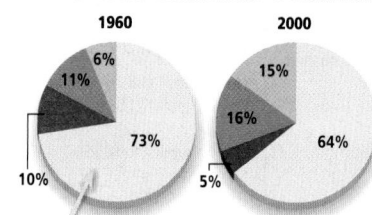

HISPANIC IMMIGRANTS TO THE UNITED STATES

Country / Region of Origin
▢ Mexico ■ Cuba ■ South America ▢ Central America

1960
6%
11%
73%
10%

2000
15%
16%
64%
5%

Source: *United States Census Bureau*

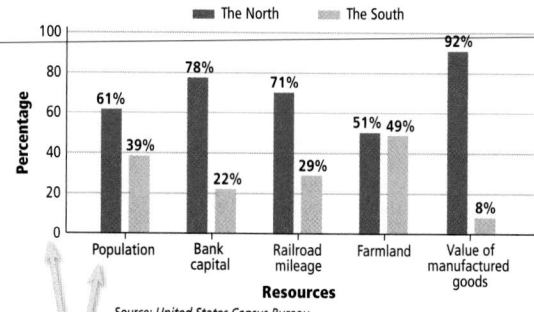

NORTHERN AND SOUTHERN RESOURCES

■ The North ▢ The South

Resources	The North	The South
Population	61%	39%
Bank capital	78%	22%
Railroad mileage	71%	29%
Farmland	51%	49%
Value of manufactured goods	92%	8%

Percentage

Source: *United States Census Bureau*

2 Read the statistics.
Compare the sizes of each piece within each graph. Then compare the pieces across the graphs.

3 Draw conclusions
Determine what the statistics tell about the subject of the pie graphs.

2 Examine the labels.
Read the horizontal and vertical axis labels. These tell what the bar graph measures and the unit of measurement.

3 Analyze the bar graph.
Compare the amounts shown on the bar graph. Draw conclusions about what this information tells about the subject.

Apply the Skill

1. What information do the pie graphs compare?
2. What information does the bar graph compare?
3. What conclusions can you draw from the data in the bar graph?

Answers

Apply the Skill **1.** *The pie graphs compare the percentage of Hispanic immigrants from their countries of origin in 1960 and 2000.*
2. *The bar graph compares the percentage of resources of the North and the South.* **3.** *The North had more industry than the South.*

Interpreting Line Graphs

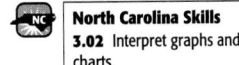

North Carolina Skills
3.02 Interpret graphs and charts.

Define the Skill

A **line graph** is a visual representation of data organized so that you can see the pattern of change over time. On a line graph, usually the **vertical axis** shows quantities and the **horizontal axis** shows time. People may use line graphs to track changes in events such as population growth or the stock market. Line graphs show time in intervals so they are not always exact and may require that you estimate quantities. Knowing how to interpret line graphs can help you recognize historical trends.

Learn the Skill

Use the following strategies to interpret a line graph.

1 Read the title of the graph.
The title tells you the subject or purpose of the graph.

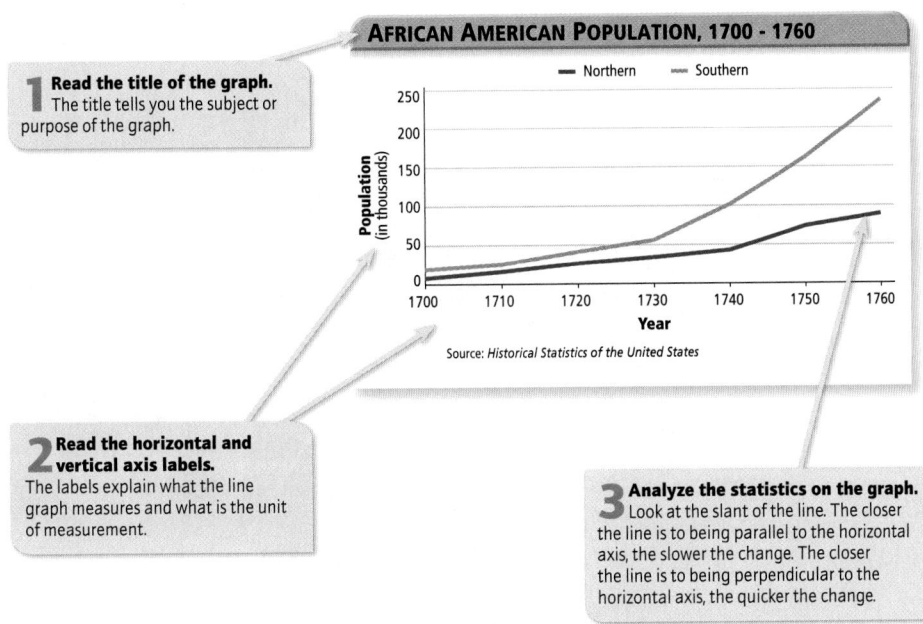

AFRICAN AMERICAN POPULATION, 1700 - 1760

— Northern   — Southern

Population (in thousands)

Year

Source: *Historical Statistics of the United States*

2 Read the horizontal and vertical axis labels.
The labels explain what the line graph measures and what is the unit of measurement.

3 Analyze the statistics on the graph.
Look at the slant of the line. The closer the line is to being parallel to the horizontal axis, the slower the change. The closer the line is to being perpendicular to the horizontal axis, the quicker the change.

Apply the Skill

1. About how big was the African American population in the South in 1740?
2. About how many more African American people lived in the South than in the North in 1760?
3. What conclusion can you draw about the African American population in the North?

Answers

Apply the Skill   1. *100,000 people;* **2.** *about 150,000 more lived in the South;* **3.** *grew much more slowly than that of the South.*

SOCIAL STUDIES SKILL

Interpreting Infographics

North Carolina Skills
2.02 Explore print and non-print materials.

Define the Skill

An **infographic** is a way of presenting a large amount of information in a graphic, or visual, form. Infographics often combine different types of information, such as text, illustrations, maps, charts, tables, graphs, and diagrams. You need to be able to understand what each piece of information is conveying on its own and how each piece works together to convey a larger point. Infographics help readers understand the importance of an event, an object, or a place. An infographic can be a two-dimensional or a three-dimensional model. Some infographics are interactive. Different types of infographics have different uses. For example, tables and charts organize information, whereas pictorial infographics are memorable and bring history to life.

Learn the Skill

Use the following strategies to interpret infographics.

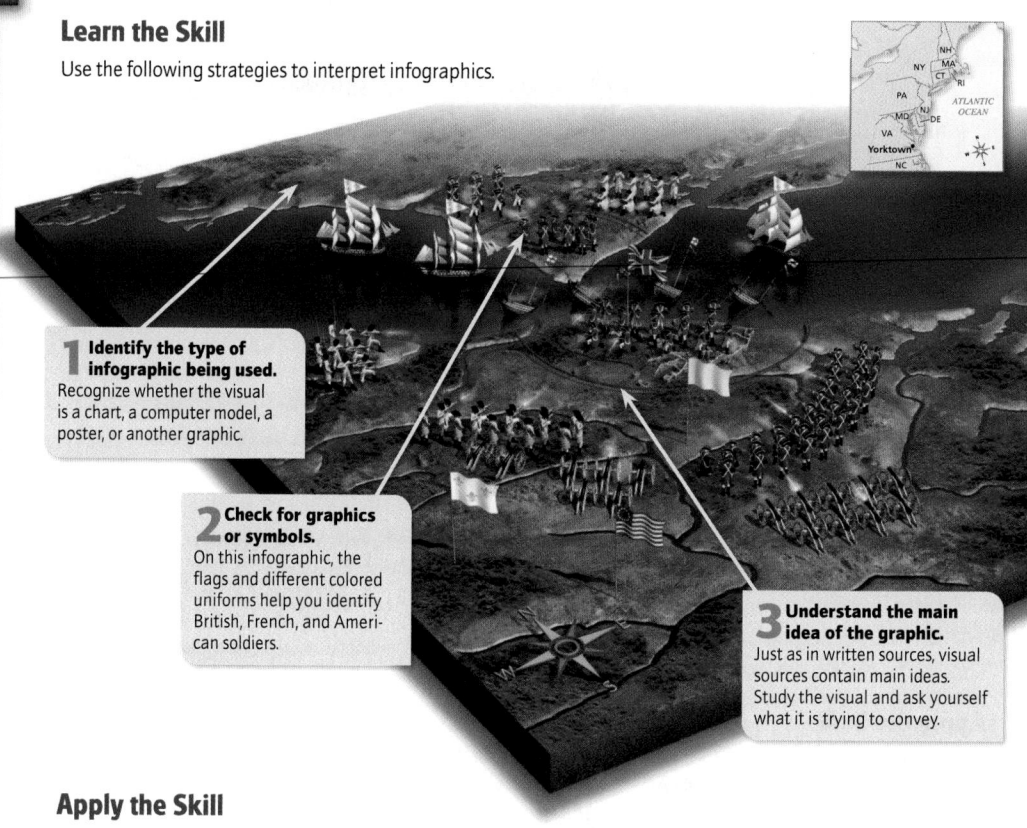

1 **Identify the type of infographic being used.**
Recognize whether the visual is a chart, a computer model, a poster, or another graphic.

2 **Check for graphics or symbols.**
On this infographic, the flags and different colored uniforms help you identify British, French, and American soldiers.

3 **Understand the main idea of the graphic.**
Just as in written sources, visual sources contain main ideas. Study the visual and ask yourself what it is trying to convey.

Apply the Skill

1. What type of infographic is this?
2. What do the ships represent?
3. Why did the British surrender at Yorktown?

H18

Answers

Apply the Skill **1.** *This is a three-dimensional computer-modeled map of the Battle of Yorktown.* **2.** *The ships are the French fleet that blockaded the Chesapeake Bay.* **3.** *They were surrounded by land and by sea.*

Interpreting Movement Maps

North Carolina Skills
3.01 Use map and globe reading skills.

Define the Skill

Different types of maps are used for different purposes. **Movement maps** show motion or travel from one point to another. They can track sea voyages, explorations, or migrations. They can span a week, a few months, or thousands of years. Understanding how to read and interpret a movement map can help you learn more about historical events, their chronology, and the geographical locations they affected.

Learn the Skill

Use the following strategies to interpret movement maps.

1 Read the title and legend to learn the subject and purpose of the map. Use that prior knowledge and the map to draw conclusions. What area does the map cover? What time period does the map cover? The legend explains what the symbols and the colors on the map mean

2 Identify and understand the patterns of movement shown on the map. Trace the path of movement from start to end. What does the map tell you about the explorers' movements?

3 Analyze the information. What do you already know about the subject?

EUROPEAN EXPLORATION OF AMERICAS 1492–1682

Apply the Skill

1. Describe the path that Magellan took.
2. What patterns can you find?
3. How do the patterns you found relate to the present-day Americas?

H19

Answers

Apply the Skill 1. *Magellan traveled southwest from Spain to a waterway that cut through the tip of South America. He then traveled north along the coast of South America before veering northwest.* **2.** *The English and French sailed to what is now North America and Canada, and Columbus stayed around what is now the Caribbean, while the Spanish sailed to what is now Mexico and Central and South America.* **3.** *The culture and languages of these areas today still reflect these early patterns; many French-speakers live in Canada, English-speakers in Canada and the United States, and Spanish-speakers in Mexico and Central and South America.*

Interpreting Historical Maps

North Carolina Skills
3.01 Use map and globe reading skills.

Define the Skill

A map is a representation of features on Earth's surface. Historians use different types of maps to locate historical events, to demonstrate how geography has influenced history, and to illustrate human interaction with the environment.

A **historical map** provides information about a place at a certain time in history. It can illustrate information such as population density, economic activity, political alliances, battles, and movement of people and goods. Knowing how to use historical maps can help you learn how places have changed over time. For example, these historical maps show how the Treaty of Paris changed North America after the French and Indian War.

Learn the Skill

Use the following strategies to interpret historical maps.

1 Read the title and legend. The title will help you identify the subject and the purpose of the map. The legend explains the meaning of the symbols and the colors on the map.

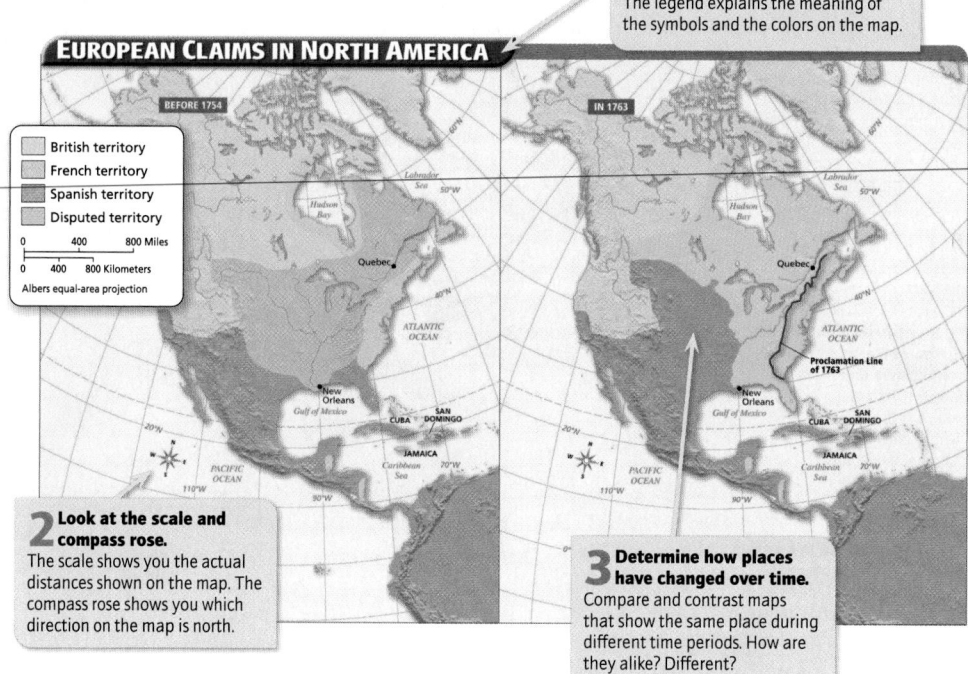

2 Look at the scale and compass rose. The scale shows you the actual distances shown on the map. The compass rose shows you which direction on the map is north.

3 Determine how places have changed over time. Compare and contrast maps that show the same place during different time periods. How are they alike? Different?

Apply the Skill

1. What is the purpose of these historical maps?
2. Which country claimed Quebec before 1754? Which country claimed Quebec in 1763?

Answers

Apply the Skill 1. *The purpose of these maps is to show how the European claims in North America changed in the 1700s.*
2. *France claimed Quebec before 1754. Britain claimed Quebec in 1763.*

Interpreting Cartograms

North Carolina Skills
3.01 Use map and globe reading skills.

Define the Skill

A distribution map show how data, such as population, is spread over a certain area. A **cartogram** is a type of distribution map that distorts the sizes and shapes of state, regions, or countries to reflect some value *other* than physical size. For example, a cartogram may display information about the population of a region or the gross national products of several countries. The cartogram is a tool for making visual comparisons. At a glance, you can see how each country, region, or state compares with another in a particular value.

Learn the Skill

Use the following strategies to interpret cartograms.

2004 ELECTORAL VOTES

1 Read the title and legend.
Identify the value illustrated by the cartogram.

Candidate	Political Affiliation	Electoral Votes
George W. Bush	Republican	286
John F. Kerry	Democratic	252
TOTAL		538

2 Determine what countries, regions, or states the cartogram shows.
Find the largest and smallest land areas on the cartogram. Compare the sizes of the land areas on the cartogram with the way they appear on a political map.

3 Analyze the information presented in the cartogram.
Using what you already know, plus the new information on the cartogram, what conclusions can you draw about the subject?

Apply the Skill

1. On the cartogram, is Pennsylvania or Missouri more distorted in size when compared with a political map?
2. What does this cartogram tell about the populations of Massachusetts and South Dakota?

Answers

Apply the Skill 1. *Missouri;* **2.** *Massachusetts had more electoral votes in 2004 than South Dakota did because Massachusetts had the larger population.*

Analyzing Costs and Benefits

North Carolina Skills
1.01 Read for literal meaning.

Define the Skill

Government officials use cost-benefit analyses to help them decide which programs to fund. A **cost-benefit analysis** is a process that measures whether a project or a policy is worthwhile by calculating and comparing its benefits with its costs to society. Basic economic indicators including employment, gross domestic product, and inflation can be used in the analysis. All costs and benefits are expressed in terms of money. Some costs and benefits, however, such as time or safety, cannot be directly measured by how much money is earned or lost. Mathematical formulas are used for these types of costs and benefits to determine how to express their monetary value. One obstacle to cost-benefit analysis is that people may sometimes disagree about the value of the costs and the benefits.

Learn the Skill

Use the following strategies to analyze costs and benefits.

1 Identify and calculate the costs.
What are the different costs of the project? Add those together to calculate the total cost.

2 Identify and calculate the benefits.
Determine the benefits of the proposed project. Calculate the total amount of money the project will save or earn for society.

3 Analyze the costs and the benefits and draw conclusions.
Compare the costs with the benefits. Divide the total benefits by the total costs to determine the benefits-to-cost ratio. If the ratio is more than 1, the project will earn money. If the ratio is less than 1, the project will lose money.

JOB CORPS: COSTS AND BENEFITS TO SOCIETY PER PARTICIPANT

Costs (1995 Dollars)	
Cost of Government-Funded Pay, Food, and Clothing for Participant	$2,361
Program Operating Costs	$14,128
Benefits (1995 Dollars)	
Participant Earns Government-Funded Pay, Food, and Clothing	$2,361
Additional Earnings and Benefits	$27,531
Reduced Crime in Community	$1,240
Reduced Use of Other Job Training Programs	$2,186

Apply the Skill

1. What is the total cost of Job Corps per participant?
2. What is one benefit of Job Corps?
3. How much money will society earn or lose for each dollar the government spends on Job Corps?
4. Will the program earn or lose money?

Answers

Apply the Skill 1. *$14,128 + $2,361 = $16,489;* **2.** *possible answer—Crime is reduced in the community.* **3.** *($2,361 + $27,531 + $1,240 + $2,186) ÷ ($14,128 + $2,361) = $2.02. For each dollar the government spends on Job Corps, society will earn $2.02.* **4.** *It will earn money.*

Evaluating Information on the Internet

North Carolina Skills
2.03 Utilize different types of technology.

Define the Skill

The **Internet** is an international computer network that connects schools, businesses, government agencies, and individuals. Every Web site on the Internet has its own address, called a **URL**. Each URL has a domain. The **domain** tells you the type of Web site you are reading. Common domains in the United States are .com, .net, .org, .edu, and .gov. A Web site with the domain .edu means that it is sponsored by an educational institution. The collection of web sites throughout the world is called the **World Wide Web**.

The Internet can be a valuable research tool. Unlike the information in books and newspapers, much of the content on the Internet is not checked for accuracy. Anyone can post information on the Web, so it is important to know how to evaluate the content of Internet resources. Evaluating the content found on the Internet will help you determine the accuracy and reliability of the information.

Learn the Skill

Use the following strategies to evaluate information on the Internet.

1 Identify the Web site's domain. Determine who sponsors the Web site. Web sites sponsored by reputable organizations, educational institutions, and government agencies usually provide accurate and reliable information.

2 Understand the purpose of the site. Find out whether the purpose of the site is to inform, to persuade, or to entertain.

3 Identify the author and check for bias. Determine the author's credentials. Is he or she an expert in the field? Decide whether the Web site presents balanced information or is overly biased towards a certain point of view.

4 Check the author's sources. For any research-based information, the author should provide a list of sources he or she used. You can also consult the author's sources for your own research.

University — Hunter-Gatherers in North America
By Dr. Jennifer Lawrence, University Professor

The first Americans were nomads who followed a hunter-gatherer way of life. Women and girls usually collected nuts, berries, wild plants, and birds' eggs. Men and boys hunted herds of animals. Hunter-gatherers followed the movements of the animals. They never stayed in one place for long.

During this time, humans found good hunting. North America was home to many large animals, such as sloths and woolly mammoths. None of these animals were used to the human hunters and they became easy prey.

References:

Michaels, Joseph. *Hunter-Gatherers Societies.* New York: University Press, 2004.

Mitchell, Stephanie. *Paleo-Indians in North America.* New York: University Press, 2004.

"Stone Age." Encyclopaedia Britannica. 2005. Enclopaedia Britannica Online. 23 Sept. 2005 <http://www.search.eb.com/eb/article-52395>

Apply the Skill

1. What is the domain of the Web site? Do you think the information on the Web site will be reliable? Why or why not?
2. Who is the author of the Web site? What are the author's credentials?
3. Do you think this Web site presents a balanced point of view or a biased point of view? Explain your response.

Answers

Apply the Skill 1. *The Web site's domain is .edu. possible answer—I believe that the information will be reliable because it comes from an educational institution.* **2.** *The author is Dr. Jennifer Lawrence. She is a university professor.* **3.** *possible answer— I believe that this Web site presents a balanced point of view because the text is based on fact. The author does not use words such as "I think" or "I believe" to present the information.*

Major Historical Concepts

To think like a historian, you need to be aware of some basic concepts of history—about how history happens and how historians think about the past. Keep these five major historical concepts in mind as you read this textbook.

Continuity and Change in History

Change happens at different rates at different times   Historical change doesn't happen at a uniform rate. Some periods see great, sweeping changes that affect the course of history for hundreds of years to come. At other times, the changes are gradual and harder to see.

Some aspects can change while others remain the same   Change happens at different rates in different places, too. Just because one part of society changes that doesn't mean all of society will change. For example, after the United States gained its independence, states in the North gradually became more industrialized and outlawed slavery, while states in the South remained largely agricultural and kept slavery.

Change is complicated   Historical change affects all areas of life, not just politics or technology. Beliefs and values are also subject to change. Once, women were not permitted to join the armed forces. Today the debate is not over whether women should be allowed to join but what role the hundreds of thousands of military women should have.

Understanding Cause and Effect in History

The limitations of cause and effect   One event may have several causes. A proximate, or immediate, cause may seem obvious, such as Germany's invasion of Poland as the proximate cause of World War II. But there also may be deeper causes, such as the war reparations that Germany was forced to pay after the Treaty of Versailles officially ended World War I. It may not always be immediately possible to identify a direct cause for an event or to identify all of the deeper causes.

What causes events? Inflation in Germany after World War I made paper money almost worthless (above left), hastening Adolf Hitler's rise to power.

The Civil Rights Movement involved millions of people and changed American politics, voting patterns, schooling, and entertainment.

H24

The destruction of the USS *Maine* may have been an act of war or it may have been a chance occurrence.

The Role of Chance in History

The impact of historical events   An explosion sunk the USS *Maine* in Havana harbor in 1898. The Spanish and the U.S. governments disagreed about the cause of the explosion, which killed all the men aboard. The Spanish-American War ensued, and "Remember the Maine!" became an American battle cry. Chance events can have unexpected and sometimes enormous consequences. Many factors may influence the direction of history, but change just one of those factors and the outcome itself may change. If the USS *Maine* had not exploded there may not have been a Spanish-American War.

Understanding Historical Events in Context

Events as they happened   Historians strive to place events in the context of their time, understanding them the way the participants would have. This means understanding the ideas and beliefs of the time and not imposing modern day values on the past. We may still disagree with the actions people took in the past, such as enslaving human beings or denying women the right to vote, but historians need to understand why people acted as they did.

Drawing Lessons from History

Comparing the present with the past   Past decisions and the consequences of historical events reverberate through our own time. Decisions made almost 150 years ago—leading up to and during the Civil War—still affect how different regions of the country view one another. Some things have changed; some have stayed the same.

Abraham Lincoln was a divisive President in his time; now he is a beloved figure.

Lessons we have learned   We can get a better sense of how to meet the challenges we face today by knowing how people in the past met or failed to meet similar challenges. For example, after the stock market crash of 1929 and the Great Depression that followed, the practice of buying stocks on borrowed money was severely restricted. Today many of the laws that make up the fabric of our nation came from lessons learned in difficult times. Historians are careful not to think the past holds all the answers. No situation is exactly like any other, and we need to be careful not to draw lessons too hastily, or too confidently.

Traders on the New York Stock Exchange are still bound by laws developed in response to the stock market crash of 1929.

Themes of History

Understanding history means understanding the connections between time, places, events, and people. Throughout *American Anthem,* you will find opportunities to make those connections and identify themes that will help you grasp the larger patterns of events across time.

Government and Democracy

The United States was founded on such ideals as human equality, limited government, and democratic representation. Today, as when our nation was founded, the American government is separated into three branches—the executive branch, the legislative branch, and the judicial branch. For over two hundred years, these three branches have worked under a system of checks and balances so that no one branch ever becomes too powerful.

Our Constitution defines the structure of our government.

Individual Rights and Responsibilities

When America was founded, only white men with property could vote in elections or hold office. Over the past two centuries, women and African Americans have fought for and won the right to vote and participate in our democracy. Today, American citizens can register to vote when they are eighteen years old. Voting is one of our most precious individual rights and responsibilities as citizens of the American democracy.

Voting is the most fundamental way citizens exercise both their rights and their responsibilities.

Economic Development

In the United States, the abundance of natural resources, a free-enterprise economic system, and government regulation protecting both private property and the public good all work together to ensure our country's economic success. The offer of social mobility and economic success through hard work has attracted immigrants to the United States from around the world.

Many innovators, such as Thomas Edison, have contributed to America's cultural and economic development.

Immigrants from many nations choose to become citizens of the United States.

Immigration and Migration

People from many nations, representing an extraordinary range of ethnic, racial, national, and religious groups, have come to the United States and become American citizens, making our country the most diverse in the world. At many times in our nation's history, people have also migrated within the country's borders, seeking new opportunities and a better way of life.

Cultural Expressions

A diverse nation has given rise to a diverse culture, drawing on the traditions of many different groups. This blending and remixing of cultural expression among ethnic, racial, and religious groups is the source of tremendous strength and creativity, but it also sometimes causes conflict.

Global Relations

Early American foreign policy reflected the country's origins as a British colony, prompting America to try to remain separate from the affairs of European nations. By the 1900s, however, the United States emerged as a world superpower, with allies and responsibilities around the world.

U.S. leaders can make an important difference in the world.

Science and Technology

A spirit of innovation in science and technology has had an enormous effect on our country's economy and culture. Throughout our history, American inventions have vastly improved quality of life and standards of living not only here but across the globe.

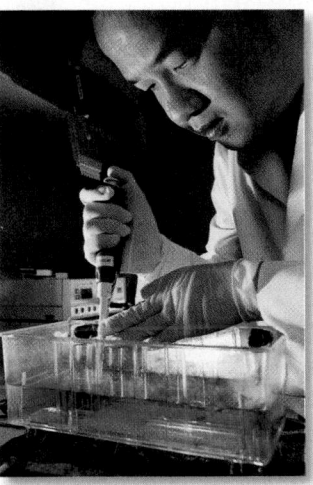

Medical and computer science are important parts of our nation's past and future.

Uniquely American art forms, such as jazz and blues music, have come from cultural diversity.

Analyzing Primary Sources

North Carolina Skills
2.01 Use appropriate sources of information.

Define the Skill

Primary sources are documents or other artifacts created by people present at historical events either as witnesses or participants. You can identify a primary source by reading for first person clues, such as *I, we,* and *our.* Quotation marks signify a speech or writing. These types of sources are valuable to historians because they give information about an event or a time period. All primary sources include a point of view because they were written or created by one person or group. Points of view may differ. For example, a Union soldier writing about a Civil War battle may have a different point of view than a Confederate soldier writing about the same battle. Historians compare primary sources to understand an event from all sides in order to write an accurate historical interpretation.

Primary sources can include:
- Letters
- Photographs
- Diaries
- Newspaper stories
- Pamphlets, books, or other writings
- Court opinions
- Autobiographies
- Pottery, weapons, and other artifacts
- Government data, laws, and statutes
- Speeches

Learn the Skill

Use the following strategies to analyze primary sources.

1 Identify the author or creator of the primary source.
There is little information given about Beverly. His role is unclear. A historian should ask more questions about this primary source.

2 Determine the historical event the primary source is describing.
Ask yourself whether Beverly's details match what you already know about Bacon's Rebellion.

Virginian Robert Beverly on Bacon's Rebellion—

"Four things may be reckoned to have been the main ingredients towards this intestine commotion [violent outbreak]. First, The extreme low price of tobacco, and the ill usage of the planter in the exchange of goods for it, which the country, with all their earnest endeavors, could not remedy. Secondly, The splitting the colony into proprieties, contrary to the original charters; and the extravagant taxes they were [charged]. Thirdly, The heavy restraints and burdens laid upon their trade by act of Parliament in England. Fourthly, The disturbance given by the Indians."

3 Compare what you already know to details in the primary source.
Often a primary source will enhance your knowledge of an event. Which detail in this source tells you something new?

Apply the Skill

1. What is Robert Beverly's point of view?
2. List two details about Bacon's Rebellion provided by this source.
3. How would this source help a historian write a historical interpretation of Bacon's Rebellion?

H28 SKILLS HANDBOOK

Answers

Apply the Skill 1. *Beverly supports the rebellion.* **2.** *The planters had four reasons for the rebellion. One reason was an Indian "disturbance."* **3.** *This source would help a historian know what someone in Virginia thought about the rebellion.*

Artifacts are also primary sources. This is a twelve shilling note from Pennsylvania, 1777.

Use the following strategies to analyze primary sources.

1 Identify the author or creator of the primary source.
In 1777, the colonies each printed their own money. The monetary system was based on a system of pounds, shillings, and pence.

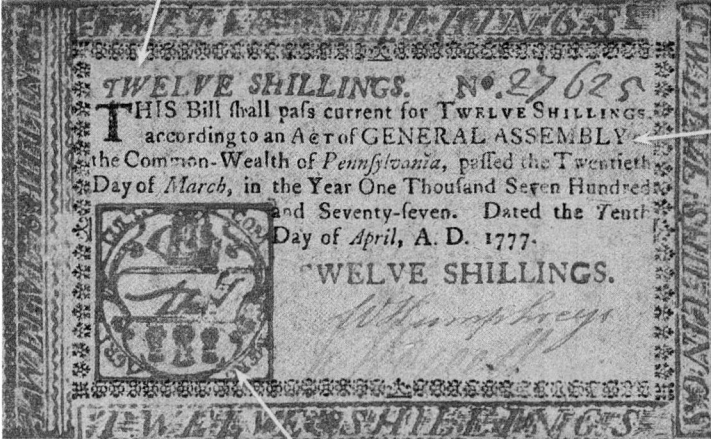

2 Determine the time period that the primary source is describing.
The paragraph printed on the money tells under whose authority it was printed. It also states when the act was passed, dating the note in 1777.

3 Compare what you already know to details in the primary source.
The seal on the note shows a ship, a plow, and bundles of wheat. What can these icons tell you about the colony of Pennsylvania?

Apply the Skill

1. Who is the creator of this primary source?
2. What can you infer about colonial money by viewing this primary source?
3. How would this source be useful to a historian?

Answers

Apply the Skill 1. *The printer is unknown, but the note was printed on the authority of the General Assembly of the Commonwealth of Pennsylvania.* **2.** *possible answer—Students may say that they can infer that the colonies used shillings instead of dollars, and that each colony issued the money rather than a federal bank.* **3.** *possible answer—Studying the way it was printed, identifying the signatures, reading the language of the paragraph, and analyzing the seal are all ways that this source would be useful to a historian.*

READING LIKE A HISTORIAN

Interpreting Visuals

North Carolina Skills
3.05 Interpret history through artifacts, arts, and media.

Define the Skill

Visuals can be important historical sources, so interpreting visuals is vital to reading like a historian. Visuals may offer an accurate portrayal of the details of a historical figure or event. Or they may represent an exaggerated or biased point of view. Knowing and understanding an artist or photographer's point of view can sometimes reveal more to a historian than the actual image itself.

To analyze an image, first determine the medium. Is the image a photograph, a piece of fine art, a poster, an advertisement, or a cartoon? What might this tell you about the image's audience? Next, look at the credit line and title, which will tell you who created the image and possibly what the artist intended it to mean. Look for details that could convey meaning. Then study the subject of the visual. Who or what is being portrayed? Are there symbols or familiar landmarks in the image? Why might those elements have been chosen? Finally, compare the image with what you know about the historical time it depicts.

Learn the Skill

Use the following strategies to analyze visuals.

1 Who or what is the subject?
Queen Elizabeth I

2 Examine the details.
What is the historical context of this picture? Behind Queen Elizabeth are images of the English fleet defeating the Spanish Armada in 1588.

4 Does the image agree or disagree with known historical facts?
The right panel behind Elizabeth shows ships sinking in bad weather, which was a historical factor in the Armada's defeat.

3 How is the subject depicted?
The queen is portrayed in a positive light, as a beautiful, poised woman in rich clothes and luxurious surroundings.

Apply the Skill

1. What symbols of power and rule are included in the picture?
2. Elizabeth was 55 years old when the English fleet defeated the Spanish Armada, yet she is portrayed as young and beautiful in this painting. Why might that be so?

H30 SKILLS HANDBOOK

Answers

Apply the Skill 1. *the globe under Elizabeth's hand and the crown;* **2.** *because she was the queen and the artist wanted to flatter her*

Interpreting Political Cartoons

North Carolina Skills
3.04 Interpret social and political messages of cartoons.

Define the Skill

Political cartoons are another kind of visual found in the historical record. These differ from visuals such as photographs and fine art because political cartoons often exaggerate characteristics of subjects or events in order to convey a specific message, either about politics in particular or society in general. Historians use political cartoons to understand how a particular person or event was perceived at the time. To interpret political cartoons, examine all the elements while considering the social, political, and historical context of the time.

Learn the Skill

Use the following strategies to interpret political cartoons.

1 Identify the cartoon's subject. This cartoon shows Congressman Preston Brooks (D, SC) attacking Senator Charles Sumner (R, MA). The two disagreed about the Kansas-Nebraska compromise over slavery.

4 Compare the message with historical knowledge. Does the cartoon agree or disagree with facts you already know? Preston attacked Sumner in a nearly empty Senate chamber, not in front of a crowd of witnesses as shown in the cartoon.

SOUTHERN CHIVALRY — ARGUMENT versus CLUB'S.

2 Read any text and study all symbols. Do they provide any clues about point of view? The caption uses the phrase "Southern Chivalry" to describe the beating; this is a use of irony, or meaning the opposite of what is actually stated.

3 Establish the cartoon's message. How is the subject portrayed? Preston Brooks is portrayed in a negative light, attacking a helpless Sumner on the floor of the Senate.

Apply the Skill

1. Does this cartoon look as though it was created by a supporter of slavery or a supporter of abolition?
2. Are there any features in this carton that are exaggerated?
3. Which of the two men is portrayed as the aggressor? Which is portrayed as the victim?

Answers

Apply the Skill 1. *Brooks is portrayed negatively, which supports abolition.* **2.** *possible answer—No, this cartoon does not exaggerate.* **3.** *Brooks is portrayed as the aggressor and Sumner as the victim.*

SKILLS HANDBOOK

SKILLS HANDBOOK

READING LIKE A HISTORIAN

Interpreting Literature as Historical Evidence

 North Carolina Skills
3.05 Interpret history through artifacts, arts, and media.

Define the Skill

Historians can sometimes use literature written during a particular time period to gain detailed insights into certain people, places, and events. For example, a novel about an upper-class New York City family in the late 1800s can provide historical details about the lifestyle of that social class. Some literature is activist, meaning that its purpose is to inspire an emotional or social response.

Learn the Skill

Use the following strategies to interpret literature.

1 Identify the author's point of view or bias.
Does the author have experiences that make the description more reliable? Reflect on what you already know about the book or author before you begin to read.

2 Look for descriptive passages.
This sentence gives descriptive details about workers in meat-packing factories. Do these details make the account historically believable?

Excerpt from *The Jungle,* by Upton Sinclair—

The men would tie up their feet in newspapers and old sacks, and these would be soaked in blood and frozen, and then soaked again, and so on until by night time a man would be walking on great lumps the size of feet of an elephant. Now and then, when the bosses were not looking, you would see them plunging their feet and ankles into the steaming hot carcass of the steer, or darting across the room to the hot-water jets.

4 Compare details in the literature with known facts about the event.
Sinclair was one of many writers in the early 1900s who investigated businesses and industry. Sinclair's work led to the passage of The Pure Food and Drug Act in 1906, to protect consumers from contaminated beef.

3 Determine whether the literature is meant to describe a certain historical event or to elicit an emotional response.
Here, the author wants to elicit an emotional response from the audience. What effect does this strategy have on the usefulness of the literature as an historical interpretation?

Apply the Skill

1. What is the author's point of view or bias?
2. What is the goal of the literature selection?
3. What can historians learn about factory work by reading this selection?

Answers

Apply the Skill **1.** *Sinclair is against the conditions in the meatpacking industry.* **2.** *to show the horrible conditions of workers in the meatpacking plant;* **3.** *possible answer—what it was really like to work in that industry at that time*

Recognizing Bias

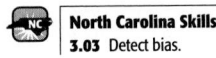

North Carolina Skills
3.03 Detect bias.

Define the Skill

To ensure an effective analysis of primary sources, historians must learn to recognize bias and the source of bias. Bias is a point of view that is slanted by personal or political beliefs. Every primary source reflects bias, from either the person who created the source or the person viewing the source. Bias appears in primary sources for a variety of reasons and gives clues about an author's intent or background.

For example, the author may be trying to justify an action or sway an opinion. Sometimes an author expresses a personal view without knowing that it is biased. Bias can help historians understand the different attitudes during a certain time in history. To avoid bias, a historian must examine different points of view and primary sources. It is important to look at many sources on the same incident or issue in order to achieve a balanced analysis.

Learn the Skill

Use the following strategies to recognize bias.

1 Identify the document.
This section gives you the context of the statement. Think about how speeches at public celebrations are different from other primary sources, such as private letters.

2 Examine the author's point of view.
What bias does the author express? Identify the author and his occupation. What can this tell you about the author's possible goals?

Dr. H. W. Harkness, Sacramento Newspaper Publisher, at the ceremony to celebrate the first transcontinental railroad—

"The east and west have come together. Never, since history commenced her record of human events, has she been called upon to note the completion of a work so magnificent."

4 Compare the primary source with historical evidence.
In what ways is the primary source different from other historical accounts? In what ways is it similar?

3 Consider the author's goal.
This claim is not a true claim. The speaker is using rhetoric, or the skill of using language effectively and persuasively. Consider whether rhetoric is appropriate for this event.

Apply the Skill

1. What is the author's goal in this statement?
2. Explain how a historian could use this document in preparing a historical account of the celebration marking the completion of the transcontinental railroad.

Answers

Apply the Skill 1. *to promote the transcontinental railroad as a great achievement;* **2.** *Harkness was a California newspaper publisher biased in favor of the railroad. A historian might be able to conclude that California political and business interests were also in favor of the transcontinental railroad.*

Evaluating Sources

North Carolina Skills
2.01 Use appropriate sources of information.

Define the Skill

Historians must constantly evaluate sources to determine their credibility. Credible sources help historians produce an accurate and reliable historical account. Historians use several criteria for evaluating sources:

- They consider the author or producer of a source.
- They think about where, when, and why a source was created.
- They assess the level of bias in a source.
- They acknowledge that sources are more reliable if the author was close in time and place to a given event.

Learn the Skill

Use the following strategies to evaluate sources.

1 Identify and learn the background of the author of the source. Quotes almost always include the name of the speaker or writer. This title also gives context information.

President Woodrow Wilson, in a speech to Congress, April 2, 1917—

❝We shall fight for the things which we have always carried nearest our hearts, for democracy. . . [and to] bring peace and safety to all nations and make the world itself at last free.❞

3 Determine whether the source was meant to be public or private. The use of quotation marks and the word "we" help show that this is a primary source. This speech was given to Congress, but who was Wilson really addressing?

2 Examine the context of the source. Consider when, in relation to the event, the source was created. In January, 1917, Germany resumed its submarine warfare. By April, they had sunk five U.S. submarines. Wilson justifies the U.S. entry into World War I by saying that the "peace and safety" of the world is at stake.

Apply the Skill

1. Who is the producer of the source?
2. What is the context of the source? Is the source meant to be public or private?
3. In what way is the source biased? What is the goal of the speaker?
4. How would you evaluate the source, on the basis of its credibility?

H34 SKILLS HANDBOOK

Answers

Apply the Skill 1. *President Woodrow Wilson;* **2.** *This is a public address to Congress.* **3.** *The excerpt is biased in favor of the United States entering the war, and President Wilson is trying to persuade people to support that action.* **4.** *This source reflects bias, but because the author is very close in time and place to the event described, it is credible.*

Analyzing Secondary Sources

 North Carolina Skills
2.01 Use appropriate sources of information.

Define the Skill

Secondary sources are accounts produced after a historical event by people who rely on primary sources. Secondary sources often contain summaries and analyses of events and time periods. Your textbook can be considered a secondary source, as can many other history books.

When a historian produces a secondary source, it often contains an interpretation of a historical event, or what the historian thinks actually happened and why. Historians build their interpretations on the basis of available facts and their own analysis. These secondary sources can be analyzed to determine whether they present a complete and accurate accounting of events.

Other kinds of secondary sources include:
- Encyclopedia entries
- Web sites
- Articles and essays by historians
- Biographies

Learn the Skill

Use the following strategies to analyze secondary sources.

1 Identify the source.
This is an encyclopedia article.

"World War I." Encyclopedia Britannica. 2005. Encyclopedia Britannica Online School Edition. 22 Sept. 2005

2 Summary
Secondary sources offer summaries of historical facts.

World War I, *also called* **First World War,** *or* **Great War**—an international conflict that in 1914–18 embroiled most of the nations of Europe along with Russia, the United States, the Middle East, and other regions. The **war** pitted the Central Powers—mainly Germany, Austria-Hungary, and Turkey—against the Allies—mainly France, Great Britain, Russia, Italy, Japan, and, from 1917, the United States. It ended with the defeat of the Central Powers. The **war** was virtually unprecedented in the slaughter, carnage, and destruction it caused.

3 Analysis
Secondary sources analyze historical facts and draw conclusions.

World War I was one of the great watersheds of 20th-century geopolitical history. It led to the fall of four great imperial dynasties (in Germany, Russia, Austria-Hungary, and Turkey), resulted in the Bolshevik Revolution in Russia, and, in its destabilization of European society, laid the groundwork for **World War II.**

4 Consequences
Since they are produced after an event is over, secondary sources can take a longer view of an event's consequences.

Apply the Skill

The first paragraph of the article offers a summary of the subject, World War I. The second paragraph contains an analysis of the importance and effects of the war. Answer these questions based on the excerpt:

1. What important information about World War I can be found in the first paragraph?
2. What are some of the consequences of World War I listed in the article?

Answers

Apply the Skill 1. *the years of the war, the countries involved, and the outcome of the war;* **2.** *the fall of four empires, the Bolshevik Revolution, and the groundwork for World War II*

Many Web sites are secondary sources, and their use is becoming more common and accepted among historians. Web sites, however, require special care in analysis. Because the World Wide Web uses open architecture, meaning that anyone can post information without any kind of review process, it is harder to determine whether information on these sites is accurate. Pay close attention to the stated source of any historical Web site, as well as the date it was last updated.

Among Web domain extensions, .gov and .edu are considered the most reliable for academic work. Some .org and .com sites are also good resources, but they require careful study to determine their credibility.

> The domain extensions that appear in a Web address can help. These include the following:
> - **.gov**—a government site
> - **.org**—usually a nonprofit organization
> - **.edu**—educational entities such as colleges and universities
> - **.com**—for-profit and commercial entities, including book publishers

Learn the Skill

Use the following strategies to analyze secondary sources.

1 What kind of secondary source is it?
This is a biography on a Web site.

2 Determine the author or the publisher of the secondary source.
What do you know about the person's or organization's credibility? The content of this biography is provided by the Smithsonian Institution, a credible source.

3 How does the author or publisher handle primary source material?
Is primary source material drawn from a range of sources for balance? The fine art portrait is identified and sourced. The biography also notes that conflicting opinions exist about General MacArthur and presents generalizations of those opinions.

4 When numbers and statistics are used, examine them carefully.
Are they offering a complete picture or just one part of the story? This biography does not use numbers or statistics, but in other historical writings, visual representations of data would need to be analyzed.

http://www.hrw.com/si/social/si_1914/index.html

SMITHSONIAN INSTITUTION

Spotlight: Biography

The Korean War

The Korean War (1950–1953) is often referred to as America's "forgotten war," because it did not capture the nation's attention as had World War II, nor did it arouse controversy as did the war in Vietnam. In fact, although the Korean War was much shorter than the Vietnam War, the casualties were almost as high, with 54,000 Americans killed and 103,000 wounded. Total casualties for the war reached 1.9 million. In 1995, more than forty years after the conflict ended, a memorial honoring the sacrifices and services of Korean War soldiers was dedicated on the Mall in Washington, D.C., directly across from the Vietnam Veterans' Memorial.

Douglas MacArthur (1880–1964)

Howard Chandler Christy (1873–1952)
Oil on canvas, 1952, NPG.78.271
National Portrait Gallery,
Smithsonian Institution, Washington, D.C.
Gift of Henry Ostrow

Though General Douglas MacArthur is perhaps best known for his participation in the Korean War, his military service actually began a half-century earlier. In fact, his was one of the longest and most controversial careers of any American military officer. Douglas MacArthur was the son of another famous soldier, Arthur MacArthur II, who led troops in the Civil War, the Spanish American War, and in the Philippines. Encouraged by his father's military successes as well as an ambitious mother, MacArthur entered the United States Military Academy at West Point and graduated at the head of

American Beginnings to 1789   American Nation from 1790 to 1865   The Expanding Nation from 1865 to 1914

Apply the Skill

1. What information do you learn about General Douglas MacArthur?
2. This source does not list an author. What information would you look at to help you determine whether this is a credible secondary source?

Answers

Apply the Skill 1. *information about his early military service;*
2. *the Web site address and the provider of this biography*

Analyzing Bias in Historical Interpretation

North Carolina Skills
1.05 Recognize bias and propaganda.

Define the Skill

When reading works of historical interpretation to determine their credibility and usefulness, it is important to read critically, looking for **bias in historical interpretation.** Most historians try to filter out their own biases when writing history. But they may not succeed, since they may not be aware of their biases. Bias can affect the way a historian tells a story, what facts are included or excluded, which events are highlighted or ignored, and how he or she treats primary sources.

Learn the Skill

Read the excerpt from Theodore Roosevelt's history of the War of 1812 between Great Britain and the United States. Then use the following strategies to analyze bias in historical interpretation.

1 Does the author have a background in the subject matter?
Theodore Roosevelt was a graduate of Harvard and a New York state Assemblyman in 1882. He would later serve as secretary of the Navy, and become President of the United States in 1901.

2 Is emotional language used to support a particular point of view?
This emotional language demonstrates Roosevelt's pro-American bias.

Theodore Roosevelt, *The Naval War of 1812*, published in 1882—

❝ But the wrongs done by the Americans were insignificant compared with those they received. Any innocent merchant vessel was liable to seizure at any moment; and when overhauled by a British cruiser short of men was sure to be stripped of most of her crew. . . . If a captain lacked his full complement there <u>was little doubt</u> as to the view he would take of any man's nationality. The <u>wrongs inflicted</u> on our seafaring countrymen by their impressment into foreign ships formed the main cause of the war. ❞

3 Are credible primary sources used to support the text?
Are footnotes or cited quotations used? This assertion is not backed up by a primary source or factual citation. The event happened more than 40 years before Roosevelt was born and he cannot have first-hand knowledge of it.

Apply the Skill

1. Who is the author? What important information is found in his background?
2. Are there examples of emotional language in the excerpt? If so, what are they?
3. Is there bias in this passage? Explain your answer.

Answers

Apply the Skill 1. *Theodore Roosevelt; was secretary of the Navy;* **2.** *yes; by using terms such as "innocent" and "wrongs inflicted";* **3.** *yes; Roosevelt's wording is biased toward the American position*

READING LIKE A HISTORIAN

Evaluating Historical Interpretation

North Carolina Skills
1.05 Recognize bias and propaganda.

Define the Skill

Historians and others evaluate historical interpretations to determine credibility, the level of bias, and the relevance of the material. A historical interpretation is a way to explain the past. These interpretations can change over time as historians learn more about the people and events of the past. Historians use several criteria for evaluating historical interpretations.

- Consider the age of the interpretation and its current relevance to the material. Some sources, such as encyclopedias, are updated periodically to include new material.
- Assess the level of bias in the interpretation.
- Determine the credibility of the interpretation.

Learn the Skill

Use the following strategies to evaluate historical interpretation.

1 **Identify the author or publisher of the source to determine credibility.**
The introduction tells you the author's name and his profession. A book by a history professor is almost always a credible source.

2 **Consider when the source was created.**
This book was published in 2003, so it probably uses current scholarship.

excerpt from *In the Presence of Mine Enemies: War in the Heart of America, 1859–1863,* by Edward L. Ayers, Professor of History, published in 2003—

Together, the stories of Augusta [County, Virginia] and Franklin [County, Pennsylvania] tell of a war both simpler and less straightforward than general accounts reveal. The Civil War was like all wars in that it elevated the worst human emotions and called them virtues. People let themselves be driven by arrogance and revenge as well as by ideology and principle. People watched themselves descend into rage and numbness, knowing themselves unworthy of their feelings. People invoked the Constitution and the Declaration of Independence against enemies invoking the same icons.

3 **Examine the level of bias in the interpretation.**
Does it detract from the overall credibility? The author's research was based on the people and public records of two counties, one in the North and the other in the South. He is using primary sources and presenting potentially opposing viewpoints. This creates a less-biased source.

Apply the Skill

1. Who is the author of the interpretation?
2. How does bias affect the interpretation?
3. Explain why the source would be valuable to current students.

Answers

Apply the Skill **1.** *The author is Professor Edward L. Ayers.* **2.** *The author seems to have a realistic view of the Civil War and includes sources from both points of view. Bias does not seem to affect Ayers' interpretation.* **3.** *Because the source is from 2003, the scholarship would be relevant to current students.*

Analyzing Alternative Interpretations of the Past

 North Carolina Skills
4.02 Examine, understand, and evaluate conflicting viewpoints.

Define the Skill

Interpretations of past events can differ in many ways. An interpretation may reflect an extreme bias for one view or another, or it may reflect two different schools of thought. Historians are often faced with alternative interpretations of a time or event in the past. When faced with opposing viewpoints, good historians do additional research to find the accuracies in each account.

Learn the Skill

Use the following strategies to analyze interpretations.

1 **Look for information about the author or the source that may give clues to possible bias.**
Andrews is a historian while Hacker is an economics professor. How could the different careers affect the authors' point of view?

Charles M. Andrews, historian—

"Primarily, the American Revolution was a political and constitutional movement and only secondarily one that was either financial, commercial or social. At bottom, the fundamental issue was the political independence of the colonies, and in the last analysis the conflict lay between the British Parliament and the colonial assemblies…"

2 **Define the main points in each argument.**
This will help you compare the interpretations.

3 **Discount rhetoric or emotional language that is not factual.**
Here, Hacker uses rhetoric to demean the "political and constitutional concepts" that Andrews supports.

Louis M. Hacker, economics professor—

"The struggle was not over high-sounding political and constitutional concepts; over the power of taxation or even, in the final analysis, over natural rights. It was over colonial manufacturing, wild lands and furs, sugar, wine, tea, and currency, all of which meant, simply, the survival or collapse of English mercantile capitalism within the imperial-colonial framework of the mercantilist system."

4 **In what ways do the interpretations differ?**
Summarize each interpretation to compare them. However, you should read additional information, opinions, or studies before you decide with which interpretation to agree.

Apply the Skill

1. Summarize the two interpretations presented above.
2. What can comparing these interpretations tell you about historical interpretation in general?

Answers

Apply the Skill 1. top: *main issue of Revolution was political;* bottom: *main issue was conflict over colonial economics;*
2. *that interpretations of the same event can vary dramatically*

Making Oral Presentations

North Carolina Skills
2.06 Create written, oral, musical, visual, and theatrical presentations of social studies information.

Define the Skill

Historians sometimes make oral presentations. These include speeches, lectures, or interviews. Oral presentations often support a version of or a conclusion about an issue and are given from outlines or note cards. They should be more dynamic than simply reading a written essay aloud. Historians must perform thorough research, make notes, and carefully organize their presentations. As a student of history, an oral presentation allows you to present information on a topic you have researched to an audience.

Learn the Skill

Use the following strategies to make oral presentations.

1 Identify a historical topic you would like to present.
Choose a central idea or theme on which to focus your research. Research the topic to gather relevant facts and vivid details. Include visual aids, such as maps, charts, or pictures, to add to your presentation.

2 Organize your information into an introduction, a body, and a conclusion.
The introduction should clearly state your topic and hypothesis while also generating interest with the listener. The body features the main points of your argument. The conclusion summarizes your main points and draws on those points to formulate a personal opinion about your topic.

3 Proofread your notes to ensure that they are well organized and grammatically correct.
Clearly label your notes. Using the terms introduction, body, and conclusion on your note cards helps you make an organized presentation.

4 Express arguments clearly and persuasively.
Write key words and clues in your notes to use as talking points. It may be helpful to structure this section in outline form. Also, look at how the opening sentence could catch the listeners' attention.

5 Practice reading your presentation aloud.
Make sure that you are comfortable speaking and that your statements are clear. Although you do not want to read directly from your notes while giving an oral presentation, it may be helpful to write sentences in your introduction to get you started.

Topic: Watergate

Introduction: On a summer night in 1972, a bungled break-in would cause the downfall of an American president. My hypothesis is that President Nixon, although a flawed person, was the victim of incompetent subordinates.

Body: Talk about Nixon's top aides
  a. H. R. Haldeman
  b. John Ehrlichman

Apply the Skill

1. Name the three parts of a well-organized oral presentation.
2. What is the topic and hypothesis of this oral presentation?
3. List two visual aids that could be used to add interest and clarity to this presentation.

H40 SKILLS HANDBOOK

Answers

Apply the Skill 1. *introduction, body, and conclusion;*
2. *The topic is Watergate and the hypothesis is that President Nixon was the victim of incompetent subordinates.* **3.** *pictures of Nixon, Haldeman, or Ehrlichman; a time line of events*

Making Written Presentations

North Carolina Skills
2.06 Create written, oral, musical, visual, and theatrical presentations of social studies information.

Define the Skill

Written presentations are one of the ways that historians present their scholarship. Historians must perform careful research and cite all sources in written presentations. They also try to write about a small part of an event. This is called narrowing the focus, and it helps historians make important points and explore new facets of history. For example, a historian might not make a written presentation about World War II, which would take thousands of pages to fully cover. He or she would probably write about one aspect of the war, such as a certain battle. As a student, a written presentation is a way for you to present information on a topic you have researched.

Learn the Skill

Use the following strategies to make written presentations.

1 Identify a historical topic. Be sure to narrow the focus of your idea or theme. Also, clearly state your topic. Make sure that any facts you include relate specifically to this topic.

2 Formulate a hypothesis. This will be the main idea of your presentation. Once you have determined your hypothesis, research will be easier. Find and organize facts, data, and details to support your hypothesis.

3 Keep a bibliography of sources as you research. A bibliography is a list of all sources used or cited in a written presentation. You must cite your sources to retain credibility and avoid plagiarism.

4 Clearly state your hypothesis and the facts that support it in your writing. This will help you organize your presentation. Good historians show both sides of any argument, so be sure to include all relevant facts.

5 Proofread your written presentation to ensure that it is well organized and grammatically correct. Proofreading your notes and your presentation is always important to prevent errors. Read your presentation aloud to make sure that your statements are clear.

Topic: The Camp David Accords, 1978

Hypothesis: The Camp David ~~Accounts~~ Accords were an important first step in establishing peace in the Middle East.

Fact: By signing the agreement, Egypt recognized Israel as a country.

Bibliography: World Book Encyclopedia, 2003 edition; Volume 1, p. 582a

Apply the Skill

1. What is the hypothesis in the written presentation notes above?
2. List an area of history you would like to research.
3. Narrow the focus to a small part of this area, and write a sample hypothesis for your written presentation.

Answers

Apply the Skill 1. *"The Camp David Accords were an important first step in establishing peace in the Middle East."* **2.** *Students' answers will vary.* **3.** *Answers will vary but should be based on the topic given in the previous answer.*

Strategies for Multiple Choice

You can improve your test-taking skills by practicing these strategies for multiple-choice questions. Read the skill-specific tips and samples on the left page. Then practice the skill on the right page. A multiple-choice question usually consists of a single *stem* and four *answer options*. Only one option is the correct answer. The other, incorrect options are *distracters*.

LEARN

1 Read the stem carefully to determine what it is asking.

2 Read carefully when a question is phrased in the negative.
Some standardized tests phrase questions in the negative. Take care with questions that contain words such as not and except.

3 Look for key words and facts within a stem.

4 Consider options such as *all of the above* and *none of the above* as you would any other possible response.
If you choose *all of the above*, ensure that all of the choices are correct.

5 If two options contradict each other, one of them is likely to be the correct answer.

6 Eliminate the answer options that you know are incorrect.

7 Watch for modifiers.
Options that include superlative words such as *always* or *never* are usually incorrect. Superlatives indicate that the correct answer must be an undisputed fact. In social studies, that is rarely the case.

① ②

Stem

1. Which of the following was *not* a cause of colonial unrest with Britain?

Answer Options

  A the Boston Massacre
  B the Olive Branch petition
  C passage of various taxes, such as the Sugar Act, on the colonies
  D the presence of British soldiers in the colonies

2. On April 18, 1775, the first shots of the Revolutionary War were fired at

> **3** Many shots were fired during the Revolution, but you are looking for those that were fired *first*.

  A Concord.
  B Lexington.
  C Philadelphia.
  D all of the above ← **4**

3. During the Revolutionary War, a Loyalist was someone who

  A remained loyal to Britain.
  B wanted freedom from Britain.   **5**
  C fought alongside the Continental Army.
  D lived mainly in New England and Virginia.

4. Many changes occurred as a result of the Revolutionary War, including

> **6** Absolute words such as *all*, *none*, and *every* often signal an incorrect option.

  A more rights for women.
  B voting rights for all men.
  C Spanish control of the colonies.
  D the formation of the United States.

> **7** You can eliminate **C** if you recall that Spain controlled Florida after the Revolutionary War.

Answers: 1 (B), 2 (B), 3 (A), 4 (D)

Directions: *Read the following questions and choose the best answer.*

1. Which of the following were considered border states in the Civil War?
   A Kentucky
   B Maryland
   C all of the above
   D none of the above

2. What existing invention was put to use in the Civil War to aid communication?
   A e-mail
   B telephone
   C the telegraph
   D the Pony Express

3. The Emancipation Proclamation freed all
   A enslaved people.
   B debtors from their debts
   C enslaved people in rebelling states.
   D enslaved people who had escaped to the North.

4. Prison camps during the Civil War did not
   A lack food.
   B have disease.
   C have overcrowding.
   D have sanitary conditions.

Answers
1. *C;* **2.** *C;* **3.** *C;* **4.** *D*

Strategies for Secondary Sources

You can improve your test-taking skills by practicing these strategies for secondary sources. Read the skill-specific tips and samples on the left page. Then practice the skill on the right page. A secondary source is a written source or a visual created after an event by a person who was not present at the event. The creators of secondary sources research primary sources and other secondary sources to learn about historical events. A biography is an example of a secondary source, as is a history textbook.

LEARN

1 Identify the type of secondary source.
Is it an encyclopedia entry, a Web site, a scholarly article, or another type of source?

2 Identify the author of the secondary source.
Note how much time has passed between the event and the time when the author writes about it. Is the author qualified to write about the topic?

3 Look at the title and topic sentence to preview the content of the passage.

4 Recognize the historical event or people involved.

5 Ask yourself whether the author uses any primary sources or other secondary sources for support.

6 Read the questions before rereading the passage so that you know what information you need to find.

①

②

—Paul Johnson, *A History of the American People*, p. 445

③

Lincoln's object was not merely to put his name and his case before the American people, as well as Illinois voters. It was also to expose the essential pantomime-horse approach of a man who tried to straddle North and South. He succeeded in both. He put to Douglas the key question: 'Can the people of a United States territory, in any lawful way, against the wish of a citizen of the United States, exclude slavery from its limits prior to the formation of a state constitution?' If Douglas said yes, to win Illinois voters, he lost the South. If he said no, to win the South, he lost Illinois. Douglas' answer was: 'It matters not what way the Supreme Court may hereafter decide as to the abstract question whether slavery may or may not go into a territory under the Constitution; the people have the lawful means to introduce it or exclude it as they please, for the reason that slavery cannot exist a day or an hour unless it is supported by the local police regulations.' This answer won Douglas Illinois but lost him the South and hence, two years later, the presidency.

④

⑤

1. Johnson uses primary source quotes to **⑥**

   A identify the two senatorial candidates.

   B show the similarities between the viewpoints of Lincoln and Douglas.

   C describe the many issues that Lincoln and Douglas debated.

   D show how Lincoln forces Douglas to state his position on slavery.

Answer: 1 (D)

Directions: *Read the following passage and use your knowledge of U.S. history to answer the questions below.*

—from *In the Presence of Mine Enemies: War in the Heart of America, 1859–1863*
By Edward L. Ayers

Michael Hanger, the young carpenter from Augusta in the 5th Virginia Infantry, described the situation he and his comrades faced [in his diary]. "5 O'Clock A.M. we can hear the cannon firing from the hills in front, and a little below us. The Yankees are endeavoring to draw us in that direction. The Junction is strongly fortified . . . in every possible direction." Put into position, Hanger and his comrades lay there for three and a half hours . . .

Things got worse the next day. "It is now raining very hard and has been all night. The wounded on the battlefield must have suffered greatly last night. It is a very muddy and disagreeable day . . ." Hanger gave no fuller evaluation of the battle. He did not say who had won and lost. He only listed the names of the men in his company who had been wounded. He did not give the name the battle was to bear. The Confederates called it Manassas, after the nearby town; the Union called it Bull Run, naming it after the nearby river, as became its custom.

1. What primary source does Ayers use?
   A accounts by Union generals
   B the diary of Michael Hanger
   C Michael Hanger's military record
   D accounts by Confederate generals

2. What historical event is Michael Hanger describing?
   A the Battle of Bull Run
   B the burning of Atlanta
   C the Battle of Yorktown
   D Michael Hanger's death

3. Ayers uses primary sources to
   A analyze the impact of the battle.
   B provide descriptive details of the battle.
   C support political viewpoints of the time.
   D give personal details about fellow soldiers.

4. How did the outcome of this battle affect the Union army?
   A The victory boosted the soldiers' morale.
   B The soldiers realized that it would be a short war.
   C The Union army decreased training for its soldiers.
   D The Union army increased training for its soldiers.

Answers
1. *B;* **2.** *A;* **3.** *B;* **4.** *D*

Strategies for Political Cartoons

You can improve your test-taking skills by practicing these strategies for political cartoons. Read the skill-specific tips and samples on the left page. Then practice the skill on the right page. Political cartoons are primary sources. They use comedic images to poke fun at political figures and issues. Cartoons can provide helpful context to the opinions and values of the time.

LEARN

1 Identify the characters and issues being portrayed.
This figure represents an anarchist.

2 Read the caption and any other labels to better understand the subject.

3 Identify any exaggerated images or ideas.
The wild character of the anarchist is a common exaggeration from the time period.

4 Identify common symbols used to help you recognize the subject of the cartoon.

5 Identify the cartoonist's point of view.
Recognize whether the subject is portrayed positively or negatively.

6 Identify the message the cartoonist wanted to send with this cartoon.
Does the cartoonist agree or disagree with the situation?

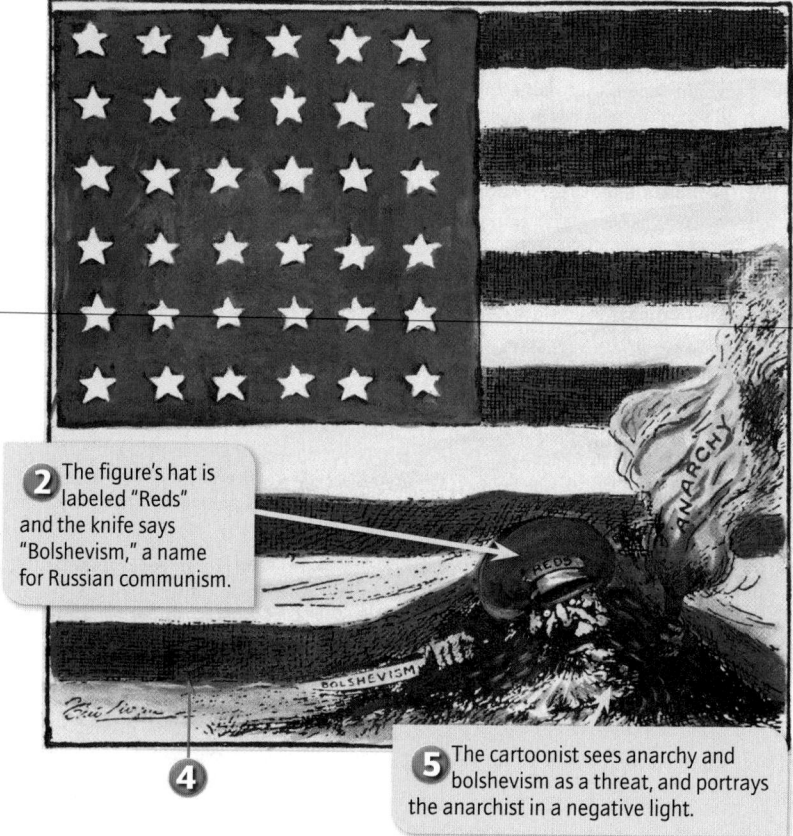

2 The figure's hat is labeled "Reds" and the knife says "Bolshevism," a name for Russian communism.

5 The cartoonist sees anarchy and bolshevism as a threat, and portrays the anarchist in a negative light.

4

1. Which sentence best summarizes the message of this cartoon?
   - **A** Immigration is anarchy.
   - **B** Anarchy is not welcome in the United States.
   - **C** Immigrants and anarchists are hiding under the U.S. flag.
   - **D** Immigration should be restricted and anarchists should be deported.

2. Which word summarizes the cartoonist opinion regarding immigration practices?
   - **A** positive
   - **B** criminal
   - **C** beneficial
   - **D** dangerous

Answers: 1 (D), 2 (D)

Directions: *Interpret the following cartoon and answer the questions below.*

1. The symbol the artist uses for the Teapot Dome oil scandal is
   A a steamship.
   B a steamroller.
   C a runaway train.
   D a horse and buggy.

2. Who might the figures running from the scandal represent?
   A ordinary citizens
   B politicians implicated or involved in the scandal
   C people harmed by the illegal oil deals
   D those who brought the scandal to the public's attention

3. What effect does the artist think the scandal will have on President Warren G. Harding?
   A It will help him.
   B It will crush him.
   C It will bypass him.
   D It will not affect him.

4. Which sentence best summarizes the message of this cartoon?
   A President Harding was a criminal.
   B Being involved with an oil company will crush politicians.
   C The Teapot Dome scandal was a minor incident.
   D The Teapot Dome scandal will negatively impact those involved.

Answers
1. *B;* **2.** *B;* **3.** *B;* **4.** *D*

Strategies for Charts

You can improve your test-taking skills by practicing these strategies for charts. Read the skill-specific tips and samples on the left page. Then practice the skill on the right page. Charts are used to organize and summarize large amounts of information. The table, one of the most common types of charts, organizes data into columns and rows.

LEARN

1 **Read the title or heading of the chart.**
Find out the topic and information covered in the chart.

2 **Find row and column headings.**
Identify the information represented, how it is organized, and how the information is related.

3 **Look for similar trends or data patterns between rows and columns.**
Also look for data that does not conform to the patterns.

4 **Make generalizations and draw conclusions from information in the chart.**
One generalization you could make from this chart is that many countries wanted to prevent future conflict.

1

PROGRAMS FOR A SAFER WORLD

As World War II came to an end, the countries of the world began seeking ways to prevent the problems and conflicts that helped lead to war. Leaders in the United States and other countries paved the way in establishing the following:

2 The first column lists the names of the programs. The second column gives details about each program's purpose.

3 The program in this row is the only one that does not relate directly to economic reconstruction.

World Bank (1944)	• Organization for providing loans and advice to countries for the purpose of reducing poverty
International Monetary Fund (1944)	• System for promoting orderly financial relationships between countries • Designed to prevent economic crises and to encourage trade and economic growth
United Nations (1945)	• Organization in which member nations agree to settle disputes by peaceful means • Replaced the League of Nations
General Agreement on Tariffs and Trade (1946)	• Agreement among member nations on rules and regulations for international trade • Focused on reducing tariffs and other trade barriers

1. Which generalization could you make from the information on this chart?

A After World War II, many countries believed that financial agreements between countries would help to limit disputes.

B After World War II, the World Bank primarily dealt with military issues.

C After World War II, these programs were developed to promote problems and conflicts between countries.

D After World War II, the wealthy countries around the world would receive loans from poorer countries.

Answer: 1 (A)

Directions: *Interpret the following chart and answer the questions below.*

JEWISH LOSSES IN THE HOLOCAUST			
	c. 1933	**c. 1950**	**Percent Decrease**
Europe	9,500,000	3,500,000	63
Selected Countries			
Poland	3,000,000	45,000	98.5
Romania	980,000	28,000	97
Germany	565,000	37,000	93.5
Hungary	445,000	155,000	65
Czechoslovakia	357,000	17,000	95
Austria	250,000	18,000	93
Greece	100,000	7,000	93
Yugoslavia	70,000	3,500	95
Bulgaria	50,000	6,500	87

Source: *United States Holocaust Memorial Museum*

1. Which of the following statements about this chart is true?
  A The data includes every country in Europe.
  B The data shows Jewish population loss in Poland during the Holocaust.
  C The data covers the years 1933 to 1980.
  D The data shows Jewish population losses around the world.

2. Which statement is NOT true about this chart?
  A Poland lost more Jews than any other country on the chart.
  B Bulgaria lost the least number of Jews of any other country on the chart.
  C From 1933 to 1950, Hungary lost more Jews than any other country shown on the chart.
  D Hungary had the smallest percentage drop in Jewish population from 1933 to 1950.

3. What trend is shown in this chart?
  A The Holocaust reduced overall Jewish population in Europe by 75 percent.
  B Jewish population losses during the Holocaust were concentrated in Central and Eastern Europe.
  C Jewish population in Europe increased during the Holocaust.
  D all of the above

4. Which generalization could you make from the data on this chart?
  A The Holocaust dramatically reduced Europe's Jewish population.
  B The Holocaust dramatically increased Europe's Jewish population.
  C The total population of Europe decreased by 65 percent.
  D The total population of Poland decreased by 98.5 percent.

Answers
1. *B;* **2.** *C;* **3.** *B;* **4.** *A*

Strategies for Line and Bar Graphs

You can improve your test-taking skills by practicing these strategies for line and bar graphs. Read the skill-specific tips and samples on the left page. Then practice the skill on the right page. Graphs are used to show the relationship among numerical data. Line graphs illustrate how quantities and trends change over time. Bar graphs compare groups of numbers within categories.

LEARN

1 **Read the title of the graph to determine its main idea.**

2 **Study the label on the vertical axis.**
The vertical axis usually indicates the type of information in the graph.

3 **Examine the label on the horizontal axis.**
The horizontal axis usually tells you the time period the graph covers.

4 **If a legend accompanies the graph, study it.**
The legend provides additional information. Legends specify what the colors, patterns, or symbols on the graph mean.

5 **Identify any trends or patterns that the graph reveals.**

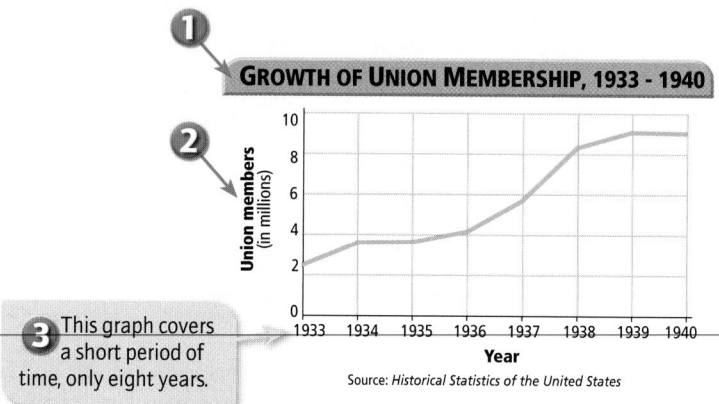

1 GROWTH OF UNION MEMBERSHIP, 1933 - 1940

3 This graph covers a short period of time, only eight years.

Source: *Historical Statistics of the United States*

1. Which statement correctly describes the trend in union membership?

A Union membership grew the most between 1933 and 1935.

B Union membership grew the most between 1934 and 1936.

C Union membership grew the most between 1936 and 1938.

D Union membership grew the most between 1938 and 1940.

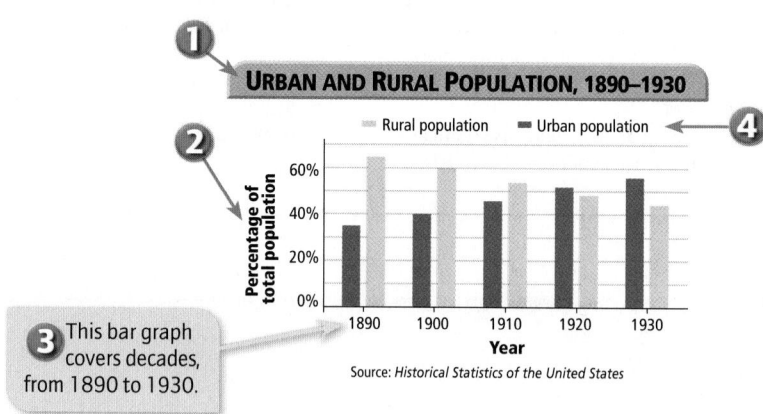

1 URBAN AND RURAL POPULATION, 1890–1930

4

3 This bar graph covers decades, from 1890 to 1930.

Source: *Historical Statistics of the United States*

2. Which of these statements describes the rural population between 1890 and 1930?

A The rural population was lower in 1890 than in 1930.

B The rural population was higher in 1890 than in 1930.

C The rural population and the urban population increased at the same rate.

D The rural population and the urban population declined at the same rate.

Answers: 1 (C), 2 (B)

Directions: *Use the line graph and the bar graph to answer the questions below.*

EUROPEAN IMMIGRATION, 1890–1930

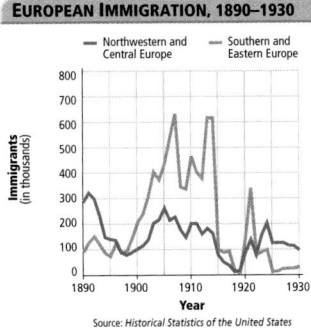

Source: *Historical Statistics of the United States*

AMERICAN INVOLVEMENT IN VIETNAM, 1965–1972

Source: *United States Department of Defense*

1. Between 1900 and 1910, most European immigrants came from

 A Southern and Eastern Europe.

 B Northern and Central Europe.

 C Southern and Central Europe.

 D Northern and Eastern Europe.

2. Which of the following describes a trend in European immigration to the United States between 1920 and 1930?

 A More European immigrants came from Northern and Eastern Europe.

 B More European immigrants came from Southern and Central Europe.

 C The number of immigrants coming from Southern and Eastern Europe decreased.

 D The number of immigrants coming from Northern and Central Europe remained about the same.

3. How did the number of U.S. military personnel in Vietnam change between 1966 and 1967?

 A It decreased by more than 100,000.

 B It increased by more than 100,000.

 C It increased by more than 200,000.

 D It decreased by more than 200,000.

4. Which of the following statements describes the number of U.S. military personnel in Vietnam from 1969 to 1972?

 A The number of U.S. military personnel in Vietnam did not change.

 B The number of U.S. military personnel in Vietnam increased slightly.

 C The number of U.S. military personnel in Vietnam decreased dramatically.

 D The number of U.S. military personnel in Vietnam increased dramatically.

Answers

1. *A;* **2.** *C;* **3.** *B;* **4.** *C*

Strategies for Pie Graphs

You can improve your test-taking skills by practicing these strategies for pie graphs. Read the skill-specific tips and samples on the left page. Then practice the skill on the right page. A pie, or circle, graph shows how parts are related to a whole. Slices of a pie graph should add up to 100% and are proportional to their percentage.

LEARN

① Read the title of the graph to learn the topic and time period it covers.
The title explains that the topic is the presidential election of 1800.

② Be sure the slices add up to 99–100%.
Compare the slices. Are they similar or do they vary widely? Pie graphs don't always indicate numbers, so you may have to estimate.

③ Look for the legend or labels to explain what the different slices represent.
The labels indicate the number of electoral votes won by each candidate.

④ If there are two graphs, compare and contrast them to identify and understand trends.

⑤ Draw conclusions about what might cause similarities or differences between slices or graphs.
The narrow margin of victory suggests that the country was evenly divided.

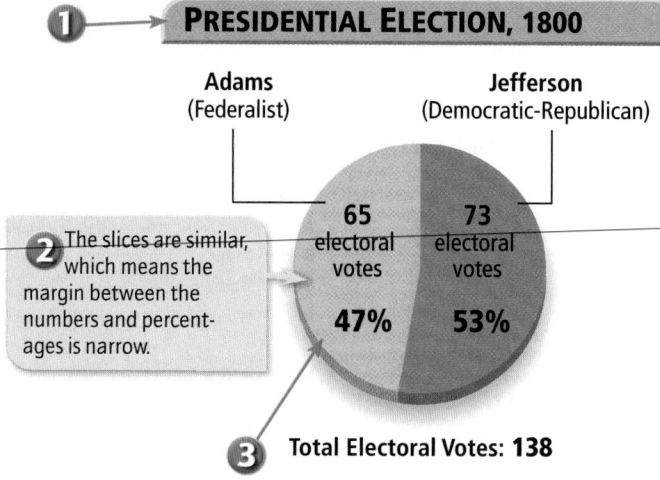

① PRESIDENTIAL ELECTION, 1800

Adams (Federalist)

Jefferson (Democratic-Republican)

② The slices are similar, which means the margin between the numbers and percentages is narrow.

65 electoral votes

73 electoral votes

47%

53%

③ Total Electoral Votes: 138

Source: *The National Atlas of the United States of America*

1. Which sentence best describes the political atmosphere surrounding the election of 1800?

A The election race was calm, as a clear Republican victory was expected.

B The election race was vicious, but a clear Federalist victory was expected.

C U.S. citizens were almost evenly divided between the two candidates

D The Federalist party had an overwhelming lead in the election race

Answer: 1 (C)

PRACTICE

Directions: *Interpret the following circle graph and answer the questions below.*

COLLEGE GRADUATES

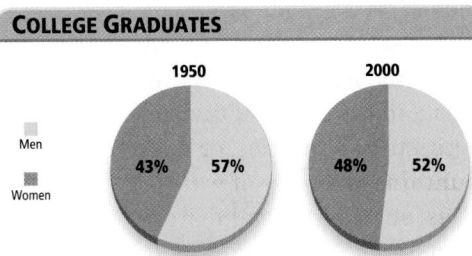

Source: *United States Census Bureau*

1. What do the different colors of the slices represent?

 A 1950 and 2000

 B men and women

 C the percentages of each slice

 D women who graduated and women who did not graduate

2. What comparison do these two graphs make?

 A the number of male versus female students who graduate from college

 B the number of women who graduate from college versus the number of women who vote

 C the gender of college graduates in 1950 versus 2000

 D the percentage of women who graduate from high school versus the percentage of women who graduate from college

3. From these graphs you can conclude that

 A More women than men graduated from college in 2000.

 B Fewer men than women graduated from college in 1950.

 C Women made up a smaller percentage of all college graduates in 2000 than in 1950.

 D Women made up a larger percentage of all college graduates in 2000 than in 1950.

4. What might explain the trend of women to close the gap on men in college graduations?

 A More men earned college degrees in 2000 than in 1950.

 B More men than women earned college degrees in 1950.

 C Women no longer thought they needed college degrees in 2000.

 D Women found a college degree more important to earn in 2000 than in 1950.

STRATEGIES FOR PIE GRAPHS **TT13**

Answers

1. *B;* **2.** *C;* **3.** *D;* **4.** *D*

Strategies for Political and Thematic Maps

You can improve your test-taking skills by practicing these strategies for political and thematic maps. Read the skill-specific tips and samples on the left page. Then practice the skill on the right page. Political maps show countries and the political divisions within them. For example, a political map might show provinces, states, counties, or major cities. They may also highlight physical features, such as mountains or bodies of water.

A thematic map shows patterns of movement, battles, or other special features. Special symbols, such as icons or arrows, are often used on these types of maps.

LEARN

1 **Read the title or heading of the map to find the topic and other information that is shown.**

2 **Find the map legend to find out what different colors or symbols on the map mean.**
Also, read any labels on the map. These can give you details about the purpose of the map.

3 **Look for any special features on the map.**
These may include a locator or an inset map. The arrows on this map show migratory patterns.

4 **Use the compass rose to find directions on the map.**
If there is no compass rose on the map, you must use your prior knowledge of geography to determine direction and location. The map scale can also help in estimating the distance between two places.

5 **Note the lines of longitude and latitude.**
These help determine location on a map.

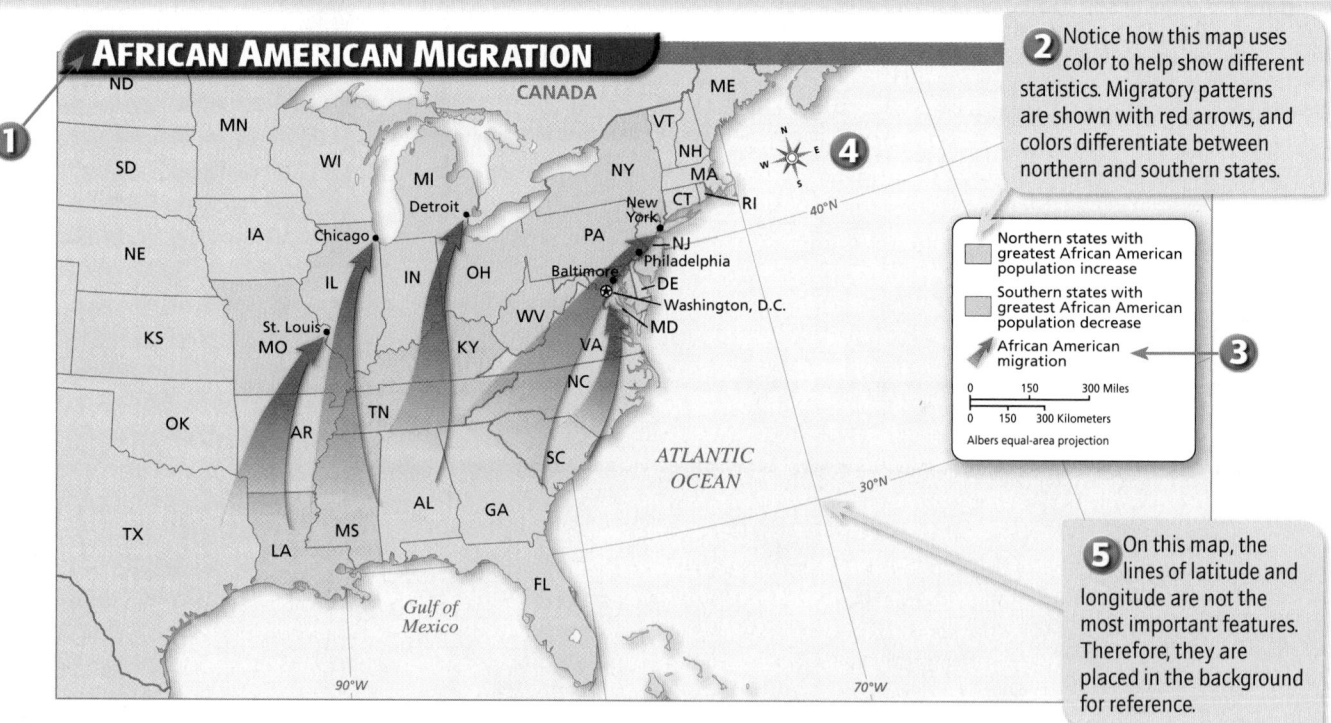

AFRICAN AMERICAN MIGRATION

2 Notice how this map uses color to help show different statistics. Migratory patterns are shown with red arrows, and colors differentiate between northern and southern states.

Northern states with greatest African American population increase

Southern states with greatest African American population decrease

African American migration

0   150   300 Miles
0   150   300 Kilometers
Albers equal-area projection

5 On this map, the lines of latitude and longitude are not the most important features. Therefore, they are placed in the background for reference.

1. Which statement about the information on the map is correct?

A Many African Americans left the East in the early 1900s.

B Many African Americans left the West in the early 1900s.

C Many African Americans left the North in the early 1900s.

D Many African Americans left the South in the early 1900s.

Answer: 1 (D)

PRACTICE

Directions: *Interpret the following thematic map and answer the questions below.*

GERMAN AGGRESSION 1938–1941

1. Which statement about the United Kingdom is correct?

   A The United Kingdom was neutral.

   B The United Kingdom was controlled jointly by the Allied and Axis powers.

   C The United Kingdom was controlled by the Axis powers.

   D The United Kingdom was controlled by the Allied powers.

2. In what year did Axis troops advance into the Union of Soviet Socialist Republics?

   A 1938

   B 1939

   C 1940

   D 1941

3. Which of the following accurately shows the order of German occupation?

   A Yugoslavia, France, Poland

   B Poland, France, Yugoslavia

   C France, Poland, Yugoslavia

   D Yugoslavia, Lithuania, France

4. All of the following statements about the map are true except:

   A Neither Bulgaria nor Finland were neutral countries.

   B Both Spain and Turkey were neutral countries.

   C Axis powers controlled most of Europe.

   D Allied powers controlled most of Europe.

Answers

1. *D;* **2.** *D;* **3.** *B;* **4.** *D*

Strategies for Time Lines

You can improve your test-taking skills by practicing these strategies for time lines. Read the skill-specific tips and samples on the left page. Then practice the skill on the right page. A time line is a type of chart which shows events as they occurred in their chronological order. Time lines are a useful visual tool for learning sequence and cause-and-effect.

LEARN

① **Read the title to learn the subject and time period of the time line.**

② **Look for the beginning and end dates on the time line.**
Think about what you already know about this time period before you begin reading.

③ **Read the events on the time line in chronological order.**
Try to understand the connections between the events.

④ **Note the intervals between events.**
Are there long or short breaks between events?

⑤ **Make inferences about the time period from the information on the time line.**

TIME LINE

Watergate

①

June 17, 1972 Burglars were caught during a break-in at the Watergate Hotel .
June 18, 1972 Carl Bernstein and Bob Woodward helped report the first in a series of stories on the break-in.

②

November 7, 1972 Nixon won re-election in a landslide.

May 18, 1973 Senate Watergate Committee began televised hearings into the scandal.

July 13, 1973 Alexander Butterfield revealed the existence of the White House taping system.

October 20, 1973 In the Saturday night massacre, Nixon fired the special prosecutor.

April 30, 1974 The White House released edited transcripts of the tapes .

July 24, 1974 The Supreme Court ruled that the White House must turn over the tapes.

August 8, 1974 Richard Nixon announced his resignation from the presidency.

③ When the Court ruled that the tapes had to be turned over, Nixon realized that he had to resign.

1. What can you infer about the reaction of the American public to Watergate?

A The public was not affected by the scandal.

B The public supported President Nixon's policies.

C The public did not think that the break-in was wrong.

D The public was disappointed and probably angered by the scandal.

Answer: 1 (D)

Directions: *Interpret the following time line and answer the questions below.*

Isolationism

1898 United States gains control of Puerto Rico, Guam, and the Philippines in the Spanish-American War.

1918 World War I ends. Isolationists in Congress defeat President Wilson's plan to join the League of Nations.

2004 NATO expands to include several countries that had once been part of the Soviet Union.

1800 — 1900 — 2000

1823 Monroe Doctrine pledges neutrality in European disputes but warns European nations not to interfere in the Western Hemisphere.

1945 World War II ends. The United States leads the effort to create the United Nations.

1949 To contain Soviet expansion during the Cold War, the United States joins eleven other nations to form the North Atlantic Treaty Organization (NATO).

1. What time period does this time line cover?
   A the 1800s
   B the 1900s
   C the 2000s
   D all of the above

2. American foreign policy in the 1800s
   A did not exist.
   B was isolationist.
   C was involved with the politics of other countries.
   D took on a leadership role to the rest of the world.

3. In what way did American foreign policy change as time passed?
   A It became more isolationist.
   B America opened relations with every country immediately.
   C America slowly became more involved with other countries.
   D The United States government thought creating a group of "united nations" would not be helpful and wanted to deal with countries on a one-on-one basis.

4. What can you infer is one reason why the United States wanted to create a group of United Nations?
   A They wanted to return to their isolationist stance.
   B They had just finished a second world war and were looking for a way to keep and encourage peace.
   C They wanted to foster trade relations.
   D They did not want to participate in any international debates.

Answers
1. *D;* **2.** *B;* **3.** *C;* **4.** *B*

Strategies for Constructed Response

You can improve your test-taking skills by practicing these strategies for constructed-response questions. Read the skill-specific tips and samples on the left page. Then practice the skill on the right page. Constructed-response questions are based on different types of documents. These can include excerpts, political cartoons, charts, graphs, maps, time lines, posters, and other visuals.

Each document is investigated through one or more open-ended, short-answer questions, which build from simple to complex and evaluate critical-thinking skills. The first question usually requires an answer that can be found in the document. The second question often asks you to connect the information presented in different parts of the document. The third question often requires an answer that is built on information that is not in the document, but is related to the subject of the document.

LEARN

1 Read the title of the document to identify the subject presented.

2 Study the document.

The callouts give you more information about the subject of the map. Each callout on this map identifies the conflict in the area.

3 Read the questions and then study the document again to locate the answers.

4 Answer the questions carefully.

Complete sentences are not necessary unless the directions say to use them.

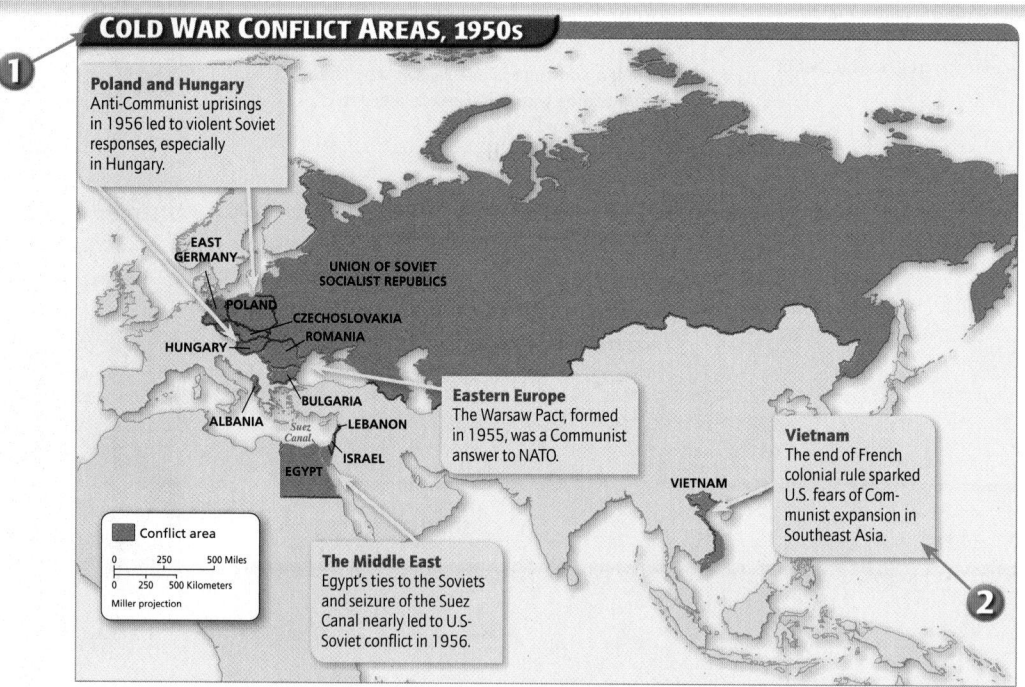

COLD WAR CONFLICT AREAS, 1950s

Poland and Hungary
Anti-Communist uprisings in 1956 led to violent Soviet responses, especially in Hungary.

EAST GERMANY

UNION OF SOVIET SOCIALIST REPUBLICS

POLAND

CZECHOSLOVAKIA

ROMANIA

HUNGARY

BULGARIA

ALBANIA

Suez Canal

LEBANON

ISRAEL

EGYPT

VIETNAM

Eastern Europe
The Warsaw Pact, formed in 1955, was a Communist answer to NATO.

Vietnam
The end of French colonial rule sparked U.S. fears of Communist expansion in Southeast Asia.

The Middle East
Egypt's ties to the Soviets and seizure of the Suez Canal nearly led to U.S.-Soviet conflict in 1956.

Conflict area

0   250   500 Miles
0   250   500 Kilometers
Miller projection

1. What was considered the Communist answer to NATO?_____ the Warsaw Pact _____

2. How was the conflict in the Middle East different than the conflicts in Poland and Hungary?
_____ In the Middle East, Egypt was friendly to the Soviet Union. _____
_____ In Poland and Hungary, there were anti-communist uprisings. _____

3. Which conflict area will the U.S. military be most involved with in the 1960s?_____ Vietnam _____

Directions: *Look at the following chart and answer the questions below.*

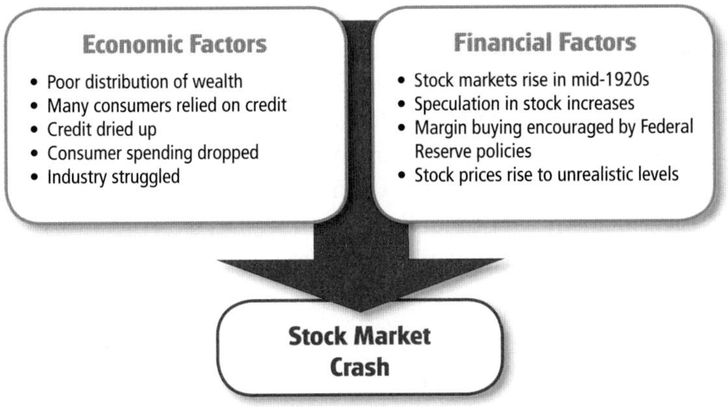

Economic Factors
- Poor distribution of wealth
- Many consumers relied on credit
- Credit dried up
- Consumer spending dropped
- Industry struggled

Financial Factors
- Stock markets rise in mid-1920s
- Speculation in stock increases
- Margin buying encouraged by Federal Reserve policies
- Stock prices rise to unrealistic levels

Stock Market Crash

1. What was one economic factor that led to the crash of the stock market?

_____

_____

2. How was credit spending both an economic and financial factor in the stock market crash?

_____

_____

3. How did the crash of the stock market affect the American economy?

_____

_____

Answers

1. *possible answer—poor distribution of wealth* **2.** *Consumers relied on credit and the Federal Reserve encouraged margin buying on the stock market.* **3.** *Unemployment increased, personal savings were lost, and many banks and businesses were closed.*

Strategies for Extended Response

You can improve your test-taking skills by practicing these strategies for extended-response questions. Read the skill-specific tips and samples on the left page. Then practice the skill on the right page. Extended-response questions usually focus on a document. Documents can be articles, historical documents, charts, graphs, photographs, political cartoons, and other information sources. Documents can be primary or secondary sources. Some extended-response questions ask you to analyze or summarize the information presented in the document. Others require you to complete a chart, graph, or diagram. In most standardized tests, a document has only one extended-response question.

LEARN

① Read the title of the document to learn what the document is about.

② Read the extended-response questions carefully.

③ Study and analyze the document.
This chart lists important New Deal programs undertaken in response to the stock market crash and the Great Depression.

④ Analyze any partial or a sample answers provided.
Your answers should take the same form as this sample answer.

⑤ Take notes and jot down ideas in outline form.
Use your notes and outline to prepare for writing an essay or other extended piece of writing.

① MAJOR NEW DEAL PROGRAMS

Relief	
Civilian Conservation Corps (CCC), 1933	provided jobs on conservation projects to young men whose families needed relief
Works Progress Administration (WPA), 1935	provided many different types of jobs on public works projects for those needing relief
Social Security Act, 1935	established pensions for retirees, unemployment benefits, and aid for certain groups of low-income or disabled people

Reform	
Securities and Exchange Commission (SEC), 1934	provided increased government regulation of the trading on stock exchanges
National Labor Relations Act, 1935	established the National Labor Relations Board (NLRB) to enforce labor laws ④

Recovery	
Tennessee Valley Authority (TVA), 1933	promoted development projects in the Tennessee River Valley
Federal Housing Administration (FHA), 1934	provided loans for renovating or building homes

1. In the right-hand column, briefly explain the function of each New Deal program listed in the left-hand column. One entry has been completed for you.

2. This chart explains several important New Deal programs introduced to respond to the stock market crash and the Great Depression. Write a short speech for Franklin D. Roosevelt discussing why these programs are necessary and what he hopes they will accomplish. ⑤

Directions: *Use the time line and your knowledge of American history to answer questions 1 and 2.*

Native American Activism and Policy

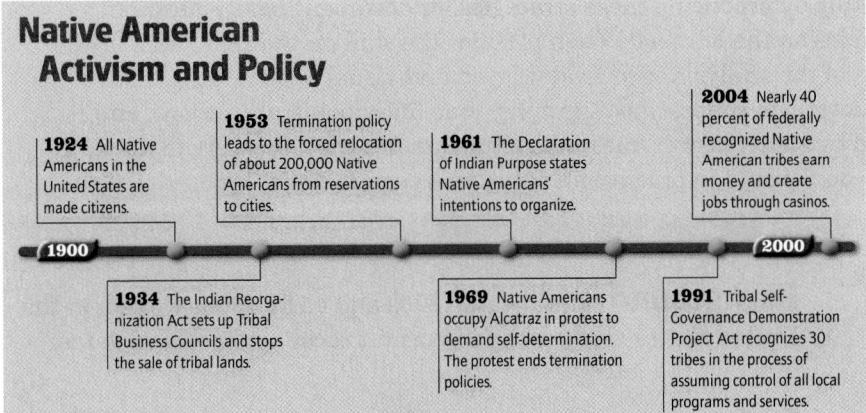

1924 All Native Americans in the United States are made citizens.

1953 Termination policy leads to the forced relocation of about 200,000 Native Americans from reservations to cities.

1961 The Declaration of Indian Purpose states Native Americans' intentions to organize.

2004 Nearly 40 percent of federally recognized Native American tribes earn money and create jobs through casinos.

1900   2000

1934 The Indian Reorganization Act sets up Tribal Business Councils and stops the sale of tribal lands.

1969 Native Americans occupy Alcatraz in protest to demand self-determination. The protest ends termination policies.

1991 Tribal Self-Governance Demonstration Project Act recognizes 30 tribes in the process of assuming control of all local programs and services.

1. Make a chart as shown below on a separate sheet of paper. Complete the chart by listing major events in Native American history since 1800 and explaining each event's significance to the relationship between Native Americans and the United States government.

Year	Event	Significance

2. Identify major changes in United States government policy toward Native Americans as shown on the time line. Write a short essay discussing the difference between Americanization and termination policies, analyzing each policy's effects on the formation of Native American social and political movements.

Answers

1. *Students' charts should list the events in chronological order and include an appropriate explanation of each event's significance.*

2. *Answers will vary, but essays should explain the difference between Americanization and termination policies and analyze the effects of each policy.*

Strategies for Document-Based Questions

You can improve your test-taking skills by practicing these strategies for document-based questions. Read the skill-specific tips and samples on the left page. Then practice the skill on the right page. A document-based question consists of the analysis of several written and visual documents. Such documents may include excerpts, quotations, maps, charts, graphs, time lines, political cartoons, and so on. These documents are followed by short-answer questions. Students use their answers to these questions and information from the documents to produce an essay on a certain topic.

LEARN

1. **Read carefully the "Background" to understand the documents that you will be analyzing.**
2. **Read the "Task" portion, which describes in detail the steps you will follow in answering document-based questions and formulating an essay about a given topic.**
3. **"Part A: Short-Answer Questions" signifies the first part of the document-based question.**
4. **Examine and study each document.**
5. **Read and answer each of the document-specific questions.**

Background In the late 1800s and early 1900s women in the United States made many important social and political gains.

Task Using information from the documents and your knowledge of United States history, answer the questions that follow each document in Part A. Your answers to the questions will help you write the Part B essay, in which you will be asked to:

> **Describe challenges facing women in the late 1800s and early 1900s.**

Part A: Short-Answer Questions

Study each document carefully. Then answer the question or questions that follow each document in the space provided.

DOCUMENT 1

> "... The women, dissatisfied as they are with this form of government, that enforces taxation without representation—that compels them to obey laws to which they have never given their consent—that imprisons and hangs them without a trial by a jury of their peers, that robs them, in marriage, of the custody of their own persons, wages and children—are this half of the people left wholly at the mercy of the other half, in direct violation of the spirit and letter of the declarations of the framers of this government, every one of which was based on the immutable [undeniable] principle of equal rights to all."

1. What were Susan B. Anthony's beliefs about women's voting rights?

She believed that women should have

the same voting rights as men.

DOCUMENT 2

6 Write your essay.
Include an introductory paragraph that frames your argument, a main body with details that explain it, and a closing paragraph that summarizes your position. Include specific details or documents to support your ideas.

Rubric
The best essays will note challenges such as voting rights (Document 1), and the tough choices relating to women's careers and home life. (Document 2).

2. What does this political cartoon represent?

It represents tough choices facing women
in their home and work lives.

Part B: Essay 6

Using the documents, your answers to the questions in Part A, and your knowledge of U.S. history, write a well-organized essay about challenges facing women in the late 1800s and early 1900s.

PRACTICE

Background In the 1920s, new forms of media emerged that enabled people to share the same information and enjoy the same pastimes.

Task Using information from the documents and your knowledge of U.S. history, answer the questions that follow each document in Part A. Your answers to the questions will help you write the Part B essay, in which you will be asked to:

> **Describe the growth of popular American culture in the 1920s.**

DOCUMENT 1

1. What does this magazine cover convey about American culture during the 1920s?

DOCUMENT 2

2. What can you tell about the popularity of films from this picture?

Part B: Essay

Using the documents, your answers to the questions in Part A, and your knowledge of U.S. history, write a well-organized essay about the growth of popular American culture in the 1920s.

Answers

1. *Films were quite popular with the American public in the 1920s, drawing large crowds to features.* **2.** *The cover conveys the increased leisure time available to and enjoyed by Americans, which included dance and the reading of popular magazines.*
Essay. *possible answer—American popular culture experienced significant growth in the 1920s. Large crowds attended films, while other Americans read and enjoyed other leisure activities such as dancing.*

UNIT 1 Beginnings of AMERICA

Beginnings–1763

Chapter 1
The World before 1600
Beginnings to 1600

Chapter 2
European Colonies in America
1500–1733

Chapter 3
Colonial Life
1650–1763

Themes

Cultural Expressions
The Native Americans' ancient ways of life changed with the arrival of European settlers. As settlements developed into colonies, colonists began to form a distinct, American culture.

Immigration and Migration
People first migrated to America many thousands of years ago and lived throughout the continent before Europeans arrived and began to form colonies.

The voyage of the Mayflower marked a new beginning for not just the settlers on board but for America as well.

THE GRANGER COLLECTION, NEW YORK

1

Unit Preview

Introducing the Unit

Explain to students that in this unit they will learn about America before it became an independent country. Have students work in pairs to create a word web, based on their previous knowledge, of statements describing the beginnings of America. Students may describe Native Americans, early European settlers, or British colonists before the Revolution. Have students retain their word webs as a study tool.

Connecting to Themes

Activity **Past and Present Challenges** Have students brainstorm a list of challenges faced by the first Europeans to come to America. Then have students brainstorm a similar list of the challenges faced by modern immigrants to the United States.
LS Verbal-Linguistic

Reading Like a Historian

Interpreting Visuals
The *Mayflower* The voyage of the *Mayflower* took 66 days, from September 16, 1620 to November 21, 1620. The ship carried 102 passengers and an unspecified number of cats. The common American Shorthair cat is descended from these first furry travelers.

Unit Resources

Planning
- Differentiated Instruction Teacher Management System: Unit Pacing Guide
- One-Stop Planner CD-ROM: Teacher Management System
- Power Presentations with Video CD-ROM

Differentiating Instruction
- Differentiated Instruction Teacher Management System: Lesson Plans for Differentiated Instruction
- Pre-AP Activities Guide for American History
- Differentiated Instruction Modified Worksheets and Tests CD-ROM

Enrichment
- Civic Participation Activities Guide
- CRF: Economics and History Activity
- CRF: Interdisciplinary Project
- American History Primary Source Library CD-ROM

Assessment
- PASS: Unit Test, Forms A & B
- Alternative Assessment Handbook
- OSP ExamView Test Generator
- HOAP Holt Online Assessment Program (in the Premier Online Edition)

The Differentiated Instruction Teacher Management System
provides a planning and instructional benchmarking guide for this unit.

Identifying Main Idea and Details

Have each student print out, make a copy of, or cut out a short article from a magazine, newspaper, or Web site about a current event. Have students write a sentence that explains the main idea of their articles. Then have students exchange their articles and main idea sentences with a partner, who should add three important details under the main idea sentence. If time permits, discard the main idea/details papers and redistribute the articles to repeat the activity.

Word Help

hierarchy different levels in an organization

Teaching Tip

Explain to students that a cable news "creep" is the scrolling band of headline-like information on the bottom of a cable news screen. Have students choose events from this unit and write "creeps" about them, as if the events were breaking news stories. Have students share their "creeps" with the class.

Skills Planner

To give students more opportunities to practice this skill, see Skills Focus activities in the teacher's edition.

Prepare to Read

Identifying Main Idea and Details

Find practice for **Identifying Main Idea and Details** in the **Skills Handbook,** p. H5

The main idea is the most important idea of a passage. Details support, illustrate, or develop the main idea.

Before You Read
Look at headings and the Reading Check questions.

While You Read
Look for topic sentences in each paragraph. These are often the main ideas.

After You Read
Ask yourself questions. What was the main idea? What was the author trying to get across?

Quakers Settle Pennsylvania

Another one of Charles II's land grants became William Penn's colony, Pennsylvania. Penn planned to build a colony that would give him and other Quakers a haven. From the king's perspective, it was an opportunity to get rid of an unpopular group.

The Quakers Of all the various groups of Nonconformists—Protestants who did not follow the Church of England—the Quakers upset people the most. Officially called the Society of Friends, their name came from their founder, George Fox. He urged them to "tremble [quake] at the name of the Lord."

Quakers believed in direct, personal communication with God. That meant no ministers and no hierarchy of priests and bishops, as in the Anglican and Roman Catholic Churches. They had no set worship service. Instead, members of the congregation spoke up in Quaker meetings. They preached their beliefs in the streets and sometimes interrupted other groups' church services

READING CHECK **Identifying Main Ideas and Details** Why did the Quakers upset members of other religious groups?

> This section head tells you the topic—how the Quakers came to settle Pennsylvania.

> **Main idea** The Quakers' religious beliefs upset the members of other groups.

> **Detail** The Quakers believed in direct communication with God, without a hierarchy priests and bishops.

Test Prep Tip

Short answer questions on tests often ask you to find details that support a passage's main idea. To find supporting details, use clue words such as *who, what, when, where, why,* and *how.* Turn section headings into questions. An example for this passage might be "Why did the Quakers settle Pennsylvania?

2 UNIT 1

Skills Focus: Identifying Main Idea and Details

At Level

Reading Skill
Identifying Main Idea and Details in Historical Texts

1. Organize students into pairs. Have each pair choose a subsection from one of the chapters in this unit.

2. Have each student read the section, including the heading. Then have students take turns quizzing each other about the main idea and details of the text section. Remind students to use the question words *who, what, when, where, why,* and *how* to identify details, and

to look at the heading for help on finding the main idea.

3. Have students choose other passages and repeat the activity as time allows. **LS Verbal-Linguistic, Intrapersonal**

📖 Alternative Assessment Handbook, Rubric 16: Judging Information

Reading like a Historian

Analyzing Primary Sources

Find practice for **Analyzing Primary Sources** in the **Skills Handbook**, p. H28

Primary sources are documents created by people who were present at historical events either as witnesses or as participants. These sources can range from letters and diary entries to newspaper stories and photographs.

Strategies historians use:

- Find clues in the text. Look for words that identify a primary source, such as *I*, or note quotation marks that indicate a passage is someone's speech or writing.
- What does the source say about the event or time period described?
- Identify the author and analyze the type of source. Is this the kind of document in which primary sources are often found?

Quotation marks, as well as the word *I*, help you determine that what you are reading is a primary source.

Benjamin Franklin is the writer. The passage describes his early life. It also tells us that people in Franklin's time learned a trade such as printing by being indentured, or legally contracted to work for someone.

❝From a child I was fond of reading, and all the little money that came into my hands was ever laid out in books…This bookish inclination at length determined my father to make me a printer, though he had already one son (James) of that profession. In 1717 my brother James returned from England with a press and letters to set up his business in Boston…[My] father was impatient to have me bound to my brother. I stood out [tried to avoid being bound] some time, but at last was persuaded, and signed the indentures when I was but twelve years old. I was to serve as an apprentice until I was twenty-one years of age…❞

— *Autobiography of Benjamin Franklin*, 1771-1790

The word *Autobiography* means "to write the story of one's own life." An autobiography is always considered a primary source.

Skills Focus — READING LIKE A HISTORIAN

As You Read Paraphrase the primary source in your own words to make sure you understand any difficult language.

As You Study Use your prior knowledge and information in the chapter to assess the source.

Analyzing Primary Sources

Explain to students that since primary sources are written by someone who witnessed or participated in a historical event, that person may be biased. Ask students why Benjamin Franklin might have chosen to record this event and what message he might have been trying to convey. Ask students if Franklin's account is biased and what evidence supports their conclusion.

Word Help

articulated pronounced

Primary Source

In his autobiography, Franklin tells about Whitefield's arrival and effect on the local clergy, as well as on his listeners: "In 1739 arrived among us from Ireland the Reverend Mr. Whitefield . . . He was at first permitted to preach in some of our churches; but the clergy, taking a dislike to him, soon refus'd him their pulpits, and he was oblig'd to preach in the fields . . . it was matter of speculation to me, who was one of the number, to observe . . . how much they admir'd and respected him, notwithstanding his common abuse of them, by assuring them that they were naturally half beasts and half devils."

— Benjamin Franklin

The Autobiography of Benjamin Franklin

Skills Focus: Analyzing Primary Sources

Above Level

Reading Like a Historian Skill
Working with Primary Sources

1. Have students find, at the library or at a reputable Internet site, two primary source quotations about the same event in American history before 1763. As examples, you might suggest the exploits of the Spanish conquistadors; the discovery of the Mississippi River, Pacific Ocean, or Hudson Bay; the landing of the Pilgrims in Massachusetts, or a battle of the French and Indian War.

2. Have students analyze their two primary sources and note how they differ and how they are similar.

3. Have volunteers share their findings. Then guide students in a discussion of how they—and historians—might evaluate the worth of different and conflicting primary sources.

LS Verbal-Linguistic

 Alternative Assessment Handbook, Rubric 30: Research

Chapter 1 Planning Guide

The World Before 1600

Chapter Overview	Reproducible Resources	Technology Resources
CHAPTER 1 pp. 4–37 **Overview:** In this chapter, students will analyze the varied cultures that called the Americas home as well as the cultures that explored the world and established colonies in the Americas.	**Differentiated Instruction Teacher Management System:*** • Instructional Benchmarking Guides • Lesson Plans for Differentiated Instruction **Interactive Reader and Study Guide:** Chapter Summary* **Chapter Resource File:*** • Focus on Writing Activity: How Europeans Viewed Native Americans • Social Studies Skills Activity: Interpreting Historical Maps • Chapter Review Activity **American History Outline Maps** **Pre-AP Activities Guide for American History***	Live Ink® Online Reading Help Student Edition on Audio CD Program Differentiated Instruction Modified Worksheets and Tests CD-ROM Interactive Skills Tutor CD-ROM United States History Primary Source Library CD-ROM Power Presentations with Video CD-ROM History's Impact: American History Video Program (VHS/DVD): The World Before 1600 Online Chapter Summaries in Spanish
Section 1: **The Early Americas** **The Main Idea:** People arrived on the American continents thousands of years ago and developed flourishing societies.	**Differentiated Instruction Teacher Management System:** Section 1 Lesson Plan* **Interactive Reader and Study Guide:** Section 1 Summary* **Chapter Resource File***	Daily Bellringer Transparency: Section 1* Map Transparency: Bering Land Bridge* Daily Test Practice Transparency: Section 1*
Section 2: **North American Cultures in the 1400s** **The Main Idea:** Complex societies existed in North America before European explorers arrived in the early 1500s.	**Differentiated Instruction Teacher Management System:** Section 2 Lesson Plan* **Interactive Reader and Study Guide:** Section 2 Summary* **Chapter Resource File***	Daily Bellringer Transparency: Section 2* Map Transparency: Native American Culture Areas* Daily Test Practice Transparency: Section 2*
Section 3: **African Cultures Before 1500** **The Main Idea:** Trade was a major factor in the development of African societies south of Sahara.	**Differentiated Instruction Teacher Management System:** Section 3 Lesson Plan* **Interactive Reader and Study Guide:** Section 3 Summary* **Chapter Resource File***	Daily Bellringer Transparency: Section 3* Map Transparency: West and Central Africa, 1100–1500* Daily Test Practice Transparency: Section 3*
Section 4: **Europe and Exploration** **The Main Idea:** Renaissance ideas inspired Europeans to explore the world.	**Differentiated Instruction Teacher Management System:** Section 4 Lesson Plan* **Interactive Reader and Study Guide:** Section 4 Summary* **Chapter Resource File***	Daily Bellringer Transparency: Section 4* Map Transparency: European Routes* Daily Test Practice Transparency: Section 4*
Section 5: **Cultures Make Contact** **The Main Idea:** Columbus's voyages to the Americas led to European colonies and an exchange of goods and ideas with Native Americans.	**Differentiated Instruction Teacher Management System:** Section 5 Lesson Plan* **Interactive Reader and Study Guide:** Section 5 Summary* **Chapter Resource File***	Daily Bellringer Transparency: Section 5* Map Transparency: Columbian Exchange* Daily Test Practice Transparency: Section 5*

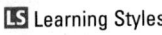

 HOLT
History's Impact
American History Video Program (VHS/DVD)
The World Before 1600

Review, Assessment, Intervention

 Quick Facts Transparency: The World Before 1600

 Spanish Chapter Summaries Audio CD Program

 Progress Assessment Support System (PASS): Chapter Test*

 Differentiated Instruction Modified Worksheets and Tests CD-ROM: Modified Chapter Test

OSP **One-Stop Planner CD-ROM:** ExamView Test Generator (English/Spanish)

HOAP **Holt Online Assessment Program (HOAP),** in the Holt Premier Online Student Edition

---

 PASS: Section 1 Quiz*

 Online Quiz: Section 1

 Alternative Assessment Handbook

 PASS: Section 2 Quiz*

 Online Quiz: Section 2

 Alternative Assessment Handbook

 PASS: Section 3 Quiz*

 Online Quiz: Section 3

 Alternative Assessment Handbook

 PASS: Section 4 Quiz*

 Online Quiz: Section 4

 Alternative Assessment Handbook

 PASS: Section 5 Quiz*

 Online Quiz: Section 5

 Alternative Assessment Handbook

 **NC RESOURCES**

The following resources were developed to help North Carolina educators teach the standards and objectives of North Carolina's eleventh grade standard course of study in United States history.

- United States history EOC Test Prep Workbook
- Teacher's Support System
- North Carolina One-Stop Planner

And be sure to direct your students to **go.hrw.com** for online access to the EOC Test Prep Workbook.

go.hrw.com
EOC Test Prep
KEYWORD: SE7 NC

 **Holt Online Learning**

go.hrw.com
Teacher Resources
KEYWORD: SD7 TEACHER

go.hrw.com
Student Resources
KEYWORD: SD7 CH1

- Document-Based Questions
- Interactive Multimedia Activities

- Current Events
- Chapter-based Internet Activities
- and more!

Holt Premier
Online Student Edition
Complete online support for interactivity, assessment, and reporting

- Interactive Maps and Notebook
- Homework Practice and Research Activities Online

The Big Picture

Jesús F. de la Teja

Whose New World? Scientists are still trying to figure out when the Americas were discovered. We'll never know who the first individual was to arrive on the shores of the Western Hemisphere, but that long-forgotten discoverer was in the vanguard of a migration that colonized two continents thousands of years before the Vikings or Iberians showed up. In the course of time the inhabitants of the Americas made many of the same discoveries as the inhabitants of Eurasia and Africa; they domesticated plants and invented the bow and arrow, and some cultures even created monumental stone architecture and invented systems of writing. They did not call themselves "Indians" and they could not form a united front against the invaders from Europe, yet in language, culture, and foodways, they are very much a part of what America is today.

The Old World Renewed From the thirteenth through the sixteenth centuries a number of technological and cultural forces transformed Europe into a dynamic center of scientific, economic, and spiritual exploration. The printing press, lateen sail, compass, astrolabe, and ship construction techniques gave European mariners unparalleled confidence in sailing into the unknown. The Spaniards' final victory over the Muslims of the Iberian peninsula made them confident that God wanted them to extend Christianity to far-off places. Expanding markets for luxury goods and spices convinced merchants and nobles alike to undertake risky ventures that promised incalculable fortunes in return. Unknown America seemed a land of endless opportunity for the people of Renaissance Europe.

Recent Scholarship

Humans Come to the New World Now in its second edition, Brian Fagan's *The Great Journey: The Peopling of Ancient America* (2004) offers the general reader a comprehensive and readable survey of the state of knowledge regarding the arrival of human beings in the New World. Among its most useful features are the presentation of competing views, a generous number of useful maps, illustrations, and photographs, and a conscientious effort to cover all the major regions of North America. Teachers will value its annotated bibliography, in which the author critically comments on some works and offers an additional list of suggested readings.

Differentiating Instruction

 Differentiated Instruction Teacher Management System
- Lesson Plans for Differentiated Instruction
- Differentiated Instructional Benchmarking Guides
- Interactive Reader and Study Guide

 Spanish Chapter Summaries Audio CD Program

 Online Chapter Summaries in Spanish

 Student Edition on Audio CD Program

 Differentiated Instruction Modified Worksheets and Tests CD-ROM
- Vocabulary Flash Cards
- Modified Vocabulary Builder Activities
- Modified Chapter Review Activity
- Modified Chapter Test

OSP One-Stop Planner CD-ROM
- ExamView Test Generator (English and Spanish)
- PuzzlePro
- Quiz Show for ExamView
- Transparencies and Videos

TE Differentiated Activities in the Teacher's Edition
- Early Cultures of North America, p. 9
- Culture Area Maps, p. 12
- Native American Traditions and Ideas, p. 16
- The Rise and Fall of Feudalism, p. 24
- Columbus's Landing, p. 31

Reading Like a Historian

Sam Wineburg

If the Past is Over Why Does History Keep Changing?

To this question, a layperson might respond, "Because historians are always making new discoveries that change our understanding." True, trunks with stuffed letters from someone's Civil War-era relative are always turning up. However, these discoveries and others like them rarely cause major shifts in our understanding.

The Artifact in Your Hands

More often, our vision of the past changes because *we* change. We put different questions to the past that direct our attention to aspects that have been there all along gathering dust. Only now, in light of our new concerns, do we pay attention to what we previously ignored.

Consider the opening chapter of the textbook you are holding. Fifty years from now historians will look back at this as an artifact of how Americans in the new millennium's first decade viewed themselves.

Beginnings

Think about beginnings, the most significant aspect of any story. Our chapter starts with an overview of the indigenous peoples of the Americas. In Section 3, the scope is expanded with information on Africa and the kingdoms of Mali and Songhai. Only after this overview do we turn our attention to Europe; the contact point between the New World and the Old appears only in our chapter's closing pages. Columbus ends—rather than begins—our story of origins.

To help students understand how history changes, consider comparing this chapter with a textbook written 30 or 40 years ago—maybe even the one you used as a high school student.

A Comparison

When I was ten years old I received a birthday present that sits on the shelf of my library to this day: the seventeen-volume *American Heritage Illustrated History of the United States* (1963). Volume I, written by University of Colorado historian Robert G. Athearn, spans roughly the same period as Chapter One of our book. Athearn's account opens with Europe's move westward. The second page shows a 1665 fresco of Christopher Columbus, his hand gripping a giant cross, gazing upward as his sailors plant the cross in the ground. Only after 20 pages is there a section called "The Aboriginal Americans," followed by a section that reviews Europe's encounter with the New World—projects of colonization by Spain, France, Holland, and England. Next comes a section delving more deeply into the context of English settlement by looking at the political and social conditions of Elizabethan England, and the flight of religious separatists from England to Holland. Nowhere in the volume is there any mention of African kingdoms, nor any attempt to catalogue America's many indigenous peoples. The book's focus is unabashedly Eurocentric.

Why the Differences?

Can we account for these differences by new historical discoveries in the last forty years? Not really. While there have doubtless been many new findings during this time, there is little in our present chapter that we did not already know in 1960. What has changed decisively is our understanding of foreground and background—what is significant and what is peripheral when beginning the American story.

The past is over, but history remains fluid because our understanding of who we are refuses to stay still. The writing of history is guided by deep assumptions about what is important. Questioning those assumptions is what historians do when reading each other's work. If we bring these assumptions to the surface for students, we can invite young people to query the past, helping them see how written histories are mirrors for who we think we are in the present.

The Big Idea and Essential Questions

To foster student understanding of this chapter's big idea, design your lesson to address each section's essential question.

Big Idea Cultures emerged in different parts of the world and began to have contact with each other.

Essential Questions

1. How did societies form on the American continents?

2. Which societies existed in North American before European explorers arrived?

3. What role did trade play in the development of African societies south of the Sahara?

4. What inspired Europeans to explore the world?

5. What were the consequences of Columbus's voyages to the Americas?

CHAPTER

1

Beginnings—1600

The WORLD Before 1600

THE BIG PICTURE During the Ice Age, nomads crossed a land bridge connecting Asia and North America. Since then, people of various cultures have made the Americas their home. Meanwhile in Europe and Africa, cultures that would one day explore the world and build colonies in the Americas were coming into contact.

North Carolina Standards

Language Arts Objectives

2.03 Demonstrate the ability to read, listen to and view a variety of increasingly complex print and non-print informational texts appropriate to grade level and course literary focus, by:
- demonstrating comprehension of main idea and supporting details.

Skills FOCUS READING LIKE A HISTORIAN

This detail from Portugal's Monument of Discovery shows Prince Henry the Navigator at the forefront of many famous Portuguese explorers. The monument is shaped like the prow of a ship and was built for the 500th anniversary of Henry's death.
Drawing Conclusions Why do you think Portugal built this monument?

See Skills Handbook, p. H12

U.S.

38,000–10,000 BC	500 BC
The first people migrate to North America.	Adena culture begins in the Ohio River Valley.

800 BC

World

4

Key to Differentiating Instruction

Below Level

Basic-level activities designed for all students encountering new material

At Level

Intermediate-level activities designed for average students

Above Level

Challenging activities designed for honors and gifted-and-talented students

Standard English Mastery

Activities designed to improve standard English usage

Introduce the Chapter

At Level

The World Before 1600

1. Tell students that in this chapter they will review centuries of history, from the first inhabitants in the Americas through the Age of Exploration.

2. Have students work in pairs to list what they remember from other history classes about the early Americas, North American cultures, early Africa, the Renaissance, Reformation, and the Age of Exploration. Have students share information from their lists with the class.

3. Have students look through the chapter and make a list of the images and maps in each section. Then have students make a list of important events that occurred before the 1500s.

4. Have students share their lists with the class and retain them as a study tool.
LS Visual-Spatial

Alternative Assessment Handbook, Rubric 11: Discussions

100 BC
Hopewell Mound Builders inherit Adena traditions.

1000
Mississippian society spreads across the southeast and southern Midwest.

200 BC —— **AD 400** —— **1000** —— **1600**

400 BC
The Maya build great stone cities in Central America.

500
Roman Empire collapses.

1440
Atlantic slave trade begins.

1492
Columbus lands on an island in the Caribbean.

5

Chapter Preview

HOLT
History's Impact
► Video Program: The World Before 1600
See the Video Teacher's Guide for strategies for using the video segment.

Reading Like a Historian

Into the Unknown Have students take a moment to examine the image on these pages. How is it possible to identify the occupations of the men? What are they? *by the instruments or objects they are holding; possible answers—explorer, church representatives, navigator, soldier*

go.hrw.com
Online Resources

Chapter Resources:
KEYWORD: SD7 CH1

Teacher Resources:
KEYWORD: SD7 TEACHER

Explore the Time Line

1. How many years passed from the time of the Mound Builders to the time the Mississippian Society had begun to spread across the southeast and southern Midwest? *1100 years*

2. When and where did the Adena culture begin? *500 BC; Ohio River Valley*

3. When did the Atlantic slave trade begin? *1440 AD*

Info to Know

The Agricultural Revolution The Agricultural Revolution started in different regions at different times. By around 5000 BC groups in what is now Mexico began growing corn. It was the beginning of the agricultural revolution in the Americas and enabled early people to settle in one place, support larger populations, and led to the development of great civilizations.

Sequencing How does the ability to grow food lead to the development of a civilization? *people can settle in one place; leads to a division of labor, population can stabilize and grow*

Answers

Reading Like a Historian
(p. 4) *possible answer—to celebrate the efforts of Prince Henry and the explorers' achievements*

5

Bellringer

The Inside Story. . . Use the **Daily Bellringer Transparency** to help students answer the question.

🖎 Daily Bellringer Transparency, Section 1

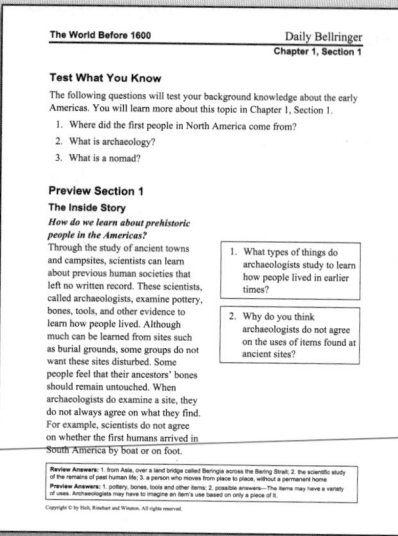

Academic Vocabulary

Review with students the high-use academic terms in this section.

distribute divide among several (p. 7)

technique method (p. 8)

🖎 CRF: Vocabulary Builder Activity, Section 1

Taking Notes

Group—Siberian nomads, Native Americans, Olmec, Maya, Toltec, Aztec, Inca, Peoples of the Southwest, Mound-Builders, Mississippian; Time—12,000 to 40,000 years ago, 2,000 years ago, 1300 BC, 400 BC, AD 900, 1400, 1400s, 2,000 years ago, 700 BC, 1250; Way of Life—hunter-gatherers, farmers, mother culture, religion and astronomy, artisans and builders, warriors and religion, vast empire, desert life and adobe buildings, clans and mound-building, advanced farming society and impressive ceremonial temple-mounds

---

The Early Americas

BEFORE YOU READ

MAIN IDEA

People arrived on the American continents thousands of years ago and developed flourishing societies.

READING FOCUS

1. According to scientists and historians, how and when did the first migration to the Americas occur?

2. What kind of cultures developed in Central and South America?

3. What characterized the earliest cultures of North America?

KEY TERMS AND PEOPLE

nomad
hunter-gatherer
agricultural revolution
Olmec
Maya
Toltec
Aztec
Inca
pueblo
clan

TAKING NOTES As you read, take notes on the changes that the first Americans gradually underwent in their ways of life. Record your notes in a chart like this one. You may need to add more rows.

Group	Time	Way of Life

The First AMERICANS

THE INSIDE STORY

How do we learn about prehistoric people in the Americas?
Prehistory means the time before written records were kept. So with no ancient scrolls or stone tablets to refer to and certainly no books or newspapers or Web sites, how do we know about the first people in our part of the world?

Information about early American cultures comes mainly from archaeology. Archaeology is the scientific study of the remains of past human life. Archaeologists carry out digs to unearth ancient towns and campsites. They examine pottery, tools, bones, and other physical evidence.

One important piece of archaeological evidence is a distinctive stone spear point called the Clovis point. Because these spear points have been found throughout the Americas, scientists have developed theories of early human migration based upon them.

Some archaeological evidence is controversial. For example, ancient burial grounds might hold valuable clues about the peoples who settled the Americas. Yet some groups do not want scientists disturbing these sites. Many Native Americans consider them sacred places and believe the bones of their ancestors should remain untouched.

▲ The discovery of artifacts like this spear straightener help researchers reconstruct the past.

Evidence may also be interpreted in different ways. As you will read, most scholars agree that the first people in North America crossed a land bridge from Siberia to Alaska. But other scholars argue that ancient humans arrived in South America by boat. A 9,000-year-old skeleton known as Kennewick Man aroused even more controversy. The skeleton did not appear to be Asian, and so certain scholars suggested that some early Americans may actually have come from Europe. Some Native American groups, however, claimed Kennewick Man as an ancestor.

All these ideas and interpretations suggest that future archaeologists will have plenty to study! ■

6 CHAPTER 1

Teach the Main Idea

The Early Americas

1. **Teach** Ask students the Reading Focus questions to teach this section.

2. **Apply** Have students create an outline of the section using the heads as main points. Have students list at least two facts under each blue subhead. **LS Verbal-Linguistic**

3. **Review** Review student outlines as a class. Have students identify the points in their outlines that they think are most important. Guide students in discussing the ways in which cultures develop.

4. **Practice/Homework** Have each student choose two of the cultures discussed in this section and write an essay in which they compare and contrast the two cultures. Direct learners having difficulty to create a chart showing similarities and differences between two of the cultures discussed in the section. **LS Verbal-Linguistic, Visual-Spatial**

🖎 Alternative Assessment Handbook, Rubric 37: Writing Assignments

Migration to the Americas

As recently as 10,000 years ago, during the last Ice Age, thick sheets of ice covered many parts of the world. So much of the earth's water was frozen that sea levels dropped, exposing land along the coasts.

Today the waters of the Bering Strait divide modern Alaska from Siberia in northeast Asia. During the Ice Age, though, a land bridge connected Asia and North America. Historians call this ancient land area Beringia.

Scholars agree that hunters from Siberia crossed the land bridge and arrived in North America. This probably took place between 12,000 and 40,000 years ago, and small groups of people crossed at different times.

Hunters and gatherers These first Americans were **nomads**, people who move from place to place. They followed a **hunter-gatherer** way of life. This meant that women and girls collected nuts, berries, wild plants, and birds' eggs. Men and boys went on extended hunts, following herds of animals. When the animals moved, the hunter-gatherers did too, never staying in one place for long.

The newcomers found good hunting in the cool grasslands along the edges of the ice sheets. North America was home to many huge animals, including giant sloths, fierce saber-toothed cats, and elephantlike woolly mammoths. Wolves and camels roamed the land, too. None of these animals were accustomed to human hunters. That made them easy prey for the hunters, who drove them off cliffs or killed them with sharp, stone-tipped spears.

The Ice Age ended as the climate grew warmer. The glaciers gradually melted away, leaving large lakes and layers of rich soil. Thick forests grew up in eastern North America.

The combination of climate change and skillful hunters wiped out most of the huge Ice Age animals. Humans had to find new food supplies, so bands of hunter-gatherers moved southward. By at least 11,000 years ago, archaeologists say, people were living in both North and South America.

The agricultural revolution Over time, Native Americans began to plant and harvest crops. Farming led them to settle into villages rather than move from place to place. This

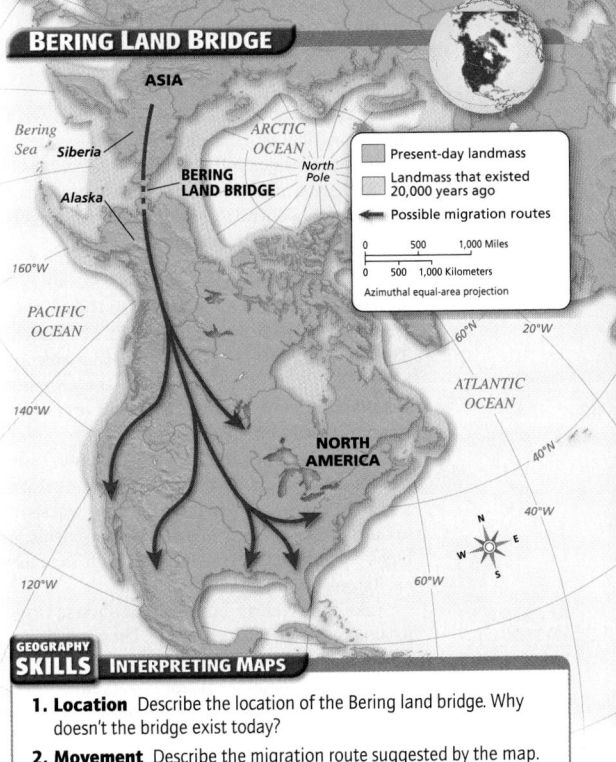

BERING LAND BRIDGE

ASIA

Bering Sea Siberia

BERING LAND BRIDGE

Alaska

160°W

PACIFIC OCEAN

140°W

120°W

ARCTIC OCEAN

North Pole

- Present-day landmass
- Landmass that existed 20,000 years ago
- Possible migration routes

0   500   1,000 Miles
0   500   1,000 Kilometers
Azimuthal equal-area projection

NORTH AMERICA

ATLANTIC OCEAN

20°W

60°N

40°N

40°W

60°W

GEOGRAPHY SKILLS INTERPRETING MAPS

1. **Location** Describe the location of the Bering land bridge. Why doesn't the bridge exist today?

2. **Movement** Describe the migration route suggested by the map.

See Skills Handbook, p. H19

dramatic change in the way people lived is called the **agricultural revolution**. Scientists believe it began in parts of the Americas at least 7,000 years ago.

By about 2,000 years ago, ancient American farming was based on three basic crops: corn (maize), beans, and squashes such as pumpkins. To supply meat, men still hunted seasonally, but they also began raising animals.

A settled way of life led to other changes in culture. With a more dependable food supply, populations grew. People developed crafts such as pottery making and weaving. Native Americans also developed ways to govern their villages and distribute wealth.

READING CHECK **Identifying Cause and Effect** How were Siberian hunters able to reach North America thousands of years ago?

ACADEMIC VOCABULARY
distribute divide among several

Reading Focus

❶ According to scientists and historians, how and when did the first migration to the Americas occur? *via a land bridge that connected Asia and North America; between 12,000 and 40,000 years ago*

Migration to the Americas

Identify Who were the first people to arrive in North America? *Siberian hunters*

Identify Cause and Effect What caused the disappearance of Ice Age animals in North America? *warmer climate; hunting*

Elaborate Do you believe that the development of farming deserves to be called a revolution? *possible answers—Yes, it completely changed the way people lived. No, it was a gradual and natural development in the lives of ancient people.*

🎞 Map Transparency: Bering Land Bridge

Skills Focus: Making Written Presentations

At Level

Reading Like a Historian Skill
Ancient Animals of North America

Research Required

1. Write the names of the following animals for students to see: American lion; camel; dire wolf; giant bear; giant vulture; ground sloth; ancient bison; mammoth; mastodon; sabre-tooth cat; tapir; western horse.

2. Tell students that these animals lived in North America at the time the first humans came from Asia.

3. Have each student select one animal to research. Have students prepare a report

summarizing their research with a map of the Americas showing the region where the animal is thought to have lived. Students should compare the ancient animal with its modern-day counterpart. Students should also try to find at least one picture of what the ancient animal may have looked like.

LS **Verbal-Linguistic, Visual-Spatial**

📖 Alternative Assessment Handbook, Rubrics 30: Research; and 37: Writing Assignments

---

Answers

Interpreting Maps 1. *between Siberia in Asia and Alaska in North America; ice melted in other areas of the world and raised water levels, burying the land bridge;* **2.** *from Asia, across the Bering Land Bridge, fanning south into North America*

Reading Check *The Ice Age exposed land along the coasts, creating a land bridge that connected Asia and North America.*

❷ What kind of cultures developed in Central and South America? *Olmec, Maya, Toltec, Aztec in Central America; Inca in South America*

Cultures of Central America and South America

Identify Which of the cultures had the largest empire, and where was it located? *Inca; Andes Mountains of South America*

Sequence How did the Mayan culture develop? *began its rise around 400 BC; established religious centers that grew into large city-states*

Activity **Time Line** Have students combine the time lines in the chapter opener and on these pages to create a single time line that shows *all* the major cultures of North and South America. Time lines should run from 1300 BC to AD 1500. **LS Visual-Spatial**

📄 CRF: Biography: Diego Durán

📄 CRF: History and Geography Activity: Tenochtitlán: Aztec Capital

Cultures of Central America and South America

Central and South America are dotted with archaeological sites from many different cultures. Three major cultures flourished in Mesoamerica, the area from present-day central Mexico into Central America. A fourth important culture arose in South America.

The Olmec The first major Mesoamerican society grew up around 1200 BC in the steamy tropical lowlands along the Gulf of Mexico. The **Olmec** culture is called the mother culture of Mesoamerica. This is because the Olmec's religion, art, agriculture, and social organization influenced later peoples.

The Olmec were engineers and artists. They were also the first in Mesoamerica to develop a writing system. Their most striking works of art are huge sculpted heads made of basalt, a black volcanic rock. Some heads weigh as much as 40 tons and stand 10 feet high.

Like many early farmers, the Olmec used a "slash-and-burn" technique. They cut down and burned the trees on a plot of land. The ashes made the soil fertile for a few years. Then the farmer moved on to a new patch of land, allowing the old plot to regain its fertility. Over time, villagers cleared large areas of land.

ACADEMIC VOCABULARY
technique method

The Maya and the Toltec Olmec culture gradually declined for reasons that remain unclear. Among the societies that succeeded it were the **Maya**, who began their rise around 400 BC. Their cities were religious centers with stone pyramids, palaces, temples, and sacred ball courts. Painted carvings of warriors, gods, and jaguars decorated the buildings.

Mayan civilization reached its height between about AD 250 and 900. Religious centers grew into city-states with thousands of people. Priests studied the stars and devised several calendars. The Maya also developed a writing system and a number system that used the concept of zero.

By about 1500, Mayan civilization had declined, but the culture never disappeared. Some 4 million Mayan-speaking people still live in southern Mexico and Guatemala today.

About AD 900, while the Maya were beginning to decline, the **Toltec** came to dominate central Mexico. These people were known for their skills as warriors, artisans, and builders. Toltec influence can be seen in the architecture of late Mayan cities such as Chichén Itzá, whose ruins still stand in southern Mexico.

The Aztec In the 1400s power in the central valley of Mexico shifted to a group of invaders from the north. These were the warlike Mexica,

TIME LINE

Early Cultures of the Americas

Long before Europeans arrived in the Americas, a wide variety of cultures existed in Mesoamerica and South America.

c. 500 BC–AD 500
The Adena and Hopewell built huge earth mounds, such as this serpent mound (right) in present-day Ohio.

Olmec

Adena and Hopewell

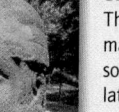

c.1200 BC–400 BC
The Olmec were the first major Mesoamerican society, influencing later cultures.

Anasazi and Hohokam

c. 200 BC–AD 1300
The Anasazi and Hohokam people lived in the Southwest. The Anasazi built multi-story adobe buildings called pueblos. This pueblo (left) built into a cliff is a distinctive example.

8 CHAPTER 1

Collaborative Learning

At Level

Cultures of Central and South America

Prep Required

1. Before class begins, write each of the following names on separate note cards: Olmec, Maya, Toltec, Aztec, Inca. Fold each note card in half with the name on the inside so that it cannot be seen.

2. Organize the class into five teams. Give each team one of the note cards. Tell the teams that the name on the note card is its secret team name. Have the members of each team work together to make a list of the major characteristics of its assigned culture group.

3. Have a volunteer from one team read its list to the class, one item at a time. After each item has been read, have the other teams try to identify the culture. When a team correctly identifies the culture, have that team explain the importance of the clues to the culture group.

4. Repeat step 3 until each team's culture has been identified. Which team was able to identify the most cultures? **LS Interpersonal**

📄 Alternative Assessment Handbook, Rubric 14: Group Activity

better known as the **Aztec.** The Aztec built their capital, Tenochtitlán (tay-nawch-teet-LAHN), on an island in a shallow lake. With canals, broad central plazas, and busy marketplaces, it was a dazzling sight. To supply food to the growing city, farmers tended floating gardens, called *chinampas,* in the lake.

The Aztec conquered many neighboring peoples. They demanded regular payments of tribute such as food, fine woods, furs, feathers, and slaves. Slaves and captives taken in war usually became victims in religious sacrifices. The Aztec, like other early peoples, believed in many gods. To honor these deities, Aztec priests ritually left offerings of food, flowers, and even human hearts. The scale of human sacrifice made many people in the empire hate their Aztec rulers.

The Inca While the Aztec were conquering Mesoamerica, a group called the **Inca** rose to power in the Andes Mountains of South America. The Inca conquered their neighbors along the coast and built a vast empire connected by roads and bridges. At its height, the Inca empire was the largest in the Americas, including perhaps 12 million people.

> **READING CHECK** **Sequencing** In what ways did Olmec culture influence later cultures in Mesoamerica?

The Earliest Cultures of North America

Early Native Americans encountered many different environments in North America—forests, deserts, and fertile land. In each region, different kinds of societies developed. Some Native Americans remained hunter-gatherers. Others settled in farming villages.

Peoples of the Southwest The early cultures of the dry Southwest probably developed more than 2,000 years ago. Trade and common ways of living linked these cultures with nearby Mexico. Groups in this region all grew corn, beans, and squash, and women typically made pottery.

The Hohokam people in south-central Arizona were one such group. To farm in the desert, they dug irrigation ditches that brought water from rivers to the fields. Some Hohokam sites had temple mounds and ball courts, like those in Mexico but simpler.

Another group, the Anasazi, settled in the area where present-day Arizona, New Mexico, Colorado, and Utah meet. Anasazi culture soon spread eastward. One of its distinctive features was multistory adobe buildings. When Spaniards arrived in the 1500s, they called the buildings **pueblos,** meaning "towns."

THE IMPACT TODAY
Government
Present-day Mexico City stands on the original site of Tenochtitlán.

c. 600–1500
The Mississippian people were an advanced farming society in the Southeast and southern Midwest.

c. 900–1500
The Toltec came to dominate what is now central Mexico as the Maya began to decline.

c.1400–1521
The Aztec empire dominated the central valley of present-day Mexico.

Aztec

Toltec

Mississippian

Maya

Inca

c. 400 BC–AD 1500
The Maya made many advances such as a writing system and a number system that used the concept of zero. This pyramid (below) was part of the Mayan city of Chichén Itzá.

c. 1100–1532
The Inca empire stretched across South America. At its height the empire included perhaps 12 million people.

Skills Focus **INTERPRETING TIME LINES**

Sequencing Which culture existed for the longest period of time?
See **Skills Handbook, p. H14**

THE WORLD BEFORE 1600 **9**

Differentiating Instruction

Above Level

Advanced Learners/GATE

Prep Required **Research Required**

1. Bring several issues of popular historical, cultural, or scientific magazines to class to share with students. Have students examine the magazines to learn how to write articles for an issue devoted to early Native American cultures in North America.

2. Organize students into three groups. Assign each group one of the following articles: "Peoples of the Southwest," "The Mound-Builders," and "Mississippian Culture." Then subdivide each of the three large groups into three smaller groups: factual researchers, photo and art researchers, and map researchers. Have each small group research information for the article and create a bibliography of the sources students used.

3. Have each group compile its research in a detailed outline with the illustrations and maps that should be included.
LS Interpersonal, Visual-Spatial

📑 Alternative Assessment Handbook, Rubrics 14: Group Activity; and 30: Research

9

10

Direct Teach

Reading Focus

The Earliest Cultures of North America

Explain What was the purpose of the mounds built by the Adena and Hopewell societies? *to bury clan members*

Draw Conclusions How do we know that the Mound Builders had an extensive trade network? *from material found in rings and ornaments that were buried with important people*

Review & Assess

Close

Have students summarize some of the early accomplishments of Native Americans.

Review

🔲 Online Quiz, Section 1

🔲 Daily Test Practice Transparency

Assess

SE Section 1 Assessment

🔲 Progress Assessment: Section 1 Quiz

🔲 Alternative Assessment Handbook

Reteach

🔲 Interactive Reader and Study Guide, Section 1

💿 Interactive Skills Tutor CD-ROM

Answers

Reading Check *dry climate; grew corn, beans, and squash; dug irrigation ditches to bring water; built on flat mesas and steep cliffs*

The Anasazi built some of their pueblos on flat mesas and on steep cliffs. Major pueblos, some with hundreds of rooms, were located in Chaco Canyon. Miles of roads linked them with distant Anasazi settlements. Traders carried food and luxuries such as turquoise.

By about 1300, the Anasazi culture was beginning to decline. So were other ancient societies of the Southwest. One reason may have been a great drought in the late 1200s. Wars or invasions may also have contributed. Dispersing eastward, some Anasazi groups settled in present-day New Mexico, becoming the ancestors of today's Pueblo Indians.

The Mound Builders Complex early societies also developed in eastern North America, from the Atlantic Ocean to the Mississippi River. These people lived in small farming villages, probably run by the leaders of **clans**, or groups of people related by blood. As these groups grew and flourished, their villages became more complex.

The Ohio River valley was the center of two highly organized farming societies, Adena and Hopewell. Both groups are known as Mound Builders because they buried clan members in large earth mounds.

Adena culture got its start sometime before 500 BC. The Adena people had a wide-ranging trade network that brought them goods from distant places. They obtained copper and pearls, for example, to adorn the rings and ornaments that were buried with important people.

By about 100 BC, Adena culture had been absorbed by the Hopewell culture. Hopewell people were skillful artists who carved realistic human statues and ceremonial pipes depicting animals. They also worked with copper, shells, mica, and other materials from as far away as the Great Lakes and the Gulf of Mexico.

By about AD 400 or 500, the trade network that linked Hopewell settlements was falling apart. Mound-building traditions, however, continued for hundreds of years.

Mississippian culture The last major mound-building culture in North America was the Mississippian. Theirs was the most advanced farming society north of Mexico. The Mississippians grew maize and beans, and they introduced a new farming tool—the hoe.

All across the Southeast and southern Midwest, the Mississippians built towns. These had impressive ceremonial temple-mounds and broad central plazas. The homes of rulers and nobles stood on pyramids around the central square. The greatest Mississippian cities were Cahokia, near present-day St. Louis, and Moundville, in Alabama.

By about 1100, Cahokia was a great population center, perhaps as large as London. Until the late 1800s, its central pyramid was the largest structure in the United States.

READING CHECK **Drawing Conclusions** How did the landscape and climate of the Southwest affect early peoples there?

SECTION 1 ASSESSMENT

Reviewing Ideas, Terms, and People

1. **a. Recall** Where did the original settlers in the Americas come from?
   b. Analyze What changes in the environment led to the **agricultural revolution**?

2. **a. Identify** What is Mesoamerica?
   b. Sequence Trace, in order, the development of different cultures in Central and South America.

3. **a. Recall** What two cultures are known as Mound Builders, and why?
   b. Make Generalizations What were the typical characteristics of the early cultures of the Southwest?
   c. Evaluate What achievements marked the Mississippians as having an advanced culture?

Critical Thinking

4. **Sequencing** Copy the chart below and fill it in to show the differences before and after the agricultural revolution.

Before	After

FOCUS ON SPEAKING

5. **Persuasive** As a member of a hunter-gatherer band long ago, write a speech explaining why a particular location will be a good place for your group to settle.

Section 1 Assessment Answers

1. **a.** Siberia
   b. The Ice Age ended as the climate grew warmer, wiping out many of the huge Ice Age animals and leaving fertile soil.

2. **a.** the area from central Mexico into Central America
   b. Olmec, Maya, Toltec, Aztec, and Inca

3. **a.** Adena and Hopewell—They buried clan members in mounds.
   b. grew corn, beans, and squash; women made pottery; linked by trade and common way of living with nearby Mexico

c. introduced the hoe; built towns; built pyramids

4. Before—people nomads, men hunted, women gathered food; After—villages spring up, farms provide food, population grows, crafts develop, government set up

5. possible answer—The climate is mild; there are many animals and food-bearing plants close by.

North American Cultures in the 1400s

BEFORE YOU READ

MAIN IDEA

A variety of complex societies existed in different regions of North America before European explorers arrived in the early 1500s.

READING FOCUS

1. How did regional differences among Native Americans shape their diverse cultures?

2. What Native American customs were shared among several groups?

3. How did trading networks link Native American societies?

KEY TERMS AND PEOPLE

Pueblo
Kwakiutl
Iroquois
longhouse
kinship
matrilineal
division of labor
shaman
barter

 TAKING NOTES As you read, take notes on the objects that Native Americans traded in their trading networks. Record your notes in a chart like this one. You may need to add more circles.

(Things traded in trading networks)

Taking Out History's TRASH

 **THE INSIDE STORY**

How do ancient trash heaps help us learn about early North Americans?
Archaeologists study ancient towns, campsites, and burial sites. They examine pottery, weapons, tools, bones, and other physical evidence. One of the best places to find useful information is an ancient trash heap, called a midden.

For years, archaeologists have studied the shell middens of the Calusa Indians at a site in Pineland, Florida. The Pineland site was a Calusa village for more than 1,500 years. Calusa Indian influence stretched across most of Florida during the sixteenth century, when Europeans arrived in North America. The Pineland site is particularly significant because it offers a distinct look at Indian life in North America before Europeans arrived.

At the Pineland site, huge shell mounds still overlook the ocean. From these mounds, archaeologists have learned many things about the Calusa. For example, they know from the large quantities of discarded shells that the Calusa people were hunter-gatherers who looked to local streams and bays for their food, rather than farming. ◢

◀ **Archaeologists unearth the secrets of the Calusa Mound Builders at Florida's Pineland site.**

North American Cultures in the 1400s

1. **Teach** Ask students the Reading Focus questions to teach this section.

2. **Apply** Have students make a table using the subheads under "Regional Differences Among Native Americans." Under each heading, have students list groups that lived in the region and briefly describe the region.

3. **Review** Guide students in a discussion of ways in which climate, physical geography, and resources of each area affected the lives of Native Americans.

4. **Practice/Homework** Have students create a table of contents for a book by a cultural historian about the Native American foods of North America. The table of contents should be organized by region. Students should also create a title page for each region listing the food items that would be included for that region. **LS Visual-Spatial, Verbal-Linguistic**

   📝 Alternative Assessment Handbook, Rubric 39: Writing to Create

   💾 Graphic Organizer Transparencies

Bellringer

The Inside Story. . . Use the **Daily Bellringer Transparency** to help students answer the question.

💾 Daily Bellringer Transparency, Section 2

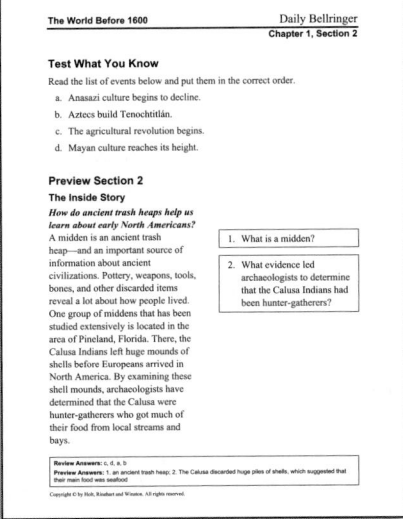

Academic Vocabulary

Review with students the high-use academic term in this section.

influence to have an effect on (p. 12)

📝 CRF: Vocabulary Builder Activity, Section 2

Taking Notes

spear points, food, flint, copper, turquoise, shells and pearls, cotton, seeds, baskets and pottery, raw materials, luxury goods, ideas

1 How did regional differences among Native Americans shape their diverse cultures? *Adapting to diverse environments, Native Americans developed a wide range of cultures.*

Regional Differences Among Native Americans

Identify Who were the Pueblo peoples? *groups of the Southwest including Zuni, Hopi, and Acoma*

Analyze Why do you think the Kwakiutl held potlatches? *possible answers—to celebrate their wealth; enjoy time with family and friends*

Evaluate Why might scientists believe that the Inuits and the Aleuts are the most recent Native Americans to come from Asia? *possible answer—because they live closest to Asia*

Teaching Tip

You might wish to visit the Web site of the National Museum of the American Indian, easily found online. One portion of the site contains an online exhibition with useful information for teachers and students.

Regional Differences Among Native Americans

ACADEMIC VOCABULARY
influence to have an effect on

The Calusa people in Florida were just one of many Native American groups scattered across the continent. North America has great differences in climate, geography, and resources. These diverse environments influenced the Native American cultures that formed across the continent.

When Europeans reached North America in the 1500s, fewer people lived there than in either Mesoamerica or South America. Historians' estimates of the population north of Mexico range from fewer than 1 million to as many as 10 million.

The Southwest The **Pueblo** peoples of the Southwest inherited many Anasazi traditions. Groups like the Zuni, Hopi, and Acoma lived in many-roomed pueblos. Each pueblo was governed by a council of religious elders. Pueblo groups grew corn, beans, squash, and cotton in the river and creek bottoms in the desert. They also made distinctive pottery and baskets.

Two groups of newcomers later arrived in the Southwest. The Apache and the Navajo were nomadic hunters from the plains farther north. Learning from their Pueblo neighbors, the Navajo gradually took up farming. They also became skillful weavers.

The Northwest Coast and California In contrast to the dry Southwest, the Northwest Coast was cool and rainy. Tall trees and wild plants grew in the moist climate. The forests supplied wild game, such as moose, deer, and bear. Abundant salmon swam in the swift rivers. Hunters went to sea in dugout canoes, using harpoons to hunt whales.

Native Americans in the Northwest Coast, including the **Kwakiutl** (kwah-kee-YOO-tuhl) and Haida (HY-duh), became skilled woodworkers. They built large, sturdy houses from cedar planks. Later, after acquiring iron tools, they began to carve totem poles, masks, and other wooden crafts.

Their rich resources made these peoples aware of wealth and luxuries. They owned luxury goods, such as fine blankets. Families also held feasts called potlatches, where they showed off their wealth by giving valuable gifts to their guests.

South of the Northwest Coast lay the California region. California was home to the Pomo, Hupa, and Yurok, among others. These people lived in small communities of 50 to 300, speaking more than 100 languages.

California had many food sources available year-round, so farming was not necessary. Instead, the people fished and hunted.

The Far North The Native Americans of the far North—also known as the Arctic and Subarctic—were probably the most recent migrants from Asia. The ancestors of modern Inuit (I-NOO-wuht) probably came by boat about 1,500 years ago. The Aleuts (a-lee-OOTs) settled much earlier on what are now the Aleutian Islands.

Much of the land in the Far North is tundra, treeless plains that are partially frozen for much of the year. Despite the lack of vegetation, animals were plentiful, so the Inuit and Aleuts lived mainly by hunting. On the coast, people hunted seals, seabirds, and whales. Inland, they hunted caribou, beaver, and bear.

Archaeological evidence from early sites in the Far North is rare. Perhaps this is because rising sea levels after the end of the Ice Age covered settlements on the coast.

The Great Basin and the Plateau Two dryland regions lay to the east of the mountain ranges of the Pacific coast. In the Great Basin, Native Americans such as the Ute (YOOT) and the Shoshones (shuh-SHOHNS) faced severe challenges—little rain, few trees, no large rivers, and little wild game.

Native Americans in the Great Basin remained hunter-gatherers. Some lived in caves. They found food by digging roots and gathering acorns, piñon nuts, and other seeds. They also hunted small animals such as rabbits. Not surprisingly, populations were small.

Although the Plateau, the high plains region to the north, is fairly arid, it gets more rain and has more forests than the Great Basin. The Plateau is crossed by rivers brimming with Pacific salmon and other fish. Groups such as the Nez Percé (NEZ PUHRS) lived in villages along these abundant rivers.

The Great Plains Some of the best-known Native American groups—the Sioux (SOO), Pawnee, and Cheyenne (shy-AN)—lived on

Differentiating Instruction

Below Level

Special Education Students; Learners Having Difficulty

Materials outline maps of Native American culture areas, colored pencils

1. Guide the class in a discussion of Native American culture areas. You might wish to ask the following questions: What makes a culture area? How did European settlement of North America affect Native American culture areas?

2. Distribute the outline maps to students. Have them follow the map in the text and create

their own culture area maps. Have students retain the maps as a study tool.

3. Guide students in a brief review of the major culture areas and characteristics of the Native American groups discussed in the section. **LS Interpersonal**

📄 American History Outline Maps: Native American Culture Areas

📄 Alternative Assessment Handbook, Rubric 20: Map Creation

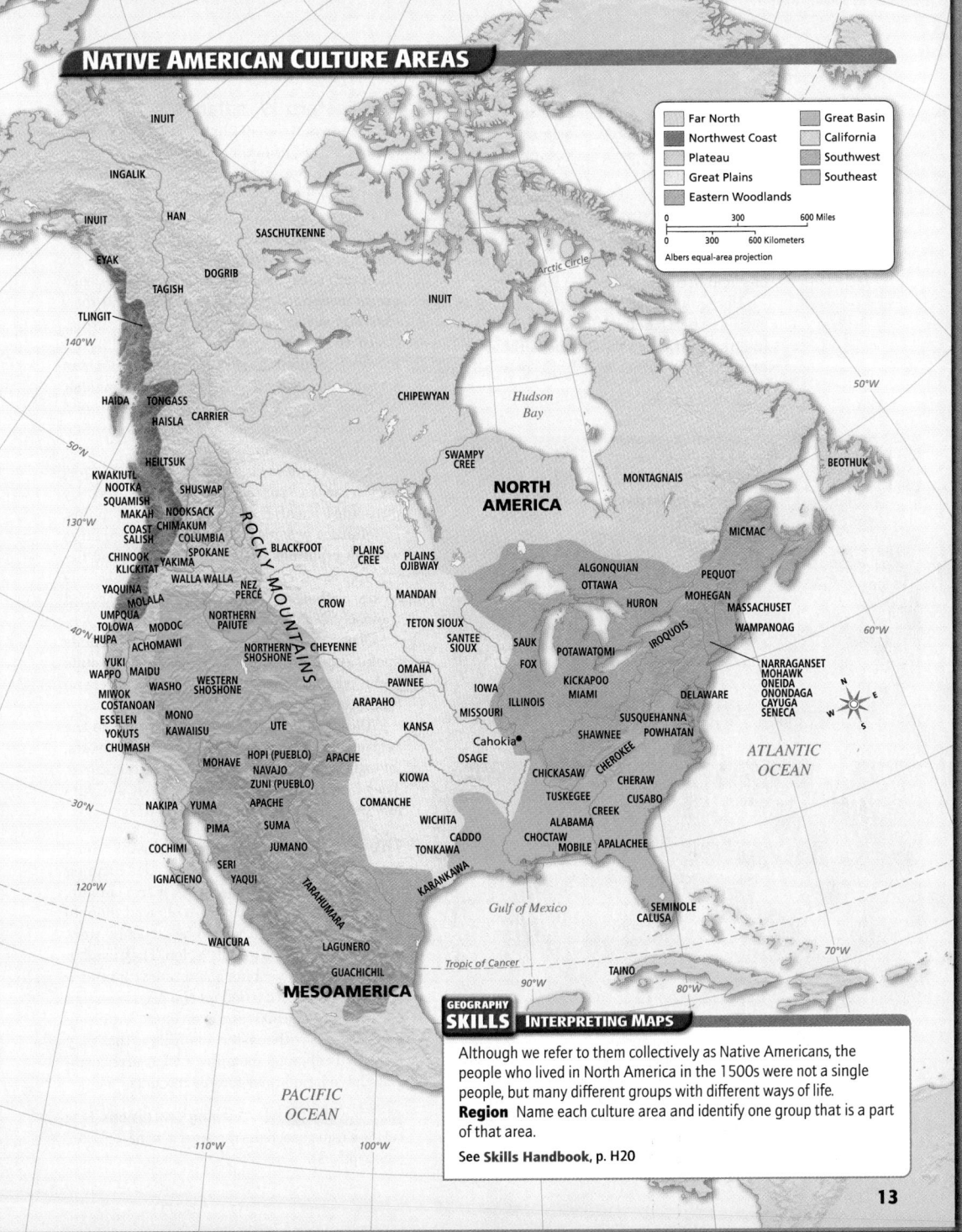

NATIVE AMERICAN CULTURE AREAS

Far North
Northwest Coast
Plateau
Great Plains
Eastern Woodlands
Great Basin
California
Southwest
Southeast

0   300   600 Miles
0 300 600 Kilometers
Albers equal-area projection

NORTH AMERICA

Hudson Bay

ROCKY MOUNTAINS

ATLANTIC OCEAN

Gulf of Mexico

MESOAMERICA

PACIFIC OCEAN

GEOGRAPHY SKILLS   INTERPRETING MAPS

Although we refer to them collectively as Native Americans, the people who lived in North America in the 1500s were not a single people, but many different groups with different ways of life.

Region Name each culture area and identify one group that is a part of that area.

See Skills Handbook, p. H20

13

Native American Culture Areas

Have students look at the map on this page. Point out that the map shows culture areas that are primarily in the United States and Canada. Ask the following questions to help the class understand the information shown on the map:

1. How many culture areas are shown on the map? *nine*

2. Which culture areas are shared by the United States and Mexico? *California and Southwest*

3. Which culture area covers the largest part of the United States? *Great Plains*

4. Which three culture areas are the smallest? *California, Northwest Coast, and Plateau*

5. How many culture areas are there in your state and what are they? *possible answer (for California)— two: California and Great Basin*

📖 American History Outline Maps: Native American Culture Areas

🗄 Map Transparency: Native American Culture Areas

Skills Focus: Interpreting Historical Maps

At Level

Research Required

Social Studies Skill
Native American Culture Areas

Materials outline maps of your state; colored pencils or markers

1. Organize the class into groups of four or five students. Give each group an outline map of your state or have groups draw their own outline maps.

2. Have each group research Native American groups in your state to determine the following: Which Native American peoples originally lived there? Where did each group live? To which

cultural group did each Native American group belong?

3. Have students mark the outline map to show the approximate boundaries of the Native American culture areas and the location of each group within the state. Have each group share its map with the class. Have groups correct their own maps, if needed. 🅛 **Interpersonal, Visual-Spatial**

📖 Alternative Assessment Handbook, Rubrics 14: Group Activity; and 20: Map Creation

Answers

Interpreting Maps *See map for possible answers.*

Regional Differences Among Native Americans

Recall What animal did the Plains Indians depend on? *the buffalo*

Identify Name two major language groups of the Eastern woodlands. *Iroquois, Algonquian*

Predict As white settlers arrived and pushed Native Americans westward, do you think it was hard for Native Americans to adapt to different environmental conditions? Explain your answer. *possible answers—No, Native Americans were used to adapting to natural conditions. Yes, moving usually required an entire change in life patterns and culture.*

Activity **Differences in Geography** Have students find pictures of Native American housing, such as the wood houses of the Kwakiutl and Haida, the thatched-roof log cabins of the Choctaw, as well as the tipi, wickiup, wigwam, and pit houses. Have students share their pictures with the class, and guide students in a discussion of housing materials and how each style of housing was suited to its builders' physical environment and way of life. **LS Kinesthetic, Visual-Spatial**

📄 CRF: Biography: Deganawidah

Answers

Reading Check *Some regions, such as the Pacific Coast, had abundant wildlife in a moist climate; other regions, such as the Great Basin, had little rain, few trees, no large rivers, and few animals.*

14

---

the Great Plains west of the Mississippi River. Prairie grasses and wildflowers grew on this flat terrain, and trees lined the wide rivers. The Plains were also home to the last of the great herds of North American animals—deer, antelope, elk, and most importantly, bison, also known as buffalo.

Because the tough roots of prairie grasses made farming difficult, the culture of early Plains Indians depended on hunting buffalo. Hunting improved after the introduction of the bow and arrow by about AD 950.

Descendants of the Mississippian culture, such as the Caddo and the Wichitas, moved into the southern Plains region. These groups brought new crops and built new villages,

Differences in Geography, Differences in Dwellings

People used the materials at hand to build their homes. In the arid Southwest, people used sun-dried clay bricks, called adobe, to build entire villages. Taos Pueblo of New Mexico (top) was built between 1000 and 1450. In contrast, longhouses of the Northeast were built of wooden frames covered with bark. The material was not as lasting as adobe, but it was plentiful. The longhouse above is a replica.

especially in the fertile valleys of the Mississippi River and its tributaries.

The Eastern Woodlands In the 1400s, thick forests covered what is now the eastern United States, from the Atlantic Ocean west to the Mississippi. Because of these forests this region is known as the Eastern Woodlands. The Native Americans in this huge area lived in distinct cultural groups, and their homelands often centered in river basins. Hills and mountain ranges made travel hard. Thus, each group developed its own traditions and tools and often a separate language.

In the Northeast, the **Iroquois** (EER-uh-kwoy) included several Native American nations, including the Mohawks and Oneidas. All these people spoke Iroquois languages, and they shared a common culture. They were often at war, however, mainly over territory.

The Iroquois lived in large villages, which were sometimes surrounded by palisades—walls of upright wood poles. **Longhouses** provided shelter. These were large wooden buildings with a central aisle and living spaces on either side. The longhouse was so key to their culture that the Iroquois called themselves "people of the longhouse."

Other groups in the Eastern Woodlands spoke Algonquian languages. These groups included the Chippewa (or Ojibwa), Fox, and Sauk (SAWK).

All woodland groups learned to make the best use of local resources. In the oak forests, for example, they made flour from bitter acorns. They hunted forest animals for meat and furs and built traps to catch fish in the rivers.

The Southeast In the Southeast, most Native Americans had lived in settled farming villages for hundreds of years. A warm climate, fertile land, and plenty of rain allowed them to grow several crops a year. The Choctaw were one of many groups in this region. They lived in thatched-roof log cabins plastered with mud.

Some peoples carried on the Mississippian culture into the 1500s and even later. One group carved shells with mysterious designs that may have had religious meaning, which archaeologists have found near temple mounds.

READING CHECK **Drawing Conclusions** How did the environment make life easier in some regions than in others?

Skills Focus: Interpreting Visuals

Below Level | **Standard English Mastery**

Reading Like a Historian Skill
Native American Housing

1. Have students carefully examine the two types of dwellings shown on this page and review the information in the text about the Pueblo and Iroquois.

2. Assign students to work in mixed-ability pairs. Have each pair choose one of the dwellings and create a detailed instruction booklet for how to construct the dwelling they have chosen, from start to finish. Written instructions should include pictures, diagrams and a list of

materials that have to be gathered and prepared before construction can begin.

3. Have pairs share their guide with another pair. The second pair should review the instructions and comment on them. Are the instructions clear? If not, why not? The pair who wrote the instructions should revise and correct their guides as needed. **LS Interpersonal, Visual-Spatial**

📄 Alternative Assessment Handbook, Rubric 39: Writing to Create

Linking TO Today

Preserving Native American Cultures

America's newest national museum is devoted to America's earliest inhabitants. The National Museum of the American Indian, a part of the Smithsonian Institution, opened in Washington, D.C., in 2004. The museum focuses on the study of Native American cultures from all over North and South America, from the oldest artifacts to current art forms.

The origins of the museum go back many years. In 1897 an electrical engineer named George Gustav Heye (HY) was working in Arizona. He became fascinated with Native American cultures. For the rest of his life, he used his wealth to build the world's largest private collection of Indian objects.

Heye spent time with various nations, including the Seneca in New York State. They named him *O'owah*, meaning "Screech Owl." In North Dakota, the Hidatsa also gave him an Indian name after he returned a sacred object lost to the nation years earlier.

In 1922 Heye opened a museum in New York City. The collections of that museum are the basis for the new Smithsonian museum.

Making Inferences Why might Heye have been able to aquire such a large number of Indian artifacts?

Northwest Indians attend a ceremony in traditional dress.

Native American Customs

Based on the records of early explorers and settlers, scholars are able to say quite a bit about how Indian societies worked before European contact. Generalizations are risky because Native Americans organized their villages and societies in different ways. Some cultures were complex, while others remained simpler. Their homes ranged from skin tents to adobe pueblos to the Iroquois longhouse. Still, Native Americans in North America shared a number of ideas and customs.

Family relations At the heart of Native American society were families. Most villages and nations were organized into clans on the basis of **kinship**, or blood relations. Sometimes kinship ties were based on the mother's family, sometimes on the father's. Kinship often determined how property would be inherited. It also determined status and who one could or could not marry.

Housing patterns and social arrangements in many societies depended on the position of women. Among the Iroquois, for example, several different clans might live in a village. But all the women in one longhouse came from a single clan. Iroquois society was **matrilineal**—property was inherited through the mother. In the longhouse, each woman and her family had their own living quarters. A man married into a particular longhouse.

Similarly, among the Hopi in the Southwest, a man went to live with his wife's family when he married. He took seeds from his mother's crops with him and raised a crop for his new household. That also helped spread different crop varieties.

Social and political structures Social organization varied greatly from group to group. Some cultures, such as the Pacific Coast and Mississippian, had strict social classes. In other groups, there was more equality.

Most clans or nations were headed by chiefs. Villages were usually run by a council of elders with wisdom and experience.

Land use Native Americans' concept of land ownership was very different from that of Europeans. Mainly, they did not believe that land should be bought and sold. Some societies viewed land as a gift of the Great Spirit to humans. It was to be used and shared by the village or group for farming or hunting.

THE WORLD BEFORE 1600 **15**

---

❸ How did trading networks link Native American societies? *Native Americans traded food, raw materials, exotic goods, and ideas.*

Trading Networks Link Native American Societies

Recall How extensive were early trading networks? *They could be very extensive; Hopewell trade network covered about two-thirds of what is now the U.S.*

Explain Why did Native American groups exchange gifts? *to show goodwill, friendship, or peace*

Develop Why did Native Americans engage in trade? *to obtain items that were not available in their own region; these items became valuable*

This does not mean that there was no sense of territoriality. For example, the Iroquois nations often went to war over hunting grounds. Other groups, however, often shared the use of an area of land.

Division of labor Even in the earliest hunter-gatherer groups, certain people did certain kinds of work. This is called **division of labor**. In ancient times, as you have read, men and boys hunted animals. Women and girls gathered plants, nuts, and berries.

With the agricultural revolution, mainly women took over planting and cultivating food crops. During years of gathering wild plants, they had learned which plants were edible and how they grew. This knowledge helped groups invent tools for farming.

In the Southwest, the division of labor was different. Both women and men were in charge of farming. Women looked after children and cooked. As artisans, women wove cloth and made pottery and baskets. Men were woodcarvers and probably metalworkers.

Religious beliefs Despite many differences in culture, Native Americans shared some spiritual and religious ideas. One was a spiritual connection to the natural world. An Indian of the Wabanaki nation in New England said, "The Great Spirit is our father, but the Earth is our mother." In many belief systems, a tree stood at the center of the earth. For the Iroquois it was a white pine; for the Sioux, a flowering tree was at the center of the sacred hoop.

Animals, particularly bears, were thought to be powerful spirits. Hunters carried out rituals to honor the spirit of an animal they were about to kill. Clans chose an animal as their symbol and spirit guide.

Native Americans told many stories. Some explained the creation of the world or the origin of their own people. Some related the deeds of heroes, often twins. Other stories were about deities or spirits, often those associated with crops, rivers, and other aspects of nature.

In many cultures, **shamans** were people believed to have spiritual and healing powers. When Europeans arrived, they called shamans medicine men.

READING CHECK Making Generalizations
How did gender differences influence the division of labor in Native American societies?

16 CHAPTER 1

Trading Networks Link Native American Societies

You might think that with different languages and different ways of living, Native American groups kept apart. What brought them together, though, was trade. From their earliest days in North America, hunting bands sometimes met during their seasonal migrations. Probably to show good will, different bands exchanged gifts and spear points. Exchanging gifts as a sign of friendship or peace became a tradition.

Later, people began to travel deliberately to exchange goods. The main trade items were food, raw materials, and luxury goods. Native Americans usually traded by a **barter** system, an exchange of goods without using money. In a few places, shells were used as money.

Reasons for trade Native Americans learned to take advantage of the unique natural resources of their own lands. That led to specialization among different peoples. For example, groups with fertile land could produce extra food to trade with areas where food was scarce. Other groups had access to desirable minerals such as flint, copper, or turquoise. People who lived near lakes or oceans collected shells and pearls. Cotton was a useful trade item in the Southwest because cloth and seeds were light and easy to carry.

Some groups mastered skills that others did not have. Basket weavers, for example, might trade with pottery makers. Exchanging handicrafts as well as raw materials helped people in different areas to meet their needs.

Trading networks In the previous section, you read that the Adena and Hopewell people, the early inhabitants of Ohio, traded widely. The Hopewell trade network was particularly vast, covering about two-thirds of what is now the United States. Exotic minerals and other goods passed from trader to trader until they reached the Hopewell heartland.

Because of the distances involved and the hardships of travel, it could take years to bring some items to Ohio. Still, the Hopewell people prized bear's teeth and obsidian, a shiny black volcanic glass, from the Rocky Mountains. They obtained copper from the Great Lakes, thin sheets of mica from the Appalachian Mountains, and shells from the Atlantic seacoast.

Advanced Learners/GATE

Research Required

1. Organize the class into small groups. Have each group research Native American traditions, beliefs, and philosophies. Have groups briefly share the results of their research with the class.

2. Have each student choose one tradition, belief, or philosophy, conduct further research if needed, and then write an essay discussing it. Introductions should provide necessary background for the topic and identify the Native Americans who believed

in that tradition or philosophy. Essays should retell the idea and explain its meaning and significance to its particular culture group.

3. Ask volunteers to read their essays to the class.

4. Guide the class in a discussion of Native American traditions, beliefs, and philosophies and their importance to Native American culture. **LS Interpersonal, Verbal-Linguistic**

📄 Alternative Assessment Handbook, Rubrics 14: Group Activity; and 30: Research

---

Answers

Reading Check *Males tended to hunt animals, while females gathered plants, nuts, and berries, took over planting and cultivating food crops; in the Southwest, men were in charge of farming and women looked after children and cooked.*

Trade Covered Thousands of Miles

Native American trading networks covered great distances. Today archaeologists find trade objects many miles from their original homes.

This Mississippian ornamental collar is made of shell. Shell objects were sometimes found many miles from the ocean.

The obsidian of this knife blade came from present-day Wyoming, but the knife blade was found in Ohio.

Native American traders used canoes to transport their wares along rivers. They also traveled on foot, carrying goods in backpacks. By the 1400s there were well-worn paths through the forests. Thousands of miles of trade networks crisscrossed North America.

One of the most famous of these trading paths began in Iroquois country and ran southward through mountain valleys as far south as present-day North Carolina. It crossed the territory of the Shawnee, Choctaw, Cherokee, and other nations.

Trading networks varied in size. In California, for example, many different bands lived in a fairly small area with very diverse environments. That encouraged an active trading network. People on the coast made trade items out of shells. They traded with people in the interior for stone objects.

Exchange of ideas Along with foodstuffs, raw materials, and more exotic goods, trade networks carried ideas from place to place. The presence of temple mounds and pyramids in Mississippian society, for example, suggests that Mississippians may have borrowed Mesoamerican building practices. In the Southwest, meanwhile, the Pueblo peoples adopted certain religious ideas that came from Mexico. They wove these ideas into their own belief systems just as they wove brilliantly colored Mexican macaw feathers into their ritual headdresses.

READING CHECK **Summarizing** What role did trade play in Native American societies?

SECTION 2 ASSESSMENT

go.hrw.com
Online Quiz
Keyword: SD7 HP1

Reviewing Ideas, Terms, and People

1. **a. Recall** What were the two main language groups in the Eastern Woodlands?
   b. Compare and Contrast What were the differences and similarities between Pacific Coast and Great Basin cultures?
2. **a. Define** Write a brief definition for each of the following terms: **kinship, division of labor**.
   b. Explain What role did **shamans** play in Native American society?
   c. Elaborate How was the natural world important in Native Americans' religious views?
3. **a. Recall** What goods did Native Americans trade?
   b. Summarize Why did Native American groups in North America trade with one another?

Critical Thinking

4. **Sequencing** Copy the flowchart below and identify the reasons why Native Americans established trading networks.

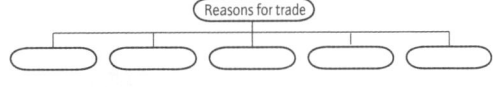

Reasons for trade

FOCUS ON SPEAKING

5. **Persuasive** As a member of a Native American group in inland California, write a speech persuading a coastal group to trade shells for your spear points.

THE WORLD BEFORE 1600 **17**

Direct Teach

Trade Covered Thousands of Miles

Explain Students will learn how widespread and important trade was from the images on this page. How was trade a motivator for European explorers? *possible answer—It gave them courage to set sail into the unknown.*

Review & Assess

Close

Guide students in a discussion of the ways in which location helped shape Native American cultures.

Review

☞ Online Quiz, Section 2
📖 Daily Test Practice Transparency

Assess

SE Section 2 Assessment
📄 Progress Assessment: Section 2 Quiz
📄 Alternative Assessment Handbook

Reteach

📄 Interactive Reader and Study Guide, Section 2
💿 Interactive Skills Tutor CD-ROM

Section 2 Assessment Answers

1. **a.** Iroquois and Algonquian
   b. Pacific Coast was cool, rainy, home to abundant wild game and plants; Great Basin had little rain, few trees, no large rivers, little wild game

2. **a.** kinship—blood relations; division of labor—tendency for certain people to do certain kinds of work
   b. thought to have spiritual and healing powers
   c. a tree stood at the center of the earth; animals thought to be powerful spirits; deities often associated with some aspect of nature

3. **a.** food, raw materials, luxury goods
   b. Native Americans took advantage of the resources of their own lands (specialization); trade helped people in different areas to meet their needs.

4. sign of friendship or peace, tradition, way to fulfill needs, desire for specialized items, exchange of ideas

5. possible answer—These arrowheads are sharper and more durable.

Answers

Reading Check *brought Native American groups together; helped people in different areas meet their needs*

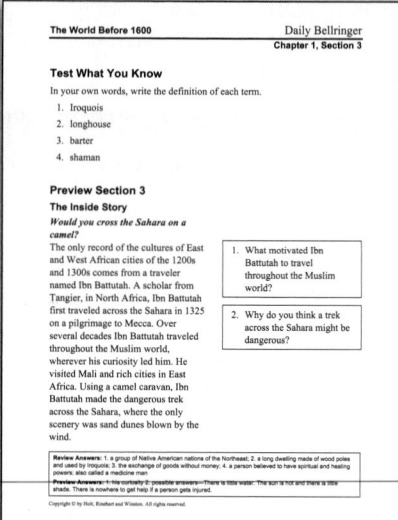
Taking Notes

Beginning—Europeans arrived in Africa and began taking Africans as guides and interpreters and then servants; Development—Europeans saw Africans used slavery already and so accepted the idea of enslaving Africans; Growth—demand for slaves increased as demand for labor in the Americas increased

---

SECTION 3 — African Cultures before 1500

BEFORE YOU READ

MAIN IDEA
Trade was a major factor in the development of African societies south of the Sahara.

READING FOCUS
1. What powerful West African trading kingdoms arose between 300 and 1500?
2. How did trade shape kingdoms in East Africa?
3. How did African society change as a result of the slave trade?

KEY TERMS AND PEOPLE
Islam
oral tradition
Mansa Musa
Muslims
Askia Muhammad
lineage
plantation

TAKING NOTES As you read, take notes on how the Atlantic slave trade developed. Use a diagram like the one here to help you organize your notes.

Beginning
Development
Growth

THE INSIDE STORY

Would you cross the Sahara on a camel? Crossing the sands of the Sahara has always been dangerous. Nevertheless, even in ancient times, traders made the trip in search of gold and other riches. One of the greatest ancient travelers, Ibn Battutah, crossed the desert mainly because he was curious. He visited Mali, the great West African trade empire, and the rich cities of East Africa. Ibn Battutah's accounts are the only record of those cultures in the fourteenth century.

Ibn Battutah was an Arab scholar from Tangier, in North Africa. His first trip, in 1325, was a pilgrimage to Mecca, the spiritual center of Islam. For almost 30 years, he traveled in the Muslim world, from Spain to India. He met rulers, merchants, scholars, and ordinary people.

Ibn Battutah made new friends wherever his travels took him. Along the way he found many different places to stay, including inns, mosques, and people's homes. Mali was his last trip across the Sahara desert. Even with a camel caravan, it was a dangerous journey. "That desert has many devils . . . ," Ibn Battutah wrote. "There is only sand blown by the wind. You see mountains of sand in a place, then you see they have moved to another." ■

West African Trading Kingdoms

Even today, the Sahara is a fearsome barrier to travelers. It divides northern Africa from the southern part of the continent. As a result, Mali and other societies south of the desert developed independently.

Crossing the Sahara

A modern-day salt caravan makes tracks across the Sahara.

18

Teach the Main Idea

At Level

African Cultures Before 1500

1. **Teach** Ask students the Reading Focus questions to teach this section.

2. **Apply** Have students create a Venn diagram showing similarities and differences between East and West African cultures before 1500. 🔲 **Visual-Spatial**

3. **Review** Review the diagrams as a class. Have students identify similarities between the cultures and explain why they might have occurred. Then have students explain the influence of Arab culture on the trading

kingdoms of East and West Africa.

4. **Practice/Homework** Have students review the information in the text on the African trading kingdoms before 1500. Have each student write a brief journal from the viewpoint of one of these traders. 🔲 **Logical-Mathematical, Verbal-Linguistic**

📝 Alternative Assessment Handbook, Rubrics 11: Discussions; and 15: Journals

📋 Graphic Organizer Transparencies

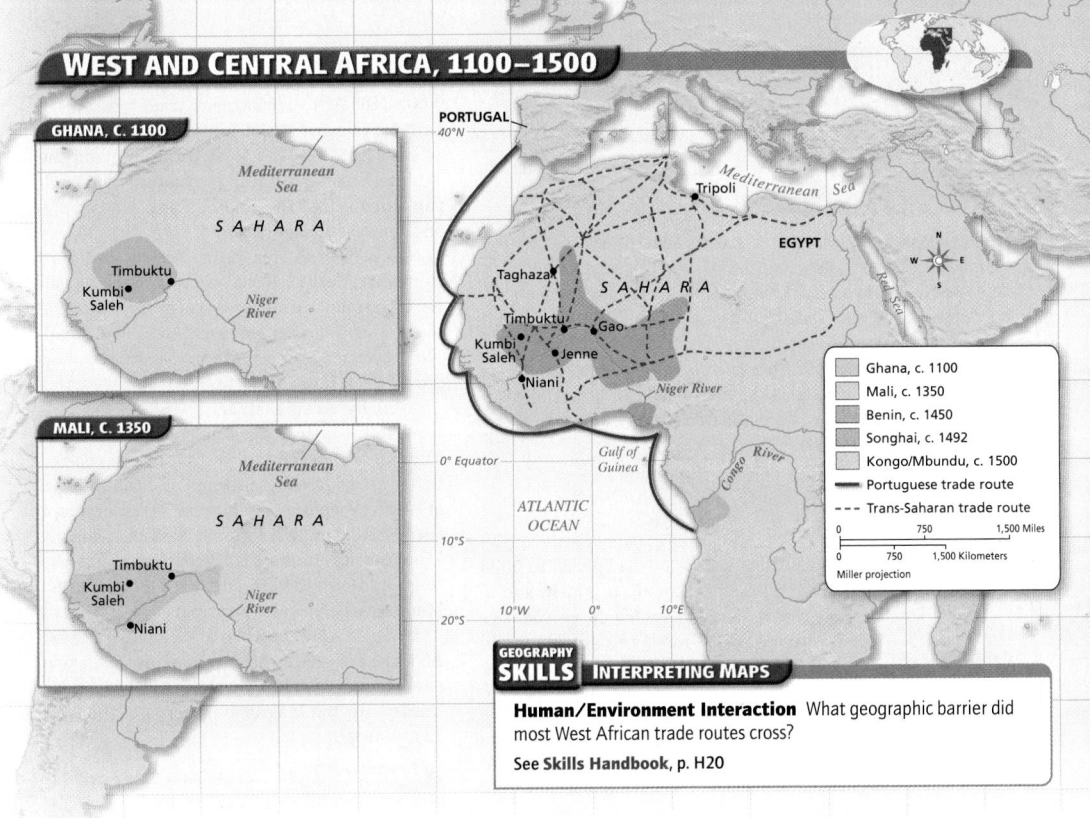

WEST AND CENTRAL AFRICA, 1100–1500

GHANA, C. 1100

MALI, C. 1350

PORTUGAL
40°N

Tripoli

EGYPT

Taghaza

Timbuktu
Gao

Kumbi
Saleh
Jenne

Niani

Niger River

0° Equator

Gulf of
Guinea

ATLANTIC
OCEAN

Congo River

10°S

20°S   10°W   0°   10°E

	Ghana, c. 1100
	Mali, c. 1350
	Benin, c. 1450
	Songhai, c. 1492
	Kongo/Mbundu, c. 1500

—— Portuguese trade route
--- Trans-Saharan trade route

0   750   1,500 Miles
0   750   1,500 Kilometers
Miller projection

GEOGRAPHY SKILLS   INTERPRETING MAPS

Human/Environment Interaction What geographic barrier did most West African trade routes cross?
See Skills Handbook, p. H20

Trans-Sahara trade Despite the dangers, trading caravans have crossed the Sahara since ancient times. The African interior had valuable resources that made the trip worthwhile. The most precious were gold and ivory. In return, Arabs from North Africa traded salt from mines in the desert. For people in the interior, salt was probably as precious as gold.

Several great trading empires in West Africa thrived thanks to gold and salt. These empires grew up in the savanna, or grasslands, near a great bend of the Niger River.

Desert traders brought something else important to West Africa—the religion of **Islam**. Founded by the prophet Muhammad, Islam began in Arabia in the 600s. Later, Arab traders brought the teachings of Islam into West Africa. Some peoples in West Africa accepted Islam. Others, however, continued to practice traditional African religions.

Ghana The earliest West African trading state was Ghana, which probably arose about AD 300. Located along the trade route for gold and salt, Ghana grew very wealthy. It also grew powerful, conquering many nearby areas.

Because African languages were not written, what we know about Ghana's early history is largely from **oral tradition**—history passed down by storytellers. These sources tell us that Ghana kept its traditional religions rather than converting to Islam.

Mali In about 1240, a great warrior named Sundiata conquered Ghana and established the new state of Mali. Mali's most famous ruler was **Mansa Musa** (MAHN-sah moo-SAH), who held power from about 1307 to 1332. Unlike the people of Ghana, the people of Mali were **Muslims**, or followers of Islam. The university in the city of Timbuktu was a center of Islamic learning.

THE IMPACT TODAY

Government

When the modern African nations of Ghana and Mali became independent, they took the names of ancient West African trading kingdoms. The modern nations do not include the same territories as the earlier states.

THE WORLD BEFORE 1600 **19**

19

2 How did trade shape kingdoms in East Africa? *traded with countries as far away as India and China; Arab influence on the coast led to the development of a new culture*

Kingdoms in East Africa

Define What is Swahili? *language that mixed Arabic words with the language patterns of the Bantu*

Explain How did Islam spread through Africa? *through Muslim traders and merchants*

Evaluate Why was there such a strong Arab influence on the cultures of East Africa? *possible answer— many Arab merchants settled in the coastal cities, shared their religion and their customs*

📄 CRF: Biography: Muhammad Askia

Faces of History
Mansa Musa

Analyze "Mansa" was originally a title meaning "emperor" or "master." Mansa Musa ruled Mali at a time of great prosperity, during which trade tripled, and Mali's land area doubled. At its height during the 14th century, the kingdom of Mali was larger than all of Europe, and second only in size to the Asian kingdom of Genghis Khan. Have students explain why Mansa Musa might be considered an enlightened ruler.

Answers

Faces of History *He encouraged education, agricultural development, industry, and trade.*

Reading Check (left) *Ghana;* **(right)** *Ships sailed across Red Sea and Indian Ocean, so Arabia, Egypt, and India became trading partners.*

20

Mansa MUSA
Died 1332

Born into a ruling family, Mansa Musa inherited the kingdom of Mali from his father in about 1307. Musa greatly influenced the lives of his people. He encouraged education, agricultural development, industry, and trade. Rich in gold, Mali grew wealthy through trade. Mansa Musa protected traders, creating a large army to guard trade routes. Mali soon expanded into a vast empire.

As a Muslim, Mansa Musa encouraged the spread of Islam in Mali, but he did not force his people to practice Islam. In 1324 he took a pilgrimage to Mecca. He brought thousands of fellow travelers and vast riches to distribute during his trip. Mansa Musa's travels made the world aware of Mali's great riches.

Explain How did Mansa Musa influence life in Mali?

THE IMPACT TODAY

Art
Mansa Musa hired artists and architects to build mosques—buildings for Muslim prayer. Some of these mosques can still be seen in West Africa today.

Mansa Musa was deeply religious. In 1324 he decided to make the hajj, a pilgrimage to the holy city of Mecca in Arabia. Mansa Musa's journey across Africa made the outside world aware of Mali's fabulous wealth.

Songhai By the mid-1400s, Mali was weakening. Another kingdom, Songhai, gained control of much of the Niger River valley. Songhai became larger than either Ghana or Mali. Its most famous ruler was **Askia Muhammad**, who reigned from 1493 until 1528. A devout man, he encouraged a revival of Muslim learning.

The power of Songhai began to fail in the late 1500s. By then, patterns of trade were shifting to routes in the coastal regions.

Coastal kingdoms By about 1300, the settlement of Benin (buh-NEEN) was becoming a powerful state. Benin grew rich from foreign trade. It eventually ruled a large area of the West African forest region. Benin was famous for its brilliant artists. They created beautiful statues of heads and other bronze artwork.

At about the same time, the kingdom of Kongo was growing up farther south, along the Congo River in Central Africa. Kongo territory spread along the Atlantic coast and far inland. The kingdom thrived in part by trading in salt and palm oil.

READING CHECK **Sequencing** What was the first great trading state in West Africa?

Kingdoms in East Africa

Across the African continent, trade was important in the growth of kingdoms. The people of East Africa looked to Egypt, India, and the Middle East for trading partners. Their trading ships sailed the Red Sea and crossed the Indian Ocean.

Like West Africa, East Africa had gold mines. Traders also sold exotic products such as cinnamon, rhinoceros horn, and tortoise shell. They shipped enslaved Africans abroad, too. In return they bought porcelain, silk, and jewels from India and China.

Nearby Arabia strongly influenced cultures in East Africa, especially along the coast. Many Arab merchants settled in the coastal cities, bringing their customs and the religion of Islam. People in the interior generally kept their traditional religions. Several wealthy Muslim city-states also grew up along the coast and on offshore islands. They included Mombasa, Kilwa, and Zanzibar.

Soon, a new culture developed in East Africa. African and Arab traders even spoke a new language. Called Swahili, it mixed Arabic words with the language patterns of the local Bantu people.

READING CHECK **Identifying Cause and Effect** How did geography affect trade in East Africa?

African Society and the Slave Trade

Visitors to Africa were amazed by the wealth and lavish lifestyles of African rulers. Most had large courts and many officials, servants, and entertainers.

Strong families were another central feature of African society. People were loyal to their clan and to those with the same **lineage**, or ancestry. They felt loyalty to their village as well. People working in certain crafts also formed tightly knit groups.

Among ordinary people, class distinctions existed, but they were not rigid. The biggest division was between people who were free and those who were not. Men and women could be enslaved if they were captured in war, found guilty of a crime, or in debt. In most African societies, however, slaves could work their way into freedom. They had social mobility, meaning that they could move from a low status to a higher one.

The Portuguese in West Africa The nature of slavery changed drastically after Europeans arrived on the African continent in the late 1400s. In the next section, you will read about the adventurous Portuguese sailors who explored the west coast of Africa. Mainly, they were looking for a sea route to India. But they had also heard stories of fabulous gold in wealthy African kingdoms. They hoped to return to Portugal with gold.

The Portuguese established trading posts and later built forts on the Atlantic coast. They found riches in an area called the Gold Coast, but many of their other ventures were not as profitable as they had hoped.

Then the Portuguese, and later the Spanish, set up **plantations**, or large-scale farms, on several islands off the African coast. During the 1500s, they also started sugar plantations on Caribbean islands and elsewhere in the Americas. It was not only the Spanish and Portuguese who launched these ventures but also the British, French, and Dutch.

Plantation agriculture requires large numbers of workers because it is so labor-intensive. Planters first tried to use Native Americans, but diseases and harsh working conditions took a heavy toll. Then Europeans turned to importing Africans.

The Atlantic slave trade begins Slavery had existed in Africa and other parts of the world for hundreds of years. Historians point out that Europeans did not deliberately come to Africa to enslave Africans. The Atlantic slave trade arose primarily in response to the demand for cheap labor. It also grew out of European views that black Africans were inferior.

Slavery was already widespread in Mediterranean countries when the Portuguese arrived in Africa in the 1400s. They began taking Africans back to Europe to show that they had actually found a new land. At first, they treated Africans well and trained them as guides and interpreters. Soon, however, the Portuguese began using Africans as servants and eventually as slaves. By one estimate, about 50,000 African captives had been sent to southern Europe by the 1550s.

The slave trade across the Atlantic began in the sixteenth century when planters in the Americas began to demand more workers for their plantations. The Portuguese and other traders in Africa persuaded a few African rulers and merchants to supply them with slaves. Merchants cooperated in order to keep the

Linking TO Today

The Door of No Return

The Atlantic slave trade affected people and societies all over the world. Today many visitors to West Africa visit the fortresses and dungeons formerly used to imprison captives before sea voyages. One of the best known is on the coastal island of Gorée (gaw-RAY) in the modern-day nation of Senegal.

Gorée is home to the House of Slaves and its Door of No Return. Some experts doubt that the House of Slaves, built in 1776, was used to hold people before they were shipped across the ocean. Historian Philip Curtin describes it as "architecturally one of the finest houses

on Gorée, certainly not a place where slaves would be kept."

Still, the Door of No Return has become a powerful symbol for tens of thousands of visitors every year. UNESCO, the UN agency that promotes cultural preservation, named Gorée a World Heritage Site in 1978. World leaders have traveled to the island, including former South African president Nelson Mandela, U.S. presidents Bill Clinton and George W. Bush, and Pope John Paul II.

Drawing Conclusions What does the Door of No Return symbolize?

The Door of No Return can be seen at the end of the dark passage flanked by the double staircase.

THE WORLD BEFORE 1600 **21**

Skills Focus: Comparing and Contrasting

Above Level

Reading Skill
African Slavery

1. Have students write two letters. The first letter will be written from the viewpoint of an African leader to a Portuguese government official explaining why slavery is evil, what slave traders are doing to his people, and arguing that the slave trade must be stopped. The second letter will be from the viewpoint of an abolitionist to the local governor of a Caribbean island arguing that slavery should not be allowed on the island.

2. Have students share their letters with the class. Guide the class in a discussion comparing and contrasting the two perspectives. What do they have in common? How might they be different? **LS Interpersonal, Verbal-Linguistic**

📋 Alternative Assessment Handbook, Rubric 37: Writing Assignments

Direct Teach

Reading Focus

3 How did African society change as a result of the slave trade? *devastated socially, economically, and politically*

African Society and the Slave Trade

Describe What class distinctions existed in African societies? *biggest division was between those who were free and those who were not; slaves could usually work their way to freedom*

Contrast How did slavery change after Europeans arrived in Africa? *People were enslaved for life to meet the demand for cheap labor.*

Info to Know

The Door of No Return Once slaves were moved into the corridor shown here and passed through the gate that led them to the sea, there was no return. Outside the gate was a loading dock where slaves were loaded onto waiting ships. Slaves who tried to escape were shot or eaten by sharks. Sharks were also fed slaves that were too sick to be loaded onto the boats.

Primary Source

"At this place [Gorée Island], liberty and life were stolen and sold. Human beings were delivered and sorted and weighed and branded with the marks of commercial enterprises and loaded as cargo on a voyage without return."
— President George W. Bush

Speech delivered at Gorée Island, July 2003

Answers

Linking to Today *There would be no return to Africa or freedom for enslaved Africans.*

21

African Society and the Slave Trade

Recall About how many slaves came to the Americas from Africa? *about 20 million*

Predict How might Africa's history have been different without the slave trade? *possible answers—It might have been more stable, had strong leaders and kingdoms, become wealthy from its natural resources, and had different political and economic development.*

● **Review & Assess** ●

Close

Guide students in a discussion of early African trading kingdoms and the development of the slave trade.

Review

⊡ Online Quiz, Section 3

⬥ Daily Test Practice Transparency

Assess

SE Section 3 Assessment

▤ Progress Assessment: Section 3 Quiz

▤ Alternative Assessment Handbook

Reteach

▤ Interactive Reader and Study Guide, Section 3

⬥ Interactive Skills Tutor CD-ROM

Answers

Reading Check *with the establishment of plantations on islands off the African coast, in the Caribbean, and in Brazil*

22

CAUSES AND EFFECTS OF THE ATLANTIC SLAVE TRADE

CAUSES

- Settlers in the Americas needed many workers for labor-intensive plantation agriculture.
- Planters wanted cheap labor.
- Europeans thought Africans were inferior.

EFFECTS

- Historians estimate that 20 million Africans landed in the Americas.
- Historians estimate that millions of Africans died on slave ships crossing the Atlantic.
- Millions were deprived of their freedom, causing tremendous human suffering.
- The American economy became dependent on slavery.
- In the nineteenth century, conflicting views over slavery led to the Civil War in the United States.

traders' business. Some rulers cooperated in exchange for European firearms. Others were motivated by a desire to weaken rival African leaders.

African suppliers did not round up all those who were enslaved, however. Europeans took some people captive during conflicts with North African Muslims. European traders also conducted slave raids and kidnappings. Some European colonists in Africa took part in these activities as well. Although the Portuguese

had begun the trade, by the 1600s the English, French, and Dutch were also heavily involved in the slave trade.

The impact on African society The Atlantic slave trade went on for 400 years and devastated societies in West Africa. Although there are no firm figures, historians estimate that some 20 million enslaved Africans were shipped to the Americas. Probably several million more were sent to Europe, Asia, and the Middle East. Countless others died while marching from the interior to the coast, or while crammed aboard slave ships crossing the Atlantic Ocean.

The human cost of the slave trade was tremendous. Slavery deprived millions of people of their basic freedom. It also affected African society in many ways. Slave hunters took some of the strongest young people—the future leaders. Slave raids made people fearful and discouraged them from planning for the future. The slave trade also interrupted normal political and economic development because parts of Africa suffered enormous losses in population.

In addition, the slave trade weakened traditional bonds and divided Africans from one another. Traders hired young men as kidnappers. Rulers conducted wars against their own people and their neighbors in order to gain captives. The forced labor of millions of Africans enriched other parts of the world—but it did not enrich Africa itself.

READING CHECK **Identifying the Main Idea** How did the demand for slave labor begin?

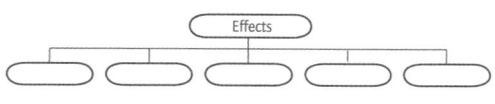

SECTION 3 ASSESSMENT

go.hrw.com
Online Quiz
Keyword: SD7 HP1

Reviewing Ideas, Terms, and People

1. a. Identify What were the great West African trading empires?
b. Analyze What kinds of products were exchanged in the trans-Sahara trade?

2. a. Describe What were the trading patterns in East Africa?
b. Make Inferences How did nearby Arabia influence cultures in East Africa?

3. a. Recall Who were the first European explorers on the Atlantic coast of Africa?
b. Explain What factors led to the Atlantic slave trade?

Critical Thinking

4. Identifying Cause and Effect Copy the chart below and list the effects of the slave trade on African societies.

(Effects)
○ ○ ○ ○ ○

FOCUS ON WRITING ✎

5. Expository As an African ruler in the 1500s, write a letter to your royal counselors explaining why you are sending all European traders out of your country.

22 CHAPTER 1

Section 3 Assessment Answers

1. a. Ghana, Mali, and Songhai
b. gold, ivory, and salt

2. a. gold, cinnamon, rhinoceros horn, tortoise shell, and enslaved Africans exported; porcelain, silk, and jewels imported
b. Arab merchants settled in the coastal cities, bringing their Muslim religion.

3. a. Portuguese
b. demand for cheap labor and European views that black Africans were inferior

4. loss of future leaders; made Africans fearful for the future; interrupted political and economic development; great losses in population; weakened traditional bonds among Africans

5. possible answer—bring strange new diseases with them and encourage slavery

SECTION 4 Europe and Exploration

BEFORE YOU READ

MAIN IDEA

Renaissance ideas changed Europeans' medieval outlook and inspired them to explore the world.

READING FOCUS

1. What changes took place in Europe during the Middle Ages?
2. What happened during the Renaissance and the Protestant Reformation?
3. What did Europeans hope to find during the Age of Exploration?

KEY TERMS AND PEOPLE

Middle Ages
Crusades
Magna Carta
Renaissance
Martin Luther
Reformation
Protestants
Queen Isabella
caravel

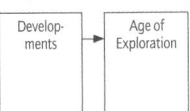
TAKING NOTES As you read, take notes on new developments that helped lead to the Age of Exploration. Record your notes in a graphic organizer like the one shown here.

| Develop-ments | → | Age of Exploration |

THE INSIDE STORY

Would you dare to sail an unknown ocean? People in medieval Europe were very superstitious. Most were uneducated and knew little about the world outside their villages. They believed in magic and witchcraft. They told stories about dragons and other fantastic monsters. They thought that evil spirits lurked in the deep dark forests around their own villages. Who could even imagine what horrible beasts might exist in places they had never seen?

Even well-educated mapmakers drew pictures of sea serpents and other fabulous creatures in unexplored parts of the world. At the edges of the Atlantic Ocean, maps said simply, "Here there be monsters."

Not surprisingly, sailors were some of the most superstitious people in the late medieval world. Uncertain of what lay beyond the horizon, most sea captains tried to stay in sight of land. But in the Age of Exploration, sea captains sailed into parts of the world that no one—as far as they knew—had ever explored.

Many sailors were afraid of these unknown waters. Some believed that the ocean water at the Equator was boiling hot and filled with sea monsters that would swallow their ships. In spite of their fears, hundreds of sailors did sign on to sail into unknown seas on the early voyages of discovery. ■

Sailing the BOILING SEAS

▶ Medieval maps often showed sea monsters, like this detail at right, illustrating sailors' fears of the unknown.

23

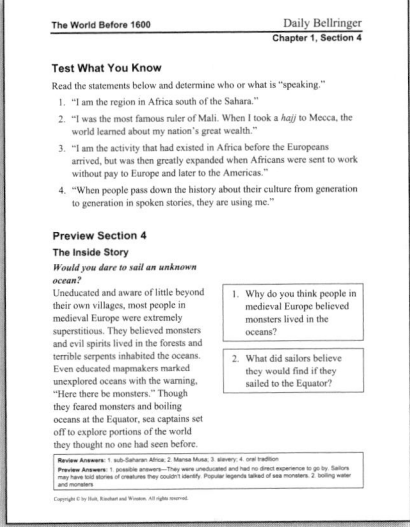
Taking Notes

Developments—the Renaissance, the Protestant Reformation, travels of Marco Polo, Prince Henry the Navigator, caravels, improved navigational instruments, desire to find a sea route to Asia

---

Teach the Main Idea

Europe and Exploration

1. **Teach** Ask students the Reading Focus questions to teach this section.

2. **Apply** Have students create a two-column, cause-and-effect chart for the Renaissance. Assign students to work in mixed-ability pairs to list factors that led to the Renaissance under CAUSES and to list the changes that took place as a result of the Renaissance under EFFECTS. **LS** Visual-Spatial

3. **Review** Have students share the information from their charts, and then discuss the Reformation and the Age of Exploration, two major historical events that resulted from the Renaissance.

4. **Practice/Homework** Have students use the information in their charts to write a summary of the Renaissance, the Reformation, and the Age of Exploration. **LS** Verbal-Linguistic

   Alternative Assessment Handbook, Rubrics 6: Cause and Effect; and 36: Time Lines

❶ What changes took place in Europe during the Middle Ages? *feudalism and the manor system developed; Catholic Church became the leading institution; nation-states emerged*

The Middle Ages

Explain How did feudalism make up for the lack of strong central governments during the Middle Ages? *lords ruled large estates, gave land to vassals and protected them in exchange for loyalty and military service*

Recall Why did Pope Urban II urge Christians to go to war in the Middle East? *Many devout believers made pilgrimages to the Holy Land, which was ruled by Muslim Turks. Pope Urban wanted to recapture the Holy Land.*

Sequence In what ways did the Crusades help bring about the end of the feudal system? *nobles lost their fortunes; a new middle class developed; towns got charters from and paid taxes to the king; led to the development of strong central government*

Info to Know

The Magna Carta The Magna Carta (Latin for "great charter") played an important role in the American Revolution. In the years before the Revolutionary War, colonists often complained that their rights as British citizens were being trampled. After the colonists won their independence, several provisions in the Magna Carta, including due process of law, made their way into the U.S. Constitution.

The Middle Ages

Monsters and boiling seas were not the only fearsome things during the **Middle Ages**, the period of European history from about AD 500 to 1500. This time, also known as the medieval period, began when the old Roman Empire collapsed, creating widespread lawlessness.

Feudalism and the manorial system

During the early Middle Ages, life was frightening for Europeans. Invaders occupied Spain and attacked other nations in central Europe. In the north, Vikings from Scandinavia raided the coasts.

Because no governments were strong enough to protect people, local nobles took over. A system of feudalism developed, mainly in France, England, and Germany. The feudal system involved interdependency between lords and vassals, or nobles of lower rank. Feudal lords ruled large estates, or manors, and gave parcels of land to vassals in exchange for their loyalty and military service.

The Crusades The Roman Catholic Church was the leading institution in medieval Europe. Religion dominated the lives of the people, most of whom had few material comforts.

Many devout believers made pilgrimages to Christian shrines and holy places. A number of these holy places were in Palestine, the area known as the Holy Land. Muslim Turks, however, ruled that region. In 1095 Pope Urban II called on Christian kings and knights to go to war to recapture those lands. Thousands answered his call. The holy wars that followed were known as the **Crusades**, and they continued until 1291.

At first the Crusaders did gain territory, but the Muslims eventually won back the region. However, the Crusades did open Europeans' eyes to the rest of the world. Soldiers who had never traveled farther than the next village suddenly experienced new lands and peoples.

The Crusades also gave a boost to trade between Europe and the Middle East. People now wanted exotic luxury goods such as fruits, spices, sugar, silks, perfumes, and carpets. Merchants in European cities, especially in Italy, made fortunes. These rich merchants, along with successful artisans, made up a growing middle class in the towns. Towns grew into bustling market centers.

New nation-states Early in the Middle Ages, Europe was divided among hundreds of nobles. Barons, earls, dukes, counts—each ruled a piece of land and hoped to rule more. By the late Middle Ages, though, things were changing. Many nobles had lost their fortunes (and even their lives) in the Crusades. At the same time, the new middle-class townspeople did not owe loyalty to a feudal lord. It was the king who gave their town a charter (a document defining its territory), and it was the king who collected taxes from them.

In England, France, and Spain, those developments allowed strong rulers to unify their lands. They began creating nation-states—countries with strong central governments and homogeneous, rather than diverse, populations. With taxes from the towns, rulers could hire their own armies. They chose royal officials from the educated middle class and made policies for all their subjects.

In England, however, some barons acted to curb the king's powers. In 1215 they forced the unpopular King John to sign the **Magna Carta**. This document established several important principles of government, such as no taxation without representation and the right to trial

24

Magna Carta

- Signed by King John in 1215
- Guaranteed certain rights to the barons
- Restricted the power of the king
- Established no taxation without representation
- Established the right to trial by jury of one's peers
- Set forth the basic principles of English and, later, American law

English-Language Learners; Special Education Students

1. Write each of the following phrases for students to see: rise of trade; need for land; rise of towns; rise of a middle class; rise of the manor system; need for protection from outsiders; lack of strong central government; growth of strong central government

2. Have students identify each phrase as a factor that contributed to the rise or fall of feudalism. *rise—need for land and protection, rise of the manor system, lack of strong central government; fall—rise of trade,* *towns, middle class, growth of strong central government*

3. Guide the class in a discussion of the impact of each of these factors on feudalism.

4. Have each student write a few sentences summarizing the factors that led to the rise and fall of feudalism. If students have difficulty, have them create a cause-and-effect diagram before writing. **LS Visual-Spatial**

📜 Alternative Assessment Handbook, Rubric 11: Discussions

by a jury "of one's peers [equals]." At first only the barons enjoyed these rights, but gradually they were extended to ordinary people.

Later in the 1200s, the English also began to develop a parliament, a representative assembly that could make laws. This evolved gradually into two "houses" that met separately. The House of Lords was a council of nobles and bishops. The House of Commons included knights and townspeople.

READING CHECK **Identifying Cause and Effect** What events helped strong nations arise toward the end of the Middle Ages?

The Renaissance and the Protestant Reformation

As the Middle Ages came to an end, the stage was set for great changes in Europe. Increased trade with the East opened people's minds to new ideas. Prosperity brought population growth and better education. In the 1300s a new era of learning and creativity began. This period is called the **Renaissance** (REN-uh-sahns), a term that comes from the French word for "rebirth."

The Renaissance The Renaissance began in the wealthy city-states of Italy. In the 1400s and 1500s, though, it spread northward to the rest of Europe.

Renaissance scholars took a fresh interest in ancient knowledge that had been lost during the Middle Ages. They studied anew the classics of ancient Greece and Rome. Inspired by those civilizations, artists and writers created works of lasting beauty. Merchants who had become rich from international trade supported their work.

The Renaissance was not just a time of intense creativity in the arts. It was truly a new beginning in ways of thinking as well. In the medieval period, many people accepted misery as their lot in life and hoped for rewards in heaven. Now people showed more interest in a meaningful life on earth. They valued individuals and their personal achievements.

Scientists also began to question long-accepted teachings of the Catholic Church—for example, the idea that the earth was at the center of the universe. It was a big change from the way people thought during the Middle Ages.

Sketch by Leonardo da Vinci

Leonardo da Vinci thought that flight would require flapping wings. This sketch shows one of his ideas for a device that would test the strength of beating wings.

Person pushed down on bar to make wing flap.

Wing flapped up and down. The greater the wingspan, the stronger the wing. Leonardo calculated that to lift a man and a flying machine weighing 400 pounds, it would take a wingspan of about 12 feet.

Skills FOCUS **READING LIKE A HISTORIAN**

1. **Interpreting Visuals** How do the wings in the sketch differ from wings on today's airplanes?
2. **Evaluating Sources** Do you think Leonardo's wings would have worked?

See *Skills Handbook*, pp. H30, H34

The Protestant Reformation It was not only scientists who challenged the authority of the church. Many people felt that some members of the clergy had become lazy and corrupt. Devout Catholics complained that the church was failing to provide proper spiritual guidance.

Discontent with the church reached its peak in northern and central Europe. In 1517 a German monk named **Martin Luther** strode to a church in the town of Wittenberg and nailed a list of arguments to the door. Luther criticized some church practices and called for a public debate. He hoped to bring about reforms, but his actions set off a religious revolution.

THE WORLD BEFORE 1600 **25**

Reading Focus

2 What happened during the Renaissance and the Protestant Reformation? *rebirth of interest in the classics of ancient Greece and Rome; church reformers broke with Catholicism and started new religions*

The Renaissance and the Protestant Reformation

Identify What was the Renaissance? *a period with renewed interest in the arts; a different way of thinking and looking at the world*

Summarize How did the way Europeans think—and the way they viewed the world—change during the Renaissance? *people wanted to have a more meaningful life on Earth; began to challenge teachings of the Church; relied more on observation and experiments*

Evaluate Why do you think the Renaissance began in Italy and not elsewhere? *possible answer—Italian merchants made fortunes from trade and banking, and they used their money to finance the Renaissance.*

Biography
Michelangelo (1475–1564)
Michelangelo, a Renaissance sculptor and painter, began to study anatomy during his teen years. He used this scientific knowledge in both his sculpture and paintings to create perfectly proportioned bodies and accurate musculature. In *David* and other works, Michelangelo captures human energy, vitality, and movement. This work also shows Michelangelo's keen observation of the human form.

Answers

Reading Like a Historian *1. their shape and material; 2. possible answer— no, not without a better system of propulsion*

Reading Check *the Crusades; the rising middle class owed loyalty to a single king, not a noble*

Skills Focus: Interpreting Time Lines | At Level

Social Studies Skill
Europe and Exploration

1. Guide students in a discussion of why time lines are important, how they can be used to show relationships between events, and how they can show a particular sequence of events.

2. Have students work in pairs to create an illustrated time line showing the following events: feudalism, the Crusades, the rise of nation-states, the Renaissance, the Reformation, the Reconquest, and the Age of Exploration. Have students include the date of each important event on their time lines.

3. Have volunteers call out the dates on their time lines, and create a class time line for all to see. Guide students in a discussion of the important turning points in history shown on the class time line.

4. Have students keep their time lines as a study tool. **LS** **Visual-Spatial**

📖 Alternative Assessment Handbook, Rubric 36: Time Lines

Direct Teach

Reading Focus

The Renaissance and the Protestant Reformation

Explain After the Reformation, how did religion divide Europe? *Protestant majority in northern Europe; Catholic Church controlled most of southern Europe; central Europe divided*

Draw Conclusions How do you think Ferdinand and Isabella would treat Protestants? *possible answer— try to force Protestants to become Catholics or punish them*

CRF: Primary Source Activity: Marco Polo Describes Japan

Info to Know

Innovation at Sea Prince Henry required his sailors to keep accurate records of their voyages. Prior to his mandate, sea captains had rarely kept logs, partly because few sailors could read and partly because they wanted to keep the best sea routes secret. Henry gathered his sailors' logs and hired a cartographer to make accurate maps from the navigational information. These maps helped the Portuguese dominate the sea trade.

go.hrw.com
Online Resources
KEYWORD: SD7 CH1
TOPIC: THE RENAISSANCE

Answers

Reading Check *scientists began to question long-accepted teachings of the Catholic Church; led to the Reformation and formation of Protestant churches*

26

Luther's calls for reform launched a movement that became known as the **Reformation**. Those who joined in protesting against the Roman Catholic Church became known as **Protestants**. They soon broke with Catholicism and formed their own churches.

Reform ideas spread beyond the German states to other parts of Europe, including Switzerland, England, Scotland, Scandinavia, and the Netherlands. By the mid-1500s Protestants began to dominate northern Europe, while the Catholic Church still controlled most of southern Europe. Central Europe was divided.

Christianity in Spain Spain was also divided along religious lines for many years. In the 700s a few small Christian kingdoms controlled northern Spain. Islam, meanwhile, had taken root in most of the Iberian Peninsula—present-day Spain and Portugal. There the Muslims, known as Moors, introduced cultural advances rare in medieval Europe.

By the 1100s, however, Muslim rule was declining. At the same time, the Crusades were inspiring Christian rulers to try to win back the Iberian Peninsula. This movement was known as the Reconquista, or Reconquest. One by one, Muslim kingdoms fell.

In 1469 a royal marriage united the two largest Christian kingdoms. **Queen Isabella** of Castile-León married King Ferdinand of Aragón. Their goal was to unite all of Spain as a Catholic kingdom. They believed that Spain could be a strong nation-state only if it had a single religion.

Granada, the last Muslim stronghold, fell in 1492. That same year, Spain's rulers ordered all Jews to convert or leave the country. In 1497 Muslims in Portugal were also ordered to convert or leave. Meanwhile, Christians suspected of defying the church risked punishment by the Spanish Inquisition, a famously harsh court.

READING CHECK **Summarizing** What happened to the Catholic Church during the Renaissance?

The Age of Exploration

The Renaissance changed the way that Europeans looked at themselves and the world around them. They had seen new places and were curious about them. Advances in science and technology encouraged people to ask questions and

think boldly. A desire to explore seized the rulers of unified nation-states—France, England, Spain, and Portugal. They dreamed of increasing their wealth and power by finding new sources of trade.

Some historians suggest that the religious spirit of the Crusades and the Reconquista also spurred the Age of Exploration that began in the 1400s. Catholic explorers hoped not only to make voyages of discovery but also to spread Christianity.

The travels of Marco Polo During the Middle Ages, some of the boldest travelers had been traders from the Italian city-states of Venice and Genoa. Many Italian merchants crossed the Mediterranean Sea to trade with Muslims, who brought spices and other goods from Asia. Only a few Europeans traveled to China and India themselves, crossing the mountains and deserts of central Asia until they finally reached the Far East. Trading trips such as these took many years.

The most famous of these travelers was a young Venetian named Marco Polo. He set out for China in 1271 with his father and uncle, who had made the trip once before. The Polos stayed in China for almost 17 years, while Marco worked for the emperor Kublai Khan.

Their return trip, partly by sea, took them to many parts of Southeast Asia and India. All along the way, Marco took note of people, places, and customs. After finally getting home to Venice, Marco dictated the story of his travels. The book became instantly popular, and it influenced later explorers.

Prince Henry the Navigator One of the leading figures in the Age of Exploration was Prince Henry of Portugal, known as the Navigator. He had heard tales of African gold, and in 1419, he set up a school and naval observatory to encourage exploration.

Henry brought in mapmakers, experienced sailors, shipbuilders, and instrument makers. He also began to sponsor many expeditions in the Atlantic Ocean and down the west coast of Africa. He hoped to find gold, compete with the Muslims for trade in Africa, and spread Christianity. He also hoped to find a sea route to India. That would let Portugal and other countries trade directly with the East instead of going through Italian merchants.

26 CHAPTER 1

Collaborative Learning

The Reformation and the Counter-Reformation

At Level
Research Required

1. Organize the class into small groups. Have each group research the Protestant Reformation and the Catholic Counter-Reformation.

2. Have each group compile its research into a table that compares major Protestant sects that developed by 1600, as well as reforms that were made in the Catholic Church. Information should include each Protestant sect, name of the founder, major leader, the location where the reform or Counter-

Reformation movement began, how it attempted to reform the church, and the distinguishing beliefs of each Protestant sect.

3. Have volunteers share their research with the class. As they share the information, create a master table for students to see.

LS Interpersonal, Logical-Mathematical

Alternative Assessment Handbook, Rubrics 14: Group Activity; and 30: Research

Graphic Organizer Transparencies

Caravel

A special type of ship called the caravel enabled European explorers to sail across huge oceans and up small rivers. Though small, caravels were sturdy. They featured important advances in sailing technology.

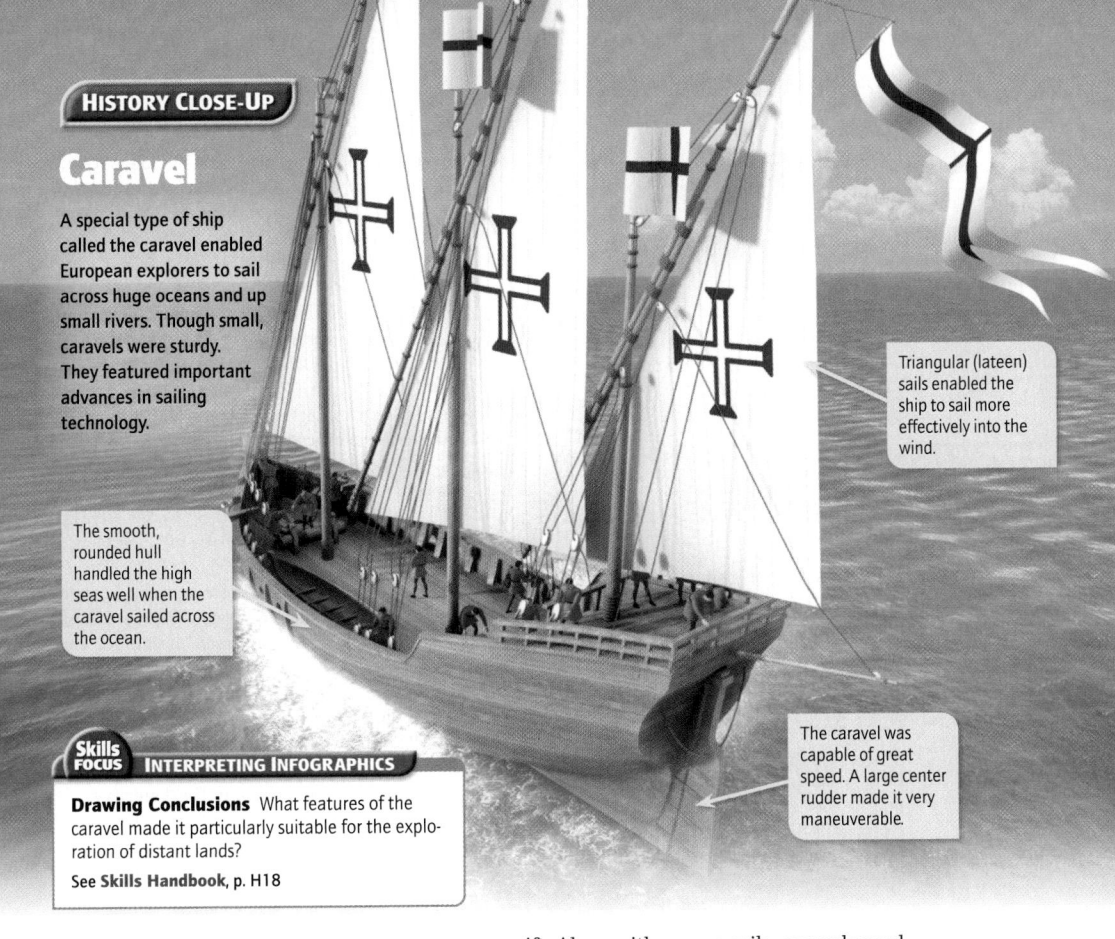

The smooth, rounded hull handled the high seas well when the caravel sailed across the ocean.

Triangular (lateen) sails enabled the ship to sail more effectively into the wind.

The caravel was capable of great speed. A large center rudder made it very maneuverable.

Skills FOCUS   INTERPRETING INFOGRAPHICS

Drawing Conclusions What features of the caravel made it particularly suitable for the exploration of distant lands?

See **Skills Handbook, p. H18**

Henry's ships traveled farther and farther south along Africa's west coast. In the 1440s, Portuguese sea captains discovered several rivers, set up colonies, made accurate maps, and brought back gold dust from West Africa. As you read in Section 3, they also began to bring Africans to Portugal as servants.

In 1448 the Portuguese set up the first European trading post in Africa. They traded for gold, ivory, pepper, and palm oil. They also started sugar plantations on the islands of Cape Verde and São Tomé.

Better sailing technology One reason that Portugal's expeditions were so successful was because sailors had a new kind of ship. Prince Henry's school in southern Portugal had developed the **caravel**, a vessel both sturdy and

swift. Along with square sails, caravels used triangular (lateen) sails, which helped them maneuver and sail against the wind. Caravels also had large cargo holds, so they could carry more goods than older ships.

There were other advances in technology, too. Previously sailors had relied on coastal landmarks to pinpoint their location. They worried about losing their way if they sailed out of sight of land. Now mariners began to use improved navigational instruments, which made longer sea voyages possible. With an astrolabe, for example, sailors could determine their latitude using the sun and stars.

Ship captains also began to use improved versions of the magnetic compass. Because the compass always showed north, they could accurately plot their course even at night or on cloudy days.

Reading Focus

3 What did Europeans hope to find during the Age of Exploration? *new sea routes to Asia*

The Age of Exploration

Identify What three technological advances helped make Portugal's expeditions successful? *caravel, astrolabe, magnetic compass*

Evaluate What would be the advantages and disadvantages of trade that did not involve Italian merchants? *possible answers—advantages: no middlemen and increased profits; disadvantages: increased danger and risk in getting goods to Europe*

Info to Know

New Technology? Much of the new sailing technology that enabled explorers to venture farther out was new only to Europeans. The astrolabe was developed by the Muslims. The Chinese invented the magnetic compass. Europeans had been using the lateen sail since the 800s, and it was probably introduced from the Persian Gulf and Indian Ocean.

About the Illustration

This illustration is an artist's conception based on available sources. Historians, however, are uncertain exactly what this scene looked like.

Skills Focus: Sequencing
At Level

Reading Skill
Sailing Technology

Organize students into four groups. Assign each group one of the following: lateen sails, the caravel, the astrolabe, and the magnetic compass. Have students create a chart like this one, listing the innovation they have been assigned, and explaining why it was created (before) and how it changed sea exploration (after). **LS Visual-Spatial**

Alternative Assessment Handbook, Rubrics 7: Charts

Graphic Organizer Transparencies

Innovation	Before	After

Answers

Interpreting Infographics *handled high seas well, sailed into the wind effectively, capable of great speed, maneuverable*

Reading Focus

The Age of Exploration

Recall How did Europeans find what is now Brazil? *A fleet led by Pedro Álvars Cabral that was bound for India sailed southwest in the Atlantic.*

Evaluate Why do you think Bartolomeu Dias sailed home instead of continuing onward after rounding the southern tip of Africa? *possible answers—tired from voyage; lack of supplies; crew forced him to turn back*

📦 Map Transparency: European Routes

Review & Assess

Close

Guide students in a discussion of the ways in which the ideas of the Renaissance led Europeans to explore the world.

Review

📦 Online Quiz, Section 4

📦 Daily Test Practice Transparency

Assess

SE Section 4 Assessment

📋 Progress Assessment: Section 4 Quiz

📋 Alternative Assessment Handbook

Reteach

📋 Interactive Reader and Study Guide, Section 4

💿 Interactive Skills Tutor CD-ROM

EUROPEAN ROUTES

Marco Polo traveled a land route to Asia. Two centuries later, Vasco da Gama discovered a sea route.

Looking for a sea route to Asia The overland trip to Asia remained long, difficult, and dangerous. Many Europeans still hoped to find a southern sea route to India. Again, Portugal led the way.

In early 1488, a Portuguese explorer named Bartolomeu Dias was sailing down Africa's west coast near the southern tip of the continent. A sudden storm blew his ships off course, and he lost sight of land for almost a month. Eventually, Dias realized that he was no longer traveling south but north. He had rounded the southern tip of Africa!

Dias returned home without going farther. He reportedly chose the name Cape of Storms for the point of land he had reached. The Portuguese king, however, signaling his pleasure in the discovery, called it the Cape of Good Hope.

About 10 years later, another Portuguese explorer, Vasco da Gama, led another historic expedition. Da Gama showed great skill at navigating. In 1498 he landed on the coast of India, finding the sea route so many had sought.

Da Gama's success was a challenge to other European rulers. The opening of a new trade route helped make Portugal a world power. It also led to the decline of trans-Sahara trade and the African trading empires.

As soon as da Gama returned to Portugal, another expedition was organized to return to India. This fleet was led by Pedro Álvars Cabral. On its way to the Cape of Good Hope, the fleet sailed southwest in the Atlantic. There the crew became the first Europeans to spot the coast of what is now Brazil. The fleet then turned eastward and continued on to India. En route, however, several ships and sailors were lost, including Bartolomeu Dias.

Though this voyage met bad luck, Cabral set up trading posts in India and brought back spices. More importantly, his sighting of Brazil gave Portugal a land claim in the Americas.

READING CHECK Identifying the Main Idea Why did the Portuguese and other Europeans want to find a sea route to India?

SECTION 4 ASSESSMENT

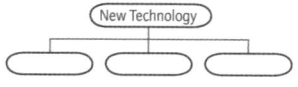
go.hrw.com
Online Quiz
Keyword: SD7 HP1

Reviewing Ideas, Terms, and People

1. **a. Describe** What were the **Crusades**?
   b. Explain What did lords and vassals offer each other under the feudal system?
   c. Elaborate What was the relationship between the growth of towns and the rise of nation-states?

2. **a. Define** Write a brief definition for each of the following terms: **Renaissance, Reformation**.
   b. Contrast How did the worldview of people in the Renaissance differ from the outlook during the **Middle Ages**?

3. **a. Recall** What were Prince Henry's contributions to the Age of Exploration?
   b. Explain What motivated the Portuguese to find a sea route to India?

Critical Thinking

4. **Sequencing** Copy the chart below and use it to show the advances in seafaring technology that aided Portuguese exploration.

New Technology

FOCUS ON WRITING ✏️

5. **Persuasive** As Prince Henry, write a letter to persuade one of your ship captains to attempt the dangerous trip around the Cape of Good Hope.

Section 4 Assessment Answers

1. **a.** holy wars between 1095 and 1291
   b. Lords gave parcels of land to vassals who gave loyalty and military service.
   c. Townships were subject to the king, and strong rulers could unify the land, leading to nation-states.

2. **a.** Renaissance—a new era of learning and creativity; Reformation—a reform movement in which individuals formed their own Christian churches
   b. Instead of hoping for rewards in heaven, individuals valued their personal

achievements and life on Earth.

3. **a.** set up a school to encourage exploration; sponsored expeditions in the Atlantic Ocean
   b. would enable Portugal to trade directly with the East

4. caravel, astrolabe, magnetic compass

5. possible answer—Portugal must find a sea route to India before other countries.

Answers

Reading Check *The overland trip to Asia remained long, difficult, and dangerous.*

BEFORE YOU READ

MAIN IDEA

Columbus's voyages to the Americas established contact with Native Americans and led to European colonies and an exchange of goods and ideas.

READING FOCUS

1. When did Vikings visit North America, and why was their stay brief?

2. Why were Columbus's voyages to the Caribbean significant?

3. What impact did European exploration have on Native Americans?

4. What was the Columbian Exchange, and how did it affect both Europe and America?

KEY TERMS AND PEOPLE

Vikings
Leif Eriksson
Christopher Columbus
Tainos
colonization
Columbian Exchange

 TAKING NOTES As you read, take notes on causes for the enslavement of the Caribbean Indians. Record your notes in a graphic organizer like the one shown below.

Cause → Effect: Enslavement of the Caribbean Indians

THE INSIDE STORY

Why did the queen of Spain sponsor Christopher Columbus's voyage? The explorer Christopher Columbus was incredibly stubborn in believing that he could reach Asia by sailing west. Still, it took many years to find someone who had enough faith to finance his expedition. That someone was Queen Isabella of Spain, one of the strongest monarchs of the time.

Columbus and Isabella came from different worlds but were somewhat alike in both looks—auburn hair and blue eyes—and personality. From their first meeting in 1486, Isabella was sympathetic to his plans. Nonetheless, the final decision took six years. Isabella named a royal committee to investigate his idea, but they advised against it. She continued to encourage Columbus, sending occasional gifts of money. She told him to try again after the Reconquista was over.

In early 1492, an impatient Columbus offered the Spanish rulers one last chance. He added other demands—property, a title, and a share of trade. They said no, so Columbus packed his maps and left. Then, at the last minute, Luis de Santangel, a royal finance official, changed Isabella's mind. The whole voyage, he said, would not cost as much as entertaining a visiting king or queen for a week! Nevertheless, Santangel said he could raise the money. Isabella quickly sent a royal guard to bring Columbus back. History had been made. ◼

▲ Christopher Columbus's persistence with Queen Isabella (seated) finally paid off in 1492.

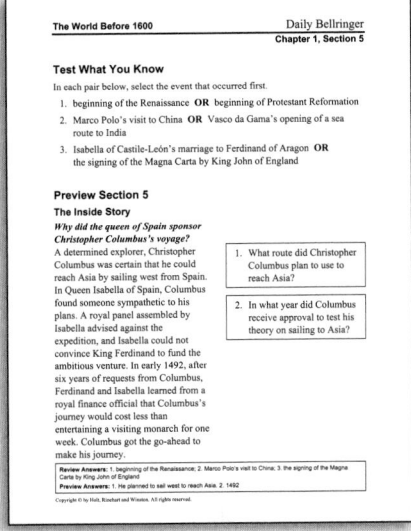

Teach the Main Idea

[At Level]

Cultures Make Contact

1. **Teach** Ask students the Reading Focus questions to teach this section.

2. **Apply** Have students create an outline of the section using the heads as main points. Students should identify at least two main ideas under each red heading or blue subheading in the section.

3. **Review** Have students identify the points in their outlines that they feel are most important. Guide students in a discussion of Columbus's trips to the Americas.

4. **Practice/Homework** Have each student make a map of North America and the Caribbean showing where the first European visitors—the Vikings and Columbus—landed during their trips, and where the first settlements were established. Have volunteers share their maps with the class.

LS **Logical-Mathematical, Visual-Spatial**

📝 Alternative Assessment Handbook, Rubrics 11: Discussions; and 20: Map Creation

Reading Focus

❶ When did Vikings visit North America, and why was their stay brief? *Greenland in the late 900s; tried to establish a colony in Vinland but left because natives were hostile*

Vikings Visit North America

Explain How did the Vikings end up on the North American mainland? *headed for Greenland, missed their destination, sailed too far west*

Analyze Why do you think the Vikings continued to visit Vinland but never tried to settle there again? *possible answers—Native Americans would let them visit, not settle; too far from home base to reinforce a settlement*

📖 CRF: Literature Activity: *The Saga of Eric the Red*

Reading Focus

❷ Why were Columbus's voyages to the Caribbean significant? *Until then, Europeans had no idea that the Americas existed.*

Columbus Voyages to the Caribbean

Describe How did Columbus prepare for his voyage? *studied sailing and navigation; made calculations of the size of the world and the width of the Atlantic*

Evaluate Do you think Columbus should be considered a hero? Explain your answer. *possible answers—Yes, he was courageous and was the first European to record his journey. No, his treatment of Native Americans does not warrant heroism.*

Answers

Faces of History *to find a new route to Asia*

Reading Check *Viking settlers left after three years because the natives were so hostile.*

30

Vikings Visit North America

Hundreds of years before Columbus planned his first voyage, the Norse from Scandinavia dominated the northern seas. The Norse, better known as **Vikings**, were sea raiders who terrorized the coasts of western Europe. The Vikings were also bold explorers in the North Atlantic Ocean.

In the late 900s, Vikings from Norway reached the island of Greenland in North America. Although Greenland today is largely ice covered, the climate was warmer then. Vikings led by Erik the Red established settlements there in 986.

In about 1000, Erik's son, **Leif Eriksson,** also headed to Greenland. He and his group missed their destination, however, and sailed further west than they had intended. Leif landed on a coast, probably in eastern Canada, where many grapevines and wild grasses grew. He named the place Vinland because of its abundant grapevines.

A few years later, other Viking explorers tried to establish a colony in Vinland. That led to the first known European contact with Native Americans. According to Scandinavian sagas—tales of legendary figures—the Viking settlers didn't find a warm welcome. Indeed, they left just three years later, after warfare with the natives. The Vikings continued to make trips to Vinland for timber, but they never settled there again.

> **READING CHECK** **Summarizing** What was the Viking experience in America?

FACES OF HISTORY

Christopher COLUMBUS
1451–1506

Christopher Columbus's first job was working with his father as a weaver. Wanting to explore the world outside the textile shop, Columbus found work as a sailor on ships in the Mediterranean.

Eventually, Columbus made his way to Portugal, where he found a job making maps. During those years Columbus met many explorers and navigators and began to hear tales of western islands rich with spices. Columbus was certain he could find the islands and earn wealth and fame.

Explain Why did Columbus sail west?

Columbus Voyages to the Caribbean

In the 1400s other Europeans knew nothing of the Vikings' journeys to North America. People in Europe had no inkling that the Americas even existed. That changed—and the whole world changed—as a result of one man's determination to find a sea route to India.

Christopher Columbus The explorer **Christopher Columbus** was born and raised in the Italian trading city of Genoa. As a young man, he went to sea and served on both merchant ships and warships. In 1476, when his ship sank in battle, he ended up in Portugal. This was a stroke of luck because the Portuguese, as you read in Section 4, were the leaders in exploration.

At the time, Vasco da Gama had not yet made his historic voyage to India. But many Portuguese mariners were sailing south along the African coast in hope of reaching the Indies. Some thought about trying a different course—sailing west. Because no one knew that the American continents were in the way, the idea of sailing west to reach Asia seemed promising. Yet no one dared venture far into the unknown Atlantic Ocean.

Columbus was the exception. He made it his life goal to lead a westward voyage. He needed ships and crews, though. As you read in the "Inside Story," it took many years before he convinced Queen Isabella of Spain to back his "Enterprise of the Indies."

In the meantime, Columbus studied sailing and navigation techniques. He also read many books dealing with travel and geography, including Marco Polo's *Travels*. After careful study, he concluded that the distance to Japan was only about 2,400 nautical miles. Unfortunately, Columbus made major errors in calculating the size of the world and the width of the Atlantic Ocean.

The first voyage On August 3, 1492, Columbus set sail. He had about 90 men, two caravels (the *Niña* and the *Pinta*), and his flagship, the *Santa Maria*. After three weeks on the open sea, the crew was frightened and restless. Some were near mutiny. Then they began to see birds and floating tree branches, which made them believe they were nearing land.

Skills Focus: Identifying Problem and Solution ⬛ At Level

Reading Skill
Financing Columbus's Voyage

1. Guide students in a discussion of Columbus's desire to explore the Atlantic and sail to Asia.

2. Have each student write a letter from Christopher Columbus to the Spanish monarchs asking for money to finance a voyage of discovery. Students' letters should include the following information: why they need the money; where they want to go; why

they think they are qualified to make the voyage; what they think they will find on their voyage; what they will do to repay the king and queen.

3. Have volunteers read their letters to the class.
   ⬛ Verbal-Linguistic

📖 Alternative Assessment Handbook, Rubrics 11: Discussions; and 37: Writing Assignments

Columbus Describes Contact

When Christopher Columbus landed in what he thought was part of Asia, he met people who had never before been seen by Europeans. Columbus's views and descriptions of these people, whom he came to call "Indians," would shape European views of Native Americans for centuries to come.

A main goal of early explorers was to convert Native Americans to Christianity.

"I gave them [Indians] a thousand good, pleasing things which I had brought, in order that they might be fond of us, and furthermore might be made Christians and be inclined to the love and service of their Highnesses and of the whole Castilian [Spanish] nation and try to help us and to give us of the things which they have in abundance and which are necessary to us."

—Columbus's Letter on His First Voyage

Columbus thought the Indians he met had gold and other riches.

 Skills FOCUS **READING LIKE A HISTORIAN**

1. **Analyzing Primary Sources** How did Columbus's goal of gaining riches for Spain affect his treatment of the Indians?

2. **Evaluating Sources** Do you think Columbus's plan worked?

See Skills Handbook, pp. H28–29

Then, before dawn on October 12, 1492, a sailor shouted, "Tierra! Tierra!," or "Land! Land!" The three ships anchored off a small island in the Caribbean. Columbus named the island San Salvador.

Because the distance he had sailed was about what he had calculated in error, Columbus believed he was in the Indies. When the local people, the **Tainos**, greeted him, Columbus called them *los Indios,* or "Indians." He gave them gifts of red caps, glass beads, and bells.

The Tainos lived simply in thatched huts in the jungle. They grew vegetables, wove cotton, and made pottery. Columbus was disappointed not to find the rich cities he expected. But he still hoped to pick up Asian spices, silks, and other treasures on the larger islands nearby.

The crews soon set off, taking six Tainos with them as guides. The local Indians promised that plenty of gold lay ahead. The fleet stopped at Cuba, then sailed to another large island, which Columbus named *La Isla Española* ("The Spanish Isle"). Today it is Hispaniola (Haiti and the Dominican Republic).

There at last they found gold, which encouraged Columbus. But the *Santa Maria* went aground on a coral reef and sank. With his two remaining ships, Columbus returned to Spain.

Columbus would later make three more trips to the Americas. Although his voyages changed history, Columbus never understood why. When he died in 1506, he still believed he had explored part of Asia.

READING CHECK **Making Inferences** Why did Columbus continue to think he was in Asia?

Impact on Native Americans

Columbus's voyages set off a wave of European **colonization** in the Americas. As you might imagine, colonization had a profound impact on the native peoples of the Americas.

Colonies in Hispaniola When the *Santa Maria* ran aground off Hispaniola in December 1492, Columbus took it as a sign from God that he was meant to establish a colony there. Because it was Christmas Day, he called it *Villa de la Navidad* ("Christmas Town") and had his men build a fort. As he departed for Spain, he told them to trade for gold, treat the natives well, and find a place to build a town.

Columbus came back to La Navidad the following year, intending to organize new colonies. But upon his return, he was shocked and

THE WORLD BEFORE 1600 **31**

31

Reading Focus

❹ What was the Columbian Exchange, and how did it affect both Europe and America? *transfer of goods and ideas; many exchanges were valuable, but some brought diseases and epidemics to the Americas*

The Columbian Exchange

Recall What tragic consequences did the Columbian Exchange have? *Diseases such as smallpox and measles, for which Native Americans had no resistance, killed thousands of people within a few years.*

Predict How would the introduction of horses from Europe affect the culture of Native Americans? *profoundly, as the horse would become central to the culture and life of the Plains Indians*

dismayed. Many of his men had behaved wildly in his absence and made the Tainos so angry that the Indians had killed them all. This incident soured relations between the Spaniards and the Tainos, who had seemed so peace-loving.

Deciding to find another site for a colony, Columbus sailed east along the coast. There he established Isabela, named after the queen. Still believing he was in Asia, Columbus hoped to set up a trading post to exchange European goods for gems, precious metals, and spices. The site was a poor choice, however. It had malaria-carrying mosquitoes and no fresh water.

Things went badly in Isabela. Columbus's brothers ran the settlement while he explored other islands. Some of the Spanish officers rebelled against them. Then, under pressure to supply more gold, Columbus and his brothers captured Indians to sell as slaves. Colonization turned into the conquest of Hispaniola. In March 1495 the Spaniards marched inland with dogs, horses, and muskets. The Indians were unable to unite against them.

BARTOLOMÉ DE LAS CASAS

Skills FOCUS **READING LIKE A HISTORIAN**

Bartolomé de Las Casas is shown at his desk. His many writings included a plea for "enlightenment to those who are in a position to do something about what has been happening."
Interpreting Visuals How is his relationship to Native Americans shown in this painting?

Eventually, Ferdinand and Isabella decided that Columbus was a better admiral than he was an administrator. He lost his post as governor of Hispaniola in 1500. Unfortunately, the people of the islands were in for more suffering under other governors.

Native American labor Columbus's first reaction to meeting the native Tainos was to note "how easy it would be to convert these people [to Christianity] and to make them work for us." That view set a pattern for later Spanish and other European explorers.

As you know, the Spaniards who came to the Caribbean were mainly interested in finding gold. Because mining required much physical labor, they recruited Indians to help. It was an easy step from forced labor to enslavement.

Slavery was also a response to pressure from Spain to make a profit from Columbus's voyages. Early in 1494, along with gold, fine woods, and parrots, Columbus sent 26 Indians back to Spain. He said that they should be taught Spanish so they could be interpreters. Columbus also suggested starting a trade in Indian slaves. Slavery was common in many societies at the time. Europeans were also receptive to the idea of enslaving non-Christians because they could then be converted.

Trade in Indian slaves Not everyone approved of enslaving Indians. One opponent was Queen Isabella, who stated that Caribbean Indians belonged to the monarchs and could not be owned by anyone else in Spain. As a result, many Indians were sent instead to plantations off the coast of Portugal. Later, after the Portuguese, French, and Dutch set up plantations on Caribbean islands, Indians who were enslaved were often kept as local labor.

The best-known defender of the Indians was a priest and friar named Bartolomé de Las Casas. He settled in Hispaniola in 1502 and later became a missionary to the Indians. He dedicated his life to protecting them from mistreatment by the settlers. Las Casas won the admiration of King Ferdinand of Spain. In the decades that followed, the Spanish government passed laws protecting the Indians, but enforcement of these laws proved difficult.

READING CHECK **Summarizing** What impact did Spanish colonization have on Native Americans?

Skills Focus: Making Generalizations

Reading Skill
The Columbian Exchange

1. Review the information about the Columbian Exchange with students. Make a class list of the items that were transferred between Europe and the Americas.

2. Guide students in a discussion of the ways in which life would have been different if the individual items on the class list had not been exchanged. For example, if tomatoes had never been taken to Italy from the Americas, many Italian foods would have been

completely different because there would have been no tomato sauce for spaghetti.

3. Have students select one item from the list and write a brief summary of how life would have been different without that particular item.

4. Have volunteers read their summaries to the class. **LS** **Interpersonal, Logical-Mathematical**

📖 Alternative Assessment Handbook, Rubrics 11: Discussions; and 37: Writing Assignments

Answers

Reading Like a Historian *close relationship reflected by close physical positions*

Reading Check *conversion to Catholicism; enslaved*

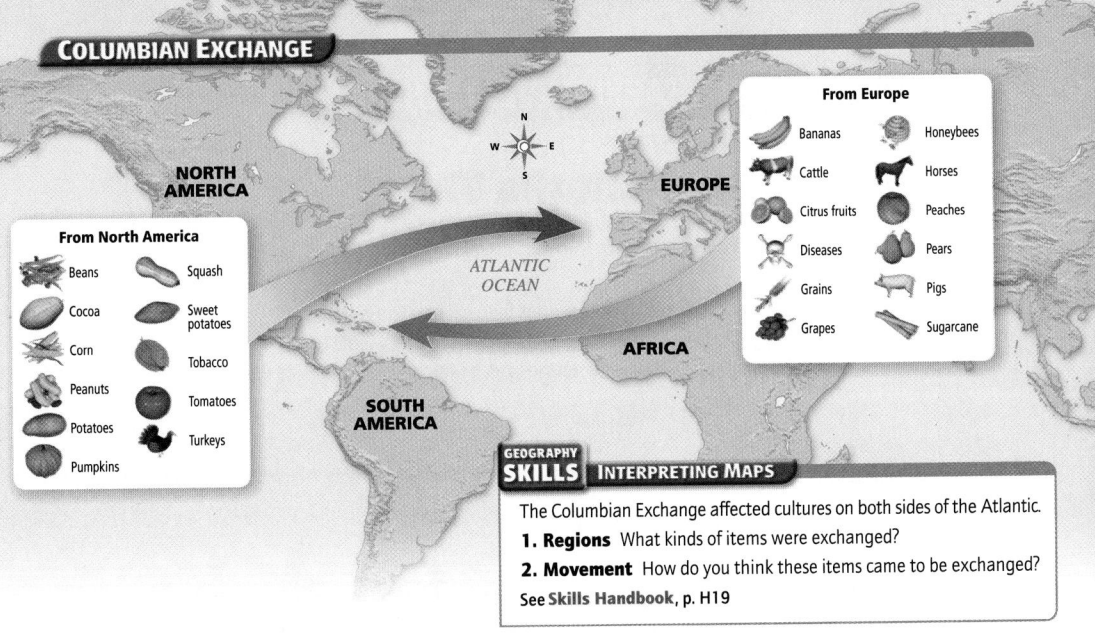

NORTH AMERICA

From North America
- Beans
- Cocoa
- Corn
- Peanuts
- Potatoes
- Pumpkins
- Squash
- Sweet potatoes
- Tobacco
- Tomatoes
- Turkeys

ATLANTIC OCEAN

EUROPE

AFRICA

SOUTH AMERICA

From Europe
- Bananas
- Cattle
- Citrus fruits
- Diseases
- Grains
- Grapes
- Honeybees
- Horses
- Peaches
- Pears
- Pigs
- Sugarcane

GEOGRAPHY SKILLS | INTERPRETING MAPS

The Columbian Exchange affected cultures on both sides of the Atlantic.
1. **Regions** What kinds of items were exchanged?
2. **Movement** How do you think these items came to be exchanged?

See **Skills Handbook**, p. H19

The Columbian Exchange

Interaction between Europeans and Native Americans—and eventually Africans—led to the exchange of plants, animals, languages, and technology. Deadly germs were exchanged, too, bringing new epidemics to the Americas. Because all these transfers came about after Columbus's voyages, they are known as the **Columbian Exchange** (see map above).

Many crops that Native Americans grew were unfamiliar in Europe. Europeans took home corn, beans, squash, tomatoes, cacao (chocolate), peanuts, and other foods when they returned from their voyages.

European explorers and settlers brought certain foods of their own to the Americas, too. Domestic animals and new technology also crossed from Europe to the Americas. Europeans brought horses, which later became central to Plains Indian culture. Indians also learned about guns from Europeans.

The Columbian Exchange had some tragic consequences as well. Native Americans had no resistance to European diseases. Thousands died of smallpox and measles.

READING CHECK **Identifying Cause and Effect** Identify one effect of the Columbian Exchange.

SECTION 5 ASSESSMENT

go.hrw.com
Online Quiz
Keyword: SD7 HP1

Reviewing Ideas, Terms, and People

1. **a. Identify** Who was **Leif Eriksson**?
   b. Explain Why didn't the **Vikings** stay in North America?
2. **a. Recall** How did **Columbus** plan to reach the Indies?
   b. Make Inferences What qualities do you suppose Columbus had?
3. **a. Recall** Where did Columbus first establish colonies?
   b. Predict How do you think the Caribbean Indians viewed Europeans?
4. **a. Define** What is meant by the term **Columbian Exchange**?
   b. Evaluate How was the Columbian Exchange both beneficial and harmful?

Critical Thinking

5. **Identifying Cause and Effect** Copy the chart below and show the factors that contributed to the enslavement of the Indians in the Caribbean.

Enslavement of Indians

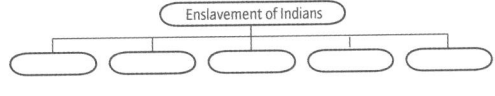

FOCUS ON WRITING

6. **Descriptive** Write a letter to a friend in Europe in the 1500s describing the fruits and vegetables you are sending from the Americas and how they can be used.

Section 5 Assessment Answers

1. **a.** Viking explorer who landed in eastern Canada
   b. The natives were too hostile.

2. **a.** by sailing west
   b. possible answer—determination, passion, intelligence, and was practical

3. **a.** Hispaniola, in the Bahamas
   b. possible answer—as threatening foreigners who were attempting to steal their land

4. **a.** interaction between Europeans and Native Americans that led to exchanges of plants, animals, languages, technology, diseases
   b. Both Europeans and Native Americans learned about new foods, technology, and languages, but they were also exposed to deadly diseases.

5. need for labor to mine gold; pressure to make a profit; desire to convert non-Christians; slavery; poor relations between Spaniards and Native Americans

6. possible answer—Peanuts and peppers can add new flavors to meals.

33

Document-Based Investigation

Migration throughout the World

Word Help

mosque Muslim place of worship
temperate mild
end purpose, intention
transacted carried out

Info to Know

Djenné and Its Great Mosque The building shown in Document 1 is the Great Mosque of Djenné, Mali. Djenné is the oldest city south of the Sahara. It was founded between 850 and 1200 AD as a trading post. In the thirteenth century, Djenné became a great market city for gold, slaves, and salt. It rivaled Timbuktu, 220 miles up the Niger River. In the seventeeth century Djenné became famous as a center of Islamic learning, attracting Muslim scholars from throughout the region. The first mosque was built in the thirteenth century when, as an expression of his faith, the ruler of Djenné had his palace destroyed and a mosque built in its place. That mosque fell into ruin, and the current mosque was built between 1905 and 1907 on the site and in the style of the original Great Mosque. It is the largest mud-brick building in the world.

Migration throughout the World

Historical Context The documents below provide information on early migration throughout the world.

Task Examine the documents and answer the questions that follow. Then you will be asked to write an essay about why people migrated, using facts from the documents and from the chapter to support the position you take in your thesis statement.

DOCUMENT 1

Many different groups have been inspired to migrate in order to spread their religious beliefs. After the founding of Islam, Arab Muslims traveled far beyond their original homeland in Southwest Asia to spread their faith. They were particularly successful in Africa, where the faith spread to key kingdoms of northern and eastern Africa, helping to solidify the Islamic Empire. This image shows one of the earliest mosques built in Africa.

DOCUMENT 2

Most scientists believe that the earliest Americans came to this continent from Asia. In all likelihood, the early migrants were looking for food. Clovis spear points like the one shown here are among the oldest artifacts found on the North American continent. They are often found in places where the earliest Americans killed woolly mammoth. This Clovis point was discovered in New Mexico and has been dated at 11,500 BC.

34 CHAPTER 1

Collaborative Learning

At Level

Reasons to Migrate

1. Guide the class in a discussion of reasons for early migration throughout the world.

2. Divide the class into small groups. Have each group collaborate in writing a skit about migrating. Students should discuss reasons for migrating, what the people hope to find in their new home, and they should describe their experiences. Students should write from the perspective of the people who are migrating, such as the first Americans or Muslims who were expanding their Islamic empire. Students may wish to conduct further research to help them lend authenticity to their skits.

3. Have each group present its skit to the class.
   LS Interpersonal, Kinesthetic

   Alternative Assessment Handbook, Rubric 33: Skits and Reader's Theater

DOCUMENT 3

The Age of Exploration was pushed in part by the desire of European nations to build their own empires. In the following letter from 1497, an Italian priest writes to the duke of Milan to report on John Cabot's trip to America and the effects it might have on England's economic power. At the time, many European leaders still thought the Americas were part of Asia. Although Cabot's exploration did not yield great riches, it did lay the foundation for later English migration to the Americas.

"[H]is Majesty [England's King Henry VII] has gained a great part of Asia without a stroke of the sword . . . And they say that the land is fertile and temperate, and think that the red wood grows there, and the silks, and they affirm that there the sea is full of fish that can be taken not only with nets, but with fishing-baskets, a stone being placed in the basket to sink it in the water . . .

[Cabot and] his partners say that they can bring so many fish that this kingdom will have no more business with Iceland, and that from that country there will be a very great trade in the fish which they call stock-fish . . . [H]e thinks of going, after this place is occupied, along the coast farther toward the east . . . where he believes all the spices of the world grow, and where there are also gems . . .

And in the spring he says that his Majesty will arm some ships, and will give him all the criminals, so that he may go to this country and plant a colony there. And in this way he hopes to make London a greater place for spices than Alexandria."

DOCUMENT 4

For the next 100 years many more explorers and migrants came to the Americas, often at great risk to themselves. The majority of these early migrants died prematurely, but they helped lay the foundation for more stable settlements. In 1604 French explorer Samuel de Champlain, who established a successful North American fur trade for his home country, commented on the many personal motivations he observed behind exploration and migration.

"The inclinations [motives] of men differ according to their varied dispositions [personalities]; and each one in his calling has his particular end in view. Some aim at gain, some at glory, some at the public weal [good]. The greater number are engaged in trade, and especially that which is transacted on the sea."

Skills Focus — READING LIKE A HISTORIAN

1. **a. Identify** Refer to Document 1. Why did Arabs build mosques in Africa?
   b. Interpret Why might someone leave their home to spread a religious faith?

2. **a. Identify** Refer to Document 2. How old is the artifact shown in this photograph?
   b. Analyze How did need for food influence migration?

3. **a. Identify** Refer to Document 3. Where did the writer think Cabot had explored?
   b. Infer Why would a country seeking to build wealth send criminals to their colonies?

4. **a. Identify** According to Champlain, what was the main personal motive of most migrants?
   b. Elaborate What do you think Champlain's personal motives probably were? Explain.

5. **Document-Based Essay Question** Consider the question below and form a thesis statement. Using examples from Documents 1, 2, 3, and 4, create an outline and write a short essay supporting your position. What motivated early world explorers to migrate to other continents?

See **Skills Handbook**, pp. H28–H29, H30

Skills Focus: Interpreting Historical Maps

Social Studies Skill

Early Explorers

Materials outline maps of North America, colored markers

1. Distribute outline maps of North America to the class.

2. Divide the class into small groups. Have each group research the early exploration and settlement of North America by John Cabot and Samuel de Champlain. Have students mark the routes of Cabot's first and second voyages of exploration along the North American coast, using a different colored marker for each. Then have students mark the areas that were explored by Champlain on his first three trips to North America, again each with a different colored marker. Finally, have students label the most important areas that were explored or settled. **LS Interpersonal, Visual-Spatial**

📝 Alternative Assessment Handbook, Rubric 21: Map Creation

Document-Based Investigation

Info to Know

Samuel de Champlain Samuel de Champlain is considered the "father of New France." He made his first visit to North America in 1603 as a geographer on a fur trading expedition. He mapped Hudson Bay and the water to the west (the Great Lakes), which he believed might be the Northwest Passage connecting the Atlantic Ocean with the Pacific Ocean. The next year he returned to establish a settlement in Acadia, a section of northeastern North America that encompassed present day Nova Scotia, as well as parts of Quebec and Maine. On his third voyage, in 1607, he founded a trading post that would become Quebec. It was the first permanent European settlement in what is now Canada. For most of the rest of his life, Champlain would spend a few months a year in Quebec, then return to France to raise money and enlist workers.

Answers

Reading Like a Historian
1. **a.** *to worship, to spread their religious beliefs;* **b.** *possible answer—because they want to convert other people to their beliefs, strengthening their religion;* 2. **a.** *approximately 13,500 years old;* **b.** *People migrated in search of new sources of food.* 3. **a.** *Asia;* **b.** *possible answer—criminals could perform the hard and dangerous work of building a colony; would eliminate need to imprison criminals within the country;* 4. **a.** *trade;* **b.** *possible answer—gain, since he established the French fur trade;* 5. *possible answer—desire to spread religious beliefs; desire for personal gain; desire to promote national interests; need for new food sources*

35

Answers

Visual Summary

Review and Inquiry Organize the class into mixed-ability groups and have them discuss the importance of trade in each culture mentioned.

🖳 Quick Facts Transparency: The World Before 1600

Reviewing Key Terms and People

1. e.
2. h.
3. f.
4. i.
5. g.
6. b.
7. j.
8. d.
9. a.
10. c.

Comprehension and Critical Thinking

11. **a.** via the Bering land bridge
    b. people settled in villages, populations grew, crafts developed, governments established

12. **a.** person with spiritual and healing powers
    b. Native Americans had a closer connection to natural world; had shamans; Christianity was dominant religion in Europe
    c. Native Americans may be willing to share the land without demanding payment

13. **a.** gold and salt
    b. Those living along the coast were nearer to Arabs who practiced and spread Islam.
    c. possible answer—hurt, because so many people were killed and captured during slavery

14. **a.** efforts by European Christians to recapture the Holy Land from Muslim Turks
    b. a new interest in ancient knowledge emerged; produced great creativity and advancement in thought

c. possible answer—the Crusades, because it opened Europeans up to a wider world

15. **a.** explorer—found a different land than he expected, though he didn't know it; governor— ineffective administrator
    b. They behaved wildly and were killed by the Tainos.
    c. possible answer—Europeans, because they acquired land and products; many Native Americans were killed by disease

Chapter Review

Visual Summary: The World Before 1600

Early Native American Cultures
- Scientists disagree on when and how the first Americans arrived.
- One theory is that the first Americans crossed a land bridge from Asia to America.
- Early Mesoamerican cultures include Olmec, Maya, and Aztec.
- Early North American cultures include Hohokam, Anasazi, Adena, Hopewell, and Mississippian.

North American Cultures in the 1400s
- Native Americans in North America establish diverse cultures based on geography.
- Some North American cultures share characteristics, including social structure, religious beliefs, and technology.
- Trading networks allow North American groups to share goods and ideas.

Africa
- Major kingdoms include Ghana, Mali, Songhai, Benin, and Kongo.
- Portuguese traders arrive in Africa in 1400s.
- European slave trade begins in late 1400s.

Europe
- Magna Carta establishes basic principles of government in 1215.
- The Renaissance begins around 1300.
- The Age of Exploration begins in the late 1400s.
- Christopher Columbus voyages to the Caribbean in 1492.
- The Reformation begins in 1517.

Reviewing Key Terms and People

Match each lettered definition with the correct numbered item below.

a. Exchange of goods without using money
b. People who move from place to place with the seasons
c. Group of people related by kinship
d. Change from hunting and gathering to farming
e. German monk who challenged the Catholic church and started the Protestant Reformation
f. Scandinavian sea raiders and explorers
g. Leader of the expedition to the Americas that included the flagship *Santa Maria*
h. The process of going to and settling in a place
i. A movement to change the Catholic church
j. Document that established several important principles of government

1. Martin Luther
2. colonization
3. Vikings
4. Reformation
5. Christopher Columbus
6. nomads
7. Magna Carta
8. agricultural revolution
9. barter
10. clan

Comprehension and Critical Thinking

SECTION 1 *(pp. 6–10)*

11. **a. Recall** How did the first people arrive in North America?
    b. Analyze What were the main effects of the agricultural revolution?

Using the Internet

16. Go to the HRW Web site and enter the keyword shown to access a rubric for this activity.

> KEYWORD: SD7 CH1

History's Impact video program
Review the video to answer the closing question:
How has American history been shaped by people
of different cultures and traditions?

SECTION 2 (pp. 11–17)

12. a. Define Write a brief definition of *shaman*.

b. Contrast What were the main differences between Native American religious beliefs and European religious beliefs?

c. Predict How could Native Americans' view of land ownership work in favor of Europeans when Europeans established colonies in the Americas?

SECTION 3 (pp. 18–22)

13. a. Identify What two valuable resources were instrumental in the development of West African trading empires?

b. Make Inferences Why were people along the African coast more heavily influenced by foreign religions, while people in the interior generally kept their traditional religions?

c. Evaluate Do you think trade with Europe ultimately helped or hurt Africa? Why?

SECTION 4 (pp. 23–28)

14. a. Recall What were the Crusades?

b. Explain In what ways was the Renaissance a rebirth for Europe?

c. Rank Of feudalism, the Crusades, the Reformation, and the Renaissance, which do you think had the biggest impact on European exploration?

SECTION 5 (pp. 29–33)

15. a. Describe Describe Columbus's career as an explorer and governor.

b. Explain How did the actions of the Spaniards cause the La Navidad colony to fail?

c. Evaluate Who do you think benefited most from the Columbian Exchange, Native Americans or Europeans? Why?

Using the Internet

go.hrw.com
Practice Online
Keyword: SD7 CH1

16. The lives and living conditions of Native Americans changed greatly after the arrival of Europeans. Using the keyword above, do research to learn about Native Americans in the United States today. Choose a group that you read about in this chapter. Then create an outline of a report that presents this information.

Analyzing Primary Sources

Reading Like a Historian This is part of Columbus's description of encountering the Tainos.

> ❝I gave them a thousand good, pleasing things which I had brought, in order that they might be fond of us, and furthermore might be made Christians and be inclined to the love and service of their Highnesses and of the whole Castilian [Spanish] nation and try to help us and to give us of the things which they have in abundance and which are necessary to us.❞
>
> —Columbus's Letter on his First Voyage

17. Identify Who was Columbus referring to when he wrote "their Highnesses"?

18. Draw Conclusions What were Columbus's goals in giving the Tainos "pleasing things"?

Critical Reading

Read the passage in Section 4 that begins with the heading "The Middle Ages." Then answer the following question.

19. According to the passage, the leading institution in medieval Europe was

  A. the military.

  B. the nation-state.

  C. the Catholic Church.

  D. the nobility.

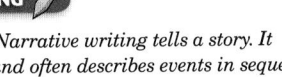
FOCUS ON WRITING

Narrative Writing *Narrative writing tells a story. It uses precise detail and often describes events in sequential order. To practice narrative writing, complete the assignment below.*

Writing Topic: How Europeans viewed Native Americans

20. Assignment Imagine that you are a European explorer who has landed in North or South America. Based on what you have read in this chapter, write a paragraph describing your first encounter with Native Americans, your reactions to these people, and your thoughts about further contact.

Answers

Analyzing Primary Sources

17. Isabella and Ferdinand

18. to make them trust the Europeans, become Christian, and aid the Spanish in the future

Critical Reading

19. C

Focus on Writing

20. possible answers—disappointed because this isn't civilization we expected, pleased with natives' friendliness; planning how to make a profit

A rubric for this activity is provided in Chapter Resource File: Focus on Writing: How Europeans Viewed Native Americans.

History's Impact Video Program

People of varying cultures and traditions have intermingled here for centuries, shaping and modifying the nation's history.

Review and Assessment Resources

Review and Reinforce

- 📝 CRF: Chapter Review Activity
- 🖥 Quick Facts Transparency: The World Before 1600
- 🔊 Spanish Chapter Summaries Audio CD Program
- 💻 Online Chapter Summaries in Spanish
- OSP Holt PuzzlePro; Quiz Show for ExamView
- 💿 Quiz Game CD-ROM

Assess

- 📝 PASS: Chapter Test, Forms A and B
- 📝 Alternative Assessment Handbook
- OSP ExamView Test Generator, Chapter Test
- 💿 Differentiated Instruction Modified Worksheets and Tests CD-ROM: Chapter Test
- HOAP Holt Online Assessment Program (in the Premier Online Edition)

Reteach/Intervene

- 📝 Interactive Reader and Study Guide
- 📝 Differentiated Instruction Teacher Management System: Lesson Plans for Differentiated Instruction
- 💿 Differentiated Instruction Modified Worksheets and Tests CD-ROM: Chapter Test
- 💿 Interactive Skills Tutor CD-ROM

go.hrw.com
Online Resources
KEYWORD: SD7 CH1

European Colonies in America

Chapter Overview	Reproducible Resources	Technology Resources
CHAPTER 2 pp. 38–69 **Overview: In this chapter, students will analyze the different reasons European nations explored and settled in the Americas, as well as the effects this had on Native Americans.**	**Differentiated Instruction Teacher Management System:*** • Instructional Benchmarking Guides • Lesson Plans for Differentiated Instruction **Interactive Reader and Study Guide:** Chapter Summary* **Chapter Resource File:*** • Writing for the SAT: Working in America • Social Studies Skills Activity: Evaluating Sources • Chapter Review Activity **American History Outline Maps** **Pre-AP Activities Guide for American History***	Live Ink® Online Reading Help Student Edition on Audio CD Program Differentiated Instruction Modified Worksheets and Tests CD-ROM Interactive Skills Tutor CD-ROM United States History Primary Source Library CD-ROM Power Presentations with Video CD-ROM History's Impact: American History Video Program (VHS/DVD): European Colonies in America Online Chapter Summaries in Spanish Graphic Organizer Transparencies
Section 1: **European Settlements in North America** **The Main Idea:** In the 1500s and 1600s, European nations continued to claim territory and build settlements in America.	**Differentiated Instruction Teacher Management System:** Section 1 Lesson Plan* **Interactive Reader and Study Guide:** Section 1 Summary* **Chapter Resource File:*** • Vocabulary Builder Activity, Section 1	**Daily Bellringer Transparency:** Section 1* **Interactive Map:** European Exploration of Americas 1492–1682* **Daily Test Practice Transparency:** Section 1* **Map Transparency:** European Exploration of the Americas 1492–1682*
Section 2: **The English in Virginia** **The Main Idea:** After several failures, the English established a permanent settlement at Jamestown, Virginia.	**Differentiated Instruction Teacher Management System:** Section 2 Lesson Plan* **Interactive Reader and Study Guide:** Section 2 Summary* **Chapter Resource File:*** • Vocabulary Builder Activity, Section 2	**Daily Bellringer Transparency:** Section 2* **Daily Test Practice Transparency:** Section 2*
Section 3: **The Northern Colonies** **The Main Idea:** The Pilgrims founded colonies in Massachusetts, while dissent led to the founding of other New England colonies.	**Differentiated Instruction Teacher Management System:** Section 3 Lesson Plan* **Interactive Reader and Study Guide:** Section 3 Summary* **Chapter Resource File:*** • Vocabulary Builder Activity, Section 3	**Daily Bellringer Transparency:** Section 3* **Daily Test Practice Transparency:** Section 3*
Section 4: **The Middle and Southern Colonies** **The Main Idea:** Events in England during and after the English Civil War led to a new wave of colonization south of New England.	**Differentiated Instruction Teacher Management System:** Section 4 Lesson Plan* **Interactive Reader and Study Guide:** Section 4 Summary* **Chapter Resource File:*** • Vocabulary Builder Activity, Section 4	**Daily Bellringer Transparency:** Section 4* **Daily Test Practice Transparency:** Section 4* **Map Transparency:** Middle and Southern Colonies*

HOLT
History's Impact
American History Video Program (VHS/DVD)
European Colonies in America

Review, Assessment, Intervention

Quick Facts Transparencies: The English Colonies in America, European Colonies in America

Spanish Chapter Summaries Audio CD Program

Progress Assessment Support System (PASS): Chapter Test*

Differentiated Instruction Modified Worksheets and Tests CD-ROM: Modified Chapter Test

OSP **One-Stop Planner CD-ROM:** ExamView Test Generator (English/Spanish)

HOAP **Holt Online Assessment Program (HOAP),** in the Holt Premier Online Student Edition

PASS: Section 1 Quiz*

Online Quiz: Section 1

Alternative Assessment Handbook

PASS: Section 2 Quiz*

Online Quiz: Section 2

Alternative Assessment Handbook

PASS: Section 3 Quiz*

Online Quiz: Section 3

Alternative Assessment Handbook

PASS: Section 4 Quiz*

Online Quiz: Section 4

Alternative Assessment Handbook

 **RESOURCES**

The following resources were developed to help North Carolina educators teach the standards and objectives of North Carolina's eleventh grade standard course of study in United States history.

• United States history EOC Test Prep Workbook
• Teacher's Support System
• North Carolina One-Stop Planner

And be sure to direct your students to **go.hrw.com** for online access to the EOC Test Prep Workbook.

go.hrw.com
EOC Test Prep
KEYWORD: SE7 NC

Holt Online Learning

go.hrw.com
Teacher Resources
KEYWORD: SD7 TEACHER

go.hrw.com
Student Resources
KEYWORD: SD7 CH2

• Document-based Questions
• Interactive Multimedia Activities

• Current Events
• Chapter-based Internet Activities
• and more!

Holt Premier
Online Student Edition
Complete online support for interactivity, assessment, and reporting
• Interactive Maps and Notebook
• Standardized Test Prep
• Homework Practice and Research Activities Online

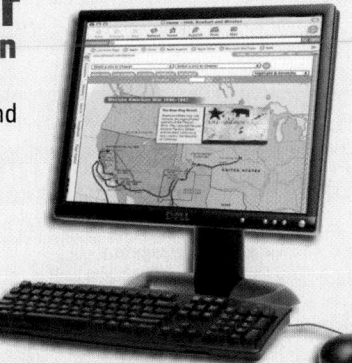

CHAPTER 2 PLANNING GUIDE

Before You Teach

The Big Picture
Jesús F. de la Teja

The First Transatlantic Empire For hundreds of years, Christian Spain had been cultivating a medieval martial spirit that in the late fifteenth century was wedded to the emerging commercial culture of the Renaissance. Cortés traveled to Mexico with a commercial purpose, although in his case military conquest was his business model. By the time the Spanish frontier reached Texas and California, Spaniards were committed to the idea of conquering people and incorporating them into the Spanish empire. Consequently, Spain's empire, unlike the later English one, did not rely so much on colonizing the land as it did conquering the people.

The English Struggle for Empire It is important to remember that in the seventeenth century absolute wealth was measured in precious metals. By that standard, Spain had found the golden goose and England and France were left to make the best of the undesirable portions of the Americas. At Roanoke and Jamestown, the first English colonists literally killed themselves in their efforts to reproduce the Spanish miracle of discovering precious metals. In time, Englishmen had to acquire gold and silver a new fashioned way—they had to grow it. Tobacco, and later rice and indigo, became the gold and silver of British North America.

An Exclusive City on a Hill By 1620 it was obvious that the principal resource of British North America was not precious metals, but the land itself. This situation suited the Pilgrims and Puritans well. Ostracized and persecuted for their ultra-reformist beliefs, those who came to America did so with the intention of showing the people back in England just what a true Christian English society could be like. Hence, early New England was not a land of religious tolerance but of exclusivity. Only when dissenters were asked to leave—leading to the formation of new colonies—was American religious pluralism really born.

Recent Scholarship

Columbus and Native Americans The Columbian quincentenary proved to be a controversial anniversary, marked by considerable soul-searching on the themes of cultural and religious chauvinism and imperialism. In *The Conquest of Paradise: Christopher Columbus and the Columbian Legacy* (1991), Kirkpatrick Sale not only challenges traditional perceptions of Columbus and the people he encountered, but goes on to note how English behavior in North America mirrored Spanish actions in the early days of colonization, to the tragic detriment of the native peoples.

Differentiating Instruction

 Differentiated Instruction Teacher Management System
- Lesson Plans for Differentiated Instruction
- Differentiated Instructional Benchmarking Guides
- Interactive Reader and Study Guide

 Spanish Chapter Summaries Audio CD Program

 Online Chapter Summaries in Spanish

 Student Edition on Audio CD Program

 Differentiated Instruction Modified Worksheets and Tests CD-ROM
- Vocabulary Flash Cards
- Modified Vocabulary Builder Activities
- Modified Chapter Review Activity
- Modified Chapter Test

OSP One-Stop Planner CD-ROM
- ExamView Test Generator (English and Spanish)
- PuzzlePro
- Quiz Show for ExamView
- Transparencies and Videos

TE Differentiated Activities in the Teacher's Edition
- The Puritans, p. 52
- Tituba of Salem Village, p. 57
- The English Civil War, p. 61

Reading Like a Historian
Sam Wineburg

Trusting Historical Accounts

In describing the settlement at Jamestown, our chapter recounts the famous story of Pocahontas and John Smith. It narrates the encounter between the young girl and the British captain this way: "As they were about to kill him, Smith said, Powhatan's young daughter Pocahontas begged her father to save him."

Two Little Words

Many students will be familiar with this story from movies and popular culture. Many will read the description and skip over two very important, but easily missed, words. Yet these two words tell us more about reading like a historian than any other two in the entire section. The words are, "Smith said."

How Do We Know?

The first question a historian asks is "How do we really know what happened in the past?" Like novelists, historians tell stories. But unlike novelists, historians claim their stories are true—and they can offer evidence to back them up. This evidence comes in many forms: physical remains, documents, letters, ship manifests, census data, archaeological findings, court testimony, probate ledgers, and countless other items that have escaped the eroding sands of time. One of the distinguishing features of the writing that historians do for each other—immediately obvious when flipping through the *Journal of American History* or the *American Historical Review*—is the division of the page into two, with the top half devoted to the story the historian wants to tell, and the bottom half, printed in a smaller type, listing the evidence (and where to find it) to support the historian's claim. It is as if the historian, anticipating a colleague's skepticism, is saying: "Don't trust me? Go to the same archive I visited, look at Box No. 2432, and you will find the basis for this statement."

Which brings us back to those two little words. How do we know that Powhatan planned to kill John Smith and that Pocahontas saved him? Because John Smith said so. But did he?

Changing Stories

In Smith's first account of his encounter with the chief, written in 1608, the same year in which the event supposedly occurred, he makes no mention of the threat to his life or of his rescue by a young woman. In this early account, Smith uses words like "friendship" and "kindness" to describe meeting Powhatan, writing, "He kindly welcomed me with such good words, and great Platters of sundry Victuals, assuring me his friendship, and my liberty within four days."

The second account, written 16 years later, uses words like "barbarous" and "fearful" and includes the claim that Pocahontas "laid her own [head] upon his to save him from death." By this time Pocahontas, who had married colonist John Rolfe, was already dead—and therefore unable to dispute Smith's story. But the plot gets thicker.

A Misunderstanding?

Let's assume that Smith was an honest man who would not fabricate stories. Even if some event had taken place in which Smith felt physically threatened, he may have grossly misunderstood its meaning. This "rescue," according to anthropologists who study Native American practices, posed no real threat to life or limb but was actually a tribal ritual meant to signify death and rebirth, symbolizing Smith's assumption of a new tribal identity under Powhatan's patronage.

So what really happened? In this instance, two words—"Smith said"—open up the intriguing puzzles of the documentary record. Who said history was over a long time ago? We are still arguing today about what happened—or didn't happen—some 400 years ago.

Chapter Preview

Standards Focus

Social Studies Competency Goals

Goal 1 The learner will identify, investigate, and assess the effectiveness of the institutions of the emerging republic.

1.02

The Big Idea and Essential Questions

To foster student understanding of this chapter's big idea, design your lesson to address each section's essential question.

Big Idea As European nations competed to establish American colonies, the English founded a group of colonies along the Atlantic Ocean seaboard.

Essential Questions

1. How did Spain establish colonies in the Americas?
2. How did the English establish their first permanent settlement in Virginia?
3. How were the New England colonies founded?
4. How were the other English colonies created?

Key to Differentiating Instruction

Below Level

Basic-level activities designed for all students encountering new material

At Level

Intermediate-level activities designed for average students

Above Level

Challenging activities designed for honors and gifted-and-talented students

Standard English Mastery

Activities designed to improve standard English usage

CHAPTER 2

1500–1733

European Colonies in America

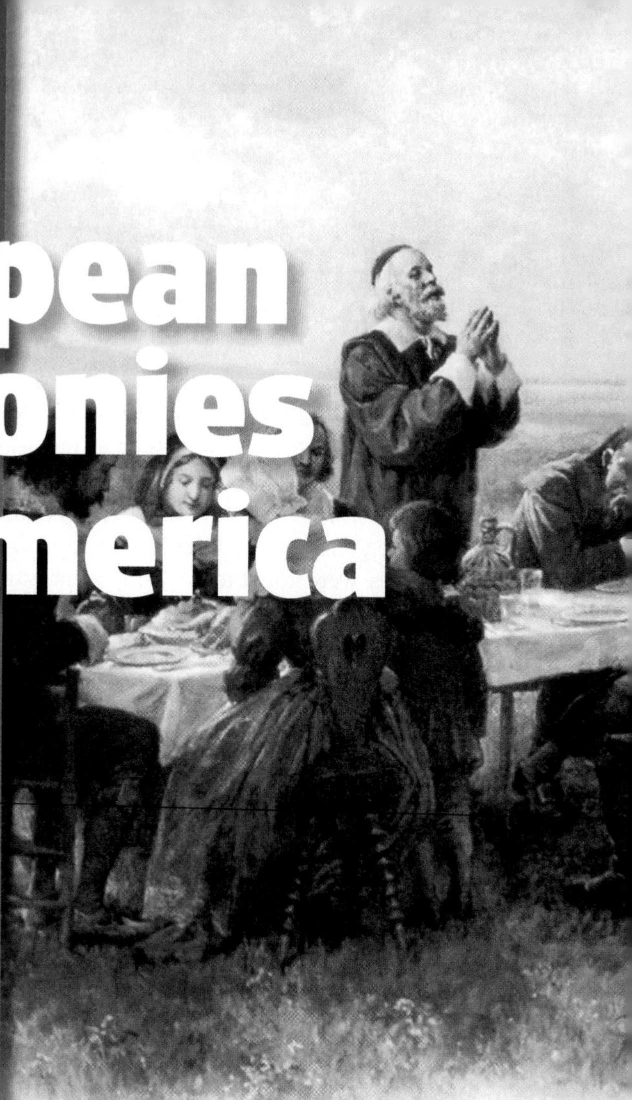

THE BIG PICTURE Following Columbus's voyages, European nations competed to establish colonies in the Americas. By 1733 the English had founded a diverse group of colonies along the Atlantic Ocean seaboard. Their efforts, however, had disastrous consequences for Native Americans.

North Carolina Standards

Social Studies Objectives

1.02 Analyze the political freedoms available to the following groups prior to 1820: women, wage earners, landless farmers, American Indians, African Americans, and other ethnic groups.

Language Arts Objectives

3.01 Use language persuasively in addressing a particular issue by:
- establishing and defending a point of view.

Skills Focus READING LIKE A HISTORIAN

Together, European colonists and Native Americans take part in a traditional harvest meal. Artist Jennie Brownscombe painted this symbolic interpretation of *The First Thanksgiving* in 1914.

Interpreting Visuals Describe the positive and negative relationship between Europeans and Native Americans shown in this painting.

See **Skills Handbook**, p. H30

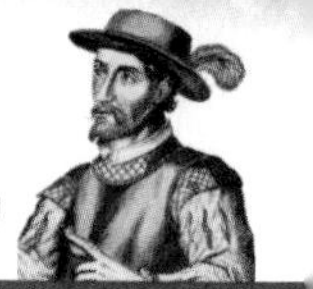

1513 Ponce de León begins exploring Florida.

1500

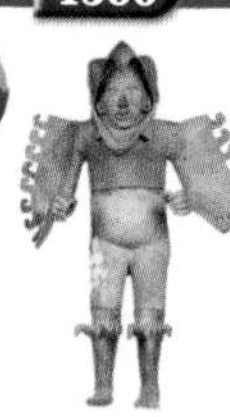

1521 Cortés conquers the Aztecs in Mexico.

1530–1536 Pizarro defeats the Incas in Peru.

38

Introduce the Chapter

At Level

Into the Unknown

1. Remind students that traveling to the New World was similar to traveling to a distant planet. Explorers and settlers had little idea what to expect, how different life might be, or what dangers lay ahead. Nor did they know if the plants and animals they knew in Europe would exist in the Americas.
2. Have students work in small groups to prepare a list of the advantages and disadvantages of traveling to a new land. Then have volunteers from each group share their lists with the class.
3. Guide students in a discussion of the ideas presented. Do the advantages of traveling to the Americas and trying to make a new life in the wilderness outweigh the disadvantages? Why or why not?
4. Tell students that in this chapter they will learn how the Americas were explored and how the first colonies were established.

Alternative Assessment Handbook, Rubric 11: Discussions

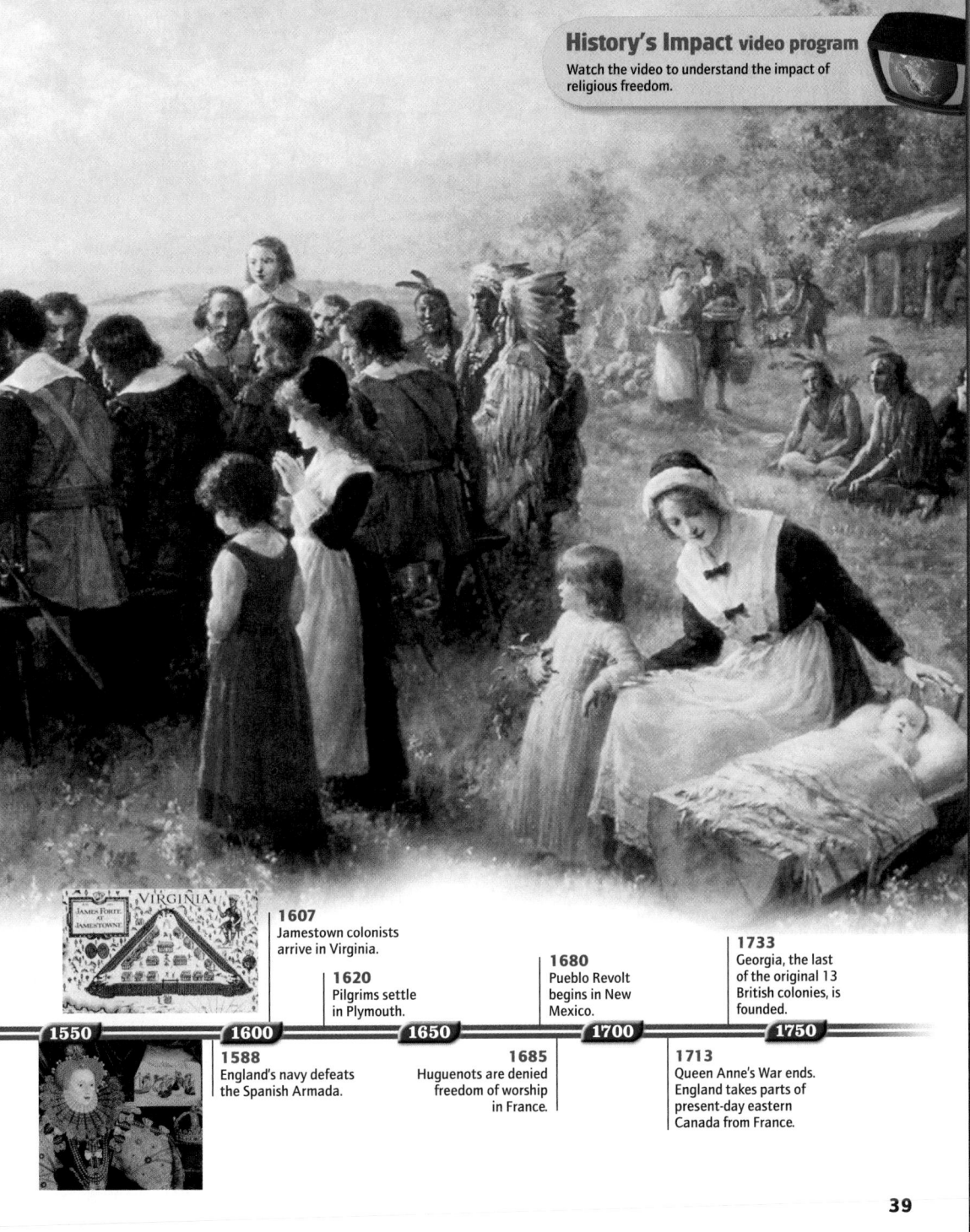

1607
Jamestown colonists arrive in Virginia.

1620
Pilgrims settle in Plymouth.

1680
Pueblo Revolt begins in New Mexico.

1733
Georgia, the last of the original 13 British colonies, is founded.

1550 | **1600** | **1650** | **1700** | **1750**

1588
England's navy defeats the Spanish Armada.

1685
Huguenots are denied freedom of worship in France.

1713
Queen Anne's War ends. England takes parts of present-day eastern Canada from France.

39

• Chapter Preview •

HOLT
History's Impact
▶ Video Program: European Colonies in America
See the Video Teacher's Guide for strategies for using the video segment.

Reading Like a Historian

Interpreting Visuals Have students take a moment to examine the image on these pages. It was painted in 1914, many years after the first Thanksgiving. Ask students what details about the painting may not accurately reflect the actual Thanksgiving meal. *possible answers—location, clothing styles, participants, tableware*

go.hrw.com
Online Resources

Chapter Resources:
KEYWORD: SD7 CH2

Teacher Resources:
KEYWORD: SD7 TEACHER

Explore the Time Line

1. When did Cortés conquer the Aztecs? *1521*
2. How many years elapsed from the founding of Jamestown until the founding of Plymouth Colony? *13 years*
3. Which was the last of the original 13 British colonies to be founded? *Georgia*
4. In what year did the English navy defeat the Spanish Armada? *1588*

Info to Know

Diseases in the Colonies Death rates were high for early colonists, especially for those in the Chesapeake region. During the 1600s, some 40 percent of colonists died within two years of their arrival from diseases such as typhoid and malaria.

Drawing Conclusions Do you think the colonists understood the great threat of disease when they decided to move to the Chesapeake region? *possible answers—Colonists may not have understood the dangers of these particular diseases, but they must have been aware of the many dangers that existed in the colonies.*

Answers

Reading Like a Historian (p. 38)
positive—some of the Native Americans are sharing the meal with colonists; negative—few Native Americans are present compared to number of colonists

Bellringer

The Inside Story. . . Use the **Daily Bellringer Transparency** to help students answer the question.

📖 Daily Bellringer Transparency, Section 1

European Colonies in America — Daily Bellringer
Chapter 2, Section 1

Test What You Know

The following questions will test your background knowledge about the first European settlements in North America. You will learn more about this topic in Chapter 2, Section 1.

1. The first explorers to arrive in the Americas in the 1500s were from what European country?
2. Who were the conquistadors?
3. What are missionaries?

Preview Section 1

The Inside Story

How did two European sea powers carve up the Americas?
After Christopher Columbus returned to Spain with news of the Americas, Queen Isabella wanted to quickly secure Spain's claims to the continent before Portugal did. She asked Pope Alexander VI for approval of Spain's claims. A Spaniard himself, Alexander agreed, and drew a line down the globe. He gave Spain claim to everything west of the line, and Portugal everything to its east. After protests from Portugal, the two nations agreed on the Treaty of Tordesillas, which gave Brazil to Portugal and all of North America to Spain.

1. What event prompted Queen Isabella's visit to the pope to request his help?
2. Why do you think Spain and Portugal wanted to claim the land in the Americas?

Review Answers: 1. Spain; 2. Spanish explorers, literally "conquerors"; 3. people who work to convert others to a particular religion.
Preview Answers: 1. the return of Christopher Columbus; 2. possible answers—They wanted to expand their empires. They hoped the new lands held gold and other riches.

Copyright © by Holt, Rinehart and Winston. All rights reserved.

Academic Vocabulary

Review with students the high-use academic term in this section.

infer to arrive at a conclusion by reasoning (p. 42)

📖 CRF: Vocabulary Builder Activity, Section 1

Taking Notes

Ponce de León explores Florida; Cortés conquers the Aztecs in Mexico; Cabeza de Vaca, De Soto, Coronado, and Cabrillo explore the Southwest for gold

---

go.hrw.com
Online Resources

KEYWORD: SD7 CH2
TOPIC: EXPLORING NORTH AMERICA

European Settlements in North America

BEFORE YOU READ

MAIN IDEA

In the 1500s and 1600s, European nations, led by Spain, continued to explore, claim territory, and build settlements in America.

READING FOCUS

1. Which Spanish conquistadors explored North America, and what were they seeking?
2. How did Spain build an empire?
3. What other nations explored North America?

KEY TERMS AND PEOPLE

Treaty of Tordesillas
conquistador
Juan Ponce de León
Hernán Cortés
Francisco Vásquez de Coronado
missionary
Popé
Sir Francis Drake

TAKING NOTES
As you read, take notes on the major explorations after those of Columbus. Record your notes in a graphic organizer like the one shown here.

Major Explorations

SPAIN or PORTUGAL?

◀ **At Tordesillas in 1494, Spain and Portugal divided the world for exploration.**

THE INSIDE STORY

How did two European sea powers carve up the Americas?
In 1493 Queen Isabella of Spain came to the pope with a problem. Columbus had just returned from his successful first voyage, and the queen wanted to move quickly to secure Spain's claim to the Americas. Spain's chief rivals, the skilled navigators of Portugal, were eager to seize land in the New World, as were other European powers. The queen wanted the Roman Catholic Church's stamp of approval on her claims before others rushed in.

Pope Alexander VI, a Spaniard himself, was happy to help. He drew an imaginary north-south line of demarcation from pole to pole in the Atlantic Ocean. Spain would control all the lands west of the line that did not have a Christian ruler. Portugal got the lands to the east.

At the time, of course, the ocean was a great mystery. Europeans did not know what lands might lie within it and across it. They did not know that Columbus had stumbled upon two giant continents. So the pope drew his line in the water, dividing the ocean's unknown lands between the two Catholic countries in the hope of keeping the peace.

King John II of Portugal protested. The line was so far east that it gave Portuguese navigators little room even to explore Africa. So in 1494, Spanish and Portuguese diplomats met at Tordesillas, Spain, and signed a treaty moving the line more than 800 miles west.

The **Treaty of Tordesillas** (tawr-day-SEE-yahs) gave Spain the best deal by far. The treaty did give Portugal a claim to Brazil, but Spain got the rest of the Americas. Not surprisingly, England, France, and Holland did not accept this division of the world. European explorers also found that other people—Native Americans—already held a claim to the Americas.

Teach the Main Idea

At Level | **Standard English Mastery**

European Settlements in America

1. **Teach** Ask students the Reading Focus questions to teach this section.

2. **Apply** Have students work in pairs to create a time line for this section. Have students find all the events that have dates and place them on their time lines in chronological order.

3. **Review** Review student time lines as a class. Have students name the events and dates in order. Create a class time line for all to see. *possible answers—(1494) Treaty of*

Tordesillas; (1513) Ponce de León claims Florida; (1519) Cortés lands in Mexico; (1588) Spanish Armada defeated; (1609) Hudson explores North America; (1680) Pueblo Revolt begins

4. **Practice/Homework** Have students write a brief summary about the search for the Seven Golden Cities. **LS Visual-Spatial, Verbal-Linguistic**

📖 Alternative Assessment Handbook, Rubrics 36: Time Lines; and 37: Writing Assignments

Spanish Conquistadors

A wave of Spanish exploration in the Americas followed the Treaty of Tordesillas. Because Columbus had landed in the Caribbean, the Caribbean islands became Spain's base for exploration in the early 1500s.

The Spanish explorers of the 1500s were called **conquistadors** (kahn-KEES-tuh-dawrz), from the Spanish for "conquerors." They traveled to lands an ocean away for "God, gold, and glory"—in other words, to spread Christianity, find wealth, and win fame. Just as the Portuguese had led the way in finding the sea route to India, Spanish conquistadors pioneered the exploration of the "New World."

Ponce de León and Florida Juan Ponce de León (wahn pahn-suh-day-lee-OHN) was a Caribbean settler who had sailed with Columbus in 1493. He explored the island of Puerto Rico and became its governor. In 1513 Ponce de León left Puerto Rico, searching not only for gold but also for a "fountain of youth." According to legend, this miraculous fountain was on an island called Bimini.

On Easter Sunday 1513, Ponce de León landed on a lush, green coast. He claimed the area for Spain, naming it "La Florida"—from *Pascua Florida,* the Spanish term for the Easter celebration. It was the first time Spanish explorers had touched mainland North America.

Cortés and the Aztec The search for gold led the conquistadors to the great Native American empires you read about earlier. In 1519 **Hernán Cortés** (ayr-NAHN cawr-TEZ) and his soldiers landed on the Gulf Coast of Mexico. Their goal was to conquer the Aztec Empire.

Remembering ancient legends, the Aztecs thought that the invaders might be messengers from the gods. Cortés took advantage of this belief as well as the resentment of peoples the Aztecs had conquered. The Spaniards marched across Mexico, gathering allies. One of Cortés's most valuable helpers was Malinche, an Aztec woman who served as his interpreter.

Moctezuma, the Aztec ruler, sent gifts of gold to welcome the Spanish. Other Aztec nobles saw the danger and tried to resist. But in 1521, after a long, violent siege, the Aztec capital, Tenochtitlán, fell to the Spanish.

The Spanish in America

Conquistadors appeared large and frightening mounted on horseback. Horses, native to Europe, had never been seen before in the Americas.

War dogs were another terrifying Spanish weapon.

Conquistadors traveled to America in the 1500s. Bringing horses and guns from Spain, they conquered huge Native American empires.

THE GRANGER COLLECTION, NEW YORK

41

Spanish Conquistadors

Identify Which explorer told stories of the Seven Golden Cities?
Cabeza de Vaca

Identify Cause and Effect What was the result of the Spanish conquest of the Aztec Empire? *conquerors brought a new culture; some aspects of Aztec culture remained, but many ancient ways disappeared*

📋 CRF: Primary Source Activity: Bartolomé de las Casas Criticizes Spanish Cruelty

Info to Know

The Aztec Empire A new emperor, Moctezuma's brother Cuitláhuac, encouraged the Aztecs to rebel against the Spanish. Historians offer different theories to explain his rise to power. Some believe that royal officials replaced Moctezuma to punish him for what they saw as his "spineless" acceptance of Cortés. Others argue that Moctezuma either suggested or accepted the replacement as a way to covertly encourage revolt. Regardless, Cuitláhuac incited the Aztecs to violence against the Spanish.

The fall of the Aztec Empire devastated Mexican peoples and their culture. Many Aztecs died, and their cities were destroyed. The conquest also brought other changes, including a new language, Spanish, and a new religion, Christianity. Some aspects of the native Mexican cultures remained, but many ancient ways disappeared forever.

Tales of golden cities Cortés's success in conquering the Aztecs inspired other quests for gold in North America. In 1527 a Spanish expedition of about 400 men landed near present-day Tampa, on the west coast of Florida. A series of misfortunes eventually reduced the expedition to just four known survivors. They included the treasurer of the expedition, Álvar Núñez Cabeza de Vaca. From the present-day Texas coast near Galveston, they traversed the continent, probably reaching present-day New Mexico and Arizona. They arrived at the Pacific coast of Mexico in 1536.

Cabeza de Vaca and his men told their stories to Spaniards when they reached Mexico. Some historians <u>infer</u> that their tales gave rise to the legend of the Seven Golden Cities of Cíbola, cities rich in gold. Later explorers in the Southwest looked for these cities in vain.

ACADEMIC VOCABULARY
infer to arrive at a conclusion by reasoning

Other Spanish explorers Several later expeditions went in search of the Seven Golden Cities. Hernando de Soto landed in Florida in 1539 and traveled through the Southeast as far north as the present-day Carolinas and Tennessee. De Soto then headed west and became the first European to see the Mississippi River. Crossing the river, he reached present-day Arkansas. In 1542 he died of a fever, and his men buried him in the Mississippi River.

Other expeditions probed the American Southwest. In search of the Seven Cities, **Francisco Vásquez de Coronado** set out in 1540. He conquered some Pueblo peoples but found no gold. His group then split up. One of Coronado's men became the first European to see the Grand Canyon. Others explored present-day Arizona, New Mexico, Texas, Oklahoma, and Kansas.

Expeditions also set out by sea from Mexico. From 1542 to 1543, Juan Rodríguez Cabrillo (cuh-BREE-oh) sailed north, exploring the coast of California. He sailed into what are now San Diego and Monterey bays, visited the Channel Islands, and spent the winter there.

The Spanish quests for gold came up empty. After finding no gold in the American Southwest, Spain then turned to mining in Mexico.

The nation's oldest city Although Ponce de León had landed in Florida in 1513, he had not established permanent settlements there. Years later, in 1565, the conquistador Pedro Menendez de Avilés founded St. Augustine in Florida. St. Augustine was strategically placed to defend the treasure that Spanish fleets were bringing to Spain. Today it is the oldest city in the United States.

READING CHECK **Identifying the Main Idea** What were the main goals of Spanish explorers?

Spain Builds an Empire

While the conquistadors were exploring North America, the government of Spain was beginning to establish colonial governments. To govern the vast areas of land they claimed, Spain set up viceroyalties. A viceroyalty was a province ruled by a representative of the monarch. The viceroyalty of New Spain included much of the American Southwest and present-day Mexico, along with Florida, Central America, part of Venezuela, and some Caribbean islands.

Social structure The Spanish conquest of the Americas caused a new social structure to emerge. Those who came from Spain, known as *peninsulares,* considered themselves superior to the *creoles.* Creoles were people born in the Americas of pure Spanish descent. Many Spanish settlers married local Native American women, and their mixed families were known as mestizos. Lower on the social scale were people of mixed Spanish and African descent, pure-blooded Indians, and Africans.

A key element of the Spanish American social structure were the **missionaries**, church members who teach and convert others to a religion. Spain sent Roman Catholic missionaries to establish missions—large plantations centered around a church—along the California coast and throughout the Southwest. There priests taught Christianity to Native Americans along with European farming, herding, and crafts. Many Native Americans came to the missions—or were forced to come—to live and work for the priests.

Skills Focus: Making Inferences | At Level

Reading Skill
The Conquistadors

1. Guide students in a discussion of the Spanish conquistadors who explored North America during the sixteenth century.

2. Have each student choose one of the Spanish conquistadors mentioned in this section, and then write five journal entries that the conquistador might have created while in the New World. Journal entries should describe the conquistador's explorations and observations about the New World.

3. Have volunteers read one journal entry for each of the conquistadors. Ask students if there was one conquistador whose adventures appealed to them more than the others. Have students explain their reasoning. 🖪 **Verbal-Linguistic**

📋 Alternative Assessment Handbook, Rubric 15: Journals

Answers

Reading Check *spread Christianity, find wealth, win fame for their adventures*

EUROPEAN EXPLORATION OF AMERICAS, 1492–1682

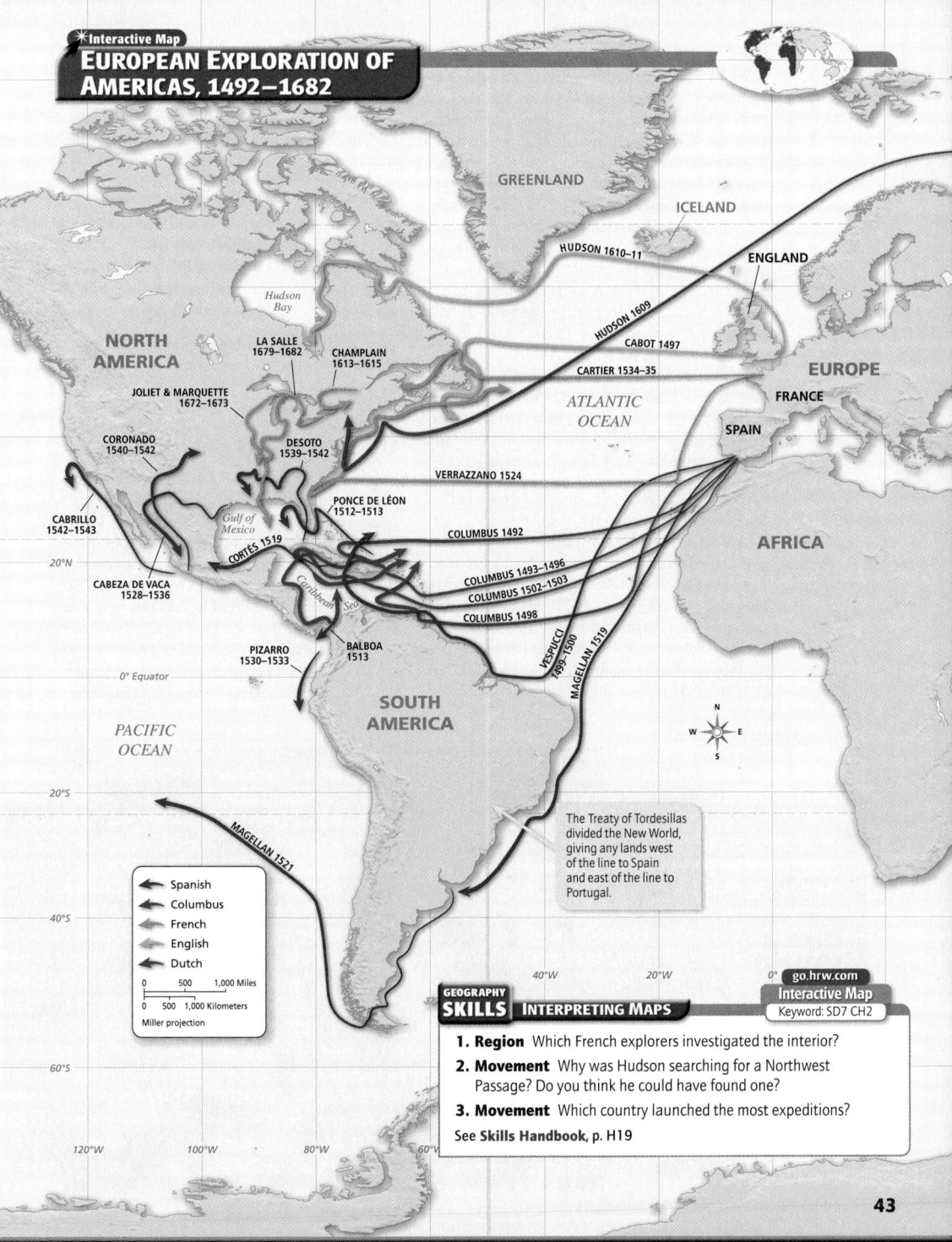

GREENLAND

ICELAND

HUDSON 1610–11

ENGLAND

Hudson Bay

HUDSON 1609

CABOT 1497

CARTIER 1534–35

EUROPE

NORTH AMERICA

LA SALLE 1679–1682

CHAMPLAIN 1613–1615

FRANCE

ATLANTIC OCEAN

JOLIET & MARQUETTE 1672–1673

SPAIN

CORONADO 1540–1542

DESOTO 1539–1542

VERRAZZANO 1524

CABRILLO 1542–1543

Gulf of Mexico

PONCE DE LÉON 1512–1513

CORTES 1519

COLUMBUS 1492

AFRICA

20°N

CABEZA DE VACA 1528–1536

Caribbean Sea

COLUMBUS 1493–1496

COLUMBUS 1502–1503

COLUMBUS 1498

PIZARRO 1530–1533

BALBOA 1513

VESPUCCI 1499–1500

MAGELLAN 1519

0° Equator

SOUTH AMERICA

PACIFIC OCEAN

N W E S

20°S

MAGELLAN 1521

The Treaty of Tordesillas divided the New World, giving any lands west of the line to Spain and east of the line to Portugal.

40°S

Spanish
Columbus
French
English
Dutch

0   500   1,000 Miles
0   500 1,000 Kilometers
Miller projection

60°S

120°W   100°W   80°W   60°

40°W   20°W   0°

GEOGRAPHY SKILLS INTERPRETING MAPS

go.hrw.com
Interactive Map
Keyword: SD7 CH2

1. **Region** Which French explorers investigated the interior?

2. **Movement** Why was Hudson searching for a Northwest Passage? Do you think he could have found one?

3. **Movement** Which country launched the most expeditions?

See **Skills Handbook, p. H19**

43

Reading Focus

❷ **How did Spain build an empire?** *Spain claimed large areas of land and established colonial governments. There were four viceroyalties, each ruled by a representative of the monarch.*

Spain Builds an Empire

Define What was a mission? *a large plantation centered on a church*

Recall Besides Christianity, what did mission priests teach Native Americans? *European farming, herding, crafts*

Rank What was the hierarchy of the social classes in Spain's colonies? *At the top were the peninsulares, who came from Spain. Below them were the creoles, people of Spanish descent born in the Americas. Next came the mestizos, people of mixed Spanish and Native American heritage. At the bottom were people of mixed Spanish and African descent, pureblooded Indians, and Africans.*

📦 Map Transparency: European Exploration of the Americas 1492–1682

📜 American History Outline Maps: Territorial Claims in North America, 1754–1763

European Exploration of Americas 1492 to 1682

Analyze Review the reasons for Spanish exploration, God, gold, and glory, with students. Have students develop a list of consequences for each of the reasons.

✳ **Interactive Map:** European Exploration of the Americas 1492–1682

Answers

Interpreting Maps 1. *Champlain, La Salle, Joliet, and Marquette;* **2.** *so that it would not be necessary to sail around the tip of South America to get to the west coast of North America via the ocean; no, one does not exist;* **3.** *Spain*

Skills Focus: Interpreting Movement Maps

At Level

Social Studies Skill
Europeans in North America

Materials outline maps of North America

1. Distribute outline maps of North America to students. Write the names of the European explorers mentioned in the text for students to see. Have students use the map on this page and information from their text to locate the places where Europeans explored or settled.

2. Guide students in a review of their maps and the explorers. Ask students to identify any

patterns they noted about places explored or settled by the Spanish and places explored or settled by explorers from other countries.

3. Place student maps on display for the class to see. **LS Visual-Spatial**

📜 Alternative Assessment Handbook, Rubric 20: Map Creation

Spain Builds an Empire

Explain How did the *encomienda* system work? *landowner controlled people of certain area, were supposed to convert Native Americans to Christianity, teach them European ways; Native Americans were to work for the landowner part of the time and to be treated humanely. In reality, Native Americans were often treated as slaves.*

Make Judgments Do you think the Pueblo Revolt was successful? Explain your answer. *possible answers—yes, because the Pueblo culture remained strong; no, the Spanish retook the area*

❸ What other nations explored North America? *England, France, Holland*

Other Nations Explore

Identify What riches did the French find in New France? *fish and furs*

Recall Who claimed Louisiana for France? *the Sieur de la Salle*

Identifying Cause and Effect How did the defeat of the Armada enable England to start building its own colonies in North America? *defeat of Spanish navy left seas and North American territory undefended and open to the English*

Answers

Art *possible answers—reign: strength of English navy symbolized by ships and hand resting on the globe; character: dominance and extravagance expressed by globe and clothing*

Reading Check *disease and ill treatment decimated the population*

Land and labor At first, Spanish colonists tried to use Native Americans as laborers. Under Spain's *encomienda* system, landowners received grants from the king, which gave them the right to control the people of a certain area. The word *encomienda* comes from the Spanish word for "entrust." Under the encomienda system, the king expected the landowners to convert the Native Americans to Christianity and teach them European ways. The Native Americans, for their part, were to work as laborers.

Officially, Native Americans were to be treated humanely. In reality, many were enslaved and worked to death on huge estates called *haciendas*. As Native American populations declined from disease and ill treatment, landowners came to depend upon the labor of enslaved Africans. Indians and Africans also were forced to work in the silver mines that came to dominate New Spain's economy.

The Pueblo Revolt In 1598 the king of Spain sent Juan de Oñate (wahn day oh-NYAH-tay) to settle New Mexico, which Coronado had abandoned a half-century before. Oñate founded the first Spanish settlements in New Mexico. Missionary work was a major part of these settlements. The Spanish missionaries wanted to replace the native religions with Christianity.

In 1680 the Pueblo Indians revolted against the Spanish missionary system. A shaman named **Popé** (poh-PAY) led the revolt, encouraging other Pueblos to rebel and take back their traditional ways of life. Many villagers joined the Pueblos.

The Pueblo Revolt began in August 1680 with an attack on Santa Fe, the Spanish capital, in what is now New Mexico. After a 10-day siege, the Spanish settlers fled the city. Popé then tried to restore traditional ways and wipe out every trace of Spanish culture.

Pueblo control of Santa Fe did not last. In 1692 Spanish soldiers retook the area. Pueblo culture, however, remained strong.

READING CHECK **Identifying Cause and Effect** What effects did Spanish conquest and colonization have on Native Americans?

Other Nations Explore

Spain soon faced competition from other European explorers in North America. England's King Henry VII sent out his country's first voyage of exploration in 1497. The captain was John Cabot, an Italian navigator. Cabot crossed the Atlantic and landed in Newfoundland. Like Columbus, Cabot thought he had reached Asia. He claimed the land for England.

By the early 1500s England had come to realize that North America was a separate continent. In 1508 Cabot's son Sebastian launched a

A Powerful Queen

Under the rule of "Good Queen Bess"—Elizabeth I—England developed a strong navy. Elizabeth I gave her sea captains unofficial permission to raid rival ships and ports. *What does this painting of the queen attempt to convey about her reign and her character? Refer to details in the painting.*

Skills Focus: Making Oral Presentations   Above Level

Reading Like a Historian Skill
Institutions of Colonization in New Spain

1. Review information in the text about missions and the *encomienda* system. Then have students develop a written historical evaluation of the intended role of missions and the *encomienda* system in extending Spanish rule in North America. In their evaluations, students should discuss the effectiveness of each of these institutions.

2. Have students use their evaluations to prepare for and conduct a debate on the relative

merits and drawbacks of the mission and the *encomienda* systems. Students should consider these questions: How well did each institution follow the rules that were established for it? If Spain had insisted on stricter enforcement of the rules, would the outcome for Native Americans have been different? **LS Verbal-Linguistic, Kinesthetic**

Alternative Assessment Handbook, Rubrics 10: Debates; and 41: Writing to Express

voyage looking for a Northwest Passage, a short-cut water route to the Pacific Ocean. A route through North America remained the goal of many later explorers because it would create a shorter sea route to Asia.

England's navy England did not act on Cabot's North American claim until the reign of Queen Elizabeth I (1558–1603). Elizabeth built England into a sea power. Her daring ship captains attacked Spanish ships to steal their gold and silver.

The most famous of these naval captains was **Sir Francis Drake.** In 1577 he circumnavigated the globe, plundering Spanish ships and towns on the Pacific coast of South America along the way.

During this time, religious conflicts between Catholic Spain and Protestant England erupted in war. In 1588 the Spanish king sent a fleet of ships, the Spanish Armada, to invade England. Bad weather and England's superior navy defeated the supposedly invincible Armada. The defeat of the Spanish Armada opened the Atlantic Ocean and North America to English colonizing expeditions.

New France France also joined the colonial rivalry in North America. In 1524 the French king sent Giovanni da Verrazano to explore the Atlantic coast. He explored from the present-day Carolinas as far north as Maine.

Ten years later, an explorer named Jacques Cartier (CAHR-tyay) discovered the St. Lawrence River and claimed the land that is now Quebec. On his second voyage, Cartier sailed up the river to an island he named Montréal.

Like so many explorers before them, the French hoped to find gold. Instead, they found that New France was rich in other resources: fish and furs. In 1608 Samuel de Champlain (sham-PLAYN) founded a fur trading post at Quebec, France's first permanent settlement in the New World.

In 1666 a French noble, the Sieur de la Salle, emigrated to become a fur trader. He explored the Great Lakes region and followed the Mississippi Valley to its mouth. He claimed the territory for France, naming it Louisiana after France's king, Louis XIV.

New Netherland The Netherlands, though a small country, had a large fleet of merchant ships that traded in Africa and Asia. After it declared independence from Spain, the Netherlands sought to explore North America.

In 1609 the Dutch sent English explorer Henry Hudson to look for a Northwest Passage. What he actually found is now called the Hudson River.

After Hudson's voyage, the Dutch claimed territory along the Atlantic coast. The colony of New Netherland drew settlers from all over northern Europe.

READING CHECK **Identifying the Main Idea** How did other nations challenge Spain's claim to North America?

SECTION 1 ASSESSMENT

go.hrw.com
Online Quiz
Keyword: SD7 HP2

Reviewing Ideas, Terms, and People

1. **a. Identify** What was the **Treaty of Tordesillas**?
   b. Contrast In what ways did the expeditions of **Ponce de León** and **Cortés** differ?
   c. Predict How might the **conquistadors'** exploration and conquest of the Americas affect the future of the region?

2. **a. Recall** What was the Pueblo Revolt?
   b. Making Inferences What differing reactions do you think Native Americans had to the encomienda system and to the Spanish **missionaries**?

3. **a. Recall** What other European nations explored North America after Spain began its explorations?
   b. Analyze What issue made England and Spain become enemies, and what happened as a result?

Critical Thinking

4. **Sequencing** Copy the chart below and make a time line of major explorations after Columbus.

   _____ _____ _____ _____ Hudson claims
   Dutch lands on
   Atlantic coast.

FOCUS ON SPEAKING

5. **Expository** Assume the role of a sea captain who must appear before a European monarch to ask the king or queen to sponsor an expedition to the Americas. Write out the petition you would make at court. Include an explanation of how the monarch will benefit from your voyage.

Section 1 Assessment Answers

1. **a.** divided Americas between Spain and Portugal; Spain got most of the land
   b. Ponce de León explored Puerto Rico and Florida, governed Puerto Rico; Cortés conquered Aztec Empire
   c. establishment of Spanish government and haciendas and mines; loss of Native American culture, religion, and identity

2. **a.** rebellion against Spanish missionary system
   b. possible answer—negative reactions, fear of a new way of life

3. **a.** French, English, Dutch
   b. the plunder of Spanish ships by the English navy; defeat of the Spanish Armada

4. possible answers—1509: Cabot searches for the Northwest Passage; 1513: Ponce de León claims Florida; 1521: Cortés conquers the Aztecs; 1534: Cartier claims what is now Quebec

5. possible answer—will spread Christianity, bring back great wealth, and gain fame and honor for the country

---

Direct Teach

Info to Know

The Elizabethan Navy Under the direction of John Hawkins, who became navy treasurer in 1577, the English began to replace their older galleons with faster, lighter, and more heavily armed ships. These new ships helped England triumph over the Spanish Armada, leading some to call Hawkins the "chief architect of the Elizabethan navy."

Review & Assess

Close

Have students summarize the early exploration and settlement of North America by the Spanish and other Europeans.

Review

Online Quiz, Section 1

Daily Test Practice Transparency

Assess

SE Section 1 Assessment

Progress Assessment: Section 1 Quiz

Alternative Assessment Handbook

Reteach

Interactive Reader and Study Guide, Section 1

Interactive Skills Tutor CD-ROM

Answers

Reading Check *England defeated the Spanish Armada, which allowed the English to build colonies in North America. France and Holland sent expeditions to explore North America and claim territory.*

Bellringer

The Inside Story. . . Use the **Daily Bellringer Transparency** to help students answer the question.

🖎 Daily Bellringer Transparency, Section 2

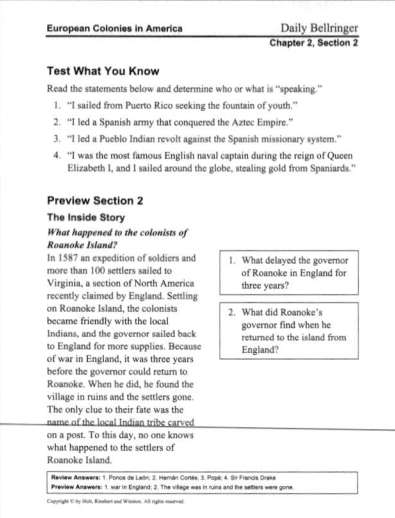

European Colonies in America   Daily Bellringer
                                              Chapter 2, Section 2

Test What You Know

Read the statements below and determine who or what is "speaking."

1. "I sailed from Puerto Rico seeking the fountain of youth."
2. "I led a Spanish army that conquered the Aztec Empire."
3. "I led a Pueblo Indian revolt against the Spanish missionary system."
4. "I was the most famous English naval captain during the reign of Queen Elizabeth I, and I sailed around the globe, stealing gold from Spaniards."

Preview Section 2
The Inside Story
What happened to the colonists of Roanoke Island?
In 1587 an expedition of soldiers and more than 100 settlers sailed to Virginia, a section of North America recently claimed by England. Settling on Roanoke Island, the colonists became friendly with the local Indians, and the governor sailed back to England for more supplies. Because of war in England, it was three years before the governor could return to Roanoke. When he did, he found the village in ruins and the settlers gone. The only clue to their fate was the name of the local Indian tribe carved on a post. To this day, no one knows what happened to the settlers of Roanoke Island.

| 1. What delayed the governor of Roanoke in England for three years? |
| 2. What did Roanoke's governor find when he returned to the island from England? |

Review Answers: 1. Ponce de León; 2. Hernán Cortés; 3. Popé; 4. Sir Francis Drake
Preview Answers: 1. war in England; 2. The village was in ruins and the settlers were gone.

Copyright © by Holt, Rinehart and Winston. All rights reserved.

Taking Notes

Settlers wanted to expand westward into land reserved for Indians; Berkeley wanted good relations with Native Americans on the frontier to protect his fur trade; Bacon hated the Indians; after Bacon's overseer was killed, he formed an army and waged war

go.hrw.com
Online Resources

KEYWORD: SD7 CH2
TOPIC: COLONIAL POPULATION GROWTH

BEFORE YOU READ

MAIN IDEA

After several failures, the English established a permanent settlement at Jamestown, Virginia.

READING FOCUS

1. Why were the first English colonies established?
2. What helped the Jamestown colony survive?
3. How did Virginia grow and change during the 1600s?

KEY TERMS AND PEOPLE

joint-stock company
John Smith
Powhatan
Pocahontas
John Rolfe
headright
House of Burgesses
indentured servant
Bacon's Rebellion

TAKING NOTES As you read, take notes on the causes of Bacon's Rebellion. Record your notes in a graphic organizer like the one below.

Cause → Bacon's Rebellion

The Lost Colony of Roanoke

THE INSIDE STORY

What happened to the colonists of Roanoke Island? Sir Walter Raleigh was an adventurer, a poet, and a favorite of Queen Elizabeth at court. With her permission, he sent several expeditions to the Atlantic coast of North America. He named the entire region Virginia—after Elizabeth, known as the "virgin queen."

Early attempts at settlement failed, but in 1587 Raleigh sent out a new expedition of soldiers and more than 100 settlers, mostly families. The group's governor, John White, wanted to create a self-sufficient colony. They settled on Roanoke Island, a three-mile-wide strip of land off present-day North Carolina, and became friendly with Manteo, leader of the local Croatoan Indians. Soon after the colonists landed on Roanoke, White's granddaughter Virginia Dare was born. She was the first English child born in North America.

The English settlers had landed too late in the season to plant crops, so White headed back to England for supplies. What happened next is one of the great mysteries in American history.

England was at war with Spain, so White had to wait three long years before obtaining a ship to return to Roanoke. In August 1590 he and his men approached Roanoke Island. They saw a light in the darkness and rowed toward it, blowing a trumpet and singing English songs to let the settlers know they were friends. There was no answer.

In the morning they landed and found the village in ruins, overgrown with trees and shrubs. The only clue White found was the word *Croatoan* carved on a post. The settlers

▲ John White puzzles over the only clue to the fate of his lost colony.

had buried chests full of pictures, books, maps, and other goods. These chests now lay strewn about, destroyed.

White hoped to find the settlers, including his family, on nearby Croatoan Island, but bad weather forced him away. No trace of the lost colony was ever found.

People have tried to solve the mystery of Roanoke Island ever since. Perhaps the settlers sought refuge with local Indians, or were killed by Indians. Maybe they were wiped out by a violent storm or severe drought. But so far, no one knows the true fate of the lost colony of Roanoke. ◼

46 CHAPTER 2

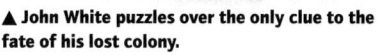

Teach the Main Idea   At Level

The English in Virginia

1. **Teach** Ask students the Reading Focus questions to teach this section.

2. **Apply** Have students create an outline of the section using the heads as main points. Have students identify at least two main ideas under each of the blue subheadings.

3. **Review** Review student outlines as a class. Then guide students in a discussion of the fluctuations in relations between the English settlers and the Powhatan people.

4. **Practice/Homework** Have students think about what may have happened to the colonists who were left on Roanoke Island. Then have each student write a short story telling what he or she thinks happened to the "lost colony" and Virginia Dare.

LS Verbal-Linguistic, Logical-Mathematical

📝 Alternative Assessment Handbook, Rubric 39: Writing to Create

The First English Colonies

Despite the tragedy on Roanoke, England continued to seek a permanent foothold in America. English settlers wanted to come to the New World for many reasons. With economic problems at home, they yearned for new opportunities. Many English farm workers were unemployed, and small farmers were struggling. In the wealthy class, large plots of land had been divided among heirs for generation after generation, until land became scarce. Some young men who did not inherit land sought new adventures in America.

King James's charter Sir Walter Raleigh never returned to North America after Roanoke was destroyed, although he still had faith that England could colonize North America. His charter rights were transferred to the London Company, a group of English merchants. Another group, the Plymouth Company, was interested in charter rights farther north.

In 1606 King James I issued a charter that divided America between the two groups. The Plymouth Company and the London Company were **joint-stock companies**, business entities in which investors pooled their money hoping to make a profit. The companies were responsible for governing and maintaining their colonies. In return, the investors got most of the colony's profit.

READING CHECK **Making Inferences** What did English settlers hope to gain by going to America?

The Jamestown Colony

Establishing a colony and outfitting an expedition was an expensive and risky venture. Several people, including Raleigh, tried and failed. Most could not afford to try again. The colonists at Jamestown, the first English colony to survive, went through many difficult years.

The first settlers Late in 1606 the London Company sent three ships and just over 100 male colonists to Virginia. After a lengthy ocean voyage, in 1607 they landed some 60 miles up the broad James River and built the Jamestown colony. The settlers named both the colony and the river after King James. One of the leaders was Captain **John Smith**, a young explorer.

Soon it became clear that Jamestown's location was a problem. It was a low, swampy area filled with malaria-carrying mosquitoes. Moreover, Jamestown was inside the territory of the powerful Powhatan Confederacy, a group of Algonquian (al-GAWN-kwee-en) peoples named for their leader, **Powhatan**.

Jamestown faced other difficulties, too. Some settlers died of malaria or dysentery from drinking unsafe water. Others became too weak to work. In addition, some of the settlers spent more time looking for treasure than growing food. Many of the adventurers were English gentlemen who were not used to physical labor. By January 1608, when more English colonists arrived, only 38 of the original settlers were alive.

Captain John Smith John Smith had become an important member of the colony. He helped trade for food with Indians, built houses, and explored the area. During one of his explorations, he later wrote, he had been captured by some Powhatans. As they were about to kill him, Smith said, Powhatan's young daughter **Pocahontas** begged her father to save him. Later, Pocahontas helped keep peace between the settlers and the Powhatans.

Smith became leader of Jamestown in 1608 and tried to impose military discipline on the colony. He laid down the law:

HISTORY'S VOICES

❝You must obey this now for a Law, that he that will not worke shall not eate (except by sickness he be disabled) for the labours of thirtie or fortie honest and industrious men shall not be consumed to maintaine an hundred and fiftie idle loyterers.❞

—John Smith, *Generall Historie of Virginia, New England, & the Summer Isles*

Smith also organized raids to steal food from the local Native Americans. The colonists got through the winter with only a few deaths, but Smith was burned in an accident with gunpowder and had to return to England.

The starving time The London Company, now called the Virginia Company, was determined to make Jamestown profitable. It sold stock to new settlers, offering free ship passage to those who would work for the company for seven years. More settlers set out in 1609—in time for one of Jamestown's worst periods.

Skills Focus: Comparing and Contrasting

At Level

Reading Skill
Methods of Colonization

1. Guide students in a discussion of the English method of colonization. Have students identify advantages and disadvantages of the English method.

2. Have students write a one-page essay explaining the differences between the English and Spanish methods of colonization in North America. In their essays have students consider how the different cultures of England and Spain might account for the differences. Students should also explain whether the differences might be due to geographic locations and natural resources of the areas each nation colonized. In their conclusions, have students tell which method they would have used, the Spanish or English model. **LS Verbal-Linguistic, Logical-Mathematical**

Alternative Assessment Handbook, Rubrics 11: Discussions; and 42: Writing to Inform

• **Direct Teach** •

Reading Focus

❶ Why were the first English colonies established? *economic problems at home; young upper-class men seeking adventure and wealth*

The First English Colonies

Identify Which two English companies had rights to establish colonies in North America? *London Company, Plymouth Company*

Recall How were the English colonies governed? *by joint-stock companies*

Evaluate Why do you think England was so determined to establish colonies in North America? *possible answers—expand its territory; provide opportunities for the unemployed and for landless upper-class men, succeed economically*

Reading Focus

❷ What helped the Jamestown colony survive? *obtaining food from Native Americans; growing tobacco for profit*

The Jamestown Colony

Recall What obstacles faced the colony at Jamestown? *poor location; malaria and dysentery; gentlemen not used to physical labor*

Explain How did John Smith become the leader of Jamestown? *provided food; built houses; explored area*

Analyzing Information Why did the Jamestown colonists steal food from local Native Americans? *They spent more time looking for gold than growing food.*

CRF: Primary Source Activity: John Smith and William Bradford Describe the Colonies

Answers

Reading Check *employment, land, wealth*

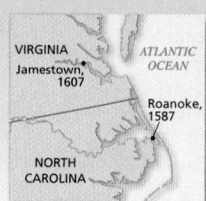

Direct Teach

The Jamestown Colony

Identify What was "the starving time"? *winter of 1609-1610; Powhatans killed the colonists' livestock, prevented colonists from hunting*

Summarize Describe relations between the early colonists at Jamestown and the Powhatan Confederacy. *generally bad; English stole food; Powhatans killed the colonists' livestock; after Pocahontas died, relations worsened again; last Powhatan attack came in 1644*

Activity **Jamestown** Have students use the Internet to conduct additional research and learn more about colonial settlement of Jamestown. Two reliable sites are http://www.jamestown1607.org and http://www.virtualjamestown.org

LS Logical-Mathematical

CRF: Biography: John Rolfe

Biography

William Strachey (1572–1621) After investing in the Virginia Company, William Strachey sailed for Virginia on the *Sea Venture* in 1609. Unfortunately, a hurricane caused the ship to run aground in Bermuda. The ship's company remained there for nine months until they were able to build two new ships. The company finally arrived in Jamestown in 1610 and Strachey was appointed secretary of the colony. An imaginative writer, Strachey recorded his experiences in the shipwreck and at the colony in a letter sent home to England. William Shakespeare's connections to both Strachey and the Virginia Company suggest that Shakespeare may have used Strachey's account in writing *The Tempest*.

Answers

Reading Check *poor land for farming; unsafe water; inside Native American territory*

A Foothold in the New World

English settlers founded Jamestown about 60 miles up the James River, out of view of Spanish ships. The fort shown in this 1607 drawing helped protect colonists from the Powhatan Indians.

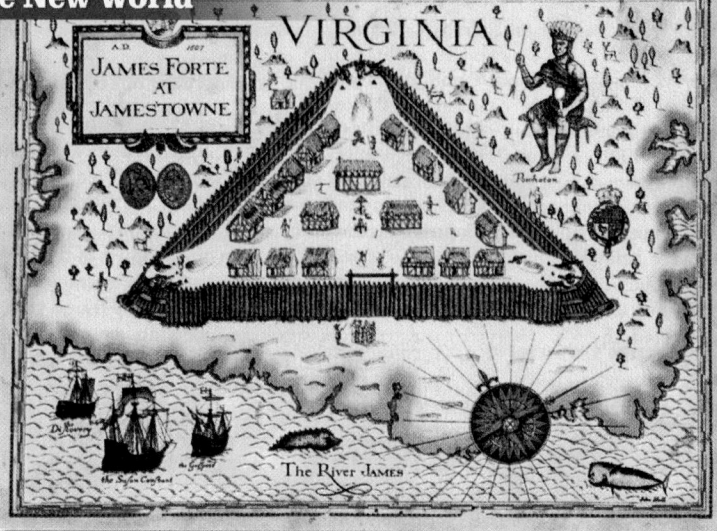

The settlers called the winter of 1609–1610 the "starving time." The Powhatan Indians, resentful of earlier raids, killed the colonists' livestock and prevented them from hunting. Many English colonists in Jamestown died that winter.

THE IMPACT TODAY

Economics

Facing declining tobacco use and increased foreign competition, modern farmers in tobacco-growing states such as Virginia, North Carolina, and Kentucky are reducing their dependence on tobacco by switching to alternative crops, from hot peppers to blueberries, with the help of federal grants.

Growing tobacco One crop finally made Jamestown and the Virginia colony profitable: tobacco. Tobacco was a native plant grown in North America and the islands of the West Indies. It was important in Native American ceremonies throughout the continent.

The first English settler to grow tobacco in Virginia was **John Rolfe**. Rolfe conducted experiments with tobacco to find out the best way to grow and cure the leafy plants, helping to make it profitable to ship the crop to England.

In 1613 while Pocahontas was being held captive by colonial officials, Rolfe proposed marriage. Pocahontas converted to Christianity, changed her name to Rebecca, and the two married. Their marriage finally secured peace between the settlers and the Powhatans.

The Virginia Company thought that the charming Pocahontas would be a good advertisement for Virginia. In 1616 she and Rolfe sailed to England, where she met the king and was welcomed in English society.

Conflicts with Native Americans By 1622, relations between the settlers and the Powhatan Confederacy had worsened. Both Pocahontas and Powhatan were dead. English farmers were taking over more and more land to grow tobacco, their profitable new crop.

In an effort to protect Indian lands, the Powhatans launched a surprise attack on Jamestown in the spring of 1622. Many settlers were killed, including John Rolfe. Continued conflict kept the colony from turning a profit, which led the king to end the Virginia Company's charter.

Still, the settlement struggled on. Attacks persisted for the next 20 years. The last Powhatan attack came in 1644. By then the Virginia settlers were strong enough to resist them.

READING CHECK **Drawing Conclusions** What was wrong with the location of Jamestown?

Virginia Grows and Changes

During its 15-year existence, the Virginia Company struggled to attract settlers and turn a profit. But persistent problems, including near-bankruptcy and perceived mismanagement, persuaded England finally to revoke the charter and make Virginia a royal colony.

Skills Focus: Interpreting Time Lines

Social Studies Skill
The English and the Native Americans

1. Guide students in a brief discussion of the ways in which the growth of Jamestown and the Virginia colony affected relations between Native Americans and English settlers. Ask: What events caused relations between the English and the Powhatans to improve? What events caused them to worsen?

2. Organize the class into pairs. Have each pair create an illustrated time line showing the fluctuations in the relations between the Powhatan Confederacy and the English settlers.

3. Have volunteers present their time lines to the class. Place all of the time lines on display for the class to see. **LS** **Interpersonal, Visual-Spatial**

Alternative Assessment Handbook, Rubric 36: Time Lines

The headright system Starting in 1618, the Virginia Company offered **headrights**, 50-acre grants of land that colonists could obtain in various ways. The head of a family received one headright for each family member and servant he had. People who paid the passage to America for another person—a new servant, for example—got an additional headright.

The Virginia Company brought in skilled artisans to help the colonial economy grow. Since most early settlers were men, the company also sent about 100 women who agreed to marry the colonists. That would make society more stable.

Soon Virginia began to thrive again. By the 1640s Virginia had a non-native population of about 8,000. Between 1640 and 1650 that number doubled.

The House of Burgesses Since the Middle Ages, English people had been proud of the political rights they had gained from Magna Carta. The first charter of Virginia promised settlers the same basic English rights. Now the Virginia Company acted on that promise.

In July 1619, representatives from the various communities in Virginia met in an assembly called the **House of Burgesses** (BUHR-juhs-ez). Membership in the House of Burgesses was granted only to white male landowners. The group had the power to raise taxes and make laws, but the governor still had the right to veto those laws.

This system was much more restrictive than the representative government we know today. Yet the House of Burgesses was significant because it was America's first legislature, or lawmaking body.

Colonial workers The majority of workers in Virginia were **indentured servants**. Employers hired indentured servants to work under contract for a certain number of years, usually four to seven. The employer, in return, would pay for food, shelter, and, most importantly, the worker's journey to America. When a servant's term of indenture expired, he or she was supposed to be given a suit of clothes as well as tools or land.

Soon indentured servants and former servants were a large part of the Virginia population. Many former indentured servants became successful farmers or artisans. But many others found themselves without a job or a good future. They were a restless group of unemployed men, moving from place to place in search of work.

About one-fourth of the indentured servants in the Chesapeake Bay region were young women. Most worked as household servants. Because men greatly outnumbered women in the colony, most women married soon after their indentures were over.

In August 1619, a Dutch ship landed at Jamestown. John Rolfe noted that it carried about 20 Africans. At first, Africans generally were regarded as indentured servants. In time, their situation changed to permanent servitude as Africans and their descendants became trapped in the institution of slavery.

By the late 1600s, the number of indentured servants was decreasing. Employers saw many advantages to using slave labor instead of indentured servants. Slaves who had been kidnapped from Africa, for example, could never go back home. Nor did the employers have to pay enslaved Africans as they had paid indentured servants. If slaves escaped, they could not blend into the white population.

Conflicts among settlers As Virginians moved westward, clashes with Native Americans continued. Conflicts among the colonists themselves also occurred.

Increasingly, settlers on the frontier had different interests from the large landholders

FACES OF HISTORY

POWHATAN

1550?–1618

When the first English colonists arrived in Virginia, Chief Powhatan ruled the Powhatan federation of Indians. Chief Powhatan controlled the territory from Jamestown to the Potomac River.

Powhatan did not welcome the English settlers. His followers led several small-scale raids on the fort and in 1608 captured Captain John Smith. Smith described Powhatan as "a tall well proportioned man." Chief Powhatan eventually let Smith return to Jamestown, and over time, relations with the colonists improved. Chief Powhatan even let his sons and his daughter, Pocahontas, visit the English settlement to trade goods.

Summarizing How did Powhatan deal with the English settlers?

Skills Focus: Making Generalizations

At Level

Reading Skill
Indentured Servitude

1. Review the information in the text about indentured servants and the role they played in early colonial life. Have each student write several diary entries describing the daily life of an indentured servant. Have students use the following questions as a guide: Why did you choose to indenture yourself in order to come to Virginia? What kind of work do you do? What is your life like? What do you plan to do when your period of indenture is over?

2. Have volunteers read their diary entries to the class.

3. Guide students in a discussion of the ways in which conditions for indentured servants differed from conditions that existed for enslaved Africans. **LS Verbal-Linguistic, Logical-Mathematical**

   Alternative Assessment Handbook, Rubric 15: Journals

Reading Focus

3 How did Virginia grow and change during the 1600s? *land grants attracted colonists; skilled artisans came; women came and married colonists*

Virginia Grows and Changes

Recall What did the first charter of Virginia do? *promised settlers same rights as Magna Carta and other English laws*

Explain What advantages were there to using slave labor rather than indentured servants? *Slaves could not complain to families back home; escaped African slaves did not easily blend into the white population.*

Evaluate Who had an easier time finding a place in colonial society after their term of indenture expired, men or women? Why? *women, because they usually married; many men found themselves without a job*

Recent Scholarship

Indians and English: Facing Off in Early America is a study of the early interactions and confrontations between the two groups. Author Karen Kupperman argues that the early interactions were not those of a stronger culture imposing its will upon a weaker one. Instead, she says that the English and Native Americans were curious about each other, and that while the English were fearful, they were also dependent upon Native Americans for survival.

Indians and English: Facing Off in Early America by Karen Kuperman. Cornell University Press, 2000

Answers

Faces of History *with violence at first, then acceptance*

Virginia Grows and Changes

Identify Who made up Nathaniel Bacon's "army"? *mostly unemployed and discontented men*

Identify Cause and Effect What were the consequences of Bacon's Rebellion? *more frontier land opened to settlers; slave labor increased*

📄 CRF: Economics and History: Tobacco in the Colonies

● Review & Assess ●

Close

Guide the class in a discussion of the first English colonies in Virginia.

Review

📱 Online Quiz, Section 2

📄 Daily Test Practice Transparency

Assess

SE Section 2 Assessment

📄 Progress Assessment: Section 2 Quiz

📄 Alternative Assessment Handbook

Reteach

📄 Interactive Reader and Study Guide, Section 2

🖱 Interactive Skills Tutor CD-ROM

Answers

Reading Like a Historian 1. *a major role—low prices of tobacco and high taxes;* **2.** *possible answer—yes, phrases such as "ill usage of the planters" and "extravagant taxes" indicate sympathy with the farmers*

Reading Check *headright system to attract new settlers, form of representative government in House of Burgesses*

50

PRIMARY SOURCES

Bacon's Rebellion

The rebellion led by farmer Nathaniel Bacon threatened the power of Virginia's colonial government. Virginian Robert Beverley later wrote about the incident and its causes.

"Four things may be reckoned to have been the main ingredients towards this intestine commotion [violent outbreak]. First, The extreme low price of tobacco, and the ill usage of the planters in the exchange of goods for it, which the country, with all their earnest endeavors, could not remedy. Secondly, The splitting the colony into proprieties, contrary to the original charters; and the extravagant taxes they were [charged]. Thirdly, The heavy restraints and burdens laid upon their trade by act of Parliament in England. Fourthly, The disturbance given by the Indians."

Skills Focus READING LIKE A HISTORIAN

1. **Drawing Conclusions** According to Beverley, what role did economics play in the rebellion?
2. **Identifying Points of View** Based on this excerpt, do you think Beverley was sympathetic to the farmers' cause? Explain your answer.

See Skills Handbook, pp. H28–H29

in the eastern tidewater region of Virginia—and from their royal government. Virginia's governor, Sir William Berkeley, wanted good relations with Native Americans on the frontier in order to protect his fur trade with them. Settlers, however, wanted to expand westward into land reserved for the Indians.

In the end, Berkeley's actions led to an uprising. Nathaniel Bacon was a well-to-do tobacco planter on the frontier. After his slave overseer was killed in an Indian attack in 1676, Bacon formed a small army and launched what became known as **Bacon's Rebellion**. Although Bacon was an aristocrat himself, his "army" was mostly former indentured servants.

Governor Berkeley declared Bacon a rebel. Bacon's army then attacked Jamestown and took control, apparently with popular support. In back-and-forth fighting, the town was burned. Berkeley fled. Then Bacon suddenly became ill and died. His rebellion collapsed.

Nevertheless, Bacon's Rebellion had lasting effects. The House of Burgesses opened more frontier land to settlers. In addition, landowners began to rely on slave labor, fearing uprisings from freed indentured servants.

READING CHECK **Summarizing** What were some key developments in the Virginia colony during the 1600s?

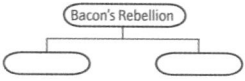

SECTION **2** ASSESSMENT

go.hrw.com
Online Quiz
Keyword: SD7 HP2

Reviewing Ideas, Terms, and People

1. **a. Identify** What was Sir Walter Raleigh's role in the colonization of Virginia?
   b. Explain What happened to the lost colony at Roanoke?
2. **a. Identify** What roles did **John Smith**, **Powhatan**, and **Pocahontas** have in the development of the Virginia colony?
   b. Summarize What factors led to hardships for the English settlers at Jamestown?
   c. Evaluate Why was it so difficult for settlers to establish a successful colony?
3. **a. Recall** What did the Virginia Company do to attract settlers to America?
   b. Explain How did the system of indentured servitude affect the population of Virginia?
   c. Predict Why was the establishment of the **House of Burgesses** important?

Critical Thinking

4. **Identifying Cause and Effect** Copy the chart below and show the aftereffects of Bacon's Rebellion.

Bacon's Rebellion

FOCUS ON WRITING ✎

5. **Persuasive** Write a newspaper editorial for a Virginia newspaper in which you argue for or against the opening of more lands in western Virginia for the growth of new English settlements.

50 CHAPTER 2

Section 2 Assessment Answers

1. **a.** sent several expeditions to the Americas, including the lost colony of Roanoke
   b. it mysteriously disappeared
2. **a.** John Smith—leader of the Jamestown settlement; Powhatan—leader of the Powhatan confederacy; Pocahontas—Powhatan's daughter, later married John Rolfe
   b. poor land for farming; unsafe drinking water; located inside Native American territory; starvation and disease
   c. possible answer—It was expensive, hard

work, and very dangerous.
3. **a.** offered headrights, which were 50–acre land grants
   b. contributed to growth, former indentured servants, now unemployed, unhappy
   c. America's first law making body
4. House of Burgesses opened more frontier land to settlers; increased use of slave labor
5. possible answer—more lands should be opened; will help colony and economy grow

SECTION 3
The Northern Colonies

BEFORE YOU READ

MAIN IDEA
The Pilgrims founded colonies in Massachusetts based on Puritan religious ideals, while dissent led to the founding of other New England colonies.

READING FOCUS
1. Why did the Puritans flee England?
2. How did dissent among the Puritans threaten the New England colonies?
3. What was life like in New England?

KEY TERMS AND PEOPLE
Mayflower Compact
Puritans
William Bradford
John Winthrop
Great Migration
Roger Williams
Anne Hutchinson
royal colony
Pequot War
King Philip's War

TAKING NOTES As you read, take notes on the Puritans' reasons for coming to New England. Record your notes in a graphic organizer like the one shown here.

> Reasons for Coming to New England

THE INSIDE STORY

How will the new colony be ruled? The passengers could scarcely wait to get off their ship and begin building their new homes on solid land in America. First, though, they had important business to conduct.

For two long months in 1620 the *Mayflower* had pitched its way across the stormy Atlantic Ocean. The ship carried English Christians who were looking for a place where they could worship as they pleased. Others on the ship simply wanted a new way of life. They would need to cooperate in order to survive in the wilderness.

The adventurers had landed too far north—at the tip of present-day Cape Cod, Massachusetts. The *Mayflower* settlers realized they were out of the jurisdiction of their Virginia charter or of any authority they knew. But they believed in the rule of law. They believed that the colony needed a government structure.

So, even before they landed, they established rules to keep order in the new settlement. On November 11, 1620, the 41 men signed the **Mayflower Compact**. Promising allegiance to England's King James, they agreed to make "just and equal laws . . . for the general Good of the Colony."

The compact was remarkable in a couple of ways. The settlers agreed to be ruled by a government chosen by the consent of the people. They agreed to obey all laws made for the good of the whole group.

Today we take these ideas for granted. Yet at a time when authority rested with kings and queens, the Mayflower Compact was a historic step toward self-government.

► **The Mayflower Compact united the Pilgrims in "a civil Body Politick."**

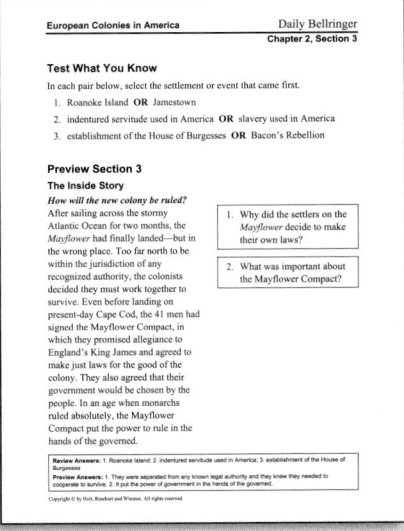

The Mayflower Compact

51

Teach the Main Idea | At Level

The Northern Colonies

1. **Teach** Ask students the Reading Focus questions to teach this section.

2. **Apply** Organize students into small groups. Have each group discuss and then list the reasons the Pilgrims came to America.

3. **Review** Guide students in a discussion of the institutions developed in New England that have had a lasting influence on what became the United States.

4. **Practice/Homework** Ask students what they think it would be like to live in a country with an "official" religion that everyone must support and at least pretend to follow or risk going to prison. Some students may have emigrated from countries with "official" religions. Then have each student write a brief essay describing why separation of church and state became a fundamental constitutional issue.

🄛 **Interpersonal, Logical-Mathematical**

📃 Alternative Assessment Handbook, Rubrics 11: Discussions; and 42: Writing to Inform

❶ Why did the Puritans flee England? *disagreed with the Church of England; were persecuted, fined, or put into prison because of their religious beliefs*

Puritans Flee To Freedom

Describe What reforms did Puritans want to make in the Church of England? *simplify church service, reduce wealth and power of bishops, remove traces of Catholicism*

Contrast How did the Puritans and Pilgrims differ? *Puritans wanted to reform Church of England; Pilgrims were Puritans and others who moved to the New World.*

Activity The Mayflower Compact Find a copy of the Mayflower Compact, distribute it to students, and have them read it. Then guide students in a discussion of the compact using the following questions: What reasons are given for establishing the colony? What do the signers promise to do? Where was the compact signed? Do references to King James seem consistent with the Pilgrims' reasons for leaving England? Why or why not?

LS Verbal-Linguistic

Puritans Flee to Freedom

The Protestant Reformation eventually led to the establishment of the Church of England, also known as the Anglican Church. The English monarch served as head of this new government-sponsored church.

The new form of worship had some elements of Roman Catholicism. Queen Elizabeth I introduced more Protestant ideas from groups such as the Calvinists. That did not satisfy some Protestants, however.

Puritans and Separatists Some English Protestants wanted to "purify" the church by making further reforms. These people were known as **Puritans**. For example, they wanted a simpler church service. They also objected to the wealth and power of bishops.

Other, more strict Puritans wished to remove all traces of Catholicism from their religious practice. The Separatists, as these people were called, wanted a total separation from the Church of England.

The Church of England, however, was the official church of the land. English subjects were required to attend services and pay taxes to support the church. Those who wanted to worship in another way were often persecuted for their beliefs. These dissenters were fined or put in prison.

Founding Plymouth Colony One group of Separatists moved to the Netherlands in 1608. Dutch society was well known for its religious tolerance. After a few years, though, the English were ready to leave. Earning a living was hard. Their children were becoming more Dutch than English. Moreover, war with Spain seemed near. The Separatists decided to move to America.

A group of merchants formed a joint-stock company to support Puritans moving to the New World. Each colonist had a share in the company. A Virginia Company charter granted them land in North America to settle. After seven years, land and profits would be divided among the colonists and the other investors.

In the end, however, only half of the Pilgrims from the Netherlands were on the small ship *Mayflower* when it set sail in September 1620. These 35 people referred to themselves as "saints." **William Bradford** headed the group. The voyagers included 66 others, many of

HISTORY CLOSE-UP

Plymouth Colony

Formed by a group of Pilgrims seeking religious freedom, Plymouth Colony was the first permanent English settlement in New England. Life in Plymouth was often difficult. The colonists had to grow their own food and build everything they needed by hand.

Plymouth houses had steeply sloped thatched roofs and small windows.

Colonists kept weapons in a central stockade, in order to protect the colony.

Pilgrims wore clothing in bright solid colors.

Plymouth had trade relations, military agreements, and some social interaction with the nearby Wampanoag Indians.

52

Differentiating Instruction

Below Level

Students Having Difficulty

1. To help students understand the problems that the Puritans faced in England, draw the graphic organizer at right for students to see. Omit the italicized answers. Have students copy the graphic organizer and complete it.

2. Have volunteers share their answers and complete the organizer for all to see. Have students correct their work and retain their graphic organizers as a study tool.

3. Guide students in a discussion about reasons why people left their homes and risked their lives

crossing the ocean to settle in a new land.

LS Visual-Spatial, Logical-Mathematical

📄 Alternative Assessment Handbook, Rubric 13: Graphic Organizers

📊 Graphic Organizer Transparencies

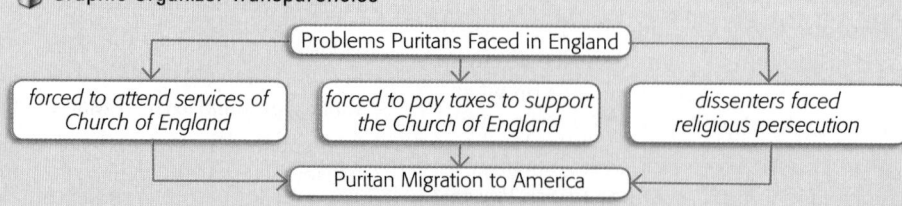

Problems Puritans Faced in England

forced to attend services of Church of England | *forced to pay taxes to support the Church of England* | *dissenters faced religious persecution*

Puritan Migration to America

whom were not Separatists. The "saints" called them strangers. Bradford later wrote about the departure from the Netherlands:

❝So they left that goodly and pleasant city which had been their resting place nearly twelve years; but they knew they were pilgrims, and looked not much on those things, but lift up their eyes to the heavens . . . and quieted their spirits.❞

—William Bradford, *Of Plymouth Plantation*

Their sponsor, the Virginia Company, had intended the expedition to land near the Hudson River. Instead, because of a storm or poor navigation, the ship had landed at Cape Cod, where they signed the Mayflower Compact. After exploring the area for several weeks, the expedition founded Plymouth Colony on a sheltered harbor just south of present-day Boston.

Winter took a toll. By the spring of 1621, about half the group had died of hunger, cold, or illness. The rest survived with the aid of the local Wampanoag (wahm-puh-NO-ahg) Indians.

The next year life improved. The first corn harvest was so successful that the Pilgrims held a harvest feast with their Wampanoag neighbors, which we now commemorate as

Skills FOCUS INTERPRETING INFOGRAPHICS

Making Inferences What does this picture tell you about life in Plymouth Colony?
See Skills Handbook, p. H18

Women baked bread in outdoor ovens.

Thanksgiving Day. Bradford was chosen governor of Plymouth in 1621. He led the colony until just before his death in 1657.

Plymouth Colony never grew very large, but it remained self-governing until 1691. Then it became part of the Massachusetts Bay Colony.

"A City upon a hill" The success of the Plymouth settlement, combined with continued religious persecution and economic hard times, encouraged thousands of other Puritans to move to "New England." Some Puritan merchants managed to get a charter from the king and organize the Massachusetts Bay Company. Its chief goals were to make a profit and to create a refuge for Puritans.

The company bought out the other investors and chose **John Winthrop** to lead the new colony. Winthrop took charge of a fleet of 11 ships and some 700 people that set out for New England in 1630. Most were families planning to make a new home. Aboard the *Arbella*, Winthrop put forth his vision of the colony as a model for the world:

❝For we must consider that we shall be as a City upon a hill. The eyes of all people are upon us.❞

—John Winthrop, *A Model of Christian Charity*

The Massachusetts Bay Colony grew faster than Plymouth. Puritan colonists soon established other towns nearby. The colony's capital was the port city of Boston. Other early towns included Salem, Watertown, and Concord.

The Massachusetts Bay Colony charter included some provisions for colonial government. It created a Massachusetts General Court, which had the ability to elect officers and make laws. Eventually, this court turned into a kind of self-government, although only male members of the court could vote or hold office. Each town elected representatives to the court. The members of the court in turn elected a council, headed by Winthrop, which held all legislative, judicial, and executive power.

The success of the Plymouth and Massachusetts Bay colonies inspired what is called the **Great Migration**. Between 1620 and 1643 some 20,000 English men and women crossed the Atlantic Ocean to settle in New England.

READING CHECK **Comparing** How were the Plymouth and Massachusetts Bay colonies founded?

Reading Focus

Puritans Flee To Freedom

Explain What happened to Plymouth Colony? *It became part of the Massachusetts Bay Colony.*

Evaluate Why do you think that the Plymouth and Massachusetts Bay Colonies remained separate for so long? *possible answer—because the Pilgrims and the Puritans had different ideas about the role of religion in society*

Primary Source

"But it pleased God to visit us then with death daily, and with so general a disease that the living were scarce able to bury the dead."

— William Bradford

From a letter to Mr. Carver, 1621, about Plymouth Plantation

Info to Know

A New Vocabulary As the colonists adjusted to life in North America, new words entered their vocabularies. They borrowed many terms from Native Americans, frequently mangling the pronunciation in the process. For example, *pawschoircora* became *hickory*. The settlers also created new words to describe the plants and animals they found in their new environment, such as *eggplant, bluebird, mockingbird, mudhen, hummingbird,* and *groundhog*.

Collaborative Learning

At Level

The Puritan Experience

1. Guide students in a discussion of the founding and early years of the Plymouth and Massachusetts Bay Colonies. Have students describe how the early settlers' life in North America would have differed from their life in England or Holland. What kinds of challenges would they have faced on a daily basis?

2. Divide the class into small groups. Have each group write a one-act play about the settlement of Plymouth Colony or the

Massachusetts Bay Colony. Allow students to choose which colony they want to write about, but make sure that they keep the facts about the two colonies straight.

3. Have each group present its play to the class.
   LS Interpersonal, Kinesthetic

   Alternative Assessment Handbook, Rubric 33: Skits and Reader's Theater

---

Answers

Interpreting Infographics *it shows how they tended to their daily needs, the type of houses they lived in, and how they defended themselves*

Reading Check *Plymouth Colony founded by Pilgrims and others led by William Bradford in 1620; Massachusetts Bay founded by Puritan-led Massachusetts Bay Company and John Winthrop in 1630*

❷ How did dissent among the Puritans threaten the New England colonies? *church and government closely linked; dissent was seen as a threat to colony's stability; dissenters chose to leave or were banished, established other colonies*

Dissent Among the Puritans

Identify What was the importance of the Fundamental Orders of Connecticut? *America's first written constitution; gave voting rights to freemen, not just church members*

Analyze How did the beliefs of Roger Williams differ from those of previous Separatists, such as the Pilgrims? *Williams wanted to keep church and government matters separate; Pilgrims wanted to separate from the established Church of England, because Pilgrims believed that the church and government were inseparable*

Evaluate Why were the Puritans so unwilling to tolerate forms of religion that differed from their own? *possible answer—Since religion and government were so closely linked, any differences in worship were seen as threats to the stability of the colony's established order.*

Counterpoints

Separation of Church and State

Define Using the quotation from Roger Williams, have students write a definition of the word *magistrate*. *possible answer—a government official in charge of administering the law*

Answers

Reading Like a Historian *because many people will be watching their actions, they should be good examples of their faith*

54

ACADEMIC VOCABULARY
fundamental original, essential
radical relating to extreme change

Dissent Among the Puritans

The Puritans came to America to find religious freedom for their form of worship, which they believed to be the true and pure religion. Their community, ways of life, and laws were deeply rooted in their religious beliefs. As in England, citizens were expected to attend church and pay taxes to support it. They obeyed strict codes of behavior, dress, and speech. Hard work and little or no play was generally the rule—and in America, they had the freedom to make their own rules and live by them.

In the Massachusetts Bay Colony, church and government were closely linked and dissent was not permitted. In time, dissenters left the colony and settled new towns in other parts of New England.

Connecticut and Rhode Island Thomas Hooker, a powerful Puritan minister, believed that "in matters which concern the common good," a government "chosen by all" was best. His differences with Winthrop's government finally led Hooker and his congregation to leave the colony. They headed west and settled in the fertile Connecticut River Valley. In 1639 the group adopted America's first written constitution: the Fundamental Orders of Connecticut. The document extended voting rights to all free men, not just church members.

Roger Williams was a man of strong convictions who clashed with authorities in Boston. A radical Separatist minister, he believed in religious tolerance. He believed that church and government matters should be separate. Williams also was a friend to the Narragansett Indians and thought that settlers should buy land, not take it. He purchased land from the Narragansetts and established a settlement he called Providence, in what is now Rhode Island. Government and church were separate, and people of all faiths, including Jews, were welcome.

Anne Hutchinson caused an even bigger uproar. She believed that people did not need a minister's teaching in order to be spiritual. Challenged by the Massachusetts governor, Hutchinson declared:

HISTORY'S VOICES

❝Now if you do condemn me for speaking what in my conscience I know to be truth, I must commit myself into the Lord.❞

—Trial of Anne Hutchinson, 1637

COUNTERPOINTS

Separation of Church and State

Roger Williams's belief that the government had no right to interfere in religious matters was considered radical and even dangerous in his day.

❝[M]agistrates, as magistrates, have no power of setting up the form of church government, electing church officers, [or] punishing with church censures . . . And on the other side, the churches as churches, have no power . . . of erecting or altering forms of civil government, electing of civil officers, [or] inflicting civil punishments.❞

Roger Williams, 1644

To John Winthrop, the colony of Massachusetts and its government were inseparable from the religious beliefs of its people.

❝We must be knit together in this work, as one man. . . For we must consider that we shall be as a City upon a hill. The eyes of all people are upon us. . . [I]f we shall deal falsely with our God in this work we have undertaken, . . . we shall be made a story and a byword throughout the world.❞

John Winthrop, 1630

Skills FOCUS READING LIKE A HISTORIAN

Analyzing Primary Sources Why does Winthrop believe the colonists' religion should guide their decisions as they build the colony?
See Skills Handbook, pp. H28–29

54 CHAPTER 2

Skills Focus: Summarizing   At Level

Reading Skill
Threats to Colonial Stability

1. Write the following events for students to see: Thomas Hooker's departure from Massachusetts; Roger Williams's departure from Massachusetts; Anne Hutchinson's banishment from Massachusetts; Salem witchcraft trials. Remind students that each event took place because of something that posed a threat to the stability of the Massachusetts Bay Colony.

2. Have each student write a paragraph about each event, explaining what caused it and what happened as a result.

3. Guide students in a discussion of life in the Massachusetts Bay Colony. What similarities and differences were there between life in Massachusetts and life in England?
🅛🅢 **Logical-Mathematical, Verbal-Linguistic**

📖 Alternative Assessment Handbook, Rubrics 9: Comparing and Contrasting; and 42: Writing to Inform

Hutchinson was imprisoned, tried, and banished from Massachusetts Bay Colony. She and her husband, Will, and other Massachusetts leaders migrated to Rhode Island.

Anne Hutchinson's brother-in-law, a minister, left Massachusetts in 1638 to start a settlement in what is now New Hampshire. In 1679 New Hampshire became a **royal colony**, under direct control of the king. It was the last of the New England colonies to be created. Maine remained part of Massachusetts until 1820.

Witchcraft trials in Salem In 1692 a series of bizarre events brought a crisis to the Massachusetts colony. It started in Salem Village, where several girls exhibited strange behaviors and claimed to have been bewitched. Belief in witches was common in the 1600s.

The girls accused several women of witchcraft, including respected church members and a West Indian servant. After some forced confessions, hysteria gripped the town. Wild rumors and hearsay led to the arrest of hundreds of people in the colony. Nineteen people were executed, and others died in jail. Then as quickly as it came, the witch scare passed. The witch trials were condemned, and the remaining prisoners were freed.

READING CHECK **Summarizing** What colonies were founded by Puritan dissenters?

Life in New England

The Puritan colonies set high ideals for themselves. Those ideals shaped their daily lives, their governments, and their school systems.

Education and public schools The American public school system began in the New England colonies. Puritans wanted their children to read well enough to understand the Bible and to have skill in a trade or craft.

In the 1640s the Massachusetts General Court passed several education laws. One gave town officials, called selectmen, the right to ensure that children and apprentices got a proper education. Other laws required towns to set up elementary and grammar schools.

Most children learned reading, writing, and some arithmetic in a "dame school," taught by a woman in her home. Often that was the only education a girl received. Boys had opportunities for

further schooling. By the early 1700s, boys could attend two New England colleges: Harvard in Massachusetts and Yale in Connecticut.

Colonial government England's colonies began with differing political arrangements. Some colonies were owned by individuals, others by joint-stock companies. During the late 1600s and early 1700s most became royal colonies under the direct rule of the English king.

The town was the center of life in the New England colonies. Typically, a town was built around a central grassy area called the common. The meeting house and schoolhouse faced the common, and cattle grazed there.

Town government was the most relevant to people's daily lives. They met in a town meeting to elect selectmen, choose delegates to the colonial assembly, set taxes, and deal with local problems such as roads. The town meeting was the closest thing to democracy in the colonies. Voting was limited to church members and property owners.

Relations with Native Americans The more the English settlements expanded, the more they came into conflict with Native Americans. Relations at first had been friendly. A Patuxet Indian named Squanto had helped the Plymouth colonists survive, for example.

By the mid-1600s, the colonists were less dependent on the Indians. Fishing, trade, and

THE IMPACT TODAY

Government
Many towns in New England have kept their town-meeting government to this day. In old town halls, set on colonial town commons, selectmen (and women) meet to make local laws and hear issues brought by citizens.

Life in New England

Explain What was the primary reason for conflict between Native Americans and settlers? *As settlers expanded and settlements multiplied, conflicts with Native Americans increased.*

Identify Cause and Effect What was the result of King Philip's War? *Settlers died in the fighting, but nearly all the Wampanoags and Narragansetts were killed and their villages destroyed. Southern New England was left open to settlers.*

• Review & Assess •

Close

Guide students in a discussion of the factors that led to the founding of the New England colonies.

Review

- Online Quiz, Section 3
- Daily Test Practice Transparency

Assess

- **SE** Section 3 Assessment
- Progress Assessment: Section 3 Quiz
- Alternative Assessment Handbook

Reteach

- Interactive Reader and Study Guide, Section 3
- Interactive Skills Tutor CD-ROM

Answers

Interpreting Maps 1. *in order to use the river for transportation* **2.** *Plymouth*
Reading Check *friendly at first and later became hostile; led to war*

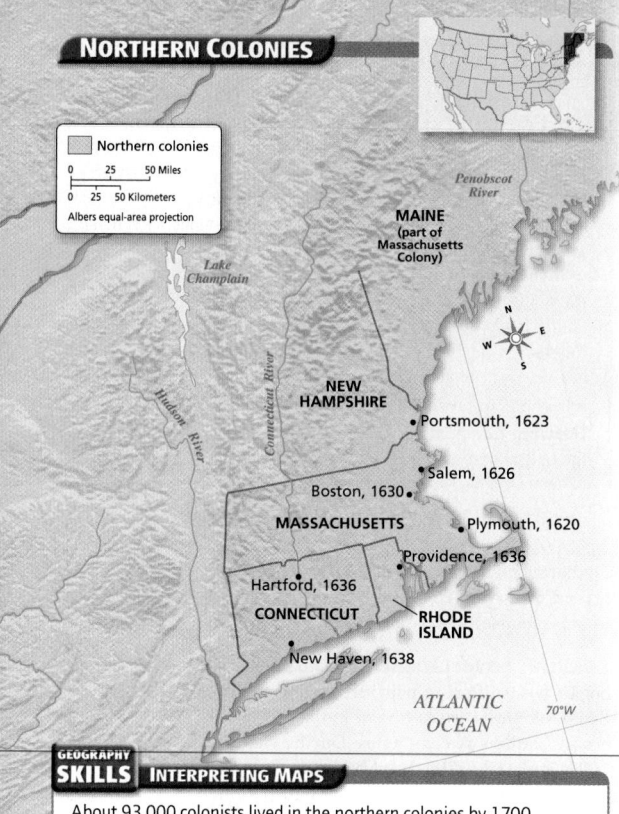

NORTHERN COLONIES

Northern colonies

0   25   50 Miles
0   25   50 Kilometers
Albers equal-area projection

MAINE
(part of Massachusetts Colony)

Penobscot River

Lake Champlain

NEW HAMPSHIRE

• Portsmouth, 1623
• Salem, 1626
Boston, 1630 •

MASSACHUSETTS

• Plymouth, 1620
• Providence, 1636

Hartford, 1636 •

CONNECTICUT   RHODE ISLAND

• New Haven, 1638

ATLANTIC OCEAN   70°W

GEOGRAPHY SKILLS **INTERPRETING MAPS**

About 93,000 colonists lived in the northern colonies by 1700.

1. **Human-Environment Interaction** Why do you think Hartford was built near a river?
2. **Location** Which colony was established first?

See Skills Handbook, p. H20

---

shipbuilding were becoming more important than the fur trade. At the same time, the Native Americans now had guns. As settlers took more land for farms and scattered the wild game, the Native Americans began to resist.

Puritan attitudes changed, too. Some still wanted to convert the Native Americans to Christianity and teach them English ways. The missionary John Eliot translated the Bible into Algonquian. But others decided that Indians were heathens and that it was their religious duty to drive them out or kill them.

In 1637 conflicts erupted in the Connecticut River Valley over land and over the Pequot Indians' trade with the Dutch. The **Pequot War** ended with a brutal massacre. Some 90 colonists, with their Narragansett and Mohegan allies, attacked a Pequot fort. They set it on fire, then killed all those who fled. The war nearly wiped out the Pequot people.

In 1675 Indians again resisted English settlers in **King Philip's War**. The Wampanoag leader Metacomet, known to the English as King Philip, led his people and others in attacks that destroyed colonial towns. In return, the colonists burned villages and crops.

The war was costly for both sides. Many settlers—perhaps 600—died in the fighting. Nearly all the Wampanoag and Narragansett Indians were killed, and their villages were destroyed. Survivors fled or were sold as slaves. The war left southern New England open to white settlers.

READING CHECK **Summarizing** How did New England colonists' relations with Native Americans change over time?

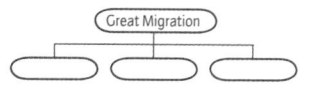

SECTION 3 ASSESSMENT

go.hrw.com
Online Quiz
Keyword: SD7 HP2

Reviewing Ideas, Terms, and People

1. **a. Describe** What was the **Mayflower Compact**?
   b. Summarize Why did the **Puritans** want to leave England?
2. **a. Identify** What did **Anne Hutchinson** and **Roger Williams** have in common?
   b. Analyze How did the treatment of dissenters both help and harm colonization in New England?
3. **a. Recall** What led to war between the New England colonists and the local Native Americans?
   b. Evaluate How did the Puritans' treatment of Native Americans conflict with their values?

Critical Thinking

4. **Identifying Cause and Effect** Copy the chart below and identify the reasons for the Great Migration.

Great Migration

FOCUS ON SPEAKING

5. **Persuasive** As a supporter of Roger Williams, write a speech urging Massachusetts Bay officials to buy rather than take land from Native Americans.

56 CHAPTER 2

Section 3 Assessment Answers

1. **a.** a document promising allegiance to King James and promising just and equal laws for the good of the colony
   b. sought religious freedom
2. **a.** disagreed with the authority of their colony
   b. possible answer—helped by creating new colonies, harmed by creating hostility toward Puritans
3. **a.** conflicts over land and trade and colonists' attitudes toward Native Americans

b. some Puritans considered them heathens, felt it was their duty to drive them out or kill them
4. Plymouth and Massachusetts Bay Colonies grow; other towns established; self-government established
5. possible answer—must maintain good relationship with Native Americans; can help each other if treat each other with respect; land is rightfully theirs

American *Literature*

About the Reading Tituba, a slave from Barbados, was among the first people accused of witchcraft in Salem. In Ann Petry's 1964 novel, *Tituba of Salem Village*, the Reverend Parris threatens and beats Tituba until she confesses to being a witch.

AS YOU READ Consider what could have prompted the witch scare.

Excerpt from

Tituba of Salem Village

by Ann Petry

I am doomed, Tituba thought. Even if the master were the kind who would risk his own life and his family's safety to protect his slave, even so he couldn't possibly save me from hanging. Anyone who saw me touch one of these girls in the middle of one of their fits, and saw them suddenly become well because I touched them, would believe me to be a witch.

"Now will you confess?" Parris asked between clenched teeth.

"What do you want me to say, master?"

"What is it you do to these children?"

"She bewitches us," Abigail said. "She and Goody Good and old Gammer Osburne. They were the first ones to come in the house after Goody Sibley baked the witch cake."

"Witch cake!" the master said, horror in his voice. "What devil's work is this?" He took hold of Abigail's arm. "What are you talking about?"

Abigail told him about the baking of the witch cake, how Goody Sibley and John had fed it to the dog, how the dog had yelped and run out of the house. Right after that, Tituba and Good and Gammer Osburne had entered the keeping room. All of them at the same time. "They were the witches, drawn to the house by the witch cake," she said primly.

"You did this in my house?" he asked scowling. "The black art was used—in my house? Why this is

The Trial of George Jacobs *painted by Tompkins Matteson in 1855 shows the hysteria over witchcraft extending into the courtroom.*

going to the Devil for help against the Devil—"

Abigail, frightened, said, "We didn't know what else to do. There have been so many things, so many strange things—We didn't mean any harm." She wept piteously and ran out of the room.

"I'll have you hanged," the master shouted, glaring at Tituba, "and Good and Osburne along with you. When this story gets out, it will ruin me in the parish."

Skills FOCUS **READING LIKE A HISTORIAN**

1. **Drawing Conclusions** Why was Reverend Parris angry at Tituba?

2. **Literature as Historical Evidence** How does this story illustrate the hysteria that took place in Salem?

See *Skills Handbook*, p. H32

Word Help

Goody shortened form of *goodwife,* used as a title for a housewife

Gammer an old woman, short for *godmother*

witch cake a cake that was supposed to break a witch's spell

keeping room a storage room or pantry

appalled horrified

cowered shrank back, cringed

unspeakable terrible, beyond description

Meet the Writer

Ann Petry (1908–1997) was a prominent African American writer. She had a middle-class upbringing in a small town in Connecticut. After her marriage in 1938, she moved to New York City, where she began a career in journalism. Her first short story appeared in 1943. With the publication of her first novel, *The Street*, Petry became the first African American woman to write a bestseller. She also wrote several books for young readers, including *Tituba of Salem Village*.

Info to Know

Witch Cakes In the winter of 1692, Betty Parris and two other girls began to behave strangely. Tituba and her husband, John, baked a "witch cake" with rye and Betty's urine and fed it to the dog. Dogs were believed to be "familiars," or witches' helpers. Upon eating the witch cake, it was believed the dog would identify the witch who had cast a spell on Betty.

Differentiating Instruction

Learners Having Difficulty
Below Level

Review with students the information in the text about the witchcraft trials in Salem. Then ask students why they think Tituba confessed to being a witch. Was her confession forced? Did she understand what the consequences might be? **LS Interpersonal**

📝 Alternative Assessment Handbook, Rubric 11: Discussions

Advanced Learners/GATE
Above Level

Have students list ways in which people react to things that are unfamiliar to them. Tituba was a foreigner, raised in a different culture. Ask students how this might have affected the villagers' interpretation of Tituba's attempts to help her master's daughter. Then have students write a summary explaining Tituba's reaction to her master. **LS Interpersonal, Logical-Mathematical**

📝 Alternative Assessment Handbook, Rubric 37: Writing Assignments

Answers

Reading Like a Historian 1. *for using what he suspected was witchcraft* **2.** *possible answer—shows the panic and fear people felt as well as the accusations and reasoning that caused the witch scare*

Jamestown and Plymouth

Info to Know

Living History Both Plymouth and Jamestown now offer visitors a chance to experience living history. At both sites, costumed actors depict the daily lives of members of the original settlement. Visitors can try their hand at grinding corn, putting on English armor, or assisting with farm chores.

Passing Through the Bay When ships sailing from England reached the shallow waters of Chesapeake Bay, they had to lighten their loads in order to pass through. Unfortunately, the practice of dumping goods overboard made the waters even shallower. Laws were eventually passed to prohibit dumping.

MISCONCEPTION ///ALERT\\\

Remind students that the English colony of Jamestown, settled in 1607, is not the oldest permanent European settlement in the continental United States. That honor belongs to St. Augustine, Florida, founded by the Spanish in 1565.

✳ Interactive
HISTORY & Geography

Jamestown and Plymouth

The historical development of any community, sometimes its very survival, depends on its geography. Does it have access to important natural resources? Is there safe and convenient access to other communities? What is the climate like? Early English colonists to North America had these and other considerations in mind when they founded their colonies. But in a new land, there was much they didn't know. They would have to adapt to their new surroundings or die.

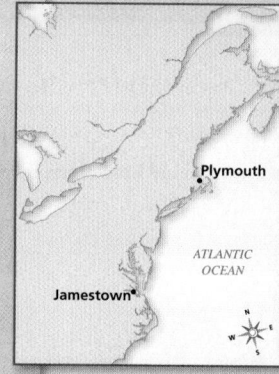

Near the Sea Plymouth and Jamestown were sited near the ocean for easy access to the ships that would carry trade goods to and from England.

ATLANTIC OCEAN

Plymouth

Jamestown•

Jamestown
Jamestown was built 36 miles upriver from the ocean. This location protected it from storm waves and enemy warships.

Williamsburg (1698)

Tobacco Virginia's warm climate and moist, well-drained soil was well-suited for tobacco growing.

Mosquitos Nearby swamps were infested with mosquitoes, which carry malaria. An epidemic broke out just two months after the colonists arrived. Frequent outbreaks of malaria eventually led colonists to move their capital to Williamsburg.

Fields The colonists grew food for themselves and tobacco for export. From 1618 to 1623, the colony's population grew from 400 to 4500 because of the tobacco boom.

Jamestown (1607)

James River

58

Skills Focus: Interpreting Historical Maps
At Level

Social Studies Skill
Mapping the New Settlements

1. Pass out outline maps of the 13 colonies to students. Have students work in mixed-ability pairs to label the location of Jamestown and Plymouth, as well as other early settlements. Students may use their text or additional resources if necessary.

2. Have volunteers share their maps with the class. Have students correct their own maps and retain them as a study tool.

3. Guide students in a discussion about why these sites were chosen. Ask students what the geographical advantages and disadvantages of these sites are.
   LS Verbal-Linguistic, Visual-Spatial

   📝 Alternative Assessment Handbook, Rubric 20: Map Creation

   📝 American History Outline Maps: The Thirteen Colonies

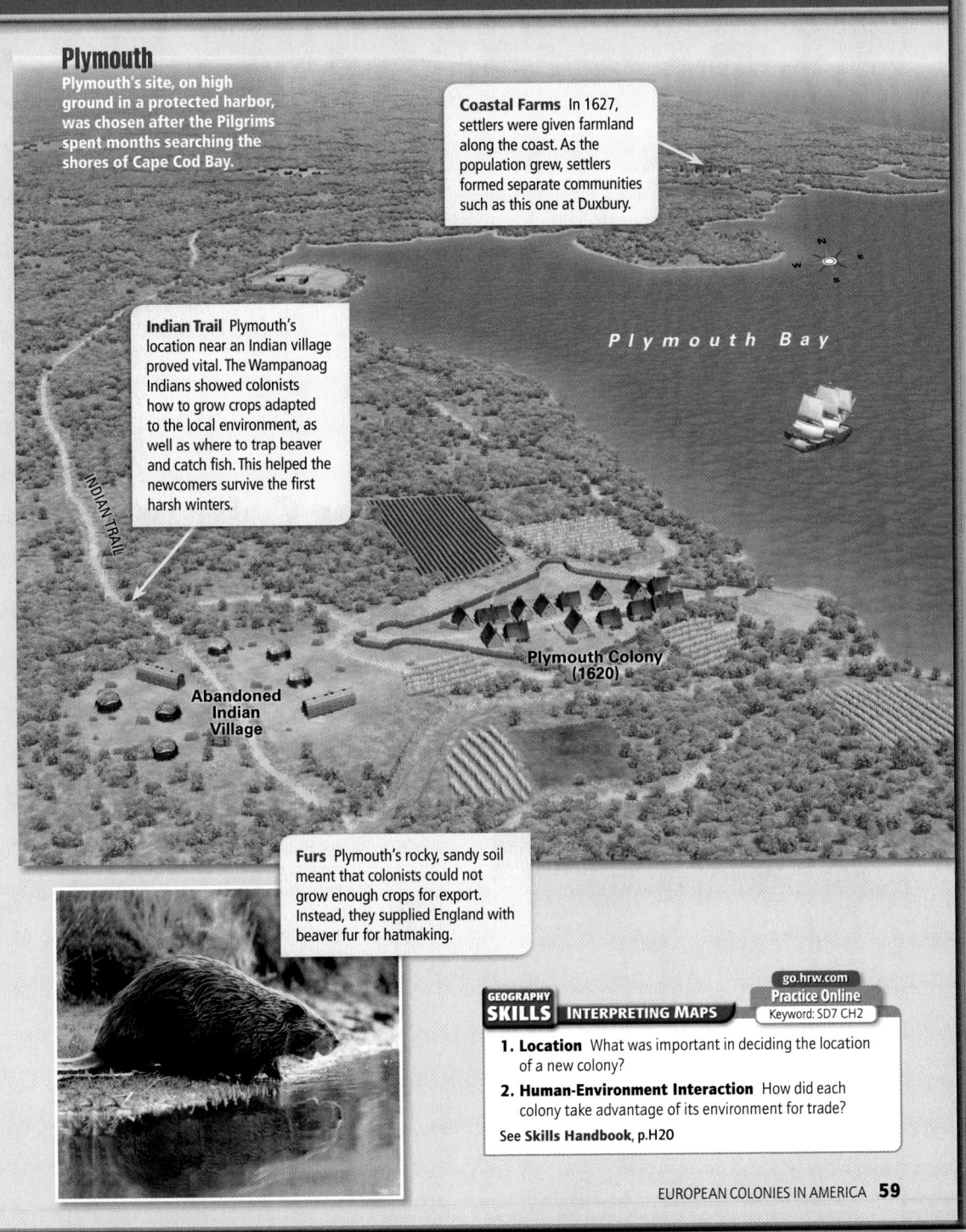

Plymouth

Plymouth's site, on high ground in a protected harbor, was chosen after the Pilgrims spent months searching the shores of Cape Cod Bay.

Coastal Farms In 1627, settlers were given farmland along the coast. As the population grew, settlers formed separate communities such as this one at Duxbury.

Plymouth Bay

Indian Trail Plymouth's location near an Indian village proved vital. The Wampanoag Indians showed colonists how to grow crops adapted to the local environment, as well as where to trap beaver and catch fish. This helped the newcomers survive the first harsh winters.

INDIAN TRAIL

Plymouth Colony (1620)

Abandoned Indian Village

Furs Plymouth's rocky, sandy soil meant that colonists could not grow enough crops for export. Instead, they supplied England with beaver fur for hatmaking.

GEOGRAPHY SKILLS — INTERPRETING MAPS

go.hrw.com
Practice Online
Keyword: SD7 CH2

1. **Location** What was important in deciding the location of a new colony?
2. **Human-Environment Interaction** How did each colony take advantage of its environment for trade?

See **Skills Handbook**, p.H20

EUROPEAN COLONIES IN AMERICA **59**

History and Geography

Info to Know

Beaver Hats By the mid-1800s, beaver hats became so popular in Europe that the animal had disappeared from all except the northernmost tip of New England. Some historians believe that the beaver might have become extinct if silk had not replaced beaver fur as a stylish and fashionable choice for clothing in the 1840s.

New England Climate England's location near the western wind belt keeps its climate rainy and mild. Rain falls throughout the year and both winters and summers tend to be temperate. New England, on the other hand, is perfectly located to bear the brunt of many storms. In New England, summers are hot and winters are cold and snowy.

Skills Focus: Analyzing Primary Sources

Reading Like a Historian Skill
Journals of the Colonists

1. Divide students into small groups. Have each group locate several primary sources written by colonists at Jamestown or Plymouth.

2. Have students analyze the documents, noting similarities and differences between the accounts. Have students also analyze whether any of the sources are biased.

3. Have a volunteer from each group share their sources and analyses with the class.

Guide the class in a discussion comparing and contrasting the experiences of settlers in Jamestown and in Plymouth. **LS Intrapersonal, Verbal-Linguistic**

📖 Alternative Assessment Handbook, Rubric 9: Comparing and Contrasting

Answers

Interpreting Maps 1. *protection from attack; good climate; access to water, natural resources, and food;* **2.** *Virginians exported tobacco, which grew in their climate and soil, while New Englanders trapped beavers for their fur.*

59

Bellringer

The Inside Story. . . Use the **Daily Bellringer Transparency** to help students answer the question.

📦 Daily Bellringer Transparency, Section 4

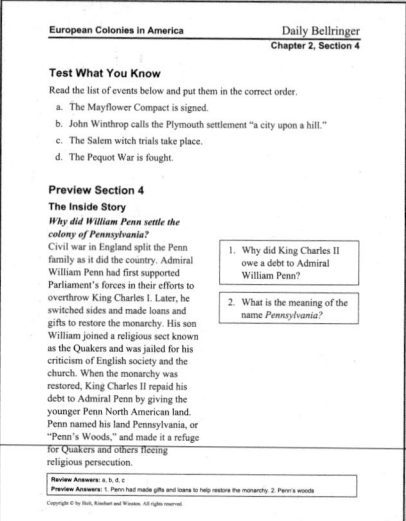

European Colonies in America — Daily Bellringer, Chapter 2, Section 4

Test What You Know

Read the list of events below and put them in the correct order.

a. The Mayflower Compact is signed.
b. John Winthrop calls the Plymouth settlement "a city upon a hill."
c. The Salem witch trials take place.
d. The Pequot War is fought.

Preview Section 4
The Inside Story
Why did William Penn settle the colony of Pennsylvania?

Civil war in England split the Penn family as it did the country. Admiral William Penn had first supported Parliament's forces in their efforts to overthrow King Charles I. Later, he switched sides and made loans and gifts to restore the monarchy. His son William joined a religious sect known as the Quakers and was jailed for his criticism of English society and the church. When the monarchy was restored, King Charles II repaid his debt to Admiral Penn by giving the younger Penn North American land. Penn named his land Pennsylvania, or "Penn's Woods," and made it a refuge for Quakers and others fleeing religious persecution.

1. Why did King Charles II owe a debt to Admiral William Penn?

2. What is the meaning of the name *Pennsylvania*?

Review Answers: a, b, d, c
Preview Answers: 1. Penn had made gifts and loans to help restore the monarchy. 2. Penn's woods

Copyright © by Holt, Rinehart and Winston. All rights reserved.

Academic Vocabulary

Review with students the high-use academic terms in this section.

distinct clearly defined (p. 61)

perspective point of view (p. 63)

📓 CRF: Vocabulary Builder Activity, Section 4

Taking Notes

Quakers from England; Small Protestant sects such as the Amish and Mennonites from Germany; Huguenots from France

go.hrw.com
Online Resources

KEYWORD: SD7 CH2
TOPIC: CREATING A NEW ENGLAND

SECTION 4
The Middle and Southern Colonies

BEFORE YOU READ

MAIN IDEA

Events in England during and after the English Civil War led to a new wave of colonization along the Atlantic coast south of New England.

READING FOCUS

1. What brought about a new era of colonization in America?

2. Why were new southern colonies founded?

3. Why did the Quakers settle Pennsylvania?

4. Why was Maryland founded?

KEY TERMS AND PEOPLE

Quaker
William Penn
Restoration
proprietary colonies
James Oglethorpe
Lord Baltimore
Toleration Act

TAKING NOTES As you read, take notes on where colonists that moved to the Pennsylvania colony came from. Record your notes in a graphic organizer like the one shown here.

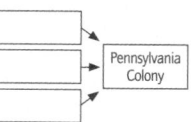

Pennsylvania Colony

William Penn's Quaker Colony

THE INSIDE STORY

Why did William Penn settle the colony of Pennsylvania? Imagine if the president and Congress each raised an army and began fighting each other. That's roughly what happened in England in the 1640s, when the armies of King Charles I clashed with the armies of Parliament in several years of civil war. Parliament's forces finally triumphed, and their strict Puritan leader, Oliver Cromwell, set up a new government. Cromwell's efforts to broadly reform government and society met with resistance, however, and after his death the monarchy was restored under King Charles II.

During the civil wars, Admiral William Penn the Elder at first supported Parliament but secretly switched sides, possibly giving ships and loans to help restore the monarchy. After the Restoration, the king knighted Admiral Penn. When Penn died in 1670, he was owed a substantial sum of money by King Charles.

Penn's son William had been a problem for his patriotic father. Inspired by a traveling preacher, the younger Penn had joined a new Christian sect known as the **Quakers**. A fervent Quaker, **William Penn** wrote dozens of books and pamphlets promoting his simple faith, social reform, and freedom of ideas. He boldly criticized power and wealth in society and in the English church. Like other Quakers, he was jailed for his beliefs.

Despite his clashes with English authorities, Penn was granted a large and valuable tract of land in North America, in payment for the debt owed to his father. Penn's land stretched across thickly forested hills west of the Delaware River. He named his new colony Pennsylvania, or "Penn's woods." It would be a refuge for Quakers and others suffering religious persecution.

◄ William Penn used pamphlets to attract settlers to his colony.

60

Teach the Main Idea

At Level

The Middle and Southern Colonies

1. **Teach** Ask students the Reading Focus questions to teach this section.

2. **Apply** Have students create an outline of the section using the heads as main points. Have students identify at least two main ideas under each of the blue subheadings.

3. **Review** Review student outlines as a class. Then guide students in a discussion of the differences between the establishment of the colonies discussed in this section and earlier colonies.

4. **Practice/Homework** Point out to students that King Charles II was using land in North America to reward his supporters. Have students write a short essay explaining why the English king thought he had the right to give away this land, and whether or not they believe he *really* had this right. **LS Verbal-Linguistic**

📓 Alternative Assessment Handbook, Rubric 37: Writing Assignments

A New Era of Colonization

During the English Civil War and the years of Oliver Cromwell's rule, little colonization occurred in America. With peace and stability came a new era of English colonization in the middle and southern part of the Atlantic coast of North America.

Charles II and the Restoration In 1660, two years after Cromwell died, a new Parliament invited the son of Charles I to become king. Charles II, "the merry monarch," rode into London, greeted by fireworks and dancing in the streets. His reign, from 1660 to 1685, is called the **Restoration** because it restored the English monarchy.

A new period of colonization began under Charles II. The king owed money and favors to those who had supported him during the civil war, including William Penn's father. What better way to repay those favors than to give gifts of land in America? Thus, the king established **proprietary colonies**, grants of land to loyal friends. The friends became Lords Proprietors of their colonies—that is, owners with executive powers. Four new proprietary colonies were established: New York, New Jersey, Carolina, and Pennsylvania. Unlike joint-stock companies, these new American colonies were governed not by investors or colonial legislatures but by their Lords Proprietors.

New Netherland becomes New York

One of Charles's first grants was to his brother James, the duke of York. It included the large swath of land between the Connecticut and Delaware rivers. The grant ignored the fact that the Dutch already claimed the area as New Netherland.

The town of New Amsterdam was a thriving settlement. Because of the Dutch colony's religious tolerance, some English settlers from New England, including Anne Hutchinson, had moved there.

Political tensions existed between England and the Netherlands, however. In addition, New Netherland had the <u>distinct</u> disadvantage of being located between English colonies in New England and those farther south. In 1664 an English fleet sailed into the harbor and demanded that New Netherland surrender.

Peter Stuyvesant, the unpopular governor of New Netherland, surrendered almost without a fight. The Dutch took the colony back briefly in 1673, but by 1674 New Netherland was firmly in English hands. James renamed it New York.

TIME LINE

Upheaval Causes English to Journey West

1642
Monarchists battled the armies of Parliament in the English Civil War, which raged until 1651.

1653
After the English Civil War, Oliver Cromwell brought unpopular reforms but encouraged tolerance of Puritans.

1640   1650   1660

1660
After the Restoration of Charles II to the monarchy, English colonization expanded in America.

Skills FOCUS   INTERPRETING TIME LINES

Upheaval delayed English colonization of America. *What events affected colonization by England?*
See Skills Handbook, p. H14

Differentiating Instruction

Above Level

Advanced Learners/GATE

Research Required

1. Organize the class into small groups. Have each group conduct research on the English Civil War. Groups should use the following questions to guide their research: What were the causes of the English Civil War? Who were the Roundheads and the Cavaliers? Who were the major participants in the English Civil War? What was accomplished by the civil war? What was life in England like under the Protectorate? What was the Restoration?

2. Have students within each group share the results of their research. Then have each group prepare an illustrated magazine feature about the English Civil War and Restoration. The feature should include a time line and a brief essay summarizing the research.

3. Have volunteers from each group share their features with the class.
   LS Interpersonal, Verbal-Linguistic

   Alternative Assessment Handbook, Rubric 19: Magazines

A New Era of Colonization

Identify What ethnic groups lived in New York? *English, Dutch, Scandinavians, Germans, French, Native Americans, and enslaved Africans*

Contrast How did New Jersey differ from other proprietary colonies? *Most proprietary colonies were grants given directly by the king. New Jersey was originally part of New York, which was granted by the king to his brother, who then gave it to two of his supporters, so they did not receive their grant directly from the king.*

📖 CRF: Biography: John Woolman

🗺 Map Transparency: Middle and Southern Colonies

Teaching Tip

Have students compare the map on this page with a modern map. How do they differ? *Carolina had not yet been split into North and South Carolina; Georgia had not been created.*

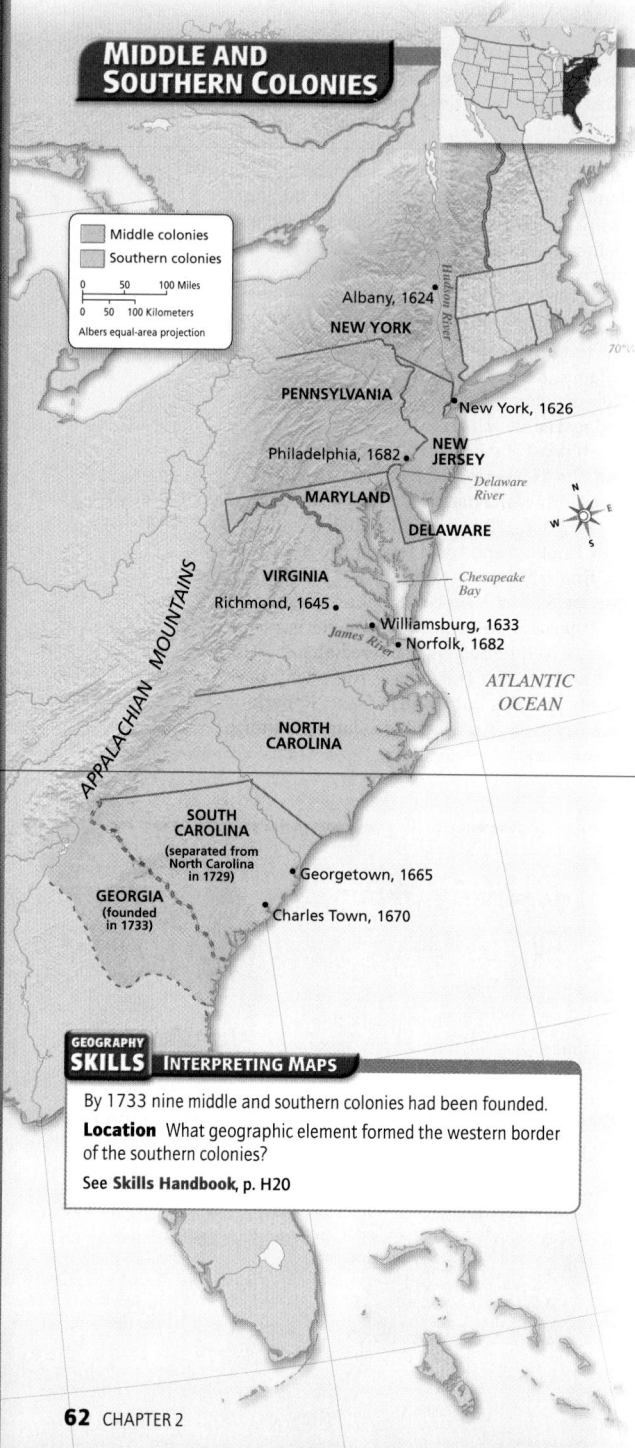

MIDDLE AND SOUTHERN COLONIES

- Middle colonies
- Southern colonies

0 50 100 Miles
0 50 100 Kilometers
Albers equal-area projection

Albany, 1624
NEW YORK
Hudson River
PENNSYLVANIA
New York, 1626
Philadelphia, 1682
NEW JERSEY
MARYLAND
Delaware River
DELAWARE
VIRGINIA
Chesapeake Bay
Richmond, 1645
Williamsburg, 1633
James River
Norfolk, 1682
ATLANTIC OCEAN
APPALACHIAN MOUNTAINS
NORTH CAROLINA
SOUTH CAROLINA
(separated from North Carolina in 1729)
Georgetown, 1665
GEORGIA
(founded in 1733)
Charles Town, 1670

GEOGRAPHY SKILLS INTERPRETING MAPS

By 1733 nine middle and southern colonies had been founded.

Location What geographic element formed the western border of the southern colonies?

See **Skills Handbook**, p. H20

New York was unusual in the diversity of its settlers. They included not only the English and Dutch but also Scandinavians, Germans, French, Native Americans, and enslaved Africans brought by the Dutch West India Company. James, a Roman Catholic, allowed religious tolerance.

At first New York did not have a representative assembly. That angered New Englanders who had settled on Long Island. Power was mainly in the hands of large land-owning families, both friends of James and the original Dutch "patroons," who had been given tracts of land in return for bringing settlers. Still, the colony grew and prospered under English rule. A treaty in 1684 made an alliance with the Iroquois, which protected the fur trade.

Soon after receiving his land, James gave a large tract of land south of the Hudson River to two proprietors. Sir George Carteret (cahr-tuh-RET) and Sir John Berkeley were his political allies. Carteret was from the Channel Island of Jersey and so named the new territory New Jersey. Over the next few years, arguments among settlers over rights and property occurred. Berkeley sold his portion of New Jersey to English Quakers, who settled the Delaware Valley. After continued disputes over land titles, the crown revoked the proprietors' charters. New York and New Jersey became royal colonies by the early 1700s.

READING CHECK **Summarizing** How did New York eventually become an English colony?

New Southern Colonies

Charles II gave large land grants to other friends and supporters. In charters issued in 1663 and 1665, eight men became the co-owners of Carolina. This land was part of the territory once claimed for Virginia, which stretched south to Spanish Florida. The name *Carolina* came from *Carolus*, the Latin form of *Charles*.

The Carolinas The new proprietors first gave themselves large estates. To attract settlers, they offered a representative assembly as well as religious toleration for all Christians. In that way, they hoped to draw settlers from other, less tolerant, colonies.

Settlement was slow, however, and some proprietors dropped out. One proprietor,

Collaborative Learning

At Level

Promoting Colonization

Materials construction paper, colored markers

1. Organize the class into five groups. Assign each group one of the colonies that began as a proprietary colony: New York, New Jersey, Carolina, and Pennsylvania. Assign one group Georgia, which was given by King George to 21 trustees.

2. Have each group use the information from the text to make a list of goals and objectives that the colonial founders, the proprietors

and trustees, had for their new colonies. Then have students create a list of actions that would be needed to achieve the goals.

3. Have each group create posters and pamphlets to attract English settlers to their new colony. Tell students to incorporate the goals and objectives they established in their posters and pamphlets. **LS Interpersonal, Visual-Spatial**

📖 Alternative Assessment Handbook, Rubrics 28: Posters; and 43: Writing to Persuade

Answers

Interpreting Maps *the Appalachian Mountains*

Reading Check *England demanded the Dutch surrender their colony of New Netherland; Duke of York established the colony of New York with his charter from King Charles.*

Anthony Ashley Cooper, persuaded others to pay to bring in boatloads of settlers. In 1670 they founded Charles Town (modern-day Charleston, South Carolina), the future capital of the colony.

The southern and northern parts of Carolina developed very differently. Southern Carolina had the port of Charles Town and the prosperous estates of aristocratic landowners. Large plantations grew up along the rivers. Rice and indigo were the major crops in Southern Carolina. They were shipped out of Charles Town along with other products.

Some plantation owners from the West Indies moved to the colony. They brought enslaved Africans with them. The colony's economy became dependent on slave labor.

By contrast, settlers in northern Carolina were mainly small farmers who did not import Africans as slaves. The region did not have a good harbor like the one at Charles Town.

In 1729 seven of the proprietors sold their interests in the land in the northern part of the colony to the Crown. The king then made North Carolina and South Carolina two separate royal colonies.

Georgia By the 1680s, English colonies lined most of the Atlantic coast south of New France. Colonists were moving steadily westward. The Spanish Empire held most of the Southeast and Southwest. Some English military experts wanted a military "buffer zone" between the Carolinas and Spanish Florida. That led to the establishment of Georgia, the last of the original 13 colonies.

The need for a buffer colony fit nicely with a plan being developed by an English general, **James Oglethorpe**. Oglethorpe was a humanitarian, a person who is interested in improving people's lives. As a member of the English Parliament, he had investigated the horrendous conditions in English prisons. He was especially concerned about honest people who were thrown in prison for being unable to pay their debts. Oglethorpe proposed starting a new colony for debtors to give them a new start in life.

In 1732 he and 20 other trustees received a charter for the Georgia colony from King George II. The next year, Oglethorpe arrived with a boatload of colonists and founded the city of Savannah, Georgia.

Unlike the founders of other colonies, the trustees of Georgia governed but did not own land or expect a profit. At first the trustees set out rigid rules for colonists regarding land ownership, slavery, and personal behavior. Eventually, those rules were relaxed. Slavery was legalized in 1751, the year before Georgia became a royal colony.

Georgia's early settlers included former debtors as well as impoverished craftspeople from Britain and religious refugees from Germany and Switzerland. The population grew, and by 1770 the colony had more than 20,000 people, nearly half of them enslaved Africans.

READING CHECK **Comparing and Contrasting** How were the colonies of Carolina and Georgia similar, and how were they different?

Quakers Settle Pennsylvania

As you have read, one of Charles II's land grants became the colony of Pennsylvania. Penn wanted the colony to be a haven for Quakers. From the king's perspective, it was a way to get rid of an unpopular group.

The Quakers Of all the various groups of Nonconformists—Protestants who did not follow the Church of England—the Quakers upset people the most. Officially called the Society of Friends, their name came from their founder, George Fox. He urged them to "tremble," or quake, "at the name of the Lord."

Quakers believed in direct, personal communication with God. They had no ministers and no hierarchy of priests and bishops, as in the Anglican and Roman Catholic churches. Instead of formal services with many rituals, Quakers held simple meetings in which members of the congregation rose to speak.

Quakers also believed in the equality of all men and women. That was a threat in a society with strict social classes based on wealth and power. Finally, they were pacifists who refused to fight in wars. For these beliefs, Quakers were jailed and persecuted in England. They were not entirely welcome in the existing American colonies, either, except in Rhode Island.

A tolerant colony Penn left for America in 1682 with a plan in mind for a "Holy Experiment" that would reflect his beliefs. He would

ACADEMIC VOCABULARY
perspective point of view

THE IMPACT TODAY

Technology
Since its construction in the early 1900s, the statue of William Penn atop Philadelphia's graceful City Hall remained the city's tallest structure. According to tradition, nothing could be taller. In 1987 the 548-foot limit was broken, as the first modern skyscraper rose above Penn.

Reading Focus

2 Why were new southern colonies founded? *Carolinas were land grants, part of the territory originally claimed for Virginia; Georgia was founded as a "buffer zone" between the Carolinas and Spanish Florida*

New Southern Colonies

Explain Why was Georgia founded? *as a buffer between English and Spanish colonies; to provide a new start in life for people who had been imprisoned for debt*

Evaluate Why do you think the northern and southern parts of Carolina attracted different types of landowners? *possible answer—southern part had port, was closer to the West Indies, easier for plantation owners to move with African slaves; north tended to be small farmers who did not use slaves*

Reading Focus

3 Why did the Quakers settle Pennsylvania? *William Penn established the colony to give fellow Quakers a haven from persecution*

Quakers Settle Pennsylvania

Identify Who was George Fox? *the founder of the Quakers*

Draw Conclusions Why would the Quakers' ideas about equality have seemed threatening to the king of England? *ideas of equality might threaten monarch and existing social order*

Skills Focus: Making Written Presentations   At Level

Reading Like a Historian Skill
A Colony for Convicts

1. Review the information in the text about the formation of Georgia with students.

2. Have students create a series of journal entries in which they weigh the pros and cons of moving from England to Georgia. Remind students that in the early 1700s living conditions in the colonies were uncertain and dangerous. For all who came to the colonies life was hard, and colonists lacked the basic amenities of city life in London or other large English cities.

3. Have volunteers share their journal entries. Then have students use the information to write a newspaper article summarizing why English citizens chose to move to Georgia.

LS Interpersonal, Verbal-Linguistic

Alternative Assessment Handbook, Rubric 23: Newspapers

Answers

Reading Check *Carolinas had wealthy landowners and small farmers; Georgia had former debtors, poor craftspeople, and religious refugees.*

63

Quakers Settle Pennsylvania

Recall Why were Germans attracted to Pennsylvania? *religious toleration for Amish and Mennonites; rich farmland*

Analyze Why did William Penn allow people of other religions to settle in Pennsylvania? *He believed in religious tolerance and wanted the colony to grow and prosper.*

❹ Why was Maryland founded? *as a haven for Catholics and source of personal wealth for Lord Baltimore*

The Founding of Maryland

Recall Where did George Calvert try to settle before he received his grant on Chesapeake Bay? *first in what is now Newfoundland in Canada, then at Jamestown*

Evaluate Which group had the most to gain by the passage of the Toleration Act, Catholics or Protestants? Why? *possible answer—Catholics; although Maryland was founded as a refuge for Catholics, the majority of the settlers were Protestants, who might have passed laws discriminating against the Catholic minority*

📄 American History Outline Maps: The Thirteen Colonies

📄 CRF: History and Geography Activity: The Thirteen Colonies

Answers

American Religious Liberty *it encouraged tolerance, since so many religious groups fled intolerance in Europe*

Reading Check *religious persecution and war throughout Europe that ruined farms and trade*

American Religious Liberty

Promoting Religious Tolerance

The Reformation in Europe triggered tense, sometimes violent conflicts among members of various Christian sects. The upheaval forced thousands of Europeans to flee their home countries. Many came to America and chose to settle in the Middle Colonies.

The Dutch were known for their religious tolerance, and Dutch settlers in New York and New Jersey continued this practice under English rule. Other settlers in these colonies included Lutherans from Sweden, Huguenots from France, and Jews from Portugal.

Pennsylvania, founded by Quakers on the principle of religious tolerance, attracted many groups, including Presbyterians, Amish, and Mennonites. In Delaware, the succession of Swedish, Dutch, and English rule, with their varying religions, promoted tolerance.

Today, the First Amendment guarantees freedom of religion. This tradition, begun in Rhode Island, was strengthened in the diverse Middle Colonies.

Making Comparisons How did changes in governing powers affect religious tolerance in the Middle Colonies?

A woman offers a religious testimony at this Quaker meeting from the mid-1600s.

build a new city, with spacious streets laid out in an orderly grid pattern. He called it Philadelphia, Greek for "City of Brotherly Love."

One enthusiastic Quaker settler, Gabriel Thomas, described how the city grew:

HISTORY'S VOICES

❝ Since that time, the Industrious (nay Indefatigable) Inhabitants have built a Noble and Beautiful City, and called it Philadelphia, which contains about two thousand Houses, all Inhabited, and most of them Stately, and of Brick, generally three Stories high, after the Mode in London, and as many as several Families in each . . . ❞

—*An Historical and Geographical Account of the Province and Country of Pennsylvania, in America* (1698)

Throughout the 1600s, while wars in Europe ruined farms and trade and religious clashes caused social upheaval, Penn advertised the colony widely. He offered opportunities and land at reasonable prices.

Members of small German Protestant sects such as the Amish and Mennonites were happy to find religious tolerance in Pennsylvania. The colony's rich farmlands attracted thousands of other Germans. Their numbers soon reached about 100,000, roughly one third of Pennsylvania's population.

After a 1685 law ended religious tolerance in France, some 15,000 French Protestants, called Huguenots, fled to America. Many of these skilled and well-educated people settled in Philadelphia and other colonial cities.

Like Roger Williams in Rhode Island, Penn recognized the Native Americans' right to the land. In 1682 he made an agreement with the Delawares, who sold him land as a way of protecting themselves against the Iroquois.

While Pennsylvania grew and prospered, some people were unhappy with Penn's one-man rule. In 1701, before returning to England, Penn granted a Charter of Liberties, which set up a representative assembly.

Delaware In 1638 a small colony of Swedes settled near what is now the city of Wilmington, Delaware. Swedish rule was brief. In 1655 the Dutch took New Sweden. The colony was later seized by England.

When William Penn received his original land grant in America, he was informed that it lacked access to the Atlantic Ocean. So in 1682 he persuaded the duke of York to make him proprietor of an area along the Delaware River and bay, which would later become the colony of Delaware. Control of these waterways would provide a major trade route for ships going in and out of the port of Pennsylvania.

READING CHECK **Identifying Cause and Effect** What events in Europe encouraged immigration to Pennsylvania?

Skills Focus: Interpreting Historical Maps
At Level

Social Studies Skill
The Pennsylvania Experiment
Research Required

1. Unlike most colonial cities, Philadelphia was a planned city. Organize the class into small groups, and have each group research the early history of Philadelphia. Students should look for a historical map that shows the plan of the city; descriptions of the early city; a list of Philadelphia "firsts." Have each group compile its information into a collage. Have students illustrate their collages with maps of the city as it was designed by William Penn and pictures of early colonial buildings.

2. Ask volunteers to share their group's collages and historical maps with the class.

3. Have students locate a modern map of Philadelphia. Compare it to see how the city has changed. **LS Interpersonal, Visual-Spatial**

📄 Alternative Assessment Handbook, Rubrics 8: Collages; and 21: Map Reading

The Founding of Maryland

The founding of the Church of England as the nation's official church made life difficult for many Roman Catholics in England. Although they were a small minority, English Catholics included some influential families. When George Calvert, the first **Lord Baltimore**, converted to Catholicism, thereby ending his political career, he sought land in America, as a haven for Catholics and for personal wealth.

In the 1620s Calvert founded a settlement in modern-day Newfoundland, Canada, but found it too cold. He traveled to Jamestown but was banned because of his religion. He then asked King Charles I for land near the broad Chesapeake Bay. He died before it was granted, but in 1632, his son Cecilius Calvert, also Lord Baltimore, received the rights. His new colony was named Maryland, perhaps for Queen Henrietta Maria or for the biblical Virgin Mary.

In fact, Maryland attracted many more Protestant settlers than Catholic ones, and clashes between the groups were common. As a result, in 1649 the colonial assembly passed the **Toleration Act**. It protected the right of all Christians to practice their religion.

READING CHECK **Making Inferences** What made English Catholics want to immigrate to America?

THE ENGLISH COLONIES IN AMERICA

Joint-stock colonies were established by groups of investors hoping to make a profit.	Virginia (settled 1607) Plymouth Colony (settled 1620)
Self-governing colonies were run independently of the king or of any joint-stock company.	Massachusetts Bay Colony (settled 1630) Rhode Island (settled 1636) Connecticut (settled 1635; Hooker 1636)
Proprietary colonies were founded by private individuals, or Lord Proprietors, who were granted the power to make and execute laws.	Maine* (settled 1623) New Hampshire (settled 1623) New York (settled 1624; English 1664) New Jersey (settled 1624; charter 1664) Maryland (charter 1632) Pennsylvania (settled 1682) Delaware (English 1664; to Penn 1682) Carolinas (charters 1663–65; divided 1712) Georgia (charter 1732) * Part of Massachusetts 1691–1820
Royal colonies were under the direct control of the king of England, who appointed a governor over the colony.	The following later became royal colonies: Virginia (1624) New Hampshire (1679) New York (1685) Massachusetts (1691) New Jersey (1702) South Carolina (1721) North Carolina (1729) Georgia (1752)

SECTION 4 ASSESSMENT

go.hrw.com
Online Quiz
Keyword: SD7 HP2

Reviewing Ideas, Terms, and People

1. a. Identify What events helped revive English colonization of America?
b. Analyze What effect did Charles II have on settlement patterns in the region south of New England?
c. Evaluate In giving proprietary colonies to his supporters, what assumptions did Charles II make about the land?

2. a. Describe What two reasons did **James Oglethorpe** have for founding the Georgia colony?
b. Compare How did the economies in the northern and southern parts of Carolina differ?

3. a. Recall Who were the **Quaker** people, and why were they persecuted in England?
b. Make Generalizations In what ways was Pennsylvania unique among the colonies?
c. Rate How important were location and natural resources in Pennsylvania's development? Explain.

4. a. Identify Who was **Lord Baltimore**?
b. Make Inferences Why do you suppose Catholics wanted to leave England after the founding of the Church of England?
c. Rate How did Maryland's **Toleration Act** compare with the practice of religious tolerance in Pennsylvania?

Critical Thinking

5. Identifying Supporting Details Copy the chart below and identify the groups of colonists in Pennsylvania.

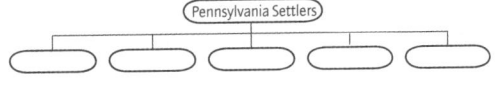

Pennsylvania Settlers

FOCUS ON WRITING

6. Persuasive Write an advertisement that will persuade new settlers to move to your colony.

EUROPEAN COLONIES IN AMERICA **65**

Section 4 Assessment Answers

1. a. the end of war in England and restoration of the monarchy
b. gave large land grants to friends and supporters
c. that it was his land to give away

2. a. wanted to protect South Carolina from Spain and provide a new life for debtors
b. South—slavery, port of Charles Town, large plantations; North—small farmers, no harbor, did not import slaves

3. a. belief in direct personal communication with God, pacifism, equality of the sexes
b. religious tolerance
c. very important; rich land helped settlers become successful farmers

4. a. founder of Maryland
b. to practice religion, avoid persecution
c. Toleration Act protected the right of all Christians to practice their religion; religious tolerance accepted all religions.

5. German Protestants, Amish, Mennonites, French Protestants, and Quakers

6. possible answer—get land at reasonable prices; opportunity for wealth, freedom

---

Representations of Pocahontas

Historical Context The documents below provide different artistic perspectives on the historical figure of Pocahontas.

Task Examine the documents and answer the questions that follow. Then you will be asked to write an essay about the portrayals of Pocahontas, using facts from the documents and from the chapter to support the position you take in your thesis statement.

Info to Know

Engraving of Pocahontas The original engraving on which this painting is based has a Latin inscription around the portrait. It refers to Pocahontas's real name, Matoaka. Pocahontas was a nickname. It means "Little Wanton," a playful, frolicsome young girl.

Pocahontas Pocahontas was a popular figure in the middle of the nineteenth century, when this painting was made. She represented the "civilizing" effect contact with Europe was supposed to have had on the American continent.

MISCONCEPTION ALERT

The story about Pocahontas saving John Smith's life comes from a memoir Smith wrote years later. It may be a complete fabrication, or it may be based on Smith's unfamiliarity with Native American rituals. The Powhatans had a traditional mock "execution and salvation" ceremony. Pocahontas's actions in saving Smith may have been a part of such a ritual.

Recent Scholarship

According to anthropologist Helen Rountree, at the time when she met Captain John Smith, Pocahontas probably would have had a shaved head. Because the women of her tribe did the hard physical labor, she would have been "built like a piano mover." And instead of wearing a deerskin minidress, at that age the real Pocahontas would probably have worn nothing.

The Colonial Gazette,
mayflowerfamilies.com

DOCUMENT **1**

Only one known image of Pocahontas was created during her lifetime. It was this engraving made in 1616, after she had married John Rolfe and moved to England. The purpose of this image was to show Pocahontas as an example of the ways in which Native Americans could become "civilized." For years this was a popular model for images of Pocahontas.

DOCUMENT **2**

This large painting by printmaker Henry Brueckner was used in a popular pamphlet about Pocahontas. The image depicts the marriage of John Rolfe and Pocahontas as a great community affair, bringing together Native American and English leaders in an elaborate ceremony in a Christian church. The painting portrays several well-known historical figures in attendance at the ceremony. In reality, most of these officials were not even in the Virginia colony at the time of Pocahontas's wedding. Although Pocahontas did become a devout Christian, her wedding was more likely a simple affair that took place in a plain wooden church, attended by few people.

Skills Focus: Analyzing Visuals

At Level

Reading Like a Historian Skill
Historical Paintings

Research Required

1. Have students search reliable Internet sites or traditional print sources for pictures illustrating the life of Pocahontas. There are pictures showing her saving John Smith, being baptized, getting married, and arriving in England.

2. Have each student choose one picture that they would like to write about. Have students print out or copy their selected picture and write an essay about the event it depicts.

In their essays students should address the historical accuracy—or lack of it—of their chosen picture. Students should also look for any symbolism that may be present in the picture.

3. Have volunteers share their pictures and essays with the class. **LS** Visual-Spatial, Logical-Mathematical

📖 Alternative Assessment Handbook, Rubrics 16: Judging Information; and 42: Writing to Inform

DOCUMENT 3

In 1995 Walt Disney Studios released a cartoon version of the Pocahontas legend. The cartoon artists consulted with many experts on Powhatan history to attempt to create images that most accurately reflected Powhatan clothing and culture at the time that Pocahontas lived.

The story, however, changed many of the facts about Pocahontas, including making her a young adult and creating a romance between her and John Smith. In reality, Pocahontas was only about 12 years old when she met Smith, and there was never any indication of a romantic relationship between them. This image from the Disney cartoon "Pocahontas" shows the heroic characters of John Smith and Pocahontas.

Skills Focus: READING LIKE A HISTORIAN

1. a. Describe Refer to Document 1. What details indicate that Pocahontas adopted English culture?

b. Interpret What conclusions might English people have drawn from this depiction of Pocahontas?

2. a. Identify Refer to Document 2. What types of people are shown attending Pocahontas's wedding?

b. Analyze Why did the artist portray the wedding as a large community affair when it probably was not?

3. a. Identify Refer to Document 3. What is significant about the items each character is holding?

b. Elaborate Why do you think the cartoonists tried to accurately reflect aspects of Powhatan culture, yet changed key events about the life of Pocahontas?

4. Document-Based Essay Question Consider the question below and form a thesis statement. Using examples from Documents 1, 2, and 3, create an outline and write a short essay supporting your position.
In what ways have images of Pocahontas been used to reflect different messages about contact between Native Americans and the English?

See **Skills Handbook,** pp. H28–H29, H30

Skills Focus: Evaluating Historical Interpretations

At Level

Reading Like a Historian Skill
Creating Legends

Background Tell students that some scholars doubt the truth of the story of Pocahontas saving the life of Captain John Smith; the version of Pocahontas's story that Disney presented took even more liberties with the truth.

1. Guide the class in a discussion of the ways in which legends grow up around historical people. Ask students what legends they can think of about people in American history.

How do these legends shape our ideas about those people? How do they teach lessons?

2. Have students think of historical figures for whom they could invent similar "legends" to help illustrate character traits. Then have each student write a fictionalized one-page account in which they create a legend. **LS** **Logical-Mathematical, Verbal-Linguistic**

📖 Alternative Assessment Handbook, Rubrics 16: Judging Information; and 41: Writing to Express

Info to Know

John Rolfe and Pocahontas John Rolfe was not Pocahontas's first husband. She was married in 1610 to a Powhatan warrior named Kocoum.

Pocahontas and John Rolfe had one son, Thomas. When Pocahontas died in 1617, during the family's visit to England, John left Thomas in England, but John returned to Virginia. They never saw each other again. Thomas did not return to Virginia until 1635, when he was 20. When Chief Powhatan died in 1618, there were rumors among his people that Thomas would become chief. This turned out to be untrue, but Powhatan did leave Thomas thousands of acres of land along the James River. Thomas Rolfe also inherited the plantation where he was born, Varina.

Answers

Reading Like a Historian
1. a. *her style of dress and adornment;* **b.** *possible answer—that Native Americans would willingly adopt English customs;* **2. a.** *Native Americans and English men and women;* **b.** *possible answers—wanted to show intermingling of cultures; make the wedding a grand affair;* **3. a.** *Pocahontas is holding a branch, possibly to symbolize peace; John Smith is holding a weapon, to symbolize aggression;* **b.** *so that the story would be more agreeable to an audience;* **4.** *possible answer—as an English lady, a Native American princess, and the heroine in a children's movie*

67

Answers

Visual Summary

Review and Inquiry Have students use the Holt outline map, Territorial Claims in North America, to point out where European colonies founded by Spain, the Netherlands, England, and France were located.

📖 American History Outline Maps: Territorial Claims in North America, 1754 and 1763

📋 Quick Facts Transparency: European Colonies in America

Reviewing Key Terms and People

1. missionary
2. Hernan Cortés
3. Francis Drake
4. Powhatan
5. indentured servants
6. Bacon's Rebellion
7. Captain John Smith
8. Roger Williams
9. Puritans
10. Great Migration
11. William Penn

Comprehension and Critical Thinking

12. **a.** spread Christianity, find wealth and win fame for their adventures; "God, gold, and glory"
    b. first as laborers, later as slaves
    c. possible answer—better than the Spanish, since the French were trading with Native Americans for furs and would want to treat them well to continue to get furs

13. **a.** bad; not enough food because of raids by Native Americans, who also prevented settlers from hunting
    b. America's first legislature
    c. possible answer—England's method and reason was better because they were not as focused on gaining wealth and fame, more concerned with providing people with better opportunities

Visual Summary: European Colonies in America

England
- Major explorers in North America: Cabot, Drake, Raleigh
- Colonies founded along Atlantic coast

France
- Major explorers in North America: Cartier, Champlain, La Salle
- Colonies founded in Quebec and Louisiana

Spain
- Major explorers in North America: Ponce de León, Cabeza de Vaca, de Soto, Coronado
- Colonies founded in American Southeast and Southwest

The Netherlands
- Major explorer in North America: Hudson
- Colonies founded in New Netherland and Delaware (both later become English colonies)

THE GRANGER COLLECTION, NEW YORK

Reviewing Key Terms and People

Identify the correct term or person from the chapter that best fits each of the following descriptions.

1. Person sent by a church to teach and convert others to a religion
2. Conquistador who conquered the Aztec peoples
3. English explorer who plundered Spanish ships and towns
4. Leader of a major Indian confederacy near the Jamestown colony
5. People who worked for a certain number of years in return for being brought to America
6. An uprising of unemployed and unhappy colonists in Virginia
7. English explorer who helped the Jamestown colony survive
8. English colonist who helped found Rhode Island
9. Protestants who wanted to purify the established Church of England
10. The flood of English immigrants who came to New England from the 1620s to the 1640s
11. English colonist who started a colony to give Quakers a refuge from religious persecution

Comprehension and Critical Thinking

SECTION 1 *(pp. 40–45)*

12. **a. Recall** What were the three main goals of the Spanish conquistadors?
    b. Analyze How did Spanish conquistadors and missionaries treat Native Americans?
    c. Predict How will French settlers probably get along with Native Americans? Why?

SECTION 2 *(pp. 46–50)*

13. **a. Describe** What was life like in Jamestown during the starving time?
    b. Make Generalizations What is the historical significance of Virginia's House of Burgesses?

14. **a.** agreed to be ruled by laws and government chosen by the group; aboard the *Mayflower*
    b. They established laws and policies that did not allow for religious freedom.
    c. government and church were separate

15. **a.** Pennsylvania and Maryland
    b. Colonies established by Charles II were proprietary and ruled by their owners rather than investors or colonial legislatures.
    c. possible answer—to create a "new" version of their home countries

History's Impact video program

Review the video to answer the closing question: How has a desire to worship freely influenced American history?

c. Rank Think about Spain's and England's reasons and methods for establishing colonies in the Americas. Was one better than the other? Why or why not?

SECTION 3 *(pp. 51–56)*

14. a. Define What was the central agreement of the Mayflower Compact, and where were the settlers when they signed it?

b. Contrast How did the Puritans' laws and government in the Massachusetts Bay Colony conflict with their reasons for moving to America?

c. Elaborate How was Rhode Island different from most of the other colonies?

SECTION 4 *(pp. 60–65)*

15. a. Identify Which two colonies were the most tolerant of other religions?

b. Contrast How were the colonies established under England's King Charles II different from earlier American colonies?

c. Evaluate The names of many towns and colonies started with "New" (New Amsterdam, New York, New Jersey). What does this say about Europeans' intentions in the Americas?

Using the Internet

go.hrw.com
Practice Online
Keyword: SD7 CH2

16. The development of each of the English colonies was shaped by its geography and by the people who lived there. Using the keyword above, do research to learn more about one of the colonies. Then, from the viewpoint of a colonist, use a word processing program to write a diary entry about how your colony is changing over time. Note how the land is being put to use. Describe how factors such as religion, culture, values, family life, and work are affecting the colony's development.

Analyzing Primary Sources

Reading Like a Historian When John Smith became the leader of Jamestown, he told the colonists:

❝You must obey this now for a Law, that he that will not worke shall not eate (except by sickness he be disabled) for the labours of thirtie or fortie honest and industrious men shall not be consumed to maintaine an hundred and fiftie idle loyterers.❞

—John Smith, *Generall Historie of Virginia, New England, & the Summer Isles*

17. Describe What problem was Smith trying to address in this passage?

18. Evaluate Was Smith's new law too harsh? Why or why not?

Critical Reading

Read the passage in Section 3 that begins with the heading "Relations with Native Americans." Then answer the question that follows.

19. The last paragraph of the passage says that King Philip's War was "costly for both sides." This means

A. the war was fast and easy for both sides.

B. the colonists suffered very little.

C. both sides lost a lot in the war.

D. Native Americans had few losses.

WRITING FOR THE SAT ✎

Think about the following issue.

During most of the 1600s and early 1700s, English subjects were required to support the Church of England by paying taxes and by attending services regularly—regardless of their personal beliefs. Many nonconformists, such as Puritans and Quakers, left England for the colonies in pursuit of religious freedom.

20. Assignment Given the uncertainty of life in the English colonies, what does it say about many colonists' religious faith that they were willing to move to the colonies? Write a short essay in which you develop your position on this issue. Support your point of view with reasoning and examples from your studies.

Answers

Using the Internet

16. Go to the HRW Web site and enter the keyword shown to access a rubric for this activity.

KEYWORD: SD7 CH2

Analyzing Primary Sources

17. lazy workers in the colony

18. possible answer—no; the colonists needed to know that in order to survive they needed to work; he was trying to motivate them to work so they could survive

Critical Reading

19. C

Writing for the SAT

20. Possible answers should include details such as strong, committed faith, willing to endure the uncertainty and danger of settling a new continent.

A rubric for this activity is provided in the CRF: Writing for the SAT Activity: Working in America.

History's Impact
Video Program

Many immigrants to America have come here in order to practice their religion and worship freely.

Review and Assessment Resources

Review and Reinforce

📋 CRF: Chapter Review Activity

📽 Quick Facts Transparencies:
The English Colonies in America, European Colonies in America

🔊 Spanish Chapter Summaries Audio CD Program

🌐 Online Chapter Summaries in Spanish

OSP Holt PuzzlePro; Quiz Show for ExamView

💿 Quiz Game CD-ROM

Assess

📋 PASS: Chapter Test, Forms A and B

📋 Alternative Assessment Handbook

OSP ExamView Test Generator, Chapter Test

💿 Differentiated Instruction Modified Worksheets and Tests CD-ROM: Chapter Test

HOAP Holt Online Assessment Program (in the Premier Online Edition)

Reteach/Intervene

📋 Interactive Reader and Study Guide

📋 Differentiated Instruction Teacher Management System: Lesson Plans for Differentiated Instruction

💿 Differentiated Instruction Modified Worksheets and Tests CD-ROM: Chapter Test

💿 Interactive Skills Tutor CD-ROM

go.hrw.com
Online Resources

KEYWORD: SD7 CH2

Chapter 3 Planning Guide

Colonial Life

Chapter Overview	Reproducible Resources	Technology Resources
CHAPTER 3 pp. 70–99 **Overview: In this chapter, students will analyze how England's colonies developed, both economically and politically, and the strains that began to appear between the colonists and Britain.**	**Differentiated Instruction Teacher Management System:*** • Instructional Benchmarking Guides • Lesson Plans for Differentiated Instruction **Interactive Reader and Study Guide:** Chapter Summary* **Chapter Resource File:*** • Focus on Writing: Tensions Between Great Britain and its Colonies • Social Studies Skills Activity: Summarizing • Chapter Review Activity **American History Outline Maps** **Pre-AP Activities Guide for American History*** **Reading Like a Historian Toolkit**	**Live Ink® Online Reading Help** **Student Edition on Audio CD Program** **Differentiated Instruction Modified Worksheets and Tests CD-ROM** **Interactive Skills Tutor CD-ROM** **United States History Primary Source Library CD-ROM** **Power Presentations with Video CD-ROM** **History's Impact: American History Video Program (VHS/DVD):** Colonial Life **Online Chapter Summaries in Spanish** **Graphic Organizer Transparencies**
Section 1: **Political Life in the Colonies** **The Main Idea:** British mercantilist policies and political issues helped shape the development of the American colonies.	**Differentiated Instruction Teacher Management System:** Section 1 Lesson Plan* **Interactive Reader and Study Guide:** Section 1 Summary* **Chapter Resource File:*** • Vocabulary Builder Activity, Section 1	**Daily Bellringer Transparency:** Section 1* **Quick Facts Transparency:** Rising Tensions Between England and America, 1651–1689* **Daily Test Practice Transparency:** Section 1*
Section 2: **The Colonial Economy** **The Main Idea:** A commerce-based economy developed in the northern colonies, while the southern colonies developed an agricultural economy.	**Differentiated Instruction Teacher Management System:** Section 2 Lesson Plan* **Interactive Reader and Study Guide:** Section 2 Summary* **Chapter Resource File:*** • Vocabulary Builder Activity, Section 2	**Daily Bellringer Transparency:** Section 2* **Map Transparency:** Triangular Trade* **Daily Test Practice Transparency:** Section 2*
Section 3: **America's Emerging Culture** **The Main Idea:** Enlightenment ideas and the Great Awakening brought new ways of thinking to the colonists, and a unique American culture developed.	**Differentiated Instruction Teacher Management System:** Section 3 Lesson Plan* **Interactive Reader and Study Guide:** Section 3 Summary* **Chapter Resource File:*** • Vocabulary Builder Activity, Section 3	**Daily Bellringer Transparency:** Section 3* **Quick Facts Transparency:** Key Political Thinkers of the European Enlightenment* **Daily Test Practice Transparency:** Section 3*
Section 4: **The French and Indian War** **The Main Idea:** The French and Indian War established British dominance in North America but put a strain on the relationship with the colonists.	**Differentiated Instruction Teacher Management System:** Section 4 Lesson Plan* **Interactive Reader and Study Guide:** Section 4 Summary* **Chapter Resource File:*** • Vocabulary Builder Activity, Section 4	**Daily Bellringer Transparency:** Section 4* **Map Transparencies:** The French and Indian War in New York, European Claims in North America* **Daily Test Practice Transparency:** Section 4*

 go.hrw.com    Print Resource    Transparency

LS Learning Styles    Audio CD   ● CD-ROM

 Video   **SE** Student Edition   **TE** Teacher's Edition

OSP One-Stop Planner CD-ROM

*also on One-Stop Planner CD-ROM

Review, Assessment, Intervention

 Quick Facts Transparencies: Rising Tensions Between England and America, Key Political Thinkers of the European Enlightenment, Colonial Life

 **Spanish Chapter Summaries Audio CD Program**

 **Progress Assessment Support System (PASS):** Chapter Test*

● **Differentiated Instruction Modified Worksheets and Tests CD-ROM:** Modified Chapter Test

OSP **One-Stop Planner CD-ROM:** ExamView Test Generator (English/Spanish)

HOAP **Holt Online Assessment Program (HOAP),** in the Holt Premier Online Student Edition

 PASS: Section 1 Quiz*
 Online Quiz: Section 1
 Alternative Assessment Handbook

 PASS: Section 2 Quiz*
 Online Quiz: Section 2
 Alternative Assessment Handbook

 PASS: Section 3 Quiz*
 Online Quiz: Section 3
 Alternative Assessment Handbook

 PASS: Section 4 Quiz*
 Online Quiz: Section 4
 Alternative Assessment Handbook

HOLT
History's Impact
American History Video Program (VHS/DVD)
Colonial Life

 **RESOURCES**

The following resources were developed to help North Carolina educators teach the standards and objectives of North Carolina's eleventh grade standard course of study in United States history.

• United States history EOC Test Prep Workbook
• Teacher's Support System
• North Carolina One-Stop Planner

And be sure to direct your students to **go.hrw.com** for online access to the EOC Test Prep Workbook.

go.hrw.com
EOC Test Prep
KEYWORD: SE7 NC

Holt Online Learning

go.hrw.com
Teacher Resources
KEYWORD: SD7 TEACHER

go.hrw.com
Student Resources
KEYWORD: SD7 CH3

• Document-based Questions
• Interactive Multimedia Activities
• Current Events
• Chapter-based Internet Activities
• and more!

Holt Premier
Online Student Edition
Complete online support for interactivity, assessment, and reporting

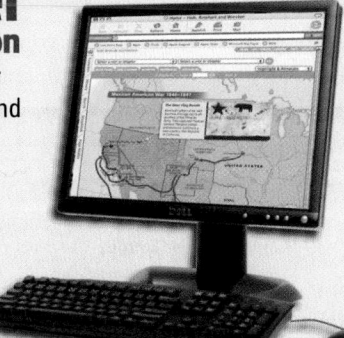

• Interactive Maps and Notebook
• Standardized Test Prep
• Homework Practice and Research Activities Online

CHAPTER 3 PLANNING GUIDE

Before You Teach

The Big Picture
Jesús F. de la Teja

Government by Dissent The religious struggles of seventeenth-century England contributed much to the development of colonial government. As English government changed hands between Catholic and Anglican kings and Puritan commonwealth, the rules, conditions, and status of the colonies changed. Colonials often found themselves having to provide for their own defense, law enforcement, and commercial regulation. In time, they came to distinguish between loyalty to England—which they approved—and submission to Parliament—which they resented.

Evolution of the Peculiar Institution When Englishmen established Jamestown, slavery had been a dead institution for centuries back home. Proof of this rests in the treatment that the first shipload of Africans to Virginia received in 1619—they were considered indentured servants. Because Africans were acquired, transported, and disposed of differently than European indentured servants, and because they obviously were not European, attitudes toward them slowly changed. Another contributing factor to the development of slavery was Africans' intrinsic value as property—they were assets against which money could be borrowed. Working and living with them made them people, but buying and selling them made them property—a peculiar institution, indeed!

Diversity in Colonial America From the beginning, America has been an amazingly diverse society. While the predominance of English culture and institutions is without question, the interactions of New and Old World peoples created a cultural dynamic in America that made it unlike anywhere else in the world. The Dutch in New York, Germans in Pennsylvania, and Africans in the southern colonies are only some of the groups that started us on the road to becoming a nation of immigrants.

Recent Scholarship

Food in the Colonies Of the three necessities of life—food, shelter, clothing—none is more diverse and culturally profuse than food. James McWilliams, in *A Revolution in Eating: How the Quest for Food Shaped America* (2005), draws out how the distinctive cuisine of each of British America's regions—New England, Chesapeake, Carolinas, and middle colonies—reflected differences in the European-origin population, the importance of African slavery and staple crops to its economy, and relations with the local native peoples. He concludes by pointing out food's role in the coming of the American Revolution. A fascinating trip through early U.S. cultural history.

Differentiating Instruction

 Differentiated Instruction Teacher Management System
- Lesson Plans for Differentiated Instruction
- Differentiated Instructional Benchmarking Guides
- Interactive Reader and Study Guide

 Spanish Chapter Summaries Audio CD Program

 Online Chapter Summaries in Spanish

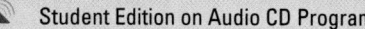 Student Edition on Audio CD Program

 Differentiated Instruction Modified Worksheets and Tests CD-ROM
- Vocabulary Flash Cards
- Modified Vocabulary Builder Activities
- Modified Chapter Review Activity
- Modified Chapter Test

OSP One-Stop Planner CD-ROM
- ExamView Test Generator (English and Spanish)
- PuzzlePro
- Quiz Show for ExamView
- Transparencies and Videos

TE Differentiated Activities in the Teacher's Edition
- Governor Andros and the Colonists, p. 74
- Northern Colonial Economics, p. 78
- The Enlightenment and the United States, p. 85
- France in North America, p. 91

Reading Like a Historian
Sam Wineburg

History and Changing Symbolism

In one of my research studies, I presented a group of high school students with pictures from the 1967 march on the Pentagon in which 50,000 antiwar demonstrators clashed with National Guardsmen in Washington, D.C. In one photo, a flower-clutching demonstrator places a carnation in the barrel of a Guardsman's rifle, inches away. While some students had no trouble understanding the symbolism—invoking the phrase "flower power" or noting the contrast between "war and peace"—others were stymied. "Someone must've died," guessed one. "It seems like he's giving a eulogy, like at a funeral," said another.

The Shelf Life of Symbols

Symbols have a shelf life, radiating meaning for a fixed time but then losing force. Like the flowers in this 1967 photo, symbolic meanings change and develop, with fashionable meanings fading and reverting to earlier, more stable ones.

A snake appears at the center of Benjamin Franklin's "Join or Die" cartoon, which appeared in the *Pennsylvania Gazette* on May 9, 1754, and which is shown on page 92 of our chapter. It is easy to grasp the basic meaning of a dismembered snake that must reconnect to survive. At the same time, few contemporary viewers will feel the resonance of this illustration in the same way as Franklin's intended readers.

The Meaning of the Snake

For many of us, the snake calls up other associations—the cunning (and later cursed) trickster that dupes Eve in the Garden of Eden; the snake as embodiment of danger, duplicity, and foreboding. Few today will gaze at the snake with the same reverence we associate with the bald eagle, our proud national symbol. Yet, this was precisely how many early Americans viewed the snake—not just any snake, of course, but the American Timber Rattlesnake, a species found only in North America.

On December 17, 1775, the *Pennsylvania Gazette* published a letter from "An American Guesser," recently identified as Franklin. In it, Franklin offers these observations on the rattler.

"I observed on one of the drums belonging to the marines . . . a Rattle-Snake, with this modest motto under it, 'Don't tread on me.' As I know it is the custom to have some device on the arms of every country, I supposed this may have been intended for the arms of America."

An Appropriate Symbol

Franklin then speculated why the rattler would be a fitting symbol for this country: it is found "in no other quarter of the world beside America"; its eyes "excelled in brightness" but it has no eyelids, making it "esteemed [as] an emblem of vigilance"; and perhaps most fitting, the rattler "never begins an attack, nor, when once engaged, ever surrenders." Franklin opposed the adoption of the eagle as national symbol, calling it "a bird of bad moral character."

The rattlesnake reappears during the American Revolution on the yellow "Gadsden flag" with the imperative "Don't Tread on Me." In 1778 it appeared again on a $20 bill from Georgia carrying the Latin motto, *Nemo me impune lacesset*, or, "No one will provoke me and get away with it."

Many students will be able to discern the basic idea of Franklin's "Join or Die" illustration. But only by digging deeper will they come to appreciate how Franklin's use of this symbol tapped into beliefs about the majesty and restraint of a creature that, today, inspires mainly fear and dread.

Standards Focus

Social Studies Competency Goals
Goal 1 The learner will identify, investigate, and assess the effectiveness of the institutions of the emerging republic.
1.03

The Big Idea and Essential Questions

To foster student understanding of this chapter's big idea, design your lesson to address each section's essential question.

Big Idea The English colonies established their own traditions of local government while maintaining ties with Great Britain.

Essential Questions

1. How did British policies and political issues shade the development of the American colonies?

2. How did the economies of the northern and southern colonies differ?

3. How did a unique American culture develop?

4. What were the effects of the French and Indian War on Britain's relationship with its colonists?

Key to Differentiating Instruction

Below Level

Basic-level activities designed for all students encountering new material

At Level

Intermediate-level activities designed for average students

Above Level

Challenging activities designed for honors and gifted-and-talented students

Standard English Mastery

Activities designed to improve standard English usage

70   CHAPTER 3

CHAPTER

3   1650–1763

Colonial Life

THE BIG PICTURE For more than 100 years, England's colonies in America grew steadily. Over time, the colonies developed their own economies, political systems, traditions of local government, and sense of self-reliance. But as time wore on, serious strains between the colonists and Britain began to appear.

North Carolina Standards

Social Studies Objectives
1.03 Assess commercial and diplomatic relationships with Britain, France, and other nations.

Language Arts Objectives
2.01 Research and analyze ideas, events, and/or movements related to United States culture by:
• locating facts and details for purposeful elaboration.

Skills FOCUS   READING LIKE A HISTORIAN

Bostonians graze their cattle and enjoy some recreation on Boston Common in this 1750 embroidery. Beacon Hill, home to many prominent residents, can be seen in the background. **Interpreting Visuals** In what ways do you think the city's common served the community?
See Skills Handbook, p. H30

70

U.S.

World

1643
Massachusetts, Plymouth, Connecticut, and New Haven colonies form the New England Confederation.

1650

1651
England passes the first of the Navigation Acts.

AN ACT
for the
Increase of Shipping
of the
NAVIGATION
NATION.

Introduce the Chapter

At Level

Colonial Life

1. Tell students that in the 1950s, the U.S. began a space program that has sent people to the moon. In 2004, President George W. Bush announced that the space program's next goal was to build a station on the moon and send people to Mars.

2. Guide students in a discussion of why Americans might someday want to establish new colonies in space. What might be gained from these colonies? Why might Americans want to move there? What challenges might new settlers face?

3. Have students write a letter to a friend in Europe from the perspective of an American colonist in the mid-1600s. Have students describe colonial life.

4. Tell students that in this chapter they will learn about life in the thirteen colonies that would eventually form the United States.
   LS Verbal-Linguistic

   Alternative Assessment Handbook, Rubrics 11: Discussions; and 25: Personal Letters

PHOTOGRAPH © 2005 MUSEUM OF FINE ARTS, BOSTON

• **Chapter Preview** •

HOLT
History's Impact
► **Video Program: Colonial Life**
See the Video Teacher's Guide for strategies for using the video segment.

Reading Like a Historian

An Embroidery of Life In early U.S. society, one of the few opportunities women had to express themselves creatively was through crafts such as embroidery, like the piece shown here. Scenes depicted in embroideries open a window to the everyday worlds of these women. African American women also produced craftwork. Pieces created for their personal use showed a strong African sense of design, allowing them to remain close to their roots even while enslaved.

1685
Charles II dies; his brother James becomes king of England.

1691
New charter makes Massachusetts, including Maine and Plymouth, a royal colony.

1701
England goes to war against Spain.

1715
After a reign of 72 years, King Louis XIV of France dies.

1739
British minister George Whitefield helps launch the Great Awakening with his preaching.

1754
The French and Indian War begins. Benjamin Franklin proposes the Albany Plan of Union to unite the colonies.

1759
Invading British forces capture the French Canadian stronghold of Quebec.

1763
The Treaty of Paris ends the Seven Years' War in Europe.

1670 | 1690 | 1710 | 1730 | 1750 | 1770

go.hrw.com
Online Resources

Chapter Resources:
KEYWORD: SD7 CH3

Teacher Resources:
KEYWORD: SD7 TEACHER

71

Explore the Time Line

1. When did England pass the first of the Navigation Acts? *1651*

2. Who proposed the Albany Plan of Union? *Benjamin Franklin*

3. Which two countries went to war in 1701? *England and Spain*

Info to Know

English Workers In the early 1600s, English laborers were paid very little. Several London workers reported that even though they and their families wore themselves out working long hard hours, they still only earned just enough to keep themselves alive.

Draw Conclusions Why might some English workers at the time have moved to a colony in North America? *possible answer—in hopes of finding a better life for themselves and their families*

Answers

Reading Like a Historian (p. 70)
possible answer—served as a marketplace, meeting space, and center of government

Bellringer

The Inside Story. . . Use the **Daily Bellringer Transparency** to help students answer the question.

📇 Daily Bellringer Transparency, Section 1

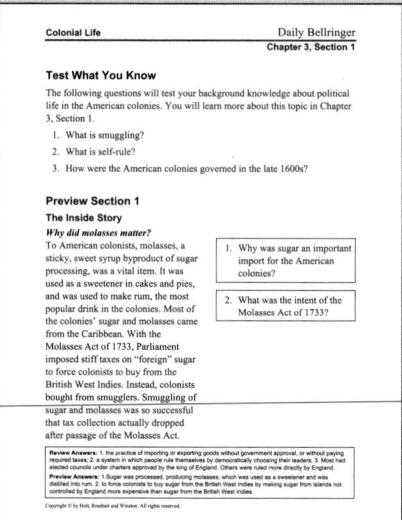

Colonial Life   Daily Bellringer
                                 Chapter 3, Section 1

Test What You Know

The following questions will test your background knowledge about political life in the American colonies. You will learn more about this topic in Chapter 3, Section 1.

1. What is smuggling?
2. What is self-rule?
3. How were the American colonies governed in the late 1600s?

Preview Section 1
The Inside Story
Why did molasses matter?
To American colonists, molasses, a sticky, sweet syrup byproduct of sugar processing, was a vital item. It was used as a sweetener in cakes and pies, and was used to make rum, the most popular drink in the colonies. Most of the colonies' sugar and molasses came from the Caribbean. With the Molasses Act of 1733, Parliament imposed stiff taxes on "foreign" sugar to force colonists to buy from the British West Indies. Instead, colonists bought from smugglers. Smuggling of sugar and molasses was so successful that tax collection actually dropped after passage of the Molasses Act.

| 1. Why was sugar an important import for the American colonies? |
| 2. What was the intent of the Molasses Act of 1733? |

Academic Vocabulary

Review with students the high-use academic terms in this section.

incentive motivational factor (p. 73)
prosperity economic well-being (p. 73)
consisted made up of (p. 76)

📝 CRF: Vocabulary Builder Activity, Section 1

Taking Notes

Increasing the amount of national wealth was the basis of mercantilism; colonies were supposed to be moneymaking institutions to build a nation's wealth; if the value of the goods a country exports is more than the value of the goods a country imports this creates a favorable balance of trade, which also contributes to national wealth

---

Political Life in the Colonies

BEFORE YOU READ

MAIN IDEA
British mercantilist policies and political issues helped shape the development of the American colonies.

READING FOCUS
1. What is mercantilism?
2. How did the Glorious Revolution and the English Bill of Rights affect political developments in the colonies?
3. How did government in the colonies change under the policy of salutary neglect?

KEY TERMS AND PEOPLE
mercantilism
balance of trade
Navigation Acts
Dominion of New England
William and Mary
Glorious Revolution
English Bill of Rights
confederation
salutary neglect

TAKING NOTES
As you read, take notes about the main principles of mercantilism. Record your notes in a graphic organizer like the one shown here.

National Wealth
Mercantilism
Colonies   Balance of Trade

THE INSIDE STORY

Why did molasses matter? Colonial merchants and ship captains knew that the rugged coast of New England had thousands of bays and coves where small boats could come ashore. That made it easy for smugglers to bring in goods and avoid certain British taxes. Smuggling made life much harder for British customs officials trying to enforce trade laws.

One of those trade laws was the Molasses Act of 1733. Molasses is a dark, sweet syrup made when raw sugar is processed. Colonists used it in cakes and pies and poured it over pancakes. Most important of all, molasses was distilled to make rum. Rum was the most popular drink in the colonies. The yearly consumption averaged more than four gallons per person! Rum was also one of the northern colonies' most valuable products, and many gallons were exported every year.

The Molasses Act made the colonists furious. They bought about half their molasses and sugar from planters in the Caribbean. The new law put a high tax on imports of such foreign sugar. Its goal was to make the colonists buy sugar from the British West Indies. Instead, smuggling became so widespread that tax revenues dropped. British officials decided not to try to enforce the act. ■

SMUGGLING MOLASSES

▼ A merchant ship loaded with goods is launched at Salem Harbor, Massachusetts.

PEABODY ESSEX MUSEUM, SALEM, MASSACHUSETTS

Teach the Main Idea

At Level

Political Life in the Colonies

1. **Teach** Ask students the Reading Focus questions to teach this section.

2. **Apply** Discuss with the class how laws relating to trade affected politics in the colonies. Organize students into small groups. Have each group discuss reasons why American merchants resented British interference, and then create a flyer protesting the Navigation Acts. Have volunteers share their flyers with the class.
LS Interpersonal

3. **Review** As you review the section, have students identify and explain the effects of English trade laws on politics in America.

4. **Practice/Homework** Have students write a brief news article for the "New England Times" about Sir Edmund Andros and his governance of the Dominion of New England. **LS Verbal-Linguistic**

📝 Alternative Assessment Handbook, Rubric 41: Writing to Express

Mercantilism

Colonists began smuggling because they felt England was taxing them unfairly. From the English perspective, however, taxing the colonies was a good way to make money. After all, profit was one of England's major incentives for establishing colonies in America.

The economic policy of **mercantilism** held that a nation's power was directly related to its wealth. The American colonies were valuable to England because the colonists could supply raw materials and could buy English goods. That would achieve another goal of mercantilism, a favorable **balance of trade**. Balance of trade is the relationship between a country's imports and exports. A country with a favorable balance of trade makes money by exporting more products than it imports.

To preserve its balance of trade, England had to prevent its colonies from trading with other nations. As a result, the interests of England and its colonies soon clashed. In theory, the mercantilist system could bring the colonies prosperity, too. The colonists, however, did not see it that way.

The English only wanted certain American products, such as fur and timber. But the colonies produced other goods, such as wheat and fish, that England did not want. In addition, colonists often could get better prices for their goods from the French, Spanish, or Dutch. They resented England's attempts to control what they could buy and sell.

The Navigation Acts Beginning in 1651, the English government passed several laws to control colonial trade and ensure the colonies

remained profitable—for England. Together, these laws are called the **Navigation Acts**.

The first act targeted trade with the Dutch. It said that all goods coming to England from Asia, Africa, or America must be carried in English ships. England did not strongly enforce this act, but it set a pattern for later laws.

In 1660 Parliament added a new provision: Not only must the ship be English, so must its captain and most of its crew. This act also listed a number of colonial products that could be sent only to England or another English colony.

Then in 1663, Parliament passed a new law. It required that almost everything being shipped to the colonies pass through England so England could tax these goods.

In 1673 Parliament tightened its control even more. Merchants now had to pay a tax, or duty, on certain goods—called "enumerated articles." Parliament sent officials to the colonies to collect these taxes.

Effects of the Navigation Acts The Navigation Acts had mixed results for both England and its colonies. For England, the laws increased revenues, but at the same time it increased the costs of law enforcement in America. For the colonists, the demand for ships stimulated certain industries, such as lumber and shipbuilding. On the other hand, the Navigation Acts also meant more English involvement in colonial affairs.

Most colonists resented the Navigation Acts. Many ignored them, and many prominent merchants took part in smuggling.

READING CHECK Identifying the Main Idea
What was the principal goal of mercantilism?

ACADEMIC VOCABULARY
incentive motivational factor
prosperity economic well-being

Rising Tensions Between England and America, 1651–1689
QUICK FACTS

THE NAVIGATION ACTS, 1651, 1660, 1663, 1673

England passed laws restricting colonial trade:
- All goods coming to England had to be carried on English ships.
- Captain and most of the crew on the ship had to be English.
- Certain products could be shipped only to England.
- American merchants had to pay a tax on certain goods.

Colonists' Reaction Some colonists began smuggling goods and refusing to pay their taxes.

PEABODY ESSEX MUSEUM, SALEM, MASSACHUSETTS

73

Direct Teach

Reading Focus

❶ What is mercantilism? *policy that holds that a nation's power is related to its wealth and balance of trade*

Mercantilism

Identify What is a balance of trade? *the relationship between a country's imports and exports*

Analyze How did England try to protect its balance of trade? *by preventing its colonies from trading with other nations*

Evaluate What effect did the Navigation Acts have on the American colonists? *raised taxes; meant more English involvement in colonial affairs; stimulated shipbuilding industry; taught colonists to ignore English laws*

Activity **Navigation Acts** Have students create a flyer protesting the Navigation Acts. **LS** Visual-Spatial

Quick Facts Transparency: Rising Tensions Between England and America, 1651–1689

CRF: Biography: Margaret Hardenbrook Philipse

Info to Know

Navigation Acts To a large degree, Parliament passed the Navigation Acts to prevent the Dutch from making economic gains in North America. On the whole, colonial merchants liked to conduct business with Dutch shippers, who offered cheap rates, good markets, and a wide range of trade goods. Over time, these Dutch shippers dominated colonial trade. As a result, Parliament passed the Navigation Acts.

Collaborative Learning

At Level

Mercantilism

1. Guide students in a discussion of mercantilism and English trade law.

2. Have students work in pairs to develop arguments defending the Navigation Acts from the viewpoint of English trade officials and opposing the Navigation Acts from the viewpoint of colonial merchants.

3. Have volunteers conduct a class debate on the following issue: Were the Navigation Acts good or bad? Have students take notes during the debate and retain them as a study tool. **LS** Interpersonal, Kinesthetic

Alternative Assessment Handbook, Rubric 10: Debates

Answers

Reading Check *to increase a nation's power by increasing its wealth and improving its balance of trade*

2 How did the Glorious Revolution and the English Bill of Rights affect political developments in the colonies? *led to several small uprisings; colonists arrested Andros and sent him back to England; end of Dominion of New England; New York gained elected assembly*

The Glorious Revolution and the English Bill of Rights

Recall Who was James II? *brother and successor to King Charles; tried to tighten control over the American colonies*

Analyze In what ways did James II try to gain control over New England? *established the Dominion of New England; made Andros governor*

Evaluate How successful was Parliament's attempt to replace James II? *very successful; Parliament invited Mary, James's Protestant daughter and her Dutch husband, William of Orange, to take the throne; James fled when the couple landed in England; Glorious Revolution was accomplished*

📄 Political Cartoons Activities for American History: Cartoon 5: Colonists React to a Royal Appointment

Teaching Tip

Have students refer to a map of the thirteen colonies in order to understand how large the Dominion of New England was.

---

go.hrw.com
Online Resources

KEYWORD: SD7 CH3
TOPIC: POLITICAL TENSION

The Glorious Revolution and the English Bill of Rights

The New England colonies, especially Massachusetts, did not behave as the English thought they should. When the English restored the monarchy under King Charles II, Puritans in Massachusetts at first refused to accept him as their king. Some even suggested that not all English laws applied to the colonies.

New Englanders also broke mercantilist laws that harmed their own economies. New England fishers competed with those from England. Some New Englanders began to compete with English manufacturers. The first successful ironworks in the colonies began at Saugus, Massachusetts, in 1646.

Royal officials looked for ways to control the colonies. First, King Charles took away Massachusetts' control over New Hampshire. In 1684, as the colony still refused to enforce the Navigation Acts, the king took back its charter and made it a royal colony.

The Dominion of New England King Charles II died in 1685. His brother James became king and tightened royal control even more. First, he created the **Dominion of New England**. It was a kind of supercolony that included all of New England, New York, and New Jersey. James's long-range plan was to divide and rule the rest of the American colonies in the same way.

The king appointed Sir Edmund Andros as governor of the Dominion. Andros was an experienced colonial governor but treated the colonists as if they were disobedient children. His arbitrary decisions soon made people angry. He demanded the return of the colonial charters. Colonists saw the charters as basic to their political rights. The new Dominion had no elected assembly, only an appointed council.

Andros infuriated the colonists in other ways, too. In Puritan Boston, he ordered Anglican services to be held in the Old South Meetinghouse. Andros also strictly enforced the Navigation Acts. He imposed new taxes on land and on imported wine, rum, and brandy.

The Glorious Revolution Meanwhile, James II was making himself equally unpopular in England. James was a Roman Catholic who hoped to make England Catholic again. He also wanted an absolute monarchy.

James's daughters Mary and Anne were Protestant. But his second wife, a Catholic, gave birth to a son in early 1688. This made leaders in Parliament fear the beginning of a Catholic dynasty. So, they invited Mary and her Dutch husband, William of Orange, to become co-rulers of England. This change of leadership became known as the **Glorious Revolution**.

The Glorious Revolution was essentially peaceful. Although William came from Holland with an army, James's supporters quickly deserted him. The ex-king fled to France.

Before being crowned, **William and Mary** jointly accepted a document that became known as the **English Bill of Rights**. This historic document allowed Parliament to set limits on

Rising Tensions, continued

THE DOMINION OF NEW ENGLAND, 1865

To gain more control over the colonies, King James II created the Dominion of New England. The Dominion combined several northern colonies under the rule of a royal governor, Edmund Andros.

Colonists' Reaction Colonists were angry because they lost their colonial charters. Used to governing themselves, they resented the king's governor, Edmund Andros.

Colonial leaders arrest Governor Andros.

74

Differentiating Instruction
Below Level | Standard English Mastery

Learners Having Difficulty; English-Language Learners

1. Review the information in the text about the Dominion of New England and Edmund Andros's actions as governor.

2. Organize students into mixed-ability pairs. Have each pair write a letter from a colonist to a relative in England, telling about Andros's treatment of colonists and the reaction of the colonists. *Students may write about how it feels to be treated as children by Andros, and/or about specific actions, such as charter revocation and the imposition of new taxes.*

3. Have volunteers read their letters to the class. Then guide students in a discussion of the ways in which government leaders treat citizens today. Do students believe that leaders treat citizens appropriately? If not, what recourse is available to citizens?

LS Verbal-Linguistic

📄 Alternative Assessment Handbook, Rubric 25: Personal Letters

the monarchs' powers. It protected freedom of speech for members of Parliament and gave them control of taxes. Later, these ideas would influence American politics.

Colonists' reactions News of the Glorious Revolution reached America in the spring of 1689. It led to several small uprisings in the colonies. Colonial leaders in Massachusetts acted quickly. They arrested Andros and his government and sent them back to England. Almost a century later, John Adams wrote, "It ought to be remembered that there was a revolution here, as well as in England, and that we, as well as the people of England, made an original, express contract with King William."

That ended the Dominion of New England. Connecticut and Rhode Island got their charters back. A new charter in 1691 made Massachusetts a royal colony that included Maine and Plymouth. Although Massachusetts was a royal colony, its colonial assembly still had a voice in choosing the governor's council.

The Glorious Revolution also sparked a rebellion in New York. Many merchants, especially the Dutch, disliked the Navigation Acts. Others were unhappy that the colony had no elected assembly.

Royal officials in New York delayed the announcement of England's new rulers. But when word of Andros' arrest came from Boston, small farmers, city workers, and others joined a rebel government. In the end, royal rule returned to New York, but the colony was at last granted an elected assembly.

READING CHECK Identifying Supporting **Details** How did Governor Andros provoke colonists' disapproval?

Government in the Colonies

Local rebellions after the Glorious Revolution showed English officials that colonists would resist arbitrary rule like that of Andros. Some colonies regained their elected assemblies. On the other hand, many more were now under tighter control as royal colonies.

Some of the colonists insisted that, as English citizens, they had all the rights that citizens enjoyed in England itself. This was not true. In fact, the English Bill of Rights did not apply in the colonies. Still, the Glorious Revolution gave colonists ideas about their rights and self-rule.

Steps toward self-rule Since the first settlements, the colonists had claimed their rights as English citizens. Colonists had taken small steps toward self-government during the English Civil War. For example, Massachusetts coined its own money, the pine-tree shilling.

The colonies even made an early move toward unity. Several joined forces to form the United Colonies of New England, also called the New England Confederation, in 1643. A **confederation** is a group in which each member keeps control of its own internal affairs. They cooperate on other actions, such as defense.

Neglect by England The Glorious Revolution had shifted considerable power to Parliament. But Parliament dealt mainly with issues in England. The monarch and his or her officials made

King William and Queen Mary accepted the English Bill of Rights and jointly ruled England.

THE GLORIOUS REVOLUTION, 1688

In England, William and Mary took the throne from King James II in a peaceful revolution.

Colonists' Reaction Colonists overthrew Governor Edmund Andros in 1689 and got their charters back.

75

ACADEMIC VOCABULARY
consisted made up of

most colonial policy. In 1696 an agency known as the Board of Trade was set up to handle colonial affairs. The board <u>consisted</u> of royal councilors and other high officials.

The Board of Trade had many roles. It had a hand in the appointment of colonial governors. It wrote laws for the colonies and sent them to Parliament for passage. It could review laws passed by colonial legislatures. It worked with other agencies to enforce the Navigation Acts.

The colonies had some say in their own government. They had agents to present their point of view to the Board of Trade. Like modern lobbyists trying to influence Congress, they tried to protect their colony's interests.

Many English officials were involved in colonial policy, but they did not rule the colonies very strictly. The politician Edmund Burke later termed this situation **salutary neglect**. In other words, the colonies benefited by being left alone.

At the same time, England's attention began to turn away from the colonies. War with Spain broke out in 1701. Later, supporters of the ex-king James II tried to put one of his relatives back on the throne. Because England's attention was focused elsewhere, colonial governments gained some independence.

THE IMPACT TODAY

Government
Many New England communities still hold town meetings to discuss local matters. A few have even tried electronic town meetings, where citizens register their opinions via the Internet.

Colonial governments in the 1700s In the colonists' daily lives, local governments were more influential than faraway English officials. New Englanders held town meetings.

In other colonies, the county or parish was the unit of local government. Many colonists saw their elected assembly as a basic right.

Most colonial assemblies were modeled on the Parliament in London. They were bicameral, that is, with two houses. The governor's council was the upper house. The council had executive and legislative powers. It was also the supreme court of the colony.

The elected assembly was the lower house, much like Parliament's House of Commons. As the Commons gained power after the Glorious Revolution, colonial assemblies also won important rights. Members had freedom of speech in debates. Most importantly, they won the right to pass money bills. That meant the governor depended on the assembly for his salary.

Each colony had a governor. In royal colonies the governor was appointed by the monarch. In proprietary colonies, the proprietor chose a governor. Members of the governor's council were chosen in the same way. They were usually rich and influential men.

On paper, colonial governors had great power. They could veto acts of the assembly. They commanded military forces, made treaties, and chose many minor officials. On the other hand, they lacked ways of backing up their decisions. No doubt many kept in mind the fate of Governor Edmund Andros.

READING CHECK **Comparing** How were colonial assemblies similar to Parliament?

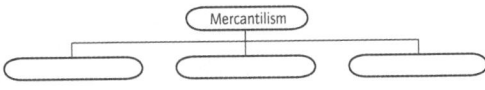

SECTION 1 ASSESSMENT

go.hrw.com
Online Quiz
Keyword: SD7 HP3

Reviewing Ideas, Terms, and People

1. **a. Identify** What were the principles behind the policy of mercantilism?
   b. Summarize What were the main provisions of the Navigation Acts?
   c. Evaluate Which benefited more from the Navigation Acts—England or the American colonies?

2. **a. Describe** What circumstances led to the Glorious Revolution in England?
   b. Make Inferences Why did colonists revolt in reaction to the Glorious Revolution?

3. **a. Recall** What early move toward unity did the New England colonies make in 1643?
   b. Analyze What was the effect of **salutary neglect**?

Critical Thinking

4. **Analyzing** Copy the chart below and show the basic principles of mercantilism.

```
        Mercantilism
    ┌───────┼───────┐
 ┌─────┐ ┌─────┐ ┌─────┐
 └─────┘ └─────┘ └─────┘
```

FOCUS ON SPEAKING

5. **Expository** Suppose you are a merchant in New England. Explain why you are resisting English law and disobeying the Navigation Acts. Read your explanation aloud to the class.

Section 1 Assessment Answers

1. **a.** A nation's power was directly related to its wealth.
   b. goods must be carried in British ships; captain, most of crew must be British; goods must pass through Britain for taxation
   c. England—became rich from trade and taxes

2. **a.** the birth of King James's son; Parliament wanted to avoid Catholic dynasty
   b. colonists wanted elected assemblies; resented royal rulers

3. **a.** formed New England Confederation
   b. colonies gained some independence and self-rule

4. brings prosperity to colonies; balance of trade; power linked to wealth

5. possible answer—taxes unfair; England suppressed competition; made goods more expensive

Answers

Reading Check *bicameral structure, with upper and lower houses*

2 The Colonial Economy

BEFORE YOU READ

MAIN IDEA

A commerce-based economy developed in the northern colonies, while the southern colonies developed an agri-cultural economy.

READING FOCUS

1. What were the characteristics of northern colonial economies?
2. What were the characteristics of southern colonial economies?
3. What was the impact of slavery in the colonies?

KEY TERMS AND PEOPLE

triangular trade
Middle Passage
cash crop
Eliza Lucas
yeoman
Olaudah Equiano
Stono Rebellion

TAKING NOTES As you read, take notes identifying the major products of the northern and southern colonies. Record your notes in a graphic organizer like the one shown here.

Northern Products	Southern Products

Slavery in the Northern Colonies

▼ Phillis Wheatley was still enslaved when she published *Poems on Various Subjects, Religious and Moral.*

THE INSIDE STORY

How did slavery affect the North?

The economies of the southern colonies came to depend on the work done by enslaved Africans. They worked on the plantations of the South, growing tobacco, rice, and indigo. But slave labor was more widespread in the northern and middle colonies than most people realize. Enslaved Africans worked in homes, workshops, and farms in New England and throughout the middle colonies.

In addition, New England ship captains were major players in the slave trade with West Africa. Even Quaker merchants in Philadelphia owned slaves, and some took part in the slave trade. The first poet of African American ancestry was Phillis Wheatley, who was kidnapped in Africa at age 7 and bought as a slave by a Boston family. Her exceptional talents made her famous, and she later gained her freedom.

Enslaved workers in the North were a smaller percentage of the population than they were in the southern colonies. In New England the percentage was less than 5 percent, but it was higher in the middle colonies, where farms were larger. In the North, enslaved Africans more often lived in urban areas and worked as household servants or artisans. Some northern farms, how-ever, were very large, with many African American workers. Most of the northern states began to abolish slavery gradually after the American Revolution, but in some places that process took many years. ◢

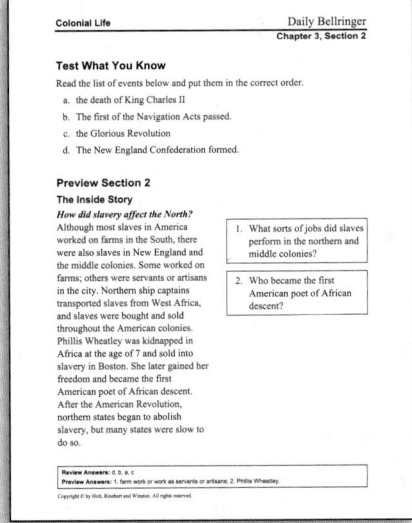

Teach the Main Idea

At Level

The Colonial Economy

1. **Teach** Ask students the Reading Focus questions to teach this section.

2. **Apply** Have students scan the section and create a graphic organizer comparing the economies of the South and the North. Have students list the primary products of each region and describe the workforce that produced them. **LS Visual-Spatial**

3. **Review** As you review the section, have students explain how climate and

soil affected the development of the colonial economies.

4. **Practice/Homework** Have students write a paragraph describing how the colonial economy might have developed if slavery had not existed. **LS Logical-Mathematical**

📑 Alternative Assessment Handbook, Rubric 13: Graphic Organizers

❶ What were the characteristics of northern colonial economies? *some farming, extracting natural resources, shipbuilding, manufacturing, trade, and commerce*

Northern Colonial Economies

Recall Why did shipbuilding flourish in New England? *available timber; Navigation Acts created heavy demand for English ships*

Analyze What was the primary reason small manufacturing operations developed in the northern colonies? *Imported English goods were very costly.*

Evaluate How did colonists benefit from the natural resources of the North? *Both fur and forest products developed into profitable exports.*

📖 American History Outline Maps: The Thirteen Colonies

🖥 Map Transparency: Thirteen Colonies, 1750

Info to Know

Whaling Whales were first hunted on a massive scale in the early seventeenth century. Many nations that were active in sea travel and trade believed that these creatures were as limitless as the ocean appeared to be. Up until the twentieth century, most whales were caught for their blubber and baleen, or a section of the mouth that filters food out of the water. The rest of the whale carcass was thrown away. Since the whale population began to drop dramatically, whaling is now conducted on a very limited scale and formal agencies regulate the practice.

Northern Colonial Economies

Agriculture was the main economic activity in colonial America. However, colonists often found that English crops and methods did not succeed in their new home. Climate, land, and other factors influenced farming in different regions. Those factors also steered some colonists into other ways of making a living.

Farming Much of the soil in New England was thin and rocky. The winters were long, and the growing season short. Many colonists practiced subsistence farming—growing just enough food for their own family. Some raised extra corn or apples or cattle to trade with their neighbors. There was rarely enough to produce an export crop.

Farther south, the middle colonies had better land and a milder climate. Farmers here grew enough wheat to sell grain and flour to other colonies and to send abroad. They also raised cattle and hogs for export.

The colonies' most productive farmers were the German colonists known as the Pennsylvania Dutch (from the word *Deutsch*, which means "German"). These settlers used fertilizer and crop rotation. As in Europe, women worked in the fields alongside men.

Natural resources For early colonists, North America's most valuable resources were its thick forests and the fur-bearing animals in them. Colonial traders got beaver furs and deerskins from Native American trappers.

The number of fur-bearing animals soon declined. Colonists turned to other resources, such as timber and fish. Lumber mills cut logs into planks, shingles, and siding for ships and houses. Timber was one of the raw materials that the colonies sent to England.

As a result of the Navigation Acts, many coastal towns became centers for shipbuilding. It was less expensive to build ships in the colonies than it was to build them in England. Shipyards built both merchant ships and small fishing boats. An estimated 33,000 colonists worked as shipbuilders, the largest single group in the work force.

Some of the fish catch was exported to Europe and the West Indies. The rest was eaten at home. New England sailors began the whaling industry in the early 1700s,

THE IMPACT TODAY

Daily Life
Today the Pennsylvania Dutch are mostly Amish and Old Order Mennonites. These groups still travel by horse and buggy and farm using teams of horses. Their use of a variation of the German language is seen as a sign of humility and a way to keep the outside world at bay.

sailing from ports such as Nantucket. Whales provided oil for lamps as well as materials used in perfumes, candles, and women's corsets.

Colonial industries Under mercantilism, colonial industries were not supposed to compete with those in England. That discouraged the growth of industries. So did a shortage of capital for investment.

Because English goods were expensive, colonists made many things at home. Small industries developed. Mills, run by waterpower, ground grain into flour. Distilling rum and brewing other alcoholic beverages were major commercial activities. Ironworks developed where there were local supplies of iron ore. Other small companies made bricks, leather goods, and glass. Importing cloth from England was too expensive for many people, so cloth making became another small-scale industry. Families wove wool and linen cloth for personal use as well as for sale to merchants.

THIRTEEN COLONIES, 1750

NEW FRANCE

NEW HAMPSHIRE (1623)

MASSACHUSETTS (Plymouth, 1620; Massachusetts Bay, 1630)

NEW YORK (1624)

RHODE ISLAND (1636)

PENNSYLVANIA (1643)

CONNECTICUT (1633)

NEW JERSEY (1660)

DELAWARE (1638)

VIRGINIA (1607)

MARYLAND (1634)

NORTH CAROLINA (1653)

SOUTH CAROLINA (1670)

GEORGIA (1733)

NEW SPAIN

ATLANTIC OCEAN

40°N

70°W

80°W

☐ Northern colonies
☐ Middle colonies
☐ Southern colonies

0   100   200 Miles
0   100   200 Kilometers
Albers equal-area projection

Differentiating Instruction

Special Education Students

1. Guide students in a discussion of natural resources found in New England. Have students focus on fur, timber, and proximity to water.

2. Organize students into mixed-ability pairs. Have each pair design a Web page that describes the importance of forests to New Englanders and to their economy. On their Web pages students should list the products that come from forests.

3. Have volunteers share their pages with the class. 🔲 **Interpersonal, Visual-Spatial**

📖 Alternative Assessment Handbook, Rubric 11: Discussions

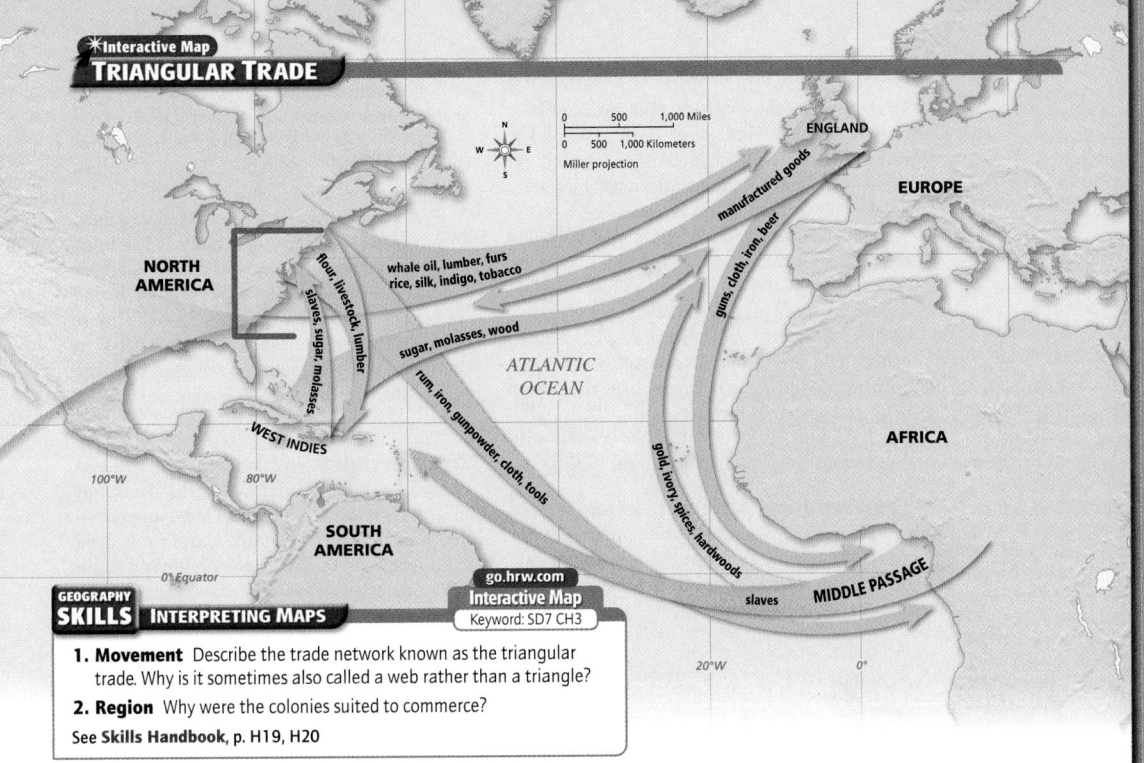

ENGLAND

EUROPE

NORTH
AMERICA

manufactured goods

guns, cloth, iron, beer

whale oil, lumber, furs
rice, silk, indigo, tobacco

flour, livestock, lumber

slaves, sugar, molasses

sugar, molasses, wood

ATLANTIC
OCEAN

AFRICA

WEST INDIES

rum, iron, gunpowder, cloth, tools

100°W   80°W

gold, ivory, spices, hardwoods

SOUTH
AMERICA

0° Equator

slaves   MIDDLE PASSAGE

20°W   0°

0   500   1,000 Miles
0   500   1,000 Kilometers
Miller projection

go.hrw.com
Interactive Map
Keyword: SD7 CH3

GEOGRAPHY
SKILLS INTERPRETING MAPS

1. **Movement** Describe the trade network known as the triangular trade. Why is it sometimes also called a web rather than a triangle?

2. **Region** Why were the colonies suited to commerce?

See Skills Handbook, p. H19, H20

Trade and commerce Good harbors, inexpensive ships, and a tradition of seafaring encouraged the development of commerce. The port cities of Boston, New York, and Philadelphia were thriving centers of trade. Merchant ships from the colonies traded along the coasts and across the Atlantic. Traders also traveled the inland rivers.

The trade routes that linked the Americas, Europe, Africa, and the West Indies are often described as the **triangular trade**. In that triangle, ships carried rum from New England to Africa to trade for enslaved Africans. Traders shipped the Africans to plantations in the West Indies and traded them for sugar and molasses. Finally, traders shipped the sugar and molasses back to New England to be made into rum.

The term **Middle Passage** is the name used by historians to describe the horrific journey that enslaved Africans made across the Atlantic. The trip from West Africa to the Indies was the middle leg of the triangle.

Historians today, however, think that real trade patterns were not that simple. They believe the patterns were more like a spider web than a neat triangle. Coastal trade linked the colonies and the West Indies. The fertile mid-Atlantic colonies sent grain, fruits, and vegetables to other colonies. Northern merchants exported flour, fish, lumber, and manufactured goods to the West Indies.

The northern colonies sent furs and timber to England. Defying the Navigation Acts, they also sold fish, fruit, and meat in southern Europe and to other colonies in the West Indies that did not belong to England. The southern colonies sent other goods to England. Overseas trade grew quickly in the 1700s. By 1770, the value of exports had increased to nearly four times the value of exports in 1700.

READING CHECK **Identifying the Main Idea**
What factors helped trade become the basis for northern colonial economies?

Direct Teach

Reading Focus

Northern Colonial Economies

Recall What was the Middle Passage? *the horrific journey enslaved Africans made across the Atlantic*

Make Judgments How important was the slave trade to the northern economy? *key component of triangular trade, gave North market for rum*

🔲 Map Transparency: Triangular Trade

✳ **Interactive Map:** Triangular Trade

MISCONCEPTION
⫻⫻⫻ALERT⫻⫻⫻

Although students may think of slavery as an exclusively southern institution, this is not the case. Slavery was widespread in the northern colonies as well. Historians and archaeologists have uncovered significant physical evidence of slavery in the North, including shackles, graves, and slave quarters. In Rhode Island, New Jersey, Pennsylvania, and New York, archival records and excavations show that many northern farmers, merchants, and landed gentry kept slaves.

Primary Source

"Shuttles in the rocking loom of history, the dark ships move, the dark ships move, their bright ironical names like jests of kindness on a murderer's mouth."

— Robert Earl Hayden

From "Middle Passage" from *Robert Hayden: Collected Poems*, edited by Frederick Glaysher. Copyright © 1985 by Emma Hayden. Reproduced by permission of **Liveright Publishing Corporation, www.liveright.com.**

Answers

Interpreting Maps 1. *goods and slaves traded among Americas, Britain, and Africa; routes were interwoven, crossed over each other;* **2.** *located near coast with access to ocean, good harbors*

Reading Check *good harbors, inexpensive ships, and a tradition of seafaring*

Skills Focus: Analyzing Primary Sources

At Level

Reading Like a Historian Skill
Triangular Trade

Research Required

1. Have students conduct outside research about the triangular trade and the brutalities endured by enslaved Africans on their journey to the Americas.

2. Have students use their research to write their own poems or song lyrics describing the conditions that enslaved Africans were forced to endure during the passage.

3. As an extension, have students expand their research to include colonial commerce by sea that was NOT part of the triangular trade. Have students write a short essay summarizing the results of their research. Have volunteers read their essays to the class.

LS **Auditory-Musical, Verbal-Linguistic**

📃 Alternative Assessment Handbook, Rubric 26: Poems and Songs

❷ **What were the characteristics of southern colonial economies?** *Southerners produced cash crops, such as tobacco, indigo, and rice. Plantations and farms worked by slave labor became dominant.*

Southern Colonial Economies

Explain Why did plantations contribute to the growth of slavery? *Large plantations required hundreds of workers to produce their crops.*

Elaborate Why did plantation owners prefer enslaved labor to indentured servants? *free workers would not work in rice fields; many Africans already knew how to grow rice; many Africans resistant to malaria*

📃 Political Cartoons Activities for American History: Cartoon 6: Rice Ready for Shipping

Info to Know

The Gullah Today, a group of African Americans from South Carolina and Georgia form a community known as the Gullah. In the 1700s, many colonists in these areas depended on the knowledge of enslaved West Africans to help them plant, harvest, and process rice. The rice-growing region of West Africa covered present-day Sierra Leone. Enslaved Africans from Sierra Leone constituted a large community in the American colonies. The Gullah, descended from this community, have managed to maintain much of their African cultural heritage because of their geographical seclusion and close-knit communities. The Gullah speak a language similar to the language used in Sierra Leone, tell African stories, make crafts in an African style, and enjoy many African dishes.

Southern Colonial Economies

Products from the southern colonies were very important in colonial trade. Still, the region remained rural, with economies based on agriculture. Unlike the northern colonies, only a few cities formed in the South.

The southern colonies produced valuable **cash crops**—agricultural products grown to be sold. One was tobacco, America's most valuable export. Indigo, a plant used to make a blue dye, and rice were also grown in the South. Southerners also produced naval stores—products such as rope, tar, and turpentine that were used to <u>maintain</u> wooden ships. There was great demand in England for these crops—and great profit to be made from them.

ACADEMIC VOCABULARY
maintain keep in an existing state

The plantation system As tobacco became an increasingly important crop, a way of life known as the plantation system developed in Virginia and Maryland. A plantation is a large farm, usually in a warm climate, with an unskilled labor force that grows one cash crop, such as sugar or tobacco. The plantation system soon became widespread through much of the South. Eventually, a wealthy and influential class of planters emerged. These planters dominated southern society and politics.

Plantations needed workers, and this need encouraged the growth of slavery. A few huge plantations had hundreds of workers, either indentured servants or slaves. Most farms were smaller and had a work force of fewer than 30. The bulk of these workers labored in the fields, although men and women on large plantations performed other necessary tasks such as shoemaking, weaving, and carpentry.

Rice and indigo While tobacco was king in Virginia, rice and indigo were the dominant crops in South Carolina. The low-lying coastline and marshes of South Carolina proved ideal for growing rice. Some historians think that enslaved West Africans brought the knowledge of rice growing to America.

HISTORY CLOSE-UP

South Carolina Rice Plantation, 1730–1750

On early rice plantations like this one, nearly all tasks were done by hand. Enslaved Africans performed the arduous work of planting, harvesting, and cultivating the rice.

Slaves lived in small, one-room buildings. The slave cabins were often built in rows.

The kitchen building was separate from the main house.

The main plantation house was usually built on high ground, facing the river.

The winnowing house was used to separate the rice from the chaff, or outer covering.

80

Skills Focus: Making Inferences

Below Level

Reading Skill
Cash Crops

1. Guide students in a discussion of the plantation system and the three main crops: rice, indigo, and tobacco.

2. Have students create a series of three advertising flyers, one for each crop. Flyers should encourage southern farmers to begin growing one of these profitable cash crops.

3. Have volunteers share their flyers with the class. **LS Visual-Spatial**

📃 Alternative Assessment Handbook, Rubric 2: Advertisements

Growing rice in swampy fields was difficult and dangerous. Mosquitoes bred in the wet coastal conditions, and they could carry malaria, a deadly disease. Free workers would not tolerate these conditions. Rice planters turned instead to enslaved Africans to do the work. Many enslaved Africans already knew successful methods of rice growing. In addition, many of them had more resistance to malaria.

The other major crop in South Carolina was indigo, a plant from the West Indies whose seeds were used to produce a deep blue dye. Indigo was widely used for military uniforms and men's coats.

The first successful indigo crop was grown in South Carolina by **Eliza Lucas**. In 1739 at about age 17, she was left to manage her father's plantations while he returned to military duty in the West Indies. Lucas experimented with crops such as ginger, figs, and indigo. She wrote about her experiences in 1740.

Tasks on a Rice Plantation

❶ **Planting** Slaves planted rice by hand in the spring.

❷ **Watering** Rice is grown in flooded fields, so rice plantations were built near natural water sources.

❸ **Canal Building** Plantation owners had slaves construct canals to direct the water to the fields. Canals and floodgates controlled the flow of water to the rice fields.

❹ **Harvesting** Slaves harvested rice in the fall.

❺ **Pounding** Getting the rice ready to sell was hard work. First, slaves pounded the rice.

❻ **Winnowing** Then they brought it to the winnowing house, where they dropped it through a grating in the floor. The rice grains fell to the ground below and were collected. Later, rice mills did this task.

❼ **Shipping** The river also provided a way to transport rice to buyers.

Skills FOCUS INTERPRETING INFOGRAPHICS

Early South Carolina rice plantations like this one were often built near natural water sources.

Making Inferences How did the location near the river help with growing rice?

See **Skills Handbook**, p. H18

❝Wrote my Father a very long letter on his plantation affairs and . . . on the pains I had taken to bring the Indigo, Ginger, Cotton . . . and had greater hopes from the Indigo (if I could have the seed earlier next year from the West Indies) than any of the rest of the things I had tryd.❞

—*Letterbook of Eliza Lucas Pinckney, 1740*

The new crop soon became profitable. Demand in England was so great that Parliament offered a bonus to indigo growers. By 1754 South Carolina exported a million pounds annually.

In 1744 Eliza Lucas married a widowed planter, Charles Pinckney. Their two sons became well-known politicians and soldiers. One was a signer of the Constitution.

Small farms Southern economies rested on the plantation system and its valuable crops. Most farmers did not live on plantations, however, but on small farms. Even small farmers sometimes had a few enslaved Africans who worked in the fields alongside them.

These independent **yeoman** (YOH-muhn) farmers raised livestock and exported beef and pork. They grew corn, wheat, fruit, and vegetables for the home market. Small-scale farmers also grew tobacco but had to sell it through the large planters.

READING CHECK **Contrasting** How did the plantation system differ from the work patterns of yeoman farmers?

The Impact of Slavery

English and Spanish settlers needed workers for their plantations and haciendas. Some colonists tried to enslave Native Americans. Due to disease and other problems, such efforts often failed. In the 1600s, indentured servants from England and Europe supplied most labor in the colonies. But former indentured servants began to pose problems in the colonies. Eventually, colonists came to depend on the work of enslaved Africans instead.

The African slave trade By the 1600s Portugal, Spain, France, Holland, and England were involved in the trans-Atlantic slave trade. Most captured Africans were taken to colonies in the Caribbean and South America, then to

Reading Focus

Southern Colonial Economies

Recall Who was Eliza Lucas? *a young woman whose experiments led to widespread cultivation of indigo in South Carolina*

Evaluate What role did slaves play in developing the rice industry in South Carolina? *Many Africans already knew how to cultivate rice, and they did the hard work necessary to do so.*

Reading Focus

❸ What was the impact of slavery in the colonies? *many colonists came to depend on the work of enslaved Africans and viewed it as an economic necessity; slavery became a permanent condition for Africans and their descendants; increasing numbers of Africans were brought to America as slaves*

The Impact of Slavery

Recall Why did colonists come to dislike the indenture system? *had trouble controlling former indentured servants*

Describe Which European countries were involved in the slave trade? *Portugal, Spain, France, Holland, England*

Skills Focus: Sequencing

At Level

Reading Skill
Growing Indigo

Materials construction paper, colored pencils

1. Organize students into small groups or mixed-ability pairs. Have each group prepare a storyboard or a multimedia presentation for a television documentary about the life and work of Eliza Lucas.

2. Have students use the information in the text about Lucas and the importance and use of

indigo. Students should also include the quote from Lucas's letterbook.

3. Have volunteers share and explain their storyboards or multimedia presentations to the class. **LS** **Visual-Spatial, Kinesthetic**

📖 Alternative Assessment Handbook, Rubric 22: Multimedia Presentations

Answers

Interpreting Infographics *rice planted in flooded fields, river also a means of transport of rice to buyers*

Reading Check *plantations—larger; many workers; grew one cash crop; yeoman farms—smaller; grew variety of products; only a few workers*

81

The Impact of Slavery

Explain What chiefly determined where most slaves lived? *the agricultural economy*

Analyze Why did slavery continue? *seen as an economic necessity*

Predict Why was the Stono Rebellion troubling to whites, and what might be its consequences? *demonstrated that slaves might turn to violence against their owners to gain freedom; might lead to very restrictive policies for African Americans*

📑 CRF: Primary Source: Olaudah Equiano Describes the Horrors of a Slave Ship

📑 CRF: Biography: Reverend Peter Fontaine

go.hrw.com

Online Resources

KEYWORD: SD7 CH3
TOPIC: THE MIDDLE PASSAGE

FACES OF HISTORY

Olaudah Equiano
1750–1797

Born in western Africa in present-day Nigeria, Olaudah Equiano was taken from his family at the age of 11 and sold into slavery.

African slave traders forced Equiano onto a slave ship sailing to the Caribbean and then to Virginia. A lieutenant in the British navy purchased Equiano from a Virginia planter. Working on ships under the command of his slaveholder, Equiano eventually earned enough money to buy his freedom in 1766. As a free man, Equiano traveled as a missionary and spoke out against slavery. He visited many countries in Europe, Latin America, and Africa, and also traveled to India. In 1789 Equiano published his autobiography, *The Interesting Narrative of the Life of Olaudah Equiano, or Gustavus Vassa, the African.* By describing the horrors of the Middle Passage, Equiano's book encouraged readers to call for an end to slavery.

Explain How did Equiano fight slavery?

North America. Only a small percentage—perhaps 5 percent—came directly to the North American colonies.

Some Africans who later gained freedom described the horrifying conditions of the passage across the Atlantic—the dreaded Middle Passage. Kidnapped Africans were chained together in dark, foul-smelling quarters below the decks of the ship. Some ship captains tried to keep their prisoners healthy to make them more valuable. Others packed men, women, and children into such a small space that they could not sit or stand.

One African, **Olaudah Equiano**, later wrote about the horrific conditions on a crowded slave ship.

HISTORY'S VOICES

> ❝The closeness of the place, and the heat of the climate... almost suffocated us.... The shrieks of the women, and the groans of the dying, rendered the whole a scene of horror almost inconceivable.❞
>
> —Olaudah Equiano, *The Interesting Narrative of the Life of Olaudah Equiano*, 1789

Three of his companions threw themselves overboard, choosing death by drowning over slavery. When Africans arrived in the Americas, they faced still more terrors—the auction block and an uncertain future.

Slavery in North and South The number of Africans in the English colonies grew quickly during the 1700s because of births as well as the slave trade. By 1760 the African population was about 250,000—10 times greater than it had been in 1700.

The agricultural economy determined where most Africans lived. Percentages were smallest in New England, Pennsylvania, and Delaware, where most people were independent yeoman farmers. There, Africans lived mainly in cities and worked as servants or artisans.

Because the Dutch had been active in the slave trade, New York and New Jersey had larger African populations. Many were skilled craftsworkers such as carpenters, shoemakers, and barrel makers.

Populations of enslaved Africans were largest in colonies with plantation agriculture. In parts of Virginia and Maryland, they made up as much as 30 percent of the population. North Carolina, with its many small farms, still had a sizable population of enslaved Africans.

In South Carolina, the large demand for workers on rice plantations caused the population of enslaved Africans to grow dramatically. By the mid 1700s, there were approximately twice as many enslaved Africans as whites in South Carolina.

Why slavery continued As you read earlier, the first Africans arrived in colonial Virginia in 1619. Many African workers were treated as indentured servants at first. Gradually, their terms of indenture grew longer until they lasted a lifetime. While white servants were freed, black servants often were not. Under the laws of several colonies, they lost other rights as well.

The line dividing blacks and whites became sharper, partly because the English settlers considered themselves naturally superior to the enslaved Africans. By the mid-1600s in Virginia and Maryland, most African servants were servants for life. Their children also became servants for life.

Historians disagree about why slavery continued for so long in the Americas. For planters, slave labor had obvious economic advantages. It cost less to hold slaves than to pay the expenses of indentured servants. The children of enslaved Africans supplied the next generation of workers. Also, the number

Skills Focus: Analyzing Primary Sources
At Level

Reading Like a Historian Skill
The Impact of Slavery

While some historians have begun to question Olaudah Equiano's account of the Middle Passage because evidence suggests that he may have been born in South Carolina, not Africa, his story still reflects the brutality of the voyage. Read the quote in the text to students and have

them write an essay describing enslaved Africans' experience on the Middle Passage.

🔲 **Verbal-Linguistic**

📑 Alternative Assessment Handbook, Rubric 42: Writing to Inform

Answers

Faces of History *by speaking out about the horrors of slavery*

of people who chose to take up indentures dropped steadily in the late 1600s.

Nevertheless, the institution of slavery troubled some colonists. But others justified the practice by pointing out that Africans themselves captured and sold their own people. Still others, such as Virginia colonist Peter Fontaine, justified slavery for economic reasons.

HISTORY'S VOICES

"... to live in Virginia without slaves is morally impossible. Before our troubles, you could not hire a servant or slave for love or money, so that, unless you are robust enough to cut wood, to go to mill, to work at the hoe, etc., you must starve. . .This of course draws us all into the original sin and curse of the country of purchasing slaves."

– Letters of Peter Fontaine, 1757

Resisting slavery Writers at the time often portrayed enslaved Africans as contented and obedient. In fact, however, many enslaved Africans physically resisted brutal treatment and abuse. Others protested by committing small acts of sabotage, such as burning a barn or breaking tools. Some ran away but were often recaptured and killed or severely punished.

Southern planters lived in fear of slave revolts. Small-scale rebellions were frequent. The major revolt in the colonial period is known as the **Stono Rebellion**. In 1739 about 100 enslaved Africans in South Carolina took weapons from a firearms shop and killed several people before they were apprehended.

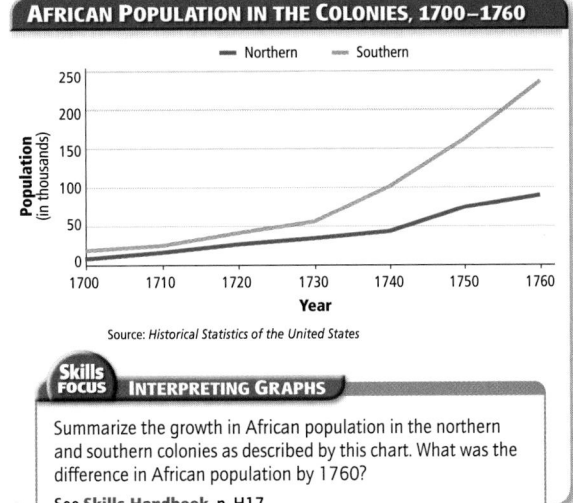

AFRICAN POPULATION IN THE COLONIES, 1700–1760

— Northern   — Southern

Source: *Historical Statistics of the United States*

Skills FOCUS   INTERPRETING GRAPHS

Summarize the growth in African population in the northern and southern colonies as described by this chart. What was the difference in African population by 1760?

See **Skills Handbook**, p. H17

Some skilled artisans escaped slavery by buying their freedom. They hired out their labor, gradually earning and saving enough money to buy freedom for themselves. Sometimes they earned enough to buy freedom for their families as well.

READING CHECK   Identifying Cause and Effect Why did the use of indentured servants decline, while slavery continued?

SECTION 2 ASSESSMENT

go.hrw.com
Online Quiz
Keyword: SD7 HP3

Reviewing Ideas, Terms, and People

1. a. Describe What is meant by the **triangular trade**?
b. Contrast Why did agriculture in the middle colonies differ from that in New England?
c. Evaluate In what ways was the ocean valuable to economies in the northern colonies?

2. a. Identify What were the four major exports of the southern colonies?
b. Explain Why did southern economies remain rural and agricultural?
c. Predict How would the value of tobacco and rice exports influence slavery in the southern colonies?

3. a. Describe What was the **Middle Passage**?
b. Sequence Trace the changes that took place in the labor force in the American colonies in the 1600s and 1700s.

Critical Thinking

4. Comparing Copy the chart below and list the major products and activities in the economies of the northern and southern colonies.

Northern Colonies	Southern Colonies

FOCUS ON WRITING

5. Descriptive As a new immigrant from England to the American colonies, write a letter home explaining which colony you would like to live in and why.

COLONIAL LIFE **83**

Section 2 Assessment Answers

1. a. trade among England, Americas, and Africa
b. better soil, milder climate in middle colonies
c. ports and harbors for shipping, fishing, trade

2. a. tobacco, rice, indigo, naval stores
b. able to grow cash crops; profited more from agricultural products
c. valuable labor-intensive crops; need for workers encouraged slavery

3. a. the passage from Africa across the Atlantic
b. Native Americans to indentured servants to enslaved Africans

4. Northern—shipbuilding, fur, timber products, fishing; Southern—tobacco, indigo, rice, plantation system, slavery

5. possible answers—northern colonies: commerce, trade, ship-building, busy ports; southern colonies: small farms, large plantations, able to grow cash crops

---

• Direct Teach •

Info to Know

The Stono Rebellion Although the cause of the Stono Rebellion is not known for certain, the trigger was most likely the passage of the Security Act. This law required all white men to bring weapons with them to church on Sundays, in order to protect themselves against the possibility of a slave rebellion. After the Stono Rebellion, laws grew even stricter. The 1739 Negro Act prohibited slaves from growing their own food, gathering together in groups, earning money on their own, or learning how to read.

• Review & Assess •

Close

Have students explain the triangular trade and how it affected both southern and northern economies.

Review

Online Quiz, Section 2

Daily Test Practice Transparency

Assess

SE Section 2 Assessment

Progress Assessment: Section 2 Quiz

Alternative Assessment Handbook

Reteach

Interactive Reader and Study Guide, Section 2

Interactive Skills Tutor CD-ROM

Answers

Interpreting Graphs *increased slowly in North and South until 1730, when began to grow quickly in South; about 150,000 more African Americans in South than in North*

Reading Check *difficult to control; more expensive than holding slaves*

83

Bellringer

The Inside Story. . . Use the **Daily Bellringer Transparency** to help students answer the question.

📽 Daily Bellringer Transparency, Section 3

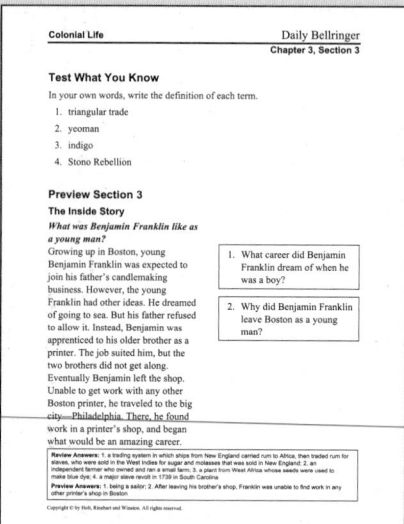

Academic Vocabulary

Review with students the high-use academic term in this section.

displaced took the place of (p. 86)

📖 CRF: Vocabulary Builder Activity, Section 3

Taking Notes

Enlightenment—influenced Declaration of Independence and Constitution; Scientific Revolution—encouraged people to look for order and method in nature; Religious Revival—increased church membership united colonies, led to creation of universities and colleges; Religious Diversity—Great Awakening led to establishment of many Protestant churches, such as Congregational, Methodist, Baptist, Presbyterian; Germans, French Huguenots, and Jews fled religious persecution to U.S.

SECTION 3
America's Emerging Culture

BEFORE YOU READ

MAIN IDEA

Enlightenment ideas and the Great Awakening brought new ways of thinking to the colonists, and a unique American culture developed.

READING FOCUS

1. What impact did the Enlightenment have in the colonies?
2. How was the Great Awakening significant?
3. How did the colonies become more diverse in the 1700s?
4. What was life like in colonial America?

KEY TERMS AND PEOPLE

Benjamin Franklin
Enlightenment
social contract
Great Awakening
Jonathan Edwards
George Whitefield

TAKING NOTES
As you read, take notes on the effects of different factors on colonial society. Record your notes in a graphic organizer like the one shown here.

Factor	Effects
Enlightenment	
Scientific Revolution	
Religious Revival	
Religious Diversity	

Benjamin Franklin's Humble Beginnings

THE INSIDE STORY

What was Benjamin Franklin like as a young man? People today remember **Benjamin Franklin** as one of the most famous Americans in history. But in 1723 he was just a 17-year-old printer's apprentice, trying to get away from a harsh older brother. As a boy, Franklin wanted to go to sea, but his father did not approve. Franklin did not want to join his father's candlemaking business, either. Since he loved to read, he was finally apprenticed to his older brother as a printer. The job suited him, but he and his brother did not get along. When Franklin decided to leave, his brother made sure that no other printer in Boston would hire him. So the young Benjamin Franklin set off alone for the big city—colonial Philadelphia.

Franklin made his way to Philadelphia by boat. Years later, in his *Autobiography*, he made fun of his first appearance in the city: "I was in my Working Dress . . . I was dirty from my Journey; my Pockets were stuff'd out with Shirts & Stockings." He had no idea of prices in the city. For three pennies at a bakery, he was surprised to get "three great Puffy Rolls." With two bread rolls under his arm, Franklin strolled down the street eating the third. He finally gave the others to a woman and child he had met on the boat. Soon, Franklin found work with a printer. It was the beginning of an amazing career. ◢

▶ **Young Benjamin Franklin, newly arrived in Philadelphia**

84 CHAPTER 3

Teach the Main Idea

At Level

America's Emerging Culture

1. **Teach** Ask students the Reading Focus questions to teach this section.

2. **Apply** Have students read the quote by Hector St. John de Crèvecoeur from *Letters from an American Farmer* History's Voices passage. Have students write a paraphrase of the quote. Then guide students in a discussion of the ways in which America's culture began to emerge and continues to change today.
LS Verbal-Linguistic

3. **Review** As you review the section, have students identify the changes that occurred in American life and culture during the period.

4. **Practice/Homework** Have students create an image depicting life in the colonies. Encourage students to address as many different aspects of colonial culture as possible. **LS Visual-Spatial**

📋 Alternative Assessment Handbook, Rubric 11: Discussions

The Enlightenment and the American Colonies

In the 1400s the Renaissance had changed Europeans' outlook on the world. Similarly, in the late 1600s, new ways of thinking changed ideas about government and human rights. These new ways of thinking gave rise to a European movement called the **Enlightenment**. Because the Enlightenment emphasized a search for knowledge, the period is also known as the Age of Reason.

The Scientific Revolution A revolution in science in the 1500s and 1600s helped lay the foundation for the Enlightenment. Using what is now called the scientific method, scientists used observation and experiments to look for natural laws that governed the universe.

For example, Sir Isaac Newton showed that certain physical laws—such as the force of gravity—seemed to operate everywhere in the universe. Other scientists looked for order and method in nature. The Swedish scientist Linnaeus devised a method for classifying plants and animals that is still the basis for scientific names today.

The Enlightenment in Europe Thinkers in Europe, especially in France and England, admired this new approach to science. They thought that logic and reason could also be used to improve society, law, and government.

In England, the philosopher John Locke wrote in defense of the Glorious Revolution. In his *Two Treatises of Government* (1690), he said that it was the duty of government to protect the citizens' natural rights. These natural rights were life, liberty, and property.

Locke also said that in a civil society, people had a **social contract** with their government. The social contract theory held that if a government (or ruler) did not protect citizens and their rights, then the people were justified in overthrowing the government.

In France, social critics admired English rights and freedoms. English laws limited the power of the ruler, while France still had an absolute monarchy. To limit the French monarchy, the Baron de Montesquieu (MOHN-tehs-kyoo) suggested that the powers of government be divided. This would prevent any person or group from gaining too much power.

Many Enlightenment thinkers were deists, who believed in God but not in traditional Christian teachings. They questioned the authority of any church to persecute those who did not accept its teachings. The French writer Voltaire used satire and wit to make fun of intolerance and prejudice.

Enlightenment philosophers such as Jean-Jacques Rousseau wanted to apply their ideas to education, which they believed would improve society. Others sought reforms in criminal justice and in conditions for the poor.

The Enlightenment in America The ideas of the Enlightenment began in the educated upper classes of Europe but soon spread beyond the European continent. Locke in particular was widely read in the American colonies. His ideas influenced Thomas Jefferson and Benjamin Franklin, among others. Jefferson used Locke's theories in 1776 when he wrote the Declaration of Independence:

HISTORY'S VOICES

❝We hold these truths to be self-evident, that all men are created equal, that they are endowed by their Creator with certain unalienable Rights, that among these are Life, Liberty and the pursuit of Happiness.❞

—The Declaration of Independence, 1776

Other early American leaders used Enlightenment ideas when they drafted the United States Constitution.

KEY POLITICAL THINKERS OF THE EUROPEAN ENLIGHTENMENT

QUICK FACTS

John Locke *Two Treatises of Government* (1690)	Developed a theory that government should protect citizens' natural rights, which included life, liberty, and property. Wrote that government and the people were bound by a social contract
Baron de Montesquieu *The Spirit of the Laws* (1748)	Outlined theories of government, including a republican democracy in which power would be divided to avoid tyranny
Jean-Jacques Rousseau *The Social Contract* (1762)	Argued that true democracy would require many people to share political power

---

Differentiating Instruction

Advanced Learners/GATE

1. Have students review the information in the text about the Enlightenment. Then have students reread the Declaration of Independence and the Preamble to the Constitution. Have students meet in small groups to discuss the effect of the European Enlightenment on colonial thinking and on the colonies' relationship with Britain.

2. Have each group create a political flyer calling for governmental reforms in the colonies based on the theory of natural rights.

3. Have volunteers present their flyers to the class and defend the ideas presented in them.

LS Kinesthetic, Interpersonal

Alternative Assessment Handbook, Rubric 28: Posters

Direct Teach

Reading Focus

1 What impact did the Enlightenment have in the colonies? *new way of thinking about government and human rights, the spirit of scientific discovery; ideas included in the Declaration of Independence and Constitution*

The Enlightenment and the American Colonies

Identify Who was Sir Isaac Newton? *scientist who showed that certain physical laws operate everywhere in the universe*

Analyze How did the ideas of John Locke contribute to American ideas on government? *Declaration of Independence echoed Locke's belief in natural rights and social contract*

Develop How did French thinkers contribute to ideas incorporated in the Declaration of Independence and the Constitution? *Montesquieu wanted to limit the powers of government by dividing authority; Voltaire satirized intolerance and prejudice; reformers like Rousseau wanted to reform education, criminal justice, and care for the poor.*

Quick Facts Transparency: Key Political Thinkers of the European Enlightenment

CRF: Interdisciplinary Project: Create a Ben Franklin Science Time Line

go.hrw.com
Online Resources
KEYWORD: SD7 CH3
TOPIC: EXEMPLIFYING THE ENLIGHTENMENT: BENJAMIN FRANKLIN

2 How was the Great Awakening significant? *increased church membership; linked colonies in a new way; led to the growth of new Protestant denominations; caused the founding of new institutions of higher learning*

The Great Awakening

Recall Who was Jonathan Edwards? *Puritan clergyman whose preaching appealed to the audience's fears and emotions*

Evaluate What concerns led clergymen to move toward a new revivalism? *Church membership was declining and tolerance for other religions was spreading. They worried that people were losing spiritual goals in the pursuit of worldly success.*

Activity Jonathan Edwards's **Revival Meeting** Have students create a flyer or two-minute speech inviting people to come to a revival where Jonathan Edwards will be speaking. **LS Auditory-Musical**

Primary Source

"Ignorance is preferable to error; and he is less remote from the truth who believes nothing, than he who believes what is wrong."

— Thomas Jefferson
Notes on the State of Virginia, 1787

Answers

Faces of History *inventor; scientist; helped guide colonies to independence*

Reading Check *used logic and reason to form rules for behavior of nature and society*

FACES OF HISTORY

THE GRANGER COLLECTION, NEW YORK

Benjamin Franklin
1706–1790

One of the most famous Americans in history, Benjamin Franklin was a man of many talents. He worked as a printer, publisher, author, inventor, scientist, politician, and diplomat. In all of these roles he helped shape American history.

As an inventor and scientist, Franklin exemplified the Enlightenment ideals of science and reason. His curious mind led him to invent bifocal glasses and the lightning rod, among other things. As a politician, Franklin helped draft the Albany Plan of Union and revised the first draft of the Declaration of Independence. During the American Revolution, Franklin served as a diplomat. Then at age 81, he was the oldest delegate at the Constitutional Convention.

Evaluate Why do you think Benjamin Franklin is one of the most famous Americans in history?

ACADEMIC VOCABULARY

displaced took the place of

Both Benjamin Franklin and Thomas Jefferson were interested in science and invention, applying reason to ask questions and find answers. Franklin was typical of the Enlightenment ideal of self-improvement and optimism. While still a printer's apprentice, he spent half his money on books, including one by Locke.

Enlightenment thinkers questioned common beliefs and deep-rooted superstitions. Benjamin Franklin, for example, did many experiments with electricity. In the most famous experiment, he flew a kite in a thunderstorm to prove that lightning was a form of electricity. Franklin was then able to collect the electricity from the lightning and conduct experiments with it. These experiments made him famous as a scientist, but they were controversial, too. Some people still did not believe that lightning was a form of electricity.

READING CHECK **Comparing** What was the connection between science and the Enlightenment?

The Great Awakening

Enlightenment ideas also led some people in the colonies to question long-accepted religious beliefs. They looked for rational, scientific explanations for how the universe worked.

At the time, many Christian denominations taught that human beings were essentially

---

wicked. Only God's grace or their own faith and good works could save them. Most Enlightenment thinkers, however, believed humankind was essentially good, or at least capable of learning to be good.

Changes in religious attitudes Such Enlightenment ideas disturbed the traditional religious establishment. Strict groups, such as the Puritans, were dismayed by the growing tolerance for other beliefs. Even in the 1700s, Puritan New England still appeared very strict to people in other colonies. But the Puritans themselves were already worried about the decline of religious fervor in their communities. Church membership was declining.

In addition, many colonies were becoming prosperous from business and trade. Some religious leaders worried that material values and concern for making money had displaced spiritual values. Clergy looked for new ways to bring people back to the church. That set the stage for one of the great social movements in American history.

A revival of religion That movement was a religious revival in the colonies known as the **Great Awakening**. Beginning in New England and New Jersey in the 1720s and 1730s, the Great Awakening eventually swept through all the colonies. One of its leaders was the Puritan minister **Jonathan Edwards**. Emphasizing the individual's personal relationship with God, Edwards appealed to his listeners' fears and emotions. His most famous sermon painted a terrifying picture of the agonies that sinners would suffer if they did not repent.

Like so many other American thinkers of the time, Edwards was influenced by the philosophies of men such as John Locke and Sir Isaac Newton. Like them, Jonathan Edwards valued rational thought. His fiery sermons displayed his belief in the rational, or logical, aspects of religion.

In 1739 a British Methodist minister, **George Whitefield**, traveled to America. As he had done in England, Whitefield held open-air meetings that were intended to move audiences to feel the religious spirit. Thousands came to hear him. Whitefield preached his way through the colonies. Unlike Edwards, he did not frighten his audiences, but his strong voice moved people to cry and confess their sins.

Skills Focus: Identifying Cause and Effect   At Level

Reading Skill
The Enlightenment and the Great Awakening

Draw the diagram shown for students to see. Have students copy the diagram and complete it, showing how the Enlightenment and the Great Awakening led to a new American culture. Have students share their answers and complete the class diagram. **LS Visual-Spatial**

📖 Alternative Assessment Handbook, Rubrics 6: Cause and Effect; and 13: Graphic Organizers

🗄 Graphic Organizer Transparencies

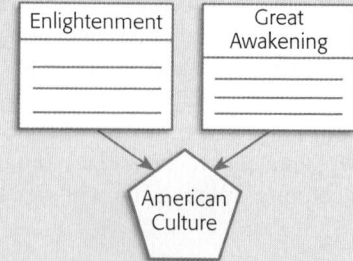

Sermon

In this 1741 sermon, clergyman Jonathan Edwards asked people to think about how God views their sinful acts.

Edwards used vivid images to stir his listeners' emotions and imaginations.

"The God that holds you over the pit of hell much as one holds a . . . loathsome insect over the fire abhors [hates] you, and is dreadfully provoked; his wrath toward you burns like fire; he looks upon you as worthy of nothing else but to be cast into the fire; he is of purer eyes than to bear you in his sight; you are ten thousand times more abominable [horrible] in his eyes than the most hateful venomous serpent is in ours. You have offended him infinitely more than ever a stubborn rebel did his prince, and yet it is nothing but his hand that holds you from falling into the fire every moment."

Great Awakening preachers believed that people would turn toward evil without the help of God.

SKILLS FOCUS — READING LIKE A HISTORIAN

1. **Analyzing Primary Sources** What imagery does Edwards use to describe his view of God's relationship with sinners?
2. **Contrasting** How does this sermon bring forth the idea of both God's anger and his forgiveness?

See *Skills Handbook*, pp. H10, H28–H29

Although Benjamin Franklin and George Whitefield did not agree about religion, they became good friends. In his *Autobiography* Franklin describes one of Whitefield's crowded meetings in Philadelphia:

HISTORY'S VOICES

❝ He had a loud and clear Voice, and articulated his Words & Sentences so perfectly that he might be heard and understood at a great Distance . . . He preached one evening from the top of the Court House Steps . . . I computed that he might well be heard by more than Thirty-Thousand. ❞

—*The Autobiography of Benjamin Franklin, 1793*

The Great Awakening led to an increase in church membership in the 1700s. It also resulted in the growth of new Protestant denominations in America. Puritan beliefs formed the basis of the Congregational Church. By the mid-1700s, the evangelistic movements of the Great Awakening helped the Methodist, Baptist, and Presbyterian churches to become well established.

The Great Awakening had other key effects on the colonies. Although its leaders sometimes disagreed on religious matters, overall the Great Awakening still forged one of the first links uniting the colonies. It also led to the creation of several respected centers of learning, including Princeton, Brown, and Rutgers colleges, as well as Dartmouth College.

READING CHECK **Summarizing** How did the Great Awakening influence religious attitudes in the colonies?

The Colonies Become More Diverse

The first colonists in New England, Virginia, and the Carolinas came primarily from England. Other colonies, especially New York and Pennsylvania, attracted people from more diverse backgrounds. Dutch influence remained strong in New York.

Non-English colonists In the early 1700s, large numbers of Scots and Scots-Irish (Scots from Northern Ireland) emigrated to the colonies. They settled mainly in the middle colonies and the Carolinas and were pioneers in settling the mountainous back country. Mostly strict Presbyterians, they had little love for the

---

Reading Focus

The Great Awakening

Contrast How did George Whitefield differ from Jonathan Edwards? *did not try to frighten audiences; encouraged them to feel religious spirit and confess their sins*

Identify Cause and Effect How did Protestant denominations benefit from the Great Awakening? *Baptist, Methodist, and Presbyterian churches became well established during the Great Awakening.*

Reading Focus

❸ How did the colonies become more diverse in the 1700s? *Non-English settlers began to arrive: Scots, Scots-Irish, Germans, French Huguenots, and Jews.*

The Colonies Become More Diverse

Describe Where did the Scots and Scots-Irish settle? *middle colonies; Carolinas; mountainous back country*

Explain Why did Germans and Jews emigrate to the Americas? *for religious freedom and tolerance*

Skills Focus: Analyzing Primary Sources

At Level

Reading Like a Historian Skill
Jonathan Edwards

1. Read the primary source excerpt from Jonathan Edwards to the class. Have students work in mixed-ability pairs to look up and define unfamiliar words. Then have each pair write a paraphrase of the excerpt.

2. Have each student write an article on Edwards's sermon for a colonial newspaper.

Students should briefly summarize Edwards's message and then predict how this sermon might affect the colonists. Have volunteers share their articles with the class.

LS Verbal-Linguistic

📖 Alternative Assessment Handbook, Rubric 23: Newspapers

Answers

Reading Like a Historian 1. *fire; insects; snakes;* **2.** *although people's sins offend God greatly, he still keeps the fires of hell away from them*

Reading Check *Church membership grew and several new denominations became well established.*

④ What was life like in colonial America? *cities were well-supplied with goods from Europe, had many social events and newspapers, communications with Europe slow; African Americans formed strong communities*

Life in Colonial America

Explain Why was city life easier for women than life on a farm? *They were freed from time-consuming farm work; wealthier women could read, write, or attend plays and concerts.*

Analyze Why did Crèvecoeur note that American culture was something new? *possible answer—The mixture of many cultures created new ways of life.*

Recent Scholarship

In *Inventing the "Great Awakening,"* Frank Lambert interprets the Great Awakening as an "invention" by the colonists who led the religious revival. According to Lambert, George Whitefield and other religious leaders developed their own understanding of the work in which they were involved, rather than waiting for later historians to analyze the significance of this movement. Lambert's book moves beyond a reexamination of the Great Awakening by investigating how a popular movement was able to develop before modern media.

Inventing the "Great Awakening" by Frank Lambert. Princeton University Press, 1999

Answers

American Civil Liberty *an important step towards freedom of the press*

Reading Check *new languages, religions, customs, and skills from Scots, Scots-Irish, French Huguenots, Germans, and Jews*

English government. They were always ready to fight for their political rights.

Religious unrest in Europe and religious tolerance in the colonies attracted Germans, French Huguenots, and Jews to America. Many German colonists were skilled farmers and artisans. They established weaving mills, ironworks, and glassworks. French colonists also brought their craft and scientific skills to the colonies. Jewish communities grew up in the cities of Newport, Philadelphia, New York, and Charleston.

THE IMPACT TODAY

Daily Life
Today, New York's population is 11 percent African American, 10 percent Puerto Rican, 9 percent Italian, 5 percent Irish, 5 percent Dominican, and 4.5 percent Chinese. The city also includes the nation's largest Jewish community.

The new American As often happens, it took a newcomer to recognize what America was becoming. Hector St. John de Crèvecoeur (krehv-CUHR) was a French immigrant who looked carefully at his adopted country.

HISTORY'S VOICES

❝What then is the American, this new man? He is neither an European, nor the descendant of an European . . . He is an American . . . Here individuals of all nations are melted into a new race of men, whose labours and posterity will one day cause great changes in the world.❞

—*Letters from an American Farmer*, 1782

READING CHECK **Identifying the Main Idea** Describe the growing ethnic, religious, and occupational diversity in colonial America.

Life in Colonial America

Early English settlers, along with newcomers from many countries, were creating a new American culture. As Hector St. John de Crèvecoeur had noticed, it was not English or European, but something new.

Colonial cities Colonial cities were lively, exciting places. Some had streets paved with cobblestones and sidewalks lit by oil lamps. Ships from foreign ports anchored in the harbors. People waited eagerly for letters from relatives. They also enjoyed the latest English newspapers and magazines with gossip and drawings of new fashions.

Many colonial cities had libraries, bookshops, and impressive public buildings. City dwellers could go to plays or concerts. They shopped in markets for country produce and luxury goods from Europe. Schools taught music, dancing, drawing, and painting as well as more traditional academic subjects.

In some ways, city life was easier for women than rural life was. They were freed from the hard work of farming, such as milking cows or working in their gardens, even though they still had many daily household tasks to perform. Women in more prosperous households had more time for reading and writing. Both men

American Civil Liberty

Freedom of the Press

Freedom of the press was not an English tradition. Instead, it developed in the American colonies. In 1734 a New York printer named John Peter Zenger printed several newspaper articles in the *New York Weekly Journal* criticizing the royal governor. Officials burned the paper and arrested Zenger.

Under English law, Zenger could have been found guilty simply for publishing the articles. But Zenger's lawyer, Andrew Hamilton, argued that the articles could not be considered libel—an unlawful attack of character—if they were true. He insisted that the jury's decision could potentially "affect every freeman that lives under a British government on the mainland of America."

The judge tried to uphold the law as written, but the jury agreed with Hamilton and freed Zenger. The case of *Crown* v. *Zenger* was an important step towards freedom of the press. The precedent it set eventually led to the acceptance of truth as a defense in cases of libel.

Identifying Cause and Effect How did the *Zenger* case influence the British colonies?

This tapestry commemorates both the *Zenger* case and victory for a free press.

Collaborative Learning

At Level

Life in a Colonial City

1. Organize the class into small groups. Have each group review and discuss the information in the text about life in a colonial city.

2. Have each group write a short play depicting life in colonial America. Students should discuss popular culture, methods of communication, influences from various cultures, and differences between city life and rural life.

3. Have volunteers perform their plays for the class. **LS Auditory-Musical, Kinesthetic**

📖 Alternative Assessment Handbook, Rubric 33: Skits and Reader's Theater

and women spent many hours writing letters to keep in touch with friends and family.

Popular culture People in colonial America worked hard but had time for play, too. Many got their work done in sociable ways, such as in quilting bees or barn raisings. Northern colonists went ice-skating and sledding in winter. Others enjoyed horse racing and hunting.

People made their own entertainments. Visiting neighbors was a favorite pastime. Social events in the colonies often included getting together with neighbors to dance or listen to music.

Colonial communications Printers in the colonies were also publishers. They printed and distributed newspapers, books, advertisements, and political announcements. The first American printer set up a printing press in Cambridge, Massachusetts. In 1640 he published the *Bay Psalm Book* for use in Puritan church services.

Communications were slow between the colonies and with England. Letters to England went by ship, taking many weeks. The ever-inventive Benjamin Franklin helped improve the postal service between colonies. The postal service also carried newspapers.

Influential newspapers were published in Boston, New York, and Philadelphia. Printing was so expensive, however, that only the most pertinent information was included in their pages. This usually meant that classified advertisements and reports of crop prices filled most columns of colonial newspapers.

Some newspaper publishers were careful not to disagree with royal officials, but others were bolder. In 1734 British royal officials arrested publisher John Peter Zenger for printing material critical of the New York governor. In the court case that followed, Zenger won the first important victory for freedom of the press in the American colonies. (See American Civil Liberty on the opposite page.)

African American culture In spite of the difficulties of their lives, enslaved Africans created their own culture and society. This was especially true on larger plantations. Their community grew to include others nearby.

African Americans tried to build a strong family structure. But the realities of slavery split husbands and wives, parents and children, who were often sold separately and sent away. Kinship networks had always been important in many African cultures. Now they became essential as a way of looking after those who had lost their real families.

Religion was another strength of the community. Many African Americans were Christians but also kept older African beliefs. The slave community preserved music and dance traditions as well. African music, foods, and other traditions gradually became a part of American culture.

READING CHECK **Summarizing** In what ways were African families in the colonies affected by slavery?

SECTION 3 ASSESSMENT

go.hrw.com
Online Quiz
Keyword: SD7 HP3

Reviewing Ideas, Terms, and People

1. **a. Define** What was the **Enlightenment**?
   b. Explain What was John Locke's view of the relationship between people and government?
   c. Elaborate How did Locke's ideas influence British colonists in North America?

2. **a. Identify** Who was **George Whitefield**, and why was he important?
   b. Compare How did **Jonathan Edwards** and Whitefield differ in their appeals to colonial audiences?
   c. Evaluate What influence did the **Great Awakening** have on colonial religion?

3. **a. Recall** Where did the Scots-Irish settle in the colonies?
   b. Make Generalizations What skills did later immigrants bring to the colonies?

4. **a. Recall** What kinds of entertainment were popular in the American colonies?
   b. Compare How did the issues in Zenger's trial compare with the issues in the arrest of Edmund Andros?

Critical Thinking

5. **Analyzing** Copy the chart below and then list the different influences on colonial culture.

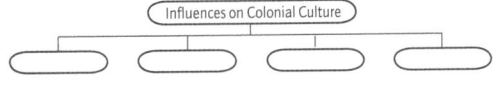

6. **Expository** Write a letter to the editor of a colonial newspaper. Explain why you think that it was right or wrong for John Peter Zenger to criticize a royal official.

COLONIAL LIFE **89**

Section 3 Assessment Answers

1. **a.** new ways of thinking about government and human rights
   b. social contract; government should protect rights of citizens
   c. caused people to question government, view human rights as basic legal rights

2. **a.** Methodist minister; popular preacher
   b. Edwards appealed to fears; Whitefield moved people to feel religious spirit
   c. increased church membership, grew new churches

3. **a.** middle colonies; Carolinas; back country
   b. weaving, ironworking, glass making; other craft and scientific skills

4. **a.** plays, concerts, sports, reading and writing, dancing
   b. both involved criticizing the government

5. Scientific Revolution, diverse population; Enlightenment; Great Awakening

6. possible answer—right, freedom of press should be protected

89

Bellringer

The Inside Story. . . Use the **Daily Bellringer Transparency** to help students answer the question.

📀 Daily Bellringer Transparency, Section 4

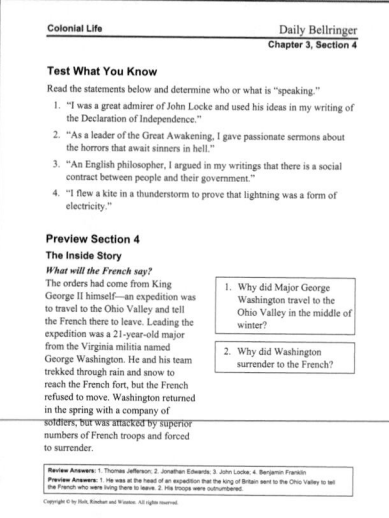

| Colonial Life | Daily Bellringer |
| | Chapter 3, Section 4 |

Test What You Know

Read the statements below and determine who or what is "speaking."

1. "I was a great admirer of John Locke and used his ideas in my writing of the Declaration of Independence."
2. "As a leader of the Great Awakening, I gave passionate sermons about the horrors that await sinners in hell."
3. "An English philosopher, I argued in my writings that there is a social contract between people and their government."
4. "I flew a kite in a thunderstorm to prove that lightning was a form of electricity."

Preview Section 4
The Inside Story

What will the French say?
The orders had come from King George II himself—an expedition was to travel to the Ohio Valley and tell the French there to leave. Leading the expedition was a 21-year-old major from the Virginia militia named George Washington. He and his team trekked through rain and snow to reach the French fort, but the French refused to move. Washington returned in the spring with a company of soldiers, but was attacked by superior numbers of French troops and forced to surrender.

1. Why did Major George Washington travel to the Ohio Valley in the middle of winter?

2. Why did Washington surrender to the French?

Review Answers: 1. Thomas Jefferson; 2. Jonathan Edwards; 3. John Locke; 4. Benjamin Franklin
Preview Answers: 1. He was at the head of an expedition that the king of Britain sent to the Ohio Valley to tell the French who were living there to leave. 2. His troops were outnumbered.

Copyright © by Holt, Rinehart and Winston. All rights reserved.

Taking Notes

Albany Plan of Union, 1754; British fail to capture Fort Duquesne, 1755; French capture Fort Oswego and Fort William Henry, 1756; French defeated British at Fort Ticonderoga, 1758; British and colonial troops recapture Fort Duquesne, 1758; Quebec, a French city, surrendered in 1759; Treaty of Paris ended war, 1763

The French and Indian War

BEFORE YOU READ

MAIN IDEA

The French and Indian War established British dominance in North America but put a strain on the relationship with the colonists.

READING FOCUS

1. How did France develop an empire in North America?
2. Why did Spain and England clash in North America?
3. What were major events in the French and Indian War?
4. What were the effects of the French and Indian War on all those involved?

KEY TERMS AND PEOPLE

George Washington
Iroquois League
Albany Plan of Union
William Pitt
Treaty of Paris
George Grenville
Pontiac
Proclamation of 1763

TAKING NOTES As you read, take notes on the major events and battles of the French and Indian War, 1754–1763. Record your notes on a graphic organizer like the one shown here. You may need to add more rows.

Major Event or Battle	Date

First Steps to FAME?

THE INSIDE STORY
What will the French say? A small expedition set out on horseback from Virginia in October 1753. It included four frontiersmen, two translators, and one 21-year-old major in the Virginia militia. The officer's name was **George Washington**. On orders from King George II, the governor of Virginia had sent Washington to the Ohio Valley to warn the French that they were on British lands and must leave.

The group traveled north through snow and rain to a French fort near Lake Erie. The French officers greeted Washington formally, but they said no to the king's message. Now Washington had to get home to Virginia in mid-winter.

A few months later, in the spring of 1754, Washington was sent back with a company of soldiers. The Virginians built a small log fort, Fort Necessity, near the French stronghold of Fort Duquesne, but they were badly outnumbered. When a much larger French force attacked, Washington had to surrender. ◢

Teach the Main Idea

At Level

The French and Indian War

1. **Teach** Ask students the Reading Focus questions to teach this section.

2. **Apply** Arrange students into small groups. Half of the groups should represent French fur traders, and the other half should represent Spanish friars heading for Florida. Each group should discuss and create a set of plans for the New World, especially how they plan to deal with English settlers in North America. Have volunteers read their plans to the class. **LS Interpersonal**

3. **Review** As you review the section, have students explain how tensions in the New World affected relationships among European countries.

4. **Practice/Homework** Have students create a brief speech asking Native Americans to fight in the French and Indian War. **LS Auditory-Musical**

📄 Alternative Assessment Handbook, Rubric 43: Writing to Persuade

France in North America

The first permanent French settlement in North America was a fur-trading post started in 1608 at Quebec by Samuel de Champlain. Later that century, La Salle claimed the Mississippi basin for France. He named the region Louisiana, after the French king Louis XIV.

To protect the fur trade, Champlain made alliances with the Algonquians and Hurons. In 1609 the French helped those allies in raids against the Iroquois Mohawks.

Instead of building towns along the coast, French fur traders and missionaries traveled deep into the interior. They formed close ties with Native American fur trappers. Traders lived in Native American villages, learned their languages, and married local women.

As early as the 1600s, English and French traders in the Great Lakes region fought over the fur trade. They also clashed over the rich fishing grounds off Nova Scotia and over islands in the Caribbean.

France had built outposts from the Great Lakes to the Mississippi Valley by the early 1700s. French forts at Detroit, Niagara, Kaskaskia, and New Orleans bordered the English colonies to the west.

While the French were forming alliances with Native Americans, the English were doing the same thing. The power struggle between the two nations and their allies meant constant battles along the frontier.

READING CHECK Identifying the Main Idea What was the basis of the economy in France's colonies in America?

Spain and England Clash

Spain and England clashed in North America, especially in the area known as La Florida. It included much of Georgia and South Carolina, the Florida peninsula, and land along the Gulf Coast.

Spain wanted its territory in La Florida as a defense against France and England. La Florida did not have gold, silver, or particularly fertile soil. But holding this territory allowed Spain to guard the sea routes for Spanish treasure ships returning from Mexico.

In the late 1500s, Franciscan friars began to establish missions along the Atlantic coast. By the mid-1600s, the Spanish were operating nearly 40 missions in Florida and Georgia.

As English colonies expanded southward, they threatened the Spanish missions and settlements. Carolina slave raiders began to attack the Spanish missions. By 1700 the Spanish presence in Florida had been reduced to the areas of St. Augustine and Pensacola.

READING CHECK Contrasting How did Florida differ from Spain's colonies in Mexico?

The French and Indian War

The French and Indian War lasted from 1754 to 1763 and became part of a larger war between France and Great Britain called the Seven Years' War. War between France and Great Britain broke out in the colonies first, then spread to the European continent. The French joined with Native Americans to attack the British in North America. Spain and its colonies were also involved.

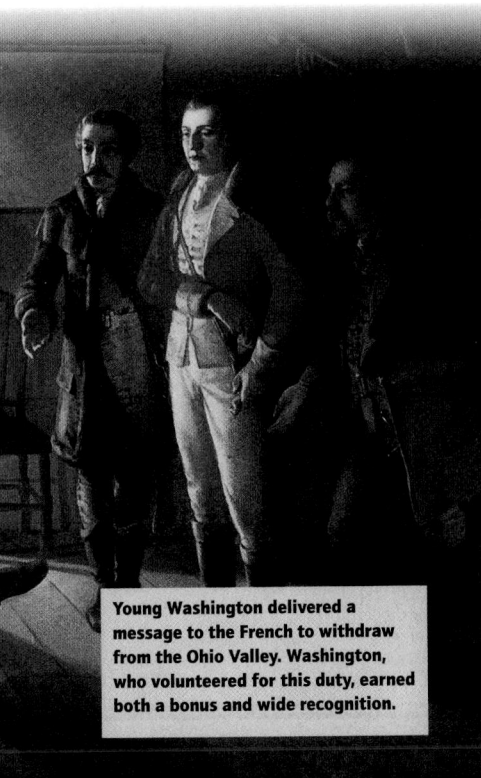

Young Washington delivered a message to the French to withdraw from the Ohio Valley. Washington, who volunteered for this duty, earned both a bonus and wide recognition.

THE IMPACT TODAY

Government
Before 1707 England and Scotland were officially separate nations. In 1707 they joined together as the Kingdom of Great Britain. Today the nation is known officially as the United Kingdom of Great Britain and Northern Ireland. The United Kingdom includes England, Scotland, Wales, and Northern Ireland.

COLONIAL LIFE **91**

Direct Teach

Reading Focus

❶ How did France develop an empire in North America? *French fur traders established relations with Native Americans; built outposts to defend the trade routes*

France in North America

Recall Why did Champlain make alliances with the Huron and Algonquian? *to protect the French fur trade*

Analyze How did French traders form close ties with Native Americans? *learned their languages; lived in their villages; married Native American women*

Reading Focus

❷ Why did Spain and England clash in North America? *Both claimed territory in "La Florida."*

Spain and England Clash

Identify What land did "La Florida" include? *parts of South Carolina, Georgia, the Florida peninsula, and land along the Gulf Coast*

Analyze Why was "La Florida" a cause of conflict between Spanish and English settlers? *Both countries claimed parts of the territory; clashes were frequent.*

📄 CRF: Primary Source Activity: The British Colonies in North America

Differentiating Instruction

Below Level   Standard English Mastery

English-Language Learners

1. Guide students in a discussion of the French fur traders in North America. Have students take notes during the discussion.

2. Have students use their notes to write a letter from a French fur trader to his family in France, describing life in the American Northeast and what life among Native Americans was like.

3. Have volunteers read their letters to the class.
LS Verbal-Linguistic, Intrapersonal

📄 Alternative Assessment Handbook, Rubric 25: Personal Letters

Answers

Reading Check (top) *fur trading;* **(bottom)** *Florida had no gold and little fertile land; it was strategically useful in defending Spain's treasure fleets.*

Reading Focus

❸ **What were major events in the French and Indian War?** *Iroquois League allied with Britain; Albany Plan was developed; British defeated at Forts Duquesne and Ticonderoga; British recaptured Fort Duquesne and captured Quebec; France surrendered*

The French and Indian War

Recall How did the Iroquois League view Europeans? *as enemies*

Analyze Why did Franklin propose the Albany Plan of Union? *He wanted to unite the colonies for military purposes.*

📄 CRF: Biography: Robert Rogers

Primary Source

"It is proposed that humble application be made for an act of Parliament of Great Britain, by virtue of which one general government may be formed in America, including all the said colonies, within and under which government each colony may retain its present constitution . . . "

Albany Plan of Union, 1754

Answers

Reading Like a Historian
1. *a divided snake;* 2. *easy to understand, even for people who could not read*

The Iroquois League An alliance of Native Americans called the **Iroquois League** allied itself with Britain. The League had formed nearly 200 years earlier in what is now upstate New York. The Mohawk, Oneida, Onondaga, Cayuga, and Seneca peoples—often at war with each other—formed an alliance in 1570. According to tradition, a prophet named Dekanawidah led the Five Nations to "plant the Tree of Great Peace" and unite as the Iroquois League. The Tuscarora joined in 1722 as the sixth nation.

The Iroquois League had a constitution and a council of leaders. Its unity allowed the Iroquois League to resist European takeover. Although most northeastern Native Americans had allied with the French, the Iroquois League saw the Europeans as enemies.

The Albany Plan In the early 1750s conflict with France erupted in the Ohio River Valley. The French built Fort Duquesne (doo-KAYN) at the point where the Allegheny and Monongahela rivers join to form the Ohio—the site of Pittsburgh today. But a Virginia-based land company planned to bring settlers there. In 1754 George Washington and his militia made an unsuccessful attempt to take this land back from France. This was the first skirmish of the French and Indian War.

Later in 1754, at the urging of British officials, delegates from New England, New York, Pennsylvania, and Maryland met in Albany. Their main goal was to win the support of the Iroquois League against the French. At the same time, they wanted to achieve some sort of unity among the colonies. Benjamin Franklin proposed the **Albany Plan of Union** as a way to colonial unity. Each colony would keep its own constitution, while a grand council would deal with military issues, Native American relations, and western settlement. Although the Albany Plan of Union was never approved, it was the first atttempt to unite the colonies.

The war continues The early war went badly for the British. Their commander, General Edward Braddock, tried again to capture

---

PRIMARY SOURCES

Political Cartoon

In 1754 Benjamin Franklin published this political cartoon to encourage support for the Albany Plan of Union.

The colonies are represented as divided parts of a snake. Some people thought Franklin chose a snake to reflect the winding eastern coastline.

JOIN, or DIE.

The slogan meant that the colonies should join together because they were on the verge of war with France.

Skills Focus | **READING LIKE A HISTORIAN**

1. **Analyzing Primary Sources** What image did Franklin use to represent the colonies?
2. **Drawing Conclusions** Why do you think Franklin chose to present his message through a cartoon?

See **Skills Handbook**, pp. H12, H28–H29

92 CHAPTER 3

Skills Focus: Analyzing Primary Sources   **Above Level**

Reading Like a Historian Skill
The Albany Plan of Union

1. Read the following quote about the Albany Plan from Benjamin Franklin, written 35 years later: "On Reflection it now seems probable, that if the foregoing Plan or some thing like it, had been adopted and carried into Execution, the subsequent Separation of the Colonies from the Mother Country might not so soon have happened, nor the Mischiefs suffered on both sides have occurred, perhaps during another Century."

2. Have students write an essay explaining what Franklin suggested in the quote. *Franklin believed that if the Albany Plan of Union had been adopted, the American Revolution might not have occurred for many years.*

LS **Verbal-Linguistic**

📄 Alternative Assessment Handbook, Rubric 40: Writing to Describe

Fort Duquesne in 1755. George Washington was his chief aide, leading about 250 Virginia militia.

In unfamiliar territory, the British soldiers were easy targets for an ambush by the French and their Native American allies. Almost 1,000 were wounded or killed, including Braddock. George Washington then assumed command of the army and proved a heroic leader, even though two horses were shot out from under him.

In New York, the Marquis de Montcalm, the French commander, won victory after victory. He captured Fort Oswego on Lake Ontario and Fort William Henry on Lake George in 1756. Montcalm's greatest battle was at Fort Ticonderoga in 1758, when his 3,800 men turned back a British force of 15,000.

William Pitt became the British secretary of state in 1757 and took control of directing the war. British officers in America began to force colonists into the army, seize supplies, and send soldiers to stay in colonists' houses. The colonists resented this and resisted. Pitt then relaxed some policies, sending more British soldiers to America.

In 1758 British and colonial troops recaptured Fort Duquesne. Their Native American allies began to desert the French. The next year the British took back Fort Ticonderoga and captured Fort Niagara and Crown Point on Lake Champlain.

Next, General James Wolfe besieged Quebec. Montcalm thought that the city's location on a steep bluff would protect it. But the British found a path up the cliff from the river. In the battle that followed, both commanders were killed. Quebec surrendered in September 1759. That was the turning point in the war, and France surrendered the following year.

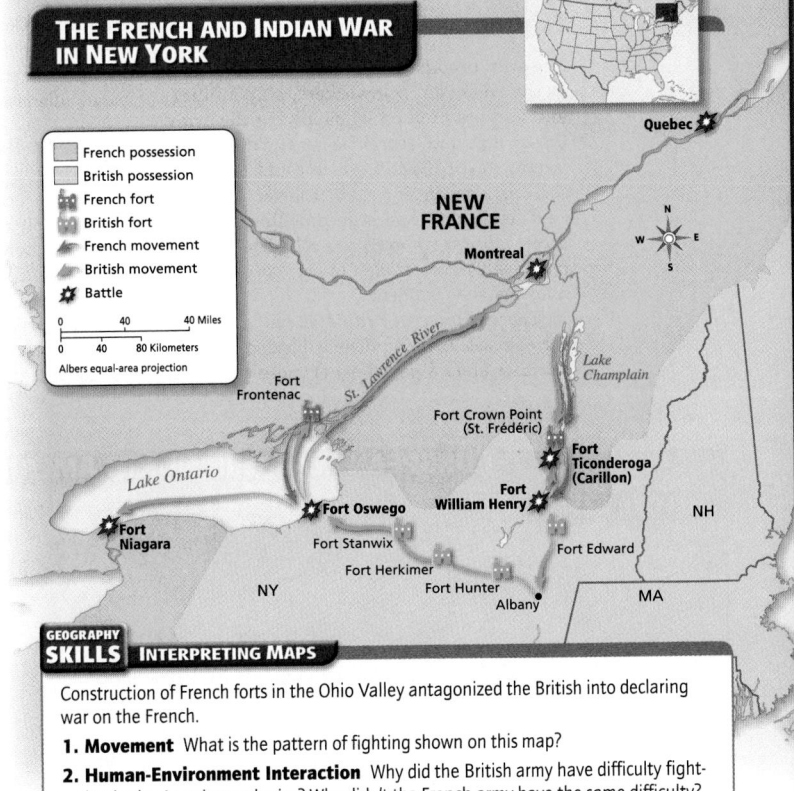

THE FRENCH AND INDIAN WAR IN NEW YORK

French possession
British possession
French fort
British fort
French movement
British movement
Battle

0   40   40 Miles
0   40   80 Kilometers
Albers equal-area projection

Quebec
NEW FRANCE
Montreal
Fort Frontenac
St. Lawrence River
Lake Ontario
Lake Champlain
Fort Crown Point (St. Frédéric)
Fort Ticonderoga (Carillon)
Fort Niagara
Fort Oswego
Fort William Henry
Fort Stanwix
Fort Herkimer
Fort Hunter
Fort Edward
Albany
NY
NH
MA

GEOGRAPHY SKILLS INTERPRETING MAPS

Construction of French forts in the Ohio Valley antagonized the British into declaring war on the French.

1. **Movement** What is the pattern of fighting shown on this map?
2. **Human-Environment Interaction** Why did the British army have difficulty fighting in the American colonies? Why didn't the French army have the same difficulty?

See **Skills Handbook**, p. H20

The peace treaty The **Treaty of Paris**, signed in 1763, ended the Seven Years' War in Europe and the French and Indian War in North America. Britain gained all French land east of the Mississippi River—including much of what is now Canada. This victory gave Britain the basis of what would become a mighty empire.

Spain gave up control of Florida to Britain but got a major prize from its ally France—the huge Louisiana Territory, including the city of New Orleans. An earlier secret treaty between the two monarchs had made the transfer, but the Treaty of Paris confirmed it. France kept two islands near Canada and regained some Caribbean islands.

READING CHECK Drawing Conclusions
What was the goal of the Albany Plan of Union?

COLONIAL LIFE **93**

Direct Teach

Reading Focus

The French and Indian War

Recall Who was Edward Braddock? *the British commanding general in America*

Analyze How well did the Marquis de Montcalm perform in the early years of the war? *He was very successful, and the French troops under his command won victory after victory; at Ticonderoga his 3,800 men defeated 15,000 British troops.*

Evaluate How well did Britain do in the Treaty of Paris? *very well; gained all French land east of the Mississippi, including much of Canada; gained Florida from Spain*

Map Transparency: The French and Indian War in New York

Skills Focus: Summarizing

Below Level

Reading Skill
The French and Indian War

1. Guide students in a discussion of the French and Indian War. Then organize the class into small groups.

2. Have each group design a Web page about the French forces in America and the importance of their Native American allies. Students should include what happened to that alliance

after British and colonial troops recaptured Fort Duquesne.

3. Have volunteers display their designs to the class. **LS** **Interpersonal, Visual-Spatial**

Alternative Assessment Handbook, Rubric 14: Group Activity

Answers

Interpreting Maps 1. *toward forts and Lake Ontario;* **2.** *British troops unfamiliar with territory, making them easy targets for ambushes; colonists resented British troops; French worked and lived with Native Americans, who knew the territory*

Reading Check *to unite the colonies for military defense*

❹ What were the effects of the French and Indian War on all those involved? *Some colonists benefited from economic opportunity and from newly acquired lands; the Ohio Valley was temporarily opened to settlers; Native Americans suffered.*

Effects of the War

Explain How did the war help unite the colonies? *They were forced to work together in common defense.*

Summarize What was the intent of the Proclamation of 1763? *to prevent settlers from moving west of the Appalachians, reserving that land for Native Americans*

Make Judgments Why do you think colonists did not feel bound by the Proclamation of 1763? *possible answers—did not respect British authority; were determined to move west*

🖳 Map Transparency: European Claims in North America: Before 1754, in 1763

Effects of the War

The war brought some important benefits to the colonists. Ironworkers, shipbuilding, and farmers profited by supplying the army. Carolinians and Georgians benefited from the acquisition of Florida, which could no longer serve as a haven for runaway slaves.

Though they had been unwilling to unite at first, the war forced the colonists to work together. Their common effort increased the colonists' self-confidence.

The war brought Britain an empire, but at a great cost. British officials decided that the colonists should pay some of those expenses.

After King George III took the throne in 1760, his new prime minister, **George Grenville**, wanted to be strict with the colonies. His policies would alienate the colonists even further.

Pontiac's Rebellion The Treaty of Paris gave Britain control over the Great Lakes region, but its native peoples resisted the take-over. Their leader was **Pontiac**, an Ottawa chief in what is now Michigan. At first Pontiac welcomed colonial and British troops who were taking over French forts. But he later realized that the British were not as friendly toward Native Americans as the French. He made a daring plan to drive them out.

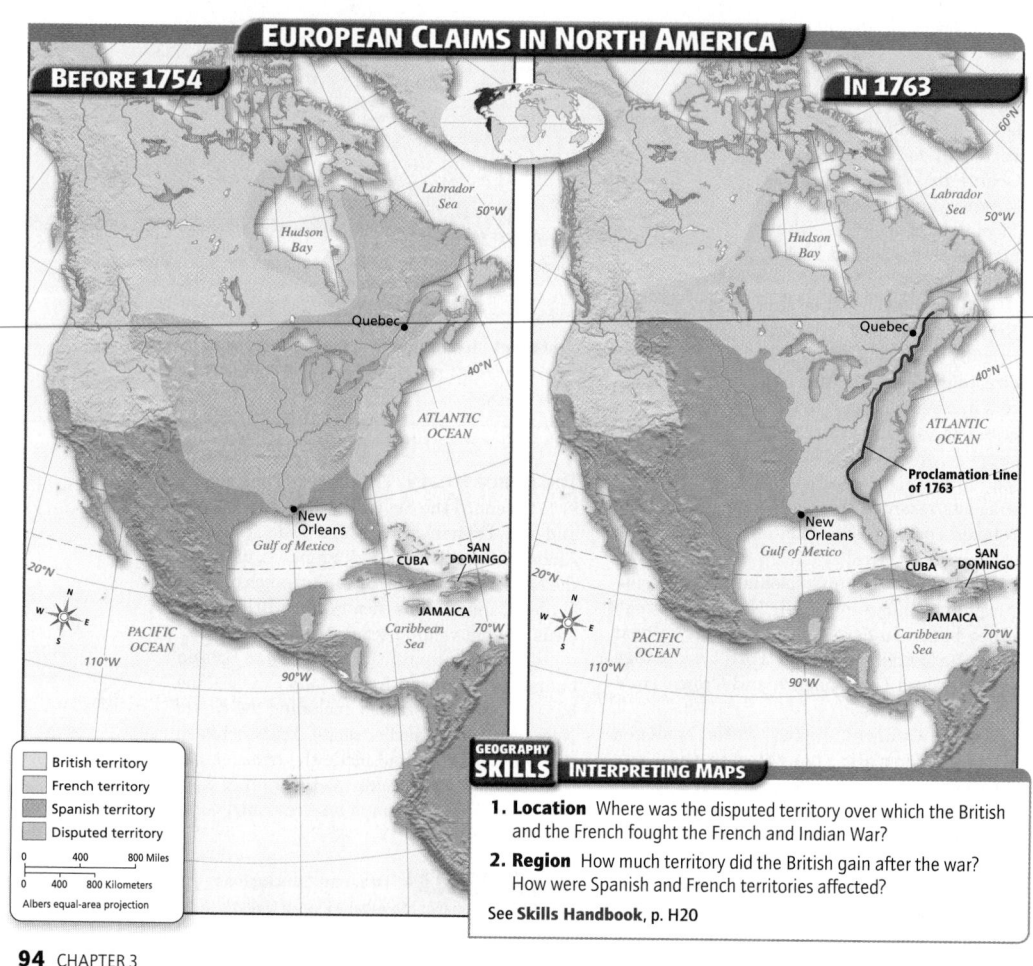

EUROPEAN CLAIMS IN NORTH AMERICA

BEFORE 1754 — IN 1763

Proclamation Line of 1763

- British territory
- French territory
- Spanish territory
- Disputed territory

0   400   800 Miles
0   400   800 Kilometers
Albers equal-area projection

GEOGRAPHY SKILLS INTERPRETING MAPS

1. **Location** Where was the disputed territory over which the British and the French fought the French and Indian War?

2. **Region** How much territory did the British gain after the war? How were Spanish and French territories affected?

See **Skills Handbook**, p. H20

94 CHAPTER 3

Answers

Interpreting Maps 1. *along the Appalachian Mountains, west of the colonies;* **2.** *all French land east of the Mississippi, including much of Canada, and Florida; Spain ceded Florida, gained Louisiana Territory; France kept two northern islands and some Caribbean islands*

Skills Focus: Analyzing Costs and Benefits   At Level

Social Studies Skill
The French and Indian War

Copy the graphic organizer for students to see. Have students work in small groups to fill in the organizer with the costs and the benefits of the French and Indian War. Have students point the needle toward whichever side is greater. 🅛 **Interpersonal, Visual-Spatial**

📄 Alternative Assessment Handbook, Rubric 13: Graphic Organizers

🖳 Graphic Organizer Transparencies

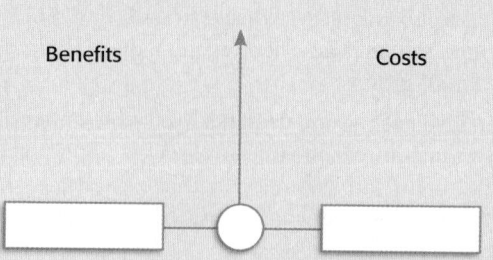

Benefits   Costs

In 1762 Pontiac put together an alliance of almost all the Native Americans in the Upper Midwest. His strategy was for each group to overcome the nearest British fort and then attack the surrounding settlements. Pontiac expected help from the French, but that help never arrived and the siege failed.

The war went on for several years. Pontiac's forces wiped out forts and settlements, but the British held on. In 1766 Pontiac agreed to a peace treaty.

The Proclamation of 1763 As soon as the French left, American traders and settlers crossed the mountains into the Ohio Valley. To avoid conflicts with the Native Americans there, officials decided to stop colonists from moving west. With the **Proclamation of 1763**, they drew a line along the Appalachian Mountains, reserving land on the western side for Native Americans.

This appealed to British officials because it gave them control of migration westward. It also slowed the movement out of cities, which were centers of trade and prosperity.

Effects on Native Americans Overall, the war was a disaster for the Native Americans of the Ohio Valley, no matter which side they had chosen. Most had supported the losing French. Even the Iroquois League, who had been allies of the British, had been weakened by the war.

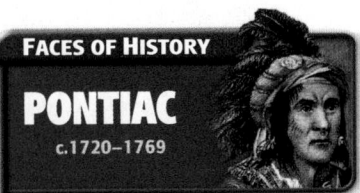

FACES OF HISTORY

PONTIAC
c.1720–1769

Pontiac was born in present-day Michigan to parents from two different Native American groups in the area, the Ottawa and the Ojibwa.

Pontiac traveled widely, meeting with various Native American groups. By 1755 he ruled as chief of a strong organization that united the Ottawas, Ojibwas and Potawatomies.

When the British began to settle in the region, Pontiac rallied the various Native American groups to oppose the newcomers. Pontiac and other Native American leaders laid siege to the British Fort Detroit for six months. While the siege was not successful, Pontiac won fame for his leadership.

Draw Conclusions Why was Pontiac considered a great leader?

The British believed the Iroquois had given only half-hearted support and no longer felt as friendly toward their former allies.

Although the Proclamation of 1763 was meant to slow western settlement, it did take away some native lands. Plus, settlers often ignored the Proclamation altogether. Later treaties continued to push the line of white settlement farther and farther west.

READING CHECK **Summarizing** What were the major effects of the French and Indian War?

SECTION 4 ASSESSMENT

go.hrw.com
Online Quiz
Keyword: SD7 HP3

Reviewing Ideas, Terms, and People

1. **a. Identify** What was the role of Samuel de Champlain in French settlement in North America?
   b. Compare How did the French colonies in North America differ from the British colonies?

2. **a. Recall** Why was Florida an important part of Spain's North American empire?
   b. Summarize What led to clashes between the British and Spanish in Florida?

3. **a. Identify** What were the roles of **George Washington**, Edward Braddock, Marquis de Montcalm, and **William Pitt** in the French and Indian War?
   b. Interpret Which country lost the most territory as a result of the French and Indian War?

4. **a. Recall** What was Pontiac's strategy to defeat the British? Did he succeed?

b. Make Inferences Why did British officials want to slow migration out of cities?
c. Predict How might the colonists' new self-confidence affect their relationship with British officials?

Critical Thinking

5. **Sequencing** Copy the chart below and make a time line of major events and battles in the French and Indian War.

The French and Indian War: 1754 — 1756 — 1758 — 1760 — 1762

FOCUS ON WRITING

6. **Persuasive** As a colonial newspaper editor, write an editorial either defending or attacking the British policy of drafting colonists and quartering soldiers in people's homes.

COLONIAL LIFE **95**

Review & Assess

Close
Have students explain what France and Great Britain gained and lost in the French and Indian War.

Review
- Online Quiz, Section 4
- Daily Test Practice Transparency

Assess
- **SE** Section 4 Assessment
- Progress Assessment: Section 4 Quiz
- Alternative Assessment Handbook

Reteach
- Interactive Reader and Study Guide, Section 4
- Interactive Skills Tutor CD-ROM

Section 4 Assessment Answers

1. **a.** established first permanent French settlement in North America
   b. French traveled into interior; established close ties with Native Americans

2. **a.** defense against France and England
   b. land disputes; English expansion

3. **a.** Braddock and Washington led British, colonial forces; Montcalm was French commander; Pitt directed war for Britain
   b. France

4. **a.** attack British forts, surrounding areas; strategy failed
   b. to avoid conflict with Native Americans
   c. possible answer—may empower them to increase demands for self-government

5. Albany Plan of Union; Fort Oswego, Fort William Henry captured by French; British recaptured Fort Duquesne; Treaty of Paris

6. possible answer—colonists should defend home country, quartering soldiers in homes civic duty

Answers

Faces of History *was able to unite various Native American groups*

Reading Check *colonists profited from supplying army, Florida acquired, united colonies, brought Britain an empire; Pontiac rebelled, Proclamation of 1763, Native Americans weakened and lost land*

Word Help

disjointed disorderly, confused
affirmations cries of agreement
devotions prayers or other religious practices

Info to Know

African Work Songs Many Africans believe that music eases the strain of repetitious and physically demanding work and makes workers more productive. In some cultures, musicians sing and play drums and stringed instruments, establishing the rhythm for tilling the soil. As if they are performing a ritual dance, rows of workers till the soil in unison, repeating the moves over and over again. Africans learn these songs at an early age. Women work the farms with their babies on their backs. The babies hear the music and feel their mothers' rhythmic movements.

The Origins of Spirituals In the American colonies, enslaved Africans attended their masters' worship services. At the time, hymns were sung in a call-and-response style. After regular worship services, slaves often stayed to sing and dance. They reworked many of the hymns for their own use, combining elements of their masters' church services, biblical passages, and their own experiences of slavery. The result was the black spiritual, which took the place of the songs that had been sung by griots, or community storytellers, in Africa. Over time, spirituals began to lose popularity, and the more upbeat forms of gospel and jazz took over as the favored forms of sacred and popular African American music.

African Traditions in the Colonies

Historical Context The documents below provide different perspectives on how Africans carried their traditions to the colonies.

Task Examine the documents and answer the questions that follow. Then you will be asked to write an essay about African culture in the colonies, using facts from the documents and from the chapter to support the position you take in your thesis statement.

DOCUMENT 1

Most African cultures have strong musical traditions. Enslaved Africans used drums for dancing and sometimes for sending coded messages. For this reason, drums were outlawed in some parts of the colonies. The drum on the left was made by an enslaved African who lived in Virginia. Created from local materials, the style of its carvings is very similar to drums found in Africa, such as the drum on the right.

DOCUMENT 2

The rhythm of the drum was often used in traditional African religious ceremonies. One of the most common types of spiritual worship that was carried to the colonies was the ring shout, in which worshippers dance and chant, often shouting as they sing. This style of worship was very different from the quieter styles typical of most European churches. Colonist John Watson commented upon observing this style of worship among a group of free blacks near Philadelphia.

"In the blacks' quarters, the coloured people get together, and sing for hours together, short scraps of disjointed affirmations, pledges, or prayers, lengthened out with long repetitious choruses. These are all sung in the merry chorus-manner of the southern harvest field, or [corn]husking-frolic method, of the slave blacks; and also very greatly like the Indian dances. With every word so sung, they have a sinking of one or the other leg of the body alternately; producing an audible sound of feet at every step . . . If some, in the meantime sit, they strike the sounds alternately on each thigh . . . [T]he example has already visibly affected the religious manner of some whites. From this cause, I have known in some camps meetings from 50 to 60 people crowd into one tent, after the public devotions have closed, and there continues the whole night, singing tune after tune, . . . scarce one of which were in our hymn books. Some of these from their nature, (having very long repetition choruses and some short scraps of matter) are actually composed as sung and are almost endless."

Skills Focus: Making Oral Presentations

At Level

Reading Like a Historian Skill

African American Musical Traditions

Research Required

1. Divide the class into small groups. Have each group choose one form of music that has its roots in African music.

2. Have each group conduct research to trace the development of its chosen type of music. Students should attempt to learn how it is related to early African American forms of music and even trace it back to African musical forms, if possible. Have students consider how the words and music reflect the conditions of African American life.

3. Have each group create a brief classroom presentation on its chosen form of music. Students should explain the origins of the genre and include brief musical selections from appropriate songs.

4. Have students make their presentations to the class. **LS Interpersonal, Auditory-Musical**

📄 Alternative Assessment Handbook, Rubric 26: Poems and Songs

DOCUMENT 3

This watercolor painting titled *The Old Plantation* was created by an unknown artist. It shows enslaved Africans from South Carolina around 1790. The image contains numerous examples of African cultural traditions that carried over to the colonies.

In African societies it was common to dance barefoot while wearing colorful head scarves. These head scarves are patterned after the style used by West African groups such as the Yoruba.

This instrument may be a Yoruba *gudugudu*, a drum made by stretching animal skin over a hollowed-out piece of wood.

This image may be showing a marriage ceremony. In some African societies, couples jumped over a stick or broom when they wed. Slaves in American societies came to refer to getting married as "jumping the broom."

This instrument is similar to the *molo*, an ancestor of the banjo, used by the Yoruba.

COLONIAL WILLIAMSBURG FOUNDATION

Skills FOCUS READING LIKE A HISTORIAN

1. **a. Identify** Refer to Document 1. How are the two drums similar?
   b. Interpret Why might some people in the colonies view drums as dangerous?

2. **a. Describe** Refer to Document 2. According to the writer, what other group has a dance style similar to that of the African Americans?
   b. Analyze In what ways did the ring shout affect white society?

3. **a. Describe** Refer to Document 3. What is happening in the image?

   b. Interpret How does the image reflect the strength of cultural traditions?

4. **Document-Based Essay Question** Consider the question below and form a thesis statement. Using examples from Documents 1, 2, and 3, create an outline and write a short essay supporting your position.
   How did African culture survive in the colonies, even under slavery?
   See Skills Handbook, pp. H28–H29, H30

COLONIAL LIFE **97**

Info to Know

Uncle Remus Not all of the traditions enslaved Africans brought with them were musical. They also brought traditional tales with them, which they continued to hand down from one generation to the next. Many of these tales were collected by an Atlanta journalist named Joel Chandler Harris. In 1879 he published "The Story of Mr. Rabbit and Mr. Fox as told by Uncle Remus." Uncle Remus was a fictional former slave. It was the first of many "Uncle Remus" stories Harris published. As he explained in prefaces to several collections of his stories, he wanted to "preserve the legends in their original simplicity, and to wed them permanently to the quaint dialect." Harris was one of the first American writers to try to capture the dialect and pronunciation of former slaves. However, these stories are often considered offensive today because of the stereotypical dialect and terminology used, even though they were derived from traditional African stories.

Skills Focus: Analyzing Primary Sources

At Level

Reading Like a Historian Skill
Perspectives on African Traditions

Research Required

1. Guide the class in a discussion of the institution of slavery and what it involved.

2. Have students use reliable Internet sites or print resources to locate a primary source dealing with African traditions in the colonies. Students may wish to use a memoir written by an enslaved African American, a free African American, or a white American.

3. Have students write a brief essay on how African traditions are described in their

source. Students should identify the writer, if possible, and include details about the experience of the writer. Students should also address any bias the writer might have had.

4. Have volunteers share their essays with the class. **LS Intrapersonal, Verbal-Linguistic**

   Alternative Assessment Handbook, Rubric 30: Research

Answers

Reading Like a Historian
1. a. *same design, made of similar materials;* **b.** *because they could be used to send coded messages, which might be used to incite rebellion;*
2. a. *American Indians;* **b.** *Some whites began to hold meetings where they sang tune after tune in a similar manner.*
3. a. *People are playing music and dancing.* **b.** *Even though the people are in America, they are still celebrating their African culture.* **4.** *possible answers—continued tradition of African song and dance; used local materials to make African musical instruments, such as the drum*

97

Visual Summary: Colonial Life

Political
- The Navigation Acts and the Dominion of New England: two attempts by England to exert more control over the colonies
- Salutary neglect of the colonies brought about colonial self-government

Economic
- Northern economy: farming, shipbuilding, trade, commerce
- Southern economy: plantation farming (tobacco, rice, indigo)
- Slavery in the northern and southern colonies provided agricultural workers, servants, and artisans.

Life in the Colonies

Military
- The French and Indian War (1754–1763): France and England clash over territory in North America
- Treaty of Paris (1763) redraws lines in North America; England and Spain claiming the most territory

Social
- The Great Awakening increased church membership
- The European Enlightenment spread to the colonies, bringing ideas of law and individual rights
- Immigration from other countries increased diversity in the colonies

Reviewing Key Terms and People

For each term or name below, write a sentence explaining its significance to colonial life.

1. mercantilism
2. balance of trade
3. Navigation Acts
4. salutary neglect
5. triangular trade
6. Middle Passage
7. Enlightenment
8. Benjamin Franklin
9. Great Awakening
10. George Washington
11. Albany Plan of Union

Comprehension and Critical Thinking

SECTION 1 *(pp. 72–76)*

12. **a. Recall** What was the Glorious Revolution?

b. Explain How were the policies of William and Mary different from those of James II?

c. Evaluate How did salutary neglect change the relationship between Britain and the colonies?

SECTION 2 *(pp. 77–83)*

13. **a. Identify** Name two major industries in the northern colonies.

b. Compare How were northern colonial economies different from southern colonial economies?

c. Evaluate Why was slavery more prevalent in the southern colonies than in the northern colonies?

History's Impact video program
Review the video to answer the closing question:
Why was victory in the French and Indian War
so important for the British?

SECTION 3 *(pp. 84–89)*

14. a. Recall What was the Enlightenment?

b. Explain How did the Great Awakening change religious life in the colonies?

c. Elaborate What were some other important aspects of colonial society?

SECTION 4 *(pp. 90–95)*

15. a. Identify What was the central conflict of the French and Indian War?

b. Summarize What were the terms of the Treaty of Paris?

c. Predict How might the terms of the Treaty of Paris continue to affect the relationship between Great Britain and the American colonies?

Using the Internet

go.hrw.com
Practice Online
Keyword: SD7 CH3

16. Colonial life was different from life today in many ways, but it was remarkably similar in others. The lack of electricity made simple tasks much more challenging. But children played games similar to those played by children today, and adults looked for ways to lighten the burdens of daily life. Using the keyword above, do research to learn more about daily life in colonial times. Then create a report that describes what you learned and how the lives of the colonists were similar to and different from our lives today.

Analyzing Primary Sources

Reading Like a Historian John Adams wrote the following passage in 1775, recalling the colonial rebellion against Governor Edmund Andros.

> **❝** It ought to be remembered that there was a revolution here, as well as in England, and that we, as well as the people of England, made an original, express contract with King William. **❞**
>
> —John Adams, *Novanglus Letters*, 1775

17. Identify What was the contract between the American colonies and King William?

18. Make Inferences In 1775 America was on the brink of revolution against Great Britain. Why was Adams referring back to the Governor Andros incident, which had happened a century earlier?

Critical Reading

Read the passage in Section 4 that begins with the heading "The Albany Plan" and study the political cartoon. Then answer the questions that follow.

19. According to the passage, the Albany Plan of Union was the idea of

A Benjamin Franklin.

B George Washington.

C the Iroquois League.

D Great Britain.

20. The passage and the political cartoon suggest that uniting the colonies was important because

A they shared one constitution.

B they were stronger together than they were apart.

C there was too much distance between the colonies.

D one colony had all the power.

21. According to the passage, the Albany Plan of Union was significant because

A it formed the framework for the Constitution.

B it was approved by the British and all the colonial assemblies.

C it was the first attempt to unite the colonies.

D it helped the colonists defeat the British.

FOCUS ON WRITING

Persuasive Writing *Persuasive writing takes a position for or against an issue, using facts and examples as supporting evidence. To practice persuasive writing, complete the assignment below.*

Writing Topic **The rising tensions between Great Britain and its colonies during the years 1650–1763**

22. Assignment Given what you have read in the chapter, were the colonists justified in protesting British policies? Write a short essay in which you develop your position on this issue. Support your point of view with reasoning and examples from your reading and studies.

COLONIAL LIFE **99**

Answers

Using the Internet

16. Go to the HRW Web site and enter the keyword shown to access a rubric for this activity.

KEYWORD: SD7 CH3

Analyzing Primary Sources

17. English Bill of Rights; that rulers would not have absolute power

18. possible answer—reminder that royal attempts to control the local governments in the colonies had failed

Critical Reading

19. A

20. B

21. C

Focus on Writing

22. possible answer—colonies justified because they had natural rights and social contract with their government. Forcing them to pay taxes unjust.

A rubric for the activity is provided in the Chapter Resource File: Focus on Writing: Rising Tensions Between Great Britain and Its Colonies, 1650–1763.

History's Impact Video Program

by defeating France, Britain took control of much of North America

Review and Assessment Resources

Review and Reinforce

▢ CRF: Chapter Review Activity

▢ Quick Facts Transparencies: Rising Tensions Between England and America; Key Political Thinkers of the European Enlightenment; Colonial Life

▢ Spanish Chapter Summaries Audio CD Program

▢ Online Chapter Summaries in Spanish

OSP Holt PuzzlePro; Quiz Show for ExamView

▢ Quiz Game CD-ROM

Assess

▢ PASS: Chapter Test, Forms A and B

▢ Alternative Assessment Handbook

OSP ExamView Test Generator, Chapter Test

▢ Differentiated Instruction Modified Worksheets and Tests CD-ROM: Chapter Test

HOAP Holt Online Assessment Program (in the Premier Online Edition)

Reteach/Intervene

▢ Interactive Reader and Study Guide

▢ Differentiated Instruction Teacher Management System: Lesson Plans for Differentiated Instruction

▢ Differentiated Instruction Modified Worksheets and Tests CD-ROM: Chapter Test

▢ Interactive Skills Tutor CD-ROM

go.hrw.com
Online Resources
KEYWORD: SD7 CH3

Unit Review

Summarizing the Unit

Remind students that although many of our country's customs and traditions come from its British roots, other peoples have also shaped American culture. Have students add to a class chart of lasting contributions from the other peoples discussed in this unit. To get them started, consider listing the ways that enslaved Africans influenced American musical traditions.

Connecting to Themes

Remind students that as the English colonies grew, they developed their own distinctive culture. Ask students what the characteristics of this culture were. Then have students decide if these characteristics have remained a part of American culture today. Have students explain their answers.

 UNIT 1 IN BRIEF Below is a chapter-by-chapter summary of the main ideas covered in Unit 1.

 CHAPTER 1 The World before 1600
Beginnings to 1600

MAIN IDEA Native Americans inhabited the Americas for thousands of years before the arrival of Europeans. Then in the 1400s, an age of exploration began in Europe. European sailors traveled to Asia, Africa, and the Americas.

SECTION 1 The first Americans developed societies in North, Central, and South America, adapting to the land and creating a way of life that remained undisturbed for thousands of years.

SECTION 2 Differences in geography shaped North American cultures prior to European settlement. Groups across North America were linked by trade.

SECTION 3 Wealthy African empires established trade routes across the Sahara. When European explorers first arrived in Africa in the 1400s, they wanted to trade for gold and other riches. Eventually, they began a slave trade from Africa that lasted for hundreds of years and caused extreme human suffering.

SECTION 4 The Renaissance in Europe was characterized by new ways of thinking and the desire to explore other worlds. Explorers set sail from Europe, hoping to find gold and spread Christianity.

SECTION 5 Searching for a westward route to Asia, Christopher Columbus landed on a new continent. The colonies he built in the Caribbean marked the beginning of European colonization in the Americas.

CHAPTER 2 European Colonies in America
1500–1733

MAIN IDEA Spain was the first European nation to claim land in the Americas. In the 1700s, however, England had joined with Scotland to form a powerful nation known as Great Britain. By 1733 Great Britain claimed 13 colonies along the Atlantic seaboard of North America.

SECTION 1 Spanish conquistadors established an empire in the Americas. France, England, Portugal, and the Netherlands also sent explorers to America.

SECTION 2 In 1607 the English established a colony at Jamestown, Virginia. It was the first permanent English settlement in North America. By the mid-1600s, the Virginia colony was thriving.

SECTION 3 To escape religious persecution in England, the Pilgrims settled Plymouth Colony in Massachusetts. Other colonies in the North soon followed.

SECTION 4 A new phase of British colonization in America began, leading to the establishment of the Middle Colonies and the Southern Colonies. These colonies were founded for a variety of reasons, from religious freedom to personal profit.

 CHAPTER 3 Colonial Life
1650–1763

MAIN IDEA Life in the colonies was shaped by the policies enforced by Great Britain, the economies that emerged in the various regions, and the distinctive American culture that was beginning to form. Struggles over territory eventually led to the French and Indian War.

SECTION 1 Great Britain's mercantilist policies gave it a strong hold over the colonies. Although the colonies formed governments, final political authority rested with Parliament and the British monarch.

SECTION 2 Colonial economies were shaped by local natural resources. Commerce and shipping dominated in the North, while the South relied on agriculture and building plantations to grow cash crops.

SECTION 3 The Enlightenment and the Great Awakening led to new ways of thinking in the colonies. During this time a unique colonial culture began to take shape in the thirteen colonies.

SECTION 4 Great Britain, France, and Spain fought for dominance in North America during the French and Indian War. Several Native American groups formed alliances with France during the war. However, Great Britain's eventual victory established a large British territory east of the Mississippi River.

100 UNIT 1 IN BRIEF

Unit Resources

Review and Reinforce

- CRF: Chapter Review Activity
- Spanish Chapter Summaries Audio CD Program
- OSP Holt PuzzlePro; GameTool for ExamView
- Quiz Game CD-ROM

Assess

- PASS: Unit Test, Forms A and B
- Alternative Assessment Handbook
- OSP ExamView Test Generator
- Differentiated Instruction Modified Worksheets and Tests CD-ROM: Chapter Tests
- HOAP Holt Online Assessment Program (in the Premier Online Edition)

Reteach/Intervene

- Interactive Reader and Study Guide
- Differentiated Instruction Teacher Management System: Lesson Plans for Differentiated Instruction
- Differentiated Instruction Modified Worksheets and Tests CD-ROM: Chapter Tests
- Interactive Skills Tutor CD-ROM

go.hrw.com
Online Resources

KEYWORDS: SD7 CH1, SD7 CH2, SD7 CH3

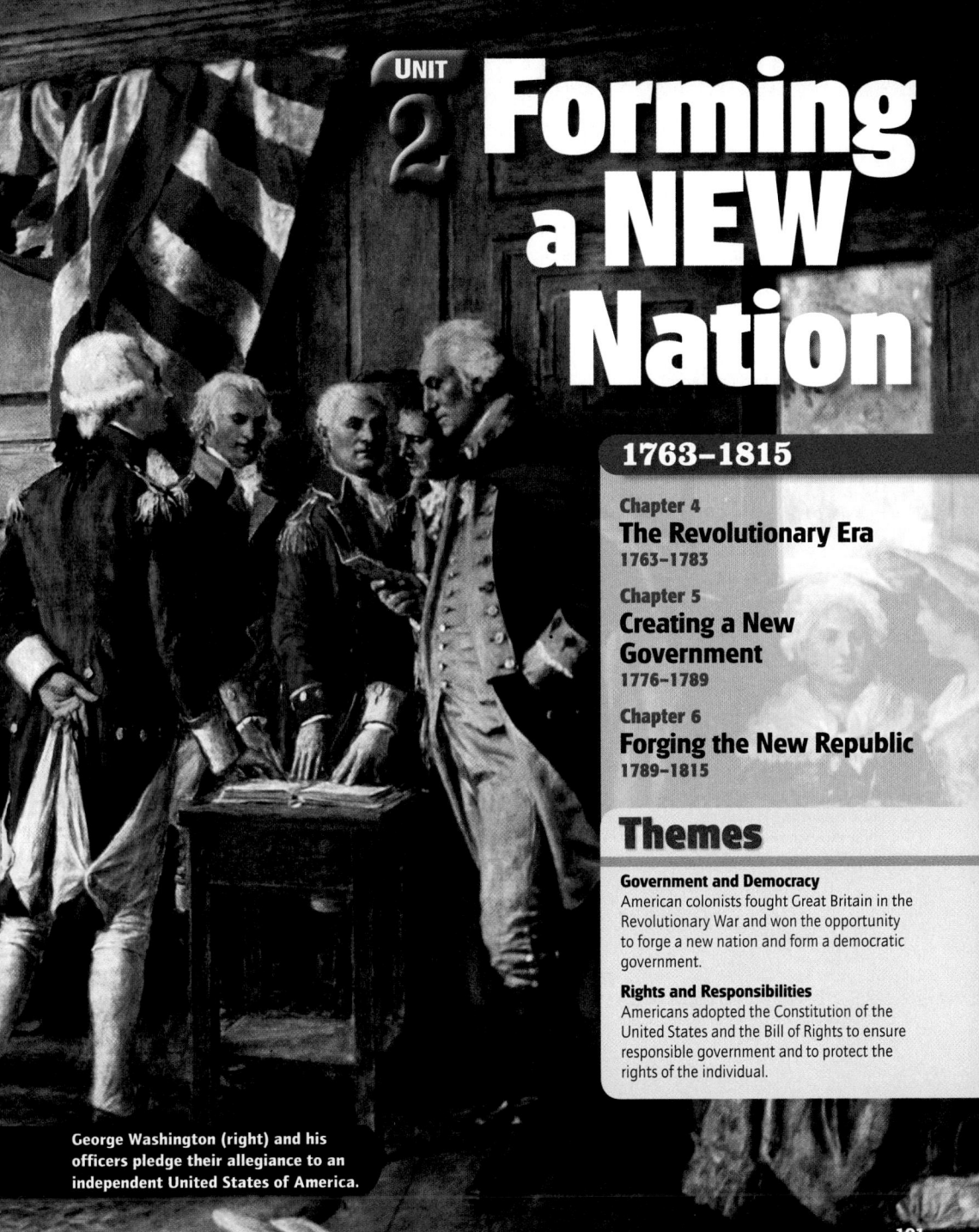

Forming a NEW Nation

1763–1815

Chapter 4
The Revolutionary Era
1763–1783

Chapter 5
Creating a New Government
1776–1789

Chapter 6
Forging the New Republic
1789–1815

Themes

Government and Democracy
American colonists fought Great Britain in the Revolutionary War and won the opportunity to forge a new nation and form a democratic government.

Rights and Responsibilities
Americans adopted the Constitution of the United States and the Bill of Rights to ensure responsible government and to protect the rights of the individual.

George Washington (right) and his officers pledge their allegiance to an independent United States of America.

101

Unit Preview

Introducing the Unit
Remind students that the war that led to American independence began as a conflict of interest between Americans and their British rulers. Ask students how the conflict might have been peacefully resolved. Then ask students if American independence could have been achieved without warfare.

Connecting to Themes
Activity Bill of Rights Discussion Explain to students that many countries do not officially list the rights retained by individual citizens. Guide students in a discussion of how the Bill of Rights has influenced how Americans think about government and society. **LS** Verbal-Linguistic

Reading Like a Historian
Interpreting Visuals Pledging Allegiance Did the Founding Fathers use the same pledge of allegiance that we use today? The answer is: no. A Baptist minister named Francis Bellamy first wrote today's pledge of allegiance in 1892. It was composed for a Columbus Day celebration honoring the 400th anniversary of the discovery of America.

Unit Resources

Planning
- Differentiated Instruction Teacher Management System: Unit Pacing Guide
- One-Stop Planner CD-ROM: Teacher Management System
- Power Presentations with Video CD-ROM

Differentiating Instruction
- Differentiated Instruction Teacher Management System: Lesson Plans for Differentiated Instruction
- Pre-AP Activities Guide for American History
- Differentiated Instruction Modified Worksheets and Tests CD-ROM

Enrichment
- Civic Participation Activities Guide
- CRF: Economics and History Activity
- CRF: Interdisciplinary Project
- American History Primary Source Library CD-ROM

Assessment
- PASS: Unit Test, Forms A & B
- Alternative Assessment Handbook
- OSP ExamView Test Generator
- HOAP Holt Online Assessment Program (in the Premier Online Edition)

The Differentiated Instruction Teacher Management System
provides a planning and instructional benchmarking guide for this unit.

● Prepare to Read ●

Summarizing

Have each student print out, make a copy of, or cut out a short article from a magazine, newspaper, or Web site about a current event. Have students write a short summary of their articles. Then have students exchange their articles and summaries with a partner, who should read and critique the summary, comparing it to the article. If time permits, redistribute the articles to repeat the activity.

Word Help

boycott refusal to associate with someone
courier messenger

Info to Know

Heroine of the Revolution Deborah Sampson's secret was almost revealed after she was wounded in the head and leg at a battle in Tarrytown, New York. Afraid she would be discovered, Sampson refused treatment on her leg wound and tried to treat it herself. It never healed properly. Shortly after, however, she came down with a fever and her true identity became known during medical treatment. On October 23, 1783, the soldier known as Robert Shurtleff received an honorable discharge from the army.

Skills Planner

To give students more opportunities to practice this skill, see Skills Focus activities in the teacher's edition.

Prepare to Read

Summarizing

Find practice for **Summarizing** in the **Skills Handbook,** p. H6

Summarizing is a way of condensing information by conveying only the most important points. Summarizing can help you recall what you read.

Before You Read
Read headings and the review questions to determine what the passage will be about.

While You Read
Identify the main idea of the passage. Then look for the key details that support it.

After You Read
To summarize the passage, restate the main idea and key supporting details in your own words.

The Role of Women

Even before independence was declared, American women had been active in boycotts and other protests. Once the fighting began, Patriot women found many other ways to take part.

A few, like Deborah Sampson, disguised themselves as men to become soldiers in the Continental Army. Mary Hays was nicknamed "Molly Pitcher" for bringing water to the troops at the battle of Monmouth in New Jersey on a blistering hot day. Stories say that she took over her husband's gun when he was overcome by the heat. Many other women also carried food and water to the soldiers on the battlefields.

Women also served as couriers, scouts, and spies. One teenager, 16-year-old Sybil Ludington, learned of a planned British attack on Danbury, Connecticut. On her horse Star, she made a 40-mile night ride to spread the alarm.

The heading tells you the topic—women's roles in the Revolutionary War.

Main Idea Patriot women contributed in many ways to the battle for independence.

Details Patriot women served as soldiers, couriers, scouts, and spies.

READING CHECK **Summarizing** In what ways did women participate in the Revolutionary War?

Test Prep Tip

Multiple choice and short answer questions on tests ask you to summarize what you have read. Try breaking lengthier text into shorter summaries by noting the main idea of each paragraph or passage as you read.

102 UNIT 2

Skills Focus: Summarizing   At Level

Reading Skill
Using an Outline to Summarize a Passage

1. Have each student choose a subsection from one of the chapters in this unit.

2. Have students read their sections. Then have students outline the text, including main ideas and details. If necessary, write a model outline form on the board for students to use.

3. Have students exchange outlines with a partner without revealing which subsection they outlined. The partner

should write a summary of the text, based on the outline only.

4. Have students compare their outlines, their summaries, and the original texts to see how accurately the outlines and summaries reflect the original text passages. **LS** **Verbal-Linguistic**

📝 Alternative Assessment Handbook, Rubric 1: Acquiring Information

Recognizing Bias in Primary Sources

Find practice for **Recognizing Bias in Primary Sources** in the **Skills Handbook,** p. H33

Bias is a point of view that is slanted by personal or political beliefs. Every primary source reflects a bias—of the person who created it. Bias may appear in primary sources for a variety of reasons. An author may be trying to argue for or justify some course of action. An author may also be expressing a personal view without knowing that it is biased.

Strategies historians use:

- Examine clues such as dates as well as words such as *our* and *we* to recognize bias in primary sources.
- Compare the primary source with other sources and with historical evidence. Is the passage consistent with other historical accounts?
- Learn about the author's background and beliefs to determine what particular bias he or she may have.

The author of this passage is justifying the action of colonists to take up arms against Great Britain.

❝We have not raised armies with ambitious designs of separating from Great Britain and establishing independent states . . . In our own native land, in defence of the freedom that is our birth-right . . . for the protection of our property, acquired solely by the honest industry of our forefathers and ourselves, against violence actually offered, we have taken up arms.**❞**

—from *Declaration of the Causes and Necessity of Taking Up Arms,* July 6, 1775

How does this account of history compare with what you already knew about it?

Dates can help you determine context. In 1775 the colonies were struggling against Great Britain. This passage was written from the colonists' point of view.

Skills FOCUS **READING LIKE A HISTORIAN**

As You Read Examine a passage once without regard to bias. Then reread the passage, looking for examples of bias. What differences did you note between your first and second readings?

As You Study Use what you know about bias to add context to important historical events. Construct a chart showing the author of a primary source, his or her point of view, and examples of bias.

FORMING A NEW NATION **103**

Prepare to Read

Recognizing Bias in Primary Sources

Have students work with a partner to create a checklist for recognizing bias in a primary source. Have volunteers share items from their checklists with the class. Students should add suggestions from others to their own checklists as appropriate. Then have students reread the passage from *A Declaration of the Causes and Necessity of Taking Up Arms*, using their checklists to evaluate this primary source.

Word Help

birth-right right from birth

solely only

Info to Know

Writing the Declaration At the request of the Second Continental Congress, Thomas Jefferson and John Dickinson wrote *A Declaration of the Causes and Necessity of Taking Up Arms*. Its purpose was to explain why the colonies had taken up arms against their rulers. Jefferson's first draft was considered too harsh, and Dickinson softened its language and argument. The final draft included ideas and text from both men.

Skills Focus: Recognizing Bias

At Level

Reading Like a Historian Skill
Detecting Bias in Primary Sources

Research Required

1. Have each student locate and copy or print out a short primary source statement about an event discussed in this unit.

2. Have students evaluate the primary source for bias. Students should determine the purpose for which the source was written and then look for words that indicate or hint at the writer's opinion on the subject.

3. Have volunteers present their evaluations to the class and explain how they detected and analyzed the writer's bias. **LS Verbal-Linguistic**

   Alternative Assessment Handbook, Rubric 12: Drawing Conclusions

Chapter 4 Planning Guide

The Revolutionary Era

Chapter Overview	Reproducible Resources	Technology Resources
CHAPTER 4 pp. 104–141 **Overview:** In this chapter, students will analyze the escalating events that led to the outbreak of war between Great Britain and the American colonists.	**Differentiated Instruction Teacher Management System:** • Instructional Benchmarking Guides • Lesson Plans for Differentiated Instruction **Interactive Reader and Study Guide*** **Chapter Resource File:*** • Writing for the SAT: Women in Combat • Social Studies Skills Activity: Interpreting Charts • Chapter Review Activity **American History Outline Maps** **Pre-AP Activities Guide for American History*** **Reading Like a Historian Toolkit**	**Live Ink® Online Reading Help** **Student Edition on Audio CD Program** **Differentiated Instruction Modified Worksheets and Tests CD-ROM** **Interactive Skills Tutor CD-ROM** **United States History Primary Source Library CD-ROM** **Power Presentations with Video CD-ROM** **History's Impact: American History Video Program (VHS/DVD):** The Revolutionary Era **Online Chapter Summaries in Spanish** **Graphic Organizer Transparencies**
Section 1: **The Road to Revolution** **The Main Idea:** Increasingly restrictive laws angered many American colonists, leading to rebellion against Britain.	**Differentiated Instruction Teacher Management System:** Section 1 Lesson Plan* **Interactive Reader and Study Guide*** **Chapter Resource File:*** • Vocabulary Builder Activity, Section 1	**Daily Bellringer Transparency:** Section 1* **Daily Test Practice Transparency:** Section 1* **Quick Facts Transparency:** Tensions between Britain and America, 1765–1775*
Section 2: **Declaring Independence** **The Main Idea:** As conflicts with Britiain continued, the Second Continental Congress declared American independence.	**Differentiated Instruction Teacher Management System:** Section 2 Lesson Plan* **Interactive Reader and Study Guide*** **Chapter Resource File:*** • Vocabulary Builder Activity, Section 2	**Daily Bellringer Transparency:** Section 2* **Daily Test Practice Transparency:** Section 2* **Quick Facts Transparencies:** The Second Continental Congress, 1775; Key Documents that Influenced the Declaration of Independence*
Section 3: **The Revolutionary War Begins** **The Main Idea:** The Revolutionary War demonstrated Washington's great leadership.	**Differentiated Instruction Teacher Management System:** Section 3 Lesson Plan* **Interactive Reader and Study Guide*** **Chapter Resource File:*** • Vocabulary Builder Activity, Section 3	**Daily Bellringer Transparency:** Section 3* **Map Transparency:** Battles of the American Revolution, 1775 to 1778* **Daily Test Practice Transparency:** Section 3*
Section 4: **An American Victory** **The Main Idea:** A strengthened Continental Army helped the colonists achieve a victory at Yorktown.	**Differentiated Instruction Teacher Management System:** Section 4 Lesson Plan* **Interactive Reader and Study Guide*** **Chapter Resource File:*** • Vocabulary Builder Activity, Section 4	**Daily Bellringer Transparency:** Section 4* **Map Transparency:** Battles of the American Revolution, 1778–1781* **Daily Test Practice Transparency:** Section 4*

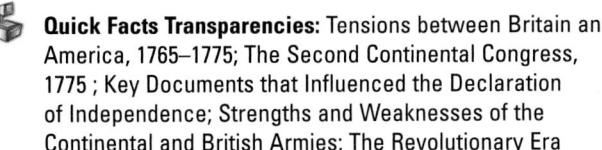

HOLT
History's Impact
American History Video Program (VHS/DVD)
The Revolutionary Era

Review, Assessment, Intervention

Quick Facts Transparencies: Tensions between Britain and America, 1765–1775; The Second Continental Congress, 1775 ; Key Documents that Influenced the Declaration of Independence; Strengths and Weaknesses of the Continental and British Armies; The Revolutionary Era

Spanish Chapter Summaries Audio CD Program

Progress Assessment Support System (PASS): Chapter Test*

Differentiated Instruction Modified Worksheets and Tests CD-ROM: Modified Chapter Test

OSP **One-Stop Planner CD-ROM:** ExamView Test Generator (English/Spanish)

HOAP **Holt Online Assessment Program (HOAP),** in the Holt Premier Online Student Edition

---

PASS: Section 1 Quiz*

Online Quiz: Section 1

Alternative Assessment Handbook

PASS: Section 2 Quiz*

Online Quiz: Section 2

Alternative Assessment Handbook

PASS: Section 3 Quiz*

Online Quiz: Section 3

Alternative Assessment Handbook

PASS: Section 4 Quiz*

Online Quiz: Section 4

Alternative Assessment Handbook

NC RESOURCES

The following resources were developed to help North Carolina educators teach the standards and objectives of North Carolina's eleventh grade standard course of study in United States history.

- United States history EOC Test Prep Workbook
- Teacher's Support System
- North Carolina One-Stop Planner

And be sure to direct your students to **go.hrw.com** for online access to the EOC Test Prep Workbook.

> **go.hrw.com**
> **EOC Test Prep**
> KEYWORD: SE7 NC

Holt Online Learning

> **go.hrw.com**
> **Teacher Resources**
> KEYWORD: SD7 TEACHER

> **go.hrw.com**
> **Student Resources**
> KEYWORD: SD7 CH4

- Document-based Questions
- Interactive Multimedia Activities

- Current Events
- Chapter-based Internet Activities
- and more!

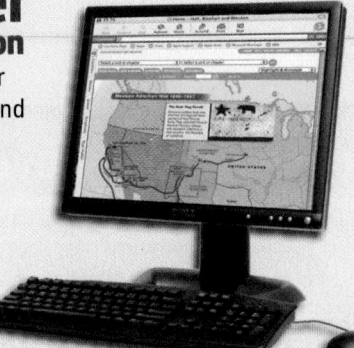

Holt Premier
Online Student Edition
Complete online support for interactivity, assessment, and reporting

- Interactive Maps and Notebook
- Standardized Test Prep
- Homework Practice and Research Activities Online

CHAPTER 4 PLANNING GUIDE

The Big Picture
Jesús F. de la Teja

A Failure to Communicate In the French and Indian War, Parliament believed that grateful colonists would appreciate the government's efforts to eliminate French support for hostile Indians on the western frontier. Colonists believed that the British government would be grateful for their decisive contribution to the victory. How shocked, then, were British North Americans to find out that Parliament intended to make them pay the military costs of maintaining this newly expanded empire while preventing them from occupying the territory they had just helped conquer. How frustrated, then, was Parliament to find colonists so disloyal as to refuse to pay their share of maintaining the empire.

Patriots and Traitors, a Personal Matter Benjamin and William Franklin are a good example of how one man's traitor can be another man's patriot. Appointed royal governor of New Jersey at the age of 32, William Franklin, Benjamin Franklin's only son, had seen adventure on the western frontier, then higher education in England. His staunch support for British rule made him increasingly unpopular among fellow New Jerseyans. After William was deposed and imprisoned in 1776 for refusing to renounce the Crown, Benjamin refused to help his son in any way, and they never reconciled. Each man held fast to what he felt were his patriotic convictions, although to the other he was a traitor.

America's Allies Why would imperial France and Spain want to support the upstart colonies in the rebellion against a fellow monarchy? After all, wouldn't a successful revolution give Spanish and French colonists ideas of their own independence? In the French and Indian War, France had lost its mainland possessions and its remaining Caribbean colonies seemed secure. Spain had lost Florida in that war, but its vast possessions in North and South America seemed equally secure. Thus, in their confrontation with Britain, the colonists benefited from one of the oldest human emotions—revenge.

Recent Scholarship

Spain and the American Revolution The American Revolution was much more than a struggle between Britain and her Atlantic seaboard colonies, as Thomas E. Chávez points out in *Spain and the Independence of the United States: An Intrinsic Gift* (2002). While the French contribution is generally known, Spanish statesmen, diplomats, soldiers, and funds were indispensable in helping to secure American independence. Chávez emphasizes events which rarely appear in textbooks, such as José de Gálvez's highly successful military campaigns in the Mississippi basin and along the Gulf of Mexico coast and Francisco de Saavedra's financing of the Yorktown campaign.

Differentiating Instruction

 Differentiated Instruction Teacher Management System
- Lesson Plans for Differentiated Instruction
- Differentiated Instructional Benchmarking Guides
- Interactive Reader and Study Guide

 Spanish Chapter Summaries Audio CD Program

 Online Chapter Summaries in Spanish

 Student Edition on Audio CD Program

 Differentiated Instruction Modified Worksheets and Tests CD-ROM
- Vocabulary Flash Cards
- Modified Vocabulary Builder Activities
- Modified Chapter Review Activity
- Modified Chapter Test

OSP One-Stop Planner CD-ROM
- ExamView Test Generator (English and Spanish)
- PuzzlePro
- Quiz Show for ExamView
- Transparencies and Videos

TE Differentiated Activities in the Teacher's Edition
- The Boston Massacre, p. 109
- Writing the Declaration, p. 118
- The Declaration of Independence, p. 121
- The Effect of the Declaration, p. 124
- An American Victory, p. 127
- Money Problems, p. 129
- Story Summary, p. 131
- Anti-British Speech, p. 131
- War in the West, p. 133

Reading Like a Historian
Sam Wineburg

Fact Into Fiction

How does fact become fiction? Our chapter provides us with one illustration of how a historical event becomes blurry over time, and meanings that fit present needs becloud—and sometimes overwhelm—historical truth.

The Battle of Lexington

The Battle of Lexington has taken on mythic proportions in the American consciousness. In 1925, for the 150th anniversary of the event, the United States Postal Service issued a commemorative stamp (based on an 1886 painting) showing defiant minutemen, fists clenched and muskets raised, standing tall against superior British forces. (This image is easily found on the Internet using the key words "Lexington," "postage stamp," and "1925.")

Comparing Images

You might ask students which image they prefer: the one appearing on the postage stamp or the lithograph by Amos Doolittle reprinted in our chapter on page 111. If they are like hundreds of students to whom I've shown these images, they will lean toward the postage stamp for several reasons. First, the image is sharper and more lifelike. Second, the stamp carries the weight and authority of the U.S. government. Finally, the stamp shows outnumbered colonists resisting their British oppressors rather than, as in the Doolittle engraving, fleeing in disarray. As historian A. S. Tourtellot noted in 1959, "Even the magnifying glass fails to reveal any member of that company in an attitude of resistance; no suggestion of a return fire or even of loading." Who wants to be remembered running for cover like rabbits?

When Doolittle's image was created several months after the events depicted, it was still in the colonists' interest to portray the encounter at Lexington as, to use Joseph Warren's words, an "inhuman proceeding . . . marks of ministerial vengeance against [Massachusetts] for refusing . . . a submission to slavery." That is why Doolittle, who based his illustration on interviews with participants, depicted fleeing colonists, mercilessly fired on with their backs turned. Casualty figures from the battle support Doolittle's image. If both sides had faced each other at close quarters, we would expect British casualties. Yet the only wounds incurred by the British were when a soldier was shot in the leg, and a horse in its flank. Given the scattershot of eighteenth-century muskets, both casualties are explained by friendly fire. The colonists, on the other hand, suffered eight deaths.

The Facts Change

Over time, fact can slowly turn to fiction for a variety of reasons. In this case, the ring of the "Massacre at Lexington" did not match how Americans wanted to remember the beginning of the Revolutionary War. Fiction had crept into American memory at least as early as 1830, when a painting by Pendleton showed colonists raising their muskets and taking aim. Ralph Waldo Emerson's lyrical 1837 description of the "embattled farmers" firing on the British at Concord further influenced public memory, and in Henry Sandham's 1886 painting (later the postage stamp), events at Lexington achieved their full transformation: not only are colonists shown firing in formation, but some are reloading their weapons while others taunt the British commander with outstretched arms.

Over the course of little more than a century, then, the American perception of Lexington changed dramatically; indeed, Doolittle's lithograph and Sandham's painting (and the postage stamp) seem to illustrate two entirely different battles.

Events in the past do not change. But the meaning we take from them can.

From *Lexington and Concord: The Beginning of the War of the American Revolution* by A. S. Tourtellot. Published by W. W. Norton, New York, 1959.

Standards Focus

Social Studies Competency Goals
Goal 1 The learner will identify, investigate, and assess the effectiveness of the institutions of the emerging republic.

 1.01

 **The Big Idea and Essential Questions**

To foster student understanding of this chapter's big idea, design your lesson to address each section's essential question.

Big Idea Small rebellions against British rule eventually led to all-out war between Great Britain and its American colonies.

Essential Questions

1. How did British laws imposed on the colonies affect relations between Britain and its colonies?

2. Why did the colonists declare independence from Great Britain?

3. What strengths and weaknesses did the British and the Americans have in the Revolutionary War?

4. How were the colonists able to achieve victory in the Revolutionary War?

Key to Differentiating Instruction

Below Level

Basic-level activities designed for all students encountering new material

At Level

Intermediate-level activities designed for average students

Above Level

Challenging activities designed for honors and gifted-and-talented students

Standard English Mastery

Activities designed to improve standard English usage

CHAPTER 4 1763–1783

The Revolutionary ERA

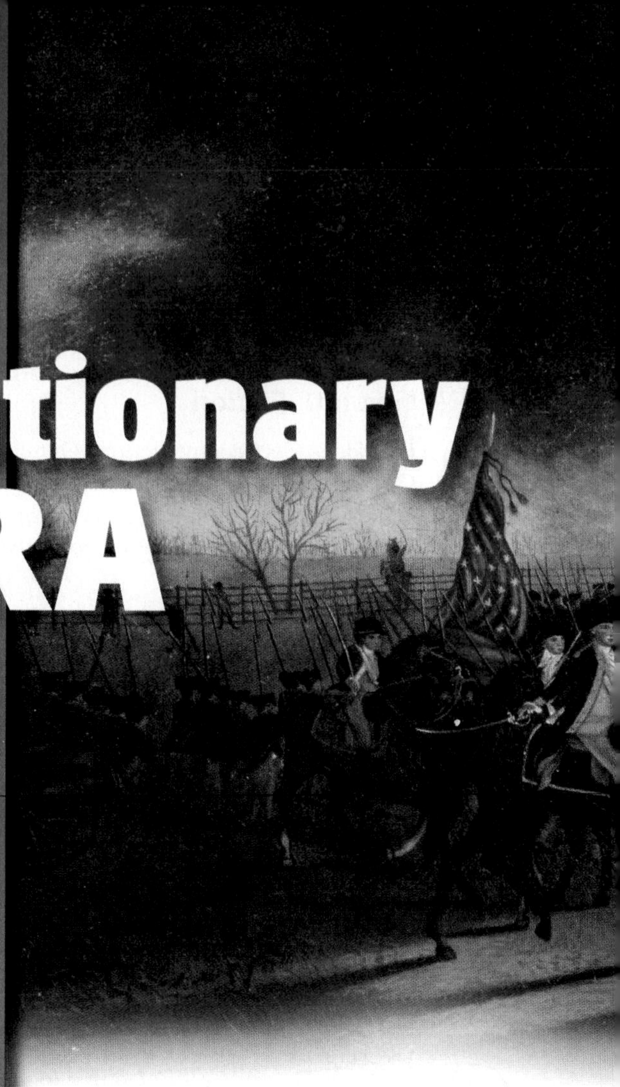

THE BIG PICTURE Great Britain began to increase taxes on the American colonists, who protested because they were not represented in Parliament. Small rebellions led to tighter controls, which triggered all-out war.

North Carolina Standards

Social Studies Objectives
1.01 Identify the major domestic issues and conflicts experienced by the nation during the Federalist Period.

Language Arts Objectives
2.03 Demonstrate the ability to read, listen to and view a variety of increasingly complex print and non-print informational texts appropriate to grade level and course literary focus, by:
  • making inferences, predicting, and drawing conclusions based on text.

Skills FOCUS READING LIKE A HISTORIAN

Cannon fire lights up the early morning sky in *The Battle of Princeton*, a 1777 painting by early American artist James Peale. The victories at Trenton and Princeton helped Americans believe that their independence was more than just words on paper.
Identifying Points of View Why do you think Peale chose to commemorate this battle?
See Skills Handbook, pp. H28–H29

104

October 1763
The Proclamation of 1763 bars colonists from settling in Indian lands west of the Appalachians.

U.S.

1765

World

1765
Parliament passes the Stamp Act, angering colonists.

Introduce the Chapter   At Level

The Revolutionary Era

1. Guide students in a discussion of the reasons that people might decide to declare war against those who govern them. Have students focus on the financial and human costs of a war, and how war affects a country's relationships with other nations.

2. Remind students that many colonists came from Britain, where they had enjoyed some basic freedoms and rights, a judicial system, and a Parliamentary form of government. In the colonies, however, they believed that

Britain did not treat them justly, and that they were subjected to unfair treatment and taxation without representation.

3. Have students list the problems the colonists faced when deciding whether or not to go to war against Britain, one of the world's most powerful nations. Then have students list the problems the colonists would face if they won the war. **LS Verbal-Linguistic**

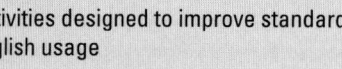 Alternative Assessment Handbook, Rubrics 11: Discussions; and 37: Writing Assignments

History's Impact video program
Watch the video to understand the impact of the Declaration of Independence today.

HOLT

History's Impact

▶ **Video Program:**
The Revolutionary Era
See the Video Teacher's Guide for strategies for using the video segment.

Reading Like a Historian

An Uncommon Success Remind students that many people never believed that the colonies would defeat the British, and the fact that a new nation was established was, in itself, revolutionary. It took great sacrifices from ordinary citizens, most of whom had never served in the military before, to defeat the British.

March 1770
Five protesters are killed by British soldiers in the Boston Massacre.

April 1775
Revolutionary War begins with battles of Lexington and Concord.

July 4, 1776
Congress approves the Declaration of Independence.

October 19, 1781
British surrender at Yorktown, ending the war.

1770 **1775** **1780** **1785**

1775
King George III issues a proclamation banning overseas trade for American colonies.

1778
Following the Battle of Saratoga, France formally recognizes the U.S. and promises military help.

1783
Treaty of Paris ends the Revolutionary War. Britain signs subsidiary treaties with America and allies France and Spain.

105

go.hrw.com
Online Resources

Chapter Resources:
KEYWORD: SD7 CH4

Teacher Resources:
KEYWORD: SD7 TEACHER

Explore the Time Line

1. How much time elapsed between the passage of the Stamp Act and the Boston Massacre? *5 years*

2. When did the Revolutionary War begin? How long did it last? *April 1775; 6 years, until October 1781*

3. What important event took place in 1778? *France formally recognized the U.S., promised help*

Info to Know

French Aid in the Revolutionary War A turning point in the war occurred when France joined the colonies in their fight against Britain. The French were still bitter about the loss of their North American holdings after the French and Indian War, and as a result, they were eager to weaken Britain's control in North America. During the Revolutionary War, the French proved to be a valuable ally to the colonists, particularly in the Battle of Yorktown, which ended the war.

Answers

Reading Like a Historian (p. 104)
possible answer—was an American victory; helped Americans realize that their struggle for independence had turned into a true war

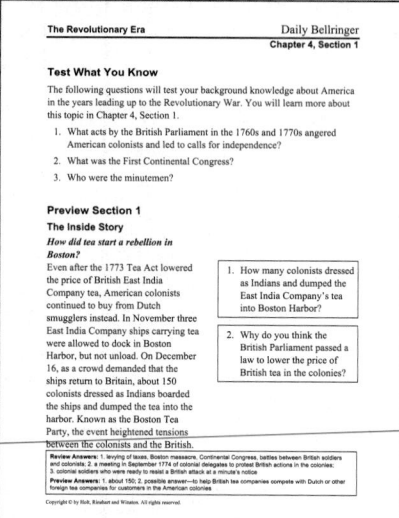
Academic Vocabulary

Review with students the high-use academic term in this section.

imported bought from another country (p. 108)

🖱 CRF: Vocabulary Builder Activity, Section 1

Taking Notes

Events—debt from French and Indian War; British military presence in the American colonies; desire for Britain to chastise the colonists; Britain wanted to raise more money; Boston Tea Party and boycotts against British goods; Britain needed to incorporate Canadian territory into their North American holdings and protect settlers from Indian attacks

Laws—Sugar Act and Stamp Act; Quartering Act; Townshend Acts; Tea Act; Intolerable Acts; Quebec Act

---

SECTION 1 — The Road to Revolution

BEFORE YOU READ

MAIN IDEA

A series of increasingly restrictive laws angered many American colonists, leading to rebellion against Britain.

READING FOCUS

1. Why did Great Britain pass new laws in America?
2. How did the colonists respond to the new laws? How did their response lead to even stricter measures?
3. Why did the First Continental Congress meet?
4. What was the significance of the battles at Lexington and Concord?

KEY TERMS AND PEOPLE

Samuel Adams
Stamp Act
writs of assistance
Boston Massacre
Committees of Correspondence
Intolerable Acts
First Continental Congress
minutemen

TAKING NOTES As you read, take notes on the events and laws that led up to the battles at Lexington and Concord. Record your notes in a graphic organizer like the one shown here.

Events	Laws

The Boston TEA PARTY

◄ Colonists in crude disguises destroy tea at Boston Harbor.

THE INSIDE STORY

How did tea start a rebellion in Boston?
In 1773 Parliament passed the Tea Act, which was designed to help a struggling British company and reduce smuggling. Because of colonial boycotts, the British East India Company had millions of pounds of unsold tea. Colonists instead were drinking smuggled Dutch tea or making "liberty tea" from dried raspberry or currant leaves.

Under the new law the East India Company was allowed to sell tea directly to the colonists. This meant East India Company tea was actually cheaper than smuggled tea. Still, the colonists resisted. In November 1773 three ships arrived in Boston Harbor. Bostonians allowed the ships to dock but not unload.

On the night of December 16, 1773, a large and angry crowd gathered in downtown Boston. They demanded that the tea ships be sent back to London. Then another group of people arrived, disguised as Indians. In fact, they were Samuel Adams and about 70 others. Protected by the crowd, they boarded the ships. They broke open the chests of tea and dumped them into the harbor. Hundreds of Bostonians watched from the shore, enjoying the Boston Tea Party. The loss of the valuable cargo infuriated British officials and brought more repressive laws. ◼

106

Teach the Main Idea

At Level

The Road to Revolution

1. **Teach** Ask students the Reading Focus questions to teach this section.

2. **Apply** Organize students into pairs and have them prepare an outline of the section using heads and subheads as the main points. Then have students create simple graphics to illustrate each head. Have students add two or three bullet point words or phrases below each subhead to fill out the outline. **LS Interpersonal**

3. **Review** Have each pair share its outline and illustrations with the class. Then guide the class in a discussion of the value of outlines in studying the section.

4. **Practice/Homework** Have each student select one of the subheads and write an editorial based on the topic. Editorials should be backed by facts and sound reasoning. **LS Verbal-Linguistic**

🖱 Alternative Assessment Handbook, Rubrics 3: Artwork; and 17: Letters to Editors

Britain Passes New Laws

By the time the Boston Tea Party took place, tensions had been rising between Great Britain and its colonies for some time. As you read in the previous chapter, colonists had rebelled against arrogant royal officials such as Edmund Andros. They had also disobeyed laws they did not like, such as the Navigation Acts.

Then the French and Indian War created even more tension between Britain and the colonies. Colonists had fought beside British soldiers, who treated them poorly and refused to learn how to fight in the American wilderness. Families also resented being forced to house British soldiers.

After the war, Parliament tried to deny the colonists access to western lands with the Proclamation of 1763. But colonists thought they had a right to those lands because they had helped defeat the French. Resentment of this and other British laws would increase over the next decade, eventually leading the American colonies to revolution.

Grenville and the Sugar Act The French and Indian War left Britain with a huge debt and with an army of 10,000 in the colonies. The British government said the troops were there to protect the colonies from lingering threats after the war. But many colonists felt the British troops were in fact there to intimidate them. Colonists also felt that they did not need British protection because they had been defending themselves for over 150 years.

The issue of British soldiers became even more of a problem for the colonists when Prime Minister George Grenville decided that the colonists should pay for the troops themselves. Grenville's plan was to tax the colonies to raise money. The first law Parliament passed to accomplish this was the Sugar Act, which put a tax on sugar and molasses imported from the French and Spanish West Indies. Northern merchants especially disliked the Sugar Act. They feared that the new tax would hurt the rum industry because the molasses used to make rum would be more expensive.

Other colonists raised a different issue. In the Boston town meeting, **Samuel Adams** said that making colonists pay taxes without a representative in Parliament changed them from being "free Subjects to the miserable state of

BOYCOTTING BRITISH GOODS

Skills Focus READING LIKE A HISTORIAN

To protest unpopular British laws, some colonial women boycotted, or refused to buy, British goods. The British illustration shown here criticized women's boycotts.

Identifying Point of View How are the women depicted here?

tributary Slaves." The cry of "no taxation without representation" became a major issue in the years before the Revolutionary War.

The Stamp Act brings protests Looking for another way to raise money, Grenville next proposed a stamp tax. Passed early in 1765, the **Stamp Act** required a government tax stamp on all legal documents, such as contracts and licenses. Newspapers, almanacs, and even printed sermons and playing cards had to have the official stamps.

The Stamp Act proved to be a very bad idea. It was the first time Parliament had taxed Americans directly, and colonists protested the law openly. In part this was because the people the Stamp Act affected most—lawyers, merchants, printers, ministers, innkeepers—were the same people who led public opinion. In many places mobs forced stamp agents to resign. In Philadelphia colonists even conducted a mock hanging of a dummy representing a stamp agent.

THE REVOLUTIONARY ERA **107**

107

Reading Focus

Britain Passes New Laws

Identify Who was Patrick Henry? *a Virginia lawyer, member of the House of Burgesses; proposed only paying taxes passed by their own assembly*

Draw Conclusions How could colonial women join the protest against taxes? *could stop buying British goods; wear homespun clothing; pressure merchants to join the boycott*

Predict What do you think will happen as a result of British officers searching homes without a search warrant? *possible answer—protests; conflict between colonists and English government*

📦 Quick Facts Transparency: Tensions Between Britain and America, 1765–1775

📄 CRF: Primary Source Activity: Benjamin Franklin Testifies Against the Stamp Act

ACADEMIC VOCABULARY
imported bought from another country

In Virginia, a young lawyer named Patrick Henry made a fiery speech to the House of Burgesses. Henry proposed that Virginians should pay only the taxes voted by their own assembly. Then the Massachusetts assembly organized the Stamp Act Congress to protest the Stamp Act. In October 1765, delegates from nine colonies met in New York to send a petition to the king and Parliament. The petition stated that Parliament did not have the right to tax the colonies without representation.

In response to the new laws, a group called the Sons of Liberty organized protests. At first this group had been made up of unskilled workers, artisans, and small farmers. Now the group included prominent citizens such as merchants and lawyers. One protest tactic was to boycott, or refuse to buy, British goods. This had started with the Sugar Act. Women joined the protests as Daughters of Liberty. They stopped buying British goods and wore clothes of homespun cloth. They also put pressure on merchants who did not join the boycott.

As merchants in Great Britain saw sales drop because of boycotts, they asked Parliament to repeal the Stamp Act. Parliament did eventually repeal the act, but still insisted it had the right to tax the colonies.

Another unpopular law passed in 1765 was the Quartering Act, which said that colonists must find quarters, or living space, for the British soldiers stationed in America. The colonists saw the Quartering Act as another attack on their rights.

Townshend Acts Many powerful people in Britain thought that Parliament was giving in to the colonists too often. So in 1767 a new government minister, Charles Townshend, came up with a new way to tax the colonies. He proposed a tax on lead, paint, paper, glass, and tea that were imported from Britain. The money raised would pay the costs of the army in America and the salaries of colonial officials. But the Townshend Acts angered the colonists. To them, it was another case of taxation without representation.

The Townshend Acts also brought back **writs of assistance**, which Parliament had used unsuccessfully in the colonies in the 1600s. A writ gave customs officers the right to search colonial homes for smuggled goods—without a search warrant. This violated the right to privacy in one's house, a cherished right in Britain. In a protest against writs, James Otis wrote:

HISTORY'S VOICES

❝A man's house is his castle; and while he is quiet, he is as well guarded as a prince in his castle. This writ, if it should be declared legal, would totally annihilate [destroy] this privilege. Customhouse officers may enter our houses when they please; we are commanded to permit their entry. Their menial servants may enter—may break locks, bars, everything in their way . . .❞

–James Otis, speech before Superior Court of Massachusetts, 1761

READING CHECK Making Inferences Why did colonists object to writs of assistance?

Tensions between Britain and America, 1765–1775

STAMP ACT, 1765	TOWNSHEND ACTS, 1767	BOSTON MASSACRE, 1770
British Action Great Britain passed a law requiring colonists to pay tax—in the form of stamps—on certain documents.	**British Action** Britain passed a series of four laws declaring its authority over the colonies. The Townshend Acts suspended one colonial representative assembly and also set up strict measures for collecting taxes in the colonies.	**British Action** British troops quartered in Boston opened fire after being harassed by an angry mob of colonists. Five colonists died.
Colonists' Reaction Refusing to use the stamps, colonists burned them and started riots. In 1765 the colonists formed a Stamp Act Congress asking Parliament to repeal the law.	**Colonists' Reaction** The colonists resented the threat to their self-government and protested what they considered "taxation without representation."	**Colonists' Reaction** Boston colonists, including Samuel Adams, demanded the removal of British troops from Boston.

108

Skills Focus: Analyzing Primary Sources

At Level

Reading Like a Historian Skill
James Otis

1. Read the following quote from James Otis to the class: " . . . Engaging in this and another popular cause has raised much resentment. But I think I can sincerely declare that I cheerfully submit myself to every odious name for conscience' sake; and from my soul I despise all those whose guilt, malice, or folly has made them my foes. Let the consequences be what they will, I am determined to proceed. The only principles of public conduct that are worthy of a gentleman or a man are to sacrifice estate, ease, health, and applause, and even life, to the sacred calls of his country."

2. Guide students in a discussion of the language used in this quote. Then have students re-write Otis's words in today's language.
   LS Interpersonal, Verbal-Linguistic

📄 Alternative Assessment Handbook, Rubric 37: Writing Assignments

Answers

Reading Check *Writs allowed customs officers to enter and search colonists' homes, a clear invasion of privacy.*

The Colonists Respond

Customs officials strictly enforced the new laws. But Boston merchants were used to avoiding customs duties. Now they joined with merchants in Philadelphia and New York in nonimportation agreements. Some southern merchants and planters joined them.

The plan worked. Most of the Townshend Acts were repealed in March 1770. Parliament kept the tax on tea, however, to show that it still had the right to tax the colonies. But by then the colonists' anger was growing. The first serious confrontation happened in Boston on the same day that the Townshend Acts were repealed, though that news had not yet reached America.

The Boston Massacre Seeing the British soldiers on their streets angered the people of Boston. The troops were a reminder of British control and arrogance. Laborers especially disliked them, since the poorly paid soldiers took part-time jobs when they were off duty. Street fights were common.

On March 5, 1770, a crowd of colonists began to throw snowballs at the sentry guarding the customs house. A British officer brought soldiers to help, but the scuffle went on. Workers taunted the British soldiers—known as Redcoats for their red uniforms—calling them "lobster scoundrels."

Accounts disagree about what happened next. Someone shouted "Fire!" and the British soldiers fired into the crowd. Five people died, including an African American sailor named Crispus Attucks, who may have led the crowd.

Colonial leaders called the event the **Boston Massacre**. They played it up as a deliberate attack on innocent civilians. The soldiers were put on trial for murder. To make sure that the law was followed, attorney John Adams (a cousin of Samuel) agreed to represent the soldiers in this unpopular case. All the soldiers were freed except for two who were given a light punishment. To avoid more violence, the troops moved out of Boston.

Samuel Adams and his fellow radicals made sure that no one would forget the Boston Massacre. A few years later, Adams introduced the idea of **Committees of Correspondence** to spread the news of British injustices from colony to colony. By communicating with each other, the committees became the basis of a political network to unify the colonies.

The first to die in the Boston Massacre, Crispus Attucks (center) became a symbol in the fight for liberty.

QUICK FACTS

TEA ACT, 1773	INTOLERABLE ACTS, 1774	BATTLES OF LEXINGTON AND CONCORD, 1775
British Action Great Britain restructured the tax on tea to give a special advantage to the British East India Company. Under the Tea Act, colonial tea merchants would lose business.	**British Action** In response to colonial protests, Britain passed a series of laws designed to punish the colonies, especially Massachusetts. The laws essentially took away the power of self-government in Massachusetts.	**British Action** 700 British troops advance toward Concord to seize the colonists' military supplies.
Colonists' Reaction In what became known as the Boston Tea Party, colonists dumped shiploads of British tea into Boston Harbor.	**Colonists' Reaction** The First Continental Congress convened in Philadelphia and sent a list of grievances to Great Britain.	**Colonists' Reaction** In Lexington, about 70 minutemen fight the British, and in Concord hundreds of colonists force the British troops to withdraw. It is the beginning of the Revolutionary War.

109

Direct Teach

Reading Focus

2 How did the colonists respond to the new laws? How did their response lead to even stricter measures? *Many agreed to nonimportation agreements; they physically resisted the Tea Act; in punishment, Great Britain passed the Intolerable Acts.*

The Colonists Respond

Identify Who was Crispus Attucks? *an African American killed in the Boston Massacre; he may have been the leader of the crowd of civilians who taunted British troops*

Draw Conclusions How was the Boston Massacre useful to colonial radicals? *It was used to organize political resistance to Great Britain.*

Activity Time Line Have students use the information on these pages to create an illustrated time line of events beginning with the repeal of the Townshend Acts. Have volunteers share their time lines with the class.

LS Visual-Spatial

CRF: Biography: Crispus Attucks

Differentiating Instruction

Above Level

Advanced Learners/GATE

Research Required

1. Organize students into small groups. Have each group research the Boston Massacre.

2. Have each group produce a news story about the Boston Massacre trial that examines the following statement by John Adams: "The Part I took in Defence of Cptn. Preston and the Soldiers, procured me Anxiety, and Obloquy[widespread condemnation] enough. It was, however, one of the most gallant, generous, manly and disinterested Actions of my whole Life, and one of the best Pieces of Service I ever rendered my Country. Judgment of Death against those Soldiers would have been as foul a Stain upon this Country as the Executions of the Quakers or Witches, anciently. As the Evidence was, the Verdict of the Jury was exactly right."

3. The news story should explain why Adams felt the way he did. **LS** Interpersonal

Alternative Assessment Handbook, Rubrics 30: Research; and 37: Writing Assignments

Reading Focus

The Colonists Respond

Identify Who was Lord North? *British prime minister who requested the Tea Act and the Intolerable Acts*

Draw Conclusions Why did some British officials oppose passage of the Intolerable Acts, or as they were called in Britain, the Coercive Acts? *They could see that harsh laws like these would more closely unite the colonies in resistance.*

Reading Focus

❸ Why did the First Continental Congress meet? *to unite the colonists against further British control*

The First Continental Congress

Recall What did the Declaration of Rights call for? *removal of British troops, repeal of taxes, repeal of the Intolerable Acts*

Analyze Why was it significant that each colony had one vote at the Continental Congress? *showed equality of representation, regardless of size or population*

Evaluate Why was the formation of the minutemen a revolutionary step for the colonies? *showed that they were prepared to fight*

Answers

Reading Check (left) *They began to resist in various ways, including boycotting British goods.* **(right)** *Colonists were of mixed opinion about the proper relationship between Britain and the colonies; however, taxation without representation was seen as unjust.*

The Tea Act and the Intolerable Acts

Another new prime minister, Lord North, took office in 1770. At first he tried policies to keep the colonies quiet. Then at his request, Parliament passed the Tea Act. As you have read, the Tea Act led to the Boston Tea Party.

The Tea Act also led to one of the earliest organized political efforts by American women. In 1774 a group of women gathered in Edenton, North Carolina, and agreed to boycott tea. A British political cartoon satirized the women because, at the time, politics was not considered a proper activity for women.

Angry officials in London wanted the colonists to pay for the Boston Tea Party. Some British politicians, such as William Pitt and Edmund Burke, warned that stricter laws would unite the colonists. But Lord North insisted. In 1774 Parliament passed a series of laws, the Coercive Acts, to punish the rebellious colonists. In the colonies, these laws were called the **Intolerable Acts**.

The first of the Intolerable Acts closed the port of Boston. Another gave the royal governor much more control over Massachusetts. He could hire and fire local officials, and limit town meetings. Still another act imposed more rules for quartering soldiers.

The Quebec Act An additional annoyance for the colonists was a law known as the Quebec Act. Britain had won French territory in Canada after the French and Indian War. Incorporating that territory into British North America proved difficult, however. Settlers in Canada were used to French law. In addition, the scattered French settlements were difficult to protect from Native Americans.

Parliament attempted to solve these problems with the Quebec Act. This act expanded the province of Quebec southward to the Ohio River and west to the Mississippi, including the scattered French settlements there. The Roman Catholic Church would be legal, and French Catholics were guaranteed their rights.

American colonists were alarmed. They assumed that the Quebec Act would limit their chances to settle on the western frontier. They also felt the act threatened their security against the French.

READING CHECK **Summarizing** How did colonists respond to increasingly strict laws from Britain?

The First Continental Congress

As some British political leaders had predicted, the Intolerable Acts brought more unity among the colonies. Other colonies sent food and money to support the people of Massachusetts. Colonists also organized boycotts.

In September 1774 delegates met in Philadelphia at the **First Continental Congress**. In attendance were Patrick Henry, George Washington, John and Samuel Adams, and John Jay. They agreed that each colony would have one vote, despite differences in size.

John Adams, who kept careful notes at the Congress, reported a speech by Patrick Henry:

HISTORY'S VOICES

❝The distinctions between Virginians, Pennsylvanians, New Yorkers, and New Englanders are no more. I am not a Virginian but an American.❞

—Patrick Henry, quoted in *The Works of John Adams*

In many ways, the First Continental Congress did bring the colonists together as Americans. All the delegates agreed that Parliament was exerting too much control. Still, their views varied from moderate to radical. One delegate suggested a plan for union under British authority, much like the Albany Plan of Union. The delegates, however, rejected that proposal by a very close vote.

The Congress then issued a Declaration of Rights protesting Great Britain's actions. This document reflected the delegates' mixed views toward Britain. In the document, the Congress accepted Parliament's right to regulate trade. But the Declaration of Rights also called for the removal of British troops and the repeal of taxes and the Intolerable Acts.

Boycotts had worked before, so the Congress used those tactics again. They agreed not to import or use British goods and to stop most exports to Britain. The Continental Congress also formed a force of **minutemen**, colonial soldiers who would be ready to resist a British attack with short notice.

After taking these actions, the Continental Congress agreed to meet again in the spring. At that time they would decide if further action was necessary.

READING CHECK **Making Inferences** Why did colonists accept British regulations on trade but not taxes?

Skills Focus: Making Generalizations

Reading Skill
The First Continental Congress Meets

1. Have students write a news story about the First Continental Congress for a 1774 issue of the "Colonial Times," a New York newspaper. Information in the story should include who attended and the outcome of the Congress.

2. Have volunteers read their stories to the class.

3. Guide students in a discussion about the role of newspapers and the importance of freedom of the press in a democratic society.
   LS **Verbal-Linguistic**
   Alternative Assessment Handbook, Rubric 40: Writing to Describe

The Battles of Lexington and Concord

Before the Continental Congress could meet again, however, war began. Minutemen in Massachusetts had been drilling on their village commons and stockpiling gunpowder and weapons. The British commander in Boston, General Thomas Gage, was waiting for reinforcements. He knew that colonial militias all across the Massachusetts countryside were preparing for a conflict.

Gage was also becoming more hostile to the unruly American colonists. He wrote to a British official that "conciliating, moderation, reasoning is over. Nothing can be done but by forceable means." In preparation Gage sent several of his officers to survey the local countryside. He also organized small groups of British soldiers to take short marches in the hopes that the colonists would see his well-trained troops and be intimidated by them.

Then in April 1775, new orders came from Great Britain. King George III wanted to take action against the colonists. The king ordered General Gage to arrest colonial leaders, particularly Samuel Adams and John Hancock. Gage also began to prepare the British troops to capture the colonists' gunpowder. The gunpowder was stockpiled in Concord, a town several miles west of Boston.

To accomplish this Gage planned a surprise attack for the night of April 18, 1775. At 10 o'clock that night, about 700 British troops crossed the Charles River in small boats and set out by road for Concord.

Battle of Lexington

The minutemen are shown leaving. Eight were killed and ten were wounded.

British troops fired at minutemen on Lexington Green.

Skills FOCUS INTERPRETING VISUALS

In this 1775 engraving American troops on Lexington Green scatter under British fire in the first battle of the Revolutionary War.

Interpreting Visuals How does this engraving show the relative experience of American and British troops?

See **Skills Handbook, p. H30**

111

Skills Focus: Analyzing Primary Sources

Below Level

Reading Like a Historian Skill
General Gage's Proclamation

1. Read the following quote from General Gage's proclamation of June 12, 1775, to the class: "In this exigency of complicated calamities, I avail myself of the last effort within the bounds of my duty, to spare the effusion of blood; to offer, and I do hereby in his Majesty's name, offer and promise, his most gracious pardon in all who shall forthwith lay down their arms, and return to the duties of peaceable subjects, excepting only from the benefit of such pardon, Samuel Adams and John Hancock . . . "

2. Guide students in a discussion of this quote.

3. Divide students into mixed-ability pairs. Have each pair write answers to the following questions: What is General Gage offering? Why do you suppose Adams and Hancock are excluded? **LS Verbal-Linguistic**

   Alternative Assessment Handbook, Rubric 40: Writing to Describe

111

The Battles of Lexington and Concord

Recall What was General Gage's purpose in sending troops to Concord? *He wanted to capture leaders of the Patriots, as well as gunpowder he knew they had stored.*

Make Judgments Do you think the British military expected strong resistance from the colonial militia? *possible answers—Yes, the British knew the militia were armed and prepared to fight. No, they probably expected that the colonists would give up when they saw that they were outnumbered.*

🗺 Map Transparency: Routes of the Alarm Riders

Spreading the alarm Colonial leaders had watched Gage's preparations, so they knew something was about to happen. A secret system of alarm riders was already in place to warn the minutemen of any unusual activity among the troops in Boston. The alarm riders were a group of about 30 men who were ready to ride their horses across the countryside to warn their fellow colonists about any action taken by the British troops.

The most famous of these riders was Paul Revere, a Boston silversmith and engraver who belonged to the Sons of Liberty. On the night of April 18, he and William Dawes learned about the British movements. They set off toward Lexington to warn Adams and Hancock.

Revere crossed the river to Charlestown, got a horse from friends, and started for Lexington. On the way, he escaped from two British guards who chased him. Revere later told how in Medford he "awaked the captain of the minute men and after that, I alarmed almost every house, till I got to Lexington."

Dawes set off from Boston. At about midnight, he met Revere in Lexington at the house

THE IMPACT TODAY
Daily Life
Each year, the Boston Marathon takes place on Patriot's Day, a day in April that commemorates Paul Revere's 1775 ride.

where Adams and Hancock were staying. They warned the two leaders, then set off for Concord. A young doctor, Samuel Prescott, another of the Sons of Liberty, caught up with them on the road. As Dawes and Prescott went to warn people in a nearby house, Revere rode on. British officers surrounded him and tried to arrest them all. Prescott and his horse jumped a low stone wall and escaped to warn the minutemen at Concord. Dawes also escaped.

The British captured Revere and continued along the route toward Lexington. But soon they heard the guns of the colonial militia. They took Revere's horse and let him go. He escaped back to the house where Adams and Hancock were staying.

Lexington and Concord The alarm riders had awakened the countryside. Alarm bells everywhere began to ring. Besides, 700 armed British soldiers could not move along a quiet country road without being heard. By the time the British reached Lexington, the militia had been waiting a long time. In fact, some colonists had already left. Still, about 70 minutemen remained waiting for the British soldiers on the Lexington town green.

When the British troops arrived, the minutemen realized they were badly outnumbered. Their captain ordered them to leave. But then, according to colonial accounts, British soldiers charged toward them. According to one account, Major Pitcairn, leading the British troops, shouted at the minutemen, "Ye villains, ye rebels, disperse!" Then from somewhere on the Lexington town green, a shot rang out.

More shots followed, and the militia fled. Eight Americans were killed, and others were wounded. The first shots of the Revolutionary War had been fired—although to this day no one is sure whether it was the colonists or the British who fired first.

The British next moved on to Concord. There the scene was very different. Hundreds of minutemen had assembled at Concord. Most of their store of gunpowder had already been used or hidden in the woods. The militia backed away from the narrow bridge as the British advanced toward them. The two sides exchanged gunfire.

Finally, the British turned and retreated toward Boston. All along the way, angry militia

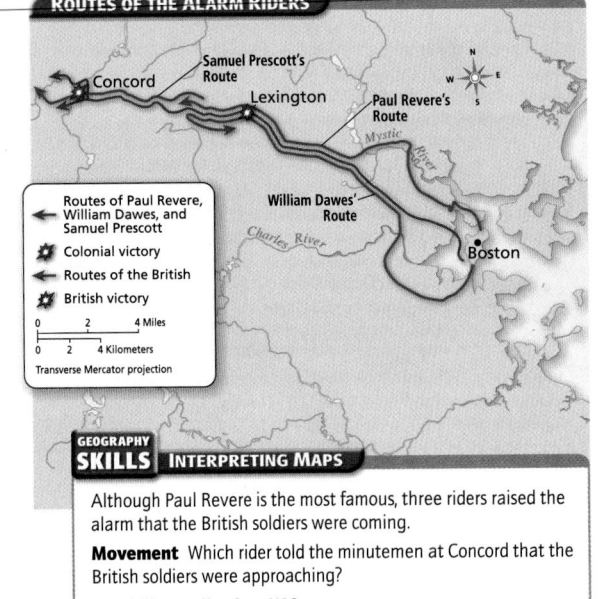

ROUTES OF THE ALARM RIDERS

Routes of Paul Revere, William Dawes, and Samuel Prescott
⚔ Colonial victory
← Routes of the British
⚔ British victory

0   2   4 Miles
0   2   4 Kilometers
Transverse Mercator projection

GEOGRAPHY SKILLS **INTERPRETING MAPS**

Although Paul Revere is the most famous, three riders raised the alarm that the British soldiers were coming.

Movement Which rider told the minutemen at Concord that the British soldiers were approaching?

See **Skills Handbook**, p. H19

Skills Focus: Making Generalizations   At Level

Reading Skill
The Patriots Prepare for War

Materials construction paper, colored pencils or markers

1. Review the Primary Sources feature, "The Battle of Lexington," with students. Then organize the class into small groups.

2. Have each group create a flyer describing the events of April 18th and 19th from the Patriot point of view. Flyers should be compelling and attractive and should create

support for the Patriots among northern and southern colonists.

3. Have volunteers from each group display their flyers to the class.

4. Guide students in a discussion about how different descriptions of events can be used to support one side or the other. 🅛 **Interpersonal, Visual-Spatial**

📄 Alternative Assessment Handbook, Rubrics 14: Group Activity; and 37: Writing Assignments

Answers
Interpreting Maps *Samuel Prescott*

The Battle of Lexington

The colonists and the British troops saw the Battle of Lexington very differently. British officer John Pitcairn gave General Gage this account of the battle.

"I gave directions to the troops to move forward, but on no account to fire, or even attempt it without orders; when I arrived at the end of the Village, I observed drawn up upon a Green near 200 rebels; when I came within about 100 yards of them, they began to file off towards some stone walls on our right flank. The Light Infantry, observing this, ran after them. I instantly called to the soldiers not to fire, but surround and disarm them, and . . . some of the rebels who had jumped over the wall fired four or five shots at the soldiers . . . and at the same time several shots were fired from a meeting house on our left. Upon this . . . the Light Infantry began a scattered fire, and continued in that situation for some little time, contrary to the repeated orders both of me and the officers that were present."

Skills FOCUS   **READING LIKE A HISTORIAN**

1. **Analyzing Primary Sources** Why do you think Pitcairn is emphasizing that the British soldiers did not fire first?
2. **Identifying Points of View** How does this source compare to other points of view you read about in this section?

See Skills Handbook, pp. H28–H29

hid behind barns, stone walls, and fences, firing at the British soldiers as they passed. At the end of the day, the number of British casualties was far greater than the number of colonial casualties.

The shot heard 'round the world Many years later, on July 4, 1837, Ralph Waldo Emerson wrote a poem for the dedication of the Battle Monument at Concord. Emerson's grandfather had fought at the Battle of Concord. In the poem, Emerson wrote an unforgettable phrase to describe the importance of the battle: "Here once the embattled farmers stood/ And fired the shot heard 'round the world."

READING CHECK   **Sequencing** Trace, in order, what happened on April 18 and April 19, 1775.

SECTION 1 ASSESSMENT

go.hrw.com
Online Quiz
Keyword: SD7 HP4

Reviewing Ideas, Terms, and People

1. **a. Identify** How did the Sons and Daughters of Liberty respond to new British laws?
   b. Analyze In what ways did the French and Indian War increase tensions between the British and the colonists?
   c. Evaluate Why did the Stamp Act anger colonists more than other taxes?

2. **a. Describe** What happened at the Boston Tea Party? Why did it happen?
   b. Make Inferences Why did colonists pay more for smuggled Dutch tea?
   c. Evaluate Were the colonists justified in dumping the British tea into Boston Harbor?

3. **a. Identify** Who were the major colonial leaders at the First Continental Congress?
   b. Summarize What actions did the First Continental Congress take?
   c. Predict Was the meeting of the Congress a final step toward independence? Why or why not?

4. **a. Recall** What did alarm riders do?
   b. Summarize Describe what happened at the Battles of Lexington and Concord.
   c. Evaluate Why did Emerson refer to the Battle of Concord as "the shot heard 'round the world"?

Critical Thinking

5. **Sequencing** Copy the chart below and make a time line of the events and laws leading up to the battles at Lexington and Concord.

_____ _____ _____ _____ → Lexington and Concord

FOCUS ON SPEAKING

6. **Persuasive** As a delegate to the First Continental Congress meeting *before* the Battles of Lexington and Concord, make a speech explaining what course you think the colonies should take next.

THE REVOLUTIONARY ERA **113**

Section 1 Assessment Answers

1. **a.** They supported resistance to the laws.
   b. British tried to keep colonists from western lands; wanted to tax colonies to pay for war
   c. first direct tax; affected public opinion

2. **a.** colonists boarded ships in Boston, dumped tea into harbor; as a protest
   b. They were boycotting British products.
   c. possible answer—No, they broke the law.

3. **a.** Washington, Henry, Jay, Samuel Adams
   b. passed Declaration of Rights; organized minutemen; agreed to meet again
   c. no, but once minutemen were organized,

armed resistance to British army more likely

4. **a.** spread word of British troop arrivals
   b. British troops met by minutemen twice, shots fired, British chased away
   c. They began the Revolutionary War, which had worldwide importance.

5. Sugar, Stamp, Townshend Acts; Boston Massacre; First Continental Congress; Gage ordered to capture colonial leaders

6. possible answer—should work together and try to negotiate with the British

Answers

Reading Like a Historian 1. *so that the British cannot be accused of initiating aggression;* **2.** *contradicts other accounts*

Reading Check *British set out for Concord; Revere and others sounded the alarm; minutemen gathered at Lexington; shots fired; Americans killed*

113

Bellringer

The Inside Story. . . Use the **Daily Bellringer Transparency** to help students answer the question.

📖 Daily Bellringer Transparency, Section 2

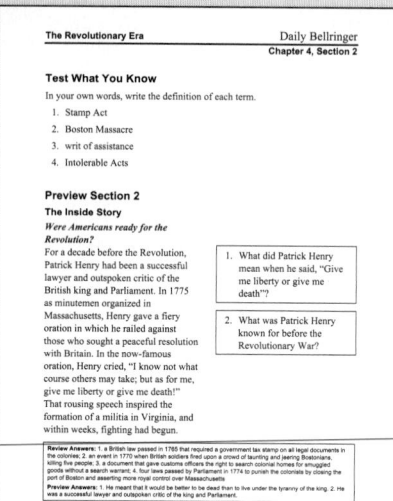

Academic Vocabulary

Review with students the high-use academic terms in this section.

differentiate make a distinction between (p. 117)

philosophy set of ideas (p. 117)

📖 CRF: Vocabulary Builder Activity, Section 2

Taking Notes

loyalty to the king; thought of themselves as British, not American; hoped for a compromise that would allow the colonies to remain British; worried that fighting against the British would expose them to Indian attacks; government oficials or Anglican Church members more likely to be Loyalists

Declaring Independence

BEFORE YOU READ

MAIN IDEA

As a revolutionary ideology grew and conflicts with Britain continued, the Second Continental Congress declared American independence.

READING FOCUS

1. What actions did the Second Continental Congress take?
2. How did violence in Boston push the colonies closer to revolution?
3. What revolutionary ideology lay behind the writing of the Declaration of Independence?
4. How did colonists' reactions to the Declaration of Independence differ?

KEY TERMS AND PEOPLE

Second Continental Congress
Thomas Jefferson
Continental Army
John Adams
Battle of Bunker Hill
Loyalist
Thomas Paine
Common Sense
Virginia Declaration of Rights
Abigail Adams

TAKING NOTES As you read, take notes on the reasons that some colonists remained Loyalists. Use a graphic organizer like the one below to organize your notes. You may need to add more circles.

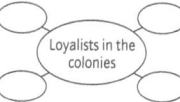

Loyalists in the colonies

"Give Me LIBERTY"

THE INSIDE STORY

Were Americans ready for the Revolution? Patrick Henry was known as a fiery speaker and a radical leader. His brilliant arguments in the courtroom made him a successful lawyer. As early as 1765, speaking against the Stamp Act, Henry criticized the king and Parliament and defended the colonies' right to self-government.

Ten years later in early 1775, Massachusetts minutemen were organizing a self-defense force. Grandfathers and teenagers were drilling with muskets on the village commons. On March 23, 1775, Patrick Henry once again stirred up his audience in the Virginia Convention of Delegates:

"Gentlemen may cry, Peace, Peace—but there is no peace. The war is actually begun! The next gale that sweeps from the north will bring to our ears the clash of resounding arms! Our brethren are already in the field! Why stand we here idle? What is it that gentlemen wish? What would they have? Is life so dear, or peace so sweet, as to be purchased at the price of chains and slavery? Forbid it, Almighty God! I know not what course others may take; but as for me, give me liberty or give me death!"

Henry's rousing speech inspired Virginians to raise a militia. Only a few weeks after his speech, as you have read, fighting began at Lexington and Concord. ◼

◀ **Patrick Henry's words fanned the flames of revolution.**

COLONIAL WILLIAMSBURG FOUNDATION

114

Teach the Main Idea

At Level

Declaring Independence

1. **Teach** Ask students the Reading Focus questions to teach this section.

2. **Apply** Organize the class into small groups. Have students in each group outline the section using the four main heads and subheads. Each subhead should have at least three bullet points of information.
   LS Visual-Spatial

3. **Review** Have volunteers review one main head aloud for the class, using their outlines

as guides, until the entire section is reviewed.

4. **Practice/Homework** Have each student design a Web page describing the highlights of the Second Continental Congress.
   LS Verbal-Linguistic

   📖 Alternative Assessment Handbook, Rubric 3: Artwork

The Second Continental Congress Takes Action

In May 1775, a few weeks after Lexington and Concord, the **Second Continental Congress** met in Philadelphia as planned. New members included Benjamin Franklin, John Hancock, and **Thomas Jefferson**. When the group convened, delegates' attitudes toward Britain was mixed. Many still felt loyalty toward King George III, blaming his ministers and Parliament for bad policies. All delegates rejected Parliament's authority to tax the colonies, but only a few actually wanted independence. During the next months they made several crucial decisions.

Creating a Continental Army War had already begun, and New Englanders and British troops were fighting around Boston. The Congress agreed to support the war, even though its members did not agree on the final goal. The Congress made the New England forces the core of a **Continental Army**.

Then in June 1775 the Congress chose George Washington to lead the new army. **John Adams** of Massachusetts suggested Washington for the position, pointing out his "skill and experience as an officer" in the French and Indian War. Adams also noted Washington's "independent fortune, great talents, and excellent universal character."

War or peace? In July the Congress issued two very different documents. The differing positions in these documents reflected the colonists' divided feelings. The first, called *A Declaration of the Causes and Necessity of Taking Up Arms*, explained why Americans were at war. It accused Parliament of having "an inordinate passion for power." It also charged General Gage with "cruel aggression." Finally, the document concluded:

HISTORY'S VOICES

❝We have not raised armies with ambitious designs of separating from Great Britain and establishing independent states. . . . In our own native land, in defence of the freedom that is our birth-right . . . for the protection of our property, acquired solely by the honest industry of our forefathers and ourselves, against violence actually offered, we have taken up arms.❞

–*A Declaration of the Causes and Necessity of Taking Up Arms*, July 6, 1775

A few days later, the Congress sent King George III what became known as the Olive Branch Petition. Its authors called themselves the king's "faithful subjects in the Colonies." They begged him to use his "royal authority and influence" to reach a "happy and permanent reconciliation."

Despite the petition, the king declared the colonies to be in rebellion. In response, Parliament passed a harsh law banning colonial trade outside the British Empire.

READING CHECK **Contrasting** How did the actions of the Second Continental Congress reflect the delegates' differences of opinion?

More Violence in Boston

Even while the Continental Congress was meeting, fighting continued in several parts of the colonies. The British at first treated these encounters as local rebellions. Then colonial forces expanded the war.

On May 10, 1775, as the Continental Congress was just beginning, the Green Mountain Boys captured the British fort at Ticonderoga in New York. The Green Mountain Boys were a local Vermont militia organized by Ethan Allen. Other members of this militia captured the fort at Crown Point a few days later. Both forts were on the strategic Lake Champlain–Lake George route to Canada.

The siege of Boston After the battles at Lexington and Concord, British troops withdrew back into Boston. Several thousand British troops occupied the town. The Americans quickly put together a larger army, bringing

---

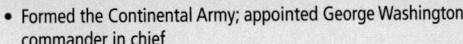

THE SECOND CONTINENTAL CONGRESS, 1775

- Formed the Continental Army; appointed George Washington commander in chief

- Issued a Continental (national) currency

- Wrote *A Declaration of the Causes and Necessity of Taking Up Arms*

- Proposed reconciliation with King George III in the Olive Branch Petition

---

Skills Focus: Analyzing Primary Sources

At Level

Research Required

Reading Like a Historian Skill
Creating a Continental Army

1. Have students research the life of George Washington. When they have finished their research, read this passage to the class, from author John E. Ferling's book about the American Revolution. It describes Washington's first encounter with his Continental Army soldiers: "Most of these men were farmers . . . . These men literally thought of themselves as the equal of one another. Washington loathed what he saw. He quietly described many of the Massachusetts officers as inept and most of the enlisted men as 'exceedingly dirty and nasty.'"

2. Have students write a short opinion about why Washington felt the way he did.
   LS Verbal-Linguistic
   Alternative Assessment Handbook, Rubric 40: Writing to Describe

---

Direct Teach

Reading Focus

❶ What actions did the Second Continental Congress take? *created a Continental Army with Washington at its head; wrote* A Declaration of the Causes and Necessity of Taking Up Arms; *issued currency; wrote the Olive Branch Petition to King George III*

The Second Continental Congress Takes Action

Recall What was the Olive Branch Petition? *an appeal to King George III to help reach a peaceful resolution of conflicts between colonists and Britain*

Analyze Why did the Congress issue the Olive Branch Petition? *Many delegates did not want to separate from Great Britain.*

🗄 Quick Facts Transparency: The Second Continental Congress, 1775

📄 Political Cartoons Activities for American History: Cartoon 7: The Colonies Throw Britain

📄 CRF: Primary Source Activity: George Washington Is Selected to Command the Colonial Army

Primary Source

Benjamin Franklin signed the Olive Branch Petition, but expected war. He wrote to a friend in Britain: "Mr. Strahan, You are a member of Parliament and one of that Majority that has doomed my country to destruction. You have begun to burn our towns, and murder our people. Look upon your hands! They are stained with the blood of your relations. You and I were long friends; you are now my enemy, and I am, yours, B. Franklin"
— Benjamin Franklin

Answers

Reading Check *They formed an army but also asked for peace.*

115

2 How did violence in Boston push the colonies closer to revolution? *The Battle of Bunker Hill gave colonists confidence that they could win a war.*

More Violence in Boston

Describe What was the outcome of the Battle of Bunker Hill? *British prevailed, but 1,000 British soldiers killed or wounded*

Make Inferences Why were the battles at Moores Creek and Sullivan's Island major victories? *discouraged British invasion of the southern colonies*

Make Judgments Was Prescott right to occupy the hills? *possible answer—yes, because colonists needed to keep the high ground around Boston in order to defend the city*

Teaching Tip

Remind students that not all Americans supported the move for independence. The term *Loyalist* refers to someone who was loyal to Britain and the king. Loyalists did not support the movement for independence.

Attack on Bunker's Hill, with the Burning of Charlestown

British troops crossed the Charles River from Boston to Charlestown to meet the colonists on Breed's Hill. After finally capturing the hill, the British set fire to Charlestown. **Why did the British nevertheless feel discouraged—and the colonists encouraged—by the outcome of this battle?**

together some 15,000 militia from all over New England. The standoff at Boston led to the first major battle of the Revolutionary War, the **Battle of Bunker Hill**.

Boston could be attacked from several hills overlooking the city. Dorchester Heights was to the south. Bunker Hill and Breed's Hill were across the river in Charlestown. General Gage was planning to occupy the hills as soon as reinforcements arrived.

But a colonial force led by Colonel William Prescott moved quickly to fortify the hills. While under attack from British cannons across the river and warships in the harbor, they hastily built a fort on Breed's Hill.

On June 17, 1775, British troops led by General William Howe tried to dislodge the colonists from the hilltop. Some 2,500 troops stormed the hill twice as the colonists fired from behind barricades. The colonists were short of ammunition and so waited until the enemy was a few yards away, then fired with deadly aim. One commander shouted the now-famous phrase, "Don't fire until you see the whites of their eyes!"

On the third British attempt, the colonists ran out of gunpowder. They were forced to retreat to nearby Bunker Hill (which gave the

battle its name). About 1,000 British soldiers and about 400 American colonists were killed or wounded.

Although the British won, the brave defense at the Battle of Bunker Hill encouraged the colonists' resistance. The battle gave them confidence in their ability to fight the better-trained and better-equipped British army.

Washington takes command Two weeks after the Battle of Bunker Hill, George Washington took command of the Continental Army in Boston. The army was seriously short of heavy weapons and gunpowder, so Washington sent Henry Knox to Fort Ticonderoga to bring back captured British weapons. Knox was a former Boston bookseller who was now in charge of artillery for the Continental Army. Using troops, horses, and oxen, Knox moved more than 50 cannons and mortars across 300 snowy miles to Boston.

As a result, by March 1776, Washington had enough guns and ammunition to recapture Boston. His troops captured and fortified Dorchester Heights. From there he forced the British to evacuate the city and the harbor. From Boston, the British sailed for Halifax, Nova Scotia, along with about 1,100 **Loyalists**,

Skills Focus: Summarizing

Reading Skill
Washington Takes Command

1. Organize students into small groups. Have each group research Henry Knox and the movement of cannons to Boston for George Washington and the Continental Army to use. Students should explore what Knox actually did and the difficulties of his task.

2. Have students create a storyboard or collage about Knox's expedition and judge whether or not he should be considered a hero.

3. Have volunteers from each group share their reports with the class. **LS Verbal-Linguistic, Logical-Mathematical**

📖 Alternative Assessment Handbook, Rubrics 8: Collages; and 30: Research

Answers

Photo *The battle showed that colonists could fight well against British troops.*

colonists whose sympathies were with the king and Britain. This first test proved Washington's ability as a general.

Other battles There were clashes in other colonies, too. In the winter of 1775–1776 Benedict Arnold led a small Continental force through the snowy wilderness in an unsuccessful attack on the city of Quebec.

In the southern colonies, colonial victories discouraged a British invasion there. In February 1776, Scottish Loyalists waving broadswords attacked a colonial force at Moores Creek, North Carolina. But well-armed colonists were waiting. Their victory ended British control in North Carolina. In June, British ships launched an attack on a fort at Sullivan's Island near Charleston, South Carolina, but the fort's commander held them off.

READING CHECK **Making Inferences** Why was the Continental Army short of gunpowder and weapons?

The Declaration of Independence

The events of 1775 pushed more American colonists toward supporting independence. They were angry at the king's reaction to the Olive Branch Petition. They also learned that the British were recruiting Native Americans and African Americans to fight against them. In addition, they heard that the king was hiring mercenary soldiers from the German state of Hesse.

By the spring of 1776, some colonists were still doubtful, but their leaders were becoming certain of their cause. When the Continental Congress met again, it opened seaports to foreign trade except with Britain.

Revolutionary ideology The colonists still thought of themselves as British. Even though they lived an ocean away, they believed they were entitled to all the rights that British citizens had claimed over the years. Those rights, such as trial by jury, went as far back as the Magna Carta. But many of Parliament's recent laws seemed to differentiate between the rights of citizens in Britain and those in America. That was why colonists refused to pay taxes imposed by a Parliament where they had no representative.

Colonial leaders knew the philosophy of Enlightenment thinkers such as John Locke. The idea of natural rights was part of their revolutionary ideology. Under Locke's theory of the social contract, the present British government was failing to protect the rights and liberties of its citizens in America. That would justify a rebellion against it.

A matter of *Common Sense* One powerful voice speaking out for independence was a British journalist who had been in America for only two years. **Thomas Paine** came to America on the advice of Ben Franklin, whom he met in London. Early in 1776 Paine published a pamphlet called ***Common Sense***. In it he condemned

ACADEMIC VOCABULARY

differentiate make a distinction between

philosophy set of ideas

PRIMARY SOURCES

Common Sense

In January 1776 many colonists were divided about their relationship with Great Britain. Then Thomas Paine published *Common Sense*, a pamphlet that stated in easy-to-understand terms why the colonies should break free from Britain. This widely read document strengthened support for the American Revolution.

"Any submission to, or dependence on, Great Britain, tends directly to involve this continent in European wars and quarrels, and set us at variance [odds] with nations who would otherwise seek our friendship, and against whom we have neither anger nor complaint. As Europe is our market for trade, we ought to form no partial connection with any part of it. 'Tis the true interest of America to steer clear of European contentions, which she can never do while by her dependence on Britain she is made the weight in the scale of British politics."

Paine used direct language to make his arguments for independence from Great Britain.

Skills FOCUS **READING LIKE A HISTORIAN**

1. **Analyzing Primary Sources** According to Paine, what is a major problem with remaining under British rule?
2. **Drawing Conclusions** Why do you think Paine named his pamphlet *Common Sense*?

See Skills Handbook, pp. H12, H28–H29

THE REVOLUTIONARY ERA **117**

Reading Focus

❸ What revolutionary ideology lay behind the writing of the Declaration of Independence? *Enlightenment thought, including the idea of natural rights and the social contract between rulers and subjects*

The Declaration of Independence

Identify Who was John Locke? *English Enlightenment philosopher who theorized about natural rights and the social contract*

Make Inferences What characteristics of some British laws in the colonies made colonists feel separated from Britain? *laws seemed to differentiate between those who lived in America and those who lived in Britain*

Recent Scholarship

David McCullough's book *1776* is a narrative of the beginnings of the American Revolution. McCullough discusses the miserable conditions both sides had to endure, the opinion of General Howe that a ragtag army could not defeat the British, the difficulties in communications, and how Washington's strategies helped the Continental Army survive and win.

1776 by David McCullough. Simon & Schuster, 2005

Collaborative Learning

At Level

The Declaration of Independence

1. Review the situation in the colonies in the spring of 1776 with students.

2. Organize students into small groups. Have each group design a Web page to inform colonists about John Locke and Thomas Paine and persuade them to join the Patriots in pushing for independence. Have students use the information in the text to make bullet points or persuasive arguments.

3. Have volunteers from each group display their Web pages to the class. Guide students in a discussion of the importance of up-to-date and accurate information in a democratic society. **LS Interpersonal, Kinesthetic**

📓 Alternative Assessment Handbook, Rubrics 3: Artwork; and 14: Group Activity

---

Answers

Reading Like a Historian 1. *It would keep the colonies involved in European wars.* **2.** *possible answer—because it stated in easy-to-understand terms the reasons for independence*

Reading Check *little money to buy supplies; army was made up of volunteers who brought their own guns*

The Declaration of Independence

Recall What evidence is there that the words of Thomas Paine were influential in launching the Revolutionary War? *Common Sense sold more than 100,000 copies in a short time.*

Explain What were the three resolutions presented by Virginia to the Continental Congress? *colonies should be independent; should seek foreign alliances; should plan to unite*

Analyze Why did the Declaration of Independence not condemn the slave trade? *because of pressure from southern colonies that depended on slave labor*

🗄 Quick Facts Transparency: Key Documents that Influenced the Declaration of Independence

📄 CRF: Biography: Robert R. Livingston

Info to Know

Signers of the Declaration George F. Scheer's and Hugh F. Rankin's 1988 book *Rebels and Redcoats: The American Revolution Through the Eyes of Those Who Fought and Lived It* asserts that the signers of the Declaration knew they had put their lives at risk: "Mr. Harrison, a delegate from Virginia, is a large portly man—Mr. Gerry of Massachusetts is slender and spare. A little time after the solemn transaction of signing the instrument, Mr. Harrison said smilingly to Mr. Gerry, 'When the hanging scene comes to be exhibited, I shall have the advantage over you, on account of my size. All will be over with me in a moment, but you will be kicking in the air half an hour after I am gone.'"

Answers

Reading Check *natural rights, social contract are the basis of the Declaration*

118

KEY DOCUMENTS THAT INFLUENCED THE DECLARATION OF INDEPENDENCE

Magna Carta (1215)	Guaranteed civil and political freedoms to feudal lords. These freedoms later became fundamental for all English citizens.
Mayflower Compact (1620)	Established the first colonial government in the colonies.
English Bill of Rights (1689)	Placed limits on the English king's power and more power in the hands of a representative government.
John Locke's *Two Treatises of Government* (1690)	Declared rights of life and property to be part of "natural law." Justified the overthrow of government if these rights were denied.
Thomas Paine's *Common Sense* (1776)	Argued that American colonists should not only rebel against unfair taxation but also declare independence from Britain.

monarchy and particularly the rule of George III. Paine called for an American declaration of independence, not just a protest against taxes.

Thomas Paine was a brilliant political writer, and his words stirred many colonists. Within a few months, the 50-page pamphlet sold more than 100,000 copies. It was one of the first American bestsellers.

THE IMPACT TODAY

Daily Life
The Continental Congress voted to declare independence on July 2. However, because the Declaration was not approved until July 4, today we celebrate Independence Day on July 4.

Virginia calls for independence In May 1776 the Virginia Convention of Delegates issued a declaration of citizens' rights called the **Virginia Declaration of Rights**. This was the first official call for American independence. It would influence not only the Declaration of Independence but also the Bill of Rights in the U.S. Constitution and many state constitutions.

Drawing on Locke's idea of natural rights, the Virginia declaration stated:

HISTORY'S VOICES

❝That all men are by nature equally free and independent and have certain inherent rights,. . . namely, the enjoyment of life and liberty, with the means of acquiring and possessing property, and pursuing and obtaining happiness and safety.❞

–Virginia Declaration of Rights

On June 7, 1776, Richard Henry Lee of Virginia then presented three resolutions to the Continental Congress. The first stated that the colonies should be independent. The second resolution stated that Americans needed to form foreign alliances for support. Finally, the third resolution recommended that the colonies form a plan for unification.

Writing the Declaration Congress discussed the Virginia proposals, and no one seriously objected. That showed how far their thinking had moved toward independence. Moderates such as John Dickinson did urge people to wait to be certain of foreign help.

Finally, the delegates named a committee to write a draft of a declaration of independence. Its members were John Adams, Robert Livingston, Roger Sherman, Thomas Jefferson, and Benjamin Franklin. Jefferson was chosen to write the draft.

Jefferson was young, but Adams wrote that he came to Congress with "a reputation for literature, science, and a happy talent of composition." In fact, Adams told him, "You can write ten times better than I can." In addition, Jefferson was a Virginian, which was an advantage to him politically.

Adams and Franklin did make some changes in Jefferson's draft, however. Then the Congress as a whole made some more. They toned down some of his language about the king. Because of pressure from some southern colonies, they also cut out an entire section attacking the slave trade. The colonial economy depended on the slave trade, so including it in the Declaration of Independence would have opened up the signers to charges of hypocrisy. Jefferson later noted that the Declaration did not present new ideas but simply stated "an expression of the American mind."

On July 2, 1776, the final document was presented to the Congress, which voted to declare independence. Two days later, on July 4, they approved the entire document. Copies were sent out and read in public. Crowds in Philadelphia, New York, Boston, and other cities cheered and rang church bells. Now, in British eyes, the colonists were all rebels.

READING CHECK **Identifying Cause and Effect** How did Enlightenment thinking influence the Declaration of Independence?

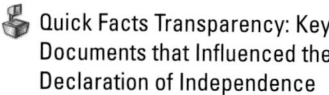

Differentiating Instruction

Above Level

Advanced Learners/GATE

Research Required

1. Organize the class into small groups. Have each group conduct outside research on both the Declaration of Independence and the Virginia Declaration of Rights, which preceded it.

2. Have each group use its research to prepare a news report discussing, with examples, the extent to which Jefferson and the others involved in the Declaration of Independence might have used the Declaration of Rights as a model.

3. Have groups present their reports to the class.
   LS Interpersonal

📄 Alternative Assessment Handbook, Rubrics 24: Oral Presentations; and 30: Research

Reactions to Independence

Not everyone was convinced of the need for American independence, however. Until the last minute, many colonists hoped for a compromise that would let the colonies remain part of Great Britain.

In addition, colonists living on the western frontier had not previously been part of political quarrels. They feared that a fight for independence would expose them to Indian attack, since any fighting against the British would draw men away from the defense of the frontier. Therefore, many frontier settlers did not support American independence.

Even after the Declaration, some colonists remained loyal to Britain. During the war, Britain would enlist the help of Loyalists to fight against the Patriots, those who supported independence. The Declaration of Independence forced the colonists to take sides. Would they be Patriots fighting for independence? Or would they be Loyalists?

The Loyalists Probably about a quarter of the colonists remained loyal to Great Britain and the king for the course of the Revolutionary War. Patriots called these Loyalists Tories, which was the name of the more conservative political party in Great Britain.

Loyalist feelings varied from region to region and from family to family. Most New Englanders and Virginians were strongly on the Patriot side. Feelings were mixed in the middle colonies and especially in New York. Loyalists were strong in southern colonies such as Georgia and South Carolina.

Close ties to Great Britain mattered, too. Loyalist sympathies were strong among people who had been government officials or belonged to the Anglican Church. Landowners, merchants, doctors and lawyers could be found on both sides. Most debtors, small farmers, and shopkeepers were Patriots.

In many places it was dangerous to be a Loyalist—at least publicly. Local Patriots sometimes harassed Loyalists, attacking their farms and

COUNTERPOINTS

Loyalist and Patriot

Benjamin Franklin's son, William Franklin, was a Loyalist who took his responsibilities as royal governor of New Jersey seriously.

❝ I think that all laws until they are repealed ought to be obeyed and that it is the duty of those who are entrusted with the executive part of government to see that they are so. ❞

William Franklin,
1771

Benjamin Franklin was a Patriot who believed that the British Parliament should not make laws in the colonies. He expressed his views in a letter to his son.

❝ I am indeed of opinion, that the parliament has no right to make any law whatever, binding on the colonies . . . I know your sentiments differ from mine on these subjects. You are a thorough government man, which I do not wonder at, nor do I aim at converting you. I only wish you to act uprightly and steadily. ❞

Benjamin Franklin,
1773

Skills FOCUS READING LIKE A HISTORIAN

Identifying Points of View How did Benjamin Franklin and William Franklin differ in their views of the British government?
See Skills Handbook, pp. H28–H29

Reactions to Independence

Identify Who was Abigail Adams?
wife of John Adams

Make Inference Why is Abigail Adams remembered to this day?
because of letters she wrote to her husband, giving both news and political advice

● **Review & Assess** ●

Close

Have students describe the actions taken by the Second Continental Congress and the consequences of those actions.

Review

📟 Online Quiz, Section 2

🎲 Daily Test Practice Transparency

Assess

SE Section 2 Assessment

📄 Progress Assessment: Section 2 Quiz

📄 Alternative Assessment Handbook

Reteach

📄 Interactive Reader and Study Guide, Section 2

💿 Interactive Skills Tutor CD-ROM

FACES OF HISTORY

Abigail ADAMS
1744–1818

Intelligent and outspoken, Abigail Adams is best known for the eloquent letters she wrote to John Adams while he was away attending to his duties.

Abigail's letters show an active interest in politics. In 1775 she encouraged her husband to support the growing independence movement. Abigail also urged him to support the education of women and the abolition of slavery. In one of her most famous letters, she reminded John to "remember the ladies" when planning the new nation's government.

Interpret What do Abigail Adams's letters tell us about her political beliefs?

property, or even driving them out of town. Families were sometimes bitterly divided. Some states passed laws taking away Loyalists' property.

During the war, several regiments of Loyalists fought with the British. Others left the country for Canada, Great Britain, or British-held islands in the Caribbean. Some simply lived quietly and avoided politics. After the American Revolution ended, perhaps 100,000 more Loyalists left the United States, mainly to settle in Canada.

A cheer for the Patriots When the news of the Declaration of Independence reached Boston in July 1776, **Abigail Adams**, the wife of John Adams, had no doubts about how she felt. In one of her famous letters to John, who was then a delegate serving in the Continental Congress, Abigail described hearing the Declaration of Independence read from the State House in Boston.

HISTORY'S VOICES

❝Great attention was given to every word. As soon as he ended, the cry from the balcony was 'God save our American States,' and then three cheers which rent the air. The bells rang . . . the cannons were discharged, the platoons followed, and every face appeared joyful . . . After dinner the King's Arms were taken down from the State House, and every vestige of him from every place in which it appeared, and burnt in King Street. Thus ends royal authority in this State. And all the people shall say Amen.❞

—Abigail Adams, letter, 1776

Abigail Adams continued to write letters to her husband throughout the Revolutionary War and later during the early years of the new American republic.

READING CHECK **Making Inferences** Why did Loyalists leave the colonies?

SECTION 2 ASSESSMENT

go.hrw.com
Online Quiz
Keyword: SD7 HP4

Reviewing Ideas, Terms, and People

1. **a. Describe** What were the delegates' points of view when the Second Continental Congress began?
   b. Evaluate Should King George III have rejected the Olive Branch Petition?

2. **a. Identify** Who were the Green Mountain Boys?
   b. Explain Explain the events at the Battle of Bunker Hill, focusing on why the battle was a British victory.
   c. Predict How did the Battle of Bunker Hill encourage the American cause?

3. **a. Recall** What British actions in 1775 pushed the colonists toward independence?
   b. Analyze What was the effect of Paine's *Common Sense* on colonial thinking?
   c. Elaborate How did ideas from the Enlightenment become part of revolutionary ideology?

4. **a. Describe** What was the position of **Loyalists** after the Declaration of Independence?

b. Make Inferences Why would a farmer or shopkeeper tend to be a Patriot?
c. Evaluate What were the strengths of the Declaration of Independence? What were some weaknesses?

Critical Thinking

5. **Contrasting** Copy the chart below and fill in reasons why someone would choose the Loyalist or Patriot side.

Loyalist	Patriot

FOCUS ON WRITING

6. **Persuasive** As a colonist writing to your family in Great Britain about the events of July 1776, explain why you have chosen to be a Patriot or a Loyalist.

Section 2 Assessment Answers

1. **a.** Some supported separation and war; others hoped for reconciliation.
   b. yes, Revolution inevitable

2. **a.** Vermont militia; captured Fort Ticonderoga
   b. British troops charged Patriots on Breed's Hill; forced them to retreat to Bunker Hill
   c. showed they could stand up to British troops

3. **a.** king rejected Olive Branch Petition; declared colonies in rebellion; British tried to recruit soldiers to fight the colonists
   b. convinced many to fight

c. natural rights, social contract justified breaking from Britain

4. **a.** Many left or lived very quiet lives.
   b. had little connection to Britain
   c. clear explanation of rights and complaints; ignored slavery

5. Loyalist—connections to Britain; belief in monarchy; Patriot—few connections to Britain; resented British policies

6. Patriot—Britain treated colonists poorly; Loyalist—tradition makes colonists British

---

Answers

Faces of History *that she was ahead of her time*

Reading Check *dangerous to remain; wanted to retain ties with Britain*

The Declaration of Independence

In Congress, July 4, 1776
The unanimous Declaration of the thirteen united States of America,

When in the Course of human events, it becomes necessary for one people to dissolve the political bands which have connected them with another, and to assume among the Powers of the earth, the separate and equal station to which the Laws of Nature and of Nature's God entitle them, a decent respect to the opinions of mankind requires that they should declare the causes which **impel** them to the separation.

We hold these truths to be self-evident, that all men are created equal, that they are **endowed** by their Creator with certain unalienable Rights, that among these are Life, Liberty, and the pursuit of Happiness. That to secure these rights, Governments are instituted among Men, deriving their just powers from the consent of the governed, That whenever any Form of Government becomes destructive of these ends, it is the Right of the People to alter or to abolish it, and to institute new Government, laying its foundation on such principles and organizing its powers in such form, as to them shall seem most likely to effect their Safety and Happiness. Prudence, indeed, will dictate that Governments long established should not be changed for light and transient causes; and accordingly all experience hath shown, that mankind are more disposed to suffer, while evils are sufferable, than to right themselves by abolishing the forms to which they are accustomed. But when a long train of abuses and **usurpations**, pursuing invariably the same Object **evinces** a design to reduce them under absolute **Despotism**, it is their right, it is their duty, to throw off such Government, and to provide new Guards for their future security.—Such has been the patient sufferance of these Colonies; and such is now the necessity which constrains them to alter their former Systems of Government. The history of the present King of Great Britain is a history of repeated injuries and usurpations, all having in direct object the establishment of an absolute **Tyranny** over these States. To prove this, let Facts be submitted to a **candid** world.

He has refused his Assent to Laws, the most wholesome and necessary for the public good.

He has forbidden his Governors to pass Laws of immediate and pressing importance, unless suspended in their operation till his Assent should be obtained; and when so suspended, he has utterly neglected to attend to them.

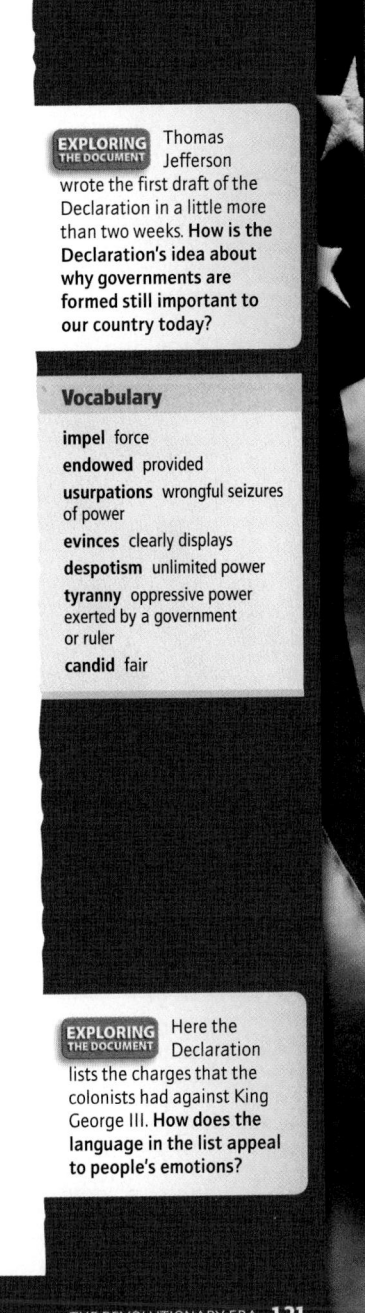

EXPLORING THE DOCUMENT Thomas Jefferson wrote the first draft of the Declaration in a little more than two weeks. **How is the Declaration's idea about why governments are formed still important to our country today?**

Vocabulary

impel force
endowed provided
usurpations wrongful seizures of power
evinces clearly displays
despotism unlimited power
tyranny oppressive power exerted by a government or ruler
candid fair

EXPLORING THE DOCUMENT Here the Declaration lists the charges that the colonists had against King George III. **How does the language in the list appeal to people's emotions?**

Direct Teach

Info to Know

Signing the Declaration On July 1, 1776, three days before the Declaration of Independence was signed, just nine of the colonies firmly supported independence. Because a vote was to be taken on July 2, supporters of independence spent the day trying to convince opposing delegates of the need for self government. One supporter, Richard Henry Lee, finally swayed South Carolina delegate Edward Rutledge, who agreed to vote for independence if the delegates from Pennsylvania and Delaware did so as well. The following morning was spent waiting for the Delaware delegate Caesar Rodney, who had been home caring for his sick wife. Rodney finally arrived, covered with mud after a frantic ride over rain-soaked roads. He cast his vote in favor of independence, and the delegates of South Carolina and Pennsylvania followed suit.

Vocabulary

relinquish release, yield
inestimable priceless
formidable causing dread
annihilation destruction
convulsions violent disturbances
naturalization of foreigners the process by which foreign-born persons become citizens
appropriations of lands setting aside land for settlement
tenure term
a multitude of many
quartering lodging, housing

He has refused to pass other Laws for the accommodation of large districts of people, unless those people would **relinquish** the right of Representation in the Legislature, a right **inestimable** to them and **formidable** to tyrants only.

He has called together legislative bodies at places unusual, uncomfortable, and distant from the depository of their Public Records, for the sole purpose of fatiguing them into compliance with his measures.

He has dissolved Representative Houses repeatedly, for opposing with manly firmness his invasions on the rights of the people.

He has refused for a long time, after such dissolutions, to cause others to be elected; whereby the Legislative Powers, incapable of **Annihilation**, have returned to the People at large for their exercise; the State remaining in the mean time exposed to all the dangers of invasion from without, and **convulsions** within.

He has endeavored to prevent the population of these States; for that purpose obstructing the Laws of **Naturalization of Foreigners**; refusing to pass others to encourage their migration hither, and raising the conditions of new **Appropriations of Lands**.

He has obstructed the Administration of Justice, by refusing his Assent to Laws for establishing Judiciary Powers.

He has made Judges dependent on his Will alone, for the **tenure** of their offices, and the amount and payment of their salaries.

He has erected **a multitude of** New Offices, and sent hither swarms of Officers to harass our people, and eat out their substance.

He has kept among us, in times of peace, Standing Armies without the Consent of our legislature.

He has affected to render the Military independent of and superior to the Civil Power.

He has combined with others to subject us to a jurisdiction foreign to our constitution, and unacknowledged by our laws; giving his Assent to their Acts of pretended legislation:

For **quartering** large bodies of armed troops among us:

For protecting them, by a mock Trial, from Punishment for any Murders which they should commit on the Inhabitants of these States:

For cutting off our Trade with all parts of the world:

For imposing taxes on us without our Consent:

For depriving us in many cases, of the benefits of Trial by Jury:

For transporting us beyond Seas to be tried for pretended offences:

EXPLORING THE DOCUMENT Colonists had been angry over British tax policies since just after the French and Indian War. **Why were the colonists protesting British tax policies?**

122 CHAPTER 4

Collaborative Learning

At Level

Grievances in the Declaration of Independence

1. Organize students into small groups, and have each group review the grievances against the king that are listed in the Declaration of Independence. Have each group create a numbered list of the grievances in simple, easy-to-understand language.

2. Have group members rank the grievances on their lists. Which British actions do they believe created the most conflict or angered the colonists the most? Have students add brief reasons or explanations to the ranked list.

3. Have a volunteer from each group share its rankings with the class. Then compare the lists. Is there consensus among the groups' rankings? Which grievances do students think were of top concern to the colonists?

LS Verbal-Linguistic, Interpersonal

Alternative Assessment Handbook, Rubric 11: Discussions

Answers

Exploring the Document *Taxes were imposed without the consent of the colonists.*

122

For abolishing the free System of English Laws in a neighboring Province, establishing therein an **Arbitrary** government, and enlarging its Boundaries so as to **render** it at once an example and fit instrument for introducing the same absolute rule into these Colonies:

For taking away our Charters, abolishing our most valuable Laws, and altering fundamentally the Forms of our Governments:

For suspending our own Legislature, and declaring themselves invested with Power to legislate for us in all cases whatsoever.

He has **abdicated** Government here, by declaring us out of his Protection and waging War against us.

He has plundered our seas, ravaged our Coasts, burnt our towns, and destroyed the lives of our people.

He is at this time transporting large armies of **foreign mercenaries** to complete the works of death, desolation and tyranny, already begun with circumstances of Cruelty & **perfidy** scarcely paralleled in the most barbarous ages, and totally unworthy the Head of a civilized nation.

He has constrained our fellow Citizens taken Captive on the high Seas to bear Arms against their Country, to become the executioners of their friends and Brethren, or to fall themselves by their Hands.

He has excited domestic **insurrections** amongst us, and has endeavored to bring on the inhabitants of our frontiers, the merciless Indian Savages, whose known rule of warfare, is an undistinguished destruction of all ages, sexes and conditions.

In every stage of these Oppressions We have **Petitioned for Redress** in the most humble terms: Our repeated Petitions have been answered only by repeated injury. A Prince, whose character is thus marked by every act which may define a Tyrant, is unfit to be the ruler of a free People.

Nor have We been wanting in attention to our British brethren. We have warned them from time to time of attempts by their legislature to extend an **unwarrantable jurisdiction** over us. We have reminded them of the circumstances of our emigration and settlement here. We have appealed to their native justice and **magnanimity**, and we have **conjured** them by the ties of our common kindred to disavow these usurpations, which, would inevitably interrupt our connections and correspondence. They too have been deaf to the voice of justice and of **consanguinity**. We must, therefore, **acquiesce** in the necessity, which denounces our Separation, and hold them, as we hold the rest of mankind, Enemies in War, in Peace Friends.

We, therefore, the Representatives of the united States of America, in General Congress, Assembled, appealing to the Supreme Judge of the world for the **rectitude** of our intentions, do, in the Name, and by Authority of the good People of these Colonies, solemnly publish and declare, That these United

THE REVOLUTIONARY ERA **123**

Vocabulary

arbitrary not based on law
render make
abdicated given up
foreign mercenaries soldiers hired to fight for a country not their own
perfidy violation of trust
insurrections rebellions
petitioned for redress asked formally for a correction of wrongs
unwarrantable jurisdiction unjustified authority
magnanimity generous spirit
conjured urgently called upon
consanguinity common ancestry
acquiesce consent to
rectitude rightness

EXPLORING THE DOCUMENT Here the Declaration calls the king a tyrant. What do you think *tyrant* means from this passage?

Info to Know

John Hancock As president of the Second Continental Congress, John Hancock was the first delegate to sign the Declaration of Independence. He signed his name in large writing, and it stands out from the other names. According to legend, Hancock wanted to make sure that King George III would see his name. As a result, the name *John Hancock* has become an informal term for a person's signature.

Primary Source

"We must all hang together, or assuredly we shall all hang separately."
— Benjamin Franklin
at the signing of the Declaration of Independence

Colonies are, and of Right ought to be Free and Independent States; that they are Absolved from all Allegiance to the British Crown, and that all political connection between them and the State of Great Britain, is and ought to be totally dissolved; and that as Free and Independent States, they have full Power to levy War, conclude Peace, contract Alliances, establish Commerce, and to do all other Acts and Things which Independent States may of right do. And for the support of this Declaration, with a firm reliance on the Protection of Divine Providence, we mutually pledge to each other our Lives, our Fortunes and our sacred Honor.

EXPLORING THE DOCUMENT Here is where the document declares the independence of the colonies. **Whose authority does the Congress use to declare independence?**

EXPLORING THE DOCUMENT The Congress adopted the final draft of the Declaration of Independence on July 4, 1776. A formal copy, written on parchment paper, was signed on August 2, 1776.

EXPLORING THE DOCUMENT The following is part of a passage that the Congress removed from Jefferson's original draft: "He has waged cruel war against human nature itself, violating its most sacred rights of life and liberty in the persons of a distant people who never offended him, captivating and carrying them into slavery in another hemisphere, or to incur miserable death in their transportation thither." **Why do you think the Congress deleted this passage?**

John Hancock	Benjamin Harrison	Lewis Morris
Button Gwinnett	Thomas Nelson, Jr.	Richard Stockton
Lyman Hall	Francis Lightfoot Lee	John Witherspoon
George Walton	Carter Braxton	Francis Hopkinson
William Hooper	Robert Morris	John Hart
Joseph Hewes	Benjamin Rush	Abraham Clark
John Penn	Benjamin Franklin	Josiah Bartlett
Edward Rutledge	John Morton	William Whipple
Thomas Heyward, Jr.	George Clymer	Samuel Adams
Thomas Lynch, Jr.	James Smith	John Adams
Arthur Middleton	George Taylor	Robert Treat Paine
Samuel Chase	James Wilson	Elbridge Gerry
William Paca	George Ross	Stephen Hopkins
Thomas Stone	Caesar Rodney	William Ellery
Charles Carroll of Carrollton	George Read	Roger Sherman
George Wythe	Thomas McKean	Samuel Huntington
Richard Henry Lee	William Floyd	William Williams
Thomas Jefferson	Philip Livingston	Oliver Wolcott
	Francis Lewis	Matthew Thornton

Differentiating Instruction

Above Level

Advanced Learners/GATE

Research Required

1. Have students conduct outside research to learn how the Declaration of Independence was received in Britain and in other countries around the world, both at the time and later. Students should use both primary and secondary sources and take notes on their research.

2. Have students use their research to write an essay in which they trace the effect of the Declaration on the quest of people around the world to separate themselves from unjust governments. In their essays students should explain American influence on groups which have tried to establish democratic reforms and on the outcomes of attempted revolutions or rebellions patterned after the American model. **LS Verbal-Linguistic**

Alternative Assessment Handbook, Rubrics 30: Research; and 42: Writing to Inform

Answers

**Exploring the Document
(top)** *"Authority of the good People of these Colonies;"* **(bottom)** *possible answers—Slavery was controversial, and many colonies, particularly those in the South, did not wish to abolish it; delegates from pro-slavery colonies would likely not have agreed to sign the Declaration if the passage had remained.*

SECTION 3
The Revolutionary War Begins

BEFORE YOU READ

MAIN IDEA
While the colonies and the British began with different strengths and weaknesses, the Revolutionary War demonstrated Washington's great leadership.

READING FOCUS
1. What groups of people played a part in the Revolutionary War?
2. What major revolutionary battles took place in the North?
3. In what ways was the Battle of Saratoga a British setback?
4. How did Washington's leadership at Valley Forge influence the course of the Revolutionary War?

KEY TERMS AND PEOPLE
Redcoats
Battle of Saratoga
Valley Forge
inflation
Marquis de Lafayette

 TAKING NOTES As you read, take notes about the advantages the Americans had in the Revolutionary War. Record your notes in a graphic organizer like the one shown below.

> American Advantages

Deborah Sampson, SOLDIER

THE INSIDE STORY

Who is that young soldier? Older soldiers in the Fourth Massachusetts Regiment felt protective toward Robert Shurtleff. The new recruit was strong, but he seemed very young to his fellow soldiers. Shurtleff was so young that he did not even have to shave! He also kept to himself, seldom joining in the teasing and rough talk that went on in camp. All the same, the young soldier proved to be brave in battle. In the fighting in New York, he was slightly wounded several times but never complained. He insisted on taking care of his wounds himself.

What the soldiers didn't realize about Robert Shurtleff was that "he" was actually a woman, Deborah Sampson. Dressed in men's breeches and shirt and with her hair cut short, the 21-year-old Sampson had joined the army posing as a man. Her disguise worked partly because she stood about 5 foot 7 inches, tall for a woman in the 1700s. She was also physically strong from doing farmwork as an indentured servant. As long as she looked and acted like a male soldier, it never occurred to anyone that Private Shurtleff was a woman. She guarded her secret until she came down with a fever. In the hospital, the truth was discovered. Sampson received an honorary discharge in October 1783, went home, and married a farmer, Benjamin Gannett. She later received a soldier's pension. ◢

▲ Sampson, shown here in the only known portrait of her, disguised herself to become a soldier.

THE REVOLUTIONARY ERA **125**

Preteach

Bellringer
The Inside Story. . . Use the **Daily Bellringer Transparency** to help students answer the question.
📖 Daily Bellringer Transparency, Section 3

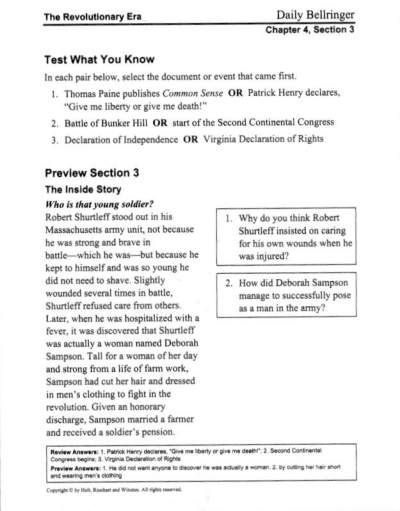

Academic Vocabulary
Review with students the high-use academic term in this section.

prospects expectations for the future (p. 126)
📄 CRF: Vocabulary Builder Activity, Section 3

Taking Notes
excellent military leaders, knowledge of home territory, allied with France, believed in their cause

---

Teach the Main Idea

[At Level]

The Revolutionary War Begins

1. **Teach** Ask students the Reading Focus questions to teach this section.

2. **Apply** Pair students and have each pair outline the section, using heads and subheads as main points. For each subhead, students should insert two or three bullet points of important information. **LS Interpersonal, Visual-Spatial**

3. **Review** Have volunteers share their outlines with the class. Discuss how the four topics in the section are related.

4. **Practice/Homework** Have each student write a short essay on the importance of believing in the cause you choose to fight for. Have students answer this question in their essays: Does an army fighting to defend its homeland have a real advantage? Why or why not? **LS Verbal-Linguistic**

📄 Alternative Assessment Handbook Rubric 37: Writing Assignments

THE REVOLUTIONARY ERA **125**

❶ What groups of people played a part in the Revolutionary War? *Continental soldiers; Redcoats; women; African Americans; Native Americans*

The People behind the American Revolution

Recall From what country did England hire soldiers to fight in America? *Germany*

Make Generalizations What was an advantage that the tiny American navy had during the war? *British ships were old and in poor condition.*

🖝 Quick Facts Transparency: Strengths and Weaknesses of the Continental and British Armies

📄 CRF: Biography: Haym Salomon

Info to Know

Women in the Revolutionary War
Some women brought vital information to Continental commanders. In Massachusetts, Deborah Champion, who was just 22 years old, traveled for two days by horseback to bring information to George Washington. Dicey Langston, a 16-year-old, crossed a deep river during the night to bring information about enemy troop movements to her brother's camp in South Carolina.

The People behind the American Revolution

After declaring independence, the colonies and the Congress next took steps toward forming a nation. The colonies adopted constitutions and established new state governments. But first, the American colonists had to win the Revolutionary War. Many people would play a role.

Continentals and Redcoats When the war began, the British seemed to have an overwhelming military advantage. Britain was a world power with an army of well-trained soldiers, known as **Redcoats** for their red uniforms.

Compared with that, American prospects looked bad. Washington's Continental Army and state militias together had only about 19,000 soldiers. He had no navy except for some merchant ships armed with guns. Raising and keeping an army was a constant problem.

Finding and paying for supplies and military equipment was even harder. Congress was always short of money. The army depended heavily on captured British guns and ammunition. Soldiers and their commanders constantly complained about shortages of food, clothes, and gunpowder.

On the other hand, the British army included many hired German soldiers. They had no loyalty to their cause, while colonists were fighting for their homes and liberty. Moreover, the Royal Navy had been allowed to decline after the French and Indian War. Many of its ships were old and in poor condition.

The role of women Even before independence was declared, American women had been active in boycotts and other protests. Once the fighting began, Patriot women found many other ways to take part.

A few, such as Deborah Sampson, disguised themselves as men to become soldiers in the Continental Army. Mary Hays was nicknamed Molly Pitcher for bringing water to the troops at the battle of Monmouth in New Jersey on a blistering hot day.

Women also served as couriers, scouts, and spies. Sybil Ludington, a 16-year-old girl, learned of a planned British attack on Danbury, Connecticut. On her horse Star, she made a 40-mile night ride to spread the alarm.

ACADEMIC VOCABULARY
prospects expectations for the future

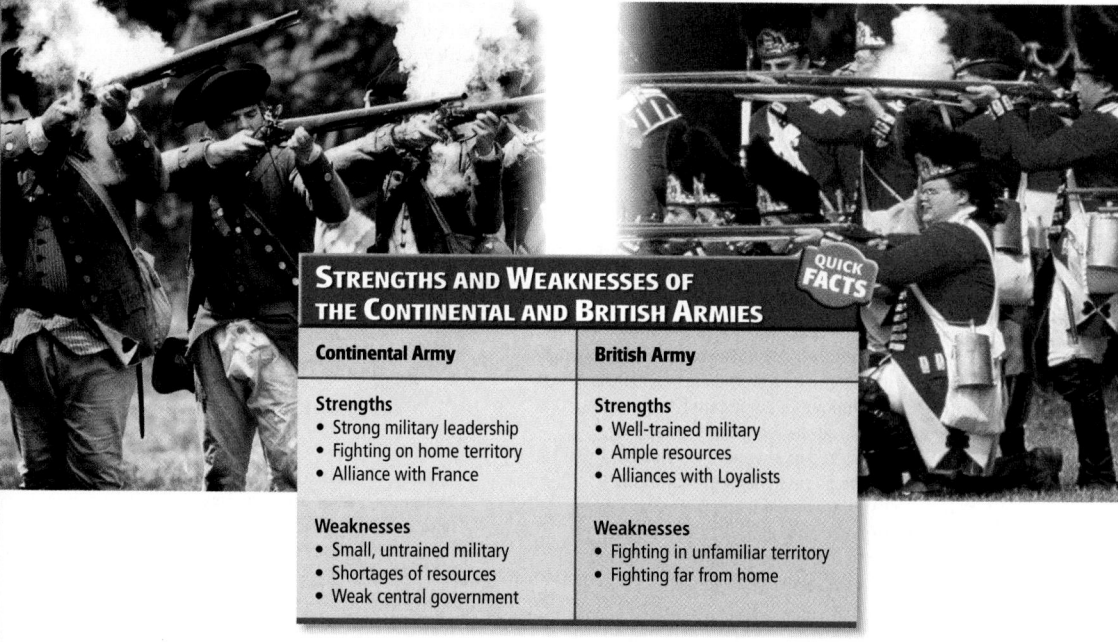

STRENGTHS AND WEAKNESSES OF THE CONTINENTAL AND BRITISH ARMIES

Continental Army	British Army
Strengths • Strong military leadership • Fighting on home territory • Alliance with France	**Strengths** • Well-trained military • Ample resources • Alliances with Loyalists
Weaknesses • Small, untrained military • Shortages of resources • Weak central government	**Weaknesses** • Fighting in unfamiliar territory • Fighting far from home

126 CHAPTER 4

Skills Focus: Summarizing   Below Level

Reading Skill
The People behind the Revolutionary War

1. Have students create a chart or Web diagram showing the different groups who participated in the Revolutionary War or helped troops who fought. Have students create one illustration showing the contribution of each group.

2. Have volunteers share their charts and illustrations with the class. **LS Visual-Spatial**

📄 Alternative Assessment Handbook, Rubrics 3: Artwork; and 7: Charts

Many women participated in the revolution in less dramatic but still vital ways. Catherine Greene, the wife of General Nathanael Greene, turned their home into a hospital. Some women in Philadelphia raised money to supply the army with food and clothing.

Many women did what was considered "women's work" such as laundry or nursing. At home, women knit wool stockings and made bandages for the troops. Some melted down their pewter pots and pitchers to make bullets. As in all wars, women kept their homes, farms, and shops running while the men were at war.

The role of African Americans African Americans, both free and enslaved, fought on both sides of the Revolutionary War. Before the war began, some British officials had tried to win over African Americans. Governor Dunmore of Virginia, for example, offered enslaved Africans their freedom if they joined the British army. As the war went on, many did. Some also enlisted in the Royal Navy. Northern Patriot militias also promised freedom in exchange for military service.

Black Americans fought at Lexington, Concord, and Bunker Hill. At first the Continental Army did not officially accept them. Soon, the need for soldiers overcame that prejudice. Volunteers were supposed to prove that they were freemen, but many recruiters did not ask.

New England regiments had the most African American soldiers because more free blacks lived there. Connecticut and Rhode Island had all-black regiments. James Middleton, the only black commissioned officer in the Continental Army, led a Massachusetts regiment.

African American soldiers generally received the same pay, clothing, and rations as whites. They served in both the army and the navy. Most African American soldiers, however, were given menial duties, kept at low ranks, and were not encouraged to re-enlist.

The role of Native Americans The Iroquois League had long been allies of the British. Now Britain expected their help. The Iroquois hoped that a British victory would slow American settlements on their lands.

But the French and Indian War had weakened the league. Only four of the Six Nations helped the British. Joseph Brant, a Mohawk leader, did become a British officer. He and his

FACES OF HISTORY

George WASHINGTON
1732–1799

Many years before he became the first president of the United States, George Washington earned a reputation as an exceptional military leader. In 1752 he joined the Virginia militia and led troops in the French and Indian War. Years later, as an early supporter of American independence, Washington began to recruit and train a militia when tensions rose with the British.

Leading the Continental Army, Washington made some early tactical mistakes, such as allowing the British to occupy New York City. Nevertheless, his ability to inspire and manage his army helped the Americans achieve victory in the end.

Predict How do you think Washington's military experience prepared him for the presidency?

sister Mary brought the Mohawks, Senecas, Onandagas, and Cayugas to help in campaigns in upstate New York. Oneidas and Tuscaroras, however, sided with the Americans.

On the frontiers, Loyalists and Native Americans sometimes fought together. In the mountains of Virginia and the Carolinas, the Cherokees attacked some settlements. Patriot militias fought back fiercely and tried to force the Cherokees to move west.

READING CHECK **Summarizing** What advantages did Britain have at the beginning of the war?

Revolutionary Battles in the North

The British reacted to the Declaration of Independence with a great show of military strength. Their losses and forced retreat from Boston in March 1776 had made them realize that they were engaged in a real war.

The British fight back After his unexpected defeat by Washington in Boston, General Howe returned to New York with a huge force. Howe was now the commander of British forces in America. More than 300 ships and approximately 30,000 British soldiers arrived in New York in August 1776. For the next few years, Revolutionary battles were centered in New York, New Jersey, and Pennsylvania.

Reading Focus

The People behind the American Revolution

Explain Why did enslaved African Americans join the British army? *promised freedom if they joined*

Summarize Why did the Continental Army begin to accept African American soldiers, and how were they treated? *needed more soldiers; received same pay, clothing, and rations as white soldiers, but were given menial duties, kept at low ranks*

Biography

Phillis Wheatley (1753–1784) Brought to America on a slave ship at age 8, Phillis Wheatley became the first critically acclaimed black poet in America. Permitted the rare privilege of learning to read and write, Wheatley quickly mastered English, Greek, and Latin. At age 14, Wheatley began to write poetry that dealt with morality and piety. In 1773, she published her first book, *Poems on Various Subjects, Religious and Moral*. Eventually, Wheatley gained her freedom, although she never succeeding in working her way out of poverty. Even after her death, abolitionists used Wheatley's work to prove the intellectual equality between blacks and whites as well as to call for better education for African Americans.

Differentiating Instruction

Above Level

Advanced Learners/GATE

Research Required

1. Have students conduct outside research using reliable Internet sites or traditional print sources to locate primary sources, particularly letters or journals, written by people who were involved in the Revolutionary War.

2. Have students meet in small groups to share the results of their research and the sources they used. Then have students choose two of the people discussed in their small groups who have differing viewpoints about the war. Students must read the letters or journals

of both individuals to gain a complete understanding of their viewpoints.

3. Have each student write an essay comparing the points of view about the war as reflected in the journals or letters of the two people.

4. Have volunteers read their essays to the class.
   LS **Verbal-Linguistic, Intrapersonal**

   📖 Alternative Assessment Handbook, Rubrics 9: Comparing and Contrasting; and 30: Research

Answers

Faces of History *learned from his mistakes; was a well-respected leader; able to inspire*

Reading Check *well trained military; ample resources; alliances with Native Americans and colonial Loyalists*

② What major revolutionary battles took place in the North? *Long Island, Harlem Heights, Trenton, Princeton, Brandywine Creek, Philadelphia*

Revolutionary Battles in the North

Describe What were the results of early battles with the British? *American troops lost most battles and had to retreat.*

Explain Why did Howe want to capture Philadelphia? *It was the American capital.*

③ In what ways was the Battle of Saratoga a British setback? *Burgoyne surrendered 5,000 troops to Gates. The outcome also convinced France to come to the aid of the Americans.*

A British Setback at Saratoga

Recall Where was General Burgoyne's military campaign? *upstate New York*

Analyze What contributed most to Burgoyne's loss at Saratoga? *lack of supplies; no reinforcements from Howe*

Answers

Reading Check (top) *Howe wanted to impress and intimidate the Americans with Britain's might.* **(bottom)** *He surrounded Burgoyne's position in Saratoga, New York, and kept badly needed supplies from arriving.*

Before the campaign began, General Howe and his brother Admiral Richard Howe tried to make peace. They wrote to Washington and offered a pardon to the rebels if they would give in and promise loyalty. Washington refused.

Howe's forces soon defeated the Americans and captured Long Island, taking many Americans prisoner. But Howe did not follow up on the victory. Washington took advantage of a heavy fog to take his remaining men across the river to Manhattan Island. As fall went on, the British moved steadily northward on the island as Washington's men retreated to the rocky heights at the northern end.

In the Battle of Harlem Heights, American forces won a few small encounters that helped their morale. Then Howe's army forced them to retreat across New Jersey. There they crossed the Delaware River into Pennsylvania.

In traditional European warfare, armies did not fight in the winter. Howe's men settled down in winter quarters at various towns in New Jersey, including Trenton and Princeton. The Hessians, the German mercenaries, were guarding Trenton, on the Delaware River.

But Washington did not follow European fighting methods. Instead, on Christmas night of 1776, he and his men crossed the icy Delaware River to Trenton. After celebrating Christmas, the Hessians were asleep. The Americans took them by surprise, occupied the town, and captured weapons and ammunition. Moving on, Washington then drove the British out of Princeton. In January 1777 the Continental Army went into winter quarters.

Campaigns in New York When fighting began again in the spring of 1777, Britain's plan was to cut New England off from the rest of the colonies. To do this, troops commanded by General John Burgoyne planned to meet General Howe's troops at Albany. But Howe changed his plans and decided to attack Philadelphia first. The city was the American capital, so Howe hoped its capture would hurt Patriot morale. He also hoped its sizeable Loyalist population would help him.

Howe took an army of 15,000 by sea from New York to Chesapeake Bay. In September he met Washington and his army of 11,000 in southeastern Pennsylvania. The British won the Battle of Brandywine Creek, but the Americans escaped without serious casualties.

THE IMPACT TODAY

Culture
At Saratoga National Historic Park in New York, people can visit the Saratoga battlefield. The Saratoga Monument stands in the nearby village of Victory.

From there Howe easily captured Philadelphia, where he and his troops settled comfortably for the winter. The Continental Congress fled the city. Washington and his exhausted troops settled into quarters at Valley Forge, Pennsylvania, for the winter of 1777–1778.

READING CHECK **Making Inferences** Why did Howe return to New York with so many ships and troops?

A British Setback at Saratoga

In the meantime, General Burgoyne was conducting a campaign in upstate New York. His strategy was to lead part of his force down the Hudson River valley to Albany. The rest would travel up the Saint Lawrence River into Lake Ontario and take the Mohawk valley. Burgoyne expected to meet Howe's army at Albany.

Things went well for the British at first. Burgoyne's army easily recaptured Fort Ticonderoga on July 5, 1777, a serious loss for the Americans. In response, Congress sent a new general, Horatio Gates, to lead the Continental Army in New York.

The other British force, however, met strong local resistance along the Mohawk River. When they attacked Fort Stanwix in early August, a band of Patriot farmers and their Oneida allies rallied to help the fort's defenders. But they were ambushed by British troops and their Iroquois allies in one of the bloodiest battles of the war. Then an American force led by Benedict Arnold arrived to hold the fort.

Burgoyne was now very short of supplies. Because of Howe's delays, no reinforcements arrived from the south. In early October, with only 5,000 men left, Burgoyne found himself at Saratoga, New York, surrounded by an American force of 17,000 under General Gates. He twice tried to break through Continental lines to reach Albany but could not. On October 17, 1777, Burgoyne surrendered to Gates.

The **Battle of Saratoga** is considered the turning point of the Revolutionary War. News of the American victory encouraged the colonists and surprised the British and Europeans. Most importantly, the victory at Saratoga convinced France to support the American cause.

READING CHECK **Summarizing** How did General Gates achieve victory at Saratoga?

Skills Focus: Sequencing
At Level

Reading Skill
A British Setback at Saratoga

1. Guide students in a discussion on the events leading up to the Battle of Saratoga.

2. Have students write an "eyewitness account" of the events that led up to the Battle of Saratoga and the reasons for the British defeat.

3. Have volunteers read their accounts to the class. Then guide students in a discussion

of the importance of war correspondents and first-hand accounts of military battles.
LS **Verbal-Linguistic**

Alternative Assessment Handbook, Rubrics 37: Writing Assignments; and 11: Discussions

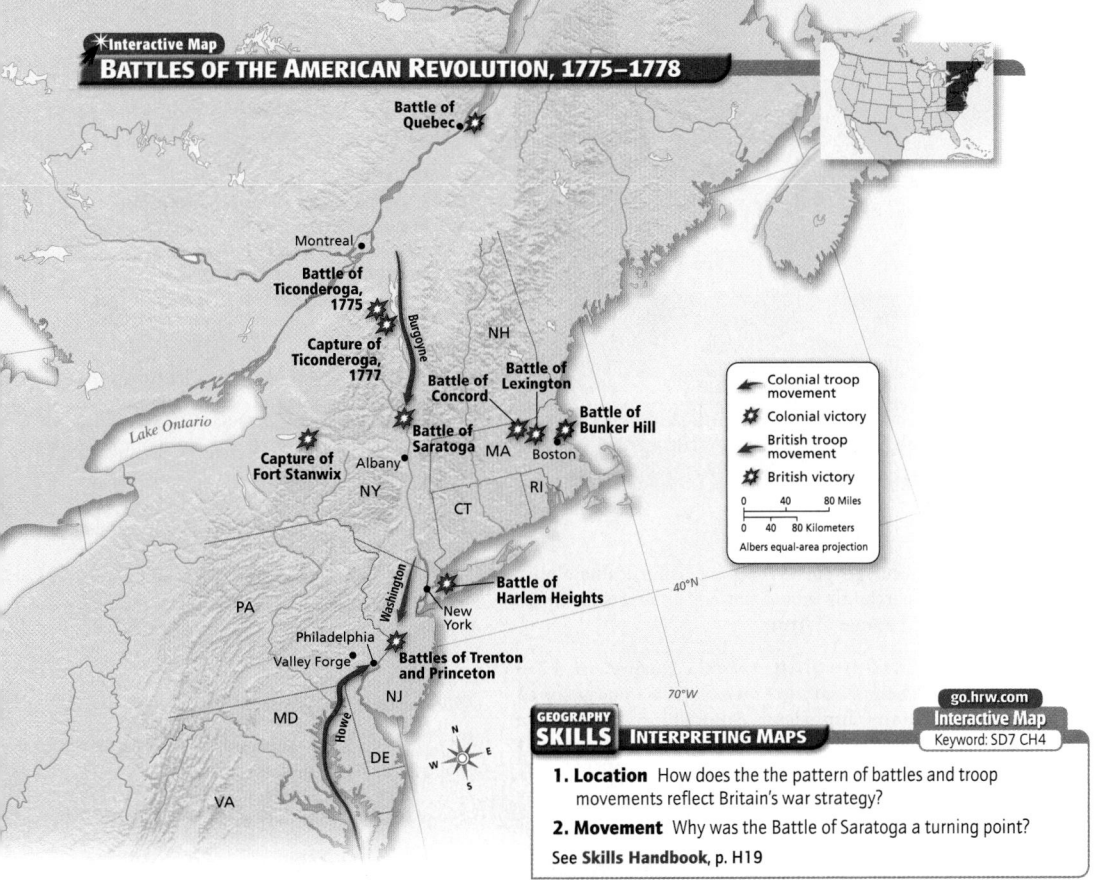

Battle of Quebec

Montreal

Battle of Ticonderoga, 1775

Burgoyne

Capture of Ticonderoga, 1777

NH

Battle of Concord

Battle of Lexington

Lake Ontario

Battle of Saratoga

MA

Battle of Bunker Hill

Boston

Capture of Fort Stanwix

Albany

NY

RI

CT

Washington

Battle of Harlem Heights

40°N

PA

New York

Philadelphia

Valley Forge

Battles of Trenton and Princeton

NJ

70°W

MD

Howe

DE

VA

Colonial troop movement
Colonial victory
British troop movement
British victory

0   40   80 Miles
0   40   80 Kilometers
Albers equal-area projection

GEOGRAPHY SKILLS   INTERPRETING MAPS

go.hrw.com
Interactive Map
Keyword: SD7 CH4

1. Location How does the the pattern of battles and troop movements reflect Britain's war strategy?

2. Movement Why was the Battle of Saratoga a turning point?

See **Skills Handbook**, p. H19

Washington's Leadership at Valley Forge

For Washington and his tired army, the winter of 1777–1778 at **Valley Forge** was a low point of the Revolution. The winter weather was bitterly cold, and some 12,000 men were housed in makeshift huts and tents. Food was scarce. Washington's soldiers shivered in worn, ragged uniforms. Many of the men became ill, and hundreds died.

The winter at Valley Forge was a tough test of Washington's leadership, but he met the challenge. His firm character and common sense helped hold his troops together. In spite of many defeats, Washington always managed to keep a national army in the field. This was in part because his men greatly admired him.

Washington enforced discipline strictly. At the same time, he was always insisting that the Congress treat the army better.

Money problems Paying for the war was an ongoing problem. Congress did not have the power to make people pay taxes. Most currencies were based on supplies of "hard money"—gold and silver—which was scarce. Congress and the states printed paper money with little to back it up. As a result, paper money became almost worthless, and prices soared. This situation is known as **inflation**.

Because Continental money was worth very little, some farmers and merchants instead chose to trade with the British, who had gold and silver coin. This caused problems. For example, the food shortages at Valley Forge

Differentiating Instruction

Below Level

English-Language Learners

1. Pair students and have each pair research the phrase "not worth a continental." Then have students write a short explanation of the origin and meaning of the phrase.

2. Have volunteers share their explanations with the class. Discuss with students how

a sound money supply would have been useful to Washington and the other Patriots fighting in the Revolutionary War.

LS Interpersonal, Verbal-Linguistic

Alternative Assessment Handbook, Rubric 37: Writing Assignments

---

Reading Focus

4 How did Washington's leadership at Valley Forge influence the course of the Revolutionary War? *Washington was able to hold his army together long enough for help to arrive.*

Washington's Leadership at Valley Forge

Recall What personal characteristics helped Washington to hold his army together that winter? *He had a firm character and common sense, and was much admired by his men.*

Make Inferences What problems did Congress have in trying to treat the army better? *inability to raise revenues; inflation*

Map Transparency: Battles of the American Revolution, 1775–1778

Info to Know

George Washington's Appearance
Scientists have researched Washington's physical characteristics with the latest scientific techniques. Using computer graphics, sculptures, paintings, and other artifacts, scientists have concluded that Washington was over 6 ft. tall, had a prominent nose, and a slim, muscular build. His eyes were gray-blue and his hair, which he often wore in a ponytail, was auburn colored.

★ Interactive Map: Battles of the American Revolution, 1775–1778

Answers

Interpreting Maps 1. *Burgoyne's troops were coming from the north, planning to meet Howe's army at Albany;* **2.** *Burgoyne had to surrender; France began to openly support Americans.*

Washington's Leadership at Valley Forge

Recall How did the writings of Thomas Paine help Washington at Valley Forge? *Washington read Paine's words to the troops to encourage them.*

Elaborate Why did European help begin to arrive in late 1776 and 1777? *American forces had begun to show that they could fight successfully against Britain.*

● Review & Assess ●

Close

Have students explain the importance of the battle of Saratoga.

Review

Online Quiz, Section 3

Daily Test Practice Transparency

Assess

SE Section 3 Assessment

Progress Assessment: Section 3 Quiz

Alternative Assessment Handbook

Reteach

Interactive Reader and Study Guide, Section 3

Interactive Skills Tutor CD-ROM

Answers

Reading Check *Many men died from the cold, lack of food, and illness.*

130

Winter at Valley Forge

George Washington (right), saw that his troops remained ready for battle, despite the harsh winter at Valley Forge. In this painting, he watches as his troops perform a series of drilling exercises. Even more important, Washington was able to inspire his men with his leadership.

occurred partly because some Philadelphia merchants would not sell their goods to the Continental Army.

Encouraging words Earlier in 1776 Thomas Paine's *Common Sense* had inspired many American colonists to support a declaration of independence from Great Britain. After the retreat across New Jersey

in 1776, Paine wrote another series of papers called *The American Crisis*. To rally his troops at Valley Forge, Washington read Thomas Paine's ringing words aloud:

HISTORY'S VOICES

❝The summer soldier and the sunshine patriot will, in this crisis, shrink from the service of their country; but he that stands it now, deserves the love and thanks of man and woman.❞

—Thomas Paine, *The American Crisis* (December 19, 1776)

Help arrives from Europe The American struggle for liberty found support in Europe. Several European officers joined the American cause. One was Baron Friedrich von Steuben of the Prussian army. In the cold, snowy winter at Valley Forge, he drilled Washington's troops. By spring, Washington's men were a well-trained fighting force.

Washington also acquired an invaluable aide, a 20-year-old French noble, the **Marquis de Lafayette**. Lafayette was like a son to Washington. In the next section you will learn how Lafayette's help became crucial in the outcome of the Revolutionary War.

READING CHECK **Summarizing** How did the winter at Valley Forge affect the army?

SECTION 3 ASSESSMENT

go.hrw.com
Online Quiz
Keyword: SD7 HP4

Reviewing Ideas, Terms, and People

1. **a. Describe** What kind of work did Patriot women undertake in the Revolution?
   b. Summarize What was the role of African Americans in the Revolution?
   c. Evaluate How did the fact that Americans were fighting for independence affect their fighting capability?
2. **a. Describe** What was Burgoyne's strategy for cutting New England off from the other colonies?
   b. Make Generalizations In general, what was the year 1776 like for the Continental Army?
3. **a. Identify** What roles did William Howe, John Burgoyne, and Horatio Gates play in the **Battle of Saratoga**?
   b. Analyze What factors contributed to the British defeat at Saratoga?
   c. Predict How do you think the victory at Saratoga will affect the course of the war?
4. **a. Identify** What factors made the winter at **Valley Forge** so difficult for the Americans?

b. Draw Conclusions What impact did Washington's character have on events at Valley Forge?

Critical Thinking

5. **Summarizing** Copy the chart below, fill it with details from the section, and then analyze the role of women, African Americans, and Native Americans in the Revolutionary War.

African Americans	Women	Native Americans

FOCUS ON WRITING

6. **Descriptive** As either a British soldier at Saratoga or an American soldier at Valley Forge, write a letter home describing one day on the battlefield to your family. Use details from the section in your description.

130 CHAPTER 4

Section 3 Assessment Answers

1. **a.** fought; served as scouts, couriers, and spies; cared for the wounded; ran farms
   b. Many fought; others did military chores.
   c. It gave them an advantage.
2. **a.** march south to meet Howe's army at Albany, pinching New England off
   b. lost ground and men; had to retreat
3. **a.** Howe, Burgoyne—British generals; Gates—American general, defeated Burgoyne
   b. Howe's delays at Philadelphia; dwindling supplies; superior American forces

   c. better morale; help from abroad
4. **a.** bitter cold; few supplies; sickness
   b. Strength, inspiration, and discipline helped Washington hold the army together.
5. African Americans—fought and did work for both sides; Women—soldiers, spies, couriers, nurses, business operators; Native Americans—many fought with Britain
6. Saratoga—supplies dwindling; no reinforcements; are surrounded; Valley Forge—bitter cold; no supplies; insufficient food

American Literature

THOMAS PAINE (1737–1809)

American Literature

About the Reading During the Revolutionary War Thomas Paine wrote a series of articles called *The American Crisis*. The following is from an article written on September 12, 1777, shortly after the Battle of Brandywine Creek.

AS YOU READ Consider how the various modes of public communication during wartime have the ability to influence public support.

Excerpt from

The American Crisis

by Thomas Paine

Gentlemen of the city and country, it is in your power, by a spirited improvement of the present circumstance, to turn it to a real advantage. Howe is now weaker than before, and every shot will contribute to reduce him. You are more immediately interested than any other part of the continent: your all is at stake; it is not so with the general cause; you are devoted by the enemy to plunder and destruction: it is the encouragement which Howe, the chief of plunderers, has promised his army . . .

Our army must undoubtedly feel fatigue, and want a reinforcement of rest though not of valor. Our own interest and happiness call upon us to give them every support in our power, and make the burden of the day, on which the safety of this city depends, as light as possible. Remember, gentlemen, that we have forces both to the northward and southward of Philadelphia, and if the enemy be but stopped till those can arrive, this city will be saved, and the enemy finally routed. You have too much at stake to hesitate. You have been invaded, have likewise driven off the invaders. Now our time and turn is come, and perhaps the finishing stroke is reserved for us. When we look back on the dangers we have been saved from, and reflect on the success we have been blessed with, it would be sinful either to be idle or to despair.

General Howe planned to stamp out both the Continental Army and the Revolution at the Battle of Brandywine Creek.

I close this paper with a short address to General Howe. You, sir, are only lingering out the period that shall bring with it your defeat. You have yet scarce began the war, and the further you enter, the faster will your troubles thicken. What you now enjoy is only a respite from ruin; an invitation to destruction; something that will lead on to our deliverance at your expense. We know the cause which we are engaged in, and though a passionate fondness may make us grieve at every injury which threatens it, yet, when the moment of concern is over, the determination to duty returns. We are not moved by the gloomy smile of a worthless king, but by the ardent glow of generous patriotism.

Skills FOCUS — READING LIKE A HISTORIAN

1. **Identifying the Main Idea** Who was Paine's audience? What were his purposes in writing?
2. **Literature as Historical Evidence** What does Paine claim motivates the British army? How might you assess the validity of these claims?

See **Skills Handbook, pp. H5, H32**

THE REVOLUTIONARY ERA **131**

Differentiating Instruction

Standard English Mastery

English-Language Learners
Below Level

Have students make a list of unfamiliar words and look them up in a dictionary. Then have students work in mixed-ability pairs to write a summary of each paragraph of the excerpt.

LS Verbal-Linguistic

Alternative Assessment Handbook, Rubric 37: Writing Assignments

Advanced Learners/GATE
Above Level

Have students use the words in the excerpt to write a speech encouraging residents of Philadelphia to stand firm against the British. Speeches should include reasons the Continental Army will prevail.

LS Verbal-Linguistic

Alternative Assessment Handbook, Rubric 24: Oral Presentations

American Literature

Excerpt from *The American Crisis* by Thomas Paine

Word Help

plunder rob, raid
lingering waiting
respite rest, break

Meet the Writer

Thomas Paine (1737–1809) Thomas Paine was born in England and held a variety of odd jobs. While he was generally unsuccessful and never earned enough to meet his living costs, he did use some of his earnings to buy books. Paine met Benjamin Franklin in London, and Franklin recommended that Paine come to America. In 1774 Paine arrived in Philadelphia where he got a job as an editor with the *Pennsylvania Magazine*, and he began to write articles, poetry, and pamphlets, including *Common Sense* and *The American Crisis*.

Info to Know

The *Crisis* Papers Thomas Paine wrote sixteen *Crisis* papers between 1776 and 1783, all in support of the Patriot cause. *The American Crisis, Number 1* was published on December 19, 1776, when George Washington's army was suffering through a brutal winter at Valley Forge.

Answers

Reading Like a Historian 1. *citizens in and near Philadelphia; wanted to encourage them to provide support to the tired troops;* **2.** *"the gloomy smile of a worthless king;" Paine is trying to encourage colonists to support their troops and the war; does not acknowledge that some British officers and soldiers might be motivated by patriotism just as he says the Americans are*

131

Bellringer

The Inside Story. . . Use the **Daily Bellringer Transparency** to help students answer the question.

📖 Daily Bellringer Transparency, Section 4

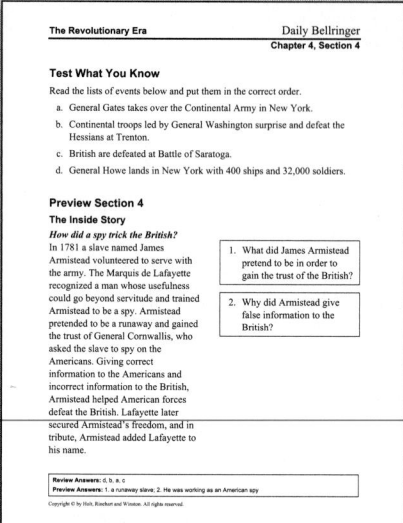

Taking Notes

Clark captures British settlements of Fort Kaskaskia and Cahokia; 1778; Clark captures British fort in Battle of Vincennes, 1779; Spain attacked British forts and troops, 1779; France sends soldiers to aid U.S., 1780; British victory at Guilford Court House, North Carolina caused great loss of British troops, 1781

An American Victory

BEFORE YOU READ

MAIN IDEA

A strengthened Continental Army, along with European allies, helped the colonists achieve a victory at Yorktown.

READING FOCUS

1. What Revolutionary War battles took place in the West and South?
2. Why did France and other European nations assist the Americans?
3. What led to the British surrender at Yorktown?
4. How did the Revolution affect American culture?

KEY TERMS AND PEOPLE

George Rogers Clark
Nathanael Greene
Charles Cornwallis
Count de Rochambeau
Bernardo de Gálvez
Battle of Yorktown
Treaty of Paris

TAKING NOTES As you read, take notes on the major events and battles leading up to the British surrender at Yorktown. Record your notes in a graphic organizer like the one shown here. You may need to add more rows.

Major Event/Battle	Date

THE INSIDE STORY

How did a spy trick the British? Like many enslaved people, James Armistead had the last name of a slaveholder. Later, he added another name—Lafayette. In 1781 Armistead volunteered to serve with the Marquis de Lafayette, expecting to be a servant. But Lafayette realized that the young African American could do much more, and Armistead became a spy. Pretending to be a runaway, he found work in the camp of Benedict Arnold, who had become a traitor. He also won the trust of British general Cornwallis, who asked him to spy on the Americans! Armistead became a double agent. He gave accurate information to the Americans and inaccurate information to the British. His efforts helped defeat the British at the crucial battle of Yorktown.

In one instance, the Americans forged a fake order for reinforcements. Armistead took the crumpled paper to Cornwallis, saying he had found it on the road. It made Cornwallis think that American forces were stronger than they actually were. After the surrender, Cornwallis visited Lafayette and was very surprised to see his spy as an aide to the French general.

Lafayette admired Armistead's courage and resourcefulness. He wrote, "His Intelligences from the Enemy's Camp were Industriously Collected and More faithfully deliver'd." He then asked the Virginia Assembly to give Armistead his freedom. When they agreed, Armistead added Lafayette's name to his own. He became a farmer in Virginia. The two met once again 40 years later when the Frenchman returned to the United States. ■

Spying for the Revolution

▶ **James Armistead (right) spied for Continental Army commander Lafayette (left) during the last phase of the Revolutionary War.**

132 CHAPTER 4

Teach the Main Idea

At Level

An American Victory

1. **Teach** Ask students the Reading Focus questions to teach this section.

2. **Apply** Pair students and have each pair create an illustrated time line of the section. **LS Interpersonal, Visual-Spatial**

3. **Review** Have volunteers share their time lines with the class. Have students identify the dates and events that they feel were

most crucial to the American victory in the Revolutionary War.

4. **Practice/Homework** Have each student write a poem commemorating the assistance from Europeans, especially the French, to the Patriot cause. **LS Auditory-Musical**

📝 Alternative Assessment Handbook, Rubrics 26: Poems and Songs; and 36: Time Lines

Revolutionary Battles in the West and South

The Revolutionary War changed in several ways after the Battle of Saratoga. The Northeast was fairly quiet, with British troops occupying New York. Washington's army—now a better, more disciplined fighting force—waited nearby. Meanwhile, the action shifted to the South and the western frontier.

War in the West In 1779 the Americans won some important victories in the area north and west of the Ohio River, largely due to the efforts of **George Rogers Clark**, a pioneer on the western frontier in Kentucky. In 1778 Clark persuaded Governor Patrick Henry of Virginia to send an expedition to deal with the British in the West. Clark led a small force down the Ohio River. His men captured the British settlements at Fort Kaskaskia and Cahokia on the Mississippi River in present-day Illinois. Although the British held the settlement of Vincennes, the people there were French and Clark won their loyalty. In 1779 he and his men captured the fort and its commander in the Battle of Vincennes.

War in the South In 1778 the British shifted their strategy. They had expected to win the war quickly and crush the rebels. Now, instead of sending more troops and supplies, British

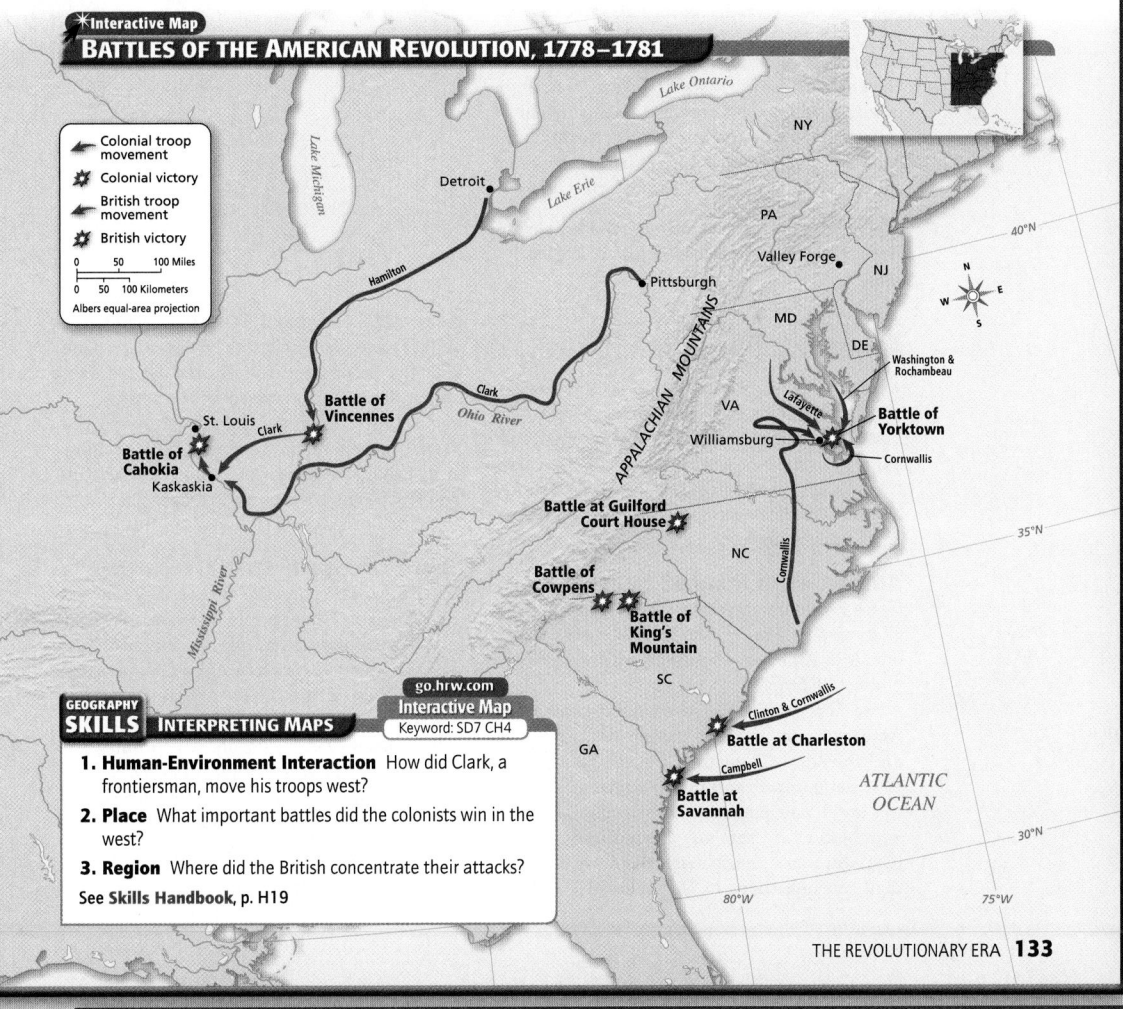

Interactive Map
BATTLES OF THE AMERICAN REVOLUTION, 1778–1781

Colonial troop movement
Colonial victory
British troop movement
British victory

0   50   100 Miles
0   50   100 Kilometers
Albers equal-area projection

GEOGRAPHY SKILLS INTERPRETING MAPS

go.hrw.com
Interactive Map
Keyword: SD7 CH4

1. **Human-Environment Interaction** How did Clark, a frontiersman, move his troops west?
2. **Place** What important battles did the colonists win in the west?
3. **Region** Where did the British concentrate their attacks?
See **Skills Handbook**, p. H19

THE REVOLUTIONARY ERA **133**

Differentiating Instruction

Below Level | Standard English Mastery

Learners Having Difficulty

1. Pair students and have each pair write a short news article telling readers in America about the exploits of George Rogers Clark and his soldiers.

2. Have volunteers read their reports to the class. Then guide students in a discussion about whether news stories like this can help or hurt a war effort. **LS Interpersonal, Verbal-Linguistic**

Alternative Assessment Handbook, Rubric 37: Writing Assignments

---

Answers

Interpreting Maps 1. *down the Ohio River;* **2.** *Cahokia, Vincennes;* **3.** *in the South*

133

Revolutionary Battles in the West and South

Recall What battles in the South helped discourage British forces? *Battle of King's Mountain, Battle of Guilford Court House*

Analyze Why did British expectations about a Loyalist uprising in the South fail to materialize? *Patriots were fierce, and Loyalists were often reluctant to get involved.*

▤ CRF: Biography: Francis Marion

❷ Why did France and other European nations assist the Americans? *They were hoping to help weaken Great Britain.*

America's European Allies

Identify Who was America's very successful representative in Paris? *Benjamin Franklin*

Evaluate How did Lafayette add to America's military strength? *He persuaded the French government to send 6,000 troops to join the fight.*

✶ **Interactive History Close-Up:** The Battle of Yorktown

About the Illustration
This illustration is an artist's conception based on available sources. Historians, however, are uncertain exactly what this scene looked like.

Answers

Reading Check (left) *They expected help from regional Loyalists.* **(right)** *Spain came into the war as an ally of France.*

134

---

officials had a different strategy. They hoped that the many Loyalists in America would rise up to support them.

Because the British believed that Loyalist sympathies were strongest in the South, they planned a campaign there. However, they discovered that Patriots were as strong and determined in Virginia as in New England. Many Loyalists lived in the Carolinas and Georgia, but they were often reluctant to help.

The British also faced frequent surprise raids by small bands of Patriots. These fighters struck quickly, then disappeared into the woods. The most famous was Francis Marion, who was nicknamed the Swamp Fox for his daring raids from the Carolina marshes.

Then at King's Mountain on the border between the Carolinas, local Patriots defeated a Loyalist force. A new American commander, **Nathanael Greene**, took charge. In March 1781 Greene and Lafayette's troops met British commander **Charles Cornwallis**'s army in a brutal battle at Guilford Court House, North Carolina. Cornwallis won, but British losses were so great that he stopped the campaign.

READING CHECK **Identifying the Main Idea** Why did the British decide to move the war into the South?

America's European Allies

Americans wanted recognition as a sovereign nation from Europe. European nations could also provide the Americans with money and supplies to fight the war. Gates's victory at Saratoga made a European alliance possible. France became America's strongest ally, but help also came from Spain and the Netherlands.

Alliance with France France was happy to see its old enemy, Great Britain, losing part of its empire. France also hoped that a British defeat in America would help restore French power in Europe.

At first the French government helped the Americans by sending gunpowder, artillery, and muskets. Then in 1776 the Americans sent Benjamin Franklin to France. In his fur cap and homespun coat, he became a favorite with both aristocrats and the ordinary people. Franklin was in Paris when the news of Saratoga reached there in December 1777. As a result of Saratoga and Franklin's diplomatic skill, France soon signed two treaties. One formally recognized the United States as a nation. The other promised military help.

In 1780 Lafayette helped persuade the French government to send a 6,000-soldier army to help the Americans against the British. The troops were led by a French general, the **Count de Rochambeau** (roh-shahm-BOH).

Help from Spain Spain did not become a direct ally of the Americans, but they did join the war in 1779 as an ally of France. At that time **Bernardo de Gálvez**, an experienced officer, was the Spanish governor of Louisiana. After Spain declared war, Gálvez began to attack British forts on the Mississippi and along the Gulf Coast in West Florida, which had once belonged to Spain. He went on to defeat the British in the southern cities of Baton Rouge, Natchez, Mobile, and Pensacola.

READING CHECK **Making Inferences** Why did the Spanish want to help the Americans?

✶ **Interactive**
HISTORY CLOSE-UP

The Battle of Yorktown

General Cornwallis brought his troops to Yorktown thinking the British navy could protect him there, but he was wrong. Instead, the combined American and French forces surrounded the British, attacking them and cutting off their support. Cornwallis surrendered on October 19, 1781.

YORKTOWN

ATLANTIC OCEAN

Yorktown

Differentiating Instruction

Above Level

Advanced Learners/GATE

Research Required

1. Organize the class into small groups. Have each group research and review the work of Benjamin Franklin in bringing France into the Revolutionary War.

2. Have each group prepare a news report in which they discuss how Franklin's personal characteristics helped his mission. *The French were fascinated by Franklin, whose colonial attire and easy way in Parisian society made him enormously popular. John Adams, also in Paris seeking help, was somewhat jealous of Franklin's successes there.*

3. Have each team present its report to the class.
   LS Interpersonal, Auditory-Musical

   ▤ Alternative Assessment Handbook, Rubrics 24: Oral Presentations; and 30: Research

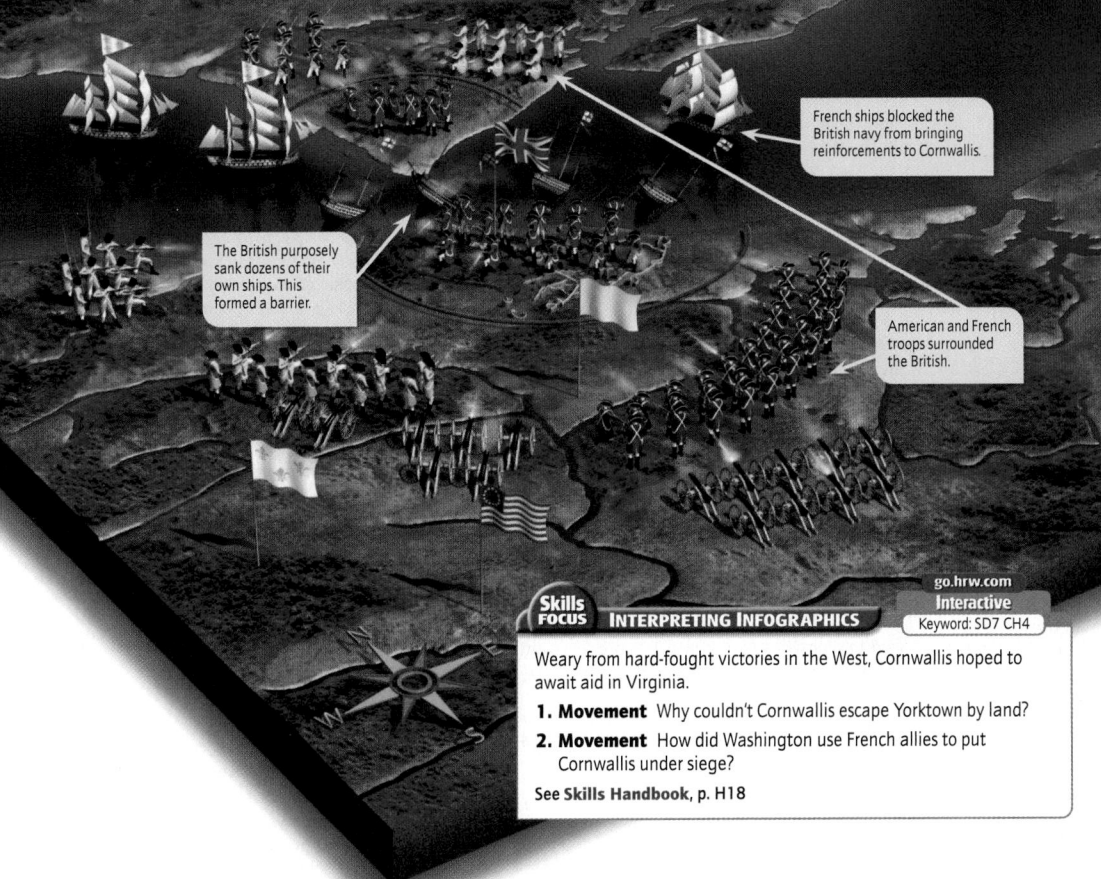

The British purposely sank dozens of their own ships. This formed a barrier.

French ships blocked the British navy from bringing reinforcements to Cornwallis.

American and French troops surrounded the British.

Skills FOCUS **INTERPRETING INFOGRAPHICS**

go.hrw.com
Interactive
Keyword: SD7 CH4

Weary from hard-fought victories in the West, Cornwallis hoped to await aid in Virginia.

1. **Movement** Why couldn't Cornwallis escape Yorktown by land?
2. **Movement** How did Washington use French allies to put Cornwallis under siege?

See Skills Handbook, p. H18

Victory at Yorktown

Washington and Rochambeau received word in January 1781 that there was trouble in Virginia. Benedict Arnold, who had been a hero for the Continental Army at Saratoga, had become a traitor. Arnold had been helping the British cause by leading British troops in raids on Patriot warehouses.

Washington was shocked and disappointed by Arnold's treachery. He sent Lafayette to Virginia to stop him. Then he and Rochambeau planned a massive march into Virginia.

After giving up his Carolina campaign, General Cornwallis moved into Virginia. But Lafayette's forces gradually forced the British to the coast. In July 1781 Cornwallis took his army to the Yorktown Peninsula in Chesapeake Bay. There they built a fort and waited for British ships to take them to Charleston or New York.

A siege at Yorktown Washington saw an opportunity to trap Cornwallis. He sent a message to Admiral de Grasse, who commanded France's Caribbean fleet. Washington asked him to establish a blockade in Chesapeake Bay (see the illustration above). The blockade would prevent British ships from rescuing Cornwallis's men.

Washington instructed Lafayette to keep Cornwallis's army trapped on the peninsula so they could not escape by land. Meanwhile, Washington and Rochambeau traveled south with a huge French and American army.

Cornwallis, with 7,000 troops, now faced a combined French and American army of more than 17,000. The **Battle of Yorktown** lasted about three weeks. With his army bombarded by land and sea, Cornwallis had little choice but to surrender. He did so on October 19, 1781, ending the fighting.

THE REVOLUTIONARY ERA **135**

Direct Teach

Reading Focus

❸ What led to the British surrender at Yorktown? *Cornwallis was trapped and surrounded by a far larger force, with little choice but to surrender.*

Victory at Yorktown

Identify What role did Admiral de Grasse play in the war? *commander of France's Caribbean fleet; blockaded Chesapeake Bay at Washington's request*

Analyze How did French naval cannons help at Yorktown? *The French bombarded Cornwallis from the sea, while Washington and Rochambeau fired from land.*

Info to Know

Marquis de Lafayette Lafayette left France against the wishes of the king and traveled to America on his own to fight for American freedom. Landing at Charleston, he soon set out by wagon, over terrible roads, for a seven hundred mile trip to Philadelphia. When he arrived, Congress, not knowing what to do with him, suggested he return to France. Lafayette wrote Congress: "After the sacrifices I have made in this cause, I have the right to ask two favors at your hands: the one is, to serve without pay, at my own expense; and the other, that I be allowed to serve, at first, as a volunteer in the ranks."

Skills Focus: Evaluating Historical Interpretations   At Level

Reading Like a Historian Skill
The War Ends

1. Read the following passage from *The War for American Independence* by Samuel B. Griffith II to students: "Six and a half years earlier, several hundred Redcoats had marched confidently from Boston to disperse rebels at Lexington. From the field at Yorktown seven thousand would march to prisoner-of-war camps."

2. Have students meet in small groups to discuss this excerpt. Do students believe it accurately

reflects the beginning and end of the war? From whose viewpoint is the excerpt written?

3. Have students design and illustrate a flyer announcing the end of the Revolutionary War and the victory of the Colonial Army. Tell students that their flyers should create mental images for the reader or viewer, just as this excerpt does. **LS Verbal-Linguistic**

🖺 Alternative Assessment Handbook, Rubric 40: Writing to Describe

Answers

Interpreting Infographics 1. *His forces were bottled up on a peninsula.* **2.** *a combined French and Continental army surrounded Cornwallis; French ships blocked the British navy from bringing reinforcements*

❹ How did the Revolution affect American culture? *broadened political rights for white males; spread the notion of equality; North began to abolish slavery; church and state separated in some colonies*

Revolution Changes America

Recall Why was there no mention of slavery in the Declaration of Independence? *Southern colonies would not accept any criticism of slavery.*

Explain What was the biggest economic problem facing the new nation? *Congress had no money to repay war debts.*

Predict What might be the effects of Jefferson's *Statute of Religious Liberty*? *possible answer—separation of church and state incorporated in the Constitution*

📑 American History Outline Maps: The Treaty of Paris 1783

In effect, the war for independence was over, although the British still occupied several American cities. It took several years to agree on the terms of a peace treaty.

The Treaty of Paris Some royal officials still hoped that America would remain part of the British Empire. But the American diplomats, who included Benjamin Franklin and John Adams, insisted on independence.

The Americans negotiated a peace treaty with Britain. The **Treaty of Paris** was signed on September 3, 1783. In it, Britain formally recognized the United States as an independent nation. The treaty also declared the Mississippi River the western boundary of the United States. Britain agreed to leave its forts in the West. Spain and France also made peace with Britain in the Treaty of Paris. In return for its help during the war, Spain regained control of Florida.

After all the trouble caused by taxes, in the Treaty of Paris the United States now promised to pay what Americans owed British merchants. The treaty also allowed Loyalists to claim property losses.

READING CHECK Making Generalizations
What territory did Great Britain lose in the Treaty of Paris?

Revolution Changes America

The American Revolution brought many changes to American society. Politics became more democratic as more men gained the right to vote. In some states, all adult male taxpayers could vote. In others, owning any kind of property—not just land—gave a man the right to vote.

The Revolution also introduced new ideas of equality. The Declaration of Independence stated that "all men are created equal." Americans never again wanted to be ruled by a monarch or an aristocratic upper class.

Women's rights Equality, however, still did not include American women. The words in the Declaration of Independence applied only to white males. Even though women had done important work during the Revolution, the war did not bring them new rights. Abigail Adams had touched on the issue of women's rights in one of her letters to John Adams. While the

THE IMPACT TODAY

Culture
The Continental Congress approved the first official American flag—the symbol of the new nation—on June 14, 1777. The original flag had thirteen stars and thirteen stripes to symbolize the thirteen original colonies. Today's flag still has thirteen stripes, but it now has 50 stars.

Continental Congress was still debating the Declaration of Independence, she had written to her husband:

HISTORY'S VOICES

❝Remember the Ladies, and be more generous and favourable to them than your ancestors. Do not put such unlimited power into the hands of the Husbands . . . If [particular] care and attention is not paid to the Ladies we are determined to foment a Rebellion, and will not hold ourselves bound by any Laws in which we have no voice, or Representation.❞
–Abigail Adams, letter of March 31, 1776

Women did not gain rights after the war, as Adams had hoped. Married women still could not sign contracts or own property. The law stated that a married woman's property belonged to her husband.

The slavery question The American struggle for freedom also raised questions about slavery. Many African Americans who had fought for the Patriot cause believed they had earned their freedom.

Worries over the morality of slavery were not new. Benjamin Franklin and Dr. Benjamin Rush had formed an antislavery organization in Philadelphia in 1775. Others in Pennsylvania, especially Quakers and Mennonites, had long opposed slavery. In 1780 Pennsylvania passed a law for the gradual abolition of slavery. During the 1780s the New England states also abolished slavery.

Such changes came more slowly in the South, however. Jefferson had written an antislavery section in the Declaration of Independence in 1776, but southern delegates removed it. After the war, both Virginia and Maryland made it easier to grant freedom to enslaved people. Several southern states also passed laws limiting the slave trade.

Impact on religion Before the war, many colonies had official churches that everyone paid taxes to support. Now changes came for many religious groups.

New laws endorsed a separation of church and state. In Virginia, Thomas Jefferson wrote a Statute for Religious Freedom (1786). It said that "no man shall be compelled to frequent [attend] or support any religious worship, place, or ministry."

136 CHAPTER 4

Reading Skill
An American Victory

Guide students in a discussion of the importance and consequences of the British defeat at Yorktown. Then write the following chart on the board. Have students copy the chart into their notes and complete it. Have volunteers share their answers with the class. 🄛 **Verbal-Linguistic, Logical-Mathematical**

📑 Alternative Assessment Handbook, Rubric 13: Graphic Organizers

🖥 Graphic Organizer Transparencies

Answers

Reading Check *lost land east of the Mississippi, as well as forts in the Northwest*

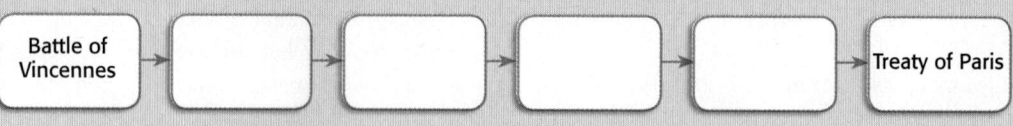

Battle of Vincennes → ▢ → ▢ → ▢ → ▢ → Treaty of Paris

The state church in Virginia and Maryland had been the Anglican Church. After the war American Anglicans reorganized as the Protestant Episcopal Church. New England states kept their relationship with the Congregational Church, but outsiders no longer had to pay to support the church.

For the Roman Catholic Church, the Revolutionary War led to a certain amount of acceptance. Catholics had often faced prejudice, but the arrival of French Catholic soldiers helped change many people's attitudes.

A new nation Economically, the war left the new nation with some problems. The Revolution had cost a lot of money, and Congress had borrowed from foreign sources and American citizens. Now the money needed to be repaid.

At the same time, the 13 colonies—now states—wanted to retain their sovereign power. They had just escaped one tyrannical government, and they did not want to create another. So, setting up a central government to deal with debt and other national issues was going to be complicated. Soon, the Continental Congress would meet again. This time the delegates would discuss economic issues and a new system of government.

READING CHECK **Making Generalizations** How did the war affect American politics?

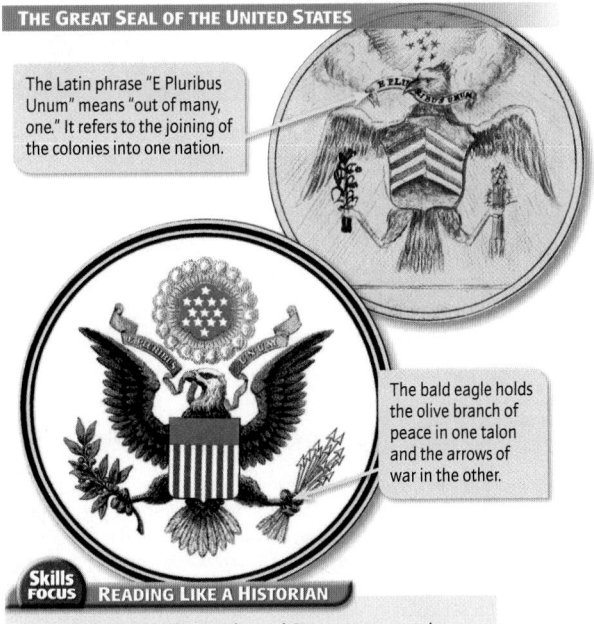

THE GREAT SEAL OF THE UNITED STATES

The Latin phrase "E Pluribus Unum" means "out of many, one." It refers to the joining of the colonies into one nation.

The bald eagle holds the olive branch of peace in one talon and the arrows of war in the other.

Skills Focus **READING LIKE A HISTORIAN**

On June 20, 1782, the Continental Congress approved an official seal of the United States. The original sketch (top) and today's seal (bottom) are shown here.

Interpreting Visuals What do the symbols in the Great Seal of the United States signify?

SECTION 4 ASSESSMENT

go.hrw.com
Online Quiz
Keyword: SD7 HP4

Reviewing Ideas, Terms, and People

1. **a. Recall** In what ways did the Revolutionary War change after the Battle of Saratoga?
   b. Explain What gains did Americans make in the West?
   c. Evaluate Was Britain's move into the South a good idea?

2. **a. Recall** What kind of aid did France give to the American Patriots?
   b. Make Inferences Why did other European nations choose to help the Americans against Great Britain?

3. **a. Identify** Who were Lafayette and **Rochambeau**, and what role did they play in the **Battle of Yorktown**?
   b. Explain How did American forces trap Cornwallis at Yorktown?
   c. Evaluate Do you think the Americans could have won the war without the help of the French?

4. **a. Recall** What actions regarding slavery did states take after the war?

b. Elaborate How did the war change colonial churches?
c. Predict What issues faced the new nation?

Critical Thinking

5. **Sequencing** Copy the chart below and make a time line of major events and battles leading up to the victory at Yorktown.

_____ _____ _____ _____ Victory at Yorktown

FOCUS ON WRITING

6. **Expository** Write an answer to Abigail Adams's letter in which you give some ideas about the status of women after the Revolutionary War.

Section 4 Assessment Answers

1. **a.** action shifted to the South and the western frontier
   b. gained control of the northwest region
   c. possible answer—no, because Loyalist support did not materialize

2. **a.** loaned money; sent troops and ships
   b. France was an enemy of Britain; Spain entered the war as an ally of France.

3. **a.** French officers; trapped British army
   b. Lafayette kept Cornwallis on the peninsula; Washington came south with troops.
   c. possible answer—no, needed supplies,

troops, and money from the French

4. **a.** some ended slavery, others restricted slave trade and made freeing slaves easier
   b. began to officially separate after war
   c. in debt, no effective central government

5. 1778 Lafayette arrives; 1779 Battle of Vincennes; 1780–1781 King's Mountain, Guilford Court House; 1780 France and Spain join Americans; 1781 Siege of Yorktown

6. agree that women deserve equal rights, but idea of equality too advanced for the time

---

• **Direct Teach** •

Info to Know

Paying for the War Congress had to fight the Revolutionary War without having the power to tax Americans to raise money. In fact, France gave the United States a loan in 1779, which provided the new nation with enough money to avoid bankruptcy.

• **Review & Assess** •

Close

Have students list the major battles of the Revolutionary War, identifying which were British victories and which were American victories.

Review

Online Quiz, Section 4

Daily Test Practice Transparency

Assess

SE Section 4 Assessment

Progress Assessment: Section 4 Quiz

Alternative Assessment Handbook

Reteach

Interactive Reader and Study Guide, Section 4

Interactive Skills Tutor CD-ROM

Answers

Reading Like a Historian *that the country is prepared for peace or war*

Reading Check *It broadened voting rights for white men, and spread ideas of equality.*

Document-Based Investigation

Patriots and Loyalists

Info to Know

Revolutionary Symbolism The image of a horse throwing its master, as seen in Document 3, was not a new symbol of rebellion. A similar image had appeared in 1774, with the title "A Political Lesson." It showed the British governor of Massachusetts, General Thomas Gage, being thrown from a horse. When he was appointed governor, Gage received orders to shut down trade in Boston until the colonists repaid the damage caused by the Boston Tea Party. Most Bostonians were forced to leave.

The Tree of Liberty In 1765, images representing two tax officials were burned into an old elm tree in Boston. The tree became a rallying site for patriotic speeches and for groups such as the Sons of Liberty. The tree, which was often decorated with flags and lanterns, soon became known as the "Liberty Tree." When the Sons of Liberty were to meet, a special flag was raised on a pole within the tree's branches. Other states from Massachusetts to Georgia soon adopted liberty trees, or sometimes liberty poles. They were usually located in the center of a town, where they served as a visible symbol of freedom. Jefferson referred to the "Tree of Liberty" in a letter to a friend: "The tree of liberty must be refreshed from time to time with the blood of patriots and tyrants."

Patriots and Loyalists

Historical Context The documents below provide different views of events during the American Revolution.

Task Examine the documents and answer the questions that follow. Then you will be asked to write an essay about Patriot and Loyalist views, using facts from the documents and from the chapter to support the position you take in your thesis statement.

DOCUMENT 1

In the years leading up to the Revolution, Patriots used tactics such as tarring and feathering to humiliate British officials without causing permanent harm to them. This image, published in 1774, expressed Loyalist horror at the tarring and feathering of British tax agent John Malcolm by suspected members of the Sons of Liberty. The Tree of Liberty, a popular image among Patriot artists, is portrayed with a hangman's noose on it to represent the hypocrisy of the Patriots.

DOCUMENT 2

The Patriots took a very different view of efforts to humiliate the British. Published in 1775, this image by a Patriot artist celebrates a New York barber who half-shaved a British officer, then forced him into the street to be laughed at by observers. The officer is shown running out of the barber shop not only half-shaven but also without his wig, which all important men wore.

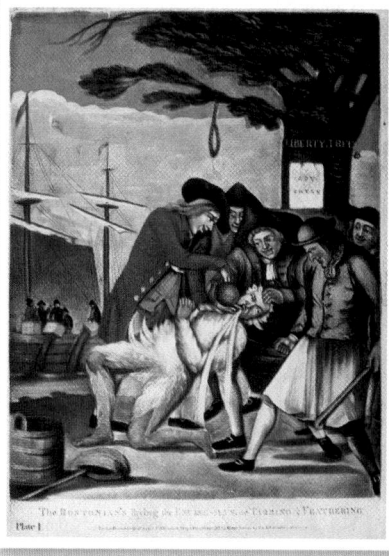

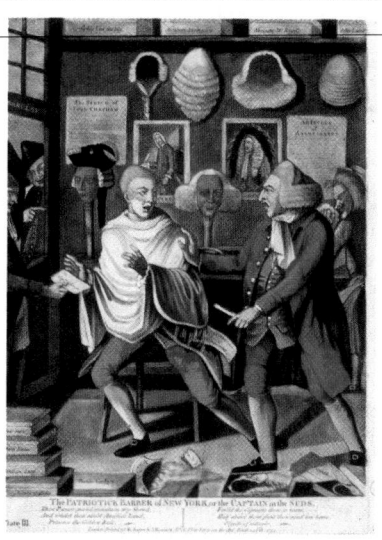

Skills Focus: Interpreting Visuals

At Level

Reading Like a Historian Skill
Revolutionary Political Cartoons

Materials construction paper, colored markers

1. Guide the class in a discussion of the three illustrations shown on these two pages. What do the images have in common? Which image probably uses the least exaggeration? What symbols are used? What do those symbols represent? Which image is the most symbolic? Why?

2. Have students work in pairs to create two political cartoons illustrating other events that

took place during the American Revolution. Cartoons should make clear the differences between the Patriots and the Loyalists, and present a single point of view. Students should try to keep their cartoons as close to the style of the period as possible.

3. Have volunteers present their cartoons to the class and explain them. **LS Interpersonal**

Alternative Assessment Handbook, Rubric 27: Political Cartoons

This image was published in 1779, three years into the war, and was titled "The Horse America Throwing his Master." It shows King George III being thrown by his horse, which represents the United States. The crop used to whip the horse is shown here as having swords, bayonets, and tomahawks on the end. These were weapons used by British soldiers and their Indian allies against the Patriots. At right, a Patriot soldier marches into the scene carrying a flag with 13 stars on it.

THE HORSE AMERICA, throwing his Master.

Skills FOCUS READING LIKE A HISTORIAN

1. **a. Describe** Refer to Document 1. What was the purpose of the actions taken against John Malcolm?
   b. Analyze Why do you think the artist saw the Patriots' actions as hypocritical?

2. **a. Identify** Refer to Document 2. Why was the British officer shown as bald in addition to being half-shaven?
   b. Elaborate Why do you think the Patriots supported humiliation as a tactic against British officials?

3. **a. Identify** Refer to Document 3. What does the flag in the image represent?

   b. Interpret Do you think this image was created by a Patriot or a Loyalist? Explain.

4. **Document-Based Essay Question** Consider the question below and form a thesis statement. Using examples from Documents 1, 2, and 3, create an outline and write a short essay supporting your position. How did Patriots and Loyalists view the American Revolution differently?

   See Skills Handbook, pp. H10, H28–29, H30, H31

Collaborative Learning

At Level

The Sons of Liberty

Research Required

1. Divide the class into small groups. Have each group conduct research on the Sons of Liberty. Tell students to use the following questions to guide their research: What were the goals of the Sons of Liberty? Who were the leaders of the Sons of Liberty? Where were the Sons of Liberty strongest? What were some of the actions the Sons of Liberty took? How did the Sons of Liberty contribute to the American Revolution?

2. Have each group use its research to write a skit dramatizing one event in the history of the Sons of Liberty.

3. Have each group present its skit to the class.
   LS Interpersonal, Kinesthetic

   Alternative Assessment Handbook, Rubric 33: Skits and Reader's Theater

---

Info to Know

The Sons of Liberty The Sons of Liberty was a vigilante group formed in Boston in 1765 in order to protest the Stamp Act. By the end of the year it had spread to other colonies. The Sons of Liberty often resorted to violence, harassing and sometimes even attacking anyone who sold or used British stamps. After the Stamp Act was repealed the next year, the Sons of Liberty formed Committees of Correspondence to coordinate action against Great Britain. Most of the participants in the 1773 Boston Tea Party were Sons of Liberty, and the next year the group was instrumental in bringing about the First Continental Congress.

Answers

Reading Like a Historian 1. a. *to humiliate him;* **b.** *possible answer— because the Patriots claim to be fighting for liberty, but they are actually harming a British official;* **2. a.** *to embarrass him;* **b.** *possible answer—did not want to cause permanent injury; lowered morale of British officials;* **3. a.** *the thirteen colonies;* **b.** *possible answer—a Patriot, because it shows the king of Britain being thrown from a horse while a Patriot marches in the background;* **4.** *possible answer—Patriots: necessary fight for liberty, getting rid of oppressive rulers; Loyalists: hypocritical and unnecessary movement against rightful British rule*

Visual Summary: The Revolutionary Era

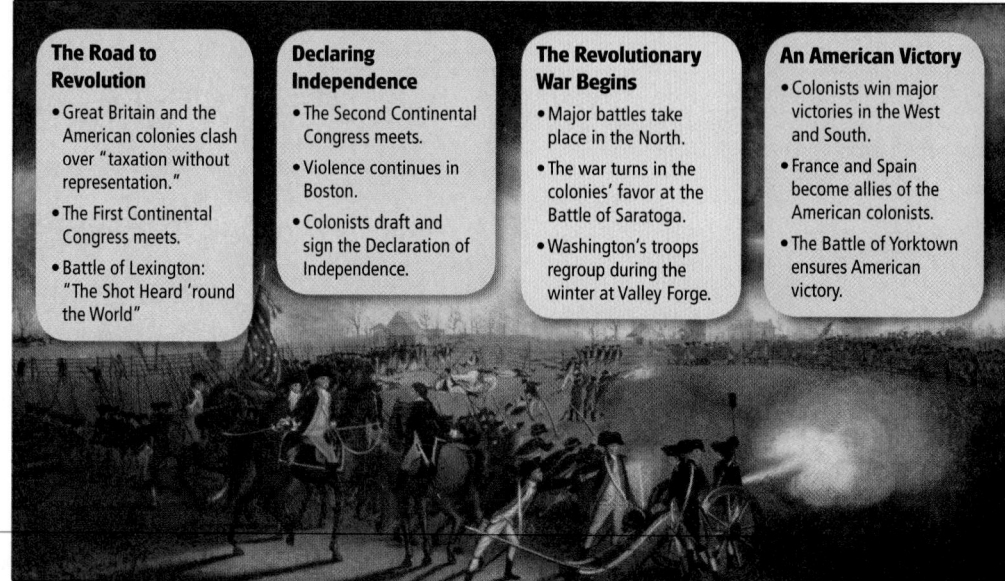

The Road to Revolution
- Great Britain and the American colonies clash over "taxation without representation."
- The First Continental Congress meets.
- Battle of Lexington: "The Shot Heard 'round the World"

Declaring Independence
- The Second Continental Congress meets.
- Violence continues in Boston.
- Colonists draft and sign the Declaration of Independence.

The Revolutionary War Begins
- Major battles take place in the North.
- The war turns in the colonies' favor at the Battle of Saratoga.
- Washington's troops regroup during the winter at Valley Forge.

An American Victory
- Colonists win major victories in the West and South.
- France and Spain become allies of the American colonists.
- The Battle of Yorktown ensures American victory.

Reviewing Key Terms and People

For each term or name below, write a sentence explaining its significance to the Revolutionary era.

1. Stamp Act
2. Intolerable Acts
3. First Continental Congress
4. battles of Lexington and Concord
5. Second Continental Congress
6. Loyalist
7. *Common Sense*
8. Thomas Jefferson
9. Battle of Saratoga
10. Valley Forge
11. Marquis de Lafayette
12. Treaty of Paris

Comprehension and Critical Thinking

SECTION 1 *(pp. 106–113)*

13. **a. Identify** What objects required stamps under the Stamp Act?

b. Sequence Create a brief time line of the events leading up to the battles of Lexington and Concord.

c. Analyze How did the American colonists win the Battle of Concord?

SECTION 2 *(pp. 114–120)*

14. **a. Recall** When did the Second Continental Congress meet?

b. Compare What were the arguments for war during the Second Continental Congress? What were the arguments for peace?

c. Evaluate Did the American colonies make the right decision in declaring their independence from Great Britain?

History's Impact video program

Review the video to answer the closing question: How does the Declaration of Independence affect American life today?

SECTION 3 *(pp. 125–130)*

15. a. Describe How did American women help with revolutionary efforts?

b. Compare What were the strengths of the Continental Army? What were the strengths of the British Redcoats?

c. Analyze Why was the Battle of Saratoga considered a turning point in the war?

SECTION 4 *(pp. 132–137)*

16. a. Recall What happened at the Battle of Yorktown?

b. Analyze How did America's European allies help shift the balance in the Revolutionary War?

c. Predict The Revolutionary War brought many changes to America. How do you think those changes affected the new nation in the years after the war?

Using the Internet

go.hrw.com
Practice Online
Keyword: SD7 CH4

17. Revolutionary battle sites still exist across the eastern seaboard of the United States. Using the keyword above, do research on a significant Revolutionary War site that tourists can visit today. Then create a brochure that teaches tourists the significance of your site and encourages them to visit.

Analyzing Primary Sources

Reading Like a Historian On July 6, 1775, the Second Continental Congress issued a document called *A Declaration of the Causes and Necessity of Taking Up Arms*, which explained why the colonists were at war. Read the excerpt below and answer the questions that follow.

❝ We have not raised armies with ambitious designs of separating from Great Britain and establishing independent states . . . In our own native land, in defence of the freedom that is our birthright . . . for the protection of our property, acquired solely by the honest industry [work] of our forefathers and ourselves, against violence actually offered, we have taken up arms. ❞

18. Identify Name three reasons why the colonists were at war.

19. Analyze How is the position of this document different from the position the colonists later took in the Declaration of Independence?

Critical Reading

Read the passage in Section 4 under the heading "Revolution Changes America." Then answer the questions that follow.

20. Which of the following statements about women's rights after the Revolution are true?

A Married women could not sign contracts or own property.

B Women could vote in Massachusetts.

C Women were not offered higher education.

D Women could not vote in any state.

21. In the years following the Revolution,

A American Anglicans reorganized as the Protestant Episcopal Church.

B women were given the right to vote.

C all men and women had the right to vote.

D Thomas Jefferson wrote the Declaration of Independence.

WRITING FOR THE SAT

Think about the following issue.

The British army in America was well trained and had access to many resources from Great Britain. In contrast, the Continental Army often lacked resources and was not as well trained. Nevertheless, the Americans were able to win independence from Great Britain in 1783.

22. Assignment Given that the British were a well-trained, well-equipped fighting force, how were the Americans able to win independence from Britain? Write a short essay in which you develop your position on this issue. Support your point of view with reasoning and examples from your reading and studies.

THE REVOLUTIONARY ERA **141**

Answers

16. a. Cornwallis trapped on a peninsula; attacked from land and sea; forced to surrender

b. Both France and Spain contributed significantly; without French help Americans might have been defeated.

c. Equality became a central part of the culture. Church and state became separated over time.

Using the Internet

17. Go to the HRW Web site and enter the keyword shown to access a rubric for this activity.

KEYWORD: SD7 CH4

Analyzing Primary Sources

18. become independent; defend freedom; protect property

19. It stopped short of declaring independence.

Critical Reading

20. A

21. A

Writing for the SAT

22. possible answer—Americans fighting for freedom; fighting on home ground; helped by European nations

A rubric for this activity is provided in the Chapter Resource File: Writing for the SAT.

History's Impact
Video Program

provides goal of equality

Review and Assessment Resources

Review and Reinforce

📃 CRF: Chapter Review Activity

🖥 Quick Facts Transparencies: Tensions Between Britain and America, The Second Continental Congress, Key Documents that Influenced the Declaration of Independence, Strengths and Weaknesses of the Continental and British Armies, The Revolutionary Era

🔊 Spanish Chapter Summaries Audio CD Program

🌐 Online Chapter Summaries in Spanish

OSP Holt PuzzlePro; Quiz Show for ExamView

💿 Quiz Game CD-ROM

Assess

📃 PASS: Chapter Test, Forms A and B

📃 Alternative Assessment Handbook

OSP ExamView Test Generator, Chapter Test

💿 Differentiated Instruction Modified Worksheets and Tests CD-ROM: Chapter Test

HOAP Holt Online Assessment Program (in the Premier Online Edition)

Reteach/Intervene

📃 Interactive Reader and Study Guide

📃 Differentiated Instruction Teacher Management System: Lesson Plans for Differentiated Instruction

💿 Differentiated Instruction Modified Worksheets and Tests CD-ROM: Chapter Test

💿 Interactive Skills Tutor CD-ROM

go.hrw.com
Online Resources
KEYWORD: SD7 CH4

Chapter 5 Planning Guide

Creating a New Government

Chapter Overview	Reproducible Resources	Technology Resources

CHAPTER 5
pp. 142–167

Overview: In this chapter, students will analyze how the weaknesses of the Articles of Confederation led to the creation of a stronger form of government.

Differentiated Instruction Teacher Management System:*
• Instructional Benchmarking Guides
• Lesson Plans for Differentiated Instruction

Interactive Reader and Study Guide:
Chapter Summary*

Chapter Resource File:*
• Focus on Writing Activity: The United States Constitution
• Social Studies Skills Activity: Making Inferences
• Chapter Review Activity

American History Outline Maps

Pre-AP Activities Guide for American History*

Live Ink® Online Reading Help

Student Edition on Audio CD Program

Differentiated Instruction Modified Worksheets and Tests CD-ROM

Interactive Skills Tutor CD-ROM

United States History Primary Source Library CD-ROM

Power Presentations with Video CD-ROM

History's Impact: American History Video Program (VHS/DVD): Creating a New Government

Online Chapter Summaries in Spanish

Graphic Organizer Transparencies

Section 1:

The Articles of Confederation

The Main Idea: In order to carry on the war and build a new nation, Americans had to create a framework of government, but their first attempt had many weaknesses.

Differentiated Instruction Teacher Management System: Section 1 Lesson Plan*

Interactive Reader and Study Guide:
Section 1 Summary*

Chapter Resource File:*
• Vocabulary Builder Activity, Section 1
• Biography Activity: Mary Katherine Goddard

Daily Bellringer Transparency: Section 1*

Quick Facts Transparency: Weaknesses of the Articles of Confederation*

Map Transparency: The Land Ordinances of 1785 and 1787*

Daily Test Practice Transparency: Section 1*

Section 2:

Drafting the Constitution

The Main Idea: The Constitutional Convention tried to write a document that would address the weaknesses of the Articles of Confederation and make compromises between large and small states and between the North and South.

Differentiated Instruction Teacher Management System: Section 2 Lesson Plan*

Interactive Reader and Study Guide:
Section 2 Summary*

Chapter Resource File:*
• Vocabulary Builder Activity, Section 2
• Biography Activity: William Paterson
• Literature Activity: *Thoughts on Government* by John Adams

Daily Bellringer Transparency: Section 2*

Quick Facts Transparencies: The Great Compromise, Checks and Balances*

Daily Test Practice Transparency: Section 2*

Section 3:

Ratifying the Constitution

The Main Idea: Federalists and Antifederalists struggled over the principles of the new Constitution. But the promise of adding a Bill of Rights brought about ratification.

Differentiated Instruction Teacher Management System: Section 3 Lesson Plan*

Interactive Reader and Study Guide:
Section 3 Summary*

Chapter Resource File:*
• Vocabulary Builder Activity, Section 3

Political Cartoons Activities for American History, Cartoons 9 and 10: Announcing the Constitution; The Temple of Liberty

Daily Bellringer Transparency: Section 3*

Map Transparency: Ratification of the Constitution*

Daily Test Practice Transparency: Section 3*

HOLT

History's Impact
American History Video Program (VHS/DVD)
Creating a New Government

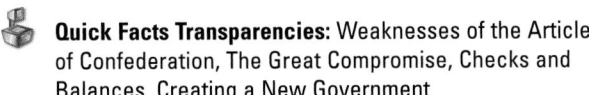

Review, Assessment, Intervention

Quick Facts Transparencies: Weaknesses of the Articles of Confederation, The Great Compromise, Checks and Balances, Creating a New Government

Spanish Chapter Summaries Audio CD Program

Progress Assessment Support System (PASS): Chapter Test*

Differentiated Instruction Modified Worksheets and Tests CD-ROM: Modified Chapter Test

OSP **One-Stop Planner CD-ROM:** ExamView Test Generator (English/Spanish)

HOAP **Holt Online Assessment Program (HOAP),** in the Holt Premier Online Student Edition

---

PASS: Section 1 Quiz*

Online Quiz: Section 1

Alternative Assessment Handbook

PASS: Section 2 Quiz*

Online Quiz: Section 2

Alternative Assessment Handbook

PASS: Section 3 Quiz*

Online Quiz: Section 3

Alternative Assessment Handbook

 **NC RESOURCES**

The following resources were developed to help North Carolina educators teach the standards and objectives of North Carolina's eleventh grade standard course of study in United States history.

• United States history EOC Test Prep Workbook
• Teacher's Support System
• North Carolina One-Stop Planner

And be sure to direct your students to **go.hrw.com** for online access to the EOC Test Prep Workbook.

go.hrw.com
EOC Test Prep
KEYWORD: SE7 NC

 **Holt Online Learning**

go.hrw.com
Teacher Resources
KEYWORD: SD7 TEACHER

go.hrw.com
Student Resources
KEYWORD: SD7 CH5

• Document-based Questions
• Interactive Multimedia Activities

• Current Events
• Chapter-based Internet Activities
• and more!

Holt Premier
Online Student Edition

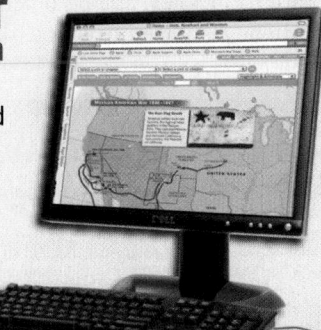

Complete online support for interactivity, assessment, and reporting

• Interactive Maps and Notebook
• Standardized Test Prep
• Homework Practice and Research Activities Online

CHAPTER 5 PLANNING GUIDE

The Big Picture

Jesús F. de la Teja

A Great Failure Under the Articles of Confederation, the first United States government proved a failure, yet it managed to achieve the country's independence and allow a successor government to take hold without civil war. The very name the Continental Congress chose for the confederation—United States of America—suggested the fundamental problem. In the eighteenth century *state* meant a sovereign political entity, what we would call a nation. In creating a United States, the Congress attempted to reconcile the need for collective action with the inherent sovereignty of each state. The experiment's failure was necessary for the states to willingly surrender enough sovereignty to create a stable and competent national government.

The Genius of Compromise The Framers were holed up in an unventilated brick meetinghouse in the middle of a Philadelphia summer, and it is amazing that the product of their efforts was as elegant and flexible as the Constitution. In the end, what saved the convention was the willingness of participants to be pragmatists rather than ideologues. In fact, the compromises entered into by slave and free, large and small, commercial and agricultural interests at the convention established a model for dealing with divisive issues that lasted until the presidential election of 1860.

The Origins of American Citizenship The Framers argued that because the states reserved to themselves all powers not explicitly granted to the United States government under the Constitution there was no need to spell out individual rights. Americans with a healthy paranoia regarding government's willingness to intrude into people's affairs remained unconvinced. In another great compromise, ratification seekers agreed that Congress would immediately set about amending the Constitution to include individual and state rights. In the process, a new form of citizenship was created; now, along with having rights as Virginians, New Yorkers, or Rhode Islanders, the citizens of the states also had rights as Americans.

Recent Scholarship

Creating the Constitution *A Brilliant Solution: Inventing the American Constitution*, by Carol Berkin (2002), covers familiar textbook ground—big vs. small states, the slavery issue, separation of powers. Berkin, however, adds depth and vitality to events by bringing the actors to life with clear, engaging prose. *A Brilliant Solution*'s story belongs not only to Madison, Hamilton, and Paterson, but to Connecticut's Roger Sherman and South Carolina's Charles Pinckney, among others. Berkin extends the story into Washington's presidency, when a real government had to be fashioned from the ideas of 1787.

Differentiating Instruction

 Differentiated Instruction Teacher Management System
- Lesson Plans for Differentiated Instruction
- Differentiated Instructional Benchmarking Guides
- Interactive Reader and Study Guide

 Spanish Chapter Summaries Audio CD Program

 Online Chapter Summaries in Spanish

 Student Edition on Audio CD Program

 Differentiated Instruction Modified Worksheets and Tests CD-ROM
- Vocabulary Flash Cards
- Modified Vocabulary Builder Activities
- Modified Chapter Review Activity
- Modified Chapter Test

OSP One-Stop Planner CD-ROM
- ExamView Test Generator (English and Spanish)
- PuzzlePro
- Quiz Show for ExamView
- Transparencies and Videos

TE Differentiated Activities in the Teacher's Edition
- The Road to Statehood, p. 148
- Constitutional Compromises, p. 154
- Federalists and Antifederalists, p. 158
- The Federalist Papers, p. 160

Reading Like a Historian
Sam Wineburg

"A Wall of Separation"

"You can't talk about religion in public school," Sylvia tells Paul. "The Constitution says so—separation of church and state!"

"A wall of separation," chimes in Shakirya.

Over the assertions of both, Paul objects: "The words 'separation of church and state' aren't even in the Constitution—look it up if you don't believe me."

Who's Right?

As Americans we love to argue about the Constitution. Sometimes we spend more time arguing about it than actually reading it. When we pause to do so, we're often surprised by what we find.

The above exchange is rooted in actual interviews we conducted with high school students in public and parochial schools (Susan Mosborg, "Speaking of History," *Cognition and Instruction*, 2002). In a narrow sense, the student who gets the last word, Paul, is right: the phrase "separation of church and state" appears nowhere in our nation's founding document.

If that's so, why are so many of us confused?

Metaphors and Understanding

Because for 200 years, the "wall of separation" metaphor has been one of the main lenses through which Article 1 of the Bill of Rights, known as the Establishment Clause—"Congress shall make no law respecting an establishment of religion, or prohibiting the free exercise thereof"—has been understood. That the originator of this metaphor was Thomas Jefferson has surely helped it achieve its near-constitutional aura.

After his 1802 election as president, Jefferson received a letter from the Danbury Baptist Association congratulating him on his victory. The Baptists, a religious minority in Connecticut, objected to taxes they paid to support Congregationalist churches, and used their letter to praise Jefferson for his bold stand on religious liberty.

In a carefully-crafted response (Jefferson circulated it among his cabinet ministers and then put it through multiple drafts), the president assured the Baptists that "religion is a matter which lies solely between man and God." He then cited the Establishment Clause, but added the following phrase after the word "thereof": "thus building a wall of separation between church and state." (In a prior draft Jefferson had written "eternal wall" but scratched it out.) He closed the letter by reciprocating the Baptists' "kind prayers for the protection and blessing of the common Father and creator of man."

The wall metaphor found its way into a Supreme Court decision in a 1878 case involving Mormon polygamy (*Reynolds* v. *United States*). But its most forceful use came in the 1947 case of *Everson* v. *Board of Education* over the legality of reimbursing parents for transporting their children to parochial schools. The Court ruled in favor of parents but not before elaborating the meaning of the Establishment Clause. Speaking for the Court, Justice Hugo Black wrote: "The First Amendment has erected a wall between church and state," adding, "that wall must be kept high and impregnable."

Problems with Metaphors

Since then, the wall metaphor has often accompanied discussions of the Establishment Clause, becoming in many people's minds conjoined. But starting in the 1980s, some members of the Supreme Court expressed doubts about the metaphor's usefulness. Indeed, the late Chief Justice William Rehnquist argued that the language of walls and separation had outlived its purpose—a "metaphor based on bad history, a metaphor which has proved useless as a guide to judging."

Metaphors permit—as well as constrain—understanding. They do so by lending us concrete images to understand abstract concepts, allowing us to communicate easily and vividly. But in this case, they also give us reason to debate and argue—something that we will surely do well into the foreseeable future.

Standards Focus

Social Studies Competency Goals

Goal 1 The learner will identify, investigate, and assess the effectiveness of the institutions of the emerging republic.

NC **1.01**

The Big Idea and Essential Questions

To foster student understanding of this chapter's big idea, design your lesson to address each section's essential question.

Big Idea Delegates from 12 states met at the Constitutional Convention and drafted a constitution which has endured for more than 200 years.

Essential Questions

1. Why did the Articles of Confederation prove to be a weak framework of government?

2. How did the delegates to the Constitutional Convention create a document that both addressed the weaknesses of the Articles of Confederation and achieved balance among the states?

3. Which principles of the new Constitution did the Federalists and Antifederalists struggle over?

CHAPTER
5 1776–1789

Creating a New GOVERNMENT

THE BIG PICTURE The Articles of Confederation, under which the thirteen colonies had united to win independence, proved insufficient to govern the new nation. Delegates from 12 states met at the Constitutional Convention in Philadelphia and fashioned a newer, stronger form of government, which has endured for more than 200 years.

 North Carolina Standards

Social Studies Objectives
1.01 Identify the major domestic issues and conflicts experienced by the nation during the Federalist Period.

Language Arts Objectives
3.02 Select an issue or theme and take a stance on that issue by:
• supporting the argument with specific reasons.

Skills FOCUS READING LIKE A HISTORIAN

The artist Junius Brutus Stearns captured the gravity of the task set before the nation's founders in his 1856 painting *Washington Addressing the Constitutional Convention.* **Interpreting Visuals** What does this painting tell you about the crafters of the Constitution?

See Skills Handbook, p. H30

142

 U.S.

November 1777 Congress adopts Articles of Confederation.

1775

 World

1778 British explorer Captain James Cook lands in Hawaii, meeting people like this Sandwich Islander.

Introduce the Chapter

At Level

Creating a New Government

1. Ask students what they believe it means to be a citizen of the United States. Make a class list of student responses. Then have students name individual rights and liberties that are granted to citizens and explain why these rights are the envy of many people around the world.

2. Have students predict what their lives might be like if they did not possess freedom of speech, freedom to assemble, freedom of religion, and a free press, or even if money issued in one state was not accepted in another state.

3. Tell students that as they study this chapter they will learn how these basic freedoms came into being, and remind students that these rights were not part of the original Constitution. **LS Verbal-Linguistic**

Alternative Assessment Handbook, Rubric 11: Discussions

• Chapter Preview •

HOLT

History's Impact

▶ **Video Program: Creating a New Government**
See the Video Teacher's Guide for strategies for using the video segment.

Reading Like a Historian

The Constitutional Convention
George Washington, who is standing, was nominated by Robert Morris of Pennsylvania to serve as president of the Constitutional Convention. Washington's election was unanimous. Have students describe how the artist shows Washington as a leader in this painting.

March 1781
Articles of Confederation go into effect.

1785
Land Ordinance of 1785 creates plan for surveying and selling land in the Northwest Territory.

May 1787
Constitutional Convention meets in Philadelphia.

1789
First U.S. Congress meets in New York.

1780

1785

1790

September 1781
Spanish settlers found the city of Los Angeles.

1784
Russians settle in the Aleutian Islands of present-day Alaska.

July 1789
The French Revolution begins with the capture of Bastille prison.

go.hrw.com
Online Resources

Chapter Resources:
KEYWORD: SD7 CH5

Teacher Resources:
KEYWORD: SD7 TEACHER

143

Explore the Time Line

1. When were the Articles of Confederation adopted, and when did they take effect? *1777; 1781*

2. When did the first U.S. Congress meet? *1789*

3. When did Russia begin to settle the Aleutian Islands? *1784*

Info to Know

Independence Hall Independence Hall in Philadelphia was built between 1732 and 1753 as the State House for the Pennsylvania colony. The U.S. Constitutional Convention met there, and the hall served as the meeting place for the U.S. Supreme Court from 1789 until 1800. It is now a World Heritage site.

Answers

Reading Like a Historian (p. 142)
They were well-dressed, well-educated, and prosperous white males.

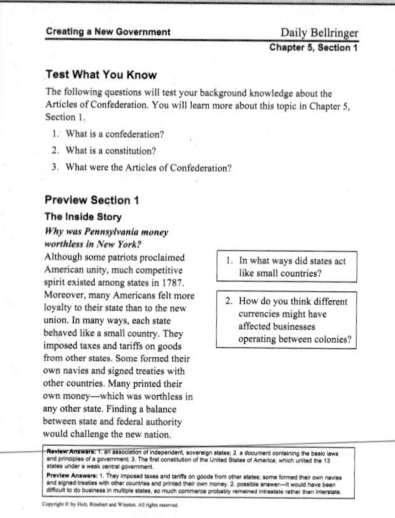

SECTION 1 — The Articles of Confederation

BEFORE YOU READ

MAIN IDEA

In order to carry on the war and build a new nation, Americans had to create a framework of government, but their first attempt had many weaknesses.

READING FOCUS

1. What were some key aspects of the new American republic?
2. What was the structure of the new national government?
3. What problems did the Confederation face?
4. What did the government accomplish in the Northwest Territory?

KEY TERMS AND PEOPLE

legislative branch
judicial branch
executive branch
republic
Articles of Confederation
Land Ordinance of 1785
Northwest Ordinance

TAKING NOTES As you read, take notes identifying the powers of government under the Articles of Confederation. Record your notes in a graphic organizer like the one shown here.

> Articles of Confederation
> ↓
> [ ]

COLLECTION OF THE AMERICAN NUMISMATIC SOCIETY, NEW YORK

The States, UNITED

◀ Almost as though they were separate nations instead of separate states, some states had their own currencies.

THE INSIDE STORY *Why was Pennsylvania money worthless in New York?* In 1774, at the First Continental Congress, Patrick Henry declared bravely: "The distinctions between Virginians, Pennsylvanians, New Yorkers, and New Englanders are no more. I am not a Virginian but an American."

Patrick Henry's words were inspiring. Yet even after the Americans won the Revolutionary War and the 13 colonies became states, they were still struggling to unite as Americans. Loyalty to one's state remained stronger than any feeling of national unity.

In many ways, each state behaved like a small country. Some had their own navies and made treaties with foreign nations. Small states and large states were at odds. Some

states, including New York and New Hampshire, argued over land claims. Trade and the economy caused most clashes among states.

Financial chaos reigned in the early years. For starters, many states printed their own paper money. If you had a pocket full of paper money printed in Pennsylvania, you could not spend it in New York or Virginia. States also imposed tariffs, or import taxes, on goods shipped from other states. An out-of-state ship that docked at a Virginia port without paying the tariff could be seized and sold.

The lack of unity made commerce especially difficult in certain states. James Madison wrote: "New Jersey, placed between Philadelphia and New York, was likened to a cask tapped at both ends; and North Carolina, between Virginia and South Carolina, to a patient bleeding at both arms."

Soon the states would attempt to come together under a new national government. If Americans were truly to unite, they would need to invent a government that would address the needs of all the states. Americans would also need to find a balance between state and national government. ◼

144 CHAPTER 5

The American Republic

While Americans were fighting for independence from Britain, they were also setting up new governments. Most of the 13 states wrote new <u>constitutions</u>. These state constitutions echoed many prized British rights, including representative government, the rule of law, limits on government power, and individual liberties.

New state governments Despite differences among the states, their governments had many similarities. Each state government had three branches. The **legislative branch** made the laws. The **judicial branch** interpreted the laws. The **executive branch**—the governor—carried out the laws. Remembering their experience with authoritarian royal governors, the states chose to limit the governor's power. Instead, elected legislatures held more power.

Republicanism Above all, Americans did not want a king or any other supreme authority over them. Going back to the ideas of John Locke, they wanted a **republic**, a political system without a monarch. It would rule "with the consent of the governed." No government in the world at that time was based on this idea. The ideal of republicanism was that hard-working, property-owning citizens would be active in government. Reality, of course, was different. Women, African Americans, Native Americans, and poor white laborers seldom owned property or took part in government.

Republican motherhood The Revolutionary War did bring a shift in women's roles. During the war, women ably managed farms and businesses. Some women fought in battle or defended their homes with axes and muskets. American women had become politically active for the first time before the war, organizing boycotts and later supporting the war effort.

The idea of republican motherhood developed from these roots. People recognized that women had the first opportunity to educate children in civic virtues and responsibilities. Republican motherhood encouraged mothers to raise their sons to be patriotic future leaders and their daughters to be intelligent, patriotic, and competent so they could run households and educate their own children.

Judith Sargent Murray, a contemporary author, maintained that young women should

REPUBLICAN MOTHERHOOD

The Sedgwick home is pictured in the background.

The book suggests the importance of education to the Sedgwick family.

SKILLS FOCUS **READING LIKE A HISTORIAN**

The Sedgwicks, a prominent Federalist family in Massachusetts, valued education. In this painting, Pamela Dwight Sedgwick is pictured with her daughter, Catharine, who became a writer.

Interpreting Visuals Why did the family choose to include a book in this portrait?
See **Skills Handbook**, p. H30

be educated in reasoning, not just household skills. After infancy, she noted, boys and girls were given very different educations:

HISTORY'S VOICES

❝ How is the one exalted, and the other depressed, by the contrary modes of education which are adopted! the one is taught to aspire, and the other is early confined and limited. As their years increase, the sister must be wholly domesticated, while the brother is led by the hand through all the flowery paths of science. ❞
—Judith Sargent Murray, quoted in *Founding Mothers*

READING CHECK **Making Inferences** Why did the states create weak executive branches?

ACADEMIC VOCABULARY

constitutions documents containing the basic laws and principles of a state or nation

---

Skills Focus: Comparing and Contrasting | At Level

Reading Skill
Republican Motherhood

1. Guide students in a discussion of the shift in women's roles that had been brought about by the Revolutionary War.

2. Organize the class into two groups. Have one group discuss and list the positive effects of republican motherhood on women's roles and opportunities. Have the other group discuss and list the negative effects.

3. Have volunteers from each group debate this statement: Republican motherhood

will provide the nation with citizens who will promote democracy and make lasting contributions to society.

4. Have each student write an essay comparing American women's roles in the early years of the republic and in the early 21st century.
LS Interpersonal, Verbal-Linguistic

Alternative Assessment Handbook, Rubrics 9: Comparing and Contrasting; and 10: Debates

Answers

Reading Like a Historian *to stress the importance of education; all children should learn to read*

Reading Check *because of their experience with authoritarian royal governors*

145

2 What was the structure of the new national government? *states kept most of their power; weak national government with only one branch, the Congress, where each state had one vote*

A New National Government

Explain Why did the states need to create a central government? *to carry on the war and make agreements with foreign governments*

Recall What were the Articles of Confederation? *first national constitution; document established association of independent states with common goals*

Predict How might the Articles of Confederation lead to problems for the nation? *lacked central executive branch, could not raise revenues or impose taxes, no federal courts*

Primary Source

"A national debt, if it is not excessive, will be to us a national blessing."
— Alexander Hamilton
from a letter to Robert Morris, April 30, 1781

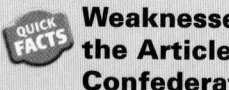 **Weaknesses of the Articles of Confederation**

Have students work in mixed-ability pairs to list one consequence of each weakness in the chart and to propose a solution to each weakness.

🖳 Quick Facts Transparency: Weaknesses of the Articles of Confederation

Answers

Reading Check *establish national policies; conduct foreign relations; borrow and coin money; set up post offices; establish an army, declare war*

146

A New National Government

The states formed their new governments quickly during the Revolutionary War, but the Continental Congress found it more difficult to agree upon a structure for a national government. Yet some kind of central government was needed to carry on the war and make agreements with foreign governments. As they worked out a plan, the Congress set up a completely new kind of government structure.

The Articles of Confederation In 1776, while one congressional committee was writing the Declaration of Independence, another committee was trying to work out a plan of union. John Dickinson of Pennsylvania led the effort. Dickinson was a moderate who had once hoped for peace with Great Britain. Now he drafted a plan for a new American government.

For more than a year Congress debated whether to adopt the **Articles of Confederation**, America's first national constitution. As its name indicates, the document established a confederation—an association of independent, sovereign states with certain common goals.

Congress formally adopted the Articles of Confederation in November 1777. It took a while longer for each of the 13 states to ratify the document because of disputes over western lands.

Powers of the new government In March 1781 the Articles of Confederation finally went into effect. The states retained most of their power under the Articles. The document provided for only a weak national government. Unlike the state governments, the central government had only one branch: the Continental Congress, which was a legislative body. There was no executive or judicial branch. Each state also had only one vote in Congress, regardless of population.

Under the Articles, Congress did have certain powers. It could establish national policies and conduct foreign relations, including relations with Native American nations. Congress could borrow and coin money and set up post offices. It also had the power to establish an army and declare war.

READING CHECK **Summarizing** Under the Articles of Confederation, what powers did the central government have?

ACADEMIC VOCABULARY
ratify officially approve
amend make changes

The Confederation Faces Problems

The powers of Congress, however, were just words on paper. It was difficult, and often impossible, for the government to make these words a reality. Nine of the 13 states had to agree on any major law. All 13 states had to agree to amend the Articles of Confederation.

Financial problems The new government's major problems involved money. Although there were large war debts to pay, the government did not have the power to impose or collect taxes. Congress did ask the states for money but only received about one-sixth of what it requested. This meant the government could not pay to support an army or navy. Nor could it repay money borrowed from foreign governments and from individual Americans during the Revolutionary War. Some soldiers who had fought in the war actually went unpaid.

In 1781 Congress set up a department of finance run by Philadelphia merchant Robert Morris and his business associate, Haym Salomon. Both men had worked hard during the war to raise money for the army. Salomon loaned thousands of dollars to the government and to several government leaders, most of which was never repaid.

Morris and others who wanted a stronger national government suggested amending the Articles of Confederation to allow Congress to place a 5 percent tax on imports. The plan

WEAKNESSES OF THE ARTICLES OF CONFEDERATION
QUICK FACTS

- Congress could not impose taxes
- Congress could not regulate trade
- Nine of 13 states needed to agree to pass laws
- All states had to agree to amend the Articles
- No executive branch to enforce laws passed by Congress
- No judicial branch to interpret laws passed by Congress

Skills Focus: Identifying Problem and Solution
At Level

Reading Skill
Creating a New Government

1. Organize the class into small groups. Have each group serve as a congressional committee that is in charge of drafting plans for the new American government. Have each group identify several economic, political, or social problems that it hopes the national government will address.

2. Have students write a plan for a new government that will address all of the problems they have listed.

3. Have volunteers share their plans with the class. Then guide the class in a discussion of how realistic these plans might be.
   LS **Interpersonal, Logical-Mathematical**

📝 Alternative Assessment Handbook, Rubrics 14: Group Activity; and 43: Writing to Persuade

The Articles of Confederation

Concerned that trouble would result from attempts to change the government, Richard Henry Lee of Virginia defended the Articles of Confederation.

❝I think Sir that the first maxim of a man who loves liberty should be, never to grant to Rulers an atom of power that is not most clearly & indispensably necessary for the safety and well being of Society . . . [T]he Confederation should not be presumptuously called an infallible system for all times and all situations . . . no change should be admitted until proved to be necessary by the fairest, fullest & most mature experience.**❞**

Richard Henry Lee, 1785

John Jay, president of the Continental Congress and part of the committee sent to negotiate peace with Great Britain, had grave misgivings about the Articles of Confederation.

❝ To oppose popular prejudices, to censure the proceedings, and expose the improprieties [wrong-doing] of states is an unpleasant task, but it must be done. Our affairs seem to lead to some crisis, some revolution. . . . [W]e are going and doing wrong, and therefore I look forward to evils and calamities. . . .**❞**

John Jay, 1786

Skills FOCUS **READING LIKE A HISTORIAN**

Identifying Points of View Both men fear "calamities" and troubles ahead, but for each, those troubles are different. What does each man fear?

See Skills Handbook, pp. H28–H29

---

failed. To amend the Articles required unanimous consent, and one state would not support the import tax.

Problems with the states Congress had very little power over the individual states. States could make their own agreements with foreign nations or Native Americans. They might set taxes on trade with neighboring states and refuse to honor contracts made in other states. As you read earlier, some states even issued their own money.

Because there was no national court system, Congress could not settle disputes between states. States sometimes refused to recognize laws or court decisions made in other states. A criminal could escape the law simply by fleeing across a state line.

Problems with foreign nations Because it was so weak, Congress also had trouble taking advantage of the territory that the United

States had won in the 1783 Treaty of Paris. The British continued to occupy their forts in the Great Lakes region. With the help of Native American allies, they kept American settlers out of parts of the Northwest Territory.

In addition, Congress had difficulty negotiating with Spain about the right to travel on the Mississippi River and use the port of New Orleans. People in the South and West, especially Kentucky and Tennessee, depended on the Mississippi River to take their produce to market. Disagreements also continued about the border with Spanish Florida.

Economic problems Money problems plagued not only the government but also private citizens and businesses in every state. The end of the war was a disaster for New England's valuable trade with Britain and the British West Indies. Traders lost the advantage of being part of the British Empire and now had to pay high customs duties.

Reading Focus

❸ What problems did the Confederation face? *could not impose or collect taxes to pay war debts; states could make their own treaties, issue their own money; problems administering territory won in the Treaty of Paris*

The Confederation Faces Problems

Recall What was the main problem the Congress faced? *money; it did not have the power to impose or collect taxes, but had large war debts to pay*

Summarize Under the new government, why were there problems in the relations between states? *Laws and contracts made in one state were often not recognized in other states, and states could impose taxes on trade with neighboring states.*

Elaborate Why was it so difficult to pass laws or amend the Articles of Confederation? *Nine of the 13 states had to agree to pass a law, while all 13 had to agree to amend the Articles of Confederation.*

📄 CRF: Biography: Mary Katherine Goddard

📄 CRF: Literature Activity: *Thoughts on Government* by John Adams

---

go.hrw.com
Online Resources
KEYWORD: SD7 CH5
TOPIC: THE NORTHWEST TERRITORY

Skills Focus: Summarizing | At Level | Standard English Mastery

Reading Skill
States and the Federal Government

1. Discuss the problems that existed between the states regarding paper money and taxation. During the discussion make a class list of documents and laws that are honored today between the states (e.g. marriage certificates, driver's licenses, Social Security cards, etc.). Discuss problems that might occur if these documents or laws were not honored.

2. Guide students in a discussion of the types of issues that are the responsibility of the federal government, such as making treaties and issuing money. Why are these best left to the federal government? Have students explain why states need to honor the laws and documents of other states and why some issues must be a federal responsibility.

LS Interpersonal, Verbal-Linguistic

📄 Alternative Assessment Handbook, Rubric 11: Discussions

Answers

Reading Like a Historian *Jay fears that states are acting improperly, country is doing wrong things; Lee fears that changes will be made granting federal government, or executive ruler, too much power.*

4 What did the government accomplish in the Northwest Territory? *passed Land Ordinance of 1785 to survey, sell, and settle land, and Northwest Ordinance, to encourage settlement and formation of new states*

The Northwest Territory

Explain What provisions were made for new states in the Articles of Confederation? *did not cover new states*

Make Inferences What did the plan for selling the land in the Northwest Territory have to do with education? *One section of each township was to be sold to support public schools.*

Contrast How did the Land Ordinance of 1785 differ from the Northwest Ordinance of 1787? *Land Ordinance of 1785 was a plan for surveying, selling, and settling the land; Northwest Ordinance dealt with legal formation of states and did not allow slavery in the territory.*

📦 Map Transparency: The Land Ordinances of 1785 and 1787

Answers

Interpreting Maps 1. *36; 1 square mile;* **2.** *160*

Reading Check *government did not have power to impose or collect taxes; paper money not backed by gold or silver, leading to inflation*

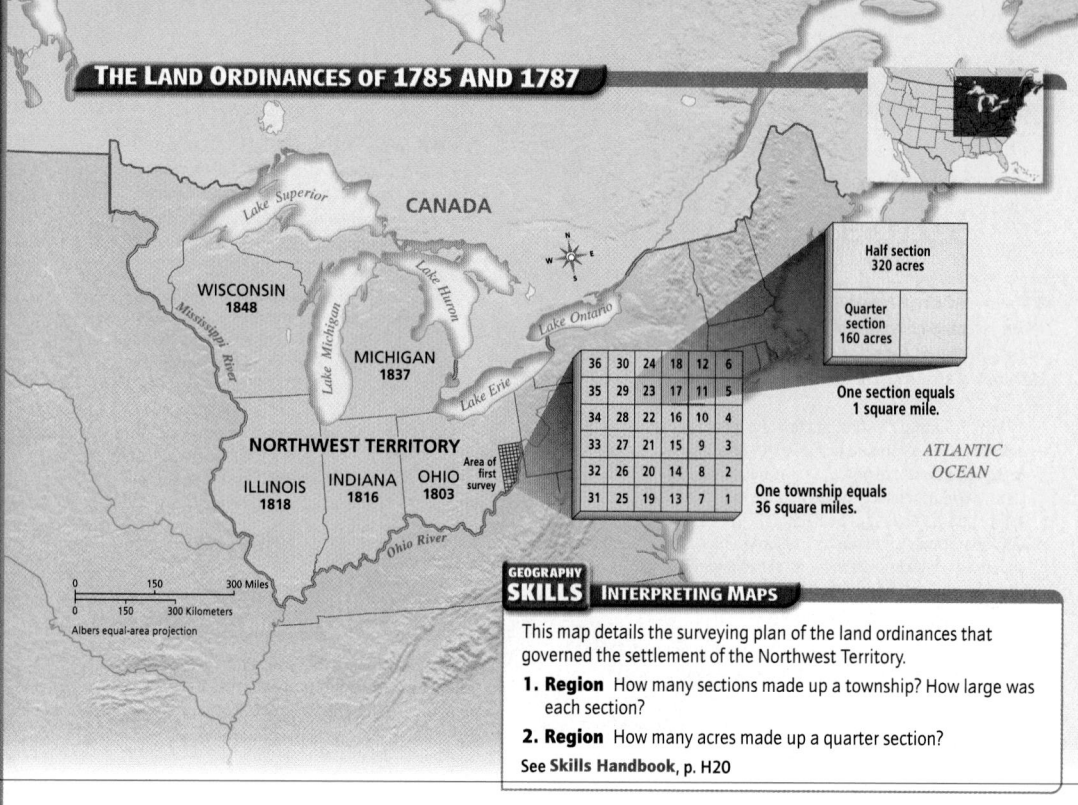

THE LAND ORDINANCES OF 1785 AND 1787

CANADA

WISCONSIN 1848

MICHIGAN 1837

NORTHWEST TERRITORY

ILLINOIS 1818   INDIANA 1816   OHIO 1803

Area of first survey

36	30	24	18	12	6
35	29	23	17	11	5
34	28	22	16	10	4
33	27	21	15	9	3
32	26	20	14	8	2
31	25	19	13	7	1

Half section 320 acres

Quarter section 160 acres

One section equals 1 square mile.

One township equals 36 square miles.

ATLANTIC OCEAN

Ohio River

0   150   300 Miles
0   150   300 Kilometers
Albers equal-area projection

GEOGRAPHY SKILLS | **INTERPRETING MAPS**

This map details the surveying plan of the land ordinances that governed the settlement of the Northwest Territory.

1. **Region** How many sections made up a township? How large was each section?

2. **Region** How many acres made up a quarter section?

See Skills Handbook, p. H20

Before the war, Great Britain had paid bonuses to support key colonial industries, such as indigo and naval stores. The end of that aid from Britain hurt southern economies. Also, because many African Americans had left during the war, there were fewer workers.

In addition, the paper money issued during the war was not backed by gold or silver. That led to inflation—a huge rise in prices as the value of paper money fell. Congress could not collect taxes, but the states could—and did. Some states required that people pay their taxes in gold or silver, not the nearly worthless paper money. People who could not pay their debts were jailed. The laws especially hurt poor farmers who were already in debt. Frustrated farmers began rebellions in several places.

READING CHECK **Summarizing** What money problems did the national government face under the Articles of Confederation?

The Northwest Territory

Even though the Confederation was a weak government, some of its actions did have long-lasting effects. One notable accomplishment was establishing a pattern for settlement in western lands.

Western land claims In colonial times, several colonies, particularly New York and Virginia, claimed huge, unmapped areas of land west of the Appalachian Mountains. But others had fixed western boundaries. They worried that western land claims would create huge neighboring states.

After the Revolutionary War, settlers streamed into the lands west of the Appalachians. People on the frontier already were at odds with people from the East over taxes and policies toward Native Americans. Now the question was how to organize settlement of the vast western lands.

Differentiating Instruction

Below Level

English-Language Learners

1. To help students understand the provisions in the Northwest Ordinance for creating new states, have students copy and complete the graphic organizer shown here. Omit the italicized answers.

2. Review student answers and discuss ways in which the Northwest Ordinance and the Land Ordinance of 1785 enabled the

government to regulate the division and development of the western lands.

LS Visual-Spatial

📓 Alternative Assessment Handbook, Rubric 13: Graphic Organizers

📦 Graphic Organizer Transparencies

The Road to Statehood

↓

| Single governor put in charge of Northwest Territory |

↓

| *Territory to be divided into 3 to 5 districts* |

↓

| *With a population of 5,000 adult males, a district could become a territory* |

↓

| *When population reached 60,000, a territory could write a constitution and apply to become a state* |

↓

| Statehood |

The Articles of Confederation did not address the question of new states. Congress had to find a way to bring western land and settlers into the political structure. Before that could happen, states had to give up their western land claims to the central government. During the 1780s and early 1790s, most states did so. Selling those lands could bring the Confederation badly needed money.

Dividing western lands In 1784 Thomas Jefferson came up with a proposal to divide the Northwest Territory—the land north and west of the Ohio River—into 10 districts. When the population in any district reached 20,000, its people would be able to send a representative to Congress. Later, the district could be admitted as a state. This original plan never fully went into effect, however.

The next year Congress drew up a plan for surveying, selling, and settling the territory. Under the **Land Ordinance of 1785**, the land would be surveyed and divided into a neat grid of townships, each 6 miles square (see map on opposite page). Within a township were 36 sections, each 1 mile square. The government would own four of the sections, while a fifth would be sold to support public schools. Surveyors planted "witness trees" to mark the corners of a section.

The Land Ordinance of 1785 changed the landscape of the Northwest Territory. As the United States expanded farther west, the same regular grid was used in other territories. This model ended many boundary disputes.

Land was to be sold at auction for at least $1 an acre. Buying a whole section was too expensive for most ordinary settlers and small farmers, who had to buy smaller parcels. Congress also sold some good land directly to land speculators.

In 1787 Congress passed another law for western settlement, the **Northwest Ordinance**. It was meant to encourage orderly settlement and the formation of new states, all controlled by law. The Northwest Ordinance also promised settlers religious freedom and other civil rights. Significantly, slavery was not allowed in the Northwest Territory.

A single governor was put in charge of the Northwest Territory, but the law said that it could later become three to five states. With a population of 5,000 adult males, a district could become a territory and send a nonvoting representative to Congress. With a population of 60,000, the territory could write a constitution and apply to become a state.

READING CHECK **Summarizing** How could a territory become a state?

THE IMPACT TODAY

Daily Life
When the Northwest Territory was divided into states, the square townships remained. Many of these townships still exist in midwestern states.

Info to Know
The Land Ordinances of 1785 and 1787 Michigan is unique among the states in that it consists of two distinct regions, separated by Lake Michigan. Originally Michigan was to consist only of the Lower Peninsula. The boundary between Michigan and Ohio was disputed, and Ohio refused to allow Michigan to be admitted to the Union until Michigan recognized Ohio's claim. In compensation, Michigan received the Upper Peninsula, which was considered worthless at the time. It turned out to have valuable timber, iron, and copper reserves.

Review & Assess

Close
Guide students in a discussion of the weaknesses of the Articles of Confederation.

Review
Online Quiz, Section 1
Daily Test Practice Transparency

Assess
SE Section 1 Assessment
Progress Assessment: Section 1 Quiz
Alternative Assessment Handbook

Reteach
Interactive Reader and Study Guide, Section 1
Interactive Skills Tutor CD-ROM

SECTION 1 ASSESSMENT

go.hrw.com
Online Quiz
Keyword: SD7 HP5

Reviewing Ideas, Terms, and People

1. a. Define What are the characteristics of a **republic**?
b. Make Inferences Why was having a written constitution so important to Americans?
c. Predict What possible changes might result from the idea of republican motherhood?

2. a. Describe What kind of government did the **Articles of Confederation** create?
b. Evaluate Was one vote per state a weakness of the new government? Why or why not?

3. a. Identify What kinds of problems did Congress face?
b. Explain Why was it so difficult to amend the Articles of Confederation?

4. a. Describe What did the survey plan for the Northwest Territory look like?
b. Interpret What were the goals of the land laws for the Northwest Territory?

c. Elaborate How might the new land laws influence settlement in the Northwest Territory?

Critical Thinking

5. Contrasting Copy the chart below and list the powers and the weaknesses of the Confederation government.

Powers	Weaknesses

FOCUS ON WRITING

6. Persuasive As a newspaper editor in a state with large western land claims, such as New York or Virginia, write an editorial in which you support or oppose giving up your state's land claims to the central government. Use details from the section to support your argument.

CREATING A NEW GOVERNMENT **149**

Section 1 Assessment Answers

1. a. no monarch; rules with consent of the governed
b. prevented anarchy; avoided tyranny of authoritarian rulers
c. women have greater role in society

2. a. association of independent, sovereign states with certain common goals
b. yes, gave small states more power; no, made all states equal, regardless of size

3. a. financial problems, problems with the states and foreign nations
b. All 13 states had to agree.

4. a. territory divided into 10 districts
b. survey, sell, and settle; eventually bring it into the Union as 3 to 5 states
c. probably encourage it; made land available, extended civil rights, education

5. Powers—establish national policies, conduct foreign relations, borrow and coin money, set up post offices, establish an army, declare war; Weaknesses—see chart in section

6. support: we cannot govern land; oppose: we can sell land, keep revenues

Answers
Reading Check *when population reached 60,000, could write a constitution and apply for statehood*

149

The Inside Story... Use the **Daily Bellringer Transparency** to help students answer the question.

📖 Daily Bellringer Transparency, Section 2

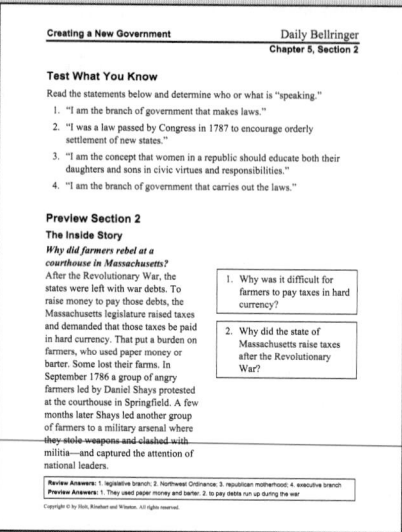

Creating a New Government   Daily Bellringer
                                             Chapter 5, Section 2

Test What You Know

Read the statements below and determine who or what is "speaking."

1. "I am the branch of government that makes laws."
2. "I was a law passed by Congress in 1787 to encourage orderly settlement of new states."
3. "I am the concept that women in a republic should educate both their daughters and sons in civic virtues and responsibilities."
4. "I am the branch of government that carries out the laws."

Preview Section 2
The Inside Story
Why did farmers rebel at a courthouse in Massachusetts?
After the Revolutionary War, the states were left with war debts. To raise money to pay those debts, the Massachusetts legislature raised taxes and demanded that those taxes be paid in hard currency. That put a burden on farmers, who used paper money or barter. Some lost their farms. In September 1786 a group of angry farmers led by Daniel Shays protested at the courthouse in Springfield. A few months later Shays led another group of farmers to a military arsenal where they stole weapons and clashed with militia—and captured the attention of national leaders.

| 1. Why was it difficult for farmers to pay taxes in hard currency? |
| 2. Why did the state of Massachusetts raise taxes after the Revolutionary War? |

Review Answers: 1. legislative branch; 2. Northwest Ordinance; 3. republican motherhood; 4. executive branch
Preview Answers: 1. They used paper money and barter. 2. to pay debts run up during the war

Copyright © by Holt, Rinehart and Winston. All rights reserved.

Academic Vocabulary

Review with students the high-use academic terms in this section.

proportion proper or equal share (p. 152)

federal national (p. 154)

📝 CRF: Vocabulary Builder Activity, Section 2

Taking Notes

Great Compromise; Three-Fifths Compromise; balance of powers

SECTION 2 Drafting the Constitution

BEFORE YOU READ

MAIN IDEA

The Constitutional Convention tried to write a document that would address the weaknesses of the Articles of Confederation and make compromises between large and small states and between the North and South.

READING FOCUS

1. What different points of view emerged at the Constitutional Convention?

2. What compromises did the delegates make at the Constitutional Convention?

3. How does a system of checks and balances prevent any one branch of the federal government from becoming too powerful?

KEY TERMS AND PEOPLE

James Madison
Constitutional Convention
Virginia Plan
New Jersey Plan
Great Compromise
Three-Fifths Compromise
checks and balances

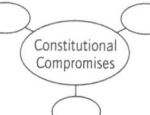

TAKING NOTES As you read, take notes identifying major compromises reached in writing the Constitution. In a diagram like the one below, list one compromise in each of the small circles.

Constitutional Compromises

THE INSIDE STORY *Why did farmers rebel at a courthouse in Massachusetts?* Times were hard after the war. To pay off the state's war debts, the Massachusetts legislature raised taxes and demanded that the taxes be paid in hard currency, not paper money. That hurt farmers in western Massachusetts, who used paper money and a barter system. Some lost their farms because they owed taxes. Some were thrown in debtors' prison.

Fed up, the farmers protested. If the courts were shut down, judges could not order the farms to be sold to pay debts. So in September 1786, Daniel Shays, a veteran who had fought at Bunker Hill, led a crowd to close the courthouse at Springfield. In January 1787, Shays led a larger group of angry farmers to break into the military arsenal at Springfield, where hundreds of guns were stored. After a short battle with Massachusetts militia, Shays and his men retreated. Four were killed.

Shays's Rebellion was only one of several taxpayers' revolts to happen during this period. The unrest alarmed some national leaders. ▪

Shays's Rebellion

▶ **Shays's forces were easily defeated, but the rebellion rang alarm bells among the nation's leaders.**

THE GRANGER COLLECTION, NEW YORK

150 CHAPTER 5

Teach the Main Idea

At Level

Drafting the Constitution

1. **Teach** Ask students the Reading Focus questions to teach this section.

2. **Apply** Have students draw three rectangles and label them with the following titles— The Great Compromise, Compromises on Slavery, and Other Compromises. Guide students in a discussion of each topic. Have students list main points of each compromise within the rectangles.

3. **Review** Discuss the provisions of the Virginia and New Jersey Plans that led to the Great Compromise.

4. **Practice/Homework** Have students write a persuasive speech in which they identify ways to solve the problems in the Articles of Confederation. Speeches should explain how the proposed changes will help preserve the nation as well as individual and states' rights. **LS Verbal-Linguistic**

📝 Alternative Assessment Handbook, Rubric 24: Oral Presentations

The Constitutional Convention

Frustration with the Articles of Confederation had been building for years, not only among farmers but also among veterans, merchants doing business between states, and creditors of the Continental Congress who had gone unpaid. A group of army officers stationed at Newburgh, New York, even launched a conspiracy in 1783 to overthrow the government, but George Washington declined the offer to lead the revolt. By fall 1786 conditions were so bad that as Shays's Rebellion began, Washington and **James Madison** were convening a meeting of five states in Annapolis, Maryland, to discuss the situation.

Washington himself had concerns about the Articles. In August 1786, he expressed these worries in a letter to John Jay, a prominent lawyer and diplomat.

HISTORY'S VOICES

❝I do not conceive we can exist long as a nation without having lodged somewhere a power, which will pervade the whole Union in as energetic a manner as the authority of the State governments extends over the several States.❞

—George Washington, Aug. 1, 1786

After the Annapolis meeting Congress called all the states to meet in Philadelphia in May 1787. According to Congress, the purpose of the Philadelphia convention was to revise the Articles of Confederation. Many states, however, sent delegates who supported a stronger central government.

A historic meeting The hot summer of 1787 was a turning point in American history. Only a few delegates arrived in Philadelphia on May 14, the day the **Constitutional Convention** was scheduled to begin. Traveling to Philadelphia over bad roads from distant states took some delegates several weeks. The meeting did not officially begin until the end of May.

Delegates from 12 states attended some or all of the meetings. (Politicians in Rhode Island opposed a stronger government and so never took part.) Each state had one vote. Decisions were made by a simple majority.

The delegates agreed to keep their discussions secret so that they could speak freely. The official secretary took only incomplete notes,

but several other delegates kept personal diaries. The best account of the convention is the detailed diary kept by James Madison. Madison took notes about the delegates, their speeches, and their votes. Because of the enormous role he played in planning and writing the final document, Madison earned the title Father of the Constitution.

The convention delegates, known today as the Framers, also included John Dickinson, Alexander Hamilton, Robert Morris, Charles Cotesworth Pinckney, and Edmund Randolph. Leading the group were George Washington and Benjamin Franklin, the most admired men in America. The convention unanimously chose Washington as its president. His strength and character made him a symbol for people in every state. His leadership would bring the convention respect and legitimacy.

The delegates were all men, and they were mostly in their thirties and forties. The youngest delegate was 26-year-old Jonathan Dayton of New Jersey. Benjamin Franklin, at 81, was the oldest.

As a group, the delegates were well-educated. Many were trained as lawyers, and about half had attended college. Others were merchants, physicians, and planters. Most had been in their state's legislature or held state office. Some had signed the Declaration of Independence. Many had served in the Revolution. Most of the delegates were wealthy.

CREATING A NEW GOVERNMENT **151**

FACES OF HISTORY

James MADISON
1751–1836

History remembers James Madison as the Father of the Constitution because of his central role at the Constitutional Convention. The detailed diary he kept during the hot summer of 1787 remains the best primary account of the Constitutional Convention. Each night Madison stayed up late to transcribe his notes, recording important speeches and votes. "Nor was I unaware of the value of such a contribution," Madison wrote, "[to] the cause of liberty throughout the world." Not only a notetaker, Madison also was one of the convention's most active participants, drafting the highly influential Virginia Plan. Later, his eloquent support of the Constitution in *The Federalist* helped bring ratification.

Interpret Why is Madison called the Father of the Constitution?

The Constitutional Convention

Recall What notable absences were there from the Constitutional Convention? *Samuel Adams, Patrick Henry, John Adams, Thomas Jefferson*

Make Inferences Why was the issue of state population troublesome for smaller states? *believed large states with more representatives might ignore the voice and wishes of small states*

Make Judgments Why do you think the New Jersey Plan called for a "plural executive" rather than a single executive? *possible answer—to keep any one person from growing too powerful and becoming a dictator*

Primary Source

"I hold it that a little rebellion now and then is a good thing, and as necessary in the political world as storms in the physical . . . An observation of this truth should render honest republican governors so mild in their punishment of rebellions as not to discourage them too much. It is a medicine necessary for the sound health of the government."

— Thomas Jefferson

on Shays's Rebellion, January 30, 1787

Biography

Royall Tyler (1757–1826) Although he served as a lawyer, teacher, and soldier, Royall Tyler is best remembered as the author of the first American comedy. A chance meeting with one of the star comedians of the American Company inspired Tyler to write *The Contrast*, which premiered in New York City in 1787. A satire of upper class customs, the play celebrated the honest patriotism of Americans and criticized the artificiality of the British. Although Tyler was unable to repeat his success with any of his other plays, *The Contrast* served as a model for future American comedies.

There were a few surprising absences from the Constitutional Convention. Several of the most fervent Patriots, such as Samuel Adams, opposed creating a stronger national government. Patrick Henry, whose fiery speeches had helped start the Revolution, also refused to attend the convention. John Adams and Thomas Jefferson did favor the convention's work but did not attend because they were on diplomatic missions abroad.

Controversial plans Almost as soon as the Constitutional Convention began, it became clear that most delegates were ready to do much more than revise the Articles of Confederation. They were ready to frame an entirely new government.

The most historic and difficult issues would involve finding a balance between the large and small states. The convention delegates would also have to find a balance between various northern and southern interests. Of tremendous importance was the emerging battle between those who wanted a strong national government and those who wanted to protect states' rights. But many smaller disagreements would make the convention long and often frustrating.

Edmund Randolph of Virginia boldly took the lead. He presented a plan that Madison had devised called the **Virginia Plan**. This plan proposed an entirely new form of national government. Many parts of Randolph's Virginia Plan were controversial, however. Government would have three separate branches: executive, legislative, and judicial. The legislature would choose an executive to carry out the laws. It would also set up a court system to interpret the laws.

Under the Virginia Plan, the national legislature would be bicameral, meaning it would have two houses, or groups of representatives. Voters would choose members of the lower house, who would then select the upper house. Members of the lower house would be chosen in proportion to each state's population. The national government would have the authority to make the states follow its laws.

THE IMPACT TODAY

Government
Today the United States has a bicameral legislature. The upper house is the Senate and the lower house is the House of Representatives. All states except Nebraska have bicameral legislatures.

ACADEMIC VOCABULARY
proportion
proper or equal share

The Constitutional Convention

Key Delegates at the Constitutional Convention

1. Roger Sherman
2. Alexander Hamilton
3. Benjamin Franklin
4. James Madison
5. George Washington
6. James Wilson

152

Skills Focus: Comparing and Contrasting · At Level

Reading Skill
Big States versus Small States

1. Organize the class into small groups. Have half of the groups prepare arguments in favor of the Virginia Plan and the other half prepare arguments in favor of the New Jersey Plan.

2. Have students use their arguments in a classroom debate on which plan would be the best to follow in creating a new national government.

3. Have each student create a handbill supporting either the Virginia Plan or the New Jersey Plan for a national government.

4. Have volunteers present their handbills to the class. **LS Kinesthetic, Visual-Spatial**

📄 Alternative Assessment Handbook, Rubrics 9: Comparing and Contrasting; and 10: Debates

Smaller states quickly objected to parts of the Virginia Plan. They were afraid of the "tyranny" of their large neighbors. For example, Virginia, the largest state in terms of population, could have 10 times as many representatives as Delaware, the smallest.

Delegates argued about Randolph's plan for several weeks. To counter it, William Paterson of New Jersey proposed a "small state" plan. The **New Jersey Plan** kept many features of the Articles of Confederation but gave Congress additional powers. The plan proposed a unicameral, or one-house, legislature. Each state would have equal representation in the legislature. The New Jersey Plan also suggested a "plural executive"—that is, two or three top executives chosen by Congress. The executive would appoint members of a supreme court. These suggestions triggered weeks of debates throughout the hot Philadelphia summer.

READING CHECK **Identifying Points of View** Why did some Patriots refuse to attend the Constitutional Convention?

Compromises at the Convention

The Virginia Plan and New Jersey Plan set the stage for major disagreements. While most delegates favored parts of the Virginia Plan, it was clear that many compromises would have to be made to satisfy smaller states.

The Great Compromise After days of argument, it looked as if the convention was at a stalemate. Some large states were hinting that they might withdraw and form their own nation. A separate committee was set up to find a way to balance the interests of large and small states.

Finally, the Connecticut delegates—Oliver Ellsworth, Roger Sherman, and Dr. William Samuel Johnson—came up with a compromise. It stated: "The two ideas . . . ought to be combined; that in one branch the people ought to be represented; in the other the States." That is, the upper house, the Senate, would

This painting shows the Framers signing the Constitution on September 17, 1787. A key accomplishment of the convention was the agreement to create a bicameral, or two-house, legislature. This agreement is called the Great Compromise.

THE GREAT COMPROMISE

Virginia Plan
(Large-state plan)
- Gave more power to state government
- Bicameral legislature
- The number of representatives for each state would be based on population.

New Jersey Plan
(Small-state plan)
- Gave more power to national government
- Unicameral legislature
- Each state would have an equal number of representatives.

THE GREAT COMPROMISE
- Bicameral legislature
- In the lower house, the number of representatives for each state is determined by population.
- In the upper house, each state has an equal number of representatives.

153

Collaborative Learning

At Level

The Great Compromise

1. Organize the class into 13 groups, each group representing one of the original 13 colonies. Assign each group a particular colony.

2. Have students in each group decide whether their colony would have supported the Virginia Plan or the New Jersey Plan. Have each group write a strong argument explaining how the plan benefits its colony and why it is the only plan the colony can support. Have a volunteer from each group read its argument to the class.

3. Have students work in their groups once more to write an explanation of the ways in which the Great Compromise benefits or hurts their assigned colony, and have students decide whether or not they can support the compromise. Again, have a volunteer from each group read its explanation to the class.

LS Verbal-Linguistic, Interpersonal

Alternative Assessment Handbook, Rubrics 14: Group Activity; and 37: Writing Assignments

153

Compromises at the Convention

Recall Which house of the legislature represents the states and which house represents the people? *Senate represents states; House of Representatives, the lower house, represents the people*

Summarize What was the effect of the Three-Fifths Compromise? *Three-fifths of the enslaved African American population in each state would be counted for both representation and taxation.*

Predict How do you think the issue of states' rights vs. federal government power will affect American history? *possible answer—The Civil War, and issues such as civil rights will pit states against the federal government.*

Activity **Three Branches of Government** Have students write a two-minute speech arguing in favor of or against the establishment of three branches of government, as proposed by Edmund Randolph. Have volunteers deliver their speeches to the class. **LS Auditory-Musical**

Teaching Tip

Remind students that because slaves were counted for taxation, they were, in essence, recognized as personal property, not as individuals. This would soon become an important issue in the history of our nation.

Answers

Reading Check *able to count part of slave population for representation and taxation*

154

---

have two representatives from each state. In the other house, representation would be based on states' population.

Today this answer may seem obvious. But it was such a major step for the convention that it is known as the **Great Compromise**. It is also called the Connecticut Compromise.

Compromises on slavery As part of the Great Compromise, delegates also had to decide on how to count population. Enslaved African Americans made up a large proportion of the population in several southern states—as much as 30 to 40 percent. Counting them in full would have given those states much greater representation in Congress. But because some taxes were based on population, it would also increase taxes.

Southern states at first wanted to count all slaves for representation purposes but none for taxation. Northern states objected. In the **Three-Fifths Compromise**, delegates agreed that all whites plus three-fifths of the slave population (referred to as "all other persons") would be counted for both representation and taxation. Native Americans were not counted.

The slavery question brought up other issues. Many people opposed slavery as immoral. Thomas Jefferson, himself a slave-holder, had tried to include a protest against it in the Declaration of Independence. Some delegates spoke eloquently about including a ban on slavery in the Constitution.

In the hope of maintaining unity between North and South, however, the delegates did not consider including a ban on slavery in the Constitution. As another compromise, they agreed to a clause allowing the slave trade to continue for 20 years. Another clause, known as the fugitive slave clause, stated that a slave who fled to another state had to be returned to his or her original state.

Other compromises Because the delegates were devising a government like no one had ever seen before, they had to consider many details. Here are some of the questions they had to answer:

- Who should choose the executive? Should the office be held by one man, or several?
- Who should be eligible to be president? How old should he be? Must the president be American-born?

ACADEMIC VOCABULARY
federal national

154 CHAPTER 5

- Who can declare war, the president or the U.S. Congress?
- What should be the term of office for the president and for members of Congress?
- Can a president be removed from office?
- Who can be a member of Congress? How old should they be? Must they be wealthy?
- Should government officials be required to belong to a certain religious faith?
- Should voters be required to own property?

Over the summer, all of these questions were raised, along with many others. Some were debated for a few hours. Other questions took weeks to resolve.

READING CHECK **Making Inferences** What benefits did the southern states gain from the Three-Fifths Compromise?

Checks and Balances

In late July 1787, a five-man committee consisting of Oliver Ellsworth, Nathaniel Gorham, Edmund Randolph, John Rutledge, and James Wilson sat down to write a final document. Their draft would include the decisions and compromises that had already been made.

By then many delegates were tired of arguing, tired of being away from home, and tired of the stiflingly hot weather. They took a 10-day holiday. George Washington and Robert Morris (in whose Philadelphia home Washington was staying) went trout fishing.

Balancing powers On August 6, delegates returned to read the draft of the Constitution that the committee had written. For more than a month they picked over the details and made changes. One big point of debate was the balance between the powers of Congress and those of the president (as the executive was now called). A related question was what powers the states should have and what powers the federal government should have.

All the delegates had taken part in a rebellion against the authority of a king. As a result, they had given much greater powers to Congress than to the president. In the first draft, Congress chose the president for one seven-year term. Popular election had been suggested, but it was voted down.

Differentiating Instruction

Below Level

Learners Having Difficulty

Remind students that the Constitution reflects compromises between large and small states and between slaveholding and free states. To help students understand the Great Compromise and the Three-Fifths Compromise, have students copy and complete the graphic organizer. Omit the italicized wording. **LS Visual-Spatial**

📓 Alternative Assessment Handbook, Rubric 13: Graphic Organizers

🖎 Graphic Organizer Transparencies

Constitutional Compromises

The Great Compromise	The Three-Fifths Compromise
Granted each state an equal voice in the upper house regardless of population	*Established that three-fifths of a state's slave population would count in determining representation and taxation*
Representation in the lower house based on state population	

Then at the end of August, James Madison said he could not support the document in its present form. This was a major blow because the entire convention had been working from his basic plan. Alarmed, they named another committee, with one delegate from each of the states. Madison represented Virginia.

The outcome was another compromise. Instead of allowing people to elect the president directly, the state legislatures would choose electors, who would then choose a president. That removed the presidency one step from the popular vote. It also took away some of the overwhelming power given to Congress.

At almost the last minute, delegates created the office of vice president. That position would go to the person who came in second in the electoral vote. (The delegates did not foresee the rise of political parties.)

These last-minute changes were important in setting up **checks and balances** among the legislative, executive, and judicial branches of government. This meant that the Constitution provided each branch with power to slow or stop an action taken by one of the other branches. These checks and balances ensured that no one branch of the government would dominate the others.

For example, the committee gave the president the power to make treaties and name judges and ambassadors. But the Senate had to give its "advice and consent" to these actions. The committee also gave the president the power to veto a law passed by Congress. But Congress could still pass any law over the president's veto provided that two-thirds of each house agreed to do so. (See the diagram on this page for more examples of checks and balances among the three branches of the federal government.)

Planning the court system The issue of the court system provoked fewer arguments. Congressional representation and the role of the president were far more divisive. But the courts were still important. Delegates wanted to keep judges and courts independent, maintaining a separation of powers.

CHECKS AND BALANCES

QUICK FACTS

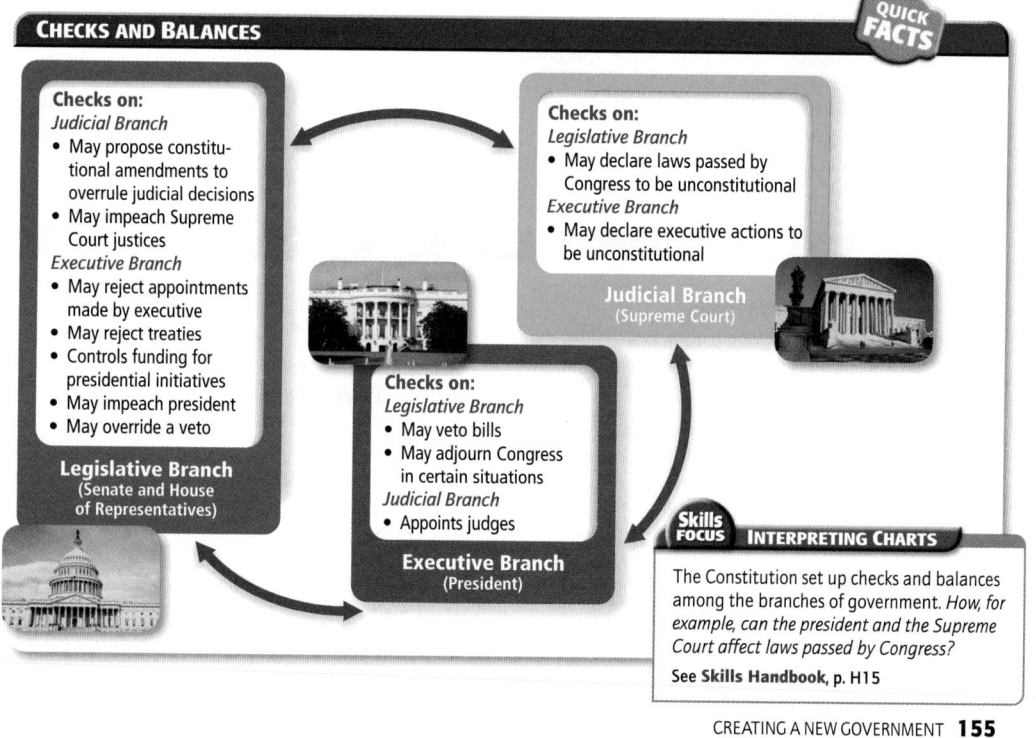

Checks on:
Judicial Branch
- May propose constitutional amendments to overrule judicial decisions
- May impeach Supreme Court justices

Executive Branch
- May reject appointments made by executive
- May reject treaties
- Controls funding for presidential initiatives
- May impeach president
- May override a veto

Legislative Branch
(Senate and House of Representatives)

Checks on:
Legislative Branch
- May declare laws passed by Congress to be unconstitutional

Executive Branch
- May declare executive actions to be unconstitutional

Judicial Branch
(Supreme Court)

Checks on:
Legislative Branch
- May veto bills
- May adjourn Congress in certain situations

Judicial Branch
- Appoints judges

Executive Branch
(President)

Skills FOCUS INTERPRETING CHARTS
The Constitution set up checks and balances among the branches of government. *How, for example, can the president and the Supreme Court affect laws passed by Congress?*
See Skills Handbook, p. H15

CREATING A NEW GOVERNMENT **155**

Skills Focus: Summarizing

Reading Skill
Checks and Balances

1. Guide students in a discussion of checks and balances and how the system works. Then have students create their own web diagrams showing the system and the relationship among the three branches. For example, Congress writes legislation; the president can veto legislation; if a law is questioned through the court system, the Supreme Court will decide if the legislation is constitutional.

2. Have volunteers present their graphic organizers to the class. Have students correct their own work and retain the diagrams as a study tool.

3. Guide students in a discussion of the ways in which checks and balances prevent abuses of power by the branches of the federal government. **LS Visual-Spatial**

📝 Alternative Assessment Handbook, Rubric 13: Graphic Organizers

📋 Graphic Organizer Transparencies

Checks and Balances

Identify Who was Gouverneur Morris? *delegate given credit for the elegant language and clarity of the Constitution*

Explain Why did some delegates choose not to sign the Constitution? *It lacked a bill of rights.*

Review & Assess

Close

Have students summarize the various compromises that had to be made by the delegates of the Constitutional Convention.

Review

- Online Quiz, Section 2
- Daily Test Practice Transparency

Assess

SE Section 2 Assessment

- Progress Assessment: Section 2 Quiz
- Alternative Assessment Handbook

Reteach

- Interactive Reader and Study Guide, Section 2
- Interactive Skills Tutor CD-ROM

Answers

Reading Check *possible answer— president makes treaties, Senate approves them; president vetoes laws, Congress can pass laws over his veto; president nominates federal judges, Senate approves them; judicial rules on constitutionality of laws*

156

At first, the delegates gave the choice of federal judges to the Senate. Then they decided to split the responsibility between the two other branches. The president would nominate judges, but the Senate would have to approve them. Judges could not be fired arbitrarily.

Final decisions As the Constitutional Convention drew to a close, a Committee on Style worked out the wording of the final draft. Madison and others gave the credit for the document's elegant language and clarity to Gouverneur Morris of Pennsylvania. Morris wrote the famous opening phrase, "We, the people of the United States."

The U.S. Constitution set out a plan of government that had never been seen before, with three separate branches. Today the basic structure of the federal government remains exactly as the Framers envisioned it over 200 years ago. The legislative branch (the House of Representatives and the Senate) makes the laws. The executive branch (the president and his advisers) carries out those laws. The judicial branch (the Supreme Court and lower courts) interprets the laws as they relate to the Constitution.

When it was time to sign the Constitution, Benjamin Franklin urged the delegates to overlook the parts of the document that they did not like because it was as close to a perfect Constitution as he thought possible:

HISTORY'S VOICES

"I confess that there are several parts of this constitution which I do not at present approve, but I am not sure I shall never approve them. For having lived long, I have experienced many instances of being obliged to change opinions even on important subjects . . . It therefore astonishes me, Sir, to find this system approaching so near to perfection as it does . . . Thus I consent, Sir, to this Constitution because I expect no better, and because I am not sure that it is not the best."

—Benjamin Franklin, quoted in James Madison's journal

Franklin urged the meeting to "act heartily and unanimously" in signing the Constitution and trying to make it work. But some of those who had worked hardest to draft the document could not, at the last minute, bring themselves to sign it. They were George Mason and Edmund Randolph of Virginia and Elbridge Gerry of Massachusetts. They would not sign because the Constitution lacked a bill of rights. Other delegates who had misgivings went ahead and signed the document anyway.

In all, 39 delegates from 12 states signed the Constitution. Then the Constitutional Convention adjourned on Monday, September 17, 1787. Now it was time for the American people to approve the document.

READING CHECK **Identifying Supporting Details** Name three instances of checks and balances in the Constitution.

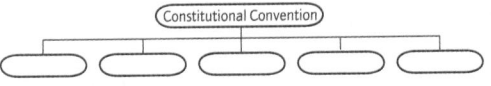

SECTION 2 ASSESSMENT

go.hrw.com
Online Quiz
Keyword: SD7 HP5

Reviewing Ideas, Terms, and People

1. **a. Recall** What were the main points of the **Virginia Plan** and the **New Jersey Plan**?
   b. Summarize How did Shays's Rebellion reveal weaknesses of the Articles of Confederation?
   c. Rate What were the most radical changes suggested in the Virginia Plan?

2. **a. Define** What was the **Great Compromise**?
   b. Explain Explain the issues the **Three-Fifths Compromise** addressed.
   c. Evaluate Did large states gain more from the Great Compromise or did small states?

3. **a. Identify** Identify the three branches of government and the role of each of them.
   b. Interpret Give one example of **checks and balances** between Congress and the president.

c. Develop How did the delegates' thinking about the office of president change during the course of the convention?

Critical Thinking

4. **Identifying Supporting Details** Copy the chart below and fill in the major issues that caused controversy at the Constitutional Convention.

Constitutional Convention

FOCUS ON SPEAKING

5. **Persuasive** As a delegate to the Constitutional Convention, write a speech in which you outline what you think ought to be the requirements for a senator.

156 CHAPTER 5

Section 2 Assessment Answers

1. **a.** Virginia—three branches of government, bicameral legislature, representation based on population; New Jersey—unicameral legislature, equal representation for all states
   b. government could not fight rebellion
   c. an independent executive; representation in legislature based on state population

2. **a.** combined ideas of Virginia and New Jersey Plans
   b. counting of slaves for taxation and representation
   c. possible answer—small states, because it

gave them equality with large states

3. **a.** legislative makes laws; executive carries out laws; judicial interprets laws
   b. Congress passes laws, but the president can veto them.
   c. initially wanted to give more power to Congress than to president

4. makeup of the legislature; state representation; role of the executive; how slaves would be counted; election of executive

5. U.S. citizen, well educated, strong leader

SECTION 3 Ratifying the Constitution

BEFORE YOU READ

MAIN IDEA

Federalists and Antifederalists struggled over the principles of the new Constitution. But the promise of adding a Bill of Rights brought about ratification.

READING FOCUS

1. What arguments for and against the Constitution were put forth by Federalists and Antifederalists?
2. What ideas were published in *The Federalist*?
3. Why was adding a Bill of Rights significant in the ratification process?

KEY TERMS AND PEOPLE

Federalist
Antifederalist
Alexander Hamilton
Brutus
Bill of Rights
Publius
The Federalist
John Jay
delegated powers
reserved powers

 TAKING NOTES As you read, take notes on the reasons for adding a Bill of Rights to the Constitution. You may want to organize your reasons in a diagram like this one.

Reasons for a Bill of Rights

A Rising Sun or a Setting Sun?

 **THE INSIDE STORY**

Will the Constitution succeed? It was the final day of the Constitutional Convention: September 17, 1787. The aging Benjamin Franklin, always a shrewd politician, knew it was important for the convention delegates to appear united. But down to the last minute, some delegates were still arguing. Local loyalties were still strong.

Franklin offered a final persuasive speech, read aloud by another delegate. He said that the new Constitution might not be perfect, but it was the best one possible.

Then the convention's oldest delegate made a motion that the meeting approve the Constitution unanimously. Although individual delegates still disagreed, every state present said yes. Delegates stepped forward, one at a time, to sign the document. Stories say there were tears in Franklin's eyes as he picked up the quill pen. He looked toward the chair where George Washington had sat to preside over the meeting. The image of a sun was painted on the back.

James Madison described the scene: Franklin remarked that painters had trouble showing the difference between a rising and a setting sun. He went on, "I have often and often in the course of Session . . . looked at that [sun] behind the president without being able to tell whether it was rising or setting. But now at length I have the happiness to know that it is a rising and not a setting Sun." ◢

◀ **The sunburst on the back of Washington's chair symbolized faith in the new Constitution.**

157

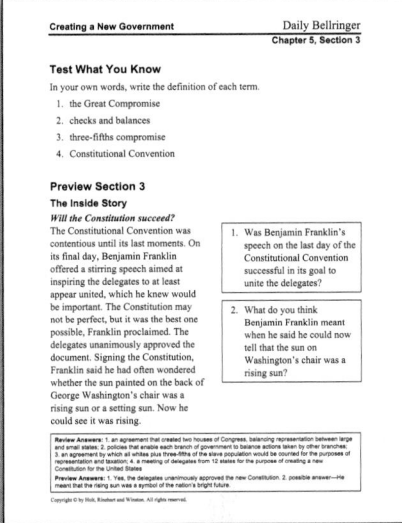

Preteach

Bellringer

The Inside Story. . . Use the **Daily Bellringer Transparency** to help students answer the question.

🖎 Daily Bellringer Transparency, Section 3

Academic Vocabulary

Review with students the high-use academic term in this section.

deviate depart from a standard or principle (p. 161)

📝 CRF: Vocabulary Builder Activity, Section 3

Taking Notes

protect basic individual liberties, protect states' interests; gain Antifederalists' support for Constitution

Teach the Main Idea

At Level

Ratifying the Constitution

1. **Teach** Ask students the Reading Focus questions to teach this section.

2. **Apply** To help students put the ratification of the Constitution in perspective, have them work in pairs to create a time line for this section. Have them include all the events in this section that have specific dates.

3. **Review** Review student time lines as a class. Have students call out the events in order, with their dates. As they do so, create a time line for the class to see. Time lines

should begin with the meeting of delegates at the Philadelphia Convention and end with the approval of the Bill of Rights.

4. **Practice/Homework** Have each student write an editorial either supporting or opposing ratification of the Constitution. Student editorials should include valid arguments in support of their positions.

🔲 Visual-Spatial, Verbal-Linguistic

📝 Alternative Assessment Handbook, Rubrics 17: Letters to Editors; and 36: Time Lines

1 What arguments for and against the Constitution were put forth by Federalists and Antifederalists?
Federalists said a strong national government was necessary for the survival of the republic. Antifederalists distrusted central authority and thought the new government favored the elites.

Federalists and Antifederalists

Explain What was the greatest fear of the Antifederalists? *that strong government would lead to tyranny and abuse of individual rights*

Analyze Why was the Federalist cause unpopular outside the cities? *The Federalists were distrusted as an educated, wealthy, urban elite.*

Evaluate Why were the Antifederalists unsuccessful in preventing the ratification of the Constitution even though they outnumbered the Federalists? *less organized and less unified than their opponents; more diverse*

Activity **Ratification Slogan**
Have students create a slogan that supports the ratification of the Constitution. **LS Verbal-Linguistic**

📰 Political Cartoons Activity for American History: Cartoon 9: Announcing the Constitution

go.hrw.com
Online Resources
KEYWORD: SD7 CH5
TOPIC: FEDERALISTS AND
ANTIFEDERALISTS

Federalists and Antifederalists

The delegates who met at Philadelphia in May 1787 expected to revise the Articles of Confederation and make the government stronger. Instead, they essentially threw out the Articles and wrote a new Constitution. The new Constitution put forth a framework for a strong national government with certain powers left to the states. It declared that the Constitution would be the "supreme law of the land."

The Philadelphia Convention had been held in secret. As the meeting continued through the summer of 1787, people wondered what it would produce. When the Constitution was finally published, the drastic changes surprised and angered some people. Many remembered British tyranny and feared the idea of a too-powerful national government. That led to a 10-month struggle over ratification.

Supporters and opponents of the new Constitution immediately began to present their arguments. Supporters of the Constitution, once called nationalists, were now known as **Federalists**. Opponents of the Constitution were called **Antifederalists**.

The Federalist viewpoint Supporters of the new Constitution had an advantage from the beginning. To begin with, they had been studying and defending their points of view all during the Constitutional Convention. They had their arguments ready.

The Federalists also had strong leaders such as Madison, John Dickinson, and the brilliant young **Alexander Hamilton**. Born in the West Indies, Hamilton had been Washington's aide during the Revolutionary War. Federalists also had the backing of George Washington and Benjamin Franklin.

Like Franklin, most Federalists admitted that the Constitution was not perfect but was the best they could do. They believed that a strong national government was necessary for the survival of the republic. They wanted government to end chaos and be a check on the kind of mob rule seen during Shays's Rebellion. At the same time, they pointed out that the separation of powers in the Constitution put limits on government power.

The Federalist cause was generally popular in the cities, but Federalists were outnumbered in the general population. Especially in the rural western parts of the states, some people saw the Federalists as an educated, wealthy, urban elite. They distrusted them.

Still, the Federalists were well organized and knew how to gather political support. As soon as the Constitution was written, they quickly began to work for its ratification.

The Antifederalist viewpoint Although they outnumbered the Federalists, those who had doubts about the Constitution were at a disadvantage. First, the term "Antifederalists" suggested that they were simply *against* something, without a plan of their own. In a sense, that was true. Many Antifederalists admitted there were flaws in the Articles of Confederation. They wanted a new government, but not the one outlined in the Constitution. Mainly, Antifederalists tried to warn people about flaws in the proposed government.

The Antifederalists were less organized and less unified than their opponents. They were more diverse, coming from different economic backgrounds and social classes. Their core consisted of farmers and planters.

Antifederalists did agree on one central issue: They distrusted any central authority. They were afraid that a strong national government would lead to a kind of tyranny—exactly what they had fought against in the Revolution. Antifederalists worried that the central government outlined in the Constitution would abuse both states' rights and individual liberties. They did not trust any government to protect the people's rights. Many also thought the new government favored the educated and wealthy over ordinary people.

Some opponents argued that a republic could not succeed in a nation as large as the United States. They also criticized specific features such as the role of the president, the number of congressional representatives, and the length of senatorial terms.

The Antifederalists had many strong leaders. Some, like Samuel Adams, Patrick Henry, and Richard Henry Lee, had opposed the convention from the beginning. Mercy Otis Warren, the colonial writer, warned it would create tyranny. In a typically fiery speech at the

Differentiating Instruction

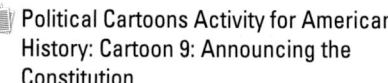

Below Level

Learners Having Difficulty

Materials construction paper, colored markers

1. Organize students into small groups. Have each group design a Web page for the Federalists and a Web page for the Antifederalists.

2. Web pages should include a title, general information about the site, and a list of links to supporting pages within the site. Linking pages might provide basic arguments of the group, key points in their arguments, or links to primary sources.

3. Have students draw their Web pages on the construction paper, and have volunteers share their Web pages with the class.

4. As an extension for at level students or advanced learners, have students create a blog about ratifying the Constitution. **LS Visual-Spatial, Kinesthetic**

📰 Alternative Assessment Handbook, Rubric 3: Artwork

Political Cartoon

This political cartoon was published soon after the ninth state, New Hampshire, ratified the Constitution.

United we stand—Divided we fall

The pillars represent the colonies in the order in which they ratified the Constitution.

A hand comes down from heaven to help hold up the pillars.

Virginia became the tenth state to ratify the Constitution, only after the addition of a bill of rights was promised.

Skills Focus READING LIKE A HISTORIAN

Identifying Points of View What does the hand supporting the pillar reflect about the artist's view of the new country and its Constitution?

See Skills Handbook, pp. H28–H29

Virginia ratifying convention, Patrick Henry even claimed that the convention delegates did not have the authority to create a completely new government.

HISTORY'S VOICES

❝My political curiosity . . . leads me to ask, who authorised them to speak the language of, *We, the People,* instead of *We, the States?* . . . The Federal Convention ought to have amended the old system—for this purpose they were solely delegated . . . You must therefore forgive the solicitation of one unworthy member, to know what danger could have arisen under the present confederation, and what are the causes of this proposal to change our Government.❞

—Patrick Henry, June 1788

George Mason, who had refused to sign the Constitution, also worked actively against its ratification. So did Robert Yates, a delegate from New York. Under the name **Brutus**, Yates wrote a number of anti-Constitution essays.

The ratification process The concerns of the Antifederalists led them to demand the addition of a **Bill of Rights**. Because they did

not trust government, they wanted to spell out some basic rights in the Constitution to make sure those rights would be protected. Adding a Bill of Rights became the main focus of the struggle over ratification.

The Framers knew that getting unanimous agreement would be hard. Article VII of the Constitution explained what must be done to bring the constitution into effect. Only 9 of the 13 states had to ratify, or approve, the Constitution. Some people thought that nine states were not enough to authorize a complete change of government. But the Confederation Congress, which was still technically the American government, approved.

To make ratification more likely, the Framers bypassed the state legislatures, which would lose considerable power to the new national government. Instead, they called for special ratifying conventions in each state. In the fall of 1787 the battle over ratification began.

READING CHECK **Drawing Conclusions** Why did their experience as colonists make some people suspicious of central government?

---

❷ What ideas were published in *The Federalist*? *explanations of the advantages that the ratification of the Constitution would bring; explanations of republican government and politics*

The Federalist Papers

Identify Who was Publius? *pen name used by James Madison, Alexander Hamilton, John Jay, who wrote* The Federalist

Summarize How did the Federalists respond to the arguments and fears of the Antifederalists? *by writing the Federalist Papers*

Elaborate Why do you think the combination of Hamilton's and Madison's writing might have helped sway opinion about the Constitution? *Madison wrote about political theory in support of the Constitution, while Hamilton gave practical arguments in favor of ratification; in this way, they were able to appeal to many people.*

📄 CRF: Primary Source Activity: Debating the New Constitution

Counterpoints

Federalist vs. Antifederalist

Antifederalist writers Tell students that both Federalists and Antifederalists published hundreds of essays and pamphlets during the debate over ratification of the Constitution. Many Antifederalist writers used pseudonyms derived from classical sources, as in the *Letters of Brutus*.

Answers

Reading Like a Historian *Words such as "precious blood," "arrayed with certain dignities," "radical," "endangered," and "relinquished" would suggest opinion. Facts include that there was a revolution, and Americans were killed; a resolution separated the colonies from Great Britain.*

Federalist vs. Antifederalist

In Federalist No. 45, James Madison argued that the states were too powerful under the Articles of Confederation.

Patrick Henry spoke against the proposed Constitution, saying it took power away from the states.

❝ Was, then, the American Revolution effected, was the American Confederacy formed, was the precious blood of thousands spilt, . . . not that the people of America should enjoy peace, liberty, and safety, but that the government of the individual States . . . might enjoy a certain extent of power, and be arrayed with certain dignities and attributes of sovereignty?" ❞

James Madison, 1787

❝ Here is a resolution as radical as that which separated us from Great Britain. It is radical in this transition; our rights and privileges are endangered, and the sovereignty of the states will be relinquished. ❞

Patrick Henry, 1788

Skills FOCUS READING LIKE A HISTORIAN

Distinguishing Fact from Opinion Which parts of these quotations are fact, and which parts are opinion?
See Skills Handbook, pp. H28–H29

THE THOMAS GILCREASE INSTITUTE OF AMERICAN HISTORY AND ART, TULSA, OKLAHOMA

The Federalist Papers

In late 1787, people in New York opened their newspapers to find a series of essays written under the pen name **Publius**. By spring, 85 essays on government had appeared. Addressed "To the People of the State of New York," they were first published in New York newspapers. Later, the essays circulated widely in other states and were collected in a book called *The Federalist*, also known as the Federalist Papers.

The anonymous Publius discussed and defended each part of the Constitution. The main goal of the essays was to persuade New York delegates to ratify the document by explaining the advantages it would bring. But they were also brilliant explanations of republican government and politics.

Writing *The Federalist* Publius was in fact three leading Federalists: James Madison, Alexander Hamilton, and **John Jay**. Their names were kept secret until 1802. Hamilton and Madison wrote most of the essays in *The Federalist*, and Jay supplied a few. Historians are still not entirely certain of the authorship of every essay in *The Federalist*.

Ideas in *The Federalist* Madison, on whose ideas the Constitution was based, wrote about political theory in his essays. Hamilton offered practical arguments for a strong government.

In *Federalist* No. 1, Hamilton introduced the series. He told his readers that the decision they were about to make was important for the whole world. He noted:

HISTORY'S VOICES

❝ . . . it seems to have been reserved to the people of this country . . . to decide the important question, whether societies of men are really capable or not of establishing good government from reflection and choice, or whether they are forever destined to depend for their political constitutions on accident and force. ❞

–The Federalist No. 1

Differentiating Instruction

Above Level

Advanced Learners/GATE

Research Required

1. Have students visit the Library of Congress Web site, thomas.loc.gov and locate Federalist Paper Number 6, which was written by James Madison. Have students read the paper, which is a four-page account on the dangers of tensions between the states. Have students take notes on the document and outline the information.

2. Have students use their notes and the document to develop an editorial response that might have appeared in a newspaper of the time. In addition, have students create a political cartoon to accompany their editorial.

3. Have volunteers share their cartoons and editorials with the class. 🄻 **Verbal-Linguistic, Intrapersonal**

📄 Alternative Assessment Handbook, Rubrics 17: Letters to Editors; and 27: Political Cartoons

Hamilton also listed the subjects of future essays, including how the Constitution would help preserve republican government, liberty, and property.

In *Federalist* No. 10, Madison warned against the dangers of factions—groups with specific, often opposing, interests. Factional fights had torn apart some European governments. But Madison argued that factions were a natural part of American society and that suppressing such groups would destroy liberty. Instead, a republican government would help balance their influence. In *Federalist* No. 51, Madison explained how the separation of powers described in the Constitution would limit government powers.

The Constitutional Convention had spent less time discussing the judiciary than the other branches. In *Federalist* No. 78, Hamilton said that the lack of a judiciary was one flaw in the Articles of Confederation. He explained the importance of an independent judiciary. He also discussed the Supreme Court's power to consider whether a law is constitutional.

READING CHECK **Summarizing** What were the main arguments made by the authors of *The Federalist*?

Adding a Bill of Rights

Even before the Constitution was signed, it was clear that the lack of a bill of rights was going to cause trouble. The three delegates who refused to sign the Constitution in Philadelphia had been the first indication that there might be problems.

For example, George Mason had written Virginia's Declaration of Rights. He said he could quickly write a national one. On the other hand, Roger Sherman of Connecticut pointed out that most state constitutions already had bills of rights and he believed that was enough. Others agreed, and the convention voted down all moves to add a bill of rights. As a result, Mason did not sign the Constitution. He never <u>deviated</u> from his opposition, hurting his friendship with Madison and Washington.

The fight for ratification When the ratification battle began, the Federalists were better prepared than their opponents. They quickly organized and gained control of several state conventions, especially in small states.

Pennsylvania's convention met first, but Delaware moved more quickly. On December 7, 1787, Delaware became the first state to ratify the Constitution, with a unanimous "yes" vote. Pennsylvania followed days later, approving it by two to one. Within the first two weeks of 1788, New Jersey, Georgia, and Connecticut also had ratified it.

Massachusetts was a bigger challenge. Elbridge Gerry led a strong opposition there. Yet the Massachusetts vote had the potential to influence delegates in other states with large Antifederalist forces, such as New York, Virginia, and North Carolina. Federalists went to work to persuade prominent men such as John Hancock. By a close 187–168 vote, Massachusetts ratified on February 6, 1788. Its resolution, however, included a number of suggested amendments.

ACADEMIC VOCABULARY
deviate depart from a standard or principle

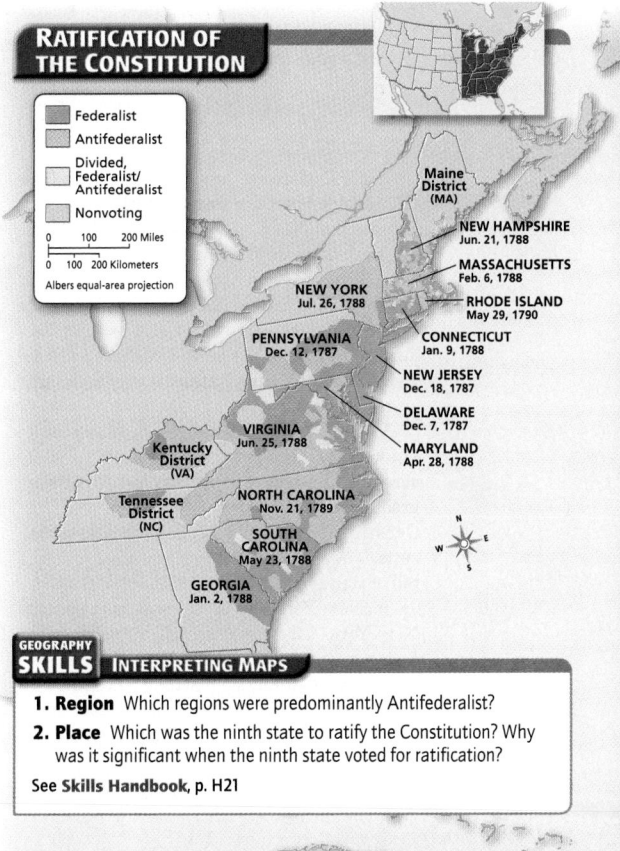

RATIFICATION OF THE CONSTITUTION

- Federalist
- Antifederalist
- Divided, Federalist/ Antifederalist
- Nonvoting

0   100   200 Miles
0   100   200 Kilometers
Albers equal-area projection

Maine District (MA)

NEW HAMPSHIRE Jun. 21, 1788

MASSACHUSETTS Feb. 6, 1788

NEW YORK Jul. 26, 1788

RHODE ISLAND May 29, 1790

PENNSYLVANIA Dec. 12, 1787

CONNECTICUT Jan. 9, 1788

NEW JERSEY Dec. 18, 1787

DELAWARE Dec. 7, 1787

VIRGINIA Jun. 25, 1788

Kentucky District (VA)

MARYLAND Apr. 28, 1788

Tennessee District (NC)

NORTH CAROLINA Nov. 21, 1789

SOUTH CAROLINA May 23, 1788

GEORGIA Jan. 2, 1788

GEOGRAPHY SKILLS **INTERPRETING MAPS**

1. **Region** Which regions were predominantly Antifederalist?
2. **Place** Which was the ninth state to ratify the Constitution? Why was it significant when the ninth state voted for ratification?

See **Skills Handbook, p. H21**

Info to Know
The Authors of the Federalist Papers
The Federalist Papers can be viewed as anonymous marketing efforts on the part of James Madison, John Jay, and Alexander Hamilton. Their writings appealed to the common man, and the trio believed in their product, the Constitution. All three served the new nation later: James Madison as president; John Jay as first Chief Justice of the Supreme Court; and Alexander Hamilton as George Washington's secretary of the treasury.

Adding a Bill of Rights

Explain What was the purpose of the Bill of Rights? *to protect individuals and states against too much government power*

Make Judgments Do you think the Framers understood how important the Bill of Rights would be? *possible answers—Yes, these amendments are a basic guarantee of rights colonists had come to expect. No, it was impossible for people to understand how these amendments would come to represent basic rights of citizens throughout the world.*

📄 CRF: Primary Source Activity: Thomas Jefferson's Act for Establishing Religious Freedom

📄 Political Cartoons Activities for American History: Cartoon 10: The Temple of Liberty

Info to Know

Antifederalists and the Bill of Rights Originally James Madison opposed the idea of a bill of rights. Only when Antifederalists in Massachusetts threatened to demand a second Constitutional Convention did he draft one. His original bill of rights included 17 amendments. That version was approved by the House of Representatives and sent on to the Senate. The Senate approved only 12 of the original 17. Of the 12 amendments sent to the states, only the ten we now know as the Bill of Rights were ratified.

Answers

American Civil Liberty *The First Amendment guarantees freedom of speech and of the press, and this amendment applies to the Internet.*

162

The First Amendment

The First Amendment protects freedom of religion, freedom of speech, freedom of the press, and the right to peaceably assemble. For over 200 years, these have been familiar rights to Americans.

In recent years, some people have wondered: Do First Amendment rights apply on the Internet? People can create Web sites on almost any topic. While many people feel some sites contain indecent or dangerous material, in the United States the First Amendment guarantees freedom of speech on the Internet.

Many other countries also encourage freedom of speech on the Internet. Some, however, strictly limit how their citizens use this technology. For example, China does not allow criticism of the government or support for oppressed religious minorities. The government of Saudi Arabia also limits Internet use. Leaders identify Web sites that they consider offensive and block access to them.

Contrasting Why is Internet access not limited in the United States as it is in some other countries?

Americans young and old exercise their First Amendment rights to assemble at a peace rally.

Federalists were less worried about New Hampshire but were unpleasantly surprised. Ratification failed on the first vote. The state did not ratify until June 1788. In the meantime, Maryland and South Carolina said yes.

That made up the nine states needed for the Constitution to go into effect. But without New York and Virginia, the United States would not be much of a country. Ratification of both large states was a must.

Virginia was oddly divided. Many large landowners opposed the Constitution, while some frontier people supported it. To Madison's great relief, the state narrowly approved "his" Constitution in June 1788. Like Massachusetts, Virginia demanded a promise to add a bill of rights.

In New York the battle was between the New York City area, which supported the Federalists, and the rest of the state. Governor George Clinton led a strong Antifederalist force, while Hamilton and his allies worked tirelessly for ratification. They even hinted that the city might secede and ratify separately. Some opponents began to see that being

outside the Union would be an economic disaster for the state. New York at last ratified in July by a vote of only 30–27.

With 11 states, the new government could now go ahead. In September 1788, the Congress of the Confederation took its final actions. It set dates in early 1789 for elections to choose members of Congress and presidential electors. The last two states, North Carolina and Rhode Island, did not join the Union until after the new government was already at work.

Constitutional amendments Several crucial states had ratified the Constitution only because they were promised a bill of rights. Once the new Congress was elected, it needed to add that bill of rights in the form of amendments to the Constitution. Article V of the Constitution gave either Congress or state conventions the right to propose amendments.

It was not only the Antifederalists who wanted a bill of rights. It was in the Federalists' interests to support one, too. Besides, most Federalists did not oppose a bill of rights. They simply did not think one was necessary.

Collaborative Learning

At Level

The Powers of Government

1. Guide students in a discussion of the concepts of delegated powers and reserved powers as they are defined in the Tenth Amendment.

2. Organize the class into small groups. Have each group make a list of personal activities that involve some level of national or state government, such as registering for the armed services, mailing letters, spending money, opening a checking account, and so on. Have volunteers from each group read their lists and create a class list of the activities.

3. Have volunteers identify each of the activities on the class list as being regulated by the national government, the state government, or both. Label those regulated by the national government as *Delegated*, those regulated by state governments as *Reserved*, and those regulated by both levels as *Concurrent*.

LS Interpersonal, Logical-Mathematical

📄 Alternative Assessment Handbook, Rubric 11: Discussions

Now Madison took charge of getting a bill of rights through Congress. In fact, he insisted on bringing up the issue. On June 8, 1789, Madison spoke to Congress and proposed some amendments. He pointed out that in England the constitution limited only the king's power, not Parliament's. These changes, he said, would protect against all abuses of power:

HISTORY'S VOICES

❝ . . . if all power is subject to abuse, that then it is possible the abuse of the powers of the General Government may be guarded against in a more secure manner than is now done. . . . We have in this way something to gain, and, if we proceed with caution, nothing to lose. ❞

–James Madison, June 8, 1789

In September 1789 Congress approved 12 amendments based on the ideas Madison had presented. As the Constitution required, they were sent to the states for approval. By the end of 1791, the state had approved 10 of them. These 10 amendments became the Bill of Rights.

The Bill of Rights The Bill of Rights protected both individuals and states against what people feared might be too much government power. The first eight amendments dealt with individual civil liberties. The Ninth Amendment stated that listing certain rights given to the people did not mean that other rights did not exist as well.

Most of the amendments echoed the rights spelled out in the Virginia Declaration of Rights. The First Amendment guaranteed civil liberties such as freedom of speech, the press, and religion. The amendments addressed problems from British colonial rule, such as the quartering of soldiers and illegal searches. Some amendments drew on rights provided in ancient English law, such as trial by jury. The complete text of the Constitution and the Bill of Rights follows this chapter.

States' rights Most of the amendments in the Bill of Rights listed things that no government, state or federal, could do. The final amendment addressed the actions that states could take. It answered Antifederalist fears about the loss of states' rights and sovereignty.

The Tenth Amendment defined two kinds of government powers. The Constitution gives certain powers to each branch of the national government. Those are the **delegated powers**. Some powers are expressly stated. Other powers are implied.

The Tenth Amendment also defined the **reserved powers**. Those are powers that the Constitution does not specifically give to the federal government or deny to the states. The Tenth Amendment says that the reserved powers belong to the states or to the people.

READING CHECK **Making Inferences** Why did Madison lead the fight for a bill of rights?

Reviewing Ideas, Terms, and People

1. **a. Identify** Identify three leaders on each side of the Federalist–Antifederalist debate.
   b. Make Generalizations What were the Antifederalists' main objections to the Constitution?
   c. Evaluate Why was the lack of the **Bill of Rights** so important in the ratification struggle?

2. **a. Recall** Who were the authors of *The Federalist*?
   b. Explain In *Federalist* No. 10, what was Madison's attitude toward factions in a republic?
   c. Predict What might Madison say about the role of factions, or political parties, in politics today?

3. **a. Recall** Which state was first to ratify the Constitution? Which states were crucial to the Constitution's success?
   b. Summarize What kinds of rights were promised in the first eight amendments to the Constitution?

c. Evaluate How has the Bill of Rights been important in American history since 1791?

Critical Thinking

4. **Identifying Supporting Details** Copy the chart below and use it to show examples of First Amendment rights.

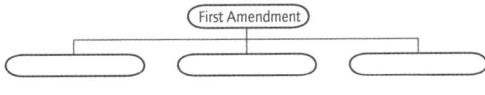

First Amendment

FOCUS ON WRITING

5. **Persuasive** As a member of the Congress elected in 1789, describe five or six amendments you would propose to add to the Bill of Rights. Explain your reasons.

Section 3 Assessment Answers

1. **a.** Federalists: James Madison, Alexander Hamilton, John Jay; Antifederalists: Samuel Adams, Patrick Henry, Richard Henry Lee
   b. distrusted central authority; worried about states' rights and individual liberties; thought new government favored elites
   c. concern over states' rights, individual liberties

2. **a.** Hamilton, Madison, Jay
   b. natural part of American society; suppressing them would destroy liberty; republican government would help balance

their influence
   c. possible answer—factional fights might tear government apart

3. **a.** Delaware; New York, Virginia
   b. individual civil liberties
   c. has protected individual and states' rights

4. freedom of speech; freedom of the press; freedom of religion

5. possible answers—any of the first ten amendments; women's right to vote; making slavery illegal

---

Direct Teach

Recent Scholarship

John Jay: Founding Father, written by lawyer Walter Stahr, is an in-depth look at one of the vital founding fathers. Jay served as president of the Continental Congress, secretary of foreign affairs, first Chief Justice of the Supreme Court, governor of New York, and was negotiator of the Treaty of Paris and one of the authors of *The Federalist*.

John Jay: Founding Father by Walter Stahr. Hambleton & London, 2005

Review & Assess

Close

Guide the class in a discussion of the arguments made by Federalists and Antifederalists over ratification of the Constitution.

Review

⬛ Online Quiz, Section 3

⬛ Daily Test Practice Transparency

Assess

SE Section 3 Assessment

⬛ Progress Assessment: Section 3 Quiz

⬛ Alternative Assessment Handbook

Reteach

⬛ Interactive Reader and Study Guide, Section 3

⬛ Interactive Skills Tutor CD-ROM

Answers

Reading Check *He knew that several crucial states had ratified the Constitution only because a bill of rights had been promised.*

163

Forming a Government

Word Help

expedient useful in bringing about a desirable result

abolition putting an end to

sanction approval

ineligible not able to be chosen

intervened came between

lay a train set the course

re-eligible re-electable

patrimony inheritance, particularly from one's father

intermission break, interruption

Info to Know

The Father of the Constitution James Madison was a small man with a high, squeaky voice. He was more at home with his books than in public—until he was inspired to greatness by the Constitutional Convention. Madison had studied the governments of the past. In preparation for the Constitutional Convention, he wrote two documents. The first was titled "Notes on Ancient and Modern Confederacies." Among the things that caught his attention were differences in the sizes of provinces, intolerance of religion, and weaknesses of a union. He then used the knowledge he had gained to write the detailed "Notes on the Confederacy" about the failings of the government that had been set up by the Articles of Confederation. In the second of these documents, he looked ahead toward a new constitution. He also began to develop the ideas about factions and large republics that would be discussed in *Federalist* No. 10.

Forming a Government

Historical Context The documents below provide different information about the debates that led to ratification of the U.S. Constitution.

Task Examine the documents and answer the questions that follow. Then write an essay about the Constitution. Use facts from the documents and from the chapter to support the position you take in your thesis statement.

DOCUMENT 1

During the Constitutional Convention, Virginia delegate James Madison took extensive notes, including these notes on whether the Constitution should ban any further importation of slaves.

"**Mr. Sherman** [Connecticut]: was for leaving the clause as it stands. He disapproved of the slave trade; yet as the States were now possessed of the right to import slaves, as the public good did not require it to be taken from them, & as it was expedient to have as few objections as possible to the proposed scheme of Government, he thought it best to leave the matter as we find it . . . He observed that the abolition of slavery seemed to be going on in the U.S. & that the good sense of the several States would probably by degrees [complete] it . . .

Mr. E[l]lsworth [Connecticut]: As he had never owned a slave could not judge of the effects of slavery on character: He said however that if it was to be considered in a moral light we ought to go farther and free those already in the Country . . . As population increases poor laborers will be so plenty as to render slaves useless. Slavery in time will not be a speck in our Country . . .

Mr. Pinckney [South Carolina]: If slavery be wrong, it is justified by the example of all the world. He cited the case of Greece Rome & other ancient States; the sanction given by France, England, Holland & other modern States . . . In all ages one half of mankind have been slaves. . . . An attempt to take away the right as proposed will produce serious objections to the Constitution which he wished to see adopted . . ."

164 CHAPTER 5

DOCUMENT 2

The delegates also discussed the powers of the presidency (the executive), which was at one point to be elected by Congress (the legislature). They debated whether to have one president or several, how long a term should be, and whether to limit the number of terms.

"**Mr. Strong** [Massachusetts]: supposed that there would be no necessity, if the Executive should be appointed by the Legislature, to make him ineligible a [second] time; as new elections of the Legislature will have intervened; and he will not depend for his [second] appointment on the same [set] of men as his first was [received] from . . .

Mr. Williamson [North Carolina]: was for going back to the original ground; to elect the Executive for 7 years and render him ineligible a second time . . . He did not like the Unity in the Executive. He had wished the Executive power to be lodged in three men taken from three districts into which the States should be divided. . . . Another objection [against] a single Magistrate [executive] is that he will be an elective King, and will feel the spirit of one. He will spare no pains to keep himself in for life, and then will lay a train for the succession of his children. It was pretty certain he thought that we should have a King; but he wished no precaution to be omitted that might postpone the event as long as possible. Ineligibility a second time appeared to him to be the best precaution. With this precaution he had no objection to a longer term than 7 years. He would go as far as 10 or 12 years . . . "

Skills Focus: Making Oral Presentations ⟨At Level⟩

Reading Like a Historian Skill
Debating the Constitution

1. Divide the class into two groups. Have one group represent the Federalists in the 1787 debate over the ratification of the Constitution. Have the other group represent the Antifederalists. Have each side prepare supporting arguments for its position.

2. Conduct a classroom debate on the ratification of the Constitution.

3. Have each student write an editorial from the perspective of either a Federalist or

Antifederalist in 1787. Student editorials should contain valid, well-supported reasoning.

4. Have volunteers read their editorials to the class. **LS Auditory-Musical, Verbal-Linguistic**
   Alternative Assessment Handbook, Rubrics 10: Debates; and 17: Letters to Editors

DOCUMENT 3

The Federalist was a collection of essays by James Madison, Alexander Hamilton, and John Jay supporting ratification of the new Constitution. In *Federalist* No. 69, Hamilton addressed fears that a strong president would be like a monarch.

"[The president] is to be elected for four years, and is to be re-eligible as often as the people of the United States shall think him worthy of their confidence. In these circumstances there is a total dissimilitude [lack of similarity] between him and a king of Great Britain, who is an hereditary monarch, possessing the crown as a patrimony descendible to his heirs forever; but there is a close analogy between him and a governor of New York, who is elected for three years, and is re-eligible without limitation or intermission . . .

The President . . . would be liable to be impeached, tried, and, upon conviction of treason, bribery, or other high crimes or misdemeanors, removed from office; and would afterwards be liable to prosecution and punishment in the ordinary course of law. The person of the king of Great Britain is sacred and inviolable; there is . . . no punishment to which he can be subjected without involving the crisis of a national revolution."

DOCUMENT 4

The table below summarizes the 10 amendments that make up the Bill of Rights.

THE BILL OF RIGHTS

1st Amendment	Protects freedom of religion, speech, press, assembly, petition
2nd Amendment	Protects the right to bear arms
3rd Amendment	Provides restrictions on quartering soldiers in citizens' homes
4th Amendment	Bans unreasonable searches or seizures
5th Amendment	Protects citizens against self-incrimination and being tried twice for the same crime; prohibits government from depriving citizens of life, liberty, or property without due process of law
6th Amendment	Protects citizens' rights to a swift and fair trial
7th Amendment	Guarantees right to trial by jury
8th Amendment	Protects citizens against cruel and unusual punishment
9th Amendment	States that citizens have rights beyond those specifically written in the Constitution
10th Amendment	States that all powers not given to the government are reserved to the states, or to the people

Skills FOCUS — READING LIKE A HISTORIAN

1. a. Identify Refer to Document 1. Which of these delegates objected most strongly to the slave trade?
b. Evaluate How does this debate reflect different attitudes toward slavery in the North and the South?

2. a. Identify Refer to Document 2. Why does Williamson think the executive should be three people?
b. Predict What problems might have developed if Williamson's plan had been adopted?

3. a. Recall Refer to Document 3. According to Hamilton, how is the United States president different from the king of Great Britain?
b. Infer Why might this essay have convinced some people to support the Constitution?

4. a. Identify Refer to Document 4. Which amendment guarantees freedom of expression?
b. Analyze Why do you think some states thought that a Bill of Rights was essential?

5. Document-Based Essay Question Consider the question below and form a thesis statement. Using examples from Documents 1, 2, 3, and 4, create an outline and write a short essay supporting your position.
What roles did debate and compromise play in the development and ratification of the Constitution?

See Skills Handbook, pp. H14, H28–29

CREATING A NEW GOVERNMENT **165**

Info to Know

The Federalist Papers Alexander Hamilton originally answered the New York opponents to the Constitution with a series of letters in newspapers signed "Caesar." When those letters seemed to have no effect, Hamilton turned to his *Federalist* collaborators, James Madison and John Jay. In writing *The Federalist*, the authors assumed that a person's main political motive was self-interest. Because of this, they argued, it was necessary to create political institutions that would make up for such human shortcomings. They believed that a strong central government was necessary to ensure law and order and prevent anarchy, such as that exhibited in Shays's Rebellion. Many of the authors' most effective arguments were directed at businessmen. The writers appealed to businessmen's self-interest, pointing out that trade would best thrive under a strong federal government. Because this interpretation of the Constitution is so brilliant, the U.S. Supreme Court has often referred to *The Federalist* in controversial cases.

Answers

Reading Like a Historian
1. a. *Mr. Ellsworth;* **b.** *possible answer—northerners hoped slavery would die out or be abolished; southerner justified slavery and saw as necessary to approval of the Constitution;*
2. a. *thought a single president would act like a king and try to hold onto power;* **b.** *possible answer—difficult to reach consensus with three different leaders;*
3. a. *president stands for re-election; king passes crown to descendants;* **b.** *president elected by people, can be removed from office, punished for crimes; very different from a monarch;*
4. a. *the 1st Amendment;* **b.** *possible answer—necessary to protect people's and states' rights;* **5.** *possible answer—significant role; Great Compromise, Three-Fifths Compromise, election of president, court system, bill of rights, Federalists, Antifederalists*

Collaborative Learning

At Level

The Bill of Rights

1. Divide the class into small groups. Have each group make a list of rights that they think should be protected by the Constitution. Students may refer to the Bill of Rights, but they should come up with their own lists and may include rights not mentioned in the Bill of Rights.

2. Have students select one of the rights from their group's list and write a brief essay

explaining why that right is important. Each student in a group should choose a different right to explain.

3. Have volunteers read their essays to the class. Then guide the class in a discussion of why the rights included in the Bill of Rights were chosen. **LS Interpersonal, Verbal-Linguistic**

📖 Alternative Assessment Handbook, Rubric 41: Writing to Express

165

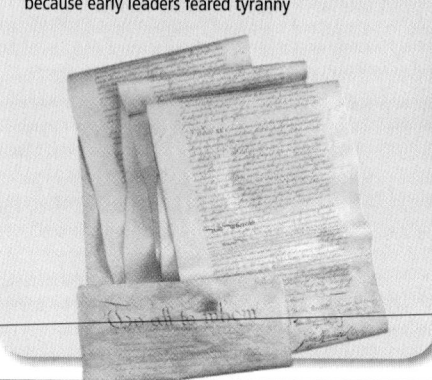

Visual Summary: Creating a New Government

The Articles of Confederation (ratified 1781)
- America's first written constitution
- A loose union of sovereign states
- Designed to make the central government weak because early leaders feared tyranny

The U.S. Constitution (ratified 1788)
- Replaced the Articles of Confederation
- Provided representation for all states
- Established three branches of government (executive, legislative, judicial) with separation of powers to avoid tyranny
- Created checks and balances among the three branches
- Bill of Rights later added (ratified 1791)

Reviewing Key Terms and People

Identify the correct term or person from the chapter that best fits each of the following descriptions.

1. The Father of the Constitution
2. Compromise at the Constitutional Convention that counted three-fifths of enslaved Africans when determining representation in Congress
3. Compromise at the Constitutional Convention that established a bicameral legislature
4. A political system without a monarch that rules with the consent of the governed
5. System that helps prevent one branch of government from becoming too strong
6. Branch of government that makes the laws
7. Branch of government that carries out the laws
8. Branch of government that interprets the laws
9. Supporters of the Constitution, also known as nationalists
10. Opponents of the Constitution
11. Name for the first 10 amendments to the Constitution
12. Name of the 1785 plan for surveying, selling, and settling the Northwest Territory
13. Series of newspaper articles in support of the proposed Constitution
14. Powers given to the branches of the national government under the Constitution

History's Impact video program
Review the video to answer the closing question:
How does the Bill of Rights protect the personal
freedoms of Americans?

Comprehension and Critical Thinking

SECTION 1 *(pp. 144–149)*

15. a. Identify What was a republican mother?

b. Explain What does it mean to *ratify* something?

c. Draw Inferences What fear led the new republic to limit the powers of its central government?

SECTION 2 *(pp. 150–156)*

16. a. Recall What was Shays's Rebellion?

b. Summarize What compromises were made at the Constitutional Convention?

c. Elaborate How do checks and balances prevent any one branch of government from becoming too powerful?

SECTION 3 *(pp. 157–163)*

17. a. Identify What were the Federalist Papers?

b. Summarize What did Federalists believe? What did Antifederalists believe?

c. Evaluate Why was the Bill of Rights necessary for ratification of the Constitution?

Using the Internet

go.hrw.com
Practice Online
Keyword: SD7 CH5

18. a. Using the keyword above, research a leader of the Constitutional Convention or a noted Federalist or Antifederalist. Then write a short biography of the person you chose. Be sure to explain why your person supported or did not support ratification of the Constitution.

b. Create a multimedia presentation that explains the proceedings of the Constitutional Convention. Profile some of the indivduals at the proceedings, the challenges they faced, and their accomplishments.

Analyzing Primary Sources

Reading Like a Historian Judith Sargent Murray wrote the following about the differences in boys' education and girls' education.

> ❝ How is the one exalted, and the other depressed, by the contrary modes of education which are adopted! The one is taught to aspire, and the other is early confined and limited. As their years increase, the sister must be wholly domesticated, while the brother is led by the hand through all the flowery paths of science. ❞
>
> —Judith Sargent Murray, quoted in *Founding Mothers*

19. Make Inferences What does the phrase "the flowery paths of science" suggest?

20. Draw Conclusions What is Judith Sargent Murray's opinion about differences in the education of boys and girls?

Critical Reading

Read the passage in Section 1 that begins with the heading "Economic problems." Then answer the questions that follow.

21. How did the end of the war with Great Britain affect the economy of the southern states?

A Southerners could now sell more indigo and naval stores to Great Britain.

B British financial aid to certain American industries ended, hurting those industries.

C Enslaved Africans who had sided with the British returned to plantation work.

D Southern plantations stopped producing indigo.

22. What led to inflation after the Revolutionary War?

A American paper money was not backed by gold or silver.

B Farmers had a lot of extra money to spend.

C The central government imposed high taxes.

D Currency in Great Britain lost value.

FOCUS ON WRITING

Expository Writing *Expository writing gives information, explains why or how, or defines a process. To practice expository writing, complete the assignment below.*

Writing Topic The U.S. Constitution

23. How was the U.S. Constitution an improvement upon the Articles of Confederation? Write a short essay in which you develop your position on this issue. Support your explanation with reasoning and examples from your reading and studies. If you have access to a computer, use a word processing program to create and format your essay.

Answers

Critical Reading

21. B

22. A

Focus on Writing

23. possible answer—The Constitution remedied many shortcomings of the Articles of Confederation. It provided a strong central government that could prevent future anarchy of the sort represented by Shays's Rebellion. It provided a three-part government that had the power to execute laws and judicial powers. It included a system of checks and balances to prevent any branch from becoming too powerful. It included the Bill of Rights, which protected individual rights.

A rubric for this activity is provided in the Chapter Resource File: Focus on Writing: The United States Constitution.

History's Impact
Video Program

lists individual civil liberties that are protected; also says that other rights may exist as well

Review and Assessment Resources

Review and Reinforce

- CRF: Chapter Review Activity
- Quick Facts Transparencies: Weaknesses of the Articles of Confederation, The Great Compromise, Checks and Balances, Creating a New Government
- Spanish Chapter Summaries Audio CD Program
- Online Chapter Summaries in Spanish
- OSP Holt PuzzlePro; Quiz Show for ExamView
- Quiz Game CD-ROM

Assess

- PASS: Chapter Test, Forms A and B
- Alternative Assessment Handbook
- OSP ExamView Test Generator, Chapter Test
- Differentiated Instruction Modified Worksheets and Tests CD-ROM: Chapter Test
- HOAP Holt Online Assessment Program (in the Premier Online Edition)

Reteach/Intervene

- Interactive Reader and Study Guide
- Differentiated Instruction Teacher Management System: Lesson Plans for Differentiated Instruction
- Differentiated Instruction Modified Worksheets and Tests CD-ROM: Chapter Test
- Interactive Skills Tutor CD-ROM

go.hrw.com
Online Resources
KEYWORD: SD7 CH5

The Constitution of the UNITED STATES

THE BIG PICTURE The Constitution has remained the central document of American government for more than two centuries. It established three branches of government—legislative, executive, and judicial. The first 10 amendments, known as the Bill of Rights, focus on personal liberties.

NC North Carolina Standards

Social Studies Objectives

1.01 Identify the major domestic issues and conflicts experienced by the nation during the Federalist Period.

Skills FOCUS READING LIKE A HISTORIAN

Tourists line up to view the Declaration of Independence and the Constitution of the United States in the rotunda of the National Archives Building in Washington, D.C. Above them hangs a mural depicting the Founders. **Interpreting Visuals** How does this photograph link the past with the present?

See Skills Handbook, p. H30

168

169

Primary Source

"The Constitution of the United States was created by the people of the United States composing the respective states, who alone had the right. "

— James Madison

September 1829

"The proposed Constitution is, in strictness, neither a national nor a federal constitution; but a composition of both."

— James Madison

The Federalist

Reading Like a Historian

Interpreting Visuals The mural shown in this image depicts Thomas Jefferson preparing to hand a draft of the Declaration of Independence to John Hancock. Another mural showing George Washington receiving a draft of the Constitution from James Madison hangs opposite the one depicted here. Both measure 14' x 35' and were created in 1936 by muralist Barry Faulkner.

Answers

Reading Like a Historian (p. 168)
The Framers are pictured in the mural; contemporary visitors are shown viewing the Constitution.

Motivate

Bring in the daily newspaper and read the headlines of several articles or editorials to the students. Ask students to explain the relationship between the headlines and the Constitution. Students should immediately note that the Constitution guarantees freedom of the press, so the newspapers can print articles that support or oppose government policies. Guide students in a discussion of the ways the Constitution affects them every day.

Building Vocabulary

Before you begin teaching the Constitution, have students make flash cards with the vocabulary that is called out in the margins of each page. Have students work in pairs to quiz each other on the terms.

Info to Know

The Preamble Although short, the Preamble was hotly debated in the state ratifying conventions. The delegates objected to the Preamble's opening phrase "We the People," because they had been appointed by the states rather than elected by the people. Patrick Henry challenged this phrase during the ratifying process in Virginia, saying "the People gave them [the delegates to the Constitutional Convention] no power to use their name. That they exceeded their power is perfectly clear."

Teaching Tip

Some students may have trouble reading the Roman numerals that appear in the Constitution. Before starting the document, spend a few minutes going over the Roman numeral system with the class. If possible, provide students with a chart defining Roman numerals through 30.

The Constitution of the United States

Preamble
The short and dignified preamble explains the goals of the new government under the Constitution.

We the People of the United States, in Order to form a more perfect Union, establish Justice, insure domestic Tranquility, provide for the common defense, promote the general Welfare, and secure the Blessings of Liberty to ourselves and our Posterity, do ordain and establish this Constitution for the United States of America.

Note: The parts of the Constitution that have been lined through are no longer in force or no longer apply because of later amendments. The titles of the sections and articles are added for easier reference.

170

Article I The Legislature

Section 1. Congress

All legislative Powers herein granted shall be vested in a Congress of the United States, which shall consist of a Senate and House of Representatives.

Section 2. The House of Representatives

1. Elections The House of Representatives shall be composed of Members chosen every second Year by the People of the several States, and the Electors in each State shall have the Qualifications requisite for Electors of the most numerous Branch of the State Legislature.

2. Qualifications No Person shall be a Representative who shall not have attained to the Age of twenty five Years, and been seven Years a Citizen of the United States, and who shall not, when elected, be an Inhabitant of that State in which he shall be chosen.

3. Number of Representatives Representatives and direct Taxes shall be apportioned among the several States which may be included within this Union, according to their respective Numbers, which shall be determined by adding to the whole Number of free Persons, including **those bound to Service**[1] for a Term of Years, and excluding Indians not taxed, three fifths of **all other Persons**.[2] The actual **Enumeration**[3] shall be made within three Years after the first Meeting of the Congress of the United States, and within every subsequent Term of ten Years, in such Manner as they shall by Law direct. The Number of Representatives shall not exceed one for every thirty Thousand, but each State shall have at Least one Representative; and until such enumeration shall be made, the State of New Hampshire shall be entitled to choose three, Massachusetts eight, Rhode-Island and Providence Plantations one, Connecticut five, New-York six, New Jersey four, Pennsylvania eight, Delaware one, Maryland six, Virginia ten, North Carolina five, South Carolina five, and Georgia three.

4. Vacancies When vacancies happen in the Representation from any State, the Executive Authority thereof shall issue Writs of Election to fill such Vacancies.

5. Officers and Impeachment The House of Representatives shall choose their Speaker and other Officers; and shall have the sole Power of impeachment.

Exploring the Document

Recall How many senators are elected from each state? *two*

Summarize What privileges are outlined in Article I, Section 6? *Senators and representatives are paid for their services out of the U.S. Treasury, and they have a number of other privileges, including immunity from arrest except in cases of treason, felony, and breach of peace.*

🎲 Quick Facts Transparency: Federal Office Terms and Requirements

Info to Know

The Seventeenth Amendment Senators are no longer "chosen by the Legislature thereof," but rather are elected by the people of their state. The Seventeenth Amendment made this change to the Constitution. Before voting, all citizens have the responsibility to learn about the candidates, such as senators and other officials.

Section 3. The Senate

1. Number of Senators The Senate of the United States shall be composed of two Senators from each State, ~~chosen by the Legislature thereof,~~ for six Years; and each Senator shall have one Vote.

2. Classifying Terms Immediately after they shall be assembled in Consequence of the first Election, they shall be divided as equally as may be into three Classes. The Seats of the Senators of the first Class shall be vacated at the Expiration of the second Year, of the second Class at the Expiration of the fourth Year, and of the third Class at the Expiration of the sixth Year, so that one third may be chosen every second Year; ~~and if Vacancies happen by Resignation, or otherwise, during the Recess of the Legislature of any State, the Executive thereof may make temporary Appointments until the next Meeting of the Legislature, which shall then fill such Vacancies.~~

3. Qualifications No Person shall be a Senator who shall not have attained to the Age of thirty Years, and been nine Years a Citizen of the United States, and who shall not, when elected, be an Inhabitant of that State for which he shall be chosen.

4. Role of Vice-President The Vice President of the United States shall be President of the Senate, but shall have no Vote, unless they be equally divided.

5. Officers The Senate shall choose their other Officers, and also a President pro tempore,[4] in the Absence of the Vice President, or when he shall exercise the Office of President of the United States.

6. Impeachment Trials The Senate shall have the sole Power to try all Impeachments.[5] When sitting for that Purpose, they shall be on Oath or Affirmation. When the President of the United States is tried, the Chief Justice shall preside: And no Person shall be convicted without the Concurrence of two thirds of the Members present.

7. Punishment for Impeachment Judgment in Cases of Impeachment shall not extend further than to removal from Office, and disqualification to hold and enjoy any Office of honor, Trust or Profit under the United States: but the Party convicted shall nevertheless be liable and subject to Indictment, Trial, Judgment and Punishment, according to Law.

The Vice President

The only duty that the Constitution assigns to the vice president is to preside over meetings of the Senate. Modern presidents have usually given their vice presidents more responsibilities.

EXPLORING THE DOCUMENT If the House of Representatives charges a government official with wrongdoing, the Senate acts as a court to decide if the official is guilty. *How does the power of impeachment represent part of the system of checks and balances?*

Vocabulary

[4] **pro tempore** temporarily

[5] **Impeachments** official accusations of federal wrongdoing

FEDERAL OFFICE TERMS AND REQUIREMENTS				
Position	**Term**	**Minimum Age**	**Residency**	**Citizenship**
President	4 years	35	14 years in the United States	natural-born
Vice President	4 years	35	14 years in the United States	natural-born
Supreme Court Justice	unlimited	none	none	none
Senator	6 years	30	state in which elected	9 years
Representative	2 years	25	state in which elected	7 years

Answers

Exploring the Document *allows one branch of government to exert power over another branch of government*

Section 4. Congressional Elections

1. Regulations The Times, Places and Manner of holding Elections for Senators and Representatives, shall be prescribed in each State by the Legislature thereof; but the Congress may at any time by Law make or alter such Regulations, except as to the Places of choosing Senators.

2. Sessions ~~The Congress shall assemble at least once in every Year, and such Meeting shall be on the first Monday in December, unless they shall by Law appoint a different Day.~~

Section 5. Rules/Procedures

1. Quorum Each House shall be the Judge of the Elections, Returns and Qualifications of its own Members, and a Majority of each shall constitute a **Quorum**[6] to do Business; but a smaller Number may **adjourn**[7] from day to day, and may be authorized to compel the Attendance of absent Members, in such Manner, and under such Penalties as each House may provide.

2. Rules and Conduct Each House may determine the Rules of its Proceedings, punish its Members for disorderly Behaviour, and, with the Concurrence of two thirds, expel a Member.

3. Records Each House shall keep a Journal of its Proceedings, and from time to time publish the same, excepting such Parts as may in their Judgment require Secrecy; and the Yeas and Nays of the Members of either House on any question shall, at the Desire of one fifth of those Present, be entered on the Journal.

4. Adjournment Neither House, during the Session of Congress, shall, without the Consent of the other, adjourn for more than three days, nor to any other Place than that in which the two Houses shall be sitting.

Section 6. Payment

1. Salary The Senators and Representatives shall receive a Compensation for their Services, to be ascertained by Law, and paid out of the Treasury of the United States. They shall in all Cases, except Treason, Felony and Breach of the Peace, be privileged from Arrest during their Attendance at the Session of their respective Houses, and in going to and returning from the same; and for any Speech or Debate in either House, they shall not be questioned in any other Place.

2. Restrictions No Senator or Representative shall, during the Time for which he was elected, be appointed to any civil Office under the Authority of the United States, which shall have been created, or the **Emoluments**[8] whereof shall have been increased during such time; and no Person holding any Office under the United States, shall be a Member of either House during his **Continuance**[9] in Office.

Vocabulary

[6] **Quorum** the minimum number of people needed to conduct business

[7] **adjourn** to stop indefinitely

[8] **Emoluments** salary

[9] **Continuance** term

Exploring the Document

Describe What bills may a president veto? *any bills passed by both houses and presented to him for approval*

Explain What is required to override a presidential veto? *two-thirds majority vote of Congress*

Analyze Why do you think a larger legislative majority is required to override a presidential veto than to pass a bill? *to balance power between the executive and legislative branches*

Activity **Political Cartoon** Ask students to find out what is meant by a "pocket veto." Then have them create a political cartoon to illustrate the purpose of this legislative maneuver and how it works. **LS** Visual-Spatial

Info to Know

The Line-Item Veto In 1996 Congress passed the line-item veto, which gave the president the power to cancel specific items in spending bills. Supporters of the law hoped that it would help stop wasteful spending by allowing the president to prevent spending that he or she considered unnecessary. However, almost immediately a group of lawmakers challenged the line-item veto on constitutional grounds. In June 1998 the Supreme Court struck down the line-item veto and confirmed a lower court's ruling that it was unconstitutional.

Vocabulary

[10] **Bills** proposed laws

EXPLORING THE DOCUMENT The Framers felt that because members of the House are elected every two years, representatives would listen to the public and seek its approval before passing taxes. *How does Section 7 address the colonial demand of "no taxation without representation"?*

EXPLORING THE DOCUMENT The veto power of the president is one of the important checks and balances in the Constitution. *Why do you think the Framers included the ability of Congress to override a veto?*

Section 7. [How a Bill Becomes a Law]

1. Tax Bills All **Bills**[10] for raising Revenue shall originate in the House of Representatives; but the Senate may propose or concur with Amendments as on other Bills.

2. Lawmaking Every Bill which shall have passed the House of Representatives and the Senate, shall, before it become a Law, be presented to the President of the United States: If he approve he shall sign it, but if not he shall return it, with his Objections to that House in which it shall have originated, who shall enter the Objections at large on their Journal, and proceed to reconsider it. If after such Reconsideration two thirds of that House shall agree to pass the Bill, it shall be sent, together with the Objections, to the other House, by which it shall likewise be reconsidered, and if approved by two thirds of that House, it shall become a Law. But in all such Cases the Votes of both Houses shall be determined by yeas and Nays, and the Names of the Persons voting for and against the Bill shall be entered on the Journal of each House respectively. If any Bill shall not be returned by the President within ten Days (Sundays excepted) after it shall have been presented to him, the Same shall be a Law, in like Manner as if he had signed it, unless the Congress by their Adjournment prevent its Return, in which Case it shall not be a Law.

3. Role of the President Every Order, Resolution, or Vote to which the Concurrence of the Senate and House of Representatives may be necessary (except on a question of Adjournment) shall be presented to the President of the United States; and before the Same shall take Effect, shall be approved by him, or being disapproved by him, shall be repassed by two thirds of the Senate and House of Representatives, according to the Rules and Limitations prescribed in the Case of a Bill.

HOW A BILL BECOMES A LAW

❶ A member of the House or the Senate introduces a bill and refers it to a committee.

❷ The House or Senate Committee may approve, rewrite, or kill the bill.

❸ The House or the Senate debates and votes on its version of the bill.

❹ House and Senate conference committee members work out the differences between the two versions.

❺ Both houses of Congress pass the revised bill.

Answers

Exploring the Document (top)
All tax bills originate in the House of Representatives whose members are elected by people from their legislative districts. **(bottom)** *to provide the legislative branch with a check on the executive branch; to prevent the president from having too much power*

Section 8.
Powers Granted to Congress

1. Taxation The Congress shall have Power To lay and collect Taxes, **Duties,**[11] **Imposts**[12] and **Excises,**[13] to pay the Debts and provide for the common Defense and general Welfare of the United States; but all Duties, Imposts and Excises shall be uniform throughout the United States;

2. Credit To borrow Money on the credit of the United States;

3. Commerce To regulate Commerce with foreign Nations, and among the several States, and with the Indian Tribes;

4. Naturalization and Bankruptcy To establish an uniform **Rule of Naturalization,**[14] and uniform Laws on the subject of Bankruptcies throughout the United States;

5. Money To coin Money, regulate the Value thereof, and of foreign Coin, and fix the Standard of Weights and Measures;

6. Counterfeiting To provide for the Punishment of counterfeiting the **Securities**[15] and current Coin of the United States;

7. Post Office To establish Post Offices and post Roads;

8. Patents and Copyrights To promote the Progress of Science and useful Arts, by securing for limited Times to Authors and Inventors the exclusive Right to their respective Writings and Discoveries;

9. Courts To constitute Tribunals inferior to the supreme Court;

10. International Law To define and punish Piracies and Felonies committed on the high Seas, and Offences against the Law of Nations;

Linking TO Today

Native Americans and the Commerce Clause

The commerce clause gives Congress the power to "regulate Commerce with . . . the Indian Tribes." The clause has been interpreted to mean that the states cannot tax or interfere with businesses on Indian reservations, but that the federal government can. It also allows Native American nations to develop their own governments and laws. These laws, however, can be challenged in federal court. Although reservation land usually belongs to the government of the Indian group, it is administered by the U.S. government.

Drawing Conclusions How would you describe the status of Native American nations under the commerce clause?

Vocabulary

[11] **Duties** tariffs

[12] **Imposts** taxes

[13] **Excises** internal taxes on the manufacture, sale, or consumption of a commodity

[14] **Rule of Naturalization** a law by which a foreign-born person becomes a citizen

[15] **Securities** bonds

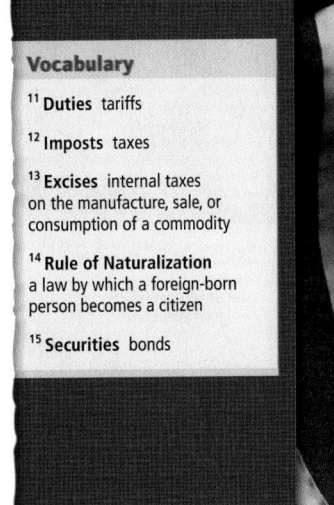

6 The president signs or vetoes the bill.

7 Two-thirds majority vote of Congress is needed to approve a vetoed bill. Bill becomes a law.

ANALYSIS SKILL **ANALYZING INFORMATION**

Why do you think the Framers created this complex system for adopting laws?

Exploring the Document

Describe What do Clauses 11–16 ensure and regulate? *control of the military*

Summarize What congressional powers are explained in Clause 17? *Congress has the power to make laws for the District of Columbia, the nation's capital. Congress also has the power to regulate use of other property belonging to the national government, such as forts and arsenals.*

Make Inferences Why do you think the Framers of the Constitution included a clause prohibiting titles of nobility? *Students might respond that the Framers wanted to make sure that no class system or aristocracy would exist in the United States as it did in Great Britain.*

Activity **The Elastic Clause** Ask students to conduct research on the minimum wage law or on the creation of military academies as examples of when the elastic clause was used to meet the changing needs of American society. Then have each student write a letter to the Framers of the Constitution. In their letters, students should use their research to explain how future government officials have used the elastic clause and their authority responsibly. **LS Verbal-Linguistic**

Vocabulary

[16] **Letters of Marque and Reprisal** documents issued by governments allowing merchant ships to arm themselves and attack ships of an enemy nation

11. War To declare War, grant **Letters of Marque and Reprisal**,[16] and make Rules concerning Captures on Land and Water;

12. Army To raise and support Armies, but no Appropriation of Money to that Use shall be for a longer Term than two Years;

13. Navy To provide and maintain a Navy;

14. Regulation of the Military To make Rules for the Government and Regulation of the land and naval Forces;

15. Militia To provide for calling forth the Militia to execute the Laws of the Union, suppress Insurrections and repel Invasions;

16. Regulation of the Militia To provide for organizing, arming, and disciplining, the Militia, and for governing such Part of them as may be employed in the Service of the United States, reserving to the States respectively, the Appointment of the Officers, and the Authority of training the Militia according to the discipline prescribed by Congress;

17. District of Columbia To exercise exclusive Legislation in all Cases whatsoever, over such District (not exceeding ten Miles square) as may, by Cession of particular States, and the Acceptance of Congress, become the Seat of the Government of the United States, and to exercise like Authority over all Places purchased by the Consent of the Legislature of the State in which the Same shall be, for the Erection of Forts, Magazines, Arsenals, dock-Yards, and other needful Buildings;—And

18. Necessary and Proper Clause To make all Laws which shall be necessary and proper for carrying into Execution the foregoing Powers, and all other Powers vested by this Constitution in the Government of the United States, or in any Department or Officer thereof.

The Elastic Clause

The Framers of the Constitution wanted a national government that was strong enough to be effective. This section lists the powers given to Congress. The last portion of Section 8 contains the so-called elastic clause.

THE ELASTIC CLAUSE

The elastic clause has been stretched (like elastic) to allow Congress to meet changing circumstances.

Section 9. Powers Denied Congress

1. Slave Trade ~~The Migration or Importation of such Persons as any of the States now existing shall think proper to admit, shall not be prohibited by the Congress prior to the Year one thousand eight hundred and eight, but a Tax or duty may be imposed on such Importation, not exceeding ten dollars for each Person.~~

2. Habeas Corpus The Privilege of the **Writ of Habeas Corpus**[17] shall not be suspended, unless when in Cases of Rebellion or Invasion the public Safety may require it.

3. Illegal Punishment No **Bill of Attainder**[18] or **ex post facto Law**[19] shall be passed.

4. Direct Taxes No **Capitation**,[20] or other direct, Tax shall be laid, unless in Proportion to the Census or enumeration herein before directed to be taken.

5. Export Taxes No Tax or Duty shall be laid on Articles exported from any State.

6. No Favorites No Preference shall be given by any Regulation of Commerce or Revenue to the Ports of one State over those of another; nor shall Vessels bound to, or from, one State, be obliged to enter, clear, or pay Duties in another.

7. Public Money No Money shall be drawn from the Treasury, but in Consequence of Appropriations made by Law; and a regular Statement and Account of the Receipts and Expenditures of all public Money shall be published from time to time.

8. Titles of Nobility No Title of Nobility shall be granted by the United States: And no Person holding any Office of Profit or Trust under them, shall, without the Consent of the Congress, accept of any present, Emolument, Office, or Title, of any kind whatever, from any King, Prince, or foreign State.

Section 10. Powers Denied the States

1. Restrictions No State shall enter into any Treaty, Alliance, or Confederation; grant Letters of Marque and Reprisal; coin Money; emit Bills of Credit; make any Thing but gold and silver Coin a Tender in Payment of Debts; pass any Bill of Attainder, ex post facto Law, or Law impairing the Obligation of Contracts, or grant any Title of Nobility.

2. Import and Export Taxes No State shall, without the Consent of the Congress, lay any Imposts or Duties on Imports or Exports, except what may be absolutely necessary for executing it's inspection Laws: and the net Produce of all Duties and Imposts, laid by any State on Imports or Exports, shall be for the Use of the Treasury of the United States; and all such Laws shall be subject to the Revision and Control of the Congress.

3. Peacetime and War Restraints No State shall, without the Consent of Congress, lay any Duty of Tonnage, keep Troops, or Ships of War in time of Peace, enter into any Agreement or Compact with another State, or with a foreign Power, or engage in War, unless actually invaded, or in such imminent Danger as will not admit of delay.

EXPLORING THE DOCUMENT Although Congress has implied powers, there are also limits to its powers. Section 9 lists powers that are denied to the federal government. Several of the clauses protect the people of the United States from unjust treatment. *In what ways does the Constitution limit the powers of the federal government?*

Vocabulary

[17] **Writ of Habeas Corpus** a court order that requires the government to bring a prisoner to court and explain why he or she is being held

[18] **Bill of Attainder** a law declaring that a person is guilty of a particular crime

[19] **ex post facto Law** a law that is made effective prior to the date that it was passed and therefore punishes people for acts that were not illegal at the time

[20] **Capitation** a direct uniform tax imposed on each head, or person

THE CONSTITUTION OF THE UNITED STATES **177**

Identify Which branch of the government is outlined in Article II? *the executive branch*

Make Inferences Why might many of the delegates to the Constitutional Convention have opposed a one-person executive? *Students might suggest that the delegates feared that they might create another monarchy, as in Great Britain.*

Summarize How are the president and vice president elected? *They are chosen by the electoral college—electors chosen by the states according to rules established by the legislatures.*

📽 Map Transparency: The Electoral College

Info to Know

The U.S. President Initially, the writers of the Constitution agreed that the president would be chosen by the national legislature for a single, seven-year term. Many delegates opposed a strong executive branch. However, when the Constitution was turned over to the Committee on Style, Gouverneur Morris, who wanted a stronger executive, reworded the article outlining the role of the president. He shortened the role of the president's term, allowed the president to run for more than one term, and altered the method by which the president would be elected. These changes passed with little debate for several reasons. For one, the delegates were ready to go home. For another, many members thought that George Washington would be the first president and believed that he would not abuse the power of the executive branch.

Executive Branch

The president is the chief of the executive branch. It is the job of the president to enforce the laws. The Framers wanted the president's and vice president's terms of office and manner of selection to be different from those of members of Congress. They decided on four-year terms, but they had a difficult time agreeing on how to select the president and vice president. The Framers finally set up an electoral system, which differs greatly from our electoral process today.

Presidential Elections

In 1845 Congress set the Tuesday following the first Monday in November of every fourth year as the general election date for selecting presidential electors.

Article II The Executive

Section 1. The Presidency

1. Terms of Office The executive Power shall be vested in a President of the United States of America. He shall hold his Office during the Term of four Years, and, together with the Vice President, chosen for the same Term, be elected, as follows:

2. Electoral College Each State shall appoint, in such Manner as the Legislature thereof may direct, a Number of Electors, equal to the whole Number of Senators and Representatives to which the State may be entitled in the Congress: but no Senator or Representative, or Person holding an Office of Trust or Profit under the United States, shall be appointed an Elector.

3. Former Method of Electing President ~~The Electors shall meet in their respective States, and vote by Ballot for two Persons, of whom one at least shall not be an Inhabitant of the same State with themselves. And they shall make a List of all the Persons voted for, and of the Number of Votes for each; which List they shall sign and certify, and transmit sealed to the Seat of the Government of the United States, directed to the President of the Senate. The President of the Senate shall, in the Presence of the Senate and House of Representatives, open all the Certificates, and the Votes shall then be counted.~~

THE ELECTORAL COLLEGE

11 Number of Electors

WA 11, OR 7, ID 4, MT 3, ND 3, MN 10, WI 10, MI 17, NY 31, VT 3, NH 4, ME 4, MA 12, RI 4, CT 7, NJ 15, DE 3, MD 10, PA 21, WV 5, VA 13, OH 20, IN 11, IL 21, IA 7, NE 5, SD 3, WY 3, NV 5, UT 5, CA 55, CO 9, KS 6, MO 11, KY 8, NC 15, TN 11, SC 8, AZ 10, NM 5, OK 7, AR 6, MS 6, AL 9, GA 15, TX 34, LA 9, FL 27, AK 3, HI 4, Washington, D.C. 3

GEOGRAPHY SKILLS INTERPRETING MAPS

Place Which two states have the most electors?

Answers

Interpreting Maps *California and Texas*

The Person having the greatest Number of Votes shall be the President, if such Number be a Majority of the whole Number of Electors appointed; and if there be more than one who have such Majority, and have an equal Number of Votes, then the House of Representatives shall immediately choose by Ballot one of them for President; and if no Person have a Majority, then from the five highest on the List the said House shall in like Manner choose the President. But in choosing the President, the Votes shall be taken by States, the Representation from each State having one Vote; A quorum for this purpose shall consist of a Member or Members from two thirds of the States, and a Majority of all the States shall be necessary to a Choice. In every Case, after the Choice of the President, the Person having the greatest Number of Votes of the Electors shall be the Vice President. But if there should remain two or more who have equal Votes, the Senate shall choose from them by Ballot the Vice President.

4. Election Day The Congress may determine the Time of choosing the Electors, and the Day on which they shall give their Votes; which Day shall be the same throughout the United States.

5. Qualifications No Person except a natural born Citizen, or a Citizen of the United States, at the time of the Adoption of this Constitution, shall be eligible to the Office of President; neither shall any Person be eligible to that Office who shall not have attained to the Age of thirty five Years, and been fourteen Years a Resident within the United States.

6. Succession In Case of the Removal of the President from Office, or of his Death, Resignation, or Inability to discharge the Powers and Duties of the said Office, the Same shall devolve on the Vice President, and the Congress may by Law provide for the Case of Removal, Death, Resignation or Inability, both of the President and Vice President, declaring what Officer shall then act as President, and such Officer shall act accordingly, until the Disability be removed, or a President shall be elected.

7. Salary The President shall, at stated Times, receive for his Services, a Compensation, which shall neither be increased nor diminished during the Period for which he shall have been elected, and he shall not receive within that Period any other Emolument from the United States, or any of them.

8. Oath of Office Before he enter on the Execution of his Office, he shall take the following Oath or Affirmation:—"I do solemnly swear (or affirm) that I will faithfully execute the Office of President of the United States, and will to the best of my Ability, preserve, protect and defend the Constitution of the United States."

EXPLORING THE DOCUMENT The youngest elected president was John F. Kennedy; he was 43 years old when he was inaugurated. (Theodore Roosevelt was 42 when he assumed office after the assassination of McKinley.) *What is the minimum required age for the office of president?*

Presidential Salary

In 1999 Congress voted to set future presidents' salaries at $400,000 per year. The president also receives an annual expense account. The president must pay taxes only on the salary.

Direct Teach

Info to Know
Presidential Qualifications Political concerns of the time determined many of the qualifications for the presidency included in the U.S. Constitution. For example, during the Constitutional Convention, a rumor spread that the delegates intended to invite a foreign king to rule the country. To squelch this rumor, the delegates included a constitutional provision requiring the president to be a natural-born citizen. In addition, the delegates added a 14-year residency requirement for the president to disqualify any Loyalists who had left during the American Revolution and then returned to the United States.

Answers
Exploring the Document
35 years old

Direct Teach

Info to Know

The First Lady The term *first lady* became common after the Civil War. Before that time, presidents' wives were referred to as Mrs. President or presidentress. Although first ladies are not mentioned in the Constitution, almost all presidents—even unmarried ones— have found someone to fill that role. For example, Dolley Madison served as first lady for widower Thomas Jefferson, before assuming that role for her own husband. Recent first ladies have done more than serve as their husbands' hostesses, however. Some first ladies—such as Eleanor Roosevelt, Betty Ford, Rosalyn Carter, and Hillary Rodham Clinton—have had highly visible roles.

go.hrw.com

Online Resources

KEYWORD: SD7 CH5
TOPIC: FIRST LADIES' BIOGRAPHIES

Commander in Chief

Today the president is in charge of the army, navy, air force, marines, and coast guard. Only Congress, however, can decide if the United States will declare war.

Appointments

Most of the president's appointments to office must be approved by the Senate.

Vocabulary

[21] **Reprieves** delays of punishment

[22] **Pardons** releases from the legal penalties associated with a crime

The State of the Union

Every year the president presents to Congress a State of the Union message. In this message, the president introduces and explains a legislative plan for the coming year.

Section 2. Powers of Presidency

1. Military Powers The President shall be Commander in Chief of the Army and Navy of the United States, and of the Militia of the several States, when called into the actual Service of the United States; he may require the Opinion, in writing, of the principal Officer in each of the executive Departments, upon any Subject relating to the Duties of their respective Offices, and he shall have Power to grant **Reprieves**[21] and **Pardons**[22] for Offences against the United States, except in Cases of Impeachment.

2. Treaties and Appointments He shall have Power, by and with the Advice and Consent of the Senate, to make Treaties, provided two thirds of the Senators present concur; and he shall nominate, and by and with the Advice and Consent of the Senate, shall appoint Ambassadors, other public Ministers and Consuls, Judges of the supreme Court, and all other Officers of the United States, whose Appointments are not herein otherwise provided for, and which shall be established by Law: but the Congress may by Law vest the Appointment of such inferior Officers, as they think proper, in the President alone, in the Courts of Law, or in the Heads of Departments.

3. Vacancies The President shall have Power to fill up all Vacancies that may happen during the Recess of the Senate, by granting Commissions which shall expire at the End of their next Session.

Section 3. Presidential Duties

He shall from time to time give to the Congress Information of the State of the Union, and recommend to their Consideration such Measures as he shall judge necessary and expedient; he may, on extraordinary Occasions, convene both Houses, or either of them, and in Case of Disagreement between them, with Respect to the Time of Adjournment, he may adjourn them to such Time as he shall think proper; he shall receive Ambassadors and other public Ministers; he shall take Care that the Laws be faithfully executed, and shall Commission all the Officers of the United States.

Section 4. Impeachment

The President, Vice President and all civil Officers of the United States, shall be removed from Office on Impeachment for, and Conviction of, Treason, Bribery, or other high Crimes and Misdemeanors.

Article III | The Judiciary

Section 1. | Federal Courts and Judges

The judicial Power of the United States shall be vested in one supreme Court, and in such inferior Courts as the Congress may from time to time ordain and establish. The Judges, both of the supreme and inferior Courts, shall hold their Offices during good Behavior, and shall, at stated Times, receive for their Services a Compensation, which shall not be diminished during their Continuance in Office.

Section 2. | Authority of the Courts

1. General Authority The judicial Power shall extend to all Cases, in Law and Equity, arising under this Constitution, the Laws of the United States, and Treaties made, or which shall be made, under their Authority;—to all Cases affecting Ambassadors, other public Ministers and Consuls;—to all Cases of admiralty and maritime Jurisdiction;—to Controversies to which the United States shall be a Party;—to Controversies between two or more States —between a State and Citizens of another State; —between Citizens of different States;—between Citizens of the same State claiming Lands under Grants of different States, and between a State, or the Citizens thereof, and foreign States, Citizens or Subjects.

2. Supreme Authority In all Cases affecting Ambassadors, other public Ministers and Consuls, and those in which a State shall be Party, the supreme Court shall have original Jurisdiction. In all the other Cases before mentioned, the supreme Court shall have appellate Jurisdiction, both as to Law and Fact, with such Exceptions, and under such Regulations as the Congress shall make.

FEDERAL JUDICIAL SYSTEM — QUICK FACTS

Supreme Court
Reviews cases appealed from lower federal courts and highest state courts

Courts of Appeals
Review appeals from district courts

District Courts
Hold trials

Judicial Branch

The Articles of Confederation did not set up a federal court system. One of the first points that the Framers of the Constitution agreed upon was to set up a national judiciary. In the Judiciary Act of 1789, Congress provided for the establishment of lower courts, such as district courts, circuit courts of appeals, and various other federal courts. The judicial system provides a check on the legislative branch: It can declare a law unconstitutional.

Exploring the Document

Identify What courts does the Constitution include in the judiciary? *Supreme Court and lower federal courts established by Congress*

Explain What power does Article III give to the third branch of government? *the power to decide court cases*

📦 Quick Facts Transparency: Federal Judicial System

Biography

John Marshall (1755–1835) The U.S. Supreme Court was considered a fairly unimportant institution in its early years. When John Marshall was appointed chief justice in 1801, the Supreme Court did not even have its own building. As chief justice, Marshall established the Supreme Court as the final interpreter of the Constitution and made the Court into an important check on the president and Congress.

Identify What is the primary subject of Article IV? *relations among states*
Explain What rights are citizens entitled to if they move to or visit another state? *the same privileges and immunities of citizens of that state*

3. Trial by Jury The Trial of all Crimes, except in Cases of Impeachment, shall be by Jury; and such Trial shall be held in the State where the said Crimes shall have been committed; but when not committed within any State, the Trial shall be at such Place or Places as the Congress may by Law have directed.

Section 3. Treason

1. Definition Treason against the United States, shall consist only in levying War against them, or in adhering to their Enemies, giving them Aid and Comfort. No Person shall be convicted of Treason unless on the Testimony of two Witnesses to the same overt Act, or on Confession in open Court.

2. Punishment The Congress shall have Power to declare the Punishment of Treason, but no Attainder of Treason shall work **Corruption of Blood**,[23] or Forfeiture except during the Life of the Person attainted.

Vocabulary

[23] **Corruption of Blood**
punishing the family of a person convicted of treason

Article IV Relations among States

Section 1. State Acts and Records

The States

States must honor the laws, records, and court decisions of other states. A person cannot escape a legal obligation by moving from one state to another.

Full Faith and Credit shall be given in each State to the public Acts, Records, and judicial Proceedings of every other State. And the Congress may by general Laws prescribe the Manner in which such Acts, Records and Proceedings shall be proved, and the Effect thereof.

Section 2. Rights of Citizens

1. Citizenship The Citizens of each State shall be entitled to all Privileges and Immunities of Citizens in the several States.

EXPLORING THE DOCUMENT The Framers wanted to ensure that citizens could determine how state governments would operate. *How does the need to respect the laws of each state support the principle of popular sovereignty?*

2. Extradition A Person charged in any State with Treason, Felony, or other Crime, who shall flee from Justice, and be found in another State, shall on Demand of the executive Authority of the State from which he fled, be delivered up, to be removed to the State having Jurisdiction of the Crime.

3. Fugitive Slaves No Person held to Service or Labour in one State, under the Laws thereof, escaping into another, shall, in Consequence of any Law or Regulation therein, be discharged from such Service or Labour, but shall be delivered up on Claim of the Party to whom such Service or Labour may be due.

Answers

Exploring the Document *If the people have the power to establish laws, they have the responsibility to follow those laws.*

FEDERALISM QUICK FACTS

National
- Declare war
- Maintain armed forces
- Regulate interstate and foreign trade
- Admit new states
- Establish post offices
- Set standard weights and measures
- Coin money
- Establish foreign policy
- Make all laws necessary and proper for carrying out delegated powers

Shared
- Maintain law and order
- Levy taxes
- Borrow money
- Charter banks
- Establish courts
- Provide for public welfare

State
- Establish and maintain schools
- Establish local governments
- Regulate business within the state
- Make marriage laws
- Provide for public safety
- Assume other powers not delegated to the national government or prohibited to the states

ANALYSIS SKILL | ANALYZING INFORMATION

Why does the power to declare war belong only to the national government?

Section 3. New States

1. Admission New States may be admitted by the Congress into this Union; but no new State shall be formed or erected within the Jurisdiction of any other State; nor any State be formed by the Junction of two or more States, or Parts of States, without the Consent of the Legislatures of the States concerned as well as of the Congress.

2. Congressional Authority The Congress shall have Power to dispose of and make all needful Rules and Regulations respecting the Territory or other Property belonging to the United States; and nothing in this Constitution shall be so construed as to Prejudice any Claims of the United States, or of any particular State.

Section 4. Guarantees to the States

The United States shall guarantee to every State in this Union a Republican Form of Government, and shall protect each of them against Invasion; and on Application of the Legislature, or of the Executive (when the Legislature cannot be convened), against domestic Violence.

EXPLORING THE DOCUMENT In a republic, voters elect representatives to act in their best interest. *How does Article IV protect the practice of republicanism in the United States?*

● **Direct Teach** ●

Info to Know

Admission of New States Although the Framers of the Constitution wanted to allow new states to be admitted, many also wanted to preserve the power of the original states. One delegate suggested that the new states' total number of House representatives should never exceed the original states' total number of representatives.

Draw Conclusions If this suggestion had become part of the Constitution, how might it have affected the current U.S. government? *States along the Atlantic coast would have a disproportionate amount of political power.*

Quick Facts Transparency: Federalism

Answers

Analyzing Information *to prevent states from declaring war on one another or on a foreign nation*

Exploring the Document *guarantees that every state will have a representative government*

183

Info to Know

Amendments to the Constitution Of the thousands of proposals for amendments to the Constitution, only 33 have obtained the required two-thirds vote in Congress. The Equal Rights Amendment was first proposed in 1923, but is still not part of the U.S. Constitution.

Activity **Researching the ERA**
Organize the class into small groups to conduct research on the Equal Rights Amendment. Assign each group one of the following research topics: the text of the Equal Rights Amendment (ERA); Alice Paul, the author of the ERA; the history of the ERA; the current political status of the amendment; and arguments for and against making the ERA part of the Constitution. Have each group present its findings to the class.
LS Interpersonal, Verbal-Linguistic

EXPLORING THE DOCUMENT America's founders may not have realized how long the Constitution would last, but they did set up a system for changing or adding to it. They did not want to make it easy to change the Constitution. *By what methods may the Constitution be amended? Under what sorts of circumstances do you think an amendment might be necessary?*

National Supremacy
One of the biggest problems facing the delegates to the Constitutional Convention was the question of what would happen if a state law and a federal law conflicted. Which law would be followed? Who would decide? The second clause of Article VI answers those questions. When a federal law and a state law disagree, the federal law overrides the state law. The Constitution and other federal laws are the "supreme Law of the Land." This clause is often called the supremacy clause.

Article V Amending the Constitution

The Congress, whenever two thirds of both Houses shall deem it necessary, shall propose Amendments to this Constitution, or, on the Application of the Legislatures of two thirds of the several States, shall call a Convention for proposing Amendments, which, in either Case, shall be valid to all Intents and Purposes, as Part of this Constitution, when ratified by the Legislatures of three fourths of the several States, or by Conventions in three fourths thereof, as the one or the other Mode of Ratification may be proposed by the Congress; Provided that ~~no Amendment which may be made prior to the Year One thousand eight hundred and eight shall in any Manner affect the first and fourth Clauses in the Ninth Section of the first Article; and that no State, without its Consent, shall be deprived of its equal Suffrage in the Senate.~~

Article VI Supremacy of National Government

All Debts contracted and Engagements entered into, before the Adoption of this Constitution, shall be as valid against the United States under this Constitution, as under the Confederation.

This Constitution, and the Laws of the United States which shall be made in Pursuance thereof; and all Treaties made, or which shall be made, under the Authority of the United States, shall be the supreme Law of the Land; and the Judges in every State shall be bound thereby, any Thing in the Constitution or Laws of any State to the Contrary notwithstanding.

The Senators and Representatives before mentioned, and the Members of the several State Legislatures, and all executive and judicial Officers, both of the United States and of the several States, shall be bound by Oath or Affirmation, to support this Constitution; but no religious Test shall ever be required as a Qualification to any Office or public Trust under the United States.

AMENDING THE U.S. CONSTITUTION

Amendments can be proposed by

Congress	National Convention

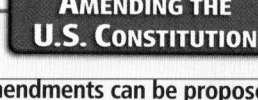

or

with a two-thirds vote in each house

called by Congress at the request of two-thirds of the state legislatures

Ratified by

Legislatures of three-fourths of the states

or

Conventions in three-fourths of the states

Amendment is added to the Constitution.

Answers

Exploring the Document *See the chart, Amending the U.S. Constitution, at right; possible answer—changes in American society or culture*

Article VII Ratification

The Ratification of the Conventions of nine States, shall be sufficient for the Establishment of this Constitution between the States so ratifying the Same.

Done in Convention by the Unanimous Consent of the States present the Seventeenth Day of September in the Year of our Lord one thousand seven hundred and Eighty seven and of the Independence of the United States of America the Twelfth In witness whereof We have hereunto subscribed our Names,

George Washington—
President and deputy from Virginia

Delaware

George Read
Gunning Bedford Jr.
John Dickinson
Richard Bassett
Jacob Broom

Maryland

James McHenry
Daniel of St. Thomas Jenifer
Daniel Carroll

Virginia

John Blair
James Madison Jr.

North Carolina

William Blount
Richard Dobbs Spaight
Hugh Williamson

South Carolina

John Rutledge
Charles Cotesworth Pinckney
Charles Pinckney
Pierce Butler

Georgia

William Few
Abraham Baldwin

New Hampshire

John Langdon
Nicholas Gilman

Massachusetts

Nathaniel Gorham
Rufus King

Connecticut

William Samuel Johnson
Roger Sherman

New York

Alexander Hamilton

New Jersey

William Livingston
David Brearley
William Paterson
Jonathan Dayton

Pennsylvania

Benjamin Franklin
Thomas Mifflin
Robert Morris
George Clymer
Thomas FitzSimons
Jared Ingersoll
James Wilson
Gouverneur Morris

Attest:
William Jackson, Secretary

Ratification

The Articles of Confederation called for all 13 states to approve any revision to the Articles. The Constitution required that 9 out of the 13 states would be needed to ratify the Constitution. The first state to ratify was Delaware, on December 7, 1787. Almost two-and-a-half years later, on May 29, 1790, Rhode Island became the last state to ratify the Constitution.

Direct Teach

Info to Know

Signers of the Constitution At 27 years of age, Jonathon Dayton was the youngest person to sign the Constitution. At 81, Benjamin Franklin was the oldest. Franklin's signature was particularly important. As one of the most renowned men in America, he lent respectability to the new document.

Bill of Rights

One of the conditions set by several states for ratifying the Constitution was the inclusion of a bill of rights. Many people feared that a stronger central government might take away basic rights of the people that had been guaranteed in state constitutions.

EXPLORING THE DOCUMENT The First Amendment forbids Congress from making any "law respecting an establishment of religion" or restraining the freedom to practice religion as one chooses. *Why is freedom of religion an important right?*

Rights of the Accused

The Fifth, Sixth, and Seventh Amendments describe the procedures that courts must follow when trying people accused of crimes.

Vocabulary

[24] **quartered** housed

[25] **Warrants** written orders authorizing a person to make an arrest, a seizure, or a search

[26] **infamous** disgraceful

[27] **indictment** the act of charging with a crime

Constitutional Amendments

Note: The first 10 amendments to the Constitution were ratified on December 15, 1791, and form what is known as the Bill of Rights.

Amendments 1–10. The Bill of Rights

Amendment I

Congress shall make no law respecting an establishment of religion, or prohibiting the free exercise thereof; or abridging the freedom of speech, or of the press; or the right of the people peaceably to assemble, and to petition the Government for a redress of grievances.

Amendment II

A well regulated Militia, being necessary to the security of a free State, the right of the people to keep and bear Arms, shall not be infringed.

Amendment III

No Soldier shall, in time of peace be **quartered**[24] in any house, without the consent of the Owner, nor in time of war, but in a manner to be prescribed by law.

Amendment IV

The right of the people to be secure in their persons, houses, papers, and effects, against unreasonable searches and seizures, shall not be violated, and no **Warrants**[25] shall issue, but upon probable cause, supported by Oath or affirmation, and particularly describing the place to be searched, and the persons or things to be seized.

Amendment V

No person shall be held to answer for a capital, or otherwise **infamous**[26] crime, unless on a presentment or **indictment**[27] of a Grand Jury, except in cases

FUNDAMENTAL LIBERTIES

Freedom of Religion   Freedom of Speech

arising in the land or naval forces, or in the Militia, when in actual service in time of War or public danger; nor shall any person be subject for the same offence to be twice put in jeopardy of life or limb; nor shall be compelled in any criminal case to be a witness against himself, nor be deprived of life, liberty, or property, without due process of law; nor shall private property be taken for public use, without just compensation.

Amendment VI

In all criminal prosecutions, the accused shall enjoy the right to a speedy and public trial, by an impartial jury of the State and district wherein the crime shall have been committed, which district shall have been previously **ascertained**[28] by law, and to be informed of the nature and cause of the accusation; to be confronted with the witnesses against him; to have compulsory process for obtaining witnesses in his favor, and to have the Assistance of Counsel for his defence.

Amendment VII

In suits at common law, where the value in controversy shall exceed twenty dollars, the right of trial by jury shall be preserved, and no fact tried by a jury, shall be otherwise reexamined in any Court of the United States, than according to the rules of the common law.

Amendment VIII

Excessive bail shall not be required, nor excessive fines imposed, nor cruel and unusual punishments inflicted.

Amendment IX

The enumeration in the Constitution, of certain rights, shall not be construed to deny or disparage others retained by the people.

Amendment X

The powers not delegated to the United States by the Constitution, nor prohibited by it to the States, are reserved to the States respectively, or to the people.

Trials

The Sixth Amendment makes several guarantees, including a prompt trial and a trial by a jury chosen from the state and district in which the crime was committed.

Vocabulary

[28] **ascertained** found out

EXPLORING THE DOCUMENT The Ninth and Tenth Amendments were added because not every right of the people or of the states could be listed in the Constitution. *How do the Ninth and Tenth Amendments limit the power of the federal government?*

Freedom of the Press

Freedom of Assembly

MR. PRESIDENT HOW LONG MUST WOMEN WAIT FOR LIBERTY

Freedom to Petition the Government

ANALYSIS SKILL **ANALYZING INFORMATION**

Which amendments guarantee these fundamental freedoms?

Review the Sixth Amendment with students

Activity **Speedy and Public Trial** Explain to students that some trials attract heavy media attention when celebrities are involved or when the crime is particularly sensational. Ask students to bring to class newspaper and magazine articles about highly publicized criminal cases. Have students use the articles to discuss the concepts of the right to a speedy and public trial by an impartial jury. Ask students to discuss how long certain cases may have been in the news. Then have students describe situations in which impartiality might be difficult to guarantee in highly publicized criminal cases. **LS Verbal-Linguistic**

Answers

Analyzing Information *Amendment 1, the First Amendment*

Exploring the Document *In the Ninth and Tenth Amendments, rights and powers not explicitly given to the federal government by the Constitution are reserved for the people and the states.*

187

Exploring the Document

Explain What does the Eleventh Amendment confirm? *No federal court may try a case in which a state is being sued by a citizen of another state or of a foreign country.*

Summarize How did the Twelfth Amendment change the electoral college? *It changed the procedure for choosing a president. The presidential electors would vote for president and vice president on separate ballots.*

Identify Cause and Effect Which three amendments do you think were a consequence of the Civil War? *Thirteenth, Fourteenth, and Fifteenth Amendments*

Reading Time Lines
Amendments to the U.S. Constitution

Activity Have each student select one amendment on the time line that is of particular interest. Ask students to conduct research on the amendment's passage and place the amendment in a matrix of events, people, time, and place. Have students use the information to create a collage of words and images that evokes the era in which the amendment was added to the Constitution. **LS Verbal-Linguistic, Visual-Spatial**

AMENDMENTS TO THE U.S. CONSTITUTION

The Constitution has been amended only 27 times since it was ratified more than 200 years ago. Amendments help the structure of the government change along with the values of the nation's people. Read the time line below to learn how each amendment changed the government.

1791
Bill of Rights
Amendments 1–10

1795
Amendment 11
Protects the states from lawsuits filed by citizens of other states or countries

1804
Amendment 12
Requires separate ballots for the offices of president and vice president

1865
Amendment 13
Bans slavery

1868
Amendment 14
Defines citizenship and citizens' rights

1870
Amendment 15
Prohibits national and state governments from denying the vote based on race

(Time line markers: 1790, 1820, 1870)

Amendments 11–27

Vocabulary

[29] **construed** explained or interpreted

President and Vice President

The Twelfth Amendment changed the election procedure for president and vice president.

Amendment XI

Passed by Congress March 4, 1794. Ratified February 7, 1795.

The Judicial power of the United States shall not be **construed**[29] to extend to any suit in law or equity, commenced or prosecuted against one of the United States by Citizens of another State, or by Citizens or Subjects of any Foreign State.

Amendment XII

Passed by Congress December 9, 1803. Ratified June 15, 1804.

The Electors shall meet in their respective states and vote by ballot for President and Vice-President, one of whom, at least, shall not be an inhabitant of the same state with themselves; they shall name in their ballots the person voted for as President, and in distinct ballots the person voted for as Vice-President, and they shall make distinct lists of all persons voted for as President, and of all persons voted for as Vice-President, and of the number of votes for each, which lists they shall sign and certify, and transmit sealed to the seat of the government of the United States, directed to the President of the Senate;—the President of the Senate shall, in the presence of the

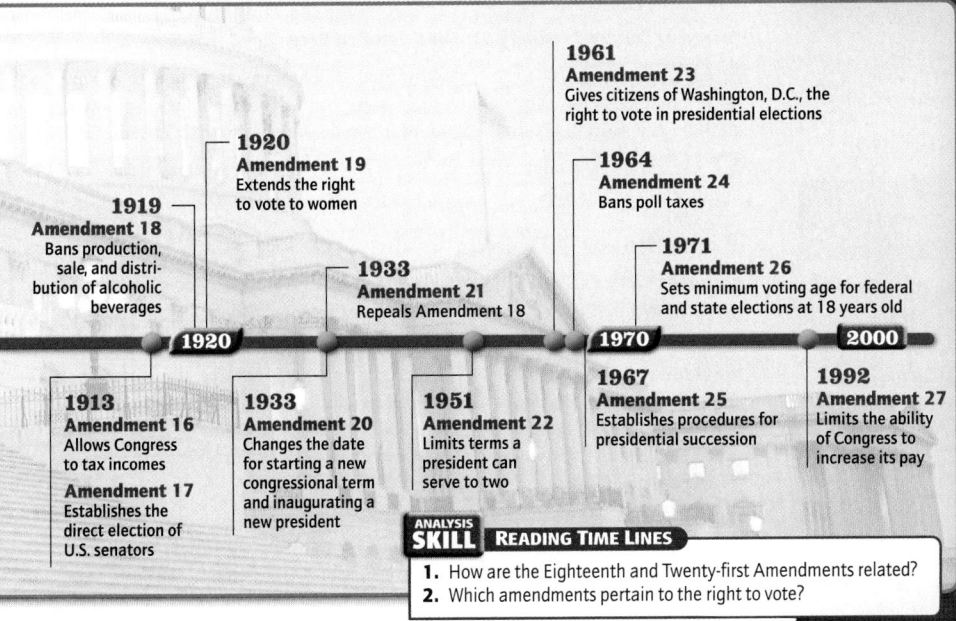

1919
Amendment 18
Bans production, sale, and distribution of alcoholic beverages

1920
Amendment 19
Extends the right to vote to women

1961
Amendment 23
Gives citizens of Washington, D.C., the right to vote in presidential elections

1964
Amendment 24
Bans poll taxes

1933
Amendment 21
Repeals Amendment 18

1971
Amendment 26
Sets minimum voting age for federal and state elections at 18 years old

1920   1970   2000

1913
Amendment 16
Allows Congress to tax incomes

Amendment 17
Establishes the direct election of U.S. senators

1933
Amendment 20
Changes the date for starting a new congressional term and inaugurating a new president

1951
Amendment 22
Limits terms a president can serve to two

1967
Amendment 25
Establishes procedures for presidential succession

1992
Amendment 27
Limits the ability of Congress to increase its pay

ANALYSIS SKILL   **READING TIME LINES**

1. How are the Eighteenth and Twenty-first Amendments related?
2. Which amendments pertain to the right to vote?

Senate and House of Representatives, open all the certificates and the votes shall then be counted;—The person having the greatest number of votes for President, shall be the President, if such number be a majority of the whole number of Electors appointed; and if no person have such majority, then from the persons having the highest numbers not exceeding three on the list of those voted for as President, the House of Representatives shall choose immediately, by ballot, the President. But in choosing the President, the votes shall be taken by states, the representation from each state having one vote; a quorum for this purpose shall consist of a member or members from two-thirds of the states, and a majority of all the states shall be necessary to a choice. ~~And if the House of Representatives shall not choose a President whenever the right of choice shall devolve upon them, before the fourth day of March next following, then the Vice-President shall act as President, as in case of the death or other constitutional disability of the President.~~—The person having the greatest number of votes as Vice-President, shall be the Vice-President, if such number be a majority of the whole number of Electors appointed, and if no person have a majority, then from the two highest numbers on the list, the Senate shall choose the Vice-President; a quorum for the purpose shall consist of two-thirds of the whole number of Senators, and a majority of the whole number shall be necessary to a choice. But no person constitutionally ineligible to the office of President shall be eligible to that of Vice-President of the United States.

Info to Know

Civil Liberties Throughout the 1900s, the U.S. Supreme Court extended the coverage of the civil liberties provided in the Bill of Rights. In earlier times, justices had ruled that the Bill of Rights did not override state laws. Although the Fourteenth Amendment stated that the states could not deprive citizens of their constitutional rights, few justices changed their opinions. In the mid-1900s, Justice Hugo Black began to reinterpret the Fourteenth Amendment. He believed that the guarantees in the Bill of Rights were absolute. The Civil Rights Act, passed in 1964, was the most far-reaching civil rights bill in the nation's history. This act forbids discrimination in public accommodations.

Activity **Civil Liberties** Have students bring to class newspaper articles related to the exercise of civil liberties. Using these articles as discussion prompts, have students describe what they think are proper and improper limitations of civil liberties.

LS Visual-Spatial, Verbal-Linguistic

Abolishing Slavery

Although some slaves had been freed during the Civil War, slavery was not abolished until the Thirteenth Amendment took effect.

Protecting the Rights of Citizens

In 1833 the Supreme Court ruled that the Bill of Rights limited the federal government but not the state governments. This ruling was interpreted to mean that states were able to keep African Americans from becoming state citizens and keep the Bill of Rights from protecting them. The Fourteenth Amendment defines citizenship and prevents states from interfering in the rights of citizens of the United States.

Vocabulary

[30] **involuntary servitude** being forced to work against one's will

Amendment XIII

Passed by Congress January 31, 1865. Ratified December 6, 1865.

1. Slavery Banned Neither slavery nor **involuntary servitude,**[30] except as a punishment for crime whereof the party shall have been duly convicted, shall exist within the United States, or any place subject to their jurisdiction.

2. Enforcement Congress shall have power to enforce this article by appropriate legislation.

Amendment XIV

Passed by Congress June 13, 1866. Ratified July 9, 1868.

1. Citizenship Defined All persons born or naturalized in the United States, and subject to the jurisdiction thereof, are citizens of the United States and of the State wherein they reside. No State shall make or enforce any law which shall abridge the privileges or immunities of citizens of the United States; nor shall any State deprive any person of life, liberty, or property, without due process of law; nor deny to any person within its jurisdiction the equal protection of the laws.

2. Voting Rights Representatives shall be apportioned among the several States according to their respective numbers, counting the whole number of persons in each State, excluding Indians not taxed. But when the right to vote at any election for the choice of electors for President and Vice-President of the United States, Representatives in Congress, the Executive and Judicial officers of a State, or the members of the Legislature thereof, is denied to any of the male inhabitants of such State, being twenty-one years of age, and citizens of the United States, or in any way abridged, except for participation in rebellion, or other crime, the basis of representation therein shall be reduced in the proportion which the number of such male citizens shall bear to the whole number of male citizens twenty-one years of age in such State.

3. Rebels Banned from Government No person shall be a Senator or Representative in Congress, or elector of President and Vice-President, or hold any office, civil or military, under the United States, or under any State, who, having previously taken an oath, as a member of Congress, or as an officer of the United States, or as a member of any State legislature, or as an executive or judicial officer of any State, to support the Constitution of the United States, shall have engaged in insurrection or rebellion against the same, or given aid or comfort to the enemies thereof. But Congress may by a vote of two-thirds of each House, remove such disability.

4. Payment of Debts The validity of the public debt of the United States, authorized by law, including debts incurred for payment of pensions and bounties for services in suppressing insurrection or rebellion, shall not be questioned. But neither the United States nor any State shall assume or pay

THE RECONSTRUCTION AMENDMENTS

The Thirteenth, Fourteenth, and Fifteenth Amendments are often called the Reconstruction Amendments. This is because they arose during Reconstruction, the period of American history following the Civil War. A key aspect of rebuilding the Union was extending the rights of citizenship to former slaves.

The Thirteenth Amendment banned slavery. The Fourteenth Amendment required states to respect the freedoms listed in the Bill of Rights, thus preventing states from denying rights to African Americans. The Fifteenth Amendment gave African American men the right to vote.

African Americans vote in an election during Reconstruction.

ANALYSIS SKILL **ANALYZING INFORMATION**
Why were the Reconstruction Amendments needed?

any debt or obligation incurred in aid of insurrection or rebellion against the United States, ~~or any claim for the loss or emancipation of any slave~~; but all such debts, obligations and claims shall be held illegal and void.

5. Enforcement The Congress shall have the power to enforce, by appropriate legislation, the provisions of this article.

Amendment XV
Passed by Congress February 26, 1869. Ratified February 3, 1870.

1. Voting Rights The right of citizens of the United States to vote shall not be denied or abridged by the United States or by any State on account of race, color, or previous condition of servitude.

2. Enforcement The Congress shall have the power to enforce this article by appropriate legislation.

Exploring the Document

Explain What did the Eighteenth Amendment ban? *the making, sale, and transport of alcohol*

Make Inferences Why do you think the Eighteenth Amendment was repealed? *Students might suggest its impracticality and enormous unpopularity.*

Elaborate What factors do you think contributed to the passage of the Nineteenth Amendment? *Students might suggest the strong leadership and determination of women as well as organized, grassroots suffrage campaigns throughout the country.*

Info to Know

Effects of Prohibition The Eighteenth Amendment may have banned the manufacture, sale, and transportation of liquor, but it also created an underground culture of bootlegging, smuggling, and organized crime. Speakeasies—illegal bars that sold alcoholic beverages—sprang up in large cities. These bars devised elaborate gadgets to hide the illegal evidence in case of police raids. New York City alone had over 30,000 speakeasies, twice the city's number of bars before Prohibition.

Amendment XVI

Passed by Congress July 2, 1909. Ratified February 3, 1913.

The Congress shall have power to lay and collect taxes on incomes, from whatever source derived, without apportionment among the several States, and without regard to any census or enumeration.

Amendment XVII

Passed by Congress May 13, 1912. Ratified April 8, 1913.

EXPLORING THE DOCUMENT The Seventeenth Amendment requires that senators be elected directly by the people instead of by the state legislatures. *What principle of our government does the Seventeenth Amendment protect?*

1. Senators Elected by Citizens The Senate of the United States shall be composed of two Senators from each State, elected by the people thereof, for six years; and each Senator shall have one vote. The electors in each State shall have the qualifications requisite for electors of the most numerous branch of the State legislatures.

2. Vacancies When vacancies happen in the representation of any State in the Senate, the executive authority of such State shall issue writs of election to fill such vacancies: *Provided,* That the legislature of any State may empower the executive thereof to make temporary appointments until the people fill the vacancies by election as the legislature may direct.

3. Future Elections This amendment shall not be so construed as to affect the election or term of any Senator chosen before it becomes valid as part of the Constitution.

Amendment XVIII

Passed by Congress December 18, 1917. Ratified January 16, 1919. Repealed by Amendment XXI.

Prohibition

Although many people believed that the Eighteenth Amendment was good for the health and welfare of the American people, it was repealed 14 years later.

1. Liquor Banned After one year from the ratification of this article the manufacture, sale, or transportation of intoxicating liquors within, the importation thereof into, or the exportation thereof from the United States and all territory subject to the jurisdiction thereof for beverage purposes is hereby prohibited.

2. Enforcement The Congress and the several States shall have concurrent power to enforce this article by appropriate legislation.

3. Ratification This article shall be inoperative unless it shall have been ratified as an amendment to the Constitution by the legislatures of the several States, as provided in the Constitution, within seven years from the date of the submission hereof to the States by the Congress.

Answers

Exploring the Document *the principle of direct representation*

WOMEN FIGHT FOR THE VOTE

To become part of the Constitution, a proposed amendment must be ratified by three-fourths of the states. Here, suffragists witness Kentucky governor Edwin P. Morrow signing the Nineteenth Amendment in January 1920. By June of that year, enough states had ratified the amendment to make it part of the Constitution. American women, after generations of struggle, had finally won the right to vote.

ANALYSIS SKILL | **ANALYZING INFORMATION**

What right did the Nineteenth Amendment grant?

Amendment XIX

Passed by Congress June 4, 1919. Ratified August 18, 1920.

1. Voting Rights The right of citizens of the United States to vote shall not be denied or abridged by the United States or by any State on account of sex.

2. Enforcement Congress shall have power to enforce this article by appropriate legislation.

Amendment XX

Passed by Congress March 2, 1932. Ratified January 23, 1933.

1. Presidential Terms The terms of the President and the Vice President shall end at noon on the 20th day of January, and the terms of Senators and Representatives at noon on the 3d day of January, of the years in which such terms would have ended if this article had not been ratified; and the terms of their successors shall then begin.

Women's Suffrage

Abigail Adams and others were disappointed that the Declaration of Independence and the Constitution did not specifically include women. It took many years and much campaigning before national suffrage for women finally was achieved.

• Direct Teach •

Biography

Elizabeth Cady Stanton The efforts of Elizabeth Cady Stanton, a tireless crusader for women's rights, contributed to the passage of the Nineteenth Amendment in 1920. At her urging, in 1878 Senator Aaron A. Sargent of California introduced a women's suffrage amendment to the Constitution. This amendment was introduced and defeated repeatedly throughout Stanton's lifetime. She died in 1902, eighteen years before the passage of the amendment for which she had worked so hard.

Primary Source

Abigail Adams, "Remember the Ladies"
In 1776, Abigail Adams wrote a letter to her husband John Adams, in which she describes women's determination to be heard and represented. "In the new code of laws which I suppose it will be necessary for you to make I desire you would remember the ladies, and be more generous and favorable to them than your ancestors. Do not put such unlimited power into the hands of the husbands. Remember all men would be tyrants if they could. If particular care and attention is not paid to the ladies we are determined to foment a rebellion, and will not hold ourselves bound by any laws in which we have no voice, or representation."

— Abigail Adams

Letter to John Adams, March 31, 1776

Answers

Analyzing Information *granted women the right to vote*

193

Biography

George W. Norris (1861–1944) During his long congressional career, George W. Norris not only created and worked to pass the Twentieth Amendment but also worked for the introduction of presidential primaries and for the direct election of senators. Though a Republican, Norris rarely voted along party lines. In defense of his independence, he claimed he "would rather be right than regular."

Info to Know

Inaugural Poems At the 1961 inauguration of John F. Kennedy, Robert Frost recited his poem "The Gift Outright." To honor Kennedy, Bill Clinton revived the tradition at his 1993 inauguration, during which Maya Angelou read her poem "On the Pulse of Morning."

Activity Inaugural Poems Have students use the library or Internet sources to locate poems read at presidential inaugurations. Ask for volunteers to read the poems aloud. Discuss what these poems convey or evoke about the significance of the moment and the promise of a new presidency.

LS Auditory-Musical, Verbal-Linguistic

Taking Office

In the original Constitution, a newly elected president and Congress did not take office until March 4, which was four months after the November election. The officials who were leaving office were called lame ducks because they had little influence during those four months. The Twentieth Amendment changed the date that the new president and Congress take office. Members of Congress now take office during the first week of January, and the president takes office on January 20.

---

2. Meeting of Congress The Congress shall assemble at least once in every year, and such meeting shall begin at noon on the 3d day of January, unless they shall by law appoint a different day.

3. Succession of Vice President If, at the time fixed for the beginning of the term of the President, the President elect shall have died, the Vice President elect shall become President. If a President shall not have been chosen before the time fixed for the beginning of his term, or if the President elect shall have failed to qualify, then the Vice President elect shall act as President until a President shall have qualified; and the Congress may by law provide for the case wherein neither a President elect nor a Vice President shall have qualified, declaring who shall then act as President, or the manner in which one who is to act shall be selected, and such person shall act accordingly until a President or Vice President shall have qualified.

4. Succession by Vote of Congress The Congress may by law provide for the case of the death of any of the persons from whom the House of Representatives may choose a President whenever the right of choice shall have devolved upon them, and for the case of the death of any of the persons from whom the Senate may choose a Vice President whenever the right of choice shall have devolved upon them.

5. Ratification ~~Sections 1 and 2 shall take effect on the 15th day of October following the ratification of this article.~~

6. Ratification ~~This article shall be inoperative unless it shall have been ratified as an amendment to the Constitution by the legislatures of three-fourths of the several States within seven years from the date of its submission.~~

Amendment XXI

Passed by Congress February 20, 1933. Ratified December 5, 1933.

1. 18th Amendment Repealed The eighteenth article of amendment to the Constitution of the United States is hereby repealed.

2. Liquor Allowed by Law The transportation or importation into any State, Territory, or Possession of the United States for delivery or use therein of intoxicating liquors, in violation of the laws thereof, is hereby prohibited.

3. Ratification ~~This article shall be inoperative unless it shall have been ratified as an amendment to the Constitution by conventions in the several States, as provided in the Constitution, within seven years from the date of the submission hereof to the States by the Congress.~~

Amendment XXII

Passed by Congress March 21, 1947. Ratified February 27, 1951.

1. Term Limits No person shall be elected to the office of the President more than twice, and no person who has held the office of President, or acted as President, for more than two years of a term to which some other person was elected President shall be elected to the office of President more than once. ~~But this Article shall not apply to any person holding the office of President when this Article was proposed by Congress, and shall not prevent any person who may be holding the office of President, or acting as President, during the term within which this Article becomes operative from holding the office of President or acting as President during the remainder of such term.~~

2. Ratification ~~This article shall be inoperative unless it shall have been ratified as an amendment to the Constitution by the legislatures of three-fourths of the several States within seven years from the date of its submission to the States by the Congress.~~

After Franklin D. Roosevelt was elected to four consecutive terms, limits were placed on the number of terms a president could serve.

Amendment XXIII

Passed by Congress June 16, 1960. Ratified March 29, 1961.

1. District of Columbia Represented The District constituting the seat of Government of the United States shall appoint in such manner as Congress may direct:

A number of electors of President and Vice President equal to the whole number of Senators and Representatives in Congress to which the District would be entitled if it were a State, but in no event more than the least populous State; they shall be in addition to those appointed by the States, but they shall be considered, for the purposes of the election of President and Vice President, to be electors appointed by a State; and they shall meet in the District and perform such duties as provided by the twelfth article of amendment.

2. Enforcement The Congress shall have power to enforce this article by appropriate legislation.

EXPLORING THE DOCUMENT From the time of President George Washington's administration, it was a custom for presidents to serve no more than two terms in office. Franklin D. Roosevelt, however, was elected to four terms. The Twenty-second Amendment restricted presidents to no more than two terms in office. *Why do you think citizens chose to limit the power of the president in this way?*

Voting Rights

Until the ratification of the Twenty-third Amendment, the people of Washington, D.C., could not vote in presidential elections.

Info to Know

Poll Taxes Congress started trying to eliminate poll taxes in 1939. These taxes had been instituted in some southern states after Reconstruction and were still in effect in five of those states in 1964. The poll tax was often explicitly adopted to discriminate against African American voters. For example, when a poll tax was passed in Virginia in 1902, one representative said, "Discrimination! Why, that is precisely what we propose."

Twenty-sixth Amendment As of 1970, four states had established a minimum voting age lower than 21. That year, Congress passed a law allowing citizens 18 and older to vote in federal elections. The U.S. Supreme Court found the law constitutional but noted that Congress did not have the power to set the voting age in state elections. To remedy any conflicts between federal and state voting standards, Congress passed the Twenty-sixth Amendment, which established 18 as the minimum voting age in all elections in the United States. The amendment was quickly ratified.

POLL TAX AMENDMENT

Poll taxes were used to deny impoverished Americans, including many African Americans and Hispanic Americans, the right to vote. Poll taxes were outlawed by the Twenty-fourth Amendment.

ANALYSIS SKILL ANALYZING INFORMATION

How did poll taxes deny poor Americans the opportunity to vote?

Presidential Disability

The illness of President Eisenhower in the 1950s and the assassination of President Kennedy in 1963 were the events behind the Twenty-fifth Amendment. The Constitution did not provide a clear-cut method for a vice president to take over for a disabled president or upon the death of a president. This amendment provides for filling the office of the vice president if a vacancy occurs, and it provides a way for the vice president—or someone else in the line of succession—to take over if the president is unable to perform the duties of that office.

Amendment XXIV

Passed by Congress August 27, 1962. Ratified January 23, 1964.

1. Voting Rights The right of citizens of the United States to vote in any primary or other election for President or Vice President, for electors for President or Vice President, or for Senator or Representative in Congress, shall not be denied or abridged by the United States or any State by reason of failure to pay poll tax or other tax.

2. Enforcement The Congress shall have power to enforce this article by appropriate legislation.

Amendment XXV

Passed by Congress July 6, 1965. Ratified February 10, 1967.

1. Succession of Vice President In case of the removal of the President from office or of his death or resignation, the Vice President shall become President.

2. Vacancy of Vice President Whenever there is a vacancy in the office of the Vice President, the President shall nominate a Vice President who shall take office upon confirmation by a majority vote of both Houses of Congress.

Answers

Analyzing Information *by requiring them to pay a fee in order to vote*

3. Written Declaration Whenever the President transmits to the President pro tempore of the Senate and the Speaker of the House of Representatives his written declaration that he is unable to discharge the powers and duties of his office, and until he transmits to them a written declaration to the contrary, such powers and duties shall be discharged by the Vice President as Acting President.

4. Removing the President Whenever the Vice President and a majority of either the principal officers of the executive departments or of such other body as Congress may by law provide, transmit to the President pro tempore of the Senate and the Speaker of the House of Representatives their written declaration that the President is unable to discharge the powers and duties of his office, the Vice President shall immediately assume the powers and duties of the office as Acting President.

Thereafter, when the President transmits to the President pro tempore of the Senate and the Speaker of the House of Representatives his written declaration that no inability exists, he shall resume the powers and duties of his office unless the Vice President and a majority of either the principal officers of the executive department or of such other body as Congress may by law provide, transmit within four days to the President pro tempore of the Senate and the Speaker of the House of Representatives their written declaration that the President is unable to discharge the powers and duties of his office. Thereupon Congress shall decide the issue, assembling within forty-eight hours for that purpose if not in session. If the Congress, within twenty-one days after receipt of the latter written declaration, or, if Congress is not in session, within twenty-one days after Congress is required to assemble, determines by two-thirds vote of both Houses that the President is unable to discharge the powers and duties of his office, the Vice President shall continue to discharge the same as Acting President; otherwise, the President shall resume the powers and duties of his office.

Amendment XXVI

Passed by Congress March 23, 1971. Ratified July 1, 1971.

1. Voting Rights The right of citizens of the United States, who are eighteen years of age or older, to vote shall not be denied or abridged by the United States or by any State on account of age.

2. Enforcement The Congress shall have power to enforce this article by appropriate legislation.

Amendment XXVII

Originally proposed September 25, 1789. Ratified May 7, 1992.

No law, varying the compensation for the services of the Senators and Representatives, shall take effect, until an election of representatives shall have intervened.

Expanded Suffrage

The Voting Rights Act of 1970 tried to lower the voting age from 21 to 18. However, the Supreme Court ruled that the act applied to national elections only, not to state or local elections. The Twenty-sixth Amendment set the minimum voting age for all elections at 18.

Close

Have students identify the amendments, or provisions, within the amendments that they believe are most important to preserving democracy.

Review/Reteach

Ask students to identify the three branches of government called out in the Constitution. Then have students explain why the Framers believed this was necessary to maintain a balance of power within the federal government.

Answers

Visual Summary

Review and Inquiry Organize students into eight groups, and assign each group one of the topics in the Visual Summary. Have each group prepare a one- to two-minute presentation explaining how its topic fits into the United States Constitution, helping to balance power and ensuring that the government will function effectively.

🗄 Quick Facts Transparency: The Constitution of the United States

Reviewing Key Terms and People

1. If the vice president is absent from the Senate, the Senate will choose a temporary, or pro tempore, president.

2. A quorum is the minimum number of people needed to conduct business.

3. Bills are drafts of proposed laws.

4. The necessary and proper clause, Section 8, Article 18, is also known as the elastic clause.

5. A writ of habeas corpus requires that the government bring a prisoner to court and explain why the person is being held.

6. An ex post facto law punishes people for actions that were not illegal at the time the actions were committed.

7. The executive branch refers to the president and vice president.

8. Every year the president gives a State of the Union address, recommending legislation and policies.

9. Federalism refers to the distribution power within government.

10. National supremacy means that laws of the national government take precedence over state laws; the Constitution and federal laws are the supreme law of the land.

11. The Bill of Rights, the first ten amendments to the Constitution, protects basic individual rights.

Visual Summary: The Constitution of the United States

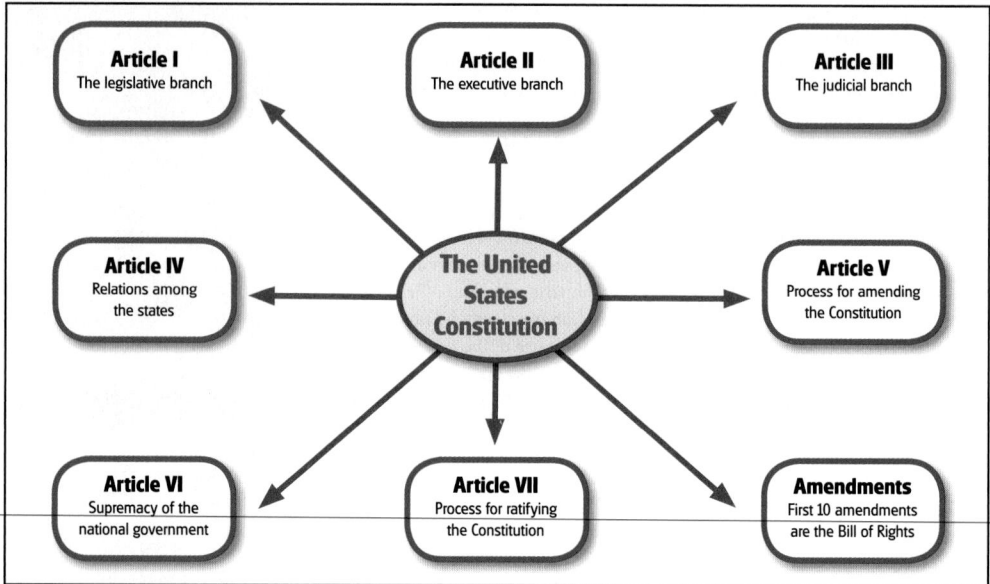

Reviewing Key Terms and People

For each term or name below, write a sentence explaining its significance to the U.S. Constitution.

1. pro tempore
2. quorum
3. bills
4. elastic clause
5. writ of habeas corpus
6. ex post facto law
7. executive branch
8. State of the Union
9. federalism
10. national supremacy
11. Bill of Rights

Comprehension and Critical Thinking

ARTICLE I *(pp. 171–177)*

12. **a. Recall** What is the focus of Article I?

    b. Make Inferences Why do you think Congress fixed the size of the House of Representatives at 435 members in 1929?

    c. Elaborate Describe how a bill becomes a law, explaining how the process is an example of checks and balances in the Constitution.

ARTICLE II *(pp. 178–180)*

13. **a. Identify** Which branch of government is the focus of Article II of the U.S. Constitution?

    b. Compare What are the main powers of the president, and how do they compare to the main powers of the legislature?

    c. Evaluate Do you think the electoral college is the best way to elect the president? Explain.

198 THE CONSTITUTION OF THE UNITED STATES

Comprehension and Critical Thinking

12. **a.** organization of Congress

    b. As population continues to grow, the number of representatives might become too large for the House to be effective.

    c. See Article 1, Section 7 and chart.

13. **a.** executive

    b. commander in chief; makes treaties with Senate concurrence; nominates ambassadors and Supreme Court justices, with Senate

concurrence; signs legislation into law

    c. possible answers—no, does not always represent the popular vote; yes, requires that popular support be distributed across country

14. **a.** judiciary

    b. decision made at district court level; decision appealed, case heard in courts of appeals; decision appealed, Supreme Court reviews cases from lower federal courts

    c. decides constitutionality of laws

ARTICLE III (pp. 181–182)

14. a. Describe Which branch of government is the focus of Article III of the U.S. Constitution?

b. Analyze How are cases appealed to the Supreme Court in the federal judicial system?

c. Elaborate How does the judicial system provide a check on the legislature?

ARTICLE IV (pp. 182–183)

15. a. Describe What is the focus of Article IV of the U.S. Constitution?

b. Analyze Why must states honor the laws of other states?

c. Evaluate How well does the system of federalism balance the powers of states and the national government?

ARTICLE V (p. 184)

16. a. Identify What does Article V of the U.S. Constitution discuss?

b. Explain What is the process for amending the U.S. Constitution?

ARTICLE VI (p. 184)

17. a. Describe What happens if a state law and a federal law conflict with each other?

b. Analyze Why do you think the idea of national supremacy was included in the Constitution?

ARTICLE VII (p. 185)

18. a. Recall How many states are needed to ratify the Constitution?

b. Compare Why was the number of states needed to ratify the Constitution different from the number of states needed to revise the Articles of Confederation?

Using the Internet

go.hrw.com
Practice Online
Keyword: SD7 CH5

19. Each of the 50 states sends representatives to the Senate and the House of Representatives. Using the keyword above, locate congressmembers representing your state or your congressional district. Then conduct research to find out if they have sponsored a bill, how they voted on recent legislation, issues that interest them, or their viewpoints on pending legislation. Create a chart to display your research.

Analyzing Primary Sources

Reading Like a Historian This poll tax receipt was issued in 1939 to a voter in Texas. Poll taxes were later outlawed by the Twenty-fourth Amendment.

20. Recall What was a poll tax?

Explain Why were poll taxes outlawed by the Twenty-fourth Amendment?

Critical Reading

Review the timeline in this section titled "Amendments to the U.S. Constitution." Consider the 27 amendments on the time line and then answer the questions that follow.

21. The purpose of Amendment 15 was

A to prohibit national and state governments from denying the vote based on race.

B to extend voting rights to women.

C to repeal Amendment 14.

D to ban production, sale, and distribution of alcoholic beverages.

22. What do the amendments have in common?

A Each amendment gave a different group of people the right to vote.

B Each amendment helped the structure of government change along with the values of the nation's people.

C Each amendment helped the Constitution remain unchanged for 200 years.

D Each amendment was eventually repealed.

FOCUS ON WRITING

Expository Writing *Expository writing gives information, explains why or how, or defines a process. To practice expository writing, complete the assignment below.*

Writing Topic **The preamble to the Constitution**

23. What does the preamble state? What does it tell you about the Framers' intentions? Write a brief paragraph that answers these questions. Include quotations from the text of the preamble.

Answers

15. a. relations among states

b. required by federal Constitution, ensure enforcement of law

c. well balanced; states' rights are respected; national government retains supremacy

16. a. how to amend the Constitution

b. See chart for complete description.

17. a. national law is upheld; state law overruled

b. to ensure supremacy of one governing body; to solve problems that arose with Articles of Confederation

18. a. nine

b. It was an attempt to help ensure ratification of the Constitution.

Using the Internet

19. Go to the HRW Web site and enter the keyword shown to access a rubric for this activity.

KEYWORD: SD7 CH5

Analyzing Primary Sources

20. a tax voters had to pay in order to vote; were used to prevent poor people, specifically African Americans, from voting

Critical Reading

21. A

22. B

Focus on Writing

23. The Preamble outlines reasons for the Constitution. Students should include appropriate quotes.

Review and Assessment Resources

Review and Reinforce

- CRF: Chapter Review Activity
- Quick Facts Transparencies: Federal Office Terms and Requirements, Federal Judicial System, Federalism, The Constitution of the United States
- Spanish Chapter Summaries Audio CD Program
- Online Chapter Summaries in Spanish
- **OSP** Holt PuzzlePro; Quiz Show for ExamView
- Quiz Game CD-ROM

Assess

- PASS: Chapter Test, Forms A and B
- Alternative Assessment Handbook
- **OSP** ExamView Test Generator, Chapter Test
- Differentiated Instruction Modified Worksheets and Tests CD-ROM: Chapter Test
- **HOAP** Holt Online Assessment Program (in the Premier Online Edition)

Reteach/Intervene

- Interactive Reader and Study Guide
- Differentiated Instruction Teacher Management System: Lesson Plans for Differentiated Instruction
- Differentiated Instruction Modified Worksheets and Tests CD-ROM: Chapter Test
- Interactive Skills Tutor CD-ROM

go.hrw.com
Online Resources
KEYWORD: SD7 CH5

Chapter 6 Planning Guide

Forging the New Republic

Chapter Overview	Reproducible Resources	Technology Resources
CHAPTER 6 pp. 200–231 **Overview:** In this chapter, students will analyze the formation of the U.S. government and the events that led to the creation of rival political parties.	**Differentiated Instruction Teacher Management System:*** • Instructional Benchmarking Guides • Lesson Plans for Differentiated Instruction **Interactive Reader and Study Guide:** Chapter Summary* **Chapter Resource File:*** • Writing for the SAT: Interpreting the Constitution • Social Studies Skills Activity: Interpreting Visuals • Chapter Review Activity **American History Outline Maps** **Pre-AP Activities Guide for American History***	**Live Ink® Online Reading Help** **Student Edition on Audio CD Program** **Differentiated Instruction Modified Worksheets and Tests CD-ROM** **Interactive Skills Tutor CD-ROM** **United States History Primary Source Library CD-ROM** **Power Presentations with Video CD-ROM** **History's Impact: American History Video Program (VHS/DVD):** Forging the New Republic **Online Chapter Summaries in Spanish** **Graphic Organizer Transparencies**
Section 1: **Washington Becomes President** **The Main Idea:** President Washington and other leaders tried to solve the new nation's economic problems.	**Differentiated Instruction Teacher Management System:** Section 1 Lesson Plan* **Interactive Reader and Study Guide:** Section 1 Summary* **Chapter Resource File:*** • Vocabulary Builder Activity, Section 1	**Daily Bellringer Transparency:** Section 1* **Daily Test Practice Transparency:** Section 1*
Section 2: **Challenges of the 1790s** **The Main Idea:** The United States tried to remain neutral when war broke out in Europe while also dealing with conflicts with Indians in the Northwest Territory.	**Differentiated Instruction Teacher Management System:** Section 2 Lesson Plan* **Interactive Reader and Study Guide:** Section 2 Summary* **Chapter Resource File:*** • Vocabulary Builder Activity, Section 2	**Daily Bellringer Transparency:** Section 2* **Map Transparency:** Northwest Territory Battles* **Daily Test Practice Transparency:** Section 2*
Section 3: **Jefferson's Presidency** **The Main Idea:** The rise of political parties influenced the election of 1800 and Thomas Jefferson's presidency.	**Differentiated Instruction Teacher Management System:** Section 3 Lesson Plan* **Interactive Reader and Study Guide:** Section 3 Summary* **Chapter Resource File:*** • Vocabulary Builder Activity, Section 3	**Daily Bellringer Transparency:** Section 3* **Map Transparency:** The Louisiana Purchase* **Daily Test Practice Transparency:** Section 3*
Section 4: **The War of 1812** **The Main Idea:** Americans faced Great Britain in another war and stopped Native Americans' attempts to resist settlers on their lands.	**Differentiated Instruction Teacher Management System:** Section 4 Lesson Plan* **Interactive Reader and Study Guide:** Section 4 Summary* **Chapter Resource File:*** • Vocabulary Builder Activity, Section 4	**Daily Bellringer Transparency:** Section 4* **Map Transparency:** War of 1812* **Daily Test Practice Transparency:** Section 4*

HOLT
History's Impact
American History Video Program (VHS/DVD)
Forging the New Republic

Review, Assessment, Intervention

 Quick Facts Transparencies: Hamilton's Economic Plan, Reactions to the XYZ Affair, The Election of 1800: Power Changes Hands, Forging the New Republic

 Spanish Chapter Summaries Audio CD Program

 Progress Assessment Support System (PASS): Chapter Test*

 Differentiated Instruction Modified Worksheets and Tests CD-ROM: Modified Chapter Test

OSP **One-Stop Planner CD-ROM:** ExamView Test Generator (English/Spanish)

HOAP **Holt Online Assessment Program (HOAP),** in the Holt Premier Online Student Edition

 PASS: Section 1 Quiz*

 Online Quiz: Section 1

 Alternative Assessment Handbook

 PASS: Section 2 Quiz*

 Online Quiz: Section 2

 Alternative Assessment Handbook

 PASS: Section 3 Quiz*

 Online Quiz: Section 3

 Alternative Assessment Handbook

 PASS: Section 4 Quiz*

 Online Quiz: Section 4

 Alternative Assessment Handbook

 **RESOURCES**

The following resources were developed to help North Carolina educators teach the standards and objectives of North Carolina's eleventh grade standard course of study in United States history.
- United States history EOC Test Prep Workbook
- Teacher's Support System
- North Carolina One-Stop Planner

And be sure to direct your students to **go.hrw.com** for online access to the EOC Test Prep Workbook.

go.hrw.com
EOC Test Prep
KEYWORD: SE7 NC

Holt Online Learning

go.hrw.com
Teacher Resources
KEYWORD: SD7 TEACHER

go.hrw.com
Student Resources
KEYWORD: SD7 CH6

- Document-based Questions
- Interactive Multimedia Activities
- Current Events
- Chapter-based Internet Activities
- and more!

Holt Premier
Online Student Edition
Complete online support for interactivity, assessment, and reporting
- Interactive Maps and Notebook
- Standardized Test Prep
- Homework Practice and Research Activities Online

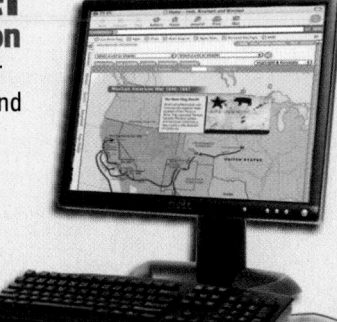

CHAPTER 6 PLANNING GUIDE

The Big Picture

Jesús F. de la Teja

Alexander Hamilton, Engineer of Government More than any other Framer, Hamilton saw the "big picture." He grasped modern economics in a way no other American leader did—using debt as an asset at the service of government, creating institutional sources of capital, using the power of government to promote economic development. Although most of his work was undone by the Jeffersonians, in the long run it was Hamilton's scheme that won the day and became the basis for the nation's political economy.

The First Party System It is hard to imagine in today's polarized political world that there was a time when the nation's leaders believed that the United States could do without political parties. The Constitution's original lack of consideration for ideological factions reflected their strong desire to see government operate in much the same way as the constitutional convention had—ideas discussed, debated, and compromised over in the best interest of the country. It quickly became clear to the founders that parties are, in fact, a natural product of government.

The War that Created America The War of 1812 was unpopular in New England, where merchants and shippers who relied on business with Britain saw disaster. It was wildly popular in the West, where folks saw an opportunity to acquire Canada and to end British support for Native American raids. Neither view proved accurate, as military stalemate led to a treaty that essentially restored the status quo. "The Star Spangled Banner" aside, the one great result was the rise of American nationalism; by 1815 New Englanders, westerners, and southerners all understood themselves to be Americans. The reality of the United States had been tested, and the country had passed the test.

Recent Scholarship

The Nation's Founders What was the greatest generation? In *Founding Brothers: The Revolutionary Generation* (2001), Joseph Ellis claims that it was the men who made the United States a reality in the aftermath of military victory and constitutional reinvention. Through a series of episodes from life in the early Republic, the author outlines how the country's political life came to be established. The rise of partisanship, the politics of compromise, the failure to deal conclusively with slavery, and the meaning of Washington's retirement from public life are among the events treated with wit and élan in this engaging and thoughtful book.

Differentiating Instruction

 Differentiated Instruction Teacher Management System
- Lesson Plans for Differentiated Instruction
- Differentiated Instructional Benchmarking Guides
- Interactive Reader and Study Guide

 Spanish Chapter Summaries Audio CD Program

Online Chapter Summaries in Spanish

Student Edition on Audio CD Program

Differentiated Instruction Modified Worksheets and Tests CD-ROM
- Vocabulary Flash Cards
- Modified Vocabulary Builder Activities
- Modified Chapter Review Activity
- Modified Chapter Test

OSP One-Stop Planner CD-ROM
- ExamView Test Generator (English and Spanish)
- PuzzlePro
- Quiz Show for ExamView
- Transparencies and Videos

TE Differentiated Activities in the Teacher's Edition
- Settling the Nation's Debts, p. 204
- The Whiskey Rebellion, p. 207
- The Louisiana Purchase Celebration, p. 218
- Tecumseh, p. 225

Reading Like a Historian
Sam Wineburg

Researching and the Prepared Mind

The advent of digital libraries presents the history teacher with unimaginable opportunities. With a few clicks of a mouse, our students are inside archives that a few years ago required multiple levels of clearance and a fat expense budget.

But all is not rosy for our novice researchers. The belief that direct contact with primary sources will lead straight to understanding can quickly get us into trouble.

The Dangers of Primary Sources

Consider some of the opportunities for making wrong turns provided by the amazing archive of the Lewis and Clark papers, hosted by the University of Nebraska, Lincoln, which may be easily found by searching for the keywords "Lewis and Clark" and "University of Nebraska." A student can search the entire corpus of Lewis and Clark's writings over their four-year journey by typing in a keyword and pressing "search."

Imagine pointing students in the direction of this digital wonderland only to have an enterprising student type "sex" in the search bar. "Look at this," our budding historian shouts across the room, pointing to Clark's entry for November 21, 1805:

"An old woman & wife to a Cheif of the Chinnooks came and made a Camp near ours. She brought with her 6 young [squaws] I believe for the purpose of gratifying the passions of the men of our party."

Interest is piqued—that's for sure. Now a group of students huddle over the computer screen, examining Clark's entry for January 5, 1805, which describes the ritual of the "Buffalo Dance" among the Mandan:

"The old men arrange themselves in a circle . . . the young men who have their wives back of the circle . . . the Girl then takes the Old man (who verry often can Scercely walk) and leads him to a Convenient place for the business . . . We sent a man to this Medisan [Dance] last night, they gave him 4 Girls."

"An expedition 'with benefits,'" chortles one student. "Where do we sign on?" snorts another.

The Need for Context

Historical study should enlarge students' perspectives by acquainting them with worlds and ways of thinking not their own. By encountering Clark's journals without the broader context of historical and anthropological research that would put these sexual encounters into context, our students may be intrigued—they may even be titillated. But they will have remained ensconced in their comfort zones and learned little.

Among the Native American peoples Lewis and Clark met, we can distinguish two broad approaches to sexuality. To the Plains Indians, whose Buffalo Dance Clark tries to understand, sexuality was a conduit of energy, a spiritual means of transmitting power between parties, with women acting as pipelines of this transmission. Now, confronted by strangers who possessed powerful medicines and dazzling technologies, sexuality was seen as one way to tap some of their amazing power.

Understanding Perspectives

Among the Chinooks of the Pacific Northwest, sexuality was used to seal a business deal—a more physical means of doing so than signing a paper. But by reading Lewis and Clark's diaries, our students will never encounter these alternative views. They will only get how these events looked from the perspective—and loins—of white explorers. If history is about learning other perspectives, students are a long way from standing in someone else's moccasins.

Digital archives are wondrous sites of possibility. But understanding is the gift of a prepared mind. Without preparation, an encounter with the past can lead nowhere, and can even confirm and harden students' worst stereotypes.

Chapter Preview

 Standards Focus

Social Studies Competency Goals
Goal 1 The learner will identify, investigate, and assess the effectiveness of the institutions of the emerging republic.
 **1.01, 1.03**

 The Big Idea and Essential Questions

To foster student understanding of this chapter's big idea, design your lesson to address each section's essential question.

Big Idea Rival political parties emerged from debates over the size and role of the federal government.

Essential Questions

1. How did attempts by American leaders to solve the nation's economic problems lead to the rise of political parties?

2. What challenges did the United States face regarding European nations and Native Americans?

3. How did Thomas Jefferson's view of the presidency differ from that of earlier presidents?

4. What military challenges from Great Britain and from Native Americans did the United States face?

CHAPTER

6 **1789–1815**

Forging the New REPUBLIC

THE BIG PICTURE In the last decade of the 1700s, debates over the size and role of the federal government led to the emergence of rival political parties. Thomas Jefferson's election as president in 1800 marked the rise of the Democratic-Republican Party.

NC **North Carolina Standards**

Social Studies Objectives
1.01 Identify the major domestic issues and conflicts experienced by the nation during the Federalist Period.
1.03 Assess commercial and diplomatic relationships with Britain, France, and other nations.

Language Arts Objectives
3.02 Select an issue or theme and take a stance on that issue by:
• supporting the argument with specific reasons.

Skills FOCUS **READING LIKE A HISTORIAN**

President George Washington celebrates his second inauguration at Independence Hall, Philadelphia, in 1793. As the country's first president, Washington not only led the nation but also set the style and tone for the office.
Interpreting Visuals What image, style, or tone does this painting suggest?
See Skills Handbook, p. H30

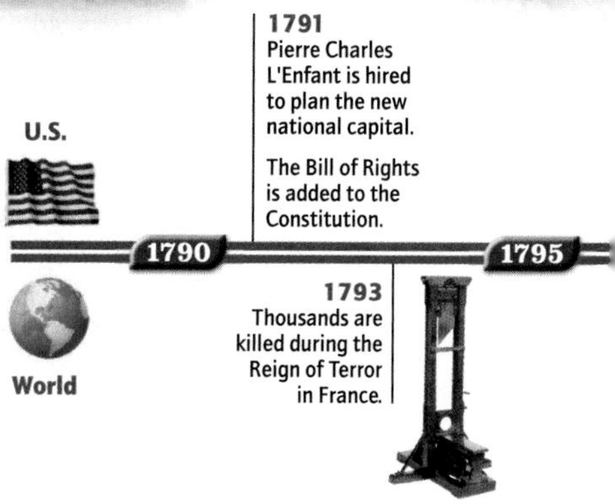

200

1791
Pierre Charles L'Enfant is hired to plan the new national capital.

The Bill of Rights is added to the Constitution.

U.S.

1790

1795

World

1793
Thousands are killed during the Reign of Terror in France.

Key to Differentiating Instruction

Below Level

Basic-level activities designed for all students encountering new material

At Level

Intermediate-level activities designed for average students

Above Level

Challenging activities designed for honors and gifted-and-talented students

Standard English Mastery

Activities designed to improve standard English usage

Introduce the Chapter

At Level

Forging the New Republic

1. Guide students in a review of what they know about George Washington, John Adams, and Thomas Jefferson, our first presidents. Then remind students that while President Washington and Congress had the Constitution to guide them, they still had to establish and organize the new government, a challenging task for each of the first presidents.

2. Have students name some of the challenges that faced the new government. As they study

the chapter, have students compare their ideas with the information in the text.

3. Have students work in pairs to answer this question: What do you think were the first tasks of the nation's new government, and how could our nation's leaders accomplish them? Write down student responses for all to see. **LS Verbal-Linguistic**

Alternative Assessment Handbook, Rubric 11: Discussions

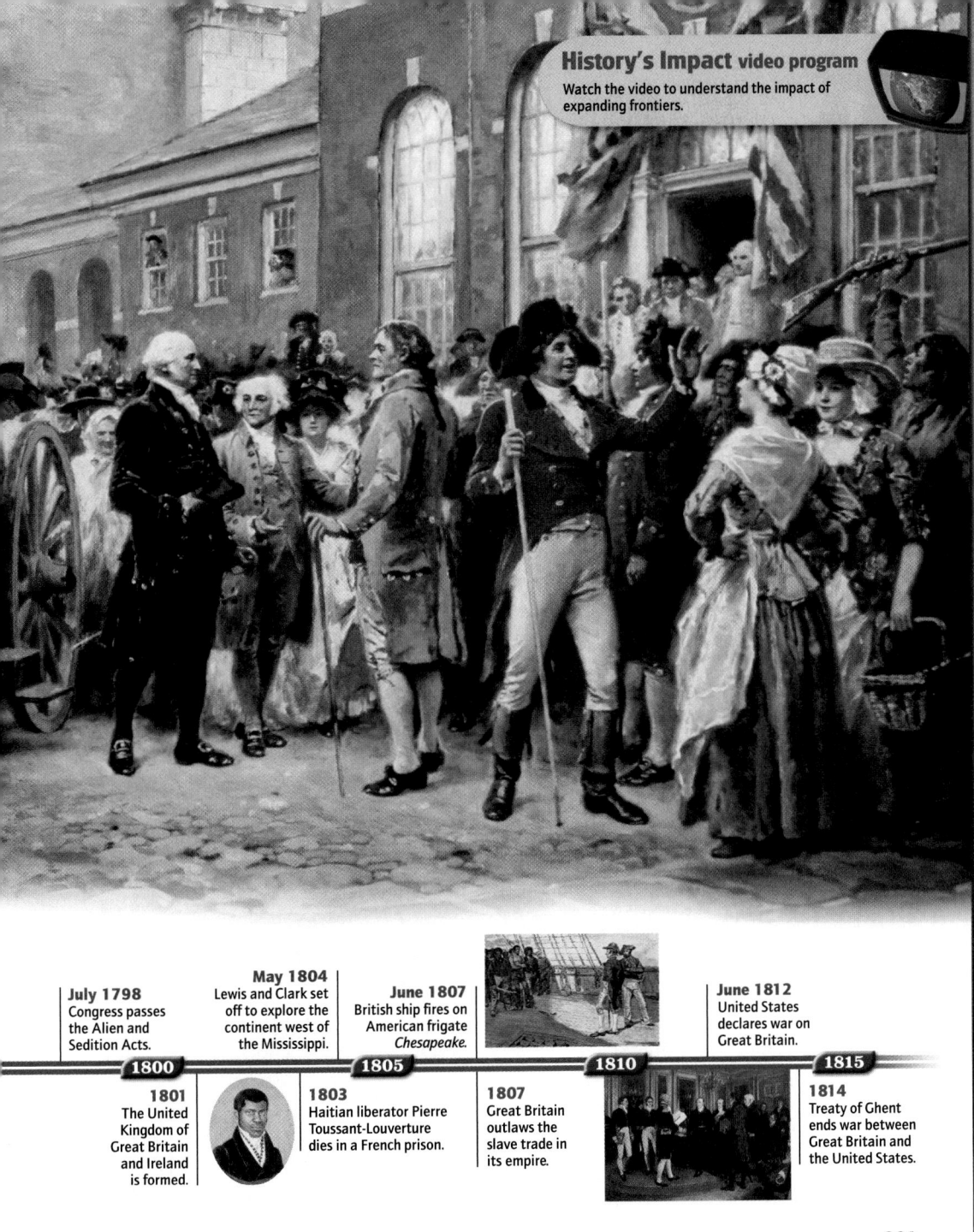

• Chapter Preview •

HOLT
History's Impact

▶ **Video Program: Forging the New Republic**
See the Video Teacher's Guide for strategies for using the video segment.

Reading Like a Historian

Washington's Second Inaugural Address During his second inauguration President Washington gave an extremely short speech, only 135 words. Have students examine the painting and name other ways in which this inauguration differed from inaugurations today. Then have students list reasons for the many changes.

July 1798
Congress passes the Alien and Sedition Acts.

May 1804
Lewis and Clark set off to explore the continent west of the Mississippi.

June 1807
British ship fires on American frigate *Chesapeake*.

June 1812
United States declares war on Great Britain.

1800

1805

1810

1815

1801
The United Kingdom of Great Britain and Ireland is formed.

1803
Haitian liberator Pierre Toussant-Louverture dies in a French prison.

1807
Great Britain outlaws the slave trade in its empire.

1814
Treaty of Ghent ends war between Great Britain and the United States.

201

go.hrw.com
Online Resources

Chapter Resources:
KEYWORD: SD7 CH6

Teacher Resources:
KEYWORD: SD7 TEACHER

Explore the Time Line

1. Who liberated Haiti? When did this person die? *Pierre Toussant-Louverture; 1803*

2. When did the Lewis and Clark expedition begin? *1804*

3. How long did war with Great Britain last? *2 years*

Info to Know

Presidential Inaugurations George Washington's first inauguration was held in New York City, his second in Philadelphia. John Adams was the first president to receive the oath of office from the Chief Justice of the Supreme Court, and Thomas Jefferson was the first president to be inaugurated at the Capitol in Washington, D.C., in March 1804.

Evaluate Why do you think the Chief Justice administers the oath of office to the president? *possible answers—to emphasize that the president's actions must fall under the Constitution*

Answers

Reading Like a Historian (p. 200)
President Washington is portrayed as a normal citizen, and while he has a military escort, he is dressed in civilian clothing, available to the throngs of citizens who came to see him. He is portrayed as an accessible person.

The Inside Story. . . Use the **Daily Bellringer Transparency** to help students answer the question.

🖥 Daily Bellringer Transparency, Section 1

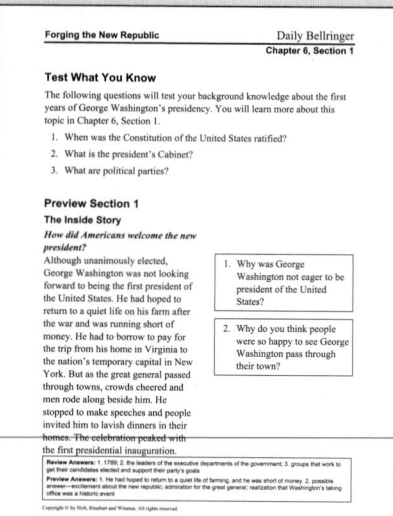

Taking Notes

Wanted a strong, centralized nation, supported growing cities and businesses, endorsed 'loose construction' interpretation of Constitution, favored national bank

---

1 Washington Becomes President

BEFORE YOU READ

MAIN IDEA
President Washington and other leaders tried to solve the new nation's economic problems. This led to the rise of political parties.

READING FOCUS
1. What steps did Congress and the president take to organize the new government?
2. What was Alexander Hamilton's plan to settle the nation's debts?
3. What was the debate over the national bank?
4. How did the first political parties form?

KEY TERMS AND PEOPLE
cabinet
Judiciary Act of 1789
strict construction
loose construction
Bank of the United States
Whiskey Rebellion
two-party system
Democratic-Republicans

TAKING NOTES As you read, take notes on the Federalist point of view on government. Record your notes on a graphic organizer like the one shown here.

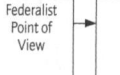

Federalist Point of View ➔

THE INSIDE STORY

How did Americans welcome the new president? The new government was slow getting started. Even after electors voted unanimously for Washington, it took months for Congress to make the results official. Washington had already packed his bags for the trip from Virginia to New York, the temporary capital. As he waited, both he and his wife, Martha, had serious doubts about the coming months.

After the war, Washington had looked forward to a quiet life as a farmer at Mount Vernon. Now it seemed that responsibility for the success of the new nation rested on his shoulders. To make things worse, he was short of money and had to borrow to pay for his trip. He wrote gloomily that he approached the presidency "with feelings not unlike those of a culprit who is going to his place of execution."

Finally, on April 14, the election results were official, and Washington set out for New York. As his coach passed through towns and villages on the trip north, enthusiastic crowds cheered him. Men on horseback rode alongside the coach, stirring up dust from the dirt roads. He stopped in small towns to make speeches. He led parades and went to lavish dinners.

The emotions of the people were almost overwhelming. At last Washington reached New York, and the joyful celebrations reached a peak on the historic day of the nation's first presidential inauguration. ◢

A Born Leader

▶ **Washington's stately image has come to symbolize the presidency.**

Teach the Main Idea

At Level | Standard English Mastery

Washington Becomes President

1. **Teach** Ask students the Reading Focus questions to teach this section.

2. **Apply** Have students draw four large ovals on their papers and label the top of each with the topics of this section in the text. Have students work in pairs to examine the visuals and charts in the section. Have students list the visuals in the ovals and write a brief explanation of the ways in which the visuals relate to the topic.

3. **Review** As you review the section, have

students explain why organizing the new government was so critical to the new nation and to the future of the country.

4. **Practice/Homework** Have students write a one-page essay in which they discuss the nation's financial debt and give suggestions about possible ways to settle the debt.

LS Logical-Mathematical, Visual-Spatial

📑 Alternative Assessment Handbook, Rubrics 13: Graphic Organizers; and 37: Writing Assignments

The President's Cabinet

Washington appointed four cabinet members, pictured with him here:

1. Henry Knox
2. Thomas Jefferson
3. Edmund Randolph
4. Alexander Hamilton
5. George Washington

THE GRANGER COLLECTION, NEW YORK

THE CABINET, 1789 TO TODAY — QUICK FACTS

Today the president's cabinet includes the vice president and the heads of 15 executive departments.

 1 **Department of War,** * 1789

2 **Department of State,** 1789

3 **Attorney general,** 1789

4 **Department of the Treasury,** 1789

Department of the Interior, 1849

Department of Justice, ** 1870

Department of Agriculture, 1889

Department of Commerce, 1903

Department of Labor, 1913

Department of Health and Human Services, 1953

Department of Housing and Urban Development, 1965

Department of Transportation, 1966

Department of Energy, 1977

Department of Education, 1979

Department of Veterans Affairs, 1988

Department of Homeland Security, 2002

* Today, this is called the Department of Defense.

** The attorney general became the head of the new Department of Justice in 1870.

Organizing the Government

No one doubted that George Washington would become the first president of the United States. The whole time that the Constitutional Convention had debated the role of the president, most people had Washington in mind for the job. Indeed, when the presidential electors met in February 1789, Washington won unanimously. John Adams, who received the second highest number of votes, became vice president.

Inauguration day, April 30, 1789, began with the sound of cannons and church bells. The streets of New York were hung with banners. Washington stepped onto the balcony of Federal Hall on Wall Street and took his oath of office. He was formally dressed in a brown suit of American-made broadcloth, to encourage American business. He also wore white silk stockings and silver-buckled shoes, and his graying hair was powdered white.

Washington spoke briefly, and then the celebrations began. Fireworks lit up the sky over New York City. The new president joined members of Congress at a church service in Saint Paul's Church.

Washington chooses a cabinet In his inaugural address, Washington spoke modestly about his lack of administrative experience. But the former commander in chief was certainly an experienced leader. His dignity and quiet power, along with his impressive height, gave him an air of authority.

Washington knew that what he did as president would set a pattern for later administrations. For example, the Constitution mentions the "heads of the executive departments" but did not specify what those departments should be. So, in 1789 Congress created the first three executive departments—state, treasury, and war. The leaders of these departments would become known as the president's **cabinet**.

For the cabinet positions, Washington chose men he knew and trusted. Henry Knox, who had been in charge of weaponry in the Revolutionary War, became secretary of war. Thomas Jefferson became secretary of state, and Alexander Hamilton became secretary of the treasury. Edmund Randolph of Virginia was attorney general, the president's legal adviser.

There were personal and political clashes in the brand-new government. Washington and

---

Organizing the Government

Recall What was John Adams's job as vice president? *to preside over the Senate*

Draw Conclusions Why did Congress pass the Judiciary Act of 1789? *Constitution had left the structure of the federal court system to Congress.*

Compare and Contrast In what ways did the Federalist vision of the nation differ from the Republican vision? *Federalists believed in a strong central government, prosperous cities with thriving businesses; Republicans believed nation should have a small central government, be more rural than urban, with a great deal of power left to the states*

🔲 Quick Facts Transparency: Hamilton's Economic Plan

Primary Source

". . . the judicial power ought to be distinct from both the legislative and executive, and independent upon both, that so it may be a check upon both, as both should be checks upon that."

— Thomas Jefferson

Letter to George Wythe, 1776

Answers

Reading Check *Democratic-Republicans wanted a small central government, more rural than urban, states powerful; Federalists supported strong central government, prosperity for cities and businesses, and limited state power*

204

THE IMPACT TODAY

Government

The Supreme Court today consists of a chief justice and eight associate justices. Chief Justice William Rehnquist served as the nation's 16th chief justice until his death in 2005. He was succeeded by John Roberts.

John Adams, the vice president, were old opponents. They avoided working closely with each other. Similarly, Hamilton and Jefferson—both brilliant men—disagreed about policies. They were also very different in personality and grew to dislike each other intensely.

Many compromises had been made in writing the Constitution. Many questions about the direction the country should take had not been answered. Deep differences remained. The Federalists, led by Hamilton, envisioned a strong centralized nation, with prospering cities and businesses and a role in world affairs. But others preferred a smaller central government, more rural than urban, with a good deal of power left to the states. Led by Jefferson and Madison, these people were known as Jeffersonian Republicans.

The first Congress Only 10 states had joined the government by this time, so the first Congress was small. The Constitution stated that Vice President Adams would preside over the Senate. That was the vice president's only job at the time.

As you read earlier, Congress quickly debated a Bill of Rights and sent proposed amendments to the states. By 1791 the 10 amendments known as the Bill of Rights became an important part of the Constitution.

The Constitution left the structure of the federal court system up to Congress. In the **Judiciary Act of 1789**, Congress organized the judicial branch. It had a six-person Supreme Court with one chief justice and five associates. Washington named John Jay as the first chief justice of the United States. Congress also created district courts and courts of appeal.

READING CHECK **Making Generalizations** What kind of government did Democratic-Republicans want and what kind did Federalists want?

Settling the Nation's Debts

The Treasury secretary, Alexander Hamilton, faced enormous problems. The new government owed money to foreign nations, to private lenders, and even to former soldiers.

Hamilton thought the secret of stable government was a wealthy aristocratic class. To win their support, he had to make the government's financial position more secure, both at home and abroad. Financial stability, he said, would help

HISTORY'S VOICES

❝to promote the increasing respectability of the American name; to answer the calls of justice; . . . to furnish new resources, both to agriculture and commerce; to cement more closely the union of the States; to add to their security against foreign attack; to establish public order.❞

—Alexander Hamilton,
Report on the Public Credit, 1790

HAMILTON'S ECONOMIC PLAN

QUICK FACTS

Alexander Hamilton developed a three-point plan to solve the nation's financial problems.

Point	Arguments For	Arguments Against
1. Pay the national debt Take on foreign and domestic debt by replacing creditors' old low-value bonds with new, interest-bearing bonds Take over most of the states' $25 million Revolutionary War debts	• Would build confidence in the new nation • Would free up state money for business and trade	• Would reward rich speculators and punish ordinary citizens who had sold their bonds at low prices • Southern states had already paid their war debts, and resented being taxed to pay the Northern debt.
2. Raise money to pay the debt Pass the Tariff of 1789 and a new excise tax	• Would raise money for the new nation and help manufacturers	• Some people resented these new taxes and tariffs
3. Standardize the banking system Create a national bank and a national mint	• Would raise money for the new nation and help manufacturers	• The Constitution did not specifically say the federal government could create a national bank.

204 CHAPTER 6

Differentiating Instruction

Below Level

Special Education Students

Materials poster paper, colored pencils or markers

1. Remind students of the problems that the nation's leaders faced in establishing a banking system and paying the nation's debts. Tell students that many organizations face similar problems today.

2. Organize students into small groups. Have each group develop a plan to help a local recreation center raise money to get a new

roof and still have a small surplus in the bank to meet future emergency needs.

3. Have groups write their plans on the poster paper.

4. Have volunteers share their plans with the class, and display their posters for the class to see. Have students discuss which plans seem most feasible. 🔷 **Visual-Spatial, Interpersonal**

📄 Alternative Assessment Handbook, Rubrics 14: Group Activity; and 28: Posters

Hamilton's economic plan Hamilton's plan had several features. He wanted the federal government to take on all debt from the Revolutionary War—including the debts of both the states and national government. To do that, he had to find ways to bring the government more income, or revenue. Finally, he wanted to establish a national bank, which would control credit and make loans to the government.

Hamilton's ideas were controversial. The government had sold bonds to merchants and farmers and army officers and soldiers, promising to pay back the money in a certain number of years. But during the hard times after the war, many people holding the bonds needed cash. They sold their bonds to speculators, who paid far less than the actual face value of the bonds. Speculators were betting that the bonds would regain their value.

Under Hamilton's plan, the government would pay the face value to the speculators who now held the bonds. The speculators would make a profit, while those people who originally held the bonds had lost money. Some people thought this was unfair.

Imposing new taxes Unlike the Articles of Confederation, the Constitution gave Congress the power to impose taxes. So far, however, most government income had come from sales of lands in the West.

To increase revenue, Hamilton proposed two different kinds of taxes. One was a tariff, a tax on imported goods. Congress quickly passed the Tariff of 1789.

In 1791 Congress also passed the first excise tax, which is a tax on the production or sale of a certain product. The 1791 tax was on liquor, sugar, snuff, and carriages. It would prove to be very unpopular.

Hamilton's plan to pay off the states' debts was also controversial. Northern states had greater debts than most of the southern states. If the national government assumed all state debts, people in the South would have to pay taxes to pay off other states' debts. Jefferson and others objected to the plan, and Congress voted it down several times.

Compromise leads to a new capital Hamilton tried to change Jefferson's mind about his economic plan. He also needed to win over southerner James Madison, who led the opposition in Congress. Over dinner, they crafted a compromise.

In 1790 the nation's capital had moved from New York to Philadelphia. But many Virginians wanted it in the South. Now the three men agreed that the capital would be moved to the new Federal City in the South by 1800. In return, southerners in Congress would allow Hamilton's debt bill to pass.

Washington was pleased because the historic bargain allowed him to choose an area on the Potomac River between Virginia and Maryland, near his Mount Vernon home. In March 1791 Washington chose a French engineer, Pierre Charles L'Enfant, to plan the new capital's layout. At Jefferson's suggestion, he named Benjamin Banneker, an African American mathematician, as a member of the planning commission.

L'Enfant conceived a grand and elegant plan for the city. The overall plan included wide boulevards radiating out from the Capitol, like spokes of a wheel. Washington, who had been a professional surveyor, admired L'Enfant's plan. Jefferson, however, had already designed and built several beautiful buildings. He disliked L'Enfant's grand, imperial style and drew his own plan for a simpler town. Although L'Enfant was eventually dismissed from the project, much of his plan was followed.

READING CHECK **Summarizing** How did Hamilton increase revenue?

FACES OF HISTORY

Benjamin BANNEKER
1731–1806

The son of a former slave, Benjamin Banneker taught himself advanced mathematics. At the age of 30, he built a precise wooden clock and, at the age of 58, he accurately predicted a solar eclipse. His scientific and mathematical skills helped him earn an appointment by George Washington to survey land for the new capital in Washington, D.C.

Banneker worked closely with Pierre L'Enfant, the architect in charge of planning the new nation's capital. When L'Enfant was dismissed from the project because of his temper, he took the plans with him. Banneker recreated the drawings from memory. These recreated plans were used to complete the work on the city.

Explain How did Banneker help build the city of Washington, D.C.?

Reading Focus

❷ What was Alexander Hamilton's plan to settle the nation's debts? *establish national bank; impose taxes*

Settling the Nation's Debts

Recall Why was the country in such poor financial condition? *owed money to foreign nations, private lenders, former soldiers*

Explain How was the Constitution different from the Articles of Confederation in terms of income generation? *Constitution gave Congress the right to impose taxes, Articles gave no such power.*

Elaborate What was Hamilton's three-pronged plan to solve the nation's financial problem? *pay off states' Revolutionary War debts; raise money through tariffs and excise taxes; create national bank to standardize banking system*

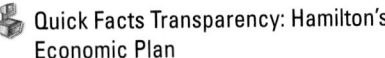 Quick Facts Transparency: Hamilton's Economic Plan

 CRF: Biography: Benjamin Banneker

Teaching Tip

Remind students that the United States is a republic, not a direct democracy. In a republic, or representative democracy, people elect representatives to carry out the work of the government for them. In a direct democracy, all voters meet to make laws and decide what actions to take.

Answers

Faces of History *Banneker worked closely with L'Enfant and recreated the city's plan after L'Enfant was dismissed from the project.*

Reading Check *tariffs and excise taxes*

Skills Focus: Making Generalizations
At Level

Reading Skill
Hamilton's Economic Plan

1. Guide students in a discussion of what it would mean for the nation to assume and then consolidate state debts. Ask students if they believe this was a wise step for a new country that was already in financial difficulty.

2. Organize students into pairs or small groups. Have each group create two political cartoons, complete with captions. One cartoon should support Hamilton's proposal to consolidate states' debts; the other cartoon should oppose his proposal.

3. Have volunteers from each group present their cartoons to the class. **LS Visual-Spatial, Interpersonal**

📋 Alternative Assessment Handbook, Rubric 27: Political Cartoons

❸ What was the debate over the national bank? *between Federalists and Republicans over how much power the central government should have*

Debating a National Bank

Recall What type of constitutional constructionist would use the phrase "whatever is necessary and proper" in determining government action? *loose constructionist*

Contrast Explain the difference between strict and loose constructionists when interpreting the Constitution. *Strict constructionists believe the government can do only those things stated within the Constitution; loose constructionists believe the government can take reasonable actions not directly stated in the Constitution, as long as the actions are not specifically prohibited.*

Summarize Why was Jefferson lukewarm about the final form of the Constitution? *believed it gave too much power to central government; wanted smaller central government, with more power reserved for states*

Counterpoints

Views of the Constitution

Summarize Have students work in mixed-ability pairs to paraphrase the statements of Hamilton and Jefferson. As an extension, organize a class debate on the two viewpoints.

Answers

Reading Like a Historian *opinions based on each person's vision of the role of government and the power of the central government*

Debating a National Bank

The most controversial part of Hamilton's plan was the national bank. The debate made clear that Jeffersonian Republicans and Federalists had opposing viewpoints about government. Like many debates during the Constitutional Convention, the disagreement centered on how much power the central government should have.

A broader debate arose over two ways of viewing the Constitution: **strict construction** and **loose construction**. People who favor strict construction believe that the government should only do what the Constitution specifically states it can do. On the other hand, those who favor loose construction think that the government can take reasonable actions that are not outlined in the Constitution—as long as those actions are not specifically prohibited.

Hamilton's bank plan The Constitution (Article I, Section 8) listed a number of specific, or expressed, powers that are granted to Congress. When Hamilton proposed a national bank, he pointed to the clause in the Constitution that allows Congress to pass all laws that are "necessary and proper" to carry out its assigned powers.

This broad interpretation of the Constitution was a prime example of loose construction. From Hamilton's point of view, the "necessary and proper" clause allowed actions that follow the intent of the Constitution even though those actions are not specifically named in the Constitution. This clause has allowed the government to expand its powers and to adjust to changing times. To this day, it is still a question for debate.

Jefferson opposes the bank Jeffersonian Republicans continued the Antifederalists' arguments against a strong central government. Jefferson himself, although he admired Washington and Madison, was lukewarm about the Constitution in its final form.

Jefferson wanted a small central government with more power left to the states. He favored limiting government powers to only

---

Views of the Constitution

Alexander Hamilton argued passionately that to constrain the powers of the federal government too much would mean to weaken it considerably.

❝ Every power vested in a Government is in its nature sovereign, and includes . . . a right to employ all the means requisite [necessary], and fairly applicable to the attainment of the ends of such power; and which are not precluded by restrictions & exceptions specified in the constitution. ❞

Alexander Hamilton,
1791

Thomas Jefferson feared that the "necessary and proper" clause would open the door to abuse of power.

❝ To take a single step beyond the boundaries thus specially drawn around the powers of Congress, is to take possession of a boundless field of power, no longer susceptible of any definition. . . . The Constitution allows only the means which are "necessary," not those which are merely "convenient" for effecting the enumerated powers. ❞

Thomas Jefferson, 1791

Skills FOCUS **READING LIKE A HISTORIAN**

Distinguishing Fact from Opinion Are the arguments presented by Hamilton and Jefferson expressions of facts or opinions? Explain your answer.

See **Skills Handbook, pp. H28–H29**

THE GRANGER COLLECTION, NEW YORK

Skills Focus: Drawing Conclusions   **At Level**

Reading Skill
Hamilton's Economic Plan

1. Guide students in a discussion about Washington's presidency and the improvements he made in the government structure. Review with students Hamilton's economic plan and the mixed reaction to its provisions.

2. Have students write a memorandum briefing President Washington on the public reaction

to Hamilton's financial plan and, in particular, to the idea of the national bank.

3. Have volunteers read their memoranda to the class. 🅛 **Verbal-Linguistic**

📃 Alternative Assessment Handbook, Rubric 42: Writing to Inform

those specifically spelled out in the Constitution—and that would not include the power to form a national bank.

Washington signs the bank bill The bank proposal made others uneasy as well. Its directors were to be private bankers, who would clearly gain more influence and wealth from it. Madison, Randolph, and others joined Jefferson in opposing it. Speaking to Congress, Madison said that the right to regulate trade had little to do with a national bank.

Despite the opposition, Congress passed the bill and sent it to the president to sign. Jefferson urged Washington to veto the bank bill. While Washington admitted that he was "greatly perplexed," he did not want to use the presidential veto.

Hamilton eventually persuaded President Washington to be flexible. Washington signed the bill to charter the first **Bank of the United States** in February 1791.

READING CHECK Summarizing Why did Jefferson oppose the national bank?

First Political Parties Form

Hamilton and Jefferson had personal differences. But their rift between the two leaders also reflected a deep split among national leaders. The people themselves were divided along the same lines as they were during the battle over ratifying the Constitution. Soon, another of Hamilton's controversial financial plans—the excise tax—led to a violent clash between supporters and opponents of strong government.

The Whiskey Rebellion Farmers and settlers in the woods and mountains of the western frontier had always resented the wealth and power of people in the East. They felt their interests were ignored. They disliked being told how to act by easterners—including the national government in Philadelphia.

In 1794 farmers on the frontier in western Pennsylvania objected violently to Hamilton's excise tax on whiskey. Their livelihoods depended on turning their surplus grain into rye whiskey. Whiskey was easier to transport

WASHINGTON REVIEWING THE WESTERN ARMY AT FORT CUMBERLAND, MARYLAND

Washington led an army of about 13,000 men.

This painting depicts Washington as a hero on a white horse.

Skills FOCUS READING LIKE A HISTORIAN

President Washington responded decisively—and in person— to the Whiskey Rebellion, leading an army to suppress it.
Interpreting Visuals How does the painting reinforce the idea of a strong federal government?

207

207

First Political Parties Form

Recall Why were Jeffersonian Republicans called Democratic-Republicans? *to emphasize that they favored popular government*

Summarize Why did President Washington personally join the effort to put down the Whiskey Rebellion? *wanted to make it clear that armed rebellions against the government would not be tolerated*

Review & Assess

Close

Have students describe the ways in which Washington and other leaders tried to solve the nation's economic problems and how this resulted in the rise of political parties.

Review

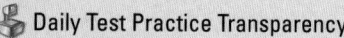 Online Quiz, Section 1

Daily Test Practice Transparency

Assess

SE Section 1 Assessment

Progress Assessment: Section 1 Quiz

Alternative Assessment Handbook

Reteach

Interactive Reader and Study Guide, Section 1

Interactive Skills Tutor CD-ROM

---

than grain and could be sold for more money. The rebel farmers led an uprising known as the **Whiskey Rebellion**.

The farmers attacked tax collectors. They burned the barns of people who gave away the location of stills where whiskey was made. A crowd of more than 2,000 angry farmers threatened Pittsburgh, then a small town. There was talk of setting up an independent nation.

Washington took command. He wanted to make it clear that armed rebellion against the national government would not be tolerated. To help the Pennsylvanians, he called out the militia from Virginia, Maryland, and New Jersey. That raised a force of some 13,000 or more men. Washington sent one last order to the rebels to stop. He and Hamilton rode west to lead the troops into Pennsylvania.

Instead of resisting the huge militia force, the surprised farmers scattered in all directions. The militia caught and arrested them. Two were later convicted of treason, but Washington eventually pardoned them. A pleased Washington said that the rebel farmers had been taught a lesson "without spilling a drop of blood." He had also shown that the federal government would take action within a state.

Political parties develop The Constitution did not anticipate political parties. Most of the Framers thought parties were dangerous to national unity. Washington opposed political

THE IMPACT TODAY

Government

Jefferson's Democratic-Republican Party eventually developed into the modern Democratic Party. The modern Republican Party was founded in the 1850s.

parties as well. In *The Federalist*, James Madison had warned about factions.

In the 1790s, however, Americans became politically divided. The Whiskey Rebellion showed that some people did not agree with Washington's policies.

Both sides—Jeffersonian Republicans and Federalists—were starting to act like political parties. The Federalists under Hamilton took the lead. They established local associations. They gave political offices and other favors to their supporters. Jeffersonian Republicans went even further than the Federalists in setting up their party organizations. In various states, Jeffersonian Republicans worked together to influence elections.

Each side justified its actions as necessary to resist what they considered the dangerous ideas of the other. By forming these two groups, early American leaders were well on their way to establishing a **two-party system**.

Jeffersonian Republicans were later called **Democratic-Republicans** to emphasize that they favored popular government. However, none of the Framers or other early leaders were in favor of a government as democratic as it eventually became. They did not completely trust the mass of ordinary and largely uneducated people.

READING CHECK **Identifying Cause and Effect** What was the main cause of the Whiskey Rebellion?

SECTION 1 ASSESSMENT

go.hrw.com
Online Quiz
Keyword: SD7 HP6

Reviewing Ideas, Terms, and People

1. **a. Identify** Who were the members of Washington's first cabinet?
   b. Explain How did Washington influence the role of future presidents?
   c. Predict What were likely to be the results of the compromises made while writing the Constitution?

2. **a. Describe** What were the main features of Hamilton's economic plan?
   b. Analyze Which leaders objected to paying the states' debts, and what were their objections?

3. **a. Recall** Why did Hamilton and Jefferson disagree on the bank bill?
   b. Compare Describe the two opposing points of view on how to interpret the Constitution.
   c. Evaluate How would the country's growth have been limited if leaders had always followed **strict construction**?

4. **a. Identify** Who were some of the leading Republicans in the 1790s?
   b. Explain What events and points of view during the 1790s showed that a **two-party system** was developing?

Critical Thinking

5. **Comparing** Copy the chart below and compare the points of view of Federalists and Republicans.

Federalists	Republicans

FOCUS ON WRITING

6. **Persuasive** As a newspaper editor in either Philadelphia or Virginia, write an editorial explaining why the national capital should be located in your region.

Section 1 Assessment Answers

1. **a.** Knox, Jefferson, Hamilton
   b. set structure of government
   c. further disputes along party lines; other amendments

2. **a.** assume states' debts; tariff and excise tax; create national bank
   b. southern states with lower debts objected to higher northern debts

3. **a.** Hamilton wanted to strengthen central government; Jefferson wanted it smaller
   b. strict constructionists—do only what Constitution says; loose constructionists—

can take actions not outlined in Constitution
   c. no new territory like that of Louisiana

4. **a.** Jefferson, Hamilton
   b. stong federal government v. weak one, urban v. rural

5. Federalists—strong, central government, favored urban development; Republicans—states' power, individual liberties, favored common man

6. region centrally located; access to good transportation

Answers

Reading Check *excise tax on whiskey*

208

SECTION 2
Challenges of the 1790s

BEFORE YOU READ

MAIN IDEA

The United States faced many challenges during the 1790s. It tried to remain neutral in European wars while dealing with conflicts with Native Americans in the Northwest Territory.

READING FOCUS

1. Why did Washington want to remain neutral in response to events in Europe?

2. What conflicts took place in the Northwest Territory?

3. What challenges did John Adams face as president, and what was the XYZ affair?

KEY TERMS AND PEOPLE

Neutrality Proclamation
Jay's Treaty
Pinckney's Treaty
Little Turtle
Battle of Fallen Timbers
Treaty of Greenville
sectionalism
XYZ affair
Alien and Sedition Acts
Virginia and Kentucky Resolutions
nullification

 TAKING NOTES As you read, take notes on what Jay's Treaty, Pinckney's Treaty, and the Treaty of Greenville accomplished for the United States. Record your notes in a graphic organizer like the one shown here.

THE INSIDE STORY

How would the Americans respond to a French Revolution? Just as the new U.S. government was getting organized, the people of France launched a revolution of their own. In France, the king had absolute power. The monarch and a few noble families owned most of the country's land and wealth. Only nobles had a voice in government.

There was an immense gap between this privileged upper class and the rest of the people. Most were poor peasants or urban laborers who paid high taxes to support the nobles' grand estates.

In early 1789 France exploded into horrific bloodshed. People protested against food shortages, high prices, and taxes. On July 14, 1789, a crowd of angry Parisians stormed the Bastille prison, a hated symbol of royal power. Soon, a revolutionary government took over. It limited the king's power and made France a constitutional monarchy.

The Americans faced a difficult question. Should they support another country's revolution against an oppressive monarchy? Or, should the United States remain neutral? ◢

Remaining Neutral

The overthrow of the French monarchy alarmed other European rulers. Austria and Prussia declared war on France. Other nations, including Great Britain and Spain, soon joined them.

But in the United States, many people celebrated the news from France. After all, help from the French military had been vital in winning the Revolutionary War. Democratic-Republicans thought that the revolution in France meant the end of monarchy and a turn toward liberty. They also feared that if the French

Revolution Abroad

▼ **French revolutionaries seize the Bastille, where arms and munitions were stored.**

209

Preteach

Bellringer

The Inside Story. . . Use the **Daily Bellringer Transparency** to help students answer the question.

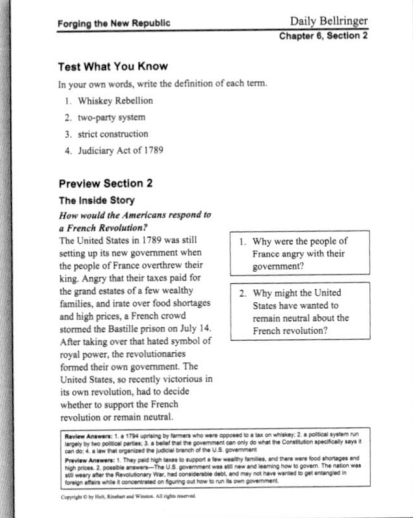 Daily Bellringer Transparency, Section 2

Academic Vocabulary

Review with students the high-use academic term in this section.

deny to refuse (p. 210)

CRF: Vocabulary Builder Activity, Section 2

Taking Notes

Jay's Treaty—British paid for damage to American ships and gave their forts in the Northwest to the U.S.; Pinckney's Treaty— settled border and trade disputes with Spain; Treaty of Greenville—Native Americans gave up claim to areas in Ohio, Indiana, Illinois, and Michigan

---

Teach the Main Idea

At Level

Challenges of the 1790s

1. **Teach** Ask students the Reading Focus questions to teach this section.

2. **Apply** Have students draw three ladders on their papers and label the top of each with one of the topics of this section in the text. Have students scan the section and list conflicts, treaties, proclamations, and government acts on the rungs of the corresponding ladders. **LS Visual-Spatial**

3. **Review** As you review the section, have students explain how these events relate to the topic.

4. **Practice/Homework** Have students write a brief report to the citizens of one of the new states, describing the victories and challenges facing the national government during this period and how these victories and challenges will affect citizens of that state. **LS Verbal-Linguistic**

Alternative Assessment Handbook, Rubric 42: Writing to Inform

Graphic Organizer Transparencies

1 Why did Washington want to remain neutral in response to events in Europe? *believed future growth and prosperity depended on staying neutral*

Remaining Neutral

Identify What was the Neutrality Proclamation? *1793 commitment to pursue friendly and impartial conduct toward nations that were at war*

Summarize Why did President Washington demand that France replace Edmund Genêt? *he defied Neutrality Proclamation; enlisted Americans to fight against the British*

Make Inferences Why do you think Jay's Treaty was unpopular? *U.S. had to agree to pay debts that it owed to Britain.*

TIME LINE

Keeping the Peace

The United States attempted to remain neutral in foreign conflicts following the French Revolution. Three agreements supported this goal:

1793 Neutrality Proclamation
The United States would be "friendly and impartial" toward France and Great Britain.

1794 Jay's Treaty
Britain relinquished control of the Northwest to the United States and agreed to pay for its attacks on American merchant ships.

1795 Pinckney's Treaty
Spain gave the United States the right to use the Mississippi River and port of New Orleans. Spain and the United States settled the northern boundary of Florida.

Skills FOCUS **INTERPRETING TIME LINES**

How might Jay's Treaty and Pinckney's Treaty have helped the United States remain neutral?

See Skills Handbook, p. H14

Revolution failed, it meant a failure of republican government everywhere.

The more conservative Federalists were horrified. Hamilton had always had a great deal of respect for monarchy and not much for democracy. But the Federalists seemed to be in the minority.

A declaration of neutrality Once war in Europe began, both France and Britain tried to draw the United States into the conflict. One crucial issue was trade by sea. Britain was a major sea power, while France was not. The French needed American ships on their side.

The new French government called on old alliances as well as public sympathy for the republican cause. Nevertheless, Washington wanted to remain strictly neutral. He did agree to recognize the new government in France, however. Jefferson explained:

ACADEMIC VOCABULARY
deny to refuse

HISTORY'S VOICES

❝We surely cannot deny to any nation the right whereon our own government is founded, that every nation may govern itself according to whatever form it pleases.❞

— Thomas Jefferson, letter to Gouverneur Morris, 1792

Washington was convinced that the future growth and prosperity of the United States depended on staying neutral. In April 1793, he issued the **Neutrality Proclamation.** It committed the United States to "pursue a conduct friendly and impartial towards the belligerent powers." He held to the Neutrality Proclamation for the rest of his presidency.

Genet defies neutrality Republican newspapers harshly attacked the president and the proclamation. They spread rumors that the Federalists wanted a return to monarchy. Then France's new ambassador to the United States, Edmund Genet, tried to convince ordinary American citizens to support the French. Pro-French mobs held street rallies. Eventually, Genet openly defied the Neutrality Proclamation. He enlisted an American crew to fight on a French ship against the British.

Washington, who had a quick temper, was furious. Even Jefferson thought that Genet had gone too far. Washington demanded that France replace Genet with a new ambassador.

More diplomatic challenges For years, Jefferson had wanted to resign as secretary of state. Now Washington could no longer convince him to stay. Jefferson's departure meant that there was no one in the cabinet to balance Hamilton's point of view.

Then close on the heels of the French crisis came trouble with Britain. In early 1794 the British began to seize American merchant ships in the West Indies, claiming they carried French goods or were sailing to a French port. They threw the American sailors into prison.

210 CHAPTER 6

Skills Focus: Making Generalizations

At Level

Reading Skill
Remaining Neutral

1. Guide students in a discussion about the reaction in the United States to the French Revolution.

2. Have students write a half-page editorial for a 1789 issue of the "New York Journal" expressing either a positive or a negative reaction to the French Revolution and the overthrow of the monarchy.

3. Have students create a political cartoon to accompany their editorials.

4. Have volunteers present their editorials and cartoons to the class. **LS Visual-Spatial, Verbal-Linguistic**

📖 Alternative Assessment Handbook, Rubrics 17: Letters to Editors; and 27: Political Cartoons

---

Answers

Interpreting Time Lines *settled boundary disputes peacefully; forced British to pay for violating American neutrality*

In addition, in the Northwest Territory the British were stirring up trouble among the Native Americans.

Washington sent Chief Justice John Jay to negotiate with the British. In **Jay's Treaty** (1794), the British agreed to pay for damages to American ships. They also agreed to leave their forts, giving the United States control of the Northwest. In return, the United States agreed to pay debts owed the British.

Jay's Treaty was wildly unpopular. It did pave the way to settle another problem, however. Spain was now worried that the United States and Britain would unite against Spain in North America. This concern aided diplomat Thomas Pinckney in his negotiations with Spain. **Pinckney's Treaty** (1795) with Spain settled many border and trade disputes between the United States and Spain.

READING CHECK **Summarizing** Why did many Democratic-Republicans sympathize with the French revolutionaries?

Conflicts in the Northwest Territory

After the Revolution, settlers poured across the Appalachians into the western lands. The Land Ordinance of 1785 and the Northwest Ordinance established patterns for dividing and settling the Northwest Territory. This land, however, was already home to many Native American nations.

The government put pressure on Iroquois, Choctaw, Chickasaw, and Cherokee leaders, sometimes forcing them to sign treaties giving up land. Other Native American nations formed confederations to resist white settlement. In the early 1790s violence broke out in Ohio and Indiana. A large force of American soldiers moved in but were turned back by a confederation of Miamis and Shawnees. Their war chief was Michikinqua, or **Little Turtle**.

In 1791 Arthur St. Clair, the governor of the Northwest Territory, brought an army to

NORTHWEST TERRITORY BATTLES

Map legend:
- Land ceded by Native Americans in Treaty of Greenville (1795)
- Native American victory
- American victory

0   100   200 Miles
0   100   200 Kilometers
Albers equal-area projection

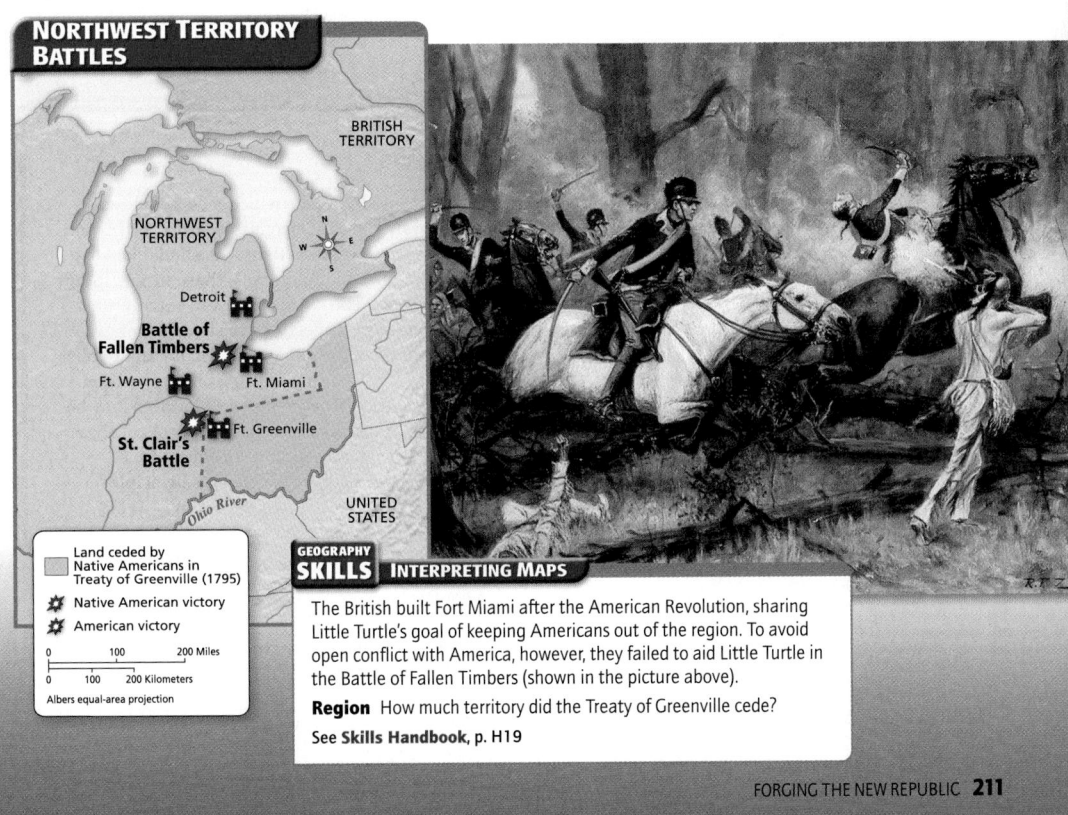

GEOGRAPHY SKILLS **INTERPRETING MAPS**

The British built Fort Miami after the American Revolution, sharing Little Turtle's goal of keeping Americans out of the region. To avoid open conflict with America, however, they failed to aid Little Turtle in the Battle of Fallen Timbers (shown in the picture above).

Region How much territory did the Treaty of Greenville cede?

See *Skills Handbook*, p. H19

FORGING THE NEW REPUBLIC **211**

See *Skills Handbook*, p. H19

211

Conflicts in the Northwest Territory

Recall What was the Battle of Fallen Timbers? *battle in 1794; decisive victory for Americans over the Miamis*

Explain What were the provisions of the 1795 Treaty of Greenville? *Miamis gave up territory in Ohio and parts of Indiana, Illinois, and Michigan; U.S. recognized Miamis' claim to land that they still possessed.*

Primary Sources

Washington's Farewell Address

~~Summarize~~ Have students make a list of unfamiliar words and look them up in a dictionary. Then have students write a paraphrase of the excerpt.

Info to Know

Fallen Timbers At Heidelberg College in Ohio, there is an archaeological project known as Fallen Timbers Battlefield. The project has two purposes: to accurately locate the battlefield so that it can be preserved, and to gain a better understanding of the lives and goals of the Native Americans who fought at Fallen Timbers.

Answers

Reading Like a Historian 1. *both support political prosperity; religion is the basis for morality;* **2.** *It is necessary to sustain stable, moral government.*

Reading Check *had to negotiate with U.S., give up large parts of their land*

---

force the Miamis, Shawnees, and Delawares to give up their lands for settlement. In November 1791 Little Turtle and his forces met St. Clair's army and won the greatest victory Native Americans had ever achieved over white armies.

U.S. General Anthony Wayne, a hero of the Revolution, then brought some 4,000 troops into the Ohio Valley. There they built forts and brought in supplies. Little Turtle realized that he could no longer expect help from the British. He urged his people to negotiate with the Americans, but he lost their support.

At the **Battle of Fallen Timbers** in 1794, the American forces won a decisive victory over the Miamis. In the **Treaty of Greenville** (1795) the Miamis gave up large territories in Ohio and parts of Indiana, Illinois, and Michigan. The treaty also recognized the Miamis' claim to the land they still had. Little Turtle himself turned to trying to maintain peace.

READING CHECK **Making Inferences** What did the loss of British support mean for Indians in the Ohio Valley?

President Adams and the XYZ Affair

In 1792 Washington reluctantly agreed to a second term in office. He was getting older and his health was not good. He wanted only to go home to Mount Vernon. In addition, Washington was no longer the universally admired hero that he had been just a few years before. His insistence on neutrality was unpopular, and many of his policies were harshly criticized by ardent Democratic-Republicans.

By 1796 nothing could persuade Washington to consider a third term as president. His Farewell Address was a long letter published in a Philadelphia newspaper. In it he continued to warn against getting involved in party politics and foreign affairs.

The election of 1796 Even though some people criticized him harshly, Washington was still a unifying symbol for the country. With his retirement, the rivalry between the two parties became more intensely political.

PRIMARY SOURCES

Washington's Farewell Address

In 1796 George Washington announced that he would not seek a third term in office. In his Farewell Address, he gave his advice on several subjects of importance to the future of the country. Following are some of his comments regarding the role of religion and politics.

"Of all the dispositions [moods] and habits which lead to political prosperity, religion and morality are indispensable supports. In vain would that man claim the tribute of patriotism who should labor to subvert these great pillars of human happiness—these firmest props of the duties of men and citizens. The mere politician, equally with the pious [religious] man, ought to respect and to cherish them. A volume could not trace all their connections with private and public felicity [truth]. . . . And let us with caution indulge the supposition that morality can be maintained without religion. Whatever may be conceded to the influence of refined education on minds of peculiar structure, reason and experience both forbid us to expect that national morality can prevail in exclusion of religious principle."

Washington emphasized the influence of religion on moral and ethical behavior.

Skills FOCUS **READING LIKE A HISTORIAN**

1. **Comparing** According to Washington, what is the relationship between religion and morality?
2. **Analyzing Primary Sources** According to Washington, what is religion's role in building the country?

See Skills Handbook, pp. H10, H28–H29

Skills Focus: Evaluating Historical Interpretations
At Level

Reading Like a Historian Skill
Washington as President
Research Required

1. Have students conduct outside research on the presidency of George Washington to answer this question: Was Washington a good president or was he a great president? Students should use both primary and secondary sources in their research.

2. Have students meet in small groups to discuss their research and their answers to the question. Have the small groups also address this question: What makes the difference between a good president and a great president, and how does the historical evaluation of a president change over time?

3. Have students write an essay in which they assess and evaluate the presidency of George Washington. **LS** **Verbal-Linguistic, Intrapersonal**

Alternative Assessment Handbook, Rubrics 30: Research; and 42: Writing to Inform

Jefferson was the clear choice as the Democratic-Republican candidate. Although Hamilton was the most prominent Federalist leader, many of his plans, including the excise tax, were unpopular. Hamilton also had no interest in the presidency. So the Federalists chose John Adams as their candidate.

Since before the Revolutionary War, Adams had been an outstanding leader. He had played a major role in creating the United States and in handling diplomacy in Europe. But to some people, Adams seemed cold, distant, and not well suited for the presidency.

As a result, while the Federalists easily won a majority of presidential electors, Adams did not have their full support. **Sectionalism**, or loyalty to one's region, played a role. Adams was best known in New England. In the South, many Federalists preferred his running mate, Thomas Pinckney of South Carolina.

The vote of the electors revealed a serious flaw in the new Constitution. Adams won with only a few votes more than Jefferson: 71 to 68. According to the Constitution, that meant that Adams's vice president would be the candidate who came in second: Jefferson, his greatest political rival.

More problems with France Relations with European nations were still a problem. Jay's and Pinckney's treaties had settled some conflicts with Britain and Spain. But Jay's Treaty made relations with revolutionary France more tense. French ships began to seize U.S. merchant vessels at sea. President Adams sent Charles Cotesworth Pinckney (older brother of Thomas) as the diplomatic representative of the United States, but the French turned him away. This was a serious insult.

Some angry Federalists wanted war. In 1797 Adams sent three distinguished American diplomats to France: Pinckney, Elbridge Gerry, and John Marshall. Again, the U.S. representatives were insulted. Rather than meeting with them, the French foreign minister, Prince Talleyrand, sent three minor diplomats who demanded bribes and a loan.

An angry President Adams sent a report to Congress, naming the three French agents as "X, Y, and Z." When the **XYZ affair** became public, many Americans wanted war. A popular slogan was: "Millions for defense but not one cent for tribute!"

Pulling back from outright war, Congress cut off trade with France. It canceled wartime treaties it had made with pre-revolutionary France, authorized building warships, and allowed the U.S. navy to capture French vessels at sea. Congress's actions persuaded the new French government, headed by a young general named Napoleon Bonaparte, to sign treaties on trade. The president and Congress had skillfully avoided a costly war with France.

Censoring free speech Indignation over the XYZ affair brought new support for the Federalists. It also brought new suspicions about the Democratic-Republicans' pro-French sympathies and a general resentment of foreigners. That mood allowed Congress to pass measures aimed at protecting the country from foreign enemies and domestic dissent during what was expected to be a war with France.

The series of four laws are known as the **Alien and Sedition Acts**. The three alien laws were aimed mainly at French and Irish refugees, most of whom supported France. Those measures increased the period of residency required for citizenship from 5 years to 14; required foreigners to register with the government; and allowed the president to jail or expel any foreigner thought to be "dangerous to the peace and safety" of the country.

FACES OF HISTORY

John **ADAMS**
1735–1826

John Adams entered Harvard College at the age of 15 and later became a respected lawyer. He rose to prominence as a Patriot during the Revolutionary War. Despite his good reputation, Adams was often critical of himself. When Thomas Jefferson pressed him to write the Declaration of Independence, Adams refused, insisting that he was "obnoxious, suspected, and unpopular." In reality, however, others respected him for his wisdom and honesty.

After serving as Washington's vice president, Adams was elected to the presidency. Although he strengthened the military and avoided war with Great Britain and France during his term, Adams's presidency is mainly remembered for its partisan conflict. Remarkably, Adams and Thomas Jefferson both died on July 4, 1826, the fiftieth anniversary of the adoption of the Declaration of Independence.

Summarize What characterized Adams's presidency?

❸ **What challenges did John Adams face as president, and what was the XYZ affair?** *threat of war with France; challenges to the federal government's authority; three minor French diplomats demanded bribes and a loan from American diplomats*

President Adams and the XYZ Affair

Explain What is sectionalism? *loyalty to one's region*

Make Inferences What factors might have contributed to some Americans' eagerness to see Washington retire? *insistence on neutrality; political divisiveness of the nation; desire for change in leadership of nation*

Summarize What provisions of the Alien and Sedition Acts were unconstitutional? *prohibited any criticism of government; restricted free speech and free press*

📃 Political Cartoons Activities for American History: Cartoon 12: A Fight in Congress

go.hrw.com
Online Resources

KEYWORD: SD7 CH6
TOPIC: ALIEN AND SEDITION ACTS

Skills Focus: Analyzing Primary Sources

Above Level

Reading Like a Historian Skill
Alien and Sedition Acts

Research Required

1. Guide students in a discussion of the XYZ Affair and the resulting Alien and Sedition Acts. Remind students that Jefferson and Madison argued that these laws were unconstitutional.

2. Have students conduct outside research to learn more about the acts and to locate and read primary sources from Jefferson and Madison discussing the acts.

3. Have students write an essay in which they summarize the arguments and present their own views about the constitutionality of the acts.

4. Have volunteers read their essays to the class. Then guide students in a discussion about if and when the government has the right to suspend civil liberties, including freedom of speech. **LS Verbal-Linguistic**

📖 Alternative Assessment Handbook, Rubrics 30: Research; and 40: Writing to Describe

Answers

Faces of History *strong military; avoidance of war with Britain and France; partisan conflict*

President Adams and the XYZ Affair

Explain Why did Jefferson and Madison draft the Virginia and Kentucky Resolutions? *so that states would nullify the Alien and Sedition Acts*

Describe What happened to the Alien and Sedition Acts? *They expired.*

Quick Facts Transparency: Reactions to the XYZ Affair

Review & Assess ●

Close

Have students identify and describe the challenges that the U.S. faced during the 1790s.

Review

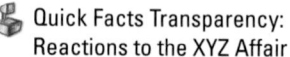 Online Quiz, Section 2

Daily Test Practice Transparency

Assess

SE Section 2 Assessment

Progress Assessment: Section 2 Quiz

Alternative Assessment Handbook

Reteach

Interactive Reader and Study Guide, Section 2

Interactive Skills Tutor CD-ROM

REACTIONS TO THE XYZ AFFAIR — QUICK FACTS

XYZ Affair
- France had attacked American merchant ships. French agents (referred to as X, Y, and Z) demanded bribes. The XYZ affair nearly brought France and the United States to war.

Alien and Sedition Acts (1798)
- The Alien Acts allowed the president to order foreigners considered to be a threat to national security to be jailed or deported.
- The Sedition Act made it a crime to speak against the government. Its target was the Democratic-Republicans, who historically had supported the French.

Virginia and Kentucky Resolutions (1798 and 1799)
- Some people saw the Alien and Sedition Acts as unconstitutional. The Virginia and Kentucky Resolutions nullified, or declared void, the Alien and Sedition Acts.

The Sedition Act outlawed any opposition to government policies by actions or by "false, scandalous, or malicious writing." In effect, it prohibited any criticism of public officials, a clear contradiction to the First Amendment rights of free speech and a free press.

Adams used the Alien and Sedition Acts cautiously. No aliens were deported, but nine Democratic-Republican newspaper editors and a member of Congress were convicted under the Sedition Act.

In an attempt to be rid of the hated laws, Jefferson and Madison drafted the **Virginia and Kentucky Resolutions**. In these resolutions, Jefferson and Madison argued that the Alien and Sedition Acts were unconstitutional.

They hoped that state legislatures would nullify the laws, or declare them void. Many supporters of states' rights believed that **nullification** of federal laws by states was legal. In the end, however, only Virginia and Kentucky passed the resolutions.

The end result of these actions was a deeper and more bitter political divide in Congress and the country. As you will read in the next section, Jefferson would eventually be elected president, and the new Congress would allow the Alien and Sedition Acts to expire.

READING CHECK **Identifying Cause and Effect** How did the XYZ affair lead to the Alien and Sedition Acts?

SECTION 2 ASSESSMENT

go.hrw.com
Online Quiz
Keyword: SD7 HP6

Reviewing Ideas, Terms, and People

1. **a. Recall** What major event occurred in France from 1789 to 1793?
   b. Compare How did Federalists and Democratic-Republicans react to the situation in France?
   c. Evaluate Was Edmund Genet's influence a threat to the United States? Why or why not?

2. **a. Identify** Who was **Little Turtle**?
   b. Summarize What happened in Ohio and Indiana as settlers moved into the Northwest Territory?

3. **a. Describe** How did Washington's retirement influence party politics?
   b. Explain What was the **XYZ affair**? How did it affect American public opinion?

   c. Rate Were the **Alien and Sedition Acts** effective weapons against foreign interference and internal turmoil? Explain.

Critical Thinking

4. **Analyzing** Copy the chart below and list the important points of each of these three treaties.

Jay's Teaty	Pinckney's Treaty	Treaty of Greenville

FOCUS ON WRITING

5. **Supporting a Position** You are a journalist who has been arrested under the Sedition Act for criticizing President Adams. Write a speech defending your right to criticize the president.

Section 2 Assessment Answers

1. **a.** French Revolution
   b. Federalists opposed; Republicans supported
   c. possible answer—yes, helped to increase divisiveness among American citizens

2. **a.** war chief of the Miamis
   b. increased conflicts with Native Americans

3. **a.** Rivalry between two parties increased
   b. three diplomats demanded loan, bribes; angered Americans, turned them against France
   c. yes, curbed outside interference; no, increased divisiveness within U.S.

4. Jay's—Britain paid for damages to U.S. ships; agreed to leave forts, gave U.S. control of Northwest; U.S. agreed to pay its debt; Pinckney's—Spain gave U.S. right to use Mississippi River; settled on northern boundary to Spanish Florida; Greenville—U.S. received territories in Ohio, Indiana, Illinois, Michigan; recognized Miamis' claim to land

5. First Amendment protects right to free speech; Sedition Act unconstitutional

Answers

Reading Check *U.S. angered and insulted by the affair; retaliated against French and Irish refugees*

3 Jefferson's Presidency

BEFORE YOU READ

MAIN IDEA

The rise of political parties influenced the election of 1800, bringing Thomas Jefferson and a new outlook to the presidency.

READING FOCUS

1. Why was the transfer of power in the election of 1800 significant?
2. What changes did Jefferson make when he took office?
3. What was the impact of the Louisiana Purchase?
4. How did the role of the Supreme Court change?

KEY TERMS AND PEOPLE

Aaron Burr
Twelfth Amendment
Louisiana Purchase
Lewis and Clark expedition
Meriwether Lewis
William Clark
Sacagawea
Zebulon M. Pike
Judiciary Act of 1801
judicial review

TAKING NOTES As you read, take notes on ways that the Louisiana Purchase might affect the United States. In each column of a diagram like the one below, fill in the kind of effect called for.

Commerce	Government	Country Size

A TIED ELECTION

THE INSIDE STORY **Will Aaron Burr be president?** Under the Constitution's plan for selecting a president, electors from each state voted for two candidates. The one with the most votes became president and the runner-up became vice president. This worked fine in the first election, because Washington was the unanimous choice. In 1796 the rise of political parties led to an uncomfortable situation. President John Adams, a Federalist, served with his political rival, Thomas Jefferson, as vice president. Politics became even more confusing in the bitterly contested election of 1800.

The Democratic-Republicans intended Jefferson to be president with Aaron Burr as vice president. In a close election, however, Jefferson and Burr each received 73 votes. A tied vote meant the House of Representatives would decide the outcome. Because Federalists were in control of the House until after the inauguration, they had to decide which Democratic-Republican they disliked less. Many despised and feared Jefferson. A few others, especially Alexander Hamilton, distrusted Burr even more.

The honorable thing for Burr to do was to concede to Jefferson, his party leader. But he did not. Over six days and nights, House members took vote after vote. Finally, on the 36th ballot, Jefferson won the presidency. Burr blamed Hamilton for his loss and never forgave him. ◾

▲ **Thomas Jefferson (left) won the election of 1800 against rival party candidate President John Adams (right) but first had to triumph over a member of his own party, Aaron Burr.**

The Election of 1800

The dawn of a new century brought many changes to the young American nation. One important political event was the presidential election of 1800. This contest marked the first time that power passed from one American political party to another.

The 1800 election matched Democratic-Republican Thomas Jefferson against Federalist John Adams, just as in the election of 1796. This time, however, **Aaron Burr** was the Democratic-Republican candidate for vice president and Charles Cotesworth Pinckney was the Federalist candidate. Each party believed that the republic's survival depended on the success of their

FORGING THE NEW REPUBLIC **215**

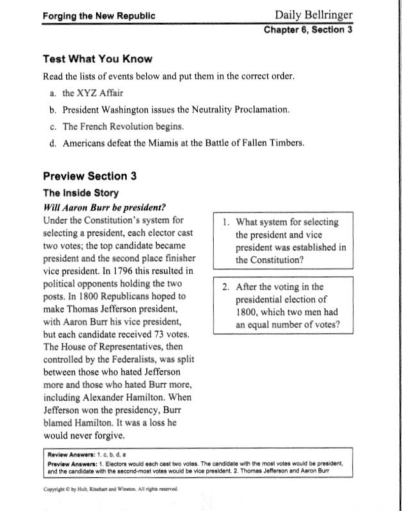

① Why was the transfer of power in the election of 1800 significant? *first time that power passed from one political party to another; led to the Twelfth Amendment*

The Election of 1800

Identify What was the purpose of the Twelfth Amendment? *established that separate ballots must be cast for president and vice president to prevent ties*

Summarize Which Federalist policies came under attack during the 1800 election? *taxes; Alien and Sedition Acts*

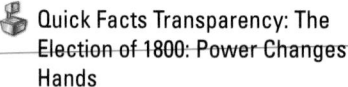 Quick Facts Transparency: The Election of 1800: Power Changes Hands

 CRF: History and Geography Activity: 1800 Presidential Election

② What changes did Jefferson make when he took office? *reduced size and influence of federal government; changed tax system*

Jefferson Makes Changes

Recall What was the central theme of Jefferson's inaugural address? *unity and tolerance*

Make Judgments Does the nation need a large army during peacetime? *possible answers—yes, needs to be prepared in case of war; no, could threaten civil liberties*

Political Cartoons Activities for American History: Cartoon 11: A Watchful Eye

Answers

Reading Check *unpopular acts that were easy targets for criticism during the election*

THE ELECTION OF 1800: POWER CHANGES HANDS

Federalists

John Adams and Charles C. Pinckney

- Wanted a strong federal government
- Thought the country should be ruled by the elite
- Emphasized manufacturing
- Believed in loose interpretation of the Constitution
- Supported Great Britain

Democratic–Republicans

Thomas Jefferson and Aaron Burr

- Wanted a limited national government that shared power with state and local governments
- Believed the country should be ruled by ordinary citizens
- Emphasized agriculture
- Believed in strict interpretation of the Constitution
- Supported France

THE IMPACT TODAY

Daily Life
One famous example of negative campaigning is Lyndon Johnson's "daisy" TV ad of 1964. It featured a small girl with a daisy, fading to the image of a nuclear explosion. It was meant to raise fears that his opponent, Barry Goldwater, would risk nuclear war.

candidates. As a result, the campaign was vicious. Supporters of each side made their arguments in letters and newspaper editorials, which often made wild accusations and spread scandalous stories.

Federalists claimed that Jefferson was dangerously pro-French. They warned that if the Democratic-Republican candidate were in office, the violence and chaos of the French Revolution would follow. Federalists also accused Jefferson of wanting to destroy organized religion because of his interest in science and philosophy.

The Democratic-Republicans attacked the Federalists as well. Unpopular Federalist policies such as the Alien and Sedition Acts were easy targets for criticism. Democratic-Republicans also claimed that Adams wanted to crown himself king and that the Federalists would try to limit Americans' rights.

When the votes were counted, the election ended in a tie. At the time, political parties did not specify who was the party's preferred candidate for president. When Jefferson and Burr each received the same number of votes, an unprecedented electoral crisis began.

The Constitution made it clear that ties would be decided by the House of Representatives. But the House was deadlocked as well. Vote after vote took place, but each ended in a tie. Alexander Hamilton urged Federalists to

---

support Jefferson and finally, on the 36th vote, Jefferson was chosen as the third president of the United States.

The problems with the voting system led Congress to propose the **Twelfth Amendment**, which was ratified in 1804. This amendment said that electors must cast separate ballots for president and vice president.

Hard feelings over the election continued for years. Burr blamed Hamilton for his loss, and when Hamilton helped prevent Burr from being elected governor of New York, Burr challenged him to a duel. In July 1804 the duel was fought, and Hamilton died. The news shocked the country and ended Burr's political career.

READING CHECK **Drawing Conclusions** How did the Alien and Sedition Acts hurt Federalists?

Jefferson Makes Changes

The election was finally decided just two weeks before inauguration day. Although both sides had bitterly fought, Jefferson's inaugural address urged unity and tolerance. He spoke of the special blessings that Americans enjoyed, and then said:

HISTORY'S VOICES

❝With all these blessings, what more is necessary to make us a happy and a prosperous people? Still one thing more, fellow-citizens—a wise and frugal government, which shall restrain men from injuring one another, shall leave them otherwise free to regulate their own pursuits of industry and improvement, and shall not take from the mouth of labor the bread it has earned.❞

—Thomas Jefferson, Inaugural Address, March 4, 1801

Jefferson considered his election victory the "revolution of 1800." His actions as president were not revolutionary, but he did succeed in reducing the size and influence of the federal government.

The members of Jefferson's cabinet shared his belief in a smaller government. His closest ally was James Madison of Virginia, who became secretary of state. Treasury Secretary Albert Gallatin had economic ideas that differed vastly from policies of the past.

Under the Federalists, Hamilton's economic plans had increased the level of public debt and established a federal tax system. In order to reduce the size of the government, the

---

Skills Focus: Making Generalizations   At Level

Reading Skill
The Press and the Election of 1800

1. Guide students in a discussion about the role of the media in shaping public opinion, especially during elections. Tell students that during the election of 1800, newspapers sometimes printed accusations or spread scandal about the candidates.

2. Have students use the information in the text to create a political attack ad either against the Federalists and their candidate John Adams or against the Democratic-Republicans and their

candidate Thomas Jefferson. Ads can be print, Web-based, or multimedia.

3. After volunteers have presented their ads to the class, guide students in a discussion of the importance of fair, balanced reporting about political candidates. **LS Visual-Spatial, Auditory-Musical**

Alternative Assessment Handbook, Rubric 2: Advertisements

Jefferson administration changed the tax system in 1802. With the new system, only customs duties and the sale of lands in the western United States produced revenue for the government. Gallatin also reduced the size of the executive department staff.

Jefferson did not think there should be a large standing army in peacetime, as the army could be a threat to civil liberties. Accordingly, he shrank the size of the army and navy, although he did help found the U.S. Military Academy at West Point in 1802.

The president later reversed course and began a naval buildup in response to the plight of merchants. Their ships started coming under attack from the so-called Barbary pirates from North Africa, who demanded tribute from U.S. merchant ships in the Mediterranean Sea.

READING CHECK **Making Inferences** How did cutting taxes fit with Jefferson's ideals?

The Louisiana Purchase

Many issues linked the United States with France. The new ruler of France was General Napoleon Bonaparte, who wanted to build a French empire. He hoped to regain France's former lands in North America to the west of the Mississippi River, a region called the Louisiana Territory. Those lands had gone to Spain in the Treaty of Paris in 1763. In 1800 in a secret treaty, Spain returned Louisiana to France along with the port city of New Orleans.

Jefferson had hoped that the United States could take control of Louisiana and New Orleans and was very concerned by this treaty. Access to New Orleans and the Mississippi River was vital to American commerce. In order to sell their products, farmers in the West needed to ship their goods down the Mississippi to New Orleans. In Pinckney's

ACADEMIC VOCABULARY

commerce purchase and sale of commodities

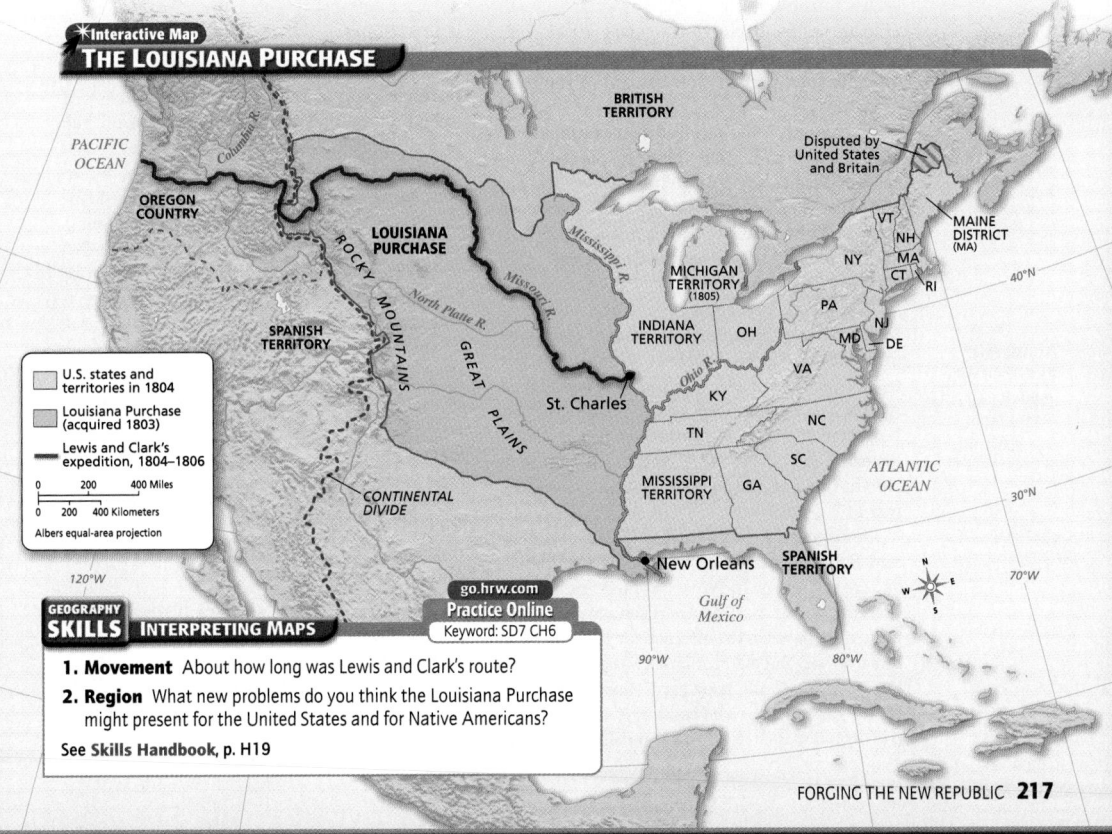

Interactive Map

THE LOUISIANA PURCHASE

Legend:
- U.S. states and territories in 1804
- Louisiana Purchase (acquired 1803)
- Lewis and Clark's expedition, 1804–1806

0   200   400 Miles
0   200   400 Kilometers
Albers equal-area projection

GEOGRAPHY SKILLS **INTERPRETING MAPS**

go.hrw.com
Practice Online
Keyword: SD7 CH6

1. **Movement** About how long was Lewis and Clark's route?
2. **Region** What new problems do you think the Louisiana Purchase might present for the United States and for Native Americans?

See *Skills Handbook*, p. H19

Direct Teach

Reading Focus

❸ What was the impact of the Louisiana Purchase? *doubled the size of the U.S.; removed French war threat; strengthened American identity*

The Louisiana Purchase

Explain How did France regain the Louisiana Territory? *secret treaty with Spain*

Draw Conclusions Why did Jefferson want Louisiana Territory? *Access to Mississippi River was vital for commerce.*

📑 American History Outline Maps: Louisiana Purchase and Exploration

🗝 Map Transparency: The Lousiana Purchase

Info to Know

Aaron Burr and Alexander Hamilton Burr and Hamilton were political enemies who ultimately settled their differences in a duel. Through a letter published in a New York newspaper, Burr learned of negative comments that Hamilton had made about him at a dinner party and challenged Hamilton to a duel. Hamilton died the day after the duel of a mortal wound. Though Burr was not physically injured, the duel ended his political career and he was charged with murder.

✳ **Interactive Map:** The Lousiana Purchase

Collaborative Learning

At Level

The Louisiana Purchase

Materials construction paper, colored markers

1. Organize students into small groups. Have each group review the information in the text about the Louisiana Purchase.
2. Have groups develop a list of pros and cons about buying the Louisiana Territory. Students should also develop a list of reasons why France should sell the territory. Then

each group should decide whether or not they believe Jefferson acted appropriately in making the purchase.

3. Have each group prepare a poster explaining its decision. **LS Interpersonal**

📋 Alternative Assessment Handbook, Rubrics 14: Group Activity; and 28: Posters

Answers

Interpreting Maps *about 2,000 miles each way; how to govern new territory; how to keep land and traditional way of life*

Reading Check *believed in a smaller government, which would need less funding*

217

The Louisiana Purchase

Recall What was the final price of the Louisiana Purchase? *15 million American dollars*

Make Judgments Do you think Monroe and Livingston were correct in signing the agreement with Napoléon? *possible answer—Yes, they had some authority from the president.*

Evaluate Was the Louisiana Purchase constitutional? Explain your answer. *possible answers—yes, it was a proper action, part of presidential powers; no, the president assumed powers that he did not have under the Constitution*

Recent Scholarship

In *Undaunted Courage: Meriwether Lewis, Thomas Jefferson, and the Opening of the American West*, historian Stephen E. Ambrose uses not only the journals of Lewis and Clark but also his own experiences to chronicle Lewis and Clark's journey to the Pacific. Ambrose, his wife, and their five children spent 20 summers following the route of the Lewis and Clark expedition. Ambrose also draws on the historical friendship between Thomas Jefferson and Meriwether Lewis to gain an understanding of Lewis as an explorer. Although Ambrose does not present new information about Lewis, he does add a personal touch to the story of an American icon.

Undaunted Courage: Meriwether Lewis, Thomas Jefferson, and the Opening of the American West, by Stephen Ambrose. Simon & Schuster, 1997

TRACING HISTORY

Westward Expansion

Of the 10 most populous cities in the United States today, six are in the West. Conquest of the West began with Spanish colonizers in the 1700s. Study the time line to learn about how the American West grew.

THE GRANGER COLLECTION, NEW YORK

1804–1806 With Sacagawea as a guide, Lewis and Clark traveled some 8,000 miles exploring the Louisiana Purchase. Fur trappers and settlers would soon follow.

1700

1700s Spanish colonizers built mission settlements in what are now Texas, New Mexico, and California.

Treaty, Spain had promised to protect American access to the river. In 1802, however, Spanish officials suddenly closed the lower Mississippi and New Orleans to American shipping. The officials soon turned over control of the area to France.

President Jefferson had to act quickly to protect American trade. He sent James Monroe to Paris to try to purchase New Orleans and West Florida. At the meeting, Monroe was stunned when French foreign minister Talleyrand offered to sell the United States all of the vast Louisiana Territory.

Napoleon had come to realize that controlling a North American empire might be difficult. The French colony of Haiti, in the Caribbean, had been taken over by enslaved Africans who revolted against French rule. Napoleon was afraid of future trouble in North America. He decided to abandon his claims in North America and to focus instead on waging war in Europe.

Jefferson had authorized James Monroe and Robert Livingston, the American ambassador, to buy only New Orleans, not all of Louisiana. But Monroe and Livingston did not have time to write to Jefferson for his approval, however, or Napoleon might change his mind. On April 30, 1803, they signed an agreement with France to buy the land. The final price of the territory included in the **Louisiana Purchase**

ACADEMIC VOCABULARY

implicit suggested or implied

was about 80 million francs, or $15 million. The purchase almost doubled the territory of the United States.

A constitutional puzzle The Louisiana Purchase was a remarkable bargain, but it raised many questions. Jefferson himself had to reconsider his long-held position in favor of strict construction of the Constitution. Jefferson believed that the Constitution should be interpreted based only on its precise meaning. Nowhere did the Constitution directly give Jefferson the authority to buy new territory for the nation, yet common sense told him that it was clearly a good idea.

Jefferson and his advisers finally decided that the right to acquire territory was implicit in the president's constitutional power to make treaties. Some Federalists in Congress, however, called the Louisiana Purchase unconstitutional. They also feared it would result in more states dominated by Democratic-Republicans. Yet even Hamilton agreed that the purchase was good for the country. Congress quickly approved it.

Lewis and Clark explore the West Americans knew very little about the people and the land of this enormous new territory to the West. In fact, they did not even know the exact size and boundaries of the land they had purchased. Jefferson wanted to learn more

218 CHAPTER 6

Differentiating Instruction

Special Education Students

Materials construction paper, colored markers

1. Guide students in a discussion about the significance of the Louisiana Purchase for the United States.

2. Have students work individually or in pairs to create a parade banner with a slogan that reflects pride about the purchase.

3. Have volunteers explain and display their banners to the class. **LS Visual-Spatial, Kinesthetic**

📝 Alternative Assessment Handbook, Rubric 34: Slogans and Banners

1838–1839 To make room for white settlers, the United States forcibly relocated thousands of Native Americans from the East to Oklahoma.

1836 Narcissa Whitman and her husband, Marcus, were among the first settlers of Oregon Territory, where they founded a mission.

1930s Route 66 became a major migration path to California for Americans fleeing an economic disaster and catastrophic Midwest dust storms.

1800

1900

about the area. He also wanted to see if there was a river route that could be taken across the country to the Pacific Ocean.

Jefferson sent out a number of expeditions to explore the West and make contact with the Native Americans there. The most famous was the Corps of Discovery, usually called the **Lewis and Clark expedition.** Its leaders were **Meriwether Lewis,** Jefferson's secretary, and **William Clark,** an experienced frontiersman. Their ultimate goal was to reach the Pacific Ocean. Jefferson wanted Lewis and Clark to map the country and survey its natural history, including plants, animals, and landforms.

The expedition, made up of about 50 skilled frontiersmen, left St. Louis in May 1804 and traveled up the Missouri River. The men made their way west across the continent, over lands that they had never before seen. They paddled along raging rivers, trudged across plains and rugged mountains, and hiked through thick forests. Along the way, they acquired a valuable guide: a young Shoshone woman, **Sacagawea,** the wife of a French Canadian fur trapper.

In November 1805 the expedition finally reached the west coast of North America. Clark called the sight of the Pacific Ocean one of "the grandest and most pleasing prospects which my eyes ever surveyed."

The group spent the winter on the coast and started home in the spring, finally reaching St. Louis in September 1806. Jefferson was delighted to hear of the expedition's success. Many Americans had feared that the entire expedition had died along the way. In fact, only one man had died—of appendicitis.

Lewis and Clark had kept detailed journals of everything they encountered, including 120 species of plants and animals that they had never seen. They sent many boxes of specimens back to Jefferson. Other members of the expedition made notes and sketches.

After the exploration and further mapping of the territory, the United States claimed ownership of land extending as far to the southwest as the Rio Grande, in what is now Texas. These land claims would later lead to disagreement between the United States and Spain.

Another explorer in the West was a young army lieutenant, **Zebulon M. Pike.** His 1805 expedition traveled 2,000 miles to explore the upper Mississippi Valley, looking for the source of the river. In 1806 Pike's group traveled to the Southwest. They explored the Arkansas and Red Rivers and gathered information about the economy and defenses of Spanish New Mexico and Texas. Pike reported back that the central plains were too dry for settlement.

READING CHECK **Identifying Problems and Solutions** What constitutional question did the Louisiana Purchase raise?

4 How did the role of the Supreme Court change? *had right to declare laws unconstitutional*

The Role of the Supreme Court Changes

Recall Who was Marbury? *one of the midnight judges who did not get his commission*

Summarize Why is *Marbury* v. *Madison* a landmark case? *The Supreme Court asserted its authority of judicial review.*

Review & Assess

Close

Have students explain the major changes that occurred in the nation during the presidency of Thomas Jefferson.

Review

Online Quiz, Section 3

Daily Test Practice Transparency

Assess

SE Section 3 Assessment

Progress Assessment: Section 3 Quiz

Alternative Assessment Handbook

Reteach

Interactive Reader and Study Guide, Section 3

Interactive Skills Tutor CD-ROM

Answers

Faces of History *kept to a simple life and habits*

Reading Check *to give Federalists more power*

FACES OF HISTORY

[#1867.306] ©COLLECTION OF THE NEW-YORK HISTORICAL SOCIETY

Thomas JEFFERSON
1743–1826

Although Thomas Jefferson is well known today as the writer of the Declaration of Independence, few people knew it at the time. As president, Jefferson sought to smooth the discord that brought him to office, declaring, "We are all Republicans—we are all Federalists."

Jefferson was a man of many talents and contradictions. He was not only a politician but also a gifted architect, scholar, scientist, and writer. He was a poor public speaker, however, and preferred to communicate in writing. Even though he was a wealthy and educated Virginia planter, he truly believed in republican simplicity. He dressed casually, walked to his inauguration, and kept state dinners informal.

Explain How did Jefferson's actions reflect his beliefs?

The Role of the Supreme Court Changes

In the election of 1800 the Federalists had lost control of both the presidency and Congress. As a result, they tried to increase their hold on the third branch of government: the judiciary. Federalist legislators in Congress passed the **Judiciary Act of 1801** shortly before their terms ended. This act created new positions in the judicial branch. Departing President John Adams hurried to fill them with Federalists.

Adams worked late into the night of March 3, 1801, to sign the commissions for these new judges. These documents had to be delivered to the new judges in order to make the appointments official. But not all were delivered before Jefferson took office the next day. James Madison, the new secretary of state, refused to deliver the remaining commissions to the so-called midnight judges.

One of the undelivered commissions was for William Marbury, who turned to the Supreme Court for help. He asked the Court to order Madison to deliver his commission.

The Court ruled that the Constitution only gave the Supreme Court the power to hear certain kinds of cases. The Constitution did not give the Court the power to force Madison to deliver Marbury's commission. Therefore, the Court said, the law that gave it that power—the Judiciary Act of 1789—was unconstitutional. *Marbury* v. *Madison* was important because it established the Supreme Court's right to declare that a law violates the Constitution. This power is known as **judicial review**.

READING CHECK **Making Inferences** Why did Adams appoint the midnight judges?

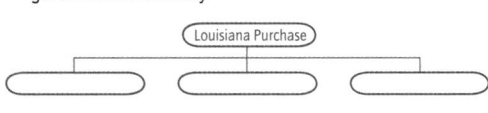

SECTION 3 ASSESSMENT

go.hrw.com
Online Quiz
Keyword: SD7 HP6

Reviewing Ideas, Terms, and People

1. **a. Recall** Why was the **Twelfth Amendment** passed?
   b. Summarize What were the issues in the election of 1800?
   c. Evaluate Why was the election important in American politics?

2. **a. Describe** What were Jefferson's goals in office?
   b. Contrast How were Adams and Jefferson different in manner and outlook?
   c. Evaluate Why do you think Jefferson urged unity and tolerance in his inaugural address?

3. **a. Identify** What roles did **Lewis**, **Clark**, **Sacagawea**, and **Pike** play in exploring the Louisiana Territory?
   b. Summarize How did the Louisiana Purchase come about?
   c. Elaborate Given Jefferson's strong feelings about strict construction, how could he justify the Louisiana Purchase?

4. **a. Recall** Who were the midnight judges?
   b. Analyze What were the main points of the Supreme Court's decision in *Marbury* v. *Madison*?

   c. Rate How did this decision relate to the system of checks and balances?

Critical Thinking

5. **Predicting** Copy the chart below and use it to show different ways in which the Louisiana Purchase would affect American government and society.

   (Louisiana Purchase)

FOCUS ON WRITING

6. **Persuasive** As a political campaign worker in 1800, write a speech promoting the campaign of either Adams or Jefferson.

220 CHAPTER 6

Section 3 Assessment Answers

1. **a.** to avoid ties in presidential elections
   b. France; taxes; Alien and Sedition Acts
   c. first time presidential power passed from one party to another

2. **a.** bringing unity to nation; reducing size and influence of federal government
   b. Adams—strong central government; Jefferson—smaller government
   c. very divisive election

3. **a.** surveyed territory; guided expedition; explored Mississippi Valley
   b. Napoléon sold to U.S. for $15 million

   c. believed it was in country's best interests; used president's implied powers

4. **a.** judges Adams appointed at end of term
   b. Judiciary Act of 1789 was unconstitutional; judicial review
   c. strengthened Supreme Court and balance of power among branches of government

5. increased image and power of U.S; gave sense of pride; doubled land size

6. with Adams, government will be strong; with Jefferson, size of federal government limited

Landmark Supreme Court Cases

Marbury v. Madison (1803)

Why It Matters *Marbury* v. *Madison* established the Supreme Court's power to decide whether laws passed by Congress are constitutional. This power, known as judicial review, remains the central job of the Supreme Court today.

Background of the Case

In the fall of 1800, President John Adams rushed to sign commissions filling 58 new government positions with members of his own party before he left office. Adams's secretary of state, John Marshall, sealed the commissions but failed to deliver 17 of them. The new secretary of state, James Madison, refused to deliver some of these commissions. One of the men who did not receive his commission, William Marbury, brought suit in the Supreme Court. He claimed that the Judiciary Act of 1789 gave the Supreme Court the power to order Madison to deliver his commission.

The Decision

In *Marbury* v. *Madison*, the Supreme Court ruled that it did not, in fact, have the power to order Madison to deliver Marbury's commission. This is because the Constitution had designated the Supreme Court an appellate court. With very few exceptions, it hears only appeals from decisions issued by other courts. Although the Judiciary Act of 1789 had tried to expand the Supreme Court's powers, that expansion violated the Constitution and could not be allowed. John Marshall, then chief justice of the Supreme Court, explained this landmark decision:

> **❝It is emphatically the province and duty of the judicial department to say what the law is.❞**

In other words, *Marbury* v. *Madison* established that the Supreme Court has the authority to declare an act of Congress unconstitutional.

THE IMPACT TODAY How the Supreme Court (shown in the artist's sketch above) interprets the Constitution through judicial review remains an issue in government today. As in Madison's day, the debate involves strict constructionists and loose constructionists.

CRITICAL THINKING

go.hrw.com
Research Online
Keyword: SS Court

1. **Analyze the Impact** Using the keyword above, find *Federalist* No. 78. Read paragraphs 9 through 14. Did Hamilton anticipate the constitutional question decided in *Marbury* v. *Madison*? Would he have agreed with Marshall's opinion?

2. **You Be the Judge** Given what you have read about checks and balances in the Constitution, do you think it is important for the Supreme Court to have the power of judicial review? How might our government be different today if the Supreme Court did not have this power?

Landmark Supreme Court Cases

Marbury v. *Madison* (1803)

Word Help

commissions appointment papers to an office
province job, responsibility

The Supreme Court and the Constitution

Article III of the Constitution states that "The Judicial Power of the United States, shall be vested in one supreme Court, and in such inferior Courts as the Congress may from time to time ordain and establish." This provided a brief sketch of the role of the Supreme Court. In 1803 in the case of *Marbury* v. *Madison*, the Court decided to take on the role of judicial review. The Court would become the "guardian of the terms of the written Constitution."

Primary Source

" . . . the courts were designed to be an intermediate body between the people and the legislature in order, among other things, to keep the latter within the limits assigned to their authority. The interpretation of the laws is the proper and peculiar province of the courts."
— Alexander Hamilton

The Federalist No. 78, June 14, 1788

Skills Focus: Identifying Problem and Solution

At Level

Reading Skill
The Supreme Court and the Balance of Power

To help students understand the importance of *Marbury* v. *Madison*, draw a Venn diagram with 3 circles, and label them judicial, executive, and legislative. Have students name responsibilities of each branch of government. Fill in the circles with student responses. Then, erase the circle representing the judicial branch. Have students predict how the government might have looked, how it might have functioned, and the problems that would have arisen between the executive and legislative branches if the Supreme Court did not exist or had not chosen to exert its authority as an equal branch. **LS Visual-Spatial**

Alternative Assessment Handbook, Rubrics 11: Discussions; and 13: Graphic Organizers

Answers

Critical Thinking 1. *While Hamilton might not have anticipated this case, most likely he would have agreed with Marshall.* **2.** *possible answer—yes, ensures balance of power; legislative and executive branches might be at odds over laws*

221

Lewis and Clark's Journey to the Pacific

Info to Know

The Cost of the Journey At President Jefferson's urging, Congress appropriated $2,500 in 1803 to fund Lewis and Clark's journey of exploration. This represents slightly more than $40,000 in today's money.

Activity **Encountering New Animals** Share these quotations with the class. Have students guess the animal the members of the expedition are describing:

"Capt. Clark joined us had killed a curious annamil resembling a Goat Willard brought it on board. it was 3 feet high resembles a Deer in some parts. the legs like a Deer. feet like a Goat. horns like a Goat only forked . . . Such an anamil was never yet known in US. States." *pronghorn antelope*

"Two of our hunters went out and killed an animal, called a prarow, about the size of a ground hog and nearly of the same colour. It has a head similar to that of a dog, short legs and large claws on its fore feet; some of the claws are an inch and an half long." *badger*

LS **Verbal-Linguistic**

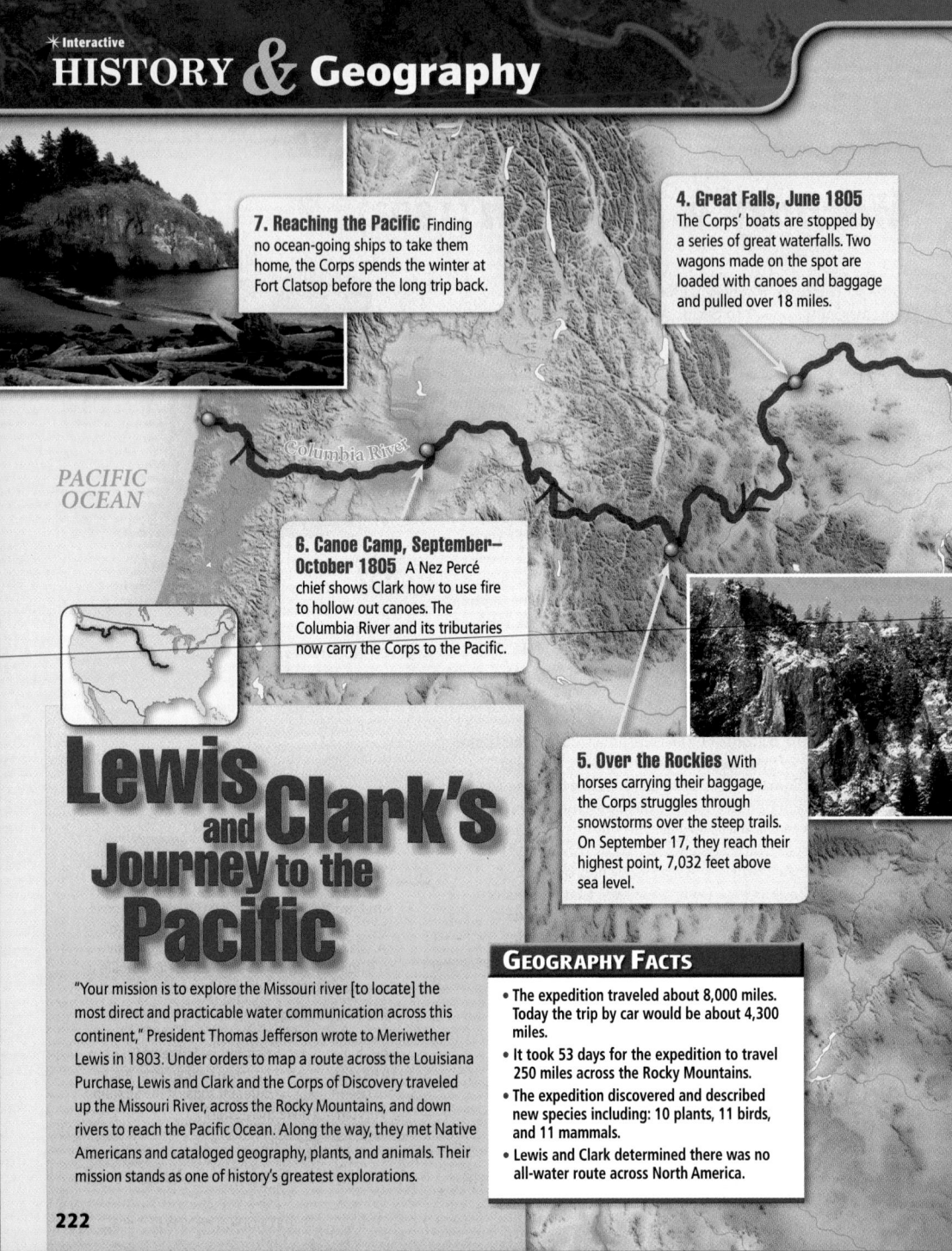

✴ Interactive
HISTORY & Geography

7. Reaching the Pacific Finding no ocean-going ships to take them home, the Corps spends the winter at Fort Clatsop before the long trip back.

4. Great Falls, June 1805 The Corps' boats are stopped by a series of great waterfalls. Two wagons made on the spot are loaded with canoes and baggage and pulled over 18 miles.

Columbia River

PACIFIC OCEAN

6. Canoe Camp, September–October 1805 A Nez Percé chief shows Clark how to use fire to hollow out canoes. The Columbia River and its tributaries now carry the Corps to the Pacific.

5. Over the Rockies With horses carrying their baggage, the Corps struggles through snowstorms over the steep trails. On September 17, they reach their highest point, 7,032 feet above sea level.

Lewis and Clark's Journey to the Pacific

"Your mission is to explore the Missouri river [to locate] the most direct and practicable water communication across this continent," President Thomas Jefferson wrote to Meriwether Lewis in 1803. Under orders to map a route across the Louisiana Purchase, Lewis and Clark and the Corps of Discovery traveled up the Missouri River, across the Rocky Mountains, and down rivers to reach the Pacific Ocean. Along the way, they met Native Americans and cataloged geography, plants, and animals. Their mission stands as one of history's greatest explorations.

GEOGRAPHY FACTS

- The expedition traveled about 8,000 miles. Today the trip by car would be about 4,300 miles.
- It took 53 days for the expedition to travel 250 miles across the Rocky Mountains.
- The expedition discovered and described new species including: 10 plants, 11 birds, and 11 mammals.
- Lewis and Clark determined there was no all-water route across North America.

222

Skills Focus: Interpreting Movement Maps
At Level

Social Studies Skill
A Long Journey

Materials outline map of Louisiana Purchase and Exploration

1. Distribute maps of the Louisiana Purchase and Exploration to students.

2. Have students locate the places described in the feature, including Camp Dubois, Council Bluffs, and Great Falls. Then have students map the journey Lewis and Clark took to the Pacific Coast. Have students reference a modern map of the U.S. in their text to see what geographical challenges the expedition faced.

3. Guide students in a discussion of how Lewis and Clark's journey influenced perceptions of the West. **LS** **Logical-Mathematical, Visual-Spatial**

Alternative Assessment Handbook, Rubric 21: Map Reading

American History Outline Maps: Louisiana Purchase and Exploration

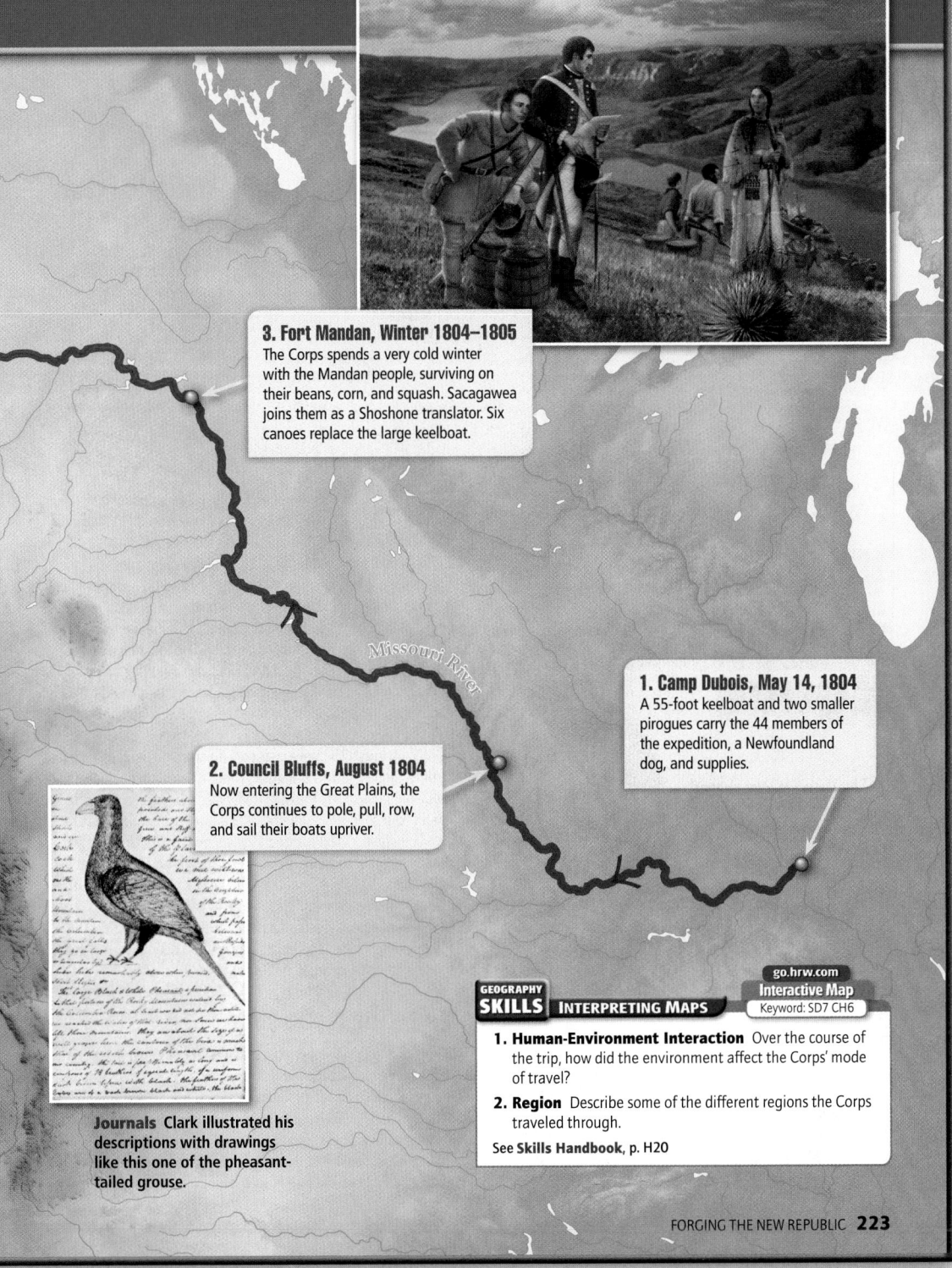

3. Fort Mandan, Winter 1804–1805
The Corps spends a very cold winter with the Mandan people, surviving on their beans, corn, and squash. Sacagawea joins them as a Shoshone translator. Six canoes replace the large keelboat.

Missouri River

1. Camp Dubois, May 14, 1804
A 55-foot keelboat and two smaller pirogues carry the 44 members of the expedition, a Newfoundland dog, and supplies.

2. Council Bluffs, August 1804
Now entering the Great Plains, the Corps continues to pole, pull, row, and sail their boats upriver.

Journals Clark illustrated his descriptions with drawings like this one of the pheasant-tailed grouse.

GEOGRAPHY SKILLS INTERPRETING MAPS

go.hrw.com
Interactive Map
Keyword: SD7 CH6

1. **Human-Environment Interaction** Over the course of the trip, how did the environment affect the Corps' mode of travel?

2. **Region** Describe some of the different regions the Corps traveled through.

See **Skills Handbook, p. H20**

Info to Know
Noteworthy Graffiti During the return trip, Lewis and Clark split up for part of the way. Taking the southern route, Clark's party came upon an unusual rock formation on the banks of the Yellowstone River. Clark named it Pompy's Tower, after Sacagawea's baby, and carved this message on the rock formation: "Wm. Clark July 25th 1806." The carving can still be seen today, about 28 miles east of Billings, Montana.

MISCONCEPTION ///ALERT\\\

Point out to students that Lewis and Clark did not "discover" the American West any more than Columbus "discovered" America. Both places had already been inhabited for thousands of years. On their journey, Lewis and Clark met almost 50 different groups of Native Americans, many of whom had lived in the area for centuries.

Collaborative Learning

At Level

Making a Mural

Research Required

1. Divide students into groups. Have each group plan and create a mural of the Lewis and Clark expedition. Students should use their textbooks and other sources of information, including primary sources, to identify scenes to recreate in their murals.

2. Have volunteers from each group present their mural to the class and explain the significance of the scenes they have illustrated.
   LS Visual-Spatial, Interpersonal
   Alternative Assessment Handbook, Rubric 3: Artwork

Answers

Interpreting Maps 1. *had to change their mode of travel depending on the environment; used different types of boats, wagons, and horses to cross rivers, prairies, and mountains;* **2.** *Great Plains were wide grassy prairies; Rockies were high mountains; Pacific Coast was rocky and forested*

Bellringer

The Inside Story. . . Use the **Daily Bellringer Transparency** to help students answer the question.

🔖 Daily Bellringer Transparency, Section 4

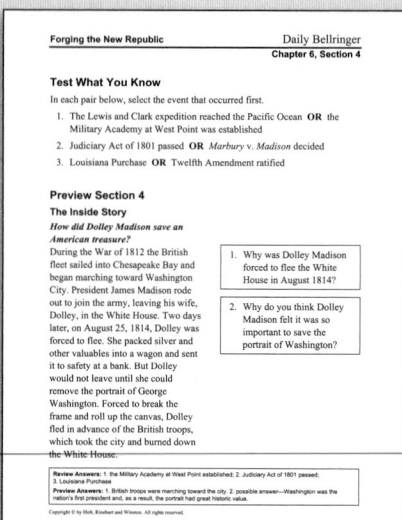

Forging the New Republic Daily Bellringer
Chapter 6, Section 4

Test What You Know

In each pair below, select the event that occurred first.

1. The Lewis and Clark expedition reached the Pacific Ocean **OR** the Military Academy at West Point was established

2. Judiciary Act of 1801 passed **OR** *Marbury* v. *Madison* decided

3. Louisiana Purchase **OR** Twelfth Amendment ratified

Preview Section 4
The Inside Story
How did Dolley Madison save an American treasure?
During the War of 1812 the British fleet sailed into Chesapeake Bay and began marching toward Washington City. President James Madison rode out to join the army, leaving his wife, Dolley, in the White House. Two days later, on August 25, 1814, Dolley was forced to flee. She packed silver and other valuables into a wagon and sent it to safety at a bank. But Dolley would not leave until she could remove the portrait of George Washington. Forced to break the frame and roll up the canvas, Dolley fled in advance of the British troops, which took the city and burned down the White House.

1. Why was Dolley Madison forced to flee the White House in August 1814?

2. Why do you think Dolley Madison felt it was so important to save the portrait of Washington?

Review Answers: 1. the Military Academy at West Point established; 2. Judiciary Act of 1801 passed; 3. Louisiana Purchase

Preview Answers: 1. British troops were marching toward the city. 2. possible answer—Washington was the nation's first president and, as a result, the portrait had great historic value.

Copyright © by Holt, Rinehart and Winston. All rights reserved.

Academic Vocabulary

Review with students the high-use academic term in this section.

prohibited did not allow (p. 225)

🔖 CRF: Vocabulary Builder Activity, Section 4

Taking Notes

August 1812, USS Constitution *and British* Guerrière; *September 1813, Battle of Lake Erie; October 1813, Battle of the Thames; March 1814, Battle of Horseshoe Bend; August 1814, Battle of Washington; September 1814, Battle of Baltimore; January 1815, Battle of New Orleans*

BEFORE YOU READ

MAIN IDEA

In the early 1800s, Americans unified to face Great Britain in war once again and to battle resistance from Native Americans over attempts to seize their lands.

READING FOCUS

1. What violations of American neutrality led to the War of 1812?

2. How did Tecumseh resist American settlers?

3. How did the War of 1812 begin? How did the war affect the new nation?

KEY TERMS AND PEOPLE

impressment
Embargo Act
William Henry Harrison
Tecumseh
War Hawks
Andrew Jackson
Battle of New Orleans
Treaty of Ghent

TAKING NOTES As you read, take notes on the major battles in the War of 1812. Record your notes in a graphic organizer like the one shown here. You may need to add more rows.

Month/Year	Battle

► Dolley Madison saved a national treasure from the British attack on the capital.

THE GRANGER COLLECTION, NEW YORK

The Burning of the White House

THE INSIDE STORY

How did Dolley Madison save an American treasure? In August 1814 the British fleet sailed into Chesapeake Bay and headed toward Washington City. Few soldiers were left to defend the capital, and government officials fled as the British approached.

On August 23 James Madison left the President's House to be with the army in the field. He left his wife, Dolley, to look after herself and the government papers in his office. The next day the First Lady was alarmed to receive two hastily written notes telling her to prepare to flee the advancing attack.

By August 25 there was still no sign of the president. Finally, Dolley found a wagon, filled it with silver and other valuables, and sent them to safety at a bank. An impatient friend had to wait while she made one last brave gesture. "I insist on waiting until the large picture of General Washington is secured, and it requires to be unscrewed from the wall." Finally, she had to break the picture frame and roll up the canvas.

The precious portrait saved, Dolley Madison fled the President's House. The British easily took the city and set fire to major buildings, including the White House. ◢

Violating Neutrality

How did the United States and Great Britain find themselves at war again so soon after the Revolution? Unresolved tensions between the two nations, both on the Northwest frontier and on the seas, caused the Americans and the British to lock in battle once again.

As early as 1803, the United States became caught in the middle of British trade disagreements. When the

---

Teach the Main Idea **At Level**

The War of 1812

1. **Teach** Ask students the Reading Focus questions to teach this section.

2. **Apply** Draw a large triangle for students to see. Label each angle with one of the topics of this section—Violating Neutrality, Tecumseh Resists American Settlers, and The War of 1812 Begins. Have students copy the diagram and use it to outline the section by adding headings and important points to each side. **LS Visual-Spatial, Logical-Mathematical**

3. **Review** As you review the section, have students identify the events and issues that led to the War of 1812.

4. **Practice/Homework** Have each student write a three- to four-minute speech explaining ways Tecumseh might have chosen to protect Native American lands. **LS Verbal-Linguistic**

🔖 Alternative Assessment Handbook, Rubric 24: Oral Presentations

Napoleonic Wars broke out between France and Great Britain, American merchant shipping was affected.

Then in 1806 and 1807, France and Britain tried to cut off each other's access to European ports. Both nations ignored American neutrality. If American ships sailed directly to Europe, the British navy might stop them. If ships stopped in Britain, the French would seize them. American captains saw the British as the more serious threat. One reason was the practice of **impressment**. Ordinary sailors in the Royal Navy were badly paid and brutally treated. To find crews, men were often impressed—kidnapped and forced to work on ships. Many deserted whenever they could.

British captains claimed they had the right to stop and search American ships for deserters. But while looking for British sailors, they often took Americans as well. In 1807 the British ship *Leopard* stopped the American frigate *Chesapeake*. When the Americans refused to let the ship be searched, the *Leopard* opened fire. The British then seized four Americans.

Americans were furious about the *Chesapeake* incident. To avoid war, President Jefferson proposed and Congress passed a drastic law. The **Embargo Act** prohibited exports to foreign countries. Many captains evaded the act, but the ban on trade was a disaster for the economy. Goods piled up in warehouses, ships sat in the harbors, people lost their jobs, and businesses failed.

The 1808 presidential election took place in the hard times after the hated Embargo Act. James Madison, Jefferson's ally, won easily. A new law reopened all trade except that with Britain and France. Still, conflicts over commerce were pushing the country toward war.

> **READING CHECK** **Summarizing** What were the consequences of the Embargo Act?

Tecumseh Resists Settlers

Another factor leading to war was the ongoing conflict between settlers and Native Americans in the Northwest Territory. Things had been fairly quiet since the the Battle of Fallen Timbers. But as anti-British feelings grew in the United States, the British tried to rebuild their old alliances with Native Americans.

New policies William Henry Harrison was a Virginian who joined the army and fought in the Indian wars. He later became the Northwest Territory's delegate to Congress.

In 1800 Harrison was named governor of the new Indiana Territory. He was supposed to carry out President Jefferson's new Native American policy. Under this policy, Native Americans could choose either to become farmers and join white society or to move west of the Mississippi. As Harrison implemented the policy, Native Americans made treaties in which they lost millions of acres of tribal lands in Michigan, Indiana, and Illinois.

New Indian leaders Two Shawnee brothers emerged as leaders who could bring Native Americans together. One was a religious leader called the Prophet, or Tenskwatawa. Thousands came to hear him speak against white culture at Prophetstown, where the Wabash River met Tippecanoe Creek in present-day Indiana. He taught his followers to reject white culture.

Tecumseh, or Shooting Star, was the Prophet's brother and an inspiring leader. In 1809 he began to unite his brother's followers. But in 1811, while Tecumseh was away, Harrison's army attacked. Both sides suffered heavy losses, and Prophetstown was burned. The Battle of Tippecanoe made Harrison a national hero. He and Tecumseh would meet again.

> **READING CHECK** **Making Inferences** Why did the British and Native Americans become allies?

ACADEMIC VOCABULARY
prohibited did not allow

③ How did the war of 1812 begin? How did the war affect the new nation? *many Americans unhappy after* Chesapeake *and* Leopold *incident; War Hawks in Congress called for war; Congress declared war; Americans proved themselves as a nation*

The War of 1812 Begins

Identify Who led the War Hawks? *Henry Clay*

Analyze What was the effect of the war on Native Americans? *many killed; lost some of their best leaders; were considered enemies*

Activity **Tecumseh** Have students write a poem or song lyrics commemorating the efforts of Tecumseh to help his people. **LS Auditory-Musical**

📝 CRF: Primary Source Activity: Felix Grundy Calls for War Against Great Britain

📦 Map Transparency: War of 1812

📦 Quick Facts Transparency: Causes and Effects of the War of 1812

Primary Source

"These lands are ours. No one has a right to remove us, because we were the first owners. The Great Spirit above has appointed this place for us . . . and here we will remain."

— Tecumseh

1810, in a message to President James Madison

Info to Know

Impressment Between 1803 and 1812, some 6,000 Americans were forced into service on British ships. Although the British government usually released Americans who could prove their citizenship, this often took years.

Answers

Interpreting Maps *removed Britain as threat in Northwest Territory; showed that U.S. was strong enough to defend itself*

The War of 1812 Begins

Ever since the incident with the *Chesapeake* and the *Leopard*, some American politicians had been calling for war. Known as **War Hawks**, most came from the western states. They were less concerned with world affairs than they were with frontier events. They hated the British and even hoped for a conquest of Canada.

War is declared Henry Clay, a leading War Hawk, became Speaker of the House in 1811. Under pressure from Congress, President Madison finally gave in. The United States declared war on Great Britain in June 1812.

The War of 1812 was fought on land and on sea, from Canada to Louisiana. Much of the war took place along the U.S.–Canadian border. The British also staged a massive blockade of the American coast and New Orleans.

Gains and losses The American navy won several surprising victories against the Royal Navy. In August 1812 the USS *Constitution* sank the British *Guerrière*. British gunfire bounced off the ship's oak hull, giving it the nickname Old Ironsides.

The naval war moved into the Great Lakes. Captain Oliver Hazard Perry hastily built new ships and gathered a small fleet. In September 1813 he anchored at the end of Lake Erie and waited for British ships to arrive. When the Battle of Lake Erie was over, Perry reported, "We have met the enemy and they are ours."

Soon after war was declared, American forces made several unsuccessful invasions of Canada. Tecumseh then joined the British in a campaign to capture Detroit and invade Ohio.

General Harrison, the hero of Tippecanoe, took command of U.S. forces in the Northwest Territory. After the American victory at Lake Erie, the British began a retreat from Detroit. Harrison's army followed them.

In October 1813, Harrison met British and Indian forces at the Battle of the Thames in

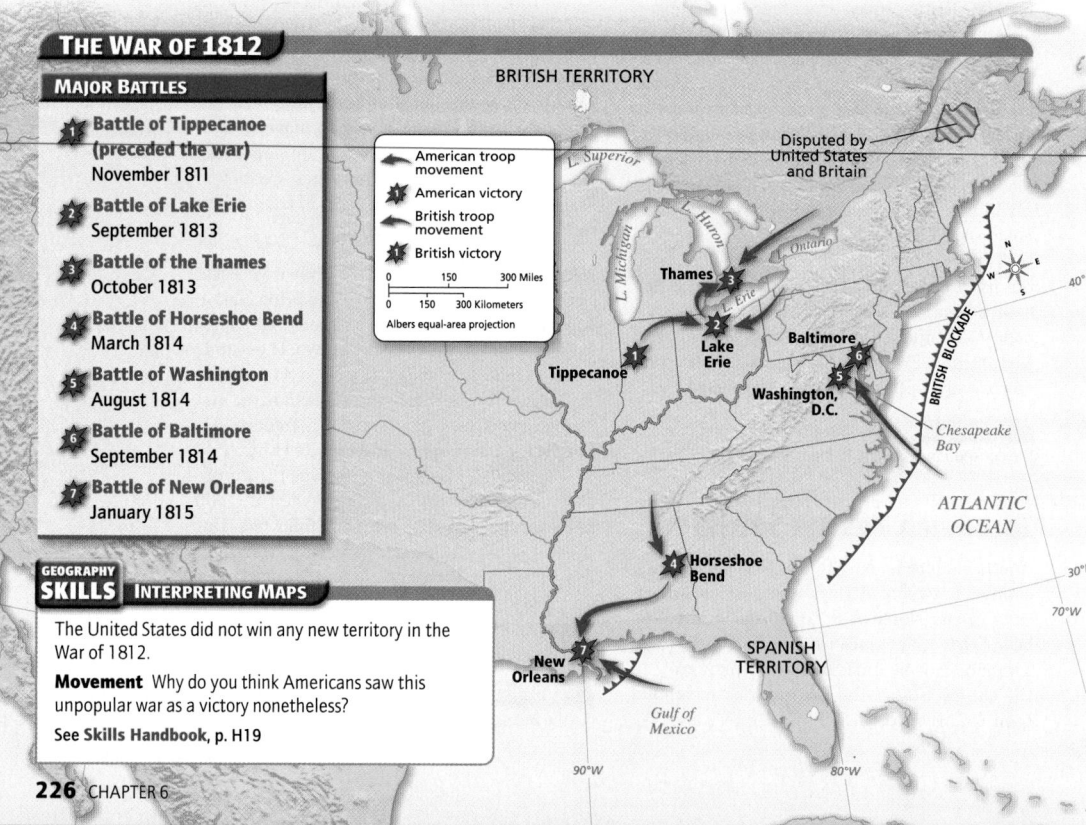

THE WAR OF 1812

MAJOR BATTLES

1. **Battle of Tippecanoe (preceded the war)** November 1811
2. **Battle of Lake Erie** September 1813
3. **Battle of the Thames** October 1813
4. **Battle of Horseshoe Bend** March 1814
5. **Battle of Washington** August 1814
6. **Battle of Baltimore** September 1814
7. **Battle of New Orleans** January 1815

→ American troop movement
⚡ American victory
→ British troop movement
⚡ British victory

0 150 300 Miles
0 150 300 Kilometers
Albers equal-area projection

GEOGRAPHY SKILLS | **INTERPRETING MAPS**

The United States did not win any new territory in the War of 1812.

Movement Why do you think Americans saw this unpopular war as a victory nonetheless?

See Skills Handbook, p. H19

226 CHAPTER 6

BRITISH TERRITORY

Disputed by United States and Britain

Thames
Lake Erie
Tippecanoe
Baltimore
Washington, D.C.
Chesapeake Bay
ATLANTIC OCEAN
Horseshoe Bend
New Orleans
SPANISH TERRITORY
Gulf of Mexico

BRITISH BLOCKADE

Collaborative Learning

At Level

The War of 1812

Materials construction paper, colored markers

1. Guide students in a discussion of the events that led to the War of 1812, including impressment.

2. Organize students into groups of two or three. Have each group create a recruitment campaign for the U.S. Navy just prior to the war. Campaigns should include slogans, banners and posters, and recruitment speeches.

3. Have volunteers present their campaign strategies, including speeches and materials, to the class. **LS Visual-Spatial, Interpersonal**

📝 Alternative Assessment Handbook, Rubric 34: Slogans and Banners

Ontario. The Americans outnumbered the enemy. Tecumseh was killed in the battle, ending the British–Native American alliance. Native Americans at once lost their greatest leader and their power in Ohio and Indiana.

Native Americans suffered another tragic loss in the South. There Tecumseh had organized the Creeks to resist settlers. Tennessee militia leader **Andrew Jackson** led a force against them. In March 1814, at the Battle of Horseshoe Bend, Jackson massacred Creek women, children, and warriors. He then seized the fort at Pensacola in Spanish Florida.

One British tactic was to make quick strikes against coastal cities. In August 1814 the British fleet sailed into Chesapeake Bay. Soldiers quickly marched to Washington, where they burned several major buildings.

The British then bombarded Fort McHenry, which guarded Baltimore harbor. After an overnight battle, a young lawyer, Francis Scott Key, was so overjoyed to see the American flag still flying that he started scribbling a poem that became America's national anthem: "The Star-Spangled Banner."

In the South, a British force landed near New Orleans in December. But Jackson got there first with an army of militia, pirates, and regular soldiers. In January 1815 the **Battle of New Orleans** made him a hero.

Treaty of Ghent By then, however, the peace treaty had been signed. In 1814 diplomats met in Ghent, Belgium, to finalize the **Treaty of Ghent**, which was signed in December. American and British diplomats were eager for peace. The Napoleonic Wars had been costly for England. In America, New Englanders were near rebellion over the war. No territory changed hands, but Americans had proved themselves as a nation.

READING CHECK **Making Inferences** Why did the War Hawks want war?

CAUSES AND EFFECTS OF THE WAR OF 1812 QUICK FACTS

CAUSES

- British impressment of American sailors
- International conflicts over commerce
- British military aid to Native Americans on the Northwest frontier

EFFECTS

- Britain and France gain respect for United States
- National pride grows
- U.S. manufacturing increases
- Native American resistance declines

SECTION 4 ASSESSMENT

go.hrw.com
Online Quiz
Keyword: SD7 HP6

Reviewing Ideas, Terms, and People

1. **a. Define** Explain the policy of **impressment** and its importance.
   b. Make Inferences What was the purpose of the **Embargo Act**?
   c. Evaluate Why were threats to merchant shipping a cause for war?

2. **a. Identify** What roles did **Tecumseh**, the Prophet, and **William Henry Harrison** play in the struggle for the western frontier?
   b. Summarize What was Jefferson's policy toward Native Americans in the Northwest Territory?
   c. Predict How did British and Native American alliances contribute to the move toward war?

3. **a. Define** What was the **Treaty of Ghent**?
   b. Analyze What losses did Native Americans suffer in the War of 1812?
   c. Evaluate Why did Americans see the end of the war as a victory?

Critical Thinking

4. **Identifying Cause and Effect** Copy the chart below and use it to make a time line of major battles in the War of 1812.

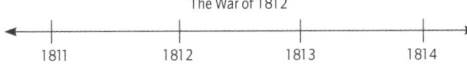

The War of 1812

| 1811 | 1812 | 1813 | 1814 |

FOCUS ON WRITING

5. **Persuasive** Prepare a speech for a debate in which you argue for or against going to war in 1812.

Direct Teach

Teaching Tip

Tell students that the term *war hawk* has come to refer to those who believe that foreign policy should be based on strong military power. *Doves*, on the other hand, are those who prefer to resolve conflict without the threat of force.

go.hrw.com
Online Resources

KEYWORD: SD7 CH6
TOPIC: THE WAR OF 1812

Review & Assess

Close

Guide students in a discussion of the new feeling of solidarity that Americans gained from the War of 1812.

Review

Online Quiz, Section 4

Daily Test Practice Transparency

Assess

SE Section 4 Assessment

Progress Assessment: Section 4 Quiz

Alternative Assessment Handbook

Reteach

Interactive Reader and Study Guide, Section 4

Interactive Skills Tutor CD-ROM

Section 4 Assessment Answers

1. **a.** British captured American sailors and drafted them into their navy; assault on U.S.
   b. to avoid war after the *Chesapeake* incident
   c. trade the livelihood of nation

2. **a.** Tecumseh, Prophet tried to hold onto Native American lands; Harrison made treaties that expanded the nation
   b. join white society or move west
   c. Americans feared their alliances

3. **a.** 1814 treaty to end War of 1812

   b. lost leaders, people, power, lands
   c. strengthened U.S. control of Northwest Territory; defeated Native Americans; destroyed British alliance

4. Lake Erie, September 1813; Thames, October 1813; Horseshoe Bend, March 1814; New Orleans, December 1814

5. possible answers—for: British have violated American neutrality; against: U.S. should not get involved in European affairs

Answers

Reading Check *They hated the British and hoped for a conquest of Canada.*

227

The First American Political Parties

Word Help

intimated suggested
discrimination bias
baneful deadly, ruinous
faction group
despotism tyranny
foments stirs up
riot disorder
insurrection rebellion

Info to Know

Political Parties Today it may seem difficult to imagine a democracy without political parties. Washington's warning against the formation of political parties actually came from ideas dating back to the ancient Greeks. According to the Greek notion of public service, a leader was expected to place the good of society as a whole above the interests of any one group. Leaders who acted to benefit only themselves or a portion of society were considered corrupt. The modern party system arose in seventeenth century England, where the Whig and Tory parties competed for political influence and control of government job appointments. In Washington's eyes, the British party system was corrupt.

Info to Know

The Federalists The Federalist Party was not originally a political party, but merely a loose coalition of individuals who wanted to create a strong national government. These individuals included Alexander Hamilton, James Madison, and George Washington, among others. Federalists dominated the national government until 1801, when Jefferson was elected. The Federalists never again won a presidential election. By 1824, the Federalist Party was essentially disbanded.

The First American Political Parties

Historical Context The documents below provide different perspectives on political parties in the federal period.

Task Examine the documents and answer the questions that follow. Then you will be asked to write an essay about the development of the first American political parties, using facts from the documents and from the chapter to support the position you take in your thesis statement.

DOCUMENT 1

In 1796 George Washington decided not to seek re-election for a third term as president of the United States. In his famous Farewell Address, Washington warned Americans to avoid divisions based on political parties and geography. Below is a short excerpt from his address.

> "I have already intimated to you the danger of Parties in the State, with particular reference to the founding of them on Geographical discriminations. Let me now … warn you in the most solemn manner against the baneful effects of the spirit of Party, generally …
>
> The alternate domination of one faction over another, sharpened by the spirit of revenge natural to party dissention … is itself a frightful despotism. …
>
> It serves always to distract the Public Council and enfeeble the Public Administration. It agitates the Community with ill founded jealousies and false alarms, kindles the animosity of one party against another, foments occasionally riot and insurrection."

DOCUMENT 2

In the election of 1800 between Thomas Jefferson and John Adams, presidential power was transferred between political parties for the first time in the young nation's history. The electoral vote was sharply divided along geographic lines, as the map below shows.

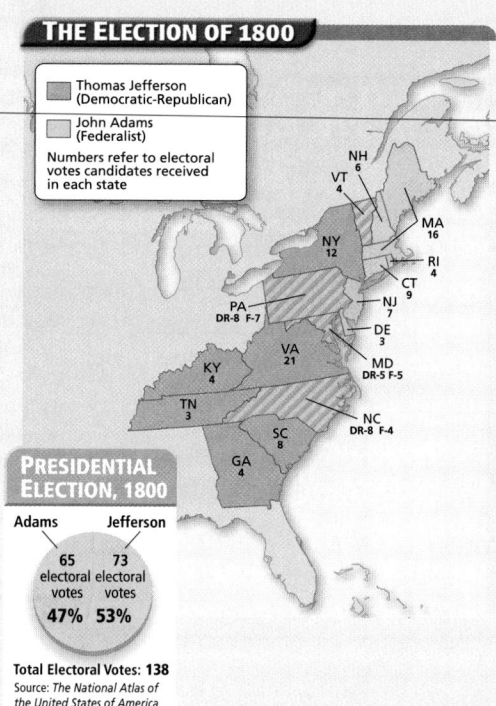

THE ELECTION OF 1800

Thomas Jefferson (Democratic-Republican)
John Adams (Federalist)
Numbers refer to electoral votes candidates received in each state

NH 6
VT 4
MA 16
NY 12
RI 4
CT 9
PA DR-8 F-7
NJ 7
DE 3
KY 4
VA 21
MD DR-5 F-5
TN 3
NC DR-8 F-4
SC 8
GA 4

PRESIDENTIAL ELECTION, 1800

Adams — 65 electoral votes — 47%
Jefferson — 73 electoral votes — 53%

Total Electoral Votes: 138
Source: *The National Atlas of the United States of America*

Skills Focus: Analyzing Primary Sources   At Level

Reading Like a Historian Skill
Washington's Farewell Address

1. Guide the class in a discussion of the excerpt from Washington's Farewell Address that makes up Document 1. Make sure that students understand all the words used.

2. Have each student write an editorial from the perspective of an American citizen in 1796. Students should take a position on Washington's warning against political parties in his Farewell Address and provide valid arguments to back up their opinions.

3. Have volunteers read their editorials to the class. Then guide the class in a discussion of what effect, if any, Washington's warning had on the American public. **LS Verbal-Linguistic, Logical-Mathematical**

   Alternative Assessment Handbook, Rubric 17: Letters to Editors

DOCUMENT 3

In 1798 one of the most controversial issues in the U.S. Congress was the passage of the Alien and Sedition Acts. The Federalist government believed that Democratic-Republican criticism of Federalist policies was disloyal and that foreigners, or aliens, would sympathize with France during war. The political cartoon below depicts Congress in 1798. Roger Griswold, a Federalist, is using his cane to attack Matthew Lyon, a Democratic-Republican, who is retaliating with tongs.

THE GRANGER COLLECTION, NEW YORK

DOCUMENT 4

The presidential campaign of 1800 was a bitter political struggle. Each party made accusations against the other. Democratic-Republicans believed the Federalist president John Adams wanted to turn the country into a monarchy. Federalists worried that Thomas Jefferson might have ties to revolutionary France. In Jefferson's Inaugural Address (1801), he called for the country to unite around common goals.

"Every difference of opinion is not a difference of principle. We have called by different names brethren of the same principle. We are all Republicans, we are all Federalists. If there be any among us who would wish to dissolve this Union or to change its republican form, let them stand undisturbed as monuments of the safety with which error of opinion may be tolerated where reason is left free to combat it . . .

Let us, then, with courage and confidence pursue our own Federal and Republican principles, our attachment to union and representative government."

Info to Know

The Revolution of 1800 George Washington's warning against political parties certainly seemed to ring true in the election of 1800. The fact that power transferred from Adams to Jefferson without any uprisings or violence was a testament to the strength of American democracy. Indeed, years later Thomas Jefferson would refer to his election as the "revolution" of 1800. The Democratic-Republicans, who drew support from small farmers, shopkeepers, and other workers, won control of both the presidency and Congress. Jefferson introduced democratic customs, such as the practice of shaking hands with the president rather than bowing to him, which the Federalists had preferred. With his inaugural address, Jefferson tried to start healing the divisions that had already come close to breaking up the young nation.

Skills FOCUS — READING LIKE A HISTORIAN

1. **a. Identify** Refer to Document 1. Name three ways Washington believed political parties could negatively affect the nation.
   b. Interpret Why might Washington have considered political parties based on geography to be dangerous?

2. **a. Identify** Refer to Document 2. According to the pie graph, what percentage of electoral votes did Jefferson receive? What percentage did Adams receive?
   b. Analyze What regional voting pattern can you identify using the map?

3. **a. Describe** Refer to Document 3. How does this cartoon characterize the political divisions in the United States in 1798?
   b. Analyze Why did the Democratic-Republicans respond so strongly against the Sedition Act? Why did the Federalists believe it was necessary?

4. **a. Recall** Refer to Document 4. What does Jefferson believe about political parties?
   b. Analyze Why might Jefferson have made this plea for unity in his inaugural address?

5. **Document-Based Essay Question** Consider the question below and form a thesis statement. Using examples from Documents 1, 2, 3, and 4, create an outline and write a short essay supporting your position.
   Explain and analyze the development of the first American political parties during the period 1794–1801. Did the presence of political parties help or harm the nation?

See **Skills Handbook**, pp. H21, H28–H29, H31

FORGING THE NEW REPUBLIC **229**

Skills Focus: Making Oral Presentations

At Level

Reading Like a Historian Skill
The Election of 1800

1. Divide the class into two groups. Have one group represent Federalists supporting President John Adams in the election of 1800. Have the other group represent Democratic-Republican supporters of Thomas Jefferson. Have each side prepare supporting arguments for its position, conducting additional research if necessary.

2. Conduct a classroom debate between the two parties. Each team of debaters should explain why their candidate would be the best choice to lead America into the new century.

3. Have students write a one-page essay telling which candidate they would have supported and why. Have volunteers read their essays to the class. **LS Logical-Mathematical, Verbal-Linguistic**

   📄 Alternative Assessment Handbook, Rubric 10: Debates

Answers

Reading Like a Historian
1. **a.** *create a spirit of revenge; lead to despotism; can incite riot and revolt;* **b.** *possible answer—They could lead to the breakup of the United States;* 2. **a.** *53 percent, 47 percent;* **b.** *North voted strongly for Adams;* 3. **a.** *Federalists and Democratic-Republicans are so divided that they are physically attacking one another;* **b.** *Many of the Democratic-Republicans sympathized with the French. The Federalists were generally distrustful of foreigners and viewed any criticism as disloyalty;* 4. **a.** *that they represent differences of opinion, not differences of principle;* **b.** *possible answer— because he was worried that the differences between Federalists and Democratic-Republicans might tear the country apart;* 5. *possible answers— help, because different opinions were presented, allowing for more discussion of government policy; harm, because political parties created division and conflict*

Visual Summary

Review and Inquiry Have students use the atlas in their text to show how much territory the United States gained during this time period. Then guide students in a review of the growing power of the federal government, and have students explain how the acquisition of territory is linked to the growing powers of the government.

Quick Facts Transparency: Forging the New Republic

Reviewing Key Terms and People

1. strict construction
2. cabinet
3. Judiciary Act of 1789
4. sectionalism
5. nullification
6. Tecumseh
7. Judicial review
8. Loose construction
9. Aaron Burr
10. Little Turtle
11. Treaty of Ghent
12. Andrew Jackson
13. Impressment

Comprehension and Critical Thinking

14. **a.** L'Enfant was the architect; Banneker recreated L'Enfant's drawings from memory after L'Enfant was fired
    b. Federalists saw country growing into strong central government with prosperous cities and businesses; Republicans saw country growing with smaller central government and being more rural than urban.
    c. He took strong military action to put down the rebellion and to teach the rebels that armed rebellion against national government would not be tolerated.

15. **a.** in favor of seeing an end to monarchy; France had helped America during Revolutionary War; insulted American diplomats,

---

Visual Summary: Forging the New Republic

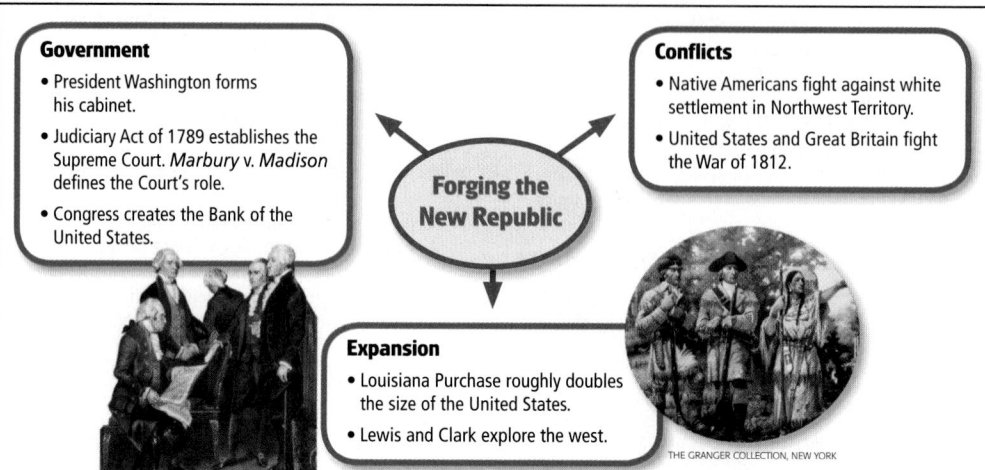

Government
- President Washington forms his cabinet.
- Judiciary Act of 1789 establishes the Supreme Court. *Marbury* v. *Madison* defines the Court's role.
- Congress creates the Bank of the United States.

Conflicts
- Native Americans fight against white settlement in Northwest Territory.
- United States and Great Britain fight the War of 1812.

Forging the New Republic

Expansion
- Louisiana Purchase roughly doubles the size of the United States.
- Lewis and Clark explore the west.

THE GRANGER COLLECTION, NEW YORK

Reviewing Key Terms and People

Complete each sentence by filling the blank with the correct term or person.

1. The idea that the powers of the central government should be limited to those specifically spelled out in the Constitution is called _____.

2. The Secretary of State, the Secretary of War, and the Secretary of the Treasury made up President Washington's _____.

3. The _____ set up the Supreme Court with one chief justice and five associates.

4. Loyalty to one's geographic region, sometimes more than to one's country, is called _____.

5. The idea that state legislatures can decide not to follow laws passed by the central government is called _____.

6. _____ led Native American forces in the Battle of Tippecanoe.

7. _____ is the right of the Supreme Court to declare that a law violates the Constitution.

8. _____ states that the central government can do certain things as long as the Constitution does not specifically prohibit them.

9. Jefferson's vice president, _____, killed Alexander Hamilton in a duel.

10. _____ tried unsuccessfully to resist the expansion of American settlement in the Northwest Territory.

11. The War of 1812 was ended by the _____.

12. _____ commanded American troops at the Battle of New Orleans.

13. _____ was the act of kidnapping men and forcing them to work on ships.

Comprehension and Critical Thinking

SECTION 1 *(pp. 202–208)*

14. **a. Identify** What roles did Pierre Charles L'Enfant and Benjamin Banneker have in the creation of Washington, D.C.?

XYZ Affair
b. with the Alien and Sedition Acts
c. possible answers—no, because violates First Amendment right to freedom of speech; yes, because necessary to protect the nation

16. **a.** reduced size of government, changed tax system, shrank the size of the military
    b. They opposed it because acquisition might lead to more pro-Republican states and diminish Federalist power in Congress.

c. possible answer—Supreme Court needs to be able to check the power of the other two branches of government.

17. **a.** Britain's impressment of American sailors; Britain tried to rebuild alliances with Native Americans against U.S.
    b. did not want to join white society; wanted to preserve their own culture; wanted to keep their land
    c. improvement in American image; defeat of Native American nations

b. Contrast What were the main differences between the Federalists and the Democratic-Republicans?

c. Predict How would President Washington's actions during the Whiskey Rebellion help determine the actions of presidents facing similar situations in the future?

SECTION 2 *(pp. 209–214)*

15. a. Recall Why were Americans generally sympathetic to France after the French Revolution? Why did those sympathies change to hostility?

b. Summarize How did the U.S. government respond to the XYZ affair?

c. Evaluate Should a democratic government be allowed to pass a law like the Sedition Act? Why or why not?

SECTION 3 *(pp. 215–220)*

16. a. Identify What changes did Jefferson make during his presidency?

b. Analyze In what ways was Federalist opposition to the Louisiana Purchase an example of party politics?

c. Evaluate Defend this statement: "The Supreme Court should have the right to declare that a law violates the Constitution."

SECTION 4 *(pp. 224–227)*

17. a. Describe What British actions helped trigger the War of 1812?

b. Make Inferences Why did Native Americans resist Jefferson's policy for Indian affairs?

c. Evaluate What was ultimately accomplished by the War of 1812?

Using the Internet

go.hrw.com
Practice Online
Keyword: SD7 CH6

18. The War of 1812 was the new country's first war against a European nation. Using the keyword above, do research to learn more about this war. Pick one topic related to the war and create a detailed report on this element or event in the conflict.

Analyzing Primary Sources

Reading Like a Historian When Native Americans in the Northwest Territory were being forced to give up their land in the early 1800s, Tecumseh mourned for his people:

66 The Great Spirit gave this great island to his red children. He placed the whites on the other side of the big water. They were not contented with their own, but came to take ours from us. They have driven us from the sea to the lakes—we can go no farther. 99

—Tecumseh, Shawnee leader

19. Identify What is "the big water"?

20. Interpret What does Tecumseh mean by "they have driven us from the sea to the lakes"?

Critical Reading

Read the passage in Section 1 that begins with the heading "Political parties develop." Then answer the following question.

21. In the third paragraph the passage reads: "Each sides justified its actions as necessary to resist the dangerous ideas of the other." Here the word *justified* means

A. claimed to be proper.

B. denied.

C. invented.

D. told many people about.

WRITING FOR THE SAT

Think about the following issue.

In his Farewell Address, George Washington warned the new nation to beware of party politics and involvement in the affairs of foreign countries.

22. Assignment Was Washington right or wrong about the danger of party politics and involvement in the affairs of other countries? Write a short essay in which you develop your position on these questions. Support your view with logical reasoning, examples from your reading, and current events.

Answers

Using the Internet

18. Go to the HRW Web site and enter the keyword shown to access a rubric for this activity.

KEYWORD: SD7 CH6

Analyzing Primary Sources

19. the Atlantic Ocean

20. White settlers have driven Native Americans westward from the ocean to the Great Lakes region.

Critical Reading

21. A

Writing for the SAT

22. possible answer—The nation is stronger with more than one voice; if there is only one party, there may be no room for criticism or other plans of action.

A rubric for this activity is provided in the Chapter Resource File: Writing for the SAT: Interpreting the Constitution.

History's Impact
Video Program

has expanded U.S. territory and led to the growth of the nation; broadened human understanding of the world

Review and Assessment Resources

Review and Reinforce

- CRF: Chapter Review Activity
- Quick Facts Transparencies: Hamilton's Economic Plan, Reactions to the XYZ Affair, The Election of 1800: Power Changes Hands, Forging the New Republic
- Spanish Chapter Summaries Audio CD Program
- Online Chapter Summaries in Spanish
- OSP Holt PuzzlePro; Quiz Show for ExamView
- Quiz Game CD-ROM

Assess

- PASS: Chapter Test, Forms A and B
- Alternative Assessment Handbook
- OSP ExamView Test Generator, Chapter Test
- Differentiated Instruction Modified Worksheets and Tests CD-ROM: Chapter Test
- HOAP Holt Online Assessment Program (in the Premier Online Edition)

Reteach/Intervene

- Interactive Reader and Study Guide
- Differentiated Instruction Teacher Management System: Lesson Plans for Differentiated Instruction
- Differentiated Instruction Modified Worksheets and Tests CD-ROM: Chapter Test
- Interactive Skills Tutor CD-ROM

go.hrw.com
Online Resources

KEYWORD: SD7 CH6

Summarizing the Unit

Remind students that the Articles of Confederation were soon found to be unsatisfactory because they gave too much power to the individual states at the expense of the federal government. Guide students in a discussion of the following questions: *What functions are best fulfilled by the federal government? What functions are best fulfilled by the states? How has this separation changed in modern times?*

Connecting to Themes

Remind students that many founders feared the development of political parties. In spite of their warnings, different ideas about government quickly led to conflict and the birth of political parties. Ask students what they feel are the benefits and disadvantages of our two-party political system today.

 **UNIT 2 IN BRIEF** Below is a chapter-by-chapter summary of the main ideas covered in Unit 2.

 CHAPTER 4 The Revolutionary Era
1763–1783

MAIN IDEA Angered by a series of new British laws, the colonists fought the Revolutionary War and eventually gained independence from Great Britain.

SECTION 1 The British Parliament passed the Stamp Act, Sugar Act, Quartering Act, and other laws to raise money in the colonies. The colonists rebelled, claiming Great Britain had no right to tax them without colonial representation in Parliament.

SECTION 2 With the Declaration of Independence, drafted by Thomas Jefferson, the colonists declared their independence from Great Britain in 1776.

SECTION 3 The Revolutionary War proved costly for both sides. Facing a better trained and equipped British army, the colonists relied on strong leadership and a fierce belief in their cause to sustain them until key victories began to turn the tide.

SECTION 4 Fighting ceased in October 1771, and the Treaty of Paris was signed in 1783, granting American independence and setting the Mississippi River as the western boundary of the United States.

 CHAPTER 5 Creating a New Government
1776–1789

MAIN IDEA Creating a new American government proved to be a difficult task. The first national constitution, the Articles of Confederation, had many weaknesses. At the Constitutional Convention, American leaders worked to build compromises between the states.

SECTION 1 The Articles of Confederation established a weak central government and left a good deal of power in the hands of individual states. Unable to impose taxes or settle disputes between the states, the Confederation government was largely ineffective.

SECTION 2 After the Articles of Confederation failed to establish an effective national government, delegates to the Constitutional Convention met to draft a new constitution. Key compromises between small and large states helped delegates agree upon the U.S. Constitution, which created a federal system of government and balanced the power of the national government among three branches.

SECTION 3 Federalists and Antifederalists began heated debates over the Constitution. Eventually, the addition of the Bill of Rights led to ratification. The Bill of Rights is the term for the first 10 amendments to the Constitution.

 CHAPTER 6 Forging the New Republic
1789–1815

MAIN IDEA In its early years, the United States faced many challenges, including the emergence of political parties and conflicts with Native Americans and Great Britain.

SECTION 1 George Washington became the first president of the United States in 1789. Disputes over the National Bank and differing views on the proper interpretation of the Constitution led to the emergence of political parties.

SECTION 2 As president, Washington maintained American neutrality in European conflicts. However, violence broke out in the western frontier in response to American settlement in Native American territory.

SECTION 3 Thomas Jefferson became president in 1800. Among his accomplishments was the Louisiana Purchase, which doubled the size of the United States in 1803.

SECTION 4 British impressment of American sailors, disputes over trade, and conflicts in the Northwest Territory led to the War of 1812. The Treaty of Ghent ended the war in 1814. The United States had proven itself as a nation once again.

232 UNIT 2 IN BRIEF

Unit Resources

Review and Reinforce

- CRF: Chapter Review Activity
- Spanish Chapter Summaries Audio CD Program
- OSP Holt PuzzlePro; GameTool for ExamView
- Quiz Game CD-ROM

Assess

- PASS: Unit Test, Forms A and B
- Alternative Assessment Handbook
- OSP ExamView Test Generator
- Differentiated Instruction Modified Worksheets and Tests CD-ROM: Chapter Tests
- HOAP Holt Online Assessment Program (in the Premier Online Edition)

Reteach/Intervene

- Interactive Reader and Study Guide
- Differentiated Instruction Teacher Management System: Lesson Plans for Differentiated Instruction
- Differentiated Instruction Modified Worksheets and Tests CD-ROM: Chapter Tests
- Interactive Skills Tutor CD-ROM

go.hrw.com
Online Resources
KEYWORDS: SD7 CH4, SD7 CH5, SD7 CH6

3 Developing a National Identity

1815–1860

Chapter 7
From Nationalism to Sectionalism
1815–1840

Chapter 8
A Push for Reform
1830–1860

Chapter 9
Expansion Leads to Conflict
1830–1860

Themes

Cultural Expressions
Americans took pride in their new nation and eagerly sought to change their lives and society through religious movements and reforms in education and other institutions.

Immigration and Migration
European immigrants flooded eastern cities, and Americans increasingly migrated to the western regions of the country.

Economic Development
The growth of factories and manufacturing established the North as an industrial power, while southern economies continued to rely mainly on agriculture.

An early steam locomotive powers a railroad in New Jersey, one of the first railroads in the country.

233

Unit Preview

Introducing the Unit
Tell students that following the War of 1812, many Americans felt a strong sense of pride in their country. This period was known as the Era of Good Feelings. Ask students if they believe that Americans today feel a sense of pride in their country. Why or why not?

Connecting to Themes
Activity **U.S. Economy**
Discussion Explain to students that in this unit they will read how key economic developments brought important changes to the United States. Ask students to name what they feel are the most important economic developments of our own time and discuss how they will affect the nation's economy and society in the years to come. **LS Verbal-Linguistic**

Reading Like a Historian
Interpreting Visuals
Early Railroads Although most people associate railroads with steam locomotives, early railways were in use before their invention. Railways were first used in Great Britain in the seventeenth century to reduce friction while moving heavily loaded wheeled vehicles. In the United States, the first "gravity road," as it was known, was built for military purposes in 1764 at the Niagara portage in Lewiston, New York.

Unit Resources

Planning
- Differentiated Instruction Teacher Management System: Unit Pacing Guide
- One-Stop Planner CD-ROM: Teacher Management System
- Power Presentations with Video CD-ROM

Differentiating Instruction
- Differentiated Instruction Teacher Management System: Lesson Plans for Differentiated Instruction
- Pre-AP Activities Guide for American History
- Differentiated Instruction Modified Worksheets and Tests CD-ROM

Enrichment
- Civic Participation Activities Guide
- CRF: Economics and History Activity
- CRF: Interdisciplinary Project
- American History Primary Source Library CD-ROM

Assessment
- PASS: Unit Test, Forms A & B
- Alternative Assessment Handbook
- OSP ExamView Test Generator
- HOAP Holt Online Assessment Program (in the Premier Online Edition)

The Differentiated Instruction Teacher Management System
provides a planning and instructional benchmarking guide for this unit.

Making Inferences

Have each student print out, make a copy of, or cut out a short article from a magazine, newspaper, or Web site about a current event. Have students write a brief paragraph on any inferences they feel are justified by the information in the text. Then have students exchange their articles with another student. Have each student make an inference in the same way about the new article. Continue the activity as time permits.

Word Help

urbanization growth of cities
evolved changed

Primary Source

A story in the *Plattsburg Republican* described the recruitment of workers for the Lowell textile mill: "One hundred girls passed through this village on the 29th ult., en route for Lowell; and some fifty for the same destination two weeks since. Agents are sent into this county, Franklin and St. Lawrence, and within the past year, more than four hundred have been 'picked up' and forwarded to the factories. Good wages are offered them, or they would not leave their homes, and great manufacturing establishments are doing a good business that will 'pay' or they would not want them."

Skills Planner

To give students more opportunities to practice this skill, see the following activity in the teacher's edition: The Abolition Movement, p. 288.

Prepare to Read

Making Inferences

Find practice for **Making Inferences** in the **Skills Handbook,** p. H7

Often meaning is implied, or hinted at in a text. When meaning is implied, good readers connect facts with their own experiences to make inferences.

Before You Read
Skim the text to determine what it will be about. Then think about what you already know about the subject.

While You Read
Note ideas directly stated in the reading, as well as those that may be implied.

After You Read
Review ideas expressed in the text and make connections to your prior knowledge. What can you infer from or about the text?

The revolution spreads

Throughout the early and middle 1800s, industrialization spread slowly from the textile to other industries in the North. In the 1830s, steam engines became better and more widely available, and their power helped make the textile industry the fastest growing part of the American economy.

Industrialization in the North led to the urbanization of the North. People left the farm and moved to cities where they could work in the mills and factories. In 1820, only 7 percent of Americans lived in cities. Within 30 years, the percentage more than doubled.

The North underwent a dramatic and rapid change. In a few decades, it evolved from a region of just small towns and farms into one including large cities and factories—all as a result of the Industrial Revolution.

READING CHECK **Making Inferences** How did industionalization change peoples' ways of life?

Implied Industrial jobs in the North offered greater opportunities than rural jobs.

Directly stated Between 1820 and 1850 the number of Americans living and working in northern cities more than doubled.

Test Prep Tip

Tests often contain passages from which you may be asked to infer meaning, such as future events or an author's purpose. Because making inferences means choosing the most likely explanation from the facts available, try to balance information in the text with prior knowledge so that you arrive at the most informed inference.

234 UNIT 3

Skills Focus: Making Inferences

`At Level`

Reading Skill
Inferences Based on Historical Texts

1. Have students work in pairs to choose a block of several paragraphs from one of the chapters in this unit.

2. Have each student read the text, including any headings. Then have students take turns making an inference from the text. Have students explain how they drew this inference and what evidence supports this inference.

3. Have students choose other passages and repeat the activity as time allows.
   LS Verbal-Linguistic, Intrapersonal
   Alternative Assessment Handbook, Rubric 16: Judging Information

Reading like a Historian

Interpreting Visuals

Find practice for **Interpreting Visuals** in the **Skills Handbook**, p. H30

Visuals such as photographs, illustrations, advertisements, or political cartoons are an important part of the historical record. These sources provide rich detail about historical events and the people who participated in them. The first **historical photographs** date from the invention of photography around 1830.

Strategies historians use:

- Identify the subject. Look for captions. Who or what is being portrayed?
- Some historical photographs are staged or posed. Others show people as they are. Both types contain important information.
- Study the visual details. What do they tell you about the image historical context?

The row of tiny houses indicates the living conditions of the people pictured.

The people in this photograph are not posing. The photo is probably an accurate record of life.

Enslaved African Americans at rest on a Sunday in 1860.

The caption tells you what the subject of this picture is.

 READING LIKE A HISTORIAN

As You Read Examine the historical photographs. Describe what they depict. How do photographs support the text? How do the photographs help you understand the material?

As You Study Compare historical photographs of different scenes and events. Look for details that will indicate historical context.

Chapter 7 Planning Guide

From Nationalism to Sectionalism

Chapter Overview	Reproducible Resources	Technology Resources
CHAPTER 7 pp. 236–263 **Overview:** In this chapter, students will analyze how such issues as slavery, economic policy, and states' rights shaped the nation after the War of 1812.	**Differentiated Instruction Teacher Management System:*** • Instructional Benchmarking Guides • Lesson Plans for Differentiated Instruction **Interactive Reader and Study Guide:** Chapter Summary* **Chapter Resource File:*** • Focus on Writing: Differences Between the North and the South • Social Studies Skills Activity: Sequencing • Chapter Review Activity **American History Outline Maps** **Pre-AP Activities Guide for American History***	Live Ink® Online Reading Help Student Edition on Audio CD Program Differentiated Instruction Modified Worksheets and Tests CD-ROM Interactive Skills Tutor CD-ROM United States History Primary Source Library CD-ROM Power Presentations with Video CD-ROM History's Impact: American History Video Program (VHS/DVD): From Nationalism to Sectionalism Online Chapter Summaries in Spanish Graphic Organizer Transparencies
Section 1: **The Rise of Nationalism** **The Main Idea:** Nationalism contributed to the growth of American culture and influenced domestic and foreign policies.	**Differentiated Instruction Teacher Management System:** Section 1 Lesson Plan* **Interactive Reader and Study Guide:** Section 1 Summary* **Chapter Resource File:*** • Vocabulary Builder Activity, Section 1	Daily Bellringer Transparency: Section 1* Daily Test Practice Transparency: Section 1* Map Transparency: Boundary Changes, 1803–1819*
Section 2: **The Age of Jackson** **The Main Idea:** President Andrew Jackson's bold actions defined a period of American history.	**Differentiated Instruction Teacher Management System:** Section 2 Lesson Plan* **Interactive Reader and Study Guide:** Section 2 Summary* **Chapter Resource File:*** • Vocabulary Builder Activity, Section 2	Daily Bellringer Transparency: Section 2* Daily Test Practice Transparency: Section 2* Map Transparency: Indian Removal, 1831–1842*
Section 3: **The Industrial North** **The Main Idea:** The North developed an economy based on industry.	**Differentiated Instruction Teacher Management System:** Section 3 Lesson Plan* **Interactive Reader and Study Guide:** Section 3 Summary* **Chapter Resource File:*** • Vocabulary Builder Activity, Section 3	Daily Bellringer Transparency: Section 3* Daily Test Practice Transparency: Section 3*
Section 4: **The Land of Cotton** **The Main Idea:** During the early 1800s, the South developed an economy based on agriculture.	**Differentiated Instruction Teacher Management System:** Section 4 Lesson Plan* **Interactive Reader and Study Guide:** Section 4 Summary* **Chapter Resource File:*** • Vocabulary Builder Activity, Section 4	Daily Bellringer Transparency: Section 4* Daily Test Practice Transparency: Section 4* Map Transparency: The Cotton Kingdom*

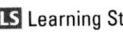

HOLT

History's Impact
American History Video Program (VHS/DVD)
From Nationalism to Sectionalism

Review, Assessment, Intervention

Quick Facts Transparency: From Nationalism to Sectionalism

Spanish Chapter Summaries Audio CD Program

Progress Assessment Support System (PASS): Chapter Test*

Differentiated Instruction Modified Worksheets and Tests CD-ROM: Modified Chapter Test

OSP **One-Stop Planner CD-ROM:** ExamView Test Generator (English/Spanish)

HOAP **Holt Online Assessment Program (HOAP),** in the Holt Premier Online Student Edition

PASS: Section 1 Quiz*

Online Quiz: Section 1

Alternative Assessment Handbook

PASS: Section 2 Quiz*

Online Quiz: Section 2

Alternative Assessment Handbook

PASS: Section 3 Quiz*

Online Quiz: Section 3

Alternative Assessment Handbook

PASS: Section 4 Quiz*

Online Quiz: Section 4

Alternative Assessment Handbook

NC RESOURCES

The following resources were developed to help North Carolina educators teach the standards and objectives of North Carolina's eleventh grade standard course of study in United States history.

- United States history EOC Test Prep Workbook
- Teacher's Support System
- North Carolina One-Stop Planner

And be sure to direct your students to **go.hrw.com** for online access to the EOC Test Prep Workbook.

go.hrw.com
EOC Test Prep
KEYWORD: SE7 NC

Holt Online Learning

go.hrw.com
Teacher Resources
KEYWORD: SD7 TEACHER

go.hrw.com
Student Resources
KEYWORD: SD7 CH7

- Document-based Questions
- Interactive Multimedia Activities

- Current Events
- Chapter-based Internet Activities
- and more!

Holt Premier
Online Student Edition

Complete online support for interactivity, assessment, and reporting

- Interactive Maps and Notebook
- Standardized Test Prep
- Homework Practice and Research Activities Online

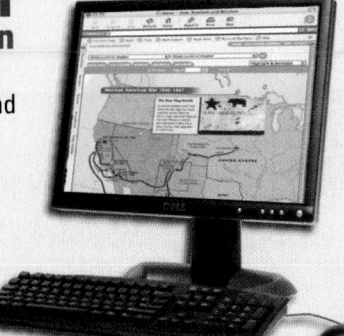

CHAPTER 7 PLANNING GUIDE

The Big Picture
Deborah Gray White

The Rise of Nationalism America emerged from the War of 1812 feeling confident about itself and its culture. Having beaten Britain for a second time, and gained true independence, there was little Americans felt they could not do. During this brief era of good feelings, white Americans reached consensus on foreign policy, internal development and expansion, and slavery.

The Age of Jackson After 1828 the expansion of democracy for some meant its contraction for others. President Andrew Jackson, the same leader who championed the rights of the common man, denied Native Americans their rights to their land, government, and families, and cruelly removed them to the West. The bank and tariff controversies underscored how difficult it would be to maintain an era of good feelings and to decide which branch of government—state or federal—best served the interest of the common man.

The Industrial North When Samuel Slater violated British law and brought plans of water-powered machines to the United States, he set off the Industrial Revolution in America. The Industrial Revolution was aided by the widespread development of transportation and communication networks, which in turn encouraged the development of urban centers.

The Land of Cotton The South developed very differently from the North. Once Eli Whitney, with the help and support of Catherine Greene, invented the cotton gin, the production of short staple cotton so dominated the southern economy that slavery was given a new lease on life. Although most southern whites did not own slaves, the southern economy and culture was built around slavery and dependent on its preservation. In the North, where slavery was illegal and the economy more variegated and dependent on technological change, life was very different than it was in the South.

Recent Scholarship

Slavery in the North It is commonly assumed that slavery was uniquely southern and that the industrializing North was removed from the horrendous institution. *The Meaning of Slavery in the North* (1998) challenges this assumption. Edited by historians David Roediger and Martin H. Blatt, this collection of essays argues that while the South's culpability regarding the horrors of slavery must be recognized, "the so-called free states of the North were full partners in the viability of the slave society of the South." In other words, that the northern and southern economies were interdependent, that slavery was a national institution, and that the prejudice that slavery generated against African Americans was likewise a national phenomenon.

Differentiating Instruction

 Differentiated Instruction Teacher Management System
- Lesson Plans for Differentiated Instruction
- Differentiated Instructional Benchmarking Guides
- Interactive Reader and Study Guide

 Spanish Chapter Summaries Audio CD Program

 Online Chapter Summaries in Spanish

Student Edition on Audio CD Program

 Differentiated Instruction Modified Worksheets and Tests CD-ROM
- Vocabulary Flash Cards
- Modified Vocabulary Builder Activities
- Modified Chapter Review Activity
- Modified Chapter Test

OSP One-Stop Planner CD-ROM
- ExamView Test Generator (English and Spanish)
- PuzzlePro
- Quiz Show for ExamView
- Transparencies and Videos

TE Differentiated Activities in the Teacher's Edition
- *Gibbons* v. *Ogden*, p. 240
- Nationalism Guides Foreign Policy, p. 241
- The Spoils System, p. 246
- The Industrial Revolution, p. 253
- A Revolution in Industry, p. 257

Reading Like a Historian
Sam Wineburg

Perspective in History

Determining what caused an event is one of the primary concerns of the historian. But often our understanding of cause will be influenced by where we stand—our perspective.

The Monroe Doctrine

Take, for example, our chapter's discussion of the Monroe Doctrine. With the defeat of Spain, Latin American countries declared their independence and threw off the Spanish yoke. But when Spain sought to reassert itself, Great Britain became worried about losing its "thriving trade with the former Spanish colonies." Great Britain was concerned about its pocketbook. What about the United States?

Rumblings by Spain "also concerned the United States. American lawmakers wanted to deter any foreign country from taking lands in the Americas that the United States might someday claim." By juxtaposing British and American interests, our chapter makes a historical claim. Britain's concern was chiefly economic. The United States, on the other hand, was concerned primarily with issues of European encroachment and territorial sovereignty.

The American Perspective

The rest of the chapter's explanation is consistent. The quotation from the Monroe Doctrine emphasizes that the American continents were not to be considered "as subjects" for European colonization, and that Europe should not interfere in American affairs. "The Monroe Doctrine was a bold statement to make to the old, great powers of Europe." In other words, the upstart U.S.A. was saying to the corrupt regimes of Europe: don't mess with us—we are not your subjects!

This explanation portrays the U.S. as a young country trying to establish itself, and warning European powers to back off. But how might the Monroe Doctrine look from another perspective? How, for example, might the same policy be viewed by countries that have lived in the shadow of American power?

A Caribbean Perspective

Consider this account from William Claypole and John Robottom's *Caribbean Story* (1994),
a textbook used in Jamaica and other Caribbean nations. The Monroe Doctrine is introduced by noting that in the aftermath of Spain's defeat by Napoleon, newly independent Latin American countries were "no longer bound to obey trading regulations" and "bought increasing amounts of goods from British and American traders." "Britain and the USA were alarmed" by the prospect of Spain returning to the Western Hemisphere. Here, then, it is not American sovereignty that is stressed but the desire to protect both British and American trade. From this perspective, U.S. economic interests come to the forefront.

A Mexican Perspective

How is the Monroe Doctrine viewed from Mexican eyes, a country which lost a major war with the United States, ceding vast tracks of New Mexico and California to its victorious neighbor? According to Mario Alfonso Rodriguez Palacios' *Mexico en la Historia* (1992), a high school textbook, by declaring the Western Hemisphere off limits to European powers in the Monroe Doctrine, the U.S. could "assume the role of protector of the young Hispano-American nations" and "under this pretext, to intervene in their politics and determine their destinies."

Which One is Right?

So, your students might ask, which cause is the right one: the desire for American sovereignty, the pursuit of economic interests, or the motivation to engage in imperialistic policies? In physics or chemistry, cause can be pinpointed by varying one factor while holding others constant. No such luck in history. Historical events are "overdetermined"—multiple causes come together in an imprecise alchemy to cause, or contribute to, major historical events. Weighing these causes—determining which are primary and which secondary—is part of the never-ending discussion that enriches our understanding of the past. Oftentimes, where we come down depends on where we stand when we begin our inquiry.

From *Caribbean Story, Book 2: The Inheritors* by William Claypole and John Robottom. Published by Carlong, Kingston, 1994.

From *Mexico en la Historia: Tercer grado, educación secu* by Mario Alfonso Rodriguez Palacios. Published by Editorial Trillas, Mexico City, 1992.

Standards Focus

Social Studies Competency Goals
Goal 2 The learner will assess the competing forces of expansionism, nationalism, and sectionalism.
🔖 **2.02, 2.03, 2.04**

The Big Idea and Essential Questions

To foster student understanding of this chapter's big idea, design your lesson to address each section's essential question.

Big Idea As a unique national identity emerged in the United States, two distinct economic systems were developing in the North and South. Sectionalism led to serious disagreements about slavery, economic policy, and states' rights.

Essential Questions

1. What was the impact of nationalism on American culture and domestic and foreign policies?

2. How did President Andrew Jackson's actions define a period of American history?

3. What was the economy of the North based upon?

4. What was the economy of the South based upon?

Key to Differentiating Instruction

Below Level

Basic-level activities designed for all students encountering new material

At Level

Intermediate-level activities designed for average students

Above Level

Challenging activities designed for honors and gifted-and-talented students

Standard English Mastery

Activities designed to improve standard English usage

CHAPTER
7 1815–1840
From Nationalism to Sectionalism

THE BIG PICTURE The War of 1812 filled Americans with national pride. Yet against the backdrop of an emerging national identity, two distinct economic systems were developing in the North and South.

North Carolina Standards

Social Studies Objectives

2.02 Describe how the growth of nationalism and sectionalism were reflected in art, literature, and language.

2.03 Distinguish between the economic and social issues that led to sectionalism and nationalism.

2.04 Assess political events, issues, and personalities that contributed to sectionalism and nationalism.

Language Arts Objectives

3.01 Use language persuasively in addressing a particular issue by:
• establishing and defending a point of view.

Skills FOCUS **READING LIKE A HISTORIAN**

Americans have been celebrating Independence Day ever since they first declared their freedom in 1776. Here they are shown celebrating in *Fourth of July at Centre Square, Philadelphia, 1819*, by John Lewis Krimmel. **Interpreting Visuals** How do you think the painting illustrates a spirit of nationalism? Give examples to support your answer.

See Skills Handbook, p. H30

COURTESY THE PENNSYLVANIA ACADEMY OF THE FINE ARTS, PHILADELPHIA

U.S.

World

1815

March 1816 James Monroe is elected president.

1815 Napoleon is defeated at the Battle of Waterloo.

236

Introduce the Chapter   At Level

From Nationalism to Sectionalism

1. Have students make a list of traits that they associate with the people of the young United States. How would they describe these Americans? Would they use terms like aggressive, young, eager, and energetic, or would they use terms like soft-spoken, traditional, and dedicated to peaceful negotiation? Make a class list of the descriptions for all to see.

2. Have students work in pairs to scan the chapter and find events that might match

each of the terms on the class list. Have volunteers share their findings with the class.

3. Tell students that in this chapter they will learn about challenges that faced the young nation, actions of the Supreme Court that helped define the country, and about the increasingly divisive issue of slavery.
LS Interpersonal, Verbal Linguistic

📖 Alternative Assessment Handbook, Rubric 11: Discussions

• Chapter Preview •

HOLT
History's Impact
► **Video Program: From Nationalism to Sectionalism**
See the Video Teacher's Guide for strategies for using the video segment.

Reading Like a Historian
July 4th, 1819, and July 4th today
Have students examine the image carefully. Have students point out contrasts in the ways people are celebrating and then explain how today's July 4th celebrations differ from those held in the early 1800s.

1820
The Missouri Compromise admits one free state and one slave state into the Union.

1821
Mexico wins independence from Spain.

1823
The Monroe Doctrine warns European powers away from the Americas.

1825
Bolivia, named for South American liberator Simón Bolívar, gains its independence.

1828
Andrew Jackson is elected president.

May 1830
The Baltimore & Ohio Railroad opens.

1832
British Reform Act gives urban centers more power.

1833
Slavery is outlawed in the British Empire.

1838
U.S. troops begin the forced removal of the Cherokee people from Georgia along the Trail of Tears.

1837
Queen Victoria begins her reign in the United Kingdom.

1840
Samuel F. B. Morse patents the telegraph.

1820   1825   1830   1835   1840

237

go.hrw.com
Online Resources
Chapter Resources:
KEYWORD: SD7 CH7
Teacher Resources:
KEYWORD: SD7 TEACHER

Explore the Time Line

1. How many years passed between the election of James Monroe and Andrew Jackson? *12*

2. How many states were admitted into the Union under the Missouri Compromise? *two*

3. What significant event occurred in 1833? *British Empire outlawed slavery*

Info to Know

Transportation Following the War of 1812, Americans began to push for better transportation. A four-horse team pulling a wagon full of goods took 75 days to make the approximately 750 mile journey from Worcester, Massachusetts, to Charleston, South Carolina.

Draw Conclusions Why might the federal government take responsibility for building roads and canals? *possible answer— They crossed state lines, helped unite the nation, and benefited all citizens.*

Answers
Reading Like a Historian (p. 236)
possible answer—The painting shows a large group of people gathering together to celebrate Independence Day.

Bellringer

The Inside Story... Use the **Daily Bellringer Transparency** to help students answer the question.

📽 Daily Bellringer Transparency, Section 1

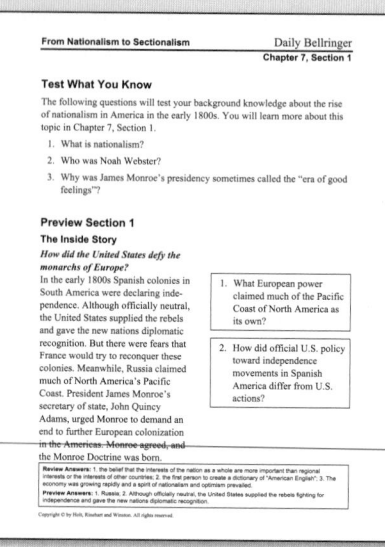

BEFORE YOU READ

MAIN IDEA
Nationalism contributed to the growth of American culture and influenced domestic and foreign policies.

READING FOCUS
1. What were the characteristics of the new American culture?
2. How did nationalism influence domestic policy?
3. How did nationalism guide foreign policy?
4. What was the Missouri Compromise?

KEY TERMS AND PEOPLE
Alexis de Tocqueville
Noah Webster
nationalism
sectionalism
McCulloch v. *Maryland*
James Monroe
John Quincy Adams
Adams-Onís Treaty
Monroe Doctrine
Missouri Compromise

 **TAKING NOTES** As you read, take notes on the different effects that growing American nationalism had on the nation's domestic and foreign policy. Create a diagram like the one shown here, and in each box list the effects.

Growing American Nationalism
Domestic Policy | Foreign Policy

Academic Vocabulary

Review with students the high-use academic terms in this section.

generation the average length of time between the birth of parents and that of their offspring (p. 239)

implement to execute or carry out (p. 241)

📄 CRF: Vocabulary Builder Activity, Section 1

Taking Notes

McCulloch *v.* Maryland *and* Gibbons *v.* Ogden *strengthened domestic policy, as did Clay's American System; the Adams-Onís Treaty and the Monroe Doctrine strengthened foreign policy.*

A Bold Move

▲ **Lady Liberty and the liberty cap and pole she carries were powerful revolutionary symbols that citizens of the young nation could rally behind.**

THE INSIDE STORY **How did the United States defy the monarchs of Europe?**
Between 1803 and 1815, a series of wars fought by or against France under the French emperor, Napoleon, had seriously threatened the monarchies of Europe. Soon after Napoleon's defeat in 1815, the major European powers, including Great Britain and Russia, formed a loose alliance known as the Concert of Europe. Their goals were to keep a balance of power in Europe and to suppress revolutionary ideas.

At the same time, revolutions were breaking out in South America, as colonies declared their independence from Spain. Although the United States declared neutrality, it supplied the rebels with ships and supplies. In 1822 President James Monroe was the first to give diplomatic recognition to the new nations. But both Great Britain and the United States were worried that France would send troops to reconquer Spain's colonies.

John Quincy Adams, Monroe's secretary of state, was an experienced diplomat who had been living abroad since he was a teenager. He was worried about territorial threats from other European nations. Russia, for example, claimed much of the Pacific Coast of North America. Adams wanted to stand up to the monarchs of Europe. He declared "that the American continents are no longer subjects for any new European colonial establishments." He also said that the United States should act on its own, instead of following like "a [rowboat] in the wake of a British man-of-war." Those brave words led to the statements made in the Monroe Doctrine, which declared the Americas off limits to European colonization. ◢

Teach the Main Idea

At Level

The Rise of Nationalism

1. **Teach** Ask students the Reading Focus questions to teach this section.

2. **Apply** Organize the class into four groups. Have each group prepare a five-minute lesson on one of the following topics: A New American Culture; Nationalism Influences Domestic Policy; Nationalism Guides Foreign Policy; and The Missouri Compromise. Have groups present their lessons to the class in the order listed. In a class discussion, have students explain how

these topics are related. **LS Interpersonal**

3. **Review** As you review the section, guide students in a discussion of the Supreme Court decisions during this period.

4. **Practice/Homework** Have students write a short essay explaining how the country might be different today without the rise of nationalism in the early nineteenth century. **LS Verbal-Linguistic**

📄 Alternative Assessment Handbook, Rubrics 24: Oral Presentations; and 42: Writing to Inform

A New American Culture

The Monroe Doctrine was a bold statement. After all, the United States was still a very young nation in 1823. Moreover, the population of the country was a tiny fraction of what it would become. There were fewer than 10 million Americans at the time. The overwhelming majority of them still lived in rural areas along or near the East Coast. The largest city, New York, was home to only about 120,000 people. The next largest cities, Philadelphia and Baltimore, were about half that size. But the young country was growing rapidly.

A country "in constant motion" Americans were hard at work building their new nation. As they went about their lives, they slowly developed their own unique culture. Culture is the ways of life of a particular group of people. It includes the group's language, art, music, clothing, food, and other aspects of daily life. The rise of a distinctly American culture during the early 1800s is important because the culture that developed then still influences the way Americans live today.

One of the most insightful observers of the emerging American culture was the French philosopher **Alexis de Tocqueville**. In his book *Democracy in America*, Tocqueville wrote of the seemingly limitless energy of Americans. He keenly observed that

HISTORY'S VOICES

❝ [Americans] all consider society as a body in a state of improvement . . . in which nothing is, or ought to be, permanent . . . America is a land of wonders, in which everything is in constant motion and every change seems an improvement. **❞**

—Alexis de Tocqueville, *Democracy in America*

Instead of imitating European cultures, as they had done for generations, Americans began doing things in a distinctly American way. A new American culture was emerging.

American art and literature The rise of American culture was especially significant in the worlds of art and literature. Before the 1800s, American artists and writers were paid little respect, even by their fellow Americans. That changed with the emergence of talented Americans whose work honored American life.

In 1825 the painter Thomas Cole helped establish the Hudson River school, a group of artists whose landscapes both depicted and celebrated the American countryside. The works of Cole and other American artists came to be admired in both America and Europe.

ACADEMIC VOCABULARY

generation the average length of time between the birth of parents and that of their offspring

A New American Style of Art

The first uniquely American style of art began with the Hudson River school, a group of landscape artists inspired by the wilderness of the Hudson River Valley. Their paintings reflected pride in the grandeur of the American landscape. *A View of the Mountain Pass Called the Notch of the White Mountains (Crawford Notch)* was painted by Thomas Cole around 1839.

The notch that is the subject of this painting allowed travelers to pass through a New Hampshire mountain range.

A tree stump was a common symbol of the Hudson River school—a reminder of the fragility of life.

People, although depicted tiny in scale, were always linked to the land.

239

❷ How did nationalism influence domestic policy? *Rulings from the Supreme Court enhanced the power of the national government, and the American System goals would further unify the country.*

Nationalism Influences Domestic Policy

Explain What is sectionalism? *the belief that one's own region or state is more important than the nation*

Analyze What belief influenced John Marshall? *a firm belief in the importance of a strong national government*

Evaluate How important were the key rulings of the Marshall Court in establishing national power? *established power of national government over states*

Info to Know

The Canal System Canals were an important new solution to transportation problems in the United States. By 1840 rivers and canals provided a web of waterways stretching from Illinois to the Atlantic Ocean. The Erie Canal reduced the cost of shipping goods between Buffalo and New York City by about 90 percent.

Answers

Reading Check *possible answer— because the Americans had not yet developed their own style*

Leaders of a Young Nation

▲ **John Quincy Adams,** as secretary of state under Monroe, extended the territory of the United States. He became the nation's sixth president.

▲ **James Monroe,** president from 1817 to 1825, secured the nation's borders with the Monroe Doctrine.

▲ **John C. Calhoun** served as Monroe's secretary of war, as vice president twice, and as a member of Congress. He was a dominant political figure and a strong advocate of states' rights.

▲ **John Marshall,** chief justice of the United States from 1801 to 1835, established the supremacy of federal law over state law.

▶ **Henry Clay** was a passionate nationalist during the several decades he spent in Congress. He proposed the American System to help unify the young nation.

240

American authors also gained respect in the early 1800s. Three writers in particular— Washington Irving, James Fenimore Cooper, and William Cullen Bryant—proved that Americans could create literature and that people on both sides of the Atlantic would respect American works.

Even Americans' unique version of the English language earned respect. In 1828 this new American English was published by lexicographer **Noah Webster** in *An American Dictionary of the English Language.* Webster's dictionary defined thousands of words that had never been included in a dictionary before. Clearly, Americans were forming a new culture—with a language all its own.

READING CHECK **Making Inferences** Why do you think Europeans initially held little respect for American writers and painters?

Nationalism Influences Domestic Policy

As a uniquely American culture developed, so too did a sense of nationalism. **Nationalism** is the belief that the interests of the nation as a whole are more important than regional interests or the interests of other countries. A spirit of nationalism replaced the tendency toward **sectionalism,** or the belief that one's own section, or region, of the country is more important than the whole.

In the early 1800s, feelings of nationalism swept the country. These feelings were soon reflected in government policies.

John Marshall John Marshall served as chief justice of the United States from 1801 until 1835—longer than any other chief justice. Marshall was a firm believer in the importance of a strong national government. His Court made two key rulings that both reflected growing feelings of nationalism and promoted nationalism by strengthening the national government.

Two key rulings In 1819 the case of *McCulloch v. Maryland* came before the Supreme Court. The case pitted the State of Maryland against the national government. In his ruling, Chief Justice Marshall sided with the national government. He made it clear that

Differentiating Instruction

Above Level

Advanced Learners/GATE

Research Required

1. Have students read the material about *Gibbons* v. *Ogden* and the American System in their text. Then have students conduct outside research to learn more about this case, the opinions of the justices, and the effect of the case on American law and policy.

2. Have students use the information from their research to conduct a court proceeding or a class debate on *Gibbons* v. *Ogden.*

3. At the conclusion of the debate, have

students write a newspaper article on ways that *Gibbons* v. *Ogden* might contribute to a successful program of national improvements in the area of roads and canals.

4. Have volunteers read their articles to the class. Then guide students in a discussion about the relationship between national power and national growth. **LS Verbal-Linguistic**

📝 Alternative Assessment Handbook, Rubrics 10: Debates; and 37: Writing Assignments

national interests were to be put above state interests. You can read more about *McCulloch v. Maryland* at the end of this section.

In 1824 the Marshall Court issued another ruling that enhanced the national government's power over the states. This case involved the cutting-edge transportation technology of the day: steamboats.

Rival steamboat companies were operating in New York. Aaron Ogden had received permission from the State of New York to run his business. Thomas Gibbons had a license from the national government to run his. Gibbons sued Ogden, and the case of *Gibbons* v. *Ogden* went to the Supreme Court.

Marshall's court ruled in favor of Gibbons, who was licensed by the national government. Thus, Marshall again declared that national law was superior to state law. Marshall further declared that the Constitution gives the national government the sole right to regulate interstate commerce, or trade between states.

In these two rulings, John Marshall's Supreme Court established the power of the national government over state governments. In matters of the Constitution, therefore, nationalism had triumphed over sectionalism.

The American System Perhaps the most nationalistic domestic policy of the early 1800s was a plan championed by Henry Clay, the speaker of the U.S. House of Representatives. His plan was called the American System. The American System sought to implement several policies to unify the young country. These policies included a tariff to protect American industries, the sale of government lands to raise money for the national government, the maintenance of a national bank, and government funding of internal improvements or public projects such as roads and canals.

The American System was never implemented as a unified policy, although the national government did establish tariffs and a bank. But the fact that it was proposed and partially put in practice demonstrates how nationalist feelings and a desire to tie the country together were very much on the minds of Americans of the early 1800s.

READING CHECK Identifying the Main Idea What domestic policies in the early 1800s promoted nationalism?

Nationalism Guides Foreign Policy

American foreign policy in the early 1800s reflected the feelings of nationalism that spread through the nation. Americans were proud of their victory in the War of 1812 and confident in the strength of their young but growing country. They were determined to take their place on the world stage.

The Era of Good Feelings In 1816 voters elected **James Monroe** to the presidency. As president, Monroe would serve from 1817 to 1825. During his presidency, the economy grew rapidly, and a spirit of nationalism and optimism prevailed. One Boston newspaper called the time the "Era of Good Feelings."

Diplomatic successes The good feelings at home were matched by successful diplomacy abroad. Monroe's administration achieved a series of brilliant diplomatic successes that helped secure the territory and borders of the United States.

In 1818 the United States concluded the Rush-Bagot Treaty with Britain. The treaty provided for the nearly complete disarmament of the eastern part of the border between the United States and British Canada. Monroe also convinced Britain to draw the western part of the border between the United States and Canada along the 49th parallel.

In 1819 Secretary of State **John Quincy Adams** reached an important agreement with Spain. Under the **Adams-Onís Treaty**, the United States acquired Florida and established a firm boundary between the Louisiana territory and Spanish territory farther to the west.

Thus Adams expanded the country to the south and east and defined its borders to the north and west. Further, Adams convinced Spain and Russia to give up their claims to the disputed Oregon Country and negotiated a treaty with Britain that would allow American settlers to travel to Oregon for 10 years.

The Monroe Doctrine Although the Monroe administration had achieved stunning diplomatic successes, the United States still faced a foreign policy problem. The problem arose in Europe but concerned hemispheric neighbors in Central America and South America.

ACADEMIC VOCABULARY
implement to execute or carry out

• **Direct Teach** •

Reading Focus

❸ How did nationalism guide foreign policy? *Treaties strengthened and expanded national boundaries; the Monroe Doctrine demanded Europe cease any new colonizing activity in the Americas.*

Nationalism Guides Foreign Policy

Identify What were some of the significant treaties of this period? *Rush-Bagot and Adams-Onís*

Draw Conclusions Why might some of the foreign policy efforts of the Monroe administration have contributed to the "era of good feelings"? *Monroe and Adams had a number of great successes, which could have made Americans proud.*

📑 American History Outline Maps: Early Roads and Canals

📑 CRF: Economics and History Activity: Pre-War Sectional Economies

Primary Source

In defense of the American System Henry Clay said, "On a general survey, we behold . . . the arts flourishing, the face of the country improved; our people fully and profitably employed, and the public countenance exhibiting tranquility, contentment, and happiness."

— Henry Clay

"Defense of the American System," 1832

Differentiating Instruction

Below Level

Special Education Students

Materials outline maps of North America

1. Distribute outline maps of North America to the class. Organize students into mixed-ability pairs. For help with this assignment, teachers may want to have students refer to the map on the following page.

2. Have each pair draw lines on their maps to mark areas covered by the Rush-Bagot Treaty and the Adams-Onís Treaty. In addition,

have students mark the location of the Oregon territory and draw an overland route from the East Coast to Oregon.

3. Display the maps for all to see, and guide students in a discussion about what these treaties meant to the developing nation.

🅻🆂 Visual-Spatial

📑 Alternative Assessment Handbook, Rubric 20: Map Creation

Answers

Reading Check McCulloch v. Maryland, Gibbons v. Ogden, American System

Nationalism Guides Foreign Policy

Recall What was the Monroe Doctrine? *a policy stating that U.S. would view any European attempts to further colonize the Americas as a threat to U.S. interests*

Explain Why did the United States issue the Monroe Doctrine? *European countries were thinking about retaking control of their former colonies.*

Map Transparency: Boundary Changes, 1803–1819

Spain had colonized Central and South America in the 1600s and 1700s. In the early 1800s Spain had neglected its colonies because it was fighting France, which, under Napoleon, was expanding in Europe. Many colonies took the opportunity to declare independence. But after Napoleon was defeated, Spain and other European powers considered retaking control of the former colonies in the Americas.

This concerned Great Britain, which had developed a thriving trade with the former Spanish colonies. It also concerned the United States. American lawmakers wanted to deter any foreign country from taking lands in the Americas that the United States might someday claim, such as the Pacific Northwest.

President Monroe and Secretary of State John Quincy Adams responded by declaring a new foreign policy for the United States. In time, it would be called the Monroe Doctrine. A doctrine is a policy. The **Monroe Doctrine** stated that the United States would view any European attempts to further colonize

the Americas "as dangerous to our peace and safety." In Monroe's message to Congress, delivered on December 2, 1823, he stated:

HISTORY'S VOICES

❝The American continents . . . are henceforth not to be considered as subjects for future colonization by any European powers.❞

—Monroe Doctrine, 1823

Monroe also stated that the United States would not "interfere in the internal concerns" of Europe. In essence, the Monroe Doctrine stated that the United States would stay out of European affairs and that it expected Europe to stay out of American affairs.

The Monroe Doctrine was a bold statement to the old, great powers of Europe. It confirmed that American nationalism was to be felt well beyond the shores of the young nation.

READING CHECK **Summarizing** What were the major diplomatic achievements of the Monroe administration?

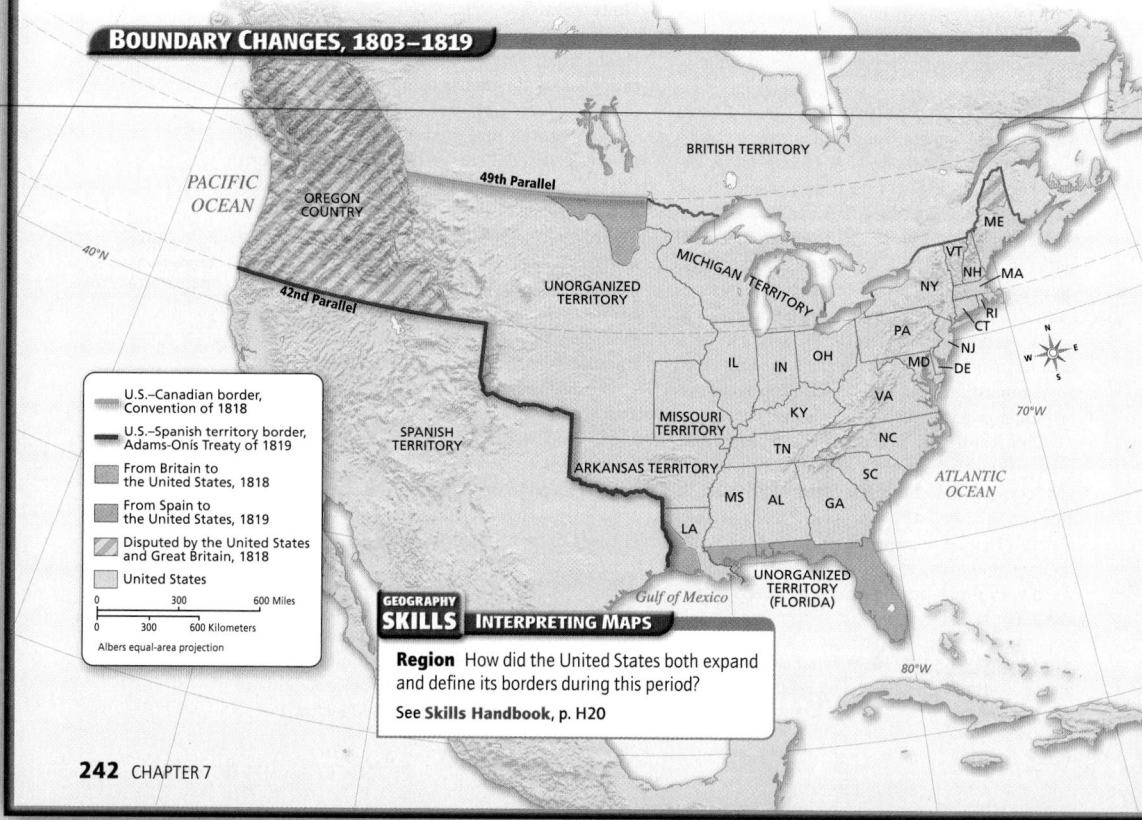

BOUNDARY CHANGES, 1803–1819

Legend:
- U.S.–Canadian border, Convention of 1818
- U.S.–Spanish territory border, Adams-Onís Treaty of 1819
- From Britain to the United States, 1818
- From Spain to the United States, 1819
- Disputed by the United States and Great Britain, 1818
- United States

0   300   600 Miles
0   300   600 Kilometers
Albers equal-area projection

GEOGRAPHY SKILLS **INTERPRETING MAPS**

Region How did the United States both expand and define its borders during this period?

See **Skills Handbook, p. H20**

242 CHAPTER 7

Skills Focus: Identifying Problem and Solution   At Level

Reading Skill
The Missouri Compromise

1. Organize the class into small groups. Have half of the groups prepare arguments supporting the admission of Missouri as a free state, and the other half as a slave state.

2. Have volunteers from each group use their group's arguments to conduct a classroom debate on the admission of Missouri to the Union as a slave or free state.

3. Have each student write a one-page essay about the Missouri Compromise explaining

why it was important to maintain a balance of power. Have students consider the following questions in their essays: Was the Missouri Compromise a long- or short-term solution? What aspects of the Missouri Compromise might be unsatisfactory to some people?

4. Have volunteers read their essays to the class.

LS **Logical-Mathematical, Verbal-Linguistic**

Alternative Assessment Handbook, Rubrics 10: Debates; and 37: Writing Assignments

---

Answers

Interpreting Maps *established 49th Parallel as border with Canada, established U.S.-Spanish border through Adams-Onís Treaty, and gained additional territories from Britain and Spain*

Reading Check *Monroe Doctrine; Rush-Bagot Treaty; Adams-Onís Treaty; settlers could travel to Oregon*

The Missouri Compromise

Americans' feelings of nationalism were fueled by the pride they took in the rapid growth of American settlement. By 1818 settlers had even spread beyond the Mississippi River into Missouri. Most newcomers to Missouri had migrated from the South. About 1 in 6 settlers were enslaved African Americans.

When the Missouri Territory applied to join the union, it caused an uproar. In 1819 there were 22 states in the Union. In half of the states—the "slave states" of the South—slavery was legal. In the other half of the states—the "free states" of the North—slavery was illegal. This exact balance between slave states and free states gave them equal representation in the U.S. Senate. If Missouri were admitted as a slave state, the balance would be upset.

The situation was resolved by what became known as the **Missouri Compromise** of 1820. Under this agreement, Missouri was admitted to the Union as a slave state and Maine was to be admitted as a free state. Thus, the balance between the number of free states and slave states was preserved. The agreement also banned slavery in the northern part of the Louisiana Territory. The Missouri Compromise

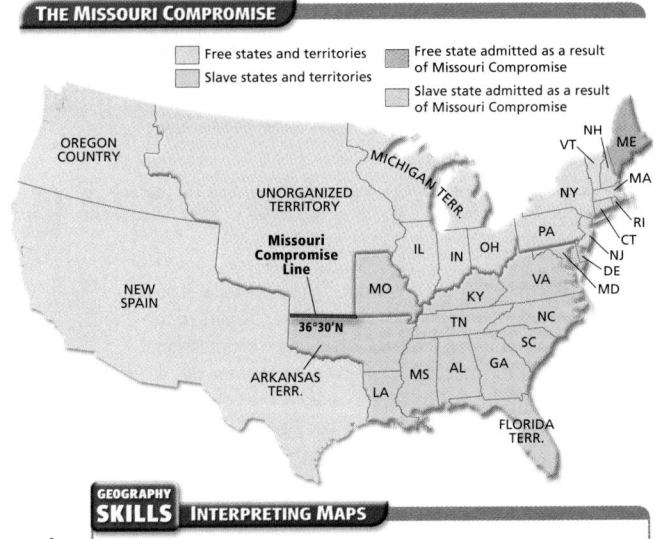

THE MISSOURI COMPROMISE

- Free states and territories
- Slave states and territories
- Free state admitted as a result of Missouri Compromise
- Slave state admitted as a result of Missouri Compromise

GEOGRAPHY SKILLS | INTERPRETING MAPS

1. Region How many slave states and free states were there before the compromise? How many were there after it?
2. Location Where is the Missouri Compromise line?

See **Skills Handbook**, p. H20

kept the balance between slave and free states. It was disturbingly clear, however, that feelings of sectionalism in the North and the South were beginning to emerge.

READING CHECK **Identifying the Main Idea** Why was the Missouri Compromise adopted?

SECTION 1 ASSESSMENT

go.hrw.com
Online Quiz
Keyword: SD7 HP7

Reviewing Ideas, Terms, and People

1. a. Describe How did **Alexis de Tocqueville** describe the American people?
b. Compare What did Thomas Cole and **Noah Webster** have in common?

2. a. Identify Who was John Marshall?
b. Compare What did *McCulloch* v. *Maryland* and *Gibbons* v. *Ogden* have in common?

3. a. Recall What was the **Adams-Onís Treaty**?
b. Analyze What was the purpose of the **Monroe Doctrine**?

4. a. Describe Why would adding only Missouri to the Union have created an imbalance in the Senate?

b. Make Inferences What does the Missouri Compromise imply about Americans' views toward slavery?

Critical Thinking

5. Identifying Cause and Effect Copy the diagram below and identify the effects of nationalism.

Nationalism

FOCUS ON WRITING

6. Expository Write a paragraph explaining why Alexis de Tocqueville's description of Americans does or does not describe Americans today. Give details that support your position.

Direct Teach

Reading Focus

❹ What was the Missouri Compromise? *Missouri entered the Union as a slave state, Maine as a free state; kept balance between slave and free states*

The Missouri Compromise

Recall What proportion of the settlers in Missouri were enslaved African Americans? *about 1 in 6*

Analyze Why was the Missouri Compromise so important? *kept balance between free and slave states*

📦 Map Transparency: The Missouri Compromise

Review & Assess

Close

Have students explain the importance of the treaties negotiated by the Monroe administration.

Review

🖥 Online Quiz, Section 1

📦 Daily Test Practice Transparency

Assess

SE Section 1 Assessment

📋 Progress Assessment: Section 1 Quiz

📋 Alternative Assessment Handbook

Reteach

📋 Interactive Reader and Study Guide, Section 1

💿 Interactive Skills Tutor CD-ROM

Section 1 Assessment Answers

1. a. in constant motion with limitless energy; seeking to improve things
b. They helped create the new American culture through art and language.

2. a. Chief Justice of the Supreme Court
b. Both decisions gave the national government more power over the states.

3. a. U.S. acquired Florida; established firm boundary between Louisiana and Spanish territories
b. create a strong U.S. presence in the

world; protect its interests; prevent foreign colonization of the Americas

4. a. would have resulted in one more slave state than free states
b. Slavery was a divisive issue.

5. American System, Monroe Doctrine

6. possible answer—does describe Americans today because U.S. is still inventing, improving way of life, especially in new fields of technology and communications

Answers

Interpreting Maps 1. *11 free, 11 slave; 12 free, 12 slave;* **2.** *36 degrees, 30 minutes north*

Reading Check *to allow states to enter the Union and maintain balance between free and slave states*

Word Help

reserves sets apart

Info to Know

The "necessary and proper" clause The last sentence of Article I, Section 8 of the Constitution grants Congress the power "To make all Laws which shall be necessary and proper for carrying into Execution the foregoing Powers, and all other Powers vested by this Constitution in the Government of the United States, or in any Department or Officer thereof." Powers exercised by the government using this so-called elastic clause are known as implied powers.

Primary Source

Chief Justice Marshall was very blunt in expressing the relative powers of the states versus the federal government: "... states have no power, by taxation or otherwise, to retard, impede, burden, or in any manner control, the operations of the constitutional laws enacted by Congress to carry into execution the powers vested in the general government. This is, we think, the unavoidable consequence of that supremacy which the Constitution has declared."

— John Marshall

McCulloch v. Maryland, 1819

LANDMARK SUPREME COURT CASES

Constitutional Issue: Federalism

McCulloch v. Maryland (1819)

Why It Matters The Constitution gives the federal government certain powers and reserves all other powers to the states. *McCulloch v. Maryland* first established congressional authority under the "necessary and proper" clause to do things that are not specifically mentioned in the Constitution but that fall within Congress's authorized powers.

Background of the Case

After the War of 1812, President Madison asked Congress to create the Bank of the United States, a national bank for the entire country. Other banks established by the states resented the competition. In 1818 the Maryland legislature put a tax on the Baltimore branch of the national bank. James McCulloch, a bank officer in the Baltimore branch, refused to pay the tax. The case raised two issues: Did Congress have the authority to create a national bank? Was Maryland's tax on the bank protected by the Constitution?

The Decision

In his ruling, Chief Justice John Marshall carefully analyzed the balance of power between the federal government and the states. The Constitution does not specifically give Congress the power to create a bank, but it does give Congress the power to collect taxes, borrow money, regulate commerce, raise an army and navy, and to make "all laws which shall be necessary and proper for carrying into execution the foregoing powers." Marshall noted that a national bank was a reasonable way for Congress to carry out its specified powers. If a state could tax the bank, Marshall argued, then it would have the power to destroy the bank, which would defeat "all the ends of government" under the Constitution. The Court ruled that Maryland's tax on the bank was therefore unconstitutional.

THE IMPACT TODAY Many federal activities are not specifically mentioned in the Constitution but are "necessary and proper" for carrying out Congress's authority. One example is Congress's power to draft Americans into military service. This power supports the constitutional authority of Congress to raise and support an army.

CRITICAL THINKING

go.hrw.com
Research Online
Keyword: SS Court

1. **Analyze the Impact** Using the keyword above, research one of the laws listed below. What is the purpose of the law? What provisions in the Constitution gave Congress the power to enact the law?
   • Americans with Disabilities Act
   • Clean Air Act of 1970

2. **You Be the Judge** Congress passed a law making it a federal crime to bribe an official of a state or local entity that receives at least $10,000 in federal funds. Does Congress have the power under the "necessary and proper" clause to create a federal crime even when there is no connection between the bribe and the federal money? Explain your answer in a short paragraph.

Skills Focus: Identifying Cause and Effect
At Level

Reading Skill
McCulloch v. Maryland

1. Tell students that not all Americans were happy with the Supreme Court ruling in *McCulloch v. Maryland*. State banks wanted no competition from a national bank. Many in the South feared that a strong national government and a national bank would interfere with states' rights.

2. Organize the class into small groups. One half of the groups should prepare arguments that support a strong national government, and the other half of the groups should support strong states' rights. Have a team of volunteers argue their positions before the class, which will serve as the justices.

3. Following the arguments, guide students in a discussion of the importance of *McCulloch v. Maryland* to U.S. history. **LS Interpersonal, Kinesthetic**

   Alternative Assessment Handbook, Rubrics 10: Debates; and 11: Discussions

Answers

Critical Thinking 1. *Americans with Disabilities Act prohibits discrimination against people with physical or mental disabilities in employment, transportation, telephone services, and public buildings. Clean Air Act sets air-quality standards and auto emissions guidelines for automakers. Both fall under the "necessary and proper" clause.*
2. *possible answer—No, only states have the authority to govern the actions of state or local officials.*

SECTION 2
The Age of Jackson

BEFORE YOU READ

MAIN IDEA

President Andrew Jackson's bold actions defined a period of American history.

READING FOCUS

1. What path led to Andrew Jackson's presidency?
2. How did the Indian Removal Act lead to the Trail of Tears?
3. Why was the national bank a source of controversy?
4. How did a conflict over the issue of states' rights lead to a crisis?

KEY TERMS AND PEOPLE

Democratic Party
Jacksonian Democracy
spoils system
Indian Removal Act
Worcester v. *Georgia*
Trail of Tears
Second Bank of the
   United States
states' rights
John C. Calhoun
secede
nullification crisis

TAKING NOTES As you read, take notes on the position of those favoring states' rights. Record your notes in a graphic organizer like the one shown here.

States' Rights

How should guests behave at the White House? Andrew Jackson won the presidency in 1828 as the candidate of the common man. Rough-hewn voters in the West and South, especially, thought of him as one of their own. So when the new president threw open the doors of the White House to anyone who wanted to attend his inaugural reception in 1829, thousands showed up to get a glimpse of their hero—and of the White House.

An estimated 20,000 well-wishers pushed and shoved their way into the White House staterooms. They trampled the carpets with muddy boots and climbed on the uphol-stered sofas and chairs. They broke china, smashed glass-ware, and bloodied more than a few noses. Finally, harried servants brought tubs of punch, ice cream, and lemonade outside, as people climbed through open windows to escape the riotous scene. The new president himself fled to the safety of a hotel.

Jackson's opponents denounced the day as "the reign of King Mob." One of Jackson's colleagues, however, was more forgiving. He called it "a proud day for the people."

Party at the WHITE HOUSE

◀ A crowd converges upon the White House to celebrate Jackson's inauguration.

Preteach

Bellringer

The Inside Story. . . Use the **Daily Bellringer Transparency** to help students answer the question.

🗂 Daily Bellringer Transparency, Section 2

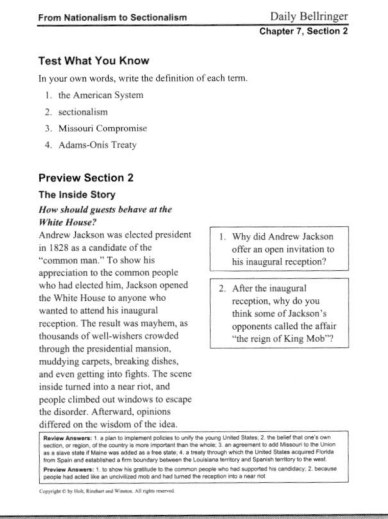

Taking Notes

supported dissolving national bank, challenged authority of tariff laws, supported nullification of federal laws that states disagreed with

go.hrw.com
Online Resources

KEYWORD: SD7 CH7
TOPIC: THE INDIAN REMOVAL ACT

Teach the Main Idea

At Level

The Age of Jackson

1. **Teach** Ask students the Reading Focus questions to teach this section.

2. **Apply** Have students name issues that might divide Americans today. Then have students explain how each of the following might have divided Americans in the 1820s: the election of 1824; Indian removal; the national bank; and tariff increases in 1824 and 1828. **LS Interpersonal**

3. **Review** As you review the section, have students explain how Jackson's fame and popularity as a military hero might have contributed to his success in elections and during his presidency.

4. **Practice/Homework** Have students create a campaign poster for Jackson for the election of 1828. Posters should include three major points for voters to consider. **LS Visual-Spatial**

📄 Alternative Assessment Handbook, Rubrics 11: Discussions; and 28: Posters

245

❶ What path led to Andrew Jackson's presidency? *successful military career; broadening voter base; Adams's problems as president*

Path to the Presidency

Explain What role did Henry Clay play in the 1824 presidential election? *was a candidate who did not win; gave his support to Adams, who then became president*

Analyze Why did the Democratic Party come into existence? *discontent over the 1824 presidential campaign*

Evaluate What effect did the easing of voter restrictions have on American politics? *Many poor Americans who supported Jackson were able to vote for the first time, helping him to win.*

🗐 Political Cartoons Activities for American History: Cartoon 14: The Spoils System

Biography

George Catlin (1796–1872) Although he was trained as a lawyer, George Catlin taught himself how to paint. In 1828, Catlin met a delegation of Plains Indians on their way to Washington, D.C.; Catlin decided to dedicate himself to recording the vanishing lifestyles and customs of Native Americans. Catlin spent years traveling throughout North and South America, sketching scenes of Native Americans working, celebrating, and playing games. Catlin's paintings, as well as his several historical accounts, chronicled Native American traditions of the 1800s and helped to generate public interest in Native American life.

Answers

Reading Check *Jackson was a military hero with a reputation for being tough, which brought him fame and votes.*

Path to the Presidency

Andrew Jackson's early life was as rambunctious as his inauguration. As a teenager, he served in the army during the Revolutionary War. As a young man, he was known to be "roaring, rollicking" and "mischievous."

Jackson moved to Tennessee in 1788. There he practiced law, became a successful land speculator, and served in a variety of government offices, including the House of Representatives and in the Senate.

The War of 1812 brought Jackson the opportunity to vent his boundless energy as a soldier. He was commissioned into the U.S. Army and ordered to march his troops toward New Orleans. Jackson drove himself and his soldiers hard. They thought their commander was tough as hickory wood, and Jackson became known as Old Hickory.

Later in the war, Jackson was given command of military operations in the South. In December 1814 and January 1815, Jackson led the American forces that drove off the British invasion at the Battle of New Orleans. The battle made Jackson nationally famous and popular as the "Hero of New Orleans." General Jackson planned to use his popularity to win the presidency.

In 1824 Jackson ran for president as a member of the Democratic-Republican Party. Other candidates of the party included John Quincy Adams and Henry Clay.

Jackson won the popular vote. But he did not win a majority of the electoral votes. As a result, the winner of the election was to be determined by a vote in the House of Representatives.

In the House vote, Clay gave his support to Adams. This gave Adams enough votes to win the election and become president in 1825. Adams immediately named Clay as his secretary of state. Jackson and his

Andrew Jackson, "man of the people," said that "the people are the government, administering it by their agents."

supporters suspected Adams and Clay had made a secret deal. They called it a "corrupt bargain." Jackson vowed to defeat Adams in the next election.

Jackson and his supporters created a new political party that came to be known, in time, as the **Democratic Party**. Adams and his supporters became the National Republicans.

Adams did not enjoy great popularity as president. His administration was weakened by scandal and by relentless criticism from Jackson's supporters. Also, Adams himself seemed to many Americans to be out of touch with the people.

In contrast, Jackson was a popular war hero who seemed very much to be "a man of the people." In the 1820s voting restrictions in many states—such as the requirement for property ownership—were being lifted, allowing poor people to become voters. These new voters were strong Jackson supporters.

In the election of 1828, Jackson easily defeated the unpopular Adams. The Age of Jackson had begun.

Andrew Jackson was supported by ordinary, working Americans. In time, such political power exercised by ordinary Americans became known as **Jacksonian Democracy**.

One of Jackson's first acts in office was to replace many officials with his supporters. Rewarding supporters in this way is called the **spoils system**. Jackson faced criticism, but in fact he only replaced about 1 in 10 officials.

READING CHECK **Identifying Cause and Effect** How did his military career help Jackson become president?

The Indian Removal Act

By the time Andrew Jackson became president, the land east of the Mississippi River was largely settled by white Americans. In the Southeast, however, huge expanses of land were still controlled by Native American groups.

Five major Native American groups lived in the southeastern United States: the Cherokee, Choctaw, Chickasaw, Seminole, and Creek. White Americans sometimes called these groups the "five civilized tribes" because many of their members had adopted aspects of European and American culture. The Cherokee,

---

Differentiating Instruction

Learners Having Difficulty

1. Guide students in a discussion of the relationship between Jackson's military career and political career. Have students name reasons Jackson might have created the spoils system, and have them explain the benefits and disadvantages of this system. Make a class list for all to see. Students should focus on whether it leads to corruption or if the spoils system is a valid way of

rewarding those who have helped an official win an election.

2. Have students work in mixed-ability pairs to create a political cartoon either favoring or opposing the spoils system. Have volunteers share their cartoons with the class. **LS Intrapersonal, Visual-Spatial**

🗐 Alternative Assessment Handbook, Rubric 27: Political Cartoons

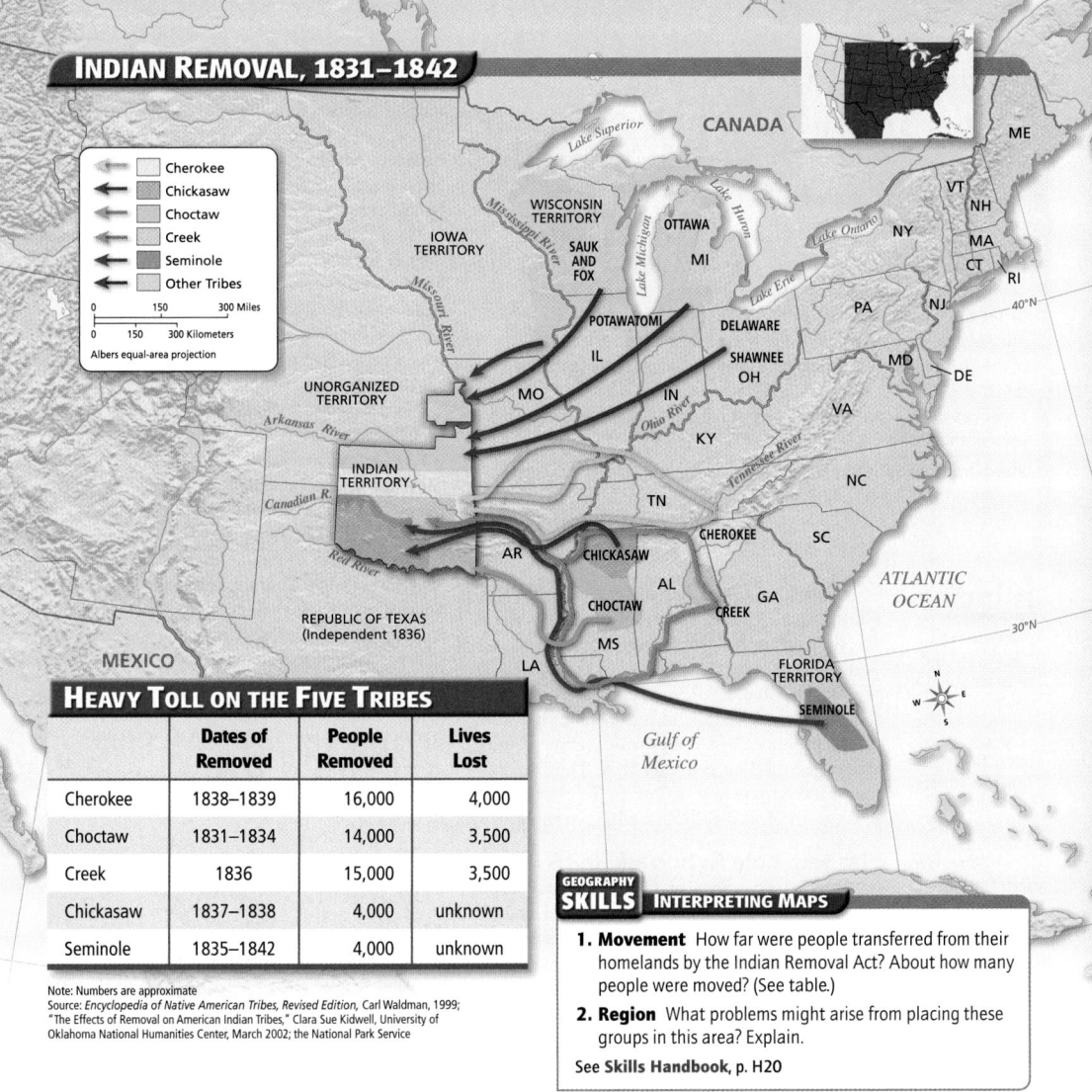

INDIAN REMOVAL, 1831–1842

Cherokee
Chickasaw
Choctaw
Creek
Seminole
Other Tribes

0   150   300 Miles
0   150   300 Kilometers
Albers equal-area projection

HEAVY TOLL ON THE FIVE TRIBES

	Dates of Removed	People Removed	Lives Lost
Cherokee	1838–1839	16,000	4,000
Choctaw	1831–1834	14,000	3,500
Creek	1836	15,000	3,500
Chickasaw	1837–1838	4,000	unknown
Seminole	1835–1842	4,000	unknown

Note: Numbers are approximate
Source: *Encyclopedia of Native American Tribes, Revised Edition,* Carl Waldman, 1999; "The Effects of Removal on American Indian Tribes," Clara Sue Kidwell, University of Oklahoma National Humanities Center, March 2002; the National Park Service

GEOGRAPHY SKILLS   INTERPRETING MAPS

1. **Movement** How far were people transferred from their homelands by the Indian Removal Act? About how many people were moved? (See table.)

2. **Region** What problems might arise from placing these groups in this area? Explain.

See Skills Handbook, p. H20

for example, learned English, built towns, and established a written constitution. A Cherokee named Sequoya created a writing system for the Cherokee language.

Although some white Americans respected these peoples, many viewed them as inferior. Above all else, though, farmland was becoming scarce in the East, and white settlers coveted the Indians' lands.

The Indian Removal Act President Jackson concluded that the best action was to relocate the nations so that the southeast would be open to white settlement. In 1830 Congress passed, and Jackson signed into law, the **Indian Removal Act**, which called for the relocation of the five nations to an area west of the Mississippi River called Indian Territory—land in what is now present-day Oklahoma.

FROM NATIONALISM TO SECTIONALISM **247**

Skills Focus: Interpreting Movement Maps

At Level

Social Studies Skill
The Move to Indian Territory

Research Required

1. Have students study the map on this page, and locate the "five civilized tribes". Have students calculate how far the groups traveled and discuss the hardships along the route.

2. Divide the class into groups, and assign each group one of the five Native American tribes. Have each group conduct research on its assigned Native American group, using the following questions as a guide: Why was the tribe removed from its original homeland?

What did the tribe experience during the removal? How did the tribe adapt to its new home in Indian Territory? Have each group prepare an illustrated report based on its research, including maps and charts.

3. Have volunteers from each group present their reports to the class. **LS Interpersonal, Visual-Spatial**

Alternative Assessment Handbook, Rubrics 3: Artwork; and 30: Research

Direct Teach

Reading Focus

2 How did the Indian Removal Act lead to the Trail of Tears? *Cherokee were forcibly removed from their homes and taken under brutal conditions to Indian Territory.*

The Indian Removal Act

Recall Who were the "five civilized tribes"? *Cherokee, Choctaw, Chickasaw, Seminole, and Creek*

Explain How did the Cherokee adopt aspects of European and American culture? *learned English; built towns; established a written constitution based on U.S. Constitution*

American History Outline Maps: Relocation of American Indian Tribes

Map Transparency: Indian Removal, 1831–1842

Recent Scholarship

Author Robert Remini, who has written an award-winning biography of Jackson, looks at the president's policies concerning Native Americans in *Andrew Jackson and His Indian Wars*. While Remini criticizes Jackson's actions, he also proposes that the forced removal may have saved many Native Americans and their nations from complete extermination.

Andrew Jackson and His Indian Wars by Robert Remini. Viking, 2001

Answers

Interpreting Maps 1. *150 to 1500 miles; 53,000;* **2.** *disputes, unfamiliarity with land and farming techniques, different weather than they were accustomed to*

The Indian Removal Act

Recall What was Indian Territory? *land in present-day Oklahoma*

Explain How did the Seminole respond to attempts to move them to Indian Territory? *with armed force; women and children hid in swamps; men conducted hit-and-run attacks on American soldiers*

Develop How did the Cherokee lose their lands, even after winning *Worcester* v. *Georgia? government officials signed treaties with Cherokee "leaders" who did not represent most of the Cherokee; army forced them off their lands*

 CRF: Biography: Osceola

CRF: Interdisciplinary Project: Create Cherokee-English Flash Cards

Primary Source

"I voted against this Indian bill, and my conscience yet tells me that I gave a good and honest vote, and one that I believe will not make me ashamed on the day of judgment . . . "
— Congressman Davy Crockett

David Crockett: His Life and Adventures by John S. C. Abbott, Chapter IX

MISCONCEPTION ///ALERT\\\

Jackson's comment " . . . John Marshall has made his decision, now let him enforce it," may have been invented by others to enhance Jackson's reputation. The remark was first reported by Horace Greeley in a newspaper, and the quote appeared in later biographies. Biographer John Spencer Bassett wrote that he believed the words to be only "popular tradition, but . . . they might have been spoken."

Answers

Faces of History *was a way to gain knowledge, and thus, independence*

Reading Check *forced off their lands; marched west; many died*

248

FACES OF HISTORY

SEQUOYA
1767?–1843

Little is known with certainty about Sequoya's early years, including when or where he was born. Settling in Georgia, he worked at various trades—farmer, trader, silversmith. Sequoya believed that knowledge was key to Cherokee independence and that written language was a way for his people to acquire that knowledge. In 1809 he set out to create a system of writing for the Cherokee language. By 1821 he had created 86 characters that represented all the syllables of the Cherokee language. Soon the Cherokee were teaching the system in their schools and publishing their own books and newspapers. Sequoya's work helped unite eastern and western Cherokee around a shared language and preserved Cherokee cultural traditions.

Summarize Why do you think Sequoya believed written language was important?

THE IMPACT TODAY

Government

Today there are three federally recognized Cherokee communities, two in Oklahoma and one in North Carolina. The largest is the Cherokee Nation of Oklahoma, which has about 125,000 members. The Cherokee are by far the largest Native American group in the United States today.

Under the supervision of the U.S. Army, the Choctaw, the Creek, and the Chickasaw were forced to march west, hundreds of miles, to Indian Territory. Conditions on the marches were miserable. Exposure, malnutrition, and disease took their toll. About one-fourth of the Choctaw and the Creek—men, women, and children—died on the long trek. The Chickasaw's forced journey to Indian Territory was shorter and less deadly, but still miserable.

The Seminole fight back The Seminole reacted to attempts at their removal with armed force. Seminole women and children hid from the soldiers in the dense Florida swamps, while Seminole men conducted hit-and-run attacks on the American soldiers. About 3,000 Seminole were forced to move to Indian Territory, but many more continued to resist. They were never officially defeated, and their descendants still live in Florida today.

The Trail of Tears While the Seminole resisted removal with armed force, the Cherokee fought in the American court system. They sued the federal government, claiming that they had the right to be respected as a foreign country. The case reached the Supreme Court in 1831. Chief Justice John Marshall, however, refused to hear the case. He ruled that the Cherokee had no right to bring suit since they were neither citizens nor a foreign country.

The Cherokee, however, had another plan of attack. Samuel Austin Worcester was a white man, a teacher, and a friend to the Cherokee. The state of Georgia, carrying out the Indian Removal Act, ordered Worcester to leave Cherokee land. He refused and brought suit on behalf of himself and the Cherokee.

In 1832 John Marshall's Supreme Court issued its decision in **Worcester v. Georgia**. Many whites were stunned when Marshall ruled against Georgia, denying them the right to take Cherokee lands. Jackson was outraged. He reportedly stated, "John Marshall has made his decision—now let him enforce it."

To get around the Court's ruling, government officials signed a treaty with Cherokee leaders who favored relocation, even though they did not represent most of the Cherokee people. Under this treaty, the Cherokee were herded by the U.S. Army, like the other nations before them, on a long and deadly march west.

Of the 16,000 Cherokee forced to leave their homes, about 4,000 died on the march to the Indian Territory. The Cherokee suffered so badly—from hunger, exposure, disease, and bandits—that their exodus became known as the **Trail of Tears**, a term that has become synonymous with all of the nations' suffering.

READING CHECK **Summarizing** How did the Indian Removal Act affect the people of the "five civilized tribes"?

The National Bank

A hotly contested issue of Jackson's presidency concerned the **Second Bank of the United States**, a national bank overseen by the federal government. Congress established the Bank in 1816 and gave it a 20-year charter. The purpose of the Bank was to regulate state banks, which had grown rapidly since the First Bank of the United States went out of existence in 1811.

Jackson and other Americans strongly opposed the Second Bank of the United States. They thought that the Constitution did not give Congress the authority to create it in the first place.

Opponents recognized that state banks were more inclined to make loans to poorer farmers in the South and West—the very people who supported Jackson. By contrast, they viewed the national bank as an institution devoted to

---

Skills Focus: Comparing and Contrasting

Above Level

Reading Skill

Research Required

Seminole and Cherokee

1. Organize students into small groups. Have half of the students in each group conduct outside research to learn how the Cherokee responded to the Indian Removal Act, and the other half conduct research to learn how the Seminole responded to the act. Have students share the results of their research with their groups.

2. Have each group use its research to develop strategies that the Cherokee and Seminole

peoples could use to fight removal from their lands. Then have each group select one member who will present the strategy to a joint Seminole-Cherokee tribal council. Have students take notes during the council, and then have each student decide which strategy might have worked best. **LS Interpersonal, Kinesthetic**

Alternative Assessment Handbook, Rubrics 24: Oral Presentations; and 30: Research

the interests of wealthy northern corporations. Jackson so despised the bank that he called it a "monster," adding, "I will kill it."

In the summer of 1832 Henry Clay and Daniel Webster, National Republicans who opposed Jackson, introduced a bill to renew the Bank's charter. The timing of the bill, during an election year, was deliberate. They hoped that Jackson's opposition to the bill would hurt his chances of reelection. Jackson promptly vetoed the bill. In the election of 1832, Clay challenged Jackson for the presidency, and the controversy over the Bank became a major campaign issue.

Nevertheless, Jackson won re-election, defeating Clay in a landslide. At the beginning of his second term, Jackson ordered his secretary of the Treasury to take the money out of the Bank and deposit it in select state banks. Critics called these banks "pet banks" because they were loyal to Jackson.

Nicholas Biddle, the president of the Second Bank of the United States, opposed the pet-bank initiative, but there was little he could do. In 1836 the Second Bank of the United States was reduced to just another state bank.

READING CHECK Identifying Points of **View** Why did Jackson oppose the Second Bank of the United States?

Conflict over States' Rights

The controversy over the Second Bank of the United States was largely a dispute over how power should be divided between the federal government and state governments. Those who favored giving more power to the states invoked the concept of **states' rights**, based on the Tenth Amendment's provision that powers "not delegated to the United States by the Constitution, nor prohibited by it to the States" are reserved to the states.

The tariff controversy In 1816 Congress passed a tariff on British manufactured goods. It raised the tariff in 1824 and 1828. The tariff was welcomed by industry leaders of the northern states. Because the tariff increased the price of British goods, it encouraged Americans to buy American goods.

The agricultural southern states despised the tariff. It forced southerners to buy northern goods instead of the less expensive British goods they were accustomed to. Moreover, southern cotton growers, who exported most of their crop to Britain, opposed interference with international trade.

The controversy over the tariff helped drive a wedge between Jackson and his vice president, **John C. Calhoun**. Calhoun, a southerner,

Battle over the National Bank

Jackson compared the Second Bank of the United States to an "undemocratic, hydra monster" and a "hydra of corruption." A hydra is a serpentlike monster in Greek mythology that grew back two heads for every one cut off. **Why did Jackson oppose the Bank?**

© COLLECTION OF THE NEW-YORK HISTORICAL SOCIETY [neg. 42459]

Collaborative Learning

At Level

The Nullification Crisis

1. Remind the class that in 1832 the nation faced a serious crisis. Divide the class into two groups, one supporting nullification and one opposing it.

2. Have each group nominate five spokespeople. Have the spokespeople from the two groups face each other. Then stage a debate on nullification. Have one spokesperson address the person opposite him or her for one minute. Then have the opposite person respond. Have students take notes during the debate.

3. Create a two-column chart for students to see. Label one column *Pro-Nullification* and the other *Anti-Nullification*.

4. Have students use their notes to identify supporting arguments for each side. Use student responses to fill in the chart.

LS Interpersonal, Visual-Spatial

Alternative Assessment Handbook, Rubrics 7: Charts; and 10: Debates

Direct Teach

Teaching Tip

Students may have difficulty understanding the meaning of nullification. Review the definition in the text—rejection—and have students list other words that have similar connotations.

Review & Assess

Close

Have students explain why some might consider the Jackson administration controversial.

Review

- Online Quiz, Section 2
- Daily Test Practice Transparency

Assess

SE Section 2 Assessment
- Progress Assessment: Section 2 Quiz
- Alternative Assessment Handbook

Reteach

- Interactive Reader and Study Guide, Section 2
- Interactive Skills Tutor CD-ROM

Answers

Reading Check *South Carolina declared a tariff law null and void and threatened to secede because of it.*

---

charged that the tariff benefited northern states at the expense of southern states. Outraged southerners referred to the 1828 tariff as the Tariff of Abominations.

Calhoun advanced the idea that a state could nullify, or reject, any law passed by Congress—such as the tariff law—that the state thought violated the Constitution or was not in the best interests of the state. The concept that states have the right to reject federal laws is called the nullification theory.

The Hayne-Webster debate The issue of nullification and states' rights was the focus of one of the most famous debates in Senate history. It took place in 1830 between Senator Robert Hayne of South Carolina and Senator Daniel Webster of Massachusetts.

Hayne maintained that the federal government was a compact, or agreement, among the states. Nullification, he said, gave states a lawful way to protest federal legislation.

Webster responded that the United States was one nation, not merely an agreement of states. His impassioned reply ended with the words, "Liberty *and* Union, now and forever, one and inseparable!" The thundering defense of the Union made Webster a nationally famous figure overnight.

The nullification crisis In 1832 Congress passed another tariff, and the nullification theory was put to the test. South Carolina declared the tariff law "null and void" and threatened to **secede**, or withdraw, from the Union if the federal government tried to enforce the tariff. This event is known as the **nullification crisis**.

Calhoun felt so strongly about the issue that he resigned the vice presidency and became a senator from his home state of South Carolina. Jackson felt just as strongly. He stated:

HISTORY'S VOICES

"I consider the power to annul a law of the United States, assumed by one State, incompatible with the existence of the Union . . ."

—Andrew Jackson, 1832

Jackson demanded and received the Force Bill from Congress that empowered him to use military force to collect the tariff in South Carolina. But South Carolina declared that bill null and void as well. The situation was resolved by Henry Clay, who worked out a compromise in which tariffs would be reduced over a period of 10 years. But the issues of nullification and of states' rights would be raised again and again in the years to come.

READING CHECK Identifying the Main Idea What was the nullification crisis?

SECTION 2 ASSESSMENT

go.hrw.com
Online Quiz
Keyword: SD7 HP7

Reviewing Ideas, Terms, and People

1. **a. Recall** How did the Battle of New Orleans help Andrew Jackson's political career?
   b. Analyze How did the "corrupt bargain" lead to the creation of a new political party?
2. **a. Identify** What were the "five civilized tribes"?
   b. Draw Conclusions What does the passage of the **Indian Removal Act** indicate about American attitudes toward Native Americans?
   c. Elaborate What do you think modern Americans should learn from the **Trail of Tears**?
3. **a. Recall** Why did Jackson want to destroy the **Second Bank of the United States**?
   b. Draw Conclusions What are two reasons that Nicholas Biddle might have had for trying to save the national bank?
4. **a. Define** What is a tariff?
   b. Contrast How did the northern and southern views of the American tariff on British manufactured goods differ?

c. Evaluate What are arguments for and against the nullification theory?

Critical Thinking

5. **Comparing and Contrasting** Copy the diagram and compare and contrast the controversies over the Second National Bank and the Tariff of Abominations.

Similarities	Differences

FOCUS ON WRITING

6. **Persuasive** Write an editorial in which you make the case for or against the concept of nullification. Support your argument with examples from the section.

250 CHAPTER 7

Section 2 Assessment Answers

1. **a.** gave him national fame as a war hero
   b. Adams, Clay agreement angered many; led Jackson to form new party
2. **a.** Cherokee, Choctaw, Chickasaw, Seminole, Creek
   b. continued refusal to honor Native American civil and legal rights
   c. possible answer—Displacing an entire population has dire consequences.
3. **a.** favored corporations; unconstitutional
   b. It supported a strong national government; it was needed to regulate state banks.

4. **a.** tax on foreign goods
   b. North—promoted purchase of their goods; South—made prices higher
   c. for—gives states the power to create their own laws; against—weakens the power of the federal government
5. both involved states vs. federal power, tariff pitted North against South, bank pitted wealthy against poor
6. possible answer—against: laws must be obeyed for the good of the entire nation

3 The Industrial North

BEFORE YOU READ

MAIN IDEA

The North developed an economy based on industry.

READING FOCUS

1. What was the Industrial Revolution?

2. How did the Industrial Revolution affect the North?

3. What advancements were made in transportation and communication?

KEY TERMS AND PEOPLE

Samuel Slater
Industrial Revolution
Francis Lowell
Lowell girls
National Road
Erie Canal
Robert Fulton
Samuel F. B. Morse
telegraph

TAKING NOTES As you read, take notes about the advantages and disadvantages of industrial work for women workers. Record your notes in a graphic organizer like the one shown here.

Advantages	Disadvantages

THE INSIDE STORY

How did a young Englishman launch America's Industrial Revolution? The man history remembers as the father of the American Industrial Revolution got his first job in the British textile industry when he was 14 years old. Born in England, **Samuel Slater** grew up in a region called Derbyshire, where the world's first water-powered textile mills were used. In 1782 Slater went to work in one of those mills. He soon learned how to manage a mill and mastered the workings of the textile machines.

In 1789 when he was 21, Slater was ready to use his skills in America. But the textile industry was so important to England's economy that English law made it illegal for the secrets of mill design, and those who knew them, to leave the country. So Slater dressed as a farm laborer and secretly boarded a ship for New York, carrying in his head the precious, forbidden knowledge.

Slater soon went to meet Moses Brown, who was trying to use English-style machines in his Rhode Island mill. Within a year they had built a successful water-powered textile mill along the Blackstone River at Pawtucket, Rhode Island. Slater's daring escape to America gave him a central role in the birth of the U.S. textile industry. ◼

Samuel Slater and the Industrial Revolution

The Blackstone River powered America's first successful textile mill.

251

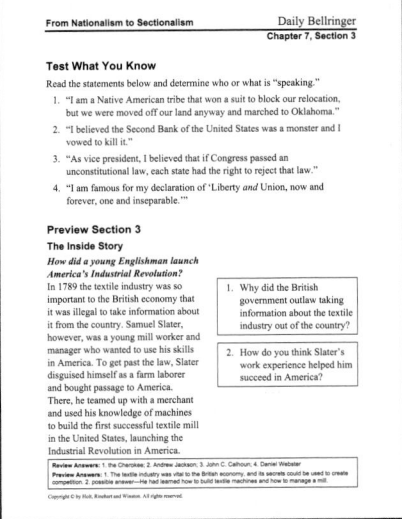

Teach the Main Idea

At Level

The Industrial North

1. **Teach** Ask students the Reading Focus questions to teach this section.

2. **Apply** Have students scan the section and then write "help wanted" posters for several industries that flourished in the early 1800s. Students should include the Lowell mills, canal building, and railroads. In a class discussion, have students predict the effect the new jobs might have on American family life as young people began to move away from farms and small towns. **LS Visual-Spatial**

3. **Review** As you review the section, have students describe the rapid economic and social changes brought about by the Industrial Revolution.

4. **Practice/Homework** Have students write an employment advertising slogan or jingle for the Lowell mills. **LS Auditory-Musical**

📄 Alternative Assessment Handbook, Rubrics 11: Discussions; and 28: Posters

Reading Focus

❶ What was the Industrial Revolution? *the birth of modern industry and the social changes that accompanied it*

The Industrial Revolution

Identify Who was James Watt? *a Scot who perfected the steam engine*

Analyze What occurred in the late 1700s to make the Industrial Revolution possible? *A number of inventions in Britain mechanized spinning and weaving.*

Reading Focus

❷ How did the Industrial Revolution affect the North? *increased urbanization; development of large cities and factories*

The North Industrializes

Recall What role did Samuel Slater play in the American textile industry? *Slater built America's first water-powered spinning mill.*

Evaluate Were the British authorities right to pass laws preventing the export of industrial knowledge? *possible answer—Yes, the knowledge was a huge financial advantage for British industries.*

go.hrw.com
Online Resources

KEYWORD: SD7 CH7
TOPIC: INDUSTRIAL ESPIONAGE

The Industrial Revolution

Samuel Slater's trip to America was an important event in one of the most dramatic changes in all of history. This change was so far-reaching that historians considered it a revolution. The **Industrial Revolution** was the birth of modern industry and the social changes that accompanied it. The Industrial Revolution occurred over a period of several decades from the middle of the 1700s to the middle of the 1800s.

The Industrial Revolution began in Great Britain's textile industry. There, for centuries, cloth had been made in workers' homes, using simple, human-powered machines. Plant fibers were spun into thread on spinning wheels. The thread was woven into cloth on looms.

Then in the late 1700s, a series of inventions radically transformed the industry. These inventions mechanized both spinning and weaving. British inventors created machines that used power from running water and steam engines to spin and weave cloth.

These powered spinning and weaving machines revolutionized the British textile industry. By 1800 textile companies had built hundreds of mills to house the new, large machines and produced volumes of cloth that could only have been dreamed of a few decades earlier. What was once a human-powered industry based in workers' homes was now a machine-powered industry based in huge mills. The Industrial Revolution had begun.

A key development of the Industrial Revolution was the replacement of human power with machine power. At the beginning of the Industrial Revolution, water power was

ACADEMIC VOCABULARY
violate to break or disregard, as in a law

far more important than steam power. But the steam engine became more and more important during the 1800s.

The steam engine was invented in England in 1698. But it didn't come into its own until the late 1700s. That's when Scottish inventor James Watt radically improved the existing engine, making it much more efficient and reliable. It was Watt's steam-engine design that powered the Industrial Revolution in Britain, and, not long after, in the United States.

READING CHECK **Sequencing** What events led to the birth of the Industrial Revolution in the British textile industry?

The North Industrializes

To keep their economic advantage, the British made it illegal for anyone with knowledge of industrial machines to leave the country or for anyone to export any industrial machines. Samuel Slater <u>violated</u> these laws when he brought knowledge of the new industrial machines to America. Slater and Moses Brown, a Pawtucket, Rhode Island, merchant, built a water-powered spinning mill on the Blackstone River. Their mill was the first successful textile mill in the country, and its construction marks the beginning of the Industrial Revolution in the United States.

Lowell The Industrial Revolution spread rapidly from Pawtucket throughout New England. By 1810 there were more than 60 mills spinning thread in New England. In 1813 in Waltham, Massachusetts, the first factory to

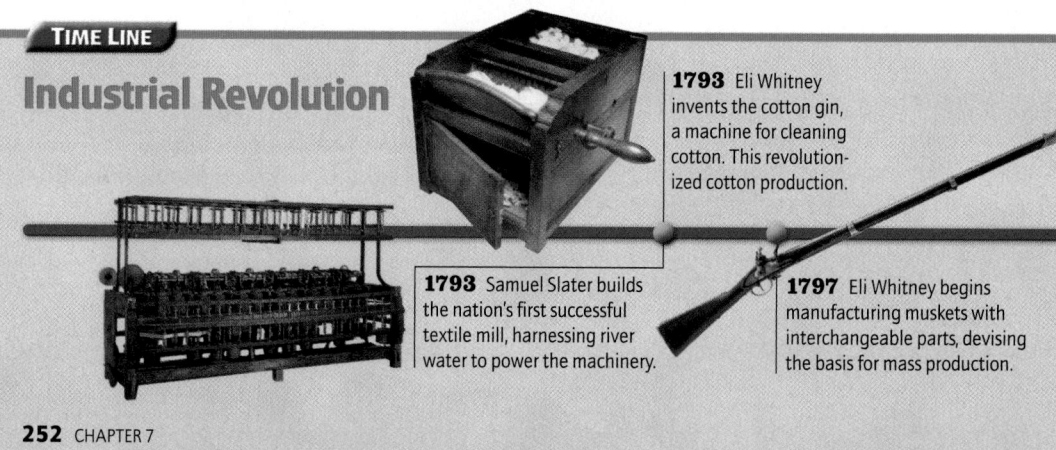

TIME LINE

Industrial Revolution

1793 Samuel Slater builds the nation's first successful textile mill, harnessing river water to power the machinery.

1793 Eli Whitney invents the cotton gin, a machine for cleaning cotton. This revolutionized cotton production.

1797 Eli Whitney begins manufacturing muskets with interchangeable parts, devising the basis for mass production.

Collaborative Learning   **At Level**

A Revolution in Industry
1. Guide students in a discussion of the British textile industry before and after the Industrial Revolution.
2. Organize the class into small groups. Have each group represent either a family working in the traditional mode to make textiles or a family employed in one of the new mills. Each group should create an illustrated

diary or storyboard that shows the family's activities on a typical workday. Encourage students to be creative.

3. Have volunteers share their diaries and illustrations with the class. **LS Interpersonal, Visual-Spatial**

📝 Alternative Assessment Handbook, Rubrics 3: Artwork; and 15: Journals

Answers

Reading Check *invention of mechanized spinning and weaving machines; improvement of the steam engine; use of steam power to replace human power*

bring all processes of cloth production under one roof was built. But it was Lowell that became the center of textile production.

The city was named for **Francis Lowell**, a wealthy Boston textile merchant. Workers began building mills and other buildings in Lowell, Massachusetts, in 1822. Within two years, the mills at Lowell were turning out great amounts of cotton cloth—and earning great profits. The city continued to grow as more and more textile firms opened mills there. Lowell soon had 40 mill buildings and 10,000 looms. People came from other countries to visit this wonder of American industry.

The majority of the workers in the Lowell mills were young women. Most of them had been recruited from local farms. They made relatively good wages for the time period, but they worked hard for it—often as long as 14 hours a day, 6 days a week.

The women's lives were strictly regulated by the ringing of bells. One worker described it this way:

HISTORY'S VOICES

❝Up before day, at the clang of the bell—and out of the mill by the clang of the bell—into the mill, and at work, to the obedience of the ding-dong bell—just as though we were so many living machines.❞

—Anonymous story in the *Lowell Offering*, a literary magazine by and for the mill girls

These hard-working young women came to be known as the **Lowell girls**. Despite their long hours, they developed a lively society in the boardinghouses in which they lived, forming friendships and clubs.

The revolution spreads Throughout the early and middle 1800s, industrialization spread slowly from the textile industry to other industries in the North. In the 1830s steam engines became better and more widely available, and their power helped make industry the fastest-growing part of the U.S. economy.

Industrialization in the North led to urbanization. People left the farm and moved to cities where they could work in the mills and factories. In 1820 only 7 percent of Americans lived in cities. Within 30 years, that percentage more than doubled.

The North underwent dramatic and rapid changes. Within a few decades, it evolved from a region of small towns and farms into one including large cities and factories—all as a result of the Industrial Revolution.

READING CHECK **Making Generalizations** What part of the United States was most affected by the Industrial Revolution?

Transportation and Communication

The development of American industry in the early 1800s went hand in hand with the development of transportation networks. Businesses needed ways to transport raw materials to their growing number of factories and mills and to ship their finished goods to market.

Roads and canals In 1811 construction began on the **National Road**. When the road was completed in 1841, it stretched 800 miles west

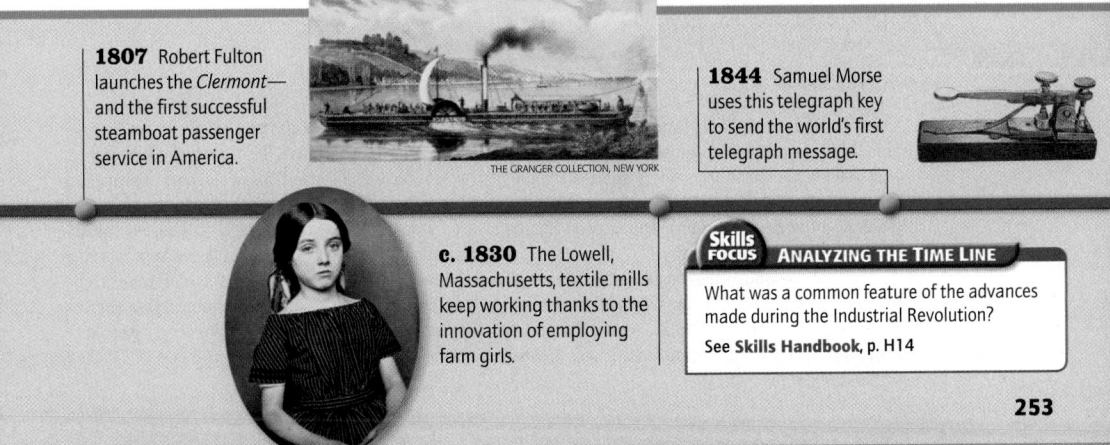

1807 Robert Fulton launches the *Clermont*—and the first successful steamboat passenger service in America.

THE GRANGER COLLECTION, NEW YORK

1844 Samuel Morse uses this telegraph key to send the world's first telegraph message.

c. 1830 The Lowell, Massachusetts, textile mills keep working thanks to the innovation of employing farm girls.

Skills FOCUS **ANALYZING THE TIME LINE**

What was a common feature of the advances made during the Industrial Revolution?

See Skills Handbook, p. H14

253

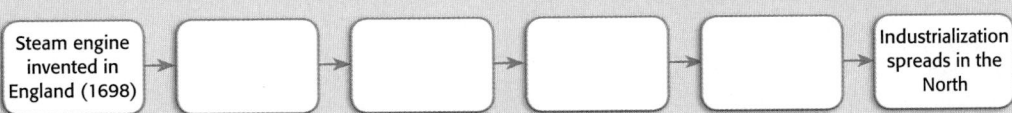

3 What advancements were made in transportation and communication? *roads, canals, steamboats, railroads, steam-powered presses, postal services, telegraph*

Transportation and Communication

Identify What was the National Road? *800 mile road from Cumberland, Maryland, to Vandalia, Illinois*

Identify Cause and Effect Why was there an urgent need for better transportation? *The nation needed better ways to transport raw materials and finished goods.*

📄 CRF: History and Geography Activity: America's First Highway

📄 CRF: Primary Source Activity: De Witt Clinton Describes the Erie Canal

Info to Know

The Maysville Road Andrew Jackson supported federal financing of the National Road. But he vetoed a pet project of Henry Clay in Kentucky. It would have financed the Maysville Road, a road entirely inside the state of Kentucky. Jackson thought local projects should be locally funded. Jackson's opponents said the veto was an abuse of presidential power.

Answers

Interpreting Infographics *It gave access to the Great Lakes, where travel could be continued on the water.*

254

HISTORY CLOSE-UP

The Erie Canal

With its endpoints in Albany and Buffalo, New York's Erie Canal linked the young nation's East and West. Canal travel encouraged trade, tourism, and western farming and settlement. After the canal opened in 1825, nearby cities and towns grew. Freight and passenger traffic, as shown in the painting below, boosted local economies.

Lumber and farm products headed east.

Manufactured goods and imports headed west.

New York City became the busiest port in America.

Skills FOCUS **INTERPRETING INFOGRAPHICS**

Drawing Conclusions How can it be said that the canal linked the eastern part of the country with the western part, when the canal was entirely in New York State?

See Skills Handbook, p. H18

COLLECTION OF THE NEW-YORK HISTORICAL SOCIETY

from Cumberland, Maryland, to Vandalia, Illinois. Most roads were not so ambitious. They were much shorter and crudely made. Still, by 1840 a network of roads connected most of the cities and towns throughout the United States, promoting travel and trade.

In 1825 the 363-mile-long **Erie Canal** opened, connecting the Great Lakes with the Hudson River—and with the Atlantic Ocean. The canal provided a quick and economical way to ship manufactured goods to the West and farm products to the East. The cost of shipping by canal barge was one-fifth of the cost of shipping by wagon, and shipping time was cut in half.

The Erie Canal also led to the establishment of New York City as a great trading city. Located where the Hudson River meets the Atlantic Ocean, New York was at the perfect geographic location to serve as a gateway between domestic and foreign trade.

254 CHAPTER 7

Skills Focus: Making Oral Presentations

At Level

Reading Like a Historian Skill

Transportation and Communication

1. Review the information in the History Close-Up feature and the text with students. Then organize students into small groups.

2. Have each group prepare a multimedia presentation or a collage showing how new trains, roads, and canals changed the speed and costs of getting goods to market. Have each group share its presentation with the class.

3. As an extension, have students compare the ways goods were shipped in the 1800s with the ways goods are shipped today.

LS Interpersonal, Verbal-Linguistic

📄 Alternative Assessment Handbook, Rubric 22: Multimedia Presentations

The success of the Erie Canal set off a canal craze in the United States. Within 15 years, more than 3,000 miles of canals formed a dense network in the northeast.

The steamboat The first successful steamboat service was run by **Robert Fulton**. In 1807 Fulton began operating a regular passenger service on the Hudson River with his boat, *The North River Steamboat of Clermont*, usually called the *Clermont*. The success of the *Clermont* inspired others to build and operate steamboats. Within a decade, dozens of steamboats were puffing up and down the Ohio, the Mississippi, and other rivers.

The railroad The first steam-powered train in the United States made its first trip in 1830. It was not a long trip, since there were only 23 miles of track in the entire country at the time. In 1831 the first scheduled passenger train service began in Charleston, South Carolina. By 1835 states had issued more than 200 contracts to build railroad lines. By 1840 there were about 3,000 miles of track in the country.

The speed, power, reliability, and carrying capacity of the railroad quickly made it a preferred means of travel and transport. The Iron Horse soon became the most important component of the American transportation network. Its success led to a general decline in roads and brought about the end of the canal craze.

Advances in communication Advances in communication rivaled advances in transportation during the early 1800s. In 1811 a German printer used steam to power a printing press. Steam-powered presses were soon built in the United States, enabling publishers to print material much faster and in much greater volumes than ever before. Another important advance in communications involved the postal service. With the growing use of steamboats and the railroad, mail delivery was faster and more widely available. In 1800 there were fewer than 1,000 post offices. By 1840 there were more than 12,000.

The greatest advancement in communication was the brainchild of **Samuel F. B. Morse**. In 1840 he patented the first practical telegraph. A **telegraph** is a device that sends messages using electricity through wires. Communication by telegraph was instantaneous, and newspapers, railroads, and other businesses were quick to grasp its advantages.

Telegraph wires would soon crisscross the nation, adding a network of rapid communication on top of an already advanced network of transportation. Thus, the Industrial Revolution was accompanied by a transportation revolution and a communications revolution.

THE IMPACT TODAY

Science and Technology
The telegraph has been replaced in most developed countries by digital information transmission that uses computer technology. Messages that once were sent by telegraph are now sent via the Internet.

READING CHECK **Summarizing** What key advancements in transportation and communication were made in the early 1800s?

SECTION 3 ASSESSMENT

go.hrw.com
Online Quiz
Keyword: SD7 HP7

Reviewing Ideas, Terms, and People
1. **a. Describe** Describe the birth of the **Industrial Revolution** in Great Britain.
   b. Analyze Why was the use of steam and water power an important part of the Industrial Revolution?
   c. Elaborate What effects of the Industrial Revolution can you identify in your own life today?
2. **a. Identify** Who were **Samuel Slater** and Moses Brown?
   b. Make Inferences Why do you think industrialization spread from the textile industry to other industries?
   c. Evaluate Do you think the **Lowell girls** were treated fairly? Explain your answer.
3. **a. Describe** What were the major economic and social effects of the **Erie Canal**?
   b. Draw Conclusions Why do you think that railroads became more important than roads and canals?

c. Evaluate What do you think was more important in the development of the nation, the transportation revolution or the communications revolution? Give reasons for your answer.

Critical Thinking
4. **Identifying Cause and Effect** Copy the diagram and identify the effects of the Industrial Revolution in the United States.

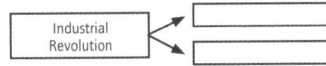

FOCUS ON WRITING

5. **Persuasive** What do you think was the most important invention of this time period? Identify and defend your choice in a persuasive paragraph.

Section 3 Assessment Answers

1. a. steam engine powered mechanized spinning and weaving machines
   b. replaced human power; led to faster production of goods
   c. urban population; national transportation systems; advanced communication systems

2. a. They built the first water-powered spinning mill in the U.S.
   b. Other industries saw they could produce goods faster and cheaper.
   c. no, worked long hours, had only one day off per week; yes, earned good wages

3. a. created a fast way to transport goods; New York City became great trading city
   b. enabled faster transportation
   c. possible answer—transportation; encouraged industry, connected country

4. transportation advances, better communication

5. telegraph, allowed instant communication

Direct Teach

Reading Focus

Transportation and Communication

Identify Who was Robert Fulton? *operator of the* Clermont, *the first passenger steamboat*

Analyze Why did the new railroads put an end to the canal-building boom? *rail was faster; could carry enormous amounts of freight*

CRF: Biography: Robert Fulton

Review & Assess

Close
Have students describe changes in the North that occurred because of the Industrial Revolution.

Review
Online Quiz, Section 3
Daily Test Practice Transparency

Assess
SE Section 3 Assessment
Progress Assessment: Section 3 Quiz
Alternative Assessment Handbook

Reteach
Interactive Reader and Study Guide, Section 3
Interactive Skills Tutor CD-ROM

Answers

Reading Check *improved roads, Erie Canal and other canals, steamboats, railroad, telegraph, steam-powered printing press, postal service*

255

Bellringer

The Inside Story. . . Use the **Daily Bellringer Transparency** to help students answer the question.

📦 Daily Bellringer Transparency, Section 4

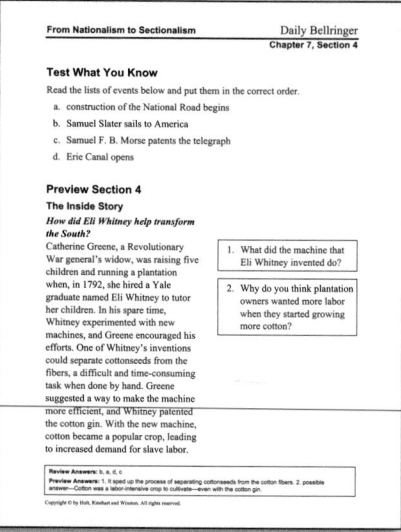

From Nationalism to Sectionalism — Daily Bellringer, Chapter 7, Section 4

Test What You Know

Read the lists of events below and put them in the correct order.

a. construction of the National Road begins
b. Samuel Slater sails to America
c. Samuel F. B. Morse patents the telegraph
d. Erie Canal opens

Preview Section 4

The Inside Story

How did Eli Whitney help transform the South?

Catherine Greene, a Revolutionary War general's widow, was raising five children and running a plantation when, in 1792, she hired a Yale graduate named Eli Whitney to tutor her children. In his spare time, Whitney experimented with new machines, and Greene encouraged his efforts. One of Whitney's inventions could separate cottonseeds from the fibers, a difficult and time-consuming task when done by hand. Greene suggested a way to make the machine more efficient, and Whitney patented the cotton gin. With the new machine, cotton became a popular crop, leading to increased demand for slave labor.

1. What did the machine that Eli Whitney invented do?

2. Why do you think plantation owners wanted more labor when they started growing more cotton?

Review Answers: b, a, d, c
Preview Answers: 1. It sped up the process of separating cottonseeds from the cotton fibers. 2. possible answer—Cotton was a labor-intensive crop to cultivate—even with the cotton gin.

Copyright © by Holt, Rinehart and Winston. All rights reserved.

Academic Vocabulary

Review with students the high-use academic term in this section.

acquire come into possession of or control of (p. 257)

📋 CRF: Vocabulary Builder Activity, Section 4

Taking Notes

Geography—good for farming; Economy—based on agriculture, use of slave labor; Technical Development—except for cotton gin, little development; Lifestyle— traditions important, rate of change slower than in the North; Organization of Society—about one-fourth of southerners owned slaves, rest were small farmers

---

The Land of Cotton

BEFORE YOU READ

MAIN IDEA

During the early 1800s, the South developed an economy based on agriculture.

READING FOCUS

1. Why was cotton king in the South?

2. How did the cultivation of cotton lead to the spread of slavery?

3. What key differences developed between the North and the South?

KEY TERMS AND PEOPLE

Eli Whitney
cotton gin
Cotton Belt
King Cotton

TAKING NOTES As you read, take notes on important features of the South. Record your notes in a graphic organizer like the one shown here.

Feature	
Geography	
Economy	
Technical Development	
Lifestyle	
Organization of Society	

Revolution in a COTTON BOX

▲ With a cotton gin, a worker could clean 50 times more cotton than by hand.

THE INSIDE STORY

How did Eli Whitney help transform the South? When Catherine Greene was 44, her husband, the Revolutionary War general Nathanael Greene, died suddenly in 1786, leaving her to raise their five children alone. Caty had a lively personality, and she was strong-willed. Determined to save her family from ruin, she faced the challenge of running the family plantation in Georgia.

In 1792, with her finances stabilized, Greene hired a young graduate of Yale University to tutor her children. In his spare time, the tutor, **Eli Whitney**, also tinkered with machines. Greene encouraged his experiments.

Not many Georgia planters at the time grew cotton because separating the seeds from the fluffy cotton fibers was so slow and expensive. In 1793, Whitney designed a wooden cylinder with teeth like a wire comb. When turned by a hand crank, it combed the seeds out of the cotton. But the sticky cotton soon jammed the machines. Greene suggested adding a stiff brush that cleaned the teeth as the cylinder turned. The cotton gin was born.

Whitney got a patent for his invention in 1794 and tried to set up a factory. Greene borrowed money to help him. But many farmers just copied the machine. In the end, neither the inventor nor his patron made any money from the cotton gin. But the South was transformed. The gin led to the spread of cotton farming throughout the region and triggered an increased demand for slave labor in the cotton-growing states. ◢

Teach the Main Idea

At Level

The Land of Cotton

1. **Teach** Ask students the Reading Focus questions to teach this section.

2. **Apply** Organize students into small groups. Have each group write a business plan for a new plantation to be started in the South in the 1820s. The plan should persuade a bank to lend money for the venture. It should describe what product is to be grown, where it will be grown, with what labor supply, and who the customers for the product will be. Have volunteers read their plans.

3. **Review** As you review the section, have students describe how the South's economy was increasingly different from that of the North, and how that might create tension.

4. **Practice/Homework** Have students write a short paragraph that gives two reasons why slaveholders came to dominate the southern economy. **LS** Verbal-Linguistic

📋 Alternative Assessment Handbook, Rubrics 14: Group Activity; and 37: Writing Assignments

"King Cotton"

The **cotton gin** (*gin* is short for *engine*) was actually quite a simple machine. It was so simple, in fact, that cotton farmers routinely built their own, copying Eli Whitney's design and infringing on his patent. Even so, the cotton gin had a major impact on life in the South.

A type of plant called long-staple cotton grew well in the West Indies, where many of the earlier cotton plantations were established. American growers were disappointed, however, when they tried the plant in the southern United States. The plants could not survive southern winters. As a result, growers turned to a hardier variety of cotton called short-staple cotton. It could stand the cold, but it was harder to clean than long-staple cotton. Whitney's cotton gin solved the problem and made the large-scale production of cotton possible.

The demand for cotton was increasing both at home and abroad. In the United States, the booming textile industry of the North bought cotton to weave into cloth to sell to the growing American population. Overseas, the greatest demand came from Great Britain. There, the mechanized textile industry, exploding in the midst of the Industrial Revolution, demanded ever-increasing amounts of cotton to feed its hundreds of mills.

The combination of the new cotton gin and the huge demand for cotton encouraged many Americans farmers to begin growing cotton. Southerners moved south and west to acquire land for cotton farms in the Carolinas, Tennessee, Georgia, Alabama, Mississippi, and Louisiana. Beginning in the 1820s, the number of acres devoted to cotton cultivation soared. A nearly uninterrupted band of cotton farms called the **Cotton Belt** stretched across the South, all the way from Virginia in the East to Texas in the West.

Growing cotton was a way to get rich relatively quickly. One man at the time described the mania for growing cotton:

ACADEMIC VOCABULARY

acquire come into possession or control of

HISTORY'S VOICES

❝Young men who come to this country, 'to make money,' soon catch the mania, and nothing less than a broad plantation, waving with the snow white cotton bolls, can fill their mental vision, as they anticipate by a few years in their dreams of the future, the result of their plans and labours.❞

—J. H. Ingram, *The South-West*

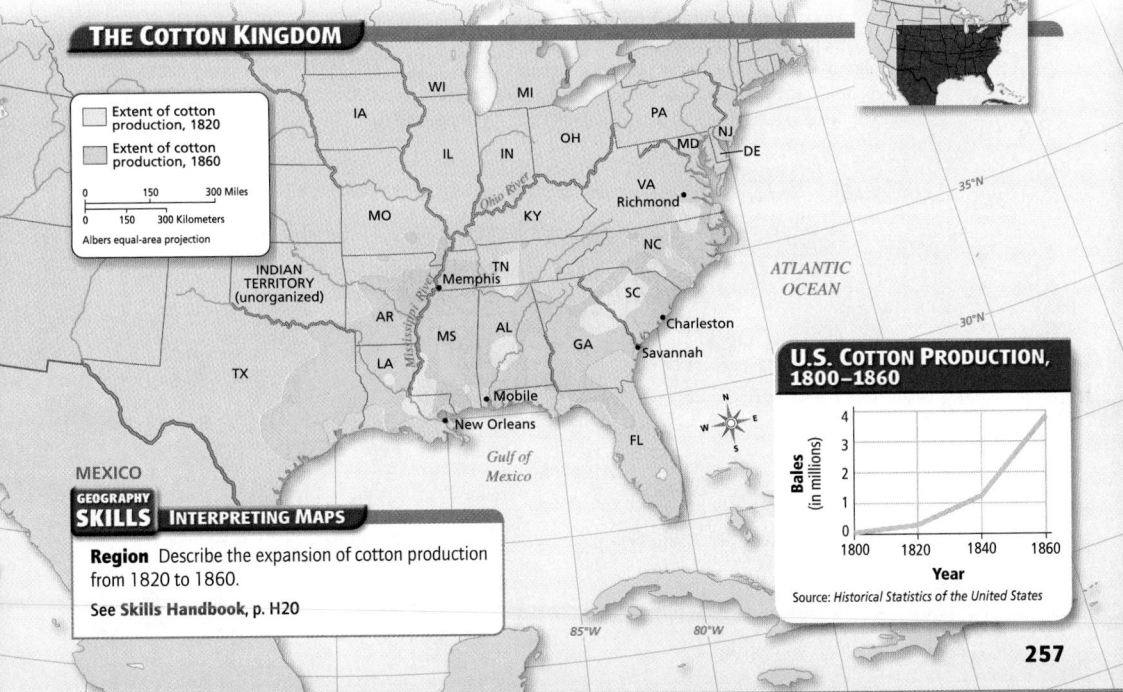

THE COTTON KINGDOM

Extent of cotton production, 1820
Extent of cotton production, 1860

0   150   300 Miles
0   150   300 Kilometers
Albers equal-area projection

WI, MI, IA, IL, IN, OH, PA, MD, NJ, DE, MO, KY, VA (Richmond), NC, TN (Memphis), INDIAN TERRITORY (unorganized), AR, MS, AL, GA, SC (Charleston), Savannah, TX, LA, Mobile, New Orleans, FL, MEXICO, Gulf of Mexico, ATLANTIC OCEAN

Ohio River, Mississippi R.

35°N, 30°N, 85°W, 80°W

U.S. COTTON PRODUCTION, 1800–1860

Bales (in millions): 0, 1, 2, 3, 4
Year: 1800, 1820, 1840, 1860
Source: *Historical Statistics of the United States*

GEOGRAPHY SKILLS   INTERPRETING MAPS

Region Describe the expansion of cotton production from 1820 to 1860.
See *Skills Handbook*, p. H20

257

Primary Source

"Without the firing of a gun, without drawing a sword, should they [northerners] make war upon us [southerners], we could bring the whole world to our feet. What would happen if no cotton was furnished for three years? . . . England would topple headlong and carry the whole civilized world with her. No, you dare not make war on cotton! No power on earth dares make war upon it. Cotton is King."

— Senator James H. Hammond of South Carolina

Speech, U.S. Senate, March 4, 1858

Answers

Interpreting Maps *The geographic area of production increased greatly throughout the South, as did amount of cotton produced.*

257

2 How did the cultivation of cotton lead to the spread of slavery? *Cotton was a labor-intensive crop to grow; as cotton farming expanded, farmers needed more workers to raise the cotton, and turned to slaves.*

The Spread of Slavery

Recall How many enslaved African Americans were there in 1840? *nearly 2.5 million*

Analyze Why did planters who used slaves become so successful? *They could clear more land, plant and pick more cotton for market, and make more money.*

Evaluate Why do you think southern whites with no slaves tolerated slavery? *possible answers— The small farmers hoped one day to be rich and own slaves; they were poor and had little power; cotton provided a better economy for all.*

📄 Political Cartoons Activities for American History: Cartoon 13: Splitting Apart Enslaved Families

📄 CRF: Literature Activity: The Farewell of a Virginia Slave Mother to Her Daughters Sold into Southern Bondage

Numbers tell the story of the cotton boom. With few exceptions, cotton was America's largest and most valuable export from 1807 until the end of the 1800s. Cotton became so important to the economy of the South that by 1855 cotton became more than a crop—it gained royal status. Senator James H. Hammond of South Carolina stood on the Senate floor and pronounced that "Cotton is king." Soon, people called the crop **King Cotton**.

READING CHECK **Identifying the Main Idea**
Why was cotton called King Cotton?

The Spread of Slavery

Even with the use of the cotton gin, farming cotton was a labor-intensive enterprise. The land had to be prepared, and the cotton seeds had to be planted. The growing plants had to be tended. Finally, of course, the crop had to be picked, cleaned, and formed into bales.

The first cotton farms were small and run by families who didn't own slaves. They were soon followed by wealthier planters who bought huge tracts of land and used enslaved African Americans to raise and pick the cotton that made the planters rich.

These wealthier planters grew cotton and other crops on plantations. As the amount of money made by growing cotton grew, so did the number of plantations. Some plantations were huge, including thousands of acres. Others were more modest.

The growth of cotton farming led directly to an increase in demand for enslaved African Americans. Although the importation of enslaved people had been banned in 1808, they were routinely smuggled into southern ports like Charleston, South Carolina, and New Orleans, Louisiana. These people, and the children of enslaved parents, were cruelly bought and sold by slave traders to provide ever more workers for the cotton fields.

In 1810 there were about 1 million enslaved African Americans in the United States. Most lived in Virginia, the Carolinas, and Tennessee. By 1840 that number had more than doubled to nearly 2.5 million.

As cotton farms spread, so too did slavery. The enslaved population grew in Georgia, Alabama, and Mississippi. Overall, enslaved African Americans accounted for about one-third of the population of the South.

Most southerners were not slaveholders. About one-fourth of the white families in the South owned slaves. Most had fewer than 20. Only a handful of large plantation owners kept hundreds of African Americans in bondage.

Planters knew that the more slaves they used as laborers, the more cotton they could grow, and the more money they could make. Thus, there was a powerful economic incentive to maintain slavery in the South.

READING CHECK **Identifying Cause and Effect** What led to the spread of slavery throughout the South?

Slavery and King Cotton
Artist William Henry Brown painted this scene of enslaved workers on a Mississippi cotton plantation in 1842. *Examine the painting carefully. What does it tell you about the lives and working conditions of enslaved African Americans?*

258

THE HISTORIC NEW ORLEANS COLLECTION

Skills Focus: Analyzing Primary Sources   Above Level

Reading Like a Historian Skill
The Economics of Slavery

1. Read the following quote from John C. Calhoun to students. "It would be well for those interested to reflect whether there now exists, or ever has existed, a wealthy and civilized community in which one portion did not live on the labor of another . . . Let those who are interested remember that labor is the only source of wealth, and how small a portion of it, in all old and civilized countries, even the best governed, is left to those by whose labor wealth is created."

2. Have students write a paraphrase of the quote and then write a brief essay in which they address this question: What do you suppose Calhoun meant by this statement in defense of slavery? **LS Verbal-Linguistic**

📄 Alternative Assessment Handbook, Rubric 37: Writing Assignments

Answers

Art *small children, men, and women all worked; no shoes, tattered clothing reveal harsh life and working conditions*

Reading Check (left) *extraordinarily important to the economy of the South; largest U.S. export;* **(right)** *growth of cotton, which was a labor-intensive crop*

Differences between the North and the South

Cotton was king in the South, but it wasn't the only crop grown there. Sugarcane, sugar beets, tobacco, and rice were also important crops. Together, these crops led the economy of the South. By 1840 the South was a thoroughly agricultural region.

In contrast, the North's economy was not nearly as reliant on agriculture. Farming was an important activity and had been since colonial times, but the Industrial Revolution made manufacturing and trade the base of the North's economy.

Different worlds The economic differences between the primarily industrial North and the primarily agricultural South led to even greater differences between the two regions. Trade and industry encourage urbanization, and so cities grew in the North much more than in the South. Moreover, the Industrial Revolution and the revolutions in transportation and communication had the greatest impact on the North. Northern businesses seized new technology in pursuit of efficiency and growth.

By contrast, in the South after the widespread use of the cotton gin, there was relatively little in the way of technological progress. Many southerners saw little need for labor-saving devices, for example, when they had an ample supply of enslaved people to do their work.

These different ways of life led to the development of different points of view. In the North, urban dwellers were exposed to many different types of people and a constantly changing landscape. They tended to view change as progress. In the South, where the landscape was less prone to change and where the population was less diverse, people tended to place a higher value on tradition.

Aggravating the differences between the North and the South was physical distance. Relatively few southerners had the means or motivation to travel extensively in the North, and relatively few northerners had ever visited the South. Thus, to most northerners, the South was a distant and different, almost foreign, place. Southerners had the same feelings about the North.

Differences over slavery The greatest difference between North and South, however, concerned slavery. In the South, where slavery was legal, it was viewed by most white people as an absolutely vital part of the economy, a natural situation, and, to many, a practice sanctioned by their Christian religion. In the North, where slavery was illegal, ever increasing numbers of people viewed it as evil.

Americans of the time were well aware of the differences between the two regions of their country. Yet few could know that the differences would eventually lead the two regions to fight each other in a bloody conflict called the Civil War.

READING CHECK **Contrasting** What were the major differences between the North and the South?

SECTION 4 ASSESSMENT

go.hrw.com
Online Quiz
Keyword: SD7 HP7

Reviewing Ideas, Terms, and People

1. a. Identify Where did the demand for cotton grown in the South come from?
b. Analyze What factors led to the establishment of the **Cotton Belt**?

2. a. Describe How did the spread of cotton farming lead to the spread of slavery?
b. Evaluate Do you think there was much opposition to slavery in the South? Why or why not?

3. a. Recall Besides cotton, what other major crops were grown in the South?
b. Compare and Contrast How were the North and the South similar and different?
c. Elaborate How did people in the South justify the continuation of the inhumane institution of slavery?

Critical Thinking

4. Comparing and Contrasting Copy the diagram and identify similarities and differences between the North and the South.

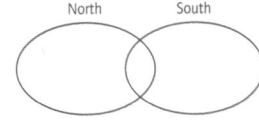

North   South

FOCUS ON WRITING

5. Expository Write a paragraph that explains why cotton became fundamental to the economy of the South.

FROM NATIONALISM TO SECTIONALISM **259**

Direct Teach

Reading Focus

❸ What key differences developed between the North and the South?
North was more industrial; South was agricultural, used slave labor

Differences between the North and the South

Explain Why did southerners see little need for labor-saving devices?
had an ample supply of enslaved laborers to do the work

Analyze Why did the North have more cities than the South?
Manufacturing and trade drew workers, creating a base for cities in the North. Many southerners were tied to their farms in rural areas.

Review & Assess

Close
Have students describe how and why the South changed after the invention of the cotton gin.

Review
Online Quiz, Section 4
Daily Test Practice Transparency

Assess
SE Section 4 Assessment
Progress Assessment: Section 4 Quiz
Alternative Assessment Handbook

Reteach
Interactive Reader and Study Guide, Section 4
Interactive Skills Tutor CD-ROM

Answers
Reading Check *North—urban, industrial society; many opposed slavery; South—rural, agricultural society; many viewed slavery as an economic necessity*

259

Section 4 Assessment Answers

1. a. textile industry in North and Great Britain
b. cotton gin; increasing demand for cotton

2. a. labor-intensive crop; increase in the number of cotton farms
b. possible answer—no, because slaves offered cheap labor

3. a. sugarcane, sugar beets, tobacco, rice
b. similarities—English language, common heritage; differences—North: urban population; economy based on manufacturing and trade; many people opposed slavery;

South: rural population; agriculture-based economy; many people supported slavery
c. vital part of the economy; believed it was sanctioned by their Christian religion

4. North—largely industrial, urban population, anti-slavery; South—largely agricultural, rural population, pro-slavery; both spoke English, similar backgrounds

5. profitable cash crop with huge demand; valuable export

Jackson and Presidential Power

Info to Know

The Hydra of Corruption According to Jackson, by reelecting him, the people of the United States had given him a mandate to break the power of the Second Bank of the United States. Jackson referred to the bank as the "hydra of corruption" and believed that the bank showed favoritism to the "moneyed capitalists" at the expense of the common people. As it turned out, Jackson had far less control over his "pet banks" than he had had over the Bank of the United States. They soon began to overextend credit by issuing currency for more money than they could back with gold and silver. In addition, new "wildcat" banks sprang up, especially in the West. Following the lead of the "pet banks," they issued currency without adequate backing. The result was runaway inflation.

Jackson and Presidential Power

Historical Context The documents below provide different information on Andrew Jackson and presidential power.

Task Examine the documents and answer the questions that follow. Then you will be asked to write an essay about how Andrew Jackson changed presidential power. Use facts from the documents and from the chapter to support the position you take in your thesis statement.

DOCUMENT 1

In his time, Andrew Jackson was an extremely popular president. The public generally supported his policies and his expansion of power. During the nullification crisis, Jackson threatened to send troops to South Carolina if necessary to force it to obey federal law. The song "Jackson and the Nullifiers" became a popular tune that reflected how much the country supported him.

When we our glorious Constitution form'd,
These Southern men declined it,
But soon they found they were unarmed,
And petitioned to sign it.
Sing Yankee doodle doodle doo,
Yankee doodle dandy,
Now like the snake torpid in a brake [lazy in a marsh],
They think Nullification it is handy.
Without their trade we are not afraid,
But we can live in peace and plenty,
But if to arms they sound alarms,
They may find it not so handy.
Sing Yankee doodle doodle doo,
Sing Yankee doodle dandy,
For Jackson he is wide awake,
He says the Union is so handy.
Our country's cause, our country's laws,
We ever will defend, Sir,
And if they do not gain applause,
My song was never penned, Sir.
So sound the trumpet, beat the drum,
Play Yankee doodle dandy,
We Jackson boys will quickly come,
And be with our rifles handy.

DOCUMENT 2

Some critics believed that Jackson had expanded the power of the presidency to a level not intended by the U.S. Constitution. This cartoon reflected those views.

Collaborative Learning

At Level

The Second Bank of the United States

Research Required

1. Tell students that some historians have charged that Jackson's policies in regard to the Second Bank of the United States were motivated more by politics than by a sincere wish to help the common people.

2. Divide the class into small groups. Have each group conduct additional research on the Second Bank of the United States and on Jackson's attempts to shut it down.

3. Have each student write an editorial from the perspective of an American citizen in 1832.

Each student should either support or oppose Jackson's attempts to shut down the Second Bank of the United States. Students may also wish to offer an alternative solution to the problem.

4. Have volunteers read their editorials to the class. **LS Interpersonal, Verbal-Linguistic**

Alternative Assessment Handbook, Rubric 17: Letters to Editors

DOCUMENT 3

One of Jackson's major goals was to destroy the Bank of the United States, which he saw as harming poor Americans. As you read in Section 2, he used his presidential power of veto and public support to end the national bank and replace it with smaller banks that he approved. This cartoon shows Jackson fighting a hydra that represents the national bank. The hydra is a mythological beast whose heads grow back when cut off. In this cartoon, the heads of the hydra are politicians who oppose Jackson's fight with the bank.

Andrew Jackson strikes the hydra with a cane labeled "veto."

Nicholas Biddle, the president of the Second Bank of the United States, is shown as the biggest head on the hydra.

THE GRANGER COLLECTION, NEW YORK

Skills FOCUS   READING LIKE A HISTORIAN

1. a. Identify Refer to Document 1. According to the song, what were the people willing to do to show their support for Jackson?
b. Analyze In the song, southern men are depicted as favoring nullification. What lines in the song express the opposite view?

2. a. Identify Refer to Document 2. To whom is Jackson being compared in this image?
b. Elaborate Do you think the cartoonist thought that Jackson's expansion of power was a positive or negative development? Explain your answer.

3. a. Identify Refer to Document 3. Who does the cartoonist seem to support in this image?
b. Interpret Why do you think Nicholas Biddle is shown as the biggest head of the hydra?

4. Document-Based Essay Question Consider the question below and form a thesis statement. Using examples from Documents 1, 2, and 3, create an outline and write a short essay supporting your position. How did Andrew Jackson change the power of the presidency?

See **Skills Handbook, pp. H28–29, H31**

Skills Focus: Making Oral Presentations   **At Level**

Reading Like a Historian Skill
The Election of 1832

1. Divide the class into two groups. Have one group represent Democrats supporting President Andrew Jackson in the election of 1832. Have the other group represent National Republican supporters of Henry Clay. Have each side prepare arguments supporting its position.

2. Conduct a classroom debate between the two groups. Each team of debaters should explain why their candidate would be the better choice.

3. Have each student write a one-page essay telling which candidate he or she would have supported. Ask students what part, if any, the candidates' stand on the Second Bank of the United States would have played in their decision.

4. Have volunteers read their essays to the class.
LS Logical-Mathematical, Verbal-Linguistic
Alternative Assessment Handbook, Rubric 10: Debates

Answers

Visual Summary

Review and Inquiry Have students work in pairs to create a jingle or song lyrics in which they describe similarities and differences between the North and the South. Have volunteers share their creations with the class.

Quick Facts Transparency: From Nationalism to Sectionalism

Reviewing Key Terms and People

1. Erie Canal
2. secede
3. Industrial Revolution
4. Samuel F.B. Morse
5. Samuel Slater
6. Robert Fulton
7. Monroe Doctrine
8. cotton gin
9. nullification crisis
10. Cotton Belt
11. Indian Removal Act

Comprehension and Critical Thinking

12. a. nationalism
   b. judicial rulings and economic policies favored strong federal government; tariffs supported American industry; diplomacy secured new territory and expanded U.S.
   c. showed how divisive slavery was and importance of maintaining a balance of power

13. a. political power exercised by ordinary Americans, not just the wealthy
   b. Seminole resisted with armed force; Cherokee appealed through the courts.
   c. drove a wedge between president and vice president; led to a crisis with South Carolina

14. a. Samuel Slater migrated, brought knowledge of English machines, and helped build the first water-powered spinning mill in the U.S.
   b. Producing textiles and manufacturing formed the basis

for the northern economy, while agriculture was the focal point of the southern economy.
   c. introduced mechanization to several industries; led to advances in communication and transportation; attracted people to the cities; northern economy became industrial

15. a. cleaned short-staple cotton; made large-scale cotton production possible
   b. The number of cotton farms grew, and labor was needed for the crop.

   c. possible answers—growing mistrust, misunderstanding, alienation or separateness; political and social disengagement; war

---

Chapter Review

Visual Summary: From Nationalism to Sectionalism

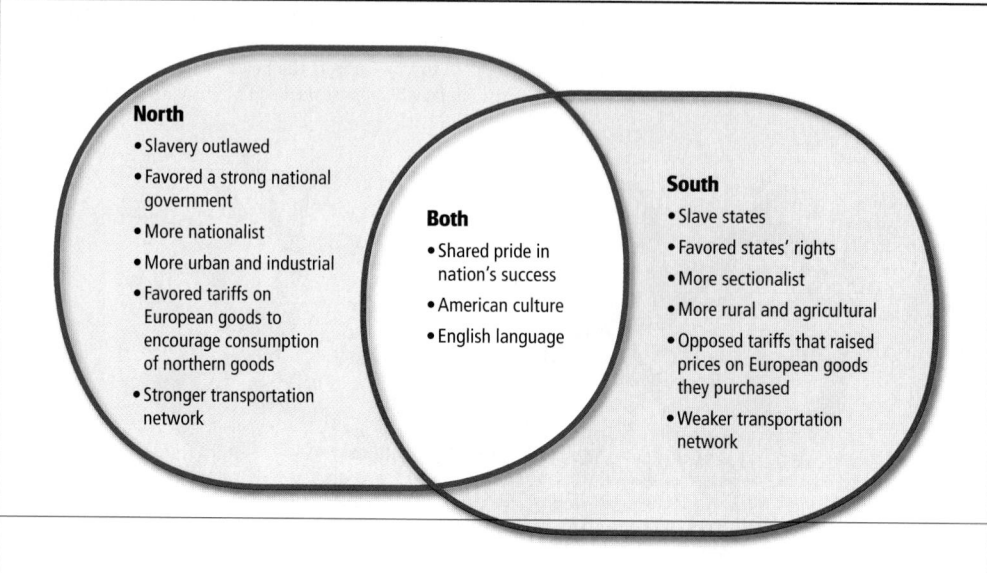

North
- Slavery outlawed
- Favored a strong national government
- More nationalist
- More urban and industrial
- Favored tariffs on European goods to encourage consumption of northern goods
- Stronger transportation network

Both
- Shared pride in nation's success
- American culture
- English language

South
- Slave states
- Favored states' rights
- More sectionalist
- More rural and agricultural
- Opposed tariffs that raised prices on European goods they purchased
- Weaker transportation network

Reviewing Key Terms and People

Identify the correct term or person from the chapter that best fits each of the following descriptions.

1. Waterway linking Great Lakes and Hudson River
2. To leave the Union
3. The birth of modern industry
4. Patented the first successful telegraph
5. Englishman who brought water-powered mill technology to the United States
6. Inventor and operator of the *Clermont*
7. United States' warning to European countries not to interfere in the Americas
8. Eli Whitney's invention
9. South Carolina's rejection of federal laws
10. Band of cotton farms in the South
11. 1830 law that resulted in the Trail of Tears

Comprehension and Critical Thinking

SECTION 1 *(pp. 238–243)*

12. a. Recall What replaced feelings of sectionalism in the early 1800s?
   b. Analyze How did growing nationalism affect foreign and domestic policies?
   c. Elaborate How did the Missouri Compromise reflect growing sectionalism in the United States?

SECTION 2 *(pp. 245–250)*

13. a. Identify What was Jacksonian Democracy?
   b. Contrast How did the Seminole and the Cherokee resist the Indian Removal Act?
   c. Elaborate How did the issues of states' rights and nullification affect Jackson's presidency?

Using the Internet

16. Go to the HRW Web site and enter the keyword shown to access a rubric for this activity.

KEYWORD: SD7 CH7

History's Impact video program
Review the video to answer the closing question:
How did the economic differences between the
North and the South help lead to the Civil War?

SECTION 3 (pp. 251–255)

14. a. Describe How did the Industrial Revolution reach the United States?

b. Make Inferences Why did the Industrial Revolution affect the North much more than it did the South?

c. Evaluate What effects did the Industrial Revolution have on the United States?

SECTION 4 (pp. 256–259)

15. a. Recall What did the cotton gin do?

b. Draw Conclusions Why did slavery spread throughout the South?

c. Predict What do you think are some likely effects of the fundamental differences between the North and the South?

Using the Internet

go.hrw.com
Practice Online
Keyword: SD7 CH7

16. During the early 1800s, Americans built thousands of miles of canals. Using the keyword above, do research to learn about the Erie Canal and its impact on New York and the rest of the country. As you do your research, find out what role New York governor DeWitt Clinton played in the development of the Erie Canal. Then create a report that describes how the Erie Canal helped New York and the rest of the country grow.

Analyzing Primary Sources

Reading Like a Historian
This work was painted in the early 1800s by John A. Woodside of Philadelphia. The woman in the painting is Lady Liberty.

17. Identify The words under the scene read "We Owe Allegiance To No Crown." What or who is meant by the word *we*?

18. Analyze Study the painting. How does the artist convey a feeling of patriotism and nationalism?

Critical Reading

Read the passage at the end of Section 1 that begins with the heading "The Missouri Compromise." Then answer the questions that follow.

19. What led to the Missouri Compromise?

   A the fact that slavery was illegal in Missouri

   B the effort to abolish slavery in the South

   C the desire to maintain a balance in the Senate between free and slave states

   D the need to admit Maine as a slave state

20. How did the Missouri Compromise affect the Louisiana Territory?

   A It banned slavery in all of the territory.

   B It allowed slavery in all of the territory.

   C It banned slavery in part of the territory and allowed it in another.

   D It left the question of slavery in the territory undecided.

FOCUS ON WRITING

Expository Writing *Expository writing gives information, explains why or how, or defines a process. To practice expository writing, complete the assignment below.*

Writing Topic Differences between the North and the South

21. Assignment Based on what you have read in this chapter, write a paragraph that explains how differences between the North and the South developed in the early 1800s. If you have access to a computer, use a word processing program to create and format your paragraph.

Answers

Analyzing Primary Sources

17. the United States; Americans

18. It shows an American proudly holding a flag and being crowned by a symbol of liberty.

Critical Reading

19. C

20. C

Focus on Writing

21. possible answer—The South's agriculture-based economy grew out of its warmer climate and fertile soil. Southerners discovered they could earn money growing cotton, sugarcane, sugar beets, rice, and tobacco. The North had a cooler climate and rocky soil. Because these conditions were not conducive to farming, northerners based their economy on the textile industry and trade. Trade and industry led to urbanization, so that northern society grew more urban, while southern society remained rural.

A rubric for this activity is provided in Chapter Resource File: Focus on Writing Activity: Differences Between the North and South.

History's Impact Video Program

northern economy relied on industry while southern economy relied on cotton farming and enslaved people for labor; differences led to rise of sectionalism and eventually to war

Review and Assessment Resources

Review and Reinforce

- CRF: Chapter Review Activity
- Quick Facts Transparency: From Nationalism to Sectionalism
- Spanish Chapter Summaries Audio CD Program
- Online Chapter Summaries in Spanish
- OSP Holt PuzzlePro; Quiz Show for ExamView
- Quiz Game CD-ROM

Assess

- PASS: Chapter Test, Forms A and B
- Alternative Assessment Handbook
- OSP ExamView Test Generator, Chapter Test
- Differentiated Instruction Modified Worksheets and Tests CD-ROM: Chapter Test
- HOAP Holt Online Assessment Program (in the Premier Online Edition)

Reteach/Intervene

- Interactive Reader and Study Guide
- Differentiated Instruction Teacher Management System: Lesson Plans for Differentiated Instruction
- Differentiated Instruction Modified Worksheets and Tests CD-ROM: Chapter Test
- Interactive Skills Tutor CD-ROM

go.hrw.com
Online Resources
KEYWORD: SD7 CH7

A Push for Reform

Chapter Overview	Reproducible Resources	Technology Resources
CHAPTER 8 pp. 264–293 **Overview:** In this chapter, students will analyze how the Second Great Awakening started a period of great social reform and how this changed the face of America.	**Differentiated Instruction Teacher Management System:*** • Instructional Benchmarking Guides • Lesson Plans for Differentiated Instruction **Interactive Reader and Study Guide:** Chapter Graphic Organizer* **Chapter Resource File:*** • Writing for the SAT: Immigration • Social Studies Skills Activity: Analyzing Primary Sources • Chapter Review Activity **American History Outline Maps** **Pre-AP Activities Guide for American History*** **Reading Like a Historian Toolkit**	Live Ink® Online Reading Help Student Edition on Audio CD Program Differentiated Instruction Modified Worksheets and Tests CD-ROM Interactive Skills Tutor CD-ROM United States History Primary Source Library CD-ROM Power Presentations with Video CD-ROM History's Impact: American History Video Program (VHS/DVD): A Push for Reform Online Chapter Summaries in Spanish Graphic Organizer Transparencies
Section 1: **New Movements in America** **The Main Idea:** A revival in religion in the early 1800s helped lead to an era of reform.	**Differentiated Instruction Teacher Management System:** Section 1 Lesson Plan* **Interactive Reader and Study Guide:** Section 1 Summary* **Chapter Resource File:*** • Vocabulary Builder Activity, Section 1	Daily Bellringer Transparency: Section 1* Daily Test Practice Transparency: Section 1*
Section 2: **Early Immigration and Urban Reform** **The Main Idea:** A wave of Irish and German immigrants entered the United States during a period of urbanization and reform.	**Differentiated Instruction Teacher Management System:** Section 2 Lesson Plan* **Interactive Reader and Study Guide:** Section 2 Summary* **Chapter Resource File:*** • Vocabulary Builder Activity, Section 2	Daily Bellringer Transparency: Section 2* Daily Test Practice Transparency: Section 2*
Section 3: **Women and Reform** **The Main Idea:** After leading reform movements to help others, some American women began to work on behalf of themselves.	**Differentiated Instruction Teacher Management System:** Section 3 Lesson Plan* **Interactive Reader and Study Guide:** Section 3 Summary* **Chapter Resource File:*** • Vocabulary Builder Activity, Section 3	Daily Bellringer Transparency: Section 3* Daily Test Practice Transparency: Section 3*
Section 4: **Fighting Against Slavery** **The Main Idea:** The movement to end slavery dominated the Reform Era.	**Differentiated Instruction Teacher Management System:** Section 4 Lesson Plan* **Interactive Reader and Study Guide:** Section 4 Summary* **Chapter Resource File:*** • Vocabulary Builder Activity, Section 4	Daily Bellringer Transparency: Section 4* Map Transparency: Major Routes to Freedom* Daily Test Practice Transparency: Section 4*

HOLT

History's Impact
American History Video Program (VHS/DVD)
A Push for Reform

Review, Assessment, Intervention

 Quick Facts Transparency: A Push for Reform

Spanish Chapter Summaries Audio CD Program

 Progress Assessment Support System (PASS):
Chapter Test*

**Differentiated Instruction Modified Worksheets and Tests
CD-ROM:** Modified Chapter Test

OSP **One-Stop Planner CD-ROM:** ExamView Test Generator
(English/Spanish)

HOAP **Holt Online Assessment Program (HOAP),** in the Holt
Premier Online Student Edition

 PASS: Section 1 Quiz*

 Online Quiz: Section 1

Alternative Assessment Handbook

 PASS: Section 2 Quiz*

 Online Quiz: Section 2

Alternative Assessment Handbook

 PASS: Section 3 Quiz*

Online Quiz: Section 3

Alternative Assessment Handbook

PASS: Section 4 Quiz*

Online Quiz: Section 4

Alternative Assessment Handbook

NC RESOURCES

The following resources were developed to help
North Carolina educators teach the standards and
objectives of North Carolina's eleventh grade standard
course of study in United States history.

- United States history EOC Test Prep Workbook
- Teacher's Support System
- North Carolina One-Stop Planner

And be sure to direct your
students to **go.hrw.com** for
online access to the EOC
Test Prep Workbook.

go.hrw.com
EOC Test Prep
KEYWORD: SE7 NC

Holt Online Learning

go.hrw.com
Teacher Resources
KEYWORD: SD7 TEACHER

go.hrw.com
Student Resources
KEYWORD: SD7 CH8

- Document-based
  Questions
- Interactive Multimedia
  Activities

- Current Events
- Chapter-based Internet
  Activities
- and more!

Holt Premier
Online Student Edition
Complete online support for
interactivity, assessment, and
reporting

- Interactive Maps and
  Notebook
- Standardized Test Prep
- Homework Practice
  and Research
  Activities Online

CHAPTER 8 PLANNING GUIDE

Before You Teach

The Big Picture
Deborah Gray White

New Movements in America The Second Great Awakening occurred during the 1820s and 1830s. Led by Protestant ministers, it spawned reform movements which lasted until the Civil War. Working on the belief that people controlled their destiny and could perfect their society, a great deal of education, temperance, and prison reform was undertaken.

Early Immigration and Urban Reform By 1860, America was home to 3 million Irish and German immigrants. The mostly poor and Catholic Irish met more discrimination than the wealthier Protestant Germans. Threatened by the Irish, nativists founded the Know-Nothings organization, which enjoyed some political success. The new urban working class lived and worked in unhealthy conditions, and efforts at reform were largely unsuccessful.

Women and Reform Although women were in the forefront of the reform movement, they were limited by their legal, economic, political, and cultural inequality. Those active in the movement to abolish slavery drew parallels between their inequality and that of the enslaved. The 1848 Seneca Falls Convention marked the beginning of the women's movement to achieve total equality with men.

Slavery and Abolition Under slavery African Americans worked endless hours and lived lives of want and fear, but nevertheless found myriad ways to survive. Some escaped alone or with the help of the Underground Railroad; a few revolted. The abolitionist movement, led first by free blacks who were subsequently joined by prominent whites, was not popular in either the North or the South. In response to abolitionism, southerners constructed elaborate arguments to justify slavery. Although first unpopular in the North, abolitionism there was gradually accepted.

Recent Scholarship

Race and Class In *Wages of Whiteness: Race and the Making of the American Working Class*, historian David Roediger connects the histories of race, labor, and immigration from 1800 to the Civil War. In this thoroughly original work, Roediger shows us how wage laborers differentiated themselves from the enslaved, how the working class defined manhood, how the Irish became accepted as white Americans, and how race came to supersede class as a major category of differentiation in America, The book helps us understand the mentality of immigrants and the American working class on the eve of the Civil War.

Differentiating Instruction

 Differentiated Instruction Teacher
Management System
- Lesson Plans for Differentiated Instruction
- Differentiated Instructional Benchmarking Guides
- Interactive Reader and Study Guide

 Spanish Chapter Summaries Audio CD Program

 Online Chapter Summaries in Spanish

 Student Edition on Audio CD Program

 Differentiated Instruction Modified Worksheets and Tests CD-ROM
- Vocabulary Flash Cards
- Modified Vocabulary Builder Activities
- Modified Chapter Review Activity
- Modified Chapter Test

OSP One-Stop Planner CD-ROM
- ExamView Test Generator (English and Spanish)
- PuzzlePro
- Quiz Show for ExamView
- Transparencies and Videos

TE Differentiated Activities in the Teacher's Edition
- Living at Walden Pond, p. 271
- Women's Roles, p. 281
- Slaves' Lives, p. 285
- African American Music in the Old South, p. 286

Reading Like a Historian
Sam Wineburg

Presentism and History

When my daughter applied for college last year she filled in a bubble form to indicate her racial status as Caucasian, African American, Hispanic American, Native American, or Pacific Islander. As I glanced at the form I couldn't help but think how she and I might have responded had this question been asked a generation or two ago.

Shifting Racial Categories

We tend to view our racial categories as biologically-determined schemes that rest on science, and students often assume an unwavering stability across time. But history shows us that such categories are more loose than fixed, more dependent on politics, culture, and ideology than any body of science.

The Irish and Racism

Section 2 of our chapter, beginning on page 272, describes the plight faced by Irish immigrants as they escaped famine in Ireland and sought refuge in the United States. We are told that the discrimination faced by the Irish was a function of their Catholicism, which rubbed the wrong way against Americans' predominant Protestantism. Another source of resentment was their willingness to take low-paying jobs, further depressing wages for other Americans. Moreover, the Irish tended to cluster in urban areas rather than fanning out across the land like "good" German immigrants. Yet there is one other intriguing factor that contributed to anti-Irish sentiment: the Irish faced racial discrimination. That's right, racial. At the turn of the century, the Irish were considered to be their own race.

The notion of a pan-white racial group—Caucasians—is a historical development that emerged and took hold over several decades before and following World War II. In postbellum America, other racial categories proliferated: Nordic, Anglo-Saxon, Negroid, Slav, Alpine, Hebrew, Mediterranean, Iberic, and Latin. A special category, "Celts," was reserved for the Irish.

Importing Ideas

Like America's legal system and many of its institutions, ideas about the Irish were British imports. Writing to his wife in 1842, the Victorian novelist Charles Kingsley (1819–1875) described a trip to Ireland in which he was still haunted by visions of the "human chimpanzees." "To see white chimpanzees is dreadful; if they were black, one would not feel it so much."

The association between the Irishman and ape became common on this side of the Atlantic. A Thomas Nast illustration published in *Harpers Weekly* in 1876 shows an African American and a hirsute Irishman, half human, half ape, sitting across from each other balancing a giant scale. The message, Nast surely hoped his readers would glean, was the equivalence in ignorance and barbarism of these two sub-human species.

Ideas about Irish racial qualities were not restricted to cartoons. In 1879 *The North American Review*, the scholarly journal edited by Henry James and his assistant Henry Cabot Lodge, published an essay arguing that Irish Catholicism was a function of Irish racial features, not vice versa. Compared to those of Anglo-Saxon ancestry, the Irish were "separate in blood, separate in religion."

Categories Change

In the years following World War II, the racial categories that seemed so natural in the 1880s and 1890s began a period of flux. Among non-Anglo-Saxon whites, differences that once determined employment or housing options would, in the words of Matthew Frye Jacobson, author of *Whiteness of a Different Color* (1998), "cease to register as *racial* at all."

In *Truth in History* (1979) Harvard's Oscar Handlin warned other historians about reading current racial divisions back onto the past. "It may or may not have been correct to speak of 'whites' or of the 'white community' in New York or Chicago of the 1960s; it was grossly inaccurate to do so for those cities before 1930." When it comes to race, the way we divide ourselves up is anything but "natural."

From *Truth in History* by Oscar Handlin. Published by Belknap Press, a division of Harvard University Press, Cambridge, MA, 1979.

From *Whiteness of a Different Color* by Matthew Frye Jacobson. Published by Harvard University Press, Cambridge, MA, 1998.

Social Studies Competency Goals

Goal 2 The learner will assess the competing forces of expansionism, nationalism, and sectionalism.

Goal 3 The learner will analyze the issues that led up to the Civil War, the effects of the war, and the impact of Reconstruction on the nation.

2.01, 3.01

The Big Idea and Essential Questions

To foster student understanding of this chapter's big idea, design your lesson to address each section's essential question.

Big Idea Reformers changed the face of America by improving conditions in prisons, factories, and cities, as well as working for women's rights and the end of slavery.

Essential Questions

1. What role did religion play in launching an era of reform?

2. What drew large numbers of Irish and German immigrants to the United States during this period?

3. How did the women's rights movement develop?

4. Why was the movement to end slavery so significant during this period?

Key to Differentiating Instruction

Below Level

Basic-level activities designed for all students encountering new material

At Level

Intermediate-level activities designed for average students

Above Level

Challenging activities designed for honors and gifted-and-talented students

Standard English Mastery

Activities designed to improve standard English usage

264 CHAPTER 8

CHAPTER 8 1830–1860

A Push for REFORM

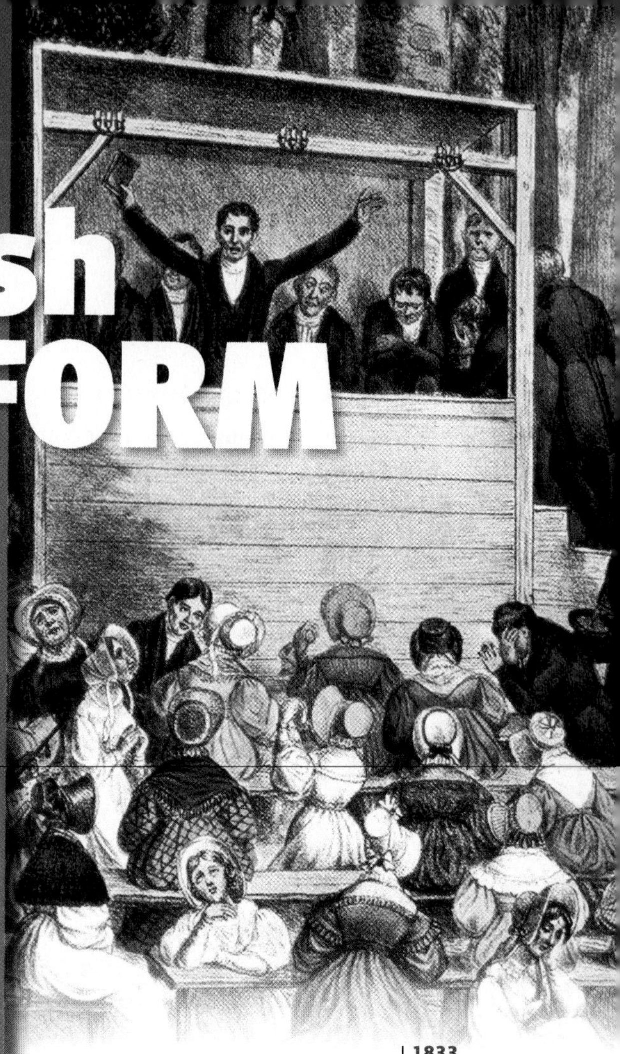

THE BIG PICTURE The religious revival called the Second Great Awakening set off one of the great periods of social reform in American history. Inspired to do good works, the reformers changed the face of America.

North Carolina Standards

Social Studies Objectives

2.05 Identify the major reform movements and evaluate their effectiveness.

2.06 Evaluate the role of religion in the debate over slavery and other social movements and issues.

Language Arts Objectives

5.01 Interpret the significance of literary movements as they have evolved through the literature of the United States by:

- evaluating the literary merit and/or historical significance of a work from Colonial Literature, the Romantic Era, Realism, the Modern Era, and Contemporary Literature.

Skills FOCUS READING LIKE A HISTORIAN

The religious fervor that swept the nation can be seen in the 1836 engraving *Methodist Camp Meeting*, by E. W. Clay. The humble settings helped drive home the preacher's message. **Interpreting Visuals** Examine the response of the people in the crowd. How are they affected by the speaker?

See Skills Handbook, p. H30

264

U.S.

1830

World

1833 Oberlin becomes the first American college to admit women.

William Lloyd Garrison founds American Anti-Slavery Society.

1835

1833 Parliament outlaws slavery throughout the British Empire.

Introduce the Chapter

At Level

A Push for Reform

1. Ask students what reforms they think might be needed to solve social problems in education, in the prison system, in growing cities, and in civil rights for women and African Americans. List student answers for all to see. Ask: How do you think ordinary people could achieve these reforms?

2. Tell students that in this chapter they are going to learn about social problems that faced the United Sates and the reform

movement that helped change and improve the country.

3. Have students write a speech in which they call on friends and neighbors to join a reform movement to make the community, and the country, a better place for all. **Verbal-Linguistic**

Alternative Assessment Handbook, Rubric 43: Writing to Persuade

[NEG. #44227] COLLECTION OF THE NEW-YORK HISTORICAL SOCIETY

1843
Dorothea Dix campaigns to improve conditions in prisons and almshouses.

1845
Abolitionist Frederick Douglass publishes his *Autobiography*.

1852
Massachusetts passes mandatory school attendance law.

1860
One in six Americans lives in a city. Some 30 percent of Americans work in manufacturing.

1840 | **1845** | **1850** | **1855** | **1860**

1845
Blight devastates Ireland's potato crop, leading to famine.

1848
Social revolutions demanding constitutional government break out across much of Europe.

1859
Charles Darwin's *On the Origin of Species* is published.

265

Chapter Preview

HOLT
History's Impact
▶ Video Program: A Push for Reform
See the Video Teacher's Guide for strategies for using the video segment.

Reading Like a Historian

Camp Meeting Have students take a moment to examine the image on these pages. Many of the attendants sitting in the pews in front of the speaker seem to be praying; the men who are praying are separated from the women. Other people around the edges of the crowd appear to be less interested in the presenter. White tents in the background indicate that the participants intended to stay for more than a day. Ask the students how might the setting of this event provide clues about it? *Possible answer—the site, in deep woods, appears remote and not usually inhabited; setting up the meeting here signals that the event was a special occasion*

go.hrw.com
Online Resources

Chapter Resources:
KEYWORD: SD7 CH8

Teacher Resources:
KEYWORD: SD7 TEACHER

Explore the Time Line

1. When were women first admitted to colleges in the United States? *1833*

2. What happened in Britain in the same year that the American Anti-Slavery Society was founded? *Slavery was outlawed throughout the British Empire.*

3. Why is 1848 a significant year in European world history? *Social revolutions, with demands for constitutional governments, broke out in much of Europe.*

Info to Know

German Aid Societies Some societies were formed to help new immigrants adjust to their new home and prosper. The German Society of New York City was this type of organization. It worked for the passage of state and federal laws to protect immigrants, and it succeeded despite heavy opposition. The German Society still exists today.

Drawing Conclusions Why do you think immigrants needed organized help when they arrived in the United States? *They faced many challenges including a new language, different customs, and discrimination.*

Answers

Reading Like a Historian (p. 264)
the people near the speaker appear to be deeply affected; those sitting farther back are interested, but not praying; those at the edge of the crowd are not paying attention

Bellringer

The Inside Story. . . Use the **Daily Bellringer Transparency** to help students answer the question.

📇 Daily Bellringer Transparency, Section 1

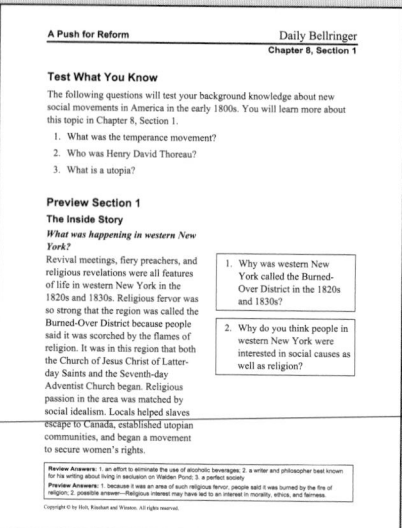

A Push for Reform   Daily Bellringer
                                    Chapter 8, Section 1

Test What You Know

The following questions will test your background knowledge about new social movements in America in the early 1800s. You will learn more about this topic in Chapter 8, Section 1.

1. What was the temperance movement?
2. Who was Henry David Thoreau?
3. What is a utopia?

Preview Section 1
The Inside Story
What was happening in western New York?
Revival meetings, fiery preachers, and religious revelations were all features of life in western New York in the 1820s and 1830s. Religious fervor was so strong that the region was called the Burned-Over District because people said it was scorched by the flames of religion. It was in this region that both the Church of Jesus Christ of Latter-day Saints and the Seventh-day Adventist Church began. Religious passion in the area was matched by social idealism. Locals helped slaves escape to Canada, established utopian communities, and began a movement to secure women's rights.

1. Why was western New York called the Burned-Over District in the 1820s and 1830s?

2. Why do you think people in western New York were interested in social causes as well as religion?

Review Answers: 1. an effort to eliminate the use of alcoholic beverages; 2. a writer and philosopher best known for his writing about living in seclusion on Walden Pond; 3. a perfect society
Preview Answers: 1. because it was an area of such religious fervor, people said it was burned by the fire of religion; 2. possible answer—Religious interest may have led to an interest in morality, ethics, and fairness.

Copyright © by Holt, Rinehart and Winston. All rights reserved.

Academic Vocabulary

Review with students the high-use academic term in this section.

ideal honorable or worthy goal (p. 270)

📄 CRF: Vocabulary Builder Activity, Section 1

Taking Notes

Temperance—eliminate use of alcoholic beverages; Education—extend and improve common schools; Prisons—change the inhumane conditions of prisons and create institutions to house and treat mentally ill people separate from criminals

SECTION 1 New Movements in America

BEFORE YOU READ

MAIN IDEA

A revival in religion in the early 1800s helped lead to an era of reform.

READING FOCUS

1. How did religion help lead to reform?
2. What role did Horace Mann play in reforming education?
3. What role did Dorothea Dix play in reforming prisons?
4. What are transcendentalism and utopianism?

KEY TERMS AND PEOPLE

Charles Grandison Finney
Second Great Awakening
Reform Era
temperance movement
Horace Mann
Dorothea Dix
transcendentalist movement
Ralph Waldo Emerson
Henry David Thoreau
utopian movement

TAKING NOTES As you read, take notes about the goals of major reform movements in the early 1800s. Record your notes in a graphic organizer like the one shown here.

Reform Movement	Goals
Temperance	
Education	
Prisons	

THE INSIDE STORY

What was happening in western New York? In the 1820s and 1830s it seemed that people in every small town were finding a new interest in religion. Crowds flocked to prayer meetings to hear fiery preachers. So many religious revivals took place that the area was called the Burned-Over District—scorched by the flames of religion. Revival meetings were personal, public, and emotional. Unlike in many traditional churches, women were welcome to pray and even preach in public.

Several religious movements began in the Burned-Over District. Joseph Smith published the Book of Mormon based on information he says he translated from golden plates delivered by an angel. Smith's teachings led to the founding of the Church of Jesus Christ of Latter-day Saints, or the Mormons. Another revivalist was William Miller, who prophesied the Second Coming of Christ. His followers developed into the Seventh-day Adventist Church. Western New York was also home to Shaker farms, utopian communities like Oneida, and advocates of Spiritualism.

Other reform movements found support too. Western New York was a stronghold for the antislavery movement. Homes and churches were "stations" on the Underground Railroad, which helped slaves escape to Canada. The movement for women's rights also took root here. ◢

FUELED BY THE Fires of Religion

▼ American Methodists flock to a camp meeting.

266

Teach the Main Idea

At Level

New Movements in America

1. **Teach** Ask students the Reading Focus questions to teach this section.

2. **Apply** Draw a time line and list Reform Era events out of chronological order.

```
├─────────────┼─────────────┤
1835        1845        1855
```

Have students copy the time line and place the events in the proper order.

3. **Review** Review student time lines as a class. Have students correct their own papers.

4. **Practice/Homework** Tell the class that the word *utopia* comes from the Greek words for "no place." Ask students to write a brief paper on the utopian movement, considering which meaning of the word— "perfect society" or "no place"—is more suitable to describe it. **LS Visual-Spatial, Verbal-Linguistic**

📄 Alternative Assessment Handbook, Rubrics 36: Time Lines; and 37: Writing Assignments

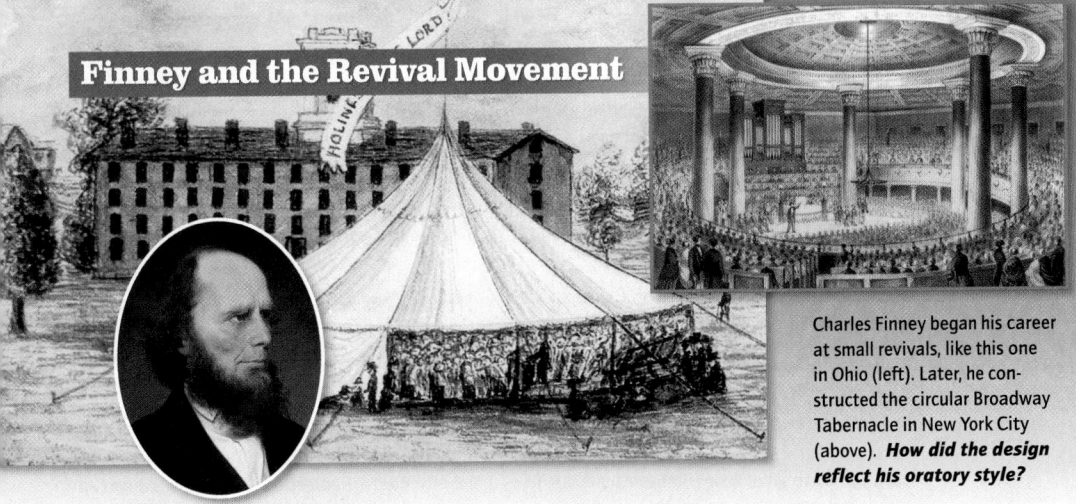

Finney and the Revival Movement

Charles Finney began his career at small revivals, like this one in Ohio (left). Later, he constructed the circular Broadway Tabernacle in New York City (above). *How did the design reflect his oratory style?*

Religion Sparks Reform

The most famous—and the most colorful—character of the Burned-Over District was a preacher named **Charles Grandison Finney**. Finney led revivals, or meetings designed to revive, or reawaken, religious feelings. Finney held revivals throughout the Burned-Over District in the 1820s and 1830s. In his memoirs, the charismatic preacher attributed his success to his way of speaking:

HISTORY'S VOICES

❝The more experience I had, the more I saw the results of my method of preaching, the more I conversed with all classes, high and low, educated and uneducated, the more was I confirmed in the fact that God had led me, had taught me, had given me right conceptions in regard to the best manner of winning souls . . . Indeed, people have often said to me: 'Why, you do not preach. You talk to the people.'❞

—Charles Grandison Finney

Finney talked to many people. At his revivals, hundreds, and sometimes thousands, of people would embrace his teachings.

The Second Great Awakening Finney was just one of many preachers who found willing audiences during the 1820s and 1830s. Across the country, but especially in the North, Americans attended revivals and joined churches in record numbers. By 1850, twice as many Americans attended church than they had at the birth of the country.

This religious movement was called the **Second Great Awakening**. A similar movement, the First Great Awakening, had taken place in the American colonies in the 1700s.

Many preachers of the Second Great Awakening were Protestant. They did not teach strict adherence to church rules, or obedience to a minister. Rather, preachers told people that "their destiny lay in their own hands." People were urged to live well and to work hard.

Further, followers were told that they had the opportunity and the responsibility to do God's work on earth. Through dedication and hard work, they were told, they could create a kind of heaven on earth. Participants in the Second Great Awakening took these beliefs to heart. Across the country, tens of thousands of Americans became determined to reform, or reshape, American life.

Thus, the Second Great Awakening helped launch a remarkable period in American history. The **Reform Era**, which lasted from about 1830 until 1860, was a time in which many Americans attempted to reshape American society. Inspired by the Second Great Awakening, the men and women who participated in the many different movements of the Reform Era are called reformers.

The temperance movement One of the main goals of the reformers was to reduce the use of alcoholic beverages. This movement is called the **temperance movement**. *Temperance* means "moderation."

A PUSH FOR REFORM **267**

Direct Teach

Reading Focus

❶ How did religion help lead to reform? *Preachers told people that they had a responsibility to do God's work on Earth.*

Religion Sparks Reform

Define What were revivals? *meetings meant to reawaken religious feelings*

Identify Cause and Effect What were some of the effects of the Second Great Awakening? *Americans joined churches; were inspired to reform American life*

Make Inferences How did the temperance movement get its name? *temperance means "moderation"; probably began as a movement to encourage moderation in drinking*

📄 CRF: History and Geography Activity: The Reform Era

Info to Know

William Miller In the 1840s a preacher named William Miller attracted some 100,000 followers with his proclamation that the apocalypse, or end of the world, would occur sometime in 1843 or 1844. When the apocalypse did not occur, Millerites revised their beliefs. Some religious denominations today have been influenced by Millerite doctrines.

go.hrw.com
Online Resources

KEYWORD: SD7 CH8
TOPIC: EARLY REFORMER: DOROTHEA DIX

Collaborative Learning

At Level

Reforms in the United States

Materials construction paper, colored markers

1. Guide students in a discussion about the Second Great Awakening and attempts to reform American society during the Reform Era.

2. Divide the class into small groups. Have each group discuss reforms they believe are needed in their school and in the United States today. Have each group make a list of reforms they believe are needed with a short explanation about the reasons why.

3. Have each group make two posters. One poster should be about school reforms; the second poster should be about national reforms.

4. Have a volunteer from each group present the group's posters to the class.
   LS Interpersonal, Visual-Spatial
   📄 Alternative Assessment Handbook, Rubric 28: Posters

Answers

Art *The design allowed a more personal experience because it was shaped so that people could gather around Finney and listen to him speak.*

2 What role did Horace Mann play in reforming education? *advocated organized system of education, mandatory attendance, normal schools*

Reforming Education

Define What were normal schools? *schools where teachers received training*

Recall What reforms in education did Horace Mann advocate? *mandatory education; the creation of normal schools; state funding for education*

Make Inferences How did *McGuffey Readers* embody Reform Era ideals? *taught moral and intellectual values*

📓 Political Cartoons Activities for American History: Cartoon 16: Anti-Prohibition Voter

Primary Sources

McGuffey Reader

Compare and Contrast What similarities and differences do you see between the *McGuffey Reader* in this picture and textbooks used today? *reader promoted morality while textbooks do not; both use excerpts from great books*

Reformers wrote books, plays, and songs about the evils of alcohol, which they linked to sickness, poverty, and the breakup of families. Reformers also founded temperance societies, or clubs, and persuaded many Americans to sign temperance pledges. In 1851 reformers persuaded legislators in the state of Maine to outlaw alcohol. Over the next several years, some 12 states followed suit.

READING CHECK **Identifying Cause and Effect** How did the Second Great Awakening help launch the Reform Era?

Reforming Education

Prior to the 1840s, American schools were either private schools or common schools—free public schools where students learned basic reading, writing, and mathematics skills. Most families could not afford private schools, and the quality of teaching in common schools was generally poor.

The common-school movement Most reform-minded Americans wanted more children to be educated. They held that educated people made better decisions and that widespread education was fundamental to a democratic society. Education reformers organized themselves into "friends of education" groups and began the common-school movement to extend and improve public schools.

Horace Mann The greatest school reformer of the Reform Era was **Horace Mann**. In 1837 he became the first secretary of education in the state of Massachusetts.

Mann advocated a new, highly organized approach to education. He envisioned systems in which states would fund and supervise locally controlled schools. Because education was so important to the individual and to society as a whole, Mann advocated compulsory attendance. He also championed the creation of so-called normal schools, where teachers would receive training.

PRIMARY SOURCES

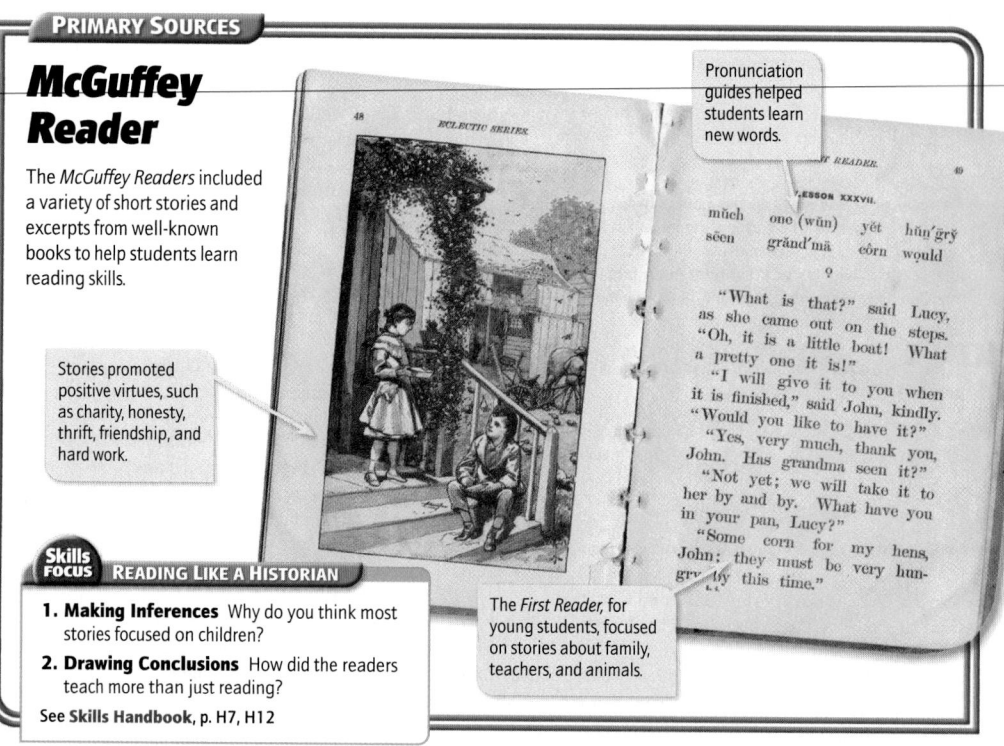

McGuffey Reader

The *McGuffey Readers* included a variety of short stories and excerpts from well-known books to help students learn reading skills.

Pronunciation guides helped students learn new words.

Stories promoted positive virtues, such as charity, honesty, thrift, friendship, and hard work.

The *First Reader*, for young students, focused on stories about family, teachers, and animals.

Skills Focus **READING LIKE A HISTORIAN**

1. **Making Inferences** Why do you think most stories focused on children?
2. **Drawing Conclusions** How did the readers teach more than just reading?

See Skills Handbook, p. H7, H12

268 CHAPTER 8

Answers

Reading Like a Historian
1. *possible answer—because stories with children would be more interesting to the children reading them;*
2. *pronunciation guides to learn new words; the stories promoted positive values such as charity and honesty*

Reading Check *teaching people that their destiny was in their own hands and that through dedication and hard work, they could create a kind of heaven on Earth*

268

Skills Focus: Making Oral Presentations

At Level

Reading Like a Historian Skill
Horace Mann and William McGuffey

1. Divide the class into small groups. Have each group write a one-act play depicting a meeting between either Horace Mann or William McGuffey and one of their contemporaries who does not support education reform. In the play, Mann and McGuffey should discuss their ideas about education. (Students may do additional, outside research if necessary.)

2. Have each group present its play for the class.

3. Guide the class in a discussion of the plays and of Mann's and McGuffey's ideas about education. What is the significance of the fact that these men who lived at the same time but became two of the most important figures in the history of American education?
LS **Interpersonal, Kinesthetic**

📓 Alternative Assessment Handbook, Rubric 33: Skits and Reader's Theater

Mann's work transformed education in Massachusetts. In 1839 Massachusetts created the country's first normal school. In 1852 it passed the first compulsory attendance law in the United States.

Other states copied Mann's education work in Massachusetts. By 1860, six in ten white children attended school—almost twice the rate of 30 years earlier. Education reform, however, did nothing to help Native American children, who lived within their tribes. Nor could it help African American children, nearly all of whom were slaves. Still, the school reformers' efforts laid the groundwork for education in the United States to the present day.

William McGuffey One of the most well known of the education reformers was William McGuffey. McGuffey wrote and published a series of textbooks called *Eclectic Readers*, which became popularly known as *McGuffey Readers*. These books, written for different grade levels, taught reading and moral and intellectual values. *McGuffey Readers* were so popular—well over 100 million were sold—that nearly every American student in the middle and late 1800s used them in school.

READING CHECK **Identifying the Main Idea** What was the goal of the common-school movement?

Reforming Prisons

Dorothea Dix was a reformer who campaigned for humane treatment of prisoners and the mentally ill. Dix visited a jail in Cambridge, Massachusetts, to teach Sunday school to prisoners in 1841. What Dix saw there appalled her. Mentally ill people and nonviolent criminals were confined with violent criminals. All were held in horribly crowded, unsanitary conditions and were often abused by their jailers.

Dix visited prisons and almshouses, or charity homes for the very poor, throughout Massachusetts. Everywhere she went, she found inhumane conditions.

In 1843 Dix petitioned the state legislature to do something about "the condition of the miserable, the desolate, the outcast" in prisons and almshouses across the state. Moved by Dix's plea, the Massachusetts legislature created state-supported institutions to house and treat mentally ill people, separate from

criminals. Dix and her supporters convinced other state governments to create similar institutions. Before Dix began her work, there were no professional treatment centers in the United States for the mentally ill. By the time of her death, more than 100 such institutions were built across the country.

READING CHECK **Summarizing** What were Dorothea Dix's main achievements?

Transcendentalism and Utopianism

One of the most remarkable movements of the Reform Era took place in New England. It was called the **transcendentalist movement**. Members of this movement believed in a philosophy called transcendentalism.

Transcendentalism is the belief that knowledge is found not only by observation of the world but also through reason, intuition, and personal spiritual experiences. Thus, by transcending, or going beyond, observation, people can have a deeper and truer understanding of the world.

Ralph Waldo Emerson The leading transcendentalist was **Ralph Waldo Emerson**. Emerson gave sermons and lectures and wrote essays and poems. In his work, Emerson expressed the transcendental belief that people should

FACES OF HISTORY

Dorothea DIX
1802–1887

A fast learner who loved to read, Dorothea Dix began teaching young students by the time she was 14. At 19 Dix opened her own school in Boston. In addition, she dedicated her spare time to helping prison inmates and the mentally ill.

While traveling in Europe, Dix met a number of reformers. Returning home, she toured a local jail where the mentally ill were chained in a dungeon. Dix demanded reforms in the treatment of prisoners and the mentally ill. She traveled the nation visiting jails and lobbying for reforms. With her support, the first state hospital was opened in New Jersey. When the Civil War erupted, Dix volunteered to lead the Army Nursing Corps for the Union.

Explain How did Dorothea Dix care for the less fortunate?

Reading Focus

❸ What role did Dorothea Dix play in reforming prisons? *petitioned Massachusetts and other state legislatures for institutions to house the mentally ill separate from criminals*

Reforming Prisons

Recall How did Dorothea Dix learn about conditions in prisons? *taught Sunday school at a jail*

Identify Cause and Effect What were the results of Dix's pleas for reform? *states created and supported institutions to house and treat mentally ill*

📄 CRF: Primary Source Activity: Dorothea Dix Pushes for Institutional Reform

Reading Focus

❹ What are transcendentalism and utopianism? *philosophy that knowledge comes from observation, reason, intuition; movement to create perfect societies*

Transcendentalism and Utopianism

Explain What is the goal of transcendentalism? *to gain a deeper understanding of the world through reason, intuition, and spiritual experiences*

Identify What transcendental belief did Ralph Waldo Emerson express in his work? *self-reliance, trust one's intuition*

Skills Focus: Identifying Cause and Effect
At Level

Reading Skill
Prison Reform

Research Required

1. Guide students in a discussion of the problems that existed in prisons at the time Dorothea Dix began her crusade, and the results of her reforms.

2. Have students conduct research on the prison system that currently exists within your state and at the national level. Students should find out how many jails and prisons exist in the U.S., the types of prisons, number of people incarcerated, and details about prison

conditions and laws that protect prisoners.

3. Have students use their research to write an essay about the prison system and any reforms they believe are needed, as well as how these reforms might be implemented. Have students include charts, graphs, and other visuals. ⬛ **Verbal-Linguistic**

📄 Alternative Assessment Handbook, Rubrics 30: Research; and 42: Writing to Inform

Answers

Faces of History *demanded reforms in the treatment of prisoners and mentally ill; led the Army Nursing Corps*

Reading Check (left) *wanted more children to be educated so they could make better decisions, which were fundamental to a democratic country;* (right) *creation of more than 100 state-supported institutions to house and treat mentally ill people separate from criminals*

269

Transcendentalism and Utopianism

Recall Which utopian communities were successful? *those established by the Shakers*

Evaluate How is Thoreau's idea of living simply connected to civil disobedience? *believed government regulations should be minimal; believed people should live simply to give their lives meaning; believed people should act according to their beliefs, even if they had to break the law*

Review & Assess

Close

Guide the class in a discussion of the Second Great Awakening and the subsequent reform movements.

Review

- Online Quiz, Section 1
- Daily Test Practice Transparency

Assess

- **SE** Section 1 Assessment
- Progress Assessment: Section 1 Quiz
- Alternative Assessment Handbook

Reteach

- Interactive Reader and Study Guide, Section 1
- Interactive Skills Tutor CD-ROM

Answers

Reading Check *similar—reform movements in the 19th century; different—Transcendentalists sought knowledge through reason, intuition, and personal spiritual experiences; Utopians believed in creating communities that would be free from social ills*

270

---

be self-reliant and trust their intuition. Such thinking, he said, would lead to a sense that all people and all of nature were connected. Thus, the transcendentalist would support social reform. Emerson's rich writing style and the power of his ideas made him one of America's most renowned and important authors.

Henry David Thoreau Another major transcendentalist was **Henry David Thoreau**. Thoreau, like Emerson, firmly believed in the power of self-reliance and individual thought.

In 1845 Thoreau began living alone in a cabin on the shore of Walden Pond, near Concord, Massachusetts. By living simply, Thoreau hoped to live a meaningful life.

Thoreau held that people should act according to their own beliefs, even if they had to break the law. In 1846 Thoreau refused to pay a tax he thought would promote slavery, and he spent a night in jail. Later, in an essay titled "Civil Disobedience," Thoreau stated "that government is best which governs least."

"Civil Disobedience" became an enormously influential essay. In the twentieth century, it inspired Mohandas Gandhi of India to develop a doctrine of nonviolent resistance that helped free his country from British rule. In the United States, civil rights leader Martin Luther King Jr. put Thoreau's and Gandhi's ideas and methods to work on behalf of African Americans in the 1960s.

ACADEMIC VOCABULARY
ideal honorable or worthy goal

Utopianism Some reformers believed in creating new communities that would be free of social ills. These communities became known as utopian communities, after the word *utopia*, which means "a perfect society." Reformers built more than 90 utopian communities in the United States during the **utopian movement** of the first half of the 1800s.

One such community was led by Robert Owen, a British social reformer. In 1825 he purchased the town of Harmonie, Indiana, and renamed it New Harmony. There he attempted to build a utopian community. Unfortunately, the residents of the community failed to implement Owen's <u>ideals</u>, and the community failed three years later.

Another famous utopian community was founded by transcendentalists in Massachusetts in 1841. Brook Farm emphasized equality among all its members. However, the community failed in 1847 due to mounting debts.

Most utopian communities were small and short-lived. A notable exception were those built by the Shakers, a Christian sect that established communities beginning in the late 1700s. In the 1830s, nearly 6,000 Shakers lived in more than a dozen communities throughout the United States.

READING CHECK **Comparing** How were the transcendentalist and the utopian movements similar and different?

SECTION 1 ASSESSMENT

go.hrw.com Online Quiz Keyword: SD7 HP8

Reviewing Ideas, Terms, and People

1. **a. Identify** Who was **Charles Grandison Finney**?
   b. Analyze How did the **Second Great Awakening** inspire the **Reform Era**?
2. **a. Identify** Who was **Horace Mann**?
   b. Evaluate How successful was the common-school movement?
3. **a. Recall** Why did **Dorothea Dix** begin her campaign?
   b. Contrast How were mentally ill people and prisoners treated differently after Dix's work?
4. **a. Identify** Who were two important members of the **transcendentalist movement**?
   b. Make Inferences How did transcendentalism support reform?
   c. Evaluate How successful was the **utopian movement**?

Critical Thinking

5. **Summarizing** Copy the chart below and identify the major movements and leaders of the Reform Era.

Movement			
Leader			

FOCUS ON WRITING

6. **Persuasive** Reformers like Dorothea Dix identified problems and then acted to solve them. Identify one aspect of American life today that you consider is a problem that should be solved. Write an editorial explaining the problem and why it should be solved. Then offer solutions to the problem. Your solutions should be feasible and realistic.

270 CHAPTER 8

Section 1 Assessment Answers

1. **a.** famous preacher
   b. taught that through hard work, people could create a kind of heaven on Earth
2. **a.** great school reformer; first secretary of education of Massachusetts
   b. very successful for white children but not for minorities; laid groundwork for today's educational system
3. **a.** visited jails and saw the inhumane conditions in which prisoners lived
   b. The mentally ill were separated from the criminals in state-funded institutions.
4. **a.** Emerson, Thoreau
   b. taught self-reliance, trusting intuition
   c. most utopian communities failed
5. Mann, common-school; McGuffey, education; Dix, prisons; Emerson, Thoreau, transcendentalist
6. possible answer—violence in schools; solutions—after-school programs, conflict resolution training for students, teachers, and parents; improved security systems; improved communication systems

American *Literature*

American Literature

About the Reading From 1845 to 1847, Henry David Thoreau, a New England transcendentalist, retreated from society to live in seclusion on Walden Pond near Concord, Massachusetts. The following excerpt is taken from a collection of Thoreau's writings from his time at Walden.

AS YOU READ Put yourself in Thoreau's place and think about the reasons why he may have wanted to live in seclusion.

Excerpt from

Walden

by Henry David Thoreau

The surface of the earth is soft and impressible by the feet of men; and so with the paths which the mind travels. How worn and dusty, then, must be the highways of the world, how deep the ruts of conformity! I did not wish to take a cabin passage, but rather to go before the mast and on the deck of the world, for there I could best see the moonlight and the mountains. I do not wish to go below now.

I learned this, at least, by my experiment; that if one advances confidently in the direction of his dreams, and endeavors to live the life which he has imagined, he will meet with a success unexpected in common hours. He will put some things behind, will pass an invisible boundary; new, universal, and more liberal laws will begin to establish themselves around and within him; or the old laws be expanded, and interpreted in his favor in a more liberal sense, and he will live with the license of a higher order of beings. In proportion as he simplifies his life, the laws of the universe will appear less complex, and solitude will not be solitude, nor poverty poverty, nor weakness weakness.

It is a ridiculous demand which England and America make, that you shall speak so that they can understand you. Neither men nor toad-stools grow so. As if that were important, and there were not enough to understand you without them. As if Nature could support but one order of understandings . . . I desire to speak somewhere *without* bounds; like a man in a waking moment, to men in their waking moments; for I am convinced that I cannot exaggerate enough even to lay the foundation of a true expression.

Skills FOCUS — READING LIKE A HISTORIAN

1. **Summarizing** What does Thoreau mean when he writes that he desires "to speak somewhere without bounds"?

2. **Literature as Historical Evidence** How does Thoreau's call for personal renewal and self-reliance reflect a larger call for reform in the 1830s and 1840s?

See **Skills Handbook**, p. H6

Walden Pond, Massachusetts, where Thoreau lived for two years

271

Word Help

Excerpt from *Walden*

insensibly without realizing

impressible may be marked with pressure

conformity endeavors in accordance with accepted behavior

license freedom

sustain support

quadruped an animal with four feet

Bright a common name for an ox

Meet the Writer

Henry David Thoreau Henry David Thoreau was born in Concord, Massachusetts, in 1817, and educated at Harvard University. After working as a teacher and tutor, he lived in the home of his friend and poet Ralph Waldo Emerson. Thoreau is best known for his book *Walden; or, Life in the Woods*, which tells of the two years he spent in a hut he built by himself on the shores of Walden Pond.

In 1846, Thoreau spent a night in jail rather than pay his poll tax. Out of that experience came his famous essay, "Civil Disobedience."

Differentiating Instruction

Below Level

English Language Learners; Learners Having Difficulty

1. Divide the class into small groups. Have each group discuss Emerson's idea of self-reliance and how Thoreau took it to heart by living at Walden Pond.

2. Guide students in a discussion of everyday life for a New Englander in the 1840s. Have each group discuss and list ways in which Thoreau's experience at Walden Pond might differ from someone's experience living apart from other people today. Then have groups explain why it would have been easier for Thoreau to make the adjustment than for someone living today. **LS Interpersonal, Visual-Spatial**

📖 Alternative Assessment Handbook, Rubric 11: Discussions

Answers

Reading Like a Historian 1. *have true freedom of speech;* **2.** *he was calling for personal reform and reevaluation at a time when people were calling for a reevaluation and reshaping of society*

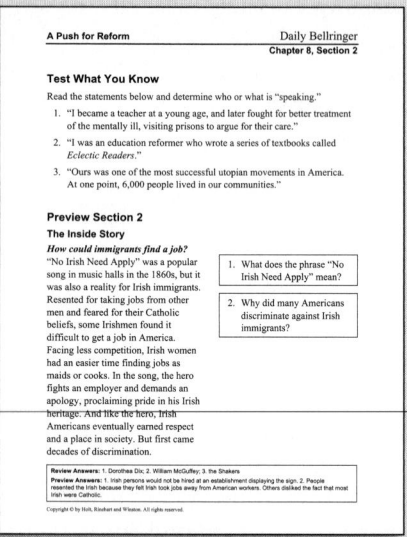

Early Immigration and Urban Reform

BEFORE YOU READ

MAIN IDEA

A wave of Irish and German immigrants entered the United States during a period of urbanization and reform.

READING FOCUS

1. Why did many Irish and Germans immigrate to the United States in the 1840s and 1850s?
2. What was life in the United States like for the new immigrants?
3. How did urbanization and industrialization lead to reform?

KEY TERMS AND PEOPLE

Great Irish Famine
push-pull model of immigration
nativism
Know-Nothings
tenements
wage earners
urban working class
labor movement
Martin Van Buren

 As you read, take notes on the Irish experience of immigration to the United States. Record your notes on the causes for Irish immigration, the treatment immigrants received, and where immigrants settled in a graphic organizer like the one shown here.

Causes   Treatment
Irish Immigration
Settlement

DISCRIMINATION Set to Music

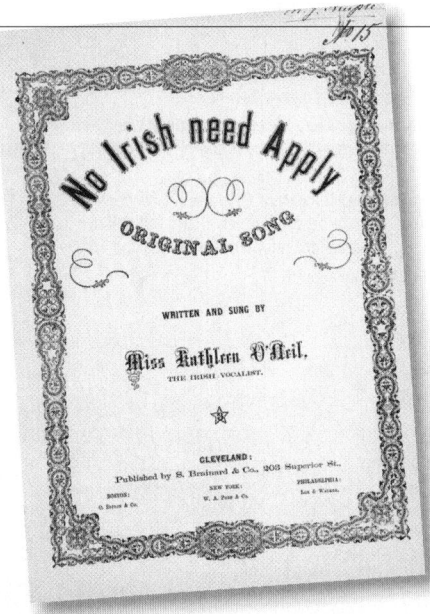

▲ This song described the discrimination that Irish immigrants sometimes faced.

THE INSIDE STORY

How could immigrants find a job? Music hall singers in the 1860s could always please an audience with the song "No Irish Need Apply." The song tells how a boy from Ireland tries to get a job, even though the ad says, "No Irish need apply." The employer insults him, but the angry young Irishman fights him and makes him apologize. In the song's chorus, he remains proud of his heritage: "But to me it is an honor / To be born an Irishman."

Irish immigrants in the mid-1800s faced widespread discrimination. Newspaper ads and signs in shop and factory windows read "No Irish need apply" or "Protestants only." Some historians question how widespread these signs actually were. But American workers resented the Irish for taking scarce jobs, especially low-paying jobs on the docks or as day laborers. Others mistrusted the Irish for being Roman Catholic. The signs were aimed mainly at Irish Catholic men. In general, Irish women found jobs as cooks or maids more easily. Eventually, Irish immigrants overcame prejudice to find their place in American society. ■

Irish and German Immigrants

The sadness of the song "No Irish Need Apply" is apparent. What makes the song even sadder, though, is that many of the Irish immigrants who faced this prejudice were desperate refugees fleeing one of the great disasters of the modern age.

Teach the Main Idea

At Level

Early Immigration and Urban Reform

1. **Teach** Ask students the Reading Focus questions to teach this section.

2. **Apply** Have students create an outline of the section using the red and blue heads as main points. Have students identify at least two main ideas under each of the blue subheadings.

3. **Review** Review student outlines as a class. Have students identify the points in their outlines that they believe are most important to immigration and reform. Guide students

in a discussion of nativism and how it affects immigration.

4. **Practice/Homework** Have each student write a brief essay comparing the patterns of immigration and experiences of Irish immigrants with those of German immigrants. **LS Logical-Mathematical, Verbal-Linguistic**

Alternative Assessment Handbook, Rubric 9: Comparing and Contrasting

Irish immigration Since the 1700s, the poor people of Ireland had relied on the potato as their staple, or major, food crop. In fact, most people of Ireland ate little else. From 1845 to 1849, a disease, or blight, struck the crop, severely restricting the potato harvest.

The results were devastating. Deprived of their primary food source and receiving little relief from the ruling British government, Ireland's poor faced starvation. By 1850 about 1 million had died during the **Great Irish Famine**.

Desperate to save themselves and their families, more than 2 million people left Ireland. By 1854, about 1.5 million of them had settled in the United States.

German immigration The other major group of immigrants to the United States in the mid-1800s were the Germans. Like the Irish, many Germans were fleeing conditions in their homeland. Unlike the Irish, they had not faced famine. Instead, they left Germany for many different reasons. Some fled economic depression and overpopulation, which made jobs scarce. Others left to escape religious persecution, harsh tax laws, or military service. Still others fled their country after a revolution in 1848 failed. Many Germans came to the United States in search of free land and business opportunities.

Pushed and pulled All immigration can be described using the **push-pull model of immigration**. In this model, factors that cause people to leave their homeland are "pushes." Factors that cause people to move to a particular country are called "pulls." Various pushes and pulls led to a record number of immigrants to the United States, including about 3 million Irish and German immigrants by 1860.

READING CHECK **Summarizing** What caused German and Irish immigrants to be pushed from their homelands?

The Lives of Immigrants

The lives that immigrants built in the United States varied widely. Wealthy people with family or other connections in the United States did well. The majority of immigrants, however,

THE IMPACT TODAY

Daily Life
In the 2000 census, about 30 million Americans indicated they had Irish ancestry and about 43 million Americans claimed German ancestry.

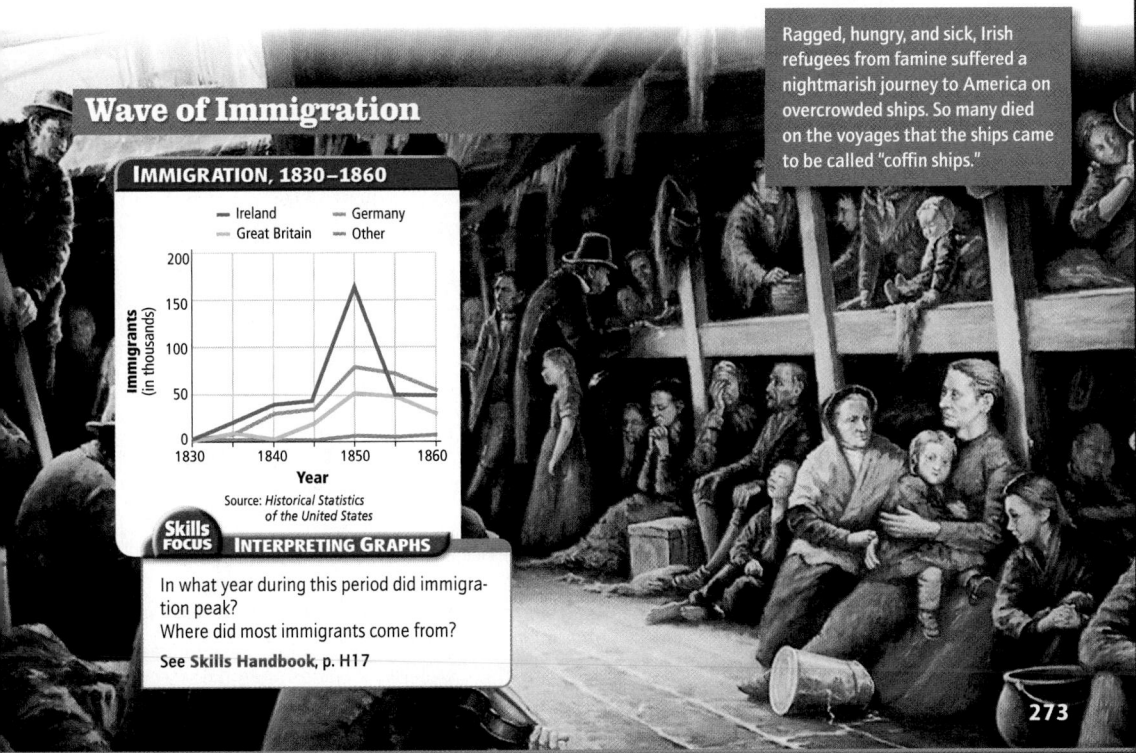

Wave of Immigration

IMMIGRATION, 1830–1860

- Ireland
- Great Britain
- Germany
- Other

Immigrants (in thousands)

Year: 1830, 1840, 1850, 1860

Source: *Historical Statistics of the United States*

Skills FOCUS **INTERPRETING GRAPHS**

In what year during this period did immigration peak?
Where did most immigrants come from?

See Skills Handbook, p. H17

Ragged, hungry, and sick, Irish refugees from famine suffered a nightmarish journey to America on overcrowded ships. So many died on the voyages that the ships came to be called "coffin ships."

273

273

2 What was life in the United States like for the new immigrants? *most Irish faced a difficult struggle, discrimination; most Germans had easier time*

The Lives of Immigrants

Identify What was the American Party? *political party organized by the Know-Nothings, a secret anti-immigrant organization*

Explain Why did German immigrants spread across the country rather than settle near ports of entry? *could afford to travel; sought free or cheap land and reunion with relatives*

Elaborate Why did many Americans believe that Roman Catholicism was at odds with democratic principles? *thought it did not acknowledge right of the people to govern, did not tolerate freedom of conscience or opinion*

Recent Scholarship

In *Strangers in the Land: Patterns of American Nativism, 1860–1925*, author John Higham argues that nativism was a constant issue throughout U.S. history, and that it had a cyclical pattern. In times of prosperity, nativism faded; in times of economic depression, it surfaced. Higham also analyzes what he sees as the three main reasons for opposition to immigration throughout American history: anti-Catholicism, anti-Semitism, and racism.

Strangers in the Land: Patterns of American Nativism, 1860–1925 by John Higham. Rutgers University Press, 2002

Answers

Reading Like a Historian *image on the right, due to his poverty*

274

---

had little or no money and often no one to turn to for help. They faced a difficult struggle to survive in, what was to them, an alien and often hostile land.

Hostility toward the Irish Many immigrant groups to the United States have faced <u>discrimination</u>. Few immigrant groups, however, met the hostility that the Irish did.

Why were the Irish treated so harshly? One reason was their sheer numbers. More than 1.3 million Irish immigrants arrived between 1846 and 1855. The country's population in that period averaged 24 million. The largest city at the time, New York, was home to only half a million people. Many Americans viewed the influx of so many people from a single foreign country as a threat to their way of life.

The Irish were also resented because of their poverty. Because desperate Irish immigrants would work for very low wages, they posed a threat to American workers.

Above all else, though, Irish immigrants were resented because they were Roman Catholic. The United States at the time was predominantly Protestant. Many Americans believed that the Roman Catholic religion was

ACADEMIC VOCABULARY

discrimination treatment based on race, class, or category rather than individual merit

at odds with democratic principles. Samuel F. B. Morse, who invented the first practical telegraph, was one such American. Describing Roman Catholicism as "Popery," he reflected the biased view of many Americans of the time.

HISTORY'S VOICES

❝Popery cannot tolerate our form of government . . . Popery does not acknowledge the right of the people to govern; but claims for itself the supreme right to govern all people and all rulers by divine right . . . It does not tolerate liberty of conscience nor liberty of opinion.❞

—Samuel F. B. Morse

As the number of Irish immigrants grew, so too did these feelings of **nativism**, or opposition to immigration. The growth of nativism was a marked change in Americans' attitudes. For generations, immigrants had been generally welcomed as adding to the population and prosperity of a growing country. Besides, most Americans were descended from immigrants—many just a generation or two in the past. But the influx of a huge number of poor, Catholic, Irish immigrants in such a short time changed many Americans' views. They began to regard immigrants as a threat to their way of life.

TWO PORTRAYALS OF IMMIGRATION

Skills FOCUS READING LIKE A HISTORIAN

These images show two portrayals of Irish immigrants.

Interpreting Visuals Which image is more likely to create bias against Irish immigrants? Explain your answer.

MUSEUM OF THE CITY OF NEW YORK

© COLLECTION OF THE NEW-YORK HISTORICAL SOCIETY

Skills Focus: Identifying Cause and Effect

At Level

Reading Skill
Nativism

1. To help students understand why some Americans responded so negatively to Irish immigration, copy the graphic organizer below for students to see. Omit the italicized answers.

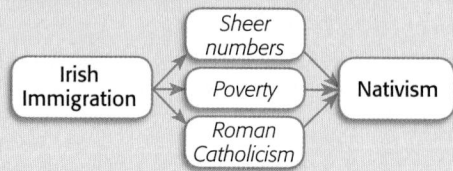

Irish Immigration → *Sheer numbers* / *Poverty* / *Roman Catholicism* → Nativism

Have students copy the graphic organizer and fill it in with the characteristics of Irish immigrants that led to the rise of nativist feelings.

2. Review student work as a class. Have students retain the graphic organizer as a study tool.

LS Visual-Spatial, Verbal-Linguistic

Alternative Assessment Handbook, Rubrics 13: Graphic Organizers; and 17: Letters to Editors

Graphic Organizer Transparencies

The Know-Nothings Anti-immigrant sentiment was promoted by well-funded and well-organized social and political groups. One such group was a secret fraternal organization called the **Know-Nothings**. The group earned its name because its members, when asked about their group's activities, answered by saying, "I know nothing."

The Know-Nothings reorganized themselves into a political party. The American Party would boast of more than 1 million members by the 1850s. They achieved remarkable political success in a short time, claiming more than 40 congressional seats. When they won elections in Massachusetts, one newspaper trumpeted the news.

HISTORY'S VOICES

❝ . . . [In Massachusetts] are heard the voices of her native born children, declaring for the perpetuity AMERICAN INSTITUTIONS, and AMERICAN LIBERTIES. The [people] have spoken in a voice of thunder, in favor of Americans ruling America . . . the warm pulsation of the people's heart beats only for FREEDOM . . . and PROTESTANTISM. ❞
—*Daily Evening Journal*, November 14, 1854

The American Party even ran a presidential candidate in 1856. Eventually disagreements over slavery and related political issues fractured the party, and it ceased to exist by the time of the Civil War.

A different German experience Nearly as many Germans as Irish immigrated to the United States in the mid-1800s. Fortunately for the Germans, they did not encounter the same hostility that greeted Irish immigrants. Why not? Whereas most Irish immigrants were poor and Catholic, most German immigrants were middle class and Protestant.

German immigrants spread across the country. They could afford to travel far inland, seeking free or cheap land, reunions with relatives, or other opportunities in the heartland. Many settled in the Midwest, but large German immigrant communities could be found from New York to Texas. German immigrants worked as farmers, artisans, factory workers, and in other occupations.

READING CHECK Contrasting How were Irish immigrants treated differently than German immigrants?

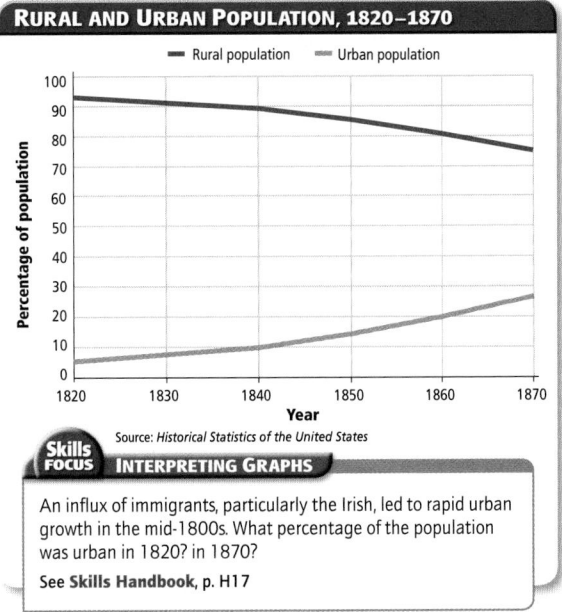

RURAL AND URBAN POPULATION, 1820–1870

— Rural population — Urban population

Percentage of population (y-axis: 0–100)
Year (x-axis: 1820–1870)

Source: *Historical Statistics of the United States*

Skills FOCUS INTERPRETING GRAPHS

An influx of immigrants, particularly the Irish, led to rapid urban growth in the mid-1800s. What percentage of the population was urban in 1820? in 1870?

See Skills Handbook, p. H17

Reform, Urbanization, and Industrialization

Immigrants to the United States in the middle 1800s arrived in a country undergoing two dramatic changes. One was urbanization. In 1800 about 1 in 20 Americans lived in urban areas; by 1860 about 1 in 6 did. The other change was industrialization. In 1800 nearly everything in the country was made by hand. By 1860 about one-third of all goods were made by machine. The parallel forces of urbanization and industrialization caused tremendous social change and resulted in important reform movements.

Growing city populations The arrival of so many Irish immigrants in the 1840s and 1850s was a major factor in the growth of some American cities. Most Irish immigrants, unable to afford to travel far from where they landed in America, settled in northeastern cities such as New York and Boston. By 1850 Irish immigrants accounted for one-fourth of the population of these cities. Even today, both have large Irish American populations.

A PUSH FOR REFORM **275**

275

Reading Focus

Reform, Urbanization, and Industrialization

Recall How did the labor movement get its start? *Artisans formed organizations to regulate their pay.*

Explain Why did the labor movement face opposition from government officials? *Many officials owned businesses or sympathized with wealthy business owners.*

Evaluate Would it have been in the best interests of business owners to reform their own workplaces or continue to try to maximize profits with long work hours and low wages? *possible answers—maximize profits: workers were replaceable, willing to work for what was offered; reform: minimize injuries and accidents, create body of loyal, trained workers who would help company profit*

📝 CRF: Biography: Sarah Bagley

Linking to Today
Aiding New Immigrants
Describe In the 1970s, Congress passed two laws designed to aid new immigrants. The Bilingual Education Act of 1974 increased funding for public schools to provide instruction to students in their primary languages while they learned English. The Voting Rights Act of 1975 required states and communities with a large number of non-English-speaking residents to print voting materials in various foreign languages.

go.hrw.com
Online Resources
KEYWORD: SD7 CH8
TOPIC: IMMIGRATION, PAST
AND PRESENT

Answers

Linking to Today *desire for a better life*

276

Linking TO Today

Immigration

In the past, most immigrants to the United States came from European nations. Today growing numbers of immigrants come from Mexico, Central America, South America, and Asia.

In 2003 more than 244,000 people born in Asia moved to the United States. Nearly 116,000 people came from Mexico, and almost 110,000 others were born in Central or South America.

No matter where immigrants are born, they leave their homes in search of a better life. They may hope to find better economic opportunities or political or religious freedom.

In earlier eras, immigrants entered the country through specific immigration centers. Europeans entered the United States at Ellis Island in New York Harbor. Asian immigrants came to Angel Island, near San Francisco. Today, immigrants arrive to the United States like any other travelers, often by plane.

Comparing What do today's immigrants share with those of the past?

Immigrants becoming U.S. citizens at a naturalization ceremony

ACADEMIC VOCABULARY
preliminary prior to the main action; introductory

Urbanization and reform By the mid-1800s, large American cities were home to some tremendously wealthy people. They had made fortunes in trade or in new industries. It was not uncommon for this richest 1 percent of the population to control more than half of the wealth of a city. The vast majority of urban Americans, however, were very poor.

Many city-dwellers lived in **tenements**, or poorly made, crowded apartment buildings. Lacking adequate light, ventilation, and sanitation, tenements were very unhealthy places to live. Disease spread rapidly in the crowded conditions.

The plight of tenement dwellers sparked preliminary efforts at reform. In some cities, local boards of health were established to set sanitation rules. Enforcement was often uneven, however, and the poorer neighborhoods—which were in the greatest need—received less attention than richer ones.

Local reform societies did what they could to alleviate the suffering but only reached a fraction of those who needed help. For the most part, the poor of America's large cities fended for themselves, helping their families, neighbors, and friends as best they could.

Conditions in the poorer districts of American cities would remain unsatisfactory throughout the mid-1800s. Serious efforts at reforming cities would not begin until late in the century.

Industrialization and reform Between 1820 and 1860, the percentage of Americans who worked in manufacturing and related fields soared from 5 percent to about 30 percent. This fundamental shift in the economy had far-reaching social effects. Previously, most Americans had worked on farms. People worked for themselves, kept the profits they earned, and made much of what they needed.

Americans who worked in factories faced a far different economic situation. They were **wage earners**. That is, instead of earning income from their own enterprise, they were paid a set amount by business owners. Instead of making the things they needed, they had to buy them—using their limited wages—from merchants in the city where they lived.

In addition to immigrants flooding the cities, many Americans were leaving farms to work in factories. A new social class arose: the **urban working class**. Most of them were poor and uneducated. Many were immigrants.

As a rule, the relatively wealthy business owners wanted to maximize their profits. The results were low wages, long hours, and unsafe working conditions for workers. In response, workers began to organize into groups to demand higher wages, shorter hours, and safer working conditions. These efforts by workers to improve their situation was one of the great reform movements of the Reform Era. It is called the **labor movement**.

Skills Focus: Making Oral Presentations

At Level

Reading Like a Historian Skill
Urbanization

Standard English Mastery

1. Review the information in the text about urban life and factory working conditions in the mid-1800s. Have students consider how these lifestyles varied from rural life. Have each student write a series of five to ten diary entries describing the daily life of someone who lives in a city tenement and works in a factory. Student entries should also consider how the life for the urban working class differed from, or might have been similar to, life for those who lived and worked on a farm.

2. Have students illustrate their diary entries and design a diary cover.

3. Have volunteers read their diaries to the class.

4. Guide students in a discussion of the living conditions that existed in cities during the mid-1800s. **LS Verbal-Linguistic, Visual-Spatial**

📝 Alternative Assessment Handbook, Rubric 15: Journals

The American labor movement began in the 1820s. During that decade skilled workers, such as carpenters and masons, formed organizations to regulate their pay. The advent of widespread factory work in the 1830s contributed to the early development of the labor movement.

Most workers' organizations were local and short-lived. Not until 1834 was an attempt made to create a national labor organization. In New York City, several smaller groups united to form the National Trades Union. It lasted only until the Panic of 1837, an economic crisis that left as many as one-third of American workers out of a job.

The labor movement faced fierce opposition from business owners. Moreover, many government officials were business owners themselves, or at least sympathized with the owners whose prosperity they thought essential to the well-being of the nation.

Labor reformers did enjoy some victories. One of their major campaigns was the Ten-Hour Movement, a campaign to limit the working day to 10 hours from the more common 12 hours—or more. In 1837 President Andrew Jackson declared a 10-hour workday for some federal employees. President **Martin Van Buren** extended the rule to others in 1840. In the mid-1840s, New Hampshire became the first state to limit the workday to 10 hours. Other states followed New Hampshire's example.

Working Conditions
A cotton mill boss whips a young worker in this 1853 woodcut. Workers in this period also faced long hours, low wages, and unsafe conditions. *How did workers try to improve their conditions?*

Despite this success, laborers remained very much at the whim of business owners. It would be decades before they made substantial progress in improving their work conditions.

READING CHECK **Identifying the Main Idea**
What reforms arose in response to urbanization and industrialization?

SECTION 2 ASSESSMENT

go.hrw.com
Online Quiz
Keyword: SD7 HP8

Reviewing Ideas, Terms, and People

1. a. Recall How did the Great Irish Famine affect the United States?
b. Draw Conclusion What factors do you think pulled Irish and German immigrants to the United States?

2. a. Recall Why were Irish immigrants discriminated against?
b. Compare Why were German immigrants treated differently than Irish immigrants?

3. a. Explain What was life like for the urban working class?
b. Evaluate What factors limited the success of the early labor movement?

Critical Thinking

4. Comparing and Contrasting Copy the diagram below and compare and contrast Irish and German immigration.

	Irish Immigrants	German Immigrants
Reasons for Immigrating		
Places Settled		
Economic Standing		
Religious Beliefs		

FOCUS ON WRITING

5. Expository Write a dialogue that might have taken place between a leader of the labor movement and a business owner in the 1830s. The dialogue should reflect each person's position on the 10-hour workday.

Section 2 Assessment Answers

1. a. many Irish immigrated to the U.S.
b. jobs, free or cheap land, economic and business opportunities, abundant resources

2. a. poor, Catholic, perceived as a threat to jobs and way of life
b. Germans not Catholic, usually wealthier

3. a. crowded and unsanitary conditions
b. Panic of 1837, fierce opposition from business owners and government officials

4. Irish—fled famine; cities on east coast; Catholic; German—fled economic depression, religious persecution, and revolution; further inland; mainly Protestant

5. possible answers—shorter workday will increase productivity because workers are rested; shorter workday will result in fewer products and lower profits

---

The Irish Famine

Info to Know

The Potato Blight Technically known as late blight, the disease that destroyed the Irish potato crop in the late 1840s was caused by a fungus. Its spores travel widely, spreading to other plants by wind, rain, and physical contact. The blight thrives in wet, windy, humid conditions, which are common in Ireland. Today, the disease is controlled by careful observation, destruction of diseased plants, the use of disease-resistant plants and seeds, and fungicides.

The Fighting Irish Recent Irish immigrants made up a significant percentage of Union troops during the Civil War. Historians estimate that more than 150,000 Irish immigrants fought for the Union, a total second only to German American immigrants. One of the best-known ethnic brigades of the war was the New York Irish Brigade. Its leader was General Thomas Meagher, a native of County Wexford, Ireland. The brigade's emerald-green flag featured a golden harp, the symbol of Ireland.

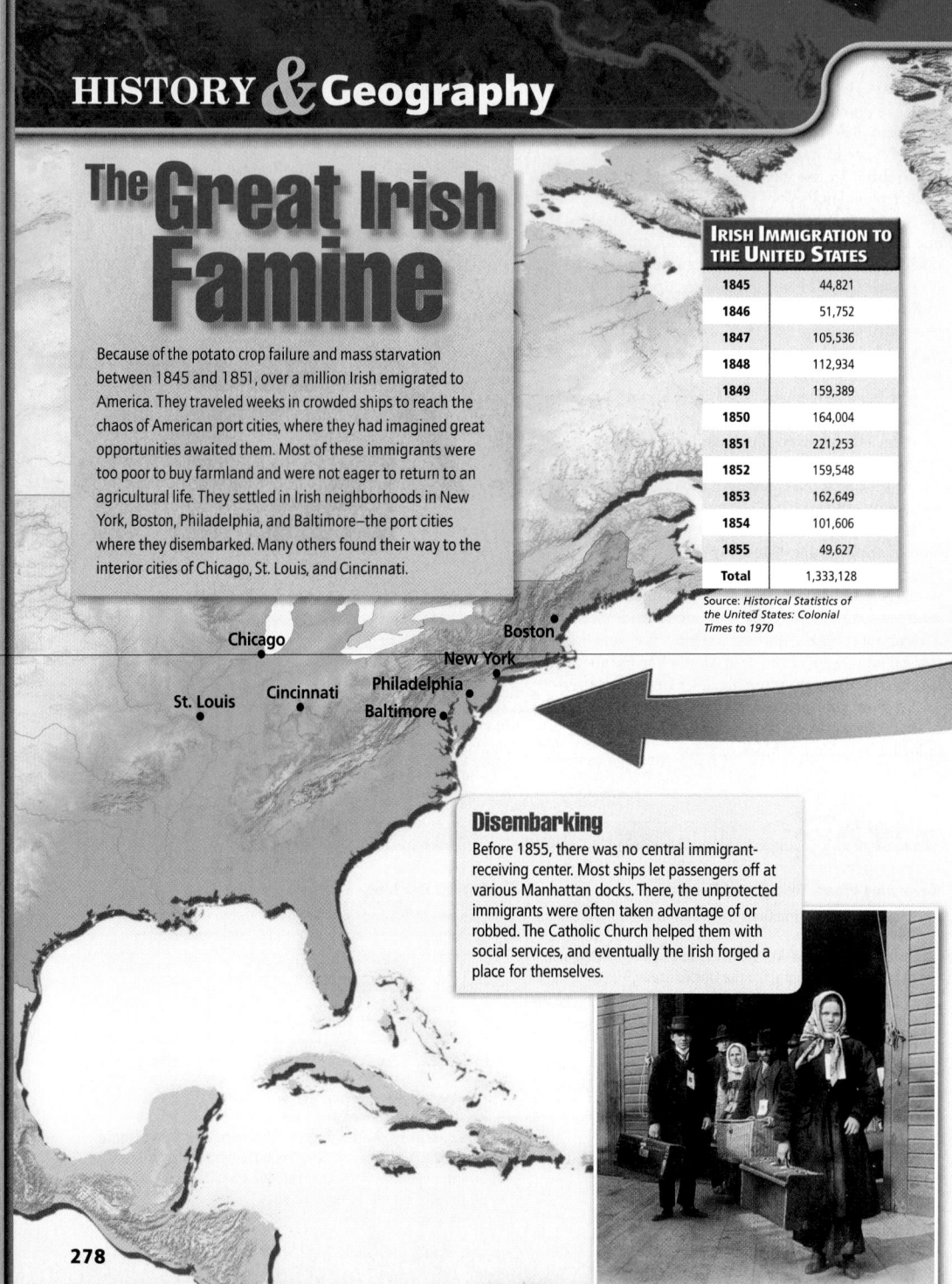

HISTORY & Geography

The Great Irish Famine

Because of the potato crop failure and mass starvation between 1845 and 1851, over a million Irish emigrated to America. They traveled weeks in crowded ships to reach the chaos of American port cities, where they had imagined great opportunities awaited them. Most of these immigrants were too poor to buy farmland and were not eager to return to an agricultural life. They settled in Irish neighborhoods in New York, Boston, Philadelphia, and Baltimore—the port cities where they disembarked. Many others found their way to the interior cities of Chicago, St. Louis, and Cincinnati.

IRISH IMMIGRATION TO THE UNITED STATES	
1845	44,821
1846	51,752
1847	105,536
1848	112,934
1849	159,389
1850	164,004
1851	221,253
1852	159,548
1853	162,649
1854	101,606
1855	49,627
Total	1,333,128

Source: *Historical Statistics of the United States: Colonial Times to 1970*

Disembarking

Before 1855, there was no central immigrant-receiving center. Most ships let passengers off at various Manhattan docks. There, the unprotected immigrants were often taken advantage of or robbed. The Catholic Church helped them with social services, and eventually the Irish forged a place for themselves.

278

Skills Focus: Analyzing Alternative Interpretations of the Past

Reading Like a Historian Skill
Voices of Irish Immigration

At Level   Research Required

1. Have students work in groups to prepare a multimedia presentation about Irish immigration to America.

2. Have students research primary sources to create an anthology of eyewitness accounts of both life in Ireland before immigration and the Irish immigrant experience in America. Encourage students to include journal entries, newspaper articles, songs, poems, visual media, and any other elements that will enhance their presentation.

3. Have each group give their presentation to the class. **LS Verbal-Linguistic, Visual-Spatial**

Alternative Assessment Handbook, Rubric 22: Multimedia Presentations

Eviction and Emigration

In the 1800s, Irish farmers rented their land from English landowners. They had little time to tend their own crops, so they came to depend on potatoes, which were easy to grow. Potatoes made up 60 percent of the Irish diet. When blight destroyed this crop several years in a row, farmers spent their money on food instead of rent. Many were then evicted and had little choice but to emigrate. Most left for North America by way of Liverpool, England.

Coffin Ships

Although laws limited the number of passengers on a ship, captains avoided the law by loading passengers at more than one port. Packed into windowless compartments, with disease spreading and food and water scarce, many passengers died during the crossing.

GEOGRAPHY SKILLS | INTERPRETING MAPS

1. **Human-Environment Interaction** How did the potato blight lead to mass Irish emigration?

2. **Movement** Describe the passage and the reception for Irish immigrants to America.

See **Skills Handbook**, p. H20

Primary Source

One well-known Irish song, "Shamrock Shore," tells of the sadness and danger of the Atlantic crossing, as well as the confusion that greeted the immigrants:

"We sailed three weeks,
we were all seasick,
Not a man on board was free
We were all confined unto our bunks
And no-one to pity poor me.
No father kind nor mother dear
To lift up my head, which was sore
Which made me think more on the lassie
I left on Paddy's green shamrock shore.
We safely reached the other side
After fifteen and twenty days,
We were taken as passengers by a man
And led round in six different ways,
Then each of us drank a parting glass,
In case we'd meet no more
And we drank a health to old Ireland
And Paddy's green shamrock shore."

Skills Focus: Comparing and Contrasting
At Level

Reading Skill
Immigration Today

1. Divide students into small groups. Have each group create a chart comparing and contrasting the Irish immigration of the mid-nineteenth century to immigration today.

2. Have students compare the causes, methods, motivations, problems, and successes of each wave of immigration.

3. Have a volunteer from each group share their findings with the class. Guide the class in a discussion of how Americans should respond to immigration. **LS Verbal-Linguistic, Logical-Mathematical**

   Alternative Assessment Handbook, Rubrics 7: Charts; and 9: Comparing and Contrasting

Answers

Interpreting Maps 1. *Many Irish depended on the potato as their main source of food; when the crop failed, they had nothing to eat, could not pay their rent, and were forced off their land.* **2.** *The passage was dangerous and difficult, and on landing, many immigrants were robbed or exploited.*

279

Bellringer

The Inside Story. . . Use the **Daily Bellringer Transparency** to help students answer the question.

📦 Daily Bellringer Transparency, Section 3

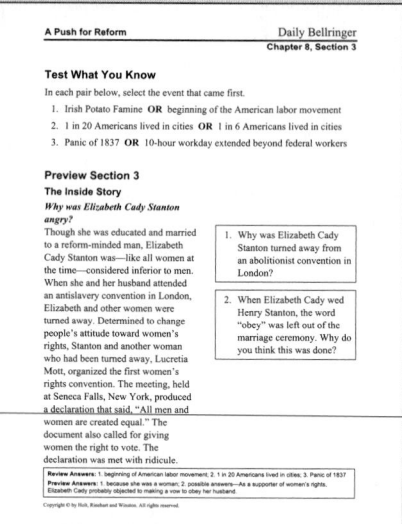

A Push for Reform
Daily Bellringer
Chapter 8, Section 3

Test What You Know

In each pair below, select the event that came first.

1. Irish Potato Famine **OR** beginning of the American labor movement
2. 1 in 20 Americans lived in cities **OR** 1 in 6 Americans lived in cities
3. Panic of 1837 **OR** 10-hour workday extended beyond federal workers

Preview Section 3
The Inside Story
Why was Elizabeth Cady Stanton angry?
Though she was educated and married to a reform-minded man, Elizabeth Cady Stanton was—like all women at the time—considered inferior to men. When she and her husband attended an antislavery convention in London, Elizabeth and other women were turned away. Determined to change people's attitude toward women's rights, Stanton and another woman who had been turned away, Lucretia Mott, organized the first women's rights convention. The meeting, held at Seneca Falls, New York, produced a declaration that said, "All men and women are created equal." The document also called for giving women the right to vote. The declaration was met with ridicule.

1. Why was Elizabeth Cady Stanton turned away from an abolitionist convention in London?

2. When Elizabeth Cady wed Henry Stanton, the word "obey" was left out of the marriage ceremony. Why do you think this was done?

Review Answers: 1. beginning of American labor movement; 2. 1 in 20 Americans lived in cities; 3. Panic of 1837
Preview Answers: 1. because she was a woman; 2. possible answers—As a supporter of women's rights, Elizabeth Cady probably objected to making a vow to obey her husband.

Copyright © by Holt, Rinehart and Winston. All rights reserved.

Academic Vocabulary

Review with students the high-use academic term in this section.

implement to carry out or accomplish (p. 282)

📄 CRF: Vocabulary Builder Activity, Section 3

Taking Notes

Legal—could not vote, hold public office, serve on juries, or enter into legal contracts; Economic—married women not allowed to own property, wages earned were property of husband; Educational—Oberlin College admits women in 1833, first women's college formed in 1837; Cultural—women were viewed as inferior to men and should attend only to household and family duties

---

Women and Reform

BEFORE YOU READ

MAIN IDEA

After leading reform movements to help others, some American women began to work on behalf of themselves.

READING FOCUS

1. What limits were placed on women's lives in the early 1800s?
2. What role did women play in the movements of the Reform Era?
3. Why was the Seneca Falls Convention important?

KEY TERMS AND PEOPLE

cult of domesticity
reform societies
Catharine Beecher
Seneca Falls Convention
Elizabeth Cady Stanton
Lucretia Mott

TAKING NOTES As you read, take notes on areas in which women's rights needed reforms. In a graphic organizer like the one shown here, fill in details about women's legal, economic, cultural, and educational rights.

Women's Rights	
Legal	
Economic	
Educational	
Cultural	

THE INSIDE STORY

Why was Elizabeth Cady Stanton angry? When Elizabeth Cady's only brother died, her father sighed, "Oh my daughter, I wish you were a boy." She tried to please him. She got the best education available to women at the time and studied law in his office. In 1840 at age 25, she married an abolitionist, Henry Stanton. Their marriage vows omitted the word *obey*.

On their honeymoon the Stantons traveled to London for a world antislavery convention, but its organizers refused to allow women to participate in convention debates. Elizabeth Cady Stanton and Lucretia Mott, another rejected delegate, decided that in order for their voices to be heard, they must work for their own rights. In 1848 they organized and directed the first women's rights convention, in Seneca Falls, New York. About 300 people attended, including abolitionist Frederick Douglass.

At the meeting, Stanton presented a Declaration of Sentiments. It echoed the Declaration of Independence—but with some important differences: "We hold these truths to be self-evident, that all men and women are created equal, that they are endowed by their Creator with certain inalienable rights . . ."

Although Lucretia Mott and Henry Stanton both objected, the Seneca Falls declaration also called for the right to vote. It said that women should have "immediate admission to all the rights and privileges which belong to them as citizens of the United States." The statement concluded that these demands were likely to meet with ridicule. Not surprisingly, that was exactly what happened. ◢

CRUSADER
for Women's Rights

▶ **Reformist Elizabeth Cady Stanton and her children, about 1848**

Teach the Main Idea

At Level

Women and Reform

1. **Teach** Ask students the Reading Focus questions to teach this section.

2. **Apply** Have students write a list of ways in which women's lives during the mid-1800s differed from women's lives today.

3. **Review** Have volunteers share their lists with the class. Then guide students in a discussion of their perceptions of women's lives during the Reform Era.

4. **Practice/Homework** Have students write

a one-page article for a current magazine about the cult of domesticity. In their articles students should explain the following: To what extent do they think the cult of domesticity was a realistic description of life in the 1800s? To what extent do they think the goals of the movement represented an ideal for women's lives? **LS Logical-Mathematical, Verbal-Linguistic**

📄 Alternative Assessment Handbook, Rubric 19: Magazines

Limits on Women's Lives

The Seneca Falls declaration was widely ridiculed. So, too, were the women who supported it. The handful of men who dared to speak out for the equal treatment of women were treated with even worse disdain. This surprised no one. A combination of legal, economic, and cultural factors limited what American women in the early 1800s could achieve.

Legal limits Legally, women in the United States were denied many of the basic rights and responsibilities of U.S. citizenship. With few exceptions, women could not vote or hold public office. Other than marraige, they could not enter into legal contracts. When married couples with children divorced, the law awarded custody of the children to the father.

Economic limits With few exceptions, married women were not allowed to own property. Real property, such as land and buildings, businesses, and even household goods, was legally owned by husbands.

In the early 1800s, many American women took jobs outside of their homes for the first time. The Industrial Revolution led to a record number of working women. In 1816 the federal government determined that more than 60,000 of the 100,000 industrial workers in the country were women. Even this did not help most women economically. Wages were low. Moreover, the wages of married women were legally the property of their husbands. Single women were expected to turn over most of their earnings to their families.

Cultural limits The legal and economic limits placed on women both reflected and promoted a widely held view that women were inferior to men. Women, most men believed, should attend only to household and family duties—and to their husbands. Matters outside the home—business, government, politics—should be the province of men, who could handle such weighty matters.

The cultural limits placed on women intensified during the Industrial Revolution. The view that "a woman's place is in the home" became more widespread. This was largely a response to the belief that industrialization was threatening family life by taking women out of the household to work. A movement arose to urge women to remain in the home environment. Books and magazines praised the virtues of women staying at home, caring for their families, and obeying their husbands. Some historians gave this movement a name: the **cult of domesticity**.

READING CHECK **Identifying the Main Idea**
What limits were placed on American women in the early 1800s?

Women in the Reform Era

Despite the many limits placed on their lives, American women often took the lead in reshaping life in the nation. They played important roles in all of the great reform movements of the Reform Era.

All of the reform movements were rooted to some degree in the Second Great Awakening. This religious revival opened many doors for women. The movement de-emphasized obedience to a minister and celebrated good works. Women were therefore able to participate more fully in religious affairs. Many formed groups, such as Bible-reading and missionary societies, that served as extensions of their involvement in churches.

Reform societies Some of these women's church societies evolved into reform societies. **Reform societies** were groups that were organized to promote social reforms. The number of reform societies grew rapidly in the 1830s and 1840s.

The New York Female Reform Society was formed in 1834.

HISTORY'S VOICES

❝It is the imperious [dominant] duty of ladies everywhere and of every religious denomination to cooperate in the great work of moral reform.❞
—Statement of the New York Female Reform Society

Similar societies sprang up throughout the Northeast. Tens of thousands of women joined these groups.

By moral reform, the groups meant promoting good behavior. Society members would visit poor neighborhoods, almshouses, jails, and other places to provide religious instruction and encouragement. Some reform society members established homes for

THE IMPACT TODAY

Economics
In 2004 about 46 percent of the American labor force consisted of women.

A PUSH FOR REFORM **281**

Direct Teach

Reading Focus

❶ What limits were placed on women's lives in the early 1800s? *legal, economic, cultural; usually could not vote or own property; were expected to perform only family duties*

Limits on Women's Lives

Recall In 1816 who formed the greater part of the industrial workforce? *women*

Evaluate Why do you think some people were concerned about women working outside the home? *concern over lack of time devoted to family and possible threat to the stability of the American family*

📄 CRF: Biography: Mary Upton Ferrin
📄 CRF: Biography: Margaret Fuller

Reading Focus

❷ What role did women play in the movements of the Reform Era? *leading role in the great reform movements*

Women in the Reform Era

Explain How did women come to play a leading role in reform movements? *formed church societies that evolved into reform societies*

Analyze Why was their emphasis on "moral reform"? *movement began in churches; these women saw social problems as moral issues*

go.hrw.com
Online Resources
KEYWORD: SD7 CH8
TOPIC: SENECA FALLS: STARTING THE WOMEN'S MOVEMENT

Answers

Reading Check *could not vote, hold public office, serve on juries, or enter into legal contracts; not allowed to own property; earned lower wages; most men expected them to attend only to household and family duties*

Differentiating Instruction   Below Level

Learners Having Difficulty; Special Education Students

Materials magazines, construction paper, scissors, glue

1. Review the meaning of the cult of domesticity and the purpose of reform societies with the class. Then guide students in a discussion of the reasons why so many women became involved in reform movements in the 1800s.

2. Divide the class into small groups. Have each group create a collage that represents women's roles in the early to mid-1800s. Have students place images pertaining to family and home life—the cult of domesticity—at the center of their collages, with images of roles beyond the domestic sphere expanding outward, toward the edges. Guide students in a discussion of whether the cult of domesticity still exists.

3. Have a volunteer from each group present its collage to the class. **LS Visual-Spatial, Interpersonal**

📄 Alternative Assessment Handbook, Rubric 8: Collages

281

Women in the Reform Era

Explain Why would the "Lowell Girls" organize a strike? *They were mill workers who wanted to improve working conditions.*

Evaluate Why do you think women led the movement to reform education? *possible answer—in order to provide the best opportunities for their children*

❸ Why was the Seneca Falls Convention important? *first women's rights convention held in U.S.; marked beginning of women's rights movement*

The Seneca Falls Convention

Explain Why did women want to obtain political power in the mid-1800s? *would allow them to advance reforms*

Identify Who was Lucretia Mott? *Quaker abolitionist; helped organize Seneca Falls Convention*

Summarize How did women's involvement in the abolitionist movement lead to the beginning of the women's rights movement? *thinking about the rights of African Americans and the injustices of slavery led to thinking about the rights of women and the injustices of gender inequality*

Answers

Reading Like a Historian
1. *possible answer—to remind readers of the Declaration of Independence's association with freedom;* **2.** *because without them women were left with no representation*

Reading Check *formed reform societies, led many reform movements, worked to improve lives of urban poor*

282

---

orphaned girls, homeless young women, and other women in need.

Education reform As in other reform movements, women led the movement to reform education. **Catharine Beecher** ran a school for women, the Hartford Female Seminary, in Massachusetts. Later, she opened the Western Female Institute in Cincinnati, Ohio. Beecher worked to create normal schools and to send teachers west to educate frontier children.

Oberlin College in Ohio became the first American college to welcome women as well as men in 1833. In 1837 Mary Lyon established the first women's college in the United States, Mount Holyoke College in Massachusetts. Many women became teachers during the Reform Era. This gave them a fundamental role in shaping American life.

ACADEMIC VOCABULARY
implement to carry out or accomplish

Other reforms Urban reforms during the Reform Era were implemented largely by female reform societies. Through visits and the establishing of homes for girls and women in need, women worked to improve the lives of the urban poor.

Women's contributions to the labor movement arose from their firsthand experiences as workers. By 1850 about 225,000 American women were at work in the country's mills and factories, toiling long hours for low wages, often in unsafe conditions. Some of the earliest labor strikes were held by women, such as the Lowell Girls, who were attempting to better their working conditions.

Many participants in the temperance movement were women. Because women were economically dependent on men, they and their children were often the victims of men's excessive alcohol consumption. Thus, they knew firsthand of the dangers of alcohol abuse.

READING CHECK **Summarizing** How did women contribute to reform?

The Seneca Falls Convention

The **Seneca Falls Convention** was held in July 1848 in Seneca Falls, New York. It was the first women's rights convention held in America. Many historians mark it as the beginning of the modern American women's movement.

PRIMARY SOURCES

Declaration of Sentiments

In 1848 women's rights supporters met in Seneca Falls, New York, and produced a document calling for greater expansion of women's rights, especially the right to vote. Modeled after the Declaration of Independence, the Declaration of Sentiments was a landmark in the women's movement.

The writer used the same words that are in the Declaration of Independence, but included women.

"We hold these truths to be self-evident: that all men and women are created equal; that they are endowed by their Creator with certain inalienable rights; that among these are life, liberty, and the pursuit of happiness; that to secure these rights governments are instituted, deriving their just powers from the consent of the governed . . .

The history of mankind is a history of repeated injuries . . . on the part of man toward woman, having in direct object the establishment of an absolute tyranny over her . . .

Having deprived her of this first right as a citizen, the elective franchise, thereby leaving her without representation in the halls of legislation, he has oppressed her on all sides."

Like the Declaration of Independence, the Declaration of Sentiments included a list of grievances.

Skills FOCUS **READING LIKE A HISTORIAN**

1. **Analyzing Primary Sources** Why do you think the writer modeled this document after the Declaration of Independence?
2. **Identifying Points of View** Why did the writer believe that voting rights were so important?

See Skills Handbook, pp. H28–29

282 CHAPTER 8

Skills Focus: Summarizing

At Level

Reading Skill
The Seneca Falls Convention

1. Ask volunteers to name the main demands of the early women's rights activists. Make a class list for students to see.

2. Have students write a newspaper editorial that could have been published in a July 1848 newspaper. In their articles students should summarize and comment upon the proceedings of the Seneca Falls Convention. Tell students to include the names of the leaders and the main demands of the Declaration of Sentiments.

3. Ask volunteers to read their articles to the class.

4. As an extension, have students create two political cartoons, one that supports the 1848 Declaration and Sentiments, and one that supports the cult of domesticity and criticizes Mott and Stanton. **LS** Logical-Mathematical, Verbal-Linguistic

📝 Alternative Assessment Handbook, Rubrics 23: Newspapers; and 27: Political Cartoons

A desire for political power Over the years, countless American women had fought for many different kinds of reforms. But the limits placed on them—especially their prohibition from participating in government by voting or holding public office—restricted their influence and accomplishments. As a result, many women wanted to obtain political power in order to advance the reforms.

Other women, however, thought that political power should be available to women, not just so that they could achieve reform but because it was fair and reasonable.

Moreover, women reformers had long worked for the rights of others. They were especially active in the abolitionist movement to end slavery. It was a short leap from thinking about racial equality to equality between the sexes. Thus, the time was right for women—who had long worked to improve the lives of others—to fight to improve their own lives.

The convention Elizabeth Cady Stanton and Lucretia Mott organized the Seneca Falls Convention. Mott was a prominent abolitionist. A Quaker, she helped found several antislavery groups and organized antislavery conventions. Stanton, like Mott, was also a dedicated and experienced abolitionist.

Mott and Stanton had attended the World's Anti-Slavery Convention in London in 1840. Mott and Stanton's husband, Henry, were official delegates. They were shocked to learn that Mott, because she was a woman, would not be allowed to participate in convention debates. Worse, women even had to be segregated from men. This experience drove Mott and Stanton to take action. They determined to call a convention on behalf of women's rights.

The women's rights convention was held near Stanton's home in Seneca Falls, New York. It was attended by about 300 people. The convention produced the Declaration of Sentiments, written by Stanton. Exactly 100 participants—68 women and 32 men—signed the Declaration of Sentiments, which publicly stated their belief that "all men and women are created equal." The struggle for the equality of American women had begun.

> **READING CHECK** **Making Inferences** How do you think the Seneca Falls Convention affected the women's movement for equal rights?

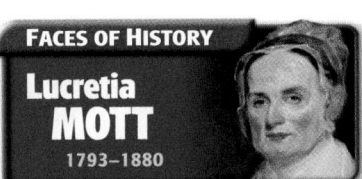

FACES OF HISTORY

Lucretia MOTT
1793–1880

THE GRANGER COLLECTION, NEW YORK

Raised as a Quaker, Lucretia Mott was strongly committed to her faith. At Quaker meetings, Mott was encouraged to speak out against social problems. In the 1830s Mott traveled the country making speeches against slavery. In 1840 Mott attended the World's Anti-Slavery Convention in England but was not allowed to speak, simply because she was a woman.

Back in the United States, Mott began to demand equal treatment for women. In 1848 Mott and Elizabeth Cady Stanton organized a convention in Seneca Falls, New York. The convention issued a Declaration of Sentiments, demanding women's equality. Throughout the rest of her life, Mott continued to fight for social justice and women's equality.

Summarize What causes did Lucretia Mott support?

SECTION 3 ASSESSMENT

go.hrw.com
Online Quiz
Keyword: SD7 HP8

Reviewing Ideas, Terms, and People

1. **a. Recall** What was the **cult of domesticity**?
   b. Draw Conclusions How did industrialization help lead to the cult of domesticity?
   c. Predict What do you think would happen to the cult of domesticity after this time period? Why?

2. **a. Describe** Describe the purpose and activities of **reform societies**.
   b. Compare What did all of the reform movements in which women participated have in common?
   c. Evaluate How important was the growth in the number of women teachers in the early 1800s? Why?

3. **a. Identify** Who organized the **Seneca Falls Convention**?
   b. Analyze What was the purpose of the Seneca Falls Convention?
   c. Evaluate Do you think the Declaration of Sentiments changed anyone's attitude toward women? Why or why not?

Critical Thinking

4. **Identifying Cause and Effect** Copy the diagram below and identify the causes of the women's rights movement.

```
┌──────────┐
│          │──┐
└──────────┘  │
┌──────────┐  │    ┌─────────────────────────────┐
│          │──┼───▶│ Effect: the women's rights movement │
└──────────┘  │    └─────────────────────────────┘
┌──────────┐  │
│          │──┘
└──────────┘
```

FOCUS ON WRITING

5. **Persuasive** Reread the excerpt from the Declaration of Sentiments on the opposite page. Then write a paragraph explaining why you think any of the grievances are or are not valid today.

A PUSH FOR REFORM **283**

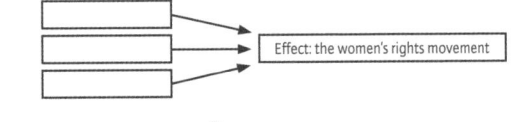

Section 3 Assessment Answers

1. **a.** a movement that encouraged women to attend only to family duties
   b. women left the home to work leading to fears about the disruption of family life
   c. possible answer—would grow because more women in the work force

2. **a.** provide religious encouragement in poor neighborhoods, jails, almshouses
   b. concerned with social issues
   c. very important, allowed them to reshape American life

3. **a.** Lucretia Mott and Elizabeth Cady Stanton
   b. to allow people interested in women's rights to meet and share ideas
   c. possible answer—no, men resented challenge to their authority

4. inability to vote or own property, men viewed them as only good for maintaining the home and raising children

5. possible answer—not valid, men no longer have tyranny over women

Answers
Faces of History *abolition, women's equality, social justice*
Reading Check *possible answer—drew more attention to the struggle for women's equality; motivated other women to join the movement*

Bellringer

The Inside Story. . . Use the **Daily Bellringer Transparency** to help students answer the question.

🔳 **Daily Bellringer Transparency, Section 4**

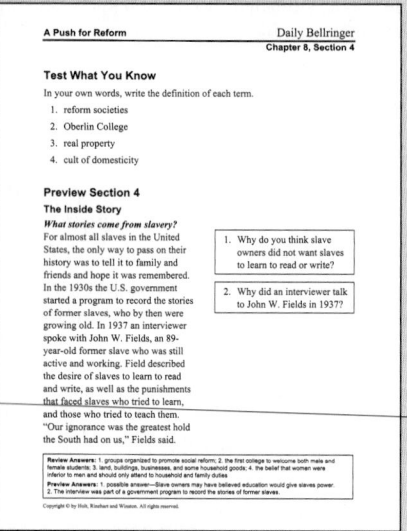

| A Push for Reform | Daily Bellringer |
| | Chapter 8, Section 4 |

Test What You Know

In your own words, write the definition of each term.

1. reform societies
2. Oberlin College
3. real property
4. cult of domesticity

Preview Section 4

The Inside Story

What stories come from slavery?
For almost all slaves in the United States, the only way to pass on their history was to tell it to family and friends and hope it was remembered. In the 1930s the U.S. government started a program to record the stories of former slaves, who by then were growing old. In 1937 an interviewer spoke with John W. Fields, an 89-year-old former slave who was still active and working. Field described the desire of slaves to learn to read and write, as well as the punishments that faced slaves who tried to learn, and those who tried to teach them. "Our ignorance was the greatest hold the South had on us," Fields said.

1. Why do you think slave owners did not want slaves to learn to read or write?

2. Why did an interviewer talk to John W. Fields in 1937?

Taking Notes

Work—hard labor was the dominant fact in their lives; Lifestyle—lived in barely tolerable conditions, with inadequate food, clothing, and shelter; medical care was nonexistent, found hope in religion, storytelling, and songs; Challenges—had no rights under the law, often harsh treatment under slavery

go.hrw.com
Online Resources

KEYWORD: SD7 CH8
TOPIC: THE LIVES OF ENSLAVED
AFRICAN AMERICANS

SECTION 4

Fighting against Slavery

BEFORE YOU READ

MAIN IDEA

The movement to end slavery dominated the Reform Era.

READING FOCUS

1. What was life like for enslaved African Americans in the South?
2. How did people in the South fight against slavery?
3. What were the major developments in the abolition movement?

KEY TERMS AND PEOPLE

free blacks
Nat Turner
Underground Railroad
Harriet Tubman
abolition movement
William Lloyd Garrison
Frederick Douglass

TAKING NOTES
As you read, take notes identifying details of what life for an enslaved person was like. Record your notes in a graphic organizer like the one shown.

Life as an Enslaved Person	
Work	
Lifestyle	
Challenges	

THE INSIDE STORY

What stories come from slavery? Most of the thousands of enslaved Africans in the Americas never had a chance to tell their stories. No one but their families and fellow slaves knew what they endured. Nevertheless, some outstanding African Americans made themselves heard. For example, abolitionist leader Frederick Douglass wrote a powerful autobiography in 1845. Opponents of slavery helped others tell their stories, either as written narratives or as oral history.

By the 1930s, during the Great Depression, African Americans who had experienced slavery were growing old. A federal government project recorded their stories. In 1937 in Lafayette, Indiana, an interviewer talked with John W. Fields, an 89-year-old former slave who was still working. Fields explained how important education was:

"In most of us colored folks was the great desire to [be] able to read and write. We took advantage of every opportunity to educate ourselves. The greater part of the plantation owners were very harsh if we were caught trying to learn or write. It was the law that if a white man was caught trying to educate a negro slave, he was liable to prosecution entailing a fine of fifty dollars and a jail sentence. We were never allowed to go to town and it was not until after I ran away that I knew that they sold anything but slaves, tobacco, and whiskey. Our ignorance was the greatest hold the South had on us." 🔳

▶ **Enslaved African Americans taking a Sunday rest by their cabins in South Carolina, 1860**

284 CHAPTER 8

Teach the Main Idea

At Level

Slavery and Abolition

1. **Teach** Ask students the Reading Focus questions to teach this section.

2. **Apply** Have students develop a paragraph describing slave life and sequencing the events leading to the abolitionist movement. Then guide students in a discussion of this question: How effective were the anti-slavery movements of the early 1800s?

3. **Review** Call on volunteers and create a class list of anti-slavery activities of the early 1800s. *slave revolts, escape,*

Underground Railroad, the abolition movement

4. **Practice/Homework** Have each student write a one-page essay discussing the links between women's rights and abolition. In their essays students should analyze why people like the Grimké sisters and Frederick Douglass were involved in both movements.

LS Verbal-Linguistic

📝 Alternative Assessment Handbook, Rubric 37: Writing Assignments

The Lives of Enslaved African Americans

Including the colonial period, slavery had been an American institution for two centuries. Enslaved African Americans were held in every colony, northern and southern. In the North, slavery continued to exist in some form until the 1840s. By 1860 nearly 4 million African Americans lived in slavery in the South. While the majority of white southerners were not slaveholders, the southern economy depended on the labor of slaves.

Some differences existed in the lives of enslaved people—where they lived, how they were treated, and what work they were made to do. Nevertheless, it is clear that work, want, fear, and hope dominated all of their lives.

A life of work Generally, slaveholders viewed slaves as property, not as people. For slaveholders, buying slaves and providing, even minimally, for them was a major expense. Slaves who could not or would not perform the tasks demanded of them were of little use to slaveholders. Therefore, work was the dominant fact in the lives of enslaved people.

Men, women, and children were expected—or forced—to work whenever the slaveholder demanded it. For most enslaved people, this meant virtually every day of their lives, from the time they were old enough to perform chores until they were too old to be of any more use to the slaveholder.

Most enslaved people lived on farms or plantations in the South, where cotton was a leading crop. Cotton farming was labor-intensive. Many slaves worked as field hands, planting, tending, picking, processing, and loading cotton. Other jobs included constructing and repairing buildings and fences, hauling water, clearing land, and doing the many other tasks needed to keep a farm or plantation running.

Other plantation slaves worked in the slaveholder's house, performing a wide variety of servant duties like cooking and cleaning. Some enslaved people were skilled artisans, and many worked as blacksmiths, bricklayers, or carpenters.

Some slaves lived in cities. There they worked in factories and mills, in offices, and in homes. Still others worked in mines or in the forest as lumberjacks.

A life of want Enslaved people lived, for the most part, in barely tolerable conditions. One man who escaped from slavery later described what life as a slave was like.

HISTORY'S VOICES

" We lodged in huts and on the bare ground . . . In a single room were huddled, like cattle, ten or a dozen persons, men, women, and children. All ideas of refinement and decency were, of course, out of the question. There were neither bedsteads, nor furniture of any description. Our beds were collections of straw and old rags, thrown down in the corners and boxed with boards, a single blanket the only covering . . . The wind whistled and the rain and snow blew in through the cracks, and the damp earth soaked in the moisture till the floor was [muddy] as a pigsty. **"**

—Josiah Henson, *Uncle Tom's Story of His Life: An Autobiography of the Rev. Josiah Henson*, 1877

The food and clothing provided to slaves were typically as inadequate as the shelter. Medical care was virtually nonexistent. Sickness rarely stopped their work. Enslaved African Americans had no rights under the law, which viewed them as property.

A PUSH FOR REFORM **285**

The Lives of Enslaved African Americans

Describe Why did most slaves fear their slaveholders? *subjected to a wide variety of brutal punishments; possibility of being separated from their families*

Explain Why was religion so important to enslaved people? *belief in better life after death; gave meaning to their lives*

❷ How did people in the South fight against slavery? *free blacks played leading role in antislavery activities; slave revolts; escape*

The Antislavery Movement in the South

Recall Why were some southern African Americans not enslaved? *freed by slaveholders; ancestors had been emancipated; escaped to freedom*

Describe How did the Underground Railroad work? *Sympathetic whites and free blacks provided escaping slaves with food, hiding places, and directions to their next destination, closer to free territory.*

Summarize What were the results of Nat Turner's revolt? *twenty rebels hanged; 100 slaves suspected of sympathizing were killed; dozens of white people killed; new laws strictly limited movements of slaves*

Answers

Reading Check (left) *possible answer—hard work, fear, tired, alone, determined, poor, enduring, hard, hopeful;* **(right)** *rebellion, escape, and the Underground Railroad*

286

A life of fear The way slaveholders treated enslaved people varied. Many slaveholders treated their slaves relatively well. But they generally did so in order to secure loyal service, not out of any great sense of humanity. Offering humane treatment did not make up for the inherently cruel condition of holding another human being as a piece of property.

Other slaveholders treated their slaves in a much harsher fashion. In addition to the cruel nature of slavery itself, some slaveholders would resort to a wide variety of punishments, such as beating, whipping, starving, and threatening a person's family members to ensure obedience.

A nightmarish reality for slaves was the threat of being separated from their families. Slaveholders and dealers routinely separated children from their parents, brothers from their sisters, and husbands from their wives, selling them to different slaveholders.

A life of hope One of the most remarkable facts about the life of African Americans under slavery was how they endured. Despite lives of backbreaking work and harsh punishments, African Americans developed ways to survive and bring some light into their lives.

Religion was a major source of comfort for enslaved people. A combination of African and Christian beliefs provided hope for a better life after death.

Drawing on their rich African oral tradition, enslaved people found pleasure in storytelling. Songs, too, provided inspiration and a brief respite from their hard lives. Many took pleasure in the dream that one day they might be free.

READING CHECK **Making Generalizations** What words would you use to describe the lives of enslaved people?

The Antislavery Movement in the South

Not all African Americans in the South were held as slaves. In 1860, about 215,000 were **free blacks**. Some were former slaves who had been emancipated, or freed, by slaveholders. More typically, some were free because their ancestors had been emancipated. These men

---

THE IMPACT TODAY

Government

Near Cuba in 1839, enslaved Africans aboard the Spanish ship *Amistad* revolted and tried to sail the ship back to Africa. They ended up sailing northward instead, where they were captured off Long Island. Both a federal court and the U.S. Supreme Court found the *Amistad* rebels innocent on charges of murder and mutiny, and in 1842, they returned to Africa. The 1997 film *Amistad* was based on the story of the revolt.

---

and women, however, faced harsh legal and social discrimination. Still, free blacks played a leading role in antislavery activities. Many aided people escaping slavery and spoke out for freedom. Some even spoke of their enslaved brethren revolting against their oppressors.

Slave revolts Between 1776 and 1860, about 200 slave uprisings and plots occurred in the United States. Most were short lived. An uprising led by **Nat Turner** in 1830 became the deadliest slave revolt in American history.

Turner and five accomplices killed Turner's slaveholder and his family. They then marched through Southampton County, Virginia, gaining as many as 75 followers and killing dozens more white people. A local militia captured the rebels and executed 20 of them, including Turner. Other white people in the area killed about 100 other slaves suspected of sympathizing with the revolt.

To try to prevent similar revolts, many southern communities stepped up their policing. New laws were enacted to strictly limit the movements and meetings of slaves.

Escape Some enslaved people chose a nonviolent way to end their enslavement: They escaped. They tried to reach the free states of the North or Canada or Mexico where slavery was illegal.

No one knows exactly how many slaves escaped. Perhaps 40,000 or more had fled the United States by 1860. Some estimates put the number at 100,000. Certainly, thousands attempted escape, and although most were soon captured, many did make it to freedom.

The Underground Railroad Over the years an informal, constantly changing network of escape routes developed. This so-called **Underground Railroad** had no formal organization. Sympathetic white people and free blacks provided escapees with food, hiding places, and directions to their next destination, closer to free territory. The most famous worker on the Underground Railroad was **Harriet Tubman**. Tubman had escaped slavery herself, and she helped many others on their journey to freedom.

READING CHECK **Identifying the Main Idea** How did enslaved people resist their captivity?

286 CHAPTER 8

Differentiating Instruction

Above Level

Advanced Learners/GATE

Research Required

1. Guide students in a discussion of the music that enslaved African Americans used to provide hope, inspiration, or respite from their hard lives. Ask if any students are familiar with any African American spirituals or work songs. Explain that songs like "Swing Low, Sweet Chariot" are part of that tradition.

2. Divide the class into small groups. Have each group conduct outside research to find five spirituals or other African American slavery-era songs to share with the class. Students should

also try to find recordings of the spirituals and songs and play them for the class.

3. Have each student choose one of the songs found by their group and write a brief essay explaining what it means and why it is historically important. In their essays, students should consider whether or not the song constitutes a primary source document.

LS **Auditory-Musical, Verbal-Linguistic**

Alternative Assessment Handbook, Rubric 42: Writing to Inform

HISTORY CLOSE-UP

The Underground Railroad

Free blacks and abolitionists helped enslaved African Americans find safety in northern states, Canada, and Mexico. This scene is an artist's re-creation showing escaped slaves reaching the house of the Reverend John Rankin. Located on the Ohio River, between free states and slaves states, the Rankin house was a key stop on the Underground Railroad.

As a "conductor," John Rankin lit a lamp in his window to tell escaping slaves that he would help them.

MAJOR ROUTES TO FREEDOM

CANADA

Boston
Detroit
Chicago
New York
Philadelphia
St. Louis
Washington, D.C.
Charleston
Savannah
New Orleans
MEXICO
Gulf of Mexico
The Everglades

- Free state
- Slave state
- Territory where slavery is permitted by local decision
- → Route to freedom
- ● Rankin House

Harriet Tubman helped hundreds of slaves escape to freedom.

Many groups and individuals helped slaves escape bondage. Religion inspired many abolitionists.

Escaping slaves used whatever means of transportation they could find, although much of their journey was on foot.

Skills FOCUS INTERPRETING INFOGRAPHICS

1. **Making Inferences** What dangers might the enslaved people have faced along their journey?
2. **Drawing Conclusions** What might have been the shortest route to freedom from the Rankin house?

See Skills Handbook, p. H7, H12, H18

A PUSH FOR REFORM **287**

• Direct Teach •

Info to Know

Special Delivery Slaves often resorted to ingenious means to gain their freedom. Some traveled north in disguise. One slave named Henry Box Brown mailed himself to freedom. In a journey lasting 26 hours, Brown shipped himself from Richmond, Virginia, to Philadelphia, Pennsylvania, in a box.

Amistad In July of 1839, the Spanish ship *Amistad* was traveling to Cuba when the 53 slaves on board, recently captured in Africa, revolted. They killed the captain and cook, but spared the navigator so that he could take them home to Sierra Leone. Instead, the navigator sailed north until the U.S. Navy captured the ship off the coast of Long Island, New York. The slaves were put on trial, pitting proslavery forces against antislavery forces. Although slavery was legal in Cuba, the importation of slaves from Africa was not. The Supreme Court ruled that the passengers aboard the ship had been kidnapped and had the right to escape. In January of 1842, the 35 surviving Africans secured passage to their homeland of Sierra Leone.

About the Illustration

This illustration is an artist's conception based on available sources. Historians, however, are uncertain exactly what this scene looked like.

Collaborative Learning

At Level

The Underground Railroad

Research Required

1. Divide the class into groups of four or five students. Have students in each group conduct outside research on the Underground Railroad, Harriet Tubman, Levi Coffin, and other conductors on the Underground Railroad. Have students in each group share their research findings.

2. Have each student use their group's research to write a one- to two-page illustrated short story about an escaping slave traveling north on the Underground Railroad or about the activities of a conductor. Short stories should have an identifiable plot and a realistic ending.

3. Have volunteers read their short stories and share their illustrations with the class.
LS Verbal-Linguistic, Visual-Spatial

Alternative Assessment Handbook, Rubric 37: Writing Assignments

Answers

Interpreting Visuals 1. *capture, violence, injury;* **2.** *traveling on the river*

287

❸ What were the major developments in the abolition movement? *Quakers condemned slavery; Second Great Awakening; The Liberator; American Antislavery Society; Frederick Douglass's writings and speeches*

The Abolition Movement

Recall How did the abolition movement grow out of the Second Great Awakening? *most religious people in the North saw slavery as a moral wrong; joined reform societies to campaign against slavery*

Explain How did southerners justify slavery? *essential to the production of cotton and the economic health of the South; tried to justify slavery in Christian terms*

Elaborate Why do you think that abolitionists also supported women's rights? *possible answer—both movements worked for equal rights; women and slaves lacked basic legal and civil rights*

📰 Political Cartoons Activities for American History: Cartoon 15: Attack on the Post Office, 1835

📄 CRF: Primary Source Activity: Letters from the Grimké Sisters

Faces of History
Terms of Slavery
Describe As a slave, Frederick Douglass hired himself out for labor in Baltimore, Maryland. He later wrote in *My Bondage and My Freedom*: "I was to be allowed all my time; to make all bargains for work; to find my own employment, and to collect my own wages; and, in return for this liberty, I was required, or obliged, to pay [to his owner] . . . three dollars at the end of each week."

📄 CRF: Literature Activity: *Narrative of the Life of Frederick Douglass, An American Slave* by Frederick Douglass

Answers

Faces of History *intelligence, communication skills*

288

The Abolition Movement

The number of slaves attempting to escape their plight increased sharply during the 1830s. They may have been encouraged by a small movement that was gaining supporters in the North. The **abolition movement** was a campaign to abolish, or end, slavery. Supporters of the abolition movement were called abolitionists.

The abolition movement was one of the the largest movement of the Reform Era of the 1830s, 1840s, and 1850s. No other movement attracted as many followers, garnered as much attention, arose such strong feelings, or had such an impact on the history of the United States. In retrospect, this is not surprising, since the lives of several million people held in slavery were at stake.

Religious roots The abolition movement had deep roots in religion. As far back as the colonial period, the Quakers condemned slavery as immoral. Elihu Embree, the son of a Quaker minister, published the first newspapers in the country devoted to the abolitionist cause. One was called *The Emancipator*. Embree proclaimed that "freedom is the inalienable right of all men." Many Quakers joined the abolitionist cause.

The rebirth of religious fervor in the Second Great Awakening also contributed to the rise of the abolition movement. Many religious people in the North saw slavery as a clear moral wrong that went directly against their beliefs. Many joined reform societies to campaign against slavery. By 1836 more than 500 such groups existed.

William Lloyd Garrison One of the most outspoken abolitionists was a Philadelphia journalist named **William Lloyd Garrison**. In 1828 he was convinced by a Quaker friend to join the abolitionist movement. Garrison soon became its leading spokesperson.

Although all abolitionists wanted an end to slavery, many favored its gradual abolition. Garrison, however, demanded that slavery be abolished immediately. In 1831 in Boston, he began publishing an abolitionist newspaper called *The Liberator*. In the first issue, he made his devotion to abolition clear.

HISTORY'S VOICES

❝I will be as harsh as truth, and as uncompromising as justice. On this subject I do not wish to think, or speak, or write, with moderation. No! No! . . . I am in earnest—I will not equivocate—I will not excuse—I will not retreat in a single inch—and I will be heard.❞

—William Lloyd Garrison

Garrison continued to publish the paper for 35 years, until slavery was abolished.

In 1833 Garrison founded the American Anti-Slavery Society, the most influential abolitionist group to call for the immediate end to slavery in the United States. By 1840, the American Anti-Slavery Society had a membership of 150,000 to 200,000.

Leading abolitionists As in other reform movements of the time, women played a significant role in the abolition campaign. Sarah and Angelina Grimké were outspoken campaigners for abolition. The daughters of a South Carolina plantation owner, the Grimké sisters witnessed the suffering of slaves firsthand. Their public outspokenness against slavery earned them the disapproval of their community. They then moved to the North, where they not only fought against slavery but also for the rights of women.

Like the Grimkés, **Frederick Douglass** supported women's rights. Douglass was a featured speaker at the Seneca Falls Convention. But he is best remembered as an abolitionist

FACES OF HISTORY

Frederick DOUGLASS
1817–1895

After escaping slavery on his second attempt, Frederick Douglass made his way to Massachusetts, where he gave a speech on the horrors of slavery, which instantly made him a leading spokesman for the abolitionist cause. For the next 50 years, he used his sharp intellect, gift for writing, and strong public speaking skills to campaign against slavery and racial prejudice in America.

During the Civil War, Douglass recruited African Americans to fight for the Union. He also met with President Abraham Lincoln to protest discrimination against black soldiers. In later years, Douglass focused on land rights for former slaves, women's rights, and the movement to end lynching.

Explain What skills made Douglass a persuasive abolitionist?

Skills Focus: Making Inferences
At Level

Reading Skill
The Abolition Movement

1. Guide students in a discussion of the roots of the abolition movement and the leaders of the movement.

2. Remind students that William Lloyd Garrison, Sarah and Angelina Grimké, and Frederick Douglass spoke publicly about the evils of slavery and they campaigned avidly for abolition. Have students select one of these abolitionists and write a speech that might have been delivered by that person arguing for the immediate abolition of slavery. In their speeches students should present valid arguments, use logical reasoning, and convey the passion that these people felt for the abolitionist cause.

3. Have students rehearse and present their speeches to the class. **LS Logical-Mathematical, Verbal-Linguistic**

📄 Alternative Assessment Handbook, Rubrics 24: Oral Presentations; and 43: Writing to Persuade

leader. Born into slavery in Maryland, Douglass escaped as a young man of 20. His intelligence and speech-making skills eventually earned him a place as a popular speaker to antislavery audiences. In 1845 Douglass published his autobiography, *Narrative of the Life of Frederick Douglass*. In writing about his quest to escape slavery, Douglass stated, "You have seen how a man was made a slave; you shall now see how a slave was made a man."

Douglass went on to publish an abolitionist newspaper, the *North Star*. His writing, his firsthand experience with slavery, and, above all, his powerful speeches made Douglass one of the most influential abolitionists.

Opposition to abolition The majority of white southerners did not own slaves. To the minority who were slaveholders, the abolition movement was an outrage. They viewed the movement as an attack on their livelihood, their way of life, and even on their religion.

Southern ministers constructed elaborate arguments attempting to justify slavery in biblical terms. Slaveholders and politicians argued that slavery was essential to the production of cotton and the health of the economy. To many, even in the North, this was a powerful argument. By 1860 cotton accounted for about 55 percent of the country's exports.

Indeed, there was support for, and toleration of, slavery in the North. To northern

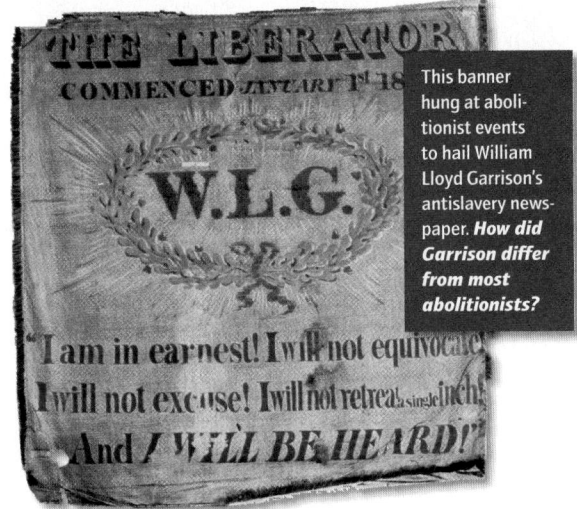

This banner hung at abolitionist events to hail William Lloyd Garrison's antislavery newspaper. **How did Garrison differ from most abolitionists?**

workers, freedom for slaves might mean more competition for jobs. Still, the pressure to abolish slavery was undeniable. Frederick Douglass said the issue of slavery was "the great, paramount, imperative, and all-commanding question for this age and nation to solve."

 **Making Inferences** What might happen as a result of the differing views of slavery in the United States?

---

go.hrw.com
Online Quiz
Keyword: SD7 HP8

Reviewing Ideas, Terms, and People

1. **a. Recall** Where did most enslaved people live?
   b. Elaborate How did enslaved people maintain their hope?
   c. Predict What do you think would bring an end to slavery in the United States?

2. **a. Describe** Describe the revolt of **Nat Turner**.
   b. Make Inferences What can you infer from the number of people who escaped from slavery?
   c. Elaborate What words do you think would best describe passage on the **Underground Railroad**?

3. **a. Identify** Who was **William Lloyd Garrison**?
   b. Contrast How was Garrison's approach to abolition different from that of earlier abolitionists?
   c. Evaluate What do you think made **Frederick Douglass** such an effective abolitionist?

Critical Thinking

4. **Identifying Cause and Effect** Copy the diagram below and identify the way groups of Americans reacted to slavery.

Group	Reactions to Slavery
Enslaved Africans and African Americans	
Abolitionists	
Slaveholders	

FOCUS ON WRITING

5. **Expository** Write a paragraph that explains what the Underground Railroad was and what its name suggests.

A PUSH FOR REFORM **289**

Section 4 Assessment Answers

1. **a.** in the South on farms or plantations
   b. religion, traditions, storytelling, songs, and dreams of freedom
   c. possible answer—changing attitudes about slavery, laws requiring freedom

2. **a.** murdered his owner, followers killed whites; eventually hanged
   b. that slavery was terrible; that some helped slaves escape
   c. possible answer—fearful, quiet, secret, done in darkness, hopeful and rewarding

3. **a.** a journalist, abolitionist
   b. demanded immediate abolition
   c. firsthand experience with slavery, intelligence, speaking skills

4. Enslaved—pain, humiliation; Abolitionists—evil that must end; Slaveholders—attack on livelihood, essential to economy

5. possible answer—a system of safe houses that offered slaves food, hiding, and assistance toward freedom

Info to Know

The Making of an Abolitionist Some white southerners supported abolition. James Birney had been a slaveholder since he received a slave as a present for his sixth birthday. After a religious conversion, however, he freed his slaves and moved to Ohio, where he published an antislavery newspaper. Later he worked for the American Anti-Slavery Society.

Review & Assess

Close

Guide the class in a discussion of the institution of slavery and the Reform Era movements to end it.

Review

Online Quiz, Section 4

Daily Test Practice Transparency

Assess

SE Section 4 Assessment

Progress Assessment: Section 4 Quiz

Alternative Assessment Handbook

Reteach

Interactive Reader and Study Guide, Section 4

Interactive Skills Tutor CD-ROM

Answers

Art *He demanded immediate abolishment of slavery.*

Reading Check *possible answer—conflict within the government, war, division of the government, and outcry of support and opposition for both sides*

289

Word Help

propagators spreaders
gross flagrant, glaring
entailed forced
sovereign independent
emancipate free

Primary Source

In *Miscellaneous Essays*, published in Philadelphia in 1830, Mathew Carey outlined proper behavior for wives: "A good wife will always receive her husband with smiles . . . She will never attempt to rule, or appear to rule her husband . . . She will, in every thing reasonable, comply with his wishes—and, as far as possible, anticipate them."

— Mathew Carey

Miscellaneous Essays, 1830

Info to Know

Henry Garnet At his speech to the national convention for free African Americans in 1843, Henry Highland Garnet shocked many of his listeners when he urged slaves to murder their masters, arguing that it was better to die fighting for freedom than to live as a slave. While many abolitionists were repelled by Garnet's radicalism, he turned toward religion and became a leading pastor. At the end of his life, Garnet worked as a minister to Liberia, advocating the return of African Americans to Africa.

CHAPTER
8 DOCUMENT-BASED INVESTIGATION

Reform Movements

Historical Context The documents below provide perspectives on different reform movements during the 1800s.

Task Examine the documents and answer the questions that follow. Then you will be asked to write an essay about reform movements in the 1800s, using facts from the documents and from the chapter to support the position you take in your thesis statement.

DOCUMENT 1

Henry Highland Garnet was born into slavery in 1815. At age nine, he escaped and made his way to the North, where he became a leader of the abolitionist movement. He gave the following speech in 1843.

"Two hundred and twenty-seven years ago, the first of our injured race were brought to the shores of America. They came not with glad spirits to select their homes in the New World . . . Neither did they come flying upon the wings of Liberty, to a land of freedom. But they came with broken hearts, from their beloved native land, and were doomed to unrequited [unpaid] toil . . .

The propagators of the system, or their immediate ancestors, very soon discovered its growing evil, and its tremendous wickedness, and secret promises were made to destroy it. The gross inconsistency of a people holding slaves, who had themselves 'ferried o'er the wave' for freedom's sake, was too apparent to be entirely overlooked . . .

The colonists threw the blame upon England. They said that the mother country entailed the evil upon them, and that they would rid themselves of it if they could. The world thought they were sincere . . . But time soon tested their sincerity.

In a few years the colonists grew strong, and severed themselves from the British Government. Their independence was declared, and they took their station among the sovereign powers of the earth . . . When the power of Government returned to their hands, did they emancipate the slaves? No; they rather added new links to our chains . . ."

DOCUMENT 2

Besides gaining voting rights, one of the main goals of the women's rights movement was to change laws regarding rights to property. This issue drew support from women like Keziah Kendall, who owned a farm with her two sisters. Kendall wrote the following letter to an opponent of women's rights, explaining her views on the subject.

"My name is Keziah Kendall. I live many miles from Cambridge, on a farm with my two sisters, one older, one younger than myself . . . [W]e have a good estate—comfortable house—nice barn, garden, orchard & such, and money in the bank besides . . . Now we are taxed every year to the full amount of every dollar we possess—town, county, state taxes—taxes for land, for moveables, for money and all. Now I don't want to go [become a] representative or anything else, anymore than I do to be a constable or a sheriff, but I have no voice about public improvements, and I don't see the justice of being taxed anymore than the revolutionary heroes did . . . I am told . . . that if a woman dies a week after she's married that her husband takes all her personal property and the use of her real estate as long as he lives—if a man dies his wife can have her thirds [one-third of the estate] . . . I think the law is in fault here . . .

Women have joined the Antislavery societies, and why? Women are kept for slaves as well as men—it is a common cause, deny the justice of it, who can!"

Collaborative Learning

At Level

Modern Reform Movements

1. Divide the class into groups of four or five students. Have each group make a list of issues that might be addressed by present-day reform movements.

2. Approve one of the possible reform movements for each group to work on. Have them come up with a strategy to bring about the reforms and write a manifesto for their reform.

3. Have each group develop and create materials that could be used to bring their cause to the public's attention. These materials could include posters and pamphlets, editorials or letters to the editor, scripts for radio and television ads, or a Web site.

4. Have each group present its reform campaign to the class. **LS Interpersonal, Logical-Mathematical**

📄 Alternative Assessment Handbook, Rubric 29: Presentations

DOCUMENT 3

The temperance movement of the 1800s focused on trying to get people to stop, or cut back on, drinking liquor. The movement used many popular images of the time to show the advantages of sobriety and the destructiveness of drunkenness. These two images show the "Tree of Temperance" and the "Tree of Intemperance," recalling the biblical story of Adam and Eve, who brought sin into the world by eating fruit from a forbidden tree. The fruits are labeled with the positive qualities of temperence and the negative qualities of drunkenness.

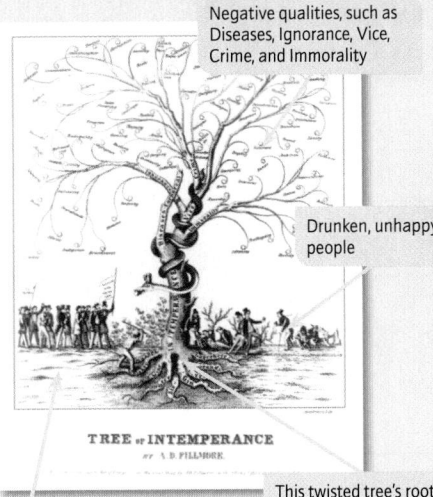

Positive qualities, such as Industry, Philanthropy, Goodwill, and Charity

Signs of a productive community

Well-dressed, happy children and adults

Negative qualities, such as Diseases, Ignorance, Vice, Crime, and Immorality

Drunken, unhappy people

Prohibitionists are celebrating the first major anti-liquor law, passed in Maine in 1851.

This twisted tree's roots represent different kinds of liquor. A serpent with an apple in its mouth and a mug of beer on its head suggests the serpent who tempted Adam and Eve.

Skills FOCUS READING LIKE A HISTORIAN

1. **a. Identify** Refer to Document 1. According to Garnet, whom did the early colonists blame for supporting slavery?
   b. Analyze In what way does Garnet see the founders of the United States as insincere?

2. **a. Identify** Refer to Document 2. To whom does Kendall compare herself when she complains about paying taxes without having a voice in government?
   b. Explain According to Kendall, why do so many women support the antislavery movement?

3. **a. Identify** Refer to Document 3. How do the two images reflect the religious background of the temperance movement?
   b. Contrast Based on these images, how was a temperate society different from an intemperate one?

4. **Document-Based Essay Question** Consider the question below and form a thesis statement. Using examples from Documents 1, 2, and 3, create an outline and write a short essay supporting your position.
   How were the reform movements of the early 1800s similar to and different from one another?

See **Skills Handbook**, pp. H28–H29

Skills Focus: Interpreting Visuals   At Level

Reading Like a Historian Skill
Temperance Then and Now

1. Guide the class in a discussion of the "Tree of Temperance" and "Tree of Intemperance" images using the following questions as a guide: What symbols of productivity are in the background of the "Tree of Temperance"? What are the roots of intemperance? What do the limbs of the "Tree of Intemperance" represent? How do the virtues that are the fruits of temperance compare with the vices that grow on the "Tree of Intemperance"? What are the people doing at the foot of the "Tree of Temperance"? What are the people doing at the foot of the "Tree of Intemperance"?

2. Pair students. Have each pair create a poster to discourage alcohol consumption that they think would be effective in today's society.

3. Display students' posters for the class to see.
   LS Visual-Spatial, Interpersonal

   Alternative Assessment Handbook, Rubrics 11: Discussions; and 28: Posters

Info to Know

Temperance America is not the only nation that has questioned the consumption of alcohol. Attempts at a legal prohibition on alcohol were made in ancient China, feudal Japan, Aztec society, Norway, Canada, Iceland, Sweden, India, and Russia. In 1919 Finland passed a prohibition law, but it was repealed in 1931. Only a few countries (primarily Muslim nations) have successfully upheld the prohibition of alcohol.

Answers

Reading Like a Historian
1. a. England; **b.** The colonists blamed England for slavery, but rather than end it upon gaining their freedom, they strengthened the institution. **2. a.** the heroes of the Revolution; **b.** because they are also treated as slaves; **3. a.** by using religious imagery, such as a serpent, an apple, and a church; by referencing the story of Adam and Eve in their titles; **b.** A temperate society was happy, productive, well-ordered, and possessed positive qualities, while an intemperate one was full of drunken, unhappy people who possessed negative qualities. **4.** Answers will vary, but students' essays may include foundations in religion, efforts to protect civil rights of all people, focus on different aspects of society, and different methods for achieving their goals.

Visual Summary

Review and Inquiry Have students list two reformers who worked in each area shown in the visual summary.

📖 Quick Facts Transparency: A Push for Reform

Reviewing Key Terms and People

1. A former slave, Frederick Douglass supported abolition through his powerful speeches and his autobiographical writings.

2. The goal of the temperance movement was to end the use of alcoholic beverages.

3. As the first Massachusetts secretary of education, Horace Mann advocated mandatory school attendance.

4. The push-pull model of immigration refers to a combination of factors that cause people to leave their homeland for a new country.

5. One of the most outspoken abolitionists, William Lloyd Garrison, published the abolitionist newspaper *The Liberator* and founded the American Anti-Slavery Society.

6. During the utopian movement, reformers created new communities that they believed would be free of social ills.

7. Dorothea Dix campaigned for the humane treatment of prisoners and for the establishment of separate institutions to house the mentally ill.

8. The Seneca Falls Convention was a meeting held in 1848 for men and women to discuss women's rights.

9. Henry David Thoreau, a transcendentalist, advocated self-reliance and individual thought; he wrote "Civil Disobedience."

10. Free blacks, or African Americans not held in slavery, played a leading role in the antislavery movement.

11. Lucretia Mott was a dedicated abolitionist and women's rights advocate who helped organize the first women's rights convention in Seneca Falls, New York.

12. Nat Turner was a slave who led an uprising against his owner and other

---

Visual Summary: A Push for Reform

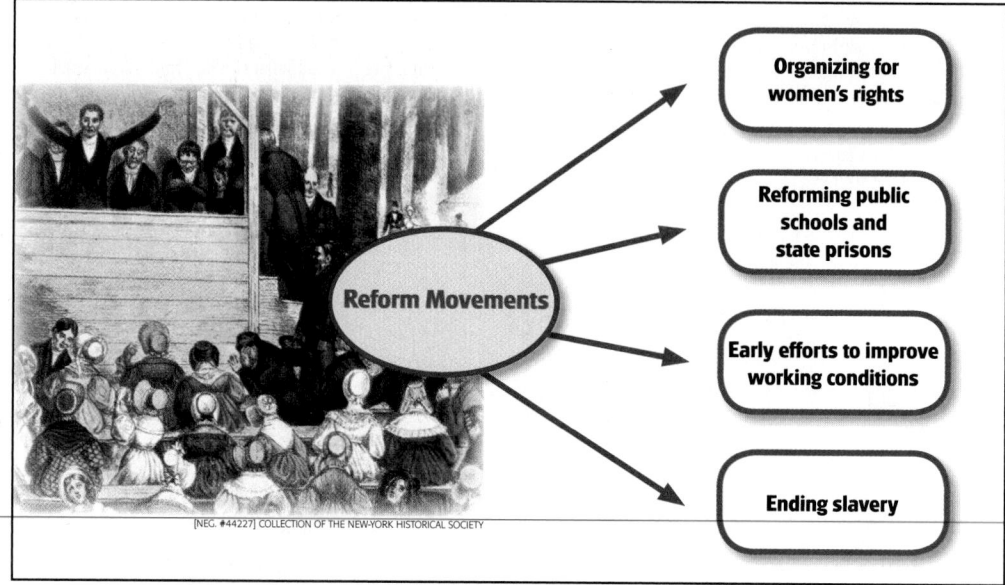

[NEG. #44227] COLLECTION OF THE NEW-YORK HISTORICAL SOCIETY

Reform Movements
- Organizing for women's rights
- Reforming public schools and state prisons
- Early efforts to improve working conditions
- Ending slavery

Reviewing Key Terms and People

For each term below, write a sentence explaining its significance to the Reform Era.

1. Frederick Douglass
2. temperance movement
3. Horace Mann
4. push-pull model of immigration
5. William Lloyd Garrison
6. utopian movement
7. Dorothea Dix
8. Seneca Falls Convention
9. Henry David Thoreau
10. free blacks
11. Lucretia Mott
12. Nat Turner

Comprehension and Critical Thinking

SECTION 1 *(pp. 266–270)*

13. **a. Recall** What was the Second Great Awakening?

b. Contrast How was it different from the First Great Awakening?

c. Evaluate Which movement of the Reform Era do you think was the most important? Why?

SECTION 2 *(pp. 272–277)*

14. **a. Define** Write a brief definition of nativism.

b. Analyze Why were Irish immigrants treated so harshly?

c. Infer What factors led many Americans to oppose immigration?

SECTION 3 *(pp. 280–283)*

15. **a. Describe** What restrictions on women existed during the 1800s?

b. Draw Conclusions Why do you think limits were placed on women?

---

white people, which ended in his own death and stricter laws to limit the movement of slaves.

Comprehension and Critical Thinking

13. **a.** a religious movement in the early 1800s that helped launch the Reform Era

b. it taught followers that their destiny lay in their own hands

c. possible answer—the common-school movement; educated people can create reforms in society

14. **a.** opposition to immigration

b. perceived as threat to American way of life and jobs; usually poor and Catholic

c. great numbers of immigrants

15. **a.** denied control over money and property; treated as inferior to men

b. possible answer—out of fear that industrialization was threatening the American family by taking women out of the household to work

History's Impact video program
Review the video to answer the closing question:
How has American life been improved by the work
of reformers?

SECTION 4 *(pp. 284–289)*

16. a. Identify What was the Underground Railroad?

b. Sequence How did the abolition movement change over the years?

c. Elaborate What did abolitionist Frederick Douglass mean when he said that the issue of slavery was "the great, paramount, imperative, and all-commanding question for this age and nation to solve"?

Using the Internet

go.hrw.com
Practice Online
Keyword: SD7 CH8

17. With the exception of Native Americans, all people who live in the United States today can trace their history back to another country. Using the keyword above, do research to learn about your family's ancestry regarding immigration. Then write a report that presents this information. Include visuals if possible.

Analyzing Primary Sources

Reading Like a Historian The American Party, also known as the Know-Nothings, opposed immigration. In 1854 they won state elections in Massachusetts. The newspaper passage below celebrates the party's victory. Read the passage and answer the questions that follow.

> **❝**The people of the Old Bay State have spoken, and from Berkshire to Cape Cod, are heard the voices of her native born children, declaring for the perpetuity AMERICAN INSTITUTIONS, and AMERICAN LIBERTIES. The descendants of the heroes of BUNKER HILL, LEXINGTON, and CONCORD, have spoken in a voice of thunder, in favor of Americans ruling America . . . the warm pulsation of the people's heart beats only for FREEDOM . . . and PROTESTANTISM.**❞**
>
> —*Daily Evening Journal*, November 14, 1854

18. Identify What does "Bunker Hill, Lexington, and Concord" refer to?

19. Interpret In addition to being against the Irish, what else is this newspaper against?

Critical Reading

Read the passage in Section 3 that begins with the heading "Limits on Women's Lives." Then answer the questions that follow.

20. According to the passage,

A. laws and culture both placed limits on women.

B. there were legal limits, but no economic limits.

C. there were some jobs in which women were paid as much as men.

D. no one challenged the limits placed on women.

21. The first paragraph says that "The handful of men who dared to speak out for the equal treatment of women were treated with even worse disdain." The word *disdain* means

A. respect.

B. contempt.

C. generosity.

D. caution.

WRITING FOR THE SAT

Think about the following issue:

In the 1800s there were many restrictions on women. In most places, they could not vote, hold public office, serve on juries, or enter into legal contracts. Most jobs were closed to them; when they worked, they did not earn as much as men. Married women could not own property; if they worked, they had to give their wages to their husbands.

22. Assignment Have conditions for women improved since the 1800s? Have women achieved complete equality with men in our society? Write a short essay in which you develop your position on this issue. Support your view with reasoning and examples from your reading and studies.

Answers

16. a. network of escape routes for enslaved people

b. Initially, abolitionists favored a gradual end to slavery; over time, demanded immediate abolition

c. possible answer—was the most urgent issue facing the nation

Using the Internet

17. Go to the HRW Web site and enter the keyword shown to access a rubric for this activity.

KEYWORD: SD7 CH8

Analyzing Primary Sources

18. battle sites from the Revolutionary War

19. Catholicism

Critical Reading

20. A

21. B

Writing for the SAT

22. possible answer—yes, women now have the same political rights as men; married women maintain control of their property and earnings; women hold jobs

A rubric for this activity can be found in the Chapter Resource File: Writing for the SAT: Immigration.

History's Impact Video Program

Americans now enjoy equal rights and privileges

Review and Assessment Resources

Review and Reinforce

- CRF: Chapter Review Activity
- Quick Facts Transparency: A Push for Reform
- Spanish Chapter Summaries Audio CD Program
- Online Chapter Summaries in Spanish
- OSP Holt PuzzlePro; Quiz Show for ExamView
- Quiz Game CD-ROM

Assess

- PASS: Chapter Test, Forms A and B
- Alternative Assessment Handbook
- OSP ExamView Test Generator, Chapter Test
- Differentiated Instruction Modified Worksheets and Tests CD-ROM: Chapter Test
- HOAP Holt Online Assessment Program (in the Premier Online Edition)

Reteach/Intervene

- Interactive Reader and Study Guide
- Differentiated Instruction Teacher Management System: Lesson Plans for Differentiated Instruction
- Differentiated Instruction Modified Worksheets and Tests CD-ROM: Chapter Test
- Interactive Skills Tutor CD-ROM

go.hrw.com
Online Resources
KEYWORD: SD7 CH8

Chapter 9 Planning Guide

Expansion Leads to Conflict

Chapter Overview	Reproducible Resources	Technology Resources
CHAPTER 9 pp. 294–315 **Overview: In this chapter, students will analyze the ideas that led thousands of Americans westward and how this expansion led to conflict with Mexico.**	**Differentiated Instruction Teacher Management System:*** • Instructional Benchmarking Guides • Lesson Plans for Differentiated Instruction **Interactive Reader and Study Guide:** Chapter Summary* **Chapter Resource File:*** • Focus on Writing: The Annexation of Mexican Land by the United States • Social Studies Skills Activity: Interpreting Movement Maps • Chapter Review Activity ~~American History Outline Maps~~ **Pre-AP Activities Guide for American History***	**Live Ink® Online Reading Help** **Student Edition on Audio CD Program** **Differentiated Instruction Modified Worksheets and Tests CD-ROM** **Interactive Skills Tutor CD-ROM** **United States History Primary Source Library CD-ROM** **Power Presentations with Video CD-ROM** **History's Impact: American History Video Program (VHS/DVD):** Expansion Leads to Conflict **Online Chapter Summaries in Spanish** **Graphic Organizer Transparencies**
Section 1: **Manifest Destiny** **The Main Idea:** Americans in large numbers followed trails to the West in the 1840s and 1850s.	**Differentiated Instruction Teacher Management System:** Section 1 Lesson Plan* **Interactive Reader and Study Guide:** Section 1 Summary* **Chapter Resource File:*** • Vocabulary Builder Activity, Section 1 • Biography Activity: Biddy Mason • Primary Source Activity: Francis Parkman on the Oregon Trail	**Daily Bellringer Transparency:** Section 1* **Map Transparency:** American Trails West* **Map Transparency:** Oregon Divided* **Internet Activity:** The Oregon Trail **Daily Test Practice Transparency:** Section 1*
Section 2: **Texas Independence** **The Main Idea:** American settlers in Texas revolted against the Mexican government and created the independent Republic of Texas.	**Differentiated Instruction Teacher Management System:** Section 2 Lesson Plan* **Interactive Reader and Study Guide:** Section 2 Summary* **Chapter Resource File:*** • Vocabulary Builder Activity, Section 2 • Biography Activity: Susanna Wilkerson Dickerson • History and Geography Activity: Southwest Expansion	**Daily Bellringer Transparency:** Section 2* **Map Transparency:** Texas Revolution* **Internet Activity:** Texas Declaration of Independence **Daily Test Practice Transparency:** Section 2*
Section 3: **War with Mexico** **The Main Idea:** Soon after annexing Texas, the United States declared war on Mexico.	**Differentiated Instruction Teacher Management System:** Section 3 Lesson Plan* **Interactive Reader and Study Guide:** Section 3 Summary* **Chapter Resource File:*** • Vocabulary Builder Activity, Section 3 • Biography Activity: Charles Francis Adams • Primary Source Activity: James Buchanan Considers the Annexation of Texas	**Daily Bellringer Transparency:** Section 3* **Map Transparency:** The Mexican-American War* **Quick Facts Transparency:** Causes and Effects of the Mexican-American War* **Internet Activity:** California: The 31st State **Daily Test Practice Transparency:** Section 3*

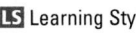 
HOLT
History's Impact
American History Video Program (VHS/DVD)
Expansion Leads to Conflict

Review, Assessment, Intervention

 Quick Facts Transparencies: Causes and Effects of the Mexican-American War, Expansion Leads to Conflict

 Spanish Chapter Summaries Audio CD Program

 Progress Assessment Support System (PASS): Chapter Test*

 **Differentiated Instruction Modified Worksheets and Tests CD-ROM:** Modified Chapter Test

OSP **One-Stop Planner CD-ROM:** Exam View Test Generator (English/Spanish)

HOAP **Holt Online Assessment Program (HOAP),** in the Premier Online Edition.

 PASS: Section 1 Quiz*

 Online Quiz: Section 1

 Alternative Assessment Handbook

 PASS: Section 2 Quiz*

 Online Quiz: Section 2

 Alternative Assessment Handbook

 PASS: Section 3 Quiz*

 Online Quiz: Section 3

 Alternative Assessment Handbook

 **RESOURCES**

The following resources were developed to help North Carolina educators teach the standards and objectives of North Carolina's eleventh grade standard course of study in United States history.
- United States history EOC Test Prep Workbook
- Teacher's Support System
- North Carolina One-Stop Planner

And be sure to direct your students to **go.hrw.com** for online access to the EOC Test Prep Workbook.

go.hrw.com
EOC Test Prep
KEYWORD: SE7 NC

Holt Online Learning

go.hrw.com
Teacher Resources
KEYWORD: SD7 TEACHER

go.hrw.com
Student Resources
KEYWORD: SD7 CH9

- Document-based Questions
- Interactive Multimedia Activities

- Current Events
- Chapter-based Internet Activities
- and more!

Holt Premier
Online Student Edition
Complete online support for interactivity, assessment, and reporting
- Interactive Maps and Notebook
- Standardized Test Prep
- Homework Practice and Research Activities Online

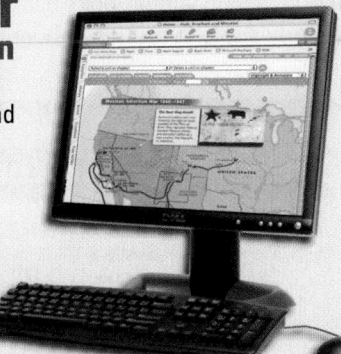

CHAPTER 9 PLANNING GUIDE

Before You Teach

The Big Picture
Jesús F. de la Teja

Manifest Destiny, the Flip Side Americans moved west for many of the same reasons that the original English colonists had come to America in the seventeenth century. Like the Puritans, the Mormons sought to escape persecution and establish an ideal society on their own terms. Like the original Jamestown colonists, thousands went west in search of quick riches, only to find that sacrifice and a lifetime of hard work were the only avenues to success. Thousands of others came, like the earlier Germans, French, and others, seeking opportunities that were denied to them back home. And, just as Englishmen were destined to displace the native peoples of the Atlantic seaboard, so were Americans destined to displace the native peoples of the West.

Mexico's Immigration Problem in Texas The years immediately following Mexican independence in 1821 coincided with the beginnings of the great push westward by Americans. Bankrupt and uncertain of itself, the newly independent nation saw Anglo American immigration to Texas as a way to develop the frontier region. The settlers, whether legal or undocumented, showed little interest in learning how to become good Mexicans. By 1830 Mexico City officials had realized what a terrible mistake they had made in allowing in the *norteamericanos,* but their efforts to turn back the tide proved too little, too late.

America's Upper Hand Less than forty years after the return of the Lewis and Clark expedition from its historic encounter with the Pacific, Yankee merchantmen and whalers were making regular visits up and down the Pacific coast. The Polk administration wanted California as much as previous administrations had wanted Texas. With a booming population, a growing industrial and mercantile economy, and a sense that the Creator wanted America to control the continent, Polk felt confident that one way or another Mexico would cede the territory that destiny manifestly wanted to be American.

Recent Scholarship

The Importance of Texas Texans have a rather high regard for their history; the decade-long Republic of Texas looms large in the state's imagination. *Crisis in the Southwest: The United States, Mexico, and the Struggle over Texas (2002)* is Richard Bruce Winders's attempt to make that importance tangible to a wider audience. While making the story of Mexican political turmoil, increasing Texan alienation, and American land hunger the central part of the narrative, the author looks back to the Louisiana Purchase and forward to the sectional crisis to shed light on manifest destiny's role in bringing about the Civil War.

Differentiating Instruction

 Differentiated Instruction Teacher Management System
- Lesson Plans for Differentiated Instruction
- Differentiated Instructional Benchmarking Guides
- Interactive Reader and Study Guide

 Spanish Chapter Summaries Audio CD Program

 Online Chapter Summaries in Spanish

 Student Edition on Audio CD Program

 Differentiated Instruction Modified Worksheets and Tests CD-ROM
- Vocabulary Flash Cards
- Modified Vocabulary Builder Activities
- Modified Chapter Review Activity
- Modified Chapter Test

 OSP One-Stop Planner CD-ROM
- ExamView Test Generator (English and Spanish)
- PuzzlePro
- Quiz Show for ExamView
- Transparencies and Videos

TE Differentiated Activities in the Teacher's Edition
- Trails West, p. 298
- Mission Life, p. 303
- Defending the Alamo, p. 306
- Alamo Movies, p. 313

Reading Like a Historian
Sam Wineburg

Remember (to watch) the Alamo

If students bring any knowledge to this chapter, all bets are on the phrase "Remember the Alamo." Even if they don't know what the Alamo is, they'll know they are supposed to remember it.

The Alamo on Film

Since the beginning of movie making, the Alamo has been the subject of 12 motion pictures—more than Gettysburg, D-Day, or any other famous battle. The latest version, by Texan John Lee Hancock—which at $90 million was by far the most expensive—features Billy Bob Thornton as Davy Crockett. In terms of sticking to the historical record, Hancock's *The Alamo* was a marked improvement over such forgettable entries as the *Martyrs of the Alamo* (1915), *Heroes of the Alamo* (1937), and *The Last Command* (1955). But the Alamo flick that has had the greatest impact on the American consciousness was shot in 1960 against the backdrop of the Cold War.

John Wayne

The 1960 version of *The Alamo* stars John Wayne as a larger-than-life Davy Crockett. Wayne financed the picture in part and viewed it as his personal mission "to re-create a moment in history which will show . . . Americans what their country really stands for . . . what some of their forebears went through to win what they had to have, or die—liberty and freedom."

In 1960 people had to go to the theatre to see John Wayne's *Alamo* but, today, access to the visual landscape has changed dramatically. We are flooded by DVDs, can watch the History Channel round the clock, or can download movie scenes from the Internet with the click of a mouse. Not even the most successful written history can compete with filmmaker Ken Burns, whose miniseries *The Civil War* reached 39 million Americans in its original broadcast and has been viewed by millions more since. Consuming filmic histories since the cradle, our students know slavery through *Amistad*, the Holocaust through *Schindler's List*, and Vietnam though *Forrest Gump*—not to mention the historical references they've picked up from Lisa, Bart Simpson's brainy little sister.

But just because our students are suffused by historical images doesn't mean they are connoisseurs about what they see. Their impulses can be dead wrong.

How Students See Movies

In a classic study, Peter Seixas, a historian at the University of British Columbia, showed excerpts from two movies to a group of adolescents. He contrasted Kevin Costner's *Dances with Wolves* (1990) with John Ford's *The Searchers* (1956), which has been called one of the "most viciously anti-Indian films ever made."

Seixas's young viewers were full of criticism for the 1956 film, noting its crude technique, grainy quality, and exaggerated acting. But when the same students turned to Costner's production, their critical faculties went on strike. Young people, Seixas wrote, "assumed that they were confronting . . . a window on the past." They could see *The Searchers* as a reflection of the biases and prejudices of the 1950s. But they viewed *Dances with Wolves*, whose norms matched their own, as the naked historical truth.

While no study has compared young people's reactions to John Wayne's *Alamo* and John Lee Hancock's, we can surmise what might happen. Many students would bristle at Wayne's soliloquies on freedom, while feasting on Hancock's admittedly more authentic and complex description of interracial interaction among Anglos, Texans, Tejanos, and Mexicans. But rather than noting how the filmmaker uses historical figures to mouth current ideas (e.g., as when one of the Tejanos whispers in Spanish, "Santa Anna just wants to rule Mexico; these disgraces want to take over the world"), students are likely to take such statements as historical truths.

How to Approach Film

Film can be a powerful classroom tool; we'd be foolish to renounce it. But if we don't teach students to approach film like any other historical product—as a reflection of its time—we stunt their analytic skills.

To show movies without first teaching students how to view them is not teaching; it's entertaining. Students get enough of that already.

Quote by John Wayne from *Gunfighter Nation: The Myth of the Frontier in Twentieth-Century America* by Richard Slotkin. Reproduced by permission of **Atheneum, a division of Random House, Inc., www.randomhouse.com.**

Standards Focus

Social Studies Competency Goals
Goal 3 The learner will analyze the issues that led up to the Civil War, the effects of the war, and the impact of Reconstruction on the nation.
 3.01, 3.02

The Big Idea and Essential Questions

To foster student understanding of this chapter's big idea, design your lesson to address each section's essential question.

Big Idea As thousands of American settlers migrated westward, souring relations between Mexico and the United States led to war and the expansion of America's borders.

Essential Questions

1. Why did large numbers of Americans move West in the 1840s and 1850s?

2. What role did American settlers play in the conflict between Texas and Mexico?

3. What were the causes and effects of the war between the United States and Mexico?

Key to Differentiating Instruction

Below Level

Basic-level activities designed for all students encountering new material

At Level

Intermediate-level activities designed for average students

Above Level

Challenging activities designed for honors and gifted-and-talented students

Standard English Mastery

Activities designed to improve standard English usage

294 CHAPTER 9

CHAPTER
9 1830–1860

Expansion Leads to Conflict

THE BIG PICTURE Between 1830 and 1860 Americans by the thousands migrated westward into the frontier wilderness. In 1846, souring relations led to war between Mexico and the United States, and the outcome defined America's borders.

North Carolina Standards

Social Studies Objectives
2.01 Analyze the effects of territorial expansion and the admission of new states to the Union.
3.01 Trace the economic, social, and political events from the Mexican War to the outbreak of the Civil War.

Language Arts Objectives
2.01 Research and analyze ideas, events, and/or movements related to United States culture by:
  • locating facts and details for purposeful elaboration.
3.01 Use language persuasively in addressing a particular issue by:
  • establishing and defending a point of view.

Skills FOCUS **READING LIKE A HISTORIAN**

Painter Albert Bierstadt spent years documenting the westward journey across the American landscape, as he did here in *Emigrants Crossing the Plains.* His popular paintings helped publicize westward expansion.
Interpreting Visuals What is the overall tone or mood of this painting?
See Skills Handbook, p. H30

294

U.S.

World

November 1830 Joseph Smith founds the Mormon Church.

1830

1834 Mexican President Antonio López de Santa Anna makes himself dictator.

Introduce the Chapter

At Level

Expansion Leads to Conflict

1. Guide the class in a discussion of why some people in the eastern United States might have wanted to move to the West during the 1800s. Create a class chart on the board. Then discuss challenges American settlers might have faced while moving to the West. Remind students that Native Americans and Mexicans were already living on some of these lands.

2. Have each student write a journal entry from the perspective of an American settler moving to the West in the early 1800s. Students should explain reasons for the move, their feelings about it, and obstacles that they might have faced.

3. Tell students that in this chapter they will learn about the westward expansion of the United States during the early 1800s, an important part of American history and culture. **LS Verbal-Linguistic**

📓 Alternative Assessment Handbook, Rubric 15: Journals

History's Impact video program
Watch the video to understand the impact of Texas and the Southwest.

| October 1835 The Texas Revolution breaks out at Gonzales. | 1843 The missionary Marcus Whitman leads a large wagon train along the Oregon Trail. | May 1846 The United States declares war on Mexico. | January 1848 Gold is discovered at Sutter's Mill in northern California. | | April 1860 Pony Express mail service begins. |

| 1836 | 1842 | 1848 | 1854 | 1860 |

| 1842 Great Britain annexes Hong Kong. | February 1848 Mexico signs the Treaty of Guadalupe Hidalgo, ceding California and much of the Southwest to the United States. | 1854 Commodore Perry and Japanese officials sign an agreement opening Japan to U.S. trade. | 1857 The first transatlantic communications cable, linking Great Britain and the United States, begins operation. |

295

Chapter Preview

HOLT

History's Impact

▶ Video Program: Expansion Leads to Conflict
See the Video Teacher's Guide for strategies for using the video segment.

Reading Like a Historian

Emigrants Crossing the Plains Have students examine the image carefully. Ask students whether this painting by Albert Bierstadt presents a positive or negative view of moving to the West. What images of the West does the artist create?

Explore the Time Line

1. When did Mexican President Antonio López de Santa Anna declare himself dictator? *1834*

2. What were the terms of the Treaty of Guadalupe Hidalgo? *Mexico ceded California and much of the Southwest to the United States.*

3. Where and when did the Texas Revolution break out? *Gonzales; October 1835*

Info to Know

The West and the American Character
American movement west affected not only the physical size of the United States but also American culture. According to historian Frederick Jackson Turner, Americans are proud of their frontier history and celebrate the qualities it took to survive and thrive in the harsh conditions of the West. These qualities included individualism, self-reliance, mobility, and optimism. To this day, Americans celebrate these qualities as part of the national character.

Answers

Reading Like a Historian (p. 294)
possible answer—peaceful; emphasizes beauty of the West

295

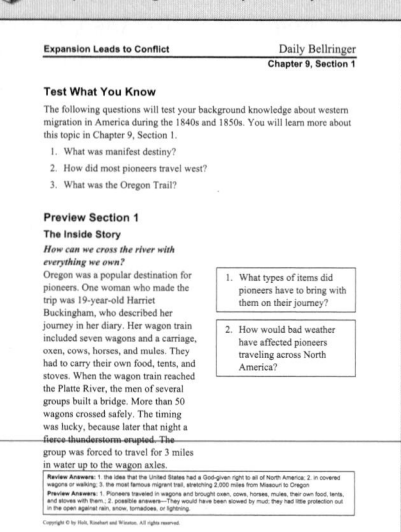
SECTION 1 Manifest Destiny

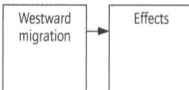

BEFORE YOU READ

MAIN IDEA

Americans in large numbers followed trails to the West in the 1840s and 1850s.

READING FOCUS

1. Why did Americans head west?
2. What were the major western trails?
3. How did the gold rush affect California?
4. What were some major effects of westward migration?

KEY TERMS AND PEOPLE

manifest destiny
entrepreneur
Santa Fe Trail
Oregon Trail
Mormon Trail
James K. Polk
gold rush
California Trail
Butterfield Trail
Pony Express

TAKING NOTES As you read, take notes identifying the effects of vast numbers of Americans migrating to the West. Record your notes in a graphic organizer like the one shown here.

| Westward migration | → | Effects |

A Day on the Trail

▲ A westward-bound family poses with their prairie schooners.

THE INSIDE STORY *How can we cross the river with everything we own?* Oregon Territory was the goal of many pioneer families. Some single women made the trip, usually traveling with a family.

Harriet Buckingham, who was just 19, kept a diary of her trip to Oregon in 1851. Buckingham was a good observer, describing the landscape and the Native American peoples she met. The wagon train included seven wagons and a carriage, along with oxen, cows, horses, and mules. They carried tents, cookstoves, and a coop full of chickens. On May 13, 1851, they reached the Platte River. One challenge was to get across the river. Another was the weather.

"We were quickly wakened this morning by the singing of the Indians. Our men all went to work with the three other companies [of wagons] building a bridge. It was completed by afternoon when we crossed. It is a matter of surprise that over 500 head of cattle & fifty wagons should cross without accident. The Waggons were all drawn over by hand & the cattle & horses swam . . . We encamped a mile from the creek. The Evening was delightful, the moon shone so clearly but before morning, it clouded up and one of the most terrifine [terrifying] storms I ever witnessed . . . The rain fell in torrents. The lightning was most vivid. We were obliged to move as soon as possible for fear of being overflown . . . we traveled on some 3 miles in water up to the axletrees." ■

296 CHAPTER 9

Teach the Main Idea

At Level

Manifest Destiny

1. **Teach** Ask students the Reading Focus questions to teach this section.

2. **Apply** To help students put the major events of America's westward expansion in perspective, have them create an outline of the section using the heads as main points. Have students identify at least two main ideas under each of the blue subheadings.

3. **Review** Review student outlines as a class, and guide students in a discussion of the various reasons Americans wanted to

migrate west.

4. **Practice/Homework** Have each student choose one conflict that was caused by westward expansion and write an essay explaining what, if anything, could have been done either to prevent the conflict or to minimize its effects. **LS Logical-Mathematical, Verbal-Linguistic**

📖 Alternative Assessment Handbook, Rubric 37: Writing Assignments

Americans Head West

Just like Harriet Buckingham, hundreds of thousands of Americans migrated west in the 1840s and 1850s. They went for many different reasons, and they settled in many different places. Yet they all shared the dream of new opportunities and a better life.

"Multiplying millions" By 1840 the American population had grown to about six times what it had been during the American Revolution. The country's area had expanded to about twice its original size. It seemed inconceivable to most Americans that the growth and expansion they had always known would stop.

In fact, many Americans of the time believed in **manifest destiny**, the idea that the nation had a God-given right to all of North America. The term was first used by newspaper editor John L. O'Sullivan. In 1845 he wrote that "our manifest destiny [is to] overspread the continent allotted by Providence [God's power] for the free development of our yearly multiplying millions." Most Americans gave little thought to how manifest destiny would affect peoples already living in regions to be added to the United States.

Reasons for westward migration Many Americans who headed west in the early and mid-1800s believed in manifest destiny. But they also had more personal reasons. Mountain men, who went west to trap and trade, were among the earliest migrants. They were followed by missionaries, who hoped to convert Native Americans to Christianity. Lumberjacks and miners headed west to capitalize on the region's natural resources.

Most pioneers in the 1840s and 1850s were farmers. They moved west to farm the vast, rich land of which earlier migrants spoke. Many of them were relatively poor. They had little to lose by leaving their homes and had a chance to gain a great deal by moving west. The farmers were followed by **entrepreneurs**, people willing to invest their money in the hope of making a profit. Shopkeepers, carpenters, and other businesspeople knew that if they were among the first to practice their trade in a new settlement, they had a greater chance for success.

READING CHECK Summarizing What types of people headed west, and for what reasons?

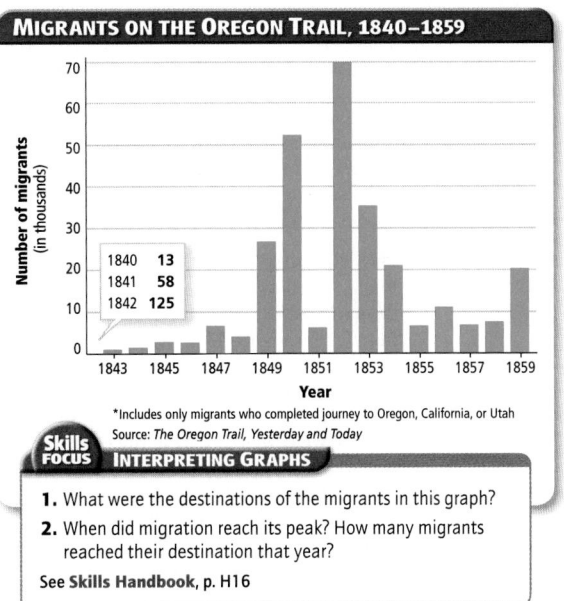

MIGRANTS ON THE OREGON TRAIL, 1840–1859

Year	Number
1840	13
1841	58
1842	125

Number of migrants (in thousands)

*Includes only migrants who completed journey to Oregon, California, or Utah
Source: *The Oregon Trail, Yesterday and Today*

Skills FOCUS INTERPRETING GRAPHS

1. What were the destinations of the migrants in this graph?
2. When did migration reach its peak? How many migrants reached their destination that year?

See Skills Handbook, p. H16

Major Western Trails

Americans who migrated west had the adventure of their lives. But for some, the trip cost them their lives.

No train tracks or smooth highways led from the East to the far West in the 1840s and 1850s. Migrants reached the West by riding in wagons pulled by oxen or horses, or by walking. Some migrants actually walked hundreds of miles to reach their new homes. They took one of several routes that were well established by 1850.

The Santa Fe Trail The first major western trail was the **Santa Fe Trail,** which led from Independence, Missouri, to the town of Santa Fe, the capital of Spanish New Mexico. The Santa Fe Trail began as a commercial route, or trade route. News of the wealth of Santa Fe motivated Americans to open trade with the people there.

In 1821 a veteran of the War of 1812 named William Becknell led a small band of traders out of Arrow Rock, Missouri, bound for Santa Fe. It took them two months to complete the difficult, 800-mile journey, but they made it and sold their goods for a huge profit.

Direct Teach

Reading Focus

1 Why did Americans head west? *for new opportunities and a better life*

Americans Head West

Recall What did the Americans who migrated west in the 1840s and 1850s have in common? *shared the dream of new opportunities and a better life*

Make Generalizations How did the idea of manifest destiny influence Americans' westward migration? *Americans believed that it was their God-given right to settle the land all the way to the Pacific Ocean.*

CRF: Biography: Biddy Mason

Reading Focus

2 What were the major western trails? *the Santa Fe, Oregon, and Mormon Trails*

Major Western Trails

Explain Without trains or highways, how did travelers reach the West in the 1840s and 1850s? *in wagons pulled by oxen or horses; walked, following one of several routes*

Analyze Why did the Santa Fe Trail begin as a commercial route? *Americans wanted to open trade with wealthy people living in the Southwest.*

go.hrw.com
Online Resources
KEYWORD: SD7 CH9
TOPIC: THE OREGON TRAIL

Answers

Interpreting Graphs 1. *Oregon, Utah, and California;* **2.** *1852; about 70,000*

Reading Check *mountain men to trap and trade; missionaries to convert Native Americans to Christianity; lumberjacks and miners to capitalize on natural resources; farmers for land; entrepreneurs to succeed in business*

297

Major Western Trails

Identify What was the longest of the trails west? *the Oregon Trail*

Contrast What was the biggest difference between the people who followed the Mormon Trail and those who followed other trails west? *The Mormons were fleeing religious persecution, while followers of other trails were looking primarily for profits or land.*

Evaluate Until they settled in Utah, why had the Mormons encountered hostile neighbors? *Mormons had some beliefs that differed from Protestant Christianity, including the practice of men having more than one wife.*

- American History Outline Maps: Western Trails
- Map Transparency: American Trails West
- CRF: Primary Source Activity: Francis Parkman on the Oregon Trail

Info to Know

Children and the Journey West After the treacherous journey west, many children were left without parents. These children were either left at a mission along the route or cared for by members of the wagon train until they reached their destination. At that point, the child was placed in an orphanage or given to a capable adult. Some orphanages refused to accept children outside a certain racial, ethnic, or religious group. While some orphanages were willing to keep children until they reached adulthood, others attempted to give the children to guardians or employers. Few children were adopted.

Answers

Interpreting Maps 1. *the Santa Fe Trail and the Butterfield Overland Trail;* **2.** *long distances, mountains, deserts*

298

Other traders followed Becknell's route. They carried cloth, books, hardware and other goods to Santa Fe and returned with Mexican silver coins, wool, animals, and other items that fetched high prices in the eastern United States. In the 1820s and 1830s, about 150 traders traveled the trail each year. By the 1840s, the trading route also began to serve as a route for migrants heading west.

The Oregon Trail The longest and most famous trail used by the migrants was the **Oregon Trail.** The 2,000-mile trail stretched from Independence, Missouri, to the rich farming lands of the Willamette Valley in what is now the state of Oregon.

Native Americans had for centuries used parts of what would become the Oregon Trail. Lewis and Clark also followed part of the route on their historic journey to the West from 1804 to 1806. Many fur traders and mountain men also knew of the route and used it when traveling to and from the West.

Migrants first used the trail in the 1840s. It was in 1843 that the Oregon Trail became established as a major trail west. In that year Dr. Marcus Whitman, who had established a mission in what was called Oregon Country, led a huge party of migrants west. The party consisted of hundreds of people. Thereafter for decades, each spring large groups of migrants started across the trail in an annual cycle.

Danger stalked migrants on their six-month journey to Oregon. Treacherous geography and harsh weather, conflict with Native Americans, and disease took the lives of some 20,000 travelers by 1859. But tens of thousands more pioneers survived. Congress organized Oregon Territory in 1848. In 1859 Oregon became the 33rd state.

The Mormon Trail In 1830 Joseph Smith founded the Church of Jesus Christ of Latter-day Saints in New York. Its members were called Mormons. In five years, Mormon missionaries had attracted some 8,000 followers.

AMERICAN TRAILS WEST

The Oregon Trail ran some 2,000 miles from Independence, Missouri, to Oregon Country.

The Santa Fe Trail was an important commercial route, transporting silver, fur, and manufactured goods.

The Old Spanish Trail was a series of footpaths and horse and mule routes that together formed a trade network between the United States and Mexico.

Butterfield Overland Trail
California Trail
Mormon Trail
Old Spanish Trail
Oregon Trail
Santa Fe Trail

0   200   400 Miles
0   200   400 Kilometers
Albers equal-area projection

GEOGRAPHY SKILLS INTERPRETING MAPS

1. Movement What trails did the Old Spanish Trail link together?

2. Human-Environment Interaction Why was overland travel to and from the West so difficult?

See Skills Handbook, p. H19

298 CHAPTER 9

Differentiating Instruction

Above Level

Advanced Learners/GATE

Research Required

1. Divide the class into small groups. Assign one of the trails to each group—the Santa Fe Trail, the Oregon Trail, and the Mormon Trail.

2. Have each group conduct research on its assigned trail. Groups should use primary and secondary sources. The following questions may help students focus their research: When was the trail first used? How was the trail's route chosen? What was life on the trail like for travelers? What kinds of transportation were most commonly used? What physical obstacles did travelers encounter? When did the last group of settlers use the trail? What happened to the trail after settlers stopped using it?

3. Have each group use the information they collected to write a skit about life on their trail. Have each group present its skit to the class. **LS Interpersonal, Kinesthetic**

- Alternative Assessment Handbook, Rubrics 30: Research; and 33: Skits and Reader's Theater

The practice of men having more than one wife was among other Mormon beliefs that differed from Protestant Christianity. It also fueled hostility. Violent mobs forced the Mormons out of New York to Ohio, out of Ohio to Missouri, and out of Missouri to Illinois. There they built the community of Nauvoo, but they again faced angry neighbors. A mob killed Joseph Smith and his brother and forced the Mormons once more to seek a new home.

Brigham Young became the new leader of the Mormons. He declared that they should migrate west to find a place where they could practice their religion freely. The Mormons abandoned Nauvoo.

Between 1847 and 1853, some 16,000 Mormons migrated to the area around the Great Salt Lake in present-day Utah. The 1,300-mile route they followed became known as the **Mormon Trail**. By 1860 the Mormons had established dozens of settlements in the region. Eventually, thousands more Mormon migrants traveled the route to new settlements in the West.

READING CHECK Comparing and Contrasting How were the Santa Fe, Oregon, and Mormon trails similar and different?

The Gold Rush

The largest single migration west—and one of the greatest migrations in U.S. history—did not occur because of manifest destiny or a desire for new farmland or a search for religious tolerance. It resulted from a hunger for gold.

Gold fever In 1848 a carpenter discovered gold in the American River at John Sutter's sawmill in northern California. Sutter tried to keep the discovery of gold on his land a secret, but word soon spread. People as far away as Asia, South America, and Europe heard the news from American sailors. Many headed to California, dreaming of striking it rich.

News reached the United States, too, but most people dismissed it as a rumor. Then on December 5, 1848, in his State of the Union address, President **James K. Polk** made an announcement that reverberated around the country. The gold mines in California "are more extensive and valuable than was anticipated," he told the Congress. "The explorations already made warrant the belief that the supply is very

The Long Tom, shown here, became a common method of placer mining by 1850. Placer mining involved separating gold deposits from other river sediment. A Long Tom took six to eight people to work and was more efficient than panning for gold.

large and that gold is found at various places in an extensive district of country."

Polk's speech was reported in newspapers across the country. Thousands of Americans caught "gold fever." When one San Francisco newspaper wrote about what happened in California, it described what soon would happen across the nation.

HISTORY'S VOICES

❝The whole country, from San Francisco to Los Angeles, and from the sea shore to the base of the Sierra Nevada resounds with the sordid cry of 'gold, GOLD, GOLD!' while the field is left half-planted, the house half-built, and everything neglected but the manufacture of shovels and pickaxes.❞
—San Francisco Californian, May 29, 1848

Rush to California The mass migration to California of miners—and businesspeople who made money off the miners—is known as the **gold rush**. The migrants who left for California in 1849 were called forty-niners. Their numbers approached a stunning 80,000.

Many more soon followed. Although the dream of finding gold brought people from around the world, 80 percent of those arriving in California came from the United States. To reach California, most people traveled over land, following the **California Trail**. Others

THE IMPACT TODAY

Science and Technology
Millions of pounds of toxic mercury used in some gold-mining processes in the mid-1800s still pollute river beds and stream beds in California today.

Reading Focus

4 What were some major effects of westward migration? *about 1.5 percent of the U.S. population moved west; treaty settled the border between U.S. and British Canada; telegraph linked East and West; lives of Native Americans changed forever*

Major Effects of Westward Migration

Identify What was the Butterfield Trail? *a major southern mail route; carried people and mail between St. Louis and San Francisco*

Summarize How were people in the East and West able to communicate with each other? *by mail, and then by telegraph*

Evaluate Why was the treaty establishing the border between the U.S. and British Canada so important? *Many Americans had settled in Oregon Country, which had been jointly controlled by the U.S. and Britain since 1818. The treaty helped prevent a possible war with Britain.*

Activity The Pony Express Have students create a flyer advertising the fast service of the Pony Express.
LS Visual-Spatial

Info to Know

George Catlin and the West After seeing a delegation of Plains Indians in Philadelphia, George Catlin decided to devote himself to creating a pictorial record of the lives and customs of Native American peoples. Over 350 of his paintings are in the collection of the National Gallery in Washington, D.C.

Answers

Reading Like a Historian *possible answers—to provide a positive or sympathetic view of Native American life and culture*

Reading Check *the discovery of gold in California; President Polk's announcement about gold*

300

---

booked passage on ships that sailed all the way around the southern tip of South America. Still others sailed south to Panama, crossed Central America by mule train, and then sailed north to California. By 1854 as many as 300,000 people had migrated to California.

Booming cities Upon reaching California, most miners moved into mining camps in the gold fields. Many others—especially businesspeople—settled in cities. San Francisco, the port nearest the gold fields, had a population of about 800 in 1848. One year later some 25,000 people lived there. By 1860 it was home to some 60,000 people.

The town of Stockton, located on the San Joaquin River on the way to the southern gold fields, boomed. Sacramento, located on the Sacramento River between San Francisco and the northern gold fields, also grew rapidly. When California became the 31st state in 1850, Sacramento became its capital.

ACADEMIC VOCABULARY
implications possible significance

READING CHECK **Sequencing** What were the major events that led to the widespread settlement of parts of California?

Skills FOCUS **READING LIKE A HISTORIAN**

Romanticizing Native American Life

George Catlin made this painting of a Mandan village from sketches, rather than memory, to capture "the thrilling panorama" he saw. Even so, like most of his paintings, it is a romanticized portrait of his subject.

Recognizing Bias Why might Catlin have painted the scene this way?

Major Effects of Westward Migration

Use of the western trails declined sharply after 1869, when railroad tracks finally ran unbroken from the east to the West Coast. By that time, however, more than 350,000 migrants had followed the overland trails to the West. Such a tremendous migration—equal to about 1.5 percent of the total American population in 1850—had significant effects.

The Oregon Treaty The presence of so many Americans in Oregon Country prompted presidential candidate James K. Polk to campaign in 1844 on the promise of securing the region for the United States. Since 1818 the United States and Britain had jointly controlled Oregon. Polk campaigned with the slogan "Fifty-four Forty or Fight!" He was referring to the line of north latitude, 54°40', that marked the northern boundary of Oregon Country. Polk's statement had dramatic <u>implications</u>. He was pledging war with Great Britain if it refused to give all of Oregon to the United States.

Skills Focus: Identifying Problem and Solution

At Level

Reading Skill
Research Required

"Fifty-four Forty or Fight!"

1. Remind students that 1844 presidential candidate James K. Polk used the campaign slogan, "Fifty-four Forty or Fight!" Polk was willing to go to war with Great Britain if Britain did not give up its claims to Oregon Country. Have each student write an editorial either supporting or opposing Polk's demands. Editorials should make logical arguments and be supported with facts and valid reasoning.

2. Have volunteers read their editorials to the class.

3. Guide the class in a discussion of the reasons students took the positions they did. Have students explain what might have happened if Polk had stuck to his demands rather than negotiate the treaty.
LS Verbal-Linguistic, Logical-Mathematical

Alternative Assessment Handbook, Rubric 17: Letters to Editors

Polk won the presidency but retreated from his pledge. Instead, he concluded a treaty with Britain that set the boundary between the United States and British Canada at the 49th parallel. This boundary, now between the United States and an independent Canada, still exists today.

Communication links Westward migration also led to the need for communication over long distances. Business and government officials in the West needed a way to stay in contact with their eastern counterparts. Individuals, likewise, wanted to stay in touch with the relatives they left behind.

The first answer to this need for communication was mail. A major southern route was the **Butterfield Trail**, over which a private stagecoach line ran. Starting in 1858 and lasting for two-and-a-half years, the Butterfield stages carried passengers and mail between St. Louis and San Francisco. The trip took more than two weeks. For about 18 months, the **Pony Express** offered somewhat quicker mail service between Missouri and California using relays of young riders on fast horses.

In 1861 the telegraph linked the East and the West. It made the Pony Express obsolete by delivering important messages much more

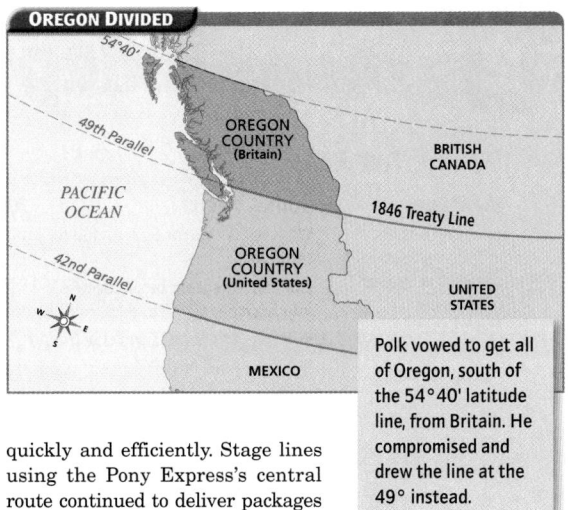

OREGON DIVIDED

Polk vowed to get all of Oregon, south of the 54°40' latitude line, from Britain. He compromised and drew the line at the 49° instead.

quickly and efficiently. Stage lines using the Pony Express's central route continued to deliver packages and routine mail, however.

In time, the greatest effect of westward migration would be on the original inhabitants of the West: Native Americans. Their lives would be forever changed.

READING CHECK Identifying the Main Idea
What were two major effects of Americans' westward migration?

SECTION 1 ASSESSMENT

go.hrw.com
Online Quiz
Keyword: SD7 HP9

Reviewing Ideas, Terms, and People

1. **a. Recall** What is **manifest destiny**?
   b. Analyze Why did many farmers and **entrepreneurs** head west in the 1840s and the 1850s?
   c. Evaluate How large a role do you think a belief in manifest destiny played in people's decisions to head west?

2. **a. Describe** How did the **Santa Fe Trail** come into existence?
   b. Make Inferences Why did the **Oregon Trail** become so heavily traveled?
   c. Evaluate How might attitudes of migrants on the Mormon Trail have been like and unlike those of other travelers west?

3. **a. Identify** What was the **gold rush**?
   b. Make Inferences Why do you think Americans who went to California took different routes there?
   c. Evaluate How did the gold rush affect the United States, California, and the people in both places?

4. **a. Recall** About how many migrants followed overland trails to the West?

   b. Make Inferences Why, do you think, did President **James Polk** retreat from his "Fifty-four Forty or Fight!" pledge?
   c. Predict What effects do you think the migration that began in the 1840s would have on Native Americans?

Critical Thinking

5. **Summarizing** Copy the chart below and complete it to summarize the causes and effects of westward migration.

Group	Cause	Effect
mountain men		
farmers		
forty-niners		
Mormons		

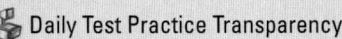
FOCUS ON WRITING

6. **Expository** Many Americans came to California to "mine the miners." Explain what this phrase means in a paragraph.

EXPANSION LEADS TO CONFLICT **301**

The Inside Story. . . Use the **Daily Bellringer Transparency** to help students answer the question.

📖 Daily Bellringer Transparency, Section 2

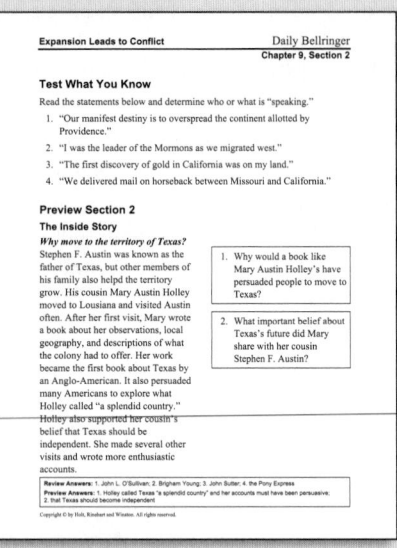

Academic Vocabulary

Review with students the high-use academic terms in this section.

criteria standards on which a decision or judgment is based (p. 303)

emphasis special consideration or insistence on something (p. 305)

📄 CRF: Vocabulary Builder Activity, Section 2

Taking Notes

Causes—settlers did not comply with conditions for receiving land; brought in slaves; April 1830 law; Mexico refused American offer to purchase Texas; confrontation at Anahuac; 1832 and 1833 conventions; new laws under Santa Anna; Battle of Gonzales

---

SECTION 2

Texas Independence

BEFORE YOU READ

MAIN IDEA
American settlers in Texas revolted against the Mexican government and created the independent Republic of Texas.

READING FOCUS
1. What system did the Spanish use to settle Texas?
2. How did Americans begin to move into Texas?
3. What were the causes and effects of the Texas Revolution?

KEY TERMS AND PEOPLE
mission system
Moses Austin
Stephen F. Austin
empresarios
Tejanos
Antonio López de Santa Anna
Texas Revolution
Sam Houston
Alamo
William Travis
Republic of Texas

TAKING NOTES As you read, take notes on the factors that caused Texans to revolt against the Mexican government. Record your notes in a graphic organizer like the one shown here.

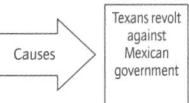

Deep in the Heart of TEXAS

THE INSIDE STORY **Why move to the territory of Texas?** Stephen F. Austin is called the father of Texas, but other members of his family also helped Texas grow. Mary Austin Holley met her younger cousin Stephen in about 1808 when he was at school in Connecticut. She was a talented and charming woman, and the two became friends. A few years after Austin established his American colony in Texas, Holley's husband died, and she moved to Louisiana to be a governess.

Soon Mary's brother Henry Austin also settled in Texas. She thought about uniting the family there, so Stephen set aside land for her on Galveston Bay. Holley visited his

colony in 1831 and loved what she saw. Soon after, she published an account of her visit—the first book about Texas by an Anglo-American. It was titled *Texas: Observations Historical, Geographical, and Descriptive, in a Series of Letters Written during a Visit to Austin's Colony.* Holley's book called Texas "a splendid country." She predicted: "There cannot be a doubt, that, in a few years, Texas will become one of the most thriving, if not the most populous, of the Mexican States."

Her book probably persuaded many Americans to come to Texas. Holley also supported her cousin's belief in Texas independence. She made several long visits to Texas and wrote more enthusiastic reports. ▪

The Spanish Settle Texas

Mary Austin Holley and the other Americans who came to Texas were far from the first people to call the region home. The original inhabitants were, of course, Native Americans. Hundreds of Native American groups had lived in Texas for thousands of years. The Indians of Texas belonged to the Plains, the Southwest, and the Southeast culture groups.

The first Europeans to visit Texas were the Spanish. Spanish explorers crossed Texas several times during the 1500s. Spain claimed Texas based on these explorations. But the Spanish, finding little wealth in the region, made little attempt to settle the land.

◀ Texas booster Mary Austin Holley attracted settlers to the state.

302

Teach the Main Idea **At Level**

Texas Independence

1. **Teach** Ask students the Reading Focus questions to teach this section.

2. **Apply** To help students learn about Texas history, have them work in pairs to create a time line for this section. Have students find all the events in this section that have specific dates and locate the events on their time lines.

3. **Review** Review student time lines as a class. Have volunteers call out the events in order, with their dates. As they do so, create a time line for the class to see.

4. **Practice/Homework** Tell students to consider the American settlement of Texas from the Mexican point of view. Have each student write a report to Mexican government officials in Mexico City describing the behavior of Americans living in Texas, recommending steps that could be taken to make the Texans abide by Mexican law and discussing the agreements the settlers made when they were given land there.

LS Interpersonal, Visual-Spatial

📄 Alternative Assessment Handbook, Rubric 36: Time Lines

In 1689, however, the Spanish discovered the fort that the French explorer René-Robert Cavelier, Sieur de La Salle, had built on the Texas coast. Local Indians had destroyed the fort, but the Spanish were alarmed. They feared the French would claim Texas. So the Spanish came up with a plan to settle Texas.

The mission system The Spanish attempted to settle Texas by building missions. Missions were small settlements designed to convert Native Americans to Catholicism and make them into loyal Spanish subjects. Missions were usually accompanied by presidios, or forts, run by soldiers who were charged with protecting the missions. The Spanish had effectively used this **mission system** in Mexico, and they expected it would work well in Texas.

Between the late 1600s and late 1700s, the Spanish built about two dozen missions and presidios in Texas. They also built the towns of San Antonio and Nacogdoches (na-kuh-DOH-chuhz). Despite Spanish hopes, the missions failed, and the towns never flourished.

Most Native Americans rejected mission life, where they were expected to give up their culture, including their religion. Moreover, they soon realized that the missions could bring death. The Spanish carried diseases that the Indians had never been exposed to. Countless thousands of Native Americans—even entire nations—were wiped out by these diseases. Some Indian groups came to view the Spanish as dangerous trespassers, and they attacked Spanish missions and towns.

The mission system ends Spain built the mission system to convert Native Americans and to counter the threat of French settlement in Texas. But France, after losing the French and Indian War, ceded much of its land claim in North America to Spain in 1762. Thus, Spain no longer faced a threat to its claim to Texas. This fact, coupled with the widespread failure of the mission system to convert Native Americans into Spanish subjects, caused Spain to all but abandon the missions. By 1800 Spain still claimed Texas, but only three Spanish settlements existed in the entire region.

READING CHECK **Identifying Cause and Effect** What caused the Spanish to implement and then abandon the mission system in Texas?

Americans Move into Texas

In 1820 **Moses Austin**, a former banker from Missouri, approached Spanish colonial officials with a plan he called the Texas Venture. Austin proposed that, in exchange for land, he would build a colony in Texas. The Spanish, eager to have the land settled, agreed. Austin died before he could start his colony. One of his last wishes was that his son, **Stephen F. Austin**, carry out his plans for a colony in Texas.

The younger Austin pursued his father's plan with a great deal of enthusiasm. He found a suitable location for the colony between the Colorado and Brazos rivers. There, well-watered land would be perfect for farming and ranching. Austin had no trouble finding American settlers for his colony, even though they had to meet strict <u>criteria</u>. Settlers were attracted by the extremely low land prices.

Austin's Colony In 1823 Austin's Colony was officially established. Austin directed the building of a small town called San Felipe de Austin. San Felipe, as it came to be called, was the administrative, commercial, and social center of the colony. By 1824 about 300 families

ACADEMIC VOCABULARY

criteria standards on which a decision or judgment is based

FACES OF HISTORY

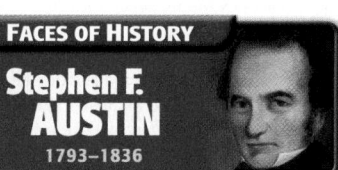

Stephen F. AUSTIN
1793–1836

Long considered the "father of Texas," Stephen F. Austin established the first Anglo-American colony in the Tejas (TAY-hahs) province of Mexico. Born in Virginia and raised in present-day Missouri, Austin traveled east at age 11 to attend college at Yale. Later, Austin returned to Missouri to help run his family's lead mine.

Stephen's father, Moses, had grander plans. He wanted to form an American settlement in Texas. He received permission from the Spanish colonial government for the project but died soon afterward, leaving his son to carry out his plan.

Stephen F. Austin worked energetically to recruit settlers and smooth over difficulties with the Mexican government. On one trip to Mexico, he was arrested on suspicion of disloyalty to Mexico. Yet even up to the outbreak of Texas Revolution, Austin worked for reconciliation between Mexico and the American settlers. The capital city of Texas is named for him.

Summarizing In what ways did Austin shape the course of American colonization of Texas?

Differentiating Instruction

Below Level

English-Language Learners

1. Guide the class in a discussion of how the mission system was supposed to work, what it was supposed to accomplish, and why it did not work in Texas.

2. Organize the class into small groups. Have each group write a skit portraying mission life from the point of view of Native Americans. Students may want to do additional research to provide them with background information for their skits.

3. Have each group create a program for the skit, with a brief description of the action and a list of cast members.

4. Have each group present its skit to the class.
   LS Interpersonal, Kinesthetic

   📋 Alternative Assessment Handbook, Rubric 33: Skits and Reader's Theater

---

Direct Teach

Reading Focus

1 What system did the Spanish use to settle Texas? *the mission system, which was intended to convert Native Americans to Catholicism and make them loyal Spanish subjects*

The Spanish Settle Texas

Identify Who were the first inhabitants of Texas? *hundreds of Native American groups from the Plains, Southwest, and Southeast culture groups*

Identify Cause and Effect Why did Native Americans reject mission life? *did not want to give up their culture and religion; realized that missions could bring death through disease*

Activity **The Mission System** Have students write an editorial opposing the mission system as a method for settling Texas. Students should use sound reasoning to back up their arguments. **LS Verbal-Linguistic**

Reading Focus

2 How did Americans begin to move into Texas? *Moses Austin devised the Texas Venture to colonize Texas, which was carried out by his son Stephen.*

Americans Move into Texas

Identify What was San Felipe? *the administrative, commercial, and social center of the colony in Texas*

Describe What was the Texas Venture? *an 1820 proposal by Moses Austin to build a colony in Texas in exchange for land from the Spanish*

Answers

Faces of History *by recruiting settlers and smoothing over difficulties with the Mexican government*

Reading Check *desire to convert Native Americans to Catholicism and make them loyal Spanish subjects; abandoned because missions were not succeeding and Spain no longer faced threat from France*

303

Americans Move into Texas

Define What was an *empresario*? *a contractor who recruited settlers and established colonies*

Make Judgments Do you think the first U.S. settlers in Texas had any intention of living permanently under Mexican rule? *possible answer—no; probably built colonies in Texas with the intention of extending U.S. control to the area*

Activity Settling Texas Have students write a letter from an American settler in Texas to a relative in the East. Students should describe life in the Mexican colony. **LS Verbal-Linguistic**

Faces of History

Santa Anna

Analyze Santa Anna changed sides in the Mexican independence movement when it became clear that the movement would succeed. He allied himself with Agustín de Iturbide, who helped lead the fight for independence. After Mexico gained independence, Iturbide proclaimed himself emperor. Santa Anna and a small group plotted against Iturbide and eventually deposed him. Ask students to explain why Iturbide might have chosen the title of emperor.

Answers

Faces of History *Switching sides during the war gave him political power in Mexico.*

Reading Check *possible answer— nervously, since the new settlers far outnumbered the Tejanos*

304

---

lived on farms and ranches throughout the colony. The population of the colony was about 1,800 people. About 400 of these settlers were enslaved Africans.

Mexican independence Moses Austin had approached Spanish officials with his original plan for settlement. By the time his son Stephen had established the colony, however, Mexico was no longer part of New Spain. After a decade-long struggle, Mexico had become an independent country in 1821.

The *empresarios* Like the Spanish government, the new Mexican government wanted Texas settled. Mexico passed a number of colonization laws offering land grants to settlers in return for becoming loyal Mexican citizens and meeting other conditions. The government assigned large amounts of land to *empresarios*, or contractors, who recruited settlers and established colonies. Stephen Austin was the most successful *empresario*. Other *empresarios*, some from Europe, also founded colonies in Texas.

By 1830 there were more than a dozen colonies in Texas. About 30,000 settlers were living there, including several thousand enslaved

THE GRANGER COLLECTION, NEW YORK

FACES OF HISTORY

Santa ANNA
1794–1876

Antonio López de Santa Anna was the ultimate political survivor. Born at a time when Mexico was still ruled by Spain, he joined the Spanish army in Mexico at age 16. When Mexico's war for independence erupted, Santa Anna at first fought for Spain against the Mexican rebels. In 1821 he switched sides and became a powerful figure by helping Mexico to secure its independence.

In 1832 Santa Anna organized a revolt against the Mexican government. The next year he was elected president, an office he held many times between 1833 and 1855.

When American settlers in Texas rebelled, Santa Anna marched an army under his command into the province. His disastrous leadership cost Mexico dearly. Santa Anna remained a dominant force in Mexican political life, however, by performing bravely in battle against an invading French force. He was finally driven from power by generals angry at his sale of land to the United States.

Making Inferences Why might Santa Anna's actions in Mexico's war for independence have benefited him personally?

304 CHAPTER 9

Africans and 4,000 **Tejanos**, or Texans of Mexican heritage. The American settlement marked a dramatic change in the region. Just a decade earlier, there were only about 2,000 non-Indian people in Texas. Most of the settlers by 1830 were from the United States.

READING CHECK **Making Inferences** How might Mexican officials have viewed the presence of so many people from the United States in Texas?

The Texas Revolution

American settlers in Texas had to agree to certain conditions in exchange for receiving land. Most important, they had to surrender their American citizenship, swear allegiance to Mexico, adopt the Roman Catholic religion, and hold the land for seven years.

In practice, the settlers did not comply and adapt. Instead, they lived much as they had in the United States. They continued to bring in large numbers of slaves, even after Mexico outlawed slavery. The settlers thought of themselves not as Mexicans, but as Americans who happened to live in Mexico. Their loyalties and economic activities remained connected to the United States. They had few dealings with the Mexican government.

Tensions in Texas The government of Mexico grew concerned about the loyalties of the American settlers in Texas. In 1827 Mexico sent General Manuel de Mier y Terán to assess the situation. As he traveled the region, he wrote to Mexico's president about the tensions there.

HISTORY'S VOICES

❝ Mexican influence is proportionately diminished until . . . it is almost nothing . . . The ratio of Mexicans to foreigners is one to ten . . . It would cause you the same chagrin [humiliation] that it has caused me to see the [extremely low] opinion that is held of our nation by these foreign colonists . . . I am warning you to take timely measures. Texas could throw the whole nation into revolution. **❞**
—Manuel de Mier y Terán, letter of June 20, 1828

The report prompted Mexico to bolster its authority in Texas. Mexican officials took steps to decrease American influence in the region. One such measure was an April 1830 law designed to halt American immigration into Texas. The law cancelled most *empresario*

Skills Focus: Identifying Problem and Solution
At Level

Reading Skill
The American Colonization of Texas

1. Guide the class in a discussion of the reasons Mexico wanted to encourage U.S. citizens to settle in Texas.

2. Have each student write an official memo on behalf of the Mexican government about immigration to Texas. Student memos should explain why immigration to Texas should be encouraged, identify potential problems related to immigration, and suggest possible solutions to those problems.

3. Have volunteers read their memos to the class. As they do so, list the potential problems and solutions that students have identified for the class to see.

4. Guide the class in a discussion of the problems and solutions. **LS Logical-Mathematical, Verbal-Linguistic**

📝 Alternative Assessment Handbook, Rubrics 5: Business Letters; and 35: Solving Problems

contracts and discouraged trade between settlers and the United States by placing a high tariff on American imports. The law also banned the importation of slaves into Texas.

The Mexican government sent troops into Texas to enforce the ban on emigration from the United States and to collect taxes. The action placed <u>emphasis</u> on the fact that settlers needed to obey Mexican law. These actions infuriated the American settlers.

International tensions The tensions within Texas heightened tensions between the United States and Mexico. Throughout the early 1800s, the United States had grown in size and wealth. Mexican government officials suspected that the United States wanted to grow even more by acquiring Texas.

The United States had originally claimed Texas as part of the Louisiana Purchase. American filibusters—people who engage in a private military action in a foreign country—had invaded Texas. Now there were tens of thousands of American settlers there. Even though the United States dropped its claim to Texas, Mexicans feared that their northern neighbor would still attempt to seize Texas from Mexico.

In 1827 Joel Poinsett, the U.S. minister to Mexico, offered on behalf of the United States to buy a large part of Texas for $1 million. Mexican officials refused, but their fears of U.S. intentions in Texas were confirmed. Poinsett reported that the Mexican people "regard the United States with distrust."

The Texas Revolution begins Tensions between settlers, now calling themselves Texans, and the Mexican government grew continually worse. In 1832, at the settlement of Anahuac, armed Texans confronted a Mexican official they felt had wrongly imprisoned two settlers. This began a protest by Texans against the government of Mexico.

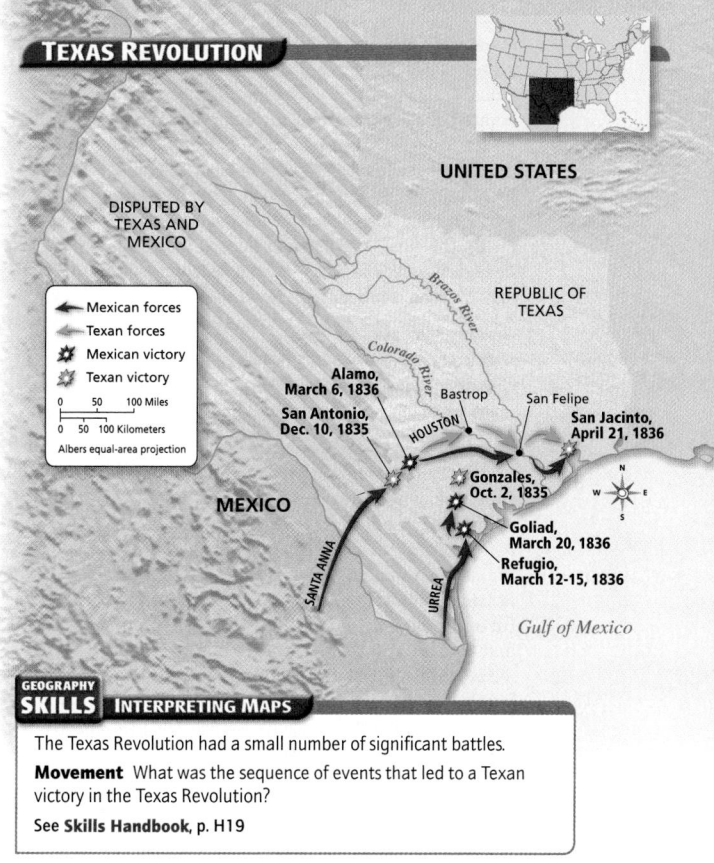

TEXAS REVOLUTION

UNITED STATES

DISPUTED BY TEXAS AND MEXICO

REPUBLIC OF TEXAS

← Mexican forces
← Texan forces
✶ Mexican victory
✶ Texan victory

0   50   100 Miles
0   50   100 Kilometers
Albers equal-area projection

Alamo, March 6, 1836
Bastrop
San Felipe
San Antonio, Dec. 10, 1835
San Jacinto, April 21, 1836
Gonzales, Oct. 2, 1835
MEXICO
Goliad, March 20, 1836
Refugio, March 12-15, 1836
Gulf of Mexico

SANTA ANNA
URREA

GEOGRAPHY SKILLS INTERPRETING MAPS

The Texas Revolution had a small number of significant battles.

Movement What was the sequence of events that led to a Texan victory in the Texas Revolution?

See **Skills Handbook**, p. H19

Protest turned bloody at the town of Velasco. Some Texans on their way to join the protest at Anahuac were transporting a cannon. When Mexican soldiers ordered them to stop, the Texans attacked. After a brief conflict, the Mexicans surrendered.

In 1832 and 1833, Texans held conventions to discuss the best course of action. Many American settlers and some Tejanos believed the situation would improve if Texas became a separate Mexican state. Austin went to Mexico City to present this plan to Mexican leaders. Instead, they felt he was threatening an armed revolt. Austin was jailed and held in Mexico City for more than a year.

To make matters worse, political strife within Mexico had produced a new president. **Antonio López de Santa Anna** assumed the

ACADEMIC VOCABULARY

emphasis special consideration or insistence on something

Reading Focus

❸ What were the causes and effects of the Texas Revolution? *causes— Americans did not want to comply with Mexico's requirements; April 1830 law limiting American immigration; effects—war between American settlers and Mexico; Texans captured Mexican president and forced him to sign treaty granting Texas independence*

The Texas Revolution

Describe What were the provisions of the April 1830 law? *designed to halt American immigration; canceled most* empresario *contracts; discouraged trade between settlers and U.S. with high tariff; outlawed importation of slaves into Texas*

Identify Cause and Effect What were the results of the Texas conventions of 1832 and 1833? *Austin went to Mexico City to present a plan for making Texas a separate Mexican state. Austin was jailed for more than a year, effectively ending chances for peaceful negotiations.*

Evaluate Why do you think Americans moved to Texas if they did not want to live by Mexican laws? *possible answer—belief in manifest destiny: hope that Texas would become part of the U.S.*

 Map Transparency: Texas Revolution

Political Cartoons Activities for American History: Cartoon 18: Volunteers for Texas

---

Skills Focus: Drawing Conclusions

At Level

Reading Skill
Tensions in Texas

1. Divide the class into small groups. Have one half of the groups represent American settlers in Texas and the other half of the groups represent Mexican government officials. Have each group develop a plan to settle the differences between American settlers in Texas and the Mexican government.

2. Have volunteers from each group conduct a class debate using arguments that might have been made by either the Texans or the Mexicans.

   Have students take notes during the debate.

3. Have students use the arguments developed in their small groups and during the class debate to write a one-page editorial telling which side they would support, and explaining their reasons for taking that position.

4. Have volunteers read their editorials to the class.

   LS Logical-Mathematical, Verbal-Linguistic

   Alternative Assessment Handbook, Rubrics 10: Debates; and 17: Letters to Editors

go.hrw.com
Online Resources

KEYWORD: SD7 CH9
TOPIC: TEXAS DECLARATION OF INDEPENDENCE

Answers

Interpreting Maps *Houston led Texas forces in retreat to the east; Santa Anna's army followed to San Jacinto; Houston led surprise attack and won quick victory; captured Santa Anna and forced him to sign a peace treaty*

The Texas Revolution

Recall Why is Washington-on-the-Brazos important in Texas history? *a group of Texans met there in November 1835 to establish a government; site where March 1836 Texas Declaration of Independence was issued*

Identify Cause and Effect What was the immediate cause of the Texas Declaration of Independence? *Mexican president Santa Anna had suspended some powers of Texas and other Mexican states in order to centralize the Mexican government; war had already broken out*

Activity Texas Independence Have students work in small groups to create two posters, one supporting Texas independence and one opposing it.

LS Visual-Spatial

🗎 CRF: History and Geography Activity: Southwest Expansion

Info to Know

The Runaway Scrape After his victory at the Alamo, Santa Anna led his troops eastward across Texas, attacking as they moved. The people who fled from Santa Anna in the "Runaway Scrape" were mostly women, children, and slaves. Desperate to escape Santa Anna's army, they abandoned everything. After the Battle of San Jacinto, the settlers returned home to find their houses looted and burned.

About the Illustration

This illustration is an artist's conception based on available sources. Historians, however, are uncertain exactly what this scene looked like.

Answers

Interpreting Infographics *possible answer—should have recognized that the battlefield was surrounded by water on three sides; high ground prevented him and his troops from seeing attacking army*

306

---

office as a supporter of the rights of Mexican states. Once in power, however, he changed sides and became the leader of those who wanted a strong central government. When Santa Anna enforced new laws banning state militias, some Mexican states revolted. Texans, including many Tejanos, were among those who felt that their liberties were threatened.

By the time Austin was released from jail, he had changed his mind about a peaceful resolution to the conflicts with Mexico.

HISTORY'S VOICES

❝War is our only recourse. There is no other remedy. We must defend our rights, ourselves, and our country by force of arms.❞

—Stephen F. Austin, 1835

War came soon enough. Violence erupted at Gonzales, when Mexican forces attempted to retrieve a cannon they had loaned Texans for defense against Native Americans. The Texans refused to return the cannon. They taunted the Mexican soldiers with a battle flag that pictured the cannon along with the phrase "Come and take it." The Texans attacked the Mexican force, and it retreated. The Battle of Gonzales, fought on October 2, 1835, was small, but it was the start of something big—it was the first battle of the **Texas Revolution**.

After Gonzales, hope for a peaceful resolution between the Texans and Mexico diminished. In November, Texans met at the settlement of Washington-on-the-Brazos. At this meeting, called the Consultation, the settlers founded a government and gave **Sam Houston** the task of raising an army.

From the Alamo to independence In December, rebel Texan forces captured the town of San Antonio, which contained a fort called the **Alamo**. In the 1700s the fort was a mission that had been converted to military use. News of its capture infuriated Santa Anna. He led an army into Texas to punish the rebels and put down the unrest there once and for all.

On February 23, 1836, Santa Anna's force of about 6,000 soldiers reached San Antonio. When some Tejanos and other Texans took refuge in the Alamo, Santa Anna demanded their surrender. The rebels' leader, **William Travis**, responded with a cannon shot.

The Mexican army laid siege to the fort. For 12 days and nights, it pounded the Alamo with cannon fire.

In the early morning hours of March 6, about 1,800 Mexican soldiers stormed the Alamo. Within four hours, they had killed nearly all of the fort's 200 defenders.

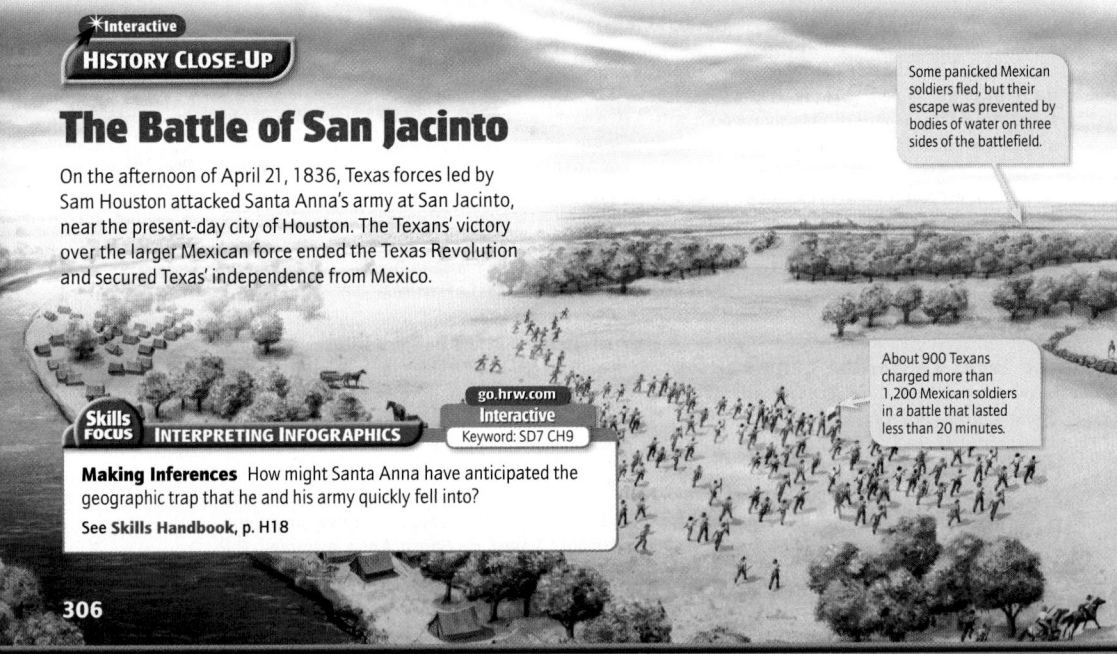

✴Interactive
HISTORY CLOSE-UP

The Battle of San Jacinto

On the afternoon of April 21, 1836, Texas forces led by Sam Houston attacked Santa Anna's army at San Jacinto, near the present-day city of Houston. The Texans' victory over the larger Mexican force ended the Texas Revolution and secured Texas' independence from Mexico.

Some panicked Mexican soldiers fled, but their escape was prevented by bodies of water on three sides of the battlefield.

About 900 Texans charged more than 1,200 Mexican soldiers in a battle that lasted less than 20 minutes.

Skills FOCUS **INTERPRETING INFOGRAPHICS**

go.hrw.com
Interactive
Keyword: SD7 CH9

Making Inferences How might Santa Anna have anticipated the geographic trap that he and his army quickly fell into?
See Skills Handbook, p. H18

306

Differentiating Instruction

Below Level | **Standard English Mastery**

Learners Having Difficulty

1. Guide students in a review of the reasons American settlers in Texas wanted independence from Mexico. Use the following questions as a guide: What steps did Texans take in their attempts to gain independence? What happened at the Alamo? What was the American reaction to the Alamo? Make a class list of the answers for all to see.

2. Have students work in mixed-ability pairs to write a letter to a friend explaining the Texan defense of the Alamo. In their letters,

students should explain the origins of the conflict with Mexico and their support for Texas independence. Encourage students to describe their feelings about the attack and the outcome of the battle.

3. Have volunteers read their letters to the class.

LS Verbal-Linguistic, Logical-Mathematical

🗎 Alternative Assessment Handbook, Rubric 25: Personal Letters

While the Alamo was under siege, a group of 57 Anglo Texans and two Tejanos met at Washington-on-the-Brazos. Unwilling to accept continued Mexican rule, they issued the Texas Declaration of Independence on March 2, 1836. Then they wrote a constitution for the new, independent nation.

Goliad and the Runaway Scrape Soon after the Alamo's fall, elements of Santa Anna's army defeated other groups of Texas rebels at the Battle of Refugio and the Battle of Coleto, near Goliad. The Mexicans held the Tejanos and Anglos captured in these and other battles in the presidio at Goliad. On March 26, following Santa Anna's orders, Mexican soldiers executed more than 340 of these prisoners.

Sam Houston, the leader of the Texas forces, was not present at the Alamo or Goliad, but he quickly learned of the disasters. Knowing his army was not well trained and organized enough to defeat Santa Anna, Houston ordered a retreat to the east.

Word of Houston's retreat, coupled with news of what was called the Goliad Massacre, set the people of Texas into a panic. In what would be called the Runaway Scrape, thousands of Texans, including many Tejanos, fled Santa Anna's advancing army.

Texans victorious Santa Anna's army followed Houston's forces to San Jacinto, near the coast. There, Houston managed to take the Mexican army by surprise. Shouting "Remember the Alamo!" and "Remember Goliad!" the Texans won a quick victory and captured Santa Anna. He was forced to sign the Treaties of Velasco, ending the war. The terms required Mexico to withdraw its troops and to recognize Texas' independence. Texas became a separate nation named the **Republic of Texas.**

The troubles between Texas and Mexico were far from over, however. Because Santa Anna was a prisoner when he signed the treaties, the Mexican government refused to honor all of their provisions. The Texas Revolution was over, but the fighting over Texas was not.

Government
In most states, the common practice is to fly the state flag below the U.S. flag. Texans, proud of their state's history as an independent nation, routinely fly the state flag—the flag of the old Republic of Texas—alone.

READING CHECK **Summarizing** What were the major events of the Texas Revolution?

High ground that separated the armies kept the Mexican troops from seeing the attack coming. They scrambled to form defenses, but it was too late.

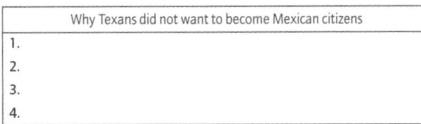

SECTION 2 ASSESSMENT

go.hrw.com
Online Quiz
Keyword: SD7 HP9

Reviewing Ideas, Terms, and People

1. **a. Describe** How was the **mission system** organized?
   b. Analyze Why did the mission system fail?
   c. Predict How might development of the American Southwest have been different if the mission system had succeeded?

2. **a. Identify** Who was **Stephen F. Austin?**
   b. Explain Why did Americans move to Texas?
   c. Evaluate Do you think it was wise for the Spanish and then the Mexican government to allow Americans to settle in Texas? Explain.

3. **a. Recall** What factors caused tensions between American settlers in Texas and the Mexican government?
   b. Compare and Contrast How were the battles at the **Alamo** and San Jacinto similar and different?
   c. Rate How important was **Antonio Lopéz de Santa Anna** as a factor in the **Texas Revolution?** Explain your assessment.

Critical Thinking

4. **Summarizing** Copy the diagram below and complete it to elaborate on the reasons that Texans did not want to become Mexican citizens.

Why Texans did not want to become Mexican citizens
1.
2.
3.
4.

FOCUS ON WRITING

5. **Persuasive** Were the Texas rebels justified in their fight for independence, or should they have honored Mexican law and government? Write a paragraph defending your position.

EXPANSION LEADS TO CONFLICT **307**

307

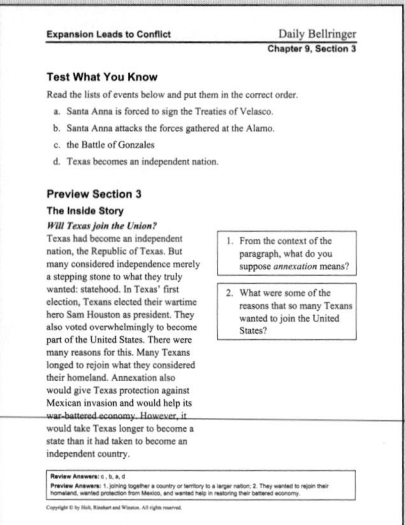

SECTION 3 · War with Mexico

BEFORE YOU READ

MAIN IDEA

Soon after annexing Texas, the United States declared war on Mexico.

READING FOCUS

1. What were the arguments for and against the annexation of Texas?
2. What created tensions between the United States and Mexico in the 1840s?
3. What were the causes and effects of the Mexican-American War?

KEY TERMS AND PEOPLE

John Tyler
Zachary Taylor
Mexican-American War
Stephen Kearny
Republic of California
Bear Flag Revolt
Winfield Scott
Treaty of Guadalupe Hidalgo
Mexican Cession

 **TAKING NOTES** As you read, take notes on the reasons that the United States declared war on Mexico. Record your notes in a graphic organizer like the one shown.

Causes ⟶ United States declares war on Mexico

From REPUBLIC to STATE

THE INSIDE STORY

Will Texas join the Union? At last, Texas was an independent nation, the Republic of Texas. Texans were proud. Yet, for many, independence was just a stepping stone to what they really wanted: statehood.

In Texas' first election, war hero Sam Houston won the presidency. His election also was the first chance for Texans to decide whether they wanted to become part of the United States. Overwhelmingly, they voted yes.

Texans voted for annexation for many reasons. Many had never considered themselves to be Mexican citizens, and they longed to be part of their homeland. Joining the United States would also bring them under the protection of the U.S. Army and Navy, which could defend them against a Mexican invasion. Texas also faced economic troubles. It was in debt, and its currency had little value. Joining the Union would help the Texas economy.

The new nation of Texas faced a new battle: the fight for statehood. It would take far longer to become a state than it had taken to become an independent country. ◢

The Annexation of Texas

Americans who believed in manifest destiny were delighted at the prospect of admitting Texas to the Union. Annexing Texas would add a large area to the country. Supporters viewed the Texas Revolution in the spirit of the American Revolution. They admired Texans for fighting for their freedom from Mexico.

▼ Lowering the Texas flag to make way for the U.S. flag

Many southerners supported annexation because Texas allowed slavery. Admitting Texas to the Union as a slave state would boost the South's political power.

Other Americans had doubts about letting Texas become a state. They were concerned that the United States would have to bear the substantial Texas debt. Many northerners opposed annexation because it would spread slavery westward and increase slave states' voting power in Congress. A major argument in Congress was that the Constitution said nothing about admitting an independent nation to the United States.

308 CHAPTER 9

Texas remained a republic for nine years. The annexation question became a significant issue in the 1844 presidential election. When James K. Polk, the pro-annexation candidate, won the presidency, Mexico warned the United States that it would consider the annexation of Texas "equivalent to a declaration of war against the Mexican Republic." However, the outgoing president, **John Tyler**, who also favored annexation, signed the joint resolution of Congress into law three days before the end of his term, in March 1845.

Meanwhile, diplomats from France, Great Britain, Mexico, and the United States maneuvered around the Texas issue. In March 1845 Congress passed the joint resolution annexing Texas to the United States. Passing such a resolution took only a simple majority in Congress. Annexing Texas by treaty with the Republic of Texas would have required two-thirds approval in the Senate, which supporters feared would be difficult to obtain.

In the fall of 1845, Texas put the question to voters once again. The results were virtually the same: more than 7,600 in favor of annexation and 430 opposed. Texas became part of the United States on December 29, 1845.

On February 19, 1846, a simple ceremony was held at the republic's capitol building in Austin. Anson Jones, the last president of Texas, lowered its tricolored flag.

"The final act of this great drama is now performed," he said. "The Republic of Texas is no more."

READING CHECK **Summarizing** Why was the annexation of Texas controversial?

Tensions between the United States and Mexico

The annexation of Texas enraged the Mexican government. Mexico still held the position that Texas had been unfairly taken from it by foreigners during the Texas Revolution.

Mexican government officials had refused to recognize the independence of the Republic of Texas. They viewed its annexation as a theft of Mexican territory. When Congress voted for the annexation of Texas, Mexico responded by breaking off diplomatic relations with the United States.

Polk and manifest destiny In March 1845 James K. Polk became president. Polk was an enthusiastic supporter of national expansion. In fact, he had set his sights on even more territory. He wanted the nation to acquire the land between Texas and the Pacific Ocean. These territories, New Mexico and California, belonged to Mexico. But Polk thought they should become part of the United States.

HISTORY'S VOICES

❝To enlarge [the United States] is to extend the dominions of peace over additional territories and increasing millions . . . my duty [is] to assert and maintain . . . the right of the United States to that portion of our territory which lies beyond the Rocky Mountains.❞
—James K. Polk, Inaugural Address, March 4, 1845

Only a handful of Americans lived in New Mexico and California. They were sparsely populated by Mexican citizens as well. In addition, the Mexican government and army had little presence in either area. Polk sought an opportunity to acquire these remote regions.

The boundary dispute Polk also sought to secure the boundary between Texas and Mexico. At first the United States recognized the Nueces River as the boundary between Mexico and the Republic of Texas. Texans, however, claimed the boundary was farther south, at the Rio Grande. When the United States annexed Texas, it also claimed the Rio Grande as the boundary. Mexico maintained that the boundary should remain at the Nueces River.

Another dispute between the United States and Mexico involved money. The United States claimed that Mexico owed American citizens $3 million for the loss of property and life during Mexico's fight for independence from Spain. Polk wanted these problems resolved. He devised a plan to settle all of these issues in one bold move.

Slidell's trip In the fall of 1845, Polk sent a special envoy, or messenger, to Mexico. The envoy, John Slidell, arrived with a U.S. offer to cancel the $3 million in claims against Mexico in exchange for Mexico's recognition of the Rio Grande as its boundary with the United States. Further, he was authorized to pay Mexico up to $30 million to purchase New Mexico and California for the United States.

EXPANSION LEADS TO CONFLICT **309**

309

Reading Focus

3 What were the causes and effects of the Mexican-American War? *causes—annexation of Texas; Mexico's refusal to meet with Polk's envoy; boundary dispute; effects—Treaty of Guadalupe Hidalgo; Mexican Cession; Gadsden Purchase*

The Mexican-American War

Recall How did the United States force Mexico to give in to American demands? *by capturing New Mexico, California, and Mexico City*

Evaluate Would Mexico have been better off if its government had accepted the offer President Polk sent by way of John Slidell? Why or why not? *possible answer—yes; might have avoided war and received twice as much money for the tract of land they were forced to cede*

Activity The Bear Flag Revolt
Have students design their own flag for the new Republic of California. Have volunteers explain their designs to the class. **LS** Visual-Spatial

- 📑 American History Outline Maps: The Mexican War
- 🖥 Map Transparency: The Mexican-American War
- 📑 CRF: Biography: Charles Francis Adams
- 📑 CRF: Primary Source Activity: James Buchanan Considers the Annexation of Texas

Answers

Interpreting Maps *Kearny moved west from Ft. Leavensworth to Bent's Fort, then southwest to Santa Fe and California; he was defeated at the battle at San Pasqual in California.*

Reading Check *Mexico believed U.S. had taken Texas unfairly; Americans believed Texas was part of the U.S.*

310

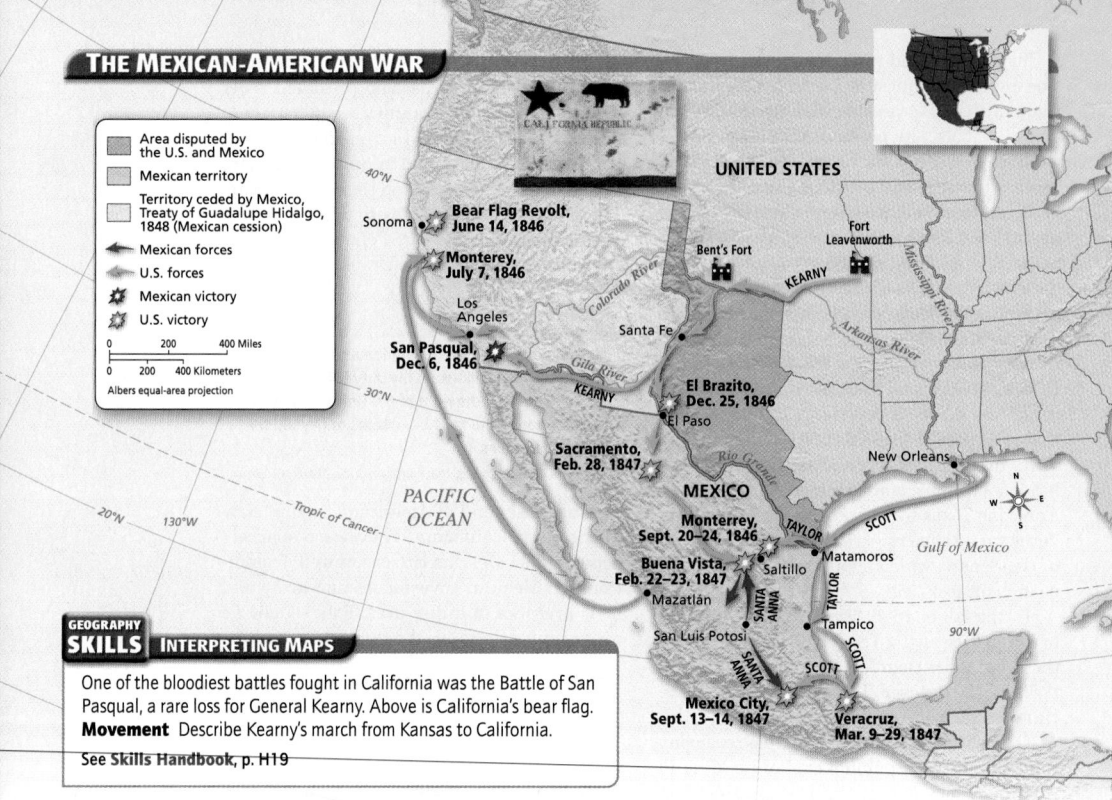

THE MEXICAN-AMERICAN WAR

GEOGRAPHY SKILLS | **INTERPRETING MAPS**

One of the bloodiest battles fought in California was the Battle of San Pasqual, a rare loss for General Kearny. Above is California's bear flag.
Movement Describe Kearny's march from Kansas to California.
See Skills Handbook, p. H19

Slidell found the Mexican government in turmoil. Neither of the rivals for Mexico's presidency would consent to meet with him. An angry Slidell recommended to Polk that Mexico be punished.

READING CHECK **Contrasting** How did the U.S. position regarding Texas differ from the Mexican position?

The Mexican-American War

While Slidell was in Mexico, Polk ordered General **Zachary Taylor** to advance with his troops into the disputed territory between the Nueces River and the Rio Grande, On April 25 some of Taylor's soldiers fought a skirmish in this region with a small party of Mexican soldiers.

Polk used this event as an excuse to request that Congress declare war on Mexico. Ignoring the fact that the boundary was in dispute, the president charged that Mexicans had "invaded our territory and shed the blood of our fellow-citizens on our own soil." The United States declared war on Mexico on May 13, 1846. The **Mexican-American War** had begun.

Fighting the war The United States used an aggressive strategy to win the war. Within weeks, General **Stephen Kearny** marched west from Kansas, bound for the New Mexico territory. He easily captured the town of Santa Fe and took control of New Mexico. Kearny then headed west, hoping to gain control of California.

In California, a small group of Americans revolted against Mexican rule. The rebels defeated a small Mexican force in the village of Sonoma and forced the Mexican leader to sign a treaty turning California over to them. On June 14, 1846, the Americans declared the independent **Republic of California**. They made

310 CHAPTER 9

Skills Focus: Making Generalizations | At Level

Reading Skill
The Treaty of Guadalupe Hidalgo

1. Guide students in a discussion of the Mexican-American War. Have students explain if they believe that the United States was justified in declaring war on Mexico. Why or why not? How did the war fit in with the American idea of manifest destiny?

2. Have students prepare two newspaper articles about the Treaty of Guadalupe Hidalgo, one from the viewpoint of a U.S. newspaper, and the other from the viewpoint of a Mexican newspaper.

3. Have volunteers read their articles to the class. Guide the class in a discussion of the terms of the treaty from both points of view.
LS Verbal-Linguistic, Logical-Mathematical
📑 Alternative Assessment Handbook, Rubric 23: Newspapers

a crude flag for their new country that had a picture of a bear on it. Because of this flag, the uprising in California became known as the **Bear Flag Revolt**.

A month later, U.S. naval forces arrived and soon gained control of California. Meanwhile, American forces under General Taylor advanced into northern Mexico and captured important towns in the region.

Another force, under General **Winfield Scott**, landed on the Gulf coast of Mexico near Veracruz. Scott led his forces inland and marched into Mexico City in September 1847.

In a matter of months, U.S. forces had captured New Mexico and California. When Mexico's capital fell, the Mexican government was forced to give in to American demands.

Results of the war Signed in 1848, the **Treaty of Guadalupe Hidalgo** ended the Mexican-American War. Under the treaty, Mexico was forced to turn over to the United States a huge tract of land known as the **Mexican Cession**. In return, the United States agreed to pay Mexico $15 million and drop the $3 million in damages. In 1853 the Gadsden Purchase clarified the treaty boundary and transferred even more land to the United States.

President Polk was pleased with America's victory. Many other Americans, however, did not feel they could be proud of this war.

CAUSES AND EFFECTS OF THE MEXICAN-AMERICAN WAR

QUICK FACTS

CAUSES
- Annexation of Texas
- Boundary dispute
- Manifest destiny and expansionism

EFFECTS
- Treaty of Guadalupe Hidalgo
- Mexican Cession
- Gadsden Purchase

THE IMPACT TODAY

Government
A 2004 government study found that the United States failed to recognize Mexican titles to millions of acres of land in the Mexican Cession, despite agreeing to do so in the Treaty of Guadalupe Hidalgo. The resulting land disputes remain a major political issue in New Mexico.

HISTORY'S VOICES

❝This is no war of defense, but one of unnecessary and offensive aggression. It is Mexico that is defending her firesides . . . not we.❞

—Henry Clay, speech of November 13, 1847

Debate continues over whether the Mexican-American War was justified, and hard feelings persist. Historians agree, however, that the war was a clear expression of America's belief in manifest destiny.

READING CHECK **Summarizing** What were the results of the Mexican-American War?

SECTION 3 ASSESSMENT

go.hrw.com
Online Quiz
Keyword: SD7 HP9

Reviewing Ideas, Terms, and People

1. a. Recall What were the major arguments for and against the annexation of Texas?
   b. Explain How did the question of slavery play a role in the annexation debate?
   c. Evaluate Which arguments for and against annexation were most powerful? Why do you think so?

2. a. Describe How did tensions between the United States and Mexico heighten during the mid-1840s?
   b. Make Inferences Why might President Polk have expected the trip to Mexico by his envoy Slidell to be a success?
   c. Evaluate Do you think Mexico was wise to break off diplomatic relations with the United States? Explain.

3. a. Identify What were the major outcomes of the Mexican-American War?
   b. Draw Conclusions Do you think the Mexican-American War was justified in terms of protecting Texas citizens? Explain.

c. Predict What effect do you think the Mexican Cession would have on tensions between the North and the South over slavery? Explain.

Critical Thinking

4. Sequencing Complete the diagram below to trace the process by which the United States expanded its borders in the 1840s.

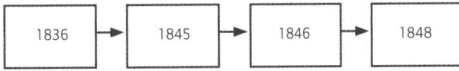

| 1836 | → | 1845 | → | 1846 | → | 1848 |

FOCUS ON SPEAKING

5. Persuasive Give a one-minute speech stating reasons to support or oppose the war between the United States and Mexico.

EXPANSION LEADS TO CONFLICT **311**

Section 3 Assessment Answers

1. a. for: manifest destiny would add land to U.S.; against: slavery, debt
   b. would increase slave states' power in Congress
   c. possible answers—for, add land; against, spread slavery

2. a. U.S. annexed Texas; disputes over boundary and money
   b. generous offer for land purchase
   c. possible answer—no, might have avoided war if they had not done so

3. a. Mexico lost a huge tract of land.
   b. possible answer—No, Americans provoked war in order to acquire more land.
   c. possible answer—might increase tensions

4. Texas declares independence; Texas annexed; California; Mexican Cession

5. possible answers—need to protect American citizens; can negotiate peaceful settlement

---

• Direct Teach •

Recent Scholarship

In *So Far from God: The U.S. War with Mexico, 1846–1848*, historian John S. D. Eisenhower examines the historical significance of the Mexican-American war and the 1848 Treaty of Guadalupe Hidalgo, in which Mexico gave up over half of its land. While discussing the political, diplomatic, and military forces behind the war, Eisenhower focuses in on three key figures: General Zachary Taylor, General Winfield Scott, and President James Polk. Eisenhower writes, "Manifest Destiny was not Polk's invention, but he was its ideal agent."

So Far from God: The U.S. War with Mexico, by John S. D. Eisenhower. Random House, 1989

Quick Facts Transparency: Causes and Effects of the Mexican-American War

• Review & Assess •

Close
Guide the class in a discussion of the causes and effects of the Mexican-American War.

Review
Online Quiz, Section 3

Daily Test Practice Transparency

Assess
SE Section 3 Assessment

Progress Assessment: Section 3 Quiz

Alternative Assessment Handbook

Reteach
Interactive Reader and Study Guide, Section 3

Interactive Skills Tutor CD-ROM

Answers

Reading Check *Mexico was forced to turn over the Mexican Cession; U.S. paid Mexico $15 million; Gadsden Purchase clarified treaty boundary and gave U.S. even more land.*

311

The "Real" Story of the Alamo

Word Help

stature status

adversity hardship

resignation acceptance

naturalist someone who is at home with nature

Info to Know

Susanna Dickinson After the battle of the Alamo, Susanna Dickinson and her daughter Angelina were interviewed by Santa Anna; like the other women who survived, they were given a blanket and two dollars in silver before being released.

📄 CRF: Biography: Susanna Wilkerson Dickinson

Primary Source

Enrique Esparza, son of Alamo defender Gregorio Esparza, survived the attack. In 1902, he shared his memories with a reporter for the San Antonio Express: "We could hear the Mexican officers shouting . . . and the families that were in the quarters just huddled up in the corners. My mother's children were near her. Finally they began shooting through the dark into the room where we were. A boy who was wrapped in a blanket in one corner was hit and killed. The Mexicans fired into the room for at least fifteen minutes. It was a miracle, but none of us children were touched."

— Enrique Esparza

San Antonio Express, 1902

The "Real" Story of the Alamo

Historical Context The documents below provide information on what happened at the Alamo, from varying points of view.

Task Examine the documents and answer the questions that follow. Then you will be asked to write an essay about differing portrayals of the Battle of the Alamo, using facts from the documents and from the chapter to support the position that you take in your thesis statement.

DOCUMENT 1

Because so few people survived at the Alamo, few records exist to tell what actually happened there. One of the few accounts by a survivor came from Susanna Dickinson, whose version of the attack was published in 1875.

"I knew Colonels [Davy] Crockett, [Jim] Bowie, and [William Barret] Travis well. Col. Crockett was a performer on the violin, and often during the siege took it up and played his favorite tunes . . .

Under the cover of darkness the [Mexicans] approached the fortifications, and planting their scaling ladders against our walls just as light was approaching, they climbed up to the tops of our walls and jumped down within, many of them to their immediate death.

As fast as the front ranks were slain, they were filled up again by fresh troops . . .

As we passed through the enclosed ground in front of the church, I saw heaps of dead and dying . . .

I recognized Col. Crockett lying dead and mutilated between the church and the two story barrack building, and even remember seeing his peculiar cap lying by his side.

Col. Bowie was sick in bed and not expected to live, but as the victorious Mexicans entered his room, he killed two of them with his pistols before they pierced him through with their sabres.

Col. Travis and Bonham were killed while working the cannon, the body of the former lay on the top of the church."

DOCUMENT 2

In 1955 a document appeared in Mexico that claimed to be Mexican officer José Enrique de la Peña's first-hand account of what happened at the Alamo. Some scholars have questioned the authenticity of the account, which is at odds with some legends of the Alamo. The following is the officer's account of Davy Crockett's death.

"Some seven men survived the general carnage and, under the protection of General [Manuel Fernández] Castrillón, they were brought before [Mexican President Antonio López de] Santa Anna. Among them was one of great stature . . . in whose face there was the imprint of adversity, but in whom one also noticed a degree of resignation and nobility that did him honor. He was the naturalist David Crockett . . . Santa Anna answered Castrillón's intervention in Crockett's behalf with a gesture of indignation [anger] and, addressing himself to the . . . the troops closest to him, ordered [Crockett's] execution. The commanders and officers were outraged at this action and did not support the order, hoping that once the fury of the moment had blown over these men would be spared; but several officers who were around the president and who . . . became noteworthy by an infamous deed, surpassing the soldiers in cruelty. They thrust themselves forward, in order to flatter their commander, and with swords in hand, fell upon these unfortunate, defenseless men just as a tiger leaps upon his prey . . . [T]hese unfortunates died without complaining and without humiliating themselves before their torturers."

Skills Focus: Analyzing Primary Sources

At Level

Reading Like a Historian Skill
The Death of Davy Crockett

Research Required

Background Long-accepted ideas of history are sometimes revised when new evidence is discovered. This seemed to be the case when de la Peña's account of the Battle of the Alamo was discovered. One of the reasons de la Peña's account has been challenged is because it contradicts the idea that Davy Crockett died in battle.

1. Have students conduct outside research and read primary sources describing the battle of the Alamo.

2. Have students use their research to write an essay explaining which version of the death of Davy Crockett is more likely to be true.

3. Ask volunteers to read their essays. Then discuss what it means to revise long-established views of history. **LS Verbal-Linguistic, Logical-Mathematical**

📄 Alternative Assessment Handbook, Rubrics 30: Research; and 42: Writing to Inform

DOCUMENT 3

The legend of the Alamo has inspired numerous books and several films. In 1960 Hollywood produced a big-budget version of the story. The film focused heavily on the American defenders, portraying the Texans as a virtually all-Anglo force. The following poster features four men, including the stars playing Jim Bowie, Davy Crockett, and William Barret Travis.

DOCUMENT 4

In 2004 filmmakers decided to retell the story of the Alamo with greater authenticity. This film version gave more attention to the Mexican view of the battle and also tried to present a more authentic portrait of the defenders, including the Tejano and African American defenders. The filmmakers worked closely with historians to make sure details such as the hair and clothing styles of the characters were accurate. This still from the film shows the actors playing Texas defenders Juan Seguín and Davy Crockett.

Skills FOCUS READING LIKE A HISTORIAN

1. a. Identify Refer to Document 1. According to Dickinson, how did William Barret Travis, Davy Crockett, and Jim Bowie die?
b. Analyze Overall, what is the impression that Dickinson gives of the attack on the Alamo?

2. a. Identify Refer to Document 2. According to José Enrique de la Peña, what happened to Crockett?
b. Compare and Contrast Refer to Documents 1 and 2. How do Dickinson and de la Peña's accounts compare to one another?
c. Evaluate Refer to Documents 1 and 2. Which one seems more reliable? Explain possible reasons.

3. a. Contrast Refer to Documents 3 and 4. What are some differences between the two film portrayals of the Texas defenders?
b. Elaborate Why do you think the film version made in 2004 was so different from the one made in 1960?

4. Document-Based Essay Question Consider the question below and form a thesis statement. Using examples from Documents 1, 2, 3, and 4, create an outline and write a short essay supporting your position.
How and why have versions of what happened at the Alamo differed?

See *Skills Handbook,* pp. H28–29, H30

EXPANSION LEADS TO CONFLICT **313**

Differentiating Instruction

Below Level

English Language Learners

Prep Required

1. Play one or two scenes from each of the two films discussed in this Document-Based Investigation, *The Alamo* (1960) and *The Alamo* (2004), for students to view.

2. Divide the class into groups of four or five students. Have each group discuss the differences they noticed between the two films and how those differences affected the way they responded to the films. You may wish to use the following list of questions as a guide:

In each film,

- does the story focus on the Mexicans or on the Americans?

- how accurate does the plot appear to be?

- how authentic are costumes, sets, and special effects?

- Overall, which film do you prefer? Why?
LS Interpersonal, Visual-Spatial

Alternative Assessment Handbook, Rubrics 14: Group Activity

313

Visual Summary: Expansion Leads to Conflict

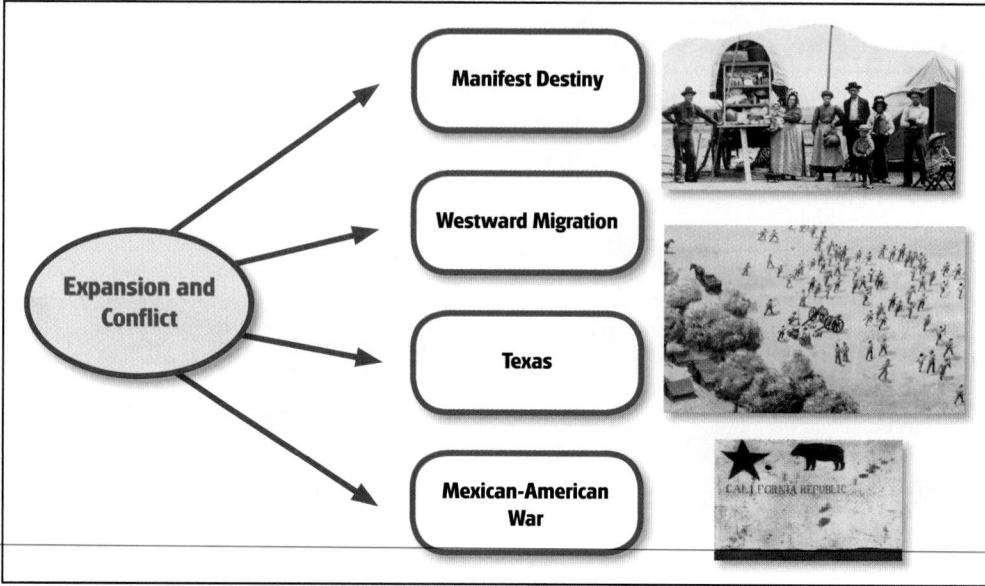

Reviewing Key Terms and People

Match each lettered definition with the correct numbered item below.

1. Catholic settlements with forts that were built by the Spanish to convert local Indians
2. Leader of American colonists in Texas
3. Land Mexico gave to the United States
4. Dictator of Mexico
5. 1846 uprising in California
6. Independent nation that resulted from the Treaties of Velasco
7. Belief that the United States should spread across the North American continent from coast to coast
8. Mexican fort in San Antonio that was important in the Texas Revolution
9. Longest, most famous migrant trail to the West
10. Process by which the Republic of Texas became part of the United States

a. manifest destiny
b. Oregon Trail
c. mission system
d. Antonio López de Santa Anna
e. Alamo
f. Republic of Texas
g. Stephen F. Austin
h. annexation
i. Bear Flag Revolt
j. Mexican Cession

314 CHAPTER 9

13. **a.** maintained that Texas had been unfairly taken from Mexico by foreigners during the Texas Revolution; still considered Texas to be Mexican territory
    b. He was furious about the fact that officials in Mexico would not agree to see him, so he recommended that Polk punish Mexico.
    c. by forcing Mexico to cede a huge tract of land, the Mexican Cession, which included California and New Mexico

Using the Internet

14. **a.** Go to the HRW Web site and enter the keyword shown to access a rubric for this activity.
    b. This keyword can also be used to access an activity about the Oregon Trail.

KEYWORD: SD7 CH9

Comprehension and Critical Thinking

SECTION 1 *(pp. 296–301)*

11. a. Identify What factor triggered the largest wave of migration to the West?

b. Analyze Why was a journey west in the 1840s and 1850s a huge adventure?

c. Predict What effect might the railroad have on the land in the western part of the United States?

SECTION 2 *(pp. 302–307)*

12. a. Recall List at least two main goals of the Spanish mission system.

b. Compare How were the tensions within Texas similar to those between the United States and Mexico?

c. Evaluate How did the American losses at the Alamo affect the Texas Revolution?

SECTION 3 *(pp. 308–311)*

13. a. Recall Why was the Mexican government angry about the annexation of Texas?

b. Make Inferences How did the recommendations of U.S. envoy John Slidell to President Polk reflect Slidell's feelings about his treatment in Mexico?

c. Elaborate How did the United States take advantage of its military victories over Mexico?

Using the Internet

go.hrw.com
Practice Online
Keyword: SD7 CH9

14. a. Marcus Whitman and his wife, Narcissa, were among the first white Americans to settle in Oregon Country. They build their mission near the Columbia River and set about converting Cayuse Indians to Christianity. Using the keyword above, do research on the Whitmans' settlement and its fate. Then create a report that describes life at the mission.

b. Using the keyword above, research some trips along the Oregon Trail taken by settlers and learn what was needed to survive the long journey. Make a list of provisions that you think would be needed to make the trip safely. Include as much detail as you can about food and supplies. Use a spreadsheet program to create a database of your provisions. What will you need to purchase? Total your purchases to find out how much money you will need to make the trip.

Analyzing Primary Sources

Reading Like a Historian President James Polk strongly supported the territorial expansion of the United States.

> ❝To enlarge [the United States] is to extend the dominions of peace over additional territories and increasing millions . . . my duty [is] to assert and maintain . . . the right of the United States to that portion of our territory which lies beyond the Rocky Mountains . . . The world beholds the peaceful triumphs of the industry of our emigrants . . . The jurisdiction of our laws . . . should be extended over them in the distant regions which they have selected for their homes.❞
>
> —President James K. Polk, Inaugural Address

15. Identify What does Polk see as his duty?

16. Draw Conclusions What reasons does Polk give to support U.S. expansion?

Critical Reading

Read the passage in Section 1 that begins with the heading "The Gold Rush." Then answer the question that follows.

17. According to the History's Voices quotation, "the whole country" refers to

A the Sierra Nevada.

B the United States.

C farmers.

D much of California.

 FOCUS ON WRITING

Persuasive Writing *Persuasive writing takes a position for or against an issue, using facts and examples as supporting evidence. To practice persuasive writing, complete the assignment below.*

Writing Topic The annexation of Mexican land by the United States

18. Assignment Based on what you have read in this chapter, write a paragraph that either supports or opposes the way the United States acquired land from Mexico. If you have access to a computer, use a word processing program to create and format your paragraph.

Answers

Analyzing Primary Sources

15. to assert and maintain the right of the U.S. to territory beyond the Rocky Mountains

16. extends peace over land and people; world is watching this successful expansion of democracy

Critical Reading

17. D

Focus on Writing

18. possible answers—opposes: The United States should have worked longer with Mexican diplomats and Texas settlers to negotiate a land settlement that met the needs of all groups involved. The U.S. could have purchased the land and negotiated a peaceful settlement to the dispute; supports: The Mexican government was unwilling to compromise and negotiate with the U.S., leaving it no option but to go to war.

A rubric for this activity is provided in the Chapter Resource File: Focus on Writing: The Annexation of Mexican Land by the United States.

History's Impact Video Program

The region's different groups have sometimes had conflicting interests; these conflicts have led to fighting and wars.

Review and Assessment Resources

Review and Reinforce

- CRF: Chapter Review Activity
- Quick Facts Transparencies: Causes and Effects of the Mexican-American War, Expansion Leads to Conflict
- Spanish Chapter Summaries Audio CD Program
- Online Chapter Summaries in Spanish
- OSP Holt PuzzlePro; QuizShow for ExamView
- Quiz Game CD-ROM

Assess

- PASS: Chapter Test, Forms A and B
- Alternative Assessment Handbook
- OSP ExamView Test Generator, Chapter Test
- Differentiated Instruction Modified Worksheets and Tests CD-ROM: Chapter Test
- HOAP Holt Online Assessment Program (in the Premier Online Edition)

Reteach

- Interactive Reader and Study Guide
- Differentiated Instruction Teacher Management System: Lesson Plans for Differentiated Instruction
- Differentiated Instruction Modified Worksheets and Tests CD-ROM: Chapter Test
- Interactive Skills Tutor CD-ROM

go.hrw.com
Online Resources
KEYWORD: SD7 CH9

Summarizing the Unit

Have students list the important reform movements discussed in this unit. Then guide students in a discussion of the following question: *Which reform movement has had the greatest influence on American society?* Have students support their answers with evidence from the text and their own knowledge.

Connecting to Themes

Review with students how Americans tried to change their society through reform movements in such areas as temperance, abolition, education, prison reform, and women's rights. Ask students what they feel are important reform movements of our own time. Ask students how these movements might affect American society and culture.

 UNIT  **3 IN BRIEF** Below is a chapter-by-chapter summary of the main ideas covered in Unit 3.

CHAPTER 7 — From Nationalism to Sectionalism
1815–1840

MAIN IDEA The outcome of the War of 1812 filled Americans with a strong sense of national pride. At the same time, the North and the South were developing very different ways of life. Sectional divisions over economic issues and slavery gradually weakened the nationalism aroused by the war.

SECTION 1 Americans' new sense of national identity was reflected in the nation's art and literature. The Monroe Doctrine and the Adams-Onís Treaty showed America's growing confidence as a nation. Despite this national pride, the Missouri Compromise in 1820 ended the Era of Good Feelings and showed that strong divisions existed over the issue of slavery.

SECTION 2 Andrew Jackson's presidency was marked by the removal of eastern Native Americans to the west of the Mississippi River. Controversies over the Second National Bank, the tariff, and states' rights showed continuing sectional divisions among Americans.

SECTION 3 Manufacturing and industry became increasingly important to the North's economy in the early 1800s. The development of roads, canals, and railroads encouraged population growth and trade.

SECTION 4 The South's economy remained heavily agricultural. The cotton gin's invention and demand for cotton in the North and Great Britain made King Cotton the South's main crop and encouraged the growth of slavery.

CHAPTER 8 — A Push for Reform
1830–1860

MAIN IDEA The mid-1800s were a time of great reform in the United States. Inspired by a religious movement, many Americans worked to make improvements in American society.

SECTION 1 The preachers of the Second Great Awakening taught that people had a responsibility to do God's work. This message led Americans to try to make society better by working for temperance, education reform, and prison reform. Some reformers formed communities to be free of society's ills.

SECTION 2 The arrival of large numbers of Irish and German immigrants in the mid-1800s brought great change, including rapid growth in the population of northern cities. Movements arose to improve conditions in factories, clean up overcrowded cities, and aid city dwellers who needed help.

SECTION 3 Despite the severe limits society put on women in the mid-1800s, they took the lead in many reform movements. Their desire to advance reform led them to demand equality and more political power in American society.

SECTION 4 The harsh lives led by slaves in the South caused an abolition movement to develop that called for an end to slavery. Some abolitionists attacked slavery in speeches, and others helped slaves escape to freedom.

CHAPTER 9 — Expansion Leads to Conflict
1830–1860

MAIN IDEA As increasing numbers of Americans moved west, the United States expanded its borders through annexation, war, and threats of war. By 1850 the nation stretched across North America from the Atlantic Ocean to the Pacific.

SECTION 1 Economic opportunity, coupled with a belief in the nation's manifest destiny, led many Americans westward in the mid-1800s. The largest migration took place over the Oregon Trail. In 1849 a gold rush drew thousands of people to California. American settlement in the West led to improved communications and changed the lives of Native Americans forever.

SECTION 2 Stephen Austin led the first American settlers into Mexico's Texas region in the 1820s. Tensions between American settlers and Mexico erupted into revolt, war, and freedom from Mexico in 1836. Texans formed an independent nation called the Republic of Texas.

SECTION 3 The United States annexed Texas in 1845. A dispute over Texas's southern border led to the Mexican War in 1846. After Mexico's defeat, the two nations signed the Treaty of Guadalupe Hidalgo in 1848. Mexico turned over a huge tract of land to the United States, including California and what is today the American Southwest.

Unit Resources

Review and Reinforce

📄 CRF: Chapter Review Activity
🔊 Spanish Chapter Summaries Audio CD Program
OSP Holt PuzzlePro; GameTool for ExamView
💿 Quiz Game CD-ROM

Assess

📄 PASS: Unit Test, Forms A and B
📄 Alternative Assessment Handbook
OSP ExamView Test Generator
💿 Differentiated Instruction Modified Worksheets and Tests CD-ROM: Chapter Tests
HOAP Holt Online Assessment Program (in the Premier Online Edition)

Reteach/Intervene

📄 Interactive Reader and Study Guide
📄 Differentiated Instruction Teacher Management System: Lesson Plans for Differentiated Instruction
💿 Differentiated Instruction Modified Worksheets and Tests CD-ROM: Chapter Tests
💿 Interactive Skills Tutor CD-ROM

go.hrw.com
Online Resources

KEYWORDS: SD7 CH7, SD7 CH8, SD7 CH9

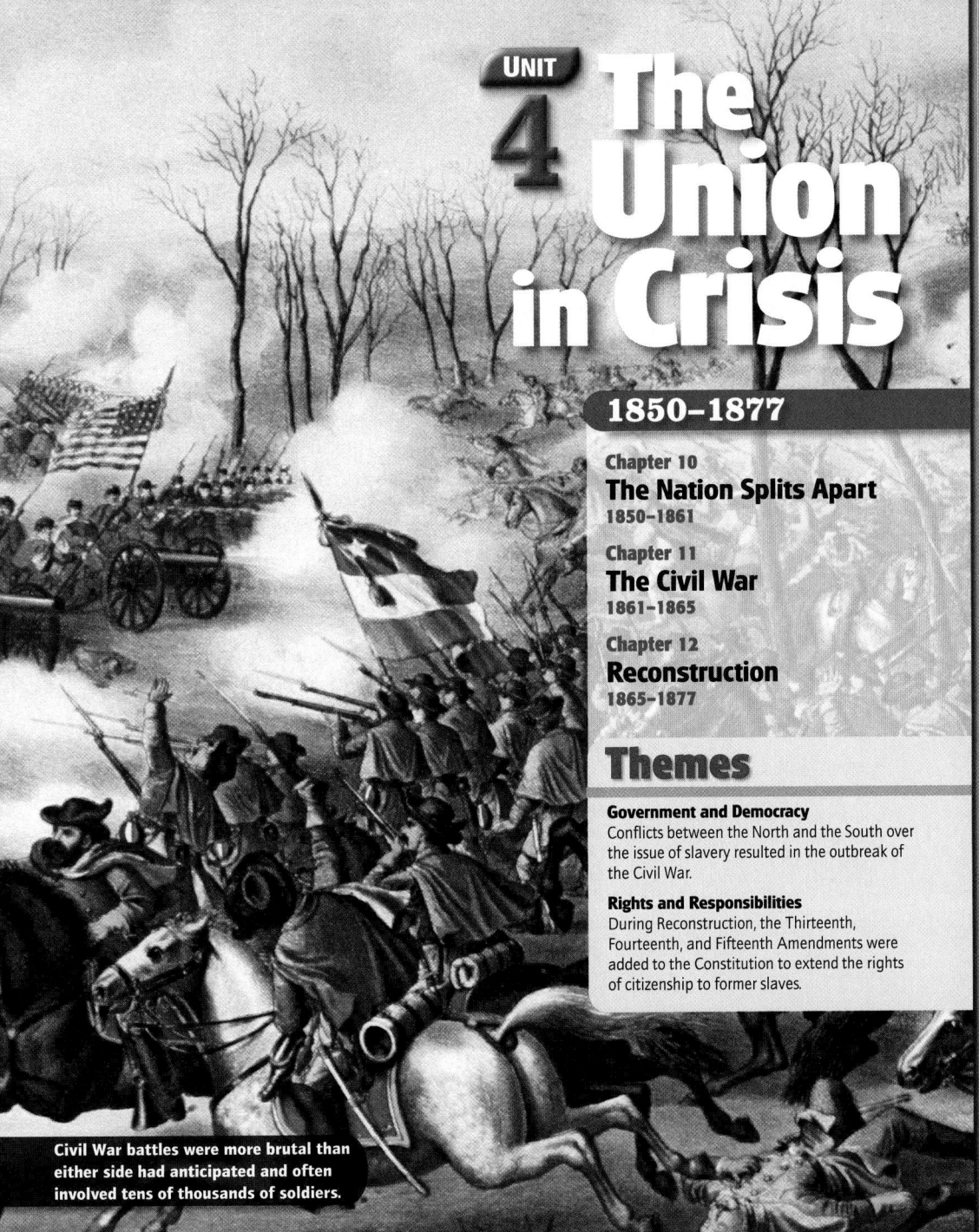

4 The Union in Crisis

1850–1877

Chapter 10
The Nation Splits Apart
1850–1861

Chapter 11
The Civil War
1861–1865

Chapter 12
Reconstruction
1865–1877

Themes

Government and Democracy
Conflicts between the North and the South over the issue of slavery resulted in the outbreak of the Civil War.

Rights and Responsibilities
During Reconstruction, the Thirteenth, Fourteenth, and Fifteenth Amendments were added to the Constitution to extend the rights of citizenship to former slaves.

Civil War battles were more brutal than either side had anticipated and often involved tens of thousands of soldiers.

317

Unit Preview

Introducing the Unit
Have the class help you fill in a word web on the Civil War. Write down words and phrases that students contribute about what they already know about the war. Have students copy the web into their notebooks and modify it as needed as they study Unit 4.

🖐 Graphic Organizer Transparencies

Connecting to Themes
Activity **Equal Rights**
Discussion Tell students that following the Civil War, citizenship rights were extended to formerly enslaved people. Then guide students in a discussion of the following questions: *Do all Americans enjoy equal rights today? If some groups of people are denied certain rights, how could this situation be corrected?*
LS Verbal-Linguistic

Reading Like a Historian
Interpreting Visuals Have students take a moment to examine the image on this page. What three types of people are participating in the conflict? What are each people's identifying characteristics? *Union soldiers, Confederates, Native Americans; Union soldiers— blue uniforms, use of cannons, American flag; Confederates—gray uniforms, use of horses and guns with bayonets, Confederate flag; Native Americans—Native clothing, use of horses and rifles*

Unit Resources

Planning
🗐 Differentiated Instruction Teacher Management System: Unit Pacing Guide
💿 One-Stop Planner CD-ROM: Teacher Management System
💿 Power Presentations with Video CD-ROM

Differentiating Instruction
🗐 Differentiated Instruction Teacher Management System: Lesson Plans for Differentiated Instruction
🗐 Pre-AP Activities Guide for American History
💿 Differentiated Instruction Modified Worksheets and Tests CD-ROM

Enrichment
🗐 Civic Participation Activities Guide
🗐 CRF: Economics and History Activity
🗐 CRF: Interdisciplinary Project
💿 American History Primary Source Library CD-ROM

Assessment
🗐 PASS: Unit Test, Forms A & B
🗐 Alternative Assessment Handbook
OSP ExamView Test Generator
HOAP Holt Online Assessment Program (in the Premier Online Edition)

The Differentiated Instruction Teacher Management System
provides a planning and instructional benchmarking guide for this unit.

• Prepare to Read •

Sequencing

On the board, write the names of 10 events that are discussed in this unit. Events might include the *Dred Scott* decision, the Battle of Antietam, or the end of Reconstruction. Have students use their textbooks to place the events in chronological order.

Teaching Tip

Divide students into mixed-ability pairs. Have each pair create a time line for a subsection in this unit. One student should read aloud while the other takes notes. Then students should work together to draw a time line with dates of the important events in the text passage.

Skills Planner

To give students more opportunities to practice this skill, see the following activities in the teacher's edition:
John Brown's Raid, p. 334;
Forming the Confederacy, p. 347.

Prepare to Read

Sequencing

Find practice for **Sequencing** in the **Skills Handbook**, p. H8

Most historical writing is organized in sequence, or the order in which events occur. Sequencing allows readers to better understand both the content and the context of what they are reading, including how one event may influence another and eventually lead to a certain outcome.

Before You Read
Examine time lines in the text. What do they tell you about the subject matter?

While You Read
Note key dates and events from the text, and use them to produce your own time line.

After You Read
Compare your time line and those in the text. How are they similar? How are they different?

Lincoln's Early Politics

As a young man, Lincoln moved to New Salem, a village about 20 miles northwest of Springfield, Illinois. He took a job as a store clerk and the next year ran for a seat in the state legislature. Lincoln lost that election, but two years later he ran again and won.

In December 1834, at age 25, Lincoln began the first of four terms in the Illinois General Assembly. During his first term he studied law at home, and in 1836 he was licensed to practice law. As a member of the state legislature, Lincoln opposed resolutions that condemned the abolition movement and that called for continuing slavery in Washington, D.C.

Lincoln met Mary Todd, the cousin of his law partner and the daughter of a wealth Kentucky slaveholder, in 1840. It was a rocky courtship because Todd flirted with another local attorney, Stephen Douglas. After a broken engagement, Lincoln and Todd made up and married in 1842. By then Lincoln had retired from the legislature to devote more time to his law practice.

READING CHECK **Sequencing** Which event occurred first? Which event occurred last?

Sequence Clue words, such as *first, next, then, before, after,* and *finally,* help indicate the order of events.

Dates, times of day, and seasons of the year are helpful clues in determining sequence.

Test Prep Tip

Multiple choice, short answer, and essay questions often ask you to determine the correct sequence of events. Sometimes, though, events can occur at the same time. Signal words such as *while, meanwhile,* and *during* tell you this.

Skills Focus: Sequencing

At Level

Reading Skill
Creating a Thematic Time Line

1. Divide students into small groups. Have each group select one of the following themes: Government and Democracy; or Rights and Responsibilities.

2. Have students skim the chapters covered in this unit, locating events that relate to their chosen theme. Then have each group create a thematic time line using events covered in this unit.

3. Have students share their time lines with the class, explaining why they included specific events. Display the thematic time lines as you study this unit. **LS Verbal-Linguistic, Visual-Spatial**

   Alternative Assessment Handbook, Rubric 36: Time Lines

Reading like a Historian

Interpreting Visuals

Find practice for **Interpreting Visuals** in the **Skills Handbook**, p. H30

Photographs capture the moment and political cartoons critique politics, but **fine art** is a type of visual created for artistic merit. Paintings created during or about points in history can provide detailed insight into certain people, places, and events. Works of fine art must be interpreted carefully for historical evidence. They are created by artists who have a point of view they wish to express.

Strategies historians use:

- Identify the subject of the piece. What event does the artist choose to portray?
- When and where does the event take place? Look for markers of time and place that aid recognition of historical context.
- What is the artist's point of view? Identify images that help identify the intended audience.

The subject of the picture is President Lincoln's tour of Richmond after that city had fallen to Union forces.

The crumbling buildings in the background help you identify the war-torn capital of Richmond.

The people in the picture appear to be celebrating President Lincoln's entrance. Therefore you can infer that the image was intended for a northern audience.

Skills FOCUS READING LIKE A HISTORIAN

As You Read Compare historical art with your reading. Do they support each other? What does art add to your understanding?
As You Study Keep in mind that art offers one interpretation of history, not necessarily the only interpretation. Be sure to balance each interpretation with known facts to arrive at the most complete historical account.

THE UNION IN CRISIS **319**

• Prepare to Read •

Interpreting Visuals

Guide students in a discussion of the following questions: *How do paintings and other forms of artwork differ from photographs as visual sources of history? How are they similar?*

Info to Know

Making Art and History The creator of this work of art is the famous illustrator Thomas Nast. Born in Germany in 1840, Nast came to America as a boy and studied art. During the Civil War, he was hired by *Harper's Weekly* magazine to make drawings of battles. His drawings were then turned into engravings and published to accompany reporting on the war. Nast was a fierce Republican and Lincoln supporter. His dramatic and powerful drawings of the war and the Union cause built support for the North and its president. Later in life, Nast created the popular symbols of the Democratic and Republican Parties, the donkey and the elephant respectively. In yet another series of illustrations, Nast developed the modern image of Santa Claus.

Chapter 10 Planning Guide

The Nation Splits Apart

Chapter Overview	Reproducible Resources	Technology Resources
CHAPTER 10 pp. 320–353 **Overview:** In this chapter, students will analyze how rising tensions over the issue of slavery led to a split in the nation and culminated in war.	**Differentiated Instruction Teacher Management System:*** • Instructional Benchmarking Guides • Lesson Plans for Differentiated Instruction **Interactive Reader and Study Guide:** Chapter Summary* **Chapter Resource File:*** • Writing for the SAT: John Brown's Raid • Social Studies Skills Activity: Interpreting Political Cartoons • Chapter Review Activity **American History Outline Maps** **Pre-AP Activities Guide for American History***	Live Ink® Online Reading Help Student Edition on Audio CD Program Differentiated Instruction Modified Worksheets and Tests CD-ROM Interactive Skills Tutor CD-ROM United States History Primary Source Library CD-ROM Power Presentations with Video CD-ROM History's Impact: American History Video Program (VHS/DVD): The Nation Splits Apart Online Chapter Summaries in Spanish Graphic Organizer Transparencies
Section 1: **The Politics of Slavery** **The Main Idea:** The issue of slavery dominated national politics during the 1850s. The federal government forged policies in attempts to satisfy both North and South.	**Differentiated Instruction Teacher Management System:** Section 1 Lesson Plan* **Interactive Reader and Study Guide:** Section 1 Summary* **Chapter Resource File:*** • Vocabulary Builder Activity, Section 1	**Daily Bellringer Transparency:** Section 1* **Map Transparency:** Upsetting the Balance, 1850* **Map Transparency:** From Compromise to Conflict* **Daily Test Practice Transparency:** Section 1*
Section 2: **Sectional Conflicts and National Politics** **The Main Idea:** Rising tensions over slavery expanded from political rhetoric into outright violence.	**Differentiated Instruction Teacher Management System:** Section 2 Lesson Plan* **Interactive Reader and Study Guide:** Section 2 Summary* **Chapter Resource File:*** • Vocabulary Builder Activity, Section 2	**Daily Bellringer Transparency:** Section 2* **Daily Test Practice Transparency:** Section 2*
Section 3: **Lincoln's Path to the White House** **The Main Idea:** After gaining national prominence in the late 1850s, Abraham Lincoln became president in 1860.	**Differentiated Instruction Teacher Management System:** Section 3 Lesson Plan* **Interactive Reader and Study Guide:** Section 3 Summary* **Chapter Resource File:*** • Vocabulary Builder Activity, Section 3	**Daily Bellringer Transparency:** Section 3* **Map Transparency:** The Election of 1860* **Daily Test Practice Transparency:** Section 3*
Section 4: **The South Secedes** **The Main Idea:** The election of Abraham Lincoln led to the secession of the southern states.	**Differentiated Instruction Teacher Management System:** Section 4 Lesson Plan* **Interactive Reader and Study Guide:** Section 4 Summary* **Chapter Resource File:*** • Vocabulary Builder Activity, Section 4	**Daily Bellringer Transparency:** Section 4* **Daily Test Practice Transparency:** Section 4*

go.hrw.com go.hrw.com	**Print Resource**	**Transparency**
LS Learning Styles	**Audio CD**	**CD-ROM**
Video Video	**SE** Student Edition	**TE** Teacher's Edition
OSP One-Stop Planner CD-ROM		

*also on One-Stop Planner CD-ROM

Review, Assessment, Intervention

Quick Facts Transparencies: Terms of the Compromise of 1850, Effects of the *Dred Scott* Decision, Effects of John Brown's Raid, Causes of Secession, The Nation Splits Apart

Spanish Chapter Summaries Audio CD Program

Progress Assessment Support System (PASS): Chapter Test*

Differentiated Instruction Modified Worksheets and Tests CD-ROM: Modified Chapter Test

OSP One-Stop Planner CD-ROM: ExamView Test Generator (English/Spanish)

HOAP Holt Online Assessment Program (HOAP), in the Holt Premier Online Student Edition

---

PASS: Section 1 Quiz*

Online Quiz: Section 1

Alternative Assessment Handbook

PASS: Section 2 Quiz*

Online Quiz: Section 2

Alternative Assessment Handbook

PASS: Section 3 Quiz*

Online Quiz: Section 3

Alternative Assessment Handbook

PASS: Section 4 Quiz*

Online Quiz: Section 4

Alternative Assessment Handbook

NC RESOURCES

The following resources were developed to help North Carolina educators teach the standards and objectives of North Carolina's eleventh grade standard course of study in United States history.

- United States history EOC Test Prep Workbook
- Teacher's Support System
- North Carolina One-Stop Planner

And be sure to direct your students to **go.hrw.com** for online access to the EOC Test Prep Workbook.

go.hrw.com
EOC Test Prep
KEYWORD: SE7 NC

Holt Online Learning

go.hrw.com
Teacher Resources
KEYWORD: SD7 TEACHER

go.hrw.com
Student Resources
KEYWORD: SD7 CH10

- Document-based Questions
- Interactive Multimedia Activities

- Current Events
- Chapter-based Internet Activities
- and more!

Holt Premier
Online Student Edition

Complete online support for interactivity, assessment, and reporting

- Interactive Maps and Notebook
- Standardized Test Prep
- Homework Practice and Research Activities Online

Before You Teach

The Big Picture

Edward L. Ayers

The Politics of Slavery Slavery had never played a more prominent role in American life than it did in the 1850s. The institution flourished and accounted for an ever-growing part of the nation's economy. The rise of a small but effective abolitionist movement in the North clashed with southern leaders insistent that slaveholders' property rights be preserved. A series of compromises in the early 1850s failed to calm the conflict.

Sectional Conflicts and National Politics In the mid-1850s the struggle between antislavery and proslavery forces broke out into harsh violence in Kansas. The territory, on the border of both North and South, became a symbol for the future of the entire country. The Supreme Court's *Dred Scott* decision fueled outrage in the North and gave the new Republican party the focus it needed. John Brown's raid in Virginia further electrified the entire nation around the issue of slavery.

Lincoln's Path to the White House Abraham Lincoln of Illinois suddenly catapulted to prominence in 1858. His debates with Senator Stephen Douglas captured the attention of Republican leaders, who found in Lincoln the sort of spokesman for whom they had been searching. Lincoln combined a firm opposition to the spread of slavery with shrewd political judgment. Nominated for the presidency, Lincoln found himself running against three other men, two representing the Democratic Party and another representing a party dedicated to compromise. Lincoln won the electoral vote, though the nation was badly divided.

The South Secedes White southerners were insulted by Lincoln's election. Leaders in South Carolina and other states in the Lower South mobilized to leave the United States and create their own nation, based on slavery. As Lincoln was inaugurated, desperate efforts at compromise failed.

Recent Scholarship

Slavery and the Civil War People never tire of debating the causes of the American Civil War and the crucial questions always turn around the role of slavery in triggering secession and the response to secession in the North. Charles B. Dew, in *Apostles of Disunion: Southern Secession Commissioners and the Causes of the Civil War* (2001), comes at the problem in a fresh way and with admirable economy. He examines the language and arguments the delegates from the new Confederacy in the Lower South used to persuade the conventions in the Upper South to join them. He finds that slavery was front and center, explicit and clear.

Differentiating Instruction

Differentiated Instruction Teacher Management System
- Lesson Plans for Differentiated Instruction
- Differentiated Instructional Benchmarking Guides
- Interactive Reader and Study Guide

 Spanish Chapter Summaries Audio CD Program

 Online Chapter Summaries in Spanish

 Student Edition on Audio CD Program

 Differentiated Instruction Modified Worksheets and Tests CD-ROM
- Vocabulary Flash Cards
- Modified Vocabulary Builder Activities
- Modified Chapter Review Activity
- Modified Chapter Test

OSP One-Stop Planner CD-ROM
- ExamView Test Generator (English and Spanish)
- PuzzlePro
- Quiz Show for ExamView
- Transparencies and Videos

TE Differentiated Activities in the Teacher's Edition
- Campaign Speeches, p. 333
- Lincoln's Path to Congress, p. 339
- Lincoln-Douglas Debates, p. 341

Reading Like a Historian

Sam Wineburg

Thinking Contextually

Consider the following words of Abraham Lincoln: "I have no purpose to introduce political and social equality between the white and black races. There is a physical difference between the two . . . I agree with Judge Douglas [that the Negro] is not my equal in many respects—certainly not in color, perhaps not in moral or intellectual endowment."

Lincoln's "Dark Side"

Modern readers are struck by the blatant racism of this comment. When I have presented this quotation to high school and college students, many have gotten angry and demanded to know why their teachers had hidden this sordid side of Lincoln's thinking. They felt they had been had.

Contextualized thinking, however, begins with different assumptions from those that guide many students' thinking. To think contextually means that words are not clear windows into the interior world of the person who has spoken them. We utter words for different reasons: to achieve specific goals, to persuade an audience with particular characteristics, to set the tone for things we'll say later. Thinking contextually means that we begin our inquiry by asking prior questions about Lincoln before leaping to conclusions about his racism. In this instance, we might begin by asking: When and where did Lincoln say these words and what might he have been trying to achieve?

What Was Lincoln Trying to Do?

Our answers help us build a context for genuine historical understanding: the occasion in which Lincoln uttered these words (a debate with Stephen A. Douglas for a fiercely contested senatorial seat in 1858), the location of this debate (Ottawa, Illinois, a hotbed of anti-black sentiment), the kinds of people who were in the audience (largely supportive of Douglas and suspicious of Lincoln), and the fact that both Lincoln and Douglas addressed these people not as prophets or moralists but as candidates courting votes. Nor can we ignore what Douglas said to spark Lincoln's response, or the words Lincoln uttered immediately after ("But in the right to eat the bread, without the leave of anybody else, which his own hand earns, [the Negro] is my equal and the equal of Judge Douglas, and the equal of every living man."). Such considerations just begin to scratch the surface of what we would need to create a historical context for Lincoln's words.

Looking for Nuances

Even equipped with this information, we miss nuances that reverberated in the 1850s, but which strike few chords today. Notice that in the above quotation, the only aspect Lincoln is willing to concede unequivocally is a physical difference in color between blacks and whites. But on the crucial question of moral and intellectual differences, Lincoln expresses doubt with his word choice, "perhaps." Nearly every student to whom I've given this document ignores this "perhaps" or attaches to it no special meaning. But in Lincoln's time, in the context of his—not our—day, to admit doubt regarding the superiority of whites was tantamount to heresy. The unquestioned superiority of white European civilization not only buttressed the institution of slavery (and its ongoing maintenance) but also guided policies toward all non-white peoples for centuries.

The Bravery of a Single Word

As historian and classicist Garry Wills argues in *Lincoln at Gettysburg*, Lincoln's "perhaps" was a courageous move that distinguished him from the accepted racism of his day. However, unless we attune our ears to the language of the 1850s and 1860s, it is a reference that we miss today—and in so doing, miss the importance and courage of our 16th president.

Standards Focus

Social Studies Competency Goals
Goal 3 The learner will analyze the issues that led up to the Civil War, the effects of the war, and the impact of Reconstruction on the nation.
 3.03

 **The Big Idea and Essential Questions**

To foster student understanding of this chapter's big idea, design your lesson to address each section's essential question.

Big Idea Divisions within the nation over slavery and states' rights led the United States to the brink of war.

Essential Questions

1. How did the federal government try to appease both North and South concerning the issue of slavery?

2. How did disagreements over slavery lead to violence in some parts of the nation?

3. How did Abraham Lincoln rise to the presidency in 1860?

4. How did the southern states respond to the election of Abraham Lincoln as president?

Key to Differentiating Instruction

Below Level

Basic-level activities designed for all students encountering new material

At Level

Intermediate-level activities designed for average students

Above Level

Challenging activities designed for honors and gifted-and-talented students

Standard English Mastery

Activities designed to improve standard English usage

320 CHAPTER 10

CHAPTER
10 1850–1861

The Nation Splits Apart

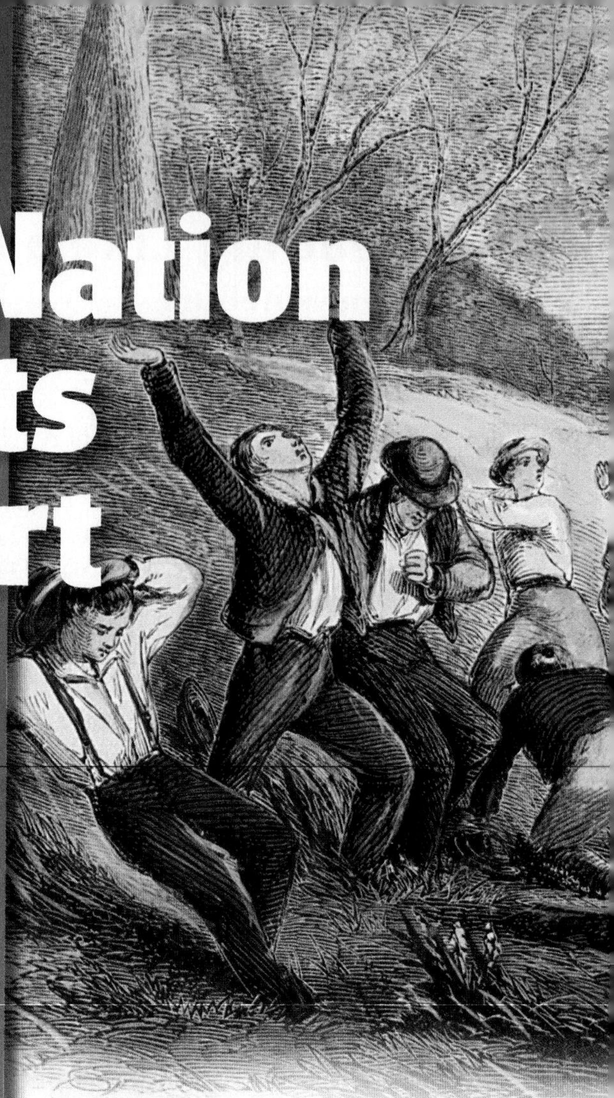

THE BIG PICTURE After the war with Mexico ended, one question stirred national politics: Would these new territories be slave or free? By 1860 the nation had split along sectional lines—North and South—and hostile camps took steps that would lead to war.

NC **North Carolina Standards**

Social Studies Objectives
3.01 Trace the economic, social, and political events from the Mexican War to the outbreak of the Civil War.
3.02 Analyze and assess the causes of the Civil War.

Language Arts Objectives
3.03 Use argumentation for:
• establishing and defending a point of view.

Skills FOCUS READING LIKE A HISTORIAN

Nowhere was the fight over slavery more pronounced than in Kansas territory. In the Marais des Cygnes Massacre, a gang of 30 pro-slavery men rounded up a group of eleven antislavery settlers and gunned them down in a small ravine, killing five and wounding four.
Interpreting Visuals Why weren't the victims of the massacre fighting back?
See Skills Handbook, p. H30

320

1850
U.S. Congress reaches the Compromise of 1850, admitting California as a free state and passing the Fugitive Slave Act.

1850

1851
World The Great Exhibition, the first World's Fair, opens in London.

Introduce the Chapter

At Level

The Nation Splits Apart

1. Ask students to list issues within their school, community, state, or the nation that are divisive, and about which there has been considerable debate.

2. Create a class list of these issues, and discuss how each issue might be resolved. Does compromise between opposing groups seem likely? Would a compromise resolve the issue and heal divisions among groups with differing views? Or is the issue best resolved through binding legislation?

3. Remind students that during the 1800s slavery was the primary divisive issue facing, and threatening, the United States.

4. Tell students that in this chapter they will learn how the issue of slavery divided the nation, how compromises failed to resolve the issue, and how this issue led to secession of the southern states. **LS Auditory-Musical**

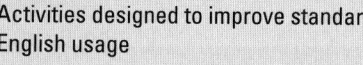 Alternative Assessment Handbook, Rubric 11: Discussions

History's Impact video program
Watch the video to understand the impact of Dred Scott.

1852
Harriet Beecher Stowe publishes *Uncle Tom's Cabin*, a novel about slave life.

May 1854
Kansas-Nebraska Act becomes law.

May 21, 1856
Proslavery group attacks antislavery stronghold of Lawrence, Kansas.

October 1859
John Brown seizes the federal arsenal at Harpers Ferry, Virginia.

1852 | **1854** | **1856** | **1858** | **1860**

1852
Republic of South Africa is established.

1854
Japan and the United States sign an agreement opening Japan to trade.

1857
Uprising against British rule in India begins with Sepoy Rebellion.

1861
Russian serfs are emancipated.

321

Explore the Time Line

1. When was the Fugitive Slave Act passed? *1850*

2. When were serfs emancipated in Russia? *1861*

3. How many months elapsed between the passage of the Kansas-Nebraska Act and the attack on Lawrence, Kansas? *24 months (2 years)*

4. Where and when did the Sepoy Rebellion begin? *India, 1857*

Info to Know

Slavery in the South Just before the Civil War, there were approximately 3.5 million slaves in the states that formed the Confederacy, just under 40 percent of the population of these states. About 31 percent of the families living in Confederate states owned slaves. During the same time period, slaves formed just under 13 percent of the total U.S. population, and under 8 percent of families living in the U.S. owned slaves.

Making Generalizations Why do you think slaveholders held so much power? *possible answers—They were rich and powerful; southern economy depended on slave labor.*

Bellringer

The Inside Story. . . Use the **Daily Bellringer Transparency** to help students answer the question.

📄 Daily Bellringer Transparency, Section 1

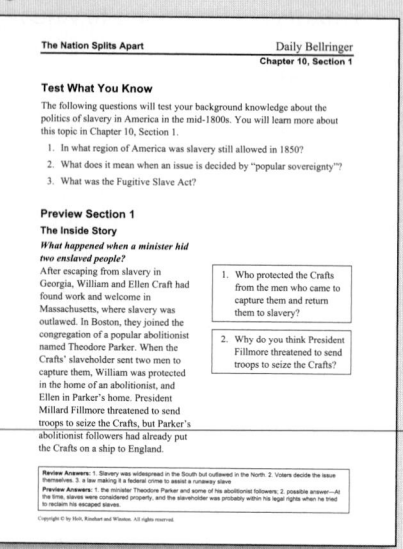

Academic Vocabulary

Review with students the high-use academic terms in this section.

ideology set of beliefs that form the basis of a culture or political system (p. 323)

valid meaningful or justifiable (p. 323)

📄 CRF: Vocabulary Builder Activity, Section 1

Taking Notes

passed the Compromise of 1850; popular sovereignty in Kansas and Nebraska; Missouri Compromise repealed

---

SECTION

1 The Politics of Slavery

BEFORE YOU READ

MAIN IDEA

The issue of slavery dominated national politics during the 1850s. The federal government forged policies in attempts to satisfy both North and South.

READING FOCUS

1. What factors made slavery in the United States an issue before 1850?

2. How did the Compromise of 1850 seek to settle issues between North and South ?

3. In what ways did the North and South each hope to benefit from the Kansas-Nebraska Act?

4. How did people in the North and South react to the Kansas-Nebraska Act?

KEY TERMS AND PEOPLE

radical
Millard Fillmore
Compromise of 1850
Fugitive Slave Act
Harriet Beecher Stowe
Uncle Tom's Cabin
Stephen Douglas
popular sovereignty
Kansas-Nebraska Act
free-soilers
Republican Party
nativism

TAKING NOTES As you read, take notes identifying actions the federal government took to satisfy the South over the issue of slavery. Record your notes in a graphic organizer like the one shown below.

Actions to Satisfy the South

A MINISTER Defies the PRESIDENT

THE INSIDE STORY

What happened when a minister hid two enslaved people? Husband and wife William and Ellen Craft escaped from slavery in Georgia in 1848 and made their way to Massachusetts, where slavery had been outlawed. William, a skilled cabinetmaker, found work in Boston.

The Crafts joined the church of well-known abolitionist Theodore Parker and lived quietly. Parker was one of the most important ministers of his day. His powerful sermons attracted so large a crowd that he preached not from a church pulpit but from the city's enormous Music Hall. Each Sunday thousands of people gathered to hear Parker denounce slavery and call for women's rights.

After learning of the Crafts' whereabouts in 1850, their slaveholder in Georgia sent two men to Boston to capture them. William fled to the home of a local African American abolitionist. There he was guarded by barrels of gunpowder that the homeowner placed on his front porch. Ellen hid in Parker's home. When President Millard Fillmore threatened to send U.S. troops to seize the Crafts, Parker's followers put them on a ship to England. "I would rather lie all my life in jail, and starve there, than refuse to protect one of these parishioners of mine," Parker angrily informed the president. "You cannot think that I am to stand by and see my church carried off to slavery and do nothing." ◼

▶ The minister Theodore Parker (above right) issued this broadside cautioning African Americans to avoid police.

CAUTION!!
COLORED PEOPLE
OF BOSTON, ONE & ALL,
You are hereby respectfully CAUTIONED and advised, to avoid conversing with the **Watchmen and Police Officers of Boston,**
For since the recent ORDER OF THE MAYOR & ALDERMEN, they are empowered to act as
KIDNAPPERS
AND
Slave Catchers,
And they have already been actually employed in **KIDNAPPING, CATCHING, AND KEEPING SLAVES.** Therefore, if you value your **LIBERTY,** and the *Welfare of the Fugitives* among you, Shun them in every possible manner, as so many **HOUNDS** on the track of the most unfortunate of your race.
Keep a Sharp Look Out for KIDNAPPERS, and have TOP EYE open.
APRIL 24, 18..

Teach the Main Idea

At Level

The Politics of Slavery

1. **Teach** Ask students the Reading Focus questions to teach this section.

2. **Apply** Have each student draw four ladders on their own paper. Have them label the tops of the ladders with the four main headings in this section: Slavery in the United States, The Compromise of 1850, the Kansas-Nebraska Act, and Reactions in North and South. Then have students list the main ideas from each heading on the rungs of the corresponding ladder. **LS Visual-Spatial**

3. **Review** Have volunteers share their main ideas with the class. Then guide students in a discussion of the more controversial components of the Compromise of 1850.

4. **Practice/Homework** Have students write a short news release that summarizes the ways in which the government attempted to satisfy both the North and the South during the 1850s. **LS Verbal-Linguistic**

📄 Alternative Assessment Handbook, Rubric 42: Writing to Inform

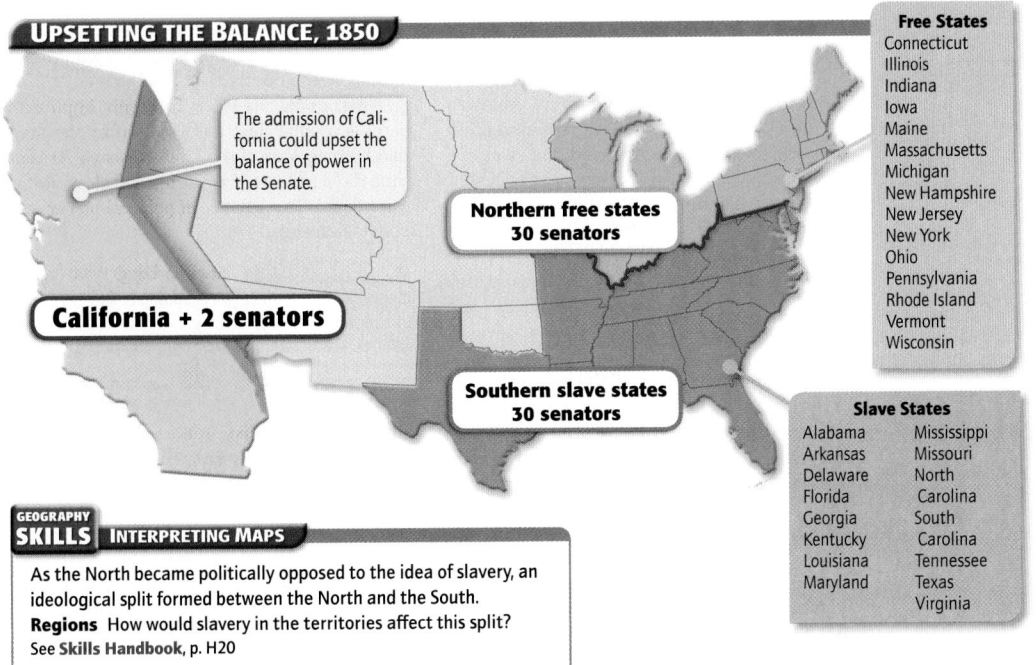

UPSETTING THE BALANCE, 1850

The admission of California could upset the balance of power in the Senate.

**Northern free states
30 senators**

California + 2 senators

**Southern slave states
30 senators**

Free States
Connecticut
Illinois
Indiana
Iowa
Maine
Massachusetts
Michigan
New Hampshire
New Jersey
New York
Ohio
Pennsylvania
Rhode Island
Vermont
Wisconsin

Slave States
Alabama   Mississippi
Arkansas   Missouri
Delaware   North
Florida   Carolina
Georgia   South
Kentucky   Carolina
Louisiana   Tennessee
Maryland   Texas
                    Virginia

GEOGRAPHY SKILLS **INTERPRETING MAPS**

As the North became politically opposed to the idea of slavery, an ideological split formed between the North and the South.
Regions How would slavery in the territories affect this split?
See **Skills Handbook**, p. H20

Slavery in the United States

By 1850 slavery had existed for more than 200 years in America. Under British rule slavery had existed in every colony, north and south. After the Revolutionary War, the northern states began to end the practice.

Freedom in the North did not always come quickly. Some northern states freed only children born after slavery had been banned. Their mothers remained enslaved. In several northern states, slavery continued to exist in some form until the 1840s.

Even at its peak, however, northern slavery never equaled that of the South. By 1790 more than 90 percent of enslaved Americans lived to the south of the Mason-Dixon line.

By 1850 the nation was divided. Two societies existed—the North where workers labored for wages and the South where a large number of workers were enslaved. Many southerners believed the health of their economy depended on slave labor. "It is, in truth, the slave labor in Virginia which gives the value to her soil and her habitations," said Virginian Thomas Dew.

The developing debate over slavery was largely one of property rights versus human rights. Those who supported slavery believed that property rights came first. "We take it for granted, that the right of the owner to his slave is to be respected," argued Dew.

To the northerners who were truly concerned about slavery, the issue was one of basic democratic <u>ideology</u>. "Shall the Government be a commonwealth where all are citizens, or an aristocracy where man owns his brother man," Theodore Parker asked. "Shall a man have a right to his own limbs, his liberty, his life?"

The treatment of slaves in the South varied widely. Northern opponents of slavery emphasized its harshness. Escaped slaves told stories of mistreatment and abuse. William Wells Brown, who had once been enslaved in Missouri, wrote that the whip was used "very frequently and freely, and a small offense on the part of the slave furnished an occasion for its use."

Those opposed to slavery believed that their arguments were <u>valid</u>. Still, many Americans in the early 1800s thought that the property

ACADEMIC VOCABULARY
ideology set of beliefs that form the basis of a culture or political system

ACADEMIC VOCABULARY
valid meaningful or justifiable

Reading Focus

1 What factors made slavery in the United States an issue before 1850?
North began ending slavery after Revolutionary War; slavery grew in the South; whether or not to allow slavery in new territories

Slavery in the United States

Recall Which American colonies permitted slavery? *permitted and existed in every colony*

Analyze Why did southerners see the debate over slavery as a battle for property rights? *Most southerners considered slaves personal property.*

Elaborate What is meant by the quote "It is . . . slave labor in Virginia which gives value to her soil and her habitations"? *Without slaves, the state and its farm owners could not prosper.*

📦 Map Transparency: Upsetting the Balance, 1850

Collaborative Learning

At Level

Slavery in the United States

1. Guide students in a discussion of slavery and its importance to the southern economy. Ask students to list arguments slaveholders used to support the practice. Then have students list arguments used by abolitionists to abolish slavery.

2. Write the words "Slaveholders" and "Abolitionists" for all students to see, and have volunteers read arguments from their own lists. Make a list of student responses. Have students add to or correct their work.

3. Organize the students into small groups. Ask students to write several sentences based on the above responses from the point of view of either a slaveholder or an abolitionist.

4. Have volunteers from each group read their sentences to the class. Have the class identify whether these sentences are written from a slaveholder's viewpoint or an abolitionist's viewpoint. **LS Interpersonal, Kinesthetic**

📖 Alternative Assessment Handbook, Rubric 24: Oral Presentations

Answers

Interpreting Maps *would upset balance between slave and free states*

323

Reading Focus

② How did the Compromise of 1850 seek to settle issues between North and South? *slavery would be decided by residents in New Mexico and Utah territories; strengthened the Fugitive Slave Act; abolished slave trade in District of Columbia*

The Compromise of 1850

Recall What prompted Daniel Webster to soften his position on abolishing slavery? *fear that the South would secede from the Union*

Analyze Why do you think John Calhoun was so opposed to compromises on the issue of slavery? *He wanted slavery to continue without any restrictions.*

Make Judgments Do you think Calhoun's threat about secession helped lead to the passage of the Compromise of 1850? Why or why not? *possible answer—perhaps; it would take more than one senator to lead to secession, but it was a serious concern*

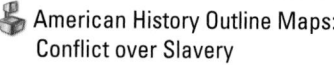 CRF: Primary Source Activity: John C. Calhoun and Daniel Webster Debate

American History Outline Maps: Conflict over Slavery

 Terms of the Compromise of 1850
Have students use the information to create an illustrated time line of the Compromise of 1850.

Quick Facts Transparency: Terms of the Compromise of 1850

Answers

Reading Check *for—human rights; against—property rights and southern economy dependent on slave labor*

324

---

rights of slaveholders were more important than the human rights of slaves. It was difficult for opponents of slavery to overcome the claim that slaveholders' rights were protected by the Constitution, just as the rights of all property owners were protected. This was one reason why the abolition movement was slow to gain popular support in the North.

After winning the Mexican-American War, the United States added more than 500,000 square miles of new territory. New states would eventually be formed from this vast area. Would these states ban or allow slavery?

The Missouri Compromise of 1820 had banned slavery in most of the northern part of the Louisiana Purchase. Now some antislavery activists wanted to do the same to this new territory. Other people, mainly southerners, wanted to allow slavery in the new lands. By 1850, the political argument over slavery no longer centered on its existence in the South. Instead, the debate shifted to the spread of slavery into places where it did not yet exist.

The question of the expansion of slavery was also a struggle for control of the Congress. New states would mean additional seats in the Senate and the House of Representatives, and these new legislators might work for or against slavery. If northern legislators could block the

expansion of slavery and gain control of Congress, laws might be passed that would end slavery in the South.

Then in March 1850, California applied to become a state, just two years after the area had become part of the United States. At that time the number of free states and slave states were equal. The balance of political power was about to change.

READING CHECK **Summarizing** What arguments existed for and against ending or limiting the institution of slavery?

The Compromise of 1850

Only about 14,000 non-Indians lived in California in 1848. So many forty-niners moved there during the gold rush, however, that by 1850 California's population had jumped to 93,000. Residents quickly approved a constitution banning slavery and applied for statehood.

This request brought the issue of slavery to the surface. In 1820 Kentucky senator Henry Clay had crafted the Missouri Compromise. Now, nearing the end of a long political career, he hoped for one more compromise between North and South. On January 29, 1850, he introduced a plan to Congress in which he proposed compromises on several slavery issues.

The Senate debate over Clay's resolutions was one of the greatest in its history. Two political giants of the time, Daniel Webster of Massachusetts and John C. Calhoun of South Carolina, faced off. Calhoun made his opposition to compromise clear. Gravely ill and unable to speak, he sat grimly in his chair while his speech was read to the other senators.

HISTORY'S VOICES

❝The South asks for justice, simple justice, and less she ought not to take . . . Nothing else can, with any certainty, finally and forever settle the question at issue, terminate agitation, and save the Union.❞

—Senator John C. Calhoun, March 4, 1850

Three days later, Webster rose to reply. He personally opposed slavery and its spread, but he was dismayed by Calhoun's threat that the South might secede, or withdraw from the Union, over this issue. He believed that the preservation of the Union was more important than the disagreement over slavery.

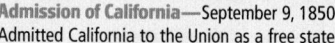

TERMS OF THE COMPROMISE OF 1850 *QUICK FACTS*

Admission of California—September 9, 1850
Admitted California to the Union as a free state.

Texas and New Mexico Act—September 9, 1850
Set the Texas-New Mexico border and organized the New Mexico Territory with slavery to be decided by its residents.

Utah Act—September 9, 1850
Organized the Utah Territory with slavery to be decided by its residents.

Fugitive Slave Act—September 18, 1850
Strengthened the Fugitive Slave Act of 1793 by imposing heavy penalties on persons who aided runaway slaves or who blocked or refused to help in their capture.

An Act Abolishing the Slave Trade in the District of Columbia—September 20, 1850
Outlawed the buying and selling of slaves, but not slavery itself, in the nation's capital.

Source: Encyclopedia of American History

324 CHAPTER 10

Skills Focus: Interpreting Historical Maps [At Level]

Social Studies Skill
The Compromise of 1850

Materials outline map of the United States, colored markers or pencils

1. Review the terms of the Missouri Compromise of 1820 and the Compromise of 1850 with students.

2. Distribute outline maps to students. Have them use three different colors to distinguish where slavery was permitted, where it was not, and in which territories slavery would

be decided by popular vote. Have students create a map key to show the significance of each color.

3. Have students compare their maps to the maps in the text, correct them as needed, and retain their maps as study tools.
LS Visual-Spatial

Alternative Assessment Handbook, Rubric 20: Map Creation

Not all northern senators agreed with Webster. New York's Senator William Seward opposed any compromise on slavery and fiercely attacked slavery itself. Seward's speech caused a stir across the nation. It established him as a **radical**, or a person with extreme views, on the slavery issue.

The debate on Clay's proposals dragged on through the summer. Calhoun's death on March 31 removed one obstacle to compromise. President Zachary Taylor, who also opposed compromise, died a few months later. His successor, **Millard Fillmore**, supported Clay's plan. Finally, in September the Senate passed five laws based on Clay's resolutions. Together, these laws formed what became known as the **Compromise of 1850**.

The Fugitive Slave Act The issues the compromise seemed to solve were soon replaced by others. One part of the compromise itself was very controversial. The **Fugitive Slave Act** made it a federal crime to assist runaway slaves. The law also allowed the arrest of escaped slaves in states where slavery was illegal. People accused of being escaped slaves had to prove that they were not, which was often difficult or impossible. In addition, escaped slaves who had lived in the North for years were returned to slavery if caught. For example, an Indiana man was turned over to a slaveholder who claimed that he had escaped 19 years earlier.

The fugitive slave law was openly resisted by people in the North. "We must trample this law under our feet," one abolitionist urged. Many northerners who had previously been quiet on slavery issues were furious. Mobs rescued slaves from northern police stations. They threatened slave catchers. In turn, the North's reaction angered southern slaveholders. By 1851 some southern leaders were again talking of seceding from the Union.

Uncle Tom's Cabin Among those angry northerners was **Harriet Beecher Stowe**, a magazine writer in Maine. Stowe had once lived in Cincinnati, Ohio, an important stop on the Underground Railroad. There she heard tales of slavery's cruelty and horror. In 1851 she wrote a series of short stories about slave life for an antislavery newspaper. A year later these stories were published as a novel called **Uncle Tom's Cabin**.

When Harriet Beecher Stowe met President Lincoln during the Civil War, he greeted her by saying, "So you're the little woman who wrote the book that made this great war."

Although Stowe had little firsthand knowledge of slavery or the South, her novel became an enormous success. Within a year, 300,000 copies were sold in the United States and nearly a million more in the rest of the world. The book outraged many southerners. They accused Stowe of writing lies about plantation life. "There never before was anything so detestable or so monstrous among women as this," a New Orleans newspaper declared angrily. Stowe's book raised tensions over slavery to a new height.

READING CHECK **Identifying Cause and Effect** How did the Fugitive Slave Act and *Uncle Tom's Cabin* add to tensions over slavery?

The Kansas-Nebraska Act

The Compromise of 1850 marked the end of an era of political leadership in Congress. Clay and Webster both died within the next two years. Their deaths allowed **Stephen Douglas**, a senator from Illinois, to gain power and influence. As a first-term senator, Douglas had led the fight for the passage of the Compromise

---

Info to Know

Harriet Beecher Stowe Harriet Beecher Stowe never visited the South; she learned about the treatment of enslaved people from an African American woman she hired. After the death of Harriet's young son, she understood what it was like to be separated from a loved one. Harriet likened this loss to the experience of slaves who were separated from their loved ones when family members were sold.

Uncle Tom's Cabin in the South
Although many southerners claimed to despise *Uncle Tom's Cabin*, it was widely read in the South. Southern writers responded to Stowe's novel by writing novels that showed slavery in a positive light. These novels included *Uncle Robin in His Cabin in Virginia, and Tom Without One in Boston; The Lofty and the Lowly;* and *The Master's House*.

📄 CRF: Biography: Harriet Beecher Stowe

📄 CRF: Literature Activity: *Uncle Tom's Cabin* by Harriet Beecher Stowe

go.hrw.com
Online Resources
KEYWORD: SD7 CH10
TOPIC: UNCLE TOM'S CABIN

Skills Focus: Making Generalizations   At Level

Reading Skill
The Fugitive Slave Act

1. Guide students in a discussion of the reasons northerners were angered by the Fugitive Slave Act.

2. Have students write an editorial protesting the law. *Students could express the sentiment of William Seward and stress the human rights issues of slavery.*

3. Have volunteers read their editorials to the class. Guide students in a discussion of the views presented in the editorials. Ask

students to name the states in which these editorials would have received a favorable response.

4. As an extension, have students prepare a rebuttal to the editorial, using arguments from the viewpoint of a southern newspaper editor.
LS **Verbal-Linguistic**
📄 Alternative Assessment Handbook, Rubric 17: Letters to Editors

Answers

Reading Check *law was resisted, northerners outraged by law and by descriptions of slave treatment in* Uncle Tom's Cabin

3 In what ways did the North and South each hope to benefit from the Kansas-Nebraska Act? *Both hoped to benefit from a railroad linking the East to California; South hoped to gain territories where slavery would be permitted.*

The Kansas-Nebraska Act

Explain What idea did Stephen Douglas propose to settle the issue of slavery in Kansas and Nebraska? *Slavery would be decided by popular sovereignty.*

Draw Conclusions In what way did Stephen Douglas further the national debate about slavery? *opened door for slavery in Kansas and Nebraska*

Evaluate Do you believe that Douglas was pleased with the Kansas-Nebraska Act? *probably not; he did not get approval for the railroad, which was the reason he proposed the legislation*

🖥 Map Transparency: From Compromise to Conflict

Biography

Stephen Foster (1826–1864) Stephen Foster was a composer who wrote many songs, hymns, arrangements, and instrumental works. Although Foster wrote many types of songs, he is best known for his minstrel songs. The lyrics of minstrel songs are often considered racist today, but many reflected the misery of slave life before the Civil War. Remembered today for songs such as "Oh! Susanna" and "Camptown Races," Foster was the first professional songwriter in the United States.

Answers

Reading Check *Douglas wanted a northern route for proposed railroad; government had to officially open land for settlement*

326

From Compromise to Conflict

The Missouri Compromise, 1820
The nation kept an uneasy balance of power by admitting Missouri as a slave state and Maine as a free state.

- Free state
- Free territory
- Slave state
- Slave territory
- Popular sovereignty

The Compromise of 1850
California's statehood would swing the balance to the North. To maintain the balance, Utah and New Mexico were allowed popular sovereignty.

THE IMPACT TODAY

Government
Today the principle of popular sovereignty is expressed in many states by initiatives and referendums. Initiatives allow voters to accept or reject laws proposed by citizen groups, and referendums enable voters to reject laws passed by the state legislature.

of 1850. By 1854 he was ready to assume the leadership role that would help earn the 5'4" politician the nickname "The Little Giant."

Among the issues that divided North and South was a proposed railroad to connect the new state of California to the rest of the nation. Southerners favored New Orleans, Louisiana, as the railroad's eastern end. Northerners opposed this route, afraid that a railroad which connected California to the South might help bring slavery into the territories organized by the Compromise of 1850.

Douglas believed the proposed railroad could transform Chicago, Illinois, into a major urban center. Before the northern route could be considered, however, the land it crossed had to be officially opened for settlement by the government. In 1854 Douglas introduced a bill into Congress to do that. He proposed that the region west of Iowa and Missouri be organized into the Kansas and Nebraska Territories.

Douglas needed southern support in order to get his bill passed. The Missouri Compromise had closed the Kansas and Nebraska region to slavery. Douglas knew that southerners would not agree to allow settlement in any territories that would someday become free states. For his solution, he turned to the Compromise of 1850. He proposed that as in New Mexico and Utah,

326 CHAPTER 10

the issue of slavery in Kansas and Nebraska should be settled by **popular sovereignty**. In other words, the people there would decide whether to allow it.

This approach got Douglas the southern support he needed. Southern senators, however, had one more demand. They wanted the Missouri Compromise repealed entirely. When Douglas changed his bill to end the Missouri Compromise's limits on slavery, it took all his political skills to hold on to northern support. In May 1854 his **Kansas-Nebraska Act** became law. Lost in the controversy over the bill was Douglas's proposed railroad to the Pacific Ocean. Congress would not approve the construction of such a railroad until 1862.

READING CHECK **Identifying the Main Idea**
Why did Douglas introduce his Kansas-Nebraska bill?

Reactions in North and South

The North's response to the Kansas-Nebraska Act was intense. Hundreds of meetings were held to protest the law. Northerners sent numerous petitions and resolutions to Congress. "This crime shall not be consummated [completed]," read one. "Nebraska, the heart of our continent, shall forever continue free."

Skills Focus: Interpreting Historical Maps   At Level

Social Studies Skill   Research Required
The Kansas-Nebraska Act

1. Ask students to use print and Internet sources to research the platforms and issues of the Democratic and Republican parties today.

2. Have each student draw a map showing which states voted for the Republican presidential candidate "red states", and which voted for the Democratic presidential candidate "blue states" during the last election.

3. Review the purple areas shown on the Kansas-Nebraska Act map. Ask students to compare

how the "red" and "blue" states line up with the "purple" states on the maps in their texts. Then ask students whether the platforms and beliefs of the "red" or the "blue" states line up with the beliefs of the "purple" states created by the Kansas-Nebraska Act.

LS **Verbal-Linguistic, Visual-Spatial**

📖 Alternative Assessment Handbook, Rubric 20: Map Creation

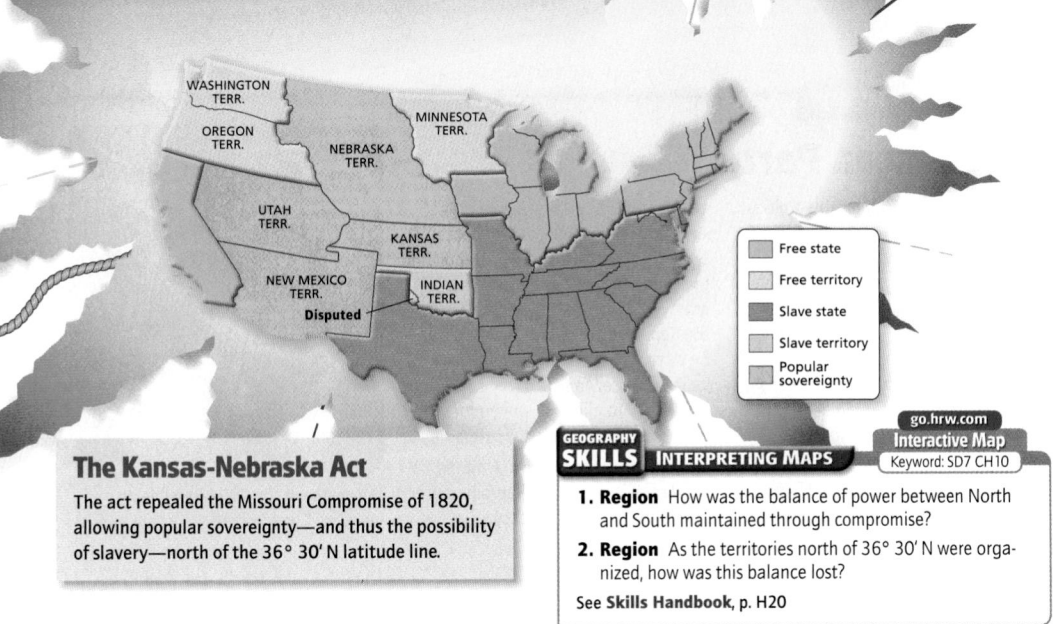

The Kansas-Nebraska Act

The act repealed the Missouri Compromise of 1820, allowing popular sovereignty—and thus the possibility of slavery—north of the 36° 30′ N latitude line.

Free state
Free territory
Slave state
Slave territory
Popular sovereignty

GEOGRAPHY SKILLS INTERPRETING MAPS

go.hrw.com
Interactive Map
Keyword: SD7 CH10

1. **Region** How was the balance of power between North and South maintained through compromise?

2. **Region** As the territories north of 36° 30′ N were organized, how was this balance lost?

See **Skills Handbook, p. H20**

Shifts in politics Some northern politicians called the Kansas-Nebraska Act a "gross violation of a sacred pledge." Such reactions caused major changes in the nation's political-party system. The controversy greatly weakened the Democratic Party. Northerners were outraged that many northern Democratic members of Congress had voted for the act. A great number of northern Democrats quit the party.

The effect on the Whig Party was even more severe. Whigs were already suffering from serious divisions. Some northern Whigs, called Conscience Whigs, opposed slavery on moral grounds. Other Whigs in both the North and the South, known as Cotton Whigs, strongly supported slavery. The deaths of Clay and Webster, the Whigs' long-time leaders, further weakened the party at a critical time in national politics.

Cotton and Conscience Whigs in Congress became bitterly divided over Douglas's proposal. After it passed, the two groups refused to work together. One Connecticut Whig resigned from the Senate in disgust. "The Whig party has been killed off . . . by that miserable Nebraska business," he complained. With their party basically dead, Cotton Whigs joined their southern Democratic allies in the Democratic Party. Many Conscience Whigs

joined northern Democrats and members of the Free-Soil Party to form a new political party in order to resist the further spread of slavery.

The rise of the Republican Party The Free-Soil Party was formed in 1848 by some northern Whigs and Democrats, and members of a small antislavery party known as the Liberty Party. The Free-Soil Party took its name because opposition to the spread of slavery was its main issue. *Free soil* was a term for land on which slavery did not exist. In fact, people of all political parties who opposed slavery's spread were often called **free-soilers**.

The Kansas-Nebraska Act caused the Free-Soil Party, northern Whigs, and others to join forces. "Rally as one man for the reestablishment of liberty and the overthrow of the Slave Power," a free-soiler urged. One such rally was held in a church at Ripon, Wisconsin, in February 1854. The rally's leaders called for a new political party to be formed. From this meeting the **Republican Party** was born. In July, at a meeting in Jackson, Michigan, the new party's name was officially adopted.

By the end of 1854, Republican groups were operating in states across the North. They worked with the Know-Nothings, members of

THE NATION SPLITS APART **327**

Direct Teach

Linking to Today
Republican Party Today
Compare and Contrast You might wish to have students visit the official Web site of the Republican Party, or print copies of the Republican Party platform, which can be found at the site. Have students write a summary of the current platform and compare it to the positions of the party in 1854.

Review & Assess

Close

Review the terms of the Compromise of 1850 with students and discuss the effects the compromise had on the nation.

Review

📘 Online Quiz, Section 1

📘 Daily Test Practice Transparency

Assess

SE Section 1 Assessment

📋 Progress Assessment: Section 1 Quiz

📋 Alternative Assessment Handbook

Reteach

📋 Interactive Reader and Study Guide, Section 1

💿 Interactive Skills Tutor CD-ROM

Answers

Linking to Today *focused on ending slavery, rebuilding the Union, limiting unfair business practices*

Reading Check *Whig Party dispersed when southern Whigs joined the Democratic Party; northern Whigs and northern Democrats joined the Free Soil Party which became the new Republican Party*

328

Linking to Today

Republican Party Today

Throughout American history, political parties have used the term *republican*. In response to the Kansas-Nebraska Act in 1854, antislavery members of several other parties joined forces. They formed the Republican Party, the same party that exists today.

The first Republican candidate for president was John C. Frémont in 1856. He lost that election, but in 1860 the Republican Party's second presidential candidate, Abraham Lincoln, was elected president of the United States.

Over time, Republican goals have shifted. During much of the nineteenth century, the party focused on rebuilding the Union, and limiting unfair business practices. During the twentieth century, the Republican Party became known for its conservative social policies and a belief in laissez-faire economic policies, which seek to minimize government interference in economic matters.

Analyzing Information How did the Republican Party gain prominence during the nineteenth century?

Delegates at the 2004 Republican National Convention

a political party officially called the American Party, to defeat Democratic candidates for Congress in the elections that year.

The Know-Nothings' **nativism**, or opposition to immigration, was troubling to some Americans. Still, the problems that the Kansas-Nebraska Act caused the Democrats and Whigs briefly gave the Know-Nothings political influence again. At first, the Republicans' association with the Know-Nothings kept

one prominent Whig, William Seward, away from the new party. Not until 1855, after he had been safely re-elected to the Senate, did Seward become a Republican. Another, much less famous northern Whig soon joined him. That politician's name was Abraham Lincoln.

READING CHECK **Summarizing** How did passage of the Kansas-Nebraska Act affect the nation's political-party system?

SECTION 1 ASSESSMENT

go.hrw.com
Online Quiz
Keyword: SD7 HP10

Reviewing Ideas, Terms, and People

1. a. Identify How was the nation divided over the institution of slavery?
b. Analyze What effect did the Mexican-American War have on the issue of slavery in the United States? Why did it have this effect?

2. a. Describe What were the terms of the **Compromise of 1850**?
b. Make Inferences Why would the Compromise of 1850 have been controversial in both the North and the South?
c. Evaluate Was the Compromise of 1850 a good solution to the conflict over slavery? Explain why or why not.

3. a. Recall What is **popular sovereignty**? Why did **Stephen Douglas** include it in his Kansas-Nebraska bill?
b. Draw Conclusions How would both the North and the South have expected to benefit from the passage of the **Kansas-Nebraska Act**?

4. a. Describe Why was the **Republican Party** founded?
b. Make Inferences Why would some northerners have been upset over the passage of the Kansas-Nebraska Act?

Critical Thinking

5. Compare and Contrast Copy the chart below and record the reasons that northerners and southerners in Congress passed the Compromise of 1850.

| Reasons for Northern Support | Compromise of 1850 | Reasons for Southern Support |

FOCUS ON WRITING

6. Expository Suppose you were a northern senator during the debate on the Kansas-Nebraska bill. Write a speech stating your position and the reasons for your stand on Senator Douglas's controversial proposal.

328 CHAPTER 10

Section 1 Assessment Answers

1. **a.** North opposed; economic necessity for South
   b. intensified debate; whether or not to allow slavery in new territory

2. **a.** See chart, Compromise of 1850.
   b. did not resolve issue of slavery
   c. possible answer—yes, allowed people living in new territories to decide slavery issue

3. **a.** a political issue decided by popular vote; needed southern support in order to get his bill passed
   b. South—potential for new slave states; North—potential slavery would become illegal;

both—railroad

4. **a.** to oppose slavery
   b. possible answer—reopened the possibility of slavery in territories

5. northern—California a free state; slave trade abolished in Washington, D.C.; southern—possibility of slavery in new territories; Missouri Compromise ban on slavery repealed; Fugitive Slave Act strengthened

6. possible answer—oppose, Kansas and Nebraska should not be open to slavery

SECTION 2
Sectional Conflicts and National Politics

BEFORE YOU READ

MAIN IDEA

Rising tensions over slavery expanded from political rhetoric into outright violence.

READING FOCUS

1. Why did popular sovereignty lead to violent struggle in Kansas?
2. In what ways did the presidential election of 1856 illustrate the nation's growing divisions?
3. What events of Buchanan's presidency further divided the nation?
4. Why was John Brown's raid on Harpers Ferry an important event in American history?

KEY TERMS AND PEOPLE

"Bleeding Kansas"
Franklin Pierce
John Brown
Pottawatomie Massacre
guerrilla war
James Buchanan
John Frémont
Dred Scott decision
Lecompton Constitution
Robert E. Lee

 TAKING NOTES As you read, take notes on the acts of violence that resulted from rising tensions between North and South. In each of the smaller circles in a diagram like the one below, identify and briefly describe one violent act.

[Diagram: central circle labeled "Rising Tensions" surrounded by empty ovals]

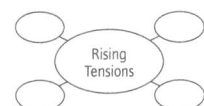

THE INSIDE STORY

What did John Doy's experience show about conditions in Kansas in the 1850s? In January 1859, John Doy and his 21-year-old son Charles, agreed to take a group of 13 escaped slaves from Lawrence, Kansas, to freedom in Iowa. Doy, an English physician, had come to Kansas in 1854 to help make the territory a free state. An active abolitionist, Dr. Doy was making the journey as a "conductor" on the Underground Railroad.

Doy and his son moved the escaped slaves in two covered wagons. They were barely 12 miles from Lawrence, however, when they were stopped by a band of slave hunters. The group seized the Doys and took them to Missouri. There Dr. Doy was tried and convicted of slave stealing and sentenced to five years in prison.

Back in Lawrence, a plan was devised to rescue Doy from jail before he could be moved to the Missouri state penitentiary. In July, a group of antislavery Kansans assembled at St. Joseph, where Dr. Doy was being held. One of them visited Doy in jail and slipped him a note about the plan to break him out. That night they

went to the jail, pretending to have captured a horse thief. Once inside, they overpowered the two jailers and freed Dr. Doy. Crossing the Missouri River in rowboats, they evaded the posse sent after them and arrived in Lawrence to a hero's welcome two days later. ■

THE RESCUE OF DR. JOHN DOY

▶ John Doy (seated) and the men who rescued him from "that vile iron box" he was jailed in.

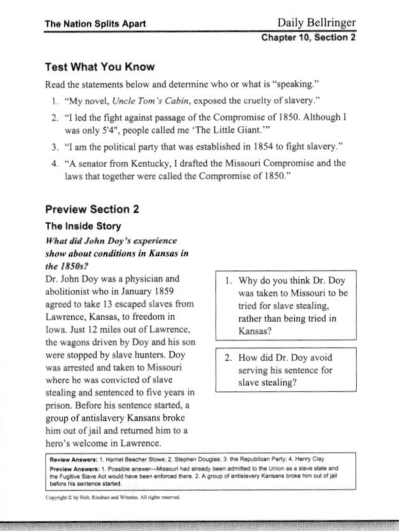
Academic Vocabulary

Review with students the high-use academic term in this section.

verified made sure that something is accurate or true (p. 331)

📄 CRF: Vocabulary Builder Activity, Section 2

Taking Notes

kidnapping of Dr. John Doy; struggle for control of Kansas; "sack of Lawrence," buildings destroyed; Pottawatomie Massacre, five proslavery settlers executed; civil war in Kansas resulted in federal intervention; John Brown's raid on Harpers Ferry resulted in the deaths of Brown and his followers

---

Teach the Main Idea

At Level

Sectional Conflicts and National Politics

1. **Teach** Ask students the Reading Focus questions to teach this section.

2. **Apply** Draw four large ovals for students to see. Label the interior of each oval with one of the four topics of this section—The Struggle for Kansas, The Election of 1856, Buchanan's Presidency, John Brown's Raid. Have students copy the diagrams and list major details from each section inside the ovals. **LS Visual-Spatial**

3. **Review** As you review the section, have the students identify the political issues that they believe were most serious for the nation.

4. **Practice/Homework** Have students review and write a summary of the criminal problems that occurred in Kansas following the Kansas-Nebraska Act. **LS Verbal-Linguistic**

📄 Alternative Assessment Handbook, Rubrics 13: Graphic Organizers; and 42: Writing to Inform

Reading Focus

❶ Why did popular sovereignty lead to violent struggle in Kansas? *proslavery and antislavery settlers fought for control*

The Struggle for Kansas

Explain Why was the election of the Kansas territorial legislature so important? *The legislature would write a constitution declaring Kansas to be a free or slave territory.*

Analyze What role did Missouri play in the Kansas elections? *Missourians came into Kansas and voted for pro-slavery candidates.*

Evaluate Do you think that the creation of two governments in Kansas was an appropriate response to the strict slave code? Explain your answer. *possible answer—no, a territory with two governments would not be accepted; could not survive for long; yes—drew attention to the problems; allowed both sides to be heard*

✴ **Interactive History Close-Up:** The Sack of Lawrence

Recent Scholarship

The Shattering of the Union: America in the 1850s, written by Eric Walther, is a readable, current analysis of the events and the ideas that led to the Civil War. Walther examines the politics, ideology, and race relations of the period and suggests that both northerners and southerners believed that they were fighting the same thing: oppression from the opposing side.

The Shattering of the Union, by Eric Walther. Rowman & Littlefield, 2003

The Struggle for Kansas

The kidnapping of Dr. John Doy was one of many acts of slavery-related lawlessness that plagued Kansas Territory. By 1856 so much violence had occurred there that the territory was being called **"Bleeding Kansas."**

Northerners and southerners alike realized what the settlement of Kansas meant for the nation. "We are playing for a mighty stake," Missouri senator David Atchison noted. "If we win we carry slavery to the Pacific Ocean, if we fail we lose . . . all the territories." Northerners were just as eager to keep Kansas free. "We will engage in competition for the virgin soil of Kansas," pledged William Seward. "God give the victory to the side which is stronger in numbers as it is in right."

Pro-slavery and free-soil forces soon were fighting for control in Kansas. Each side intended to control the territory's elections and, later, a vote on a state constitution. Free-soil settlers flooded into the territory. Groups opposed to slavery raised money to help volunteers move there. People in slaveholding states also formed emigrant groups. Atchison took a leave of absence from the Senate to lead the effort to establish slavery in the new territory.

Popular sovereignty Settlement of the slavery issue by popular sovereignty did not require settlers to vote on whether to allow it. Instead, the question was settled indirectly. The voters would elect a territorial legislature, which would then pass laws on the subject. Later, a constitution had to be written and approved by voters before the territory could become a state. That constitution would either permit or ban slavery. It was through these processes that Kansas would eventually enter the Union as a slave state or as free soil.

The first election was held in November 1854 to choose the territory's delegate to Congress. About 1,700 armed Missourians crossed into Kansas and threatened violence if they were not allowed to vote. A pro-slavery delegate was elected.

Even greater voting fraud took place in elections for the territorial legislature in March 1855. In some districts the number of

✴ **Interactive**
HISTORY CLOSE-UP

The Sack of Lawrence

On May 21, 1855, a pro-slavery posse arrived in Lawrence, Kansas, to arrest leaders of the "rebel" antislavery government. The posse looted and destroyed much of the town.

When posse members could not destroy the Free State Hotel with cannon shots, they set it on fire.

The posse burned the office of *The Free State*, one of Lawrence's anti-slavery newspapers.

330

Collaborative Learning

At Level

Bleeding Kansas

1. Guide students in a review of the causes and effects of the violent acts that occurred in Kansas during 1855 and 1856. Have students list these acts and note how each act would be viewed differently by northerners and by southerners.

2. Make a list of student responses for all to see, and have students add to and correct their own lists.

3. Organize the class into small groups. Have each group prepare newspaper articles on the violence for publication in two newspapers: one proslavery, the other antislavery. Have students incorporate the ideas from their lists in their articles.

4. Have volunteers from each group present their articles to the class. **LS** **Interpersonal**

📃 Alternative Assessment Handbook, Rubric 23: Newspapers

ballots cast was more than twice the number of registered voters. A legislature of 36 pro-slavery candidates and 3 free-soilers was elected. "Missourians have nobly defended our rights," declared an Alabama newspaper.

The legislature met in the town of Lecompton and quickly passed a strict slave code into law. Outraged free-soilers refused to accept the new legislature. They elected an antislavery governor and legislature and set up their own government. By 1856 two governments were passing and carrying out laws, each claiming to be the legal government of Kansas.

The Sack of Lawrence By 1855 the town of Lawrence had become a center of antislavery activity in the territory. In November, shootings of pro-slavery settlers near the town brought some 1,500 Missourians across the border. Nearby federal troops waited for the president's order to keep peace in the area. No such order was issued. The Missourians decided against attacking Lawrence only when they <u>verified</u> that it was defended by a heavily armed force of free-soilers.

Although President **Franklin Pierce** was a New Hampshire Democrat, he seemed to be under the influence of pro-slavery elements in Congress. In January 1856 Pierce condemned the free-soil government in Kansas as rebels. This prompted pro-slavery Kansas officials to charge free-soil leaders with treason.

On May 21 a pro-slavery sheriff and about 800 men rode into Lawrence to arrest them. The posse destroyed the offices of the town's two antislavery newspapers, burned the hotel and the free-soil governor's house, and looted stores and homes. Antislavery newspapers labeled the raid the Sack of Lawrence in an effort to paint the raiders as barbarians and inflame public opinion in the North.

The Pottawatomie Massacre A related event soon inflamed public opinion in the South. Fifty-six-year-old **John Brown** was a committed abolitionist. As a young man, he had used his Pennsylvania home as a station on the Underground Railroad. After several business failures, Brown followed several of his sons to Kansas in 1855. All hoped to obtain land and

ACADEMIC VOCABULARY
verified made sure that something is accurate or true

Posse members took the printing press from the office of the antislavery newspaper *The Herald of Freedom* and dumped it in a nearby river.

Members of the posse looted homes and businesses, making off with whatever they could carry.

go.hrw.com
Interactive
Keyword: SD7 CH10

Skills FOCUS **INTERPRETING INFOGRAPHICS**

1. **Drawing Conclusions** Why did the posse want to destroy the two antislavery newspapers in Lawrence?
2. **Making Inferences** Why did some members of the posse loot private homes and businesses?

See Skills Handbook, p. H18

331

• **Direct Teach** •

Reading Focus

The Struggle for Kansas

Recall Why did Missourians decide not to attack people living in Lawrence, Kansas? *The town was defended by an armed group of free-soilers.*

Make Judgments Do you think President Pierce should have taken a different approach to problems in Kansas? *possible answers—yes, his condemnation of free-soil government led to violence; no—he lent support to proslavery government, which he must have felt was legitimate*

📝 Political Cartoons Activities for American History: Cartoon 19: Settlers Oppose Slavery

📝 CRF: Biography: Clara Brown

About the Illustration
This illustration is an artist's conception based on available sources. Historians, however, are uncertain exactly what this scene looked like.

go.hrw.com
Online Resources

KEYWORD: SD7 CH10
TOPIC: BLEEDING KANSAS

Skills Focus: Drawing Conclusions

Below Level

Reading Skill
The Sack of Lawrence

1. Have students examine the images and captions in the History Close-Up "The Sack of Lawrence." Remind students that President Pierce had condemned Kansas's free-soil government.

2. Have students write a brief summary of the events that led up to the "sack of Lawrence." Have volunteers read their summaries to help ensure that all students understand the event.

3. Guide students in a discussion of the way

free-soilers must have felt following the sack of the town.

4. Have students write song lyrics commemorating the free-soilers who lived in Lawrence during the sacking of the town. Have volunteers share their lyrics with the class. **LS Auditory-Musical**

📝 Alternative Assessment Handbook, Rubric 26: Poems and Songs

Answers

Interpreting Infographics 1. *posse was proslavery; by destroying newspapers, strong antislavery voices would be stopped;* **2.** *to punish or vandalize those who were antislavery*

The Struggle for Kansas

Recall What two events led to the civil war in Kansas? *sacking of Lawrence; Pottawatomie Massacre*

Analyze Why do you think it took federal troops four months to end the civil war in Kansas? *possible answers—not used to guerrilla warfare; it was a large territory*

Info to Know

Brooks' Cane vs. Sumner's Pen The typical way for gentlemen to settle disputes during this period was to duel. Congressman Brooks, however, chose to approach Senator Sumner on the floor of the Senate and attack him with a type of walking cane that was often used to keep unruly dogs in line. Although there was an attempt to expel Brooks from Congress after the attack, the motion did not get the necessary two-thirds vote. Brooks resigned.

Critical Thinking Why do you think the motion to expel Brooks failed? *possible answers—He had support from voters and fellow southerners; he defended himself before the House.*

Answers

Reading Check *fraudulent election of a proslavery government; creation of a separate antislavery government; "Sack of Lawrence"; the Pottawatomie Massacre*

---

help make the territory a free state. Brown settled at the free-soil town of Osawatomie and appointed himself a captain of the local antislavery militia.

Outraged by the Sack of Lawrence, Brown sought bloody revenge. On the night of May 24, 1856, he and a small group of followers dragged five pro-slavery settlers out of their cabins along Pottawatomie Creek and executed them. This brutal act of terrorism became known as the **Pottawatomie Massacre**.

"Bleeding Kansas" The violent events at Lawrence and Pottawatomie Creek ignited a civil war in Kansas. A civil war is a war that involves opposing groups of citizens of the same country. For the next four months, large bands of pro-slavery and antislavery forces ranged over the territory. Several battles took place. Many settlers on both sides saw their property looted or destroyed. An antislavery settler from New Hampshire described that terrible summer.

HISTORY'S VOICES

❝We are in the midst of war—war of the most bloody kind—a war of extermination. Freedom and slavery are interlocked in a deadly embrace, and death is certain for one or the other . . . and only God knoweth where it will end.❞
—Julia Louisa Lovejoy, August 25, 1856

In September, federal troops finally brought the major fighting to an end. Peace did not return, however. A **guerrilla war**—fighting marked by sabotage, ambushes, and other surprise attacks—continued.

"The Crime Against Kansas" Violence over Kansas also spilled into the halls of Congress. In May 1856, reacting to the raid on Lawrence, Massachusetts senator Charles Sumner delivered an angry two-day speech in the Senate. Sumner called his speech "The Crime Against Kansas."

Sumner's speech also attacked several southern senators who had played key roles in passing the Kansas-Nebraska Act. He directed some of his most vicious remarks at South Carolina's Andrew Butler, who was absent from the Senate at the time.

Two days later, Congress member Preston Brooks walked into the Senate. Brooks was also from South Carolina and was Andrew Butler's

nephew. The chamber was nearly deserted because the Senate had finished business for the day. Sumner had remained, however, and was at his desk writing letters. Shouting angrily at the senator, Brooks beat him some 30 times with a heavy gold-handled walking stick. Sumner collapsed to the floor, his head covered in blood.

Northerners were incensed by the brutal attack. "Has it come to this, that we must speak with bated breath in the presence of our southern masters?" asked the *New York Evening Post*. "Are we to be chastised [punished] as they chastise their slaves?" Northerners were equally outraged that southerners in the House of Representatives blocked efforts to expel Brooks from Congress for his deed.

Sumner was so badly injured that he could not return to the Senate for more than three years. During that time northerners kept his empty chair on display in the Senate as a reminder of the attack. Meanwhile, southerners sent Brooks hundreds of canes to replace the one he had broken in the assault.

READING CHECK **Sequencing** What events led to "Bleeding Kansas"?

The Election of 1856

The controversy over Kansas dominated the presidential election of 1856. Some southern Democrats supported Pierce for a second term. Others favored Stephen Douglas. Disgusted northern Democrats refused to support either candidate. The Democratic Party settled on **James Buchanan**, a former senator from Pennsylvania, as its nominee. Buchanan had been out of the country serving as U.S. minister to Great Britain for years. He had no involvement in the battles in Congress over slavery.

As its first presidential candidate, the new Republican Party chose war hero and California senator **John Frémont**, who had led the force across the Rocky Mountains that helped seize California for the United States during the Mexican-American War. The American Party, or Know-Nothings, nominated former president Millard Fillmore as its candidate.

Buchanan won the election for two main reasons: The North's heavily immigrant population was repelled by the Know-Nothings' nativism, and the Democrats painted the

---

Skills Focus: Comparing and Contrasting At Level

Reading Skill
Creating Political Cartoons

1. Review with students the events that led to the attack on Senator Sumner. Guide students in a discussion of the political cartoon about this event.

2. Ask students to name current political or economic issues that might cause a state or federal official to become angry enough to verbally strike out at another official. *possible answer—closing schools; budget cuts, etc.* Make a class list for all to see.

3. Have each student create two political cartoons; one of the cartoons should depict the violence of "Bleeding Kansas." The other cartoon should depict one of the current issues from the class list.

4. Have volunteers display and explain their cartoons to the class. **LS Visual-Spatial, Intrapersonal**

📝 Alternative Assessment Handbook, Rubric 27: Political Cartoons

Political Cartoon

As tensions over slavery increased, violence even broke out in Congress. In 1856 South Carolina representative Preston Brooks attacked Massachusetts senator Charles Sumner over an anti-slavery speech Sumner had made.

Although the Senate chamber was nearly empty when the attack occurred, the artist added observers in this portrayal.

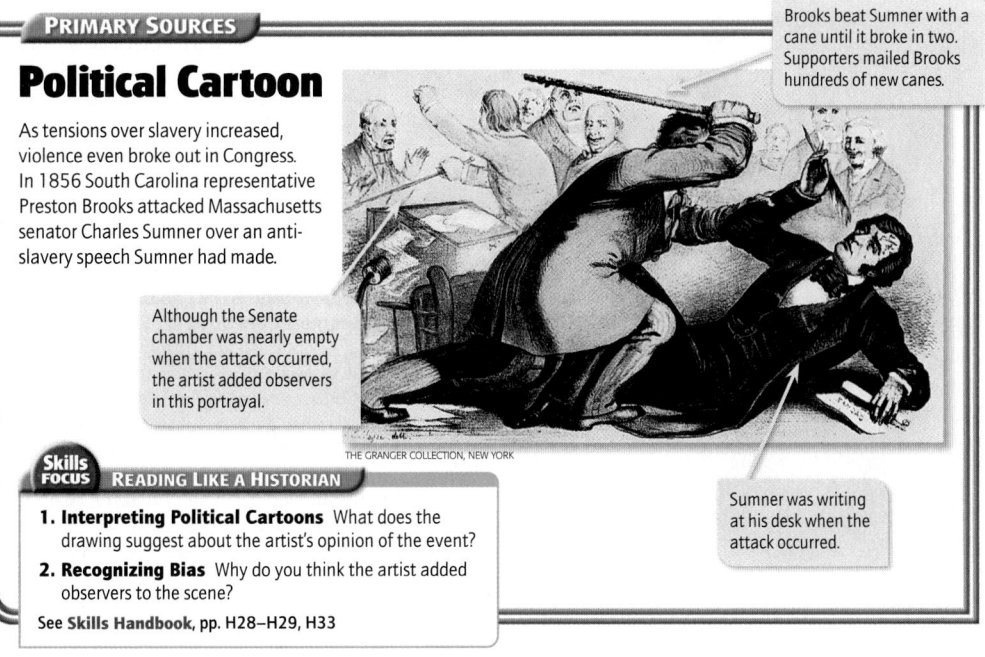

Brooks beat Sumner with a cane until it broke in two. Supporters mailed Brooks hundreds of new canes.

THE GRANGER COLLECTION, NEW YORK

Sumner was writing at his desk when the attack occurred.

Skills FOCUS   READING LIKE A HISTORIAN

1. **Interpreting Political Cartoons** What does the drawing suggest about the artist's opinion of the event?
2. **Recognizing Bias** Why do you think the artist added observers to the scene?

See Skills Handbook, pp. H28–H29, H33

Republicans as extremists on the issue of slavery. "The Union is in danger and the people everywhere know it," Buchanan warned. Some southerners helped his cause by hinting at secession if the Republicans won. "The election of Frémont," warned one southern senator, "would be the end of the Union and ought to be." As a result, Buchanan was the voters' choice in both North and South. Frémont, however, won all the states of the Upper North.

READING CHECK **Identifying Cause and Effect** Why did James Buchanan win the presidential election of 1856?

Buchanan's Presidency

In his inaugural address, Buchanan renewed his support for popular sovereignty in the territories and his pledge to not interfere with slavery where it already existed. Coupled with the decreased violence in Kansas, his words gave many Americans hope that the crisis was finally past. Such hopes were fleeting, however. Two events soon reignited the passions over slavery that were tearing the nation apart.

The *Dred Scott* decision Two days after Buchanan took office, the Supreme Court announced its long-awaited decision in the *Dred Scott* case. (See *Scott* v. *Sandford* at the end of this section.) Dred Scott, a slave, had sued for his freedom. Scott had lived on free soil during much of the 1830s. His argument was that by living where slavery was illegal, he had become free.

In a complicated decision, a deeply divided Court ruled against Scott in 1857. Chief Justice Roger Taney noted that, among other things, the Fifth Amendment to the Constitution protected the property rights of persons who held others as slaves.

The political firestorm that erupted over the *Dred Scott* decision rivaled that of the Kansas-Nebraska Act. Southerners viewed it as a wonderful victory. Northerners feared that slavery could now not be barred in any territory. Republicans, in particular, worried that the Court's decision had stripped their party of its main issue—blocking the spread of slavery. The decision actually helped the Republican Party, however, by widening divisions between northern and southern Democrats.

THE IMPACT TODAY

Recent Scholarship Republican William Seward charged that President Buchanan secretly tried to influence the Supreme Court to decide the case in favor of the South. Republicans at the time labeled Seward's charge as outrageous. Modern historical research, however, has shown it was true.

THE NATION SPLITS APART **333**

Differentiating Instruction

Above Level

Advanced Learners/GATE

Research Required

1. Have students locate and read several recent presidential campaign speeches. Guide students in a discussion of similarities among the speeches. Ask students these questions: How did the candidates reach out to the voters? What themes or approaches did the candidates take? Did they use recurring slogans? What made the speeches effective, appealing, or interesting?

2. Have students use their research to write a campaign speech for Buchanan. Students

should include some of the techniques used in recent presidential campaign speeches.

3. Have volunteers read their campaign speeches to the class.

4. Guide students in a discussion of the views presented in the speeches. Would the information about the candidate persuade them to vote for Buchanan?

LS Verbal-Linguistic

Alternative Assessment Handbook, Rubric 43: Writing to Persuade

---

Direct Teach

Reading Focus

2 In what ways did the presidential election of 1856 illustrate the nation's growing divisions? *three candidates: Buchanan, Frémont, and Fillmore; Democrats initially divided, settled on Buchanan*

The Election of 1856

Describe Why was the 1856 election campaign considered two campaigns? *Buchanan vs. Fillmore in the South; Buchanan vs. Frémont in the North*

Summarize How did James Buchanan ultimately win the election? *had not been involved in battles over slavery; painted Republicans as extremists; used threat of secession to his advantage*

Reading Focus

3 What events of Buchanan's presidency further divided the nation? Dred Scott *decision; Lecompton Constitution*

Buchanan's Presidency

Explain Why was Buchanan's inaugural address well received? *support for popular sovereignty; promised not to interfere with existing slave states*

Draw Conclusions Do you think Buchanan led Americans to believe that the crisis in Kansas was over? *possible answer—yes, he was optimistic; Americans wanted to believe it was over*

Answers

Reading Like a Historian 1. *the attack was unprovoked, Brooks is a violent man;* **2.** *possible answer—to make the attack seem even worse than it was*

Reading Check *opposition to Buchanan split between Millard Fillmore in the South and John Frémont in the North; Buchanan painted Republicans as extremists on slavery*

333

Reading Focus

Buchanan's Presidency

Explain Why did Dred Scott believe that he should be free? *He had lived in territory where slavery was illegal.*

Draw Conclusions In what ways did the *Dred Scott* decision help Democrats and Republicans? *Democrats—protected the rights of slaveholders; Republicans—drove deep wedge between Democrats, weakening the party*

Predict How did the Lecompton Constitution contribute to the coming Civil War? *encouraged southerners to threaten secession to protect slavery*

 Quick Facts Transparency: Effects of the *Dred Scott* Decision

Reading Focus

4 Why was John Brown's raid on Harpers Ferry an important event in American history? *U.S. forces fought abolitionists; raised possibility of a slave revolt and may have united white southerners*

John Brown's Raid

Explain How did John Brown differ from most abolitionists? *Brown did not share their belief in nonviolence.*

Draw Conclusions Why did southerners want Brown executed? *his ideas were treasonous; threatened southern way of life; fear of slave revolts*

CRF: Primary Source Activity: A Hostage Describes John Brown's Raid

Answers

Reading Check *Only a special part of the constitution about allowing new slavery was submitted to a vote; free-soilers refused to vote on the proposal*

334

Dred Scott "had no rights which the white man was bound to respect," ruled Chief Justice Roger Taney.

 QUICK FACTS

Effects of the *Dred Scott* Decision

- Increased northern opposition to slavery
- Deprived free African Americans of citizenship if they were descendants of slaves
- Increased tensions between North and South
- Widened divisions in the Democratic Party

The Lecompton Constitution By late 1857 the controversy over slavery in Kansas Territory boiled over once again. An election of delegates to a constitutional convention in June gave the pro-slavery forces control over the writing of a state constitution. In supervised elections in October, however, free-soilers gained a majority of the seats in both houses of the territory's legislature.

Pro-slavery leaders recognized that in a fair election, voters would never approve the constitution they had written. Therefore, they refused to submit the **Lecompton Constitution** to a vote. Instead, they proposed that voters decide only a special provision on slavery. If approved, it would allow slavery in Kansas. If defeated, further importation of slaves would be banned, but enslaved African Americans already in Kansas would remain in slavery.

Northerners were again outraged. Even Steven Douglas viewed the proposal as a mockery of popular sovereignty. Buchanan, however, decided to let the vote proceed. When free-soilers in Kansas refused to take part, the provision passed. In their own election in January 1858, the free-soilers rejected the provision, and the entire constitution. Some southerners again threatened secession if Congress accepted the second set of results.

Bowing to southern pressure, Buchanan submitted the Lecompton Constitution to Congress and called for the admission of Kansas as a slave state. The Senate quickly approved the measure, but the House blocked it.

In May a compromise was found. Congress decided to require that Kansans vote on the constitution again. If it passed, the territory would be admitted as a slave state. If not, statehood for Kansas would be delayed until its population reached 90,000. In August 1858, Kansas voters overwhelmingly rejected the Lecompton Constitution. That vote and the *Dred Scott* decision finally put the Kansas issue to rest.

Controversy over the Lecompton Constitution further deepened the sectional divisions in the Democratic Party. Douglas's break with President Buchanan over the Lecompton Constitution weakened the senator's position as a party leader. His opposition to the Lecompton Constitution also cost him support among southern Democrats. Finally, the controversy encouraged the belief of some radical southerners that making threats of secession would get the South its way.

READING CHECK **Making Inferences** Why was the Lecompton Constitution controversial?

John Brown's Raid

While the Congress debated the Lecompton Constitution, one Kansas settler hatched an idea. John Brown never shared the belief of most abolitionists in nonviolence. "Talk! Talk! Talk! That will never free the slaves," he proclaimed. "What is needed is action—action." In May 1858 Brown and some followers agreed on a plan to establish a nation of freed slaves in the southern Appalachian Mountains.

Brown then approached leading abolitionists to get support for his plan. Theodore Parker and several others agreed to finance a raid on a U.S. arsenal, a place where guns are stored, at Harpers Ferry, Virginia. Brown planned to use the guns to arm a slave revolt in the area.

Brown rented a farm in Maryland, across the Potomac River from the town of Harpers Ferry, in the summer of 1859 and prepared for the attack. Frederick Douglass tried to convince him the plot was unlikely to succeed, but Brown refused to listen.

Skills Focus: Sequencing   Below Level

Reading Skill
John Brown's Raid

Have students work individually or in mixed-ability pairs to create a flow chart showing the main events of John Brown's raid. Students should add as many boxes to their charts as needed to show the complete sequence of events that led to Brown's execution. Have students share and explain their flow charts, and create a class chart for all to see. Have students correct their own work as needed and retain the charts

as a study tool. **LS Visual-Spatial, Logical-Mathematical**

Alternative Assessment Handbook, Rubric 13: Graphic Organizers

Graphic Organizer Transparencies

On the night of October 16, Brown and 21 followers, including five African Americans, easily captured the arsenal. Brown then sent members of his group to spread the word to the area's slaves to rise up in revolt. They returned with a few hostages, but no slaves were willing to run away and join Brown's revolt.

In the morning local townspeople with guns trapped Brown's group inside the arsenal. Several of his followers were killed in the fight that followed, and some others escaped. That night a company of U.S. Marines arrived. They were commanded by Colonel **Robert E. Lee**. The next morning, October 18, the marines stormed the arsenal. They captured what remained of Brown's group without bringing any harm to the hostages.

Brown and his six surviving followers were tried in Virginia. All were sentenced to hang. John Brown's sentence was carried out on December 2, 1859. He remained committed to his cause to the end.

HISTORY'S VOICES

❝If it is deemed necessary that I should forfeit my life for the furtherance of the ends of justice, and mingle my blood further with the blood of my children and with the blood of millions in this slave country whose rights are disregarded by wicked, cruel, and unjust enactments, I say, let it be done.❞

—John Brown, November 2, 1859

Effects of John Brown's Raid

- Aroused widespread support for Brown in the North
- Increased southern fears that abolitionists would inspire slave revolts
- United white southerners in support of the South
- Probably speeded the coming of the Civil War

John Brown used violence to oppose slavery.

For southerners, John Brown's raid was at the same time unifying, strengthening, and frightening. In the North, although some questioned Brown's sanity, many people viewed him as a hero. Church bells tolled across the North on Brown's execution day.

READING CHECK **Identifying the Main Idea**
Why did John Brown launch his raid?

SECTION 2 ASSESSMENT

go.hrw.com
Online Quiz
Keyword: SD7 HP10

Reviewing Ideas, Terms, and People

1. **a. Identify** Why was Kansas called "Bleeding Kansas"?
   b. Make Inferences Why did violence erupt in Kansas?
   c. Evaluate Was the exercise of popular sovereignty in Kansas a success or a failure? Explain why.

2. **a. Recall** Who were the candidates for president in 1856?
   b. Analyze In what ways did the presidential election of 1856 demonstrate the nation's deep sectional divisions?
   c. Predict How might the nation's history have been different if the Republican had won the 1856 election?

3. **a. Describe** For what reason did Dred Scott believe that he should be freed from slavery?
   b. Draw Conclusions How did the *Dred Scott* decision affect tensions over slavery? Explain why.
   c. Predict How would the controversy over slavery have been affected if the Supreme Court had ruled in favor of Dred Scott?

Critical Thinking

4. **Identifying Cause and Effect** Copy the chart below and complete it with details to explain how the raid of **John Brown** affected relations between North and South.

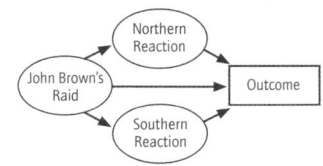

FOCUS ON WRITING

5. **Expository** Write a letter to the editor of a northern antislavery newspaper explaining why John Brown's raid on Harpers Ferry was or was not justified.

THE NATION SPLITS APART **335**

Section 2 Assessment Answers

1. **a.** so much violence had occurred in Kansas
   b. Proslavery and free-soil forces were fighting for control.
   c. possible answer—failure because significant voting fraud took place

2. **a.** James Buchanan; John Frémont; Millard Fillmore
   b. campaign was actually two campaigns, Buchanan vs. Fillmore in the South and Buchanan vs. Frémont in the North
   c. a Republican might have supported abolition, rejected Lecompton Constitution

3. **a.** had lived on free soil
   b. inflamed tension; northerners feared slavery could not be barred in any territory
   c. possible answer—southerners outraged; northerners might have pushed for complete ban on slavery

4. North—some viewed him as hero; South—unified proslavery forces; divisions deepened

5. possible answer—not justified; violence is not an acceptable method of protest

---

Scott v. Sandford

Word Help

dismissed rejected

Info to Know

Dred Scott Historians believe that Dred Scott was born around 1795, although the exact date is unknown. He was called Sam during his youth, but at some point he became known as Dred Scott. Some historians believe that the name is a corruption of the nickname "Great Scott" given to Sam because his small stature, under five feet, was the opposite of General Winfield Scott.

Media coverage of the case

Newspapers from both North and South followed the *Scott* v. *Sandford* case closely. They highlighted the issues and gave thorough coverage to the outrage that followed the decision. After the case had been argued, the abolitionist newspaper *New York Tribune* printed an account of the Court's secret deliberations, as well as the position of each justice. Apparently Justice John McLean was leaking information to a *Tribune* reporter. This was a very unusual practice at the time.

Primary Source

"[The *Dred Scott* decision] may well be regarded as the most important case that has ever been brought before that tribunal [Supreme Court]."

New York Courier, December 28, 1856

LANDMARK SUPREME COURT CASES

Constitutional Issue: Equal Protection

Scott v. Sandford (1857)

Why It Matters As the country expanded during the first half of the nineteenth century, arguments over the role of slavery in the new territories became especially bitter. The Supreme Court's decision in the *Dred Scott* case brought the nation closer to civil war.

Background of the Case

Dred Scott was born a slave in Virginia around 1795. During the 1830s, Dr. John Emerson, the owner of Scott and his wife, Harriet, brought them to live in the free state of Illinois and to the free Wisconsin Territory, where slavery was prohibited under the Missouri Compromise of 1820. The Emersons later returned to St. Louis with the Scotts. In 1846, the Scotts sued for their freedom in the Circuit Court of St. Louis, Missouri. They argued that their years of living in free territories had freed them from slavery. After losing in the Missouri Supreme Court, the Scotts sued in federal court, where they again lost. They then appealed to the U.S. Supreme Court.

The Decision

Chief Justice Roger B. Taney wrote the majority opinion. He concluded that because Scott was black he was not a citizen and therefore could not sue in federal court. Taney reviewed prior cases to show that slaves were not considered citizens in the Constitution as originally adopted and had not been granted citizenship since that time. Since only a citizen could sue in the federal courts, Scott did not have the right to sue.

Justice Taney's opinion could have stopped there, with the case dismissed because Scott could not sue. But he went on to consider the constitutionality of the entire Missouri Compromise. Taney concluded that by making slavery illegal in certain territories, Congress had exceeded its authority under the Constitution. The decision was popular with southern slave owners but upset many northerners. Instead of resolving the controversy, the case increased the intensity of the conflict over slavery in the country.

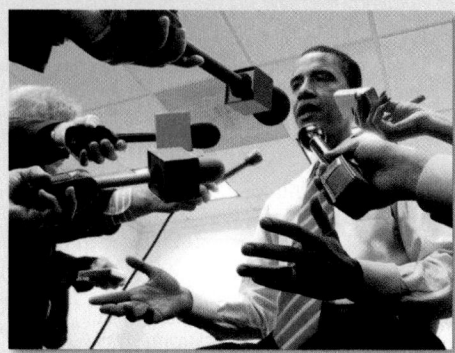

THE IMPACT TODAY In 1868 the *Dred Scott* decision was overturned by the Fourteenth Amendment, which declared that all persons born or naturalized in the United States are citizens. African Americans continued to work to gain the full rights of citizenship. Today they actively take part in civic and political life. Above, U.S. Senator Barack Obama talks to reporters.

go.hrw.com
Research Online
Keyword: SS Court

CRITICAL THINKING

1. **Analyze the Impact** Before he became Chief Justice in 1930, Charles Evans Hughes described the *Dred Scott* decision as a "self-inflicted wound" that harmed the Court's reputation for at least a generation. Explain what you think Hughes meant by this description.

2. **You Be the Judge** In the 2004 presidential election decision *Bush* v. *Gore*, the Supreme Court intervened in the Florida ballot recount, leading to George W. Bush's election. Justice Stephen Breyer wrote in dissent that the Court's decision risked "a self-inflicted wound—a wound that may harm not just the Court, but the Nation." Do you agree or disagree? Is his implied comparison to *Dred Scott* justified? Explain your answer in a short paragraph.

Skills Focus: Analyzing Primary Sources

Above Level

Reading Like a Historian Skill
Scott v. Sandford

Research Required

1. Have students read historical accounts, including both primary and secondary sources, about Dred Scott's attempt to be free and the court cases involved. Students should be able to find newspaper accounts, Roger Taney's opinion, McLean's dissent, and other primary and secondary sources.

2. Have students write a short essay summarizing Scott's appeal to the different courts.

3. Have students write a legal amicus curiae (friend of the court) brief supporting the argument that Dred Scott should be free because he lived in free territory.

4. Have volunteers share their briefs with the class. **LS Verbal-Linguistic**

   📓 Alternative Assessment Handbook, Rubric 43: Writing to Persuade

---

Answers

Critical Thinking 1. *possible answer—showed the Court to be biased and racist, involved in political decisions outside of Constitution; Justice Taney's ruling went beyond the actual court case;* **2.** *possible answer—agree, Supreme Court should not be involved in political issues, should work to maintain balance of power among branches of government; the Bush v. Gore case, however, did not harm an entire population as the Dred Scott decision did.*

Lincoln's Path to the White House

BEFORE YOU READ

MAIN IDEA
After gaining national prominence in the late 1850s, Abraham Lincoln became president in 1860.

READING FOCUS
1. How did Lincoln's personal views on slavery differ from his political position on the subject?
2. How did the Lincoln-Douglas debates benefit Lincoln's political career?
3. What circumstances resulted in Lincoln's election as president in 1860?

KEY TERMS AND PEOPLE
Abraham Lincoln
Lincoln-Douglas debates
Freeport Doctrine
platform
John C. Breckinridge
John Bell

TAKING NOTES As you read, take notes on the reasons why Abraham Lincoln won national prominence in the 1850s. Record your notes in a graphic organizer like the one shown here.

Cause → Lincoln wins national prominence

Debate or Sideshow?

THE INSIDE STORY

How did the Lincoln-Douglas debates differ from political debates today? Political debates in the 1850s were quite different from the televised debates of modern times. Instead of being media events, they were a mix of carnival and public-speaking contest. The seven great debates of 1858 between Abraham Lincoln and Stephen A. Douglas were no exception.

The Lincoln-Douglas debates were open-air events. People arrived on foot, on horseback, and in wagons and carriages from throughout the countryside. They brought picnic baskets and turned the debates into all-day family outings. Banners flew and bands played as supporters of each candidate tried to outdo each other. Douglas arrived for one debate at the head of a mile-long parade.

The debates themselves were long affairs. The first speech lasted an hour, followed by a 90-minute speech by the opponent. The opening speaker then gave a 30-minute

▲ Crowds gathered to witness debates between Lincoln (in white jacket) and Douglas (in dark suit).

reply. Each speaker's remarks were peppered with applause and cheers from supporters, and with groans and heckling from supporters of the other side. The crowd shouted questions and challenged the speakers' claims. Election politics in the 1850s was typical of the turmoil of the times. ▪

THE NATION SPLITS APART **337**

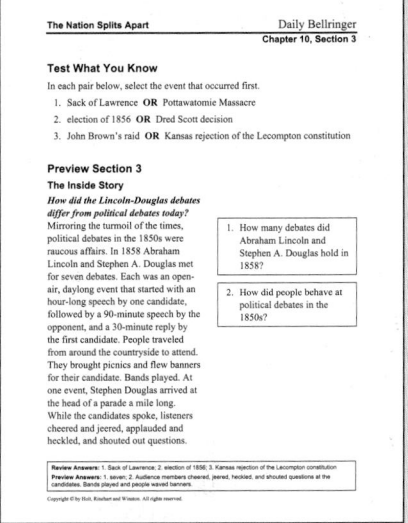

Preteach

Bellringer
The Inside Story. . . Use the **Daily Bellringer Transparency** to help students answer the question.

📋 Daily Bellringer Transparency, Section 3

The Nation Splits Apart — Daily Bellringer — Chapter 10, Section 3

Test What You Know
In each pair below, select the event that occurred first.
1. Sack of Lawrence OR Pottawatomie Massacre
2. election of 1856 OR Dred Scott decision
3. John Brown's raid OR Kansas rejection of the Lecompton constitution

Preview Section 3
The Inside Story
How did the Lincoln-Douglas debates differ from political debates today?
Mirroring the turmoil of the times, political debates in the 1850s were raucous affairs. In 1858 Abraham Lincoln and Stephen A. Douglas met for seven debates. Each was an open-air, daylong event that started with an hour-long speech by one candidate, followed by a 90-minute speech by the opponent, and a 30-minute reply by the first candidate. People traveled from around the countryside to attend. They brought picnics and flew banners for their candidate. Bands played. At one event, Stephen Douglas arrived at the head of a parade a mile long. While the candidates spoke, listeners cheered and jeered, applauded and heckled, and shouted out questions.

1. How many debates did Abraham Lincoln and Stephen A. Douglas hold in 1858?

2. How did people behave at political debates in the 1850s?

Review Answers: 1. Sack of Lawrence; 2. election of 1856; 3. Kansas rejection of the Lecompton constitution
Preview Answers: 1. seven; 2. Audience members cheered, jeered, heckled, and shouted questions at the candidates. Bands played and people waved banners.

Copyright © by Holt, Rinehart and Winston. All rights reserved.

Academic Vocabulary

Review with students the high-use academic term in this section.

context the circumstances in which something happens or is to be considered (p. 340)

📋 CRF: Vocabulary Builder Activity, Section 3

Taking Notes

Causes—member of Congress, organization of Illinois Republican Party, house divided speech, debates with Douglas

---

go.hrw.com
Online Resources

KEYWORD: SD7 CH10
TOPIC: LINCOLN'S RISE TO PROMINENCE

Teach the Main Idea

At Level

Lincoln's Path to the White House

1. **Teach** Ask students the Reading Focus questions to teach this section.

2. **Apply** Draw three large boxes for students to see. Label the top of each box with one of the three topics of this section: Lincoln, Politics, and Slavery; Lincoln and Douglas Clash; The Election of 1860. Guide students in a discussion of each topic. As you discuss each topic, use the boxes as a graphic organizer and list the main ideas for each topic within the related box.

3. **Review** Have students identify one issue that they believe to be the most serious problem facing the nation in the 1850s.

4. **Practice/Homework** Have students write a short essay describing the Freeport Doctrine, the key events surrounding it, and its significance in the 1860 presidential election. **LS Visual-Spatial, Verbal-Linguistic**

📋 Alternative Assessment Handbook, Rubrics 13: Graphic Organizers; and 40: Writing to Describe

❶ How did Lincoln's personal views on slavery differ from his political position on the subject? *political—favored popular sovereignty, believed Congress did not have the authority to end slavery within a state; personal—antislavery*

Lincoln, Politics, and Slavery

Explain What events led to Lincoln's antislavery views? *parents' opposition, witnessing slave auction and treatment of slaves*

Summarize What major issues faced Lincoln regarding slavery? *whether states should decide slavery for themselves; whether slavery should expand to new territories; whether Congress should decide issue of slavery in new territories and in Washington, D.C.*

Make Judgments Do you think compensated emancipation would have worked? *possible answers—no, too expensive and plantations would have lost labor force; yes, it was a fair solution because slaveholders would have been paid for their slaves*

History's Voices

Remind students that in the nineteenth century, Negro was an accepted term for African Americans.

Lincoln, Politics, and Slavery

For **Abraham Lincoln**, the debates with Stephen Douglas marked the end of a long road toward national politics. Lincoln, who once summarized his early life as "the short and simple annals [record of events] of the poor," had less than a year of formal schooling. His mother, Nancy, encouraged him to educate himself by learning on his own. "All that I am or ever hope to be I owe to her," he said.

A frontier upbringing Abraham Lincoln was born in 1809 in a one-room cabin near Louisville, Kentucky. About 1,000 slaves lived in the area at the time. His parents were poor, however, and like most white southerners, they held no slaves. It is not clear when Lincoln's distaste for slavery began. His mother was a deeply religious woman. The minister of the family's church thought slavery was wrong, and the boy probably heard his parents speak against it at home. "I am naturally antislavery," Lincoln observed years later. "I cannot remember when I did not so think and feel."

His parents' opposition to slavery was one reason the Lincolns moved from Kentucky to Indiana Territory in 1816. They settled near the Ohio River, about 75 miles west of Louisville. The boy helped his father build a cabin and clear enough land for a small farm. The slavery issue continued to swirl around his family, however. Although slavery was banned in Indiana, not all the region's settlers were opposed to the institution. In addition, slave catchers frequented the area, hunting down runaways who had crossed the Ohio River seeking freedom.

In 1828 Lincoln took a job on a boat moving farm produce down the Ohio and Mississippi rivers from Indiana to New Orleans. There the curious 19-year-old had his first direct contact with slavery when he attended a slave auction. He witnessed men and women bought and sold like livestock. "I saw it all [for] myself," Lincoln recalled in 1851, "and the horrid pictures are in my mind yet."

On another trip down river, a similar scene greatly disturbed Lincoln.

HISTORY'S VOICES

❝A gentleman had purchased twelve Negroes in different parts of Kentucky and was taking them to a farm in the South. They were chained six and six together . . . like so many fish upon a trot-line. In this condition they were being separated forever from the scenes of their childhood, their friends, their fathers and mothers, and brothers and sisters, and many of them, from their wives and children.❞

—Abraham Lincoln, 1841

Lincoln's Early Life

Lincoln lived his early years in a small cabin (reconstructed above). Self-educated, he began practicing law in 1836. Six years later, he married Mary Todd (right), an educated woman from a prominent Kentucky family.

338 CHAPTER 10

Skills Focus: Comparing and Contrasting   At Level

Reading Skill
Lincoln's Family

1. Remind students that Lincoln was born in Kentucky, a slave state, but his family did not own slaves. Ask students how this may have contributed to Lincoln's personal antislavery views.

2. Guide students in a discussion of how the views of slaveholders might be at odds with southerners who did not own slaves.

3. Have students write a well-reasoned speech from the perspective of a loyal southerner who does not own slaves and who opposes slavery. Students should explain their views and propose ways to end slavery and, at the same time, provide ways for plantation owners to continue to farm profitably.

4. Have volunteers share their speeches with the class. ⬛ **Verbal-Linguistic**

📝 Alternative Assessment Handbook, Rubric 41: Writing to Express

Lincoln's early politics As a young man, Lincoln moved to New Salem, a village about 20 miles northwest of Springfield, Illinois. He took a job as a store clerk, and the next year he ran for a seat in the state legislature. Lincoln lost that election, but two years later he ran again and won.

In December 1834, at age 25, Lincoln began the first of four terms in the Illinois General Assembly. During his first term he studied law at home and was licensed to practice law in 1836. As a member of the state legislature, Lincoln protested a resolution passed overwhelmingly by the legislature that denounced abolitionist societies.

Lincoln met Mary Todd, the cousin of his law partner and the daughter of a wealthy Kentucky slaveholder, in 1840. It was a rocky courtship because of differences in temperament and the opposition of Todd's sisters. After a broken engagement, Lincoln and Todd made up and married in 1842. By then Lincoln had retired from the legislature to devote more time to his law practice.

Lincoln in Congress In 1846 Lincoln returned to politics and successfully ran for Congress. He took his seat in 1847 as the Mexican-American War was underway. He soon gained attention by charging President Polk, a slaveholding Democrat, with starting the war in order to spread slavery. Just two weeks into his term, Lincoln introduced a resolution in Congress challenging the president to identify the place where American blood had been shed, which justified going to war.

Lincoln did not take part in the debates on the Wilmot Proviso to ban slavery in territory gained from Mexico. However, he favored the proposal. Each time David Wilmot introduced his amendment in the House, Lincoln voted for it. He believed Congress could regulate slavery in the territories and in Washington, D.C. Lincoln maintained that only the states had the right to decide on slavery within their borders. He believed Congress did not have the authority to end slavery within a state.

In 1849 Lincoln proposed ending slavery in Washington, D.C., by paying slaveholders to free their slaves. This approach to ending slavery, called compensated emancipation, was favored by some abolitionists. It was one solution to slaveholders' arguments that slavery was protected by the Fifth Amendment guarantee of property rights. However, the amendment also states " . . . nor shall private property be taken for public use without just compensation." Some people who supported compensated emancipation believed this statement allowed Congress to act against slavery so long as slaveholders were paid for their loss. In 1849, however, this idea was too radical for many members of Congress, and Lincoln's proposal got little support.

Lincoln worked hard to help elect the Whig candidate Zachary Taylor as president in 1848. He expected a job in the Taylor administration as a reward and was bitterly disappointed when he was not offered the position he sought. He resigned from Congress in 1849 and returned home to practice law. Lincoln's second retirement from politics, however, turned out to be no longer than his first.

READING CHECK **Identifying the Main Idea** Why did Lincoln not seek the abolition of slavery, even though he personally opposed it?

Lincoln and Douglas Clash

The Kansas-Nebraska Act stirred Lincoln from retirement in 1854. He described himself as "thunderstruck and stunned" by the law's passage. The renewed controversy over slavery in the territories energized him to return to public life. In a speech in Peoria, Illinois, Lincoln clarified his opposition to Stephen Douglas's position on popular sovereignty.

HISTORY'S VOICES

❝Near eighty years ago we began by declaring that all men are created equal; but now from that beginning we have run down to the other declaration, that for some men to enslave others is a 'sacred right of self-government.' These principles cannot stand together.❞

—Abraham Lincoln, October 16, 1854

This speech and many of Lincoln's other remarks expressed the basic beliefs and principles of the newly founded Republican Party. Yet Lincoln still considered himself a Whig. He was elected as a Whig to another term in the state legislature in 1854. However, he resigned in February 1855 because he had decided to seek one of Illinois's two seats in the United States Senate.

Reading Focus

❷ How did the Lincoln-Douglas debates benefit Lincoln's political career? *competently argued with Douglas; attained national name recognition, seen as a leader*

Lincoln and Douglas Clash

Explain Why did the Kansas-Nebraska Act motivate Lincoln to return to politics? *he was angered that the law passed; wanted to be in public life again*

Identify Cause and Effect What part of Lincoln's 1854 speech guaranteed him negative reaction in the South? *statement that all men are created equal*

Info to Know

Mary Todd Lincoln Mary Todd Lincoln got involved in her husband's career early on. When Abraham Lincoln was first elected to Congress, his wife went with him to Washington, D.C. This was highly unusual in the 1850s. When Abraham Lincoln campaigned for the Senate, Mary lobbied for him, watched how he was treated by the press, and attended the last of the Lincoln-Douglas debates.

Differentiating Instruction

Below Level

English-Language Learners; Learners Having Difficulty

Materials construction paper, colored markers

1. Guide students in a discussion about Lincoln's early life and career. Ask the students what Lincoln said or did to show that he was against slavery. *moved to an area that did not have slavery; supported abolition movement; voted for legislation that banned slavery in new territory*

2. Make a list of student responses for all to see. Have students copy the information onto their own papers.

3. Have students create two congressional campaign posters for Lincoln, one that would appeal to abolitionists and one that would appeal to those who supported popular sovereignty for slavery.

4. Have volunteers share their campaign posters with the class. **LS** **Visual-Spatial**

    📖 Alternative Assessment Handbook, Rubric 28: Posters

Answers

Reading Check *Lincoln believed that states should decide the issue and that Congress did not have the authority to end slavery within a state.*

Lincoln and Douglas Clash

Identify What were the main issues of Lincoln's 1858 Senate campaign? *Kansas-Nebraska Act; Dred Scott decision; spread of slavery*

Analyze How did the debates with Stephen Douglas help Lincoln's future bid for the presidency? *national press coverage; national name recognition*

Evaluate Do you think Lincoln realized, in advance, the commotion that his "house divided" speech would create? *possible answer—Yes; this is a strong, clear antislavery statement.*

Counterpoints

Lincoln-Douglas Debates

Analyze Stephen Douglas was short in stature, while Lincoln was very tall. Ask students to explain how Douglas's style of presentation at the debates might have helped him offset Lincoln's height advantage. *Douglas spoke loudly, used strong gestures, and made himself appear as "big" as Lincoln.*

Info to Know

The Lincoln Library and Museum

The Lincoln Library and Museum in Springfield, Illinois, opened in October 2004 and was formally dedicated in April 2005. Both the library and museum contain information about all aspects of Lincoln's life. The museum displays many of Lincoln's writings, including the Gettysburg Address.

Answers

Reading Like a Historian *the U.S. Constitution*

Lincoln-Douglas Debates

Democratic senator Stephen A. Douglas believed that each state or territory should decide for itself whether or not to allow slavery.

❝ When this government was established by Washington and Madison and Jay and Hamilton, . . . it was composed of free States and slave States, bound together by our common Constitution. We have existed and prospered from that day to this, divided into these free and slave States. ❞

Stephen A. Douglas,
September 18, 1858

Abraham Lincoln challenged Douglas for the Illinois seat in the Senate. He countered that the framers had intended a gradual end to slavery.

❝ [T]he fathers of the government intended and expected [slavery] to come to an end . . . It is not true . . . that [they] made this government part slave, and part free . . . The exact truth is that they found the institution existing among us and they left it as they found it . . . because of the . . . absolute impossibility of the immediate removal of it. ❞

Abraham Lincoln,
October 15, 1858

Skills Focus READING LIKE A HISTORIAN

Analyzing Primary Sources According to Senator Douglas, what united the states during the early days of the republic?
See Skills Handbook, pp. H28–H29

"A house divided" By the mid-1850s the Whigs were nearly dead as a political party. Lincoln needed a new party if he hoped to reenter national politics. The Republicans seemed more in line with his beliefs than the Democratic Party did. With these thoughts in mind, Lincoln helped organize the Illinois Republican Party in 1856. Later that year, Illinois Republicans tried but failed to put him on the ticket with John Frémont as the party's candidate for vice president.

In 1858 Lincoln decided to oppose Douglas's bid for a third term in the U.S. Senate. His acceptance of the Republican nomination produced one of the most important speeches of his political career. It focused on what Lincoln planned to make the main issue of his campaign—the controversy over the Kansas-Nebraska Act, the *Dred Scott* decision, and the spread of slavery.

Addressing the delegates at the state Republican convention, Lincoln quoted from the Bible and made a dire prediction.

ACADEMIC VOCABULARY
context the circumstances in which something happens or is to be considered

HISTORY'S VOICES

❝ 'A house divided against itself cannot stand.' I believe this government cannot endure, permanently half *slave* and half *free*. I do not expect the Union to be *dissolved*—I do not expect the house to *fall*—but I do expect it will cease to be divided. It will become *all* one thing or *all* the other. ❞
—Abraham Lincoln, June 16, 1858

Many viewed this statement as the most radical stance against slavery yet taken by a Republican leader. It suggested that Lincoln's goals went far beyond limiting slavery's spread. For months afterward, he tried to explain the remark's context—that he was making a prediction, not stating a position. From that point on, however, many slaveholders were convinced that Lincoln secretly was an abolitionist.

The Lincoln-Douglas debates Lincoln's "house divided" speech attracted national attention, and despite the problems it caused, it gave him national name recognition. Weeks later, when he and Douglas debated the issues

340 CHAPTER 10

Skills Focus: Comparing and Contrasting

At Level

Reading Skill

Consequences of the Lincoln-Douglas Debates

1. Draw a two-circle Venn diagram for students to see. Label one circle Lincoln, and the other circle Douglas. Have students copy the diagram onto their own paper.

2. Have students use the diagram to compare and contrast the consequences of the Lincoln-Douglas debates. *Both—made clear their positions on slavery; national media coverage; Lincoln—national name recognition; alarmed southerners; gained*

northern support; lost election; Douglas—lost southern support; won Senate seat

3. Have volunteers share the information in their diagrams and complete the class diagram. Have students correct any errors they may have made, and have them retain their diagrams as a study tool. 🄻🄢 **Visual-Spatial, Logical-Mathematical**

📋 Alternative Assessment Handbook, Rubric 13: Graphic Organizers

in their Senate campaign, their remarks were reported in newspapers across the nation. The **Lincoln-Douglas debates** took place from late August to mid-October 1858. Seven debates were held in all, in towns across the state of Illinois. Thousands of people gathered at each place to hear the two men speak.

Lincoln and Douglas were very different in appearance and style. Douglas spoke with great flair, clenching his fists and stamping his feet for emphasis. Lincoln's manner was mild, and he sprinkled his remarks with humor. His strength lay not in theatrics but in the logic and reasoning of his ideas.

The Freeport Doctrine The second debate, at Freeport, Illinois, turned out to be the most critical of the seven. A crowd of 15,000 people gathered to hear the exchange. Lincoln spoke first. He challenged Douglas to explain how people could use popular sovereignty to keep slavery out of a place when the *Dred Scott* decision had said they could not. Douglas's reply came to be known as the **Freeport Doctrine**.

HISTORY'S VOICES

❝Slavery cannot exist a day or an hour anywhere unless it is supported by the local police regulations. Those police regulations can only be established by the local legislature, and if the people are opposed to slavery they will elect representatives to that body who will by unfriendly legislation . . . prevent the introduction of it into their midst.❞
—Stephen Douglas, August 27, 1858

In the first debates, Douglas had fired back at Lincoln's claim that the nation could not continue half slave and half free. He painted Lincoln as a dangerous radical. If the states "cannot endure thus divided," Douglas noted, then Lincoln "must strive to make them all free or all slave, which will inevitably bring about a dissolution of the Union." He called Lincoln's beliefs "revolutionary and destructive of the existence of this government."

Lincoln's social views Lincoln also emphasized the immorality of slavery in the debates, calling the institution "a moral, a social, and a political wrong." Douglas evaded the morality issue but attacked Lincoln's other arguments.

Douglas continually referred to Lincoln's party as the Black Republicans and painted what was, to Douglas, the unpleasant image of

a society where the races were equal. Douglas pressed his opponent on this point. "Are you in favor of conferring upon the negro the rights and privileges of citizenship?" he challenged.

Backed into a corner, a frustrated Lincoln made his position clear in the fourth debate, held at Charleston, Illinois.

HISTORY'S VOICES

❝I will say then that I am not, nor have ever been, in favor of bringing about in any way the social and political equality of the white and black races.❞
—Abraham Lincoln, September 18, 1858

The debates' significance The debates illustrated the sharp differences between Lincoln and Douglas on slavery. Deciding who won is difficult. Most historians judge Lincoln to have been the winner even though Douglas retained his Senate seat. (The voters did not elect U.S. senators until 1913. Before then each state's senators were chosen by its legislature.) In the fall election, the Illinois legislature returned Douglas to the Senate.

Even in electoral defeat Lincoln had achieved a victory. He had argued the more famous Douglas to a draw and in the process made himself a national political figure. Douglas's Freeport Doctrine and his opposition to the Lecompton Constitution caused him to lose the support of southern Democrats. This loss proved critical when he faced Lincoln again in the presidential election two years later.

Lincoln's moderate positions increased his standing among northerners. At the same time, however, nothing in the debates gave southerners cause to shed their growing belief that Lincoln was a serious threat to slavery.

Perhaps most importantly, even though the state legislature decided the Senate race, Lincoln and Douglas had taken their arguments directly to the people. By focusing on the most controversial topic of the times, they made clear to the entire nation the issues that were tearing the country apart. In addition, the outcome of the debates directly affected the presidential election of 1860. These factors rank the Lincoln-Douglas debates among the great political events of U.S. history.

READING CHECK **Identifying the Main Idea** Why were the Lincoln-Douglas debates such important events?

Reading Focus

Lincoln and Douglas Clash

Recall Which of Lincoln's arguments about slavery did Stephen Douglas not refute? *that it was immoral*

Analyze What was Douglas saying in the Freeport Doctrine? *that slavery could exist only in a territory or state where people wanted it; if people did not want slavery they would elect a legislature that would vote against it*

Develop Following the debates, why did some people consider Lincoln a moderate and others see him as a radical? *possible answers—moderate, he did not argue for full citizenship rights for enslaved people; radical because he was solidly antislavery*

Teaching Tip

The full text of the Lincoln-Douglas debates can be found online at www.nps.gov/liho/debates.htm. The site also contains a map of Illinois showing the places where the debates took place.

Differentiating Instruction

Above Level

Advanced Learners/GATE

Research Required

1. Remind students that the Lincoln-Douglas debates received national newspaper coverage and that thousands of people came to hear the two candidates debate.

2. Have students create a journal or diary entry about the 1858 debate of the two candidates in Freeport. Students should include what the two men looked like, how they acted during the debate, the comments they made, and the reaction of the crowd to their arguments. Ask students to use vivid imagery and include

all the details available in the text about the styles of the two men. Students should also express their opinion about who they think won the debate.

3. Have volunteers share their journals with the class. **LS Visual-Spatial, Logical Mathematical**
   📖 Alternative Assessment Handbook, Rubric 15: Journals

Answers

Reading Check *debates focused on slavery, issue that was tearing the country apart; illustrated the sharp differences between the two men on slavery; Lincoln gained national recognition*

3 What circumstances resulted in Lincoln's election as president in 1860? *Democratic Party split; Republicans chose Lincoln because he was more moderate than Seward; Lincoln won every northern state*

The Election of 1860

Recall How did northern Democrats and southern Democrats differ in their goals for the 1860 national convention? *northern Democrats supported Douglas and popular sovereignty; southern Democrats wanted to block Douglas and protect the extension of slavery*

Develop Do you think it was reasonable for the *New York Herald* to state that slaves would run away if Lincoln were elected president? *possible answers—No, newspapers should be unbiased. Yes, this was a real possibility, and it was a Democratic newspaper.*

Primary Source

"Shall I tell you what this collision [between slave and free labor] means? . . . It is an irrepressible conflict between opposing and enduring forces, and it means that the United States must and will . . . become entirely a slave-holding nation or entirely a free-labor nation."

— William H. Seward

Rochester, New York, October 25, 1858

Drawing Conclusions Do you think that William Seward believed that the nation would engage in a civil war over the issue of slavery? Explain your answer. *possibly; he understood exactly how divisive the issue was for the nation and how North and South were becoming more resolute*

Answers

Reading Like a Historian *Lincoln was stronger candidate, stood up for his beliefs*

342

Political Cartoon

This cartoon tries to show why Lincoln won the election of 1860. The four candidates are portrayed as baseball players, with Lincoln, the victor, standing on home base.

The bat of Stephen Douglas is labeled, "Non Intervention," reflecting his position that the government should leave slavery up to the states.

Southern Democrat John C. Breckinridge took the most extreme position. His bat says "Slavery Extension" and his belt "Disunion Club."

Lincoln's bat is shown as a rail, stronger than his opponents' regular bats.

Skills FOCUS READING LIKE A HISTORIAN

Interpreting Political Cartoons What is the artist's point of view about why Lincoln won the election?

See Skills Handbook, pp. H28–H29

The Election of 1860

Stephen Douglas had his eyes on the presidency at the time of the Lincoln-Douglas debates. After the debates, Lincoln did too. Each faced a hard battle to become his party's nominee.

The Democratic convention Both the nation and the Democratic Party were seriously divided in the spring of 1860. The Democrats held their national convention in Charleston, South Carolina, in April. Southern Democrats arrived with two main goals—to block the nomination of Douglas and to adopt a party **platform** that protected slavery and its spread. (A platform is a declaration of the principles for which a group stands.) Northern Democrats supported Douglas and popular sovereignty.

Amid much bitterness, the northerners managed to push their platform through. The convention could not agree on a candidate, however, and many southerners walked out. The remaining delegates met again in Baltimore in June and chose Douglas as the party's candidate. Later that month southern Democrats nominated Vice President **John C. Breckinridge** of Kentucky as their presidential

candidate. The split in the Democratic Party was complete. Southern moderates formed the Constitutional Union Party and nominated Tennessee senator **John Bell** for president.

The Republican convention William Seward seemed to be the leading candidate for the nomination when the Republicans met in Chicago in May. However, many Republicans feared that Seward's abolitionist views were too radical for most northern voters. The Republicans settled on Lincoln as the candidate with the most strengths and fewest weaknesses.

The party's platform opposed the spread of slavery. To attract midwestern farmers, factory workers, and northern industrialists, the platform called for free land in the West, improved wages, and tariff increases. In addition, it expressed a firm commitment to the preservation of the Union.

The 1860 campaign As in 1856, the election of 1860 was really two sectional elections. In the North it was Lincoln versus Douglas. In the South the contest was between Breckinridge and Bell. Lincoln's name did not even appear on the ballot in several southern states. Douglas

342 CHAPTER 10

Skills Focus: Interpreting Political Cartoons   At Level

Reading Like a Historian Skill
Creating a New Political Cartoon

1. Have students examine the political cartoon on this page. Then guide the class in a discussion about the images depicted in the cartoon and the national divisions that existed during the 1860 campaign.

2. Ask students to name current political issues that are divisive and might cause a large-scale national division. Make a class list of these issues for all to see.

3. Have each student choose one topic from the class list and create a political cartoon explaining the issue and showing why it is divisive.

4. Have students display and explain their cartoons to the class. **LS Visual-Spatial, Verbal-Linguistic**

   Alternative Assessment Handbook, Rubric 27: Political Cartoons

tried to portray himself as the candidate of national unity. However, many southerners viewed him as a traitor because of the positions he had taken on the Lecompton Constitution and in the Lincoln-Douglas debates.

Democrats in the North sought to appeal to voters with an openly racist campaign. The *New York Herald*, the nation's largest Democratic newspaper, predicted that a Lincoln victory would bring "hundreds of thousands" of runaway slaves north to "their friends—the Republicans . . . and be placed by them side by side in competition with white men." Republicans branded the Democrats as corrupt and promised that "Honest Abe Lincoln" would restore good government.

The vote in November was largely along sectional lines. Lincoln won nearly every northern state. In the South, Breckinridge and Bell split the vote, with the Lower South going entirely to Breckinridge. The split in the Democratic Party allowed Lincoln to be elected president with less than 40 percent of the popular vote nationwide. Of the nearly 2 million votes Lincoln received, only 26,000 came from slave states. These election results would spell trouble for the Union.

Many northerners celebrated Lincoln's victory. "The great revolution has finally taken place," one free-soiler wrote. "The country has once and for all thrown off the domination of the slaveholders." Many southerners looked at the election results with concern. "A party founded on the . . . hatred of African slavery is

now the controlling power," the *New Orleans Delta* warned the slaveholding South.

READING CHECK **Identifying the Main Idea** What was the main issue in the 1860 presidential election campaign?

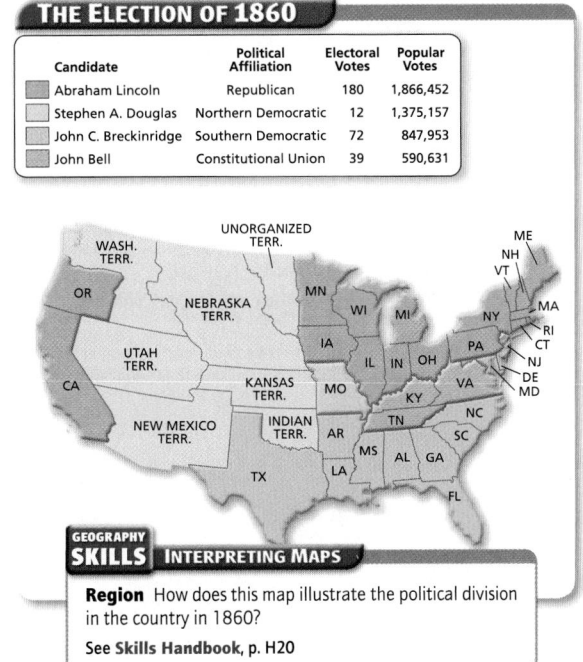

THE ELECTION OF 1860

Candidate	Political Affiliation	Electoral Votes	Popular Votes
Abraham Lincoln	Republican	180	1,866,452
Stephen A. Douglas	Northern Democratic	12	1,375,157
John C. Breckinridge	Southern Democratic	72	847,953
John Bell	Constitutional Union	39	590,631

GEOGRAPHY SKILLS **INTERPRETING MAPS**

Region How does this map illustrate the political division in the country in 1860?

See Skills Handbook, p. H20

SECTION 3 ASSESSMENT

go.hrw.com
Online Quiz
Keyword: SD7 HP10

Reviewing Ideas, Terms, and People

1. **a. Define** What was **compensated emancipation**?
   b. Predict Do you think slaveholders would have accepted compensated emancipation as a way of settling the slavery controversy? Why or why not?

2. **a. Describe** What were **Abraham Lincoln**'s personal views of slavery and on social equality for African Americans?
   b. Evaluate Was Lincoln an abolitionist? Explain.

3. **a. Identify** What was the **Freeport Doctrine**?
   b. Compare and Contrast How did the views of Lincoln and Douglas differ? In what areas were they similar?
   c. Elaborate How did the Freeport Doctrine affect Douglas's chances to become president? Why did it have this effect?

4. **a. Identify** Who were the presidential candidates in 1860?

b. Make Inferences How did the election of 1860 illustrate the nation's deep divisions?

Critical Thinking

5. **Sequencing** Copy the chart below and complete it to trace Lincoln's rise in politics from state legislator to president of the United States.

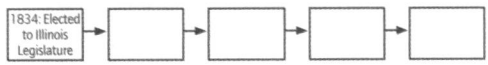

1834: Elected to Illinois Legislature → ☐ → ☐ → ☐

FOCUS ON WRITING

6. **Expository** Write a short essay explaining how the **Lincoln-Douglas debates** affected the presidential election of 1860.

THE NATION SPLITS APART **343**

Bellringer

The Inside Story. . . Use the **Daily Bellringer Transparency** to help students answer the question.

📧 Daily Bellringer Transparency, Section 4

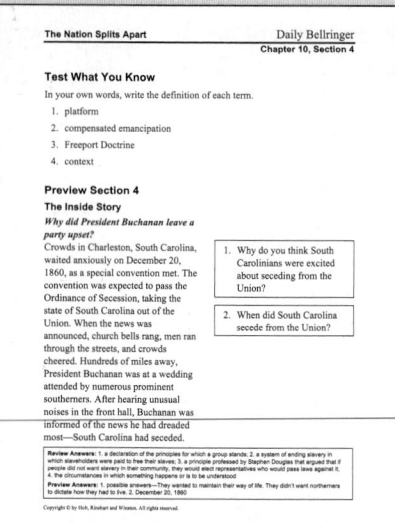

Taking Notes

Southern—most states not universal in their support of secession; some wanted to secede only if federal government did not meet final set of demands; some wanted to give Lincoln a chance to prove his claims of good intentions towards the South; many believed united resistance was essential; Northern—some thought nation was better off without slave states; some bore southerners no ill will and wanted South to go in peace; others worried about the long-term effects of secession

The South Secedes

BEFORE YOU READ

MAIN IDEA

The election of Abraham Lincoln led to the secession of the southern states.

READING FOCUS

1. What led to the secession of the states of the Lower South from the Union?

2. How and why was the Confederacy formed?

3. Why did compromises and other attempts to save the Union fail?

KEY TERMS AND PEOPLE

Jefferson Davis
provisional
Confederate States of America
Crittenden Compromise
Peace Convention

TAKING NOTES As you read, take notes on the varying points of view people in the South and in the North held on southern secession.

Southern Points of View on Secession	Northern Points of View on Secession

Breaking Bad News to the President

THE INSIDE STORY *Why did President Buchanan leave a party upset?* Everyone in Charleston, South Carolina, was waiting for the news. Soon, a special convention would pass the Ordinance of Secession, taking the state out of the Union. On the morning of December 20, 1860, crowds began to gather in the streets. Finally, the news was announced. "The whole city was wild with excitement as the news spread like wildfire," an eyewitness wrote. "Old men ran shouting down the street." Cannons were fired, and church bells rang. The shouts of the crowd drowned out the trumpets and drums of military bands.

On that same December day, President James Buchanan was at a wedding reception in Washington, D.C. The groom was a Louisiana congressman, and many guests were prominent southerners. Buchanan, now a "lame duck" president after Abraham Lincoln's election, was talking with Sara Pryor, the wife of a congressman from South Carolina. When the president heard unusual noises in the front hall, Sara Pryor went to check. Another South Carolina congressman was waving a telegram. "South Carolina has seceded!" he said excitedly.

Sara hurried inside and whispered the news to Buchanan. Quickly ordering his carriage, the president drove back to the White House. The news was not yet official, but he knew it was true. The thing he dreaded most had occurred. ■

▲ South Carolinians wave a "states' rights" flag to celebrate secession.

Teach the Main Idea

At Level

The South Secedes

1. **Teach** Ask students the Reading Focus questions to teach this section.

2. **Apply** Draw three large boxes for students to see. Label the boxes with the main topics of this chapter: Secession!; Forming the Confederacy; Compromise Fails. Guide students in a discussion of the three topics. As you discuss each topic, have students identify and then list supporting details for each topic in the corresponding box. Have students copy the graphic organizer.

3. **Review** As you review each section, have students identify the attempt and the failure of compromise to hold the Union together.

4. **Practice/Homework** Have students write a balanced account of the challenges facing the Union and the South in 1860. The accounts should include ideas about how to resolve the problems. **LS Verbal-Linguistic**

📝 Alternative Assessment Handbook, Rubric 42: Writing to Inform

Secession!

The United States began breaking apart on November 13, 1860. On that day, one week after Abraham Lincoln's election, the South Carolina legislature called a state convention to consider withdrawing from the Union. "Black Republicans triumphant—radical Southerners equally so," one woman wrote in her diary.

The 169 convention delegates met at Columbia, the state capital, in December. The air around them was filled with excitement. In this atmosphere, they unanimously passed the following resolution:

HISTORY'S VOICES

❝We the people of the State of South Carolina, in convention assembled, do declare and ordain . . . that the union now subsisting between South Carolina and the other states under the name of the 'United States of America' is hereby dissolved.❞

—Ordinance of Secession, December 20, 1860

Four days later the South Carolina delegates issued a statement of the reasons for secession. It noted that the Declaration of Independence established the people's right to abolish an abusive government and create a new one. Among the many abuses the statement claimed was that the federal government had failed to properly protect slavery and safeguard the property rights of slaveholders.

Following South Carolina's lead, the other states of the Lower South quickly withdrew from the Union. Mississippi seceded on January 9, 1861, followed by Florida the next day and Alabama the day after. Georgia, Louisiana, and Texas had also seceded from the United States by February 1. Four other southern states—Virginia, North Carolina, Tennessee, and Arkansas—warned that if the federal government made any attempt to use force against a state, they also would withdraw from the United States.

Southerners and secession Despite all the excitement, southerners' support for secession was by no means universal. In each of the states that seceded, the action was taken by a state convention made up of delegates. Only in South Carolina's convention was the vote unanimous. In some conventions, between 30 and 40 percent of the delegates voted against secession.

Texas, Virginia, and Tennessee were the only states to later submit their conventions' action to a vote by the people. About 3 in 10 Tennesseans opposed leaving the Union. Texas Governor Sam Houston led the opposition.

HISTORY'S VOICES

❝You may, after the sacrifice of countless millions of treasure and hundreds of thousands of lives, as a bare possibility, win Southern independence . . . But I doubt it . . . the North is determined to preserve this Union.❞

—Sam Houston, 1859

CAUSES OF SECESSION

CAUSES

The Compromise of 1850
- Admitted California as a free state, ending the balance between the number of free and slave states in the Union
- Tried to settle the dispute over the expansion of slavery into the Mexican Cession by using popular sovereignty

The Kansas-Nebraska Act (1854)
- Applied the popular sovereignty principle to settle the question of slavery in Kansas Territory
- Caused the North and South to compete to settle the territory
- Led to guerrilla warfare between pro- and antislavery settlers

The Lincoln-Douglas Debates (1858)
- Emphasized the divisions over the Kansas-Nebraska Act and the *Dred Scott* decision
- Brought Lincoln's opposition to slavery's spread to a national audience
- Caused Douglas to lose support in the North and the South

The Election of 1860
- Split in Democratic Party allowed Lincoln's election as president
- Left both houses of Congress in northern hands with an opponent of slavery heading the executive branch

Secession (1860–1861)
- Fears in South Carolina that a northern-controlled government would act against slavery; South Carolina withdrew from the Union
- Several other slave states followed South Carolina's lead and formed the Confederate States of America

---

Skills Focus: Comparing and Contrasting   `At Level`

Reading Skill
Secession

1. Guide the students in a discussion about the causes of secession. Make a list of student responses for all to see and have students copy the information onto their own paper.

2. Organize the students into four groups. Assign each group *one* cause: Compromise of 1850; Kansas-Nebraska Act of 1854; Lincoln-Douglas Debates of 1858; Election of 1860. Have the groups prepare a detailed outline about how their assigned cause was viewed by southerners and by northerners.

3. Have volunteers from each group present their outlines to the class. Have students take notes during the presentations.

4. Review the historical, economic, and social differences between North and South, and how these differences led to secession.
   LS Interpersonal, Kinesthetic
   📖 Alternative Assessment Handbook, Rubric 14: Group Activity

---

Reading Focus

❶ What led to the secession of the states of the Lower South from the Union? *exercised their right to abolish an abusive government; believed federal government failed to protect slavery and slaveholders' property rights*

Secession!

Identify Which was the first state to secede? *South Carolina*

Analyze Why do you think Sam Houston was able to understand the cost of the Civil War even before it began? *possible answer—He understood the determination of the North to preserve the Union and foresaw how much money and how many lives a war would cost.*

Evaluate Do you think the decision to secede should have been put to popular vote? Why or why not? *possible answer—yes, decision meant a major change in people's lives*

🗳 Quick Facts Transparency: Causes of Secession

MISCONCEPTION ///ALERT

Bonded Labor . . . Modern-Day Slavery Students may believe that slavery no longer exists; however, that is not the case. Modern-day slavery often takes the form of bonded labor. In certain regions of the world such as South Asia and West Africa, people who cannot repay loans are forced or tricked into the position of bonded laborers. They must work for no pay, often for the rest of their lives. Although bonded labor is illegal in most countries today, it still exists and is considered a form of slavery. The UN Working Group on Contemporary Forms of Slavery estimated that in 1999 almost 20 million people were held in bonded labor around the world. Bonded workers are treated as property and have few rights. Some governments have been lax about enforcing laws that make the practice illegal.

Secession!

Explain What was Lincoln's view of secession? *that it was illegal*

Analyze After southern states seceded, what was the key question facing the Union? *whether the minority has the right to leave*

Develop Why do you think that northerners had such varied reactions to secession? *possible answers—it had never happened before; some just wanted the nation to be at peace; glad that the conflict might be over*

Info to Know

Harper's Weekly **on the Secession of Mississippi** The edition of *Harper's Weekly* that carried the report of Mississippi's secession had a picture of the Mississippi delegation on the cover. Jefferson Davis, head of Mississippi's state armed forces and a strong candidate for a role in a new government, was shown at the top of the picture, which was sketched by the artist Winslow Homer.

Primary Source

"I see now around me some with whom I have served long; there have been points of collision . . . I carry with me no hostile remembrance. Whatever offense I have given which has not been redressed . . . I have, Senators, in this hour of our parting, to offer you my apology for any pain which, in heat of discussion, I have inflicted . . . Mr. President, and Senators, having made the announcement which the occasion seemed to me to require, it only remains to me to bid you a final adieu."

— Jefferson Davis
resignation from Congress, January 21, 1861

Answers

Reading Like a Historian *the United States; possible answer—going to war, rather than allowing secession and the break-up of the nation*

THE EAGLE'S NEST

ANNIHILATION TO TRAITORS.

Skills FOCUS READING LIKE A HISTORIAN

The slogan about preserving the Union was a popular rallying cry in the North following secession of the southern states.
Interpreting Political Cartoons What does the eagle represent? What sort of resolution regarding secession does this cartoon suggest? Explain.

THE IMPACT TODAY

Government
In 1933 the president's inauguration was changed from March to January by the Twentieth Amendment. The change was intended to allow a new president to deal with a crisis more quickly. In 1933 the crisis was the Great Depression.

Some southerners wanted their states to issue a final set of demands to the federal government and secede only if those demands were not met. Others asked that Lincoln be given a chance to prove his claims of good intentions toward the South. The radical secessionists prevailed, however. "You might as well attempt to control a tornado as to attempt to stop them," a moderate southerner complained.

Even those who opposed secession thought united resistance to the U.S. government was important, whatever form that resistance might take. "Cooperation before secession was the first object of my desire," a Mississippi moderate noted. "Failing this I am willing to take the next best, . . . cooperation after secession." In mid-January a Georgian worried that four states had already seceded. "In order to act with them, we must secede with them," he urged.

Northern response In the North, the reaction to secession was as varied as it was in the South. Some northerners felt the nation would be better off with the slave states gone.

"If the Union can only be maintained by new concessions to the slaveholders," said African American abolitionist Frederick Douglass, "let the Union perish."

Other northerners bore southerners no ill will. They merely wanted the South to go in peace. "If the Cotton States shall become satisfied that they can do better out of the Union than in it, we insist on letting them go," wrote Horace Greeley in an editorial in the *New York Tribune*. "We hope to never live in a republic whereof one section is pinned to the residue [remainder] by bayonets."

Still other northerners worried about the long-term effects of letting secession proceed. "If any minority have the right to break up the government at pleasure, because they have not had their way, there is [the] end of all government," a northern newspaper warned. President-elect Lincoln seemed to agree. "No state can, in any way lawfully, get out of the Union, without the consent of the others," he observed in a letter to a Republican leader.

Lincoln waits In the 1800s, a president's term of office began in March, not in January as it does today. Newspapers pressed Lincoln for a public statement that would calm the nation's fears during this period. Lincoln worried that any public statement might make matters worse. Privately, however, he tried to convince southern leaders that the South had nothing to fear. He wrote to one Georgia leader:

HISTORY'S VOICES

❝Do the people of the South really entertain fears that a Republican administration would . . . interfere with their slaves, or with them about their slaves? If they do, I wish to assure you . . . that there is no cause for such fears.❞
—Letter to Alexander Stephens, December 22, 1860

Lincoln was also committed to preserving the Union. He told Republican Party leaders, "We must settle this question now, whether in a free government the minority have the right to break up the government whenever they choose."

In the meantime, the outgoing president Buchanan did little to ease the crisis. He agreed that secession was illegal. He also claimed that the Constitution gave the federal government no power to prevent it. "No state has the right to secede unless it wishes to," joked Seward of

Skills Focus: Interpreting Political Cartoons   At Level

Reading Like a Historian Skill
Keeping the Union Together

1. Have students study the political cartoon on this page. Then guide students in a discussion about the cartoon's message.

2. Organize students into mixed-ability pairs. Have them create a new cartoon that conveys the same message as the cartoon on this page, the Union view of secession.

3. Have students create a new cartoon that shows the Confederate view of secession.

4. Have volunteers display and explain their cartoons to the class. **LS** **Visual-Spatial, Verbal-Linguistic**

   Alternative Assessment Handbook, Rubric 27: Political Cartoons

Buchanan's views, adding, "It is the President's duty to enforce the laws, unless somebody opposes him."

Buchanan did take a stand, however, when South Carolina's governor demanded that all federal property within the state be turned over to state authorities. This included two island forts in Charleston Harbor, Fort Moultrie and Fort Sumter. Buchanan rejected the request but promised that he would not attempt to reinforce the forts. Meanwhile, the forts' commander moved all his troops to the stronger Fort Sumter. He believed that if war came, it would likely start in this place.

READING CHECK **Summarizing** How were feelings about secession similar in North and South?

Forming the Confederacy

In early February 1861, representatives of the seven seceded states met at Montgomery, Alabama, to form a new nation. The convention worked to have a government in place before Lincoln took office. In five days it had written a constitution and selected former Mississippi senator **Jefferson Davis** as **provisional**, or temporary, president. The convention's delegates chose Georgia's Alexander Stephens as vice president. They appointed themselves to serve as the nation's legislature until elections could be held in the fall.

The new nation's constitution was rapidly written because it was modeled on the U.S. Constitution. Two important differences existed, however. The new constitution specifically recognized and protected slavery. Secondly, it recognized the "sovereign and independent" nature of each state. In effect, the delegates created a nation like what the United States had been under the Articles of Confederation. They named their new nation the **Confederate States of America**.

Davis becomes president Jefferson Davis was at home on his plantation near Vicksburg, Mississippi, when the telegram arrived that he had been chosen to be the president of the Confederacy. He was not pleased with the news. He did not want the presidency. A sense of duty drove him to accept, however. The next day he left for Montgomery, stopping briefly at Vicksburg to bid its people goodbye.

FACES OF HISTORY

Jefferson DAVIS
1808–1899

Jefferson Davis received a classical education and graduated from West Point. He served in the U.S. Army on the frontier before moving to Mississippi to run a plantation. In 1845 Davis won a seat in the House of Representatives but resigned the next year to fight in the Mexican War. After the war, Davis served in the Senate and as secretary of war.

In 1861 Davis resigned from the Senate and was elected president of the Confederate States. He closely controlled military matters and the policies of the Confederacy. After the South's surrender, he was charged with treason and imprisoned. Two years later, the charges were dropped, and Davis was released without going to trial.

Summarizing How did Davis serve the nation before the Civil War?

HISTORY'S VOICES

❝Our safety and honor required us to dissolve our connection with the United States. I hope that our separation may be peaceful. But whether it be so or not, I am ready . . . to redeem my pledge to you and the South by shedding every drop of my blood in your cause.❞

—Jefferson Davis, February 11, 1861

Getting to Montgomery was hard because there was no direct railroad connection. Davis arrived on February 16 and took the oath of office two days later. He gave an encouraging inaugural address to an enthusiastic crowd. Privately, he worried. "We are without means, without machinery, and threatened by a powerful opposition," he wrote to his wife.

Confederate government In many ways Davis's assessment seemed accurate. His office in Montgomery was marked by a sheet of paper pinned on the door. The secretary of the treasury had to buy his own desk and chair. The new nation had no currency or even a press capable of making some. The job of printing Confederate money at first was contracted out to a company in New York.

Davis held his first cabinet meeting in a hotel room. Some of the cabinet members had opposed secession. "There is a perfect magazine [a storehouse for explosives] of discord and discontent," Mary Chesnut, the wife of a former South Carolina senator, said of the leaders of the Confederate government.

Reading Focus

❷ How and why was the Confederacy formed? *seven states joined together; wrote constitution similar to U.S. Constitution; to protect slavery, honor states' rights*

Forming the Confederacy

Identify What were the two main differences between the Union and the Confederate constitutions? *Union did not protect slavery, Confederacy did; Union represented an alliance among the states; Confederacy saw each state as sovereign and independent*

Draw Conclusions Why did Jefferson Davis think there would be problems in the Confederacy? *states not unified; lacked manufacturing and industrial base, North had means to wage war*

Make Judgments Do you think Jefferson Davis should have refused the Confederate presidency? *possible answers—yes, he did not want the job, knew it would be dangerous; no, it was his duty to serve and he was well qualified*

📰 Political Cartoons Activities for American History: Cartoon 20: The South Secedes

---

Skills Focus: Sequencing

Below Level

Reading Skill
Forming the Confederacy

1. Draw a large time line for students to see. Give the chart the title: Forming the Confederacy

2. Have the students copy the time line and add the date and a brief description of each event in the formation of the Confederate States of America. Students should begin with South Carolina's secession in December 1860 and end with President Jefferson Davis's oath of office on February 18, 1861.

3. Have volunteers complete the large class time line. Have students correct their work and keep the time lines as a study tool.

4. As an extension, have students illustrate their time lines. **LS Visual-Spatial, Logical-Mathematical**

📰 Alternative Assessment Handbook, Rubric 36: Time Lines

📄 Graphic Organizer Transparencies

Answers

Faces of History *in the U.S. Army, in Congress, and as secretary of war*

Reading Check *mixed in both the North and South; some supporting it, others opposing it*

347

3 Why did compromises and other attempts to save the Union fail? *the South was determined to promote slavery; Lincoln's election as president*

Compromise Fails

Recall What were the main provisions of the Crittenden Compromise? *ban slavery north of old Missouri Compromise line; slavery would continue south of that line*

Drawing Conclusions Why do you think the Peace Convention failed? *leaders did not represent current ideas; unable to come up with new solution to the slavery issue*

~~**Make Judgments**~~ Why do you think Lincoln's public reaction to the Crittenden Compromise differed from his private reaction to it? *possible answers—did not want to influence the vote; personally opposed to extension of slavery; feared the effect the vote would have on his presidency and his party*

📄 CRF: Biography: John Jordan Crittenden

Info to Know

Slavery in the South Just before the Civil War began, most southerners did not own slaves; about 75,000 slaveholders owned one slave; about 140,000 slaveholders owned 2 to 5 slaves; about 130,000 slaveholders owned between 6 and 19 slaves. Very few slaveholders owned more than 100 slaves, and, of the 15 slaveholders in the United States who owned more than 500 slaves, 8 lived in South Carolina.

Answers

Reading Like a Historian 1. *southerners;* **2.** *two sides have much in common*

Reading Check *seceded; representatives met to write a constitution; elected a provisional president and vice-president; appointed a temporary legislature*

348

No issue seemed too petty to debate. Less than a week after Davis's inauguration, some critics were already accusing the new congress of violating the constitution by providing the president with a house in which to live. The Confederacy did not seem to be getting off to a promising start.

READING CHECK **Sequencing** What steps did southern leaders take to create a new nation?

Compromise Fails

Even after the Confederacy had formed, the U.S. Congress made efforts to keep the Union together. In December 1860 the House and Senate had appointed a special committee to study the situation and possible solutions to it. Eventually, more than 30 plans for compromise were introduced into Congress. Some called for splitting the nation into districts. Others proposed separate presidents for the North and the South.

The Crittenden Compromise In January 1861 a plan came from Senator John Crittenden of Kentucky. The **Crittenden Compromise** proposed amending the U.S. Constitution to ban slavery north of the old Missouri Compromise line and guarantee that it would not be interfered with south of that line.

Crittenden's plan also proposed an amendment to pay slaveholders for their loss when officers were prevented from arresting escaped slaves. Another amendment would prohibit Congress from interfering with the transportation of slaves from one state to another. A final proposed amendment guaranteed that none of these amendments could ever be repealed by a future amendment.

Powerful leaders in both the North and South opposed the Crittenden Compromise. For many southerners, no compromise could undo their main reason for secession—Lincoln's election as president. "No human power can save the Union, all the cotton states will go," wrote Jefferson Davis, who was still a member of the Senate at the time. Louisiana senator Judah Benjamin agreed that "a settlement [is] totally out of our power to accomplish."

Lincoln remained publicly silent on the ideas for compromise. Privately, however,

---

PRIMARY SOURCES

Lincoln's Inaugural Address

By the time Abraham Lincoln was sworn into office, the country was already being torn apart. As the nation sat on the brink of civil war, the new president appealed to secessionists.

Lincoln warned the seceded states that he could not let them break up the nation.

"In your hands, my dissatisfied fellow-countrymen, and not in mine, is the momentous issue of civil war. The Government will not assail [attack] you. You can have no conflict without being yourselves the aggressors. You have no oath registered in heaven to destroy the Government, while I shall have the most solemn one to 'preserve, protect, and defend it.'. . . We are not enemies, but friends. We must not be enemies. Though passion may have strained it must not break our bonds of affection. The mystic chords of memory, stretching from every battlefield and patriot grave to every living heart and hearthstone all over this broad land, will yet swell the chorus of the Union, when again touched, as surely they will be, by the better angels of our nature."

Lincoln placed responsibility for the future on the South.

Lincoln reminded southerners that like northerners, their parents and grandparents had fought and died creating the nation in the American Revolution.

Skills Focus **READING LIKE A HISTORIAN**

1. **Analyzing Primary Sources** In Lincoln's view, who will be to blame if war breaks out?
2. **Evaluating Information** Why does Lincoln believe the two sides should remain together?

See Skills Handbook, pp. H28–H29

348 CHAPTER 10

Skills Focus: Identifying Problem and Solution

At Level

Reading Skill
The South Secedes

1. Tell students that in 1861, state legislators met in Georgia and Louisiana and decided to secede from the Union. Guide students in a discussion about the events leading up to secession, including the Compromise of 1850. Focus the discussion on how the state legislators might have used these events to support their belief that secession was the only choice for their state, and that it was a justifiable, constitutionally correct decision.

2. Have students prepare a speech from the legislators' point of view explaining and justifying the secession of their state from the Union. Remind students that citizens of these two states did not get to vote about the decision to secede, and that many southerners did not hold slaves. **LS Verbal-Linguistic**

📄 Alternative Assessment Handbook, Rubric 35: Solving Problems

he opposed any plan that allowed the extension of slavery. "There is no possible compromise upon it," he told one Republican in Congress. "On that point hold firm, as with a chain of steel."

In particular, Lincoln feared what effect accepting the Crittenden Compromise would have on his presidency and his party. Even the radical Seward urged him to consider it, but Lincoln refused to budge. "We have just carried an election on principles fairly stated to the people," Lincoln wrote to key Republican leaders. "If we surrender, it is the end of us."

Without the president-elect's support, the Crittenden Compromise had little chance of passage. The Republicans on the Senate special committee made sure the committee did not support it. Crittenden then took his plan directly to the Senate floor. A woman in the Senate gallery witnessed his desperate plea for the survival of the nation.

HISTORY'S VOICES

❝Mr. Crittenden spoke to-day in a trembling voice and with tearful eyes, beseeching those who could to save the Union . . . It was sad to see that old white-haired man, who had devoted his best years to the country, find himself powerless to help it [now].❞

—diary of Mrs. Eugene McLean, January 16, 1861

In the March 1861 vote, Crittenden's plan was defeated by a vote of 25–23. Although most southern senators refused to vote, all 25 "no" votes came from Republican senators.

The Peace Convention As Confederate leaders met at Montgomery, a **Peace Convention** began on February 4, 1861, in Washington, D.C. Most of the northern states were represented, as were all the remaining slave states except Arkansas. Led by the former president John Tyler, it was nicknamed the Old Gentlemen's Convention. Like Tyler, many of its members were leaders from a time that was long past in America.

After a month of debate, the best the Peace Convention could offer was a proposal much like the Crittenden Compromise. Just two days before Lincoln was to take office, the Senate rejected the Peace Convention's plan. Once again, compromise was defeated mainly by Republican votes.

Lincoln's inauguration On March 4, 1861, Abraham Lincoln became president of the United States. In his inaugural address, he quoted the provisions of the Constitution that protected slavery and offered this assurance. "I have no purpose, directly or indirectly, to interfere with the insitution of slavery in the states where it exists," he pledged. "I believe I have no lawful right to do so."

"What more does any reasonable southern man expect or desire?" asked Representative John Gilmer of North Carolina. But would Lincoln's pledge be enough to save the Union?

READING CHECK **Identifying Problems and Solutions** What were Lincoln's views on compromise?

SECTION 4 ASSESSMENT

go.hrw.com
Online Quiz
Keyword: SD7 HP10

Reviewing Ideas, Terms, and People

1. **a. Recall** Why did the states of the Lower South withdraw from the United States?
   b. Make Inferences What was the level of public support for secession in the states that seceded?
   c. Elaborate How similar were attitudes about secession in northern and southern states? How do you account for this?

2. **a. Identify** Why was **Jefferson Davis** important to the **Confederate States of America**?
   b. Compare and Contrast How was the Confederacy's government similar to and different from that of the United States?
   c. Predict How might the Confederate constitution have limited the nation's ability to handle a national crisis?

3. **a. Describe** What was the **Crittenden Compromise**?
   b. Analyze Why did attempts to find compromises to save the nation fail?

Critical Thinking

4. **Sequence** Copy the chart below and complete it to record the secession of the states of the Lower South.

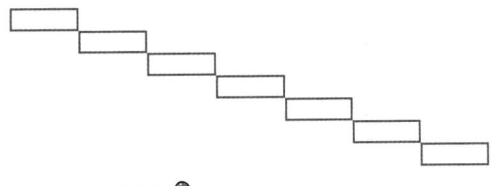

FOCUS ON WRITING

5. **Decision Making** If you had been President-elect Lincoln, would you have supported the Crittenden Compromise? Write a paragraph explaining why or why not.

Was Secession Justified?

Word Help

domestic native

incited stirred up

servile of slaves

insurrection rebellion

judicious sensible

conserve preserve

impracticable unworkable

endeavors efforts

Primary Source

"Our present political position has been achieved in a manner unprecedented in the history of nations. It illustrates the American idea that governments rest on the consent of the governed, and that it is the right of the people to alter or abolish them at will whenever they become destructive of the ends for which they were established. . . . The impartial and enlightened verdict of mankind will vindicate the rectitude of our conduct; and He who knows the hearts of men will judge the sincerity with which we have labored to preserve the Government of our fathers in its spirit."

— Jefferson Davis
Inaugural Address, 1861

Was Secession Justified?

Historical Context The documents below provide different perspectives on the secession of the southern states from the Union.

Task Examine the documents and answer the questions that follow. Then you will be asked to write an essay about secession, using facts from the documents and from the chapter to support the position you take in your thesis statement.

DOCUMENT 1

South Carolina led the way in calling for secession from the Union. In December 1860 the state's leaders issued the Declaration of Immediate Causes, spelling out their complaints and explaining why they felt that secession was the only solution.

"Thus were established the two great principles asserted by the Colonies, namely: the right of a State to govern itself; and the right of a people to abolish a Government when it becomes destructive of the ends for which it was instituted . . .

We affirm that these ends for which this Government was instituted have been defeated, and the Government itself has been made destructive of them by the action of the non-slaveholding States. Those States have assume[d] the right of deciding upon the propriety of our domestic institutions; and have denied the rights of property established in fifteen of the States and recognized by the Constitution; they have denounced as sinful the institution of slavery . . . They have encouraged and assisted thousands of our slaves to leave their homes; and those who remain, have been incited . . . to servile insurrection . . .

We, therefore, the People of South Carolina, by our delegates in Convention assembled, appealing to the Supreme Judge of the world for the rectitude [rightness] of our intentions, have solemnly declared that the Union heretofore existing between this State and the other States of North America, is dissolved, and that the State of South Carolina has resumed her position among the nations of the world, as a separate and independent State; with full power to . . . contract alliances, establish commerce, and to do all other acts and things which independent States may of right do."

350 CHAPTER 10

DOCUMENT 2

In the months after South Carolina's secession, other slave states followed suit. Several, like Tennessee, cautiously waited until fighting had broken out before seceding. Four slave states never left the Union.

The editorial below appeared in the Tennessee newspaper *The Republican Banner* in January 1861. It urged caution and support for the Crittenden Compromise, which proposed to restore the division between slave and free states that had been established in the Missouri Compromise.

"That the sympathies of Tennessee are emphatically Southern, no one will deny. She will take no course . . . against the interest of her Southern sisters. But the question for her to decide—and it is a question upon which hangs her own and the destiny of the South and the Union—is what course is most judicious, most patriotic, and best calculated to conserve the interests of her Southern sisters, and if possible preserve the Union? Upon this question there is a difference of opinion. Some are for . . . secession. Others for maintaining our present attitude, prepared, when the time comes, to act as mediators upon the basis of the Crittenden [Compromise]. If the policy of the former party is pursued, we lose the advantage of our position as pacificators [peacemakers], and gain nothing that we could not gain at a future time, when it shall be demonstrated, as it unfortunately may be, that a settlement is impracticable. We are therefore opposed to hasty action. We do not think the friends of a fair and honorable settlement, in the seceding States, desire Tennessee to follow their example until all honorable endeavors to secure such a settlement are exhausted . . . "

Skills Focus: Making Oral Presentations   At Level

Reading Like a Historian Skill

The Secession Debate

1. Divide the class into two halves. Have one half represent the southerners in 1860 who want to do whatever is necessary to avoid secession. Have the other half represent southerners in 1860 who feel that the only solution left is secession.

2. Conduct a classroom debate on the desirability of seceding. Tell students that this debate should be about states' rights, not slavery. Debaters should consider the possible economic, political, and social consequences of secession.

3. Have students write a letter to the editor of a southern newspaper in 1860. Students should either support or oppose secession and give the reasons for their positions.

4. Ask volunteers to read their letters to the class.
   LS Logical-Mathematical, Verbal-Linguistic

The following political cartoon appeared in a New York publication after seven of the southern states had seceded from the Union. Titled "Little Bo Peep and her Foolish Sheep," it portrays the seceded states as sheep who have run into the woods, only to become the prey of wolves, representing European powers. Little Bo Peep represents the United States, trying to protect her remaining sheep (states), including ones clearly labeled for slave states that were wavering, such as Virginia.

LITTLE BO-PEEP AND HER FOOLISH SHEEP.
" Little Bo-peep, she lost her sheep, | Let 'em alone, and they'll all come home,
And didn't know where to find 'em ; | With their tails hanging down behind 'em."

Skills FOCUS READING LIKE A HISTORIAN

1. a. Identify Refer to Document 1. What are the two great rights it says were established by the colonies?
b. Analyze What is the main argument in favor of South Carolina's secession?
c. Evaluate Which southerners would be most attracted, and least attracted, to the argument in this document?

2. a. Describe Refer to Document 2. What role does the newspaper believe Tennessee should play in the crisis?
b. Analyze According to the writer, what is the main goal that needs to be achieved?

3. a. Identify Refer to Document 3. What is happening to the "foolish sheep"?
b. Interpret What message is the artist sending in drawing this cartoon?

4. Document-Based Essay Question Consider the question below and form a thesis statement. Using examples from Documents 1, 2, and 3, create an outline and write a short essay supporting your position. Was secession justified?

See **Skills Handbook**, pp. H28–H29, H31

Skills Focus: Analyzing Primary Sources   At Level

Reading Like a Historian Skill
The Constitutionality of Secession

1. Tell students that when Virginia ratified the Constitution of the United States, it reserved the right to rescind the ratification "whensoever the same shall be perverted to their injury or oppression." According to Article IV, Section 2 of the Constitution, "The Citizens of each State shall be entitled to all Privileges and Immunities of Citizens in the several States."

2. Guide the class in a discussion of the constitutional issues involved in secession. If Virginia reserved the right to secede when it approved the Constitution, does Article IV give other states the same right? If the states had the right to secede, was the federal government behaving in bad faith by not allowing this?

3. Ask students whether or not the states today should be able to secede. Have students write a brief essay arguing either for or against a state's right to secede. Ask volunteers to share their essays with the class. **LS Logical-Mathematical, Verbal-Linguistic**

Info to Know

The Legality of Secession In 1869, just four years after the Civil War ended, the Supreme Court was asked to decide the meaning of "state" and of "Union" in *Texas* v. *White*. The case concerned U.S. bonds that had been sold off by the Confederate government of Texas during the Civil War. The Court ruled that the actions of the Confederate government were irrelevant because secession itself was unconstitutional. Chief Justice Salmon P. Chase explained the decision: "When, therefore, Texas became one of the United States, she entered into a [sic] indissoluble relation. All the obligations of perpetual union, and all the guaranties of republican government in the Union, attached at once to the State. The Act which consummated her admission into the Union was something more than a compact; it was the incorporation of a new member into her political body. And it was final."

Texas v. *White* in *Congressional Quarterly's Guide to the Supreme Court*, p. 296

Answers

Reading Like a Historian
1. a. *the right of a state to govern itself; the right of a people to abolish a destructive government;* **b.** *that the government has violated the property rights of the states by denouncing slavery, encouraging slaves to run away, and inciting the remaining slaves to revolt;* **c.** *most strongly appeal—those who own slaves; least influenced—those who do not own slaves; slaves themselves;* **2. a.** *should act as a mediator and attempt to secure a compromise; should only secede after all other avenues have been exhausted;* **b.** *the conservation of southern interests;* **3. a.** *They are running into the woods, where wolves await them.* **b.** *that the seceding states are running away from the protection of the Union and will be vulnerable to attack by European powers;* **4.** *possible answers—yes, because the Declaration of Independence gives the states the right to separate from an oppressive government; no, because the states cannot separate from the Union just because they do not agree with some of its policies*

Visual Summary

Review and Inquiry Review the information in the web diagram with students. Then have students work in pairs to create an antislavery newspaper headline for each of the bulleted items. When students have written their headlines, have them create a political cartoon that illustrates the issue in each headline. Have volunteers share their headlines and cartoons with the class.

Quick Facts Transparency: The Nation Splits Apart

Reviewing Key Terms and People

1. arsenal
2. radical
3. Compromise of 1850
4. Fugitive Slave Act
5. Free-soilers
6. guerrilla war
7. *Dred Scott* decision
8. platform
9. James Buchanan
10. John Brown
11. Jefferson Davis
12. nativism
13. civil war
14. Abraham Lincoln
15. Crittenden Compromise
16. Kansas-Nebraska Act

Comprehension and Critical Thinking

17. **a.** balance of power between North and South, antislavery and proslavery groups
   b. many northerners resisted law, which angered southerners
   c. Douglas would benefit from creation of a northern route for the proposed transcontinental railroad

18. **a.** For four months in 1856, proslavery and antislavery forces battled over the territory, looting and destroying property. In September, federal troops brought an end to the major fighting, but a guerrilla war continued.

Visual Summary: The Nation Splits Apart

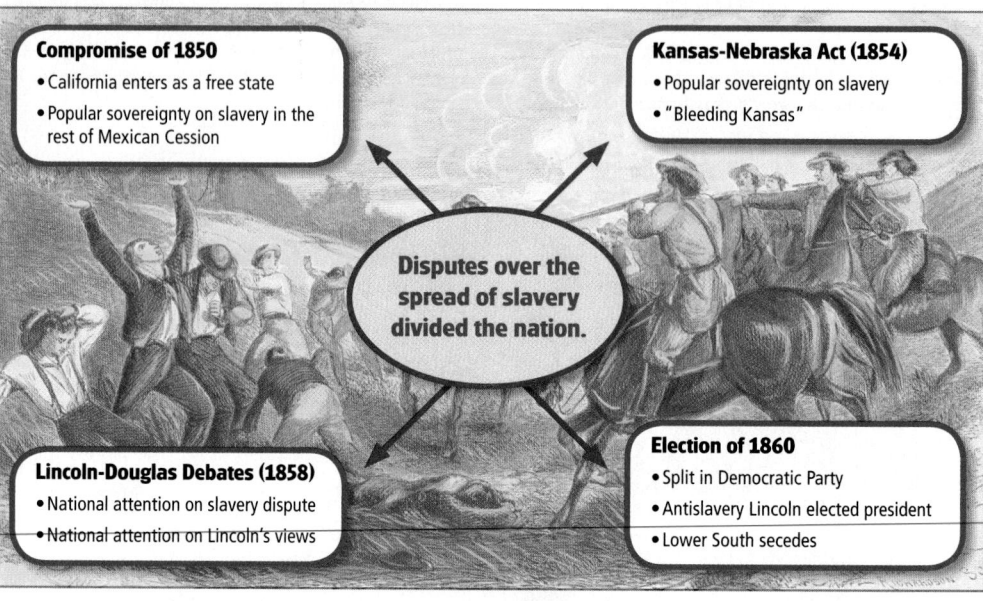

Compromise of 1850
- California enters as a free state
- Popular sovereignty on slavery in the rest of Mexican Cession

Kansas-Nebraska Act (1854)
- Popular sovereignty on slavery
- "Bleeding Kansas"

Disputes over the spread of slavery divided the nation.

Lincoln-Douglas Debates (1858)
- National attention on slavery dispute
- National attention on Lincoln's views

Election of 1860
- Split in Democratic Party
- Antislavery Lincoln elected president
- Lower South secedes

Reviewing Key Terms and People

Complete each sentence by filling in the blank with the correct term or person.

1. An army's guns are stored in an _____ .
2. A person who holds extreme views is sometimes called a _____.
3. The _____ resulted from proposals made by Henry Clay to settle the nation's issues regarding slavery.
4. The _____ made it illegal to help runaway slaves.
5. _____ were people who wanted land to be closed to the practice of slavery.
6. A _____ involves fighting from ambush and surprise attacks.
7. The Supreme Court's ruling in the _____ widened the nation's divisions over slavery.
8. A _____ is a statement of principles.

9. In 1856, the divisions between North and South helped _____ _____ to win a three-way election for president.
10. _____ _____ was a radical settler who thought that abolitionists should use violence.
11. The convention that formed the Confederate States of America elected _____ _____ as the new nation's first president.
12. A person who supports _____ is opposed to immigrants and to immigration.
13. Fighting that involves opposing groups of citizens from the same country is called a _____ .
14. The presidential candidate who received the least votes in the South in the election of 1860 was _____ _____.
15. The _____ proposed protecting slavery by restoring the Missouri Compromise.
16. The _____ , which would have allowed slavery in Kansas, widened sectional divisions.

---

b. the fear of southern secession and the dissolution of the Union
c. possible answers—negotiations and compromises were no longer effective; drastic action would be taken to resolve the issue

19. **a.** passage of the Kansas-Nebraska Act; renewed controversy over slavery in the territories
   b. Lincoln predicted that the Union could not endure with both free states and slave states; viewed by many slaveholders as a radical threat

c. possible answer—Lincoln received less than 40 percent of the popular vote; few southerners voted for him; Lincoln would receive limited support for his actions

20. **a.** Beginning with South Carolina, several southern states decided to secede.
   b. Lincoln opposed any plan that allowed the extension of slavery, and he feared the effect of the Crittenden Compromise on his presidency and Republican Party.
   c. mixed; except for South Carolina, state convention delegates did not unanimously vote for secession

History's Impact video program
Review the video to answer the closing question:
What immediate effect did the Dred Scott decision have on the United States?

Comprehension and Critical Thinking

SECTION 1 (pp. 322–328)

17. a. Identify What issue was behind the question of the expansion of slavery after the Mexican War?

b. Analyze How did the Fugitive Slave Act cause more divisions between the North and South?

c. Evaluate What were Stephen Douglas's motives in pushing through the Kansas-Nebraska Act?

SECTION 2 (pp. 329–335)

18. a. Describe Give a description of the civil war that developed in Kansas.

b. Draw Conclusions What underlying fear caused voters to turn to James Buchanan for president in the election of 1856?

c. Predict How did John Brown's raid foreshadow future events?

SECTION 3 (pp. 337–343)

19. a. Recall Why did Abraham Lincoln re-enter politics after his second retirement?

b. Analyze How did Lincoln's acceptance speech for the Republican nomination for the U.S. Senate create a national issue?

c. Predict Why would the circumstances of Lincoln's election as president 1860 suggest major problems in the future?

SECTION 4 (pp. 344–349)

20. a. Describe What happened to the Union after the election of Abraham Lincoln as president?

b. Draw Conclusions Why didn't Lincoln support the Crittenden Compromise?

c. Evaluate How strong was the movement for secession on the South? Explain.

Using the Internet

go.hrw.com
Practice Online
Keyword: SD7 CH10

21. Harriet Beecher Stowe's novel *Uncle Tom's Cabin* inflamed passions on both sides before the Civil War. Using the keyword above, find excerpts from the book that you think help explain its impact on people of the 1850s. Write a review in which you analyze whether Stowe was concerned with accuracy in the characters and events she created.

Analyzing Primary Sources

Reading Like a Historian In 1859 Texas governor Sam Houston made a speech opposing secession.

> ❝You may, after the sacrifice of countless millions of treasure and hundreds of thousands of lives, as a bare possibility, win Southern independence . . . But I doubt it . . . the North is determined to preserve this Union.❞
>
> —Sam Houston, 1859

22. Identify What sacrifice is Houston referring to?

23. Make Inferences Why is Houston convinced that secession cannot succeed?

Critical Reading

Read the passage in Section 2 that begins with the heading "The Sack of Lawrence." Then answer the questions that follow.

24. According to the passage, the attack on the free-soil government of Kansas was set off by remarks made by

  A. William Seward.

  B. Franklin Pierce.

  C. John Brown.

  D. Charles Sumner.

25. In the last paragraph in this section, the term *barbarians* means

  A. illegal voters.

  B. fighters who conduct guerrilla war.

  C. people who act in an uncivilized manner.

  D. persons who support slavery.

WRITING FOR THE SAT

Think about the following issue:

Congress hoped that the Compromise of 1850 would settle disagreements between the North and South and keep the Union together.

26. Assignment: Did the Compromise of 1850 have a chance of succeeding? Write a short essay in which you develop your position on this issue. Support your point of view with reasoning and examples from your reading and studies.

Answers

Using the Internet

21. Go to the HRW Web site and enter the keyword shown to access a rubric for this activity.

KEYWORD: SD7 CH10

Analyzing Primary Sources

22. people's lives and money

23. because the North is determined to keep the Union together regardless of southern opposition

Critical Reading

24. B

25. C

Writing for the SAT

26. possible answers—yes, it was fair to both pro- and antislavery groups, was democratic in that it allowed voters to decide issue; might have maintained balance between North and South; no—issue of slavery would not go away, regardless of the compromise; slavery was immoral and had to end
A rubric for this activity can be found in the Chapter Resource File: Writing for the SAT: John Brown's Raid

History's Impact Video Program

led to increasing division over slavery

Review and Assessment Resources

Review and Reinforce

- CRF: Chapter Review Activity
- Quick Facts Transparencies: Terms of the Compromise of 1850, Effects of the *Dred Scott* Decision, Effects of John Brown's Raid, Causes of Secession, The Nation Splits Apart
- Spanish Chapter Summaries Audio CD Program
- Online Chapter Summaries in Spanish
- OSP Holt PuzzlePro; Quiz Show for ExamView
- Quiz Game CD-ROM

Assess

- PASS: Chapter Test, Forms A and B
- Alternative Assessment Handbook
- OSP ExamView Test Generator, Chapter Test
- Differentiated Instruction Modified Worksheets and Tests CD-ROM: Chapter Test
- HOAP Holt Online Assessment Program (in the Premier Online Edition)

Reteach/Intervene

- Interactive Reader and Study Guide
- Differentiated Instruction Teacher Management System: Lesson Plans for Differentiated Instruction
- Differentiated Instruction Modified Worksheets and Tests CD-ROM: Chapter Test
- Interactive Skills Tutor CD-ROM

go.hrw.com
Online Resources
KEYWORD: SD7 CH10

Chapter 11 Planning Guide

The Civil War

Chapter Overview	Reproducible Resources	Technology Resources
CHAPTER 11 pp. 354–399 **Overview:** In this chapter, students will analyze the technologies and strategies used to fight the Civil War, the soldiers who fought, and the effects the war had on the nation.	**Differentiated Instruction Teacher Management System:*** • Instructional Benchmarking Guides • Lesson Plans for Differentiated Instruction **Interactive Reader and Study Guide:** Chapter Summary* **Chapter Resource File:*** • Focus on Writing: The Emancipation Proclamation • Social Studies Skills Activity: Identifying Cause and Effect • Chapter Review Activity **American History Outline Maps** **Pre-AP Activities Guide for American History***	**Live Ink® Online Reading Help** **Student Edition on Audio CD Program** **Differentiated Instruction Modified Worksheets and Tests CD-ROM** **Interactive Skills Tutor CD-ROM** **United States History Primary Source Library CD-ROM** **Power Presentations with Video CD-ROM** **History's Impact: American History Video Program (VHS/DVD):** The Civil War **Online Chapter Summaries in Spanish**
Section 1: **Preparing for War** **The Main Idea:** The attack on Fort Sumter led both the North and the South to prepare for war in earnest.	**Differentiated Instruction Teacher Management System:** Section 1 Lesson Plan* **Interactive Reader and Study Guide*** **Chapter Resource File***	**Daily Bellringer Transparency:** Section 1* **Map Transparency:** Secession, 1860–1861* **Daily Test Practice Transparency:** Section 1*
Section 2: **Fighting Erupts** **The Main Idea:** Widespread fighting occurred during the first two years of the Civil War.	**Differentiated Instruction Teacher Management System:** Section 2 Lesson Plan* **Interactive Reader and Study Guide*** **Chapter Resource File***	**Daily Bellringer Transparency:** Section 2* **Map Transparencies:** The War in the West 1862–1863*, The War in the East 1861–1863* **Daily Test Practice Transparency:** Section 2*
Section 3: **The War Behind the Lines** **The Main Idea:** The Civil War created hardships, challenges, and opportunities for people in the North and the South.	**Differentiated Instruction Teacher Management System:** Section 3 Lesson Plan* **Interactive Reader and Study Guide*** **Chapter Resource File***	**Daily Bellringer Transparency:** Section 3* **Daily Test Practice Transparency:** Section 3*
Section 4: **The War Continues** **The Main Idea:** Important fighting occurred in all sections of the country as well as at sea.	**Differentiated Instruction Teacher Management System:** Section 4 Lesson Plan* **Interactive Reader and Study Guide*** **Chapter Resource File***	**Daily Bellringer Transparency:** Section 4* **Interactive Map:** Three Days at Gettysburg **Map Transparency:** Three Days at Gettysburg* **Daily Test Practice Transparency:** Section 4*
Section 5: **The Final Phase** **The Main Idea:** Southerners continued to hope for victory in 1864, but military and political events caused those hopes to fade.	**Differentiated Instruction Teacher Management System:** Section 5 Lesson Plan* **Interactive Reader and Study Guide*** **Chapter Resource File***	**Daily Bellringer Transparency:** Section 5* **Map Transparency:** Final Campaigns 1864–1865* **Daily Test Practice Transparency:** Section 5*

go.hrw.com	Print Resource	Transparency
 **LS** Learning Styles	 Audio CD	CD-ROM
Video	**SE** Student Edition	**TE** Teacher's Edition

OSP One-Stop Planner CD-ROM

*also on One-Stop Planner CD-ROM

Review, Assessment, Intervention

 Quick Facts Transparencies: The Generals, Causes and Effects of the Civil War, The Civil War

 Spanish Chapter Summaries Audio CD Program

Progress Assessment Support System (PASS): Chapter Test*

 Differentiated Instruction Modified Worksheets and Tests CD-ROM: Modified Chapter Test

OSP **One-Stop Planner CD-ROM:** ExamView Test Generator (English/Spanish)

HOAP **Holt Online Assessment Program (HOAP),** in the Premier Online Edition.

 PASS: Section 1 Quiz*

 Online Quiz: Section 1

Alternative Assessment Handbook

 PASS: Section 2 Quiz*

Online Quiz: Section 2

Alternative Assessment Handbook

PASS: Section 3 Quiz*

Online Quiz: Section 3

Alternative Assessment Handbook

PASS: Section 4 Quiz*

Online Quiz: Section 4

Alternative Assessment Handbook

PASS: Section 5 Quiz*

Online Quiz: Section 5

Alternative Assessment Handbook

 **NC** RESOURCES

The following resources were developed to help North Carolina educators teach the standards and objectives of North Carolina's eleventh grade standard course of study in United States history.

• United States history EOC Test Prep Workbook
• Teacher's Support System
• North Carolina One-Stop Planner

And be sure to direct your students to **go.hrw.com** for online access to the EOC Test Prep Workbook.

go.hrw.com
EOC Test Prep
KEYWORD: SE7 NC

Holt Online Learning

go.hrw.com
Teacher Resources
KEYWORD: SD7 TEACHER

go.hrw.com
Student Resources
KEYWORD: SD7 CH11

• Document-based Questions
• Interactive Multimedia Activities

• Current Events
• Chapter-based Internet Activities
• and more!

Holt Premier
Online Student Edition

Complete online support for interactivity, assessment, and reporting

• Interactive Maps and Notebook
• Standardized Test Prep
• Homework Practice and Research Activities Online

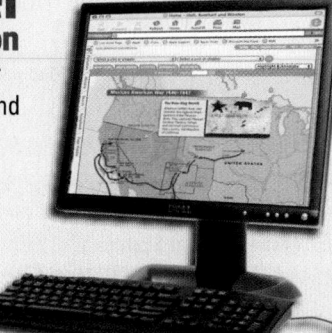

CHAPTER 11 PLANNING GUIDE

The Big Picture
Edward L. Ayers

Preparing for War Soon after Lincoln's inauguration, he learned that the supplies at Fort Sumter were about to run out. After the Confederates fired on the ship that brought supplies, Lincoln called for volunteers to defend the United States. The Upper South slaveholding states had to decide where their loyalties lay. Virginia, Arkansas, Tennessee, and North Carolina went with the Confederacy; Maryland, Missouri, and Kentucky stayed in the Union. The evenly balanced sides sought to take advantage of their strengths, with the North relying on its navy and the South relying on defensive war and the power of cotton to win allies.

Fighting Erupts Both the North and the South scrambled to mobilize as many men as possible. The United States succeeded early in the war in controlling the rivers of the South and took massive amounts of territory in Tennessee and Louisiana. In Virginia, however, the Confederacy checked the efforts of the United States to drive the war to an early victory.

Behind the Lines African Americans were eager to fight for the Union. When they were finally permitted to do so in early 1863, they made an immediate and enduring impact. The Emancipation Proclamation changed a war for union into a war to destroy slavery.

A Widespread War The Civil War stretched from the ports of Virginia and South Carolina to California and New Mexico. In 1863 the United States won major victories in Vicksburg, Gettysburg, and Chattanooga, but the Confederacy showed few signs of giving up.

The Final Phase Grant and Lee fought one horrible battle after another against each other in Virginia. After Sherman's march and Lincoln's re-election in the fall of 1864, however, the Confederacy saw its hopes fade and its prospects darken. In the spring of 1865, Robert E. Lee surrendered.

Recent Scholarship

Lee and the Confederacy Why did the North win the Civil War? To many people, the answer seems obvious: more men, more guns, and more factories. But Gary Gallagher, a leading historian of the war, reminds us in *The Confederate War* (1997) that the Confederacy fought for a remarkably long time, and several times came close to defeating its larger and better-equipped foe. Focusing on the centrality of Robert E. Lee and his Army of Northern Virginia, Gallagher shows that the army itself became, for many white southerners, the embodiment of the Confederacy. As long as Lee was in the field, the nation lived. Gallagher's brisk analysis helps frame important issues.

Differentiating Instruction

 Differentiated Instruction Teacher Management System
- Lesson Plans for Differentiated Instruction
- Differentiated Instructional Benchmarking Guides
- Interactive Reader and Study Guide

 Spanish Chapter Summaries Audio CD Program

 Online Chapter Summaries in Spanish

Student Edition on Audio CD Program

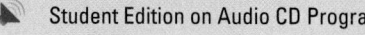 Differentiated Instruction Modified Worksheets and Tests CD-ROM
- Vocabulary Flash Cards
- Modified Vocabulary Builder Activities
- Modified Chapter Review Activity
- Modified Chapter Test

OSP One-Stop Planner CD-ROM
- ExamView Test Generator (English and Spanish)
- PuzzlePro
- Quiz Show for ExamView
- Transparencies and Videos

TE Differentiated Activities in the Teacher's Edition
- The Anaconda Plan, p. 360
- The Battle of Shiloh, p. 366
- The Mississippi River Campaign, p. 367
- Wartime Medicine, p. 374
- Prison Camps, p. 375
- The Civil War at Sea, p. 381
- Battle of Gettysburg, p. 384
- Grant versus Lee, p. 391
- Confederate Hopes Fade, p. 393

Reading Like a Historian
Sam Wineburg

The Problem with Words

A colleague who teaches in Ireland once told me about a class in which he gave students a document written by England's Queen Elizabeth I (1533–1603). In it, Elizabeth refers to her Irish subjects as "mere Irish." Never missing an opportunity to take umbrage, students interpreted this as an insult. They understood mere as "insignificant," as in "a mere drop in the ocean" or a "mere pittance."

"Mere," however, has a long and distinguished history. The *Oxford English Dictionary* lists the use "mere wine" from 1545, when mere meant "pure or not mixed with water." Applied to people, the OED explicitly lists the entry "mere Irish" but adds this warning: "now often misunderstood as term of disparagement."

Historical Meaning

Words have histories, which makes understanding primary sources particularly difficult. Just think how hard it would be if we stopped at every word to investigate its historical meaning. Reading would be so tedious that it would hardly be worth the trouble. On the other hand, the assumption that words have fixed meanings across time also gets us into trouble. How do we get around this dilemma?

Consider an address Abraham Lincoln delivered before a group of free black men at the White House on August 15, 1862, some 16 months into the war. The topic under discussion was a proposal to establish a colony for freed blacks in Central America, an idea Lincoln had long favored and which Congress had approved, allocating $600,000 toward it. The president said, "It is exceedingly important that we have men at the beginning [of establishing the colony] capable of thinking as White men, and not those who have been systematically oppressed."

The Dilemma

Here the dilemma over words confronts us directly: What did Lincoln mean when he claimed—in front of his black audience—that the colony needed men "capable of thinking as White men"? Was his audience aghast at the insult, or did the phrase pass unnoticed because it was widely understood by his audience in a way that now escapes us? As eavesdroppers on a conversation that occurred 150 years ago, how can we ever be sure?

Several years ago I presented this dilemma to a historian who had written several books on Lincoln. I asked this expert to read Lincoln's address and to "think aloud" as he did so. As expected, he alighted on "capable of thinking as White men," calling it "an unfortunate choice of words" and speculating that Lincoln was using the term "White men" synonymously with "free men."

How to Make Judgments

He then paused to explain to me that we had two choices for judging Lincoln, either using the measuring stick of "present day standards" or appealing to what he called the "historical way." Using the former gauge, Lincoln surely exposed himself to criticism—guilty as charged of using injudicious language.

What about the "historical way"? Choosing this path means that we have to ask not what these words mean to us but what they might have meant to Lincoln in 1862. If in Lincoln's world, the word "white" was widely equated with "free," then the president can hardly be blamed for using a phrase whose meaning was clear to his listeners.

Linguistic Context

The historian described a way of thinking about context—a linguistic context—novel to most students but not altogether different from the use of the *Oxford English Dictionary* above. He suggested that we should examine the literature of abolitionists in the 1800s—both black and white. If we found that "White men" was widely equated with "free men" it would be unfair to indict Lincoln for using the linguistic tools of his world.

This is not only a problem when thinking about Lincoln. It is, as someone from 1545 might say, a "mere problem" for all historical research. Words have contexts too.

Standards Focus

Social Studies Competency Goals
Goal 3 The learner will analyze the issues that led up to the Civil War, the effects of the war, and the impact of Reconstruction on the nation.
3.04, 3.05

The Big Idea and Essential Questions

To foster student understanding of this chapter's big idea, design your lesson to address each section's essential question.

Big Idea The Civil War resulted in the preservation of the United States and the freedom of African Americans, but at a staggering cost, both in terms of lives lost and destruction of property.

Essential Questions

1. What event led the North and South to prepare for war in earnest?

2. What were the significant events of the first two years of the Civil War?

3. How did the Civil War affect people in the North and South?

4. What were the important land and sea battles of the second half of the Civil War?

5. Why did Southerners begin to lose hope for victory in 1864?

Key to Differentiating Instruction

Below Level

Basic-level activities designed for all students encountering new material

At Level

Intermediate-level activities designed for average students

Above Level

Challenging activities designed for honors and gifted-and-talented students

Standard English Mastery

Activities designed to improve standard English usage

354 CHAPTER 11

CHAPTER
11
1861–1865

The CIVIL WAR

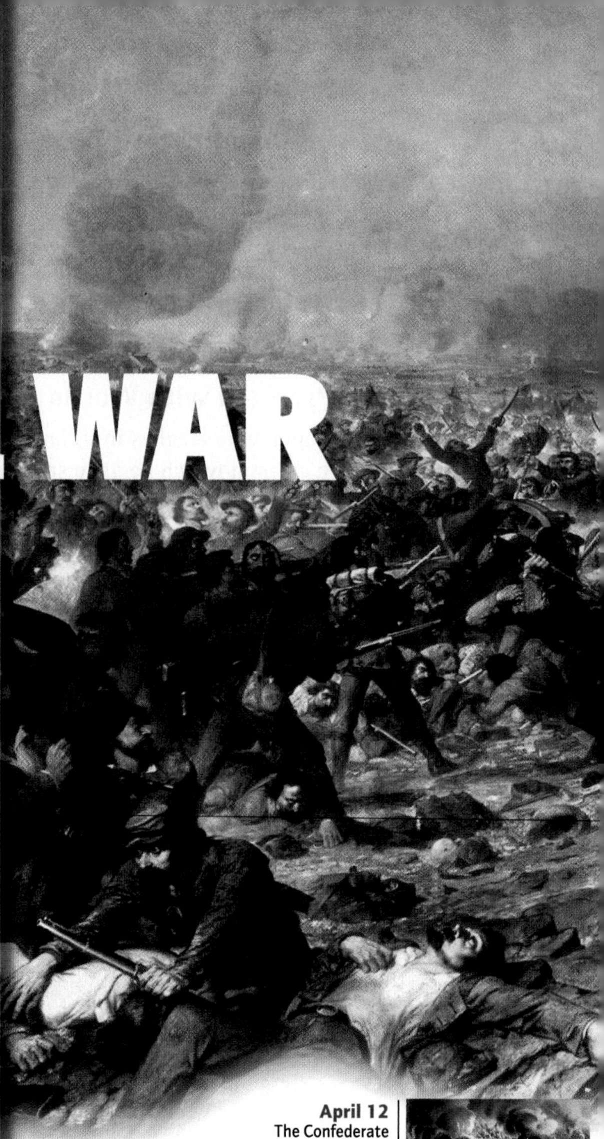

THE BIG PICTURE The Civil War resulted in freedom for some 4 million enslaved people and the preservation of a nation. The costs were staggering—more than 600,000 lives lost and about $5 billion in property damaged or destroyed.

North Carolina Standards

Social Studies Objectives
3.03 Identify political and military turning points of the Civil War and assess their significance to the outcome of the conflict.

Language Arts Objectives
5.01 Interpret the significance of literary movements as they have evolved through the literature of the United States by:
- evaluating the literary merit and/or historical significance of a work from Colonial Literature, the Romantic Era, Realism, the Modern Era, and Contemporary Literature.

Skills FOCUS   READING LIKE A HISTORIAN

Peter Frederick Rothermel completed this painting of Pickett's Charge, part of a bloody battle in Gettysburg, Pennsylvania, in 1871. The painting, which hangs in the state museum, is 32 feet wide and more than 16 feet high. **Interpreting Visuals** What impact do you think seeing this painting on such a large scale would have? Explain.

See Skills Handbook, p. H30

U.S.

World

April 12 The Confederate bombardment of Fort Sumter became the opening engagement of the Civil War.

1861

1861 Louis Pasteur invented pasteurization.

Benito Juárez elected president of Mexico.

354

Introduce the Chapter

At Level

Chapter Main Ideas

Section 1 The attack on Fort Sumter led both the North and the South to prepare for war in earnest.

Section 2 Widespread fighting occurred during the first two years of the Civil War.

Section 3 The Civil War created hardships, challenges, and opportunities for people in the North and the South.

Section 4 Important fighting occurred in all sections of the country as well as at sea.

Section 5 Southerners continued to hope for victory in 1864, but military and political events caused those hopes to fade.

January 1
President Lincoln issues the Emancipation Proclamation.

July 4
Confederate stronghold of Vicksburg surrenders after a siege.

November 15
Sherman burns Atlanta and begins March to the Sea.

April 9
Lee surrenders to Grant at Appomattox.

| 1862 | 1863 | 1864 | 1865 |

1863
French troops capture Mexico City and install Austria's Archduke Maximilian as emperor.

The International Red Cross is established.

1864
Denmark surrenders disputed territory to Prussia and Austria.

1865
British surgeon Joseph Lister develops the use of antiseptics in surgery.

355

• Chapter Preview •

HOLT
History's Impact
► **Video Program: The Civil War**
See the Video Teacher's Guide for strategies for using the video segment.

Reading Like a Historian
New Weapons Tell students that in this chapter they will learn about the new weapons that were developed during this time, and the terrible consequences that occurred when new weapons met old-style battle tactics.

Explore the Time Line

1. When did Louis Pasteur invent the process of pasteurization? *1861*

2. In what year did President Lincoln issue the Emancipation Proclamation? *1863*

3. How much time elapsed between the burning of Atlanta and the surrender at Appomattox? *five months*

Info to Know

Response to the Fall of Fort Sumter News of the Confederate attack on Fort Sumter in April 1861 spread quickly throughout the North and the South. In the North, people were stunned by the news, and in Boston, church bells tolled sorrowfully all day. In much of the South, people celebrated. The secretary of war for the Confederacy proclaimed that the Confederate flag would "float over the dome of the old Capitol in Washington" by May.

Answers

Reading Like a Historian (p. 354)
horror or amazement at the devastation and deaths

355

Bellringer

The Inside Story. . . Use the **Daily Bellringer Transparency** to help students answer the question.

📖 Daily Bellringer Transparency, Section 1

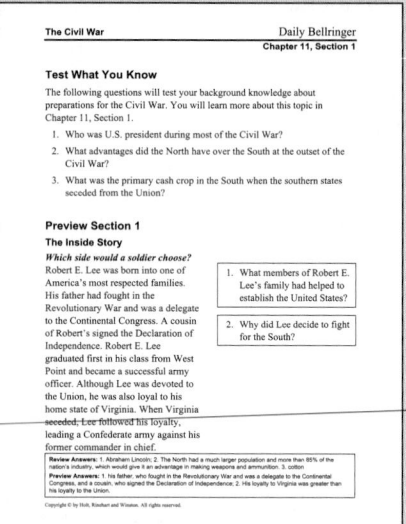

The Civil War — Daily Bellringer
Chapter 11, Section 1

Test What You Know

The following questions will test your background knowledge about preparations for the Civil War. You will learn more about this topic in Chapter 11, Section 1.

1. Who was U.S. president during most of the Civil War?
2. What advantages did the North have over the South at the outset of the Civil War?
3. What was the primary cash crop in the South when the southern states seceded from the Union?

Preview Section 1
The Inside Story

Which side would a soldier choose? Robert E. Lee was born into one of America's most respected families. His father had fought in the Revolutionary War and was a delegate to the Continental Congress. A cousin of Robert's signed the Declaration of Independence. Robert E. Lee graduated first in his class from West Point and became a successful army officer. Although Lee was devoted to the Union, he was also loyal to his home state of Virginia. When Virginia seceded, Lee followed his loyalty, leading a Confederate army against his former commander in chief.

| 1. What members of Robert E. Lee's family had helped to establish the United States? |
| 2. Why did Lee decide to fight for the South? |

Review Answers: 1. Abraham Lincoln; 2. The North had a much larger population and more than 85% of the nation's industry, which would give it an advantage in making weapons and ammunition. 3. cotton
Preview Answers: 1. his father, who fought in the Revolutionary War and was a delegate to the Continental Congress, and a cousin, who signed the Declaration of Independence. 2. His loyalty to Virginia was greater than his loyalty to the Union.

Copyright © by Holt, Rinehart and Winston. All rights reserved.

Academic Vocabulary

Review with students the high-use academic term in this section.

rebellion violent resistance to established government or authority (p. 358)

📝 CRF: Vocabulary Builder Activity, Section 1

Taking Notes

Northern Goals—keep border states in Union, preserve the Union; Northern Strategies—take advantage of lack of manufacturing resources in the South, blockade

1 Preparing for War

BEFORE YOU READ

MAIN IDEA

The attack on Fort Sumter led both the North and the South to prepare for war in earnest.

READING FOCUS

1. How did the fall of Fort Sumter lead to war?
2. Why did many northerners and southerners eagerly rush to war?
3. Why was the loyalty of the border states important, and how did Lincoln obtain it?
4. What were Union and Confederate goals and strategies for the war?

KEY TERMS AND PEOPLE

Robert Anderson
artillery
border states
martial law
Anaconda Plan
cotton diplomacy
embargo

TAKING NOTES As you read, take notes identifying and describing the goals and strategies of the North in fighting the war. Record your notes in a graphic organizer like the one shown here.

Northern Goals	Northern Strategies

The Reluctant Warrior

THE INSIDE STORY

Which side would a soldier choose? Robert E. Lee's family was one of the oldest and most distinguished families in Virginia. His father, "Light-Horse Harry" Lee, was an outstanding cavalry officer in the Revolutionary War, a delegate to the Continental Congress, and a friend of George Washington. Richard Henry Lee, a great uncle, had signed the Declaration of Independence. Robert E. Lee, born in 1807, lived up to the family's proud traditions. In 1829 he graduated second in his class from the U.S. Military Academy at West Point. In the Mexican-American War, General Winfield Scott called Lee "the very best soldier I ever saw in the field." He was handsome, good-humored, and a natural leader.

As war between the North and the South came nearer, Lee's loyalties were torn between his country and his state. From an army post in Texas, he wrote to his son: "I can anticipate no greater calamity for the country than a dissolution of the Union . . . I am willing to sacrifice every thing but honour for its preservation." His native state of Virginia had not yet seceded, but it did so after President Lincoln called for volunteers for the army in April 1861.

President Lincoln asked Lee to command the forces the federal government was gathering to put down the rebellion. Although Lee opposed secession, he refused Lincoln's offer. Saying that he could not take part in invading the South, Lee regretfully resigned from the U.S. Army and became commander of Virginia's state forces. In 1862 Lee assumed overall command of one of the Confederacy's main armies, the Army of Northern Virginia. ■

◄ **Gentleman and soldier Robert E. Lee**

356

THE MUSEUM OF THE CONFEDERACY, RICHMOND, VIRGINIA

Teach the Main Idea

At Level

Preparing For War

1. **Teach** Ask students the Reading Focus questions to teach this section.

2. **Apply** Organize the class into pairs. Have students work together to create an outline of the section, with three bullet points for each subhead. Have students use their outlines to create a chart comparing and contrasting the preparedness of the North and South for war. 🤝 **Interpersonal**

3. **Review** Have each pair share its chart with the class. Then guide students in a

discussion of the economic, military, and political differences between the North and South at the outset of the war.

4. **Practice/Homework** Have each student select one subhead from their outlines and write an editorial based on the information under the subhead. Editorials should be backed by facts and sound reasoning. 🗣️ **Verbal-Linguistic**

📝 Alternative Assessment Handbook, Rubrics 7: Charts; and 17: Letters to Editors

The Fall of Fort Sumter

On April 12, 1861, Confederate guns fired on Fort Sumter in the harbor of Charleston, South Carolina, and the Civil War began. This bloody, four-year conflict tore the nation apart and changed the course of American history.

Crisis at Fort Sumter The crisis at Fort Sumter actually began about a month earlier, on March 5. On that day, President Abraham Lincoln's first full day in office, he received a desperate message from the commander of Fort Sumter, **Robert Anderson**. Confederate leaders had demanded that he surrender the fort or face an attack. The fort's supplies were running low, and Anderson needed help.

Confederate troops had seized many forts, arsenals, and other federal government property throughout the states that had seceded. Fort Sumter was one of the few such places still in Union hands. It had become a target of the Confederate revolt. If President Lincoln turned over the fort, his surrender might reassure southerners that the North did not want war. On the other hand, it would also anger many people in the North who did not want to treat the Confederacy as if it were a separate, legitimate nation.

Lincoln made a clever decision. He would not surrender Fort Sumter. Instead, he told the Confederates that he would send only food and other nonmilitary supplies to the fort to feed the soldiers trapped there.

Now Confederate president Jefferson Davis faced a difficult decision. If he allowed the fort to be resupplied, it could hold out indefinitely and would continue to be a symbol of federal authority in the South. If he attacked the fort, however, war would begin.

The attack on Fort Sumter Davis decided to act before the supplies arrived. "You will at once demand [the fort's] evacuation," he ordered the Confederate commander in Charleston. "If this is refused, proceed, in such manner as you may determine, to reduce [destroy] it."

In the early morning of April 12, Confederate **artillery**, or large mounted guns, opened fire on the fort. The fort's defenses were no match for these massive guns, and it surrendered the next day. On April 14 the U.S. flag flying over the fort was replaced with a southern flag.

READING CHECK **Identifying the Main Idea** Why was the dispute that arose over Fort Sumter significant?

Confederates unleash cannon fire upon Fort Sumter. Captain Abner Doubleday of the U.S. Army said, "Their explosion shook the fort like an earthquake."

357

357

Reading Focus

❷ Why did many northerners and southerners eagerly rush to war? *Both sides were confident, and all expected the war to end quickly.*

The Rush to War

Recall How did Delaware and Maryland respond to Lincoln's call for troops? *ignored his request*

Analyze Why did one southern paper write that "Blood is thicker than water"? *to help convince southerners that they should side with the rest of the South in the war*

Elaborate Why do you think the South was so confident that it could easily raise an army? *possible answer— angered by Northern response, defiant, confident*

📖 CRF: Primary Source Activity: Charleston, South Carolina

The Rush to War

ACADEMIC VOCABULARY

rebellion violent resistance to established government or authority

In response to the fall of Fort Sumter, President Lincoln called for 75,000 volunteers to serve for 90 days in order to put down the <u>rebellion</u>. Lincoln's old political enemy Stephen Douglas supported this action. "There are only two sides to the question," Douglas told a huge crowd in Chicago. "There can be no neutrals in this war, only *patriots—or traitors*."

Northerners rushed to enlist in the military. A woman in Boston reported people's eagerness to fight.

HISTORY'S VOICES

❝Hastily formed companies marched to camps of rendezvous, the sunlight flashing from gun-barrel and bayonet ... Merchants and clerks rushed out from stores ... saluting them as they passed ... I had never dreamed that New England could be fired with so warlike a spirit.❞

—Mary Ashton Livermore in *Voices of the Civil War*

Reaction in the South was very different. Lincoln's call for volunteers forced the eight slave states that remained in the Union to choose a side. "We must either identify ourselves with the North or the South," a Virginia newspaper wrote. "The South must go with the South," a North Carolina paper argued. "Blood is thicker than water."

All the slave states that remained in the Union refused to provide troops to fight against fellow southerners. "Not one man will the State of Missouri furnish to carry on any such unholy

FACES OF HISTORY

Abraham LINCOLN
1809–1865

Throughout his time in office, Abraham Lincoln struggled with personal tragedies while striving to hold his family and the nation together during the Civil War. In 1862 Abraham and Mary Todd Lincoln's 11-year-old son William died of typhoid fever in the White House.

Struck with grief over the loss of their son, the Lincolns sank into depression. The first lady took William's death especially hard. The president struggled in the midst of a war that was going badly to care for his wife and to grieve the loss of his son. Lincoln often resorted to humor and storytelling to overcome his grief. He explained to a friend "if it were not for these stories [and] jokes ... I should die."

Summarize Why was Lincoln's presidency especially difficult?

358 CHAPTER 11

crusade," its governor informed the president. The governors of Arkansas, Kentucky, North Carolina, Tennessee, and Virginia sent similar replies. Delaware and Maryland ignored Lincoln's request.

In the Confederate states, anger ran high. "Lincoln may bring his 75,000 troops against us," Confederate vice president Alexander Stephens said defiantly. "We can call out a million of peoples if need be, and when they are cut down we can call another."

On April 17 Virginia seceded. In May, the states of Arkansas, Tennessee, and North Carolina followed Virginia into the Confederacy. Meanwhile, leaders on both sides wondered what Delaware, Kentucky, Maryland, and Missouri would do.

READING CHECK **Making Generalizations** How did southerners react to Lincoln's call for troops to put down the rebellion?

The Border States

Delaware, Kentucky, Maryland, and Missouri were known as **border states**—slaveholding states that remained in the Union and formed its border with the Confederacy. Delaware had few slaves and slaveholders, and most people believed it would remain in the Union. In the other border states, however, secessionist sympathies were strong. Each of these states had great geographic and military importance.

Martial law in Maryland Maryland was perhaps the most critical border state. If it seceded, Washington, D.C., would be completely surrounded by Confederate territory. When some pro-secession Marylanders began burning bridges and cutting telegraph lines to harm the Union war effort, Lincoln acted quickly to ensure they did not do more damage.

For much of 1861 federal troops guarded sites in Maryland that had military value. Maryland churches were forced to fly the American flag. Newspapers that supported secession were shut down, and their editors were jailed or banished to the South.

Lincoln also placed parts of Maryland under **martial law**. This is a type of rule in which military commanders are in control and citizens' rights and freedoms are suspended. In November 1861 the military supervised new elections

Answers

Faces of History *Lincoln had personal family tragedies to deal with in addition to the war.*

Reading Check *southerners were outraged at Lincoln's call for troops; threatened to raise more troops than the North*

358

Skills Focus: Analyzing Primary Sources

Above Level

Reading Like a Historian Skill
Maryland and the Writ of *Habeas Corpus*

Background: President Lincoln saw that pro-Confederacy activity in Maryland, including the destruction of railroad bridges and attacks on federal troops, might result in the state's secession. He authorized suspension of the writ of *habeas corpus* for parts of Maryland, so that troublemakers could be arrested and detained. Lincoln wrote: "Are all the laws but one [the right of *habeas corpus*], to go unexecuted, and the government itself go to pieces, lest that one be violated?"

Read the passage to the class, and have them copy it onto their own papers. Have each student write an opinion piece about Lincoln's action and his words. Then have students draw a political cartoon about this excerpt. Cartoons should express approval or disapproval for Lincoln. Have students read their opinion pieces and share their cartoons with the class. 🅛 **Visual-Spatial, Verbal-Linguistic**

📖 Alternative Assessment Handbook, Rubrics 14: Group Activity; and 27: Political Cartoons

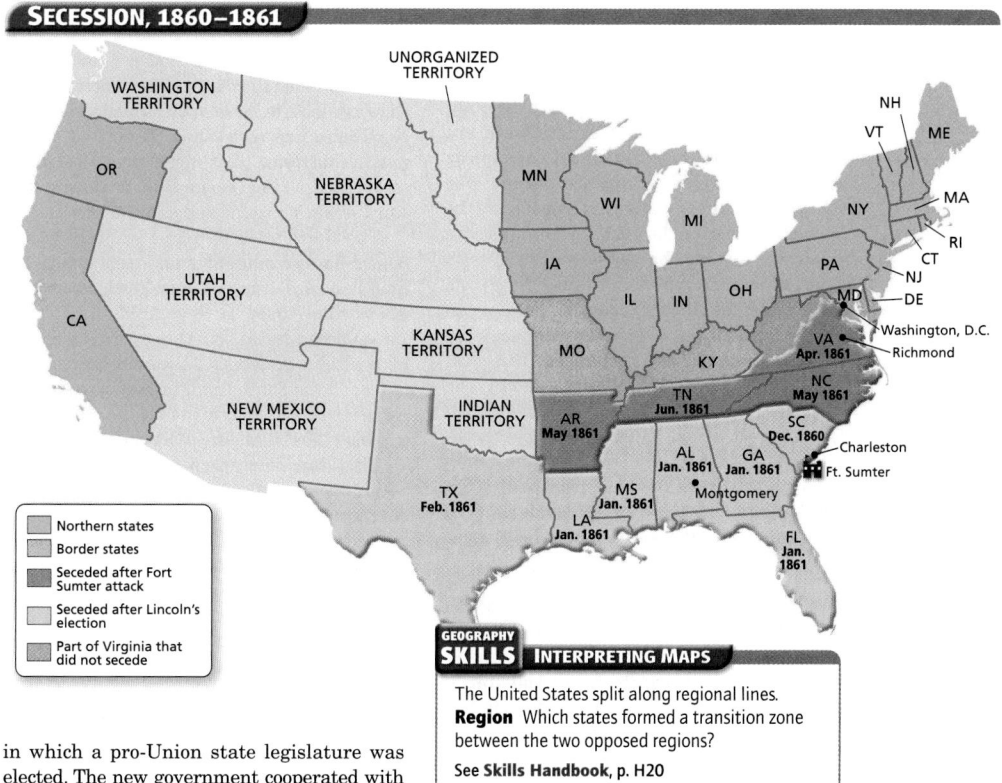

SECESSION, 1860-1861

WASHINGTON TERRITORY
OR
UTAH TERRITORY
CA
NEBRASKA TERRITORY
UNORGANIZED TERRITORY
KANSAS TERRITORY
NEW MEXICO TERRITORY
INDIAN TERRITORY
MN
WI
IA
IL
MO
AR May 1861
TX Feb. 1861
LA Jan. 1861
MS Jan. 1861
MI
IN
OH
KY
TN Jun. 1861
AL Jan. 1861
GA Jan. 1861
FL Jan. 1861
NH
VT
ME
NY
MA
CT
RI
PA
NJ
MD
DE
VA Apr. 1861
NC May 1861
SC Dec. 1860
Washington, D.C.
Richmond
Charleston
Ft. Sumter
Montgomery

Northern states
Border states
Seceded after Fort Sumter attack
Seceded after Lincoln's election
Part of Virginia that did not secede

GEOGRAPHY SKILLS INTERPRETING MAPS

The United States split along regional lines.
Region Which states formed a transition zone between the two opposed regions?

See Skills Handbook, p. H20

in which a pro-Union state legislature was elected. The new government cooperated with federal officials for the rest of the war.

Divisions in Missouri Missouri was important because it could control the lower Mississippi River. Missourians' loyalties were divided. Many government officials and the state's slaveholders supported secession, but most Missourians did not. Pro-Union citizens formed a militia and organized a rival government. Lincoln sent troops to aid the pro-Union forces against the secessionists. The Confederates aided the other side. The secessionists, however, never gained enough control over the state to withdraw it from the Union.

Divided loyalties in Kentucky Control of Kentucky meant control of some 700 miles of the Ohio River that formed its northern border. If Kentucky were in Confederate hands, a large part of the Union would be open to the threat of invasion. "I hope to have God on my side, but I must have Kentucky," Lincoln reportedly said.

Most of the state's government officials opposed secession, but many citizens favored joining the Confederacy. As a result, Kentucky's governor declared that the state would not choose a side in the war. Eventually, Kentucky sided with the Union after the state was invaded by Confederate troops in September 1861.

No matter which side the border states took, they all had some citizens fight for the North and others fight for the South. Nowhere was this more true than in Kentucky. One of Kentucky senator John Crittenden's sons was a Union general and the other was a general in the Confederate army. First Lady Mary Todd Lincoln, a Kentucky native, had four brothers in Confederate armies.

READING CHECK Summarizing Why was it important to the Union that the border states remain loyal?

❹ What were Union and Confederate goals and strategies for the war?
North—preserve the Union, blockade and seal off the South from rest of world, divide it along the Mississippi; South—be left alone with slavery, fight for home and family, use cotton as a diplomatic weapon

Goals and Strategies

Identify Who was Winfield Scott? *commander of the Union Armies; thought southerners would rise up against the Confederacy*

Analyze Why did northern newspapers advocate that Scott march into Richmond? *wanted a quick, decisive end to the war*

📋 American History Outline Maps: Union and Confederacy

Info to Know

Ersatz Commodities Ersatz is a German word meaning "substitute." As the war progressed, people in the South were deprived of many common items, and so they learned to make do with ersatz. They substituted sawdust for soap, stuffed their mattresses with tree leaves, used okra seeds to make coffee beans, and some even used gourds for cups. Women who were unable to obtain cloth were forced to make clothing from scraps of old material, blankets from carpets, and even shoes from leather saddles and parts of furniture.

Answers

Interpreting Graphs 1. *the North; population—22 percent more; bank capital—56 percent more; railroad mileage—42 percent more; farmland— 2 percent more; value of manufactured goods—84 percent more;* **2.** *possible answers—greater ability to produce weapons, more fighting men, more efficient transportation of goods and troops*

360

Goals and Strategies

As both sides prepared to fight, their leaders announced their goals for the war. Lincoln had to define the Union's goals very carefully. He knew that most northerners were not abolitionists and that they would not support a war that centered around the dispute over slavery. He also feared that making slavery the issue in the war might push the border states to secede. Instead, he asked northerners to fight for patriotic reasons—to save the Union, not to settle the slavery issue.

The South's war goals were simple: to be left alone with slavery unchanged. This position shaped the South's military strategy. The Confederates prepared to defend the South against an invasion by the North. Southerners believed that if they held off the invading armies, northerners would soon get tired of the fighting and withdraw. Many people on both sides doubted that the war would last longer than 90 days.

The North's strategy While the South could plan a defensive war, the North faced a much more difficult task. Unless southerners returned their states to the Union voluntarily, northern armies would need to invade the South in order to crush the rebellion.

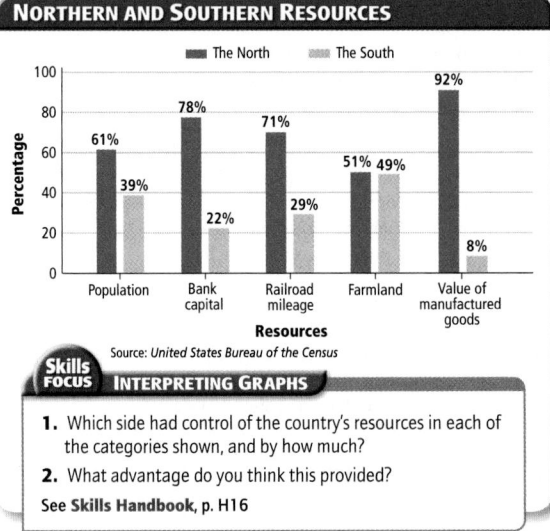

NORTHERN AND SOUTHERN RESOURCES

■ The North ▨ The South

Source: United States Bureau of the Census

Skills Focus **INTERPRETING GRAPHS**

1. Which side had control of the country's resources in each of the categories shown, and by how much?
2. What advantage do you think this provided?

See **Skills Handbook**, p. H16

360 CHAPTER 11

In many ways, however, the North was better equipped than the South for such a war. For example, the North had a much larger population than the South, so more northerners were available to serve in the armed forces. The North also had more than 85 percent of the nation's factories. This meant that the North would have a much easier time producing war supplies such as guns and ammunition.

The North tried to take advantage of the South's lack of industries and resources in its first plan for fighting the war. The Union strategy was developed by General Winfield Scott, the commander of the Union armies and a hero of the war against Mexico. Scott planned to seal off the South from the rest of the world. He believed this would end the rebellion with less bloodshed than any other means.

First, the Union navy would blockade the South's ports. This would prevent the Confederacy from importing the manufactured goods it so desperately needed. It would also prevent the South from exporting the cotton and other products it sold to the rest of the world. Then a fleet of Union gunboats would move down the Mississippi River and cut the Confederacy in two. With the Confederacy divided and weakened, Scott believed that southerners who did not support secession would rise up and overthrow the Confederate leaders.

Scott's plan had major flaws, however. For one thing, it was based on the false belief that most southerners did not support secession and were under the control of radical leaders. It would also take a great deal of time to form an effective blockade and capture and control the Mississippi River. Scott's plan failed to recognize that most northerners believed in and wanted a short war.

Northern journalists thought Scott's strategy absurd. They called it the **Anaconda Plan**, after the snake that slowly squeezes its victims to death. Instead, they urged Scott to send an army to capture the new capital of the Confederacy—Richmond, Virginia—which was close to Union territory. "On to Richmond!" northern newspapers cried, and a quick end to the war.

The South's strategy While the Confederates had far fewer resources than northerners, they essentially made up for this with their support for the cause. White southerners believed themselves to be fighting for their freedom and

Differentiating Instruction
Above Level

Advanced Learners/GATE

1. Have students analyze the information in the text about the Anaconda Plan and why General Scott thought his plan the best way to fight the war. Students may wish to conduct outside research to learn more about General Scott and his plans.

2. Have students prepare for a debate in which they analyze why Scott thought his plan was the best and why many others thought it would

not work effectively. Have volunteers debate the issue before the class. Then guide students in a discussion about Scott's reasoning. Do students agree that Scott's Anaconda Plan would not have worked? If not, why not?

LS **Logical-Mathematical, Kinesthetic**

📋 Alternative Assessment Handbook, Rubric 10: Debates

their homeland, as the Patriots had done in the Revolutionary War. They fought to defend their new nation even though three-fourths of them did not hold slaves.

"Thank God! We have a country at last," a Mississippian declared, "to live for, pray for, fight for, and, if necessary, to die for." Many southerners viewed Union troops as vandals who were being sent to plunder the South. "Our men *must* prevail in combat, or lose their property, country, freedom, everything," one Confederate wrote.

Southerners also placed great value on their bravery and fighting ability. They were convinced of their military superiority over the armies of the North.

HISTORY'S VOICES

❝The army of the South will be composed of the best material that ever made up an army; while that of Lincoln will be gathered from the sewers of the cities...who will serve for pay and will run away as soon as they can when danger threatens.❞

—*Raleigh Banner*, Raleigh, North Carolina

In fact, the South's military leaders did give the Confederacy a strong advantage over the North. Many of the nation's most talented and promising army officers were southerners. Like Robert E. Lee, most sided with their home states and fought for the Confederacy.

Cotton diplomacy Many southerners believed that their greatest strength and advantage over the North was their cotton. The South had long exported enormous amounts of cotton to the textile mills of Great Britain and France. Southerners were convinced that if war disrupted this supply, both nations would come to the Confederacy's aid to restore the cotton trade. They expected that the powerful British navy would break through any Union blockade of southern ports.

"If those miserable Yankees try to blockade us, and keep you from our cotton," one southern merchant told a British journalist, "you'll just send their ships to the bottom and acknowledge us." By "acknowledge us" he meant that Britain would recognize the Confederacy as an independent nation.

Propaganda Map

At the start of the war, General Winfield Scott developed a plan to surround the South and cut off its supplies. This 1861 map cartoon expressed confidence in Scott's plan.

Scott's strategy was called the Anaconda Plan, after the South American snake that wraps around and suffocates its prey.

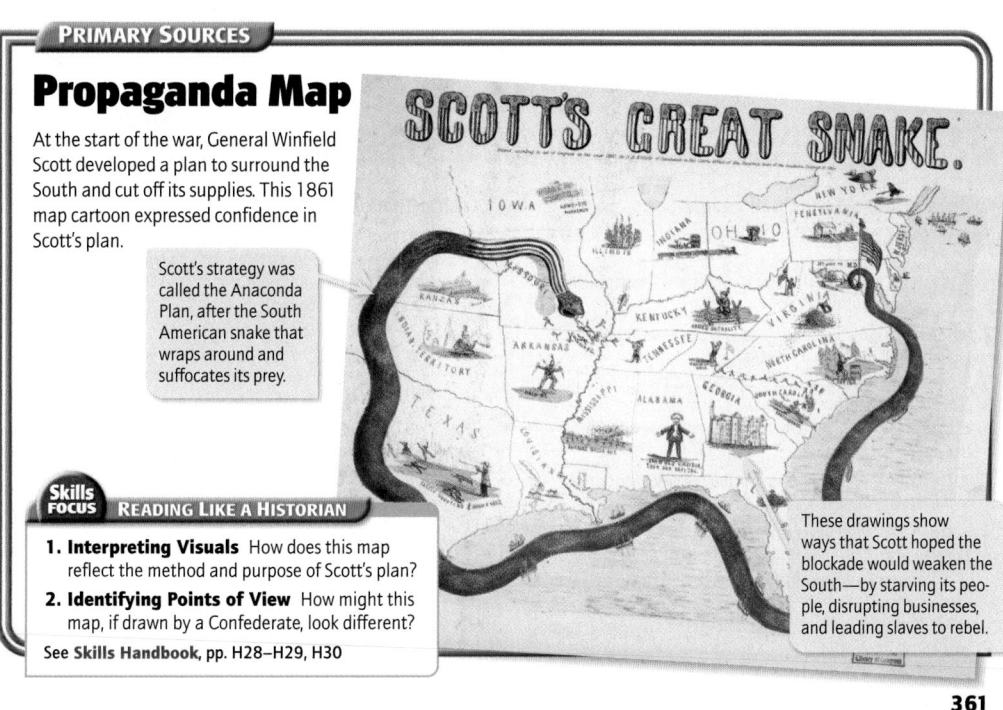

SCOTT'S GREAT SNAKE.

These drawings show ways that Scott hoped the blockade would weaken the South—by starving its people, disrupting businesses, and leading slaves to rebel.

Skills FOCUS READING LIKE A HISTORIAN

1. **Interpreting Visuals** How does this map reflect the method and purpose of Scott's plan?
2. **Identifying Points of View** How might this map, if drawn by a Confederate, look different?

See Skills Handbook, pp. H28–H29, H30

361

Goals and Strategies

Explain Why did cotton diplomacy anger the British? *resented attempt to blackmail their economy*

Describe What countries began to supply Europe with cotton? *Egypt and India*

Review & Assess

Close

Close Guide students in a discussion of the differences in attitudes about war as the North and South prepared for battle.

Review

 Online Quiz, Section 1

Daily Test Practice Transparency

Assess

SE Section 1 Assessment

Progress Assessment: Section 1 Quiz

Alternative Assessment Handbook

Reteach

Interactive Reader and Study Guide, Section 1

Interactive Skills Tutor CD-ROM

Answers

Reading Check *mill owners had stockpiled cotton, imported it from Egypt and India; refused to be blackmailed by the South*

362

Receiving foreign aid and the recognition of southern independence became important goals in the South's war strategy. Southerners believed that their cotton was the key to making this happen. "Our cotton is . . . the tremendous lever by which we can work our destiny," Confederate vice president Alexander Stephens declared in July 1861. This use of cotton as a tool of Confederate foreign policy was known as **cotton diplomacy**.

When Britain and France failed to recognize the Confederacy as an independent nation early in the war, Confederates deliberately stopped shipping cotton to those countries. The *Memphis Argus* instructed planters to **embargo**, or totally restrict, their export of cotton to markets overseas.

HISTORY'S VOICES

❝Keep every bale of cotton on the plantation. Don't send a thread to New Orleans or Memphis until England and France have recognized the Confederacy—not one thread.❞

—*Memphis Argus*, Memphis, Tennessee

"The cards are in our hands," the *Charleston Mercury* boasted, "and we intend to play them out to the bankruptcy of every cotton factory in Great Britain and France for the recognition of our independence."

Cotton diplomacy failed, however, in part because the British deeply resented the Confederacy's attempt to blackmail them. "[If southerners] thought they could extort our cooperation by the agency of king cotton, they had better think again," warned the London *Times*. "No English Parliament could do so base [dishonorable] a thing," Britain's foreign minister declared.

More importantly, a huge cotton crop in 1860 had allowed overseas mill owners to stockpile southern cotton. In addition, the end of southern exports raised cotton prices worldwide. These higher prices encouraged farmers in Egypt and India to grow more cotton to sell to European countries. When mill owners in Britain and France exhausted their reserves of southern cotton, they turned to Egypt and India for a new supply.

By the time southerners realized that cotton diplomacy had failed, the North's blockade had tightened, making the export of cotton nearly impossible. Further efforts to gain or block foreign involvement in the conflict, however, remained important to the actions and strategies of both sides during the Civil War.

READING CHECK **Summarizing** For what reasons did cotton diplomacy fail?

SECTION 1 ASSESSMENT

go.hrw.com
Online Quiz
Keyword: SD7 HP11

Reviewing Ideas, Terms, and People

1. **a. Identify** Where did the first battle of the Civil War take place?
   b. Analyze Why was this place important to both the North and the South?

2. **a. Identify** Which states joined the Confederacy after Lincoln's call for troops?
   b. Make Inferences Why did Lincoln's call for troops force the slave states that remained in the Union to choose a side?
   c. Elaborate Why were many men eager to enlist at the beginning of the war?

3. **a. Describe** What made the **border states** important?
   b. Analyze Why was Maryland the most critical border state?

4. **a. Describe** What was **cotton diplomacy**?
   b. Compare How were many southerners' views during the Civil War similar to those of Patriots during the Revolutionary War?
   c. Predict Which side do you think was better prepared for war, the North or the South? Explain why you think so.

Critical Thinking

5. **Comparing and Contrasting** Review your notes on Civil War goals and strategies. Then copy the graphic organizer below and use it to compare and contrast the North's and the South's goals and strategies.

Northern Goals and Strategies	Southern Goals and Strategies

FOCUS ON SPEAKING

6. **Persuasive** Suppose that you lived in a border state in 1861. Give a speech that makes an argument and provides reasons for or against your state seceding and joining the Confederacy.

362 CHAPTER 11

Section 1 Assessment Answers

1. **a.** Fort Sumter, Charleston, South Carolina
   b. represented federal authority in state that had seceded

2. **a.** Virginia, Arkansas, Tennessee, North Carolina
   b. send troops, side with North; refuse, side with South
   c. thought war would end quickly

3. **a.** slave states that remained in Union; controlled strategic roads and rivers
   b. If it seceded, Confederacy would surround Union capital.

4. **a.** southern use of cotton as tool of foreign policy
   b. thought they could beat a larger foe, gain assistance from Europe, fighting for independence
   c. the North; more men, more industrial assets

5. North—save Union; blockade South; South— left alone, fighting for home, cotton to bring in allies

6. for—must join our neighbors; against—will lead to destruction, cannot win against industrial North

Fighting Erupts

BEFORE YOU READ

MAIN IDEA
Widespread fighting occurred during the first two years of the Civil War.

READING FOCUS
1. What factors made the major battles in the war so bloody?
2. How did the Union carry out its strategy in the Mississippi Valley?
3. What led to the Confederate successes in the war in the East?
4. Why did Confederate forces invade the Union, and with what result?

KEY TERMS AND PEOPLE
Stonewall Jackson
infantry
First Battle of Bull Run
casualties
George McClellan
cavalry
ironclads
Ulysses S. Grant
Battle of Shiloh
Battle of Antietam

TAKING NOTES As you read, take notes on major battles fought during the first two years of the Civil War. Record your notes in a graphic organizer like the one shown here.

Battle	Date	Outcome
First Battle of Bull Run		
Battle of Shiloh		
Second Battle of Bull Run		
Battle of Antietam		
Battle of Fredericksburg		

THE INSIDE STORY

Why was an audience watching a battle? In the summer of 1861, northerners and southerners both expected victory by the fall. In July, Lincoln sent an army southward from Washington toward Richmond, Virginia. On July 21 the Union army attacked Confederate forces about 30 miles south of Washington, near a creek called Bull Run.

Enthusiasm for the war was high in Washington. Many men and women, including members of Congress, packed picnic baskets and rode out to watch the battle. The Union army made gains at first, but fresh Confederate troops arrived, forcing the Union army to retreat.

Then a Confederate artillery shell blew up a wagon on a bridge, creating a bottleneck along the march route. The orderly retreat turned into chaos as panicked Union soldiers began to run. Terrified civilians joined the stampede away from the battlefield.

Edmund Clarence Stedman, a reporter for the *New York World,* described the scene: "Hosts of federal troops . . . were fleeing along the road . . . Army wagons, sutlers' teams [merchants' wagons], and private carriages choked the passage, tumbling against each other amid clouds of dust . . . Hacks [hired carriages], containing unlucky spectators . . . were smashed like glass . . . Those on foot who could catch [horses] rode them bareback, as much to save themselves from being run over as to make quicker time." ◼

Picnic on the BATTLEFIELD

▼ The First Battle of Bull Run plunges into chaos, a signal to both sides that a long and bloody war is to come.

Teach the Main Idea
`At Level`

Fighting Erupts

1. **Teach** Ask students the Reading Focus questions to teach this section.

2. **Apply** Have students use their own paper to make flash cards for each of the battles discussed in the section. On the front, have students write the name of the battle, and on the back students should list pertinent details about the battle, including dates, who won, which generals were involved, and where, or in which state, the battle took place. **LS Visual-Spatial**

3. **Review** Have students work in pairs or in small groups and use their flash cards to quiz each other on the battles.

4. **Practice/Homework** Have each student write a news story for a southern newspaper about the Confederate successes in the East.
   LS Verbal-Linguistic
   Alternative Assessment Handbook, Rubric 23: Newspapers

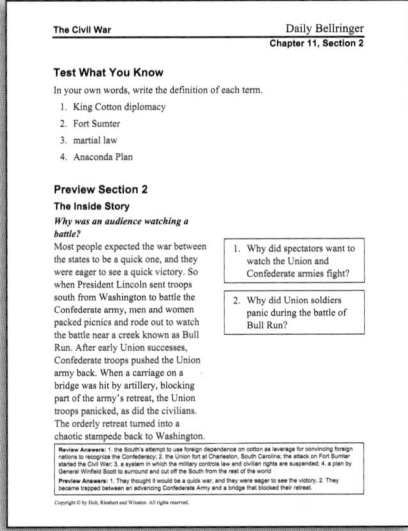

① What factors made the major battles in the war so bloody? *old battlefield strategies and deadly new weapons*

The Major Battles Begin

Identify Where is Bull Run? *in Virginia, near Manassas Junction*

Analyze Why did the Confederacy nearly win the war at Bull Run? *routed Union army, could probably have pursued and destroyed it*

Predict How would the Confederate victory at Bull Run change the northern view of the war? *It became clear that the war would be a long one and that the southern troops were determined to fight.*

Activity **Battle Slogan** Have students compose a slogan for the Confederate army based on their victory at Bull Run. **LS** **Auditory-Musical**

📄 CRF: Biography: Stonewall Jackson

Biography

Julia Ward Howe (1819–1910) Although she dedicated most of her life to humanitarian causes, Julia Ward Howe is best remembered for writing "Battle Hymn of the Republic." Raised in a wealthy family, Howe published several volumes of poetry without any success. Then, in 1861, Howe wrote "Battle Hymn of the Republic" while visiting an army camp near Washington, D.C. The poem was published, set to the tune of an old folk song, and quickly became the favorite song of the Union Army. Prior to the Civil War, Howe was an active abolitionist; after the war, she devoted herself to women's rights. Howe continued to write travel books, poetry, essays, and biographies throughout her life. In 1908, Howe became the first woman elected to the American Academy of Arts and Letters.

HISTORY CLOSE-UP

The New Weapons of War

Civil War soldiers used several weapons that were new to America. Although some had been developed in Europe, the American Civil War was their first major test in battlefield conditions.

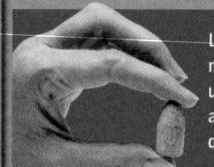

Large bullets called minié balls were used by both sides and did great damage on impact.

Union balloons rose 3,500 feet and allowed observers to see up to 6 miles.

Several types of ironclads, ships covered with iron plates of armor, were used by both sides in the war.

The Major Battles Begin

General Irvin McDowell warned President Lincoln that the Union army was not ready to fight. The 90-day enlistments of the North's volunteers were nearly over, however. There would soon be no army. "You are green [inexperienced] it is true," Lincoln noted, "but they [the Confederate troops] are green, also; you are all green alike." He decided that the army must attack.

On July 16, 1861, General McDowell began to march his 35,000-man army into Virginia. Blocking his path to Richmond were 22,000 Confederate troops located near the small town of Manassas Junction. The Confederates positioned themselves on the south side of a stream called Bull Run and waited.

McDowell's troops took two and a half days to march the 25 miles between Washington and Manassas. "They were not used to journeys on foot," he later explained. Their slow pace allowed the Confederate commander, P. G. T. Beauregard, to bring in 11,000 more troops by train. By the time the Union army arrived, the two forces were about equal in size.

First Battle of Bull Run Beauregard and McDowell had each planned carefully, but their inexperienced armies could not carry out the plans. The battle became a chaotic free-for-all. At first, the Union troops pushed the Confederates back. Then some Virginia soldiers

THE IMPACT TODAY

Culture
The battlefield at Bull Run is today a national park. It is one of 384 Civil War battlefields that have been designated as historic sites by the U.S. or state governments.

led by General Thomas Jackson rushed onto the field and stopped the Union advance. "There stands Jackson like a stone wall!" Confederate general Barnard Bee shouted to his troops. "Rally behind the Virginians!" Bee was killed soon after, but **Stonewall Jackson** had earned his famous nickname.

By late afternoon the Union troops began to fall back. When Beauregard ordered his entire line of **infantry**, or foot soldiers, to charge, the Union retreat turned into a stampede. Soldiers tossed away guns, packs, and anything else that might slow them down as they ran from the battlefield.

If the Confederates had pursued the fleeing troops, they might have been able to destroy the Union army. Instead, as one Confederate general put it, "our army was more disorganized by victory than that of the United States by defeat." The exhausted victors stayed on the battlefield after the **First Battle of Bull Run**. The Confederate army had suffered nearly 2,000 **casualties**, the military term for those killed, wounded, or missing in action. Union casualties numbered about 2,900.

The Battle of Bull Run ended most northerners' hopes for a short war. Lincoln called for a million more volunteers willing to serve for three years. The president also replaced McDowell with a brilliant 34-year-old general, **George McClellan**. McClellan immediately set about turning some 100,000 of these three-year volunteers into a real army.

Skills Focus: Analyzing Primary Sources | At Level |

Reading Like a Historian Skill
The Battle of Bull Run

1. Provide students the following account of the flight of Union soldiers at Bull Run: "When a mounted officer galloped into the mass, and yelled that the Rebels 'were upon us,' the Federals who heard him 'started like a flock of sheep, with every man for himself and the devil take the hindermost.' The New Jersey troops in Theodore Runyan's division tried to stop the flight, but their efforts failed."

2. Have students use this quote to write two reports for newspapers of the time about the end of the Battle of Bull Run. One report should be for the "Charleston Courier" and the other for the "Boston Daily."

3. Have volunteers read their accounts to the class. **LS** **Verbal-Linguistic**

📄 Alternative Assessment Handbook, Rubric 40: Writing to Describe

The Union's Gatling gun, an early machine gun, could fire 200 times per minute.

The Confederate *Hunley* was the first submarine to sink an enemy vessel. The explosion sank the *Hunley*, too.

THE MUSEUM OF THE CONFEDERACY, RICHMOND, VIRGINIA

Skills Focus **INTERPRETING VISUALS**

Making Inferences How were ironclads an advantage over wooden ships?

See **Skills Handbook, p. H30**

Tactics and technology Most of the top generals on each side in the war had been trained at the U.S. Military Academy at West Point. The predominant instruction was based on the wars conducted by Napoleon in his conquest of Europe a half-century before. Such tactics often involved sending a force of infantry or **cavalry**, soldiers on horseback, to charge an enemy position. These methods had worked well in the Mexican-American War. Many Civil War generals had served in that war as young officers.

The weapons on Civil War battlefields, however, were far more deadly than those used in the 1840s. In the Mexican War, the average musket had a range of 250 yards and was accurate only to a distance of about 80 yards. In addition, it took about 25 seconds to reload the weapon. A charging enemy often could overwhelm defenders before they could fire again.

By the 1850s, however, weapon makers found that bullet-shaped ammunition traveled through the air in a much straighter line than a round ball. They also discovered that cutting a spiral groove inside a gun barrel, called rifling, made the bullet rotate after it was fired. Both changes increased range and accuracy. Rifles, as the new guns were called, were accurate to 500 yards. New systems for reloading allowed a soldier to fire about 10 times a minute.

The killing power of artillery also increased. The solid iron cannonballs of earlier years were

replaced by shrapnel—shells that exploded in the air over a target, or when they struck a target. Fragments of these exploding shells ripped into any troops nearby. If enemy troops were close to defenders, cannon could fire canister—shells filled with small bits of metal. Canister turned artillery into giant shotguns that mowed down advancing troops.

Attacks against military forces with these modern weapons produced huge numbers of casualties. This clash of tactics and technology is why some historians call the Civil War the last old-time war and first modern one.

New devices of war The Civil War was the first time observation balloons were used to direct artillery fire. This gave rise to the first use of camouflage to disguise tents and guns from airborne observers. Other devices that saw limited use for the first time include machine guns, wire entanglements, flamethrowers, and gas shells called stink bombs.

Existing devices were put to new uses as well. The telegraph, invented by Samuel F. B. Morse in the 1840s, allowed generals in the field to communicate quickly with government leaders. The Civil War also marked the first time in history that railroads were used to move large numbers of troops.

READING CHECK **Summarizing** How did tactics, technology, and inexperience shape the fighting in the Civil War?

ACADEMIC VOCABULARY
predominant most noticeable or important

❷ **How did the Union carry out its strategy in the Mississippi Valley?** *Grant fought along rivers to the Mississippi and headed south; Farragut's fleet penetrated southern defenses south of New Orleans and moved up the Mississippi to capture New Orleans, Baton Rouge, and Natchez.*

The Fight for the Mississippi Valley

Explain How did Grant cause a sensation in both South and North early in 1862? *by capturing Forts Donelson and Henry, opening the way to the Mississippi*

Evaluate How did Grant assess the likely length of the war after his victory at Shiloh? *Even though he won, the Confederates fought so well that it was obvious the South was nowhere near collapsing.*

📑 CRF: History and Geography Activity: The Battle of Shiloh

Info to Know

General Grant Grant was a generous man in victory, and after the Confederate surrender at Fort Donelson, he gave permission for Confederates to cross the lines to bury their dead. Grant wrote: ". . . I have no doubt many got beyond our pickets and went on [ran away]. The most of the men who went that way no doubt thought they had had war enough, and left with the intention of remaining out of the army. Some came to me and asked permission to go, saying that they were tired of the war and would not be caught in the ranks again, and I bade them go."

The Fight for the Mississippi Valley

Among the most successful new weapons of the Civil War were the Union's **ironclads**. These armored gunboats were critical to the North's campaign in the Mississippi River valley. Covered with heavy iron plates up to three inches thick, the boats were nearly invincible to Confederate cannon fire.

As McClellan trained the new Army of the Potomac in Washington, D.C., other Union soldiers began to carry out General Scott's plan to take control of the Mississippi River. Southern leaders expected the Union's attack to come down the Mississippi River. To resist this tactic, they invaded western Kentucky and fortified the bluffs above the river. However, the Union attacked from the Tennessee River instead.

Grant moves south In February 1862 seven Union gunboats and 15,000 troops led by General **Ulysses S. Grant** moved up the Tennessee River. The gunboats pounded Fort Henry, a Confederate fort near the Kentucky-Tennessee line, into a quick surrender.

Grant then marched his troops cross-country to capture Fort Donelson on the Cumberland River. After holding out for three days, the fort's commander tried to negotiate. Grant refused. "No terms except unconditional and immediate surrender can be accepted," he said. The fort's 12,000 defenders gave up, and the North had a much-needed victory. When newspapers reported Grant's tough remark, northerners also had a hero.

Grant's capture of Forts Henry and Donelson caused a sensation in both North and South. Two major rivers into the western Confederacy were wide open. In addition, Confederate defenses along the Mississippi River were now vulnerable to attack.

Another Union army under General Don Carlos Buell quickly advanced up the Cumberland River to capture Nashville, the capital of Tennessee. Meanwhile, Grant and about 38,000 soldiers continued south along the Tennessee River toward Corinth, Mississippi, an important railroad center.

The Battle of Shiloh By late March 1862 more than 40,000 Confederate troops from across the region had gathered at Corinth

to block the Union advance. Grant, however, stopped at Pittsburg Landing, Tennessee, a small river town some 20 miles away. He was waiting for 25,000 more troops that Buell had sent from Nashville. The Confederates decided to attack before Grant's army got larger.

On April 6, 1862, the southerners surprised the Union soldiers, who were camped at Shiloh Church outside Pittsburg Landing. *Shiloh* means "place of peace" in Hebrew, but it was far from peaceful that day. After hours of fighting, the Confederates pushed the Union forces back against the Tennessee River. By nightfall the Confederates were confident they would finish off Grant's army in the morning. When Union officers suggested that their army retreat, Grant replied, "Retreat? No. I propose to attack at daylight and whip them."

Buell's troops finally arrived that night and, true to his word, Grant attacked the next morning. Now facing an army much larger than their own, the Confederates were driven back. By 2:30 p.m. the **Battle of Shiloh** was over, and the Confederate army was in retreat.

This two-day battle produced some of the bloodiest fighting yet seen in the war. About one of every four soldiers was killed or wounded. The Union army suffered some 13,000 losses, while Confederate casualties totaled more than 10,000.

The Battle of Shiloh also ended northern hopes that the rebellion would collapse on its own. Grant wrote later that after this battle, "I gave up all idea of saving the Union except by complete conquest."

The Mississippi River campaign The Battle of Shiloh opened the way for Union forces to split the Confederacy and gain complete control of the Mississippi River. Union generals began massing more than 100,000 troops at Pittsburg Landing, preparing to move south along the river. Meanwhile, a Union fleet of 24 wooden ships entered the river from the Gulf of Mexico and pushed north to capture New Orleans, Louisiana, the South's largest city. Admiral David Farragut commanded the fleet. Aboard some of his ships were 15,000 army troops led by General Ben Butler.

Two forts guarded New Orleans on opposite sides of the Mississippi River just south of the city. "Nothing afloat could pass the forts," claimed one New Orleans citizen. Indeed,

---

Differentiating Instruction

Advanced Learners/GATE

1. Have students research the Battle of Shiloh and read primary source documents from the perspective of the soldiers on either side. Ambrose Bierce, among others, wrote of his time there.

2. Have students use their research to write a detailed letter to a family in the South or North as if they had just survived the battle, describing what it was like to take part in such a furious battle.

3. Have volunteers read their letters to the class.

4. Ask students if they believe written descriptions accurately portray what such an experience was like. **LS Verbal-Linguistic**

📑 Alternative Assessment Handbook, Rubric 41: Writing to Express

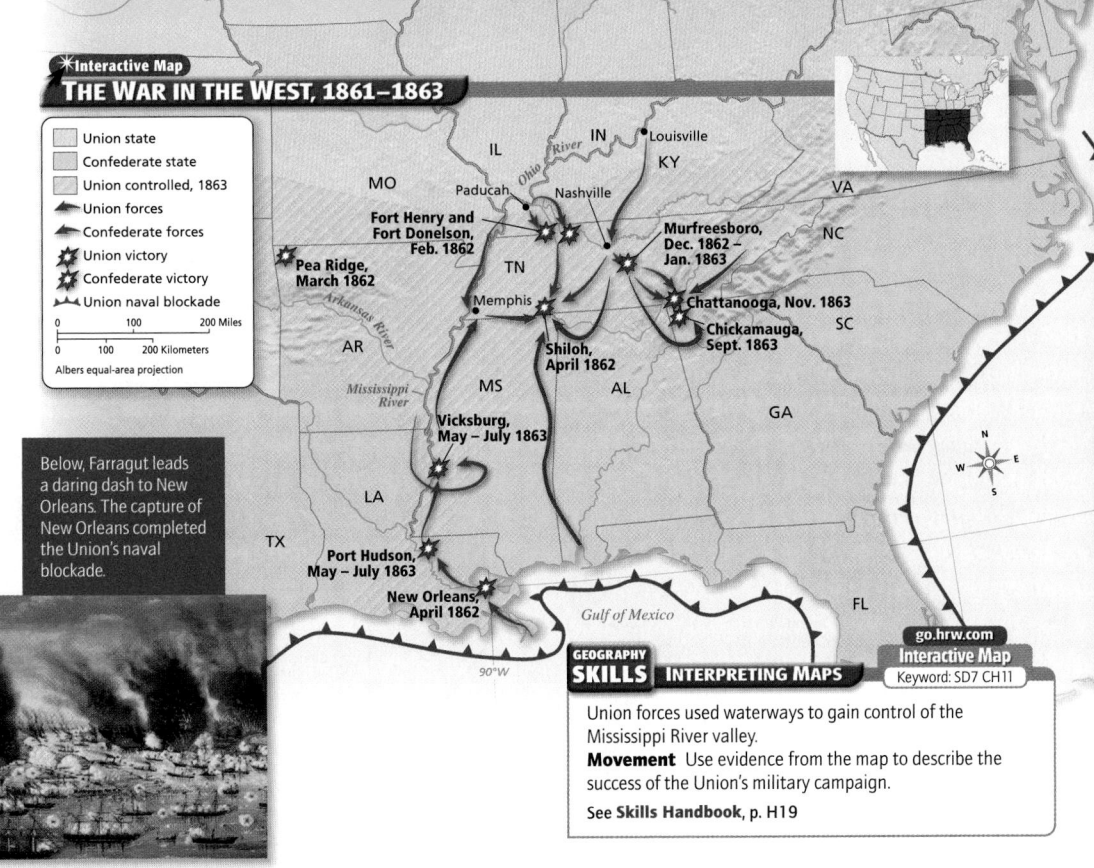

Union state
Confederate state
Union controlled, 1863
Union forces
Confederate forces
Union victory
Confederate victory
Union naval blockade

0   100   200 Miles
0   100   200 Kilometers
Albers equal-area projection

IL
IN
Louisville
MO
KY
Paducah
Nashville
Fort Henry and
Fort Donelson,
Feb. 1862
Murfreesboro,
Dec. 1862 –
Jan. 1863
VA
NC
Pea Ridge,
March 1862
TN
Memphis
Chattanooga, Nov. 1863
Chickamauga,
Sept. 1863
SC
AR
Shiloh,
April 1862
Vicksburg,
May – July 1863
MS
AL
GA
LA
TX
Port Hudson,
May – July 1863
New Orleans,
April 1862
Gulf of Mexico
FL
90°W

Below, Farragut leads a daring dash to New Orleans. The capture of New Orleans completed the Union's naval blockade.

GEOGRAPHY
SKILLS | INTERPRETING MAPS

go.hrw.com
Interactive Map
Keyword: SD7 CH11

Union forces used waterways to gain control of the Mississippi River valley.
Movement Use evidence from the map to describe the success of the Union's military campaign.
See **Skills Handbook**, p. H19

after six days of heavy fire from the Union ships the forts remained standing. Finally, Farragut decided on a bold plan—to slip past the forts under the cover of darkness. At two o'clock on the morning of April 24, the Union vessels began to move. Then the moon rose and disaster struck. The Confederate soldiers in the forts saw the ships and opened fire with artillery. The lead vessel was heavily battered, but most of the ships managed to make their way past the forts.

After sinking several Confederate warships further upriver, Farragut's fleet arrived at New Orleans on April 25. The nearly undefended city quickly surrendered.

Many southerners were concerned about what the fall of New Orleans might mean for the Confederacy's future. Mary Chesnut, who was married to a Confederate general, wrote about her fears in her diary.

HISTORY'S VOICES

❝New Orleans gone—and with it the Confederacy. Are we not cut in two? The Mississippi ruins us if lost...Death, not life, seems to be our fate now.❞

—Mary Chesnut, April 27, 1862

Farragut soon pushed north to capture the cities of Baton Rouge, Louisiana, and Natchez, Mississippi. In June, another Union fleet came downriver from Missouri and seized Memphis, Tennessee. The town of Vicksburg, Mississippi, high on a bluff, was the major river stronghold, and it remained in Confederate hands. "Ships . . . cannot crawl up hills 300 feet high," Farragut noted. An army would be needed. That assignment would fall to General Grant.

READING CHECK **Sequencing** By what process did Union forces gain control of nearly all of the Mississippi River in 1862?

THE CIVIL WAR **367**

• ● Direct Teach ● •

Reading Focus

The Fight for the Mississippi Valley

Recall How did Farragut get past the heavy cannon protecting New Orleans? *sailed under cover of darkness*

Make Generalizations What did the fall of New Orleans mean to the South? *their largest city was captured, Mississippi would come under Federal control, splitting the Confederacy*

Map Transparency: The War in the West, 1861–1863

✷ Interactive Map: The War in the West, 1861–1863

go.hrw.com
Online Resources
KEYWORD: SD7 CH11
TOPIC: CIVIL WAR TECHNOLOGY

Differentiating Instruction

Below Level | Standard English Mastery

English-Language Learners

Research Required

1. Organize the class into small groups. Have each group review the capture of New Orleans by Admiral David Farragut. Teams should use the text and reliable Internet sites for their research.

2. Have each group prepare a poster or storyboard about the battle for New Orleans, including a sketch of the river where Farragut had to pass the southern forts.

3. Have volunteers from each group share their posters with the class. Guide students in a discussion about whether Farragut and his men should be considered heroes.
LS **Interpersonal**
Alternative Assessment Handbook, Rubric 28: Posters

Answers

Interpreting Maps *Using rivers, the North is making great strides toward controlling the all-important Mississippi River Valley.*

Reading Check *Grant moved along secondary rivers to the Mississippi, where he captured Confederate forts. Meanwhile, Farragut moved up the Mississippi, capturing New Orleans, Baton Rouge, and Natchez.*

3 What led to the Confederate successes in the war in the East? *McClellan was very slow to attack, giving Lee and Jackson opportunities to operate freely.*

The War in the East

Identify Who was commander of the Union army in the East? *General McClellan*

Analyze How did McClellan propose to attack Richmond? *from the east, where it was less heavily defended*

Predict What would be the result of McClellan's hesitancy? *Lee would be handed the opportunity to defeat the Union again at the Second Battle of Bull Run.*

📦 Map Transparency: The War in the East, 1861–1863

✴ Interactive Map: The War in the East, 1861–1863

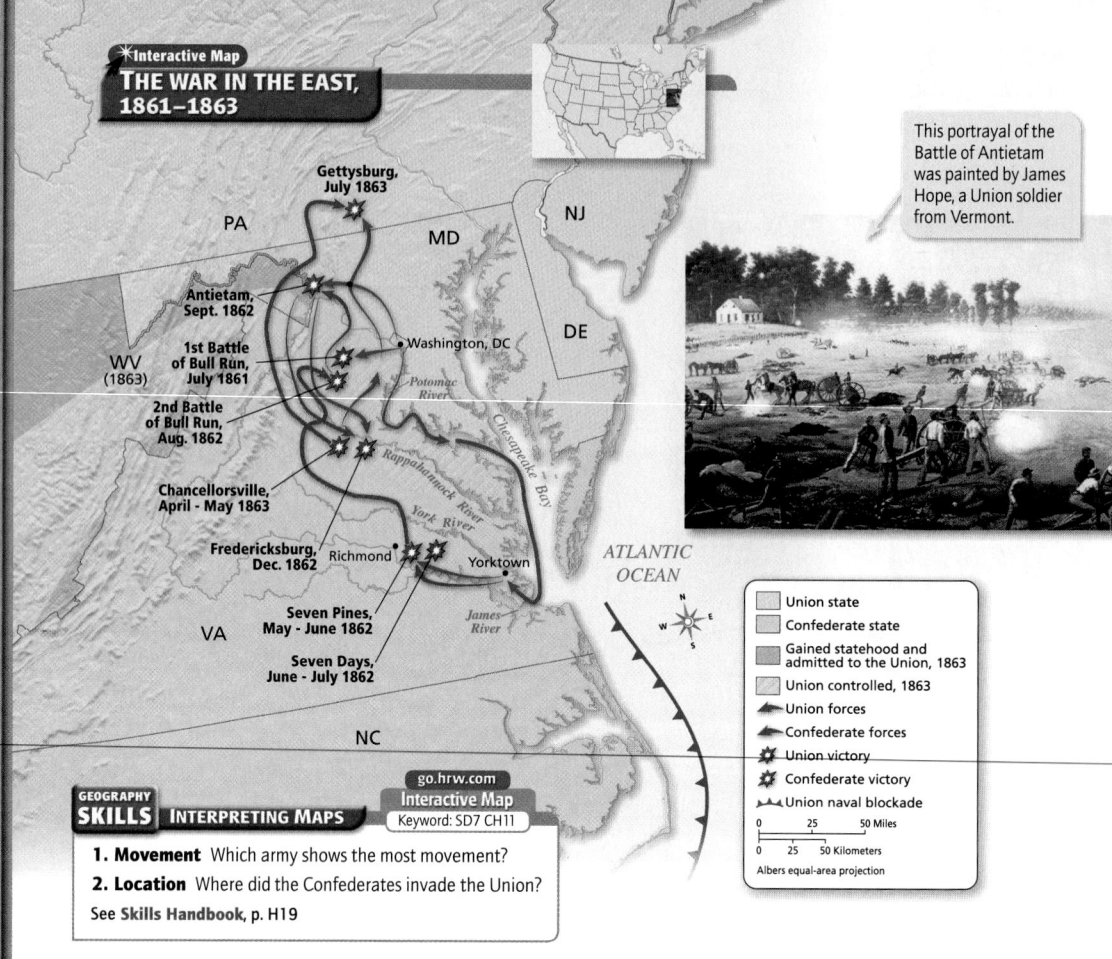

✴ Interactive Map
THE WAR IN THE EAST, 1861–1863

This portrayal of the Battle of Antietam was painted by James Hope, a Union soldier from Vermont.

Gettysburg, July 1863
PA
NJ
MD
Antietam, Sept. 1862
Washington, DC
DE
WV (1863)
1st Battle of Bull Run, July 1861
Potomac River
2nd Battle of Bull Run, Aug. 1862
Rappahannock River
Chesapeake Bay
Chancellorsville, April - May 1863
York River
ATLANTIC OCEAN
Fredericksburg, Dec. 1862
Richmond
Yorktown
VA
Seven Pines, May - June 1862
James River
Seven Days, June - July 1862
NC

☐ Union state
☐ Confederate state
☐ Gained statehood and admitted to the Union, 1863
☐ Union controlled, 1863
← Union forces
← Confederate forces
✶ Union victory
✶ Confederate victory
⚓ Union naval blockade

0   25   50 Miles
0   25   50 Kilometers
Albers equal-area projection

GEOGRAPHY SKILLS | **INTERPRETING MAPS**
go.hrw.com
Interactive Map
Keyword: SD7 CH11

1. Movement Which army shows the most movement?
2. Location Where did the Confederates invade the Union?
See Skills Handbook, p. H19

The War in the East

As Grant moved south through Tennessee, McClellan's army in the East was finally ready for action. General McClellan had a clever plan. Rather than march directly toward Richmond, he planned to move his army by boat down the Potomac River and across Chesapeake Bay. He would then attack the Confederate capital from the east, where its defenses were weaker. It was a good plan, but McClellan never seemed ready to fight. As the months passed and still he did not move, Lincoln lost patience. "How *long* would it require to actually get in motion?" the president asked McClellan in December 1861.

The peninsula campaign In March 1862 McClellan finally began to move his 100,000-man army. In early April the advancing Union soldiers came upon 15,000 Confederates at Yorktown, about 60 miles from Richmond. The Confederates' defenses were weak, but McClellan delayed an attack in order to ask Lincoln for more troops. The president refused. A Confederate force of 20,000 men led by Stonewall Jackson was causing trouble for Union troops elsewhere in Virginia. Lincoln was afraid that if he sent additional troops to help McClellan, those soldiers might later be needed to defend Washington. Instead, the president sent his general a clear warning.

368 CHAPTER 11

Collaborative Learning

At Level

The War in the East

1. Organize the class in small groups, and have each group review the information in the text about the war in the East.

2. Have each group develop Union battle plans, including generals who could lead the Union army, for the war in the East. Plans should include maps and estimates of number of troops needed to carry out the plans. Have

each group include advice to President Lincoln about ways to implement these plans and help ensure Union victory.

3. Have each group share its plans with the class. **LS** **Interpersonal, Kinesthetic**

📋 Alternative Assessment Handbook, Rubrics 14: Group Activity; and 20: Map Creation

Answers

Interpreting Maps 1. *Confederate;*
2. *in Maryland, Pennsylvania*

❝It is indispensable to *you* that you strike a blow ...The country will not fail to note—is now noting—that the present hesitation to move upon an entrenched enemy is but the story of Manassas [Bull Run] repeated...I have never written to you, or spoken to you, in greater kindness of feeling than now...*But you must act.***❞**

—Abraham Lincoln, April 9, 1862

McClellan ignored the president's advice. After spending another month waiting outside Yorktown, he finally attacked. The Confederates offered no resistance. Instead, they retreated toward Richmond. McClellan's delay, however, had given the Confederate commander, General Joseph Johnston, time to gather more troops.

Suddenly, on May 31, the Confederates turned and attacked the much larger Union army at a moment when the Union forces were divided by a river. Neither side won the Battle of Seven Pines, but both sides suffered heavy casualties. Johnston was among the Confederates who were wounded. General Robert E. Lee took command of Johnston's army and renamed it the Army of Northern Virginia.

As McClellan again waited for Lincoln to send more troops, the Confederates again took advantage of their opponent's caution. Although Lee's army was still greatly outnumbered by the Union forces, he sent some of his troops to help Stonewall Jackson fight in the Shenandoah Valley. Lee was gambling that McClellan would not attack while these soldiers were gone. With his now larger force, Jackson pretended that he was going to attack Washington. Lincoln ordered McClellan's reinforcements to stay and protect the capital.

This was exactly what Lee had hoped for. Jackson quickly moved his army from the Shenandoah Valley to join Lee. In late June their combined armies attacked McClellan in a series of bloody clashes called the Seven Days' Battles. Although McClellan won four of the five battles, he retreated.

The Second Battle of Bull Run While McClellan's army sat motionless to the southeast of Richmond, Lincoln turned to General John Pope, who was forming a new Union army near Washington. In mid-July, Pope moved into northern Virginia with about 50,000 troops. Lincoln ordered McClellan to renew his attack in order to trap Lee's forces between the two Union armies. Once again McClellan did nothing. Lincoln then ordered him to withdraw his army from the Virginia peninsula and join Pope's troops.

Lee decided to act before the two Union armies could unite and create an overwhelming force. On August 29 he lured Pope into battle near Manassas, on almost the same ground where the Confederates had beaten McDowell's army a year before. At the Second Battle of Bull Run, Pope met the same fate. After Pope's defeat, Lincoln put McClellan back in command. When members of his cabinet protested, Lincoln explained, "We must use what tools we have."

READING CHECK **Identifying Cause and Effect** Why were Confederate forces able to defeat the larger Union armies that invaded Virginia?

The Union Is Invaded

The series of defeats in Virginia brought morale in the North to a new low. "The nation is rapidly sinking just now," a New Yorker wrote in his diary. "Disgust with our present government is certainly universal." In the Confederacy, General Lee sensed this situation, and an opportunity. He wrote to Confederate president Jefferson Davis, "The present seems to be the most propitious [favorable] time . . . for the Confederate army to enter Maryland."

Davis agreed. A victory on Union soil might prompt the North to ask for peace. If not, Confederate leaders hoped such a victory would at least convince Britain and France to recognize southern independence. In addition, moving the war out of Virginia would give farmers there the chance to harvest what remained of their crops, which were much needed by the troops and civilian population.

In early September 1862 Lee's army crossed the Potomac River into western Maryland, with McClellan's army in pursuit. Then a Union soldier found a copy of Lee's marching orders that had been lost by a careless Confederate officer. Now that he knew Lee's plans, McClellan exclaimed, "If I cannot whip Bobbie Lee, I will be willing to go home." When he telegraphed his good news to Lincoln, the delighted president replied, "God bless you and all with you. Destroy the rebel army, if possible."

THE CIVIL WAR **369**

Skills Focus: Summarizing | **At Level**

Reading Skill
Second Bull Run and Antietam

1. Review the invasion of the North with students. Guide students in a discussion of how the loss at Bull Run and the losses at Antietam may have increased the negative feelings northerners already had about war and about the president's ability to lead.

2. Have each student write a speech for President Lincoln in which he tries to explain and justify to the nation what happened both at the Second Battle of Bull Run and at Antietam.

The speech should try to ease citizens' fears and to create support for the Union army.

3. Have volunteers from each group read their speeches to the class. Ask students to try to read as they imagine President Lincoln might have sounded. **LS Auditory-Musical**

📖 Alternative Assessment Handbook, Rubric 24: Oral Presentations

Direct Teach

Reading Focus

The Union is Invaded

Recall Why did President Lincoln relieve McClellan of his command?
refusal to pursue Confederate army

Describe What was the outcome of the Battle of Fredericksburg?
Lee won easily; Union lost more than 13,000 soldiers

Review & Assess

Close

Close Have students describe Union and Confederate victories and losses beginning with the First Battle of Bull Run and ending with Fredericksburg.

Review

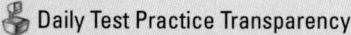 Online Quiz, Section 2

Daily Test Practice Transparency

Assess

SE Section 2 Assessment

Progress Assessment: Section 2 Quiz

Alternative Assessment Handbook

Reteach

Interactive Reader and Study Guide, Section 2

Interactive Skills Tutor CD-ROM

The Battle of Antietam McClellan caught up with Lee near the town of Sharpsburg, Maryland, and prepared for battle. His 70,000 Union troops dwarfed Lee's army of 40,000. Yet again, the ever-cautious McClellan delayed for 16 hours before beginning his attack. This gave the Confederates time to organize their defenses. Finally, on September 17, 1862, the **Battle of Antietam** took place. Named after a creek that crossed the battlefield, Antietam was the bloodiest single-day battle of the Civil War—and of U.S. history.

Time and time again the Union troops charged the Confederate defenses. The savage fighting ended in late afternoon, when both sides became too exhausted to continue. Union and Confederate casualties combined exceeded 23,000. Lee lost almost a third of his army. McClellan had as many as 25,000 troops waiting in reserve, but he did not use them.

Had McClellan attacked Lee again the next day he would have followed Lincoln's command to "destroy the rebel army." But he did not. Instead, that night the Confederate troops began a slow retreat back to Virginia. Lincoln ordered McClellan to "cross the Potomac and give battle." Again, McClellan would not move. In early November 1862, President Lincoln relieved the general of command for the second and final time.

The Battle of Fredericksburg Lincoln replaced McClellan with General Ambrose Burnside. Soon, Burnside was marching a massive army of 110,000 men toward Richmond. He found his path blocked, however, by Lee and 75,000 Confederate soldiers on the south side of the Rappahannock River at Fredericksburg. Lee expected the Union army to cross the river above or below the town. Burnside decided instead to surprise Lee by crossing directly in front of the Confederate army.

The only thing that surprised Lee was Burnside's terrible judgment. Burnside ordered five pontoon bridges built across the river and sent his army over them to attack. He believed his superior numbers could force Lee to retreat.

On December 13, 1862, at the Battle of Fredericksburg, Burnside ordered his troops to charge Lee's army 14 times. Only the approach of darkness and the pleas of Burnside's commanders halted the horrible slaughter. The Union army lost nearly 13,000 men, more than twice the number of Confederate losses.

The disaster at Fredericksburg plunged the North into gloom. When Lincoln heard the terrible news, he said, "If there is a worse place than Hell, I am in it."

READING CHECK **Drawing Conclusions**
Why was the Battle of Antietam an especially significant battle in the Civil War?

SECTION 2 ASSESSMENT

go.hrw.com
Online Quiz
Keyword: SD7 HP11

Reviewing Ideas, Terms, and People

1. a. Describe What was the outcome of the **First Battle of Bull Run**?
b. Predict Although they had many new weapons, Civil War generals relied on old battlefield strategies. How might such weapons and tactics affect the outcomes of battles?

2. a. Identify What were **ironclads**? How did the North use them?
b. Analyze Why were **Ulysses S. Grant**'s early victories in the Mississippi River valley important?

3. a. Describe What happened at the Second Battle of Bull Run?
b. Contrast How was the war in the East different from the war in the West?
c. Elaborate How would you describe **George McClellan** as a battlefield commander? Give reasons for your answer.

4. a. Recall Why did Lee cross into Maryland in 1862?
b. Evaluate Do you think Lincoln was right to relieve McClellan of his command after the **Battle of Antietam**?

Critical Thinking

5. Categorizing Review your notes on major Civil War battles. Then copy the graphic organizer below and use it to list Union and Confederate victories.

Union Victories	Confederate Victories

FOCUS ON WRITING

6. Expository Suppose you are President Lincoln. Write a letter to a friend describing your personal thoughts and feelings about the progress of the war.

370 CHAPTER 11

Section 2 Assessment Answers

1. a. major Confederate victory
b. deadly; many more soldiers killed

2. a. armored ships; used on rivers in the Mississippi River campaign
b. opened a path for Union control of the Mississippi

3. a. North was soundly defeated.
b. West, fought along rivers to gain control of territory; East, fought to destroy armies
c. overly cautious, ineffective, reluctant to fight

4. a. to move the war out of Virginia, discourage the North, attract foreign support, hoped North would ask for peace
b. yes; his failures led to great loss of life, prolonged war

5. Union—Fort Henry, Fort Donelson, Shiloh, New Orleans, Antietam; Confederate—Bull Run, Second Battle of Bull Run, Fredericksburg

6. war is not going well; great loss of human life; McClellan will not fight

Answers

Reading Check *stopped Lee's invasion of the North*

The War behind the Lines

BEFORE YOU READ

MAIN IDEA

The Civil War created hardships, challenges, and opportunities for people in the North and the South.

READING FOCUS

1. How did the Emancipation Proclamation affect the Civil War?

2. How did African Americans contribute to the war effort?

3. What was life like in the military?

4. What similarities and differences existed on the home front in the North and South?

KEY TERMS AND PEOPLE

Emancipation Proclamation
emancipation
freedmen
conscription
Copperheads
habeas corpus
Clara Barton

TAKING NOTES As you read, take notes identifying reasons people supported the Emancipation Proclamation. Record your notes in a graphic organizer like the one shown here.

Reasons for Supporting the Emancipation Proclamation

▼ President Lincoln reads to the members of his cabinet the Emancipation Proclamation he has written.

The Decision That CHANGED a Nation

THE INSIDE STORY

What great change did Lincoln make in the nation? The retreat of the Confederate army from Maryland in September 1862 allowed Abraham Lincoln to call the Battle of Antietam a victory for the North. Lincoln needed a victory because he planned a drastic action he hoped would help end the war. He had been waiting for the right time to announce this measure to the nation and the world.

The president called his cabinet together on September 22, the Monday after the battle. "I wish that we were in a better condition," he observed. "The action of the army against the rebels has not been quite what I should have best liked. But they have been driven out of Maryland."

President Lincoln then pulled from a pocket a paper he had written. He told the cabinet members in advance that he did not seek their advice about "the main matter" because he had already made up his mind, but he was willing to listen to any suggestions they might have about the wording he had used.

Then Lincoln began to read aloud from the paper he held. Finally, he reached the historic words that changed a nation—that on January 1, 1863, "all persons held as slaves within any state, or part of a state, the people whereof shall then be in rebellion against the United States shall be then, thenceforward, and forever free." ◢

THE CIVIL WAR **371**

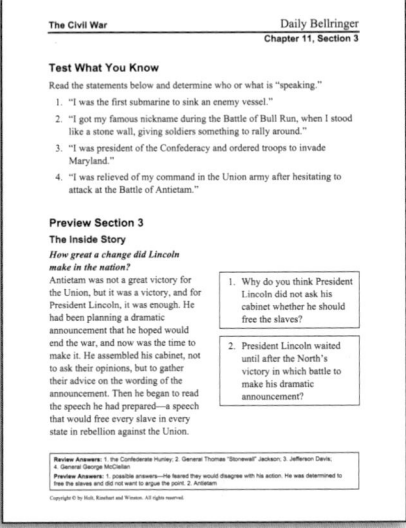

Preteach

Bellringer

The Inside Story. . . Use the **Daily Bellringer Transparency** to help students answer the question.

🖋 Daily Bellringer Transparency, Section 3

Academic Vocabulary

Review with students the high-use academic term in this section.

credit the sum of money provided by a lender (p. 376)

📑 CRF: Vocabulary Builder Activity, Section 3

Taking Notes

would help shorten the war; would lead to end of slavery; former slaves could join the Union army

---

Teach the Main Idea

At Level

The War behind the Lines

1. **Teach** Ask students the Reading Focus questions to teach this section.

2. **Apply** Have students create a Web diagram or chart showing the effect of the war on African Americans, troops, women, and other civilians. **LS Visual-Spatial**

3. **Review** Have volunteers share their diagrams with the class. Discuss whether living conditions behind the lines can significantly change a war effort or its outcome.

4. **Practice/Homework** Have student write a short analysis of what they believe was the most important difference between life in the North and life in the South during the Civil War. **LS Logical-Mathematical**

📝 Alternative Assessment Handbook Rubric 37: Writing Assignments

🖋 Graphic Organizer Transparencies

The Emancipation Proclamation

Recall Why was Lincoln reluctant to issue the Emancipation Proclamation? *He did not think he had constitutional authority to do so.*

Make Generalizations Why were some northerners opposed to the emancipation of slaves? *They feared competition for scarce jobs.*

Evaluate Was Lincoln right to limit the proclamation to those slaves living in rebellious states? *probably; he still needed the border states, which allowed slavery, on his side*

Primary Source

Lincoln wrote, in an open letter: *"My paramount object in this struggle is to save the Union, and it is not either to save or destroy slavery. If I could save the Union without freeing any slave, I would do it, and if I could save it by freeing all the slaves, I would do it, and if I could save it by freeing some and leaving others alone I would also do that . . . I have here stated my purpose according to my view of my official duty, and I intend no modification of my oft-expressed personal wish that all men every where could be free."*
— Abraham Lincoln
Letter to Horace Greeley, August 11, 1862

Answers

Reading Check *slavery became a war issue; generally boosted support for the war in the North; ended possibility of British aid to the South*

372

The Emancipation Proclamation

As the fighting dragged on and casualties increased, northern attitudes about the war began to change. Some northerners came to believe that just saving the Union was not enough. They did not want the nation restored to what it had been before the war. These northerners argued that the South, which they blamed for causing the bloodshed and horrors of the war, should be punished by freeing its enslaved people.

Lincoln did not think that the Constitution gave him the power to take such action. Gradually, however, others convinced him that he could. They did so by noting that slavery provided the labor the South needed to continue the war. "This rebellion has its source and life in slavery," one influential Republican in Congress declared. This reasoning allowed Lincoln to use his constitutional power as commander in chief of the armed forces to end slavery in the rebelling states.

On January 1, 1863, Lincoln issued the **Emancipation Proclamation**. This document freed the slaves in all areas that were in rebellion against the United States.

Reaction to **emancipation**—the act of freeing someone from slavery—was mixed in the North. Many abolitionists were upset that the Emancipation Proclamation allowed slavery to continue in states that were not in rebellion. It did not even apply to areas of the Confederacy that had already been conquered by Union armies.

Some northerners opposed emancipation because they feared increased competition for jobs in the North. When the government had used former slaves to help harvest crops in Illinois in 1862, for example, riots broke out in protest. Calm was not restored until the government returned the former slaves to south of the Ohio River. Riots against black workers also took place in Cincinnati, Ohio; Brooklyn, New York; and several other northern cities.

Many northerners supported the Emancipation Proclamation, however, because they thought it would help shorten the war. A Cincinnati newspaper expressed pleasure that Lincoln was trying to destroy "the compulsory labor system *which feeds the enemy*." Reactions in Union armies generally reflected those in northern society. Few soldiers were abolitionists, an Indiana colonel noted, but they were eager "to destroy everything that . . . gives the rebels strength."

Reaction overseas was also mixed. In Great Britain, where the abolition movement was strong, many felt that Lincoln had not gone far enough. "Where he has no power, Mr. Lincoln will set the negroes free," the London *Times* critically wrote. "Where he retains power he will consider them as slaves." Nevertheless, Lincoln's action ended whatever hope remained in the South for British intervention in the war. The British government was not willing to take the side of a slave power in a war that was now about ending slavery.

READING CHECK **Identifying Cause and Effect** In what ways did the Emancipation Proclamation affect the Civil War?

African American Union Soldiers
About 10 percent of the Union forces were African American. Their performance in battle proved to doubters their valor.

NOW IN CAMP AT READVILLE!
54th REGIMENT!
AFRICAN DESCENT
Col. ROBERT G. SHAW
Colored Men, Rally 'Round the Flag of Freedom!
BOUNTY $100!
AT THE EXPIRATION OF THE TERM OF SERVICE.
Pay, $13 a Month!
Good Food & Clothing!
State Aid to Families!
RECRUITING OFFICE,
COR. CAMBRIDGE & NORTH RUSSELL STS.
BOSTON.
Lieut. J. W. M. APPLETON, Recruiting Officer.

Juneteenth

The Emancipation Proclamation took effect on January 1, 1863—except in Texas. News of freedom did not reach African Americans there until June 19, 1865. Today that date marks a celebration that is known as Juneteenth. It is the oldest celebration of the ending of slavery in the United States.

In 1980 Juneteenth became a state holiday in Texas. It is not an official holiday anywhere else, but it is celebrated by people in Louisiana, Oklahoma, and other states.

Some of the largest Juneteenth events take place in Minneapolis, Minnesota, and Milwaukee, Wisconsin.

Juneteenth festivities take many forms. Early events included prayer services as well as family gatherings. Today Juneteenth is also celebrated with speeches, parades, picnics, and rodeos.

Drawing Conclusions Why do you think Juneteenth is celebrated so widely, even though it is an official holiday only in Texas?

Civil War re-enactors celebrate Juneteenth with a parade through Austin, Texas.

African Americans and the War

Enslaved African Americans made important contributions to the South's war effort. Their work on farms and plantations provided much of the food the South needed and released white males from labor so they could fight in Confederate armies. Many of the armies' non-combat jobs, such as cooking, nursing, driving wagons, and building defenses, were performed by slaves.

Even before the Emancipation Proclamation, thousands of slaves escaped to the safety of invading Union troops. Many were then hired by the Union army. They drove wagons, built forts, served as guides for invading forces, and performed a variety of other jobs.

The Proclamation encouraged **freedmen** (the term for emancipated slaves) to join the Union army and navy. Black sailors had been serving in the Union navy since the beginning of the war, but at first the Union army did not accept black volunteers. By the time the Emancipation Proclamation took effect, however, escaped slaves and free African Americans had been formed into Union army regiments in Louisiana, South Carolina, and Kansas. Black abolitionists called on all African American men to join in the fight.

HISTORY'S VOICES

❝ Let the black man get upon his person the brass letters, U.S.; let him get an eagle on his button, and a musket on his shoulder and bullets in his pocket, and there is no power on earth which can deny that he has earned the right to citizenship. ❞

—Frederick Douglass, *Douglass' Monthly*, August 1863

African American soldiers served in segregated units that were usually commanded by white officers. At first, black regiments were used mainly for labor and guard duty, thereby freeing white soldiers to fight. In May and July of 1863, however, African American troops fought heroically in attacks at Port Hudson on the Mississippi River and at Fort Wagner in South Carolina. In both battles the African American regiments suffered terrible losses. The 54th Massachusetts Infantry, which led the charge on Fort Wagner, became one of the most famous units of the Civil War.

Nearly 180,000 African Americans served in the Union armies. More than half had been in slavery when the war began. At the end of the war, more than a tenth of Union soldiers were African American. Black troops took part in some 200 battles. More than 38,000 died serving the Union.

READING CHECK **Summarizing** What contributions did northern and southern African Americans make in the Civil War?

THE CIVIL WAR **373**

③ What was life like in the military? *mostly boring while in camp; infectious disease, poor sanitation, ineffective medicines; much worse in the prison camps*

Life in the Military

Recall What was the United States Sanitary Commission? *organization of volunteer women who served as nurses and ambulance drivers; also advised on sanitation and nutrition*

Develop How did new military technology contribute to greater death rates? *The new minié balls struck with greater force, shattering bones and contributing to infections.*

📄 CRF: Biography: Clara Barton
📄 CRF: Biography: Mathew Brady

go.hrw.com

Online Resources

KEYWORD: SD7 CH11
TOPIC: CIVIL WAR PHOTOGRAPHY

Life in the Military

Most of the troops who died during the Civil War did not die on the battlefield or from wounds suffered there. Disease was by far the greatest killer of soldiers. For every death that resulted from battle, about two more soldiers died from disease.

Wartime medicine In a time before vaccinations and antibiotics, epidemics of mumps, measles, and smallpox swept through army camps. Soldiers who escaped infectious diseases were often sickened by conditions such as dysentery, cholera, and typhoid fever, which resulted from poor sanitation and polluted water supplies. At times, as many as one-third of an army's soldiers might be too sick to fight.

In Europe, scientists were learning that tiny organisms, today called bacteria, could spread disease, infect food and water, and enter the bloodstream through open wounds. Civil War doctors, however, knew none of these things. Doctors often went days without washing their instruments, or even their hands, passing germs from one patient to another. Soldiers sometimes tried to conceal wounds to avoid seeing the doctor.

Battlefield wounds, however, were often difficult to conceal. The minié bullet, or "minnie ball," was the most common ammunition on both sides. This heavy lead bullet inflicted great damage. Shots to an arm or leg usually shattered any bones the bullet struck. The bullets also carried dirt and germs into the wound, which often caused infection.

President Lincoln approved the creation of the United States Sanitary Commission in 1861. Within two years it had 7,000 branches across the North, staffed mainly by women volunteers. The Sanitary Commission provided nurses and ambulance drivers to the army. Its workers also collected and distributed food, clothing, and medical supplies. They inspected hospitals and army camps and offered advice on sewage disposal, hygiene, disease prevention, and nutrition.

PRIMARY SOURCES

Photograph

Civil War soldiers spent much more time in camp than on the battlefield. Camp life was boring but also dangerous due to frequent epidemics of disease.

Many soldiers had strong opinions about the war. Newspapers kept them informed about the war's progress and the political issues involved.

Writing letters home was probably the major leisure time activity in camp. Although mail delivery was often slow, letters helped morale.

Skills FOCUS   READING LIKE A HISTORIAN

Analyzing Visuals What evidence in the photograph indicates that soldiers had to do their own housekeeping while in camp?

See **Skills Handbook**, p. H30

374 CHAPTER 11

Differentiated Learning

Above Level

Advanced Learners/GATE

Research Required

1. Organize the class into small groups. Have each group research the Women's Central Association of Relief (WCAR).

2. Have each group prepare a multimedia study of the WCAR that includes its origins and purpose, and what took its place as the Civil War progressed. *precursor to the U.S. Sanitary Commission; run by women, collected supplies to be used for the care of wounded northern soldiers; dissolved when the U.S. Sanitary Commission was formed*

In their reports students should present information and an analysis of the effectiveness of women's efforts in the Civil War.

3. Have each group share its presentation to the class.

4. Then guide students in a discussion of the role of voluntary organizations and whether or not they can and should influence or direct government policy. **LS Visual-Spatial**

📄 Alternative Assessment Handbook, Rubrics 14: Group Activity; and 30: Research

Answers

Reading Like a Historian *soldier mending his own clothing*

374

Camp life On average, soldiers spent about 75 percent of their time in camp. Conditions were often horrible. In wet weather, camps were a sea of mud. In dry weather, they were filled with clouds of dust. Soldiers crammed into tents that were designed for far fewer people. As canvas for tents became scarce in the South, Confederate soldiers were often forced to sleep on the open ground.

Days in camp were long and boring. They typically began at 5 a.m. in summer and 6 a.m. in winter. After breakfast, the men took part in up to five daily drills. During these two-hour sessions they learned and practiced battlefield maneuvers. Between drills, the troops cleaned the camp, gathered firewood, wrote letters home, and played games. Boxing matches, baseball, and card games were popular.

Troops on both sides ate well at first. In camp, soldiers' daily rations consisted of bread, fresh or salted pork or beef, coffee, and beans. When on the march, however, hard bread biscuits called hardtack and coffee or water were the main sources of nourishment. Soldiers often added to their diets whatever they could find in the area. A large army could strip the countryside of crops and livestock.

Prison camps As hard as army life was, conditions for prisoners of war were much worse. At first, neither North nor South kept large numbers of captured soldiers. Many prisoners were released if they promised to go home instead of back to their army. Others were exchanged for prisoners held by the other side.

When African Americans began joining the Union army in 1863, however, this changed. Confederate leaders declared that captured black soldiers would be enslaved or executed. This threat caused Union leaders to end prisoner exchanges. As a result, the number of prisoners held by each side increased.

Good treatment of prisoners was never a high priority for either side. The end of prisoner exchanges led to overcrowding in prison camps in both the North and the South. This caused conditions to worsen. A large number of major battles in 1863 and 1864 also overwhelmed camps that were already inadequate.

Andersonville and Elmira To handle the growing number of prisoners, in 1864 Confederate leaders erected a stockade in an open field near the town of Andersonville, Georgia. Built to hold 10,000 Union soldiers, by July 1864 it held more than 30,000 men within its 20-foot log walls. A single stream ran though the enclosure, serving as a sewer as well as providing water for bathing and drinking. Under these terrible conditions, about 100 prisoners died each day in the hot sun.

When word of conditions at Andersonville reached the North, Union leaders responded by limiting Confederate prisoners' food to only bread and water. As a result, the death rate at the Union's most notorious prison camp at Elmira, New York, approached that of Andersonville. Prisoners at Elmira ate rats in order to get some meat in their diets.

READING CHECK Making Generalizations What was a soldier's life like?

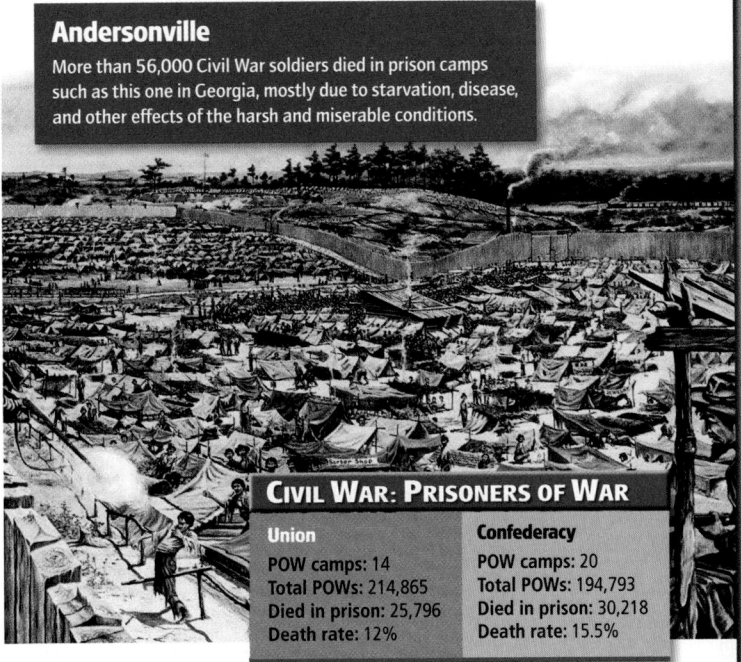

Andersonville
More than 56,000 Civil War soldiers died in prison camps such as this one in Georgia, mostly due to starvation, disease, and other effects of the harsh and miserable conditions.

CIVIL WAR: PRISONERS OF WAR

Union	Confederacy
POW camps: 14	POW camps: 20
Total POWs: 214,865	Total POWs: 194,793
Died in prison: 25,796	Died in prison: 30,218
Death rate: 12%	Death rate: 15.5%

Source: The Civil War Day by Day

THE IMPACT TODAY
Government
Humane treatment of prisoners of war is now required by the fourth Geneva Convention, an international agreement reached in 1949.

THE CIVIL WAR **375**

Reading Focus

Life in the Military

Recall What did troops do in camp? *ate, drilled, cleaned, wrote letters, and played games to relieve the boredom*

Compare How did the Union respond after word got out of the terrible conditions in Andersonville, the Confederate prison? *by punishing Confederate soldiers at the notorious Elmira prison*

Elaborate When did prison camps become especially crowded and cruel? *following the Emancipation Proclamation, when Confederates threatened to execute or enslave captured African Americans, when prisoner exchanges ended*

Answers

Reading Check *most of time in camp, routine, boring; hard, lack of supplies*

④ What similarities and differences existed on the home front in the North and South? *South suffered shortages of manufactured goods and food, and inflation, North did not. Both sides resorted to a military draft that was resented and seen as unfair, and anti-draft riots occurred in the North. Both sides imposed martial law or the suspension of habeas corpus.*

Life on the Home Front

Recall What was the effect of inflation in the South? *hardship, food riots, soldiers deserted*

Draw Conclusions Why did thousands of Confederate soldiers feel justified in deserting? *needed to go home and take care of their families and farms*

Elaborate Why did conscription so offend many in the South? *They felt they were fighting a war against an unjust and coercive national government, and did not want to be coerced by their own.*

📰 Political Cartoons Activities for American History: Cartoon 22: Southern "Volunteers"

Life on the Home front

Families on both sides made sacrifices and endured hardships as a result of the war. Still, life on the home front was quite different in the North and the South.

The southern home front Shortages made life difficult for southerners. With few factories, the South had little ability to manufacture needed goods. Food production dropped as invading Union armies made farming difficult. As a result, the costs of everyday items soared. A pair of shoes that sold for $18 in 1862 cost up to $800 by 1865. Bread sold for $25 a loaf in some places.

Scarcity was only one reason for high prices, however. Another was inflation, an increase in prices resulting from an increased supply of money. To pay for the war, the Confederate government printed huge sums of paper money. Since the South had little gold to back this money, by 1863 a Confederate paper dollar was worth only about 20 cents. The Confederate government also borrowed money by selling bonds and thus fought the war on <u>credit</u>.

High prices and shortages brought hardship. In 1863 about 1,000 women looted shops in Richmond for food, shoes, cloth, and other items. Food riots took place in several other southern cities. Such conditions led thousands of soldiers to desert. "Men cannot be expected to fight for the government that permits their wives and children to starve," one Confederate leader noted. "Poor men have been compelled to leave the army to come home to provide for their families," a Mississippi soldier explained. "We are poor men and willing to defend our country but our families [come] first."

The Confederate draft As the one-year enlistments of the original volunteers expired, southern leaders grew concerned about maintaining the armies. Many soldiers shared the views of one Virginian, who in January 1862 wrote, "If I live this twelve months out, I intend to try mighty hard to keep out [of the army]."

Reacting to such sentiments, the Confederate Congress enacted the first military draft in American history in April 1862. The law extended the volunteers' enlistments for two more years and required three years' service from other white males aged 18 to 35. (By 1864 the ages had been changed to 17 and 50.) Men in jobs critical to the war effort at home were excused as were slave overseers on large plantations and holders of 20 or more slaves.

This **conscription**, or forced service in the military, was extremely unpopular. It seemed to violate the very principles of states' rights

ACADEMIC VOCABULARY
credit the sum of money provided by a lender

Women on the Home Front

Women took over family farms and businesses while the men were away at war. These northern women (right) are part of a local militia, prepared to defend themselves against southern invaders. *The Return to Fredericksburg after the Battle* (far right) shows southern life during the war. **What does the painting show about the effects of the war on the home front?**

376 CHAPTER 11

Skills Focus: Making Inferences

At Level

Reading Skill
Recruiting Confederate Soldiers

1. Have students review the information in the text about the southern home front and the Confederate draft. You might wish to remind students of the quote from Alexander Stephens, Confederate vice president, which appears in the first section: "We can call out a million of peoples if need be, and when they are cut down, we can call another."

2. Have each student create two political cartoons, one lamenting the change in the South since the war began and the other protesting the Confederate draft.

3. Have students display their cartoons to class.
LS Visual-Spatial

📰 Alternative Assessment Handbook, Rubric 27: Political Cartoons

Answers

Photo *Women stepped up to defend themselves, if necessary.*

and limited national power for which southerners were fighting. A Texas senator defended the draft against such complaints.

Many southerners found little comfort in this reasoning. A North Carolina soldier observed that "when we hear men comparing the despotism [unlimited power] of the *Confederacy* with that of the Lincoln government —*something must be wrong.*"

The governors of Georgia and North Carolina did not support the draft and attempted to block it in their states. The draft's exemption of slaveholders also provided reasons for soldiers to desert. Many agreed with a poor farmer who deserted because he would not be forced "to fight for the rich men while they were at home having a good time."

Groups of draft evaders and deserters blocked Confederate government authority in some regions of the South. Government officials placed some areas under martial law to restore order.

Copperheads and the Union draft

Although northerners did not suffer the supply shortages that southerners did, they experienced some of the other problems that plagued the South. When the Union needed more soldiers in March 1863, it also turned to the draft to find them.

Like the Confederate draft law, the Union law allowed men who could afford to do so to hire substitutes to fight in their place. In addition, those drafted could be excused by paying a $300 fee. This amount was more than seven months' wages for the average worker. As in the South, northern critics accused the draft of turning the war into a poor man's fight.

Antidraft riots erupted across the North. The worst took place in New York City in July 1863. For four days, mobs attacked draft offices and African Americans. Shouting, "There goes a $300 man," rioters even attacked well-dressed white men. The violence left more than 100 people dead.

The draft fueled an antiwar movement that had already emerged in the North. Opposition to the war was led by some members of the Democratic Party in Congress and in several state legislatures. Their supporters referred to them as Peace Democrats. Critics called them **Copperheads**, comparing them to the poisonous snake of the same name.

Copperhead newspapers called on Union troops to desert. "It is to emancipate slaves . . . that you are used as soldiers," an Iowa newspaper wrote. "Are you, as soldiers, bound by patriotism, duty, or loyalty to fight in such a cause?" These tactics seriously threatened the war effort. As a result, the federal government arrested and jailed without trials some of the most vocal critics who opposed the war, the draft, or emancipation.

These government actions were possible because in September 1862 and again a year later Lincoln suspended **habeas corpus** across the entire country. Habeas corpus is the constitutional right of an arrested person to appear in court charged with a crime. Lincoln also suspended habeas corpus in specific places at other times during the war. He justified his actions by saying that he was willing to violate the Constitution in order to save the nation. During the war, tens of thousands of people were arrested for opposing government policy.

THE CIVIL WAR **377**

Info to Know

Mary Walker Dr. Mary Walker's Congressional Medal of Honor has been somewhat controversial, in part because she earned it through service, not combat activities. Two years before she died, the government asked for it to be returned. But sixty years after that, it was awarded to her again.

• Review & Assess •

Close

Have students create a chart contrasting life in the North and the South during the Civil War.

Review

Online Quiz, Section 3

Daily Test Practice Transparency

Assess

SE Section 3 Assessment

Progress Assessment: Section 3 Quiz

Alternative Assessment Handbook

Reteach

Interactive Reader and Study Guide, Section 3

Interactive Skills Tutor CD-ROM

FACES OF HISTORY

Mary WALKER
1832–1919

Born into an abolitionist family, Mary Edwards Walker was encouraged by her father to pursue an education. In 1855 she graduated from Syracuse Medical College, the only woman doctor in her class.

When the Civil War began, Walker tried to join the Union army but was denied a position as a medical officer. She managed to serve as an unpaid assistant surgeon, becoming the first woman surgeon in the U.S. Army. Walker worked as a field surgeon near the Union front lines for almost two years. She earned the Congressional Medal of Honor for her wartime service—the only woman to be so honored.

Make Inferences How did Walker show her support for the Union?

Women in the Civil War Women in the North and South contributed to the war in many ways. Several hundred disguised themselves as men and enlisted in the army. A few served as spies. Most women, however, filled less dramatic but more important roles. Women on both sides took over farms, plantations, stores, and other businesses while their fathers, husbands, and sons served in armies. They worked as bankers and steamboat captains. Northern women produced huge amounts of food with the help of new farm equipment such as the McCormick reaper.

The need for clothes, shoes, and other supplies created about 100,000 jobs for women in northern factories. Women also worked in the South's few factories, and women on both sides performed dangerous work making ammunition for the troops.

Women formed thousands of societies to gather and send supplies to their armies. They made bandages, shirts, and bedclothes for soldiers. After the war hundreds of female teachers went south to educate former slaves.

Many women found new occupations. Hundreds were hired by the Union government as clerks. They became the first women to hold federal government jobs. Women also staffed government offices in the South. Like clerical work, nursing was a man's job before the war. During the war, however, about 3,000 women served the Union army as paid nurses.

Some women, like **Clara Barton**, who later founded the American Red Cross, cared for the wounded on the battlefield. Thousands of female volunteers worked on hospital ships or in hospitals behind the lines. In the South women nurses served as volunteers at first. In 1862 the Confederate Congress passed a law permitting women to be hired as army nurses.

READING CHECK **Comparing and Contrasting** What similarities and differences existed in conscription in the North and South?

SECTION 3 ASSESSMENT

go.hrw.com
Online Quiz
Keyword: SD7 HP11

Reviewing Ideas, Terms, and People

1. **a. Recall** What is emancipation?
   b. Predict How do you think the Emancipation Proclamation will affect people's attitudes toward the war?

2. **a. Describe** Who were freedmen?
   b. Make Inferences Why do you think the Union army did not accept African American volunteers at first?

3. **a. Identify** What did most Civil War soldiers die from?
   b. Draw Conclusions What do you think Union leaders hoped to accomplish by ending prisoner exchanges?
   c. Predict How could camp conditions have been improved for soldiers?

4. **a. Describe** What is habeas corpus, and what role did it play in the Civil War?
   b. Analyze Why was the war often called a poor man's fight?
   c. Elaborate How did the war change some women's lives?

Critical Thinking

5. **Identifying Points of View** Review your notes on the Emancipation Proclamation. Then copy the graphic organizer below and use it to identify reasons people supported or opposed the Emancipation Proclamation.

Reasons to Oppose the Emancipation Proclamation	Reasons to Support the Emancipation Proclamation

FOCUS ON WRITING

6. **Narrative** Suppose that you live in either the North or the South during the Civil War. Write a diary entry that describes your life and experiences on the home front and your feelings about the war.

378 CHAPTER 11

Section 3 Assessment Answers

1. **a.** set someone free from slavery
   b. possible answer—will see it as a war about slavery because it frees slaves in the Confederacy

2. **a.** freed slaves
   b. possible answer—prejudice, racism

3. **a.** disease
   b. punish Confederacy for execution policy
   c. clean water, food, clothing, shelter

4. **a.** right of a prisoner to go to court and hear the charges; suspended to arrest and hold

   troublemakers criticizing U.S. policy
   b. well-off could hire someone to replace them or pay fee to avoid serving
   c. worked; volunteered to help soldiers; became spies, nurses, soldiers; lost loved ones

5. oppose—opposed a war to free slaves, government lacked power to issue it; support—damaged southern economy; moral grounds

6. have to work, shortages of goods, poverty, hardships, men dying

---

Answers

Faces of History *worked as a surgeon*

Reading Check *similarities—unpopular, seen as unfair, some were exempt; differences—southern draft was first in American history, seen as violation of states' rights*

About the Reading Louisa May Alcott is most commonly known for writing *Little Women* (1868–69). When the Civil War began, Alcott volunteered as a nurse until she contracted typhoid and was sent home. *Hospital Sketches* (1863) is a published collection of letters from her time as a nurse and was one of her first significantly recognized works.

AS YOU READ Consider how difficult it must have been for hospital staff to care for injured soldiers under such poor conditions.

Excerpt from

Hospital Sketches

by Louisa May Alcott

In they came, some on stretchers, some in men's arms, some feebly staggering along propped on rude crutches, and one lay stark and still with covered face, as a comrade gave his name to be recorded before they carried him away to the dead house. All was hurry and confusion; the hall was full of these wrecks of humanity, for the most exhausted could not reach a bed till duly ticketed and registered; the walls were lined with rows of such as could sit, the floor covered with the more disabled, the steps and doorways filled with helpers and lookers on; the sound of many feet and voices made that usually quiet hour as noisy as noon; and, in the midst of it all, the matron's motherly face brought more comfort to many a poor soul, than the cordial draughts she administered, or the cheery words that welcomed all, making of the hospital a home.

The sight of several stretchers, each with its legless, armless, or desperately wounded occupant, entering my ward, admonished me that I was there to work, not to wonder or weep; so I corked up my feelings, and returned to the path of duty, which was rather a "hard road to travel" just then. The house had been a hotel before hospitals were needed, and many of the doors still bore their old names; some not so inappropriate as might be imagined, for that ward was

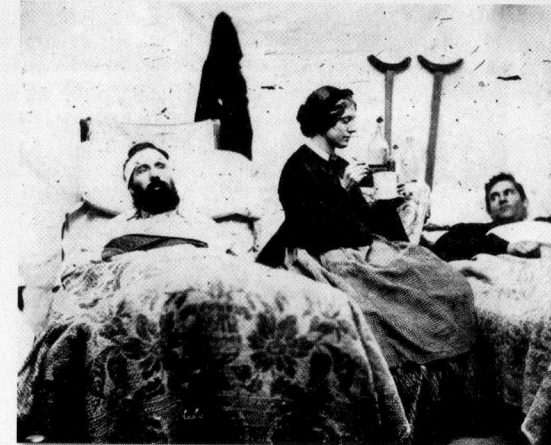

Nurse Ann Bell tends to wounded soldiers in a federal hospital in Nashville, Tennessee.

in truth a *ballroom,* if gun-shot wounds could christen it. Forty beds were prepared, many already tenanted by tired men who fell down anywhere, and drowsed till the smell of food roused them. Round the great stove was gathered the dreariest group I ever saw— ragged, gaunt and pale, mud to the knees, with bloody bandages untouched since put on days before; many bundled up in blankets, coats being lost or useless; and all wearing the disheartened look which proclaimed defeat. . .

Skills FOCUS   READING LIKE A HISTORIAN

1. **Making Inferences** What critical role did women play during the Civil War?

2. **Literature as Historical Evidence** What inferences can be made from the excerpt about the Union army and the conditions under which soldiers fought?

See Skills Handbook, p. H32

Skills Focus: Interpreting Literature as Historical Evidence   **At Level**

Reading Like a Historian Skill
Civil War Hospitals

1. Have students make a list of words that are new to them and make flash cards with the definitions. Have students work in small groups to quiz each other on the words.

2. Have students work individually to list words that provide the description of the wounded and the crowded conditions within the hospital.

3. Have volunteers share their word lists with the class, then guide students in a discussion. Ask students if they believe that the picture created by Alcott is realistic, and have them explain their reasoning.

LS Interpersonal, Intrapersonal

Alternative Assessment Handbook, Rubrics 1: Acquiring Information; and 11: Discussions

---

Excerpt from *Hospital Sketches* by Louisa May Alcott

Word Help

feebly weakly, sickly
admonished warned
tenanted filled
gaunt very thin

Meet the Writer

Louisa May Alcott (1832–1888) After the Civil War began, Louisa May Alcott volunteered as a nurse, and it was her letters home that were published in 1863 as *Hospital Sketches*. Alcott is best known, however, for the classic *Little Women*, an autobiographical novel about a New England family. Alcott's father was a transcendentalist, and Alcott spent most of her life in Boston and Concord, Massachusetts, where the family knew both Ralph Waldo Emerson and Henry David Thoreau. Alcott became a writer to help support her family, and it was her children's works like *Little Women* that brought her fame.

Answers

Reading Like a Historian
1. *They cared for wounded soldiers under incredibly difficult circumstances.*
2. *The army was unprepared to care for its wounded; war was horribly deadly*

379

Bellringer

The Inside Story. . . Use the **Daily Bellringer Transparency** to help students answer the question.

Daily Bellringer Transparency, Section 4

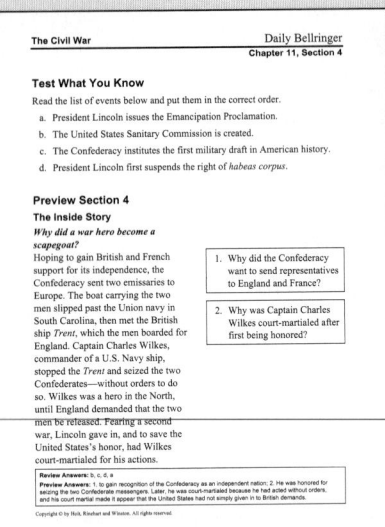

Taking Notes

Chancellorsville—Union army was attacked from both sides, Confederate victory; Gettysburg—Union army takes hills and ridges, direct attack, Union victory; Vicksburg—Union forces besiege city, try to starve city into surrender, Union victory

BEFORE YOU READ

MAIN IDEA

Important fighting occurred in all sections of the country as well as at sea.

READING FOCUS

1. In what ways was the war at sea an important part of the Civil War?
2. What were each side's goals in the West, and how were events there influenced by the rest of the war?
3. What three major battles took place in 1863, and why was each important?
4. Why was the fighting around Chattanooga, Tennessee, important to the outcome of the war?

KEY TERMS AND PEOPLE

Trent affair
Battle of Glorieta Pass
Battle of Pea Ridge
Stand Watie
Battle of Chancellorsville
George Meade
Battle of Gettysburg
James Longstreet
Pickett's Charge
Battle of Chickamauga

TAKING NOTES As you read, take notes on three crucial battles fought in 1863. Record your notes in a graphic organizer like the one shown here.

Battle	Key Strategy	Outcome
Battle of Chancellorsville		
Battle of Gettysburg		
Siege of Vicksburg		

THE INSIDE STORY

Why did a war hero become a scapegoat? It was no secret that Confederate leaders planned to send two of their number to Europe to seek British and French recognition of southern independence. So when a boat carrying James Mason and John Slidell slipped past the Union blockade of Charleston, South Carolina, in October 1861, the U.S. Navy was embarrassed. Reaching Cuba, the two men then boarded the *Trent*, a British ship bound for England. Captain Charles Wilkes, commander of the U.S. warship *San Jacinto*, decided to redeem the navy's honor. On November 8, even though he had no specific order to do so, Wilkes stopped the unarmed *Trent* at sea and seized Mason and Slidell.

Wilkes's action made him a hero in the North. Congress voted him a commendation. However, Britain demanded that Mason and Slidell be released. When Lincoln hesitated, the British government sent troops to Canada. Facing the prospect of war with Britain, Lincoln allowed the two Confederates to resume their journey. "One war at a time," the president explained. His advisers, however, did not want the United States to be humiliated by appearing to give in to a British threat. A way was found to save the nation's honor. Captain Wilkes, the recent national hero, was court-martialed for what now was labeled his great misdeed. ■

One War at a Time

◀ **A Union warship chases a Confederate blockade runner.**

380

Teach the Main Idea

At Level

The War Continues

1. **Teach** Ask students the Reading Focus questions to teach this section.

2. **Apply** Have students create a time line of the events discussed in the section.

3. **Review** Have volunteers share their time lines with the class, and have students explain the significance of each event they included. **LS** **Visual-Spatial**

4. **Practice/Homework** Have each student write a poem about the Civil War at sea.
   LS **Auditory-Musical**
   Alternative Assessment Handbook Rubric 26: Poems and Songs
   Graphic Organizer Transparencies

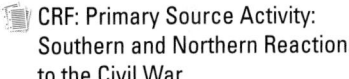

Clash of the Ironclads
The battle between the *Monitor* (right) and the *Virginia* (left), also known by its former name, the *Merrimack*, tested the capabilities of ironclad ships.

The Civil War at Sea

As the *Trent* affair illustrates, the Civil War was a world event. The war's most obvious international impact was its effect on trade. In particular, the Union's naval blockade disrupted the South's trade with the rest of the world.

Blockade runners At the beginning of the war, slipping through, or "running," the Union blockade was fairly easy. Once the Union navy obtained more ships, however, the blockade became tighter and tighter. By the summer of 1862, Union warships guarded most southern ports.

To get supplies from overseas, the South depended on ships known as blockade runners. Blockade runners were built for speed. They were low, sleek vessels painted gray to make them less visible. To make the vessels even harder to see, attempts to run the blockade often took place at night, without lights. Many blockade runners burned anthracite coal for fuel, which produces no smoke.

When leaving the South, these ships were packed full of cotton. They brought this valuable material to Bermuda, the Bahamas, or Cuba, where it was unloaded and shipped to Europe. On the return trip, the blockade runners carried silk, soap, pepper, and other goods that brought high prices in the South. Later in the war, when supplies in the South were desperately low, the Confederate government required that blockade runners be at least half full of medicine, food, and military supplies.

The scarcity of many goods in the South meant that prices were high, and successful blockade runners could make enormous profits. A ship that ran the blockade could pay for itself in just one round trip. A captain could earn $5,000 in gold and a crew member $250 for the voyage. Crew members were often British citizens because, if captured, they were quickly released. Confederates who were captured trying to run the blockade faced long prison terms.

The *Monitor* and the *Merrimack* The Confederates could run the Union blockade, but they hoped to destroy it. To do so, they created a powerful ironclad ship by repairing the damaged USS *Merrimack*, which they had captured. Then they covered it with thick iron plates for armor and renamed it the *Virginia*.

When word reached the North that the Confederates were building the *Virginia*, Union officials hurried to complete their own seagoing ironclad, which they had been building in New York. On March 9, 1862, the Union's ironclad *Monitor* arrived off the Virginia coast to confront the *Virginia*.

The two ships fought for hours in the world's first battle between ironclads. Neither was able to seriously damage the other, but engine problems forced the *Virginia* to return to port. Although the battle had no winner, it changed naval warfare forever. In May the Confederates destroyed the *Virginia* to prevent its capture by McClellan's invading Union army.

Reading Focus

1 In what ways was the war at sea an important part of the Civil War? *Union navy tried to disrupt the South's trade; South tried to "run" the blockade.*

The Civil War at Sea

Recall What was the bulk of the cargo on ships sailing from the South? *cotton*

Make Generalizations Why would blockade runners risk their ships and their lives to bring goods to southern ports? *Profits were enormous for those who got through.*

Analyze Why did the first battle between two ironclads end in a draw? *Neither ironclad was able to sufficiently damage the other.*

📖 CRF: Primary Source Activity: Southern and Northern Reactions to the Civil War

---

Differentiating Instruction

Below Level

Special Education Students

1. Have students use the information in the text to sketch the battle between the *Monitor* and the *Virginia*. Have students label the battleships, and write a brief statement telling what happened.

2. Have volunteers share their illustrations and statements with the class.

3. As an extension, have students research and create a pictorial history of ironclads and the evolution of battleships to the modern day.
   LS Visual-Spatial

   📖 Alternative Assessment Handbook, Rubric 3: Artwork

Confederate raiders Unable to match the Union navy's strength, the South turned to unconventional tactics to battle the North at sea. Confederate leaders paid for the construction of 29 commerce raider ships in Europe. These vessels then roamed the world's oceans attacking Union merchant ships and disrupting the North's foreign trade.

The most famous of the Confederate commerce raiders was the CSS *Alabama*. Launched from Britain in May 1862, the *Alabama* terrorized Union shipping across the Atlantic and Pacific oceans. It was finally caught and sunk by the USS *Kearsarge* off the coast of France in June 1864. By that time, however, the *Alabama* had done enormous damage to Union trade. It captured 68 northern merchant ships during its 22 months at sea. Another of the raiders, the *Shenandoah*, captured 36 vessels.

READING CHECK **Summarizing** How did the South try to overcome the North's advantages at sea?

The War in the West

While the most important battles of the Civil War took place east of the Mississippi River, Union and Confederate forces clashed to the west of the Mississippi as well. About 90 engagements were fought in the West.

California and the territories Congress admitted Kansas to the Union as a free state in 1861 and quickly added the Dakota, Colorado, and Nevada territories as well. Between 1862 and 1864 Congress created the Idaho, Arizona, and Montana territories. Lincoln appointed pro-Union officials to head each of the new territorial governments. These actions were intended to secure the West for the Union.

To help further ensure western loyalty, Lincoln did not enforce the draft in the West or pressure the region for volunteers. Nevertheless, some 17,000 Californians joined the Union army. The state's main contribution, however, was its gold. Mines in California and in the new territories provided vast amounts of gold and silver, which helped the Union pay the costs of fighting the war.

Because the need for soldiers in the East was so great, few Union troops were available to defend the West. In early 1862 about 4,000 Confederate troops in Texas marched north.

The Confederates' goal was to conquer the lightly defended Union territories and capture their valuable mines.

Union troops and volunteers from California, Colorado, and Kansas stopped the Confederate invasion in the **Battle of Glorieta Pass** in northern New Mexico on March 28, 1862. The Confederates actually won the day-long battle. Some Colorado soldiers, however, slipped around the Confederate army during the fighting and destroyed the Confederate supply wagons. The loss of their supplies forced the invaders back to Texas. Their retreat secured the West for the Union.

Native Americans and the war More than 10,000 Native Americans took part in the Civil War. Many Cherokees fought for the Confederacy, but the war bitterly divided the Cherokees—and other nations as well—over issues of loyalty and slavery.

Some nations saw the transfer of soldiers from western forts to eastern battlefields as a chance to take back land they had lost. In 1862, for example, Sioux in Minnesota and Dakota Territory began a revolt.

When the Union moved its soldiers from Indian Territory to the East, Confederate agents soon arrived. They negotiated treaties with the Cherokees, Creeks, Choctaws, Chickasaws, and several smaller tribes. These four tribes, with aid from the Seminoles, raised about 5,000 Indian troops for the Confederate army.

Despite the treaties, most Cherokees, Creeks, and Seminoles supported the Union. Some of them tried to escape to Kansas but were attacked by Confederate Indian troops and Texas cavalry. In Kansas, Union officers organized the survivors and other Native Americans into two regiments.

About 1,000 Native Americans were among the 14,000 Confederates who took part in the war's biggest battle west of the Mississippi. This was the **Battle of Pea Ridge**, which occurred in Arkansas in March 1862. Although the Union army won the battle, Indian troops commanded by Cherokee leader **Stand Watie** fought bravely. Watie was later promoted to general, the only Native American on either side to hold this rank in the war.

Victory at the Battle of Pea Ridge helped the Union's plan to conquer the Mississippi River valley. It also exposed Indian Territory to attack. In June 1862 and again in 1863, Union Indians and other troops invaded Indian Territory and defeated the Confederate Indians. Many Indians then abandoned their treaty with the South and pledged loyalty to the Union. Watie, however, continued to resist. He waged a guerrilla campaign for the rest of the war. In fact, Watie was the last Confederate general to surrender when the war ended.

READING CHECK **Identifying Problems and Solutions** Why would some Indians have viewed the war as an opportunity and have sided with the South?

Three Major Battles

After being crushed at the Battle of Fredericksburg in December 1862, the Union Army of the Potomac was ready to fight again by spring. General Joseph Hooker was now in command.

The Battle of Chancellorsville Leaving 40,000 men at Fredericksburg to keep Confederate General Robert E. Lee's attention, Hooker moved more than 70,000 troops west and then south across the Rappahannock River, hoping to surprise the Confederates from behind.

Lee expected this and marched 40,000 soldiers west. He ordered the 10,000 troops he left in Fredericksburg to light many campfires at night so Union forces would think a much larger army was still there. Then Lee divided his army again and sent Stonewall Jackson and about 30,000 troops on a daylong march around Hooker's army to attack its right side. At 6 p.m. on May 2, 1863, Jackson's troops charged out of the woods at Hooker's troops as they cooked dinner in their camps, near a crossroads named Chancellorsville. The attack was a complete surprise. If darkness had not halted the fighting, the Union army might have been destroyed.

Reading Focus

❸ What three major battles took place in 1863, and why was each important? *Chancellorsville, major victory for Lee, gave South hope; Gettysburg, a terrible defeat for the South; Vicksburg, great victory for Grant, gave the Union total control of the Mississippi*

Three Major Battles

Recall What was Hooker's strategy for attacking Lee's forces at Chancellorsville? *Hooker would go west, then south, to attack Lee from the rear.*

Analyze What was the major problem with Hooker's strategy? *Lee had anticipated his move.*

Battle of Chancellorsville

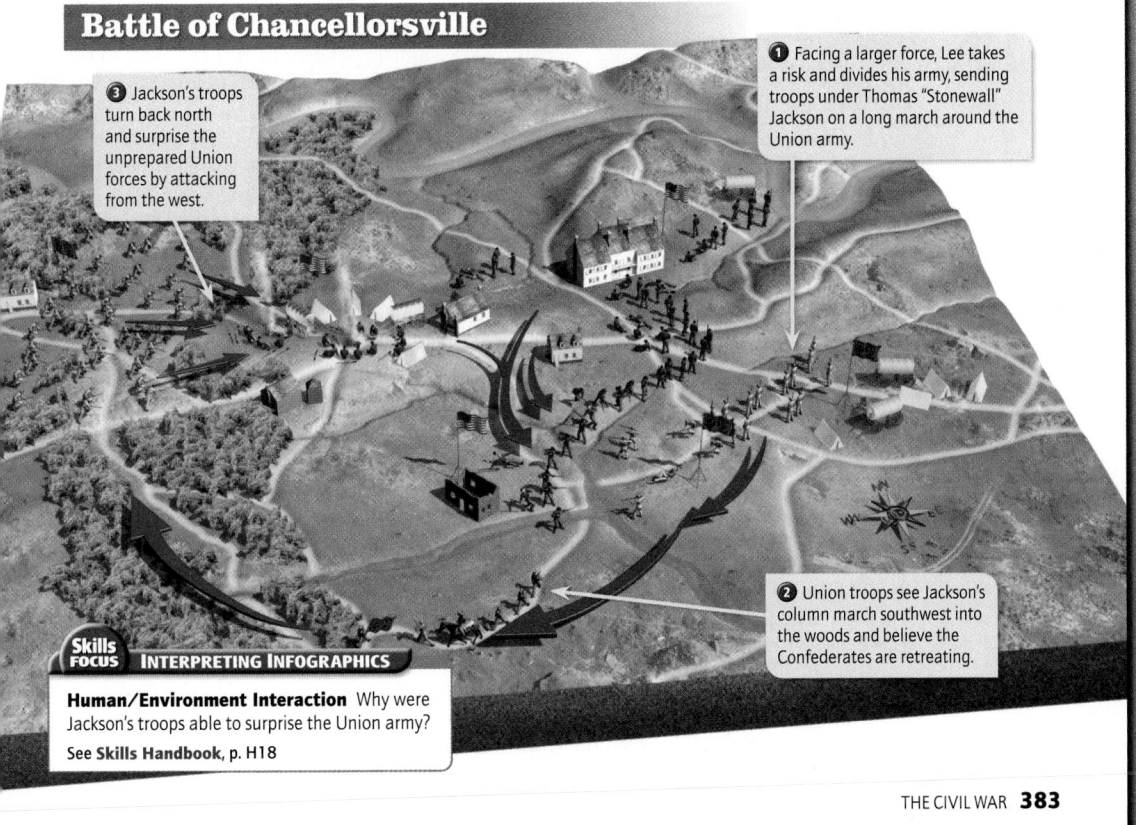

❸ Jackson's troops turn back north and surprise the unprepared Union forces by attacking from the west.

❶ Facing a larger force, Lee takes a risk and divides his army, sending troops under Thomas "Stonewall" Jackson on a long march around the Union army.

❷ Union troops see Jackson's column march southwest into the woods and believe the Confederates are retreating.

Skills Focus **INTERPRETING INFOGRAPHICS**

Human/Environment Interaction Why were Jackson's troops able to surprise the Union army?
See Skills Handbook, p. H18

THE CIVIL WAR **383**

Skills Focus: Analyzing Primary Sources

Reading Like a Historian Skill
Chancellorsville

1. Read the following words of General Hooker to the class: *"Our artillery had always been superior to that of the rebels, as was also our infantry, except in discipline; and that for reasons not necessary to mention, never did equal Lee's army; with a rank and file vastly inferior to our own, intellectually and physically, that army has, by discipline alone, acquired a character for steadiness and efficiency unsurpassed, in my judgment, in ancient or modern times. We have not been able to rival it, nor has there been any near approximation to it in the other rebel armies."*

2. Have students write a brief essay in which they answer the following questions: why was Lee's army so much more steady and efficient than Hooker's? How does Hooker view the southern soldier? **LS Linguistic-Verbal**

 Alternative Assessment Handbook, Rubric 12: Drawing Conclusions

Answers

Interpreting Infographics *Union forces thought Jackson's army was still in Fredericksburg.*

Reading Check *Union army often used against Native Americans; some thought fighting against the Union would enable them to regain lost territory.*

Reading Focus

Three Major Battles

Recall How did the Battle of Gettysburg begin? *accidentally, as a few southern soldiers looking for shoes came across a Union scouting party*

Analyze Why had Lee decided to invade the North again? *Lee was confident after Chancellorsville; wanted to carry the war to the North hoping to persuade them to sue for peace and end the blockade that was starving the South.*

Activity **Gettysburg** Have students use the information about the three days at Gettysburg to create their own sequencing chart for the battle.

LS Visual-Spatial

Map Transparency:
Three Days at Gettysburg

✳ **Interactive Map:**
Three Days at Gettysburg

Recent Scholarship

In *Gettysburg*, Civil War historian Stephen Sears provides an in-depth examination of the battle at Gettysburg, beginning with the initial planning in May 1863 and ending with the defeat and retreat of the Army of Northern Virginia. Sears provides clear account of how 60,000 men became casualties, and he argues that Lee was never fully in charge of the army during the battle.

Gettysburg by Stephen Sears. Houghton Mifflin, 2003

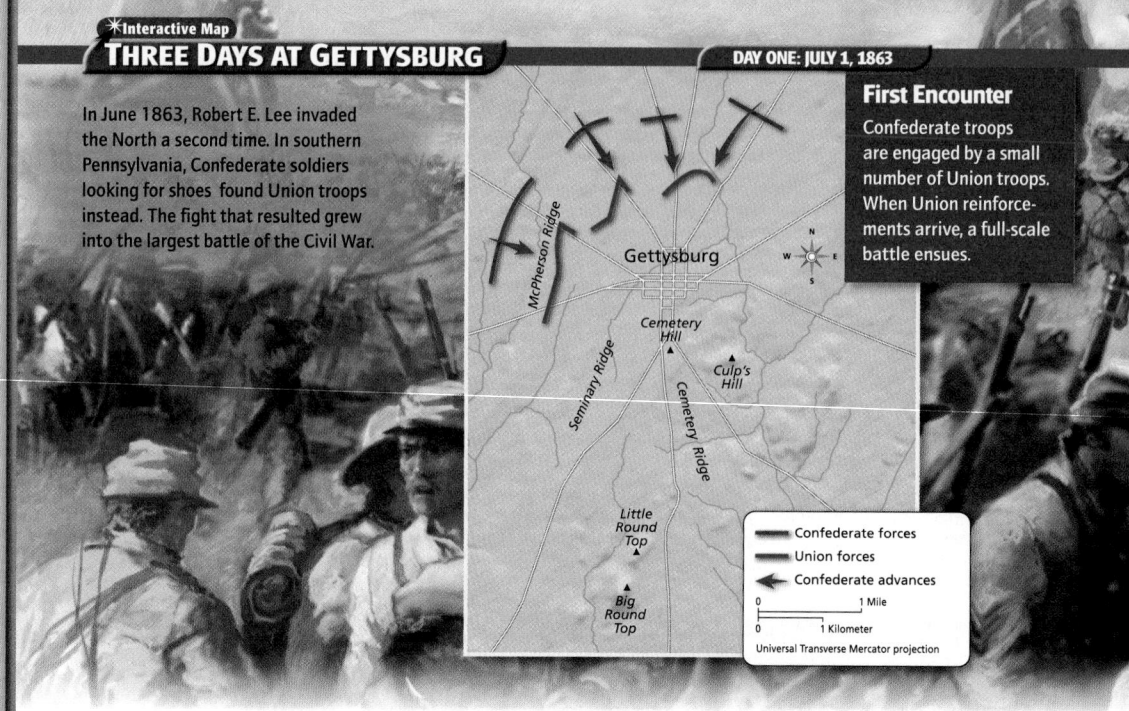

✳Interactive Map
THREE DAYS AT GETTYSBURG

DAY ONE: JULY 1, 1863

In June 1863, Robert E. Lee invaded the North a second time. In southern Pennsylvania, Confederate soldiers looking for shoes found Union troops instead. The fight that resulted grew into the largest battle of the Civil War.

First Encounter
Confederate troops are engaged by a small number of Union troops. When Union reinforcements arrive, a full-scale battle ensues.

- Confederate forces
- Union forces
- Confederate advances

0   1 Mile
0   1 Kilometer
Universal Transverse Mercator projection

The **Battle of Chancellorsville** lasted two more days. Then on May 5 Hooker retreated, having suffered more than 17,000 casualties. Lee lost nearly 13,000 men. Among them was Stonewall Jackson, the man Lee called his "strong right arm." Jackson was mistakenly shot by his own troops as he returned from scouting enemy lines on the first night of the battle. On May 10 he died from his wounds.

Chancellorsville was Lee's greatest and most brilliant victory. Defeating a force about twice its size lifted the spirits of his army. In the North, morale sank even lower. The antiwar Copperheads pointed to Chancellorsville as proof that the war could not be won.

For these reasons and others, Lee decided the time was right to invade the North again. The Union blockade and the South's shortages were beginning to seriously weaken his army. He hoped a major victory on Union soil would cause the North to finally quit the war.

The Battle of Gettysburg In June 1863 Lee marched his army north. Hooker's army moved too, keeping itself between the enemy

force and Washington, D.C. However, Hooker did not try to block the Confederates from entering Union territory on June 24. Convinced that Hooker was as indecisive as McClellan, Lincoln replaced him with General **George Meade**.

Meanwhile, a Confederate general learned about a supply of shoes rumored to be in the nearby town of Gettysburg, Pennsylvania. His troops desperately needed shoes. On July 1 he ordered some soldiers into the town to locate and seize the shoes. There they came upon Union cavalry units who were looking for Lee's army. The skirmish that took place developed into the largest battle ever fought in North America, the three-day **Battle of Gettysburg**.

When the fighting began, both sides rushed reinforcements to Gettysburg. By early afternoon about 24,000 Confederate and 19,000 Union troops were involved. When the day ended, the southerners had pushed the Union army back onto some hills south of the town.

That night Lee and Meade arrived. General **James Longstreet** had become Lee's most trusted commander after Jackson's death. Longstreet warned Lee that the Union positions were too

Differentiating Instruction

Below Level

English-Language Learners
Battle of Gettysburg

1. Review the events leading to the Battle of Gettysburg.

2. Read the following homily to students: *For want of a nail, a shoe was lost; For want of a shoe, a horse was lost; for want of a horse, a battle was lost.*

3. Have students write a poem or song lyrics about how little things influenced the course

of history, as in the battle at Gettysburg. In this case, the Battle of Gettysburg began because of a "little thing" like needing shoes, rather than establishing a plan of attack at a time or a place Lee or the Union commanders might have chosen. **LS Auditory-Musical**

Alternative Assessment Handbook, Rubric 26: Poems and Songs

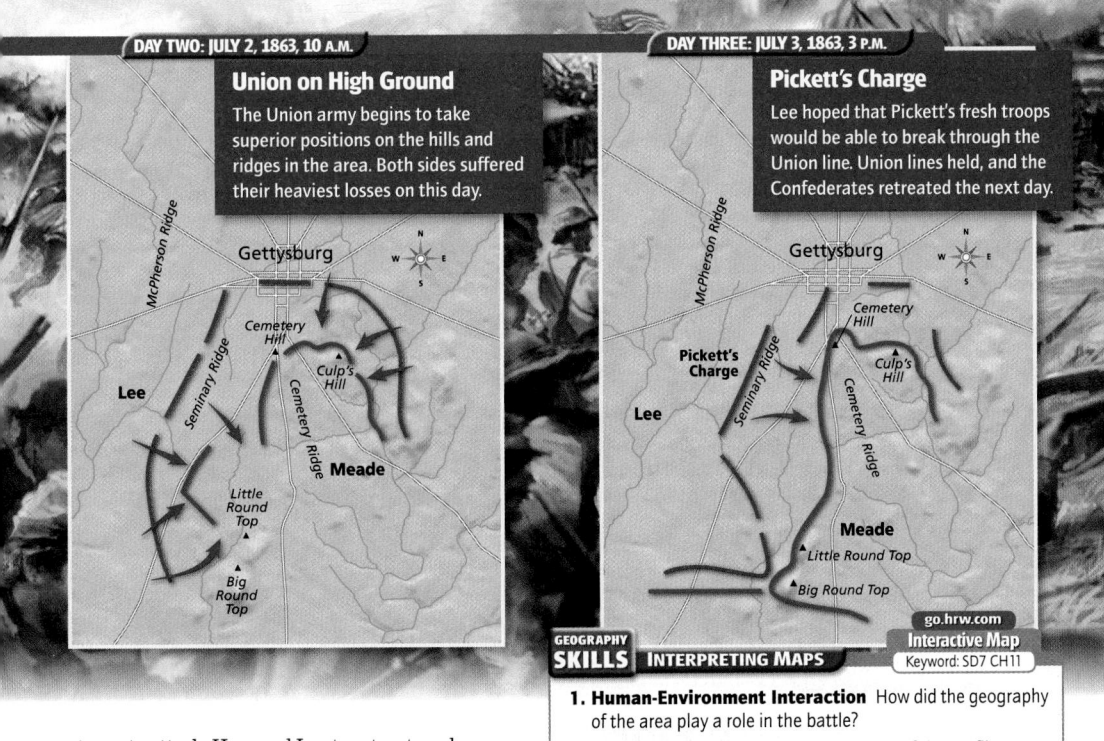

DAY TWO: JULY 2, 1863, 10 A.M.

Union on High Ground
The Union army begins to take superior positions on the hills and ridges in the area. Both sides suffered their heaviest losses on this day.

DAY THREE: JULY 3, 1863, 3 P.M.

Pickett's Charge
Lee hoped that Pickett's fresh troops would be able to break through the Union line. Union lines held, and the Confederates retreated the next day.

GEOGRAPHY SKILLS | INTERPRETING MAPS

go.hrw.com
Interactive Map
Keyword: SD7 CH11

1. **Human-Environment Interaction** How did the geography of the area play a role in the battle?
2. **Movement** Trace the mounting severity of the conflict from July 1 to July 2. What were the Confederate and Union strategies? Who had the advantage by July 3? Explain.

See **Skills Handbook**, p. H18

strong to attack. He urged Lee to retreat, make the Union army chase him, and fight the battle on ground of his own choosing.

After Chancellorsville, however, Lee had great confidence in his army. "The enemy is there and I intend to attack him there," he said, pointing to the Union lines. "If he is there, it will be because he is anxious that we should attack him," Longstreet replied, "a good reason, in my judgment, for not doing so." Ignoring this warning, Lee ordered an attack the next day.

July 2 saw some of the bloodiest fighting of the entire war. Confederate troops broke through Union defenses and tried to seize Little Round Top, an undefended hill just south of the Union's lines. The 20th Maine regiment rushed to the hill in time for a heroic defense. The day's fighting cost the Confederates some 9,000 casualties, but Lee was determined not to leave Pennsylvania without a victory. He ordered 15,000 fresh troops to attack the center of the Union lines on Cemetery Ridge the next day.

Longstreet objected. Again Lee would not be persuaded. The next day a great artillery duel took place as the Confederates tried to soften up the Union defenses for the assault. The thunder of the guns was heard in Pittsburgh, some 200 miles away.

Then in mid-afternoon, the guns fell silent. Longstreet was with one of his officers, General George Pickett, when the order came to attack. Pickett later recalled their exchange.

HISTORY'S VOICES

❝He looked at me for a moment, then held out his hand. Presently clasping his other hand over mine without speaking, he bowed his head...I saw tears glistening on his cheeks and beard. The stern old war-horse, God bless him, was weeping for his men.❞
—General George Pickett in a letter to his fiancée

Then Pickett's troops, a line of soldiers a mile wide and three rows deep, began marching toward the Union positions a mile away. As

THE CIVIL WAR **385**

Three Major Battles

Recall How many men took part in Pickett's Charge? *15,000*

Evaluate How did Lee finally indicate that he understood how he had failed and took responsibility for that failure? *He rode among his men and said "It's all my fault. It is I who lost this fight."*

Analyze Why was the surrender of Vicksburg so important to the Union? *It was the last Confederate stronghold on the Mississippi; its fall split the South east and west.*

📋 CRF: Interdisciplinary Project: Calculate and Interpret Civil War Data

Info to Know

Vicksburg General Grant's 12-year-old son Fred accompanied his father to war. Following a battle near Vicksburg, he later wrote: [I] *"joined a detachment which was collecting the dead for burial—but sickening at the sights I made my way with another one which was gathering the wounded to a log house which had been appropriated for a hospital. Here the scenes were so terrible that I became faint and ill, and making my way to a tree, I sat down, the most wobegone twelve-year-old in America."*

MISCONCEPTION ///ALERT\\\

While popular legend has it that President Lincoln hurriedly wrote the Gettysburg Address on the back of an envelope, this is not the case. Lincoln wrote two drafts of his speech and made further changes to it as he spoke. Later on, Lincoln made copies of his remarks.

Answers

Reading Like a Historian 1. *to see if a nation conceived in liberty and dedicated to the belief that all men are created equal can survive;* **2.** *deaths of soldiers means that nation must continue its efforts, the living must finish the jobs those soldiers began*

386

---

the Confederates moved across the open field that separated the two armies, a storm of bullets and artillery shells tore huge holes in their ranks. About 300 Confederate soldiers briefly reached the Union defenses, but they were driven back or killed.

Of the 15,000 soldiers who carried out **Pickett's Charge**, less than half returned to the Confederate lines. Lee told Pickett to ready his division in case the Union army launched a counterattack. "General Lee, I have no division," Pickett replied. Finally understanding the extent of the slaughter, Lee apologized as he rode among his troops. "It's all my fault," he said. "It is I who lost this fight."

The next day, July 4, the Confederates began their retreat. Lee had suffered 28,000 casualties among his 75,000 troops. The Union had about 23,000 casualties out of some 85,000 soldiers. As Lee's battered army made its way back to Virginia, word reached Richmond that Vicksburg, the Confederate stronghold on the Mississippi River, had fallen to the Union.

The Siege of Vicksburg After several attempts to capture Vicksburg, Grant began one of his most brilliant campaigns. In April 1863 he marched his army down the west bank of the Mississippi River past Vicksburg. South of the city, Grant crossed the river and moved inland, where he fought and won five battles in 17 days. Then in May, having driven the other Confederate forces from the region, he began a siege to starve Vicksburg and its 32,000 defenders into surrender. (You can read more about Vicksburg in the History and Geography feature that follows this section.)

For weeks, Grant's artillery and Union gunboats on the river kept up a constant shelling of the city. Vicksburg's citizens dug caves into the sides of hills and moved into them to escape the rain of death and destruction. As they exhausted their food supplies, they ate horses, mules, dogs, and rats to stay alive.

On July 4, the forty-eighth day of the siege and the day Lee began his retreat from Gettysburg, the Confederate commander at Vicks-

The Gettysburg Address

Lincoln made this speech to dedicate a cemetery for the soldiers killed in the Battle of Gettysburg. He used the occasion to remind a war-weary nation why it was fighting.

Fourscore and seven years ago our fathers brought forth on this continent a new nation, conceived in liberty and dedicated to the proposition that all men are created equal.

Now we are engaged in a great civil war, testing whether that nation or any nation so conceived and so dedicated can long endure. We are met on a great battlefield of that war. We have come to dedicate a portion of it as a final resting place for those who died here that the nation might live. It is altogether fitting and proper that we should do this.

But, in a larger sense, we can not dedicate—we can not consecrate—we can not hallow—this ground. The brave men, living and dead, who struggled here, have consecrated it, far above our poor power to add or detract. The world will little note nor long remember what we say here, but it can never forget what they did here.

It is for us the living, rather, to be dedicated here to the unfinished work which they who fought here have thus far so nobly advanced. It is rather for us to be here dedicated to the great task remaining before us—that from these honored dead we take increased devotion to that cause for which they here gave the last full measure of devotion—that we here highly resolve that these dead shall not have died in vain, that this nation shall have a new birth of freedom, and that government of the people, by the people, for the people shall not perish from the earth.

Skills FOCUS | **READING LIKE A HISTORIAN**

1. **Analyzing Primary Sources** For what reason does Lincoln say the Union is fighting the war?

2. **Identifying Points of View** How does he connect the soldiers' deaths to the need to continue the war?

See Skills Handbook, pp. H28–H29

Skills Focus: Analyzing Primary Sources   At Level

Reading Like a Historian Skill
The Siege of Vicksburg

1. Read the following description of civilian life in Vicksburg during the siege: *"Mother and I were standing in the tent, she brushing my hair, when we heard the report of the mortar, heard the shell rattling over, and knew it was near. We looked at each other, and Mother exclaimed, 'That sounds very near. Get into the cave!' She did get in, but I had only time to jump into a small hole we children had dug out into the side of the hill, when a piece of the shell came down into the tent, demolishing the wash-stand by which we had stood."*

2. Have students discuss why primary sources like these, written by civilians, provide a view of the Civil War that might otherwise be unavailable to historians. **LS Interpersonal**

📋 Alternative Assessment Handbook, Rubric 11: Discussions

burg surrendered the city and his army of 31,000 troops to Grant. Four days later, Port Hudson, Louisiana, the last Confederate fort on the Mississippi River, also surrendered to Union forces.

READING CHECK **Identifying Cause and Effect** What set of events led to the huge, three-day Battle of Gettysburg?

The Chattanooga Campaign

The losses at Gettysburg, Vicksburg, and Port Hudson plunged southerners into gloom. Their spirits improved only slightly when a Confederate army led by General Braxton Bragg won a major victory at the **Battle of Chickamauga** in northwest Georgia in September 1863. The battle resulted from a Union campaign to capture Chattanooga, an important railroad center on the Georgia-Tennessee border.

General William Rosecrans, the Union commander, had lured the Confederate army out of Chattanooga, planning to destroy it on open ground. Instead, it was the Union army that was nearly destroyed. As the Union soldiers retreated, they found the Confederates had left the road to Chattanooga unprotected. This allowed the Union army to flee to the very city it hoped to capture. By the time Bragg pursued

them, Union troops were ready to defend the city. Bragg's forces dug in on the hills around Chattanooga and tried to starve them out.

In late October, Grant arrived and opened a supply line to feed the Union troops trapped in Chattanooga. By late November 1863, he had gathered enough troops to end the Confederate siege. In the Battle of Lookout Mountain and the Battle of Missionary Ridge, his forces drove the Confederates from their positions overlooking the city. A northern journalist described the Union attack on Missionary Ridge.

HISTORY'S VOICES

❝They creep up [the mountain], hand over hand, loading and firing, and wavering and halting... Plunging shot tear away comrades on left and right...but our brave mountaineers are clambering steadily on.❞

—B.F. Taylor, November 25, 1863

These victories gave the Union forces control of Chattanooga, an important first step in Grant's plan to invade Georgia, the heart of the Lower South. Southerners were also aware of what the battles meant. "Unless something is done," one Confederate official wrote, "we are irretrievably [hopelessly] gone."

READING CHECK **Identifying Main Idea and Details** What did the Union hope to accomplish in the Battle of Chickamauga, and with what result?

THE IMPACT TODAY

Culture
Chickamauga was the first Civil War battlefield to become a national park, earning that designation in 1890. Gettysburg became a national park in 1895.

SECTION 4 ASSESSMENT

go.hrw.com
Online Quiz
Keyword: SD7 HP11

Reviewing Ideas, Terms, and People

1. **a. Identify** What was the *Trent* affair?
   b. Draw Conclusions How did the battle between the *Monitor* and the *Virginia* change naval warfare?

2. **a. Describe** How did Lincoln encourage loyalty to the Union in the West?
   b. Elaborate What factors might have influenced Native Americans to choose a side in the war?

3. **a. Recall** Why did Lee decide to invade the North in 1863?
   b. Draw Conclusions Why were Vicksburg and Port Hudson important locations?
   c. Evaluate Do you agree that Lee was responsible for the loss of the **Battle of Gettysburg**? Why or why not?

4. **a. Identify** Who was Braxton Bragg?
   b. Make Inferences Why was control of Chattanooga important to the North?
   c. Elaborate By the end of 1863, what was the general feeling about the war in the South? Why?

Critical Thinking

5. **Comparing and Contrasting** Review your notes on major Civil War battles. Then copy the graphic organizer below and use it to identify similarities and differences between them.

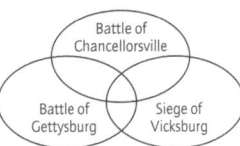

Battle of Chancellorsville

Battle of Gettysburg

Siege of Vicksburg

FOCUS ON WRITING

6. **Descriptive** Suppose you are a newspaper reporter who has witnessed one of the major battles discussed in this section. Write a news story that provides an account of the battle for readers in either the North or the South.

THE CIVIL WAR **387**

387

The Battle for Vicksburg

Info to Know

A State Divided The Civil War divided communities and states, as well as the nation. The state of Missouri sent 39 regiments to fight in the Battle for Vicksburg; 22 regiments fought for the Union and 17 fought for the Confederacy. By the time the war ended, every state except South Carolina had sent troops to fight for the North.

Primary Source

Dora Miller, a resident of Vicksburg during the siege, recorded the following in her diary: "Today we are down in the cellar again; provisions so nearly gone . . . that a few more days will bring us to starvation. Martha says rats are hanging dressed in the market for sale with mule-meat; there is nothing else."

— Dora Miller

Diary entry, July 3, 1863

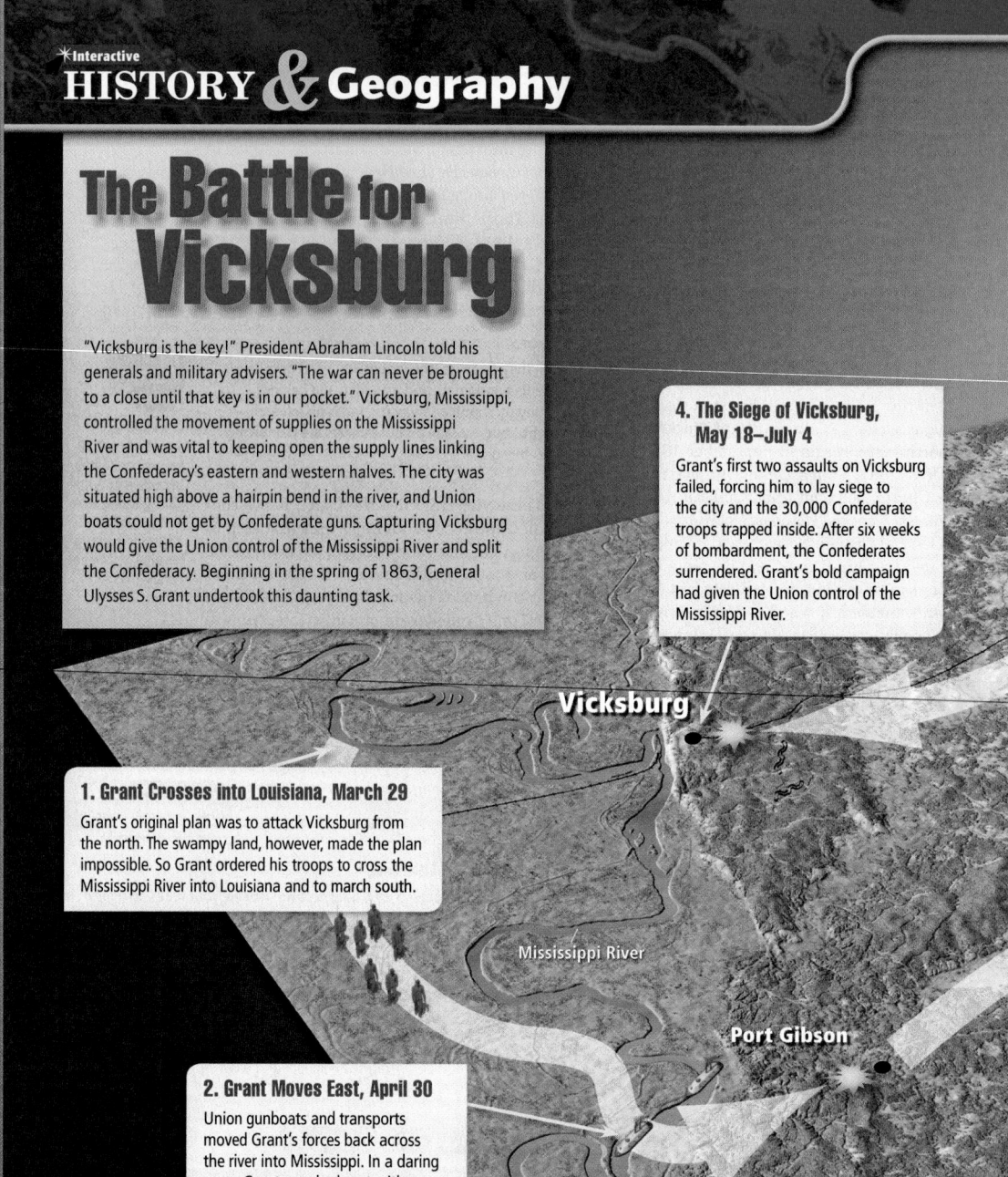

*Interactive
HISTORY & Geography

The Battle for Vicksburg

"Vicksburg is the key!" President Abraham Lincoln told his generals and military advisers. "The war can never be brought to a close until that key is in our pocket." Vicksburg, Mississippi, controlled the movement of supplies on the Mississippi River and was vital to keeping open the supply lines linking the Confederacy's eastern and western halves. The city was situated high above a hairpin bend in the river, and Union boats could not get by Confederate guns. Capturing Vicksburg would give the Union control of the Mississippi River and split the Confederacy. Beginning in the spring of 1863, General Ulysses S. Grant undertook this daunting task.

4. The Siege of Vicksburg, May 18–July 4

Grant's first two assaults on Vicksburg failed, forcing him to lay siege to the city and the 30,000 Confederate troops trapped inside. After six weeks of bombardment, the Confederates surrendered. Grant's bold campaign had given the Union control of the Mississippi River.

Vicksburg

1. Grant Crosses into Louisiana, March 29

Grant's original plan was to attack Vicksburg from the north. The swampy land, however, made the plan impossible. So Grant ordered his troops to cross the Mississippi River into Louisiana and to march south.

Mississippi River

Port Gibson

2. Grant Moves East, April 30

Union gunboats and transports moved Grant's forces back across the river into Mississippi. In a daring move Grant marched east without a supply line, allowing his troops to move quickly.

388

Collaborative Learning

Below Level

The Battle for Vicksburg

Materials poster paper, colored markers

1. Pair students. Have each pair design a poster from the Confederate perspective, encouraging residents of Vicksburg to wait out the siege. Students should focus on the strategic importance of the city and the necessity of keeping it in Confederate control.

2. Display students' posters for the class to see.

3. Guide the class in a discussion of the Battle for Vicksburg. How was Grant able to successfully attack the city? Would the war have ended differently if Grant had not succeeded? **LS Interpersonal, Visual-Spatial**

Alternative Assessment Handbook, Rubric 28: Posters

Ironclads

Union ironclads were vital to the Vicksburg campaign. These gunboats protected Grant's troops when they crossed the Mississippi. Later, they bombarded Vicksburg during the siege of the city.

Jackson

3. The Battle of Jackson, May 14

Union troops defeated a Confederate army at Jackson, Mississippi, before moving on to Vicksburg. The Union victory kept Confederate forces from reinforcing Vicksburg.

Missouri · Kentucky · Virginia · Arkansas · Tennessee · North Carolina · South Carolina · Alabama · Georgia · VICKSBURG · Mississippi · Louisiana · GULF OF MEXICO

UNION CONTROL

CONFEDERATE CONTROL

GEOGRAPHY SKILLS INTERPRETING MAPS

go.hrw.com
Interactive Map
Keyword: SD7 CH11

1. Location How did Vicksburg's location make it the "key" to winning the war?

2. Place Why would Grant want to split the Confederacy?

See Skills Handbook, p. H20

THE CIVIL WAR **389**

Primary Source

" . . . now on this Fourth of July just past, when a gigantic rebellion has risen in the land, precisely at the bottom of which is an effort to overthrow that principle 'that all men are created equal,' we have a surrender of one of their most powerful positions and powerful armies forced upon them on that very day. And I see in the succession of battles in Pennsylvania, which continued three days, so rapidly following each other as to be justly called one great battle, fought on the first, second and third of July; on the *fourth* the enemies of the declaration that all men are created equal had to turn tail and run."

— Abraham Lincoln

"Independence Day Address," July 7, 1863

Info to Know

Shunning a Holiday July 4, the day of the city's final surrender, became an infamous date in Vicksburg. Independence Day was not celebrated in the city for another 81 years.

Skills Focus: Analyzing Primary Sources

Research Required | Above Level

Reading Like a Historian Skill
Journals of the Siege

1. Have students do an Internet search to find primary source materials on the siege of Vicksburg. Students should attempt to locate sources from both the residents of Vicksburg and the Union soldiers who attacked the city.

2. Have students write a brief essay discussing the sources, identifying concerns the authors

expressed, and evaluating the materials' validity and usefulness as historical documents.

3. Have volunteers share their essays with the class. **LS Verbal-Linguistic, Intrapersonal**

Alternative Assessment Handbook, Rubrics 30: Research; and 41: Writing to Express

Answers

Interpreting Maps 1. *It could give the Union control of the Mississippi River.* **2.** *could cut off supply lines between halves of Confederacy*

Bellringer

The Inside Story. . . Use the **Daily Bellringer Transparency** to help students answer the question.

🖥 Daily Bellringer Transparency, Section 5

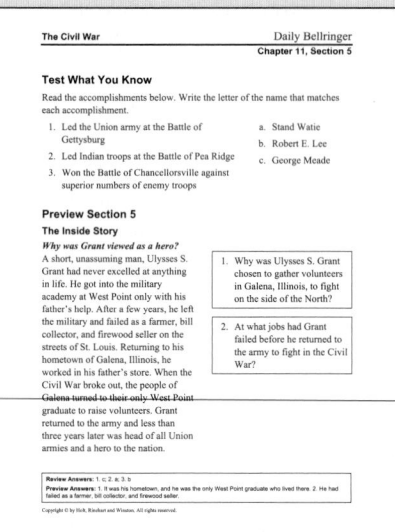

Academic Vocabulary

Review with students the high-use academic term in this section.

phase a stage in a process of change or development (p. 393)

📑 CRF: Vocabulary Builder Activity, Section 5

Taking Notes

Confederate army short of both troops and supplies; high casualties; destruction of Atlanta; Sherman's march and total destruction; Lee's army surrounded by Grant's forces

---

The Final Phase

BEFORE YOU READ

MAIN IDEA

Southerners continued to hope for victory in 1864, but military and political events caused those hopes to fade.

READING FOCUS

1. What tactics did Grant use against Lee to change the course of the war?

2. How did the election of 1864 affect Confederate hopes for victory in the Civil War?

3. How did the actions of Sherman and Grant help bring the war to an end?

KEY TERMS AND PEOPLE

William Tecumseh Sherman
Battle of the Wilderness
Battle of Spotsylvania
Battle of Cold Harbor
Battle of Atlanta
Thirteenth Amendment

TAKING NOTES As you read, take notes identifying events late in the war that helped bring on the southern surrender. Record your notes in a graphic organizer like the one shown here.

Causes ➡ The South Surrenders

A CALL TO GREATNESS

THE INSIDE STORY

Why was Grant viewed as a hero? The people in the lobby of Washington's Willard Hotel did not notice the short, rumpled man and the teenage boy as they checked in. However, the desk clerk snapped to attention as the man signed the guest register: "U.S. Grant and son, Galena, Illinois." Word spread quickly that the new head of all Union armies was in town. That evening Grant walked to the White House to call on the president, who happened to be holding a reception. Cheering erupted as the guests pushed forward to get a glimpse of the great general. Secretary of State Seward helped him stand on a sofa to be better seen.

Grant had shown absolutely no signs of greatness as a young man. His father had gotten him into West Point, hoping that a military career might provide a living for his unexceptional son. Grant left the army after the Mexican War, however, and then failed at farming, bill collecting, and even selling firewood on the streets of St. Louis. Finally, he went to work in his father's store in Galena, Illinois. Because he was Galena's only West Point graduate, the town put him in charge of raising volunteers when the Civil War began. Grant rejoined the army and never looked back. Now, less than three years later, as a reception guest noted, "The little, scared-looking man who stood on a crimson sofa was the idol of the hour." ■

◀ The war revealed in Grant a talent for military leadership.

390

Teach the Main Idea

The Final Phase

1. **Teach** Ask students the Reading Focus questions to teach this section.

2. **Apply** Have students scan the chapter and create a sequencing diagram of the battles and events that led to the end of the Civil War. Have students include a key point or detail about each battle or event in their diagrams. **LS Visual-Spatial**

3. **Review** Have volunteers share their diagrams with the class.

4. **Practice/Homework** Have students write a short essay on the importance of the election of 1864 to the war and how Sherman's capture of Atlanta affected the election. **LS Logical-Mathematic, Verbal-Linguistic**

📑 Alternative Assessment Handbook Rubric 37: Writing Assignments

🖥 Graphic Organizer Transparencies

Grant versus Lee

Ulysses S. Grant's victory over Confederate forces at Chattanooga in November 1863 convinced President Lincoln that the Union finally had a general who could crush the Confederates. In March 1864 Lincoln brought Grant to Washington and gave him command of all Union armies. Grant named one of his top officers, General **William Tecumseh Sherman**, to replace him as commander on the western front of the war.

Confederate leaders still had some hope for victory in 1864. It was a presidential election year in the North. If the South could hold out until the November election, northerners might be so tired of war that they would reject Lincoln. A new president might accept southern independence in return for peace. Robert E. Lee's plan was not necessarily to win battles but to make the cost of fighting so high for the North that Lincoln would lose the election.

Grant hoped to end the war before November. He knew that the South was running short of men and supplies. Grant told Sherman to attack the Confederate army that he was facing. "Break it up," Grant ordered, "and get into the interior of the enemy's country as far as you can, inflicting all the damage you can against their war resources."

The Wilderness and Spotsylvania

In May, Grant moved the Army of the Potomac toward Richmond. Almost at once, Lee's 61,000 troops forced about 100,000 Union soldiers into another battle near Chancellorsville. Fighting in the two-day **Battle of the Wilderness** was so fierce that the dense forest caught fire from the shooting. Many of the wounded were burned to death. Despite losses nearly twice as high as Lee's, Grant pushed south. His troops' spirits rose. For the first time, the Union army was staying on the attack after a battle.

Two days later, the armies of Grant and Lee met again in an 11-day series of clashes known as the **Battle of Spotsylvania**. The fiercest fighting took place on May 12, when Union troops attacked the strongest part of the Confederate defenses, a place that became known as the Bloody Angle. The two armies battled for some 20 hours in fighting so heavy that rifle fire cut down trees nearly two feet thick. A Union officer described the scene.

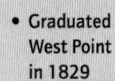

HISTORY'S VOICES

❝ Rank [a row of troops] after rank was riddled by shot and shell and bayonet thrusts, and finally sank, a mass of torn and mutilated corpses; then fresh troops rushed forward to replace the dead; and so the murderous work went on. ❞
—Colonel Horace Porter in *Voices of the Civil War*

Casualties were appalling. From May 5 to May 12, the Union army suffered 32,000 killed, wounded, or missing. Lee's losses totaled 18,000. Yet, the worst was to come.

Cold Harbor and Petersburg

Grant continued to push toward Richmond. In early June the armies fought yet again. In the first 30 minutes of fighting at the **Battle of Cold Harbor**, the charging Union soldiers suffered about 7,000 casualties. "It was not war," a Confederate general recalled later. "It was murder."

Following a month of marching and fighting, the Union army's high spirits were gone. Many soldiers at Cold Harbor pinned their names and addresses on their uniforms before the battle so their bodies could be more easily identified. "The men feel at present a great horror and dread of attacking earthworks [fortifications] again," one Union officer observed. So after failing to capture Petersburg, a rail center just south of Richmond, Grant began a siege of the

---

Final Campaigns

Importance of Atlanta Guide students in a discussion about the importance of Atlanta, and why it was such a strategic target for the North and a vital stronghold for the South.

🗺 Map Transparency: Final Campaigns, 1864–1865

Primary Source

"If [southerners] raise a howl against my barbarity and cruelty, I will answer that war is war, and not popularity-seeking. If they want peace, they and their relatives must stop the war."

— William T. Sherman

Letter to General Halleck, September 4, 1864

✳ **Interactive Map:** Final Campaigns, 1864–1865

Interactive Map
FINAL CAMPAIGNS, 1864–1865

General Sherman hoped to hasten the end of the war by destroying the Confederacy's economic base and crushing its citizens' spirits.

1. Movement Trace Sherman's path of destruction. How long did he wage his so-called total war?

2. Region About how many miles did Sherman's march cover?

See Skills Handbook, p. H19

go.hrw.com
Interactive Map
Keyword: SD7 CH11

392 CHAPTER 11

Skills Focus: Interpreting Movement Maps   At Level

Social Studies Skill
Movement Maps

1. Have students examine the map carefully and list the cities that Sherman encountered on his march to the sea. Then have students calculate how far the army had to march from one city to the next.

2. Guide students in a discussion of the "total war" philosophy Sherman employed in his march. Have students predict how this philosophy and widespread destruction might affect the relations between North and South after the war. **LS Verbal-Linguistic**

📖 Alternative Assessment Handbook Rubric 21: Map Reading

Answers

Interpreting Maps 1. *from Nashville, Tennessee, through Atlanta and Savannah, Georgia, to Columbia, South Carolina, to Bentonville, North Carolina; from July 1864 to March 1865;* **2.** *about 600 miles*

392

city. He knew that if he prevented food from passing through Petersburg to the Confederate capital, Richmond eventually would have to surrender. Lee was content to dig in his troops and wait for the November election.

Sherman on the move As Grant pressured Lee's army in Virginia, the next <u>phase</u> of the war began when Sherman set out from Chattanooga on his long-expected invasion of Georgia. The Union army marched toward Atlanta, an important southern manufacturing and transportation center. About 60,000 Confederate troops, led by General Joseph Johnston, stood between Sherman's 100,000 troops and their objective. Johnston's army slowed Sherman's advance but could not stop it. By mid-July the Union army was just eight miles from the city.

At this point, President Jefferson Davis replaced Johnston with the more aggressive General John Hood. Hood attacked the Union army immediately. This was exactly what Sherman was hoping for. In the Battle of Peachtree Creek on July 20 and the **Battle of Atlanta** on July 22, Hood desperately threw his troops against the Union forces. The two battles cost him nearly a quarter of his army.

Hood pulled his weakened forces back behind Atlanta's defenses, hoping to hold out until the North's presidential election. Sherman laid siege to the city, shelling it daily with his artillery. Finally, he was able to close the last railroad line into Atlanta, forcing Hood's troops to abandon the city on September 1. The next day the Union army entered Atlanta. "Atlanta gone," Mary Chesnut wrote in her diary. "No hope. We will try to have no fear."

> **READING CHECK** **Making Inferences** Why were Grant and Sherman eager for the armies opposing them to fight?

Confederate Hopes Fade

While Sherman was besieging Atlanta, the Democratic Party held its national convention in Chicago. The Democrats chose General George McClellan as their presidential candidate. They adopted a party platform that called for an immediate end to the war. Southerners found new hope in these events. Confederate vice president Alexander Stephens called them

"the first ray of real light I have seen since the war began." In South Carolina, the *Charleston Mercury* predicted that McClellan's election would "lead to peace and our independence."

The Republicans, hoping to broaden Lincoln's appeal, dropped Vice President Hannibal Hamlin of Maine from the ticket. In his place they chose Andrew Johnson, a pro-Union Democrat from Tennessee. Many believed it would not be enough. The Emancipation Proclamation and Grant's huge losses in Virginia had made the war highly unpopular in the North. "The people are wild for peace," a Republican Party leader reported. Lincoln himself expected to lose the election. "I am going to be beaten," he predicted gloomily, "and unless something changes, *badly* beaten."

Sherman's capture of Atlanta provided the change Lincoln hoped for. It allowed the president to defeat McClellan easily in the November election. Even soldiers in the Union army gave Lincoln a huge margin of victory. "We all want peace . . . but an *honorable* one," wrote one soldier, a Democrat, to explain why troops did not vote for the popular general.

Lincoln's victory also enabled Congress to pass the constitutional amendment that Republicans had been seeking since 1862. The **Thirteenth Amendment** to end slavery in the United States finally passed the House of Representatives on January 31, 1865. It was ratified by the states and became part of the Constitution in December 1865.

As Lincoln began his second term in March, the war seemed nearly over to all except the most die-hard secessionists. To those who called for harsh punishment of the South, Lincoln announced his intention to be forgiving.

HISTORY'S VOICES

> ❝With malice toward none, with charity for all, with firmness in the right as God gives us to see the right, let us strive on to finish the work we are in, to bind up the nation's wounds.❞
> —Lincoln's Second Inaugural Address, March 4, 1865

Meanwhile, the task of completing what Lincoln called "the work we are in" continued on the battlefields as the long and bloody war entered its final phase.

> **READING CHECK** **Identifying the Main Idea** Why did Confederate hopes for success in the war rise and then fall in 1864?

ACADEMIC VOCABULARY
phase a stage in a process of change or development

THE CIVIL WAR **393**

Reading Focus

❷ How did the election of 1864 affect Confederate hopes for victory in the Civil War? *Southern hopes were dashed.*

Confederate Hopes Fade

Explain What was the purpose of the Thirteenth Amendment? *abolish slavery*

Evaluate How did Sherman's capture of Atlanta help Lincoln's election chances? *It greatly enhanced northern expectations of victory in the war, and helped Lincoln win reelection.*

Differentiating Instruction

Above Level

Advanced Learners/GATE

Research Required

Confederate Hopes Fade

1. Have each student conduct outside research on the election of 1864, focusing on the Chicago convention of 1864 and the "Peace Plank."

2. Have each student write an analysis of the campaign and the convention. In their

analyses, students should explain why McClellan firmly rejected his party's Peace Plank. **LS Verbal-Linguistic**

▢ Alternative Assessment Handbook, Rubrics 30: Research; and 37: Writing Assignments

Answers

Reading Check (left) *South had little manpower and few supplies in reserve.* **(right)** *expected that McClellan would beat Lincoln, giving them hope for peace*

❸ How did the actions of Sherman and Grant help bring the war to an end? *Sherman's troops savaged a wide swath of Georgia and South Carolina, while Grant relentlessly moved on Richmond and on Lee's weak army.*

The War Comes to an End

Explain How did both Grant and Lee demonstrate dedication to restoring the Union at Appomattox? *Lee advised his soldiers to return home, obey the laws, and become good citizens; Grant reminded his troops that the war was over, and "the Rebels are our countrymen again."*

Analyze Would Sherman's actions in Georgia and South Carolina be described in today's terms as terrorism? *They were mostly directed against a helpless civilian population and designed to strike fear into southern hearts; some might call it terrorism.*

Draw Conclusions How was Grant so easily able to move into Richmond? *The small, weakened Confederate army had retreated in the face of Grant's powerful forces.*

🗄 Quick Facts Transparency: Causes and Effects of the Civil War

The War Comes to an End

One of Sherman's first acts after entering Atlanta in September 1864 was to force its citizens to leave the city. When Atlanta's mayor protested the harshness and cruelty of this order, the general replied:

HISTORY'S VOICES

❝War is cruelty, and you cannot refine it. And those who brought war into our country deserve all the curses...a people can pour out...The only way the people of Atlanta can hope once more to live in peace and quiet at home is to stop the war.❞
—William Tecumseh Sherman in *Voices of the Civil War*

THE IMPACT TODAY

Economics
In the decades following the Civil War, Atlantans rebuilt their ruined city into what today is the major commercial center of the South.

Sherman's March Sherman remained in Atlanta until after the November election. Then he set out with some 60,000 troops to march across Georgia and capture Savannah. As he abandoned Atlanta, his troops burned much of the city.

During Sherman's March to the Sea, the Union army cut a swath of destruction 300 miles long and 50 to 60 miles wide across the heart of Georgia. The soldiers slaughtered livestock, destroyed crops, tore up railroad tracks, and looted homes and businesses.

Sherman's tactics were designed to show that Union armies could now do as they wished in the South and that further resistance was hopeless. He also wanted to destroy food supplies needed by Lee's troops at Petersburg.

Arriving outside Savannah, Georgia, on December 10, Sherman began a siege of the city. Its 10,000 defenders soon slipped away, and on December 21, Union troops entered Savannah. Sherman telegraphed a holiday greeting to President Lincoln in Washington. "I beg to present you, as a Christmas gift, the city of Savannah," Sherman's telegram read.

In January 1865 Sherman brought his army north into South Carolina, which had been the first state to secede. "The whole army is burning with . . . desire to wreak vengeance on South Carolina," Sherman wrote. "I almost tremble at her fate."

In Georgia, Union troops burned relatively few private homes. In South Carolina, however, few homes in their path escaped destruction. The destruction of civilian property finally stopped when the army entered North Carolina in late February.

The fall of Richmond Sherman's army was headed north in order to join Grant at Petersburg, where the siege had been going on since June 1864. With Sherman's army added to his own, Grant hoped to surround Lee without spreading Union forces so thin that the Confederates could break through and escape. As it turned out, Grant's plan was not necessary.

By late March 1865 the number of defenders at Petersburg had shrunk to about 35,000. They were low on food, ammunition, and other supplies. Grant realized that he could break through Lee's defenses without waiting for Sherman, and on April 2 he did. With nothing now standing between Grant's army and Richmond, Confederate leaders fled the city. Union troops entered Richmond on the next day.

Meanwhile, Lee tried to escape with what was left of his army. He hoped to join another Confederate force that was retreating from Sherman in North Carolina. Grant's army pursued Lee's 13,000 remaining troops, however, and blocked their escape. When the Union forces surrounded the Confederates at the town of Appomattox Court House, Virginia, Lee decided to surrender.

Surrender at Appomattox Lee and Grant met in a home in Appomattox Court House on Sunday, April 9. The two generals chatted briefly about their service as young officers in the Mexican-American War. Then Grant presented the terms of the surrender. They were extremely generous for a conflict that had been so long, bloody, and bitter. Lee's troops merely had to turn over their weapons and leave.

Grant then offered food for Lee's starving troops. "It will be a great relief, I assure you," Lee responded. After a few more minutes of conversation, Lee, Grant, and other officers signed the surrender. Lee then returned to his troops to tell them that the war was over.

HISTORY'S VOICES

❝I have done for you all that it was in my power to do. You have done all your duty. Leave the result to God. Go to your homes and resume your occupations. Obey the laws and become as good citizens as you were soldiers.❞
—Robert E. Lee, April 9, 1865

In the Union army's camps, the troops began firing artillery to salute the victory. Grant ordered the guns silenced. "The war is over," he

Skills Focus: Analyzing Primary Sources [At Level]

Reading Skill
The War Comes to an End

1. Organize students in small groups, and then read the following passage from a book about Lee's surrender at Appomattox when Lee was preparing to go and meet Grant: *"He was dressed in a suit of new uniform, sword and sash, a handsomely embroidered belt, boots and a pair of gold spurs. At first approach his compact figure appeared as a man in the flush vigor of forty summers, but as I drew near, the handsome apparel and brave bearing failed to conceal his profound depression."*

2. Have groups write a story about Lee at the moment of surrender. Stories should answer the following questions. Why was Lee dressed so finely? How does he look at first glance? Why would he wear gold spurs? How does Lee really feel? 🄻 **Verbal-Linguistic, Interpersonal**

📝 Alternative Assessment Handbook, Rubrics 33: Skits and Reader's Theater; and 40: Writing to Describe

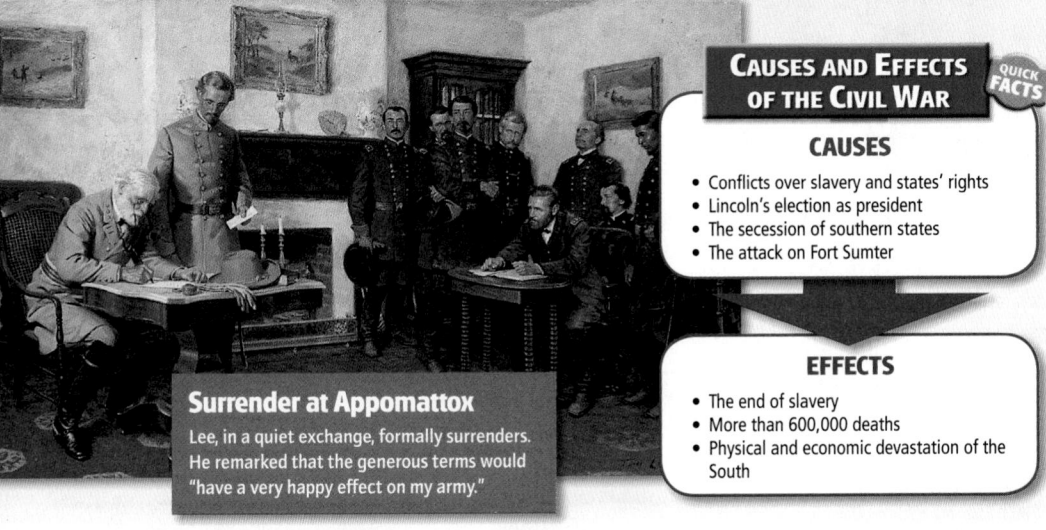

CAUSES AND EFFECTS OF THE CIVIL WAR

QUICK FACTS

CAUSES

- Conflicts over slavery and states' rights
- Lincoln's election as president
- The secession of southern states
- The attack on Fort Sumter

Surrender at Appomattox
Lee, in a quiet exchange, formally surrenders. He remarked that the generous terms would "have a very happy effect on my army."

EFFECTS

- The end of slavery
- More than 600,000 deaths
- Physical and economic devastation of the South

---

said. "The rebels are our countrymen again." In cities across the North, however, news of Lee's surrender brought wild, joyful celebration.

In Washington, a huge crowd gathered outside the White House. Too tired for a speech, Lincoln said instead that he'd always liked "Dixie," an old tune that had become a popular song among Confederates. "We fairly captured it [yesterday]," he joked. "I now request the band to favor me with its performance."

It was not until May 26, 1865, however, that the last of the Confederate forces finally surrendered. Tragically, President Lincoln did not live to see the official end of the war. His death would change the course of American history in the months and years following the war.

READING CHECK **Sequencing** What series of events in Georgia, the Carolinas, and Virginia brought the Civil War to an end?

SECTION 5 ASSESSMENT

go.hrw.com
Online Quiz
Keyword: SD7 HP11

Reviewing Ideas, Terms, and People

1. **a. Recall** What strategy did Lee adopt in 1864, and what was his goal?
   b. Analyze Why did Lincoln put Grant in command of all the Union armies?
   c. Evaluate Was Grant's strategy as a commander effective? Why or why not?

2. **a. Identify** What did the **Thirteenth Amendment** do?
   b. Elaborate Why did Lincoln expect to be beaten for re-election in 1864? What might have changed his mind?
   c. Predict How might the nation's history be different if **William Tecumseh Sherman** had failed to capture Atlanta before the 1864 election?

3. **a. Describe** What was Sherman's march across Georgia like?
   b. Contrast How did Sherman's army behave differently in South Carolina than in Georgia?
   c. Elaborate Why do you think Grant offered Lee such generous surrender terms?

Critical Thinking

4. **Identifying Cause and Effect** Review your notes on the South's surrender. Then copy the graphic organizer below and use it to identify causes and effects of the South's surrender.

The South Surrenders

Cause	Effect

 **FOCUS ON WRITING**

5. **Expository** Lincoln and Grant both favored generous, forgiving treatment of the South after the war. Write a paragraph explaining why you agree or disagree with their ideas about dealing with the South.

THE CIVIL WAR **395**

Section 5 Assessment Answers

1. **a.** make cost of war so high that Lincoln would lose the election
   b. Grant was an aggressive, successful military leader.
   c. Yes. He ruined the South and wore Lee's army out.

2. **a.** banned slavery in the United States
   b. war had not gone well; Sherman's taking Atlanta
   c. Lincoln might have lost; some kind of peace established

3. **a.** destroyed goods, supplies, livestock, property, burned cities
   b. totally destroyed civilian property
   c. respect for Lee, wanted to restore the Union

4. Causes—South was crushed; Lee's army broken; Effects—joy in the North, depression in the South

5. possible answer—agree because Union needs to be reunited, harmonious relations needed

---

Close
Have students summarize the effect of Sherman's march on the South.

Review
Online Quiz, Section 5
Daily Test Practice Transparency

Assess
SE Section 5 Assessment
Progress Assessment: Section 5 Quiz
Alternative Assessment Handbook

Reteach
Interactive Reader and Study Guide, Section 5
Interactive Skills Tutor CD-ROM

Answers

Reading Focus *Sherman's march through Georgia and South Carolina and Grant's pursuit and defeat of Lee's forces in Virginia.*

395

Attitudes toward the Civil War

Word Help

sage pudding a mushy food usually made with flour, in this case seasoned with the herb sage

scanty meager; thin

Info to Know

Early Photography For people used to digital cameras, even film cameras seem old-fashioned. But for over a hundred years, they represented the state of the art, and were a vast improvement over earlier methods of photography. The first means of taking pictures that became popular were daguerreotype, ambrotype, and tintype. They produced images on sheets of copper, glass, or iron, respectively. Each image was one of a kind. The development of glass negative plates allowed many prints to be made from a single glass negative. Several photographers used this process to chronicle the Civil War. It was not until 1889 that George Eastman introduced the roll-film negatives that dominated photography until the digital age.

Photographing the Civil War By the time of the Civil War, Mathew Brady was already known as one of America's greatest photographers. He had opened a studio in Washington, D.C., in 1856 so that he could photograph famous men and women. Today he is best remembered as the man who chronicled the Civil War in photographs. Brady did not actually shoot most of the photos that bear his name, but supervised a team of photographers. In order to make his collection as complete as possible, he also bought photographs by other photographers. When they were published, they were all labeled "Photograph by Brady." His battlefield photographs shocked many Americans. It was the first time many people had witnessed "the terrible reality and earnestness of war."

Attitudes toward the Civil War

Historical Context The documents below provide different information on communication between soldiers and civilians during the Civil War.

Task Examine the documents and answer the questions that follow. Then you will be asked to write an essay about attitudes toward the Civil War, using information from the documents and the chapter to support the position you take in your thesis statement.

DOCUMENT 1

The Civil War was the first major American military conflict after the invention of photography. As a result, an extensive photographic record of the battlefield experience exists. Also, many men on each side had portraits taken of themselves before they left home for military service. Usually it was the first, and sometimes the only, photo they had ever had taken. Below are portraits of two soldiers. The photograph on the left is of a young Confederate enlisted man. The young Union soldier on the right was probably an officer.

Skills Focus: Interpreting Visuals

Research Required At Level

Reading Like A Historian Skill
Picturing the Civil War

1. Divide the class into small groups. Have each group conduct research to find photographs of the Civil War.

2. Have students make copies of their photographs and categorize them by theme. Have each group make a list of all the themes they found.

3. Have volunteers share their lists of themes.

4. Have each student select a theme and write an essay explaining how the photographs illustrate this theme. Students should include an analysis of the ways in which each photograph contributes to their understanding of that aspect of the Civil War.

5. Have volunteers share their essays and photographs with the rest of the class.
   LS Visual-Spatial, Logical-Mathematical

   Alternative Assessment Handbook, Rubric 37: Writing Assignments

DOCUMENT 2

As the war dragged on, life became more difficult for Confederate soldiers, and mail service was often disrupted. This letter was written by Georgia soldier Zachariah H. J. Benefield to his wife, Sarah Jane, in April 1864. At the time, he was fighting in Tennessee.

"Jane, I have no news of interest to write to you, only [that] we have had a hard march. We marched five days. It snowed and rained everyday we were camped at Zolicofer, Tennessee, eleven miles from the [state] line of Virginia . . . On Tuesday the 22 of March the snow fell two feet deep here & it has been snowing & raining ever since. We are on our road to Virginia, I think.

Jane we are faring very bad for something to eat. We get flour with the bran in it & it is half oats & [a] man can't hardly eat it. We don't get half enough of it. We steal a little . . . We can't buy nothing [because] our money [is not worth anything]. Jane, this is the fifth letter I have written to you & got no answer yet. Jane, I don't know what to think. Jane, you said you would write to me every week. If you have written to me I ain't got your letter. Jane, if you knew how bad I want to hear from you, you would write to me . . . Jane, tell brother that I am looking for a letter from him. They say that the Yankees is advancing on Richmond. Again we have to go and defend it. We are falling back out of east Tennessee. Jane, we saw a bad time, marching through the snow & rain."

DOCUMENT 3

By the final months of the war, people on both sides were growing weary of the suffering. Following are several diary entries by Union nurse Rebecca Usher, written in the spring of 1865. At the time she was stationed at a hospital in Virginia, where the fighting was still active.

"**Sat. [Jan. 21st]** – The men come in for all sorts of stores as usual and many of them complain of being hungry—they say they do not have enough to satisfy their appetites. . . . We do all we can for them—give one man a cup of tea and a slice of dry toast, another corn starch, another sage pudding, another crackers, anything we can think of to eke out their scanty meals. . . .

Thursday 16th – . . . A train filled with Rebel deserters came in last evening. It is said there were 500. One of them said they had fought us well before now but they had become convinced it was no use to hold out any longer. . . .

March 22—A man came in yesterday from Conn., who said it was the first time he had spoken to a woman in a year. The tears came into his eyes, his voice trembled, & he was entirely overcome by his feelings.

A boy from Michigan who was an orphan & had lost 3 brothers in the army came in with one of our Maine boys. He had lost his voice from the measles & was the only one of his family left. We got him a [bag of donated goods]. It seemed a great comfort to him. He smiled & appeared as pleased as a child as he examined its contents. He found a letter in it from a Yarmouth girl, which pleased him more than all."

Skills FOCUS — READING LIKE A HISTORIAN

1. a. Describe Refer to Document 1. How would you describe the two men?
b. Analyze How do you think having a photograph of soldiers affected their families back home?

2. a. Identify Refer to Document 2. What were the main problems facing Benefield's unit?
b. Interpret How would lack of mail have affected soldiers' morale and people's attitudes back home?

3. a. Identify Refer to Documents 2 and 3. What problems did Union soldiers share with the Confederates?

b. Elaborate How do you think the Civil War had changed the soldiers that Usher described?

4. Document-Based Essay Question Consider the question below and form a thesis statement. Using examples from Documents 1, 2, and 3, create an outline and write a short essay supporting your position.
How did connections between the homefront and frontlines affect civilians and soldiers during the Civil War?

See **Skills Handbook, pp. H28-H29, H30**

Collaborative Learning

[At Level]

Recruiting Nurses

Materials construction paper, colored markers

1. Tell students that not all Civil War nurses were women. For example, the poet Walt Whitman was a nurse during the Civil War.

2. Divide the class into small groups. Have each group come up with ideas for recruiting men and women to serve as nurses in the Civil War.

3. Have each group put their ideas into effect, and create posters, advertisements, editorials, sermons, or skits that could have been used during the Civil War.

4. Have each group present its recruitment campaign to the class. **LS Interpersonal**

   Alternative Assessment Handbook, Rubric 2: Advertisements

Info to Know

Mail During the Civil War During the Civil War, soldiers had a hard time sending and receiving mail. When they were encamped for several weeks, it was fairly easy to find soldiers for mail delivery. Much of the time, however, armies were on the move and delivering mail became a challenge. Because soldiers often did not have any way to buy stamps, their letters were frequently marked "postage due," with the cost paid by the recipients, who were eager for word from their loved ones. Families that were divided by the South's secession had an even harder time staying in touch. Northern mail addressed to the Confederacy was returned to the sender, and Confederate stamps were not recognized by the Union. Mail could be sent through foreign ports or carried across the border by blockade runners. While such methods took a long time to get to their destinations, they still allowed people to keep in touch in a divided land.

Answers

Reading Like a Historian

1. a. *both are young soldiers who seem eager to defend their beliefs;*
b. *possible answer—it probably made them proud;* **2. a.** *hard marches, bad weather, not enough to eat, no mail;*
b. *lack of mail would lower soldiers' morale and worry the people back home;*
3. a. *hunger and lack of contact with family members;* **b.** *possible answer— made them desperate;* **4.** *answers will vary but should include mail service that was slow or lacking altogether, and the fact that lack of communication made things worse*

Answers

Visual Summary

Review and Inquiry Organize students into small groups. Have each group explain how the first three boxes led to the events in the last two.

🖐 Quick Facts Transparency: The Civil War

Key Terms and People

1. f.
2. j.
3. l.
4. g.
5. k.
6. d.
7. e.
8. a.
9. c.
10. b.
11. h.

Comprehension and Critical Thinking

12. a. Scott's plan to surround the South, cut it off from outside trade, and squeeze it to death.
b. South would fight a defensive war on home ground; North would have to invade
c. No, they would have to take the war to the North or be worn down by blockades and invasions.

13. a. They made the war extremely deadly.
b. realized sides were evenly matched, would not be a short war
c. The war might have ended sooner as Grant surely would have vigorously attacked the Confederate army.

14. a. compulsory military service
b. created great scarcity of manufactured goods; caused prices to rise sharply
c. feared causing trouble in border states and other parts of the North

Visual Summary: The Civil War

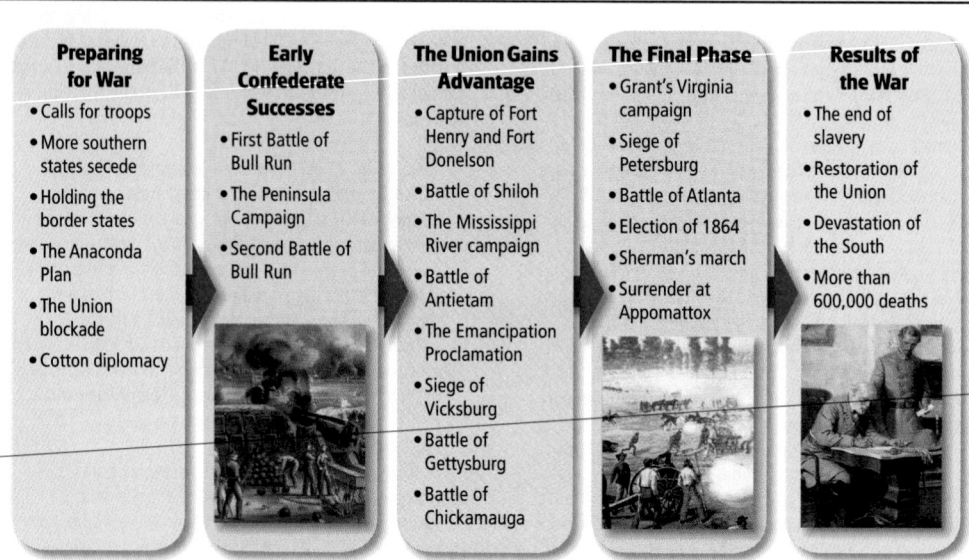

Preparing for War	Early Confederate Successes	The Union Gains Advantage	The Final Phase	Results of the War
• Calls for troops • More southern states secede • Holding the border states • The Anaconda Plan • The Union blockade • Cotton diplomacy	• First Battle of Bull Run • The Peninsula Campaign • Second Battle of Bull Run	• Capture of Fort Henry and Fort Donelson • Battle of Shiloh • The Mississippi River campaign • Battle of Antietam • The Emancipation Proclamation • Siege of Vicksburg • Battle of Gettysburg • Battle of Chickamauga	• Grant's Virginia campaign • Siege of Petersburg • Battle of Atlanta • Election of 1864 • Sherman's march • Surrender at Appomattox	• The end of slavery • Restoration of the Union • Devastation of the South • More than 600,000 deaths

Reviewing Key Terms and People

Match each numbered definition with the correct lettered item at right.

1. Type of rule in which military commanders are in control and citizens' rights and freedoms are suspended
2. Southern general whose nickname reflected his bravery in battle
3. Union general who boosted the North's morale with early victories
4. Group of Democrats who opposed the war
5. Northern general who frustrated Lincoln with his hesitancy to fight
6. Announcement freeing enslaved African Americans in all areas that were in rebellion against the United States
7. Southern general who urged Lee to withdraw at Gettysburg
8. Increase in prices
9. Person who helped with the war effort by caring for soldiers wounded in battle
10. Northern general in command at Gettysburg
11. Union general who helped end the war with his invasion of Georgia

a. inflation
b. George Meade
c. Clara Barton
d. Emancipation Proclamation
e. James Longstreet
f. martial law
g. Copperheads
h. William Tecumseh Sherman
j. Stonewall Jackson
k. George McClellan
l. Ulysses S. Grant

15. a. Battles of Chancellorsville, Gettysburg, siege of Vicksburg
b. Some wanted to see U.S. power diminished; some were concerned about trade with the South.
c. He could have saved his troops, chosen a better location for fighting, and defeated the Union army again.

16. a. captured Atlanta
b. Grant on the offensive; Lee in a holding strategy, waiting for the election
c. Lee wanted the country united peacefully.

History's Impact video program

Review the video to answer the closing question: How did the Civil War divide and ultimately unify the nation?

Comprehension and Critical Thinking

SECTION 1 *(pp. 356–362)*

12. a. Identify What was the Anaconda Plan?

b. Contrast How were the initial military strategies of the North and South different?

c. Evaluate Was the South's strategy for fighting the war a good one? Why or why not?

SECTION 2 *(pp. 363–370)*

13. a. Describe How did the new weapons used in the war affect the fighting?

b. Analyze How did the First Battle of Bull Run change the way people viewed the war?

c. Predict What might have happened if Lincoln had replaced McClellan with Grant earlier in the war?

SECTION 3 *(pp. 371–378)*

14. a. Define What is the draft?

b. Analyze How did the blockade affect the South?

c. Elaborate Why did Lincoln free slaves only in areas in rebellion against the United States?

SECTION 4 *(pp. 380–387)*

15. a. Identify What major events of the war occurred in 1863?

b. Draw Conclusions Why were Britain and other nations concerned about the Civil War?

c. Predict How might the war have been different if Lee had decided not to fight at Gettysburg?

SECTION 5 *(pp. 390–395)*

16. a. Recall How did Sherman help Lincoln win re-election in 1864?

b. Contrast In what ways were Grant's and Lee's strategies different in 1864?

c. Elaborate Why do you think Lee encouraged his soldiers to go home and become good citizens?

Using the Internet

go.hrw.com
Practice Online
Keyword: SD7 CH11

17. The Civil War was a long conflict marked by many complex battles. Using the keyword above, do research to learn more about one of the most important battles of the war. Then create a report on the fighting, people involved, or consequences of the Battle of Gettysburg.

Analyzing Primary Sources

Reading Like a Historian Read the History's Voices passage in Section 5 from Abraham Lincoln's Second Inaugural Address that begins: "With malice toward none, with charity for all."

18. Identify What is the "work we are in" that Lincoln refers to?

19. Make Inferences How do Lincoln's words show his attitude toward the South?

Critical Reading

Read the passage in Section 5 that begins with the heading "Sherman's March." Then answer the questions that follow.

20. According to the passage, one of Sherman's main reasons for being so destructive was that he

A wanted revenge on Robert E. Lee.

B was trying to show Grant he was a good general.

C wanted to destroy the South's ability to fight.

D was trying to make Britain and France stop supporting the South.

21. In the second paragraph of the passage, "Sherman's army cut a swath . . . across the heart of Georgia," the term *swath* means

A a strike or blow.

B an important victory.

C an exchange of goods or services.

D a long, broad band or strip.

FOCUS ON WRITING

Persuasive Writing *Persuasive writing takes a position for or against an issue, using facts and examples as supporting evidence. To practice persuasive writing, complete the assignment below.*

Writing Topic **The Emancipation Proclamation**

22. Assignment Based on what you have read in this chapter, write a paragraph that argues whether or not the Emancipation Proclamation was effective. If you have access to a computer, use a word processing program to create and format your paragraph.

THE CIVIL WAR **399**

Review and Assessment Resources

Review and Reinforce

- CRF: Chapter Review Activity
- Quick Facts Transparencies: The Generals; Causes and Effects of the Civil War; The Civil War
- Spanish Chapter Summaries Audio CD Program
- Online Chapter Summaries in Spanish
- OSP Holt PuzzlePro; Quiz Show for ExamView
- Quiz Game CD-ROM

Assess

- PASS: Chapter Test, Forms A and B
- Alternative Assessment Handbook
- OSP ExamView Test Generator, Chapter Test
- Differentiated Instruction Modified Worksheets and Tests CD-ROM: Chapter Test
- HOAP Holt Online Assessment Program (in the Premier Online Edition)

Reteach/Intervene

- Interactive Reader and Study Guide
- Differentiated Instruction Teacher Management System: Lesson Plans for Differentiated Instruction
- Differentiated Instruction Modified Worksheets and Tests CD-ROM: Chapter Test
- Interactive Skills Tutor CD-ROM

go.hrw.com
Online Resources
KEYWORD: SD7 CH11

Chapter 12 Planning Guide

Reconstruction

Chapter Overview	Reproducible Resources	Technology Resources
CHAPTER 12 pp. 400–431 **Overview:** In this chapter, students will analyze the effects that Reconstruction had on the nation.	**Differentiated Instruction Teacher Management System:*** • Instructional Benchmarking Guides • Lesson Plans for Differentiated Instruction **Interactive Reader and Study Guide:** Chapter Summary* **Chapter Resource File:*** • Writing for the SAT: Who Should Lead Reconstruction Efforts? • Social Studies Skills Activity: Recognizing Bias • Chapter Review Activity **American History Outline Maps** **Pre-AP Activities Guide for American History***	**Live Ink® Online Reading Help** **Student Edition on Audio CD Program** **Differentiated Instruction Modified Worksheets and Tests CD-ROM** **Interactive Skills Tutor CD-ROM** **United States History Primary Source Library CD-ROM** **Power Presentations with Video CD-ROM** **History's Impact: American History Video Program (VHS/DVD):** Reconstruction **Online Chapter Summaries in Spanish** **Graphic Organizer Transparencies**
Section 1: **Plans for Reconstruction** **The Main Idea:** Northern leaders had differing ideas for dealing with the many issues and challenges of restoring the southern states to the Union.	**Differentiated Instruction Teacher Management System:** Section 1 Lesson Plan* **Interactive Reader and Study Guide:** Section 1 Summary* **Chapter Resource File:*** • Vocabulary Builder Activity, Section 1	**Daily Bellringer Transparency:** Section 1* **Daily Test Practice Transparency:** Section 1*
Section 2: **Congressional Reconstruction** **The Main Idea:** Congress took control of Reconstruction as a new, radical branch of the Republican Party was emerging.	**Differentiated Instruction Teacher Management System:** Section 2 Lesson Plan* **Interactive Reader and Study Guide:** Section 2 Summary* **Chapter Resource File:*** • Vocabulary Builder Activity, Section 2	**Daily Bellringer Transparency:** Section 2* **Map Transparency:** Military Districts, 1867* **Daily Test Practice Transparency:** Section 2*
Section 3: **Republicans in Charge** **The Main Idea:** Republican Reconstruction had a significant impact on life in the South.	**Differentiated Instruction Teacher Management System:** Section 3 Lesson Plan* **Interactive Reader and Study Guide:** Section 3 Summary* **Chapter Resource File:*** • Vocabulary Builder Activity, Section 3	**Daily Bellringer Transparency:** Section 3* **Quick Facts Transparency:** Hopes Raised and Denied* **Daily Test Practice Transparency:** Section 3*
Section 4: **Reconstruction Collapses** **The Main Idea:** A variety of events and forces led to the end of Reconstruction, which left a mixed legacy for the nation.	**Differentiated Instruction Teacher Management System:** Section 4 Lesson Plan* **Interactive Reader and Study Guide:** Section 4 Summary* **Chapter Resource File:*** • Vocabulary Builder Activity, Section 4	**Daily Bellringer Transparency:** Section 4* **Map Transparency:** The Election of 1876* **Daily Test Practice Transparency:** Section 4*

HOLT

History's Impact
American History Video Program (VHS/DVD)
Reconstruction

Review, Assessment, Intervention

 Quick Facts Transparencies: Hopes Raised and Denied, Reconstruction

Spanish Chapter Summaries Audio CD Program

Progress Assessment Support System (PASS): Chapter Test*

Differentiated Instruction Modified Worksheets and Tests CD-ROM: Modified Chapter Test

OSP **One-Stop Planner CD-ROM:** Exam View Test Generator (English/Spanish)

HOAP **Holt Online Assessment Program (HOAP),** in the Premier Online Edition.

PASS: Section 1 Quiz*

Online Quiz: Section 1

Alternative Assessment Handbook

PASS: Section 2 Quiz*

Online Quiz: Section 2

Alternative Assessment Handbook

PASS: Section 3 Quiz*

Online Quiz: Section 3

Alternative Assessment Handbook

PASS: Section 4 Quiz*

Online Quiz: Section 4

Alternative Assessment Handbook

NC RESOURCES

The following resources were developed to help North Carolina educators teach the standards and objectives of North Carolina's eleventh grade standard course of study in United States history.

- United States history EOC Test Prep Workbook
- Teacher's Support System
- North Carolina One-Stop Planner

And be sure to direct your students to **go.hrw.com** for online access to the EOC Test Prep Workbook.

go.hrw.com
EOC Test Prep
KEYWORD: SE7 NC

Holt Online Learning

go.hrw.com
Teacher Resources
KEYWORD: SD7 TEACHER

go.hrw.com
Student Resources
KEYWORD: SD7 CH12

- Document-based Questions
- Interactive Multimedia Activities

- Current Events
- Chapter-based Internet Activities
- and more!

Holt Premier
Online Student Edition
Complete online support for interactivity, assessment, and reporting

- Interactive Maps and Notebook
- Standardized Test Prep
- Homework Practice and Research Activities Online

The Big Picture

Edward L. Ayers

Plans for Reconstruction Even before the Civil War ended many people were planning ahead for freedom—especially the people who formerly had been enslaved. Lincoln had only a sketchy plan in place when he was assassinated, however, and even that plan came under attack from both Democrats and Republicans. Andrew Johnson had none of Lincoln's clout or skill and Johnson found his plans for leniency for most white southerners sharply attacked by Republicans.

Congressional Reconstruction The former Confederate states changed as little about slavery as they could, and whites worked to reimpose their control over black southerners through laws and violence. White southern resistance fueled demands in the North for a more rigorous Reconstruction, and the Radical Republicans launched such an effort in March 1867. Johnson resisted, and was impeached by his Republican opponents.

Republicans in Charge Under Radical Reconstruction, new groups came to power in the South: southern scalawags and northern carpetbaggers, black and white alike. This alliance proved fragile and uneasy, but nevertheless saw the enactment of important changes in the laws and institutions of the South. The Republicans did not attempt land redistribution, however, and most black southerners languished in dependence and poverty.

Reconstruction Collapses White southerners resisted Reconstruction in every way they could, through means both legal and illegal. In one state after another, Reconstruction came to an end. By 1876, only South Carolina, Louisiana, and Florida remained in Republican hands. After the disputed presidential election of that year, the Republicans removed the last federal troops from the South and Reconstruction came to an official and disheartening end.

Recent Scholarship

Reconstruction and Reconciliation Reconstruction is often treated as a discrete period in American history. After the end of the disputed presidential election of 1876, the South and southern race relations are often forgotten. But David Blight, in *Race and Reunion: The Civil War in American Memory* (2001), one of the most honored books on American history in the last decade, shows us that the issues unleashed by the Civil War, emancipation, and Reconstruction lived on in American life and politics long after 1876. In a series of beautifully rendered portraits, Blight shows how white Americans, northern and southern, reconciled with one another by "forgetting" the rights and hopes of black Americans.

Differentiating Instruction

 Differentiated Instruction Teacher Management System
- Lesson Plans for Differentiated Instruction
- Differentiated Instructional Benchmarking Guides
- Interactive Reader and Study Guide

 Spanish Chapter Summaries Audio CD Program

 Online Chapter Summaries in Spanish

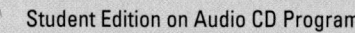 Student Edition on Audio CD Program

 Differentiated Instruction Modified Worksheets and Tests CD-ROM
- Vocabulary Flash Cards
- Modified Vocabulary Builder Activities
- Modified Chapter Review Activity
- Modified Chapter Test

OSP One-Stop Planner CD-ROM
- ExamView Test Generator (English and Spanish)
- PuzzlePro
- Quiz Show for ExamView
- Transparencies and Videos

TE Differentiated Activities in the Teacher's Edition
- Wartime Construction, p. 404
- Congress Takes Control of Reconstruction, p. 412
- Schools and Segregation, p. 419
- New Lives for Freedmen, p. 420
- Abandoning the South, p. 424

Reading Like a Historian
Sam Wineburg

Prior Assumptions

Reading is guided by our prior assumptions. Yet prior knowledge poses a particular problem when trying to understand the past. Knowledge brought from the present is an inescapable but often fallible guide to building historical understanding.

Take our chapter's description of the experiments in Reconstruction on South Carolina's Sea Islands, on pages 404–405. It was at Port Royal, South Carolina, that the first school was set up for freed slave children. This educational experiment became famous because of the literary talents of one of its teachers, Charlotte L. Forten. On October 27, 1862, Forten journeyed from Philadelphia to South Carolina to help establish the school, and later published her impressions in a series of magazine articles in the *Atlantic Monthly*. Consider Forten's first impressions on arrival in South Carolina:

A Southern School

"The first day at school was rather trying . . . Some children were too young to learn the alphabet . . . I never before saw children so eager to learn, although I had had several years' experience in New England schools.

"Of course there are some stupid ones, but these are the minority. The majority learn with wonderful rapidity. It is wonderful how a people who have been so long crushed to the earth . . . can have so great a desire for knowledge, and such a capability for attaining it.

"I told them about Toussaint [L'Ouverture], thinking it well that they should know what one of their own color had done for his race. They listened attentively, and seemed to understand . . . It is necessary to interest them every moment, in order to keep their thoughts from wandering."

Forming Impressions

Based on these excerpts, many readers will have formed an impression of Charlotte Forten. Based on her use of the word "stupid" to describe some children (and the racist connotations that seemingly brings up), the sophistication of her language, her experience as a teacher in New England at a time when few women benefited from higher education, and the prestige of the *Atlantic Monthly*, many readers will assume that Forten was a white aristocrat from a patrician Philadelphia family—a "charity-lady" do-gooder. Here, however, is an instance where background knowledge leads us astray.

Charlotte Forten (1837–1914) was an African American woman, highly educated, and a member of a wealthy Philadelphia family of prosperous free blacks. In her spare time she wrote poetry and studied the works of her favorite authors—Byron, Phyllis Wheatley, and Chaucer. Her grandfather, James Forten, himself born of free blacks, was a sailmaker who outfitted American forces during the War of 1812 and become one of the richest men in the city. Her family lived in a brick house on Philadelphia's fashionable Lombard Street and was part of the social circle that included William Lloyd Garrison and other abolitionists who founded the American Anti-Slavery Society.

Few students will be acquainted with the variety and richness of African American life before the Civil War. Even fewer will be familiar with northeastern communities of free blacks, some of whom amassed great wealth. (Fifty million dollars is a conservative estimate of the wealth of free blacks on the eve of the Civil War.)

The Dangers of Background Knowledge

Our prior conceptions allow us to glimpse the past—they are the lenses through which we form an initial image. But prior knowledge imported from the present distorts as well as aids. There is no way to get around this double-edged sword. An encounter with history, however, teaches caution, a heightened sensitivity to a world more complicated and more fascinating than one we could ever imagine.

Standards Focus

Social Studies Competency Goals
Goal 2 The learner will assess the competing forces of expansionism, nationalism, and sectionalism.
2.05, 2.06

The Big Idea and Essential Questions

To foster student understanding of this chapter's big idea, design your lesson to address each section's essential question.

Big Idea The federal government implemented a plan to rebuild the South which lasted 12 years and resulted in only limited gains for southern African Americans.

Essential Questions

1. What different kinds of ideas did Northern leaders have about restoring the South to the Union?

2. How did Reconstruction change when Congress took control of it?

3. How did Reconstruction affect the lives of people in the South?

4. What were the lasting effects of Reconstruction?

Key to Differentiating Instruction

Below Level

Basic-level activities designed for all students encountering new material

At Level

Intermediate-level activities designed for average students

Above Level

Challenging activities designed for honors and gifted-and-talented students

Standard English Mastery

Activities designed to improve standard English usage

400 CHAPTER 12

CHAPTER
12 1865–1877

Reconstruction

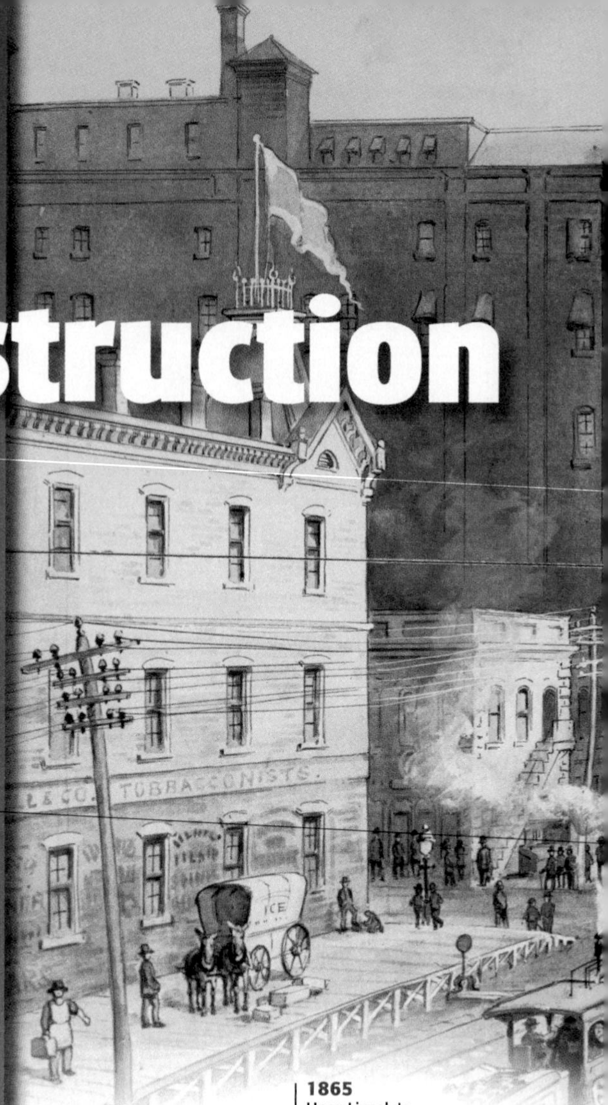

THE BIG PICTURE Following the Civil War, Congress implemented a plan to reconstruct the South. After 12 years, and in response to fierce resistance from many white southerners, the federal government declared Reconstruction over.

North Carolina Standards

Social Studies Objectives

3.04 Analyze the political, economic, and social impact of Reconstruction on the nation and identify the reasons why Reconstruction came to an end.

3.05 Evaluate the degree to which the Civil War and Reconstruction proved to be a test of the supremacy of the national government.

Language Arts Objectives

3.01 Use language persuasively in addressing a particular issue by:
• establishing and defending a point of view.

3.03 Use argumentation for:
• establishing and defending a point of view.

Skills FOCUS READING LIKE A HISTORIAN

Much of Atlanta had been burned during the Civil War, but following the war it became Georgia's new state capital and a center of Reconstruction activity.
Interpreting Visuals What evidence of Atlanta's revival can you see in this Reconstruction-era painting?
See Skills Handbook, p. H30

400

1865
U.S.
Upon Lincoln's death, Andrew Johnson becomes president. Johnson launches his own Reconstruction plan.

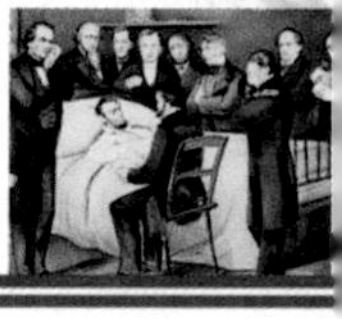

1865

World

1866
Swedish chemist Alfred Nobel invents dynamite.

Introduce the Chapter

At Level

Reconstruction

1. Have students work in small groups to develop a plan to reconstruct a city or region that has been devastated by a natural disaster, such as a hurricane, tornado, or earthquake. Have students prepare a list of what services and businesses they would want first restored, and which would have lower priorities.

2. Have volunteers share their plans with the class.

3. Tell students that immediately following the Civil War, plans to rebuild the South and unify the nation were begun. It was not an easy process and different groups had very different ideas about what the South should look like following Reconstruction.
LS Verbal-Linguistic, Kinesthetic
Alternative Assessment Handbook, Rubrics 11: Discussions; and 14: Group Activity

February 1869
Congress passes the Fifteenth Amendment, assuring African American men the right to vote.

February 1870
Hiram R. Revels becomes the first African American U.S. Senator.

1876
Supreme Court limits Fourteenth and Fifteenth Amendments, weakening Reconstruction.

1877
Compromise of 1877 gives Rutherford B. Hayes presidency, ending Reconstruction.

1870

1875

1880

1869
The Suez Canal is completed.

1871
German states, united under Prussia, defeat France in the Franco-Prussian War.

1873
Canada's famed Mounted Police force is established.

1877
The tenth Russo-Turkish War begins.

401

Chapter Preview

HOLT
History's Impact
▶ **Video Program:**
Reconstruction
See the Video Teacher's Guide for strategies for using the video segment.

Reading Like a Historian
After the Civil War Have students examine the painting carefully, and explain the contrast between this image and the devastation of southern cities, businesses, and railroads immediately following the Civil War.

go.hrw.com
Online Resources
Chapter Resources:
KEYWORD: SD7 CH12
Teacher Resources:
KEYWORD: SD7 TEACHER

Explore the Time Line

1. How long did Reconstruction last? *12 years, from 1865 to 1877*

2. How did the Supreme Court weaken Reconstruction? *limited the Fourteenth and Fifteenth Amendments*

3. When was dynamite invented? By whom? *1866; Alfred Nobel*

Info to Know

The Suez Canal While the United States was trying to solve its own domestic problems of reuniting and rebuilding the South, events were happening overseas. In 1869 the Suez Canal opened, connecting the Mediterranean and Red seas. This channel is just over 100 miles in length. Because the levels of both seas are relatively equal, there was no need to build locks to raise and lower ships. The Suez Canal reduced the voyage from Europe to the Indian Ocean by about 5,000 miles. By 1945 the number of annual shipments through the canal peaked at 984,000. In recent years, however, traffic through the canal has dropped.

Answers

Reading Like a Historian (p. 400)
busy city street indicates a prosperous community; buildings, streets, and telegraph lines look undamaged; American flags flying indicates pride in heritage

Bellringer

The Inside Story. . . Use the **Daily Bellringer Transparency** to help students answer the question.

📖 Daily Bellringer Transparency, Section 1

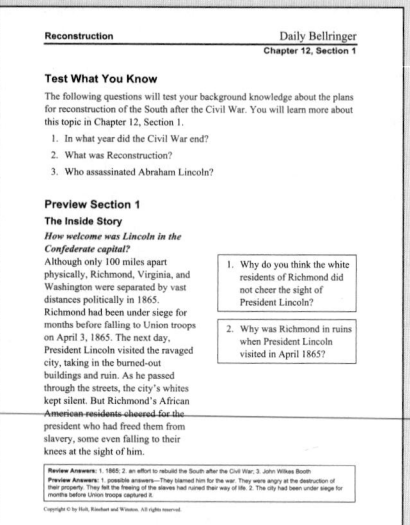

Academic Vocabulary

Review with students the high-use academic term in this section.

contract an official legal agreement between two parties (p. 405)

📄 CRF: Vocabulary Builder Activity, Section 1

Taking Notes

Lincoln's Plan—appointed temporary military governors for parts of Confederacy in Union hands; issued a Proclamation of Amnesty and Reconstruction, which allowed a state to rejoin the Union when 10 percent of its voters had taken a loyalty oath (the Ten Percent Plan); vetoed Wade-Davis Bill; Johnson's Plan—similar to Lincoln's plan at first, though his did not require a set percentage of voters to take a loyalty oath

Plans for Reconstruction

BEFORE YOU READ

MAIN IDEA

Northern leaders had differing ideas for dealing with the many issues and challenges of restoring the southern states to the Union.

READING FOCUS

1. What challenges faced the South after the Civil War?

2. What actions did Union leaders take during wartime to reconstruct the nation after the war's end?

3. How did Lincoln's assassination affect the nation?

4. Why did President Johnson and Congress differ over Reconstruction?

KEY TERMS AND PEOPLE

Freedmen's Bureau
Ten Percent Plan
Thaddeus Stevens
Wade-Davis Bill
pocket veto
John Wilkes Booth
Andrew Johnson

TAKING NOTES As you read, take notes on Lincoln's and Johnson's plans for reconstruction of the South. Record your notes in a graphic organizer like the one shown below.

Lincoln's Plan	Johnson's Plan

An Unexpected Visitor

THE INSIDE STORY

How welcome was Lincoln in the Confederate capital? Less than 100 miles separate Richmond, Virginia, and Washington, D.C. In 1865, one city was the U.S. capital, the other the capital of the Confederacy. By early April, Richmond had been under siege for months. On April 3, Union forces finally captured the city. The next day, President Lincoln decided to pay a visit. Richmond lay in ruins. Skeletons of burned-out buildings lined the streets.

Lincoln reached the city on a navy ship with his son Tad. It was Tad's 12th birthday. They walked through the ruined streets with a small guard of soldiers. One witness said that Lincoln "was walking with his usual long, careless stride, and looking about with an interested air and taking in everything." The president visited Jefferson Davis's house and was curious about everything in it. He met with Confederate officials who remained and then toured the city.

As Lincoln, in his trademark stovepipe hat, walked the streets, most of Richmond's white citizens kept an angry silence. The newly freed African Americans reacted very differently. Hundreds emerged from the ruins. Some fell on their knees as they recognized the president, crying "Glory, hallelujah!" An African American Union soldier wrote: "It was a great deliverer among the delivered. No wonder tears came into his eyes." Lincoln told the Union commander to treat all Richmonders with compassion. ◾

In the late 1800s an artist painted a different version of Lincoln's visit to Richmond.

402

Teach the Main Idea

At Level

Plans for Reconstruction

1. **Teach** Ask students the Reading Focus questions to teach this section.

2. **Apply** Draw four large rectangles for students to see. Label the top of each with one of the four topics of this section. Have students work in pairs to identify the significant details of each topic. Have volunteers name the details and use the rectangles as a graphic organizer. Have students copy the organizer and use it as a study tool. **LS Visual-Spatial**

3. **Review** As you review the section, have students explain whether Confederates should have been punished or forgiven for starting war and how the Freedmen's Bureau could have been more effective.

4. **Practice/Homework** Have students create a two-column table and complete it by listing hopes and challenges for freed African Americans in the South. **LS Visual-Spatial**

📄 Alternative Assessment Handbook, Rubric 7: Charts

📖 Graphic Organizer Transparencies

Richmond, Virginia, 1865

This view of Richmond shows the level of destruction from which parts of the South needed to recover.

The South after the War

President Lincoln's visit to Richmond showed him some of the challenges facing the nation at the end of the Civil War. Richmond was in ruins, as were many other southern cities and towns. Large parts of the countryside had been devastated by the fighting and by armies passing through them. The loss of farm buildings, machinery, work animals, and other livestock was widespread.

Furthermore, formerly enslaved African Americans faced an uncertain future. Although they were now free, they had very few job opportunities, and many were unable to make a living.

Property losses In the years after the war, farms and plantations in the South were worth only about half of what they were in 1860. Farms and plantations that did survive the war suffered from neglect. This was because many small farmers died fighting the war, leaving their farms without proper care. In total, more than one-fifth of the South's white male population perished.

Plantations suffered from the loss of workers. Some slaves escaped during the war; others left after the war's end. "All was lost, except my debts," one Confederate general complained about his once prosperous plantation.

Property losses were not limited to cities and farms, however. War damage or neglect also left the South's transportation network in poor shape. Long stretches of railroad lines were useless. In Alabama, a government survey described the condition of one railroad.

HISTORY'S VOICES

❝ From Pocahontas to Decatur, one-hundred and fourteen miles, almost entirely destroyed, except the road-bed and iron rails, and they in very bad condition—every bridge and trestle destroyed, cross-ties rotten, buildings burned . . . and track grown up in weeds and bushes . . . About forty miles of the track was burned . . . and rails bent and twisted in such a manner as to require great labor to straighten. ❞

—House Report 34, 39th Congress, 1865

Challenges for African Americans The nearly 4 million African Americans living in the former Confederacy had won their freedom. But they faced other problems after the war. Most had no money or education. The condition of the South's economy made job prospects bleak. Former owners needed workers but often could not afford to pay them. The South needed to find a new labor system that would replace slavery, put people to work, and make the region productive again.

Many former slaves were no longer willing to work the long hours that been required under slavery. Some women resisted work in the fields and tried to enroll their children in school instead. They wanted an education, too, and to devote more time to their families. Ways had to be found to provide educational and economic opportunities for all formerly enslaved African Americans.

RECONSTRUCTION **403**

② What actions did Union leaders take during wartime to reconstruct the nation after the war's end? *created Freedmen's Bureau; implemented Reconstruction experiments to help freedmen; Ten Percent Plan*

Wartime Reconstruction

Recall What was the Freemen's Bureau? *organization created by Congress to help blacks and southern whites uprooted by the war*

Compare and Contrast How did some northerners believe the Confederate states should be treated, and how did this view differ from Lincoln's view? *Some northerners believed states should be treated harshly; Lincoln believed that they should be treated with charity.*

Elaborate Why were the Sea Islands considered a significant Reconstruction experiment? *Whites had fled; land divided up; freed slaves hired to farm it.*

Activity Freedmen's Bureau Ad
Have students design a poster advertising the Freedmen's Bureau. Remind students that the vast majority of slaves in the South did not know how to read or write. **LS** Visual-Spatial

📄 CRF: Primary Source Activity: Report of the South Carolina Freedmen's Bureau

Primary Source

"Strip the proud nobility of their bloated estates, reduce them to a level with plain republicans, send forth to labor, and teach their children to enter the workshops or handle the plow, and you will thus humble proud traitors."
— Thaddeus Stevens

Answers

Interpreting Graphs 1. *total property wealth;* **2.** *nearly as many as all other wars*

Reading Check *in ruins; farms, buildings, machinery, livestock destroyed, land was devastated; no prospects for jobs*

How to treat the South The nation also needed to answer many legal and political questions. What place would African Americans have in political life in the South? What was the status of the Confederate states? Were they conquered territories, or were they once again states in the Union? If they were not states, how could they become states? Should Confederates be forgiven? Or, should they be punished for seceding and starting the war?

READING CHECK Identifying the Main Idea
What were conditions like in the South in the aftermath of the Civil War?

Wartime Reconstruction

Union leaders began addressing these issues even before the South's formal surrender. For example, in March 1865 Congress created the **Freedmen's Bureau** to provide help to the thousands of black and white southerners uprooted by the fighting. The Bureau continued to function throughout the Reconstruction era, which lasted from 1865 to 1877.

Northerners disagreed over how to treat the conquered Confederacy. Many, including some members of Congress, shared the view of abolitionist Wendell Phillips. "We have a right to trample it [the South] under the heels of our boots," Phillips declared. "That is the meaning of the war." Lincoln, however, stated in his second inaugural address in 1865 that he hoped to treat the South "with malice toward none, with charity for all."

Reconstruction experiments Even before the war ended, northern leaders tested possible roles for freed African Americans in the South's economy. When planters fled regions that came under Union control, the army often seized their plantations. Sometimes, the army hired freed slaves to work on the plantations for pay. In a few cases, former slaves rented plantations. This allowed them to farm the land and to keep or sell the crops they raised. In this way, some former slaves saved enough money to buy land of their own.

The most famous wartime reconstruction experiment took place on the Sea Islands off the coast of South Carolina. When Union forces captured these islands early in the war, nearly all the white population fled to the mainland. The federal government seized their plantations, sold some of the land, and hired former slaves to farm the rest of it.

In January 1865 General Sherman divided this and other land along the South Carolina and Georgia coasts into 40-acre plots. He offered a plot to any formerly enslaved family who wanted land. By the end of the war more than 40,000 freedmen were farming in the region,

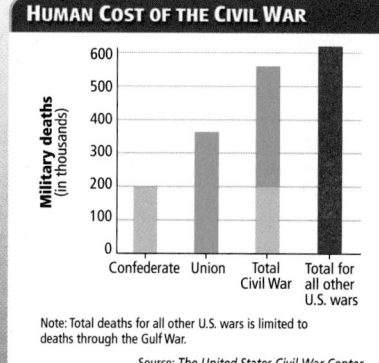

The Costs of the Civil War

HUMAN COST OF THE CIVIL WAR

Military deaths (in thousands)

Confederate · Union · Total Civil War · Total for all other U.S. wars

Note: Total deaths for all other U.S. wars is limited to deaths through the Gulf War.

Source: *The United States Civil War Center*

FINANCIAL COST OF THE CIVIL WAR

Southern livestock killed: 40 percent

Southern farm machinery destroyed: 50 percent

Drop in South's total property wealth: 66 percent

Total national wealth held by the South, 1860: 30 percent

Total national wealth held by the South, 1870: 12 percent

Skills FOCUS INTERPRETING GRAPHS

1. According to the chart, what was the South's worst financial loss of the war?
2. According to the graph, how do Civil War deaths compare with the total for all other U.S. wars?

See Skills Handbook, pp. H15, H16

Differentiating Instruction

Below Level

Learners Having Difficulty

1. Organize the students into small groups. Have each group review and list the Reconstruction experiments discussed in the section.

2. Have students discuss and rate each experiment using the terms poor, good, very good, or excellent.

3. Have each group create a report card and assign a letter grade to each experiment. Then have groups complete the report card

by adding evaluation comments about each experiment.

4. Have volunteers from each group share the report cards with the class. **LS** Visual-Spatial, Interpersonal

📄 Alternative Assessment Handbook, Rubric 11: Discussions

Freedmen's Village

Union troops provided building materials to help these former slaves transform an abandoned Sea Islands plantation into a village.

on land they considered their own. Northern religious groups and other organizations sent teachers to coastal Georgia and South Carolina to start schools for the former slaves.

In Louisiana another large reconstruction experiment provided former slaves as paid workers to planters who took Lincoln's loyalty oath. The freedmen signed a <u>contract</u> to work for a year. In return, the planter agreed to provide housing, food, and medical care in addition to wages. But the planter sometimes deducted these basic items from the freedmen's wages. Little money was left over, so many freedmen could not afford to leave the plantation when their contracts ended.

Lincoln's Reconstruction plans In 1862 Lincoln appointed military governors temporarily to rule parts of the Confederacy that were already in Union hands. To prepare these and other conquered regions for rejoining the Union, he issued a Proclamation of Amnesty and Reconstruction in December 1863.

Lincoln's proclamation offered forgiveness for the rebellion to all southerners (except high-ranking Confederate leaders) who pledged loyalty to the Union and support for emancipation. When 10 percent of a state's voters had taken this oath, they could organize a new state government. The new government was then required to ban slavery. Once these steps

were complete, Lincoln would recognize it as the state's legal government, even if the state's Confederate government was still functioning.

This procedure for readmitting seceded states became known as the **Ten Percent Plan**. Before the war ended, Lincoln had accepted three southern states back into the Union. By early 1865, Arkansas, Louisiana, and Tennessee had formed pro-Union governments and sent senators and representatives to take seats in Congress.

Opposition to Lincoln's plan Lincoln's actions set off a great debate in Congress over who would control Reconstruction. Some members noted that admitting states to the Union was a power of Congress. They claimed it was not up to the president to make the rebel states part of the Union again. Lincoln's supporters pointed out that since secession was unlawful, the Confederate states had never legally left the Union in the first place. Therefore, Congress did not need to readmit them.

Many members of Congress did not support readmitting southern states. Massachusetts senator Charles Sumner argued that the southern states had given up their status as states when they seceded. Other members claimed that the parts of the Confederacy controlled by Union armies were conquered

ACADEMIC VOCABULARY

contract an official legal agreement between two parties

• **Direct Teach** •

Reading Focus

Wartime Reconstruction

Explain What was the Ten Percent Plan? *Lincoln's plan to admit Confederate states back into the Union*

Summarize What were the major constitutional issues that plagued the Union as it created plans for Reconstruction? *whether the president or Congress should control Reconstruction; how to readmit states*

Make Judgments Why do you think that President Lincoln took a lenient position toward the states that had seceded? *wanted the nation to be reunited; wanted to end bitter divisiveness*

Info to Know

Louisiana Louisiana was the first Confederate state to meet the requirements of the Ten Percent Plan. Occupied by Union military forces during the war, the state held a convention in 1864 and drafted a new constitution that outlawed slavery. Despite the state's having met the president's requirements for readmission to the Union, Congress refused to allow Louisiana's representatives to take their seats in the U.S. Congress.

Collaborative Learning

At Level

Wartime Reconstruction

1. Organize the students into small groups to prepare for a class debate on Reconstruction.

2. Have one-third of the groups prepare arguments supporting President Lincoln's plan for Reconstruction, one-third supporting President Johnson's plan, and the other one-third supporting Congress's plans.

3. Have one volunteer from each group open the debate by summarizing the group's Reconstruction plan. Then conduct a class

debate on which plan best serves the South and the nation. Have class members take notes on the arguments presented.

4. Guide students in a discussion of which side presented the most convincing arguments.

LS Verbal-Linguistic, Kinesthetic

Alternative Assessment Handbook, Rubric 10: Debates

Wartime Reconstruction

Recall What were the provisions of the Wade-Davis Bill? *required that a majority of state's white males pledge loyalty to the Union before elections could be held*

Make Inferences Why do you think President Lincoln ignored the Wade-Davis Bill, rather than veto it outright? *did not want to confront northerners, but wanted a more lenient policy for readmitting southern states*

Make Judgments What role do you think the president should take in introducing legislation and helping ensure its passage? *possible answer— president can work with Congress to help see that legislation is introduced; however, it is the Congress's duty to make laws*

Activity **Wade-Davis Bill** Have students refer to the Constitution in their textbooks and cite the articles that Wade and Davis refer to in their 1864 manifesto. **LS** **Verbal-Linguistic**

CRF: Biography: Thaddeus Stevens

Counterpoints

Views on Reconstruction

Analyze What types of punishment might Thaddeus Stevens have thought appropriate for the states, and the people that lived in the states that seceded from the Union? *possible answers—taxes, fines, reparations, loss of citizenship*

Activity **Reconstruction Political Cartoons** Have students create a political cartoon expressing their opinion about Thaddeus Stevens's view that southerners be treated as a conquered people. **LS** **Visual-Spatial**

Answers

Reading Like a Historian *was a southerner from Tennessee; wanted to treat fellow southerners fairly*

Reading Check *Lincoln viewed Confederate states with compassion; some Congress members wanted to punish Confederacy for leaving Union*

---

territories. According to this reasoning, Congress would decide on their admission to the Union as it did with all territories that became states.

Some members of Congress objected to the Ten Percent Plan as much too lenient. Republican **Thaddeus Stevens** of Pennsylvania noted that allowing just 10 percent of a state's voters to form a government violated the nation's principles. "The democratic doctrine that the majority shall rule is discarded and dangerously ignored," he observed. "When the doctrine that the *quality* and not the *number* of voters is to decide the right to govern, then we no longer have a republic."

For these reasons and others, Congress refused to allow senators and representatives from states organized under Lincoln's plan to take their seats. Instead, Congress responded with its own Reconstruction plan in 1864 by passing the **Wade-Davis Bill**. The bill required a majority of a state's white male citizens to pledge loyalty before elections could be held.

Lincoln, however, thought this tougher requirement would make southerners more committed to continuing the war. He killed the Wade-Davis Bill with a **pocket veto**. This is a presidential power to prevent a bill passed in the last 10 days of a legislative session from becoming law by simply ignoring it. The bill's outraged Republican sponsors, Benjamin Wade and Henry Davis, wrote a stinging criticism of Lincoln's action.

HISTORY'S VOICES

❝[The president] must understand that our support is of a cause and not of a man; that the authority of Congress is paramount and must be respected; . . . and if he wishes our support, he must confine himself to his executive duties— to obey and execute, not make the laws— to suppress by arms armed rebellion, and leave political reorganization to Congress.❞

—The Wade-Davis Manifesto, August 5, 1864

This attack by members of his own party hurt Lincoln deeply. It was just the first indicator, however, of the struggle that was to come.

READING CHECK **Contrasting** How did Lincoln's views on Reconstruction differ from the views of some members of Congress?

COUNTERPOINTS

Views on Reconstruction

Representative Thaddeus Stevens, a Radical Republican leader, insisted that the South be treated as a conquered territory.

❝ [W]e hold it the duty of the Government to inflict . . . punishment on the rebel belligerents, and so weaken their hands that they can never again endanger the Union . . . This can be done only by treating and holding them as a conquered people.❞

Thaddeus Stevens, 1865

President Andrew Johnson, a southerner, argued that the southern states should not be denied their rights.

❝ [T]he policy of military rule over a conquered territory [implies] that the States [who took] part in the rebellion had by the act . . . ceased to exist. But the true theory is that all pretended acts of secession were from the beginning null and void.❞

Andrew Johnson, 1865

Skills FOCUS **READING LIKE A HISTORIAN**

Recognizing Bias Why might President Johnson have been biased in favor of the South?

See **Skills Handbook, p. H33**

Skills Focus: Analyzing Primary Sources
Below Level

Reading Like a Historian Skill
Standard English Mastery
Reconstruction Viewpoints

1. Guide students in a discussion about Reconstruction and the views of Thaddeus Stevens and Andrew Johnson as expressed in the Counterpoints feature.

2. Have students work in mixed-ability pairs to write a paraphrase of each quote, and have volunteers share their paraphrases with the class.

3. Have students write a paragraph explaining how the difference in point of view over Reconstruction policy reflected different views about the South and the Civil War.
   LS **Interpersonal**

   Alternative Assessment Handbook, Rubrics 9: Comparing and Contrasting; and 37: Writing Activity

Lincoln's Assassination

Lincoln's popularity as a victorious wartime leader might have allowed him to win the battle with Congress for control of Reconstruction. But the president did not live long enough.

Less than a week after General Lee's surrender in Virginia, **John Wilkes Booth** shot Lincoln while the president watched a play at Ford's Theater in Washington, D.C. on April 14, 1865. Lincoln died the next morning.

Booth, a southerner, strongly supported secession and the Confederacy. His first plan had been to kidnap the president and exchange him for Confederate prisoners of war. Booth organized a group to help carry out the kidnapping. The plot failed when Lincoln's schedule changed and he did not appear at the place Booth intended to seize him. Booth decided to kill Lincoln instead.

Other plotters were assigned to assassinate Secretary of State William Seward and Vice President **Andrew Johnson** the same night. Booth hoped this would create chaos within the government and help the Confederacy win the war. Only Booth carried out his assignment successfully, however. He escaped into Virginia where he was located by Union troops and killed when he refused to surrender.

Lincoln's death produced one of the greatest outpourings of grief in the nation's history. A train carried his body back to Illinois for burial. Huge crowds gathered to pay respects at stops along the train's nearly two-week journey.

White southerners reacted to Lincoln's death with more concern than grief. They feared the effect the assassination might have on the Reconstruction program. Some southern leaders disliked Andrew Johnson even more than they disliked Lincoln. The vice president was a southerner who had sided with the Union during the war. In the eyes of many white southerners, this made him a traitor. Now this traitor to their cause would become president of the United States.

READING CHECK **Sequencing** Trace the events that led to Lincoln's assassination.

Lincoln's funeral procession traveled by train across more than 1,600 miles of countryside, making stops in major cities such as New York (above). "Now he belongs to the ages," Secretary of War Edwin Stanton said upon Lincoln's death. *Why do you think so many people were given an opportunity to participate in the funeral?*

ANNE S.K. BROWN MILITARY COLLECTION, BROWN UNIVERSITY LIBRARY

Johnson and Congress Differ over Reconstruction

Andrew Johnson was sworn in as president a few hours after Lincoln's death. The two men shared a common background. Both had been raised in poverty without much formal schooling. Both men overcame their humble beginnings to achieve success. Johnson had been governor of Tennessee and a U.S. senator. When Lincoln sought re-election in 1864, the Republicans picked Johnson to run for vice president. Like Lincoln, Johnson never forgot his roots.

Early relations with Congress Even though Johnson was a Democrat, Republican leaders in Congress at first thought they could work with him. "Treason is a crime and crime must be punished," Johnson told Senator Wade. Senator Sumner also met with Johnson and described his attitude as excellent. "There is no difference between us," Sumner reported.

Wade, Sumner, and other Republican leaders failed to understand Johnson's views. The new president held no ill will toward the South or toward southerners. He merely despised the wealthy planter class. In addition, although Johnson opposed secession, he had always supported states' rights and limits on

---

Reading Focus

❸ How did Lincoln's assassination affect the nation? *produced one of greatest outpourings of grief in nation's history*

Lincoln's Assassination

Explain How did white southerners react to Lincoln's death? *with concern about the effect on Reconstruction*

Make Inferences What emotions do you feel freedmen experienced at Lincoln's death? *sadness, fear that gains made during Lincoln's presidency would be taken away, loss of hope*

Reading Focus

❹ Why did President Johnson and Congress differ over Reconstruction? *Congress believed South should be punished; Johnson held no ill will toward the South, supported states' rights*

Johnson and Congress Differ over Reconstruction

Describe What prior public serviced experience did Andrew Johnson have? *governor of Tennessee, U.S. senator*

Compare How were Johnson and Lincoln's background alike? *poor family, little formal education, overcame beginnings to achieve success; never forgot roots*

Collaborative Learning

At Level

Reconstruction Plans

Have students copy the chart onto their own paper and complete it by listing the following events and providing Confederate and Union reactions to the event: Freedmen's Bureau, Reconstruction experiments, Ten Percent Plan, veto of Wade-Davis Bill. **LS Visual-Spatial**

📄 Alternative Assessment Handbook, Rubric 7: Charts

📊 Graphic Organizer Transparencies

Event	Former Confederacy	Union

Answers

Art *popular president; nation mourned the loss*

Reading Check *Reconstruction plans proposed; Booth involved in conspiracy to create chaos in Union government to help Confederacy win war; Booth was to kidnap Lincoln, decided to kill him*

407

Johnson and Congress Differ over Reconstruction

Recall Why did Johnson launch his Reconstruction plan while Congress was in recess? *did not want to wait until Congress returned from lengthy recess*

Contrast How did Johnson's Reconstruction plan differ from Lincoln's? *did not have percentage requirement; presidential pardon required for those owning property valued at more than $20,000*

● Review & Assess ●

Close

Have students compare and contrast the plans for Reconstruction.

Review

Online Quiz, Section 1

Daily Test Practice Transparency

Assess

SE Section 1 Assessment

Progress Assessment: Section 1 Quiz

Alternative Assessment Handbook

Reteach

Interactive Reader and Study Guide, Section 1

Interactive Skills Tutor CD-ROM

---

the power of the national government. He was not about to give Congress the control it sought over the affairs of the rebel states.

Johnson's Reconstruction plan Practical matters also convinced Johnson to keep Reconstruction under presidential control. Congress was in recess when he took office as president. Its new session did not begin until December. Johnson believed it was important to have a program to reunite the nation in place before that time.

Johnson launched his Reconstruction plan in late May. Like Lincoln's plan, it restored the rights of white southerners who took an oath of loyalty to the United States.

Johnson added to Lincoln's list of exceptions, however. Southerners who owned property worth more than $20,000 would also have to apply to the president for a pardon, just like former Confederate military and political leaders. This added measure allowed President Johnson to decide personally the punishment the planters would receive.

Unlike the Wade-Davis Bill and Lincoln's plan, the Johnson plan did not set a percentage of loyal voters that was needed to form a state government. It merely required that pledge-takers call a convention to repeal secession, amend the state constitution to abolish slavery,

THE IMPACT TODAY

Government

When Johnson took office in April 1865, Congress was in recess for most of the remainder of the year. Congress today is in session for much longer. In 2004 the Senate convened for 133 days and the House for 110 days, passing a total of more than 1,400 bills.

and refuse to pay the debts of the Confederate government. When these steps were complete, the state could elect a governor and legislature and send representatives to Congress.

Concern over Johnson's plan Sumner, Stevens, and other leading Republicans in Congress were troubled by the president's plan. One concern was that it contained no provisions for giving freedmen a role in southern state government. Another was that once a state had qualified under Johnson's plan to hold elections, any voter could take part.

Stevens wrote Johnson in July to request that he suspend his plan. "Can you not hold your hand and wait the action of Congress?" Steven asked the president. Johnson did not even bother to answer Stevens's letter. The new president ignored one of the most powerful members of Congress and continued to push forward on his own.

When Congress met in December, Johnson told it that every former Confederate state except Texas had met his conditions for Reconstruction and had been restored to the Union. Many members of Congress were far from satisfied. A battle for control of Reconstruction was about to begin.

READING CHECK **Identifying the Main Idea** What was President Johnson's plan for Reconstruction?

SECTION 1 ASSESSMENT

go.hrw.com
Online Quiz
Keyword: SD7 HP12

Reviewing Ideas, Terms, and People

1. **a. Recall** What happened to southern farms and plantations during the Civil War?
   b. Contrast How did conditions differ for African Americans before and after the Civil War?
   c. Evaluate Do you think it was necessary to punish the former Confederate states for seceding?

2. **a. Identify** State the importance of each of the following: Freedmen's Bureau, Thaddeus Stevens.
   b. Interpret How well did wartime Reconstruction experiments work in employing freed African Americans?
   c. Elaborate Why did Congress feel that Reconstruction was a congressional task and not a presidential task?

3. **a. Recall** Who was John Wilkes Booth?
   b. Predict What effect do you think Lincoln's assassination had on Reconstruction?

4. **a. Describe** For what reasons did Congress oppose the Reconstruction plan put forward by **Andrew Johnson**?

b. Compare and Contrast In what ways were Lincoln and Johnson similar?

Critical Thinking

5. **Evaluating** Fill in the chart below, listing the major aspects of the three different Reconstruction plans. Which do you think was the best Reconstruction plan? Why?

Ten Percent Plan	Wade-Davis Bill	Johnson's Plan

FOCUS ON WRITING

6. **Expository** Write a letter to the Freedmen's Bureau in which you explain your opinion about work contracts between freed African Americans and planters. Use details from the section to support your position.

Section 1 Assessment Answers

1. **a.** devastated; land and animals destroyed
   b. no longer enslaved, few jobs available
   c. no, devastation of war punishment enough

2. **a.** Bureau—helped get freedmen and southern whites back on feet after war; Stevens—senator who thought South should be punished
   b. gave a few paid work and hope of land ownership
   c. considered Confederacy to be conquered territory; Congress had power to admit states

3. **a.** Confederate sympathizer who killed Lincoln
   b. great; direction of Reconstruction changed

4. **a.** plan was too lenient on South
   b. from poor families; little formal education; never forgot roots

5. Ten Percent—when 10 percent of state voters take loyalty oath, state could begin establishing new governments; Wade-Davis—increased percentage of citizens who should take loyalty oath; Johnson—similar to Lincoln's plan, added exceptions; Ten Percent Plan provided quickest restoration of South

6. Contracts were similar to slavery.

Answers

Reading Check *restore rights to white southerners who took loyalty oath; those owning property valued at more than $20,000 had to apply for pardon; repeal secession by convention; amend state constitution to abolish slavery; refuse to pay Confederate government's debts*

Ex Parte Milligan (1866)

Why It Matters Criminal defendants have fewer constitutional protections in military courts than in civil courts. In 1866 the Supreme Court limited the power of military courts to try civilians for violating criminal law.

Background of the Case

An army court found Lambden Milligan guilty of disloyal activities during the Civil War and sentenced him to death. Milligan was not in the military and he lived in Indiana, which was not part of the Confederacy. Because his trial was run under the direction of the Indiana military commander, he did not receive some constitutional protections, such as a public trial and a trial by jury, that would have been available to him in a civilian court. On appeal, Milligan argued that the military court had no authority to try him.

The Decision

The Supreme Court held that the Constitution is not suspended during times of emergency. Even in wartime, citizens are entitled to civil trials. If a wartime commander had the right to suspend all civil rights of citizens and substitute military law for civilian law, then military law would be superior to civilian law. This was not what the Constitution intended, the justices said.

During wartime the government must have more flexibility to protect the country, the justices agreed. Martial law can be declared when the courts and civil authorities of a community no longer function. However, the Court observed that the Civil War was not being fought in Indiana, and that civil courts were available to try alleged wrongdoers. The military court, therefore, had no authority over civilians like Milligan, and the Supreme Court granted his request for discharge from confinement.

THE IMPACT TODAY After the terrorist attacks on America on September 11, 2001, the U.S. military began imprisoning suspected terrorists at a military base at Guantánamo Bay, Cuba. They were held indefinitely and interrogated without access to lawyers or courts. In 2004 the U.S. Supreme Court ruled that American-born Yaser Esam Hamdi could challenge his treatment at Guantánamo in a U.S. court.

CRITICAL THINKING

go.hrw.com
Research Online
Keyword: SS Court

1. **Analyze the Impact** Milligan wanted legal protections he could not get in a military court. Other Court cases have defined what protections are required in a civil trial. Using the keyword above, study *Gideon* v. *Wainwright*. What rule did that case create to protect the rights of criminal defendants?

2. **You Be the Judge** Should foreigners accused of terrorism be tried in civil courts or in military tribunals? What parts of *Milligan* suggest a right to trial in civil courts? In what ways is *Milligan* different, so that military tribunals might be allowed?

Landmark Supreme Court Cases

Ex Parte Milligan

Word Help

antagonism hostility, conflict
irreconcilable impossible to settle

Info to Know

Military Law and *Habeas Corpus*
Ex Parte Milligan was a challenge to the suspension of the writ of *habeas corpus*, Article I, Section 9 of the Constitution. The Supreme Court split 5–4 in deciding if Congress had the power to authorize military trials in cases like Milligan's. In its decision the Court ruled that martial law must be limited to "the theater of active military operations." The court ruled that the president did not have the power to require that civilians be tried in military courts in regions where regular courts were functioning. Justice Davis, whom President Lincoln had nominated to the Supreme Court, wrote the opinion.

Primary Source

"The Constitution of the United States is a law for rulers and people, equally in war and in peace, and covers with the shield of its protection all classes of men, at all times and under all circumstances."

— Justice David Davis

Ex Parte Milligan, 1866

Skills Focus: Analyzing Primary Sources

At Level

Reading Like a Historian Skill
The Supreme Court and L. P. Milligan

1. Have students conduct outside research to read more about the Court decision in this case. Students should read both Justice Davis's opinion and the dissenting opinion.

2. Have students work in small groups to share the results of their research and discuss the opinions. Have each group decide if they would have sided with the majority or the minority in this case.

3. Have volunteers from each group use the small group discussion and their research to present a class debate on the case.

Research Required

LS Kinesthetic, Verbal-Linguistic
📖 Alternative Assessment Handbook, Rubrics 24: Oral Presentations; and 30: Research

Answers

Critical Thinking 1. *due process; Court ruled that states must provide legal assistance for defendants charged with serious crimes;* **2.** *Constitution applies to U.S. citizens, so Milligan is different; also depends upon whether regular courts are available; if nation is at war, military tribunals might be allowed*

409

Bellringer

The Inside Story. . . Use the **Daily Bellringer Transparency** to help students answer the question.

Daily Bellringer Transparency, Section 2

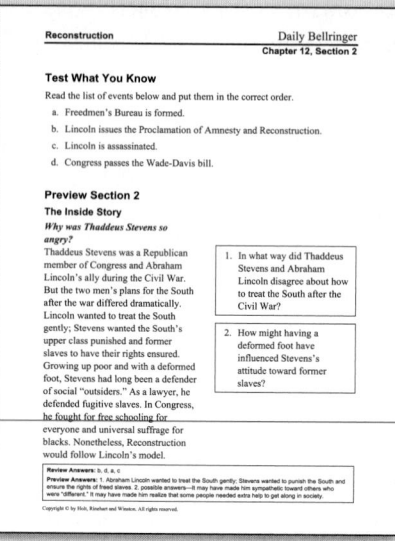

Reconstruction — Daily Bellringer
Chapter 12, Section 2

Test What You Know

Read the list of events below and put them in the correct order.
a. Freedmen's Bureau is formed.
b. Lincoln issues the Proclamation of Amnesty and Reconstruction.
c. Lincoln is assassinated.
d. Congress passes the Wade-Davis bill.

Preview Section 2
The Inside Story
Why was Thaddeus Stevens so angry?
Thaddeus Stevens was a Republican member of Congress and Abraham Lincoln's ally during the Civil War. But the two men's plans for the South after the war differed dramatically. Lincoln wanted to treat the South gently; Stevens wanted the South's upper class punished and former slaves to have their rights ensured. Growing up poor and with a deformed foot, Stevens had long been a defender of social "outsiders." As a lawyer, he defended fugitive slaves. In Congress, he fought for free schooling for everyone and universal suffrage for blacks. Nonetheless, Reconstruction would follow Lincoln's model.

1. In what way did Thaddeus Stevens and Abraham Lincoln disagree about how to treat the South after the Civil War?

2. How might having a deformed foot have influenced Stevens's attitude toward former slaves?

Review Answers: b, d, a, c
Preview Answers: 1. Abraham Lincoln wanted to treat the South gently; Stevens wanted to punish the South and ensure the rights of freed slaves. 2. possible answers—It may have made him sympathetic toward others who were "different." It may have made him realize that some people needed extra help to get along in society.

Copyright © by Holt, Rinehart and Winston. All rights reserved.

Academic Vocabulary

Review with students the high-use academic terms in this section.

prejudice a judgment or opinion about a person or group that is formed in ignorance (p. 411)

utilize use (p. 414)

CRF: Vocabulary Builder Activity, Section 2

Taking Notes

extended life of Freedmen's Bureau, 1866; Civil Rights Act, 1866; Fourteenth Amendment, proposed 1866 (ratified 1868); Reconstruction Acts, 1867; Fifteenth Amendment, proposed 1869 (ratified 1870)

SECTION 2 Congressional Reconstruction

BEFORE YOU READ

MAIN IDEA
Congress took control of Reconstruction as a new, radical branch of the Republican Party was emerging.

READING FOCUS
1. How did the South respond to Reconstruction under President Johnson?
2. Why did Congress take control of Reconstruction, and what changes did it make?
3. How did Radical Reconstruction differ from earlier Reconstruction plans, and what were its effects?

KEY TERMS AND PEOPLE
Black Codes
Ku Klux Klan
Radical Republicans
Civil Rights Act
Fourteenth Amendment
Reconstruction Acts
impeachment
Fifteenth Amendment

TAKING NOTES As you read, take notes on the major acts passed under Congressional Reconstruction. Record your notes in a graphic organizer like the one shown here. You may need to add more rows.

Act	Date

Clashing over Reconstruction

THE INSIDE STORY

Why was Thaddeus Stevens so angry? Thaddeus Stevens's strong, controversial opinions made him deeply hated—and deeply admired. Stevens grew up in poverty and had a deformed foot, which he hid with a special boot. This background helped give him deep sympathy for other social "outsiders." He hated slavery and, as a lawyer, defended fugitive slaves. As a Republican member of Congress, he became one of its leaders during the Civil War.

Although a wartime ally of President Lincoln, Stevens disagreed with Lincoln's plans for the South after the war. Stevens wanted to treat the South like a defeated nation, punishing the planter class and ensuring the rights of freed slaves. His ideas were radical for the time: free schools for everyone and universal suffrage for African Americans. Until those rights were secure, he did not want to allow the southern states to rejoin the Union.

When President Andrew Johnson adopted Lincoln's forgiving approach to Reconstruction after Lincoln's death, Stevens was outraged. In September 1865 he lashed out at Johnson's gentle handling of the South: "The foundation of their institutions—political, municipal, and social—must be broken up and relaid or all our blood and treasure have been spent in vain. This can only be done by treating and holding them as conquered people." ▪

▶ **Stevens viewed white southerners as "conquered rebels."**

410 CHAPTER 12

Teach the Main Idea

At Level

Congressional Reconstruction

1. **Teach** Ask students the Reading Focus questions to teach this section.

2. **Apply** Have students scan the section and create a list of the conflicts, challenges, and problems the nation faced during the time period covered in the section. Then have students work in pairs or small groups to compare their lists. LS **Visual-Spatial**

3. **Review** Have students share their lists with the class. Create a class list for all to see, and have students identify the issue that they believe to be most threatening to the nation.

4. **Practice/Homework** Have students write a speech for President Johnson explaining to Congress and the nation why he chose to veto the bill extending the life of the Freedmen's Bureau and the Civil Rights Act. LS **Auditory-Musical**

Alternative Assessment Handbook, Rubric 24: Oral Presentations

Reconstruction under President Johnson

Representative Thaddeus Stevens may have been unhappy with Johnson's handling of the Reconstruction program, but most white southerners welcomed Johnson's approach. They were relieved that he did not intend to punish them for the rebellion. In particular, they were pleased that his plan let them form new governments on their own terms.

Many white southerners wanted their society and government to remain much as they were before the war. They wanted to rebuild their society with all the advantages they had enjoyed before the war. Although the fighting had stopped, deep-rooted prejudice against African Americans did not simply vanish. Most white southerners did not intend to concede equality to the former slaves.

Johnson himself made it clear that while African Americans had rights, those rights did not include a role in government. "White men alone must manage the South," he declared.

State governments President Johnson pardoned nearly every planter and former Confederate leader who applied. So the states he restored to the Union generally restored to power their prewar leaders. They sent to Washington nine Confederate generals, two Confederate cabinet members, and Alexander Stephens, the vice president of the Confederacy. Not surprisingly, Congress refused to seat these former Confederates.

The Black Codes Southern state leaders could not restore slavery after the ratification of the Thirteenth Amendment in December 1865. But they wanted to preserve the unequal relationship between white and black southerners. Southern state legislatures passed **Black Codes**, which were laws designed to keep freedmen in a slavelike condition and to give planters a supply of cheap labor. However, these laws did allow freedmen certain rights, such as the right to marry or own property.

The Black Codes varied from state to state. In most states, former slaves were required to sign contracts requiring the freedman, and sometimes his family, to work for his employer for one year. If a freedman quit before the end of his contract, he forfeited his wages. Further-

more, it was illegal for any employer to hire a freedman while he was under contract with another employer.

To discourage freedmen from starting businesses, the Black Codes forbade them from renting property in cities or towns. In some states, freedmen who worked at a job other than field hand or servant had to pay a tax.

Any freedman refusing to sign a labor contract or who left his job during his contract could be arrested for being jobless. Such offenses were punished by fines. If a freedman could not pay the fine, he or she had to perform forced labor for up to a year.

In some states, freedmen could not own guns. In others, their guns and dogs were taxed. This was to prevent freedmen from hunting as a source of food. All these laws were designed keep freedmen dependent on the plantations for their existence.

ACADEMIC VOCABULARY

prejudice a judgment or opinion about a person or group that is formed in ignorance

---

Reconstruction under President Johnson

Explain What was the purpose of the Ku Klux Klan? *to terrorize African Americans and whites who were loyal to the U.S. government*

Make Inferences Why do you think members of the Ku Klux Klan were rarely prosecuted? *Their actions were silently supported by other whites.*

❷ Why did Congress take control of Reconstruction, and what changes did it make? *wanted to improve Johnson's Reconstruction program; extended life of Freedmen's Bureau and passed Civil Rights Act*

Congress Takes Control of Reconstruction

Recall Why did northerners initially support President Johnson? *eager to put Civil War behind them and reunite nation*

Summarize What was the position of the Radical Republicans? *wanted to reshape southern society; wanted freed slaves to have economic opportunity and political participation*

Answers
Reading Check *provide cheap labor supply; restrict freedmen*

Southern defiance Because the Black Codes helped retain a familiar way of life, local sheriffs and Civil War veterans supported and enforced these laws. They invaded African Americans' homes and seized guns and other property. They also abused freedmen who refused to sign labor contracts.

These activities inspired white citizens to form their own private groups, supposedly to help keep order in the South. Among these groups was the **Ku Klux Klan**. This group began as a social club in Tennessee in 1866 but soon began terrorizing African Americans and whites who were loyal to the U.S. government. Similar groups sprang up in other southern states. Local officials rarely prosecuted whites who committed violence against blacks.

READING CHECK **Summarizing** What was the purpose of the Black Codes?

Congress Takes Control of Reconstruction

At first, most northerners supported President Johnson's Reconstruction plan. They were eager to put the Civil War behind them and reunite the nation. Johnson's program seemed the easiest way to do that.

Northern opposition grows As time passed, however, northerners became disturbed by what was happening in the South. "Public sentiment [there] is still as bitter and unloyal as in 1861," the *New York Times* reported. The return of former Confederates to power seemed to confirm this view. "[The] reptile spirit of secession is still alive," a New Jersey newspaper warned, "and ready to display its fangs at any moment."

Northerners were even more troubled by the Black Codes. Most white northerners still cared little about African American rights. Many believed, however, that if southern states were allowed to abuse freedmen, the North's victory would be diminished.

Congress fights back Northern response to the Black Codes strengthened a group of senators and representatives who wanted a more thorough Reconstruction program for the South. The so-called **Radical Republicans** favored much tougher requirements for restoring the southern states' governments and wanted to reshape southern society.

Radical Republicans had pushed Lincoln to make the end of slavery a Union goal during the war. They now wanted freed slaves to have economic opportunity and political equality after the war.

The Freedmen's Bureau

The Freedmen's Bureau aided former slaves in many ways. It was most successful in founding schools, like this one in Virginia. The Freedmen's Bureau also built hospitals and provided medical assistance to freedmen.

412

Differentiating Instruction

Below Level | **Standard English Mastery**

English-Language Learners

1. Write the following statements for the students to see: 1) The main goal of Reconstruction is to create a new South and give African Americans the right to vote. 2) The main goal of Reconstruction is to restore the southern states to the Union, keep former Confederates out of government, and give African Americans some rights. Have the students copy the statements into their notes.

2. Have students determine if the statements represent the views of Radical Republicans

or moderate Republicans, and then label each statement. *First statement represents Radical Republicans; the second represents moderate Republicans.*

3. As an extension, have students write one or two paragraphs explaining how these political issues affected the Republican Party during the Reconstruction period. 🔲 **Visual-Spatial, Verbal-Linguistic**

📝 Alternative Assessment Handbook, Rubric 37: Writing Assignments

American Civil Liberty

The Right to Vote

The Thirteenth Amendment ended slavery, and the Fourteenth Amendment granted citizenship to former slaves. Voting, however, remained under the control of the states. Although southern states had to grant African Americans voting rights in order to rejoin the Union, many whites objected. Many northern states also avoided granting voting rights to blacks.

In 1870 the Fifteenth Amendment established that "the right of citizens of the United States to vote shall not be denied or abridged by the United States or by any State on account of race, color, or previous condition of servitude."

Still, states set other requirements that kept many African Americans from voting. Also, the Fifteenth Amendment did not give the vote to women. Native Americans could not vote because they were not considered citizens. Women were not granted the vote nationwide for another 50 years, and Native Americans did not have the right to vote until after World War II.

Making Generalizations Why was the Fifteenth Amendment necessary?

Freedmen cast their votes, 1867

"The whole fabric of southern society must be changed," proclaimed Stevens, a leader of the Radical Republicans in the House.

HISTORY'S VOICES

❝We have turned loose . . . four million slaves without . . . a cent in their pockets. The infernal laws of slavery have prevented them from acquiring an education . . . This Congress is [determined] to provide for them until they can take care of themselves . . . If we leave them to the legislation of their late masters, we had better had left them in bondage.❞

—Thaddeus Stevens, September 18, 1865

When Congress reconvened in December 1865, it ignored Johnson's announcement that Reconstruction was complete. Instead, moderate Republicans, who still controlled both the House and Senate, decided to continue but improve Johnson's Reconstruction program.

Johnson versus Congress The moderates did not share the Radicals' desire to force a social revolution on the South. Yet they did see a need to help the freedmen and protect their civil rights. With this in mind, the moderates proposed two bills in January 1866.

The first bill extended the life and expanded its duties of the Freedmen's Bureau, which was about to close. The bill allowed the Bureau to continue building schools, finding land, and providing other aid to freedmen. It also gave the Bureau authority in legal disputes between whites and African Americans. The intent of this change was to remove such cases from southern state courts.

The second bill was an attack on the Black Codes. The **Civil Rights Act** gave African Americans citizenship and "equal benefit of all laws and proceedings for the security of person and property, as is enjoyed by white citizens." Anyone who denied freedmen these rights would be tried in federal courts.

Both bills easily passed Congress. President Johnson vetoed them, however, claiming they were unnecessary and unconstitutional. When Congress modified the Freedmen's Bureau Bill in response to Johnson's objections, he vetoed it again. Congressional Republicans then united to pass both bills over the president's veto.

Johnson's rigid actions in the fight over the Freedmen's Bureau and the Civil Rights Act ended all attempts by moderate Republicans to work with him. They decided instead to help the Radical Republicans to take control of Reconstruction.

READING CHECK **Identifying Cause and Effect** What developments led Congress to take control of Reconstruction?

Direct Teach

Reading Focus

Congress Takes Control of Reconstruction

Recall What did the Civil Rights Act provide? *gave African Americans citizenship and benefits of all laws that affected white citizens*

Draw Conclusions What was at the root of the North's opposition to the happenings in the South? *pride, believed that the abuse of freedmen diminished the North's war victory*

Make Inferences Why do you think that Congress was motivated to pass the Civil Rights Act? *strong reaction to abuses of Black Codes*

Teaching Tip

Remind students that impeachment does not mean removal from office, nor does it mean that the official is guilty of a crime. An official who has been impeached will have a trial in the U.S. Senate.

go.hrw.com
Online Resources
KEYWORD: SD7 CH12
TOPIC: JOHNSON'S IMPEACHMENT

Collaborative Learning

Above Level

Civil Rights Legislation

Research Required

Materials butcher paper, colored markers, magazines, scissors, glue

1. Organize the class into small groups. Assign each group to research the history of civil rights legislation in the United States, beginning with the 1866 Civil Rights Act. Students should include recent legislation, including the Americans with Disabilities Act. In their research students should learn who proposed the legislation, who supported and who opposed it, how long it took for the legislation to be passed, and who is affected by the legislation.

2. Have each group prepare an illustrated collage that traces the history of civil rights legislation.

3. Have each group present its collage to the class. **LS Visual-Spatial, Interpersonal**

Alternative Assessment Handbook, Rubric 8: Collages

Answers

American Civil Liberty *to ensure that African American males would be able to vote*

Reading Check *Johnson vetoed the Freedmen's Bureau Bill and the Civil Rights Act, convincing even moderate Republicans that they could not work with him.*

❸ How did Radical Reconstruction differ from earlier Reconstruction programs, and what were its effects? *wanted to reshape South economically, socially, and politically; Fourteenth Amendment; military to help implement programs*

Radical Reconstruction

Recall What was the purpose of the Fourteenth Amendment? *granted citizenship to all persons born or naturalized in U.S.; granted citizens equal protection of the laws; barred states from depriving anyone of life, liberty or property without due process*

Draw Conclusions What was the primary reason for the Republicans' victory over Johnson's congressional candidates? *violent riots in Memphis and New Orleans where white mobs attacked African Americans*

Make Judgments Why do you think the U.S. military was used to enforce civilian rights? *possible answer—Local police and elected officials did not protect citizens.*

📑 Map Transparency: Military Districts, 1867

📄 CRF: Biography: Sojourner Truth

📄 CRF: History and Geography Activity: The Fourteenth Amendment

Radical Reconstruction

Johnson claimed that the Civil Rights Act threatened the constitutional rights of the states. Congressional Republicans worried that the Supreme Court might agree and overturn the law or that a future Congress might weaken or repeal it. To prevent this, Congress passed the **Fourteenth Amendment** in June 1866 and submitted it to the states for approval.

The amendment required states to grant citizenship to "all persons born or naturalized in the United States." It promised citizens "equal protection of the laws" and barred states from depriving anyone of "life, liberty, or property without due process of law." In effect, it wrote the Civil Rights Act into the Constitution.

ACADEMIC VOCABULARY
utilize use

The election of 1866 Some northerners thought the Fourteenth Amendment went too far. Johnson saw the chance to block Congress by making control of Reconstruction an issue in the 1866 congressional elections. He toured the North, campaigning for candidates who supported his policies.

Johnson's views were discredited, however, by riots that took place in Memphis, Tennessee, and New Orleans, Louisiana, in 1866. In both cities, white mobs attacked African American soldiers and freedmen, killing dozens of people and injuring hundreds more. "You may judge [Johnson] by the terrible massacre at New Orleans," proclaimed Charles Sumner, a Radical Republican leader in the Senate. The Republicans won an overwhelming victory over the candidates favored by Johnson.

The Reconstruction Acts The election of 1866 gave the Radicals the votes in Congress to take control of Reconstruction. They quickly passed, over Johnson's veto, the first of four **Reconstruction Acts** in March 1867. This law divided the South into five military districts under the control of the U.S. Army. Only Tennessee, which Congress had readmitted to the Union in 1866, was exempt from the law.

The act required the remaining states to ratify the Fourteenth Amendment, to write new state constitutions that guaranteed freedmen the right to vote, and to form new state governments elected by all male citizens, including African Americans. A state would not be eligible for readmission to the Union until these three conditions were met.

Congress passed three more Reconstruction Acts in 1867 and 1868. These laws authorized the army to register African Americans to vote. Military commanders could also remove any elected official who did not cooperate.

Since these laws placed much of Congress's program in the hands of the army, Republican leaders worried that President Johnson might <u>utilize</u> his power as commander in chief to interfere with Reconstruction. To prevent this, Congress passed the Tenure of Office Act in March 1867. This law required Senate permission to remove any official whose appointment had required Senate approval.

President Johnson's impeachment The Tenure of Office Act set off the final battle between Johnson and the Republicans. The dispute centered around Lincoln's secretary of war, Edwin Stanton, who had stayed on in

MILITARY DISTRICTS, 1867

- Military district I
- Military district II
- Military district III
- Military district IV
- Military district V
- Not part of a military district

Dates refer to year of readmission to the Union

VA (1870)
TN (1866)
NC (1868)
AR (1868)
SC (1868)
MS (1870)
AL (1868)
GA (1870)
TX (1870)
LA (1868)
FL (1868)

CANADA
ATLANTIC OCEAN
MEXICO
Gulf of Mexico
30°N
80°W
90°W

0   150   300 Miles
0   150   300 Kilometers
Albers equal-area projection

GEOGRAPHY SKILLS | INTERPRETING MAPS

1. **Regions** Into how many military districts was the South divided? What states made up each district?

2. **Location** In what order were the states readmitted to the Union?

See **Skills Handbook**, p. H20

Skills Focus: Drawing Conclusions   At Level

Reading Skill
Radical Republicans

1. Have students write a short speech honoring the actions of a Radical Republican senator as he retires from Congress.

2. In their speeches, students should include a brief resumé of the acts and laws that the senator worked to pass on behalf of African Americans.

3. Have volunteers share their speeches with the class. **LS Verbal-Linguistic, Auditory-Musical**

📄 Alternative Assessment Handbook, Rubric 24: Oral Presentations

Answers

Interpreting Maps 1. *five: Texas and Louisiana; Arkansas and Mississippi; Florida, Georgia, and Alabama; North and South Carolina; Virginia;* **2.** *Tennessee; Arkansas, Florida, North Carolina, South Carolina, Louisiana, Alabama; Virginia, Mississippi, Texas, Georgia*

the Johnson cabinet. Stanton was a strong supporter of congressional Republicans. It was difficult for Johnson to undermine Congress's program with Stanton in charge of the army.

When Johnson fired Stanton, the House of Representatives voted in February 1868 to impeach the president for violating the Tenure of Office Act. **Impeachment** is the process set forth in the Constitution for charging the president or another federal official with a crime. Once impeached by the House, the president is tried by the Senate, where a two-thirds vote is needed for conviction.

After a two-month trial, the Senate fell just one vote short of convicting President Johnson and removing him from office. The verdict allowed Johnson to remain in office.

Although his control of Reconstruction had ended, Johnson continued to issue pardons. By the end of 1868 the rights of almost all Confederate leaders had been restored.

The Fifteenth Amendment While the Senate was deciding Johnson's fate, Republicans nominated General Ulysses Grant as their presidential candidate. The election in November 1868 was close, but a half million African American votes in the South gave Grant a comfortable victory in the electoral college.

When Republicans realized that most white southern voters had supported Grant's Democratic opponent, Horatio Seymour, they pushed the **Fifteenth Amendment** through Congress. The amendment, which stated that people could not be denied the right to vote because of their race, became part of the Constitution in March 1870. Many white northerners opposed the amendment because it applied to their states as well. Women also criticized the amendment because it did not give them voting rights.

Still, by extending suffrage to all African American males, the Fifteenth Amendment brought millions of potential new voters to the Republican Party. It also aimed to protect freedmen from the growing political power of pardoned former Confederates. This protection turned out to be temporary, however, because the amendment did not ban denial of suffrage for reasons other than race.

READING CHECK Making Inferences Why was President Johnson impeached?

DEFYING THE TENURE OF OFFICE ACT

THE LITTLE BOY WOULD PERSIST IN HANDLING BOOKS ABOVE HIS CAPACITY.

AND THIS WAS THE DISASTROUS RESULT.

THE GRANGER COLLECTION, NEW YORK

Skills FOCUS READING LIKE A HISTORIAN

Johnson ignored the Tenure of Office Act, arguing that the law was unconstitutional.
Identifying Points of View What outcome did the cartoonist predict for the impeachment trial? What was the actual outcome?

SECTION 2 ASSESSMENT

go.hrw.com
Online Quiz
Keyword: SD7 HP12

Reviewing Ideas, Terms, and People

1. **a. Recall** What events showed continuing prejudice against African Americans?
   b. Interpret Why were violent acts against African Americans often not punished?
   c. Predict What were some possible social effects of the **Black Codes**?
2. **a. Define** Write a brief definition of **Radical Republicans**.
   b. Analyze Why did President Johnson think the **Civil Rights Act** was unconstitutional?
3. **a. Recall** What did the four **Reconstruction Acts** do?
   b. Predict How do you think women might have used the **Fifteenth Amendment** to fight for their own voting rights?

Critical Thinking

4. **Recognizing Cause and Effect** Copy the chart below and record the events that led to the passage of the Fifteenth Amendment.

```
_____  _____  _____  _____  →  Passage of
                                      the Fifteenth
                                      Amendment
```

FOCUS ON SPEAKING

5. **Persuasive** Present a speech that Thaddeus Stevens might have given in the House of Representatives. Argue for or against President Johnson's approach to Reconstruction, using supporting details from the section.

RECONSTRUCTION **415**

Direct Teach

Reading Focus

Radical Reconstruction

Explain What was the Tenure of Office Act? *Senate permission required to remove official whose appointment had required Senate approval*

Describe What was the purpose of the Fifteenth Amendment? *to ensure that males were not denied right to vote based on race*

- CRF: Primary Source Activity: The Impeachement Trial of Andrew Johnson
- Political Cartoons Activities for American History: Cartoon 23: David and Goliath

Review & Assess

Close
Have students explain how Radical Republicans emerged.

Review
- Online Quiz, Section 2
- Daily Test Practice Transparency

Assess
- **SE** Section 2 Assessment
- Progress Assessment: Section 2 Quiz
- Alternative Assessment Handbook

Reteach
- Interactive Reader and Study Guide, Section 2
- Interactive Skills Tutor CD-ROM

Answers

Reading Like a Historian *that Johnson would be voted out of office; he stayed in office*

Reading Check *final stage in battle between Congress and president; Johnson violated Tenure of Office Act; fired Stanton without Congress's approval*

415

Bellringer

The Inside Story. . . Use the **Daily Bellringer Transparency** to help students answer the question.

📖 Daily Bellringer Transparency, Section 3

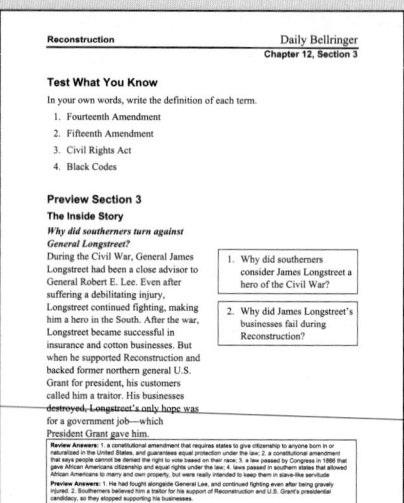

Reconstruction   Daily Bellringer
                                  Chapter 12, Section 3

Test What You Know

In your own words, write the definition of each term.

1. Fourteenth Amendment
2. Fifteenth Amendment
3. Civil Rights Act
4. Black Codes

Preview Section 3

The Inside Story

Why did southerners turn against General Longstreet?

During the Civil War, General James Longstreet had been a close advisor to General Robert E. Lee. Even after suffering a debilitating injury, Longstreet continued fighting, making him a hero in the South. After the war, Longstreet became successful in insurance and cotton businesses. But when he supported Reconstruction and backed former northern general U.S. Grant for president, his customers called him a traitor. His businesses destroyed, Longstreet's only hope was for a government job—which President Grant gave him.

| 1. Why did southerners consider James Longstreet a hero of the Civil War? |
| 2. Why did James Longstreet's businesses fail during Reconstruction? |

Review Answers: 1. a constitutional amendment that requires states to give citizenship to anyone born in or naturalized in the United States, and guarantees equal protection under the law; 2. a constitutional amendment that says people cannot be denied the right to vote based on their race; 3. a law passed by Congress in 1866 that gave African Americans citizenship and equal rights under the law; 4. laws passed in southern states that allowed African Americans to marry and own property, but were really intended to keep them in slave-like servitude

Preview Answers: 1. He had fought alongside General Lee, and continued fighting even after being gravely injured. 2. Southerners believed him a traitor for his support of Reconstruction and U.S. Grant's presidential candidacy, so they stopped supporting his businesses.

Copyright © by Holt, Rinehart and Winston. All rights reserved.

Taking Notes

Political—joined with carpetbaggers and scalawags to elect delegates to constitutional conventions; more than 1,500 African Americans held state and local offices; repealed Black Codes; outlawed racial discrimination; guaranteed right to vote; Economic—searched for employment, usually obtained low-paying jobs; some went west; Educational—public and private schools quickly established; vocational schools and colleges also established

---

Republicans in Charge

BEFORE YOU READ

MAIN IDEA

Republican Reconstruction had a significant impact on life in the South.

READING FOCUS

1. What changes did Republican government bring to the South?
2. What was life after slavery like for African Americans?
3. How did Reconstruction affect patterns of land ownership and land use in the South?

KEY TERMS AND PEOPLE

scalawag
carpetbagger
Hiram Revels
Southern Homestead Act
sharecropping
tenant farming

TAKING NOTES As you read, take notes on ways life changed for newly freed African Americans under Reconstruction. Record your notes in a graphic organizer like the one shown here.

Changes under Reconstruction	
Political	
Economic	
Educational	

Civil War Hero— and Scalawag

General James Longstreet suffered because of the choices he made after the Civil War.

THE INSIDE STORY

Why did southerners turn against General Longstreet? At first, James Longstreet was a war hero in the South. He had been an important aide to General Lee, who called him "my old war horse." Although seriously wounded and paralyzed in one arm, he served with Lee until the Confederate surrender at Appomattox.

After the war Longstreet quickly became wealthy as a cotton broker and head of an insurance company. But his hero status—and his economic fortunes—soon changed. A practical businessperson, he supported Reconstruction, believing that the best way for the South to rebuild was to cooperate with the victors. In addition, he joined the Republican Party and backed General Grant, an old friend and his wife's cousin, for president in 1868.

To many white southerners, Longstreet went from a war hero to a **scalawag**—a scoundrel and a traitor in the eyes of former Confederates. His businesses failed, and he was forced to turn to the Republican Party in order to make a living. President Grant gave Longstreet a government job in New Orleans. He later held other federal posts, including U.S. ambassador to Turkey and U.S. marshal for Georgia. ◼

Republican Government Brings Change to the South

As Congress and the army took control of Reconstruction, political power shifted in the South. General Longstreet and other white "scalawags" chose to support this change. For Longstreet, becoming a scalawag changed his life dramatically. He had to rely on the Republican Party for government jobs until he died in 1904.

Teach the Main Idea

At Level

Republicans in Charge

1. **Teach** Ask students the Reading Focus questions to teach this section.

2. **Apply** Have students work in pairs to create a sequencing chart of the changes that occurred in the lives of southern African Americans during the time period discussed in the section. **LS** **Visual-Spatial, Logical-Mathematical**

3. **Review** As you review the section, have students identify issues that were most promising for improving the lives of African Americans after the Civil War.

4. **Practice/Homework** Have students prepare a half-page encyclopedia entry on the impact of Republican Reconstruction on southern life. **LS** **Verbal-Linguistic**

   📝 Alternative Assessment Handbook, Rubric 42: Writing to Inform

Scalawags and carpetbaggers Many scalawags were farmers who had never owned slaves and had opposed secession and the war. Many also lived in areas where the population was mostly white. They joined the Republicans to prevent the old planter class from returning to power. In addition, some scalawags were planters and other formerly wealthy southerners who had been financially ruined by the war. They hoped that the new state governments would pass laws to protect them from their debts. Still others were business leaders who wanted to end the South's long dependence on plantation agriculture.

The scalawags allied with northern Republicans who came south to take part in the region's political and economic rebirth. Southern critics called these northerners **carpetbaggers**, a reference to a type of cheap suitcase made of carpet. The newcomers were scorned as low-class persons who could carry everything they owned in a carpetbag.

In fact, many carpetbaggers were educated people. Like the scalawags, they came from a variety of backgrounds, ranging from political and business leaders to teachers, Freedmen's Bureau officers, and former soldiers. Some were African American. Many carpetbaggers

Reading Focus

1 What changes did Republican government bring to the South? *U.S. Army and Congress took control of Reconstruction; political power shifted; African Americans served in public office*

Republican Government Brings Change to the South

Recall Why did scalawags join the Republican Party? *to prevent planters and former wealthy southerners from reclaiming power*

Evaluate Would it be correct to say that carpetbaggers were scalawags from the North? *yes, many similarities; they came to South to participate in political rebirth, and they both came from a variety of backgrounds*

Political Cartoons Activities for American History: Cartoon 24: Carpetbaggers

---

PRIMARY SOURCES

Political Cartoon

A bitter war of political cartoons raged throughout the Reconstruction era. In this 1880 cartoon in the magazine *Puck*, James Albert Wales depicts the view of many traditional southern whites toward Radical Reconstruction under President Ulysses S. Grant.

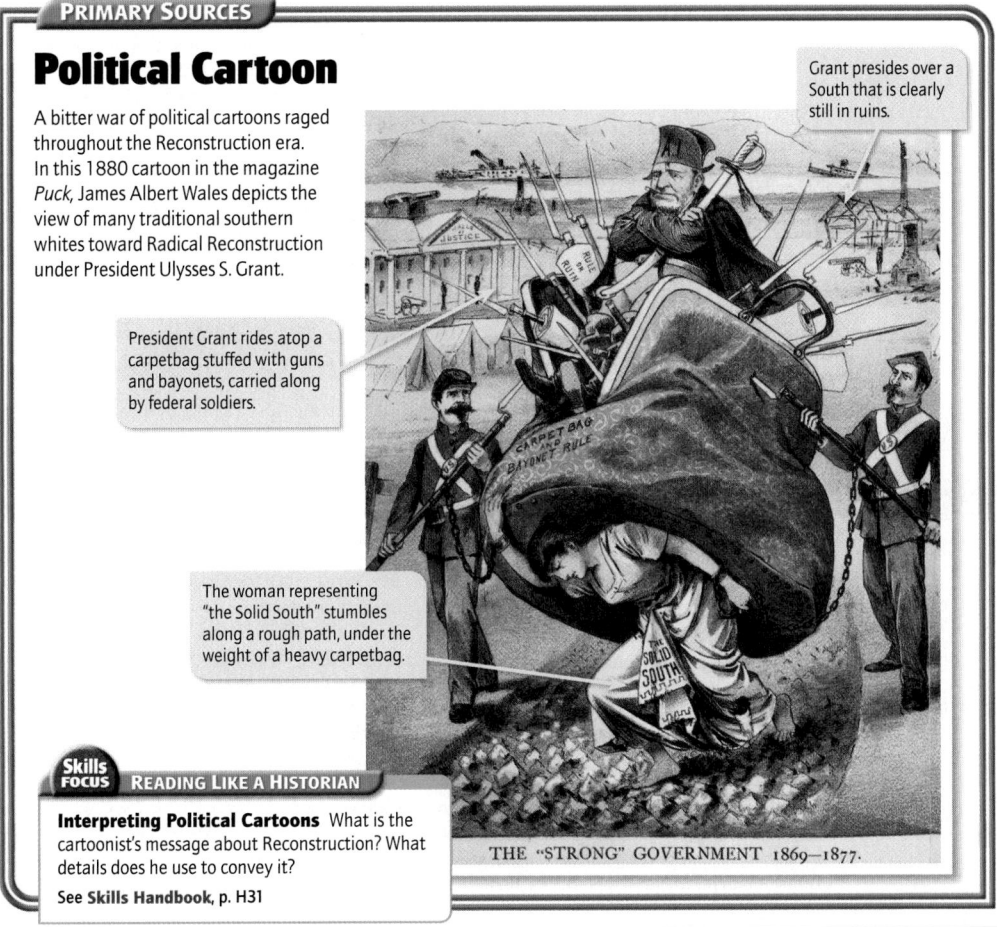

Grant presides over a South that is clearly still in ruins.

President Grant rides atop a carpetbag stuffed with guns and bayonets, carried along by federal soldiers.

The woman representing "the Solid South" stumbles along a rough path, under the weight of a heavy carpetbag.

THE "STRONG" GOVERNMENT 1869–1877.

Skills FOCUS   READING LIKE A HISTORIAN

Interpreting Political Cartoons What is the cartoonist's message about Reconstruction? What details does he use to convey it?

See Skills Handbook, p. H31

RECONSTRUCTION **417**

Biography

Winslow Homer (1836–1910) Winslow Homer is best known for his paintings and watercolors of outdoor scenes, especially those that feature the sea. Homer's mother was a painter who encouraged her son's artistic talent, and at age 19, Homer became an apprentice in a lithography firm in Boston. During the Civil War, Homer was an artist-correspondent, but his drawings focused on scenes of camp life, not on the battles. After the war, Homer studied in Europe and when he returned he began to paint scenes of New England and became renowned for his watercolors. Most of Homer's paintings and water-colors focus on nature and human isolation in the face of natural forces.

Skills Focus: Interpreting Political Cartoons   At Level

Reading Like a Historian Skill
Republican Government Brings Change to the South

1. Have the students study the political cartoon on this page. Then guide students in a discussion about the images and message depicted in the cartoon. Have students identify the point of view and the bias of the cartoonist.

2. Review the purpose of political cartoons with the class. Then have students create their own political cartoons that illustrate the Republican government from the perspective

of those who firmly believed that northern Republicans came to the South to help restore the economy and would help move the South in an industrial, progressive direction.

3. Have volunteers display their cartoons and explain them to the class. **LS Verbal-Linguistic, Interpersonal**

Alternative Assessment Handbook, Rubric 27: Political Cartoons

Answers

Reading Like a Historian *negative; U.S. Army and president riding rough-shod on back of the South*

417

Reading Focus

Republican Government Brings Change to the South

Explain What was Hiram Revels's background? *had served in and recruited troops for Union Army; established churches and schools*

Elaborate In what ways did the Republican government help improve the South's infrastructure and economy? *built schools and hospitals, thousands of miles of new railroads; reduced taxes on poor farmers*

Reading Focus

❷ What was life after slavery like for African Americans? *somewhat better; some moved, searched for jobs; started businesses; went to school; established churches*

Life after Slavery for African Americans

Describe What did both cities in the North and South offer freedmen? *segregation, low-paying jobs, poor housing*

Draw Conclusions What hopes did Reconstruction awaken in freedmen? *economic improvement, equal rights*

📖 CRF: Biography: Robert Ball Anderson

Answers

Faces of History *helped establish schools and churches; served in U.S. Senate*

Reading Check *Most scalawags were southern farmers who had opposed the war; carpetbaggers were northerners who came to help rebuild the South; they joined together to help rebuild the South politically and economically.*

418

FACES OF HISTORY

Hiram REVELS
1822–1901

Born free as the son of former slaves in North Carolina, Hiram Revels attended seminaries (schools for the training of ministers) in the North. He recruited African American soldiers and served as a Union army chaplain during the Civil War. After the war, Revels moved to Mississippi to help establish new churches and schools. He became involved in politics and in 1868 became the first African American to serve in the U.S. Senate. After a year in office, he returned to Mississippi, where he continued his ministry and educational work.

Summarize What contributions did Revels make to Mississippi?

---

bought abandoned land cheaply or formed partnerships with planters and helped rebuild the South's economy.

African Americans in government The carpetbaggers and scalawags allied to control southern state governments. They were joined by freedmen, who were eager to exercise the rights they had gained from the Civil Rights Act and the Fourteenth Amendment. In South Carolina and Louisiana, African American delegates outnumbered whites in the constitutional conventions that the Reconstruction Acts required. In other states, about 25 percent of the delegates were African American.

African Americans formed the largest group of Republican voters in the South. As a result, nearly 700 African Americans served in southern state legislatures during Reconstruction. Sixteen African Americans served in Congress. They included **Hiram Revels**, who took the Senate seat held by Confederate president Jefferson Davis before the war. In all, more than 1,500 African Americans held state and local offices during Radical Reconstruction.

New state governments The state governments established under Radical Reconstruction brought many changes to the South. New state constitutions guaranteed male freedmen the right to vote. Republican governments created the region's first public school systems. They also built many hospitals as well as institutions for orphans and people with mental

THE IMPACT TODAY

Government
The 109th Congress included 42 African Americans in the House and 1 in the Senate. Only 5 African Americans, including Hiram Revels, have served in the Senate.

---

disabilities. These schools and other facilities were open to all southerners, although they were usually segregated by race.

The new governments eliminated property requirements for voting and officeholding. They modernized divorce laws and expanded the rights of married women. State legislatures in the Lower South enacted laws making it illegal for railroads, hotels, and other public facilities to discriminate against African Americans. The Black Codes were repealed in every state.

To help the South's economy grow, the Republicans built thousands of miles of new railroads. Railroad companies got grants of land and money from state governments. The government raised this money by increasing taxes on large landowners. At the same time, they reduced taxes on poor farmers.

Many of these changes angered the planters and Democratic Party politicians who had controlled the South for so long. Some of the freedmen were unhappy too, because the Republican governments did little to help them obtain their own land.

READING CHECK **Identifying the Main Idea** Who were scalawags and carpetbaggers? What did they join together to do?

Life after Slavery for African Americans

Freedom meant a variety of things to formerly enslaved African Americans in the South. For some, it meant the chance to search for long-lost relatives who had been sold during slavery. Many freedmen traveled thousands of miles to reunite with family members.

Seeking economic opportunity Other freedmen searched for employment, often by moving to urban areas. The African American population of the South's 10 largest cities doubled by 1870. A smaller number of freedmen moved to the North. Cities in both North and South usually offered only segregation, poor housing, and low-paying jobs.

Some former slaves went west, where they started businesses or worked as miners, soldiers, and cowboys. Most freedmen remained in the rural South, however. Whether they continued to work for their former slaveholders

---

Skills Focus: Summarizing   Below Level

Reading Skill
Hiram Revels

Materials construction paper, colored markers

1. Review the information in the text about Hiram Revels, the first African American to serve in the U.S. Senate.

2. Have students design a banner and a postage stamp honoring Hiram Revels' achievements.

3. Have students share their banner and postage stamp designs with the class.

🅛🅢 **Visual-Spatial, Kinesthetic**

📖 Alternative Assessment Handbook, Rubrics 3: Artwork; and 34: Slogans and Banners

African Americans and Reconstruction

During the early days of Reconstruction, new doors opened for African Americans in the South. Not only did they gain political power in state legislatures and in Congress, but they were also able to enjoy the simple human privileges and joys of daily life unknown to them under slavery.

Economic Freedom A store owner (in the apron) celebrates Emancipation Day—and his economic freedom—in 1888.

Freedom of Worship African American families pose for a photograph at a church picnic.

Political Representation Blanche Bruce fled slavery. After the war, he became the first African American to serve a full term in the U.S. Senate.

Educational Opportunity Students attend the Hampton Institute in Virginia, ca. 1899. The institute was founded in 1868 to provide moral training and industrial education to freedmen.

Skills FOCUS **INTERPRETING INFOGRAPHICS**

These scenes, like snapshots out of a family album, would have been virtually unimaginable to generations of families trapped in slavery. Life during Reconstruction wasn't easy, but it brought hope.

Contrasting How might the people in each of these photographs have described the changes in their circumstances after the war?

See Skills Handbook, p. H18

419

Direct Teach

History Close-Up

African Americans and Reconstruction

Analyze Have students work in pairs to explain which constitutional right is being exercised in each of the photos in the feature.

Activity **Education** Have students design a brochure advertising a school for freed children. In their brochures students should explain and illustrate the importance of education for all people, especially for formerly enslaved African Americans. **LS Visual-Spatial**

MISCONCEPTION ALERT

Remind students that African Americans did not flock to the North after gaining their freedom. Most had no means to travel. Many freedmen did move to southern towns where African American schools and churches created a sense of community. Others chose to remain near the plantations and farms that had been their homes.

go.hrw.com
Online Resources

KEYWORD: SD7 CH12
TOPIC: AFRICAN AMERICANS
DURING RECONSTRUCTION

Differentiating Instruction

Above Level

Advanced Learners/GATE

Research Required

1. Point out to students that in the South it would have been highly unusual for whites to attend the new schools that were established for freedmen, a pattern of educational segregation that continued for almost a century.

2. Have students conduct outside research to learn more about the pattern of school segregation in the South and in the North, culminating in the Supreme Court cases

Brown v. *Board of Education* and *Brown II*, in which the Supreme Court ruled that segregation was illegal and that public schools would be integrated.

3. Have students present the results of their research in an illustrated time line or in a multimedia presentation. **LS Visual-Spatial**

Alternative Assessment Handbook, Rubrics 30: Research; and 36: Time Lines

---

Answers

Interpreting Infographics *life improved; had ability to start own business; achieved educational goals; able to exercise right to assemble in groups; enjoyed political participation*

419

Life after Slavery for African Americans

Explain What was the significance of Hampton Institute? *provided vocational education for freedmen; became model for most black colleges in the South*

Make Inferences What do you think the transition from slave to freedman was like for African Americans? *possible answer—difficult and fearful; African Americans had nothing with which to start their new lives; whites still saw African Americans as easy, cheap supply of labor*

Info to Know

Howard University Howard University in Washington, D.C., was named for Oliver O. Howard, the first commissioner of the Freedmen's Bureau. The university opened in May 1867 to provide educational opportunities for freed people. The original goal of the school was "training for preachers and teachers." From its beginnings, Howard University was open to men and women of all races. Today the university has schools of law, dentistry, medicine, social work, and business.

depended on how they had been treated as slaves. If the slaveholder had been violent, few of his workers were likely to remain.

One such slaveholder tried to convince a former slave family who had moved to Ohio to return to the plantation. The husband wrote back with this reply:

HISTORY'S VOICES

❝We have concluded to trust your sincerity by asking you to send us our wages for the time we served you. This will make us forget and forgive old scores, and rely on your justice and friendship in the future.❞

—Jourdan Anderson, August 7, 1865

Education and religion Denied schooling under slavery, freed African American slaves eagerly sought education. By 1877 more than 600,000 African Americans had enrolled in elementary schools in the South. The Freedmen's Bureau alone started more than 4,000 schools.

Many northern groups, both black and white, sponsored schools. A general who had commanded black troops during the war started Hampton Institute in Virginia in 1868. Hampton's system of vocational education became the model for most black colleges in the South. The American Missionary Association founded seven colleges, including Fisk University in Nashville, Tennessee. Fisk was unique at the time because it stressed higher education for freedmen instead of job training.

African Americans established other institutions themselves, especially churches. Under slavery they had been forced to worship in their slaveholders' churches. During Reconstruction freedmen founded their own churches. These churches became centers of community life for African Americans, and ministers became community leaders.

Some black churches also started schools. Morehouse College was founded in 1867 by Springfield Baptist Church in Augusta, Georgia, to prepare African Americans for careers as ministers and teachers. Morehouse moved to Atlanta in 1879. It became best known for educating Dr. Martin Luther King Jr.

The meaning of freedom Freedmen created a wide variety of other organizations to help themselves and one another. These included debating clubs, drama societies, trade associations, fire companies, and mutual aid societies. African Americans in Nashville, Atlanta, New Orleans, and other southern cities raised money to establish orphanages, soup kitchens, employment agencies, and funds to aid the poor.

Robert Fitzgerald, a black carpetbagger in Virginia, was encouraged to see freedmen taking the lead to improve themselves and gain control of their lives.

HISTORY'S VOICES

❝They tell me before Mr. Lincoln made them free they had nothing to work for, to look up to, now they have everything, and will, by God's help, make the best of it.❞

—Robert Fitzgerald, diary entry

READING CHECK **Summarizing** What were some new educational opportunities for African Americans in the 1860s and 1870s?

Reconstruction and Land Ownership

The main symbol of personal freedom and economic independence to many former enslaved African Americans was their own land. At first former slaves often claimed a right to plantation land because of the years of unpaid labor they had provided. For some freedmen, the redistribution of the planters' land seemed a logical step after emancipation.

Hopes for land fade In Section 1 you read about land redistribution in Georgia and South Carolina. Freedmen hoped this would be repeated elsewhere. But President Johnson soon returned land in the South to its original white owners.

Although some Radical Republicans wanted to give the planters' land to their former slaves, most considered this proposal too extreme. Instead, Congress passed the **Southern Homestead Act** in June 1866. This law set aside 45 million acres of government-owned land in southern states to provide free farms for African Americans. Few freedmen had the means to buy seed, animals, and equipment, however. As a result, only about 4,000 families took advantage of the offer, and the law was repealed in 1872.

Differentiating Instruction | **Above Level**

Advanced Learners/GATE

1. Organize students into small groups. Have each group write a play about the opportunities available to freedmen and the challenges and prospects of their new lives.

2. Plays should last about ten minutes and should focus on educational, political, social, or economic changes in the lives of freedmen. Remind the students to address the obstacles

that the freedmen faced and how they might have overcome the problems.

3. Have each group present its play, or a videotape of the play, to the class.

LS **Interpersonal, Kinesthetic**

Alternative Assessment Handbook, Rubric 33: Skits and Reader's Theater

Answers

Reading Check *vocational colleges and Fisk University were established; churches also established colleges*

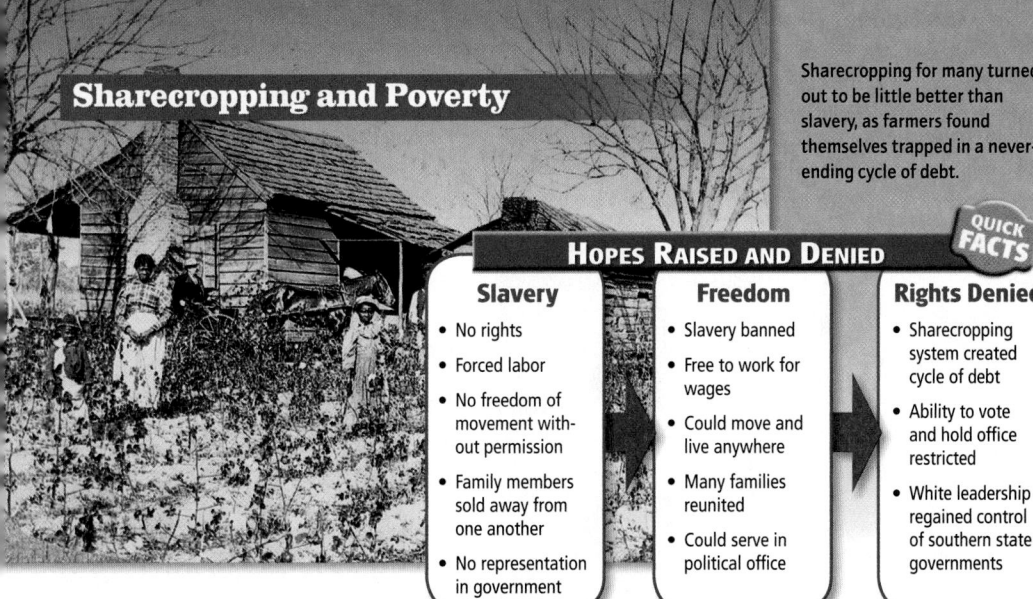

Sharecropping and Poverty

Sharecropping for many turned out to be little better than slavery, as farmers found themselves trapped in a never-ending cycle of debt.

HOPES RAISED AND DENIED

QUICK FACTS

Slavery	Freedom	Rights Denied
• No rights	• Slavery banned	• Sharecropping system created cycle of debt
• Forced labor	• Free to work for wages	• Ability to vote and hold office restricted
• No freedom of movement without permission	• Could move and live anywhere	
• Family members sold away from one another	• Many families reunited	• White leadership regained control of southern state governments
• No representation in government	• Could serve in political office	

Freedmen who did have money to buy land often found landowners unwilling to sell to them. In part, this was because white southerners did not want to lose their supply of cheap labor. Land ownership would give former slaves economic independence. "Freedom and independence are different things," a Mississippi planter wrote in his diary. "A man may be free and yet not independent."

Still, some freedmen found ways to buy farms and other land. In Mississippi, for example, 1 in every 12 African American families owned land by 1870.

Sharecroppers and tenant farmers
Most freedmen were not content to work for the low wages planters were willing—and in many cases able—to pay. They also disliked working in supervised groups as they had under slavery. As a result, a new system gradually arose to replace the wage labor system. Instead of working for wages, freedmen began receiving a share of their employer's crop. This arrangement was known as **sharecropping**. By the end of the 1870s most freedmen and many poor white southerners were sharecroppers.

Under the sharecropping system, the employer provided land, seed, tools, a mule, and a cabin. The sharecropper provided the labor. Employers benefited because they no longer had to pay their workers. In turn, sharecroppers benefited by having a specific plot of land to farm.

A sharecropper who did well and saved some money might switch to **tenant farming**. Tenant farmers rented the land they farmed from the landowner. This arrangement allowed tenant farmers to grow whatever crops they chose. Many preferred growing food crops to cotton. Food crops increased freedmen's independence by providing not only a source of income but also food for their families as well.

Several factors combined to keep most sharecroppers and tenant farmers in poverty, however. Neither group had any income until harvest time. To meet their everyday needs, they had to promise their crop to local merchants, who then sold them other goods on credit. If the sale of the crop did not produce enough money to pay for their purchases, the merchant added the remaining debt to the next year's bill.

This system made it difficult for many sharecroppers and tenant farmers to get out of poverty and gain true independence. It also helped keep the South's economy tied to one-crop agriculture. Merchants generally gave credit only to farmers who grew certain crops. Most often they were only interested in extending credit to farmers who grew cotton.

RECONSTRUCTION **421**

● Direct Teach ●

Reading Focus

❸ How did Reconstruction affect patterns of land ownership and land use in the South? *freedmen received some land from redistribution of plantations; President Johnson returned land in South to original owners; Southern Homestead Act temporarily gave freedmen opportunity to own land*

Reconstruction and Land Ownership

Explain Why wasn't the Southern Homestead Act successful? *freedmen could not afford the necessary tools, animals, and supplies to take advantage of opportunity*

Analyze Why did both sharecroppers and tenant farmers often end up in lifelong debt? *Crops did not make a profit; debt accrued from one year to the next.*

Make Judgments Do you think that it would be better to be a tenant farmer or a sharecropper? *possible answer—tenant farmer has more autonomy; may be less dependent upon land owner*

📋 CRF: Economics and History: Value of U.S. Cotton Exports

📦 Quick Facts Transparency: Hopes Raised and Denied

Skills Focus: Comparing and Contrasting

At Level

Reading Skill
Homestead Act and Habitat for Humanity

Research Required

1. Remind students that the Southern Homestead Act of 1866 was an early government attempt to provide homes and farms to those in need. Today, Habitat for Humanity is a charitably funded organization whose goal is to provide homes for those in need. Have students conduct outside research to learn more about Habitat for Humanity, how people qualify for a home, and what they must do to contribute to the effort.

2. Have students create a chart in which they compare the Southern Homestead Act and Habitat for Humanity. Then have students use the information in the chart to write a brief essay comparing and contrasting the goals and purposes of the two. 🄻 **Verbal-Linguistic**

📋 Alternative Assessment Handbook, Rubrics 9: Comparing and Contrasting; and 30: Research

Review & Assess

Close

Guide students in a discussion about problems and challenges that faced southern African Americans during Reconstruction.

Review

Online Quiz, Section 3

Daily Test Practice Transparency

Assess

SE Section 3 Assessment

Progress Assessment: Section 3 Quiz

Alternative Assessment Handbook

Reteach

Interactive Reader and Study Guide, Section 3

Interactive Skills Tutor CD-ROM

Rise of Southern Industry

Workers process cloth in a cotton factory in North Carolina. In 1860 about 324,000 spindles turned in southern cotton mills. By 1900 that number rose to nearly 4.4 million.

A nationwide depression caused cotton prices to fall steeply in the 1870s. This prompted southern farmers to grow more cotton in an attempt to raise their incomes. Crop surpluses drove prices even lower, plunging sharecroppers and tenant farmers deeper into debt.

Industrial growth in the South Even as the rural South suffered economically, southern cities grew rapidly. As Radical Republican governments improved the South's railroad system and linked it to northern lines, Atlanta and other cities gradually became important business centers. Southern business leaders joined with northern investors to build textile mills and other manufacturing ventures.

Most of the South's industrial growth occurred after Reconstruction ended. The growth did not greatly benefit African Americans or other poor southerners. Industrial workers in the South earned far lower wages than northern workers. Most southern African Americans could not find factory work at all.

In some industries, workers lived in houses provided by their employer and bought goods on credit at the company store. Like sharecroppers and tenant farmers, they often found themselves locked in a cycle of debt.

READING CHECK **Contrasting** How did sharecropping and tenant farming differ?

SECTION 3 ASSESSMENT

go.hrw.com
Online Quiz
Keyword: SD7 HP12

Reviewing Ideas, Terms, and People

1. **a. Identify** Who was **Hiram Revels**?
   b. Explain What did the new state governments accomplish under Radical Reconstruction?
   c. Rate Do you think the new governments were successful in bringing change to the South?

2. **a. Describe** What organizations were created in the 1860s and 1870s to help African Americans take advantage of their freedom?
   b. Analyze Among formerly enslaved African Americans, why did freedom mean different things to different people?

3. **a. Recall** What was the **Southern Homestead Act**?
   b. Explain Why did the system of **sharecropping** make it difficult for freedmen to become economically independent?
   c. Evaluate Why was land ownership a key issue for African Americans at this time?

Critical Thinking

4. **Comparing and Contrasting** Copy the chart below and fill in some details about African American workers as sharecroppers, tenant farmers, and industrial workers. Use details from Section 3 to fill in the chart. What does your completed chart tell you about opportunities for African American workers during this time?

African Americans as sharecroppers	African Americans as tenant farmers	African Americans as industrial workers

FOCUS ON WRITING

5. **Descriptive** Write a letter from a freedman to a planter looking for workers. Describe the conditions under which you will return to work for the planter. Use details from this section in your letter.

422 CHAPTER 12

Section 3 Assessment Answers

1. **a.** first African American to serve in Senate
   b. created schools, guaranteed males right to vote, modernized laws, repealed Black Codes, improved infrastructure
   c. yes, temporarily

2. **a.** schools, churches, trade associations, mutual aid societies
   b. different individuals wanted different things, educational, political, economic opportunities, freedom to worship, civil rights

3. **a.** law that gave government-owned land to freedmen
   b. received no wages; could not choose crops; led to a cycle of debt
   c. would give them the ability to farm land and receive benefits of their work

4. sharecroppers—received no wages, did not own land; tenant farmers—rented land, could plant what they wanted; industrial workers—low wages, lived in company housing; all locked in cycle of debt and poverty

5. will work hard for fair wages

Answers

Reading Check *sharecropper had no choice in crop planted, received share of crop instead of wages; tenant farmer rented land, could plant crop of choice for income and food*

SECTION 4
Reconstruction Collapses

BEFORE YOU READ

MAIN IDEA

A variety of events and forces led to the end of Reconstruction, which left a mixed legacy for the nation.

READING FOCUS

1. What problems caused support for Reconstruction to decline?
2. What events brought Reconstruction to an end?
3. What was Reconstruction's legacy for the South and for the rest of the nation?

KEY TERMS AND PEOPLE

Enforcement Acts
Liberal Republicans
Redeemers
Rutherford B. Hayes
Compromise of 1877
New South
Solid South

 TAKING NOTES As you read, take notes on the challenges of the Reconstruction era. Record your notes in a graphic organizer like the one shown here.

Challenges to Reconstruction

In the Shadow of Slavery

THE GRANGER COLLECTION, NEW YORK

▲ Many African Americans after the Civil War met with violence and oppression from whites.

THE INSIDE STORY

What was life like for African Americans in the South after the Civil War? Violence erupted in much of the Reconstruction-era South. Some angry southerners attacked newly freed African Americans and the white Americans who supported the freedmen's right to equality.

Violence was both personal and political. The Ku Klux Klan began as a social group but soon became a terrorist organization. It was the most widespread white supremacist group, but not the only one. Others included the White Liners, the White League, and the Knights of the White Camelia. These groups all used tactics such as threats, beatings, whippings, and even torture and murder. They burned down schools and churches. Race riots broke out in cities and towns.

George Houston, a tailor born in slavery, was a political activist in Alabama and a member of the state legislature. In August 1869, members of the Klan paid him a visit. A Klansman wounded his son, broke down the door, and shot him in the leg.

Houston put up a fight. He had only a gun for shooting squirrels, but "[I] cocked the barrel and shot at his head at fifteen steps . . . My wife jumped and fastened the window. Then they shot the window full of holes and the side of the house beside that. As she shut the window the balls came in the house like rain. They shot the whole side of the house."

Unlike many unfortunate victims, the Houstons were rescued eventually. After the terrifying incident, they moved away, but George Houston remained defiant: "I say the Republican party freed me, and I will die on top of it. I don't care who is pleased. I vote every time." ■

Bellringer

The Inside Story. . . Use the **Daily Bellringer Transparency** to help students answer the question.

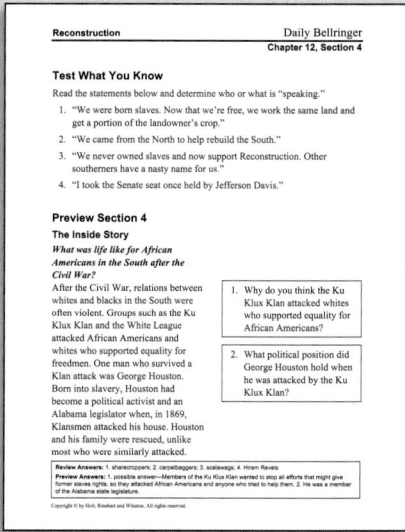

Academic Vocabulary

Review with students the high-use academic term in this section.

hierarchy a body of persons in authority (p. 424)

📄 CRF: Vocabulary Builder Activity, Section 4

Taking Notes

Threatened by terrorist groups like the Ku Klux Klan; Northern support declined; Liberal Republicans helped Democrats gain power in the Senate; the Redeemers took back control of the government in the South through violence and intimidation

go.hrw.com
Online Resources

KEYWORD: SD7 CH12
TOPIC: RECONSTRUCTION LAWS

Teach the Main Idea
At Level

Reconstruction Collapses

1. **Teach** Ask students the Reading Focus questions to teach this section.

2. **Apply** Draw three ladders for students to see. Label the top of each ladder with the topics of this section—Problems with Reconstruction, The End of Reconstruction, and Reconstruction's Legacy. Have students copy the ladders and write the main points of each topic on the corresponding rungs of each ladder. ⬛ **Visual-Spatial**

3. **Review** As you review the section, have students explain the successes and failures of Reconstruction for whites and for African Americans.

4. **Practice/Homework** Have students write a letter to the editor of the "Atlanta Gazette" in the 1870s condemning the actions of white terrorist groups, such as the Ku Klux Klan. ⬛ **Verbal-Linguistic**

📄 Alternative Assessment Handbook, Rubrics 13: Graphic Organizers; and 17: Letters to Editors

① What problems caused support for Reconstruction to decline? *anti-Reconstruction violence; southerners believed Enforcement Acts threatened individual freedom; African Americans still in poverty*

Problems with Reconstruction

Recall How pervasive was the Ku Klux Klan in the South? *very few active members; others supported their goals*

Explain What does the quote "made a neighbor a disguised assassin" mean? *Members of terrorist groups put on disguises and murdered their African American and white neighbors.*

Analyze Who were the targets of the Ku Klux Klan? *white Republicans, successful African Americans, white and black members of Freedmen's Bureau*

📖 CRF: Literature Activity: Testimony of Elias Hill

Info to Know

Exodusters As the terrorist groups of the South became bolder in their lawlessness, a number of African Americans migrated to Kansas to take advantage of the Homestead Act of 1862. These emigrants were called exodusters. Their goal was to free themselves from the discrimination and difficult conditions of the South and make a better life for themselves and their families.

Answers

Reading Like a Historian 1. *Grant in barrel with whiskey frauds and other scandals; barrel itself suggests whiskey; Grant's hand touching one of the scandals implies his closeness to the corruption; the barrel held together by rings could imply Grant's support of and affiliation with political rings;* **2.** *corruption by Grant or in his administration*

Problems with Reconstruction

Despite the efforts to control it, violent opposition to Reconstruction plagued the South through much of the Reconstruction era.

Terrorist groups in the South The hooded and disguised night riders of the Ku Klux Klan were the most active terrorists, but many similar organizations existed. Their members included planters, merchants, and poor white farmers and laborers. They were united by a common desire to undo the South's new hierarchy and restore the old political and social order. Although only a small minority of white southerners were members of these groups, many others supported their goals.

The groups' main target was African Americans, especially local leaders. But both blacks and whites were terrorized by threats, house burnings, and much worse. Members of these groups beat Freedmen's Bureau

teachers, women as well as men. They murdered an Arkansas member of Congress and three members of the Georgia legislature, along with thousands of other people. Many state and local officials resigned in fear. A carpetbagger in North Carolina described the situation.

HISTORY'S VOICES

❝Of the slain, there were enough to furnish forth a battlefield, and all from those three classes, the negro, the scalawag, and the carpet-bagger—all killed with deliberation . . . shot, stabbed, hanged, drowned . . . And almost always by an unknown hand . . . execution without warning, mercy, or appeal . . . in the treachery which made a neighbor a disguised assassin.❞

—Albion Tourgée, *A Fool's Errand*, 1879

The groups did not limit their attacks to white Republicans and politically active African Americans, however. They also assaulted and killed African Americans whom they regarded as too economically successful.

PRIMARY SOURCES

Political Cartoon

During the Grant administration, corruption plagued the federal government. Many politicians used their offices for financial gain. Grant was not directly involved in any scandals, but many people felt that they reflected his lack of leadership.

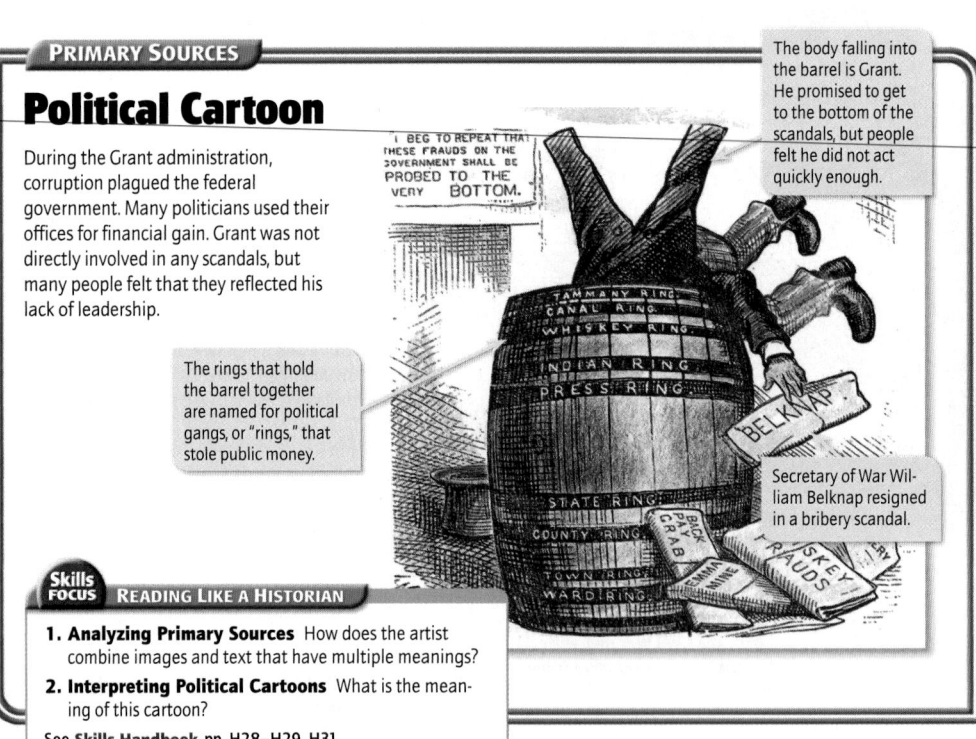

The body falling into the barrel is Grant. He promised to get to the bottom of the scandals, but people felt he did not act quickly enough.

The rings that hold the barrel together are named for political gangs, or "rings," that stole public money.

Secretary of War William Belknap resigned in a bribery scandal.

Skills FOCUS **READING LIKE A HISTORIAN**

1. **Analyzing Primary Sources** How does the artist combine images and text that have multiple meanings?
2. **Interpreting Political Cartoons** What is the meaning of this cartoon?

See **Skills Handbook**, pp. H28–H29, H31

424 CHAPTER 12

Differentiating Instruction

Below Level **Standard English Mastery**

English-Language Learners

1. Guide students in a discussion and review of the information about terrorist groups in the South during Reconstruction. Ask students to explain why the groups were effective in instilling fear and why they were rarely punished. Have students take notes during the discussion.

2. Have students use the information in the text and from their class notes to write a letter from a northern carpetbagger to his family in the North explaining why he has decided to return home. **LS Verbal-Linguistic, Intrapersonal**

📝 Alternative Assessment Handbook, Rubric 25: Personal Letters

When state governments proved unable to control this violence, Congress passed three **Enforcement Acts** in 1870 and 1871. These laws set heavy penalties, including imprisonment, for anyone attempting to prevent a qualified citizen from voting. They also banned the use of disguises to deprive any person of rights. The laws empowered the army and federal courts to capture and punish Ku Klux Klan members. Although the Klan's power was soon broken, many similar groups continued to operate.

Support for Reconstruction declines

White southerners claimed the Enforcement Acts threatened individual freedom. The laws also caused support for Reconstruction to decline in the North. Many northerners were dismayed that after so many years the army was still needed to keep peace in the South and that the Republican state governments were so ineffective. This reaction was exactly what the terrorist groups wanted.

Even southern Republicans began losing faith in Reconstruction. African Americans remained unhappy about their widespread poverty and the lack of land reform. Southerners of both races were discouraged by the region's poor overall economic condition, despite the Republicans' costly building programs and other reforms. These programs raised taxes and plunged the states into debt. Some programs, especially railroad building, also raised charges that the Reconstruction governments were inefficient and corrupt.

Conditions in the South strengthened the **Liberal Republicans**. This group broke with the party over the Enforcement Acts and the scandals that plagued the Grant administration. Although they could not block Grant's reelection in 1872, Liberal Republicans helped Democrats regain control of the House of Representatives in 1874. The Republican majority in the Senate was cut almost in half.

Economic factors also weakened support for Reconstruction. A severe five-year depression began in 1873, taking a toll on the South's economy as it was struggling to rebuild. The depression's impact in the North caused Republican leaders to pay less attention to Reconstruction and more to economic issues.

READING CHECK **Summarizing** What caused support for Reconstruction to decline?

The End of Reconstruction

By the mid-1870s it was clear to northerners and southerners alike that Reconstruction was on the decline. The most determined leaders of Reconstruction, Representative Thaddeus Stevens and Senator Charles Sumner, had died, and decisions of the Supreme Court were weakening key provisions of Reconstruction.

In 1873 the Supreme Court ruled in the *Slaughterhouse Cases* that most civil rights and freedoms remained under state control and were therefore not protected by the Fourteenth Amendment. Three years later, in *United States* v. *Cruikshank*, the Court ruled that the Fourteenth Amendment did not empower the federal government to punish whites who suppressed African Americans.

In *United States* v. *Reese* (1876), the Court determined that the Fifteenth Amendment did not protect voting rights if they were denied for some other reason than race. These three Supreme Court decisions combined to seriously weaken the goals and operations of Reconstruction.

"Redeeming" the South As support for Reconstruction declined in both the North and the South, southern Democratic leaders and their supporters grew stronger and bolder. Lawlessness and terrorism increased as they tried to regain control of their governments.

Terrorists publicly threatened, beat, and even murdered Republican candidates and their supporters in broad daylight. On election days armed Democrats stole or destroyed ballot boxes and drove African American voters from the polls. When Mississippi's governor asked for federal help to solve these problems in 1875, President Grant refused, saying that the northern public was "tired out" by the South's continuing problems.

By 1876 only South Carolina, Louisiana, and Florida remained under Republican rule. The Democrats who controlled the other southern states called themselves the **Redeemers** for having redeemed, or won back, their states from the Republicans. Many Redeemers were former Confederate leaders. Inspired by the Redeemers, Democrats in South Carolina, Louisiana, and Florida were determined to regain control of their states from the Republican leaders of Reconstruction, too.

The End of Reconstruction

Summarize What was the Compromise of 1877? *Hayes became president; federal troops removed from the South*

Draw Conclusions Who had the biggest win as a result of the 1877 Compromise? *Republican won presidency; southern Democrats saw end of Reconstruction; major victories for both*

🖻 Map Transparency: The Election of 1876

📝 CRF: Biography: Lucy Webb Hayes

Recent Scholarship

History professor Eric Foner's *Reconstruction: America's Unfinished Revolution, 1863–1877* did more than win the Los Angeles Times Book Award, the Bancroft Prize, and the Parkman Prize: it redefined how Reconstruction was viewed by historians everywhere. Dr. Foner's book has become a classic work on this initially promising, but ultimately disappointing, period in American history.

Reconstruction: America's Unfinished Revolution, 1863–1877 by Eric Foner. Harper & Row, 1988

THE ELECTION OF 1876

Rutherford B. Hayes

Samuel J. Tilden

Candidate	Political Affiliation	Electoral Votes	Popular Votes
Rutherford B. Hayes	Republican	165	4,036,298
Samuel J. Tilden	Democratic	184	4,300,590
Disputed		20	

GEOGRAPHY SKILLS | INTERPRETING MAPS

1. **Region** What regional voting patterns can you identify on the map?
2. **Location** In which states were the electoral votes disputed?

See Skills Handbook, p. H20

THE IMPACT TODAY

Government

Close presidential election results in 2000 and 2004 resulted in claims of fraud, including alleged efforts to prevent African Americans from voting or to exclude their votes from the count. No fraud prosecutions resulted, but various federal, state, and private commissions formed to recommend election reforms.

The election of 1876 Southern Democrats' efforts in South Carolina, Louisiana, and Florida had a direct effect on the presidential election of 1876. The election pitted Ohio's Republican governor, **Rutherford B. Hayes**, against Democrat Samuel J. Tilden, the governor of New York.

Tilden narrowly won the popular vote. He also finished ahead in the electoral college vote, 184–165. Yet he was still one vote short of the majority he needed to win the election. This was because 20 electoral votes were disputed. All but one of the disputed votes were from the three southern states the Republicans still controlled. Tilden needed only one more electoral vote to win the majority and become president. Hayes, the Republican candidate, needed all 20 of the disputed votes.

Charges flew that massive voting fraud had taken place in Louisiana, South Carolina, and Florida. Republicans claimed that Democrats in those states had prevented African Americans from voting. Democrats complained that

election officials appointed by the Republican governments in Louisiana, South Carolina, and Florida had thrown out large numbers of votes cast by Democrats.

Nearly everyone agreed that Oregon's disputed electoral vote should go to Hayes. But each side claimed the 19 votes from Louisiana, South Carolina, and Florida. Democrats threatened to put Tilden in the White House by force if necessary. "Tilden or War," Democratic newspapers proclaimed.

Congress could not resolve the crisis on its own. In January 1877 it established an Electoral Commission to decide which candidate deserved each vote. After some political maneuvering, the Republicans gained an 8–7 majority on the 15-member commission. Not surprisingly, this commission awarded all 20 of the disputed votes to the Republican candidate, Hayes.

To get the Democratic-controlled House of Representatives to accept the Electoral Commission's decision, Democratic and Republican

Skills Focus: Summarizing

At Level

Reading Skill
The Election of 1876

1. Guide students in a discussion about the election of 1876, including the anger and accusations of both parties.

2. Have students create two newspaper op-ed pieces and two editorial cartoons about the election. One op-ed piece and one cartoon should support Democratic candidate Tilden as president; the other should support Republican candidate Hayes.

3. Have volunteers share their opinion pieces and editorial cartoons with the class.
   🄻 **Visual-Spatial, Verbal-Linguistic**

   📝 Alternative Assessment Handbook, Rubrics 17: Letters to Editors; and 27: Political Cartoons

Answers

Interpreting Maps 1. *Democrats, the South and most of Mid-Atlantic; Republicans, West, Midwest, New England;* **2.** *Oregon, Louisiana, Florida, South Carolina*

leaders negotiated the **Compromise of 1877**. In return for Hayes becoming president, Republicans agreed to withdraw the remaining federal troops from the South. Without the protection of the federal government, the last of the Republican state governments collapsed and Reconstruction came to an end.

READING CHECK **Identifying Cause and Effect** How did the election of 1876 contribute to the end of Reconstruction?

Reconstruction's Legacy

Reconstruction and its collapse deeply affected the nation's future development. The Fourteenth and Fifteenth Amendments began permanent change in both the South and the North. These amendments, which were part of the Radicals' program to make former slaves citizens and guarantee them the right to vote, established citizenship and voting rights for northern African Americans as well. Passage of the Fifteenth Amendment also increased calls for women to have the right to vote, too.

After Reconstruction, some southerners referred to their region as the **New South**. This was because the late 1800s and early 1900s were a time of industrialization and economic change in the South. In other ways, however, the South remained as it had been before

the Civil War. The Supreme Court's decisions weakening the protections of the Fourteenth and Fifteenth Amendments encouraged those who preferred the old southern way of life.

The Redeemers, for example, found ways to return African Americans to what one white southerner called "an era of second slavery." You will learn more about the Redeemers' actions in a later chapter.

If the Civil War was fought to settle the issue of states' rights, the experience of Reconstruction showed that it failed to do so. White southerners deeply resented that the federal government controlled their states for more than a decade after the war. This resentment continued in the South for much of the next century.

Reconstruction also intensified the hostility that many white southerners had felt toward the Republican Party before and during the Civil War. For a century after Reconstruction ended, the South was so strongly Democratic that it was known as the **Solid South**. Not until the 1970s did the Republican Party begin to regain the level of support in the South that it enjoys today.

READING CHECK **Comparing and Contrasting** What changes did Reconstruction bring to the South? In what ways did the South remain unchanged?

• Direct Teach •

Reading Focus

❸ What was Reconstruction's legacy for the South and for the rest of the nation? *led to profound change, strong southern Democratic Party support, argument over states' rights continued*

Reconstruction's Legacy

Identify What is meant by the Solid South? *South was strongly Democratic for many years*

Describe How did the New South resemble the old South? *civil rights weakened; African Americans not much better off*

• Review & Assess •

Close

Have students compare and contrast the South before and after Reconstruction.

Review

Online Quiz, Section 4

Daily Test Practice Transparency

Assess

SE Section 4 Assessment

Progress Assessment: Section 4 Quiz

Alternative Assessment Handbook

Reteach

Interactive Reader and Study Guide, Section 4

Interactive Skills Tutor CD-ROM

SECTION 4 ASSESSMENT

go.hrw.com
Online Quiz
Keyword: SD7 HP12

Reviewing Ideas, Terms, and People

1. a. Recall What terrorist groups operated in the South after the Civil War? What kinds of actions did they take to oppose Reconstruction?
b. Analyze Did the **Enforcement Acts** help to carry out Reconstruction? Why or why not?
c. Evaluate Do you think northerners were right to stop supporting Reconstruction? Why or why not?

2. a. Identify Which leaders of Reconstruction had died by 1877?
b. Summarize What did the Supreme Court decide in the *Slaughterhouse Cases*, *United States v. Cruikshank*, and *United States v. Reese*?
c. Evaluate Do you think the **Compromise of 1877** was a good idea? Why or why not?

3. a. Define Write a brief definition for the following terms: New South, Solid South.

b. Analyze Why did Reconstruction bring back issues of states' rights?
c. Predict What do you think happened in the South after the end of Reconstruction?

Critical Thinking

4. Sequencing Copy the chart below and fill in the events in the North, South, and entire nation that contributed to the end of Reconstruction.

_____ _____ _____ _____ Reconstruction ends

FOCUS ON SPEAKING

6. Persuasive Suppose you are a member of the House of Representatives in 1877. Present a speech urging your fellow House members to accept or reject the Compromise of 1877.

Section 4 Assessment Answers

1. a. Ku Klux Klan, White Liners, White League, Knights of the White Camelia; used violence and threats
b. yes, stopped Klan but other groups continued
c. possible answer—no, violence continuing, troops still needed in the South

2. a. Thaddeus Stevens, Charles Sumner
b. civil rights under state control; government did not punish those suppressing African Americans; voting rights not protected
c. possible answer—yes, satisfied both parties

3. a. South after Reconstruction; strong

Democratic Party in South
b. Supreme Court rulings, resentment of federal troops
c. "business as usual"; African Americans in cycle of debt and poverty

4. anti-Reconstruction violence; Enforcement Acts; Supreme Court decisions; 1876 election; Compromise of 1877

5. accept; will end turmoil

Answers

Reading Check (left) *led to Compromise of 1877, which put an end to Reconstruction* **(right)** *change—civil rights, citizenship, industrialization and economic change; same—southern hostility toward Republican Party; belief in states' rights*

427

Changed Lives during Reconstruction

Historical Context The documents below provide different information on how Reconstruction changed people's lives in the South.

Task Examine the documents and answer the questions that follow. Then you will be asked to write an essay about how Reconstruction changed people's lives, using facts from the documents and from the chapter to support the position you take in your thesis statement.

Word Help

disposed willing
concluded decided
monopolize take over completely

Info to Know

New Roles in Government In 1870, Hiram Revels became the first African American man to be elected to the United States Senate. Revels represented Mississippi in the seat that had been last held by Jefferson Davis. Blanche K. Bruce, also from Mississippi, was the only other African American to serve in the United States Senate during the 1800s.

Embracing Education Most slaves were prohibited from learning how to read or write. After the Civil War, many formerly enslaved African Americans embraced their newfound freedom to educate themselves. People of all ages, from the very young to the very old, flocked to school. Many women from the North traveled to the South in order to help educate formerly enslaved African Americans. By the beginning of the twentieth century, most African Americans could read and write.

DOCUMENT 1

Many southerners fully expected their former slaves to continue to work for them and were shocked when they left to seek opportunities elsewhere. In this letter, freedman Jourdan Anderson, living in Dayton, Ohio, responds to a request from his former master to come back to Tennessee and work on the plantation.

"I am doing tolerably well here; I get $25 a month, with [food] and clothing; have a comfortable home for [my wife] Mandy (the folks here call her Mrs. Anderson), and the children, Milly, Jane, and Grundy, go to school and are learning well ... We are kindly treated ... Now, if you will write and say what wages you will give me, I will be better able to decide whether it will be to my advantage to move back again ...

Mandy says she would be afraid to go back without some proof that you are sincerely disposed to treat us just and kindly—and we have concluded to test your sincerity by asking you to send us our wages for the time we served you ... I served you faithfully for thirty-two years and Mandy twenty years. At $25 a month for me, and $2 a week for Mandy, our earnings would amount to $11,680. Add to this the interest for the time our wages has been kept back and deduct what you paid for our clothing and three doctor's visits to me, and pulling a tooth for Mandy, and the balance will show what we are in justice entitled to ... If you fail to pay us for faithful labors in the past we can have little faith in your promises in the future."

DOCUMENT 2

The Reconstruction era saw many new opportunities for poor whites as well as for black southerners. The use of slaves had limited the amount of work for wages that was needed and available in the South. Now, African Americans and poor whites often competed for similar work. In the following article, a newspaper in Petersburg, Virginia, noted the changes Reconstruction brought to service employment in the city.

"Formerly a white drayman [hauler of heavy goods] or cartman or hack [buggy] driver was a sight unknown in our streets, now they share these employments with the blacks, and eventually will monopolize them ... Formerly most, if not all, of our bars were tended by colored men, though owned by whites, now the [drinks] are mixed, as well as the rent paid, and the stock kept up by white men in many instances. Formerly the restaurants of Petersburgh were almost exclusively in the hands of the colored people; now, we believe, there is but one establishment of the sort in the city. Formerly we had only colored barbers; now, the native whites seek, generally, barbers of their own color, and eventually they will do so exclusively."

Collaborative Learning

At Level

Reconstructing the South

1. Divide the class into small groups. Have each group brainstorm ideas for reuniting the nation and rebuilding the South after the Civil War. Students may look to the actual policies followed during Reconstruction as a model, but should come up with their own ideas.

2. Have each group write a plan of action for reconstructing the South. Tell students to differentiate between short-term and long-term goals as well as to prioritize between their goals.

3. Have volunteers from each group present their plan to the class. Then guide the class in a discussion of how practical and effective these policies might have been.
   LS Interpersonal, Logical-Mathematical
   Alternative Assessment Handbook, Rubric 14: Group Activity

DOCUMENT 3

Former slaves were often eager to seek new lives for themselves and their families. The photograph on the left shows enslaved people and their living quarters on a Georgia plantation around 1860. The photograph on the right shows a family of formerly enslaved people in Mississippi around 1870.

Skills FOCUS: READING LIKE A HISTORIAN

1. a. Describe Refer to Document 1. What does Anderson ask his former master to do to prove that his offer of a job is sincere?
b. Analyze How does Anderson's letter reflect the changing expectations that former slaves had about their treatment by whites?

2. a. Identify Refer to Document 2. What had changed in Petersburg?
b. Interpret How might some whites use this information to try to convince former slaves to remain on their old plantations?

3. a. Describe Refer to Document 3. Describe the scenes in the two photographs.
b. Compare How do these two photographs reflect changes in dignity for African Americans under slavery and during Reconstruction?

4. Document-Based Essay Question Consider the question below and form a thesis statement. Using examples from Documents 1, 2, and 3, create an outline and write a short essay supporting your position. How did Reconstruction change the lives of African American and white southerners?

See Skills Handbook, pp. H28–29

RECONSTRUCTION **429**

Skills Focus: Comparing and Contrasting

At Level

Reading Skill
Life After Slavery

1. Guide the class in a discussion of the conditions of life for a slave. Ask students how the lives of former slaves changed after the Civil War.

2. Have each student write an essay comparing and contrasting the two photographs on this page. Ask students whether African Americans had achieved true freedom by 1870. Why or why not?

3. Have volunteers read their essays to the class.
LS Visual-Spatial, Logical-Mathematical

Alternative Assessment Handbook, Rubrics 9: Comparing and Contrasting; and 37: Writing Assignments

---

Visual Summary

Review and Inquiry Divide the class into six groups, and assign each group one of the six topics in the summary. Have each group prepare a two-minute oral summary of its assigned topic. Students should explain, when appropriate, how the bulleted item came into being and what its consequences were.

🔊 Quick Facts Transparency: Reconstruction

Reviewing Key Terms and People

1. i.
2. g.
3. e.
4. h.
5. d.
6. f.
7. j.
8. c.
9. b.
10. a.

Comprehension and Critical Thinking

11. a. farms, businesses, and infrastructure in ruins; how to regain entry into Union
b. felt it was too lenient; believed it violated the democratic doctrine of majority rule; believed president had no authority to readmit states
c. lenient to southern states; returned former Confederates to power

12. a. gave them what they wanted: power in hands of states
b. leniency with South and Black Codes led to stricter rules, Army troops
c. did not include women nor recognize that states might try other ways to disenfranchise African Americans

Visual Summary: Reconstruction

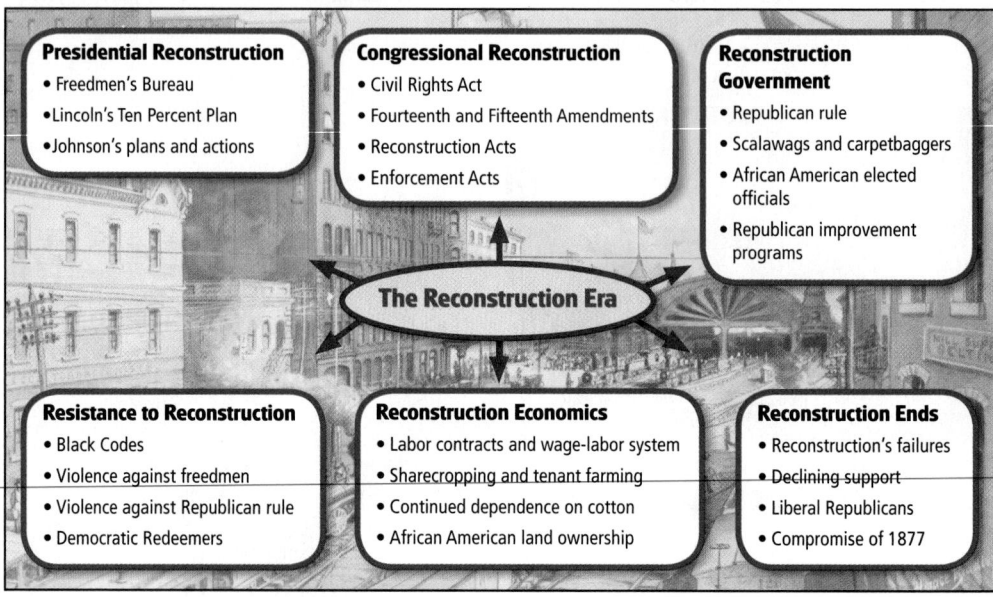

Presidential Reconstruction
• Freedmen's Bureau
• Lincoln's Ten Percent Plan
• Johnson's plans and actions

Congressional Reconstruction
• Civil Rights Act
• Fourteenth and Fifteenth Amendments
• Reconstruction Acts
• Enforcement Acts

Reconstruction Government
• Republican rule
• Scalawags and carpetbaggers
• African American elected officials
• Republican improvement programs

The Reconstruction Era

Resistance to Reconstruction
• Black Codes
• Violence against freedmen
• Violence against Republican rule
• Democratic Redeemers

Reconstruction Economics
• Labor contracts and wage-labor system
• Sharecropping and tenant farming
• Continued dependence on cotton
• African American land ownership

Reconstruction Ends
• Reconstruction's failures
• Declining support
• Liberal Republicans
• Compromise of 1877

Reviewing Key Terms and People

Match each lettered definition with the correct numbered item at right.

a. Leader of the Radical Republicans
b. White citizens that terrorized African Americans
c. Organization to assist uprooted southerners after the Civil War
d. Man who became president after Lincoln's death
e. Southerners who supported changes brought by Reconstruction
f. Northern Republicans who came to the South to take part in the region's rebirth
g. African American who became a senator
h. An attempt to provide land ownership to freed African Americans
i. A farming system that replaced the wage labor system
j. Agreement that brought Reconstruction to an end

1. sharecropping
2. Hiram Revels
3. scalawags
4. Southern Homestead Act
5. Andrew Johnson
6. carpetbaggers
7. Compromise of 1877
8. Freedmen's Bureau
9. Ku Klux Klan
10. Thaddeus Stevens

13. a. Fourteenth and Fifteenth Amendments; Reconstruction Acts passed; divided South into 5 districts under control of U.S. Army
b. made their lives more uncertain; gave them hope that land ownership was possible; established schools and churches
c. tied them to the landowner through accumulating debts; became a source of cheap labor

14. a. Supreme Court decisions weakened rights won during Reconstruction and left rights unprotected.
b. contested election led to Compromise of 1877 and end of Reconstruction, what Democrats wanted
c. slavery ended; some were better off, most were not; had schools and churches; those who stayed in the South, were usually tied to a cycle of poverty that resembled slavery

Comprehension and Critical Thinking

SECTION 1 *(pp. 402–408)*

11. a. Describe What major problems did the South face after the Civil War?

b. Analyze Why did some members of Congress oppose Lincoln's Ten Percent Plan?

c. Predict Why was Johnson's Reconstruction plan likely to provoke problems with Congress?

SECTION 2 *(pp. 410–415)*

12. a. Recall Why did the South welcome Johnson's Reconstruction plan?

b. Draw Conclusions How did Johnson's views help lead to Radical Reconstruction efforts?

c. Evaluate What were some shortcomings of the Fifteenth Amendment?

SECTION 3 *(pp. 416–422)*

13. a. Identify What changes did the new state governments make under Radical Reconstruction?

b. Analyze How did freedom change the lives of African Americans in the South?

c. Elaborate How did the sharecropping system limit the freedom of African Americans?

SECTION 4 *(pp. 423–427)*

14. a. Describe How did legal challenges contribute to the decline of Reconstruction?

b. Drawing Conclusions In what ways was the election of 1876 a victory for the Democrats?

c. Evaluate How much better off were African Americans after Reconstruction than they had been before the Civil War?

Using the Internet

go.hrw.com
Practice Online
Keyword: SD7 CH12

15. A main goal of freed African Americans after the Civil War was to get an education. Using the keyword above, do research to find out more about schools started by the Freedmen's Bureau for African Americans in the South. Then create a report analyzing the impact of these schools.

History's Impact video program
Review the video to answer the closing question: How did the three amendments passed after the Civil War help the civil rights movement a century later?

Analyzing Primary Sources

Reading Like a Historian The damage and destruction of property in the South that resulted from the Civil War was severe. In addition, many places had been neglected as people went to war or fled from areas where fighting was taking place. Re-read the History's Voices passage in Section 1 that begins, "From Pocahontas to Decatur, one hundred and fourteen miles . . ."

16. Identify What does this primary source describe?

17. Predict How would these conditions likely affect the economy of the South?

Critical Reading

Re-read the passage in Section 4 that begins with the heading "Terrorist groups in the South." Then answer the question that follows.

18. When this passage states, "The hooded and disguised night riders of the Ku Klux Klan were the most active terrorists," the term *terrorists* means

A people who favor enslaving African Americans.

B people who use violence to further their goals.

C people who are the targets of attacks.

D people who use disguises and ride at night.

WRITING FOR THE SAT

Think about the following issue:

Three constitutional amendments—the Thirteenth, Fourteenth, and Fifteenth—were passed during Reconstruction. Under Johnson's Reconstruction program, however, the southern states passed Black Codes restricting the rights of African Americans. Subsequent laws passed by the Redeemers and rulings by the Supreme Court continued to weaken the impact of the Reconstruction amendments.

19. Assignment Did Reconstruction ultimately help African Americans gain more rights? Write a short essay in which you develop your position on this issue. Support your point of view with reasoning and examples from your reading and studies.

RECONSTRUCTION **431**

Review and Assessment Resources

Review and Reinforce

- CRF: Chapter Review Activity
- Quick Facts Transparencies: Hopes Raised and Denied, Reconstruction
- Spanish Chapter Summaries Audio CD Program
- Online Chapter Summaries in Spanish
- OSP Holt PuzzlePro; Quiz Show for ExamView
- Quiz Game CD-ROM

Assess

- PASS: Chapter Test, Forms A and B
- Alternative Assessment Handbook
- OSP ExamView Test Generator, Chapter Test
- Differentiated Instruction Modified Worksheets and Tests CD-ROM: Chapter Test
- HOAP Holt Online Assessment Program (in the Premier Online Edition)

Reteach/Intervene

- Interactive Reader and Study Guide
- Differentiated Instruction Teacher Management System: Lesson Plans for Differentiated Instruction
- Differentiated Instruction Modified Worksheets and Tests CD-ROM: Chapter Test
- Interactive Skills Tutor CD-ROM

go.hrw.com
Online Resources
KEYWORD: SD7 CH12

Unit Review

Summarizing the Unit

In the famous opening of his novel *A Tale of Two Cities*, Charles Dickens wrote, "It was the best of times; it was the worst of times . . . " Ask students how the Civil War and its aftermath might represent both the best and the worst of the country at the time.

Connecting to Themes

Guide students in a discussion of the following question: *Although the Civil War was the most divisive event in the nation's history, do you think that in some ways it made the nation stronger and more united?* Have students explain their answers.

 UNIT 4 IN BRIEF Below is a chapter-by-chapter summary of the main ideas covered in Unit 4.

CHAPTER 10 — The Nation Splits Apart
1850–1861

MAIN IDEA Slavery moved to the forefront of national politics in the 1850s. Despite efforts to find compromises between the North and the South over slavery, southern states eventually seceded from the Union and created the Confederate States of America.

SECTION 1 In passing the Compromise of 1850 and the Kansas-Nebraska Act, Congress attempted to please both the North and the South. Despite these compromises, many northerners and southerners remained at odds over issues related to slavery.

SECTION 2 Tensions over slavery in Kansas erupted into violence in the mid-1850s. The *Dred Scott* decision in 1857 and Buchanan's actions as president widened the nation's divisions. John Brown's raid on a government arsenal in Virginia in the hope of arming a slave revolt helped to unite southerners in defense of slavery.

SECTION 3 Abraham Lincoln rose in politics in the 1840s and 1850s by opposing the spread of slavery. Lincoln won the presidency in 1860 in an election that not only widened the divisions between North and South but also split the Democratic Party as well.

SECTION 4 Following Abraham Lincoln's election as president, South Carolina seceded from the Union in December 1860. Other states of the Lower South soon followed South Carolina's lead, resulting in the creation of the Confederate States of America in 1861.

CHAPTER 11 — The Civil War
1861–1865

MAIN IDEA The Civil War pitted the North against the South in the bloodiest war the United States had yet seen. Fighting on many fronts, the Union eventually defeated the Confederacy in 1865.

SECTION 1 The Confederacy attacked Fort Sumter in April 1861. President Lincoln called for troops to put down the rebellion, and both sides prepared for war.

SECTION 2 The Civil War began with decisive victories for the Confederacy in Virginia and for the Union in the Mississippi Valley. The Confederates' success in Virginia prompted Lee to invade the Union in 1862, only to be defeated at the Battle of Antietam.

SECTION 3 Hoping to weaken the Confederates' ability to fight, Lincoln granted freedom to slaves in unconquered areas of the South in 1863. Both sides resorted to unpopular drafts to raise more troops. Opposition to the war became strong in the North and in the South as well, where the hardships of war were especially harsh.

SECTION 4 The Civil War raged at sea as well as on land, where the fighting reached west of the Mississippi River and involved Native Americans. Union victories at Gettysburg and Vicksburg in July 1863 became a turning point in the war.

SECTION 5 Grant's battles with Lee in Virginia and Sherman's march through Georgia and the Carolinas weakened the South. Lincoln's re-election in 1864 ended the South's remaining hopes for victory. Lee finally surrendered to Grant in April 1865.

CHAPTER 12 — Reconstruction
1865–1877

MAIN IDEA Reconstruction of the South following the Civil War went through many phases and brought many changes to the region.

SECTION 1 Even before the war ended, Union leaders developed reconstruction plans for the South. These plans fell apart after the war and Lincoln's assassination, as President Johnson and Congress differed over how the defeated South should be treated.

SECTION 2 Southern resistance to Reconstruction and the introduction of Black Codes led to Congress taking control of Reconstruction. Led by Radical Republicans, Congress passed laws to change southern society, protect the rights of the newly freed slaves, and take control from former Confederates.

SECTION 3 Former slaves enjoyed new rights and freedoms as southern state governments came under Radical Republican control. Despite much rebuilding, black and white southerners alike continued to suffer from economic problems.

SECTION 4 As northern interest in Reconstruction declined, white southerners regained control in the South. Reconstruction was ended as part of a compromise between Republicans and Democrats to settle the disputed presidential election of 1876.

Unit Resources

Review and Reinforce

- CRF: Chapter Review Activity
- Spanish Chapter Summaries Audio CD Program
- OSP Holt PuzzlePro; GameTool for ExamView
- Quiz Game CD-ROM

Assess

- PASS: Unit Test, Forms A and B
- Alternative Assessment Handbook
- OSP ExamView Test Generator
- Differentiated Instruction Modified Worksheets and Tests CD-ROM: Chapter Tests
- HOAP Holt Online Assessment Program (in the Premier Online Edition)

Reteach/Intervene

- Interactive Reader and Study Guide
- Differentiated Instruction Teacher Management System: Lesson Plans for Differentiated Instruction
- Differentiated Instruction Modified Worksheets and Tests CD-ROM: Chapter Tests
- Interactive Skills Tutor CD-ROM

go.hrw.com
Online Resources

KEYWORDS: SD7 CH10, SD7 CH11, SD7 CH12

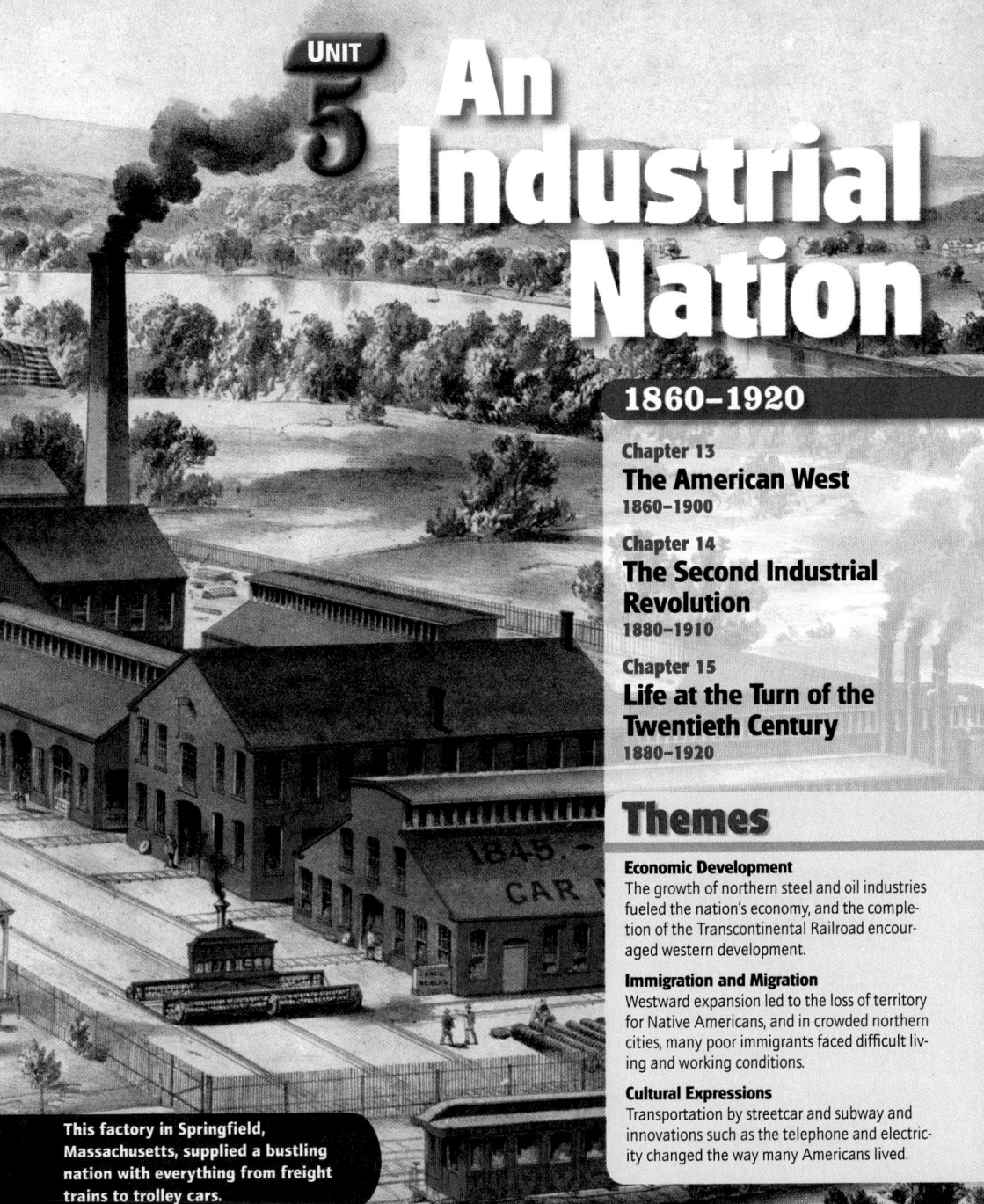

1860–1920

Themes

Economic Development
The growth of northern steel and oil industries fueled the nation's economy, and the completion of the Transcontinental Railroad encouraged western development.

Immigration and Migration
Westward expansion led to the loss of territory for Native Americans, and in crowded northern cities, many poor immigrants faced difficult living and working conditions.

Cultural Expressions
Transportation by streetcar and subway and innovations such as the telephone and electricity changed the way many Americans lived.

This factory in Springfield, Massachusetts, supplied a bustling nation with everything from freight trains to trolley cars.

433

Unit Preview

Introducing the Unit
The Old West has captured the imagination of millions, both in America and around the world, through books, movies, paintings, television, and other media. Have students make a list of things they think they know about the Old West and the source of their knowledge. Have volunteers share some of their responses. Have students keep their lists and return to them after they have studied this unit to see how their perceptions may have changed.

Connecting to Themes
Activity Industry Development Tell students that they will soon read about the growth of several key industries, such as steel and oil, along with the construction of a nationwide railroad network. All of these developments fueled a second industrial revolution in the United States. Ask students what they know about the current status of these industries and transportation network. Have students draw conclusions about how the economy of a nation can change over time. **LS Verbal-Linguistic**

Reading Like a Historian
Interpreting Visuals Have students take a moment to examine the image on this page. What types of transportation are taking place? Where? *Boats on river, railroad car on track, horse-drawn wagon unloading railcar, mechanized cart travels back and forth among buildings*

Unit Resources

Planning
- Differentiated Instruction Teacher Management System: Unit Pacing Guide
- One-Stop Planner CD-ROM: Teacher Management System
- Power Presentations with Video CD-ROM

Differentiating Instruction
- Differentiated Instruction Teacher Management System: Lesson Plans for Differentiated Instruction
- Pre-AP Activities Guide for American History
- Differentiated Instruction Modified Worksheets and Tests CD-ROM

Enrichment
- Civic Participation Activities Guide
- CRF: Economics and History Activity
- CRF: Interdisciplinary Project
- American History Primary Source Library CD-ROM

Assessment
- PASS: Unit Test, Forms A & B
- Alternative Assessment Handbook
- OSP ExamView Test Generator
- HOAP Holt Online Assessment Program (in the Premier Online Edition)

The Differentiated Instruction Teacher Management System
provides a planning and instructional benchmarking guide for this unit.

Identifying Cause and Effect

Have students work together to find causes and effects in a subsection from this unit. Students should take turns explaining to each other how a single cause can have multiple effects and how a single effect can stem from multiple causes. As an example of a cause and effect, point out that the discovery of gold and silver lured settlers west, which caused conflict between Native Americans and settlers. Have volunteers explain other connections.

Word Help

blacklisted unable to be hired

Info to Know

A Holiday Is Born Although the railroad workers' union was destroyed by President Cleveland's firm response to the Pullman strike, American workers gained another kind of victory just six days later. Criticism of Cleveland's use of troops to break the strike was widespread, and the president felt he needed to do something to appease angry workers. Both houses of Congress unanimously passed a bill creating Labor Day, and Cleveland felt forced to sign it into law.

Skills Planner

To give students more opportunities to practice this skill, see the following activities in the teacher's edition: Destruction of the Buffalo, p. 439; Industrial Innovation, p. 461.

Identifying Cause and Effect

Find practice for **Identifying Cause and Effect** in the **Skills Handbook**, p. H9

As students of history, you want to know why certain events occurred. By learning to identify causes and effects, you can better understand how historical events influence one another.

Before You Read
Skim the review questions in the reading. List what you already know about the subject matter and what you would like to know about it after the reading.

While You Read
Create a table that lists the causes and effects of various events. Keep in mind that a cause may have many effects, and an effect may have more than one cause.

After You Read
Compare the two lists. How are they alike or different?

The Pullman Strike

Other unions suffered setbacks too. In 1893 the Pullman Company laid off more than half its employees. It cut the wages of the remaining employees as much as 50 percent, but it did not lower their rents.

That led to the decision by workers to go on strike with the support of **Eugene V. Debs**, the leader of the American Railway Union (ARU). He urged the members of the ARU not to work on any trains that included Pullman cars.

The government soon stepped in. It ordered the union to call off the strike because it was interfering with the delivery of U.S. mail. When ARU officials refused, many of them were jailed. Meanwhile, President Grover Cleveland called in federal troops, and the strike collapsed. As a result of their participation in the strike, most of the workers who had taken part wound up fired or blacklisted.

READING CHECK **Identifying Cause and Effect** What events led to the Pullman Strike?

Cause Employees were displeased about layoffs and wage cuts at the Pullman Company.

Effect Employees decided to go on strike against the Pullman Company.

Test Prep Tip

Multiple choice and short answer questions ask you to identify cause and effect. Signal words such as *because* and *led* to show causes. Words such as *therefore, so,* and *since* show effects. An example of an effect in this passage might be, "As a result of their participation in the strike, most of the workers who had taken part were fired or blacklisted."

Skills Focus: Identifying Cause and Effect
Below Level

Reading Skill
Cause-and-Effect Charts

1. Draw on the board several boxes connected by arrows pointing from left to right. Explain to students that a good way to identify cause and effect is to make a similar chart.

2. Have students copy the chart onto their notes. Fill in the first box with "Employees were unhappy about layoffs and wage cuts." Fill in the second box with "Employees went on strike." Explain to students that the first event caused the second event.

3. Have students fill in the rest of the boxes with events from the Pullman strike. Students may fill in as many boxes as necessary.

4. Have volunteers share their answers with the class. Fill in the chart on the board with appropriate answers. Have students correct their own charts and retain them as a study tool. **LS** **Verbal-Linguistic, Visual-Spatial**

   Alternative Assessment Handbook, Rubric 7: Charts

Reading like a Historian

Evaluating Sources

Find practice for **Evaluating Sources** in the **Skills Handbook**, p. H34

Historians understand that although certain sources are more reliable than others, bias can influence any historical source. Therefore, historians must evaluate all sources. Sources report what writers believe to have happened or what writers want readers to know. Both point of view and personal experience affect sources. Understanding how bias influences a source allows historians to know how, or whether, they will use it.

> **Strategies historians use:**
> - Who created the source? Is the author impartial in his or her writing, or influenced by his or her interests?
> - What is the purpose of the source? Is it supposed to convey public or private information? Does the writer want to inform or persuade others?
> - Compare the source with other sources of information, including both primary and secondary sources. Are they consistent?

Social Darwinism

A professor and minister, William Graham Sumner was the leading proponent of social Darwinism in the United States.

> **"**If . . . men were <u>willing</u> to set to work with energy and courage . . . all might live in plenty and prosperity. But if they insist on remaining in the slums of great cities . . . there is no device . . . which can prevent them from falling victims to poverty and misery or from succumbing in the competition of life to those who have <u>great command</u> of capital.**"**

Note the background of each speaker. Sumner was a professor and a minister. As such, he probably lived in a middle-class setting, unlike Rauschenbusch, who lived among impoverished people.

Look for clue words such as *willing* that might indicate bias. Identify how bias affects each source.

Walter Rauschenbusch, lived among the poor. He found fault with the attitude of the rich toward the working class.

> **"**Progress slackens when a single class appropriates the social results of the common labor, fortifies its <u>evil</u> rights by unfair laws, throttles the masses by political centralization and suppression, and consumes in luxury what it has taken in <u>covetousness</u> . . . Exploitation creates poverty, and poverty is followed by physical degeneration.**"**

Does the source present logical arguments? Are the cause-and-effect relationships sound? Are conclusions rational or emotional?

 READING LIKE A HISTORIAN

As You Read Evaluate each source and decide whether you would use it to draw conclusions or make generalizations about the historical period or subject.

As You Study After you have evaluated the source, determine the extent to which it relates to your study. Then decide how the source contributes to your historical understanding.

AN INDUSTRIAL NATION **435**

Prepare to Read

Evaluating Sources

Have volunteers suggest things to look for when evaluating a text. Create a class list on the board and have students copy it into their notes. Then have students reread the two passages on social Darwinism, using the class list to evaluate the sources.

Word Help

device way, method
succumbing being defeated by
slackens weakens
appropriates takes over
fortifies strengthens
throttles strangles
covetousness greed
exploitation taking advantage of
degeneration decay

Teaching Tip

Guide the class in a discussion of which source provides a more accurate description of the reasons for poverty. Which writer's experiences better qualify him to draw conclusions about the lives of poor people? Have students explain and support their answers.

Skills Focus: Evaluating Sources

At Level

Reading Like a Historian Skill

Evaluating Sources of Historical Information

Research Required

1. Have students perform an Internet search to find a primary source quotation about one of the historical events discussed in this unit. Students might focus on the settling of the West, the second industrial revolution, or the increase in immigration at the turn of the century.

2. Have students write a brief paragraph evaluating their source. Students should explain who wrote the source, the author's background and connections to the event, the purpose of the account, and other relevant elements.

3. Have volunteers share their sources and evaluations with the class. **LS Intrapersonal, Verbal-Linguistic**

   Alternative Assessment Handbook, Rubric 16: Judging Information

Chapter Overview	Reproducible Resources	Technology Resources
CHAPTER 13 pp. 436–457 **Overview:** In this chapter, students will analyze the expansion of the United States into the West and the effects this movement had on Native Americans and the various Americans who settled there.	**Differentiated Instruction Teacher Management System:*** • Instructional Benchmarking Guides • Lesson Plans for Differentiated Instruction **Interactive Reader and Study Guide:** Chapter Summary* **Chapter Resource File*** • Focus on Writing Activity: The Settlement of the West • Social Studies Skills Activity: Interpreting Infographics • Chapter Review Activity **American History Outline Maps** **Pre-AP Activities Guide for American History*** **Reading Like a Historian Toolkit**	Live Ink® Online Reading Help Student Edition on Audio CD Program Differentiated Instruction Modified Worksheets and Tests CD-ROM Interactive Skills Tutor CD-ROM United States History Primary Source Library CD-ROM Power Presentations with Video CD-ROM History's Impact: American History Video Program (VHS/DVD): The American West Online Chapter Summaries in Spanish Graphic Organizer Transparencies
Section 1: **The Fight for the West** **The Main Idea:** Native Americans fought the movement of settlers westward, but the U.S. military and the persistence of American settlers proved too strong to resist.	**Differentiated Instruction Teacher Management System:** Section 1 Lesson Plan* **Interactive Reader and Study Guide:** Section 1 Summary* **Chapter Resource File*** • Vocabulary Builder Activity, Section 1 • Biography Activity: Mary Lucinda Bonney • Primary Source Activity: Rules for Indian Schools • History and Geography Activity: The Battle of Little Bighorn	Daily Bellringer Transparency: Section 1* Map Transparency: Major Battles and Native American Territory in the West, 1890* Daily Test Practice Transparency: Section 1* Internet Activity: Native American Leaders
Section 2: **Mining and Ranching** **The Main Idea:** Many people sought fortunes during the mining and cattle booms of the American West.	**Differentiated Instruction Teacher Management System:** Section 2 Lesson Plan* **Interactive Reader and Study Guide:** Section 2 Summary* **Chapter Resource File*** • Vocabulary Builder Activity, Section 2 • Biography Activity: Nat Love • Primary Source Activity: Montana Cattle Country	Daily Bellringer Transparency: Section 2* Map Transparency: Cattle Trails* Daily Test Practice Transparency: Section 2* Internet Activity: The Gold Rush
Section 3: **Farming the Plains** **The Main Idea:** The government promoted the settlement of the West, offering free or cheap land to those willing to put in the hard work of turning the land into productive farms.	**Differentiated Instruction Teacher Management System:** Section 3 Lesson Plan* **Interactive Reader and Study Guide:** Section 3 Summary* **Chapter Resource File*** • Vocabulary Builder Activity, Section 3 • Biography Activity: James Oliver • Literature Activity: Covered Wagon Women: Diaries and Letters from Western Trails, 1854–1860	Daily Bellringer Transparency: Section 3* Daily Test Practice Transparency: Section 3* Internet Activity: Moving West

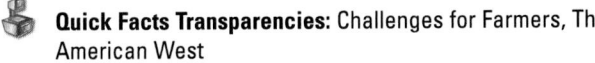

go.hrw.com	Print Resource	Transparency
LS Learning Styles	Audio CD	CD-ROM
Video	SE Student Edition	TE Teacher's Edition
OSP One-Stop Planner CD-ROM		

*also on One-Stop Planner CD-ROM

Review, Assessment, Intervention

Quick Facts Transparencies: Challenges for Farmers, The American West

Spanish Chapter Summaries Audio CD Program

Progress Assessment Support System (PASS): Chapter Test*

Differentiated Instruction Modified Worksheets and Tests CD-ROM: Modified Chapter Test

OSP **One-Stop Planner CD-ROM:** ExamView Test Generator (English/Spanish)

HOAP **Holt Online Assessment Program (HOAP),** in the Holt Premier Online Student Edition

 **PASS:** Section 1 Quiz*

 **Online Quiz:** Section 1

Alternative Assessment Handbook

PASS: Section 2 Quiz*

Online Quiz: Section 2

Alternative Assessment Handbook

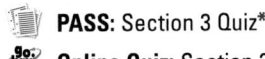 **PASS:** Section 3 Quiz*

Online Quiz: Section 3

Alternative Assessment Handbook

NC RESOURCES

The following resources were developed to help North Carolina educators teach the standards and objectives of North Carolina's eleventh grade standard course of study in United States history.

- United States history EOC Test Prep Workbook
- Teacher's Support System
- North Carolina One-Stop Planner

And be sure to direct your students to **go.hrw.com** for online access to the EOC Test Prep Workbook.

go.hrw.com
EOC Test Prep
KEYWORD: SE7 NC

Holt Online Learning

go.hrw.com
Teacher Resources
KEYWORD: SD7 TEACHER

go.hrw.com
Student Resources
KEYWORD: SD7 CH13

- Document-based Questions
- Interactive Multimedia Activities

- Current Events
- Chapter-based Internet Activities
- and more!

Holt Premier
Online Student Edition

Complete online support for interactivity, assessment, and reporting

- Interactive Maps and Notebook
- Standardized Test Prep
- Homework Practice and Research Activities Online

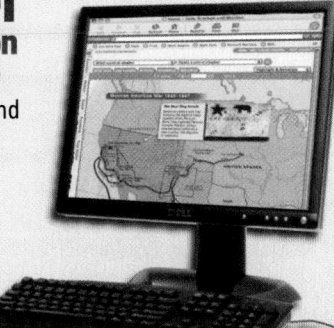

The Big Picture

Edward L. Ayers

The Fight for the West During the Civil War and Reconstruction, the Native Americans of the West struggled to defend their way of life against the soldiers and settlers of the United States. The steady incursion of outsiders onto the Plains threatened the culture and the means of subsistence of the Plains Indians, as buffalo were exterminated in massive numbers. A series of bloody battles and massacres heightened the stakes of the struggle over the West. Slowly, one people after another were conquered and contained on reservations.

Mining and Ranching The West proved to be rich in gold and silver. Throughout the second half of the nineteenth century, one mining discovery after another brought prospectors, miners, traders, and businessmen to hastily built boom towns throughout the West. At the same time, the cattle business reached its peak of profitability and folklore as cattle ranches sprawled across the Great Plains. Many migrants to the West found the going tough, but enough succeeded to keep the fever high.

Farming the Plains Americans from the East, as well as immigrants from Europe and Asia, showed a never-ending fascination and hunger for land in the West. In 1862 Congress passed three acts to turn public land in the West into private property. Though agriculture proved to be harder in much of the region than people had expected, the support of the government and of railroads continued to bring settlers to the Plains, and in 1890 the U.S. Census Bureau declared that the frontier no longer existed.

Recent Scholarship

The True West Patricia Limerick's *The Legacy of Conquest: The Unbroken Past of the American West* (1987) continues to stimulate all who struggle with the history of the American West. In a passionate, sometimes opinionated narrative, Limerick turns most of the familiar images of the West on their head. Instead of independence, individualism, optimism, and unbounded opportunity, Limerick finds reliance on government, big business, and subjugation of the environment and Native Americans. Teachers and students will find much to discuss and debate in this account.

Differentiating Instruction

 Differentiated Instruction Teacher Management System
- Lesson Plans for Differentiated Instruction
- Differentiated Instructional Benchmarking Guides
- Interactive Reader and Study Guide

 Spanish Chapter Summaries Audio CD Program

 Online Chapter Summaries in Spanish

 Student Edition on Audio CD Program

 Differentiated Instruction Modified Worksheets and Tests CD-ROM
- Vocabulary Flash Cards
- Modified Vocabulary Builder Activities
- Modified Chapter Review Activity
- Modified Chapter Test

OSP One-Stop Planner CD-ROM
- ExamView Test Generator (English and Spanish)
- PuzzlePro
- Quiz Show for ExamView
- Transparencies and Videos

TE Differentiated Activities in the Teacher's Edition
- Indian Wars Time Line, p. 440
- The Lure of Gold and Silver, p. 445
- The Closing of the Frontier, p. 452

Reading Like a Historian
Sam Wineburg

The Past is a Foreign Country

The easiest thing we can do when reading about long-departed figures is to condemn them—particularly when they espouse views that strike us as racist, backward, or just plain dumb. Put in a time machine and transported to the same situation, we assume that our own actions would be more enlightened and humane.

Moral Superiority

Our chapter's descriptions of policies toward Native Americans in the 1870s provide grist for feelings of moral superiority. "Americanization," we are told, "entailed a wholesale attack on Native American beliefs and practices." The chapter goes on to quote a Bureau of Indian Affairs directive that ordered Native Americans to cut their hair and renounce tribal garb.

As part of the Dawes Act, the federal government created special boarding schools that separated Native American children from their parents. At one of these schools, Superintendent H. M. Beadle recommended that a fence "12 feet high, enclosing a space 200 by 300 yards" be erected. By walling off children from their parents, Beadle hoped to achieve an environment in which children would be separated "from the demoralizing influences" of their surroundings. Their "progress toward civilization" would be "correspondingly accelerated."

Guided by Convictions

What kind of people were these, who acted so coldly toward Native Americans? Often, they were well-meaning citizens, motivated by a genuine concern with improving the conditions of those history had wronged. Like us, these people were guided by convictions that seemed so patently true they were considered common sense. As historian Patricia Limerick writes in *The Legacy of Conquest: The Unbroken Past of the American West*, one of these convictions was that "inside every Indian was a white American citizen and property holder, waiting to be set free."

Consider a statement by a group calling itself "The Friends of the Indian," which convened every summer, starting in 1883, in Lake Monhonk, New York. Members traveled considerable distances, volunteering their time and financial resources, to deliberate over the fate of the American Indian. Members were socially prominent, uniformly white, and often rich. What brought them together was a heightened social conscience and a desire to ease human suffering. They were acquainted with the deplorable conditions on the reservation and believed that the way to help Native Americans was to make them become more like white socialites—which meant, according to their beliefs, "get[ing] the Indian out of the blanket and into trousers—and trousers with a pocket in them, and with a pocket that ache[d] to be filled with dollars!"

Trying to Understand

Condemning such views comes easily, abhorrent as they are to contemporary modes of thought. But a bigger challenge is to try to understand the beliefs that well-meaning, kind, and socially upstanding citizens must have held that would lead them to make policies that, viewed from our perch, seem callous and cruel.

The geographer and historian David Lowenthal calls the past a "foreign country." By this he means that the past is a strange place whose norms defy current logic. No one can silence the part of the brain that makes snap judgments—including snap judgments about the past. But if we stop there, self-satisfied with the verdicts we issue, we will gain little knowledge and even less understanding about this "foreign country" on the other side of time.

From *The Legacy of Conquest: The Unbroken Past of the American West* by Patricia Nelson Limerick. Published by W. W. Norton & Company, New York, 1987.

Standards Focus

Social Studies Competency Goals
Goal 4 The learner will evaluate the great westward movement and assess the impact of the agricultural revolution on the nation.
🔲 4.01, 4.02, 4.04

The Big Idea and Essential Questions

To foster student understanding of this chapter's big idea, design your lesson to address each section's essential question.

Big Idea As the federal government forcibly relocated Native Americans to reservations, Americans and immigrants settled on the new frontier as miners, ranchers, and farmers.

Essential Questions

1. In what ways did Native Americans respond to the efforts of American settlers to move westward?

2. How did the mining industry and cattle ranching develop in the West?

3. How did agriculture develop in the West?

Key to Differentiating Instruction

Below Level

Basic-level activities designed for all students encountering new material

At Level

Intermediate-level activities designed for average students

Above Level

Challenging activities designed for honors and gifted-and-talented students

Standard English Mastery

Activities designed to improve standard English usage

436   CHAPTER 13

CHAPTER
13   1860–1900

The American WEST

THE BIG PICTURE   In the late 1800s, the federal government relocated Native Americans to vastly smaller homelands. Immigrants, African Americans, and white Americans eagerly moved into the new frontier to mine, ranch, and establish farms.

NC **North Carolina Standards**

Social Studies Objectives

4.01 Compare and contrast the different groups of people who migrated to the West and describe the problems they experienced.

4.02 Evaluate the impact that settlement in the West had upon different groups of people and the environment.

4.04 Describe innovations in agricultural technology and business practices and assess their impact on the West.

Language Arts Objectives

2.01 Research and analyze ideas, events, and/or movements related to United States culture by:
  • locating facts and details for purposeful elaboration.

Skills FOCUS **READING LIKE A HISTORIAN**

A family of homesteaders traveling west pauses to pose for a photograph beside their covered wagon in Loup Valley, Nebraska, in 1886.
Interpreting Visuals Using clues from the photograph, describe what the journey might have been like.
See Skills Handbook, p. H30

436

U.S.

1860

World

1868 Sioux sign a treaty agreeing to live on a reservation.

1864 The Taiping Rebellion in China leaves 20 million Chinese dead and causes mass emigration.

Introduce the Chapter   `At Level`

The American West

1. List the three main ideas of the chapter for students to see. Assign students to work in pairs and list what they already know about each topic.

2. Have students share the information in their lists, and write it under each main idea.

3. Guide students in a discussion of the ideas. Which seem to be correct, factual historical ideas, and which seem to be folklore about the West?

4. Tell students that in this chapter they will learn how the American West was transformed from unsettled territories to ranches, farms, and towns. **LS Verbal-Linguistic**

📖 Alternative Assessment Handbook, Rubric 11: Discussions

1871
Some 600,000 cattle are driven to market on the Chisholm Trail.

June 1876
Native Americans, led by Sitting Bull, defeat a U.S. Cavalry force at the Battle of Little Bighorn.

April 1889
Thousands lay claim to land during the Oklahoma Land Run.

July 1897
The Klondike gold rush begins.

1870   **1880**   **1890**   **1900**

1871
Prussia consolidates German states into a unified nation.

1875
Industrial revolution causes 1 million to crowd Berlin.

1880
Crop failures and a troubled economy cause millions of Italians to emigrate to America.

1895
Guglielmo Marconi invents the radio.

437

Explore the Time Line

1. When was the Oklahoma Land Run? *April 1889*

2. When was the radio invented? *1895*

3. What was happening in Germany about the same time as the Battle of Little Bighorn in the United States? *Industrial revolution was drawing people to cities like Berlin.*

Info to Know

The Dawes General Allotment Act of 1887
Although the initial intent of the Dawes Act was to help Native Americans, amendments added by Congress provided that any land that remained after the allotments were made to Native Americans would be available for public sale. Through various techniques including sale and swindle, by 1932, whites had acquired two-thirds of the 138,000,000 acres that had been held by Native Americans in 1887.

● **Chapter Preview** ●

HOLT

History's Impact
▶ **Video Program:**
The American West
See the Video Teacher's Guide for strategies for using the video segment.

Reading Like a Historian
Homesteaders in Nebraska
In 1854, when the Nebraska territory was opened to settlement, the government established a reservation for the Omaha Indians in the northeastern part of Nebraska. Between 1866 and 1877 the Nebraska State Board of Immigration hired an agent in Europe to recruit settlers to come to Nebraska, and the railroads also encouraged new immigrants to settle in the region. Many of the early homesteaders were immigrants who came from Germany, Scandinavia, and Bohemia.

Evaluate Why do you think immigrants from Northern Europe would have been attracted to Nebraska? *possible answer—cheap farm land, used to long, cold winters*

go.hrw.com
Online Resources

Chapter Resources:
KEYWORD: SD7 CH13

Teacher Resources:
KEYWORD: SD7 TEACHER

Answers

Reading Like a Historian (p. 436)
possible answers—lack of water, no way to resupply, loss of livestock, no way to treat illnesses

Bellringer

The Inside Story. . . Use the **Daily Bellringer Transparency** to help students answer the question.

🖙 Daily Bellringer Transparency, Section 1

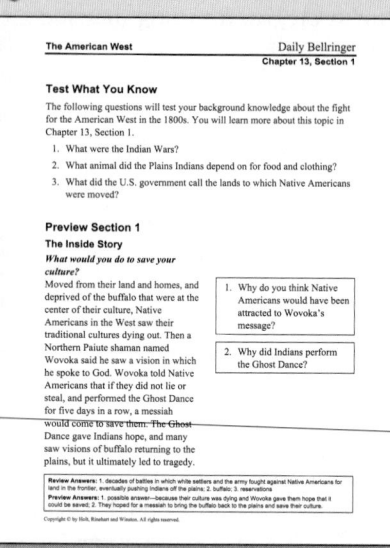

The American West — Daily Bellringer
Chapter 13, Section 1

Test What You Know

The following questions will test your background knowledge about the fight for the American West in the 1800s. You will learn more about this topic in Chapter 13, Section 1.

1. What were the Indian Wars?
2. What animal did the Plains Indians depend on for food and clothing?
3. What did the U.S. government call the lands to which Native Americans were moved?

Preview Section 1
The Inside Story
What would you do to save your culture?

Moved from their land and homes, and deprived of the buffalo that were at the center of their culture, Native Americans in the West saw their traditional cultures dying out. Then a Northern Paiute shaman named Wovoka said he saw a vision in which he spoke to God. Wovoka told Native Americans that if they did not lie or steal, and performed the Ghost Dance for five days in a row, a messiah would come to save them. The Ghost Dance gave Indians hope, and many saw visions of buffalo returning to the plains, but it ultimately led to tragedy.

1. Why do you think Native Americans would have been attracted to Wovoka's message?

2. Why did Indians perform the Ghost Dance?

Review Answers: 1. decades of battles in which white settlers and the army fought against Native Americans for land in the frontier, eventually pushing Indians off the plains; 2. buffalo; 3. reservations

Review Answers: 1. possible answer—because their culture was dying and Wovoka gave them hope that it could be saved; 2. They hoped for a messiah to bring the buffalo back to the plains and save their culture.

Copyright © by Holt, Rinehart and Winston. All rights reserved.

Academic Vocabulary

Review with students the high-use academic terms in this section.

policy plan, course of action (p. 439)

traditional established, customary (p. 442)

🖙 CRF: Vocabulary Builder Activity, Section 1

Taking Notes

Fort Kearney, Bozeman Trail closed, Second Treaty of Fort Laramie; Little Bighorn, Sioux victory; Palo Duro Canyon, U.S. victory, Comanches forced onto reservation; Wounded Knee massacre, end of conflict with Plains Indians; Nez Percé, Chief Joseph captured; Apache, Geronimo captured

---

The Fight for the West

BEFORE YOU READ

MAIN IDEA

Native Americans fought the movement of settlers westward, but the U.S. military and the persistence of American settlers proved too strong to resist.

FOCUS QUESTIONS

1. How was the stage set for conflict between white settlers and Native Americans in the West?
2. What were the Indian Wars and their consequences?
3. How did Native American resistance to white settlement end?
4. What was life like on the Indian reservations?

KEY TERMS AND PEOPLE

Sand Creek Massacre
Sitting Bull
George Armstrong Custer
Battle of the Little Bighorn
Wounded Knee Massacre
Chief Joseph
Geronimo
Americanization
Bureau of Indian Affairs
Dawes Act

TAKING NOTES As you read, take notes on the outcomes of clashes between Americans and Native Americans. Record your notes in a graphic organizer like the one shown here.

Battle	Outcome

The Ghost Dance

◄ **Some Plains Indians hoped the Ghost Dance would help them reclaim their former ways of life.**

THE INSIDE STORY

What would you do to save your culture? By the 1890s Native Americans and their cultures faced extinction. People had lost their land, homes, and food sources. In utter desperation, many Indians turned to traditional religion—and to a prophet with a new message of hope.

Wovoka, a shaman of the Northern Paiute in Nevada, became known as a healer who could bring rain. Working for white farmers, Wovoka learned about Christianity and its belief in a messiah, or savior. In 1889 he had a vision that he spoke with God in heaven, where he saw many who had died. The dream, he said, told him to bring the Indians a new message and a sacred dance. According to most surviving accounts, the message was that the people should get along and not steal or lie or go to war. They were to perform the special Ghost Dance five nights in a row. Wovoka promised that a messiah would come to save only the Indians.

Wovoka's message, and the Ghost Dance movement, spread across the central Plains. During the frenzied dances people saw visions of buffalo herds returning and white settlers leaving the West. The Ghost Dance offered hope. But as you will read, it ultimately led to tragedy. ■

Stage Set for Conflict

The Ghost Dance was an expression of deepest grief about the loss of Native Americans' ways of life. As white settlers began streaming into the West, Native Americans and white settlers clashed over control of the land. U.S. government actions compounded the tensions.

Culture of the Plains Indians The Sioux, Blackfoot, and Cheyenne of the northern Plains and the Kiowa and Comanche of the southern Plains thrived thanks to the abundance of wild buffalo, their main source of food, clothing, shoes, shelter, and supplies. The Plains Indians lived a nomadic lifestyle, traveling the great grasslands on horseback as they followed the migrations of the buffalo herds. They did not believe that land should be bought and sold.

Most white settlers were farmers or town dwellers. They believed that land should be divided and claims given to people to farm or establish businesses. If

---

Teach the Main Idea

At Level

The Fight for the West

1. **Teach** Ask students the Reading Focus questions to teach this section.

2. **Apply** Organize the class into mixed-ability pairs. Have each pair write two newspaper headlines that support key changes in U.S. government policy toward Native Americans during the mid-1800s. Then have each pair write two headlines that oppose proposed policy changes. **LS Interpersonal, Verbal-Linguistic**

3. **Review** Have each pair share its headlines with the class, and write them for all students to see.

4. **Practice/Homework** Have each student select one of the headlines and write an editorial based on the position expressed in the headline. Editorials should be backed by facts and sound reasoning. **LS Verbal-Linguistic**

🖙 Alternative Assessment Handbook, Rubric 23: Newspapers

Native Americans would not settle down in one place, many Americans believed, then their lands were available for the taking.

Government policy In the mid-1800s the United States government's Indian policy underwent a key change. Previously the Army had forcibly removed Native Americans from the East and relocated them farther west. By the 1850s growing numbers of white settlers wanted to move into those western lands as well. So instead of pushing the Indians further westward, the government began seizing their land and sending them to reservations. The goal was to break the power of the Plains Indians and open up their lands for settlement. Americans generally agreed with this new policy.

Destruction of the buffalo For Plains Indians, being confined to reservations threatened their buffalo-centered way of life. Yet the vast herds that had supported them for countless generations now were being driven to extinction. In 1800 some 60 million buffalo had lived on the Plains. Remarkably, by 1894 perhaps as few as 25 buffalo remained. The

catastrophe had several causes. White settlement reduced buffalo grazing lands and cut off migration routes. Settlers' livestock carried diseases that destroyed buffalo herds.

Yet other more deliberate actions by whites hastened the catastrophe. The U.S. Army adopted a policy of encouraging the destruction of the buffalo. It sought to wipe out the Plains Indians' food supply to force them onto reservations.

One of the most dramatic causes of destruction was the hunting of buffalo for sport and profit. With the expansion of railroads across the Plains, buffalo hides could easily be shipped east, where demand for them increased in the 1870s. Hides were used to make belts for factory machines and fashionable buffalo robes.

For pleasure, railroads offered "hunting specials," allowing passengers to shoot buffalo from the train. The slaughter was so massive that in one summer, several railroads had to cancel their hunting specials. The stench of buffalo carcasses sickened passengers.

ACADEMIC VOCABULARY
policy plan, course of action

READING CHECK **Identifying Problems and Solutions** How did Americans deal with Indians that stood in the way of their westward expansion?

HUNTING ON THE PLAINS

Hunters used spears and arrows to bring down the huge beasts. Families then harvested the skin, bones, meat, and tissue, wasting little.

Strength, speed, agility, and accuracy made Plains horsemen skilled hunters, highly respected in their communities.

Skills FOCUS **READING LIKE A HISTORIAN**

Artist John Mix Stanley had a keen sense that he was chronicling a vanishing way of life as he painted *Buffalo Hunt on the Southwestern Prairies* in 1845.
Interpreting Visuals What qualities does Stanley convey about the hunters?

THE AMERICAN WEST **439**

Skills Focus: Identifying Cause and Effect

At Level

Reading Skill
Destruction of the Buffalo

1. Have students draw a cause-and-effect diagram like the one shown here. Omit the italicized answers.

2. Have students complete the chart by listing the reasons for the decline in the buffalo population between 1800

and 1894. Complete the chart and have students correct their work.
LS Visual-Spatial

📓 Alternative Assessment Handbook, Rubric 6: Cause and Effect

🖥 Graphic Organizer Transparencies

Causes

Settlers' oxen and horses ate the buffalos' food supply

Settlers' livestock brought diseases that killed buffalo

Increased demand for buffalo hides

Railroads offered buffalo "hunting specials"

Effect

Only about 25 buffalo survived by 1894

440

The Indian Wars

Tensions between the settlers and the Plains Indians escalated into decades of violence that swept the Indians from most of the West. The conflicts are known as the Indian Wars.

The Sand Creek Massacre In Colorado Territory, a band of Cheyenne raided nearby ranches in 1864. Army officials offered amnesty, or forgiveness, if they returned to their reservation at Sand Creek. Cheyenne chief Black Kettle wanted peace. He led his people back.

Before dawn on November 29, Army colonel John M. Chivington arrived at Sand Creek with about 700 troops. Black Kettle raised an American flag and a white flag as a sign of peace. But Chivington did not want peace. "It is simply not possible for Indians to obey or even understand any treaty," he said. "[T]o kill them is the only way we will ever have peace . . . in Colorado."

Chivington's troops opened fire and killed about 150 people, mostly women, children, and elderly people. After burning the camp to the ground, the troops returned to Denver with scalps, which they displayed to cheering crowds. News of the **Sand Creek Massacre** outraged many Americans. Congressional investigators condemned Chivington's actions as atrocities, but they did not punish him.

Treaties After the Sand Creek Massacre, enraged Cheyenne stepped up raids. The Sioux did as well. A swelling stream of travelers along the Bozeman Trail were passing through sacred Sioux hunting grounds. The Sioux chief Red Cloud had tried without success to negotiate an end to white encroachment in this area. In December 1866 the Sioux attacked a supply wagon train outside newly built Fort Kearny. When a patrol of some 80 soldiers tried to drive off the war party, the Sioux killed the entire group of soldiers.

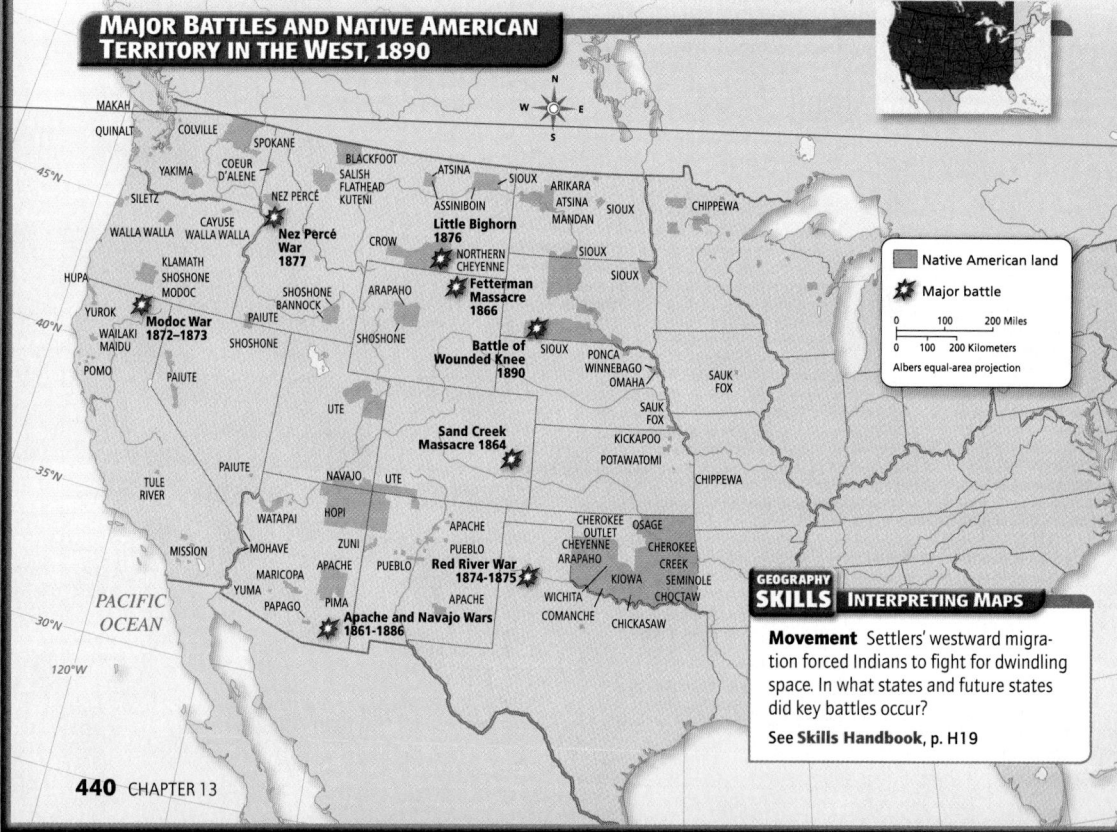

MAJOR BATTLES AND NATIVE AMERICAN TERRITORY IN THE WEST, 1890

Native American land

Major battle

0   100   200 Miles
0   100   200 Kilometers
Albers equal-area projection

PACIFIC OCEAN

GEOGRAPHY SKILLS INTERPRETING MAPS

Movement Settlers' westward migration forced Indians to fight for dwindling space. In what states and future states did key battles occur?

See Skills Handbook, p. H19

440 CHAPTER 13

Differentiating Instruction

Below Level

Learners Having Difficulty

1. Draw the time line below for students to see:

1860   1870   1880   1890

2. Write the names of the following events for students to see. Omit the italicized dates. Battle of Little Bighorn *June 1876*; Battle of Palo Duro Canyon *fall 1874*; Final capture of Geronimo *September 1886*; Ghost Dance movement begins *1889*; Relocation of the Nez Percé *1877*; Sand Creek Massacre *November 1864*; Wounded Knee Massacre *December 1890*; Second Treaty of Fort Laramie *1868*; Medicine Lodge Treaty *1867*

3. Have students copy the time line onto their own paper. Then have them use their text to help them place the events listed above in chronological order on their time lines. Ask students to call out the events and the dates in the correct order. Complete the class time line. **LS Visual-Spatial, Logical-Mathematical**

📋 Alternative Assessment Handbook, Rubric 36: Time Lines

Finally, the government agreed to close the Bozeman Trail. In exchange, officials pressured the Sioux to sign the Second Treaty of Fort Laramie in 1868. The Sioux agreed to live on a reservation along the Missouri River.

Meanwhile, U.S. officials forced the Comanche, Kiowa, Cheyenne, and other southern nations to sign the Medicine Lodge Treaty in 1867. Those nations would be moved to reservations in what is now western Oklahoma.

Battle of the Little Bighorn For years the Lakota Sioux conducted raids against white settlers who had moved into Sioux lands. In response, the U.S. government ordered all Lakota Sioux to return to their reservation by January 31, 1876. They refused. The situation was turned over to the military.

About 2,000 Sioux, Cheyenne, and Arapaho gathered near the Little Bighorn River. The leader of the Sioux, **Sitting Bull**, conducted a ceremonial sun dance. He reportedly had a vision of a great victory over soldiers.

The brash leader of the U.S. Army troops, Lieutenant Colonel **George Armstrong Custer**, predicted victory as well. On June 25, 1876, Custer led his troops into a headlong attack against superior numbers. Custer and his troops were quickly encircled and slaughtered. The **Battle of the Little Bighorn** was a tremendous victory for the Sioux—but a temporary one. Now the U.S. government was even more determined to put down the Indian threat to settlers.

The Battle of Palo Duro Canyon In the Texas Panhandle, Colonel Ranald McKenzie caught Comanches, Kiowas, and Cheyennes preparing a winter encampment in the fall of 1874. He sent in his cavalry. Some Indians fled; others defended their scattered camps. Then McKenzie's men slaughtered more than 1,000 Indian ponies and destroyed all food stores. Starving Comanches led by Quanah Parker had no choice but to move onto the reservation in Indian Territory the following spring. The Indian Wars in the southern Plains were over.

The Ghost Dance As you read earlier, word spread that a Paiute shaman, Wovoka, had received a powerful vision in 1889. Wovoka declared that the Indian dead would live again, the buffalo would return, and the settlers would leave. Wovoka's vision developed into a

religious movement. Known to outsiders as the Ghost Dance, it inspired hope among Native Americans who were suffering terribly.

In August 1890 newspapers began suggesting that the Ghost Dance was a sign of a coming uprising. A small but very vocal group of whites began asking the government for help.

In December 1890 the U.S. military ordered the arrest of Sitting Bull, who had joined the Ghost Dance movement. A skirmish broke out, and Sitting Bull was killed. Many of Sitting Bull's band of Sioux fled west. The weary Sioux surrendered to U.S. troops, who took them to Wounded Knee Creek, in modern-day South Dakota, to make camp.

The Wounded Knee Massacre The next morning, Colonel James Forsyth of the 7th Cavalry ordered the Sioux to give up their rifles. One young man named Black Coyote did not want to give up his gun, and in his struggle with the soldiers, the gun went off. Instantly, the Sioux and the soldiers began shooting.

About half of the Sioux men were killed right away. Women and children fled, but soldiers pursued them. By the end of the fight, about 300 Sioux men, women, and children lay dead. Bodies of women and children were found as far as three miles from the camp.

The **Wounded Knee Massacre** shocked many Americans. General Nelson Miles was so outraged that he removed Forsyth from command. Others in the army did not share Miles' concern, however. Three officers and 15 enlisted men received the Medal of Honor for their actions.

Wounded Knee marked the end of the bloody conflict between the army and the Plains Indians. Black Elk, a survivor of the massacre, came to realize what the loss truly meant:

HISTORY'S VOICES

❝I did not know then how much was ended. When I look back now from this high hill of my old age, I can still see the butchered women and children . . . as plain as when I saw them with eyes still young. And I can see that something else died there in the bloody mud, and was buried in the blizzard. A people's dream died there. It was a beautiful dream . . .❞

—From "Black Elk Speaks," ca. 1932

READING CHECK Identifying the Main Idea
What were the U.S. Army and the Plains Indians fighting over in the Indian Wars?

THE IMPACT TODAY

Culture
To this day Wounded Knee remains a symbol of injustice toward Native Americans. In 1973, so-called "Wounded Knee II," a standoff between the U.S. military and Indians protesting discrimination, ended in the deaths of two Indian activists.

Info to Know
George Armstrong Custer Although he was a popular general, George Armstrong Custer had a mixed military record. He graduated at the bottom of his class at West Point, and in 1867 he was court-martialed and temporarily suspended from command for a number of offenses, including overmarching his troops and leaving his post without permission.

Biography
Charles Russell (1864–1926) Charles Russell, whose paintings of the West give us an enduring glimpse into the lives of cowboys and the Plains Indians, was the first "Western" artist who actually lived in the West. Russell admired the culture of the Northern Plains Indians and spent time during the summer of 1888 with the Blood Indians in Alberta, Canada. Russell mourned the impact that white settlement had on Native Americans, and he shows this in his paintings. In a letter to a friend, he once wrote, "The Red Man was the true American. The history of how they fought for their country is written in blood, a stain that time cannot grind out."

go.hrw.com
Online Resources
KEYWORD: SD7 CH13
TOPIC: NATIVE AMERICAN LEADERS

Collaborative Learning | At Level

Resolving Conflicts
1. Organize the class into groups of four. Have students within each group identify and list the sources of conflict between the Plains Indians and the government. *Sources of conflict might include killing buffalo; land use and reservations; outrage over massacres of Native Americans; raids on white settlements by Native Americans; failure to honor promises and treaties; and the Ghost Dance movement.*

2. Have each group develop treaties to bring the conflicts to an end. Treaties should include specific provisions to satisfy both Native Americans and the U.S. government. Treaties should be written, and their provisions numbered. Treaties should address the major sources of conflict between the groups.

3. Ask each group to read its treaty to the class, and have the class assess the recommendations considering both fairness and practicality.
LS Interpersonal
☐ Alternative Assessment Handbook, Rubric 14: Group Activity

Answers
Reading Check *The Plains Indians were fighting to protect their lands and their way of life against settlers moving west.*

441

❸ How did Native American resistance to white settlement end? *Native Americans were moved to reservations, captured, or defeated.*

Resistance Ends in the West

Explain Why did the government take back 90 percent of the Nez Percé reservation land? *The land was desired by settlers and gold miners.*

Evaluate Why do you think Geronimo and his followers went back to raiding settlements soon after returning to reservation life? *possible answer—being restricted to life on the reservation reminded the Apache how bad life was there, how free they used to be*

📄 CRF: Biography: Mary Lucinda Bonney

📄 Political Cartoons Activities for American History: Cartoon 25: Indian Agent

Faces of History
Chief Joseph
Summarize Use a large map to show students how far Chief Joseph led the Nez Percé and how close they came to Canada before capture. Have students calculate the miles the group traveled.

📄 American History Outline Maps: Relocation of American Indian Tribes

Answers

Faces of History *to preserve the Nez Percé way of life; to prevent his people from having to live on a small reservation*

Reading Check *Native Americans were forced to surrender; tribes were moved onto reservations*

442

ACADEMIC VOCABULARY
traditional
established, customary

Resistance Ends in the West

West of the Great Plains, Native Americans struggled to maintain their <u>traditional</u> ways of life. Their stories ended in tragedy as well.

Resistance in the Northwest In 1855 the Nez Percé (NEZ PUHRS) agreed to move onto a reservation in Idaho and Oregon. But in 1863, as gold miners and settlers began streaming onto the reservation, the U.S. government took back nine tenths of the Nez Percé land.

In 1877 the Indians were ordered to abandon the last portion of their Oregon homeland and move into a small section of Idaho. Their leader, **Chief Joseph,** reluctantly agreed. In the meantime, hostilities broke out among settlers and some young Nez Percé. The Indians—warriors, women, and children—were forced to flee, with the army in close pursuit.

The Nez Percé headed to Canada, fighting major battles as they fled. Less than 40 miles from the Canadian border, Joseph and his people were forced to surrender to the U.S. Army.

HISTORY'S VOICES

❝I am tired of fighting. Our chiefs are killed. . . It is cold, and we have no blankets. The little children are freezing to death. . . My heart is sick and sad. From where the sun now stands I will fight no more forever.❞
–Chief Joseph, statement at his surrender, 1877

FACES OF HISTORY
Chief JOSEPH
1840–1904

Chief Joseph became the leader of the Nez Percé in 1871. He struggled to preserve his people's way of life and their homeland in the forested Wallowa Valley. In 1877 when the U.S. government ordered the Nez Percé to relocate to a reservation, Joseph at first agreed, but then was forced to flee. He attempted to escape into Canada with about 750 of his people. On a historic journey across Idaho, Montana, Oregon, and Washington, they defeated pursuing troops who greatly outnumbered them. Traveling with families, low on supplies, the warriors managed to evade the U.S. Army for more than three months.

Ultimately, though, Chief Joseph saw that resistance was futile. To protect his hungry and exhausted people, Joseph surrendered. In the years that followed, the Nez Percé leader continued to speak out against the injustices of U.S. policy toward Native Americans.

Drawing Conclusions Why did Joseph hope to reach Canada?

Chief Joseph and his people were taken first to eastern Kansas and then to Indian Territory (present-day Oklahoma), where many died. Half of the Nez Percé were eventually returned to Idaho, but Chief Joseph and many others were sent to northern Washington State.

Resistance in the Southwest In the 1870s the government had moved the Apache peoples to the San Carlos Reservation along the Gila River in Arizona. Soldiers had forcefully stopped a religious gathering there in 1881. The Apache leader **Geronimo** fled the reservation with dozens of others.

Geronimo's band of Apache led raids on both sides of the Arizona-Mexico border for years. Geronimo briefly returned to reservation life in 1884. But soon he resumed raiding settlements. Captured one last time in September 1886, Geronimo and his followers were sent to an Apache internment camp in Florida as prisoners of war. Geronimo's surrender marked the end of armed resistance in the Southwest.

READING CHECK **Summarizing** How did Native American resistance end in the Northwest and Southwest regions?

Life on the Reservations

The U.S. government had two reasons for creating Indian reservations. First, it wanted control over all the western territories. Second, many Americans wanted Native Americans to abandon their traditional culture and religions and live like white Americans.

Americanization Starting in about 1870, the government's Indian policy changed yet again. Most government officials and reformers began to believe that Native Americans would be better off if they abandoned their culture and adopted the culture of white America. The new thinking was that instead of removal, treaties, reservations, or war, the government should pursue a policy of **Americanization**.

Americanization entailed a wholesale attack on Native American beliefs and practices, starting with tribal identity. The federal agency that managed the Native American reservations, the **Bureau of Indian Affairs** (BIA), began issuing wide-ranging orders that left few aspects of Indian culture untouched.

442 CHAPTER 13

Skills Focus: Making Written Presentations
At Level

Reading Like a Historian Skill
History Makers
Research Required

1. Have students select one person from the following list to research. Students should focus their research on the person's experience in the West and on the conflict in the region. Students will then create an illustrated biography of the person they have chosen: Black Elk; Black Kettle; Chief Joseph; George Armstrong Custer; Geronimo; James Forsyth; John M. Chivington; Quanah Parker; Ranald McKenzie; Sitting Bull; Wovoka

2. Biographies should describe how the person was regarded during his lifetime as well as how he is remembered today. Illustrations can be photocopies or hand-drawn illustrations of the person and key events in his life.

3. Ask volunteers to share their finished biographies and their illustrations with the class. 🄻🄢 **Verbal-Linguistic, Visual-Spatial**

📄 Alternative Assessment Handbook, Rubrics 4: Biographies; and 30: Research

❝You are therefore directed to induce your male Indians to cut their hair, and both sexes to stop painting [their faces]. . . The wearing of citizens' clothing, instead of the Indian costume and blanket, should be encouraged.❞

–BIA letter to Greenville Indian School, California, 1902

The government built schools for Native American children, often hundreds of miles away from the students' homes. In these schools, students could only speak English and could not wear their traditional clothing. Every effort was made to discourage students from practicing their own culture so that they might learn to live like white Americans.

The Dawes Act Congress took a significant step in the Americanization process when it passed the **Dawes Act** in 1887. The new law broke up most reservations and turned Native Americans into individual property owners. Each head of family received 160 acres. Each single person over 18 years old received 80 acres, and each child would receive 40 acres. Any land left over would be sold.

The BIA and reformers, some well-intentioned, believed this shift would transform the Indians' relationship to the land. Ownership would provide incentives to succeed, they thought—and then the federal government could slash support for reservations.

The Carlisle Indian Industrial School was a school for assimilation in Pennsylvania. Boys and girls were taught to read, write, and learn industrial and domestic activities of white American culture. The left photo shows some Lakota boys upon their arrival at the school. **What changes do you see in them in the right photo, after they have spent some time at the school?**

The government, however, gave the less productive land to the Indians and sold off the best land. Many Native Americans received near-desert lands unsuitable for farming. But even when Indians received good land, many could not afford the tools, animals, seed, and other supplies necessary to start farms.

READING CHECK **Identifying Supporting Details** What was the Dawes Act?

SECTION 1 ASSESSMENT

go.hrw.com
Online Quiz
Keyword: SD7 HP13

Reviewing Ideas, Terms, and People

1. **a. Explain** Why was the destruction of the buffalo significant to the lives of Native Americans on the Plains?
   b. Evaluate How did U.S. government policies bring the army into conflict with Plains Indians?

2. **a. Define** What were the Indian Wars?
   b. Compare How did Americans and Indians react to the **Sand Creek Massacre** and the **Wounded Knee Massacre**?

3. **a. Identify** Which events marked the end of armed resistance by Native Americans in the Northwest and the Southwest?
   b. Draw Conclusions What factors brought about the end of the Indian resistance?

4. **a. Describe** What was the process of **Americanization**?
   b. Make Inferences What did Americanization reveal about white Americans' views of Native Americans?

Critical Thinking

5. **Identifying Cause and Effect** Copy the chart below and record causes and effects of the Battle of the Little Bighorn.

Causes → Battle of the Little Bighorn → Effects

FOCUS ON WRITING

6. **Expository** Suppose you have been living among the Lakota Sioux. Newspapers have frightened local settlers by suggesting that the Ghost Dance is a sign of a coming Indian uprising. Write a letter to the editor explaining the true meaning of the Ghost Dance.

THE AMERICAN WEST **443**

Section 1 Assessment Answers

1. **a.** lost food source, means to build shelters and to make clothing
   b. government seized lands, forced Indians onto reservations

2. **a.** a long period of violence between Indians and settlers and the U.S. Army
   b. with anger, outrage at U.S. Army

3. **a.** Northwest—surrender of Nez Percé; Southwest—surrender of Geronimo
   b. deprived of food, shelter, and land; unable to continue fighting the U.S. Army

4. **a.** forcing Native Americans to adopt white culture
   b. showed lack of respect or understanding of Native Americans

5. Lakota Sioux raids against white settlers, Sioux refuse to return to reservation, Sitting Bull has vision of victory over U.S. Army; Indian camps, food supplies, and animals destroyed; Indians forced back onto reservation

6. possible answer—the dance expresses wish to return to traditional way of life

---

443

444 CHAPTER 13

Bellringer

The Inside Story. . . Use the **Daily Bellringer Transparency** to help students answer the question.

📖 Daily Bellringer Transparency, Section 2

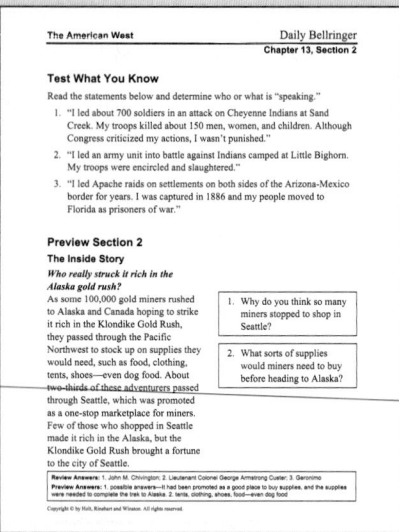

Academic Vocabulary

Review with students the high-use academic terms in this section.

invest put money into in order to gain a financial return (p. 446)

Taking Notes

Rise—cattle ranching offered a way to profit off prairie grasses, Texas longhorn bred, demand for beef rises, ranching as big business, invention of barbed wire; Fall— severe winters combined with drift fences killed thousands of cattle

---

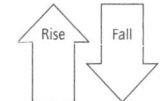

SECTION 2 Mining and Ranching

BEFORE YOU READ

MAIN IDEA

Many people sought fortunes during the mining and cattle booms of the American West.

FOCUS QUESTIONS

1. How did mining lead to new settlements in the West?
2. Why did mining become big business?
3. How and why did the cattle boom come to an end?

KEY TERMS AND PEOPLE

Comstock Lode
placer mining
hydraulic mining
hard-rock mining
Chisholm Trail
Joseph Glidden

TAKING NOTES As you read, take notes on the rise and fall of the cattle boom in the West. Record your notes in a graphic organizer like the one shown here.

Rise | Fall

Seattle Strikes it RICH

▲ Miners seeking gold in the Klondike stocked up on provisions in Seattle.

THE INSIDE STORY

Who really struck it rich in the Alaska gold rush? Gold in the Klondike! As the news spread, some 100,000 miners raced to Alaska. Several cities in the Pacific Northwest became boomtowns, but the richest by far was Seattle, Washington. Some two thirds of the prospectors passed through Seattle. Its merchants were ready, offering everything from tents to miners' shoes to "Alaska Dog Feed."

"The stores are ablaze with Klondike goods; men pass by robed in [odd] garments," a local newspaper reported in 1897. It observed "teams of trained dogs, trotting about with sleds; men with packs upon their backs, and a thousand and one things which are of use in the Klondike trade." Women could even get advice on choosing the right outfit.

The city's success was no accident. Erastus Brainerd, a former Boston museum curator, led an energetic campaign to promote Seattle as the one-stop marketplace for miners.

Few miners hit it rich in Alaska, of course. But the Klondike Gold Rush brought a fortune to the city of Seattle. ◢

444

Teach the Main Idea

At Level

Mining and Ranching

1. **Teach** Ask students the Reading Focus questions to teach this section.

2. **Apply** Have students work in pairs to create an outline of the section using the heads as main points. Have students identify and record at least two ideas under each main point in their outlines. **LS Interpersonal**

3. **Review** Review student outlines as a class. Have students identify the points in their outlines that they feel are most important to the mining industry and the cattle boom.

Discuss similarities and differences between mining and ranching.

4. **Practice/Homework** Have students decide whether they would have preferred the life of a miner or a rancher. Then have each student write a diary entry telling which way of life he or she would have preferred, and why. **LS Interpersonal, Logical-Mathematical**

📝 Alternative Assessment Handbook, Rubrics 11: Discussions; and 37: Writing Assignments

Striking Gold and Silver

The California gold rush of 1849 had captured the imaginations of many Americans. New mining strikes inspired thousands of people to rush to the West in search of fortune.

As the news of each new discovery spread, miners raced from one gold or silver strike to the next—to Idaho, Montana, the Black Hills of the Dakota Territory, Arizona, and to Cripple Creek, Colorado. Miners were excited by reports of others finding riches.

Discovering gold and silver After the California gold rush, the first promising mining discovery occurred in Colorado. In 1858 prospectors found gold near Pikes Peak. Thousands flocked to the area. Most left disappointed.

In 1859 prospectors found silver in the Carson River valley of present-day Nevada. Thousands of miners rushed to this mine, which became known as the **Comstock Lode**. Over the next 20 years, miners took about $500 million worth of silver from the Comstock Lode.

The Klondike gold rush "Gold! Gold! Gold!" shouted the headline of the *Seattle Post Intelligencer* on July 17, 1897. A huge gold strike had been made along the Klondike River in Canada's remote Yukon Territory near the Alaska border. Soon gold was discovered on the Alaska side of the border as well. Over the next year, about 100,000 Americans stampeded to the Klondike in search of riches.

Getting to the Klondike was treacherous. Canadian officials required that miners bring enough provisions for a year—nearly a ton of goods. Prospectors brought groceries, clothing, hardware, tents, packsaddles, camp stoves, bedding, and sleds. Prospectors made slow progress, having to move a year's worth of supplies—weighing as much as a ton—over rough terrain. One miner wrote about the hardship.

HISTORY'S VOICES

" My feet are sore, my heels are blistered, my legs sore and lame, my hands, neck, shoulders, sore and chafed from rope. But boys, don't think I'm discouraged. . . there is a golden glimmer in the distance. "

–Prospector Fred Dewey

Like the majority of gold seekers in previous gold rushes, most of the prospectors who reached the Klondike came away disappointed. The best gold-bearing creeks had already been claimed, and the reports of "gold for the taking" had been greatly exaggerated.

Mining camps Most prospectors were men. They came from all over the United States as well as from other nations. Thousands poured into mining areas from Mexico, England, Ireland, China, and many other countries.

Almost as soon as gold was discovered, prospectors would swarm into the region. They set up camps that were little more than groups of tents or hastily built shacks. Most camps had no law enforcement. Since miners were competing against each other for gold, the intense rivalry frequently led to violence.

Some people formed their own vigilante committees to combat theft and violence, but

PRIMARY SOURCES

Letter

Many of the gold seekers were like Hunter Fitzhugh, an unemployed young man who left Kentucky for Alaska in 1897. He gave up his quest after three years. This letter describes life in his mining camp.

"I am sitting in my flannel shirt sleeves . . . at our . . . dining table, by a little bit of window made of celluloid instead of glass . . . I am the cook this week, and am at present cooking peas, evaporated potatoes, evaporated eggs, tomatoes, and cornstarch pudding . . . I washed my shirt and my other pair of socks [yesterday evening], so don't have to repeat the performance for at least two months. The sun never sets now, and all night is just the same as all day . . . To be sure I long for home and civilization, . . . but on the other hand if I was in the States I would be under the eye and hand of a boss, or out of a job . . . I may get next to a claim this year that will net me $125,000.00 . . . who knows."

Skills FOCUS READING LIKE A HISTORIAN

1. **Making Inferences** What does Fitzhugh believe the future holds for him?

2. **Analyzing Primary Sources** What does Fitzhugh's description tell you about supplies and sanitary conditions in the mining camps?

See Skills Handbook, p. H28–29

THE AMERICAN WEST **445**

445

Mining as Big Business

Describe How did hard-rock mining change the mining industry? *It turned mining into an industry, and miners became employees of the companies.*

Analyze What conditions led miners to start unions? *dangerous working conditions*

Evaluate What made placer mining popular? *It could be done with simple hand tools; possibility of great wealth*

Info to Know

Looking for Gold High boat fares forced most prospectors to the Klondike to travel through Alaska on foot. Once there, the extreme conditions forced many to give up their dreams of riches and return to the United States. Historians estimate that more than 50,000 people who embarked on the trip turned around before they reached the Klondike.

Answers

Photo *prevented adequate water supply for crops, sent sediment into rivers, choked rivers, caused floods*

Reading Check (left) *Stores and other businesses quickly developed in the camps; families moved to camps and began to establish churches, newspapers, and town life;*
(right) *Large-scale mining techniques created dangerous working conditions. Miners had to dig mine shafts, build and work in tunnels. They faced cave-ins, underground fires, explosions, and flooded mines.*

446

ACADEMIC VOCABULARY
invest put money into in order to gain a financial return

their methods were often excessively violent. An accused criminal could be hanged after a speedy and unofficial "trial" of sorts.

Camps become towns Some of the sprawling mining camps developed into towns. These early towns had dirt streets, wooden sidewalks, and hastily constructed buildings. Stores and saloons sprang up, seemingly overnight.

As towns developed, more women and children came to join the men. The arrival of families often turned rough-and-tumble towns into prosperous, respectable communities. Townspeople established churches, schools, newspapers—even opera houses.

> **READING CHECK** **Sequencing** How did Western mining camps evolve into towns?

Mining as Big Business

In the early days of the Gold Rush, individual prospectors worked with hand tools. Some found gold through **placer mining**, in which minerals are found in loose sand or gravel. The simplest form of placer mining was panning for gold. It was a cheap but tough way for an individual to try to make money.

When the surface deposits of gold ran out, miners needed more sophisticated equipment to extract gold from deeper within the earth.

Large companies were formed to <u>invest</u> in this expensive equipment. By the 1880s, mining was dominated by these big companies.

Mining companies used two methods to extract the ore. **Hydraulic mining** used water under high pressure to blast away dirt, exposing the minerals underneath. This method sent sediment into rivers, choking them and causing floods. **Hard-rock mining** required cutting deep shafts in solid rock to extract the ore.

Miners became employees of mining companies rather than lone prospectors. They dug mine shafts, built tunnels, and drilled and processed ore. For some it was better than relying on their own luck. Yet it carried plenty of risks. Countless miners died in cave-ins, underground fires, explosions, and flooded mines.

In some towns, miners began to organize unions to negotiate for safer working conditions and better pay. The mining companies bitterly resisted these efforts. In Cripple Creek, Colorado, violent conflict broke out in 1903 between members of the Western Federation of Miners and corporate mining interests determined to crush the union. When it was over, 30 men had been killed in numerous gun battles, and the union was defeated.

> **READING CHECK** **Contrasting** How did working conditions for miners change once mining companies took over?

Hydraulic mining was a large-scale form of placer mining. Miners diverted water from a high to a low elevation. The water exited a small nozzle, called a monitor, at 5,000 pounds of pressure. Hydraulic mining was banned in 1884 because of its negative effects on farmers. *How did hydraulic mining affect farmers?*

446 CHAPTER 13

Skills Focus: Summarizing
At Level

Reading Skill
The Business of Mining

1. Have students describe and explain the changes that took place in mining, from individuals working with hand tools to the time when large corporations took over the mining industry.

2. Have each student write a letter to friends living on the East Coast from the viewpoint of a miner who had been self-employed but now works for a large mining company. The letter should tell of the changes that took place when mining companies took over and how those changes affected individual miners. Students should use facts from the textbook in writing their letters.

3. To adapt this activity for English-Language Learners, have students create a storyboard rather than write a letter.
LS Verbal-Linguistic, Visual-Spatial

Alternative Assessment Handbook, Rubrics 6: Cause and Effect; and 37: Writing Assignments

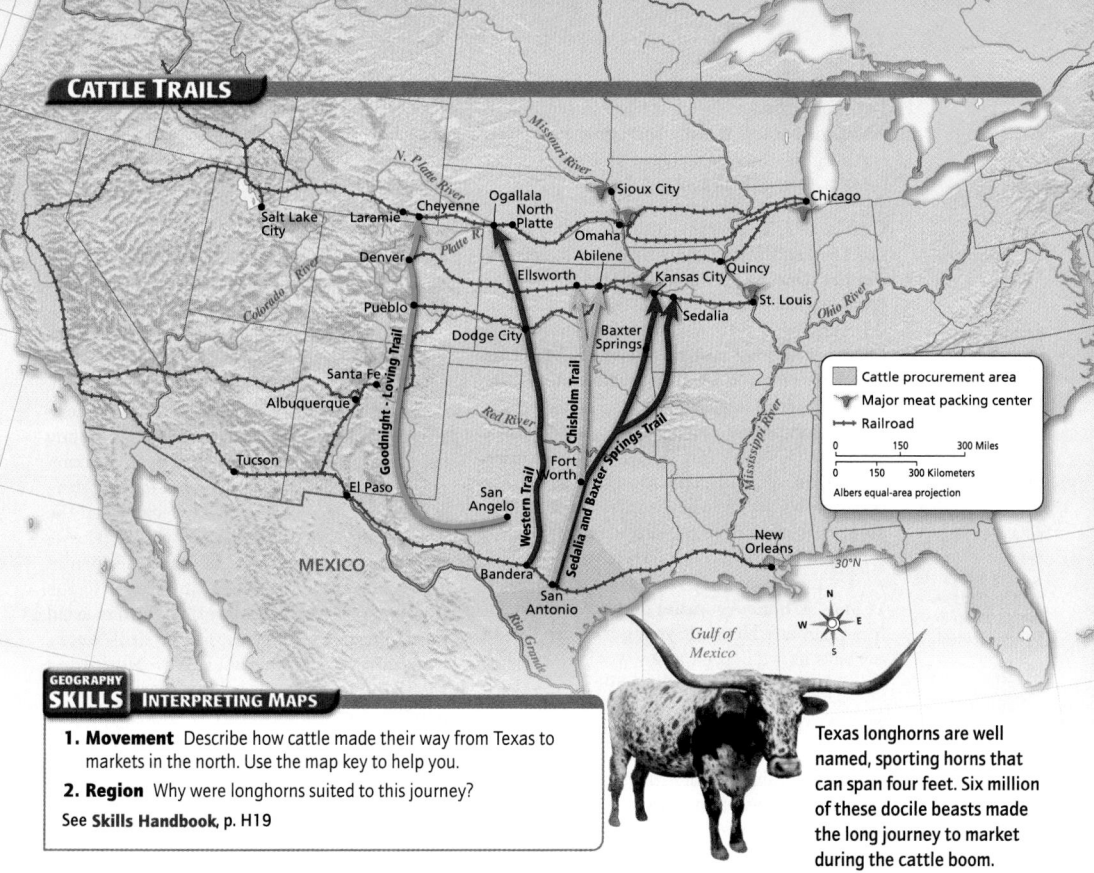

CATTLE TRAILS

Cattle procurement area
Major meat packing center
Railroad

0   150   300 Miles
0   150   300 Kilometers
Albers equal-area projection

Texas longhorns are well named, sporting horns that can span four feet. Six million of these docile beasts made the long journey to market during the cattle boom.

The Cattle Boom

In the decades after the Civil War, with the buffalo hunted to near extinction and most Native Americans confined to reservations, a new business came to dominate the economy of the Plains. Cattle ranching offered a way to "mine" the lush prairie grasses for profit.

Origins of Western ranching The first ranchers in the West were the Spanish, who brought cattle to the New World from Spain in the 1500s. The Spanish, and later the Mexicans, became adept at raising cattle under dry and difficult environmental conditions.

These ranchers interbred Spanish and English cattle to develop a new breed that thrived on the Plains: the Texas longhorn. Unlike other breeds, the Texas longhorn were hardy, could travel long distances without much water, and

could live on grass alone. They also had immunity to Texas fever, a disease that was deadly to other breeds of cattle.

The Spanish also introduced sheep ranching to the West. In the Southwest, Navajos and Pueblos raised sheep as well. After the Civil War, New England mills increased their demand for raw wool to produce cloth. Sheep ranchers responded to that demand by raising new breeds of sheep that produced more wool.

Cowboys complained that sheep ruined the grass for cattle by eating the roots. Conflicts between sheep owners and cattle owners sometimes became violent as they competed for grazing land on the open range.

Demand for beef After the Civil War, cities in the East clamored for beef to feed their growing populations. By 1866 a steer that might sell for as little as $4 in Texas could bring $40 up

THE AMERICAN WEST **447**

447

The Cattle Boom

Recall Who worked as cowboys on the cattle drives? *white teenage boys between the ages of 12 and 18, African American and Hispanic young men, some women*

Elaborate How did barbed wire affect cattle ranching? *grazing lands enclosed; privately owned cattle ranches; led to the deaths of thousands of cattle between 1885–1887*

📝 CRF: Primary Source Activity: Montana Cattle Country

Review & Assess

Close

Guide students in a discussion of the ways in which mining and cattle booms helped lure people west.

Review

🖥 Online Quiz, Section 2

🗄 Daily Test Practice Transparency

Assess

SE Section 2 Assessment

📝 Progress Assessment: Section 2 Quiz

📝 Alternative Assessment Handbook

Reteach

📝 Interactive Reader and Study Guide, Section 2

💿 Interactive Skills Tutor CD-ROM

Answers

Reading Check *Spanish and Mexican ranchers breed Texas longhorn cattle, who thrive in dry conditions; cities in East demand beef; subjugation of Native Americans creates safe areas for ranching to develop*

448

---

north. The age of the cattle drives had begun. Ranchers hired cowboys to drive the cattle to railheads, or towns with railroads, where the cattle could then be shipped to meatpacking centers such as Chicago.

Cattle trails Several different cattle trails ran from cattle country in Texas to major rail centers. One of the most important was the **Chisholm Trail**, which began in San Antonio, ran through Fort Worth, and ended in the Kansas towns of Abilene and Ellsworth. By 1871 as many as 600,000 cattle traveled along the Chisholm Trail in a single year.

The long drive north usually lasted three months. Cowboys gently urged the cattle northward, allowing them to graze along the trail for 10 or 12 miles a day. Pushing the animals faster risked causing a stampede.

About two thirds of the cowboys on the trail were white teenage boys between the ages of 12 and 18, but substantial numbers of African American and Hispanic young men worked as cowboys as well. Even a few women—usually disguised as men—rode the trails.

Ranching as big business Cattle owners often had trouble keeping track of their herds on the open range. By the 1870s, however, a new invention allowed ranchers to enclose some of their grazing lands. **Joseph Glidden** of De Kalb, Illinois, received a patent for barbed wire, a fencing material made of sharp, pointed pieces

THE IMPACT TODAY

Economics

Battles over land use continue today. Often they center on whether companies should be allowed to drill for oil and natural gas or to conduct logging operations in wilderness areas previously off-limits to development.

of wire, or barbs, wrapped around a strand of wire. Barbed wire made excellent fences on the Plains, where wood and stone were scarce.

Privately owned cattle ranches spread quickly across the Great Plains. Between 1882 and 1886, more than 400 cattle corporations sprang up in Wyoming, Montana, Colorado, and New Mexico. Most of these were backed by eastern and European investors. This transformed the cattle business into big business.

The enclosure of the open range led to conflicts between landless cattle owners and the ranchers and farmers who enclosed the land. Some ranchers were reckless with their enclosures, stringing barbed wire across public lands or other people's property, even blocking public roads. This set off a wave of fence cutting in 1883, which slowed the next year when the Texas legislature made fence cutting a felony.

The severe winters of 1885–1886 and 1886–1887 brought staggering losses to the cattle industry. Cattle migrating south to avoid harsh blizzards were trapped by drift fences, which stretched from eastern New Mexico and across the Texas Panhandle to Indian Territory (modern-day Oklahoma). The drift fences had been built to prevent the spread of cattle with Texas fever, but they proved deadly. Trapped by the fences, thousands of cattle perished in a disaster cattle owners called the "Big Die-up."

READING CHECK **Identifying Cause and Effect** What factors caused the Western cattle boom?

SECTION 2 ASSESSMENT

go.hrw.com
Online Quiz
Keyword: SD7 HP13

Reviewing Ideas, Terms, and People
1. **a. Recall** What difficulties did miners face in reaching the mining districts of the Klondike?
   b. Summarize How did mining lead to the establishment of new towns in the West?
2. **a. Describe** What resources did mining companies have that individual prospectors did not?
   b. Contrast How did **placer mining, hydraulic mining,** and **hard-rock mining** differ?
3. **a. Identify** What was the importance of the Texas longhorn?
   b. Make Generalizations How did ranching become established in the West?
4. **a. Describe** How did cowboys move cattle from ranch lands in southern Texas to the railroads in Kansas?

b. Evaluate What could have been done to avoid the problems that struck the Western cattle industry?

Critical Thinking
5. **Sequencing** Copy the chart below and record the sequence of events that led to the rise and fall of the cattle drives.

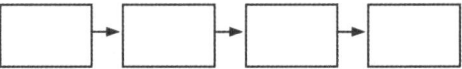

FOCUS ON WRITING ✏

6. **Expository** Take the position of a cattle owner who owned land in Texas or one who did not. Based on your position, write a letter arguing for or against the use of barbed wire on the open range.

448 CHAPTER 13

Section 2 Assessment Answers

1. **a.** far away; hard to reach; supplies had to be brought in over difficult terrain
   b. Miners congregated; stores and saloons sprang up; families came; towns developed.
2. **a.** well financed; able to buy machinery
   b. placer—minerals found in loose sand or gravel; hydraulic—water under high pressure blasts away dirt, exposing minerals; hard-rock—deep shafts cut into solid rock to reach and extract ores
3. **a.** well suited to dry climate; made ranching profitable

b. Spanish and Mexicans were skilled at raising cattle in the West; demand for beef increased; cattle ranches spread.

4. **a.** drove large herds along established trails
   b. providing ways to protect cattle

5. more land; Texas longhorn; increased demand for beef; barbed wire fences

6. for—protects grass, ensures adequate water supply; against—public lands should be open to all

3 Farming the Plains

BEFORE YOU READ

MAIN IDEA

The government promoted the settlement of the West, offering free or cheap land to those willing to put in the hard work of turning the land into productive farms.

READING FOCUS

1. What incentives encouraged farmers to settle in the West?
2. Which groups of people moved to the West, and why did they do so?
3. What new ways of farming evolved in the West?

KEY TERMS AND PEOPLE

sod house
Homestead Act
Pacific Railway Act
Morrill Act
Frederick Jackson Turner
Benjamin "Pap" Singleton
Exoduster
dugout
James Oliver
bonanza farm

TAKING NOTES As you read, take notes on government policies intended to encourage settlement of the West. Record your notes in a graphic organizer like the one shown here.

Policy	How It Encouraged Settlement

"Home, Sweet Soddie"

▶ The humble sod house had the advantage of being cool in the summer and warm in the winter. Notice the cow grazing on the roof.

THE INSIDE STORY *Could you live in a house made of dirt?* Uriah Oblinger, a Civil War veteran, staked his claim in Fillmore County, Nebraska, and began to build what he called his "sod mansion." Oblinger, along with his wife, Mattie, and their baby daughter, were among the thousands of pioneer families whose first home in the West was a **sod house**, or "soddie."

Sod is a strip or block of dense grass with the roots and soil attached. The tough roots of the prairie grasses made ideal sod. With some effort it could be cut and stacked like bricks to make thick-walled homes that stayed warm in harsh prairie winters and cool in the blazing summers. In the treeless Plains, sod was a popular building material.

In a letter home, Uriah reported proudly that in nine days, he had hauled the sod, built walls, and put in window and door frames. All that was left was to put on a roof and level the floor. Most soddies had dirt floors. People sometimes smoothed and whitewashed the inside walls.

In 1873, Mattie wrote to her family in Indiana: "At Home in our own house, and a sod at that! . . . I suppose you would like to see us in our sod house. It is not quite so convenient as a nice frame, but I would as soon live in it as the cabins I have lived in. And then we are at home which makes it more comfortable." Some women hated the constant fight with insects, dirt, and leaky roofs. Others, like Mattie, were just happy to have a home that they owned. ◼

THE AMERICAN WEST **449**

Preteach

Bellringer

The Inside Story. . . Use the **Daily Bellringer Transparency** to help students answer the question.

📰 Daily Bellringer Transparency, Section 3

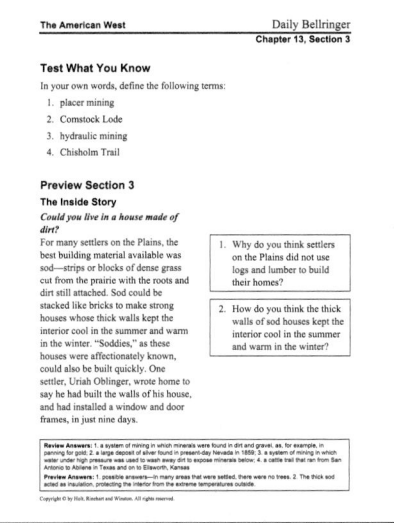

Academic Vocabulary

Review with students the high-use academic term in this section.

thesis a proposition put forth for argument (p. 451)

📄 CRF: Vocabulary Builder Activity, Section 3

Taking Notes

Policy—Homestead Act, Pacific Railway Act, Morrill Act, opening of Oklahoma to settlers; How It Encouraged Settlement—allowed any head of household to claim land and own it after five years, gave land to railroad companies to aid in the construction of railroad and telegraph lines, gave land to states to build colleges of agriculture and mechanic arts, thousands of settlers claimed land

---

Teach the Main Idea

At Level

Farming the Plains

1. **Teach** Ask students the Reading Focus questions to teach this section.

2. **Apply** Have students create a graphic organizer showing the provisions of the Homestead Act, the Pacific Railway Act, and the Morrill Act. **LS** **Verbal-Linguistic**

3. **Review** Review graphic organizers with the class. Ask students the following questions: What role did each act play in the economic development of the West?

   How did each of the three acts work either directly or indirectly to increase settlement?

4. **Practice/Homework** Have students select one of the acts and create a poster that shows potential benefits of the act. Display the finished posters for the class to see. **LS** **Visual-Spatial**

   📝 Alternative Assessment Handbook, Rubrics 13: Graphic Organizers; and 28: Posters

❶ What incentives encouraged farmers to settle in the West? *Homestead Act, opening of Oklahoma territory*

Incentives for Settlement

Explain Why was the Morrill Act significant? *It was the first time the federal government provided assistance for higher education.*

Summarize How did the railroad companies encourage settlement of the West? *They sold land they received from federal, state, and local government; advertised in Eastern newspapers and in Europe.*

Predict How do you think Native Americans might have reacted to the government decision to open Indian Territory to settlers? *possible answers—with resignation, regret, anger*

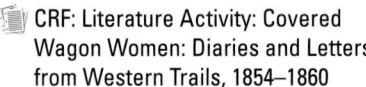 CRF: Literature Activity: Covered Wagon Women: Diaries and Letters from Western Trails, 1854–1860

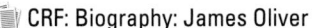 CRF: Biography: James Oliver

Info to Know

Bureau of Indian Affairs In 1775 the Continental Congress created a Committee on Indian Affairs with three departments, and both Benjamin Franklin and Patrick Henry served as departmental commissioners. In 1824 Secretary of War John Calhoun created the Office of Indian Affairs, and in 1834 Congress officially established the Department of Indian Affairs.

THE IMPACT TODAY

Science and Technology
Today, land-grant colleges make higher education widely accessible. Famous universities such as Michigan State and Texas A&M are at the forefront of technological research and innovation.

Incentives for Settlement

Major Stephen H. Long, an early visitor to the Great Plains, called the region "the Great American Desert." He believed the area was "unfit for cultivation, and of course uninhabitable by a people depending upon agriculture for their subsistence." A few decades later, with encouragement from the government, people began pouring onto the Plains to build farms.

New legislation Congress passed three acts in 1862 to turn public lands into private property. The **Homestead Act** allowed any head of household over the age of 21 to claim 160 acres of land. Each homesteader had to build a home on the land, make improvements, and farm the land for five years before being granted full ownership of the land by the government. Nearly 2 million people applied for land claims under this act. Most of the best land awarded under the Homestead Act was claimed before 1900, but the last homesteader received land in 1988.

The **Pacific Railway Act** of 1862 gave land to railroad companies to encourage the construction of railroad and telegraph lines. The **Morrill Act**, also passed by Congress in 1862, gave land to the states to provide colleges for "agriculture and the mechanic arts." Not all states actually built colleges on the land they received. Instead, many sold the land and used the proceeds to fund education. The Morrill Act was significant because it was the first time the federal government provided assistance for higher education.

Railroads encourage settlement Railroad companies lured settlers to the West. Within a few years of the passage of the Pacific Railway Act, the federal government had given the railroads some 125 million acres of public land. State and local governments had given nearly 100 million more acres.

Railroad companies reaped profits by selling some of the land to settlers. They placed ads in eastern newspapers, as well as in Europe, singing the praises of the American West. In the early 1900s railroads advertised that Montana was a farmer's paradise. In response to the ads, some 40,000 homestead claims were filed in Montana between 1906 and 1918, making it the favorite destination of homesteaders.

The Oklahoma Land Run of 1889 By the 1870s, treaties had resulted in the relocation of a number of Native American nations to Indian Territory (present-day Oklahoma). In

---

HISTORY CLOSE-UP

Oklahoma Land Rush

Between 1889 and 1895, five land runs drew thousands of new settlers to Oklahoma. The largest land run occurred in 1893. Settlers claimed seven million acres of land in an area known as the Cherokee Outlet on September 16, 1893.

Homesteaders await the trumpet calls, gunshots, and even cannon blasts that will signal the start of the land run.

Around 100,000 settlers rushed to claim land in the Cherokee Outlet.

450

Skills Focus: Comparing and Contrasting

At Level

Reading Skill
The Government's Role in the West

1. Write the following opinion for students to see: Government subsidies, not individual initiatives, were the main factor in the development of the American West.

2. Guide the class in a discussion of what this statement means. Ask students to identify and describe the government subsidies they have read about in this section.

3. Divide the class into two groups. Have one group write arguments that support the statement. Have the other group write arguments that disagree with the statement.

4. Conduct a class debate on the statement. After the debate, have students write a brief paragraph explaining and supporting their own position. **LS Logical-Mathematical**

Alternative Assessment Handbook, Rubrics 10: Debates; and 11: Discussions

1879, however, a Cherokee activist discovered that some 2 million acres in central Oklahoma had not been assigned to any nation. For 10 years settlers tried to move into these unassigned lands, despite presidential proclamations forbidding unlawful entry into Indian Territory. By the late 1880s, however, a political movement arose to open this area, and in 1889, it was opened to settlers.

On April 22, 1889, thousands of eager settlers lined up along the perimeter of these unassigned lands. At noon, federal troops gave the signal, and some 50,000 people rushed into the Oklahoma interior to stake their claim. A magazine described the founding of one town:

HISTORY'S VOICES

❝The city of Guthrie was built in . . . an afternoon. At twelve o'clock on Monday, April 22nd, the resident population of Guthrie was nothing; before sundown it was at least ten thousand. In that time streets had been laid out, town lots staked off, and steps taken toward the formation of a municipal government. At twilight the campfires of ten thousand people gleamed on the grassy slopes of the Cimarron Valley, where, the night before, the coyote, the gray wolf, and the deer had roamed undisturbed.❞

–William Willard Howard, *Harper's Weekly*, May 1889

Between 1889 and 1895, five different land runs brought countless settlers to live in Oklahoma. Not everyone who rushed there to claim land was fully prepared to settle, however. Some arrived with few provisions and no money. Many hopeful settlers became quickly discouraged and left once they realized they could not survive until the next year's crops came in.

Closing of the frontier For decades the U.S. Census Bureau had monitored the extent of American settlement. The frontier, according to the bureau, existed at a point where the population totaled fewer than 2 people per square mile.

In 1890 the Census Bureau issued a momentous report. It stated that "at present the unsettled area has been so broken into by isolated bodies of settlement that there can hardly be said to be a frontier line." In simpler terms, the federal government had declared the frontier closed.

The historian **Frederick Jackson Turner** seized on the news. Jackson believed that the existence of the frontier had made the United States distinctive. He explained his frontier thesis in an 1893 essay.

ACADEMIC VOCABULARY

thesis proposition put forth for argument

Like many frontier towns, Perry, Oklahoma, began to emerge within days of the opening of the Cherokee Outlet.

Skills FOCUS INTERPRETING VISUALS

Chaotic settlement patterns led to some conflicts between homesteaders and the people known as boomers and sooners. These were people who staked claims before the territory was legally opened to settlers. **Making Inferences** What other types of conflicts do you think might have arisen in the land rush?

See Skills Handbook, p. H7

THE AMERICAN WEST **451**

Primary Source

Kate Dunlap was a pioneer from Iowa who went to Montana in 1864. Her diary entries support the railroad companies' claims that Montana was a farmer's paradise:

"In N.W. Montana some of the vallies have a milder climate than Bannack, and the soil is very productive . . . Farming has been well tested, and the yield is much larger for wheat and potatoes than in Iowa. They have herds of cattle and horses, and the latter is the finest stock in the territory. It is reported . . . that as high as 60 bushels of wheat to the acre have been raised in favorable seasons. The yield of potatoes along the Bitter Root is enormous, at least three times greater than in Iowa. Fall and spring wheat do equally well, also oats."

— Kate Dunlap

Letter, January 30, 1865

Info to Know

Native American Population In the 1870s the Native American population in the West alone was approximately 300,000; between 1890 and 1910, the *total* Native American population of the United States had dropped to about 250,000.

go.hrw.com
Online Resources

KEYWORD: SD7 CH13
TOPIC: MOVING WEST

Skills Focus: Drawing Conclusions

At Level

Reading Skill
The Oklahoma Land Rush

1. Ask students to reread the information about the Oklahoma Land Rush. Have each student make a list of reasons to give the land to settlers and a list of reasons not to give the land away. *reasons to give land to settlers—to spur development, prevent possible violence; reasons not to give land to settlers—it was part of Indian Territory even though it had never been assigned to any tribe, President Hayes had issued a proclamation forbidding unlawful entry into the territory*

2. Have students evaluate their lists and decide which position they support.

3. Have each student create a political cartoon supporting his or her position about the land rush.

4. Have students share and explain their cartoons. **LS Verbal-Linguistic, Visual-Spatial**

📋 Alternative Assessment Handbook, Rubric 27: Political Cartoons

Answers

Interpreting Visuals *disputes over water, grazing rights; precise dividing lines between farms*

451

Reading Focus

② Which groups of people moved to the West, and why did they do so? *white settlers, cheap land; African Americans fled violence and oppression in the South; Europeans, economic opportunity; Chinese immigrants, gold rush and jobs building railroads*

Migrating West

Recall Where did most of the white settlers who moved west come from? *states in the Mississippi valley*

Summarize What happened when federal troops withdrew from the South in 1877? *segregation laws were passed; violent attacks on African Americans; many migrated*

Draw Conclusions Why do you think Chinese were prohibited from owning land? *possible answers—to help ensure that they would return to China; racism*

📰 Political Cartoons Activities for American History: Cartoon 26: African American Migration During and After Slavery

Faces of History
Benjamin Singleton

Elaborate Remind students of the importance of Kansas prior to and during the Civil War. Then ask why they think Singleton chose Kansas as the state to establish communities for African Americans.

Answers

Faces of History *protected runaway slaves; helped establish farming communities for former slaves*

Reading Check (left) *allowed any head of household over 21 to claim 160 acres of land; homesteader had to farm for 5 years before gaining full ownership of the land;* **(right)** *better economic opportunities; to acquire farmland for farming; to find jobs, including working on the railroads*

452

HISTORY'S VOICES

❝Up to our own day American history has been in a large degree the history of the colonization of the Great West. The existence of an area of free land, its continuous recession [moving back], and the advance of American settlement westward, explain American development.❞

–Frederick Jackson Turner

For more than a century, historians debated Turner's idea. Today most dispute it. Some point to other factors—such as slavery, immigration, and industrialization—as being more important to the country's development. Others question whether the term *frontier* should even apply to an area that was already inhabited by Native Americans.

READING CHECK **Summarizing** What did the Homestead Act do?

Migrating West

After the Civil War, most of the people moving West belonged to one of three major groups: white Americans from the East, African Americans from the South, and immigrants from foreign countries.

White settlers Most of the white settlers who moved West came from states in the Mississippi Valley, which had once been the frontier. So many people had moved to those states that cheap land was getting difficult to find. Still, those who went west were mostly middle-class farmers or businesspeople. They could afford the money for supplies and transportation.

African American settlers In the late 1870s, African Americans began a massive migration west. Some were inspired by the words of **Benjamin "Pap" Singleton**, a community builder and former slave who urged African Americans to build their own communities in the West. Others fled because of violence and oppression in the South. The withdrawal of federal troops from the South in 1877 led to segregation laws and violent attacks from groups such as the Ku Klux Klan.

Rumors soon spread throughout the South that the federal government would set aside Kansas for former slaves. The rumor turned out to be false, but some 15,000 African Americans moved to Kansas within the year in search of a peaceful life. The settlers became known as **Exodusters**. Tens of thousands of these Exodusters left the South and settled in Kansas, Missouri, Indiana, and Illinois.

European settlers The lure of economic opportunity brought thousands of Europeans to the west. Scandinavians from Sweden, Norway, and Finland poured onto the northern Plains in the 1870s, seeking farmland. Many Irish who had come to help build the railroads decided to stay and settle on the Plains. Many Russian Mennonites, members of a Protestant religious sect, brought their experience of farming on the Russian steppes, or grasslands, to the Great Plains. Huge numbers of Germans came to the United States as well. Many moved to the central part of Texas, creating a distinctive culture in that area.

Chinese settlers By the 1880s some of the Chinese immigrants who had come for the California gold rush or to build railroads had turned to farming, especially in California. Those who had experience as farmers in China introduced innovative techniques, helping to establish California's fruit industry. Although some Chinese farmed their own land, most ended up as farm laborers, usually because of laws that barred Chinese from owning land.

READING CHECK **Drawing Conclusions** Why did European immigrants move to the West?

FACES OF HISTORY

Benjamin SINGLETON
1809–1892

Born in Nashville, Tennessee, Benjamin Singleton escaped slavery and settled in the North. There, he protected runaway slaves. After the Civil War, Singleton returned to Tennessee determined to help the newly freed African Americans there purchase farmland. But white landowners refused to sell their land at fair prices.

Singleton found an answer. He established settlements in Kansas and encouraged former slaves to move west. Thousands did. These former slaves became known as Exodusters. The exodus peaked in 1879 two years after Reconstruction ended. Later in life, Singleton unsuccessfully tried to help resettle African Americans in Africa.

Sequence What steps did Singleton take to try to help African Americans gain better lives?

452 CHAPTER 13

Differentiating Instruction   **Above Level**

Advanced Learners/GATE   **Research Required**

1. Have students read more about Frederick Jackson Turner and his thesis that it was the existence of the frontier that made the U.S. distinctive. They may want to read the first chapter of his book *The Frontier in American History*, where he summarizes his views.

2. Have each student write an essay in which he or she takes a position in regard to Jackson's thesis, either agreeing with it or disagreeing with it. Students who disagree should tell which factor or factors they think were most important in making the United States what it is. All students should back their opinions with valid arguments. Have volunteers read their essays.

3. Ask students if they agreed or disagreed with Jackson. Ask those who disagreed what they think the leading factors were in making the U.S. distinct from other countries.

LS Logical-Mathematical, Verbal-Linguistic

📄 Alternative Assessment Handbook, Rubric 37: Writing Assignments

New Ways of Farming

The journey west was expensive and full of hardships. But once farmers staked a claim on a homestead, they faced new challenges.

First, the climate was harsh. Winters could be bitterly cold as snowstorms rushed down from Canada. Summers were fiercely hot, causing crops to shrivel and die.

Water was scarce, forcing farmers to dig wells and install windmill-driven pumps. In the Southwest, some settlers used Hispanic and Native American irrigation techniques. Their farms stretched out in strips from water sources so that each would have water access.

Without lumber to build houses, many settlers used the earth itself. Some early settlers built **dugouts**, shelters dug into the sides of hills. They soon replaced dugouts with sturdy sod houses.

Farming in a new environment New kinds of farming equipment helped farmers meet the challenge of farming on the Plains. **James Oliver** developed a new plow with a sharper edge that helped Plains farmers plow their fields with much less effort. Machines called combine harvesters cut wheat, separated the grains from the stalks, and removed the husks from the grains all in one operation. Such equipment was expensive, and many small farmers went into debt to buy it.

Challenges for Farmers — QUICK FACTS

- **Harsh climate:** from bitter snowstorms to fierce heat and drought
- **Scarce water:** low rainfall and few rivers
- **Lumber shortage:** few wood sources for home-building or heating

Pumps powered by windmills drew water from deep underground.

Farming as big business Large companies soon saw a business opportunity on the Plains. They created giant **bonanza farms**. These farms operated like factories, with expensive machinery, professional managers, and laborers who performed specialized tasks.

Owners of bonanza farms reaped great profits during good growing seasons. During bad growing seasons, they struggled to maintain equipment and pay workers. Small family farmers with fewer expenses often handled the boom-and-bust cycles better than the big companies. By the 1890s, most bonanza farms had been broken up.

READING CHECK **Identifying Problems and Solutions** How did farmers deal with the harsh environment of the Great Plains?

---

go.hrw.com
Online Quiz
Keyword: SD7 HP13

SECTION 3 ASSESSMENT

Reviewing Ideas, Terms, and People

1. **a. Define** Write a brief definition of the following terms: Homestead Act, Pacific Railway Act, Morrill Act
   b. Evaluate Do you think the West would have been settled as quickly without U.S. government incentives? Explain.
2. **a. Identify** Which groups of people decided to move West?
   b. Explain Why did the **Exodusters** leave the South, and why did they choose to move to Kansas?
   c. Predict Which kinds of people do you think would be most successful in establishing a new farm on the Plains?
3. **a. Recall** What factors made farming different in the West than in the East?
   b. Compare and Contrast How were **dugouts** and **sod houses** similar? How were they different?
   c. Evaluate How did farmers adapt their lives because of the scarcity of resources?

Critical Thinking

4. **Comparing** How did the government and the railroads promote settlement in the West?

Government	Railroads

FOCUS ON WRITING

5. **Descriptive** Suppose you and your family are living on the prairie. Write a letter to your friend back East describing the challenges of living in a sod house.

THE AMERICAN WEST **453**

Section 3 Assessment Answers

1. **a.** Homestead Act—allowed head of household to claim 160 acres of land; Pacific Railway Act—gave land to railroad companies; Morrill Act—gave land to states for colleges
   b. no, free or cheap land was key

2. **a.** middle-class farmers and businesspeople; African Americans; European immigrants
   b. to escape violence and oppression, to purchase their own farmland
   c. people used to harsh climates, long winters, who knew how to farm; those with enough resources to support themselves

3. **a.** water was scarce; soil hard to plow; climate was harsh
   b. similar—small, created from the earth; different—dugouts were shelters dug out of the sides of hills; sod houses were above ground, built with squares of turf and prairie soil
   c. dug wells, built windmills, used irrigation; used resources other than wood for building

4. Homestead Act, Pacific Railway Act, Morrill Act; opened parts of Oklahoma to settlers; railroad companies advertised to sell land

5. small, made of earth, little light

Direct Teach

Reading Focus

3 What new ways of farming evolved in the West? *new machinery, bonanza farms*

New Ways of Farming

Explain How did settlers in the Southwest adapt their farming methods to the dry conditions? *They used irrigation, dividing land in long strips along water sources so that each farmer would have access to water.*

Contrast Why were bonanza farms more susceptible to boom-and-bust cycles than family farms? *bonanza farms required expensive machinery and hired laborers; family farmers were smaller, did not have to pay for labor or large amount of equipment*

Quick Facts Transparency: Challenges for Farmers

Review & Assess

Close

Have students summarize the ways in which the government promoted the settlement of the West.

Review

Online Quiz, Section 3

Daily Test Practice Transparency

Assess

SE Section 3 Assessment

Progress Assessment: Section 3 Quiz

Alternative Assessment Handbook

Reteach

Interactive Reader and Study Guide, Section 3

Interactive Skills Tutor CD-ROM

Answers

Reading Check *They dug water wells; built dugouts and sod houses; used new types of farming equipment, including plows.*

453

Word Help

improvements changes or additions

privations lack of ordinary necessities of life

Primary Source

"A might nation moving west,
With all its steely sinews set
Against the living forest.
Hear the shouts, the shots of pioneer,
The rended forests, rolling wheels."

— Joaquin Miller

Westward Ho!, 1871

Info to Know

Farming the Great Plains After the Civil War, new inventions started a revolution in farming. Barbed wire reduced the cost of fencing, redesigned windmills brought water from underground, and improved farm machinery cut labor costs. Under the Homestead Act, farmers could obtain 160 acres of land. Soon farms of every size dotted the Plains. As the number of farms grew, the price of crops began to fall. Between 1867 and 1896, prices fell by over 50 percent. Struggling to get out of debt, farmers planted more crops, driving prices ever lower. To add insult to injury, it often cost farmers more to transport their crops to market than the produce was worth.

Influences on Homesteaders

Historical Context The documents below provide different perspectives on why homesteaders moved west.

Task Examine the documents and answer the questions that follow. Then, you will be asked to write an essay about the reasons homesteaders moved west, using facts from the documents and from the chapter to support the position you take in your thesis statement.

DOCUMENT 1

People moved west for a great variety of reasons. Some were drawn there by so-called "pull factors"—aspects of the West that attracted people. Other people were motivated by "push factors"—conditions that made them want to leave their homes and start a new life elsewhere. Many people picked up and headed west to escape desperate poverty in eastern cities.

DOCUMENT 2

Many people who migrated west wrote letters back home to tell family members about their experiences. Uriah Oblinger was an impoverished young man from Indiana who fell in love with Mattie Thomas. To earn enough money to support a family, he kept moving farther west, looking for job opportunities and land. After they finally married in 1869, Uriah and Mattie settled a homestead in Nebraska, taking advantage of the opportunities created by the Homestead Act of 1862. During their years on the farm, Mattie wrote many letters to her family back in Indiana telling them about the opportunities in Nebraska.

"I think George & Grizzie would do well to come west if their money will not go far enough there for them . . . [W]e will be as well off as they are in a few years. We can say now that we own 160 [acres] and all it wants is improvements and I am sure it is a healthy place. Poor little Earny! It is too bad he must have the chills so much. If I was them I would be willing to sacrifice some of my enjoyments to endure a few privations for the sake of having health in my family. I am very sure they would be healthier here, but I shall not urge them to come for fear they would not be satisfied & then we would be to blame. Do you ever hear how Al Shoap likes the west? Is he in the grasshopper region? Tell Doc we will write to him soon to be patient & wait."

Collaborative Learning

At Level

Push-Pull Factors

1. Create a chart on the board with a column labeled *Push* and a column labeled *Pull*. Have students copy the chart into their notes.

2. Divide the class into small groups. Have each group fill in the chart with factors that made homesteaders want to leave their homes and factors that attracted homesteaders to the West.

3. Have volunteers fill in the class chart. Have students correct their charts and retain them as a study tool.

4. Guide students in a discussion of the factors that let to migration west. Did *push* or *pull* factors play a greater role? Which factor do students think provided the biggest motivation for migration? **LS Interpersonal, Logical-Mathematical**

   Alternative Assessment Handbook, Rubric 7: Charts

DOCUMENT 3

The U.S. government and land agents used advertisements such as posters and fliers to encourage people to move west. The following advertisement was for an offer of land being sold by a railroad company.

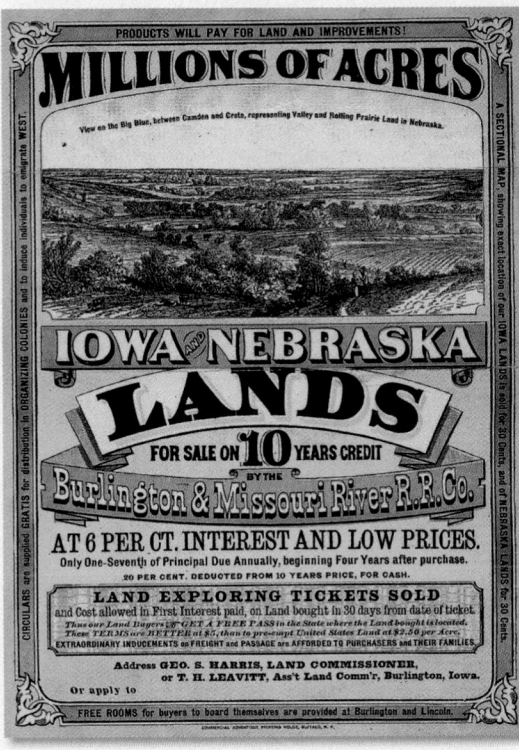

SKILLS FOCUS **READING LIKE A HISTORIAN**

1. **a. Describe** Refer to Document 1. Would the situation shown in the photograph be a push factor or a pull factor for westward migration?
   b. Analyze How do you think life would be different for these families if they moved west?

2. **a. Identify** Refer to Document 2. How does the experience of the Oblingers illustrate both push factors and pull factors?
   b. Elaborate Do you think that Mattie Oblinger's arguments for moving west are persuasive? Explain.

3. **a. Identify** Refer to Document 3. What is the purpose of this advertisement?
   b. Interpret How might people like those in Document 1 have been influenced by the ad in Document 3?

4. **Document-based Essay Question** Consider the question below and form a thesis statement. Using examples from Documents 1, 2, and 3, create an outline and write a short essay supporting your position.
   Why did people move west in the late 1800s?
   See Skills Handbook, pp. H28–29, H30

Skills Focus: Making Inferences

At Level

Reading Skill
Homestead Life

1. Guide the class in a discussion of the Homestead Act of 1862. How did it affect western migration? What part did railroads play in the settling of the West?

2. Have each student write a letter from a homesteader to a relative back East. Students should describe their reasons for moving west and compare life on a prairie homestead to life in the East. Have volunteers read their letters to the class.

3. As an extension, have students exchange letters and write a letter in response.
   LS Verbal-Linguistic

   Alternative Assessment Handbook, Rubric 25: Personal Letters

Visual Summary

Review and Inquiry Review the information in the chart with the students and discuss each effect. Point out to students that each of the effects shown in the chart could be considered a cause that had its own effects. Have students create another cause and effect chart using the effects shown here as causes. Then have them work in pairs to list effects of each new cause. *possible answers—Native American culture destroyed; towns develop from mining camps; ranchers suffer economic hardship during severe winters and from depending upon single crop; frontier is gone, forests and plains disappear as towns and cities develop*

📦 Quick Facts Transparency: The American West

Reviewing Key Terms and People

1. d.
2. k.
3. i.
4. h.
5. m.
6. g.
7. f.
8. e.
9. b.
10. j.
11. c.
12. a.
13. l.

Comprehension and Critical Thinking

14. a. Cheyenne under Chief Black Kettle returned to their Sand Creek reservation where U.S. troops killed 150 Indians, mainly women, children, and elderly, and burned their camp; outrage
b. U.S. forces became determined to confine Native Americans on reservations to free up land for white settlers.
c. Some tribes fought to keep white settlers from traveling through or taking their land; some tribes

Visual Summary: The American West

Cause
• Westward Expansion

Effects
• Native Americans were massacred, sent to reservations, their lands stolen, their culture destroyed
• Mining boom created new towns and businesses
• Cattle boom created new trails and ranches
• Farmers settled the Plains, building communities

Reviewing Key Terms and People

Match each lettered definition with the correct numbered item below.

a. A breed of cattle that thrived under the harsh conditions of the Great Plains
b. A law that allowed any adult head of household to claim 160 acres of land
c. Homes built on the prairie from squares of turf and soil
d. The process used to force Native Americans to abandon their traditional ways of life
e. A method used to extract minerals by cutting deep ridges in solid rock
f. African Americans who moved from southern states to Kansas after the end of Reconstruction
g. Homes built into the sides of hills on the prairie
h. One of the most important routes used to drive cattle from Texas to rail centers in Kansas

i. The federal agency that managed the Native American reservations
j. A method used to extract minerals by using water under high pressure
k. The last Sioux victory in battle against the U.S. Army
l. The violent event that marked the end of the war between the Plains Indians and the U.S. Army
m. The law that divided reservation land among individual Native Americans

1. Americanization
2. Battle of the Little Bighorn
3. Bureau of Indian Affairs
4. Chisholm Trail
5. Dawes Act
6. dugouts
7. Exodusters
8. hard-rock mining
9. Homestead Act
10. hydraulic mining
11. sod houses
12. Texas longhorn
13. Wounded Knee Massacre

fought hard against U.S. troops; other tribes moved, or were forcibly moved, onto reservation lands set aside for them.

15. a. working with hand tools to find gold in loose sand or gravel
b. When surface deposits gave out, miners needed very expensive equipment to continue mining. Placer mining did not yield great riches.
c. Placer mining was quickly exhausted. Big businesses could afford the expensive machinery needed to extract gold. Companies were large and well-financed.

16. a. Pacific Railway Act—gave federal land to railroad companies for construction of railroads and telegraph lines; Morrill Act—gave federal land to states for colleges
b. possible answer—Railroads provided the means for expanding settlements, building the basis for new industries, linking the country from coast to coast, creating one nation.
c. possible answer—opened up vast amount of land to ranching and farming

History's Impact video program
Review the video to answer the closing question:
How have forms of communication changed over time?

Comprehension and Critical Thinking

SECTION 1 *(pp. 438–443)*

14. a. Identify What was the Sand Creek Massacre, and how did people react to it?

b. Analyze How did the Indian Wars reflect changes in U.S. government policy toward Native Americans that occurred when white Americans began moving onto the Great Plains?

c. Elaborate Describe the differing responses of Native Americans and their leaders to the actions of the U.S. Army during the Indian Wars.

SECTION 2 *(pp. 444–448)*

15. a. Recall What was placer mining?

b. Draw Conclusions Why did very few individuals become rich through mining?

c. Analyze What factors caused western mining to become dominated by large corporations rather than individual prospectors?

SECTION 3 *(pp. 449–453)*

16. a. Describe What was the purpose of the Pacific Railway Act and the Morrill Act?

b. Make Inferences Why was the federal government interested in helping the railroad companies expand throughout the West?

c. Evaluate What effects did the expansion of the railroads have on the economy, land use, and population of the West?

Using the Internet

**go.hrw.com
Practice Online
Keyword: SD7 CH13**

17. During the gold and silver rushes of the late 1800s, people often abandoned mining towns as soon as the mineral deposits were exhausted. Using the keyword above, do research to learn about ghost towns of the West. Then create a report that tells the story of one town, from its founding to its decline.

Analyzing Primary Sources

Reading Like a Historian

18. Describe What do you think the stacked bags may be?

19. Draw Conclusions Why was this moment important enough to be photographed?

Critical Reading

Read the passage in Section 3 that begins with the heading "The Oklahoma Land Run of 1889." Then answer the questions that follow.

20. Why was land in Oklahoma Territory made available to settlers in 1889?

A The federal government had purchased the land from Native Americans.

B The Homestead Act made the land available.

C The government gave in to pressure from settlers to open the unassigned lands.

D Railroad companies sold the land to pay for expansion of the railroads.

21. How did the unassigned lands change at noon on April 22, 1889?

A All lands had been claimed by that time.

B Thousands of people rushed into the unassigned lands to stake their claims.

C The town of Guthrie had been laid out by noon.

D Municipal government had been formed.

FOCUS ON WRITING

Expository Writing *Expository writing gives information, explains why or how, or defines a process. To practice expository writing, complete the assignment below.*

Writing Topic The settlement of the West

22. Based on what you have read in this chapter, write a paragraph that explains how Americans settled the West in the late 1800s and how the region changed as a result.

Answers

Using the Internet

17. Go to the HRW Web site and enter the keyword shown to access a rubric for this activity.

KEYWORD: SD7 CH13

Analyzing Primary Sources

18. supplies for miners

19. The large amount of supplies shows the massive number of miners trying to find gold.

Critical Reading

20. C

21. B

Focus on Writing

22. possible answer—moved to West as miners, farmers, ranchers; began to farm and ranch; government provided free land to settlers; railroads built, towns established.

A rubric for this activity is provided in Chapter Resource File: Focus on Writing: The Settlement of the West.

History's Impact Video Program

Communication has become much faster as forms of communication have grown more technologically advanced.

Review and Assessment Resources

Review and Reinforce

📓 CRF: Chapter Review Activity

💾 Quick Facts Transparencies: Challenges for Farmers; The American West

🔊 Spanish Chapter Summaries Audio CD Program

🌐 Online Chapter Summaries in Spanish

OSP Holt PuzzlePro; Quiz Show for ExamView

💿 Quiz Game CD-ROM

Assess

📓 PASS: Chapter Test, Forms A and B

📓 Alternative Assessment Handbook

OSP ExamView Test Generator, Chapter Test

💿 Differentiated Instruction Modified Worksheets and Tests CD-ROM: Chapter Test

HOAP Holt Online Assessment Program (in the Premier Online Edition)

Reteach/Intervene

📓 Interactive Reader and Study Guide

📓 Differentiated Instruction Teacher Management System: Lesson Plans for Differentiated Instruction

💿 Differentiated Instruction Modified Worksheets and Tests CD-ROM: Chapter Test

💿 Interactive Skills Tutor CD-ROM

**go.hrw.com
Online Resources**

KEYWORD: SD7 CH13

Chapter 14 Planning Guide

The Second Industrial Revolution

Chapter Overview	Reproducible Resources	Technology Resources
CHAPTER 14 pp. 458–485 **Overview:** In this chapter, students will analyze the causes of the Second Industrial Revolution and the effects it had on American businesses and people.	**Differentiated Instruction Teacher Management System:*** • Instructional Benchmarking Guides • Lesson Plans for Differentiated Instruction **Interactive Reader and Study Guide:** Chapter Summary* **Chapter Resource File:*** • Writing for the SAT: Innovation • Social Studies Skills Activity: Interpreting Literature as Historical Evidence • Chapter Review Activity **American History Outline Maps** **Pre-AP Activities Guide for American History***	**Live Ink® Online Reading Help** **Student Edition on Audio CD Program** **Differentiated Instruction Modified Worksheets and Tests CD-ROM** **Interactive Skills Tutor CD-ROM** **United States History Primary Source Library CD-ROM** **Power Presentations with Video CD-ROM** **History's Impact: American History Video Program (VHS/DVD):** The Second Industrial Revolution **Online Chapter Summaries in Spanish** **Graphic Organizer Transparencies**
Section 1: **Industry and Railroads** **The Main Idea:** During the late 1800s, new technology led to rapid industrial growth and the expansion of railroads.	**Differentiated Instruction Teacher Management System:** Section 1 Lesson Plan* **Interactive Reader and Study Guide:** Section 1 Summary* **Chapter Resource File:*** • Vocabulary Builder Activity, Section 1	**Daily Bellringer Transparency:** Section 1* **Interactive Map:** Railroads Built By 1910* **Map Transparency:** Railroads Built By 1910* **Daily Test Practice Transparency:** Section 1*
Section 2: **The Rise of Big Business** **The Main Idea:** Corporations run by powerful business leaders became a dominant force in the American economy.	**Differentiated Instruction Teacher Management System:** Section 2 Lesson Plan* **Interactive Reader and Study Guide:** Section 2 Summary* **Chapter Resource File:*** • Vocabulary Builder Activity, Section 2	**Daily Bellringer Transparency:** Section 2* **Daily Test Practice Transparency:** Section 2*
Section 3: **Workers Organize** **The Main Idea:** Grim working conditions in many industries led workers to form unions and stage labor strikes.	**Differentiated Instruction Teacher Management System:** Section 3 Lesson Plan* **Interactive Reader and Study Guide:** Section 3 Summary* **Chapter Resource File:*** • Vocabulary Builder Activity, Section 3	**Daily Bellringer Transparency:** Section 3* **Daily Test Practice Transparency:** Section 3*
Section 4: **The Age of Invention** **The Main Idea:** Important innovations in transportation and communication occurred during the Second Industrial Revolution.	**Differentiated Instruction Teacher Management System:** Section 4 Lesson Plan* **Interactive Reader and Study Guide:** Section 4 Summary* **Chapter Resource File:*** • Vocabulary Builder Activity, Section 4	**Daily Bellringer Transparency:** Section 4* **Daily Test Practice Transparency:** Section 4*

 go.hrw.com  Print Resource  Transparency

LS Learning Styles  Audio CD CD-ROM

VIDEO Video **SE** Student Edition **TE** Teacher's Edition

OSP One-Stop Planner CD-ROM

*also on One-Stop Planner CD-ROM

HOLT

History's Impact
American History Video Program (VHS/DVD)

The Second Industrial Revolution

Review, Assessment, Intervention

 Quick Facts Transparency: The Second Industrial Revolution

 Spanish Chapter Summaries Audio CD Program

 Progress Assessment Support System (PASS): Chapter Test*

Differentiated Instruction Modified Worksheets and Tests CD-ROM: Modified Chapter Test

OSP **One-Stop Planner CD-ROM:** ExamView Test Generator (English/Spanish)

HOAP **Holt Online Assessment Program (HOAP),** in the Holt Premier Online Student Edition

 PASS: Section 1 Quiz*

 Online Quiz: Section 1

 Alternative Assessment Handbook

 PASS: Section 2 Quiz*

 Online Quiz: Section 2

 Alternative Assessment Handbook

 PASS: Section 3 Quiz*

 Online Quiz: Section 3

 Alternative Assessment Handbook

PASS: Section 4 Quiz*

Online Quiz: Section 4

Alternative Assessment Handbook

NC RESOURCES

The following resources were developed to help North Carolina educators teach the standards and objectives of North Carolina's eleventh grade standard course of study in United States history.

- United States history EOC Test Prep Workbook
- Teacher's Support System
- North Carolina One-Stop Planner

And be sure to direct your students to **go.hrw.com** for online access to the EOC Test Prep Workbook.

go.hrw.com
EOC Test Prep
KEYWORD: SE7 NC

Holt Online Learning

go.hrw.com
Teacher Resources
KEYWORD: SD7 TEACHER

go.hrw.com
Student Resources
KEYWORD: SD7 CH14

- Document-based Questions
- Interactive Multimedia Activities
- Current Events
- Chapter-based Internet Activities
- and more!

Holt Premier
Online Student Edition
Complete online support for interactivity, assessment, and reporting

- Interactive Maps and Notebook
- Standardized Test Prep
- Homework Practice and Research Activities Online

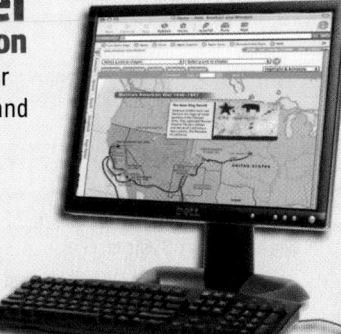

CHAPTER 14 PLANNING GUIDE

Before You Teach

The Big Picture

Edward L. Ayers

Industry and Railroads Factories and railroads had emerged in the United States in the first half of the nineteenth century, but both spread and developed rapidly after the Civil War. Steel and oil were new arrivals on the scene, produced with innovative technologies and put to new uses. Railroads became the engines that drove much of the new economy, transforming every part of the country. Much westward migration took place on railroads, not in wagons.

The Rise of Big Business Many Americans, impressed with the transformative power of the new industries and forms of transportation, thought it best to let them grow unchecked by government oversight. In this environment, innovation and monopoly went hand-in-hand as capitalists with virtually unlimited means quickly dominated the most rapidly growing industries, accumulating unprecedented fortunes in the process.

Workers Organize Faced with stagnant wages, child labor, dangerous conditions, competition from immigrants, and little help from the government, American workers renewed their efforts to organize themselves to win what they considered their due. In a series of major strikes, they attempted to use their numbers to weigh against employers who seemed to hold all the cards. Despite impressive successes in organizing, workers won few long-term victories.

The Age of Invention With vast amounts of capital available for investment and spending, Americans innovated feverishly in the late nineteenth and early twentieth centuries. In both transportation and communication, in particular, the United States became a world leader in its creativity and effectiveness in getting new products to market.

Recent Scholarship

Causes of Industrialization Industrialization is often seen as a process distinct from the American landscape, an urban phenomenon that had defined itself by its distance from rural people and ways of life. William Cronon's remarkable book *Nature's Metropolis: Chicago and the Great West* (1991) shows that, in fact, the rise of an industrial America stretched far from the cities and deep into the life of the countryside. Through ingenious research and revealing maps, Cronon reveals that railroads, cattle, wheat, banking, and other aspects of industrial life transformed vast areas of the Midwest.

Differentiating Instruction

 Differentiated Instruction Teacher Management System
- Lesson Plans for Differentiated Instruction
- Differentiated Instructional Benchmarking Guides
- Interactive Reader and Study Guide

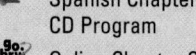 Spanish Chapter Summaries Audio CD Program

Online Chapter Summaries in Spanish

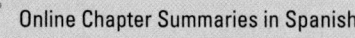 Student Edition on Audio CD Program

 Differentiated Instruction Modified Worksheets and Tests CD-ROM
- Vocabulary Flash Cards
- Modified Vocabulary Builder Activities
- Modified Chapter Review Activity
- Modified Chapter Test

OSP One-Stop Planner CD-ROM
- ExamView Test Generator (English and Spanish)
- PuzzlePro
- Quiz Show for ExamView
- Transparencies and Videos

TE Differentiated Activities in the Teacher's Edition
- Social Darwinism, p. 467
- Advances in Transportation, p. 478
- Lewis Hine's Photographs, p. 483

Reading Like a Historian
Sam Wineburg

Interpreting Cartoons

We often assume that editorial cartoons are easy for students because they convey their message with a picture and few words. Viewing an image of smoking towers alongside a turbaned figure, we get the message instantly. Yet the very aspect that makes a contemporary image accessible is often what renders images from the past inscrutable. We do not get the joke.

The Problem

But there's another problem. Because we can often generate a reasonable meaning when viewing a picture, we tend to think we do get the joke. We end up with the illusion of understanding, when all we've done is inject a familiar meaning into something foreign.

Questions of Context

The child labor cartoon on page 483, in the Document-Based Investigation feature, is a deceptively simple illustration. As with every historical document, we should begin by asking basic questions of context—when and where did this image appear? *When* is impossible to answer from the image alone, although the text helpfully supplies the date of August 1910.

The question of *where* will be an enigma to most students. The cartoon is identified as having appeared in *Puck* magazine, but few will recognize the name of the widely popular humor magazine, a forerunner to today's *Mad* or *National Lampoon*. Historians will discern the telltale style and coloring as "Puckish" (literally, "childishly mischievous"), for *Puck* was the first weekly to use full-color lithography, with a color front and back and double-page centerfold.

Subtle Overtones

Although some students will pick up on the issue of forced labor—defenseless children held in tow by a whip-touting overlord ("Greed")—others will fail to connect this figure to his referent: corporate America, tone-deaf to the cries of the suffering and motivated solely by Mammon.

Fewer still will detect the image's racial overtones. Not only are the children uniformly white, but their whiteness is highlighted by shadow and light. Embraced by early Progressive reformers, the cause of child labor focused almost exclusively on white children; the exploitation of African American children was not yet part of the Progressive's consciousness. To be sure, the cartoon pivots on notions of slavery, but not of the American plantation type. Here the allusion is to galley slavery, in which impressed (white) sailors could eventually earn their freedom. Indeed, "white slavery" was a common theme during this period, figuring prominently in such films as D. W. Griffith's *The Fatal Hour* (1908), in which Chinese traders abduct and traffic in white women. Here, corporate America is made more threatening by assuming the guise of a sandal-clad Semitic Levantine, complete with head covering and whip.

Opening Doors

Editorial cartoons open doors to attitudes and codes that were discerned by a broad audience at the time in which they were created but which often escape us today. To understand these images' effectiveness, we must treat them as legitimate historical documents, asking not what they mean now but what they meant to people in the past. Only then can we be stretched by the past rather than squeezing it to fit our preconceived notions.

Social Studies Competency Goals
Goal 5 The learner will describe innovations in technology and business practices and assess their impact on economic, political, and social life in America.
5.02, 5.03, 7.04

The Big Idea and Essential Questions

To foster student understanding of this chapter's big idea, design your lesson to address each section's essential question.

Big Idea Fueled by the growth of the railroad industry, the United States became the world's manufacturing leader during the Second Industrial Revolution.

Essential Questions

1. What impact did new technology have on American industry?

2. How did the organization of business change in the late 1800s?

3. How did workers respond to increasingly difficult working conditions?

4. How did the transportation and communication industries develop in the late 1800s?

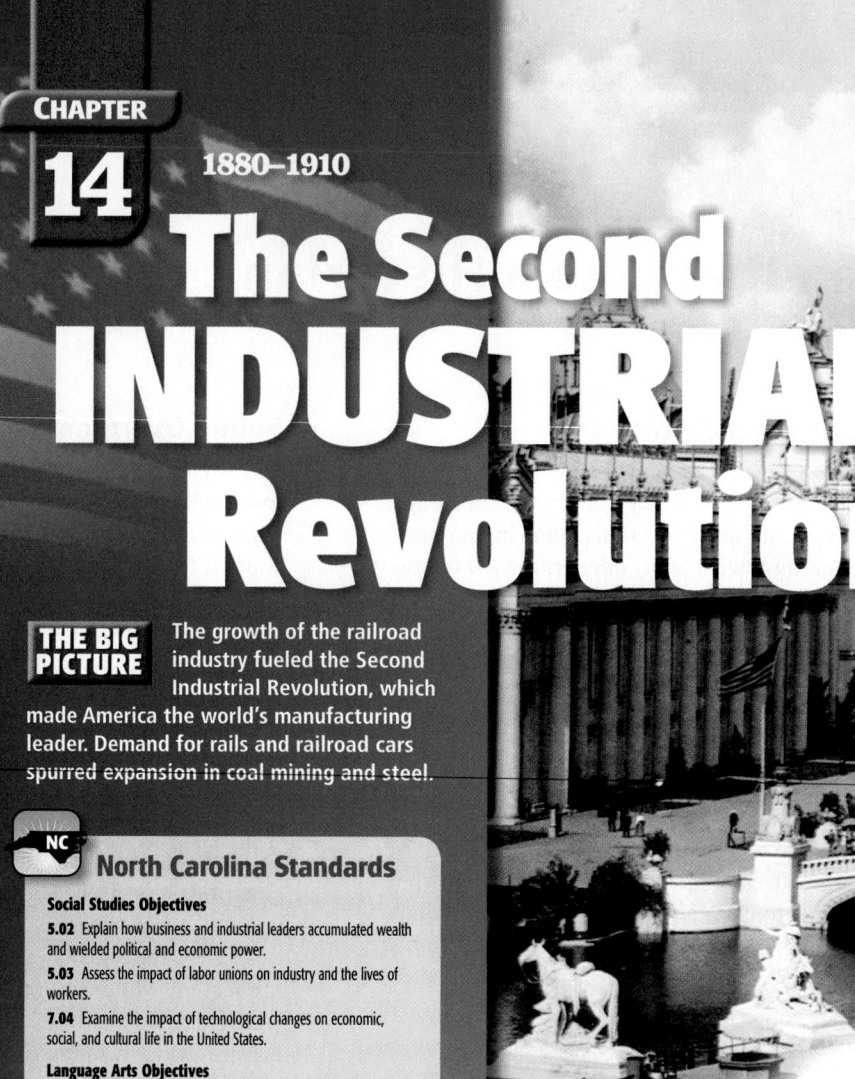

CHAPTER
14   **1880–1910**

The Second INDUSTRIAL Revolution

THE BIG PICTURE The growth of the railroad industry fueled the Second Industrial Revolution, which made America the world's manufacturing leader. Demand for rails and railroad cars spurred expansion in coal mining and steel.

North Carolina Standards

Social Studies Objectives
5.02 Explain how business and industrial leaders accumulated wealth and wielded political and economic power.
5.03 Assess the impact of labor unions on industry and the lives of workers.
7.04 Examine the impact of technological changes on economic, social, and cultural life in the United States.

Language Arts Objectives
2.01 Research and analyze ideas, events, and/or movements related to United States culture by:
• locating facts and details for purposeful elaboration.

Skills Focus **READING LIKE A HISTORIAN**

In 1904 the St. Louis World's Fair celebrated the nation's progress since the Louisiana Purchase. Nearly 20 million visitors toured the fair's grand buildings to view such technological innovations as air conditioning and cars.
Making Inferences What can you infer from the fact that so many people toured the fair?
See Skills Handbook, p. H7

U.S.
1880

1881
The Pullman Palace Car Company creates the town of Pullman, Illinois, to house its employees.

World

1882
Italy, Austria-Hungary, and Germany form the Triple Alliance for mutual defense.

458

Key to Differentiating Instruction

Below Level
Basic-level activities designed for all students encountering new material

At Level
Intermediate-level activities designed for average students

Above Level
Challenging activities designed for honors and gifted-and-talented students

Standard English Mastery
Activities designed to improve standard English usage

Introduce the Chapter   At Level

The Second Industrial Revolution

1. Guide students in a discussion of the ways in which modern appliances and inventions have made their lives easier. For example, with computers they no longer have to write papers by hand; they probably take washing machines, dryers, and dishwashers for granted.

2. Have students make a chart of modern appliances and conveniences that are available to Americans today. Ask students to organize items on their lists into three categories: transportation, communication, and daily life. Ask volunteers to share their charts with the class.

3. Explain to students that in this chapter they will be learning about how these inventions came into being and the changes that occurred in American society during the late 1800s, the time of the Second Industrial Revolution. **LS Verbal-Linguistic**

   Alternative Assessment Handbook, Rubric 11: Discussions

History's Impact video program

Watch the video to understand the impact of the U.S. as the world's most powerful industrial nation.

● Chapter Preview ●

HOLT

History's Impact

▶ **Video Program: The Second Industrial Revolution**
See the Video Teacher's Guide for strategies for using the video segment.

Reading Like a Historian

The World's Fair Have students take a moment to examine the image on these pages. This photograph shows a few of the over 1,500 buildings that were constructed for the fair. During the seven months that the fair was open, exhibits were staged by the U.S. government, 43 states, and 62 foreign countries. What can be inferred from the fact that so many large, elaborate buildings were built for the fair? *possible answer—that the ideas of progress and innovation were important, and that many visitors were expected*

May 1886
Strikes take place across the nation.

The Haymarket Riot occurs in Chicago.

1890
Congress passes the Sherman Antitrust Act.

1895
Sears, Roebuck and Company produces a 532-page mail-order catalog.

December 1903
The Wright brothers make the first airplane flight.

1885
German engineer Gottlieb Daimler patents a version of the modern gas engine.

1890

1900
The Boxer Rebellion breaks out in China.

1900

1905
The Russo-Japanese War ends, and Japan emerges as a major world power.

1910

1910
Four former British colonies unite as the Union of South Africa.

459

go.hrw.com

Online Resources

Chapter Resources:
KEYWORD: SD7 CH14

Teacher Resources:
KEYWORD: SD7 TEACHER

Explore the Time Line

1. When did the Wright brothers make their first airplane flight? *December 1903*

2. What was happening in China in 1900? *the Boxer Rebellion*

3. Which company built a town to house its own employees? *Pullman Palace Car*

4. When and where did the Haymarket Riot occur? *May 1886; Chicago*

Info to Know

Time of Tycoons Some of the wealthiest Americans in U.S. history started their careers during the Second Industrial Revolution. By 1913 John D. Rockefeller had a total wealth of about $900 million, equivalent to about $190 billion today; Andrew Carnegie accumulated a fortune worth $475 million, about $100 billion today.

Answers

Reading Like a Historian (p. 458)
possible answer—It was a showcase for innovation, a source of national pride, and a tourist attraction.

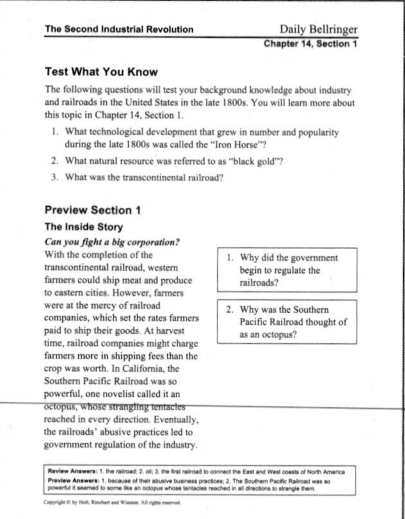

Preteach

Bellringer

The Inside Story. . . Use the **Daily Bellringer Transparency** to help students answer the question.

📎 Daily Bellringer Transparency, Section 1

Taking Notes

Effects—provided thousands of jobs, united East and West Coasts, allowed for quicker travel, promoted trade, increased settlement of the West, standardized time zones

SECTION 1 Industry and Railroads

BEFORE YOU READ

MAIN IDEA
During the late 1800s, new technology led to rapid industrial growth and the expansion of railroads.

READING FOCUS
1. What new industries emerged in the late 1800s, and why were they important?
2. Why did railroads expand, and what changes resulted?

KEY TERMS AND PEOPLE
Bessemer process
Edwin L. Drake
wildcatter
transcontinental railroad

 TAKING NOTES As you read, take notes on the effects of the expansion of the railroads. Record your notes in a graphic organizer like the one shown here.

"TENTACLES OF STEEL"

THE INSIDE STORY

Can you fight a big corporation? In May 1869 officials from the Union Pacific and Central Pacific railroads met at Promontory Summit, Utah. They pounded a symbolic golden spike into a railroad tie. The first transcontinental railroad was complete! Railroads quickly expanded.

The railroad—the Iron Horse— linked California with the rest of the country. It gave many people jobs. It let farmers ship fresh produce and meat to eastern cities. Railroad companies thus had tremendous political and financial power. All too often, though, they used their power unfairly.

One issue was rates for shipping freight. Railroads charged different rates to different shippers. They raised rates at harvest time, charging more than the crop would sell for. Nevertheless, farmers had to depend on them.

Many California farmers resented the situation. The Southern Pacific Railroad was the biggest corporation and the largest employer in the state. To farmers, the railroad was an octopus whose tentacles were reaching in all directions to strangle them.

In 1901 novelist Frank Norris published *The Octopus.* The book describes the uneven struggle between California wheat farmers and the railroads. One character in the book sees the railroad as "the terror of steel and steam . . . with tentacles of steel clutching into the soil, the soulless Force, the iron-hearted Power, the monster, the Colossus, the Octopus." Eventually, the railroads' abuses of power would lead to government regulation of their business practices. ◾

460 CHAPTER 14

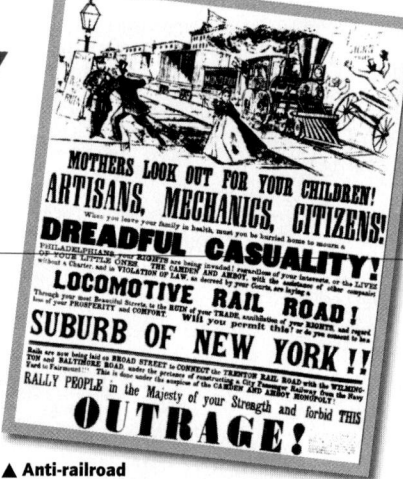

▲ Anti-railroad poster from 1843

New Industries Emerge

As you read earlier, the United States began its Industrial Revolution in the early 1800s. Water or steam power replaced animal and human sources of power. Workers made goods in factories instead of in small workshops or private homes.

In the late 1800s, new technologies helped industry grow to new heights. Electrical power replaced steam and water power. Factories became larger and produced more and more goods. Faster transportation helped move people and goods more cheaply. Industrial growth was so dramatic in the late 1800s that the period is sometimes called the Second Industrial Revolution.

Teach the Main Idea

At Level

Industry and Railroads

1. **Teach** Ask students the Reading Focus questions to teach this section.

2. **Apply** Have students work in pairs to create a graphic organizer showing causes and effects of the growth of the steel, oil, and railroad industries. **LS Verbal-Linguistic**

3. **Review** Review students' graphic organizers as a class. You may wish to create a class graphic for all students to see. Then guide students in a discussion of the ways in which industrial growth

helped railroads expand, and the effects that expansion had on the nation.

4. **Practice/Homework** Ask students which of the industries—steel, oil, or railroad—has the greatest impact on our lives today. Have each student write an essay explaining his or her choice, whether that industry will continue to be important in the future, and why. **LS Interpersonal, Logical-Mathematical**

📝 Alternative Assessment Handbook, Rubrics 13: Graphic Organizers

Making steel In the 1850s two inventors an ocean apart were working on a new way to make steel. In the United States, William Kelly used a blast of hot air to purify molten iron and convert it to steel. Working independently in England, Henry Bessemer developed a similar method, which he quickly patented.

Using the so-called **Bessemer process**, American steel mills began working faster and more cheaply than ever before. In 1873 the United States turned out about 115,000 tons of steel. By 1910 output had soared to 24 million tons, making America the world's top producer.

Why did this matter? Steel helped transform the United States into a modern industrial economy. Steel was stronger, less brittle, and more easily shaped than iron. Thus railroads found steel to be a superior material for locomotives and rails. With steel, construction companies could build bigger bridges and taller buildings. The low cost of steel also made it desirable for ordinary items such as nails and wire.

The start of the oil industry Oil became another key commodity in the late 1800s, valued both as a fuel source and as a lubricant for factory machinery. For generations, people had been finding oil on the surface of coastal waters and lakes. It was not until the mid-1800s, though, that people put it to good use, refining it into kerosene to light lamps.

As demand for kerosene skyrocketed, companies sought to profit. One of them hired **Edwin L. Drake** to extract oil from the ground in Pennsylvania. At first people mocked Drake's drilling efforts as "Drake's Folly." Then in August 1859, his crew hit a crevice deep in the rock. As oil seeped up, the men scrambled to collect it in a bathtub. Edwin Drake had drilled the first commercial oil well. He was soon steadily pumping "black gold" to the surface.

The output from Drake's oil well was modest, but it drew plenty of **wildcatters,** or oil prospectors, to the area. Wildcatters looked for oil in other regions, too. In January 1901, a group led by Anthony F. Lucas struck a rich oil pocket

Texas Leads the Oil Boom

U.S. OIL PRODUCTION, 1880–1910

Barrels (in millions) / Year

Source: *Historical Statistics of the United States*

Skills FOCUS INTERPRETING GRAPHS

Wooden derricks line Spindletop's Boiler Avenue in Texas in 1903. After Spindletop gushed, speculators rushed to buy area land. *About how many more barrels of oil were produced in 1910 than in 1880?*

See **Skills Handbook, p. H17**

461

Boiler Avenue

Direct Teach

Reading Focus

1 What new industries emerged in the late 1800s, and why were they important? *steel—helped transform U.S. into a modern industrial economy; oil—new source of energy, fueled transportation and industry*

New Industries Emerge

Identify What technological changes in the late 1800s helped industry grow? *electrical power; the Bessemer process for steel; improved transportation; crude oil and petroleum*

Explain How did steel help transform the U.S. into a modern industrial economy? *for railroads, better locomotives and rails; for construction companies, bigger bridges and taller buildings; factories used steel machinery to manufacture more goods*

Develop What do you think was the driving force behind the dramatic increase in the amount of oil produced between 1900 and 1910? *possible answer—rise of industry*

Political Cartoons Activities for American History: Cartoon 28: The Railroad in California

go.hrw.com
Online Resources

KEYWORD: SD7 CH14
TOPIC: STEELWORKERS

Answers

Interpreting Graphs *about 200,000*

Skills Focus: Identifying Cause and Effect

Below Level

Reading Skill
Industrial Innovation

1. Guide students in a discussion of the effects that new processes for making steel and refining petroleum had on those industries. *Bessemer process allowed steel mills to work faster and more cheaply. Petroleum could be refined for use as kerosene to light lamps.*

2. To help students understand how these improved processes might have affected industrial growth in the 1800s, draw the graphic organizer at right for students to see.

Omit the italicized answers.

3. Have each student copy the graphic organizer and complete it.

4. Ask volunteers to call out their answers, and then write each answer in the graphic organizer for the class to see. **LS Visual-Spatial**

Alternative Assessment Handbook, Rubrics 6: Cause and Effect; and 13: Graphic Organizers

Graphic Organizer Transparencies

New Processes

Steel | **Oil**

Effects on Industry
• *allowed expansion of railroad industry*
• *provided material for building bridges and taller buildings*
• *allowed construction of machinery for factories*

Effects on Industry
• *used as a lubricant for factory machinery*
• *resulted in production of kerosene for light*
• *led to development of gasoline and other fuels*

461

Reading Focus

2 Why did railroads expand, and what changes resulted? *The federal government gave land to railroad companies, and steel prices dropped. The railroads promoted trade, provided jobs, sped up the settlement of the West, and led to the adoption of standard time.*

Railroads Expand

Recall How did the railroad companies use the land they were given by the federal government? *used some for new routes; sold some to finance construction*

Explain Why was construction of the Central Pacific more difficult than construction of the Union Pacific? *the terrain was tougher; crews had to cross deserts, blast through mountains, face attacks by Native Americans*

Evaluate Why do you think accurate timekeeping was so important to railroads? *possible answer—They had to be able to set and keep schedules.*

📖 CRF: Biography: C.F. Dowd

🖥 Map Transparency: Railroads Built By 1910

✳ **Interactive Map:** Railroads Built By 1910

Answers

Interpreting Maps 1. *4;* **2.** *Central Time Zone; possible answer—major trading cities located in the time zone*

Reading Check *Steel allowed superior railroads, buildings, bridges, and other goods to be built at a cheaper price. Oil was used for kerosene and would lead to other major sources of energy.*

462

---

at Spindletop Hill near Beaumont, Texas. The oil gushed nearly 100 feet in the air for nine days before it could be capped.

The discovery at Spindletop kicked off an oil boom in Texas. Spindletop Hill bristled with oil derricks, jammed in so closely they nearly touched each other. Spindletop produced more than 17 million barrels of oil in 1902. With so many wells, though, production began to decline rapidly. By 1904 Spindletop produced only about 20 percent of what it had in 1902.

This first oil boom in Texas lasted less than 20 years, but it had long-term consequences. Many of the world's leading oil companies, such as Exxon Mobil, Gulf Oil, and Texaco, got their start at Spindletop. They would refine crude oil not only into kerosene, but also into gasoline and other fuels. These new petroleum products would become major sources of energy, fueling a revolution in transportation and industry.

READING CHECK **Drawing Conclusions** Why did steel and oil become important industries?

Railroads Expand

In the 1850s train tracks already crisscrossed the Northeast and reached into the Southeast and the Great Lakes area. In the following decades, rail service spread even farther. Between 1865 and 1890, the number of miles of railroad track jumped nearly fivefold.

The federal government aided this growth by giving thousands of acres of land to railroad companies. They used some of it for new routes and sold some to finance construction. Cheap steel also helped the railroads expand. Steel rails cost only about $12 a ton in the late 1890s, down from $50 a ton in 1877.

A transcontinental railroad In 1862 Congress authorized two companies to build rail lines to the West Coast. For the next six

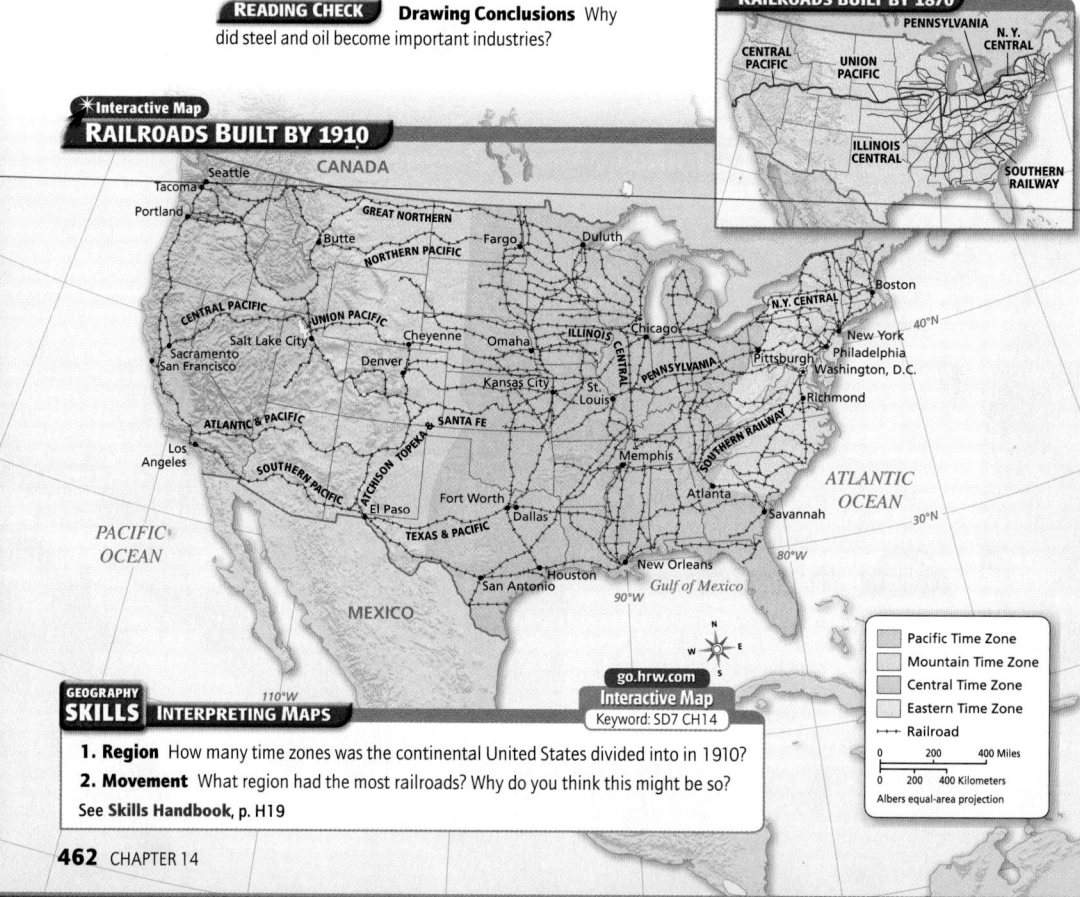

✳ **Interactive Map**
RAILROADS BUILT BY 1910

RAILROADS BUILT BY 1870

GEOGRAPHY SKILLS INTERPRETING MAPS

1. Region How many time zones was the continental United States divided into in 1910?

2. Movement What region had the most railroads? Why do you think this might be so?

See *Skills Handbook*, p. H19

go.hrw.com
Interactive Map
Keyword: SD7 CH14

Pacific Time Zone
Mountain Time Zone
Central Time Zone
Eastern Time Zone
Railroad

0   200   400 Miles
0   200   400 Kilometers
Albers equal-area projection

462 CHAPTER 14

Skills Focus: Comparing and Contrasting   At Level

Reading Skill   **Research Required**
Building the Transcontinental Railroad

1. Have students research the experiences of the people who built the transcontinental railroad. You may wish to have students work in mixed-ability pairs to conduct research.

2. Guide the class in a discussion of the different challenges faced by workers on the Union Pacific and the Central Pacific railroads.

3. Have each student use the information from their research to write five diary entries from

the point of view of a worker on the Central Pacific Railroad in the late 1860s.

4. Ask volunteers to read their diaries to the class. **LS Verbal-Linguistic**

📖 Alternative Assessment Handbook, Rubrics 15: Journals; and 30: Research

and a half years, workers raced to complete the first **transcontinental railroad**—one that would cross the whole country.

The Union Pacific laid tracks westward from Omaha, Nebraska. It hired thousands of Irish, German, English, African American, and Native American workers to build its part of the line. These workers could make progress fairly quickly because much of the land was prairie or gently rolling hills.

Workers for the Central Pacific laid track toward the east, starting in Sacramento, California. These workers—primarily Chinese—labored on tougher terrain. They had to cross deserts and blast through the granite mountains on the California-Nevada border. They also faced attacks by Native Americans.

On May 10, 1869, the two rail lines met at Promontory Summit in Utah Territory. At the ceremony celebrating the completion of the railroad, an official praised the achievement:

HISTORY'S VOICES

❝The east and west have come together. Never, since history commenced her record of human events, has she been called upon to note the completion of a work so magnificent.❞

—Dr. H. W. Harkness

The first transcontinental railroad was soon followed by others. Regional railroads expanded, too, uniting the country both physically and economically.

The effects of expansion The creation of a vast railroad network had several important effects. On the economic front, the railroads promoted trade and provided many jobs. In addition, the demand for rails and railcars gave a boost to steel and train manufacturers.

The railroads also sped up settlement of the West. A journey to the West Coast once took months. Now travelers could go from the Atlantic to the Pacific in just a few days. As a result, parts of the country that had been sparsely populated began to fill with residents. Wherever railroads were built, new towns sprang up and existing towns grew into bigger cities.

Railroads also led to the adoption of what we call standard time. Earlier, people kept time according to the position of the sun. When it was noon in Chicago, it was 12:07 p.m. in Indianapolis and 12:31 p.m. in Pittsburgh. The state of Michigan had at least 27 different local times. Wisconsin had even more—38!

Running a railroad, however, required accurate timekeeping. A New York school principal, C. F. Dowd, was the first to propose dividing the earth into time zones. All communities within a single time zone would set their clocks alike. Railroad officials enthusiastically embraced this idea in 1883. In 1918 Congress adopted standard time for the nation as a whole.

THE IMPACT TODAY

Economics
Rail travel has declined since the advent of cars and planes. Most U.S. trains now carry freight instead of passengers.

READING CHECK **Identifying Problems and Solutions** Why did railroads adopt standard time?

---

go.hrw.com
Online Quiz
Keyword: SD7 HP14

SECTION 1 ASSESSMENT

Reviewing Ideas, Terms, and People

1. **a. Describe** How did the **Bessemer process** change steel making in the United States?
   b. Explain Why is **Edwin L. Drake** an important figure in the history of the oil industry? Why was the discovery at Spindletop important?
   c. Elaborate How did the growth of the steel industry affect other industries?

2. **a. Recall** What role did the U.S. government play in the expansion of railroads during the late 1800s?
   b. Analyze How did the **transcontinental railroad** affect the settlement of the West?
   c. Evaluate How did the expansion of the railroads change life for all Americans?

Critical Thinking

3. **Sequence** Copy the time line below and use it to record key events in the oil and railroad industries.

1855 ———————————————————— 1905

FOCUS ON WRITING

4. **Descriptive** You live in a small town in the late 1800s. You know that a railroad company is planning to build tracks in your general area. Write a letter to a distant friend describing how people feel about the coming of the railroad and what benefits or drawbacks it will have for the town.

Railroads Built By 1910

Have students examine the map "Railroads Built By 1910." Ask them to name geographic features that made building railroads to California difficult. *mountains, deserts*

📄 American History Outline Maps: Western Railroads and Cattle Trails

● **Review & Assess** ●

Close

Guide the class in discussing the technological developments that spurred industrial growth in the late 1800s.

Review

🔲 Online Quiz, Section 1

🔲 Daily Test Practice Transparency

Assess

SE Section 1 Assessment

📄 Progress Assessment: Section 1 Quiz

📄 Alternative Assessment Handbook

Reteach

📄 Interactive Reader and Study Guide, Section 1

⊙ Interactive Skills Tutor CD-ROM

Section 1 Assessment Answers

1. **a.** produced steel faster, cheaper
   b. drilled the first oil well; offered a new energy source; began oil boom in Texas
   c. led to growth of building and transportation industries

2. **a.** government gave land to railroad companies; sponsored the transcontinental railroad
   b. led to growth; helped create towns; made it easier to travel long distances
   c. made it easier to travel, ship goods and resources; expanded settlement; united nation; provided jobs; standard time

3. 1855, Bessemer process invented;
   1859, Drake discovers oil in Pennsylvania;
   1869, Transcontinental railroad completed;
   1901, Oil discovered in Texas

4. possible answers—increases area's population and development; provides jobs; makes transporting people, resources, and goods faster

Answers

Reading Check *needed accurate timekeeping for railroad schedules*

Railroads Transform Chicago

Info to Know

The Birthplace of Modern Architecture
In 1888, a young civil engineer from Wisconsin got a job at one of Chicago's leading architectural firms, Adler and Sullivan. Although he worked as an assistant to Louis Sullivan, the young man soon began to apply his own ideas to the plans he was drawing. In 1893, he left the company to start his own firm. Combining ideas from many different sources, he eventually became the most famous architect of the twentieth century. Many of his buildings still stand in Chicago and other cities around the world. His name was Frank Lloyd Wright.

Mail-Order Houses During the first half of the 1900s, Sears customers could purchase a mail-order house. More than 100,000 homes, from near-mansions to simple cottages, were sold all over the country. Customers could even design their own homes and submit the blueprints to Sears. Once they received the building materials, customers could construct their dream homes.

★ Interactive
HISTORY & Geography

Railroads Transform Chicago

By 1900, railroads had transformed Chicago into the hub of the nation's transportation system. The city was the primary place where eastern manufactured goods were sold and then shipped to the smaller towns of the West. It was also the place where western farm produce, lumber, and other products were processed before being shipped to distant markets around the world. Large industries and retailing businesses, eager to exploit the city's transportation advantages, took root in the city. As industries grew, so did the population, forcing the city to grow upwards and outwards.

Meatpacking Industry
The Union Stock Yards covered more than a square mile. Railroads brought in cattle and hogs from as far away as Texas. Huge packing companies processed meat and shipped it out across the country over the rails.

464

Skills Focus: Analyzing Primary Sources
At Level

Reading Like a Historian Skill
Life in Chicago
Research Required

1. Divide students into small groups. Have each group locate several primary sources written by individuals living in Chicago in the early 1900s.

2. Have students analyze the documents, noting similarities and differences between the accounts. Have students also analyze whether any of the sources are biased in any way.

3. Have a volunteer from each group share the group's sources and analyses with the class. Guide the class in a discussion comparing and contrasting the experiences of individuals living in Chicago. How do these accounts reflect the growing role of industry and transportation? **LS Interpersonal, Verbal-Linguistic**

📖 Alternative Assessment Handbook, Rubric 9: Comparing and Contrasting

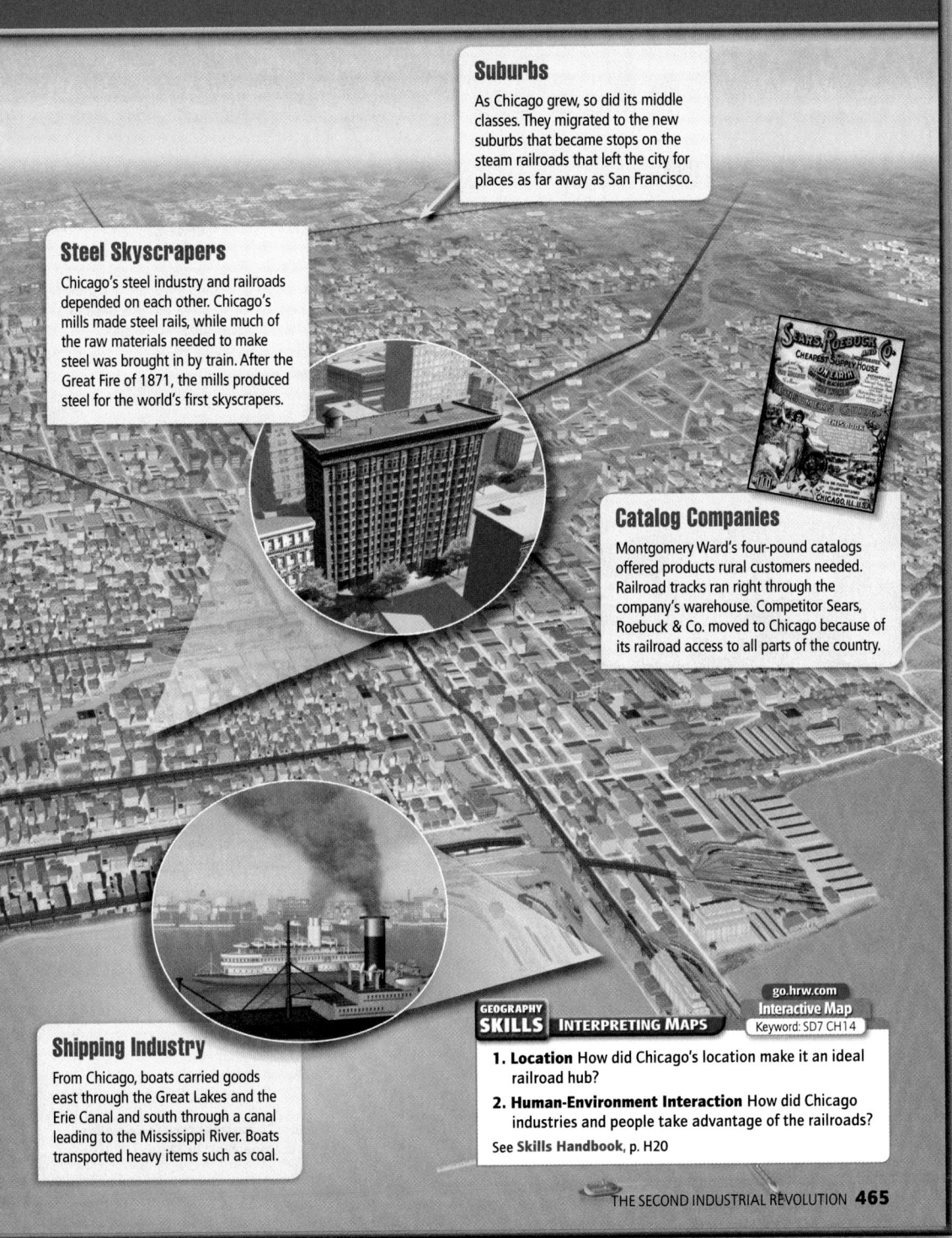

Suburbs

As Chicago grew, so did its middle classes. They migrated to the new suburbs that became stops on the steam railroads that left the city for places as far away as San Francisco.

Steel Skyscrapers

Chicago's steel industry and railroads depended on each other. Chicago's mills made steel rails, while much of the raw materials needed to make steel was brought in by train. After the Great Fire of 1871, the mills produced steel for the world's first skyscrapers.

Catalog Companies

Montgomery Ward's four-pound catalogs offered products rural customers needed. Railroad tracks ran right through the company's warehouse. Competitor Sears, Roebuck & Co. moved to Chicago because of its railroad access to all parts of the country.

Shipping Industry

From Chicago, boats carried goods east through the Great Lakes and the Erie Canal and south through a canal leading to the Mississippi River. Boats transported heavy items such as coal.

GEOGRAPHY SKILLS **INTERPRETING MAPS**

go.hrw.com
Interactive Map
Keyword: SD7 CH14

1. **Location** How did Chicago's location make it an ideal railroad hub?
2. **Human-Environment Interaction** How did Chicago industries and people take advantage of the railroads?

See **Skills Handbook**, p. H20

THE SECOND INDUSTRIAL REVOLUTION **465**

History and Geography

Primary Source

"HOG Butcher for the World, Tool Maker, Stacker of Wheat, Player with Railroads and the Nation's Freight Handler; Stormy, husky, brawling, City of the Big Shoulders:"

— Carl Sandburg

Chicago, 1916

Skills Focus: Identifying Cause and Effect

At Level

Reading Skill
The Transformation of Chicago

1. Create a cause and effect chart on the board. Have students copy it into their notes.

2. Have students work in small groups to fill in the chart with the causes and effects of new forms of transportation on the development of Chicago. Remind students to consider both water and rail transportation.

3. Have volunteers share their answers with the class. Fill in the class diagram. Guide students in a discussion of how advances in transportation have altered life in America today. **LS Verbal-Linguistic, Visual-Spatial**

📖 Alternative Assessment Handbook, Rubrics 6: Cause and Effect; and 7: Charts

📇 Graphic Organizer Transparencies

Answers

Interpreting Maps 1. *located in the middle of the country; connected to the Great Lakes and the Mississippi River;* **2.** *industries received raw materials by rail and water; Sears and Montgomery Ward shipped items to customers all over the country; suburbs spread quickly along rail lines; meatpackers received animals from the West and shipped meat throughout the country*

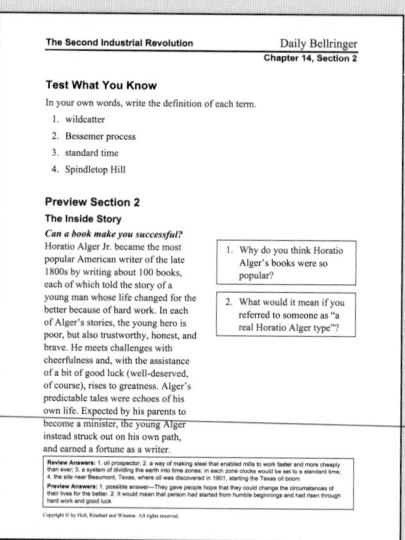

SECTION 2 — The Rise of Big Business

BEFORE YOU READ

MAIN IDEA

Corporations run by powerful business leaders became a dominant force in the American economy.

READING FOCUS

1. What conditions created a favorable climate for business during the late 1800s?
2. How did business structures change?
3. Who were the leading industrial tycoons, and what did they achieve?
4. How did mass marketing change the way goods were sold?

KEY TERMS AND PEOPLE

entrepreneur
capitalism
laissez-faire
social Darwinism
monopoly
John D. Rockefeller
vertical integration
horizontal integration
Andrew Carnegie
Cornelius Vanderbilt

TAKING NOTES As you read, take notes on different kinds of business organizations in the late 1800s. Record your notes in a graphic organizer like the one shown here. You may need to add more circles.

Business Organizations

From Rags to Riches

THE INSIDE STORY

Can a book make you successful? "Strive and succeed!" That was the lesson that thousands of American boys learned from the popular novels of Horatio Alger Jr. It was also the title of one of his 100 or so books. Alger was one of the most popular American writer of the late 1800s. His stories inspired hundreds of young men to strive for success.

The Horatio Alger hero was poor but honest, brave, and trustworthy. He faced hardships but eventually found a good job, and sometimes fame and fortune. He was cheerful even when faced with difficulties. He worked hard, too, but it was usually sudden good luck (which he of course deserved) that brought the final happy ending.

Alger had his own success story. Born in 1832, he was the son of a Unitarian minister. His family expected him to become a clergyman, but he really wanted to be a writer. In 1867, he found his own formula for success. He released *Ragged Dick, or Street Life in New York*, first as a magazine serial and then as a book. This story of a streetwise shoeshine boy was an immediate hit. Many other tales followed. Their plots were all very similar; only the hero's name was different. Here are a few Alger titles: *Bound to Rise, or Live and Learn; The Train Boy, or Up the Ladder; Struggling Upward, or Luke Larkin's Luck.* ■

◀ **This is one of 70 rooms in business tycoon Cornelius Vanderbilt II's summer cottage, built in 1895.**

466 CHAPTER 14

A Favorable Climate for Business

Horatio Alger's novels showcased an American ideal—self-reliant individualism. His characters went from rags to riches through their own hard work. Similarly, many people in the late 1800s believed that a strong work ethic made one successful. The business world welcomed **entrepreneurs**—risk takers who use their money and talents to launch new ventures.

Belief in free markets American entrepreneurs were working within the capitalist system. **Capitalism** is an economic system in which private businesses run most industries. Competition determines prices and wages.

By the late 1800s most business leaders believed in **laissez-faire** (le-say-FER) capitalism. The term *laissez-faire* is French for "to let do." Laissez-faire capitalism allows companies to conduct business without intervention by the government. Business leaders believed that government <u>regulation</u> would destroy individual self-reliance, reduce profits, and harm the economy.

Social Darwinism Americans understood that there were inequalities under capitalism. But many thinkers believed that inequalities were part of a natural order. To explain why some people prospered while others did not, economists and business leaders embraced the philosophy of **social Darwinism.** This philosophy adapted the ideas of the British scientist Charles Darwin and applied them to human society.

Darwin had studied plants and animals and concluded that members of a species compete for survival. Those best adapted to their environment thrive. Less well adapted members gradually die out. Darwin called this process natural selection.

Social Darwinists believed that natural selection also applied to society. Stronger people, businesses, and nations would prosper. Weaker ones would fail. Social Darwinists believed that what they called "survival of the fittest" strengthened society as a whole. They opposed any interference with the process.

READING CHECK **Summarizing** What beliefs did social Darwinists hold?

ACADEMIC VOCABULARY
regulation rules or legal oversight

Social Darwinism

A professor and minister, William Graham Sumner advocated social Darwinism.

" If . . . men were willing to set to work with energy and courage . . . all might live in plenty and prosperity. But if they insist on remaining in the slums . . . there is no device . . . which can prevent them from falling victims to poverty and misery or from succumbing in the competition of life to those who have greater command of capital. "

William Graham Sumner, c. 1885

THE GRANGER COLLECTION, NEW YORK

Walter Rauschenbusch, also a minister, lived among the poor in New York City. He found fault with the attitude of the rich toward the working class.

" Competitive commerce exalts selfishness to the dignity of a moral principle. It pits men against one another in a gladiatorial game in which there is no mercy and in which ninety percent of the combatants finally strew the arena. . . . If the rich had only what they earned, and the poor had all that they earned, . . . life would be more sane. "

Walter Rauschenbush, 1908

Skills Focus **READING LIKE A HISTORIAN**

Identifying Points of View How does each man find fault with either the working class or the wealthy?
See Skills Handbook, pp. H28–H29

THE SECOND INDUSTRIAL REVOLUTION **467**

Differentiating Instruction

Above Level

Advanced Learners/GATE

Research Required

1. Organize the class into two groups. Have each group research social Darwinism as it applies to business. One group should focus on the arguments made by proponents of social Darwinism, while the other group should focus on the arguments made by critics of the theory.

2. Using the arguments of social Darwinists or their opponents, have members of the two groups debate the theory of social Darwinism.

3. Following the debate, guide the class in a discussion of the ethical implications of social Darwinism. Ask students to consider what problems might arise when people try to apply the laws of nature to social issues.

LS Interpersonal, Verbal-Linguistic

Alternative Assessment Handbook, Rubrics 10: Debates; 14: Group Activity; and 30: Research

---

Reading Focus

❶ What conditions created a favorable climate for business during the late 1800s? *entrepreneurs working in capitalist system; competition determined prices and wages*

A Favorable Climate for Business

Recall Why did business leaders oppose government regulation? *thought it would destroy self-reliance, reduce profits, harm the economy*

Analyze Why did business leaders want to apply Darwin's theory of natural selection to human society? *It was an attempt to justify inequalities.*

Evaluate What were the implications of social Darwinism? *weak deserved to fail, the strongest to prosper; government regulation would upset the natural order*

Counterpoints
Social Darwinism

Summarize Give one example of the way in which Sumner attempts to blame the poor for their poverty. In what way might his argument be flawed? *implies that the poor "insist on remaining in the slums"* How do the words Rauschenbusch use show that he is trying to arouse emotions? *phrases like "exalts," "pits men," "gladiatorial game"*

go.hrw.com
Online Resources
KEYWORD: SD7 CH14
TOPIC: ENTREPRENEURS

Answers

Identifying Points of View *Sumner—working class lacks energy and courage; Rauschenbusch—wealthy exploit the working class*

Reading Check *stronger people, businesses, and nations prosper; survival of the fittest strengthened society*

467

② How did business structures change? *They changed from privately owned proprietorships and partnerships to corporations owned by stockholders.*

Business Structures Change

Describe Describe the business structures that were most common at the end of the Civil War. *proprietorships; partnerships*

Elaborate How did trusts and monopolies stifle competition? *They bought other companies, controlled prices, eliminated competition.*

Recent Scholarship

Titan: The Life of John D. Rockefeller, Sr., written by Ron Chernow, provides a fascinating view of John D. Rockefeller both as the business tycoon and as an eccentric original. The work describes Rockefeller's fierce fight to make and keep Standard Oil a powerful trust. The work differs from other biographies in that it also documents Rockefeller's life as a temperance advocate, a devout Christian, and a very generous philanthropist.

Titan: The Life of John D. Rockefeller, Sr. by Ron Chernow. Vintage, 2004

Answers

Interpreting Charts *vertical— acquiring suppliers; horizontal— acquiring similar companies*

Reading Check *proprietorships— owned and managed by individuals, owners responsible for all debts; corporations—owned by stockholders, run by board of directors, can raise money through stock sales, not dependent on owner for existence*

468

Business Structures Change

ACADEMIC VOCABULARY

complex complicated; made up of many parts

In the late 1800s industrialization continued on a massive scale. Businesses became larger and more complex. This led to changes in the way businesses were organized.

Proprietorships and partnerships At the end of the Civil War, most businesses were small. Some were run by individual owners— an arrangement called a proprietorship. Other companies were owned by two or more people in a partnership. In both proprietorships and partnerships, the owners of the company were personally responsible for all debts and obligations of the business.

Corporations The massive industries of the late 1800s needed more expert management. These industries began organizing as corporations. A corporation is a business with the legal status of an individual. It is owned by stockholders—people who buy shares of the company, or stock. The major business decisions of a corporation are made by a board of directors. The board in turn hires corporate officers to run the day-to-day operations.

A corporation has several advantages. It can raise large sums of money by selling stock. That money can be used to expand the business. Also, stockholders have limited responsibility for the corporation's debts. They can lose only the amount of money they have invested in the business. Finally, a corporation is not dependent on a single owner for its existence. It can continue to function long after its original founders leave.

Trusts and monopolies In the late 1800s competition in the marketplace was fierce. To gain dominance, some competing companies formed trusts. The companies agreed to merge and turn over their separate stocks to a board of trustees. The trustees then ran the group of companies as if it were a single corporation, and all the participants split the profits.

When a trust gained complete control over an industry, it held a **monopoly.** That meant it had no competition from other firms. It could raise prices on its products or lower quality much more freely than it otherwise might.

READING CHECK **Contrasting** How were proprietorships and corporations different?

VERTICAL AND HORIZONTAL INTEGRATION

Vertical Integration
Purchase of companies producing the supplies and the services upon which the main business depends

Railroad tanker cars

Pipelines

Refineries   Refineries ← Refineries

Horizontal Integration
Purchase of competing companies in the same industry

Barrel factories

Oil-storage facilities

Oil fields

Skills FOCUS **INTERPRETING CHARTS**

Rockefeller integrated, or combined, businesses both vertically and horizontally to increase profits. *How do vertical and horizontal integration differ?*

See Skills Handbook, p. H15

468 CHAPTER 14

Industrial Tycoons

As businesses grew ever larger in the late 1800s, many corporate leaders amassed staggering fortunes. Three of them—John D. Rockefeller, Andrew Carnegie, and Cornelius Vanderbilt—were wealthier than any Americans before them.

Rockefeller and oil John D. Rockefeller entered the oil business in 1863 and proved himself to be a superb business leader. His company, Standard Oil, started as a refinery. To increase profits, though, Rockefeller engaged in **vertical integration**—acquiring companies that supplied his business. Rockefeller bought barrel factories, oil fields, oil-storage facilities, pipelines, and railroad cars. This allowed him to keep his costs low and profits high.

To expand his business, Rockefeller also practiced **horizontal integration.** This meant taking over other companies producing the same product. Rockefeller bought as many refineries as he could. By 1879 Standard Oil refined 90 percent of all U.S. oil.

Reading Skill
Big Business

1. Have students work in mixed-ability pairs. Have each student create a flow chart showing how businesses became larger and more complex after the Civil War and how this growth led to the development of trusts and monopolies. *Flow charts should show how businesses developed from proprietorships and partnerships to corporations to trusts to monopolies.*

2. Display student work for all students to see.

3. Guide the class in a discussion of the characteristics of each type of business structure.

4. Ask students to try to name past and current examples of each type of business structure.

LS Visual-Spatial, Logical-Mathematical

Alternative Assessment Handbook, Rubric 7: Charts

Political Cartoon

This 1901 drawing portrays John D. Rockefeller as ruling the oil industry.

Standard Oil owned interests in all parts of the industry, including drilling, refining, and storage of oil.

Rockefeller got special rates from railroad companies, lowering his transport costs.

Rockefeller's fortune rested on Standard Oil.

SKILLS FOCUS   READING LIKE A HISTORIAN

1. **Interpreting Political Cartoons** What images suggest Rockefeller's wealth and power?
2. **Contrasting** How does this depiction of Rockefeller contrast with his position as a generous philanthropist?

See Skills Handbook, pp. H10, H31

Rockefeller tried to limit competition in other ways as well. He made special deals with railroads and shipping companies to get the lowest possible price for transporting his oil. Rockefeller could now sell his oil much more cheaply than his competitors could. In this way, he drove rival firms out of business.

At one point, Rockefeller's fortune approached $900 million. He gave away over half of it to worthy causes, though. Rockefeller donated more than $80 million to the University of Chicago. He channeled millions more into education and other good works through his Rockefeller Foundation.

Carnegie and steel Andrew Carnegie lived a true rags-to-riches story. Born in Scotland to parents that hit hard economic times when he was about 9, Carnegie immigrated to the United States when he was 12. He advanced quickly in his early jobs and began investing in the iron, oil, railroad, and telegraph industries. He soon founded his own company and rose to the top of the steel business.

Carnegie held down costs by using vertical integration, buying supplies in bulk, and producing items in large quantities. By the end of the century the Carnegie Steel Company dominated the U.S. steel industry. In 1901 Carnegie sold the company to banker J. P. Morgan for $480 million. After retiring, Carnegie began to devote his time to philanthropy, or charity.

Carnegie gave away some $350 million over his lifetime, mostly to support education. He built public libraries, financed scientific work, and established what is now Carnegie Mellon University in Pittsburgh. He also built Carnegie Hall, the famous concert site in New York City, and funded international peace efforts.

THE IMPACT TODAY

Culture
The Rockefeller Foundation is now active across the globe, supporting cultural activities and projects in health, agriculture, and urban development.

Skills Focus: Analyzing Alternative Interpretations of the Past

Reading Like a Historian Skill   **At Level**
Kings of Capitalism

1. Have students review the information on John D. Rockefeller, Andrew Carnegie, Cornelius Vanderbilt, and George Pullman. Have students compare how they made their fortunes, business practices that helped them succeed, innovations that they introduced, and how generous they were to educational institutions and philanthropic causes. Remind students that these businessmen were highly successful, shrewd, and at times ruthless.

2. Have students debate how these business tycoons should be remembered. Should they be depicted as "robber barons" or "captains of industry," or somewhere between the two extremes?

3. Have students create a political cartoon that expresses their opinion about these four men.
   LS Verbal-Linguistic, Visual-Spatial
   Alternative Assessment Handbook, Rubrics 10: Debates; and 27: Political Cartoons

---

Reading Focus

❸ **Who were the leading industrial tycoons, and what did they achieve?** *John D. Rockefeller, Standard Oil, refined half of all oil in U.S.; Andrew Carnegie, Carnegie Steel Company, dominated the steel industry; Cornelius Vanderbilt controlled more than 4,500 miles of railroad; George Pullman designed and built railroad cars*

Industrial Tycoons

Explain Which of John D. Rockefeller's business practices might be viewed as ruthless? *vertical and horizontal integration; making deals to get lowest price for transporting oil*

Summarize How did Rockefeller and Carnegie use their wealth to do good? *Both men gave substantial amounts to universities. Carnegie built public libraries, Carnegie Hall, financed scientific work and international peace efforts.*

CRF: Primary Source Activity: Standard Oil Cartoon

Biography

Emily Dickinson (1830–1886) Although Emily Dickinson lived at the same time as John D. Rockefeller and Andrew Carnegie, her life was antithesis of these captains of industry. Dickinson was not a recluse, but she rarely left her home in the village of Amherst, Massachusetts. She lived her life very simply and made no effort to acquire wealth or great fame. The themes of Dickinson's poems include love, war, death, and religious beliefs, which reflect her understanding of humanity. Few of Dickinson's poems were published during her lifetime, yet in their sharpness, length, and imagery, her poems served as precursors to modern poetry.

Answers

Reading Like a Historian 1. *his crown, clothing;* **2.** *His stern expression doesn't make him seem generous.*

Reading Focus

Industrial Tycoons

Identify What was the Gospel of Wealth? *Andrew Carnegie's philosophy that wealthy people had a duty toward the rest of society*

Evaluate How did George Pullman's "company town" prove to be a mixed blessing? *comfortable homes, shops, a church, and a library; no local newspapers, no self-government, and anyone who spoke out against company policies could be evicted*

Reading Focus

4 How did mass marketing change the way goods were sold? *by targeting advertisements to women, by using new approaches to win customers, and by making shopping easier*

Mass Marketing

Explain How did department stores make shopping easier? *sold many different products under one roof*

Develop In addition to the methods described in this section, what other way do retailers today appeal to potential customers? *possible answer— through the Internet, television*

CRF: Biography: Richard Warren Sears

Carnegie believed that wealthy people had a duty toward the rest of society. He explained his philosophy, known as the Gospel of Wealth, in 1889:

HISTORY'S VOICES

❝This, then, is held to be the duty of the man of Wealth: . . . to consider all surplus revenues which come to him simply as trust funds . . . to produce the most beneficial result for the community.❞

—Andrew Carnegie

Railroad tycoons Other industrial leaders rode the railways to success. **Cornelius Vanderbilt** began investing in railroads during the Civil War. By 1872 he owned the New York Central Railroad. Soon his holdings stretched west to Michigan and north to Canada. At the height of his career, he controlled more than 4,500 miles of railroad track. He also invested heavily in steamship lines and dominated shipping along the Atlantic Coast.

Unlike Rockefeller and Carnegie, Vanderbilt supported few charities. His greatest donation was a $1 million gift to Central University in Nashville, Tennessee, which was later renamed Vanderbilt University. When Vanderbilt died in 1877, he left an estate of $100 million.

Another railroad man, George Pullman, made his fortune by designing and building railroad cars. His Pullman Palace Car Com-

ACADEMIC VOCABULARY

maximize make as large as possible

FACES OF HISTORY

Andrew CARNEGIE
1835–1919

Andrew Carnegie began his working career in the United States in a textile factory, but he soon found a job as a telegraph operator. From there he became the assistant to a Pennsylvania Railroad official. With his savings and a small loan, Carnegie made his first investment in iron manufacturing. Carnegie also advanced his career at the railroad. He soon earned enough to invest in a variety of industries. In 1865 he resigned his job to devote himself to his business ventures. Carnegie's business boomed when he turned to steel manufacturing. His eye for efficiency and close partnerships with railroad companies made Carnegie the king of steel. In 1901 he sold his company and turned to philanthropy. His charities established over 2,500 libraries in the United States and in other English-speaking countries.

Make Inferences How do you think Carnegie's background influenced his drive for success and his charitable activities?

---

pany, founded in Chicago in 1867, was known for creating sleeper cars that made long-distance travel more comfortable.

In 1881 Pullman built an entire town south of Chicago for his employees. He believed that happy workers would be productive workers. The town of Pullman had comfortable homes with indoor plumbing—a luxury for working-class families. Residents also enjoyed shops, a church, and a library.

At the same time, the Pullman Company controlled many aspects of life in the town. There were no local newspapers and no self-government. Those who spoke out against company policies might find themselves evicted from their homes.

A mixed legacy Some Americans came to view the business tycoons of the late 1800s as "robber barons." Critics have argued that these entrepreneurs profited unfairly by squeezing out competitors and using other tough tactics. Their huge mansions and luxurious lifestyles seemed like ill-gotten rewards.

Other people, though, saw men like Rockefeller, Carnegie, and Vanderbilt as "captains of industry." Admirers credited these tycoons with using their business skills to make the American economy more productive. That in turn made the American economy stronger. In addition, Rockefeller and Carnegie won praise for their generous contributions to charity.

READING CHECK **Identifying Supporting Details** How did Rockefeller and Carnegie gain a competitive edge?

Mass Marketing

The industrial tycoons of the day were not the only people bringing changes to American business. Retailers, too, looked for new ways to maximize their profits.

Many companies that advertised in popular magazines began targeting their messages to women. They realized that women made most purchasing decisions about household goods.

Advertisers also tried new approaches to win customers. Food companies often used wholesome farm images to convey a sense of purity. Some companies came up with clever brand names, such as Uneeda Biscuit crackers, to help customers remember their products.

Skills Focus: Making Generalizations
Below Level

Reading Skill
Mass Marketing

1. Guide students in a discussion of the types of stores available to consumers today, and where they tend to be located.

2. Review with students how a downtown area of a small town might have looked in the 1880s. Have students make a list of the types of stores that would have been located in the town. Have volunteers share their lists.

3. Ask students to list the advantages and disadvantages of shopping today at a department store or a "big-box" store. Have volunteers share their lists with the class.

4. Have students write an editorial either opposing or supporting the opening of a large modern department store in a town during the 1880s. Have students use the information from their lists and their texts to support their position. **LS Interpersonal, Visual-Spatial**

Alternative Assessment Handbook, Rubric 17: Letters to Editors

---

Answers

Faces of History *possible answer— It motivated him to better his own conditions and the conditions of others.*

Reading Check *Rockefeller practiced vertical and horizontal integration, made special deals with railroads and shipping companies. Carnegie used vertical integration, buying supplies in bulk, produced items in large quantities.*

In the cities a new kind of store emerged that made shopping easier. This was the department store, where retailers sold many different products under one roof, grouping them into separate departments for clothing, shoes, cookware, and so on. No longer did customers have to trudge from shop to shop to purchase a variety of goods. They loved the convenience of one-stop shopping—and they loved department store prices. Because these stores bought in bulk, they could pass on the savings to their customers.

Rural dwellers, meanwhile, could purchase a huge variety of goods from mail-order companies. In 1895 Sears, Roebuck and Company produced a 507-page catalog offering everything from slippers to stoves to saddles. The 1904 Montgomery Ward catalog weighed a hefty four pounds and was mailed to roughly 3 million homes.

Mail-order customers simply made their selections, sent in their payments, and waited for the merchandise they ordered to arrive by rail or post. Now even Americans living in the countryside could buy a wide range of manufactured goods—wider than ever before—without having to travel to cities.

READING CHECK Identifying the Main Idea
How did companies make their products available to more people in the late 1800s?

House in the Mail

Mass marketers sold affordable, ready-to-assemble houses through their catalogs (below). Right, a modern couple enjoys living in one of these now historic homes.

The CARLIN No. 3031 "Already Cut" and Fitted. $1,172.00

SECTION 2 ASSESSMENT

go.hrw.com
Online Quiz
Keyword: SD7 HP14

Reviewing Ideas, Terms, and People

1. **a. Define** What was laissez-faire capitalism?
   b. Analyze Why did business leaders oppose government regulation of business?

2. **a. Recall** Why did corporations arise?
   b. Draw Conclusions Do you think the public generally welcomed or feared monopolies? Explain.

3. **a. Describe** What does vertical integration involve? What does horizontal integration involve?
   b. Evaluate How would you assess the contributions—both positive and negative—made by tycoons such as John D. Rockefeller and Andrew Carnegie?

4. **a. Recall** How did companies market their products in the late 1800s?
   b. Explain What was innovative about the department store?
   c. Predict How might the rise of department stores and mail-order catalogs have affected Americans' spending habits?

Critical Thinking

5. **Comparing and Contrasting** Copy the chart below and record the main characteristics of the following types of businesses: proprietorships, partnerships, and corporations.

Proprietorship	Partnership	Corporation

FOCUS ON WRITING

6. **Expository** You are a small business owner or a consumer living in the late 1800s. You believe that trusts and big corporations have accumulated too much power. You think there should be more competition in the marketplace. Write an article for your local newspaper explaining how large corporations dominate the business world and how this affects ordinary people like you.

THE SECOND INDUSTRIAL REVOLUTION **471**

471

Bellringer

The Inside Story. . . Use the **Daily Bellringer Transparency** to help students answer the question.

🖥 Daily Bellringer Transparency, Section 3

The Second Industrial Revolution   Daily Bellringer
                                                         Chapter 14, Section 3

Test What You Know

Read the statements below and determine who or what is "speaking."

1. "I believed in a philosophy I called the Gospel of Wealth—that rich people had a duty to use their money for society's good."

2. "I believed that happy workers would be more productive, so I built a whole town for my workers."

3. "I used both vertical and horizontal integration to build my oil company. At one point, my company refined half the oil in America."

4. "We are companies owned by shareholders rather than individuals, and we are run by a board of directors."

Preview Section 3

The Inside Story

Could you live on $133 a year?
One aspect of the Industrial Revolution that was often ignored was the life of the workers. That changed in 1883 when a Senate committee investigated labor conditions. They heard from out-of-work textile laborer Thomas O'Donnell, who said he could not find work because factories were hiring children to work the new, smaller machines. The day he spoke, O'Donnell was literally penniless. He had earned only $133 that year—not enough to buy clothes and food for himself, his wife, and two children.

| 1. How did factory owners fill the new demand for smaller workers caused by the development of smaller machines? |
| 2. On average, how much would someone working every day and who earned $133 in a year earn per day? |

Review Answers: 1. Andrew Carnegie; 2. George Pullman; 3. John D. Rockefeller; 4. corporations
Preview Answers: 1. They hired children to work in factories. 2. a little over 36¢

Copyright © by Holt, Rinehart and Winston. All rights reserved.

Academic Vocabulary

Review with students the high-use academic term in this section.

labor work performed for wages (p. 473)

📑 CRF: Vocabulary Builder Activity, Section 3

Taking Notes

Knights of Labor founded, 1869; Great Railroad Strike, 1877; Haymarket Riot, 1886; American Federation of Labor formed, 1886; Homestead Strike, 1892; Pullman Strike, 1893

SECTION 3 Workers Organize

BEFORE YOU READ

MAIN IDEA

Grim working conditions in many industries led workers to form unions and stage labor strikes.

READING FOCUS

1. What was the relationship between government and business in the late 1800s?

2. What were working conditions like for industrial workers?

3. How did workers seek changes?

KEY TERMS AND PEOPLE

Sherman Antitrust Act
sweatshop
Knights of Labor
Terence V. Powderly
xenophobia
blacklist
Samuel Gompers
American Federation of Labor
Eugene V. Debs
Grover Cleveland

TAKING NOTES As you read, take notes on major events in the development of the labor movement in the late 1800s. Record your notes in a graphic organizer like the one shown here. You may need to add more rows to your organizer.

Event	Date

THE INSIDE STORY

Could you live on $133 a year? When the Industrial Revolution began, businesses did pretty much as they pleased. Few officials worried about the workers, and by the late 1800s there were more workers than jobs.

In October 1883 Thomas O'Donnell, a part-time textile worker, appeared before a Senate committee looking into labor conditions. He was one of many who could not find full-time work. O'Donnell's worn clothes contrasted with the formal dress of the senators. He painted a devastating picture of life for the working poor. New machines required smaller workers, encouraging the use of child labor. Factories fired adults and hired men who had sons who could work. "Whoever has a boy has work," O'Donnell said, "and whoever has no boy stands no chance."

"How much money have you got?" a senator asked. "I have not got a cent in the house," O'Donnell answered, "didn't have when I came out this morning." In fact, he, his wife, and two children had lived on only $16 for the past three months. Over the entire year, the family income had amounted to about $133 from a few weeks' work in the textile mill. O'Donnell dug clams for food and picked up wood for heating. His children were often sickly because they lacked food or clothes or shoes. For workers like O'Donnell, there seemed to be no way to escape from these conditions. ■

"NOT A CENT IN THE HOUSE!"

▼ Too small for the job, these child workers climb onto the machinery at a Georgia textile mill in 1909.

Teach the Main Idea   At Level

Workers Organize

1. **Teach** Ask students the Reading Focus questions to teach this section.

2. **Apply** Have students make a list of the labor unions discussed in the section. Have each student write a brief summary of each union, its goals, its members, and its purpose. 📖 **Verbal-Linguistic**

3. **Review** Review the union information with the class. Guide students in a discussion of the early years of the labor movement. Ask them how successful they think the labor movement was in its early years.

4. **Practice/Homework** Have students select one grievance that labor might have had against employers in the 1800s, such as long hours or dangerous working conditions. Have students write a speech from the perspective of a labor leader explaining the problem and what should be done to correct it. 📖 **Verbal-Linguistic, Auditory-Musical**

📑 Alternative Assessment Handbook, Rubric 37: Writing Assignments

Government and Business

In the late 1800s the government maintained a hands-off attitude toward business. Most politicians, like business leaders, insisted that regulating business would harm the economy.

Nonetheless, as corporations expanded, the government grew uneasy about the power of these giants. In 1890 Congress passed the **Sherman Antitrust Act**. This act made it illegal to form trusts that interfered with free trade. It also prohibited monopolies and activities that hindered competition in the marketplace.

At first the government did not prosecute many companies under this act. Between 1890 and 1901 just 18 suits were brought, and four of those were against labor unions. The law was vague, and for a time the government stopped trying to enforce the Sherman Act.

The government paid even less attention to workers. After all, industrialization was raising the standard of living for all Americans. Yet income inequality was increasing too. By 1890 just 10 percent of the population controlled 75 percent of the nation's wealth. This meant that the rich were exceedingly rich. At the same time, many industrial workers were barely scraping by, earning less than $500 per year.

READING CHECK Drawing Conclusions
How did government policies affect business?

Industrial Workers

The growth of industry in the late 1800s required huge numbers of workers to keep the factories running. Who were these people whose labor fueled American industry?

The workforce Many factory workers were immigrants. Many others were rural Americans who came to the cities to earn a living. The best factory jobs went to native-born whites or European immigrants. African Americans found more opportunities as laborers or household help, but those jobs usually paid less than factory work.

Many industrial workers were children. By 1900 about one in six children between the ages of 10 and 15 held a job outside the home. Even children as young as five sometimes worked to help make ends meet.

Working conditions Most unskilled laborers typically worked 10 hours per day, six days a week. They had no paid vacation, no sick leave, and no compensation for injuries suffered on the job. Employers pressured these tired, low-paid laborers to work as fast as possible to speed up production. This often led to terrible accidents. Most employers felt no responsibility to help those who were injured. They simply hired new workers to replace them.

Some of the worst exploitation occurred in cramped workshops set up in shabby tenement buildings. These so-called **sweatshops** were especially common in the garment industry:

HISTORY'S VOICES

❝In [the tenements] the child works unchallenged from the day he is old enough to pull a thread. There is no such thing as a dinner hour; men and women eat while they work, and the 'day' is lengthened at both ends far into the night. Factory hands take their work with them at the close of the lawful day to eke out their scanty earnings by working overtime at home.❞

—Jacob Riis

Some garment workers toiled in their own apartments instead of in sweatshops. But this meant that the workers—not the employers—were paying for the rent, heat, and light needed to make the clothing.

READING CHECK Making Inferences Why would workers agree to work in difficult conditions?

ACADEMIC VOCABULARY
labor work performed for wages

THE IMPACT TODAY

Government
The federal government and all 50 states now have child labor laws to protect minors. These laws set minimum ages for different kinds of work and limit the hours that children may work.

THE SECOND INDUSTRIAL REVOLUTION **473**

473

Reading Focus

❸ How did workers seek changes? *by joining together to form unions*

Workers Seek Changes

Explain How did the Knights of Labor hope to achieve their ends without strikes? *by using boycotts and negotiating with employers*

Recall What evidence is there to suggest that xenophobia had a part in the arrests made following the Haymarket affair? *those who were arrested had foreign-sounding names; there was no evidence to connect men to the crime*

Evaluate When do you think the federal government should use military troops to end a strike? *possible answer—when the strike threatens the public welfare*

📖 CRF: Biography: Harriet Hanson Robinson

Info to Know

The Knights of Labor When the Knights of Labor drafted the preamble to their constitution, they wrote that they were "calling upon all who believe in securing 'the greatest good to the greatest number' to aid and assist us." The preamble emphasizes the importance of workers' minds as well as the safety and financial value of their physical work. The constitution asks for "the reduction of the hours of labor to eight per day, so that the laborers may have more time for social enjoyment and intellectual improvement."

go.hrw.com
Online Resources
KEYWORD: SD7 CH14
TOPIC: LABOR UNIONS

TRACING HISTORY

The Labor Movement

Union membership has declined since the late 1940s as traditionally unionized industries lost jobs and as employment in non-unionized high-tech and service industries grew. Study the time line to learn about key events in the American labor movement.

◄ Early 1800s New England factory

1834 Young mill girls in Lowell, Massachusetts, form a union, the Factory Girl's Association, to protest wage cuts.

1700

1800

1794 Shoemakers in Philadelphia establish the first trade union in the United States.

► American Federation of Labor emblem

1886 Violence breaks out between police and union supporters in Chicago's Haymarket Square. Samuel Gompers founds the American Federation of Labor (AFL).

Workers Seek Changes

By the late 1800s working conditions were so dismal that workers began organizing in ever-increasing numbers. By banding together, they hoped to pressure employers into making the workplace safer and paying reasonable wages.

Early organizing The labor movement had gotten its start in the late 1700s. In 1794 a group of Philadelphia shoemakers formed a trade union to protect their interests. Over the next few decades, skilled workers in other trades—carpenters, printers, blacksmiths, and so forth—also organized. These early unions remained mostly small and local, however.

National unions After the Civil War, the labor movement began to grow. The National Labor Union (NLU) organized in 1866 as a federation of small, local unions. The NLU pushed to shorten the workday to eight hours. Unsuccessful in this effort, the NLU folded in 1872.

The **Knights of Labor**, founded in Philadelphia in 1869, was a more effective group. Under the leadership of **Terence V. Powderly** in the 1880s, the Knights of Labor began to accept unskilled workers, women, African Americans, and even employers as members. It excluded only bankers, gamblers, lawyers, liquor sellers, physicians, and stockholders. By 1886 the group had more than 700,000 members.

With the motto "An injury to one is a concern of all," the Knights of Labor campaigned for many reforms. The group's constitution outlined its general goals:

HISTORY'S VOICES

❝To secure to the toilers [workers] a proper share of the wealth that they create; more of the leisure that rightfully belongs to them; more society advantages; . . . in a word, all those rights and privileges necessary to make them capable of enjoying, appreciating, defending and perpetuating the blessings of good government.❞
—Preamble to the Constitution of the Knights of Labor

The Knights of Labor also worked for the eight-hour workday, the end of child labor, and equal pay for equal work. In its early years, the organization discouraged the use of strikes, preferring boycotts and negotiation with employers. Yet soon enough, strikes would become commonplace.

The Great Railroad Strike The first major rail strike happened in 1877. Times were tough, and several northern railroads cut wages that year. Workers for the Baltimore and Ohio Railroad protested by walking off the job and blocking several freight trains. Pennsylvania Railroad employees blocked the movement of all trains on their rail lines. The strikes quickly spread to other railroads, stopping most freight traffic for more than a week.

474 CHAPTER 14

Skills Focus: Identifying Problem and Solution
Below Level

Reading Skill
Organizing Workers
Standard English Mastery

1. Guide students in a discussion of the Knights of Labor. You may wish to use the following questions: What were the union's strengths and weaknesses? What would be the advantages and disadvantages of accepting employers in the union? What would be the advantages and disadvantages of discouraging the use of strikes?

2. Organize the class into small groups. Tell students that they are to plan a new union to rival the Knights of Labor. Have each group name its union and create a three-fold illustrated brochure to recruit potential members. The brochures should show why the Knights are failing to meet workers' needs and how the new union can do a better job of helping workers.

3. Have volunteers present their brochures to the class. Then have students vote for the union they would join. **LS Visual-Spatial**

📝 Alternative Assessment Handbook, Rubrics 14: Group Activity; and 43: Writing to Persuade

◀ Air traffic controllers on the picket line

1981 President Ronald Reagan fires most of the nation's striking air-traffic controllers.

◀ Service Employees International president Andy Stern (right) announces the union's split from the AFL-CIO.

1994 Despite union protests that jobs will relocate to lower-wage Mexican factories, the North American Free Trade Agreement (NAFTA) takes effect between the United States, Canada, and Mexico.

2005 The Teamster and Service Employees International Union splits from the AFL–CIO. Shortly after, the United Food and Commercial Workers also leaves.

1900

2000

Several governors called out their state militias to put down the strikes. In Baltimore, the militia fired into crowds, killing 10 people. Troops in Pittsburgh killed 20 civilians, including 3 children. Protestors reacted angrily to this bloodshed. Mobs in Pittsburgh set train engines, buildings, and equipment on fire, causing more than $4 million in damage.

The arrival of U.S. Army troops put an end to the Great Railroad Strike of 1877. But the violence on the part of both strikers and the government had led to the deaths of more than 100 people.

The Haymarket Riot The United States experienced a year of more intense strikes and turmoil in 1886. Wage cuts in many industries caused workers across the nation to go on strike. Labor demonstrations were common that year, some involving violent clashes with police. One of the worst confrontations was the Haymarket Riot.

In Haymarket Square in Chicago, crowds gathered to protest violent police action at a strike the day before. Suddenly, someone threw a bomb into the crowd. People panicked, and gunfire rang out. Before the situation calmed down, 11 people had lost their lives and more than 100 suffered injuries.

People immediately blamed foreign-born unionists for the violence. The press fanned the flames of this **xenophobia** (zeh-nuh-FO-bee-uh), or fear of foreigners. Police arrested numerous suspects and eventually charged eight men with conspiracy and murder. All had foreign-sounding names.

No evidence existed to connect these men to a crime. In fact, five of them were not even in Haymarket Square when the bomb went off. But all eight were convicted and sentenced to death. Four were hanged, and one killed himself in prison. In 1893 the new governor of Illinois pardoned the last three, believing that their guilt had not been proven.

The American Federation of Labor Following the Haymarket Riot, employers struck back at organized labor. Increasingly, they forced employees to sign documents saying they would not join unions. Employers made and shared **blacklists**—lists of people perceived as troublemakers, whom they refused to hire. When workers protested by striking, employers replaced them with "scabs," or strikebreakers. These scabs were often African Americans or others who had been excluded by the unions.

Union members did not stop organizing, despite the risks. In 1886 a group of skilled workers led by **Samuel Gompers** formed the **American Federation of Labor** (AFL). Using strikes and other tactics, the AFL won wage increases and shorter work weeks.

THE IMPACT TODAY

Economics
In 1955 the AFL merged with another powerful union, the Congress of Industrial Organizations. Today the AFL-CIO represents more than 9 million American workers.

THE SECOND INDUSTRIAL REVOLUTION **475**

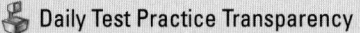
Workers Seek Changes

Recall How did the Homestead Strike end? *governor called in state militia to end strike*

Analyze Do you think the federal government was correct in ordering an end to the Pullman Strike? *possible answers—yes, strike interfered with public services; no, a settlement could have been reached*

Review & Assess

Close

Guide the class in a discussion of the factors that led to the rise of the labor movement.

Review

- Online Quiz, Section 3
- Daily Test Practice Transparency

Assess

- **SE** Section 3 Assessment
- Progress Assessment: Section 3 Quiz
- Alternative Assessment Handbook

Reteach

- Interactive Reader and Study Guide, Section 3
- Interactive Skills Tutor CD-ROM

Answers

Interpreting Graphs *Union membership decreased immediately afterward.*

Reading Check *with violence; federal troops often called in to stop strike*

476

THE GROWTH OF UNIONS, 1880–1910

- Total nationwide union membership
- American Federation of Labor membership
- Knights of Labor membership

1886 Haymarket Riot

Year (x-axis): 1880, 1885, 1890, 1895, 1900, 1905, 1910
Members (y-axis): 0, 500,000, 1,000,000, 1,500,000, 2,000,000, 2,500,000

Sources: *Growth of American Trade Unions, 1880–1923; Ebb and Flow of Trade Unionism*

Skills FOCUS **INTERPRETING GRAPHS**

What effect did the Haymarket Riot seem to have on labor union membership?

See Skills Handbook, p. H17

The Homestead strike Although unions made some gains, conflicts with employers continued. In 1892 workers at the Carnegie Steel Company in Homestead, Pennsylvania, protested when the manager wanted to step up production. They refused to work faster, and the manager tried to lock them out. The workers then seized the plant.

Days later, gunfire erupted when private guards hired by the company tried to take control. A fierce battle raged for 14 hours, leaving 16 people dead. The governor called out the state militia to restore order, and within months, the steelworkers' union withered.

The Pullman strike Other unions suffered setbacks, too. In 1893 the Pullman Company laid off a third of its employees. It cut the wages of the remaining employees an average of 25 percent, but it did not lower their rents.

The workers went on strike with the support of **Eugene V. Debs**, the leader of the American Railway Union (ARU). He urged the members of the ARU not to work on any trains that included Pullman cars.

The government soon stepped in. It ordered the union to call off the strike because it was interfering with delivery of the U.S. mail. When ARU officials refused, many of them were jailed. Meanwhile, President **Grover Cleveland** called in federal troops, and the strike collapsed. Workers who would not quit the ARU wound up fired or blacklisted.

For the next several decades, unions struggled for progress. They would eventually gain considerable power, but the late 1800s remained the era of big business.

READING CHECK **Making Generalizations** How did employers and political leaders generally respond to the labor strikes of the late 1800s?

SECTION 3 ASSESSMENT

go.hrw.com
Online Quiz
Keyword: SD7 HP14

Reviewing Ideas, Terms, and People

1. **a. Identify** What was the **Sherman Antitrust Act**?
   b. Analyze Did the Sherman Antitrust Act curb the power of big business? Explain.

2. **a. Describe** What groups of people went to work in factories during the Second Industrial Revolution?
   b. Make Inferences Why might some employers have preferred child workers to adult workers?

3. **a. Recall** Why did more and more workers begin organizing in the late 1800s?
   b. Contrast How did the **Knights of Labor** and the **AFL** differ from earlier unions?
   c. Evaluate You read that violence often accompanied labor union strikes. Do you think this helped or hurt the cause of workers? Explain.

Critical Thinking

4. **Identifying Cause and Effect** Copy the chart below and record the causes and effects of key labor incidents.

Incident	Cause	Effect

FOCUS ON SPEAKING

5. **Persuasive** You are a factory owner and that your workers want higher wages and shorter hours. You believe that meeting these demands will drive you out of business. Give a talk to your workers to try to persuade them to accept your terms and refrain from striking.

476 CHAPTER 14

Section 3 Assessment Answers

1. **a.** a federal law making it illegal to form trusts that interfere with free trade
   b. No; companies found ways to evade the law.

2. **a.** immigrants, children, and rural Americans who moved to the cities
   b. paid less, were obedient

3. **a.** to protest poor working conditions
   b. Knights of Labor and AFL were larger, better organized; Knights accepted unskilled workers

   c. possible answer—hurt; employers and the government became less tolerant of violence and disruption

4. Great Railroad Strike—wages cut; many people died, property damaged; Homestead Strike—manager wanted increased production; many people died; Pullman Strike—wages cut, rent not cut; federal troops called in, workers fired

5. business can stay open only if profitable; if workers strike, replacement workers will be hired

The Age of Invention

BEFORE YOU READ

MAIN IDEA

Important innovations in transportation and communication occurred during the Second Industrial Revolution.

READING FOCUS

1. What advances in transportation were made in the late 1800s?
2. What inventions led to a communications revolution?
3. How did Thomas Edison help shape the modern world?

KEY TERMS AND PEOPLE

mass transit
Orville and Wilbur Wright
telegraph
Alexander Graham Bell
Thomas Alva Edison

TAKING NOTES As you read, take notes on new developments in transportation and how they changed life in American cities. Record your notes in a graphic organizer like the one shown here.

Development	How It Changed Life

THE INSIDE STORY

How did two bicycle mechanics change the world? On a windy December day in 1903, a one-man airplane flew over the dunes near Kitty Hawk, North Carolina. The pilot was Orville Wright. Orville and his older brother Wilbur had always been clever with machines. Bicycling was a new craze in the 1890s, and the Wrights started a successful business designing and making bicycles. Wilbur began to read about experiments with gliders—light airplanes that have no motors but are carried by the wind. In 1899 the Wright brothers began to build and test gliders. Soon they turned to powered flight.

On the morning of December 17, the brothers took turns piloting their tiny 745-pound plane. On Orville's first flight, the plane lurched up and down, stayed in the air for 12 seconds, and then nosed into the ground. It was the first true flight in an airplane. The brothers made three more flights that day. Orville's diary described the fourth trip: "The machine started off with its ups and downs as it had before, but by the time he [Wilbur] had gone over three or four hundred feet he had it under much better control and was traveling on a fairly even course." The plane traveled 852 feet in 59 seconds. The Wrights had flown into history. ◢

A Flight Into History

▼ Orville Wright makes the first flight as his brother Wilbur watches.

477

The Age of Invention

1. **Teach** Ask students the Reading Focus questions to teach this section.

2. **Apply** Have students create a list of inventions discussed in the section. Next to each item, have students note whether or not the device is still in use, and if not, what modern device has replaced it.

3. **Review** Review student lists as a class. Discuss the advances in transportation and communications that took place during the late 1800s. Ask students to name the

invention that they think was the most significant or changed life the most.

4. **Practice/Homework** Have students select one of Edison's inventions and write a newspaper article from the viewpoint of a reporter living in the late 1800s. The article should explain what the invention does and why it is revolutionary.
LS Logical-Mathematical, Verbal-Linguistic
Alternative Assessment Handbook, Rubric 37: Writing Assignments

---

Bellringer

The Inside Story. . . Use the **Daily Bellringer Transparency** to help students answer the question.

Daily Bellringer Transparency, Section 4

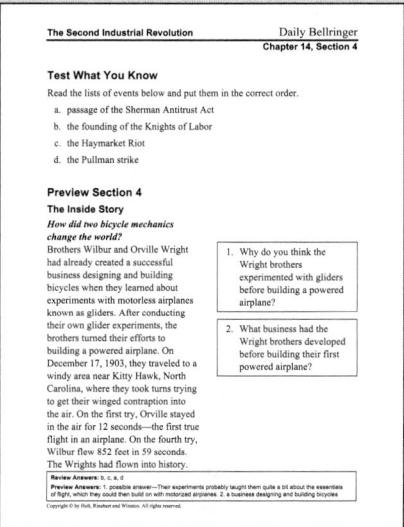

Taking Notes

streetcars, allowed riders to travel at the speed of a horse; cable cars, used electricity to propel vehicles up hills; subways, avoided traffic at street-level; automobiles, faster transportation; airplanes, faster transportation over great distances

❶ What advances in transportation were made in the late 1800s? *streetcars, subways, automobile*

Advances in Transportation

Explain How did cable cars work? *Cars latched onto an underground cable that was kept in motion by a steam engine.*

Identify Who built the first practical motorcar in the United States? *Charles and J. Frank Duryea*

Elaborate How did mass transit develop? *rose from need; horsecars, then streetcars were used; traffic became a problem, which led to the development of the subway*

Teaching Tip

Many people confuse cable cars and trolleys. Trolleys get their power from electrical wires *overhead*. Cable cars use an *underground* cable to move them.

Answers

Linking to Today *possible answers— in appearance, both use overhead electricity*

478

Cable Cars to Light Rail

The late 1800s were the heyday of cable cars and electric streetcars in urban America. But with the rise of the automobile, many systems declined or were dismantled by the 1950s.

Today more cities are turning to light rail trains. These are electrically powered by overhead trolley wires or an electrified third rail. Los Angeles, for example, has a light-rail network linking its downtown with outlying areas.

Supporters of light rail emphasize its benefits in reducing traffic and pollution. Opponents argue that too few people use these systems.

Comparing How are some light-rail systems like old-fashioned trolleys?

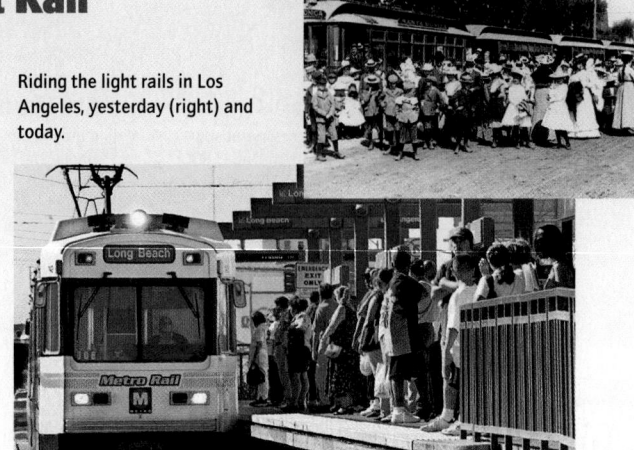

Riding the light rails in Los Angeles, yesterday (right) and today.

Advances in Transportation

Railroads allowed people to travel long distances quite easily. But Americans also needed local forms of transportation. As cities grew larger in the 1800s, walking everywhere became impractical. Workers wanted faster ways of getting to and from their jobs. People wanted easier access to stores and attractions. Residents in distant neighborhoods felt isolated from the city center.

Cities responded by devising means of **mass transit**. These are public transportation systems that carry large numbers of people and make regular stops along established routes.

Streetcars The first forms of mass transit were horse-drawn passenger vehicles. By the 1830s these horsecars were rolling along rails in the street, and they became known as streetcars. Rails made the ride smoother and allowed horses to pull larger and heavier loads.

In cities with steep hills, though, streetcars needed more power than horses could provide. Andrew Smith Hallidie solved the problem in San Francisco by building the first cable car line in 1873. The cars could climb up the hills

by latching onto a moving cable underground. The cable was kept in motion by a steam engine in a central station.

Soon the cable cars became a symbol of San Francisco. One visitor wrote about them admiringly in 1888:

HISTORY'S VOICES

❝If any one should ask me what I consider the most distinctive, progressive feature of California, I should answer promptly, its cable-car system . . . A point of perfection [is] the amazing length of the ride that is given you for . . . a nickel. I have circled this city of San Francisco . . . for this smallest of . . . coins.❞

—Harriet Harper, 1888

Other cities began to build cable car lines, but they quickly became outdated. By 1900 most had been replaced by streetcars powered by overhead electrical wires. Electric streetcars, or trolleys, were cheaper to build and faster to run than cable cars.

Subways As American cities continued to expand rapidly, traffic became a serious problem. In urban centers such as Boston and New York, traffic sometimes came to a complete

---

Differentiating Instruction

Below Level

English-Language Learners

Research Required

Materials plain paper and colored pencils or markers

1. Have students work in pairs or small groups. Assign one of the following means of transportation to each group of students: streetcars, subways, light rail, automobiles, and airplanes.

2. Have each pair look for illustrations showing early forms of their assigned means of transportation.

3. Have each pair make a poster showing a picture of its form of transportation and explaining how it changed people's lives when it was invented.

4. Display the posters for the class to see.
   LS Interpersonal, Visual-Spatial

   Alternative Assessment Handbook, Rubrics 14: Group Activity; and 28: Posters

standstill, with horses and electric streetcars competing for space on narrow roads. Then Boston found a solution. The city unveiled the nation's first subway line in 1897, attracting more than 100,000 riders on opening day. The local newspaper reported the event proudly:

HISTORY'S VOICES

❝It was a great success. . . . The regularity with which the cars were run, the haste with which they were occupied and emptied at the . . . terminal and the machine-like precision with which they arrived and departed were undoubtedly wonderful.❞

—Boston Daily Globe, 1897

New York opened its subway in 1904 to even bigger crowds. On its first day, some 350,000 New Yorkers eagerly rode the new underground trains.

Automobiles While mass transit was taking off, inventors were also experimenting with vehicles for personal use. A breakthrough came when Nikolaus A. Otto, a German engineer, invented the internal combustion engine in 1867. Soon inventors in Europe and the United States were trying to adapt that engine to power a "horseless carriage." In 1893 Charles and J. Frank Duryea built the first practical motorcar in the United States.

The early automobiles were for the wealthy few who could afford expensive playthings. A new car cost about $2,500—at a time when the average worker made roughly $500 a year.

Airplanes Human beings had tried for hundreds of years to discover a way to fly. During the Renaissance, the Italian artist Leonardo da Vinci designed—but did not build—a flying machine. It was not until 1903 that two American brothers crafted a successful airplane.

Orville and Wilbur Wright were Ohio bicycle makers who tackled the challenge systematically. They made kites to test their wing designs. They built a wind tunnel to study the forces of wind on the wings. They figured out how to power their plane with an engine and how to control it.

On December 17, 1903, the Wright brothers tried out their airplane at Kitty Hawk, North Carolina. In freezing temperatures and a strong wind, Orville climbed into the pilot's seat. The plane took off across the beach, flying just inches above the ground and landing 120

feet from where it had started. This short trip—12 seconds in all—was the first true flight in an airplane. The Wright brothers quickly followed this success with even longer flights.

READING CHECK **Summarizing** What innovations in the late 1800s changed the way people moved from place to place?

Communications Revolution

Inventors also changed the way Americans communicated in the 1800s. In earlier times, people had face-to-face contact or relied on handwritten letters or printed materials. Communicating over long distances meant physically carrying a document from one place to another. Technology changed all this.

The telegraph In 1837 Samuel F. B. Morse patented his method of communicating by sending messages over wires with electricity. He called his invention the **telegraph.** Telegraph operators tapped out patterns of long and short signals that stood for letters of the alphabet. Using this system, known as Morse code, an operator could send a message to distant locations in mere minutes.

After the Civil War, the telegraph grew with the railroads. Telegraph wires were strung on poles along the railroad tracks. Train stations had telegraph offices inside them. Telegraphs became the fastest way to send messages.

The telephone Elisha Gray and **Alexander Graham Bell** both developed devices that could transmit voices using electricity. In 1876 the two men brought their designs to the patent office within hours of each other. Bell, however, got his design patented first. Today he is known as the inventor of the telephone.

Companies quickly found telephones to be an essential business tool. People wanted them in their homes, too. By 1900 more than a million telephones had been installed in offices and households across the nation.

The typewriter Inventors in many nations made attempts to create a writing machine. Christopher Latham Sholes, a Milwaukee printer, developed the first practical typewriter in 1867, with the help of Carlos Glidden and Samuel Soulé. Sholes later improved upon his

THE IMPACT TODAY

Daily Life
New York's subway system is one of the world's busiest, carrying an average of 4.5 million people every weekday. The system includes more than 840 miles of track—enough to reach to Chicago if it were laid end to end.

Skills Focus: Analyzing Bias in Historical Interpretation — At Level

Reading Like a Historian Skill
Communications Innovations

1. Divide the class into three groups. Assign one of the following inventions to each group: the telegraph, the telephone, or the typewriter.

2. Have each group prepare an advertising campaign for its assigned product that includes a newspaper ad, a magazine ad, and a slogan or jingle encouraging businesspeople to adopt this new invention. Ads, slogans, and jingles should describe the possible effects that the new invention may have on business.

3. Have volunteers from each group share their advertising campaign with the class.

4. Guide the class in a discussion of the revolution in communications. How did each of these inventions evolve into its modern form? **LS** **Auditory-Musical, Verbal-Linguistic**
   Alternative Assessment Handbook, Rubrics 2: Advertisements; and 14: Group Activity

---

Reading Focus

❷ What inventions led to a communications revolution? *telegraph, telephone, typewriter*

Communications Revolution

Explain What was Morse Code and how did it work? *system of long and short signals that stood for letters of the alphabet; telegraph operators used it to send messages over wires with electricity*

Compare and Contrast Name one similarity and one difference between the telegraph and the telephone. *Both use electricity to communicate over distances. The telegraph transmits code, whereas the telephone transmits voices.*

📄 CRF: Biography: Elijah McCoy
📄 Political Cartoons Activities for American History: Cartoon 27: The Atlantic Telegraph Cable

Info to Know

Western Union In the early days of the telegraph, there were six major companies. They agreed to divide the national market into six regions. By 1866 Western Union had taken over all of the other companies, creating a monopoly. This allowed Western Union to standardize its rates, equipment, and language, and led to a reduction in telegraph costs.

go.hrw.com
Online Resources
KEYWORD: SD7 CH14
TOPIC: INVENTIONS

Answers

Reading Check *mass transit, streetcars, subways, and automobiles; made traveling faster and more practical*

❸ **How did Thomas Edison help shape the modern world?** *by inventing the light bulb, phonograph, motion picture camera, and projector*

Thomas Edison

Recall Why did Edison sometimes view his hearing impairment as a blessing? *because it helped him concentrate on his work*

Draw Conclusions? Why wasn't the electric light bulb an immediate success? *Electricity was not widely available.*

Info to Know

Thomas Edison Thomas Edison did not fit in well at school; he was hard of hearing, which made school difficult. He was, however, an avid reader. Edison quit school when he was 12 and started working for the railroad. Four years later, in 1863, he began working as a telegraph operator, and he worked for several different companies. Edison was repeatedly fired from these companies for experimenting with the office equipment without permission; by 1869 he had created the duplex telegraph and a printer. His career as an inventor had begun.

Answers

Reading Like a Historian 1. *Bottles, work tables, and scientific equipment are used by inventors.* **2.** *They could collaborate and bounce ideas off each other.*

Reading Check *made it faster and easier*

480

---

machine by designing the QWERTY keyboard, which is still the standard in computers today. The name QWERTY comes from the first few letters found at the top left. Sholes purposely placed the most frequently used letters far apart so the keys wouldn't jam when struck.

The typewriter could produce legible documents very quickly. Businesses began to hire women as typists to manage company correspondence. This opened up new job opportunities for many American women.

READING CHECK Identifying the Main Idea
How did technology improve communication during the Second Industrial Revolution?

Thomas Edison

Inventors and innovators in the late 1800s were obsessed with the idea of progress. They made things work better, faster, and more cheaply. They turned seemingly impossible dreams into profit-making ventures.

One of the most amazing inventors of the era was **Thomas Alva Edison**. As a child, he had an unstoppable curiosity about how everything worked. Although he lost almost all his hearing when he was about 12, Edison did not let this discourage him. In fact, he sometimes looked upon it as a blessing because it helped him concentrate on his work.

At the age of 22, Edison declared himself an inventor. His early successes included an improved telegraph. In 1876, in a pioneering move, Edison opened his own research laboratory in Menlo Park, New Jersey. He hired several assistants to work with him, choosing men with scientific and technical expertise. He provided them with materials and equipment, and he encouraged them to think creatively.

Edison also encouraged hard work. As he said, "Genius is 1 percent inspiration, 99 percent perspiration." Laboring right alongside his assistants, Edison spent long hours testing out ideas and tinkering with designs. Even failures didn't phase him:

HISTORY'S VOICES

❝I never quit until I get what I'm after. Negative results are just what I'm after. They are just as valuable to me as positive results.❞
—Thomas Alva Edison

Menlo Park Lab

Thomas Alva Edison's greatest invention may have been the modern industrial research laboratory. In Menlo Park, New Jersey, Edison brought together inventors who shared ideas and helped design hundreds of inventions. Following the Menlo Park model, young companies like Bell Telephone and Eastman Kodak quickly set up their own research labs. Such facilities are now common in most industries.

In 1879 the lab became the first building ever to be equipped for electric lighting.

Another great Menlo Park invention was the phonograph, developed in 1877. On this phonograph, sound was recorded by a stylus inscribing a piece of tinfoil wrapped around a cylinder which was turned by cranking the large wheel shown here.

Thomas Edison built Menlo Park when he was 29.

Gathering groups of inventors together to work under one roof was unheard of before Edison's time.

Skills FOCUS **READING LIKE A HISTORIAN**

1. **Interpreting Visuals** How does this image reflect the type of work carried on at Menlo Park?
2. **Making Inferences** What would be the advantage of bringing together many inventors under one roof?

See **Skills Handbook, pp. H7, H30**

Skills Focus: Making Inferences
Above Level

Reading Skill
Edison's Laboratory

1. Tell students that in 1876, Thomas Edison opened his research laboratory in Menlo Park, New Jersey. He placed classified advertisements in newspapers around the country to find assistants with scientific and technical expertise.

2. Have each student write a letter applying for a position at Edison's laboratory. Students should also prepare a professional resume to accompany their letters. Students should try to convince Edison to hire them by explaining characteristics that have made them innovative thinkers and that will help them come up with new ideas and work out problems in flawed designs. In their resumes, students should document their experiences and support the information in their letters.

LS **Verbal-Linguistic**

Alternative Assessment Handbook, Rubric 43: Writing to Persuade

Within four years of setting up shop, Edison and his team had invented the first phonograph, or record player, and a telephone transmitter. Other inventions poured out of the lab so quickly that Edison became known as the Wizard of Menlo Park.

Edison's greatest bit of "wizardry" was probably his development of practical electric lighting. He first came up with an incandescent bulb that could safely illuminate homes and streetlamps. Edison realized, though, that his lightbulb wouldn't be widely used until electricity became widely available. So in 1880 he undertook a new challenge—bringing electricity to New York City.

Edison first had to design and produce by hand all the parts necessary for an electricity network—sockets, fuses, switches, power meters, and generators. In 1882 he was ready. Near Wall Street, he installed a lighting system powered by his own electric power plant. The plant could deliver electricity only to homes and offices within a square mile. Luckily, within that square mile lay some very influential customers, including the New York Stock Exchange and the major New York newspapers. Electric power plants soon arose all over the country, and new investors flocked to Edison.

In 1887 Edison built an even larger laboratory in West Orange, New Jersey. He hired hundreds of brilliant technicians for his "invention

factory." There, Edison and his team improved the phonograph, invented the motion picture camera and projector, and developed stronger and more powerful batteries. Over his lifetime, Edison earned more than 1,000 U.S. patents.

READING CHECK **Making Inferences** Why was Edison's lightbulb so important?

FACES OF HISTORY
Thomas EDISON
1847-1931

Thomas Alva Edison prefered self instruction to formal schooling. He read widely in history, literature, and the sciences. In his spare time he built complicated models, including a working sawmill and a steam-powered railroad engine.

At the age of 14, he was earning $10 a day producing and selling his own newspaper. At the age of 20, Edison created his first invention, an electric vote-counting machine. Disappointed because few politicians were interested, Edison vowed that from then on, he would invent only things that people would buy.

Edison's next invention, a new stock ticker for reporting sales and purchases of stocks, earned him $40,000. He used the money to set up his Menlo Park laboratory. Edison also established businesses to manufacture his gadgets.

Elaborate How was the commercial failure of Edison's vote-counting machine a blessing in disguise?

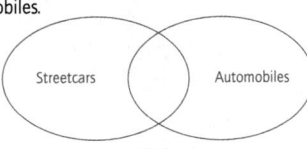

SECTION 4 ASSESSMENT

go.hrw.com
Online Quiz
Keyword: SD7 HP14

Reviewing Ideas, Terms, and People

1. **a. Recall** Name three different kinds of mass transit vehicles used in the 1800s.
   b. Explain Why were cable cars replaced in many cities by 1900?
   c. Elaborate Why would cars and airplanes be useful forms of transportation?

2. **a. Describe** How did the **telegraph** improve communication between people?
   b. Rank Which invention do you think was more significant, the telegraph or the telephone? Explain.

3. **a. Identify** What were some of the major inventions created by **Thomas Alva Edison**?
   b. Draw Conclusions How did Edison's inventions change the way Americans lived?

Critical Thinking

4. **Comparing and Contrasting** Copy the chart below and record the similarities and differences between streetcars and automobiles.

Streetcars   Automobiles

FOCUS ON WRITING

5. **Expository** You are a city official working to develop the first subway system in Boston. Write an announcement explaining how this new mode of transportation works and how it will benefit residents and visitors.

THE SECOND INDUSTRIAL REVOLUTION **481**

Section 4 Assessment Answers

1. **a.** horsecars; streetcars; subways
   b. Electric streetcars were cheaper and faster.
   c. Cars allow people to make their own routes; airplanes and cars allow people to travel great distances more quickly.

2. **a.** Messages could be sent in minutes.
   b. possible answer—the telephone, because interaction became immediate

3. **a.** phonograph; incandescent bulb; motion picture camera and projector; storage battery for cars; vote-counting machine

b. could stay up after dark; music at home; communicate immediately; watch movies

4. similar—transported people; different—streetcar: transported large number of people, fueled by electricity or horsepower, inexpensive, accessible; automobile: transported a few people, fueled by gasoline, expensive to buy and operate

5. cheap, fast, clean, convenient

The Rights of Workers

Historical Context The documents below provide different information about the rights of workers and the needs of businesses in the 1800s.

Task Examine the documents and answer the questions that follow. Then you will be asked to write an essay about why workers and business owners were at odds in the 1800s, using facts from the documents and the chapter to support the position you take in your thesis statement.

Word Help

permeating filling
dividends bonuses

Info to Know

Mother Jones Mary Harris "Mother" Jones faced several tragedies in her own life before she advocated on behalf of workers' rights. Within the span of one week in 1867, Jones lost her husband and all four of their young children. Only four years later, Jones lost everything she owned in the great Chicago fire of 1871. A dynamic speaker, Jones gained a well-earned reputation as an agitator; in her own words, "I'm not a humanitarian. I'm a hell-raiser."

Primary Source

Andrew Carnegie was no stranger to child labor. At the age of 13, Carnegie earned $1.20 a week as a bobbin boy in a cotton factory. Carnegie later wrote about that time in his life: "I began to learn what poverty meant. It was burnt into my heart then that my father had to beg for work. And then and there came the resolve that I would cure that when I got to be a man."

— Andrew Carnegie

Autobiography of Andrew Carnegie, 1920

DOCUMENT 1

Mary Harris "Mother" Jones was a passionate supporters of workers' rights. She championed labor unions from the 1870s until the 1920s, when she was more than 90 years old. The speech below, given to a group of striking coal miners in Charlestown, West Virginia, on August 15, 1912, reflects her sympathy for workers' struggles.

"Come with me and see the horrible pictures, see the horrible condition the ruling class has put these women in. Aye, they destroy women. Look at those little children, the rising generation, yes, look at the little ones, yes . . .

Go into our factories, see how the conditions are there, see how women are ground up for the merciless money pirates, see how many of the poor wretches go to work with crippled bodies . . .

I talked with a mother who had her small children working. She said to me, "Mother, they are not of age, but I had to say they were; I had to tell them [the employers] they were of age so they could get a chance to help me to get something to eat . . . "

There is a great revolution going on in the industrial world . . . The small business man is beginning to be eliminated. He has got to get down, he can't get up . . .

This fight that you are in is the great industrial revolution that is permeating the heart of men over the world."

DOCUMENT 2

One of Mother Jones's main targets was steel magnate Andrew Carnegie, whom she criticized for exploiting workers. In his autobiography, Carnegie wrote that he believed in paying workers well. He also blamed the violent Homestead strike on a handful of unreasonable union members. Below is an excerpt from *The Autobiography of Andrew Carnegie*, written in 1920.

"Taking no account of the reward that comes from feeling that you and your employees are friends and judging only from economical results, I believe that higher wages to men who respect their employers and are happy and contented are a good investment, yielding, indeed, big dividends . . .

The unjust demands of the few union men, and the opinion of the three thousand non-union men that they were unjust, very naturally led [the Homestead factory supervisor] into thinking there would be no trouble . . .

Nothing I have ever had to meet in all my life, before or since, wounded me so deeply. No pangs remain of any wound received in my business career save that of Homestead. It was so unnecessary. The men were outrageously wrong. The strikers, with the new machinery, would have made from four to nine dollars a day under the new scale—thirty per cent more than they were making with the old machinery."

Collaborative Learning

At Level

Mother Jones and Andrew Carnegie

Research Required

1. Divide the class into groups of four or five students. Have students conduct outside research to familiarize themselves more fully with the attitudes of Mother Jones and Andrew Carnegie. Encourage students to locate primary sources.

2. Have each group write a short scene in which Mother Jones and Andrew Carnegie meet and discuss their ideas about business ownership and labor. Students may also incorporate actual quotations from their research into their scripts.

3. Have members of each group present their scene to the class. Guide the class in a discussion of what compromises these two leaders might agree on. **LS Interpersonal, Kinesthetic**

📖 Alternative Assessment Handbook, Rubric 33: Skits and Reader's Theater

DOCUMENT 3

One of the most controversial practices of the industrial era was using child labor. Young workers saved factory owners a lot of money because they were cheaper to hire than adults. Many adult factory workers could not earn enough to support their families unless their children also worked.

Labor leaders and social reformers called for both the end of child labor and wages that workers could live on. Many business owners resisted these changes, however, fearing they would cut into profits. This cartoon, titled "The Galley," appeared in *Puck* magazine on August 4, 1910.

THE GALLEY.

Skills FOCUS — READING LIKE A HISTORIAN

1. a. Explain Refer to Document 1. Why did the mother lie to let her children work?
b. Elaborate According to Mother Jones, how do modern working conditions "destroy" women?

2. a. Identify Refer to Document 2. What kind of worker does Carnegie think should be rewarded with good wages?
b. Analyze According to Carnegie, in what way were the strikers being shortsighted?

3. a. Describe What image does the cartoonist use to depict working conditions for children?

b. Interpret How does the cartoonist imply that factory owners are being cruel? What motive is suggested for their behavior?
c. Evaluate Where do the cartoonist's sympathies lie?

4. Document-Based Essay Question Consider the question below and form a thesis statement. Using examples from Documents 1, 2, and 3, create an outline and write a short essay supporting your position.
How were the needs of workers and business owners at odds in the Second Industrial Revolution?

See **Skills Handbook**, pp. H31, H34

THE SECOND INDUSTRIAL REVOLUTION **483**

Info to Know

Child Labor Laws In the early 1800s, one-third of U.S. factory workers were children between the ages of 7 and 12. Despite repeated attempts at legislation throughout the century, employment of children grew rapidly during the expansion of industry after the Civil War. Today, American children are protected by a combination of state and federal laws.

Evaluate Why do you think it took so long to get laws passed regulating child labor? *possible answer— because businesses had the money to fight legislation*

Differentiating Instruction

Above Level

Advanced Learners/GATE

Research Required

Background In the early 1900s, the National Child Labor Committee hired Lewis Hine to photograph and report on child labor throughout the country. Hine used his photographs to convince the public and the federal government to fight against child labor.

1. Divide the class into small groups. Have each group locate several of Lewis Hine's photographs of child laborers.

2. Have each student choose one photograph and write an essay comparing Document 3

with the photograph he or she has selected. Students should consider whether the cartoonist exaggerates and which medium (cartoon or photograph) presents a more pitiable picture of child labor.

4. Ask volunteers to read their essays to the class. **LS Visual-Spatial, Verbal-Linguistic**

📖 Alternative Assessment Handbook, Rubric 40: Writing to Describe

Answers

Reading Like a Historian 1. a. *so that they could help her get something to eat;* **b.** *possible answer—because pay was so low, working conditions were so poor, and workers had no other options;* **2. a.** *employees who respect their employers and are happy and contented;* **b.** *They would have made 30 percent more with the new machinery than they had made with the old machinery.* **3. a.** *a slave ship;* **b.** *children are tied to oars; overseer has whip; greed;* **c.** *with the children;* **4.** *Answers will vary, but students' essays should address the fact that business owners increased their profits by giving workers low wages, long hours, and unsafe working conditions.*

483

Answers

Visual Summary

Review and Inquiry Show the visual summary transparency for all students to see. Have students work individually or in small groups to brainstorm and write down as many details as they can about each of the topics in the Web diagram. When students are finished, have them call out the information. Have students add to or correct their information as needed.

Quick Facts Transparency: The Second Industrial Revolution

Reviewing Key Terms and People

1. entrepreneur
2. telegraph
3. free enterprise or laissez-faire
4. Sherman Antitrust Act
5. social Darwinism
6. vertical integration
7. Bessemer process
8. American Federation of Labor (AFL)
9. Thomas Edison
10. wildcatter
11. sweatshop
12. John D. Rockefeller
13. blacklist
14. Alexander Graham Bell

Comprehension and Critical Thinking

15. **a.** steel and oil
    b. possible answer—to bring settlers into the newly acquired west
    c. Its strength and low cost allowed for quick production of railroads.

16. **a.** proprietorships, partnerships, corporations, trust, monopolies
    b. Rockefeller—oil; Carnegie—steel; Vanderbilt—railroads; Pullman—railroad cars
    c. stronger people and businesses prosper, weaker ones fail

---

Chapter Review

Visual Summary: The Second Industrial Revolution

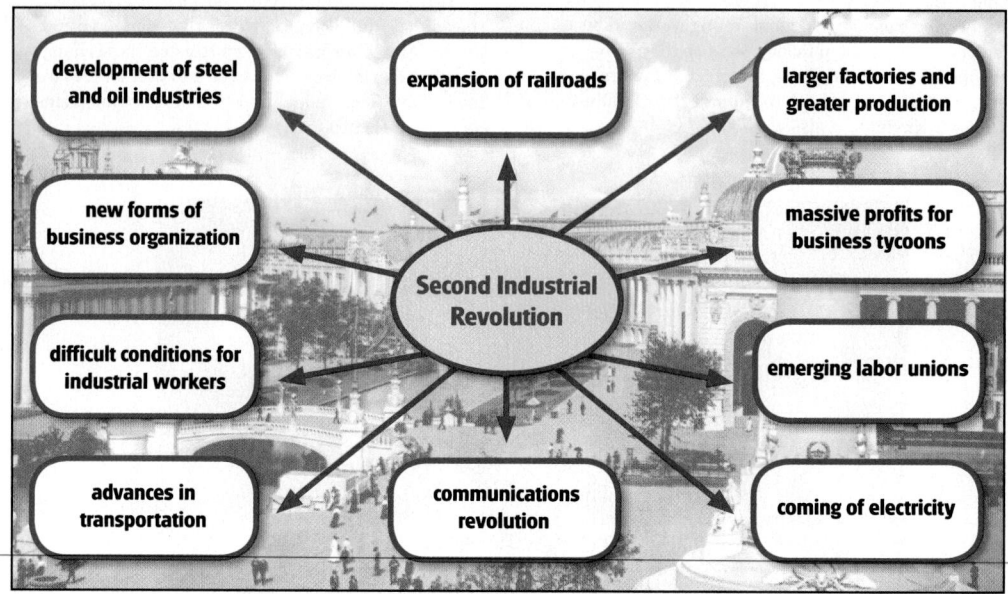

- development of steel and oil industries
- expansion of railroads
- larger factories and greater production
- new forms of business organization
- **Second Industrial Revolution**
- massive profits for business tycoons
- difficult conditions for industrial workers
- emerging labor unions
- advances in transportation
- communications revolution
- coming of electricity

Reviewing Key Terms and People

Identify the correct term or person from the chapter that best fits each of the following descriptions.

1. Someone who invests money and takes risks to start a new business
2. A device for sending coded messages over wires with electricity
3. A form of capitalism in which the government does not intervene
4. An 1890 law that prohibited trusts from interfering with free trade
5. A philosophy holding that people compete in society and those who are stronger and more capable are the ones who prosper
6. A process of acquiring companies that provide many of the supplies and services needed for a particular industry
7. A technique developed in the 1850s for making steel faster and cheaper
8. A union of skilled workers led by Samuel Gompers in the 1880s
9. The so-called Wizard of Menlo Park, whose inventions included practical electric lighting, the phonograph, and the movie camera
10. An oil prospector
11. A tenement workshop where employees toil long hours under poor conditions for little pay
12. The owner of the Standard Oil Company and a leading philanthropist
13. A list of perceived troublemakers whom employers won't hire
14. The inventor of the telephone

484 CHAPTER 14

---

17. **a.** crowds protesting police action in Chicago, bomb killed 11 people
    b. long hours, unsafe workplaces; improve working conditions
    c. possible answers—belief in social Darwinism; desire to maximize profits

18. **a.** transportation systems that carry large numbers of people
    b. possible answer—His inventions affect everyday life for most of the world.
    c. possible answer—will bring goods to market and people to their destinations quicker, allow people to collaborate over distances

History's Impact video program
Review the video to answer the closing question:
How did the Second Industrial Revolution change
life in the United States?

Comprehension and Critical Thinking

SECTION 1 *(pp. 460–463)*

15. a. Identify What new industries spurred America's industrial growth in the late 1800s?

b. Make Inferences Why do you think the federal government helped finance the first transcontinental railroad?

c. Elaborate How was steel linked to the expansion of the railroads?

SECTION 2 *(pp. 466–471)*

16. a. Recall What new kinds of business structures arose during the late 1800s?

b. Explain Name four industrial tycoons of the day and explain how they made their fortunes.

c. Develop How did American economic principles and the ideas of social Darwinists encourage the growth of big business?

SECTION 3 *(pp. 472–476)*

17. a. Describe What was the Haymarket Riot?

b. Make Generalizations What were conditions like for factory workers, and what goals did union organizers have?

c. Evaluate Why do you think employers and government officials were generally unsympathetic to the labor movement in the late 1800s?

SECTION 4 *(pp. 477–481)*

18. a. Define What is mass transit?

b. Analyze Why is Thomas Alva Edison regarded as one of the greatest inventors in history?

c. Predict How do you think American productivity was affected by advances in transportation and communication? Discuss some specific examples in your answer.

Using the Internet

go.hrw.com
Practice Online
Keyword: SD7 CH14

19. During the late 1800s, many of the captains of industry donated millions of dollars to charitable organizations. Using the keyword above, do research to learn about Andrew Carnegie's involvement with public libraries. Then create a report that tells the story of the Carnegie libraries. Find out whether your town received funds to build a Carnegie public library.

Analyzing Primary Sources

Reading Like a Historian
From 1908 to 1912 photographer Lewis Hine documented the dangerous and difficult conditions in which child laborers worked.

20. Explain Why are these boys standing on this spinning machine?

21. Draw Conclusions What opportunities for injury can you see in this photograph?

Critical Reading

*Reread the passage with the heading "Making steel."
Then answer the question that follows.*

22. Why was the new way to make steel known as the Bessemer process and not the Kelly process?

A Bessemer's method worked, but Kelly's did not.

B Bessemer bought the rights to the technique from Kelly.

C Bessemer did a better job of promoting the use of his method.

D Bessemer was quick to secure a patent for his technique.

WRITING FOR THE SAT

Think about the following issue:

Social Darwinists believed that the process of natural selection made society stronger as a whole. Therefore, they opposed any intervention that would interfere with that process.

23. Assignment Did the social Darwinists have the right or wrong idea about how society becomes stronger and better? Write a short essay in which you develop your position on this issue. Support your point of view with reasoning and examples from your reading and studies.

Answers

Using the Internet

19. Go to the HRW Web site and enter the keyword to access a rubric for this activity.

KEYWORD: SD7 CH14

Analyzing Primary Sources

20. They are too short to reach working area.

21. hands, feet, clothing caught in machine; cuts from equipment; hearing loss from loud noise of machine

Critical Reading

22. D

Writing for the SAT

23. possible answer—wrong idea, because intervention is needed to protect consumers from unfair and unsafe business practices

A rubric for this activity is provided in the Chapter Resource File: Writing for the SAT: Innovation.

History's Impact
Video Program

Innovation in manufacturing and business led to countless new inventions that changed daily life.

Review and Assessment Resources

Review and Reinforce

- CRF: Chapter Review Activity
- Quick Facts Transparency: The Second Industrial Revolution
- Spanish Chapter Summaries Audio CD Program
- Online Chapter Summaries in Spanish
- **OSP** Holt PuzzlePro; Quiz Show for ExamView
- Quiz Game CD-ROM

Assess

- PASS: Chapter Test, Forms A and B
- Alternative Assessment Handbook
- **OSP** ExamView Test Generator, Chapter Test
- Differentiated Instruction Modified Worksheets and Tests CD-ROM: Chapter Test
- **HOAP** Holt Online Assessment Program (in the Premier Online Edition)

Reteach/Intervene

- Interactive Reader and Study Guide
- Differentiated Instruction Teacher Management System: Lesson Plans for Differentiated Instruction
- Differentiated Instruction Modified Worksheets and Tests CD-ROM: Chapter Test
- Interactive Skills Tutor CD-ROM

go.hrw.com
Online Resources
KEYWORD: SD7 CH14

Chapter 15 Planning Guide

Life at the Turn of the 20th Century

Chapter Overview	Reproducible Resources	Technology Resources
CHAPTER 15 pp. 486–515 **Overview:** In this chapter, students will analyze life at the turn of the century for Americans, including the hardships and discrimination that many faced.	**Differentiated Instruction Teacher Management System:*** • Instructional Benchmarking Guides • Lesson Plans for Differentiated Instruction **Interactive Reader and Study Guide:** Chapter Summary* **Chapter Resource File:*** • Focus on Writing Activity: U.S. Policy on Inspection of Immigrants • Social Studies Skills Activity: Comparing and Contrasting • Chapter Review Activity **American History Outline Maps** **Pre-AP Activities Guide for American History*** **Reading Like a Historian Toolkit**	Live Ink® Online Reading Help Student Edition on Audio CD Program Differentiated Instruction Modified Worksheets and Tests CD-ROM Interactive Skills Tutor CD-ROM United States History Primary Source Library CD-ROM Power Presentations with Video CD-ROM History's Impact: American History Video Program (VHS/DVD): Life at the Turn of the 20th Century Online Chapter Summaries in Spanish Graphic Organizer Transparencies
Section 1: **New Immigrants** **The Main Idea:** A new wave of immigrants came to the United States in the late 1800s, settling in cities, and troubling some native-born Americans.	**Differentiated Instruction Teacher Management System:** Section 1 Lesson Plan* **Interactive Reader and Study Guide:** Section 1 Summary* **Chapter Resource File:*** • Vocabulary Builder Activity, Section 1	Daily Bellringer Transparency: Section 1* Daily Test Practice Transparency: Section 1* Quick Facts Transparency: Old and New Immigrants*
Section 2: **Urban Life** **The Main Idea:** In cities in the late 1800s, people in the upper, middle, and lower classes lived different kinds of lives because of their different economic situations.	**Differentiated Instruction Teacher Management System:** Section 2 Lesson Plan* **Interactive Reader and Study Guide:** Section 2 Summary* **Chapter Resource File:*** • Vocabulary Builder Activity, Section 2	Daily Bellringer Transparency: Section 2* Daily Test Practice Transparency: Section 2*
Section 3: **Politics in the Gilded Age** **The Main Idea:** Political corruption was common in the late 1800s, but reformers began fighting for changes to make government more honest.	**Differentiated Instruction Teacher Management System:** Section 3 Lesson Plan* **Interactive Reader and Study Guide:** Section 3 Summary* **Chapter Resource File:*** • Vocabulary Builder Activity, Section 3	Daily Bellringer Transparency: Section 3* Daily Test Practice Transparency: Section 3*
Section 4: **Segregation and Discrimination** **The Main Idea:** The United States in the late 1800s was a place of great change—and a place in need of even greater change.	**Differentiated Instruction Teacher Management System:** Section 4 Lesson Plan* **Interactive Reader and Study Guide:** Section 4 Summary* **Chapter Resource File:*** • Vocabulary Builder Activity, Section 4	Daily Bellringer Transparency: Section 4* Daily Test Practice Transparency: Section 4*

Review, Assessment, Intervention

📀 **Quick Facts Transparencies:** Old and New Immigrants, Life at the Turn of the 20th Century

🔊 **Spanish Chapter Summaries Audio CD Program**

📄 **Progress Assessment Support System (PASS):** Chapter Test*

💿 **Differentiated Instruction Modified Worksheets and Tests CD-ROM:** Modified Chapter Test

OSP **One-Stop Planner CD-ROM:** ExamView Test Generator (English/Spanish)

HOAP **Holt Online Assessment Program (HOAP),** in the Holt Premier Online Student Edition

---

📄 **PASS:** Section 1 Quiz*

go.hrw.com **Online Quiz:** Section 1

📄 **Alternative Assessment Handbook**

📄 **PASS:** Section 2 Quiz*

go.hrw.com **Online Quiz:** Section 2

📄 **Alternative Assessment Handbook**

📄 **PASS:** Section 3 Quiz*

go.hrw.com **Online Quiz:** Section 3

📄 **Alternative Assessment Handbook**

📄 **PASS:** Section 4 Quiz*

go.hrw.com **Online Quiz:** Section 4

📄 **Alternative Assessment Handbook**

NC RESOURCES

The following resources were developed to help North Carolina educators teach the standards and objectives of North Carolina's eleventh grade standard course of study in United States history.

- United States history EOC Test Prep Workbook
- Teacher's Support System
- North Carolina One-Stop Planner

And be sure to direct your students to **go.hrw.com** for online access to the EOC Test Prep Workbook.

> **go.hrw.com**
> **EOC Test Prep**
> KEYWORD: SE7 NC

Holt Online Learning

> **go.hrw.com**
> **Teacher Resources**
> KEYWORD: SD7 TEACHER

> **go.hrw.com**
> **Student Resources**
> KEYWORD: SD7 CH15

- Document-based Questions
- Interactive Multimedia Activities

- Current Events
- Chapter-based Internet Activities
- and more!

Holt Premier
Online Student Edition

Complete online support for interactivity, assessment, and reporting

- Interactive Maps and Notebook
- Standardized Test Prep
- Homework Practice and Research Activities Online

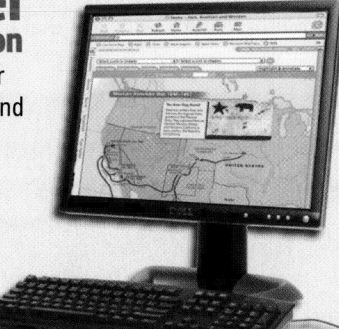

Before You Teach

The Big Picture
Deborah Gray White

New Immigrants in an Urban America Massive numbers of immigrants came to the United States between 1880 and 1910. Most were from southern and eastern Europe. Coming in search of religious freedom and economic opportunity, they traveled to America under conditions that threatened their health. Immigrants who arrived at Ellis Island had a stressful experience passing health tests, but the Chinese who arrived at Angel Island were often detained in prison-like conditions. Both Chinese and Japanese immigrants experienced severe discrimination, and the Chinese Exclusion Act of 1882 and further legislation in 1902 banned Chinese immigration entirely.

Politics in the Gilded Age The growth of cities and industrialization gave rise to different types of politics. Machine politics dominated cities, while rural areas saw the growth of farmer movements. Corruption became widespread in both government and business, setting off reform movements. Many Americans blamed the depression of 1893 on the unscrupulous dealings of the rich. The Populist Party formed with the idea that ordinary people could fight the corruption of elites and politicians, but their 1896 free-silver platform was not enough to beat William McKinley.

Segregation and Discrimination African Americans were deprived of the right to vote by a variety of means, and faced the terror of the lynch mob if they did anything to anger whites. In 1896 segregation was legalized in *Plessy* v. *Ferguson*. African Americans resisted by forming the NAACP and by shoring up their economic position. Other minorities experienced similar legal and social discrimination.

Recent Scholarship

The Struggle at the Turn of the Century The Gilded Age and Progressive period are usually treated as separate eras. In Nell Irvin Painter's *Standing at Armageddon: The United States, 1877–1919* (1987), the two periods are combined. Perhaps the first book to integrate all dispossessed groups into a social and political history of the period, *Standing at Armageddon* argues that the era was marked by a monumental struggle between elites who espoused patriotism and law and order, and the many dispossessed who fought for equality of opportunity. Integrating the histories of labor, farmers, African Americans, immigrants, and women, Painter creates a picture of turn-of-the-twentieth-century America that has resonance today.

Differentiating Instruction

 Differentiated Instruction Teacher Management System
- Lesson Plans for Differentiated Instruction
- Differentiated Instructional Benchmarking Guides
- Interactive Reader and Study Guide

 Spanish Chapter Summaries Audio CD Program

Online Chapter Summaries in Spanish

Student Edition on Audio CD Program

 Differentiated Instruction Modified Worksheets and Tests CD-ROM
- Vocabulary Flash Cards
- Modified Vocabulary Builder Activities
- Modified Chapter Review Activity
- Modified Chapter Test

OSP One-Stop Planner CD-ROM
- ExamView Test Generator (English and Spanish)
- PuzzlePro
- Quiz Show for ExamView
- Transparencies and Videos

TE Differentiated Activities in the Teacher's Edition
- Nativist Response, p. 493
- How Different Classes Lived, p. 497
- Federal Corruption, p. 502
- Legalized Discrimination, p. 508
- *Plessy* v. *Ferguson*, p. 511

Reading Like a Historian
Sam Wineburg

Columbus and New Immigrants

On July 21, 1892, President Benjamin Harrison issued a proclamation setting aside October 12 of that year as "Discovery Day," a national holiday in honor of the "400th anniversary of the discovery of America by Columbus." Buried on page eight of the *New York Times*, Harrison's proclamation stated that Columbus "stood in his age as the pioneer of progress and enlightenment." The president urged Americans to gather in their "churches and in the other places of assembly" to express their "gratitude to Divine Providence for the devout faith of the Discoverer."

Columbus the Pioneer?

The claim that Columbus was a "pioneer of progress and enlightenment" caught the eye of 16-year-old Eric, an articulate high school junior finishing up a year-long Advanced Placement class. Eric participated in one of my research studies and read the Harrison document aloud in my presence. "From what I've learned [Columbus's] goals were not entirely noble," he opined. "Just get rich, whatever."

When I shared Eric's reaction to this document with a group of student teachers, they nodded approvingly at his "critical thinking," his ability to stand back from a presidential proclamation and present an alternative view of the "Discoverer." "How can we get our own students to think this way?" one wanted to know.

A Different Approach

For this same study, I also interviewed historians and advanced graduate students. Melvin, a 30-year-old historian, had a completely different approach to this same document. He began:

"Okay, it's 1892 . . . Harrison is the president . . . It is the beginning of the Progressive Era . . . 'progress and enlightenment' . . . 'universal education,' all the Progressive Era buzzwords . . . Also an era of intense immigration . . . Are they trying to use this holiday for national identity?"

In his comments, Eric focuses on Columbus; Melvin, not at all. For Melvin, the document is not about the events of 1492, but life in 1892. What was going on then, Melvin asked, that merited the establishment of a new holiday?

A Changing America

In 1792 the tercentenary had been a smallish event—restricted almost entirely to the Northeast, and then only in urban areas. But as our chapter describes, 1890s America was in the midst of a facelift as a new kind of immigrant was reaching America's shores. These Italians, Poles, Portuguese and others joined a large Irish contingent to form a new bloc: urban Catholics. And who better than Columbus, that devout Catholic, to make into the symbol of the American ideal?

Catholic immigrants needed a hero and Columbus was their man. On March 29, 1882, reacting to anti-Catholic fever in urban areas (the "Catholic menace"), an Irish priest in New Haven, Connecticut, organized a band of men to create a new fraternal organization: the Knights of Columbus.

Confronting a Historical Document

In the final result, Eric's reaction to the Harrison document tells us more about Eric than about the document he read. By criticizing Columbus, he repeated today's accepted beliefs. But acting as the mouthpiece for conventional wisdom hardly qualifies as "critical thinking."

Eric never paused to ask why a proclamation was issued, or what might have been going on in America that prompted it. He never considered why the proclamation might have been a prudent political move by Harrison, or which groups backed it.

Only questions, not pronouncements, pry open the door to critical thinking.

Social Studies Competency Goals

Goal 4 The learner will evaluate the great westward movement and assess the impact of the agricultural revolution on the nation.

Goal 5 The learner will describe innovations in technology and business practices and assess their impact on economic, political, and social life in America.

Goal 7 The learner will analyze the economic, political, and social reforms of the Progressive Period.

4.03, 5.01, 5.04, 7.03

The Big Idea and Essential Questions

To foster student understanding of this chapter's big idea, design your lesson to address each section's essential question.

Big Idea Government at all levels was plagued by corruption, and immigrants from Southern and Eastern Europe settled in the cities.

Essential Questions

1. How did immigrants change American cities in the late 1800s?

2. What were living conditions like for Americans in the upper, middle, and lower classes?

3. How did reformers respond to corruption in government?

4. How did society regulate relations between African Americans and white Americans in the late 1800s?

 **Key to Differentiating Instruction**

Below Level

Basic-level activities designed for all students encountering new material

At Level

Intermediate-level activities designed for average students

Above Level

Challenging activities designed for honors and gifted-and-talented students

Standard English Mastery

Activities designed to improve standard English usage

CHAPTER

15 1880–1920

Life at the Turn of the 20th Century

THE BIG PICTURE In the late 1800s waves of immigrants from Southern and Eastern Europe settled in the cities. Government at all levels was plagued by corruption.

 North Carolina Standards

Social Studies Objectives

4.03 Describe the causes and effects of the financial difficulties that plagued the American farmer and trace the rise and decline of Populism.

5.01 Evaluate the influence of immigration and rapid industrialization on urban life.

5.04 Describe the changing role of government in economic and political affairs.

7.03 Evaluate the effects of racial segregation on different regions and segments of the United States' society.

Language Arts Objectives

3.01 Use language persuasively in addressing a particular issue by:
- establishing and defending a point of view.

Skills FOCUS READING LIKE A HISTORIAN

New York City's Mulberry Street in 1900 was home to a tightly knit community of Italian immigrants struggling to survive under difficult living conditions.
Interpreting Visuals What does this photograph tell you about the way immigrants lived?

See Skills Handbook, p. H30

486

1881
Tennessee passes the first Jim Crow law.

1880

1885
Calling for greater local participation, the Indian National Congress is founded in British-ruled India.

Introduce the Chapter

At Level

Focus on Industry and Technology

1. Discuss with students how industrialization changed life in the U.S. Ask students how industrialization might affect businesspeople, the government, and workers differently.

2. Have students create a chart with two columns. In the first column, have them list technological innovations we may take for granted, such as electricity, the telephone, etc. In the second column, have students explain how these technologies have affected American society. *possible answer—*

E-mail and cell phones have improved communication.

3. Ask volunteers to share their lists with the class, then review some of the changes brought on by industrialization and increased immigration in the late 1800s. Ask students to identify why an immigrant may have wanted to come to the United States in the late 1800s. **LS Verbal-Linguistic**

Alternative Assessment Handbook, Rubric 9: Comparing and Contrasting

May 1893
Stock market crashes, triggering depression in which 3 million lose their jobs.

February 1905
W.E.B. DuBois and others found the Niagara Movement, an early civil rights organization.

January 1910
Immigration station opens at Angel Island in San Francisco Bay.

February 1917
Congress approves a literacy test for immigrants.

1890 — 1900 — 1910 — 1920

1889
The Eiffel Tower opens in Paris.

1893
New Zealand becomes the first country to allow women to vote.

1907
Japan stops issuing passports to laborers headed to the U.S.

1910
Over 2 million Italians have left for the United States over 10 years.

1911
Sun Yat-sen becomes the first persident of the Republic of China.

487

Chapter Preview

HOLT
History's Impact
▶ **Video Program: Life at the Turn of the 20th Century**
See the Video Teacher's Guide for strategies for using the video segment.

Reading Like a Historian
Mulberry Street, 1900 Have students take a moment to examine the image on these pages. The Italian immigrants shown here are involved in many activities: some are buying produce, some are talking, some are playing, and some are working in what seems to be a typical, busy day in New York City at the turn of the century. How might the lives of the children pictured differ from the lives of children in today's American cities? *possible answer—children in image in street, no playgrounds visible, no signs of games or other entertainment*

go.hrw.com
Online Resources

Chapter Resources:
KEYWORD: SD7 CH15

Teacher Resources:
KEYWORD: SD7 TEACHER

Explore the Time Line

1. How many years passed between the passage of the first Jim Crow law and the founding of the Niagara Movement? *24*

2. When was the Angel Island immigration station opened? *1910*

3. What was the first country to allow women to vote? When? *New Zealand, 1893*

4. When did the Eiffel Tower open? *1889*

Info to Know

Settlement House Samuel Augustus Barnett established the first settlement house in London in 1884. A clergyman, Barnett invited university students to spend their holidays in poor neighborhoods in order to learn about social problems. With the support generated by this project, Barnett established a residence for graduates in a poor area; graduates participated in local life, collected social data, and improved local conditions. The residence, known as Toynbee Hall, continues to serve London's East End today.

Answers

Reading Like a Historian (p. 486)
in crowded, noisy, polluted areas

487

Bellringer

The Inside Story. . . Use the **Daily Bellringer Transparency** to help students answer the question.

📖 Daily Bellringer Transparency, Section 1

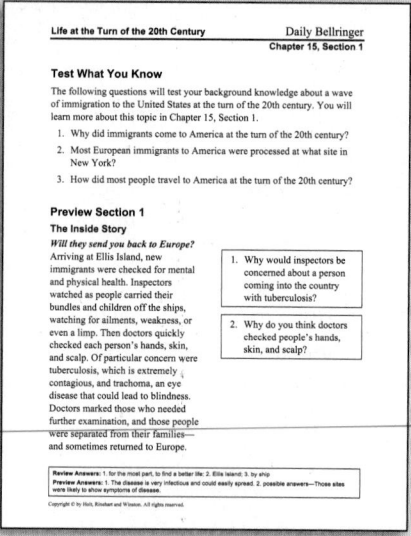

Life at the Turn of the 20th Century — Daily Bellringer
Chapter 15, Section 1

Test What You Know

The following questions will test your background knowledge about a wave of immigration to the United States at the turn of the 20th century. You will learn more about this topic in Chapter 15, Section 1.

1. Why did immigrants come to America at the turn of the 20th century?
2. Most European immigrants to America were processed at what site in New York?
3. How did most people travel to America at the turn of the 20th century?

Preview Section 1

The Inside Story

Will they send you back to Europe? Arriving at Ellis Island, new immigrants were checked for mental and physical health. Inspectors watched as people carried their bundles and children off the ships, watching for ailments, weakness, or even a limp. Then doctors quickly checked each person's hands, skin, and scalp. Of particular concern were tuberculosis, which is extremely contagious, and trachoma, an eye disease that could lead to blindness. Doctors marked those who needed further examination, and those people were separated from their families—and sometimes returned to Europe.

1. Why would inspectors be concerned about a person coming into the country with tuberculosis?
2. Why do you think doctors checked people's hands, skin, and scalp?

Review Answers: 1. for the most part, to find a better life; 2. Ellis Island; 3. by ship
Preview Answers: 1. The disease is very infectious and could easily spread; 2. possible answers—Those sites were likely to show symptoms of disease.

Copyright © by Holt, Rinehart and Winston. All rights reserved.

Academic Vocabulary

Review with students the high-use academic term in this section.

immigration the movement of people into foreign countries (p. 489)

📄 CRF: Vocabulary Builder Activity, Section 1

Taking Notes

Getting Here—separation from people they loved and culture they knew, families worked to save money to send one member over who would work and save to bring the rest, difficult to get to port city, had to have proof they could board the ship, underwent medical examination before boarding, traveled steerage; Being Allowed In—had to pass medical inspections at Ellis Island, some Chinese immigrants faced harsh prison-like conditions at Angel Island; Nativist Response—helped pass Chinese Exclusion Act, Japanese students segregated in San Francisco, literacy test instituted

go.hrw.com
Online Resources

KEYWORD: SD7 CH15
TOPIC: IMMIGRATION CHALLENGES

New Immigrants

BEFORE YOU READ

MAIN IDEA

A new wave of immigrants came to the United States in the late 1800s, settling in cities and troubling some native-born Americans.

READING FOCUS

1. How did patterns of immigration change at the turn of the century?
2. Why did immigrants come to America in the late 1800s, and where did they settle?
3. How did nativists respond to the new wave of immigration?

KEY TERMS AND PEOPLE

Ellis Island
Angel Island
benevolent society
Denis Kearney
Chinese Exclusion Act
Gentlemen's Agreement
literacy test

TAKING NOTES As you read, take notes on the challenges of the immigrant experience in the late 1800s. Record your notes in a graphic organizer like the one shown below.

Getting Here	Being Allowed In	Nativist Response

THE INSIDE STORY

Will they send you back to Europe? At the immigration checkpoint at Ellis Island in New York Harbor, families huddled nervously. Inspectors were waiting to check each newcomer for any disease or defect, mental or physical. They would decide whether a person would be admitted to the United States—or sent back to Europe.

Most people didn't realize that the first test came as they climbed the stairs, carrying children and bundles. Doctors were watching carefully. Did that woman seem sickly? Did that man limp? Any sign of weakness could be trouble.

The physical checkup took only a few minutes. Doctors looked at the way people spoke, walked, and behaved. They examined hands, skin, and scalp. They especially looked for diseases, such as tuberculosis, which could spread to other people. What many people feared most was the test for trachoma, an eye disease. With his fingers or with an instrument like a buttonhook, the "eye man" turned the eyelid inside-out to look for signs. Trachoma, which could lead to blindness, meant rejection.

To identify people who needed a closer look, doctors marked their shoulders with blue chalk. The letter *B* meant back, *H* meant heart, *L* meant lameness, *X* meant mental problems. Families were terribly upset when one member was sent for further tests. It could mean they would be separated, perhaps forever. ◼

Buttonhook Men and Blue Chalk

▶ An immigrant undergoes an eye exam at Ellis Island, 1905.

Teach the Main Idea

At Level

A New Wave of Immigration

1. **Teach** Ask students the Reading Focus questions to teach this section.

2. **Apply** Discuss the differences between the old immigrants and the immigrants who came to the U.S. after 1880. Have students design a series of Web pages that contrast the old immigrants with the new. The pages should list typical characteristics of the immigrants, and show the kind of economic opportunities that awaited them in the U.S.

3. **Review** Have students present their Web pages to the class.

4. **Practice/Homework** Have students create a flyer for incoming immigrants that tells them what to expect as they begin their new lives in the U.S. **LS Logical-Mathematical, Verbal-Linguistic, Visual-Spatial**

📄 Alternative Assessment Handbook, Rubric 3: Artwork

Changing Patterns of Immigration

It has been said that the United States is a nation of immigrants. During the history of this country, Native Americans were the only ones who did not come from somewhere else originally. All other Americans, at some point in their family history, came to the United States as immigrants.

The old immigrants Between 1800 and 1880, more than 10 million immigrants came to the United States. These people became known as the old immigrants. Most came from Northern and Western Europe—primarily from the United Kingdom, the Netherlands, the German states, Sweden, and Norway. Most of these immigrants were Protestant Christians. Their cultures were fairly similar to those of the original American settlers.

Why did the old immigrants come to the United States? Some came to have a voice in their government. Others came to escape political turmoil. Still others sought religious freedom. Some, like the Irish, came to escape poverty and starvation.

Most immigrants, however, came in search of economic opportunity. They had limited prospects in their home countries, where jobs were scarce and nobles and the church controlled most of the land. The huge supply of open farming land in the United States—and the easy access to it—attracted millions of Northern and Western Europeans in the decades before 1880.

Europeans, however, were not the only ones to come to the United States during these early waves of immigration. About 25,000 Chinese immigrants arrived to seek their fortunes in the late 1840s and early 1850s, lured by news of the California gold rush.

After the gold rush faded, more Chinese immigrants came to help build the nation's railroads, especially the first transcontinental railroad. Many later found employment as farmers, miners, or domestic servants.

The new immigrants From 1880 to 1910, a new wave of immigration brought some 18 million people to America. Their arrival would further transform the United States.

Unlike the old immigrants, most of these new immigrants came from Southern and Eastern Europe. Many were Czech, Greek, Hungarian, Italian, Polish, Russian, or Slovak. Furthermore, most of these new immigrants were not Protestant Christians. Many were Roman Catholics, Orthodox Christians, or Jews. Arab, Armenian, and French Canadian immigrants also poured in by the thousands.

Smaller numbers of new immigrants came from East Asia. Chinese communities had flourished for decades in the western United States. Severe immigration laws in the 1880s reduced new Chinese arrivals to a trickle. However, an estimated 90,000 people of Chinese descent lived in the country in 1900.

Meanwhile, Japanese immigrants were beginning to appear. The earliest came around 1885, when Japan decided to let laborers leave to work on sugar plantations in the Hawaiian Islands. From Hawaii, many Japanese moved to the United States. By 1904 about 10,000 Japanese lived in the United States.

The massive flood of new immigrants dramatically changed the makeup of the American population. The United States became more diverse than ever before. In fact, by 1910 about 1 in 12 Americans had been born in a foreign country.

READING CHECK **Contrasting** How did the new immigrants differ from the old immigrants?

ACADEMIC VOCABULARY

immigration
the movement of people into foreign countries

OLD AND NEW IMMIGRANTS — QUICK FACTS

Old Immigrants	New Immigrants
• Arrived before 1880	• Arrived 1880–1910
• Came from Northern and Western Europe	• Came from Southern and Eastern Europe
• Were mainly Protestant Christians	• Were mainly Catholics, Jews, or Orthodox Christians
• Were culturally similar to the original American settlers	• Were often culturally different from the original American settlers
• Settled both in cities and in rural areas	• Generally settled in cities

---

Reading Focus

1 How did patterns of immigration change at the turn of the century? *Previously, most immigrants were Northern and Western Europeans; now, most immigrants were Southern and Eastern Europeans.*

Changing Patterns of Immigration

Recall How many immigrants arrived in the U.S. between 1880 and 1910? *nearly 18 million*

Analyze How did the California Gold Rush influence immigration? *Some Chinese immigrants came to seek their fortunes.*

Predict How might Americans view the new wave of immigrants? *possible answers—threatening because of large numbers, different cultures, increased competition for jobs and land*

 Quick Facts Transparency: Old and New Immigrants

Info to Know

Chinese Immigrants By 1851, 25,000 Chinese had come to California, a land some called "gold mountain." They came to strike it rich in the California Gold Rush. Most Chinese immigrants who arrived in California never located the "gold mountain." Instead they discovered that mining was hard work, and they quickly learned that local people did not generally welcome them. New arrivals found it hard to survive, and with no money, they were cut off from their families. They could not afford to pay for their families to join them in California, nor could they afford to go back home.

Answers

Reading Check *different cultures, languages, religions; new immigrants came from Southern and Eastern Europe*

489

Collaborative Learning

Below Level | **Standard English Mastery**

The New Immigrants

1. Review the information in the text about the old and new immigrants. Have students use a world map from the atlas in their text to point out where the new immigrants came from, or use a large classroom map to point out the countries identified in the text.

2. Organize the class into small groups. Have each group create both a chart that compares and contrasts old immigrants with new immigrants and a world map that shows the countries of origin of old and new immigrants.

3. Have students use the information in the charts and maps to write a short essay comparing and contrasting old and new immigrants. **LS** **Interpersonal, Verbal-Linguistic**

Alternative Assessment Handbook, Rubrics 7: Charts; and 9: Comparing and Contrasting

❷ Why did immigrants come to America in the late 1800s, and where did they settle? *to escape religious persecution, for better economic opportunity; many settled in northeastern and midwestern cities*

Coming to America

Recall What did U.S. immigration authorities want to know about each immigrant after 1893? *that they had proper identification documents, no incurable diseases or disabilities, $30 in cash, had never been in prison, a poorhouse, or mental institution*

Explain Why would a father or eldest son leave his family to come to the United States? *Families could only afford one ticket; he would save money and send tickets back for the rest of the family.*

▢ CRF: Biography: Emma Lazarus

▢ Political Cartoons Activities for American History: Cartoon 30: Immigration

Info to Know

Ellis Island In just one day in 1907, Ellis Island's peak immigration year, over 11,000 immigrants passed through Ellis Island. By 1924 the numbers had begun to decrease.

Tracing History
Immigration

(Activity) **Identify** Guide students in a discussion of U.S. immigration. Ask students what patterns, if any, they can identify in the ways that America has dealt with immigrants. Ask students how America should deal with immigrants who come to America today. Have students explain their reasoning. **LS Verbal-Linguistic**

Immigration

The number and origins of immigrants coming to the United States have been influenced by many factors, including political and economic changes abroad, as well as U.S. policies that alternately encourage or restrict immigration.

1845–1850 Some 500,000 people flee famine in Ireland to come to America.

1800

1892 Ellis Island immigration station opens in sight of the Statue of Liberty in New York Harbor.

Coming to America

The decision to move to the United States was agonizing for many immigrants. Leaving their homeland meant separation from the people they loved and the culture they knew. What brought them here?

Desire for a better life John F. Kennedy, an Irish American who became president in 1961, wrote in his book *A Nation of Immigrants*, "There were probably as many reasons for coming to America as there were people who came." Most of the new immigrants, like their predecessors, were seeking a better life. But the reasons they left their homelands varied.

Russian Jews fled to the United States in search of freedom from religious persecution. Entire villages of Jews were forced out of Russia and Eastern Europe by pogroms, organized attacks that were often encouraged by local authorities. Many of these Jews came to the United States not only to practice their religion but also to save their lives.

Many immigrants left Southern and Eastern Europe because of desperate poverty and little economic opportunity. Europe's population was rising fast. Too many people competed for too little land and too few jobs. Many Europeans heard that America was the land of opportunity. In America, it was said, all people needed to do was work hard and save their money, and they would prosper.

The journey to America The decision to come to the United States often involved the entire family. One family member—usually a father or an eldest son—might make the journey first. The family would pool their resources to buy his passage on a ship. He would then come to the United States and work, saving his earnings so he could send prepaid tickets back to the rest of his family.

For many immigrants, just getting to a departure point was a journey in itself. Travelers made their way to port cities by train, wagon, or foot. Once at the docks, they might have to wait weeks for a departing ship.

After a U.S. immigration law went into effect in 1893, immigrants had to be approved by the steamship authorities before they were allowed to come on board. They had to provide identifying information, show that they had at least $30 in cash, and indicate whether they had ever been in prison, a poorhouse, or a mental institution.

Immigrants faced one last hurdle before boarding the ship: the medical examination. Doctors employed by the steamship lines examined immigrants for any obvious diseases

490 CHAPTER 15

Skills Focus: Identifying Problem and Solution

Above Level

Reading Skill
The Bureau of Immigration

1. Explain to students that after the Civil War individual states had begun to pass immigration laws. As a result, in 1875 the Supreme Court declared that regulating immigration was a federal responsibility. Congress began to issue laws affecting immigration, and in 1891 the Bureau of Immigration was established.

2. Have students write a speech that might have been given by a member of Congress supporting or opposing the creation of the Bureau of Immigration. Students should explain why they do or do not believe a government agency is needed and whether regulating immigration should be a state or federal responsibility.

3. Ask volunteers to give their speeches to the class. **LS Verbal-Linguistic**

▢ Alternative Assessment Handbook, Rubric 24: Oral Presentations

1910 The Angel Island immigration center opens in San Francisco Bay, processing mainly Asian immigrants.

1900

2000

2000–2003 Almost 3 million legal immigrants come to the United States.

Coming to America

Recall Why did so many immigrants travel in steerage? *It was the cheapest way to travel.*

Analyze Why do you think steerage passengers were required to go through immigration at Ellis Island? *possible answers—because they were poor, not given same respect and treatment as wealthier passengers; there were thousands more of them; might be sick, dirty*

📄 CRF: Primary Source Activity: Immigrants at Ellis Island

or defects. They then vaccinated all immigrants, disinfected them and their baggage, and allowed the immigrants to board the ship.

Most immigrants traveled in steerage, the cheapest way to travel. Steerage passengers were held in the bottom of the steamships in crowded and unsanitary conditions. A government report in 1911 explained how terrible these conditions were.

HISTORY'S VOICES

❝The ventilation is almost always inadequate, and the air soon becomes foul. The unattended vomit of the seasick, the odors of not too clean bodies, the reek of food and the awful stench of the nearby toilet rooms make the atmosphere of the steerage such that it is a marvel that human flesh can endure it . . . All of these conditions are naturally aggravated by the crowding.❞
—*Reports of the Immigration Commission*, 1911

Immigrants who survived the awful ocean crossing faced one last test before they could begin their new lives in America. They had to make it through the immigration station.

Ellis Island The U.S. government opened an immigration station in 1892 on **Ellis Island** in New York Harbor. Over the next 62 years, some 112 million immigrants would pass through Ellis Island on their way to begin a new life.

Immigrants had to pass inspection before being allowed to enter the United States. For those who traveled in first or second class, inspectors came aboard ship to check their health and review their papers.

Those who traveled in steerage had to make their way through the immigration checkpoint at Ellis Island. The inspection process usually took up to five hours. Immigrants waited nervously, fearful they would be sent back home. Doctors would scan each passenger for signs of serious disease or disability. Immigrants who did not pass the medical inspection were sent back, some penniless and without their families.

In peak years, as many as 20 percent of immigrants were held for weeks or longer at Ellis Island before being allowed to land. Sick passengers stayed at the island's hospital until they recovered. Those whose papers did not pass review were held for a hearing. About five out of every six passengers who were detained were eventually cleared to enter.

After passing inspection, immigrants were free to enter the United States and begin their new lives. Some headed off on their own, while others met family members already in the United States. One Russian Jewish immigrant remembered meeting her father for the first time, in 1910.

THE IMPACT
TODAY

Daily Life
It is estimated that nearly half of all Americans today can trace their family origins to at least one immigrant who entered the country at Ellis Island.

Info to Know
Steamships to the United States
By the 1890s steamships had reduced travel time from Europe to the United States from three months to two weeks. Large shipping lines such as Cunard and White Star competed fiercely for immigrant passengers, who they viewed as profitable, self-loading cargo. Steamships could pack up to two thousand passengers into steerage, the lower decks of the ship.

Skills Focus: Comparing and Contrasting　　　At Level

Reading Skill
Ellis Island

1. Organize the class into small groups. Have each group develop a factual article, a political cartoon, and an editorial for a 1901 edition of a New York newspaper. In their work, students should compare and contrast the treatment officials gave to immigrants who traveled in steerage with the treatment given to immigrants who traveled in first or second class, and present their opinions about the differences in treatment.

2. Have volunteers from each group present their articles, editorials, and cartoons to the class.

3. Guide students in a discussion about whether or not such different treatment might have been justified. Remind students about the differences in fare. **LS Interpersonal, Verbal-Linguistic**

📄 Alternative Assessment Handbook, Rubric 23: Newspapers

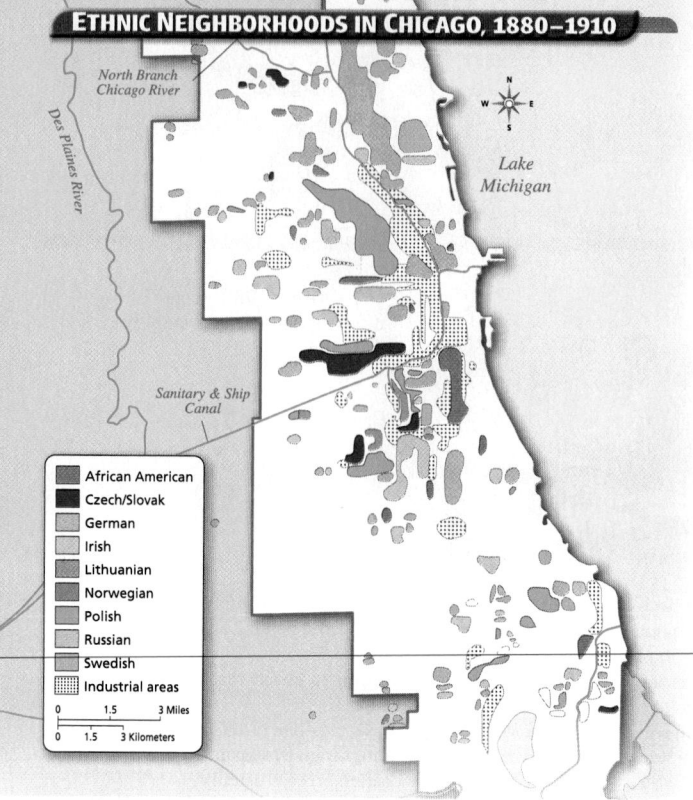
Coming to America

Recall What was Angel Island? *immigration station in San Francisco Bay*

Make Inference What evidence is there that Chinese immigrants had a powerful desire to come to the United States? *Chinese immigrants continued to arrive; endured detention and harsh treatment; understood that many would be sent back*

Evaluate Why do you think many immigrants wanted to keep their own traditions, language, and culture? *possible answers—wanted to remember their homes, way of life, practice their traditional religious faiths; maintain sense of community*

ETHNIC NEIGHBORHOODS IN CHICAGO, 1880–1910

North Branch Chicago River

Des Plaines River

Lake Michigan

Sanitary & Ship Canal

- African American
- Czech/Slovak
- German
- Irish
- Lithuanian
- Norwegian
- Polish
- Russian
- Swedish
- Industrial areas

0   1.5   3 Miles
0   1.5   3 Kilometers

GEOGRAPHY SKILLS | **INTERPRETING MAPS**

Around the turn of the century, three-quarters of Chicago's population consisted of immigrants and their children.
Place What were the two largest ethnic groups in Chicago at this time?
See Skills Handbook, p. H20

HISTORY'S VOICES

"I saw a man coming forward and he was so beautiful I didn't know he was my father . . . Later on I realized why he looked so familiar to me. He looked exactly like I did . . . But that's when I met him for the first time. And I fell in love with him and he with me."

—Katherine Beychok, *Ellis Island History*

Angel Island After 1910, newcomers arriving on the West Coast were processed at **Angel Island**, an immigration station in San Francisco Bay. Some immigrants passed through Angel

Island fairly quickly. But many Chinese immigrants were detained for weeks or months while awaiting a ruling on whether or not they could stay.

The people detained at Angel Island faced prisonlike conditions. Much of the time they were locked in barracks to prevent escape and were allowed outside only for supervised recreation. To relieve the boredom of life at Angel Island, some Chinese immigrants wrote poetry on the walls of their barracks. Their poems often expressed resentment and despair over their treatment.

HISTORY'S VOICES

"Imprisoned in the wooden building day after day,

My freedom withheld; how can I bear to talk about it?

I look to see who is happy but they only sit quietly.

I am anxious and depressed and cannot fall asleep . . .

After experiencing such loneliness and sorrow,

Why not just return home and learn to plow the fields?"

—Anonymous Chinese immigrant

For those immigrants who were finally allowed to settle in the United States, a stressful ordeal was over. Yet for many, the hard times were just beginning. Poverty and discrimination faced many new arrivals.

Building urban communities Many immigrants found themselves better off in the United States than they had been. Still, they typically experienced hardships. Most immigrants settled in crowded cities. Most could find only low-paying, unskilled jobs. As a result, new immigrants generally had no choice but to live in poor housing in teeming slums—frequently near the factories where they worked.

In the cities of the Northeast and Midwest, immigrants usually settled near others from their homeland or even their home city or province. Surrounded by people who spoke their language and shared their culture, newcomers

492 CHAPTER 15

Skills Focus: Analyzing Secondary Sources

At Level

Reading Like a Historian Skill
Building Community

Research Required

1. Organize the class into small groups and have each group use secondary sources, such as encyclopedias or Web sites, to research benevolent societies and how they helped immigrants.

2. Have each group create a brochure that describes the services offered by a benevolent society. The brochure should target a particular immigrant group, and include reasons why immigrants should use the society's services. Brochures must be illustrated, since many immigrants did not know how to read.

3. Have each group present its brochure to the class.

4. Discuss the importance of benevolent societies to new immigrants. **LS Interpersonal, Verbal-Linguistic**

   📓 Alternative Assessment Handbook, Rubrics 3: Artwork; and 40: Writing to Describe

Answers

Interpreting Maps *Polish and German*

492

found companionship and got help adapting to their new lives. Meanwhile, the cities became a patchwork of ethnic clusters.

In these immigrant neighborhoods, residents built institutions to keep their cultures alive. They established churches and synagogues so they could practice their religious faith. Many religious organizations provided their members with economic assistance, training courses, and child care.

In a number of cities, residents formed **benevolent societies**, aid organizations to help immigrants. Some benevolent societies helped immigrants obtain jobs, health care, or education. Some collected a few cents from members every month. In return, members received financial support if they became too ill to work, and they were buried when they died.

These benevolent societies made a huge difference in helping immigrants through difficult times. At the time, there were no state-sponsored programs to help poor and needy people. The benevolent societies filled this void. At the same time, they helped build a sense of community among immigrants.

READING CHECK **Contrasting** How did Ellis Island and Angel Island differ?

Nativists Respond

The immigrants who settled in the United States strengthened the American economy. Immigrant labor kept the factories running and helped build cities.

Many native-born Americans, however, saw the new immigrants as a threat to society. Many thought the newcomers were simply too different to fit in. Others blamed immigrants for problems such as crime, poverty, and violence. Americans who opposed immigration were known as nativists.

Nativists believed that immigrants also posed a threat to the economy. Immigrants accepted lower wages for their work. The result, claimed nativists, was a loss of jobs for native-born Americans and lower wages for everyone. Nativists opposed further immigration. They began pressing for laws that would close America's doors to newcomers.

Limiting Chinese immigration For many years people had tolerated Chinese workers, although they did not welcome them. After 1873, though, the economy worsened. Many American citizens blamed Chinese immigrants for taking away needed jobs.

PRIMARY SOURCES

Political Cartoon

This cartoon appeared in 1893. Its caption reads: "They would close to the new-comer the bridge that carried them and their fathers over."

These successful old immigrants stand opposed to new immigration.

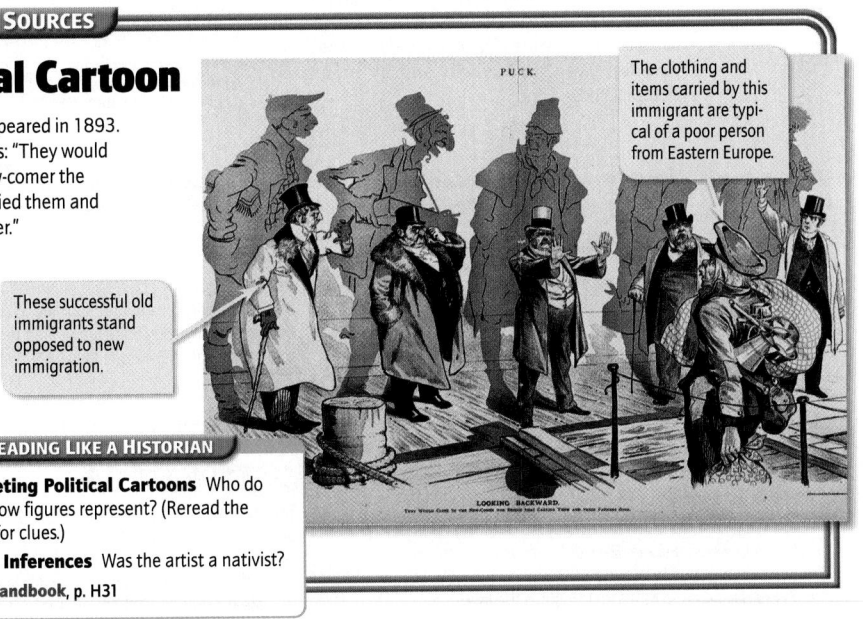

The clothing and items carried by this immigrant are typical of a poor person from Eastern Europe.

PUCK.

LOOKING BACKWARD.

Skills FOCUS **READING LIKE A HISTORIAN**

1. **Interpreting Political Cartoons** Who do the shadow figures represent? (Reread the caption for clues.)
2. **Making Inferences** Was the artist a nativist?

See Skills Handbook, p. H31

LIFE AT THE TURN OF THE 20TH CENTURY **493**

Direct Teach

Reading Focus

❸ How did nativists respond to the new wave of immigration? *opposed further immigration and called for restrictions*

Nativists Respond

Describe What is a nativist? *someone who opposes immigration*

Summarize Why did nativists believe immigrants posed an economic threat? *Nativists believed immigrants would work for lower wages, decreasing wages for everyone and taking jobs away from native-born citizens.*

Make Judgments Do you believe that immigrants cause wages to fall when they take low-paying jobs? *possible answers—no, immigrants take jobs that no one else wants; yes, immigrants lower the average wage level, allowing employers to offer less money to all workers*

📰 CRF: Primary Source Activity: Labor Union Flyer in Butte, Montana

Primary Source

Mark Twain once wrote about the Chinese in California, "*They are a kindly disposed, well-meaning race, and are respected and well treated by the upper classes, all over the Pacific coast. No Californian gentleman or lady ever abuses or oppresses a Chinaman, under any circumstances . . . Only the scum of the population do it . . .*".
— Samuel L. Clemens (Mark Twain)
Roughing It, p. 397

Differentiating Instruction

Below Level

Learners Having Difficulty

1. Have students work in mixed-ability pairs to review the information about the nativist response to immigration.
2. Have students copy the table at right. Omit the italicized answers. Have students complete the table listing the reasons nativists objected to immigration.
3. Have volunteers share the information from their charts and complete the class chart for all to see. Have students correct their own

work and retain the table as a study tool.
LS **Visual-Spatial**
📄 Alternative Assessment Handbook, Rubric 7: Charts
📇 Graphic Organizer Transparencies

too different to fit in
increased crime
increased poverty
were an economic threat

Answers

Reading Like a Historian
1. *ancestors of these wealthy men who were once poor immigrants themselves;*
2. *no, the artist is criticizing the unfair treatment of new immigrants*

Reading Check *Ellis Island—East Coast; most immigrants came from Europe; detained those whose health or document status was uncertain; Angel Island—West Coast, detained Chinese, passed others through quickly*

493

Nativists Respond

Recall Who was Denis Kearney? *Irish immigrant who strongly opposed Chinese immigration*

Analyze Why do you believe Congress passed the Chinese Exclusion Act? *possible answers—response to political pressure, California had already limited Chinese from holding certain jobs and living wherever they wished, prejudice against Asian people*

• Review & Assess •

Close

Guide students in a discussion of the ways in which immigration changed the United States.

Review

Online Quiz, Section 1

Daily Test Practice Transparency

Assess

SE Section 1 Assessment

Progress Assessment: Section 1 Quiz

Alternative Assessment Handbook

Reteach

Interactive Reader and Study Guide, Section 1

Interactive Skills Tutor CD-ROM

Answers

Reading Check *saw new immigrants as an economic threat; blamed them for crime, poverty, violence; thought they were too different to fit in*

In the late 1870s a group of unemployed workers organized the Workingmen's Party of California to oppose Chinese immigration. Their leader was **Denis Kearney**, an Irish immigrant. Kearney ended many of his speeches with the angry cry, "The Chinese must go!"

In 1879 California adopted a new state constitution that prohibited Chinese workers from holding state jobs. The new constitution also allowed local governments to ban the Chinese from their communities or to restrict them to certain districts.

Soon this anti-Chinese sentiment spread to the federal level. In 1882 Congress passed the **Chinese Exclusion Act.** This law banned Chinese immigration for 10 years. It also declared that none of the Chinese who were already in the United States could become citizens. The law was renewed in 1892. Then in 1902 Congress banned Chinese immigration indefinitely.

This ban did not completely stop Chinese immigration to the United States. Some exceptions were made. Overall, though, Chinese immigration declined sharply after 1882.

Limiting Japanese immigration The nativists on the West Coast resented Japanese immigrants as well. As a result, in 1906 the San Francisco school board segregated its schools. Japanese students were then required to attend a separate school from white children. The Japanese government angrily protested this discrimination.

THE IMPACT TODAY

Daily Life
The Chinese Exclusion Act was repealed in 1943, and the Immigration Act of 1965 ended other discriminatory policies toward the Chinese. Today Chinese Americans are the largest Asian group in the country, numbering some 2.7 million in the 2000 census.

The matter went to President Theodore Roosevelt, who in 1907 negotiated the **Gentlemen's Agreement** with Japan. Japan agreed to prevent unskilled workers from immigrating to the United States. In exchange, San Francisco stopped the practice of segregating Japanese schoolchildren.

Deterring other immigrants Some nativists opposed immigration not only from Asia but also from Southern and Eastern Europe. They claimed that those immigrants could not blend into American society because they were poor, illiterate, or non-Protestant.

Many nativists called for immigrants to pass a **literacy test**, an exam to determine whether the test takers could read English. They wanted the test to keep many of these immigrants out. In 1917 Congress passed the Literacy Test Act over President Woodrow Wilson's veto.

Americanization Not all native-born Americans wanted to prevent immigrants from coming to the United States. Some people wanted to teach the newcomers American ways to help them assimilate into American society. Schools and voluntary organizations taught immigrants English literacy skills and subjects needed for citizenship, such as American history and government.

READING CHECK **Summarizing** Why did nativists oppose immigration?

SECTION 1 ASSESSMENT

go.hrw.com
Online Quiz
Keyword: SD7 HP15

Reviewing Ideas, Terms, and People

1. **a. Describe** Who were the new immigrants?
   b. Analyze Why did the United States seem to offer immigrants a promising future?
   c. Predict Of all the differences between new and old immigrants, which ones do you think would pose the most tensions between the two groups? Explain your reasoning.

2. **a. Recall** Where were **Ellis Island** and **Angel Island** located?
   b. Compare How were Ellis Island and Angel Island similar?
   c. Elaborate How did the practices at Angel Island reveal a bias against certain immigrants?

3. **a. Identify** Who was **Denis Kearney**?
   b. Make Generalizations How did nativists view the new wave of immigrants in the late 1800s?
   c. Evaluate How did nativism influence the law?

Critical Thinking

4. **Sequencing** Copy the chart below and record the steps taken by most immigrants in their journey to the United States. Begin with the decision to leave their homeland and end with their approval to enter the United States.

Decide to leave homeland → → → → → Enter the United States

FOCUS ON WRITING

5. **Persuasive** Suppose you are an American citizen who opposes nativist legislation such as the **Chinese Exclusion Act**. Write a letter to the editor to support your position. Consider the contributions of immigrants to U.S. history and the reasons for anti-immigrant sentiments.

494 CHAPTER 15

Section 1 Assessment Answers

1. **a.** people from Southern and Eastern Europe, China, and Japan
   b. U.S. "land of opportunity"
   c. possible answer—cultural differences, new immigrants may be perceived as too different from rest of American society

2. **a.** New York Harbor; San Francisco Bay
   b. ports of entry, in harbors of coastal cities; detained some immigrants
   c. Chinese detained in prison-like conditions

3. **a.** opposed Chinese immigration
   b. immigrants threatened economy, were too

   different and too many of them; blamed for crime and poverty
   c. Chinese prohibited from state jobs; Chinese Exclusion Act; ban on Chinese immigration; Gentlemen's Agreement with Japan

4. to leave homeland; find seaport; pass inspection; travel to America; taken to Ellis or Angel Island; pass inspection; enter U.S.

5. possible answer—discriminatory law; immigrants enrich America with culture; hard work strengthens economy

SECTION 2 — Urban Life

BEFORE YOU READ

MAIN IDEA
In cities in the late 1800s, people in the upper, middle, and lower classes lived different kinds of lives because of their different economic situations.

READING FOCUS
1. How did American cities change in the late 1800s?
2. How did class differences affect the way urban dwellers lived?
3. How did the settlement house movement work to improve living conditions for immigrants and poor Americans?

KEY TERMS AND PEOPLE
Elisha Otis
Frederick Law Olmsted
settlement house
Jane Addams
Lillian Wald
Social Gospel

TAKING NOTES As you read, take notes on improvements and problems in turn-of-the-century society. Record your notes in a graphic organizer like the one shown here.

The Social Gospel	Social Darwinism

THE INSIDE STORY

Do you enjoy a walk in the park? If so, thank Frederick Law Olmsted. He and his firm planned and built many of America's most beautiful public parks. His ideas had a strong influence on park design throughout the country.

Before becoming a landscape architect—a term he invented—Olmsted studied engineering, ran a farm, and worked as a journalist. In 1850, when he was 28, Olmsted and some friends took a walking tour of Europe. There he admired the many public and private parks as well as the elegant layouts of country estates.

By 1856 the City of New York had acquired 840 acres on what was then the edge of town. Olmsted and architect Calvert Vaux won a competition to design the city's new Central Park. Their plan kept the feel of a natural landscape but added walks and parkways so that people could stroll comfortably and enjoy the area.

Central Park was one of the first large U.S. city parks. Olmsted thought that expanses of green space and trees improved the quality of city life. "A park is a work of art," he said. Every detail—every blade of grass—mattered.

During the Civil War, Olmsted was in charge of medical supplies and sanitation for the Union army. After the war he returned to park design. For the next 30 years he created peaceful havens in Philadelphia, Detroit, Chicago, Boston, Montreal, and other cities. His firm also designed landscapes for the U.S. Capitol and White House grounds and for national parks from Maine to California. ■

▼ Frederick Law Olmsted designed a series of parks for the city of Boston, Massachusetts, known collectively as the Emerald Necklace.

"A Park Is a Work of Art"

495

Teach the Main Idea

At Level

Urban Life

1. **Teach** Ask students the Reading Focus questions to teach this section.

2. **Apply** Discuss the differences between the upper class and the working class in a typical large city. Divide students into groups of three. Ask each group to prepare a brief, illustrated magazine article entitled "How the Other Folks Live." The article and the illustrations should contrast the lives of the upper class and the working class.

3. **Review** Guide students in a discussion of the ways in which American society was becoming divided along class lines.

4. **Practice/Homework** Ask students to create a series of visuals illustrating how new technologies transformed American cities in the late 1800s. **LS Interpersonal, Verbal-Linguistic, Visual-Spatial**

   Alternative Assessment Handbook, Rubrics 3: Artwork; and 19: Magazines

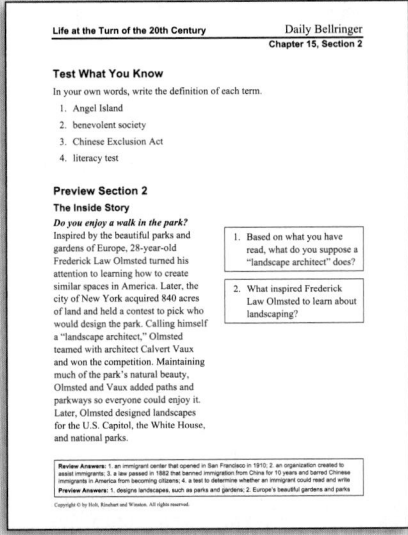

❶ How did American cities change in the late 1800s? *tall buildings, mass transit, urban planning; parks*

American Cities Change

Recall Who was Frederick Law Olmstead? *landscape architect; designed New York City's Central Park*

Analyze What effect did mass transit systems have on the working class in cities? *little, as they could not afford to move from the city center*

Evaluate What was the benefit of the new urban planning? *sought best use of space in cities, helped ensure some amount of green space*

Recent Scholarship

In *Settlement Houses Under Siege*, authors Michael Fabricant and Robert Fisher provide a critique of the complex role that settlement houses played in major U.S. cities in the early 1900s. The book focuses on the ways in which settlement houses built a strong sense of community for immigrants. The authors then look at settlement houses today and examine the roles that they could play in building community in cities like New York.

Settlement Houses Under Siege by Michael Fabricant and Robert Fisher. Columbia University Press, 2001

HISTORY CLOSE-UP

Early Skyscrapers

The Reliance Building Reaching 14 stories in 1894, the Reliance Building in Chicago seemed to defy gravity. Its steel skeleton supported an exterior made mostly of windows. The Reliance Building helped usher in the era of the skyscraper.

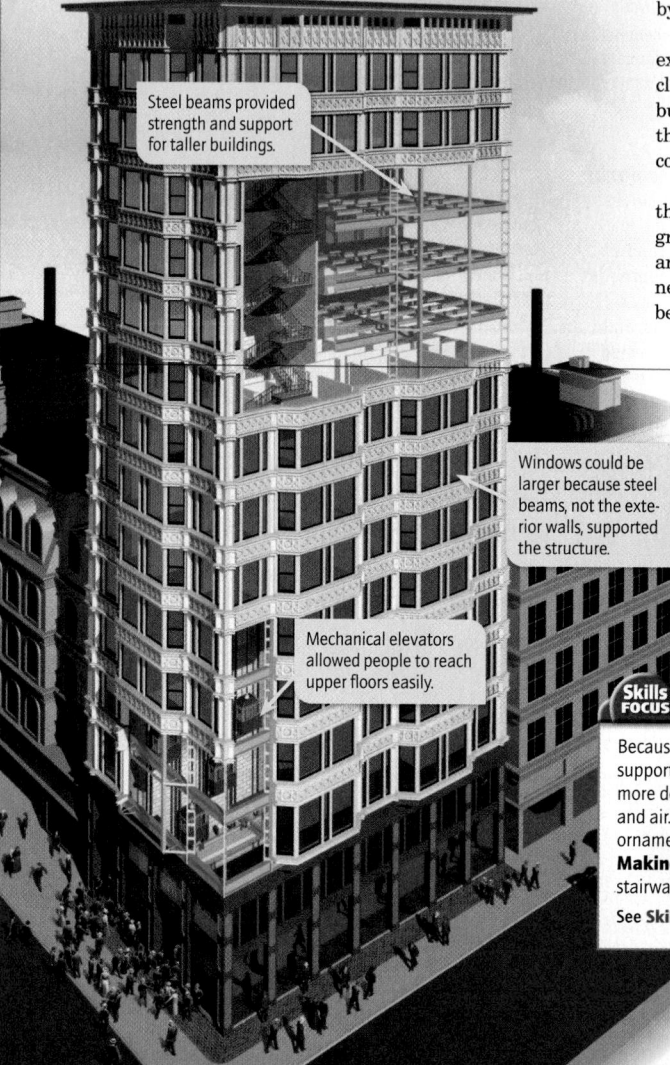

Steel beams provided strength and support for taller buildings.

Windows could be larger because steel beams, not the exterior walls, supported the structure.

Mechanical elevators allowed people to reach upper floors easily.

496

American Cities Change

Before industrialization, cities were compact. Few buildings stood taller than four stories. Most people lived within walking distance of their workplaces, schools, shopping districts, and places of worship. But in the late 1800s, cities began to run out of buildable space. Instead of spreading out, they began to build up. Architects started using strong steel frames, which allowed them to build taller buildings than ever before. The safety elevator, invented by **Elisha Otis,** made taller buildings practical.

With the coming of mass transit, cities expanded as people moved farther away. Middle class and wealthy people could work in the city but leave the noises and smells behind when they went home. The working poor, however, could not afford to move from the city center.

As cities grew, some people began to fear that urban areas would no longer have any green spaces. The new field of urban planning arose to deal with this challenge. Urban planners and civil engineers tried to map out the best use of space in cities. Landscape architects such as **Frederick Law Olmsted** designed city parks to provide city residents with a sense of the countryside. Olmsted designed New York City's Central Park as well as a network of Boston parks known as the Emerald Necklace and other urban parks.

READING CHECK
Identifying Cause and Effect How did the use of steel change the way architects designed buildings?

Skills FOCUS **INTERPRETING INFOGRAPHICS**

Because an internal steel skeleton provided structural support, the outside of the Reliance Building could be more decorative. Larger-than-usual windows let in light and air. Exterior details, such as the bands of terra cotta ornamentation, gave it an intricate look.
Making Inferences Why did the Reliance Building need stairways when it already had mechanized elevators?
See Skills Handbook, p. H18

Skills Focus: Making Generalizations
At Level

Reading Skill
Changing Cities

1. Guide students in a discussion of the changes mass transit made to American cities and how it enabled suburbs to develop and grow.

2. Have each student think about what life would have been like in a suburb and in the city in the late 1800s. Have students write two letters concerning life in the late 1800s. One letter should describe daily life in the city to a friend who has moved to the suburbs. The

other letter should describe life in the suburbs to someone who lives in the city.

3. Have volunteers read their letters to the class. Ask students if, based on the letters, they would have preferred city or suburban life.
LS Verbal-Linguistic
Alternative Assessment Handbook, Rubric 25: Personal Letters

Answers

Interpreting Infographics *possible answer—in case a fire or technical difficulties prevented the elevator from functioning*
Reading Check *Buildings could be taller, making efficient use of ground space.*

Class Differences

America's booming cities provided bountiful opportunities for success in life. But the opportunities varied tremendously depending on one's status in society.

The wealthy The richest Americans in the late 1800s did not all come from old-money families with inherited wealth. Instead, they made their fortunes in industry and business. Many of these newly rich made a point of conspicuously displaying their wealth. Because of their excesses, the period from the 1870s to the 1890s is sometimes called the Gilded Age.

The well-to-do spent vast sums of money on housing. Affluent New Yorkers lined Fifth Avenue with grand houses resembling medieval castles and Italian Renaissance palaces. In the summer, they left their city homes for magnificent country estates. The oldest grandson of industrialist Cornelius Vanderbilt, for example, built a palatial summer home in Newport, Rhode Island. His "cottage" had 70 rooms.

High-society women read instructive literature that outlined proper behavior for ladies and gentlemen. The guides glorified the ideal woman as a homemaker. Her role was to organize and decorate her home, entertain, supervise a staff of servants, and offer moral and social guidance to her family. Most wealthy women stayed busy with these private activities. Some, however, lent their time and occasionally their money to social reform efforts.

The middle class The growth of new industries resulted in an increase in the urban middle class. The rise of modern corporations also caused the middle class to swell as more and more people became accountants, clerks, managers, and salespeople.

Industry and business, as well as a growing population, created a need for educated workers such as teachers, engineers, lawyers, and doctors. Before the late 1800s, however, few standards existed to ensure that these workers had appropriate qualifications. During the 1870s and 1880s, schools and organizations began to standardize the skills and knowledge needed for certain occupations. This process became known as professionalization. It brought new respect to professions such as medicine, law, and education.

Few professions accepted women as members. But women found other opportunities to work outside the home. Businesses hired women as salesclerks, secretaries, and typists.

When young, middle-class women married, they usually stopped working outside the home. Yet managing a home now involved less labor than it had previously. Women could buy many of the items their mothers had formerly made themselves, such as clothing. In addition, many middle class households employed at least one servant to manage the housework.

With less time spent on housework, many middle class women had time for other activities. Some participated in reform movements. Others joined reading clubs and other social groups. By taking part in activities outside the home, middle class women began to expand their influence into the public world.

The working class Many people in the cities lived in terrible poverty. As more people moved to the cities in search of work, the growing population kept wages low. Housing shortages meant that most workers lived in cramped conditions. In New York City, for example, about half of the population crowded into tenements, or run-down apartment buildings.

Tenements were usually within walking distance of the factories, stockyards, and ports where many of the urban poor worked. This meant that at home, as well as on the job, they had to endure pollution and filth. Sickness and untimely death were common.

Tenements lacked <u>sufficient</u> light and ventilation. Only the rooms facing the street and the back of the building had windows, and even these were a mixed blessing. They let in sunlight but also the stench from trash and sewage and the pollution from belching factories.

Housekeeping was laborious in a tenement. With no indoor plumbing, women and children had to haul water from an outdoor water pump for laundry, bathing, and cooking. Women washed clothes by boiling them on the stove and then hanging them to dry on lines strung between buildings or in the kitchen. On top of their difficult housekeeping tasks, many working-class women also labored in low-paying jobs outside the home.

ACADEMIC VOCABULARY
sufficient enough, adequate

THE IMPACT TODAY
Government
Today all 50 states have laws requiring licensing for many occupations, from practicing medicine to doing electrical work to cutting hair in a barbershop or beauty salon.

READING CHECK **Contrasting** How did life in the cities differ for wealthy and working-class people?

Differentiating Instruction

Advanced Learners/GATE

1. Guide students in a discussion of how different classes lived in the United States during the late 1800s.

2. Have students write an article or prepare a PowerPoint presentation from the perspective of a modern social critic writing about American social classes during the 1890s. Students should address the following question: Were American cities better or worse off following the changes brought by growth and the new technologies? Students

may wish to conduct outside research to provide examples and support arguments they make in their articles or presentations.

3. Have volunteers present their articles to the class.

4. After the presentations, guide students in a discussion about the nature of social change.
LS Verbal-Linguistic

Alternative Assessment Handbook, Rubrics 29: Presentations; and 30: Research

---

Reading Focus

2 How did class differences affect the way urban dwellers lived? *upper class—conspicuous consumption, luxurious homes, women managed house and servants; middle class—educated workers, women involved in social or reform activities; working class—poverty, harsh living and working conditions, many women worked outside the home for low wages*

Class Differences

Define What is conspicuous consumption? *public display of wealth*

Make Generalizations Who were the new professionals? *doctors, teachers, lawyers, mostly men*

Evaluate What caused the quick development of the middle class? *growth of new industries; rise of the modern corporation, which needed accountants, clerks, salespeople, and managers*

Biography

William Dean Howells (1837–1920)
William Dean Howells, literary critic and novelist, helped the American public to appreciate such influential writers as Henry James and Mark Twain. In the more than thirty novels he wrote himself, Howells realistically depicted everyday aspects of American life, ranging from the failure of a marriage to the rise of a self-made businessman. At a time when Americans were adjusting to an urban society, Howells recognized the overwhelming social and economic divisions that came with industrialization.

Answers

Reading Check *upper class—lavish homes, servants, and country estates; working class—crowded, unsanitary homes; faced disease, industrial pollution and filth*

❸ How did the settlement house movement work to improve living conditions for immigrants and poor Americans? *taught skills they would need to help themselves out of poverty*

The Settlement House Movement

Recall Who were the founders of Chicago's Hull House? *Jane Addams and Ellen Gates Starr*

Analyze How did religion play a role in settlement house activity? *Many reformers and workers believed that religious faith should be expressed through good works.*

📄 CRF: Biography: Janie Porter Barrett

● Review & Assess ●

Close

Guide students in a discussion of changes that occurred in U.S. cities and how some Americans tried to solve the problems of the working poor.

Review

📄 Online Quiz, Section 2

📦 Daily Test Practice Transparency

Assess

SE   Section 2 Assessment

📄 Progress Assessment: Section 2 Quiz

📄 Alternative Assessment Handbook

Reteach

📄 Interactive Reader and Study Guide, Section 2

💿 Interactive Skills Tutor CD-ROM

Answers

Faces of History *founded Hull House; pushed for reforms in city government; advocated progressive reforms, such as women's suffrage*

Reading Check *taught people skills needed to lift themselves out of poverty, offered English, job training*

498

FACES OF HISTORY

Jane ADDAMS
1860–1935

Jane Addams grew up in privileged circumstances in Illinois, but she found her calling in serving the disadvantaged. With her father's encouragement, she attended college and became part of the first generation of American women to gain higher education.

In the 1880s Addams toured Europe and visited a settlement house in London. Inspired, she returned to Chicago and founded Hull House to serve poor immigrants and the working class. Addams also pushed for reforms in city government, championed voting rights for women, and spoke out against racial discrimination and war. In 1931 Addams became the second woman to receive the Nobel Peace Prize.

Summarize How did Addams work to improve her community?

The Settlement House Movement

With poverty a desperate problem, some American reformers turned to Great Britain for inspiration. In 1884 London reformers had founded the first **settlement house**, a place where volunteers provided a variety of services to people in need.

Instead of just giving handouts, settlement houses taught immigrants many skills they could use to help themselves out of poverty. They offered English classes and job-training courses. They also provided social activities, such as clubs and sports.

Soon, settlement houses began appearing in U.S. cities. One of the first was Hull House in Chicago, founded by **Jane Addams** and Ellen Gates Starr in 1889. The settlement house movement spread quickly. In New York City, **Lillian Wald** founded the Henry Street Settlement. Janie Porter Barrett established the Locust Street Social Settlement in Hampton, Virginia, the first settlement house for African Americans. By 1910 there were 400 settlement houses in U.S. cities.

Most settlement house workers were middle-class, college-educated women who lived among the people they served. In a society that barred women from working in many professions, the settlement houses gave women new opportunities to lead, organize, and improve life for others.

Many workers in the settlement houses held strong religious views. They believed in the **Social Gospel**, the idea that religious faith should be expressed through good works. They believed that churches had a moral duty to help solve society's problems.

Social Darwinists, however, criticized the Social Gospel movement. Social Darwinists such as sociologist William Graham Sumner viewed existence as a competitive struggle in which only the fittest would survive. People were poor, Sumner said, because of their own deficiencies. Therefore, social reforms could not help them.

READING CHECK **Summarizing** How did the settlement house movement work to address poverty?

SECTION 2 ASSESSMENT

go.hrw.com
Online Quiz
Keyword: SD7 HP15

Reviewing Ideas, Terms, and People

1. **a. Identify** Who was Elisha Otis?
   b. Draw Conclusions How did elevators and steel change the way cities looked?
2. **a. Describe** What were conditions in tenements like?
   b. Explain How did professionalization meet the needs of the developing American economy?
   c. Develop How did women's roles vary from one social class to another?
3. **a. Recall** What was the **settlement house** movement?
   b. Make Inferences Why did middle-class women get involved in the settlement house movement?
   c. Elaborate How did the settlement house movement differ from earlier attempts to relieve poverty?

Critical Thinking

4. **Contrasting** Copy the table below and record the differences between the Social Gospel concept and social Darwinism.

Social Gospel	Social Darwinism

FOCUS ON WRITING ✎

5. **Descriptive** Suppose you are a settlement house worker around 1900. Write a letter to a friend describing the people you serve, their needs, and their neighborhood.

498 CHAPTER 15

Section 2 Assessment Answers

1. **a.** inventor of the safety elevator
   b. buildings taller with larger windows and more decoration
2. **a.** crowded, dirty, dark
   b. standardized occupations
   c. financial and educational differences, roles in the home, need to work
3. **a.** reformers taught skills to help immigrants combat poverty
   b. educated; strong religious beliefs; wanted to help society

   c. taught people skills instead of just giving handouts
4. Social Gospel—express religious faith through good works; churches have moral duty to help society; Social Darwinism—people poor because of deficiencies; only fittest survive
5. possible answer—dark, crowded buildings; no water or indoor plumbing; near polluted factories, stockyards, and ports; diseases common

Politics in the Gilded Age

BEFORE YOU READ

MAIN IDEA

Political corruption was common in the late 1800s, but reformers began fighting for changes to make government more honest.

READING FOCUS

1. How did political machines control politics in major cities?
2. What efforts were made to reduce federal corruption?
3. How did the Populist movement give farmers political power?

KEY TERMS AND PEOPLE

William Marcy Tweed
Thomas Nast
James A. Garfield
Chester A. Arthur
National Grange
Populist Party
William McKinley

TAKING NOTES As you read, take notes on major developments in the rise of the Populist movement in the United States. Record your notes in a graphic organizer like the one shown here.

Rise of the Populist Movement
1867
1870s on
1892

THE INSIDE STORY

Who runs the city? James Pendergast owned a hotel and saloon in an area of tenements and small factories in Kansas City, Missouri. In 1892 "Big Jim" won a seat representing this tough ward on the City Council. This became his base for building a powerful political machine—a network of friends who helped him control city government.

Pendergast spoke out for underpaid workers, such as firefighters. He made sure that poor families had food and heat. He could count on their support in return. "All there is to it," he said, "is having friends, doing things for people, and then later on they'll do things for you."

Not all of Pendergast's buddies were upstanding citizens. Some ran illegal gambling and liquor operations. But Pendergast's cronies in the police department protected them.

When "Big Jim" died in 1911, his brother Tom took over and extended machine control over the entire state Democratic Party. The Pendergast machine grew more and more corrupt. It finally collapsed in the 1930s as Tom Pendergast and others went to prison. ■

▶ **These down-at-the-heels citizens gladly exchanged their votes for a pair of new shoes.**

Politics and Friendship

499

Teach the Main Idea

At Level

Politics in the Gilded Age

1. **Teach** Ask students the Reading Focus questions to teach this section.

2. **Apply** Discuss the workings of political power during the Gilded Age. Draw a teeter totter for students to see. Have students copy it and list the beneficial results of political power in cities in the late 1800s on one end of the bar. On the other end, students should list the negative results of it.

3. **Review** Have volunteers share their completed graphic organizers with the class.

4. **Practice/Homework** Have students create two illustrated flyers, one protesting corruption in city government, and the other denouncing the hardships experienced by farmers in the late 1800s. **LS Visual-Spatial**

   Alternative Assessment Handbook, Rubrics 3: Artwork; and 13: Graphic Organizers

---

● Preteach ●

Bellringer

The Inside Story. . . Use the **Daily Bellringer Transparency** to help students answer the question.

🖎 Daily Bellringer Transparency, Section 3

Life at the Turn of the 20th Century	Daily Bellringer
	Chapter 15, Section 3

Test What You Know

Read the statements below and determine who or what is "speaking."

1. "We are crowded apartment buildings where poor workers live in the city."
2. "I invented the safety elevator."
3. "I founded Hull House in Chicago, a settlement house where immigrants could learn skills they would need in America."
4. "We are a class of people that grew during the late 1800s. Many of us are accountants, clerks, and salespeople."

Preview Section 3
The Inside Story
Who runs the city?
James Pendergast was a hotel and saloon owner in a tough ward of Kansas City, Missouri, when he won a seat on the City Council in 1892. "Big Jim" built a political machine through which he controlled city government. He had a large base of support because he fought for the rights of underpaid workers and made sure the poor had food and heat. When Pendergast died in 1911, his brother Tom took over the political machine. However, the operation grew more corrupt and finally collapsed in the 1930s when Tom went to prison.

1. What was James Pendergast's occupation before he got a seat on the City Council of Kansas City?

2. How did James Pendergast maintain support for his political machine?

Review Answers: 1. tenements; 2. Elisha Otis; 3. Jane Addams; 4. the middle class
Preview Answers: 1. He was a saloon and hotel owner. 2. He fought for better pay for underpaid workers, and he made sure the poor had food and heat.

Copyright © by Holt, Rinehart and Winston. All rights reserved.

Academic Vocabulary

Review with students the high-use academic term in this section.

objective goal (p. 503)

📝 CRF: Vocabulary Builder Activity, Section 3

Taking Notes

1867—foundation of the National Grange; 1870s on—regulation of railroad rates, Interstate Commerce Act and Interstate Commerce Commission enacted, Farmers' Alliances, Gold and Silver Standards; 1892—foundation of Populist Party, Panic of 1893, defeat of Populist-supported Bryan in 1896 election

go.hrw.com
Online Resources

KEYWORD: SD7 CH15
TOPIC: GOVERNMENT CORRUPTION IN THE GILDED AGE

❶ How did political machines control politics in major cities? *exchanged money and assistance for votes; used corrupt methods, including election fraud, bribes, payoffs*

Political Machines

Recall Why did cities need professional politicians? *City problems, including crime, water supplies, and sanitation, became large and complicated.*

Evaluate How did growing numbers of immigrants contribute to the evolution of political machines? *immigrants needed help finding jobs, housing, food and other resources; were more easily controlled by machine bosses*

Activity Have students design a flyer inviting immigrants to a community meeting with their city's bosses. Flyers should explain why immigrants should attend and how their local city bosses can help them. **LS** **Visual-Spatial**

Primary Sources

Political Cartoon
Describe Guide students in a discussion of the political cartoon to ensure that they understand its message. Ask students how Nast's role in turning public opinion against William Tweed might have affected the way the public viewed political cartoonists. Then ask students what effect Nast's cartoons may have had on modern political cartoons.

Answers

Reading Like a Historian *public money was being stolen by the Tammany Hall political machine; possible answers— his expression, presence of his enforcers*

500

Political Machines

Before the Civil War, most cities were small and easily managed by part-time politicians. By the late 1800s, however, cities faced challenges that part-timers could not handle. Problems such as crime, inadequate water supplies, and poor sanitation needed professionals to solve them.

The solution in many cities was the political machine, an informal group of professional politicians who controlled local government. Political machines sorted out some of the biggest urban problems. However, they often resorted to corrupt methods.

Immigrants and political machines By the late 1800s, political machines controlled many major U.S. cities. They made a special point of reaching out to immigrants. They helped newcomers find jobs or housing, supplied coal in winter, and provided turkeys for holiday dinners. Machine politicians also helped immigrants become naturalized citizens. In return, these elected officials expected the people they assisted to vote for them and rally broader community support.

James Pendergast was a popular political boss in Kansas City, Missouri. He gained the loyalty of local immigrants by doing favors such as giving money to those in need. He used his connections to run for alderman. By 1900 he controlled Kansas City politics.

Political machines sometimes dominated entire counties. Stephen Powers and James B. Wells Jr. set up a political machine in Cameron County, Texas, in the 1870s. In exchange for votes, they helped Mexican Americans pay for weddings, funerals, and living expenses during hard times.

In some cities, immigrants not only backed the political machine but also became part of it. Irish Americans rose through the ranks of Boston's political machine. Two second-generation Irish immigrants even became mayor: John F. Fitzgerald (President John F. Kennedy's grandfather) and James Michael Curley.

Political Cartoon

Thomas Nast's biting political cartoons helped expose the corrupt Tammany Hall political machine. Here Boss Tweed takes money from the public, while a sign above him says tauntingly, "What are you going to do about it?"

Tweed, behind the table, collects payments from both rich and poor.

A police officer with a nightstick enforces Tweed's shady business.

Skills FOCUS **READING LIKE A HISTORIAN**

Identifying Points of View What message was Nast trying to send about public money?
Interpreting Political Cartoons What makes Tweed look corrupt?

See Skills Handbook, pp. H28–H29, H31

500 CHAPTER 15

Collaborative Learning

At Level | Standard English Mastery

Political Machines

1. Guide students in a review of political machines, how they operated, and the services they provided to immigrants.

2. Organize the class into mixed-ability pairs. Have each pair select a U.S. city that had a political machine. Several cities are listed in the text. It is their job to represent the city's political machine and meet immigrant families as they arrive for the first time in the city. Have each pair write a list of things they will tell the new immigrants and what support

and help the political machine can offer the family.

3. Have volunteers read their lists to the class.

4. Have students prepare a speech that might have been given by a political boss to new immigrants describing the help the city's political machine can provide. Have students read their speeches to the class.
LS **Interpersonal, Verbal-Linguistic**

Alternative Assessment Handbook, Rubric 24: Oral Presentations

Corruption It is appropriate for politicians to help their constituents and ask for their support. But political machines became famous for using illegal tactics to maintain control.

Machine bosses bought voter support with jobs and favors. They also engaged in election fraud. Sometimes they hired men to vote several times in an election. The hired voters would change coats or shave off their beards so they could vote more than once without detection. Hence the old Chicago joke, "Vote early and vote often."

Many machine politicians practiced graft—using their position to gain money and power dishonestly. They demanded bribes and payoffs in exchange for contracts or jobs. For example, one Chicago business leader routinely paid members of the City Council to let him maintain a monopoly over the city's streetcar system. Like other business leaders, he considered the payoffs part of the cost of doing business.

The Tweed Ring The most notorious political machine was Tammany Hall, which ran the Democratic Party in New York City. In 1863 **William Marcy Tweed** became the powerful head of Tammany Hall.

Like other political bosses, Boss Tweed used his position to rake in riches for himself and his friends, a group known as the Tweed Ring. In one case the city paid $13 million to build a new courthouse, which was several times the actual construction cost. The difference went into the pockets of Tweed and his associates.

Tweed controlled elections, corrupt judges, and big business in the city. His power seemed unbreakable—until 1871. That's when a new bookkeeper for the county gave evidence to the *New York Times* that proved how much the Tweed Ring had stolen.

Thomas Nast, a political cartoonist, attacked this corruption in *Harper's Weekly* magazine in 1871. Week after week, Nast's cartoons sharply criticized Tweed and Tammany Hall. As public opinion turned against Tweed, he is said to have demanded that the cartoons be stopped.

HISTORY'S VOICES

❝I don't care so much what the papers write about me—my constituents can't read, but they can see the . . . pictures.❞

—William Marcy "Boss" Tweed, 1871

Tweed was convicted for fraud and extortion in 1873. He was sentenced to 12 years' imprisonment. Tweed later escaped but was caught in Spain. Officials there recognized him from one of Nast's drawings. In 1878 Tweed died in a New York City jail.

READING CHECK **Drawing Conclusions** Why do you think corruption flourished in New York City for so long without a public outcry?

Federal Corruption

The dominant image of government in the late 1800s was the smoke-filled back room—the clubs and parlors where corrupt politicians and business leaders made deals to enrich themselves. Much dirty business was conducted in this way, out of public view. The problem extended to the highest levels of government.

Scandals of the Grant administration
Ulysses S. Grant, the Union army's commanding general at the end of the Civil War, became president in 1869. His presidency was marred by several scandals that outraged the nation.

One of the most significant dramas was the Crédit Mobilier scandal. In the 1860s the Union Pacific Railroad set up a construction company called Crédit Mobilier to build part of the transcontinental railroad. Crédit Mobilier charged American taxpayers about $23 million more than it actually cost to build the railroad. That $23 million went into the bank accounts of the Union Pacific directors and the Crédit Mobilier stockholders.

In 1872 the *New York Sun* revealed that Crédit Mobilier had given stock to members of Congress and even to Vice President Schuyler Colfax. Corruption now tainted some of the nation's foremost leaders.

Another scandal erupted in 1875 when a new treasury secretary revealed a conspiracy to divert tax collections into private hands. The Whiskey Ring, a group that included Grant's private secretary, whiskey distillers, distributors, and government officials, stole millions of dollars of taxpayers' money. Whiskey producers paid bribes to government officials. In exchange, officials allowed them to keep millions of dollars in liquor taxes that should have gone to the federal treasury.

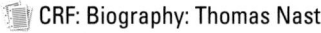
• **Direct Teach** •

Reading Focus

Political Machines

Recall Who was Thomas Nast? *political cartoonist who attacked Tweed and Tammany Hall*

Draw Conclusions Why did Tammany Hall become more notorious than other city political machines? *because of the amount of extortion and theft; exposure by the media*

📄 CRF: Biography: Thomas Nast

📄 Political Cartoons Activities for American History: Cartoon 29: Boss Tweed

Reading Focus

❷ What efforts were made to reduce federal corruption? *federal employees prohibited from managing political parties or campaigns; law required promotions to be based on merit*

Federal Corruption

Identify What was Crédit Mobilier? *railroad-building company that defrauded the federal government of millions*

Analyze Why did Crédit Mobilier bribe government officials? *possible answer—wanted a free hand to steal from government without fear of prosecution*

Skills Focus: Evaluating Historical Interpretation   At Level

Reading Like a Historian Skill   Standard English Mastery
The Crédit Mobilier Scandal

1. Review with students the information in the text about the Crédit Mobilier scandal.

2. Organize the class into small groups and have each group discuss why it was wrong for Crédit Mobilier to offer and for members of Congress and the vice president to accept shares of stock in the company. Each group should write a list of their reasons.

3. Have students use the information from their group's list to write a letter to President

Ulysses S. Grant expressing their concern and anger over the scandal. In their letters students should propose reforms that would prevent this type of scandal from recurring.

4. Have volunteers read their letters to the class. Then guide students in a discussion about whether corruption in government is a problem today. 🔵 **Verbal-Linguistic**

📄 Alternative Assessment Handbook, Rubric 25: Personal Letters

Answers

Reading Check *political machines had controlled elections, judges, big business, but helped immigrants, who then supported them*

Federal Corruption

Identify Who was Roscoe Conkling? *political boss and Republican senator from New York who wanted to retain spoils system*

Analyze Why did the Stalwarts oppose reform? *wanted to continue to control access to federal jobs and maintain power over government affairs*

Make Judgments Do you think the spoils system would have been reformed in the 1880s if President Garfield had not been assassinated? *possible answers—yes, Garfield supported reform and because of government scandals, there was significant push for reform; no, the Republican Party was split on reform issues*

❸ How did the Populist movement give farmers political power? *The Grange and Farmers' Alliances lobbied for reform; Populist Party began direct political campaigns.*

The Populist Movement

Identify Who paid the highest prices to transport their crops to market? *the smallest farmers*

Draw Conclusions Why do you think farmers believed that businesses were profiting from their labor, while they struggled to survive? *possible answer—merchants, bankers, and railroad companies grew rich; charged farmers excessive prices*

Answers

Photo *to ensure that government employees were qualified for their jobs*

Reading Check *Hayes issued an executive order banning political activity by federal employees; Arthur pushed through the Pendleton Civil Service Act, which reformed the spoils system.*

502

Many state and local governments, along with the federal government, adopted civil service reform. Here Chicago police are taking a civil service exam. **What was the purpose of the exams?**

President Hayes and reform These scandals moved reformers to action. They wanted to end the fraud under the spoils system, a long-standing practice of filling government jobs with the winning political party's supporters.

When Republican Rutherford B. Hayes became president in 1877, he wanted reform. He issued an executive order that prohibited government employees from managing political parties or campaigns. At the New York Customhouse, where corrupt Republicans controlled the jobs, two top officials ignored the order. Hayes fired them.

This outraged Roscoe Conkling, a political boss and Republican senator from New York. Conkling and his supporters, known as the Stalwarts, wanted to continue the spoils system. Reformers in the Republican Party wanted to end it.

In 1880, when Hayes decided not to run for a second term, the Republicans split over whom to nominate. They finally compromised on Ohio senator **James A. Garfield**.

Garfield's short presidency Garfield won the election, but he soon angered the Stalwarts by failing to give Conkling a cabinet appointment. The feud did not last long, however. Four months into his term, in July 1881, Garfield was shot in a Washington, D.C., railroad station. The president died in September.

502 CHAPTER 15

The man who killed Garfield was Charles Guiteau (guh-TOH), an unstable character who had been denied a job in Garfield's administration. Guiteau believed that killing the president would help the Stalwart cause. However, the opposite happened. Garfield was succeeded by the vice president, **Chester A. Arthur**. Although Arthur had formerly supported the Stalwarts, he now turned against the spoils system.

Civil service reform President Arthur surprised many people by acting independently of the Republican Party that helped him into office. In 1883 he helped secure passage of the Pendleton Civil Service Act. The law required that promotions be based on merit, not on political connections. Although the Pendleton Act initially applied to only 10 percent of federal jobs, it was an important first step in reducing corruption in the federal government.

READING CHECK **Summarizing** How did Presidents Hayes and Arthur begin civil service reform?

The Populist Movement

Calls for reform also arose from another direction. Farmers began a movement for reform that would challenge both of the major political parties.

Farmers' hardships Farmers in the late 1800s were in a desperate situation. Crop prices were falling. Many farmers borrowed large sums to buy new equipment or more land so they could grow more crops. The resulting oversupply of farm products caused prices to fall even further. A farmer who planted 24 acres of cotton in 1894 made less money than a farmer who planted only 9 acres in 1873.

Indebted farmers found it increasingly difficult to repay their loans. Even worse, railroads began to charge enormous fees to transport crops to market. The smallest farmers often had to pay the highest shipping prices.

To many farmers, it seemed that everyone else was making money at their expense. The merchants who sold the farm equipment profited. The banks and the railroads got richer and richer. But the farmers who worked all day every day were nearly penniless. Outraged farmers decided to fight this unjust situation.

Differentiating Instruction

Below Level

Special Education Students; Learners Having Difficulty

1. Review and discuss with students the information in this section about political machines, corruption at the city and federal levels, government scandals, and the subsequent reforms.

2. Have students work individually or in mixed-ability pairs to create a sequencing chart showing the series of events that led to the Pendleton Civil Service Act.

3. Have volunteers share their charts with the class, and create a class chart for all students

to see. Have students correct their work and retain the charts as a study tool.

4. Have students create one visual to illustrate each event on their charts. **LS Interpersonal, Visual-Spatial**

📖 Alternative Assessment Handbook, Rubrics 3: Artwork; and 13: Graphic Organizers

The National Grange With no one else to help them, farmers organized to help themselves. Local groups formed to provide emergency aid and other assistance to individual farmers. In time, local groups merged to form nationwide organizations.

The first major farmers' organization was the Order of Patrons of Husbandry, more commonly known as the **National Grange**. Founded in 1867 by Oliver Hudson Kelley, the Grange began as a social group. Kelley had surveyed farming conditions in the South immediately after the Civil War, and he saw how downtrodden many farmers were. He decided to create an organization in which farmers could support each other.

HISTORY'S VOICES

❝1. United by the strong and faithful tie of Agriculture, we mutually resolve to labor for the good of our Order, our country, and mankind.

2. We heartily endorse the motto: 'In essentials, unity; in non-essentials, liberty; in all things, charity.'❞

—1874 Declaration of Purposes of the National Grange

The Grange campaigned to unite farmers from across the nation, transcending regional rivalries. The organization declared that "in our agricultural brotherhood and its purposes, we shall recognize no North, no South, no East, no West."

Within a few years, membership in the Grange exploded. Farmers began to realize that to save their livelihoods, they would have to fight against the railroads and operators of grain elevators who made huge profits at their expense. An 1874 Grange document urged farmers to act boldly to protect their interests.

HISTORY'S VOICES

❝Choke monopolies, break up rings, vote for honest men, fear God and make money. So shalt thou prosper and sorrow and hard times shall flee away.❞

—"The Ten Commandments of the Grange,"
Oshkosh (WI) Weekly Times, December 16, 1874

Around this time, the focus of the Grange shifted toward fighting for political reform. The organization's first target was railroad rates. By the late 1870s, the Grange had succeeded in persuading the state legislatures in Illinois, Iowa, Minnesota, and Wisconsin to regulate railroads and operators of grain elevators. The

business opposed regulation because it took a bite out of their profits. They challenged these Granger laws in the courts.

In 1877 the Supreme Court agreed with the Grange. In the case of *Munn* v. *Illinois,* the Court declared that state legislatures did have the right to regulate businesses that involved the public interest.

Nine years later the Court ruled again on the issue of business regulation. In the 1886 case *Wabash* v. *Illinois,* the Court ruled that the federal government had the power to regulate railroad traffic moving across state boundaries.

The *Wabash* case led Congress to approve the Interstate Commerce Act in 1887. Passage of the law had great historic significance. It marked the first time that the federal government had regulated an industry.

The objective of the Interstate Commerce Act was to make railroad rates fair for all customers by requiring the rates to be "reasonable and just." The act prohibited railroads from giving more favorable rates or special rebates to large shippers. It also forbade railroads from charging more for short hauls than for long hauls over the same rail line. To oversee the railroads, the act created the Interstate Commerce Commission (ICC).

ACADEMIC VOCABULARY
objective goal

The National Grange was founded in 1867. In less than a decade, more than 21,000 granges were organized on the state, county, and local levels.

Reading Focus

The Populist Movement

Describe What was the Colored Farmers' Alliance? *alliance of African American farmers that worked for same reforms as Southern Alliance; also worked to fight prejudice*

Analyze In what way was the power of the Interstate Commerce Commission limited? *unable to enforce the provisions of the Interstate Commerce Act*

Make Judgments Do you think that expanding the money supply would have created a better economic situation for farmers? *possible answers—yes, because inflation would ease farmers' debt burden; no, because prices would also rise and farmers would still not have enough money*

Info to Know

National Grange Today The National Grange remains active today, with programs focused on lessening the isolation of life on a farm and providing insurance in case of natural disasters. The Grange also pursues its original goals by working toward the passage of legislation to alleviate the economic conditions of many farmers. In 2000, the Grange had approximately 300,000 members with close to 4,000 local groups operating in the United States.

Answers

Interpreting Charts *It created a need to mechanize farming, which set off a chain reaction.*

504

Congress did not, however, give the ICC the power to enforce the provisions of the law. The ICC did not gain enforcement power until 1906, under President Theodore Roosevelt. Nonetheless, the ICC would later serve as a model for government regulation of private businesses.

The Alliance movement Other farmers' organizations formed in Texas and New York in the 1870s. As they grew and established links, they became known as the Farmers' Alliance.

Like the Grange, the Farmers' Alliance began as a way to help farmers with practical needs such as buying equipment or marketing farm products. Soon, the Alliance also began lobbying for banking reform and regulation of railroad rates.

The Alliance movement spread quickly. By 1890 more than 1 million farmers from different regions of the country had joined.

In the South, however, leaders of the Southern Alliance restricted membership to white farmers only. African American farmers therefore formed their own organization, the Colored Farmers' Alliance.

In 1890 the Colored Farmers' Alliance had more than 1 million members. It worked for the same kinds of reforms as the Southern Alliance. In addition, the Colored Farmers'

Alliance fought prejudice. It urged its members to become economically strong by avoiding debt and owning their own farms. Like other African American organizations of the time, it advocated hard work and sacrifice as the keys to gaining equality in society.

The money supply issue In order to create better economic conditions for farmers, the Farmers' Alliances wanted to expand the money supply. In other words, they wanted the government to print more money. They thought that more money in circulation would inflate prices, including the prices for crops. The resulting inflation would ease farmers' debt burden.

Paper money was originally redeemable for either gold or silver coins. But in 1873 Congress voted to adopt the gold standard, a monetary system in which the standard unit of exchange is a certain amount of gold. Under the gold standard, the government promised to redeem any bill for gold. In addition, there could only be as much money in circulation as there was gold in the treasury to back it up.

The gold standard reduced the number of dollars in circulation, and this alarmed many farmers. In the hope of expanding the supply of money, farm groups urged that money once

Growth of the Populist Movement

The Populist movement began among struggling farmers in the Midwest, South, and West. Eventually laborers joined with farmers to press for new government policies that would benefit ordinary working people. The Populist movement reached its height in the 1890s with the formation of the Populist Party.

THE POPULIST MOVEMENT

- Industrial Revolution mechanizes farming
  - Farmers go into debt to buy equipment
  - Crop production increases; prices fall
- Railroads charge excessively high rates
- Farmers organize to pressure state legislatures for railroad regulation
- Alliance movement seeks regulation of business, expansion of the money supply
- Populist Party forms to press for reforms at the national level

Skills Focus INTERPRETING CHARTS

What role did the Industrial Revolution play in the formation of the Populist Party?

See Skills Handbook, p. H15

504 CHAPTER 15

Skills Focus: Making Generalizations   Below Level

Reading Skill

The Populist Movement

Materials construction paper, colored markers

1. Organize students into small mixed-ability groups.

2. Have each group use a large piece of paper to draw a political cartoon and write a caption depicting farmers and the National Grange's struggle with the railroads. Then have students draw another large political cartoon showing industry's view of government regulation of private business.

3. Have each group display its cartoons to the class.

4. Guide students in a discussion about whether the Grange was effective in its campaign to establish fair shipping rates for large and small farmers. **LS Interpersonal, Visual-Spatial**

📖 Alternative Assessment Handbook, Rubric 27: Political Cartoons

again be backed by silver as well as gold. They pressured Congress to pass laws requiring the government to buy some silver to mint coins. However, the silver did not have much impact on the money supply.

This sharply disappointed Alliance members. In the elections of 1890, they became very politically active. They stood behind any candidate who supported their position on monetary policy, and they had remarkable success. Alliance-backed candidates won more than 40 seats in Congress and four governorships.

The Populist Party Encouraged by their clout in the elections, Alliance leaders decided to form a national political party. At a convention in Omaha, Nebraska, in July 1892, the People's Party was born. This coalition of farmers, labor leaders, and reformers became more commonly known as the **Populist Party**.

The Populist Party supported National Grange and Alliance demands. The party platform called for an income tax, bank regulation, government ownership of railroad and telegraph companies, and the free (unlimited) coinage of silver. In pushing this agenda, the Populists claimed to speak for the common people rather than the ruling elite.

HISTORY'S VOICES

❝We seek to restore the government of the Republic to the hands of the 'plain people,' with which class it originated. We assert our purposes to be identical with the purposes of the National Constitution . . . We believe that the power of government—in other words, of the people—should be expanded . . . to the end that oppression, injustice, and poverty shall eventually cease in the land.❞

—Preamble to the 1892 Platform of the Populist Party

In the 1892 presidential election, the Populists backed James B. Weaver against the Republican incumbent, Benjamin Harrison, and the Democratic candidate, Grover Cleveland. Cleveland won the election, but the Populist Party won several seats in Congress as well as several state offices. This was remarkable success for a new party.

The Panic of 1893 Soon after the election, the nation plunged into an economic depression. In May 1893 one of the leading railroad companies failed. This triggered the Panic of

1893: investors pulled out of the stock market and thousands of businesses collapsed. By year's end, some 3 million people had lost their jobs. Strikes and protests swept the country.

There were many causes for this national depression, including a worldwide financial slump. President Cleveland focused on one of many causes: the Sherman Silver Purchase Act of 1890.

This law required the government to pay for silver purchases with paper money redeemable in either gold or silver. But new discoveries of silver decreased its value, and people rushed to exchange their paper money for gold. This put a huge strain on the treasury's gold reserves. To protect the gold standard and to restore confidence in the economy, Cleveland called for Congress to repeal the Sherman Silver Purchase Act. Congress did so in October 1893. Because of Cleveland's actions, the country stayed on the gold standard.

The election of 1896 Silver continued to be a controversial issue. In the presidential election of 1896, the Republicans nominated Ohio governor **William McKinley**, who believed that the gold standard was the key to the nation's prosperity. The Democrats, meanwhile, did not want President Cleveland to seek re-election because the Panic of 1893 had made him so unpopular. Instead, they nominated William Jennings Bryan, a former two-term U.S. congressman from Nebraska.

FACES OF HISTORY

Mary Elizabeth LEASE
1853–1933

Daughter of an Irish immigrant activist, Mary Elizabeth Lease became an activist as well. Lease moved west to Kansas for a teaching job and soon joined the temperance movement. She became more involved in politics when she joined the Populist Party.

In the 1890 election Lease traveled the country giving more than 160 speeches. A riveting speaker, she was nicknamed Mary "Yellin" Lease by her opponents. Lease spoke out unceasingly in favor of popular election of U.S. senators, government control of railroads, regulation of corporations, women's right to vote, and monetary reforms. She also opposed the efforts of Populists who wanted to merge with the Democratic Party.

Make Generalizations What kinds of causes did Lease support?

THE IMPACT TODAY

Economics
President Richard Nixon took the United States off the gold standard in 1971, and the dollar has been allowed to "float" according to market value ever since.

● **Direct Teach** ●

Reading Focus

The Populist Movement

Recall What name was given to the People's Party? *the Populist Party*

Analyze Why did many farmers oppose the gold standard? *because it limited the amount of dollars in circulation*

Make Judgments Do you believe that the Populist Party, which only lasted a few years, made a difference in American politics and policies? *possible answers—no, because unable to elect president and power faded after 1896 election; yes, because later politicians adopted populist ideas and language*

Teaching Tip

Have students copy the quote from the Oshkosh *Weekly Times* from page 503 onto their own papers. Have them underline the verbs, and then have students rewrite the quote as a series of simple sentences.

Skills Focus: Analyzing Secondary Sources
Above Level

Reading Like a Historian Skill
The Election of 1892
Research Required

1. Organize the class into groups of three. Within each group, assign each student one of the 1892 presidential candidates: James Weaver, Benjamin Harrison, and Grover Cleveland. Each student will be responsible for researching the candidate and the issues in the 1892 presidential election. Encourage students to conduct outside research to supplement the information in the text.

2. Have students use their research to develop a campaign strategy, a slogan, and a speech with three to five major points that could have been delivered by their assigned candidate.

3. Have volunteers present their speeches and campaign materials to the class.

4. As an extension, have students prepare for and present a presidential campaign debate of the issues. **LS Interpersonal, Verbal-Linguistic**

📖 Alternative Assessment Handbook, Rubrics 24: Oral Presentations; and 30: Research

Answers

Faces of History *temperance, popular election of senators, government control of railroads, regulation of corporations, women's right to vote, monetary reform*

505

Reading Focus

The Populist Movement

Recall Who won the presidential election of 1896? *William McKinley*

Explain How did the Panic of 1893 affect the 1896 election? *President Cleveland was so unpopular that his own party, the Democrats, chose William Jennings Bryan as their candidate.*

● **Review & Assess** ●

Close

Guide students in a discussion of the ways city political machines and the Populist Party changed American politics.

Review

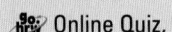 Online Quiz, Section 3

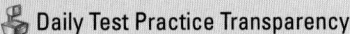 Daily Test Practice Transparency

Assess

SE Section 3 Assessment

Progress Assessment: Section 3 Quiz

Alternative Assessment Handbook

Reteach

Interactive Reader and Study Guide, Section 3

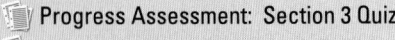 Interactive Skills Tutor CD-ROM

Answers

Reading Like a Historian *by waving the crown of thorns and prominently displaying the cross*

Reading Check *Alliance formed to help farmers, began lobbying for reform, had success in 1890 elections, Alliance leaders decided to form Populist Party in 1892*

506

Skills Focus **READING LIKE A HISTORIAN**

The caption of this Republican cartoon called Bryan unfit to be president because he made "sacrilegious" use of Christian symbols—the cross and crown of thorns—in his speeches. **Interpreting Political Cartoons** How does the image suggest Bryan's lack of respect?

Bryan hailed the free coinage of silver as the key to prosperity. In a famous speech, he vowed to resist the gold standard alongside business people, workers and farmers.

HISTORY'S VOICES

❝If they [Republicans] dare to come out in the open field and defend the gold standard as a good thing, we will fight them to the uttermost. Having behind us the producing masses of this nation and the world, supported by the commercial interests, the laboring interests and the toilers everywhere, we will answer their demand for a gold standard by saying to them: You shall not press down upon the brow of labor this crown of thorns, you shall not crucify mankind upon a cross of gold.❞

—William Jennings Bryan, speech to the Democratic National Convention, July 9, 1896

The Democratic Party's adoption of the free-silver platform caused the Populists to throw their support to Bryan as well. Worried that Bryan was picking up votes, many business leaders contributed millions of dollars to the Republican campaign. McKinley subsequently won the election. Free silver had not been a strong enough issue for a national victory.

The election of 1896 was the high point of influence for the Populist Party, which soon faded away. Even so, the party's platform laid the groundwork for reforms that the government would later enact. Populist language also became a mainstay in politics. Many politicians have tried to craft populist messages that suggest they are on the side of ordinary people and not special interests.

READING CHECK **Sequencing** How did the Farmers' Alliance give rise to the Populist Party?

SECTION 3 ASSESSMENT

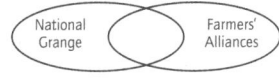

go.hrw.com
Online Quiz
Keyword: SD7 HP15

Reviewing Ideas, Terms, and People

1. **a. Describe** What was the relationship between **William Marcy Tweed** and **Thomas Nast**?
   b. Summarize How did political machines gain power?
   c. Evaluate Do you think political machines did more harm than good? Explain.

2. **a. Recall** How did the **Crédit Mobilier scandal** tarnish the Grant administration?
   b. Elaborate In what way did the **Pendleton Civil Service Act** affect federal corruption?

3. **a. Identify** Who were **William McKinley** and William Jennings Bryan?
   b. Analyze How did farmers raise their issues from the local level to national politics?
   c. Evaluate What was the impact of the **Populist Party**?

Critical Thinking

4. **Comparing and Contrasting** What were the main similarities and differences between the **National Grange** and the Farmers' Alliances?

National Grange   Farmers' Alliances

FOCUS ON SPEAKING

5. **Persuasive** Imagine you are a leader of the Populist Party. Deliver a short speech in which you explain why the issue of free silver is so important to your cause.

506 CHAPTER 15

Section 3 Assessment Answers

1. **a.** Nast criticized Tweed
   b. supported and helped immigrants in exchange for votes
   c. possible answers—harm, impeded democratic process, acted illegally; good, helped immigrants find jobs, housing, provided food, improved living conditions

2. **a.** some members of Congress and vice president implicated in it
   b. promotions based on merit, not political connections

3. **a.** presidential candidates in 1896
   b. took on industries with government support
   c. laid the groundwork for future reform

4. similarities—support groups for farmers; lobbied for railroad regulation; differences—Grange transcended regional differences; Alliance for whites only; fought against gold standard

5. possible answer—put more money into circulation; more goods and services available; crop prices would inflate, easing farmers' debt

SECTION 4

Segregation and Discrimination

BEFORE YOU READ

MAIN IDEA

The United States in the late 1800s was a place of great change— and a place in need of even greater change.

READING FOCUS

1. What kinds of legalized discrimination did African Americans endure after Reconstruction?

2. What informal discrimination did African Americans experience?

3. Who were the most prominent black leaders of the period, and how did their views differ?

4. In what ways did others suffer discrimination in the late 1800s?

KEY TERMS AND PEOPLE

poll tax
grandfather clause
Jim Crow law
Plessy v. *Ferguson*
racial etiquette
lynching
Booker T. Washington
W. E. B. Du Bois
NAACP
debt peonage

TAKING NOTES As you read, take notes on laws, policies, and legal decisions that discriminated against African Americans. Record your notes in a graphic organizer like the one shown below. You may need to add more circles.

Discrimination against African Americans

THE INSIDE STORY

Why did a dinner invitation cause controversy? In October 1901, soon after he became president, Theodore Roosevelt invited a national leader to dine at the White House. The invitation made headlines because that leader was an African American: Booker T. Washington. Roosevelt often consulted with him about political appointments in the South because he knew that Washington understood the complicated relationships in the region. The dinner was a small occasion with the president, his family, and a few guests. To some people, that social closeness was even more upsetting. At the time, many restaurants would not serve black people.

Washington was not the first African American to visit the White House. President Lincoln had welcomed Sojourner Truth and Frederick Douglass to discuss abolition. Black entertainers performed there in the late 1800s. But a social invitation to dinner was another matter.

When Washington died in 1915, the *New York Times* obituary noted, "Most of the criticism fell upon Colonel Roosevelt, but the incident [the White House dinner] served also to injure Dr. Washington's work in some parts of the South." ◼

▶ **Appearing side by side, Roosevelt and Washington made a powerful statement to both the black and the white communities.**

ROOSEVELT AND BOOKER T. WASHINGTON

LIFE AT THE TURN OF THE 20TH CENTURY **507**

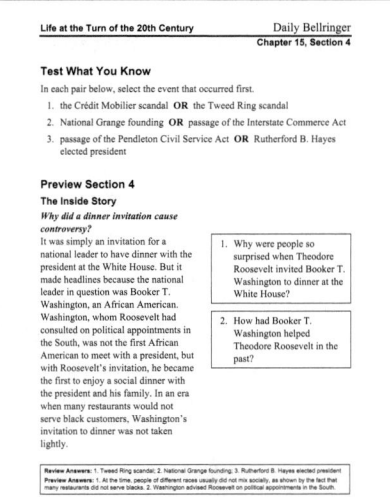
Teach the Main Idea

At Level

Segregation and Discrimination

1. **Teach** Ask students the Reading Focus questions to teach this section.

2. **Apply** Have students create a series of five diary entries describing what journalists from the late 1800s might have observed about the lives of African Americans while traveling in the South.

3. **Review** Have volunteers read entries from their travel diaries to the class. Then guide students in a discussion of the ways in which discrimination toward minority

groups in the late 1800s might affect American life today.

4. **Practice/Homework** Have students write an essay in which they compare and contrast discrimination faced by Mexican Americans, Asian Americans, and Native Americans in the late 1800s with today.

LS Verbal-Linguistic

📃 Alternative Assessment Handbook, Rubric 15: Journals

507

① What kinds of legalized discrimination did African Americans endure after Reconstruction? *prevented from voting; segregation*

Legalized Discrimination

Recall What was a poll tax? *tax voters had to pay in order to vote*

Describe What was the purpose of Jim Crow laws? *to create and enforce segregation of African Americans*

Evaluate How did the Supreme Court contribute to legalized discrimination? *overturned 1875 Civil Rights Act;* Plessy v. Ferguson *declared separate facilities constitutional*

Primary Source

"Any person . . . who shall be guilty of printing, publishing or circulating . . . arguments or suggestions in favor of social equality or of intermarriage between whites and negroes, shall be guilty of a misdemeanor and subject to fine not exceeding five hundred dollars or imprisonment not exceeding six months or both."

— Former Mississippi State Law

Info to Know

Brown* v. *Board of Education In the Supreme Court case *Brown* v. *Board of Education*, racial segregation in public schools was declared illegal. The decision was issued on May 17, 1954.

Answers

Reading Check *Jim Crow laws; poll taxes; grandfather clauses; literacy tests*

508

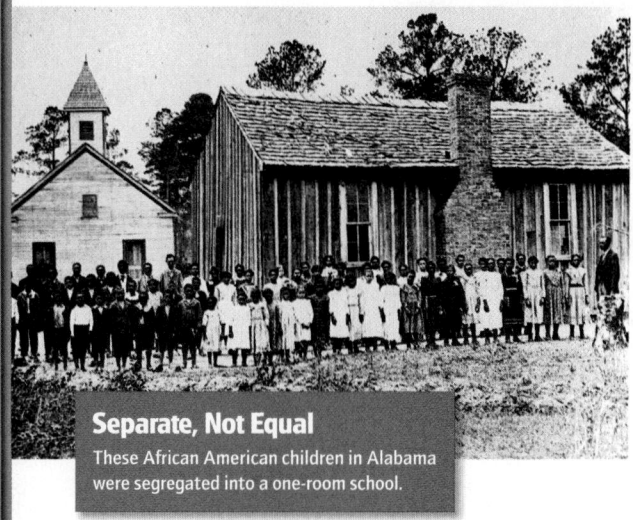

Separate, Not Equal
These African American children in Alabama were segregated into a one-room school.

Legalized Discrimination

As you know, the Fourteenth and Fifteenth Amendments were meant to guarantee the rights of African Americans. Yet that did not happen. In the late 1800s, prejudice persisted throughout the country, and in the South, new laws made discrimination legal.

Restricting the right to vote By the time Reconstruction ended, white Democrats had regained control over the southern state legislatures. They went to great lengths to make sure that African Americans could not exercise their right to vote. One tactic was to require voters to pay a **poll tax** and pass a literacy test. These measures kept most African Americans from voting. Most were too poor to afford the poll tax, and many had been denied the education needed to pass the literacy test.

The laws prevented some poor or illiterate white men from voting. However, many southern state legislatures had written **grandfather clauses** into their constitutions. The clauses stated that a man could vote if he, his father, or his grandfather had been eligible to vote before January 1, 1867. That date is significant. Before that time, only white men had the right to vote. Freed slaves had not yet achieved that right. The grandfather clause, therefore, made sure that African Americans could not vote.

508 CHAPTER 15

Legalized segregation Southern state legislatures also passed a series of laws designed to create and enforce segregation. These provisions were called **Jim Crow laws**. The name Jim Crow came from a stereotypical character in a minstrel song of the 1820s. By the 1890s the term was used for the laws discriminating against African Americans.

The first of these laws, passed in Tennessee in 1881, required separate railway cars for African Americans and whites. By the 1890s southern states had segregated many public places and services, including schools.

African Americans filed lawsuits against railroads, hotels, and theaters that refused to serve them. They wanted equal treatment under the Civil Rights Act of 1875.

HISTORY'S VOICES

❝All persons . . . shall be entitled to full and equal enjoyment of the accommodations, advantages, facilities, and privileges of inns, public conveyances on land or water, theaters, and other places of public amusement.❞

—Civil Rights Act of 1875

In 1883, however, the Supreme Court declared that the Civil Rights Act of 1875 was unconstitutional. The Court ruled that the Fourteenth Amendment—which guarantees equal protection of the law—applied only to state governments. Congress could prevent the states from denying African Americans their rights, but Congress could not outlaw discrimination by private individuals or businesses.

Thirteen years later, another key case came before the Supreme Court. This time the matter involved a Louisiana state law requiring railroads to provide "equal but separate accommodations for the white and colored races." Homer Plessy, an African American man, sat in a whites-only train compartment to test the law. He was arrested, but he appealed based on the Fourteenth Amendment.

In ***Plessy* v. *Ferguson*** (1896) the Court upheld the practice of segregation. The Court ruled that "separate but equal" facilities did not violate the Fourteenth Amendment. Only one justice, John Marshall Harlan, disagreed with the majority. The *Plessy* decision allowed legalized segregation for nearly 60 years.

READING CHECK **Summarizing** How did southern states limit the rights of African Americans?

Learners Having Difficulty; English-Language Learners

1. Have students reread the information about legalized discrimination against African Americans.

2. Have students use the information to make a two-column chart about segregation and discrimination. In the first column students should list actions taken by southern states and the Supreme Court to legalize segregation and discrimination, such as poll taxes, Jim Crow laws, and *Plessy* v. *Ferguson*. In the second column students should list the

consequences of those actions and laws.

3. Have students write a summary of the information in their charts describing how African Americans in the South were prevented from obtaining basic civil rights and gaining any political power.

4. Have volunteers share their summaries either in small groups or with the class. **⑤ Visual-Spatial, Verbal-Linguistic**

📄 Alternative Assessment Handbook, Rubrics 13: Graphic Organizers; and 37: Writing Assignments

Informal Discrimination

Laws were not the only source of racial barriers. Strict rules of behavior, called **racial etiquette**, governed social and business interactions. African Americans were supposed to "know their place" and defer to whites in every encounter. If they failed to speak respectfully or acted with too much pride or defiance, the <u>consequences</u> could be serious.

The worst consequence was **lynching**—the murder of an individual, usually by hanging, without a legal trial. Between 1882 and 1892, nearly 900 African Americans lost their lives to lynch mobs. Lynchings declined after 1892, but they continued into the early 1900s.

Lynchings could be sparked by the most minor offenses, or perceived offenses. Many, if not most, victims were innocent of any crime, and few of the killers were ever punished.

READING CHECK **Drawing Conclusions**
Why did African Americans usually go along with the system of racial etiquette?

Prominent Black Leaders

Near the turn of the century, two different approaches emerged for improving the lives of African Americans. **Booker T. Washington,** born into slavery, believed that African Americans should accept segregation for the moment. He thought they could best prosper by acquiring farming and vocational skills. He founded the Tuskegee Institute in Alabama to teach African Americans practical skills for self-sufficiency.

W. E. B. Du Bois, a Harvard-trained professor, believed in speaking out against prejudice and striving for full rights immediately. African Americans, he said, should be uplifted by the "talented tenth," their best-educated leaders. Du Bois launched the Niagara Movement in 1905 to protest discrimination. Four years later, he helped found an even more influential organization, the National Association for the Advancement of Colored People (**NAACP**).

READING CHECK **Contrasting** How did the views of Washington and Du Bois differ?

ACADEMIC
VOCABULARY
consequence
something that logically follows an action

COUNTERPOINTS

Overcoming Discrimination

Booker T. Washington walked a fine line between helping African Americans to advance and trying to avoid angering white Americans.

To W. E. B. Du Bois, equality meant opportunities to achieve at the highest levels.

66 No race can prosper till it learns that there is as much dignity in tilling a field as in writing a poem . . . The opportunity to earn a dollar in a factory just now is worth infinitely more than the opportunity to spend a dollar in an opera-house. 99

Booker T. Washington,
1895

66 Industrial and trade teaching is needed . . . [but] it is not needed as much as thorough common school training and the careful education of the gifted in higher institutions. 99

W. E. B. Du Bois,
1904

Skills FOCUS **READING LIKE A HISTORIAN**

Identifying Points of View For those who favored gradual social change, whose approach would be more appealing? Explain your reasoning.
See Skills Handbook, pp. H28–H29

LIFE AT THE TURN OF THE 20TH CENTURY **509**

Direct Teach

Reading Focus

2 What informal discrimination did African Americans experience? *the system of racial etiquette; lynching*

Informal Discrimination

Identify What was the name given to rules of behavior between white and black Americans? *racial etiquette*

Make Judgments Why do you think so few of those who took part in lynchings were punished? *possible answers—authorities did not prosecute; identities kept secret*

Reading Focus

3 Who were the most prominent black leaders of the period, and how did their views differ? *Booker T. Washington— accepted segregation for time being; W. E. B. Du Bois—fought segregation*

Prominent Black Leaders

Recall Who created the Tuskeegee Institute? Why? *Booker T. Washington—to teach African Americans practical skills*

Make Judgments Do you think Washington's or Du Bois's response to discrimination was more effective? *possible answer—Washington's, because it helped more people*

Skills Focus: Making Written Presentations

At Level

Reading Like a Historian Skill
Combatting Discrimination

1. Remind students that both W. E. B. Du Bois and Booker T. Washington believed strongly in their own approach to solving problems of discrimination and racial segregation.

2. Ask students to decide which approach they believe would have been more effective in the late 1800s. Then have students write an essay explaining whether they would have supported Booker T. Washington's point

of view or W. E. B. Du Bois's point of view. In their essays students should attempt to persuade and convince the reader that their position is justified.

3. Have volunteers read their essays to the class.
   LS **Verbal-Linguistic, Logical-Mathematical**
   Alternative Assessment Handbook, Rubric 43: Writing to Persuade

Answers

Reading Like a Historian
Washington's approach because sought to avoid angering white Americans by advocating small steps toward ending discrimination

Reading Check (left) *They could be severely punished or killed for not complying.* **(right)** *Washington accepted segregation for the moment; Du Bois fought for immediate equality.*

509

4 In what ways did others suffer discrimination in the late 1800s? *Mexican Americans—debt peonage, menial jobs, little pay; Asian Americans—segregation, bans on immigration; Native Americans—denied citizenship, right to vote, traditional way of life; few economic opportunities*

Others Suffer Discrimination

Recall What types of jobs were open to Mexican immigrants? *jobs in mines, railroads, farms*

Evaluate What evidence do you see that only whites were allowed full economic and political opportunities in the United States in the late 1890s? *widespread discrimination against African Americans, Mexican Americans, Asian Americans, Native Americans*

Close

Guide students in a discussion of Jim Crow laws, *Plessy* v. *Ferguson*, and discrimination faced by other minority groups in the late 1800s.

Review

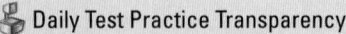 Online Quiz, Section 4

Daily Test Practice Transparency

Assess

SE Section 4 Assessment

Progress Assessment: Section 4 Quiz

Alternative Assessment Handbook

Reteach

Interactive Reader and Study Guide, Section 4

Interactive Skills Tutor CD-ROM

Answers

Reading Check *all groups faced legal and social discrimination; limited economic opportunities*

510

Mexican American workers, like these railway workers in Texas, were routinely the lowest paid of any ethnic group.

Others Suffer Discrimination

African Americans were not the only people to face racial prejudice. Mexican Americans, Asian Americans, and Native Americans all experienced legal and social discrimination in the late 1800s.

Mexican Americans Many Mexican Americans and Mexican immigrants encountered hostility from white Americans. They often did not speak English well and had to take the most menial jobs for little pay. Some worked in the mines or on railroads. Most, however, worked on farms.

Many Mexican immigrants became trapped in their jobs because of a system brought from Mexico called **debt peonage**. In this system, workers were tied to their jobs until they could pay off debts they owed their employer. Debt peonage was finally made illegal in 1911.

Asian Americans Earlier in this chapter, you read about laws that limited immigrants from Asia and denied Chinese Americans citizenship. But discrimination went further. Chinese and Japanese Americans had to live in segregated neighborhoods and attend separate schools. Esther Wong, a Chinese immigrant, noted that "only a very few Chinese could find houses in American districts, for most house owners do not want Chinese tenants." Several states also forbade marriage with whites.

Native Americans Native Americans, too, endured injustices, including continuous government efforts to stamp out their traditional ways of life. Children were sometimes sent away from their parents to be "Americanized." People living on reservations had few opportunities for economic advancement. Many Native Americans were also excluded from political activity. In a number of states, they were not considered citizens until the passage of the Indian Citizenship Act of 1924.

READING CHECK **Comparing** How were the experiences of minority groups similar?

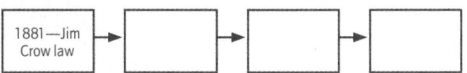

go.hrw.com
Online Quiz
Keyword: SD7 HP15

SECTION 4 ASSESSMENT

Reviewing Ideas, Terms, and People

1. **a. Define** What was a **grandfather clause**?
   b. Draw Conclusions What was the real purpose of **poll taxes**, literacy tests, and the grandfather clause?
2. **a. Describe** What was **racial etiquette**?
   b. Explain What could happen to African Americans who defied the rules of racial etiquette?
3. **a. Identify** Who was **Booker T. Washington**?
   b. Analyze What did **W. E. B. Du Bois** expect of the group he called "the talented tenth"?
   c. Predict For the time period of this chapter, do you think Washington's or Du Bois's approach would have been most beneficial for African Americans? Explain.
4. **a. Recall** What was **debt peonage**?
   b. Make Inferences How do you think segregation affected the people who were subjected to it?

Critical Thinking

5. **Sequencing** Copy the chart below and record the sequence of legal milestones from the passage of the first Jim Crow law in Tennessee to the Supreme Court's decision 15 years later in *Plessy* v. *Ferguson*. Be sure to include dates.

   1881—Jim Crow law → □ → □ → □

FOCUS ON WRITING

6. **Expository** Imagine that you are a newspaper editor in 1896. Write an editorial explaining what you think of the Supreme Court's decision in *Plessy* v. *Ferguson*. Address the "separate but equal" argument.

510 CHAPTER 15

Section 4 Assessment Answers

1. **a.** a man could vote if his grandfather eligible to vote before 1867
   b. to prevent African Americans from voting
2. **a.** rules of behavior between white and black Americans
   b. fear of consequences, including lynching
3. **a.** ex-slave, founded school
   b. protest discrimination
   c. Washington's—would help more people
4. **a.** remain in jobs until debts paid

b. possible answer—humiliating, limited economic advancement

5. Jim Crow law first passed, 1881; lawsuit in 1883 under Civil Rights Act of 1875 fails; Louisiana law requires separate railway cars; Supreme Court declares segregation legal

6. possible answer—segregation is unjust; Fourteenth Amendment guarantees equal treatment; separate facilities will not be equal

Plessy v. Ferguson (1896)

Why It Matters By the 1890s southern states had laws enforcing segregation in most aspects of daily life. *Plessy* v. *Ferguson* upheld the states' rights to regulate social and economic matters within their borders.

Background of the Case

Homer Plessy was convicted of sitting in a whites-only railway car. He had white parents and white grandparents but was considered black because he had a black great-grandparent. Plessy argued that Louisiana's Separate Car Act of 1890 violated the Thirteenth Amendment, which abolished slavery, and the Fourteenth Amendment, which requires all people to be treated equally under the law.

The Decision

The Court upheld the Separate Car Act. Justice Henry Brown maintained that the abolition of slavery did not prevent states from making legal distinctions between races. A law can recognize the obvious differences between races, he wrote, without violating their legal equality.

The Court noted that the Fourteenth Amendment requires legal equality but does not eliminate all racial distinctions and does not force people to accept a social "commingling of the races upon terms unsatisfactory to either." The lone dissenter, Justice John Marshall Harlan, wrote:

> ❝Our Constitution is color-blind, and neither knows nor tolerates classes among citizens. In respect of civil rights, all citizens are equal before the law. The humblest is the peer of the most powerful. The law regards man as man, and takes no account of his surroundings or of his color when his civil rights as guaranteed by the supreme law of the land are involved.❞

THE IMPACT TODAY Nearly 60 years passed before *Plessy* was formally overturned in *Brown* v. *Board of Education* (1954). Even then, segregation did not disappear overnight. Today, however, people of all races mix freely in public accommodations, as these airplane travelers are doing.

go.hrw.com
Research Online
Keyword: SS Court

CRITICAL THINKING

1. **Analyze the Impact** Using the keyword above, read about the *Brown v. Board of Education* decision, which overruled *Plessy*. What did the Court in *Brown* say about the "separate but equal" doctrine in *Plessy*? Why was the reasoning in *Brown* so significant in ending legal segregation?

2. **You Be the Judge** Until 1997 the Virginia Military Institute was an all-male, state-supported military college with a long tradition of rigorous "adversarial" training to mold character and develop leadership. Did excluding women violate the Constitution? Would it matter if Virginia also had an all-female military school? Explain.

City Life

Historical Context The documents below provide information on city life near the turn of the century.

Task Examine the documents and answer the questions that follow. Then you will be asked to write an essay about city life around 1900, using facts from the documents and from the chapter to support the position you take in your thesis statement.

Word Help

propaganda spreading of ideas to help a cause

conviction strong belief

tolerance open-mindedness

Primary Source

"Without comprehension, the immigrant would forever remain shut—a stranger in America. Until America can release the heart as well as train the hand of the immigrant, he would forever remain driven back upon himself, corroded by the very richness of the unused gifts within his soul."

— Anzia Yezierska

How I Found America, 1920

Info to Know

Hull House Today Although the original Hull House was sold during the 1960s, the organization relocated and continues to work toward Jane Addams's vision of providing assistance to needy families. Today, Hull House serves several hundred thousand people in the Chicago area.

DOCUMENT 1

Beginning in the late 1800s, more immigrants began to arrive in the United States from Eastern and Southern Europe. Few of these immigrants spoke English, and most of them settled in major cities such as New York, Boston, and Chicago. There they created ethnic neighborhoods that made the cities very diverse.

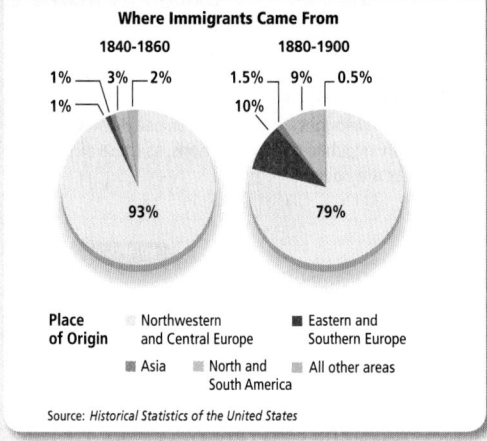

SHIFTING PATTERNS OF IMMIGRATION

Where Immigrants Came From

1840-1860: 1% / 3% / 2% / 1% / 93%

1880-1900: 1.5% / 9% / 0.5% / 10% / 79%

Place of Origin:
- Northwestern and Central Europe
- Eastern and Southern Europe
- Asia
- North and South America
- All other areas

Source: *Historical Statistics of the United States*

DOCUMENT 2

In some cities, settlement houses took the lead in trying to help poor immigrants with basic needs, such as housing, education, and job training. Hull House founder Jane Addams explained how her organization viewed its role in Chicago.

"The Settlement then, is an experimental effort to aid in the solution of the social and industrial problems which are engendered [created] by the modern conditions of life in a great city. It insists that these problems are not confined to any one portion of a city. It is an attempt to relieve, at the same time, overaccumulation at one end of society and the destitution [poverty] at the other; but it assumes that overaccumulation and destitution is most sorely felt in the things that pertain to social and educational privileges. From its very nature it can stand for no political or social propaganda ... It must be open to conviction and must have a deep and abiding sense of tolerance. It must be hospitable and ready for experiment. ... It must also be grounded in a philosophy whose foundation is the solidarity of the human race ... Its residents must be emptied of all conceit of opinion and all self-assertion, and ready to arouse and interpret the public opinion of their neighborhood. They must be content to live quietly side by side with their neighbors, until they grow into a sense of relationship and mutual interests."

Skills Focus: Identifying Problem and Solution

At Level

Reading Skill

Settlement Houses

1. Guide the class in a discussion of the goals of settlement houses. What other institutions, if any, can students think of that help meet these goals today?

2. Divide the class into groups of four or five students. Have each group write a plan for a settlement house in their community that will help immigrants with their needs.

What services will they offer? Who will be eligible? What kind of facilities will be needed? How will they recruit workers and fund their enterprise?

3. Ask volunteers to share their plans with the rest of the class. **LS Interpersonal, Logical-Mathematical**

DOCUMENT 3

Around 1890 British writer Rudyard Kipling visited San Francisco. He was fascinated by the city's cable cars, which seemed able to effortlessly navigate steep hills and sharp turns.

"The cable cars have for all practical purposes made San Francisco a dead level. They take no count of rise or fall, but slide equally on their appointed courses from one end to the other of a six-mile street. They turn corners almost at right angles, cross other lines, and for [all] I know may run up the sides of houses. There is no visible agency of their flight, but once in awhile you shall pass a five-storied building humming with machinery that winds up an everlasting wire cable, and the initiated will tell you that here is the mechanism. I gave up asking questions. If it pleases Providence [God] to make a car run up and down a slit in the ground for many miles, and if for twopence halfpenny [two and a half cents] I can ride in that car, why shall I seek the reasons of the miracle?"

DOCUMENT 4

This photograph shows cable car passengers traveling along San Francisco's Sutter Street in 1905. Women were expected to take seats, but men had the option of standing and hanging onto special poles.

Skills FOCUS   READING LIKE A HISTORIAN

1. a. Describe Refer to Document 1. How did immigration patterns change in the late 1800s?
b. Analyze How did this change affect major cities?

2. a. Identify Refer to Document 2. According to Addams, what was the purpose of the settlement house?
b. Draw Conclusions What kind of relationship did Addams expect settlement house residents to have with their neighbors?

3. a. Recall Refer to Documents 3 and 4. What were some of the features of cable cars?

b. Interpret Did Kipling really imagine that cable cars could "run up the sides of houses"? What point was he trying to make?

4. Document-Based Essay Question Consider the question below and form a thesis statement. Using examples from Documents 1, 2, 3, and 4, create an outline and write a short essay supporting your position. How did immigrants and new technology change American cities around 1900?
See Skills Handbook, pp. H15, H28–H29, H30

LIFE AT THE TURN OF THE 20TH CENTURY   **513**

Collaborative Learning

At Level

Public Transportation

Materials poster paper and colored markers

1. Pair students. Have each pair design a poster to encourage people to use public transportation. Tell them that their goal is to make public transportation appeal to everyone, from the wealthy to the poor.

2. Display students' posters for the class to see.

3. Guide the class in a discussion of public transportation. Does it operate as a "leveler" of social classes? Why or why not? Why might cable cars have been a greater social leveler than other types of public transportation? **LS Interpersonal, Visual-Spatial**

513

Answers

Visual Summary

Review and Inquiry Have students copy the Web diagram onto their own papers. Have students add spokes to each oval and add two details or people to each of the ovals. Have students share their details and people with the class.

Quick Facts Transparency: Life at the Turn of the 20th Century

Reviewing Key Terms and People

1. i.
2. b.
3. d.
4. h.
5. g.
6. c.
7. f.
8. j.
9. a.
10. e.

Comprehension and Critical Thinking

11. **a.** in cities
    b. Both limited immigration from Asia.
    c. possible answer—American citizens opposed immigrants who were different in appearance and customs; they wanted people who blended in with existing U.S. society.

12. **a.** landscape architect who designed New York City's Central Park
    b. Social Gospel was idea that religious faith includes good works; most settlement house workers strongly religious
    c. possible answer—no, much poverty existed

13. **a.** economic system in which the standard unit of exchange is a certain amount of gold
    b. to increase the amount of paper currency and ease their debt burden
    c. helped poor and immigrants find jobs, housing; harmed public by expecting votes in return for assistance

14. **a.** African American advocates for better treatment of blacks
    b. legal—Jim Crow laws, poll taxes, literacy tests; informal—racial etiquette, lynching
    c. possible answer—courageous, faced strong opposition and possible violence

Using the Internet

15. Go to the HRW Web site and enter the keyword shown to access a rubric for this activity.

KEYWORD: SD7 CH15

Visual Summary: Life at the Turn of the Twentieth Century

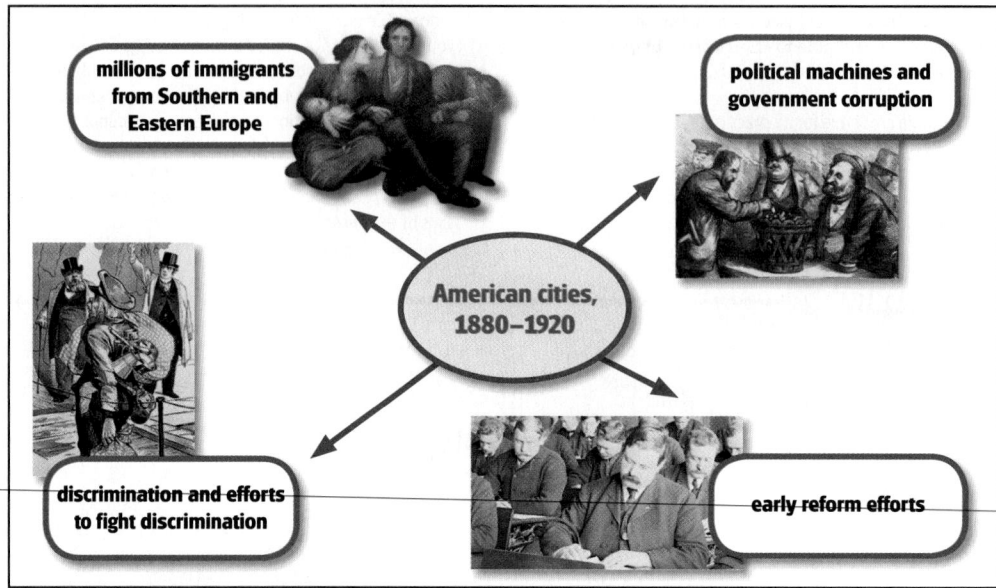

millions of immigrants from Southern and Eastern Europe

political machines and government corruption

American cities, 1880–1920

discrimination and efforts to fight discrimination

early reform efforts

Reviewing Key Terms and People

Match each lettered definition with the correct numbered item below.

  a. Angel Island
  b. Jane Addams
  c. James A. Garfield
  d. debt peonage
  e. Ellis Island
  f. Jim Crow laws
  g. National Grange
  h. poll tax
  i. Thomas Nast
  j. Social Gospel

1. political cartoonist who helped expose the corrupt dealings of the Tweed Ring
2. activist who founded Chicago's Hull House

3. system in which workers were tied to their jobs until they had paid off money that they owed to their employer
4. fee that citizens had to pay before voting
5. organization founded to fight for issues important to the nation's farmers
6. Ohio senator who won the presidency in 1880, but who was assassinated just four months into his term.
7. legislation that created and enforced segregation
8. idea that religious faith should be expressed through good works
9. immigration station in San Francisco Bay through which most Asian immigrants entered the United States
10. immigration station in New York Harbor through which most European immigrants entered the United States

Analyzing Primary Sources

16. an eye exam to see if she has trachoma, an eye disease
17. to prevent diseases from other countries from being brought into the U.S.

Critical Reading

18. B

Comprehension and Critical Thinking

SECTION 1 *(pp. 488–494)*

11. a. Describe Where did new immigrants to America typically settle?

b. Compare What did the Gentlemen's Agreement and the Chinese Exclusion Act have in common?

c. Elaborate Why do you think that Congress passed laws banning some groups of immigrants and not others?

SECTION 2 *(pp. 495–498)*

12. a. Identify Who was Frederick Law Olmsted?

b. Explain How were the settlement house movement and the Social Gospel movement connected?

c. Develop Did all Americans live equally well during the Gilded Age? Explain.

SECTION 3 *(pp. 499–506)*

13. a. Recall What was the gold standard?

b. Analyze Information Why did farmers organize in the late 1800s?

c. Evaluate How did political machines both help and harm the public?

SECTION 4 *(pp. 507–511)*

14. a. Identify Who were Booker T. Washington and W. E. B. Du Bois?

b. Summarize In what ways did African Americans suffer both legal and informal discrimination in the late 1800s?

c. Evaluate Do you think Homer Plessy was rash or courageous for challenging the law requiring separate rail cars for African Americans and whites? Explain.

Using the Internet

go.hrw.com
Practice Online
Keyword: SD7 CH15

15. Thousands of immigrants crowded into American cities in the late 1800s and early 1900s. Using the keyword above, do research to learn about immigrants' lives in their new homes. Where did they live? How did they live? In what ways did they maintain their old traditions, and in what ways did they adapt to American society? Write a description of the ways in which immigrants tried to make their difficult living conditions more bearable.

Analyzing Primary Sources

Reading Like a Historian
Photographers captured the tension of immigrants, such as this woman at Ellis Island, trying to enter the United States.

16. Identify What is happening in this picture?

17. Draw Conclusions Why did the government undertake this process?

Critical Reading

Read the passage in Section 3 under the heading "The Populist Party." Then answer the question that follows.

18. Which of the following statements is true?

A The Populist Party began as a coalition of farmers, laborers, and business leaders.

B The Populist Party campaigned for an income tax, government regulation of business, and unlimited coinage of silver.

C Populist candidates fared poorly in the elections of 1892.

D Populists believed that government regulation of banks and railroads would harm the economy.

FOCUS ON WRITING

Persuasive Writing *Persuasive writing takes a position for or against an issue, using facts and examples as supporting evidence. To practice persuasive writing, complete the assignment below.*

Writing Topic **U.S. policy on inspection of immigrants**

19. Assignment U.S. officials believed that wealthier immigrants were less likely to become a social burden than poor ones. First and second class passengers arriving in New York underwent a quick inspection aboard ship. Steerage passengers faced medical and legal inspections on Ellis Island. Do you think this was a reasonable policy? Write a paragraph in which you develop your position.

LIFE AT THE TURN OF THE 20TH CENTURY **515**

Focus on Writing

19. possible answers—no, because all passengers could become a burden in case of illness, death, or disability; poorer immigrants would be more motivated to work harder and create better lives for themselves; yes, because wealthier passengers could use their resources to contribute to American economy; healthier and better educated

A rubric for this activity is provided in the CRF: Focus on Writing: U.S. Policy on Inspection of Immigrants.

History's Impact Video Program

The decision legalized segregation, and would deny civil rights to African Americans for many years to come.

Review and Assessment Resources

Review and Reinforce

- CRF: Chapter Review Activity
- Quick Facts Transparencies: Old and New Immigrants, Life at the Turn of the 20th Century
- Spanish Chapter Summaries Audio CD Program
- Online Chapter Summaries in Spanish
- OSP Holt PuzzlePro; Quiz Show for ExamView
- Quiz Game CD-ROM

Assess

- PASS: Chapter Test, Forms A and B
- Alternative Assessment Handbook
- OSP ExamView Test Generator, Chapter Test
- Differentiated Instruction Modified Worksheets and Tests CD-ROM: Chapter Test
- HOAP Holt Online Assessment Program (in the Premier Online Edition)

Reteach/Intervene

- Interactive Reader and Study Guide
- Differentiated Instruction Teacher Management System: Lesson Plans for Differentiated Instruction
- Differentiated Instruction Modified Worksheets and Tests CD-ROM: Chapter Test
- Interactive Skills Tutor CD-ROM

go.hrw.com
Online Resources
KEYWORD: SD7 CH15

Summarizing the Unit

Write the following opinion on the board: *Conflicts between settlers and Native Americans, and the destruction of the Native American way of life, were impossible to avoid.* Have students write a brief paragraph either supporting or opposing this position, using evidence to support their reasoning.

Connecting to Themes

Tell students that sociologists, historians, and others have documented that Americans move more than other people, that we are a "mobile society." Guide students in a discussion of the following questions: *Why do you think Americans are more mobile than most other people? What relationship might this mobility have to the westward movement and the immigrations in the period you just read about?*

UNIT 5 IN BRIEF

Below is a chapter-by-chapter summary of the main ideas covered in Unit 5.

CHAPTER 13 The American West
1860–1900

MAIN IDEA In the late 1800s Americans moved West in increasing numbers. They established mining, ranching, and farming operations, but in the process they also destroyed the traditional way of life of the Native Americans they encountered.

SECTION 1 Native Americans resisted the movement of Americans westward. Nevertheless, the power of the U.S. military and the persistence of American settlers eventually proved too strong to resist.

SECTION 2 The lure of gold and silver drew thousands of miners westward, though few found the wealth they dreamed of. Meanwhile, ranchers established a thriving cattle industry on the Great Plains.

SECTION 3 The government promoted the settlement of the West by offering free or cheap land to those willing to establish productive farms. The government also gave land to railroad companies, which could either use it to extend the railroads or sell to settlers.

CHAPTER 14 The Second Industrial Revolution
1880–1910

MAIN IDEA In the late 1800s innovations in business and industry occurred at an ever-more rapid pace. Business leaders made vast sums of money as they consolidated their holds over industry, but ordinary workers continued to work and live in dangerous and difficult conditions.

SECTION 1 The rise of the oil and steel industries transformed industry in the late 1800s. The railroads were a direct beneficiary of these innovations.

SECTION 2 Powerful business leaders consolidated their hold over industries by developing new business structures and strategies. This often resulted in cheaper manufactured goods for consumers but also less competition in the market.

SECTION 3 While businesses made huge profits—largely free of government regulation—workers toiled in dangerous conditions for scandalously low wages. With government turning a blind eye to the condition of workers, many workers began to organize in an effort to improve their situations.

516 UNIT 5 IN BRIEF

SECTION 4 Innovations in transportation and communications went hand in hand with other business transformations in the late 1800s. Automobiles, streetcars, subways, telephones, and electricity changed the way Americans lived.

CHAPTER 15 Life at the Turn of the Twentieth Century
1880–1920

MAIN IDEA In the late 1800s waves of immigrants were arriving from southern and eastern Europe. Government was plagued by corruption, although reformers began to make efforts to restore honesty to government. Discrimination was a daily reality for African Americans, Asian Americans, Hispanic Americans, and Native Americans.

SECTION 1 A new wave of immigrants from southern and eastern Europe came to America. They settled mainly in cities, where they lived in often squalid conditions.

SECTION 2 The middle class was growing, while a small number of wealthy people enjoyed lavish lifestyles. Most urban dwellers, however, lived in deep poverty, and reformers began working to improve their living conditions.

SECTION 3 Major cities were controlled by political machines, and corruption even crept into national government. Reforms began at the national level to restore honest government. Meanwhile, a farmer's movement to reform railroad practices soon led to a political movement at the national level.

SECTION 4 In the late 1800s African Americans experienced tremendous discrimination. Jim Crow laws enforced segregation and restricted African American voting rights, while informal racial etiquette reinforced their lower status in society. Meanwhile, Hispanic Americans, Asian Americans, and Native Americans experienced discrimination in employment, housing, and education.

Unit Resources

Review and Reinforce

- CRF: Chapter Review Activity
- Spanish Chapter Summaries Audio CD Program
- OSP Holt PuzzlePro; GameTool for ExamView
- Quiz Game CD-ROM

Assess

- PASS: Unit Test, Forms A and B
- Alternative Assessment Handbook
- OSP ExamView Test Generator
- Differentiated Instruction Modified Worksheets and Tests CD-ROM: Chapter Tests
- HOAP Holt Online Assessment Program (in the Premier Online Edition)

Reteach/Intervene

- Interactive Reader and Study Guide
- Differentiated Instruction Teacher Management System: Lesson Plans for Differentiated Instruction
- Differentiated Instruction Modified Worksheets and Tests CD-ROM: Chapter Tests
- Interactive Skills Tutor CD-ROM

go.hrw.com
Online Resources

KEYWORDS: SD7 CH13, SD7 CH14, SD7 CH15

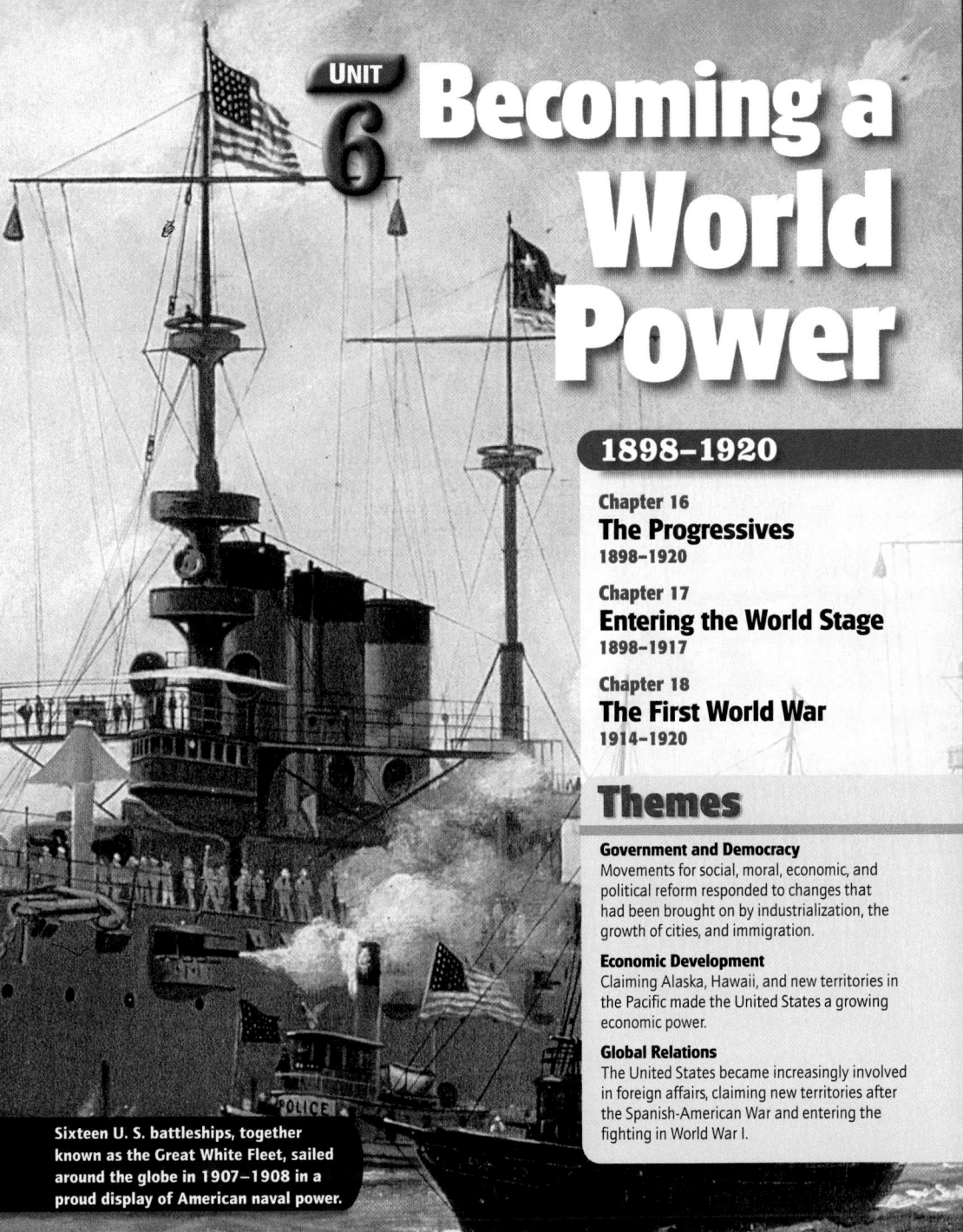

UNIT 6

Becoming a World Power

1898–1920

Chapter 16
The Progressives
1898–1920

Chapter 17
Entering the World Stage
1898–1917

Chapter 18
The First World War
1914–1920

Themes

Government and Democracy
Movements for social, moral, economic, and political reform responded to changes that had been brought on by industrialization, the growth of cities, and immigration.

Economic Development
Claiming Alaska, Hawaii, and new territories in the Pacific made the United States a growing economic power.

Global Relations
The United States became increasingly involved in foreign affairs, claiming new territories after the Spanish-American War and entering the fighting in World War I.

Sixteen U. S. battleships, together known as the Great White Fleet, sailed around the globe in 1907–1908 in a proud display of American naval power.

517

Unit Preview

Introducing the Unit
During the Progressive Era, many people came to believe that the federal and state governments had a responsibility to correct the wrongs of society. Ask students if they think most Americans still feel this way. Why or why not?

Connecting to Themes
Activity **Discussing America's Role** Tell students that in this unit they will learn how the United States first became a power on the world's stage. Guide students in a discussion of how economic development and the changing role of the government are affecting America's role in the world today. **LS Verbal-Linguistic**

Reading Like a Historian
Interpreting Visuals
The Great White Fleet Sixteen battleships of the U.S. Atlantic Fleet, along with their attending auxiliary ships, made up Theodore Roosevelt's Great White Fleet—a show of U.S. military strength and pride. Each ship was painted white, save for gilded bows. The ships stopped in the ports of Spain, Brazil, Chile, Peru, Mexico, New Zealand, Australia, the Philippine Islands, China, Ceylon, Egypt, and Gibraltar before heading home to Hampton Roads, Virginia.

Unit Resources

Planning
- Differentiated Instruction Teacher Management System: Unit Pacing Guide
- One-Stop Planner CD-ROM: Teacher Management System
- Power Presentations with Video CD-ROM

Differentiating Instruction
- Differentiated Instruction Teacher Management System: Lesson Plans for Differentiated Instruction
- Pre-AP Activities Guide for American History
- Differentiated Instruction Modified Worksheets and Tests CD-ROM

Enrichment
- Civic Participation Activities Guide
- CRF: Economics and History Activity
- CRF: Interdisciplinary Project
- American History Primary Source Library CD-ROM

Assessment
- PASS: Unit Test, Forms A & B
- Alternative Assessment Handbook
- OSP ExamView Test Generator
- HOAP Holt Online Assessment Program (in the Premier Online Edition)

The Differentiated Instruction Teacher Management System
provides a planning and instructional benchmarking guide for this unit.

Comparing and Contrasting

Ask students to name two current national political figures. Draw a Venn diagram on the board and ask students to compare and contrast the two figures. Write characteristics they have in common in the overlapping section and those they do not share in each figure's own circle. Then have students use the completed Venn diagram to compose sentences that compare and contrast the figures.

Word Help

exclusively entirely, only
aligned associated

Primary Source

Victoria Woodhull knew that her candidacy would meet with strong opposition from many people. She explained, "I am well aware that in assuming this position I shall evoke more ridicule than enthusiasm at the outset. But this is an epoch of sudden changes and startling surprises. What may appear absurd today will assume a serious aspect tomorrow."

— Victoria Woodhull

Skills Planner

To give students more opportunities to practice this skill, see the following activities in the teacher's edition: Regulating Big Business, p. 538; End of the Monarchy, p. 555; Readiness for War, p. 586.

Prepare to Read

Comparing and Contrasting

Find practice for **Comparing and Constrasting** in the **Skills Handbook,** p. H10

Historians can describe people and events by comparing and contrasting them. Good readers identify similarities and differences in the text and use them to gain better understanding of a passage's overall context.

Before You Read
Skim the headings and visuals to determine what you will be reading about.

While You Read
Compare and contrast the reading with the headings and visuals. How are they alike or different?

After You Read
Compare and contrast what you previously knew about the subject matter with what you have learned about it.

Political Organizing

The failure of women to gain the vote urged suffragists to action. In 1869 Elizabeth Cady Stanton and Susan B. Anthony helped form the National Woman Suffrage Association (NWSA). The NWSA focused its efforts on campaigning for a constitutional amendment to give women the vote. But it also dealt with other issues that concerned women, such as labor organizing. In 1872 the NWSA supported Victoria Woodhull, the first woman candidate for U.S. president.

Similarly, the American Woman Suffrage Association (AWSA) was founded in 1869 with Henry Ward Beecher as its president. Unlike the NWSA, the American Woman Suffrage Association focused exclusively on winning the right to vote on a state-by-state basis. It also aligned itself with the Republican party.

READING CHECK **Comparing** In what ways was the NWSA similar to the AWSA?

Compare Both the NWSA and the AWSA were founded in 1869 and worked for suffrage.

Identify signal words such as *similarly* and *likewise* for comparison and *but* and *unlike* for contrast.

Contrast Unlike the NWSA, which dealt with various issues affecting women, the AWSA focused solely on suffrage.

Test Prep Tip

Some essay questions on tests will ask you to compare and contrast historical people, places, and events. As a prewriting activity, create and complete a word web or Venn diagram about the subject matter. Then use your findings to develop an outline for the essay.

Skills Focus: Comparing and Contrasting
At Level

Reading Skill
Analyzing Historical Texts
Research Required

1. Divide students into mixed-ability pairs. Have each pair skim one of the chapters in this unit and choose one section.

2. Have students create a chart with two columns on their papers. Have each pair fill in the chart with similarities and differences between two people, places, groups, or ideas contained within their section.

3. Have students use their lists to write a paragraph that compares and contrasts the topics within their sections. Ask volunteers to share their paragraphs with the class.
   LS Verbal-Linguistic

   Alternative Assessment Handbook, Rubrics 7: Charts; and 9: Comparing and Contrasting

Reading like a Historian

Interpreting Political Cartoons

Find practice for **Interpreting Political Cartoons** in the **Skills Handbook**, p. H31

Political cartoons are visual information sources that present messages about issues or people in funny or ironic ways. Political cartoons can portray a subject in either a positive or a negative light. Cartoonists often communicate a message through the use of symbols and caricature, or the drawing of subjects with distorted physical features. Labels, speech balloons, and captions can clarify the meaning of political cartoons.

Strategies historians use:
- Determine the cartoon's subject, reading all text and studying all symbols and caricatures.
- Establish the cartoon's message. Does it portray its subject in a positive or a negative light?
- Compare the cartoon's message with historical information you already know.

By portraying President Theodore Roosevelt as the popular figure Uncle Sam, the cartoonist may be trying to persuade readers to follow Roosevelt's leadership.

The yellow smoke symbolizes the dangers connected with the meat industry.

The cartoon supports Roosevelt's actions because the text says that the job must be done. The cartoon's message is that Roosevelt deserves support.

This cartoon refers to unsanitary conditions in meat factories in the early 1900s.

A NAUSEATING JOB, BUT IT MUST BE DONE
(President Roosevelt takes hold of the investigating muck-rake himself in the packing-house scandal.)

Skills FOCUS — READING LIKE A HISTORIAN

As You Read Make and complete a two-column chart in which you record reasons to support or contradict the cartoonist's message.
As You Study Use the two-column chart to compare the cartoonist's message with other information from this historical period. What conclusions can you draw from this comparison?

BECOMING A WORLD POWER **519**

BECOMING A WORLD POWER **519**

Chapter 16 Planning Guide

The Progressives

Chapter Overview	Reproducible Resources	Technology Resources
CHAPTER 16 pp. 520–549 **Overview: In this chapter, students will analyze the Progressive movement and how it changed America.**	**Differentiated Instruction Teacher Management System:*** • Instructional Benchmarking Guides • Lesson Plans for Differentiated Instruction **Interactive Reader and Study Guide:** Chapter Summary* **Chapter Resource File:*** • Writing for the SAT: Consumer Protection: Federal or State? • Social Studies Skills Activity: Identifying Main Idea and Details • Chapter Review Activity **American History Outline Maps** **Pre-AP Activities Guide for American History***	Live Ink® Online Reading Help Student Edition on Audio CD Program Differentiated Instruction Modified Worksheets and Tests CD-ROM Interactive Skills Tutor CD-ROM United States History Primary Source Library CD-ROM Power Presentations with Video CD-ROM **History's Impact: American History Video Program (VHS/DVD):** The Progressives Online Chapter Summaries in Spanish
Section 1: **Progressivism** **The Main Idea:** Progressives focused on easing the suffering of the urban poor, improving working conditions, and reforming government.	**Differentiated Instruction Teacher Management System:** Section 1 Lesson Plan* **Interactive Reader and Study Guide:** Section 1 Summary* **Chapter Resource File:*** • Vocabulary Builder Activity, Section 1	**Daily Bellringer Transparency:** Section 1* **Daily Test Practice Transparency:** Section 1* **Internet Activity:** Urban Changes
Section 2: **Women and Public Life** **The Main Idea:** Women during the Progressive Era actively campaigned for reforms in education, children's welfare, temperance, and suffrage.	**Differentiated Instruction Teacher Management System:** Section 2 Lesson Plan* **Interactive Reader and Study Guide:** Section 2 Summary* **Chapter Resource File:*** • Vocabulary Builder Activity, Section 2	**Daily Bellringer Transparency:** Section 2* **Daily Test Practice Transparency:** Section 2* **Internet Activity:** Women in College
Section 3: **Theodore Roosevelt's Square Deal** **The Main Idea:** Theodore Roosevelt used the power of the presidency to push for progressive reforms.	**Differentiated Instruction Teacher Management System:** Section 3 Lesson Plan* **Interactive Reader and Study Guide:** Section 3 Summary* **Chapter Resource File:*** • Vocabulary Builder Activity, Section 3	**Daily Bellringer Transparency:** Section 3* **Map Transparency:** Conservation Lands* **Daily Test Practice Transparency:** Section 3* **Internet Activity:** Consumer Protections
Section 4: **Taft and Wilson** **The Main Idea:** Progressive reforms continued during the Taft and Wilson presidencies.	**Differentiated Instruction Teacher Management System:** Section 4 Lesson Plan* **Interactive Reader and Study Guide:** Section 4 Summary* **Chapter Resource File:*** • Vocabulary Builder Activity, Section 4	**Daily Bellringer Transparency:** Section 4* **Map Transparency:** 1912 Election* **Daily Test Practice Transparency:** Section 4* **Internet Activity:** The Election of 1912

HOLT

History's Impact
American History Video Program (VHS/DVD)
The Progressives

Review, Assessment, Intervention

 Quick Facts Transparency: The Progressives

 Spanish Chapter Summaries Audio CD Program

 **Progress Assessment Support System (PASS):**
Chapter Test*

 **Differentiated Instruction Modified Worksheets and Tests CD-ROM:** Modified Chapter Test

OSP **One-Stop Planner CD-ROM:** ExamView Test Generator (English/Spanish)

HOAP **Holt Online Assessment Program (HOAP),** in the Holt Premier Online Student Edition

 PASS: Section 1 Quiz*

 Online Quiz: Section 1

 Alternative Assessment Handbook

 PASS: Section 2 Quiz*

 Online Quiz: Section 2

 Alternative Assessment Handbook

 PASS: Section 3 Quiz*

 Online Quiz: Section 3

 Alternative Assessment Handbook

 PASS: Section 4 Quiz*

 Online Quiz: Section 4

 Alternative Assessment Handbook

 **RESOURCES**

The following resources were developed to help North Carolina educators teach the standards and objectives of North Carolina's eleventh grade standard course of study in United States history.

- United States history EOC Test Prep Workbook
- Teacher's Support System
- North Carolina One-Stop Planner

And be sure to direct your students to **go.hrw.com** for online access to the EOC Test Prep Workbook.

go.hrw.com
EOC Test Prep
KEYWORD: SE7 NC

Holt  **Online Learning**

go.hrw.com
Teacher Resources
KEYWORD: SD7 TEACHER

go.hrw.com
Student Resources
KEYWORD: SD7 CH16

- Document-based Questions
- Interactive Multimedia Activities

- Current Events
- Chapter-based Internet Activities
- and more!

Holt Premier
Online Student Edition
Complete online support for interactivity, assessment, and reporting

- Interactive Maps and Notebook
- Standardized Test Prep
- Homework Practice and Research Activities Online

Before You Teach

The Big Picture
Deborah Gray White

Progressivism Industrialization brought with it a host of new problems that Progressives sought to address. They pressed for reforms in housing, health care, and civil rights. They fought to prohibit child labor and improve working conditions for laborers. Commission and city manager style of governments curbed corruption and delivered expert oversight. Progressives endorsed direct primaries, the initiative, referendum and recall, and the successful Seventeenth Amendment, which gave voters the power to elect senators.

Women, Public Life, and the Vote With increased opportunities to be educated and to find work, women became some of the most dedicated reformers. They worked for a variety of reforms, including Prohibition. Excluded from white women's groups, African American women organized separately and added civil rights to their cause. The political skills women gained from their reform efforts were put to use in the suffrage fight.

Theodore Roosevelt's Square Deal When William McKinley was assassinated in 1901, Theodore Roosevelt became president. During his administrations he initiated his Square Deal to balance the interest of individuals, workers, and business. He actively pursued labor arbitration, anti-trust legislation, business regulation, consumer protection, and conservation of the environment.

Taft and Wilson William Howard Taft supported the income tax amendment but broke with Progressives when he signed a high tariff bill and allowed businessmen to buy public land in Alaska. As part of his New Freedom program, Woodrow Wilson lowered taxes, reformed the nation's banking system, strengthened anti-trust legislation, created the Federal Trade Commission, and supported the successful suffrage amendment. Despite the successes of progressivism, it achieved little in the way of civil rights for African Americans. In fact, the actions of Roosevelt and Wilson actually hurt that cause.

Recent Scholarship

Gender, Race, and Civilization American modernization was not achieved without a distressing amount of anxiety. The changes in gender roles and class, ethnic, and racial relationships disrupted established beliefs and ways of doing things. In *Manliness and Civilization: A Cultural History of Gender and Race in the United States, 1880–1917* (1995), Gail Bederman uses the changing definition of manhood to analyze the tensions of the period and examine the reconfiguration of ideas that connected race, class, and gender to so-called progressive notions of civilization.

Differentiating Instruction

 Differentiated Instruction Teacher Management System
- Lesson Plans for Differentiated Instruction
- Differentiated Instructional Benchmarking Guides
- Interactive Reader and Study Guide

 Spanish Chapter Summaries Audio CD Program

 Online Chapter Summaries in Spanish

 Student Edition on Audio CD Program

 Differentiated Instruction Modified Worksheets and Tests CD-ROM
- Vocabulary Flash Cards
- Modified Vocabulary Builder Activities
- Modified Chapter Review Activity
- Modified Chapter Test

OSP One-Stop Planner CD-ROM
- ExamView Test Generator (English and Spanish)
- PuzzlePro
- Quiz Show for ExamView
- Transparencies and Videos

TE Differentiated Activities in the Teacher's Edition
- *The Jungle* and Working Conditions, p. 528
- Meatpacking Plant Worker's Journal, p. 528
- Women's Reform Issues, p. 531
- Safeguarding the Environment, p. 539
- President Wilson's Reforms, p. 543

Reading Like a Historian

Sam Wineburg

Photos and Truth

In the midst of Hurricane Katrina's devastation in 2005, a controversy ricocheted in the press over two photographs showing similar scenes. Both images depicted residents clutching bags of food as they waded, chest-deep, through the flooded streets of New Orleans. What sparked the controversy was not the images themselves, but their captions. In one picture, the two white (or light skinned) flood victims are described as "finding" food; in the second, the protagonist, a young African American man, is described as having "looted" the food.

Photographic "Reality"

Photographs are not innocent. The caption that accompanies them, the book that reprints them, the Web site that distributes them, all frame the interpretation that viewers adopt. The camera's shutter selects, accentuates, and blots out parts of the world we ultimately see. Nor is this a new development in photography's history; it has been present from the moment Louis Daguerre announced a way to etch images on a copper plate.

The pictures of Jacob Riis are prime examples of how photography has been marshaled to advance social causes. Riis did not set up his camera and wait for reality to unfold. Like a hunter with a keen sense of prey, Riis set out in search of images he knew would jar the well-to-do citizens who attended his public lectures. When he couldn't find those images, he did what photographers before and since have done: he staged them.

One of the most famous images to appear in *How the Other Half Lives* showed two young boys (Riis called them "street Arabs") accosting a drunk and emptying his pockets. As this image seems to have been shot in broad daylight, we might wonder how Riis secured the permission of these delinquents to be photographed in the act. The answer, according to University of Delaware historian James Curtis (whose essay "Making Sense of Documentary Photographs" can be downloaded at http://historymatters.gmu. edu/mse/Photos/photos.pdf) is that Riis hired these youngsters, plying them with cigarettes so as to gain their cooperation in his photographic "expose."

Motivation and Meaning

As with our modern caption writer, Riis knew that photos do not stand alone. Another Riis image, captioned "Bandit's Roost," shows a dimly lit alley with a dozen different people engaged in various activities. Riis argued that the crowded conditions of urban life served as the breeding ground for crime, lawlessness, and untoward social behavior. But without considering Riis' caption, what do we actually discern from the photo? In the foreground, several menacing looking characters look squarely into the camera (were they told to "look tough"?—we don't know); in the background a woman leans out a window with her small child. Other figures stand in front of clotheslines with hanging laundry.

Is this alley crime's incubator, as Riis told the audiences who attended his lantern-slide lectures at churches, social clubs, civic organizations and reform societies? Or did these people—often immigrants from Southern and Eastern Europe, people who looked differently from the Danish immigrant Riis—arouse suspicion by their very foreignness? The text of *How the Other Half Lives* provides some clues about how Riis viewed his subjects. Jews: "Money is their God. Life itself is of little value compared to even the leanest bank account." Irish: "Wherever he is mustered in force the saloon is the gorgeous center of political activity." Italians: "Lighthearted"…"content to live in a pig-sty."

Seeing and Believing

Confronted with photographic "pieces of reality," students let their eyes deceive. For seeing, the saying goes, is believing. But more often than not, what we see is carefully crafted, cropped, backlit—and sometimes even posed. Rather than the world shown to us unfiltered, photos, like all documents, betray the human hand.

Chapter Preview

Standards Focus

Social Studies Competency Goals

Goal 7 The learner will analyze the economic, political, and social reforms of the Progressive Period.

7.01, 7.02

The Big Idea and Essential Questions

To foster student understanding of this chapter's big idea, design your lesson to address each section's essential question.

Big Idea In the early 1900s, reformers known as Progressives campaigned to make the United States economically and politically fairer.

Essential Questions

1. On which major areas of reform did Progressives focus their efforts?
2. How did Progressive women make important contributions to reform movements?
3. How did President Theodore Roosevelt use the power of his position to promote reform?
4. What kinds of reforms were made during the Taft and Wilson presidencies?

CHAPTER 16 1898–1920

The Progressives

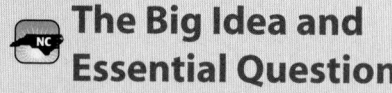

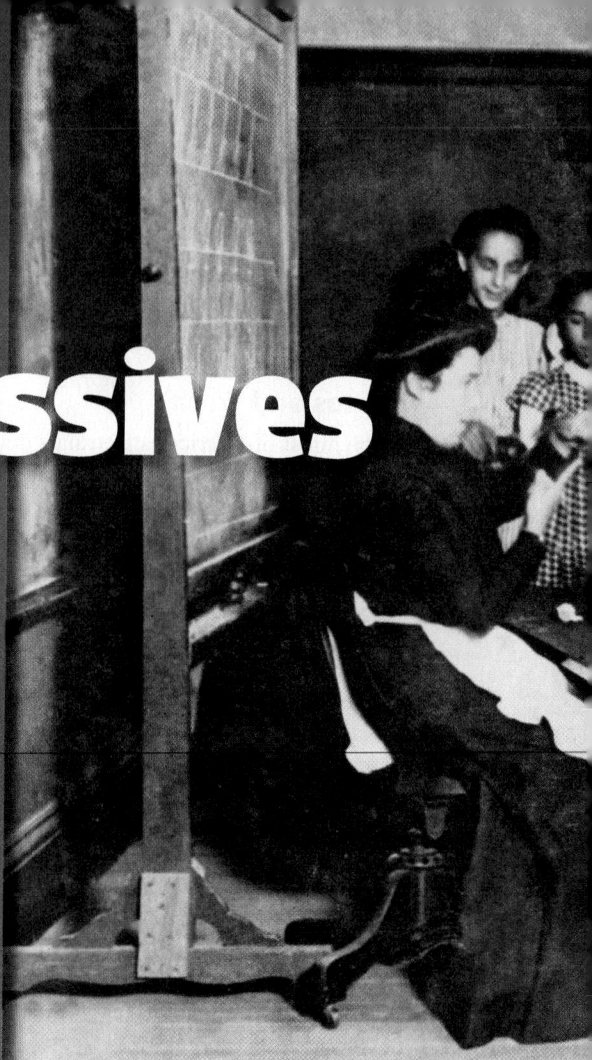

THE BIG PICTURE As the 1900s dawned, activists called Progressives fought to make America's economic and political systems fairer. Some fought for women's suffrage. Others attacked a wide range of societal ills.

North Carolina Standards

Social Studies Objectives

7.01 Explain the conditions that led to the rise of Progressivism.

7.02 Analyze how different groups of Americans made economic and political gains in the Progressive Period.

Language Arts Objectives

5.01 Interpret the significance of literary movements as they have evolved through the literature of the United States by:

- evaluating the literary merit and/or historical significance of a work from Colonial Literature, the Romantic Era, Realism, the Modern Era, and Contemporary Literature.

Skills Focus READING LIKE A HISTORIAN

Improving the living conditions of urban immigrants became a major priority for many Progressives. In this 1909 photograph, immigrant students receive instruction at the Hancock School in Boston.

Making Inferences What special challenges do you think immigrant students faced?

See **Skills Handbook**, p. H7

U.S.

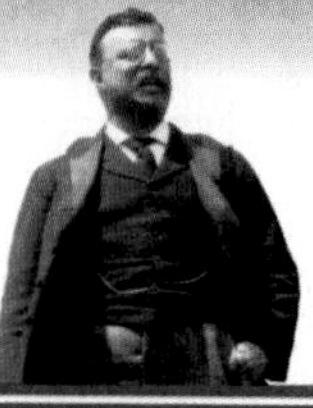

September 1901 Theodore Roosevelt becomes president after McKinley is assassinated.

1900

World

1901 First Nobel Prize is awarded.

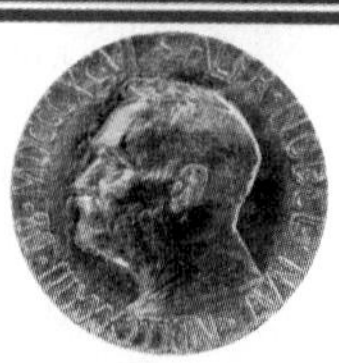

520

Key to Differentiating Instruction

Below Level
Basic-level activities designed for all students encountering new material

At Level
Intermediate-level activities designed for average students

Above Level
Challenging activities designed for honors and gifted-and-talented students

Standard English Mastery
Activities designed to improve standard English usage

Introduce the Chapter — At Level

The Progressives

1. Guide students in a discussion of laws that they know about that regulate food, drugs, medicine, and working conditions. Ask students if they feel current laws adequately protect Americans from harmful substances in their food, and if they believe that labor laws sufficiently protect both rights of businesses and working people.
2. Tell students that in the late 1800s there were very few laws designed to protect consumers and workers. Government did not regulate what went into the food supply, drugs, or medicine. Nor did the government regulate working conditions in factories.
3. In this chapter students will learn about many turn-of-the-century reforms, how and why they came about, and how these reforms have improved living and working conditions for all Americans. **LS Verbal-Linguistic**

Alternative Assessment Handbook, Rubric 11: Discussions

• **Chapter Preview** •

HOLT
History's Impact
▶ **Video Program: The Progressives**
See the Video Teacher's Guide for strategies for using the video segment.

Reading Like a Historian
Women in the Classroom Ask students to examine the photo carefully. Have students describe differences between this classroom and classrooms of today. *all students are female; script on blackboard; all in dresses; different style of desks* Remind students that until the late 1800s few women were able to attend college and become teachers, like the one pictured here.

1904
Muckraker Lincoln Steffens exposes government corruption in *The Shame of the Cities.*

May 1909
Civil rights activists found the NAACP.

1913
Anti-Defamation League is formed to fight anti-Semitism.

January 1919
Eighteenth Amendment bans alcoholic beverages.

August 1920
Nineteenth Amendment gives women the right to vote.

1904	1908	1912	1916	1920	1924

1906
Workers form the British Labour Party.

1913
Dr. Albert Schweitzer opens hospital in the French Congo to battle diseases such as leprosy and the plague.

1915
Mohandas K. Gandhi returns to India after leading a nonviolent campaign against discrimination in South Africa.

1923
Mustafa Kemal establishes the Republic of Turkey.

521

go.hrw.com
Online Resources

Chapter Resources:
KEYWORD: SD7 CH16

Teacher Resources:
KEYWORD: SD7 TEACHER

Explore the Time Line

1. How many years elapsed between the formation of the NAACP and Mohandas Gandhi's return to India? *6 years*

2. When was the NAACP founded? *1909*

3. Which amendment granted women the right to vote, and when was it ratified? *Nineteenth; 1920*

Info to Know

Women's Suffrage The Nineteenth Amendment, granting women the right to vote, was ratified in 1920, 50 years after the ratification of the Fifteenth Amendment, which stated that the "right of citizens of the United States to vote shall not be denied or abridged . . . on account of race, color, or previous condition of servitude."
Analyze Why did it take so long after the Fifteenth Amendment for women to get the right to vote? *possible answers—strong opposition in most states to women voting; was considered improper; women had not organized into a strong national voice for equal rights*

Answers

Reading Like a Historian (p. 520)
may not have spoken English, confronted by different culture and beliefs than they were used to

Bellringer

The Inside Story. . . Use the **Daily Bellringer Transparency** to help students answer the question.

📖 Daily Bellringer Transparency, Section 1

The Progressives   Daily Bellringer
                        Chapter 16, Section 1

Test What You Know

The following questions will test your background knowledge about progressivism. You will learn more about these topics in Chapter 16, Section 1.

1. What was progressivism?
2. What was the Seventeenth Amendment?
3. What was the NAACP?

Preview Section 1

The Inside Story

How did a photographer help the nation's urban poor?

Jacob Riis wanted to tell about the lives of immigrants in New York City, so he went to the tenements of the Lower East Side. He wrote about living conditions that included overcrowded rooms with beds made of old boxes and straw, broken stoves leaking smoke, and piles of rubbish rotting in corners. But words were not enough to describe the squalor, so Riis used a camera to photograph what he found. His 1889 article in *Scribner's* magazine, "How the Other Half Lives," later became a best-selling book. Riis impelled the city to clean up slums and build parks and schools.

1. Why do you think immigrants would have had to live in such awful conditions?

2. What was the title of the book that both described the conditions that Riis found and helped him in his fight to improve them?

Review Answers: 1. a wide-ranging movement to improve living conditions of the poor, working conditions, and responsiveness of government 2. gave voters the power to directly elect U.S. senators; 3. National Association for the Advancement of Colored People, a group established to fight for the rights of African Americans
Preview Answers: 1. possible answer—it was probably all that they could afford. 2. *How the Other Half Lives*

Copyright © by Holt, Rinehart and Winston. All rights reserved.

Academic Vocabulary

Review with students the high-use academic term in this section.

concrete specific, particular (p. 524)

📄 CRF: Vocabulary Builder Activity, Section 1

Taking Notes

dangerous conditions in factories; squalid living conditions for working families; political and business corruption; insurance and stock manipulation; exploitation of child labor; slum conditions; racial discrimination

---

BEFORE YOU READ

MAIN IDEA

Progressives focused on three areas of reform: easing the suffering of the urban poor, improving unfair and dangerous working conditions, and reforming government at the national, state, and local levels.

READING FOCUS

1. What issues did Progressives focus on, and what helped energize their causes?
2. How did Progressives try to reform society?
3. How did Progressives fight to reform the workplace?
4. How did Progressives reform government at the national, state, and local levels?

KEY TERMS AND PEOPLE

Jacob Riis
progressivism
muckrakers
Ida Tarbell
Lincoln Steffens
Robert M. La Follette
Seventeenth Amendment
initiative
referendum
recall

 As you read, takes notes identifying various problems that the Progressives targeted. Create a diagram like the one below. Fill in each of the small circles with one of the problems. You may need to add more circles.

(Progressives' Targets)

How the OTHER HALF Lives

MUSEUM OF THE
CITY OF NEW YORK

◀ **Jacob Riis photographed a part of America that people did not know existed—or did not want to know.**

522 CHAPTER 16

THE INSIDE STORY

How did a photographer help the nation's urban poor? When **Jacob Riis** wrote about the lives of impoverished immigrants in New York City, he was telling a familiar story: his own. Riis emigrated from Denmark in 1870, at the age of 21. He had trouble finding jobs and lived in poverty. By 1877, however, he was a police reporter for the *New York Tribune*, a voice for social reform.

Riis went to places that were comfortably out of view of most Americans: the tenements of the Lower East Side. "Someone had to tell the facts; that is one reason I became a reporter," he said. He described a room where six adults and five children lived: "One, two, three beds are there, if the old boxes and heaps of foul straw can be called by that name; a broken stove with crazy pipe from which the smoke leaks at every joint . . . piles of rubbish in the corner. The closeness and smell are appalling."

Words could barely describe the squalor. So Riis learned to use a camera. With a new invention, flash powder, he photographed dingy rooms and hallways. He showed his photos in public lectures. His 1889 article in *Scribner's Magazine*, "How the Other Half Lives," became a best-selling book. Riis's fame helped him press the city to improve living conditions for the poor and to build parks and schools. ◼

Teach the Main Idea

At Level

Progressivism

1. **Teach** Ask the students the Reading Focus questions to teach this section.

2. **Apply** Draw four computer monitors (rectangles with bases) for students to see. Label each computer screen with each of the main topics of this chapter: What was Progressivism? Reforming Society; Reforming the Workplace; Reforming Government. Guide students in a discussion of the four main topics. Use the computer screens as a graphic organizer.

3. **Review** As you review each topic in the section, have students identify the one issue that they believe posed the most serious problem at the time.

4. **Practice/Homework** Have each student write a report on one problem of this period and what should be done to solve it.
   LS Verbal-Linguistic

📄 Alternative Assessment Handbook, Rubric 37: Writing Assignments

What Was Progressivism?

Jacob Riis's book *How the Other Half Lives* stunned Americans with its photographs of desperate urban poverty. In the late 1800s, a reform movement known as **progressivism** arose to address many of the social problems that industrialization created. The reformers, called Progressives, sought to improve living conditions for the urban poor. They questioned the power and practices of big business. Progressives also called for government to be more honest and responsive to people's needs.

Reform-minded writers were the first to expose many of the social ills that Progressives targeted. Popular magazines printed journalists' firsthand accounts of injustices and horrors they had witnessed. These journalists were known as **muckrakers** because they "raked up" or exposed the filth of society.

Most of the muckrakers' articles focused on business and political corruption. **Ida Tarbell** wrote a scathing report condemning the business practices of the Standard Oil Company in *McClure's Magazine*. Tarbell revealed how John D. Rockefeller crushed his competition in his quest to gain control over the oil business. Tarbell's reports appealed to a middle-class readership increasingly frightened by the unchecked power of large businesses such as Standard Oil.

Other muckrakers wrote about insurance and stock manipulation, the exploitation of child labor, slum conditions, and racial discrimination. **Lincoln Steffens** exposed the corruption of city governments in *The Shame of the Cities* (1904). Frank Norris described the strangling power of a monopolistic railroad in his 1901 novel *The Octopus: A Story of California*. The muckrakers helped prepare the way for many reforms in the United States.

> **READING CHECK** Sequencing How important were the writings of the muckrakers in the Progressive movement, and what did they write about?

Reforming Society

By 1920, more than half of all Americans lived in cities. As cities continued to grow, they were increasingly unable to provide the services people needed: garbage collection, safe housing, and police and fire protection.

Ida Tarbell

Journalist Ida Tarbell's 1903 exposé of the business practices of the Standard Oil Company was one of the triumphs of muckraking. Here Tarbell comments on the company's 1880 victory over independent oil producers who were pressured into giving up their lawsuits against Standard Oil.

"Now, what was this loose and easily discouraged organization [of independent oil producers] opposing? A compact body of a few able, cold-blooded men—men to whom anything was right that they could get, men knowing exactly what they wanted, men who loved the game they played because of the reward... The withdrawal of the [law]suits was a great victory for Mr. Rockefeller. There was no longer any doubt of his power in defensive operations. Having won a victory, he quickly went to work to make it secure."

Skills Focus READING LIKE A HISTORIAN

1. **Analyzing Primary Sources** How does Tarbell describe the leaders of Standard Oil?
2. **Identifying Points of View** What do you think Tarbell hoped to achieve by publishing her articles?

See Skills Handbook, pp. H28–H29

Housing reforms For the reformers, these conditions provided an opportunity. In New York City, for example, activists such as Lillian Wald worked vigorously to expand public health services for the poor. Progressives scored an early victory in New York State with the passage of the Tenement Act of 1901. This law forced landlords to install lighting in public hallways and to provide at least one toilet for every two families. Outhouses were eventually banned from New York City slums.

These simple steps helped create a healthier environment for impoverished New Yorkers. Within 15 years, the death rate in New York dropped dramatically. Housing reformers in other cities and states pushed for legislation similar to New York's law.

Fighting for civil rights Some progressives also fought prejudice in society. In 1909 Ida Wells-Barnett, W. E. B. Du Bois, Jane Addams,

THE PROGRESSIVES **523**

❸ How did Progressives fight to reform the workplace? *campaigned to prohibit child labor, limit working hours, initiate minimum wage laws*

Reforming the Workplace

Describe What was the major difference between the outcomes of *Lochner* v. *New York* and *Muller* v. *Oregon? In Lochner, court sided with business owners; in Muller, court sided with workers.*

Summarize Briefly summarize the New York and Oregon labor cases. *New York (Lochner)—court refused to limit bakers' workday to 10 hours; Oregon (Muller)—established 10-hour workday for women working in laundries and factories; Oregon (Bunting)—protected 10-hour workday limit for men working in mills and factories*

📄 CRF: Primary Source Activity: Women and Children Working in a Food Processing Plant

Info to Know

Ida Tarbell Ida Tarbell was the daughter of an independent oil producer in western Pennsylvania. Due to the business practices of Standard Oil under John D. Rockefeller, Tarbell's father lost his business. Later, as a journalist, Ida Tarbell investigated Standard Oil and exposed the company's monopoly of the oil industry. Her articles were balanced, yet hard hitting. She praised Rockefeller for bringing stability to the oil industry but condemned him for his unfairness.

Answers

Reading Check *The NAACP and the ADL fought against injustices and inequality.*

524

---

and other activists formed the multiracial National Association for the Advancement of Colored People (NAACP). Its purpose was to fight for the rights of African Americans.

The NAACP fought on a number of fronts. In 1913 it protested the introduction of segregation into the federal government. Two years later, the NAACP protested the film *Birth of a Nation*, by D.W. Griffith, because of its hostile stereotyping of African Americans. Attempts to ban or censor the film met with little success.

In 1913 Sigmund Livingston, a Jewish man living in Chicago, founded the Anti-Defamation League (ADL). The mission of the ADL was to fight anti-Semitism, or hostility toward Jews.

ADL began by combatting the use of negative stereotypes of Jews in print, on stage, and in films. Adolph S. Ochs, publisher of *The New York Times* and a member of the ADL, wrote a memo to newspaper editors nationwide discouraging the use of negative references to Jews. By 1920 the practice in newspapers had nearly stopped.

ACADEMIC VOCABULARY
concrete specific, particular

READING CHECK **Comparing** How were the missions of the NAACP and the ADL similar?

Reforming the Workplace

By the end of the 1800s, labor unions were actively campaigning for the rights of adult male workers. Progressive reformers took up the cause of working women and children. In 1893 Florence Kelley helped persuade Illinois to prohibit child labor and to limit the number of hours women were forced to work.

In 1904 Kelley helped found the National Child Labor Committee. The committee's mission was to persuade state legislatures to ban child labor. Yet many employers continued hiring children, and not all states enforced child labor laws.

Progressives also organized state-by-state campaigns to limit women's workdays. Kelley led a successful effort in Oregon that limited the workday in laundries to 10 hours. Utah also passed a law limiting workdays to eight hours in some women's occupations.

But unskilled workers, men and women alike, were still paid extremely low wages. In 1900 about 40 percent of working-class families lived in poverty. Labor unions and Progressives both worked to secure laws ensuring

---

workers a minimum wage. In 1912 Massachusetts became the first state to pass such a law. Congress did not pass a national minimum-wage law until 1938.

Courts and labor laws Business owners began to fight labor laws in the courts. In the early 1900s, the Supreme Court ruled on several cases concerning state laws that limited the length of the workday. In the 1905 case *Lochner* v. *New York*, the Supreme Court sided with business owners. The Court refused to uphold a law limiting bakers to a 10-hour workday on the grounds that it denied workers their right to make contracts with employers.

But in 1908 the Court sided with workers. In the case *Muller* v. *Oregon*, the Court upheld a state law establishing a 10-hour workday for women in laundries and factories. Louis D. Brandeis, the attorney for the state of Oregon and a future Supreme Court justice, argued the state's case. He maintained that concrete evidence showed that working long hours harmed the health of women. This research convinced the Supreme Court to uphold the Oregon law.

His defense, known as the Brandeis brief, became a model for the defense of other labor laws. It was used in the 1917 case *Bunting* v. *Oregon*, in which the Court upheld a law that extended the protection of a 10-hour workday to men working in mills and factories.

The Triangle Shirtwaist Company Fire A gruesome disaster in New York in 1911 galvanized Progressives to fight for safety in the workplace. About 500 young women worked for the Triangle Shirtwaist Company, a high-rise factory that made women's blouses. One Saturday, just as these young workers were ending their six-day workweek, a fire erupted, probably from a discarded match.

Within moments, the eighth floor was ablaze, and the flames quickly spread to two other floors. Escape was nearly impossible. Many doors were locked to prevent theft. The flimsy fire escape broke under the weight of panic-stricken people, sending its victims tumbling to their deaths. With flames at their backs, dozens of workers leaped from the windows.

More than 140 women and men died in the Triangle Shirtwaist Company fire. Union organizer Rose Schneiderman commented on the senseless tragedy.

Skills Focus: Interpreting Time Lines
Below Level

Social Studies Skill
Reforming the Workplace

1. Draw a time line for students to see that begins in 1893 and ends in 1938.

2. Have students copy the time line onto their own paper. Have students review the section Reforming the Workplace and have them label their time lines with the key dates of workplace reform and the major events and legislation of the period.

3. Have students share information from their time lines and complete the class time line for students to see. Have students correct their time lines and keep them as a study tool.

LS Visual-Spatial, Logical-Mathematical

📄 Alternative Assessment Handbook, Rubric 36: Time Lines

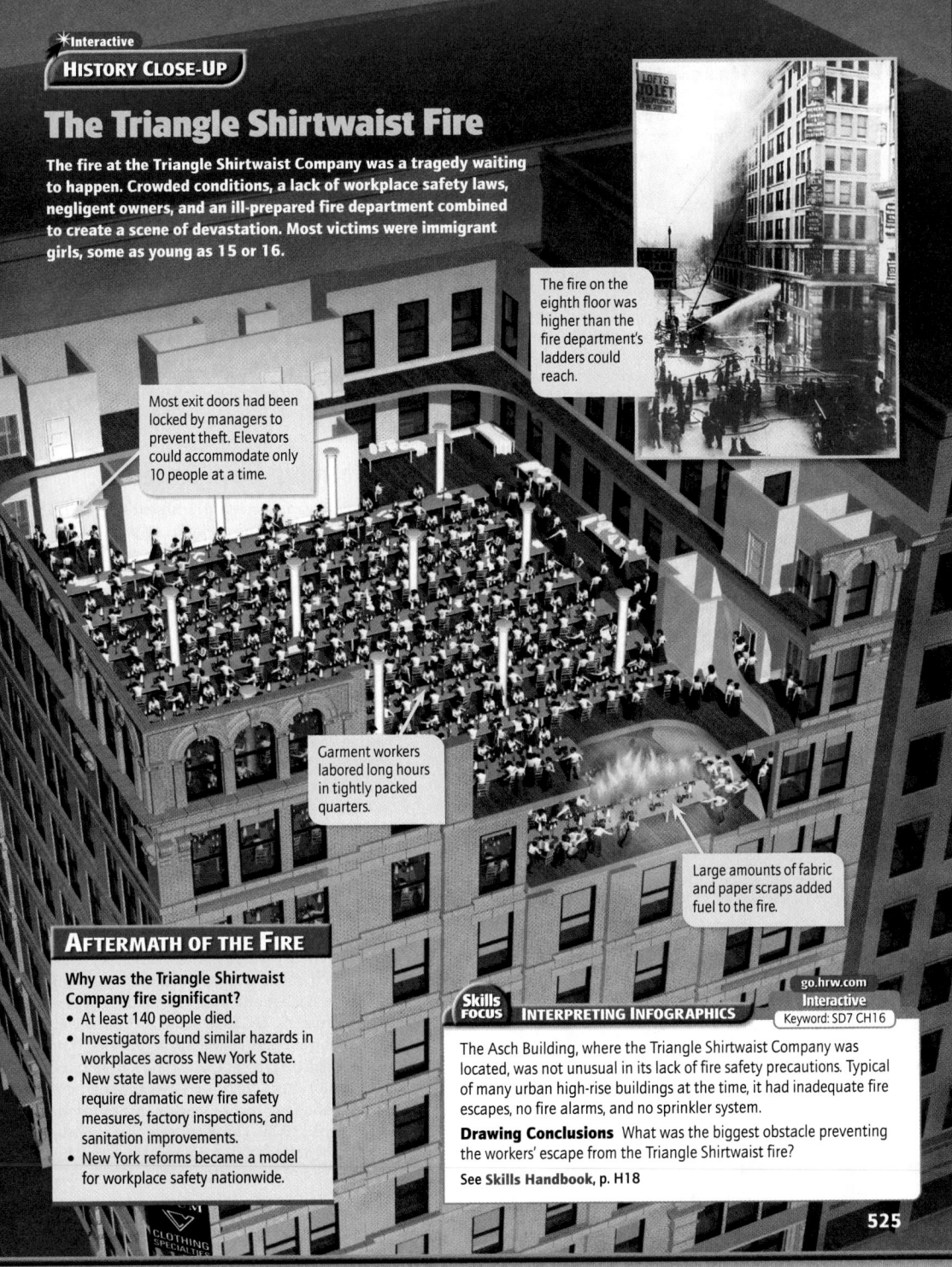

HISTORY CLOSE-UP
*Interactive

The Triangle Shirtwaist Fire

The fire at the Triangle Shirtwaist Company was a tragedy waiting to happen. Crowded conditions, a lack of workplace safety laws, negligent owners, and an ill-prepared fire department combined to create a scene of devastation. Most victims were immigrant girls, some as young as 15 or 16.

The fire on the eighth floor was higher than the fire department's ladders could reach.

Most exit doors had been locked by managers to prevent theft. Elevators could accommodate only 10 people at a time.

Garment workers labored long hours in tightly packed quarters.

Large amounts of fabric and paper scraps added fuel to the fire.

AFTERMATH OF THE FIRE

Why was the Triangle Shirtwaist Company fire significant?
- At least 140 people died.
- Investigators found similar hazards in workplaces across New York State.
- New state laws were passed to require dramatic new fire safety measures, factory inspections, and sanitation improvements.
- New York reforms became a model for workplace safety nationwide.

Skills FOCUS INTERPRETING INFOGRAPHICS

go.hrw.com
Interactive
Keyword: SD7 CH16

The Asch Building, where the Triangle Shirtwaist Company was located, was not unusual in its lack of fire safety precautions. Typical of many urban high-rise buildings at the time, it had inadequate fire escapes, no fire alarms, and no sprinkler system.

Drawing Conclusions What was the biggest obstacle preventing the workers' escape from the Triangle Shirtwaist fire?

See Skills Handbook, p. H18

525

Skills Focus: Identifying Problem and Solution

At Level

Reading Skill

Research Required

The Triangle Shirtwaist Fire

1. Have students conduct outside research on the Triangle Shirtwaist fire and the laws that were passed after the fire to prevent such a tragedy from happening again.

2. Have students use the information from their research and from the text to write a letter to the New York City mayor and the fire chief at the time explaining why fire prevention regulations and reforms are needed and how such precautions and regulations might save lives.

3. Have volunteers share their letters with the class. Guide students in a discussion of the effectiveness of these regulations today and how businesses are regularly checked to ensure that they meet fire safety regulations. Ask students about fire hazards that they have observed and what regulations might address those hazards. **LS Verbal-Linguistic**

Alternative Assessment Handbook, Rubric 43: Writing to Persuade

---

• Direct Teach •

History-Close Up
Triangle Shirtwaist Fire
The doors at the Triangle Shirtwaist Company that were not locked opened inwards. As workers rushed to those doors, they were held shut by the panicked workers themselves. When the fire engines arrived, water from the fire hoses only reached the 7th floor, and the ladder reached only between the 6th and 7th floor, providing no means of escape for the trapped workers.

Info to Know
New York Tenement Houses In order to address the housing shortage in New York, the *Plumber and Sanitary Engineer* magazine sponsored a housing design contest in 1879. James Ware won the prize. His design was called the "dumbbell." It consisted of two tenement buildings connected by a long hallway and had airshafts that ran through the middle of the building to permit light. Housing 300 people, each "dumbbell" was 6 stories high and had 84 rooms. Inadequate space, poor ventilation, and improper waste and garbage disposal that forced residents to throw their garbage into the airshafts made the "dumbbell" a haven for foul smells and filth.

✷ **Interactive History Close-Up:**
The Triangle Shirtwaist Factory Fire

About the Illustration
This illustration is an artist's conception based on available sources. Historians, however, are uncertain exactly what this scene looked like.

go.hrw.com
Online Resources

KEYWORD: SD7 CH16
TOPIC: URBAN CHANGES

Answers
Interpreting Infographics *locked exit doors*

525

4 How did Progressives reform government at the national, state, and local levels? *Progressives attacked government corruption at all levels.*

Reforming Government

Identify What characterized the secret ballot? *printed all candidates' names on a single piece of paper, instead of each political party printing its own ballot on colored paper*

Summarize In what ways was Robert La Follette's Wisconsin Idea ambitious? *called for direct primary election; limits on campaign spending; created regulatory commissions for railroads and utilities; formed commissions to oversee transportation, civil service, and taxation*

Make Judgments Why was the Texas hurricane of 1900 a mixed blessing for Galveston? *city suffered severe damage; commission of honest, efficient experts appointed to govern city during disaster; commission model adopted by many American cities*

⬛ CRF: Biography: Mother Jones

HISTORY'S VOICES

❝This is not the first time girls have been burned alive in the city. Every week I must learn of the untimely death of one of my sister workers. Every year thousands of us are maimed. The life of men and women is so cheap and property is so sacred.❞

—Rose Schneiderman, April 2, 1911

THE IMPACT TODAY

Government
In 1970, about 60 years after the Triangle Shirtwaist fire, the federal Occupational Safety and Health Administration (OSHA) was created.

The Triangle Shirtwaist fire was a turning point for reform. With the efforts of Schneiderman and others, New York State passed the toughest fire-safety laws in the nation.

The unions During the Progressive Era, energetic new labor unions joined the fight for better working conditions. The International Ladies' Garment Workers Union (ILGWU) was founded in 1900. Unlike the American Federation of Labor (AFL), which allowed only skilled workers as members, the ILGWU organized unskilled workers. In 1909 the garment workers called a general strike known as the "Uprising of the 20,000." The strikers won a shorter workweek and higher wages. They also attracted thousands of workers to the union.

Meanwhile, the Industrial Workers of the World (IWW), founded in 1905, opposed capitalism altogether. Under the leadership of William "Big Bill" Haywood, the IWW organized the unskilled workers that the AFL ignored. Known as "Wobblies," IWW members

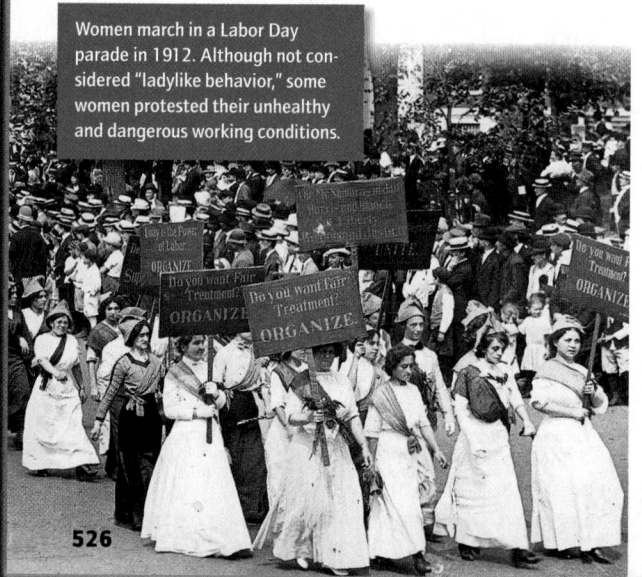

Women march in a Labor Day parade in 1912. Although not considered "ladylike behavior," some women protested their unhealthy and dangerous working conditions.

526

not only used traditional strategies such as strikes and boycotts but also engaged in more radical tactics, including industrial sabotage.

At the height of its strength in 1912, the IWW led some 20,000 textile workers on strike in Lawrence, Massachusetts, to protest pay cuts. After a bitter, well-publicized 10-week strike, the mill owners gave in and raised wages.

But the IWW's success was brief. Several later strikes were terrible failures. Fearing the union's revolutionary goals, the government cracked down on the IWW's activities. Disputes among its leaders also weakened the union. Within a few years, it declined in power.

READING CHECK **Identifying Cause and Effect** What factors produced reforms in wages and workplace safety?

Reforming Government

Progressives targeted government for reform as well. They wanted to eliminate political corruption and make government more efficient.

City government reforms Cleaning up government often meant winning control of it. One of the most successful reform mayors was Tom Johnson of Cleveland, Ohio. He set new rules for the police, released debtors from prison, and supported a fairer tax system. In Toledo, Ohio, Mayor Samuel M. Jones overhauled the police force, improved municipal services, set a minimum wage for workers, and opened kindergartens for children.

Progressives also promoted new government structures as a means to improve efficiency. In 1900 a massive hurricane struck Galveston, Texas. The traditional city government proved unable to cope with the disaster, so the Texas legislature set up a five-member commission to govern the city. The commissioners were experts in their fields rather than party loyalists. Galveston's city commission was more honest and efficient than its previous government. By 1918 some 500 American cities adopted the commission plan of city government.

Another new form of government, the council-manager model, began in Staunton, Virginia, in 1908. The city council appoints a professional politician to run the city. The reform inspired cities nationwide to follow suit.

Skills Focus: Making Generalizations

At Level

Reading Skill
Reforming Government

1. Review with students the information in the text on Robert La Follette's election as governor of Wisconsin in 1900.

2. Have students prepare the governor's inaugural speech announcing the reforms expressed in the Wisconsin Idea. Remind students that it is their job to convince the state legislature, as well as the various business interests in the state, that they should support the proposed reforms.

3. Have volunteers read their speeches to the class. Have students respond with possible rebuttals from various business interests in the state. Guide the class in a discussion of the reforms and the obstacles that La Follette may have faced in getting these reforms through the legislature. 🖪 **Verbal-Linguistic**

⬛ Alternative Assessment Handbook, Rubric 24: Oral Presentations

---

Answers

Reading Check *terrible tragedies like the Triangle Shirtwaist fire helped spur reforms in safety while unions helped increase wages for many workers*

State government reforms The fight for Progressive reforms extended to the state level. In Wisconsin, a progressive governor named **Robert M. La Follette** pushed through an ambitious agenda of reforms that became known as the Wisconsin Idea.

Elected in 1900, La Follette called for electoral reforms, such as limits on campaign spending. He created state commissions to regulate railroads and utilities. He also formed commissions to oversee transportation, civil service, and taxation.

Other governors pushed for reforms in their states. In New York Charles Evans Hughes regulated public utilities and pushed through a worker safety law. In Mississippi James Vardaman limited the use of convict labor. Vardaman's reforming spirit, however, was marred by extreme racism. He exploited prejudices of poor white farmers toward African Americans to gain support for his policies.

Election reforms Progressives wanted to reform elections to make them fairer and to make politicians more accountable to voters. They pushed for the direct primary, an election in which voters choose candidates to run in a general election. Mississippi adopted the direct primary in 1903. Most other states followed.

Progressives also backed the **Seventeenth Amendment**, ratified in 1913. The amendment gave voters, rather than state legislatures, the power to directly elect their U.S. senators. Progressives believed that direct elections would undermine the influence of party bosses.

Progressives also fought for the use of the secret ballot, which printed all candidates' names on a single piece of paper. Previously, each political party printed its own ballot on colored paper, making it easy to see how people voted and to pressure them to support certain candidates. By 1900 almost all states had adopted the secret ballot.

Finally, Progressives urged states to adopt three additional election reform measures: the initiative, the referendum, and the recall. These measures have become powerful tools with which voters can influence public policy.

An **initiative** allows voters to put a proposed law on the ballot for public approval. The **referendum** allows citizens to place a recently passed law on the ballot, allowing voters to approve or reject the measure. The **recall** enables citizens to remove an elected official from office by calling for a special election. Each measure was designed to make politicians more accountable to voters.

READING CHECK **Contrasting** How does the city commission form of government differ from the city manager form?

PROGRESSIVE ELECTION REFORMS

- **direct primary** voters select a party's candidates for public office

- **17th Amendment** voters elect their senators directly

- **secret ballot** people vote privately without fear of coercion

- **initiative** allows citizens to propose new laws

- **referendum** allows citizens to vote on a proposed or existing law

- **recall** allows voters to remove an elected official from office

---

go.hrw.com
Online Quiz
Keyword: SD7 HP16

SECTION 1 ASSESSMENT

Reviewing Ideas, Terms, and People

1. a. Identify What was **progressivism**?
b. Summarize What were some areas of reform that the Progressives targeted?
c. Evaluate If the **muckrakers** had not done their work, do you think reforms would have occurred? Explain.

2. a. Explain Why was the Triangle Shirtwaist fire important?
b. Contrast How did the tactics of the **ILGWU** differ from those of the IWW?

3. a. Recall What are the differences between an **initiative**, a **referendum**, and a **recall**?
b. Rank Which of the election reforms do you think had the greatest impact on American voters? Explain.

Critical Thinking

4. Identifying Cause and Effect Copy the chart below and record the effects of the work of the Progressives in three broad categories: society, workplace, and government.

FOCUS ON WRITING

5. Descriptive Suppose you are a New York newspaper reporter in 1911. Describe the events of the Triangle Shirtwaist fire.

THE PROGRESSIVES **527**

Direct Teach

Progressive Election Reforms
Review the six bulleted items in the chart with students. Have volunteers explain the significance of each item to the democratic election process. Then ask students to choose the one that they believe has contributed most to ensuring honest elections in the U.S. today.

Quick Facts Transparency: Progressive Election Reforms

Review & Assess

Close
Guide students in a discussion of the social and political reforms of this period, including labor laws, fire regulations, and voting reforms.

Review
Online Quiz, Section 1
Daily Test Practice Transparency

Assess
SE Section 1 Assessment
Progress Assessment: Section 1 Quiz
Alternative Assessment Handbook

Reteach
Interactive Reader and Study Guide, Section 1
Interactive Skills Tutor CD-ROM

Section 1 Assessment Answers

1. a. reform movement addressing social problems
b. housing; public health; civil rights; workplace safety; government
c. possible answer—no, because they exposed corrupt practices in society

2. a. exposed unsafe working conditions
b. ILGWU used strikes; IWW used strikes and boycotts but also engaged in sabotage

3. a. initiative—people propose new laws; referendum—people vote on proposed or existing law; recall—people remove elected official from office

b. possible answer—Seventeenth Amendment allowed voters to have a more direct voice

4. Society—exposed slum conditions and racial discrimination; Workplace—exposed child labor, poor safety and health conditions; Government—exposed corruption, need for electoral reforms

5. fire erupts on eighth floor and spreads; exits locked; fire escape breaks; many jump to their deaths

Answers

Reading Check *commission—people who were experts in their field; city manager—a professional administrator rather than an amateur politician*

527

American Literature

Excerpt from *The Jungle* by Upton Sinclair

Word Help

rheumatism painful inflammation of muscles and joints

carcass dead body

Meet the Writer

Upton Sinclair Upton Sinclair had written several novels before *The Jungle*, but this novel was his first popular success. A weekly newspaper had asked Sinclair to investigate working conditions in the stockyards, and the resulting exposé of unsanitary conditions and impurities in meat brought him instant fame. Sinclair later became involved in politics, and even ran for governor of California.

Linking to Today

Modern Muckraking

Unhealthy Diets A book called *Fast Food Nation* by Eric Schlosser was published in 2002. Like *The Jungle*, it addressed issues of concern in the food processing industry. Additionally, a 2004 film documentary called *Super Size Me* featured an individual whose sole diet consisted of fast food for an entire month. The documentary showed the ill-effects of such a diet.

Answers

Reading Like a Historian

1. *Workers faced freezing cold temperatures and accidents with knives. The food faced the danger of contamination from knives and the men.*
2. *possible answer—poor working conditions*

UPTON SINCLAIR (1878–1968)

American *Literature*

About the Reading The muckraking novel *The Jungle* exposed the horrific working conditions and unsanitary manufacturing practices in the meatpacking industry. The book prompted a huge federal probe and the passage of the Meat Inspection Act of 1906.

AS YOU READ Think about the risks these factory workers dealt with on the job every day.

Excerpt from

by Upton Sinclair

Sinclair exposed the nation's meatpacking plants, where workers operated in dangerous, grueling, disease-ridden conditions.

There was no heat upon the killing-floor. The men might exactly as well have worked out of doors all winter. For that matter, there was very little heat anywhere in the building, except in the cooking-rooms and such places—and it was the men who worked in these who ran the most risk of all, because whenever they had to pass to another room they had to go through ice-cold corridors, and sometimes with nothing on above the waist except a sleeveless undershirt. In summer time the chilling-rooms were counted deadly places, for rheumatism and such things; but when it came to winter the men envied those who worked there—at least the chilling rooms were kept at a precise temperature, and one could not freeze to death. On the killing-floor you might easily freeze, if the gang for any reason had to stop for a time. You were apt to be covered with blood, and it would freeze solid; if you leaned against a pillar you would freeze to that, and if you put your hand upon the blade of your knife, you would run a chance of leaving your skin on it. The men would tie up their feet in newspapers and old sacks, and these would be soaked in blood and frozen, and then soaked again, and so on until by night time a man would be walking on great lumps the size of feet of an elephant. Now and then, when the bosses were not looking, you would see them plunging their feet and ankles into the steaming hot carcass of the steer, or darting across the room to the hot-water jets. The cruelest thing of all was that nearly all of them—all of those who used knives—were unable to wear gloves,

and their arms would be white with frost and their hands would grow numb, and then of course there would be accidents. Also the air would be full of steam, from the hot water and the hot blood, so that you could not see five feet before you; then, with men rushing about at the speed they kept up on the killing-floor, and all with butcherknives, like razors, in their hands —well, it was to be counted as a wonder that there were not more men slaughtered than cattle.

Skills FOCUS READING LIKE A HISTORIAN

1. **Identifying Supporting Details** What dangers to workers and to food does Sinclair describe?
2. **Literature as Historical Evidence** What does *The Jungle* suggest about reasons workers formed unions?

See Skills Handbook, pp. H5, H32

Differentiating Instruction

English-Language Learners   Below Level

1. After reading about unsanitary working conditions in *The Jungle*, President Theodore Roosevelt was determined to see the 1906 Meat Inspection Act signed into law. The act was one of the first aimed at protecting consumers.

2. Have students reread the excerpt and explain differences between killing-rooms and chilling-rooms. Then have students develop a list of the problems faced by men working in the killing-rooms. **LS Visual-Spatial**

Advanced Learners/ GATE   Above Level

Have students create a series of ten journal entries from the viewpoint of a worker in a meatpacking plant in 1905. Journal entries should describe working conditions in the killing-rooms during summer and winter, family interaction away from work, and details about their poverty. Remind students to use vivid images and clear descriptions. **LS Verbal-Linguistic**

Alternative Assessment Handbook, Rubric 15: Journals

Women and Public Life

BEFORE YOU READ

MAIN IDEA

Women during the Progressive Era actively campaigned for reforms in education, children's welfare, temperance, and suffrage.

READING FOCUS

1. What opportunities did women have for education and work outside the home during the late 1800s?

2. How did women gain political experience through participation in reform movements?

3. How did the women's suffrage movement campaign for the vote?

KEY TERMS AND PEOPLE

Prohibition
Woman's Christian Temperance Union
Frances Willard
Carry Nation
Eighteenth Amendment
National Association of Colored Women
Susan B. Anthony
National American Woman Suffrage Association

TAKING NOTES As you read, take notes on organizations that supported women's suffrage and their goals. Record your notes in a graphic organizer like the one shown below. You may need to add more rows.

Organization	Goals

THE INSIDE STORY

How did some African American women break barriers in the late 1800s? Most African American women of the 1800s could only dream of going to college. Two women dreamed it, and then did it. Alberta Virginia Scott (1875–1902) and Otelia Cromwell (1874–1972) both graduated from prestigious women's colleges.

Scott was the first known African American to graduate from Radcliffe College in Cambridge, Massachusetts. She entered Radcliffe in 1894, studying science and classics. After graduating, Scott felt she should teach in the South. In 1900 Booker T. Washington invited her to teach at Tuskegee Institute, but sadly, after a year she became ill and died.

Otelia Cromwell had a long and distinguished career as an educator. She transferred from Howard University to Smith College in Northampton, Massachusetts. After graduating in 1900, she taught public school in Washington, D.C. She then went back to school, earning a master's degree from Columbia University and a Ph.D. from Yale.

Professor Cromwell became head of the literature department at Miner Teachers College in Washington. She wrote and edited several books and articles, including a respected biography of suffragist Lucretia Mott. She retired in 1944, and in 1950 she received an honorary degree from Smith. Today Smith College hosts an annual Otelia Cromwell Day, featuring lectures, films, and workshops.

Educational PIONEERS

▶ Otelia Cromwell was honored for her career in education.

THE PROGRESSIVES **529**

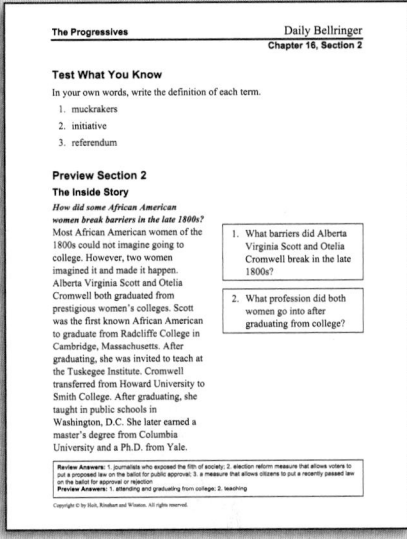

1 What opportunities did women have for education and work outside the home during the late 1800s? *By 1870, 20 percent of college students were women; many women put their skills to work in reform movements; some women worked as bookkeepers, secretaries, typists, or shop clerks.*

Opportunities for Women

Identify What types of jobs were available to women without a high school education? *industry jobs; garment industry*

Contrast In terms of wages, what did employers assume about working women and men? *assumed women were single, supported by father; assumed men were supporting families, so paid them more*

Activity **Female factory workers** Have students write a paragraph to a supervisor from the point of view of a female factory worker in the early 1800s. Students should ask for equal wages for equal work. Ask students what arguments the supervisor might have used to deny the increase.

LS Verbal-Linguistic

CRF: Literature Activity: *The Yellow Paper* by Charlotte Perkins Gilman

Primary Source

"The women's trade union leagues, national and state, are not only valuable because of support given to the workers, but because they make it possible for women other than wage-earners to identify themselves with working people . . . and thus the realization of the ideals of democracy can be advanced."

— Lillian Wald

The House on Henry Street, 1915

Opportunities for Women

By the late 1800s, women were finding more opportunities for education and employment. With greater opportunities came a desire for greater involvement in the life of the community. Many women turned outward, beyond the home, to work for change and reform in society. They sought to use their talents and skills to make life better for others as well as for themselves. In the process, women became a greater political force.

Higher education Throughout the early 1800s, women had limited opportunities for higher education. It wasn't until 1833, for example, that a college, Oberlin College in Ohio, began admitting women as well as men. Later in the century, more colleges opened their doors to women. By 1870 about 20 percent of all college students were women. By 1900 that number had increased to more than one-third.

Most of the women who attended college at this time were members of the middle or upper classes. They wanted to be able to use their knowledge and skills after graduating. However, many professional opportunities were still denied them. The American Medical Association, for example, did not admit women members until 1915. Denied access to their professions, many of these women put their talents and skills to work in various reform movements. These movements would be the training grounds for later political activism.

Employment opportunities Job opportunities for educated middle class women expanded in the late 1800s. Women worked as teachers and nurses—the traditional "caring professions"—but they also entered the business world as bookkeepers, typists, secretaries, and shop clerks.

In addition, businesses such as newspapers and magazines began to hire more women as artists and journalists. The businesses wanted to cater to the interests of the growing consumer group formed by educated and employed women. By 1900 the census counted 11,207 female artists, up from 412 in 1870, and 2,193 female journalists, up from a mere 35 some three decades before.

Working class women and those without high school educations found jobs available to them in industry. Women poured into the garment industry, where they took positions that paid less than men's jobs did. Employers usually assumed that women were single and were being supported by their fathers. They also

TRACING HISTORY

Women's Rights

Efforts to expand women's rights began long before the Progressive Era and continued beyond it. Study the time line to learn about key events in the history of women's rights.

1848 Delegates to the historic Seneca Falls Convention, led by Elizabeth Cady Stanton (right), issue a bold declaration calling for equal rights for women.

1700

1800

1776 Shortly before the Declaration of Independence was drafted, Abigail Adams wrote her husband, John, urging that the new nation protect women's liberties.

1869 Women living in Wyoming Territory become the first American women to win the right to vote.

530 CHAPTER 16

Skills Focus: Drawing Conclusions
Below Level   Standard English Mastery

Reading Skill
Women, Public Life, and the Vote

1. Guide students in a discussion about areas of interest for progressive American women during this period. Make a class list for students to see. *education, children's welfare, temperance, right to vote*

2. Ask students why they think women focused on these areas. *these topics affected them personally; areas where they felt reform would improve family life*

3. Organize students into small groups and have them discuss the obstacles that blocked women in their efforts to achieve reform in these areas. Have each group make a list of barriers faced by female reformers.

4. Have students use their lists to write a paragraph about problems women faced and advances they made during this period.

LS Verbal-Linguistic

Alternative Assessment Handbook, Rubric 42: Writing to Inform

assumed that male employees were supporting families. Employers used these assumptions as reasons to pay women lower wages.

By the late 1800s these opportunities in public life began to change the way many middle-class women viewed their world. They began to see that they had a role to play in their communities and in society beyond the home.

READING CHECK **Summarizing** What new opportunities did women find outside the home in the late 1800s?

Gaining Political Experience

As in earlier times, women became the backbone of many reform movements during the Progressive Era. Women learned how to organize, how to persuade other people, and how to publicize their cause. Furthermore, participation in these movements taught women that they had the power to improve life for themselves, their families, and their communities.

Children's health and welfare Some women gained experience while campaigning for the rights of children. Many Progressive reformers worked to end child labor, improve children's health, and promote education.

Lillian Wald, founder of the Henry Street Settlement in New York City, believed the federal government had a responsibility to tend to the well being of children. She campaigned tirelessly for the creation of a federal agency to meet that goal. She was successful when the Federal Children's Bureau opened in 1912.

Prohibition Progressive women also gained political experience by participating in the **Prohibition** movement, which called for a ban on making, selling, and distributing alcoholic beverages. Reformers believed alcohol was often responsible for crime, poverty, and violence against women and children.

Two major national organizations, the **Woman's Christian Temperance Union** (WCTU) and the Anti-Saloon League, led an organized crusade against alcohol. **Frances Willard** headed the WCTU from 1879 to 1898. Willard made the WCTU a powerful force for temperance and for the rights of women.

Many reformers spread the anti-alcohol message in Protestant churches. Billy Sunday, a former baseball player turned Presbyterian evangelist, preached that the saloons were "the parent of crimes and the mother of sins." Starting in 1900, evangelist **Carry Nation** took her campaign right to the source. With a hatchet

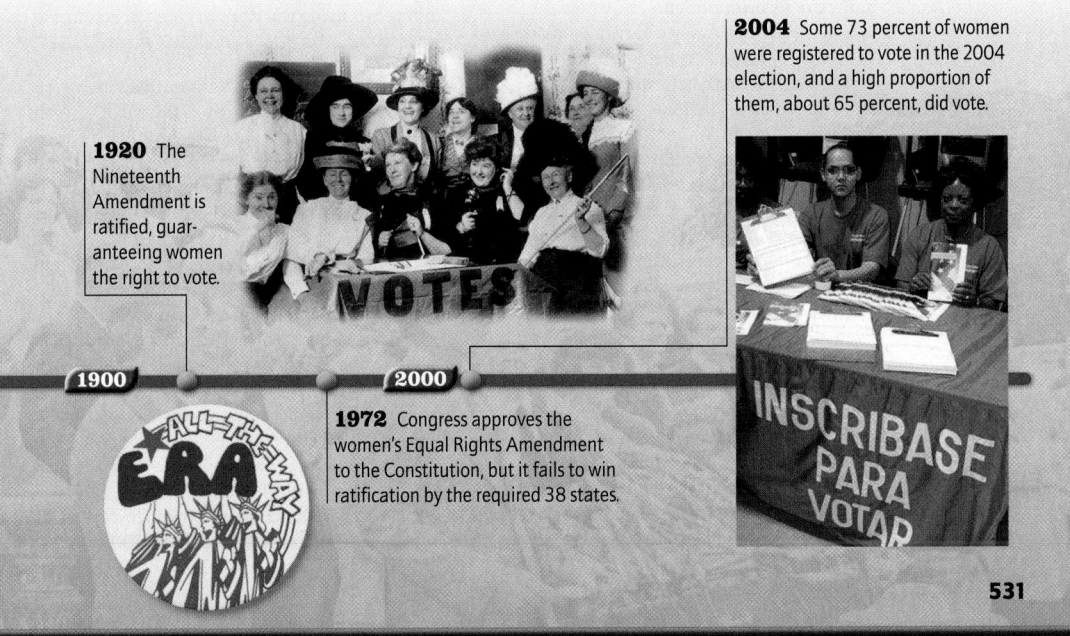

1920 The Nineteenth Amendment is ratified, guaranteeing women the right to vote.

2004 Some 73 percent of women were registered to vote in the 2004 election, and a high proportion of them, about 65 percent, did vote.

1900

2000

1972 Congress approves the women's Equal Rights Amendment to the Constitution, but it fails to win ratification by the required 38 states.

531

❸ How did the women's suffrage movement campaign for the vote? *organized political groups, tried to register to vote, worked for a constitutional amendment*

Women's Suffrage Movement

Recall What was the main purpose of the NWSA? *to campaign for a constitutional amendment to give women the right to vote*

Contrast Discuss the difference in focus between the NWSA and the AWSA. *NWSA—obtaining right to vote through federal government; AWSA—obtaining right to vote through state governments*

Draw Conclusions Why do you think the AWSA aligned with the Republican Party? *possible answer— Republicans had supported voting rights for African Americans, which resulted in the Fifteenth Amendment, and the AWSA hoped they would support women's right to vote as well.*

Info to Know

Anti-lynching Laws Federal anti-lynching legislation was never passed by Congress. In February 2005, the U.S. Senate offered a formal apology, Senate Resolution 39, "Apologizing to the victims of lynching and the descendants of those victims for the failure of the Senate to enact anti-lynching legislation."

Answers

Reading Check *organization, persuasion, how publicity works*

Carry Nation's theatrical hatchet-wielding protests made her a big attraction. This poster spelled her name as "Carrie."

in one hand and a Bible in the other, she smashed up saloons in Kansas and urged other women to do the same. Nation's fiery speeches, dramatic raids, and canny sense of publicity made her a national figure in the temperance cause.

Prohibitionists eventually won Congress to their cause. In 1917 Congress proposed the **Eighteenth Amendment**, which prohibited the manufacture, sale, and distribution of alcoholic beverages.

The states ratified the amendment in 1919. The Eighteenth Amendment proved so unpopular, however, that it was repealed in 1933.

Civil rights African American women fought for many of the same causes as white women, such as ending poverty, promoting child welfare, fighting for better wages and safer workplace conditions, and fighting alcohol abuse. Yet these women had the added burden of waging their battles in an atmosphere of discrimination.

Many African American women discovered that they were not welcome in most reform organizations. So they formed their own.

One of the largest organizations of African American women was founded in 1896. The **National Association of Colored Women** (NACW) included some of the most prominent women within the African American community, such as antilynching activist Ida B. Wells-Barnett and Margaret Murray Washington of the Tuskegee Institute. Harriet Tubman, the famous conductor on the Underground Railroad during the 1850s, who had remained active in civil rights causes, also became a member. By 1916 the organization had more than 100,000 members.

The NACW campaigned against poverty, segregation, and lynchings. It fought against the persistence of Jim Crow laws that denied African Americans the right to vote. Eventually, the NACW also began to

campaign for temperance and women's suffrage. The organization formed settlement houses, hospitals, and schools.

READING CHECK **Identifying the Main Idea** What did women learn through their reform work that would be useful to them politically?

Rise of the Women's Suffrage Movement

When the delegates to the Seneca Falls Convention met in 1848 to campaign for women's rights, little did they know how long it would take for women to win the right to vote. It took 72 more years of organizing, campaigning, and persuading before they won the right to vote.

The Fifteenth Amendment After the Civil War, suffragists, who had supported abolition, called for granting women the vote as well as newly freed African American men. They were told that women would have to wait. Abolitionist Horace Greeley urged them to "remember that this is the Negro hour and your first duty is to go through the state and plead his claims." Suffragists waited.

Many of these suffragists were not satisfied by the ratification of the Fifteenth Amendment in 1868. The amendment gave the vote to African American men but not to women. It prohibited denying the right to vote "on account of race, color, or previous condition of servitude."

Women organize Now suffragists were spurred to action. In 1869 Elizabeth Cady Stanton and **Susan B. Anthony** formed the National Woman Suffrage Association. The NWSA campaigned for a constitutional amendment to give women the vote. It dealt with other issues that concerned women as well, such as labor organizing. In 1872 some NWSA members supported Victoria Woodhull, the first woman presidential candidate.

Meanwhile, the American Woman Suffrage Association (AWSA) was founded in 1869, with Henry Ward Beecher as its president. Unlike the NWSA, the American Woman Suffrage Association focused exclusively on winning the right to vote on a state-by-state basis. It also aligned itself with the Republican Party.

Very soon, suffragists began to rejoice at some victories in the West. In 1869 Wyoming

Skills Focus: Making Oral Presentations
At Level

Reading Like a Historian Skill
Rise of the Women's Suffrage Movement

1. Have students review the information in the text and in the Women's Rights time line. Have students use the time line to find out how many years it took women to win the right to vote. Guide students in a discussion of the obstacles women faced in gaining the right to vote.

2. Have students write a short speech for a meeting of the NWSA in 1869. In their speeches, students should demand that

women be given the right to vote and explain why they should not be deprived of this basic right. Students should also include a slogan.

3. Have students share their speeches with the class. 🄻🅂 **Verbal-Linguistic**

📖 Alternative Assessment Handbook, Rubrics 28: Posters; and 34: Slogans and Banners

Territory became the first to grant women the vote. Utah Territory followed a year later. Before women nationwide won the vote, legislators in 12 states granted women the right to vote.

Susan B. Anthony tests the law A tireless campaigner for the women's suffrage cause, Susan B. Anthony wrote pamphlets and made speeches. She also testified before every Congress between 1869 and 1906 on behalf of women's suffrage. In 1872 she and three of her sisters staged a dramatic protest. They registered to vote, and on Election Day they voted in Rochester, New York. Two weeks later they were arrested for "knowingly, wrongfully and unlawfully" voting for a representative to the Congress of the United States.

Before her trial began, Anthony delivered an address in which she spelled out many reasons that justice required that women be given the right to vote.

HISTORY'S VOICES

❝One-half of the people of this nation to-day are utterly powerless to blot from the statute books an unjust law, or to write there a new and a just one. The women, dissatisfied as they are with this form of government, that enforces taxation without representation—that compels them to obey laws to which they have never given their consent—that imprisons and hangs them without a trial by a jury of their peers, that robs them, in marriage, of the custody of their own persons, wages and children—are this half of the people left wholly at the mercy of the other half, in direct violation of the spirit and letter of the declarations of the framers of this government, every one of which was based on the immutable [undeniable] principle of equal rights to all.❞

—Susan B. Anthony, 1872

At her trial, the judge refused to allow Anthony to testify on her own behalf, ruled her guilty, and fined her $100. Anthony refused to pay the fine, hoping to force the judge to

THE IMPACT TODAY

Government
Some 65 women served as representatives and 14 as senators in the 2005–2006 U.S. Congress. Representative Nancy Pelosi of California was minority leader in the House, the highest-ranking position ever held by a woman in Congress.

PRIMARY SOURCES

Political Cartoon

In 1912 cartoonist Laura E. Foster addressed an issue faced by even more women today: the tough choices relating to careers and home life.

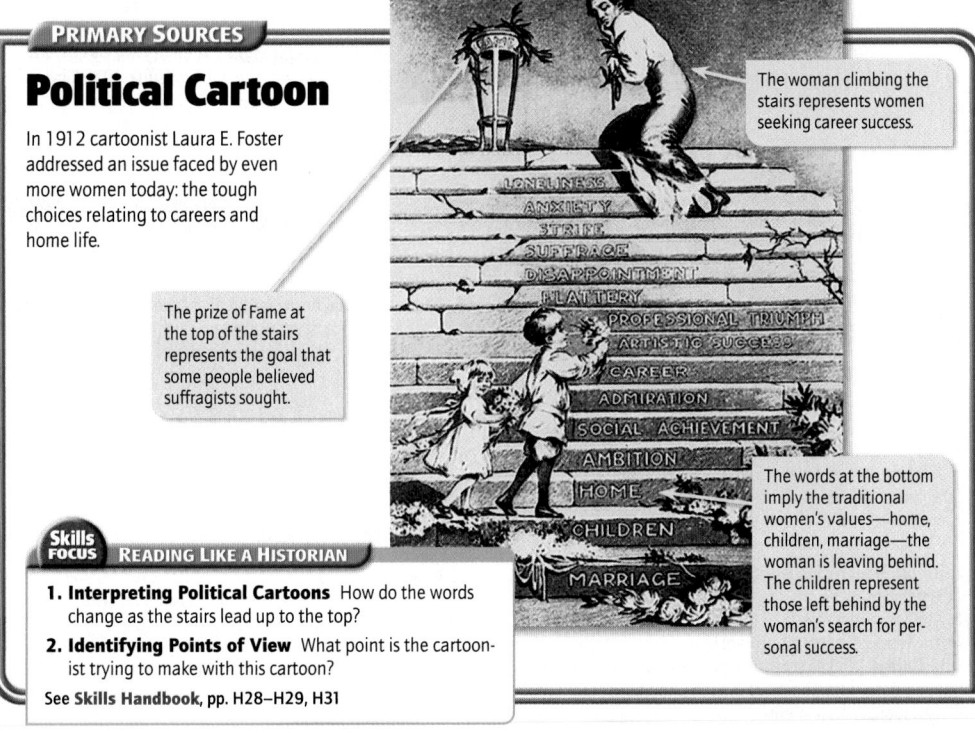

The woman climbing the stairs represents women seeking career success.

The prize of Fame at the top of the stairs represents the goal that some people believed suffragists sought.

The words at the bottom imply the traditional women's values—home, children, marriage—the woman is leaving behind. The children represent those left behind by the woman's search for personal success.

Skills FOCUS READING LIKE A HISTORIAN

1. **Interpreting Political Cartoons** How do the words change as the stairs lead up to the top?
2. **Identifying Points of View** What point is the cartoonist trying to make with this cartoon?

See Skills Handbook, pp. H28–H29, H31

THE PROGRESSIVES **533**

Skills Focus: Sequencing

At Level

Reading Skill
Rise of the Women's Suffrage Movement

1. Guide students in a discussion of Susan B. Anthony's campaign for women's right to vote, her decision to vote illegally, and her subsequent arrest.

2. Have students create a series of cartoons showing Anthony voting, her arrest, the judge fining Anthony, and Anthony refusing to pay her fine.

3. Have students share their cartoons with the class.

4. Then ask students why they believe the judge did not want Anthony to have the opportunity to appeal her case. *possible answer—it was his way of ending the matter; did not want to give Anthony basis to further publicize her cause* **LS** **Visual-Spatial**

📋 Alternative Assessment Handbook, Rubric 3: Artwork

● **Direct Teach** ●

Reading Focus

Women's Suffrage Movement

Recall Why was Susan B. Anthony arrested? *for voting in a congressional election*

Analyze Why do you think the Supreme Court ruled that the right to vote should be left to individual states? *possible answer—citizens register to vote within a state, so this was a matter best left to the states*

📋 Political Cartoons Activities for American History: Cartoon 32: Pursuing Women's Votes

Primary Sources
Women in the Workplace
Compare Guide students in a discussion of the political cartoon to ensure that they understand its message. Then guide students in a discussion of today's equivalent, a "glass ceiling," or an obstacle to career advancement. Do students believe that this ceiling still exists? Have them explain their reasoning.

Teaching Tip

Some students will have difficulty understanding the quote from Susan B. Anthony. Review difficult words and phrases with the class. Then have students work in mixed-ability pairs; have groups identify the subject and verb of each sentence and then paraphrase the quote in their own words.

Answers

Reading Like a Historian 1. *they become negative;* **2.** *that the farther up the career ladder a woman goes, the farther she is from her family and from happiness*

533

Reading Focus

Women's Suffrage Movement

Explain Why did businesses oppose women's suffrage? *liquor industry feared temperance movement; business owners feared women would vote for regulations that would drive up their costs*

Drawing Inferences Why was it beneficial for the NWSA and AWSA to merge? *more power in larger numbers; could unite efforts to publicize cause; more members meant the group was less likely to be ignored*

Review & Assess

Close

Guide students in a discussion of the reasons that the suffragists decided to adopt a state-by-state strategy instead of putting efforts toward a constitutional amendment for women's suffrage.

Review

Online Quiz, Section 2

Daily Test Practice Transparency

Assess

SE Section 2 Assessment

Progress Assessment: Section 2 Quiz

Alternative Assessment Handbook

Reteach

Interactive Reader and Study Guide, Section 2

Interactive Skills Tutor CD-ROM

Answers

Reading Check *urged suffragists into action*

534

---

arrest her and create a case that could be tried through the courts. The judge, however, did not imprison Anthony for refusing to pay the fine, thus denying her the right to appeal her case to a higher court.

In 1875 the Supreme Court ruled that even though women were citizens, citizenship did not give them the right to vote. The Court decided it was up to the states to grant or withhold that right. Suffrage associations therefore continued their strategy of trying to persuade each state legislature to grant women the vote.

Anti-suffrage arguments Opponents of the suffrage movement put forth a variety of arguments. Some believed that voting would interfere with women's duties at home or would destroy families altogether. Others claimed that women did not have the education or experience to be competent voters. Still others believed the <u>notion</u> that most American women did not want to vote. They said that it was unfair for suffragists to try to force the vote on those unwilling women.

Significant business interests also opposed women's suffrage. The liquor industry feared that women would vote for Prohibition. As women became more active in other reform movements—such as food and drug safety,

ACADEMIC
VOCABULARY
notion idea

worker safety, and child labor—business owners feared that women would vote for regulations that would drive up business costs.

Even some churches and clergy members spoke out against women's suffrage. They argued that marriage was a sacred bond in which the entire family was represented by the man. In that case, they believed that women did not need the vote.

Two organizations merge In 1890 the National Woman Suffrage Association and the American Woman Suffrage Association merged. They formed the **National American Woman Suffrage Association** (NAWSA) under the leadership of Elizabeth Cady Stanton. Susan B. Anthony served as NAWSA's president from 1892 to 1900. Anthony died in 1906. Her final public statement was "Failure is impossible."

Like Susan B. Anthony, most of the early suffragists did not live long enough to cast their ballots. In fact, when women nationwide finally won the vote in 1920, only one signer of the Seneca Falls Declaration—Charlotte Woodward, age 92—was still alive.

READING CHECK **Identifying Cause and Effect** What effect did the passage of the Fifteenth Amendment have on suffragists?

SECTION 2 ASSESSMENT

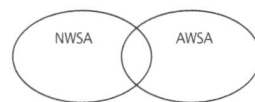
go.hrw.com
Online Quiz
Keyword: SD7 HP16

Reviewing Ideas, Terms, and People

1. **a. Describe** In the 1800s, what new opportunities did women in various social classes have outside the home?
   b. Explain How did new opportunities change the way many women viewed their place in the public world?

2. **a. Identify** Write a sentence describing each of the following: **Prohibition, Carry Nation, Frances Willard, National Association of Colored Women**.
   b. Analyze Why did many women choose to join the temperance movement?
   c. Elaborate How were women's reform causes related to traditional roles in the home?

3. **a. Recall** What happened to **Susan B. Anthony** when she attempted to vote?
   b. Analyze What effect did the Fifteenth Amendment have on the women's rights movement?
   c. Elaborate Why do you think many suffragists decided to adopt a state-by-state strategy, rather than campaign for a constitutional amendment?

534 CHAPTER 16

Critical Thinking

4. **Comparing and Contrasting** Copy the Venn diagram below and fill it out to show the ways in which the National Woman Suffrage Association and the American Woman Suffrage Association were similar and different.

NWSA AWSA

FOCUS ON WRITING

5. **Persuasive** Suppose you are a woman who has gained political experience in the abolitionist movement. Write a letter to the editor explaining your opposition to the exclusion of women from the proposed Fifteenth Amendment. Be sure to provide details to support your argument.

Section 2 Assessment Answers

1. **a.** higher education and employment
   b. saw they had a role beyond the home

2. **a.** Sentences should reflect Key Term definitions in the section.
   b. believed alcohol was responsible for crime, poverty, and violence against women
   c. improved lives of families and communities

3. **a.** later arrested and pronounced guilty for voting

   b. made women fight harder and organize
   c. possible answer—reform is easier on a smaller scale

4. similar—focused on giving women the right to vote; different—NWSA focused on constitutional amendment, AWSA focused on state approval

5. possible answer—women as capable and intelligent as men

3 Theodore Roosevelt's Square Deal

BEFORE YOU READ

MAIN IDEA

Theodore Roosevelt used the power of the presidency to push for progressive reforms in business and in environmental policy.

READING FOCUS

1. What was Theodore Roosevelt's view of the role of the president?
2. How did Roosevelt attempt to regulate big business?
3. What was Roosevelt's philosophy about conserving the environment, and how did he carry out his philosophy?

KEY TERMS AND PEOPLE

Theodore Roosevelt
bully pulpit
Square Deal
Elkins Act
Hepburn Act
Upton Sinclair
Meat Inspection Act
Pure Food and Drug Act
John Muir
Newlands Reclamation Act
Gifford Pinchot

TAKING NOTES As you read, take notes on the various reforms that Theodore Roosevelt supported during his presidency. Record your notes in a graphic organizer like the one shown here:

Regulating Business	Protecting the Environment

THE INSIDE STORY

Cowboy or politician? No one who knew "Teedie" Roosevelt at age 9 would have recognized the sturdy athlete who later cleaned up a corrupt New York City police department and led the Rough Riders in Cuba during the Spanish-American War. The young Roosevelt was sickly and shy. Family doctors forbade any sports or strenuous activity, so Teedie spent his time reading and studying natural history. Then as a teenager, **Theodore Roosevelt** energetically set about making himself into a new person. He took up boxing, tennis, horseback riding, and rowing. He fashioned an optimistic, vigorous personality that was to make him a successful politician.

Roosevelt came from a prominent New York family and attended Harvard University, but he grew to love the outdoors. He spent time in northern Maine and in the rugged Badlands of the Dakota territory, where he rode horses and hunted buffalo. When Roosevelt was 26, tragedy struck. Both his wife and his mother died unexpectedly. Trying to forget his grief, Roosevelt returned to his ranch in Dakota Territory.

For two years, Roosevelt lived and worked with cowboys, who came to admire his toughness as he rode in roundups and hunted bear, elk, and mountain lions. The westerners also liked the way he stood up to bullying rustlers who called him "four eyes" because of his thick glasses. After two years, Roosevelt's western adventure was over. He returned to New York and to politics. ◾

▶ **A young Theodore Roosevelt in 1880**

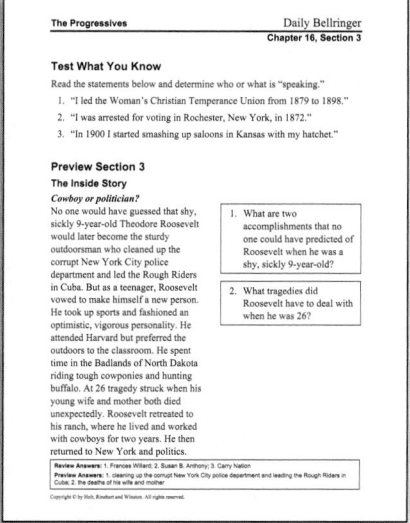

Prelude to the Presidency

Theodore Roosevelt's Square Deal

1. **Teach** Ask the students the Reading Focus questions to teach this section.

2. **Apply** Review the reformers that students have studied and what actions these individuals might have taken if they became president. Have students share their predictions with the class. Then, as students read the section, have them compare their predictions with the actions taken by President Theodore Roosevelt. **LS Verbal-Linguistic**

3. **Review** Have students identify issues they think were most important for the president and Congress to address.

4. **Practice/Homework** Remind students that much of the reform legislation enacted during this time is still in place. Have students write a brief summary of the reform actions taken by President Roosevelt and the results of those actions. **LS Verbal-Linguistic**

    Alternative Assessment Handbook, Rubric 42: Writing to Inform

Academic Vocabulary

Review with students the high-use academic term in this section.

framework the basic concepts that constitute a way of viewing reality (p. 536)

   CRF: Vocabulary Builder Activity, Section 3

Taking Notes

Regulating Business—busting "bad" trusts, Elkins Act, Hepburn Act, Meat Inspection Act, Pure Food and Drug Act; Protecting the Environment—Newlands Reclamation Act, U.S. Forest Service, Antiquities Act, National Park Service

❶ What was Theodore Roosevelt's view of the role of the president? *He used the power of the office to publicize and seek support for important issues.*

Roosevelt's View of the Presidency

Identify What was the reason for the 1902 coal strike? *Miners wanted higher wages, shorter hours, and recognition of their union.*

Describe Discuss Roosevelt's strategy to settle the coal strike. *urged arbitration; threatened that government would take over the mines*

Evaluate In what way did the coal strike agreement represent a square deal? *labor and business gained some, lost some, consumers benefited*

Biography

Jack London (1876–1916) Jack London was an American writer whose works dealt with man's struggle for survival. After unsuccessfully seeking his fortune in the Klondike gold rush, London published two of his most critically acclaimed novels, *The Call of the Wild* and *White Fang*. His autobiography, *Martin Eden*, conveyed London's rigorous work ethic. Known throughout the world for his rich imagery, vivid language, and thrilling storylines, London remains one of America's most important authors of the period.

Answers

Reading Check *belief that the needs of workers, business, and consumers should be balanced*

Roosevelt's View of the Presidency

Theodore Roosevelt's rise to the governorship of New York in 1898 spelled big trouble for the Republican political machine in New York. To rid themselves of the Progressive reformer, party bosses came up with a clever plan: They got Roosevelt nominated as vice president, a job with little power at the time.

Taking office However, the party bosses—and the nation—were shocked when anarchist Leon Czolgosz (CHAWL-gawsh) fatally shot President William McKinley in 1901. Theodore Roosevelt, the energetic reformer, now held the highest office in the land.

Roosevelt was just 42 years old when he took office—the youngest person ever to become president. During the late 1800s, most presidents had taken a hands-off approach to governing. Not Teddy Roosevelt. He saw the White House as a **bully pulpit**—a powerful platform to publicize important issues and seek support for his policies. With great enthusiasm and energy, Roosevelt brought new momentum to the Progressive movement.

The coal strike of 1902 Soon after the new president took office, some 150,000 Pennsylvania coal miners struck for higher wages, shorter hours, and recognition of their union. The strike gave Roosevelt an opportunity to define his view of the presidency.

As winter neared, Roosevelt feared what might happen if the strike were not resolved. Northern cities depended on Pennsylvania coal for heating. The president felt compelled to use his influence "to bring to an end a situation which has become literally intolerable."

Roosevelt urged the mine owners and the striking workers to accept arbitration. In the arbitration process, two opposing sides agree to allow a third party to settle a dispute. The workers agreed to accept arbitration, but the mine owners refused. As winter drew nearer, Roosevelt threatened to take over the mines. The threat finally convinced the mine owners to agree to his arbitration plan.

After a three-month investigation, the arbitrators announced their decision. They gave the workers a shorter workday and higher pay but did not require the mining companies

ACADEMIC VOCABULARY

framework the basic concepts that constitute a way of viewing reality

to recognize the union. For the first time, the federal government had intervened in a strike to protect the interests of the workers and the public. Satisfied, Roosevelt pronounced the compromise a "square deal."

The Square Deal The **Square Deal** became Roosevelt's 1904 campaign slogan and the framework for his entire presidency. He promised to "see that each [person] is given a square deal, because he is entitled to no more and should receive no less." Roosevelt's promise revealed his belief that the needs of workers, business, and consumers should be balanced. Roosevelt's Square Deal called for limiting the power of trusts, promoting public health and safety, and improving working conditions.

The popular president faced no opposition for the nomination with his party. In the general election Roosevelt cruised to victory, easily defeating his Democratic opponent, Judge Alton Parker of New York.

READING CHECK **Identifying the Main Idea** What was Roosevelt's Square Deal?

Regulating Big Business

Roosevelt believed that big business was essential to the nation's growth, but he also believed companies should behave responsibly.

HISTORY'S VOICES

❝We demand that big business give the people a square deal; in return we must insist that when anyone engaged in big business honestly endeavors to do right he shall himself be given a square deal.❞

—Theodore Roosevelt

Roosevelt focused a great deal of attention on regulating large corporations. Addressing Congress in 1902, Roosevelt stated, "We are . . . determined that they [corporations] shall be so handled as to subserve [serve] the public good. We draw the line against misconduct, not against wealth."

Trust-busting In 1901 tycoons J. P. Morgan, James J. Hill, and E. H. Harriman joined their railroads together to eliminate competition. Their company, the Northern Securities Company, dominated railroad shipping from Chicago to the Northwest.

Collaborative Learning

At Level | **Standard English Mastery**

The Square Deal

1. Guide students in a discussion of the reasons for the 1902 coal strike and Roosevelt's concept of a Square Deal.

2. Organize the students into small groups. Have students in half the groups represent mine workers and union activists during the 1902 coal strike. Have the other half represent mine owners and business leaders. Have students in each group prepare a detailed outline that describes their demands and why they believe that these demands are reasonable. Have

volunteers from each group read their outlines to the class.

3. Have volunteers from each group conduct a class debate over the primary arbitration issues of the coal strike.

4. Have students use their debate notes and group outlines to write an essay expressing their position about the arbitration and outcome of the coal strike. **LS Kinesthetic**

📝 Alternative Assessment Handbook, Rubric 10: Debates

The following year, President Roosevelt directed the U.S. attorney general to sue the Northern Securities Company for violating the Sherman Antitrust Act. In 1904 the Supreme Court ruled that the monopoly did violate the Sherman Antitrust Act, and it ordered the corporation dissolved.

The ruling proved to be a watershed. An encouraged Roosevelt administration launched a vigorous trust-busting campaign. It filed dozens of lawsuits against monopolies and trusts that it believed were not in the public interest.

The size of the trust was not the issue. What mattered was whether a particular trust was good or bad for the American public. The Roosevelt administration went after the bad trusts: the ones that sold inferior products, competed unfairly, or corrupted public officials.

Regulating the railroads Another way to ensure that businesses competed more fairly was through regulation. Railroads commonly granted rebates to their best customers. This meant that huge corporations

Bully Pulpit

NO MOLLY-CODDLING HERE

THE GRANGER COLLECTION, NEW YORK

Skills Focus READING LIKE A HISTORIAN

Far left, Roosevelt is making good use of the bully pulpit. The cartoon shows Roosevelt as a man who will not "mollycoddle," or indulge, big business.

1. **Interpreting Political Cartoons** What does the reference to big business mean?

2. **Identifying Points of View** What does the cartoon say about Roosevelt's efforts? Explain.

See **Skills Handbook**, p. H28–H29, H31

THE PROGRESSIVES **537**

Reading Focus

❷ How did Roosevelt attempt to regulate big business? *through legislation; trust-busting; railroad regulations; Meat Inspection and Pure Food and Drug Acts*

Regulating Big Business

Explain What is trustbusting? *breaking up monopolies and trusts that do not serve the public interest*

Draw a Conclusion Explain President Roosevelt's view of trusts. *trusts are not necessarily bad; good trusts, those that serve the public interest, should be allowed to exist*

Make Judgments Do you think filing lawsuits or passing new laws was the best way to break up monopolies and trusts? *possible answer—passing new laws because they established high standards for future generations*

📄 CRF: Primary Source Activity: President Theodore Roosevelt Calls for Trust Regulation

📄 Political Cartoons Activities for American History: Cartoon 31: The Wrestling Match

Skills Focus: Interpreting Political Cartoons   At Level

Reading Like a Historian Skill
Regulating Big Business

1. Have students examine the political cartoon on this page. Have students work in mixed-ability pairs to help ensure that they understand what the cartoon shows.

2. Guide students in a discussion of how Roosevelt's actions led to the breakup of the Northern Securities Company.

3. Have students create two new political cartoons. One cartoon should show Roosevelt breaking up Northern Securities Company; the other cartoon should defend the company or portray the viewpoint of the company leaders. Have students write captions or slogans for each of the cartoons.

4. Have students share their cartoons, and display their work for the class. **LS Visual-Spatial**

📄 Alternative Assessment Handbook, Rubric 3: Artwork

Answers

Reading Like a Historian 1. *large corporations and trusts;* **2.** *He is vigorous and effective.*

537

Regulating Big Business

Recall Which two acts regulated shipping rates within the railroad industry? *Elkins Act; Hepburn Act*

Identify Cause and Effect What caused improvements within meat-packing and drug industries? *The Jungle; reports from Secretary of Agriculture*

Evaluate Why do you think it took so long for reforms to occur within the food and drug industries? *possible answers—No one had reported on the conditions; big business interests had little desire to reform their practices.*

Info to Know

Meat Inspection Act In order to ensure public safety, the processing of beef, pork, mutton, and lamb for human consumption was strictly regulated. The slaughterhouses were now under strict cleanliness guidelines. In addition to federal inspection before slaughter, there were inspections of animals after slaughter as well. In 1957, the Poultry Products Inspection Act was enacted, so that the poultry industry would also be inspected and regulated.

Answers

Faces of History *He continually sought challenges, and met them with enthusiasm and perseverance.*

Reading Check *Elkins Act, Hepburn Act, Meat Inspection Act, Pure Food and Drug Act*

538

FACES OF HISTORY
Theodore ROOSEVELT
1858–1919

Author, athlete, and Nobel Prize–winning statesman, Theodore Roosevelt forged a presidential style that was an extension of the fascinating life he had led. Doing battle with corporate trusts and crusading for the environment were just other adventures for the battle-ready hero and nature lover.

Roosevelt embraced the "strenuous life" in what he called "the arena" of public service. Whether reforming the New York City police department, defying corrupt party bosses, or leading soldiers in the Spanish-American War, Roosevelt was always, in his words, "daring greatly." As president, Roosevelt focused on "trust-busting" and environmental conservation at home and pursued a "muscular" foreign policy, using an enlarged U.S. Navy to project American power. His intervention in Central America led to the founding of Panama and, later, the building of the Panama Canal.

"TR" even survived a brush with death in 1912. Shot in the chest by a would-be assassin, he proceeded to give a 90-minute campaign speech. He told the stunned crowd, "It takes more than that to kill a bull moose."

Interpret How did Roosevelt's life affect his style of leadership?

Many drug companies were equally unconcerned for their customer's welfare. Some sold medicines that simply did not work. Others marketed patent, or nonprescription, medicines containing dangerous narcotic drugs. Products such as Dr. James' Soothing Syrup, intended to soothe babies' teething pain, contained the drug heroin. Gowan's Pneumonia Cure contained the addictive painkiller opium.

Few industries fell into greater public disrepute than the meatpacking business. The novelist **Upton Sinclair** exposed the wretched and unsanitary conditions at meatpacking plants in his 1906 novel *The Jungle*.

HISTORY'S VOICES

❝There would be meat stored in great piles in rooms; and the water from leaky roofs would drip over it, and thousands of rats would race about on it. . . . A man could run his hand over these piles of meat and sweep off handfuls of the dried dung of rats. . . . The packers would put poisoned bread out for them; they would die, and then rats, bread, and meat would go into the hoppers together.❞
—Upton Sinclair, *The Jungle*, 1906

Sinclair's novel ignited a firestorm of criticism aimed at meatpackers. Reformers and an outraged public called for change. Roosevelt ordered Secretary of Agriculture James Wilson to investigate the conditions in the packing houses. Wilson's final report made for gruesome reading.

"We saw meat shoveled from filthy wooden floors, piled on tables rarely washed, pushed from room to room in rotten box carts. In all of which processes it [the meat] was in the way of gathering dirt, splinters, floor filth, and the expectoration [saliva] of tuberculous and other diseased workers."

The Wilson report shocked the U.S. Congress into action. In 1906 it enacted two groundbreaking consumer protection laws. The first, the **Meat Inspection Act**, required federal inspection of meat shipped across state lines. The **Pure Food and Drug Act** forbade the manufacture, sale, or transportation of food and patent medicine containing harmful ingredients. The law also required food and medicine containers to carry accurate ingredient labels.

READING CHECK **Summarizing** What measures did the Roosevelt administration take to regulate business and protect consumers?

---

paid significantly less to ship their products than small farmers or small businesses. In 1903 Congress passed the **Elkins Act**, which prohibited railroads from accepting rebates. The Elkins Act ensured that all customers paid the same rates for shipping their products.

The **Hepburn Act** of 1906 strengthened the Interstate Commerce Commission (ICC), giving it the power to set maximum railroad rates. It also gave the ICC the power to regulate other companies that were engaged in interstate commerce.

Protecting consumers Roosevelt also responded to growing public dismay about practices of the food and drug industries. Some food producers, drug companies, and meat packers were selling dangerous products to an unknowing public.

Food producers, for example, resorted to clever tricks to pass off tainted foods. Some poultry sellers added formaldehyde, a chemical used in embalming dead bodies, to old eggs to hide their foul odor. Unwary consumers bought the tainted food and were tricked into thinking it was healthy.

THE IMPACT TODAY
Government
The Pure Food and Drug Act was the forerunner of today's Food and Drug Administration, which regulates food, drugs, cosmetics, and medical products.

Skills Focus: Comparing and Contrasting   At Level

Reading Skill   Research Required
Regulating Big Business

1. Have students review the excerpt from *The Jungle* that appears in this chapter and the quotes by Upton Sinclair and James Wilson.

2. Have students conduct research on food and drug regulations and legislation passed subsequent to the 1906 Meat Inspection and Pure Food and Drug Acts. Then have students write a report comparing and contrasting conditions in food and drug processing plants

before 1906 with conditions in food and drug processing plants after the laws were passed.

3. Ask volunteers to read their reports to the class. Guide students in a discussion of ways the government helps to ensure that Americans are protected from unsafe food and medicines. 🇱🇸 **Verbal-Linguistic**

📰 Alternative Assessment Handbook, Rubric 9: Comparing and Contrasting

Environmental Conservation

In the late 1800s people acted as if the United States had an unending supply of natural resources. Lumber companies cleared large tracts of forest lands. Farmers plowed up the Great Plains. Ranchers' cattle and sheep overgrazed the prairies. Mining companies clogged rivers and cluttered the land with their refuse. Cities dumped sewage into rivers and garbage onto the land.

Roosevelt, however, believed that each generation had a duty to protect and conserve natural resources for future generations.

HISTORY'S VOICES

❝We of an older generation can get along with what we have, . . . but in your full manhood and womanhood you will want what nature once so bountifully supplied and man so thoughtlessly destroyed; and because of that want you will reproach us, not for what we have used, but for what we have wasted.❞

—Theodore Roosevelt

Before Roosevelt's presidency, the federal government had left the nation's natural resources largely unregulated. Business needs had always taken priority over the environment. But Roosevelt recognized that natural resources were limited, and he believed their use needed to be controlled.

In 1903 Roosevelt joined famed naturalist **John Muir** for a camping trip in Yosemite National Park in California. Muir had played a pivotal role in convincing the government to protect and preserve Yosemite. "Unfortunately, God cannot save trees from fools," Muir had observed. "Only the government can do that."

Despite their friendly camping trip, Muir and Roosevelt held different views about conservation. Muir wanted the entire wilderness to be preserved in its natural state. Roosevelt believed that conservation involved the active management of public lands for a variety of uses. Some lands should be preserved as wilderness. Other lands should be put to more directly economical productive uses.

The **Newlands Reclamation Act** of 1902 reflected Roosevelt's beliefs. It allowed the federal government to create irrigation projects to make dry lands productive. The projects would be funded from money raised by selling off public lands. The Roosevelt administration launched more than 20 reclamation projects.

Linking TO Today

National Park System

Theodore Roosevelt will be remembered as the first champion of conservation. Yet before him, some Americans worked to protect natural wonders.

In 1872 Congress passed a law that set aside land in Wyoming, Montana, and Idaho as Yellowstone National Park. Yellowstone became the world's first national park.

Over time, the federal government founded more national parks across the country. In 1919 parts of the Grand Canyon in Arizona became a national park. Shenandoah National Park in Virginia was founded in 1935. Biscayne National Park in Florida was established in 1980, and Cuyahoga Valley National Park in Ohio was created in 2000.

While many parks preserve land and wildlife, other parks throughout the world preserve cultural history. Mesa Verde National Park in Colorado is famous for its Cliff Palace, a settlement built by ancestral Pueblo Indians about 800 years ago. In the Caribbean, Virgin Islands National Park is home to ancient ruins and Danish sugar plantations from the 1700s and 1800s.

In the Yellowstone tradition, national parks have been created in many countries. Meanwhile, debate continues over how to both save and use public lands.

Making Generalizations Why do some national parks preserve cultural elements as well as natural ones?

Visitors enjoy the wonders of Colorado's Mesa Verde National Park.

540

Review & Assess

Close

Guide students in discussion of the reforms initiated by President Theodore Roosevelt and the effects of these reforms.

Review

go.hrw.com Online Quiz, Section 3

Daily Test Practice Transparency

Assess

SE Section 3 Assessment

Progress Assessment: Section 3 Quiz

Alternative Assessment Handbook

Reteach

Interactive Reader and Study Guide, Section 3

Interactive Skills Tutor CD-ROM

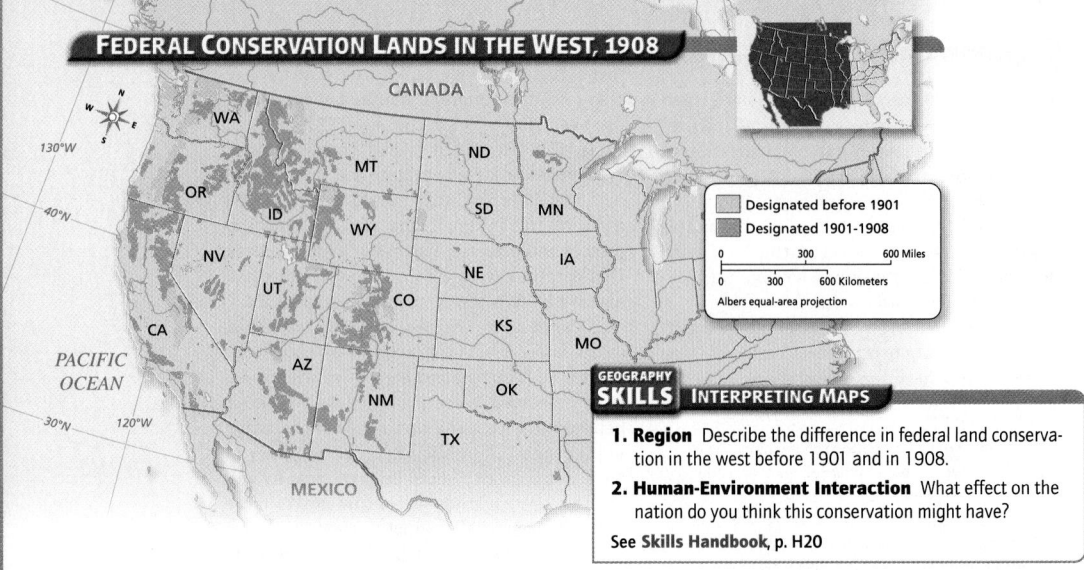

FEDERAL CONSERVATION LANDS IN THE WEST, 1908

Designated before 1901
Designated 1901–1908

0 300 600 Miles
0 300 600 Kilometers
Albers equal-area projection

GEOGRAPHY SKILLS INTERPRETING MAPS

1. **Region** Describe the difference in federal land conservation in the west before 1901 and in 1908.

2. **Human-Environment Interaction** What effect on the nation do you think this conservation might have?

See **Skills Handbook**, p. H20

Another conservationist, **Gifford Pinchot** (PIN-shoh), shared Roosevelt's view. Pinchot first came up with the word *conservation* to describe the need to protect the country's natural environment. He wrote: "The conservation of natural resources is the key to the future. It is the key to the safety and prosperity of the American people." Pinchot believed scientific management of natural resources was crucial to sustaining them to serve the nation's needs.

In 1905 the Roosevelt administration established the U.S. Forest Service with Pinchot as its chief. During Roosevelt's presidency, the Forest Service added nearly 150 million acres to the national forests, controlled their use, and regulated their harvest.

The Antiquities Act of 1906 led to the creation of 18 national monuments during Roosevelt's presidency. For many historians, environmental conservation is Roosevelt's greatest legacy.

READING CHECK **Contrasting** How did Roosevelt's and Muir's views of natural resources differ?

SECTION 3 ASSESSMENT

go.hrw.com
Online Quiz
Keyword: SD7 HP16

Reviewing Ideas, Terms, and People

1. **a. Recall** How did Roosevelt use the **bully pulpit** to promote the **Square Deal**?
   b. Evaluate How was Roosevelt's response to the coal strike symbolic of his view of the presidency?

2. **a. Describe** How did Roosevelt engage in trust-busting?
   b. Draw Conclusions Why did the food companies knowingly sell spoiled food?
   c. Predict What impact would Roosevelt's policies have on consumer protection in America?

3. **a. Identify** Who was **Gifford Pinchot**?
   b. Contrast How did Roosevelt's view of natural resources differ from the policies of past presidents?

Critical Thinking

4. **Summarizing** Copy the chart below and record major legislation regulating business during Roosevelt's presidency.

Law	Purpose

FOCUS ON WRITING

5. **Persuasive** As a consumer in 1906, write a letter to Congress supporting the Pure Food and Drug bill.

540 CHAPTER 16

Section 3 Assessment Answers

Answers

Interpreting Maps 1. *The amount of conserved land was much greater in 1908 than before 1901.* **2.** *possible answer— natural wonders might otherwise have been destroyed*

Reading Check *Roosevelt—some lands should be preserved and others should be managed in order to serve the nation's needs; Muir—wilderness should be completely preserved in its natural state*

1. **a.** publicized and gained support for issues
   b. used arbitration to win compromises

2. **a.** filed lawsuits against monopolies and trusts; passed laws regulating business practices, such as rebates
   b. It was cheaper than using fresh products.
   c. possible answer—paved the way for the protection of consumers

3. **a.** first head of U.S. Forest Service
   b. Roosevelt recognized that natural resources were limited and should be protected

4. Elkins Act, prohibited railroads from accepting rebates; Hepburn Act, authorized ICC to set maximum railroad rates; Meat Inspection Act, required federal inspection of meat shipped across state lines; Pure Food and Drug Act, forbade manufacture, sale, or transportation of food and patent medicine containing harmful ingredients

5. possible answer—bill protects consumer health

SECTION 4 — Taft and Wilson

BEFORE YOU READ

MAIN IDEA

Progressive reforms continued during the Taft and Wilson presidencies, focusing on business, banking, and women's suffrage.

READING FOCUS

1. How did Taft's approach to progressivism split the Republican Party?
2. What was Wilson's New Freedom reform plan?
3. How did women gain the right to vote in national elections?
4. How did progressivism affect African Americans?

KEY TERMS AND PEOPLE

William Howard Taft
Sixteenth Amendment
Hiram W. Johnson
Woodrow Wilson
New Freedom
Federal Reserve Act
Clayton Antitrust Act
Alice Paul
Nineteenth Amendment
Brownsville incident

TAKING NOTES As you read, takes notes on laws passed under President Wilson's New Freedom. In a chart like the one shown below, identify each law and its goal. You may need to add more rows.

Law	Goals

THE INSIDE STORY

Can politics and friendship mix? In 1904 Theodore Roosevelt told the country he would not seek re-election as president. He kept his word. Instead, when the 1908 election approached, Roosevelt put forth a successor: his friend and close adviser **William Howard Taft**.

The two men were very different. Roosevelt was an energetic crusader for reform. He held an expansive view of the president's powers and was not afraid to set new precedent. Taft was an easygoing, cautious lawyer with a more restrained view of the presidency. He expressed some discomfort at Roosevelt's activism, saying that Roosevelt "ought more often to have admitted the legal way of reaching the same ends." Still, he served the president loyally for four years as secretary of war and, though his main ambition was to become the chief justice of the Supreme Court, he agreed to run.

Taft didn't enjoy the campaign. He called it "one of the most uncomfortable four months of my life." But he pledged loyalty to the Roosevelt program, and with the president's strong backing he won the 1908 election. In March of 1909 the reluctant candidate found himself living in the White House.

Roosevelt soon regretted his decision. He believed that Taft departed from Progressive ideals on tariffs and the environment. Roosevelt charged that Taft "completely twisted around the policies I advocated." The onetime friends were to become bitter foes. ◢

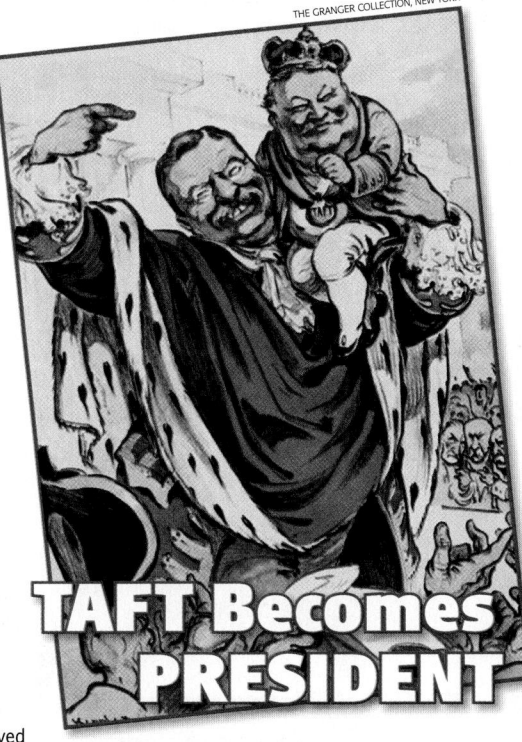

THE GRANGER COLLECTION, NEW YORK

TAFT Becomes PRESIDENT

▲ Roosevelt crowns his successor, believing Taft will carry on his work.

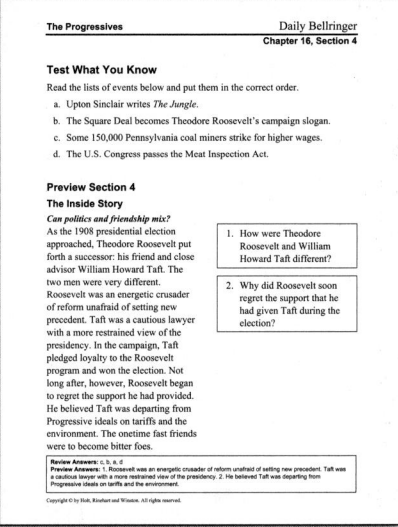
Taking Notes

Law—Underwood Tariff Act, Federal Reserve Act, Clayton Antitrust Act, Federal Trade Commission, Nineteenth Amendment; Goals—reduced tariffs, created a central fund for banks to borrow from during a financial panic, clarified and extended Sherman Antitrust Act, enforced antitrust laws and launched investigations of businesses, gave women full voting rights

Teach the Main Idea

At Level

Taft and Wilson

1. **Teach** Ask students the Reading Focus questions to teach this section.

2. **Apply** Have students create a detailed time line of this section beginning with the presidential election of 1908 and ending with the outbreak of World War I in 1914.

3. **Review** Guide students in a discussion of the four main topics in this section. During the discussion have students read dates and events from their time lines.

4. **Practice/Homework** Have students write five questions that a journalist might ask President Taft or President Wilson. Have students work in pairs to supply the answers to the questions. Have volunteers present their "interviews" to the class. **LS Verbal-Linguistic, Visual-Spatial**

📝 Alternative Assessment Handbook, Rubric 37: Writing Assignments

❶ How did Taft's approach to progressivism split the Republican Party? *tried to consolidate reforms, but limited progressivism; signed high tariff bill; lacked commitment to environment*

Progressivism Under Taft

Identify What was the main provision of the Sixteenth Amendment? *allowed Congress to tax individual's income*

Make Inferences Why do you think Pinchot reacted so strongly to Richard Ballinger's sale of the Alaskan timberland? *Pinchot had devoted his life to forest preservation.*

📃 CRF: Biography: Hiram Johnson

Recent Scholarship

The election of 1912 was a critical one for the nation. In *1912: Wilson, Roosevelt, Taft, and Debs—The Election that Changed the Country*, historian and professor of international relations James Chace brings the issues and the candidates to life. Chace argues that this election was "a defining moment in American history," and the book is an excellent examination of the electoral process. Chace also contends that Roosevelt and Wilson changed the presidency by increasing the powers of the executive office.

1912: Wilson, Roosevelt, Taft, and Debs

go.hrw.com
Online Resources

KEYWORD: SD7 CH16
TOPIC: THE ELECTION OF 1912

Answers

Interpreting Maps *won the vast majority of electoral votes (435)*

542

Progressivism under Taft

In the election of 1908, Taft faced three-time Democratic candidate William Jennings Bryan. The Democrats lost the election by a wide margin in the electoral college and by nearly 1.27 million popular votes.

A cautious man, President Taft worked to secure Roosevelt's progressive reforms rather than to build upon them. Still, he supported several reforms, such as creating a Department of Labor to enforce labor laws and increasing national forest reserves.

The Taft administration also is credited with passage of the **Sixteenth Amendment**. Introduced during the Taft years but ratified in 1913 after Taft left office, the Sixteenth Amendment granted Congress the power to levy taxes based on an individual's income. Progressives had supported a nationwide income tax as a way to pay for government programs more fairly.

Despite these reforms, President Taft lost the support of most Progressive Republicans.

The trouble began early, in April 1909, with the passage of a bill on tariffs, or taxes charged on imports or exports.

The House had passed a version of the bill, which lowered tariffs on imported goods. When the bill went to the Senate, though, Senator Nelson Aldrich of Rhode Island and others added so many amendments that it became a high-tariff bill. Nevertheless, Taft signed the Payne-Aldrich Tariff into law. Progressives were outraged because they saw tariff reduction as a key step in lowering the prices of consumer goods.

Taft also alienated Progressive supporters of conservation. His secretary of the interior, Richard Ballinger, was accused of impeding a government fraud investigation of public coal-land deals in Alaska. When Gifford Pinchot, head of the U.S. Forest Service, charged Ballinger with sabotaging conservation efforts, Taft fired Pinchot.

Progressives believed that the Ballinger-Pinchot affair showed Taft's lack of commitment to conservation. Theodore Roosevelt, who had put forth Taft for the presidency, refused to support Taft after the Ballinger-Pinchot affair.

Split in the Republican Party In the 1910 congressional elections, Roosevelt campaigned for Progressive Republicans who opposed Taft. Roosevelt proposed a program called New Nationalism, a set of laws to protect workers, ensure public health, and regulate business.

Some reformers saw the New Nationalism as a revival of the progressive spirit. Roosevelt's help on the campaign trail was not enough to ensure a Republican victory, though. Republicans lost control of the House of Representatives for the first time in 16 years.

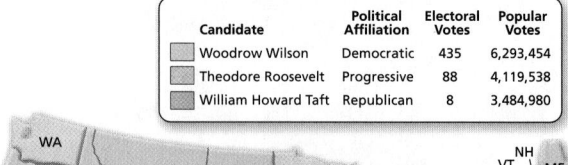

THE ELECTION OF 1912

Candidate	Political Affiliation	Electoral Votes	Popular Votes
Woodrow Wilson	Democratic	435	6,293,454
Theodore Roosevelt	Progressive	88	4,119,538
William Howard Taft	Republican	8	3,484,980

GEOGRAPHY SKILLS INTERPRETING MAPS

Taft made the poorest showing of any president seeking reelection. Wilson won with only about 42 percent of the popular vote.

Region In comparison, how did Wilson fare in the electoral vote?

See **Skills Handbook**, p. H21

542 CHAPTER 16

Skills Focus: Making Inferences
At Level

Reading Skill
Progressivism Under Taft

1. Guide the students in a discussion about Taft's presidency. Ask students to explain how Taft's philosophy and actions differed from Roosevelt's.

2. Make a list of student responses and have students copy the information onto their own paper.

3. Ask students to write a letter from President Taft to Gifford Pinchot thanking him for his work with the U.S. Forest Service and explaining why he is being fired from his position.

4. As an extension, have students create a reform-minded political cartoon depicting the Ballinger-Pinchot affair. **LS Verbal-Linguistic, Visual-Spatial**

📃 Alternative Assessment Handbook, Rubrics 42: Writing to Inform; and 3: Artwork

By the presidential election of 1912, the Republican Party was badly fractured. Many Republicans continued to support Taft. When the Republican Party nominated Taft as its presidential candidate, the more Progressive Republicans broke away to form the new Progressive ("Bull Moose") Party. Theodore Roosevelt led the ticket, and the popular governor of California, **Hiram W. Johnson**, was their candidate for vice president.

With the Republicans split between Taft and Roosevelt, Democrat **Woodrow Wilson** glided to victory. Wilson received 435 electoral votes, while Roosevelt received 88 and Taft received 8. Socialist candidate Eugene V. Debs won more than 900,000 popular votes but no electoral votes.

READING CHECK **Identifying Cause and Effect** What effect did the split in the Republican Party have on the election of 1912?

Wilson's New Freedom

Wilson came to office with a reputation as a zealous reformer. As governor of New Jersey, he had fought political machines, approved a law permitting direct primaries, and enacted a program to compensate injured workers. During the campaign, he proposed an ambitious plan of reform that he called the **New Freedom**. The New Freedom platform called for tariff reductions, banking reform, and stronger antitrust legislation—causes dear to the hearts of Progressives.

Tariff reduction Wilson's first priority as president was to lower tariffs. Wilson waged a tireless campaign to persuade Congress. He even appeared at a joint session of Congress, the first president since John Adams to do so. In October 1913 Congress passed the Underwood Tariff Act. This law reduced tariffs to their lowest levels in more than 50 years.

Tariff reduction meant that the government had less income, however. How would the nation make up the shortfall?

The answer was an income tax. The Underwood Tariff Act also introduced a graduated income tax, which would assess people at different rates according to their income levels. Wealthier people would pay more; poorer people would pay less.

Banking reform President Wilson's next target for reform was the banking system. Historically bank failures had been common. Banks collapsed when too many people withdrew their deposits at the same time. What could be done to keep the banks' doors open, while still allowing people to withdraw their money when they wanted to?

The answer was the **Federal Reserve Act**. This law, passed in 1913, created a central fund from which banks could borrow to prevent collapse during a financial panic.

The Federal Reserve Act created a three-tier banking system. At the top was the Federal Reserve Board, a group of officials appointed by the president and charged with running the system. On the second level were 12 Federal Reserve banks, which served other banks rather than individuals. On the third level were the private banks, which could borrow from the Federal Reserve banks as they needed to. The Federal Reserve Act put the nation's banking system under the supervision of the federal government for the first time.

Stronger antitrust laws Congress had passed the Sherman Antitrust Act in 1890 to limit the power of monopolies. But lax enforcement and loopholes in the law allowed a number of unfair business practices to persist.

At President Wilson's urging, Congress passed the **Clayton Antitrust Act**, which clarified and extended the Sherman Antitrust Act. Passed in 1914, the Clayton Antitrust Act prohibited companies from buying the stock of competing companies in order to form a monopoly. The law also supported workers by making strikes, boycotts, and peaceful picketing legal for the first time.

In another effort to make business fairer, Wilson supported the creation of the Federal Trade Commission (FTC) by Congress in 1915. The FTC enforced antitrust laws and got tough on companies that used deceptive advertising. It also had the power to undertake special investigations of businesses. Progressives were displeased, however, when Wilson appointed to the commission a number of people who were sympathetic to business.

READING CHECK **Identifying Problems and Solutions** What were the three major areas of reform in Wilson's New Freedom?

THE PROGRESSIVES **543**

3 How did women gain the right to vote in national elections? *followed British tactics; gave strong support to war effort; actively campaigned for the vote at state and national levels*

Women Gain the Vote

Explain How did the goals of the National Woman's Party differ from those of the NAWSA? *National Woman's Party focused on constitutional amendment to gain suffrage; NAWSA favored state-by-state approach.*

Analyze Why do you think NAWSA's membership grew even though no state passed legislation allowing women to vote? *efforts gained national attention and momentum; support for suffrage was growing*

Activity **Campaign Slogans**
Have students create membership campaign slogans for the NAWSA and the National Woman's Party.
LS **Auditory-Musical**

Info to Know

The League of Women Voters Carrie Chapman Catt founded the League of Women Voters in 1920 with a mission to help 20 million newly enfranchised American women carry out their responsibility as voters. The League has always been a nonpartisan organization. Initially, however, members were encouraged to lobby for government and social reform legislation. Today the League continues to have an influential voice in public policy.

Answers

Reading Like a Historian
Chapman—women should work with lawmakers, Paul—women should picket, strike, and be imprisoned

Reading Check *NAWSA—used patriotism to generate support; NWP—used civil disobedience and hunger strikes*

544

How to Win the Vote

Alice Paul believed that picketing, imprisonment, and hunger strikes would win suffrage.

❝ Every day that the Government sends women to prison for holding harmless banners . . . makes the position of the Government more indefensible and therefore strengthens our position. ❞

Alice Paul,
1917

Suffragist Carrie Chapman Catt believed that women had to work with lawmakers to win the vote.

❝ When thirty-six state associations . . . [agree] to get the Amendment submitted by Congress and ratified by their respective state legislatures; when they live up to their compact by running a red-hot, never ceasing campaign . . . we can get the Amendment through. ❞

Carrie Chapman Catt,
1916

Skills FOCUS **READING LIKE A HISTORIAN**

Identifying Points of View Summarize each woman's approach to the struggle for voting rights.
See Skills Handbook, p. H28–H29

Women Gain the Vote

The struggle for women's suffrage took some dramatic turns during Wilson's time in office, highlighted by a split in the ranks of suffrage supporters over the best way to win the vote. The National American Woman Suffrage Association (NAWSA) favored a state-by-state approach. But by 1901 just four western states had given women full voting rights.

Frustrated by this slow progress, in 1913 two activists, **Alice Paul** and Lucy Burns, broke away from NAWSA and formed the Congressional Union for Woman Suffrage. Renamed the National Woman's Party (NWP) in 1916, the group focused on passage of a federal constitutional amendment for women's suffrage. Paul and Burns used new tactics learned from the British suffrage movement. The NWP members picketed the White House in January 1917, chaining themselves to the railings. Many were arrested. Some went on hunger strikes in prison. The dramatic efforts of the NWP protesters brought renewed attention to the suffrage cause.

Meanwhile, the state-by-state approach was gaining momentum. In 1915 Massachusetts, New Jersey, New York, and Pennsylvania held special referendums on women's suffrage. The motions were all defeated, but NAWSA's membership grew to nearly 2 million.

Under the energetic leadership of Carrie Chapman Catt, NAWSA launched a new strategy in 1916 to campaign for suffrage on both the state and federal levels. When the United States entered World War I in 1917, leaders of the movement—along with millions of American women—lent strong support to the war effort. Women's patriotism helped weaken opposition to suffrage.

The work of suffragists convinced members of the House and Senate to support a constitutional amendment. Even President Wilson lent his support, in a speech in 1918. Proposed by Congress in 1919 and ratified in 1920, the **Nineteenth Amendment** finally gave women full voting rights.

READING CHECK **Contrasting** Explain how the tactics used by NAWSA and the NWP differed.

Skills Focus: Evaluating Information on the Internet ▸ **Above Level**

Social Studies Skill **Research Required**
The Nineteenth Amendment

1. Have students conduct outside research so that they fully understand the differences between the NAWSA and the National Woman's Party. Explain to students how to determine the credibility of an online source.

2. Have students use the information from their research to create two recruitment speeches: one for the NAWSA, and the other for the National Woman's Party.

3. Have students rehearse and deliver their speeches to the class.

4. As an extension, have students research the process through which a constitutional amendment is proposed, brought to Congress, and ratified. Guide students in a discussion of how the Nineteenth Amendment was ratified.
LS **Verbal-Linguistic**

📓 Alternative Assessment Handbook, Rubric 24: Oral Presentations

Progressivism and the Rights of African Americans

The Progressive movement achieved some remarkable successes. But progressive efforts at reform had limits, particularly when it came to securing the rights of African Americans.

Theodore Roosevelt compiled a mixed record concerning the treatment of African Americans. In 1901 he invited Booker T. Washington to the White House, becoming the first U.S. president to entertain an African American as a dinner guest there. Roosevelt also refused to bow to pressure to withdraw his appointment of an African American collector of tariffs in South Carolina.

HISTORY'S VOICES

❝ I cannot consent to take the position that the doorway of hope—the door of opportunity—is to be shut upon any man, no matter how worthy, purely upon the grounds of race or color. Such an attitude would, according to my contentions, be fundamentally wrong. **❞**

—Theodore Roosevelt

However, Roosevelt's reaction to an event in 1906 in Brownsville, Texas, disappointed African Americans. Twelve members of the African American 25th Infantry were accused of going on a shooting spree in town. The members of the 25th were told that if no one accepted responsibility, they would all be dishonorably discharged. None came forward. Roosevelt signed the papers discharging 167 African American soldiers, denying them all back pay and canceling their pensions. Years later, the truth came out that the soldiers involved in the **Brownsville incident** had been falsely accused. It wasn't until 1972 that their records were corrected to read "honorable discharge."

President Woodrow Wilson had a worse record on civil rights. He opposed a federal anti-lynching law and maintained that the matter should be dealt with at the state level. He also allowed cabinet members to segregate their offices, which had been desegregated since Reconstruction. In addition, during Wilson's administration, Congress passed a law making it a felony for blacks and whites to marry in the District of Columbia.

The outbreak of World War I in Europe in 1914 brought an end to the Progressive Era. As the United States edged closer to war, reformers found that Americans were more interested in the war and less eager to devote their energies to the reform movement. World War I, not progressivism, dominated President Wilson's second term in office.

READING CHECK **Drawing Conclusions** How would you characterize Roosevelt's and Wilson's records in regard to African Americans' rights?

SECTION 4 ASSESSMENT

go.hrw.com
Online Quiz
Keyword: SD7 HP16

Reviewing Ideas, Terms, and People

1. **a. Identify** What was the **Sixteenth Amendment**?
   b. Explain What did Progressives like and not like about Taft?
   c. Evaluate Do you think Roosevelt should have run for a third term, run as the Bull Moose candidate, or not run again?

2. **a. Recall** What was the **New Freedom**?
   b. Compare How did the **Clayton Antitrust Act** expand on the Sherman Antitrust Act?
   c. Predict How might the Federal Reserve Act protect the nation in the future?

3. **a. Identify** What was the **Nineteenth Amendment**?
   b. Elaborate How did the tactics of both NAWSA and the NWP succeed?

4. **a. Recall** What was the **Brownsville incident**?
   b. Make Inferences What do you suppose Wilson's reasons were for not supporting an antilynching law?

Critical Thinking

5. **Analyzing Information** Copy the chart below and record examples of the major elements of Wilson's New Freedom.

Wilson's New Freedom		
Tariff reduction	Banking reform	Antitrust legislation

FOCUS ON SPEAKING

6. **Persuasive** In 1913 Congress debated the bill that would become the Underwood Tariff Act. Suppose you are a member of Congress. Write a short speech in which you support or oppose a graduated income tax. Provide specific examples to support your argument.

THE PROGRESSIVES **545**

Section 4 Assessment Answers

1. **a.** placed taxes on individuals' income
   b. Liked—increasing nation's forest reserves, Department of Labor; Disliked—Payne-Aldrich Tariff, Ballinger-Pinchot affair
   c. should have run, Taft did not share his stand on tariffs, environment

2. **a.** reform plan, tariff reductions, banking reform, stronger antitrust laws
   b. prohibited companies from buying stock of competitors to form a monopoly; made strikes, boycotts, picketing legal
   c. might prevent banking collapse

3. **a.** gave women full voting rights
   b. rallied support for women's rights; Nineteenth Amendment passed

4. **a.** African Americans wrongly accused of shooting spree and dishonorably discharged from army
   b. possible answer—state issue

5. Underwood Tariff Act—Federal Reserve Act—Clayton Antitrust Act

6. all citizens should help pay for government; wealthier people should pay more

---

● **Direct Teach** ●

Reading Focus

❹ How did progressivism affect African Americans? *did not benefit much from reforms*

Progressivism and the Rights of African Americans

Recall What was the Brownsville incident? *dishonorable discharge of African American soldiers after they were falsely accused of a shooting spree*

Describe What was President Wilson's record on civil rights? *opposed federal anti-lynching law; renewed segregation in executive offices; passed law prohibiting interracial marriage in Washington, D.C.*

● **Review & Assess** ●

Close

Guide students in a discussion of the problems reformers faced and the achievements they made during the Taft and Wilson administrations.

Review

Online Quiz, Section 4

Daily Test Practice Transparency

Assess

SE Section 4 Assessment

Progress Assessment: Section 4 Quiz

Alternative Assessment Handbook

Reteach

Interactive Reader and Study Guide, Section 4

Interactive Skills Tutor CD-ROM

Answers

Reading Check *possible answer—Roosevelt had a mixed record, Wilson was much worse*

545

Impact of Progressivism

Word Help

commercialism extreme concern with profit

bootblack someone who polishes shoes

compulsory required

Info to Know

Muckraker In John Bunyan's *Pilgrim's Progress*, the "Man with the Muckrake" was offered the crown of heaven in exchange for his muckrake, but he continued to look down and rake the muck. In a 1906 speech, President Theodore Roosevelt compared the journalists who wrote about social problems to the "Man with the Muckrake," both of whom could only look down at the filth beneath them. Journalists took the comparison as a compliment and the term *muckraker* was born.

Impact of Progressivism

Historical Context The documents below provide different types of information about the muckrakers, turn-of-the-century journalists and activists who publicized corruption and urban problems.

Task Examine the documents and answer the questions that follow. Then you will be asked to write an essay about the goals of muckrakers, using facts from the documents and from the chapter to support the position you take in your thesis statement.

DOCUMENT 1

The muckrakers got their nickname from a tool used to scrape up sewage and other unwanted garbage. The cartoon below reflects President Theodore Roosevelt's investigation into unsanitary conditions in meat packing plants. The investigation was sparked by muckraker Upton Sinclair's book *The Jungle*.

A NAUSEATING JOB, BUT IT MUST BE DONE
(President Roosevelt takes hold of the investigating muck-rake himself in the packing-house scandal.)

Collaborative Learning

At Level

Modern Muckrakers

Research Required

Background Muckraking still exists, although today it usually goes by a different name: investigative reporting. Modern television programs routinely feature exposés that would make their muckraking predecessors proud.

1. Divide the class into groups of four or five students. Have each group conduct research into businesses, industries, or institutions that have recently been subjects of investigations.

2. Have each group select one modern muckraking investigation to report on. Then have them write a report using the following questions as a guide: Why was the investigation conducted? What were the findings of the investigation? What, if any, reforms were put into place as a result of the investigation?

3. Have volunteers from each group read their reports to the class. **LS Interpersonal, Verbal-Linguistic**

📋 Alternative Assessment Handbook, Rubric 30: Research

DOCUMENT 2

One leading muckraker was Lincoln Steffens, who wrote several articles on city corruption between 1902 and 1904. He published the collection as a book titled *The Shame of the Cities*. In this introduction to the book, he reflects on the central problem that faced all of the cities he studied.

"[P]olitics is business. That's what's the matter with it . . . But there is hope, not alone despair, in the commercialism of our politics. If our political leaders are to be always a lot of political merchants, they will supply any demand we may create. All we have to do is to establish a steady demand for good government . . . If we would leave parties to the politicians, and would vote not for the party, not even for men, but for the city, and the State, and the nation, we should rule parties, and cities, and States, and nation. If we would vote in mass on the more promising ticket, or, if the two are equally bad, would throw out the party that is in, and wait till the next election and then throw out the other party that is in—then, I say, the commercial politician would feel a demand for good government and he would supply it. That process would take a generation or more to complete, for the politicians now really do not know what good government is. But it has taken as long to develop bad government, and the politicians know what that is. If it would not 'go', they would offer something else, and, if the demand were steady, they, being so commercial, would 'deliver the goods.'"

DOCUMENT 3

Florence Kelley was a social worker and lawyer who published numerous studies on urban problems. The following is from a study she conducted with Alzina P. Stevens on child labor in Chicago. It led to the first Illinois laws limiting work hours for women and children.

"The Ewing Street Italian colony furnishes a large contingent to the army of bootblacks and newsboys; lads who leave home at 2:30 A.M. to secure the first edition of the morning paper, selling each edition as it appears, and filling the intervals with blacking boots and tossing pennies, until, in the winter half of the year, they gather in the Polk Street Night-School, to doze in the warmth, or torture the teacher with the gamin [street kid] tricks acquired by day. For them, school is "a lark," or a peaceful retreat from parental beatings and shrieking juniors at home during the bitter nights of the Chicago winter.

There is no body of self-supporting children more in need of effective care than these newsboys and bootblacks. They are ill-fed, ill-housed, ill-clothed, illiterate, and wholly untrained and unfitted for any occupation. The only useful thing they learn at their work in common with the children who learn in school, is the rapid calculation of small sums in making change; and this does not go far enough to be of any practical value."

Skills FOCUS — READING LIKE A HISTORIAN

1. **a. Describe** Look at the political cartoon in Document 1. Describe what is going on.
   b. Interpret Do you think the artist sees the work of muckrakers as positive or negative? Explain.

2. **a. Compare** Refer to Document 2. To what does Steffens compare politics?
   b. Interpret Steffens blames the public for urban problems. Why?
   c. Evaluate Would Steffens's reform work? Explain.

3. **a. Recall** Refer to Document 3. What kinds of work do the boys do?

b. Analyze Why do you think the boys see no importance in going to school?

4. **Document-Based Essay Question** Consider the question below and form a thesis statement. Using examples from Documents 1, 2, and 3, create an outline and write a short essay supporting your position.
   How did muckrakers change government and society?
   See *Skills Handbook*, p. H28–H29, H31–H33

THE PROGRESSIVES **547**

Differentiating Instruction

Advanced Learners/GATE

1. Divide the class into small groups. Have each group conduct research on modern laws regulating child labor and compulsory education, paying special attention to the laws in your state. Have students use the following questions to guide their research: When were laws regulating child labor and compulsory education first passed in your state? How do the dates of passage compare with the dates of similar laws in other states? How do the laws regarding the minimum number of years

of education vary from state to state? How do laws regarding child labor vary from one state to another?

2. Have each group write a report on their findings.

3. Have students explain how child labor laws and compulsory school attendance work together to protect young people.
   LS Interpersonal, Logical-Mathematical

   Alternative Assessment Handbook, Rubric 30: Research

Visual Summary: The Progressives

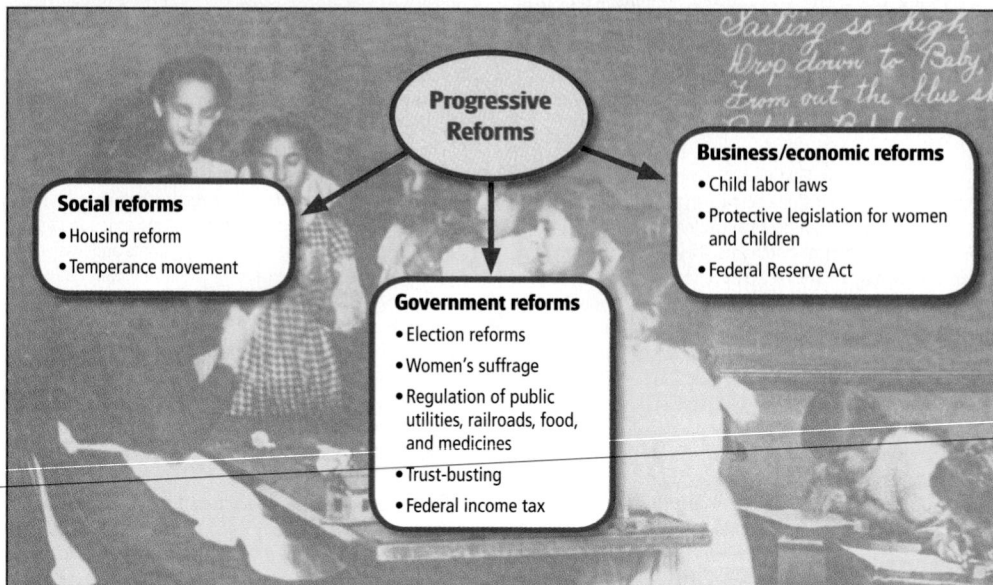

Progressive Reforms

Social reforms
• Housing reform
• Temperance movement

Government reforms
• Election reforms
• Women's suffrage
• Regulation of public utilities, railroads, food, and medicines
• Trust-busting
• Federal income tax

Business/economic reforms
• Child labor laws
• Protective legislation for women and children
• Federal Reserve Act

Reviewing Key Terms and People

Match each lettered definition with the correct numbered item.

a. A law that gave American women the right to vote

b. A reform that gives voters the power to put a proposed law on the ballot for public approval

c. A law that allowed Congress to levy taxes based on an individual's income

d. A law giving voters power to elect senators directly

e. A law that banned the manufacture and sale of alcoholic beverages in the United States

f. A women's organization that fought poverty, segregation, lynchings, and Jim Crow laws

g. Theodore Roosevelt's plan to balance the needs of workers, business, and consumers fairly

h. A law that created a central fund from which banks could borrow to prevent collapse

i. A women's suffrage group that favored a state-by-state approach

1. Eighteenth Amendment
2. Federal Reserve Act
3. initiative
4. National Association of Colored Women
5. National American Woman Suffrage Association
6. Sixteenth Amendment
7. Seventeenth Amendment
8. Nineteenth Amendment
9. Square Deal

Using the Internet

14. **a.** Go to the HRW Web site and enter the keyword shown to access a rubric for this activity.
    b. This keyword can also be used to access an activity in which students create a multimedia presentation about women in college.

KEYWORD: SD7 CH16

History's Impact video program
Review the video to answer the closing question:
What impact have labor laws had on American workers and industries?

Comprehension and Critical Thinking

SECTION 1 *(pp. 522–527)*

12. a. Analyze How did the commission plan make city government more effective?

b. Evaluate Why do you think that the city manager plan of government eventually became more popular than the commission plan?

SECTION 2 *(pp. 529–534)*

13. a. Recall What strategy did major women's suffrage organizations use to campaign for the vote?

b. Draw Conclusions How did the Supreme Court influence the decision to use this strategy?

c. Evaluate What were some possible advantages and disadvantages of adopting this strategy?

SECTION 3 *(pp. 535–540)*

14. a. Define What was the Elkins Act?

b. Analyze Why did the U.S. attorney general sue the Northern Securities Company?

c. Elaborate Why do you think that regulating the railroads was such a high priority for Roosevelt?

SECTION 4 *(pp. 541–545)*

15. a. Identify What were the three main reforms called for in the New Freedom?

b. Make Inferences How did all of those reforms relate to business in the United States?

c. Evaluate Why would the president be so concerned about business practices?

Using the Internet

go.hrw.com
Practice Online
Keyword: SD7 CH16

16. a. Upton Sinclair's novel *The Jungle* had a powerful effect on readers, including President Roosevelt. Using the keyword above, research Roosevelt's reaction to the novel. Then write a paragraph explaining how the novel moved Roosevelt to act.

b. Research a college or university that opened its doors to women in the late 1800s. Then create a multimedia presentation that gives the history of the institution, including why it was founded as well as when and why women were first admitted. What famous alumnae does the college claim? Be sure to include graphics and other key facts in your presentation.

Analyzing Primary Sources

Reading Like a Historian
This political cartoon shows President Theodore Roosevelt's support for William Howard Taft as his successor.

THE GRANGER COLLECTION, NEW YORK

17. Describe What relationship does the cartoon show?

18. Analyze Do you think the cartoonist supports Roosevelt's action?

Critical Reading

Read the passage in Section 4 that begins with the heading "Women Gain the Vote." Then answer the question that follows.

19. How did Alice Paul and Lucy Burns change the American women's suffrage movement?

A Their decision to adopt a state-by-state approach split the main suffrage organization.

B Their support of NAWSA led to success.

C Their use of tactics from the British movement focused new attention on the suffragists' cause.

D Their attention-getting tactics turned supporters away from the women's suffrage movement.

WRITING FOR THE SAT

Think about the following issue:

Roosevelt believed in achieving a balance between conservation and management of the nation's wilderness areas. He thought that some land should be kept in its natural state and some should be used to meet the nation's needs.

20. Assignment Do you agree with Roosevelt's beliefs about the proper use of the nation's wilderness areas? Write a short essay in which you develop your position on this issue. Support your point of view with reasoning and examples from your reading and studies.

Analyzing Primary Sources

15. Taft is portrayed as the successor (prince) while Roosevelt is the king.

16. possible answer—No, the expressions on the characters' faces are false.

Critical Reading

17. C

Writing for the SAT

18. possible answers—yes, humans depend on natural resources for fuel, heat, construction, and food; need to ensure next generation will have resources; proper management of natural resources can fulfill human needs and preserve nature; no, America has abundant resources; conservation not necessary because there will always be more land, animals, and fuel for humans to use

A rubric for this activity is provided in the Chapter Resource File: Writing for the SAT: Consumer Protection: Federal or State?

History's Impact Video Program

They have protected employees from exploitation and helped ensure safety on the job.

Review and Assessment Resources

Review and Reinforce

- CRF: Chapter Review Activity
- Quick Facts Transparencies: Progressive Election Reforms; The Progressives
- Spanish Chapter Summaries Audio CD Program
- Online Chapter Summaries in Spanish
- OSP Holt PuzzlePro; Quiz Show for ExamView
- Quiz Game CD-ROM

Assess

- PASS: Chapter Test, Forms A and B
- Alternative Assessment Handbook
- OSP ExamView Test Generator, Chapter Test
- Differentiated Instruction Modified Worksheets and Tests CD-ROM: Chapter Test
- HOAP Holt Online Assessment Program (in the Premier Online Edition)

Reteach/Intervene

- Interactive Reader and Study Guide
- Differentiated Instruction Teacher Management System: Lesson Plans for Differentiated Instruction
- Differentiated Instruction Modified Worksheets and Tests CD-ROM: Chapter Test
- Interactive Skills Tutor CD-ROM

go.hrw.com
Online Resources
KEYWORD: SD7 CH16

Chapter 17 Planning Guide

Entering the World Stage

Chapter Overview	Reproducible Resources	Technology Resources
CHAPTER 17 pp. 550–579 **Overview:** In this chapter, students will analyze the causes and effects of the United States' transformation into a world power.	**Differentiated Instruction Teacher Management System:*** • Instructional Benchmarking Guides • Lesson Plans for Differentiated Instruction **Interactive Reader and Study Guide:** Chapter Summary* **Chapter Resource File:*** • Focus on Writing Activity: U.S. Imperialism in the Late 1800s and Early 1900s • Social Studies Skills Activity: Evaluating Information on the Internet • Chapter Review Activity **American History Outline Maps** **Pre-AP Activities Guide for American History***	Live Ink® Online Reading Help Student Edition on Audio CD Program Differentiated Instruction Modified Worksheets and Tests CD-ROM Interactive Skills Tutor CD-ROM United States History Primary Source Library CD-ROM Power Presentations with Video CD-ROM History's Impact: American History Video Program (VHS/DVD): Entering the World Stage Online Chapter Summaries in Spanish
Section 1: **The Lure of Imperialism** **The Main Idea:** The United States expanded its power and influence in the Pacific.	**Differentiated Instruction Teacher Management System:** Section 1 Lesson Plan* **Interactive Reader and Study Guide:** Section 1 Summary* **Chapter Resource File:*** • Vocabulary Builder Activity, Section 1	Daily Bellringer Transparency: Section 1* Daily Test Practice Transparency: Section 1*
Section 2: **The Spanish–American War** **The Main Idea:** A quick victory in the Spanish–American War gave the United States a new role as a world power.	**Differentiated Instruction Teacher Management System:** Section 2 Lesson Plan* **Interactive Reader and Study Guide:** Section 2 Summary* **Chapter Resource File:*** • Vocabulary Builder Activity, Section 2	Daily Bellringer Transparency: Section 2* Map Transparency: The Spanish American War, 1898* Daily Test Practice Transparency: Section 2*
Section 3: **Roosevelt and Latin America** **The Main Idea:** The United States exerted influence over Latin America after the Spanish–American War.	**Differentiated Instruction Teacher Management System:** Section 3 Lesson Plan* **Interactive Reader and Study Guide:** Section 3 Summary* **Chapter Resource File:*** • Vocabulary Builder Activity, Section 3	Daily Bellringer Transparency: Section 3* Map Transparency: Imperialism, c. 1900* Daily Test Practice Transparency: Section 3*
Section 4: **Wilson and the Mexican Revolution** **The Main Idea:** American intervention in Mexico's revolution caused strain between the countries.	**Differentiated Instruction Teacher Management System:** Section 4 Lesson Plan* **Interactive Reader and Study Guide:** Section 4 Summary* **Chapter Resource File:*** • Vocabulary Builder Activity, Section 4	Daily Bellringer Transparency: Section 4* Daily Test Practice Transparency: Section 4*

HOLT

History's Impact
American History Video Program (VHS/DVD)
Entering the World Stage

Review, Assessment, Intervention

 Quick Facts Transparencies: Causes of U.S. Expansionism, Entering the World Stage

 Spanish Chapter Summaries Audio CD Program

 Progress Assessment Support System (PASS): Chapter Test*

● **Differentiated Instruction Modified Worksheets and Tests CD-ROM:** Modified Chapter Test

OSP **One-Stop Planner CD-ROM:** ExamView Test Generator (English/Spanish)

HOAP **Holt Online Assessment Program (HOAP),** in the Holt Premier Online Student Edition

---

 PASS: Section 1 Quiz*

 Online Quiz: Section 1

 Alternative Assessment Handbook

 PASS: Section 2 Quiz*

 Online Quiz: Section 2

 Alternative Assessment Handbook

 PASS: Section 3 Quiz*

Online Quiz: Section 3

 Alternative Assessment Handbook

 PASS: Section 4 Quiz*

Online Quiz: Section 4

Alternative Assessment Handbook

RESOURCES

The following resources were developed to help North Carolina educators teach the standards and objectives of North Carolina's eleventh grade standard course of study in United States history.

- United States history EOC Test Prep Workbook
- Teacher's Support System
- North Carolina One-Stop Planner

And be sure to direct your students to **go.hrw.com** for online access to the EOC Test Prep Workbook.

go.hrw.com
EOC Test Prep
KEYWORD: SE7 NC

Holt Online Learning

go.hrw.com
Teacher Resources
KEYWORD: SD7 TEACHER

go.hrw.com
Student Resources
KEYWORD: SD7 CH17

- Document-based Questions
- Interactive Multimedia Activities

- Current Events
- Chapter-based Internet Activities
- and more!

Holt Premier
Online Student Edition
Complete online support for interactivity, assessment, and reporting

- Interactive Maps and Notebook
- Standardized Test Prep
- Homework Practice and Research Activities Online

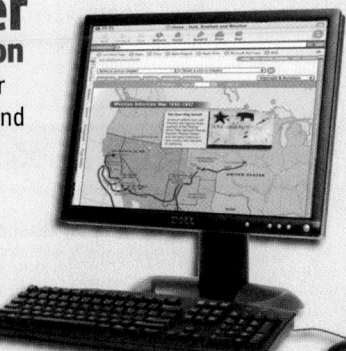

CHAPTER 17 PLANNING GUIDE

The Big Picture

Jesús F. de la Teja

The Second Age of Empire In *The Wealth of Nations* (1776), Adam Smith critiqued mercantilism and, consequently, the type of imperial system practiced by Britain, Spain, and France up to that time. Yet colonies were still useful when they could supply the raw materials or other strategic resources that would allow the mother country to better compete on the world economic stage. And so, in the late nineteenth century, as the United States watched Britain, France, Germany, Belgium, and the Netherlands scramble for such colonies, it too felt compelled to enter the game.

Uneasy Imperialists Throughout the nineteenth century the United States had been growing into its role as an imperialist power. In the Monroe Doctrine it had staked out a sphere of influence; in the Mexican War it had acquired territory from another country through military means. The purchase of Alaska and growing influence in Hawaii saw the United States expanding its interests globally. Although many Americans felt uneasy about incorporating non-European peoples into the American orbit, and others were uncomfortable with the United States ruling territories that would never become states, American industrialists demanded a global U.S. presence, and the government proved more than willing to comply.

The Mexican Revolution in the U.S. For the United States, Mexico posed a greater challenge than Cuba, Puerto Rico, or the Philippines. American investment in Mexico in the last third of the nineteenth century linked the two economies. Mexican timber and ores traveled north, while American manufactured goods traveled south. In the years just before the revolution American petroleum companies acquired important stakes in Mexican oil fields. Additionally, Mexican labor was indispensable to the development of the American West. Strong as the United States was, Pancho Villa's successful evasion of General Pershing and the need to shift resources to the war in Europe showed the limits to American power.

Recent Scholarship

The Spanish American War *The War of 1898: The United States and Cuba in History and Historiography* (1998), by Louis A. Pérez Jr., is a revisionist look at the war that launched the United States as a world power seen through the narrow perspective of the Cuban campaign. Pérez argues that the traditional American historical perspective on causes and outcomes of the war inadequately explains what happened, dependent as it is almost exclusively on U.S. and European sources. Controversial for a harsh assessment of the McKinley administration and for the American usurpation of what was about to become a Cuban victory, Pérez's sophisticated arguments deserve serious attention.

Differentiating Instruction

 Differentiated Instruction Teacher Management System
- Lesson Plans for Differentiated Instruction
- Differentiated Instructional Benchmarking Guides
- Interactive Reader and Study Guide

 Spanish Chapter Summaries Audio CD Program

 Online Chapter Summaries in Spanish

 Student Edition on Audio CD Program

 Differentiated Instruction Modified Worksheets and Tests CD-ROM
- Vocabulary Flash Cards
- Modified Vocabulary Builder Activities
- Modified Chapter Review Activity
- Modified Chapter Test

OSP One-Stop Planner CD-ROM
- ExamView Test Generator (English and Spanish)
- PuzzlePro
- Quiz Show for ExamView
- Transparencies and Videos

TE Differentiated Activities in the Teacher's Edition
- Taking Hawaii, p. 554
- China: An Economic Giant, p. 556
- Cuban Revolt, p. 559
- Land and Sea Battles in Cuba, p. 562
- The Panama Canal, p. 567
- Drawing the Lock System, p. 571

Reading Like a Historian
Sam Wineburg

Emphasis

Many students don't see their textbook as offering one of several possible versions of the past, but 'the' version. As Derek, a student I once interviewed, explained, the textbook offers "straight information, just saying what happened." To Derek, finding out "what happened" requires no more effort than looking up something in the phonebook.

Becoming a Reading Detective

It isn't so easy to help Derek and countless others like him to become critical readers. Although professional historical writing openly displays the seams of interpretation—footnoted references to the documentary record—textbooks hide them. But if we look closely, we can still find these seams. To do so, however, students must become reading detectives, paying as much attention to the words of their history books as they would to a poem in Language Arts class. For many students, this will be a different kind of reading from what they're used to.

Consider our chapter's description of the war in Cuba. Beginning on page 561, seven paragraphs describe the defeat of Spanish forces in Cuba (eight if we include "History's Voices"). Overall, the names Teddy Roosevelt and the Rough Riders appear nine times. On the other hand, the African American "Buffalo Soldiers" are mentioned only twice. Most textbooks place a similar emphasis on Roosevelt and the Rough Riders when describing the Battle of San Juan Hill, mentioning the Buffalo Soldiers only in passing. But a clue awaits the reading detective in our two mentions.

Look carefully at the sentence in which the Buffalo Soldiers first appear. They "led the charge," we are told, "supported by the Rough Riders." This sentence conjures up a picture in which the Buffalo Soldiers are at the center, and somewhere alongside them in a secondary or subsidiary role are the Rough Riders.

And then the chapter goes on to reveal an intriguing fact that most textbooks omit. When medals were awarded for this battle, the Buffalo Soldiers earned three times as many Medals of Honor as Roosevelt's group of celebrities, socialites, and journalists.

Emphasis and Interpretation

This fact should give us pause. Not even forty years since the end of slavery, this was a time when deep-seated prejudice against blacks was a regular feature of white society, and the officers handing out these medals were all white. To overcome the strikes against them, these Buffalo Soldiers must have done something absolutely extraordinary that day on San Juan Hill.

This was exactly the conclusion of their white commander, John J. Pershing, the same Pershing who later led the American Expeditionary Force in World War I. As for Roosevelt, Pershing's assessment was less enthusiastic. To Pershing, Roosevelt and his pampered group of celebrities (Roosevelt's khaki uniform had been tailored at Brooks Brothers) were what we might call today a hyped-up media event.

While Pershing would have heartily concurred with our description of the Buffalo Soldiers leading the charge, if he had written our textbook he doubtless would have inverted the emphasis, mentioning the Buffalo Soldiers more than the Rough Riders and substituting his own words for Roosevelt's in "History's Voices." For him—as well as the commanders who awarded medals—it was the courageous black units of the Ninth and Tenth Cavalries who should have been given the most credit. In this version of the past, different aspects are given emphasis. It is the Buffalo Soldiers who appear in the center of the picture, with the Rough Riders relegated to the periphery.

Social Studies Competency Goals
Goal 6 The learner will analyze causes and effects of the United States emergence as a world power.
🔲 6.01, 6.02, 6.03

The Big Idea and Essential Questions

To foster student understanding of this chapter's big idea, design your lesson to address each section's essential question.

Big Idea The global competition for empire at the end of the 1800s resulted in the emergence of the United States as a world power.

Essential Questions

1. How did the United States gain power and influence in the Pacific region?

2. How did the Spanish-American War change the role of the United States in the world?

3. How did the United States begin to exert its influence over Latin America?

4. Why did the United States intervene in the Mexican Revolution?

Key to Differentiating Instruction

Below Level

Basic-level activities designed for all students encountering new material

At Level

Intermediate-level activities designed for average students

Above Level

Challenging activities designed for honors and gifted-and-talented students

Standard English Mastery

Activities designed to improve standard English usage

550 CHAPTER 17

CHAPTER 17
1898–1917

Entering the WORLD STAGE

THE BIG PICTURE At the end of the nineteenth century, global competition for empire led the United States into war against Spain and into military conflicts in Mexico. The United States had forged a new role as a world power.

NC North Carolina Standards

Social Studies Objectives

6.01 Examine the factors that led to the United States taking an increasingly active role in world affairs.

6.02 Identify the areas of United States military, economic, and political involvement and influence.

6.03 Describe how the policies and actions of the United States government impacted the affairs of other countries.

Language Arts Objectives

3.01 Use language persuasively in addressing a particular issue by:
- establishing and defending a point of view.

3.03 Use argumentation for:
- establishing and defending a point of view.

Skills Focus **READING LIKE A HISTORIAN**

In the Battle of San Juan Hill, future president Theodore Roosevelt leads a band of rough-and-ready volunteers in a famous charge in a war against Spain.
Interpreting Visuals What kind of leader does this painting suggest Roosevelt was? What kind of president do you think he would make?

See Skills Handbook, p. H30

550

U.S. **February 1898**
USS Maine explodes in Havana Harbor, triggering the Spanish-American War.

1900

World **1900** Radicals in China stage the Boxer Rebellion to drive away foreigners.

Introduce the Chapter

At Level

The United States Enters the World Stage

1. For some nations, the 1800s was a time of empire building. The U.S. decided that it too needed to look beyond its shores for new territories and markets for its goods.

2. Have students develop a list of the potential benefits for the U.S. if it changed its foreign policy to one of expansion. Then have students develop a list of reasons why the U.S. should steer clear of foreign entanglements and concentrate on development within its existing borders.

3. Create a class list of the benefits of expansion and reasons not to expand for students to see; use it as a basis for discussion about expansion and imperialism.

4. Tell students that in this chapter they will learn how the United States came to control Hawaii, other islands in the Pacific, and the Panama Canal. **LS Verbal-Linguistic**

📝 Alternative Assessment Handbook, Rubric 11: Discussions

550 CHAPTER 17

History's Impact video program
Watch the video to understand the impact of the Panama Canal.

1904
The United States begins construction of the Panama Canal.

1903
Panama declares independence from Colombia.

1905
Japan wins the Russo-Japanese War.

1911
President Taft promotes "dollar diplomacy."

1910
The Mexican Revolution begins.

April 1914
U.S. troops intervene in the Mexican Revolution, occupying Veracruz, Mexico.

August 1914
Panama Canal opens.

1917
Russian Revolution begins.

1903 · 1906 · 1909 · 1912 · 1915 · 1918

551

HOLT

History's Impact

▶ **Video Program: Entering the World Stage**
See the Video Teacher's Guide for strategies for using the video segment.

Reading Like a Historian

The Rough Riders The Rough Riders, led by Theodore Roosevelt, were critical to U.S. success in the Spanish-American War in Cuba. Tell students that as they read this chapter they will learn more about the Rough Riders, what made them unusual, and how their efforts led to victory at the Battle of San Juan Hill.

Interpreting Visuals Have students explain how the artist shows courage and leadership, as well as the horrors of war in this image. *Men are advancing through fire, moving up the hill. Some soldiers have been killed.*

Explore the Time Line

1. When did the U.S. begin building the Panama Canal? *1904*

2. When did the Mexican Revolution begin and when did the United States become involved? *1910; 1914*

3. Why did a group of radicals in China stage the Boxer Rebellion? *to drive away foreigners*

Info to Know

The Great White Fleet At the end of the Russo-Japanese War, western nations began to fear the growing power of Japan. President Theodore Roosevelt wanted to send the U.S. Navy, nicknamed the Great White Fleet, on a worldwide tour as a display of American strength. Congress refused to approve funding for the voyage, but Roosevelt ordered the fleet to set sail anyway. Congress later authorized the funding.

Answers

Reading Like a Historian
(p. 550) *an energetic, courageous, involved one; possible answer—one who is not afraid to lead in difficult times*

Bellringer

The Inside Story. . . Use the **Daily Bellringer Transparency** to help students answer the question.

📽 Daily Bellringer Transparency, Section 1

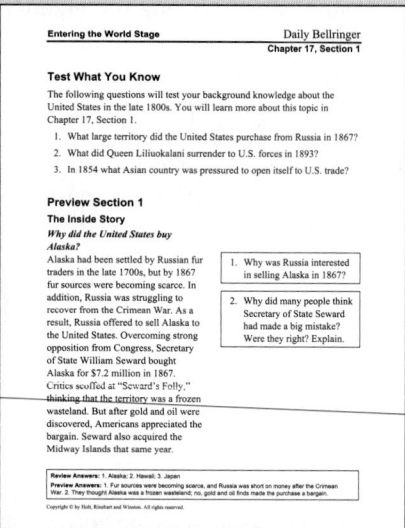

Academic Vocabulary

Review with students the high-use academic term in this section.

ideology set of ideas about human life or culture (p. 553)

📄 CRF: Vocabulary Builder Activity, Section 1

Taking Notes

restricted king's power; deprived most Hawaiians of the vote; gave Pearl Harbor to the United States; allowed sugar planters political control over Hawaii

---

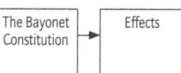

SECTION 1 — The Lure of Imperialism

BEFORE YOU READ

MAIN IDEA
The United States entered the imperialist competition late, but it soon extended its power and influence in the Pacific region.

READING FOCUS
1. What inspired the imperialist activity of the late 1800s?
2. How did the United States take control of Hawaii?
3. How did the United States gain influence in China?
4. How did the United States exert influence in Japan?

KEY TERMS AND PEOPLE
imperialism
bayonet constitution
Liliuokalani
Sanford B. Dole
sphere of influence
Open Door Policy
Boxer Rebellion
Russo-Japanese War

TAKING NOTES   As you read, take notes on the effects of the bayonet constitution in Hawaii. Record your notes in a graphic organizer like the one shown here.

The Bayonet Constitution → Effects

The FRUITS of Imperialism

▲ Uncle Sam did not have to look far to pluck new territories. This political cartoon suggests that the nation continued to eye neighboring countries.

THE INSIDE STORY

Why did the United States buy Alaska? In the 1890s the United States seemed to be off to a late start in the scramble for colonial possessions. European nations were already busily adding new colonies to their empires. The United States, though, had actually taken its first step toward imperialism back in 1867. While European nations were looking toward Africa and Asia, the United States was expanding in North America and the Pacific.

The huge Alaska landmass lies at the northwestern edge of North America, almost touching northeastern Russia. Russian fur traders were the first foreigners to settle there, in 1784. With a charter from Czar Paul I, the Russian-American Company served as Alaska's government after 1799. Russian, British, and American fur traders all competed amicably. But by 1867, sea otters, which had the most valuable fur, were becoming scarce. In addition, Russia was struggling to recover from the Crimean War. Russia offered to sell the territory to the United States.

At the time, William H. Seward was secretary of state for President Andrew Johnson. He had visions of an American empire and was eager to buy Alaska. He thought it had potential as a resource for fur, timber, and metals. He faced opposition from Congress, though. Unaware of Alaska's rich mineral resources, many people regarded the territory as a frozen wasteland.

Seward finally succeeded in buying Alaska for $7.2 million. Critics joked about Seward's Folly and Seward's Icebox. Later, though, after gold and oil were discovered in Alaska, Americans came to appreciate the bargain they'd gotten.

Alaska was not Seward's only smart acquisition. The very same year—1867—he snapped up the Midway Islands, strategically located west of Hawaii. ◼

Teach the Main Idea   At Level

Imperialist Activity

1. **Teach** Ask students the Reading Focus questions to teach this section.

2. **Apply** Draw four rectangles for students to see. Label the rectangles with the main topics of this section: Imperialist Activity; Taking Control of Hawaii; Influence in China; and Influence in Japan. Guide students in a discussion of the four topics. As students name the main points in each topic, record them in the rectangles. Have students copy the completed graphic organizer.

3. **Review** Have students identify one significant issue under each heading and explain how it relates to imperialism.

4. **Practice/Homework** Have students write a balanced essay about the growing strength of the United States in the early 1900s.
   LS Verbal-Linguistic

📄 Alternative Assessment Handbook, Rubric 37: Writing Assignments

📽 Graphic Organizer Transparencies

Imperialist Activity

From the 1870s to the 1910s, a few industrialized nations actively competed for territory in Africa, Asia, and Latin America. This scramble for territorial control was part of the imperialist mind-set. **Imperialism** involves the extension of a nation's power over other lands.

By the late 1800s, nations such as Great Britain, France, Belgium, Germany, and Japan had all embraced the imperialist spirit. Soon, beginning in Hawaii, the United States would also pursue imperialist policies. What led to this quest for empire?

Economic interests The Industrial Revolution had brought great prosperity to the Western powers. Industrialized nations had flooded their own countries with goods and investment capital. Now they looked to other nations for new customers and new places to invest. Industrialists also began to look to Africa, Asia, and Latin America for new sources of raw materials for their factories.

Military needs Industrialized nations created strong navies to defend their shores and protect their trading interests. But navies needed bases where ships could refuel and make repairs. Industrialized nations sought foreign territory so they could build these coaling stations in strategic places.

Ideology Two popular ideologies also contributed to imperialism. One was a strong sense of nationalism, or love of one's country. Many people felt that territorial conquests enhanced a nation's power and prestige.

The other ideological motive was a feeling of cultural superiority. Because Africa, Asia, and Latin America had less industry and urban development, they seemed "backward" to many Europeans and Americans in the late 1800s.

Social Darwinism fed into this view. Social Darwinists believed that when nations competed against one another, only the fittest would survive. Some people therefore considered it a social responsibility to "civilize" the inhabitants of less developed countries and spread the benefits of Western society. In addition, Protestant Christian missionaries felt they had a moral duty to convert others to their beliefs.

The scramble for territory By the late 1800s, European imperial powers had taken control of vast territories in Africa and Asia, and dominated the economy of Latin America. The British Empire alone ruled about one-quarter of the world's land and population. France, Belgium, Germany, and Japan also controlled huge areas overseas.

Many Americans began to believe it was time for the United States to claim its own territories abroad. The prospect of new markets and military advantages was a powerful attraction. Some Americans, too, wanted to spread the Christian faith and democratic values. Josiah Strong, a Protestant clergyman, expressed this viewpoint eloquently.

HISTORY'S VOICES

❝The two great needs of mankind . . . are, first, a pure, spiritual Christianity, and second, civil liberty. Without controversy, these are the forces which, in the past, have contributed most to the elevation of the human race . . . It follows, then, that the Anglo-Saxon [person of British descent], as the great representative of these two ideas . . . is divinely commissioned to be, in a peculiar sense, his brother's keeper.❞

—Josiah Strong, *Our Country*, 1885

In the mid-1800s, Americans had believed it was their manifest destiny to expand westward to the Pacific Ocean. Now people sought to move even beyond the shoreline, to claim distant islands farther west.

READING CHECK **Summarizing** What were the three main reasons that industrialized nations became imperialist nations?

ACADEMIC VOCABULARY
ideology set of ideas about human life or culture

CAUSES OF U.S. EXPANSIONISM
QUICK FACTS

CAUSES

- **Economic** Desire for new markets and raw materials
- **Military** Desire for naval bases and coaling stations
- **Ideological** Desire to bring Christianity, western-style culture, and democracy to other peoples

United States expansionism

Skills Focus: Making Inferences

At Level

Reading Skill
The Lure of Imperialism

1. Guide students in a discussion about the causes and effects of imperialism.

2. Make a list of the student responses for all to see, and have students copy the information.

3. Have students write a speech from the viewpoint of a 19th century U.S. senator expressing the opinion that the United States should become an imperialistic world power. Have students use the four reasons for expansion to support their position.

4. Have volunteers read the speeches to the class.

5. As an extension, have students prepare a speech expressing the opposite view, and organize a class debate on the issue: Should the United States become an imperial power?
LS Interpersonal, Kinesthetic

Alternative Assessment Handbook, Rubric 24: Oral Presentations

---

553

Reading Focus

② How did the United States take control of Hawaii? *took over land and economy; bayonet constitution; forced queen to surrender; annexed the territory*

Taking Control of Hawaii

Explain Why was Hawaii an ideal acquisition for the United States? *good place for coaling stations and naval bases; profitable sugar industry*

Make Inferences In what ways did Captain James Cook's visit to Hawaii have both good and bad results? *good—imperialist nations learned about a valuable Pacific port; bad—Hawaiians faced the spread of disease and a serious threat to their independence*

📋 CRF: Primary Source Activity: William Jennings Bryan on Imperialism

📋 Political Cartoons Activities for American History: Cartoon 34: U.S. Imperialism

Info to Know

Captain James Cook Captain James Cook was one of the first sea captains who insisted on a proper diet for his sailors so that they avoided scurvy, the disease that results from a deficiency of Vitamin C. Sailors under Cook's command ate vegetables, sauerkraut, and a type of orange extract, which helped prevent the disease while the men were at sea.

go.hrw.com
Online Resources

KEYWORD: SD7 CH17
TOPIC: IMPERIALISM

Taking Control of Hawaii

American expansionists became interested in acquiring Hawaii in the late 1800s. Located some 2,000 miles west of California, Hawaii was an ideal spot for coaling stations and naval bases for ships traveling to and from Asia.

Early contact Americans were not the first outsiders to show interest in Hawaii. A British explorer, Captain James Cook, had visited the islands in 1778. Great Britain did not claim Hawaii then, but Captain Cook's voyage brought Hawaii to the attention of the outside world.

Shortly after Cook's arrival, Hawaii's Chief Kamehameha (kah-MAY-hah-MAY-hah) united the eight major islands under his leadership. He established a monarchy and began a profitable trade in sandalwood. In the 1820s U.S. ships began arriving with some frequency, bringing traders and missionaries. Many of the missionaries had come from New England to convert Hawaiians to Christianity. Soon, the missionaries and their families began to settle down and raise crops, particularly sugarcane.

The foreigners also brought diseases, to which Hawaiians had no immunity. The population of Hawaii declined from about 300,000 in the 1770s to about 40,000 by 1893.

Sugar interests gain power As more and more Americans came to the islands, investors in the sugar industry began increasing their control. Americans had a sweet tooth, and sugar planters grew very rich. To keep the sugarcane plantations running, planters needed workers. With so few native Hawaiians left, planters brought in workers from China, Japan, and the Philippines.

Kalakaua became king in 1874. By this time, Americans had gained control over Hawaii's land and economy. But Kalakaua was strongly nationalistic. He resented the Americans' influence over his government and promised to put native Hawaiians back into power.

HISTORY'S VOICES

❝Do not be led by the foreigners; they had no part in our hardships, in gaining the country. Do not be led by their false teachings.❞

—Kalakaua, "Proclamation," 1872

Early in his reign, King Kalakaua allied himself with landowners in his desire to strengthen the Hawaiian economy. He negotiated a treaty in 1875 that allowed Hawaiian sugar to enter the United States tax free. This

Pineapple Industry
James Dole, Sanford Dole's cousin, began growing pineapples in Hawaii in 1901. By the 1930s Dole supplied 90 percent of the world's canned pineapple.

554

HAWAIIAN PINEAPPLE

Differentiating Instruction

Below Level

English-Language Learners

Standard English Mastery

1. Have students review the information in the text about how and why the United States decided to annex Hawaii.

2. Have students create a time line showing the steps to annexation, beginning with Cook's visit to the islands in 1778 and ending with U.S. annexation.

3. Have students illustrate their time lines with visuals that represent each event.

4. Have students present and explain their time lines to the class. Have students correct their work and retain the time lines as a study tool. Finally, have students write a brief summary of the U.S. takeover of Hawaii. **LS** **Visual-Spatial, Verbal-Linguistic**

📋 Alternative Assessment Handbook, Rubrics 36: Time Lines; and 40: Writing to Describe

made Hawaiian sugar cheaper than sugar from other places. The treaty gave a real boost to the Hawaiian sugar industry. But the more money that the sugar tycoons made, the more power they wanted over Hawaiian affairs.

Plotting against the king A group of American business leaders, planters, and traders formed a secret society called the Hawaiian League. Its purpose was to overthrow the monarchy and establish a democracy in Hawaii under the control of Americans.

Conflicts between these American business leaders and the king escalated in 1886. The United States wanted the port of Pearl Harbor in exchange for renewing the sugar treaty. But King Kalakaua refused to give up the independence of any part of Hawaii.

Angered, the Hawaiian League forced King Kalakaua to sign a new constitution at gunpoint in July 1887. The king angrily called it the **bayonet constitution**. It severely restricted his power and deprived most Hawaiians of the vote. King Kalakaua was now forced to give Pearl Harbor to the United States. This gave U.S. warships a permanent port in Hawaii.

American sugar planters now had political control over Hawaii. But the economy suffered a heavy blow in 1890. The United States revoked the sugar treaty in order to support sugar producers on the U.S. mainland. American sugar producers in Hawaii believed they had only one option to protect their businesses—become part of the United States. Secretly, they began talks with U.S. officials about annexation.

End of the monarchy When King Kalakaua died in 1891, his sister **Liliuokalani** (LI-lee-uh-woh-kuh-LAHN-ee) became queen. Queen Liliuokalani was a Hawaiian nationalist who wanted to do away with the bayonet constitution. In January 1893, she announced her plan to restore the power of the Hawaiian monarchy. In response, members of the business community plotted to overthrow her. They wanted the islands to be governed as a territory of the United States.

John L. Stevens, the American minister to Hawaii, decided he would help the rebel sugar planters. Without authorization, he ordered four boatloads of U.S. Marines to go ashore. They took up positions around the royal palace, aiming machine guns and cannons at the

building. The rebels then declared an end to the monarchy. Queen Liliuokalani surrendered under protest on January 17, 1893.

The rebel leaders quickly formed a new regime with **Sanford B. Dole**, a sugar tycoon, as president. John L. Stevens, acting on his own once again, formally recognized the new Republic of Hawaii. He also proclaimed Hawaii to be under U.S. protection, while the Senate considered a treaty to annex the islands.

Annexation Troubled by the events in Hawaii, President Grover Cleveland put the treaty on hold and ordered an investigation. The investigator's report condemned the revolt against Liliuokalani and proposed restoring her to the throne. Cleveland agreed, but Dole refused to step down.

Cleveland was unwilling to use military force to back Liliuokalani. Yet he would not support annexation, either. The matter remained at a standstill until the next president, William McKinley, took office. McKinley favored annexation, and Congress narrowly voted its approval in 1898. Hawaii became an American territory and eventually—in 1959—the fiftieth state. In 1993 Congress apologized for the U.S. role in overthowing Liliuokalani.

READING CHECK **Sequencing** How did American sugar interests gain so much power in Hawaii?

FACES OF HISTORY

Queen LILIUOKALANI
1838–1917

Born into a royal Hawaiian family, Lydia Liliuokalani grew up proud of her heritage. Although she studied with foreign missionaries, learned to speak English, and married the son of a Boston sea captain, she did not want Hawaii to become part of the United States.

After ascending to the throne in 1891, Liliuokalani tried to fortify the islands through a political movement called Oni Pa'a (Stand Firm). Nonetheless, she was soon overthrown by American business owners. Accused of attempting to revolt against the new government, Liliuokalani was arrested in 1895 and jailed for more than a year. After being released, the queen continued to live quietly in Hawaii, a beloved figure to her people.

Make Inferences What can you infer about the goals of Queen Liliuokalani's Oni Pa'a movement?

Skills Focus: Comparing and Contrasting   [At Level]

Reading Skill
End of the Monarchy

1. Guide students in a discussion of the monarchy of Queen Liliuokolani. Remind students that she had a loyal following of Hawaiians who supported her and the monarchy. Then review the establishment of the Republic of Hawaii with Sanford Dole as its president. Finally review the sentiments of President Grover Cleveland, President William McKinley, and Congress toward annexation.

2. Have students create a series of political cartoons, one that supports the Hawaiian monarchy; one that shows Liliuokalani's imprisonment; one that shows support for Dole's presidency, and one that shows support for U.S. annexation of Hawaii.

3. Have volunteers display and explain their cartoons to the class. **LS** **Visual-Spatial**

   Alternative Assessment Handbook, Rubric 27: Political Cartoons

555

❸ How did the United States gain influence in China? *proposed Open Door Policy; sent in troops to put down the Boxer Rebellion; forced China to sign a settlement agreement*

Influence in China

Describe How did the Boxer Rebellion ultimately help the United States? *increased support for Open Door Policy*

Identify Cause and Effect What motivated the Boxers to attack foreigners in Beijing? *resentment and anger over foreign influences; desire to push foreigners out*

Evaluate What effect did the Open Door Policy have on China? *possible answers—allowed foreigners to have great influence over economy, exploit the country's resources; allowed missionaries to work*

THE BOXER REBELLION

Skills FOCUS READING LIKE A HISTORIAN

Chinese forces take European enemy generals prisoner in this Chinese print of the Boxer Rebellion.
Interpreting Visuals How are the foreigners depicted in the image?

Influence in China

Early on, Hawaii had attracted American interest because it was a convenient place to stop for fuel and supplies on the journey to China. American traders had been traveling to China since 1784.

Even so, China stayed nearly isolated from the rest of the world. It strictly controlled foreign trade, allowing foreigners only in the port of Guangzhou. Then in 1842, the British forced China to open five ports to British trade. Two years later, the United States received broader trading privileges as well. For the next 50 years, China's rulers struggled to keep foreign interests from overrunning the country.

The threat was not just from Western nations, however. In 1895 Japan took over the island of Taiwan and tried to seize the Liaotung Peninsula too. European powers—Russia, France, Germany, and Great Britain—quickly carved out their own **spheres of influence** in China. A sphere of influence is a geographic area where an outside nation exerts special economic or political control.

The United States was too late to secure a sphere of influence in China. American leaders feared that the United States would be shut out of the valuable China trade. As a result, Secretary of State John Hay proposed the **Open Door Policy** in 1899. The aim was to give all nations equal trading rights in China. As Senator Henry Cabot Lodge of Massachusetts declared, "We ask no favors; we only ask that we shall be admitted to that great market upon the same terms with the rest of the world."

Hay sent notes recommending the Open Door Policy to Great Britain, Germany, Russia, Japan, France, and Italy. None of them agreed to it, but none rejected it outright. Therefore, Hay felt he could announce in March 1900 that the Open Door Policy had been approved.

With foreign countries now vying for business in China, antiforeigner sentiments grew. A secret group called the Society of Righteous and Harmonious Fists—known to westerners as Boxers—began attacking foreign missionaries and Chinese Christians. In June 1900 the Boxers laid siege to the capital city of Beijing in what became known as the **Boxer Rebellion**.

Western nations rushed 20,000 troops—including 2,000 Americans—to China. They soon quelled the rebellion, and a year later, in September 1901, China signed a humbling settlement agreement.

The Boxer Rebellion increased support for Hay's Open Door Policy. Western nations realized that competition among themselves would hurt their ability to exploit the China trade.

READING CHECK **Identifying Problem and Solution** Why did Hay propose the Open Door Policy?

Differentiating Instruction

Above Level

Advanced Learners/GATE

Research Required

1. Guide students in a discussion of China's economic importance in the late 1800s and review reasons why foreign nations wanted to trade with and have access to China's ports.

2. Have students use the Internet, newspapers, or magazines to examine current economic and trade relations between the United States and China. Have students use their research to write an essay analyzing trade relations between the two countries. Students should discuss types of goods traded and the balance of trade, as well

as problems, and how they are being resolved. Students should include charts and graphs to support their findings and conclusions. Reports must also include a bibliography.

3. Have volunteers share their reports with the class. Finish the activity with a discussion of the importance of China as a world economic power. **LS Verbal-Linguistic, Logical-Mathematical**

📃 Alternative Assessment Handbook, Rubric 38: Writing to Classify

Answers

Reading Like a Historian *as subservient*

Reading Check *The United States was too late to secure a sphere of influence in China, and American leaders feared they would not be able to take part in trade with China.*

Influence in Japan

Until Japan seized Taiwan from China in 1895, no one would have thought of the Japanese as imperialists. Since the late 1630s, the country had been inward-looking, shutting itself off from nearly all foreign contact.

By the mid-1800s, though, Japan had come under U.S. pressure to open its ports to trade. In 1853 President Millard Fillmore sent Commodore Matthew Perry with a fleet of four ships into Edo (Tokyo) Bay. Japan was not yet industrialized, and Japanese people had never seen steamships before. They were awed by the demonstration of American naval strength.

The Japanese government knew that it could not defend itself against a modern navy. It also realized that it could no longer maintain its isolated position in the world. So in 1854 its leaders agreed to a treaty that opened Japan to trade with the United States.

Japan then embarked on a program of rapid modernization. It transformed itself into an industrial power and built a strong military. After taking over Taiwan, Japan began eyeing Korea and the Chinese province of Manchuria. Russia, meanwhile, also wanted these lands.

In 1904 the **Russo-Japanese War** broke out. The conflict took a toll on both sides, and by the following spring, both sides had had enough.

At Japan's request, President Theodore Roosevelt helped negotiate a peace treaty. He met with representatives of the two countries in Portsmouth, New Hampshire, and hammered out a compromise. Roosevelt received the Nobel Prize for Peace for his efforts in negotiating the Treaty of Portsmouth.

Japan was the clear victor in the war with Russia, and it emerged as a major power. It was now the strongest power in East Asia and a rival to the United States for influence in China and the Pacific region. American leaders knew that Japan remained hungry for territory. It had fewer natural resources than the other imperialist nations. In addition, the Japanese government wanted to expand territorially in order to counterbalance U.S. expansion in the Pacific.

Roosevelt decided to impress upon Japan—and the rest of the world—just how powerful the U.S. military was. In 1907 he sent four squadrons of battleships, known as the Great White Fleet, on a 43,000-mile, around-the-world journey. Led by Rear Admiral Charles Sperry, the fleet stopped at 20 ports on six continents, including a port in Japan, before returning home in 1909.

READING CHECK **Identifying the Main Idea** How did the United States influence Japan's economic policies and its imperialist ambitions?

SECTION 1 ASSESSMENT

go.hrw.com
Online Quiz
Keyword: SD7 HP17

Reviewing Ideas, Terms, and People

1. **a. Define** What is **imperialism**?
   b. Summarize What were the main incentives for countries to seek new territories?
   c. Evaluate Do you think imperialists who wanted to spread western culture were arrogant or well meaning? Explain.

2. **a. Recall** Why did its location make Hawaii attractive to Americans?
   b. Draw Conclusions What role did sugar play in the desire of many Americans to control Hawaii?
   c. Elaborate How did American sugar planters go outside the law to gain control over Hawaii?

3. **a. Describe** What was the **Open Door Policy**?
   b. Explain Why did Americans think they might be at a disadvantage in trading with China?
   c. Predict What would have been the likely consequences for the United States if other western powers had divided China into colonies instead of accepting the Open Door Policy?

4. **a. Identify** Who was Commodore Perry?
   b. Analyze Why did the United States want to impress Japan in particular with the Great White Fleet?

Critical Thinking

5. **Identifying Cause and Effect** Copy the chart below and record the effects of key events in Hawaii's history.

Event	Effect

FOCUS ON WRITING

6. **Expository** Write an essay about the different perspectives that a Chinese native and a Christian missionary might have had on the Boxer Rebellion. Explain how each might have viewed the Boxers' goals and their means of achieving them.

ENTERING THE WORLD STAGE **557**

Direct Teach

Reading Focus

❹ How did the United States exert influence in Japan? *by displaying military might; negotiating treaty to end Russo-Japanese War*

Influence in Japan

Explain Why did the Russo-Japanese War begin? *Both Japan and Russia wanted Korea and Manchuria.*

Analyze How did Japan become a world power? *opened itself to foreigners; modernized; built military and industry*

Review & Assess

Close

Guide students in a discussion of the circumstances that led to U.S. intervention into the internal affairs of Hawaii, China, and Japan.

Review

Online Quiz, Section 1

Daily Test Practice Transparency

Assess

SE Section 1 Assessment

Progress Assessment: Section 1 Quiz

Alternative Assessment Handbook

Reteach

Interactive Reader and Study Guide, Section 1

Interactive Skills Tutor CD-ROM

Section 1 Assessment Answers

1. **a.** extension of a nation's power over other lands
   b. economic interests; military bases
   c. possible answer—arrogant, assumed other cultures needed Western culture

2. **a.** ideal for naval bases
   b. Sugar planters wanted to protect their businesses and land.
   c. formed Hawaiian League, forced king to sign a new constitution; ordered Marines ashore

3. **a.** gave nations equal trading rights in China

   b. did not have own sphere of influence
   c. possible answer—would not have been able to take part in trade

4. **a.** naval officer, led fleet to Japan in 1853
   b. to remind them of U.S. military strength

5. king signs bayonet constitution, monarchy restricted, Hawaiians lose right to vote; queen removed from power, monarchy ends; Hawaii annexed, becomes U.S. territory

6. possible answers—Chinese, Boxer Rebellion was only way to get foreign powers out of China; missionary, we are here to help

Answers

Reading Check *by making Japan aware of modern world; by displaying U.S. naval strength*

557

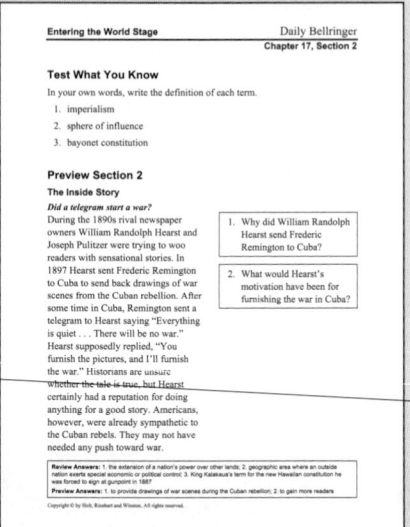
The Spanish-American War

BEFORE YOU READ

MAIN IDEA

A quick victory in the Spanish-American War gave the United States a new role as a world power.

READING FOCUS

1. How did simmering unrest in Cuba lead to rebellion?
2. Why did Americans get war fever?
3. What happened in the course of the Spanish-American War?
4. Why was annexing the Philippines controversial?

KEY TERMS AND PEOPLE

José Martí
William Randolph Hearst
Joseph Pulitzer
yellow journalism
de Lôme letter
George Dewey
Emilio Aguinaldo
Rough Riders
Battle of San Juan Hill

TAKING NOTES As you read, take notes identifying arguments for the United States to annex the Philippine Islands. Record your notes in a graphic organizer like the one shown here.

For Annexation

"You Furnish the PICTURES, I'll Furnish the WAR"

THE INSIDE STORY

Did a telegram start a war? In the 1890s rival newspapers owned by William Randolph Hearst and Joseph Pulitzer were competing fiercely. They tried to woo readers with sensational stories and blaring banner headlines.

How far would Hearst go? In January 1897 he sent an artist and reporter team to cover the Cuban rebellion against Spanish rule. Frederic Remington was to send drawings of war scenes. Richard Harding Davis would write the dramatic stories. According to one account, Remington spent some time in Cuba and found that not much was happening in the way of a war. He sent this telegram: "W. R. Hearst, *New York Journal*, N.Y.: Everything is quiet. There is no trouble here. There will be no war. I wish to return. Remington."

Supposedly Hearst answered: "Remington, Havana: Please remain. You furnish the pictures, and I'll furnish the war. W. R. Hearst."

Is the story true? One historian points out that the only source was a journalist named James Creelman, who wrote a book about his life as a foreign correspondent for Hearst. Hearst always denied a role in "manufacturing" the war, but the tale fit with people's belief that he would do anything for a good story. Certainly both the *Journal* and its rival, the *New York World*, played up every incident in Cuba. But Americans were already sympathetic to the Cuban rebels, and perhaps they did not need a push toward war. ■

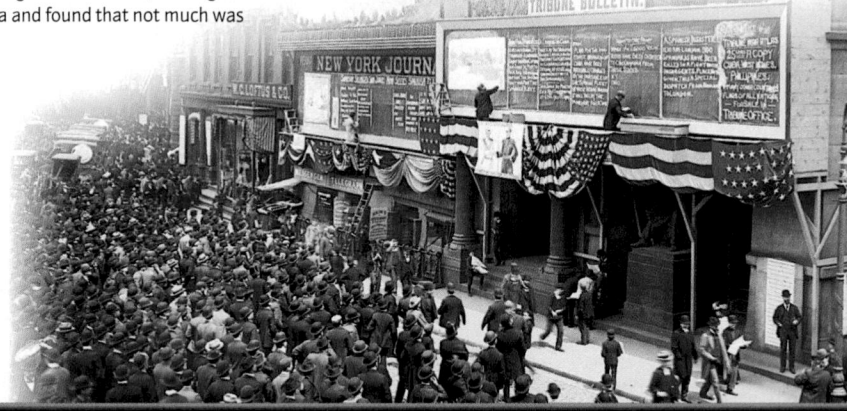

▶ War news draws a crowd outside the *New York Journal* offices.

558

Teach the Main Idea

At Level

The Spanish-American War

1. **Teach** Ask students the Reading Focus questions to teach this section.

2. **Apply** Have students look at the atlas in their text and locate Cuba and the Philippine Islands. Ask students to predict why the United States was interested in these countries. Then have students work in pairs to list benefits to the U.S. if it was able to gain control of Cuba and the Philippines.

3. **Review** Guide students in a review of the reasons for imperialism. Then have students explain the role yellow journalism played in the history of this period.

4. **Practice/Homework** Have students write a balanced article explaining the growing strength of the United States and its desire to acquire new territories. Tell students to direct their explanations to those who prefer fair, unbiased reporting to sensationalism.
LS Verbal-Linguistic

📝 Alternative Assessment Handbook, Rubric 42: Writing to Inform

Simmering Unrest in Cuba

By the 1890s Spain had lost all of its colonies in the Western Hemisphere except for Cuba and Puerto Rico. Cubans in particular were not happy to be part of Spain's empire. Since 1868, Cubans had launched a series of revolts against Spanish rule. Spain responded by exiling leaders of the independence movement.

José Martí was one such leader, exiled in 1878. He moved to New York City, where he continued to promote independence and inspire his fellow Cubans. Through newspaper articles and poetry, Martí urged Cubans to fight for their freedom. He also founded the Cuban Revolutionary Party in 1892 and made preparations to return to his homeland.

Cubans rose once more in revolt against Spain in February 1895. Martí joined them in April, but a month later he was killed in battle. By dying for his country, José Martí immediately became one of Cuba's greatest heroes.

As the revolt raged on, Spain sent General Valeriano Weyler to suppress the rebels in 1896. Weyler forced thousands of civilians into camps controlled by the Spanish army to keep them from aiding the rebels. However, nearly one-third of the Cubans in the camps died from starvation or disease. Weyler's mistreatment of these civilians shocked Americans.

READING CHECK **Summarizing** How did José Martí inspire other Cubans to seek independence?

Americans Get War Fever

Many Americans were already sympathetic to the Cuban cause. They believed the Cubans' struggle was similar to their own during the American Revolution. They became even more supportive after learning how Cuban civilians were suffering under General Weyler.

The media's role In this era before radio, television, or the Internet, most people got their news from daily or weekly newspapers. At one point, New York City had as many as 15 daily newspaper editions.

Two of the most widely read papers were the *New York Journal*, published by **William Randolph Hearst**, and the *New York World*, published by **Joseph Pulitzer**. Both papers told scandalous stories and splashed large,

shocking illustrations across their pages. This style of sensationalist reporting became known as **yellow journalism**, named after the "Yellow Kid," a popular comic strip that ran in the *World*. Determined to compete with the *World* in every way, the *Journal* created its own "yellow kid" comic, and the rivalry between the two papers became a competition between the two "yellow kids."

The *Journal* threw its support behind the Cuban rebels and refused to use any Spanish sources for news stories. Relying only on Cuban sources made the *Journal*'s stories biased, but it also made for exciting reading—and sold more papers.

Not to be left behind, the *World* abandoned all attempts at objectivity. It used the same strategy as the *Journal*, and newspaper sales went up. People could not get enough of the dramatic stories printed daily.

The explosion of the *Maine* Hearst felt strongly that the United States should intervene in Cuba. As a result, the *Journal* continued the drumbeat for war. In 1897 Hearst sent artist Frederic Remington to Cuba to create illustrations showing Spanish cruelty. Hearst printed those drawings in his papers to stir up more support for war with Spain.

President William McKinley was reluctant at first to involve the United States in the conflict. Events soon changed McKinley's

THE IMPACT TODAY

Culture
Today's most prestigious award in journalism is the Pulitzer Prize, funded by Joseph Pulitzer in his will.

FACES OF HISTORY

William R. HEARST
1863–1951

An outgoing and controversial man, William Randolph Hearst built a vast publishing empire. He began his career managing the *San Francisco Examiner*. At the height of his success, he owned 28 major newspapers and 18 magazines, along with various news services, radio stations, and movie companies. Hearst even served in the House of Representatives but was defeated in his efforts to become the mayor of New York City, and later the governor of New York State.

Orson Welles's 1941 film *Citizen Kane* depicted Hearst's extravagant life. It became one of the most popular films of all time.

Drawing Conclusions Many film critics consider *Citizen Kane* to be one of the best movies ever made. Why might Hearst's life make an interesting story?

Reading Focus

❶ How did simmering unrest in Cuba lead to rebellion? *Cubans unhappy with Spanish rule; series of revolts; leaders exiled; José Martí encouraged another revolt*

Simmering Unrest in Cuba

Identify Who was José Martí? *led Cuban rebellion against Spain*

Analyze Why did General Valeriano Weyler's attempt to suppress the Cuban rebellion backfire? *By mistreating Cubans, he directed international attention to their misfortunes.*

Reading Focus

❷ Why did Americans get war fever? *Newspapers created sensational accounts of events in Cuba; supported Cuban rebels.*

Americans Get War Fever

Explain What was yellow journalism? *sensationalized reporting designed to attract readers*

Make Inferences Why could William Randolph Hearst and Joseph Pulitzer be considered part of the Cuban revolt? *Sensationalist newspaper accounts created support for Cuban freedom.*

CRF: Primary Source Activity: Beginning and Ending the Spanish-American War

---

Differentiating Instruction

Below Level

Special Education Students

Materials butcher paper or large construction paper, colored markers

1. Draw a cause-and-effect diagram for students to see. Guide students in a discussion about the causes and effects of Cuba's revolt against Spain. Fill in the graphic organizer with student responses.

2. Organize the class into small groups. Have each group prepare a poster which chronicles the events in Cuba, beginning with the 1868 revolts and ending with the peace treaty

signed with Spain in 1898. Students may include illustrations and descriptions on their posters.

3. Have groups share their storyboards with the class.

4. As an alternative for at-level or above-level students, have students develop a PowerPoint presentation chronicling these events.

Visual-Spatial

Alternative Assessment Handbook, Rubric 3: Artwork

Answers

Faces of History *because of his business success and political endeavors*

Reading Check *wrote newspaper articles and poetry; founded Cuban Revolutionary Party*

559

Americans Get War Fever

Describe Why did the de Lôme letter raise such an outcry? *criticized and ridiculed President McKinley*

Draw Conclusions Do you think the Spanish minister was justified in writing about the U.S. president? *possible answers—Yes, his job was to keep his government informed. No, the remarks were overly critical and insulting.*

Activity **The de Lôme Letter**
Have students write a newspaper headline and a lead paragraph for an article about the de Lôme letter for a newspaper like the *New York Journal* or *New York World*. **LS** Verbal-Linguistic

Primary Sources

On the *Maine*

Identify Have students read the editorial from the *New York Journal* and then write an unbiased newspaper report of the *Maine* explosion.

MISCONCEPTION ALERT

USS *Maine* There have been many theories and several scientific investigations regarding the sinking of the USS *Maine*. Today, experts and historians, using advanced technology, still have not been able to give a definitive, universally accepted explanation for the cause of the explosion.

Answers

Reading Like a Historian 1. *the United States;* **2.** *choice of words such as "starved or otherwise murdered" and "an accident of a remarkably convenient kind for Spain"*

Reading Check *tensions between the two countries; the de Lôme letter*

560

Editorial

The *New York Journal* published this editorial on February 17, 1898, after the *Maine* exploded.

"To five hundred thousand Cubans starved or otherwise murdered have been added an American battleship and three hundred American sailors lost as the direct result of the dilatory [slow] policy of our government toward Spain. If we had stopped the war in Cuba when duty and policy alike urged us to do[,] the *Maine* would have been afloat today . . .

It was an accident, they say. Perhaps it was, but . . . it was an accident of a remarkably convenient kind for Spain. Two days ago we had five battleships in the Atlantic. Today we have four. A few more such accidents will leave us at the mercy of a Spanish fleet."

Skills Focus **READING LIKE A HISTORIAN**

1. **Analyzing Primary Sources** Whom does the *Journal* blame for the deaths on the *Maine*?

2. **Recognizing Bias** What suggests that the *Journal* is biased against Spain?

See Skills Handbook, pp. H28–H29, H33

mind. On February 9, 1898, the *Journal* published a letter written by Enrique Dupuy de Lôme, Spain's minister to the United States. The letter had fallen into the hands of a Cuban spy who sold it to Hearst. The **de Lôme letter** ridiculed McKinley for being "weak and catering to the rabble." Americans were outraged at the remarks. The *Journal* called it "the worst insult to the United States in its history."

Furious Americans began clamoring for war with Spain. Then came the final straw: a violent tragedy in Havana Harbor that brought relations with Spain to a breaking point. The battleship USS *Maine* had been sent to Havana to protect American lives and property. On February 15, 1898, the *Maine* mysteriously blew up, killing 260 sailors.

"DESTRUCTION OF THE WAR SHIP MAINE WAS THE WORK OF AN ENEMY!" screamed the *Journal*'s headline, although

---

there was no proof of this. Some historians now believe that a fire in a coal storage room caused the explosion. At the time, however, Americans blamed Spain. "Remember the *Maine*!" became the rallying cry of war supporters.

At the time, an inquiry into the explosion confirmed public perceptions, blaming a Spanish mine for destroying the *Maine*. In late March, President McKinley demanded that Spain grant Cuba its independence. When Spain refused, Congress declared a state of war on April 25, 1898. The Spanish-American War had begun.

READING CHECK **Making Inferences** Why did the *Journal* jump to the conclusion that the Spanish were responsible for the explosion of the *Maine*?

The Course of the War

Although its impact would be felt for years, the Spanish-American War lasted only about four months. It was fought on two fronts: Cuba and the Philippines.

War in the Philippines The Philippines are a group of islands located east of Vietnam between the Philippine Sea and the South China Sea. Spain had claimed the islands since the 1500s.

Before the United States declared war on Spain, Theodore Roosevelt (then the assistant secretary of the navy) sent secret orders to Commodore **George Dewey**, the commander of the U.S. Navy's Asiatic Squadron. If war broke out between the United States and Spain, Dewey's assignment was to attack the Spanish fleet in the Philippines.

Once Dewey received word that war had been declared, his squadron rushed to Manila Bay in the Philippines. Early on the morning of May 1, 1898, the Spanish fleet opened fire, but the American forces were out of range. Dewey had his sailors hold their fire for nearly half an hour, until they came within striking distance of the Spanish ships. Dewey did not want to waste ammunition, because the nearest American point of resupply was in California, some 7,000 miles away.

Finally, Commodore Dewey quietly told Charles Gridley, the captain of the flagship *Olympia*, "You may fire when ready, Gridley." The Americans had the advantage of modern ships with iron and steel hulls, as well as

---

Skills Focus: Drawing Conclusions

Reading Skill
Rebels and the War in Cuba

1. Guide students in a discussion about how Cuban rebels might have reacted when the USS *Maine* was sunk and the United States was deciding whether or not to go to war with Spain over the incident. The rebels can either join the United States, or they can remain independent and try to continue their fight against Spanish domination without foreign support. Remind students of the risks of either course of action.

2. Have students decide which course of action they believe would have been most effective in gaining Cuban independence. Then have students write a speech from the viewpoint of a Cuban rebel in which they try to convince other Cuban rebels to join them in the struggle. Have volunteers read their speeches to the class. **LS** Verbal-Linguistic

Alternative Assessment Handbook, Rubrics 24: Oral Presentations; and 42: Writing to Inform

superior weaponry. They were soon inflicting heavy damage on the old-fashioned wooden ships of the enemy.

Then two hours into the battle, Captain Gridley reported that the *Olympia* was low on ammunition. Dewey decided to withdraw from battle so that the ships could redistribute their remaining supplies. To keep morale up, he told his men they were taking a break to eat breakfast. During the break, however, Dewey learned that the report about the ammunition was incorrect. The *Olympia* had plenty of supplies for the rest of the battle.

The Americans continued fighting shortly before noon. Soon the entire Spanish fleet was ablaze and sinking. In a matter of hours, the United States had won a decisive victory. Not a single American life was lost, but nearly 400 Spaniards were injured or killed in the Battle of Manila Bay.

Dewey then began planning an attack on the capital city of Manila. He found a willing partner in **Emilio Aguinaldo**, leader of a rebel army of Filipino patriots. Filipinos had been fighting for independence from Spain for two years. While Dewey's warships remained in the harbor, Aguinaldo's army captured Manila. Cut off by Dewey's fleet and surrounded by Aguinaldo's rebels, Spanish forces in the Philippines surrendered on August 14, 1898.

The war in Cuba Days before declaring war, Congress had recognized Cuba's independence and adopted the Teller Amendment. This stated that once Cuba freed itself from Spanish rule, the United States would "leave the government and control of the Island to its people."

Victory in Cuba proved difficult to achieve, however. The U.S. War Department was not as prepared as it should have been for the conflict.

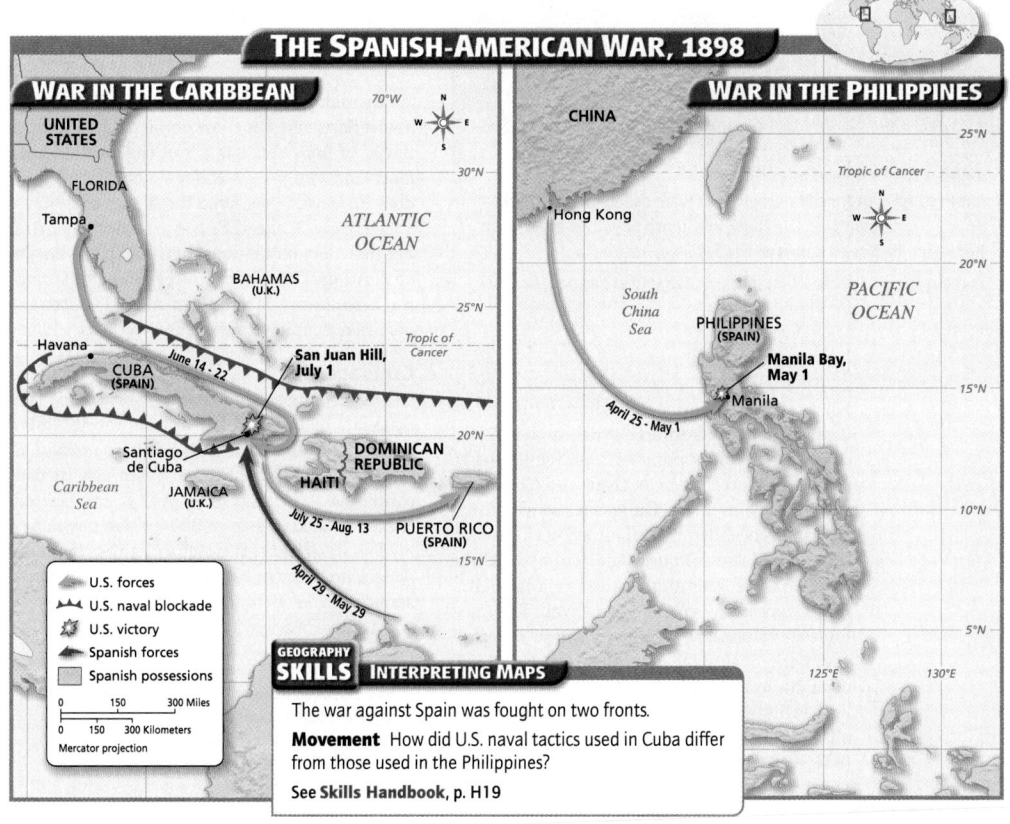

THE SPANISH-AMERICAN WAR, 1898

WAR IN THE CARIBBEAN

UNITED STATES
FLORIDA
Tampa
ATLANTIC OCEAN
BAHAMAS (U.K.)
Havana
June 14 - 22
San Juan Hill, July 1
CUBA (SPAIN)
Santiago de Cuba
July 25 - Aug. 13
Caribbean Sea
JAMAICA (U.K.)
HAITI
DOMINICAN REPUBLIC
PUERTO RICO (SPAIN)
April 29 - May 29

U.S. forces
U.S. naval blockade
U.S. victory
Spanish forces
Spanish possessions

0   150   300 Miles
0   150   300 Kilometers
Mercator projection

WAR IN THE PHILIPPINES

CHINA
Hong Kong
Tropic of Cancer
South China Sea
PHILIPPINES (SPAIN)
PACIFIC OCEAN
Manila Bay, May 1
Manila
April 25 - May 1

GEOGRAPHY SKILLS | **INTERPRETING MAPS**

The war against Spain was fought on two fronts.
Movement How did U.S. naval tactics used in Cuba differ from those used in the Philippines?
See Skills Handbook, p. H19

ENTERING THE WORLD STAGE **561**

Direct Teach

Reading Focus

❸ What happened in the course of the Spanish-American War? *U.S. defeat of Spanish navy in Manila Bay; land and sea victory for U.S. in Cuba; defeat of Spanish troops in Puerto Rico*

The Course of the War

Recall How long did the Spanish-American War last? *about four months*

Analyze Why do you think the U.S. chose the Philippines as one of the locations to attack the Spanish? *islands have excellent strategic location in the Pacific*

📰 CRF: Literature Activity: "The Price of the Harness," by Stephen Crane

The Spanish-American War, 1898

Identify Have students use the atlas in their text to locate the sites of some of the key battles in the Spanish-American War. *Students should locate Manila Bay, Santiago, and San Juan Hill.*

📰 American History Outline Maps: The Spanish-American War

🖥 Map Transparency: The Spanish-American War, 1898

go.hrw.com
Online Resources

KEYWORD: SD7 CH17
TOPIC: YELLOW JOURNALISM

Skills Focus: Comparing and Contrasting   At Level

Reading Skill
"A Splendid Little War"

1. Review the text about the Spanish-American War with the students. Point out how quickly the United States Navy was able to defeat the Spanish fleet.

2. Have students create two editorial cartoons that might have appeared in a U.S. newspaper celebrating the victories. One cartoon should focus on the U.S. victory in the Philippines; the other should focus on the U.S. naval victory in Cuba.

3. Then have students write an editorial for a Spanish newspaper lamenting Spain's defeat, the humbling of its navy, and the end of one of the world's great imperial powers.

4. Have students share their work with the class. Guide students in a discussion of the points of view presented in their work. **LS Visual-Spatial, Verbal-Linguistic**

📰 Alternative Assessment Handbook, Rubric 27: Political Cartoons

Answers

Interpreting Maps *In Cuba, the U.S. used a naval blockade and had a close point of resupply. The tactic in the Philippines was a decisive and direct attack on the port in Manila Bay.*

561

The Course of the War

Explain Why was fighting in Cuba so difficult? *U.S. soldiers forced to deal with old, inappropriate uniforms and supplies, and bad food*

Making Inferences What was unusual about the troops who fought in the Spanish-American War? *The U.S. troops were diverse: African American soldiers led the charge at San Juan Hill; Native Americans served with the Rough Riders.*

Evaluate What do you think John Hay and Henry Cabot Lodge meant when they said the war began with the highest motives and that it had world-wide meaning? *highest motives—U.S. went to war to help free Cuba; worldwide meaning—gained territory for the U.S.; gave notice that the U.S. was a strong military force, and would use military means to achieve goals*

CRF: Biography: Buffalo Soldiers

Biography

William Glackens (1870–1938) William Glackens helped to bring realism into American art with his paintings of street scenes and urban life. In 1898, Glackens worked as a special correspondent for *McClure's Magazine* in Cuba, creating images of the fighting that many historians consider accurate representations of the Spanish-American War. Traveling with other artists known collectively as "The Eight," Glackens became increasingly adept at depicting life in the early 1900s. Today, Glackens is remembered as a pioneer in the style known as social realism.

Answers

Reading Like a Historian *They are holding an American flag.*

562

BUFFALO SOLDIERS AND ROUGH RIDERS

Skills Focus READING LIKE A HISTORIAN

Some 10 African American regiments were called to serve in the Spanish-American War. The Ninth and Tenth Cavalries are shown here with the Rough Riders at the Battle of Kettle Hill.

Interpreting Visuals What marks these soldiers as Americans?

For example, it equipped soldiers with woolen uniforms for a summer war in a tropical climate. The mess pans—tin plates issued to soldiers—were left over from the Civil War. The canned meat in Cuba was so sickening that soldiers called it "embalmed beef."

Most of the soldiers who fought in Cuba were enlisted men (also called regulars), but there were many volunteers as well. The most famous volunteers were the **Rough Riders**, a regiment organized by Theodore Roosevelt after he left his navy post. Adventurous college athletes, cowboys, ranchers, and miners all joined the Rough Riders. They expected to fight on horseback, but because the transport ships to Cuba were overbooked, they had to leave their horses behind in America. The Rough Riders ended up functioning as foot soldiers instead of as a cavalry.

The American strategy in Cuba was to capture the port city of Santiago. U.S. troops needed to control the hills around the city. On July 1, one U.S. division seized the hill at El Caney after a four-hour fight.

That same day, some 8,000 U.S. soldiers fought to take control of Kettle and San Juan hills. Experienced African American soldiers of the Ninth and Tenth Cavalries—known as Buffalo Soldiers—led the charge, supported by the Rough Riders and regulars. Theodore Roosevelt described how the Rough Riders stayed the course.

HISTORY'S VOICES

❝ We were still under a heavy fire and I got together a mixed lot of men and pushed on . . . , driving the Spaniards through a line of palm-trees, and over the crest of a chain of hills. When we reached these crests we found ourselves overlooking Santiago. **❞**

—Theodore Roosevelt, *The Rough Riders*, 1902

By nightfall, U.S. troops controlled the ridge above Santiago. For their heroic actions in the **Battle of San Juan Hill**, six of the Buffalo Soldiers and two Rough Riders—including Theodore Roosevelt—received the Medal of Honor.

On July 3, the U.S. Navy sank the entire Spanish fleet off the coast of Cuba in the Battle of Santiago. Two weeks later, Spanish troops in Cuba surrendered. Soon after, U.S. troops defeated Spanish forces in Puerto Rico.

Consequences of the war The terms of the peace treaty proved costly for Spain. The Spanish had to give up all claims to Cuba and cede Puerto Rico and the Pacific island of Guam to the United States. Spain also turned control of the Philippines over to the United States in exchange for a $20 million payment.

For Americans, the victory in the Spanish-American War was sweet. John Hay, the ambassador to Great Britain, summed up his view in a letter to Theodore Roosevelt.

HISTORY'S VOICES

❝ It has been a splendid little war; begun with the highest motives, carried on with magnificent intelligence and spirit, favored by that fortune which loves the brave. **❞**

—John Hay, letter to Theodore Roosevelt

Differentiating Instruction

Below Level

Learners Having Difficulty

1. Remind students that U.S. newspapers covered the Spanish-American War thoroughly and even sent artists like Frederic Remington to provide illustrations.

2. Have students examine the photo of the Rough Riders on this page. Then have students create two black and white illustrations, one that shows the Battle of San Juan Hill as described by Theodore Roosevelt, and the other showing the U.S. Navy fleet in the Battle of Santiago.

Remind students that they should attempt to show what actually happened.

3. Have students share their visuals with the class. **LS Visual-Spatial**

Alternative Assessment Handbook, Rubric 3: Artwork

Still, the United States paid a heavy toll for the war. The monetary costs amounted to roughly $250 million. In addition, some 2,000 soldiers died, not from battle wounds but from yellow fever.

Despite the lives lost and the dollars spent, the Spanish-American War had a huge payoff for the United States. Senator Henry Cabot Lodge of Massachusetts noted that although the war was very brief, "its results were many, startling, and of world-wide meaning."

The United States now moved into the ranks of imperialist nations. Its new overseas territories gave it more bases for trade and for resupplying its navy. Within a year, it would capitalize on its new economic and military strength to acquire the Pacific island of Samoa. Expansionists expressed delight over the country's growing power, but the quest for empire troubled many Americans.

READING CHECK Making Generalizations
How did the United States benefit from the war?

Annexing the Philippines

After the Spanish-American War, a controversy raged in the United States over whether to annex the Philippines. Some Americans were uneasy with the idea of controlling overseas territories. Others believed that imperialism not only made the United States stronger but also benefited those under colonial rule.

Arguments for annexation Some people who favored annexation believed that the United States had a duty to spread its values overseas. President McKinley, for example, spoke of the need "to educate the Filipinos, and uplift and civilize and Christianize them."

Other Americans wanted the Philippines for their economic and strategic value. Located on the route to China, the Philippines would be useful as a place to refuel and resupply ships. For that reason, many expansionists wanted to annex the Philippines before they fell into the hands of Germany, Japan, or another nation.

❹ Why was annexing the Philippines controversial? *some Americans uneasy about expansionism; others believed added territories made U.S. stronger*

Annexing the Philippines

Recall What two reasons were used to justify annexation of the Philippines? *U.S. duty to spread its values; economic and strategic value*

Predict Why might other nations have gone to war against the United States to gain control of the Philippines? *possible answers— natural resources; location; new market for goods*

COUNTERPOINTS

Annexation of the Philippines

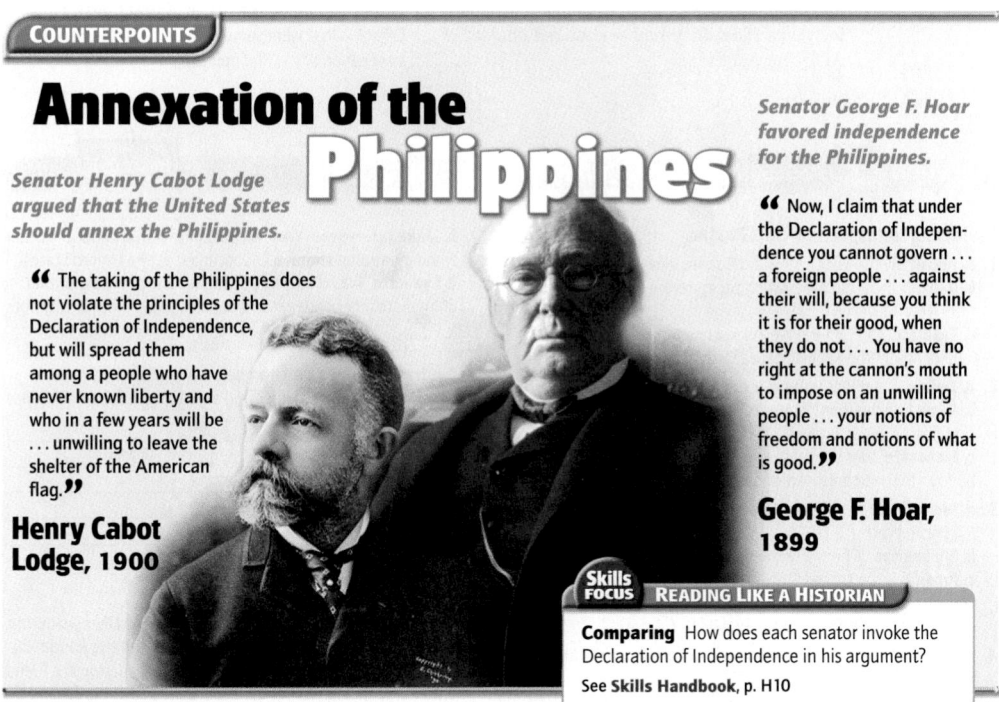

Senator Henry Cabot Lodge argued that the United States should annex the Philippines.

Senator George F. Hoar favored independence for the Philippines.

❝ The taking of the Philippines does not violate the principles of the Declaration of Independence, but will spread them among a people who have never known liberty and who in a few years will be ...unwilling to leave the shelter of the American flag. ❞

Henry Cabot Lodge, 1900

❝ Now, I claim that under the Declaration of Independence you cannot govern ... a foreign people ... against their will, because you think it is for their good, when they do not ... You have no right at the cannon's mouth to impose on an unwilling people ... your notions of freedom and notions of what is good. ❞

George F. Hoar, 1899

Skills FOCUS READING LIKE A HISTORIAN

Comparing How does each senator invoke the Declaration of Independence in his argument?
See Skills Handbook, p. H10

ENTERING THE WORLD STAGE **563**

Counterpoints
Annexation of the Philippines
Compare Have students reread the U.S. Declaration of Independence in their texts. Guide students in a discussion of the viewpoints and interpretations of the Declaration presented in the feature.

Reading Like a Historian Skill   **Research Required**
Philippine Annexation

1. Have students conduct outside research on the 1890s debate within the United States about annexing the Philippines. Students should look for primary sources.

2. Have students write and present summaries of their research to the class. Guide students in a discussion of the expansionist and anti-imperialist viewpoints that prevailed at the time.

3. Have students decide, based on their research and the class discussion, whether or not they believe the United States should have pursued annexing the Philippine Islands.

4. Have students prepare for and conduct a class debate about this issue. **LS Verbal-Linguistic, Kinesthetic**

Alternative Assessment Handbook, Rubrics 1: Acquiring Information; and 10: Debates

Answers

Reading Like a Historian *Lodge says that by annexing the Philippines, the principles of the Declaration would be spread to the people there who have never known freedom. Hoar argues that the Declaration cannot be used to govern a foreign people against their will.*

Reading Check *gained new territories which were used to resupply navy, as bases for trade, and which allowed for future territorial gain*

Annexing the Philippines

Explain Why did some groups in the U.S. oppose annexing the Philippines? *believed annexation would violate American ideals of self-government; believed country should be correcting racial problems at home; feared increased immigration*

Analyze Did the U.S. honor its stated goal of preparing Philippines for independence? *Yes, but it took over four decades.*

Close

Guide students in a discussion of the Spanish-American War.

Review

Online Quiz, Section 2

Daily Test Practice Transparency

Assess

SE Section 2 Assessment

Progress Assessment: Section 2 Quiz

Alternative Assessment Handbook

Reteach

Interactive Reader and Study Guide, Section 2

Interactive Skills Tutor CD-ROM

Answers

Reading Check *fighting broke out and Filipino fighters battled U.S. forces for three years; resulted in the deaths of hundreds of thousands of people*

ACADEMIC VOCABULARY
foundation
underlying principle

Opponents' views Americans who opposed annexing the Philippines felt strongly, too. Some reasoned that annexation would violate the ideal of self-government—the foundation of the American system. They formed the Anti-Imperialist League in June 1898.

Many African Americans worried about exporting oppression to the Philippines. A group of activists called the Colored Citizens of Boston argued that with racism and violence still painfully common at home, "the duty of the President and country is to reform these crying domestic wrongs and not attempt the civilization of alien peoples by powder and shot."

Other Americans feared that annexing the Philippines would open the doors to a flood of new immigrants. Samuel Gompers, the leader of the American Federation of Labor, believed that this would hurt American workers.

American rule After a fierce debate, the Senate narrowly approved the treaty calling for annexation of the Philippines. The measure passed on February 6, 1899.

Filipino nationalists were infuriated. They had been fighting for independence from Spain for years. Now they had exchanged one set of rulers for another.

Emilio Aguinaldo had already set up a government and proclaimed himself president of the new Philippine Republic. He warned that he was prepared to take military action if the United States tried to assume control of the Philippines.

To no one's surprise, fighting broke out. For three years, Filipino independence fighters battled U.S. soldiers. Aguinaldo was finally captured by the Americans and forced from power in 1901. By the time the rebellion ended, more than 4,000 U.S. soldiers and some 220,000 Filipinos had died, many from disease.

In taking over the Philippines, the stated goal of the United States was to prepare the islands for independence. Therefore, although Congress put a U.S.-appointed governor in charge, Filipinos were also allowed a voice in governing. At first they could only elect members to the lower house of their legislature. Then in 1916, Filipino voters won the right to elect both houses of their legislature. Three decades later, on July 4, 1946, the United States finally granted full independence to the Philippines.

READING CHECK **Identifying Cause and Effect** What were some of the effects of American annexation of the Philippines?

SECTION 2 ASSESSMENT

go.hrw.com
Online Quiz
Keyword: SD7 HP17

Reviewing Ideas, Terms, and People

1. **a. Recall** By the 1890s, how did Cubans view Spanish rule?
   b. Explain How did **José Martí** promote the Cuban cause from New York City?
   c. Evaluate Did General Weyler's actions toward civilians help or hinder the Spanish cause? Explain.
2. **a. Define** What was **yellow journalism**?
   b. Draw Conclusions Why was the sinking of the USS *Maine* significant?
   c. Elaborate Was the press irresponsible in covering the buildup to the Spanish-American War? Why or why not?
3. **a. Identify** What were the key battles during the Spanish-American War?
   b. Summarize What were the terms of the peace treaty?
   c. Predict If the United States had lost the Spanish-American War, do you think it would have been more or less likely to continue its quest for empire? Explain.
4. **a. Recall** Why were the Philippines of strategic importance to the United States?

b. Make Inferences Why might **Emilio Aguinaldo** and other Filipino nationalists have felt betrayed by the United States?
c. Evaluate Was the United States justified in not granting immediate independence to the Philippines? Why or why not?

Critical Thinking

5. **Contrasting** Copy the chart below and record the reasons why some Americans supported annexation of the Philippines and others opposed it.

Supporters	Opponents

FOCUS ON WRITING

6. **Narrative** Imagine that you were aboard the *Olympia* during the Battle of Manila Bay or that you were with the Rough Riders during the Battle of San Juan Hill. Write a letter to a friend back home telling about your experiences and your feelings.

564 CHAPTER 17

Section 2 Assessment Answers

1. **a.** resented it, wanted independence
   b. founded the Cuban Revolutionary Party; writing urged Cubans to fight
   c. hinder; his actions drew U.S. into conflict
2. **a.** a sensational style of reporting
   b. promoted U.S. entry into war
   c. yes, it was fictionalized, unbalanced
3. **a.** Manila Bay; San Juan Hill
   b. Spain gave up Cuba, ceded Puerto Rico and Guam, gave up Philippines for $20 million
   c. possible answer—more likely because loss would have motivated it to try again

4. **a.** located on the route to China; could be used as a base to refuel and resupply ships
   b. believed U.S. would help them; ended up exchanging one set of rulers for another
   c. possible answer—yes, country needed time to develop democratic process
5. Supporters—U.S. had duty to spread its beliefs; useful for naval bases; Opponents—annexation violates the U.S. ideals; U.S. should address problems at home
6. possible answer—San Juan Hill was dangerous, filled with heroics

SECTION 3

Roosevelt and Latin America

BEFORE YOU READ

MAIN IDEA

The United States began to exert its influence over Latin America in the wake of the Spanish-American War.

READING FOCUS

1. How did the United States govern Cuba and Puerto Rico?
2. Why and how was the Panama Canal built?
3. What was the Roosevelt Corollary?
4. How did Presidents Taft and Wilson reshape U.S. diplomacy?

KEY TERMS AND PEOPLE

Platt Amendment
protectorate
Foraker Act
Roosevelt Corollary
dollar diplomacy

 TAKING NOTES As you read, take notes on U.S. intervention in Latin America. In each of the small circles in a diagram like the one below, identify one way the United States intervened in Latin America. You may need to add more circles.

Intervention in Latin America

SANTO DOMINGO

CARIBBEAN SEA

DEBT COLLECTOR

MEXICO

CUBA

THE GRANGER COLLECTION, NEW YORK

▲ Roosevelt uses a "big stick" to control the Caribbean region.

"Speak Softly and Carry a Big Stick"

THE INSIDE STORY *How did President Roosevelt get the Canal Zone?*

Theodore Roosevelt was a man of action with a vigorous foreign policy. He often quoted a West African proverb: "Speak softly and carry a big stick; you will go far."

Roosevelt's "big stick" was naval power. As president, he built up the Great White Fleet. It helped achieve his dream—a canal that would let ships sail between the Atlantic and the Pacific without going around South America. The canal site was in Panama, which was then a province of Colombia.

Under pressure, Colombian diplomats agreed to lease a canal zone across Panama for a one-time payment of $10 million and a yearly fee of $250,000. The Colombian senate, however, rejected the deal and demanded more money.

Then various groups with a stake in the canal stepped in to encourage a revolution in Panama. In November 1903, the USS *Nashville* lingered off the coast. American marines landed to "maintain order," preventing Colombian troops from stopping the rebels. Within three days, the government of newly independent Panama agreed to the original treaty. Work on the canal could begin! ■

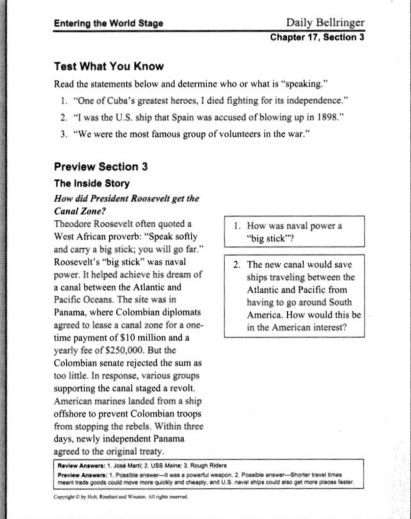
---

❶ How did the United States govern Cuba and Puerto Rico? *Cuba—Platt Amendment made it a U.S. protectorate; Puerto Rico—governed as a territory; Foraker Act allowed U.S. to appoint governor and upper house of legislature; gave U.S. citizenship to Puerto Ricans*

Cuba and Puerto Rico

Explain What benefits did the United States receive as a result of the Platt Amendment? *right to intervene in Cuban affairs; rights to buy or lease land for naval bases and coaling stations*

Contrast How did Puerto Rico become a U.S. territory, while Cuba became a protectorate? *U.S. had promised in Teller Amendment in 1898 that Cuba would not be annexed; no such promise was made to Puerto Rico*

📄 CRF: Biography: Walter Reed

Cuba and Puerto Rico

After the Spanish-American War, the United States began to expand its power in Latin America. To restore order in Cuba and Puerto Rico after the war—and to protect American investments—President William McKinley set up military governments on each island.

Yellow fever in Cuba President McKinley appointed Leonard Wood as governor of Cuba in 1899. During Wood's term in office, scientists made significant steps toward eliminating yellow fever. The disease had reached epidemic levels among American troops in Cuba. As many as 85 percent of the people infected with yellow fever died.

U.S. Army doctors Walter Reed and William C. Gorgas studied the problem. Cuban doctor Carlos Juan Finlay had theorized that mosquitoes spread yellow fever. Within a year, Reed and Gorgas had proven Finlay's theory. Then Gorgas organized a plan to drain all pools of standing water, where mosquitoes bred. Within six months, yellow fever had been virtually eliminated from the city of Havana.

THE IMPACT TODAY
Government
Since the terrorist attacks of September 11, 2001, the base at Guantánamo has housed prisoners suspected of terrorist activity.

U.S. control over Cuba Wood also oversaw the drafting of a new Cuban constitution in 1901. The United States had already declared with the Teller Amendment of 1898 that it would not annex Cuba. After the Spanish-American War, however, the United States feared that other imperialist nations might try to take control of Cuba or undercut American business interests there.

As a result, the United States forced Cuba to include the **Platt Amendment** as part of its new constitution. The amendment limited Cuba's ability to sign treaties with other nations. At the same time, it gave the United States the right to intervene in Cuban affairs. The amendment also required Cuba to sell or lease land to the United States for naval and coaling stations. This last clause led to the establishment of a U.S. naval base at Guantánamo Bay.

The Platt Amendment made Cuba a U.S. **protectorate**—a country under the control and protection of another country. After Cuba accepted the Platt Amendment, U.S. troops withdrew. The amendment was eventually repealed, but the United States retained its lease on the naval base at Guantánamo Bay.

Political Cartoon

This cartoon reflects the debate at the end of the Spanish-American War over what should be done with new U.S. territories.

In the caption Uncle Sam says, "These little shavers [kids] seem to like it here. I wonder had I better keep 'em all in the family?"

The children at the table represent lands taken over by the United States in the 1890s.

Lady Liberty was often paired with Uncle Sam in political cartoons, representing America's ideal parents.

THE GRANGER COLLECTION, NEW YORK

SKILLS FOCUS **READING LIKE A HISTORIAN**

1. **Interpreting Political Cartoons** Why do you think the artist used a Thanksgiving scene?
2. **Recognizing Bias** How does this cartoon portray the peoples of the acquired lands?

See Skills Handbook, pp. H31, H33

Skills Focus: Analyzing Bias in Historical Interpretation   At Level

Reading Like a Historian Skill
Roosevelt and Latin America

1. Have students examine the political cartoon on this page. Ask students the following questions: How are the "children" dressed and what are their expressions? Why are the nations represented as children?

2. Review the meaning of the word *bias* with the students. Remind students that historical documents and interpretations can be biased, depending upon the author's background, political views, belief system, and the

historical period in which a document was created.

3. Have students list details in this cartoon that show the cartoonist's bias. Then ask students how this cartoon might have been regarded by leaders such as Queen Liliuokalani, José Martí, or Emilio Aguinaldo.

📄 Alternative Assessment Handbook, Rubric 16: Judging Information

Answers

Reading Like a Historian
1. *possible answers—turkey represents new territory to be 'carved up'; Americans thankful war is over so quickly; that the territories were now part of the American 'family';* **2.** *as little children who need to be looked after by America*

Governing Puerto Rico The United States did not make Puerto Rico a protectorate. Instead, it governed Puerto Rico as a territory, as it did the Philippines. The **Foraker Act** of 1900 established that the United States would appoint Puerto Rico's governor and the upper house of its legislature. Puerto Rican voters would elect the lower house.

A 1917 law granted U.S. citizenship to Puerto Ricans. It also allowed Puerto Rican voters to elect all of their legislative representatives. In 1952 Puerto Rico became a self-governing commonwealth of the United States. Today the Puerto Rican government has power over most of its domestic affairs. The U.S. government still controls certain matters though—interstate trade, immigration, and military affairs—just as it does for U.S. states.

READING CHECK **Summarizing** How did Cuba become a U.S. protectorate?

The Panama Canal

For decades, people had dreamed about a faster way to move between the Atlantic and Pacific oceans without having to travel all the way around South America. In the 1880s a French company tried to solve this problem. It began building a canal across the 50-mile-wide Isthmus of Panama, which was then part of the Republic of Colombia. Facing many obstacles, the company eventually went bankrupt and abandoned the canal.

U.S. interest in a canal In 1902 the United States bought the rights to the French canal property and equipment. Secretary of State John Hay began negotiations with Colombia to gain permanent use of the strip of land that the canal would cut through. By 1903 a treaty for a canal zone had been drafted, but Colombia's senate would not ratify it.

Panama's revolution President Theodore Roosevelt had a keen interest in building the canal. Meanwhile, Panamanian revolutionaries were plotting to break free of Colombian

rule. Roosevelt supported the rebellion, and on November 2, it began. The next day, Panama declared its independence, and the United States swiftly recognized the Republic of Panama. Soon afterward, a new treaty with Panama gave the United States complete and unending sovereignty over a 10-mile-wide Canal Zone.

Building the Panama Canal American work on the Panama Canal began in May 1904. Harsh working conditions and shortages of labor and materials hampered construction efforts. The situation grew worse when a serious outbreak of yellow fever hit.

To put the project back on track, Roosevelt appointed John F. Stevens as chief engineer and architect. Stevens tackled the technical problems while the army colonel Dr. William C. Gorgas focused on improving sanitation and health. Wiping out yellow fever was one goal, but malaria was an even greater threat. Unlike yellow fever, which gave survivors immunity, malaria could strike people again and again. During the first month of U.S. construction activity, nearly the entire workforce had been stricken with malaria.

Eliminating the mosquitoes that spread malaria was a huge task. Sanitation workers drained swamps, cleared vegetation, spread oil

Hardships Faced by Canal Workers
- Yellow fever and malaria
- Accidents
- Lost equipment
- Extreme heat
- Estimated death toll of more than 30,000 workers

Direct Teach

Reading Focus

② Why and how was the Panama Canal built? *create shorter route between Atlantic and Pacific; started by French company, finished by U.S. with 44,000 workers, 60 giant steam shovels, Stevens as chief*

The Panama Canal

Explain What was the first attempt to build the canal? *in 1880s French company began canal across Isthmus of Panama, went bankrupt*

Summarize How did U.S. secure rights to build the Panama Canal? *U.S. supported Panamanian rebellion against Colombia; received control of the Canal Zone as part of treaty with Panama*

Elaborate What obstacles did the United States face in building the Panama Canal, and how were they handled? *harsh working conditions; disease; John Stevens handled engineering and logistical problems; Dr. William Gorgas worked to eradicate yellow fever and malaria*

🗐 CRF: History and Geography Activity: A Canal Across Panama

go.hrw.com
Online Resources

KEYWORD: SD7 CH17
TOPIC: PANAMA CANAL

Differentiating Instruction

Below Level

Special Education Students

Materials construction paper, colored markers

1. Guide students in a discussion about the events that led up to the building of the Panama Canal. Have students study the photo and then discuss the hardships that faced all those who worked to build the canal.

2. Organize the class into small groups. Have each group work together to write a poem and design a poster to honor the hard-working people who built the canal. Have students

draw their posters on the construction paper and write their poems at the bottom of the poster.

3. Have volunteers share their posters and poems with the class. **LS Visual-Spatial, Auditory-Musical**

🗐 Alternative Assessment Handbook, Rubrics 3: Artwork; and 26: Poems and Songs

Answers

Reading Check *Platt Amendment made Cuba a U.S. protectorate.*

❸ What was the Roosevelt Corollary? *doctrine that threatened use of U.S. military force to prohibit further European involvement in Latin America*

The Roosevelt Corollary

Recall What proverb inspired President Roosevelt's corollary to the Monroe Doctrine? *"Speak softly and carry a big stick; you will go far."*

Analyze What financial situation made Latin American nations particularly vulnerable to forceful takeover? *They were in debt and unable to repay the loans.*

Making Inferences Why were European lenders so eager to invest in Latin America? *gave Europeans power in Latin American countries; area had many laborers, consumers, and raw materials*

Activity Giving Loans Have students make a chart showing the cause and effect of foreign loans to Latin American countries.
LS Visual-Spatial

Map Transparency, Imperialism, 1900

Imperialism, 1900

Compare Have students use the map to determine how much foreign territory the U.S. held compared to Great Britain.

Answers

Interpreting Maps *Africa; South America; that it was quite effective*

Reading Check *The U.S. wished to continue building a canal across the Isthmus of Panama, but Colombia would not ratify the treaty.*

on pools of standing water, and bred spiders, ants, and lizards to feed on the adult mosquitoes. By 1913 malaria was almost eliminated.

Meanwhile, John F. Stevens resigned in 1907, and Lt. Col. George W. Goethals continued the mammoth task of coordinating the construction—not just the canal but all the housing and other facilities needed for workers. His efforts led him to be called the Genius of the Panama Canal.

More than 60 giant steam shovels bit into the land, digging out hundreds of train-car loads of earth each day. Up to 44,000 workers, many recruited from the British West Indies, labored on the project at a time. There were frequent accidents, lost equipment, and deaths—but there was also progress. In August 1914 the SS *Ancon* became the first ship to pass officially through the Panama Canal.

READING CHECK **Drawing Conclusions** Why did the United States get involved in Panama's rebellion against Colombian rule?

The Roosevelt Corollary

The Monroe Doctrine, proclaimed in 1823, declared the Western Hemisphere off-limits to further colonization by European nations. For much of the 1800s, however, the Monroe Doctrine was only an idle threat.

After the Spanish-American War, however, presidents began to back up the Monroe Doctrine with military strength. They wanted to protect American economic interests in Latin America.

In the late 1800s Europeans and Americans invested large sums of money in Latin America, which had a wealth of laborers, consumers, and raw materials. Much of this investment came in the form of high-interest bank loans, which many Latin American countries found difficult to repay. Foreign powers often intervened to collect the loans.

In 1904 the Dominican Republic was unable to repay its European lenders. Fearing that the Europeans would use force to collect

IMPERIALISM, c. 1900

Map legend:
American, Belgian, British, Chinese, Danish, Dutch, French, German, Italian, Japanese, Ottoman, Portuguese, Russian, Spanish, Independent country

0   2,500   5,000 Miles
0   2,500   5,000 Kilometers
Miller projection

GEOGRAPHY SKILLS **INTERPRETING MAPS**

Region Which continent was most affected by imperialism? least?
Human/Environment Interaction What can you infer from the map about the effectiveness of the Roosevelt Corollary?

See Skills Handbook, p. H20

Skills Focus: Analyzing Secondary Sources   At Level

Reading Like a Historian Skill
The Roosevelt Corollary

1. Have students conduct outside research on the Panamanian rebellion and the way in which the United States gained rights to the Panama Canal Zone. Have students locate and use primary and secondary sources in their research.

2. Have students write a well-reasoned one-page letter to President Theodore Roosevelt, either praising or condemning his actions in securing the rights to build the Panama Canal.

Students should defend their position with information gained from their research. Have students develop and attach a bibliography to their written letters.

3. Have volunteers read their letters to the class. Then guide students in a discussion of the ideas and arguments presented in the letters.
LS Verbal-Linguistic

Alternative Assessment Handbook, Rubrics 25: Personal Letters; and 30: Research

the debts, President Roosevelt decided to take a tough policy stand. Without seeking approval from any Latin American nation, he issued the **Roosevelt Corollary** to the Monroe Doctrine.

HISTORY'S VOICES

❝Chronic wrongdoing . . . in the Western Hemisphere . . . may force the United States, however reluctantly . . . to the exercise of an international police power.❞

—Theodore Roosevelt, Roosevelt Corollary, 1904

Roosevelt was putting into practice one of his favorite proverbs: "Speak softly and carry a big stick; you will go far." Applying this "big stick" policy to the situation in the Dominican Republic, the United States pledged to use armed forces to prevent any European country from seizing Dominican territory.

Roosevelt hoped to avoid a military confrontation. To ensure that the Europeans were repaid, the United States took control of collecting all Dominican customs duties.

The Roosevelt Corollary succeeded in bringing more stability to the region and keeping other nations out. But America's willingness to use its police power made many Latin Americans uneasy. They worried about continued U.S. involvement in their affairs.

READING CHECK **Identifying Problems and Solutions** Why did Roosevelt decide to announce the Roosevelt Corollary?

Reshaping U.S. Diplomacy

During the presidency of William H. Taft, U.S. influence in Latin America deepened. Taft believed in advancing U.S. interests in other countries through **dollar diplomacy**, a policy of promoting American economic interests in other countries and using that economic power to achieve American policy goals.

To reduce the chances of European interference in Latin America, Taft suggested that Americans buy out European loans. By 1914 Americans had invested more than $1.6 billion in Latin America, mainly in mines, railroads, and banana and sugar plantations.

Dollar diplomacy, however, caused resentment. In Nicaragua, for example, American banks made loans to the government and became heavily involved in the economy. In 1912 President Taft had to send in U.S. troops to quell an uprising against the authorities.

President Woodrow Wilson, who succeeded Taft in 1913, rejected the <u>concept</u> of dollar diplomacy in favor of moral diplomacy, the use of persuasion and American ideals to advance the nation's interests abroad. Nonetheless, he did send in troops when civil unrest shook Haiti in 1915 and the Dominican Republic in 1916. In both cases, U.S. Marines occupied the countries for years.

ACADEMIC VOCABULARY
concept abstract notion or idea

READING CHECK **Contrasting** How did Taft and Wilson differ in their patterns of diplomacy?

SECTION 3 ASSESSMENT

go.hrw.com
Online Quiz
Keyword: SD7 HP17

Reviewing Ideas, Terms, and People

1. **a. Recall** How did the United States govern Puerto Rico?
   b. Draw Conclusions Why did the United States make Cuba a **protectorate**?

2. **a. Identify** What was the Panama Canal Zone?
   b. Explain Why was it important to control malaria and yellow fever in Panama?
   c. Predict What effect do you think the Panama Canal had on American military capabilities?

3. **a. Identify** What was the **Roosevelt Corollary**?
   b. Contrast What did the Roosevelt Corollary do that the Monroe Doctrine had not done?

4. **a. Recall** Which president favored **dollar diplomacy**?
   b. Evaluate How effective do you think dollar diplomacy was in Nicaragua?

Critical Thinking

5. **Organizing Information** Copy the table below and fill in the names of Latin American lands discussed in this chapter. Then briefly note how the United States became involved in each.

Country or Territory	U.S. Involvement

FOCUS ON WRITING

6. **Descriptive** Imagine you are a worker helping to build the Panama Canal. Write a diary entry giving details about the task you're doing, the hardships you face, and why you think the project is worthwhile.

ENTERING THE WORLD STAGE **569**

Section 3 Assessment Answers

1. **a.** as a territory
   b. so that no other nation could take control

2. **a.** 10-mile-wide region alongside canal
   b. They were sickening and killing workers.
   c. possible answer—U.S. ships could move quickly between Atlantic and Pacific

3. **a.** pledge that U.S. would police Western Hemisphere
   b. threatened the use of military force

4. **a.** Taft
   b. possible answer—not very effective, since Taft had to send in American troops

5. Cuba, Platt Amendment; Puerto Rico, Foraker Act, Colombia and Panama, Panama Canal

6. possible answer—work is brutal, many accidents, unbearable heat, diseases; it will shorten trip between Atlantic and Pacific

● **Direct Teach** ●

Reading Focus

❹ How did Presidents Taft and Wilson reshape U.S. diplomacy? *Taft—used economic power; Wilson—tried to nurture constitutional governments, used military force when needed*

Reshaping U.S. Diplomacy

Explain How did President Taft use dollar diplomacy? *encouraged Americans to buy out European loans in Latin American countries*

Analyze Why did President Wilson send troops into Haiti and the Dominican Republic? *may have believed they would come under foreign control*

● **Review & Assess** ●

Close
Guide students in a discussion of U.S. foreign policy and involvement in Latin America.

Review
Online Quiz, Section 3
Daily Test Practice Transparency

Assess
SE Section 3 Assessment
Progress Assessment: Section 3 Quiz
Alternative Assessment Handbook

Reteach
Interactive Reader and Study Guide, Section 3
Interactive Skills Tutor CD-ROM

Answers

Reading Check (left) *President Roosevelt feared that since the Dominican Republic was unable to repay its European lenders, the Europeans would use force to collect the loans.* **(right)** *Taft believed in dollar diplomacy while Wilson believed in nurturing constitutional governments.*

569

Building the Panama Canal

Info to Know

Malaria Although the disease was controlled during the building of the canal, malaria is still one of the world's leading health threats, along with HIV/AIDS and tuberculosis. The United Nations' World Health Organization maintains that people who live in tropical and subtropical regions, some 40 percent of the world's population, are at risk for the disease. Prevention has been hampered by several factors. The malaria parasite has grown resistant to drugs that treat the disease itself. In addition, insecticides that kill the mosquitoes that carry the disease gradually lose their effectiveness.

MISCONCEPTION ///ALERT\\\

The Panama Canal was not the first transportation link across the strategic isthmus. In 1846, the government of Colombia, which ruled Panama, proposed a railroad link between the Atlantic and Pacific oceans. It suggested that the United States assume responsibility for protecting the access to and neutrality of the railroad. The United States successfully built the railroad, finishing it in 1855.

*Interactive

HISTORY & Geography

Caribbean Sea

Lake Gatún
Created by damming the Chagres River, this lake's water feeds the lock system and was once the world's largest human-made lake.

Gaillard Cut
At the continental divide, the canal route cuts through the lowest point between two hills, 335.5 feet above sea level. For nearly 9 miles, workers blasted loose the rock. Steam shovels loaded the spoil onto railroad cars to be hauled away.

San Francisco   New York

5,200 miles

13,000 miles

Building the Panama Canal

Sailors had dreamed of a canal through Central America since the 1500s, but it wasn't until the early 1900s that engineers had the technology to build it. The canal's planners and builders faced considerable geographic obstacles along the 50-mile path.

570

Skills Focus: Analyzing Visuals   Below Level

Reading Like a Historian Skill
A Canal Quiz

1. Have students work with a partner to examine the illustration of the canal on this spread. Have students write five questions for a quiz based on the visual portrayal of the Panama Canal, the lock system, the Western Hemisphere map, and the text support.

2. Have each pair exchange quizzes with another pair and answer the questions, using the illustration and text as aids.

3. Have the two pairs check their answers and resolve any disagreements. **LS Verbal-Linguistic, Visual-Spatial**

   Alternative Assessment Handbook, Rubric 35: Solving Problems

Madden Lake and Dam
The lake is used to provide more water to the canal system.

How Canal Locks Work

1. A ship enters a lock chamber where the water is level with the body of water the ship is leaving.

2. Gates close behind the ship, and the water level in the chamber rises until level with the next body of water.

3. The gates in front of the boat open to let the vessel pass.

Swamps
When research showed that the malaria-carrying mosquito could not fly far without feeding on vegetation, hundreds of acres were cleared near housing and work sites. To kill the larvae, over 100 square miles of swamps were drained and thousands of gallons of oil were sprayed on the remaining water.

Pacific Ocean

GEOGRAPHY SKILLS INTERPRETING MAPS

go.hrw.com
Interactive Map
Keyword: SD7 CH17

1. **Location** What made this part of Panama a good location for a canal?

2. **Human/Environment Interaction** What obstacles made the canal's construction difficult?

See Skills Handbook, p. H20

History and Geography

Building the Panama Canal

Activity **Savings from the Panama Canal** Have students calculate how many miles the Panama Canal saved sailors traveling from the East Coast to the West Coast of the U.S. Have students first find how many miles the journey from New York to San Francisco took before and after the construction of the canal. *13,000; 5,200* Then have students calculate the total miles saved by the construction of the canal for that journey. *13,000 – 5,200 = 7,800* Finally, have students compute the percentage savings this represents. *7,800/13,000 = 60 percent savings*
LS Logical-Mathematical

Info to Know

Planning the Panama Canal Much of the initial planning for the Panama Canal was done by a French noble, Ferdinand de Lesseps. Earlier in his career, he had supervised the building of the Suez Canal in Egypt, which opened in 1869. When he was 74, he turned his attention to the Isthmus of Panama. An international organization chose him to lead the effort in 1879, and work began two years later. However, the work was much more difficult than in Egypt. The land to be crossed was hilly and rocky, and many workers died from tropical diseases such as malaria. After eight years and 50 million cubic meters of excavation, de Lesseps gave up. However, his group's equipment, including buildings, trains, and maps, was sold to the United States in 1904.

Differentiating Instruction

At Level

Learners Having Difficulty

Research Required

Materials paper, colored pencils

1. Divide students into small groups. Have each group make a detailed drawing of the lock system.

2. Have students share their drawings with the class, explaining the different parts of the lock system and how they work. Display the drawings in the classroom as you read about the Panama Canal.

3. As an extension, have students construct models of the way canal locks work to raise and lower water levels. **LS** Visual-Spatial, Kinesthetic

📖 Alternative Assessment Handbook, Rubric 3: Artwork

Answers

Interpreting Maps 1. *relatively narrow strip of land; near lakes and rivers that could be used as part of the canal;* **2.** *mosquitoes carried malaria; some of the land above sea level; had to blast rock out of the way; difficulty constructing locks*

571

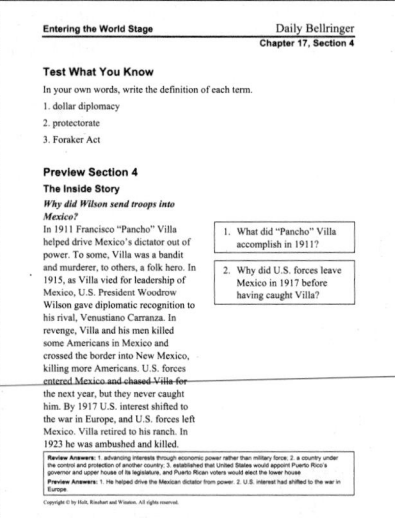

Wilson and the Mexican Revolution

BEFORE YOU READ

MAIN IDEA

American intervention in Mexico's revolution caused strained relations between the two neighbors.

READING FOCUS

1. How did the Díaz dictatorship spark a revolution in Mexico?

2. How and why did the United States intervene in the Mexican Revolution?

3. How did the Mexican Revolution conclude?

KEY TERMS AND PEOPLE

Porfirio Díaz
Francisco Madero
Mexican Revolution
Emiliano Zapata
Francisco "Pancho" Villa
Victoriano Huerta
Tampico incident
Battle of Veracruz
John J. Pershing

TAKING NOTES As you read, take notes identifying major events of the Mexican Revolution. Record your notes in a graphic organizer like the one shown below. You may need to add more rows.

Event	Date

THE INSIDE STORY

Why did Wilson send troops into Mexico? To many people, Francisco "Pancho" Villa was a bandit, a cattle rustler, even a murderer. To many others, he was a folk hero, a kind of Mexican Robin Hood. Legends and ballads told about his deeds. Villa was a brilliant horse rider, leading a cavalry force called Los Dorados ("Golden Ones") in northern Mexico. In 1911 he helped drive Mexico's dictator out of power.

Two years later, Villa was again at the center of a power struggle. This time he was vying with Venustiano Carranza to lead Mexico. When U.S. president Woodrow Wilson recognized Carranza as president, Villa was furious. In 1916 Villa and his men killed a group of American mining engineers in Mexico, and then crossed the border to Columbus, New Mexico. In an attack there, Villa's followers killed more Americans.

Wilson was outraged by the raid on American territory. He sent General John J. Pershing into Mexico with a "punitive expedition." With vehicles and even airplanes, they chased Villa through northern Mexico for almost a year. They never caught him.

By 1917 the United States was preoccupied with war in Europe. American forces left Mexico, and Pancho Villa retired to his ranch. In 1923, however, Villa was ambushed and killed. He died as dramatically as he had lived.

PANCHO VILLA WAGES WAR

◀ **Pancho Villa rides to revolution on horseback.**

572

Dictatorship Sparks a Revolution

When Mexico erupted in revolution in the early 1900s, the United States was drawn into the conflict because of its economic ties with Mexico. But what led to the revolution in the first place?

The Díaz dictatorship For most of the period from 1877 to 1910, the dictator **Porfirio Díaz** ruled Mexico. When Díaz came to power, he brought order to Mexico, which had endured decades of war and unrest. However, order came at a price. Díaz jailed his opponents. He did not permit freedom of the press. He used the army to maintain peace at any cost.

Díaz also got money from foreign investors, including many Americans. Their investments helped modernize Mexico very quickly. Railroads expanded. Production of factory goods doubled. Cotton production also doubled. Still, most Mexicans did not enjoy the benefits of modernization. Wealth became concentrated in the hands of foreign investors and a small Mexican elite. Most Mexicans lived in poverty, and opposition to Díaz grew steadily.

Overthrowing Díaz In 1910 Porfirio Díaz ran for re-election. As in earlier elections, Díaz controlled the outcome. Just before the voting began, he jailed his opponent **Francisco Madero**, a wealthy landowner but a reform-minded idealist. When the ballots were counted, Díaz claimed he had earned a million votes and Madero had earned fewer than 200.

After being released from jail in September 1910, Madero fled over the border to Texas. There he declared himself president of Mexico and called for a revolution. When Madero returned to Mexico in November, he found bands of rebels already active.

The **Mexican Revolution** unfolded as a series of uprisings in different parts of the country. In the south, **Emiliano Zapata** and his army of mostly Native American peasants—known as Zapatistas—wanted land to be returned to the native peoples. They began to seize land by force. Meanwhile, in northern Mexico, **Francisco "Pancho" Villa** and Pascual Orozco led a large-scale revolt against Díaz. Rebellion spread, and in May 1911, Díaz resigned and went into exile in France.

Shaky leadership In November 1911, Francisco Madero was elected president of Mexico. He tried to establish a democratic government, but he was quickly overwhelmed by the very forces he had unleashed in toppling Díaz. Madero faced challenges from all sides. Even the commander of the government troops, **Victoriano Huerta** (WEHR-tah), proved disloyal. In 1913 Huerta overthrew Madero, imprisoned him, and had him executed soon thereafter. Huerta named himself president of Mexico, but immediately four armies rose up to fight him. The situation in Mexico grew dire.

READING CHECK **Sequencing** What major events occurred between the Mexican election of 1910 and the declaration of Huerta as president?

Turmoil in Mexico

Conflicting visions for Mexico's future led to a series of violent government overthrows.

Porfirio Díaz ruled Mexico as an oppressive dictator from 1877 to 1910. He modernized the country, but kept most of the people impoverished.

Emiliano Zapata led the revolt against Díaz in the south. He and his fellow Zapatistas wanted land returned to Native Americans.

After Díaz fled in the face of revolt, Francisco Madero became president of Mexico. He tried to establish a democratic government.

Victoriano Huerta executed Madero and named himself president. He faced opposition from Mexicans and the United States.

573

Direct Teach

Reading Focus

❶ How did the Díaz dictatorship spark a revolution in Mexico? *civil rights limited; opponents jailed; used army to maintain peace; widespread poverty*

Dictatorship Sparks a Revolution

Sequence How did Francisco Madero become Mexico's president? *ran against Díaz, was jailed; fled to U.S. and declared himself president of Mexico; returned to Mexico, rebels forced out Díaz, and Madero was elected president*

Analyze Why did Díaz imprison Madero? *Madero was a threat to his rule.*

Develop Why do you think Huerta was unable to control the armies? *Huerta had executed elected president; armies were fighting for democracy.*

📄 CRF: Biography: Sara Estela Ramirez

Teaching Tip

Have students copy and add a column to the chart of Mexico's rebel leaders during the revolution. Then have students add one detail about each leader to help them follow the sequence of the Mexican Revolution.

Collaborative Learning

At Level

Dictatorship Sparks a Revolution

Materials construction paper, colored markers, scissors

1. Guide students in a discussion of the overthrow and resignation of Porfirio Díaz. Ask students why they think foreign investors and wealthy Mexicans did not try to keep Díaz's government in power. Then have students give reasons to support Díaz's overthrow.

2. Make a list of the responses for all students to see, and have students copy the list onto their own paper.

3. Organize the students into small groups. Have each group design a campaign rally with posters, banners, slogans, and speeches to attract followers to overthrow Díaz.

4. Have volunteers read their speeches and share their campaign materials with the class.
LS **Interpersonal, Kinesthetic**

📄 Alternative Assessment Handbook, Rubrics 24: Oral Presentations; and 34: Slogans and Banners

Answers

Reading Check *Madero fled to U.S. then returned to Mexico to start revolution, Zapata seized land, Villa and Orozco led revolt, Díaz resigned, Madero elected president, Huerta overthrew Madero and had him executed*

573

❷ How and why did the United States intervene in the Mexican Revolution? *sent troops and occupied Veracruz; did not recognize Huerta's claim to presidency; Tampico incident; Germans were sending arms to Huerta*

The United States Intervenes

Recall What started the Tampico incident? *U.S. sailors arrested by soldiers loyal to Huerta in Tampico, Mexico*

Summarize Why did the United States believe that it was justified in seizing Veracruz? *German ship loaded with arms for Huerta en route to Veracruz*

Primary Source

". . . therefore I come to ask your approval that I should use the armed forces of the United States in such ways and to such an extent as may be necessary to obtain from General Huerta . . . the fullest recognition of the rights and dignity of the United States . . ."
— Woodrow Wilson
Address to Congress, April 20, 1914

go.hrw.com
Online Resources
KEYWORD: SD7 CH17
TOPIC: MEXICAN REVOLUTION

Answers

Photo *mediation by Argentina, Brazil, and Chile*

Reading Check *President Wilson thought Huerta had no legitimate claim to power.*

574

The United States Intervenes

Many European nations recognized Huerta's government, but the United States did not. President Woodrow Wilson viewed Huerta as an assassin with no legitimate claim to power. In February 1914 Wilson authorized arms sales to Huerta's enemies. For a time, Wilson followed a policy of "watchful waiting." Then came an incident that let him move openly against Huerta.

The Tampico incident On April 9, 1914, nine crew members of the USS *Dolphin* went ashore for supplies in the Mexican port of Tampico. There they were arrested by soldiers loyal to Huerta. The Americans were quickly released unharmed, and Mexican officials apologized. However, U.S. Admiral Henry Mayo demanded more than a formal apology from the Mexican government. He also insisted that the Mexicans give the American flag a 21-gun salute within 24 hours. Huerta refused this humiliating demand.

Because of the **Tampico incident**, the president asked Congress on April 20 to authorize the use of armed forces against Mexico. Congress approved the request on April 22, but events in Mexico moved faster.

Occupying Veracruz While waiting for Congress to act, President Wilson learned some alarming news. A German ship loaded with weapons for Huerta was heading for the Mexican port city of Veracruz. Without deliberating further, Wilson ordered the U.S. Navy to seize the city.

Under the cover of a naval bombardment, U.S. Marines then landed at Veracruz. They were met by gunfire from Mexican soldiers, and a violent battle erupted. The Americans had expected to seize control with little bloodshed. Instead, 17 Americans and some 300 Mexicans died during the **Battle of Veracruz**.

For the next six months, U.S. troops occupied the city. The occupation threatened to plunge the United States and Mexico into war. Crisis was avoided, though, thanks to mediation by Argentina, Brazil, and Chile.

Meanwhile, Huerta struggled to stay in power. In June the mediators called for Huerta's resignation and for the creation of a provisional government. Huerta refused. Pressure mounted against him within Mexico and beyond. In July he resigned and fled to Spain.

READING CHECK **Identifying Cause and Effect** Why did the United States take action against Huerta's government?

The Battle of Veracruz
American sailors aboard a battleship use field artillery to attack Veracruz from their position off the coast. *What prevented the Battle of Veracruz from turning into a full-scale war between the United States and Mexico?*

574 CHAPTER 17

Reading Skill
The United States Intervenes

1. Guide students in a review of the information concerning President Wilson's belief in nurturing democracies and his decision to send the U.S. Marines to Veracruz.

2. Have students consider the options available to the United States and Congress following the unrest in Mexico and the Tampico incident. *U.S. could accept the Mexican apology; could decide to support the Huerta government; could refuse to recognize its* *legitimacy; could declare war*

3. Have students select one of the options and write a letter to a member of Congress supporting and justifying the position they have taken.

4. Have students present their letters to the class.
🔲 **Verbal-Linguistic, Kinesthetic**

The Revolution Concludes

With Huerta gone from Mexico, Venustiano Carranza stepped in and declared himself the leader of the Mexican Revolution in August 1914. He faced opposition from Pancho Villa and Emiliano Zapata, however. For some time, it appeared that Villa and Zapata would triumph. This worried American leaders, who feared that U.S. economic interests would be harmed by the land redistribution that Zapata and Villa wanted. President Wilson decided to support the more moderate Carranza.

Pancho Villa retaliated with violence. In March 1916 he led hundreds of troops across the U.S. border to the small, isolated town of Columbus, New Mexico. Striking at dawn, Villa's troops burned the town and killed 17 Americans. This was the first armed invasion of the continental United States since the War of 1812.

Pursuing Pancho Villa President Woodrow Wilson quickly ordered a military expedition to hunt down Villa. Within a week, General **John J. Pershing** led more than 10,000 U.S. troops into Mexico. They searched for 11 months but were never able to capture Pancho Villa. The farther Pershing went into Mexican territory, the more the Mexicans resented the Americans.

By early September 1916, nearly 150,000 U.S. National Guard members were stationed along the Mexican border. Wilson realized that the threat of war increased each day that U.S. troops remained in Mexico. Furthermore, America's attention was shifting to Europe, where World War I was raging. In late January 1917, the president called off the search for Pancho Villa and withdrew U.S. troops from Mexico. Nonetheless, for the rest of Wilson's presidency, relations between Mexico and the United States remained strained.

A new constitution for Mexico In December 1916, Venustiano Carranza called a constitutional convention. A new constitution went into effect on February 5, 1917. The constitution contained the ideas of all the revolutionary groups. It protected the liberties and rights of citizens.

Despite the new constitution, fighting continued in Mexico until 1920. Mexico's economy suffered terribly. Agriculture was disrupted, mines were abandoned, and factories were destroyed. Many Mexican men and women immigrated to the United States in search of work and a more stable life.

THE IMPACT TODAY

Daily Life
More than 25 million people of Mexican descent now live in the United States.

READING CHECK **Summarizing** How did Pancho Villa cause trouble for the United States?

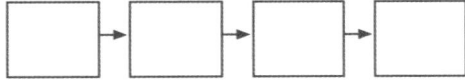

 go.hrw.com
Online Quiz
Keyword: SD7 HP17

Reviewing Ideas, Terms, and People

1. **a. Identify** Who was **Porfirio Díaz**?
   b. Explain Why did Mexicans rise up against Díaz?
   c. Elaborate Why do you think that **Francisco Madero** and **Victoriana Huerta** both faced challenges after they claimed Mexico's presidency?

2. **a. Recall** What was the **Tampico incident**?
   b. Analyze How did the Tampico incident draw the United States into armed conflict with Mexico?
   c. Evaluate Was the United States justified in launching the **Battle of Veracruz**? Why or why not?

3. **a. Describe** What made **Pancho Villa** decide to lead a raid into New Mexico?
   b. Draw Conclusions Why was President Wilson so eager to capture Pancho Villa?
   c. Predict How do you think the expedition to find Pancho Villa affected relations between Mexicans and Americans?

Critical Thinking

4. **Sequencing** Copy the flowchart below and record the major sequence of events of the Mexican Revolution, from the overthrow of Díaz to the Constitution of 1917. Add as many boxes as you need.

$$\square \rightarrow \square \rightarrow \square \rightarrow \square$$

FOCUS ON SPEAKING

5. **Persuasive** Imagine that you are a Mexican revolutionary in 1911, while Porfirio Díaz is still clinging to power. Prepare a speech to give to people in your community, explaining why you oppose Díaz and whom you support in his place. Encourage your listeners to join you in the fight to overthrow Díaz and bring better leadership to Mexico.

Section 4 Assessment Answers

1. **a.** Mexican dictator from 1877 to 1910
   b. civil rights restricted; widespread poverty; use of military force
   c. neither could gain the support of the entire nation

2. **a.** arrest of nine crew members of the USS *Dolphin* who went into Tampico
   b. Mexican government refused U.S. demand for 21-gun salute to American flag
   c. possible answer—no, U.S. was fighting against civilians, not the Mexican army

3. **a.** U.S. supported Carranza instead of Villa.
   b. Villa burned American town and killed U.S. citizens.
   c. possible answer—caused Mexicans to resent Americans and Americans to blame Mexicans

4. See Turmoil in Mexico. Huerta resigned; Carranza took power

5. possible answer—Díaz is cruel, should be overthrown

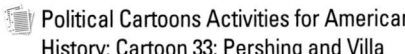 **Direct Teach**

Reading Focus

3 How did the Mexican Revolution conclude? *U.S. withdrew troops; new Mexican constitution put into effect; Wilson supported Carranza as new Mexican leader*

The Revolution Concludes

Identify Who led the opposition to Carranza? *Pancho Villa; Emiliano Zapata*

Explain Why was the U.S. determined to find Pancho Villa? *He attacked a U.S. town and killed 17 Americans; he was a threat to Carranza's government.*

📖 Political Cartoons Activities for American History: Cartoon 33: Pershing and Villa

Review & Assess

Close

Have students make a chronological list of the events and leaders discussed in this section.

Review

📕 Online Quiz, Section 4

🖨 Daily Test Practice Transparency

Assess

SE Section 4 Assessment

📖 Progress Assessment: Section 4 Quiz

📖 Alternative Assessment Handbook

Reteach

📖 Interactive Reader and Study Guide, Section 4

💿 Interactive Skills Tutor CD-ROM

Answers

Reading Check *Villa crossed the U.S. border and burned Columbus, New Mexico, killing 17 Americans*

575

Views on American Expansionism

Word Help

wail cry
imperative necessary
paramount main, primary
sloth laziness
nought nothing
cloak cover, conceal

Info to Know

Liliuokalani Queen Liliuokalani was educated by missionaries and even toured the West before ascending the throne. From an early age, Liliuokalani showed a talent for music. She wrote over 160 poetic melodies and chants during her lifetime, including one of the four Hawaiian national anthems.

Primary Source

Princess Kaiulani made her plea directly to President Cleveland. In her book *Hawaii's Story by Hawaii's Queen*, Queen Liliuokalani expressed her gratitude to Cleveland for his efforts to help her: "The Hawaiian people almost worship the name of President Cleveland; for he has tried to do what was right, and it was only because he was not supported by Congress that his efforts were not successful . . . [M]y grateful people will always remember that, in his message to Congress and in his official acts, Mr. Cleveland showed the greatest anxiety to do that which was just, and that which was for the honor of the nation over which he had been elected chief ruler. He has always had from me the utmost respect and esteem."

— Liliuokalani, Queen of Hawaii

Hawaii's Story by Hawaii's Queen, Chapter XLI, 1898

Views on American Expansionism

Historical Context The documents below provide information about attitudes regarding American expansion in the late 1800s.

Task Examine the documents and answer the questions that follow. Then write an essay about interaction between imperialists and local peoples. Use facts from the documents and the chapter to support the position you take in your thesis statement.

DOCUMENT 1

Princess Kaiulani, niece of Hawaii's Queen Liliuokalani, visited Washington, D.C., in 1893 to plead for a restoration of the monarchy.

"Seventy years ago, Christian Americans sent over Christian men and women to give religion and civilization to Hawaii. Today, three of the sons of the missionaries are at your capitol, asking you to undo their fathers' work. Who sent them? Who gave them the authority to break the constitution which they swore they would uphold? Today, I, a poor, weak girl, with not one of my people near me and all these statesmen against me, have the strength to stand up for the rights of my people. Even now I can hear their wail in my heart, and I am strong . . . strong in the faith of God, strong in the knowledge that I am right, strong in the strength of seventy million people who in this free land will hear my cry and will refuse to let their flag cover dishonor to mine!"

DOCUMENT 2

John L. Stevens was the U.S. minister to Hawaii in 1893, when Queen Liliuokalani was forced from the throne. That year, he wrote "The Hawaiian Situation. II. A Plea for Annexation."

"The Hawaiian monarchy being thus extinct, and the Hawaiian Islands being not sufficient to constitute an independent nation, all who really understand their situation know that good government is now the first and imperative need . . . [T]hese Islands have become thoroughly Americanized . . . For sixty years the Islands have had the American school system . . . The two principal daily newspapers are edited, owned, and published by Americans. The principal lawyers at the bar and on the bench are Americans . . . and educated in American colleges. More than eighty percent of the trade, amounting to more than twenty million dollars per year, is with the United States. American newspapers, magazines, and books are in as familiar use in the Islands as in the United States . . .

A paramount reason why annexation should not be long postponed is that, if it soon takes place, the crown and government lands will be cut up and sold to American and Christian Caucasian people, thus preventing the Islands from being submerged and overrun by Asiatics, putting an end to Japanese ambitions stimulated by our strong European rival."

Skills Focus: Making Oral Presentations
At Level

Reading Like a Historian Skill
The Annexation of Hawaii

1. Divide the class into groups of five students. Remind students that in 1893 President Grover Cleveland had to decide whether to support or oppose the annexation of Hawaii.

2. Have each group study the arguments for and against annexation. Then have each group split into two opposing two-person teams. Have one team support the annexation of Hawaii and the other oppose annexation and favor the restoration of the monarchy.

3. Have each group conduct a debate, with the fifth group member serving as moderator. Students may use information from their textbooks, or they may conduct additional research to help them support their arguments for or against annexation. When each group has finished its debate, ask the moderators to announce the winning position. **LS Interpersonal**

Alternative Assessment Handbook, Rubric 10: Debates

DOCUMENT 3

Puck was a political magazine that often used humor and satire to address social and political issues. In this magazine cover, the annexation of Hawaii is shown as a marriage between a Hawaiian woman and Uncle Sam. President William McKinley is depicted as a minister, and Alabama senator John T. Morgan stands behind the couple with a shotgun.

ANOTHER SHOTGUN WEDDING, WITH NEITHER PARTY WILLING.

Primary Source

In 1993, the 100th anniversary of the overthrow of the kingdom of Hawaii, a joint resolution of the United States Congress officially apologized to the people of Hawaii: "The Congress . . . apologizes to Native Hawaiians on behalf of the people of the United States for the overthrow of the Kingdom of Hawaii on January 17, 1893 with the participation of agents and citizens of the United States, and the deprivation of the rights of Native Hawaiians to self-determination; expresses its commitment to acknowledge the ramifications of the overthrow of the Kingdom of Hawaii, in order to provide a proper foundation for reconciliation between the United States and the Native Hawaiian people . . ."

United States Public Law 103–150, 103d Congress Joint Resolution 19, Nov. 23, 1993

Skills Focus: READING LIKE A HISTORIAN

1. a. Recall Refer to Document 1. Why does Kaiulani feel that she will be successful?
b. Contrast In Kaiulani's view, how are the sons of the early missionaries different from their fathers?

2. a. Identify Refer to Document 2. What reasons does Stevens give for annexing Hawaii to the United States?
b. Predict How might Stevens have responded to a statement like that made by Kaiulani?

3. a. Identify Refer to Document 3. What expression is shown on the woman's face?

b. Evaluate How would you describe the cartoonist's opinion of annexation?

4. Document-Based Essay Question Consider the question below and form a thesis statement. Using examples from Documents 1, 2, and 3, create an outline and write a short essay supporting your position.
What factors influenced the decision to annex Hawaii?

See **Skills Handbook**, pp. H28–H29, H31

Skills Focus: Interpreting Political Cartoons

At Level

Reading Like A Historian Skill
Perspectives on Annexing Hawaii

Research Required

1. Organize the class into small groups. Have each group look for five political cartoons that address American annexation of Hawaii. Students should try to locate political cartoons that illustrate different points of view.

2. Have students write a brief analysis for each cartoon. Students should explain what message the political cartoon conveys and what bias, if any, the artist demonstrates.

3. Have volunteers share their cartoons and analyses with the class. Then guide the class in a discussion of the positive and negative effects of the U.S. annexation of Hawaii.
LS Interpersonal, Visual-Spatial

Alternative Assessment Handbook, Rubric 27: Political Cartoons

Answers

Reading Like a Historian
1. a. *She thinks that she is morally right and that the American people will support her appeal.* **b.** *She thinks that the fathers brought religion and civilization to Hawaii, while their descendants want to undo their work.*
2. a. *the islands are Americanized already; to keep them from being taken over by the Japanese;* **b.** *possible answer—Missionaries civilized Hawaii, which is equivalent to making it American.* **3. a.** *anger and sadness;* **b.** *negative, forced upon the people;* **4.** *possible answers—desire of imperialists to control the government, economy, education, religion, and labor of local peoples.*

Answers

Visual Summary

Review and Inquiry Review the graphic visual summary with students. Then have students work in pairs to write a headline and a "yellow journalism" paragraph with at least two supporting details for each box. Have volunteers read their paragraphs to the class.

📖 Quick Facts Transparency: Entering the World Stage

Reviewing Key Terms and People

1. bayonet constitution
2. spheres of influence
3. Open Door Policy
4. yellow journalism
5. Platt Amendment
6. dollar diplomacy
7. Porfirio Díaz
8. Tampico incident
9. Battle of Veracruz

Comprehension and Critical Thinking

10. a. queen of Hawaii
b. American sugar producers believed the only way to protect their businesses was to become part of the U.S., but Queen Liliuokalani wanted to reassert Hawaiian independence.
c. possible answer—they were probably impressed; yes

11. a. a letter written by Spain's minister to the U.S. which ridiculed McKinley and outraged Americans
b. Spain gave up all claims to Cuba, ceded Puerto Rico and Guam to U.S., and turned control of the Philippines over to U.S. for a $20 million payment.
c. possible answer—The media was extremely influential because it portrayed the Spanish as ruthless and Cubans as victims. As a result, Americans wanted the U.S. to intervene.

Visual Summary: Entering the World Stage

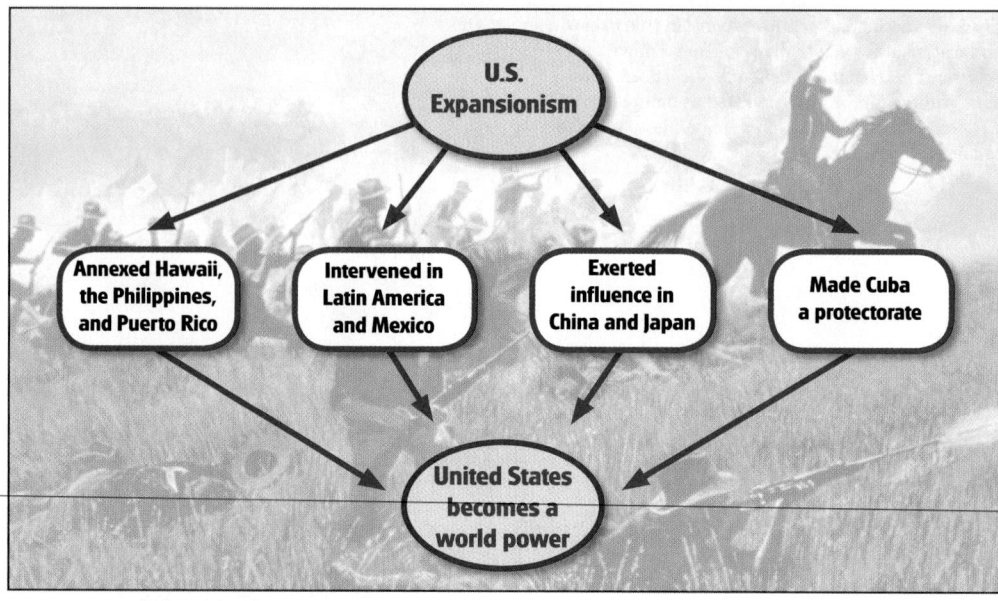

Reviewing Key Terms and People

Complete each sentence by filling the blank with the correct term or name.

1. In 1887 King Kalakaua was forced to sign the _____, which severely restricted his power and denied most Hawaiians the right to vote.
2. Imperialist nations carved out _____ in China—geographic areas where they dominated politics or the economy.
3. The _____ was intended to give all nations equal trading rights in China.
4. The sensationalist style of news coverage called _____ helped sway U.S. public opinion in favor of war with Spain.
5. The _____ gave the United States the right to intervene in Cuban affairs and to buy or lease land for naval and coaling stations.
6. In Latin America and Asia, President Taft practiced _____, a policy of substituting economic power for military force.
7. The Mexican Revolution began as an effort to overthrow the dictator _____.
8. The _____ occurred on April 9, 1914, when nine U.S. sailors were mistakenly arrested by Mexican soldiers.
9. The _____ took place after the United States seized a German ship that was carrying weapons to Mexican president Victoriano Huerta.

Comprehension and Critical Thinking

SECTION 1 *(pp. 552–557)*
10. a. Identify Who was Queen Liliuokalani?
b. Explain Why did Liliuokalani's plans for strengthening the monarchy alarm the American business community in Hawaii?
c. Predict How do you think the Japanese reacted to the Great White Fleet? Do you think the fleet had the effect that President Roosevelt wished?

578 CHAPTER 17

12. a. U.S. pledge to use armed forces to prevent any European country from seizing territory in the Western Hemisphere
b. use of military force and economic power, such as support for the rebels in Panama and the building of the canal
c. possible answer—The U.S. began to view itself as an international police force, playing a central role in regulating international affairs.

13. a. Mexican revolutionary leader
b. Díaz was a cruel dictator while Madero tried to establish a democratic government
c. possible answer—His attention was focused on World War I in Europe and as a result could not commit the troops to a war with Mexico.

SECTION 2 (pp. 558–564)

11. a. Recall What was the de Lôme letter?

b. Summarize What were the consequences of the Spanish-American War?

c. Evaluate How much influence did the media have in building public support for the Spanish-American War? Explain.

SECTION 3 (pp. 565–569)

12. a. Describe What was the Roosevelt Corollary?

b. Analyze In what various ways did the United States exert its power in Latin America?

c. Evaluate How did the acquisition of overseas territory affect the way the United States viewed its role in the world?

SECTION 4 (pp. 572–575)

13. a. Identify Who was Pancho Villa?

b. Contrast As government leaders, how did Porfirio Díaz and Francisco Madero differ?

c. Elaborate Why do you think President Wilson wished to avoid war with Mexico?

Using the Internet

go.hrw.com
Practice Online
Keyword: SD7 CH17

14. On December 31, 1999, the United States returned control of the Panama Canal and the 10-mile-wide Canal Zone to the government of Panama. Using the keyword above, do research to learn about the events that led to this historic handover. Then create a report that analyzes the reasons why the United States gave up the canal and the Canal Zone to Panama.

Analyzing Primary Sources

Reading Like a Historian This painting shows a pineapple plantation in Hawaii, where pineapples were typically harvested by hand.

15. Analyzing Visuals How are the pickers protecting themselves against the tropical heat?

16. Making Inferences Why do you suppose one man is on horseback?

Critical Reading

Read the passage in Section 1 that begins with the heading "Influence in China." Then answer the questions that follow.

17. Why did the United States propose the Open Door Policy?

A The United States wanted to prevent China from refusing to trade with western nations.

B The United States was protesting Japan's seizure of Taiwan.

C The United States hoped the Open Door Policy would help resolve the Boxer Rebellion.

D Without a sphere of influence of its own, the United States was afraid of being cut out of the China trade.

18. Which of the following is a true statement about the Boxer Rebellion?

A Members of a secret martial arts group in China demanded more respect for their sport.

B Foreign missionaries and Chinese Christians in Beijing came under attack.

C An large international military force stopped the rebellion in 1900 and occupied China for many years afterward.

D The Boxer Rebellion caused western nations to reject the Open Door Policy.

FOCUS ON WRITING

Persuasive Writing *Persuasive writing takes a position for or against an issue, using facts and examples as supporting evidence. To practice persuasive writing, complete the assignment below.*

Topic U.S. imperialism in the late 1800s and early 1900s

19. Assignment Write a paragraph in which you take a position on the overseas activities of the United States in the late 1800s and early 1900s. Was the United States justified in annexing foreign territories and expanding its control over other nations during this period? Support your point of view with reasoning and examples from your reading and studies.

Answers

Using the Internet

14. Go to the HRW Web site and enter the keyword shown to access a rubric for this activity.

KEYWORD: SD7 CH17

Analyzing Primary Sources

15. hats and long-sleeved clothing

16. He is the boss.

Critical Reading

17. D

18. B

Focus on Writing

19. possible answers—no, not justified; was motivated by a sense of cultural superiority and interest in own economic and military needs; in Hawaii, the Philippines, and Mexico, U.S. intervention took away national independence and frequently led to war

A rubric for this activity is provided in the Chapter Resource File: Focus on Writing: U.S. Imperialism in the Late 1800s and Early 1900s.

History's Impact Video Program

allowed ships to sail directly between Atlantic and Pacific oceans; strengthened American military position in Latin America; symbolized American ingenuity and engineering skills

---

Review and Assessment Resources

Review and Reinforce

- CRF: Chapter Review Activity
- Quick Facts Transparencies: Causes of U.S. Expansionism, Entering the World Stage
- Spanish Chapter Summaries Audio CD Program
- Online Chapter Summaries in Spanish
- OSP Holt PuzzlePro; Quiz Show for ExamView
- Quiz Game CD-ROM

Assess

- PASS: Chapter Test, Forms A and B
- Alternative Assessment Handbook
- OSP ExamView Test Generator, Chapter Test
- Differentiated Instruction Modified Worksheets and Tests CD-ROM: Chapter Test
- HOAP Holt Online Assessment Program (in the Premier Online Edition)

Reteach/Intervene

- Interactive Reader and Study Guide
- Differentiated Instruction Teacher Management System: Lesson Plans for Differentiated Instruction
- Differentiated Instruction Modified Worksheets and Tests CD-ROM: Chapter Test
- Interactive Skills Tutor CD-ROM

go.hrw.com
Online Resources
KEYWORD: SD7 CH17

Chapter 18 Planning Guide

The First World War

Chapter Overview	Reproducible Resources	Technology Resources
CHAPTER 18 pp. 580–615 **Overview:** In this chapter, students will analyze the events and ideas that pushed the United States into World War I and the efforts the nation took to help the Allies win the war.	**Differentiated Instruction Teacher Management System:*** • Instructional Benchmarking Guides • Lesson Plans for Differentiated Instruction **Interactive Reader and Study Guide:** Chapter Summary* **Chapter Resource File:*** • Writing for the SAT Activity: Deadly Technology • Social Studies Skills Activity: Analyzing Secondary Sources • Chapter Review Activity **American History Outline Maps** **Pre-AP Activities Guide for American History***	**Live Ink® Online Reading Help** **Student Edition on Audio CD Program** **Differentiated Instruction Modified Worksheets and Tests CD-ROM** **Interactive Skills Tutor CD-ROM** **United States History Primary Source Library CD-ROM** **Power Presentations with Video CD-ROM** **History's Impact: American History Video Program (VHS/DVD):** The First World War **Online Chapter Summaries in Spanish**
Section 1: **A World Crisis** **The Main Idea:** Rivalries among European nations led to the outbreak of war in 1914.	**Differentiated Instruction Teacher Management System:** Section 1 Lesson Plan* **Interactive Reader and Study Guide*** **Chapter Resource File:*** • Biography Activity: Erich Maria Remarque	**Daily Bellringer Transparency:** Section 1* **Map Transparency:** World War I, 1914–1917* **Quick Facts Transparency:** Major Battles* **Daily Test Practice Transparency*** **Internet Activity:** New Technology and Tactics
Section 2: **The United States in World War I** **The Main Idea:** The United States helped turn the tide for an Allied victory.	**Differentiated Instruction Teacher Management System:** Section 2 Lesson Plan* **Interactive Reader and Study Guide*** **Chapter Resource File:*** • Primary Source Activity: Woodrow Wilson's Second Inaugural Address • Literature Activity: *The Marne*	**Daily Bellringer Transparency:** Section 2* **Map Transparency:** World War I, 1917–1918* **Daily Test Practice Transparency*** **Internet Activity:** From Neutrality to War
Section 3: **The Home Front** **The Main Idea:** The United States mobilized a variety of resources to wage World War I.	**Differentiated Instruction Teacher Management System:** Section 3 Lesson Plan* **Interactive Reader and Study Guide*** **Chapter Resource File:*** • Economics and History Activity: Mobilizing the Economy for World War I	**Daily Bellringer Transparency:** Section 3* **Daily Test Practice Transparency*** **Internet Activity:** Wartime Propaganda
Section 4: **Peace Without Victory** **The Main Idea:** The Allies determined the terms for peace in the postwar world.	**Differentiated Instruction Teacher Management System:** Section 4 Lesson Plan* **Interactive Reader and Study Guide*** **Chapter Resource File:*** • Biography Activity: Fannie Fern Phillips Andrews	**Daily Bellringer Transparency:** Section 4* **Map Transparency:** Europe and the Middle East, 1915, 1919* **Quick Facts Transparency:** Wilson's Fourteen Points and the Treaty of Versailles* **Daily Test Practice Transparency***

HOLT

History's Impact
American History Video Program (VHS/DVD)
The First World War

Review, Assessment, Intervention

 Quick Facts Transparencies: Major Battles, Fourteen Points and the Treaty of Versailles, The First World War

 Spanish Chapter Summaries Audio CD Program

 **Progress Assessment Support System (PASS):** Chapter Test*

 **Differentiated Instruction Modified Worksheets and Tests CD-ROM:** Modified Chapter Test

OSP **One-Stop Planner CD-ROM:** ExamView Test Generator (English/Spanish)

HOAP **Holt Online Assessment Program (HOAP),** in the Holt Premier Online Student Edition

---

 PASS: Section 1 Quiz*

 Online Quiz: Section 1

 Alternative Assessment Handbook

 PASS: Section 2 Quiz*

 Online Quiz: Section 2

 Alternative Assessment Handbook

 PASS: Section 3 Quiz*

 Online Quiz: Section 3

 Alternative Assessment Handbook

 PASS: Section 4 Quiz*

 Online Quiz: Section 4

 Alternative Assessment Handbook

NC RESOURCES

The following resources were developed to help North Carolina educators teach the standards and objectives of North Carolina's eleventh grade standard course of study in United States history.

- United States history EOC Test Prep Workbook
- Teacher's Support System
- North Carolina One-Stop Planner

And be sure to direct your students to **go.hrw.com** for online access to the EOC Test Prep Workbook.

go.hrw.com
EOC Test Prep
KEYWORD: SE7 NC

Holt Online Learning

go.hrw.com
Teacher Resources
KEYWORD: SD7 TEACHER

go.hrw.com
Student Resources
KEYWORD: SD7 CH18

- Document-based Questions
- Interactive Multimedia Activities

- Current Events
- Chapter-based Internet Activities
- and more!

Holt Premier
Online Student Edition
Complete online support for interactivity, assessment, and reporting

- Interactive Maps and Notebook
- Standardized Test Prep
- Homework Practice and Research Activities Online

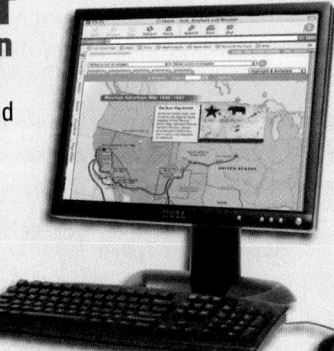

CHAPTER 18 PLANNING GUIDE

Before You Teach

The Big Picture
Edward L. Ayers

A World Crisis In retrospect, we can see that the conditions for war had been building in Europe for generations. Flush with prosperity, confidence, and colonialism, the nations of Europe imagined themselves as the pinnacle of civilization. They built massive armies and aligned with one another in military alliances. One event that upset the balance could throw the entire continent into chaos—and, of course, that is exactly what happened with the assassination of Archduke Franz Ferdinand. The Germans, in particular, thought that their new technologies would quickly win any war. They were wrong. The trench warfare, poison gas, tanks, and airplanes unleashed the most destructive war the world had ever seen.

The United States in World War I Although the United States inclined toward the British and the Allies, many Americans demanded that their country remain neutral. The sinking of the *Lusitania* and the intercepted Zimmermann Note radically altered people's opinions, however, and the nation entered the war.

The Home Front The United States, building on the remarkable industrialization, urban growth, and population movement that had marked the preceding half century, proved itself a formidable power. American workers generated vast stores of goods, and played an important role in bringing the war to a more rapid close and in defeating Germany and the Axis Powers.

Peace Without Victory A triumphant Woodrow Wilson, suddenly a leader on the world stage, came into France with a plan to rebuild Europe. His Fourteen Points offered a blueprint for a new order, but the victorious nations could not bring themselves to accept sacrifice or compromise. Moreover, many in the United States were wary of involvement in the affairs of other places—and of a plan put forward by a president of the other party—and even the United States did not support the League of Nations.

Recent Scholarship

Wilson and the League of Nations One of the crucial questions in any discussion of the period after World War I is the fate of the League of Nations. Some historians blame Wilson for the failure, while others blame his opponents. In *Breaking the Heart of the World: Woodrow Wilson and the Fight for the League of Nations* (2001), John Milton Cooper Jr. examines the issues from all sides and concludes that "For all their decency and intelligence, Wilson's opponents were wrong. For all his flaws and missteps, Wilson was right." This book is useful in providing sufficient background for a full discussion of the issue.

Differentiating Instruction

 Differentiated Instruction Teacher Management System
- Lesson Plans for Differentiated Instruction
- Differentiated Instructional Benchmarking Guides
- Interactive Reader and Study Guide

 Spanish Chapter Summaries Audio CD Program

 Online Chapter Summaries in Spanish

Student Edition on Audio CD Program

 Differentiated Instruction Modified Worksheets and Tests CD-ROM
- Vocabulary Flash Cards
- Modified Vocabulary Builder Activities
- Modified Chapter Review Activity
- Modified Chapter Test

OSP One-Stop Planner CD-ROM
- ExamView Test Generator (English and Spanish)
- PuzzlePro
- Quiz Show for ExamView
- Transparencies and Videos

TE Differentiated Activities in the Teacher's Edition
- World War I Battles, p. 585
- Raising an Army, p. 593
- *Farewell to Arms* Mural, p. 597
- *Farewell to Arms* Play, p. 597
- Recovering from the War, p. 610

Reading Like a Historian
Sam Wineburg

Historical Context

Our chapter describes the clash between President Woodrow Wilson and Senator Henry Cabot Lodge over the ratification of the Treaty of Versailles. The Senate's defeat of the treaty on November 19, 1919, and again the following March, dashed Wilson's dream of creating a "League of Nations" with the United States at its helm.

When History Gets Personal

To view this conflict solely in political terms—Wilson's "internationalism" versus Lodge's "isolationism"—ignores the intense personal rivalry between these two men. Just as events have contexts, so, too, do men. "I think it is safe to say," remarked Wilson expert Thomas J. Knock, "that Woodrow Wilson and Henry Cabot Lodge hated each other's guts." We must first understand the personal feud between Wilson and Lodge before we can understand their failure to reach political compromise.

The two men competed from the very start. They both had earned the PhD degree (Lodge from Harvard, Wilson from Johns Hopkins) and both were schooled in statecraft and government. Until Wilson arrived on the scene, Lodge shone as the rising academic star. But few people could match Wilson's prodigious output and piercing intellect (indeed, his dissertation, *Congressional Government*, remains in print well over 100 years after it first appeared). Lodge turned toward politics. Wilson, the academic wunderkind, assumed the presidency of Princeton.

Political Disagreements

No doubt part of their ill will had to do with political differences. In the early years of the war, Wilson tried to be a fair broker between the warring European states, while Lodge, as early at 1915, sought to throw the weight of the United States behind Britain and France, thus bringing Germany to its knees. Lodge saw Wilson as weak and unmanly. For his part,

Wilson viewed Lodge and his followers ("bungalow minds") as men of limited imagination. It is rumored that Wilson once compared Lodge's intellect to the soil of his home state of Massachusetts: barren but highly cultivated.

In leaving to represent the United States at the Paris peace talks in February 1919, Wilson made a tactical error. In forming the American contingent he bypassed the Senate—and with it the ranking member of the Senate's Foreign Relations Committee, Henry Cabot Lodge. It was an insult Lodge would never forget.

With Wilson's return to the United States, the treaty's ratification seemed like a done deal. The only thing Lodge could do was delay. And that he did. During the sweltering period between July 14 and 28, 1919, Lodge stood in the chambers of Congress reading—first in French and then in English—all 264 pages of the Treaty of Versailles. And, as if to taunt Wilson's "Fourteen Points," Lodge labeled his own objections to the treaty, "Fourteen Reservations."

Refusing to Compromise

Wilson, who had achieved fame as a skillful negotiator and artful compromiser, refused to move an inch toward Lodge. Wilson's friend and campaign backer Barnard Baruch tried to convince the president that "half a loaf is better than no bread." Wilson preferred to go hungry, telling his wife Edith, "Better a thousand times to go down fighting than to dip your colors to dishonorable compromise."

When the Senate Foreign Relations committee chose Henry Cabot Lodge to represent them at Wilson's state funeral in 1924, Edith Wilson learned of the plan and conveyed the following message to the senator: "Realizing that your presence would be embarrassing to you and unwelcome to me, I write to request that you do not attend." Lodge honored Wilson's spirit and stayed home. Only in death did these two rivals achieve compromise.

Quote by Thomas J. Knock from *Woodrow Wilson: The Film & More*. Published by KCET, 2001.

Quote by Woodrow Wilson from *My Memoir* by Edith B. Wilson. Published by Bobbs-Merrill, Indianapolis, 1939.

Standards Focus

Social Studies Competency Goals
Goal 8 The learner will analyze United States involvement in World War I and the war's influence on international affairs during the 1920's.
8.01, 8.02, 8.03

 The Big Idea and Essential Questions

To foster student understanding of this chapter's big idea, design your lesson to address each section's essential question.

Big Idea The United States tried to stay neutral in World War I, but after it joined the Allies in 1917, the nation quickly mobilized for war.

Essential Questions

1. What led to the outbreak of war in Europe in 1914?
2. How did the United States affect the outcome of World War I?
3. How did the United States make contributions to the war effort?
4. How did World War I end?

CHAPTER
18 1914–1920
The First WORLD WAR

THE BIG PICTURE The United States tried to stay neutral when war swept Europe. Once the United States joined the Allies in 1917, however, the nation quickly mobilized for war.

North Carolina Standards

Social Studies Objectives
8.01 Examine the reasons why the United States remained neutral at the beginning of World War I but later became involved.
8.02 Identify political and military turning points of the war and determine their significance to the outcome of the conflict.
8.03 Assess the political, economic, social, and cultural effects of the war on the United States and other nations.

Language Arts Objectives
5.01 Interpret the significance of literary movements as they have evolved through the literature of the United States by:
• understanding influences that progress through literary movements of the United States.

Skills Focus **READING LIKE A HISTORIAN**
Artist Frank Schoonover captured a spirit of optimism and determination in the faces of these young Allied soldiers in *Doughboys First*. (A "doughboy" is an infantry member.) The painting was one of a series painted for *The Ladies' Home Journal*.
Interpreting Visuals What do you think the artist wanted to accomplish with this painting?
See Skills Handbook, p. H30

U.S.
August 1914 President Wilson declares American neutrality in World War I.

1914

World
June 1914 Archduke Franz Ferdinand is killed in Sarajevo.

August 1914 German troops invade Belgium, and Great Britain declares war on Germany.

580

Introduce the Chapter
At Level

The First World War

1. Tell students that in this chapter they will learn about events in Europe and Russia that led the United States to abandon its long-standing policy of neutrality and send forces to fight with the Allies in World War I.

2. Have students make a list of the advantages and disadvantages of remaining neutral during a major war. Have volunteers share their lists with the class.

3. Then have students scan the chapter and make a brief outline and a list of the charts and maps that appear in the chapter.

4. Guide students in a discussion of how involvement in World War I might affect America. Ask students to predict the impact on the American economy and society, as well as on the relationship between America and Europe. **LS Visual-Spatial**

Alternative Assessment Handbook, Rubric 11: Discussions

May 1915
German U-boat sinks the *Lusitania*, killing 128 Americans.

April 1917
President Wilson asks Congress to declare war against Germany.

January 1918
President Wilson presents his 14-point plan for world peace.

August 1920
The Nineteenth Amendment, giving women the right to vote, is ratified.

Mr. President WHAT WILL YOU DO FOR WOMAN SUFFRAGE

| 1915 | 1916 | 1917 | 1918 | 1919 | 1920 |

February 1915
Germany sets up a submarine blockade of England.

November 1917
Lenin's Bolsheviks take control of Russia.

November 11, 1918
The Allies and Germany sign an armistice.

June 1919
The Treaty of Versailles officially ends World War I.

581

HOLT

History's Impact

▶ **Video Program: The First World War**
See the Video Teacher's Guide for strategies for using the video segment.

Reading Like a Historian

Off to War Have students take a moment to examine the image on these pages. How do these soldiers differ from today's soldiers? *possible answer—no women, different uniforms and weapons, no minorities*

Interpreting Visuals U.S. soldiers in World War I were called 'doughboys.' The meaning of that term is unclear, but it was in use as far back as the 1600s, when it referred to boiled flour dumplings, otherwise known as donuts. During the U.S. Civil War the name applied to infantrymen who wore large round buttons on their uniforms.

Explore the Time Line

1. When was the *Lusitania* destroyed? *May 1915*

2. When did President Wilson ask Congress to declare war? *April 1917*

3. When was the armistice signed? *November 11, 1918*

4. How long after the armistice was signed was the official end of the war? *seven months*

Info to Know

What is a GI? Tons of supplies were sent to U.S. troops serving in Europe. Each item was inspected before it was shipped, and each crate was marked with the letters "GI," which stood for "Government Issue." Europeans began to call American troops GIs, and the name stayed with the soldiers when they returned home.

Evaluate Why do you think all items were inspected? *to ensure uniformity, quality control*

Answers

Reading Like a Historian
1. *possible answer—show youthfulness of soldiers; contrast young soldiers' attitudes with those of seasoned officers*

581

Bellringer

The Inside Story. . . Use the **Daily Bellringer Transparency** to help students answer the question.

📖 Daily Bellringer Transparency, Section 1

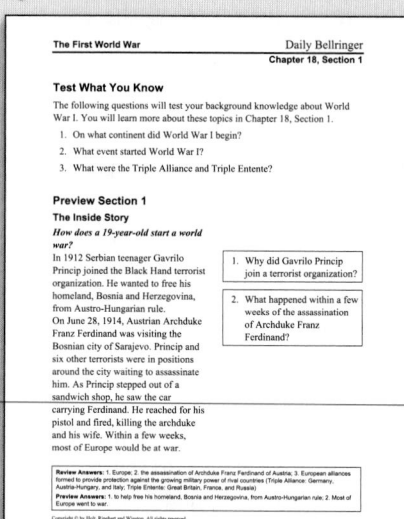

The First World War | Daily Bellringer
Chapter 18, Section 1

Test What You Know

The following questions will test your background knowledge about World War I. You will learn more about these topics in Chapter 18, Section 1.

1. On what continent did World War I begin?
2. What event started World War I?
3. What were the Triple Alliance and Triple Entente?

Preview Section 1

The Inside Story

How does a 19-year-old start a world war?

In 1912 Serbian teenager Gavrilo Princip joined the Black Hand terrorist organization. He wanted to free his homeland, Bosnia and Herzegovina, from Austro-Hungarian rule. On June 28, 1914, Austrian Archduke Franz Ferdinand was visiting the Bosnian city of Sarajevo. Princip and six other terrorists were in positions around the city waiting to assassinate him. As Princip stepped out of a sandwich shop, he saw the car carrying Ferdinand. He reached for his pistol and fired, killing the archduke and his wife. Within a few weeks, most of Europe would be at war.

1. Why did Gavrilo Princip join a terrorist organization?
2. What happened within a few weeks of the assassination of Archduke Franz Ferdinand?

Review Answers: 1. Europe. 2. the assassination of Archduke Franz Ferdinand of Austria; 3. European alliances formed to provide protection against the growing military power of rival countries (Triple Alliance: Germany, Austria-Hungary, and Italy; Triple Entente: Great Britain, France, and Russia)

Preview Answers: 1. to help free his homeland, Bosnia and Herzegovina, from Austro-Hungarian rule; 2. Most of Europe went to war.

Copyright © by Holt, Rinehart and Winston. All rights reserved.

Academic Vocabulary

Review with students the high-use academic term in this section.

subsequent following in time or order (p. 583)

📝 CRF: Vocabulary Builder Activity, Section 1

Taking Notes

rise of nationalism; imperialism and competition for overseas colonies; rise of militarism; alliances between nations

go.hrw.com
Online Resources

KEYWORD: SD7 CH18
TOPIC: NEW TECHNOLOGY
AND TACTICS

BEFORE YOU READ

MAIN IDEA

Rivalries among European nations led to the outbreak of war in 1914.

READING FOCUS

1. What were the causes of World War I?
2. How did the war break out?
3. Why did the war quickly reach a stalemate?

KEY TERMS AND PEOPLE

Archduke Franz Ferdinand
Kaiser Wilhelm II
militarism
Triple Alliance
Triple Entente
balance of power
Central Powers
Allied Powers
trench warfare

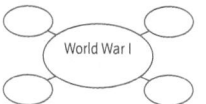

TAKING NOTES As you read, take notes on the causes of World War I. Write one cause in each small circle. Record your notes in a graphic organizer like the one shown here. You may need to add more circles.

World War I

◀ Soldiers arrest Archduke Ferdinand's young assassin.

A WRONG TURN INTO History

THE INSIDE STORY *How does a 19-year-old start a world war?* In 1912 Serbian teenager Gavrilo Princip joined the Black Hand terrorist organization. Princip wanted to free his home country, Bosnia and Herzegovina, from Austro-Hungarian rule. He was already a good shot with a pistol—a handy skill for a terrorist.

After years of training and planning, the Black Hand leaders came up with a terrorist plot that they hoped could lead to an independent Bosnia. They heard that **Archduke Franz Ferdinand** of Austria was going to visit the Bosnian city of Sarajevo. The Black Hand ordered a team of assassins to kill the archduke.

On June 28, 1914, Princip and six other terrorists positioned themselves around Sarajevo as Ferdinand and his wife toured the city in a convertible sedan. Princip was hungry, so he went to buy a sandwich. As he stepped out of the sandwich shop, he could not believe his eyes. There, stopped in front of him, was the car carrying the archduke. Princip dropped his sandwich, reached for his pistol, and fired, killing the archduke and his wife. This single act would propel most of Europe into war within weeks. ◀

Teach the Main Idea

At Level

A World Crisis

1. **Teach** Ask students the Reading Focus questions to teach this section.

2. **Apply** Have students create an outline of the section. Have students identify at least two main ideas under each subheading.

3. **Review** Review student outlines as a class. Then guide students in a discussion of the early days of the war.

4. **Practice/Homework** Have students use the map of World War I to determine which European nations were neutral during the war. Then have students write an essay in which they explain what neutrality means. In their essays, have students identify nations whose neutrality was violated.

LS Visual-Spatial

📄 American History Outline Maps: World War I in Europe

📄 Alternative Assessment Handbook, Rubrics 21: Map Reading; and 37: Writing Assignments

Causes of World War I

Some 3,000 miles away from Sarajevo, most Americans cared little about the news of Archduke Franz Ferdinand's death. A North Dakota newspaper reported, "One archduke more or less makes little difference." In Europe, however, the death of this archduke made a huge difference. Most of Europe plunged into war within five short weeks. But how could one assassination start a world war?

Long before Princip fired his pistol, a series of political changes in Europe made war almost unavoidable. By 1914 Europe was ripe for war.

Nationalism Nationalism is an extreme pride or devotion that people feel for their country or culture. The spirit of nationalism led to the formation of new nations, such as Germany and Italy during the 1870s. It also led to competition for power.

This struggle for greater power was most visible in the Balkans, a region of southeastern Europe populated by a great number of ethnic groups. The Ottoman Empire, which had ruled the Balkans for hundreds of years, was starting to fall apart during the 1800s. The Austro-Hungarian Empire saw an opportunity to expand and began to push into the region, annexing provinces such as Bosnia and Herzegovina. Many Slavic peoples there, such as the Serbs, rejected the rule of these outsiders.

Some Serbs encouraged other Slavic peoples to revolt against Austria-Hungary, and they received support from Russia, another European power. Russia saw itself as the protector of the Slavs and argued with the Austro-Hungarian rulers about the future of Serbia and control of the Balkans. By the early 1900s tensions in the region were high.

Imperialism Austria-Hungary was not the only nation trying to expand during the late 1800s. Growing nationalism also led nations to compete for overseas colonies. This quest for colonial empires was known as imperialism.

By the late 1800s Great Britain and France already had colonial empires in Africa, the Middle East, and Asia. Colonies provided markets and rich natural resources, so the German emperor, **Kaiser Wilhelm II**, wanted colonies for Germany, too. And to get them, Germany would need a stronger military.

Militarism The world soon also saw the rise of **militarism**—the policy of military preparedness and building up weapons. In 1900 Germany began to build a navy that could take on the world's strongest sea power—Great Britain's Royal Navy.

At the same time, Germany had also enlarged its army. It supplied its troops with the latest weapons, including machine guns and larger artillery.

German army officials also began to draw up war strategies. One such strategy, the Schlieffen Plan, provided precise instructions for waging a two-front war against France and Russia at the same time. The Schlieffen Plan also called for a surprise invasion of France by passing through Belgium, with a subsequent attack on Russia.

Aware of Germany's growing supply of weapons, Great Britain, France, and Russia worried about Germany's intentions. Each country began to build its own military in order to defend itself should war break out.

Many Europeans believed that strong military forces would prevent countries from attacking one another. British admiral Jackie Fisher explained, "I am not for war, I am for peace. That is why I am for a supreme Navy. The supremacy of the British Navy is the best security for the peace of the world."

Alliances For protection, some nations formed alliances, or partnerships. These alliances were created to maintain peace, but they would lead Europe directly into war.

Germany formed a military alliance with Austria-Hungary and Italy. This alliance became known as the **Triple Alliance**. Fearful of Germany's growing power, France and Russia formed a secret alliance with each other. Meanwhile, Great Britain also began to worry about Germany's expanding navy and allied itself with France. Soon Britain, France, and Russia formed the **Triple Entente** (AHN-TAHNT).

ACADEMIC VOCABULARY

subsequent following in time or order

ALLIANCES, 1914

▢ Triple Entente	▢ Triple Alliance
① Great Britain	④ Germany
② France	⑤ Austria-Hungary
③ Russia	⑥ Italy

Causes of World War I

Recall What single event triggered the war? *assassination of Archduke Franz Ferdinand*

Evaluate Why didn't the balance of power in Europe prevent World War I? *National tensions, imperial rivalries, and military expansion were too great to overcome.*

2 How did the war break out? *assassination of Archduke Ferdinand; set in motion the system of alliances across Europe*

War Breaks Out

Identify What other country joined Germany and Austria-Hungary to form the Central Powers? *Ottoman Empire*

Predict Why do you think World War I was known as the Great War? *It involved most of the major powers of Europe, and another 30 nations*

CRF: History and Geography Activity: Alliances in Europe in 1914

Answers

Reading Check *nationalism, imperialism, militarism, and alliances*

The word *entente* come from French and means "understanding.")

Some European leaders believed that these alliances created a **balance of power**, in which each nation or alliance had equal strength. Many leaders thought that the alliance system would help decrease the chances of war. They hoped that no single nation would attack another out of fear that the attacked nation's allies would join the fight.

The assassination of Archduke Franz Ferdinand exposed the flaws in this thinking. The major European powers' long history of national tensions, imperial rivalries, and military expansion proved too great for alliances to overcome. After this single attack on Austria-Hungary, Europe exploded into war.

READING CHECK **Summarizing** What issues led Europe to the brink of war in 1914?

War Breaks Out

After the assassination, Princip was immediately arrested. While investigating Princip's background, Austro-Hungarian officials learned that the Serbian government had supplied the assassins with bombs and weapons. Furious, Austria-Hungary blamed Serbia for Ferdinand's murder and declared war.

Russia had promised to protect Serbian Slavs. Therefore, the Russian army quickly began to mobilize, or prepare for war. Germany viewed Russia's mobilization as an act of aggression against its ally Austria-Hungary and declared war on Russia. Then Germany declared war on France, Russia's ally. All-out war was about to begin.

The Germans take Belgium Germany made the first move in the war, following the Schlieffen Plan. On August 4, 1914, German troops crossed the border into the neutral country of Belgium. Kaiser Wilhelm II believed Germany needed to make this first move in order to catch Belgium and France by surprise.

Germany's invasion of Belgium drew a new, powerful nation into the conflict. Because the British had pledged to defend Belgium, Great Britain declared war on Germany.

With the entry of Great Britain into the war, most of the major powers of Europe had chosen sides. On one side were Germany,

Austria-Hungary, and the Ottoman Empire, fighting together as the **Central Powers**.

On the other side of the conflict were Great Britain, France, and Russia, who united as the **Allied Powers**, or Allies. Before the conflict's end, another 30 nations, including Italy, would join in what became known as the Great War. Later generations would call it World War I.

At first the Schlieffen Plan worked well for Germany. With only six divisions of troops, Belgian forces were no match for the 38 divisions of the German army, totaling a massive 700,000 soldiers. The tiny Belgian army fought bravely and put up an unexpectedly strong defense, but they were only able to delay the German advance briefly.

The German attack on Belgium was fierce. Germans burned entire villages to the ground. Civilians caught in the fighting, including women and children, were executed. German field marshall Helmuth von Moltke admitted,

MAJOR BATTLES

1 Battle of Tannenberg, Aug. 1914
Russia's worst defeat in World War I

2 1st Battle of the Marne, Sept. 1914
Allies halted the German advance and saved Paris from occupation

3 1st Battle of Ypres, Oct.–Nov. 1914
Last major German offensive until 1918

3 3rd Battle of Ypres (Passchendaele), July–Nov. 1917
British forces advanced just five miles at a cost of about 300,000 lives

4 Battle of Gallipoli, April–Dec. 1915
Failed attempt of the Allies to knock the Ottoman Empire out of World War I

5 Battle of Verdun, Feb.–Dec. 1916
Longest battle of World War I with huge loss of life

6 Battle of the Somme, July–Nov. 1916
First major offensive for the British; remembered for its staggering loss of life

7 Battle of Caporetto, Oct.–Nov. 1917
Tremendous victory for the Central Powers

Skills Focus: Summarizing

Reading Skill
Early Strategies of World War I

1. Review the Schlieffen Plan with the class. What was the Schlieffen Plan? What did it call for?

2. To help students understand the results of the strategy used during the early days of World War I, draw the graphic organizer at right for students to see. Omit the italicized answers. Have students copy and complete the chart.

3. Have volunteers provide the answers, and have students correct their own charts. Then guide students in a discussion of the Schlieffen Plan. **LS Logical-Mathematical, Visual-Spatial**

Alternative Assessment Handbook, Rubric 13: Graphic Organizers

Graphic Organizer Transparencies

Early World War I Strategy and Response

Central Powers	Allied Powers
Germany, Austria-Hungary, Ottoman Empire	*Great Britain, France, Russia*

Early Strategy	Allied Response
Schlieffen Plan: Invade neutral Belgium to attack France; defeat France quickly; attack Russia	*Sent troops to support Belgium; counterattack at Marne River gave Russia time to mobilize for war*

"Our advance in Belgium is certainly brutal... all who get in the way must take the consequences."

A new kind of warfare Word of the German invasion of Belgium quickly spread to France and other European countries. French troops mobilized and rushed to meet the approaching German divisions. The French troops who marched to the front looked much as French soldiers had looked more than 40 years earlier, wearing bright red uniforms and heavy brass helmets. The Germans, on the other hand, dressed in gray uniforms that worked as camouflage to help them blend into the battlefield.

French war strategy had also not changed much since the 1800s. In Belgium, French soldiers marched row by row onto the battlefield. With bayonets mounted to their field rifles,

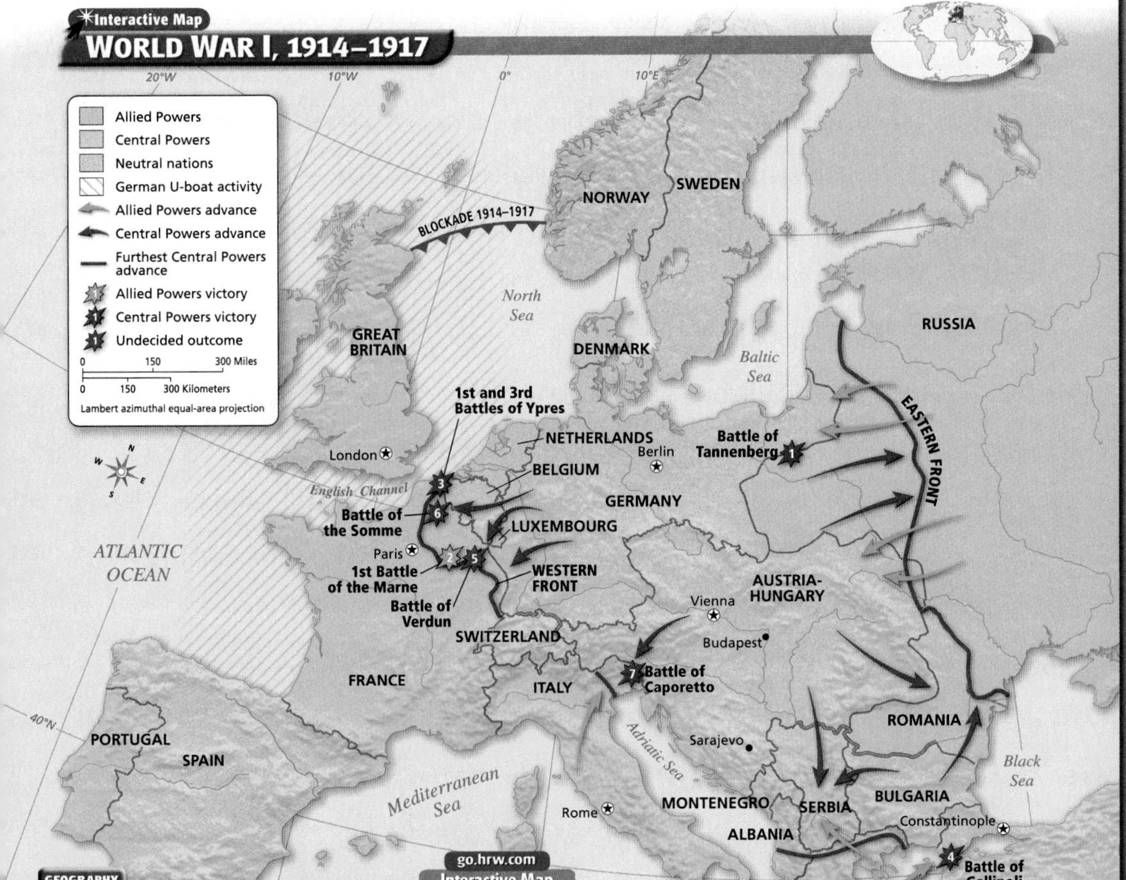

Interactive Map
WORLD WAR I, 1914–1917
Allied Powers
Central Powers
Neutral nations
German U-boat activity
Allied Powers advance
Central Powers advance
Furthest Central Powers advance
Allied Powers victory
Central Powers victory
Undecided outcome
0 150 300 Miles
0 150 300 Kilometers
Lambert azimuthal equal-area projection
20°W
10°W
0°
10°E
40°N
BLOCKADE 1914–1917
NORWAY
SWEDEN
RUSSIA
North Sea
Baltic Sea
GREAT BRITAIN
DENMARK
1st and 3rd Battles of Ypres
NETHERLANDS
Berlin
Battle of Tannenberg
EASTERN FRONT
London
English Channel
BELGIUM
GERMANY
Battle of the Somme
LUXEMBOURG
ATLANTIC OCEAN
Paris
1st Battle of the Marne
WESTERN FRONT
AUSTRIA-HUNGARY
Vienna
Battle of Verdun
SWITZERLAND
Budapest
FRANCE
Battle of Caporetto
ITALY
ROMANIA
PORTUGAL
SPAIN
Sarajevo
Adriatic Sea
Black Sea
Mediterranean Sea
Rome
MONTENEGRO
SERBIA
BULGARIA
Constantinople
ALBANIA
Battle of Gallipoli
GREECE
Aegean Sea
OTTOMAN EMPIRE
go.hrw.com
Interactive Map
Keyword: SD7 CH18

GEOGRAPHY SKILLS INTERPRETING MAPS

Location Where was the Western Front of the war located at this time? What were the outcomes of the major battles fought there?
Movement Describe the movement of the Central Powers. Why did the war have two fronts?

See **Skills Handbook**, p. H20

Direct Teach

QUICK FACTS Major Battles

Have students use information from the accompanying map of World War I to determine which side was victorious in each of the major battles in the table.

Quick Facts Transparency: Major Battles

Interpreting Maps

World War I, 1914–1917

Point out to students that with their furthest advance, the Central Powers controlled all of central Europe from the North Sea down through the Balkans and into Asia Minor. Their territory was contiguous. The territory controlled by the Allies, however, was divided by territory held by the Central Powers. Guide students in a discussion of the advantages and disadvantages of holding contiguous territory versus holding divided territory.

Map Transparency: World War I, 1914–1917

Interactive Map: World War I, 1914–1917

Info to Know

Bosnia Bosnia was ruled by various kingdoms before gaining its independence in about 1200. It remained independent until 1463, when it was conquered by the Ottoman Turks. In 1878 Austria-Hungary took control of Bosnia from the Ottoman Empire. At the end of World War I, Bosnia joined Serbia and other Balkan nations to create Yugoslavia, with Serbia's leader as the new nation's king. Bosnia and Herzegovina finally gained its independence in 1992, but not without a bloody war.

Differentiating Instruction

Above Level

Advanced Learners/GATE

Research Required

1. Organize the class into five groups. Assign each group one of the major battles on the Quick Facts table except the First Battle of the Marne. Have each group conduct outside research on its assigned battle.
2. Have each group write a report on its assigned battle, providing the following information, plus any other information about the battle (such as "firsts"): details of the battle's location, including maps; dates; nations involved; importance of the battle; number of casualties on both sides; final outcome.
3. Have volunteers from each group present their reports to the class. **LS Interpersonal, Verbal-Linguistic**

Alternative Assessment Handbook, Rubrics 20: Map Creation; and 40: Writing to Describe

Answers

Interpreting Maps *northeastern France and Italy; three Central Powers' victories, one Allied victory, one undecided; to the east, west, and south Germany had decided to invade Russia and France*

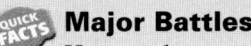

War Breaks Out

Explain Why did European leaders think that the war would be short? *because of the advanced military technology*

Make Judgments Which nation was better prepared for war, France or Germany? Explain your answer. *possible answer—Germany because had detailed plans, machine guns; soldiers wore camouflaged uniforms*

📄 CRF: Literature Activity: *The Marne* by Edith Wharton

History Close-Up
Fighting in the Trenches
Identify Students can "experience" trench warfare with "Over the Top," an online interactive game on the Canadian War Museum Web site: http://www.civilization.ca/cwm/overtop/index_e.html
The phrase "over the top" referred to going over the sandbags that lined the top of the trenches in the front and into the line of fire.

✳ **Interactive History Close-Up:**
Fighting in the Trenches

Info to Know

Taxicabs to the Front During the First Battle of the Marne, French officers experienced a shortage of automobiles and train cars. They ordered Paris taxi drivers to transport soldiers to the front. The taxis, along with various other kinds of vehicles, carried thousands of soldiers to the battle.

About the Illustration
This illustration is an artist's conception based on available sources. Historians, however, are uncertain exactly what this scene looked like.

---

they were prepared for close combat with the Germans. But when French officers drew their swords and ordered their troops to charge, they were met by a hail of machine gun bullets.

The French military had purchased a small number of machine guns and other new weapons such as the 75-millimeter artillery gun. They were not prepared for Germany's massive firepower.

A well-trained German machine gun team could set up its equipment in just four seconds, and each machine gun's firepower equaled that of 50 to 100 French rifles. Machine guns could fire up to 600 bullets per minute and mow down thousands of troops. In early battles, some 15,000 French soldiers died per day. In short, the Germans were prepared to fight a new kind of war. The French were not.

Many European leaders thought that these modern advances in military technology would result in a short war. German military advisers confidently predicted that France would be defeated in two months.

When the war began in midsummer, Kaiser Wilhelm II promised his German soldiers that they would be home "before the leaves had fallen." The European powers would soon learn that this new kind of war would last much longer than expected, and its devastation would be much more terrible.

The First Battle of the Marne The German army quickly advanced through northern France. After only one month of fighting, the German army was barely 25 miles from Paris. Still, the French troops refused to surrender.

Fighting in the Trenches

Protected by rows of barbed wire, sandbags, and armed soldiers, trenches were very difficult to capture. Neither side could advance on the Western Front without losing thousands of men in the attack.

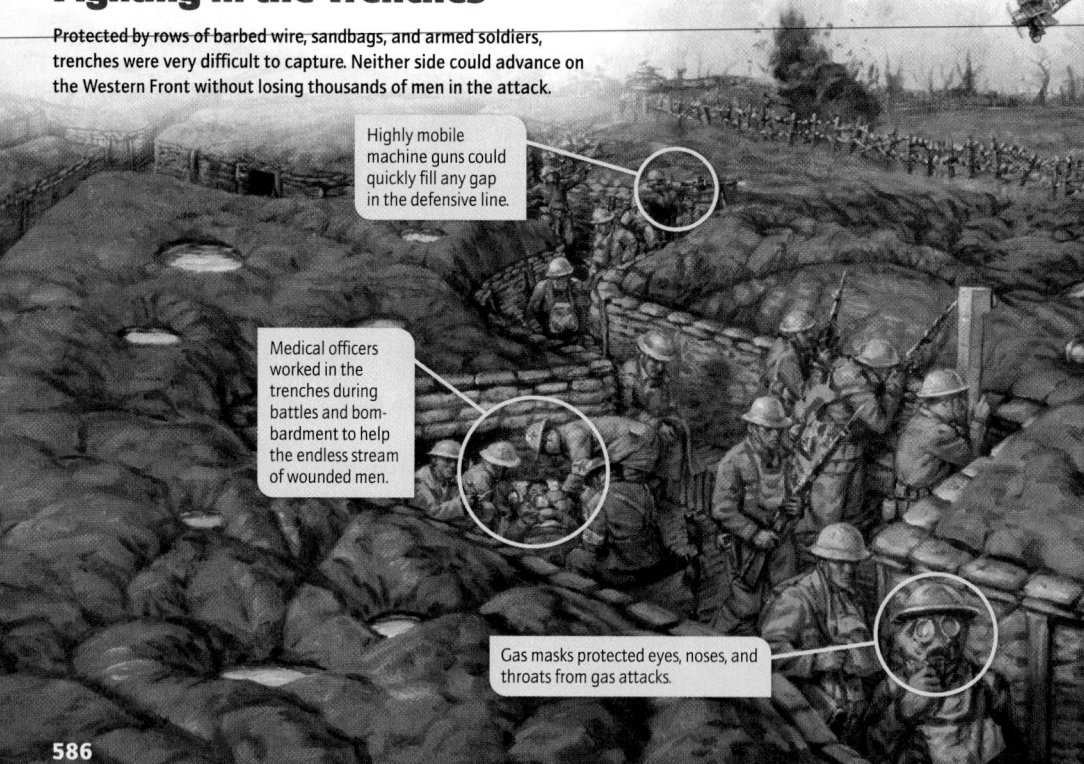

Highly mobile machine guns could quickly fill any gap in the defensive line.

Medical officers worked in the trenches during battles and bombardment to help the endless stream of wounded men.

Gas masks protected eyes, noses, and throats from gas attacks.

586

Skills Focus: Comparing and Contrasting
Below Level

Reading Skill
Readiness for War

Standard English Mastery

1. Have students write the words *France* and *Germany* on their own papers, and then write them for all students to see. Have students fill in facts about the state of French military preparedness at the outbreak of World War I. Ask volunteers for their answers and write their responses under the heading *France*. Then have students fill in facts about the state of German military preparedness at the beginning of World War I. Write their

responses under the heading *Germany*.

2. Have students use the information in their tables to write a brief analysis predicting the outcome of a war between France and Germany based on the state of each country's preparedness. **LS Logical-Mathematical, Verbal-Linguistic**

📄 Alternative Assessment Handbook, Rubrics 13: Graphic Organizers; and 42: Writing to Inform

📋 Graphic Organizer Tranparencies

Desperate for a victory, the French launched a daring counterattack along the Marne River east of Paris on September 7, 1914. In what became known as the First Battle of the Marne, 2 million men fought along a battle-front that stretched 125 miles. After five days and 250,000 lives lost, the French had rallied and pushed the Germans back some 40 miles.

The French had paid a heavy price. A French journalist walking on the battlefield saw what he thought was a field of red poppies. However, these bright patches of red were actually the uniforms of countless fallen French troops.

Despite the cost of the French counterattack, it helped the Allies by giving Russia more time to mobilize for war. Once Russia mobilized, Germany had to pull some of its troops out of France. It needed those troops to fight Russia along the Eastern Front, which stretched from the Black Sea to the Baltic Sea.

READING CHECK **Drawing Conclusions** Why was World War I considered a new kind of war?

The War Reaches a Stalemate

The First Battle of the Marne ended in a standoff. Both French and German soldiers dug trenches, or deep ditches, to seek protection from enemy fire and to defend their positions. By the late fall of 1914, two massive systems of trenches stretched for some 400 miles across western Europe. These battle lines of the Western Front extended from Switzerland to the North Sea.

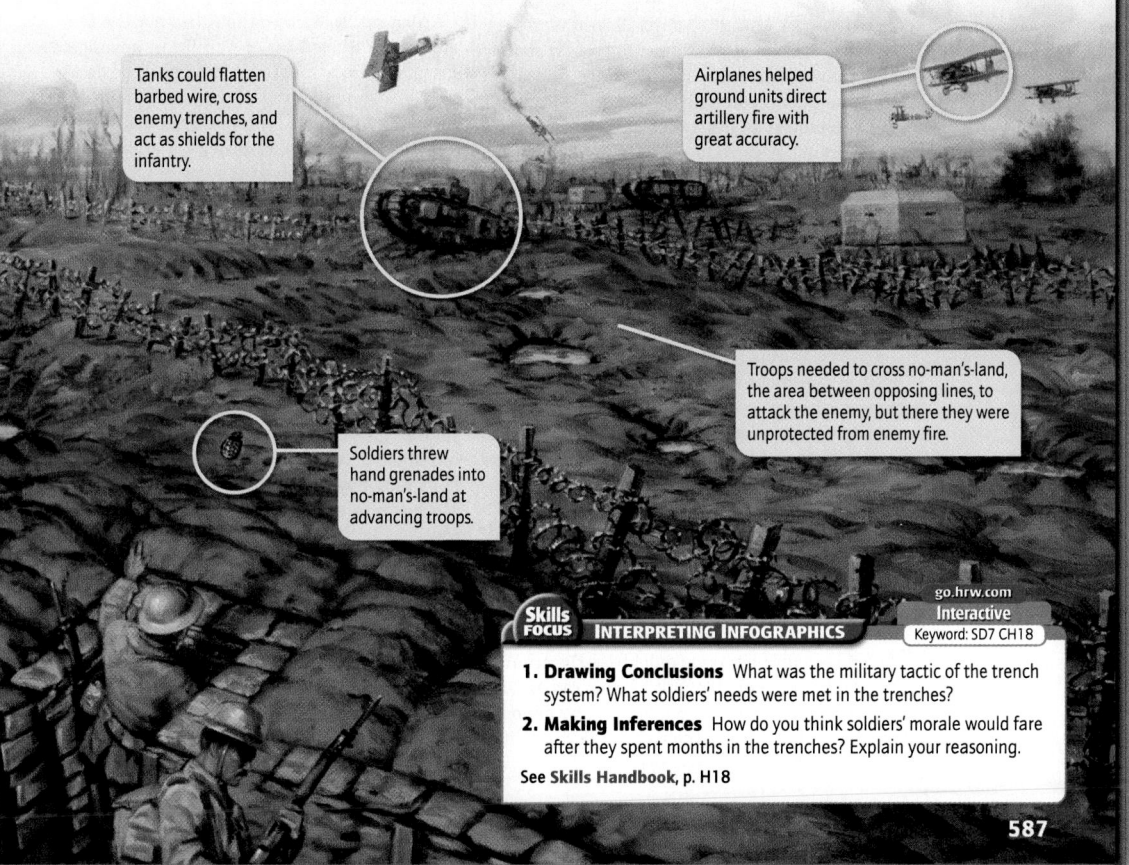

Tanks could flatten barbed wire, cross enemy trenches, and act as shields for the infantry.

Airplanes helped ground units direct artillery fire with great accuracy.

Troops needed to cross no-man's-land, the area between opposing lines, to attack the enemy, but there they were unprotected from enemy fire.

Soldiers threw hand grenades into no-man's-land at advancing troops.

Skills Focus **INTERPRETING INFOGRAPHICS**

go.hrw.com
Interactive
Keyword: SD7 CH18

1. **Drawing Conclusions** What was the military tactic of the trench system? What soldiers' needs were met in the trenches?
2. **Making Inferences** How do you think soldiers' morale would fare after they spent months in the trenches? Explain your reasoning.

See Skills Handbook, p. H18

587

Direct Teach

Reading Focus

The War Reaches a Stalemate

Identify What new weapons were developed during World War I? *poison gas, armored tanks, airplanes*

Recall Why did some military officers object to the use of poisonous gas as a weapon? *They thought it was an unfair and barbarous way to fight.*

Draw Conclusions Was trench warfare an effective strategy during World War I? Why or why not? *possible answer—no, because it led to stalemates*

📁 CRF: Biography: Erich Maria Remarque

Casualties of War

Review the numbers of casualties in the Battle of the Somme with students. Ask students to name cities in the United States whose population is about 1.2 million. *Dallas, Detroit, Philadelphia, Phoenix, San Antonio* Remind students that this is the number of casualties from just one battle of the war.

Info to Know

Shell Shock The intense, bloody fighting of World War I left some soldiers with a nervous disorder called shell shock. The term described a wide range of symptoms—from headaches to comas to suicidal depression. Shell shock was widespread during the war. In many cases, some doctors argued, the symptoms were brought on by horrible experiences that were beyond soldiers' ability to absorb.

The Battle of the Somme

The British made little progress against the Germans' heavy barbed wire and trenches during the Battle of the Somme. After months of fighting, they had advanced only six miles, and hundreds of thousands of soldiers had lost their lives (see table below).

SOMME STATISTICS

Duration of battle: July 1–Nov. 18, 1916

Total Allied casualties: about 630,000

British casualties on day 1: about 57,000

Total German casualties: about 650,000

THE IMPACT
TODAY

Science and Technology
Since World War I, improvements in technology have made trench warfare nearly obsolete. Because the military today uses long-distance weapons, radar, and air surveillance, there is less direct combat.

Fighting in the trenches Trench warfare, or fighting from trenches, was not a new strategy. Years earlier American armies had dug trenches during some Civil War battles, including Petersburg. In other wars, armies had dug some trenches in Asia decades before World War I.

However, no soldiers had ever experienced trench warfare on the scale that European forces now did. All across the Western Front, soldiers lived in the trenches, surrounded by machine gun fire, flying grenades, and exploding artillery shells.

Many European military officers thought that a well-motivated army could easily capture the enemy's trenches. They were wrong. Opposing forces had their machine guns aimed at enemy trenches at all times. Any time a helmet or rifle appeared along the trench line, the opposing troops would fire.

Occasionally, soldiers would go over the top to fire at the enemy, but this meant they also lost the protection the trench provided. Soldiers would jump out of their trenches and run across the area between opposing trenches—called no-man's-land—as quickly as they could to attack the other side. But as they ran, thousands of men were chopped down by enemy machine gun fire. No-man's-land became littered with bodies.

As a result, neither the Allies nor the Germans were able to make significant advances. Trench warfare created a stalemate, or deadlock. With the fighting bogged down, both the Allied and Central Powers began looking for new ways to gain an advantage. Many of these new strategies involved the use of new weapons and technology.

New weapons Scientists for both the Allied and Central Powers developed new weapons during World War I in an attempt to win an advantage. German military scientists had been experimenting with poisonous gas as a possible weapon to defeat the Allies.

Although gas seemed to be a breakthrough in military technology, actually using the poisonous gas as a weapon on the battlefield remained a very risky maneuver. Soldiers did not know how much gas to use in an attack. Moreover, a quick change in wind direction could blow the gas back into the troops who had launched it.

The German military eventually found ways to overcome these obstacles, however. In April 1915 German soldiers fired canisters of poisonous gas into Allied trenches. A yellow-green cloud of chlorine gas miles wide enveloped the Allied soldiers. The gas quickly destroyed the soldiers' lungs, and many of them panicked.

588 CHAPTER 18

Collaborative Learning

At Level

World War I Innovations

Research Required

1. Organize the class into small groups. Assign each group one of the following types of new weapons that were used in World War I: chemical warfare (poison gas), firearms (machine guns and other new types of firearms), tanks, and airplanes.

2. Have each group write a report about its assigned weapon type. Reports should discuss the development and use of each type of weapon and why it was important. Students should also include illustrations or detailed diagrams with their reports.

3. Have volunteers from each group present the reports to the class. 🅛🅢 **Interpersonal, Verbal-Linguistic**

📁 Alternative Assessment Handbook, Rubrics 30: Research; and 38: Writing to Classify

Some traditional military officers felt that using poisonous gas was an unfair and barbaric way to fight the war. Even the German commander at the April 1915 attack regretted using the gas, saying, "The plan of poisoning the enemy with gas just as if they were rats . . . disgusted me."

Nevertheless, the Allies could not let the Germans gain an advantage. So British and French forces soon began to develop and use the poisonous gas in their attacks against the Germans as well.

Gas, however, had little effect on the outcome of battles. Soldiers on both sides began to carry gas masks for protection against this new kind of chemical warfare. The gas masks worked well. As long as the soldiers could see the colored gas cloud approaching, they could survive a poisonous gas attack simply by putting on their gas masks.

Once again facing a stalemate, both the Allied and Central Powers began to look for other weapons that could help them win the war. British forces soon developed a motorized armored tank which could maneuver through the dangerous no-man's-land.

These tanks, however, had limited success. In the first battle in which tanks were used, 18 out of 48 tanks became stuck in the mud. Although the tanks frightened the German troops, German military planners were not as impressed. They soon developed strategies to destroy the tanks with artillery fire.

Airplanes proved to be even more useful than tanks. Both sides used airplanes to map enemy positions and trenches and to attack the trenches from above. At first, airplane pilots dropped bricks and heavy objects on enemy troops. Soon, mechanics also figured out how to mount machine guns on planes and launch bombs from the air.

Skilled French and British pilots, or aces, fought German pilots in spectacular air battles called dogfights. Using daring rolls and dives, Allied pilots dueled German aces such as the notorious Baron Manfred von Richthofen, who was known as the Red Baron. The Red Baron shot down 80 Allied planes before he himself was finally shot down in 1918.

Nevertheless, none of the new technologies used in battle gave the Allied or Central Powers the advantage they hoped for. The miserable form of battle known as trench warfare continued. Clearly something would have to change before either side could declare victory in the war.

READING CHECK **Summarizing** Why were the new weapons not very effective in ending trench warfare?

SECTION 1 ASSESSMENT

go.hrw.com
Online Quiz
Keyword: SD7 HP18

Reviewing Ideas, Terms, and People

1. **a. Identify** What was **militarism**?
   b. Explain How did the assassination of **Archduke Franz Ferdinand** lead so many nations into war?
   c. Elaborate Why do you think that European nations were willing to go to war so quickly?

2. **a. Recall** What kinds of military technology were new in World War I?
   b. Draw Conclusions At the beginning of the war, how did the new military technology affect the way European leaders thought about the war?
   c. Evaluate Was it reasonable for European leaders to believe the war would be quick? Why or why not?

3. **a. Identify** What was **trench warfare**?
   b. Draw Conclusions How did trench warfare affect the progress of the war?
   c. Elaborate How did soldiers try to overcome the limitations of trench warfare?

Critical Thinking

4. **Identifying Cause and Effect** Copy the chart below and record the four main causes of World War I. Below each cause list two supporting examples.

Cause			
Example			
Example			

FOCUS ON WRITING

5. **Persuasive** Write a letter to the editor of a newspaper that argues either for or against using poison gas and other new military technologies in World War I. Write your letter as if you are a soldier in the war. Use information from the chapter to support your position.

THE FIRST WORLD WAR **589**

Info to Know

Cavalry in World War I Horses were still being used during World War I. But the new weapons of war proved devastating to both the horses and their riders as they fell under the spray of machine guns. The days when horses were useful in battle had come to an end, and the deaths of millions of horses had greatly reduced the total number of horses in the world.

Review & Assess

Close

Guide the class in a discussion of the conditions that led to the outbreak of war in 1914.

Review

- Online Quiz, Section 1
- Daily Test Practice Transparency

Assess

SE Section 1 Assessment
- Progress Assessment: Section 1 Quiz
- Alternative Assessment Handbook

Reteach

- Interactive Reader and Study Guide, Section 1
- Interactive Skills Tutor CD-ROM

Section 1 Assessment Answers

1. **a.** military preparedness; arms build up
   b. countries had created alliances involving most of Europe; countries agreed to come to each other's aid
   c. believed they possessed superior military power; thought they could win

2. **a.** camouflaged uniforms, machine guns, artillery guns, poison gas
   b. thought new technology would result in short war
   c. possible answer—no, because the military advances were not enough to give one nation a substantial advantage

3. **a.** fighting from deep ditches
   b. created a stalemate
   c. with poison gas, tanks, and airplanes

4. nationalism—new nations of Germany and Italy, tension in the Balkans; imperialism—British and French colonies, German quest for colonies; militarism—German navy buildup, creation of Schlieffen Plan; alliances—Triple Entente, Triple Alliance

5. possible answer—it is uncivilized, hurts soldiers

Answers

Reading Check *soldiers could live and hide in the trenches; used gas masks; tanks got stuck in the mud*

589

Bellringer

The Inside Story. . . Use the **Daily Bellringer Transparency** to help students answer the question.

🖺 Daily Bellringer Transparency, Section 2

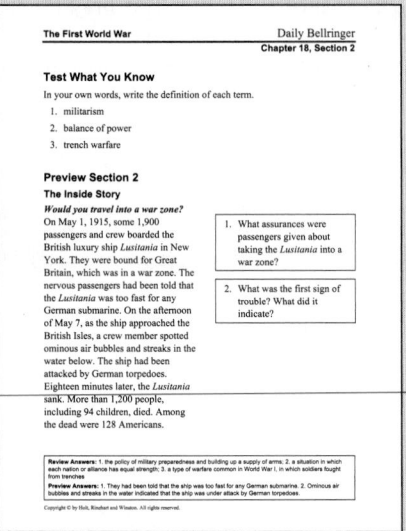

Academic Vocabulary

Review with students the high-use academic terms in this section.

neutral not aligned with either side in a war or dispute (p. 591)

factor something that contributes to a result (p. 595)

📝 CRF: Vocabulary Builder Activity, Section 2

Taking Notes

U.S. had close ties with the Allies; German submarine warfare angered Americans; sinking of Lusitania *and Sussex; Wilson asks for authority to install guns on U.S. merchant ships; Zimmermann Note; more Americans supportive of Allies after Russian czar lost power; U-boats sink American merchant ships*

go.hrw.com
Online Resources

KEYWORD: SD7 CH18
TOPIC: FROM NEUTRALITY TO WAR

The United States in World War I

BEFORE YOU READ

MAIN IDEA
The United States helped turn the tide for an Allied victory.

READING FOCUS
1. Why did the United States try to stay neutral in the war?
2. Which events showed that America was heading into war?
3. What contributions did Americans make in Europe?
4. How did the war end?

KEY TERMS AND PEOPLE
Lusitania
isolationism
U-boats
Sussex pledge
Zimmermann Note
Selective Service Act
convoy system
Communists

 **TAKING NOTES** As you read, take notes on events and activities that pushed the U.S. to enter World War I. Record your notes in a graphic organizer like the one shown here.

Causes → United States Enters World War I

THE INSIDE STORY   *Would you travel into a war zone?* In New York Harbor on Saturday, May 1, 1915, some 1,900 passengers and crew boarded the British luxury ship *Lusitania* and headed for a war zone. The ship's destination was Great Britain. A spokesperson for the ship's company reassured the nervous passengers, "The *Lusitania* ... is too fast for any German submarine."

In the early afternoon of May 7, 1915, the *Lusitania* approached the British Isles. Crew member Leslie Morton spotted ominous air bubbles and streaks in the water below. He grabbed a megaphone and shouted, "Torpedoes coming!" But it was too late. A torpedo slammed into the ship's right side. Passengers scrambled for life jackets and lifeboats when the ship began to lean and take on water. As the *Lusitania* slid beneath the waves, parents tried to hold their children above water. Some even tied their children to deck chairs and

wreckage in a futile attempt to save them. As Morton later described the scene, "The turmoil of passengers and life jackets, many people losing hold on the deck and slipping down and over the side ... [created] a horrible and bizarre orchestra of death."

The *Lusitania* sank only 18 minutes after it was torpedoed. About 1,200 people died. Among the dead were 128 Americans. ◼

Sailing INTO WAR

▶ **The sinking of the *Lusitania* killed more than 1,200 people.**

Teach the Main Idea
          At Level

The United States in World War I

1. **Teach** Ask students the Reading Focus questions to teach this section.

2. **Apply** Have students work in pairs to create a time line for this section. Have students include all the events that have specific dates on their time lines.

3. **Review** Review student time lines as a class. Ask students to call out the events in order, with their dates. As they do so, create a time line for the class to see.

4. **Practice/Homework** Have each student write a letter to the editor of a newspaper explaining how he or she thinks the United States should have responded to the Zimmermann Note in 1917. 🔲 **Visual-Spatial, Verbal-Linguistic**

📝 Alternative Assessment Handbook, Rubrics 17: Letters to Editors; and 36: Time Lines

United States Stays Neutral

Before the sinking of the *Lusitania*, Americans thought of the war as a European conflict that had little effect on life in the United States. Just after the war began, President Woodrow Wilson declared that the United States would remain <u>neutral</u>. Wilson's response to the war reflected a long-standing American tradition of isolationism—a policy of not being involved in the affairs of other nations.

Leaning toward the Allies Privately, Wilson favored the Allied cause. He was extremely concerned about Germany's war tactics and its invasion of Belgium. Furthermore, the United States historically had greater political, cultural, and commercial ties to Great Britain and France than to Germany.

Financially, the United States was far from neutral. The British fleet had blockaded German ports and transportation routes, and few American businesses could sell goods to German forces. It was far easier, however, to supply the Allies. By 1917 Britain was purchasing nearly $75 million worth of war goods from American businesses each week.

German submarine warfare Germany suffered greatly under the British blockade, and the German navy began to develop a plan to strike back at Great Britain. Germany planned to wage its naval war with **U-boats**—small submarines named after the German word *Unterseeboot*, which means "undersea boat."

In February 1915 the German government announced that the waters around Great Britain would be a war zone in which Germany would destroy all enemy ships. Germany warned the United States that neutral ships might be attacked as well. This policy of having submarines attack all ships was called unrestricted submarine warfare.

The German plan for unrestricted submarine warfare angered most Americans. Wilson believed that Germany's actions violated the laws of neutrality. He warned Germany that he would hold the nation responsible if American lives were lost. Tensions between the United States and Germany were rising.

> **READING CHECK** **Drawing Conclusions**
> Why did American businesses do more business with the Allies than with Germany?

Heading Toward War

ACADEMIC VOCABULARY
neutral not aligned with either side in a war or dispute

As you read in the "Inside Story," the American public was outraged by the 1915 sinking of the *Lusitania*. President Wilson demanded an end to unrestricted submarine warfare.

Facing international criticism, the German government agreed to attack only supply ships. But less than one year later, Germany attacked the French passenger ship *Sussex* on March 24, 1916, killing about 80 people. After this attack, Wilson threatened to end diplomatic relations with Germany unless it stopped killing innocent civilians. German officials feared that the United States might enter the war, so Germany issued the **Sussex pledge**, which included a promise not to sink merchant vessels "without warning and without saving human lives."

Wilson's re-election As he campaigned during the election of 1916, Wilson assured Americans that he would not send their sons to die in Europe. Wilson's chief rival, Republican candidate Charles Evans Hughes, took a stronger pro-war stance. The election was very close. In the end, Wilson won by little more than 3 percent of the popular vote.

Once re-elected, Wilson began to work for a peace settlement. In January 1917 he asked the Allied and Central Powers to accept a "peace without victory." This request angered

THE FIRST WORLD WAR **591**

591

Heading Toward War

Recall Why did the Allies reject President Wilson's "peace without victory" plan? *They blamed the Central Powers for starting the war and wanted them to pay for wartime damage and destruction.*

Make Inferences How did the United States intend to "make the world safe for democracy" when most of the European countries on both sides of the war were monarchies? *France was a republic; Britain, with its Parliament, was a constitutional monarchy; and Russia had a new government based on republican ideals.*

Predict How do you think history might have been different if Mexico had entered World War I as an ally of the Central Powers? *possible answer—Mexico wouldn't have posed much of a threat to the United States, but a war on the southern border might have kept the U.S. from entering the war in Europe until later, allowing the Central Powers to win there.*

📄 CRF: Interdisciplinary Project: Debate a Declaration of War

📄 CRF: Primary Source Activity: Senator George Norris Opposes U.S. Entry into the War

From Neutrality to War

Remind students that all presidential candidates make campaign promises. However, once elected, presidents must do what they believe is best for the nation, even if that contradicts earlier promises.

Primary Source

"The world must be made safe for democracy. Its peace must be planted upon the tested foundations of political liberty."

— Woodrow Wilson
Address to Congress, April 2, 1917

---

the Allies. They blamed the Central Powers for starting the war and wanted them to pay for wartime damage and destruction.

Any hope for peace ended when Germany resumed unrestricted submarine warfare on February 1, 1917. Two days later, the United States ended diplomatic relations with Germany. Wilson asked Congress for the authority to install guns on U.S. merchant ships.

The Zimmermann Note Meanwhile, German foreign secretary Arthur Zimmermann sent a telegram to a German official in Mexico. The **Zimmermann Note** proposed an alliance between Germany and Mexico. "We shall make war together, make peace together," the telegram offered. "[In exchange] Mexico is to reconquer the lost territory in New Mexico, Texas, and Arizona." The Germans hoped that an American war with Mexico would keep the United States out of the war in Europe. Since Mexico expressed no interest in fighting, this German strategy backfired.

The British had intercepted the Zimmermann Note, decoded it, and sent it to American officials. On March 1, American newspapers printed excerpts from the telegram. More Americans began to call for war against Germany. Yet Wilson continued to resist, hoping to bring about a lasting peace in Europe.

The United States declares war In mid-March, dramatic events in Russia raised new questions for the United States. An uprising in Russia forced Czar Nicholas II to give up his absolute power over the government. Rebel leaders set up a government based on republican ideals.

These changes made Russia more democratic but also raised questions about how long the new Russian government would continue to fight on the Eastern Front. Many Americans—who believed that the American role in world politics should be to promote democracy—became more supportive of the Allies and the war after the Russian czar lost power.

Then in mid-March 1917, German U-boats sank three American merchant ships. Outraged about the violation of American neutrality, President Wilson called a meeting with his cabinet. Each cabinet member argued for war. On April 2, Wilson asked Congress to declare war on Germany so that the world could "be made safe for democracy."

HISTORY'S VOICES

❝We shall fight for the things which we have always carried nearest our hearts, for democracy ... [and to] bring peace and safety to all nations and make the world itself at last free.❞

—Woodrow Wilson, Speech to Congress, April 2, 1917

From Neutrality to War

Remaining Neutral

Below, a German U-boat prowls the seas. President Wilson opposed the use of unrestricted submarine warfare, but he campaigned for re-election in 1916 (right) with promises to keep America out of the war.

592

Skills Focus: Sequencing

At Level

Reading Skill
The U.S. Enters the War

1. To help students identify the events that led to U.S. entry into World War I, have them create a graphic organizer showing the significance of each of these events:
   • March 1916: Germany attacks the passenger ship *Sussex*
   • February 1917: Germany resumes unrestricted submarine warfare
   • March 1917: American newspapers publish excerpts from the Zimmermann Note

   • April 1917: German U-boats sink three American merchant ships

2. After students have finished their graphic organizers, have them rank the events in order of importance. Have volunteers share their answers with the class. 🄻🅂 **Visual-Spatial, Verbal-Linguistic**

📄 Alternative Assessment Handbook, Rubric 13: Graphic Organizers

📄 Graphic Organizer Transparencies

Congress approved President Wilson's request. On April 6, 1917, the United States joined the war on the side of the Allies.

READING CHECK **Drawing Conclusions**
How did the United States respond to war in Europe?

Americans in Europe

Now the United States military began quickly preparing for battle. An army needed to be raised, new recruits needed to be trained for combat, and troops and supplies needed to be shipped to the front.

Raising an army On May 18, 1917, Congress passed the **Selective Service Act**, which required men between the ages of 21 and 30 to register to be drafted into the armed forces. Most young men willingly participated in the draft. A small number of men asked to be classified as conscientious objectors—members of certain religious groups, such as the Quakers, whose moral or religious beliefs prevented them from fighting in a war. But few local draft boards accepted their applications. Once rejected, these men had to take combat positions or face prison.

In the summer of 1917, the new recruits reported for training but found almost nothing ready for them. Many soldiers slept in tents until barracks could be hastily built. Supplies had been ordered but had not yet arrived.

Nevertheless, the training was intense. New recruits spent most of their days learning military rules and practices, marching, and preparing for inspections. Because of a shortage of rifles, they practiced with wooden sticks. Instead of horses, the trainees pretended to ride wooden barrels.

African American soldiers were segregated into separate divisions and trained in separate camps. Many white Army officers and southern politicians objected to the training of African American soldiers to use weapons. They feared that these black soldiers might pose a threat after the war. Because of these beliefs, only a few black regiments were trained for combat.

Latinos also experienced discrimination. Some Hispanic soldiers faced scorn from other American troops and were often assigned menial tasks. Some Latinos who were eager to serve in the war did not speak English fluently. The federal government did not reject them. Instead, the military established special programs in New Mexico and Georgia to help them improve their English skills. After completing such training, the soldiers would fight alongside other American troops.

THE IMPACT TODAY
Government
The Selective Service Act remains in effect today. All men between the ages of 18 and 25 must register to be selected randomly for military service. However, the draft has not been instituted since 1973.

Joining the War

After the United States declared war in 1917, General John J. Pershing led U.S. forces in Europe. Below, Pershing arrives in France with the first soldiers. He spent months establishing the American Expeditionary Forces (right) and setting up communications and supply lines.

593

Americans in Europe

Identify Who made up the American Expeditionary Force?
American soldiers who went overseas, including soldiers from the regular army, the National Guard, and new volunteers and draftees

Make Judgments Do you think General Pershing's decision to train his troops in Europe rather than have them join the Allies who desperately needed help was a wise decision? Explain your answer.
possible answers—yes, he did not want them to get killed; no, it only prolonged the war and the suffering endured by the Allies.

CRF: Biography: James Reese Europe

America at War

African American soldiers faced officially sanctioned discrimination. It was suggested that they should work solely as laborers, which would free up white soldiers to train for battle. Despite this discrimination, many African Americans supported the war effort and welcomed the opportunities for travel, education, and honor that sometimes accompanied the experience.

Info to Know

African American Soldiers Remind students that the U.S. military forces were segregated until after the end of World War II when President Truman issued an executive order ending the practice.

Arriving in Europe The American soldiers who went overseas formed the American Expeditionary Forces (AEF), led by General John J. Pershing. The AEF included soldiers from the regular army, the National Guard, and a new larger force of volunteers and draftees.

The first U.S. troops arrived in France in late June 1917. To transport forces safely, Pershing relied on the **convoy system**, in which troop-transport ships were surrounded by destroyers or cruisers for protection. The convoy system reduced the number of ships sunk and limited the loss of troops and supplies.

When American troops arrived in France, the Allies' situation was grim. German troops occupied all of Belgium and part of northeastern France. Along the Eastern Front, Russia was struggling to defend itself against Germany. The Russians were facing famine and civil war. If Russia fell, many German troops could be sent to fight in France. The Allies desperately needed help and wanted the Americans to start fighting as soon as they arrived.

General Pershing had other plans. He wanted his soldiers to fight as American units and not as individuals in different European regiments. Pershing also wanted to give his troops more training. The American general believed that sending inexperienced soldiers

into battle was the same as sending them to die. As a result, Pershing sent his troops to training camps in eastern France.

Allied setbacks Meanwhile, the Allies suffered another blow. In November 1917 a group known as the Bolsheviks took control of Russia's government. The Bolsheviks were **Communists**—people who seek the equal distribution of wealth and the end of all private property. The new government, led by Vladimir Ilich Lenin, withdrew the Russian army from the Eastern Front and signed a peace agreement with the Central Powers. Now Germany was free to focus on fighting in the west.

In March 1918, German soldiers launched a series of tremendous offensives against the Allies. The Germans were backed by some 6,000 artillery pieces, including "Big Berthas"—massive guns capable of firing a 2,100-pound shell almost 75 miles. By late May the Germans had pushed the Allies back to the Marne River, just 70 miles northeast of Paris.

U.S. troops in action Almost 12 months after arriving in France, American troops finally saw combat. Reaching the front lines, they quickly learned the Allied war strategy. They dug extensive trenches to protect themselves from German gunfire. When Company A

From Neutrality to War, *continued*

Fighting in the War

In June 1918, Belleau Wood, France, became the proving grounds for American soldiers (below). Although a U.S. victory, 8,000 American casualties at the Battle of Belleau Wood made it America's bloodiest battle thus far in the war.

594

Skills Focus: Analyzing Primary Sources

At Level

Reading Like a Historian Skill

Waiting to Fight

Research Required

1. Have students conduct outside research and find letters or other primary source documents written by American World War I soldiers who served in Europe.

2. Have volunteers read their letters to the class or make a class set for all students to read.

3. Discuss the information in the documents with the students. Then discuss General Pershing's decision to delay the entry of U.S. troops into the fighting. Based on

the information in the primary source documents, do students believe that delaying the American soldiers' entry into the war by nearly a year was worth it in the long run? How might the delay have prolonged the war? Do students believe that American lives were spared at the expense of European lives?

LS Verbal-Linguistic, Logical-Mathematical

Alternative Assessment Handbook, Rubrics 11: Discussions; and 30: Research

of the 82nd Division reached the front lines, for example, its members had to dig 3,000 yards of trenches and set up 12,000 yards of barbed wire. The soldiers worked in the middle of the night to avoid detection by the enemy. As dawn broke, the exhausted soldiers returned to their temporary shelters. They were covered in mud, and their uniforms were torn to shreds by barbed wire.

Life in the trenches was a painful ordeal. The soldiers stood in deep mud as rats ran across their feet. Enemy planes dropped bombs, artillery shells exploded nearby, and clouds of mustard gas floated into the trenches. "It was an eerie feeling down in that dugout [trench]," one soldier recalled. "No one knew what was going to happen next."

The American troops were a major <u>factor</u> in the war. While defending Paris in June 1918, U.S. troops helped the French stop the Germans at Chateau-Thierry. In northern France, a division of U.S. Marines recaptured the forest of Belleau Wood and two nearby villages. After fierce fighting, the Allies finally halted the German advance. Paris was saved.

American military women The vast majority of Americans who served in the military were men, but some women also signed up to serve overseas. The U.S. Army Signal Corps recruited French-speaking American women to serve as switchboard operators. Known as the Hello Girls, they served a crucial role in keeping communications open between the front line and the headquarters of the American Expeditionary Forces.

During the war, more than 20,000 nurses served in the U.S. Army in the United States and overseas. Women also served in the navy and marines, usually as typists and bookkeepers, although some became radio operators, electricians, or telegraphers.

READING CHECK Identifying the Main Idea Why did it take so long for U.S. troops to enter combat?

The War Ends

On July 15, 1918, the Germans launched their last, desperate offensive at the Second Battle of the Marne. During the fighting, the U.S. 3rd Division blew up every bridge the Germans had built across the Marne. The German army retreated on August 3, having suffered some 150,000 casualties.

The Allies began a counterattack in September 1918. For the first time, Americans fought as a separate army. The AEF defeated German troops at Mihiel, near the French-German border.

ACADEMIC
VOCABULARY
factor something that contributes to a result

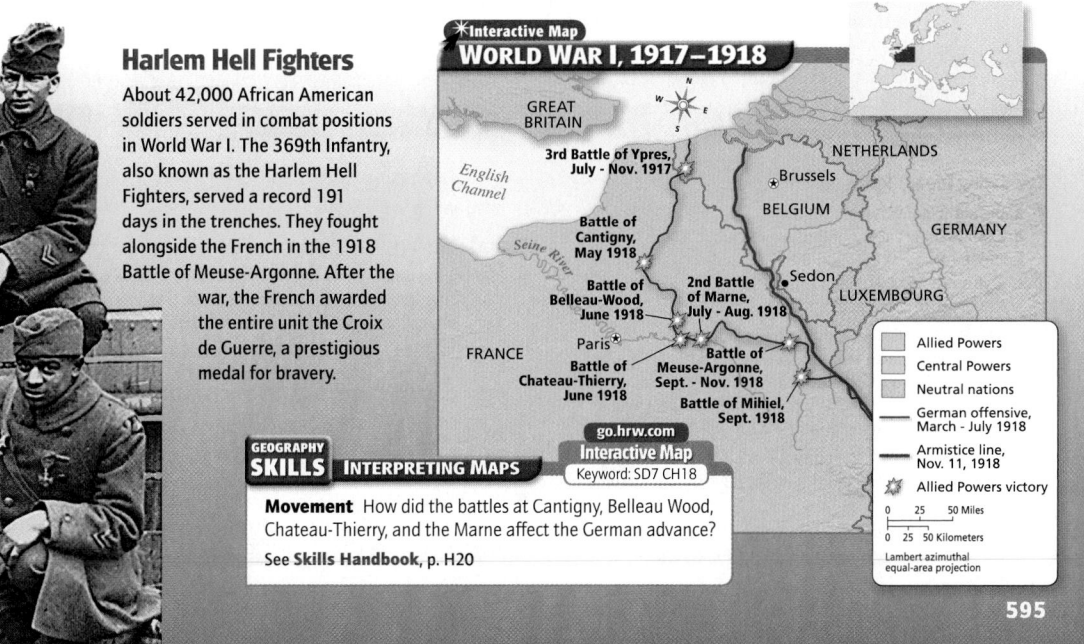

Harlem Hell Fighters

About 42,000 African American soldiers served in combat positions in World War I. The 369th Infantry, also known as the Harlem Hell Fighters, served a record 191 days in the trenches. They fought alongside the French in the 1918 Battle of Meuse-Argonne. After the war, the French awarded the entire unit the Croix de Guerre, a prestigious medal for bravery.

Interactive Map
WORLD WAR I, 1917–1918

GREAT BRITAIN
English Channel
3rd Battle of Ypres, July - Nov. 1917
Brussels
NETHERLANDS
BELGIUM
Seine River
Battle of Cantigny, May 1918
GERMANY
Battle of Belleau-Wood, June 1918
2nd Battle of Marne, July - Aug. 1918
Sedon
LUXEMBOURG
FRANCE
Paris
Battle of Chateau-Thierry, June 1918
Battle of Meuse-Argonne, Sept. - Nov. 1918
Battle of Mihiel, Sept. 1918

Allied Powers
Central Powers
Neutral nations
German offensive, March - July 1918
Armistice line, Nov. 11, 1918
Allied Powers victory
0   25   50 Miles
0   25   50 Kilometers
Lambert azimuthal equal-area projection

go.hrw.com
Interactive Map
Keyword: SD7 CH18

GEOGRAPHY
SKILLS INTERPRETING MAPS

Movement How did the battles at Cantigny, Belleau Wood, Chateau-Thierry, and the Marne affect the German advance?

See **Skills Handbook, p. H20**

595

The War Ends

Summarize What demands did the Allies make of Germany in return for an armistice? *that Germany leave all territories it occupied, surrender military equipment, and allow the Allies to occupy some German territory*

Evaluate Why do you think World War I was referred to as "the war to end all wars"? *possible answer—It caused so much death and destruction that people never wanted to experience another war.*

Review & Assess

Close

Have students summarize the events that led to the United States' entry into World War I and how it helped to turn the tide.

Review

Online Quiz, Section 2

Daily Test Practice Transparency

Assess

SE Section 2 Assessment

Progress Assessment: Section 2 Quiz

Alternative Assessment Handbook

Reteach

Interactive Reader and Study Guide, Section 2

Interactive Skills Tutor CD-ROM

Answers

Reading Check *Allied victories; war crippled German economy; Central Powers could not recruit soldiers; Austria-Hungary signed peace agreement with Allies; German delegation negotiated with France*

596

Alvin York's bravery—and capture of 132 Germans—made him the most famous hero of the war.

After the victory, the Allies continued their advance toward the French city of Sedan on the Belgian border. The railway there was the main supply line for German forces. Other Allied forces advanced all along the front.

For more than a month the Allies pushed northward through the rugged Argonne Forest, facing artillery explosions and deadly machine gun fire every step of the way. In the Battle of the Argonne Forest the Americans suffered some 120,000 casualties. By November, however, the Allies reached and occupied the hills around Sedan.

The armistice By late 1918 the war was crippling the German economy; many civilians lacked food and supplies. Food riots and strikes erupted in Germany, and revolution swept across Austria-Hungary. The Central Powers had difficulty encouraging their soldiers to fight. Some soldiers even ran away.

Lacking the will to keep fighting, the Central Powers began to surrender. In early November, Austria-Hungary signed a peace agreement with the Allies. On November 7 a German delegation entered French territory to begin peace negotiations.

The Allies demanded that Germany leave all territories it had occupied. Germany surrendered its aircraft, heavy artillery, tanks, and U-boats. The Allies also forced Germany to allow Allied troops to occupy some German territory. On November 11, 1918, the armistice went into effect, and the guns of war fell silent. An Allied soldier later described the moment when the Great War ended.

HISTORY'S VOICES

" There came a second of expectant silence, and then a curious rippling sound ... It was the sound of men cheering from the Vosges [mountain range] to the sea. **"**

—John Buchan, *The King's Grace*, 1935

War tragedies muted some of the celebration. When asked what the armistice meant, one British soldier replied, "Time to bury the dead." People around the world had grown weary of death. Some 8.5 million people had been killed. People everywhere hoped that the Great War would be "the war to end all wars." World leaders soon turned their attention to healing what the American writer W.E.B. Du Bois referred to as the "wounded world."

READING CHECK **Sequencing** What events led to the armistice?

SECTION 2 ASSESSMENT

go.hrw.com
Online Quiz
Keyword: SD7 HP18

Reviewing Ideas, Terms, and People

1. **a. Define** What was **isolationism**?
   b. Explain Why did the United States pursue a policy of isolationism?
   c. Elaborate How did Germany's actions make the United States begin to consider abandoning isolationism?

2. **a. Recall** What was the **Zimmermann Note**?
   b. Draw Conclusions How did the Zimmermann Note affect American public opinion about the war?
   c. Evaluate Which event do you think was the most significant in convincing Americans to join the war? Why?

3. **a. Identify** What was the **convoy system**?
   b. Explain What effect did U.S. troops have on the outcome of the war?

4. **a. Describe** What was the Battle of the Argonne Forest?

b. Analyze How did the economic effects of the war help bring an end to the fighting?

Critical Thinking

5. **Identifying Cause and Effect** Copy the timeline below. Using information from the section, place on the timeline the major events that led the United States to declare war against Germany.

FOCUS ON WRITING

6. **Expository** What caused the United States to enter World War I? Write a short paragraph in which you explain the events that led the United States to declare war.

596 CHAPTER 18

Section 2 Assessment Answers

1. **a.** staying out of other nations' affairs
   b. long-standing tradition; belief that war had little effect on life in U.S.
   c. Germany's war tactics, use of unrestricted submarine warfare angered Americans

2. **a.** note from Germany to Mexico proposing an alliance
   b. More Americans began to call for war.
   c. possible answer—the sinking of U.S. merchant ships

3. **a.** troop-transport ships were surrounded by destroyers or cruisers for protection

b. played a major role in helping French troops stop the German advance on Paris

4. **a.** month-long Allied push northward through the Argonne Forest; eventual Allied victory
   b. cost crippled the German economy; German food riots and strikes hurt Central Powers' ability to continue the fight

5. Zimmermann Note; merchant ships sunk

6. possible answer—U.S. ties to Allies, sent supplies to Britain; Zimmermann Note and sinking of U.S. merchant ships

About the Reading Ernest Hemingway based his novel *A Farewell to Arms* (1929) on his experiences as an ambulance driver for the American Red Cross in World War I. His novel tells the story of Frederic Henry, an American serving with the Italian ambulance service, who falls in love with Catherine Barkley, a British nurse. In the following passage Frederic describes an atmosphere of confusion and uncertainty as he works to help the wounded.

AS YOU READ Notice how the narrator remains distant from the "great battle."

Excerpt from

A Farewell to Arms

by Ernest Hemingway

The wounded were coming into the post, some were carried on stretchers, some walking and some were brought on the backs of men that came across the field. They were wet to the skin and all were scared. We filled two cars with stretcher cases as they came up from the cellar of the post and as I shut the door of the second car and fastened it I felt the rain on my face turn to snow. The flakes were coming heavy and fast in the rain.

When daylight came the storm was still blowing but the snow had stopped. It had melted as it fell on the wet ground and now it was raining again. There was another attack just after daylight but it was unsuccessful. We expected an attack all day but it did not come until the sun was going down. The bombardment started to the south below the long wooded ridge where the Austrian guns were concentrated. We expected a bombardment but it did not come. It was getting dark. Guns were firing from the field behind the village and the shells, going away, had a comfortable sound.

We heard that the attack to the south had been unsuccessful. They did not attack that night but we heard that they had broken through to the north.

American snipers on the outskirts of a French town take potshots at German soldiers from the shelter of a shattered building.

In the night word came that we were to prepare to retreat. The captain at the post told me this. He had it from the Brigade. A little while later he came from the telephone and said it was a lie. The Brigade had received orders that the line of the Bainsizza should be held no matter what happened. I asked about the break through and he said he had heard at the Brigade that the Austrians had broken though the twenty-seventh arms corps up toward Caporetto. There had been a great battle in the north all day.

Skills FOCUS — READING LIKE A HISTORIAN

1. **Drawing Conclusions** How reliable is the information about the distant battle that the narrator receives?
2. **Literature as Historical Evidence** What larger statement do you think Hemingway is trying to make about the nature of warfare in the twentieth century?

See **Skills Handbook,** pp. H12, H32

THE FIRST WORLD WAR **597**

American Literature

A Farewell to Arms
Word Help

bombardment attack

Meet the Writer

Ernest Hemingway (1899–1961) was born in Oak Park, Illinois, where he spent his early years. During World War I, he volunteered to serve as an ambulance driver in Italy, but he later transferred to the Italian infantry and was severely wounded. Before and after the war, he was a reporter for American and Canadian newspapers. During the 1920s he was a member of the American expatriate community in Paris. Among his friends there was Gertrude Stein, a writer and patron of the arts who encouraged him to write fiction. He was a reporter in Spain during that country's civil war, and later served as a newspaper correspondent in Europe during World War II. In addition to his wartime experiences, Hemingway drew on his love of fishing, hunting, and bullfights in his writing. He received the Nobel Prize for literature in 1954. He died in Idaho in 1961.

Info to Know
Writers Who Served During the War
Hemingway was just one of many American writers who volunteered their services as ambulance drivers during World War I. Other writers included Dashiell Hammett, John Dos Passos, E. E. Cummings, and Gertrude Stein.

Differentiating Instruction

Learners Having Difficulties   Below Level

Materials construction or butcher paper, colored markers

Divide the class into small groups. Have each group discuss this passage to make sure that they understand it. Have each group create a mural illustrating a portion of the passage.
LS Interpersonal, Visual-Spatial

Advanced Learners/GATE   Above Level

Divide the class into small groups. Have each group write a script for a play based on the passage. Scripts should include a list of characters, dialogue, a list of props, a description of the set, stage directions, and sound effects. Have each group present its play to the rest of the class.
LS Interpersonal, Verbal-Linguistic

Alternative Assessment Handbook, Rubrics 3: Artwork; and 33: Skits and Reader's Theater

Answers
Reading Like a Historian 1. *unreliable because source had already given incorrect information;* **2.** *that war was nonstop; no one knew when or what to expect; confusion of war*

Bellringer

The Inside Story. . . Use the **Daily Bellringer Transparency** to help students answer the question.

📦 Daily Bellringer Transparency, Section 3

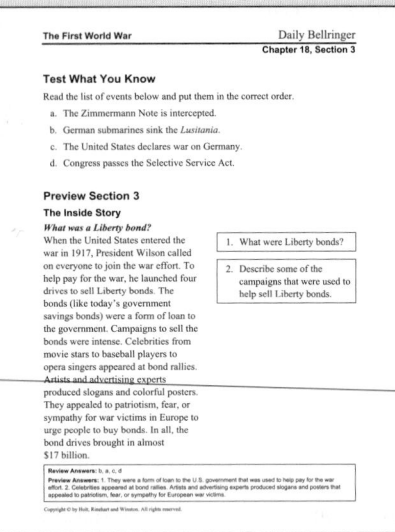

The First World War	Daily Bellringer
	Chapter 18, Section 3

Test What You Know

Read the list of events below and put them in the correct order.

   a. The Zimmermann Note is intercepted.
   b. German submarines sink the *Lusitania*.
   c. The United States declares war on Germany.
   d. Congress passes the Selective Service Act.

Preview Section 3
The Inside Story
What was a Liberty bond?
When the United States entered the war in 1917, President Wilson called on everyone to join the war effort. To help pay for the war, he launched four drives to sell Liberty bonds. The bonds (like today's government savings bonds) were a form of loan to the government. Campaigns to sell the bonds were intense. Celebrities from movie stars to baseball players to opera singers appeared at bond rallies. Artists and advertising experts produced slogans and colorful posters. They appealed to patriotism, fear, or sympathy for war victims in Europe to urge people to buy bonds. In all, the bond drives brought in almost $17 billion.

| | 1. What were Liberty bonds? |
| | 2. Describe some of the campaigns that were used to help sell Liberty bonds. |

Review Answers: b, a, c, d
Preview Answers: 1. They were a form of loan to the U.S. government that was used to help pay for the war effort. 2. Celebrities appeared at bond rallies. Artists and advertising experts produced slogans and posters that appealed to patriotism, fear, or sympathy for European war victims.

Copyright © by Holt, Rinehart and Winston. All rights reserved.

Taking Notes

creation of regulatory boards for industry and agriculture that allowed military first pick of supplies; Lever Food and Fuel Control Act set prices and production controls for food and fuel; Food Administration managed and increased food production; prohibition on alcohol; Fuel Administration set production goals and prices for fuels

go.hrw.com
Online Resources
KEYWORD: SD7 CH18
TOPIC: WARTIME PROPAGANDA

BEFORE YOU READ

MAIN IDEA

The United States mobilized a variety of resources to wage World War I.

READING FOCUS

1. How did the government mobilize the economy for the war effort?
2. How did workers mobilize on the home front?
3. How did the government try to influence public opinion about the war?

KEY TERMS AND PEOPLE

Liberty bonds
Bernard Baruch
National War Labor Board
Committee on Public Information
George Creel
propaganda
Schenck v. United States

TAKING NOTES As you read, take notes on ways the United States managed food, fuel, and other supplies for the war effort. Use a diagram like the one below to organize your notes.

Managing Supplies for the War Effort

Pocketbook PATRIOTISM

THE INSIDE STORY

What was a Liberty bond? When the United States entered the war in 1917, President Wilson called on everyone to join the war effort. To help pay for the war, he launched four drives to sell **Liberty bonds**. The bonds, like today's government savings bonds, were a form of loan to the government. In schools, children filled Liberty Books with 25-cent stamps until they were full and could be exchanged for a bond. The slogan was "Lick a Stamp and Lick the Kaiser."

Campaigns to sell bonds were intense. Organizers sent out workers to sell in workplaces, neighborhoods, and theaters. Celebrities from movie stars to baseball players to opera singers appeared at rallies flanked by doughboys in uniform and asked their audiences to buy bonds. Some of the largest rallies were held in Manhattan. In one skit, movie actor Douglas Fairbanks—known for playing swashbuckling heroes—wore boxing gloves labeled Victory and Liberty Bonds as he knocked out the Kaiser.

Artists and advertising experts produced slogans and colorful propaganda posters. They appealed to patriotism, fear, or sympathy for war victims in Europe. One famous poster showed a woman refugee and her children. It read: "Must Children Die and Mothers Plead in Vain—Buy More Liberty Bonds." Another showed a smiling little girl hugging a bond: "My daddy bought me a government bond of the Third Liberty Loan. Did Yours?" In all, the bond drives brought in almost $17 billion. ■

598 CHAPTER 18

OVER THE TOP FOR YOU

Buy U.S. Gov't Bonds
THIRD LIBERTY LOAN

Teach the Main Idea

At Level

The Home Front

1. **Teach** Ask students the Reading Focus questions to teach this section.

2. **Apply** Organize the class into groups of four or five students. Have each group discuss the ways in which life changed on the home front during World War I, making a list of the changes during the discussion.

3. **Review** Review student lists of wartime changes with the class. Which of these changes had lasting effects? In what ways? *possible answer—Women's war efforts*

finally earned them the right to vote.

4. **Practice/Homework** Have students write an essay comparing the kinds of changes that took place in the United States during World War I with changes that took place in the U.S. following the attacks of September 11, 2001. 🄻 **Interpersonal, Verbal-Linguistic**

📋 Alternative Assessment Handbook, Rubrics 9: Comparing and Contrasting; and 14: Group Activity

Mobilizing the Economy

Going to war was an enormous—and enormously expensive—undertaking. One of the first things that President Wilson and his advisers had to do after joining the war was figure out how to pay for it. First, Congress passed the War Revenue Act of 1917. This law established very high taxes and taxed the wealthiest Americans as much as 77 percent of their annual incomes. It increased federal revenues by 400 percent within two years.

The government also borrowed money to pay for the war. The national debt grew from $1.2 billion in 1916 to $25.5 billion in 1919. More than $20 billion of that debt was owed to Americans who had purchased Liberty bonds. These bonds were essentially a loan from the American people to the federal government.

Regulating industry To make sure that the troops received all the supplies they needed, the Wilson administration prepared the nation's industries for war. Congress created hundreds of administrative boards to regulate both industrial and agricultural production and distribution.

One of the most powerful boards was the War Industries Board (WIB). It had the authority to regulate all materials needed in the war effort. Wall Street business leader **Bernard Baruch**, head of the WIB, explained the board's power: "No steel, copper, cement, rubber, or other basic materials could be used without our approval."

The policies and rules of the WIB managed to increase American industrial production by about 20 percent. The military could select any of the goods that were produced. Once the military's needs were met, any remaining goods could be used by civilians.

Regulating food To make sure that the troops would have plenty of food and supplies, Congress passed the Lever Food and Fuel Control Act. This law gave the government the power to set prices and establish production controls for food and for the fuels needed to run military machines.

Wilson's administration also created agencies to manage and increase food production. Herbert Hoover led the Food Administration, whose slogan was "Food Can Win the War." Hoover's goals were to increase the production of crops and to conserve existing food supplies for the military and for American allies.

Financing the War

Colorful posters that spoke to Americans' sense of patriotism (left), parades (below), and appeals by movie stars such as Charlie Chaplin, Mary Pickford, and Douglas Fairbanks (right), all encouraged the purchase of war bonds. *What other attempts did the government make to finance the war?*

BUY LIBERTY BONDS
BUY NOW

THE FIRST WORLD WAR **599**

Skills Focus: Identifying Cause and Effect

Below Level

Reading Skill
Preparing for War

1. Guide students in a discussion of ways in which the U.S. government prepared the nation for war, such as raising money, making sure that there were adequate supplies, and creating public support.

2. Have each student select one of the following areas in which the United States prepared for war: raising revenue; regulating industry; regulating food and fuel; mobilizing workers; influencing public opinion. Have students write a brief essay about their selected topic, explaining what was done and why it was important.

3. Have volunteers read their paragraphs to the class. **LS Logical-Mathematical, Verbal-Linguistic**

📝 Alternative Assessment Handbook, Rubric 42: Writing to Inform

Direct Teach

Reading Focus

1 How did the government mobilize the economy for the war effort? *raised taxes, borrowed money through Liberty bonds to finance the war, regulated industry, food, and fuel in order to supply the troops*

Mobilizing the Economy

Identify What was the War Revenue Act of 1917? *a law establishing very high taxes; it taxed the wealthiest Americans as much as 77 percent of their annual income*

Describe What was the function of the War Industries Board? *It had the authority to regulate all materials needed for the war effort. Only after the military's needs were met could remaining goods be used by civilians.*

Make Judgments Why do you think it was necessary for the government to set prices and production controls for food and fuel during the war? *possible answer—to prevent food and fuel producers from "price gouging," or charging consumers too much because of shortages caused by the war*

📄 CRF: Economics and History Activity: The Economics of World War I

Info to Know

Taxes During War In times of war, taxes are often raised to help pay for the war and to prevent businesses from taking advantage of any increases in government and consumer spending. The United States adopted an excess profits tax in 1917, with the rates continuing to increase until 1921.

Answers

Photo *War Revenue Act of 1917 raised taxes, also borrowed money*

Mobilizing the Economy

Recall What steps did the Fuel Administration take to encourage fuel conservation? *It introduced daylight saving time, promoted "gasless Sundays" and "heatless Mondays."*

Elaborate How did patriotism play a part in the passage of the Eighteenth Amendment? *The temperance movement was opposed to alcohol, which is made from crops such as grapes and wheat. The alcoholic content of wine and beer was limited by Congress so that these crops could be used for food instead. As the war continued, the temperance movement grew stronger, and in 1919 the Eighteenth Amendment was ratified.*

Activity **Eighteenth Amendment** Have students write a campaign slogan supporting the Eighteenth Amendment as a means to help feed the troops and win the war. **LS** **Auditory-Musical, Verbal-Linguistic**

Info to Know

Food Conservation Under Herbert Hoover's direction, the United States pushed to bring children into the war effort, especially in the area of food conservation. The Food Administration devised poems, slogans, and songs to interest children in the issue, even reworking popular nursery rhymes.

In order to encourage wartime production, he promised farmers higher prices for their crops. Farm production soared.

Hoover asked Americans to plant vegetables at home in "victory gardens." He also urged Americans to eat less by participating in "meatless Mondays" and "wheatless Wednesdays." His efforts paid off. By 1918 the United States had so much surplus food that it exported three times as much food as it had prior to the war.

Another proposal to conserve food supplies was a prohibition, or ban, on alcohol. Most alcohol is made with food crops such as grapes and wheat. Days after entering the war, Congress limited the alcohol content of wine and beer so that these crops could be used for food production instead.

Some progressives tried to discourage Americans from drinking beer by linking German Americans to the brewing industry. The progressives hoped that anti-German feelings would lead Americans to stop drinking beer.

As the war continued, the temperance, or anti-alcohol, movement gained strength. In 1919 the Eighteenth Amendment was rati-

fied, banning the "manufacture, sale or transportation" of alcohol in the United States. In 1919 Congress passed the Volstead Act, giving the government the authority to enforce this prohibition on alcohol.

Regulating fuel After the passage of the Lever Food and Fuel Control Act, the Fuel Administration was established to set production goals and prices for fuels. Its purpose was to make sure that military needs for fuel could always be met.

Harry Garfield, the son of former president James A. Garfield, headed the Fuel Administration. To encourage fuel conservation, Garfield introduced daylight saving time in order to extend daylight hours for those who worked long shifts in the factories. He promoted fuel conservation in other ways, such as through publicity campaigns calling for "gasless Sundays" and "heatless Mondays."

Supplying U.S. and Allied troops By creating these various boards and agencies, the federal government was quickly able to produce and collect the supplies needed for the

Working for the War Effort

600

Promoting the War Effort

1. Divide the class into small groups. Have each group select one particular administration or program involved in the war effort, such as the War Industries Board, the Food Administration, "victory gardens," or "meatless Mondays."

2. Have each group develop an advertising campaign to promote its chosen agency or program. Campaigns should use a variety of

media, including newspaper and magazine advertisements, posters, and scripts for personal appearances by celebrities. (Remind students that there was no radio or television, and that movies did not yet have sound.)

3. Have each group present its campaign to the class. **LS** **Interpersonal, Verbal-Linguistic**

Alternative Assessment Handbook, Rubrics 28: Posters; and 34: Slogans and Banners

war effort. It was not just American soldiers who benefited from these supplies. The United States also became the major supplier for the Allied Powers. During the war Great Britain alone received more than 1 billion rounds of ammunition, 1.2 million rifles, and more than half a million tons of explosives from the United States. The power of U.S. manufacturing and farming became a much-needed boost for the struggling Allies and a boost for the American economy as well.

READING CHECK **Drawing Conclusions** How did the Wilson administration change the U.S. economy for the war effort?

Mobilizing Workers

During the war, the profits of many major industrial corporations skyrocketed. This was because the corporations sold their products to the federal government. In turn, the federal government used those products in the war effort. In this way the war created enormous profits for stockholders of industries such as chemicals, oil, and steel.

Women in a gun factory (left) assemble soldiers' pistols in 1918. Below, men at a steel plant make shell casings in 1917. After many male workers went off to fight in the war, women supplied much-needed labor. **How did Wilson aid this transition?**

Wages for factory workers increased as well. The rising cost of food and housing, however, meant that workers were hardly better off than they had been before the war.

Meanwhile, war demands led to laborers working long hours, sometimes in increasingly dangerous conditions. The urgent need to produce materials for the war—and the great financial incentive for companies to do so—led to a faster pace of production.

These harsher working conditions led many workers to join labor unions. Union membership increased by about 60 percent between 1916 and 1919. Union activities boomed as well, with more than 6,000 strikes being held during the war.

National War Labor Board Massive industrial production was essential to the war effort. Leaders feared that industrial protests such as strikes would disrupt the war effort. To keep disruptions to a minimum, the Wilson administration created the **National War Labor Board** in 1918. This board judged disputes between workers and management. During the short time that the board was in operation (less than a year), it handled some 1,200 cases involving 700,000 workers.

The National War Labor Board also set policies that sought to improve working conditions for all Americans. The board established the eight-hour workday, urged that businesses recognize labor unions, and promoted equal pay for women who did equal work.

Women's war efforts As men left their jobs to fight on the war front, women moved into those jobs to keep the American economy moving. Women took on many jobs traditionally held by men. They worked on railroads, at docks, and in factories. They also built ships and airplanes.

Other women filled more traditional jobs, working as teachers and nurses. Some took on volunteer positions that ranged from helping to sell Liberty bonds to digging victory gardens. In all, about 1 million women entered the workforce during World War I. After the war ended, however, most women left the jobs they had taken. Many women left by choice, but others were forced to leave by employers who wanted to return the jobs to men who had served in the war.

THE FIRST WORLD WAR **601**

Skills Focus: Analyzing Primary Sources

At Level

Reading Like a Historian Skill
Women in the Workforce

Research Required

1. Have students find primary sources such as diaries or memoirs written by women who joined the labor force during World War I. If students have trouble finding primary sources, allow them to use secondary sources.

2. Have students develop their own projects on the topic of women in the workplace. For example, they might write war diaries from the point of view of a female worker

or design a poster urging women to do their part for the war effort.

3. Have each student complete his or her project and present it to the class.

4. Guide the class in a discussion of the ways in which World War I changed women's lives.

LS Logical-Mathematical

📖 Alternative Assessment Handbook, Rubrics 30: Research; and 37: Writing Assignments

● **Direct Teach** ●

Reading Focus

2 How did workers mobilize on the home front? *Laborers worked long hours to produce war materials. Women moved into jobs vacated by men who were sent to the front.*

Mobilizing Workers

Recall What were some of the policies set by the National War Labor Board? *It established an eight-hour workday, urged businesses to recognize labor unions, and promoted equal pay for women doing equal work.*

Make Inferences What can you infer from the fact that profits of many major industrial corporations skyrocketed because they sold their products to the federal government? *possible answer—companies were able to take advantage of the huge new demand for their products during the war*

Identify Cause and Effect How did war demands lead to an increase in union membership? *hours were long, companies increased the pace of production, making working conditions increasingly dangerous; as a result workers turned to labor unions for protection*

Info to Know

Munitions Tax The 1916 revenue law included a munitions tax levied on manufacturers of military equipment. It was meant to prevent war profiteering, as well as to satisfy Americans who were opposed to U.S. involvement in the war.

Answers

Photo *instituted the National War Labor Board to improve pay and working conditions, and handle disputes*

Reading Check *raised taxes, regulated industrial and agricultural production and distribution; Lever Food and Fuel Control Act*

601

Mobilizing Workers

Describe How did the influenza epidemic affect American life? *increased fear; public events were canceled; rumors spread about cause of disease*

Sequence How did the influenza epidemic spread? *spread across the Western Front; a soldier in Fort Riley, Kansas, complained of flu-like symptoms on March 11, 1918; by the end of the week more than 500 soldiers had come down with it; by August, influenza was reported in Philadelphia and Boston*

Info to Know

Committee on Public Information
George Creel started his career as a muckraking journalist. During President Wilson's re-election campaign, Creel supported Wilson by writing favorable political tracts. Wilson repaid Creel by making him the head of the Committee on Public Information. In that role, Creel blanketed the country with pro-war propaganda, distributing some 75 million pamphlets and 14,000 drawings.

Answers

Linking to Today *Travelers can infect many people on their trips, who then infect others where they live.*

Reading Check *to judge disputes between industrial workers and company management and to keep labor disruptions to a minimum*

Linking TO Today

Epidemics

In 1918 and 1919, an influenza epidemic killed millions of people, including some 675,000 Americans. Influenza also spread around the world, killing at least 20 million, and perhaps as many as 40 million people. Travelers carried the disease between countries.

In 2002 a respiratory virus called Severe Acute Respiratory Syndrome (SARS) emerged in China. It also spread to the United States. As with influenza in 1918, travelers are believed to have carried the disease.

Making Inferences How can travel affect the spread of disease?

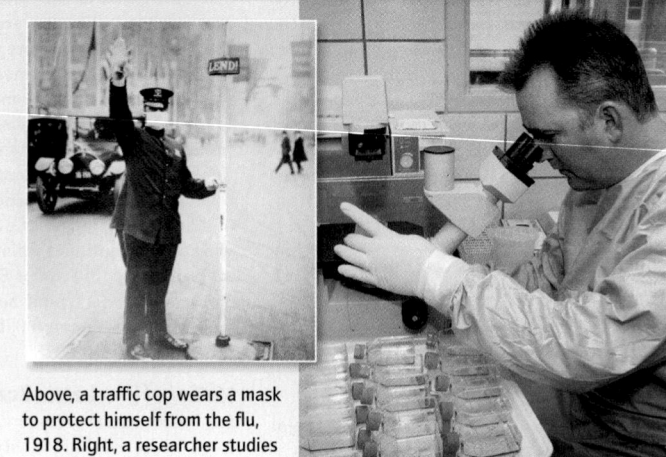

Above, a traffic cop wears a mask to protect himself from the flu, 1918. Right, a researcher studies the SARS virus.

The contributions that women made to the war effort did not go unnoticed. Women's suffrage advocates used these contributions as further justification for granting women the vote. President Wilson also acknowledged women's role in the war effort.

HISTORY'S VOICES

❝ This war could not have been fought ... if it had not been for the services of women rendered in every sphere. ❞

—President Woodrow Wilson, 1918

Influenza epidemic on the home front

The war's effort was seriously affected by an extremely severe flu epidemic that broke out between 1918 and 1919. In Europe the disease quickly spread across the Western Front, where crowded and unsanitary trenches were perfect breeding grounds for the disease. In fact, of all the American troops who lost their lives in World War I, about half of them died from influenza.

Soldiers on the front lines, however, were not the only ones to suffer from influenza. On March 11, 1918, an army private in Kansas complained of flulike symptoms. By the end of that week, more than 500 soldiers had come down with influenza. By August, influenza was reported in Philadelphia and Boston.

THE IMPACT TODAY

Science and Technology
Scientists have reconstructed the 1918 influenza virus and found it to be a bird flu that was transmitted directly to humans. The research team analyzed lung tissue from two people who died in the 1918–1919 epidemic.

This was no ordinary flu. Most forms of influenza were simply uncomfortable and unpleasant. But this form of influenza was deadly. It killed healthy people within days. During the month of October 1918 alone, influenza killed nearly 200,000 Americans.

Panicked city leaders canceled public gatherings, but the disease still spread. Rumors spread almost as quickly. Many people, such as Lieutenant Colonel Philip Doane, wrongly blamed Germans for causing the disease. Doane remarked, "It would be quite easy for one of these German agents to turn loose influenza germs in a theater or some other place where large numbers of persons are assembled."

By the time this wave of influenza passed, some 675,000 Americans had lost their lives. It was the deadliest epidemic in U.S. history.

READING CHECK **Identifying the Main Idea** Why did the Wilson administration create the National War Labor Board?

Influencing Public Opinion

President Wilson moved quickly to build public support after Congress declared war. Many Americans had been in favor of the U.S. position of neutrality. Now Wilson had to convince these

602 CHAPTER 18

Skills Focus: Analyzing Secondary Sources
Above Level

Reading Like a Historian Skill
Research Required

Deadly Influenza

1. Organize the class into small groups. Have each group conduct additional research on the influenza epidemic that began in 1918 using the following questions as a guide: Why was this strain of influenza so deadly? Where did it begin and how did it spread from one continent to another? How many people died on each continent? How many people died from the epidemic each month in the United States? How many people died altogether?

2. Have each student write a brief summary and analysis of the epidemic, including charts and graphs to illustrate their summaries. Have each student include a world map that shows the spread of the disease and the number of people who died on each continent.

LS **Interpersonal, Verbal-Linguistic**

Alternative Assessment Handbook, Rubrics 20: Map Creation; and 37: Writing Assignments

Americans that it was their duty to support the war. "It is not an army that we must shape for war … it is a nation," he said.

Winning American support Wilson created the **Committee on Public Information** (CPI) less than two weeks after the United States declared war. He appointed newspaper reporter and political reformer **George Creel** to head the CPI.

Creel began a nationwide campaign of **propaganda**—posters, newspaper stories, speeches, and other materials designed to influence people's opinions. This campaign was meant to encourage Americans to support the war. Creel hired popular movie stars such as Mary Pickford and Douglas Fairbanks to speak on behalf of the war effort.

The CPI also hired artists to create patriotic posters and pamphlets. These posters included James Montgomery Flagg's famous image of Uncle Sam pointing to the viewer and demanding, "I Want You for the U.S. Army."

As many Americans became more patriotic and supportive of the war, some began to distrust all things German as well. Some tried to eliminate all German influence from American culture. Many schools stopped teaching the German language to their students. Many symphonies stopped playing music written by German composers. Even German-sounding items were renamed to sound patriotic. For example, sauerkraut became liberty cabbage, dachshunds became liberty pups, and hamburger became known as liberty steak.

Anti-German feelings continued to grow after reports spread that secret agents from Germany were operating in the United States. In one of the worst acts of sabotage, German agents planted a bomb at a ship-loading terminal in New York City. The bomb destroyed $20 million worth of supplies for the war, killed three dock workers, and shattered windows in buildings across lower Manhattan.

Acts such as these led some Americans to question the loyalty of German Americans in their communities. As a result, some German Americans experienced discrimination and violence. In April 1918, for example, a mob in Illinois lynched socialist coal miner Robert Prager because townspeople suspected him of being a German spy.

PRIMARY SOURCES

Propaganda Poster

To gain support for the war effort, officials in the United States hired skilled artists to create posters that would build public support and increase recruitment. This poster was designed by artist James Montgomery Flagg.

The use of the word *you* as well as Uncle Sam looking and pointing at the viewer makes it clear that the U.S. Army is asking each individual to serve.

Uncle Sam's red, white, and blue clothing tells young men that joining the army is an act of patriotism.

I WANT YOU for the U.S. ARMY ENLIST NOW

Skills FOCUS READING LIKE A HISTORIAN

1. **Drawing Conclusions** What is the main message of this propaganda poster?
2. **Interpreting Visuals** How effective do you think this poster was?

See Skills Handbook, p. H30

603

Primary Source

" . . . while there is a lower class, I am in it, and while there is a criminal element I am of it; and while there is a soul in prison, I am not free . . . I look upon the Espionage Act as a despotic enactment in flagrant conflict with democratic principles and with the spirit of free institutions . . . "

— Eugene V. Debs

during his trial, September 1918

● Review & Assess ●

Close

Guide students in a discussion of the ways in which the United States mobilized resources for the war effort.

Review

Online Quiz, Section 3

Daily Test Practice Transparency

Assess

SE Section 3 Assessment

Progress Assessment: Section 3 Quiz

Alternative Assessment Handbook

Reteach

Interactive Reader and Study Guide, Section 3

Interactive Skills Tutor CD-ROM

Limiting antiwar speech Prominent Americans, such as reformer Jane Addams and Senator Robert La Follette, spoke out against the war. Addams, a pacifist, also founded the Women's International League for Peace and Freedom. As the Wilson administration built public support, it also tried to limit this public opposition to the war.

In 1917 Congress passed the Espionage Act, which punished people for aiding the enemy or refusing military duty. The next year, Congress passed a related law called the Sedition Act. This law made it illegal for Americans to "utter, print, write, or publish any disloyal … or abusive language" criticizing the government, the flag, or the military.

More than 1,000 opponents of the war were jailed under these laws. Robert Goldstein, who directed a film on the American Revolution called *The Spirit of '76*, was jailed for three years because he refused to remove scenes of British brutality from the movie.

In another case, Socialist Party leader Eugene V. Debs was sentenced to prison for 10 years for criticizing the United States government's prosecution of Americans under the Espionage Act. After the war ended, however, Debs was released from prison by a presidential order.

Some Americans believed that the Espionage Act and the Sedition Act violated the First Amendment. Others, however, thought these laws were essential to protect military secrets, the safety of American soldiers, and the overall U.S. war effort.

The Supreme Court also struggled to interpret the Espionage Act and the Sedition Act. The defining case came when Charles Schenck, an official of the American Socialist Party, was convicted of violating the Espionage Act. Schenck had organized the printing and distribution of some 15,000 leaflets opposing government war policies. He challenged the conviction as a violation of his constitutional right to free speech.

In its first decision interpreting the First Amendment, the Supreme Court upheld Schenck's conviction. Justice Oliver Wendell Holmes Jr. wrote the Court's unanimous opinion in *Schenck v. United States*, explaining the limits to free speech.

In his written opinion, Holmes went on to explain that many things that can safely be said in peacetime can cause problems for the government and danger for soldiers in wartime. For that reason, Holmes argued, some limits needed to be placed on individual free-speech rights during wartime to ensure the country's overall safety. You will read more about *Schenck* v. *United States* on the following page.

READING CHECK **Drawing Conclusions** Why did the Wilson administration place wartime limitations on free speech?

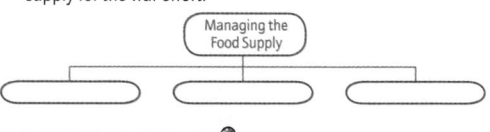

SECTION 3 ASSESSMENT

go.hrw.com
Online Quiz
Keyword: SD7 HP18

Reviewing Ideas, Terms, and People

1. **a. Identify** What were **Liberty bonds**?
   b. Explain In what two ways did the United States pay for its war effort?

2. **a. Describe** What happened to the profits of many major corporations during the war?
   b. Compare and Contrast Did workers prosper in the same way that major companies did during the war? Why or why not?
   c. Elaborate Why would the government consider it necessary to get involved in disputes between workers and management?

3. **a. Recall** What was the **Committee on Public Information**?
   b. Contrast How did the government try to persuade people to support the war and discourage them from opposing it?

c. Evaluate Was the government justified in trying to suppress opposition to the war? Why or why not?

Critical Thinking

4. **Identifying Supporting Details** Copy the chart below and record the ways in which the United States managed its food supply for the war effort.

```
        Managing the
         Food Supply
    ┌─────────┼─────────┐
 ┌──────┐  ┌──────┐  ┌──────┐
 └──────┘  └──────┘  └──────┘
```

FOCUS ON WRITING

5. **Expository** Write a short paragraph in which you explain the contributions American women made to the war effort.

604 CHAPTER 18

Section 3 Assessment Answers

1. **a.** war bonds that were a form of loan to the government
   b. increased taxes; Liberty bonds

2. **a.** Profits skyrocketed as companies sold their products to the federal government.
   b. no, wages increased, but rising costs meant that they weren't any better off
   c. to keep disruptions such as strikes to a minimum

3. **a.** led a nationwide campaign of propaganda to encourage Americans to support the war

   b. promotion of propaganda and limits on antiwar speech
   c. possible answers—no, because the laws violated the First Amendment; yes, because government believed all Americans needed to support war effort completely

4. increased farm production; victory gardens; agencies to regulate food supply

5. Many women left their homes to join the workforce and to replace men who were fighting the war.

Answers

Reading Check *to build public support by limiting public opposition to the war*

Schenck v. United States (1919)

Why It Matters Schenck was the first major Supreme Court case to consider limits on the First Amendment right of free speech. According to the decision, speech can be limited when it poses a "clear and present danger."

Background of the Case

During World War I, the Espionage Act made it a crime to interfere with the war effort. Charles Schenck, general secretary of the American Socialist Party, distributed thousands of leaflets urging men to oppose the draft. Schenck was convicted of violating the Espionage Act, and he appealed. He argued that the First Amendment protected his right to speak out on this subject.

The Decision

The Supreme Court ruled unanimously against Schenck. Writing for the Court, Justice Oliver Wendell Holmes Jr. looked both at what Schenck said and at the circumstances in which he said it. The Constitution does not protect speech that causes danger to others. For example, the First Amendment

> **"**. . . would not protect a man in falsely shouting 'Fire' in a theatre and causing a panic. . . . The question in every case is whether the words used . . . create a clear and present danger . . .**"**
>
> — Justice Oliver Wendell Holmes Jr.

Certain things that might safely be said during peacetime could be dangerous when the country was at war. Congress can place some limits on the right of free speech in order to protect the country's safety. Schenck's intent was to interfere with the draft, and the First Amendment does not protect this activity.

THE IMPACT TODAY War protesters march in California to mark the first anniversary of the 2003 invasion of Iraq. If this demonstration had taken place in 1919 or 1920, the group could have been arrested under the Espionage Act or the Sedition Act.

CRITICAL THINKING

go.hrw.com
Research Online
Keyword: SS Court

1. **Analyze the Impact** Using the keyword above, research the decision in *Texas* v. *Johnson*. How do the facts in *Johnson* differ from those in *Schenck*? Why did the Court decide in Johnson's favor?

2. **You Be the Judge** While U.S. troops were fighting in Vietnam, Afghanistan, and Iraq, some Americans argued that it is unpatriotic to oppose an ongoing war. Others said that the right to disagree with government policy is essential to democracy. Can Congress constitutionally restrict Americans' right to speak against military actions? Explain your answer.

Info to Know

The First Amendment "Congress shall make no law respecting an establishment of religion, or prohibiting the free exercise thereof; or abridging the freedom of speech, or of the press; or the right of the people peaceably to assemble, and to petition the Government for a redress of grievances."

Info to Know

The Espionage Act The Espionage Act was passed in June 1917, two months after the United States entered World War I. Most of the act dealt with espionage. Section 3, however, dealt with those who "obstruct[ed] the recruiting or enlistment service" when the United States was at war. In May 1918 Congress passed an amendment to the original act, greatly expanding the range of actions that were prohibited in time of war. Under the amended act, it was illegal to say or print anything against the government, Constitution, armed forces, or flag of the United States when the United States was at war. Displaying the flag of a foreign enemy in time of war was outlawed. It was also made illegal to "advocate, teach, defend, or suggest the doing of any of the acts or things enumerated."

Skills Focus: Identifying Cause and Effect

At Level

Reading Skill
Schenck v. United States

1. Read the annotation about the Espionage Act to students. Guide the class in a discussion of the implications of the act.

2. Have students suggest statements that might have brought punishment under the Espionage Act. Write their responses for the class to see.

3. Have students write an essay giving their

views on the Espionage Act. Students should back their support of the act or opposition to it with logical arguments.

4. Have volunteers read their essays to the class.
   LS **Logical-Mathematical, Verbal-Linguistic**

   📝 Alternative Assessment Handbook, Rubric 41: Writing to Express

Answers

1. *U.S. was at war when Schenck protested, but not when Johnson protested; Court viewed Schenck's comments as threatening to U.S. security, but Johnson's flag burning as not threatening;* **2.** *possible answers— no, because First Amendment rights deserve complete protection; yes, because Congress needs to protect its military troops*

Bellringer

The Inside Story. . . Use the **Daily Bellringer Transparency** to help students answer the question.

📑 Daily Bellringer Transparency, Section 4

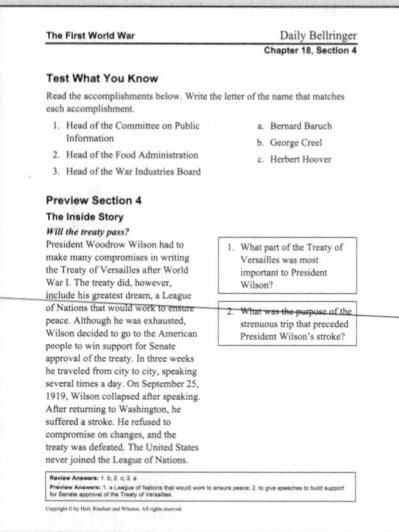

Academic Vocabulary

Review with students the high-use academic term in this section.

component a part of something (p. 607)

📑 CRF: Vocabulary Builder Activity, Section 4

Taking Notes

U.S.—emerged as world's leading economic power, increased inflation, passage of Nineteenth Amendment, many African Americans moved north; World—millions dead and disabled, overthrow of monarchies, rise of Bolsheviks in Russia, France in ruins, Great Britain in debt to the U.S., Germany crippled by reparations, anger and hostility remained

go.hrw.com
Online Resources

KEYWORD: SD7 CH18
TOPIC: A PLAN FOR PEACE

SECTION 4 Peace without Victory

BEFORE YOU READ

MAIN IDEA:
The Allies determined the terms for peace in the postwar world.

READING FOCUS
1. What was President Wilson's Fourteen Points plan for peace?
2. What was resolved at the Paris Peace Conference?
3. Why did Congress fight over the treaty?
4. What was the impact of World War I on the United States and the world?

KEY TERMS AND PEOPLE
Fourteen Points
self-determination
League of Nations
David Lloyd George
Georges Clemenceau
Big Four
reparations
Treaty of Versailles
Henry Cabot Lodge

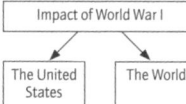
TAKING NOTES As you read, take notes on the ways World War I affected the United States and the world. Make a diagram like the one below to organize your notes.

Impact of World War I

The United States | The World

THE INSIDE STORY

Will the treaty pass? President Woodrow Wilson had to make many compromises at the peace conference after World War I. The Treaty of Versailles did, however, include his greatest dream—a League of Nations, an international organization that would work to ensure peace. "America shall in truth show the way," Wilson told the Senate, which still had to approve the treaty.

Although he was worn out, Wilson decided to go to the people for support. He set out on an exhausting cross-country speaking tour. In three weeks he traveled 8,000 miles by train from city to city, speaking several times a day. His speeches were eloquent, but they ignored some of the harsh provisions of the treaty. Western audiences were welcoming, which encouraged Wilson to push himself harder.

After speaking in Pueblo, Colorado, on September 25, 1919, Wilson collapsed. A few days later, after returning to Washington, he suffered a stroke that left him partially paralyzed. He carried on some duties but was an invalid, often angry and bitter, for the rest of his presidency. He cut off ties with old friends and political allies. He was openly angry at his opponents. He refused to compromise on changes, and the treaty was defeated. The United States never joined the League of Nations. Perhaps Wilson's only real reward was the 1919 Nobel Peace Prize, which called the League "a design for [bringing] a fundamental law of humanity into present-day international politics." ■

▶ **President Wilson rides through the streets of San Francisco on his tour to promote the League of Nations.**

A Plan for Peace

Teach the Main Idea

At Level

Peace Without Victory

1. **Teach** Ask students the Reading Focus questions to teach this section.

2. **Apply** Divide the class into small groups. Have each group discuss and rank President Wilson's Fourteen Points in the order that they believe is most important for ensuring world peace. Then have students make a list of the points that were included in the Treaty of Versailles.

3. **Review** Guide the class in a discussion of the Fourteen Points. Which point did

Wilson consider the most important? Why did that point prevent the United States from ratifying the Treaty of Versailles?

4. **Practice/Homework** Have students write essays explaining why President Wilson thought the League of Nations was so important. **LS Interpersonal, Verbal-Linguistic**

📑 Alternative Assessment Handbook, Rubrics 13: Graphic Organizers; and 37: Writing Assignments

The Fourteen Points

As World War I drew to a close, the scale of destruction and massive loss of life was shocking. President Woodrow Wilson wanted a "just and lasting peace" to ensure that a war like the Great War would never happen again.

Wilson outlined his vision of world peace in a speech he made to the U.S. Congress in January 1918, before the war ended. His plan for peace was called the **Fourteen Points**.

HISTORY'S VOICES

❝What we demand … is that the world be made fit and safe to live in; and particularly that it be made safe for every peace-loving nation which, like our own, wishes to live its own life, determine its own institutions, be assured of justice and fair dealing by the other peoples of the world as against force and selfish aggression.❞

—President Woodrow Wilson, Fourteen Points speech, 1918

Wilson's first four points called for open diplomacy, freedom of the seas, the removal of trade barriers, and the reduction of military arms. The fifth point proposed a fair system to resolve disputes over colonies. The next eight points dealt directly with **self-determination**, or the right of people to decide their own political status. For example, Wilson wanted the different ethnic groups within Austria-Hungary to be able to form their own nations.

The fourteenth point, which Wilson believed was the most important, called for the establishment of the **League of Nations**. The League would be an organization of nations that would work together to settle disputes, protect democracy, and prevent future wars.

The components of the Fourteen Points expressed a new philosophy for U.S. foreign policy. The Fourteen Points applied the principles of progressivism to foreign policy. The ideals of free trade, democracy, and self-determination sprang from the same ideals that Progressive reformers supported within the United States. Most importantly, the Fourteen Points declared that the foreign policy of a democratic nation should be based on morality—not just on what was best for that nation.

READING CHECK Identifying the Main Idea
What did President Wilson hope to accomplish with his Fourteen Points?

Paris Peace Conference

President Wilson led the group of American negotiators who attended the peace conference that began in Paris in January 1919. By doing so, he became the first U.S. president to visit Europe while in office.

Republicans and others back home criticized Wilson's decision to leave the country. They argued that it was more important for Wilson to stay and help the nation restore its economy after the war than to work toward peace in Europe.

Wilson had a dream of international peace, though, and he wanted to make that dream a reality. He believed that a lasting peace required a fair and unbiased leader, such as himself, to attend the Paris Peace Conference. Otherwise he felt sure that the European powers would continue to squabble over land and colonial rights.

The American delegation arrived in France a few weeks before the conference was scheduled to begin. President Wilson enjoyed a hero's welcome in Paris, when thousands of Parisians lined the streets to cheer his arrival. Before the conference began, Wilson also traveled to London and Rome, and in each city, he received the same heartfelt welcome.

The conference opens The Paris Peace Conference began on January 12, 1919. Leaders from 32 nations—representing about three-quarters of the world's population—attended the conference.

The leaders of the victorious Allies dominated the negotiations. Those leaders—President Woodrow Wilson of the United States, British prime minister **David Lloyd George**, French premier **Georges Clemenceau**, and Italian prime minister Vittorio Orlando—became known as the **Big Four**. Germany and the other Central Powers nations, however, were not invited to participate.

Conflicting needs The delegates arrived at the Paris Peace Conference with competing needs and desires. President Wilson had a vision of a better world where nations dealt with each other openly and traded with each other fairly, while at the same time reducing their arsenals of weapons. Many of the other Allies, however, wanted to punish Germany

THE FIRST WORLD WAR **607**

THE IMPACT TODAY

Government
The League of Nations failed to prevent future wars, in part because the United States and Germany were not members. After World War II, the United Nations (UN) formed to solve many of the same problems. The United States has been a member of the UN since 1945.

ACADEMIC VOCABULARY

component a part of something

Reading Focus

Paris Peace Conference

Identify Who were the Big Four? *British prime minister David Lloyd George, French premier Georges Clemenceau, Italian prime minister Vittorio Orlando, U.S. president Woodrow Wilson*

Draw Conclusions Why do you think that the Central Powers were excluded from the Paris Peace Conference? *They had lost the war; Allies wanted to punish and humiliate Germany.*

Make Judgments Do you think that France would really have taken military action if Germany had refused to sign the Treaty of Versailles? Why or why not? *possible answer—no, the United States and other nations would have prevented it, because it might have started another war*

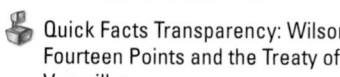 Quick Facts Transparency: Wilson's Fourteen Points and the Treaty of Versailles

---

for its role in the war. Georges Clemenceau explained the French view in a speech at the conference in June 1919.

HISTORY'S VOICES

❝The conduct of Germany is almost unexampled in human history. The terrible responsibility which lies at her doors can be seen in the fact that not less than seven million dead lie buried in Europe, while more than twenty million others carry upon them the evidence of wounds and sufferings, because Germany saw fit to gratify her [desire] for tyranny by resort to war.❞

—Georges Clemenceau

Other leaders came to the Paris Peace Conference seeking independence. Some wanted to build new nations, such as Yugoslavia and Czechoslovakia. Delegates from Poland, which had been divided between Germany and Russia during the war, wanted to re-establish their nation. A young Vietnamese chef named Ho Chi Minh who worked at the Paris Ritz hotel asked the peacemakers to grant his nation independence from France. Ho Chi Minh would later lead his people in taking Vietnamese independence by force.

The Treaty of Versailles The Allies eventually reached an agreement and presented their peace treaty to Germany in May. The final treaty was much harsher than Wilson had wanted. The treaty forced Germany to disarm its military forces. It required Germany to pay the Allies **reparations**—payments for damages and expenses caused by the war. This amount far exceeded what the German government could actually afford to pay. The Allies also demanded that Germany accept sole responsibility for starting the war.

The treaty did include some of Wilson's Fourteen Points. It would establish a League of Nations. Some ethnic groups in parts of

---

Wilson's Fourteen Points and the Treaty of Versailles

Some—but not all—of President Wilson's Fourteen Points were reflected in the Treaty of Versailles.

THE FOURTEEN POINTS

1. Public diplomatic negotiations and an end to secret treaties
2. Freedom of navigation on the seas
3. Free trade among nations
4. Reduction of armaments to the level needed for domestic safety
5. Fair resolution of colonial claims that arose because of the war
6. Evacuation of Russia and restoration of its conquered territories
7. Preservation of Belgium's sovereignty
8. Restoration of France's territory, including Alsace-Lorraine
9. Redrawing Italy's borders according to nationalities
10. Divide up Austria-Hungary according to nationalities
11. Redraw the borders of the Balkan states according to nationalities
12. Self-determination for Turks and the other nationalities under Turkish rule
13. Creation of an independent Polish nation
14. Creation of a League of Nations

MAJOR PROVISIONS OF THE TREATY OF VERSAILLES

Military Changes
- Limited the German army to 100,000 men, with no tanks or heavy artillery.
- Limited the German navy to 15,000 men.
- Banned Germany from having an air force.

Territory Changes
- Required Germany to cede land to France, Denmark, Poland, Czechoslovakia, and Belgium.
- Required Germany to surrender all colonies to the control of the League of Nations.
- Germany and Austria were prohibited from uniting.

War-Guilt Provisions
- Held Germany solely responsible for all losses and damages suffered by the Allies during the war.
- Required Germany to pay reparations of 269 billion gold marks, later reduced to 132 billion.

Establishment of the League of Nations
- Did not initially permit Germany to join the League.

608 CHAPTER 18

Skills Focus: Making Oral Presentations

Above Level

Reading Like a Historian Skill
The Paris Peace Conference

Research Required

1. Divide the class into four groups. Have each group represent one of the Big Four—David Lloyd George, Georges Clemenceau, Vittorio Orlando, and Woodrow Wilson. Have each group conduct outside research to learn more about its leader's position at the Paris Peace Conference.

2. After students have finished their research, regroup them into groups of four, with each group having one of each of the Big Four as a member. If there are any students left over, have them serve as moderators for the groups.

3. Have each group re-enact the Paris Peace Conference, complete with discussions and negotiations. Circulate among the groups that don't have moderators to help moderate their discussions. **LS Interpersonal, Logical-Mathematical**

📓 Alternative Assessment Handbook, Rubrics 30: Research; and 33: Skits and Reader's Theater

The League of Nations

President Wilson exhausted himself traveling the country to win support for the League.

The man who most strongly voiced the opposition to the League was Senator Henry Cabot Lodge.

❝ Why, my fellow citizens, this is one of the great charters of human liberty, and the man who picks flaws in it . . . forgets the magnitude of the thing, forgets the majesty of the thing, forgets that the counsels of more than twenty nations combined . . . in the adoption of this great instrument. **❞**

Woodrow Wilson, 1919

❝ We would not have our politics distracted and embittered by the dissensions of other lands. We would not have our country's vigour exhausted or her moral force abated, by everlasting meddling and muddling in every quarrel, great and small, which afflicts the world. **❞**

Henry Cabot Lodge, 1919

Skills FOCUS **READING LIKE A HISTORIAN**

Identifying Points of View Wilson and Lodge had very different views on the role of the United States in the world. How does each quotation about the League of Nations reflect the speaker's view of relationships between nations?

See **Skills Handbook,** p. H28–H29

Germany, Austria-Hungary, and Russia would receive the right of self-determination. The treaty would create nine new nations, including Czechoslovakia, Poland, and Yugoslavia. The Central Powers also had to surrender control of their colonies to the Allies. The treaty placed some of the colonies under the temporary control of Allied nations until the colonies were deemed ready for independence.

Germany strongly protested the terms of the treaty. Threatened with French military action, however, German officials signed the **Treaty of Versailles** on June 28, 1919. Wilson was disappointed at the treaty's harshness but believed that the League of Nations could resolve any problems the treaty had created.

READING CHECK **Summarizing** How did the Allied leaders at the Paris Peace Conference react to the Fourteen Points?

The Fight over the Treaty

President Wilson returned to the United States on July 8, 1919, and formally presented the treaty to the U.S. Senate two days later. Wilson needed the support of both Republican and Democratic senators to ratify, or approve, the treaty. The Republicans had won control of the Senate in 1918, and getting their support proved difficult for the Democratic president.

The senators quickly divided into three groups. The first consisted of Democrats who supported immediate ratification of the treaty. The second group was the so-called irreconcilables, who urged the outright rejection of U.S. participation in the League of Nations. The last group was the reservationists, who would ratify the treaty only if changes were made.

The reservationists focused their criticism on the part of the League of Nations charter that required its members to use military force to carry out the League's decisions. Some Republicans believed that this conflicted with the constitutional power of the United States Congress to declare war. Senator **Henry Cabot Lodge,** head of the Committee on Foreign Relations, led the reservationists.

Wilson refused to compromise with the reservationists. He took his case directly to the

THE FIRST WORLD WAR **609**

Skills Focus: Sequencing

Below Level

Reading Skill
The Treaty of Versailles

To help students understand the terms of the Treaty of Versailles and why the U.S. Senate rejected it, copy the chart for students to see. Omit the italicized suggested answers. Have students complete the chart, and have volunteers fill in the class chart for all to see.

LS Visual-Spatial

📝 Alternative Assessment Handbook Rubric 13: Graphic Organizers

🖥 Graphic Organizer Transparencies

THE TREATY OF VERSAILLES	
The Terms of the Treaty:	**The Senate's Objections:**
• *Forced Germany to disarm* • *Created a League of Nations* • *reparations*	• *Irreconcilables completely rejected the League of Nations* • *military force in League*

• **Direct Teach** •

Reading Focus

❸ **Why did Congress fight over the treaty?** *Most of the opposition centered on U.S. participation in the League of Nations; one group opposed it outright, while another had reservations about some of the provisions of the League's charter.*

The Fight over the Treaty

Describe How was the Senate divided by the fight over the Treaty of Versailles? *one group supported immediate ratification; another group wanted changes before ratification; another group urged outright rejection of the treaty*

Make Judgments Do you think the reservationists were right in refusing to ratify the Treaty of Versailles? Explain. *possible answer—no, it was too late to make changes in the treaty, since it had already been signed by other nations*

📄 Political Cartoons Activities for American History: Cartoon 36: Tied Down

---

Counterpoints
League of Nations

Henry Cabot Lodge During the administration of President Theodore Roosevelt, Henry Cabot Lodge backed Roosevelt's wish to see the United States take a larger part in international affairs. However, because of his opposition to U.S. membership in the League of Nations, he is now remembered primarily as an isolationist.

Answers

Reading Like a Historian *Wilson—believes nations must work together; Lodge—believes nations should not become involved in the business of other countries*

Reading Check *Allied leaders were more concerned with punishing Germany than with the Fourteen Points.*

609

4 What was the impact of World War I on the United States and the world? *left millions of people dead; cost billions of dollars; monarchies were overthrown; European economies devastated; U.S. emerged as leading economic power*

The Impact of World War I

Recall What casualties resulted from World War I? *more than 14 million people killed; 7 million men permanently disabled*

Identify Cause and Effect How did World War I have a lasting effect on American society? *Nineteenth Amendment gave women right to vote; African Americans moved to northern cities, changing the population patterns and leading to new race relations.*

Evaluate What was the condition of the U.S. economy after the war? *U.S. was the world's leading economic power, but faced economic challenges; increased demand for consumer goods fueled inflation; farmers were hit hard by the drop in demand for their products*

Map Transparency: Europe and the Middle East, 1915, 1919

EUROPE AND THE MIDDLE EAST, 1915

EUROPE AND THE MIDDLE EAST, 1921

Allied Powers
Central Powers
Neutral nations

0   250   500 Miles
0 250 500 Kilometers
Lambert azimuthal equal-area projection

New nations and mandates
Allied-occupied zones

0   250   500 Miles
0 250 500 Kilometers
Lambert azimuthal equal-area projection

GEOGRAPHY SKILLS   INTERPRETING MAPS

The map of Europe changed after World War I ended (right). Boundaries changed, and many new nations were created.

Region Where were new nations created? Name them.

See Skills Handbook, p. H20

American people. In 22 days Wilson traveled 8,000 miles and gave 32 major speeches, urging the public to pressure Republican senators to ratify the treaty. He warned of serious consequences if the world's nations did not work together in the future.

HISTORY'S VOICES

❝I can predict with absolute certainty that within another generation there will be another world war if the nations of the world do not concert [agree upon] the method by which to prevent it.❞

—President Woodrow Wilson

As you read in the "Inside Story," Wilson's speaking schedule took a heavy toll on his health. After a speech in Pueblo, Colorado, on September 25, 1919, he collapsed. He suffered a stroke in early October and never fully recovered. Wilson spent the rest of his term living privately in the White House, cut off from everyone except his wife and his closest aides.

In November 1919, Senator Lodge presented the treaty to the U.S. Senate for ratification. He included a list of 14 reservations, or con-

cerns about the treaty. Wilson was unwilling to compromise. Following Wilson's instructions, the Senate rejected Lodge's revised treaty on November 19 and again in March 1920.

After Wilson left office in 1921, the United States signed separate peace treaties with Austria, Germany, and Hungary. The United States never joined the League of Nations. Without the United States, the League's ability to keep world peace was uncertain.

READING CHECK   Making Inferences Why did some Americans oppose the Treaty of Versailles?

The Impact of World War I

World War I was a devastating conflict that shocked the world with its staggering cost. By the end of the war, combat, disease, and starvation had killed more than 14 million people. The war left some 7 million men permanently disabled. The war had cost more than $280 billion—significantly more than any previous war in history.

Differentiating Instruction

Above Level

Advanced Learners/GATE

1. Guide students in a discussion of the global impact of World War I. Then have students decide what was, in their opinion, the most devastating human or economic cost of World War I.

2. Have each student write a proposal outlining a plan for economic and political recovery in Europe after the war.

3. Have volunteers present their plans to the class.

4. Following the presentations, guide students in a discussion of the different approaches to recovery. **LS Logical-Mathematical**

Alternative Assessment Handbook, Rubric 24: Oral Presentations

---

Answers

Interpreting Maps *in Eastern Europe and the Middle East; Finland, Estonia, Latvia, Lithuania, East Prussia, Poland, Czechoslovakia, Austria, Hungary, Yugoslavia, Syria, Iraq, Lebanon, Palestine, Trans-Jordan*

Reading Check *fearful of the part of the League's charter that required members to use military force to carry out the League's decisions*

When the war ended, Americans were eager to return to normal life. But the war had changed the world, and there was no going back to the way things had once been.

Political impact The consequences of World War I were felt far beyond the battlefield. The war led to the overthrow of the monarchies in Russia, Austria-Hungary, Germany, and the Ottoman Empire. It contributed to the rise of the Bolsheviks to power in Russia in 1917. It fanned the flames of revolts against colonialism in the Middle East and in Southeast Asia.

Economic impact World War I devastated European economies. As a result, the United States emerged as the world's leading economic power.

Despite this new financial power, the United States still faced economic challenges at home. The demand for consumer goods increased as Americans raced to buy items that had been in short supply during the war. This increased demand led to inflation, and many Americans struggled to afford ordinary, day-to-day items.

Farmers, who had increased production to meet the needs of European markets during the war, were particularly hard hit when postwar markets no longer need to buy their food. Despite these economic setbacks, most Americans looked forward to the new decade as a time of peace and prosperity.

Social impact The war had drawn more than a million women into the American workforce. Their service to the nation contributed to the passage of the Nineteenth Amendment in 1919, which gave women the right to vote. In 1920 the states ratified the amendment.

The war also encouraged many African Americans to move to northern cities in search of factory work. This changed the population patterns of northern cities and led to new and often uneasy race relations.

Impact in Europe The effects of the war in Europe were devastating. European nations had lost almost an entire generation of young men. France, where most of the combat took place, was in ruins. Great Britain was deeply in debt to the United States and lost its position as the world's financial center. The reparations imposed on Germany by the Treaty of Versailles were crippling.

World War I would not be the "war to end all wars," as many had hoped. Too many issues were left unresolved, and too much anger and hostility would remain. Within a generation, conflict would again break out in Europe, pulling the United States and the rest of the world back into war.

READING CHECK **Summarizing** What economic effects did World War I have on the United States?

SECTION 4 ASSESSMENT

go.hrw.com
Online Quiz
Keyword: SD7 HP18

Reviewing Ideas, Terms, and People

1. a. Define What was Wilson's **Fourteen Points** plan?
b. Explain Why did Wilson believe the Fourteen Points should be the basis for peace talks?
c. Elaborate How did the Fourteen Points explain a new philosophy of U.S. foreign policy?

2. a. Recall What are **reparations**?
b. Contrast Why did the other Allies reject much of Wilson's plan?
c. Evaluate Whose plan do you believe was most justified—Wilson's or the other Allies? Explain.

3. a. Identify Who were the reservationists in the U.S. Senate?
b. Drawing Conclusions Why did the reservationists believe that some provisions of the League of Nations were dangerous?
c. Predict What might be the consequence of the United States not joining the League of Nations?

4. a. Describe What are two ways in which World War I made a political impact on the world?
b. Analyzing Information How did World War I propel the United States into a position of greater power in the world?

Critical Thinking

5. Compare Copy the chart below and record examples of the major ways in which World War I had a lasting impact.

	Political Impact	Economic Impact	Social Impact
United States			
The World			

FOCUS ON WRITING

6. Persuasive Should the United States have joined the League of Nations? Write a paragraph supporting your position.

Section 4 Assessment Answers

1. a. plan for world peace after World War I
b. wanted to preserve international peace
c. used principles of progressivism

2. a. payments for damages and expenses
b. wanted to punish Germany
c. possible answer—Wilson's because it would prevent future wars

3. a. group that agreed to ratify the peace treaty if changes were made
b. military force required to carry out League's decisions; believed this conflicted with Congress's power to declare war

c. possible answer—The League of Nations might lose power and credibility.

4. a. led to overthrow of monarchies; rise of the Bolsheviks in Russia
b. devastated European economies, U.S. became world's leading economic power

5. U.S.—world leader; World—changes in government; devastated economies; enormous loss of life

6. yes, the U.S. should lead the way in peace

Close
Have students summarize the conflicts that took place in trying to build a lasting peace following World War I.

Review
Online Quiz, Section 4
Daily Test Practice Transparency

Assess
SE Section 4 Assessment
Progress Assessment: Section 4 Quiz
Alternative Assessment Handbook

Reteach
Interactive Reader and Study Guide, Section 4
Interactive Skills Tutor CD-ROM

Answers

Reading Check *U.S. emerged as world's leading economic power; increased inflation; farmers suffered*

Perspectives on Trench Warfare

Word Help

garrison troops

apoplexy stroke or cerebral hemorrhage

parapet wall used to screen troops from enemy fire

Info to Know

Remarque At the age of 18, Erich Maria Remarque was drafted into the German army. During the course of the war, Remarque was wounded five times and suffered permanent injuries to his lungs as a result of poison gas. *All Quiet on the Western Front*, Remarque's novel based on his experiences, was an immediate international sensation and was made into an American film in 1930. Though Remarque continued to write on his wartime experiences, none of his other novels were able to achieve the same level of success.

Perspectives on Trench Warfare

Historical Context The three documents below provide different perspectives of trench warfare in World War I.

Task Read the selections and answer the questions that follow. Then write an essay about soldiers' experiences in trench warfare, using facts from the documents provided and from the chapter to support the position you take in your thesis statement.

DOCUMENT 1

In 1929 German author Erich Maria Remarque wrote *All Quiet on the Western Front*, an autobiographical account of the war that became the most celebrated novel of its time. Remarque immigrated to the United States in 1939 after his books were banned by the Nazis and his citizenship was revoked. In the excerpt below, the book's main character, a soldier in whose voice the novel is told, describes a visit home on a leave. Here, he is visiting his mother who is ill in bed.

Suddenly my mother seizes hold of my hand and asks falteringly: "Was it very bad out there, Paul?"

Mother, what should I answer to that! You would not understand, and never realize it. And you never should realize it. Was it bad, you ask.—You, Mother,—I shake my head and say: "No, Mother, not so very. There are always a lot of us together so it isn't so bad."

"Yes, but Heinrich Bredemeyer was here just lately and he said it was terrible out there now, with the gas and all the rest of it."

It is my mother who says that. She says: "With the gas and all the rest of it." She does not know what she is saying, she is merely anxious for me. Should I tell her how we once found three enemy trenches with their garrison all stiff as though stricken with apoplexy? Against the parapet, in the dug-outs, just where they were, the men stood and lay about, with blue faces, dead.

"No, Mother, that's only talk," I answer, "there's not very much in what Bredemeyer says."

DOCUMENT 2

Stull Holt was an American soldier in World War I, fighting in the trenches of France. Below is a letter he wrote home after a frightening experience in which he left his trench and was knocked down by a shell. His gas mask fell off and he was affected by the poison gas.

Sept. 1, 1917
Dear Lois,

At last the long delayed and promised letter. You mustn't complain tho because I wrote to no one . . .

I had a very close call with gas . . . I and this other fellow crawled in a trench alongside the road and waited. We huddled there a long time getting splashed several times by mud thrown by shells exploding, when gas shells started to come in great numbers . . . We started crawling throwing ourselves flat, crawling again (gas masks on of course) . . . I was about buried by a shell and a few seconds later a big gas shell went off within 20 ft of me. Something hit me on the head, making a big dent in my helmet . . . I was dazed, knocked down and my gas mask knocked off. I got several breathes of the strong solution right from the shell before it got diluted with much air. If it hadn't been for the fellow with me I probably wouldn't be writing this letter because I couldn't see, my eyes were running water and burning, so was my nose and I could hardly breathe. I gasped, choked and felt the extreme terror of the man who goes under in the water and will clutch at a straw. The fellow with me grabbed me and led me the hundred yards or so to the post . . . where I felt alright again in a few hours . . . I think the hardest thing I ever did was to go back alone the next night."

Skills Focus: Comparing and Contrasting

At Level

Reading Skill
Two Perspectives on Trench Warfare

1. Guide the class in a discussion of Documents 1 and 2. Point out that Document 1 was written by a German, a member of the Central Powers, and Document 2 was written by an American, a member of the Allied Powers. Ask them to look specifically for differences and similarities in the point of view of the two soldiers.

2. Divide the class into groups of four or five students. Have each group write a script portraying an imaginary meeting after the war between the two soldiers in Documents 1 and 2. Ask students to think about how the two men might relate to each other during peacetime.

3. Have each group present its script to the class.
   LS Interpersonal, Kinesthetic

   Alternative Assessment Handbook, Rubric 9: Comparing and Contrasting

This photograph from March 17, 1918, shows U.S. troops of the 168th infantry in the trenches near the town of Badonville, France.

Skills FOCUS READING LIKE A HISTORIAN

1. a. Recall Refer to Document 1. What does the soldier think to himself and not tell his mother?
b. Interpret *All Quiet on the Western Front* is a novel, but its author, Erich Maria Remarque, drew upon his experiences as a German soldier to write it. In your opinion, which parts of this excerpt might be based on Remarque's own experiences, and which parts of the excerpt might be fiction?

2. a. Recall Refer to Document 2. How was Stull Holt's gas mask knocked off?
b. Make Inferences Why do you think Stull Holt says that walking back alone was the hardest thing he had ever done?

3. a. Identify Refer to Document 3. Then review the labeled illustration of trench warfare in Section 1.

Identify the following items in Document 3: machine gun, no-man's-land.
b. Make Inferences What is happening in this photograph? Is there a battle under way? Explain your answer using information in the photograph.

4. Document-Based Essay Question Consider the question below and form a thesis statement. Using examples from Documents 1, 2, and 3, create an outline and write a short essay supporting your position.
What challenges might soldiers face when they returned to peacetime life at home?
See **Skills Handbook**, p. H28–29, H30, H32

Collaborative Learning

At Level

The Soldiers of World War I

1. Divide the class into groups of four or five students. Have each group conduct research to find additional photographs of World War I that give an idea of what a soldier's life was like. Have students make copies of their selected photographs.

2. Have each student write a journal entry or letter from the perspective of one of the soldiers in their photographs. Students should describe what their daily life is like and their feelings on the war.

3. Ask volunteers to share their journal entries or letters and the photographs that inspired them with the rest of the class.
LS Interpersonal, Visual-Spatial

Alternative Assessment Handbook, Rubric 15: Journals

Document-Based Investigation

Primary Source

After fighting for the British in World War I, Patrick MacGill remembered his experiences by quoting these lyrics from a popular soldier's tune, *Sing Me to Sleep*:
"Sing me to sleep where bullets fall,
Let me forget the war and all;
Damp is my dug-out, cold my feet,
Nothing but bully and biscuits to eat.
Over the sandbag helmets you'll find
Corpses in front and corpses behind"
— Patrick MacHill

The Great Push; An Episode of the War

Analyzing Visuals

Activity Have students look for memoirs, diaries, or letters home describing life in the trenches. Have each student find a passage that seems to describe what is happening in the photograph that comprises Document 3.
LS Visual-Spatial, Verbal-Linguistic

Info to Know

The "Splendid Little War" Both sides initially thought that the war that began in 1914 would be a "splendid little war" that would be over by the end of the year. The war quickly bogged down into stalemate, becoming a war of attrition. Battles took months, as each side tried to outlast the other, and the war dragged on for four years. It left an entire generation permanently scarred by its brutality.

Answers

Reading Like a Historian
1. a. *He thinks of the horrors he has experienced in the war;* **b.** *possible answer—sightings of enemy soldiers real; conversation with mother fictional;*
2. a. *Something hit him on the head after a gas shell went off;* **b.** *possible answer—because there would be no one to save him if he was exposed to gas again;* **3. a.** *soldier holding machine gun; area beyond trench;* **b.** *possible answer—waiting for battle to begin;*
4. *Answers will vary, but students' essays may include difficulty relating to those who did not fight in war; injuries from war*

Visual Summary

Review and Inquiry Review the cause and effect chart with students. Then have students work in pairs to write three important supporting facts or details about each of the events on the chart. Have volunteers share their facts and details with the class.

Quick Facts Transparency: The First World War

Reviewing Key Terms and People

1. l.
2. c.
3. j.
4. g.
5. h.
6. b.
7. a.
8. k.
9. i.
10. e.
11. f.
12. d.

Comprehension and Critical Thinking

13. **a.** nationalism, imperialism, militarism, and alliances
b. Their obligations to their allies forced them to declare war.
c. possible answer—alliances because nations could be pulled into war without any direct interest in the conflict

14. **a.** attacked all ships, including those from neutral nations, within a given war zone
b. unrestricted submarine warfare, the sinking of the *Lusitania*, the Zimmermann Note, and the sinking of three American merchant ships
c. major factor in the war, assisting French troops in pushing German forces back to the Belgian border

15. **a.** gave the government the power to set prices and establish production controls for food and

---

Visual Summary: The First World War

European rivalries lead to the outbreak of war in 1914.
- Nationalism
- Militarism
- Imperialism
- Alliances

The United States enters the war in 1917 and helps turn the tide for an Allied victory.
- Victory in the Battle of Chateau-Thierry
- Stopped German advance at Belleau Wood
- Defeated Germans' last offensive in the Second Battle of the Marne

With the Treaty of Versailles, the Allies determine the terms for peace in the postwar world.
- Forced Germany to pay massive reparations
- Created the League of Nations
- Treaty not ratified by U.S. Senate
- United States did not join the League of Nations

Reviewing Key Terms and People

Match each lettered definition with the correct numbered item below at right.

a. a communication that proposed an alliance between Germany and Mexico to help the Central Powers in case the United States declared war on Germany

b. a military alliance among Germany, Austria-Hungary, and Italy

c. a policy of not being involved in the affairs of other nations

d. payments for damages and expenses caused by the war

e. a military alliance among Great Britain, France, and Russia

f. an extreme pride or devotion that people feel for their country or culture

g. the expansion of arms and the policy of military preparedness

h. posters, newspaper stories, speeches, and other materials designed to influence people's opinions, often during wartime

i. the right of people to decide their own political status

j. the name given to Germany, Austria-Hungary, and the Ottoman Empire during World War I

k. the German promise not to sink merchant vessels without warning

l. the name given to Great Britain, France, and Russia during World War I

1. Allied Powers
2. isolationism
3. Central Powers
4. militarism
5. propaganda
6. Triple Alliance
7. Zimmermann Note
8. *Sussex* pledge
9. self-determination
10. Triple Entente
11. nationalism
12. reparations

---

for the fuels needed to run military machines
b. to make sure that the troops would have plenty of food and supplies
c. gave a major and much needed boost to the Allies

16. **a.** payments for damages and expenses caused by war
b. Wilson wanted to create a better world where nations dealt with each other openly, traded with each other fairly, and

reduced their arsenals of weapons. The other Allies wanted to punish Germany for its role in the war.
c. the establishment of a League of Nations, self-determination for several ethnic groups in parts of Germany, Austria-Hungary, and Russia, and the surrender of the Central Powers' control over their colonies

History's Impact video program

Review the video to answer the closing question: How does the Supreme Court's decision in *Schenck v. United States* explain the limits to free speech?

Comprehension and Critical Thinking

SECTION 1 *(pp. 582–589)*

13. a. Identify What were the main causes of World War I?

b. Analyze How did European leaders discover that a balance of power did not decrease the chances for war among them?

c. Evaluate Which cause of World War I do you believe was the most dangerous? Explain.

SECTION 2 *(pp. 590–596)*

14. a. Recall What did Germany do with its U-boats that violated laws of neutrality?

b. Sequencing Which German actions helped shift U.S. public opinion toward supporting the Allies in the war?

c. Elaborate What effect did U.S. troops have on the Allied fight against the Central Powers?

SECTION 3 *(pp. 598–604)*

15. a. Describe What did the Lever Food and Fuel Control act do?

b. Analyze Why did the U.S. government impose so many regulations on industrial and food production during the war?

c. Elaborate What impact did U.S. industrial and food production have on the war effort for the Allies?

SECTION 4 *(pp. 606–611)*

16. a. Recall What are reparations?

b. Contrasting How did Wilson's goal for the peace treaty differ from that of the other Allies?

c. Elaborate What provisions from Wilson's Fourteen Points were included in the Treaty of Versailles?

Using the Internet

> **go.hrw.com**
> **Practice Online**
> Keyword: SD7 CH18

17. The influenza epidemic of 1918 was the deadliest in U.S. history. Using the keyword above, do research to learn about the origins, progression, and final conclusion of this tragic epidemic. Then create a time line of the major events in the progression of the epidemic.

Analyzing Primary Sources

Reading Like a Historian
Propaganda posters like this one encouraged Americans to buy Liberty bonds to support the war effort.

18. Identify What does "Over the Top" mean?

19. Analyze Do you think this was an effective poster? Why or why not?

Critical Reading

Read the passage in Section 1 that begins with the heading "War Breaks Out." Then answer the following question.

20. What was one effect of the German invasion of Belgium?

A It led Russia to join the Central Powers.

B It failed miserably, as Belgium pushed the German forces back across the border.

C It drew Britain into the war against Germany.

D It led the French to surrender to Germany out of fear of being attacked like Belgium.

WRITING FOR THE SAT

Think about the following issue:

The United States had a long-standing foreign-policy tradition of isolationism. As European nations went to war, the United States tried to stay neutral. Eventually, it began leaning toward the Allied side, until in 1917 it joined the war on the side of the Allies.

21. Assignment Given its history of neutrality, was the United States justified in going to war against Germany and the other Central Powers? Write a short essay in which you develop your position on this issue. Support your point of view with reasoning and examples from your reading and studies.

THE FIRST WORLD WAR **615**

Using the Internet

17. Go to the HRW Web site and enter the keyword shown to access a rubric for this activity.

> KEYWORD: SD7 CH18

Analyzing Primary Sources

18. that U.S. soldiers are fighting hard for their fellow Americans

19. possible answer—effective, reminds viewers that their country needs their help

Critical Reading

20. C

Writing for the SAT

21. possible answers—no, the U.S. would have done better to maintain neutral position and not become involved, would have saved lives and been a more ethical path; yes, the U.S. had a moral obligation to help its traditional friends in Europe, stop invasion of other nations, and help maintain European democratic traditions.

A rubric for this activity is provided in Chapter Resource File: Writing for the SAT: Deadly Technology.

History's Impact Video Program

limiting free speech is sometimes necessary to protect military secrets, public safety, and war effort

Review and Assessment Resources

Review and Reinforce

- CRF: Chapter Review Activity
- Quick Facts Transparencies: Major Battles, Wilson's Fourteen Points and the Treaty of Versailles, The First World War
- Spanish Chapter Summaries Audio CD Program
- Online Chapter Summaries in Spanish
- OSP Holt PuzzlePro; Quiz Show for ExamView
- Quiz Game CD-ROM

Assess

- PASS: Chapter Test, Forms A and B
- Alternative Assessment Handbook
- OSP ExamView Test Generator, Chapter Test
- Differentiated Instruction Modified Worksheets and Tests CD-ROM: Chapter Test
- HOAP Holt Online Assessment Program (in the Premier Online Edition)

Reteach/Intervene

- Interactive Reader and Study Guide
- Differentiated Instruction Teacher Management System: Lesson Plans for Differentiated Instruction
- Differentiated Instruction Modified Worksheets and Tests CD-ROM: Chapter Test
- Interactive Skills Tutor CD-ROM

> **go.hrw.com**
> **Online Resources**
> KEYWORD: SD7 CH18

Summarizing the Unit

In this unit, students read about how important changes in the nation and the world helped the United States to assume a major global role. Ask students which change they feel has had the greatest effect on how Americans live and think about their country. Have students support their answers with evidence from the unit.

Connecting to Themes

Have students focus on the theme of Global Relations and on the events they read about in this unit that affected America's role in the world. Point out that, as the United States grew more powerful militarily and economically, the nation began to gain influence among other countries, an influence that has continued to expand. Ask students if they feel it has been an overall benefit or disadvantage to the United States to be the world leader it is today. Have students explain their answers.

UNIT 6 IN BRIEF

Below is a chapter-by-chapter summary of the main ideas covered in Unit 6.

CHAPTER 16 The Progressives
1898–1920

MAIN IDEA During the early 1900s the Progressive movement arose to redress the negative impact of industrialization. Progressives achieved many wide-reaching reforms that affected American political, social, and economic life.

SECTION 1 Progressives focused their attentions on improving the lives of the urban poor, changing dangerous and unfair working conditions, and reforming government.

SECTION 2 Most American women did not have the right to vote in national elections. Nevertheless, many were politically active in reform campaigns for education, children's welfare, temperance, and the vote.

SECTION 3 President Theodore Roosevelt pushed for many Progressive reforms in business and the environment. His program, called the Square Deal, sought to balance the needs of business and industry leaders and those of workers and consumers.

SECTION 4 Progressive reforms continued during the Taft and Wilson presidencies, focusing on business, banking, and certain civil rights reforms. During this time, women won the vote. Despite the many reforms that Progressives campaigned for, they did not fight for the civil rights of African Americans.

CHAPTER 17 Entering the World Stage
1898–1917

MAIN IDEA Global competition for empire led the United States into war against Spain and into military conflicts in Mexico. The United States emerged with a new role as a world power.

SECTION 1 The United States joined other industrialized nations in the scramble for empire. For economic, military, and nationalistic reasons, the United States annexed Hawaii and extended its influence in China and Japan.

SECTION 2 The Spanish-American War resulted in a resounding defeat for Spain and the relinquishing of Cuba, Puerto Rico, Guam, and the Philippines to U.S. control. In the aftermath of war, American expansionists and anti-imperialists debated whether to annex the Philippines.

SECTION 3 The United States began to exert its influence over Latin America in the wake of the Spanish-American War. It made Cuba a protectorate and governed Puerto Rico as a territory. Meanwhile, the United States undertook the mammoth task of building the Panama Canal.

SECTION 4 When Mexico exploded into revolution, the United States became drawn into the conflict to protect its economic interests.

CHAPTER 18 The First World War
1914–1920

MAIN IDEA The United States stayed neutral when European nations went to war in 1914. After the United States joined the Allies in 1917, however, the U.S. government quickly mobilized the economy and built public support for the war.

SECTION 1 Rivalries among European nations led to the outbreak of war in 1914. The assassination of an Austrian archduke led to rapid declarations of war, and soon most of Europe was drawn into World War I. Changes in military technology and strategies made World War I a new and deadlier kind of war.

SECTION 2 The United States tried to stay neutral in World War I, but hostile German acts soon convinced President Wilson and Congress that war was inevitable. The United States sent troops to France, where they helped turn the tide for the Allies. The Central Powers agreed to an armistice on November 11, 1918.

SECTION 3 The U.S. government mobilized its resources for the war effort. It sold Liberty bonds to pay for the war and regulated industry to fulfill the needs of the troops overseas. It encouraged women to take on the jobs left vacant by men who joined the military. The government also campaigned to win the support of public opinion and minimize dissent.

SECTION 4 At the Paris Peace Conference, the Allies hammered out a peace treaty. Some, but not all, of Wilson's Fourteen Points were included in the Treaty of Versailles. The treaty also called for Germany to pay heavy reparations for its role in the war. In the United States, the Senate hotly debated the treaty. Many senators objected to the idea of the United States joining the League of Nations, and eventually the Senate rejected the treaty.

616 UNIT 6 IN BRIEF

Unit Resources

Review and Reinforce

- CRF: Chapter Review Activity
- Spanish Chapter Summaries Audio CD Program
- OSP Holt PuzzlePro; GameTool for ExamView
- Quiz Game CD-ROM

Assess

- PASS: Unit Test, Forms A and B
- Alternative Assessment Handbook
- OSP ExamView Test Generator
- Differentiated Instruction Modified Worksheets and Tests CD-ROM: Chapter Tests
- HOAP Holt Online Assessment Program (in the Premier Online Edition)

Reteach/Intervene

- Interactive Reader and Study Guide
- Differentiated Instruction Teacher Management System: Lesson Plans for Differentiated Instruction
- Differentiated Instruction Modified Worksheets and Tests CD-ROM: Chapter Tests
- Interactive Skills Tutor CD-ROM

go.hrw.com
Online Resources

KEYWORDS: SD7 CH16, SD7 CH17, SD7 CH18

Themes

Government and Democracy
The nation struggled with postwar labor unrest, radical political ideas, and later, high unemployment brought on by the Great Depression.

Economic Development
Americans experienced a period of great productivity and prosperity, followed by a devastating economic downturn.

Cultural Expressions
The growth of mass media and popular culture, a rebirth in the arts, and the development of a consumer society marked a period of cultural change.

New York City's Times Square is ablaze with electric lights and other signs of progress and prosperity in this 1925 painting.

617

Unit Preview

Introducing the Unit

In the years following the end of World War I, many Americans enjoyed great prosperity. However, many also felt fearful after experiencing the trauma of war. Guide students in a discussion of whether or not Americans today experience similar feelings.

Connecting to Themes

Activity **Popular Culture** Tell students that during the years covered by this unit the United States developed its first real mass media and a lively popular culture. Ask students what these terms mean to them. What kinds of mass media and popular culture can students recall from earlier times?
LS Verbal-Linguistic

Reading Like a Historian

Interpreting Visuals
Times Square The famous Times Square, located at Broadway and 7th Avenue in New York City, was once called Longacre Square. In the late 1800s, immigrant Oscar Hammerstein began transforming the area into an entertainment complex. In 1904, *The New York Times* newspaper held a New Year's celebration to commemorate their successful effort to rename Longacre Square, where their headquarters now stood. The New Year's celebration has continued every year since.

Unit Resources

Planning

- Differentiated Instruction Teacher Management System: Unit Pacing Guide
- One-Stop Planner CD-ROM: Teacher Management System
- Power Presentations with Video CD-ROM

Differentiating Instruction

- Differentiated Instruction Teacher Management System: Lesson Plans for Differentiated Instruction
- Pre-AP Activities Guide for American History
- Differentiated Instruction Modified Worksheets and Tests CD-ROM

Enrichment

- Civic Participation Activities Guide
- CRF: Economics and History Activity
- CRF: Interdisciplinary Project
- American History Primary Source Library CD-ROM

Assessment

- PASS: Unit Test, Forms A & B
- Alternative Assessment Handbook
- OSP ExamView Test Generator
- HOAP Holt Online Assessment Program (in the Premier Online Edition)

> **The Differentiated Instruction Teacher Management System**
> provides a planning and instructional benchmarking guide for this unit.

Identifying Problems and Solutions

Have volunteers list on the board problems that Americans face today. Then ask students how the government should respond to each of these problems.

Word Help

unnerving frightening
assets holdings
precautions steps

Info to Know

Protecting American Deposits

The agency that insures Americans' bank deposits is the Federal Deposit Insurance Corporation. It insures deposits up to $100,000 per person held in most kinds of bank accounts. It is funded by premiums that banks pay to take part in the insurance program.

Skills Planner

To give students more opportunities to practice this skill, see the following activities in the teacher's edition: What If?, p. 676; Saving the World Economy, p. 678; Preventing Bank Failures, p. 681; Herbert Hoover's Philosophy, p. 688; Hoover Tries to End the Depression, p. 690; The Second Bonus Army, p. 701.

Prepare to Read

Identifying Problems and Solutions

Find practice for **Identifying Problems and Solutions** in the **Skills Handbook,** p. H11

Historical texts frequently discuss problems that people in the past encountered and the solutions they adopted. Identifying problems and solutions can help you understand what you are reading.

Before You Read
Skim headings to determine a passage's content. What problem do you think will be discussed in this passage?

While You Read
Note the problem cited in the text and the reasons it occurred.

After You Read
Review the problem and the solutions offered.

Bank Failures

As you have read, the collapse of the stock market strained the financial resources of many banks. In the weeks following the crash, a number of banks failed. For ordinary Americans, the collapse of banks was unnerving. Most people did not have money invested in banks, but many had entrusted their savings to banks.

Today, insurance from the federal government protects most people's deposits in the event of bank failure. That is, most Americans do not have to worry that they will lose their savings if their bank goes out of business. In addition, laws today require that a bank keep a greater percentage of its assets in cash, to be paid out to depositors on request.

READING CHECK **Identifying Problems and Solutions** What precautions has the federal government taken to safeguard people's money in banks?

Identify the problem
If the problem is large, organize it in smaller parts.

Problem The collapse of banks unnerved many Americans who had entrusted their savings to them.

Solution Federal insurance and laws help protect people's finances today.

Test Prep Tip

Some tests may require you to identify a problem and its solution. In such instances, first try to recognize the problem and its cause and then to identify possible options and solutions for that problem. Then evaluate the effectiveness of the solution.

618 UNIT 7

Skills Focus: Identifying Problems and Solutions | At Level

Reading Skill
Examining Historical Problems

1. Divide students into small groups. Have each group select a section from one of the chapters in this unit. Have each group identify one of the major problems of the time period discussed in their section.

2. Have each group write a paragraph explaining their problem as well as what solutions are described in the text. Have students also propose two different solutions of their own.

3. Have volunteers share their paragraphs with the class. Have students retain their paragraphs and use them at the end of the unit to evaluate the success of the solutions.
LS Verbal-Linguistic

Alternative Assessment Handbook, Rubric 35: Solving Problems

Interpreting Literature as Historical Evidence

Find practice for **Interpreting Literature as Historical Evidence** in the **Skills Handbook,** p. H32

Literature can be an important source of historical information. It can tell us what life was like in the past and what people believed. But it needs to be read with caution. The author is creating a fictional story not recording facts. Be sure to use your prior knowledge and information from reliable primary and secondary sources when assessing literature as historical evidence.

Strategies historians use:

- Look for descriptive passages that help you understand what life was like in that time and place.
- Examine the author's point of view and any biases by contrasting the types of words used to describe different events.
- Determine whether the literature is meant to describe a certain historical event or to elicit an emotional response.

> Steinbeck is describing the migration of people from the Plains to California in the 1930s along Route 66, "the great cross-country highway."

The cars of the migrant people crawled out of the side roads onto the great cross-country highway, and they took the migrant way to the West. In the daylight they scuttled like bugs to the westward; and as the dark caught them, they clustered like bugs near to shelter and to water. And because they were lonely and perplexed, because they had all come from a place of sadness and worry and defeat, and because they were all going to a new mysterious place, they huddled together; they talked together; they shared their lives, their food, and the things they hoped for in the new country. Thus it might be that one family camped for the spring and for company, and a third because two families had pioneered the place and found it good. And when the sun went down, perhaps twenty families and twenty cars were there.

—from *The Grapes of Wrath* by John Steinbeck, 1939

> Words like *lonely* and *perplexed* describe how the migrants heading west to California felt. You could check these words against other sources.

> The description of families gathering together is fairly neutral. It doesn't seem to betray any bias.

READING LIKE A HISTORIAN

As You Read List historical evidence found in the literature. Then compare the evidence with known facts to arrive at the most complete account of history.

As You Study Use literature to help you understand political and social movements in history. Determine whether the literature recounts history, makes an activist appeal, or has some other purpose.

A MODERN NATION **619**

• Prepare to Read •

Interpreting Literature as Historical Evidence

Ask students to name novels and stories that they feel accurately describe our own time and place. Then have students evaluate whether the literature is also intended to inspire an emotional or social response. What is this response? How do they know? What techniques does the author use to create this response?

Word Help

perplexed uncertain, puzzled
pioneered settled

Teaching Tip

Ask students if they believe this excerpt from *The Grapes of Wrath* is meant to inspire an emotional or social response, or whether Steinbeck only wanted to describe a certain historical time and place. Have students give evidence from the excerpt to support their answers.

Skills Planner

To give students more opportunities to practice this skill, see the following activity in the teacher's edition: *The Grapes of Wrath*, p. 686.

Skills Focus: Interpreting Literature as Historical Evidence

Reading Like a Historian Skill
Evaluating Historical Fiction

Research Required   **At Level**

1. Have students choose a novel or short story from the school or classroom library that is set in the past. Encourage students to ask a librarian for suggestions.

2. Have students read either their short story or the first chapter of their novel. Have students take notes on how the author represents the time period and historical setting of the story. Have students note details in the setting, language the

characters use, activities they perform, and other fictional elements.

3. Have students share their notes with the class. Have students evaluate whether or not the author is trying to elicit an emotional response to the fiction. Have students explain their answers. **LS Verbal-Linguistic**

   Alternative Assessment Handbook, Rubric 16: Judging Information

From War to Peace

Chapter Overview	Reproducible Resources	Technology Resources
CHAPTER 19 pp. 620–643 **Overview:** In this chapter, students will analyze the dangers and changes the nation faced after World War I.	**Differentiated Instruction Teacher Management System:*** • Instructional Benchmarking Guides • Lesson Plans for Differentiated Instruction **Interactive Reader and Study Guide:** Chapter Summary* **Chapter Resource File:*** • Focus on Writing Activity: Impact of the Assembly Line • Social Studies Skills Activity: Interpreting Line Graphs • Chapter Review Activity **American History Outline Maps** **Pre-AP Activities Guide for American History***	**Live Ink® Online Reading Help** **Student Edition on Audio CD Program** **Differentiated Instruction Modified Worksheets and Tests CD-ROM** **Interactive Skills Tutor CD-ROM** **United States History Primary Source Library CD-ROM** **Power Presentations with Video CD-ROM** **History's Impact: American History Video Program (VHS/DVD):** From War to Peace **Online Chapter Summaries in Spanish**
Section 1: **Postwar Havoc** **The Main Idea:** Although the end of World War I brought peace, it did not ease the minds of many Americans, who found much to fear in the postwar years.	**Differentiated Instruction Teacher Management System:** Section 1 Lesson Plan* **Interactive Reader and Study Guide:** Section 1 Summary* **Chapter Resource File:*** • Vocabulary Builder Activity, Section 1 • Biography Activity: John L. Lewis • Primary Source Activity: Representative Parish Discusses Immigration	**Daily Bellringer Transparency:** Section 1* **Daily Test Practice Transparency:** Section 1* **Internet Activity:** Sacco and Vanzetti
Section 2: **A New Economic Era** **The Main Idea:** New products, new industries, and new ways of doing business expanded the economy in the 1920s, although not everyone shared in the prosperity.	**Differentiated Instruction Teacher Management System:** Section 2 Lesson Plan* **Interactive Reader and Study Guide:** Section 2 Summary* **Chapter Resource File:*** • Vocabulary Builder Activity, Section 2 • Biography Activity: Alfred P. Sloan • Primary Source Activity: Automobiles and Buses Change City Life • History and Geography: Growth of Cities in the 1920s • Literature: *Main Street* by Sinclair Lewis	**Daily Bellringer Transparency:** Section 2* **Daily Test Practice Transparency:** Section 2* **Internet Activity:** Automobiles of the 1920s
Section 3: **The Harding and Coolidge Presidencies** **The Main Idea:** The nation's desire for normalcy and its support for American business was reflected in Presidents Harding and Coolidge.	**Differentiated Instruction Teacher Management System:** Section 3 Lesson Plan* **Interactive Reader and Study Guide:** Section 3 Summary* **Chapter Resource File:*** • Vocabulary Builder Activity, Section 3 • Biography Activity: Robert La Follette	**Daily Bellringer Transparency:** Section 3* **Quick Facts Transparency:** Effects of World War I* **Daily Test Practice Transparency:** Section 3* **Internet Activity:** Warren G. Harding

HOLT

History's Impact
American History Video Program (VHS/DVD)
From War to Peace

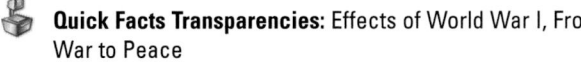
Review, Assessment, Intervention

Quick Facts Transparencies: Effects of World War I, From War to Peace

Spanish Chapter Summaries Audio CD Program

Progress Assessment Support System (PASS): Chapter Test*

Differentiated Instruction Modified Worksheets and Tests CD-ROM: Modified Chapter Test

OSP **One-Stop Planner CD-ROM:** ExamView Test Generator (English/Spanish)

HOAP **Holt Online Assessment Program (HOAP),** in the Holt Premier Online Student Edition

---

PASS: Section 1 Quiz*

Online Quiz: Section 1

Alternative Assessment Handbook

PASS: Section 2 Quiz*

Online Quiz: Section 2

Alternative Assessment Handbook

PASS: Section 3 Quiz*

Online Quiz: Section 3

Alternative Assessment Handbook

 **RESOURCES**

The following resources were developed to help North Carolina educators teach the standards and objectives of North Carolina's eleventh grade standard course of study in United States history.

• United States history EOC Test Prep Workbook
• Teacher's Support System
• North Carolina One-Stop Planner

And be sure to direct your students to **go.hrw.com** for online access to the EOC Test Prep Workbook.

go.hrw.com
EOC Test Prep
KEYWORD: SE7 NC

Holt
Online
Learning

go.hrw.com
Teacher Resources
KEYWORD: SD7 TEACHER

go.hrw.com
Student Resources
KEYWORD: SD7 CH19

• Document-based Questions
• Interactive Multimedia Activities

• Current Events
• Chapter-based Internet Activities
• and more!

Holt Premier
Online Student Edition

Complete online support for interactivity, assessment, and reporting

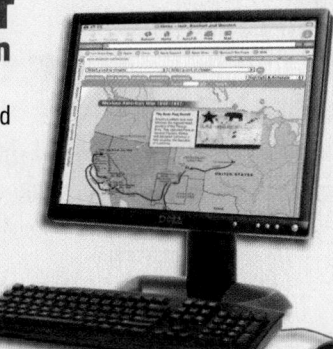

• Interactive Maps and Notebook
• Standardized Test Prep
• Homework Practice and Research Activities Online

CHAPTER 19 PLANNING GUIDE

Before You Teach

The Big Picture

Edward L. Ayers

Postwar Havoc Americans who expected the peace after World War I to bring peace at home were disappointed. Not since the Civil War had the United States seen such dissension and anxiety. The rise of the Bolsheviks in Russia coincided with the reassertion of labor's calls for justice, creating the impression among many that the two were related, and the resulting Red Scare scarred the nation. The rise of nativism, caused in part by the Red Scare and competition for scarce jobs, led to federal legislation limiting immigration as well as a rebirth of the Ku Klux Klan.

A New Economic Era The postwar era saw the rapid development and adoption of the automobile, a machine that transformed all of American society in one way or another. Everything from the assembly line to installment buying to the growth of suburbs was spurred by the car, and American life would never be the same. Yet the economy of the so-called Roaring Twenties had serious weaknesses.

The Harding and Coolidge Presidencies American voters apparently got what they wanted in the presidency in the 1920s: men who stayed out of the way. Harding's anti-government, pro-business policies proved popular, but at the time of his death his administration was beset by scandals. Coolidge shared Harding's faith in the power of business to fuel American growth, and his sterling reputation for honesty helped him get through the fallout of the Harding scandals. The decade saw retrenchment both at home and abroad, despite the high-flying words of the Kellogg-Briand Pact.

Recent Scholarship

Exploring the Scopes Trial Few subjects capture the imagination of students like the Scopes trial—and few subjects are harder to teach well, especially with the reappearance of debates over the teaching of evolution. Edward Larson's *Summer for the Gods: The Scopes Trial and America's Continuing Debate Over Science and Religion* (1997) is an award-winning book that presents this politically charged story in a fresh way and with rare balance. Stooping neither to ridicule nor defense, Larson shows the powerful cultural forces that culminated in Dayton, Tennessee, in 1925.

Differentiating Instruction

 Differentiated Instruction Teacher Management System
- Lesson Plans for Differentiated Instruction
- Differentiated Instructional Benchmarking Guides
- Interactive Reader and Study Guide

 Spanish Chapter Summaries Audio CD Program

 Online Chapter Summaries in Spanish

Student Edition on Audio CD Program

 Differentiated Instruction Modified Worksheets and Tests CD-ROM
- Vocabulary Flash Cards
- Modified Vocabulary Builder Activities
- Modified Chapter Review Activity
- Modified Chapter Test

OSP One-Stop Planner CD-ROM
- ExamView Test Generator (English and Spanish)
- PuzzlePro
- Quiz Show for ExamView
- Transparencies and Videos

TE Differentiated Activities in the Teacher's Edition
- Causes and Effects of Labor Unrest, p. 625
- Role of Automobiles, p. 630
- Advertising for a New Product, p. 632
- Economic Effect of War on Europe, p. 638

Reading Like a Historian
Sam Wineburg

The Vividness Effect and Historical Analysis

How can we gauge Thomas Edison's effect on American life? One way is to look at how Edison's inventions changed the daily habits of ordinary Americans.

Thanks to the Library of Congress's digital collection "American Memory," we can now view a personal letter to Edison from Mrs. W. C. Lathrop, a woman living in Norton, Kansas, written on March 5, 1921. (The letter may be seen at http://memory.loc.gov/learn/lessons/99/edison/images/mrs2.gif)

"It is not always the privilege of a woman to thank personally the inventor of articles which make life liveable for her sex," the letter begins. "I am a college graduate and probably my husband is one of the best known surgeons between Topeka and Denver . . . [Our] house is lighted by electricity. I cook on a Westinghouse electric range, wash dishes in an electric dish washer. An electric fan even helps to distribute heat all over the house . . . I wash clothes in an electric machine and iron on an electric mangle and with an electric iron. I clean house with electric cleaners . . . Then start the Victrola and either study Spanish for a while or listen to Kreisler and Gluck and Galli . . . I know I am only one of many under the same debt of gratitude to you."

How Typical Was She?

Recently I observed a class of 11th graders who examined this letter, using it to address the question, "How did Edison's inventions change American life?" Carried away by Mrs. Lathrop's exuberance, students gushed, "In every way," "A lot," "They made life easier—especially for women." Not until the teacher interrupted by asking students, "How typical was Mrs. Lathrop—how much can we say from this one letter?" did these young people move from glib first impressions to the real work of historical analysis.

While 90 percent of large cities had electricity by 1930, in rural areas the figure was less than 10 percent, and nine years before, when Mrs. Lathrop wrote, even less than that. "Where is Norton, Kansas?" one student asked. (Answer: In the northwest corner of Kansas, far from the population centers of Kansas City and Topeka.) Other questions followed: What kind of place was Norton—wealthy or poor, urban or rural? How would we find out?

In ways no less dramatic than the invention of the light bulb, we can now sit at our own desks and with a few clicks be inside the 1920 federal census.

The census tells us that in 1920, Norton County accounted for 11,423 residents of Kansas's population of 1,769,257. To place Mrs. Lathrop's college degree in context, we can find out how many people among Norton's 18- to 20-year-olds attended college or university—117, or just over 1 percent of its 2000 residents. From other sources on the web, we learn that women earned 18 percent of the college degrees issued at this time (mostly as teachers). From these figures, we get a rough sense of just how exceptional Mrs. Lathrop was for her time and place.

The Vividness Effect

Social psychologists talk about a "vividness effect" in which the color and immediacy of data skew our judgments of typicality and representativeness. To be sure, Mrs. Lathrop's letter provides a vivid peek inside her life—as a source, it is expressive and memorable, and with a handwritten note by Edison at the top it possesses an authenticity shared with few secondary sources.

But the qualities that attract us to this letter can also lead us astray. Mrs. Lathrop's letter tells us how Edison's inventions transformed the life of one unusual woman of status, privilege, and culture who, in 1921, owned appliances that even today—cheaper and more easily obtained—are lacking in many American households.

No doubt Edison's inventions transformed Mrs. Lathrop's life. But it would be many years before these changes affected the lives of ordinary Americans—particularly those living in outlying rural areas. One letter tells us about Mrs. Lathrop; it does not tell us about the country as a whole.

Standards Focus

Social Studies Competency Goals
Goal 8 The learner will analyze United States involvement in World War I and the war's influence on international affairs during the 1920's.

Goal 9 The learner will appraise the economic, social, and political changes of the decades of "The Twenties" and "The Thirties."
 8.03, 9.01, 9.02

The Big Idea and Essential Questions

To foster student understanding of this chapter's big idea, design your lesson to address each section's essential question.

Big Idea As the United States returned to peacetime, fears of dangers seen and unseen troubled the nation, but a booming economy seemed to smooth the transition from war to peace.

Essential Questions

1. Why did Americans face new fears in the years after World War I?

2. How did the American economy change in the 1920s?

3. What were the main characteristics of the Harding and Coolidge administrations?

Key to Differentiating Instruction

Below Level

Basic-level activities designed for all students encountering new material

At Level

Intermediate-level activities designed for average students

Above Level

Challenging activities designed for honors and gifted-and-talented students

Standard English Mastery

Activities designed to improve standard English usage

620 CHAPTER 19

CHAPTER 19 1919–1928

From WAR to PEACE

THE BIG PICTURE The end of the war brought peace to Americans, but not peace of mind. Dangers seen and unseen troubled the nation—until a new president in the White House and a booming economy seemed to smooth the transition from war to peace.

North Carolina Standards

Social Studies Objectives
8.03 Assess the political, economic, social, and cultural effects of the war on the United States and other nations.
9.01 Elaborate on the cycle of economic boom and bust in the 1920's and 1930's.
9.02 Analyze the extent of prosperity for different segments of society during this period.

Language Arts Objectives
2.01 Research and analyze ideas, events, and/or movements related to United States culture by:
  • locating facts and details for purposeful elaboration.

Skills Focus **READING LIKE A HISTORIAN**

This photo, taken in 1924 by the Electric Club of Louisville, Kentucky, shows a few of this appliance store's products. These people are members of the club or employees of the store. **Analyzing Primary Sources** What does the fact that Louisville had an Electric Club tell you about how American consumers felt about modern electrical appliances during the 1920s?
See Skills Handbook, pp. H28–H29

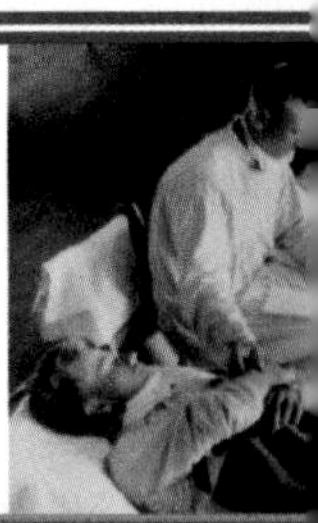

620

U.S.

1918

WORLD

1919 Attorney General Palmer launches anti-radical raids.

1918–1919 Influenza epidemic kills millions of people worldwide.

Introduce the Chapter

At Level

From War to Peace

1. Tell students that the period following the end of World War I was a time of leadership change and a time of innovation in the United States.

2. Have students scan the chapter and make a table of notable individuals discussed in the chapter and their accomplishments. Have volunteers share the information from their tables and create a class table for all to see.

3. When students have finished studying this chapter, have them choose one individual and write a brief, illustrated summary of the person's life. **LS Verbal-Linguistic, Visual-Spatial**

   Alternative Assessment Handbook, Rubrics 3: Artwork; and 42: Writing to Inform

1920
Promising normalcy, Warren G. Harding wins the presidency.

1924
The U.S. government imposes strict limits on immigration.

1928
Coolidge opts not to seek re-election.
The United States signs the Kellogg-Briand Pact.

1920 — 1922 — 1924 — 1926 — 1928 — 1930

1920
Bolsheviks win a civil war and take control of Russia.

1922
Benito Mussolini establishes a Fascist regime in Italy.

1927
The German stock market collapses.

1928
Scottish doctor Alexander Fleming discovers penicillin.

621

• Chapter Preview •

HOLT

History's Impact

► **Video Program: From War to Peace**
See the Video Teacher's Guide for strategies for using the video segment.

Reading Like a Historian

New Consumer Goods In 1908 the Hurley Machine Company in Chicago introduced one of the first electric washing machines. During the 1920s, electricity and plumbing became more available, and washing machines became popular.

Contrast How do modern washing machines differ from this 1920s model? *larger, front or top loading, wringer mechanism is inside the machine*

go.hrw.com
Online Resources

Chapter Resources:
KEYWORD: SD7 CH19

Teacher Resources:
KEYWORD: SD7 TEACHER

Explore the Time Line

1. When did the United States begin to set strict limits on immigration? *1924*

2. In what year did the German stock market collapse? *1927*

3. When did the Bolsheviks take control of Russia? *1920*

Info to Know

The influenza epidemic of 1918–1919 was the most destructive in recorded history. Between 20 and 40 million people died from the disease worldwide, including some 600,000 Americans. This is more than were killed during World War I, World War II, the Korean War, and the Vietnam War combined.
Draw Conclusions How do you think the disease traveled so quickly? *possible answers— returning soldiers came into contact with many other people; people were moving after the war*

Answers

Reading Like a Historian *interested in the possibilities of these new inventions*

621

The Inside Story. . . Use the **Daily Bellringer Transparency** to help students answer the question.

🖥 Daily Bellringer Transparency, Section 1

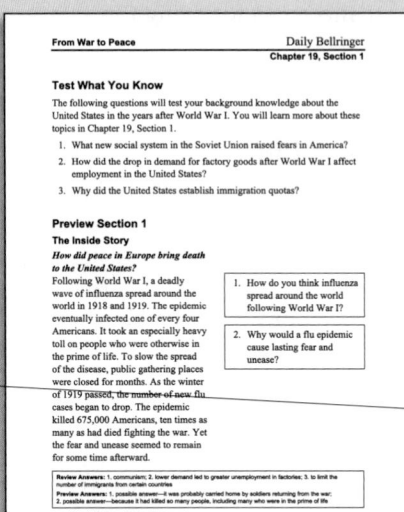

From War to Peace · Daily Bellringer
Chapter 19, Section 1

Test What You Know

The following questions will test your background knowledge about the United States in the years after World War I. You will learn more about these topics in Chapter 19, Section 1.

1. What new social system in the Soviet Union raised fears in America?
2. How did the drop in demand for factory goods after World War I affect employment in the United States?
3. Why did the United States establish immigration quotas?

Preview Section 1

The Inside Story

How did peace in Europe bring death to the United States?
Following World War I, a deadly wave of influenza spread around the world in 1918 and 1919. The epidemic eventually infected one of every four Americans. It took an especially heavy toll on people who were otherwise in the prime of life. To slow the spread of the disease, public gathering places were closed for months. As the winter of 1919 passed, the number of new flu cases began to drop. The epidemic killed 675,000 Americans, ten times as many as had died fighting the war. Yet the fear and unease seemed to remain for some time afterward.

1. How do you think influenza spread around the world following World War I?

2. Why would a flu epidemic cause lasting fear and unease?

Review Answers: 1. communism; 2. lower demand led to greater unemployment in factories; 3. to limit the number of immigrants from certain countries

Preview Answers: 1. possible answer—it was probably carried home by soldiers returning from the war; 2. possible answer—because it had killed so many people, including many who were in the prime of life

Copyright © by Holt, Rinehart and Winston. All rights reserved.

Academic Vocabulary

Review with students the high-use academic term in this section.

status one's standing in society relative to that of others (p. 625)

🖥 CRF: Vocabulary Builder Activity, Section 1

Taking Notes

Radicals—fear, distrust; Labor—suspicion; Immigrants—distrust, fear, discrimination

---

SECTION 1 Postwar Havoc

BEFORE YOU READ

MAIN IDEA
Although the end of World War I brought peace, it did not ease the minds of many Americans, who found much to fear in the postwar years.

READING FOCUS
1. What were the causes and effects of the first Red Scare?
2. How did labor strife grow during the postwar years?
3. How did the United States limit immigration after World War I?

KEY TERMS AND PEOPLE
Bolshevik
communism
Red Scare
A. Mitchell
  Palmer
Palmer raids
alien
deportation
anarchist

TAKING NOTES As you read, take notes on Americans' attitudes toward radicals, organized labor, and immigrants following World War I. Record your notes in a graphic organizer like the one shown here.

Radicals	Labor	Immigrants

A DEADLY Epidemic

▼ In March 1918, soldiers in Camp Funston, Kansas, became the first U.S. influenza victims.

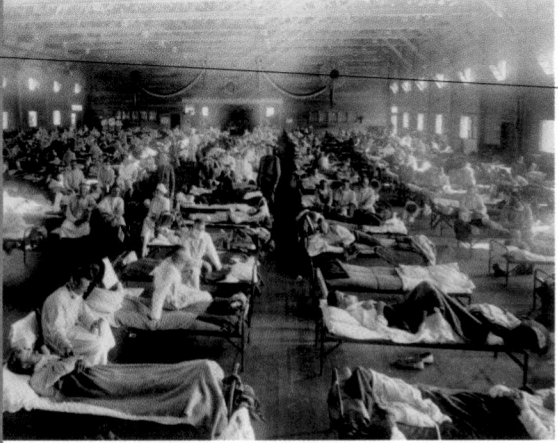

THE INSIDE STORY
How did peace in Europe bring death to the United States? Influenza found breeding grounds in the military camps and the trenches, where soldiers lived in close quarters. It invaded the United States, traveling on troop ships among the healthy and the wounded. In the streets, as hopeful Americans gathered to celebrate the end of World War I, the infection spread quickly. Soon, many were sick and dying—victims of a worldwide influenza epidemic

in 1918 and 1919 that would kill some 10 times as many Americans as died in battle in World War I.

Even in the early 1900s, the flu was not generally a serious disease. It caused unpleasant symptoms, and it could be dangerous to the very old and very young. Healthy adults might feel ill for a few days, but they usually recovered quickly. In 1918, however, a powerful new strain of influenza struck with deadly force, eventually infecting more than 1 in 4 Americans. It took an especially heavy toll on men and women in their twenties and thirties. Some victims died within a day or two of getting sick.

The nation's hospitals, already strained with large numbers of wounded soldiers, suddenly had thousands of new patients at their doorsteps. Cities and towns suffered shortages of doctors, nurses, and beds for the sick.

As the winter of 1919 passed, the number of new flu cases began to drop. The crisis had passed, but more than half a million Americans had perished.

As society began to return to normal in the postwar world, many people remained fearful and uneasy. The world was at peace, but Americans were not. As you will read, this feeling would continue for some time. ◼

The First Red Scare

The end of World War I in 1918 brought great rejoicing in America, but it was just the beginning of new problems at home. Besides a terrifying medical crisis, the nation faced economic and political turmoil that cast a dark shadow over the postwar recovery.

Farms and factories that had buzzed with activity during the war now lay silent, as demand for their products suddenly fell. In the slowing economy, returning soldiers had difficulty finding jobs. People began to

---

Teach the Main Idea | At Level

Postwar Havoc

1. **Teach** Ask students the Reading Focus questions to teach this section.

2. **Apply** Draw a large triangle for students to see. Label the angles *Red Scare, Labor Unrest,* and *Immigration.* Guide students in a discussion of the three topics of this section. Have students name ways in which each of these topics is related to the other two topics. Write student answers along the sides of the triangle that connect the related topics. 🖳 **Visual-Spatial, Logical-Mathematical**

3. **Review** As you review the section, have students identify the one issue that they believe posed the most real and serious problem at the time.

4. **Practice/Homework** Have each student write a newspaper editorial about what he or she thinks is the biggest challenge facing the United States, and what should be done about it. 🖳 **Verbal-Linguistic**

🖳 Alternative Assessment Handbook, Rubric 41: Writing to Express

Terrorism in the United States

Around noon on September 16, 1920, a horse-drawn cart stopped in front of the offices of financier J.P. Morgan, on Wall Street in New York City. Suddenly, the cart—which had been packed with dynamite—exploded. More than 30 people were instantly killed, and some 300 were injured. Of the cart and horse, only hooves remained.

Detectives took the horseshoes to thousands of stables, but they found no more evidence. Some officials suspected labor organizers and political radicals. Although many people were questioned and even arrested, no one was ever brought to trial.

At about 9 a.m. on April 19, 1995, a homemade bomb exploded inside a truck parked in front of the Alfred P. Murrah Federal Building in Oklahoma City. Nearly 170 people were killed, including children, and more than 500 were injured.

Investigators learned that the Oklahoma City bombing was carried out by two men who opposed earlier government actions against an armed group in Texas. Both were tried and convicted. One received the death penalty, and the other was sentenced to life in prison.

Contrasting How did the outcomes of the two investigations differ?

The 1995 Oklahoma City bombing collapsed the front of the federal building. At the time the bombing was the worst terrorist attack that had occurred on American soil.

---

realize that in many ways, they had traded a painful war for a troubling peace.

HISTORY'S VOICES

> ❝I felt that when peace came we'd all be so joyful that nothing would weigh upon us again. I find, however, the problems of reconstruction loom so large that we are as much occupied with them as we have been with the problems of war.❞
>
> —Illinois governor Frank Lowden, quoted in *The Harding Era* by Robert K. Murray

The emotional turmoil of the times had disturbing political effects. While World War I had stirred deep feelings of patriotism, it had also ignited hatred toward Germans. These sentiments gave rise to a movement known as 100 Percent Americanism. It celebrated all things American while it attacked ideas—and people—it viewed as foreign or anti-American.

The rise of the Bolsheviks Americans worried about a new foreign enemy. In 1917 a violent revolution had ripped across Russia. The Red Army of the **Bolsheviks**, which was led by Vladimir I. Lenin, eventually gained control. Five years later Russia would become part of a new nation called the Soviet Union.

Lenin and the Bolsheviks dreamed of establishing a new social system for their people—and for the world. This system, called **communism**, would have no economic classes and no private property. Lenin believed all people should share equally in society's wealth.

American reaction Many Americans were baffled and frightened by communism. The Soviets called for the overthrow of capitalism. But most Americans embraced the ideals of capitalism, including the freedom to own property. They valued the opportunity to better themselves by hard work or ingenuity.

Lenin predicted that communism would inspire workers throughout the world to rise up and crush capitalism. To some Americans, the threat seemed more ominous than the traditional conflicts of the past.

Throughout World War I, the American public had focused its fear and hatred on "the Hun." Now, public anxiety became fixed on a new target: Communists and others who held radical ideas. They were known as Reds.

Communist parties formed in the United States after the war. Some of their members promoted the violent overthrow of the government. In fact, radicals may have played a role in a 1919 plot in which bombs were mailed to government officials. The plot failed, however. Most historians agree that an internal

FROM WAR TO PEACE **623**

Direct Teach

Reading Focus

❶ What were the causes and effects of the first Red Scare? *causes—fear of communism; formation of Communist parties in the U.S.; exaggerated newspaper reports; effects—crime to call for overthrow of government; socialists barred from office; Palmer raids; aliens deported*

The First Red Scare

Identify What problems faced the United States after World War I? *the medical crisis (influenza); economic and political turmoil*

Analyze How did 100 Percent Americanism combine feelings of both pride and prejudice? *celebrated all things American; attacked foreign ideas and people*

Develop Why do you think capitalism is considered fundamental to American life? *owning property is a fundamental constitutional right; American belief in advancement through hard work*

　📖 CRF: Literature Activity: *Main Street* by Sinclair Lewis

Linking to Today

Terrorism in the United States
The PATRIOT Act Have students research the USA PATRIOT Act (H.R. 3162), which was passed following the terrorist attacks on September 11, 2001. Guide students in a discussion of the ways in which the act limits some civil liberties and tries to guarantee others.

Collaborative Learning

Above Level

The Red Scare

1. Guide the class in a discussion of communism and the American reaction to it following World War I. Ask students why communism might appeal to some people, and to what groups it would be most likely to appeal. Then ask students to consider which groups might find communism threatening, and why this might be.

2. Make a list of student responses for all students to see. Have them copy the information onto their own papers.

3. Organize the class into small groups. Have each group write a play reflecting attitudes of the time, including the fear of communism, and that shows how communism might be defeated. Have students incorporate ideas from the lists into their plays.

4. Have students present their plays for the class. As an extension, you might ask students to videotape their plays. **LS Kinesthetic**

　📖 Alternative Assessment Handbook, Rubric 33: Skits and Reader's Theater

---

Answers

Linking to Today *In 1920 investigators were unable to find evidence leading them to the criminals; in 1995 investigations led to trials and convictions.*

623

The First Red Scare

Explain How did the U.S. government react to the Red Scare? *used wartime laws to arrest suspected radicals; deported aliens*

Identify Cause and Effect What caused the Red Scare to die down? *predictions about the radical threat were not coming true; Communist movements in Germany and Hungary were failing, lessening worldwide threat of communism*

Make Judgments Do you think the media acted correctly in reporting the Red Scare? *possible answer—No, the media have a responsibility to investigate honestly, not to exaggerate.*

📖 U.S. History Political Cartoon Activity: Cartoon 37: Bolshevism

---

PRIMARY SOURCES

Political Cartoon

Hundreds of political cartoons, including this one titled "Put Them Out and Keep Them Out," fueled Red Scare fears. This cartoon originally appeared in the *Philadelphia Inquirer* in October 1919, when the U.S. government was trying to deport many suspected Communist sympathizers.

THE GRANGER COLLECTION, NEW YORK

Political cartoonists often portrayed Communist sympathizers as bearded, sinister-looking characters carrying torches and sometimes weapons.

The torch of anarchy represents the destructive nature of communism. The knife represents the dangers of Bolshevism.

Skills FOCUS READING LIKE A HISTORIAN

1. **Drawing Conclusions** What do you think the title "Put Them Out and Keep Them Out" means?

2. **Interpreting Political Cartoons** Why do you think the artist showed the character peeking out from under the American flag?

See **Skills Handbook**, p. H12, H31

THE IMPACT TODAY

Government

Between 1917 and 1920, many Americans were willing to give up some civil liberties in order to achieve security. The American Civil Liberties Union (ACLU), founded in 1920, works to defend the constitutional rights of citizens. The ACLU has fought to protect civil liberties, even in times of national emergencies.

Communist threat to the nation was probably never great. Yet at the time, the threat seemed very real.

A **Red Scare**, or widespread fear of communism, gripped the nation. One official noted, "I believe it has been 'scared up' considerably by the newspapers, which relate every arrest and incident . . . by printing large scary headlines."

The government took the threat seriously. New York state legislators voted to bar five legally elected socialists from office. New York also passed a law making it a crime to call for the overthrow of the government. In *Gitlow* v. *New York* (1925) the Supreme Court upheld the New York law. But it also held that the Fourteenth Amendment prohibited states from depriving citizens of the right to free speech.

The Palmer raids **A. Mitchell Palmer**, had been one of the targets of the 1919 bombing plot. Later that year, as attorney general of the United States, Palmer became a key leader of the federal government's anti-Communist campaign. He led an attack on suspected radicals known as the **Palmer raids**.

To justify the raids, Palmer used wartime laws that gave the government broad powers against suspected radicals. For **aliens**—citizens of other countries living in the United States—just belonging to certain groups considered radical could lead to deportation. **Deportation** means removing an alien from one country and sending him or her to another country.

In late 1919 Palmer's forces arrested thousands of members of suspected radical groups. In December 1919, a naval vessel named the *Buford* set sail carrying nearly 250 aliens who were being deported. Many Americans cheered Palmer's actions. Said Leonard Wood, a Republican leader, "I believe we should place them all in ships of stone, with sails of lead."

In time, the Red Scare died down. It became clear that predictions about the radical threat to the country were not coming true. At the same time, Communist movements in Germany and Hungary were failing. These failures dampened fears of worldwide revolution. The nation's anxiety was reduced, but it was not eliminated.

READING CHECK **Sequencing** Who replaced "the Hun" as the object of American fear and hatred?

Skills Focus: Interpreting Political Cartoons   `At Level`

Reading Like a Historian Skill

Creating a New Political Cartoon

1. Have students study the political cartoon on this page. Then lead a discussion about the images depicted in the cartoon.

2. Ask students what issue or issues today might cause the same sort of fear that the Red Scare caused in the period following World War I. *possible answer—terrorists or terrorism*

3. Organize the class into groups of five or six students. Have each group work together to create a political cartoon that presents the

modern-day issue in a way that would inspire a similar sense of fear. If more than one issue was mentioned, allow students to choose a topic that appeals to them.

4. Call on volunteers to display and explain their cartoons to the class. 🔲 **Interpersonal, Visual-Spatial**

📖 Alternative Assessment Handbook, Rubrics 14: Group Activity; and 27: Political Cartoons

---

Answers

Reading Like a Historian 1. *to deport aliens and prevent them from reentering the United States;* **2.** *possible answer—Foreigners might be trying to sneak into the United States, create anarchy, disrupt or overthrow the government and American way of life.*

Reading Check *Communists and others who held radical ideas; Reds*

Labor Strife Grows

The year 1919 was one of the most explosive times in the history of the American labor movement. Some 4 million workers took part in more than 3,000 strikes nationwide. In nearly every case, labor lost. Wartime successes and peacetime disappointments set the stage for this catastrophic year for workers.

Postwar difficulties Workers' raised expectations helped create the crisis. During the war, President Wilson had sought good relations with workers who were keeping the troops clothed and equipped. Organized labor won many gains, including shorter hours and higher wages. When the war ended, labor leaders hoped to build on what they had achieved. They were disappointed.

A number of factors combined to frustrate labor's high hopes. Wilson, now focused on promoting his peace plan, paid less attention to events at home and did little to promote workers' causes. Meanwhile, the sinking postwar demand for factory goods hurt many industries. Returning soldiers expected to take their place on the factory floor, but the jobs just weren't there. Unhappy workers, especially strikers, were replaced.

The Red Scare further weakened labor by damaging its reputation. Communism's call to workers to rise up and overthrow their government made many people suspicious of organized labor. Opponents linked labor with the radical ideas that so many people feared.

Labor's losses The showdown between labor and management in 1919 devastated organized labor. Unions lost members and national political power. It would take another decade—and another national crisis—to restore organized labor's reputation, status, and bargaining power in the United States.

Major strikes of the era Among the thousands of union strikes that rocked the country in 1919, a few hold a place in labor history. In Seattle, Washington, labor unrest at the shipyards spread citywide, igniting what became the nation's first major general strike—one in which workers in all industries take part.

The conflict virtually shut down the city. Yet the Seattle general strike of 1919 failed to achieve any gains for workers. In fact, it did great harm. For years afterward, industry, and its jobs, stayed away from Seattle.

On the opposite coast, the city of Boston descended into chaos when its police force went on strike in September 1919 to protest low wages and poor working conditions. Eventually, Massachusetts governor Calvin Coolidge called in the state's militia to end the strike.

ACADEMIC VOCABULARY
status one's standing in society relative to that of others

Major Strikes, 1919

- **Seattle general strike—** February 6–11
- **Boston police strike—** September 9–13
- **Nationwide steel-workers strike—** September 22, 1919– January 1920

625

❸ How did the United States limit immigration after World War I? *1921 law established immigration quotas; the National Origins Act of 1924 set even stricter quotas, almost eliminated immigration from Asian countries*

Limiting Immigration

Identify How did immigrants before and after 1900 differ? *Before 1900— Protestant Christians from northern and western Europe; after 1900— Catholics and Jews from eastern and southern Europe*

Identify Cause and Effect Why did labor unions join nativists in pushing for restrictions on immigration? *new immigrants willing to work for low wages; unions saw them as a threat*

Evaluate Do you think the convictions of Sacco and Vanzetti were justified? *possible answers—no, evidence against the men was weak; on trial for views, not burglary and murder; execution seems extreme*

📑 CRF: Primary Source Activity: Representative Parish Discusses Immigration

📑 CRF: History and Geography Activity: Growth of Cities in the 1920s

📑 CRF: Social Studies Skills Activity: Interpreting Line Graphs

go.hrw.com
Online Resources
KEYWORD: SD7 CH19
TOPIC: SACCO AND VANZETTI

Answers

Interpreting Graphs *Following a sharp rise in 1920–1921, immigration from southern and eastern Europe declined.*

Reading Check *organized labor failed to make progress in improving working conditions, lost members and status; strikes unsuccessful; federal government helped industry owners, hurt labor movement*

It was another loss for labor, but a great political boost for the Republican governor. In a telegram to the famous labor leader Samuel Gompers, Coolidge wrote, "There can be no right to strike against the public safety by anybody, anywhere, anytime."

The words echoed across a nervous country and made Coolidge a hero. His sudden fame as a champion of law and order elevated his career to the national stage and eventually landed him in the White House.

Other notable strikes hit the steel industry and the coalfields of the eastern United States. The United Mine Workers had kept a "no strikes" pledge during the war. Under the tough new leadership of John L. Lewis, the striking union won a large wage increase.

The workers failed, however, to win other key demands, such as a reduction of their workweek to five days. Lewis recognized the limitations of the union's power at that time.

"We cannot fight the government," the labor leader declared. His miners, like union members throughout the country, would have to wait to press their demands for shorter hours and safer workplaces.

READING CHECK **Summarizing** How successful were the postwar labor strikes?

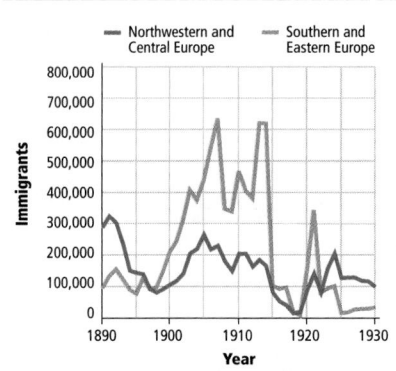

EUROPEAN IMMIGRATION, 1890–1930

— Northwestern and Central Europe
— Southern and Eastern Europe

Source: *Historical Statistics of the United States*

Skills FOCUS **INTERPRETING GRAPHS**

How did the immigration quotas of the 1920s change the pattern of European immigration?

See Skills Handbook, p. H14

Limiting Immigration

Competition for scarce jobs, combined with the Red Scare, triggered an ugly backlash against foreigners in the postwar period. The rise of nativism, or distrust of foreigners, produced a culture clash between the nation's earlier immigrants and its newer ones.

Many nativists were Protestant Christians who had their roots in northern and western Europe, the source of most immigration before 1900. The nativists targeted newer arrivals from southern and eastern Europe, many of whom were Catholics and Jews. Immigrants from these areas of Europe, nativists argued, were less willing to become "Americanized," and should not be welcomed.

Labor leaders, along with the nativists, pushed for immigration restrictions on these groups. New arrivals, often poor and alone, were willing to work for low wages. Unions saw them as a threat.

Immigration control The federal government responded to nativist concern by passing laws to limit immigration. A 1921 law established a quota—an established number—of immigrants to be allowed into the United States from various nations.

The National Origins Act of 1924 went even further. It set quotas for each country at 2 percent of the number of people from that country living in the United States in 1890. The goal was clearly to reduce immigration to the United States from certain countries—mainly southern and eastern European countries. The act also nearly eliminated all immigration from Asian countries.

Nativism also produced a revival in the 1920s of the Ku Klux Klan. The Klan had started as a terror group that targeted African Americans in the South. It reemerged in the postwar years with a broader mission. The hate group now targeted Jews, Catholics, and radicals of all types.

A Klan slogan of the 1920s characterized the group's vision of the nation: "Native white, Protestant supremacy." The new Ku Klux Klan of the 1920s also moved out of the South into other parts of the United States.

Sacco and Vanzetti In the 1920s a court case in Massachusetts dramatically illustrated

---

Skills Focus: Drawing Conclusions

At Level

Reading Skill
The Trial of Sacco and Vanzetti

1. Review the information about Sacco and Vanzetti with students. Have each student write a short editorial explaining the public interest in the trial of the two men. Students should explain to what extent, or in what ways, if any, the Red Scare and hostility toward immigrants played a part in the trial. *Students should note that Americans were deeply divided over the trial.*

2. Have volunteers read their editorials to the class.

3. Guide the class in a discussion of the views presented in the editorials. Do students feel that Sacco and Vanzetti received a fair trial? What could have been done at the time to ensure fairness? 🅛🅢 **Verbal-Linguistic, Logical-Mathematical**

📑 Alternative Assessment Handbook, Rubric 40: Writing to Describe

the nation's struggle with nativist and anti-radical feelings. In May 1920, two men, Nicola Sacco and Bartolomeo Vanzetti, were arrested for armed robbery and murder. The two men were Italian immigrants. More importantly, they proclaimed that they were **anarchists**—radicals who sought the destruction of government.

At the trial, it became clear that the evidence against the two men was weak. It also was apparent that Sacco and Vanzetti were on trial for their political beliefs as well as for bank robbery and murder.

Amid great publicity and protests in Europe and South America as well as in the United States, the two men were convicted and sentenced to die. They were executed in 1927.

Historians still argue over the guilt or innocence of Sacco and Vanzetti. Many agree, however, that the men's political ideas played a prominent role in the trial.

Bartolomeo Vanzetti expressed these same ideas before his trial.

HISTORY'S VOICES

❝My conviction is that I have suffered for things I am guilty of. I am suffering because I am a radical, and indeed I am a radical; I have suffered because I was an Italian, and indeed I am Italian.❞
—Bartolomeo Vanzetti in court, 1927

The executions of Sacco and Vanzetti were highly controversial at the time. By then, how-

Skills FOCUS READING LIKE A HISTORIAN

The artist Ben Shahn based this painting of Sacco and Vanzetti, like many subjects of his paintings, on a newspaper photograph.

Making Inferences Why do you think Shahn chose to use newspaper images?

ever, the nation had largely recovered from the Red Scare and the turmoil of the postwar years. The 1920s would be very different from the previous decade.

READING CHECK **Identifying Cause and Effect** How did Congress respond to the growing concern about immigration?

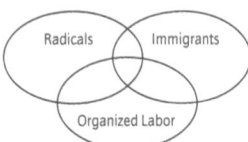

SECTION 1 ASSESSMENT

go.hrw.com
Online Quiz
Keyword: SD7 HP19

Reviewing Ideas, Terms, and People

1. a. Define What was the Red Scare?
b. Compare How did American attitudes toward "the Hun" relate to attitudes toward Reds?
c. Evaluate Why do you think Americans were able to quickly transfer their feelings about Germans to Communists and radicals?

2. a. Describe Why did labor strife increase after the war?
b. Contrast How did labor fare after the war compared to during the war?

3. a. Define Write a brief definition for each of the following terms: **alien, anarchist**
b. Explain What change in immigration in recent decades appeared to concern many Americans in the postwar years?
c. Elaborate How do you think nativism might have related to the Red Scare?

Critical Thinking

4. Comparing and Contrasting Copy the chart below and compare and contrast the public attitudes about radicals, organized labor, and immigrants in the post–World War I era.

Radicals   Immigrants

Organized Labor

FOCUS ON WRITING

5. Persuasive Write a letter to a member of Congress in which you argue for or against the idea that simply holding a "radical" idea should be against the law.

FROM WAR TO PEACE **627**

Preteach

Bellringer

The Inside Story. . . Use the **Daily Bellringer Transparency** to help students answer the question.

🔖 Daily Bellringer Transparency, Section 2

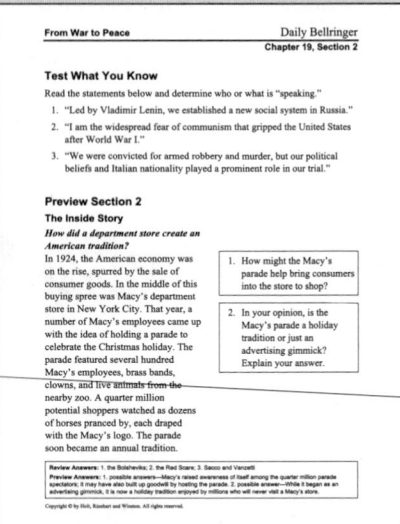

Taking Notes

assembly line, competition in auto industry, new industries, new products such as the radio and electrical appliances, rise of advertising, installment buying and credit

---

SECTION 2 · A New Economic Era

BEFORE YOU READ

MAIN IDEA

New products, new industries, and new ways of doing business expanded the economy in the 1920s, although not everyone shared in the prosperity.

READING FOCUS

1. What role did the Ford Motor Company and Henry Ford play in revolutionizing American industry?
2. How did both the auto industry and the nation change during the 1920s?
3. What were some qualities of the new consumer of the 1920s?
4. What were some weak parts of the economy in the 1920s?

KEY TERMS AND PEOPLE

Henry Ford
assembly line
productivity
welfare capitalism
suburb
installment buying
credit

TAKING NOTES As you read, take notes on why the U.S. economy boomed during the 1920s. Record your notes in a graphic organizer like the one shown here.

Causes ➡ A Booming Economy

THE INSIDE STORY

How did a department store create an American tradition?

In 1924 Americans were on a shopping spree. The U.S. economy was on the rise, spurred by the American consumer, who was busy spending money on a wide range of exciting new products.

In the middle of this national buying frenzy was Macy's department store in New York City. By 1924 Macy's aisles and displays filled some 1 million square feet of New York real estate. It was said to be the largest store in the world.

In 1924 some Macy's employees came up with the idea to hold a Christmas parade. Many of the employees were recent immigrants from Europe, and they wanted to share their holiday traditions as a gift to the people of their new country. It wasn't a bad idea for the store, either. The parade would provide an opportunity for Macy's to unveil its enormous Christmas window displays along 34th Street.

The parade kicked off on Thanksgiving Day, 1924, featuring about a thousand employees of the store. Brass bands, clowns, and zoo animals enlivened the scene. Along the route, a quarter million potential shoppers took in the sights and sounds.

The first Macy's parade was a great success. In 1925, on Thanksgiving Day, marchers once again delighted the crowds and welcomed the holiday season. Soon the parade—and the department store itself—was a tradition shared not just by the people of New York but also by visitors from around the world.

Meanwhile, the American consumers who had helped make Macy's a success in New York continued their postwar shopping spree. Indeed, as you will read, for Macy's and other American businesses, the 1920s provided much to be thankful for and to celebrate. ◢

▼ Macy's first big Christmas parade was held on November 27, 1924.

Let the PARADE Begin

628 CHAPTER 19

Teach the Main Idea

At Level

A New Economic Era

Materials colored markers, construction paper

1. **Teach** Ask students the Reading Focus questions to teach this section.

2. **Apply** Organize the class into groups of four or five students. Have each group choose one of the new products mentioned in this chapter, then design a magazine advertisement for it. Students should use words and pictures to try to create a demand for the product. Ads should be colorful and show the product's features.

3. **Review** Have volunteers present each group's advertisement to the class. Then guide the class in a discussion of the strategies that each group used to create a demand for the product.

4. **Practice/Homework** Have each student write a script for a radio commercial or a jingle for one of the products. **LS Verbal-Linguistic, Auditory-Musical**

📄 Alternative Assessment Handbook, Rubrics 2: Advertisements; 14: Group Activity

Ford Revolutionizes Industry

The black automobiles that chugged and sputtered their way down the streets of New York and other cities represented the latest in American technology. During the 1920s, the Ford Model T automobile, like the Macy's parade, would become a fixture of American life.

The first cars appeared in America in the late 1800s, but they remained a toy for the rich through the early 1900s. That changed when a young entrepreneur, **Henry Ford**, began selling his Model T in 1908. It wasn't much to look at. However, it changed American society forever. Ford spelled out his revolutionary vision:

HISTORY'S VOICES

❝I will build a motor car for the great multitude. It will be large enough for the family but small enough for the individual to run and care for. It will be constructed of the best materials, by the best men to be hired, after the simplest designs that modern engineering can devise. It will be so low in price that no man making a good salary will be unable to own one.❞

—Henry Ford, announcing plans for his Model T

The assembly line Imagine how expensive cars would be today if every one were custom-made! Ford began by making his cars identical and simple. That brought the cost down, but not enough. So he studied manufacturing processes, from interchangeable parts to the moving belts in meatpacking plants that brought the work to the workers. Then he hired scientific management expert Frederick Winslow Taylor to determine how workers should move, and at what speed, to be most productive.

These ideas combined to produce the first large-scale moving **assembly line**, a production system in which the item being built moves along a conveyor belt to various workstations. On Ford's assembly line, each worker had one of 84 specific jobs, often requiring simple skills.

Ford explained, "The man who puts on a bolt does not put on a nut. The man who puts on the nut does not tighten it." In its first year, the Ford assembly line produced a car every hour and a half.

The car sold for under $500, about half the cost of the first Model Ts. The price was not cheap in its day, but many people could afford it. By the 1920s Ford was rolling out a car every

minute, and the price had dropped even lower. By 1929 about 22 million cars bumped along the nation's mostly unpaved roads. People loved the Model T. They wrote songs about it. They formed automobile driving clubs.

Ford realized that his workers also were potential car buyers. He raised his workers' pay to $5 a day, far above average factory wages. This enabled his workers to buy cars.

Workers did pay a price, however. Ford bitterly opposed unions and dealt ruthlessly with anyone who tried to organize workers. Organizers pointed out the boring, repetitive tasks in Ford's clockworklike assembly lines. One labor leader remarked, "Ford workers are not really alive, they are half dead."

The effect on industry During the first quarter of the century, the Ford Motor Company dominated automaking. In the 1920s, more than half the cars in the United States were Fords. Competitors such as General Motors and Chrysler tried to improve on Ford's formula. In an effort to keep costs low, Ford refused to change the Model T's design until 1927, after some 15 million had rolled off the assembly line. New competitors General Motors and Chrysler arose to challenge that formula, bringing out new designs and colors each year. Competition helped the entire industry grow.

Other industries also learned from Ford. Manufacturers of all kinds of consumer goods

THE IMPACT TODAY

Science and Technology
Automakers still use assembly lines to make cars. Industrial robots, instead of people, perform much of the repetitive work. Each machine performs a specific task, much as in Ford's assembly line.

FACES OF HISTORY

Henry FORD
1863–1947

Since he was a young boy, Henry Ford loved to tinker with machines. As a young man, Ford worked as a machinist at the Edison Company plant in Detroit. In 1896 Ford built his first automobile. A few years later, Ford quit his machinist job to start an automobile company. Ford wanted to make cars more affordable. By developing the assembly line and using standardized parts, Ford drastically lowered the cost of manufacturing cars. In turn, he sold his cars at a price the average American could afford. Ford's strategy worked. In 1908 Ford designed the Model T. By 1927, Ford sold more than 15 million Model Ts, transforming American life.

Explain How did Ford build more affordable cars?

FROM WAR TO PEACE **629**

Direct Teach

History Close-Up

The General Motors Corporation

General Motors Corporation (GM) began as a risky business venture. Organized in 1908, GM first acquired small car companies that were unable to compete on their own. By the end of 1909 it had acquired more than 20 small companies. Over the next decade, GM struggled to finance and coordinate these holdings. The company did not fully succeed until Alfred P. Sloan took control in 1920 and reorganized it into five basic manufacturing divisions: Buick, Cadillac, Chevrolet, Oldsmobile, and Pontiac.

CRF: Biography: Alfred P. Sloan

go.hrw.com
Online Resources
KEYWORD: SD7 CH19
TOPIC: AUTOMOBILES OF THE 1920s

Answers

Interpreting Infographics *several; more jobs and different types of work; women in the workplace; travel for pleasure*

HISTORY CLOSE-UP

Autos Drive the Modern Age

The automobile fostered many changes in American industry, business, and culture.

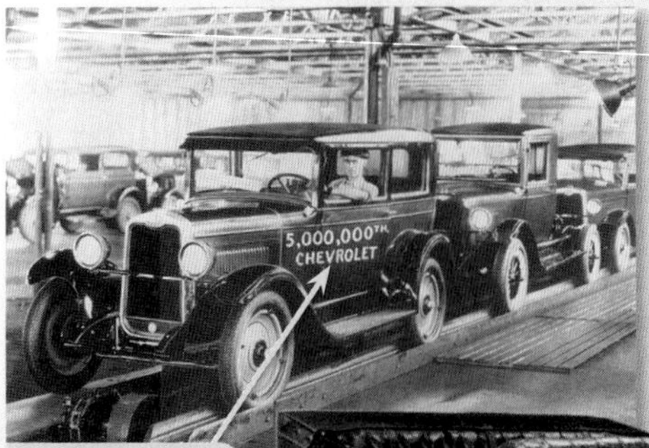

The Model T had its competitors—as many as 107 at one time. By the end of the 1920s, however, three competitors dominated the market: General Motors, Chrysler, and Ford.

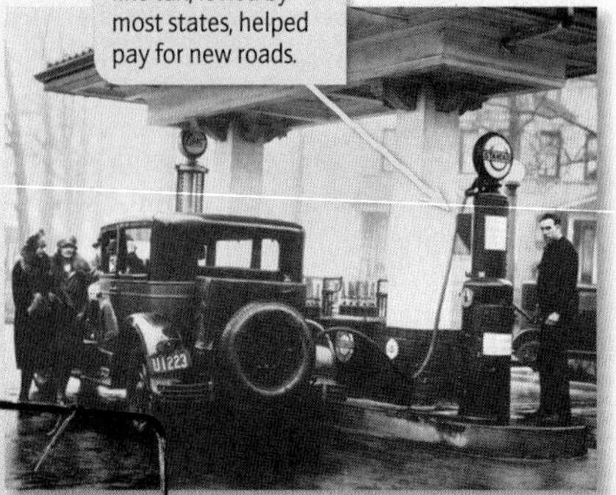

Service stations gassed up American cars, and the gasoline tax, levied by most states, helped pay for new roads.

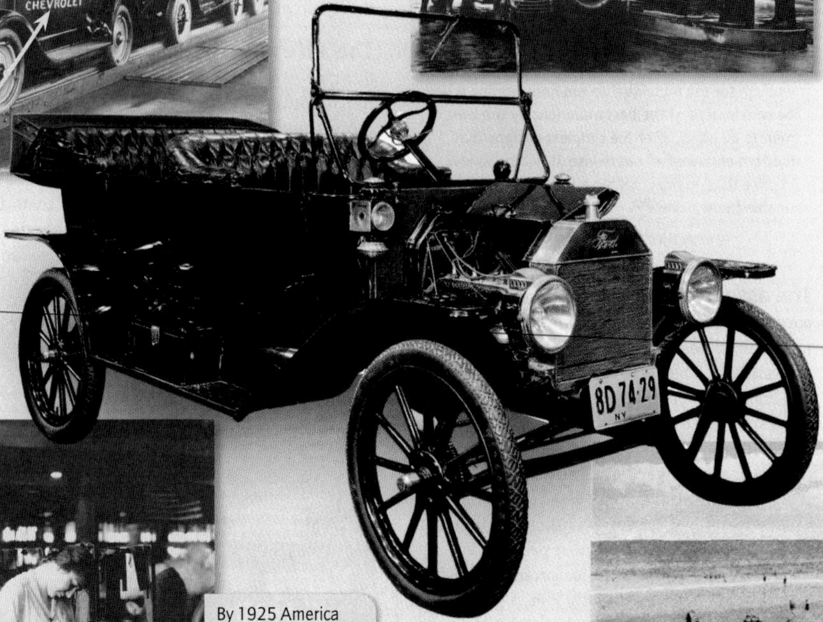

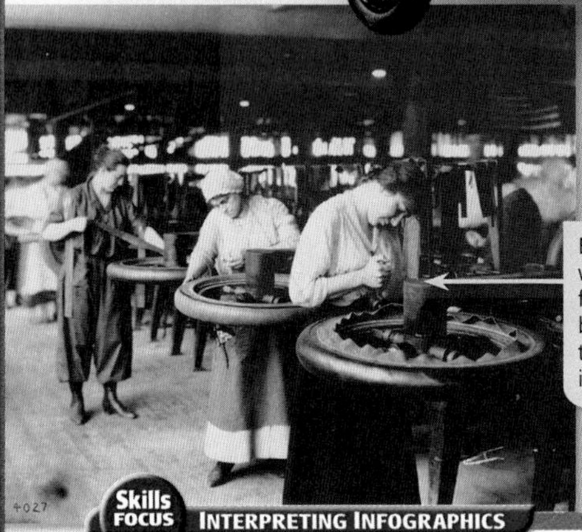

By 1925 America was producing about five times the number of car and truck tires that it was making a decade earlier.

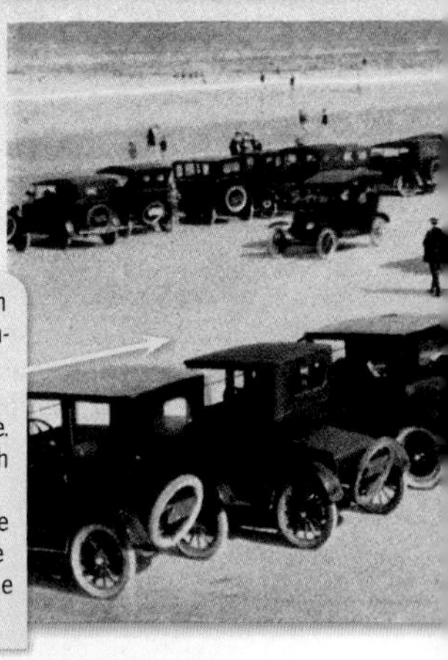

Like many Americans in the 1920s, these beachgoers in Jacksonville, Florida, took to their cars in pursuit of leisure. America's romance with the open road had its tragic side, too. The rate of traffic fatalities more than doubled during the decade.

Skills Focus INTERPRETING INFOGRAPHICS

Mass production of the automobile affected Americans' lives in many ways. ***How many can you identify by examining these pictures?***

See **Skills Handbook**, p. H30

Differentiating Instruction

Below Level

Learners Having Difficulty

Materials newspapers and magazines, large sheets of paper, scissors, glue

1. Organize the class into small groups. Have each group find photographs, articles, and ads in current newspapers and magazines that depict automobiles and related products and services. These may include, but are not limited to, photographs of automobile accidents, articles about gasoline prices, tire advertisements, car rental ads, etc. Have students cut out each item they find.
2. Have students create a collage with their materials. Display student work.
3. Lead a discussion of the ways in which automobiles continue to play a large role in daily life and U.S. economy.
4. Have students examine the economics of the automobile industry, how it affects their community and the nation. **LS Visual-Spatial**

Alternative Assessment Handbook, Rubrics 11: Discussions; and 14: Group Activity

began using assembly-line techniques to make goods in large quantities and at lower costs. In the 1920s productivity rose by 60 percent. **Productivity** is a measure of output per unit of input such as labor. American workers were producing more in less time.

The success of business in the 1920s led to a growth of what is called **welfare capitalism**, a system in which companies provide benefits to employees in an effort to promote worker satisfaction and loyalty. For example, many companies offered company-paid pensions—payments made to workers when they retire. Others set up recreation programs for workers. In return, business owners hoped that welfare capitalism would encourage workers to shun unions and accept lower pay. Many did.

READING CHECK Drawing Conclusions
What innovation by Henry Ford helped transform American industry?

Industry Changes Society

Every time motorists turned the crank handle to start their cars, other industries benefited. Demand for steel, glass, rubber, and other automobile materials soared. Automobile repair shops and filling stations sprang up in cities and towns. Motels and restaurants arose to meet the needs of car travelers.

The simple engines ran on gasoline, a by-product of petroleum. A few of the landowners who found petroleum on their property became rich practically overnight.

Automaking put the city of Detroit, Michigan, on the map. Henry Ford based his manufacturing operations there, and other carmakers followed. In 1910 fewer than 500,000 people lived in Detroit. Within 20 years the population had tripled.

The growth in manufacturing caused a boom in other Midwest cities. Akron, Ohio, the center of the rubber and tire industry, grew from fewer than 70,000 people in 1910 to nearly 210,000 in 1920. For the decade, it was the fastest-growing city in the United States.

As cities grew, so did their **suburbs**, the smaller towns located outside urban areas. Many suburbs had been established since the late 1800s, thanks in part to the construction of trolley lines that carried workers back and forth between home and workplace. Car travel, however, allowed people to live at even greater distances from their jobs. Trolley enterprises, however, suffered during the 1920s, even as suburbs expanded.

Freedom to travel also produced a new tourist industry. Before the auto boom, Florida had a few resorts that attracted mainly wealthy visitors. Automobiles brought tourists by the thousands to discover warm, sunny Florida. Buyers snatched up land, causing prices to rise sharply. Some Florida swamps were drained to put up new housing.

READING CHECK Identifying Cause and Effect How did the growth of the auto industry affect related industries?

The New Consumer

During the 1920s Americans witnessed an explosion of new products, new experiences, and new forms of mass communication on a scale never seen before. People were getting into the buying habit and liking it. Companies were happy to supply more new products for them to buy.

New products Using cost-efficient, new manufacturing processes, factories turned out a variety of new electrical appliances, such as refrigerators and vacuum cleaners. The

FROM WAR TO PEACE **631**

Collaborative Learning   At Level

Computers Drive the Modern Age

1. Remind students that like the automobile, the personal computer has had a major effect on American life. Organize the class into small groups. Have each group list ways computers are used in daily life. Have each group create a chart grouping computer uses into logical categories such as *Education, Entertainment,* and *Communication.*

2. Draw a master chart for students to see. Across the top, write the categories students created. Then have students read the uses

under each category, and write each use under the appropriate heading.

3. The computer industry created many new industries, including computer components, products, and services. Ask the class to name as many new industries as they can think of, and write them for students to see.

4. Guide students in a comparison with the early automobile industry. **LS Interpersonal**

Alternative Assessment Handbook, Rubrics 7: Charts; and 14: Group Activity

Answers

Reading Check (left) *the assembly line;* **(right)** *boom in many auto-related industries, including steel, glass, rubber, petroleum, motels, restaurants; land developers also prospered*

631

③ What were some qualities of the new consumer of the 1920s? *eager to buy new electrical appliances; bought on credit*

The New Consumer

Explain How did advertising change the American marketplace? *created demand for consumer goods*

Make Inferences How was the public hurt and helped by advertisements? *encouraged Americans to go into debt; kept costs of magazines and newspapers down; helped make radio programs available*

Make Judgments Do you think Americans would have bought as many appliances if they had not been advertised? *no, advertising created demand, encouraged people to use credit*

Biography

Willa Cather (1873–1947) Willa Cather is considered to be one of the greatest American writers of the early 20th century. When she was nine, she moved with her family from Virginia to Nebraska, where she grew up among the rugged immigrants from Europe—Swedes, Bohemians, Russians, and Germans—who were breaking the land on the Great Plains. Cather later described the move as being "thrown onto a land as bare as a piece of sheet iron." She used her experiences in Nebraska and her observations of immigrant life in her famous novel *My Antonia*, published in 1918. Cather often wrote about the spirit and courage of settlers on the American plains.

Answers

Consumer Culture *everyone is buying; prosperous lifestyle*

Reading Check *New products became widely available; consumers purchased items on credit.*

---

electrification of new areas of the country enabled more people to use the latest home conveniences.

Perhaps the favorite new electronic home technology was the radio. By the end of the 1920s, 4 homes in 10 had a radio. Like the televisions and computers that followed it, the radio opened new worlds to American families. Now, families gathered in the evenings to hear news from around the world as well as dramas and comedy shows.

Radio connected the world as never before. So did a new form of public transportation: the airplane. Aviation had made great advances during World War I. The first passenger airlines appeared over American skies in the 1920s.

The early flights offered little comfort—some passengers wore goggles and helmets. Planes were uninsulated and unpressurized; they couldn't fly over mountains or at night. In fact, for cross-country travel, trains were more comfortable as well as cheaper. For some Americans, though, the thrill of air travel outweighed the early discomforts.

Creating demand Buy! Buy! Buy! On the sidelines of the great American spending spree, advertisers became the cheerleaders. During the 1920s, persuasive advertising gained a major role in the economy. Advertisers paid for space in publications. Companies sponsored popular radio shows, such as the Palmolive Hour and the Maxwell House Concert. Advertising money made these publications and shows available to the public, and advertising gave wide exposure to consumer products.

New ways to pay In the early 1900s, most Americans paid for items in full when they bought them. They might borrow money to buy a house, a piano, or a sewing machine. But as one economist noted, "People who made such purchases didn't talk about them." Borrowing money was not considered respectable.

Setting the stage for today's credit-card society, the generation of the 1920s turned to **installment buying**—paying for an item over time in small payments. They bought on **credit**, which is, in effect, borrowing money.

Consumers took quickly to installment buying to purchase the new products on the market. By the end of the decade, 90 percent of durable goods, or long lasting goods such as cars and appliances, were bought on credit. Advertisements encouraged the use of credit, telling consumers they could "get what they want now" and assuring them that with small payments they would "barely miss the money."

READING CHECK **Summarizing** How did life change for consumers in the 1920s?

The advertising industry expanded after World War I. With the help of psychologists, advertising produced glamorous ads that tempted Americans with exciting new products. New payment methods convinced people they could afford to buy them. *What image of Americans is the advertisers portraying?*

Differentiating Instruction

Above Level

Advanced Learners/GATE

1. Organize the class into groups of four or five students. Ask each group to come up with an idea for a new product, and then develop plans for the product using drawings and descriptions.

2. Have each group plan a sales strategy for their product. Students should name their product so that consumers will understand what it is and how it is used. They will need to decide where the product will be sold. Will it be sold in stores? If so, what kind of stores?

3. Have students plan an advertising campaign for the product. How and where will it be advertised? Have each group create at least one advertisement for its product.

4. Have each group present its advertisement(s) to the class, and discuss the effectiveness of the ads. Do they create a demand for a product that might not otherwise be considered necessary? **LS Visual-Spatial**

📖 Alternative Assessment Handbook, Rubrics 2: Advertisements; and 14: Group Activity

Weaknesses in the Economy

The era that brought the boom in cars, consumer goods, radio, and advertising earned the nickname the Roaring Twenties. The name captured a certain excitement of the times. Today, however, historians tend to avoid that nickname because it gives the false impression that all Americans were prosperous and free-wheeling. In fact, many Americans suffered deeply in the postwar period.

American farmers had experienced good times during World War I. Demand for their products was high, and competition from European farmers was low. After the war, however, demand slowed. European farmers returned to their fields. A glut of farm products hit the market. As a result, U.S. farm prices plunged, and American farmers entered a decade of extreme hardship. Farm failures increased. The income of farmers and even the value of farmland declined.

The federal government tried to help. A 1921 tariff made foreign farm products more expensive, which helped raise prices for U.S. products. Yet these measures failed to fully relieve the problems.

In some places, nature added to farmers' woes. An infestation of an insect called the boll weevil destroyed cotton crops throughout the South. As a popular song of the era observed, this plague hit struggling sharecroppers especially hard.

HISTORY'S VOICES

❝Well, the merchant got half the cotton.
The boll weevils got the rest.
Didn't leave the poor farmer's wife
but one old cotton dress.
And it's full of holes, all full of holes.❞

—Carl Sandburg, *the Boll Weevil Song*

Disaster also struck the South in 1927, when the great Mississippi River flooded. Up to a thousand people died, and countless more were left homeless.

In Florida the wild land boom came to a sudden and disastrous end. Demand for land peaked, then collapsed. Then came "The Big Blow"—the strongest hurricane recorded up to that time. The hurricane had winds of 150 miles per hour, and it killed 243 people. Few people heard the warning on South Florida's only radio station. The hurricane was one of the most destructive ever. As a result, Florida sunk into an economic depression even as other parts of the nation enjoyed prosperity.

READING CHECK **Making Generalizations** What was one group that missed out on the booming economy of the 1920s?

SECTION 2 ASSESSMENT

go.hrw.com
Online Quiz
Keyword: SD7 HP19

Reviewing Ideas, Terms, and People

1. **a. Define** What was the **assembly line**?
   b. Explain How did the assembly line affect Ford's ability to make automobiles?
   c. Predict What potential problems might result from industry's rapid increase in **productivity**?

2. **a. Describe** What was the effect of the boom in the auto industry on other industries?
   b. Interpret Why could industrial changes be said to change the map of the United States?
   c. Predict How do you think the rise of the automobile will affect rural areas?

3. **a. Define** Write a brief definition for each of the following terms: **installment buying, credit**
   b. Contrast What change occurred in consumer attitudes in the 1920s compared to earlier times?
   c. Elaborate How did the changes in consumer behavior make possible the growth of the American economy in the 1920s?

4. **a. Identify** What part of the American economy did not enjoy prosperity in the 1920s?
   b. Summarize What factors explain the economic plight of farmers?

Critical Thinking

5. **Sequencing** Copy the chart below and then place events in the chapter in the diagram in the order in which they occurred.

☐ → ☐ → ☐ → ☐

FOCUS ON WRITING

6. **Persuasive** Write a letter to the editor of your local newspaper arguing for or against the use of credit for the purchase of desired goods, such as cars and appliances.

FROM WAR TO PEACE **633**

Section 2 Assessment Answers

1. **a.** manufacturing process in which each worker performed a single, specific task
   b. produced cars quickly and cheaply
   c. possible answers—increased or decreased demand for workers

2. **a.** New industries grew quickly.
   b. Industrial cities and suburbs grew quickly.
   c. Rural areas will begin to disappear.

3. **a.** installment buying—paying for an item over a period of time; credit—borrowing money to pay for an item over time
   b. not embarrassed to buy items on credit
   c. consumers bought more goods; increase in demand and in production

4. **a.** agriculture
   b. European crops; increased competition drove down prices; insects and natural disasters hurt farmers

5. assembly line; growth of industries related to automobile; increased demand for consumer goods, buying on credit; farm problems

6. for—people should enjoy available consumer goods; against—people should save to buy consumer goods, not go into debt

---

Direct Teach

Reading Focus

❹ What were some weak parts of the economy in the 1920s? *farming; land development in Florida*

Weaknesses in the Economy

Identify Why did American agriculture suffer after World War I? *demand dropped; increased competition from Europe hurt American farmers*

Identify Cause and Effect How did low prices for crops affect farmers? *farm failures increased; farmland values and farmers' incomes went down*

Review & Assess

Close

Guide students in a discussion of new processes and products that were introduced in the 1920s and the effects they had on the economy.

Review

📖 Online Quiz, Section 2
📀 Daily Test Practice Transparency

Assess

SE Section 2 Assessment
📋 Progress Assessment: Section 2 Quiz
📋 Alternative Assessment Handbook

Reteach

📋 Interactive Reader and Study Guide, Section 2
💿 Interactive Skills Tutor CD-ROM

Answers

Reading Check *farmers*

Bellringer

The Inside Story. . . Use the **Daily Bellringer Transparency** to help students answer the question.

📖 Daily Bellringer Transparency, Section 3

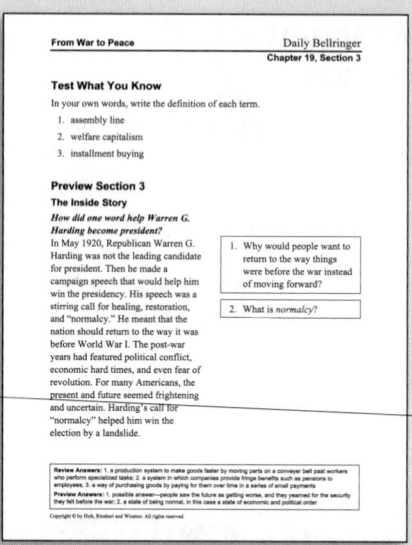

Academic Vocabulary

Review with students the high-use academic terms in this section.

coherent clear and logical (p. 635)

motive reason to take action (p. 636)

📄 CRF: Vocabulary Builder Activity: Section 3

Taking Notes

Harding's Presidency—Fordney-McCumber Tariff, Ohio Gang, Teapot Dome scandal; Coolidge's Presidency—ended corruption scandals, Indian Citizenship Act, promoted business

---

The Harding and Coolidge Presidencies

BEFORE YOU READ

MAIN IDEA

The nation's desire for normalcy and its support for American business was reflected in two successive presidents it chose—Warren G. Harding and Calvin Coolidge.

READING FOCUS

1. What political events and ideas marked the Warren G. Harding presidency?

2. What political events and ideas marked the Calvin Coolidge presidency?

3. What were the lingering effects of World War I on politics in the 1920s?

KEY TERMS AND PEOPLE

Warren G. Harding
Teapot Dome
Calvin Coolidge
reparation
arms race
Charles Evans Hughes
Billy Mitchell
Kellogg-Briand Pact

TAKING NOTES As you read, take notes identifying major events in the presidencies of Harding and Coolidge. Record your notes in a graphic organizer like the one shown here.

Harding's Presidency	Coolidge's Presidency

A New Time and a New PRESIDENT

THE INSIDE STORY

How did one word help Warren G. Harding become president?
The Ohio senator was not known for being an intellectual giant. But behind his appearance of lazy good humor, Warren G. Harding had political smarts. In 1920 he sensed something about the country. He sensed the longing that people have, in times of fear and chaos, for the things that seem familiar and safe. With typical Harding flair, he used a word coined shortly before the Civil War, *normalcy,* rather than the more accepted word *normality.*

Harding was running in the 1920 presidential race when he made a speech in May, in Boston. To recover from World War I, he said, the nation needed healing, restoration, and . . . "normalcy." What did he mean by normalcy? What did it mean to Americans?

People were weary of the great sacrifices they had made during World War I. Soldiers had witnessed unspeakable horrors in the trenches and on the battlefields, and many citizens wondered what the country had gained from

▲ In a 1920 speech, Harding spoke about America's need for "normalcy."

it all. After a year of violent labor conflicts and fears of Communist revolution, with factories and family farms in trouble, normalcy—whatever it meant—sounded good to many Americans.

Democrats made fun of what they called Harding's "pompous phrases." But voters wanted a "return to normalcy" nonetheless. They swept Harding into office and inaugurated a decade of Republican rule. ◾

Teach the Main Idea

At Level

The Harding and Coolidge Presidencies

1. **Teach** Ask students the Reading Focus questions to teach this section.

2. **Apply** Pair students and have each pair create a two-column, two-row chart. Columns should be labeled *Harding* and *Coolidge*. Rows should be labeled *Similarities* and *Differences*. Have students complete the chart comparing the presidential administrations of Warren G. Harding and Calvin Coolidge. **LS Interpersonal, Visual-Spatial**

3. **Review** Draw a large, master chart for students to see. Have students share the information in their charts with the class, and as each similarity or difference is read, write it in the appropriate place on the chart.

4. **Practice/Homework** Have each student write a short analysis of the ways in which Harding's approach to governing affected his administration. **LS Verbal-Linguistic**

📄 Alternative Assessment Handbook, Rubrics 7: Charts; 14: Group Activity

The Harding Presidency

In Marion, Ohio, where newspaper publisher **Warren G. Harding** grew up, people were proud of their small-town values. They did not expect or want the government to solve their problems. They believed in taking care of one another and working hard.

In his political career, however, Harding is not remembered for his work ethic. In fact, his notorious love of leisure produced quite a casual approach to governing. Elected as the U.S. senator from Ohio in 1914, Harding actually skipped more sessions than he attended. He missed historic Senate debates on Prohibition and on women's suffrage. As president, he regarded the job as largely ceremonial and told friends that the job was beyond his skills. On the other hand, his friendly, backslapping manner—and his tendency to avoid taking positions on issues—made him quite popular.

The election of 1920 As Woodrow Wilson's term came to a chaotic end, Republicans knew they had an opportunity to win the White House. At first, Harding was not a leading candidate for his party's nomination. However, he offered a <u>coherent</u> message, one highly appealing to the public. A high point for Harding was inventing the normalcy slogan in his campaign speech in Boston. Harding's candidacy also was aided by the lack of a dominant leader among the Republicans. Theodore Roosevelt, the heart and soul of the party in the early 1900s, had died the year before. Teddy Roosevelt had no clear successor.

Out of this uncertainty, the Republicans named Harding as their candidate. Democrats nominated James Cox, also of Ohio. In the campaign, voters overwhelmingly preferred Harding's vision of normalcy. Harding also helped himself by skillfully avoiding taking a firm stand for or against the League of Nations. The result was a landslide. Harding won more than 60 percent of the vote.

Harding's policies President Harding's answer to the nation's postwar economic troubles was his campaign slogan, "Less government in business and more business in government." To help achieve his pro-business goal, Harding sought to cut the federal budget and to reduce taxes on the wealthiest Americans. Harding and his advisers believed that

ACADEMIC VOCABULARY

coherent clear and logical

PRIMARY SOURCES

Political Cartoon

As the Teapot Dome scandal unfolded, many people began to take a closer look at the illegal activities of the Harding cabinet. This cartoon, titled "Juggernaut," was published in 1924 during the height of the scandal. A "juggernaut" is an indestructible force that crushes everything in its path.

The oil scandal at the heart of Teapot Dome is portrayed as a steamroller.

The steamroller is headed towards the White House.

THE GRANGER COLLECTION, NEW YORK

Skills FOCUS READING LIKE A HISTORIAN

1. **Identifying Points of View** What does the artist's choice of title and imagery say about the power of the scandal?

2. **Making Inferences** What effect does the artist think the scandal might have on the Republican administration?

See **Skills Handbook**, p. H7, H28–H29

Direct Teach

Reading Focus

❶ What political events and ideas marked the Warren G. Harding presidency? *pro-business policies; Fordney-McCumber Tariff; Teapot Dome Scandal*

The Harding Presidency

Recall How did Harding's tendency to avoid taking positions on issues affect his presidency? *made him popular*

Analyze In what way did the Fordney-McCumber Tariff backfire? *made it harder for Europeans to pay war debts*

Evaluate Considering Harding's position about business and government, should the Teapot Dome scandal have been a surprise? *possible answers— Yes, bribes are never acceptable; no, the administration's pro-business attitude created a climate in which scandals could happen.*

CRF: Biography: Robert La Follette

U.S. History Political Cartoon Activity: Cartoon 38: Harding's Bid for Reelection

go.hrw.com

Online Resources

KEYWORD: SD7 CH19
TOPIC: WARREN G. HARDING

Collaborative Learning

At Level

The Teapot Dome Scandal

1. Organize the class into small groups. Have students plan a documentary about the Teapot Dome scandal. They should look for the following information: maps showing the location of Teapot Dome; how the naval oil reserves came to be under the Department of the Interior; what transactions took place; the people who participated in the transactions; what happened to the participants after the transactions became known; and what happened to Teapot Dome.

2. Have each group create a graphic storyboard sequencing the major events that they would include in their documentary.

3. Have volunteers from each group present their group's storyboard, providing narration about the events depicted in each graphic.
   LS Interpersonal, Visual-Spatial

   Alternative Assessment Handbook, Rubrics 3: Artwork; 14: Group Activity; and 30: Research

Answers

Reading Like a Historian 1. *possible answer—Anyone in the way of the steam roller will get caught; people are trying to get out of the way as the steam roller makes its way into the White House;* **2.** *The scandal will touch everyone in the administration.*

The Harding Presidency

Identify Name three respected members of Harding's cabinet and the positions they filled. *Andrew Mellon, Secretary of the Treasury; Charles Evans Hughes, Secretary of State; Herbert Hoover, Secretary of Commerce*

Summarize Why did the Teapot Dome incident cause a scandal? *Secretary of the Interior Albert Fall accepted bribes in return for allowing oil companies to drill on federally owned land.*

Info to Know

Harding Asks for Advice When rumors of the Teapot Dome scandal reached him, President Harding asked Secretary of Commerce Herbert Hoover for advice: "If you knew of a great scandal in our administration, would you for the good of the country and the party expose it publicly or would you bury it?" Hoover urged him to make the scandal public, but Harding was worried about how it would affect his political career.

Answers

Faces of History *mother died when he was a child; had to work on family farm and go to school; failed his first college entrance exam*

Reading Check *to create a climate in which business could prosper, with little government interference*

---

it was the wealthy who started and expanded businesses. By taxing them less, the thinking went, business would grow and pull the nation out of the hard times.

To farmers, Harding offered little. He did sign the high Fordney-McCumber Tariff soon after taking office. His <u>motive</u> was to help American farmers by raising the cost of foreign-grown farm products. As the costs for foreign products rose, so did the prices for American products. This helped U.S. farmers in the short term. Yet it also hurt Europeans by making it harder for them to pay back war debts.

The tariff was the only measure Harding would take to help American agriculture. "The farmer," he said, "requires no special favors at the hands of government."

ACADEMIC VOCABULARY

motive reason to take action

Scandal and sudden death Whatever he lacked in governing skills, Harding attempted to compensate for by appointing highly skilled people to his cabinet. One of his most gifted and respected advisers was Treasury Secretary Andrew Mellon, a multimillionaire business person and philanthropist. Mellon proceeded to reform the nation's tax system during more than a decade in the office. Harding's cabinet included two other highly respected men: Secretary of State Charles Evans Hughes and Commerce Secretary Herbert Hoover.

FACES OF HISTORY

Calvin & Grace COOLIDGE
1872–1933 and 1879–1957

When Calvin Coolidge was only 12 years old, his mother died. Coolidge had to take over many duties on the family farm while going to school. He had another setback when he failed a college entrance exam. He studied hard and finally passed. Coolidge's determination helped him rise in politics from city council member in Northampton, Massachusetts, to president of the United States.

Grace Coolidge's warm, outgoing personality greatly benefited her husband's political career. As first lady, Grace had a striking memory for names and faces. She enjoyed entertaining artists, actors, and writers at the White House. Grace's colorful personality was a welcome contrast to Calvin's quiet demeanor.

Summarize What challenges did Calvin Coolidge overcome?

Unfortunately, not all of Harding's choices were so wise. He named a number of old friends from Ohio to lower-level government posts. Some members of this so-called Ohio Gang were later convicted of taking bribes.

The worst Harding-era scandal involved Secretary of the Interior Albert Fall. Fall accepted bribes in return for allowing oil companies to drill federal oil reserves on a piece of federal land known as **Teapot Dome** in Wyoming. Fall was eventually convicted and sent to jail.

Harding was never found to be personally connected to Teapot Dome or the Ohio Gang incidents, and he did not live to see their effects. Distressed by the rumors of scandals, Harding and his wife took a trip to Alaska.

While giving a speech in Seattle at the end of his trip, Harding collapsed. His doctor first diagnosed indigestion. The *New York Times* reassured readers "Harding . . . Rallies From a Slight Indigestion." He had, however, suffered a heart attack. Harding himself expressed concern. "I am worn out," he told his sister at the Palace Hotel in San Francisco, "can't stand the heavy responsibilities and physical work too." In bed that evening, he shuddered and died.

At the time of his death, Harding's popularity was high. Over time, however, the corruption of his administration and Harding's own failings soured his reputation.

READING CHECK **Drawing Conclusions** What was Harding's goal with regard to business when he became president?

The Coolidge Presidency

"I was awakened by my father coming up the stairs calling my name. I noticed his voice trembled," **Calvin Coolidge** later recalled. To the vice president and the whole country, the news of Harding's death was a shock.

Coolidge received the message after he had gone to bed on the evening of August 2. He walked across town to the nearest telephone to call Secretary of State Charles Evans Hughes, who urged Coolidge to take the oath of office. In the early hours of the morning, by the light of an oil lamp, John Coolidge, a notary public, administered the oath of office to his son, John Calvin Coolidge—now the thirtieth president of the United States.

Skills Focus: Analyzing Primary Sources   At Level

Reading Like a Historian Skill
Working Together

Background When Warren G. Harding accepted the Republican nomination, he called for cooperation between industry and workers: "I want the employers in industry to understand the aspirations, the convictions, the yearnings of the millions of American wage-earners, and I want the wage-earners to understand the problems, the anxieties, the obligations of management and capital, and all of them must understand their relationship to the people and

their obligation to the republic . . . I am speaking as one who has counted the contents of the pay envelope from the viewpoint of the earner as well as the employer."

Have students explain Harding's last sentence. How does this qualify him to say what he says? Do Harding's policies reflect his call for cooperation? **S Verbal-Linguistic**

Alternative Assessment Handbook, Rubric 11: Discussions

American Civil Liberty

Native Americans and Citizenship

President Coolidge (left) poses with members of the Blackfoot nation.

Citizenship and voting rights have expanded throughout U.S. history. By 1869 nearly everyone born in the United States, except Native Americans, was a citizen.

The 1887 Dawes Act granted citizenship to some Native Americans, and the Indian Naturalization Act, passed in 1890, allowed Indians to apply for citizenship. In 1901 Congress granted citizenship to Native Americans living on reservations in Oklahoma.

At this time, possibly one-third of Native Americans were not U.S. citizens. In spite of this, thousands of Indians served in the U.S. military during World War I or supported the war effort at home. Still it was not until 1924 when President Coolidge signed the Indian Citizenship Act, that all Indians born in the United States were granted citizenship.

Sequencing What steps did Congress take toward granting citizenship to all Native Americans?

Coolidge's background The Coolidges' rural Vermont home was modest. Calvin Coolige's father ran a store and was active in the local Republican Party. These two interests, business and politics, would stick with Calvin Coolidge throughout his life.

After graduating from college in Amherst, Massachusetts, Coolidge took up law and politics, working his way up the ranks of the Republican Party. Elected governor of Massachusetts in 1918, he achieved national fame for his role in the Boston police strike, as you read in Section 1. The event ignited Coolidge's national career, earning him the vice presidential slot on the 1920 Republican ticket with Harding.

Coolidge in office Coolidge's reputation for honesty helped him deal with the erupting Harding administration scandals. He quickly got rid of officials suspected of corruption. His success overcoming the scandals was proven when he easily defeated Democrat John W. Davis in the 1924 election.

Coolidge's presidency was characterized by his unshakable faith in the power of business and industry. "Those who build a factory build a temple of worship," he said. "Those who work in the factory, worship there."

Business, he believed, would provide the energy and resources to fuel America's growth. Business would promote the arts and sciences. It would fund charities to help society.

The president's faith in the positive power of business was matched by his strong belief that the role of government should be strictly limited. Government, he thought, did not produce things of value and only took away resources that could be used to build businesses. Coolidge believed in lowering taxes and reducing the federal budget. In fact, there were no major budget increases between 1923 and 1929.

One observer noted Coolidge's "active inactivity." Indeed, the president proposed few laws or policies. Among his chief initiatives were efforts to stop congressional plans to help farmers. He also vetoed a bill to provide a bonus to World War I veterans. The costs, he felt, were too great. Coolidge also worked to weaken regulations on industry.

Coolidge the man Serious and straightforward, Coolidge was known as "Silent Cal." He hated small talk, although he did enjoy playing practical jokes on White House staff. His style—and the fairly good times of his era—made him popular at the time.

In his quiet, no-nonsense fashion, Coolidge stunned the nation as the presidential election of 1928 approached. While on vacation he declared, "I do not choose to run for President in 1928."

READING CHECK **Comparing** How did Coolidge's basic beliefs compare to Harding's?

FROM WAR TO PEACE **637**

Reading Focus

❷ What political events and ideas marked the Calvin Coolidge presidency? *pro-business policies; limited government regulation of business and industry*

The Coolidge Presidency

Identify What did Coolidge see as the driving force in the growth and development of the nation? *business*

Explain How was Calvin Coolidge able to avoid being tainted by the scandals that had surfaced in the Harding administration? *Coolidge had a reputation for honesty; he worked quickly to get rid of those in government suspected of wrongdoing.*

American Civil Liberty

Native Americans and Citizenship

In the 1920s Native Americans successfully organized to fight the Harding administration's attempt to buy back all tribal land.

Evaluate Do you think the Harding administration would have tried to gain control of all tribal land if Native Americans had been citizens? Why or why not? *possible answer—No, because Native Americans would have then had equal rights under the law.*

Collaborative Learning   **Below Level**

Presidential Campaign '24

Materials construction paper, colored markers, scissors, glue

1. Organize the class into small groups. Have each group write an outline for a platform for Calvin Coolidge's re-election campaign. Have students use material from the section on "The Coolidge Presidency" to create their platforms. *Platforms should indicate that Coolidge will work to limit the damage from the scandals; will restore the reputation of the presidency; will promote pro-business*

policies, promote arts and sciences; fund charities. Coolidge will also limit the role of government.

2. Have each group create campaign buttons, posters, and slogans for the 1924 presidential election using ideas from their platforms.

3. Have volunteers from each group share their platforms and campaign materials with the class. **LS Interpersonal, Visual-Spatial**

📖 Alternative Assessment Handbook, Rubrics 2: Advertisements; and 14: Group Activity

American Civil Liberty *1901, U.S. citizenship granted to Native Americans living on reservations in Oklahoma; 1924, citizenship granted to all Native Americans born in U.S.*

Reading Check *beliefs about business, limited government, taxes, and the federal budget were very similar*

637

❸ What were the lingering effects of World War I on politics in the 1920s? *U.S. had to loan money to Germany; U.S. navy reduced in size; Kellogg-Briand Pact signed*

The Lingering Effects of World War I

Recall What was the purpose of the Washington Naval Conference of 1921? *head off an arms race; try to prevent another war*

Explain How did lending money to Germany indirectly benefit the United States after World War I? *helped Germany pay its war debt to the Allies so they could pay their war debts to the U.S.*

Make Judgments Do you think most Americans of the time agreed with Hughes's comment about the agreement reached at the Naval Conference? *possible answer—Yes, Americans were optimistic, and no one wanted another war.*

🗄 Quick Facts Transparency: Effects of World War I

The Past is Behind Us
The Future is Ahead
Let us all strive to
make the future
better and brighter
than the past ever was.

U.S. DEPARTMENT OF LABOR
W.B. WILSON
Secretary of Labor

This 1918 poster expressed the hope of many Americans that postwar life would soon return to normal.

The Lingering Effects of World War I

The fighting on the battlefields of World War I ended in 1918, yet the war's effects on national and international politics endured throughout a whole generation and several presidencies. The fight over Wilson's peace plans and the League of Nations consumed the final years of Wilson's presidency. Other questions about the peace played a major role in 1920s politics.

The question of war debt During World War I, the warring nations of Europe had borrowed more than $10 billion from the United States. Americans expected that, when the fighting stopped, the Europeans would repay the money. For the war-torn nations of Europe, this proved very difficult.

The high Fordney-McCumber Tariff made the task that much harder. Europeans had trouble selling their goods in the United States and so could not earn the dollars they needed to pay off their debts. Instead, countries turned to Germany and demanded that it pay extremely high **reparations**, or payments designed to make up for the damage of the war.

Germany was unable to pay what the Allies demanded. This, in turn, left the Allies unable to pay off their war debts. To solve this problem, the United States began to lend money to Germany. In this way, the United States assumed the role of banker to Europe. The loans continued throughout the 1920s, until the German reparations were sharply reduced.

The Washington Naval Conference Peacetime brought considerable public pressure to reduce the size of U.S. armed forces to save money and reduce the threat of war. On the other hand, people feared that the naval powers of the world, especially Great Britain and Japan, were on the verge of a naval arms race. In an **arms race**, competing nations build more and more weapons in an effort to avoid one nation gaining a clear advantage.

Hoping to head off an arms race, the U.S. government organized the Washington Naval Conference in 1921. The major naval powers of the world were invited. At the conference, the parties agreed to cut back sharply on the size of their navies. Countries actually scrapped existing ships and some that were under construction. The conference also led to agreement

Differentiating Instruction

Below Level

English-Language Learners

1. Pair students and have each pair create a flow chart showing how the Fordney-McCumber Tariff, war debts, and reparations affected the United States. *Tariff made it difficult for the Allies to sell their goods in the U.S.; without the revenues from these sales, Allies could not earn money they needed to pay their war debts to the U.S. To make their payments, the Allies demanded harsh reparations from Germany. Germany was unable to pay what the Allies demanded. This left the Allies unable to pay off their war debts. To solve this problem, the U.S. began to lend money to Germany.*

2. As an extension, have students write a letter describing the effect of war debts and reparations on European countries. Students should express their opinions and feelings about the situation in Europe in their letters.
LS Interpersonal, Visual-Spatial

📖 Alternative Assessment Handbook, Rubrics 6: Cause and Effect; and 40: Writing to Describe

on several issues that threatened world peace. These included plans to avoid competition among the world's military powers for the control of China.

Many Americans considered the conference a great success. Secretary of State **Charles Evans Hughes** reported, "We are taking perhaps the greatest forward step in history to establish the reign of peace." As you will read, however, it would not be long before world tensions were rising and nations were again building ships of war.

Billy Mitchell argues for air power

While the United States was scuttling some of its fleet, Brigadier General **Billy Mitchell** was arguing that the United States should invest more in building up its air power. Mitchell had commanded the U.S. air combat operations in World War I. He was a firm believer in the military potential of aircraft.

To demonstrate his point, Mitchell conducted tests in which he used planes to sink two battleships. This, Mitchell thought, proved the superiority of air power over naval power. Other military officials were not convinced. Mitchell's confrontational style hurt him. He was eventually punished for accusing them of "almost treasonable administration of the national defense." He left the military and continued to promote air power until his death in the 1930s.

The Kellogg-Briand Pact

Though the United States had refused to join the League of Nations, a strong interest remained in preventing another catastrophic war. So, when the French proposed a treaty with the United States that would outlaw war between two nations, the United States responded with a bigger idea. Secretary of State Frank Kellogg proposed an agreement that would involve many countries.

The **Kellogg-Briand Pact** was the result. It stated the following:

HISTORY'S VOICES

> 66 The High Contracting Parties solemnly declare in the names of their respective peoples that they condemn recourse to war for the solution of international controversies, and renounce it, as an instrument of national policy in their relations with one another. 99

—Kellogg-Briand Pact, Article I, 1928

In a world where war had raged across continents throughout human history—a world that had viewed war as a necessity, even a game—the pact represented a high ideal. More than 60 nations signed on. Yet the pact had no system for enforcement. The only thing holding nations to their promise was their word. As you will read, that would not be enough.

READING CHECK **Summarizing** How did America demonstrate its wish to disarm in the 1920s?

THE IMPACT TODAY

Science and Technology
Today the U.S. Air Force is central to the nation's military capability and security. Air power has been a decisive factor in military conflicts such as Afghanistan and Iraq.

SECTION 3 ASSESSMENT

go.hrw.com
Online Quiz
Keyword: SD7 HP19

Reviewing Ideas, Terms, and People

1. **a. Identify** What was Teapot Dome?
   b. Analyze What do you think Harding meant when he said that the United States needed "normalcy"?
   c. Evaluate Why do you think so many voters were drawn to Harding's message of normalcy and a return to values of the past?

2. **a. Recall** Why is Calvin Coolidge known as "Silent Cal"?
   b. Compare How did Coolidge's policies compare to those of Harding?
   c. Rank Who do you think would have had a more positive impression of Coolidge: a farmer or a business owner? Explain.

3. **a. Define** Write a brief definition for the following term: reparation
   b. Make Inferences Why do you think Billy Mitchell was unable to get a strong commitment to air power in the 1920s?

c. Evaluate Why do you think the United States signed the Kellogg-Briand Pact but did not join the League of Nations?

Critical Thinking

4. **Sequencing** Copy the chart below, using information from the chapter to complete the diagram.

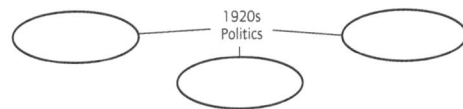
1920s Politics

FOCUS ON WRITING

5. **Persuasive** Write a memo to the president in which you argue for or against the agreements made in the Washington Naval Conference.

FROM WAR TO PEACE **639**

639

Tactics of the Red Scare

Word Help

belfry bell tower

aliens foreign-born residents of a country who have not yet become citizens

nice precise

Info to Know

ACLU In response to Attorney General Palmer's restraints on civil liberties, the American Civil Liberties Union (ACLU) was formed in 1920. Roger Baldwin and other social reformers, such as Clarence Darrow, Jane Addams, and Helen Keller, created the group as an extension of the American Union Against Militarism, an organization that sought amnesty for conscientious objectors during World War I. In working to protect the civil liberties guaranteed in the Bill of Rights, the ACLU has initiated some of the most influential court cases of the twentieth century. Currently, the ACLU has 400,000 members and over 300 chapters across the nation.

Info to Know

IWW In 1905 representatives of 43 trade unions met in Chicago to found the Industrial Workers of the World (IWW), an organization aimed at including all industrial workers. The IWW reached its peak between 1912 and 1917, with 60,000 to 100,000 members, or "Wobblies." After the Red Scare of 1920, membership dwindled and the IWW no longer played a significant role in the labor movement.

Tactics of the Red Scare

Historical Context The documents below provide several different perspectives on the U.S. government's actions during the Red Scare.

Task Examine the documents and answer the questions that follow. Then, you will be asked to write an essay about the government's tactics during the Red Scare, using facts from the documents and from the chapter to support the position you take in your thesis statement.

DOCUMENT 1

Attorney General A. Mitchell Palmer led the government's attack on suspected radicals. He was one of several public officials who had been targeted by bombs suspected of being sent by violent radicals. Among his more controversial policies was the jailing or deportation of people for speech or writings that might lend support for radical actions. In the following magazine article, he explained why people should be arrested for speech, not just actions, against the government.

> Like a prairie-fire, the blaze of revolution was sweeping over every American institution of law and order a year ago. It was eating its way into the homes of the American workman, its sharp tongues or revolutionary heat were licking the altars of the churches, leaping into the belfry of the school bell, crawling into the sacred corners of American homes ... burning up the foundations of society. ...
>
> Upon these two basic certainties, first that the "Reds" were criminal aliens, and secondly that the American Government must prevent crime, it was decided that there could be no nice distinctions between the theoretical ideals of the radicals and their actual violations of our national laws. ... Any theory which excuses crime is not wanted in America.

DOCUMENT 2

Not all government officials supported the tactics used to crackdown on suspected Communists. Georgia Senator Thomas W. Hardwick had also been a target of radical bombings. He, his wife, and a maid had all been injured when a mailed bomb exploded in his home. Although Hardwick supported tightening some immigration laws to keep suspected radicals out of the country, he spoke out against Red Scare laws aimed mainly at weakening the power of labor unions, especially the Industrial Workers of the World (IWW). Laws against radical speech were often used against union members who criticized anything about the capitalist system.

> I understand that the real, in fact practically the only, object of this [legislation] is to get some men called I.W.W.'s who are operating in a few of the Northwestern states, and you Senators from those states have been exceedingly solicitous [concerned] to have legislation of this kind enacted ... I dislike to be confronted by a situation in which in the name of patriotism we are asked to justify the fundamental rights and liberties of 100,000,000 American people in order to meet a situation in a few Northwestern states."

Skills Focus: Making Oral Presentations   At Level

Reading Like a Historian Skill
Limiting Free Speech

1. Divide the class into two groups. Have one half represent supporters of Attorney General Palmer's policies of jailing or deporting people for speech or writings that might lend support to radical actions. Have the other half represent supporters of Senator Hardwick's view that laws that limited speech were a violation of the fundamental rights and liberties of American citizens. Have each side prepare supporting arguments for its position.

2. Conduct a classroom debate between members of the opposing sides.

3. Have each student write a one-page paper telling which position he or she would personally take and why. **LS Logical-Mathematical, Verbal-Linguistic**

    Alternative Assessment Handbook, Rubric 10: Debates

DOCUMENT 3

This political cartoon refers to the deportation of alien radicals that occurred in December 1919. The ship, the USS *Buford*, pictured in the cartoon, was nicknamed the "Soviet Ark." The bear in the lower left hand corner was a feature that the artist Clifford K. Berryman used in all his cartoons.

A. Mitchell Palmer and J. Edgar Hoover spent four months rounding up alleged alien radicals and others for deportation. In the end, fewer than 300 of the thousands detained were deported. Because they were not citizens, aliens could be deported without a trial or indictment. Most, but not all, of those deported were members of the Union of Russia Workers and supported the Bolshevik revolution in Russia. Emma Goldman, a well known radical and publisher of *Mother Earth* magazine, was among those deported.

Primary Source

Emma Goldman arrived in the Soviet Union expecting to find a new, liberated society. After less than two years, she left, determined to share with the world the harsh political and economic conditions she had witnessed: "All my life I fed on the wonderful spirit of Russia, then to have found it prostrate, kicked into the gutter, attacked on all sides, enduring tortures Dante's inferno did not contain. Above all, stabbed in the heart by its own friends. And then not to be able to help even a little bit . . . but it was impossible."

Skills FOCUS: READING LIKE A HISTORIAN

1. **a. Describe** Refer to Document 1. To what does Palmer compare the spread of revolution in the United States?
   b. Analyze What is his main justification for the jailing of people for speech?

2. **a. Identify** Refer to Document 2. What region of the country does Hardwick argue will be affected the most from Red Scare laws targeted at labor?
   b. Analyze Why does Hardwick oppose such laws?

3. **a. Identify** Refer to Document 3. How does the cartoonist depict the people on the boat?

   b. Interpret What is the message the cartoonist is trying to send?

4. **Document-Based Essay Question** Consider the question below and form a thesis statement. Using examples from Documents 1, 2, and 3, create an outline and write a short essay supporting your position.
   Were the Red Scare policies of the U.S. government appropriate responses to fears of a Bolshevik revolution?

See Skills Handbook, p. H28–H29, H31

FROM WAR TO PEACE **641**

Collaborative Learning

At Level

The Voyage of the *Buford*

1. Divide the class into groups of four or five students. Have each group develop a project to help them learn more about the voyage of the *Buford*. Some ideas for projects might include pretending to be a reporter covering the deportation, writing diary entries from the point of view of deportees, or writing a script for a play about the deportation.

2. Have each group submit its project idea for approval before beginning work. If necessary, help students fine-tune their ideas.

3. Have each group work on its project, conducting additional research if necessary.

4. Have each group to present its project to the class. **LS Interpersonal**

Answers

Reading Like a Historian
1. a. *a "prairie-fire";* **b.** *that the U.S. government must prevent crime and that there is no difference between ideas and actions;* **2. a.** *the Northwest;* **b.** *He dislikes curbing the rights of all Americans because of problems created by a few people.* **3. a.** *as a gift from the U.S. to Russia;* **b.** *possible answer—that the U.S. is getting rid of the people it does not want by sending them to Russia;* **4.** *possible answers—no, they violated First Amendment rights of all Americans; yes, necessary to protect American government from potential threat*

Answers

Visual Summary

Review and Inquiry Have students write at least one sentence explaining the significance of each illustration in the visual summary.

🖼️ Quick Facts Transparency: From War to Peace

Reviewing Key Terms and People

1. Red Scare
2. credit
3. Warren G. Harding
4. reparations
5. Calvin Coolidge
6. assembly line
7. Bolsheviks
8. deportation
9. Henry Ford
10. Teapot Dome

Comprehension and Critical Thinking

11. a. the Red Scare, labor strikes, immigration restrictions, rise of the Ku Klux Klan
b. slowing economy, exaggerated newspaper accounts, Palmer raids, low wages, unemployment
c. distrust of foreigners, fear that immigrants were taking jobs and promoting the overthrow of the government

12. a. assembly line—goods could be produced quickly and cheaply; welfare capitalism—companies provided fringe benefits to factory workers to help offset low wages and keep unions out; installment buying—consumers were able to buy factory-made goods that they could not have afforded without using credit
b. Agriculture suffered; crop prices were low, insects and natural disasters contributed to farming problems.
c. Consumers could buy appliances and autos on credit, creating new demands and increasing factory productivity. Consumers' need for jobs and better wages to pay off their growing debt would become a problem.

Visual Summary: From War to Peace

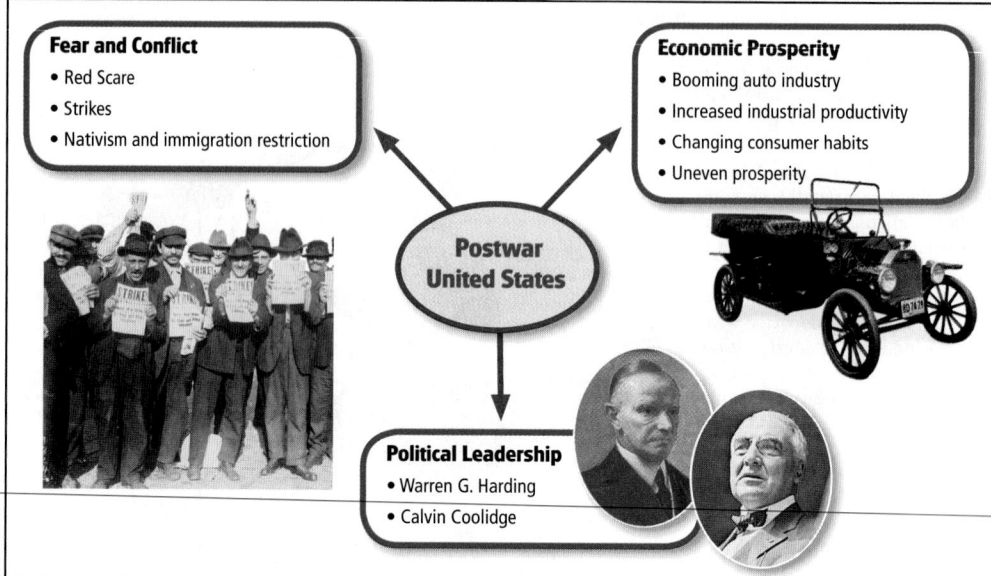

Fear and Conflict
- Red Scare
- Strikes
- Nativism and immigration restriction

Economic Prosperity
- Booming auto industry
- Increased industrial productivity
- Changing consumer habits
- Uneven prosperity

Postwar United States

Political Leadership
- Warren G. Harding
- Calvin Coolidge

Reviewing Key Terms and People

Complete each sentence by filling the blank with the correct term or person.

1. Following World War I, a heightened fear of radicals, or a _____ , gripped the nation.
2. Increasingly, consumers in the 1920s paid for purchases with _____ rather than with cash.
3. _____ became president in 1920 by promising a return to normalcy.
4. The United States government helped Germany pay its high _____ .
5. Vice President _____ skillfully avoided being tainted by the scandals of the Harding administration.
6. The _____ allowed cars to be made in large numbers and at a relatively low cost.
7. The _____ wanted to establish a new social system in their country and in the world.

8. A. Mitchell Palmer's raids led to the _____ of many aliens.
9. _____'s dream was to build a car that the average American could afford.
10. Harding's secretary of the interior was involved in a scandal over a place called _____ .

Calvin Coolidge
Bolsheviks
deportation
Teapot Dome
Henry Ford
credit
Warren G. Harding
reparations
assembly line
Red Scare

13. a. Warren G. Harding; Calvin Coolidge
b. low business taxes; limited government involvement in and regulation of business
c. They did not support labor strikes or violent labor actions; believed that businesses would fuel the nation's growth, that business would fund charities to help the needy.

History's Impact video program
Review the video to answer the closing question:
How did American women win the right to vote?

Comprehension and Critical Thinking

SECTION 1 *(pp. 622–627)*

11. a. Describe What are some examples of postwar havoc in the United States?

b. Summarize What factors contributed to the postwar havoc?

c. Evaluate Why do you think many Americans reacted to the difficulties of the postwar years by targeting immigrants?

SECTION 2 *(pp. 628–633)*

12. a Describe Describe the significance of the following terms in the 1920s economy: assembly line, welfare capitalism, installment buying.

b. Compare How did the economic performance of agriculture compare to that of industry in the 1920s?

c. Evaluate What was the role of consumer credit in the expansion of the 1920s economy, and why might this pose a problem in the future?

SECTION 3 *(pp. 634–639)*

13. a. Recall Who were the two U.S. presidents who served between 1920 and 1928?

b. Make Generalizations What kind of relationship did the American political leaders of the 1920s promote between business and government?

c. Evaluate Why do you think many people in the United States were so willing to support the pro-business policies of the federal government in the 1920s?

Using the Internet

go.hrw.com
Practice Online
Keyword: SD7 CH19

14. The decade after World War I was a turbulent one. Americans feared the spread of communism. They also were experiencing many political, social, and economic changes at home. Using the keyword above, do research to learn about the changes that were occuring in the United States during the years 1919–1928. Then create a report that describes how political, social, and economic forces combined to create such a sense of uneasiness in the decade after World War I.

Analyzing Primary Sources

Reading Like a Historian
The vacuum cleaner was one of the many new products sold to consumers, often on installment plans, in the 1920s.

15. Identify Who was the primary audience for this advertisement?

16. Analyze Based on the woman's facial expression in the ad, what do you think the ad is claiming the vacuum cleaner will do?

Critical Reading

Read the passage in Section 1 that begins with the heading "American Reaction." Then answer the questions that follow.

17. According to the passage, the fear of Reds in the United States was a continuation of

A wartime prosperity.

B the fight over the League of Nations.

C hatred of "the Hun."

D the rise of labor.

18. In the fourth paragraph of the passage, the text reads, "Some of their members promoted the violent overthrow of the government." In this sentence, the word *promoted* means

A opposed.　　**C** achieved.

B stopped.　　**D** advocated.

 FOCUS ON WRITING

Expository Writing *Expository writing gives information, explains why or how, or defines a process. To practice expository writing, follow the directions below.*

Writing Topic The impact of the assembly line

19. Assignment Based on what you have read in this chapter, write a paragraph that explains how Ford's assembly line revolutionized the automobile industry and other industries.

Using the Internet

14. Go to the HRW Web site and enter the keyword shown to access a rubric for this activity.

KEYWORD: SD7 CH19

Analyzing Primary Sources

15. middle-class women and families

16. make housework easy and pleasant

Critical Reading

17. C

18. D

Focus on Writing

19. possible answer—Because of the assembly line, cars could be produced inexpensively and quickly. On an assembly line, workers had to learn only one skill. This was a major change from hand-produced items, which required a skilled worker who might be responsible for a piece from its beginning to its final stage. The assembly line quickly spread to other industries, as it saved money, reduced the need for highly skilled workers, and led to increased profits.

A rubric for this activity is provided in the Chapter Resource File: Focus on Writing Activity: The Impact of the Assembly Line

History's Impact Video Program

protests and activism over many years

Review and Assessment Resources

Review and Reinforce

- CRF: Chapter Review Activity
- Quick Facts Transparencies: Effects of World War I; From War to Peace
- Spanish Chapter Summaries Audio CD Program
- Online Chapter Summaries in Spanish
- OSP Holt PuzzlePro; Quiz Show for ExamView
- Quiz Game CD-ROM

Assess

- PASS: Chapter Test, Forms A and B
- Alternative Assessment Handbook
- OSP ExamView Test Generator, Chapter Test
- Differentiated Instruction Modified Worksheets and Tests CD-ROM: Chapter Test
- HOAP Holt Online Assessment Program (in the Premier Online Edition)

Reteach/Intervene

- Interactive Reader and Study Guide
- Differentiated Instruction Teacher Management System: Lesson Plans for Differentiated Instruction
- Differentiated Instruction Modified Worksheets and Tests CD-ROM: Chapter Test
- Interactive Skills Tutor CD-ROM

go.hrw.com
Online Resources
KEYWORD: SD7 CH19

Chapter 20 Planning Guide

The Roaring Twenties

Chapter Overview	Reproducible Resources	Technology Resources
CHAPTER 20 pp. 644–669 **Overview:** In this chapter, students will analyze the rapid and radical change American culture underwent in the 1920s.	**Differentiated Instruction Teacher Management System:*** • Instructional Benchmarking Guides • Lesson Plans for Differentiated Instruction **Interactive Reader and Study Guide:** Chapter Summary* **Chapter Resource File:*** • Interdisciplinary Project: Harlem Renaissance Poetry • Writing for the SAT Activity: The Constitution and Prohibition • Social Studies Skills Activity: Interpreting Pie and Bar Graphs • Chapter Review Activity **American History Outline Maps** **Pre-AP Activities Guide for American History***	**Live Ink® Online Reading Help** **Student Edition on Audio CD Program** **Differentiated Instruction Modified Worksheets and Tests CD-ROM** **Interactive Skills Tutor CD-ROM** **United States History Primary Source Library CD-ROM** **Power Presentations with Video CD-ROM** **History's Impact: American History Video Program (VHS/DVD):** The Roaring Twenties **Online Chapter Summaries in Spanish**
Section 1: **American Life Changes** **The Main Idea:** The United States experienced many social changes during the 1920s.	**Differentiated Instruction Teacher Management System:** Section 1 Lesson Plan* **Interactive Reader and Study Guide:** Section 1 Summary* **Chapter Resource File:*** • Vocabulary Builder Activity, Section 1 • Biography Activity: Alice Paul	**Daily Bellringer Transparency:** Section 1* **Daily Test Practice Transparency:** Section 1* **Internet Activity:** Urbanization
Section 2: **The Harlem Renaissance** **The Main Idea:** Transformations in the African American community contributed to a blossoming of black culture centered in Harlem, New York.	**Differentiated Instruction Teacher Management System:** Section 2 Lesson Plan* **Interactive Reader and Study Guide:** Section 2 Summary* **Chapter Resource File:*** • Vocabulary Builder Activity, Section 2 • Biography Activity: Blues and Jazz: Bessie Smith and Duke Ellington	**Daily Bellringer Transparency:** Section 2* **Map Transparency:** African American Migration, 1910–1920* **Daily Test Practice Transparency:** Section 2* **Internet Activity:** The Harlem Renaissance
Section 3: **A New Popular Culture is Born** **The Main Idea:** New technologies helped produce a new mass culture in the 1920s.	**Differentiated Instruction Teacher Management System:** Section 3 Lesson Plan* **Interactive Reader and Study Guide:** Section 3 Summary* **Chapter Resource File:*** • Vocabulary Builder Activity, Section 3 • Biography Activity: David Sarnoff	**Daily Bellringer Transparency:** Section 3* **Daily Test Practice Transparency:** Section 3* **Internet Activity:** 1920s Culture

HOLT
History's Impact
American History Video Program (VHS/DVD)
The Roaring Twenties

Review, Assessment, Intervention

Quick Facts Transparency: The Roaring Twenties

Spanish Chapter Summaries Audio CD Program

Progress Assessment Support System (PASS):
Chapter Test*

Differentiated Instruction Modified Worksheets and Tests CD-ROM: Modified Chapter Test

OSP One-Stop Planner CD-ROM: ExamView Test Generator (English/Spanish)

HOAP Holt Online Assessment Program (HOAP), in the Holt Premier Online Student Edition

PASS: Section 1 Quiz*

Online Quiz: Section 1

Alternative Assessment Handbook

PASS: Section 2 Quiz*

Online Quiz: Section 2

Alternative Assessment Handbook

PASS: Section 3 Quiz*

Online Quiz: Section 3

Alternative Assessment Handbook

 NC RESOURCES

The following resources were developed to help North Carolina educators teach the standards and objectives of North Carolina's eleventh grade standard course of study in United States history.

- United States history EOC Test Prep Workbook
- Teacher's Support System
- North Carolina One-Stop Planner

And be sure to direct your students to **go.hrw.com** for online access to the EOC Test Prep Workbook.

go.hrw.com
EOC Test Prep
KEYWORD: SE7 NC

Holt Online Learning

go.hrw.com
Teacher Resources
KEYWORD: SD7 TEACHER

go.hrw.com
Student Resources
KEYWORD: SD7 CH20

- Document-based Questions
- Interactive Multimedia Activities

- Current Events
- Chapter-based Internet Activities
- and more!

Holt Premier
Online Student Edition

Complete online support for interactivity, assessment, and reporting

- Interactive Maps and Notebook
- Standardized Test Prep
- Homework Practice and Research Activities Online

CHAPTER 20 PLANNING GUIDE

The Big Picture

Deborah Gray White

American Life Changes The 1920s were marked by enormous social change. The automobile revolutionized social relationships and brought rural and urban America closer together. Women got the vote and the entrance of women into the labor force fueled their changing roles. The social changes of the era were resisted by some who feared the erosion of religion and traditional American values like hard work and self-reliance; this resistance to change was marked in part by the rise of racism and fundamentalism, and support of Prohibition. The government waged an unsuccessful war against the criminal empires that Prohibition gave rise to.

The Harlem Renaissance The call for workers in the war industries prompted the move of African Americans out of the South. Like many immigrants, African American migrants moved to the North for greater freedom and economic opportunity. Harlem, the home of the NAACP and its rival organization, Marcus Garvey's Universal Negro Improvement Association, became the unofficial capital of the black political world. The congregation of so many artists, musicians, poets, performers, and novelists in Harlem also made it the center of black cultural production.

A New Popular Culture is Born New types of entertainment both enriched and changed American culture. Use of the radio expanded when music was added to the airwaves. Technological advances, including the addition of sound, expanded the movie industry and gave rise to a new class of celebrities—movie stars. Americans gained new heroes like Charles Lindbergh and Amelia Earhart, and new artists, whose creativity spawned new novels, poetry, and music for Americans to consume.

Recent Scholarship

The Modern Temper: American Culture and Society in the 1920s (1995), Lynn Dumenil's synthesis of this anxious decade, dislodges the notion that it was one of gaiety. In addition to the rural/urban, fundamentalist/liberal divides, Dumenil takes a close look at the different ways the working and middle-classes consumed. She argues that changing sexual mores and gender roles were not easily accepted, nor did corporate America easily reconcile itself with worker autonomy. Her inclusion of minorities, including Japanese, Chinese, Catholics, Jews, Mexicans, and African Americans, makes this narrative a standout.

Differentiating Instruction

 Differentiated Instruction Teacher Management System
- Lesson Plans for Differentiated Instruction
- Differentiated Instructional Benchmarking Guides
- Interactive Reader and Study Guide

 Spanish Chapter Summaries Audio CD Program

Online Chapter Summaries in Spanish

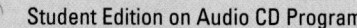 Student Edition on Audio CD Program

 Differentiated Instruction Modified Worksheets and Tests CD-ROM
- Vocabulary Flash Cards
- Modified Vocabulary Builder Activities
- Modified Chapter Review Activity
- Modified Chapter Test

OSP One-Stop Planner CD-ROM
- ExamView Test Generator (English and Spanish)
- PuzzlePro
- Quiz Show for ExamView
- Transparencies and Videos

TE Differentiated Activities in the Teacher's Edition
- Changes in Rural & Urban Areas, p. 649
- History of NAACP, p. 656
- Lindbergh's Accomplishment, p. 662

Reading Like a Historian
Sam Wineburg

Reading the Silences

There have been many views on the prosecution of John T. Scopes, the sandy-haired science teacher from Dayton, Tennessee. Some commentators cast the trial as a showdown between the forces of progressivism and rationalism, embodied by Clarence Darrow, against the weight of tradition and down-home common sense, characterized by the "Great Communicator," William Jennings Bryan. Others see it as a conflict between local control and outside meddling. Shelves of books have been written about the "trial of the century." The case even served as the basis for director Stanley Kramer's 1960 American classic film "Inherit the Wind," whose title was taken from Proverbs 11:29: "He that troubleth his own house shall inherit the wind."

At the time, the trial dominated press coverage and became the first in American history to be broadcast live over a national radio network. Possibly more has been written about the Scopes trial than any other in American history. Everyone, it seems, has weighed in.

Overlooked Perspectives

It is in such instances that historians engage in a practice known as "reading the silences." Given this cacophony of perspectives, historians ask, are there any that have been hidden, silenced, or systematically overlooked?

According to the 1920 census, one in every five Tennesseans was black. At first glance, the issue of race does not seem to play any part in our story. In Frederick Lewis Allen's *Only Yesterday*, the best-selling book about the 1920s read by millions of Americans, the Scopes trial is featured prominently, but race fits nowhere in the telling. Not only is race not part of our chapter's narrative of the trial but it is largely absent from the historical writing about the case. Yet, as University of Kansas historian Jeffrey Moran shows

in *The Scopes Trial, a Brief History with Documents* (2002), black newspapers of the day interpreted the trial like few others. According to their editorials, the effort to ban the teaching of evolution had at its core a racial motive. How so?

Race and the Scopes Trial

According to the *Chicago Defender*, which by World War I had become America's most influential black weekly with a circulation over 100,000, at the heart of white Tennessee's opposition to evolution was the Darwinian notion that all humans come from the same common ancestor. "Admit that premise," claimed a *Chicago Defender* editorial writer, "and they will have to admit that there is no fundamental difference between themselves and the race they pretend to despise." This stance was echoed by the white journalist W. J. Cash, an observer at the trial and the author of *The Mind of the South* (1941): "One of the most stressed notions which went around was that evolution made a Negro as good as a white man—that is, threatened White Supremacy."

Another theme noted by the black press: the hypocrisy of the white establishment, which on one hand bristled at the notion of being associated with animals, but on the other hand, engaged in inhumane behavior with reckless abandon. A cartoon in the June 20, 1925 *Chicago Defender* showed two monkeys frightfully grasping each other on a limb, while observing a raucous crowd gathered around a dangling body at a lynching. "Joe," one monkey, aghast, says to the other, "do you believe fiends like those are descendants of ours?"

For African Americans during the 1920s—a time of lynchings, Jim Crow, and institutional racism—this trial was anything but a laughing matter.

From *The Mind of the South* by W. J. Cash. Published by Alfred A. Knopf, a division of Random House, Inc., 1941.

BEFORE YOU TEACH

Standards Focus

Social Studies Competency Goals
Goal 9 The learner will appraise the economic, social, and political changes of the decades of "The Twenties" and "The Thirties."

 **9.03, 9.04**

The Big Idea and Essential Questions

To foster student understanding of this chapter's big idea, design your lesson to address each section's essential question.

Big Idea American culture underwent dramatic changes in the 1920s as large population shifts and new technologies transformed the nation from rural to urban and from traditional to modern.

Essential Questions

1. What kinds of social changes did the United States experience in the 1920s?

2. What was the significance of the Harlem Renaissance?

3. How did a new mass culture arise in the 1920s?

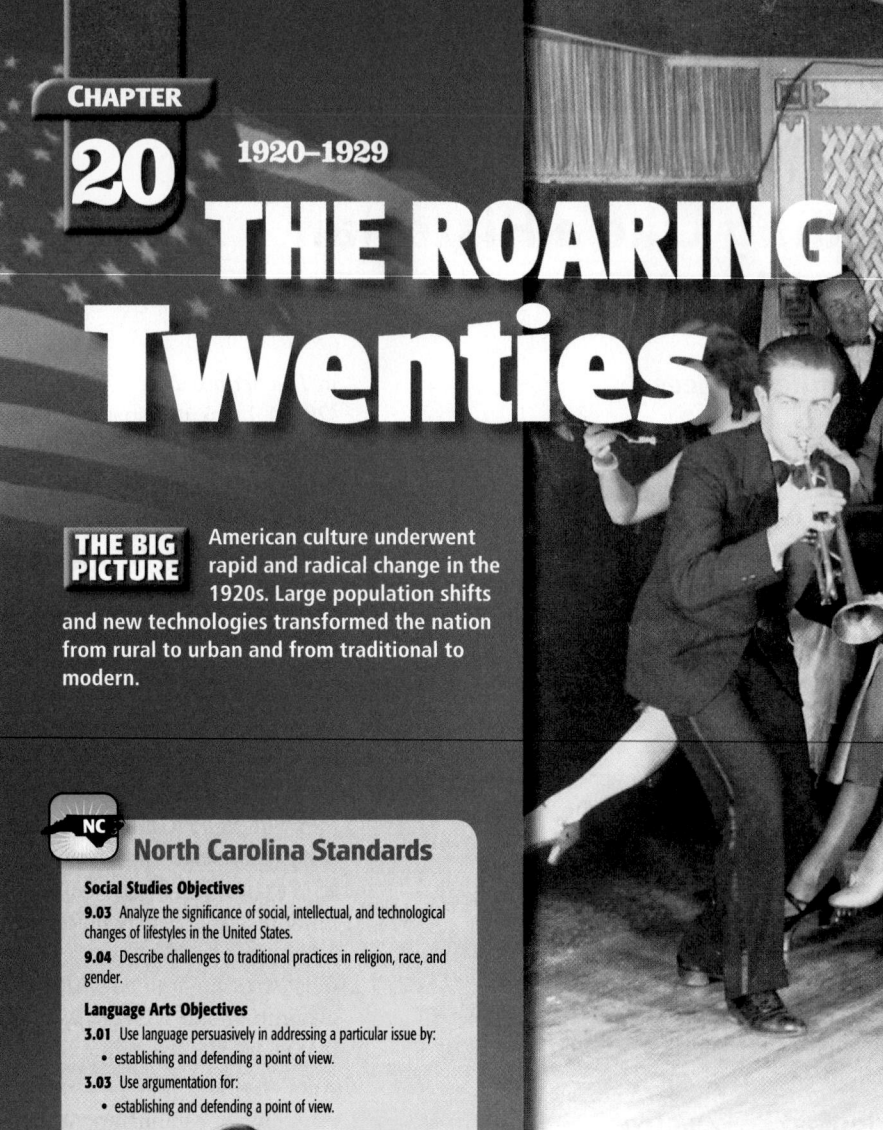

CHAPTER
20 1920–1929
THE ROARING Twenties

THE BIG PICTURE American culture underwent rapid and radical change in the 1920s. Large population shifts and new technologies transformed the nation from rural to urban and from traditional to modern.

North Carolina Standards

Social Studies Objectives
9.03 Analyze the significance of social, intellectual, and technological changes of lifestyles in the United States.
9.04 Describe challenges to traditional practices in religion, race, and gender.

Language Arts Objectives
3.01 Use language persuasively in addressing a particular issue by:
 • establishing and defending a point of view.
3.03 Use argumentation for:
 • establishing and defending a point of view.

Skills FOCUS **READING LIKE A HISTORIAN**

This jazz band is supplying not only music but also some food and drink to competitors in a Charleston endurance contest. The Charleston was a new dance that was all the rage in the 1920s.
Interpreting Visuals What words would you use to describe the mood of the scene captured in this photograph?
See Skills Handbook, p. H30

U.S.

1920 First corporate radio station offers music and news.

1920

World

1920 League of Nations holds first meeting in Paris, France.

644

Key to Differentiating Instruction

Below Level
Basic-level activities designed for all students encountering new material

At Level
Intermediate-level activities designed for average students

Above Level
Challenging activities designed for honors and gifted-and-talented students

Standard English Mastery
Activities designed to improve standard English usage

Introduce the Chapter   **At Level**

Changes during the 1920s

1. Guide students in a discussion of the political changes that occurred in the nation following World War I.

2. Remind students that during the 1920s, social, economic, and technological changes occurred in the country as well.

3. Ask students to name some of the changes that occurred or to suggest images that they have of the 1920s. List student responses for all to see and discuss the ideas with the class.

4. Tell students that in this chapter they will learn about the social changes, literary movements, and heroes of the decade.
LS Verbal-Linguistic
Alternative Assessment Handbook, Rubric 11: Discussions

1924
Nellie Tayloe Ross is elected in Wyoming as the nation's first woman governor.

1926
Langston Hughes publishes *The Weary Blues*, his first book of poetry.

1927
Charles Lindbergh completes his solo flight across the Atlantic Ocean.

1922 | 1924 | 1926 | 1928 | 1930

1924
Soviet leader Vladimir Lenin dies.

1926
Ruins of Mayan cities reported found in Mexico.

1929
The National Revolutionary Party is established in Mexico.

645

Explore the Time Line

1. When did the first corporate radio station begin broadcasting? *1920*

2. When was the nation's first woman governor elected? *1924*

3. When did Charles Lindbergh fly solo across the Atlantic Ocean? *1927*

Info to Know

Prohibition The Eighteenth Amendment, instituting Prohibition, was ratified in January 1919. The 21st Amendment, which repealed Prohibition, was ratified in December 1933.

Make Generalizations Should the government amend the Constitution in an attempt to change social behaviors? *possible answer—yes, if it is for the common good*

Chapter Preview

HOLT

History's Impact
▶ **Video Program: The Roaring Twenties**
See the Video Teacher's Guide for strategies for using the video segment.

Reading Like a Historian

Dancing Flappers Have students take a moment to examine the image on these pages. Where are the women in this photo? *They are enjoying themselves in what looks like a dance hall filled with musicians.*

go.hrw.com
Online Resources

Chapter Resources:
KEYWORD: SD7 CH20

Teacher Resources:
KEYWORD: SD7 TEACHER

Answers

Interpreting Visuals (p. 644) *These young women are smiling and dancing. They seem to be relaxing and enjoying the freedom that shorter skirts and good music can provide.*

Bellringer

The Inside Story. . . Use the **Daily Bellringer Transparency** to help students answer the question.

Daily Bellringer Transparency, Section 1

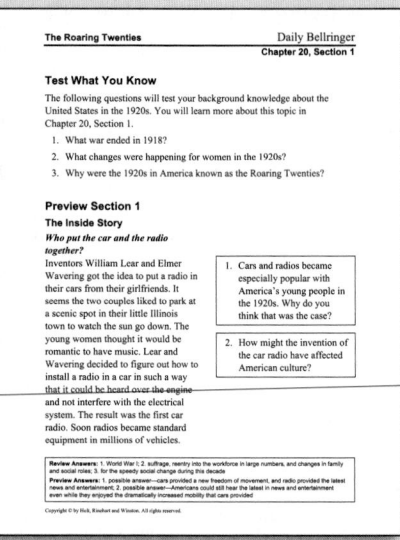

The Roaring Twenties	Daily Bellringer
	Chapter 20, Section 1

Test What You Know

The following questions will test your background knowledge about the United States in the 1920s. You will learn more about this topic in Chapter 20, Section 1.

1. What war ended in 1918?
2. What changes were happening for women in the 1920s?
3. Why were the 1920s in America known as the Roaring Twenties?

Preview Section 1
The Inside Story
Who put the car and the radio together?

Inventors William Lear and Elmer Wavering got the idea to put a radio in their cars from their girlfriends. It seems the two couples liked to park at a scenic spot in their little Illinois town to watch the sun go down. The young women thought it would be romantic to have music. Lear and Wavering decided to figure out how to install a radio in a car in such a way that it could be heard over the engine and not interfere with the electrical system. The result was the first car radio. Soon radios became standard equipment in millions of vehicles.

1. Cars and radios became especially popular with America's young people in the 1920s. Why do you think that was the case?
2. How might the invention of the car radio have affected American culture?

Review Answers: 1. World War I; 2. suffrage, reentry into the workforce in large numbers, and changes in family and social roles; 3. for the speedy social change during this decade
Preview Answers: 1. possible answer—cars provided a new freedom of movement, and radio provided the latest news and entertainment; 2. possible answer—Americans could still hear the latest in news and entertainment even while they enjoyed the dramatically increased mobility that cars provided

Copyright © by Holt, Rinehart and Winston. All rights reserved.

Academic Vocabulary

Review with students the high-use academic terms in this section.

mode style or fashion (p. 648)
stability consistency; resistance to change (p. 651)

CRF: Vocabulary Builder Activity, Section 1

Taking Notes

Social Behavior—more women in the workforce, more women in college, new attitudes toward women and the home, rise of the flapper, bootleggers and illegal smuggling of alcohol; Laws— Nineteenth Amendment, Eighteenth Amendment, Volstead Act; Religion— rise of fundamentalism, evolution vs. fundamentalism

---

SECTION 1

American Life Changes

BEFORE YOU READ

MAIN IDEA

The United States experienced many social changes during the 1920s.

READING FOCUS

1. What were the new roles for American women in the 1920s?
2. What were the effects of growing urbanization in the United States in the 1920s?
3. In what ways did the 1920s reveal a national conflict over basic values?
4. What was Prohibition, and how did it affect the nation?

KEY TERMS AND PEOPLE

flapper
values
Billy Sunday
fundamentalism
Aimee Semple McPherson
evolution
Clarence Darrow
William Jennings Bryan
bootlegger
speakeasy

TAKING NOTES As you read, take notes identifying major change in American social behavior, laws, and religion during the 1920s. Record your notes in a graphic organizer like the one shown here.

Social Behavior	Laws	Religion

THE INSIDE STORY

Who put the car and the radio together? By the early 1920s cars and radio were well on their way to becoming key features of American life. For young people especially, cars meant freedom. Radio meant access to music, news, sports, and a blossoming American popular culture.

Inventors William Lear and Elmer Wavering were two young Americans who enjoyed cars and music. It was their girlfriends, however, who gave them the idea to put a radio inside a car. The two couples liked to park at a scenic spot

in their little Illinois town to watch the sun go down. When the young women suggested that it would be wonderful to have music on these evenings, Lear and Wavering decided to figure out how to install a radio inside a car in such a way that it could be heard over the car's engine and would not interfere with the car's electrical system. The result was the invention of the first practical car radio.

Within a few years the car radio would become standard equipment in millions of automobiles. The world of the American teenager would never be the same. ■

A Match Made in Heaven

◄ Before radios were installed into cars, people used portable radios powered by the car's battery. The bulky size didn't stop people from carrying them along.

Teach the Main Idea

At Level

American Life Changes

1. **Teach** Ask the students the Reading Focus questions to teach this section.

2. **Apply** Tell students that changes in society often result from economic change, social problems, and technological advances. Have students name changes that occurred during the 1920s and decide what caused them.

3. **Review** Have students identify the one change that they believe had the greatest impact on society during the 1920s. Have students explain their choice.

4. **Practice/Homework** Journalists working for large city newspapers during the 1920s often wrote editorial-opinion pieces. Have students write an editorial discussing a change they have identified and whether it will have a positive or negative effect on society. **LS Verbal-Linguistic**

Alternative Assessment Handbook, Rubric 23: Newspapers

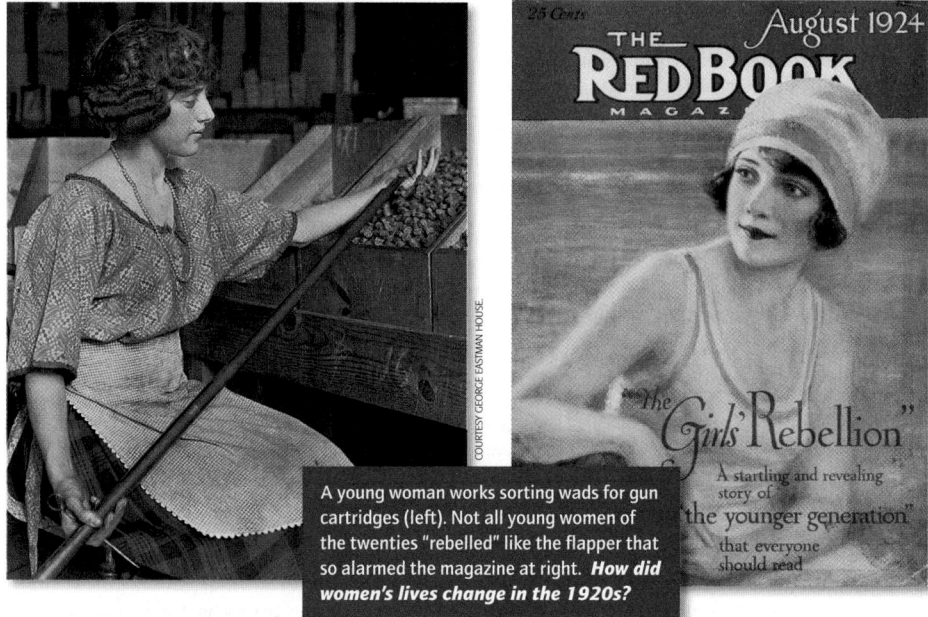

A young woman works sorting wads for gun cartridges (left). Not all young women of the twenties "rebelled" like the flapper that so alarmed the magazine at right. **How did women's lives change in the 1920s?**

New Roles for Women

The invention of the car radio was just one example of the many cultural changes that took place in the 1920s. The decade itself became known as the Roaring Twenties for the speedy social change it brought to the United States. Women were especially affected.

New opportunities As you have read, the states ratified the Nineteenth Amendment in 1920. After a decades-long struggle, women could finally vote. As a result, women were soon elected to state and local offices. In Wyoming, Nellie Tayloe Ross became the nation's first woman governor when she won election in 1924 to complete the term of her husband, William B. Ross, who had died in office. Miriam "Ma" Ferguson was elected governor of Texas that same year.

In general, however, women voters did not make their presence felt at the ballot box and bring about sweeping changes in the national government, as some advocates for women's suffrage had expected. In fact, women in the 1920s tended to vote much as their husbands, fathers, or other men in their lives voted. As a result, they did not yet represent a unique group of voters with a distinct point of view.

American women also saw changes in their workplace roles during the 1920s. While many women had taken jobs outside the home during World War I, most lost these wartime jobs when the troops returned to the United States. During the economic boom of the 1920s, however, women again joined the workforce in large numbers. They filled a greater range of jobs than ever before. Still, nearly all women in the workforce held jobs in a handful of the lowest-paying professions, including nurses, teachers, and domestic servants.

Also during the 1920s, Americans began attending college in greater numbers than ever before. Many of these new students were women from middle- and upper-class families.

New family roles In part because of these changing opportunities for women, the 1920s brought about a shift in many people's attitudes concerning the relationship between men and women. The basic rules that defined proper female behavior were beginning to change. American women did continue to have primary responsibility for caring for the home and children, and most still depended on men for financial support. An increasing number, however, sought a greater sense of equality in their relationships with men.

Direct Teach

Reading Focus

❶ What were the new roles for American women in the 1920s? *gained the right to vote, were elected to state and local offices, entered the work force, attended college*

New Roles for Women

Explain What was the purpose of the Nineteenth Amendment? *gave women the right to vote*

Analyze Why do you think women tended to vote as their husbands or fathers did? *possible answers—had same political views, were from similar backgrounds*

Develop How do you think World War I changed women's lives? *began to work outside the home, became more independent, wanted to break away from traditional roles*

📄 CRF: Biography: Alice Paul

Skills Focus: Interpreting Visuals   Below Level

Reading Like a Historian Skill
Women's Roles
Materials plain paper, colored pencils or markers

1. Guide the class in a discussion about the new opportunities women gained during the 1920s. List student responses for all to see.

2. Have students examine the two images of young women on this page. Guide students in a discussion of the differences between the two. Then ask how these differences reflect changing societal values.

3. Guide students in a discussion of women's roles today. Have students list opportunities that women have now but did not have in the 1920s. List student responses for all to see.

4. Have students use this list to create a magazine cover that shows the role of women in today's society. **LS Visual-Spatial**

📄 Alternative Assessment Handbook, Rubrics 3: Artwork; and 11: Discussions

Answers

Photo *gained the right to vote, were given increased access to jobs and education*

New Roles for Women

Describe How were supporters of women's rights different from flappers? *They wanted to advance women's causes; flappers were perceived as frivolous in attitude and behavior.*

Evaluate Why do you think flappers lived mostly in urban areas? *Small towns and rural areas usually held traditional attitudes.*

❷ What were the effects of growing urbanization in the United States in the 1920s? *shifts in values; greater interaction between rural and urban populations; more young people going to school*

Effects of Urbanization

Identify What surprising information was revealed in the 1920 census? *More people lived in urban areas than in rural areas.*

Analyze How did the automobile change life in rural areas? *People living in rural areas spent time in towns and became urban in outlook and values.*

Evaluate Why do you think increasing educational opportunities changed rural populations? *more people went to high school, on to college or to city jobs; did not return to the farm*

📰 CRF: Social Studies Skills Activity: Interpreting Pie and Bar Graphs

Answers

Reading Check *Flappers represented greater freedom and independence for women.*

The flapper One popular image that reflects many of the changes affecting women in the 1920s is the **flapper**. The term refers to young women of the era who defied traditional ideas of proper dress and behavior. Flappers shocked society by chopping off their hair, raising their hemlines, wearing makeup, smoking cigarettes, drinking alcohol, and going dancing in nightclubs. Not all flappers did all of these things, of course. The new <u>mode</u> of dress, however, was particularly popular among rebellious girls.

ACADEMIC VOCABULARY

mode style or fashion

HISTORY'S VOICES

❝ Not since 1820 has feminine apparel been so frankly abbreviated [shortened] as at present … Nor is this merely the sensible half of the population dressing as everyone ought to, in hot weather. Last winter's styles weren't so dissimilar, except that they were covered up by fur coats and you got the full effect only indoors. ❞

—Bruce Bliven, *The New Republic*, September 9, 1925

In general, the term *flapper* suggested a certain lifestyle of great independence and freedom. As writer Dorothy Parker slyly noted about the modern woman, "She's not what Grandma used to be."

Although flappers became a symbol of the 1920s, they were hardly representative of all women of their time. Not all American women were flappers. In fact, in many parts of the United States, including small towns and rural areas, women merely read about flappers in magazines. They either disapproved of them or would not dare to be so bold or reckless. Indeed, many older supporters of women's rights believed that the flappers were more interested in having fun than in advancing the cause of women.

Disapproving of the face powder that flappers wore, Charlotte Perkins Gilman wrote, "A generation of white-nosed women who wear furs in summer cannot lay claim to any real progress." So while the flapper did represent some very real shifts taking place in American society, she certainly did not represent all American women.

READING CHECK **Summarizing** In what ways did flappers represent the changes American women were experiencing in the 1920s?

Effects of Urbanization

The flapper craze took hold mainly in American cities. In many ways the flapper phenomenon represented the growing divide between the nation's booming cities and the countryside.

As you have read, the 1920s was a time of great economic prosperity in the United States. One segment of the economy, however, did not share in the good times. Farming took a hard

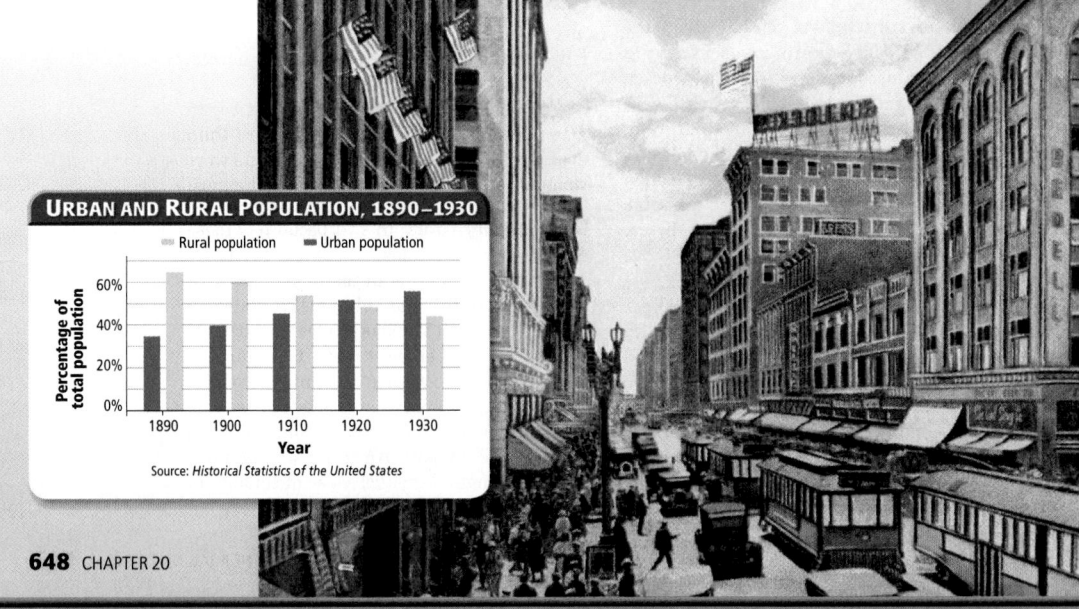

URBAN AND RURAL POPULATION, 1890–1930

Rural population ■ Urban population

Percentage of total population

60%

40%

20%

0%

1890 1900 1910 1920 1930

Year

Source: *Historical Statistics of the United States*

Skills Focus: Comparing and Contrasting

Above Level

Reading Skill
Modern Trends

1. Remind students that the flapper was a popular symbol of the Roaring Twenties. Images of flappers were used in advertising, movies, and literature of the period. Have students explain why they think the flapper, a controversial image and lifestyle, became such a well known, representative image.

2. Guide students in a discussion about how new trends and cultural changes can result in conflict over traditional values. Have students name modern trends and images that have created conflicts in society.

3. Have students select one image that they believe represents a current social trend and write a short essay explaining and analyzing the image, how it reflects the trend, and why the image and trend are significant. **LS** **Verbal-Linguistic**

📰 Alternative Assessment Handbook, Rubrics 11: Discussions; and 37: Writing Assignments

hit in the post-World War I years, as wartime demand for food dropped off. Hard times in agriculture contributed to a loss of rural population, as people sought jobs in the cities. The 1920 census showed that for the first time ever, more Americans lived in urban areas than in rural areas. Three fourths of all workers worked somewhere other than a farm.

The rise of the automobile also helped shift the geographic borderline between rural and urban America. As more rural people acquired cars, the distances that had once separated them from the cities shrank. Rural people were now more likely to spend time in town interacting with each other and joining in the urban culture. Even if they continued to live in the country, they became less isolated and more urban in their outlook and attitudes.

Related to the rural-to-urban population shift was an increase in education in the United States. By the 1920s many states had passed laws requiring young people to attend school. These laws helped force children out of the workplace and into the classroom. Requiring children to attend school was also a way to teach immigrants about American life.

Interestingly, school attendance increased along with the growth of American industry. Why? As industry grew, the earnings of American workers also rose. More families could afford to send their children to school instead

America Moves to the Cities

Los Angeles, California, shown here in a 1920s postcard, grew from a city of just over 50,000 in 1890 to a city with a population of more than 1 million by 1930. *According to the chart, during what decade did the United States become a nation of urban dwellers?*

of sending them to the textile mills and other factories. As a result, high school and college enrollment increased.

READING CHECK **Contrasting** How did the relationship between rural America and urban America change in the 1920s?

Conflicts Over Values

The shift from a mostly rural America to a mostly urban one was highly significant. Americans were living in larger communities. This population change also produced important shifts in **values**, the key ideas and beliefs a person holds. The values of many urban Americans in the 1920s differed greatly from the traditional values of rural dwellers.

Urban and rural America differed significantly in the kinds of values that were dominant in those places. In the minds of some people, rural America represented the traditional spirit of the nation: hard-working, self-reliant, religious, and independent. Cities, on the other hand, represented changes that threatened those values.

As you read in an earlier chapter, the Ku Klux Klan grew dramatically in the 1920s. The new Klan drew many of its new members from rural America. Most new Klan members were workers, farmers, and small business owners. They saw their own status declining while the size and cultural influence of urban America was increasing. They believed the Klan could help them preserve their place in society.

Members of the new Klan continued to use violent tactics. The Klan targeted not only African Americans but also recent immigrants, especially Catholics and Jews. In the 1920s, however, the Klan also focused on influencing politics. Although founded in the South, the Klan had members nationwide in the 1920s. At its peak, membership was in the millions. Membership declined in the late 1920s because of a series of scandals affecting top Klan leaders. But the social divisions that the Klan had taken advantage of still remained.

The rise of fundamentalism The uncertainty that comes with changing times caused many Americans to turn to religion for answers. One key religious figure of the time was a tough-talking former ballplayer named

THE IMPACT TODAY

Daily Life
Urbanization continued throughout the century. According to the 2000 U.S. Census, the country's population was 79.2 percent urban and 20.8 percent rural.

THE ROARING TWENTIES **649**

• **Direct Teach** •

Reading Focus

3 In what ways did the 1920s reveal a national conflict over basic values? *conflicts between urban and rural values, rise of fundamentalism, growth of Ku Klux Klan, Scopes trial*

Conflicts Over Values

Describe What were the traditional values of rural America? *religious, hard-working, self-reliant, independent*

Evaluate Why do you think the Ku Klux Klan began targeting recent immigrants in addition to African Americans? *Many were Catholics or Jews, holding different religious values and ethnic traditions.*

📰 CRF: Primary Source Activity: The Ku Klux Klan Marches in Washington, D.C.

📰 CRF: History and Geography Activity: From Rural to Urban America

Answers

Photo *1920*

Reading Check *decreased separation between rural and urban areas, population shift to urban areas*

Differentiating Instruction

Below Level

Special Education Students; Learners Having Difficulty

1. Organize the class into mixed-ability pairs or have students work independently. Have the students reread the information about the effects of urbanization.

2. Draw the table at right for all students to see. Omit the answers.

3. Have students copy the table and complete it with information from the text. Ask volunteers to share their answers and complete the table for all students to see.

Have students correct their tables as needed and use them as a study guide.

4. As an extension, have students write a letter to a friend living in the city in the 1920s explaining why they would like to leave the farm to come to live in the city. **LS Verbal-Linguistic**

📰 Alternative Assessment Handbook, Rubric 41: Writing to Express

📰 Graphic Organizer Transparencies

Rural Areas	Urban Areas
loss of population, limited jobs, spending more time in cities, changing values	growing populations, better educational opportunities; better-paying jobs

Conflicts Over Values

Recall What was the issue at the heart of the Scopes trial? *whether or not evolution could be taught in public schools*

Explain Why did fundamentalists want to ban teaching evolution in schools? *believed teaching evolution undermined religious faith*

Develop Why do you think Clarence Darrow was arguing about freedom of speech in the Scopes case? *possible answer—because he thought it was the main issue*

Info to Know

The Scopes trial The Scopes trial was the first trial that was brought to the public through live radio broadcasts. Outside the Dayton courthouse where the trial took place, enterprising vendors sold Bibles and toy monkeys as well as hot dogs and lemonade.

The Scopes Trial

THE GRANGER COLLECTION, NEW YORK

Key figures in the Scopes trial were Clarence Darrow (above left), representing John Scopes, and William Jennings Bryan (above right), leading the prosecution. At right, Scopes stands to receive his guilty verdict. Political cartoons like the one at left portrayed the case as a "monkey trial" because it focused on a theory that humans may have descended from an ape-like species.

Billy Sunday. Ordained as a minister in 1903, Sunday rose to national prominence as a powerful revivalist preacher. Reflecting the values of many white, rural Americans, Sunday condemned radicals and criticized the changing attitudes of women.

Sunday's Christian beliefs were based on a literal interpretation of the Bible, which is called **fundamentalism**. While many people believe that certain stories in the Bible were meant to be symbolic rather than literal, fundamentalists believe that historic events occurred exactly as the Bible describes.

Another leading fundamentalist preacher of the time was **Aimee Semple McPherson**. McPherson presented a much more sophisticated image than Billy Sunday did. In fact, she seemed to embrace the kind of glamour that many other fundamentalists warned about. Her religion, however, was firmly in the fundamentalist tradition. She was especially well known for healing the sick through prayer.

The Scopes trial As fundamentalism gained strength in the 1920s, it came into sharper conflict with the teachings of modern science. A leading example of this conflict centered on the theories of the 19th-century scientist Charles Darwin. The most controversial of Darwin's ideas is known as **evolution**. The theory of

THE IMPACT TODAY

Science and Technology
The teaching of evolution in public schools continues to be a controversial issue. More than 80 years after the Scopes trial, debate continues about what to teach in the public schools about the origin of life.

evolution holds that inherited characteristics of a population change over generations and that as a result of these changes, new species sometimes arise.

According to Darwin, the human species may have developed from an ape-like species that lived long ago. Fundamentalists believed that this theory went against the biblical account of how God created humans. Further, many fundamentalists believed that teaching evolution undermined religious faith.

Fundamentalists worked hard to prevent evolution from being taught in public schools. In several states, they succeeded in having laws passed which outlawed the teaching of Darwin's ideas or the inclusion of evolution in classroom materials. One of these states was Tennessee, where a 1925 law made it a crime to teach evolution to students.

Opponents of the Tennessee law were quick to challenge it. One group persuaded a young science teacher named John Scopes to agree to violate the law and get himself arrested. This set the stage for one of the most dramatic trials in American history.

Skills Focus: Identifying Main Idea and Details ⟨At Level⟩

Reading Skill
The Scopes Trial

1. Guide students in a discussion about the issues involved in the Scopes trial. Have students identify and explain the key points of the trial and its outcome. List student answers for all to see. Have students copy the information onto their own paper.

2. Have students use the information to write a speech about the Scopes trial. Each student should take a position in favor of or against the decision to convict John Scopes of

violating the Tennessee law.

3. Have volunteers read their speeches to the class. Some students may wish to create a videotape and present it to the class.

4. Following the presentations, guide students in a discussion of the views presented in the various speeches. **LS Verbal-Linguistic**

📝 Alternative Assessment Handbook, Rubric 29: Presentations

The trial took place in the little town of Dayton, Tennessee, but people around the country followed the events. The nation riveted its attention on the two distinguished, colorful lawyers who squared off against one another.

Representing Scopes was **Clarence Darrow**, perhaps the most famous criminal lawyer in the country. **William Jennings Bryan**, the three-time candidate for president, led the prosecution. Beloved as an orator who championed farmers and rural values, Bryan had become a major figure in the fundamentalist movement. In fact, he had influenced public opinion in Tennessee against evolution.

The guilt of John Scopes was never really in doubt. In the trial, both sides focused on larger issues. Bryan called it a contest between the competing ideas of Christianity and evolution. The defense openly stated that it was trying to make a point about freedom of speech.

The key moment in the trial occurred when Darrow called Bryan to testify as an expert witness on religion. Darrow asked Bryan an exhausting series of questions about events described in the Bible. Bryan said that in his view, some biblical events may not have happened exactly as described. Yet he stood by his basic beliefs. "If I am not able to explain it, I will accept it," he declared.

The trial ended, as expected, with Scopes's conviction. He was fined $100. Scopes's fate, however, was not the only story. This occurred five days after the trial, when Bryan died in his sleep. To many fundamentalists, he died a hero, giving his life for a sacred cause.

Darrow's team had hoped to appeal the decision and test the constitutionality of the Tennessee law. They never got the chance. A higher court overturned Scopes's conviction because the judge had committed a technical violation of the law.

The Tennessee law remained in place into the 1960s. Meanwhile, other states that passed similar laws soon repealed them.

READING CHECK **Identifying the Main Idea**
For what crime was Scopes tried and convicted?

Prohibition

Throughout the history of the United States, groups such as the Woman's Christian Temperance Union had fought to outlaw alcohol. To many people, alcohol was the source of much unhappiness. It hurt families, and it promoted crime, they said. Outlawing alcohol, they argued, would promote family <u>stability</u>. Over the years, a number of states passed anti-alcohol laws.

The drive to outlaw alcohol gained strength in the early 1900s, as Progressives joined the effort to curb the harmful effects of liquor on society. World War I aided the cause. The war-time need for discipline among the troops—and the need for grain, from which different types of alcohol are made—were two arguments in favor of banning alcohol nationally.

The fight against alcohol also borrowed from the bias against immigrants that was increasing in the World War I era. Some people who opposed immigration portrayed certain immigrant groups as abusers of alcohol. Small-town Americans also tended to view alcohol and its evils as a city problem—one that was growing more serious as the nation became more urban. Protestant religious groups and fundamentalists were among those who favored a liquor ban.

The Eighteenth Amendment For these and other reasons, by 1917 more than half the states had passed some form of law restricting alcohol use. In that year, Congress proposed an amendment to the Constitution that made it illegal to manufacture, transport, or sell alcohol in the United States. Ratification of this amendment—the Eighteenth Amendment—followed in 1919. Congress then passed

ACADEMIC VOCABULARY
stability consistency; resistance to change

Prohibition

Recall How did Americans obtain alcohol during Prohibition? *from smugglers, made their own, prescribed as medicine*

Identify Cause and Effect How did the passage of the Eighteenth Amendment and the Volstead Act lead to the rise of organized crime? *demand for alcohol remained high, led to organized crime controlling the smuggling and illegal sales of alcohol*

Make Judgments Why do you think law enforcement officials were unsuccessful in enforcing the Volstead Act? *too few agents; gangsters too powerful, lack of full, strong public support*

📝 U.S. History Political Cartoon Activity: Cartoon 39: Politicians and Prohibition

Info to Know

AAPA A group of wealthy industrialists formed the Association Against the Prohibition Amendment (AAPA), which sponsored anti-Prohibition meetings and supported "wet" political candidates. AAPA members argued that Prohibition represented a needless encroachment on individual rights by a federal government that had become too powerful. The AAPA played a key role in persuading legislators to vote for the Twenty-first Amendment.

Counterpoints

For and Against Prohibition

Have students use the dictionary to look up words in the quotes that are unfamiliar to them. Then have students work in pairs to rewrite the quotes in their own words.

Answers

Reading Like a Historian *White believed that personal liberty should be sacrificed to ensure public safety; Sabine believed government should not regulate personal conduct.*

652

---

a law known as the Volstead Act to enforce the amendment. Prohibition, as the new ban on alcohol was known, became the law of the land in 1920.

Prohibition in practice Supporters of Prohibition believed it would have many positive effects on American society. To be sure, Prohibition did reduce the amount of alcohol Americans consumed. Enforcing the new law, however, proved to be virtually impossible.

While making, transporting, and selling alcohol was illegal, drinking it was not. Many people continued to drink liquor during Prohibition—and those who wanted alcohol had little trouble getting it.

Prohibition gave rise to huge smuggling operations. Large amounts of alcohol slipped into the country through seaports and across the border from Canada. It was said that in Detroit, Michigan, located on the Canadian border, liquor smuggling was the second largest industry after automobile manufacturing. Newspaper headlines followed the high drama of the hunt for **bootleggers**, or liquor smugglers. Bootleggers—from the slang term for smuggling items inside boots—were highly skilled at avoiding capture. Government officials estimated in 1925 that they had stopped only 5 percent of all the liquor entering the country illegally.

In addition to smuggled liquor, many people simply made their own illegal alcohol using homemade equipment. Others drank alcohol that was intended for use in medicines or other products. At the time, doctors were allowed to prescribe alcohol to their patients for medical reasons.

The illegal liquor business also became the foundation of great criminal empires. The most notorious Prohibition-era gangster was Chicago's Al Capone. After brutally destroying

COUNTERPOINTS

For and Against Prohibition

William Allen White was a journalist who supported many social causes, including Prohibition.

At first a prohibitionist, Pauline Sabine later spoke against the Eighteenth Amendment.

❝ [I]t is the duty of the nine people who do not overdrink, as it seems to me, to give up their liberties so far as drink goes for the good not of the one man who abuses the privilege but for the ten thousands who are his potential victims. That is the whole philosophy of prohibition. ❞

William Allen White, 1927

❝ Prohibition ... has led to more violations of and contempt for law ... than anything else in our national life ... To tell citizens what they must or must not do in their strictly personal conduct as long as public safety is not affected is a function which government should not attempt. ❞

Pauline Sabine, 1929

Skills FOCUS READING LIKE A HISTORIAN

Contrasting How do White and Sabine's views on personal liberty differ?

See Skills Handbook, p. H10

652 CHAPTER 20

Skills Focus: Identifying Problem and Solution   At Level

Reading Skill
Enforcing the Law

1. Read the quote by Albert Einstein about law enforcement to the class. Make sure that all students understand the quote.

2. Remind students of John Adams's statement, "the only good government is a nation of laws, not men," and that all Americans have a responsibility to obey our laws. Guide students in a discussion of what this means.

3. Have students work in pairs to identify current laws that they believe are not easily

enforced. Examples might include speeding on turnpikes or freeways. Have pairs share their answers and make a class list.

4. Have each student select one law from the list. Have students write a paragraph summarizing the law, how it is violated, and what steps law enforcement officials might take to correct the situation. **LS** Interpersonal

📝 Alternative Assessment Handbook, Rubric 37: Writing Assignments

his competition, he used the alcohol trade to build a business that earned tens of millions of dollars a year.

With these resources, Capone and other gangsters were able to frighten off and pay off the law-enforcement agents who threatened them. The federal government, which never had more than 3,000 Prohibition agents working nationwide, found it difficult to compete with the criminals. Still, many agents worked diligently to enforce the law. They shut down **speakeasies**, the illegal bars where alcohol was served. They destroyed barrels of captured liquor and the equipment that gangsters used to make alcohol. Yet they could not keep up with the criminals.

In spite of its problems, Prohibition continued through the 1920s. More and more people, however, questioned whether this experiment was succeeding. The scientist Albert Einstein voiced the concerns of many Americans:

HISTORY'S VOICES

❝ The prestige of government has undoubtedly been lowered considerably by the Prohibition law. For nothing is more destructive of respect for the government and the law of the land than passing laws which cannot be enforced.❞

—Albert Einstein,
"My First Impression of the U.S.A.," 1921

Agents created a red river in the streets of Los Angeles as they destroyed 900 gallons of wine one day in 1920. *How effective were agents in controlling the distribution of alcohol?*

Even as millions of Americans violated the spirit of the Eighteenth Amendment, Prohibition remained in force. It would be several more years before it came to an end.

READING CHECK **Making Generalizations** In what ways did Prohibition cause more problems than it solved?

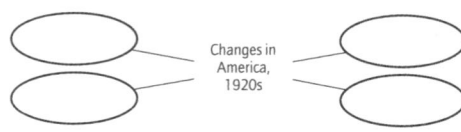

SECTION 1 ASSESSMENT

go.hrw.com
Online Quiz
Keyword: SD7 HP20

Reviewing Ideas, Terms, and People

1. **a. Define** What was a **flapper**?
   b. Make Generalizations How were women's roles changing in the 1920s?
   c. Evaluate How do you think people who did not embrace the changes of the 1920s might have reacted to the flappers?

2. **a. Recall** What significant change in the distribution of the American population became known in 1920?
   b. Analyze How did rural and urban areas of the United States differ in terms of **values**?

3. **a. Define** Write a brief definition for each of the following terms: **fundamentalism, evolution**
   b. Make Inferences Why did fundamentalism gain popularity in the 1920s?
   c. Elaborate How did the Scopes trial reflect the tensions and conflicts taking place in American society in the 1920s?

4. **a. Identify** What was **Prohibition**?
   b. Sequence Briefly trace the history of the effort to outlaw alcohol in the United States.

c. Predict Do you think Prohibition would have been different if drinking alcohol had been outlawed completely?

Critical Thinking

5. **Identifying the Main Idea** Copy the chart below and place events in the chapter in the diagram that support the main idea.

Changes in America, 1920s

FOCUS ON WRITING

6. **Persuasive** Write a letter to one of your government representatives that argues either for or against a prohibition on alcohol. Use information from the chapter to support your position.

Section 1 Assessment Answers

1. **a.** young woman who defied traditional ideas
   b. able to vote, better opportunities
   c. negative reaction to their lifestyle

2. **a.** More people lived in urban areas.
   b. rural—religion, hard-work, self-reliance; urban—change and modernity

3. **a.** belief in strict interpretation of the Bible; theory that modern species developed over time
   b. concern over changing values
   c. reflected conflict between fundamentalists and those who believed in modern science

4. **a.** ban on making, selling, transporting alcohol
   b. several states restricted use of alcohol; Progressives joined effort; World War I; 18th Amendment passed
   c. possible answer—yes, enforcing law might have been easier; no, people would still have gotten alcohol

5. growing role of women; increased urbanization; rise of fundamentalism; Prohibition

6. possible answer—alcohol should be prohibited because it endangers everyone

---

Close

Guide a discussion on how rapid social changes led to a growing gap between rural and urban America.

Review

Online Quiz, Section 1

Daily Test Practice Transparency

Assess

SE Section 1 Assessment

Progress Assessment: Section 1 Quiz

Alternative Assessment Handbook

Reteach

Interactive Reader and Study Guide, Section 1

Interactive Skills Tutor CD-ROM

Answers

Photo *not very effective*

Reading Check *law widely disregarded; illegal bars flourished; gangsters founded crime empires*

Bellringer

The Inside Story. . . Use the **Daily Bellringer Transparency** to help students answer the question.

🖎 Daily Bellringer Transparency, Section 2

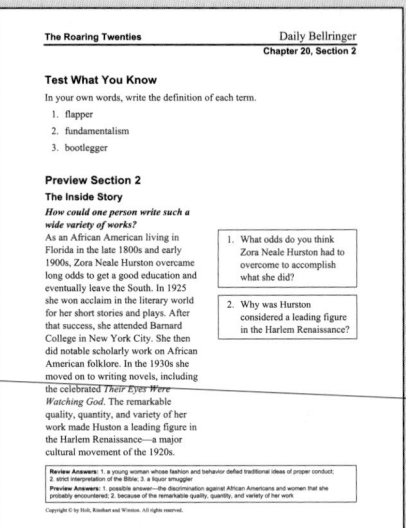

Taking Notes

Great Migration, settlement in Harlem, NAACP, publication of The Crisis, *creation of the UNIA*

SECTION 2
The Harlem Renaissance

BEFORE YOU READ

MAIN IDEA

Transformations in the African American community contributed to a blossoming of black culture centered in Harlem, New York.

READING FOCUS

1. What was the Great Migration, and what problems and opportunities faced African Americans in the post–World War I era?
2. What was Harlem, and how was it affected by the Great Migration?
3. Who were the key figures of the Harlem Renaissance?

KEY TERMS AND PEOPLE

Zora Neale Hurston
Great Migration
Harlem Renaissance
Marcus Garvey
James Weldon Johnson
Langston Hughes
Paul Robeson
jazz
Louis Armstrong
Bessie Smith

TAKING NOTES As you read, take notes identifying the major events that helped bring about the Harlem Renaissance. Record your notes in a graphic organizer like the one shown here.

Zora Neale HURSTON

▲ Hurston wanted "a busy life, a just mind and a timely death."

THE INSIDE STORY

How could one person write such a wide variety of works? If a "Renaissance man" is a person with a wide range of knowledge and abilities, **Zora Neale Hurston** was a Renaissance woman. As an African American girl living in Florida in the late 1800s and early 1900s, she overcame long odds to get a good education and eventually leave the South.

In 1925 Hurston won acclaim in the literary world by writing short stories and plays. After that success, she attended Barnard College in New York City, where she studied anthropology, the study of human cultures. With this training, she did important scholarly work on the subject of African American folklore. In the 1930s she moved on to writing novels, including the celebrated *Their Eyes Were Watching God*. Later still, she wrote nonfiction, including an autobiography and essays about politics.

Zora Neale Hurston's life is remarkable for the quality, quantity, and variety of the work she produced. Indeed, she was one of the leading figures in a major cultural movement that was centered in New York City's Harlem neighborhood in the 1920s: the Harlem Renaissance. ◼

The Great Migration

Beginning around 1910 Harlem, a neighborhood in upper Manhattan, became a favorite destination for black Americans migrating from the South. Life in the South was very difficult for African Americans. Many had little choice but to work as sharecroppers or in other low-paying jobs. Segregation laws kept southern African Americans in a separate and unequal world. For these people, racial violence was a constant threat.

Teach the Main Idea

At Level

The Harlem Renaissance

1. **Teach** Ask students the Reading Focus questions to teach this section.

2. **Apply** Organize the class into mixed-ability pairs. Have students work together, but have each student write three summaries: the major changes in African American demographics, what life was like in Harlem, and the cultural flowering that occurred within the African American community. **LS Interpersonal, Verbal-Linguistic**

3. **Review** Have volunteers share their summaries with the class.

4. **Practice/Homework** Have each student create an illustration for each of the three summaries, one for each of the main heads in the section. **LS Visual-Spatial**

📝 Alternative Assessment Handbook, Rubrics 3: Artwork; and 37: Writing Assignments

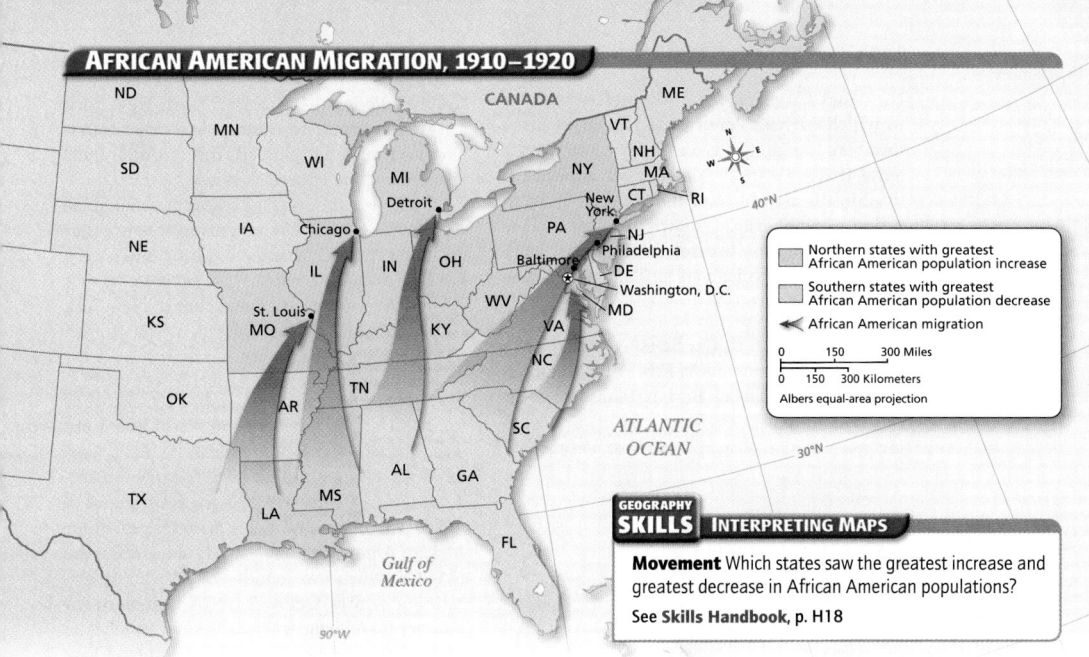

AFRICAN AMERICAN MIGRATION, 1910–1920

Northern states with greatest African American population increase

Southern states with greatest African American population decrease

African American migration

0   150   300 Miles

0   150   300 Kilometers

Albers equal-area projection

GEOGRAPHY SKILLS | **INTERPRETING MAPS**

Movement Which states saw the greatest increase and greatest decrease in African American populations?

See **Skills Handbook, p. H18**

Many African Americans looked to the North with hope of finding the freedom and economic opportunities unavailable to them in the South. These hopes came true with the outbreak of World War I. Suddenly, demand for war equipment and supplies surged, and northern factories had more jobs than they could fill. Employers eagerly looked to the South for a new supply of workers. African American newspapers, such as the *Chicago Defender*, helped spread the word about the economic opportunities. The papers, in turn, fielded many requests for information. "I don't want you to loan me another 1 cent," wrote one Mississippi man, "but help me to find an occupation there in your town."

By the thousands, southern African Americans streamed into northern cities such as Chicago and Detroit. Black populations of these communities rose sharply. This major relocation of African Americans is known as the **Great Migration**.

African Americans after World War I

African Americans moved North with high hopes. Many found opportunities there, but they did not escape the effects of racism.

Racial tensions were especially severe after World War I. You have read about the economic adjustments that followed the return home of American soldiers. The shortage of jobs created tension between whites and African American workers.

This tension contributed to a wave of racial violence in the summer of 1919. The deadliest riot occurred in Chicago, Illinois. There, a dispute at a public beach led to rioting that left 38 people dead and nearly 300 people injured. Racially motivated riots occurred in some two dozen other cities in 1919.

Another factor that added to racial conflict was the changing expectations of African Americans. Many believed that they had earned greater freedom by helping fight for freedom overseas in World War I.

Unfortunately for African Americans, not everyone agreed that their war service had earned them greater freedom. In fact, some whites were determined to strike back against the new African American attitude.

READING CHECK **Identifying Cause and Effect** Why did many African Americans decide to move to the North in the early 1900s?

Reading Focus

1 What was the Great Migration, and what problems and opportunities faced African Americans in the post-World War I era? *Thousands of African Americans moved to the North to escape segregation and violence; problems—racism and racial tension; opportunities—better jobs and higher wages*

The Great Migration

Explain Why did northern industries recruit workers from the South? *During World War I factories could not find enough workers to fill jobs.*

Summarize What factors contributed to racial tension in northern cities? *shortage of jobs after the war; changing expectations*

Develop Why do you think African Americans moved to Detroit, Chicago, New York, and Washington, D.C.? *possible answer—These cities had large industries with available jobs.*

🗺 Map Transparency: African American Migration, 1910–1920

Skills Focus: Identifying Cause and Effect

At Level

Reading Skill
Decision to Migrate North

1. It was difficult for young adult sharecroppers living in the South during the early 1900s to make a living from the land. Family/friends send copies of "Want Ads" from the *Chicago Defender* advertising jobs in the Chicago area that sound wonderful.

2. Have each student make a chart listing the advantages and disadvantages of leaving the South to pursue a job in the North. *advantages—better life, escape from poverty and segregation; disadvantages—unfamiliar place, leaving family, job might not be available*

3. Have students weigh the advantages and disadvantages and then decide whether to stay in the South or migrate North. Have students write an explanation of their decision.
    LS Logical-Mathematical

   📝 Alternative Assessment Handbook, Rubrics 7: Charts; and 42: Writing to Inform

---

Answers

Interpreting Maps *increase—Missouri, Illinois, Indiana, Ohio, West Virginia, Michigan, Pennsylvania, New York, New Jersey, Maryland; decrease—Louisiana, Mississippi, Tennessee, Kentucky*

Reading Check *freedom and economic opportunities*

655

② What was Harlem, and how was it affected by the Great Migration? *African American neighborhood in New York City; became the center for African American culture and activism*

Life in Harlem

Describe What was the purpose of the NAACP? *to end discrimination and mistreatment of African Americans*

Contrast How did the NAACP differ from the UNIA? *NAACP founded by African Americans and whites to end discrimination and mistreatment of African Americans; UNIA founded by African Americans, wanted them to look out for their own interests, did not want white involvement*

Develop Why do you think poor African Americans were attracted to UNIA? *possible answer—charismatic leader, appealed to African American self-interests, wanted to maintain racial purity of Africans*

Activity *The Crisis* Have students examine the two covers of *The Crisis* shown on this page. Have students sketch their own cover for a current issue of the magazine. **LS** **Visual-Spatial**

Biography

Jean Toomer (1894–1967) Jean Toomer, a poet and novelist of mixed race, said that he was of the "human race." His grandfather was the first U.S. governor of African American descent, and Toomer attended both all-white and all-black schools. He was a central and dominant figure in the African American literary community. His most famous work, *Cane*, celebrated African American culture and identity in both the North and the South. This influential work of poems and prose put Toomer at the forefront of the Harlem Renaissance.

Life in Harlem

New York City was one of the northern cities to which African Americans moved in large numbers during the Great Migration. By the early 1920s, about 200,000 African Americans lived in the city. Most of these people lived in a single neighborhood known as Harlem. This neighborhood soon became the unofficial capital of African American culture and activism in the United States.

The role of W.E.B. Du Bois A key figure in the rise of Harlem was W.E.B. Du Bois, about whom you read earlier. Born in Massachusetts, the well-educated Du Bois had been a leading voice in the African American community for many years. In 1909 he helped found the National Association for the Advancement of Colored People—the NAACP—in New York City. This group worked to end discrimination and mistreatment of African Americans throughout the United States.

Du Bois also served as editor of a magazine called *The Crisis*. The magazine was a major outlet for African American writing and poetry. Du Bois and *The Crisis* helped promote a great African American arts movement in New York City in the 1920s. The movement was known as the **Harlem Renaissance**.

The rise of Marcus Garvey Another famous Harlem figure of the World War I era was **Marcus Garvey**. A Jamaican by birth, Garvey took great pride in his African heritage. Through his Universal Negro Improvement Association, or UNIA, he encouraged other African Americans to do the same. Unlike the NAACP, which was founded by African Americans and whites, Garvey's UNIA promoted self-reliance for African Americans. Garvey believed that African Americans could and should look out for their own interests, without involvement from whites. Garvey looked forward to the day when Africans from around the world could return to Africa and create a new empire. UNIA's slogan was "Back to Africa."

"We have no animus [hatred] against the white man," Garvey said. "All that we have as a race desired is a place in the sun."

In order to achieve that goal, Garvey declared, African Americans needed to build a base of economic success. This he hoped to achieve by operating a number of business enterprises. The most significant was the Black Star Line, which promoted trade among Africans around the world.

Some 2 million people, mostly impoverished African Americans, joined UNIA. Garvey held colorful parades and wore military-style uniforms to help build enthusiasm.

Garvey was highly critical of W.E.B. Du Bois and the NAACP. Garvey believed that the NAACP undermined and discouraged African American pride and self-confidence. He felt that the NAACP goal of breaking down the barriers between blacks and whites threatened the racial purity of Africans.

For their part, Du Bois and the NAACP were suspicious of Garvey and his organization.

The Crisis Magazine

First published by the NAACP in 1910, *The Crisis* was a forum for African American literary talent as well as discussion of race relations. It helped launch the careers of such Harlem Renaissance figures as Langston Hughes and Countee Cullen. It remains the official publication of the NAACP today.

Differentiating Instruction

Above Level

Advanced Learners/GATE

Research Required

1. Tell students that the NAACP still exists and is a strong voice for African Americans in the United States.

2. Have students research the history and current activities of the NAACP. Using traditional print and Internet sources, students should examine how effective the NAACP was during the civil rights movement; they should also learn about the NAACP today, the name and background of the current president, how the NAACP is organized, and what issues and problems currently face the organization.

3. Have students present their findings in the form of a poster or in a media presentation.

4. When students have finished their presentations, guide the class in a discussion of the issues that are of the most concern to the NAACP today. **LS** **Intrapersonal, Visual-Spatial**

📖 Alternative Assessment Handbook, Rubrics 29: Presentations; and 30: Research

Du Bois published in *The Crisis* the results of a thorough investigation of the UNIA. The Federal Bureau of Investigation (FBI) kept the UNIA under close watch. In 1923 the FBI had collected enough evidence to charge Garvey with mail fraud. Garvey went to prison in 1925. When he was released in 1927 he was forced to leave the country. With Garvey gone, the UNIA collapsed as an organization. The Harlem it left behind, however, remained a vital and exciting place.

READING CHECK **Contrasting** How did the views of W.E.B. Du Bois and Marcus Garvey differ?

A Renaissance in Harlem

Harlem in the 1920s bristled with creative energy. The growing New York City neighborhood became home to tens of thousands of African Americans. To some, Harlem was their first experience living outside of the South. They felt a strong sense of racial pride and identity. This spirit attracted a historic influx of talented African American writers, thinkers, musicians, and artists.

The result was a flowering of African American arts that came to be known as the Harlem Renaissance. The term *renaissance* comes from a French word that means "rebirth" or "revival."

Harlem writers and poets A great number of African American poets and writers burst onto the scene during the Harlem Renaissance. Their literary achievements were astounding. This is especially true given the fact that before this era, little African American literature had been published. But in 1924 the National Urban League's magazine *Opportunity* sponsored a dinner at the New York Civic Club to bring together prominent publishers and editors with up-and-coming black writers. This helped propel African American writers into the mainstream of American literature.

One notable Harlem Renaissance figure was **James Weldon Johnson**. A man of many talents, he had worked early in life as a journalist, educator, and lawyer. Johnson expressed a musical side as well: In 1900 he and his brother wrote the song "Lift Every Voice and Sing." Two decades later, Johnson had risen to the top leadership post of the NAACP, and his song

FACES OF HISTORY

Langston HUGHES
1902–1967

Langston Hughes began writing poetry as a teenager. As a young man, he traveled to Mexico, Africa, and Europe, writing about the things he saw. In 1926 he published *The Weary Blues,* his first book of poetry. He used the money he earned to complete college.

After college, Hughes settled in Harlem, where he soaked up the rhythms of jazz music and incorporated them into his writing. In characteristic images and jangling language, Hughes's poetry described the rich culture of African American life, capturing the joys, suffering, and speech of the people he knew. Hughes had a major impact on the Harlem Renaissance and on American literature.

Predict How might Hughes's travels affected his view of America?

became that organization's official anthem. In addition to his NAACP work, Johnson continued to write and to collect and publish the work of other poets of the Harlem Renaissance. In 1927 he published a book of poetry called *God's Trombones*, which many regard as his finest work.

A common theme among Harlem Renaissance writers was defiance or resistance in the face of white prejudice. The great poet Claude McKay wrote this poem, one of his most famous, following the 1919 race riots.

HISTORY'S VOICES

"If we must die, let it not be like hogs
Hunted and penned in an inglorious spot,
While round us bark the mad and hungry dogs,
Making their mock at our accursed lot.
If we must die, O let us nobly die,
So that our precious blood may not be shed
In vain; then even the monsters we defy
Shall be constrained to honor us though dead!
O kinsmen! we must meet the common foe!
Though far outnumbered let us show us brave,
And for their thousand blows deal one deathblow!
What though before us lies the open grave?
Like men we'll face the murderous, cowardly pack,
Pressed to the wall, dying, but fighting back!"
—Claude McKay, "If We Must Die," 1919

Langston Hughes, another celebrated Harlem Renaissance poet and writer, wrote of black defiance as well, but he also wrote of hope. His works recorded the distinctive culture of Harlem during the 1920s itself.

History Close-Up
The Harlem Renaissance

The Cotton Club opened in Harlem in 1923; the name was supposed to remind people of a stylish Southern plantation. While guests were white, the entertainers were African American. Many jazz stars, including Duke Ellington, Ethel Waters, and Lena Horne, got their start at the club.

Harlem Stomp! A Cultural History of the Harlem Renaissance written by Laban Carick Hill contrasts the South's violence and frustration with the hopes of African Americans in the 1920s. The book explores these factors as reasons for the Great Migration. The text then focuses on New York City, which became the center of the Harlem Renaissance, attracting writers, artists, and musicians. Of interest is the coverage of everyday events in African American life: the role of the church, funeral processions, and rent parties. The book also examines the infighting within the African American community.

Harlem Stomp! A Cultural History of the Harlem Renaissance by Laban Carick Hill. Megan Tingley, 2004.

Answers
Interpreting Visuals *five—music, singing, theater, art, literature; possible answers—gave them pride in their heritage and means of creative expression*

658

HISTORY CLOSE-UP

The Harlem Renaissance

During the 1920s, the numerous African American writers, artists, and musicians in Harlem inspired one another to reach new heights of creativity. The work produced during this time of enormous literary and artistic achievement often reflected a strong and growing sense of racial pride and confidence.

Literature
Claude McKay's *Home to Harlem*, a novel about daily life in Harlem, was published in 1928 and quickly became a bestseller. It was the first novel by a Harlem writer to reach the bestseller list.

Performing Arts
Paul Robeson, Bessie Smith, and Louis Armstrong (from left to right) were just a few of the influential performers and musicians of the Harlem Renaissance.

Fine Arts
Artist Aaron Douglas used elements of African design and subject matter in his murals for public buildings, illustrations for publications, and paintings such as "Into Bondage" (below). Douglas also created the cover for *Home to Harlem*.

AARON DOUGLAS, "INTO BONDAGE", 1936. OIL ON CANVAS, 60 3/8 x 60 1/2 IN. CORCORAN GALLERY OF ART, WASHINGTON, D.C.

Skills FOCUS INTERPRETING INFOGRAPHICS

African American writer and philosopher Alain Locke said of Harlem that "culturally and spiritually it focuses a people."

Drawing Conclusions How many art forms are represented in these pictures? How do you think this flourishing of the arts affected African Americans in general?

See **Skills Handbook**, p. H30

658 CHAPTER 20

Skills Focus: Comparing and Contrasting

Below Level

Reading Skill
Jazz

Prep Required

1. Before class, locate and bring to class recordings of jazz musicians and singers who were popular during the 1920s. Recordings and videotapes of these artists can usually be found at the local library.

2. Have students identify major African American performing artists today, actors, musicians, or artists. Ask students to identify the area in which the artist excels. Write the list for all to see.

3. Play the recordings or videotapes for the class. Tell students to listen carefully and take notes about the style, the lyrics, and other things that catch their attention.

4. Guide students in a discussion of the similarities and differences between the artists of the 1920s and those on the class list.
LS Musical-Auditory

Alternative Assessment Handbook, Rubric 11: Discussions

Harlem artists Black American artists also won fame and recognition during the Harlem Renaissance. Among the best known were William H. Johnson, Aaron Douglas, and Jacob Lawrence. Each of these artists often focused on the experiences of African Americans in their work. Later artists such as Loïs Mailou Jones drew inspiration from the works of the Harlem Renaissance.

Performers and musicians The Harlem Renaissance helped create new opportunities for African American stage performers. Historically, black actors, musicians, and other performers were not given serious roles on the American stage. That began to change in the 1920s. One of the key figures in this development was the multitalented **Paul Robeson**.

Robeson had originally come to New York to practice law but won fame on the stage. He performed in a number of movie and stage productions, the most famous of which was Shakespeare's *Othello*, in which he played the lead character. This role won him acclaim around the country and the world.

Robeson also had a rich singing voice. One of his earliest performances was in the groundbreaking 1921 musical show *Shuffle Along*, which featured an all-black cast. Another cast member was a young woman named Josephine Baker. She would go on to a remarkable career as a singer and dancer, much of it in Europe.

Audiences in France and elsewhere in Europe tended to be more accepting of black performers than white Americans were.

Harlem was also a vital center for **jazz**. This music blended several different musical forms from the Lower South into a wholly original American form of music that was new, different, and very exciting. While a jazz song might start with a known melody or theme, much of the music was improvised, or composed on the spot. Jazz could be fast or slow, and it was easy to dance to. In short, jazz was not defined by clear rules but rather by its spirit and creativity. "Man, if you have to ask what it is," said legendary jazz musician **Louis Armstrong**, "you'll never know."

Louis Armstrong was a leading performer on the Harlem jazz scene, which was centered at clubs such as the Savoy Ballroom and the Cotton Club. The audience was made up in large part of white jazz fans. They flocked to Harlem to hear Armstrong and other leading performers, including Cab Calloway, composers Duke Ellington and Fats Waller, and the great blues singer **Bessie Smith**.

Jazz music was not limited to Harlem. As you will read, it was part of a wider cultural movement spreading throughout the United States in the 1920s.

THE IMPACT TODAY

Daily Life
The Cotton Club closed its doors in 1940 and the site was later demolished. After decades of decline, Harlem is again on the rise, and a new, relocated Cotton Club serves up jazz, swing, and gospel music to multi-ethnic audiences.

READING CHECK **Identifying the Main Idea**
What happened during the Harlem Renaissance?

SECTION 2 ASSESSMENT

go.hrw.com
Online Quiz
Keyword: SD7 HP20

Reviewing Ideas, Terms, and People

1. a. Recall What was the **Great Migration**?
b. Draw Conclusions Why do you think the Great Migration occurred when it did?
c. Design Create an poster that would encourage southern African Americans to move to the North in the early 1900s.

2. a. Identify What was the role of the **NAACP** and UNIA in the growth of Harlem?
b. Contrast How did W.E.B. Du Bois and **Marcus Garvey** differ in their views about the future of African Americans?
c. Elaborate Why do you think Du Bois and Garvey were so critical of each other's ideas?

3. a. Identify Briefly describe the contributions of **James Weldon Johnson** and **Zora Neale Hurston**.
b. Explain What role did *The Crisis* play in the **Harlem Renaissance**?

c. Evaluate Why do you think there were so few published African American writers prior to the Harlem Renaissance?

Critical Thinking

4. Sequence Copy the chart below and place events in the chapter in the diagram to complete the sequence of events.

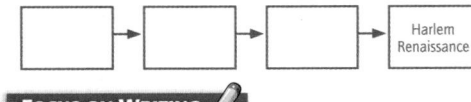

FOCUS ON WRITING

5. Persuasive Write a letter to a publisher urging him or her to publish more African American writers. Write your letter as if you are living in the 1920s. Use information from the section to support your argument.

THE ROARING TWENTIES **659**

Section 2 Assessment Answers

1. a. Thousands of African Americans moved north.
b. With the war, northern industries needed workers.
c. possible answer—"Find economic opportunity in the North"

2. a. Both promoted pride and an end to discrimination.
b. Garvey believed African Americans should return to Africa; Du Bois believed they should work toward equal status in the U.S.
c. possible answer—trying to reach the same

population but had opposing ideas

3. a. Johnson—led the NAACP and published his work and the work of other poets; Hurston—gifted author
b. major outlet for African American writing
c. possible answer—racial barriers limited recognition and opportunities

4. Great Migration, NAACP, *The Crisis*

5. The blossoming of African American literature has created new forms of expression interesting to the public.

● **Direct Teach** ●

Reading Focus

A Renaissance in Harlem

Describe What is jazz? *a musical form known for improvisation, spirit and creativity*

Predict What influence might the Harlem Renaissance have on future aspiring African American artists and writers? *possible answer—understanding that African Americans could be heard and achieve fame in their chosen careers*

📄 CRF: Biography: Blues and Jazz: Bessie Smith and Duke Ellington

● **Review & Assess** ●

Close
Name the major figures of the Harlem Renaissance discussed in the section and have students explain how these people gained fame.

Review
📄 Online Quiz, Section 2
📄 Daily Test Practice Transparency

Assess
SE Section 2 Assessment
📄 Progress Assessment: Section 2 Quiz
📄 Alternative Assessment Handbook

Reteach
📄 Interactive Reader and Study Guide, Section 2
💿 Interactive Skills Tutor CD-ROM

Answers

Reading Check *African Americans developed a strong sense of racial pride and identity, encouraged by the blossoming of African American literature, art, theater, and music.*

659

Bellringer

The Inside Story. . . Use the **Daily Bellringer Transparency** to help students answer the question.

Daily Bellringer Transparency, Section 3

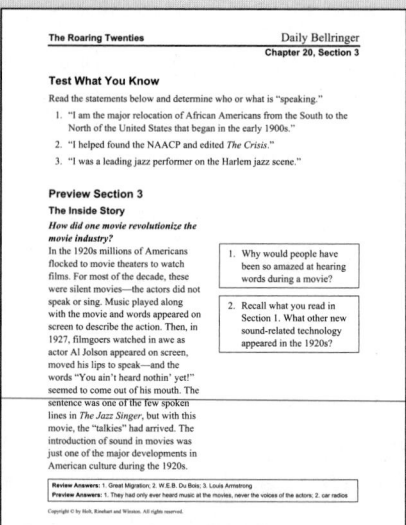

Academic Vocabulary

Review with students the high-use academic term in this section.

media forms of communication (p. 661)

CRF: Vocabulary Builder Activity, Section 3

Taking Notes

Entertainment—rise of radio and movies; Heroes—rise of movie stars, Charles Lindbergh, Amelia Earhart, sports stars; Arts—authors Fitzgerald, Lewis, Millay, and Barton, music of Gershwin

---

A New Popular Culture Is Born

BEFORE YOU READ

MAIN IDEA

New technologies helped produce a new mass culture in the 1920s.

READING FOCUS

1. How did mass entertainment change in the 1920s?
2. Who were the cultural heroes of the 1920s?
3. How was the culture of the 1920s reflected in the arts and literature of the era?

KEY TERMS AND PEOPLE

D. W. Griffith
Charlie Chaplin
Charles A. Lindbergh
transatlantic
Amelia Earhart
F. Scott Fitzgerald
George Gershwin

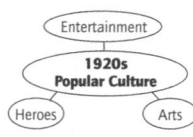 **TAKING NOTES** As you read, take notes identifying major developments in popular culture in the United States during the 1920s. Record your notes in a graphic organizer like the one shown here.

Entertainment

1920s Popular Culture

Heroes   Arts

THE INSIDE STORY *How did one movie revolutionize the movie industry?* In the 1920s, Americans by the millions flocked to movie theaters to watch films. For most of the decade these films were silent. Printed words on the screen narrated the story and gave the dialogue.

Then in 1927 filmgoers watched in awe and amazement as actor Al Jolson appeared on screen, moved his lips to speak, and the words "You ain't heard nothin' yet!" came right out of his mouth.

▼ *The Jazz Singer premiered at Warners' Theatre in New York City.*

 **The Jazz Singer Talks**

That sentence was one of only a few spoken lines of dialogue in the film, called *The Jazz Singer*. The movie also included many songs and the traditional onscreen printed explanations of events. But to the moviegoing public, the "talkies" had arrived. *The Jazz Singer* was a huge success and made millions of dollars for its producers. It also helped change the movie industry forever. As you will read, the introduction of sound in movies was one of the major developments in a decade of enormous change in American popular culture. ■

660

Teach the Main Idea

At Level

A New Popular Culture Is Born

1. **Teach** Ask students the Reading Focus questions to teach this section.

2. **Apply** Have students develop an outline of this section, using the main headings as major points. Students should include the blue headings in their outlines as well. Under each blue head, students should list two supporting details and names of the individuals who are discussed in the section.

3. **Review** Review student outlines as a class. Guide students in a discussion of the

contributions of each individual named in the outlines.

4. **Practice/Homework** Have students create an illustration for each of the blue heads in this section. Organize the class into small groups and have students share and explain their illustrations.

LS Interpersonal, Visual-Spatial

Alternative Assessment Handbook, Rubrics 3: Artwork; and 14: Group Activity

Mass Entertainment in the 1920s

The American people have always sought ways to entertain and inform themselves. In the 1920s, new <u>media</u> created whole new types of entertainment. These technologies were able to reach a growing share of the nation's population. Increasingly, people all across the country were sharing the same information and enjoying the same pastimes. A new American popular culture was emerging.

Radio One driving force in the development of this popular culture was the radio. During the 1920s, this device went from being a little-known novelty to being standard equipment in the American home.

Guglielmo Marconi invented radio in the late 1800s. In the early 1900s the military and ships at sea used the technology to aid in communications. Radio was also popular with a small number of hobbyists around the country. As the 1920s dawned, however, few Americans owned a radio. No regular programming was on the airwaves for people to listen to.

Radio's breakthrough occurred in 1920. In that year a radio hobbyist living near Pittsburgh, Pennsylvania, began to play records over his radio. His audience was made up of the small but growing number of people with radios within range of his equipment.

The growing popularity of these simple broadcasts caught the attention of the Westinghouse Company, which manufactured radios. Westinghouse realized that more people would buy its product if there was good programming on the airwaves. In October 1920 Westinghouse started the first corporate radio station in the United States. The station's call letters were KDKA. The station played music and provided news—including the results from the 1920 presidential election.

KDKA was quickly joined by hundreds of radio stations across the nation. By 1922 the United States had 570 stations broadcasting all types of programming. Listeners enjoyed music, news, and broadcasts of religious services and sporting events. Children tuned in to hear bedtime stories.

Technical improvements in radios increased their popularity. A new device called the vacuum tube greatly increased the quality of radio sound. Radios became portable with the invention of battery-powered units.

Like the automobile, the radio helped break down barriers that had once separated country people from city folk. Now Americans everywhere could hear the same news and listen to the same music. They heard the same advertisements and bought the same products. In short, the radio helped create a shared culture that included a growing number of Americans.

Movies Movies were another form of mass entertainment that exploded in popularity during the 1920s. Several factors explain this development. One was a change in the type of films available to viewers. In earlier years

ACADEMIC VOCABULARY

media forms of communication

Mass Media in the 1920s

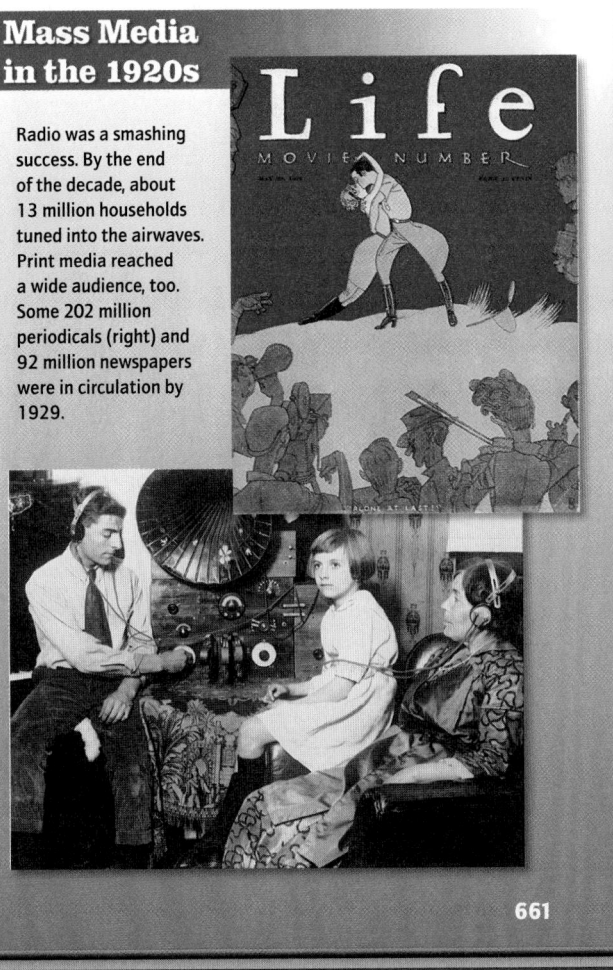

Radio was a smashing success. By the end of the decade, about 13 million households tuned into the airwaves. Print media reached a wide audience, too. Some 202 million periodicals (right) and 92 million newspapers were in circulation by 1929.

661

Direct Teach

Reading Focus

❶ How did mass entertainment change in the 1920s? *radio and movies reached many Americans, created a common culture*

Mass Entertainment in the 1920s

Identify What were the first uses of the radio? *military and ships at sea, hobbyists*

Analyze How did radio help create a common culture in the U.S.? *People throughout the country heard the same news, ads, and music.*

Elaborate Do you think a common culture would have evolved without national media? *possible answers— No, people would not easily know what others were thinking and doing. Yes, with the change from rural to urban, people had already started to create a common culture.*

📰 CRF: Biography: David Sarnoff

Collaborative Learning

At Level

The History of the Radio and Movies

Research Required

1. Organize the class into groups of four or five students. Assign each student in a group a 20-year time span beginning with 1920. One student would be responsible for 1920–1940; another for 1941–1960, etc.

2. Have students conduct independent research on radio and movies, including programming, innovations, and technical advances that occurred during their assigned time span.

3. When students have finished their research, have each group create an illustrated time

line showing the history of radio, radio programming, and the movie industry since their inception in the 1920s to the current day.

4. Post the time lines for all students to see. Guide students in a discussion of the variety of programming available today on the radio and the languages in which radio programs are broadcast. 🅛 **Interpersonal, Visual-Spatial**

📰 Alternative Assessment Handbook, Rubrics 14: Group Activity; 30: Research; and 36: Time Lines

2 Who were the cultural heroes of the 1920s? *Chaplin, Lindbergh, Earhart*

An Era of Heroes

Recall What characteristics made Lindbergh an American hero? *He was daring, skilled, determined, and courageous.*

Make Generalizations What do the successes of Lindbergh and Earhart reveal about American technology? *Technology was advanced enough to make planes that could fly for long distances and long periods of time.*

Rank What other American achievements might be equal to Lindbergh's flight across the Atlantic? *possible answers—man on the moon, the Space Shuttle, invention of the computer microchip*

Activity Acknowledge a Triumph Read the quote about Lindbergh to the students. Have students write their own poem or song celebrating Amelia Earhart's flight across the Atlantic. **LS Auditory-Musical**

CRF: Primary Source Activity: Senator Henry Myers Calls for Censorship of the Movies

Info to Know

The Ten Commandments This movie produced by Cecil B. DeMille was his first biblical epic, and it was the top-grossing film of the 1920s.

Answers

Photo *The movie industry had created a new group of heroes for Americans to follow: movie stars.*

Reading Check *Both experienced technical improvements that widened the audience, creating a shared cultural experience for Americans.*

662

---

most movies were short, simple pieces. During World War I, however, filmmaker **D. W. Griffith** produced the powerful *The Birth of a Nation*. This film's content was, and still is, highly controversial. By standards then and today, it includes themes and images that many people consider racist. Yet the film's impact on the movie industry is undeniable. *The Birth of a Nation* introduced many advanced filmmaking techniques. It helped establish film as an art form and widened the audience for movies. Viewers included President Woodrow Wilson. "It's like writing history with lightning," he is said to have remarked after a screening of the movie.

Another important movie innovation of the 1920s was the introduction of films with sound. In 1928, a year after the release of *The Jazz Singer*, a filmmaker named Walt Disney released an animated film called *Steamboat Willie*. It featured a character named Mickey Mouse, and a new type of movie star—a cartoon character—was born.

THE IMPACT TODAY

Daily Life
Movies help diffuse popular culture worldwide. American films are translated into foreign languages and widely distributed overseas, often reaching much larger audiences than in the United States.

What did the public reaction to Rudolph Valentino's death show about the role of the movie industry in American life?

Rudolph Valentino

JESSE L. LASKY Presents
GEORGE MELFORD'S PRODUCTION
"THE SHEIK"
WITH
AGNES AYRES and RUDOLPH VALENTINO
From the novel by EDITH M. HULL
Scenario by MONTE M. KATTERJOHN
It's a Paramount Picture

662 CHAPTER 20

The popularity of the movies was enormous. By the end of the decade, experts estimated that Americans bought 100 million tickets a week. At the time, the entire population of the United States was about 123 million people. As with radio, movies provided the nation with a shared experience.

READING CHECK **Comparing** What qualities did movies and radio have in common?

An Era of Heroes

The great popularity of movies in the 1920s helped to create a new type of celebrity: the movie star. Indeed, the 1920s produced a whole new group of heroes for Americans to follow. The public responded with enthusiasm.

Film stars One of the brightest stars of the 1920s was the silent film actor **Charlie Chaplin**. Millions loved his signature character, a tramp with ragged clothes and a derby hat.

Rudolph Valentino was also a superstar of the silent movies. This dashing leading man made his name in romantic films such as *The Sheik*. When he died unexpectedly in 1926, tens of thousands of women visited the funeral home where his body lay.

Like Valentino, Clara Bow became a movie sex symbol. Nicknamed the "It Girl," she starred in a number of films that helped her build a highly popular image. Actress Mary Pickford was beloved as "America's Sweetheart." She was married to Douglas Fairbanks Jr., a major star of swashbuckling action films. Their magnificent home, called Pickfair, was located in Hollywood, California, the center of the motion picture industry.

Lucky Lindy On May 21, 1927, a small, single-engine airplane touched down on an airfield in Paris, France. In the cockpit was a lone pilot, **Charles A. Lindbergh**. Thirty three and one-half hours earlier, he had taken off from a muddy airfield in New York on a nonstop flight across the Atlantic Ocean.

Several pilots had attempted this daring **transatlantic** flight, but no one had succeeded—until Lindbergh. With his triumph, Lindbergh achieved what one newspaper called "the greatest feat of a solitary man in the history of the human race."

Differentiating Instruction

Below Level

English-Language Learners

Standard English Mastery

1. Review the information about Lindbergh with the class. Have students make a list of any words under the heading "Lucky Lindy" that are unfamiliar to them. Either have students look up the definitions in a dictionary or, as a class, define the words.

2. Remind students that when Lindbergh completed his flight in 1927, he was considered to be an American hero, and as the text says, the press celebrated his accomplishment.

3. Have students write a newspaper headline and a brief newspaper article explaining Lindbergh's accomplishment. In their articles students should tell how many hours the flight across the Atlantic took, the name of the airplane, and other details they feel are significant.

4. Have volunteers share their articles with the class. **LS Verbal-Linguistic**

Alternative Assessment Handbook, Rubric 23: Newspapers

The Spirit of St. Louis

Lindbergh modified the *Spirit of St. Louis* for his transatlantic flight. He lightened the aircraft as much as he could to compensate for the weight of the fuel needed for the long voyage. He even replaced the leather pilot's seat with a wicker one.

Because he placed the main fuel tank in front of the pilot's seat, Lindbergh needed a periscope to see ahead.

Extra fuel tanks occupied the cabin space.

The wingspan was increased to accommodate the weight of the fuel.

Lindbergh became perhaps the most beloved American hero in an era of heroes. There were many reasons for his popularity. Young, tall, and handsome, Lindbergh simply looked like a hero. His down-to-earth, humble manner seemed to represent many of the qualities Americans admired. A true pioneer, he had triumphed alone against overwhelming odds. He had achieved his goal with a powerful combination of skill, daring, and determination.

The public adoration of Lindbergh was astounding. Songwriters published hundreds of songs about him and his flight.

HISTORY'S VOICES

❝Lucky Lindy, up in the sky
Fair or windy,
He's flying high
Peerless, fearless, knows every cloud,
The kind of a son makes a mother feel proud.❞
— "Lucky Lindy!" by L. Wolfe Gilbert and Abel Baer, 1927

Before attempting his famous flight, Lindbergh had won some fame as a daredevil pilot. He had practiced his skills working as an airmail pilot, a dangerous job that had claimed the lives of 31 of the first 40 pilots employed in the service. When he learned about a $25,000 prize for the first aviator to fly nonstop between New York and Paris, he resolved to win. He rejected the commonly held belief that this flight would require a large plane with multiple engines. Instead, he developed a single-engine craft with room for only one pilot. Then he removed every ounce of unnecessary weight and added as much gasoline as the plane could carry.

The myth of Lindbergh was not far from the reality. He truly was a courageous man who risked much to expand the nation's frontiers.

Amelia Earhart A little over a year after Lindbergh's famous flight, **Amelia Earhart** became the first woman to fly across the Atlantic. She too returned to the United States as a hero. Earhart went on to a legendary career as a pilot in which she set a number of speed and distance records. In 1937 she was most of the way through another record-breaking attempt—a flight around the world—when she disappeared over the Pacific Ocean. No definitive trace of her remains has ever been found.

Sports heroes The American people's fascination with movie stars was matched in the 1920s by their devotion to sports heroes.

THE IMPACT TODAY

Technology
On March 3, 2005, millionaire Steve Fossett landed his Virgin Atlantic GlobalFlyer at the Kansas airport where he had taken off 67 hours before, becoming the first person to fly nonstop, solo, around the world without refueling. Fossett flew 23,000 miles (36,800 kilometers).

❸ How was the culture of the 1920s reflected in the arts and literature of the era? *Artistic and literary works reflected the changing social and economic culture of the country.*

Arts of the 1920s

Identify Which authors wrote about their experiences during World War I? *Ernest Hemingway and John Dos Passos*

Summarize What were some of the common themes of literature written in the 1920s? *social concerns, business success, glamorous lifestyle of the wealthy*

Make Judgments Why do you think authors glamorized the "Roaring Twenties" lifestyle and, at the same time, criticized it? *It was an exciting, enviable lifestyle; it also represented a major shift in American values.*

📄 CRF: Literature Activity: "Bernice Bobs Her Hair" by F. Scott Fitzgerald

📄 U.S. History Political Cartoon Activity: Cartoon 40: Social Changes

Sports Heroes of the 1920s

◀ The "Galloping Ghost" swept like a shadow across college football fields. Red Grange turned professional after college—a bit shocking for the time.

▶ Helen Wills played powerful tennis, winning 31 major tournaments and two Olympic gold medals. Nerves of steel earned her the nickname "Little Miss Poker Face."

◀ Bobby Jones won golf's first Grand Slam—that is, he won the game's four major tournaments. He remains the only golfer to earn a Grand Slam for tournaments won in the same calendar year.

▶ The "Sultan of Swat," Babe Ruth, was legendary on the field for his home runs.

BABE RUTH Right Field

664 CHAPTER 20

Radio helped inflame public passion for sports. Americans by the millions tuned in to broadcasts of ballgames and prize fights. Millions more attended events in person. In the process, American athletes were the top performers among the most famous and wealthy individuals in the world.

READING CHECK **Identifying the Main Idea** What types of heroes did Americans idolize in the 1920s?

Arts of the 1920s

The 1920s was a decade of great economic and social change. These themes offered novelists a rich source of material. You have read already about the writers of the Harlem Renaissance. A number of other American authors produced important works in this decade.

F. Scott Fitzgerald may be the writer most closely linked with the 1920s. His works include stories such as "Bernice Bobs Her Hair," which helped create the image of the flapper, and *Tales of the Jazz Age*, which provided a lasting nickname for the decade. His novel *The Great Gatsby* explored the lives of the rich and critically examined the values of the wealthy.

Sinclair Lewis's novel *Babbitt* also underscored the costs of success in America. Unlike Fitzgerald's glamorous characters, however, Lewis's Babbitt illustrated the emptiness of middle-class life.

HISTORY'S VOICES

❝ He was forty-six years old now, in April, 1920, and he made nothing in particular, neither butter nor shoes nor poetry ... He who had been a boy very credulous of life was no longer greatly interested in the possible and improbable adventures of each new day. ❞

—Sinclair Lewis, *Babbitt*, 1922

Edna St. Vincent Millay wrote beautiful poetry that ranged from celebrations of youthful spirit to concern over leading social issues of the day. For example, she was deeply involved in the effort to prevent the executions of Italian immigrants Sacco and Vanzetti, which you read about earlier.

Women also held a prominent place in the field of fiction writing. Willa Cather and Edith Wharton produced some of the era's most notable works of literature.

Skills Focus: Comparing and Contrasting
Below Level

Reading Skill
Sports: Then and Now

1. Have students examine the four sports pictures. Guide students in a discussion of the accomplishments of these four individuals.

2. Have students create four separate Venn diagrams, one for each sport: football, tennis, golf, and baseball.

3. Have students complete the diagrams comparing and contrasting styles of clothing, prominent sports heroes, and the way these games are played, then and now.

4. Call on volunteers to share their diagrams with the class. **LS** **Visual-Spatial, Verbal-Linguistic**

📄 Alternative Assessment Handbook, Rubric 13: Graphic Organizers

📦 Graphic Organizer Transparencies

Answers

Reading Check *film stars, pilots, and sports heroes*

World War I had a deep impact on American writers, including Ernest Hemingway and John Dos Passos. Both were war veterans, and both wrote powerfully about their experiences. Hemingway's *A Farewell to Arms* and Dos Passos's *Three Soldiers* are major works of the era. Hemingway and Dos Passos were also included among the so-called Lost Generation. The term, invented by writer Gertrude Stein, referred to the group of American writers who chose to live in Europe following World War I. It included F. Scott Fitzgerald, who lived part time in Paris in the 1920s.

Some literature celebrated the booming business and popular culture of the time period. In 1925 advertising executive Bruce Barton published *The Man Nobody Knows*. In it, he compared the biblical figure of Jesus to a modern-day business executive. Hard-driving business and advertising, Barton argued, was consistent with Christianity.

George Gershwin was another writer, but of music rather than of literature. He is especially remembered for his composition *Rhapsody in Blue*. This orchestral piece showed the powerful impact of jazz music, which was gaining great popularity in the 1920s. Gershwin is also beloved for his popular songs, many of which were written with his brother, Ira.

READING CHECK **Contrasting** How did the writings of Fitzgerald and Lewis differ?

PRIMARY SOURCES

The Great Gatsby

F. Scott Fitzgerald published *The Great Gatsby* in 1925. The novel details the selfish, reckless, and ultimately meaningless lives of the very rich—an image that became associated with the Jazz Age. Here he describes a party on a Long Island estate.

By seven o'clock the orchestra has arrived, no thin five-piece affair, but a whole pitful of oboes and trombones and saxophones and viols and cornets and piccolos, high and low drums. The last swimmers have come in from the beach now and are dressing upstairs; the cars from New York are parked five deep in the drive, and already the halls and salons and verandas are gaudy with primary colors, and hair shorn in strange new ways ... The bar is in full swing, and floating rounds of cocktails permeate the garden outside, until the air is alive with chatter and laughter, and casual innuendo and introductions forgotten on the spot, and enthusiastic meetings between women who never knew each other's names."

Skills FOCUS **READING LIKE A HISTORIAN**

1. **Drawing Conclusions** What details indicate showy excess at the party?

2. **Interpreting Literature** What message is Fitzgerald conveying about the Jazz Age?

See *Skills Handbook*, p. H28–H29

SECTION 3 ASSESSMENT

go.hrw.com
Online Quiz
Keyword: SD7 HP20

Reviewing Ideas, Terms, and People

1. **a. Recall** What two major developments in mass entertainment took place in the 1920s?
   b. Make Generalizations How did the development of mass entertainment affect American culture?
   c. Evaluate Do you think the new mass entertainment would have a greater effect in urban areas or in rural ones?

2. **a. Identify** Briefly describe the significance of the following: Charlie Chaplin, Charles A. Lindbergh, Amelia Earhart
   b. Make Inferences What can you infer from the fact that some 300 songs were written about Lindbergh's 1927 flight?
   c. Rate Judge which of the heroes discussed in this chapter had the most lasting influence on life in the United States.

3. **a. Identify** Briefly describe the contributions of the following: F. Scott Fitzgerald, George Gershwin
   b. Contrast Contrast the points of view of Sinclair Lewis and Bruce Barton as described in the section.

c. Evaluate Why do you think economic and social changes in the 1920s affected American literature?

Critical Thinking

4. **Support the Main Idea** Copy the diagram below. Complete the diagram using details that support the main idea.

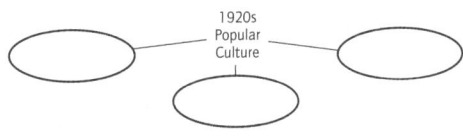

1920s Popular Culture

FOCUS ON WRITING

5. **Persuasive** Write an advertisement for a radio. The ad should seek to persuade potential buyers of the possible benefits of owning a radio in the 1920s.

665

The 1920s Flapper

Word Help

dingy dirty-looking, shabby

Info to Know

Dorothy Parker During the 1920s, Dorothy Parker co-founded the Algonquin Round Table, an informal group of writers who met for lunch daily at the Algonquin Hotel in New York City. In the conversations that ensued, Parker launched her reputation as one of New York's wittiest conversationalists. Remembered for her quick wit and intelligent mind, Parker symbolized the liberated woman of the 1920s.

Primary Source

In "A Flapper's Appeal to Parents," Ellen Welles Page asked the older generation to accept the lifestyle of flappers: "You! You parents, and grandparents, and friends, and teachers, and preachers—all of you . . . We are the Younger Generation. The war tore away our spiritual foundations and challenged our faith. We are struggling to regain our equilibrium . . . Help us to put our knowledge to the best advantage. Work with us! That is the way!"

The 1920s Flapper

Historical Context The documents below provide different perspectives on new fashions of the 1920s. As you read in this chapter, some young American women of the era were captivated by new trends in nightlife, fashion, and music.

Task Examine the documents and answer the questions that follow. Then you will be asked to write an essay about American reactions to new styles in the 1920s, using facts from the documents and from this chapter to support the position you take in your thesis statement.

DOCUMENT 1

Well-known poet Dorothy Parker lived from 1893 to 1967. Her poetry is known for its witty, quotable lines and its insightful social criticism. Below is the first stanza of Parker's poem "The Flapper." You will notice the French phrase *au contraire*, which means "on the contrary" or "just the opposite."

> The Playful flapper here we see,
> The fairest of the fair.
> She's not what Grandma used to be, –
> You might say, au contraire.
> Her girlish ways may make a stir,
> Her manners cause a scene,
> But there is no more harm in her
> Than in a submarine.

DOCUMENT 2

Not all women during the 1920s were flappers, and not everyone was captivated by the flapper lifestyle. Below is an excerpt from a 1923 commentary in a newspaper called *The New York World*.

> There is nothing inspiring in seeing an extremely tired pretty girl in a worn bathrobe, dingy white stockings in rolls about scruffy felt slippers, her eyes held shut, her arms hung over her partner's shoulders, drag aching feet that seemed glued to the floor in one short, agonizing step after another, dancing to the sounds of what they call jazz . . .

Skills Focus: Making Inferences   At Level

Reading Skill
The Lifestyle of a Flapper

1. Guide the class in a discussion of the 1920s using the following questions as a guide:

   • Why would people have been shocked about the way flappers dressed?

   • Why did some people consider jazz to be "noise" rather than music?

   • Why would the lifestyle of the Roaring Twenties have worried older generations?

   • To what extent were the new styles a result of behavioral changes?

2. Have each student write an editorial from the perspective of a newspaper editor in the 1920s. Students should either criticize or support the lifestyle of the flapper and explain why. **LS Logical-Mathematical, Verbal-Linguistic**

   Alternative Assessment Handbook, Rubrics 11: Discussions; and 17: Letters to Editors

DOCUMENT 3

John Held Jr. was an artist and cartoonist who is best known for his cartoons depicting the flappers of the 1920s. Below is a cover from *Life* magazine. The woman shown here is dressed in typical flapper style, with short (bobbed) hair, a loose dress, and heavy makeup.

DOCUMENT 4

This 1925 article was printed in a magazine called *The New Republic*. The author describes a 19-year-old woman named Jane who dresses in the flapper style. Part of the article is an interview with Jane, in which she describes her reasons for dressing the way she does.

> Jane's a flapper. That is a quaint, old-fashioned term, but I hope you remember its meaning. . . .
>
> Let us take a look at the young person as she strolls across the lawn of her parents' suburban home, having just put the car away after driving sixty miles in two hours. She is, for one thing, a very pretty girl. Beauty is the fashion in 1925. She is frankly, heavily made up, not to imitate nature, but for an altogether artificial effect—pallor mortis [deathly paleness], poisonously scarlet lips, richly ringed eyes . . .
>
> "In a way," says Jane, "it's just honesty. Women have come down off the pedestal lately. They are tired of this mysterious-feminine-charm stuff. Maybe it goes with independence, earning your own living and voting and all that."

Primary Source

At the end of the article in Document 4, Jane makes a link between the liberated clothing styles of the day and women's then-new rights and freedoms: "That fact is," as Jane says, "that women to-day are shaking off the shreds and patches of their age-old servitude. 'Feminism' has won a victory so nearly complete that we have even forgotten the fierce challenge which once inhered in the very word. Women have highly resolved that they are just as good as men, and intend to be treated so . . . They don't intend to be debarred from any profession or occupation which they choose to enter."

Skills FOCUS: READING LIKE A HISTORIAN

1. **a. Identify** Refer to Document 1. What does the line "She's not what Grandma used to be" tell you about the differences between flappers and women of previous generations?
   b. Analyze Does the poem present a positive or negative view of the flapper?

2. **a. Describe** Refer to Document 2. What activity is this passage criticizing?
   b. Analyze What is the main argument the writer makes against the flapper lifestyle?

3. **a. Describe** Refer to Document 3. Name three characteristics of the woman in the cartoon.
   b. Interpret What message does this cartoon present about flappers?

4. **a. Describe** What does Jane look like?
   b. Judge Do you think flapper fashions were connected to women's growing independence? Why or why not?

5. **Document-Based Essay Question** Consider the question below and form a thesis statement. Using examples from Documents 1, 2, 3, and 4, create an outline and write a short essay supporting your position. Did American reactions to flappers in the 1920s reflect tensions between old attitudes and new trends?
   See **Skills Handbook**, pp. H31, H32

THE ROARING TWENTIES **667**

Skills Focus: Comparing and Contrasting

At Level

Reading Skill
Young People of the 1920s

1. Guide the class in a discussion of modern fashion. Ask students if they have ever been criticized for the way they dress or wear their hair. Ask them what about their appearance has been criticized.

2. Pair students. Have each pair make a list of similarities and differences between young people of the 1920s and young people of today.

3. Ask volunteers to share their lists of similarities and differences with the class.

4. Have each student write a paragraph telling whether he or she thinks that young people of the 1920s were more similar to young people today or more different. Have students explain the reasons for their answers.
   LS Interpersonal, Verbal-Linguistic

   📋 Alternative Assessment Handbook, Rubrics 9: Comparing and Contrasting

Answers

Reading Like a Historian
1. **a.** *Flappers are edgy, modern women, as opposed to the sweet, old-fashioned types that "Grandma" represents.*
   b. *possible answer—negative because compares flappers to submarines, which could be lethal; positive because she is beautiful;* 2. **a.** *dancing;* **b.** *image presented by flappers is not attractive or inspiring;* 3. **a.** *short dress, short hair, flamboyant, free attitude;* **b.** *They live fun-filled lives, not restrained by traditional view of women;* 4. **a.** *She is heavily made up, with an artificial pallor, scarlet lips, and lots of eye makeup.*
   b. *possible answer—yes, because new outfits allowed women much more freedom and mobility;* 5. *possible answer—yes, because older generation had difficulty accepting new clothing, hairstyles, and freedoms embraced by younger generation*

Visual Summary

Review and Inquiry Review the information in the Visual Summary with students and then organize students into groups of three. Have each group create a political cartoon for each of the three topics in the summary: social developments, the Harlem Renaissance, and a new popular culture. Have groups share and explain their cartoons with the class.

📇 Quick Facts Transparency: The Roaring Twenties

Reviewing Key Terms and People

1. f.
2. e.
3. i.
4. a.
5. c.
6. g.
7. d.
8. j.
9. h.
10. b.

Comprehension and Critical Thinking

11. a. first time this had happened in U.S. history; demonstrated significant shift in values and in lifestyles
b. The Scopes trial represented conflict between fundamentalism and modern scientific theory; Prohibition represented conflict over whether or not alcohol should be legal.
c. fundamentalism appealed to rural Americans who saw a decline in their own status reflected in changing values; was a response to 1920s city lifestyle

12. a. The Great Migration meant that large numbers of African Americans lived in the same neighborhoods, allowing for the coming together of many talented African American writers and thinkers. An African American identity started to emerge.

Visual Summary: The Roaring Twenties

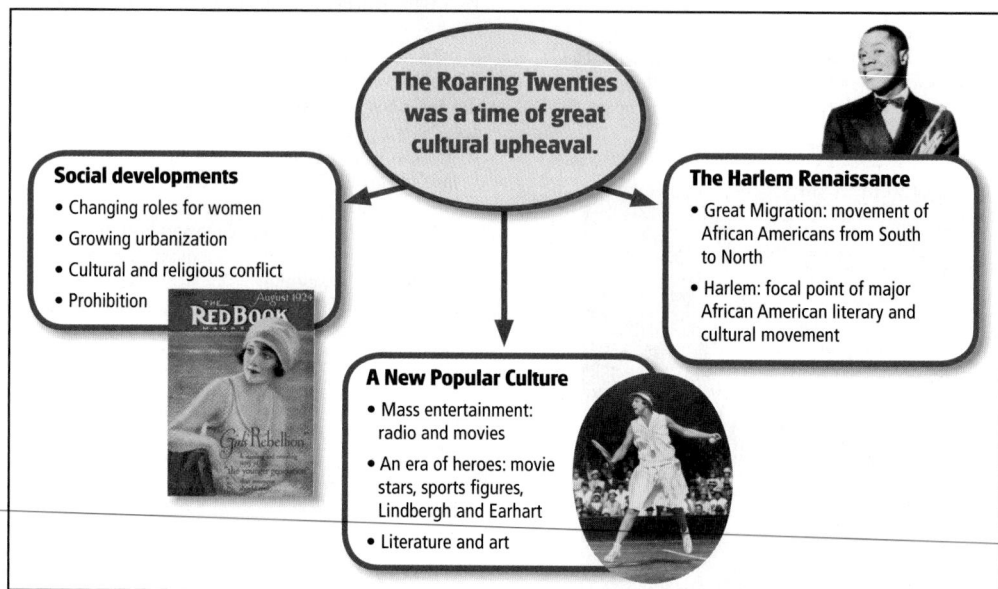

The Roaring Twenties was a time of great cultural upheaval.

Social developments
• Changing roles for women
• Growing urbanization
• Cultural and religious conflict
• Prohibition

The Harlem Renaissance
• Great Migration: movement of African Americans from South to North
• Harlem: focal point of major African American literary and cultural movement

A New Popular Culture
• Mass entertainment: radio and movies
• An era of heroes: movie stars, sports figures, Lindbergh and Earhart
• Literature and art

Reviewing Key Terms and People

Match each numbered definition with the correct numbered item from the list below.

a. African American literary flowering during the 1920s
b. a system of religious belief based on a strict interpretation of the Bible
c. pilot whose solo crossing of the Atlantic Ocean made him a national hero
d. the large-scale movement of African Americans from the South to the North in the early 1900s
e. founder of the Universal Negro Improvement Association (UNIA)
f. an African American woman writer who produced novels and many works of nonfiction
g. the lawyer who defended John Scopes in the trial about teaching evolution in Tennessee schools
h. writer from the 1920s who wrote *The Great Gatsby*

i. term for the nation's experiment with outlawing the manufacture and sale of alcohol
j. a young woman of the 1920s who adopted a certain style of dress and behavior

1. Zora Neale Hurston
2. Marcus Garvey
3. Prohibition
4. Harlem Renaissance
5. Charles A. Lindbergh
6. Clarence Darrow
7. Great Migration
8. flapper
9. F. Scott Fitzgerald
10. fundamentalism

b. Racial barriers had prevented African Americans from publishing their works and receiving recognition.
c. The term *renaissance* comes from a French word meaning *rebirth* or *revival*; it suggested a resurgence of African American culture in American life.

13. a. Movies and radio provided the nation with a shared experience, creating an increasingly large and common culture.

b. New media allowed Americans to share the same information and learn about the same events, which enabled Americans to share admiration of various individuals.
c. Lindbergh represented many of the qualities Americans valued most; he was handsome, humble, skillful, daring, and determined.

History's Impact video program
Review the video to answer the closing question: How did young Americans change society during the 1920s?

Comprehension and Critical Thinking

SECTION 1 *(pp. 646–653)*

11. a. Recall What was the significance of the fact that the 1920 census showed that the United States population was more urban than rural?

b. Analyze Identify at least two events that represent the conflict over values taking place in America in the 1920s.

c. Evaluate How was rising fundamentalism related to changing American values in the 1920s?

SECTION 2 *(pp. 654–659)*

12. a. Describe How did the Great Migration relate to the development of the Harlem Renaissance?

b. Draw Conclusions Why do you think so few African Americans had achieved literary success before the Harlem Renaissance?

c. Evaluate Why was *renaissance* an appropriate term to describe what took place in Harlem in the 1920s?

SECTION 3 *(pp. 660–665)*

13. a. Identify What effects did the development of radio and motion pictures have on American culture?

b. Analyze Why did the development of mass culture contribute to the creation of widespread adoration of heroes, such as movie stars, sports figures, and Charles Lindbergh?

c. Evaluate Why do you think Charles Lindbergh captured the imagination of the American people perhaps more than other heroes of the age?

Using the Internet

go.hrw.com
Practice Online
Keyword: SD7 CH20

14. American movies became incredibly popular during the 1920s, as films added sound and grew more sophisticated. Using the keyword above, do research to learn more about changes in American films during the 1920s. Then create an illustrated report that describes these changes, including references to important films, actors, and directors.

Analyzing Primary Sources

Reading Like a Historian During the 1920s radio went from being a little-known novelty to standard equipment in the American home. The photograph at right shows a family listening to their radio.

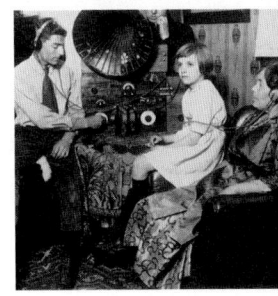

15. Describe How is this radio different from modern radios?

16. Interpret What does the placement of chairs and people around the radio suggest about its importance to the family?

Critical Reading

Read the passage in Section 1 under the heading "Effects of Urbanization." Then answer the questions that follow.

17. Which of the following is true of rural America in the 1920s?

A It was prospering economically.

B It was losing population compared with urban America.

C It was gaining population compared with urban America.

D It was attracting millions of immigrants.

WRITING FOR THE SAT

Think about the following issue.

The 1920s in the United States was a time of much social change. To some people, rural America represented the traditional spirit of the nation, while cities represented changes that threatened traditional values.

18. Assignment Did the social changes of the 1920s threaten traditional American values? Write a short essay in which you develop your position on the issue. Support your point of view with reasoning and examples from your readings and studies.

Answers

Using the Internet

14. Go to the HRW Web site and enter the keyword shown to access a rubric for this activity.

KEYWORD: SD7 CH20

Analyzing Primary Sources

Reading Like a Historian

15. The radio is much bigger and requires the use of headphones.

16. very important, because the people are gathered around it

Critical Reading

17. B

Writing for the SAT

18. possible answers—yes, people who lived in urban areas did not share the values of hard work, strong religious beliefs, and self-reliance that made the country strong, and this did threaten traditional American values; no, values would have changed anyway; over time values and lifestyles change; this does not represent a challenge to the traditional values of a nation

A rubric for this activity is provided in the CRF: Writing for the SAT Activity: The Constitution and Prohibition.

History's Impact Video Program

new beliefs, changed U.S. culture

Review and Assessment Resources

Review and Reinforce

- CRF: Chapter Review Activity
- Quick Facts Transparency: The Roaring Twenties
- Spanish Chapter Summaries Audio CD Program
- Online Chapter Summaries in Spanish
- OSP Holt PuzzlePro; Quiz Show for ExamView
- Quiz Game CD-ROM

Assess

- PASS: Chapter Test, Forms A and B
- Alternative Assessment Handbook
- OSP ExamView Test Generator, Chapter Test
- Differentiated Instruction Modified Worksheets and Tests CD-ROM: Chapter Test
- HOAP Holt Online Assessment Program (in the Premier Online Edition)

Reteach/Intervene

- Interactive Reader and Study Guide
- Differentiated Instruction Teacher Management System: Lesson Plans for Differentiated Instruction
- Differentiated Instruction Modified Worksheets and Tests CD-ROM: Chapter Test
- Interactive Skills Tutor CD-ROM

go.hrw.com
Online Resources
KEYWORD: SD7 CH20

The Great Depression Begins

Chapter Overview	Reproducible Resources	Technology Resources
CHAPTER 21 pp. 670–695 **Overview:** In this chapter, students will analyze the economic boom in the 1920s and the causes and effects of the stock market crash.	**Differentiated Instruction Teacher Management System:*** • Instructional Benchmarking Guides • Lesson Plans for Differentiated Instruction **Interactive Reader and Study Guide:** Chapter Summary* **Chapter Resource File:*** • Focus on Writing Activity: Hoover's Response to the Great Depression • Social Studies Skills Activity: Identifying Problem and Solution • Chapter Review Activity **American History Outline Maps** **Pre-AP Activities Guide for American History*** **Reading Like a Historian Toolkit**	**Live Ink® Online Reading Help** **Student Edition on Audio CD Program** **Differentiated Instruction Modified Worksheets and Tests CD-ROM** **Interactive Skills Tutor CD-ROM** **United States History Primary Source Library CD-ROM** **Power Presentations with Video CD-ROM** **History's Impact: American History Video Program (VHS/DVD):** The Great Depression Begins **Online Chapter Summaries in Spanish**
Section 1: **The Great Crash** **The Main Idea:** The stock market crash of 1929 revealed weaknesses in the American economy and helped trigger a spreading economic crisis.	**Differentiated Instruction Teacher Management System:** Section 1 Lesson Plan* **Interactive Reader and Study Guide:** Section 1 Summary* **Chapter Resource File:*** • Vocabulary Builder Activity, Section 1 • Biography Activity: Jesse Livermore • Primary Source Activity: Free Soup, Coffee, and Doughnuts	**Daily Bellringer Transparency:** Section 1* **Quick Facts Transparency:** Warning Signs* **Daily Test Practice Transparency:** Section 1* **Internet Activity:** The Great Crash
Section 2: **Americans Face Hard Times** **The Main Idea:** The Great Depression and the natural disaster known as the Dust Bowl produced economic suffering on a scale the nation had never seen before.	**Differentiated Instruction Teacher Management System:** Section 2 Lesson Plan* **Interactive Reader and Study Guide:** Section 2 Summary* **Chapter Resource File:*** • Vocabulary Builder Activity, Section 2 • Biography Activity: John Beecher • Primary Source Activity: Political Activist Describes Migrant Housing in California	**Daily Bellringer Transparency:** Section 2* **Map Transparency:** The Dust Bowl* **Quick Facts Transparencies:** Distribution of Wealth, 1929*; Causes of the 1929 Stock Market Crash* **Daily Test Practice Transparency:** Section 2* **Internet Activity:** The Dust Bowl
Section 3: **Hoover as President** **The Main Idea:** Herbert Hoover came to office with a clear philosophy of government, but the events of the Great Depression overwhelmed his responses.	**Differentiated Instruction Teacher Management System:** Section 3 Lesson Plan* **Interactive Reader and Study Guide:** Section 3 Summary* **Chapter Resource File:*** • Vocabulary Builder Activity, Section 3 • Biography Activity: The Bonus Army	**Daily Bellringer Transparency:** Section 3* **Daily Test Practice Transparency:** Section 3* **Internet Activity:** The Hoover Dam

go.hrw.com   Print Resource   Transparency

LS Learning Styles   🔊 Audio CD   💿 CD-ROM

📹 Video   **SE** Student Edition   **TE** Teacher's Edition

OSP One-Stop Planner CD-ROM

*also on One-Stop Planner CD-ROM

Review, Assessment, Intervention

 Quick Facts Transparencies: Distribution of Wealth, 1929; Causes of the 1929 Stock Market Crash; Economic Impact of the Great Depression; The Great Depression Begins

 **Spanish Chapter Summaries Audio CD Program**

 **Progress Assessment Support System (PASS):** Chapter Test*

 **Differentiated Instruction Modified Worksheets and Tests CD-ROM:** Modified Chapter Test

OSP **One-Stop Planner CD-ROM:** ExamView Test Generator (English/Spanish)

HOAP **Holt Online Assessment Program (HOAP),** in the Holt Premier Online Student Edition

 PASS: Section 1 Quiz*
 Online Quiz: Section 1
Alternative Assessment Handbook

 PASS: Section 2 Quiz*
 Online Quiz: Section 2
Alternative Assessment Handbook

 PASS: Section 3 Quiz*
 Online Quiz: Section 3
Alternative Assessment Handbook

 RESOURCES

The following resources were developed to help North Carolina educators teach the standards and objectives of North Carolina's eleventh grade standard course of study in United States history.
- United States history EOC Test Prep Workbook
- Teacher's Support System
- North Carolina One-Stop Planner

And be sure to direct your students to **go.hrw.com** for online access to the EOC Test Prep Workbook.

go.hrw.com
EOC Test Prep
KEYWORD: SE7 NC

Holt Online Learning

go.hrw.com
Teacher Resources
KEYWORD: SD7 TEACHER

go.hrw.com
Student Resources
KEYWORD: SD7 CH21

- Document-based Questions
- Interactive Multimedia Activities

- Current Events
- Chapter-based Internet Activities
- and more!

Holt Premier
Online Student Edition
Complete online support for interactivity, assessment, and reporting
- Interactive Maps and Notebook
- Standardized Test Prep
- Homework Practice and Research Activities Online

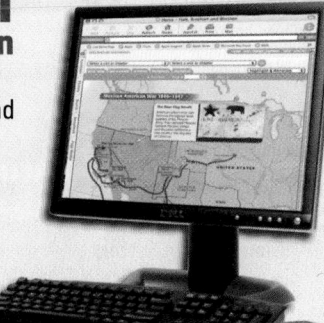

CHAPTER 21 PLANNING GUIDE

Before You Teach

The Big Picture

Deborah Gray White

The Great Crash The good times of the 1920s were fueled by a booming economy. The gross national product rose, the stock market expanded, and faith in business and government was high. Yet the decade was also marked by uneven distribution of wealth and the rise of debt. When the economy slumped at the end of the 1920s, the credit pyramid that had been created by stock market investors, brokers, and banks crumbled swiftly. The American economy, and then the world economy, crashed.

Americans Face Hard Times The ripple effect of the stock market crash spread hardship throughout the nation. Bank failures wiped out ordinary people's savings. Americans went hungry, and as the demand for food decreased, farms foreclosed. Companies failed, causing massive unemployment. Hoboes roamed the country and the unemployed and homeless built shantytowns called Hoovervilles. In the Great Plains region, drought and dust storms compounded people's misery. Migrants from the Dust Bowl, called Okies, met discrimination as they fled the natural disaster.

Hoover As President Hoover's response to the catastrophe was grounded in his philosophical belief in rugged individualism and cooperation between business and government. There was little cooperation, however, as individuals lost the means to help themselves and state and local governments made decisions based on their own interests. Hoover's actions brought little relief. The high tariff, increased income taxes, and opposition to paying the veteran's bonus made Hoover appear unsympathetic to the people's plight. In 1932 voters went to the polls intent on replacing Hoover with a more capable and sympathetic president.

Recent Scholarship

In *Building Hoover Dam: An Oral History of the Great Depression* (1993), Andrew J. Dunar and Dennis McBride make the experiences of people during the Depression come alive, and at the same time give a first person account of the building of one of America's architectural wonders. A fascinating look at the social and cultural worlds of men and women of all races, this bottom-up analysis also doubles as a community study of Boulder City and Las Vegas, Nevada, during the depression.

Differentiating Instruction

 Differentiated Instruction Teacher Management System
- Lesson Plans for Differentiated Instruction
- Differentiated Instructional Benchmarking Guides
- Interactive Reader and Study Guide

Spanish Chapter Summaries Audio CD Program

 Online Chapter Summaries in Spanish

Student Edition on Audio CD Program

 Differentiated Instruction Modified Worksheets and Tests CD-ROM
- Vocabulary Flash Cards
- Modified Vocabulary Builder Activities
- Modified Chapter Review Activity
- Modified Chapter Test

OSP One-Stop Planner CD-ROM
- ExamView Test Generator (English and Spanish)
- PuzzlePro
- Quiz Show for ExamView
- Transparencies and Videos

TE Differentiated Activities in the Teacher's Edition
- Indicators of Prosperous Economy, p. 675
- Description of Hoovervilles, p. 682
- *Grapes of Wrath* Mural, p. 686
- Migration Comparison, p. 686
- Cooperative Movement Discussion, p. 690

Reading Like a Historian
Sam Wineburg

Exploring Causality

Not content to chronicle what happened in the past, historians toil under the weight of *why*. Why did things happen as they did? What caused major events to occur?

Understanding causality poses a perennial stumbling block to students. Unlike physics, where students can perform a clever experiment to get at the cause of a particular action, historical events have multiple—often competing—causes, many of which resist simplification and elimination. Indeed, philosophers of history refer to historical explanations as "over-determined," by which they mean that for every major event there are more causes available than are needed to explain it. An overabundance of causes.

A Question of Interpretation

Causal explanations in history have a greater similarity to the grainy and uneven texture of a literary interpretation than to the cold sleekness of a mathematical proof. We judge their adequacy by their ability to (a) account for the available evidence, and (b) cohere into an integrated whole, their "verisimilitude" or feeling of truthfulness and trustworthiness. Two historians can agree on the same facts about what led up to a historical event, but disagree endlessly on how these facts come together as a causal explanation.

Our chapter offers a ripe opportunity to explore these issues. Cause comes to the forefront in Section 1, under the heading "Economic Weaknesses," beginning on page 675 where our authors lay out their explanation for the stock market's abrupt fall. Two main causes are adduced: first, the unequal distribution of wealth between rich and poor, and second, the availability of easy credit ("buying on margin"), which led to wild speculation. While not a foolproof guide, the amount of space authors assign an explanation can signal its relative importance. In our case, the second cause receives double the coverage as the first.

Comparing Explanations

While the causes given by our authors are accepted by most historians, some believe that other factors were equally—or more—important. In economist John Kenneth Galbraith's *The Great Crash 1929* (1954), for example, Galbraith also gives pride of place to the unequal distribution of wealth. But he dismisses the availability of credit as a cause, instead listing such contributing causes as a flawed corporate structure; the 1920s as a time of "an exceptional number of promoters, grafters, swindlers, imposters, and frauds"; a weak banking structure, in which bankers fell victim to the same optimism as ordinary investors; an unfavorable balance of trade (a factor also noted by our chapter); and the poor state of economic intelligence, part of which was the widespread belief that "ordinary people were meant to be rich."

Other writers mention still more contributing factors to the stock market collapse, including the federal government's management of monetary policy, a contracting money supply, consumers' purchasing decisions, falling demand for products, and more.

Explanation and Ambiguity

Faced with competing causal accounts, our students—often intolerant of ambiguity—will demand to know, "Which one is right?" The only legitimate retort can be a question of our own: "So, which explanation best accounts for the available evidence?" It is this question that will lead to more learning and engage students in building causal accounts of their own.

Standards Focus

Social Studies Competency Goals
Goal 9 The learner will appraise the economic, social, and political changes of the decades of "The Twenties" and "The Thirties."

9.01, 9.02

The Big Idea and Essential Questions

To foster student understanding of this chapter's big idea, design your lesson to address each section's essential question.

Big Idea The underlying weaknesses of the U.S. economy were exposed when the stock market collapsed in 1929, and the nation plunged into the worst economic depression in its history.

Essential Questions

1. What did the stock market crash of 1929 reveal about the American economy?

2. What were the effects of the Great Depression and the Dust Bowl on the American economy and people?

3. How did President Herbert Hoover respond to the events of the Great Depression?

Key to Differentiating Instruction

Below Level

Basic-level activities designed for all students encountering new material

At Level

Intermediate-level activities designed for average students

Above Level

Challenging activities designed for honors and gifted-and-talented students

Standard English Mastery

Activities designed to improve standard English usage

670 CHAPTER 21

CHAPTER
21 1929–1933

The Great DEPRESSION Begins

THE BIG PICTURE The boom times of the 1920s had never reached into all sectors of the economy. In 1929 the economy's underlying weaknesses were exposed when the stock market collapsed, and the nation plunged into the worst economic depression in its history.

North Carolina Standards

Social Studies Objectives
9.01 Elaborate on the cycle of economic boom and bust in the 1920's and 1930's.
9.02 Analyze the extent of prosperity for different segments of society during this period.

Language Arts Objectives
5.01 Interpret the significance of literary movements as they have evolved through the literature of the United States by:
- evaluating the literary merit and/or historical significance of a work from Colonial Literature, the Romantic Era, Realism, the Modern Era, and Contemporary Literature.

Skills FOCUS READING LIKE A HISTORIAN

Employees of the *Chicago Defender*, an African American newspaper, prepare food supplies to donate to needy families at Thanksgiving, 1931. Thousands of Americans had to rely on such generosity to survive the Great Depression.
Interpreting Visuals Do these workers seem to be victims of the Great Depression? Explain.

See **Skills Handbook**, p. H30

670

U.S.

March 1929 President Herbert Hoover takes office.

1929

World

August 1929 German dirigible *Graf Zeppelin* begins round-the-world flight.

Introduce the Chapter

At Level

The Great Depression Begins

1. Write the following scenario for students to see. *Banks are closed forever, and families have no way to get any money. All working members of the family have lost their jobs. Bills are due, and the family has no way to pay any bills. How and where are family members going to find new jobs? If they cannot pay rent, where are they going to live? If they lose their cars because they cannot afford the car payment, how will they look for work?*

2. Ask: How would you feel if this were to occur? How would you respond? During the Depression people reacted with anger, feelings of despair and hopelessness, and they hoped that the government would help.

3. Tell students that in this chapter they will learn about the greatest economic crisis in U.S. history—the Great Depression.
LS Verbal-Linguistic

Alternative Assessment Handbook, Rubric 11: Discussions

● Chapter Preview ●

HOLT
History's Impact
► Video Program: The Great Depression Begins
See the Video Teacher's Guide for strategies for using the video segment.

Reading Like a Historian
Interpreting a Photograph Have students take a moment to examine the image on these pages. Guide students in a discussion about what the appearance of the people reveals about them. *They don't appear to be suffering from the effects of the Depression.*

October 29, 1929 Stock market crashes on "Black Tuesday."	**1931** Drought that helps produce the Dust Bowl begins on the Great Plains.	**June 1932** World War I veterans' "Bonus Army" sets up camp in Washington, D.C.	

1930　　1931　　1932　　1933

1931 Japanese army invades Manchuria.	**1932** Ibn Saud proclaims himself king of newly created Saudi Arabia.	**January 1933** Adolf Hitler becomes chancellor of Germany.

671

go.hrw.com
Online Resources

Chapter Resources:
KEYWORD: SD7 CH21

Teacher Resources:
KEYWORD: SD7 TEACHER

Explore the Time Line

1. When did Ibn Saud become king of Saudi Arabia? *1932*

2. When did Adolf Hitler become chancellor of Germany? *January 1933*

3. Who was president when the stock market crashed on "Black Tuesday"? *Herbert Hoover*

4. What event began in 1931 that added to the misery of the Depression? *drought on the Great Plains*

Info to Know

Stock Market, 1929 On September 3, 1929, the Dow Jones Industrial Average reached its 1929 peak. On October 24, 1929, stock prices fell sharply, and a new record was set when almost 13 million shares of stock were sold. Then on October 29, 1929, over 16 million shares of stock were sold off. This record lasted for 39 years.

Draw Conclusions Why do you think so many people rushed to sell their stocks on the same day? *possible answer—They were concerned that they would lose even more money if they did not sell.*

Answers

Interpreting Visuals (p. 670) *No, they appear to be clean, well-fed, and well-clothed.*

671

Bellringer

The Inside Story. . . Use the **Daily Bellringer Transparency** to help students answer the question.

📖 Daily Bellringer Transparency, Section 1

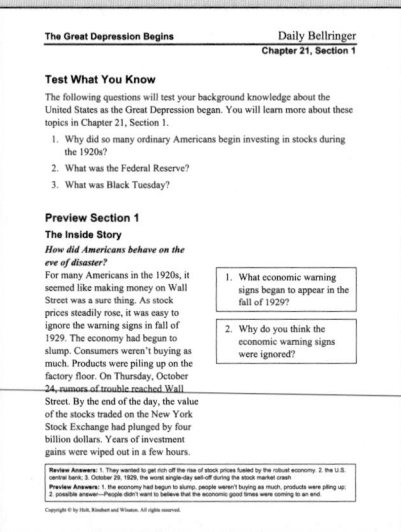

| The Great Depression Begins | Daily Bellringer |
| | Chapter 21, Section 1 |

Test What You Know

The following questions will test your background knowledge about the United States as the Great Depression began. You will learn more about these topics in Chapter 21, Section 1.

1. Why did so many ordinary Americans begin investing in stocks during the 1920s?
2. What was the Federal Reserve?
3. What was Black Tuesday?

Preview Section 1

The Inside Story

How did Americans behave on the eve of disaster?

For many Americans in the 1920s, it seemed like making money on Wall Street was a sure thing. As stock prices steadily rose, it was easy to ignore the warning signs in fall of 1929. The economy had begun to slump. Consumers weren't buying as much. Products were piling up on the factory floor. On Thursday, October 24, rumors of trouble reached Wall Street. By the end of the day, the value of the stocks traded on the New York Stock Exchange had plunged by four billion dollars. Years of investment gains were wiped out in a few hours.

| 1. What economic warning signs began to appear in the fall of 1929? |
| 2. Why do you think the economic warning signs were ignored? |

Review Answers: 1. They wanted to get rich off the rise of stock prices fueled by the robust economy. 2. the U.S. central bank; 3. October 29, 1929, the worst single-day sell-off during the stock market crash

Preview Answers: 1. the economy had begun to slump, people weren't buying as much, products were piling up; 2. possible answer—People didn't want to believe that the economic good times were coming to an end.

Copyright © by Holt, Rinehart and Winston. All rights reserved.

Academic Vocabulary

Review with students the high-use academic term in this section.

specific particular (p. 673)

📄 CRF: Vocabulary Builder Activity, Section 1

Taking Notes

Causes—uneven wealth distribution; easy credit; buying stock on margin; Stock Market Crash of 1929; Effects—people in debt; bank failures; businesses failed

---

The Great Crash

BEFORE YOU READ

MAIN IDEA

The stock market crash of 1929 revealed weaknesses in the American economy and helped trigger a spreading economic crisis.

READING FOCUS

1. What economic factors and conditions made the American economy appear prosperous in the 1920s?
2. What were the basic economic weaknesses in the American economy in the late 1920s?
3. What events led to the stock market crash of October 1929?
4. What were the effects of the crash on the economy of the United States and the world?

KEY TERMS AND PEOPLE

gross national product
Herbert Hoover
buying on margin
Federal Reserve System
Black Tuesday

TAKING NOTES

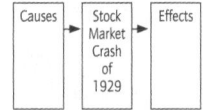 As you read, take notes on the causes and effects of the stock market crash of 1929. Record your notes in a graphic organizer like the one shown here.

Causes → Stock Market Crash of 1929 → Effects

Calm Before the Storm

THE INSIDE STORY

How did Americans behave on the eve of disaster? For many people in the 1920s, investing in the stock market was one big joyride. Week after week, month after month, stock prices steadily rose. After a while, it seemed like making money on Wall Street was a sure thing.

With so many fortunes being made, it was easy to ignore the warning signs that began to appear in the fall of 1929. The economy had began to slump. Consumers weren't buying as much. Products were piling up on factory floors. A handful of experts whispered that trouble lay in store for the stock market.

On Thursday, October 24, 1929, those whispers became reality. By the end of the day, the value of the stocks traded on the New York Stock Exchange had plunged by 9 percent. Years of investment gains—billions of dollars—were wiped out in a few hours.

Major banks and stockbrokers tried to rally the market on Friday. They bought large numbers of stocks, hoping to keep prices from dropping still more. Over the anxious weekend of October 26 and 27, stockbrokers worked quietly to reassure investors. They made phone calls and wrote letters to major investors urging them to buy stocks when the markets reopened on Monday. But nothing could answer the questions on everyone's minds. On Monday morning, which way would prices go—up or down? Were the good times about to come to an end? 🔲

▲ **Stockholders anxiously gather outside the New York Stock Exchange after news of the crash on October 29, 1929.**

Teach the Main Idea

At Level

The Great Crash

1. **Teach** Ask students the Reading Focus questions to teach this section.
2. **Apply** Have students create an outline of the section using the red and blue heads as main points. Have students identify at least two main ideas under each of the blue subheadings. **LS** Verbal-Linguistic
3. **Review** Review student outlines as a class. Have students identify the points in their outlines that they believe are most important. Ask students to explain if the

1920s were a time of true prosperity.

4. **Practice/Homework** Have each student make a table with four columns showing how the stock market crash affected each of the following: individuals, banks, business, and the rest of the world. **LS** Mathematical-Logical, Verbal-Linguistic

📄 Alternative Assessment Handbook, Rubrics 7: Charts; and 11: Discussions
📖 Graphic Organizer Transparencies

An Appearance of Prosperity

The 1920s may not have been good times for everyone. Most farmers, for instance, saw their incomes drop. But for the economy as a whole, the "Roaring Twenties" were a period of impressive and sustained growth. Between 1922 and 1928, the **gross national product** (GNP)—the total value of goods and services produced in a nation during a specific period—rose by 30 percent. At a time when most people's understanding of economic matters was relatively limited, such rapid growth triggered a feeling of optimism that proved contagious. That optimism, however, led to reckless activities.

The explosive growth of American manufacturing, particularly the new automobile industry, helped drive the expansion of the American economy. By 1929 one in five Americans owned a car. Industries that made products related to automobile production—including steel, oil, and rubber—enjoyed unprecedented business opportunities. Overall, the automobile industry and related industries employed nearly 4 million workers.

As corporate profits swelled, companies hired additional factory workers to keep up with production needs. Unemployment between 1923 and 1929 remained very low, averaging around 3 percent. Low unemployment, in turn, slowed the growth of organized labor. Union membership dropped as employers expanded welfare capitalism programs.

As you read earlier, welfare capitalism is a term for various benefits, such as employer-paid insurance, which companies provide to employees as a way of improving worker loyalty and satisfaction. Such programs helped increase workers' sense of prosperity and well-being in the 1920s.

This feeling of prosperity encouraged many workers to purchase the new products coming off the nation's assembly lines. With their shorter work hours and bigger paychecks, Americans flocked to movie theaters, sporting events, and other leisure activities. Times, it seemed, were good.

Stock market expansion While Americans generally were feeling good about the economy in the 1920s, those who invested in the stock market were overjoyed. The stock market is a place where stocks are bought and sold. *Stock* is ownership in a company, and it is sold in *shares*. In other words, by buying shares of stock, a person is able to buy a piece of a corporation. If the corporation succeeds, its value may rise. This means that the value of its stock also rises. If the corporation does not do well, it may lose value. This would drive the value of the stock down.

ACADEMIC VOCABULARY
specific particular

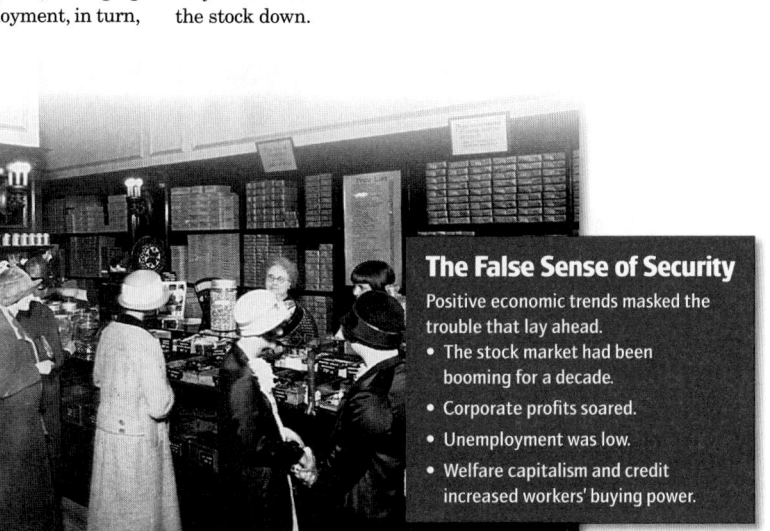

The False Sense of Security

Positive economic trends masked the trouble that lay ahead.

- The stock market had been booming for a decade.
- Corporate profits soared.
- Unemployment was low.
- Welfare capitalism and credit increased workers' buying power.

THE GREAT DEPRESSION BEGINS **673**

An Appearance of Prosperity

Recall How did Coolidge and Harding view the relationship between business and government? *Government should support, not interfere, with business practices.*

Analyze In what ways did the election of 1928 represent a conflict over values? *Hoover and Smith represented different backgrounds, religions, ideas; each appealed to different groups of Americans.*

Make Judgments Do you think that the president should be responsible when calamity strikes the nation? *possible answers—Yes, as the leader in charge, president is responsible; no—president cannot be responsible for all problems within a country.*

📄 CRF: Economics and History Activity: From "Prosperity" to Depression

📄 CRF: Biography: Jesse Livermore

Info to Know

Stock investors Many Americans invested in the stock market because they had heard stories of ordinary citizens earning fortunes. In one popular tale, a peddler turned $4,000 into $250,000. In addition, many people saw the market as a safe way to make money. In spite of this, historians have estimated that just 3 million Americans, or less than 2.5 percent of the nation's population, owned stocks in 1928.

Answers

Interpreting Maps *Republican; the South*

674

The American stock market performed spectacularly during the 1920s. Although stocks increased at different rates, the general trend in stock prices was sharply upward. Between 1920 and 1929 the overall value of stocks traded at the nation's stock markets quadrupled.

The steep rise in stock prices changed the way many people thought about buying stocks. Since the market never seemed to go down in the 1920s, many people began to act as though it never would.

A growing number of ordinary Americans began to make stock investments. To *invest* means to put money into stocks, land, or some other location in the hope that the value of this money will grow.

The number of shares being traded in the United States rose sharply during the 1920s. The number rose from 318 million in 1920 to more than 1 billion in 1929. Many investors were encouraged by the words of men such as John Raskob, a leader of General Motors.

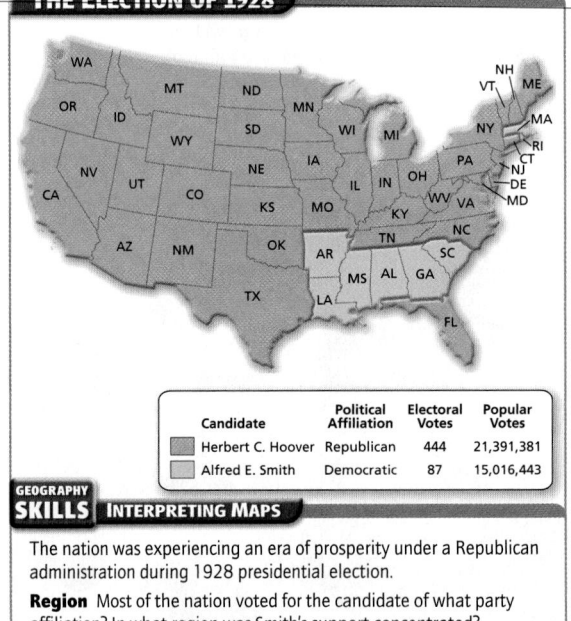

THE ELECTION OF 1928

Candidate	Political Affiliation	Electoral Votes	Popular Votes
Herbert C. Hoover	Republican	444	21,391,381
Alfred E. Smith	Democratic	87	15,016,443

GEOGRAPHY SKILLS INTERPRETING MAPS

The nation was experiencing an era of prosperity under a Republican administration during 1928 presidential election.

Region Most of the nation voted for the candidate of what party affiliation? In what region was Smith's support concentrated?

See Skills Handbook, p. H20

674 CHAPTER 21

Faith in business and government For many Americans, the prosperity of the 1920s demonstrated the triumph of American business. Presidents Harding and Coolidge favored policies that gave businesses the maximum freedom to achieve and succeed. As Coolidge once famously remarked, "The chief business of the American people is business."

This approach was popular with the majority of voters. Harding had won a clear victory in the 1920 election, and Coolidge did the same in 1924. Coolidge in particular remained widely popular throughout his term in office. Public confidence in the federal government and in its pro-business policies remained very high.

The election of 1928 Coolidge decided not to run for reelection in 1928, so the Republicans chose **Herbert Hoover** as their candidate. Hoover had never held elective office, but he had an impressive record of public service. He had overseen America's food production during World War I and later directed relief efforts in Europe. He also served as the secretary of commerce under Harding and Coolidge.

By 1928 Hoover had built an outstanding reputation as a businesslike administrator—just the sort of leader who could guide the prosperous nation. Indeed, people thought so highly of Hoover that it troubled him. "They have a conviction that I am sort of superman, that no problem is beyond my capacity," he once said. "If some unprecedented calamity should come upon the nation . . . I would be sacrificed to the unreasoning disappointment of a people who expected too much."

Hoover and the Democratic candidate, Al Smith, presented the nation with a stark contrast. Smith was an outgoing and natural politician. Hoover was quiet and shy by comparison. Smith was a Catholic—the first ever to run for president—and drew much of his support from Catholic urban immigrant

---

Skills Focus: Comparing and Contrasting

Reading Skill
Selecting a New President in 1928

1. Organize the class into small groups. Have students develop campaign strategies for the 1928 presidential election. Half of the groups should represent Republicans campaigning for Hoover. The other half should represent Democrats campaigning for Smith.

2. Students should carefully study each candidate's positions on the issues and prepare a campaign strategy for their candidate. Students should prepare

strategies and slogans that appeal both to the candidate's base and to those who might be less willing to vote for their candidate.

3. Have groups present their campaign strategies and slogans to the class. Then guide students in a discussion of the candidates. 🔲 **Visual-Spatial**

📄 Alternative Assessment Handbook, Rubric 14: Group Activity

populations. Hoover was a Quaker, and many of his supporters did not trust Catholics. His support was strongest in small towns.

The two men also differed on Prohibition. Smith supported alcohol sales, while Hoover supported Prohibition. In short, the contest represented many of the cultural conflicts that had divided the nation in the 1920s. Hoover won an easy victory.

READING CHECK **Identifying Cause and Effect** How did the rise of the stock market affect American investors?

Economic Weaknesses

The economic prosperity of the 1920s helped define the decade. Yet while many Americans celebrated their financial good fortune, a number of serious problems bubbled just beneath the surface.

Wealth distribution One troubling aspect of the American economy was the vastly uneven distribution of the new wealth that was being created. Despite the boom in business in the 1920s, a surprisingly small number of people had truly prospered. As a group, the wealthiest 1 percent of the population had seen their share of the national income grow 60 percent between 1920 and 1929. Most workers, however, experienced much smaller pay increases—about 8 percent for most job categories.

Workers in certain industries, such as farming and coal mining, were hit particularly hard. By 1929 more than 70 percent of the nation's families had an income below the level they needed for a good standard of living. The personal savings rate declined noticeably during the decade as well.

For much of the decade, the easy availability of credit had allowed many Americans to buy the automobiles, radios, vacuum cleaners, and other products rolling quickly off the nation's assembly lines. By the end of the decade, however, many consumers were reaching the limits of their credit. The pace of purchases slowed. Warehouses became filled with factory goods that no one could afford to buy.

Credit and the stock market Installment credit was not just a tool for buying consumer products. Investors also used credit to purchase

stocks. This risky practice increased during the 1920s as the stock market rose sharply.

Here is how it worked: Imagine an investor wanted to buy 100 shares of stock in Company A at $10 a share. The total purchase price would be $1,000. To make this purchase, the investor would pay just a portion of the $1,000—say, for example, $500. The investor would borrow the other $500 from a stockbroker. The understanding was that the investor would pay off the loan when he or she sold the stock. Buying stocks with loans from stockbrokers is known as **buying on margin.**

As enthusiasm for investing in the stock market grew, brokers began to require lower and lower margins for stock purchases, giving bigger and bigger loans to investors. In 1929 an investor could purchase a stock with as little as a 10 percent margin. In a time when many stocks were gaining value by the day, margin buying seemed like an easy way to make money.

Buying on margin, however, involved enormous risks. Returning to the example of Company A, say its stock price rose to $15 a share. The investor then could sell the stock

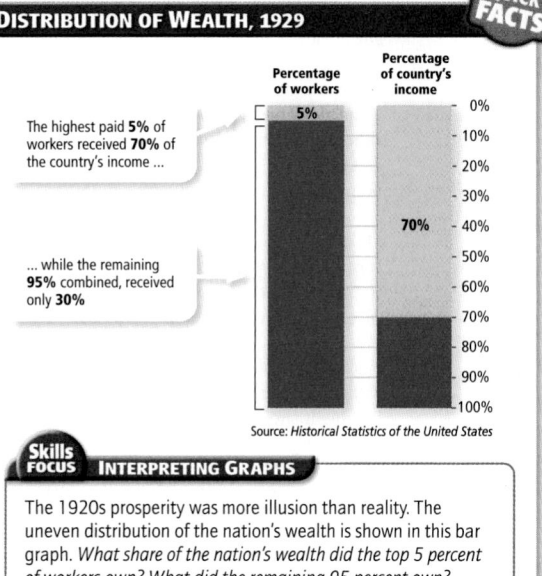

DISTRIBUTION OF WEALTH, 1929

QUICK FACTS

Percentage of workers

Percentage of country's income

The highest paid **5%** of workers received **70%** of the country's income ...

5%

... while the remaining **95%** combined, received only **30%**

70%

0%
10%
20%
30%
40%
50%
60%
70%
80%
90%
100%

Source: *Historical Statistics of the United States*

Skills FOCUS **INTERPRETING GRAPHS**

The 1920s prosperity was more illusion than reality. The uneven distribution of the nation's wealth is shown in this bar graph. *What share of the nation's wealth did the top 5 percent of workers own? What did the remaining 95 percent own?*

See **Skills Handbook**, p. H16

THE GREAT DEPRESSION BEGINS **675**

Direct Teach

Reading Focus

2 What were the basic economic weaknesses in the American economy in the late 1920s? *uneven distribution of wealth; easy credit; too easy to buy stock on margin*

Economic Weaknesses

Describe How did most Americans fare during the 1920s? *not well; most had only small increases in salary*

Analyze In what way was the easy availability of credit a blessing and a curse? *allowed Americans to buy products, fueled economic growth; when consumers could not pay their debts, purchasing slowed; warehouses were filled with goods*

Evaluate Do you think that advertising played a significant role in mounting consumer debt? *Yes, people wanted to buy things that were advertised.*

Quick Facts Transparency: Distribution of Wealth, 1929

Answers

Interpreting Graphs *70%; 30%*

Reading Check *Many people began to invest because they thought the market would not go down.*

Economic Weaknesses

Define What was a margin call? *demand for payment of a margin loan if a stock's value fell below a certain point*

Evaluate Why do you think many people ignored Babson's warnings of a stock market crash? *possible answer—because the economy had been so strong they probably thought any slump would be temporary*

Primary Sources

The Crash

John Hersch, an investment broker, described Thursday, October 24, 1929—the first day the stock market began to plummet. "I had about $3,000 in the stock market, which was all the money I had. On Black Friday—Thursday, was it?—that margin account went out of the window. I may have had about $62 left. My wife had a colossal $125 a week job . . . That night, she came home . . . and she said, 'Guess what happened today?' I said, 'What?' She said, 'I quit.' I was making $60 a week and she was making $125. Two-thirds of our income and all of our savings disappeared that day."

go.hrw.com
Online Resources
KEYWORD: SD7 CH21
TOPIC: THE GREAT CRASH

for $1,500. In this case, the investor would get back the original $500 investment, be able to repay the $500 loan, and still have a $500 profit—doubling the original investment. But if the stock price dropped to $5 a share, the sale then would bring in just $500. All of this would go to pay off the loan. The investor would have no profit and be out the original $500 as well.

The terms of a margin loan made the gamble even riskier for the investor. Under these terms, brokers could force investors to repay their loans if the stock's value fell below a certain point. Such a demand was called a margin call. In theory, margin calls ensured that brokers would get their loans repaid. Margin calls also meant that investors could be in big trouble if their stocks lost value suddenly.

THE IMPACT TODAY

Economics
Today the Federal Reserve Board places strict limits on the practice of buying on margin.

The Federal Reserve The nation's fascination with stocks and with buying on margin drew the concern of the governing board of the **Federal Reserve System**, which serves as the nation's central bank. The Federal Reserve Board takes actions and sets policies to regulate the nation's money supply in order to promote healthy economic activity. In the late 1920s, the Federal Reserve Board decided to make it more difficult and more costly for brokers to offer margin loans to investors.

The Federal Reserve's move was partly successful, at least at first. Borrowing from banks by brokers began to decrease, but it was replaced by money from a new source. Large American corporations began providing brokers with the cash to make margin loans to investors. As a result, the run-up of the stock market continued despite the Federal Reserve's actions.

In September 1929, economist Roger Babson sounded a warning note. "Sooner or later," he said, "a crash is coming, and it may be terrific." The crash he was anticipating was a sudden drop in stock prices, which could devastate those who had borrowed heavily to buy stock.

Many experts, however, dismissed Babson's worries. In October, banker Charles E. Mitchell responded to the warnings of people such as Babson. Mitchell said, famously, "I see no reason for the end-of-the-year slump which some people are predicting." He could not have been more wrong.

READING CHECK **Summarizing** What were some of the weaknesses of the economy in the 1920s?

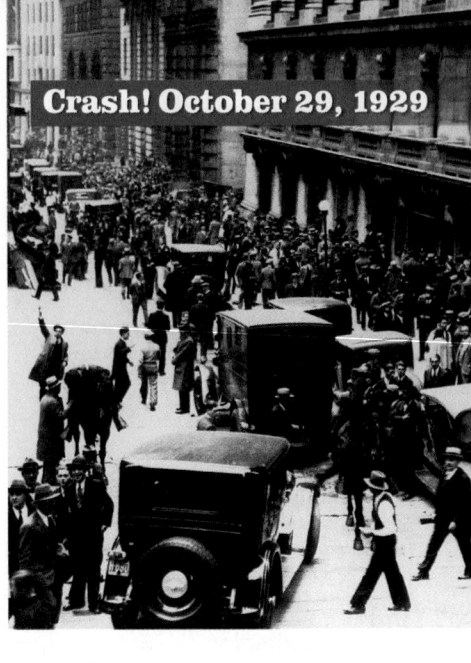

Crash! October 29, 1929

The Stock Market Crashes

While Babson and Mitchell were making their contrasting predictions about the future of the stock market, American investors looked back on several years of fantastic success. The steady growth of the early and mid-1920s had given way to truly astounding gains as the decade neared its end. One leading measure of the market's value showed a 50 percent gain in 1928 alone. During the following year, 1929, the market gained another 27 percent before reaching its high point on September 3.

Many people in the financial world, however, were beginning to recognize increasing signs of trouble in the economy. Sales of some manufactured goods were sagging badly. Rumors spread that some big investors were getting ready to take their money out of the market. Fears began to grow that current stock prices could soon collapse. The stage was set for an economic disaster.

On Thursday, October 24, 1929, some nervous investors began selling stocks. As others noticed the increased activity, they joined in the selling, afraid to be left behind. A huge sell-off had begun. With few people willing to buy the millions of stocks flooding the market,

---

Skills Focus: Identifying Problem and Solution
Above Level

Reading Skill
What If?

1. Organize the class into small groups. Tell students that in the 1920s people began to buy stock on margin. The Federal Reserve Board became concerned about the trend and began to develop a set of guidelines about stock buying in an effort to protect the nation's economy.

2. Have each group develop regulations for the buying and selling of stocks that could be used by the Federal Reserve Board.

3. Have volunteers from each group share their regulations with the rest of the class.

4. Guide the class in a discussion of the proposed regulations. Were any of the regulations suggested by all groups? If so, what were they? **LS** **Interpersonal, Logical-Mathematical**

Alternative Assessment Handbook, Rubrics 14: Group Activity; and 37: Writing Assignments

---

Answers

Reading Check *uneven distribution of wealth, dependence on credit, and buying stock on margin*

Weaknesses in the general economy, combined with unsound financial practices, set the stage for the stock market crash. Worried investors (at left) crowded Wall Street on Black Tuesday to await news.

CAUSES OF THE 1929 STOCK MARKET CRASH

Economic Factors
- Poor distribution of wealth
- Many consumers relied on credit
- Credit dried up
- Consumer spending dropped
- Industry struggled

Financial Factors
- Stock markets rise in mid-1920s
- Speculation in stock increases
- Margin buying encouraged by Federal Reserve policies
- Stock prices rise to unrealistic levels

Stock Market Crash

stock prices plunged, triggering an even greater panic to sell. One newspaper described it as "the most terrifying stampede of selling ever experienced on the New York Stock Exchange."

HISTORY'S VOICES

❝Traders on the floor of the Stock Exchange shrieked and howled their offers for desperate minutes before they found takers. Such a roar arose from the Stock Exchange floor that it could be heard for blocks up and down Broad and Wall Streets.❞
—*Seattle Post-Intelligencer*, October 25, 1929

Toward the end of this terrible day, a number of leading bankers joined together to buy stocks and prevent a further collapse in their prices. This effort succeeded in stopping the panic—for a time. The market returned to normal trading on Friday, and some stocks actually gained value.

When traders returned to work on Monday, however, the good feelings from Friday had completely evaporated. As trading began that day, the market sank like a stone. The next day—Tuesday, October 29—was the worst of all. As panic completely overcame the markets, investors dumped more than 16 million shares of stock. While the sell-offs of earlier days had

affected mainly the stocks of weaker businesses, the collapse on **Black Tuesday** affected the stock of even the most solid companies.

The damage was widespread and catastrophic. During October, the stock market dropped in value by about $16 billion. This represented nearly one-half of the market's pre-crash value.

"It was like a thunderclap," one investment banker recalled. "Everybody was stunned."

Devices called ticker-tape machines communicated a steady stream of falling stock prices. One reporter described the scene on October 29 as horrified investors watched the ticker tape.

HISTORY'S VOICES

❝[T]he crowds about the ticker tapes, like friends about the bedside of a stricken friend, reflected in their faces the story the tape was telling. There were no smiles. There were no tears either. Just the camaraderie of fellow-sufferers. Everybody wanted to tell his neighbor how much he had lost. Nobody wanted to listen. It was too repetitious a tale.❞
—*The New York Times*, October 30, 1929

READING CHECK **Sequencing** Briefly describe the events of the stock market crash from October 24 through October 29, 1929.

THE GREAT DEPRESSION BEGINS **677**

Direct Teach

Reading Focus

❸ What events led to the stock market's crash in October 1929? *sale of consumer goods declined; rumors spread; fears grew; investors began selling stocks; stock prices plunged*

The Stock Market Crashes

Explain Why did some people expect economic trouble in 1929? *sales were declining; rumors that big investors were going to take money out of the market*

Sequence How did the big sell-off of stocks begin? *Some investors began selling; others joined in; with no buyers, stock prices fell.*

Predict Do you think a stock market crash could occur today? *possible answers—Yes, large numbers of people could sell stock and prices would plunge; no, there are safeguards to prevent it.*

Answers

Reading Check *investors began selling stocks, huge sell-off began; bankers joined together to buy stocks and returned the market to normal; on October 29, the market crashed*

Skills Focus: Sequencing

Below Level

Reading Skill
The Stock Market Crashes

1. Copy the graphic organizer for students to see. Omit the italicized answers.

2. Have students copy the graphic organizer onto their own paper, and have them fill in the blank boxes.

3. Have volunteers read the factors from their completed graphic organizers. As students read their answers, fill in the master graphic organizer for students to see. Make sure that all steps are in the correct order.

4. Guide students in a discussion of the causes of the stock market crash. Ask: What were the signs of trouble that worried investors? What was done to try to prevent a further collapse in stock prices? Were efforts to prevent further collapse successful? Why or why not?

LS Visual-Spatial, Logical-Mathematical

Alternative Assessment Handbook, Rubrics 11: Discussions; and 13: Graphic Organizers

Graphic Organizer Transparencies

Factors that Caused the Stock Market Crash

Signs of trouble in the economy worry some investors
↓
Investors sell stocks
↓
Stock prices plunge
↓
Panic to sell more stock
↓
The Crash

677

❹ What were the effects of the crash on the economy of the United States and the world? *banks failed; investors lost money; consumers stopped buying; nearly three million Americans lost their jobs; rest of the world affected*

The Effects of the Crash

Recall What impact did the stock market crash have on individual investors? *almost all suffered; lost savings; went into debt*

Explain Why were banks affected by the stock market crash? *depositors withdrew money; lost money from stocks and from loans made to stockbrokers*

Predict Do high tariffs end up hurting or helping world economies? *possible answer—hurt more than help because goods become more expensive*

🗐 U.S. History Political Cartoon Activity: Cartoon 41: Victim of Bank Failures

Gross National Product
In the aftermath of the crash, U.S. GNP fell by nearly one half—from $103.1 billion in 1929 to $55.6 billion in 1933.

Banking Crisis
The stock market crash triggered a banking crisis. By 1933 more than 5,000 banks had shut their doors.

World Economy
The effects of stock market crash rippled through the world economy. In Germany, industrial productivity plunged by more than 40 percent.

Fallen on Hard Times
A Wall Street speculator (above) tries to sell his car after losing his wealth in the stock market crash. Margin calls left many such investors desperate for cash. *What other effects did the stock market crash have on individuals?*

The Granger Collection, New York

The Effects of the Crash

In the aftermath of the crash, business and political leaders rushed to calm the panic and reassure the nation. One business executive wrote optimistically in the days following Black Tuesday, "The recent collapse of stock market prices has no significance as regards the real wealth of the American people as a whole." President Hoover also downplayed the effects of the crash. He and many others firmly believed that the economy would soon recover from the shock and return to prosperity.

The impact on individuals No one denied, however, that the stock market collapse had ruined many individual investors. Some had lost years of gains. Huge fortunes disappeared before their eyes.

Margin buyers were particularly hard hit. When stock prices began to fall, brokers demanded that they pay back the borrowed money. To meet these margin calls, investors were forced to sell their shares for far less than they had paid for them. Some lost their entire savings trying to make up the difference. In the end, investors often owed enormous amounts of money to their brokers for stocks they had been forced to sell below cost.

Effects on banks The stock market crash triggered a banking crisis. Frightened depositors rushed to withdraw their money, draining banks of funds. Worse, many banks had themselves invested, directly or indirectly, in the stock market. They had purchased stock in companies whose shares were now crumbling in value. In addition, banks had made loans to stockbrokers, who in turn had loaned the money to investors on margin. When individual investors failed to cover their margins, the banks absorbed losses, too.

These loan failures eventually drove many banks out of business. As you will read in the next section, the struggles of the banks would have a deep impact on the American people.

Skills Focus: Identifying Problem and Solution `Above Level`

Reading Skill
Saving the World Economy

1. Have students review information about the causes of the 1929 stock market crash. Remind students that President Hoover downplayed the effects of the crash.

2. Have students develop strategies to protect the stock market and to convince the American people that the crash was an aberration, that the economy is still strong, and that it will quickly recover.

3. Have students write a speech that the

president will deliver to the nation presenting this information. Have volunteers read their speeches to the class.

4. Have students discuss and analyze the strategies and plans presented in the speeches. Which speeches presented an effective plan? Which speech was most convincing?
LS Interpersonal, Logical-Mathematical

🗐 Alternative Assessment Handbook, Rubrics 14: Group Activity; and 37: Writing Assignments

Answers

Photo *many individuals owed money to brokers; could not pay debts; lost all savings*

Effects on business The crash delivered a crushing blow to already struggling businesses. With money scarce, banks and investors were suddenly unwilling or unable to provide industry with the money it needed to grow and expand.

At the same time, consumers cut back their spending on everything but essential purchases. With consumers spending less, many companies began to lay off workers. Unemployed workers had even less money to make purchases, and the cycle of layoffs and reduced consumer spending accelerated quickly.

In the year that followed the great crash, Americans saw their wages drop by a total of $4 billion. Nearly 3 million people lost their jobs. Faced with an uncertain future and lower incomes, consumers, who had driven the prosperity of the 1920s, simply stopped spending.

Effects overseas The crisis that began in the United States soon rippled throughout the industrialized world. The fragile economies of Europe, still recovering from World War I, were thrown backward. American banks that had lent heavily to European businesses and governments now called in those loans.

In many cases businesses and governments alike simply did not have the money to pay back the loans. Moreover, with buying power down in the United States, foreign businesses were less able to export their products here. They responded by laying off workers. Just as in the United States, laying off workers in Europe meant that there was less money in the hands of consumers to buy products.

Governments in the United States and in countries around the world moved to protect their own industries by passing high tariffs. A high tariff would make imported goods more expensive than those made at home. Leaders in each country hoped that high tariffs would benefit their local manufacturers.

Unfortunately, the high tariff actually did more harm than good to the American and world economies. As you will read, the decline in world trade that took place in the 1930s created misery around the world. It was one of the several factors that contributed to the nation's slide into what came to be called the Great Depression.

THE IMPACT TODAY

Economics

Today an international organization called the World Trade Organization (WTO) oversees many trade agreements between nations. Its goal is to reduce trade barriers such as tariffs.

READING CHECK **Identifying Cause and Effect** How did the stock market crash affect banks?

SECTION 1 ASSESSMENT

go.hrw.com
Online Quiz
Keyword: SD7 HP21

Reviewing Ideas, Terms, and People

1. **a. Define** Write a brief definition for the following term: gross national product
   b. Identify Cause and Effect What effect did America's mood have on individuals' financial decisions?
   c. Evaluate Defend the widespread American investment in stocks in the 1920s.

2. **a. Recall** Name two signs of weakness in the American economy in the 1920s.
   b. Analyze Why is it significant that much of the nation's wealth was owned by a small number of people?
   c. Predict How might the lack of available credit hurt the nation's economy in the 1930s?

3. **a. Identify** What was Black Tuesday?
   b. Sequence Describe how the drop in the stock market brought ruin to so many investors.
   c. Elaborate Why would an investor who had not bought stocks on margin have been in a better position to survive the crash than one who had?

4. **a. Describe** How did the crash affect individual investors, brokers, and banks?

   b. Summarize Why did the stock market crash have such a powerful impact on the overall economy?
   c. Evaluate Defend Hoover's belief that the economy would soon recover.

Critical Thinking

5. **Understanding Cause and Effect** Copy the chart below and use information from the section to identify effects of the stock market crash on the American economy.

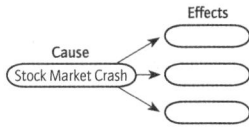

Cause
Stock Market Crash

Effects

FOCUS ON WRITING

6. **Persuasive** Write a letter to a friend in which you urge him or her to be careful about making stock market investments. Use information from the chapter to support your position.

THE GREAT DEPRESSION BEGINS **679**

679

Bellringer

The Inside Story. . . Use the **Daily Bellringer Transparency** to help students answer the question.

📦 Daily Bellringer Transparency, Section 2

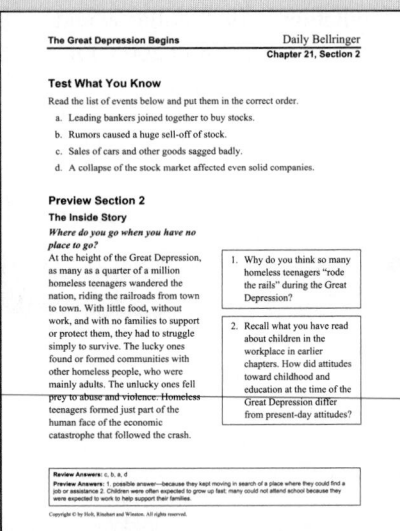

The Great Depression Begins — Daily Bellringer — Chapter 21, Section 2

Test What You Know

Read the list of events below and put them in the correct order.

a. Leading bankers joined together to buy stocks.

b. Rumors caused a huge sell-off of stock.

c. Sales of cars and other goods sagged badly.

d. A collapse of the stock market affected even solid companies.

Preview Section 2

The Inside Story

Where do you go when you have no place to go?

At the height of the Great Depression, as many as a quarter of a million homeless teenagers wandered the nation, riding the railroads from town to town. With little food, without work, and with no families to support or protect them, they had to struggle simply to survive. The lucky ones found or formed communities with other homeless people, who were mainly adults. The unlucky ones fell prey to abuse and violence. Homeless teenagers formed just part of the human face of the economic catastrophe that followed the crash.

1. Why do you think so many homeless teenagers "rode the rails" during the Great Depression?

2. Recall what you have read about children in the workplace in earlier chapters. How did attitudes toward childhood and education at the time of the Great Depression differ from present-day attitudes?

Review Answers: c, b, a, d

Preview Answers: 1. possible answer—because they kept moving in search of a place where they could find a job or assistance 2. Children were often expected to grow up fast; many could not attend school because they were expected to work to help support their families.

Copyright © by Holt, Rinehart and Winston. All rights reserved.

Academic Vocabulary

Review with students the high-use academic terms in this section.

asset financial holdings or resources (p. 681)

plight bad situation (p. 685)

📝 CRF: Vocabulary Builder Activity, Section 2

Taking Notes

Causes—stock market crash, bank failures; Effects—unemployment, farm failures, poverty

---

Americans Face Hard Times

BEFORE YOU READ

MAIN IDEA

The Great Depression and the natural disaster known as the Dust Bowl produced economic suffering on a scale the nation had never seen before.

READING FOCUS

1. How did the Great Depression develop?

2. What was the human impact of the Great Depression?

3. Why was the Dust Bowl so devastating?

KEY TERMS AND PEOPLE

hobo
Great Depression
foreclosure
Hooverville
drought
Dust Bowl
Okie
Woody Guthrie

TAKING NOTES As you read, take notes to identify the causes and effects of the Great Depression. Record your notes in a graphic organizer like the one shown here.

Causes
↓
| Great Depression |
↓
| Effects |

Teenage HOBOES

THE INSIDE STORY *Where do you go when you have no place to go?* Some of them decided on their own to leave home. Others were told to leave by their parents because there simply was no money to care for them. In either case, tens of thousands of teenagers faced a stark reality during the Great Depression. They had to find their future on the road.

At the height of the Great Depression, as many as a quarter of a million teenagers were wandering the nation, riding the railroads from town to town. With no families to support or protect them, they joined the ranks of the jobless, homeless wanderers known as **hoboes**.

For the young hoboes of the Depression—boys and girls, black and white, some less than 16 years old—the daily task was to survive. The lucky ones found or formed communities with other homeless people, who were primarily adults. The unlucky ones fell prey to abuse and violence.

Young women often disguised themselves as boys in order to reduce the dangers they faced. African Americans often had the threat of racial violence added to the hardships of the road.

Homeless teenagers riding the rails or walking the back roads became a familiar sight in the years of the Great Depression. Along with millions of others, they formed part of the human face of the economic catastrophe that followed the crash. ◼

◀ **Thousands of youths experienced the grim life of a hobo.**

Teach the Main Idea

At Level

Americans Face Hard Times

1. **Teach** Ask students the Reading Focus questions to teach this section.

2. **Apply** Have students create a Web diagram showing the main points of this section. Have students create a center circle and label it the Great Depression. Then have students list the effects of the Depression on the spokes. **LS Visual-Spatial**

3. **Review** Review student diagrams as a class. Then guide students in a discussion of the emotional impact of the Great Depression. How might it have shaped people's attitudes and expectations for the rest of their lives?

4. **Practice/Homework** Have students write lyrics for a song about living conditions during the Great Depression. **LS Auditory-Musical**

📝 Alternative Assessment Handbook, Rubric 26: Poems and Songs

📦 Graphic Organizer Transparencies

The Development of the Great Depression

With the crash of the stock market, the boom times of the 1920s came to an end. The crash and its aftermath revealed serious flaws in the American economy. These flaws helped transform a stock market crisis into the **Great Depression**, the most severe economic downturn in the history of the United States.

Bank failures As you have read, the collapse of the stock market strained the financial resources of many banks. In the weeks following the crash, a number of those banks failed. For ordinary Americans, the collapse of banks was an especially unnerving new development. Most people did not have money invested in stocks, but many had entrusted their savings to banks.

Today, most Americans do not have to worry that they will lose their savings if their bank goes out of business. Insurance from the federal government protects most people's deposits in the event of bank failure. In addition, laws today require that a bank keep a greater percentage of its <u>assets</u> in cash, to be paid out to depositors on request.

In 1929 there was no such deposit insurance, and with little cash on hand, banks were vulnerable to "runs." A run occurred when nervous depositors, suspecting a bank might be in danger of failing, rushed to withdraw their savings. A run could quickly drain a bank of its cash reserves and force the bank to close.

In the months following October 1929, bank runs struck across the country. Hundreds of banks failed. In late 1930 the rate of failures turned from frightening to disastrous. In December alone almost 350 banks closed. Included was the enormous Bank of the United States, which once had boasted about 400,000 depositors. By 1933 U.S. bank failures had wiped out billions of dollars in savings, on top of losses from the stock market crash.

Farm failures The hard times farmers had faced in the 1920s only worsened with the onset of the Great Depression. Widespread joblessness and poverty reduced Americans' ability to buy food. Many people simply went hungry. With farmers producing more than they could sell, farm prices sank. By 1933 prices were down more than 50 percent from their already low 1929 levels. Lower prices meant lower income for farmers.

ACADEMIC VOCABULARY

asset financial holdings or resources

Economic Impact of the Great Depression

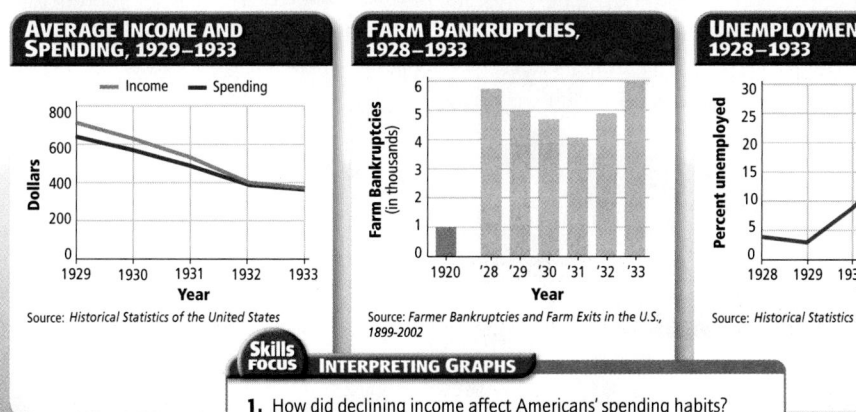

Source: *Historical Statistics of the United States*

Source: *Farmer Bankruptcies and Farm Exits in the U.S., 1899–2002*

Source: *Historical Statistics of the United States*

Skills FOCUS INTERPRETING GRAPHS

1. How did declining income affect Americans' spending habits?
2. Compare unemployment rates in 1928 and 1933.

See Skills Handbook, p. H16, H17

THE GREAT DEPRESSION BEGINS **681**

❷ What was the human impact of the Great Depression? *People lost jobs and homes; some ended up in shanty-towns, others became hoboes. People were filled with shame or anger.*

The Human Impact of the Great Depression

Identify Who provided relief to the poor during the Great Depression? *local charities and some municipal and state governments*

Describe How did the Great Depression affect the minds and spirits of Americans? *many felt that they had failed as individuals; widespread feeling that the nation had failed its citizens*

Make Judgments Considering the dangers, why do you think some young men became hoboes rather than try to find a place to settle? *thought they could find work; unable to live in shame and poverty of shantytowns*

📖 CRF: Literature Activity: *Yonnondio: From the Thirties* by Tillie Olsen

📖 CRF: Primary Source Activity: *Free Soup, Coffee, and Doughnuts*

It was typical for farmers to borrow money from banks to pay for land and equipment. As their incomes dropped, many farmers were unable to make the payments on their loans. In 1933 alone, some 364,000 farms went bankrupt or suffered foreclosure. **Foreclosure** occurs when a bank or other lender takes over ownership of a property from an owner who has failed to make loan payments.

Unemployment The year following the crash of October 1929 saw a sharp drop in economic activity and a steep rise in unemployment. Such negative trends are not uncommon in a time of economic downturn. What made the Great Depression different was the extent and the stubborn duration of these trends.

By 1933 the gross national product had dropped more than 40 percent from its pre-crash levels. Unemployment reached a staggering 25 percent. In some places and among some groups, the number was even higher. In the African American neighborhood of Harlem in New York City, for example, unemployment reached 50 percent in 1932.

READING CHECK **Making Generalizations**
What happened to the economy in the early 1930s?

The Human Impact of the Great Depression

The Great Depression was an economic catastrophe. Yet statistics tell only part of the story. The true measure of the disaster lies in how it affected the American people.

Hoovervilles and hoboes With millions of people out of work, the competition for jobs became fierce. Thousands of workers would apply for a handful of jobs, and the winners knew they were lucky.

HISTORY'S VOICES

❝I'd get up at five in the morning and head for the waterfront. Outside the Spreckles Sugar Refinery, outside the gates, there would be a thousand men. You know dang well there's only three or four jobs. The guy would come out … 'I need two guys for the bull gang. Two guys to go into the hole.' A thousand men would fight like a pack of Alaskan dogs to get through there.❞
—Ed Paulson, quoted in Studs Terkel's *Hard Times*

For millions of Americans during the Great Depression, the loss of a job meant a quick slide into poverty. To survive, some people begged from door to door. Unable to provide food for

HISTORY CLOSE-UP

Life in a Hooverville

As desperate poverty engulfed people from coast to coast, many formed makeshift communities that they nicknamed Hoovervilles.

The lack of running water and power made tasks such as cooking and cleaning much more difficult and messy.

Most male residents of Hoovervilles had been used to a life of work. For many, idleness led to deep feelings of uselessness and despair.

682

Differentiating Instruction

Below Level **Standard English Mastery**

Learners Having Difficulty

1. Organize the class into mixed-ability pairs. Have each group review the descriptions and examine the images of Hoovervilles in this section.

2. Have each pair write a newspaper headline and a brief newspaper article describing the living conditions in a Hooverville. Remind students that Hooverville shanties provided only the most basic shelter, usually had only

one room, no electricity, plumbing, or floors. Also remind students to be unbiased in their article and their headline.

3. Ask volunteers from each group to share their newspaper articles with the class.

LS Interpersonal

📖 Alternative Assessment Handbook, Rubrics 14: Group Activity; and 23: Newspapers

Answers

Reading Check *severe economic downturn—banks failed, farms failed, unemployment rose, and poverty grew*

themselves, some relied on soup kitchens or breadlines—or simply went without.

In the early 1930s, no federal government programs provided food or money to the poor. Local charities and some municipal and state governments provided relief, but these programs were unable to meet the need. In 1932 only 1 in 4 families needing unemployment relief received it.

With no jobs or income, many Americans lost their homes. Property owners evicted tenants who couldn't pay rent, and banks foreclosed on homeowners. In many communities, sprawling neighborhoods of shacks sprang up on the outskirts of town or in public parks to house the newly homeless. These shantytowns came to be known as **Hoovervilles**. This was a bitter reference to President Hoover, whom many people blamed for the Great Depression.

On the streets of America's great cities, some unemployed workers took to selling apples. Charging a nickel an apple, a seller might earn $1.15 on a good day. In the fall of 1930 more than 6,000 unemployed workers sold apples on the streets of New York City alone.

Other Americans took to the road in search of work. Hoboes hopped trains to travel from town to town, often taking their lives in their hands. Not only was boarding a moving train very dangerous, it was also illegal. Many railroads hired "bulls," or guards, to chase hoboes off the trains.

Wherever hoboes went, finding food was a constant challenge. Townspeople often had little food to spare. Approaching homes to beg or steal, hoboes were sometimes met with violence. Across the country, hoboes developed a system of sign language to alert each other to good opportunities—and warn of possible dangers—in a particular town or home.

Most hoboes were men. Many had left behind families that they could no longer care for. During the Great Depression, some families simply broke apart under the strains of poverty and homelessness.

The emotional toll The greatest toll of the Great Depression may have been on the minds and spirits of the American people. Even though millions of people shared the same fate, many of the unemployed saw their situation as a sign of a personal failure. Accepting handouts deeply troubled many proud Americans.

"Shame? You tellin' me?" recalled one person who lived through the Depression. "The only scar it left on me was my pride, my pride." The

For people living in a Hooverville, reminders of their former homes and the lives they used to lead often were important. Here, pictures provide a touch of beauty to an otherwise grim environment.

Hooverville shacks were generally thrown together with whatever building materials could be found. They were often leaky and drafty.

Skills FOCUS **INTERPRETING INFOGRAPHICS**

Hoovervilles, like this one in New York, were cobbled together with whatever people could salvage.

Drawing Conclusions What hardships might the men in this photograph have endured?

See **Skills Handbook, p. H18**

683

History Close-Up

Life in a Hooverville

Construction and Locations Shantytowns knows as Hoovervilles were built from discarded materials like crates, cardboard, and flattened tin cans. They sprang up throughout the U.S.; one even sat in the middle of New York's Central Park.

Info to Know

Help for the unemployed Although city governments and charities tried to provide assistance to poor people, they simply could not meet the needs of the unemployed. New York City, for example, spent $79 million on relief in 1932—an amount that totaled only one month's wages for the city's unemployed. In 1931 Chicago spent $100,000 a day on relief in an effort to replace lost wages that totaled some $2 million per day.

Biography

Dorothea Lange (1895–1965) Dorothea Lange was one of the most talented photographers of the Depression era. She began taking photographs of homeless men wandering the streets of San Francisco and later photographed migrant farm workers in California. Her photographs document the poverty and suffering, as well as the dignity, of the workers and their families.

Skills Focus: Analyzing Primary Sources

Above Level

Reading Like a Historian Skill

Research Required

Life in the Great Depression

1. Have each student develop a list of at least ten questions about life for ordinary Americans during the Great Depression. Have students find and read primary sources that answer their questions. Students should record the answers to each of their questions.

2. Have volunteers read their questions and the answers they found, citing the sources they used. Ask students if the primary sources presented conflicting images and answers

to the questions, or if there were similarities among the sources. Have students propose reasons that might account for the similarities and the differences.

3. Guide students in a discussion of the importance of analyzing and contrasting information found in various sources.

LS Interpersonal, Verbal-Linguistic

Alternative Assessment Handbook, Rubrics 1: Acquiring Information; and 30: Research

Answers

Interpreting Infographics *loss of work, separation from families, emotional problems, poor health, and hunger*

Reading Focus

❸ Why was the Dust Bowl so devastating? *long period of drought; destroyed farmland and lives of farming families*

Devastation in the Dust Bowl

Define What was the Dust Bowl? *parts of Oklahoma, Kansas, Colorado, New Mexico, and Texas that were hardest hit by drought*

Recall What caused the Dust Bowl? *drought; agricultural practices that led to severe erosion*

Evaluate Why do you think people in California were hostile to migrants from the Great Plains? *did not want any more competition in the job market; to discourage others from coming*

Recent Scholarship

In *Rethinking the Great Depression: A New View of Its Causes and Consequences*, Gene Smiley, Professor of Economics at Marquette University, uses economic analytical techniques to give readers a better understanding of what happened during the Great Depression and why it happened.

Rethinking the Great Depression: A New View of Its Causes and Consequences by Gene Smiley. Ivan R. Dee, 2003.

go.hrw.com
Online Resources
KEYWORD: SD7 CH21
TOPIC: THE DUST BOWL

Answers

Interpreting Maps 1. *California, Northwest, Midwest;* **2.** *Kansas, Oklahoma, Texas, New Mexico, and Colorado*

Reading Check *fought for jobs, begged, relied on charity, went without; some became hoboes*

684

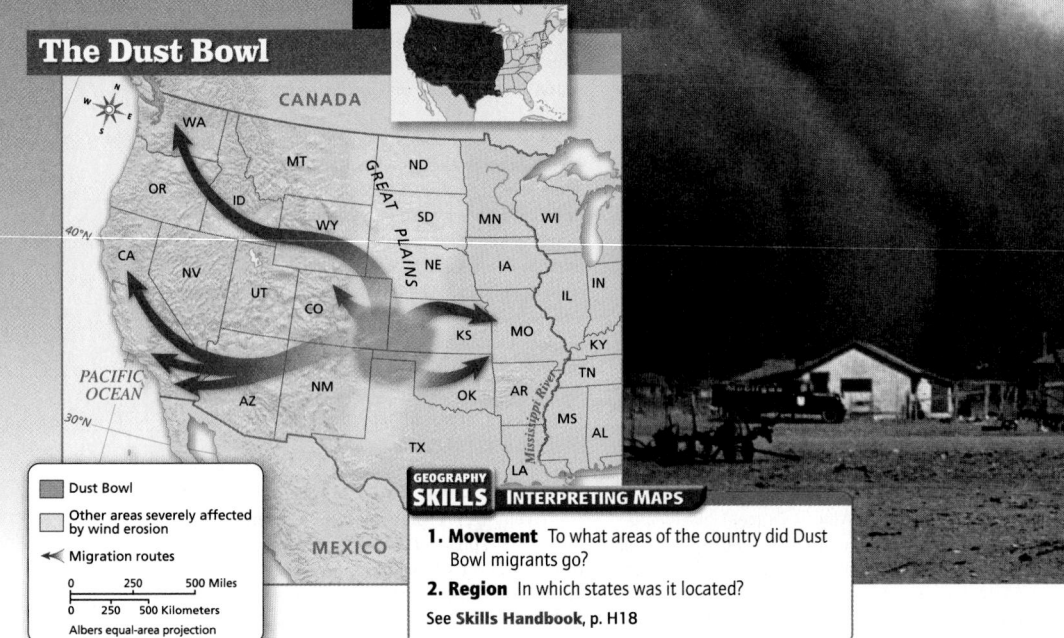

The Dust Bowl

GEOGRAPHY SKILLS | **INTERPRETING MAPS**

1. **Movement** To what areas of the country did Dust Bowl migrants go?
2. **Region** In which states was it located?

See Skills Handbook, p. H18

Legend:
- Dust Bowl
- Other areas severely affected by wind erosion
- Migration routes

0   250   500 Miles
0   250   500 Kilometers
Albers equal-area projection

---

grim despair people felt was reflected in a rise in suicide rates in the early 1930s.

Other people were simply angry. There was a widespread feeling that the nation had failed its hardworking citizens. One popular song of the era summed up the mixture of defiance and shame this way:

HISTORY'S VOICES

❝Once I built a railroad, I made it run, made it race against time,

Once I built a railroad; now it's done. Brother, can you spare a dime?❞

—"Brother, Can You Spare a Dime,"
Yip and Gorney Harburg, 1931

READING CHECK **Summarizing** In what ways did the Great Depression affect many Americans?

Devastation in the Dust Bowl

In the midst of the economic disaster, nature delivered a cruel blow. Around 1931 much of the Great Plains region entered a long, severe dry spell. This **drought**, or period of below-average rainfall, lasted for several years. By the time it lifted, millions of people had fled the area.

684 CHAPTER 21

The great dust storms Drought is a part of a weather cycle, naturally occurring on the Great Plains every few decades. By the 1930s, however, careless agricultural practices had left the region vulnerable. Land once covered with grasses now lay bare to the sky with no vegetation to hold the soil in place.

When wind storms came, they stripped away the topsoil and blew it hundreds of miles away. In some of the worst storms, dust reached as far as the Atlantic Coast. Drifting mounds of dust choked crops and buried farm equipment. The fine dust blew into homes through drafty windows and under doors. Year after year, storms came and wreaked destruction. The hardest hit area—including parts of Oklahoma, Kansas, Colorado, New Mexico, and Texas—became known as the **Dust Bowl**.

Fleeing the Plains The terrible drought and dust storms robbed many farmers of their livelihood. Some simply packed up what little they had and moved. By the end of the 1930s, about 2.5 million people had left the Great Plains states. Many headed west along Route 66 to California, where they settled in camps and sought work in farms and orchards.

Skills Focus: Making Inferences
Above Level

Reading Skill
The Dust Bowl

1. Have each student write a short story describing what life is like in the 1930s on a farm in the middle of the Dust Bowl. Ask students to use vivid imagery and accurate details. You may wish to assign students to conduct additional research to find more details to help them with their stories.

2. Have volunteers read their stories to the class. Then take a vote, asking students if they would have tried to stay on their farms or if they would have left the area to go elsewhere and try to start a new life. What would be the advantages and disadvantages of each choice?

3. As an extension, you may wish to organize students into mixed-ability pairs and have students illustrate the short stories. **LS** **Verbal-Linguistic**

📖 Alternative Assessment Handbook, Rubric 40: Writing to Describe

Pitch-black dust storms, like this one in Springfield, Colorado, drove people out of the Plains on migration routes shown by the arrows on the map. Decades of farming had removed the natural vegetation that had held the soil in place.

The migrants were called **Okies**, after the state of Oklahoma. The term was inaccurate, since the migrants came from a number of different states. It was also meant to be insulting. The Great Plains migrants were often met by resistance and outright discrimination.

The plight of the migrants captured the imagination of some of America's greatest writers and artists, including author John Steinbeck and singer-songwriter **Woody Guthrie**. Guthrie's songs about the Dust Bowl describe the disaster's effect on the people it touched.

HISTORY'S VOICES

❝It's a mighty hard row my poor hands have hoed;
My poor feet have traveled this hot dusty road
Out of your dustbowl and westward we rolled,
Your desert was hot and your mountains were cold.
I've worked in your orchards of peaches and prunes,
Slept on the ground by the light of the moon
On the edge of your city you've seen us and then,
We come with the dust and we're gone with the wind.❞

—Woody Guthrie, "Pastures of Plenty"

Guthrie's lyrics speak to the hardships and struggles not only of the migrants who left the Dust Bowl but also of all Americans hit hard by the Great Depression. For much of the decade the Depression seemingly defied most government efforts to defeat it. The American people were forced to fend for themselves.

READING CHECK **Identifying the Main Idea**
How did the Dust Bowl affect Americans?

ACADEMIC VOCABULARY
plight bad situation

go.hrw.com
Online Quiz
Keyword: SD7 HP21

SECTION 2 ASSESSMENT

Reviewing Ideas, Terms, and People

1. **a. Identify** Briefly describe the **Great Depression** and its main effects.
   b. Explain What is the significance of the fact that there were few government relief programs in the early 1930s?
   c. Predict How do you think the federal government will respond to the Great Depression?

2. **a. Define** Write a brief definition for the following term: Hooverville
   b. Make Inferences What can you infer from the fact that the shantytowns of homeless Americans came to be known as Hoovervilles?
   c. Predict What do you think the political effect of the Great Depression on President Hoover will be? Explain.

3. **a. Identify** Who were the **Okies**?
   b. Compare How were the Okies similar to **hoboes**?

   c. Elaborate Do you think those affected by the Dust Bowl were victims of nature or responsible for their own fate?

Critical Thinking

4. **Understand Cause and Effect** Copy the chart below and use information from the section to identify effects of the Great Depression.

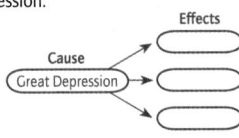

FOCUS ON WRITING

5. **Expository** Write an essay in which you describe the causes and effects of the Great Depression. Use details from the section to support your account.

THE GREAT DEPRESSION BEGINS **685**

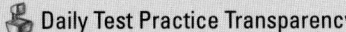
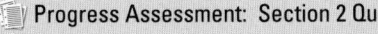

American *Literature*

Excerpt from *The Grapes of Wrath* by John Steinbeck

Word Help

perplexed confused
awestruck fascinated

Meet the Writer

John Steinbeck Steinbeck is best known for his novels about common people. *The Grapes of Wrath* aroused sympathy for the plight of migrant farm workers and won the Pulitzer Prize and the National Book Award. Like much of Steinbeck's writing before and immediately after World War II, *The Grapes of Wrath* has elements of social criticism. Steinbeck received the Nobel Prize for literature in 1962.

Info to Know

Route 66 The "great cross-country highway" referred to in this selection is Route 66, which stretched from Chicago to Oklahoma through largely rural communities. From Oklahoma, it followed a southern course onward to Los Angeles. For the Joads, and others like them, Route 66 symbolized the road to opportunity.

About the Reading Drought, dust storms, and new technology combined to displace tenant farmers during the 1930s. In his Pulitzer Prize-winning 1939 novel *The Grapes of Wrath*, John Steinbeck tells the story of the Joads, a family who lost everything during the Great Depression. Like many other families, the Joads begin migrating from Oklahoma toward California in search of work and a fresh start.

AS YOU READ Think about the challenges facing farmers and their families as they leave their homes in search of new beginnings.

Excerpt from

The Grapes of Wrath

by John Steinbeck

Migrant workers, like this family on the road in California's San Joaquin Valley in 1935, were the lowest paid in the nation.

The cars of the migrant people crawled out of the side roads onto the great cross-country highway, and they took the migrant way to the West. In the daylight they scuttled like bugs to the westward; and as the dark caught them, they clustered like bugs near to shelter and to water. And because they were lonely and perplexed, because they had all come from a place of sadness and worry and defeat, and because they were all going to a new mysterious place, they huddled together; they talked together; they shared their lives, their food, and the things they hoped for in the new country. Thus it might be that one family camped for the spring and for company, and a third because two families had pioneered the place and found it good. And when the sun went down, perhaps twenty families and twenty cars were there.

In the evening a strange thing happened: the twenty families became one family, the children were the children of all. The loss of home became one loss, and the golden time in the West was one dream. And it might be that a sick child threw despair into the hearts of twenty families, of a hundred people; that a birth there in a tent kept a hundred people quiet and awestruck through the night and filled a hundred people

with birth-joy in the morning. A family which the night before had been lost and fearful might search its goods to find a present for a new baby. In the evening, sitting about the fires, the twenty were one. They grew to be units of the camps, units of the evenings and the nights. A guitar unwrapped from a blanket and tuned—and the songs, which were all of the people, were sung in the nights.

> **Skills FOCUS** READING LIKE A HISTORIAN
>
> **Analyze** Do you think Steinbeck was a social activist?
> **Literature as Historical Evidence** In the 1930s many people believed that collective action could be more effective than individual action. How does the excerpt express that point of view?
> See **Skills Handbook**, p. H32

686 CHAPTER 21

Skills Focus: Interpreting Literature as Historical Evidence

Reading Like a Historian Skill   **At Level**
The Grapes of Wrath

1. Have students reread the passage, taking notes on the way in which Steinbeck represents the time period and historical setting of the story. Have students note details in the setting, language, actions of characters, and other fictional elements.

2. Have volunteers share items from their notes. Create a class list of images that Steinbeck creates of life during the Great Depression.

3. Guide students in a discussion of the passage

using the following questions as a guide: Does Steinbeck create an accurate picture of life during the Great Depression? Why or why not? What bias might Steinbeck have? Is this passage a valid source for historical information? Why or why not? **LS** **Verbal-Linguistic**

📝 Alternative Assessment Handbook, Rubric 11: Discussions

Answers

Reading Like a Historian *possible answer—yes, because he brought sympathy and attention to the plight of migrant workers; possible answer— Suffering was not limited to a single family but was shared by an entire section of American society.*

3 Hoover as President

BEFORE YOU READ

MAIN IDEA

Herbert Hoover came to office with a clear philosophy of government, but the events of the Great Depression overwhelmed his responses.

READING FOCUS

1. What was President Hoover's basic philosophy about the proper role of government?
2. What actions did Hoover take in response to the Great Depression?
3. How did the nation respond to Hoover's efforts?

KEY TERMS

associative state
Hoover Dam
cooperative
Reconstruction Finance Corporation
Smoot-Hawley Tariff Act

TAKING NOTES As you read, takes notes identifying President Hoover's responses to the Great Depression. Record your notes in a graphic organizer like the one shown here.

Great Depression → Hoover's Response

Hoover Seals his DOWNFALL

THE INSIDE STORY

How did a ragtag army help defeat President Hoover? In 1932 the United States was nearing the low point of the Great Depression. By now Americans had become used to scenes of homeless, jobless people camped out in cardboard shacks in public areas. But the group of some 15,000 World War I veterans who set up camp near the nation's capital in May 1932 was not just another group of men who were down on their luck.

These veterans had come to Washington for a reason. They were trying to put pressure on the federal government to pay them the veteran's bonus, a cash award they had been promised for their service during the war. The bonus, $1.25 for each day served overseas and $1 a day for U.S. service, was not supposed to be paid until 1945. But the men needed the money now, and they believed their request was fair.

The campers settled in, laying out orderly streets and sanitation facilities. As May turned to June, the numbers of so-called Bonus Marchers grew. When Congress failed to agree to their demands, some of the Bonus

Marchers left town, but a core of them remained, along with women and children. In July police and U.S. Army soldiers began clearing the area of the veterans. Violence erupted, and soon the Bonus Marchers' main camp was in flames. Hundreds were injured, and two of the veterans were killed.

Many Americans were deeply disturbed by the sight of U.S. soldiers using weapons against homeless veterans. For President Herbert Hoover, who was already facing complaints that he did not care enough about the plight of the nation's poor, the impact was devastating. As you will read, the Bonus Marchers incident helped complete the public view of Hoover as heartless and helpless in the face of the nation's suffering. ■

▼ **Bonus Army marchers from Columbus, Georgia, begin their trek to Washington, D.C.**

687

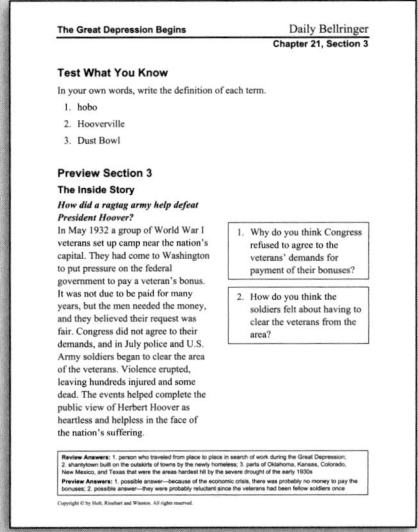
Teach the Main Idea

At Level

Hoover as President

1. **Teach** Ask students the Reading Focus questions to teach this section.

2. **Apply** Divide the class into groups of four or five students. Have each group analyze Herbert Hoover's philosophy toward business and government and then determine how his philosophy affected his response to the Great Depression. Have each group write its analysis.

3. **Review** Ask volunteers from each group to share their findings with the class. Guide the

class in a discussion of the ways in which the nation responded to Hoover's handling of the Great Depression.

4. **Practice/Homework** Select one of Hoover's responses to the Great Depression. Have each student write a short newspaper article discussing the ways in which it reflected his philosophy. **LS Interpersonal, Verbal-Linguistic**

Alternative Assessment Handbook, Rubrics 14: Group Activity; and 23: Newspapers

① What was President Hoover's basic philosophy about the proper role of government? *favored government policies that interfered as little as possible in business*

Herbert Hoover's Philosophy

Explain How was the associative state supposed to work? *Businesses would form voluntary associations, and government specialists would work with them.*

Make Inferences How might the construction of the Hoover Dam have tested Hoover's belief in the associative state? *possible answer—The amount of cooperation needed between the government and independent companies was huge, and had never been faced before by a president.*

Evaluate What do you think Hoover meant by "rugged individualism"? *possible answer—a person's power to take responsibility for his or her own life; to fend for oneself*

📄 CRF: Primary Source Activity: A Political Source Activity: A Political Activist Describes Migrant Housing in California

📄 CRF: History and Geography Activity: Herbert Hoover's Dam

go.hrw.com
Online Resources
KEYWORD: SD7 CH21
TOPIC: THE HOOVER DAM

Answers

Photo *six companies designed and built it; federal government provided funding; dam provided electricity and water to parts of seven states*

Reading Check *government should play as little a role as possible in the affairs of business; voluntary partnerships between business associations and government*

688

Herbert Hoover's Philosophy

Herbert Hoover came to the presidency with a set of core beliefs that he had formed over a long career in business and government service. He knew just how he planned to run the country. Yet after less than a year in office, Hoover's plans were upset by the massive stock market collapse. In responding to the growing crisis, Hoover drew on his experience and on the core beliefs that had guided him.

THE IMPACT TODAY

Government
In modern times, Republican presidents from Ronald Reagan to George W. Bush have also sought to limit government regulation on businesses.

"Rugged individualism" Hoover had served in the administrations of both Warren G. Harding and Calvin Coolidge. He shared many of their ideas about the proper relationship among government, business, and the people. In short, he favored a federal government that played as little role as possible in the affairs of business.

Hoover believed that unnecessary government not only threatened prosperity but also dimmed the very spirit of the American people. A key part of this spirit was what he called "rugged individualism."

The Hoover Dam took 21,000 men five years to complete at a cost of $165 million. **How did the project exemplify the associative state?**

688

HISTORY'S VOICES

❝One of the great problems of government is to determine to what extent the Government itself shall interfere with commerce and industry and how much it shall leave to individual exertion . . . By adherence to the principles of . . . opportunity and freedom to the individual, our American experiment has yielded a degree of well-being unparalleled in all the world.❞

—Herbert Hoover, speech, October 1928

Hoover did not reject the idea of government oversight or regulation of certain business. Nor did he advocate letting people and businesses do exactly as they pleased. Yet he believed deeply that it was vital for the nation's well-being not to destroy people's belief in their own responsibility and power.

The associative state Individualism did not rule out cooperation in Hoover's view. Businesses, he believed, should form voluntary associations that would make the economy fairer and more efficient. Skilled government specialists would then "cooperate with these various associations for the accomplishment of high public purposes." Hoover had a term for his vision of voluntary partnerships between business associations and government. He called it the **associative state**.

As secretary of commerce in the Harding and Coolidge administrations, Hoover had put these beliefs into practice. He often called together meetings of business leaders and experts to discuss ways to achieve key national goals. He continued to call such conferences after he became president.

Hoover's beliefs were dramatically tested in the construction of what came to be called the **Hoover Dam**. The dam would harness the Colorado River to provide electricity and a safe, reliable water supply to a vast area that included parts of seven states. The federal government provided funding for the project, which was approved in the 1920s and built in the 1930s. A group of six independent companies joined together to design and construct it. For Hoover, the project's success demonstrated the creative power of partnerships between private business and the federal government.

READING CHECK **Identifying the Main Idea** Briefly describe the two key features of President Hoover's main beliefs about government.

Skills Focus: Identifying Problem and Solution **Above Level**

Reading Skill
Herbert Hoover's Philosophy

1. Have each student write a few sentences explaining President Hoover's philosophy concerning the proper relationship among government, business, and working people. *"rugged individualism"; unnecessary government threatened prosperity; private businesses and federal government could work together*

2. Have students review the information in the chapter and then write a position paper supporting or opposing Hoover's position on the roles of government, business, and the people. Have volunteers read their position papers.

3. Organize a class debate between students who supported Hoover's economic policies and philosophy and students who opposed them.

📝 **Logical-Mathematical, Verbal-Linguistic**

📄 Alternative Assessment Handbook, Rubrics 11: Discussions; and 37: Writing Assignments

Hoover's Response to the Great Depression

Hoover's core beliefs shaped many of his early actions as president. Government, Hoover believed, should not provide direct aid. It should find ways to help people help themselves.

Voluntary cooperation Hoover put these beliefs into practice before the stock market crash, when he looked for ways to assist the nation's struggling farmers. He pushed for a program of loans to create and strengthen farm cooperatives. A **cooperative** is an organization that is owned and controlled by its members, who work together for a common goal. The idea behind farmers' cooperatives was that large groups of farmers could buy materials such as fertilizer at lower prices than individual farmers could. Cooperatives also could help farmers market crops in ways that would raise crop prices and increase farmers' income.

After the stock market crash, Hoover continued to rely on his basic belief in voluntary action and cooperation between business and government. He called together many of the nation's top business and government leaders and urged them not to lay off workers or cut wages. If these groups cooperated, Hoover reasoned, workers would have plenty of money to spend on consumer goods, and the worst of the economic crisis would soon pass.

Direct action Unfortunately, the president found it difficult to rally cooperation. In the face of economic disaster, individuals made decisions according to their own economic interests. Businesses cut jobs and wages. State and local governments stopped their building programs, throwing many people out of work. Consumers stopped spending. As a result, the economy plunged into the Great Depression.

The growing crisis eventually persuaded Hoover to break somewhat with his beliefs. At his urging, Congress created in early 1932

Political Cartoon

Most Hoover officials believed the effects of the Great Crash would eventually ease without drastic government action. Treasury Secretary Ogden L. Mills was especially reluctant to fund relief programs. This cartoon appeared three weeks before the 1932 presidential election.

President Herbert Hoover, an engineer by training, is unsure how to put the car back together again.

Treasury Secretary Ogden L. Mills attempts to reassure the driver, "U.S. public," that repairs are underway.

"IT WON'T BE LONG NOW?"
—By Jerry Doyle

Skills FOCUS READING LIKE A HISTORIAN

Interpreting Political Cartoons What message is the cartoonist trying to convey, and what details in the drawing support that message?
See Skills Handbook, p. H31

THE GREAT DEPRESSION BEGINS **689**

Primary Source

"Economic depression cannot be cured by legislative action or executive pronouncement. Economic wounds must be healed by the action of the cells of the economic body—the producers and consumers themselves."

— Herbert Hoover
Message to Congress, December 1930

❸ How did the nation respond to Hoover's efforts? *He came under attack; Democrats won seats in Congress.*

The Nation Responds to Hoover

Explain Why did Hoover have a problem with credibility? *He continued to make optimistic claims about the economy as the nation slid deeper into depression.*

Make Judgments Do you think that Hoover should have been more concerned about a balanced federal budget or about overspending and expanding government to help people? Why? *possible answer—overspending; the budget could be balanced when the economy recovered*

Answers

Faces of History *poorly; he seemed unable to address or fix problems*

Reading Check *he pushed for loans to help farms, urged business and government leaders not to cut workers and wages, authorized the Reconstruction Finance Corporation and signed the Smoot-Hawley Tariff Act*

ACADEMIC VOCABULARY
clause separate section of writing

the **Reconstruction Finance Corporation** (RFC). A key <u>clause</u> in the RFC legislation authorized up to $2 billion in direct government loans to struggling banks, insurance companies, and other institutions. Later that year, Hoover asked Congress to create the Federal Home Loan Bank. The new program encouraged home building and reduced the number of home foreclosures. These measures marked a historic expansion of the role of the federal government in the business of the American people. Still, for many citizens, Hoover's actions were too little, too late.

The Smoot-Hawley Tariff Act One of Hoover's major efforts to address the economic crisis backfired badly. In 1930 he signed the **Smoot-Hawley Tariff Act**. The new tariff raised the cost of imported goods for American consumers, making it more likely that they would purchase the cheaper American goods.

The Smoot-Hawley Tariff Act was a disaster. The tariff rates were set at historically high levels. When European nations responded with tariffs on American goods, trade plunged. By 1934 global trade was down roughly two thirds from 1929 levels.

> **READING CHECK** **Summarizing** What actions did Hoover take to improve the economy during the Great Depression?

FACES OF HISTORY

Herbert HOOVER
1874–1964

Few presidents have entered office seemingly as well prepared and qualified as Herbert Hoover, yet the Great Depression proved too great a challenge for him to master. As an engineer, successful businessman, and humanitarian, Hoover had never met a problem he could not solve through sheer brilliance and dogged hard work. But his failure to make headway againt the Depression combined with his reluctance to provide public relief spelled electoral disaster.

Following his defeat, Hoover wrote books and continued to serve with distinction on various government commissions into the 1950s. His work streamling the executive branch for presidents Truman and Eisenhower demonstrated a still potent talent for administration.

Rate How did Hoover's performance as president compare with his earlier public service?

The Nation Responds to Hoover

Hoover had entered office believing that government should seek to avoid direct involvement in the lives of individuals and businesses. Under the pressure of events, he modified his beliefs and began to push for some forms of direct relief. In spite of his efforts, however, Hoover increasingly came under attack for his handling of the Great Depression.

The president loses favor Hoover's frequent optimistic claims about the economy slowly undermined his credibility with voters. Early in the crisis, as millions of people were losing their jobs, he proclaimed the basic economic foundation of the nation to be sound. "I am convinced," he told the nation, "that we have passed the worst." In fact, the worst was yet to come.

Hoover later spoke glowingly about the efforts being made to deal with the Depression. "Industry and business have recognized their social obligation," he said in February 1931. "Never before in a great depression has there been so systematic a protection against distress." Millions of jobless Americans did not share Hoover's assessment of the situation.

Worse, many Americans came to question Hoover's compassion. As economic conditions grew worse, his unwillingness to consider giving direct relief to people became harder and harder for Americans to understand. When Hoover finally broke with his stated beliefs and pushed for programs such as the Reconstruction Finance Corporation, many people wondered why he was willing to give billions of dollars to banks and businesses but nothing to individuals.

Bonus March The Bonus March incident further damaged Hoover's reputation. The photographs of armed soldiers fighting with unarmed, unemployed veterans deeply troubled many observers. As one newspaper of the time observed, "If the Army must be called upon to make war on unarmed citizens, this is no longer America."

Hoover's opposition to paying the Bonus Army marchers stemmed partly from a concern about the federal budget. Hoover believed that the government must have a balanced

---

Reading Skill
Hoover Tries to End the Depression

1. Have the class brainstorm and develop two or three measures that they believe might have promoted economic recovery in the early 1930s. Then have students review the information in the text about Hoover's attempts to help end the Depression.

2. To help students understand how the Hoover administration tried to bring the United States out of the Great Depression, copy the chart on the right for students to see. Have students

copy and complete it.

3. Guide the class in a discussion of Hoover's attempts to help the nation recover. How successful were they? How did they compare with the ideas students came up with during their brainstorming session? **LS Intrapersonal, Verbal-Linguistic**

📓 Alternative Assessment Handbook, Rubric 7: Charts

Hoover and the Great Depression	
Effort	**Description**
associative state	
cooperatives	
Reconstruction Finance Corporation (RFC)	
Federal Home Loan Bank	
Smoot-Hawley Tariff Act	

budget—that is, it must spend no more money than it takes in—in order to achieve financial health. To meet this goal, Hoover pushed for and got a large tax increase in 1932. At a time when people were suffering and asking for government relief, a larger tax burden was highly unpopular.

The voters react The 1930 midterm congressional elections provided an early sign that the public was growing dissatisfied with Hoover's policies. The Republican Party had controlled Congress during the boom years of the 1920s. In 1930, however, Democrats managed to win a majority of the seats in the U.S. House of Representatives. They also came within one seat of matching the Republicans in the Senate.

By the 1932 presidential election, it seemed certain that the voters would reject Hoover at the polls. The Great Depression showed little sign of ending, and Hoover's ability to influence events was nearly gone. The president didn't even bother campaigning until October, little

After Congress refused to approve payment to the Bonus Army marchers, stunned protestors began a "Death March" in front of the Capitol. Finally Hoover moved to disband the camp, and violence broke out. *How did the public respond?*

more than a month before the election. The main question now was who the Democrats would pick to run against him, and what that candidate would do to end the nation's grief.

READING CHECK **Identifying Supporting Details** What were some actions—taken or not taken—that made voters believe Hoover did not care?

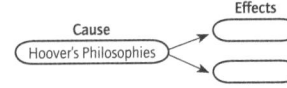 **SECTION 3 ASSESSMENT**

go.hrw.com
Online Quiz
Keyword: SD7 HP21

Reviewing Ideas, Terms, and People

1. **a. Identify** What were two key ideas that helped shape Hoover's core beliefs?
   b. Compare In what ways were Hoover's basic beliefs similar to those of Presidents Harding and Coolidge?
   c. Evaluate What is your opinion about Hoover's belief in the importance of rugged individualism?

2. **a. Define** Write a brief definition for each of the following terms: **cooperative, Reconstruction Finance Corporation, Smoot-Hawley Tariff Act**
   b. Analyze How effective was President Hoover's preferred approach to government in responding to the hardships of the Great Depression?
   c. Rate Defend Hoover's commitment to avoiding direct relief to individuals.

3. **a. Describe** What was the general reaction of the American people to Hoover's performance?
   b. Contrast How did Hoover's core beliefs contrast with what many Americans wanted?

   c. Design What are some relief programs that Hoover's Democratic opponent might suggest?

Critical Thinking

4. **Understanding Cause and Effect** Copy the chart below and use information from the section to identify effects of Hoover's personal philosophy on government.

Cause
Hoover's Philosophies

Effects

FOCUS ON WRITING

5. **Persuasive** Write a letter to the editor in which you either defend or criticize Herbert Hoover's approach to the stock market crash and the depression that followed. Use details from the section to support your position.

THE GREAT DEPRESSION BEGINS **691**

Word Help

communal shared

Info to Know

"No One Has Starved" In 1932 artist Reginald Marsh made an etching showing men standing in a bread line. He gave it the title "No One Has Starved," after a comment that had been made by Herbert Hoover. His etching, like the photograph in Document 1, illustrated the dehumanizing and humiliating aspects of unemployment. Hoover's comment also served as the title of an article in the September 1932 issue of *Fortune* magazine. According to the article, "The director of the President's Organization on Unemployment Relief, Mr. Walter S. Gifford of the American Telephone and Telegraph co., was forced to acknowledge before a subcommittee of the Senate in January, 1932, that he did not know, nor did his Organization know, how many persons were out of work and in need of assistance in the U.S. nor even how many persons were actually receiving aid at the time of his testimony."

Info to Know

The Rise of Social Work At the beginning of the Great Depression, most social work was done by private charitable organizations. As the number of unemployed people grew, private agencies found themselves overwhelmed. Local governments tried to step in, but had to appeal to the states, which in turn appealed to the federal government.

Life During the Great Depression

Historical Context The documents below provide different types of information on the life during the Great Depression.

Task Examine the documents and answer the questions that follow. Then you will be asked to write an essay about life during the Great Depression, using facts from the documents and from the chapter you just read to support the position you take in your thesis statement.

DOCUMENT 1

During the Depression many families found themselves standing helplessly in lines to get donated food and clothing. A great many of these people never imagined they would be in such a situation. The photograph below shows people standing in a relief line in San Antonio, Texas, to receive aid.

DOCUMENT 2

Charities did what they could to help the needy, but it was often not enough. Social worker Nell Blackshear of Atlanta, Georgia, recalled the relief lines in her city and her experiences providing help to others through a government program.

"That was a sad time when there was a soup line. Men, women, and children would come and go through the soup line once a day—it was bad. They had a black soup line, of course. There was no such thing as just hungry people. Even on relief you had to remember that you were black and they were white. They would have hot soup and sometimes just coffee and bread that was donated from some of the bakeries . . .

[As part of a government program,] I had to buy milk for the families. Even had to buy clothes. We would take the mothers to the stores on Edgewood Avenue . . . We would buy the clothing, then order and pay for the coal, twenty-five-cent bags of coal.

I remember the rear of 210 Butler Street. This was a long tenement house. I would have to go get some groceries in the house, or take coal to give them to make a fire in those little rooms. Sometimes seven or eight people would live in one room. They had a communal toilet outside. It was a deplorable [horrible] sort of thing. And that's where our clients lived, this is the kind of relief and work with families that I started off doing."

Collaborative Learning
At Level

Social Work in the Great Depression

1. Divide the class into small groups. Have each group make a needs assessment, or a list of problems that people faced during the Great Depression. Then have students make a relief plan, or a list of services to provide relief for each of the problems.

2. Have each group share its needs assessment and relief plan with the class. Create a class list on the board.

3. Have each student write a letter to a member of Congress from the perspective of a social worker during the Great Depression. Students should use their needs assessments and relief plans to help convince their congressperson to vote to fund relief efforts.

4. Have volunteers read their letters to the class.
   LS Interpersonal, Verbal-Linguistic

   Alternative Assessment Handbook, Rubric 43: Writing to Persuade

DOCUMENT 3

Like African Americans, Asian Americans were targets of discrimination. In California, many Asian American communities were segregated from their white neighbors. They relied heavily on one another. During the 1930s many survived by sharing resources. The photograph at right shows Japanese American migrant workers picking broccoli in Guadalupe, California.

DOCUMENT 4

People showed remarkable generosity during the hard times. Kitty McCulloch, a young seamstress, recalled her experiences.

"There were many beggars, who would come to your back door, and they would say they were hungry. I wouldn't give them money because I didn't have it. But I did take them in and put them in my kitchen and give them something to eat.

One elderly man that had white whiskers and all, he came to my back door. He was pretty much of a philosopher. He was just charming. A man probably in his sixties. And he did look like St. Nicholas, I'll tell you that. I gave him a good, warm meal. He said, 'bring me a pencil and paper and I'll draw you a picture.' So he sketched. And was really good. He was an artist.

A man came to my door. . . He said, 'You don't suppose you could have a couple of shirts you could give me, old shirts of your husband's?' I said, 'Oh, I'm so very sorry, my husband hasn't anything but old shirts, really. That's all he has right now and he wears those.' He said, 'Lady, if I get some extra ones, I'll come back and give them to you.'"

Info to Know

California's Migrants Many migrant workers faced discriminatory attitudes from California farmers. As new white refugees arrived from the Dust Bowl, farmers and other employers often replaced Latino and Asian workers with whites. In answer to pressure from white farm owners, state and local governments began to "repatriate" Mexicans, sending them back to Mexico by the busload. The authorities did not distinguish between Mexican citizens and Mexican American U.S. citizens. Many of the Latino workers who remained organized labor unions with Asian Americans and members of other races in an attempt to protect their jobs from discriminatory practices.

Skills Focus — READING LIKE A HISTORIAN

1. a. Describe Refer to Document 1. Describe the expressions on the people's faces.
b. Elaborate How do you think these people felt about having to go on relief?

2. a. Identify Refer to Document 2. What did Blackshear do as part of her job with the government?
b. Interpret What did Blackshear mean when she said, "There was no such thing as just hungry people?"

3. a. Identify Refer to Document 3. What are the people in the photograph doing?
b. Analyze How do the field workers reflect the community spirit of Japanese Americans in the 1930s?

4. a. Identify Refer to Document 4. What were the beggars who came to McColluch's door seeking?
b. Elaborate How did the beggars' responses to McColluch reflect the spirit of the times?

5. Document-Based Essay Question Consider the question below and form a thesis statement. Using examples from Documents 1, 2, 3, and 4, create an outline and write a short essay supporting your position.
How did the Great Depression bring people together?

See Skills Handbook, p. H28–29, H30

THE GREAT DEPRESSION BEGINS **693**

Skills Focus: Interpreting Visuals

At Level

Reading Like a Historian Skill
Migrant Workers in the Great Depression

Research Required

1. Organize the class into small groups. Have each group look for five photographs of migrant workers during the Great Depression. Students should try to find photographs that illustrate different aspects of the lives of migrant workers.

2. Have students write a caption for each photo. Captions should attempt to explain what is going on in the photograph, or they may provide a running commentary that will link

the photographs, turning it into a graphic essay or story.

3. Have volunteers share their photos and their captions with the class. Then guide the class in a discussion of what images these photos create of life for migrant workers during the Great Depression ⬛ **Visual-Spatial, Verbal-Linguistic**

📓 Alternative Assessment Handbook, Rubric 14: Group Activity

Answers

Reading Like a Historian
1. a. *possible answer—frustrated, anxious;* **b.** *possible answer—embarrassed, humiliated;* **2. a.** *She had to buy milk, clothing, and coal, and deliver them to families on relief.* **b.** *soup lines were segregated;* **3. a.** *picking broccoli;* **b.** *Families appear to be working together and looking after one another.* **4. a.** *food, clothing;* **b.** *kind; trying to help each other;* **5.** *possible answer—many people relied on relief from the community and government; families lived together, worked together, and helped one another to survive*

Answers

Visual Summary

Review and Inquiry Have students work in mixed-ability pairs and examine the cause-and-effect diagram. Then have students work individually to write a newspaper headline and a lead-in sentence for a newspaper article for each bulleted effect.

Quick Facts Transparency: The Great Depression Begins

Reviewing Key Terms and People

1. Black Tuesday
2. associative state
3. Hooverville
4. cooperative
5. hobo
6. Okies
7. Smoot-Hawley Tariff Act
8. Dust Bowl
9. buying on margin
10. Reconstruction Finance Corporation
11. Federal Reserve System
12. drought
13. foreclosure
14. Woody Guthrie
15. gross national product

Comprehension and Critical Thinking

16. a. stock market was very profitable; increasing numbers of Americans invested in stocks
b. As the stock market grew, Americans bought stock on margin, betting that they could use future profits to repay loans to brokers.
c. collapse of the stock market shook faith in the economy; caused consumers to stop spending; businesses laid off workers; banks failed

17. a. lost savings when banks failed; lost jobs, homes, and farms; quick descent into poverty
b. Many Americans felt that they had failed as individuals. They also suffered from hurt pride and from anger. Some became hoboes, others moved to shantytowns.

Visual Summary: The Great Depression Begins

Great Depression Begins
• Stock market crashes; banks, businesses fail
• Widespread joblessness and suffering occur
• Drought and dust storms add to suffering

Hoover Responds
• Relies on cooperation, voluntary action
• Later begins using power of government
• Fails to curb spreading economic crisis

Reviewing Key Terms and People

Identify the correct term or person from the chapter that best fits each of the following descriptions.

1. The term for the decisive drop in the stock market at the end of October 1929
2. Hoover's vision of a partnership between private business associations and government
3. The nickname given to a settlement of homeless people during the Great Depression
4. An organization owned and controlled by its members, who work together for a common goal
5. A person who rode the railroads from town to town in search of work
6. The nickname given to refugees from the dust storms of the early 1930s
7. Law originally meant to protect American businesses but that ended up harming the United States and world economies
8. The nickname for the central Plains region struck by a terrible drought and dust storms in the 1930s
9. The widespread practice during the 1920s that increased the danger to investors from a drop in the stock market
10. An organization created by the Hoover administration to aid struggling banks
11. The central bank of the United States
12. A prolonged period of below-normal rainfall
13. What can happen to a home or farm when the owner fails to pay off loans taken to buy the property
14. A singer who described the effects of the Dust Bowl
15. the total value of goods and services produced in a nation during a specific period of time

c. possible answer—They believed they should be able to take care of themselves and their families, and find jobs if they really tried.

18. a. The government should encourage individualism and not interfere in the affairs of its citizens.
b. As economic conditions worsened, Americans increasingly favored direct relief from the government, while Hoover favored as little a role for the government as possible. Hoover eventually recognized the limits of his beliefs and pushed for some forms of direct relief.
c. possible answer—Yes, because his tactics were not working and government needed to step in to ease the crisis.

Using the Internet

19. Go to the HRW Web site and enter the keyword shown to access a rubric for this activity.

KEYWORD: SD7 CH21

Comprehension and Critical Thinking

SECTION 1 *(pp. 672–679)*

16. a. Recall What was the general experience of investors in stocks in the United States in the mid-1920s?

b. Explain How did the success of the American stock market also increase the dangers of investing in the market?

c. Elaborate How did the collapse of the stock market come to hurt so many people who did not have money invested in stocks?

SECTION 2 *(pp. 680–685)*

17. a. Describe How did the Great Depression affect ordinary Americans?

b. Summarize How did victims of the Great Depression cope with the effects of homelessness and joblessness?

c. Evaluate Why do you think so many people blamed themselves for their misfortune during the Great Depression, in spite of the fact that millions of Americans were in a similar situation?

SECTION 3 *(pp. 687–691)*

18. a. Identify What was President Hoover's basic belief about the proper relationship of citizens to their government?

b. Analyze Why did the Great Depression greatly test Hoover and his fundamental philosophy about how to govern?

c. Evaluate Do you think it was reasonable to expect Hoover to change his philosophy and tactics in response to the crisis the nation faced in the Great Depression? Explain.

Using the Internet

go.hrw.com
Practice Online
Keyword: SD7 CH21

19. The worst day of the Great Crash of 1929 was "Black Tuesday," October 29. During a catastrophic series of workdays preceding Black Tuesday, the American stock market lost nearly one half of its value. Using the keyword above, do research to learn more about what happened to the American economy in October 1929. Then create a report that traces the aftereffects of the stock market crash and explains how it quickly came to affect people throughout the nation, even those who had not invested in stocks.

History's Impact video program

Review the video to answer the closing question: How do changes made after the 1929 stock market crash help protect the American economy today?

Analyzing Primary Sources

Reading Like a Historian
This photograph shows an automobile being sold by an investor following the stock market crash of October 1929.

20. Describe What is the significance of the moment shown in this photograph?

21. Draw Conclusions What does this image tell you about how Americans were affected by the crash?

Critical Reading

Read the passage in Section 1 that begins with the heading "An Appearance of Prosperity." Then answer the question that follows.

22. The heading "An Appearance of Prosperity" suggests that

A. there was no prosperity in the United States at all.

B. every American prospered in the 1920s.

C. overall, the economy seemed to be performing very well.

D. in fact, only the auto industry was performing well.

FOCUS ON WRITING

Expository Writing *Expository writing gives information, explains why or how, or defines a process. To practice expository writing, complete the assignment below.*

Writing Topic **Herbert Hoover's Response to the Great Depression**

23. Assignment Based on what you have read in this chapter, write a paragraph that discusses why so many Americans were dissatisfied with Hoover's response to the Great Depression. If you have access to a computer, use a word processing program to create and format your paragraph.

THE GREAT DEPRESSION BEGINS **695**

Analyzing Primary Sources

20. The stock market crash left investors desperate for cash.

21. Americans were financially and emotionally devastated by the crash.

Critical Reading

22. C

Focus on Writing

23. possible answer—Americans had lost jobs, savings, farms, and homes; they had no way to support themselves. Hoover's claim that the worst was over and his belief that it was not the role of government to help individuals led to great dissatisfaction.

A rubric for this activity is provided in the Chapter Resource File: Focus on Writing Activity: Hoover's Response to the Great Depression.

History's Impact Video Program

Securities and Exchange Commission and other acts limit the damage a stock market crash today could cause; laws protect banks deposits

Review and Assessment Resources

Review and Reinforce

- CRF: Chapter Review Activity
- Quick Facts Transparencies: Distribution of Wealth, 1929; Causes of the 1929 Stock Market Crash; Economic Impact of the Great Depression; The Great Depression Begins
- Spanish Chapter Summaries Audio CD Program
- Online Chapter Summaries in Spanish
- OSP Holt PuzzlePro; Quiz Show for ExamView
- Quiz Game CD-ROM

Assess

- PASS: Chapter Test, Forms A and B
- Alternative Assessment Handbook
- OSP ExamView Test Generator, Chapter Test
- Differentiated Instruction Modified Worksheets and Tests CD-ROM: Chapter Test
- HOAP Holt Online Assessment Program (in the Premier Online Edition)

Reteach/Intervene

- Interactive Reader and Study Guide
- Differentiated Instruction Teacher Management System: Lesson Plans for Differentiated Instruction
- Differentiated Instruction Modified Worksheets and Tests CD-ROM: Chapter Test
- Interactive Skills Tutor CD-ROM

go.hrw.com
Online Resources
KEYWORD: SD7 CH21

Chapter 22 Planning Guide

The New Deal

Chapter Overview	Reproducible Resources	Technology Resources
CHAPTER 22 pp. 696–731 **Overview:** In this chapter, students will analyze the causes and effects of President Roosevelt's New Deal programs.	**Differentiated Instruction Teacher Management System:*** • Instructional Benchmarking Guides • Lesson Plans for Differentiated Instruction **Interactive Reader and Study Guide:** Chapter Summary* **Chapter Resource File:*** • Writing for the SAT Activity: The Minimum Wage • Social Studies Skills Activity: Analyzing Bias in Historical Interpretation • Chapter Review Activity **American History Outline Maps** **Pre-AP Activities Guide for American History***	**Live Ink® Online Reading Help** **Student Edition on Audio CD Program** **Differentiated Instruction Modified Worksheets and Tests CD-ROM** **Interactive Skills Tutor CD-ROM** **United States History Primary Source Library CD-ROM** **Power Presentations with Video CD-ROM** **History's Impact: American History Video Program (VHS/DVD):** The New Deal **Online Chapter Summaries in Spanish**
Section 1: **Launching the New Deal** **The Main Idea:** In 1933 Franklin Delano Roosevelt became president of a suffering nation. He quickly sought to address the country's needs, with mixed results.	**Differentiated Instruction Teacher Management System:** Section 1 Lesson Plan* **Interactive Reader and Study Guide*** **Chapter Resource File:*** • Vocabulary Builder Activity, Section 1	**Daily Bellringer Transparency:** Section 1* **Map Transparency:** The Election of 1932* **Daily Test Practice Transparency:** Section 1*
Section 2: **The Second New Deal** **The Main Idea:** A new wave of government initiatives starting in 1935 resulted in some strong successes and stunning defeats for President Roosevelt.	**Differentiated Instruction Teacher Management System:** Section 2 Lesson Plan* **Interactive Reader and Study Guide*** **Chapter Resource File:*** • Vocabulary Builder Activity, Section 2	**Daily Bellringer Transparency:** Section 2* **Quick Facts Transparency:** Major New Deal Programs* **Daily Test Practice Transparency:** Section 2*
Section 3: **Life During the New Deal** **The Main Idea:** The Great Depression and the New Deal had a deep impact on American culture during the 1930s.	**Differentiated Instruction Teacher Management System:** Section 3 Lesson Plan* **Interactive Reader and Study Guide*** **Chapter Resource File:*** • Vocabulary Builder Activity, Section 3	**Daily Bellringer Transparency:** Section 3* **Daily Test Practice Transparency:** Section 3*
Section 4: **Analyzing the New Deal** **The Main Idea:** The New Deal had mixed success in rescuing the economy, but it fundamentally changed Americans' relationship with their government.	**Differentiated Instruction Teacher Management System:** Section 4 Lesson Plan* **Interactive Reader and Study Guide*** **Chapter Resource File:*** • Vocabulary Builder Activity, Section 4	**Daily Bellringer Transparency:** Section 4* **Quick Facts Transparency:** Unemployment and Deficit Spending, 1933–1940 **Daily Test Practice Transparency:** Section 4*

 go.hrw.com    Print Resource    Transparency

 Learning Styles   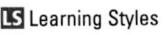 Audio CD   CD-ROM

 Video   **SE** Student Edition   **TE** Teacher's Edition

OSP One-Stop Planner CD-ROM

*also on One-Stop Planner CD-ROM

Review, Assessment, Intervention

 Quick Facts Transparency: The New Deal

 Spanish Chapter Summaries Audio CD Program

 **Progress Assessment Support System (PASS):** Chapter Test*

 **Differentiated Instruction Modified Worksheets and Tests CD-ROM:** Modified Chapter Test

OSP **One-Stop Planner CD-ROM:** ExamView Test Generator (English/Spanish)

HOAP **Holt Online Assessment Program (HOAP),** in the Holt Premier Online Student Edition

---

 PASS: Section 1 Quiz*

 Online Quiz: Section 1

 Alternative Assessment Handbook

 PASS: Section 2 Quiz*

 Online Quiz: Section 2

 Alternative Assessment Handbook

 PASS: Section 3 Quiz*

 Online Quiz: Section 3

 Alternative Assessment Handbook

 PASS: Section 4 Quiz*

 Online Quiz: Section 4

 Alternative Assessment Handbook

HOLT

History's Impact
American History Video Program (VHS/DVD)
The New Deal

NC RESOURCES

The following resources were developed to help North Carolina educators teach the standards and objectives of North Carolina's eleventh grade standard course of study in United States history.

- United States history EOC Test Prep Workbook
- Teacher's Support System
- North Carolina One-Stop Planner

And be sure to direct your students to **go.hrw.com** for online access to the EOC Test Prep Workbook.

go.hrw.com
EOC Test Prep
KEYWORD: SE7 NC

Holt Online Learning

go.hrw.com
Teacher Resources
KEYWORD: SD7 TEACHER

go.hrw.com
Student Resources
KEYWORD: SD7 CH22

- Document-based Questions
- Interactive Multimedia Activities

- Current Events
- Chapter-based Internet Activities
- and more!

Holt Premier
Online Student Edition
Complete online support for interactivity, assessment, and reporting

- Interactive Maps and Notebook
- Standardized Test Prep
- Homework Practice and Research Activities Online

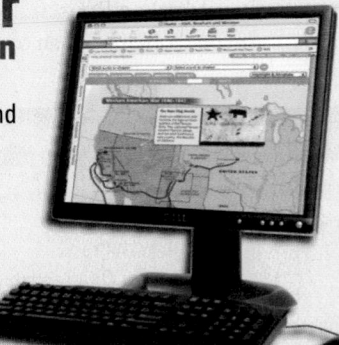

CHAPTER 22 PLANNING GUIDE

THE NEW DEAL   **695b**

Before You Teach

The Big Picture

Edward L. Ayers

Launching the New Deal The triumph of Franklin Roosevelt set the United States on a new path in 1933. Aided more by his wife Eleanor than by a clear plan, Roosevelt set out on a series of experiments that restored some confidence, if not prosperity. The Hundred Days saw unprecedented activity in the federal government and the creation of powerful new "alphabet" agencies.

The Second New Deal In the spring of 1935, the nation still in the trough of the Great Depression, Roosevelt set out upon the Second Hundred Days, focusing more on relief than on industrial recovery. The Works Progress Administration and the Social Security Administration provided unprecedented support for Americans in need, while organized labor set out upon a successful campaign to bring in new union members and to use that power to win concessions from industry. The president's plans were hurt by his attempt to expand the Supreme Court, damaging his reputation and costing his plans momentum.

Life During the New Deal African Americans used the opportunity to claim a new ally in Roosevelt, though his support was weakened by his need to keep white Southerners loyal to the Democrats. The ferment of reform in the New Deal, and the sheer extent of suffering, unleashed a wave of creativity among photographers and writers eager to document the situation Americans faced. In radio and on the screen, however, most artists and most audiences lived in a world of escape and imagination.

Analyzing the New Deal In retrospect, we can see that the New Deal changed much, but left much in place. Roosevelt's plans helped ease hunger and hopelessness, but did not lift the nation out of the Depression. That would be the ironic result of the vast war that would soon descend upon the world.

Recent Scholarship

The Politics of the New Deal It is sometimes difficult to see the familiar stories of these years as a whole, to see how the various pieces form a coherent picture. In his compassionate, deeply researched, and beautifully written volume *Freedom From Fear: The American People in Depression and War, 1929–1945* (1999), David Kennedy provides the fullest account we have of the important issues that any teacher would want to address. Kennedy, while neither denigrating Hoover nor mindlessly celebrating Roosevelt, chronicles the real successes of the New Deal and their transformative role in American history. Anyone looking for an overview of politics and diplomacy during these years should begin with this volume.

Differentiating Instruction

 Differentiated Instruction Teacher Management System
- Lesson Plans for Differentiated Instruction
- Differentiated Instructional Benchmarking Guides
- Interactive Reader and Study Guide

 Spanish Chapter Summaries Audio CD Program

 Online Chapter Summaries in Spanish

 Student Edition on Audio CD Program

 Differentiated Instruction Modified Worksheets and Tests CD-ROM
- Vocabulary Flash Cards
- Modified Vocabulary Builder Activities
- Modified Chapter Review Activity
- Modified Chapter Test

OSP One-Stop Planner CD-ROM
- ExamView Test Generator (English and Spanish)
- PuzzlePro
- Quiz Show for ExamView
- Transparencies and Videos

TE Differentiated Activities in the Teacher's Edition
- New Deal Posters, p. 702
- TVA Benefits, p. 707
- New Deal Programs, p. 712
- Limitations of the New Deal, p. 726
- The 1932 Election, p. 729

Reading Like a Historian
Sam Wineburg

Telling True Stories

During the 1930s, clouds of dust swept across a drought-stricken region of the Great Plains, forcing people off their farms and causing unimaginable suffering. Consider the various ways the story of the Dust Bowl has been told:

"The Dust Bowl was the darkest moment in the twentieth-century life of the southern plains . . . It cannot be blamed on illiteracy or overpopulation or social disorder. It came about because the culture was operating in precisely the way it was supposed to . . . The Dust Bowl . . . was the inevitable outcome of a culture that deliberately, self-consciously, set itself [the] task of dominating and exploiting the land for all it was worth."

Or this account:

"The story of the dust bowl was the story of people, people with ability and talent, people with resourcefulness, fortitude, and courage . . . During those hard years they continued to build their churches, their businesses, their schools . . . They grew closer to God and fonder of the land . . . Because they stayed during those hard years and worked the land and tapped her natural resources . . . the nation today enjoys a better standard of living."

Different Stories

The first account tells the story of people disregarding the rhythms of the earth, ignoring the signs of doom because greed beclouded their judgment. The second tells a different tale: one of human courage and resourcefulness, of people who weathered adversity and grew because of it.

It is not just the feel of these two accounts that differs; each seems to be telling a different story. Each excerpt is drawn from a major study on the Dust Bowl, Donald Worster's *Dust Bowl: The Southern Plains in the 1930s* and Paul Bonnifield's *The Dust Bowl: Men, Dirt, and Depression*. Both books came out in 1979, but each has a different plot line, narrative structure, and set of heroes and villains. The themes of the two books—in Worster's case, a fall from grace caused by hubris; in Bonnifield's, the indomitable human spirit that triumphs over adversity—are like the positive and negative poles of a battery, the opposite charges of a single entity.

History as Literature?

You'll notice I'm using a metaphor, the poles of a battery, and terms—theme, plot, character, narrative—more common to a Language Arts class than a history class. Are such terms appropriate? Should we impose literary constructs on the past so that we can understand it?

The philosopher of history, Louis O. Mink, believed that "the past is not an untold story." For Mink, stories are human constructions that obey structures that simplify but also disfigure the past's complexity. To take one small example: past events that occurred simultaneously must be rendered by the historian sequentially because the act of writing demands putting one thing before another.

What, then, makes historians different from novelists? It was this question that environmental historian William Cronon addressed in an article, "A Place for Stories: Nature, History, and Narrative," in the 1992 volume of the *Journal of American History*.

How Historians Differ

Cronon distinguished three ways historians part company with their fiction-writing colleagues: (1) The historian's story must accord with known facts; (2) the historical account must accord with the laws of physical reality and (3) historical stories must be judged by the community of scholars who police each other's work, guarding the profession's standards.

Historians, in other words, are storytellers. But what makes historians different is that their stories are supposed to be true.

From *The Dust Bowl: Men, Dirt, and Depression* by Paul Bonnifield. Published by University of New Mexico Press, Albuquerque, 1979.

From *Dust Bowl: The Southern Plains in the 1930s* by Donald Worster. Published by Oxford University Press, New York, 1979.

Standards Focus

Social Studies Competency Goals
Goal 9 The learner will appraise the economic, social, and political changes of the decades of "The Twenties" and "The Thirties."

 9.01, 9.02, 9.05

The Big Idea and Essential Questions

To foster student understanding of this chapter's big idea, design your lesson to address each section's essential question.

Big Idea President Franklin D. Roosevelt's plan for overcoming the Great Depression—a plan known as the New Deal—achieved varied levels of success and represented a basic change in American society.

Essential Questions

1. How did President Franklin D. Roosevelt respond to the Great Depression soon after taking office?

2. What were the successes and failures of government initiatives that began in 1935?

3. How did the Great Depression and the New Deal affect American culture?

4. How did the New Deal shape Americans' relationship with their government?

Key to Differentiating Instruction

Below Level

Basic-level activities designed for all students encountering new material

At Level

Intermediate-level activities designed for average students

Above Level

Challenging activities designed for honors and gifted-and-talented students

Standard English Mastery

Activities designed to improve standard English usage

696 CHAPTER 22

CHAPTER 22 1933–1940

The NEW DEAL

THE BIG PICTURE The New Deal was President Franklin D. Roosevelt's plan for overcoming the Great Depression. Although New Deal programs achieved varied levels of success, they did represent a basic change in American society.

NC North Carolina Standards

Social Studies Objectives
9.01 Elaborate on the cycle of economic boom and bust in the 1920's and 1930's.
9.02 Analyze the extent of prosperity for different segments of society during this period.
9.05 Assess the impact of New Deal reforms in enlarging the role of the federal government in American life.

Language Arts Objectives
3.01 Use language persuasively in addressing a particular issue by:
  • establishing and defending a point of view.
3.03 Use argumentation for:
  • establishing and defending a point of view.

Skills FOCUS READING LIKE A HISTORIAN

Artist Ben Shahn painted this mural for the community center of Jersey Homesteads. The panel shown here celebrates the planning of the New Jersey town, which was built as part of a New Deal program for garment workers.
Interpreting Visuals Why do you think Shahn included a poster of Roosevelt among the symbols in the mural?

See Skills Handbook, p. H30

696

U.S.

March 1933 President Franklin Delano Roosevelt is inaugurated.

1933

1934

World

March 1933 Germans elect Adolf Hitler as chancellor.

Introduce the Chapter

At Level

What Was the New Deal?

1. Write the following scenario for students to see. *The United States government has decided to take whatever steps it can to end the Great Depression. The government has never had a job program before, nor has it ever undertaken programs to help the needy. The government's goals are to put people back to work, improve the nation's infrastructure, and get the country moving forward.*

2. Have students discuss possible actions that the government could take. Have students consider the economics of the situation: the government does not have much money, and to create successful programs would require enormous amounts of capital and planning.

3. In this chapter students will learn about President Roosevelt's plans to solve the Depression, how they were implemented, and whether or not they were effective.
LS Verbal-Linguistic

Alternative Assessment Handbook, Rubric 11: Discussions

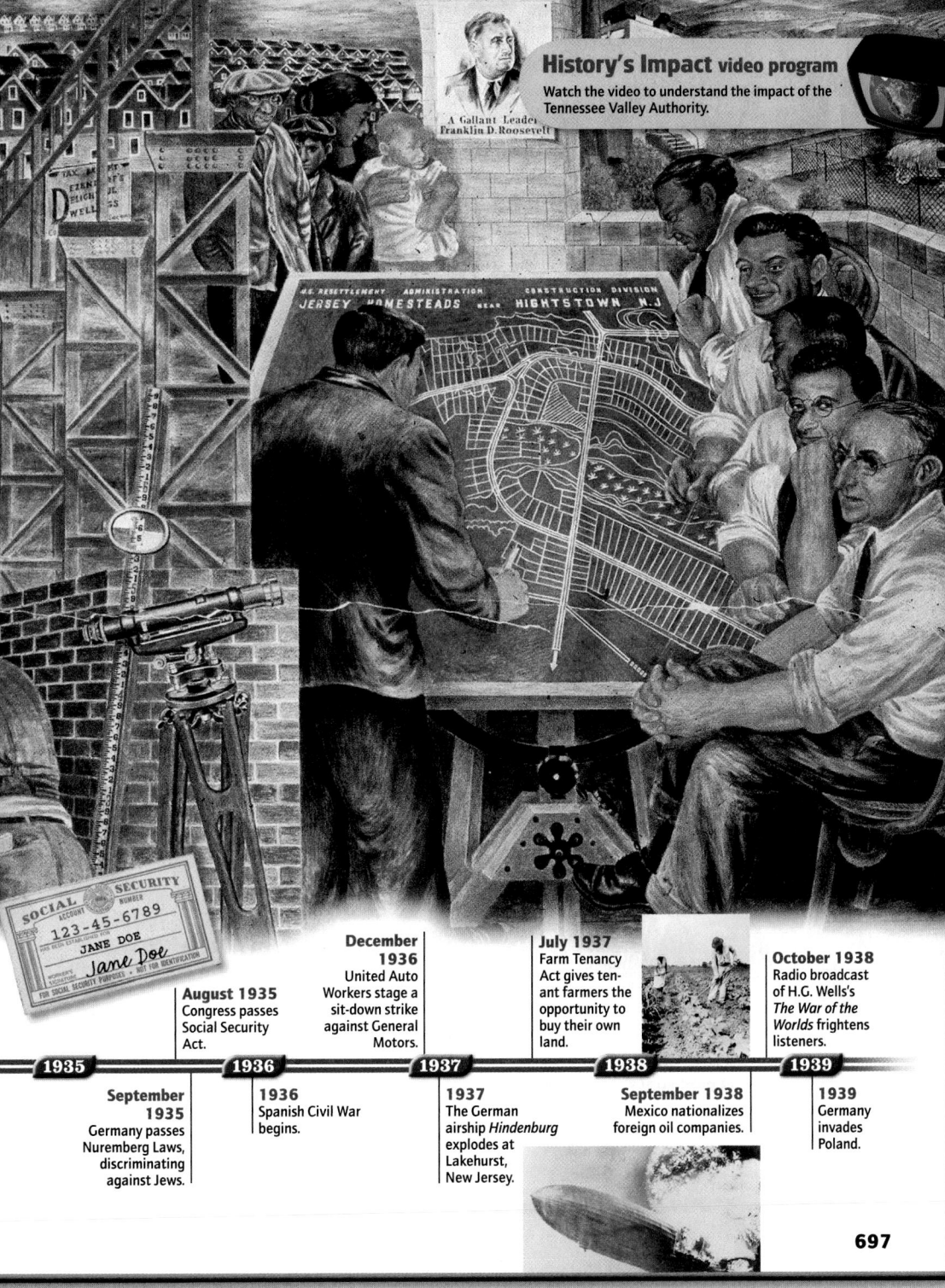

A Gallant Leader
Franklin D. Roosevelt

History's Impact video program
Watch the video to understand the impact of the Tennessee Valley Authority.

● **Chapter Preview** ●

HOLT
History's Impact
▶ **Video Program: The New Deal**
See the Video Teacher's Guide for strategies for using the video segment.

Reading Like a Historian

Town Planning If this mural was painted about a planned development today, what might be different about it? *possible answers—The workers might include women and minorities; hair and clothing styles would differ; the technology represented would include computers, and other symbols of modern technology.*

SOCIAL SECURITY
ACCOUNT NUMBER
123-45-6789
JANE DOE
Jane Doe
FOR SOCIAL SECURITY PURPOSES • NOT FOR IDENTIFICATION

December 1936
United Auto Workers stage a sit-down strike against General Motors.

August 1935
Congress passes Social Security Act.

July 1937
Farm Tenancy Act gives tenant farmers the opportunity to buy their own land.

October 1938
Radio broadcast of H.G. Wells's *The War of the Worlds* frightens listeners.

| 1935 | 1936 | 1937 | 1938 | 1939 |

September 1935
Germany passes Nuremberg Laws, discriminating against Jews.

1936
Spanish Civil War begins.

1937
The German airship *Hindenburg* explodes at Lakehurst, New Jersey.

September 1938
Mexico nationalizes foreign oil companies.

1939
Germany invades Poland.

697

go.hrw.com
Online Resources

Chapter Resources
KEYWORD: SD7 CH22

Teacher Resources
KEYWORD: SD7 TEACHER

Explore the Time Line

1. Who was chosen to lead Germany about the same time Roosevelt was inaugurated as president? *Adolf Hitler*

2. When was the Social Security Act passed? *August 1935*

3. How much time elapsed from Hitler's election as chancellor until the Nuremburg Laws were passed? *two years*

Info to Know

The Common Man Although Franklin D. Roosevelt came from a wealthy background, he understood the plight of ordinary working Americans suffering through the Depression. With his strong leadership and reforms, he changed the role of the presidency and expanded the federal government.

Draw Conclusions Why might some Americans have supported Roosevelt's expansion of the government? *possible answers—created jobs; initiated social programs like Social Security; supported labor movement*

Answers

Reading Like a Historian *to acknowledge Roosevelt's part in the planning of the town*

697

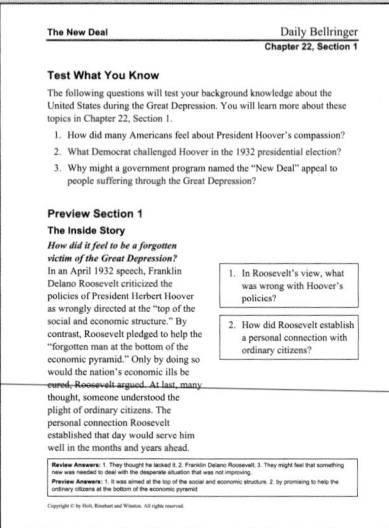

BEFORE YOU READ

MAIN IDEA

In 1933 Franklin Delano Roosevelt became president of a suffering nation. He quickly sought to address the country's needs, with mixed results.

READING FOCUS

1. What were the key events of the presidential election of 1932?
2. What was the nature of Franklin and Eleanor Roosevelt's political partnership?
3. What initial actions did Roosevelt take to stabilize the economy?
4. How did the New Deal run into trouble in Roosevelt's first term?

KEY TERMS AND PEOPLE

Franklin Delano Roosevelt
public works
fireside chat
Eleanor Roosevelt
Hundred Days
New Deal
subsidy
Huey P. Long
Father Charles Coughlin
Dr. Francis Townsend

TAKING NOTES As you read, take notes on major actions taken by the government in the Hundred Days after Franklin Delano Roosevelt took office. Record your notes in a graphic organizer like the one shown here.

> The Hundred Days
> ↓
> ☐

▲ Roosevelt's "forgotten man" speech was as powerful as Maynard Dixon's 1934 painting of the same name.

THE INSIDE STORY

How did it feel to be a forgotten victim of the Great Depression?

Franklin Delano Roosevelt seemed to know. In 1932 Roosevelt was one of several candidates seeking the Democratic presidential nomination. Some critics dismissed him as "an amiable man... without very strong convictions." But in an April 1932 speech, Roosevelt took a strong stand. He criticized the policies of President Hoover as ineffective and wrongly directed at only the "top of the social and economic structure." By contrast, Roosevelt pledged to help the "forgotten man at the bottom of the economic pyramid." Only by helping these people, Roosevelt claimed, would the nation's economic ills be cured.

Roosevelt's speech included few specific proposals. Yet that did not seem to matter to the Depression-weary citizens reading his words or watching the newsreels at the movie houses. Here at last was someone who understood the plight of ordinary citizens. He remembered them, he cared about them, and he seemed to understand that their fate was key to the nation's recovery.

The personal connection Roosevelt established was something few Americans felt they had with Herbert Hoover. It would serve Roosevelt well in the months and years ahead. ■

Teach the Main Idea

At Level

Launching the New Deal

1. **Teach** Ask students the Reading Focus questions to teach this section.

2. **Apply** Organize students into mixed-ability pairs, and have each pair write short newspaper articles on the following: the election of President Roosevelt; the growing role of the First Lady; the Civilian Conservation Corps, the Agricultural Adjustment Act, the National Industrial Recovery Act, the Tennessee Valley Authority, and the Civil Works Administration.

3. **Review** Have volunteers read their articles to the class. Guide students in a discussion of the New Deal programs.

4. **Practice/Homework** Have each student write a brief speech from the viewpoint of a representative of one of the New Deal agencies created to promote recovery. The speech should detail the goals and plans of the agency. **LS Verbal-Linguistic**

Alternative Assessment Handbook, Rubric 23: Newspapers

The Election of 1932

The 1932 presidential election presented the Democrats with a great opportunity to recapture the White House for the first time in 12 years. With joblessness mounting and banks collapsing in record numbers, many Americans placed the blame squarely on President Hoover. Eager to unseat him, Democrats competed fiercely for their party's nomination. **Franklin Delano Roosevelt** emerged the victor.

Roosevelt's rise Franklin Roosevelt was a distant relative of former president Theodore Roosevelt. He had served as assistant secretary of the navy under Woodrow Wilson. He had also run unsuccessfully for vice president in 1920.

Soon after, the ambitious young politician was stricken with polio. The disease nearly killed him and left him without full use of his legs. Yet Roosevelt rebounded from that experience to become governor of New York in 1929. Many considered Roosevelt's record as governor impressive. He launched a groundbreaking relief program to aid the state's many victims of the Great Depression. By 1932 Roosevelt's program had provided help to 1 of every 10 New York families. His record stood in stark contrast to Hoover's insistence on limited government action.

The 1932 campaign During the campaign, Roosevelt offered some general ideas about what he would do as president. He promised relief for the poor and more **public works** programs—government-funded building projects—that would provide jobs. He also talked about lowering tariffs.

Mainly, though, Roosevelt attacked Hoover and the Republicans for their response to the Great Depression. "For at least two years after the crash," Roosevelt railed in an October 1932 speech, "the only efforts made by the national administration to cope with the distress of unemployment were to deny its existence." At the same time, Roosevelt criticized Hoover for spending too much money, and he promised to cut the federal budget. In general,

his speeches laid out the case for change at the White House without tying him down to specific promises or policies.

Though Roosevelt's speeches were vague and sometimes contradictory, they alarmed Hoover. Considering the prospect of Roosevelt's election, he predicted disaster. "The grass will grow in the streets of a hundred cities," cried Hoover. "The weeds will overrun the fields of millions of farms."

A landslide victory Hoover's warnings failed to stir many voters. On election day, the voters handed Roosevelt a clear victory. Roosevelt received more than 57 percent of the popular vote and swept the electoral vote in all but six states. In addition, the Democrats gained 90 seats in the House of Representatives and 13 seats in the Senate to take control of both houses of Congress.

READING CHECK **Making Generalizations**
What was Franklin Roosevelt's campaign strategy in the election of 1932?

THE ELECTION OF 1932

Candidate	Political Affiliation	Electoral Votes	Popular Votes
F. D. Roosevelt	Democratic	472	22,821,857
Herbert Hoover	Republican	59	15,761,841

GEOGRAPHY SKILLS **INTERPRETING MAPS**

Roosevelt won by a landslide in 1932.

Region What region was the Republican stronghold? How many electoral votes went to the Republican candidate, and how many to the Democratic candidate?

See Skills Handbook, p. H21

Reading Focus

❶ What were the key events of the presidential election of 1932? *Many Americans blamed Hoover for economic problems; Roosevelt promised relief and public works programs to provide jobs*

The Election of 1932

Recall What government jobs did Roosevelt hold before running for president? *assistant secretary of navy; governor of New York*

Explain How did Roosevelt plan to turn the economy around? *relief for the poor; public works programs; lowering tariffs*

Evaluate Do you think as a presidential candidate, Roosevelt should have clearly described his plans to end the Depression? *possible answers—yes, should have communicated ideas and plans; no, without congressional approval, plans could not be put into action*

The Election of 1932

Have students locate and use election maps to compare the results of the 1932 and 2004 presidential elections. Guide students in a discussion of the conditions that may lead to a landslide victory. *possible answer—president in office has either remarkable failure or success*

Collaborative Learning

At Level

The 1932 Presidential Election

Research Required

1. Organize the class into small groups. Explain to students that in the 1932 presidential election, Republicans backed Herbert Hoover and Democrats backed Franklin D. Roosevelt. Half of the groups should represent the Republicans and the other half should represent the Democrats.

2. Have each group develop a campaign strategy for its candidate, with slogans and detailed plans. Remind groups to design their campaigns to draw support from citizens who

seem most likely to vote for their candidate and from those who are undecided. Have each group select a campaign manager to present the group's plans and slogans.

3. Ask students which slogans they believe best represented the candidate and which plans seemed most realistic in solving the problems of the Depression. **🅂 Interpersonal**

📝 Alternative Assessment Handbook, Rubrics 34: Slogans and Banners

Answers

Interpreting Maps *northeast; Republican: 59; Democratic: 472*

Reading Check *promised relief for the poor and more public works; attacked Hoover for his handling of the Great Depression*

699

2 What was the nature of Franklin and Eleanor Roosevelt's political partnership? *Their marriage played a vital role in the president's political career. Eleanor served as Franklin's "eyes and ears," and he valued her insight.*

A Political Partnership

Explain How did Roosevelt turn his disability into a strength? *people identified with his struggles; admired his courage*

Analyze What is Roosevelt saying about government's role in the History's Voices quote? *Government's role should be expanded to help solve social problems.*

Develop How did Eleanor Roosevelt transform the role of the First Lady? *became involved in social issues; spoke publicly about injustices*

📰 CRF: Primary Source Activity: A Fireside Chat with Franklin Roosevelt

Faces of History
Franklin Delano Roosevelt

Evaluate How did Roosevelt's performance as governor give Americans confidence that he could be an effective president? *He was able to ease the suffering of New Yorkers.*

go.hrw.com
Online Resources
KEYWORD: SD7 CH22
TOPIC: THE ROOSEVELTS

Answers

Faces of History *It provided him with valuable experience in assisting those hardest hit by the Depression.*

700

Franklin Delano ROOSEVELT
1882–1945

Raised in a wealthy New York family, Franklin Roosevelt had private tutors and traveled to Europe frequently. He won election in 1910 to the New York State Senate, but he resigned in 1913 to serve as President Wilson's assistant secretary of the navy.

Roosevelt's career seemed over when he contracted polio in 1921. With the help of his wife, Eleanor, Roosevelt returned to public service. In 1928 he won the race for governor of New York, serving during the early years of the Depression. His work in easing New Yorkers' suffering helped him win the 1932 Democratic presidential nomination.

Explain How did Roosevelt's experience in New York help him nationally?

A Political Partnership

As a politician, Roosevelt's greatest asset may have been his personality. He had an appealing blend of cheerfulness, optimism, and confidence. These qualities were illustrated by his response to the illness that had left him unable to walk without assistance.

Rather than giving in to his disability, Roosevelt had worked tirelessly to regain strength in his legs and to continue his public career. In this era before television, most Americans were unaware of Roosevelt's handicap. However, his personal struggle gave him a strength that many found very reassuring. In this way, Roosevelt took a personal challenge and turned it into one of his greatest political strengths.

Roosevelt also possessed a warmth and charm that made him an effective communicator. As president, he used the radio to great effect, particularly in his **fireside chats**. As the name suggests, these addresses were meant to sound as though Roosevelt were in the listener's living room, speaking personally with the family. He spoke calmly and clearly and in a way that ordinary people could understand. He conveyed real concern and gave reassurance to millions of troubled Americans.

"I never saw him," recalled one Depression survivor, "but I knew him." This ability to help people feel better during their time of hardship won Roosevelt lasting support with voters.

Roosevelt's philosophy As you have read, Roosevelt sent some unclear signals during his 1932 presidential campaign. Sometimes he attacked Hoover for not doing enough to fight the Depression—and sometimes for doing too much. At heart, however, Roosevelt was a reform-minded Democrat in the tradition of Woodrow Wilson and the Progressives who came before him.

As he had demonstrated as governor of New York, Roosevelt believed that it was the government's job to take direct action to help its people. His basic faith in the ability of government to solve economic and social problems and to help people in need ran deep.

HISTORY'S VOICES

❝I assert that modern society, acting through its Government, owes the definite obligation to prevent the starvation or the dire want of any of its fellow men and women who try to maintain themselves but cannot.❞

—Franklin D. Roosevelt, Campaign Speech, October 13, 1932

Eleanor Roosevelt While still in law school, Franklin Roosevelt had married his distant cousin, **Eleanor Roosevelt**. Their marriage would play a central role in Franklin Roosevelt's political success.

Throughout her husband's career, but especially following his bout with polio in the 1920s, Eleanor served as her husband's "eyes and ears." With his mobility impaired, Franklin Roosevelt relied on his wife to collect and share information gained in her wide travels. He deeply valued his wife's keen insight.

In her own right, Eleanor became a powerful political force. She threw her energies into several major social issues, including the campaign to stop the lynching of African Americans. In the process, she helped change the role of First Lady.

During her husband's presidency, Eleanor began writing her own newspaper column, called "My Day." She received thousands of letters every week. These letters demonstrate the trust and affection many Americans held for the First Lady. They also revealed people's faith in her influence. "Thank you very much for helping me to keep my house," wrote one admirer. "If it wasn't for you, I know I would have lost it."

Skills Focus: Making Inferences   At Level

Reading Skill
Interviewing the Roosevelts

1. Tell students that in 1932, after Franklin D. Roosevelt was elected, reporters questioned the Roosevelts about the president's plans for his administration and the role Eleanor Roosevelt would play as First Lady.

2. Have each student write ten to fifteen questions that a reporter might ask the Roosevelts. Students should write questions for both Franklin and Eleanor.

3. Have volunteers read their questions, and

ask students how the Roosevelts might have answered.

4. Guide the class in a discussion of the Roosevelts' working relationship, how it compares to presidents and their spouses today, and what students believe to be the appropriate role for a First Spouse. 🔲 **Verbal-Linguistic**

📰 Alternative Assessment Handbook, Rubric 1: Acquiring Information

Not everyone was a fan of Eleanor Roosevelt and her active political role. She was a frequent target of the enemies of her husband's administration. Yet even her critics agreed that no First Lady had ever played such an important role in the government of the nation.

READING CHECK **Summarizing** What did President Roosevelt believe was the proper role of government in the lives of American citizens?

Roosevelt Takes Action

By the time Roosevelt was inaugurated in March 1933, four months had passed since the election. Hoover had struggled during that time to prevent a worsening of the economy. As the loser of the presidential race, however, Hoover had little power to accomplish anything. The crisis deepened.

Rescuing the nation's banking system presented the most immediate challenge facing Roosevelt when he took office. The problems facing the nation's banks had gotten so bad that when leaders gathered in Washington, D.C., for Roosevelt's March 4 inauguration, hotels would not accept checks from out-of-town guests. The hotels feared that the guests' banks might fail before the hotels were able to receive payment.

The banking crisis Roosevelt could see that the nation faced a critical loss of confidence. He wasted no time in addressing the situation. In his inaugural address, the new president sought to calm the public.

HISTORY'S VOICES

❝ So, first of all, let me assert my firm belief that the only thing we have to fear is fear itself—nameless, unreasoning, unjustified terror which paralyzes needed efforts to convert retreat into advance. ❞

—Franklin D. Roosevelt, First Inaugural Address, March 4, 1933

Two days later, Roosevelt took action. The shaky state of the nation's banks had led many people to withdraw all their money from their accounts. They feared losing their savings if the bank collapsed. Such large-scale withdrawals could—and did—ruin even healthy banks. This created more panic, more withdrawals—and more bank failures. To stop this cycle, Roosevelt issued an executive order temporarily closing all of the nation's banks. The president called it a bank holiday.

Next, the president called Congress into emergency session and pushed through the Emergency Banking Act. The law gave government officials power to examine each bank,

"Hoover sent the army; Roosevelt sent his wife."
A World War I veteran

FACES OF HISTORY

Eleanor ROOSEVELT
1884–1962

Orphaned at the age of 10, Eleanor Roosevelt was raised by her mother's relatives. A sad and shy teenager and a serious and scholarly young woman, she married the fun-loving, outgoing Franklin D. Roosevelt.

Eleanor grew into her roles in life, becoming one of the most respected women in America. With dynamic energy, she labored for charities, traveled the world making speeches, and spoke out for women's rights and against racial discrimination. After her husband died in office, Eleanor began a new chapter in life. She served as a delegate to the United Nations, chaired President John F. Kennedy's Commission on the Status of Women, and remained active in American politics.

Make Inferences What choices did Eleanor Roosevelt make in life, and what did those choices reflect about her character?

When a second Bonus Army came to Washington in 1933, Roosevelt sent Eleanor to investigate. Her tour of their camp in Virginia ended in a sing-along.

THE NEW DEAL **701**

701

Reading Focus

Roosevelt Takes Action

Describe What was the goal of the Tennessee Valley Authority? *to transform the region by developing the resources of the Tennessee River*

Analyze How did the public benefit from the Federal Securities Act? *companies had to share certain financial information with the public; helped investors make wiser choices and restored confidence in the fairness of the markets*

Predict How do you think the NIRA will affect interactions between labor unions and businesses? *possible answer—Unions will be more successful in receiving benefits from businesses because of federal protection.*

- CRF: Biography: Walter Lippmann
- U.S. History Political Cartoon Activity: Cartoon 43: Farm Relief
- U.S. History Political Cartoon Activity: Cartoon 44: A New Deal

Relief, Reform, Recovery

Analyze Which of the three goals of the New Deal was intended to have the most immediate effect? Why? *relief; provided help for those suffering from the effects of the Depression*

Teaching Tip

Remind students that the Square Deal was Theodore Roosevelt's plan to balance the interests of business, labor, and consumers. The New Deal was Franklin D. Roosevelt's series of programs to end the Depression.

go.hrw.com
Online Resources

KEYWORD: SD7 CH22
TOPIC: THE NEW DEAL

Relief, Reform, Recovery

determine its soundness, take steps to correct problems, and, if necessary, close it. To explain to the worried public what was going on, Roosevelt gave the first of his famed fireside chats.

The plan worked. Within days, banks began to reopen with government assurances that they were on solid footing. Ordinary people, who had been frantically taking money out of their banks, started to return funds. Some banks never did reopen, but the crisis was over. In just over a week, the nation had regained crucial confidence in its financial system.

In the days ahead, Congress enacted additional banking reforms. The Glass-Steagall Act of 1933 created the Federal Deposit Insurance Corporation, or FDIC. This provided government insurance for depositors' savings. Individual depositors no longer needed to fear losing their savings if their bank collapsed.

Reassured by the new law, even more depositors took the money they had stuffed in home safes and under their mattresses and returned it to the banking system. Within a month, about $1 billion in new deposits flowed into the system.

The Hundred Days The resolution of the banking crisis was just the beginning of a critical period of government activity that came to be known as the **Hundred Days**. During this time, Roosevelt pushed Congress to put in place many of the key parts of his program—what he called the **New Deal**.

Roosevelt first used the phrase in a campaign speech in which he promised "a new deal for the American people." The New Deal came to include a wide range of measures aimed at accomplishing three goals:

(1) *relief* for those suffering the effects of the Great Depression;

(2) *recovery* of the depressed economy;

(3) *reforms* that would help prevent serious economic crises in the future.

The Civilian Conservation Corps, or CCC, was typical of the reform programs passed during the Hundred Days. Established in March 1933, it sought to address an immediate problem: unemployment among young men 18 to 25 years old.

Americans enrolled in the CCC were paid to work on a variety of conservation projects, such as planting trees and improving parks. CCC workers lived in army-style camps and were required to send most of their earnings to their families.

Two key recovery programs sought to reinforce the twin pillars of the economy—agriculture and industry. The Agricultural Adjustment Act, or AAA, gave farmers a **subsidy**, or government payment, to grow fewer crops. A smaller

Differentiating Instruction

Below Level | Standard English Mastery

English-Language Learners

Materials construction paper, colored markers

1. Organize students into mixed-ability pairs. Have each pair create two posters that provide information about New Deal programs. Posters should tell citizens about programs such as the Civilian Conservation Corps, the Public Works Administration, or the Civil Works Administration. Posters should also show who will benefit from the program, and what the program is supposed to accomplish. Each poster should tell about only one program.

2. Display student posters in the classroom. Have the class view all posters. Then guide students in a discussion of the programs covered by the posters. Help students evaluate how well the posters conveyed the purposes of the programs, and whether or not they would be effective in reaching their target audience.

LS Interpersonal, Visual-Spatial

Alternative Assessment Handbook, Rubric 28: Posters

Civilian Conservation Corps workers replant a clear-cut Oregon hillside with seedlings in 1939 (left). The CCC brought immediate relief to families and provided work for 3 million young men. Businesses following fair-practice business codes displayed the NRA's blue eagle emblem (above).

supply of crops on the market would increase demand for those crops. This would drive prices up and help farmers earn more.

The National Industrial Recovery Act (NIRA) mandated that businesses in the same industry cooperate with each other to set prices and levels of production. In the days of Theodore Roosevelt, government had viewed such cooperation as a violation of antitrust laws. Now, with the NIRA, government sought to promote it as a way of helping business.

The NIRA also included $3.3 billion for public-works programs. These were managed through a new agency called the Public Works Administration, or PWA. (The New Deal was famous for creating an "alphabet soup" of government agencies known by their initials.) Labor unions benefited, too, from the NIRA. For the first time, labor got federal protection for the right to organize.

The Federal Securities Act emerged as a major reform effort of the Hundred Days. The measure forced companies to share certain financial information with the public. The purpose was to help investors and to restore confidence in the fairness of the markets.

In 1934 Congress established the Securities and Exchange Commission. The SEC would serve as a government watchdog over the nation's stock markets.

One of the most far-reaching and ambitious programs of the New Deal was the Tennessee Valley Authority, or TVA. Created in May 1933, this massive program was charged with developing the resources of the entire Tennessee River Valley, a vast region in the Southeast United States.

The TVA built dams and other projects along the Tennessee River and its tributaries. These dams controlled floods, aided navigation and shipping along the river, and provided hydroelectric power to be used by industries. (See the History and Geography feature on the TVA at the end of this section.)

Beyond the Hundred Days President Roosevelt had campaigned promising action and "bold, persistent experimentation." He had delivered. Many Americans applauded his efforts. Journalist and former Roosevelt critic Walter Lippmann wrote, "In the hundred days from March to June we became again an organized nation confident of our power."

Amid the successes, there was also much to criticize. Even Roosevelt admitted in a fireside chat, "I do not deny that we make mistakes." Comparing himself to a baseball player, he said, "I have no expectation of making a hit every time we come to bat."

Yet FDR and the Congress kept trying, passing significant legislation in the period after the Hundred Days. In November 1933, for example, the Civil Works Administration (CWA) was created. This agency provided winter employment to 4 million workers. CWA crews built miles of highways and sewer lines, hundreds of airports, and more.

In June 1934 Congress passed the Indian Reorganization Act. It reversed previous policies by recognizing the tribe as the key unit of social organization for Native Americans. It limited the sale of Indian lands and provided assistance to native groups in developing their resources, economy, and culture. It also granted some limited rights of self-rule.

Many Native Americans hailed the new direction. Others viewed it more skeptically, as just another instance of outsiders telling them what to do.

ACADEMIC VOCABULARY
mandate require

READING CHECK **Identifying Supporting Details** What were the three main categories of the programs and actions of Roosevelt's New Deal?

● **Direct Teach** ●

Info to Know

The NRA The head of the National Recovery Administration (NRA) tried to win support for his agency by associating compliance with NRA codes with patriotism. When labor leaders, liberals, and Progressives complained that the NRA catered to big business, President Roosevelt created a review board to investigate their complaints. The head of the review board soon agreed that the NRA was dominated by monopolies and was not solving any economic problems.

Native Americans In the late 1920s, a report on Native American life listed numerous problems. Native Americans argued that their culture had been stripped away by measures like the Dawes Act of 1887, which had ended tribal government and resulted in great losses of tribal land. The Indian Reorganization Act reversed the Dawes Act policy and tried to revive tribal rule. It provided funds to start tribal businesses and to pay for the college education of young Native Americans. The bill also ordered Congress "to promote the study of Indian civilization and preserve and develop . . . Indian arts, crafts, skills, and traditions."

CRF: Primary Source Activity: CWA Workers Building a Road in California

Answers

Reading Check *relief, recovery, reform*

Skills Focus: Identifying Cause and Effect

At Level

Reading Skill
Transforming the Tennessee River Valley

1. To help students understand the goals for the Tennessee River Valley, have each student copy the organizer and complete it. Omit the answers. Have volunteers call out the answers, and fill in the master graphic organizer for the class to see. Have students correct their own charts.

2. Guide students in a discussion of the Tennessee Valley Authority, using the following questions as a guide: What other benefits would have come from the project? Why might people have criticized the TVA in spite of its efforts to improve the quality of life in the region? Should the government or the private sector be responsible for improving the quality of life in impoverished regions? **LS** **Visual-Spatial, Logical-Mathematical**

Alternative Assessment Handbook, Rubric 13: Graphic Organizers

Graphic Organizer Transparencies

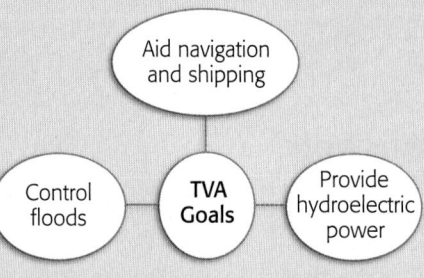

④ How did the New Deal run into trouble in Roosevelt's first term? *Liberals thought it didn't do enough; conservatives thought it went too far; some provisions were struck down by the Supreme Court.*

Trouble for the New Deal

Recall What did Huey P. Long's Share Our Wealth Society want to do? *raise taxes on the wealthy; give every family $5,000 to buy a home plus an income of $2,500 a year*

Analyze Why did the American Liberty League appeal to both Democrats and Republicans? *Conservatives in both parties felt the New Deal had gone too far.*

Evaluate Do you think the New Deal went too far or not far enough? Why? *possible answer—not far enough because Roosevelt did not do enough to assist certain groups of Americans, such as the poor and the elderly*

Info to Know

Long's Power Grab Huey P. Long held populist ideas from the beginning of his career, when he attacked Standard Oil and opposed the Ku Klux Klan. As governor of Louisiana, Long abolished his state's local governments and personally controlled the courts, the militia, police forces, schools, and the tax assessors. Due to his unprecedented accumulation of power, Long faced impeachment by the state legislature but was not convicted.

Answers

Reading Like a Historian
1. *possible answer—Uncle Guinea Pig is being experimented upon by the New Deal.* 2. *possible answer—no, the New Deal is a dangerous experiment on a sleeping nation.*

704

ACADEMIC VOCABULARY
significant meaningful

Trouble for the New Deal

The New Deal marked a significant shift in the relationship between government and the American people. Never before had government assumed such a central role in the business and personal lives of its citizens. Not surprisingly, this shift triggered strong reactions.

Some reformers and radicals believed the New Deal had not gone far enough in reforming the economy. They wanted a complete overhaul of capitalism. The New Deal, they complained, merely propped up the old banking system and gave new freedoms to business. These, critics charged, were the same people and powers that had led the nation into the Great Depression in the first place.

Conservatives, on the other hand, attacked the New Deal as a radical break with traditional American ideals. Senator Carter Glass of Virginia lamented in 1933 that "Roosevelt is driving this country to destruction faster than it has ever moved before."

Leading critics of the New Deal Over time, several leading critics of the New Deal emerged. Perhaps the most powerful of these was Senator **Huey P. Long** of Louisiana, who believed Roosevelt's policies were too friendly to banks and businesses.

In 1934 Long set up his own political organization, the Share Our Wealth Society. Long's idea, reflected in the slogan "Every Man a King," was to give every family $5,000 to buy a home, plus an income of $2,500 a year. To pay for this, Long proposed heavy taxes on wealthy Americans. Long's organization attracted millions of followers. Roosevelt's advisers feared his possible role in the 1936 election.

Father Charles Coughlin, a Catholic priest, was another one-time Roosevelt supporter who turned against the president. At the peak of Coughlin's popularity, one-third of the nation tuned in to the weekly radio broadcasts of the "radio priest." His program, featuring religious messages and political commentary, was sharply critical of the nation's bankers and financial leaders. When Coughlin concluded that the president was not doing enough to curb their power, he called the president "Franklin Double-Crossing Roosevelt."

Coughlin also began to attack leading Jewish figures in the administration and elsewhere. As his speeches became more extreme,

---

PRIMARY SOURCES

Political Cartoon

The New Deal represented a great change in the role of the federal government in the lives of Americans. Government agencies became involved in people's business and personal lives in many new ways—and not everyone was pleased with the results.

This long line of eager scholars represent government officials carrying out New Deal programs.

The United States is depicted as a patient under anesthesia.

Skills FOCUS **READING LIKE A HISTORIAN**

1. **Interpreting Political Cartoons** What does this cartoon suggest is happening to Uncle Guinea Pig?
2. **Drawing Conclusions** Does this cartoon present a positive view of the New Deal? Explain.

See Skills Handbook, p. H31

704 CHAPTER 22

Skills Focus: Comparing and Contrasting   `At Level`

Reading Skill
Criticism of the New Deal

1. Remind students that New Deal measures were criticized by both liberals and conservatives. Ask students why criticism of the New Deal might have been so widespread. *Some people thought the administration wasn't doing enough to help the poor and elderly; business interests felt threatened by what they viewed as anti-business policies.*

2. Guide students in a discussion of liberal and conservative people and groups that opposed and supported the New Deal. Have students make a list of liberals and conservatives who opposed New Deal policies.

3. Have volunteers share their lists with the class. Then have each student write a brief description or summary of reasons why those on the class list opposed the New Deal.
LS **Visual-Spatial, Logical-Mathematical**

Alternative Assessment Handbook, Rubric 9: Comparing and Contrasting

Coughlin began to lose influence with the American people. Eventually, the Catholic Church forced him to end his radio program.

Dr. Francis Townsend criticized the New Deal for not doing enough for older Americans. He proposed a plan for providing pensions to people over the age of 60. Like Long and Coughlin, Townsend attracted millions of followers. Some of his ideas would later help shape the thinking and policies of President Roosevelt.

The American Liberty League spoke for many conservatives who felt the New Deal had gone too far. The League drew members from both parties, including former Democratic presidential candidate Al Smith. It also included a number of wealthy business leaders, who believed the New Deal's policies were antibusiness. But despite spending thousands of dollars to defeat New Deal candidates in elections, the League met with little success.

Opposition from the courts The American people supported the New Deal's attempts to bring change to the economy. The courts, however, were more skeptical.

The New Deal changed in basic ways the relationship between the American people and their government. It also threatened to alter the balance of power among the president, the Congress, and the courts. Critics feared that the New Deal gave the president too much power over other branches of government. Presidentially appointed administrators, rather than Congress, were now making rules affecting millions of people. Some critics argued that these changes violated the Constitution.

By 1935 New Deal cases were making their way to the Supreme Court. Their decisions delivered a series of sharp blows to Roosevelt's program. For example, in May 1935, the Supreme Court issued a ruling in *Schechter Poultry Corporation* v. *United States* that destroyed key parts of the NIRA. (See the Landmark Supreme Court Cases feature at the end of this section.) In 1936 the court's ruling in *United States* v. *Butler* found a key part of the AAA—the tax used to raise the money for farmer subsidies—unconstitutional.

The courts managed do what the New Deal's critics had failed to accomplish over the course of two years. As Roosevelt faced re-election in 1936, he continued to enjoy wide popularity among voters. Yet parts of his ambitious economic program were in shambles. Meanwhile, the Great Depression remained a grim fact of life for millions of Americans.

READING CHECK **Summarizing** What were the two major types of complaints about the New Deal during Roosevelt's first term in office?

SECTION 1 ASSESSMENT

go.hrw.com
Online Quiz
Keyword: SD7 HP22

Reviewing Ideas, Terms, and People

1. a. Define Write a brief definition for the following term: public works
   b. Explain What factors made Roosevelt a good choice for the Democratic nomination in 1932?
   c. Evaluate Defend Roosevelt's campaign strategy in 1932.

2. a. Describe What were Roosevelt's **fireside chats**?
   b. Analyze How did Franklin Roosevelt's beliefs about government represent a change from those of Hoover?
   c. Compare Compare **Eleanor Roosevelt** to First Ladies who came before her.

3. a. Define Write a brief definition of the following terms: **Hundred Days, New Deal, subsidy**
   b. Draw Conclusions Why do you think Roosevelt's first act as president was to try to restore confidence in the nation's banking system?
   c. Rank Of the three main goals—relief, recovery, and reform—which do you think was most important? Explain.

4. a. Identify Identify at least three major critics of the New Deal in its early years.
   b. Compare What viewpoint did **Huey P. Long, Father Coughlin,** and **Dr. Francis Townsend** share in common?
   c. Predict How do you think the decisions of the Supreme Court will affect Roosevelt in the future?

Critical Thinking

5. Sequence Copy the chart below and use information from the section to record events in sequence.

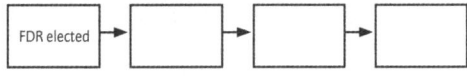

FDR elected → □ → □ → □

FOCUS ON WRITING

6. Persuasive Write a letter to the editor in which you either defend or criticize Roosevelt's New Deal programs. Use details from the section to support your position.

THE NEW DEAL **705**

Section 1 Assessment Answers

1. a. government-funded building projects
   b. promised relief for the poor
   c. possible answer—Most Americans agreed that Hoover had failed.

2. a. radio addresses to the American people
   b. believed government should take direct action to help its people
   c. active role, addressed social issues

3. a. Hundred Days—critical first days of Roosevelt's administration; New Deal—relief, recovery, reform measures; subsidy—government payment

   b. needed to stabilize banks and prevent collapse of the banking system
   c. possible answer—relief; people needed help

4. a. Long, Coughlin, Townsend
   b. All criticized Roosevelt for not doing enough.
   c. possible answer—They will limit Roosevelt's ability to pass new legislation.

5. economy worsened; banks closed; Hundred Days began

6. possible answers—New Deal offered hope; relief, reform, recovery

---

Review & Assess

Close
Have students summarize Roosevelt's election to the presidency and actions he took during the Hundred Days.

Review
Online Quiz, Section 1

Daily Test Practice Transparency

Assess
SE Section 1 Assessment

Progress Assessment: Section 1 Quiz

Alternative Assessment Handbook

Reteach
Interactive Reader and Study Guide, Section 1

Interactive Skills Tutor CD-ROM

Answers
Reading Check *Government didn't do enough. Government programs went too far.*

The Tennessee Valley Authority

Activity **Exploring the Tennessee Valley** Have students find a detailed map that shows the area served by TVA power and the Tennessee River watershed. Have students use the scale on the map to estimate the total area served by the TVA, the length of rivers such as the Cumberland and Tennessee, and how far a barge would have to travel from one key point to another on the river system. **LS Logical-Mathematical**

Info to Know

Contributing to the War Effort Although the TVA was created in 1933, much of its hydroelectric capacity was built in the early 1940s. During World War II, the United States required vast amounts of aluminum to build bombs and airplanes. Aluminum plants, in turn, needed electricity. To provide power to make this critical material, TVA started one of the largest hydropower construction programs in American history. By 1942, 12 hydroelectric projects and a steam plant were under construction. About 28,000 people worked on the project that year.

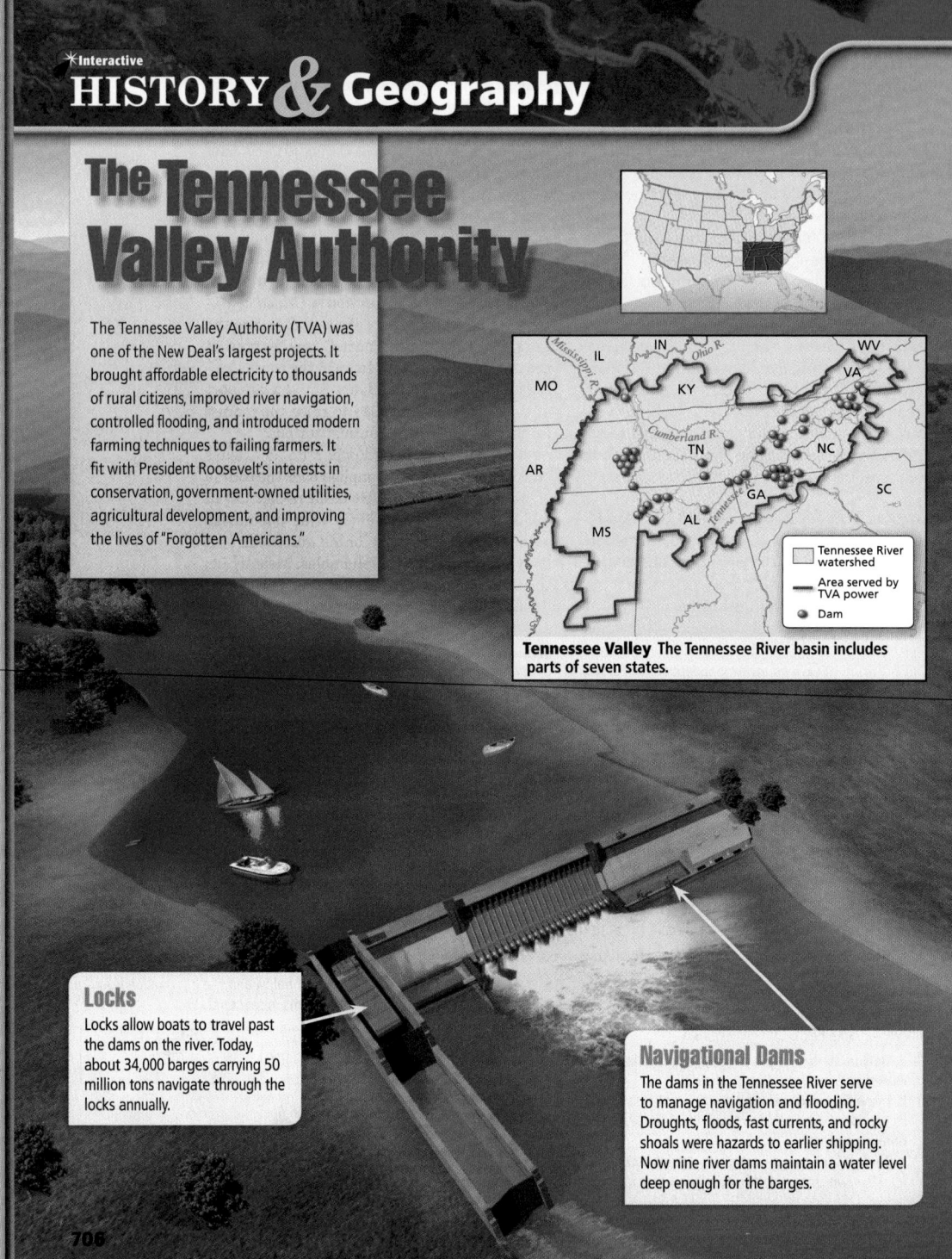

*Interactive

HISTORY & Geography

The Tennessee Valley Authority

The Tennessee Valley Authority (TVA) was one of the New Deal's largest projects. It brought affordable electricity to thousands of rural citizens, improved river navigation, controlled flooding, and introduced modern farming techniques to failing farmers. It fit with President Roosevelt's interests in conservation, government-owned utilities, agricultural development, and improving the lives of "Forgotten Americans."

Tennessee Valley The Tennessee River basin includes parts of seven states.

Tennessee River watershed
Area served by TVA power
Dam

Locks
Locks allow boats to travel past the dams on the river. Today, about 34,000 barges carrying 50 million tons navigate through the locks annually.

Navigational Dams
The dams in the Tennessee River serve to manage navigation and flooding. Droughts, floods, fast currents, and rocky shoals were hazards to earlier shipping. Now nine river dams maintain a water level deep enough for the barges.

706

Skills Focus: Drawing Conclusions
At Level

Reading Skill
The Government's Role

1. Guide students in a discussion of how the TVA coincided with President Roosevelt's beliefs about the proper role of the government. List student answers on the board.

2. Have students write an editorial about whether or not Roosevelt's beliefs are appropriate for the government today. Have volunteers share their responses with the class. **LS Verbal-Linguistic**

Alternative Assessment Handbook, Rubric 17: Letters to Editors

Electricity for Farms

By the 1930s, only 10 percent of rural dwellers had electricity, while 90 percent of urbanites did. Isolated farmers couldn't keep food cold or turn on a light. The Roosevelt Administration thought the government should provide electricity to citizens not yet served by private companies.

Hydroelectric Dams

The dams built on the rivers that flow into the Tennessee River are high dams backed by huge reservoirs. These dams generated the cheap electricity needed to improve lives and lure industries that would provide jobs to the region.

Farming Practices

Many Tennessee Valley farmers used methods that depleted and eroded the soil. The TVA taught farmers how to use crop rotation and plants like alfalfa and clover to enrich and conserve the soil.

GEOGRAPHY SKILLS INTERPRETING MAPS

go.hrw.com
Interactive Map
Keyword: SD7 CH22

1. Location Why was the Tennessee Valley a good location for this New Deal project?

2. Movement How did the TVA help boats navigate the river?

See **Skills Handbook,** p. H20

Differentiating Instruction

Below Level

Learners Having Difficulty

1. Write a sample costs/benefits chart on the board. Have students copy the chart into their notes and fill it in with information on TVA.

2. Have students use the information in this feature, from the text discussion, and from their previous knowledge to list ways the TVA project was beneficial and ways it may have been harmful.

3. Guide students in a discussion of whether TVA's benefits were worth its costs and disadvantages. **LS** **Verbal-Linguistic, Logical-Mathematical**

📖 Alternative Assessment Handbook, Rubric 7: Charts

Info to Know

Green Power TVA offers its customers the option of buying electrical power that has been generated by "green" sources, such as the sun, wind, or methane gas recaptured from sewage-treatment plants. Customers pay a small extra charge per month to buy blocks of TVA's green power. Currently, TVA has the capacity to provide 54,000 homes and many businesses with green electrical power.

MISCONCEPTION ALERT

Students may be surprised to know that, although TVA is best known as a source of hydroelectric power, 30 percent of its electricity is generated by nuclear power plants. The three nuclear plants, located near Athens, Alabama, Soddy-Daisy, Tennessee, and Spring City, Tennessee, generate about 5,700 megawatts of electricity. This is enough electricity to power more than three million homes in the Tennessee Valley.

Answers

Interpreting Maps 1. *one of largest river basins in U.S.; several good sites for dams; need for electricity and agricultural development;* **2.** *maintained water level deep enough for barges; controlled flooding; eliminated hazards like fast currents and shoals*

707

LANDMARK SUPREME COURT CASES

Constitutional Issue: Powers of the President

Word Help

mandatory required, obligatory
compulsory required, enforced

Info to Know

The Constitutional Grounds for the *Schechter* Decision The first of the grounds for finding the compulsory code system unconstitutional is found in Article I, Section 1 of the Constitution:

"All legislative Powers herein granted shall be vested in a Congress of the United States, which shall consist of a Senate and House of Representatives."

The second of the grounds the Supreme Court cited in the *Schechter* case was the Commerce Clause (Article I, Section 8, Clause 3), which states that Congress shall have power:

"To regulate Commerce with foreign Nations, and among the several States, and with the Indian Tribes."

Schechter Poultry Corporation v. United States (1935)

Why It Matters Can Congress broadly delegate its lawmaking authority to the administrative agencies of the executive branch? That was the question the Court faced in *Schechter*. The Court's negative ruling temporarily derailed President Franklin D. Roosevelt's New Deal program. However, it also forced Roosevelt and Congress to tailor future legislation more narrowly.

Background of the Case

In 1933 President Roosevelt created the National Recovery Administration (NRA). The NRA supervised the development of mandatory industry-wide codes for production, prices, and wages. The standards carried the force of law. The Schechter Corporation appealed after it was convicted of violating the minimum wage and maximum hour provisions of the code for the live poultry industry.

The Decision

In its unanimous decision, the Court cited two grounds for finding the mandatory code system unconstitutional. First, it ruled that the delegation of rule-making authority to an agency of the executive branch violated the constitutional separation of powers. The Constitution places all legislative power in the Congress. Rules or codes having the force of law could only be made by Congress, not by the executive branch.

Second, the Court ruled that the activities of the Schechter Corporation were not subject to congressional regulation. Under the commerce clause, Congress can regulate interstate commerce (conducted in more than one state), not intrastate commerce (conducted entirely within a single state). The Schechter Corporation bought and sold its chickens almost exclusively within New York State. So the commerce clause did not apply to the way that Schecter conducted business.

THE IMPACT TODAY The Supreme Court later took an expanded view of the commerce clause and gave Congress more authority to delegate lawmaking authority to administrative agencies. Today there is widespread governmental regulation of business and economic matters. Much of the regulation is done by administrative agencies within the executive branch. Above, President George W. Bush meets with Senate leaders to discuss energy policy.

CRITICAL THINKING

go.hrw.com
Research Online
Keyword: SS Court

1. **Analyze the Impact** Using the keyword above, read about the Interstate Commerce Commission. What does the Commission do? If *Schechter* had been ruled differently, what aspects of the commission today would have created constitutional problems?

2. **You Be the Judge** The Gun Free School Zones Act of 1990 made it a federal crime for an individual knowingly to possess a firearm in a school zone. Does the act exceed Congress's power to legislate under the Commerce Clause? State the arguments for and against the law's constitutionality.

Skills Focus: Drawing Conclusions
At Level

Reading Skill
Fair Labor Standards Act

Background: In 1938 Congress passed the Fair Labor Standards Act, which included provisions for a national minimum wage as well as maximum working hours.

1. Ask students what significant difference there is between the Fair Labor Standards Act (FLSA) and the regulations passed down by the National Recovery Administration (NRA). *Although the FLSA and the NRA were both passed by Congress, the NRA was written by members of an agency.*

2. Recently there has been discussion about whether employers should be able to exempt teenage employees from the minimum wage. Conduct a class debate in which students argue for and against exempting teens from minimum wage laws. **LS Verbal-Linguistic**

Alternative Assessment Handbook, Rubric 10: Debates

Answers

Critical Thinking 1. *It regulates commerce that occurs in more than one state; government agencies might have less regulatory power.* **2.** *for—Schools receive federal funding and federal law takes precedence over state law. against—The law does not fall in the realm of commerce, so it is therefore unconstitutional.*

SECTION 2 The Second New Deal

BEFORE YOU READ

MAIN IDEA
A new wave of government initiatives starting in 1935 resulted in some strong successes and stunning defeats for President Roosevelt.

READING FOCUS
1. What were the key programs in the Second Hundred Days?
2. How did New Deal programs help to revive organized labor?
3. What were the key events of the 1936 election?
4. Why was 1937 a troubled year for Roosevelt and the Second New Deal?

KEY TERMS AND PEOPLE
Second New Deal
Social Security
John L. Lewis
CIO
sit-down strike
deficit
John Maynard Keynes

 **TAKING NOTES** As you read, take notes identifying the major pieces of the Second New Deal. Record your notes in a graphic organizer like the one shown here.

The Second New Deal

THE INSIDE STORY

How do you restore hope to the hopeless? The New Deal did not end the Great Depression. Yet the sense of forward movement it created helped give people hope.

Starting in 1935, government increased its commitment to work relief. Earlier programs such as the Civilian Conservation Corps (CCC) had shown how such programs provided not just a source of income but also a sense of purpose and dignity. One worker described how hard work in the CCC transformed his body and mind: "[Y]ou must go through the actual experience before you can really understand the hopeless state of mind most of the prospective members of the CCC were in when we put on our 'G.I.' clothing and

tramped half-heartedly into the forests and fields to plant and cut trees, build dams,… fire breaks and trails, control insect pests, tree diseases, and risk our lives… protecting the forests from the most efficient of destructive forces—Fire. But our don't-care-what-happens attitude didn't last long…. I am making my own way and that is sufficient for the present. What is probably more important is the fact that I am not the undernourished, furtive-eyed, scared kid that went in … over five years ago. Instead, my eyes are clear and my mind is receptive to whatever the future has in store. In short, the CCC has equipped me with the weapons necessary to cope with the innumerable problems that are bound to obstruct my path through life and that must be surmounted before success can be attained."

Working for Dignity

▼ Millions of Americans were uplifted by New Deal work-relief programs.

Teach the Main Idea

At Level

The Second New Deal

1. **Teach** Ask students the Reading Focus questions to teach this section.

2. **Apply** Have students create an outline of the section using the red and blue heads as main points. Have students identify at least two main ideas under each of the blue subheadings.

3. **Review** Ask students to identify the points in their outlines that they feel are most important regarding the Second New Deal.

4. **Practice/Homework** Have each student write a short essay describing labor's revival with the passage of the National Labor Relations Act, the organization of the Committee of Industrial Organization (CIO), and groundbreaking strikes against General Motors and United States Steel.
   LS Verbal-Linguistic, Logical-Mathematical
   Alternative Assessment Handbook, Rubric 42: Writing to Inform

Preteach

Bellringer
The Inside Story. . . Use the **Daily Bellringer Transparency** to help students answer the question.

Daily Bellringer Transparency, Section 2

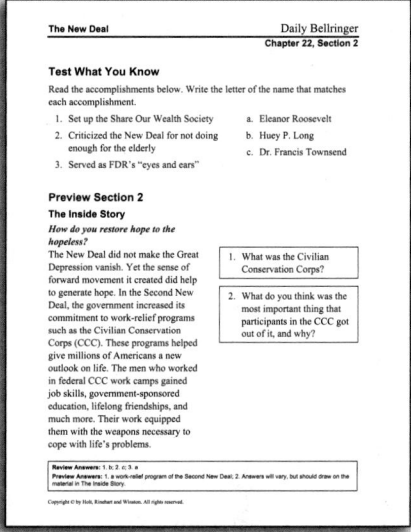

Academic Vocabulary
Review with students the high-use academic term in this section.
classical well known, original (p. 716)
CRF: Vocabulary Builder Activity, Section 2

Taking Notes
WPA, Social Security, Wagner Act (NLRB)

❶ What were the key programs in the Second Hundred Days? *the Works Progress Administration, Social Security*

The Second Hundred Days

Recall What were the provisions of the Social Security Act? *provided a pension for many Americans age 65 and older; included a system of unemployment insurance*

Explain Why might critics of the first New Deal have favored the Second New Deal? *required people to work for their pay*

Make Judgments Do you think that Herbert Hoover would have agreed or disagreed with the quotation from Roosevelt's 1935 State of the Union Address? Explain your answer. *possible answer—agreed, because Hoover believed in self-reliance*

📄 CRF: Biography: Ellen Sullivan Woodward

Info to Know

Surplus Food The Second New Deal introduced a plan to provide surplus food to people who were eligible for federal work relief. This plan allowed participants to buy orange-colored food stamps. For each dollar of orange stamps purchased, the buyer would be given 50 cents' worth of blue stamps. Orange stamps could be used to buy any kind of food, but blue stamps could be used only for surplus foods.

go.hrw.com
Online Resources
KEYWORD: SD7 CH22
TOPIC: THE WPA

The Second Hundred Days

With public support for the president and the New Deal running high, the Democratic Party rolled to an unprecedented victory in the congressional elections of 1934. For the first time in U.S. history, the party in control of the White House gained seats in both houses of Congress in a midterm election.

When the new Congress took office in 1935, Democrats held three-quarters of all seats. It was a clear vote of confidence in Roosevelt. As one journalist remarked, "He has been all but crowned by the people."

Roosevelt's victory, however, threatened to be a hollow one. The courts were in the process of finding major parts of the New Deal unconstitutional. The economy was proving stubbornly resistant to recovery. Meanwhile, more-liberal elements in the country were clamoring for the president to do more.

And he did do more. In a flurry of activity in the spring of 1935, during a period called the Second Hundred Days, Roosevelt launched the so-called **Second New Deal**. In short order, Congress passed laws extending government oversight of the banking industry and raising taxes for the wealthy. It funded new relief programs for the still-struggling population.

Emergency relief The major relief legislation of the Second New Deal marked a shift from Roosevelt's earlier programs. The Emergency Relief Appropriations Act largely did away with direct payments to Americans in need. As you have read, the Second New Deal expanded on what had been a small but successful part of the first New Deal: work relief. From now on, said the president, people should work for pay.

HISTORY'S VOICES

❝[C]ontinued dependence upon relief [brings about] a spiritual and moral disintegration . . . destructive to the national fiber. To dole out relief in this way is to administer a narcotic, a subtle destroyer of the human spirit.❞

—Franklin Delano Roosevelt,
State of the Union Address, 1935

The new Works Progress Administration (WPA), created in 1935, was the largest peacetime jobs program in U.S. history. It eventually employed 8.5 million Americans on all kinds of public-works projects at a cost of about $11 billion.

WPA workers built roads, subways, airports, even zoos. They worked in offices, schools, museums, and factories. They ventured into the fields to record the oral histories of former

Murals of the New Deal

Men operating air drills and rope work the dangerously steep slopes of the canyon.

Workers operating a heavy crane hoist a huge conduit above a canyon.

710 CHAPTER 22

Collaborative Learning

At Level

The Legacy of the WPA

Research Required

1. Organize the class into small groups. Have each group conduct research on WPA projects and make a list of the WPA projects that were done locally or in a nearby state.

2. Have each student write a brief magazine article entitled "The Legacy of the WPA" about one of the local WPA projects. Students should use the following questions to guide them: What was the project? Who was employed on it? What impact did the project

have on the community at the time? Is the product of the project still in existence? What was the lasting importance of the project? If possible, students should include pictures, photographs, and other illustrations with their articles.

3. Have volunteers share their articles with the class. **LS** **Interpersonal, Verbal-Linguistic**

📄 Alternative Assessment Handbook, Rubric 19: Magazines

slaves. The WPA even funded the efforts of artists, writers, composers, and actors. A number of soon-to-be-famous figures got their starts in the program, including artist Jackson Pollock and writers Ralph Ellison, Richard Wright, and Eudora Welty.

At its peak, the WPA employed some 3.4 million formerly jobless Americans. This amounted to nearly a fourth of the unemployed people in the country.

As Roosevelt had hoped, getting the opportunity to earn a paycheck rather than get a handout lifted people's spirits. As one worker put it, "You worked, you got a paycheck and you had some dignity."

Social Security A centerpiece of the Second New Deal was the Social Security Act, signed in August 1935. This law created a system called **Social Security**, which provided a pension, or guaranteed, regular payments, for many people 65 and older.

With the creation of Social Security, many retired workers no longer needed to fear hunger and homelessness once they became too old to work. The Social Security Act also included a system of unemployment insurance run jointly by the federal government and the states. This program provided payments to workers who

The WPA paid artists to create public art. *Construction of the Dam,* a mural by William Gropper, shows workers on a WPA construction project.

A group of muscular men put together a large section of steel framework.

lost their jobs, giving them a financial cushion while they looked for new work. To fund the programs, Congress passed new taxes that affected both workers and employers.

In promoting Social Security, Roosevelt responded to a number of his critics. For example, in helping older Americans, Roosevelt hoped to undermine the attacks of Dr. Francis Townsend, the California doctor whose plan for older Americans had attracted so many supporters. The president hinted to nervous lawmakers that his own plan was preferable to Townsend's more radical design.

Funding Social Security, however, posed problems. To avoid a huge tax hike that could hamper economic recovery, Roosevelt agreed to exclude certain workers from the new program. "Everybody ought to be in on it," Roosevelt had argued. In the end, millions of Americans, including farmworkers, household workers, and government employees, were left out of Social Security.

READING CHECK **Summarizing** What were two major elements of the Second New Deal?

Reviving Organized Labor

After setbacks during the 1920s, the passage of the NIRA during the first New Deal marked a major step forward for organized labor. It guaranteed workers the right to form unions and bargain collectively. Yet many businesses ignored the new rules, vigorously battling the growth of unions. In 1934, unions lost a number of major strikes, as labor-related violence increased.

A cautious FDR was unwilling to push business too hard to accept labor's new powers. In addition, under NIRA's terms, government had little power to force business cooperation.

When NIRA was fatally weakened by the Supreme Court's ruling in *Schechter*, Roosevelt recognized the need to act on behalf of labor. He threw his support behind a new labor law, the Wagner Act (named for its sponsor, Senator Robert Wagner of New York).

The law, also known as the National Labor Relations Act, was stronger than NIRA. The act outlawed a number of antilabor practices, such as the creation of company-sponsored unions. It also established a powerful new National Labor Relations Board. The NLRB was given

THE IMPACT TODAY

Government
The public today has come to depend heavily on Social Security. The cost to workers and employers for funding this program have risen steadily, and payments have risen as more and more Americans live longer and longer lives.

Reading Focus

2 How did New Deal programs help to revive organized labor? *established the National Labor Relations Board; outlawed antilabor practices; gave workers the right to form unions and bargain collectively*

Reviving Organized Labor

Recall Why was the NIRA considered prolabor? *guaranteed workers right to form unions and bargain collectively*

Explain What was the National Labor Relations Board empowered to do? *conduct voting in workplaces to determine whether employees wanted union representation*

MISCONCEPTION ALERT

Although New Deal programs provided many jobs in the 1930s, unemployment stayed around 10 percent, a relatively high figure.

Info to Know

Social Security Begins Providing monthly pensions to retired people or their survivors is the best-known Social Security program. The first person to receive a monthly Social Security check was Ida May Fuller of Ludlow, Vermont. Her first check, for $22.54, arrived January 31, 1940. Since its beginning in the 1930s, Social Security has been expanded to cover children, people with disabilities, and many others. Social Security also manages numerous welfare programs, including subsidized school lunches.

Answers

Reading Check *Works Progress Administration (WPA); Social Security Act*

Collaborative Learning

Above Level

Social Security Today

Research Required

1. Organize the class into small groups. Have each group conduct research on Social Security to see how it has grown and changed since it was first introduced during the Great Depression. Students should also examine how different presidential administrations have addressed the funding of Social Security.

2. Tell students that one of the recent solutions suggested for the funding of Social Security has been to replace it, or parts of it, with private retirement accounts. Have students

read media accounts and economic analyses of this and other proposed changes and how they might affect the Social Security system.

3. Have students write a letter to the editor of the local newspaper expressing his or her opinion about how the funding for Social Security could be improved.

4. Have volunteers read their letters to the class.
LS Interpersonal, Verbal-Linguistic

📝 Alternative Assessment Handbook, Rubric 17: Letters to Editors

Reviving Organized Labor

Describe What advantage did a sit-down strike have over a traditional strike? *Management could not bring in security forces to scatter picketers, nor could it use traditional strike-breaking techniques.*

Recall What events helped establish the CIO as a major force in American labor? *United Auto Workers sit-down strike against General Motors beginning in December 1936; successful action against the United States Steel Corporation in 1937*

Contrast What was the major difference between the AFL and the CIO? *The AFL was a collection of smaller unions representing skilled workers, organized within specific crafts. The CIO was made up largely of unskilled workers organized across industries, such as the automobile industry.*

Major New Deal Programs

Analyze Why do you think that most of the programs listed under Relief in the table are no longer in existence? *They were temporary measures intended to provide immediate help to people during the Depression.*

Quick Facts Transparency: Major New Deal Programs

MAJOR NEW DEAL PROGRAMS

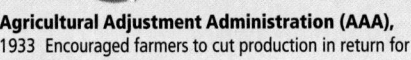

Relief

Civilian Conservation Corps (CCC), 1933 Provided jobs on conservation projects to young men whose families needed relief

Federal Emergency Relief Administration (FERA), 1933 Provided grants to states for direct relief to the needy

Public Works Administration (PWA), 1933 Provided public-works jobs for many of those needing relief

Civil Works Administration (CWA), 1933 Provided public-works jobs for many of those needing relief

Works Progress Administration (WPA), 1935 Provided public-works jobs on a wide range of projects for many of those needing relief

Social Security Act, 1935 Established pensions for retirees, unemployment insurance, and aid for certain groups of low-income or disabled people

Farm Security Administration (FSA), 1937 Provided assistance to tenant farmers to help them purchase land or establish cooperatives

Reform

Emergency Banking Act, 1933 Gave federal government power to reorganize and strengthen banks

Federal Deposit Insurance Corporation (FDIC), 1933 Established an insurance program for deposits in many banks

Securities and Exchange Commission (SEC), 1934 Provided increased government regulation of the trading on stock exchanges

National Labor Relations Act (NLRB), 1935 Established the National Labor Relations Board to enforce labor laws

Fair Labor Standards Act (Wages and Hours Law), 1938 Established minimum wages and maximum hours for many workers

Recovery

Agricultural Adjustment Administration (AAA), 1933 Encouraged farmers to cut production in return for a subsidy

Tennessee Valley Authority (TVA), 1933 Promoted development projects for the Tennessee River Valley—for example, to improve navigation, produce electricity, and control floods

National Industrial Recovery Act (NIRA), 1933 Encouraged cooperation among businesses in establishing production and labor practices

Federal Housing Administration (FHA), 1934 Encouraged loans for renovating or building homes

Rural Electrification Administration (REA), 1935 Encouraged the delivery of electricity to rural areas

Programs in red are still in existence.

---

the authority to conduct voting in workplaces to determine whether employees wanted union representation. The NLRB could require businesses to accept the voting results. With these new legal tools, organized labor membership surged by millions in the years to come.

The CIO is born The passage of the Wagner Act roughly coincided with a major change in the American labor movement. A new union devoted to the interests of industrial workers arose to challenge the traditional hold of the nation's largest union, the American Federation of Labor (AFL).

The AFL was created as a collection, or federation, of smaller unions representing the interests of skilled workers. These smaller unions were organized within specific crafts rather than across broad industries, such as the auto or steel industries. In general, the AFL looked down on unskilled factory workers, many of whom were immigrants.

The growth of mass production in the 1920s, however, greatly swelled the ranks of unskilled workers. **John L. Lewis**, head of the United Mine Workers, recognized this opportunity. He sought to take advantage of it.

A fiery speaker and organizer, Lewis led a group that broke away from the AFL in 1935 to form the Committee for Industrial Organization, or **CIO**. (The CIO later changed its name to the Congress of Industrial Organizations.) It was not long before Lewis and his new organization would make their mark.

Differentiating Instruction

Learners Having Difficulty

Materials blank 3" x 5" note cards (17–18 per student)

1. Have students create note cards for the New Deal programs. Have students write the name of one program on the front of the card and the date the program was put into effect and a brief description of the program on the back.

2. Have students review the New Deal programs using their cards. You might wish to organize students into pairs or small groups and have them use their cards to quiz each other on the programs.

3. Guide students in a discussion of the New Deal programs using the following questions: Which types of programs are no longer in existence? Why? *relief; they were temporary measures;* Which category has the largest percentage of programs still in existence? Why? *reform; they were designed to prevent another Depression;* What similar programs have been put into place since the Great Depression? *OSHA, farm subsidies, Medicare*

LS Kinesthetic

The GM sit-down strike In December 1936 the United Auto Workers, which was part of the CIO, launched a new kind of strike. Workers at the General Motors (GM) plant in Flint, Michigan, simply sat down inside the factory and stopped working.

A **sit-down strike**, as it was called, required the strikers to stay at the factory day and night until the dispute was resolved. They relied on supporters outside the factory to provide food and to look after their families at home.

The sit-down strike created a complicated situation for GM. It could not use traditional methods of strike breaking—bringing in security forces to scatter the picket line and hiring non-union "scab" labor to run the factory. Any effort to take back the factory might turn violent. Valuable property inside the factory could be destroyed, and the risk of negative publicity, such as images of workers being beaten or killed, was too high.

GM asked the state government for help in removing the workers, but Michigan's governor refused. The company tried shutting off heat and water to the factory, but the strikers stayed on. When the police tried shutting off food deliveries to the factory, workers rioted. A brief battle raged between striking workers and the police until the police withdrew.

The sit-down strike was hard on the workers, but it was harder still on GM. The shutdown cost the automaker tens of millions of dollars a week in sales. After a tense six weeks, GM finally gave in and agreed to recognize the union. The workers had won.

It was an enormous victory for labor—and for the CIO. Along with a successful action against the United States Steel Corporation in 1937, the General Motors strike helped establish the CIO as a major force in American organized labor.

HISTORY'S VOICES

❝When [GM executive William] Knudsen put his name to a piece of paper and says that General Motors recognizes UAW-CIO—until that moment we were non-people, we didn't even exist. That was the big one.❞

—Bob Stinson, sit-down striker, recorded in *Hard Times*

The CIO and other labor unions did not win every confrontation with American business in the 1930s. Indeed, unions suffered some serious losses later in the decade. Yet union membership continued to grow. By the early 1940s, nearly one-fourth of the American workforce was unionized.

READING CHECK **Identifying Cause and Effect** How did the Wagner Act work to revive labor?

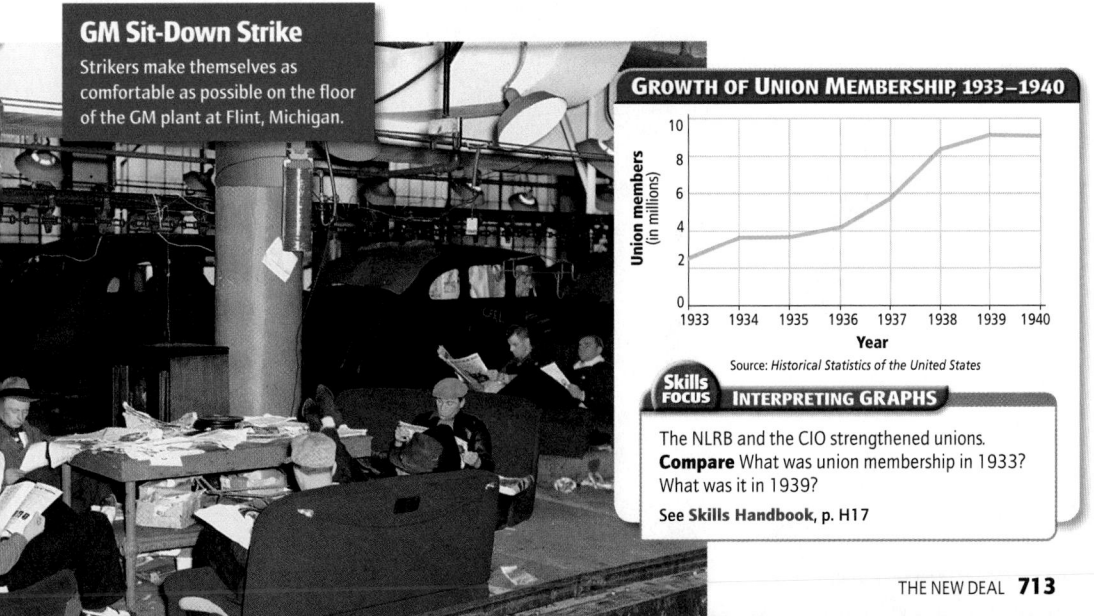

GM Sit-Down Strike
Strikers make themselves as comfortable as possible on the floor of the GM plant at Flint, Michigan.

GROWTH OF UNION MEMBERSHIP, 1933–1940

Union members (in millions) — vertical axis: 0, 2, 4, 6, 8, 10
Year — horizontal axis: 1933, 1934, 1935, 1936, 1937, 1938, 1939, 1940

Source: *Historical Statistics of the United States*

Skills FOCUS **INTERPRETING GRAPHS**

The NLRB and the CIO strengthened unions.
Compare What was union membership in 1933? What was it in 1939?

See Skills Handbook, p. H17

GM Sit-Down Strike

Analyze Why do you think union membership made its sharpest rise in the year 1937? *The GM sit-down strike and a successful action against the United States Steel Corporation were resolved that year.*

Info to Know

Founding the Committee for Industrial Organization (CIO) Observers remember great excitement among industrial workers in response to the founding of the CIO. The *CIO News* editor wrote, "The workers were waiting for the CIO, pounding on its doors long before the CIO was ready for them." An organizer recalled, "It is difficult to impart on ordinary paper the magic that surrounded the letters *C-I-O* in 1937." A song that soon became popular explained some of the CIO's popularity:

"A union for the masses
To include every craft,
Better wages for each worker,
In CIO there is no class."

For many Americans, the CIO represented an end to divisions based on social rank because it gave every worker the opportunity to demand fair treatment.

Skills Focus: Evaluating Information on the Internet
Above Level

Social Studies Skill   **Research Required**
Labor Unions and Strikes

1. Review the information in the text about labor unions and strikes. Have students research a recent strike, preferably a local one. You may either assign a single strike for all students to research or allow students to choose from several recent strikes. Encourage students to look for sources on the Internet and explain to them how to decide which sources are credible.

2. Have each student write a brief essay on the strike providing the following information:

the name of the employer; the name of the union; the grievance(s) that caused the strike; attempts made by the employer and workers to negotiate; date the strike began, ended, and outcome. Have students conclude their essays with a paragraph explaining which side they would have supported, labor or management.

LS **Logical-Mathematical, Verbal-Linguistic**

🖊 Alternative Assessment Handbook, Rubric 40: Writing to Describe

Answers

Interpreting Graphs *slightly over 2 million; about 9 million*

Reading Check *Wagner Act outlawed many antilabor practices, established National Labor Relations Board, which could require businesses to accept unions.*

713

The Election of 1936

Explain Why was the Rural Electrification Act important for farmers? *electricity brought to rural areas where for-profit power companies had been unwilling to put in power lines*

Identify What major shift in American politics took place in 1936? *Northern African Americans switched to the Democratic Party.*

Elaborate How might the results of the 1936 election have been different if Huey Long had not been assassinated the year before? *possible answer—Long might have been the Union Party candidate for president; his party probably would have done much better; he might have defeated Roosevelt.*

📝 CRF: History and Geography Activity: Presidential Election of 1936

The Election of 1936

As President Roosevelt entered the election year of 1936, he could look back on a productive 1935. He also knew there was more to be done before he faced the voters in November.

Rural electricity One goal was to provide additional help to rural Americans. Toward this end, Roosevelt in May signed the Rural Electrification Act. It empowered the Rural Electrification Administration (REA) to loan money to farm cooperatives and other groups trying to bring electricity to people living outside of cities and towns. In many areas, for-profit power companies had been unwilling to put in the miles of power lines needed to serve remote, sparsely settled areas. Under the REA, the numbers of rural homes with electricity grew from 10 percent to 90 percent in about a decade. Millions of farmers were finally able to enjoy the benefits of electricity.

Americans re-elect Roosevelt President Roosevelt campaigned on a solid record of legislative achievement. He also pointed to significant improvements in the economy. Unemployment, though still high, had been sliced in half. Personal incomes and corporate earnings were up sharply. New Deal programs had given hope and help to millions, even if they had not brought about full economic recovery.

In the 1936 campaign, Roosevelt virtually ignored the Republican nominee, Governor Alf Landon of Kansas. Landon's mildly reformist positions supporting organized labor and aid to the unemployed and elderly posed no serious threat. Roosevelt also faced no serious competition from the Union Party, a new party formed by Father Charles Coughlin and Dr. Francis Townsend.

Appealing to potential Union Party supporters, Roosevelt gave speeches thundering against big business. Business leaders responded with alarm, again pouring money into the American Liberty League. To some of them, the New Deal amounted to a revolution.

THE IMPACT TODAY

Technology
In what is seen as a parallel to rural electrification in the 1930s, Congress has earmarked funds to help bring high-speed Internet service to rural America today.

HISTORY'S VOICES

"The history of these past three years will be written in the future as the history of an American revolution which was engineered and carried on under the unseeing eyes of one hundred and thirty million citizens."
—Senator Lester Dickinson, *The American Mercury*, February 1936

In a bitterly waged campaign, Republicans attacked Roosevelt's New Deal for being overly bureaucratic and creating a planned economy.

On election day, however, the American voters again handed Roosevelt a tremendous victory. Landon carried only two states. The ineffective Union Party candidate polled less than 2 percent of the popular vote. The Democrats again gained in both houses of Congress. They also won 26 of the 33 races for governor.

The electoral landslide also confirmed a momentous shift in American politics. African Americans in the North switched from the party of Lincoln to the Democratic Party.

READING CHECK Identifying **Supporting Details** What evidence can you find to suggest that the 1936 election showed widespread support for Roosevelt and the New Deal?

Historically, African Americans had supported the Republicans, the party of Lincoln. In 1936, however, a majority of African American voters chose Roosevelt and the Democrats—a shift in loyalty that has continued to this day.

714

Skills Focus: Making Generalizations

At Level

Reading Skill
The 1936 Election

Research Required

1. Divide students into small groups. Have students create a political cartoon that supports one of the three 1936 presidential candidates and criticizes the other two. Assign one of the following candidates to each group: Democrat Franklin D. Roosevelt, Republican Alf Landon (who was endorsed by the American Liberty League), and the Union Party's candidate, William Lemke. Have students complete outside research to review the positions of

their candidate on the principal campaign issues.

2. Have students share their cartoons with the class. Guide students in a discussion of the reasons they found to back each candidate and why Roosevelt and the Democratic Party won by such a wide margin in most races held in 1936. 🆂 **Verbal-Linguistic, Logical-Mathematical**

📝 Alternative Assessment Handbook, Rubric 27: Political Cartoons

Answers

Reading Check *Roosevelt was re-elected in a landslide.*

Political Cartoon

President Roosevelt was very upset when the Supreme Court struck down some of the key provisions of the New Deal. To protect his new reforms, he attempted to "pack" the Court by adding more justices. Congress stopped this effort, marking one of the few great political defeats for the popular president. Many critics feared that such a change would threaten the balance of powers as spelled out in the U.S. Constitution. The following political cartoon originally included a caption that read, "Oh, So That's the Kind of a Sailor He Is!"

 Skills FOCUS **READING LIKE A HISTORIAN**

1. **Contrasting** How do the expressions of the captain and the sailor reflect different views of the court-packing plan?
2. **Interpreting Political Cartoons** Why do you think the artist chose this imagery?

See Skills Handbook, pp. H10, H31

On a ship, if a compass showed that the vessel was sailing in the wrong direction, the captain would change course, not demand a new compass.

THAT COMPASS DOESN'T POINT THE WAY I WANT TO GO. CHANGE IT. NOW!

The nation is frequently referred to as the "ship of state." The captain of the ship represented Roosevelt. The cartoonist may also have been referring to Roosevelt's early career as assistant secretary of the navy.

The sailor, whose instinct is to obey the ship's captain, represents the Democrat-controlled Congress, which here is shown reacting in alarm.

A Troubled Year

Never before had Roosevelt seemed more in command than when he began his second term. His determination to overcome obstacles to his programs, however, led to a serious misstep.

The court-packing plan Frustrated that the courts had struck down many New Deal programs, Roosevelt surprised Congress with a plan to reorganize the nation's courts. The plan would give the president power to appoint many new judges and expand the Supreme Court by up to six justices. The president argued that changes were needed to make the courts more efficient. Most observers, however, saw it as a clumsy effort to "pack" the Supreme Court with friendly justices—and a dangerous attempt to upset the constitutional balance of power. Even the president's supporters were troubled.

The battle over Roosevelt's proposal occupied Congress for much of 1937. Even members of the president's own party began to desert him. In the end, the president who had begun the year looking invincible ended it with a crushing loss.

HISTORY'S VOICES

❝Roosevelt moved against the court more boldly and directly than any other President had ever done. Public opinion then swung to the defense of the court, and F.D.R. suffered the most humiliating defeat of his career.❞

—Merlo J. Pusey, *American Heritage*, April 1958

Moving forward President Roosevelt lost much of the year in his doomed battle over expanding the Supreme Court. Congress, however, did enact some major legislation in 1937.

The Farm Tenancy Act aided some of the poorest of the nation's poor—tenant farmers and sharecroppers. Many had been forced off the land as a result of New Deal programs that paid landowners to take fields out of production. The new law gave tenants and sharecroppers a chance to buy land of their own.

Roosevelt also won some important victories in an unlikely place—the Supreme Court. Even as he was trying to push through his court-packing plan, the Court handed down rulings that favored key New Deal programs. In March 1937 the Court upheld a rather

THE NEW DEAL **715**

Direct Teach

Reading Focus

④ Why was 1937 a troubled year for Roosevelt and the Second New Deal? *attempt to reorganize the courts was controversial; Democrats rebelled; sharp drop in the stock market; 2 million Americans lost their jobs*

A Troubled Year

Identify What was the Farm Tenancy Act? *bill that gave tenants and sharecroppers a chance to buy land*

Summarize What was the result of Roosevelt's attempt to reorganize the courts? *rebellion within Democratic Party; a major political loss for Roosevelt*

Info to Know

The Court-packing Plan Although Roosevelt's attempt to "pack" the Supreme Court angered some Americans, others supported his action. Thomas F. Konop, dean of the Notre Dame Law School, said that the Court was "usurping the power of Congress and the President. It . . . has been destroying laws providing for a better life, more liberty and equality, social justice, and the pursuit of happiness of 130,000,000 people."

Skills Focus: Making Written Presentations   **At Level**

Reading Like a Historian Skill
"Packing" the Court

1. Review with students Roosevelt's court-packing plan. Have each student write a letter to a U.S. senator supporting or opposing the president's plan. Students should describe what Roosevelt planned to do and why. Tell students to predict the possible results of packing the Supreme Court as the basis for their support or opposition to the plan. *Roosevelt asked Congress to give him the power to expand the Supreme Court by up to six justices to make*

the Court more efficient. Supporters may argue that this is the only way to keep the Supreme Court from overturning New Deal programs. Opponents may argue that it would upset the constitutional balance of power and could result in a dictatorship.

2. Have volunteers read their letters to the class.
   LS Verbal-Linguistic, Logical-Mathematical

   Alternative Assessment Handbook, Rubrics 16: Judging Information; and 17: Letters to Editors

Answers

Reading Like a Historian 1. *The captain looks confident and at ease; the sailor looks horrified.* **2.** *possible answers—because the public was familiar with the role of crewmen on sailing vessels, and because the country was sailing into uncharted waters during the New Deal*

715

A Troubled Year

Explain How did Roosevelt respond to the new wave of unemployment in late 1937 and early 1938? *by seeking large sums of money to fund programs, thus increasing the deficit*

Make Judgments Do you think Roosevelt's court-packing attempts affected the Supreme Court rulings in favor of the Wagner and Social Security Acts? Why or why not? *possible answers—Yes, the justices thought that if they seemed too unwilling to work with the president, public opinion might give Roosevelt the support he needed to "pack" the court; no, because the Supreme Court is independent.*

📖 Quick Facts Transparency: Gross National Product, 1933–1938

Close

Guide the class in a discussion of the initiatives of the Second New Deal.

Review

📖 Online Quiz, Section 2

📖 Daily Test Practice Transparency

Assess

SE Section 2 Assessment

📖 Progress Assessment: Section 2 Quiz

📖 Alternative Assessment Handbook

Reteach

📖 Interactive Reader and Study Guide, Section 2

💿 Interactive Skills Tutor CD-ROM

Answers

Interpreting Graphs *1937*

Reading Check *The economy suffered a setback and the court-packing plan resulted in loss of support.*

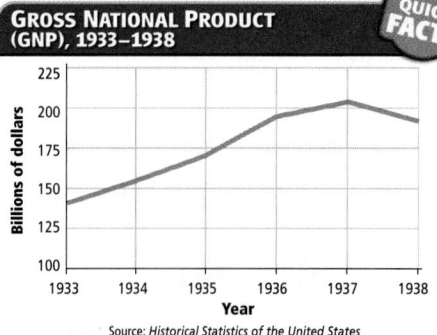

GROSS NATIONAL PRODUCT (GNP), 1933–1938

Source: Historical Statistics of the United States

Skills FOCUS **INTERPRETING GRAPHS**

The economy made some progress during Roosevelt's time in office. Which year between 1933 and 1938 saw the worst performance?

See Skills Handbook, p. H17

ACADEMIC VOCABULARY

classical well known, original

controversial Washington State law requiring a minimum wage for workers. The ruling signaled a new willingness to let legislatures regulate the economy—a decision with clear implications for the New Deal.

In April the Court also ruled clearly in favor of a key element of the Wagner Act. In May it declared Roosevelt's Social Security plan to be constitutional.

The favorable rulings pleased Roosevelt. They effectively killed any remaining support for his court-packing plan, however.

Recovery in doubt In the fall of 1937, the nation's economy suffered another setback. It began in a familiar way with a sharp drop in the stock market. By the time the year was over, about 2 million more Americans had lost their jobs.

The return of hard times changed Roosevelt's plans. He had hoped to cut back on government spending, fearing the growing federal budget **deficit**. A deficit occurs when a government spends more money than it takes in through taxes and other income. But as unemployment rose in late 1937 and early 1938, Roosevelt again found himself seeking large sums of money to help the unemployed.

Roosevelt may have been troubled by deficits, but the new spending was supported by the theories of British economist **John Maynard Keynes**. Contrary to <u>classical</u> economic theory, which stressed balanced budgets, Keynes argued that deficit spending could provide jobs and stimulate the economy.

In fact, the economy did begin to rebound in the summer of 1938. By then, however, the positive feelings about Roosevelt and the New Deal had begun to fade.

READING CHECK **Sequencing** What events made 1937 a troubled year for President Roosevelt?

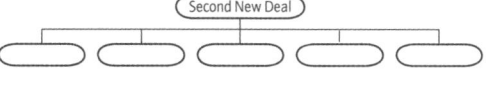

SECTION 2 ASSESSMENT

go.hrw.com
Online Quiz
Keyword: SD7 HP22

Reviewing Ideas, Terms, and People

1. **a. Identify** Identify the significance of the following terms: Second New Deal, Social Security
   b. Make Inferences What lessons did Roosevelt draw from the 1934 election?
   c. Evaluate What do you think of Roosevelt's decision to cut back on programs that provided relief without work?

2. **a. Identify** What was the CIO?
   b. Explain What factors contributed to labor's growth after 1935?
   c. Rank Which do you think was more important in labor's success: the passage of the Wagner Act or the success of the sit-down strikes? Explain.

3. **a. Recall** What was Roosevelt's 1936 election strategy?
   b. Summarize What were the results of the 1936 election?

4. **a. Identify** Identify the significance of the following: deficit, John Maynard Keynes
   b. Summarize Why did the court-packing plan cause so much damage to Roosevelt?

Critical Thinking

5. **Understand Cause and Effect** Copy the chart below and use information from the section to fill it in.

> Second New Deal

FOCUS ON SPEAKING

6. **Persuasive** Deliver a speech in which you argue for or against Roosevelt's court-reorganization plan.

Section 2 Assessment Answers

1. **a.** new laws and new programs to aid suffering; provided a pension for Americans 65 or older and unemployment insurance
   b. public approved of his actions
   c. possible answer—helped restore people's hopes and self-esteem

2. **a.** labor union for unskilled workers
   b. formation of CIO; success of GM sit-down strike; success of U.S. Steel action
   c. possible answer—Wagner Act: outlawed antilabor practices and enforced labor laws

3. **a.** to reach voters from the Union Party

b. Democrats won both houses of Congress, 26 governor's races; Roosevelt reelected.

4. **a.** negative balance in budget; British economist who believed deficit spending helped economy
   b. People believed Roosevelt was trying to upset the constitutional balance of power.

5. WPA; Social Security; NLRB; Rural Electrification Act; Farm Tenancy Act

6. for—would help get legislation passed; increases Court's efficiency; against—violates constitutional separation of powers

3 Life during the New Deal

BEFORE YOU READ

MAIN IDEA

The Great Depression and the New Deal had a deep impact on American culture during the 1930s.

READING FOCUS

1. How did the public roles of women and African Americans change during the New Deal?

2. How did artists and writers of the era tell the story of the Great Depression?

3. What forms of popular entertainment were popular during the Great Depression?

KEY TERMS AND PEOPLE

Frances Perkins
Black Cabinet
Mary McLeod Bethune
Dorothea Lange
swing

TAKING NOTES As you read, take notes on the arts and popular culture in the 1930s. Record your notes in a graphic organizer like the one shown here.

Showing Social Problems Realistically	Escaping the Problems of the Depression

Bellringer

The Inside Story. . . Use the **Daily Bellringer Transparency** to help students answer the question.

Daily Bellringer Transparency, Section 3

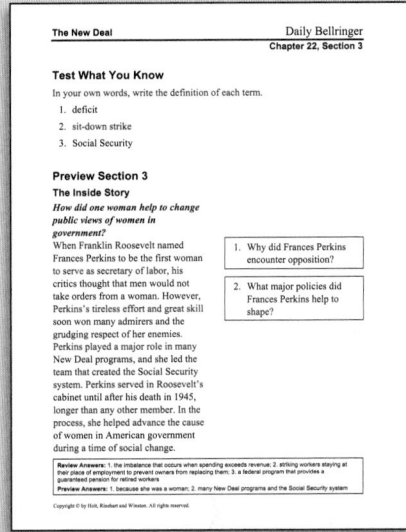

Taking Notes

Showing Problems—The Grapes of Wrath, music, work of Lange, Agee, and Evans; *Escaping Problems*—radio programs, movies, swing music, sports

▼ Labor Secretary Frances Perkins on the job

The Best Woman for the Job

How did one woman help to change public views of women in government?

"[M]en will take advice from a woman, but it is hard for them to take orders from a woman." That was a bit of counsel Franklin Roosevelt received when he was considering naming Frances Perkins to a key post in his administration.

Women's suffrage was not yet a decade old when Roosevelt, as New York's governor, made Perkins the top labor official in the state. When Roosevelt became president, he named Perkins to be his secretary of labor—the first woman ever to serve in the cabinet.

Born in Boston, Massachusetts, Perkins was already a social reformer when she witnessed the Triangle Shirtwaist Factory fire in New York City in 1911. That gruesome tragedy, in which 146 people died, spurred her interest in working to improve conditions in the workplace.

During her time in Washington, her tireless efforts and great skill won her many admirers—and the grudging respect of her enemies. Perkins played a central role in the creation of many New Deal programs, and she led the White House team that created the Social Security system.

Perkins served in Roosevelt's cabinet from 1933 until after his death in 1945. Her example advanced the cause of women in government. ■

Teach the Main Idea

At Level

Life During the New Deal

1. **Teach** Ask students the Reading Focus questions to teach this section.

2. **Apply** Have students make a list of the key terms and people, the images, and the main red headings in the section. Then divide the class into small groups. Have each group create two drawings to illustrate each heading.

3. **Review** Have each group present its illustrations to the class. Guide students in a discussion of the gains women and African

Americans made under the New Deal, and the challenges and discrimination that both groups still faced.

4. **Practice/Homework** Ask students to think about the similarities and differences between popular entertainment in the 1930s and today. Have each student write a short essay discussing the similarities and differences. **LS Visual-Spatial, Verbal-Linguistic**

Alternative Assessment Handbook, Rubrics 3: Artwork; and Rubric 9: Comparing and Contrasting

1 How did the public roles of women and African Americans change during the New Deal? *offered women and African Americans hope for expanded role in public life; they served in prominent government posts*

New Roles for Women and African Americans

Explain Why was Roosevelt concerned about angering southern Democrats in Congress? *afraid they would block his bills*

Summarize How did women fare in the New Deal workforce? *A few held prominent government posts, most faced discrimination, received lower wages, had fewer job opportunities than men.*

Make Inferences Why was Eleanor Roosevelt often ahead of her husband in championing civil rights? *Franklin was concerned about political repercussions, and was reluctant to antagonize southern Democrats.*

Info to Know

A Symbol of Change Before her appointment as secretary of labor, Frances Perkins was a social worker. She had worked with a variety of progressive reformers and groups. Despite the fact that she held some conservative ideas, such as a distrust of labor unions, Perkins was a symbol of the New Deal's liberal policies.

Answers

Faces of History *She founded an educational institution that remains today, advised four presidents, and was the first African American to head federal agency.*

718

FACES OF HISTORY

Mary McLeod BETHUNE
1875–1955

The fifteenth child of former slaves, Mary McLeod Bethune rose from the cotton fields of South Carolina to be a pioneer in several fields.

In 1902, with borrowed furniture and $1.50, Bethune opened a school for African American girls in Daytona, Florida. This effort reflected her belief in the power of education as a means of advancement. Her little school later became Bethune-Cookman College.

Fiercely determined, a stirring speaker, and a tireless fundraiser, Bethune eventually gained national prominence. She worked for the voting rights of African Americans and women. An adviser to four presidents, she was the first African Amercan woman to head an agency of the federal government

Summarize How did Mary McLeod Bethune make a lasting impact?

New Roles for Women and African Americans

The New Deal brought great change in American life and society. Under the pressure of an economic emergency, old ways of doing things gave way to new. For women and African Americans, these changes brought hope for an expanded role in public life.

Women in the New Deal As you read in Section 1, Eleanor Roosevelt played a major role in her husband's administration. In addition to her tireless support for her husband's programs, she actively pursued issues of importance to women, helping leaders of women's groups gain access to the president.

THE IMPACT TODAY

Government
Today it is commonplace for women, African Americans, and members of other minorities to fill cabinet and other top government posts. They continue, however, to hold a relatively small share of these positions.

HISTORY'S VOICES

❝When I wanted help on some definite point, Mrs. Roosevelt gave me the opportunity to sit by the president at dinner and the matter was settled before we finished our soup.❞

—Molly Dewson, quoted in *Beyond Suffrage* by Susan Ware, 1981

Other women besides the First Lady served in prominent government posts during the New Deal, none more so than Secretary of Labor **Frances Perkins**. As the first woman to head an executive department, Perkins played a leading role in the formation of major New Deal policies. This included, as you have read, the

Social Security system. Perkins, however, was not the only prominent woman in the government. Ruth Bryan Owen, daughter of three-time presidential candidate William Jennings Bryan, served as minister to Denmark. Roosevelt also appointed women to such posts as director of the U.S. Mint and assistant secretary of the Treasury. Women served as leaders in several New Deal agencies. In short, Roosevelt's record at promoting and recognizing women was simply unmatched for his time.

Still, women faced challenges and discrimination. New Deal programs, for example, generally paid men higher wages than women in work-relief jobs. Men continued to enjoy far more work opportunities. The attitude in the wider world to women in the workforce ranged from grudging acceptance to outright hostility. For example, one journalist put forward his idea for solving unemployment: "Simply fire the women, who shouldn't be working anyway, and hire the men. Presto! No unemployment."

African Americans in the New Deal Roosevelt's administration also broke new ground in appointing African Americans. William Hastie, for example, became the first black federal judge in U.S. history. African Americans were also hired to fill posts in the government. A group of these officials, known as the **Black Cabinet**, met under the leadership of **Mary McLeod Bethune**, director of Negro Affairs in the National Youth Administration.

The Black Cabinet acted as unofficial advisers to the president. They stood as a powerful symbol of rising African American influence in government. In addition, First Lady Eleanor Roosevelt visibly championed civil rights, frequently staking out bold positions in advance of what her husband felt he could take.

Still, African Americans continued to face tremendous hardships in the 1930s. New Deal programs left largely unchallenged the discrimination that African Americans faced in the larger society. In addition, thousands of African American sharecroppers and tenant farmers suffered terribly. Many never saw real benefit from any New Deal program.

Roosevelt often explained his record with respect to African Americans by saying he was at the mercy of southern Democrats in Congress. Many of these legislators strongly opposed efforts to aid African Americans.

Skills Focus: Comparing and Contrasting
[Below Level]

Reading Skill
Women and African Americans

1. Organize students into mixed-ability pairs, and have each pair create a two-column chart. One column should be labeled *Women*; the other column *African Americans*. Then have students compare and contrast how the Roosevelt administration addressed the concerns of these two groups. Have volunteers present their charts to the class.

2. As an extension, have students conduct research and report on the challenges and

discrimination still faced by women and minority groups. What gains have they made since Roosevelt's administration? What obstacles still remain? 🖪 **Interpersonal, Logical-Mathematical**

📝 Alternative Assessment Handbook, Rubric 13: Graphic Organizers

🖥 Graphic Organizer Transparencies

Roosevelt felt that angering southern Democrats would jeopardize the entire New Deal. "They will block every bill I ask Congress to pass to keep America from collapsing," he told the head of the NAACP when he was pressed to support an antilynching law. "I just can't take that risk."

Although President Roosevelt's record was not perfect, African American voters apparently decided that their best hopes lay with the Democratic Party. Staunchly Republican since the Civil War, a majority of African Americans for the first time in history voted Democratic in the 1934 midterm elections. As you have read, this support continued in the 1936 presidential election as well.

READING CHECK **Making Generalizations**
What was the overall effect of Roosevelt's policies on women and African Americans in the 1930s?

Telling the Story of the Depression

Responding to unprecedented economic calamity, artists showed a new interest in social problems and activism. Painters and sculptors fashioned works depicting the struggles of the working class. Authors and playwrights focused on the plight of the rural and urban poor. For example, you read in the last chapter about John Steinbeck's moving tale of Dust Bowl refugees, *The Grapes of Wrath*. Songwriter Woody Guthrie celebrated the grandeur of America and the lives of ordinary people.

The work of Dorothea Lange Photographer **Dorothea Lange** was another celebrated chronicler of the Great Depression. In her hometown of San Francisco, Lange recorded images of jobless people. Yet her most famous subjects were the rural poor, who were especially hard hit in the 1930s.

Starting in 1935, Lange worked on behalf of the Farm Security Administration. This organization focused on the lives of tenant farmers and sharecroppers. One of her most famous photographs appears at right. These and other pictures helped raise awareness about the poorest of the poor. Indeed, in 1937 the federal government finally began to provide help to tenant farmers and sharecroppers.

IMAGES OF THE GREAT DEPRESSION

Ella Watson, a Washington, D.C. charwoman, with her three children

Gordon Parks

© THE OAKLAND MUSEUM, THE CITY OF OAKLAND

Dorothea Lange

Destitute mother of seven children in California

Skills FOCUS **READING LIKE A HISTORIAN**

Photographers like Gordon Parks and Dorothea Lange were hired to document the plight of the poor and, through their images, gain public support for Roosevelt's New Deal programs.

Interpreting Visuals Do you think these photographs succeed in showing a sympathetic view of their subjects? Explain.

THE NEW DEAL **719**

719

Reading Focus

❸ What forms of popular entertainment were popular during the Great Depression? *movies; radio; jazz and swing music*

Popular Entertainment in the 1930s

Explain Why did Americans in the 1930s like movies that showed luxurious life styles? *helped them escape from their problems*

Compare Compare the role of radio in people's lives during the 1930s with the role television plays in our lives today. *possible answer—Radio provided many of the kinds of information and entertainment that television now provides.*

Develop What is significant about the fact that it was white big-band leaders who brought jazz to new audiences? *possible answer—White audiences might have been unwilling to listen to African American band leaders.*

📖 CRF: Biography: Frank Capra

📖 CRF: Literature Activity: *The Daring Young Man on the Flying Trapeze* by William Saroyan

go.hrw.com
Online Resources
KEYWORD: SD7 CH22
TOPIC: LIFE IN THE 1930S

HISTORY CLOSE-UP

Going to the Movies

At an average of 25 cents a ticket, movies were one of the most affordable forms of entertainment in the 1930s. More than that, movies served the public's emotional needs.

▲ Comedian Charlie Chaplin wrestles with machinery in *Modern Times*, a film that criticized the dehumanizing effects of industry.

Agee, Evans, and *Famous Men* Writer James Agee and photographer Walker Evans also depicted the lives of sharecroppers in the Lower South. Their work, *Let Us Now Praise Famous Men,* focused on a group of families in rural Alabama. This work received little notice when it was first published. Yet Evans's compassionate and unblinking images and Agee's powerful descriptions form a moving record of the reality of rural poverty and the great dignity of those who struggled against it.

READING CHECK **Comparing** How did artists such as Lange, Parks, Agee, and Evans seek to tell the story of the Great Depression?

Popular Entertainment in the 1930s

Despite the hard times of the 1930s, Americans still found the handful of pennies it cost to go to a movie theater. Radio also continued to

grow in popularity in the 1930s. A large majority of American households had a radio, and a wide range of programming, including sports, was available.

Movies One study in 1935 showed that nearly 80 million of the nation's 127 million Americans attended a movie each week. Throughout the decade, movie studios produced some 5,000 feature-length films.

A few of these movies focused on the hardships of life during the Great Depression. For example, Steinbeck's *The Grapes of Wrath* was turned into a successful Hollywood film in 1940. Another example of a successful Depression-themed film was *I Am a Fugitive from a Chain Gang.* This told the tale of a jobless man who is lured into a life of crime. *Make Way for Tomorrow* portrayed the financial hardships of an older couple.

For the most part, however, films of the 1930s steered clear of troubling reminders of the hard times gripping the nation. Indeed,

Collaborative Learning

At Level

Escaping Problems in the Great Depression

Research Required

Materials colored pens or markers, poster board

1. Organize students into small groups. Have each group research the different kinds of movies that were popular during the Depression, focusing on the types that offered people an escape from their problems, such as gangster movies, horror films, Westerns, comedies, and musicals. Have each group select a topic, a title, and create a storyboard for a new movie designed to take people's minds off their troubles. Explain to students

that a storyboard is a series of panels that outlines the major events in the plot of a movie. Based on their research, students should also suggest a possible cast for their movie.

2. Have volunteers from each group share their storyboards with the class. **LS Interpersonal, Visual-Spatial**

📖 Alternative Assessment Handbook, Rubrics 3: Artwork; and 37: Writing Assignments

Answers

Reading Check *by depicting the rural poor*

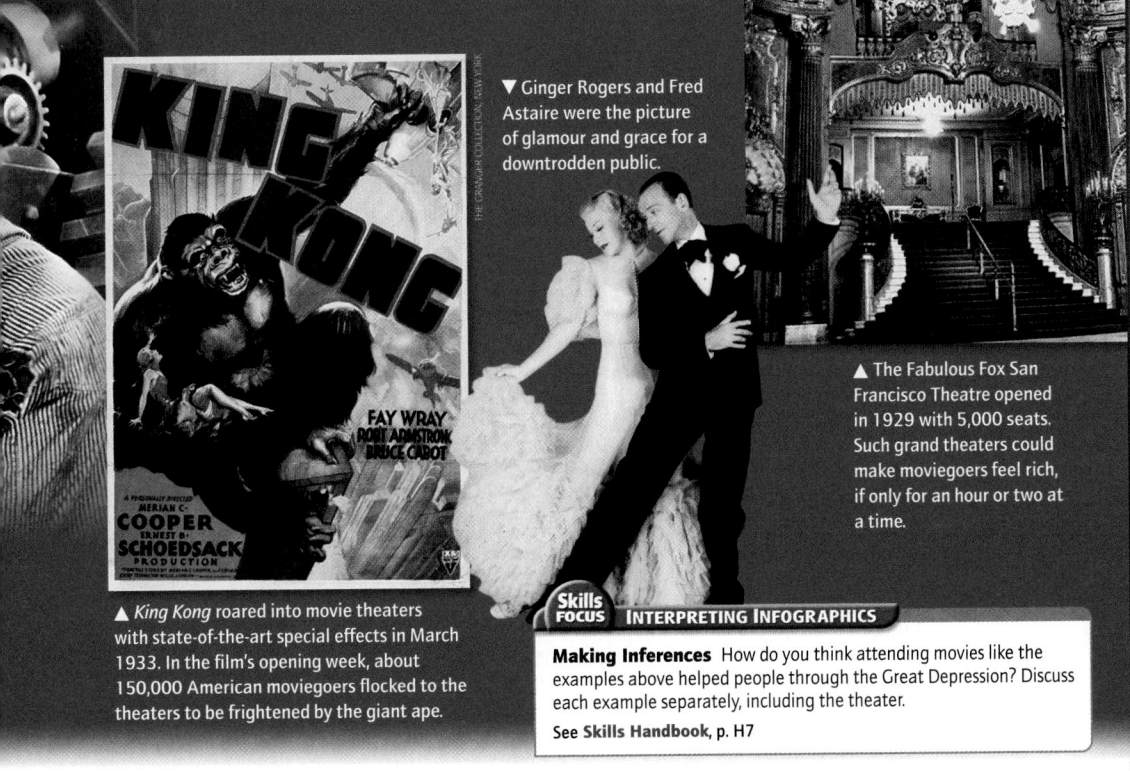

King Kong roared into movie theaters with state-of-the-art special effects in March 1933. In the film's opening week, about 150,000 American moviegoers flocked to the theaters to be frightened by the giant ape.

▼ Ginger Rogers and Fred Astaire were the picture of glamour and grace for a downtrodden public.

▲ The Fabulous Fox San Francisco Theatre opened in 1929 with 5,000 seats. Such grand theaters could make moviegoers feel rich, if only for an hour or two at a time.

Skills FOCUS INTERPRETING INFOGRAPHICS

Making Inferences How do you think attending movies like the examples above helped people through the Great Depression? Discuss each example separately, including the theater.

See **Skills Handbook**, p. H7

filmmakers seemed to realize that most Americans went to the movies in an attempt to escape from their own problems—even if only for a couple of hours.

Highly popular in the 1930s were grand musicals featuring glamorous dancers gliding across lavish sets or living it up at posh nightclubs. In the exciting, imaginary lives of characters played by actors such as Fred Astaire and Ginger Rogers, viewers got a glimpse of a life they could only dream about.

Comedy was another popular choice for the public. The Marx Brothers used a zany style to produce a string of hits in the 1930s. Charlie Chaplin continued to be popular. Not only did he make the transition to talkies successfully but he also continued to produce silent movies. The classic *Modern Times* took a hilarious look at a serious subject—the dehumanizing effect of industrial life.

Director Frank Capra captured the spirit of the times in films that combined social themes with a sentimental and comic view of life. Films

such as *Mr. Deeds Goes to Town* and *Mr. Smith Goes to Washington* told of the triumph of the "little guy."

The 1930s also saw the introduction of some new moviemaking techniques. For example, Walt Disney's *Snow White and the Seven Dwarfs* was history's first full-length animated feature. It drew huge audiences. *The Wizard of Oz* delighted audiences not only with its charming story and performances but also with the use of color photography and special effects. *Gone with the Wind*, which came out the same year as *The Wizard of Oz*, was also a color blockbuster.

Radio Radio had an important role in American politics. From President Roosevelt's fireside chats to Father Coughlin's rants against the New Deal, radio brought a variety of news and views into millions of American homes.

Of course, radio also provided listeners with religion, music, sports, and other forms of entertainment. Though by today's standards

Close

Guide the class in a discussion of life in the United States during the New Deal.

Review

Online Quiz, Section 3

Daily Test Practice Transparency

Assess

SE Section 3 Assessment

Progress Assessment: Section 3 Quiz

Alternative Assessment Handbook

Reteach

Interactive Reader and Study Guide, Section 3

Interactive Skills Tutor CD-ROM

the sound quality was poor, families in living rooms across the country were enthralled by action shows such as *The Lone Ranger* and comedies such as *Fibber McGee and Molly*.

Radio's power to captivate listeners was dramatically demonstrated in October 1938. The actor Orson Welles produced a radio broadcast of the H. G. Wells science fiction tale *The War of the Worlds* that was so realistic, it convinced many panicked listeners that Earth was actually under attack by spaceships from Mars.

Radio helped broaden the appeal of jazz. This vibrant form of music had its roots in African American communities in New Orleans and other big cities. It had spread northward and taken root in cities such as New York. There, performers such as Louis Armstrong dazzled audiences with their ability at improvising.

A new, highly orchestrated type of jazz known as **swing** swept the country in the 1930s. This music tended to feature larger groups of musicians known as big bands. Audiences often danced to the music, performing such steps as the jitterbug or the Lindy Hop (named after Charles Lindbergh).

Swing had its share of African American stars. Duke Ellington and Count Basie were two famous big-band leaders. At the same time, white big-band leaders such as Benny Goodman and the Dorsey Brothers reached audiences that had been untouched by the jazz masters of the 1920s.

Joyous or soulful, the unrestrained moods of jazz were medicine for the times. Said one critic, "This was the Depression. It was not an easy period. And this was a music that was just pure pleasure. Pure physical pleasure."

Sports in the 1930s The 1920s is widely regarded as the golden age of sports. The Great Depression did limit the ability of many Americans to buy tickets and attend events in person. Nevertheless, interest in sports remained quite strong.

Baseball remained a popular attraction. The legendary Babe Ruth, who had become a huge star in the 1920s, continued his career until the mid-1930s. He was soon replaced on the roster of the New York Yankees by a new star—the great Joe DiMaggio.

Meanwhile, former Ruth teammate Lou Gehrig stirred the emotions of the nation when, stricken with a terrible illness that would soon end his life, he ended his record streak of consecutive games played.

Sports fans also thrilled to the exploits of Babe Didrikson Zaharias. A multisport star, Zaharias won fame for her talents in softball, golf, basketball, and track and field.

Boxing was hugely popular in the 1930s. The big star was heavyweight fighter Joe Louis. His 1938 bout against German Max Schmeling came to represent the growing conflict between Germany and the United States. You will read more about this contest in the next chapter.

READING CHECK **Identifying the Main Idea** How did popular entertainment help Americans cope with the stresses of the Great Depression?

SECTION 3 ASSESSMENT

go.hrw.com
Online Quiz
Keyword: SD7 HP22

Reviewing Ideas, Terms, and People

1. **a. Identify** Who were Frances Perkins and Mary McLeod Bethune?
   b. Make Generalizations How did women and African Americans fare under the policies of the Roosevelt administration?

2. **a. Identify** Who was Dorothea Lange?
   b. Make Generalizations Why do you think Lange, Evans, and Agee focused on the plight of sharecroppers and tenant farmers?

3. **a. Define** Write a brief definition of the following term: swing
   b. Draw Conclusions What can you conclude about the importance of movies in American life based on the average weekly audience in the 1930s?

Critical Thinking

4. **Find Supporting Details** Copy the chart below and use information from the section to find supporting details for the main idea given.

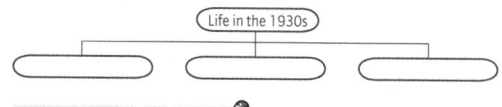

FOCUS ON WRITING

5. **Descriptive** Write a brief description of American popular entertainment in the 1930s, using examples from your reading of the chapter.

722 CHAPTER 22

Section 3 Assessment Answers

1. **a.** Perkins—first woman to head an executive department; McLeod Bethune—director of Negro Affairs in the National Youth Administration
   b. better than before; more opportunities available

2. **a.** photographer who chronicled the Depression
   b. to inspire social action; these people were among hardest hit by the Depression

3. **a.** form of jazz music
   b. provided entertainment, escape, and hope

4. expanding role for women and African Americans; artists and writers addressed social problems; growing popularity of movies and radio

5. Radio, movies, swing, baseball, boxing provided escape.

Analyzing the New Deal

BEFORE YOU READ

MAIN IDEA
The New Deal had mixed success in rescuing the economy, but it fundamentally changed Americans' relationship with their government.

FOCUS QUESTIONS
1. What was the impact of the New Deal on the nation in the 1930s?
2. In what ways was the impact of the New Deal limited?
3. How did the New Deal come to an end?

KEY TERMS AND PEOPLE
Marian Anderson
minimum wage
incumbent

TAKING NOTES As you read, take notes on the impact of the New Deal. In each box in a diagram like the one below, fill in examples of the New Deal's effects in the area indicated.

```
        Impact of the
         New Deal
         /        \
  Government    Economy
```

THE INSIDE STORY

How far would white society go to battle racial discrimination in the 1930s? As a musically gifted African American child, **Marian Anderson** got her vocal training the only way she could: singing in the choir at the local church. In time, her talents took her from the choir box to some of the world's most famous concert halls.

Like many African American performers of her day, Anderson went to Europe first to build up her reputation. She returned to America as an international star. But success did not protect her from discrimination at home.

In 1939 Anderson's manager tried to book a concert for her at Constitution Hall in Washington, D.C. The owners of the hall, a prestigious group called the Daughters of the American Revolution (DAR), turned him down, citing a contract clause that said "concert by white artists only."

Many Americans were outraged. Eleanor Roosevelt and other prominent women resigned from the DAR. The First Lady then arranged for Anderson to hold a concert on the steps of the Lincoln Memorial in Washington. Some 75,000 people turned out, hearing Anderson's glorious voice sing the words, "My country, 'tis of thee, sweet land of liberty." Millions heard the national radio broadcast. Anderson later gave a private concert at the White House.

Eleanor Roosevelt's actions on behalf of Marian Anderson were typical of her efforts to aid African Americans. However, the incident also illustrated just how widespread racism was in 1930s America. A principled stand, a public cry of outrage, and groundbreaking symbolism went far in changing attitudes. Indeed, within four years, Constitution Hall changed its whites-only policy and invited Anderson to sing there. Meanwhile, however, there was no move to legally challenge the injustice done to Anderson or the racism it represented. The architects of the New Deal, including President Roosevelt, chose not to fight that battle. ◢

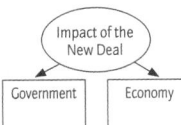

"OF THEE I SING..."

▶ **Marian Anderson performs on the steps of the Lincoln Memorial.**

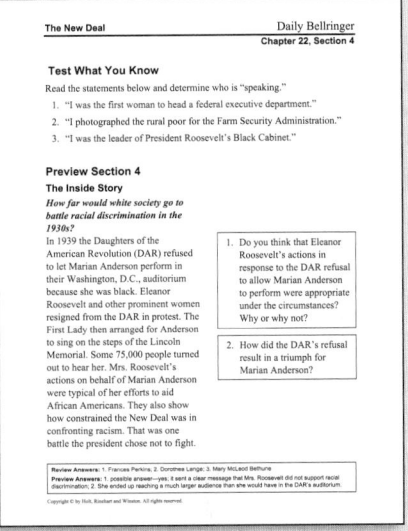

724

Direct Teach

Reading Focus

❶ What was the impact of the New Deal on the nation in the 1930s? *helped poor Americans; less successful in delivering economic recovery; changed relationship between citizens and government; government became much bigger*

The Impact of the New Deal

Recall What was the physical legacy of the WPA? *new roadways, bridges, dams, public buildings, public art*

Rate In which area—relief, recovery, or reform—do you think the New Deal was most successful? Why? *possible answer—Reform, because programs such as the FDIC and SEC restored faith in banks and stock market; FDIC and SEC still function today.*

Make Judgments As a result of the New Deal, Americans began to look regularly to government for help. Do you think this is a good or bad trend? Why? *possible answers—a good thing, because governments should try to make their citizens' lives better; a bad thing, because it undermines people's self-reliance*

Unemployment and Deficit Spending

Elaborate Why do you think deficit spending dropped so drastically in 1938 and then returned to its former level? *possible answer—growing power of Roosevelt's opponents in Congress due to the economic downturn in the fall of 1937*

🔲 Quick Facts Transparency: Unemployment and Deficit Spending, 1933–1940

Answers

Interpreting Graphs 1. *It dropped.*
2. *Unemployment rose as deficit spending dropped.*

QUICK FACTS

UNEMPLOYMENT, 1933–1940

Source: Historical Statistics of the United States

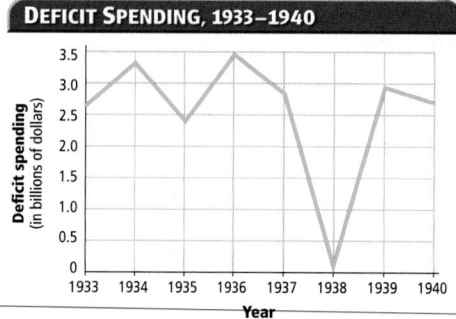

DEFICIT SPENDING, 1933–1940

Source: Historical Statistics of the United States

Skills FOCUS **INTERPRETING GRAPHS**

1. What was the overall trend of unemployment between 1933 and 1940?
2. What was significant about 1938?

See **Skills Handbook, p. H17**

The Impact of the New Deal

From the moment he took office, Franklin Roosevelt knew he faced an economic crisis—and a crisis of spirit. Though he could not hope to please everyone, he knew he had to take action. "Take a method and try it," he said, describing his approach. "If it fails, admit it frankly and try another. But above all, try something."

Relief, recovery, and reform What was the record of the New Deal? Was the promise of relief, recovery, and reform met?

Certainly, the relief programs enacted in 1933 and 1935 put billions of dollars into the pockets of poor Americans. Millions of people

---

enjoyed some form of help, from direct relief to jobs that provided a steady paycheck. Programs such as Social Security and unemployment insurance, moreover, became a fixture of American government.

The New Deal was less successful in delivering economic recovery. Joblessness initially fell from a high of 13 million in 1933 to about 9 million by 1936. Wages, factory output, and other economic indicators rose to levels at or even above those of 1929. Unfortunately, many early gains were wiped out in the downturn of 1937 and 1938. At decade's end, some 10 million workers remained unemployed.

Historians continue to debate the reasons for the New Deal's mixed results. Some argue that Roosevelt's policies, which were never popular with big business, hurt business confidence and slowed the pace of recovery. Others believe that the New Deal was too timid and that real unemployment reduction would have required spending billions more.

New Deal reforms proved more successful—and long-lasting. For example, the Federal Deposit Insurance Corporation helped restore public confidence in the safety of the nation's banks. This was a critical step in stopping the nation's slide into chaos in 1933. The FDIC has continued to serve the nation's economy ever since. Similarly, the Securities and Exchange Commission, established in 1934, helped the public regain faith in the stock markets. Investors today continue to rely on SEC oversight.

The New Deal also left an impressive legacy in the form of thousands of roadways, bridges, dams, and public buildings. The WPA built 2,500 hospitals and nearly 6,000 schools. WPA artists painted over 2,500 murals and erected nearly 18,000 sculptures in public places.

Changing relationships Americans have long argued about whether the New Deal was good or bad for the nation. What is undeniable is that the New Deal changed some basic relationships in American society.

In general, the New Deal changed the link between the American people and their government. The leaders of the 1920s had promoted business as the best way to achieve progress, and they generally viewed government as a barrier to progress. Roosevelt believed that government could help businesses and individuals achieve a greater level of economic security.

Skills Focus: Analyzing Bias in Historical Interpretation　**Above Level**

Reading Like a Historian Skill　　　　　　　　　　　　**Research Required**
The Impact of the New Deal

1. Guide students in a discussion about whether Roosevelt's New Deal helped or hindered recovery and whether the economy would have recovered without any government intervention.

2. Have students research this issue, distinguishing between fact and opinion in the sources they use. Then have each student write a two-page essay discussing the impact they think the New Deal had on economic

recovery. Students should back their opinions with valid reasoning, and cite sources for factual information.

3. Have volunteers read their essays to the class.

4. Have students conduct a formal debate on the issue of Roosevelt's policies and their effect on economic recovery. **🆂 Verbal-Linguistic**

📝 Alternative Assessment Handbook, Rubrics 1: Acquiring Information; and 42: Writing to Inform

The new role for government meant a much bigger government. Dozens of new programs and agencies put people in contact with their government in ways they had not experienced before. Americans now began to look regularly to government for help. Roosevelt and the New Deal were both praised and hated for this. For some, this change brought a welcome shift from the laissez-faire policies of the 1920s. To others, it threatened the basic character that had always held the country together.

HISTORY'S VOICES

“ It cannot be successfully denied that whatever the merits of the New Deal policies, they have, as a whole, caused an appreciable drift away from individual responsibility and self-reliance. They have brought about an excessive, utterly [false] and dangerous reliance upon government. ”

—*Saturday Evening Post*, November 6, 1936

READING CHECK Making Generalizations
How did the New Deal impact relationships among important segments of American society?

Limits of the New Deal

The New Deal was never as sweeping as its supporters or its opponents claimed. In practice, New Deal programs often compromised—some might say contradicted—Roosevelt's desire to build "a country in which no one is left out."

Relief programs provide a clear example. While they gave aid to millions of people, these programs were never meant to be a permanent solution to joblessness. Nor were they able to provide jobs to all those who needed them.

Roosevelt had hoped the federal government would assist all but about 1.5 million "unemployable" people, who would be left to the states to care for, but some 4.7 million went unserved. Work-relief programs could only provide temporary help. In addition, pay scales were very low. An unskilled worker might make a mere third of what the government deemed a minimum family income. Government leaders did not want wages to be so high that workers would be discouraged from seeking nongovernment jobs.

Info to Know

The WPA During the WPA's building program, 116,000 buildings, 78,000 bridges, and 651,000 miles (1,047,000 km) of roads were constructed. Nearly 10,000 drawings, paintings, and sculptures were produced through the WPA. WPA murals decorated many public buildings, especially post offices. An average of 4,000 musical performances were presented each month under the project. Writers in the WPA produced a valuable series of state and regional guidebooks.

Recent Scholarship

In his 2003 book, *FDR's Folly: How Roosevelt and His New Deal Prolonged the Great Depression*, Jim Powell, historian and senior fellow at the Cato Institute, argues that the New Deal did not help solve the economic crisis of the Great Depression. Instead, Powell contends that New Deal programs prolonged the crisis and added to the nation's problems. Powell says that Social Security and new labor laws increased unemployment; he also explains how the New Deal added costly expenses to the government's budget.

FDR's Folly: How Roosevelt and His New Deal Prolonged the Great Depression by Jim Powell. Crown Forum, 2003.

COUNTERPOINTS

Role of Government in Everyday Life

Although Charles McNary of Oregon was a Republican, he supported most New Deal programs, including the Social Security Act.

“ I am confident that once the magnitude of this problem is clearly recognized, once we face squarely the fact that it has passed beyond the ability of the individual to master, and is distinctly national in its character, we shall set ourselves to the task of its solution. ”

Senator Charles McNary, 1935

Daniel Reed of New York took a strong stand against Social Security.

“ I was taught and the people I have the honor to represent believe that the greatest heritage of a free people is the right to transmit that freedom to their children. I loathe this attempt to deceive and betray industry and labor and further fasten upon them this foreign system of regimentation [strict rule]. ”

Representative Daniel Reed, 1935

Skills FOCUS READING LIKE A HISTORIAN

Analyzing Primary Sources Why does McNary believe that Social Security is needed? Why does Reed oppose it?

See Skills Handbook, pp. H28–29

THE NEW DEAL **725**

Collaborative Learning

Below Level

The Government in Everyday Life

1. Organize the class into small groups. Have each group brainstorm and list ways in which the government plays a part in everyday life today.

2. Have volunteers share their lists with the class. Make a class list for all to see.

3. Guide the class in a discussion of the various roles government plays in everyday life and how those roles have expanded over the past decades. What other government roles are there that may not be on the class list?

Try to help students determine which level of government—federal, state, or local—each represents. *possible answers—schools (federal, state, local), traffic regulations (federal, state, local), sales tax (state, local)* Ask students if they believe the government should be more involved or less involved than it is now. **LS Interpersonal, Logical-Mathematical**

Alternative Assessment Handbook, Rubric 11: Discussions

Answers

Reading Like a Historian *McNary— national problem, not a problem for individuals; Reed—it restricts freedom*

Reading Check *closer contact between American people and their government; bigger role for government in social programs and in relationship between businesses and individuals*

❷ In what ways was the impact of the New Deal limited? *never reached all the people it was intended to help; jobs programs didn't pay well; permitted discrimination*

Limits of the New Deal

Explain Why did the government keep WPA wages low? *to provide relief while encouraging people to find nongovernment jobs*

Make Judgments Do you think that Roosevelt should have pushed harder to end discrimination in New Deal programs? Why or why not? *possible answers—yes, because there was an opportunity to end discrimination in exchange for government money; no, because in doing so Roosevelt might have doomed those programs*

Limits of the New Deal

The New Deal did not lift everyone out of poverty. Many working families, such as these migrant workers in Minnesota (right) or these homesteaders in New Mexico (far right) had little choice but to make the best out of the cramped and impoverished conditions in which they lived.

The level of government assistance also varied by state. For example, under Aid to Families with Dependent Children, a child in Massachusetts might receive more than $60 a month, while one in Arkansas might get $8.

In addition, New Deal programs sometimes permitted discrimination against African Americans, Hispanic Americans, women, and others. New Deal leaders, Roosevelt included, were unwilling to irritate local populations by requiring programs to go against "local standards"—including discriminatory ones.

READING CHECK **Summarizing** What were some of the limits of the New Deal?

The End of the New Deal

The sense of optimism accompanying Roosevelt's victory in 1936 withered by 1937. The fight over court-packing cost the president some of his support within his party and with the American public. The economic downturn of 1937–1938 delivered a further blow to his efforts. By the end of 1938, the New Deal era of reform launched in 1933 was, in reality, over.

Weakening support Roosevelt's setbacks emboldened his opponents in Congress. In late 1937, a group of anti–New Deal senators made up of Republicans and southern Democrats issued a direct challenge to Roosevelt's policies. They called on the president to cut taxes, balance the budget, and return more power to the states. This group was strong enough to stop most legislation they disliked.

One target of this group's opposition was the president's plan to reorganize the executive branch of the government. Roosevelt said his goal was to help make the executive branch work more smoothly.

Critics, however, complained that the measure gave too much power to the president. As one member of Congress stated, "This is just a step to concentrate power in the hands of the president and set up a… form of dictatorship." Such a charge carried real weight after the court-packing episode.

Only one major piece of legislation emerged from Congress in 1938: the Fair Labor Standards Act. This law established a **minimum wage**—the lowest wage an employer can legally pay a worker. It also set the maximum number of required hours for a work week at 44. (This was later lowered to 40.) The Fair Labor Standards Act also included a requirement that workers receive the overtime rate of time-and-a-half—payment at one-and-a-half times their normal rate for any hours over the weekly maximum.

Differentiating Instruction

Below Level

Reading Skill

Standard English Mastery

Limitations of the New Deal

1. Have students work in pairs to write a few sentences about the limitations of the New Deal. *jobless programs did not reach all who needed help; pay was often too low to help; discrepancies in levels of relief from one state to another; programs permitted discrimination*

2. Have volunteers read their sentences to the class.

3. Have students use the sentences to write a paragraph summarizing the limitations of the New Deal. Students should support or oppose the justifications given for these limitations. Then ask if students believe that it is better to hold out for equal treatment and risk losing everything, or is it better to try to make the best deal for as many people as possible?

LS Verbal-Linguistic

Alternative Assessment Handbook, Rubric 43: Writing to Persuade

Answers

Reading Check *relief programs were a temporary solution that left out many Americans; level of government assistance varied by state; programs permitted discrimination against women and minorities*

The new law did not cover many large groups, such as farmworkers. Still, it marked a major victory for millions of workers.

Southern Democrats opposed the bill. Southern industry, they argued, depended on paying workers less than in other parts of the country. But Roosevelt worked hard to win passage of the bill. Although he did not know it, the bill would be the last major New Deal law.

The 1938 elections Facing opposition in Congress, President Roosevelt decided his best hope lay in defeating his opponents in the 1938 congressional elections. This included opponents within his own party. He handpicked candidates to fight for the Democratic nominations in several southern states.

President Roosevelt traveled to the South to tell voters he needed new senators to help pass his program. The embattled senators responded by enflaming white fears that African Americans were becoming politically empowered, sponsored by Roosevelt.

Georgia senator Walter George was among those targeted by Roosevelt. He compared the president's attempt to influence the election to the U.S. Army's occupation of the South during post–Civil War Reconstruction. "We answered this question before when federal bayonets stood guard over the ballot box," he observed.

Roosevelt's efforts backfired. In each case, his candidate lost, and the **incumbent** senator—the one presently in office—won the nomination and the November election. In addition, Republicans made gains in the House and Senate, further swelling the ranks of New Deal opponents.

After the New Deal Following the 1938 elections, President Roosevelt lacked the support he needed to pass more New Deal–style laws. Opposition was simply too strong for Roosevelt to overcome.

At the same time, Congress, the president, and the American public turned their attention away from the long struggle against the Great Depression. The possibility of a different kind of struggle lay ahead.

Now Europe appeared to be marching relentlessly toward another war. American factories now began to gear up to arm those who would fight the battles. By the millions, workers returned to the assembly lines and workshops. In a period of months in 1939 and 1940, international conflict produced what years of political struggle had failed to achieve: an end to the Great Depression.

READING CHECK **Sequencing** What events marked the end of the New Deal?

---

go.hrw.com
Online Quiz
Keyword: SD7 HP22

SECTION 4 ASSESSMENT

Reviewing Ideas, Terms, and People

1. **a. Describe** On what grounds did people praise and criticize the New Deal?
   b. Contrast How did Roosevelt's views about the role of government differ from presidents of the 1920s?
   c. Rate Do you think the positive impact of the New Deal outweighed the negative impact? Explain.

2. **a. Recall** Did the New Deal bring an end to the Depression?
   b. Make Inferences Why were New Deal programs able to provide only limited support to the needy?
   c. Evaluate Defend the New Deal's approach of honoring local customs in establishing levels of aid.

3. **a. Define** Write brief definitions of the following terms: minimum wage, incumbent
   b. Explain How did Roosevelt's effort to get rid of disloyal Democrats backfire?
   c. Elaborate How might Roosevelt have tried to improve relations with Congress and win more support for his efforts?

Critical Thinking

4. **Find Supporting Details** Copy the chart below and use information from the section to find supporting details for the main idea given.

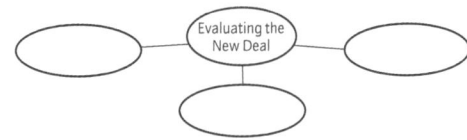
Evaluating the New Deal

FOCUS ON WRITING

5. **Narrative** Write a narrative account of the final year of the New Deal. Be sure to include details from the section about the failures and rare successes of Roosevelt as well as the reasons for the end of the New Deal.

THE NEW DEAL **727**

Section 4 Assessment Answers

1. **a.** brought relief and reform; did not end Depression; increased government's role and size
   b. thought government should take an active role in business and people's lives
   c. positive—brought some relief and many reforms; negative—government increased in size, deficit spending

2. **a.** no
   b. low pay; government assistance varied by state; permitted discrimination
   c. Programs would have faced more resistance if they did not honor local customs.

3. **a.** the lowest wage an employer can legally pay a worker; person currently in office
   b. Roosevelt's chosen candidates all lost, and incumbents won.
   c. possible answer—He could have supported laws Congress wished to pass.

4. provided money and jobs; reduced unemployment; passed lasting legislation, improved infrastructure

5. Court-packing plan, attempt to reorganize executive branch; Fair Labor Standards Act

Perceptions of Roosevelt

Word Help

perception view, understanding

intermittent irregular; on-again, off-again

doff take off, remove

straddling seeming to favor two different sides of an issue

consummately completely, perfectly

hiss show disapproval of something or someone by making a hissing noise

Primary Source

"When our children's children read the story of the 20th century, they will see that above all, it is the story of freedom's triumph . . . And they will see that the embodiment of that triumph, the driving force behind it, was President Franklin Delano Roosevelt . . . Even though Franklin Roosevelt was the architect of grand designs, he touched tens of millions of Americans in a very personal way . . . To ordinary Americans, Roosevelt was always more than a great President, he was part of the family."

— Bill Clinton

"Captain Courageous," *Time*, Jan. 3, 2000

Perceptions of Roosevelt

Historical Context The documents below provide different information on perceptions of Franklin Roosevelt.

Task Examine the documents and answer the questions that follow. Then you will be asked to write an essay about perceptions of Franklin Roosevelt, using facts from the documents and from the chapter to support the position you take in your thesis statement.

DOCUMENT 1

To his admirers, Franklin Roosevelt's appeal lay in both his policies and his personality. His energy and enthusiasm helped reassure a country that was going through hard times. Tom Vinciguerra, who grew up during the Great Depression, recalled his family's perceptions of Roosevelt.

> "'Depression' was fast becoming a household word to all six of us children. Mother's pretty and usually smiling face now turned grim almost daily. The '29 crash destroyed my father's car-repair business. Survival was dependent on Dad's intermittent part-time jobs, plus welfare. Coal money ran out fast, and we weren't always warm. Hand-me-downs and leftover store bread warded off stark desperation.
>
> In 1931, my nonpolitical mother surprised us with an announcement that the family would attend an election eve rally for Roosevelt in Camden, N.J. At the rally, I watched my mother smile and sing. I was so happy for her. As the troubled '30s rolled on, Roosevelt's alphabet soup—PA, CCC, etc. —worked its magic. Our lives improved.
>
> In 1939, at age 13, I heard the loud wail of sirens while walking to my part-time busboy job in downtown Camden. It was Roosevelt's reelection motorcade. As it reached me, the president doffed his famous hat in my direction. Thrilled, I ran home. When I told my mother, she hugged me. I felt her tremble as she sobbed. Then she looked at me as if through me she could express her deep gratitude to the president. My brothers and sisters treated me like a celebrity. I did not bus dishes that day."

DOCUMENT 2

Some critics argued that Roosevelt's charisma sometimes gave people false hope and hid the details of his political plans. The following editorial appeared in *The Nation* magazine after one of Roosevelt's 1936 speeches, as he was preparing for his re-election.

> "Mr. Roosevelt's amazing radio message to Congress has undoubtedly strengthened his campaign fortunes, but leaves his program as unclear as ever. Politically adroit [skilled], and from the standpoint of radio oratory a magnificent achievement, it was intellectually a confused and straddling performance. . . The common man wanted to be let in on a dramatic occasion, and he had his wish. He wanted a fighting speech, and he got it. He was tuning in on history-in-the-making, and the President took pains to make it a good show . . . The President has again used some sort of magic to increase his stature, and by comparison every Presidential possibility on the Republican side seems puny and frustrate[d]. . . .
>
> But a sober rereading of the speech shows how consummately Mr. Roosevelt displayed his talent for leaving almost all the important things unsaid. . . .
>
> In the domestic field Mr. Roosevelt's message was better as a manifesto [a public statement] than as a preface [introduction] to legislative action. It was here that the speech became… a political rally, with the business of state being transacted under the klieg lights [bright lights used in making motion pictures]."

728 CHAPTER 22

Skills Focus: Analyzing Primary Sources
At Level

Reading Like a Historian Skill
Differing Perspectives on Roosevelt

1. Organize the class into four groups. Assign each group one of the documents.

2. Have each group analyze the document and then write a summary of the message conveyed by the document. Remind students that visual art and political cartoons convey messages that can be as strong, or stronger, than messages in written documents.

3. Have a volunteer from each group present its summary to the class. Guide students in a discussion of the different views of Roosevelt presented in the documents.

4. Have students write a brief essay expressing their impression of Roosevelt based on the four documents and the class discussion.

LS Verbal-Linguistic, Visual-Spatial

Alternative Assessment Handbook, Rubric 41: Writing to Express

DOCUMENT 3

Although he grew up wealthy and privileged, President Roosevelt had a strong appeal among many poor Americans, who felt he understood their suffering. The following cartoon reflects this idea.

"Yes, you remembered me."

DOCUMENT 4

Some of Franklin Roosevelt's harshest critics were the wealthy, who resented his efforts to redistribute wealth by taxing the rich to help the poor. Some accused him of betraying his class. In this cartoon, a group of wealthy New Yorkers are going to the Trans-Lux, a popular movie theater on Madison Avenue in New York City that showed newsreels about the president.

"Come along. We're going to the Trans-Lux to hiss Roosevelt."

Skills FOCUS   READING LIKE A HISTORIAN

1. a. Identify Refer to Document 1. What was the writer's impression of Roosevelt?
b. Analyze How did Roosevelt change this family's life in multiple ways?

2. a. Describe Refer to Document 2. According to the writer, what was the main purpose of Roosevelt's speech?
b. Interpret Why was the writer critical of the president for having strong speaking abilities?

3. a. Identify Refer to Documents 3 and 4. What are the two different types of people responding to Roosevelt?

b. Contrast What do these two cartoons reflect about the personal appeal of President Roosevelt?

4. Document-Based Essay Question Consider the question below and form a thesis statement. Using examples from Documents 1, 2, 3, and 4, create an outline and write a short essay supporting your position. How did President Franklin Roosevelt's personality shape public perceptions of his presidency?

See Skills Handbook, pp. H28–H29, H31

Info to Know

Roosevelt accepts the 1932 nomination
When the Democratic national convention began, Roosevelt was just a few votes short of the presidential nomination. At last, he received the votes he needed. He then flew to Chicago to accept the nomination in person. This was a break with tradition, but Roosevelt wanted to show the nation that he was strong and energetic, and that polio had not and would not slow him down.

Primary Source

"Franklin D. Roosevelt is no crusader. He is no tribune of the people. He is no enemy of entrenched privilege. He is a pleasant man who, without any important qualifications for the office, would very much like to be president."

— Walter Lippman

Interpretations, 1931–1932, ed. Allan Nevins, p. 262

Answers

Reading Like a Historian
1. a. *idolized Roosevelt; saw him as a miracle worker;* **b.** *provided moral encouragement and support;* **2. a.** *to encourage ordinary citizens to vote for him;* **b.** *felt Roosevelt did not convey a real message, that people did not listen to the message, but were captivated by the delivery;* **3. a.** *Document 3—poor Americans; Document 4—wealthy Americans;* **b.** *possible answer— Roosevelt appealed more to the common man than to the wealthy.* **4.** *possible answer—public viewed him as inspirational and heroic; poor Americans felt he understood and supported them; wealthy Americans felt betrayed by Roosevelt's programs to redistribute wealth*

Differentiating Instruction

Above Level

Advanced Learners/GATE

1. Tell students that Roosevelt campaigned very hard to get the 1932 Democratic Party nomination for president and that he then conducted an effective campaign. Remind students that although President Herbert Hoover was unpopular, he still had support among many Americans.

2. Have students conduct outside research on the 1932 campaign. Have students focus on how Roosevelt got the nomination and on his presidential campaign speeches. Students

should use primary and secondary sources.

3. Have students write an in-depth report of the 1932 election. Student reports should include a complete summary, quotes, supporting documentation, and an evaluation of the election results. Students should include a bibliography with their reports.

4. Have volunteers read their reports to the class.
   LS Intrapersonal, Verbal-Linguistic

   Alternative Assessment Handbook, Rubrics 30: Research; and 42: Writing to Inform

Visual Summary

Review and Inquiry Have students review the image. Ask these questions: What did the New Deal consist of initially? Where did criticism and resistance come from? What was the lasting impact of New Deal programs? Have students write the answers to these questions.

Quick Facts Transparency: The New Deal

Reviewing Key Terms and People

1. Public works projects provided jobs.

2. Fireside chats were weekly radio addresses.

3. The Hundred Days was the time when Roosevelt began his program for relief, recovery, and reform.

4. Huey P. Long was the powerful Democratic governor of Louisiana.

5. Social Security provides a government pension plan for the elderly.

6. The CIO was a labor union for unskilled workers.

7. A deficit occurs when a government spends more money than it collects.

8. John Maynard Keynes believed deficit spending would stimulate the economy.

9. The Black Cabinet were African Americans who held posts in cabinet departments and New Deal agencies.

10. Frances Perkins was secretary of labor.

11. Mary McLeod Bethune was director of Negro Affairs in the National Youth Administration.

12. The minimum wage is the lowest wage an employer can legally pay a worker.

Comprehension and Critical Thinking

13. **a.** Franklin D. Roosevelt
b. liked—attempt to improve economy; disliked—radical change between people and government
c. No plan is without critics.

Visual Summary: The New Deal

The New Deal
- Two major plans—in 1933 and 1935
- Established many new government programs
- Popular at first, but limited in its success

Criticism and Resistance
- Political opposition from right and left
- Supreme Court opposition

Lasting Impact
- Forever changes relationship between people and government
- Introduces programs such as Social Security that are still functioning today
- Still controversial

Reviewing Key Terms and People

For each term or name below, write a sentence explaining its significance to the New Deal.

1. public works
2. fireside chat
3. Hundred Days
4. Huey P. Long
5. Social Security
6. CIO
7. deficit
8. John Maynard Keynes
9. Black Cabinet
10. Frances Perkins
11. Mary McLeod Bethune
12. minimum wage

Comprehension and Critical Thinking

SECTION 1 *(pp. 698–705)*

13. **a. Recall** Who did the Democratic Party choose as its candidate in 1932?

b. Contrast What did the American people seem to like most about Roosevelt's programs? What did they find fault with?

c. Evaluate What can you conclude from the fact that Roosevelt and the New Deal were criticized both for doing too much and for doing too little?

SECTION 2 *(pp. 709–716)*

14. **a. Identify** What was the Second New Deal?

b. Draw Conclusions What factors undermined support for Roosevelt and his programs?

c. Evaluate Explain this statement: In some ways, President Roosevelt's success contributed to his failure in the late 1930s.

14. **a.** new wave of government initiatives
b. alienation of business, inability to reduce unemployment, attempt to pack courts
c. became powerful, creating mistrust; to fund programs federal debt grew

15. **a.** appointed them to powerful positions; did not take a strong stand on civil rights.
b. She did not have to worry about losing votes.
c. possible answer—brought more women and minorities into government positions; failed to work against discrimination

16. **a.** initially helped; economic downturn reversed many early gains
b. success—restored faith in economy; provided economic relief; lowered unemployment; created lasting reforms; failure—economic downturn reversed gains; many did not receive aid
c. Students can take either position above.

SECTION 3 *(pp. 717–722)*

15. a. Recall How did the Roosevelt administration treat women and African Americans?

b. Make Inferences Why do you think Eleanor Roosevelt was able to take a firmer stand for the rights of women and African Americans than her husband did?

c. Rate How do you think Franklin Roosevelt should be evaluated historically in terms of his treatment of women and minorities?

SECTION 4 *(pp. 723–727)*

16. a. Describe What effects did New Deal programs have on the major problems of the Great Depression, such as unemployment?

b. Summarize On what grounds can the New Deal be considered a success? a failure?

c. Rate In your opinion, was the New Deal a success or a failure? Explain.

Using the Internet

go.hrw.com
Practice Online
Keyword: SD7 CH22

17. Photographer Dorothea Lange used a camera to tell stories of life during the Great Depression. Her photographs convey many different moods, show different groups of people and different types of circumstances. Yet the pictures have much in common. Using the keyword above, research Lange's life and study some of her photographs. Then answer these questions: (a) How did Lange's own life affect her work? (b) What do her photographs reveal about the lives of people during the Depression? In your answers, refer to at least two specific photographs by their titles.

Analyzing Primary Sources

Reading Like a Historian This photograph shows Eleanor Roosevelt meeting with several members of the Bonus Army that formed during the early years of the Roosevelt administration.

18. Describe How would you describe the interaction between Eleanor Roosevelt and the Bonus Army marchers?

19. Contrast How did Eleanor Roosevelt's interaction with the Bonus Army differ from Hoover's treatment of the Bonus Army of 1932?

Critical Reading

Read the passage in Section 2 that begins with the heading "The Second Hundred Days." Then answer the question that follows.

20. The issue of Social Security is most closely associated with the criticisms of

A Congress.

B Dr. Francis Townsend.

C voters in 1936.

D African Americans.

WRITING FOR THE SAT

Think about the following issue.

Franklin Roosevelt and the New Deal set off one of the most fundamental debates about government in the nation's history. Not since the debates between the Federalists and Antifederalists had the country seen such diverging viewpoints as those between Roosevelt and his conservative opponents. The debate is as strong as ever today.

21. Assignment How far should government go to try to improve the lives of citizens? Is it appropriate to use deficit spending when necessary to relieve suffering? What standards would you apply to decide how much help is too little or too much? Support your point of view with reasoning and examples from the chapter.

Answers

Using the Internet

17. Go to the HRW Web site and enter the keyword shown to access a rubric for this activity.

KEYWORD: SD7 CH22

Reading Like a Historian

18. warm and respectful

19. She met with them instead of sending troops against them.

Critical Reading

20. B

Writing for the SAT

21. possible answers—government should be willing to use deficit spending to help Americans who are suffering; government should not intervene in the private sector by controlling business; should provide job opportunities in the government; assistance should go to poorest Americans; purpose of government is to improve the lives of its citizens

A rubric for this activity is provided in the Chapter Resource File: Writing for the SAT: The Minimum Wage.

History's Impact Video Program

controlled flooding, brought electricity, improved farmland

Review and Assessment Resources

Review and Reinforce

- CRF: Chapter Review Activity
- Quick Facts Transparencies: Major New Deal Programs, Gross National Product, 1933–1938, Unemployment and Deficit Spending, 1933–1940, The New Deal
- Spanish Chapter Summaries Audio CD Program
- Online Chapter Summaries in Spanish
- OSP Holt PuzzlePro; Quiz Show for ExamView
- Quiz Game CD-ROM

Assess

- PASS: Chapter Test, Forms A and B
- Alternative Assessment Handbook
- OSP ExamView Test Generator, Chapter Test
- Differentiated Instruction Modified Worksheets and Tests CD-ROM: Chapter Test
- HOAP Holt Online Assessment Program (in the Premier Online Edition)

Reteach/Intervene

- Interactive Reader and Study Guide
- Differentiated Instruction Teacher Management System: Lesson Plans for Differentiated Instruction
- Differentiated Instruction Modified Worksheets and Tests CD-ROM: Chapter Test
- Interactive Skills Tutor CD-ROM

go.hrw.com
Online Resources
KEYWORD: SD7 CH22

Summarizing the Unit

Remind students that the New Deal was a large-scale government response to a severe social crisis. Have students discuss these questions: *Is the United States today facing any challenges severe enough to need a government program similar to the New Deal? If so, what form should the program take? If not, what are other ways Americans can overcome the challenges they face?*

Connecting to Themes

Have students focus on the economy during the first half of the twentieth century. Guide students in a discussion that compares the economy in the early 1900s to the economy today. In what ways are the periods similar? In what ways are they different?

 **UNIT 7 IN BRIEF** Below is a chapter-by-chapter summary of the main ideas covered in Unit 7.

CHAPTER 19 From War to Peace
1919–1928

MAIN IDEA The years following World War I brought unease over the apparent spread of radical influences. The American people sought leaders who offered a return to peaceful times—and they eagerly contributed to a booming, consumer-driven economy.

SECTION 1 Far from feeling safe and at peace, many Americans in the postwar years saw threats in a variety of forms, including labor unrest, rising immigration, and radical political ideas.

SECTION 2 The increasing availability of consumer goods—from cars to household appliances—helped inspire a growing economic boom in the 1920s.

SECTION 3 Warren G. Harding captured the national mood—and the White House—with his calls for normalcy. His pro-business agenda was expanded upon by his successor, Calvin Coolidge.

CHAPTER 20 The Roaring Twenties
1920–1929

MAIN IDEA The 1920s was a time of widespread cultural change. Music, art, literature, and popular culture reflected dramatic demographic and cultural developments.

SECTION 1 The changing American culture of the 1920s was reflected in new roles for women and an increase in urbanization.

SECTION 2 Centered in New York City's Harlem community, African American culture experienced a renaissance of literature, music, and art.

SECTION 3 The growing popularity of the radio and the movies helped contribute to the rise of a mass popular culture in the 1920s. Americans idolized the stars, both on the screen and off, that emerged from these new forms of entertainment.

CHAPTER 21 The Great Depression Begins
1929–1933

MAIN IDEA Following an era of apparent prosperity, the Great Depression began in 1929. Soon millions of Americans were suffering, and the political landscape of the United States stood on the brink of great change.

SECTION 1 The American stock markets, which had ballooned in value and helped fuel the economic optimism of the 1920s, collapsed in 1929. The crash had effects far beyond the losses by investors.

SECTION 2 In the Great Depression that followed the 1929 stock market crash, millions of people lost their jobs, their savings, and their homes. In some parts of the country, environmental catastrophe added to the suffering.

SECTION 3 President Herbert Hoover believed in limited government action to address the growing national crisis. For many Americans, he came to be the target of much anger and unhappiness.

CHAPTER 22 The New Deal
1933–1940

MAIN IDEA Swept into office in 1932 on his promises of help for the victims of the Great Depression, Franklin Delano Roosevelt pushed forward a series of programs that came to be called the New Deal. These programs met with some success as well as some criticism.

SECTION 1 As president, Roosevelt quickly sought to address the fears of the nation. New Deal laws helped repair the banking system and provide relief for the jobless, though they met with significant criticism.

SECTION 2 The Emergency Relief Appropriation Act and Social Security helped set the pace for the Second New Deal, which helped Roosevelt win re-election as president in 1936.

SECTION 3 The New Deal provided some new opportunities for women and minority groups. It also helped shape the popular and artistic culture of the decade.

SECTION 4 The New Deal had mixed results in solving the economic problems of the Great Depression. However, it unquestionably changed the relationship between the people and their government.

Unit Resources

Review and Reinforce
- CRF: Chapter Review Activity
- Spanish Chapter Summaries Audio CD Program
- OSP Holt PuzzlePro; GameTool for ExamView
- Quiz Game CD-ROM

Assess
- PASS: Unit Test, Forms A and B
- Alternative Assessment Handbook
- OSP ExamView Test Generator
- Differentiated Instruction Modified Worksheets and Tests CD-ROM: Chapter Tests
- HOAP Holt Online Assessment Program (in the Premier Online Edition)

Reteach/Intervene
- Interactive Reader and Study Guide
- Differentiated Instruction Teacher Management System: Lesson Plans for Differentiated Instruction
- Differentiated Instruction Modified Worksheets and Tests CD-ROM: Chapter Tests
- Interactive Skills Tutor CD-ROM

go.hrw.com
Online Resources

KEYWORDS: SD7 CH19, SD7 CH20, SD7 CH21, SD7 CH22

8 A Champion of Democracy

1939–1960

Chapter 23
World War II Erupts
1939–1941

Chapter 24
The United States in World War II
1941–1945

Chapter 25
The Cold War Begins
1945–1953

Chapter 26
Postwar America
1945–1960

Themes

Global Relations
The United States and the Allies defeated the Axis Powers in World War II, but tensions between the United States and its former ally the Soviet Union led to a long-running Cold War.

Government and Democracy
The United States fought against regimes that opposed democracy during World War II and the Cold War.

Japan formally surrendered aboard the USS *Missouri* on September 2, 1945, bringing World War II to an end.

733

Unit Preview

Introducing the Unit
In the 1950s many schools held "drop drills," in which students were instructed to drop to the floor and crawl beneath their desks to protect themselves from nuclear fallout. Ask students if they would react similarly today to these types of drills.

Connecting to Themes
Activity **Consequences** In this unit you will learn about World War II and its consequences. As you read each chapter, think about how the themes of Global Relations, Economics, and Science and Technology are discussed, and how the world changed during this time period. **LS Verbal-Linguistic**

Reading Like a Historian
Interpreting Photographs
Japan Surrenders After Japan officially surrendered, ceremonies involving representatives of both Japanese and U.S. governments were held aboard the *Missouri*, as shown here. The ceremony included the signing of a document called an Instrument of Surrender and concluded with U.S. Navy carrier planes that flew in formation above the ship.

Unit Resources

Planning
- Differentiated Instruction Teacher Management System: Unit Pacing Guide
- One-Stop Planner CD-ROM: Teacher Management System
- Power Presentations with Video CD-ROM

Differentiating Instruction
- Differentiated Instruction Teacher Management System: Lesson Plans for Differentiated Instruction
- Pre-AP Activities Guide for American History
- Differentiated Instruction Modified Worksheets and Tests CD-ROM

Enrichment
- Civic Participation Activities Guide
- CRF: Economics and History Activity
- CRF: Interdisciplinary Project
- American History Primary Source Library CD-ROM

Assessment
- PASS: Unit Test, Forms A & B
- Alternative Assessment Handbook
- OSP ExamView Test Generator
- HOAP Holt Online Assessment Program (in the Premier Online Edition)

The Differentiated Instruction Teacher Management System
provides a planning and instructional benchmarking guide for this unit.

Drawing Conclusions

Learning from the Past Ask students to bring in a newspaper or magazine article about a subject that interests them. Have students read their articles and write down several facts about their articles. Then have students write down two or three inferences based on those facts. Have students draw logical conclusions based on their facts and inferences and write them in a short paragraph.

Word Help

converted changed

Primary Source

WASP Members of the Women's Airforce Service Pilots were a clear example of the changing roles of women in World War II, as this quote by Annelle Henderson Bulechek shows: "You don't need legislation to prove something . . . you can be whatever you set your heart and head to be, and don't let anybody tell you you can't be, because 1,078 women pilots did it in World War II."

—Annelle Henderson Bulechek

Skills Planner

To give students more opportunities to practice this skill, see the following activities in the teacher's edition: Women in the Workplace, p. 761; World War II: The Final Costs, p. 806; The Costs of the Korean War, p. 840.

Drawing Conclusions

Find practice for **Drawing Conclusions** in the **Skills Handbook,** p. H12

Good readers can use clues and their own prior knowledge to draw conclusions about various people places, and events mentioned in text. Drawing conclusions helps you remember what you read.

Before You Read
Skim chapter titles, section headings, and visuals to determine what the chapter will be about. Make a mental list of what you already know about the subject matter.

While You Read
Identify facts and ideas in the text. Then look for connections between those facts, ideas and what you already know.

After You Read
Briefly summarize what you have read. Then form a conclusion that makes a decision, judgment, or opinion about what the facts and ideas mean to you.

> The section head tells you that the passage will be about how science and industry were mobilized for war.

Mobilizing Industry and Science

The enthusiasm of American fighting forces was important. In order to defeat the Axis armies, however, American troops would need the proper equipment. The nation responded quickly to this need. Many factories that made consumer goods were quickly converted to the production of war supplies.

> **Fact** To win, American troops needed equipment.

Rosie the Riveter Producing enough supplies to fight the war required many workers. At the same time, American men were leaving their factory jobs by the millions to join the armed forces.

Women helped provide a solution to this problem. During the war, the number of women working outside the home rose dramatically. Many of these eight million new workers took industrial jobs that had never been open to women before.

> **Fact** Factories needed workers, but men were leaving to be soldiers.

READING CHECK **Drawing Conclusions**
How were working women important to the war effort?

Test Prep Tip

Short answer and essay questions on tests frequently ask you to draw a conclusion about something you have read. But conclusions are not always stated directly. Try restating a passage from the text as a question that begins, "Why was it important that…?" For example, "Why was it important that many of the eight million new [women] workers took industrial jobs?"

734 UNIT 8

Skills Focus: Drawing Conclusions | At Level

Reading Skill | **Research Required**
Analyzing Historical Text

1. Remind students that when reading historical text, it is important to identify facts and ideas in the text and make connections to what they already know. It is also important to ask questions about the text in order to draw sound conclusions about the reading.

2. Have students choose three paragraphs in a section of one of the chapters in this unit. After students have read the paragraphs, have them note the page number and heading of the text at the top of their papers, then write at least five questions about the material. Questions may relate directly to information in the text, or they may be questions that would require additional research.

3. Have students exchange papers with a partner and see if the other student can answer the questions. **LS Verbal-Linguistic**

Alternative Assessment Handbook, Rubric 37: Writing Assignments

Interpreting Visuals

Find practice for **Interpreting Visuals** in the **Skills Handbook,** p. H30

Many visuals are created for a specific reason. A newspaper photograph may be intended to inform readers, but a war-time **poster** may be a piece of propaganda used to convey a message or a point of view. By interpreting visuals, you can gain insight into different perspectives on historical events.

Strategies historians use:
- Find clues to the artist's point of view. Is the subject treated in a positive or negative light?
- Reflect on who the author's audience might have been.
- Think about the historical context of the image.

The word "Victory" is in large type, and is a different color. this indicates it is more important than the other words on the poster.

The basket is over-flowing with fresh food. This creates an impression of abun-dance, even during a time of shortage.

The woman is dressed as a civilian, but wears a military cap. This calls atten-tion to the war effort at home.

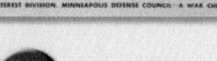

Skills Focus • READING LIKE A HISTORIAN

As You Read Examine how the visuals on each page relate to the text that you are reading. How do details in the visuals explain more about those historical events?

As You Study Compare and contrast the visuals in each chapter. Use the visuals to help you understand the progression of historical events.

A CHAMPION OF DEMOCRACY **735**

• **Prepare to Read** •

Interpreting Visuals

Word Help

propaganda ideas, facts, or rumors spread deliberately to further a cause or damage an opposing cause

Teaching Tip

Explain to students that many governments have used propaganda to sway public opinion or to move people to action. For example, Hitler used propaganda as a way to gain popularity. To influ-ence Americans to support the war, the U.S. government used propaganda, including films and posters.

Skills Focus: Interpreting Visuals
At Level

Reading Like a Historian Skill
Analyzing World War II Posters

Materials poster board, colored markers

1. Tell students that many government posters during World War II urged citizens to aid the war effort.

2. Have students conduct research using online or print sources to find World War II posters. (The Smithsonian National Museum of American History has an online collection) Have students choose three posters and record the central issues to which the illustration and wording refer.

3. Have students create their own World War II posters, choosing an issue they have learned about from their research. Posters should include a catchy phrase or slogan in support of the war effort. **LS Visual-Spatial**

    Alternative Assessment Handbook, Rubric 28: Posters

Chapter 23 Planning Guide

World War II Erupts

Chapter Overview	Reproducible Resources	Technology Resources
CHAPTER 23 pp. 736–767 **Overview:** In this chapter, students will analyze the events that led to the outbreak of World War II.	**Differentiated Instruction Teacher Management System:*** • Instructional Benchmarking Guides • Lesson Plans for Differentiated Instruction **Interactive Reader and Study Guide:** Chapter Summary* **Chapter Resource File:*** • Focus on Writing Activity • Social Studies Skills Activity: Evaluating Historical Interpretations • Chapter Review Activity **American History Outline Maps** **Pre-AP Activities Guide for American History***	Live Ink® Online Reading Help Student Edition on Audio CD Program Differentiated Instruction Modified Worksheets and Tests CD-ROM Interactive Skills Tutor CD-ROM United States History Primary Source Library CD-ROM Power Presentations with Video CD-ROM History's Impact: American History Video Program (VHS/DVD): World War II Erupts Online Chapter Summaries in Spanish
Section 1: **The Rise of Dictators** **The Main Idea:** The effects of World War I set the stage for a new generation of leaders in Europe.	**Differentiated Instruction Teacher Management System:** Section 1 Lesson Plan* **Interactive Reader and Study Guide:** Section 1 Summary* **Chapter Resource File:*** • Vocabulary Builder Activity, Section 1	Daily Bellringer Transparency: Section 1* Daily Test Practice Transparency: Section 1*
Section 2: **Europe Erupts in War** **The Main Idea:** Far from being appeased by France and Great Britain, Germany triggered the start of World War II.	**Differentiated Instruction Teacher Management System:** Section 2 Lesson Plan* **Interactive Reader and Study Guide:** Section 2 Summary* **Chapter Resource File:*** • Vocabulary Builder Activity, Section 2	Daily Bellringer Transparency: Section 2* Map Transparency: German Aggression 1938–1941* Daily Test Practice Transparency: Section 2*
Section 3: **The United States Enters the War** **The Main Idea:** Axis aggression eventually destroyed isolationist feelings in the United States and pushed it into war.	**Differentiated Instruction Teacher Management System:** Section 3 Lesson Plan* **Interactive Reader and Study Guide:** Section 3 Summary* **Chapter Resource File:*** • Vocabulary Builder Activity, Section 3	Daily Bellringer Transparency: Section 3* Daily Test Practice Transparency: Section 3*
Section 4: **Mobilizing for War** **The Main Idea:** The outbreak of World War II spurred the mobilization of American military and industrial might.	**Differentiated Instruction Teacher Management System:** Section 4 Lesson Plan* **Interactive Reader and Study Guide:** Section 4 Summary* **Chapter Resource File:*** • Vocabulary Builder Activity, Section 4	Daily Bellringer Transparency: Section 4* Daily Test Practice Transparency: Section 4*

HOLT

History's Impact
American History Video Program (VHS/DVD)
World War II Erupts

Review, Assessment, Intervention

 Quick Facts Transparency: World War II Erupts

 Spanish Chapter Summaries Audio CD Program

 Progress Assessment Support System (PASS):
Chapter Test*

 Differentiated Instruction Modified Worksheets and Tests CD-ROM: Modified Chapter Test

OSP **One-Stop Planner CD-ROM:** ExamView Test Generator (English/Spanish)

HOAP **Holt Online Assessment Program (HOAP),** in the Holt Premier Online Student Edition

 PASS: Section 1 Quiz*

 Online Quiz: Section 1

 Alternative Assessment Handbook

 PASS: Section 2 Quiz*

 Online Quiz: Section 2

 Alternative Assessment Handbook

 PASS: Section 3 Quiz*

 Online Quiz: Section 3

 Alternative Assessment Handbook

 PASS: Section 4 Quiz*

 Online Quiz: Section 4

 Alternative Assessment Handbook

NC RESOURCES

The following resources were developed to help North Carolina educators teach the standards and objectives of North Carolina's eleventh grade standard course of study in United States history.

- United States history EOC Test Prep Workbook
- Teacher's Support System
- North Carolina One-Stop Planner

And be sure to direct your students to **go.hrw.com** for online access to the EOC Test Prep Workbook.

go.hrw.com
EOC Test Prep
KEYWORD: SE7 NC

Holt Online Learning

go.hrw.com
Teacher Resources
KEYWORD: SD7 TEACHER

go.hrw.com
Student Resources
KEYWORD: SD7 CH23

- Document-based Questions
- Interactive Multimedia Activities

- Current Events
- Chapter-based Internet Activities
- and more!

Holt Premier
Online Student Edition
Complete online support for interactivity, assessment, and reporting

- Interactive Maps and Notebook
- Standardized Test Prep
- Homework Practice and Research Activities Online

CHAPTER 23 PLANNING GUIDE

Before You Teach

The Big Picture
Robert D. Schulzinger

Origins of World War II World War I left a legacy of bitterness in many European nations. In the years after the war, European and Asian nationalist leaders gained popular support by promising to restore their nations' glory through military conquest. In the 1930s Fascist Italy attacked Ethiopia, Nazi Germany defied the Versailles peace treaty of 1919 by rearming and annexing Austria, and Japan attacked China. The League of Nations did little to stop this aggression. When Adolf Hitler demanded that the northern portion of Czechoslovakia be ceded to Germany in 1938, British and French leaders sought to appease the Nazi dictator to avoid war. But appeasement failed, and in September 1939 Germany launched a blitzkrieg against Poland.

American Neutrality Many Americans regretted their country's participation in the Great War and vowed to remain neutral in the face of new threats to peace. President Franklin D. Roosevelt sympathized with the victims of aggression and with Britain and France, but he wanted to avoid arousing a popular backlash among isolationists. He declared his goal of making the United States the arsenal of democracy, and he coordinated diplomatic and military policy with British prime minister Winston Churchill.

The United States Enters World War II War came suddenly to America on the morning of Sunday, December 7, 1941, when Japanese planes bombed the U.S. Navy's Pacific fleet at Pearl Harbor, Hawaii. Japan's military leaders hoped a crippling blow to the United States military would permit Japan to dominate Asia and the Pacific. Instead, the surprise attack united American public opinion in favor of war against Japan in the Pacific and Germany and Italy in Europe. The United States mobilized for war. Millions entered the armed forces, and science, industry, and labor joined to produce the tools needed to win.

Recent Scholarship

Evaluating Roosevelt President Franklin D. Roosevelt has been praised as a supreme realist who masterfully managed American foreign relations, and condemned as a devious manipulator and an incompetent manager. Most historians endorse the conclusion reached by Warren F. Kimball in *The Juggler: Franklin Roosevelt as Wartime Statesman* (1991), which argues that Roosevelt skillfully adjusted to the international and political realities of his day in order to contain Hitler and aid Britain. Frank Freidel argues in *Franklin D. Roosevelt: A Rendezvous with Destiny* (1990), that the president moved the United States toward collective security while trying to avoid entry into the war.

Differentiating Instruction

 Differentiated Instruction Teacher Management System
- Lesson Plans for Differentiated Instruction
- Differentiated Instructional Benchmarking Guides
- Interactive Reader and Study Guide

 Spanish Chapter Summaries Audio CD Program

 Online Chapter Summaries in Spanish

Student Edition on Audio CD Program

 Differentiated Instruction Modified Worksheets and Tests CD-ROM
- Vocabulary Flash Cards
- Modified Vocabulary Builder Activities
- Modified Chapter Review Activity
- Modified Chapter Test

OSP One-Stop Planner CD-ROM
- ExamView Test Generator (English and Spanish)
- PuzzlePro
- Quiz Show for ExamView
- Transparencies and Videos

TE Differentiated Activities in the Teacher's Edition
- Hitler's Rise to Power, p. 741
- The Fall of France, p. 748
- Opportunities and Challenges for African Americans, p. 762

Reading Like a Historian

Sam Wineburg

History and Truth

In April 2005, demonstrations rocked China. In Beijing, 20,000 jeering protesters stormed the Japanese embassy, pelting it with eggs and water bottles. In Shenzhen, in China's Guangdong province, rioters defaced Japanese-owned businesses, scuffling with police and demanding a boycott of Japanese goods. Behind this rage was an unlikely cause: a high school history textbook.

"An Incident"

In the early months of 2005, Japan's Ministry of Education had approved a text that glossed over the Japanese atrocities in Nanjing, China, from 1937–38, during which (according to our chapter's estimate) some 300,000 Chinese citizens were raped, butchered, and killed. According to the Japanese account, Nanjing was merely "an incident."

Faced with conflicting factual statements, some students will be confused. There will be those who seek refuge in relativism, concluding that history is unknowable and that differences in interpretation can be explained simply by knowing where a person "comes from."

Such positions endanger democratic principles. If getting to the bottom of things doesn't matter, if truth's nothing more than a language game, then Orwell's Ministry of Truth—where four extended fingers equals five—awaits us at the next exit.

The figure of 200,000 to 300,000 deaths at Nanjing was the conclusion of Allied tribunals conducted in Japan and China at the war's end. Five Japanese officers were sentenced to death for their roles in these atrocities.

History is Whitewashed

But by the mid-1970s, political winds had changed in Japan and ultra-nationalists, once again, began to rumble. Seeking to whitewash Japan's wartime aggression, they issued wholesale denials of these crimes. The title of Suzuki Akira's best-selling book left no doubt where he stood: *The Illusion of the "Nanjing Massacre."* The attempt to cleanse Japanese history even reached official levels. A 500-page army history of WWII, published in 1975, provided no mention of Nanjing in its main text, relegating these events to a ponderous footnote.

But something unpredictable started to happen. The more time elapsed, the more historians started to learn. Japanese soldiers, veterans of these atrocities, began to grow older and their consciences started to beat louder. They began to unburden their guilt by telling their stories in public. Likewise, diaries by high-ranking military officers, long hidden in dusty attics or dank cellars, began to surface, and with them came candid admissions of official culpability in these events.

What remains in dispute is the exact number of people who lost their lives in Nanjing, and the exact chain of command that lead to these events. But other questions can be considered settled. Whereas in 1990, George Washington University historian Daquing Yang despaired that truth would "never be found," a decade later he revised his position, announcing an "emerging convergence" shared by historians from China, the United States—and Japan. The question of whether "Japanese troops committed a variety of atrocities on a massive scale in Nanjing some sixty years ago" was now, wrote Yang, "beyond any doubt."

History's Dark Side

If that's the case, why does a government-approved textbook seek to minimize Japan's role? One reason is there are still government censors in Japan who monitor and approve the content of all history textbooks. But even deeper is the cultural belief that sharing the dark side of one's history with young people will lessen their love of country and loyalty to it.

Chalmers Johnson, president of University of San Francisco's Japan Policy Research Institute and former Berkeley professor, called this stance "one of the most curiously self-defeating policies of any former belligerent government." For truth, like a running brook, must eventually find its outlet. And when it does, when citizens realize they've been willfully misled by their government, their love of country is not enhanced, but diminished beyond measure.

From essay: "Some Thoughts on the Nanjing Massacre" by Chalmers Johnson from *Japan Policy Research Institute Critique,* vol. VI, no. 1, January 2000. Published by University of San Francisco Center for the Pacific Rim, San Francisco, 2000.

From essay: "Convergence or Divergence? Recent Historical Writings on the Rape of Nanjing" by Daquing Yang from *The American Historical Review,* vol. 104, no. 3, June 1999.

Standards Focus

Social Studies Competency Goals
Goal 10 The learner will analyze United States involvement in World War II and the war's influence on international affairs in following decades.
 10.01, 10.02, 10.03

The Big Idea and Essential Questions

To foster student understanding of this chapter's big idea, design your lesson to address each section's essential question.

Big Idea In the uneasy peace following World War I, Germany, Italy, and Japan fell under the sway of leaders promising power and glory. Their aggression would plunge the world into war once more by the end of the 1930s.

Essential Questions

1. How did the effects of World War I lead to the rise of new kinds of aggressive leaders in Europe and Asia?

2. How did German actions lead to the outbreak of World War II?

3. How was the United States eventually drawn into World War II?

4. What effect did U.S. entry have on American industry and the military?

CHAPTER
23 1939–1941

World War II ERUPTS

 THE BIG PICTURE The Treaty of Versailles ending World War I created an uneasy peace. Germany, Italy, and Japan fell under the sway of leaders promising order and glory. By the end of the 1930s, their aggression would plunge the world once more into war.

NC

North Carolina Standards

Social Studies Objectives

10.01 Elaborate on the causes of World War II and reasons for United States entry into the war.

10.02 Identify military, political, and diplomatic turning points of the war and determine their significance to the outcome and aftermath of the conflict.

10.03 Describe and analyze the effects of the war on American economic, social, political, and cultural life.

Language Arts Objectives

2.01 Research and analyze ideas, events, and/or movements related to United States culture by:
• locating facts and details for purposeful elaboration

3.01 Use language persuasively in addressing a particular issue by:
• establishing and defending a point of view.

 Skills FOCUS **READING LIKE A HISTORIAN**

A crowd salutes German dictator Adolf Hitler as he leads a Reich Party Day celebration in the city of Nuremberg. The annual rallies were held in the city from 1933 to 1938. *Reich* is the German word for *empire*.
Interpreting Visuals What is the focus of this event? What might its purpose be?
See Skills Handbook, p. H30

736

U.S.

September 1939 Congress passes cash-and-carry law to ease the sale of arms to countries at war.

1939

 World

September 1939 Germany invades Poland.

Introduce the Chapter

At Level

World War II Erupts

1. Review with students the way in which World War I began and ended with an Allied victory. Remind students that the war was very expensive in financial and human costs. It had been called the "war to end all wars."

2. Ask students how they might feel if their family had lost members in a war, the family had lost its savings and jobs during the ongoing Depression, and another war seemed about to break out in Europe.

3. Have students suggest reasons Americans might have wanted to steer clear of any further involvement in a European war.

4. Tell students that this was the situation facing the nation in the late 1930s. When Pearl Harbor was bombed, however, the U.S. declared war and joined its Allies in the battle for democracy. **LS Verbal-Linguistic**

Alternative Assessment Handbook, Rubric 11: Discussions

History's Impact video program
Watch the video to understand the impact of isolationism.

March 1941
Congress establishes the lend-lease program to deliver arms to Great Britain on credit.

December 1940
President Roosevelt declares the United States an "arsenal of democracy."

December 7, 1941
Japanese bomb the U.S. Navy's Pacific Fleet at Pearl Harbor, Hawaii.

1940

1941

May 1940
Winston Churchill becomes UK prime minister.

May–June 1940
Germany conquers the Netherlands, Belgium, and France.

October 1940
Battle of Britain ends with Hitler's forces rebuffed.

September 1940
Japan joins Axis alliance with Germany and Italy.

October 1941
General Hideki Tojo becomes Japanese prime minister.

737

Chapter Preview

Reading Like a Historian

Hitler and his Commanders Have students take a moment to examine the image on these pages. What do the figures' uniforms and facial expressions reveal about the German military? What does the location of the photo reveal about the status of the German military in the government? *possible answers—neat, well-tailored uniforms give an impression of orderliness; facial expressions reveal that the military takes itself seriously; location in front of building draped with Nazi flag shows that the military's status in government is high*

Explore the Time Line

1. What events took place in 1941? *U.S.—Lend-Lease Act; Pearl Harbor; Japan—Tojo becomes prime minister*

2. What happened from May to June 1940 in the Netherlands, Belgium, and France? *conquered by Germany*

3. Who was president of the U.S. during World War II? *Franklin D. Roosevelt*

Info to Know

Chamberlain and Appeasement Neville Chamberlain became British prime minister in 1937. In 1938 Chamberlain visited Germany three times, and after the Munich Agreement in which France and Great Britain granted Hitler most of his demands, Chamberlain returned to England as a hero who had secured peace. In 1939, however, Chamberlain gave up the policy of appeasement, and when Germany invaded Poland, Great Britain declared war against Germany.

Answers

Reading Like a Historian *Hitler and his military commanders at a Reich Party Day celebration; to encourage German loyalty to the government*

738 CHAPTER 23

Preteach

Bellringer

The Inside Story. . . Use the **Daily Bellringer Transparency** to help students answer the question.

📦 Daily Bellringer Transparency, Section 1

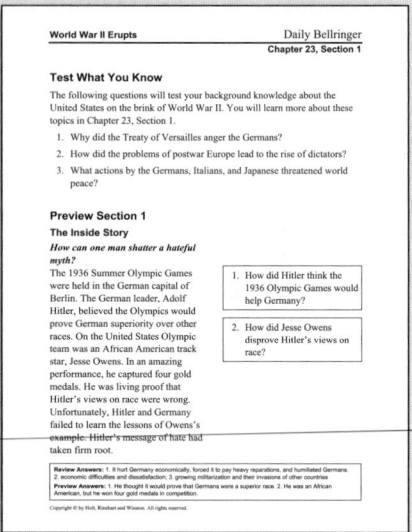

Academic Vocabulary

Review with students the high-use academic term in this section.

ethnic relating to a large group of people sharing a common racial, national, linguistic, or cultural heritage (p. 745)

📝 CRF: Vocabulary Builder Activity, Section 1

Taking Notes

deaths of millions; destruction of numerous cities and farms; nations left unhappy with Treaty of Versailles; Germans lost control of land, had to make payments to other countries, deal with inflation and political turmoil; totalitarian governments arose

---

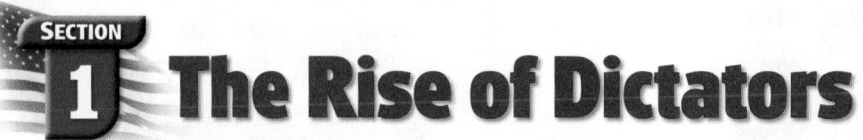

SECTION 1 — The Rise of Dictators

BEFORE YOU READ

MAIN IDEA

The shattering effects of World War I helped set the stage for a new, aggressive type of leader in Europe and Asia.

READING FOCUS

1. How did the aftermath of World War I contribute to political problems in Europe?

2. How did the problems facing Europe in the postwar years lead to the rise of totalitarian leaders?

3. What events exemplify the growing use of military force by totalitarian regimes in the 1930s?

4. What alarming actions did Adolf Hitler take in the mid-1930s?

KEY TERMS AND PEOPLE

inflation
Benito Mussolini
fascism
dictatorship
totalitarian
Adolf Hitler
Francisco Franco
Joseph Stalin
Haile Selassie
Neville Chamberlain

TAKING NOTES As you read, take notes on postwar problems in Europe. Record your notes in a graphic organizer like the one shown here.

Postwar Problems in Europe

THE INSIDE STORY

How can one man shatter a hateful myth? The 1936 Summer Olympic Games were held in the German capital of Berlin. For German leader Adolf Hitler, the event presented a golden opportunity. Hitler had risen to power telling of the greatness of the German people—and of the racial inferiority of certain other groups, such as Africans. The Olympic Games, many Germans believed, would provide proof of this racist idea for the whole world to see.

The U.S. Olympic team included many African American athletes. Among them was track star Jesse Owens. In an amazing performance, he captured gold medals in the 100- and 200-meter dashes, the long jump, and a relay. As he stood on the podium before the German crowd, he was living proof that Hitler's views on race were wrong.

Unfortunately, Hitler and Germany failed to learn the lessons of Owens's example. Hitler's hold on the German people was strong, and his message of hate, anger, and false pride had taken firm root. As you will read, he was merely one of several powerful and ruthless leaders to emerge during this time of turmoil and uncertainty. ◼

▶ **Jesse Owens (center) stands above his competitors at the 1936 Olympic Games.**

The "Master Race" Loses the Race

738 CHAPTER 23

Teach the Main Idea

At Level

The Rise of Dictators

1. **Teach** Ask students the Reading Focus questions to teach this section.

2. **Apply** Have students scan the section and create a time line of the major events discussed. Students should begin their time lines with Mussolini becomes leader of Italy's government in 1922 and end with *Anschluss* in 1938. You may wish to assign students to work in mixed-ability pairs for this activity.

3. **Review** Review student time lines as a class. Have students correct their work and retain the time lines as a study tool.

4. **Practice/Homework** Have students create illustrations that depict each event on their time lines. Have volunteers present and explain their illustrations to the class.
   LS Visual-Spatial, Verbal-Linguistic

📝 Alternative Assessment Handbook, Rubric 36: Time Lines

Europe after World War I

In an earlier chapter, you read about some of the difficulties facing the United States after World War I. Economic problems, social change, and the threat of communism helped produce a Red Scare—a fear of aliens and radicals.

Europe faced even more challenges at the end of the war. The war had caused the deaths of millions and the destruction of numerous cities and farms. The European economy was in ruins. It would take years to recover.

Problems with peace The Treaty of Versailles (ver-SY), which had brought the war to an end, left many European nations dissatisfied. France in particular had hoped to use the peace settlement to severely weaken Germany. They felt the treaty was not harsh enough on the Germans. Italy was also unhappy with the treaty. The Italians had been on the winning side in the war. They had hoped to be rewarded with territory as part of the treaty. Instead, they were largely ignored during the peace talks.

German outrage Germany suffered the most as a result of the Treaty of Versailles. Its terms did serious damage to the German economy. It also left the German people—and the German military—feeling humiliated. This helped usher in a period of political upheaval.

The treaty forced Germany to give up control of some of its land, including major industrial regions. As you read earlier, the treaty also required Germany to make heavy reparation payments to other countries. In the early 1920s, these factors helped bring about a period of severe **inflation,** or rising prices. Prices for goods increased at an incredible rate. The chart on this page shows the effects of this economic disaster. By 1923 German currency had simply ceased to have any meaningful value. For millions of Germans, a lifetime's worth of hard work and savings had vanished.

Germany also experienced political turmoil after the war. As you have read before, Communists and Socialists tried to take control of Germany in 1918 and early 1919. This effort failed, and Germany soon established a democratic system of government led by less radical elements. This government was known as the Weimar (VY-mahr) Republic, after the German city where it was established.

German money lost so much value in the early 1920s that children used currency as building blocks.

TALES OF GERMAN HYPERINFLATION

One American dollar could buy about 9 German marks in 1919. At the height of the panic, a dollar could buy more than 4 trillion marks.

By 1923, some 300 paper mills and 2,000 printing presses were working around the clock to print money.

Prices rose extremely fast. One customer at a cafe ordered a cup of coffee at 5,000 marks. By the time he ordered his second, the price had risen to 7,000 marks.

A typical loaf of bread cost about 1 mark in 1920. By November 1, 1923, that bread might cost 3 billion marks. Two weeks later, the price for the bread would have risen to 80 billion marks.

The Weimar Republic, however, was not a very strong government. It faced opposition from the political far left—Communists—and from the far right, which was antidemocratic. Another problem was unhappiness in the German military. It had been greatly reduced in size and power as part of the Treaty of Versailles. These factors helped make the Weimar Republic weak and unstable.

READING CHECK Identifying Cause and Effect How did the Treaty of Versailles affect Europe after World War I?

2 How did the problems facing Europe in the postwar years lead to the rise of totalitarian leaders? *They expressed people's anger; promised return to greatness; people were willing to give up basic freedoms in return for the hope of future glory.*

Totalitarian Leaders Arise

Identify Name three things that Mussolini and Hitler had in common. *Any three of the following: outraged by the Treaty of Versailles; dynamic speakers; strong leaders; stressed nationalism; used political skills and violence when necessary to gain power; glorified by citizens; totalitarian dictators*

Summarize What is the myth of the Aryan master race? *Hitler's idea that the Germanic people were superior*

Evaluate Why do you think there was not more support for democratic governments in Italy and Germany? *possible answers—people were looking for new leaders; wanted problems solved; felt democracy had failed them*

📄 CRF: Biography: Kurt Weill

📄 CRF: Literature Activity: "Nightmare at Noon" by Stephen Vincent Benét

Totalitarian Leaders Arise

European struggles and dissatisfaction during the postwar years had a major effect on European politics. In some countries, a certain type of leader emerged—one who reflected and expressed the people's bitterness and anger. These leaders promised a return to greatness for their nations. This vision was so appealing to their unhappy people that many were willing to give up basic freedoms in return for the hope of future glory.

Mussolini and the birth of fascism

The first of these new leaders to emerge in Europe was the Italian **Benito Mussolini**. He had begun his public life in the early 1900s as a member of a Socialist party in Italy. Unlike many of his fellow Socialists, however, he supported Italy's entry into World War I. By the war's end, Mussolini had moved to the far right of Italian politics. He strongly opposed socialism and communism.

Outraged by the Treaty of Versailles, Mussolini founded a new Italian political party—the National Fascist Party. The term *fascist* comes from a Latin word for "a bundle of rods tied together." The ancient Romans had used this bundle as a symbol of their state. The single rod, Roman thinking went, could be easily broken. When tied together with other rods, however, it was strong.

For Mussolini, **fascism** was a system of government that stressed the glory of the state. He summed up the principle of fascism with the slogan, "Everything in the State, nothing outside the State, nothing against the State." The rights and concerns of individuals were of little importance.

HISTORY'S VOICES

❝ Anti-individualistic, the Fascist conception of life stresses the importance of the State and accepts the individual only in so far as his interests coincide with those of the State. ❞

—Benito Mussolini and Giovanni Gentile, *The Doctrine of Fascism*, 1932

After World War I, Mussolini used his dynamic public speaking skill to win a seat in Italy's parliament. His vision of a strong, orderly Italy appealed to many people. He also encouraged the use of violence against Communists and Socialists, whom many Italians blamed for the disorder of postwar Italy. By these means, Mussolini gained wide support. In 1922 he became leader of the government.

Europe's New Dictators

Skills Focus: Making Inferences   `At Level`

Reading Skill

Interviewing Mussolini

1. Guide students in a discussion of Mussolini's rise to power.

2. Have students prepare an interview with Benito Mussolini for a profile in a news magazine that could have been published in 1922.

3. Have each student write ten questions that they would ask Mussolini about his rise to power and his plans for Italy. Then have

students use the material in the text to write Mussolini's answers to those questions.

4. Ask volunteers to read their "interviews" to the class. As an extension, ask pairs of students to enact their interviews. **LS Verbal-Linguistic, Kinesthetic**

📄 Alternative Assessment Handbook, Rubric 19: Magazines

Once in power, Mussolini established a **dictatorship**—government by a leader or group that holds unchallenged power and authority. He allowed no other political parties and ruthlessly crushed opponents. His government controlled newspapers, schools, and businesses. All power flowed through the man Italians referred to as *Il Duce* (il DOO-chay)—"the leader." Under this **totalitarian** regime, Mussolini had total control over daily life in Italy.

Hitler's rise to power Another of Europe's aggressive new leaders was Austrian-born **Adolf Hitler**, who had an unremarkable early life. An unsuccessful art student, he was rejected by the Austrian military because they thought him too weak to carry a weapon. With the start of World War I, however, Hitler volunteered for the German army. There he built a solid record as a soldier.

Hitler's anger about the Treaty of Versailles led him into politics. He joined a small political party known as the National Socialists, or Nazis. The party attracted many former soldiers and others who were unhappy with conditions in Germany. It was during this time that

Hitler (left) and Mussolini (above) both used cunning, violence, and repression to achieve and maintain power. Both also possessed a theatrical speaking style that enabled them to achieve great influence over their audiences.

Hitler discovered his talent for public speaking and leadership. Under his guidance, the Nazis gained influence in German politics.

Hitler, however, was impatient for change. In 1923 he organized an effort to seize power in Germany by force. This revolt failed. As a result, Hitler was imprisoned for nine months of a five-year sentence.

While in prison, he produced a book called *Mein Kampf*—German for "My Struggle." The book outlined Hitler's major political ideas. Like Mussolini, Hitler stressed nationalism and devotion to the state. He dreamed of uniting all the Germans of Europe in a great empire. "Germany will either be a world power or there will be no Germany," he wrote.

In *Mein Kampf*, Hitler expressed a belief in the racial superiority of Germanic peoples, whom he called Aryans. In addition, he blamed Jews for many of Germany's problems and believed that they threatened the purity of the Aryan race. (You will read more about Hitler's beliefs in the next chapter.)

HISTORY'S VOICES

❝If we pass all the causes of the German collapse in review, the ultimate and most decisive remains the failure to recognize the racial problem and especially the Jewish menace.❞
—Adolf Hitler, *Mein Kampf*, 1924

When he got out of prison, Hitler was determined to gain power through peaceful means. Seizing on public discontent and offering an appealing vision of German greatness, Hitler gradually built support. By 1933 the Nazis were the most powerful party in the nation. Hitler became Germany's chancellor, a top position in the government.

Hitler now moved to establish himself as a totalitarian dictator. Using his political skills—and violence when necessary—he managed to eliminate his political opponents. Meanwhile, Hitler continued to spread the myth of Aryan greatness and the coming German empire. At the center of this myth was Hitler himself. As with Mussolini in Italy, Hitler the man was glorified above all other Germans.

Hitler also began secretly to build up the German armed forces. He knew that these would be useful to him as he sought to fulfill his goal of expanding German territory. The German people, Hitler explained, needed more "living space" in which to grow and prosper.

Direct Teach

Differentiating Instruction

Learners Having Difficulty

Below Level

1. Draw the graphic organizer at right for students to see. Omit the italicized answers.

2. Have students work in pairs to fill in the graphic organizer with the steps that led to Hitler becoming a totalitarian dictator.

3. Have volunteers list the steps that led to Hitler becoming dictator of Germany. Complete the master chart for the class to see. Have students correct their work and retain the chart as a study tool. **LS Interpersonal, Visual-Spatial**

Alternative Assessment Handbook, Rubric 13: Graphic Organizers

Graphic Organizer Transparency

Hitler's views win him many supporters

Hitler becomes chancellor of Germany

Nazis become most powerful party

Hitler becomes dictator by eliminating political opponents

Totalitarian Leaders Arise

Recall What other countries had powerful and nationalistic regimes prior to World War II? *Spain, Soviet Union, Japan*

Contrast What was the major difference between the totalitarian regimes in the Soviet Union and those in Italy and Germany? *The Soviet Union had a Communist regime; Italy and Germany were Fascist states.*

Linking to Today

Identify What present-day countries are governed by powerful and controlling regimes? *possible answers—China, Cuba, Libya, Syria, Vietnam*

Info to Know

Joseph Stalin Stalin was born Iosif Dzhugashvili in 1879. He took the name Stalin, which means "steel," in 1912, when he began writing articles for a Communist newspaper.

Answers

Linking to Today *possible answer—No, because dictators often suppress their people and country in many ways; some democratic nations will not trade with totalitarian regimes.*

Reading Check *social, political, and economic unrest from World War I; charismatic leaders gained support for their causes*

Linking TO Today

Totalitarian Dictators

Totalitarian governments are not just a part of the historical past. Today a number of countries are controlled by dictatorial governments.

In Africa, the former British colony of Rhodesia became the independent nation of Zimbabwe in 1980. A guerrilla fighter turned politician named Robert Mugabe gained power.

At first, many people saw him as a reformer. As time passed, however, Mugabe came under sharp criticism. His land-redistribution policies drove out white farm owners and broke up large farms into small plots of land. In recent years, Mugabe has used fear and violence to limit voting rights.

North Korea also has a totalitarian government. Ruled by Kim Jong Il, the government controls all television and radio broadcasts. It does not permit any criticism of the nation's so-called Dear Leader. Rigid economic policies have led to more than 10 years of famine.

In Myanmar, also called Burma, the totalitarian government is run by a group of military officers. The government has suppressed prodemocracy movements since 1988 and ignored the results of a legislative election in 1990.

Drawing Conclusions Would you expect a country with a totalitarian government to have a thriving economy? Explain.

North Korean leader Kim Jong Il

Other regimes Some of the same forces that helped Mussolini and Hitler gain totalitarian power also helped create powerful regimes in other countries. For example, Spain erupted in civil war in the 1930s. Out of this conflict, Fascist general **Francisco Franco** came to power. You will read more about the Spanish Civil War shortly.

In the Soviet Union, communism was already established when **Joseph Stalin** came to power in the mid-1920s. Communism and fascism represent opposite political extremes. Yet there were similarities between the Soviet system under Stalin and the Fascist systems. Like the Fascists, Stalin violently crushed his political opponents.

Also like Hitler and Mussolini, Joseph Stalin created a myth of his own greatness. Throughout the Soviet Union, towns and cities were renamed for him. His portrait was displayed everywhere. "[W]e regard ourselves as the happiest of mortals," gushed one writer in the newspaper *Pravda*, "because we are the contemporary of a man who never had an equal in world history." Stalin's domination of all aspects of Soviet life made him one of the era's most notorious totalitarian dictators.

Japan was another country torn by political and economic conflict. In the early 1930s, military leaders used violence to gain control over the government. They, too, were inspired by nationalistic dreams of Japanese greatness. Such dreams would soon lead to war.

READING CHECK **Comparing** What common factors contributed to the rise of the totalitarian leaders who emerged after World War I?

Totalitarian Governments and Military Force

A common feature of the powerful postwar leaders was a willingness to use violence to gain power. Many were also willing to use military force against other nations.

Japan and Manchuria Among the problems facing Japan in the 1920s was the limited size of its territory. The islands of Japan were growing crowded. Many Japanese wanted to expand their territory and gain greater access to wealth and resources. This desire grew even stronger as a result of the worldwide economic depression of the 1930s.

THE IMPACT TODAY

Government

In 2003 the American-led attack on Iraq was meant in part to remove the totalitarian dictator Saddam Hussein. Like Mussolini, Hitler, and Stalin, Saddam glorified himself with statues and portraits throughout Iraq.

742 CHAPTER 23

Skills Focus: Comparing and Contrasting

Below Level

Reading Skill

Standard English Mastery

Stalin and Hitler

1. Have students work in mixed-ability pairs to create a chart that shows similarities and differences between Stalin and Hitler.

2. Have volunteers share the information with the class. Create a class chart, and have students correct their work.

3. Have students use the information in their charts to write a short essay in which they

compare and contrast the two dictators.

4. Have volunteers read their essays to the class.

LS **Interpersonal, Visual-Spatial**

Alternative Assessment Handbook, Rubric 9: Comparing and Contrasting

Graphic Organizer Transparency

At this time, Japan's government was under civilian control. Many Japanese, however, were unhappy with their leaders. Dissatisfaction was especially high among members of the military who held strong nationalist beliefs.

Some Japanese generals decided it was time to act. In 1931 the army invaded the Chinese province of Manchuria—without the approval of the Japanese government. The goal was to seize Manchuria's land and resources for the use of the Japanese people. Japan's government ordered the army to end the action. The army officers simply refused to obey the order.

The takeover of Manchuria demonstrated the weakness of the Japanese government and the strength of Japan's nationalists. Over the next several years, the military would expand its influence over the government, in part by assassinating its political enemies. In general, the Japanese public supported the increasingly powerful military. As in Germany and Italy, the Japanese people were beginning to believe in the nationalists' dream of expansion.

The League of Nations strongly criticized Japan for the invasion of Manchuria. In response, Japan simply withdrew from the League of Nations, which was unable or unwilling to take any strong action against Japan. The powerlessness of the League was clear for the world to see.

Italy invades Ethiopia The weakness of the League was soon confirmed by events elsewhere. In 1935 Mussolini's Italy invaded the East African nation of Ethiopia.

Italy's history with Ethiopia was several decades old. Italian efforts to establish a colony there in the late 1800s had ended in a crushing military defeat at the hands of the Ethiopians.

Italy did manage to keep several smaller colonies in East Africa. Some Italians, however, held on to bitter feelings toward Ethiopia for decades.

Those feelings resurfaced when Mussolini came to power with grand plans to rebuild an Italian empire. In 1935 he used a dispute about the border between Ethiopia and an Italian colony as an excuse to launch an invasion.

The Ethiopians were unable to resist the more powerful Italian forces, and Italy soon conquered the country. Ethiopian emperor **Haile Selassie** personally asked the League of Nations for help.

HISTORY'S VOICES

❝It is collective security. It is the very existence of the League of Nations. It is the confidence that each State is to place in international treaties. It is the value of promises made to small States that their integrity and their independence shall be respected and ensured.... In a word, it is international morality that is at stake.❞

—Haile Selassie, Speech to League of Nations, June 1936

Selassie's words failed to sway the League. Again, the international community was unwilling to take a strong stand against aggression.

American leaders, meanwhile, spoke out against Italy's actions, but there was little public support for doing more. President Franklin Roosevelt was unwilling to take formal steps to punish Mussolini.

The Spanish Civil War Spain in the mid-1930s was troubled by fierce political conflict. On the left were Communists. On the right were Fascists and Nationalists. Most Spaniards held political views somewhere in between these extremes.

In 1936 this conflict led to civil war. The war soon attracted interest and involvement from

THE SPANISH CIVIL WAR

Spanish Civil War
1,000,000 DEAD
$20,000,000,000 LOST
32 MONTHS OF TERROR
RUINED CITIES
WRECKED HOMES
BOMBED FACTORIES
LOST TREASURES
FARMS INJURED

Skills FOCUS READING LIKE A HISTORIAN

The skeleton is dressed in traditional Spanish clothing.

Interpreting Political Cartoons What point is being made by the skeleton's list?

See **Skills Handbook**, p. H31

• **Direct Teach** •

Reading Focus

❸ What events exemplify the growing use of military force by totalitarian regimes in the 1930s? *Japanese invasion of Manchuria; the Italian invasion of Ethiopia; Spanish Civil War*

Totalitarian Governments and Military Force

Identify What is Manchuria? *Chinese province that was taken over by Japan in 1931*

Analyze Why do you think the Japanese army was able to take over Manchuria? *possible answer—because the Chinese army was weak, while the Japanese army was growing in strength*

Make Inferences Why didn't the League of Nations take action when Japan took control of Manchuria and Italy invaded Ethiopia? *League of Nations had no military arm or power to force member nations to obey international law.*

Info to Know

Spanish Civil War Approximately 3,000 Americans joined the fight against fascism. Although these Americans came from every part of the United States, most of them came from urban, industrial areas where they had been exposed to radical political ideas. The Americans, many of whom fought in a group called the Abraham Lincoln Battalion, were not well-trained soldiers. They suffered high casualty rates; about one third of the American volunteers were killed.

Skills Focus: Interpreting Political Cartoons

At Level

Reading Like a Historian Skill
Ethiopia and Spain

1. Have students review the information in the text about the Italian invasion of Ethiopia and the Spanish Civil War. Discuss the political cartoon about the Spanish Civil War with students to ensure that students have interpreted it correctly.

2. Have students create two political cartoons. One cartoon should be about the costs and losses endured during the Spanish Civil War. The second cartoon should represent the

viewpoint of Ethiopians, whose country has been invaded.

3. Have volunteers present and explain their cartoons to the class.

4. Guide students in a discussion of the costs of war to a nation and the failure of the League of Nations to help Ethiopia. **LS Interpersonal, Visual-Spatial**

📖 Alternative Assessment Handbook, Rubric 27: Political Cartoons

Answers

Reading Like a Historian *the high price of the Spanish Civil War*

④ What alarming actions did Adolf Hitler take in the mid-1930s? *rebuilt military; sent troops into the Rhineland, Austria, and the Sudetenland*

Hitler Takes Action

Explain How did Hitler justify rebuilding Germany's military? *said that he was helping stop spread of communism*

Define What was Anschluss? *forced union of Austria with Germany*

Evaluate Why do you think the British and French were so eager to avoid war that they allowed Hitler to violate the Treaty of Versailles and international law? *possible answers—devastation of World War I; determination to avoid another war; maintain peace; thought each violation would be the last one*

Teaching Tip

Students will be familiar with the term *civil war* in reference to the American war between the Union and the Confederacy. Tell students that the term refers to any war between geographic regions or political factions within the same country.

Answers

Reading Like a Historian *possible answer—Chamberlain did not believe that Britain should reject cooperation with dictators if it led to peace.*

Reading Check *did nothing; League was powerless to take strong action against aggression*

744

Appeasement

Prime Minister Chamberlain declared himself "a man of peace to the depths of my soul."

When Chamberlain returned from his meeting with Hitler declaring "peace for our time," Churchill voiced a quite different opinion of events.

❝ [W]e should seek by all means in our power to avoid war, by analyzing possible causes, by trying to remove them, by discussion in a spirit of collaboration and good will. I cannot believe that such a programme would be rejected by the people of this country, even if it does mean the establishment of personal contact with dictators. ❞

Neville Chamberlain, 1938

❝ The Prime Minister desires to see cordial relations between this country and Germany.... You must have diplomatic and correct relations, but there can never be friendship between the British democracy and the Nazi Power. ❞

Winston Churchill, 1938

Skills FOCUS **READING LIKE A HISTORIAN**

Drawing Conclusions How does Chamberlain's comment hint at why Churchill's warnings went unheeded in 1938?

See Skills Handbook, p. H12

---

many other countries in Europe and in North America. For example, Fascist Italy and Nazi Germany sent forces and equipment to fight for the Nationalists, who were led by General Francisco Franco. Opposing the Nationalists were the the so-called Republicans, who controlled the government at the start of the war. They had the support of the Soviet Union, which provided arms and equipment. In addition, volunteers from the United States and many other countries joined the fight on the Republican side.

The fighting in the Spanish Civil War was bloody and brutal. Many hundreds of thousands of people died. This included several hundred American participants in the fighting. By 1939, however, Franco's Nationalists had defeated the Republicans. Spain came under the control of a Fascist dictator.

READING CHECK **Summarizing** How did the League of Nations respond to Japan's and Italy's use of military force?

Hitler Takes Action

As soon as Hitler gained power in Germany, he secretly began to rebuild the German military. Before long, however, he was openly stating his plan to re-arm Germany. This was in direct violation of the Treaty of Versailles. Despite this, Hitler managed to convince Great Britain and France to tolerate his actions. In 1935, for example, the British agreed to allow Germany to rebuild its naval forces, including submarines. Hitler claimed that he was building German military strength in order to resist the spread of communism. This was a goal the British supported. In fact, he was already committed to using war to expand his nation.

Militarizing the Rhineland Under the Treaty of Versailles, Germany was required to keep its troops out of an area in the Rhine River valley along the French border. This was meant to protect France against possible German aggression. In 1936, however, Hitler violated

---

Skills Focus: Analyzing Bias in Historical Interpretation [At Level]

Reading Like a Historian Skill
Anschluss

1. Guide students in a discussion of Hitler's early actions that violated the terms of the Treaty of Versailles, including moving troops into the Rhineland, forcing a union with Austria, and annexing the Sudetenland.

2. Have students write two journal entries. One entry should be from the viewpoint of a high school student living in Austria in 1938 who supports *Anschluss*. The second entry should be written from the viewpoint of an

Austrian student who supports the Austrian government's position and who believes that *Anschluss* will lead to a disaster for Austria.

3. Have volunteers read their journal entries to the class. **[LS]** **Verbal-Linguistic, Logical-Mathematical**

📖 Alternative Assessment Handbook, Rubric 15: Journals

the treaty by sending German troops into the Rhineland. As an excuse, Hitler claimed that a recent French military agreement with the Soviet Union threatened Germany.

France was greatly alarmed by the German action. It was unwilling, however, to take military action against Germany. Britain, for its part, had no interest in going to war over the matter. Germany's troops remained in the Rhineland, and Hitler grew bolder.

The *Anschluss* Two years later, Hitler took action to gain control of neighboring Austria. Hitler was an Austrian by birth. He had long dreamed of uniting all <u>ethnic</u> Germans, including the Austrians. In 1938 he tried to force the Austrian government to agree to *Anschluss* (AHN-shloos)—union with Germany. When the Austrian government refused, Hitler sent troops into the country.

The *Anschluss* was popular among the people of Austria. It was, however, another German violation of the Treaty of Versailles. Germany's neighbors issued strongly worded protests. But they did nothing more to stop Hitler.

The Sudetenland By now, Hitler was confident that no one would act to stop him. Soon after the *Anschluss*, he began plans to gain control of a German-speaking portion of Czechoslovakia called the Sudetenland. First, he encouraged Germans in the Sudetenland to protest against Czechoslovakian rule. Then he began threatening a military attack.

Hoping to end the crisis, British prime minister **Neville Chamberlain** and French premier Edouard Daladier met with Hitler. As in the past, the British and French seemed most interested in avoiding armed conflict. At a meeting in Munich, Chamberlain and Daladier agreed to allow Hitler to annex the Sudetenland—that is, make it part of Germany. Czechoslovakia, which had no representative at the Munich meeting, protested the agreement. Chamberlain, however, boasted of having achieved "peace for our time." In reality, the world was on the verge of war.

ACADEMIC VOCABULARY
ethnic relating to a large group of people sharing a common racial, national, linguistic, or cultural heritage

READING CHECK **Summarizing** Explain how France and Great Britain responded to Hitler's actions in the early to mid-1930s.

go.hrw.com
Online Quiz
Keyword: SD7 HP23

SECTION 1 ASSESSMENT

Reviewing Ideas, Terms, and People

1. a. Describe How did the conclusion of World War I affect the political climate in Europe?
   b. Make Inferences How did the severe **inflation** in Germany affect the population?
   c. Evaluate Why do you think it is important for a peace agreement, such as the Treaty of Versailles, to be regarded as fair by all sides?

2. a. Define Write a brief definition for each of the following terms: **fascism, dictatorship, totalitarian**
   b. Compare What did **Mussolini, Hitler,** and **Stalin** all share in common?
   c. Elaborate Why do you think the three totalitarian dictators worked so hard to build public adoration of themselves?

3. a. Identify What was the significance of Manchuria, Ethiopia, and Spain in the 1930s?
   b. Make Generalizations How did other nations react to the aggression of the Japanese and the Italians?
   c. Evaluate Why do you think the League of Nations was unwilling to stand up to the aggression of the Japanese and the Italians?

4. a. Describe How did Hitler respond to Germany's obligations under the Treaty of Versailles when he became Germany's leader?

b. Compare How did the reaction of Great Britain and France toward Germany compare to their reaction toward Italy and Japan?
c. Predict How do you think the failure to enforce rules of the League of Nations and the Treaty of Versailles will affect Germany in the future?

Critical Thinking

5. Identifying Cause and Effect Copy the chart below and use information from the section to identify the effects of the rise of dictators.

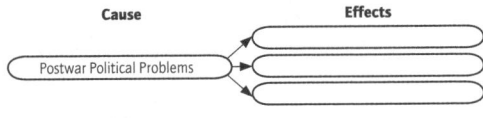

Cause		Effects
Postwar Political Problems		

FOCUS ON WRITING

6. Persuasive Assume the position of a delegate to the League of Nations and deliver a speech in which you argue for or against firm action to enforce the League's promises of protection for places such as Manchuria and Ethiopia.

Europe Erupts in War

Bellringer

The Inside Story. . . Use the **Daily Bellringer Transparency** to help students answer the question.

🖥 Daily Bellringer Transparency, Section 2

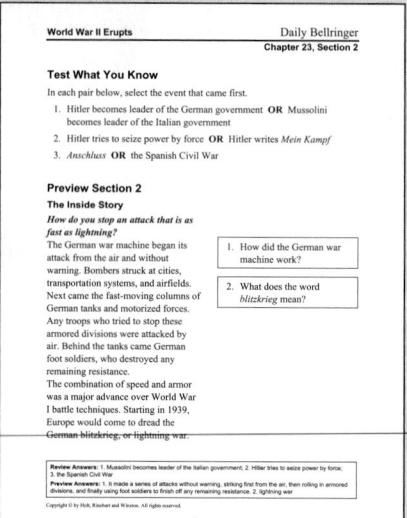

World War II Erupts · Daily Bellringer · Chapter 23, Section 2

Test What You Know

In each pair below, select the event that came first.

1. Hitler becomes leader of the German government **OR** Mussolini becomes leader of the Italian government

2. Hitler tries to seize power by force **OR** Hitler writes *Mein Kampf*

3. *Anschluss* **OR** the Spanish Civil War

Preview Section 2

The Inside Story

How do you stop an attack that is as fast as lightning?

The German war machine began its attack from the air and without warning. Bombers struck at cities, transportation systems, and airfields. Next came the fast-moving columns of German tanks and motorized forces. Any troops who tried to stop these armored divisions were attacked by air. Behind the tanks came German foot soldiers, who destroyed any remaining resistance.

The combination of speed and armor was a major advance over World War I battle techniques. Starting in 1939, Europe would come to dread the German blitzkrieg, or lightning war.

1. How did the German war machine work?

2. What does the word *blitzkrieg* mean?

Review Answers: 1. Mussolini becomes leader of the Italian government; 2. Hitler tries to seize power by force; 3. the Spanish Civil War
Preview Answers: 1. It made a series of attacks without warning, striking first from the air, then rolling in armored divisions, and finally using foot soldiers to finish off any remaining resistance. 2. lightning war

Copyright © by Holt, Rinehart and Winston. All rights reserved.

Academic Vocabulary

Review with students the high-use academic term in this section.

security the promise of safety (p. 747)

🖥 CRF: Vocabulary Builder Activity, Section 2

Taking Notes

German Invasions—Poland, Denmark and Norway, Netherlands and Belgium, France, Air raids on Britain; Allied Response—Germany was too quick, Allies were surprised by quick attack, Allied troops trapped at Dunkirk, France falls, Britain stops the Luftwaffe; Japanese Aggression—brutal war with China, took control of French Indochina

BEFORE YOU READ

MAIN IDEA

Far from being satisfied by the actions of France and Great Britain, Germany turned to force and triggered the start of World War II.

READING FOCUS

1. How did Germany's actions in 1939 trigger the start of World War II?

2. Where did German forces turn after overrunning Poland in 1939?

3. What developments increased tensions between the United States and Japan in East Asia?

KEY TERMS AND PEOPLE

appeasement
Winston Churchill
blitzkrieg
the Allies
Vichy France
Charles de Gaulle
Luftwaffe
Axis Powers
Hideki Tojo

TAKING NOTES As you read, take notes on events that propelled the United States to enter World War II. Record your notes in a graphic organizer like the one shown here.

German Invasions	
Allied Response	
Japanese Aggression	

THE INSIDE STORY

How do you stop an attack that is as fast as lightning? The German war machine began its attack from the air and without warning. Bombers struck at cities, transportation systems, and airfields. Roads became choked with panicked citizens.

Next came the fast-moving columns of German tanks and motorized forces, stabbing deep into the enemy countryside. Defending troops who went out to meet the armored German forces often were attacked by air.

After the tanks came German foot soldiers, fanning out across the land their tanks had just rumbled through. They destroyed or scattered any remaining resistance.

The German method of attack was devastating. The combined effect of speed and armor represented a major innovation over battle techniques used just two decades before in World War I. Starting in 1939, Europe would come to dread the German blitzkrieg, or lightning war. 🖥

HISTORY CLOSE-UP

Blitzkrieg

Aircraft bombed airfields, transportation systems, and cities, crippling defenses.

Fast-moving armored columns struck quickly, driving deeply into enemy territory.

746

Teach the Main Idea
At Level

Europe Erupts in War

1. **Teach** Ask students the Reading Focus questions to teach this section.

2. **Apply** Have students create a sequence chart showing the events that led to World War II and Germany's early military moves.

3. **Review** Have students share their charts with the class, and have students identify turning points in the early stages of the war. Then guide students in a discussion of what effect appeasement may have had on the war.

4. **Practice/Homework** Leaders of other European countries were surprised when Hitler and Stalin signed a nonaggression pact. Have each student write a journal entry about the pact from the viewpoint of a citizen of the Soviet Union living in Moscow in 1939. **LS Visual-Spatial, Logical-Mathematical**

🖥 Alternative Assessment Handbook, Rubrics 13: Graphic Organizers; and 15: Journals

World War II Starts

British prime minister Neville Chamberlain believed that his policy toward Hitler of **appeasement**, or giving in to aggressive demands to maintain peace, had prevented the outbreak of a needless war. "How horrible, fantastic, incredible it is," Chamberlain said after meeting Hitler in Munich, "that we should be digging trenches and trying on gas masks here because of a quarrel in a faraway country." Yet others believed that Hitler was not going to stop after gaining the Sudetenland, as he had promised Chamberlain. One such critic was a rival politician named **Winston Churchill**. He condemned Chamberlain's appeasement as cowardly and likely to lead to war.

Hitler's early moves Churchill was correct. In March 1939 Hitler sent his troops into what remained of Czechoslovakia, capturing it without a fight. Now even Chamberlain realized that Hitler could not be trusted—and that his aggression was far from over.

Hitler's next move was to build alliances that he hoped would help him in the future. First, he established a pact with Italy. Then in August 1939, he announced a nonaggression pact with Stalin's Soviet Union.

With this pact, Hitler had shrewdly won Stalin's agreement to stay out of Germany's way as it continued to expand. In return, Hitler promised not to attack the Soviet Union. He also secretly agreed to give the Soviet Union parts of soon-to-be-conquered territory in Eastern Europe. "I have the world in my pocket!" Hitler triumphantly declared when Stalin agreed to the deal.

This development shocked many in Europe. The British and French had thought that tensions between the Soviets and Germans were rising. They had hoped that Stalin would stand with them against a possible German attack. In fact, the Soviets did fear Hitler's intentions. Stalin, however, believed the deal with the Nazis offered the greatest <u>security</u>.

Hitler attacks Poland Within days of the Nazi-Soviet agreement, Hitler was ready to launch his next strike—the invasion of Poland. To provide an excuse for the attack, Hitler had a German criminal dressed in a Polish military uniform. The man was taken to the German-Polish border and shot. The next morning—September 1, 1939—Germany claimed it had been attacked by Poland, using the dead criminal as proof. German troops immediately launched a massive invasion of Poland.

ACADEMIC VOCABULARY

security the promise of safety

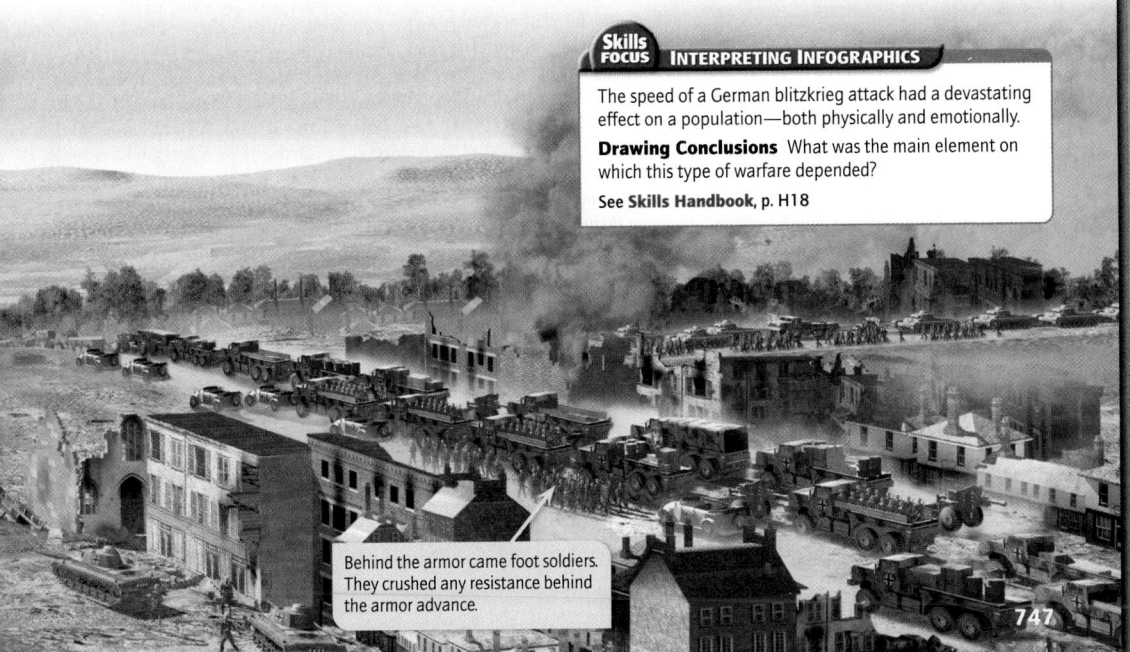

Skills FOCUS — **INTERPRETING INFOGRAPHICS**

The speed of a German blitzkrieg attack had a devastating effect on a population—both physically and emotionally.

Drawing Conclusions What was the main element on which this type of warfare depended?

See **Skills Handbook**, p. H18

Behind the armor came foot soldiers. They crushed any resistance behind the armor advance.

747

Skills Focus: Making Oral Presentations

Reading Like a Historian Skill

Appeasement

1. Have students conduct outside research on the British House of Commons and parliamentary debate. Remind students that parliamentary debate differs from U.S. congressional debate.

2. Divide the class into two groups. Have all students develop speeches that might have been given in Parliament in 1938 when it was debating appeasement. Have one group support Neville Chamberlain and appeasement. The other group will support Winston Churchill,

who opposed appeasement.

3. Have each student develop a strategy, along with the speech, to help convince others to support Chamberlain or Churchill.

4. Conduct a parliamentary debate in class over the issue of appeasement. Have students use their speeches in the debate. **LS Interpersonal, Logical-Mathematical**

Alternative Assessment Handbook, Rubric 10: Debates

❷ Where did German forces turn after overrunning Poland in 1939? *to western Europe*

German Forces Turn to the West

Recall What took place during the *sitzkrieg*? *German military leaders developed plans to invade France through the Ardennes Forest.*

Sequence What countries did Germany overrun between the fall of Poland and the Battle of Britain? *Denmark, Norway, the Netherlands, Belgium, and France*

Predict What might have happened in Western Europe if the Allies had attacked Hitler in 1939 or early 1940? *possible answers—might have been able to save some European countries from Nazi control; might have lost even more troops and equipment*

📄 CRF: Biography: Jan Nowak-Jezioranski

📄 CRF: History and Geography Activity: British Children and the Blitz

Primary Source

"France has lost a battle. But France has not lost a war."

— Charles de Gaulle

Speech, June 18, 1940, London

Info to Know

Churchill and Roosevelt Winston Churchill and Franklin D. Roosevelt met briefly in London in 1918. They began corresponding by letter and telegram in 1939, and by 1945 they had exchanged 1,949 messages.

Answers

Reading Check *March 1939, captured Czechoslovakia; pact with Italy; September 1939, nonaggression pact with the Soviet Union, invasion of Poland*

Earlier you read about German military tactics. The **blitzkrieg**, German for "lightning war," featured an overwhelming combination of air attack and fast-moving armored strikes to drive deep into enemy territory.

The well-trained Germans used the blitzkrieg to devastating effect in Poland. Although the Poles fought bravely, they could not resist the German onslaught. The Polish landscape offered few natural barriers to slow the speedy invasion, and Polish troops were no match for German armor. In some battles, Polish soldiers on horseback carried swords into battle against German tanks. By the end of the month, Poland was in German hands.

READING CHECK **Sequencing** Outline Hitler's actions in 1939 which led to war.

German Forces Turn to the West

On September 3, 1939, Great Britain and France declared war on Germany. They became known as **the Allies**. There was little they could do, however, to slow Hitler in Poland. And even before the fighting there had ended, Hitler was planning his attack on his new enemies.

The Allies, meanwhile, had been forming their own strategy. They decided not to attack Germany. Instead, they would wait for Hitler's next move. They hoped German forces would weaken by trying to break through what they thought were France's strong defenses.

Allied leaders were surprised that Germany did not attack in the winter of 1939–1940. This period of inaction came to be known as the *sitzkrieg*, or the phony war. In fact, German military leaders were busily making plans for an invasion through the dense Ardennes (ahr-DEN) Forest in northern France and Belgium. Thinking that the forest was too rugged for an army to pass through, the French had concentrated their defenses elsewhere. Some troops were stationed to the north of the Ardennes, along France's border with Belgium. French defenses to the south of the Ardennes featured the famed Maginot (MA-zhuh-noh) Line. This was a string of bunkers and fortresses that lined part of the French-German border.

The lull in the fighting ended in April 1940, when Hitler sent his forces into Denmark and

---

Norway. This move was aimed at improving Germany's access to the Atlantic Ocean. Both countries fell with little resistance. The surprised Allies were unable to do much to help. With Denmark and Norway secured, Hitler was now ready to focus on France.

The Netherlands and Belgium fall The Germans finally made their expected strike toward France in May 1940. Their plan worked to perfection. One group of German troops quickly conquered the Netherlands and stormed into Belgium. There they were met by Belgian, British, and French units.

These forces, however, were unable to stop the German assault. By early June, the Germans had trapped hundreds of thousands of Allied soldiers at the French port of Dunkirk. Included were nearly all British forces in France. In a heroic rescue, Allied ships and hundreds of civilian boats plucked nearly 340,000 troops from the coast and carried them to Great Britain. These rescued forces would prove vital to Great Britain's defense.

France falls France, however, was doomed. While Hitler's troops were capturing the Netherlands and Belgium, more German soldiers were carrying out the planned surprise attack through the Ardennes. When they broke through the forest, they easily overwhelmed the thin French force waiting there. The Maginot Line had simply been bypassed.

Having shattered France's defensive plan, Hitler's troops now raced toward Paris, the capital. By the end of June, France had surrendered to Germany and Italy, which had joined the war earlier that month. German forces now occupied much of France. The rest was placed under the control of French officials who cooperated with Hitler. This unoccupied part of France was known as **Vichy** (VEE-shee) **France**. Many other French leaders, led by General **Charles de Gaulle**, fled to Great Britain. There they organized resistance to German and Vichy control of France.

The Battle of Britain Now Great Britain stood alone against what appeared to be an unstoppable German war machine. The nation was now led by Winston Churchill, who had a great gift for inspiring courage and confidence among the British people.

748 CHAPTER 23

Differentiating Instruction

Advanced Learners/GATE

1. Organize the class into small groups. Have each group conduct research on France's fate in June 1940. Have students address the following questions: How much of France, and which parts of it, were under direct German rule? Why was unoccupied France called Vichy France? Who were the leaders of Vichy France and why did they cooperate with Hitler? Who were the Free French, and where were they based? What territories did they control?

2. Have each group create a map showing which parts of France were under German control and which parts were under Vichy control.

3. Have each student write a series of diary entries from the perspective of a high school student living in Vichy France in June 1940. Students should discuss the takeover of France and how life differs under Vichy control. 🅛 **Visual-Spatial, Verbal-Linguistic**

📄 Alternative Assessment Handbook, Rubrics 20: Map Creation; and 15: Journals

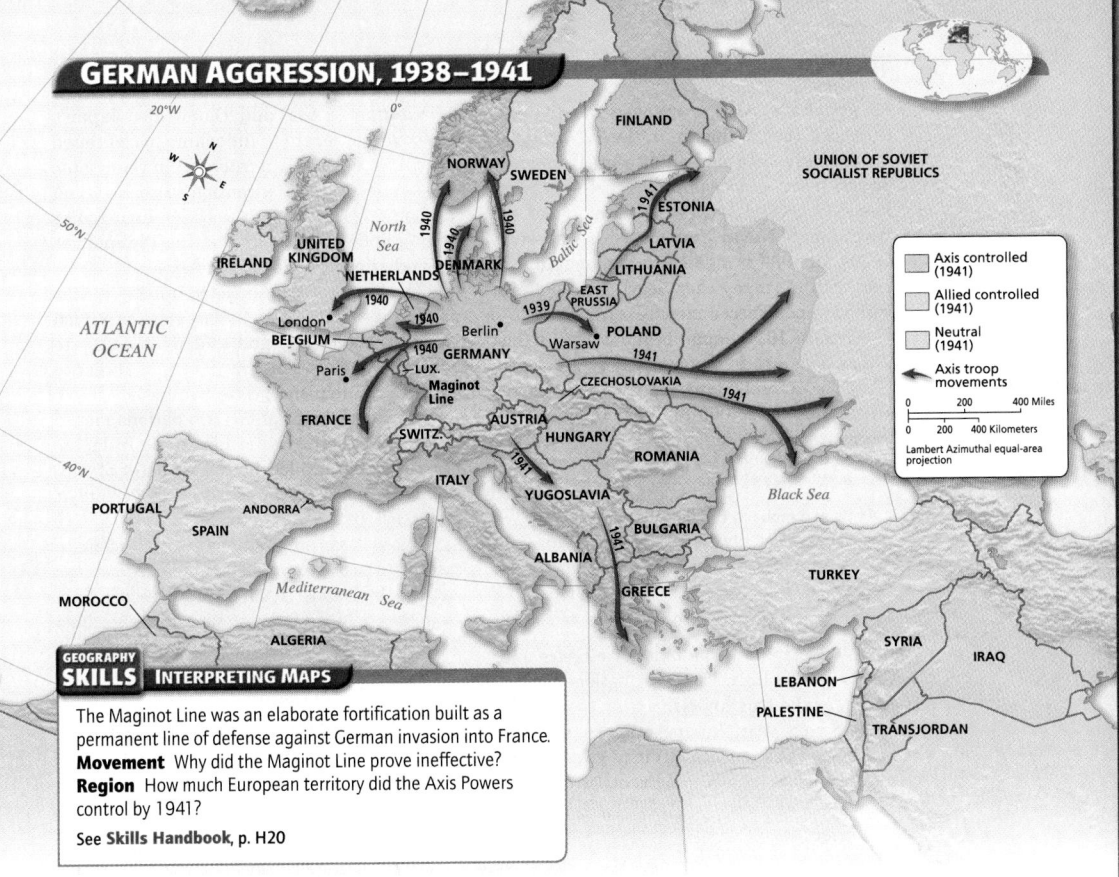

GERMAN AGGRESSION, 1938–1941

FINLAND
NORWAY
SWEDEN
UNION OF SOVIET SOCIALIST REPUBLICS
North Sea
UNITED KINGDOM
IRELAND
DENMARK
ESTONIA
LATVIA
LITHUANIA
EAST PRUSSIA
NETHERLANDS
London
BELGIUM
Berlin
POLAND
Warsaw
GERMANY
Paris
LUX.
Maginot Line
CZECHOSLOVAKIA
FRANCE
SWITZ.
AUSTRIA
HUNGARY
ITALY
ROMANIA
YUGOSLAVIA
Black Sea
BULGARIA
ATLANTIC OCEAN
PORTUGAL
ANDORRA
SPAIN
ALBANIA
TURKEY
GREECE
MOROCCO
Mediterranean Sea
ALGERIA
SYRIA
IRAQ
LEBANON
PALESTINE
TRANSJORDAN

Axis controlled (1941)
Allied controlled (1941)
Neutral (1941)
Axis troop movements

0   200   400 Miles
0   200   400 Kilometers
Lambert Azimuthal equal-area projection

GEOGRAPHY SKILLS   INTERPRETING MAPS

The Maginot Line was an elaborate fortification built as a permanent line of defense against German invasion into France.
Movement Why did the Maginot Line prove ineffective?
Region How much European territory did the Axis Powers control by 1941?
See **Skills Handbook**, p. H20

HISTORY'S VOICES

❝We shall defend our island whatever the cost may be; we shall fight on beaches, landing grounds, in fields, in streets and on the hills. We shall never surrender...❞

—Winston Churchill, speech before the House of Commons, June 4, 1940

As promised, Churchill refused even to consider trying to negotiate a peace agreement with Germany. Hitler, meanwhile, prepared to invade Great Britain.

The first stage of the German plan was to destroy the British Royal Air Force, or RAF. For the first time in the war, the Germans failed. Using radar, a new technology that used radio waves to detect approaching airplanes, the RAF inflicted heavy damage on German planes. As the battle wore on, the German air force, or

Luftwaffe, began bombing London. The goal was to terrorize the public so that they would lose the will to fight. Though thousands of civilians died in the raids, Churchill helped keep the nation's spirits up. "Little does [Hitler] know the spirit of the British nation," he said, "or the tough fiber of the Londoners."

Americans followed the Battle of Britain through the thrilling radio reports of Edward R. Murrow. He was an American reporter stationed in London. His live broadcasts described the air raids as bombs exploded around him.

By late 1940, the Battle of Britain was over. The British had stopped the Luftwaffe. Hitler was forced to call off the attempted invasion.

READING CHECK   **Summarizing** What was Hitler's experience when he turned his forces to the West in 1940?

THE IMPACT TODAY

Science and Technology
Radar continues to be a major tool in modern armies and navies. Radar allows not only the tracking of enemy aircraft, but also other functions, including detailed weather prediction and guidance for missile systems.

WORLD WAR II ERUPTS **749**

Skills Focus: Making Generalizations   **Below Level**   **Standard English Mastery**

Reading Skill
The Battle of Britain

1. Guide students in a discussion of the Battle of Britain. Remind students that Germany had quickly conquered Poland, the Netherlands, Belgium, and most of France. Have students list reasons why Germany was unsuccessful in conquering England. Make a class list for all to see.

2. Have students write a magazine article about the Battle of Britain and the courage of the British people from the viewpoint of an

American journalist in the fall of 1940. Have volunteers read their magazine articles to the class.

3. As an extension, have students research primary sources from the Battle of Britain, including illustrations and maps, and include quotes and visuals in their articles. **LS Verbal-Linguistic, Logical-Mathematical**

  Alternative Assessment Handbook, Rubric 19: Magazines

---

3 What developments increased tensions between the United States and Japan in East Asia? *military alliance with Germany and Italy, takeover of French Indochina*

Tensions in East Asia

Recall Which three nations formed the Axis Powers? *Germany, Italy, Japan*

Explain Why was the U.S. concerned about the Japanese takeover of French Indochina? *threatened British and American interests in the region*

Make Judgments Should the U.S. have tried to reach a compromise with Japan? *possible answers—no, Japan was on aggressive course that would have conflicted with U.S. interests no matter what; yes, would have saved thousands of lives*

Review & Assess

Close

Review the German reaction to appeasement.

Review

🔲 Online Quiz, Section 2

🔲 Daily Test Practice Transparency

Assess

SE Section 2 Assessment

🔲 Progress Assessment: Section 2 Quiz

🔲 Alternative Assessment Handbook

Reteach

🔲 Interactive Reader and Study Guide, Section 2

🔲 Interactive Skills Tutor CD-ROM

Answers

Reading Check *It caused Japan's government to resign and a group favoring war gained power.*

750

Tensions in East Asia

As you have read, Japanese nationalists expanded their influence in the 1930s. Japan increasingly viewed itself as a great imperial power. In 1934 it began expanding its naval forces. This violated promises made at the Washington Naval Conference in the early 1920s. In 1936 it signed an anticommunism pact with Germany that clearly linked Japan with Europe's Fascist menace.

Then in 1937, Japan began a war against China. The attack was marked by great brutality. For example, Japanese troops massacred an estimated 200,000 to 300,000 Chinese in the capital of Nanjing.

HISTORY'S VOICES

❝There is probably no crime that has not been committed in this city today…. How many thousands were mowed down by guns or bayoneted we shall probably never know.❞

—Minnie Vautrin, recorded in her diary, 1937

In 1940 Japan formed a military alliance with Germany and Italy. The three nations became known as the **Axis Powers**.

The next year, Japanese forces, with the agreement of the French Vichy government, moved to take control of French Indochina.

This was a French colony in Southeast Asia that included the modern-day countries of Vietnam, Laos, and Cambodia. Japan's takeover of French Indochina threatened British and American interests in the region. It signaled Japan's intention to seek the oil and other resources of the Dutch East Indies (today known as Indonesia), the Philippines, and other parts of Southeast Asia.

The United States reacted quickly to this move. President Roosevelt took steps to punish Japan economically and to deny it access to vital oil supplies. This was a serious threat to Japan's future plans.

Representatives of the two nations met to try to settle their growing differences. In Japan, a powerful group led by the minister of war, General **Hideki Tojo**, pushed the government not to accept any compromise.

Tojo was a strong nationalist. He was quite willing to go to war in order to build a Japanese empire. In October 1941, strong pressure from Tojo forced Japan's government to resign. Tojo took control of the country. American leaders did not yet realize it, but the time for compromise with Japan was over.

READING CHECK **Identifying Cause and Effect** How did rising tension between the United States and Japan affect politics in Japan?

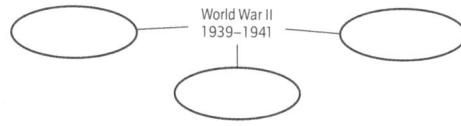

SECTION 2 ASSESSMENT

go.hrw.com
Online Quiz
Keyword: SD7 HP23

Reviewing Ideas, Terms, and People

1. a. Define Write a brief definition for each of the following terms: **appeasement**, **blitzkrieg**
   b. Compare What factor made Germany's blitzkrieg so different from the tactics used in World War I?
   c. Develop Based on what you have read about the blitzkrieg, how do you think the Poles might have better defended against it?

2. a. Identify What was the significance of the **Allies**, **Vichy France**, and **Luftwaffe**?
   b. Compare Why do you think the British were able to defend themselves against the Germans but the French were not?
   c. Rate Why do you think the leadership abilities of Winston Churchill were so important to the British during the Battle of Britain?

3. a. Describe Briefly describe the relationship between Japan and the United States in the late 1930s and early 1940s.
   b. Make Inferences Why do you think the United States was so concerned about Japanese expansion into Southeast Asia?

c. Evaluate Do you think the United States did the right thing by drawing a firm line against Japanese aggression? Explain.

Critical Thinking

4. Identifying the Main Idea Copy the chart below and use information from the section to identify and record key details about the early stages of World War II.

World War II
1939–1941

FOCUS ON WRITING

5. Descriptive Write a description of what you imagine life was like in Great Britain just before and during the Battle of Britain.

750 CHAPTER 23

Section 2 Assessment Answers

1. a. giving into the demands of another nation; lightning war
   b. used air attacks and armored vehicles
   c. strong barricades, modern weapons

2. a. Allies—Great Britain and France; Vichy France—portion of France governed by French officials who cooperated with Germany; Luftwaffe—the German air force;
   b. possible answer—geography; Britain is an island, attacked only by air
   c. possible answer—determined leader kept the nation's spirit up

3. a. strained; Japanese takeover of French Indochina threatened American interests; Americans upset by Japan's military alliance with Germany and Italy
   b. feared for its economic interests in the area, concerned about Japanese empire
   c. possible answer—Yes. The U.S. demonstrated that it would not accept aggression.

4. German victory over France, Battle of Britain, Japanese aggression in East Asia

5. possible answer—difficult to face bombings

The United States Enters the War

BEFORE YOU READ

MAIN IDEA

Isolationist feeling in the United States was strong in the 1930s, but Axis aggression eventually destroyed it and pushed the United States into war.

READING FOCUS

1. Why was a commitment to isolationism so widespread in the 1930s?

2. How did Roosevelt balance American isolationism with the need to intervene in the war?

3. What did the United States do to prepare for war in 1940 and 1941?

4. What were the causes and effects of the Japanese attack at Pearl Harbor?

KEY TERMS AND PEOPLE

pacifist
Neutrality Act
neutral
Quarantine Speech
cash-and-carry
Wendell Willkie
Lend-Lease Act
Atlantic Charter

TAKING NOTES As you read, take notes on events that propelled the United States to enter World War II. Record your notes in a graphic organizer like the one shown here.

Event	Date

THE INSIDE STORY

Lindbergh and "AMERICA FIRST"

What threat made even Lucky Lindy nervous?
Ever since his historic 1927 solo flight across the Atlantic, Charles Lindbergh held a place as perhaps the greatest of all American heroes. People admired him not just for his bravery but also for his knowledge about aviation. When he spoke, people listened.

In the early days of World War II, Lindbergh was speaking a lot. Back in the United States after several years living in Europe, the great American flying hero was working hard to keep the country out of the war.

Getting involved in the fighting would be a disaster for the United States, Lindbergh argued. We were safe here in the United States as long as we built our own defenses and minded our own business, he claimed. Danger waited if we got mixed up in the bloody affairs of Europe. There, Lindbergh argued, the mighty German nation, with its superior air force, was poised to win. Lindbergh himself had inspected their aircraft and came away deeply impressed. He concluded that lending support to Hitler's foes was a lost cause that might end up costing us dearly. Americans, Lindbergh insisted, should put "America first." It must avoid giving in to the cries for help from the British and the other doomed people of Europe.

Lindbergh was a powerful voice in American society. His message was well received by millions of people, including many leading politicians. It would take one of the most shocking events in American history to drown it out. ◼

◀ **A soldier snatches a sign from an antiwar demonstrator at the White House in 1941.**

WORLD WAR II ERUPTS **751**

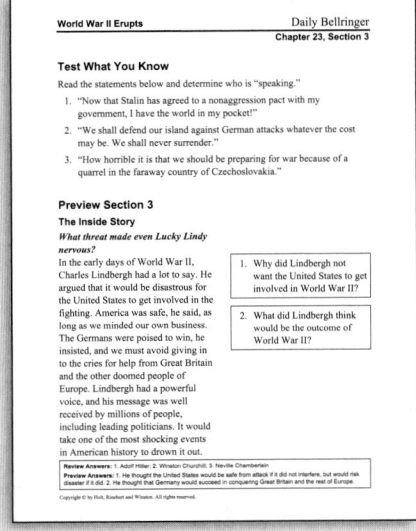

Preteach

Bellringer

The Inside Story. . . Use the **Daily Bellringer Transparency** to help students answer the question.

📦 Daily Bellringer Transparency, Section 3

Academic Vocabulary

Review with students the high-use academic terms in this section.

liberal favoring political reform; progressive (p. 752)

conservative tending to preserve established traditions or policies (p. 752)

circumstances happenings or facts, especially those that affect other people or events (p. 753)

📄 CRF: Vocabulary Builder Activity, Section 3

Taking Notes

Japan invades China, 1937; Germany invades Poland, 1939; German victories, 1940; Atlantic Charter, 1941; attack on Pearl Harbor, 1941

Teach the Main Idea

At Level

The United States Enters the War

1. **Teach** Ask students the Reading Focus questions to teach this section.

2. **Apply** Have students create an outline of the section using the red and blue heads as main points. Have students identify at least two main ideas under each of the blue subheadings.

3. **Review** Review student outlines as a class. Have students identify the points in their outlines that they feel are most important. Guide students in a discussion of U.S.

isolationist policy and the U.S. decision to enter into World War II.

4. **Practice/Homework** Have students write a brief essay explaining why Germany attacked U.S. naval vessels and Japan attacked Pearl Harbor when both nations must have known that their actions would draw the U.S. into the war. **LS Logical-Mathematical, Verbal-Linguistic**

📝 Alternative Assessment Handbook, Rubric 42: Writing to Inform

Reading Focus

1 Why was a commitment to isolationism so widespread in the 1930s? *After World War I, many Americans were afraid of being drawn into future foreign wars.*

American Isolationism

Identify What foreign policy matter did President Roosevelt address while he was focusing on his New Deal programs? *The U.S. established diplomatic relations with the Soviet Union.*

Evaluate Why do you think the Neutrality Act prohibited the export of arms, ammunition, or any other tools of war to any country that was at war? *possible answers—might lead that country's enemies to attack the U.S., draw U.S. into war; aiding nations at war is a form of participation in the war*

📄 CRF: Biography: Jeannette Rankin

Info to Know

Henry Ford While Henry Ford is remembered primarily for his pioneering work with the assembly line and the development of the Model-T, during his lifetime he was also known for his social views and his firm belief in isolationism. Ford vigorously opposed U.S. involvement in World War I, and in 1915 he chartered an ocean liner to take a group of pacifists to Europe in an effort to end the war. In 1918 Ford bought the newspaper *The Dearborn Independent* and proceeded to publish a number of attacks on Jews, whom he accused of financing World War I. After public protests, Ford formally retracted those attacks and sold the paper.

Answers

Reading Check *Americans were horrified by World War I and burdened by the Depression, so they wished to avoid involvement in foreign armed conflict.*

American Isolationism

Many Americans had questioned what the Allies' costly victory in World War I had actually achieved. These feelings helped explain why the U.S. Senate was unwilling for America to join the League of Nations. Many feared that the League might drag the United States into future wars. Anti-League feelings remained strong in the 1920s and 1930s.

The desire to avoid involvement in foreign wars was known as isolationism. This view was shared by both liberals and conservatives in the 1930s. Isolationists were not necessarily **pacifists**, or people who do not believe in the use of military force. Most Americans remained ready to defend their country and its interests. Isolationists simply wanted to preserve America's freedom to choose the time and place for such action.

Franklin D. Roosevelt was not an isolationist. After World War I, for example, he had supported entry into the League of Nations. Though this remained an unpopular position in 1932, Roosevelt easily defeated the staunch isolationist Herbert Hoover in that year's election. This was largely because

ACADEMIC VOCABULARY

liberal favoring political reform; progressive

conservative tending to preserve established traditions or policies

voting took place in the depths of the Great Depression. Most voters were more concerned with economic issues than with foreign policy.

In his first term, Roosevelt only rarely focused on foreign-policy matters. The United States did establish diplomatic relations with the Soviet Union in 1933. Nearly all of Roosevelt's attention, however, went to his New Deal programs. Meanwhile, when Congress discussed foreign affairs, it was generally to pass isolationist measures, such as the first **Neutrality Act**. Passed in 1935, this law was meant to prevent the nation from being drawn into war as it had been in 1917.

HISTORY'S VOICES

❝Upon the outbreak or during the progress of war between, or among, two or more foreign states...it shall thereafter be unlawful to export arms, ammunition, or [tools] of war to any port of such [warring] states.❞

—Neutrality Act, 1935

Over the next several years, Congress strengthened the Neutrality Act. For example, it outlawed making loans to warring countries.

READING CHECK **Summarizing** Why was isolationism widespread in the years after World War I?

TRACING HISTORY

Isolationism

From the nation's founding, many American leaders have sought to isolate the nation from international politics. Since World War II, however, the United States has increasingly formed alliances with other nations. Study the time line to learn how international events challenged American isolationist impulses.

The USS *Maine* blows up in Havana Harbor.

1898 United States gains control of Puerto Rico, Guam, and the Philippines in the Spanish-American War.

1800

UNITED STATES
MONROE DOCTRINE PROCLAIMED 1823

THE GRANGER COLLECTION, NEW YORK

1823 Monroe Doctrine pledges neutrality in European disputes but warns European nations not to interfere in the Western Hemisphere.

Political cartoon supporting the Monroe Doctrine

752 CHAPTER 23

Skills Focus: Identifying Cause and Effect

At Level

Reading Skill

Research Required

The Neutrality Act

1. Divide the class into small groups. Have each group research the Neutrality Act of 1935 and the amendments and revisions that were made to it between 1936 and 1941. Have each group make a chart showing the provisions of the act, amendments, and revisions, and listing the reasons for each provision.

2. Have each group present and explain its chart.

3. Guide students in a discussion of the Neutrality Act, its amendments, and revisions.

Ask students if the act and its provisions were effective in doing what it originally intended: keeping the U.S. out of the conflict. Were there backdoor ways of letting the U.S. participate? Do students think the U.S. should adopt similar policies today? Have them explain their reasoning. **LS Interpersonal, Visual-Spatial**

📄 Alternative Assessment Handbook, Rubrics 13: Graphic Organizers; and 11: Discussions

Balancing Isolationism and Intervention

While many Americans focused on their own problems in the 1930s, <u>circumstances</u> overseas were taking an alarming turn. Italy's 1935 invasion of Ethiopia disturbed Roosevelt deeply. He viewed Italy as a dangerous aggressor. Citing the Neutrality Act, he halted arms sales to the two warring countries. This, Roosevelt knew, would hurt only Italy, for Ethiopia was unable to afford weapons. He further urged businesses to voluntarily end oil shipments to Italy. Few listened. Roosevelt, however, could do little more. He feared that taking a stronger stance against Italy would anger isolationists, whose political support he still needed. The isolationists wanted the United States to remain **neutral**—that is, not aid one side or the other.

Other events of the mid-1930s also challenged Roosevelt and his relationship with the isolationists. During the Spanish Civil War, strict neutrality meant not supplying either warring party with arms. Remaining truly neutral, however, was not a simple matter for the United States. Not aiding either side clearly gave an advantage to the Fascists, who were being well supplied by the Italians and Germans. Even the isolationists were unclear how to solve this dilemma.

Another problem was that deep down, President Roosevelt did not want to be neutral. He was deeply disturbed by the increasingly aggressive actions of the world's new group of totalitarian dictators. His willingness to avoid conflict with isolationists in the government was beginning to fade.

After Japan invaded China in 1937, President Roosevelt decided that it was time to speak out. In a speech he delivered in Chicago, he offered his views on recent world events.

ACADEMIC VOCABULARY

circumstances happenings or facts, especially those that affect other people or events

HISTORY'S VOICES

❝The peace, the freedom, and the security of 90 percent of the population of the world is being jeopardized by the remaining 10 percent who are threatening a breakdown of all international order and law.❞

—Franklin D. Roosevelt, October 5, 1937

Roosevelt compared the spread of war to the spread of a contagious disease. Such diseases can be stopped, he said, by a quarantine. This means identifying the sick and separating them from the healthy. Roosevelt urged the United

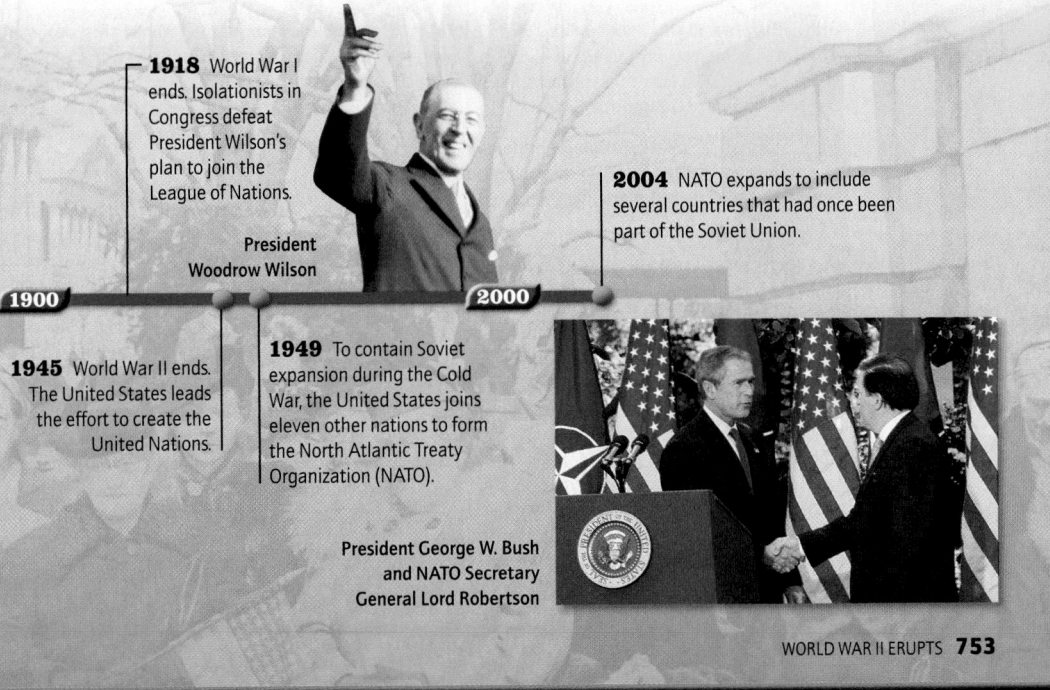

1918 World War I ends. Isolationists in Congress defeat President Wilson's plan to join the League of Nations.

President Woodrow Wilson

1900

1945 World War II ends. The United States leads the effort to create the United Nations.

1949 To contain Soviet expansion during the Cold War, the United States joins eleven other nations to form the North Atlantic Treaty Organization (NATO).

2004 NATO expands to include several countries that had once been part of the Soviet Union.

2000

President George W. Bush and NATO Secretary General Lord Robertson

WORLD WAR II ERUPTS **753**

Reading Focus

❸ What did the United States do to prepare for war in 1940 and 1941? *traded surplus ships to Britain for military bases; started to build new warships; passed the Lend-Lease Act*

Preparing for War

Identify What was the Lend-Lease Act? *act of Congress that allowed U.S. to send weapons to Great Britain whether Britain could pay for them or not*

Analyze Do you think Roosevelt should have made stronger attempts to convince isolationists of the need for the U.S. to enter the war? *possible answers—Yes, Roosevelt needed all Americans on his side. No, in his speeches and actions he clearly stated his views, and isolationists should have rallied to protect the U.S. and help its allies.*

Make Judgments Do you think that the U.S. should "police a world that chooses to follow insane leaders"? Why or why not? *possible answers— Yes, it is better to eliminate them before they attack us. No, the U.S. alone cannot police the world.*

Primary Sources

Have students study the cartoon. Ask them to explain why Democracy is on her knees pleading with Uncle Sam.

Answers

Reading Like a Historian 1. *stay out of the events in Europe;* **2.** *possible answer—believed that if the U.S. gets involved, America could be defeated and democracy could end*

Reading Check *At first, Roosevelt publicly supported isolationist policies; in 1937, he urged the U.S. to become more involved in stopping the spread of war.*

Political Cartoon

After the outbreak of World War II, many Americans were sympathetic to the Allies, but few wanted to get involved in another global war. *Chicago Tribune* cartoonist Carey Orr produced this cartoon recommending the American course of action.

"STAY OUT! STAY OUT FOR MY SAKE, AS WELL AS YOUR OWN!"

WAR MAP EUROPE

AMERICA THE LAST REFUGE OF DEMOCRACY

DEMOCRACY

The character of Uncle Sam represents the government of the United States.

Across the Atlantic lies Europe.

The character of Democracy pleads with Uncle Sam to stay out of the war.

THE GRANGER COLLECTION, NEW YORK

Skills Focus **READING LIKE A HISTORIAN**

1. **Interpreting Political Cartoons** What is the artist recommending the United States do?
2. **Drawing Conclusions** Why do you think the artist took this position?

See Skills Handbook, pp. H12, H28–H29, H31

States to work with peace-loving countries to quarantine aggressive nations and stop the spread of war. For this reason, the speech was referred to as the **Quarantine Speech**.

READING CHECK **Identifying Problems and Solutions** How did Roosevelt strike a balance between isolationism and intervention in the 1930s?

Preparing for War

Roosevelt's Quarantine Speech upset many isolationists. They predicted that his policies would lead to war. North Dakota senator Gerald P. Nye attacked the speech as a "call...upon the United States to police a world that chooses to follow insane leaders." Still, others applauded Roosevelt. Indeed, the president seemed to be gaining strength against the isolationists.

In early 1938, for example, Roosevelt sought from Congress money for building new naval vessels. Isolationists saw warships mainly as a means of fighting wars far from the United

States. Some complained about this proposal. Nevertheless, Congress approved the request.

But Adolf Hitler's aggressive actions strengthened Roosevelt's position. Isolationists had cheered Chamberlain's appeasement at Munich. When German forces later invaded Poland, however, Roosevelt got Congress to change the nation's neutrality laws. The change established a new policy known as **cash-and-carry**. Under this policy, countries at war were allowed to purchase American goods as long as they paid cash and picked up their orders in American ports.

Roosevelt had hoped that the cash-and-carry policy would allow the Allies to slow Hitler's advances. German victories in 1940, however, convinced the president that he needed to do more.

As a result, Roosevelt urged a policy of "all aid short of war." The president agreed to trade fifty aging American warships for eight British military bases. Isolationists opposed the deal but were too weak to stop it.

Skills Focus: Comparing and Contrasting ▸ At Level

Reading Skill
Policing the World

1. Guide students in a discussion of Roosevelt's Quarantine Speech and the reactions to it, particularly Senator Gerald Nye's comment that it was a "call . . . upon the United States to police a world that chooses to follow insane leaders."

2. Ask students to name instances since World War II when the United States has helped to police the world. Make a list of student responses. Can students name any instances

since World War II in which citizens of a country have *chosen* to follow an "insane" leader? What difficulties has the U.S. faced when policing the world?

3. Have each student write an essay reviewing the U.S. policy of policing the world after World War II. 🖪 **Verbal-Linguistic**

📝 Alternative Assessment Handbook, Rubric 9: Comparing and Contrasting

The election of 1940 As Europe was erupting into war, Roosevelt decided to seek a third term as president. Though no one had ever been elected to more than two terms, Roosevelt felt that the world situation required experience in the White House. His opponent was business leader **Wendell Willkie**. In terms of foreign policy, Willkie's views were similar to Roosevelt's. The voters decided to stick with Roosevelt for another term.

Following his re-election, Roosevelt continued his drive to provide aid to the Allies in their fight against Hitler's armies. In a speech at the end of December 1940, Roosevelt declared his goal of making the United States the "arsenal of democracy." An arsenal is a place where weapons are stored. Soon afterward, Congress passed the **Lend-Lease Act**. This allowed the nation to send weapons to Great Britain regardless of its ability to pay.

Ties between the United States and Britain were further strengthened in August 1941. Roosevelt and British leader Winston Churchill met secretly on a ship off the coast of Canada. There the two leaders agreed to the **Atlantic Charter**. This agreement proclaimed the shared goals of the United States and Britain in opposing Hitler and his allies.

Isolationists reacted strongly to these developments. They viewed them as steps leading directly to war. Charles Lindbergh and the America First Committee, which you read about earlier, became leading critics of the president's actions.

In spite of their complaints, however, the United States was looking more and more like a nation at war. Indeed, armed conflict was already taking place on the open seas. As the United States sought to deliver war supplies under the terms of the Lend-Lease Act, German U-boats tried to stop them. In October 1941, torpedoes struck the American destroyer USS *Kearny*. Eleven Americans died. Two weeks later, a German U-boat sank the USS *Reuben James*, killing more than 100 sailors.

Despite the attacks on their ships, many Americans continued to oppose entry into the war. That, however, was about to change.

> **READING CHECK** **Identifying Cause and Effect** Why did the conflict between Roosevelt and the isolationists grow as the United States prepared for the coming war?

Japan Attacks Pearl Harbor

While the situation in Europe troubled many Americans, an even bigger threat to peace was taking shape in the Pacific Ocean. Indeed, by late fall of 1941, American leaders were convinced that war between the United States and Japan was likely. The two nations had earlier come into conflict over French Indochina. Japan had also forged an alliance with Germany and Italy, and Japan's new prime minister, Hideki Tojo, was hostile toward the United States.

The key remaining question was how and where the fighting would start. American officials believed that Japan might attack American bases in the Philippines or British territory in Southeast Asia. In any case, American officials were determined not to fire the first shot. They continued to negotiate with the Japanese. At the same time, they warned American forces throughout the world to be prepared for a possible Japanese attack.

The attack on Pearl Harbor American officials were correct: Japan had decided on war. For months, Japanese military leaders had been developing plans for a surprise attack on the American naval base at Pearl Harbor, Hawaii. This base was home to the United States Navy's Pacific Fleet. The Japanese plan called for aircraft carriers to approach the island of Oahu, where Pearl Harbor was located, from the north. Japanese war planes loaded with bombs and torpedoes would lift off from the carriers and destroy as many American ships and planes as possible.

American military planners had for months believed that an attack on Pearl Harbor was a possibility. In December 1941, however, forces at the base were unready to defend it. This was in part because no single commander was in charge of Pearl Harbor's defenses. In the resulting confusion, routine defensive steps, such as using airplanes to watch for approaching ships, were not in place. The Japanese attack force was able to approach Pearl Harbor undetected.

As the sun rose on Sunday morning, December 7, 1941, the Japanese strike force went into action. The raid was a complete surprise to the Americans. Most American fighter planes in Hawaii never got off the ground. Hundreds were severely damaged or

Reading Focus

❹ What were the causes and effects of the Japanese attack at Pearl Harbor? *causes—conflict over French Indochina, Japan joining Axis Powers; U.S. refusal to sell oil to Japan; effects—severe damage to U.S. Pacific Fleet and aircraft; U.S. declaration of war*

Japan Attacks Pearl Harbor

Recall Why was Pearl Harbor targeted by the Japanese? *It was home to U.S. Navy's Pacific Fleet.*

Explain How were Japanese airplanes able to approach Pearl Harbor without being detected? *Routine defensive measures were not in place.*

Design What should have been done to minimize the destruction that occurred when the Japanese attacked Pearl Harbor? *possible answer—The U.S. should have acted on belief that Japan would attack; defense should have been prepared and coordinated; there should have been regular drills to prepare for an attack.*

📝 CRF: Primary Source Activity: The Atlantic Charter

Differentiating Instruction   Below Level

Learners Having Difficulty

1. Remind students that the attack on Pearl Harbor in December 1941 stunned the nation. Have students reread the information in the text about the attack on Pearl Harbor and the reaction to the attack.

2. Then have students write an editorial for a December 1941 newspaper. Students should denounce the attack, give details

about American losses, and comment on President Roosevelt's address to the nation on December 8.

3. Have volunteers share their headlines and read their articles to the class. **LS** **Verbal-Linguistic**

📝 Alternative Assessment Handbook, Rubric 23: Newspapers

Answers

Reading Check *As Roosevelt gave more aid to the Allies, isolationists feared that the U.S. would enter the war.*

755

Reading Focus

Japan Attacks Pearl Harbor

Recall How long did the Japanese attack on Pearl Harbor last? *two hours*

Compare and Contrast List the similarities and differences between the attacks on Pearl Harbor on December 7, 1941, and the attacks on the United States on September 11, 2001. *possible answers—similarities: Both were surprise attacks; resulted in destruction and loss of life; resulted in U.S. military reprisals; differences: attack on Pearl Harbor was a military attack by a foreign government; September 11 attacks were carried out by terrorists using civilian aircraft on civilian and military targets*

Evaluate Do you think the Japanese would have dared attack the United States mainland? Why or why not? *possible answers—no, because it was too far from Japan and Japanese couldn't expect to surprise or succeed; yes, because Japanese wanted to inflict as much damage as possible on their enemies*

📦 Map Transparencies: Pearl Harbor Invasion; U.S. Ships at Pearl Harbor

✹ **Interactive Maps:** Pearl Harbor Invasion; U.S. Ships at Pearl Harbor

HISTORY CLOSE-UP

Attack on Pearl Harbor

In December 1941 military officials throughout the Pacific were on alert for a possible Japanese attack. Yet Pearl Harbor was not considered the most likely target, and the Japanese strike force approached Hawaii undetected. In one stroke, they destroyed the American Pacific battleship fleet. Below, the USS *West Virginia* sinks as sailors rescue a survivor in the water.

go.hrw.com
Interactive Map
Keyword: SD7 CH23

PEARL HARBOR INVASION

PACIFIC OCEAN

First Wave 7:55 AM
Second Wave 8:55 AM

Fighters   Oahu   Fighters

Dive Bombers   Wheeler Field   Dive Bombers

Torpedo Bombers   Kaneohe

High-Level Bombers   Pearl Harbor   High-Level Bombers

0 4 Miles
0 4 Kilometers

Hickam Field

U.S. SHIPS AT PEARL HARBOR

Utah

U.S. Naval Air Station

Arizona   Nevada
Tennessee
Maryland   West Virginia
Oklahoma
California

Ford Island

Pearl Harbor

Pennsylvania

◯ Undamaged   ◯ Battleship
◖ Damaged   ⊙ Other ship
● Sunk

Skills FOCUS: INTERPRETING INFOGRAPHICS

1. **Making Inferences** What types of ships do you think the Japanese were targeting in their attack?

2. **Interpreting Visuals** How do you think the images of the destruction to the American fleet may have affected the American public?

See **Skills Handbook**, pp. H7, H18, H30

756

Skills Focus: Making Generalizations   At Level

Reading Skill
"A Date Which Will Live in Infamy"

1. Guide students in a discussion of the events that led to the Japanese attack on Pearl Harbor, the actual attack, and the American reaction to the attack.

2. Ask students to describe how Americans might have felt when they first learned about the attack. Have students write several journal entries for December 1941 in which they describe how Americans might have reacted to the attack, fears they might have had about

the future, and what they think will happen in the U.S. Then have volunteers read their journal entries to the class.

3. Have students compare and contrast the attack on Pearl Harbor and the terrorist attacks that occurred on September 11, 2001. 🔳 **Verbal-Linguistic, Logical-Mathematical**

📝 Alternative Assessment Handbook, Rubric 15: Journals

Answers

Interpreting Infographics 1. *battleships, aircraft carriers;* **2.** *angered, outraged them; convinced Americans to enter the war*

destroyed where they sat. Meanwhile, Japanese bombs and torpedoes took a heavy toll on the American warships anchored in the harbor.

The Japanese attack lasted barely two hours. By the time it was over, however, the Pacific Fleet was a tangled mass of smoking metal. "We felt like crying," said one sailor who survived the raid. "We could see our beautiful fleet upside down and burning up."

The destruction was enormous. All eight battleships in the harbor suffered damage. Four were sunk. Nearly 200 aircraft were completely destroyed, and more were damaged. Some 2,400 Americans were dead. Japan, meanwhile, lost only a handful of submarines and fewer than 30 aircraft. It was a complete defeat for the United States.

American reaction Americans reacted to the devastating attack with anger and fear. Rumors spread that Japanese troops would soon invade the West Coast. Nervous Californians reported seeing submarines off their shores. They strung beaches with barbed wire. As you will read in the next chapter, some people became afraid that Japanese Americans would secretly assist an invasion of the United States mainland.

Roosevelt had expected a Japanese strike, but he also expected a formal declaration of war by Japan. Indeed, Japan's ambassadors had scheduled an appointment to deliver just such a message on the day of the attack. By the time they arrived, however, Pearl Harbor was in flames. Roosevelt was furious that Japan had meant to deceive the United States. On December 8, 1941, he asked Congress for a declaration of war.

HISTORY'S VOICES

❝Yesterday, December 7, 1941—a date which will live in infamy—the United States of America was suddenly and deliberately attacked by naval and air forces of the Empire of Japan.... Always will we remember the character of the onslaught against us. No matter how long it may take us to overcome this..., the American people in their righteous might will win through to absolute victory.❞
—Franklin Roosevelt, December 8, 1941

America was now at war with Japan. Three days later, Germany and Italy declared war on the United States. The nation had entered World War II as one of the Allies.

READING CHECK **Drawing Conclusions** What made Japan's attack on Pearl Harbor so devastating?

THE IMPACT TODAY

Daily Life
The terrorist attacks of September 11, 2001 in the United States are often compared to the attack on Pearl Harbor. Both took the nation completely by surprise and caused reactions of fear and anger. Both triggered strong surges of patriotism and a commitment to defeat our foes.

SECTION 3 ASSESSMENT

go.hrw.com
Online Quiz
Keyword: SD7 HP23

Reviewing Ideas, Terms, and People

1. **a. Define** Write a brief definition for each of the following terms: pacifist, Neutrality Act
   b. Analyze How did World War I contribute to isolationist feeling in the 1920s and 1930s?

2. **a. Describe** Why were some isolationists skeptical of Roosevelt's foreign policy during his campaign for president?
   b. Sequence How did Roosevelt's position toward isolationism change over time?
   c. Elaborate Why do you think Roosevelt increasingly came into conflict with isolationists?

3. **a. Recall** What events explain Roosevelt's continuing shift away from isolationism in the late 1930s?
   b. Compare Describe cash-and-carry and the Lend-Lease Act and how they differed from one another.
   c. Evaluate Do you think the isolationists were correct in arguing that Roosevelt's policies, including lend-lease, would increase the likelihood of war? Explain.

4. **a. Describe** What was the attack on Pearl Harbor?
   b. Summarize What was the significance of this battle?

Critical Thinking

5. **Sequencing** Copy the chart below and use information from the section to identify and record the sequence of events that led the United States away from its isolationist position and into World War II.

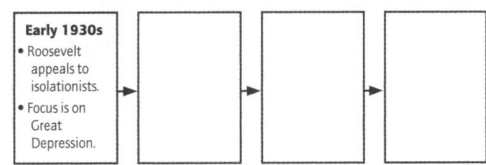

Early 1930s
• Roosevelt appeals to isolationists.
• Focus is on Great Depression.

FOCUS ON WRITING

6. **Persuasive** Write a letter to the editor of a local newspaper from the perspective of a citizen in October 1941, in which you argue either for or against isolationism. Be sure to refer to information from this section and elsewhere in the chapter to support your view.

WORLD WAR II ERUPTS **757**

757

Bellringer

The Inside Story. . . Use the **Daily Bellringer Transparency** to help students answer the question.

📋 Daily Bellringer Transparency, Section 4

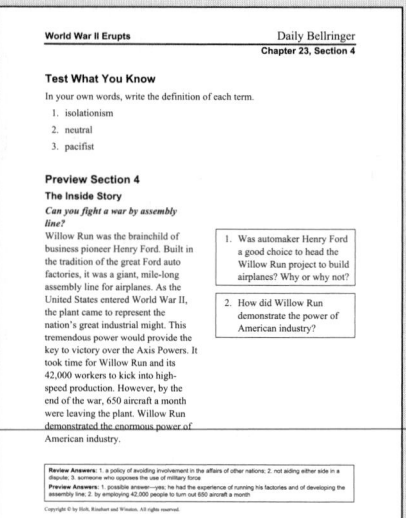

Taking Notes

Armed Forces—increased military spending, expanded the draft, many young men and women volunteered, built new military bases; Industry—federal government spent billions of dollars on weapons, supplies, and ships, created agencies to ensure needs of armed forces were met, women took over men's jobs, NWLB established; Science— Manhattan Project

SECTION 4 Mobilizing for War

BEFORE YOU READ

MAIN IDEA

The outbreak of World War II spurred the mobilization of American military and industrial might.

READING FOCUS

1. How did the U.S. armed forces mobilize to fight World War II?

2. What role did American industry and science play in mobilizing to fight World War II?

3. How did mobilization challenge the nation's ideals of freedom?

KEY TERMS AND PEOPLE

George C. Marshall
Oveta Culp Hobby
Rosie the Riveter
Manhattan Project
atomic bomb
J. Robert Oppenheimer
A. Philip Randolph
Bracero Program
zoot suit riots

TAKING NOTES As you read, take notes on ways the United States mobilized for World War II. Record your notes in a graphic organizer like the one shown here.

Mobilizing for War

Armed Forces	Industry	Science

THE INSIDE STORY *Can you fight a war by assembly line?* Reporters had never seen anything like Willow Run. Inside the giant structure, a person could scarcely see from end to end. "Like infinity," noted an observer, "it stretches everywhere into the distance."

The building these people were describing was the brainchild of business pioneer Henry Ford. Built in the tradition of the great Ford auto factories, Willow Run was a giant, mile-long assembly line for airplanes. As the United States entered World War II, the plant stood as a symbol of the nation's great industrial might. Indeed, the tremendous power of American industry would provide the key to victory against the Axis menace.

It took time for Willow Run to get up to speed. Finding tens of thousands of employees was difficult. Lack of housing was another issue. Over time, however, Ford and the government resolved these problems. Willow Run and its 42,000 workers kicked into high-speed production. By the end of the war, 650 aircraft per month were coming off the Willow Run line.

Willow Run demonstrated the enormous power of American industry—and the mighty effort of American business and government leaders to harness it. As you will read, this was just one part of the nationwide effort to get ready to fight World War II. 🖥

▲ B-24 bombers roll off the assembly line in the Willow Run factory.

758 CHAPTER 23

Teach the Main Idea

[At Level]

Mobilizing for War

1. **Teach** Ask students the Reading Focus questions to teach this section.

2. **Apply** Have students create their own graphic organizers showing how the United States mobilized the armed forces, science, and industry.

3. **Review** Review student graphic organizers as a class. Guide students in a discussion of how the U.S. began its mobilization program and how it helped end the Great Depression.

4. **Practice/Homework** Mobilization provided new opportunities for African Americans and Latinos but they still faced widespread discrimination. Have students write a short essay about one challenge African Americans or Latinos faced and how they dealt with it. **LS Visual-Spatial, Logical-Mathematical**

📝 Alternative Assessment Handbook, Rubrics 13: Graphic Organizers; and 38: Writing to Classify

Mobilizing the Armed Forces

The Japanese bombs and torpedoes that fell on Pearl Harbor had destroyed not only ships and planes, but also most of the remaining isolationist feeling in the United States. Now that the country had entered the war, it had to mobilize, or bring its forces into readiness. This was a huge job.

Fortunately, the United States had made something of a head start. Starting in 1940 the government had sharply increased military spending. This spending, in fact, was largely responsible for ending the Great Depression. Thousands found work in the now-busy factories, making supplies for the military.

The leader of the mobilization effort was Army Chief of Staff, General **George C. Marshall**. Marshall worked closely with President Roosevelt to plan for war. He ensured that American soldiers were well equipped and properly trained. Marshall would also play an important role in developing the nation's military strategy.

Finding soldiers In addition to equipment and supplies, the United States needed soldiers and sailors to fight the Axis Powers. Following Pearl Harbor, the government expanded the draft, which Roosevelt had reinstated in 1940. Many young men, however, did not wait to be called into service. Eager to defend their country, they volunteered by the millions.

HISTORY'S VOICES

❝I wanted to be in it. I was fifteen.... I lied about my age and tried to get in in '43. I was sixteen now. My mother wouldn't sign. ... Then I passed the air corps test at Oak Park High.... Then I figured... you're gonna be two years training, the war'll be over. Go in the Marine Corps.❞

—Roger Tuttrup, quoted in
"The Good War": An Oral History of World War Two, by Studs Terkel

Eventually, some 16 million Americans would enter the armed forces.

Women and the armed forces Although they were not permitted to take part in combat, American women filled a variety of vital roles in the military. Their service helped make more men available for fighting. For example, 10,000 women joined the Women Accepted for Volunteer Emergency Service, or WAVES. This was a navy program in which women did

---

Reading Focus

❶ How did the U.S. armed forces mobilize to fight World War II? *increased spending; military draft; Women's Army Corps; new military bases*

Mobilizing the Armed Forces

Explain How did the United States get the soldiers and sailors needed to fight in the war? *in 1940 expanded the draft; many young men volunteered*

Recall How did WAVES help the war effort? *by doing clerical work, thus freeing men for battle*

Evaluate How do you think increased military spending during 1940 and 1941 contributed to ending the Great Depression? *possible answers—new jobs in the defense industry and in military; money pumped into economy because of increased government spending*

Propaganda Poster

During World War II the U.S. government produced a wide variety of posters to encourage recruitment and support for the war. This poster for the Army Air Corps was created by artist James Montgomery Flagg, who also created the famous image of Uncle Sam during World War I.

P-38 Lightnings were one of the most popular fighter aircraft used in the war.

The man is clearly enthusiastic to join the fight.

This man's gear identifies him as a pilot.

Coming Right Up!

Skills FOCUS   READING LIKE A HISTORIAN

1. **Analyzing Primary Sources** What was the purpose of this image?
2. **Interpreting Visuals** Do you think the image accurately reflects fighter pilots during World War II? Explain.

See **Skills Handbook, pp. H28–H29, H30**

Skills Focus: Analyzing Primary Sources   At Level

Reading Like a Historian Skill
The Armed Forces in World War II

1. Divide the class into groups of five or six students. Have each group develop a series of questions to ask someone who remembers U.S. involvement in World War II.

2. Have each student identify someone they could interview, such as grandparents, great-grandparents, neighbors, people at a senior center, or people at a local Veterans of Foreign Wars. Students may use primary sources to answer their questions.

3. Have students conduct their interviews using the pre-written questions as a starting point. Students should encourage the person they are interviewing to tell his or her story. Students may either record the interview or take detailed notes. Afterwards, they should edit interview results and prepare a written summary of the interview. **LS Interpersonal, Verbal-Linguistic**

📝 Alternative Assessment Handbook, Rubrics 16: Judging Information; and 40: Writing to Describe

Answers

Reading Like a Historian
1. *encourage enlistment and public support for war;* 2. *possible answer— No, combat was probably frightening and not fun.*

759

Mobilizing the Armed Forces

Explain Why did the military need so many new bases? *to house and train millions of new military troops*

Contrast What was the difference between the WAACs and the WACs? *WAACs worked with, but were not part of, the Army; WACs were full-fledged members of the Army.*

Draw Conclusions How did military bases help transform the southern United States? *possible answers—rural areas grew with the influx of young people; economic development*

📑 Political Cartoons Activities for American History: Cartoon 46: Pulling Together for Defense

Info to Know

World War II Advances in Medicine and Technology During World War II advances in medicine and technology helped save lives. New blood transfusion methods allowed for stored blood to be used to stabilize wounded soldiers at the front lines until they could be evacuated to hospitals. In addition, the development of helicopters with air evacuation equipment allowed for quicker transportation of wounded soldiers from the battlefield.

Answers

Reading Check *recruiting and providing for soldiers; building military bases*

760

---

necessary clerical work that would otherwise have to be performed by men. Some 1,000 women joined the Women Airforce Service Pilots, or WASPs. They tested and delivered aircraft. Nearly 40 WASPs gave their lives serving the country.

By far the largest women's unit was the Women's Army Corps, or WAC, in which 150,000 women served. At the start of the war, the unit was known as the Women's Army Auxiliary Corps, or WAAC. Its members worked with, but were not part of, the army. The WAACs repaired equipment, worked as electricians, and performed many other jobs.

By 1943 demand for their services was so great that the army created the Women's Army Corp. WACs were full-fledged members of the army. As such, they were entitled to full army protection and benefits and could serve overseas on nearly every task except combat. They were led by **Oveta Culp Hobby**, who was given the rank of colonel.

New military bases The millions of Americans entering the armed forces all needed training and housing. This required building hundreds of new military bases.

In general, the military looked to build new bases in rural areas where there was plenty of open land. Life on a rural, isolated base often required a big adjustment, especially for those who came from larger cities. It also required some getting used to by local citizens. They had to cope with the presence of thousands of young men in their once quiet neighborhoods.

The military buildup transformed many parts of the country. California became home to more military bases than any other state. Florida, with its warm weather and plentiful land, was also an excellent location for military training. Camp Blanding, with its 55,000 soldiers, became the fourth largest city in Florida almost overnight.

Texans saw 1.2 million troops train at their army bases, including Camp Hood. Some 200,000 air pilots trained at Texas air bases, such as Randolph Air Field. In addition, Texas was a temporary home to over 50,000 German, Italian, and Japanese prisoners of war.

READING CHECK **Identifying Problem and Solution** What were the challenges of mobilizing the armed forces?

Mobilization

Women were essential to the war mobilization effort. They filled many jobs once reserved for men, such as riveting (above).

Mobilizing Industry and Science

The enthusiasm of American fighting forces was important. In order to defeat the Axis armies, however, American troops would need the proper equipment. The nation responded quickly to this need. Many factories that made consumer goods were quickly converted to the production of war supplies.

The federal government spent tens of billions of dollars on weapons and supplies in the months following the outbreak of war. Shortly after Pearl Harbor, Roosevelt set the ambitious goal of building 60,000 new planes in 1942 and a further 125,000 aircraft the following year. He asked for 120,000 new tanks over the same time period. Thanks to the efforts of people such as Henry Ford and the workers of Willow Run, American industry met these goals.

The United States not only had to produce all of these war supplies, it also had to ship them to the armed forces overseas. Cargo

---

Collaborative Learning

At Level

Military Bases in the United States

Research Required

1. Divide the class into small groups. Have each group conduct research and make a list of military bases established during the World War II era in California, Florida, Texas, or your own state.

2. Have each group conduct additional research to find out how many of these World War II bases are still in use. Ask students to investigate how the bases contribute to the economies of the surrounding areas and to the state as a whole.

3. Have each group draw a map of the state showing major cities and military bases. Have students use a star to indicate bases still in use, and a circle to indicate bases that have been closed. Have a volunteer from each group display its map for the class to see.

4. Guide students in a discussion of the ways in which military bases continue to affect community and state economies. **LS Interpersonal**

📑 Alternative Assessment Handbook, Rubric 20: Map Creation

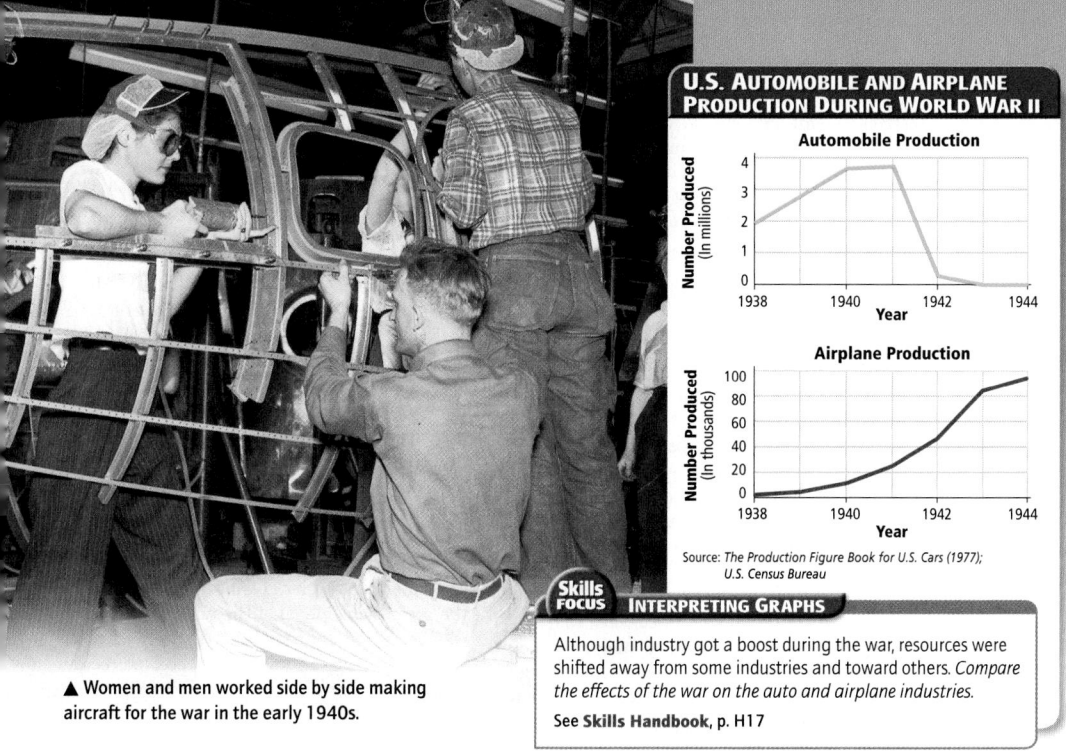

U.S. AUTOMOBILE AND AIRPLANE PRODUCTION DURING WORLD WAR II

Automobile Production

Airplane Production

Source: *The Production Figure Book for U.S. Cars* (1977); U.S. Census Bureau

Skills FOCUS **INTERPRETING GRAPHS**

Although industry got a boost during the war, resources were shifted away from some industries and toward others. *Compare the effects of the war on the auto and airplane industries.*

See **Skills Handbook, p. H17**

▲ Women and men worked side by side making aircraft for the war in the early 1940s.

ships, however, were a main target of enemy submarines. Early in the war, submarines took a terrible toll on American shipping. To replace these losses, American shipyards turned out 5,500 vessels over the course of the war.

About half of these ships were the so-called liberty ships built by Henry Kaiser. Before the war, Kaiser was known for such projects as Hoover Dam. He had never built a ship. Yet he created a shipyard in California and used assembly-line techniques to produce massive cargo ships at an astounding rate. His workers once produced a liberty ship in a mere four and a half days.

The federal government created several new agencies to help ensure that American industry would be able to meet the needs of the armed forces. These agencies regulated what products factories produced, what prices they could charge, and how the nation's raw materials would be used. The wartime agencies were staffed in part by American business and labor leaders. Key figures included William Knudsen and Sidney Hillman, who led the

Office of Production Management, and Donald Nelson, who headed the government's War Production Board.

Rosie the Riveter Producing enough supplies to fight the war required many workers. At the same time, American men were leaving their factory jobs by the millions to join the armed forces.

Women helped provide a solution to this problem. During the war, the number of women working outside the home rose dramatically. Many of these 6.5 million new workers took industrial jobs that had never been open to women before.

"I was a woman doing a 'man's job'!" recalled one of these women workers. "I was also very proud of the fact that I was contributing, even in a small way, to the war efforts." Working women of the war came to be represented by the symbolic figure known as **Rosie the Riveter**.

Labor in World War II Government spending during World War II helped end the Great Depression and created millions of new

Reading Focus

2 What role did American industry and science play in mobilizing to fight World War II? *Factories began to produce war supplies; scientists worked to develop new weapons, including the atomic bomb.*

Mobilizing Industry and Science

Define What was a liberty ship? *a quickly built cargo ship built in Henry Kaiser's factories using assembly-line techniques*

Summarize How did the role of the federal government grow during the early days of the war? *New regulatory agencies were created.*

Evaluate Why do you think the character of Rosie the Riveter was so important? *possible answer—showed that women could do jobs previously held only by men*

📃 CRF: Biography: Henry John Kaiser

Biography

Richard Wright (1908–1960) Richard Wright was an African American author who grew up in the segregated South and later moved to Chicago where he began a career as a writer. His most famous novel, *Native Son,* led many Americans to question the treatment of African Americans within U.S. society. The novel was the first best-selling novel written by an African American. In his autobiography *Black Boy* Wright discusses what it was like to grow up in the South under Jim Crow laws.

Skills Focus: Drawing Conclusions

At Level

Reading Skill
Women in the Workplace

1. Have students make a list of the kinds of jobs they think women might have held before World War II. Then have students make a list of jobs they think opened to women during the war. Make a class list for all to see.

2. Guide students in a discussion of the new job opportunities for women. Ask students to predict if new ideas about what women could do in the workplace might change women's expectations in other areas of life.

3. Ask students to consider whether women should continue to work in their new jobs when the war ends, or whether jobs should be given back to men returning from military duty. Have each student write a letter to a newspaper editor expressing their opinions on the subject. **LS Interpersonal, Logical-Mathematical**

📃 Alternative Assessment Handbook, Rubric 17: Letters to Editors

Answers

Interpreting Graphs *Automobile production fell sharply, while airplane production rose steadily.*

761

Mobilizing science

Recall What was the Manhattan Project? *project to build atomic bomb*

Analyze Why was this project the most important science project of the war? *The U.S. wanted to be first to build an atomic bomb.*

❸ How did mobilization challenge the nation's ideals of freedom? *Minority groups faced significant discrimination at the same time that they were being asked to serve their country; women and minorities began to take jobs previously closed to them.*

Fighting for Freedom at Home

Identify What was the Bracero Program? *gave Mexican workers the chance to work temporarily in U.S.*

Interpret How did African Americans serving in the armed forces help break down racial barriers? *first African American marines enlisted; Navy commissioned its first black officers*

Draw a Conclusion Why would Roosevelt's executive order outlawing discrimination in government or defense jobs affect sleeping car porters? *possible answer—because during the war, rail transportation was considered vital to national defense*

📖 CRF: Primary Source Activity: World War II Joe Louis Poster

Answers

Photo *issued an executive order that outlawed discrimination in government and defense jobs*

Reading Check *spent billions on weapons and supplies; created new agencies to help American industries meet the needs of the armed forces; supported the Manhattan Project*

jobs. Many of these workers joined labor unions, but the federal government was concerned that strikes might hamper the war effort.

Just weeks after the nation declared war on Japan, President Roosevelt established the National War Labor Board to help settle labor disputes. In 1943 Congress passed the Smith-Connally Act, giving the president power to take over vital industries in the event of strikes. These measures helped reduce—but not end—labor disputes in the early war years.

Mobilizing science War planners knew that technology would play an important role in World War II. The **Manhattan Project**, with laboratories in Los Alamos, New Mexico, was the most significant scientific program of World War II. This was a top-secret American program to build an **atomic bomb**, a powerful weapon that used energy released by the splitting of atoms.

Research into building an atomic bomb had begun in 1939, motivated by concern that Germany was already working on such a weapon. As you will read later, American scientists led by physicist **J. Robert Oppenheimer** would win this race. The result would shape world history for decades to come.

READING CHECK **Identifying the Main Idea** What steps did the U.S. government take to mobilize industry and science?

Fighting for Freedom at Home

As in World War I, the United States faced the challenge of fighting for freedom overseas. The nation also faced the challenge of ensuring freedom for Americans at home.

African Americans in the military Hundreds of thousands of African Americans served with honor during World War II. In the process, they broke down barriers that had long blocked their way. For example, the war saw the enlistment of the first African American marines in U.S. history. The navy commissioned the first African American officers during the war.

At the same time, African Americans continued to suffer discrimination. They were forced to serve in segregated units. Their bravery often went unrecognized. Not a single African American soldier of World War II received the prestigious Medal of Honor. This oversight was corrected nearly 50 years after the fact, when seven African Americans received recognition for their remarkable bravery in battle.

African Americans in the workforce The war created an enormous demand for factory workers. White women took many of these jobs. African Americans found new opportunities as well. As factories increased

Seeking Equal Opportunity
African American workers wanted an equal opportunity to contribute to the nation's mobization effort and to benefit from the opportunities it created. *How did President Roosevelt respond to African American demands for fair treatment?*

Differentiating Instruction

Below Level **Standard English Mastery**

English-Language Learners

1. Have students work in mixed-ability pairs to make a list of the new opportunities that were open to African Americans and women in the U.S. armed forces and in the workforce during World War II. Then have each pair make a list of the problems that African Americans and women still faced.

2. Have pairs share their lists with the class.

3. Have each student use the information from their lists to write a short essay comparing and contrasting the treatment of African Americans during World War II with the treatment of women. **LS Interpersonal, Logical-Mathematical**

📖 Alternative Assessment Handbook, Rubric 9: Comparing and Contrasting

war production, thousands found jobs that had in the past been unavailable to them. Yet even with these new opportunities came harsh reminders of widespread racist attitudes. For example, African Americans were often forced to take the lowest-paying jobs, regardless of their skills or experience.

Union leader **A. Philip Randolph**, head of the Brotherhood of Sleeping Car Porters, noted these developments. In 1941 he called for a march on Washington, D.C., to protest unfair treatment of African Americans. Only after President Roosevelt issued an order outlawing discrimination in government or defense jobs did Randolph call off the march.

Challenges for Hispanic Americans Hispanic Americans experienced opportunities and challenges during World War II. For example, the demand for farm labor led the U.S. and Mexican governments to establish the **Bracero Program** in 1942. This gave some Mexican workers the chance to work temporarily in the United States.

In some communities, unfortunately, the arrival of thousands of Hispanic workers led to increased ethnic tensions. In California, such tensions boiled over into violence. In the **zoot suit riots** of June 1943, white sailors stationed in Los Angeles fought with groups of Mexican American youths during a week of terrible violence. The riot was named after the zoot suit, a flashy style of clothing favored by some Mexican American young men.

In spite of the conflicts, Hispanic Americans remained deeply loyal to the United States and sought opportunities to serve.

HISTORY'S VOICES

❝We know that us Mexican-American boys and girls can do a lot of things to win the war if someone will give us a chance.... [D]iscrimination is the thing that makes the other Americans divide from us.❞

—Letter from Youth Committee for the Defense of Mexican American Youth to Vice President Henry Wallace

Like members of other minority groups, many Hispanic Americans served bravely in the armed forces. They also shared a strong commitment to victory and freedom.

READING CHECK **Identifying Cause and Effect** Explain how mobilization triggered a fight for freedom among minority groups in the United States.

SECTION 4 ASSESSMENT

go.hrw.com
Online Quiz
Keyword: SD7 HP23

Reviewing Ideas, Terms, and People

1. a. Describe Briefly describe the significance of the following to the mobilization effort during World War II: **George C. Marshall**, **Oveta Culp Hobby**
   b. Explain What effect did the bombing of Pearl Harbor have on the nation's mobilization effort?
   c. Evaluate How do you think the changing roles of women in the United States were reflected in their experiences during wartime?

2. a. Define Write a brief definition of each of the following terms: **Rosie the Riveter**, **Manhattan Project**, and **atomic bomb**
   b. Summarize Why was mobilization of American industry considered so important to the war effort?
   c. Evaluate Do you think the decision of the U.S. government to expand its oversight of American industry would help or hurt industry's ability to meet its goals? Explain

3. a. Recall How did African American military personnel and workers fare during World War II?

b. Draw Conclusions Why do you think World War II created so many opportunities for women and members of minority groups?
   c. Predict How do you think the end of the war, when it comes, will affect minority groups? Explain your answer.

Critical Thinking

4. Identifying Supporting Details Copy the chart below and use information from the section to identify and record the details that support the main idea.

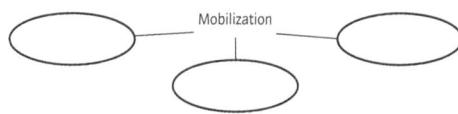

Mobilization

FOCUS ON WRITING

5. Descriptive The preparations for World War II brought major changes to life in the United States. Assume the point of view of an American citizen in late 1941 to early 1942. Write a journal entry in which you describe the changes taking place around you.

Section 4 Assessment Answers

1. a. Marshall—Army Chief of Staff; Hobby—led the Women's Army Corps
   b. Millions volunteered for the military.
   c. Women were given a variety of new jobs.

2. a. symbol for World War II working women; program to build an atomic bomb; a weapon of mass destruction
   b. workers needed to produce supplies
   c. possible answer—help, government could ensure that necessary supplies were available

3. a. greater opportunities for jobs and military positions, still faced discrimination
   b. possible answer—Most young white males fought in the war, which created job openings for women and minority groups.
   c. might face job loss and discrimination

4. finding soldiers; developments in industry; opportunities for women and minorities

5. possible answer—young men are volunteering for the armed forces; women are working in factories; factories are now producing war supplies

---

Direct Teach

Seeking Equal Opportunity
Recall Remind students that during the Depression, African Americans were particularly hard hit, and that unemployment rates were very high. Guide students in a discussion of the difficulty of all Americans, but especially African Americans, in finding jobs that paid living wages.

Review & Assess

Close
Guide students in a discussion of the mobilization that had begun even before the United States entered the war and its effect on the economy.

Review
Online Quiz, Section 4
Daily Test Practice Transparency

Assess
SE Section 4 Assessment
Progress Assessment: Section 4 Quiz
Alternative Assessment Handbook

Reteach
Interactive Reader and Study Guide, Section 4
Interactive Skills Tutor CD-ROM

Answers

Reading Check *Minority groups faced significant discrimination at the same time that they were being asked to serve their country.*

Reactions to Pearl Harbor

Word Help

infamy disgrace
onslaught attack
premeditated planned
righteous blameless
uttermost utmost
unbounded unlimited
contingent group

Activity **Roosevelt Reacts** Roosevelt's speech to Congress was broadcast to the nation, and was recorded. Copies of the recording are widely available on the Internet. Find a recording of the address and play it to the class.
LS Auditory-Musical

Primary Source

Listeners to NBC radio heard an eyewitness account of the attack on Pearl Harbor as Japanese planes still swarmed overhead. A reporter at the Honolulu affiliate climbed to the roof of a downtown building carrying a microphone. "The city of Honolulu has . . . been attacked and considerable damage done. This battle has been going on for nearly three hours . . . It's no joke, it's a real war."

— Radio Report, Dec. 7, 1941

Michigan State University, G. Robert Vincent Voice Library

Make Inferences Why do you think the reporter felt it was necessary to tell his listeners that his report was not a joke? *possible answer—because most people would not believe that the Japanese had actually attacked the U.S.*

Reactions to Pearl Harbor

Historical Context The documents below provide information on different reactions to the Japanese bombing of Pearl Harbor in Hawaii.

Task Examine the documents and answer the questions that follow. Then you will be asked to write an essay about reactions to the Pearl Harbor attack, using facts from the documents and information from the chapter to support the position you take in your thesis statement.

DOCUMENT 1

The day after the attack on Pearl Harbor, President Franklin Roosevelt asked Congress to declare war on Japan. His simple speech reflected the shock that most Americans felt about the attack.

"Yesterday, December 7, 1941—a date which will live in infamy—the United States of America was suddenly and deliberately attacked by naval and air forces of the Empire of Japan.…

Always will we remember the character of the onslaught against us. No matter how long it may take us to overcome this premeditated invasion, the American people in their righteous might will win through to absolute victory.

I believe I interpret the will of the Congress and of the people when I assert that we will not only defend ourselves to the uttermost but will make very certain that this form of treachery shall never endanger us again.

Hostilities exist. There is no blinking at the fact that our people, our territory and our interests are in grave danger.

With confidence in our armed forces—with the unbounded determination of our people—we will gain the inevitable triumph—so help us God."

DOCUMENT 2

The government used memories of Pearl Harbor to encourage support for the war. The poster below was created to encourage support for war-related work, such as making munitions.

Differentiating Instruction

Above Level

Advanced Learners/GATE

1. Ask each student to think of someone who would remember hearing about the attack on Pearl Harbor at the time it happened. Possibilities include grandparents or great-grandparents, neighbors, or people at a senior center. If students cannot find someone to interview, they may use primary sources.

2. Have students interview their chosen person for an oral history. They should encourage the person they are interviewing to tell what they were doing at the time, how they reacted,

and what they thought in the next few days. Students may want to record the interviews, but they should be written down and edited before being turned in. Have volunteers read their interviews to the class.

3. Collect the interviews for an oral history of Pearl Harbor Day. **LS** Interpersonal, Verbal-Linguistic

📖 Alternative Assessment Handbook, Rubric 29: Presentations

DOCUMENT 3

Most Americans found out about the Pearl Harbor attacks from the radio. Duane T. Brigstock of Battle Creek, Michigan, recalled his reactions upon hearing the news.

"Along with a large contingent [group] of Battle Creek bowlers, I was participating in the Central States tournament in Toledo, Ohio, that fateful Sunday afternoon. As the news broke, the message was relayed to us over the P.A. system: 'The Japanese are bombing Pearl Harbor!' We listened in shocked disbelief and activity halted on the busy alleys. Our first reaction was anger—followed by a great surge of patriotism. Bowling scores were quickly forgotten. As we checked out of our hotel, someone softly started to sing "God Bless America" and soon everyone joined in.

We were a quiet group driving home as we listened to bits of information on our car radios. We dug out our draft registration cards from our billfolds to recheck our numbers and wonder when we would be called up. There was no question in our minds that we would serve—only when."

DOCUMENT 4

While many people reacted to the war by joining the military, those who worked on the home front never forgot the event. Just a few weeks after the attack, these war-production workers took a break from their night shift on New Year's Eve to celebrate the coming year. Instead of shouting "Happy New Year," they shouted "Remember Pearl Harbor!"

Skills FOCUS   READING LIKE A HISTORIAN

1. a. Identify Refer to Document 1. Why does Roosevelt call December 7, 1941, a "date which will live in infamy?"
b. Analyze How does Roosevelt try to warn and also to reassure the nation after the attack?

2. a. Describe Refer to Document 2. What is going on in this image?
b. Interpret What kind of effect do you think this image had on wartime workers?

3. a. Identify Refer to Document 3. What feelings did the attack immediately stir up for this writer?
b. Elaborate How do you think that day changed the lives of those who heard about it on the radio?

4. a. Identify Refer to Document 4. How did these workers celebrate the new year?
b. Analyze Why do you think the workers chose that cheer to mark the new year?

5. Document-Based Essay Question Consider the question below and form a thesis statement. Using examples from Documents 1, 2, 3, and 4, create an outline and write a short essay supporting your position.
How did Americans react to the attack on Pearl Harbor?

See **Skills Handbook**, pp. H28–H29, H30

WORLD WAR II ERUPTS   **765**

Collaborative Learning

The Effect of Pearl Harbor on Life in America

At Level

Research Required

1. Divide the class into small groups. Have each group choose two of the documents to use as a jumping-off point for further research into reactions to Pearl Harbor.

2. Have each group conduct research into the ways the attack on Pearl Harbor affected American life. For example, one group might use Documents 2 and 3 as a starting point, then look at the ways the attack on Pearl Harbor affected mass media and popular culture.

3. Have each group prepare a class presentation about its research. Students may present recordings of music or news broadcasts, excerpts from movies or radio programs, or additional posters or photographs that show how Americans responded to Pearl Harbor.

LS Interpersonal, Visual-Spatial

Alternative Assessment Handbook, Rubrics 24: Oral Presentations; and 30: Research

---

Info to Know

The Japanese Attack On the same day they attacked Pearl Harbor, the Japanese also launched attacks on Guam, the Philippines, Wake Island, Midway Island, Hong Kong, Thailand, and British Malaya. The following day, the United States was joined by all of the Allies in declaring war on Japan.

Primary Source

A newspaper article published on December 8, 1941, recorded the anger and fear felt by many Americans: "Japan assaulted every main United States and British possession . . . in a hasty but evidently shrewdly-planned prosecution of a war she began Sunday without warning . . . From that moment, each tense tick of the clock brought new and flaming accounts of Japanese aggression in her secretly launched war of conquest or death for the land of the Rising Sun . . . Thus the war that Adolf Hitler started in September, 1939, exploded at last into a real World War."
Associated Press, December 8, 1941

Answers

Reading Like a Historian
1. a. *because Roosevelt believed that Americans would always remember the unprovoked attack;* **b.** *warns of grave danger to America, but asserts that Americans will win a complete victory;* **2. a.** *Uncle Sam is waving his fist in anger at the Japanese bombers;* **b.** *possible answer—would inspire them with patriotism and a sense of duty;* **3. a.** *disbelief, anger, and patriotism;* **b.** *possible answer—knew that war was inevitable; everyone would have to serve their country;* **4. a.** *by shouting "Remember Pearl Harbor!"* **b.** *possible answer—wanted to honor memory of those who had been killed and those who were now fighting as a result of Pearl Harbor;* **5.** *Answers will vary, but students' essays may include outrage; shock; surge of patriotism; desire to go to war to defend America.*

Visual Summary: World War II Erupts

Rise of Dictators
• Dictators, taking advantage of widespread fear, uncertainty and despair, emerge in the post–World War I era.

Aggression and War
• Aggressive dictators use war to promote their tyrannical goals.

The United States: From Isolationism to War
• Isolationism gives way to the call for war when the United States comes under direct attack.

Mobilizing for War
• The United States musters its tremendous industrial and human might to fight the war.

Reviewing Key Terms and People

Complete each sentence by filling in the blank with the correct term or person.

1. Benito Mussolini introduced a political philosophy known as _____.
2. In the 1930s, many Americans supported _____ rather than an active involvement in affairs overseas.
3. Neville Chamberlain is associated with the _____ of Hitler at Munich.
4. The German attack of Poland demonstrated a tactic known as _____.
5. The symbol for women factory workers during the war was _____ _____ _____.
6. Germany, Italy, and Japan formed the _____ _____.
7. In order to aid the British, Roosevelt promoted the policy of _____.

8. In 1933 _____ _____ became the chancellor of Germany.
9. The _____ _____ was a top-secret program to build an atomic bomb.
10. In the _____ _____, Roosevelt likened the spread of aggression to the spread of disease.
11. The _____ _____ provided an opportunity for workers from Mexico to work in the United States temporarily.

Comprehension and Critical Thinking

SECTION 1 *(pp. 738–745)*

12. **a. Identify** Who were the major totalitarian dictators to emerge following World War I?
b. Summarize What were the key features of the postwar totalitarian regimes?
c. Elaborate What do you think was the appeal of fascism, and why did it spread in the post–World War I era?

History's Impact video program
Review the video to answer the closing question:
Why did so many Americans favor isolationism
before the United States entered World War II?

SECTION 2 *(pp. 746–750)*

13. a. Recall What countries did Germany attack in 1939 and 1940?

b. Make Inferences Based on the events of 1940, what can you infer about the Allies' evaluation of German military strength at the start of World War II?

c. Evaluate Do you think Hitler would have behaved differently had the British and French not appeased him in Munich? Explain.

SECTION 3 *(pp. 751–757)*

14. a. Describe During the 1930s, what was the general attitude among the American public toward events taking place in Europe, Africa, and Asia?

b. Sequence Describe the change in American attitudes toward world events in the period between the late 1930s and the end of 1941.

c. Develop How would you counter the isolationist argument in the late 1930s? Write a brief statement to explain your idea.

SECTION 4 *(pp. 758–763)*

15. a. Describe Describe the key steps in mobilizing the nation for war.

b. Explain What does it mean to say that mobilization created "opportunities and challenges" for minority groups?

c. Predict How do you think a mobilization effort such as the one that occurred in the early 1940s would affect the United States today? Explain your answer.

Using the Internet

> go.hrw.com
> **Practice Online**
> Keyword: SD7 CH23

16. Why did people put their faith in totalitarian dictators who propelled their nations into war? Using the keyword above, do some research on the Internet to find some answers to this question. Then create a chart to compare and contrast the reasons why many German, Italian, and Japanese people supported totalitarian dictators in their nations.

Analyzing Primary Sources

Reading Like a Historian
This photograph shows a worker at a defense plant during World War II.

17. Identify What term was used to identify the type of worker shown in this picture?

18. Analyze What is the significance of the fact that this worker is a woman?

Critical Reading

Read the passage in Section 2 that begins with the heading "World War II Starts." Then answer the questions that follow.

19. Winston Churchill believed that

A. appeasement would lead to war.

B. it was foolish to get involved in foreign conflicts.

C. Hitler would stop at the Sudetenland.

D. Chamberlain correctly handled Hitler.

20. The passage suggests that in return for giving into Chamberlain's demands, Hitler

A. threatened to invade Great Britain.

B. promised to support Chamberlain.

C. promised not to seek further territorial gains.

D. agreed that Chamberlain was a coward.

FOCUS ON WRITING

Narrative Writing *Narrative writing tells a story. It uses precise detail and often describes events in sequence. To practice narrative writing, complete the assignment below.*

Writing Topic **Isolationism in the 1930s**

21. Assignment Based on what you have read in this chapter, write a narrative paragraph that retells the story of the rise and fall of isolationist feeling in the United States between World War I and World War II.

WORLD WAR II ERUPTS **767**

Answers

Using the Internet

16. Go to the HRW Web site and enter the keyword shown to access a rubric for this activity.

> KEYWORD: SD7 CH23

Analyzing Primary Sources

17. Rosie the Riveter

18. Women took industrial jobs that had never been open to them before.

Critical Reading

19. A

20. C

Focus on Writing

21. possible answer—World War I made many believe that the U.S. should stay out of international disputes; Neutrality Act passed; Roosevelt's Quarantine Speech; cash-and-carry policy to aid Allies; Lend-Lease Act and Atlantic Charter supported Britain; Japanese attacked Pearl Harbor

A rubric for this activity is provided in Chapter Resource File: Focus on Writing Activity: American Isolationism in the 1930s.

History's Impact Video Program

They remembered the horrors of World War I, and did not want the U.S. to become involved in another foreign war.

Review and Assessment Resources

Review and Reinforce

- CRF: Chapter Review Activity
- Quick Facts Transparency: World War II Erupts
- Spanish Chapter Summaries Audio CD Program
- Online Chapter Summaries in Spanish
- OSP Holt PuzzlePro; Quiz Show for ExamView
- Quiz Game CD-ROM

Assess

- PASS: Chapter Test, Forms A and B
- Alternative Assessment Handbook
- OSP ExamView Test Generator, Chapter Test
- Differentiated Instruction Modified Worksheets and Tests CD-ROM: Chapter Test
- HOAP Holt Online Assessment Program (in the Premier Online Edition)

Reteach/Intervene

- Interactive Reader and Study Guide
- Differentiated Instruction Teacher Management System: Lesson Plans for Differentiated Instruction
- Differentiated Instruction Modified Worksheets and Tests CD-ROM: Chapter Test
- Interactive Skills Tutor CD-ROM

> go.hrw.com
> **Online Resources**
> KEYWORD: SD7 CH23

Chapter 24 Planning Guide

The United States in World War II

Chapter Overview	Reproducible Resources	Technology Resources
CHAPTER 24 pp. 768–813 **Overview: In this chapter,** students will analyze the events of World War II along with the effect these events had on the lives of Americans.	**Differentiated Instruction Teacher Management System:*** • Instructional Benchmarking Guides • Lesson Plans for Differentiated Instruction **Interactive Reader and Study Guide*** **Chapter Resource File:*** • Social Studies Skills Activity: Reading Time Lines • Chapter Review Activity **American History Outline Maps** **Pre-AP Activities Guide for American History***	**Live Ink® Online Reading Help** **Student Edition on Audio CD Program** **Differentiated Instruction Modified Worksheets and Tests CD-ROM** **History's Impact: American History Video Program (VHS/DVD):** The United States in World War II **Online Chapter Summaries in Spanish**
Section 1: **The War in Europe and North Africa** **The Main Idea:** The United States focused first on the war in Europe.	**Differentiated Instruction Teacher Management System:** Section 1 Lesson Plan* **Interactive Reader and Study Guide** **Chapter Resource File:*** **Political Cartoons Activities***	**Daily Bellringer Transparency:** Section 1* **Map Transparency:** World War II in Europe and North Africa, 1941–1944* **Daily Test Practice Transparency*** **Internet Activity:** D-Day
Section 2: **The Holocaust** **The Main Idea:** Germany's Nazi government systematically murdered some 6 million Jews and 5 million others.	**Differentiated Instruction Teacher Management System:** Section 2 Lesson Plan* **Interactive Reader and Study Guide** **Chapter Resource File:*** • Biography Activity: Sala Garncarz Kirschner	**Daily Bellringer Transparency:** Section 2* **Map Transparency:** The Holocaust* **Daily Test Practice Transparency*** **Internet Activity:** The Holocaust
Section 3: **The War in the Pacific** **The Main Idea:** After early defeats in the Pacific, the United States gained the upper hand and began to fight its way to Japan.	**Differentiated Instruction Teacher Management System:** Section 3 Lesson Plan* **Interactive Reader and Study Guide** **Chapter Resource File:*** • Primary Source Activities • History and Geography Activity: Island-Hopping	**Daily Bellringer Transparency:** Section 3* **Map Transparency:** World War II in the Pacific, 1942–1945* **Daily Test Practice Transparency*** **Internet Activities**
Section 4: **The Home Front** **The Main Idea:** Americans on the home front were making contributions of their own to the war effort.	**Differentiated Instruction Teacher Management System:** Section 4 Lesson Plan* **Interactive Reader and Study Guide** **Chapter Resource File:*** • Literature Activity: Farewell to Manzanar • Economics and History Activity **Political Cartoons Activities*** **U.S. Supreme Court Case Studies***	**Daily Bellringer Transparency:** Section 4* **Daily Test Practice Transparency*** **Internet Activity:** Rosie the Riveter
Section 5: **World War II Ends** **The Main Idea:** The Allies completed the defeat of the Axis Powers and made plans for the postwar world.	**Differentiated Instruction Teacher Management System:** Section 5 Lesson Plan* **Interactive Reader and Study Guide** **Chapter Resource File:*** • Biography Activity: Leo Szilard	**Daily Bellringer Transparency:** Section 5* **Quick Facts Transparency*** **Daily Test Practice Transparency*** **Internet Activity:** The Atomic Bomb

HOLT

History's Impact
American History Video Program (VHS/DVD)

The United States in World War II

Review, Assessment, Intervention

 Spanish Chapter Summaries Audio CD Program

 Progress Assessment Support System (PASS): Chapter Test*

 Differentiated Instruction Modified Worksheets and Tests CD-ROM: Modified Chapter Test

OSP **One-Stop Planner CD-ROM:** ExamView Test Generator (English/Spanish)

HOAP **Holt Online Assessment Program (HOAP),** in the Premier Online Edition.

 PASS: Section 1 Quiz*

 Online Quiz: Section 1

Alternative Assessment Handbook

 PASS: Section 2 Quiz*

 Online Quiz: Section 2

Alternative Assessment Handbook

 PASS: Section 3 Quiz*

 Online Quiz: Section 3

Alternative Assessment Handbook

 PASS: Section 4 Quiz*

 Online Quiz: Section 4

Alternative Assessment Handbook

 PASS: Section 5 Quiz*

 Online Quiz: Section 5

Alternative Assessment Handbook

NC RESOURCES

The following resources were developed to help North Carolina educators teach the standards and objectives of North Carolina's eleventh grade standard course of study in United States history.

- United States history EOC Test Prep Workbook
- Teacher's Support System
- North Carolina One-Stop Planner

And be sure to direct your students to **go.hrw.com** for online access to the EOC Test Prep Workbook.

go.hrw.com
EOC Test Prep
KEYWORD: SE7 NC

Holt Online Learning

go.hrw.com
Teacher Resources
KEYWORD: SD7 TEACHER

go.hrw.com
Student Resources
KEYWORD: SD7 CH24

- Document-based Questions
- Interactive Multimedia Activities

- Current Events
- Chapter-based Internet Activities
- and more!

Holt Premier
Online Student Edition

Complete online support for interactivity, assessment, and reporting

- Interactive Maps and Notebook
- Standardized Test Prep
- Homework Practice and Research Activities Online

The Big Picture

Robert D. Schulzinger

Fighting the War Germany and Japan seemed triumphant when the United States entered the war. The Allies concentrated first on defeating Germany in Europe and then on forcing the surrender of Japan. By mid-1944, the Allies were moving from east and west toward Germany itself. In the Pacific, the Allies hopped from island to island, and in 1945 their troops approached Japan. Germany and Japan surrendered in 1945. At least fifty million people were killed in the most destructive war in history.

The Holocaust One horror stood above the rest: the Nazi extermination of millions of Jews and others. In the 1930s the Nazi government took ever stricter measures against Jews, many of whom desperately sought to leave Germany, but neither the United States nor other countries welcomed Jewish refugees. After the fighting began, Nazi troops rounded up Jews and others considered to be enemies of Hitler's regime and sent them to concentration camps. There Hitler's forces gassed, starved, and worked to death millions of men, women, and children in an organized mass murder that became known as the Holocaust. During the war the Allies did not highlight the suffering of the Holocaust, but they later tried some of the Nazi leaders thought to be responsible for it.

The Home Front At home millions of Americans sacrificed in support of the war effort by conserving vital resources, buying war bonds, and going to work in defense plants. The power and reach of the federal government expanded. In the midst of panic after the attack on Pearl Harbor, President Roosevelt ordered the internment of 110,000 Japanese Americans, who then endured years of hardship in remote camps. Decades later the federal government formally apologized to the internees.

Recent Scholarship

The Decision to Drop the Bomb The United States' decision to drop atomic bombs on Japan is one of the most controversial events of the twentieth century. Some historians argue that the bomb shortened the war and saved hundreds of thousands of American lives. Others counter that the bombing was unnecessary to force Japan to surrender. J. Samuel Walker's *Prompt and Utter Destruction: Truman and the Use of the Atomic Bomb* (1997) pursues a middle ground. He concludes that the atomic bomb was not necessary to end the war in a short time, but it saved thousands—not hundreds of thousands—of American lives.

Differentiating Instruction

 Differentiated Instruction Teacher Management System
- Lesson Plans for Differentiated Instruction
- Differentiated Instructional Benchmarking Guides
- Interactive Reader and Study Guide

 Spanish Chapter Summaries Audio CD Program

 Online Chapter Summaries in Spanish

 Student Edition on Audio CD Program

 Differentiated Instruction Modified Worksheets and Tests CD-ROM
- Vocabulary Flash Cards
- Modified Vocabulary Builder Activities
- Modified Chapter Review Activity
- Modified Chapter Test

OSP One-Stop Planner CD-ROM
- ExamView Test Generator (English and Spanish)
- PuzzlePro
- Quiz Show for ExamView
- Transparencies and Videos

TE Differentiated Activities in the Teacher's Edition
- Life on a U-Boat, p. 771
- German Advance Across Russia, p. 772
- Memorial for Those Killed at Auschwitz, p. 781
- *Night,* p. 784
- Turning Points in the War in the Pacific, p. 788
- Propaganda Posters, p. 795
- Island Hopping Maps, p. 809
- Drawings of Military Life, p. 811

Reading Like a Historian
Sam Wineburg

Historical Context

Our chapter asks, "Why did the Nazi government single out Jews especially for mistreatment?"

If we consider historical context, we might question this statement's premise. We might argue that Nazis no more "singled out Jews especially for mistreatment" than someone singles out an umbrella for a rainstorm. A small minority in the sea of European Christendom, the Jews had long been singled out as alien and different.

Jews as the "Other"

The Jews constituted the quintessential "other," an easily identified group whose adherents rejected Jesus and who were often accused of "deicide," the killing of Christ. From Constantine's conversion in 312 AD to the first Crusade in 1095, much of this antagonism was theological and doctrinal, rooted in the differences between the parent religion, Judaism, and the new faith, Christianity.

St. John Chrysostom (344–407 AD) explained why God had seemed to reject the Jews, "Through your madness against Christ you have committed the ultimate transgression. This is why you are being punished worse now than in the past." Jews were perceived as blind to the truth, stubborn in their ways, and willfully ignorant of the true God.

It was with the Crusades that traditional antagonism against Jews took on otherworldly dimensions. No longer just an adherent of a rival faith, the Jews became evil incarnate in partnership with the devil. Throughout medieval Europe, Jews were accused of "desecrating the host"—burning or stabbing the wafer used in the mass service. The first massacre on this charge occurred in 1243 in Berlitz, near Berlin, when the city's Jewish population was burned alive. Similarly, many Jews lost their lives in riots caused by the trumped up "blood libel," in which Jews allegedly murdered Christian children and then used their blood to make the unleavened bread eaten during Passover.

With the Protestant Reformation, Martin Luther fully expected Europe's Jews to embrace a "reformed" Christianity. When they didn't, he turned against them, urging rulers to set "fire to their synagogues," raze their houses, and forbid rabbis from teaching.

The Rise of Modern Anti-Semitism

The French Revolution ultimately led to the Jews' "emancipation," the removal of legal restrictions barring them from civil society. But with emancipation came a virulent strain of anti-Semitism. Judaism was no longer viewed as an act of belief but a racial characteristic, something "in the blood." By the 1880s, anti-Semitism had become a political movement attracting some of the most educated members of society. Adolf Stoecker, the court chaplain to Kaiser Wilhelm, organized the Christian Social Labor Party in 1879, which advocated curtailing the Jews' civil rights and barring them from public office. In 1879 the Prussian nationalist historian Heinrich von Treitschke coined the phrase that the Nazis later adopted: "The Jews are our misfortune" ('Die Juden sind unser Unglück').

In his three-volume history *The Destruction of European Jewry* (1985), Raul Hilberg argued that Nazi racial legislation had roots in an earlier period. The decree requiring Jews to wear the yellow star originated in the Fourth Lateran Council. Laws barring Jews from universities and forcing them into ghettos began during the Council of Basel in 1431–1445. For most of European history, the Jew was told, "You cannot live as Jews among us," which required them to live in ghettos. They were told, "You cannot live among us," which required their expulsion. The Nazis brought the hatred of Jews to a new level. Hitler's Final Solution simply said, "You have no right to live."

Christianity did not cause the Holocaust. Yet, as Dennis Prager and Joseph Telushkin argue in *Why the Jews: The Reason for Antisemitism* (2003), it is impossible to understand the appeal of the Nazis' racial policies without understanding the history of European anti-Semitism. The Nazis followed in others' footsteps in viewing the Jew as evil incarnate. Where the Nazis innovated was in bringing the technological and bureaucratic power of the modern state to the wholesale murder to the Jewish people.

Standards Focus

Social Studies Competency Goals
Goal 10 The learner will analyze United States involvement in World War II and the war's influence on international affairs in following decades.

🔖 **10.02, 10.03**

The Big Idea and Essential Questions

To foster student understanding of this chapter's big idea, design your lesson to address each section's essential question.

Big Idea The Allies, including the United States, defeated the Axis Powers in Europe and the Pacific in World War II.

Essential Questions

1. Where did the United States focus its attention after entering World War II?

2. What was the impact of the Nazi government's actions during the Holocaust?

3. How did the war develop in the Pacific?

4. What contributions to the war effort did Americans make on the home front?

5. How did World War II end?

Key to Differentiating Instruction

Below Level

Basic-level activities designed for all students encountering new material

At Level

Intermediate-level activities designed for average students

Above Level

Challenging activities designed for honors and gifted-and-talented students

Standard English Mastery

Activities designed to improve standard English usage

CHAPTER
24 1941–1945
The United States in WORLD WAR II

THE BIG PICTURE The United States succeeded along with the Allies to defeat the Axis powers in Europe and the Pacific. Yet the cost of victory and the discovery of the full horrors of World War II were staggering.

🔖 North Carolina Standards

Social Studies Objectives

10.02 Identify military, political, and diplomatic turning points of the war and determine their significance to the outcome and aftermath of the conflict.

10.03 Describe and analyze the effects of the war on American economic, social, political, and cultural life.

Language Arts Objectives

3.03 Use argumentation for:

• establishing and defending a point of view.

Skills FOCUS   READING LIKE A HISTORIAN

U.S. soldiers in Germany pose on top of an enormous cannon captured from the Germans. These guns were called railway guns because they required one or even two sets of railroad tracks to move their bulk. **Interpreting Visuals** What do the soldiers' poses tell you about their attitudes?

See Skills Handbook, p. H30

768

U.S.

World

1941

January 6 Roosevelt delivers the Four Freedoms speech about the future of the world.

December 7 Japan attacks Pearl Harbor.

June 22 Germany begins its invasion of the Soviet Union.

Introduce the Chapter

At Level

The United States in World War II

1. Tell students that in this chapter they will learn about the most devastating war in recent history. It began with the rise of totalitarian governments in Europe and ended with dropping the atomic bomb on two cities in Japan.

2. To help students understand that this was a world war, have them use the atlas in their texts to create their own maps of the world. Have students scan the chapter, refer to the maps in the text, and identify the countries and regions that were involved in World War II. Have students color and code their own maps showing the land and sea areas that were affected by and involved in the war.

3. Have volunteers share their maps with the class, and guide students in a discussion of the global nature of World War II. **LS Visual-Spatial**

📝 Alternative Assessment Handbook, Rubrics 20: Map Creation; and 37: Writing Assignments

June 4
Americans destroy four Japanese aircraft carriers in the Battle of Midway.

January
Americans win the Battle of Guadalcanal.

July 10
Allies invade Sicily.

June 6
Allies launch invasion of France.

August 15
After the bombings of Hiroshima and Nagasaki, the Japanese surrender.

1942 • 1943 • 1944 • 1945

1942
Hitler and the Nazis formalize plans for exterminating Europe's Jews.

February
The Soviet Union finally defeats the Germans in the Battle of Stalingrad.

June
French Resistance forces aid the Allied invasion of France.

April 30
Adolf Hitler commits suicide in Berlin.

769

Chapter Preview

HOLT

History's Impact
▶ Video Program: The United States in World War II
See the Video Teacher's Guide for strategies for using the video segment.

Reading Like a Historian

World War II Soldiers Have students take a moment to examine the image on these pages. Where do they think these soldiers might be? Tell students that as they study the chapter they will learn about the battle to take the Atlantic Ocean, the D-Day offensive, and the Allied victory over Germany.

go.hrw.com
Online Resources

Chapter Resources:
KEYWORD: SD7 CH24

Teacher Resources:
KEYWORD: SD7 TEACHER

Explore the Time Line

1. When was the attack on Pearl Harbor?
December 7, 1941

2. When did World War II finally end?
August 15, 1945

3. How much time elapsed between the Soviet victory at Stalingrad and the Allied invasion of France? *16 months*

Info to Know

Free French forces More than 100,000 Free French soldiers fought with British and American troops in Italy, and at the time of the D-Day invasion, more than 300,000 Free French troops were fighting in the war.

Draw Conclusions Why do you think it was difficult for the French to organize an army? *France had been invaded, troops had scattered; some had been forced to serve with the Vichy government.*

Answers

Reading Like a Historian (p. 768)
confident and relaxed; undoubtedly proud of their accomplishments in the hard-fought battles across Europe

769

Bellringer

The Inside Story. . . Use the **Daily Bellringer Transparency** to help students answer the question.

🖳 Daily Bellringer Transparency, Section 1

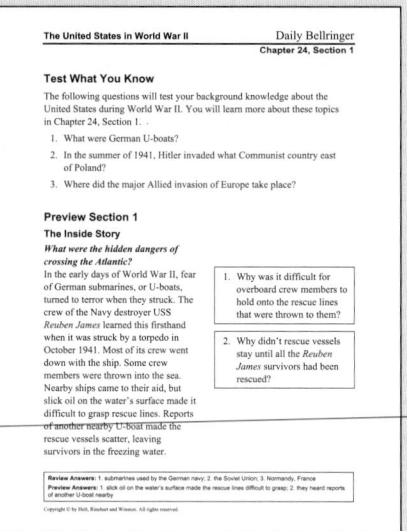

| The United States in World War II | Daily Bellringer |
| | Chapter 24, Section 1 |

Test What You Know

The following questions will test your background knowledge about the United States during World War II. You will learn more about these topics in Chapter 24, Section 1. . .

1. What were German U-boats?
2. In the summer of 1941, Hitler invaded what Communist country east of Poland?
3. Where did the major Allied invasion of Europe take place?

Preview Section 1

The Inside Story

What were the hidden dangers of crossing the Atlantic?

In the early days of World War II, fear of German submarines, or U-boats, turned to terror when they struck. The crew of the Navy destroyer USS *Reuben James* learned this firsthand when it was struck by a torpedo in October 1941. Most of its crew went down with the ship. Some crew members were thrown into the sea. Nearby ships came to their aid, but slick oil on the water's surface made it difficult to grasp rescue lines. Reports of another nearby U-boat made the rescue vessels scatter, leaving survivors in the freezing water.

| 1. Why was it difficult for overboard crew members to hold onto the rescue lines that were thrown to them? |
| 2. Why didn't rescue vessels stay until all the *Reuben James* survivors had been rescued? |

Review Answers: 1. submarines used by the German navy; 2. the Soviet Union; 3. Normandy, France
Preview Answers: 1. slick oil on the water's surface made the rescue lines difficult to grasp; 2. they heard reports of another U-boat nearby

Copyright © by Holt, Rinehart and Winston. All rights reserved.

Academic Vocabulary

Review with students the high-use academic term in this section.

logical based on correct reasoning (p. 773)

🖳 CRF: Vocabulary Builder Activity, Section 1

Taking Notes

Atlantic Ocean—fight for control, U-boats give Germany early edge, American ships overcome U-boat advantages, Allies break German code; Europe—Germany invades Soviet Union, bloody battles and harsh winter halt German advance, Allies invade Italy and France; North Africa—British and Italian forces fight, British defeat Germans at El Alamein, Americans defeat Rommel's forces

---

SECTION 1

The War in Europe and North Africa

BEFORE YOU READ

MAIN IDEA

After entering World War II, the United States focused first on the war in Europe.

READING FOCUS

1. How and why did the Allies fight the Battle of the Atlantic?
2. What were the key events of the war in the Soviet Union?
3. What did American forces accomplish in North Africa and Italy?
4. What were the events and significance of the Allies' D-Day invasion of France?

KEY TERMS AND PEOPLE

wolf pack
Erwin Rommel
Operation Torch
Dwight D. Eisenhower
Tuskegee Airmen
Operation Overlord
Omar Bradley
D-Day
Battle of the Bulge
George S. Patton

TAKING NOTES As you read, take notes on the war in the Atlantic Ocean, Europe, and North Africa. Write your notes in a graphic organizer like the one shown below.

Atlantic Ocean	Europe	North Africa

The Sinking of the Reuben James

▲ The *Reuben James*, the first U.S. vessel destroyed by enemy fire in World War II, lost more than 100 of its crew.

THE INSIDE STORY

What were the hidden dangers of crossing the Atlantic? For ships traveling across the Atlantic Ocean in the early days of World War II, the danger of German submarine attack was always present. Unable to tell whether U-boats, or submarines, were lurking nearby, ships' crews lived in constant fear of attack. When submarines struck without warning, that fear turned to terror.

The crew of the Navy destroyer USS *Reuben James* learned this firsthand in October 1941. At the time, the United States had not yet entered the war. Its ships, however, were serving as escorts to convoys carrying goods from American ports to Great Britain. It was while on such a mission that the *Reuben James* was attacked by a German U-boat. Following a torpedo strike, the ship's ammunition exploded. The *Reuben James* sank quickly. Most of its crew, including all officers, went down with the ship.

A number of crew members, however, were thrown into the sea. They struggled to stay afloat in the freezing water, which was covered with a thick, black layer of oily fuel from the *Reuben James*. Nearby ships rushed to their aid, but the slick oil made it difficult for the sailors to grasp the rescue lines. Reports of another nearby U-boat made the rescue vessels scatter—leaving survivors still bobbing in the sea.

The terrible story of the *Reuben James* would be repeated often in the months ahead. As you will read, the first battles the United States would fight were not on dry land but on the high seas. There it would take time before the United States and its allies would find effective ways to fight their hidden enemy—the German U-boat. ■

Teach the Main Idea

At Level

The War in Europe and North Africa

1. **Teach** Ask students the Reading Focus questions to teach this section.

2. **Apply** Have students create a time line of the events in this section beginning with the defeat of German forces in North Africa in May 1943 and ending with the Allied victory at the Battle of the Bulge in January 1945.

3. **Review** Have volunteers identify dates and events on their time lines and create a class

time line for all to see. Guide students in a discussion of the significance of each of the events on the class time line.

4. **Practice/Homework** Have students write a brief newspaper article describing the suffering that the citizens of Leningrad endured during the 900-day German siege of the city. **LS Verbal-Linguistic, Visual-Spatial**

🖳 Alternative Assessment Handbook, Rubrics 36: Time Lines; and 40: Writing to Describe

The Battle of the Atlantic

For the United States and the Allies, defeating the Axis Powers depended largely on control of the seas. It was only by sea that the United States could deliver soldiers and supplies to the hard-pressed opponents of Hitler. If the Atlantic was not kept safe for shipping, the Axis would soon win the war.

Germany entered World War II with a navy powerful enough to challenge for control of the seas. It featured several new surface ships. Foremost among these was the giant *Bismarck*, the pride of the German fleet. After Great Britain managed to sink the *Bismarck* in 1941, however, Germany began to rely on a familiar weapon—the U-boat.

U-boat attacks In World War I the Allies had learned to protect ships against U-boats by forming convoys. Early in World War II, however, the British (and the Americans) did not have enough vessels to form effective convoys. This made it easy for U-boats to attack supply ships bound for Great Britain. The Germans also developed new tactics to increase U-boat

effectiveness. One example was the so-called **wolf pack**, in which U-boats hunted in groups and often attacked at night.

The German U-boat fleet enjoyed what it referred to as the "happy time" in 1940 and 1941. U-boats sent hundreds of ships and tons of supplies to the bottom of the sea. At the same time, the German navy lost only a few dozen U-boats.

After Germany declared war on the United States, U-boat attacks on American shipping increased. German submarines even patrolled the waters off the East Coast of the United States. There they made easy pickings of merchant ships that sailed from American ports without the protection of a full convoy. In a few short months, 360 American ships were sunk compared to just eight German U-boats.

The Allies fight back Despite early losses, America's entry into the war would help turn the tide in the Battle of the Atlantic. Energized American shipyards began producing new ships at an amazing rate. These were used to form larger, better-equipped convoys, which helped cut down on the effectiveness of U-boat

Reading Focus

1 How and why did the Allies fight the Battle of the Atlantic? *Ships crossed in convoys protected by aircraft and radar. It was only by sea that the U.S. could deliver soldiers and supplies to Europe.*

The Battle of the Atlantic

Recall Why was it so easy for German U-boats to attack British supply ships at the beginning of World War II? *The British did not have enough ships to form effective convoys.*

Identify Cause and Effect How did America's entry into the war help turn the tide in the Battle of the Atlantic? *American shipyards produced new ships at an amazing rate, and these ships were used to form larger, better protected convoys.*

Evaluate Which do you think was more important in helping the Allies protect shipping lines, breaking the Enigma code or use of better protected convoys? *possible answer—breaking the code so that the Allies knew where to expect attacks and could protect ships*

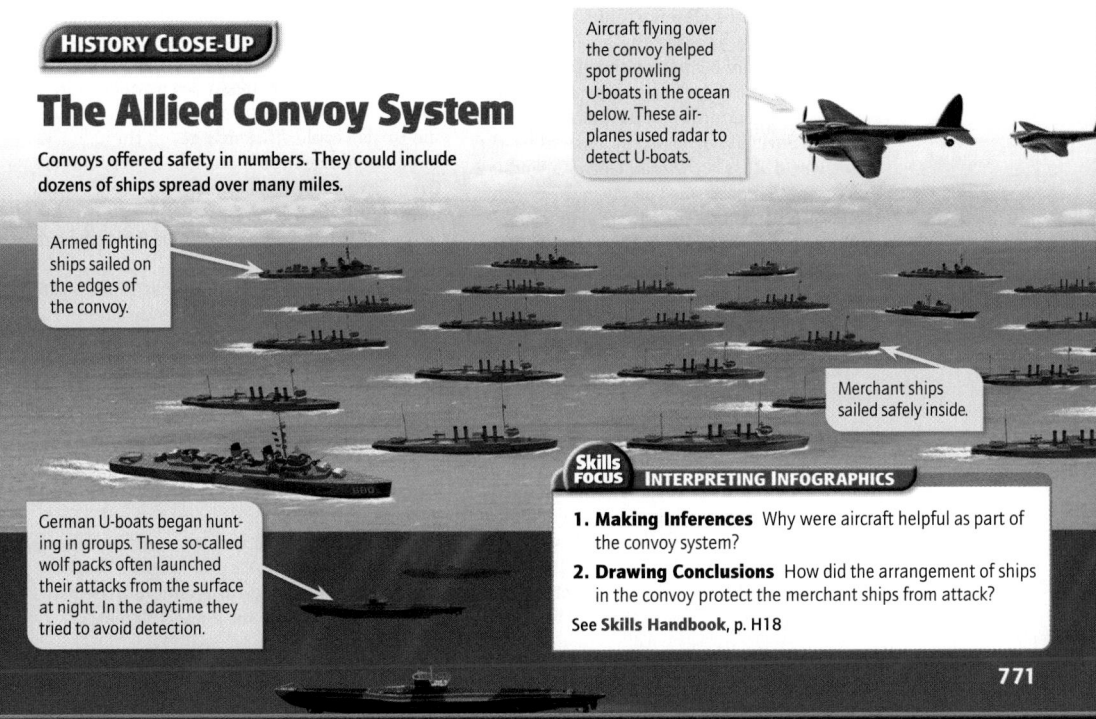

HISTORY CLOSE-UP

The Allied Convoy System

Convoys offered safety in numbers. They could include dozens of ships spread over many miles.

Aircraft flying over the convoy helped spot prowling U-boats in the ocean below. These airplanes used radar to detect U-boats.

Armed fighting ships sailed on the edges of the convoy.

Merchant ships sailed safely inside.

German U-boats began hunting in groups. These so-called wolf packs often launched their attacks from the surface at night. In the daytime they tried to avoid detection.

Skills FOCUS INTERPRETING INFOGRAPHICS

1. **Making Inferences** Why were aircraft helpful as part of the convoy system?
2. **Drawing Conclusions** How did the arrangement of ships in the convoy protect the merchant ships from attack?

See Skills Handbook, p. H18

771

Differentiating Instruction

Above Level

Advanced Learners/GATE

Research Required

1. Organize the class into small groups. Have each group conduct research about life on a German U-boat during the war. Students should include at least one primary source (such as journals, diaries, or letters from men who served on a U-boat). Students may wish to use the school library, the local public library, or the Internet to find reliable sources and documents.

2. Based on their research, have each group write a script for a skit about life on a U-boat.

3. Have each group present its skit for the rest of the class.

4. After all of the skits have been presented, lead the class in a discussion of the skits. How did the skits differ? What similarities were there? What did students learn about life on a U-boat? **LS Interpersonal, Kinesthetic**

Alternative Assessment Handbook, Rubrics 14: Group Activity; 30: Research; and 33: Skits and Reader's Theater

Answers

Interpreting Infographics 1. *airplanes spotted U-boats;* **2.** *The fighting ships formed a barrier between the U-boats and the merchant ships.*

② What were the key events of the war in the Soviet Union? *siege of Leningrad; battle of Stalingrad*

The War in the Soviet Union

Describe Why was Stalingrad a major target for the Germans? *It was an important industrial center.*

Summarize How did the Russian winter help save the Soviet Union from falling to the Germans? *German soldiers and equipment performed poorly in freezing temperatures; severe weather slowed the invasion.*

Develop What might have happened if the Germans had taken Stalingrad? *With access to an industrial base, they could have built more weapons and heavy equipment. Soviets might have been demoralized and had little means to stop German advance.*

Have students use the map of Europe and North Africa in their texts to understand how far German troops traveled to reach Stalingrad.

Answers

Reading Check (left) *larger, better protected convoys; air protection; advances in radar; broke the German code system;* **(right)** *German troops quickly advance; suffer during bitterly cold winter; siege of Leningrad; Soviet victory in Stalingrad; Soviet forces gradually push German troops back*

772

---

attacks. At the same time, new Allied aircraft protected convoys from the air. The aircraft and escort ships used radar and other technologies to find and destroy more U-boats.

Another factor in the Allied success was the breaking of Germany's code system, which was called Enigma. After cracking Enigma in 1941, the Allies began to gain vital information about the locations and plans of U-boat formations.

These factors began to give the Allies an advantage over German U-boats. German sailors were soon referring to their ships as "iron coffins." By war's end, some 70 percent of the Germans who had served on a submarine were dead. The Atlantic belonged to the Allies.

READING CHECK **Identifying Problems and Solutions** How did the Allies overcome the German U-boats and win the Battle of the Atlantic?

The War in the Soviet Union

In the summer of 1941, Hitler broke his nonaggression pact with Stalin and sent his forces into the Soviet Union. (The Soviets thus joined the Allies as enemies of the Axis Powers.) For the next several months, German forces stormed across the Soviet countryside. As they had in Poland and France, German tanks, planes, and soldiers steadily pressed the attack. Stalin's forces seemed unable to stop the blitzkrieg.

Though the Soviet Union appeared close to collapse, it did not fall. As autumn came and went, the Soviets were joined by a new ally—the bitterly cold Russian winter. German soldiers and equipment performed poorly in the freezing temperatures, and their invasion slowed.

Still, the Germans held a huge portion of the western Soviet Union. They had also besieged the city of Leningrad. The suffering of the people there was extreme. With little food and fuel, some 200,000 residents died in January and February alone. Hundreds of thousands more would perish in the months ahead.

The Battle of Stalingrad When spring returned to the Soviet Union, the German armies renewed their assault. One major target was the city of Stalingrad, a major industrial center on the Volga River. The Germans attacked Stalingrad in August 1942. In some of the bloodiest fighting in the history of warfare, the Soviets refused to let Stalingrad fall.

Not only did the Germans fail to take Stalingrad, they also exposed themselves to a Soviet counterattack. In the fighting that followed, 250,000 Axis soldiers were trapped by Soviet forces. The surviving Axis troops were forced to surrender in early 1943. Hitler had suffered a stunning defeat.

Stalingrad marked the beginning of Germany's collapse in the Soviet Union. Thereafter, Soviet forces began to push German forces back toward Germany. The fighting took a terrible toll. Hitler's forces suffered losses of some 2 million, and the Soviets paid an even higher price—12 million soldiers. Millions of civilians also died. In Leningrad alone, as many as 800,000 civilians perished before the siege there was finally lifted in January 1944. Yet the Soviet Union had survived. Now it was fighting toward the final defeat of the Axis.

READING CHECK **Sequencing** Briefly describe the sequence of events of the war in the Soviet Union.

American Forces in North Africa and Italy

Soon after the fall of France in June 1940, the British and Italians began a battle for North Africa. This territory was vital to the Allies. By controlling it, the British could protect shipping on the Mediterranean Sea against Italian attack. This shipping was a lifeline by which the British could efficiently get oil through the Suez Canal from the Middle East. Without oil Great Britain would not be able to defend itself, much less defeat the Axis.

In the early fighting, Italian forces based in Libya tried to drive the British from their stronghold in Egypt. They failed. In fact, the Italians were beaten badly and driven backwards. Hitler was forced to send troops to support the Italians in early 1941. At the head of these forces was the famed German general **Erwin Rommel**. Throughout 1941 and 1942, Rommel's forces and the British fought a backand-forth battle for control of North Africa. Though Rommel led brilliantly—it was here he earned the nickname Desert Fox—the British ultimately gained control. At the battle of El Alamein (el-a-luh-MAYN), fought about the same time as the Battle of Stalingrad, the British handed the Germans a major defeat.

772 CHAPTER 24

Learners Having Difficulty

Materials colored markers, drawing paper, map of Europe showing Soviet Union

1. Organize the class into mixed-ability pairs. Have each pair create its own map of the Soviet Union. Maps should show the cities of Leningrad and Stalingrad.

2. Have each pair draw the German advance across the Soviet Union on their maps. Maps should also include a key showing the dates of the German siege of both cities.

3. Have students include the length of the siege on their map keys.

4. Have volunteers share their maps with the class. Have students, especially struggling readers, keep the maps as a study tool.

LS Interpersonal, Logical-Mathematical

Alternative Assessment Handbook, Rubric 20: Map Creation

WORLD WAR II IN EUROPE AND NORTH AFRICA, 1941–1944

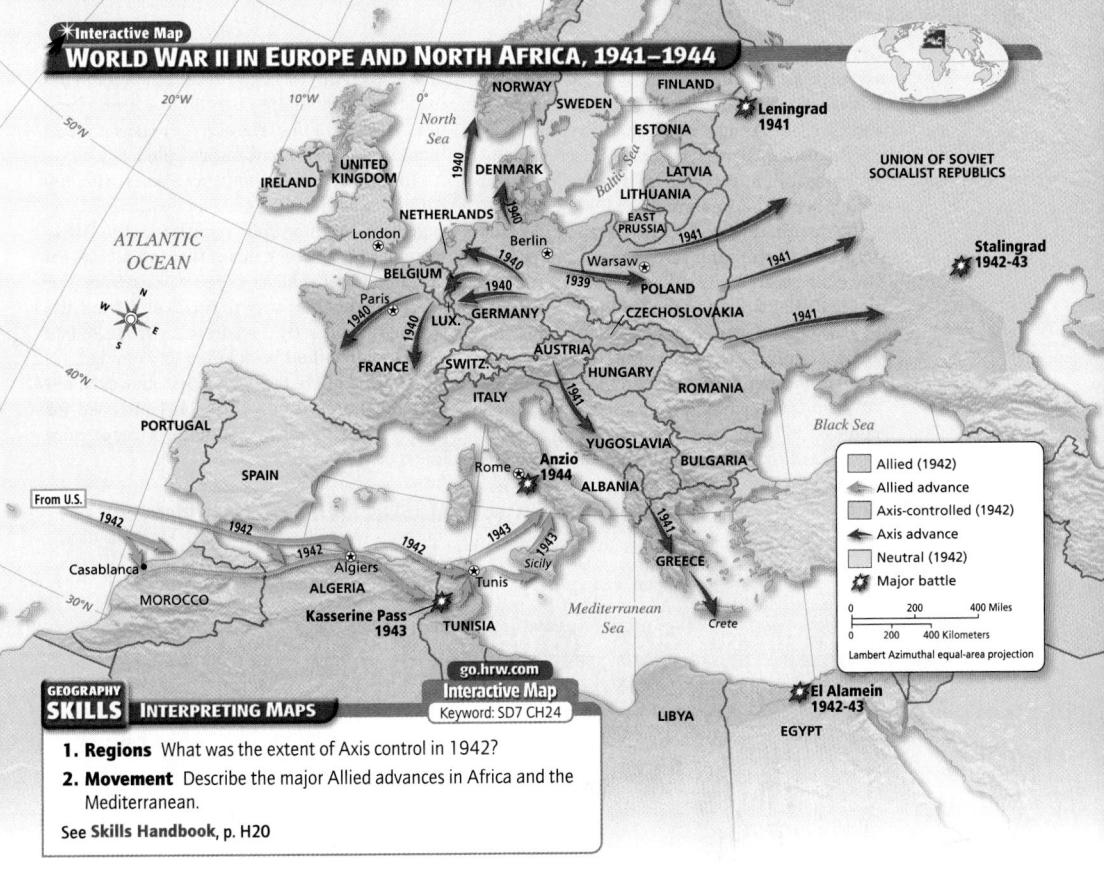

GEOGRAPHY SKILLS INTERPRETING MAPS

go.hrw.com
Interactive Map
Keyword: SD7 CH24

1. **Regions** What was the extent of Axis control in 1942?
2. **Movement** Describe the major Allied advances in Africa and the Mediterranean.

See **Skills Handbook**, p. H20

Map legend:
- Allied (1942)
- Allied advance
- Axis-controlled (1942)
- Axis advance
- Neutral (1942)
- Major battle

0   200   400 Miles
0   200   400 Kilometers
Lambert Azimuthal equal-area projection

Operation Torch When the United States entered the war in late 1941, President Roosevelt was anxious to make a contribution quickly. Stalin wanted the Allies to invade Europe, to help divide Hitler's attentions. Other Allied leaders, however, resisted calls to rush into Europe unprepared. North Africa, it was decided, was the logical place for American soldiers to enter the fray.

The commander of what came to be called **Operation Torch** was a U.S. lieutenant general named **Dwight D. Eisenhower**. The plan called for American forces to invade the North African countries of Morocco and Algeria in November 1942. France had controlled this territory before 1940. After the fall of France, Vichy leaders were installed there. Still, the Allies hoped that the French in North Africa

would side with them in battle. Indeed, the Allies met little resistance upon landing, and French forces soon joined them.

After landing, Allied forces turned east to fight the Germans. In battles at places such as Kasserine Pass, Americans gained valuable combat experience. Some 20,000 Americans were killed or wounded in the six months of North Africa fighting. But by May 1943, they had helped defeat Rommel's forces.

While this fighting was taking place, Allied leaders focused on the war's next phases. Stalin continued to push for a European invasion, and in the planning stages was a massive invasion of France. In early 1943, however, such an operation was still a year away. For now, Allied leaders prepared to cross the Mediterranean and knock the Italians out of the war.

ACADEMIC VOCABULARY
logical based on correct reasoning

THE UNITED STATES IN WORLD WAR II **773**

Direct Teach

Reading Focus

3 What did American forces accomplish in North Africa and Italy? *helped drive the Axis out of North Africa; used it as a base for invading Italy*

American Forces in North Africa and Italy

Explain Why was Erwin Rommel sent to North Africa? *Italians were beaten; Hitler sent Rommel and German troops to continue the battle.*

Make Inferences Why did the Italians and Germans want to drive the British out of North Africa? *Axis Powers wanted to cut off the oil supply to Britain.*

Make Judgments Why do you think French soldiers in North Africa joined Allied forces in North Africa? *possible answers—The Nazis had installed the military leaders; French soldiers' allegiance may have been with the Allies, not the Nazis.*

📋 American History Outline Maps: World War II in Europe

💻 Map Transparency: World War II in Europe and North Africa, 1941–1944

✳ **Interactive Map:** World War II in Europe and North Africa, 1941–1944

Skills Focus: Interpreting Historical Maps

Below Level

Social Studies Skill
World War II in Europe and North Africa

1. Have the class study the map of Europe and North Africa at the top of the page. Ask students to identify which of the nations shown on the map were neutral in 1942. Ask students what it means to be neutral. *Ireland, Switzerland, Sweden, Portugal, Spain, Turkey, and Egypt; to be neutral means not to take sides*

2. Have students use their own paper to create a chronological list, from earliest to latest, of the major battles shown on the map.

3. Have volunteers read their lists of battles. Write the battles for students to see. Then ask students which side, either Allied or Axis, won each battle and write the correct answer for students to see. 🄻🅂 **Visual-Spatial**

📋 Alternative Assessment Handbook, Rubric 21: Map Reading

Answers

Interpreting Maps 1. *Axis Powers controlled most of North Africa except Egypt; most of Europe except Sweden, Switzerland, Spain, United Kingdom, Ireland, Portugal, and Turkey.* **2.** *east through Morocco and Algeria, to Tunis, then Italy*

On to Italy

Recall How did the Italian people respond to the Allied invasion of Sicily? *They turned against Mussolini and forced him from power.*

Draw Conclusions Why are the Tuskegee Airmen remembered? *They were the first African Americans to receive training as pilots, and they overcame widespread discrimination.*

Develop Why was Anzio a significant victory for Allied forces? *It gave the Allies their first foothold in Europe.*

📄 CRF: Biography: Groups That Made a Difference

Info to Know

The Tuskegee Airmen During World War II, most African American soldiers served in noncombat positions. The Tuskegee Airmen, an all-black unit of fighter pilots, engaged in their first combat mission in June 1943, when they launched an assault on a small Italian island. During the next two years they escorted bombing missions and attacked Axis air fields, supply centers, and communication lines. By the end of the war the Tuskegee Airmen were the only U.S. escort group that had not lost a single bomber to enemy planes.

Answers

Reading Check *fierce fighting, significant losses, eventual victory*

On to Italy The first major step in this assault was the July 1943 invasion of the island of Sicily. Soon after the attack began, Roosevelt and Churchill issued a message to the Italian people asking them "whether they want to die for Mussolini and Hitler or live for Italy and civilization." The Italians chose life. By the end of the month, they had turned against dictator Benito Mussolini and forced him from power. The Allies took Sicily a few weeks later. They planned next to occupy the Italian Peninsula.

Hitler, however, was not going to let the Allies simply march through Italy and into Europe. German forces rushed to stop them.

Despite German resistance, the Allies made steady progress at first. Taking part in the fighting were the **Tuskegee Airmen**. This was a segregated unit of African Americans, the first ever to receive training as pilots in the U.S. military.

After its early success, the Allied invasion slowed as it approached Rome. To keep it moving, the Allies planned to land a large force behind enemy lines. The site they chose for this landing was a seafront resort called Anzio.

In late January, the first of some 100,000 Allied soldiers went ashore at Anzio. Fighting raged for the next four months as the Allies were unable to break out of their small coastal beachhead. Finally, Allied forces from the south fought their way to Anzio and freed the trapped soldiers. By then, from 25,000 to 30,000 Allied soldiers had been killed or wounded.

The end of the battle at Anzio, however, did not end the fighting in Italy. It continued for nearly a year. Some 300,000 Allied troops were killed or wounded there.

READING CHECK **Summarizing** What did American forces experience in North Africa and Italy?

Americans in North Africa and Italy

The Tuskegee Airmen's 99th Pursuit Squadron (left) provided air support in both North Africa and Italy. Among their numerous awards, their fighter group was honored for "outstanding performance and extraordinary heroism." In all, the Tuskegee Airmen completed 15,500 missions. Below, elite U.S. Army Rangers charge up an Italian hillside. Rangers, specially trained volunteers who had been serving in Northern Ireland, spearheaded the push through Italy.

Skills Focus: Identifying Problem and Solution | At Level

Reading Skill
The Allies on the Offensive

1. Have students use the map of Europe and North Africa to identify where the Allied invasion in Europe began. From where did the Allies launch their offensive attacks? *the island of Sicily; from North Africa*

2. Tell students that military leaders prepare detailed battle plans before any major operation. Have each student prepare a one-page military brief suggesting Sicily and the mainland of Italy as the starting point for the Allied invasion of Europe. Students' briefs should discuss the advantages and disadvantages of that choice.

3. Have volunteers read their briefs to the class, then guide the class in a discussion of the briefs. Ask students why they think the Allies started by invading Italy rather than France.
   LS Logical-Mathematical, Verbal-Linguistic

📄 Alternative Assessment Handbook, Rubric 37: Writing Assignments

D-Day: The Invasion of France

The fighting in Italy was slow and difficult partly because the Allies could not devote all their fighting resources to the battle. Many of these resources were being held for the planned invasion of France. This plan came to be known as **Operation Overlord**.

Planning Operation Overlord To end the war as quickly as possible, the Allies wanted to launch a large invasion of mainland Europe. Careful planning was vital. The Allies worked for months to select a location for Operation Overlord. They finally settled on the beaches of Normandy, in northern France.

The Allies had to assemble huge numbers of troops, weapons, and other equipment necessary for an invasion. Eisenhower commanded the mission and chose General **Omar Bradley** to lead the American troops. The top British commander was Bernard Montgomery.

While good planning was important, speed was also vital. Of particular concern to the Allies was the expected introduction of two new German weapons, the V1 flying bomb and the V2 rocket. The Allies were able to destroy some rocket-launch sites, but fears of these dangerous weapons forced the Allies onward.

The landing at Normandy By early June 1944, the Allied force of 3.5 million soldiers was ready for action. Tension ran high. The soldiers knew they had to succeed—and that success was uncertain. They knew that at Normandy they would meet a determined German force.

After a short delay caused by bad weather, **D-Day** finally arrived on June 6, 1944. The attack began with soldiers parachuting behind the German lines to try to secure key sites. Ships offshore rained shells on the coastline to destroy German defenses. Allied aircraft filled the sky to provide cover for the wave of troops to come. A variety of amphibious craft helped deliver equipment and soldiers to the beaches.

In the end, however, the success of Operation Overlord came down to the courage of the individual soldiers who would make the landing. Their job was to wait for their landing-craft gate to open—then to move forward toward shore. By the thousands, they waded through the surf till they hit the sand and then raced through obstacles, wounded and dead comrades, and a hail of gunfire to find something to hide behind. Then those who managed to get that far gathered their courage, got to their feet, and went forward again. All was chaos and confusion. Little went according to plan. Still, soldiers stuck to their assigned tasks.

HISTORY'S VOICES

❝It's amazing what you can do when you're called upon to do it. There was just an overwhelming demand for me to do my duty. Patriotism—that was there. But more, I was filled with a sense of duty. This was my duty, my assigned duty. This is what was expected of me.❞

—Frank Walk, recorded in *War Stories*, by Elizabeth Mullener

Fortunately for the Allies, the Germans were slow to respond to the invasion. Thanks in part to Allied deceptions, Hitler feared that the assault on Normandy was just a trick and that another invasion would take place elsewhere. For precious days, German leaders delayed in sending backup forces to the area. By the time they realized their mistake, the Allies had established a beachhead.

Though the costs were high—an estimated 10,000 Allied casualties, including 6,600 Americans—D-Day had been a success. With each day, more troops and equipment came ashore. By early July, the Allies had landed almost a million soldiers and nearly 180,000 vehicles. The landing area was considered secure enough to send in members of the Women's

---

FACES OF HISTORY

Dwight EISENHOWER
1890–1969

Dwight D. Eisenhower was known for his logical mind, a talent for organizing, and an outgoing yet diplomatic attitude. He proved to be the ideal person to lead the Allied military force in World War II.

From his humble childhood in the small farm town of Abilene, Kansas, Eisenhower rose steadily through the ranks of the army. During World War II, General George C. Marshall chose Eisenhower to be Supreme Allied Commander in Europe. In this position Eisenhower planned and commanded Operation Overlord (D-Day), the invasion of France. He also accepted Germany's surrender in 1945.

Explain In what ways do you think Eisenhower's personality helped make him a good leader in World War II?

Skills Focus: Making Inferences

Reading Skill
D-Day Disaster

1. Organize the class into small groups. Have each group make a list of things that could have gone wrong on D-Day. *German aircraft could have sunk Allied ships and Allied aircraft shot down preventing paratroopers from being dropped inland. German defenses could have kept the beaches secure.*

2. Guide students in a discussion of what might have happened if the Allies' D-Day invasion of France had failed. Have each group write a scenario about what might have happened if the Germans had responded more quickly to the invasion.

3. Have volunteers from each group read their scenarios to the class. **LS Interpersonal, Verbal-Linguistic**

📝 Alternative Assessment Handbook, Rubrics 14: Group Activity; and 37: Writing Assignments

Reading Focus

The Battle of the Bulge

Explain How did the Battle of the Bulge get its name? *from the bulge in the Allied battle lines created by the German advance*

Rank Which do you think was more important to Allied victory in Europe, the victory on D-Day or at the Battle of Bulge? *possible answers—D-Day because it gave the Allies a foothold in Europe; Battle of the Bulge because Germany was badly defeated*

Info to Know

Operation Fortitude Operation Fortitude was the code name for the elaborate campaign of deception that preceded Operation Overlord. Months before the invasion at Normandy, U.S. commanders created a "phantom" army. Allied planes also dropped tons of bombs on the northeastern coast of France, and on the night before D-Day thousands of soldiers gathered near a "fleet" of unseaworthy landing craft in British ports across the English Channel from Calais. This dummy invasion force was equipped with cardboard tanks that were made by members of the American and British film industries.

About the Illustration

This illustration is an artist's conception based on available sources. Historians, however, are uncertain exactly what this scene looked like.

✴ **Interactive History Close-Up:** D-Day, June 6, 1944

Answers

Reading Check *difficult logistics; Allies had to work together; equipment had to be brought together for the invasion; troops had to be trained*

✴ Interactive
HISTORY CLOSE-UP

D-Day, June 6, 1944

Allied forces landed at five separate sites at Normandy on D-Day of the invasion of France. Omaha Beach was one of two beaches invaded by U.S. forces (see map opposite). As American soldiers moved toward the nearly 100-foot-high cliffs, German guns at the top rained a deadly fire down on them.

Allied aircraft provided cover for the invading forces.

Allied warships fired shells on German positions before and during the landing.

Army Corp. They were to supply support for the forces that would soon fight their way past German defenses at Normandy. This breakthrough occurred in late July. As the German commander reported, "The whole western front has been ripped open."

The Allies were now on the march in France. By the end of August, Paris had been freed from the Germans. Hitler's once mighty war machine was now in full retreat.

The Battle of the Bulge Throughout the fall of 1944, the Allies moved eastward. The Germans fought well in places. For example, the Battle of Hürtgen Forest claimed thousands of Allied lives. Overall, however, the Germans appeared near collapse. As one of Eisenhower's advisers put it in early December, "The battle is over and the German army has had it."

This judgment, it turned out, was premature. On December 16, 1944, the Germans launched a surprise offensive of their own. The attack was known as the **Battle of the Bulge**. This referred to the bulge in the Allied battle

lines created by the German advance. For several days, Hitler's forces threatened to win back vital ground from the Allies.

A key moment in the battle came at the Belgian city of Bastogne. This was an important crossroads, and the Germans were determined to take it. Even more determined was the small force of American defenders. Surrounded by Germans, shivering in below-zero temperatures and low on supplies, the Americans clung to survival. But survive they did. On December 26, troops led by Lieutenant General **George S. Patton** arrived to provide relief for the American force. The victory at Bastogne helped blunt the German offensive. It also became a symbol of American strength and determination.

By the end of January 1945, the bulge created by the German offensive had been rolled back. Once again the Allies set their sights on Germany and the defeat of Hitler. Victory was close at hand.

READING CHECK Drawing Conclusions
Why did the planning for D-Day take so long?

776 CHAPTER 24

Collaborative Learning

At Level

First-Person Accounts

Research Required

1. Organize the class into small groups. Have each group find primary source materials written by American soldiers who served in Europe or North Africa during the war. Assign each group one of the following: Battle of the Atlantic; Operation Torch; Invasion of Sicily; Battle of Anzio; Operation Overlord; Battle of the Bulge. Each student should find at least one primary source, and all of the sources selected by the group should be written by different people.

2. Have each group analyze the primary sources and make a list of similarities and differences. Next have each group find additional first-person accounts of the same battle written by Axis soldiers. Have students answer these questions: How do Axis soldiers' accounts differ from Allied soldiers' accounts? How are they similar?

3. Have volunteers read their analyses.
   LS Interpersonal, Logical-Mathematical

   📖 Alternative Assessment Handbook, Rubrics 14: Group Activity

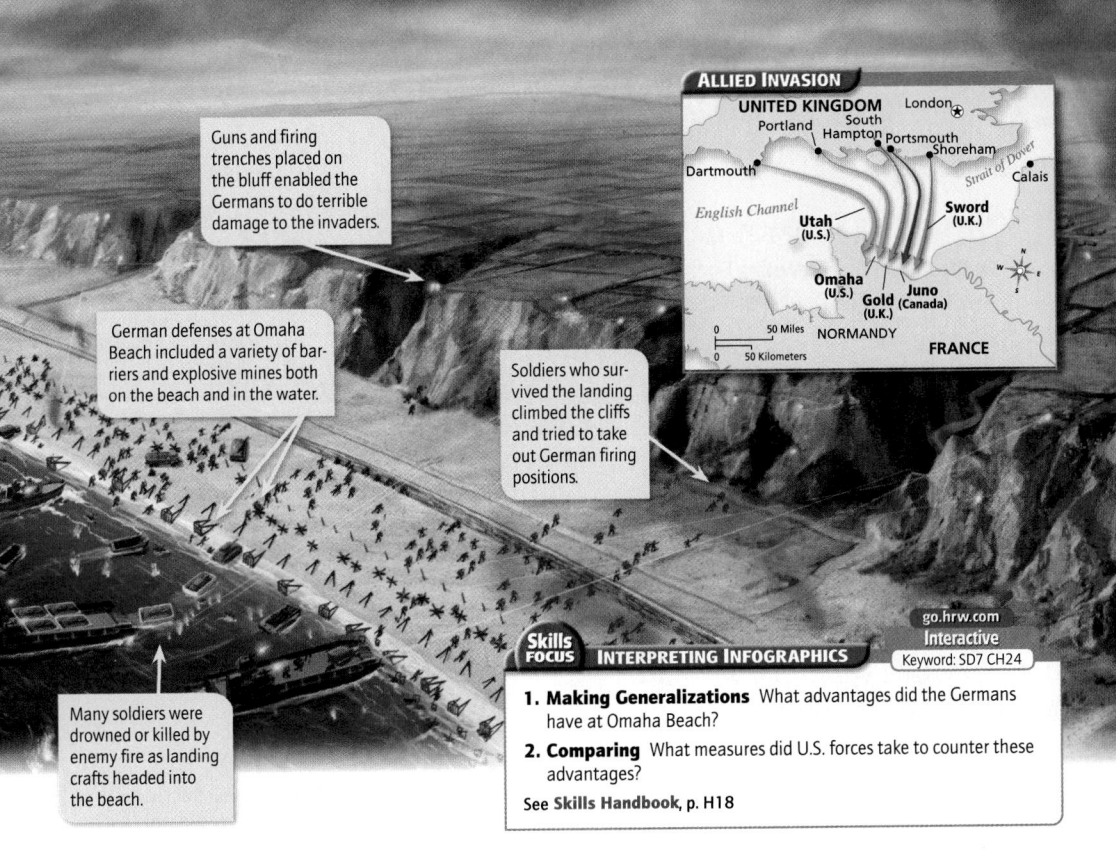

Guns and firing trenches placed on the bluff enabled the Germans to do terrible damage to the invaders.

German defenses at Omaha Beach included a variety of barriers and explosive mines both on the beach and in the water.

Soldiers who survived the landing climbed the cliffs and tried to take out German firing positions.

Many soldiers were drowned or killed by enemy fire as landing crafts headed into the beach.

ALLIED INVASION

UNITED KINGDOM
Portland — South Hampton — London
Dartmouth — Portsmouth — Shoreham
Strait of Dover — Calais
English Channel
Utah (U.S.) — Sword (U.K.)
Omaha (U.S.) — Gold (U.K.) — Juno (Canada)
0 50 Miles NORMANDY
0 50 Kilometers FRANCE

Skills FOCUS INTERPRETING INFOGRAPHICS

go.hrw.com
Interactive
Keyword: SD7 CH24

1. **Making Generalizations** What advantages did the Germans have at Omaha Beach?

2. **Comparing** What measures did U.S. forces take to counter these advantages?

See Skills Handbook, p. H18

SECTION 1 ASSESSMENT

go.hrw.com
Online Quiz
Keyword: SD7 HP24

Reviewing Ideas, Terms, and People

1. **a. Describe** Briefly describe the Battle of the Atlantic.
   b. Explain Why was control of the seas so important for the Allies and the Axis?

2. **a. Identify** Why was the Battle of Stalingrad significant?
   b. Summarize Write one sentence that summarizes the fighting in the Soviet Union between 1941 and 1944.

3. **a. Define** Write brief definitions of the following terms: **Operation Torch, Tuskegee Airmen**
   b. Make Inferences What can you infer from the fact that the Americans' initial battles with the Germans can be described as "learning experiences"?

4. **a. Define** Write brief definitions of the following terms: **Operation Overlord, D-Day, Battle of the Bulge**
   b. Contrast How did Operation Overlord compare to the landing at Anzio?

Critical Thinking

5. **Identifying Cause and Effect** Copy the chart. Use it to identify major battles in the Soviet Union, North Africa, and Europe between 1941 and 1944 and the result of each battle.

Battle	Result
1.	
2.	
3.	
4.	

FOCUS ON WRITING

6. **Expository** Was Operation Overlord a major turning point in the European war? Write a short essay in which you develop your position on this issue.

THE UNITED STATES IN WORLD WAR II **777**

Bellringer

The Inside Story... Use the **Daily Bellringer Transparency** to help students answer the question.

🗐 Daily Bellringer Transparency, Section 2

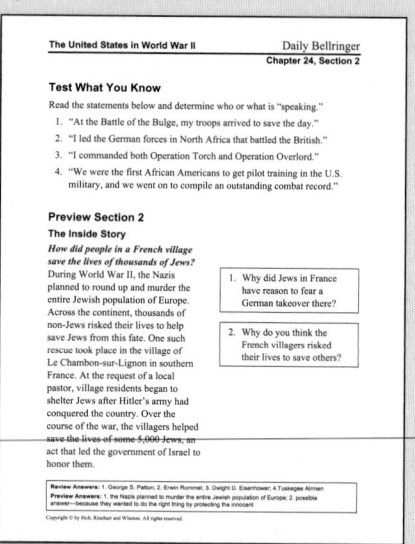

Academic Vocabulary

Review with students the high-use academic term in this section.

established created or brought into being (p. 779)

📋 CRF: Vocabulary Builder Activity, Section 2

Taking Notes

Holocaust—Hitler promotes anti-Semitism, establishes Nuremberg Laws, Kristallnacht, Jews placed in concentration camps and ghettos, Nazis enact the Final Solution; U.S. Response—limits on immigration due to scarcity of jobs, initially unaware that many lives were at stake, doubtful upon first hearing of Final Solution, troops and focus concentrated elsewhere, creation of War Refugee Board, liberation of concentration camps

---

SECTION 2 The Holocaust

BEFORE YOU READ

MAIN IDEA

During the Holocaust, Germany's Nazi government systematically murdered some 6 million Jews and 5 million others in Europe.

READING FOCUS

1. What was the history of Nazi anti-Semitism?
2. What was the Nazi government's Final Solution?
3. How did the United States respond to the Holocaust?

KEY TERMS AND PEOPLE

anti-Semitism
Kristallnacht
concentration camp
ghetto
genocide
Final Solution
War Refugee Board
Holocaust
Hermann Göering

TAKING NOTES As you read, take notes on the Holocaust and the U.S. response to it. Write your notes in a graphic organizer like the one shown below.

Holocaust	United States Response

◄ **During the Holocaust, the Nazi government targeted European Jews.**

A Life-Saving EFFORT

THE INSIDE STORY *How did people in a French village save the lives of thousands of Jews?* In 1940 Hitler's German army was rampaging across Europe. By June it had conquered France. The Jewish population there found itself facing what Jews in Germany and Poland had already come to know—government-sponsored persecution, hatred, and brutal mistreatment at the hands of Germany's Nazi Party. Scenes like the one shown above took place throughout France, as Nazis and their followers rounded up Jews and sent them to prison camps far from home. These Jews' futures—and their chances of survival—were extremely grim.

During World War II, thousands of non-Jews risked their lives to help save Jews from the Nazis. One such rescue took place in the village of Le Chambon-sur-Lignon (luh shahm-BOHN-soor-leen-yohn) in southern France. In 1942 André Trocmé, the pastor of a local church, called on village residents to give shelter to Jews who asked for help. The residents began to hide Jews in their homes and farms and help them escape to safety in Switzerland. France's Nazi-controlled government demanded that the pastor end the rescue effort. He responded by saying, "These people came here for help and for shelter. I am their shepherd. A shepherd does not desert his flock . . . We do not know what a Jew is; we only know people."

Over the course of the war, the people of Le Chambon helped some 5,000 Jews escape Nazi capture. This was a life-saving effort. As you will read in this section, the persecution of Jews was part of a terrible Nazi plan to murder the entire Jewish population of Europe.

In 1963 the government of Israel began a program to honor those who risked their lives to save Jews. Among those honored were the people of Le Chambon. ◢

Teach the Main Idea

At Level

The Holocaust

1. **Teach** Ask students the Reading Focus questions to teach this section.

2. **Apply** Organize the class into small groups. Have each group define the Holocaust and make a list of the factors that allowed it to happen. *systematic murder of European Jews and others; factors include German ideas of superiority, anti-Semitism, Nazi propaganda, many Jews had no means to flee, many countries limited immigration* **LS Interpersonal**

3. **Review** Have volunteers from each group read their definitions and lists to the class. After each group has presented its definition and list of factors, guide the class in a discussion of the Holocaust.

4. **Practice/Homework** Have students write a one-page essay about whether the Holocaust, or something similar to it, could happen today. **LS Verbal-Linguistic, Interpersonal**

📝 Alternative Assessment Handbook, Rubrics 14: Group Activity; and 37: Writing Assignments

Nazi Anti-Semitism

Why did the Nazi government single out Jews especially for mistreatment? The answer has to do with **anti-Semitism**, which is hostility toward or prejudice against Jews.

As you have read, Germany after World War I suffered blows to its economy and pride. Adolf Hitler rose to power in part by promising to return Germany to its former glory. He also told the Germans that they came from a superior race—the Aryans. The idea that Germans had descended from the mythical Aryan people was not new. It was found in German folktales and music. Hitler, however, was effective at using the notion to build support.

In addition to appealing to German pride, Hitler also provided a scapegoat—someone to blame for Germany's woes. The group he singled out was the Jews.

In fact, Jews had lived in Germany for 1,600 years. Christian hostility toward Jews had existed since the Middle Ages. Indeed, many of the anti-Jewish Nazi laws recalled medieval efforts to humiliate Jews. For example, a Nazi law that forced Jews to wear the Jewish Star of David was similar to a 1215 decree that told Jews to dress differently than Christians.

Nazi anti-Semitism combined this medieval Christian hostility with modern—but false—scientific ideas about racial inferiority. Another Nazi law defined anyone with a Jewish grandparent as a Jew, even if the person had no connection with Judaism. Under the Nazis, anti-Semitism changed from prejudice based on religion to hatred based on ancestry.

Hitler in power Hitler began his campaign against Germany's Jews soon after becoming chancellor in 1933. Over the next few years, his Nazi government established a series of anti-Semitic laws. The purpose was to drive the Jews from Germany. For example, in 1935, the Nuremberg Laws stripped Jews of German citizenship and took away most civil and economic rights. The laws also defined who was a Jew and who was an Aryan German.

Attacks on Jews Some Germans were repelled by Hitler's actions. Yet many other people supported his anti-Semitic ideas.

Jewish shopkeepers in Berlin pick up the pieces of their shattered businesses after the destruction of Kristallnacht. **What prompted Germans to attack their Jewish neighbors?**

Discrimination against Jews continued. Violent attacks against Jews also increased.

In 1938, on the nights of November 9 and 10, anti-Jewish riots broke out across Germany. The attack came to be called *Kristallnacht* (KRIS-tahl-nahkt)—the "night of broken glass." The Nazis claimed the attacks were a spontaneous reaction to the assassination of a Nazi official by a Jewish teenager. In fact, the Nazis encouraged the violence. During the rampage, thousands of Jewish businesses and places of worship were damaged. Thugs killed nearly 100 Jews. Over 26,000 more were sent to **concentration camps**—labor camps meant to hold what Hitler called enemies of the state. The Nazis blamed the Jews for Kristallnacht and held them financially responsible. Jews were fined a total of 1 billion marks.

Flight from Germany Kristallnacht sent a strong message to those Jews still in Germany: "Get out!" Over 100,000 managed to leave Germany in the months following the attacks. Many others, however, found it difficult to leave the country. Nazi laws had left many German Jews without money or property, and most countries were unwilling to take in poor immigrants. Other countries, such as the United States, had limited the number of Germans who could enter the country.

ACADEMIC VOCABULARY
established
created, or brought into being

READING CHECK **Summarizing** Briefly trace the history of Nazi anti-Semitism.

THE UNITED STATES IN WORLD WAR II **779**

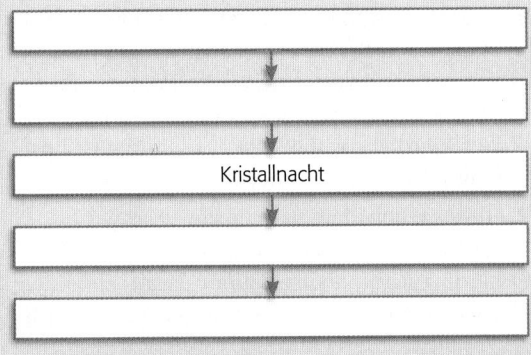

Reading Focus

❷ What was the Nazi government's Final Solution? *plan to murder all Jews in Europe and the Soviet Union*

Toward the Final Solution

Describe What were conditions in the Nazi concentration camps like? *horrific; inmates died of starvation and overwork; cruel medical experiments often ended in death; punishment was deadly*

Develop Why do you think the Nazis were so determined to exterminate Jews and other groups? *They wanted to create a pure race; Jews were seen as Germany's most serious problem.*

Primary Source

"That's the difficulty in these times: ideals, dreams and cherished hopes rise within us, only to meet the horrible truth and be shattered. It's really a wonder that I haven't dropped all my ideals, because they seem so absurd and impossible to carry out. Yet I keep them, because in spite of everything I still believe that people are really good at heart."

— Anne Frank

The Diary of Anne Frank: The Revised Critical Edition, p. 716 (Saturday 15 July 1944)

Info to Know

White Rose Society In 1942, five German students at the University of Munich joined together with one of their professors to protest the Nazi government. The group began to distribute leaflets that condemned the actions of Hitler and of any Germans who did not object to Hitler's actions: "[The White Rose] will not be silent. We are your bad conscience. The White Rose will not leave you in peace!" The Gestapo, or Nazi police, quickly discovered the uprising and killed the leaders. A 1983 German film commemorated the bravery of the members of the White Rose Society.

Toward the Final Solution

When Hitler came to power, Europe was home to 9 million Jews. Few of these people lived under German control. That changed with the outbreak of World War II. As Hitler's armies blazed across Europe, many European Jews came under the control of the Nazi SS. This was the feared police and military force that carried out terror activities for the Nazis. SS treatment of the Jews was overwhelmingly brutal. In the words of one SS leader, the goal was to "incarcerate [jail] or annihilate" the Jews.

Concentration camps and ghettos The first concentration camps were created in Germany before the start of World War II. These were basically prisons for Jews and others who were considered enemies of Hitler's regime. After the outbreak of World War II, the Nazis established many more camps to hold Jews from the countries that Germany had invaded and occupied. Camps were also set up to house prisoners of war.

As German forces took control of an area, they would arrest the Jews living there. The local population sometimes helped shelter their Jewish neighbors. *The Diary of Anne Frank* is a famous book that tells the story of a young Jewish girl living in the Netherlands whose family hid successfully for two years with the help of neighbors. Like many Jews in German-occupied lands, the Franks were eventually discovered and sent to concentration camps.

Conditions in the Nazi camps were horrific. Inmates received little food and were often forced to perform grueling labor. This combination of overwork and starvation was deliberately designed to kill. Punishment for even the most minor offenses was swift, sure, and deadly. In short, there were many ways to die in a concentration camp. Yet as you will read, the Nazis had only just begun to develop their ghastly killing methods.

Another tactic used by the Nazis to control and punish Jews was to establish **ghettos**. These are neighborhoods in a city to which a group of people are confined. As in the concentration camps, life in a Jewish ghetto was desperate. Walls or fences kept Jews inside. Those trying to get out were shot. Food was scarce. Diseases spread quickly in the crowded conditions, and many Jews fell ill.

The worst ghetto was in Warsaw, Poland. There, a half-million Jews were crammed into an area less than 1.5 miles square. They lived on a daily ration of thin soup and a slice of bread. In 1941 alone, 43,000 died of hunger. Recalled one survivor, "Every day was men with hand wagons picking up the dead ones from the corners who died of hunger or cold."

In 1943, most of the ghetto residents were sent off to Treblinka, a concentration camp. Those who remained decided to fight back. A group called the Jewish Fighting Organization attacked the Germans with crude weapons. For many Jews it was a proud moment.

HISTORY'S VOICES

❝ For the first time since the occupation, we saw Germans clinging to walls, crawling on the ground, running for cover, hesitating before taking a step in the fear of being hit by a Jewish bullet. ❞

—Tuvia Borzykowski, recorded in *The Second World War: A Complete History*, by Martin Gilbert

The Warsaw uprising lasted nearly a month. In the end, however, it was crushed. The residents were killed or shipped to concentration camps, where most would die.

The Final Solution From the first days of World War II, instances of Nazi mass-killings of Jews and other civilians occurred. In many Polish towns, German soldiers rounded up Jews and shot them on the spot. In Bedzin, soldiers forced several hundred Jews into the local synagogue, or Jewish house of worship, and set it on fire. Stories such as these were repeated across Poland.

The German invasion of the Soviet Union in 1941 raised the killing of Jews to a new level. Now Hitler called for the total destruction of all of Europe's Jews. What he proposed—the killing of an entire people—is called **genocide**. At first, the bloody work was carried out by mobile killing units—*Einsatzgruppen* (EYEN-sahtz-GROOP-uhn). In one incident in the fall of 1941, over 33,000 people were massacred in two days. The bodies were piled into a ravine at Babi Yar, near the Ukrainian city of Kiev.

As bloody as the work of the *Einsatzgruppen* was, Nazi leaders were not satisfied. For them, the killing was not going quickly enough. It was also proving difficult on the men who performed it. Thus, Nazi officials adopted a plan known as the **Final Solution**. This involved

Skills Focus: Analyzing Primary Sources

Above Level

Reading Like a Historian Skill

Research Required

The Holocaust

1. Have each student find primary source materials about the Holocaust written by a victim or survivor. Primary sources should tell about the writer's experiences of the Holocaust in ghettos or concentration camps, hiding from Nazi authorities, or as refugees.

2. Have each student write a short essay about their primary sources to serve as an introduction to the selection. Essays should provide background material on the writers if possible. Students should also explain what can be learned about the Holocaust by reading the selection.

3. Collect student essays and copies of their primary sources. Put them together in a loose-leaf binder to create a book of readings on the Holocaust. Essays should precede the primary source documents. **LS Verbal-Linguistic**

📝 Alternative Assessment Handbook, Rubrics 30: Research; and 37: Writing Assignments

THE HOLOCAUST, 1939–1945

GEOGRAPHY SKILLS INTERPRETING MAPS

The Nazis expanded the number of camps as their conquests brought more Jews under their control.

1. **Place** Which country had the greatest number of camps?

2. **Location** Why do you think the Nazis built so many camps there?

See Skills Handbook, p. H20

Major concentration camp
Concentration camp
Extent of German control

0   150   300 Miles
0   150   300 Kilometers
Albers equal-area projection

the establishment of six new camps. These were to be extermination camps for the widespread murder of Jews. Unlike the concentration camps you read about earlier, nearly all inmates at the extermination camps were murdered upon their arrival. The method of killing was by exposure to poison gas in specially built gas chambers. Inmates might also be selected for cruel medical experiments, which often ended in death. Some were also forced to perform labor.

Some 3 million Jews died in Nazi extermination camps. Another 3 million died at Nazi hands by other means. Nazis murdered men, women, and children alike. Wrote Nazi leader Heinrich Himmler, "I did not feel justified in exterminating the men... while allowing the avengers, in the form of their children, to grow up."

In addition to the Jews, the Nazi death machine killed about 5 million others. Among these victims were prisoners of war, disabled people, and the Romany, an ethnic group also known as Gypsies.

READING CHECK Identifying the Main Idea
What was the purpose of the Final Solution?

JEWISH LOSSES IN THE HOLOCAUST

	c. 1933	c. 1950	Percent Decrease
Europe	9,500,000	3,500,000	63
Selected Countries			
Poland	3,000,000	45,000	98.5
Romania	980,000	28,000	97
Germany	565,000	37,000	93.5
Hungary	445,000	155,000	65
Czechoslovakia	357,000	17,000	95
Austria	250,000	18,000	93
Greece	100,000	7,000	93
Yugoslavia	70,000	3,500	95
Bulgaria	50,000	6,500	87

Source: *United States Holocaust Memorial Museum*

❸ How did the United States respond to the Holocaust? *The U.S. was slow to respond. Immigration rules limited the number of Jews who were able to move to the U.S. In January 1944, the War Refugee Board was formed.*

The American Response

Recall How did Americans first get proof of Hitler's Final Solution? *In 1942 the head of a major Jewish organization in Switzerland gave American officials information about it.*

Summarize What conditions did American and British forces discover at the Nazi concentration camps? *appalling scenes; at one camp, bodies of victims lay in piles; survivors barely alive; at another camp, 13,000 died after being freed*

Evaluate Considering the number of deaths in the concentration camps, do you think justice was carried out when only 22 Nazis were tried for war crimes? *possible answer—yes, these were the ones involved in the decision making; others were just carrying out orders; no, all those involved should have been tried and punished.*

Concentration Camp Liberation

As the Allied forces pushed westward across Europe, they came upon the concentration camps that held victims of the Holocaust. Many of the survivors were barely alive. Gerda Weissman was a Jewish prisoner in a Czechoslavakian camp. She recalled the day that American soldiers liberated her camp.

Skills FOCUS **READING LIKE A HISTORIAN**

1. **Analyzing Primary Sources** Why was Gerda Weissman so surprised by the soldier's question?

2. **Drawing Conclusions** What did Weissman mean when she said the soldier's gesture "restored me to humanity"?

See Skills Handbook, pp. H28–H29

"All of a sudden I saw a strange car coming down the hill, no longer green, not bearing the swastika, but a white star. It was sort of a mud-splattered vehicle but I've never seen a star brighter in my life. And two men sort of jumped out, came running toward us and one came toward where I stood. He was wearing battle gear… I would say it was the greatest hour of my life. And then he asked an incredible question. He said, 'May I see the other ladies?' You know, what… what we have been addressed for six years and then to hear this man. He looked to me like a young god… He held the door open for me and let me precede him and in that gesture restored me to humanity."

The American Response

THE IMPACT TODAY

Government American leaders continue to face pressure to help populations under attack by their own governments. In the early 2000s, the United States worked to end what was seen as a government-supported effort to destroy the population in Darfur, a region of the African nation of Sudan.

In the 1930s American immigration rules limited the number of Jews who could move to the United States. Although many Americans had read of Kristallnacht and knew about Hitler's policies toward the Jews, they were unwilling to allow large numbers of foreign workers enter the United States during a time when jobs were already scarce. At the time, few truly understood that millions of lives were at stake.

The start of the war eventually brought an end to the economic problems facing American workers, but it did not change American feelings about immigration. That began to change in 1942, when American officials started to learn the horrifying details of what was taking place in Europe. The head of a major Jewish organization in Switzerland told American officials what he had heard about Hitler's Final Solution. The Americans were doubtful at first. One official wrote to another, "The report has earmarks of war rumor inspired by fear." Soon, however, the reality began to sink in.

The fate of Europe's Jews was just one of many issues that preoccupied the United States and its leaders. As you have read, 1943 was a year of difficult fighting in Italy and a time for planning the D-Day invasion. The United States was also fighting hard in the Pacific. These were vital steps in the effort to defeat Hitler and the Axis Powers, which, some argued, might help save millions of lives.

It was not until January 1944 that President Roosevelt announced the creation of the **War Refugee Board.** This organization was told to "take all measures to rescue victims of enemy oppression in imminent [immediate] danger of death." Through the board, the United States was able to help 200,000 Jews who might otherwise have fallen into the hands of the Nazis.

Liberating the Nazi camps As you have read, Allied forces in 1942 started to push back the German advances gained in the beginning of the war. The Soviets made the greatest early progress. In 1944 Soviet troops began to discover some of the Nazi camps that had been set up to house and kill Jews in Poland. In early 1945, they reached the huge extermination camp at Auschwitz. Their reports of the conditions at these camps finally gave the American people proof of Hitler's terrible plan.

American and British forces also encountered death camps. In April 1945 American soldiers came upon several, including the camp

Rallying Support for Hitler's Victims

1. Organize the class into small groups. Have each group select a leader. Have each group consider, and then list what Americans might have heard in 1942 about Nazi actions toward Jews and others in Europe. You may wish to review each group's list.

2. Each leader's task is to coordinate efforts within his or her group to convince the U.S. government to take action to stop Hitler's plans for the Final Solution. Leaders should work with their groups to plan a campaign,

assigning volunteers within the group to write letters to editors, write speeches or skits, create posters, and do anything else that they think will help get their point across.

3. Have each group present its campaign to rally support for Hitler's victims. When each group has finished, lead the class in a discussion of the effectiveness of their campaigns.

LS Interpersonal, Verbal-Linguistic

Alternative Assessment Handbook, Rubrics 14: Group Activity; and 22: Multimedia Presentations

Answers

Reading Like a Historian 1. *She was addressed politely as a lady, not insulted as a Jew;* **2.** *It was undoubtedly the first time since being sentenced to the camp that the woman had been treated humanely.*

at Buchenwald. This was one of the first and largest concentration camps established in Germany. During its existence, some 240,000 prisoners spent time at the camp. Of those, at least 43,000 died. Another 10,000 were shipped elsewhere to be killed.

The Nazis had abandoned Buchenwald shortly before the Americans arrived. Many of the camp's prisoners, however, remained behind. The scenes were appalling. The bodies of victims lay in piles throughout the camp. Many of the survivors were themselves barely alive. One American soldier who was among the first to enter the camp recalled, "They were just one step from their last breath. They weren't able to feel happy. They were so skinny—just skin and bones." Many of these rescued victims were so ill that they could not be saved. At the Bergen-Belsen concentration camp, 13,000 inmates died after they were set free by the British.

Some of the inmates were strong enough to celebrate their freedom. At Dachau, surviving inmates broke out of their prison to meet the approaching American tanks. "Everybody was running—everybody who could run," recalled one survivor. "It looked like somebody from heaven came." Yet within the camp fences was the same horror—the piles of bodies and a great many starving inmates.

HISTORY'S VOICES

❝I was a hardened soldier. I had been in combat since 1944, and I had seen death and destruction that was unparalleled in modern times. But this—there are no words to describe this.❞

—Reid Draffen, recorded in *War Stories*, by Elizabeth Mullener

The Nuremberg trials Following World War II, many Nazis faced trial for their roles in what is now called the **Holocaust**—the genocidal campaign against the Jews during World War II. The court, located at Nuremberg, Germany, was called the International Military Tribunal. It was organized by the United States, Great Britain, France, and the Soviet Union.

A total of twenty two Nazis were tried for war crimes. Included were some of the leading Nazis, such as **Hermann Göering** (GEH-ring). Twelve were sentenced to die. Several others served long prison terms.

After Nuremberg, several Nazis have been captured and tried in different courts, including in Israel. These trials demonstrate the commitment of people around the world to remember the Holocaust and the millions of victims of Nazi brutality during World War II.

READING CHECK **Summarizing** How did the United States respond to the reports that the Nazis were attempting to kill all of Europe's Jews?

THE IMPACT TODAY

Government
After World War II, many surviving European Jews were sent to displaced persons' camps. Many made their way to Palestine, where in the late 1940s they took part in the creation of the Jewish nation of Israel.

SECTION 2 ASSESSMENT

go.hrw.com
Online Quiz
Keyword: SD7 HP24

Reviewing Ideas, Terms, and People

1. **a. Recall** What term describes Hitler's racist attitudes toward the Jews?
   b. Explain Why do you think the German people supported Hitler's anti-Semitic attitudes?
   c. Evaluate Why do you think observers of events in Germany did not do more to help Germany's Jews?

2. **a. Define** Write brief definitions of the following terms: ghetto, Final Solution
   b. Make Generalizations What was the experience of Jews living in territories conquered by the Germans?
   c. Develop How can you explain the participation of so many Germans in the campaign to destroy the Jews?

3. **a. Identify** What was the significance of the **War Refugee Board**?
   b. Make Inferences Why did it take the United States so long to offer direct help to Europe's Jews?

c. Evaluate Do you think that the best way to help Europe's Jews was to defeat Hitler as quickly as possible? Or should the United States have taken a different approach? Explain.

Critical Thinking

4. **Identifying Supporting Details** Copy the chart below and use information from the section to find supporting details for the main idea given.

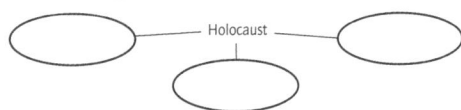

Holocaust

FOCUS ON SPEAKING

5. **Persuasive** Could the United States have done more to prevent the Holocaust? Write a persuasive speech in which you present your position.

THE UNITED STATES IN WORLD WAR II **783**

Section 2 Assessment Answers

1. **a.** anti-Semitism
   b. historic hostility; propaganda; belief in Hitler's views
   c. possible answers—did not know of the atrocities or believe reports

2. **a.** ghetto—a confined neighborhood; Final Solution—mass killings of Jews
   b. arrested, shipped to concentration camps, tortured, forced labor, starved, killed
   c. possible answers—afraid to disobey orders; propaganda; agreed with Hitler

3. **a.** helped rescue many Jews

b. possible answers—believed information was based on rumor; had to focus on the war
   c. possible answers—Allies had to focus on war, had no way of getting to the camps; Allies could have taken action before the war

4. anti-Semitism; police, civilian, and military actions against Jews; Jews arrested, sent to camps, and killed

5. possible answers—The U.S. should have helped Jews escape before the war began. The U.S. had no way to gain access to the camps.

Excerpt from *Night* by Elie Wiesel

Word Help

whirlpool a pool of water, rapidly moving in a circle

glimmer small, faint glow

void empty space

halt stop

corpse dead body

Meet the Writer

Elie Wiesel (1928–) Elie Wiesel and his family were sent from their home in Hungary to Auschwitz in May 1944. Once there Wiesel was assigned to Buna-Monowitz, the slave labor part of the camp. In January 1945 Wiesel and his father were sent on a death march to Buchenwald where Wiesel's father died. Elie Wiesel, however, survived the ordeal and was liberated in April 1945. *Night,* published in 1958, is his story of Auschwitz. Many critics consider *Night* to be the finest piece of work about the Holocaust ever written. Wiesel became a noted lecturer about the Holocaust. His work in condemning violence, hatred and oppression brought him worldwide fame, and in 1986, he was awarded the Nobel Peace Prize.

Info to Know

Night In 1956 Wiesel wrote this book in Yiddish. Its title was *And the World Has Remained Silent. Night* is the abridged title given to the work in 1958. **Evaluate** Ask students which title they feel best represents the work and ask them to explain the significance of the first title.

Answers

Reading Like a Historian *provides a first-hand account of the events and suffering endured by the victims*

784

American *Literature*

ELIE WIESEL (1928–   )

About the Reading Elie Wiesel was born in the small town of Sighet, Romania, in 1928. In 1944 the Nazis began deporting Jewish families from his hometown. In his autobiography, *Night* (1958), he recounts his experiences during his time in Nazi concentration camps. Wiesel became an American citizen in 1963. In this excerpt from *Night*, he describes his journey by train to the camp in Auschwitz, Poland.

AS YOU READ **Think about the reasons why we study the Holocaust today.**

Excerpt from

Night
by Elie Wiesel

Survivors at Buchenwald after their liberation in 1945. Elie Wiesel is on the second bunk from the bottom, seventh from the left.

Pressed up against the others in an effort to keep out the cold, head empty and heavy at the same time, brain a whirlpool of decaying memories. Indifference deadened the spirit. Here or elsewhere—what difference did it make? To die today or tomorrow, or later? The night was long and never ending.

When at last a gray glimmer of light appeared on the horizon, it revealed a tangle of human shapes, heads sunk upon shoulders, crouched, piled one on top of the other, like a field of dust-covered tombstones in the first light of the dawn. I tried to distinguish those who were still alive from those who had gone. But there was no difference. My gaze was held for a long time by one who lay with his eyes open, staring into the void. His livid face was covered with a layer of frost and snow.

My father huddled near me, wrapped in his blanket, his shoulders covered with snow. And was he dead, too? I called him. No answer. I would have cried out if I could have done so. He did not move.

My mind was invaded suddenly by this realization—there was no more reason to live, no more reason to struggle. The train stopped in the middle of a deserted field. The suddenness of the halt woke some of those who were asleep. They straightened themselves up, throwing startled looks around them.

Outside, the SS went by, shouting:

784 CHAPTER 24

"Throw out all the dead! All corpses outside!"

The living rejoiced. There would be more room. Volunteers set to work. They felt those who were still crouching.

"Here's one! Take him!"

They undressed him, the survivors avidly sharing out his clothes, then two "gravediggers" took him, one by the head and one by the feet, and threw him out of the wagon like a sack of flour.

From all directions came cries:

"Come on! Here's one! This man next to me. He doesn't move."

Skills FOCUS READING LIKE A HISTORIAN

Literature as Historical Evidence How does the personal testimony of survivors such as Wiesel help us understand the Holocaust?

See Skills Handbook, p. H32

Differentiating Instruction   **Below Level**

Special Education Students; English-Language Learners

Materials colored markers

1. Organize the class into mixed-ability pairs. Have students reread the passage to ensure that they understand the excerpt. Have pairs write a sentence or two summarizing each paragraph of the passage. Ask for volunteers to share their summaries. Have students correct their work.

2. Have each student create a series of drawings that illustrate the passage. Students may use their summaries to help them sequence the information. Have volunteers share and discuss their drawings. **LS Visual-Spatial**

3. To extend this activity for Advanced Learners/GATE, have students write a script based on the excerpt, prepare the skit, and videotape it for the class to see. **LS Verbal-Linguistic, Kinesthetic**

   📖 Alternative Assessment Handbook, Rubrics 3: Artwork; and 37: Writing Assignments

The War in the Pacific

BEFORE YOU READ

MAIN IDEA

After early defeats in the Pacific, the United States gained the upper hand and began to fight its way island by island to Japan.

READING FOCUS

1. Why did the Allies experience a slow start in the Pacific?

2. How did the Allies bring about a shift in their fortunes in the Pacific?

3. What were the major events that marked Allied progress in the late stages of the Pacific war?

KEY TERMS AND PEOPLE

Douglas MacArthur
Bataan Death March
James Doolittle
Chester Nimitz
Battle of Midway
code talker
kamikaze
Battle of Iwo Jima
Battle of Okinawa

TAKING NOTES As you read, take notes on the war in the Pacific theater. Write your notes in a graphic organizer like the one shown below.

Japan Advances	Turning Points	U.S. Advances

THE INSIDE STORY

Why was it so hard to capture a tiny island? Iwo To lies 750 miles south of Japan. The small island, known as Iwo Jima (EE-woh-JEE-muh) until 2007, covers barely eight square miles. Yet during World War II over 100,000 soldiers fought for a month to capture this tiny scrap of land. It was some of the heaviest fighting of the war.

On February 19, 1945, the U.S. Marines stormed the beaches of the island then called Iwo Jima. The marines made easy targets for the Japanese, who had dug miles of tunnels and built dozens of hidden concrete bunkers throughout the island. From these hiding places they could pick off American troops without being exposed.

Also deadly for the Americans were the Japanese guns mounted high on the slopes of Mount Suribachi, an extinct volcano on the southern tip of the island. The Americans knew that they must capture Suribachi or be blown off the island.

On the morning of February 23, a group of Marines finally made it to the top of Mount Suribachi and raised the American flag as thousands of soldiers below watched and cheered. A few hours later a larger flag was raised. This second flag raising is shown in the famous photograph on this page.

Raising the Flag at Iwo Jima

The American flag now flew over Iwo Jima, but fierce fighting lasted for another month before the Americans finally captured the island. An estimated 25,000 American soldiers were killed or wounded. Among the dead were three of the six men who raised the flag atop Mount Suribachi. ■

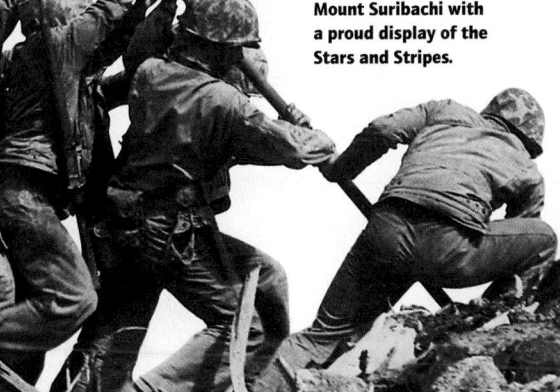

◀ **U.S. Marines claim Mount Suribachi with a proud display of the Stars and Stripes.**

785

Preteach

Bellringer

The Inside Story. . . Use the **Daily Bellringer Transparency** to help students answer the question.

🖳 Daily Bellringer Transparency, Section 3

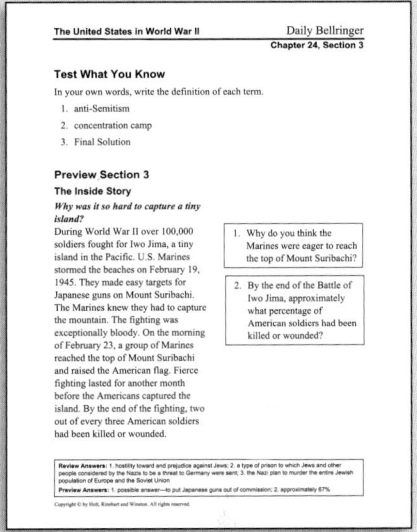

Academic Vocabulary

Review with students the high-use academic term in this section.

strategy plan of action (p. 791)

📝 CRF: Vocabulary Builder Activity, Section 3

Taking Notes

Japan Advances—victories at Wake Island, Guam, Hong Kong, Singapore, Dutch East Indies, British Borneo, Battle of Java Sea, Burma, Philippines; Turning Points—Doolittle's air raid of Tokyo, victory at Coral Sea, Midway; U.S. Advances—victories at Guadalcanal, Gilbert, Marshall, Caroline, Mariana islands, Philippines, Iwo Jima, and Okinawa, use of code talkers

---

Teach the Main Idea

At Level

The War in the Pacific

1. **Teach** Ask students the Reading Focus questions to teach this section.

2. **Apply** Have students work in pairs to create an outline of the section using the heads as main points. Have students list all the major events in the Pacific war, along with the dates.

3. **Review** Review student outlines as a class. Have students identify the points in their outlines that they feel are most important or most interesting. Ask them to identify the

event that they believe changed the course of the Pacific war. **LS Interpersonal**

4. **Practice/Homework** Have each student write a brief essay on what might have happened if Japan had defeated the Allies in the Pacific. Ask volunteers to read their essays to the class. **LS Verbal-Linguistic, Logical-Mathematical**

📝 Alternative Assessment Handbook, Rubric 37: Writing Assignments

785

① Why did the Allies experience a slow start in the Pacific? *because of the losses suffered during the attack on Pearl Harbor and the decision to concentrate major efforts on the war in Europe*

A Slow Start for the Allies

Identify What territories was Japan able to conquer early in World War II? *Wake Island, Guam, Hong Kong, Singapore, the Dutch East Indies, Burma, and positions in the South Pacific*

Analyze In what ways did the Japanese attack on Pearl Harbor backfire? *It inspired a firm resolve in Americans to fight; led U.S. to increase production of war materials*

Evaluate Why do you think there was only a small American military force in the Philippines when the Japanese attacked in December 1941? *possible answer—The United States had just entered the war and had not had an opportunity to station more troops there.*

🗐 CRF: Primary Source Activity: Presidential Address on the Declaration of War on Japan

MISCONCEPTION
///**ALERT**\\\

Pearl Harbor Most historians agree the attack on Peal Harbor was not a complete surprise, as is often reported. The U.S. knew the Japanese were planning a major attack on Allied forces somewhere in the Pacific on December 7, 1941, but neither Roosevelt nor Churchill believed that Japanese pilots could reach the Hawaiian Islands. The devastation of the Pacific Fleet, however, came as a complete surprise to both leaders.

Answers

Photo *Bataan was defended by a small number of Americans and poorly trained and equipped Filipino soldiers.*

A Slow Start for the Allies

The attack on Pearl Harbor had been a tremendous success for the Japanese. They had dealt a blow to the U.S. Pacific Fleet that would take months to overcome. The damage to American sea power—combined with the Allies' decision to focus their energy and resources on defeating the Axis in Europe—would for a time limit the ability of the United States to strike back at the Japanese.

Pearl Harbor also had an enormous emotional impact. For the Japanese, it provided a major boost to national pride and encouraged them to continue their assault. For Americans, it inspired a firm resolve to fight. Some Japanese leaders seemed to sense the dual danger of Japanese confidence and American anger.

HISTORY'S VOICES

❝ The fact that we have had a small success at Pearl Harbor is nothing . . . Personally, I do not think it is a good thing to whip up propaganda to encourage the nation. People should think things over and realize how serious the situation is. ❞

—Japanese admiral Isoroku Yamamoto, quoted in *The Second World War: Asia and the Pacific,* Thomas E. Griess, Ed.

Japanese advances In the early days of the war, the Japanese saw little reason to heed Admiral Yamamoto's warning. After all, following Pearl Harbor, Japanese forces won a quick string of impressive victories. In late 1941 they drove American forces from Wake Island and Guam. Elsewhere, they captured the British stronghold at Hong Kong. Then they launched a campaign against the British base at Singapore. The British had believed that this mighty fortress would never fall to invaders. It took the Japanese just two weeks to capture it. In the process, they handed the British what Winston Churchill called "the greatest disaster and capitulation [surrender] in British history."

At the same time, other Japanese forces were easily taking control of the Dutch East Indies (today known as Indonesia) and British Borneo. In the Battle of Java Sea, they caused much damage to the Allied navies. The Japanese also conquered British-controlled Burma as well as a number of key positions in the South Pacific. In this way, they gained control of rich oil reserves, which were vital to their military plans. They also established strategic bases for future operations.

Bataan Death March
Some 70,000 American and Filipino prisoners were force-marched 63 miles in tropical heat with little food or water in the Bataan Death March. Some 7,000 to 10,000 died. The surrender at Bataan was the largest in U.S. history. *Why were the forces defending Bataan so vulnerable?*

786

Skills Focus: Identifying Problem and Solution | Above Level

Reading Skill
Stopping Japanese Advances

1. Display a current map of the Pacific for students to see. Ask volunteers to use the map to point out the farthest extent of Japanese control in the Pacific.

2. Have students review the information in the text about Japanese military strengths. Then have students write a memorandum informing the president of the strengths of the Japanese military in the months following the U.S. entry into the war.

3. Have volunteers read their memorandums and briefs to the class.

4. Guide the class in a discussion of possible American strategies to stop Japanese advances. 🅛🅢 **Visual-Spatial, Verbal-Linguistic**

🗐 Alternative Assessment Handbook, Rubric 42: Writing to Inform

The Allies were stunned by the rapid success of the Japanese military in the months after Pearl Harbor. They had not realized that Japanese soldiers were so highly skilled and well trained. The Japanese military also had excellent equipment. For example, Japanese fighter aircraft were as good as—or better than—anything the Allies could produce. Japanese ships and torpedoes were also of high quality. These factors gave the Japanese an important advantage early in the war.

The British were the first to discover the true strength of Japan's military in Hong Kong, Singapore, and Burma. American soldiers were about to learn the same lesson.

The Philippines Japan's attacks on Hong Kong, Singapore, the Dutch East Indies, and Burma were part of a large offensive that had one other major target: the American-controlled islands of the Philippines. General **Douglas MacArthur** led the defense of that island chain. He commanded a small force of Americans, plus a number of poorly trained and equipped Filipino soldiers. In fact, MacArthur's troops were no match for the Japanese invaders, who came ashore in December 1941.

As the Japanese gained ground, MacArthur planned a retreat to the Bataan Peninsula. There he hoped to hold off the Japanese for as long as possible. Simply getting his troops into this defensive position, however, took hard fighting and brilliant leadership. Once there, the soldiers found that food, medicine, and other supplies were terribly short. MacArthur urged Allied officials to send ships to help relieve his starving troops. War planners, however, decided that such a move was too risky. As Secretary of War Henry Stimson grimly noted, "There are times when men have to die."

MacArthur and his forces fought on bravely. Soon, however, illness and hunger began to take their toll. In March 1942 MacArthur was ordered to leave his men. He did so reluctantly, promising, "I shall return." Less than a month later, 10,000 American and 60,000 Filipino troops on Bataan surrendered.

The fighting was over, but the suffering of the soldiers was just beginning. For five days and nights, the Japanese forced the already starving and sick soldiers to march through the steaming forests of Bataan. Those who dropped out of line were beaten or shot. Those

who fell were left for dead. The Japanese provided little food or water. Thousands of soldiers perished on this so-called **Bataan Death March**. Those who completed this terrible journey did not fare much better. In the Japanese prison camp, lack of food and medicine claimed hundreds more American and Filipino lives.

READING CHECK **Drawing Conclusions** Why did the Allies experience a slow start in the war in the Pacific?

Fortunes Shift in the Pacific

The loss of the Philippines was a low point for the United States in the Pacific war. Days later, however, Americans finally got some good news. On April 18, 1942, Army Lieutenant Colonel **James Doolittle** led a group of 16 American bombers on a daring air raid of Tokyo and several other Japanese cities. The airplanes had been launched from an aircraft carrier several hundred miles off the coast of Japan.

Doolittle's raid, as the event came to be known, did not do major damage to the Japanese targets. It did, however, have some significant effects. One was to finally give the American people something to celebrate. The other effect was to worry and anger Japan's leaders. Their outrage—and their concern about future attacks—would cloud their judgment and lead to major military mistakes in the months ahead.

THE UNITED STATES IN WORLD WAR II **787**

Fortunes Shift in the Pacific

Explain What was the significance of the Battle of Coral Sea? *It was the first time in the war that the Japanese advance had been halted.*

Summarize How did the Japanese plan to destroy what remained of the American fleet? *They planned to lure the Americans into a large sea battle by attacking the American-held Midway Island; they hoped the attack would pull the American fleet into the area where they could destroy it.*

Evaluate How important was breaking Japanese codes to the overall success of Allied forces? *possible answer—very important, gave the Allies a key advantage; not very important, Allies would have won anyway because they had superior military material and the ability to replace ships and planes*

The Battle of Coral Sea Americans got something else to cheer about in May 1942, when news reached home about the Battle of Coral Sea. This battle featured the one part of the Pacific fleet that had not been badly damaged at Pearl Harbor—the aircraft carriers.

The Battle of Coral Sea took place as Japanese forces were preparing to invade the British controlled Port Moresby on the island of New Guinea. To prevent this attack, U.S. Admiral **Chester Nimitz** sent two aircraft carriers on the attack. In the battle that followed, the American and Japanese navies both suffered damage. For the Americans, this included the loss of an aircraft carrier and several dozen aircraft. Yet they had stopped the Japanese attack. For the first time, the Japanese advance had been halted.

The Battle of Midway As you have read, Doolittle's raid had troubled Japan's leaders. They were determined to stop any future attacks on the Japanese mainland. To do this, they knew they had to destroy what remained of the United States naval power.

Japanese military planners decided to try to lure the Americans into a large sea battle. The first step would be to attack the American-held Midway Island, which sat in the middle of the Pacific Ocean. They hoped the attack would pull the American fleet into the area. Then the Japanese could destroy it.

The Japanese had a large advantage in the number of ships and carriers they could bring to the battle. The Americans, however, had one great advantage. Naval intelligence officers had broken a Japanese code and learned about the plans for attacking Midway. Americans knew the date for the planned attack—June 3, 1942. They also knew the direction from which the Japanese ships would approach.

The Americans also benefited from the carelessness of Japanese war planners. These planners had recognized possible flaws in their plan. Yet they chose to ignore them. It seemed as though their recent success had led them to believe they could not be defeated.

They were wrong. Using his advance knowledge of Japanese plans, Admiral Nimitz placed his three available aircraft carriers carefully. His goal was to stop a Japanese landing at Midway and to avoid contact with the larger Japanese fleet.

Nimitz's plan worked perfectly. Just as he had expected, the Japanese launched their attack in the early morning hours of June 4, 1942. The first stage was an air attack, meant to prepare Midway Island for a future landing by Japanese forces. The attacking Japanese planes took off from a group of four aircraft carriers that were leading the assault on Midway. American air defenses were waiting and managed to fight off the air raid.

The surviving Japanese planes raced back to their carriers to refuel and rearm. They were followed by American aircraft. The Japanese desperately fought off dozens of American bombers. Finally, several planes from the USS *Enterprise* broke through the Japanese defenses.

HISTORY'S VOICES

❝The terrifying scream of the dive bombers reached me first, followed by the crashing of a direct hit. There was a blinding flash and then a second explosion, much louder than the first... I watched the fires spread, and I was terrified at the prospect of induced explosions, which would surely doom the ship.❞

—Mitsuo Fuchido, quoted in *The Pacific War*, by John Costello

The American bombs severely damaged three of the four carriers. The decks of these ships had been cluttered with returning planes, bombs and torpedoes, and fuel, which blew up in the American attack. As Fuchido had predicted, these fires and explosions destroyed all three ships. American aircraft later destroyed the fourth carrier in this group.

During the battle, Japanese planes did manage to destroy one of the American carriers, the USS *Yorktown*. Nimitz, however, had placed the rest of his ships perfectly. The surviving ships of the Japanese battle fleet were too far away to threaten them. As the **Battle of Midway** ended, it was clear the Americans had won a tremendous victory.

Differentiating Instruction

Below Level

English-Language Learners

1. Have students give the names and dates of the early turning points of the war in the Pacific. Write student responses for the class to see.

2. Display a current map of the Pacific Ocean. Ask volunteers to indicate the location of each of the battles.

3. Organize the class into six groups, two groups for each battle. Assign one of the battles to each group. Have three groups develop a radio news report of its battle. Have the other three groups create an illustrated newspaper

account of its battle. Each report or account should include the five "Ws" of the battle: Who, What, When, Where, and Why it was significant.

4. Have volunteers present their radio reports and newspaper accounts to the class. Then guide the class in a discussion of the three battles. **LS Interpersonal, Verbal-Linguistic**

📖 Alternative Assessment Handbook, Rubric 14: Group Activity

The plan to invade Midway had been stopped, and Japan's navy had suffered a terrible blow. Japan's once great advantage on the seas no longer existed.

READING CHECK Sequencing What events helped shift the Americans' fortunes in the Pacific?

The Allies Make Progress

The Battle of Midway had changed the entire balance of power in the Pacific. Japanese naval power, which had been a key to its early success, was greatly reduced. Now on a more equal footing with the Japanese, the Americans began to make plans of their own in the Pacific.

Guadalcanal A first step was to win control of territory in the Solomon Islands. The Japanese had moved into these islands in the spring of 1942. This threatened nearby Australia, which was fighting alongside the Allies in the Pacific. An Allied presence in the Solomons would help protect Australia. It would also provide a base for further efforts to push back the Japanese.

A key goal in the Solomons was the capture of an island called Guadalcanal (GWAHD-uhl-KUH-NAL). The Japanese had nearly completed an airfield there, making it a tempting target. The rest of the island, however, offered little. It was covered by swamps and dense jungles. Daytime temperatures regularly reached into the 90s. Millions of disease-carrying insects filled the air. It was a miserable place to fight.

In spite of this, American forces came ashore on Guadalcanal in August 1942. For the next six months, they fought in bloody combat with Japanese forces. The battle took place on land, at sea, and in the air. Each side won small victories until finally, in February 1943, Japanese forces fled the island. It was a key moment in the war. "Before that," recalled one soldier, "we weren't looking for the Japanese, they were looking for us. . . . But from there on out, the Japanese were on the run."

The Allies press on The Allied victory at Guadalcanal set a pattern that was repeated in the coming months. The Allies would use a powerful combination of land, sea, and air forces to capture key islands. These would then

The American Victory at the Battle of Midway

Devastator torpedo bombers lie in wait for the Japanese fleet aboard the USS *Enterprise* (left). Above, a Japanese battle cruiser is destroyed by a hail of American bombs. After Midway, the *Enterprise* received the first Presidential Unit Citation ever awarded to a carrier, the Navy Unit Commendation, and 20 battle stars.

789

World War II in the Pacific

Guide students in a discussion of the differences in climate and geography between Europe and the Pacific islands where the war was fought. Tell students that fighting in the Pacific presented its own challenges and differed from fighting in Europe. Food and rations spoiled in the tropical heat and humidity of the Pacific islands. Packages deteriorated and cans rusted, making their contents useless. In addition shoes and clothes wore out more quickly than they did in Europe, and they rotted in storage. Salt spray and the coral found on many islands took their toll on supplies and equipment.

- Map Transparency: World War II in the Pacific
- American History Outline Maps: World War II in the Pacific
- **Interactive Map:** World War II in the Pacific

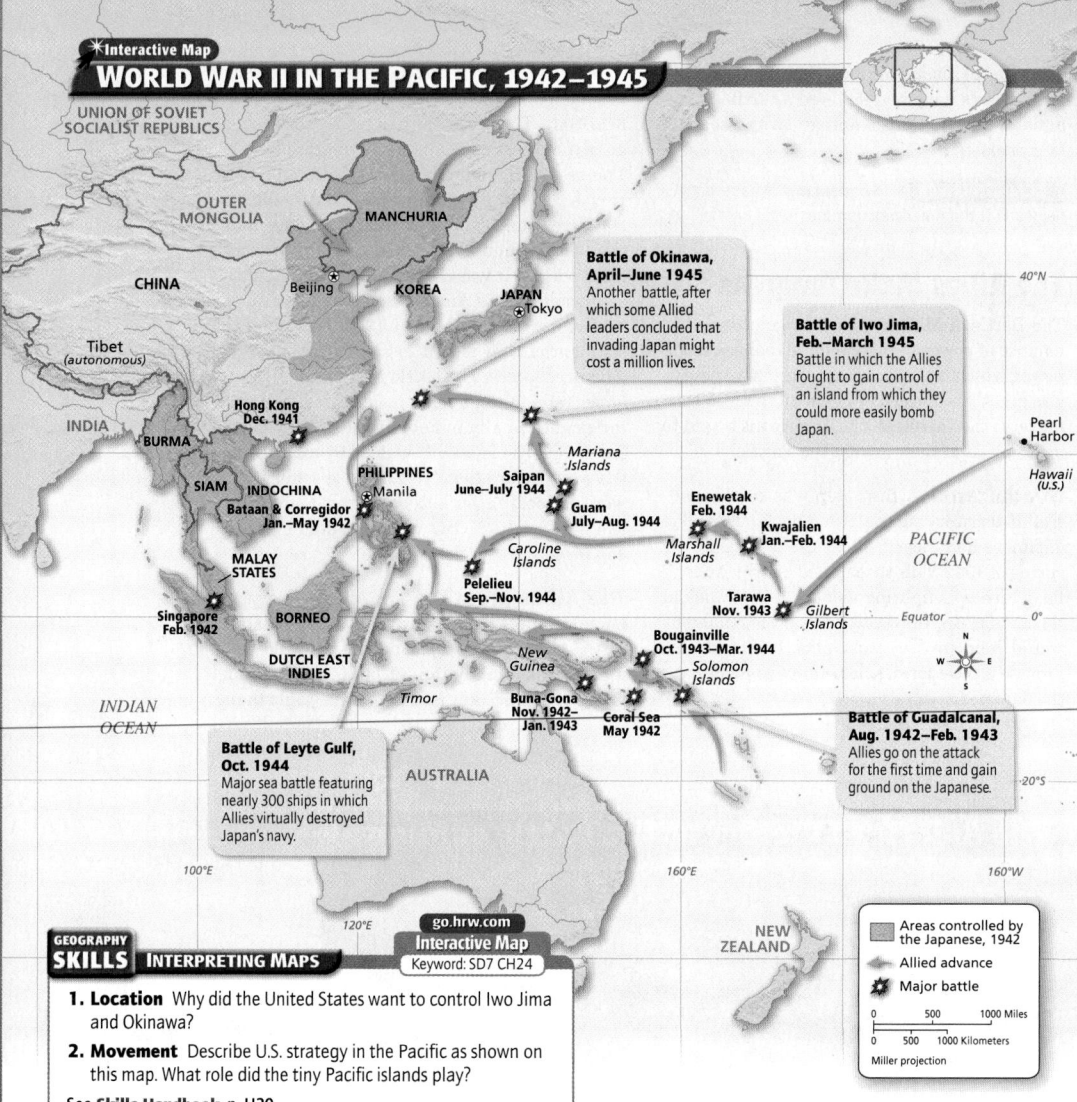

Interactive Map
WORLD WAR II IN THE PACIFIC, 1942–1945

Battle of Okinawa, April–June 1945 Another battle, after which some Allied leaders concluded that invading Japan might cost a million lives.

Battle of Iwo Jima, Feb.–March 1945 Battle in which the Allies fought to gain control of an island from which they could more easily bomb Japan.

Battle of Leyte Gulf, Oct. 1944 Major sea battle featuring nearly 300 ships in which Allies virtually destroyed Japan's navy.

Battle of Guadalcanal, Aug. 1942–Feb. 1943 Allies go on the attack for the first time and gain ground on the Japanese.

GEOGRAPHY SKILLS INTERPRETING MAPS

go.hrw.com
Interactive Map
Keyword: SD7 CH24

1. **Location** Why did the United States want to control Iwo Jima and Okinawa?
2. **Movement** Describe U.S. strategy in the Pacific as shown on this map. What role did the tiny Pacific islands play?

See **Skills Handbook,** p. H20

- Areas controlled by the Japanese, 1942
- Allied advance
- Major battle

0   500   1000 Miles
0   500   1000 Kilometers
Miller projection

become the stepping-stones for future military actions. The Allies focused on Japanese weak spots and simply skipped over strongholds. In this way, the Allies made steady progress in the Southwest Pacific in 1943. In 1944 the Allies captured locations in the Gilbert, Marshall, Caroline, and Mariana islands. You can trace this progress in the map above.

The Allies also began to take advantage of America's tremendous industrial power. The fighting in the Pacific was extremely costly, and both sides lost dozens of ships and thousands of aircraft. These were losses the Japanese were unable to replace. Busy American factories, meanwhile, produced planes and ships at an amazing rate.

Skills Focus: Identifying Main Idea and Details   At Level

Reading Skill
Island-Hopping in the Pacific

1. Have students analyze the advantages, disadvantages, and dangers of the island-hopping strategy. Then have students write a one-page military brief explaining and justifying the strategy. *The Allies used island-hopping first to stop the Japanese advance, then to capture islands that would provide a base for further efforts to push back the Japanese, and finally to gain important launching pads for an invasion of Japan.*

2. Ask volunteers to read their briefs to the class.

3. Have students look at the map on this page. Ask them if they can think of any other effective strategy besides island-hopping to defeat Japan. Have students share their responses. **LS Verbal-Linguistic, Logical-Mathematical**

- Alternative Assessment Handbook, Rubric 37: Writing Assignments

Answers

Interpreting Maps 1. *Allies wanted islands within reach of Japan;* **2.** *jump from one island to another; they were integral to attacking Japanese forces*

790

American fighters in the Pacific also benefited from Allied gains in Europe. Early in the war, Allied leaders had followed the strategy of focusing their efforts on Europe first. This cut down on the numbers of soldiers, sailors, and supplies available for the Pacific war. Then the Soviets began to push back German advances, and the Allies made gains in North Africa, Italy, and France. This allowed Allied war planners to send more resources to the Pacific.

American ingenuity and diversity also played a role in the Allied success. One example was the hundreds of Native Americans of the Navajo nation who served in the Marines as **code talkers**. Their main job was translating messages into a coded version of the Navajo language. This unwritten language is so complex that the Japanese code-breakers were never able to figure it out. Navajo code talkers could quickly and accurately transmit vital information about troop movements, enemy positions, and more. Their contributions helped the Allies win many major battles.

Back to the Philippines Ever since leaving the Philippines in early 1942, General MacArthur had looked forward to the day when he could fulfill his promise to return. By the middle of 1944, that day was at hand. Allied forces had fought to within striking distance of the Philippines. After much planning, MacArthur was ready to attack.

The first major action took place on the seas—the Battle of Leyte (LAY-tee) Gulf. Here nearly 300 ships took part in the largest naval battle ever fought. By this time, the Allies held a huge advantage in numbers of ships. When the battle was over, the Japanese had lost four carriers, three battleships, and a number of other vessels. What little was left of their fleet would play no major role in the rest of the war.

The Battle of Leyte Gulf also saw the first major use of a new Japanese weapon—the **kamikaze** attack. The term *kamikaze* is a Japanese word meaning "divine wind." It refers to a famous event in Japanese history—a sudden storm that drove off a fleet preparing to invade Japan in the 1200s. In World War II, however, a kamikaze was a pilot who loaded his aircraft with bombs and deliberately crashed it into an enemy ship. It was understood that the attack would lead to the death of the pilot. As a Japanese admiral explained, such tactics were "the only way of assuring our meager strength will be effective to the maximum degree." The kamikaze attacks did not change the outcome of the Battle of Leyte Gulf, but the Allies would come to fear these suicidal attacks.

In late October 1944, MacArthur waded ashore to fulfill his promise to return to the Philippines. It would take his soldiers many more months of tough fighting to gain full control of the islands.

ACADEMIC VOCABULARY
strategy plan of action

THE IMPACT TODAY

Recent Scholarship
The work of the Navajo code talkers was kept secret for years. It was not until recently that they received public recognition. In 2001 the 29 original code talkers received the Congressional Gold Medal for their service.

Linking TO Today

Return to Iwo Jima

Iwo Jima was one of the bloodiest battles of the war in the Pacific. On the 60th anniversary of the battle, it was the site of a reunion of former enemies.

After the month-long battle in early 1945, nearly 7,000 Americans had been killed, along with three times as many Japanese fighters. Around 1,000 Japanese soldiers were captured.

In 2005 American and Japanese veterans returned to Iwo Jima to remember the battle and show how the world has changed. Following World War II, Japan and the United States became close allies. The two nations have a strong trade relationship and work together on international issues.

"Today, 60 years after the battle of Iwo Jima, it gives me deep awe to see Japan and the United States cooperate in fighting terrorism," said Yoshitaka Shinda, whose grandfather was the island's last Japanese commander.

Drawing Conclusions Would Yoshitaka Shinda's grandfather agree with his statement? Explain.

Honoring the war dead on the 60th anniversary of the Battle of Iwo Jima

THE UNITED STATES IN WORLD WAR II **791**

Iwo Jima and Okinawa

Explain What was significant about the Battle of Iwo Jima? *For the first time, Japanese troops were defending land that had been a part of their nation before the war began.*

Predict What do you think might have happened if Japanese troops had surrendered on Okinawa and Iwo Jima? *The war might have ended earlier; the U.S. might not have dropped atomic bombs on Japan.*

📁 CRF: Biography: Ernie Pyle

● Review & Assess ●

Close

Have students summarize the progress of the war in the Pacific from the bombing of Pearl Harbor to the capture of Okinawa.

Review

🖥 Online Quiz, Section 3

📦 Daily Test Practice Transparency

Assess

SE Section 3 Assessment

📓 Progress Assessment: Section 3 Quiz

📓 Alternative Assessment Handbook

Reteach

📓 Interactive Reader and Study Guide, Section 3

💿 Interactive Skills Tutor CD-ROM

Answers

Reading Check *Allies used air, land, and sea power to force Japanese troops to retreat; attacked weak spots; U.S. continued to produce new warships and planes*

792

Iwo Jima and Okinawa Beginning in late 1944 the massive new American B-29 bomber began making regular raids on Japanese cities. Allied bombers dropped many tons of explosives on Tokyo and other centers.

In order to provide a better base from which to launch these raids, American forces set out in February 1945 to capture Iwo Jima. This tiny volcanic island lay some 750 miles south of Tokyo, the capital of Japan. The island's rugged terrain was heavily guarded by Japanese soldiers. American troops greatly outnumbered the defenders. For the first time in the war, however, the Japanese troops were fighting for land that was actually part of Japan. Hidden in caves and tunnels and protected by concrete bunkers, they fought ferociously.

Early in the **Battle of Iwo Jima**, marines managed to capture the island's tallest point, Mount Suribachi. You read about this moment earlier in this section. Some Americans thought that the capture of Mount Suribachi meant that the battle was over, but the Japanese troops refused to surrender. The fighting raged on for several more weeks. By the time it was over, nearly 7,000 Americans were dead and many more were wounded. More than 20,000 Japanese defenders had been on Iwo Jima when the Americans landed. All but a thousand of them fought to the death.

The next American target was Okinawa (OH-kee-NAH-wah). Only 350 miles from Japan, this island was to be the launching pad for the final invasion of Japan itself. First, however, it had to be captured. This would be the bloodiest task the Americans would face in the Pacific.

Allied troops invaded Okinawa on April 1, 1945. The Japanese forces retreated to the southern tip of the island to plan their response. Five days later, they attacked. The island of Okinawa was filled with caves and tunnels. Japanese soldiers used these skillfully to hide and to launch deadly assaults. Over 12,000 Americans died in the **Battle of Okinawa**, and thousands more were injured.

The Japanese lost a staggering 110,000 troops in the fighting. As on Iwo Jima, their willingness to fight on when death was certain filled the Americans with amazement—and dread. "I see no way to get them out," noted one American general, "except to blast them out yard by yard."

In spite of the terrible losses, the Americans finally gained control of the island in June 1945. As you will read, the lessons learned on Okinawa would have a major impact on the final days of the war.

READING CHECK **Summarizing** What factors allowed the Allies to advance in 1944 and 1945?

SECTION 3 ASSESSMENT

go.hrw.com
Online Quiz
Keyword: SD7 HP24

Reviewing Ideas, Terms, and People

1. **a. Recall** What events led up to the **Bataan Death March**?
   b. Analyze What were the key reasons for the early success of the Japanese?
   c. Evaluate How do you think the fighting in Europe may have affected events taking place in the Pacific?

2. **a. Identify** Describe the significance of the following people in World War II: James Doolittle, Chester Nimitz
   b. Explain What was the importance of the American victory at the **Battle of Midway**?
   c. Predict At Iwo Jima and Okinawa, Japanese troops refused to surrender even when facing certain defeat. How might this reluctance to give in affect the end of the war?

3. **a. Identify** Describe the significance of the following: **code talkers, kamikaze**
   b. Make Generalizations How would you describe the performance of the Japanese in the later battles of the war in the Pacific?

792 CHAPTER 24

c. Elaborate What is your opinion about the actions of the kamikaze?

Critical Thinking

4. **Identifying Supporting Details** Copy the chart below and use information from the section to find supporting details for the main idea given.

Slow start	Fortunes shift	Progress

FOCUS ON WRITING ✐

5. **Persuasive** In the early years of the war, should the Allies have committed more resources to the fighting in the Pacific? Write a short essay in which you develop your position on the issue. Include references to events in Europe.

Section 3 Assessment Answers

1. **a.** Americans unable to hold off Japanese, retreated, surrendered
   b. most of U.S. Pacific fleet destroyed; Japanese were well supplied, well organized, well-trained
   c. Allies focused on war in Europe.

2. **a.** Doolittle—led raid on Tokyo; Nimitz—won Battles of Coral Sea and Midway
   b. U.S. stopped the Japanese advance.
   c. The war would continue.

3. **a.** code talkers—Navajos who created unbroken code; kamikaze—Japanese pilots

who flew their planes into U.S. ships
   b. They were fierce, determined fighters.
   c. possible answers—brave, determined to defend their country; the missions were futile

4. more effort spent on war in Europe; Allies gain control of Pacific islands; plan to attack Japan

5. possible answers—The U.S. did not have sufficient resources to fight on two fronts; Japanese grew stronger, established bases in the Pacific, cost many Americans their lives.

The Home Front

BEFORE YOU READ

MAIN IDEA
While millions of military men and women were serving in World War II, Americans on the home front were making contributions of their own.

READING FOCUS
1. What sacrifices and struggles did Americans at home experience?
2. How did the U.S. government seek to win American support for the war?
3. What was Japanese internment?
4. How did World War II help expand the role of the government in the lives of the American people?

KEY TERMS AND PEOPLE
rationing
Ernie Pyle
Bill Mauldin
internment

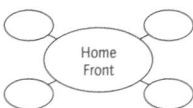 **TAKING NOTES** As you read, take notes on challenges Americans faced on the home front. Write your notes in a graphic organizer like the one shown below.

Home Front

Gardening for Victory

THE INSIDE STORY *How did vegetable gardens help to win a war?* World War II placed huge demands on the United States. Not only did millions of Americans serve in the armed forces, but people at home had to make do with less—including less food and less fuel for harvesting and transporting crops.

To help overcome these shortages and preserve precious resources for the military, Americans by the millions planted "victory gardens." In small towns and large cities, any spare piece of land was likely to be used to grow food. People gardened on the rooftops of apartment buildings and in flower boxes outside their windows. School yards, ball fields, and vacant lots were plowed under. Government agencies and private businesses encouraged the effort with posters, seeds, and instructions for gardening.

Many victory gardens were small and humble but combined they produced big results. In 1943 the nation's 20 million victory gardens yielded an astounding 8 million tons of produce. Grace Bracker's Wisconsin garden was typical. She canned over 400 quarts of fruits and vegetables her first year—more than she and her family could eat.

Victory gardens also helped unite communities. Very young children and older men and women could all help in the preparation, planting, weeding, and harvesting of vegetables. Indeed, the victory gardens became a popular expression of patriotism. They helped Americans at home stay strong during the difficult days of the bloodiest war in human history. ◢

► A few simple tools, some seed, some fertilizer, and a patriotic spirit were nearly all a person needed to grow a victory garden.

THE UNITED STATES IN WORLD WAR II **793**

Bellringer

The Inside Story. . . Use the **Daily Bellringer Transparency** to help students answer the question.

🗄 Daily Bellringer Transparency, Section 4

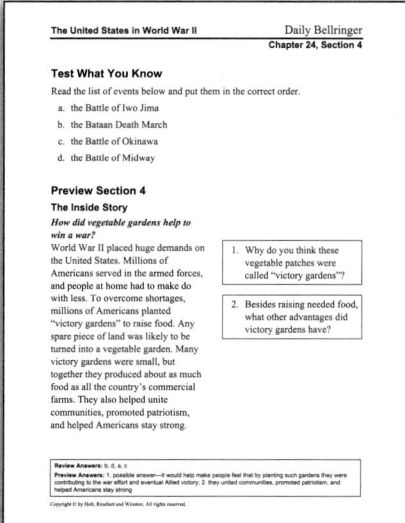

Academic Vocabulary

Review with students the high-use academic term in this section.

civic public or community (p. 795)

📄 CRF: Vocabulary Builder Activity, Section 4

Taking Notes

meeting food needs of military, rationing, shortages of materials, losing loved ones, Japanese Americans faced internment and discrimination

Teach the Main Idea

At Level

The Home Front

1. **Teach** Ask students the Reading Focus questions to teach this section.

2. **Apply** Have students create a list of ways in which they think life in the U.S. during World War II differed from life in the U.S. today.

3. **Review** Ask volunteers to share their lists with the class. Then guide the class in a discussion of its perceptions of life during World War II.

4. **Practice/Homework** Have students check their predictions about life in the United States during World War II with the reality as it is described in this section. Have students note which of their ideas were correct and which were incorrect. **LS Logical-Mathematical, Verbal-Linguistic**

📝 Alternative Assessment Handbook, Rubric 11: Discussions

1 What sacrifices and struggles did Americans at home experience? *rationing and shortages of consumer commodities, absence and death of those fighting in the military*

Sacrifice and Struggle at Home

Identify What kinds of materials were collected in scrap drives? *tin cans, bits of rubber and glass, women's silk and nylon stockings*

Summarize How did rationing work? *Each member of a family received a ration book entitling that person to a certain amount of rationed goods.*

Predict If Americans had not purchased war bonds, how might the U.S. have financed the war effort? *possible answers—increased federal debt; increased taxes*

📄 CRF: Biography: Hazel Ying Lee and the WASP

American Support for the War Effort

Recall Guide students in a discussion of the ways Americans were encouraged to buy bonds.

Sacrifice and Struggle at Home

You have read about the amazing courage and sacrifice of the Allied soldiers, sailors, and pilots. By the millions, they risked life and limb so that others could enjoy freedom. Many spilled their blood so that others could live.

World War II, however, made demands of every American. The women, children, and men who remained in the United States played a key role in ensuring success overseas.

HISTORY'S VOICES

❝Not all of us can have the privilege of fighting our enemies in distant parts of the world ... But there is one front and one battle where everyone in the United States is in action. That front is right here at home.❞
—Franklin D. Roosevelt, radio address, April 28, 1942

As you read earlier, millions of Americans made contributions to the war effort by taking jobs in factories or offices. In addition, life in the American home changed significantly as citizens of all ages did their part to help the cause of victory in Europe and the Pacific.

Conserving food and other goods Meeting the food needs of the military took top priority in the United States. The planting of victory gardens, which you read about in the "Inside Story," was one way in which Americans filled these needs.

Victory gardens alone did not solve all the nation's food needs. Some foods could not be produced in home gardens, and there was simply not enough of certain products to go around. As a result, the United States began rationing food shortly after the nation entered the war. **Rationing** means limiting the amount of a certain product each individual can get.

During the war, the government rationed products such as coffee, butter, sugar, and meat. Each member of the family received a ration book, which entitled that person to a certain amount of certain foods. Most people willingly accepted the system. Penalties for breaking the rationing rules could be severe.

The war effort also meant shortages of other materials, such as metal, glass, rubber, and gasoline. Gasoline was rationed. Americans helped meet the demand for other materials by holding scrap drives, in which citizens col-

American Support for the War Effort

These children (right) drum up support for the war with a scrap metal drive. Communities enthusiastically responded to such drives by contributing everything from old pots and pans to the statues in their town squares. People also turned out for war bond rallies, such as this one at a navy shipyard in Chicago in 1944 (below). The promotional efforts of movie stars and artists helped sell war bonds to tens of millions of Americans.

794

Skills Focus: Analyzing Primary Sources

At Level

Reading Like a Historian Skill
Life on the Home Front

1. Organize the class into groups of five or six students. Have each group develop a series of questions that they would like to ask about life in the United States during World War II.

2. Have students contact someone who could answer the questions developed by the group. Possibilities include grandparents or great-grandparents, neighbors, retired military personnel and their families, or people at a senior center.

3. Have students conduct an interview using their questions. Students should take notes, but they may want to tape-record the interviews. Questions and answers should be edited before being turned in.

4. Have volunteers read their interviews to the class. Discuss the similarities and differences in the subjects' experience. **LS Interpersonal**

📄 Alternative Assessment Handbook, Rubrics 14: Group Activity; and 18: Listening

lected waste material of all sorts that might be used in the war efforts. Empty tin cans, bits of rubber and glass—anything that could be useful was salvaged. Even women's silk and nylon stockings were recycled to make parachutes.

Scrap drives provided a way for young Americans to help with the war effort. Scouts and other youth organizations helped lead the way in this important national effort.

Investing in victory Americans supported the war effort not just with their trash but also with their treasure. They did this by buying billions of dollars worth of war bonds. The money invested by millions of ordinary citizens helped pay for the the vast quantities of shipping, aircraft, and other weaponry being produced in American factories.

Throughout the war, magazines and newspapers were filled with ads encouraging people to do their <u>civic</u> duty and support the war effort. Inspirational pictures and messages helped promote patriotism and self-sacrifice. "Our fighting forces will do their stuff," promised one ad, "but we at home must do ours."

The result of these appeals was amazing. By war's end, 85 million Americans had purchased war bonds. This represented well over half of the entire population of the country. The total raised was nearly $185 billion. This amount was twice what the entire federal government spent in the year 1945.

Paying the personal price Americans willingly put up with many hardships and made do without many comforts during the war. For many, the hardest part was dealing with the absence of loved ones.

HISTORY'S VOICES

❝At first you feel abandoned and you feel angry because they took him when you needed him more at home ... [B]ut he went and he was doing his duty, and we figured that was part of our job to give our husband to the war effort and to do the best we could without him.❞

—Jean Lechnir, quoted in *Women Remember the War,* Michael E. Stevens, Ed.

Across the country, families with loved ones in the service showed their sacrifice by displaying a flag with a blue star. If the service member was killed, the blue star was replaced with a gold one.

Families followed the news of the war with great interest. Millions of Americans read the newspaper columns of writer **Ernie Pyle**, who covered the war from the point of view of the men in the field. **Bill Mauldin**, whose cartoons featured two ordinary soldiers named Willie and Joe, also gave folks on the home front a soldier's view of life in the army.

READING CHECK Identifying Problems and Solutions What were some of the sacrifices and struggles facing people on the home front?

Winning American Support for the War

American leaders were well aware that public support for the war effort was vital to its success. In the words of one government publication of the time, "Each word an American utters either helps or hurts the war effort." For this reason, the government made a great effort to shape public attitudes and beliefs.

This effort to win American support for the war effort began even before the United States entered the war. In January 1941, President Roosevelt gave a speech in which he observed that the challenge facing the world was a struggle for basic American values. By supporting its allies overseas, Roosevelt argued, the nation would be working to protect what he called the "four freedoms." These were the freedom of speech, freedom of worship, freedom from want, and freedom from fear.

The Office of War Information When the United States officially entered the war, the federal government's need to influence the thoughts, feelings, and actions of the public became even greater. In June 1942, the government created the Office of War Information (OWI). This agency was responsible for spreading propaganda, or information and ideas designed to promote a cause.

The OWI produced dozens of posters and films during the war. Many of these encouraged a positive vision of the United States and stressed positive actions. For example, many posters and films encouraged men to join the fighting forces and women to take jobs in war industries. Others encouraged positive goals, such saving gasoline and working for racial

ACADEMIC VOCABULARY
civic public or community

Reading Focus

❷ How did the U.S. government seek to win American support for the war? *President Roosevelt called for support for the "four freedoms;" Office of War Information was created*

Winning American Support for the War

Identify What were Roosevelt's "four freedoms"? *freedom of speech, freedom of worship, freedom from want, and freedom from fear*

Evaluate Do you think that the government needed to create an agency to build support for the war effort? Explain your answer. *possible answers—yes, everyone needed to support the war effort, government had to get its message to the people; no, Americans would have supported the war effort without propaganda.*

Activity The Four Freedoms Have each student create a list of the four to six freedoms that are most important to them, along with their reasons for choosing these particular rights. Have volunteers share their lists with the class. **LS** Logical-Mathematical

Teaching Tip

Explain to students what a war bond was—an interest-bearing certificate that was purchased to help finance the war. Students may be familiar with government savings bonds, which are similar.

Differentiating Instruction

Below Level

Learners Having Difficulty

Materials poster paper, colored pencils, markers

1. Organize the class into small groups. Have each group think of an idea for a poster and a slogan to encourage U.S. citizens to support the war effort. Ideas may include encouraging the following activities: planting victory gardens, conserving gasoline, collecting scrap materials, buying war bonds, joining the armed forces, etc.

2. Have a volunteer from each group share the group's poster idea. Help groups fine-tune

their slogans. For example, to encourage people to pay their taxes, you might suggest "Pay Your Taxes to Beat the Axis!"

3. Have each group create a poster using its slogan. Posters should be colorful, and artwork should fit the slogan. **LS** Interpersonal, Visual-Spatial

Alternative Assessment Handbook, Rubrics 14: Group Activity; and 28: Posters

Answers

Reading Check *rationing and shortages of consumer commodities including food and gasoline; absence and death of those fighting in the military*

795

Reading Focus

Winning American Support for the War

Summarize What part did the Hollywood film industry play in the war effort? *Studios made patriotic films that featured soldiers and workers on the home front. Movie stars helped sell war bonds and provided entertainment to the troops at home and overseas.*

Evaluate Why did the Jehovah's Witnesses challenge a law requiring students to salute the American flag? *the law went against their religious teachings*

📰 CRF: Literature Activity: Farewell to Manzanar

📰 CRF: Economics and History Activity: Mobilization Ends the Depression

Primary Sources

Propaganda Poster

Describe Guide students in a discussion of the images and messages on the poster. Ask students if they believe that this poster would have been effective at the time. Where do students think posters like this might have been displayed?

Answers

Reading Like a Historian 1. *The hand is putting the puzzle pieces together; once the puzzle is complete the Nazis will know Allied plans.* **2.** *One should be vigilant about not talking about possible war plans or leaking any bits of information that could be put together to reveal war plans.*

---

harmony. Another famous poster series illustrated the four freedoms that Roosevelt had talked about. These featured paintings by the popular artist Norman Rockwell.

The OWI also issued stark warnings to the public about the dangers they faced. Drawings of Nazi or Japanese soldiers threatening small children were meant to inspire fear in Americans—and the desire to take action against the Axis nations. "We're fighting to prevent this," declared one headline. Below the words was a picture of a giant Nazi boot crushing a little white church.

Another technique was to show the harmful outcomes of improper actions and attitudes, such as talking about sensitive military information. "Someone talked!" accused a drowning American sailor in one poster, moments before he slipped beneath the waves. Films such as *Safeguarding Military Information* dramatized the same ideas.

Hollywood helps out Movies remained enormously popular during the war years. In the early 1940s, some 90 million Americans visited the movie theater each week. As a result, the nation's film industry became a major producer of wartime propaganda.

In general, Hollywood was a willing helper in the war effort. The big movie studios made a series of patriotic films that featured soldiers and workers on the home front. To assist the studios, the OWI produced a guide called "The Government Information Manual for the Motion Picture." This offered tips to ensure that Hollywood films helped promote what the government felt were the right attitudes about the war. The OWI also reviewed movie scripts for the proper messages.

Many leading movie stars devoted time and energy to the war cause. They helped sell war bonds and provided entertainment to the troops at home and overseas.

PRIMARY SOURCES

Propaganda Poster

Office of War Information propaganda posters used bold graphics and simple text to convey their messages. This poster was issued in 1943. It addressed a key priority: the need to safeguard sensitive war-related information when nearly everyone in society was involved in the war effort.

The hand with the swastika suggests that Nazi spies might be hidden in America.

The poster compares bits of information with puzzle pieces that, if combined, could reveal a damaging secret.

BITS OF CARELESS TALK ARE PIECED TOGETHER BY THE ENEMY

England

Convoy sails for tonight

Skills FOCUS READING LIKE A HISTORIAN

1. **Interpreting Visuals** What is the hand doing, and why?
2. **Drawing Conclusions** What is the main message of this poster?

See Skills Handbook, p. H12, H30

796 CHAPTER 24

Skills Focus: Identifying Main Idea and Details   Above Level

Reading Skill
Keeping up Morale

1. Conduct a brief discussion on the ways in which the U.S. government tried to keep wartime morale high. *created the Office of War Information, which was responsible for spreading propaganda; produced posters and films encouraging a positive vision of the U.S. and stressing positive actions; gave tips to the film industry to ensure that films helped promote what the government felt were the right attitudes about the war*

2. Have each student write a proposal for a movie that supports the war effort and boosts wartime morale. Each script proposal should include the movie title and a brief plot summary.

3. Have volunteers share their proposals.

4. As an extension, have students create a PowerPoint presentation for their proposals.
   LS Verbal-Linguistic

📄 Alternative Assessment Handbook, Rubric 37: Writing Assignments

The *Barnette* ruling While most Americans willingly supported the war effort, the drive to influence public attitudes sometimes led to conflict. For example, in West Virginia, members of the Jehovah's Witness religious group challenged a law that required students in school to salute the American flag. The Jehovah's Witnesses felt that this requirement went against their religious teachings. In 1943 the Supreme Court of the United States agreed that Americans could not be forced to salute the flag. In *West Virginia Board of Education v. Barnette*, the Court wrote that "no official … can prescribe [require] what shall be orthodox [standard or required belief] in politics, nationalism, religion or other matters of opinion."

READING CHECK **Identifying Supporting Details** What was the mission of the Office of War Information in influencing public opinion?

Japanese Internment

After Pearl Harbor, government officials began to fear that people of German, Italian, and especially Japanese descent would help the enemy. Many Italians and Germans who had immigrated to the United States were forced to carry identification cards. Thousands were placed in prison camps. But the worst treatment was reserved for Japanese Americans.

Executive Order 9066 Right after the bombing of Pearl Harbor, military officials began to investigate the Japanese American community for signs of spying or other illegal activity. They found no evidence of wrongdoing. In spite of this finding, General John L. DeWitt, the Army officer in charge of the western United States, still recommended that all people of Japanese background be removed from the West Coast. "The very fact that no sabotage or espionage has taken place," he warned, "is disturbing and confirming indication that such action will take place."

In response to warnings such as this, President Roosevelt issued Executive Order 9066 on February 19, 1942. This order gave the armed forces the power to establish military zones. It also gave them the power to force people or groups to leave these zones. The clear goal of the order was to remove people of Japanese heritage from the western United States.

The order affected all people of Japanese heritage living in the military zone. Within weeks of the order, soldiers were rounding up Japanese Americans in California, Washington, Oregon, and Arizona. Two-thirds of the 110,000 people affected were American citizens. Many had been born in the United States and had lived here for decades. No hearings or trials were conducted to determine if an individual posed a real threat. The only factor considered was the person's racial background. The Japanese Americans were told they would be taken to one of several camps somewhere in the West. There they would be forced to live for as long as the military decided it was necessary.

This forced relocation and confinement to the camps was called **internment**. It placed many hardships on Japanese Americans. They were allowed to bring only those belongings they could carry. Everything else—homes, businesses, and other property—had to be left behind or sold. Sometimes people were given just days to get rid of their property. As a result, they were forced to accept very low prices for their belongings or were unable to sell them at all. In this way, many Japanese Americans lost their homes and businesses. Confined to camps they were unable to work and pay off loans.

Life in the camps was hard. Many camps were located in barren desert areas with a harsh climate. Barbed wire and armed guards surrounded the facility. Families lived in cramped quarters with few furnishings. Facilities for education and health care were poor.

Japanese American loyalty While interned, Japanese Americans were required to answer questions about their loyalty to the United States. Though German Americans and Italian Americans also faced restrictions during the war, they were not forced to answer such questions.

For many Japanese in America, the desire to prove their loyalty to the country was strong. A number of young people from the camps joined the armed forces to help fight the Axis powers. Many became part of the 442nd Regimental Combat Team, made up entirely of Japanese Americans. This unit fought in Europe and had an outstanding record in battle. For the length of time it served, this unit received more medals and awards than any other of its size in American military history.

Skills Focus: Analyzing Primary Sources

At Level

Reading Like a Historian Skill
Japanese Internment

Research Required

1. Have students conduct research to find accounts of internment written by Japanese Americans who were interned.

2. Have each student select one account and write a one-page report based on it. Students should summarize the account and include biographical information about the person who wrote it. Students should also indicate the type of account they used—whether it was a letter, diary, oral history, etc.

3. Have volunteers read their reports to the class. Then guide students in a discussion of the reports. Ask them to compare the experiences of Japanese Americans who were interned with the experiences of Nazi concentration camp prisoners. **LS Verbal-Linguistic, Logical-Mathematical**

   Alternative Assessment Handbook, Rubrics 30: Research; and 37: Writing Assignments

Reading Focus

❸ What was Japanese internment?
People of Japanese heritage who lived in the West Coast area were rounded up and forced to stay in government camps.

Japanese Internment

Explain What did Executive Order 9066 do? *It gave the armed forces the power to establish military zones and to force people or groups to leave these zones. Its goal was to remove people of Japanese heritage from the West Coast area.*

Make Inferences Why do you think some Japanese Americans were interned in barren areas, far from their homes? *to prevent them from spying or providing the enemy with information*

Elaborate Why do you think only Japanese Americans and not German Americans or Italian Americans, were singled out for internment? *possible answer—because of racism and the attack on Pearl Harbor*

Biography

Bing Crosby (1903–1977) Bing Crosby made his first film in 1931 and quickly gained fame as a singer and an actor. One of his most famous songs, *White Christmas,* was recorded on December 25, 1941, and the desire for a Christmas "just like the ones we used to know" had immediate appeal to a nation at war. Crosby sang for military troops during the war, and *White Christmas* was a usual request. Following a tour of Europe in the fall of 1944 where he entertained troops, Crosby expressed surprise on the remarkable effect the song had on the audience, sometimes bringing soldiers to tears.

Answers

Reading Check *It spread pro-war propaganda, posters, information, and films to increase support for the war effort.*

④ How did World War II help expand the role of the government in the lives of the American people? *size and power of the government grew; boards and offices that instituted controls over many parts of American lives were established; income tax was extended to include most workers*

A New Role for the Federal Government

Explain How did the federal government raise money to help pay for the war effort? *sold war bonds; increased income tax rates, began taxing millions of Americans who had not previously paid income taxes*

Make Inferences What was the connection between the War Production Board and the fashion industry? *The War Production Board placed limits on clothing manufacturers in order to ensure a plentiful supply of fabrics.*

Japanese American Internment

Once an elegant race track, California's Santa Anita Assembly Center held Japanese Americans during the war. Internees were instructed to bring personal effects and small household goods, such as plates, utensils, and linens. Here they awaited transportation to more permanent relocation centers. **Why did the government intern Japanese Americans?**

Other inmates of the internment camps demonstrated their loyalty in different ways. For some, the greatest statement they could make was in keeping faith in the future and in the promise of the country that had imprisoned them.

HISTORY'S VOICES

❝We are ever hoping that the time will come soon when we can all re-enter the America beyond the relocation camps in order that we make our contributions and be considered as an integral part of the American way of living.❞

—Yoshiko Uchiyama, letter reprinted in the *University of Washington Daily*, January 1943

Not all Japanese Americans accepted their internment peacefully. Incidents of violence and resistance occurred at the camps. In addition, a number of legal challenges were mounted against Japanese internment. One was *Korematsu* v. *United States*, a landmark Supreme Court case that you will read about at the end of this section.

After the war some Japanese Americans continued to speak out against the injustice of their internment. Decades later, the federal government formally acknowledged that it had

acted unjustly. Survivors of the internment received letters of apology and a payment from the government.

READING CHECK Identifying Supporting **Details** What was life like in the internment camps?

A New Role for the Federal Government

During the 1930s, the federal government faced the crisis of the Great Depression. With the New Deal, the government grew to have a much larger role in the lives of average Americans than it had in the past. The trend that began in the Great Depression continued during World War II.

You have read about wartime rationing. This program was run by the Office of Price Administration (OPA). The OPA also placed limits on the prices businesses could charge for products and materials.

The War Production Board was another agency involved in the war effort. It was created to make sure that the military got the products and resources it needed to fight the

---

Skills Focus: Identifying Problem and Solution   Above Level

Reading Skill   **Research Required**
Federal Income Tax

1. Remind students that there was a major change in the tax law during the war, and that for the first time many Americans were required to pay income tax. Have students research the format and language used by President Roosevelt during his "fireside chats" with the American people.

2. Have students write a "fireside chat" for President Roosevelt in which he will announce the changes in the tax law to the

American public. In the speech the president must make Americans aware of the necessity of the new income tax and make it acceptable to them.

3. Have volunteers deliver their speeches to the class in the form of a "fireside chat."
   LS Interpersonal, Visual-Spatial

   Alternative Assessment Handbook, Rubric 24: Oral Presentations

---

Answers

Photo *concern about possible espionage*

Reading Check *difficult; camps guarded, surrounded by barbed wire; cramped living quarters; poor facilities*

war. As part of this effort, the board promoted the scrap drives you read about earlier. The War Production Board also placed limits on clothing manufacturers in order to ensure a supply of fabrics, such as cotton, wool, silk, and nylon. Jackets were only allowed to be a certain length. Skirts and dresses were limited in size as well. It was these restrictions on clothing that played a role in the zoot suit riots you read about in the last chapter.

Government spending during the war rose sharply. As you can see from the graph on this page, the high cost of waging war meant a steep increase in the federal budget. Almost all of this increase went to the armed forces.

To help pay for the war effort, the federal government increased income tax rates. Before the war, income taxes had been just for the wealthy, but now millions of Americans paid income taxes for the first time. As one observer noted, "the Kansas wheat farmer, the lumberjack, and the boys around the cracker barrel in the corner grocery are going to have to pay the tax bill this time." As a result Ameri-

can tax revenues jumped from $7.4 billion in 1941 to $43 billion in 1945.

READING CHECK Identifying Supporting **Details** Why did income tax rates increase during World War II?

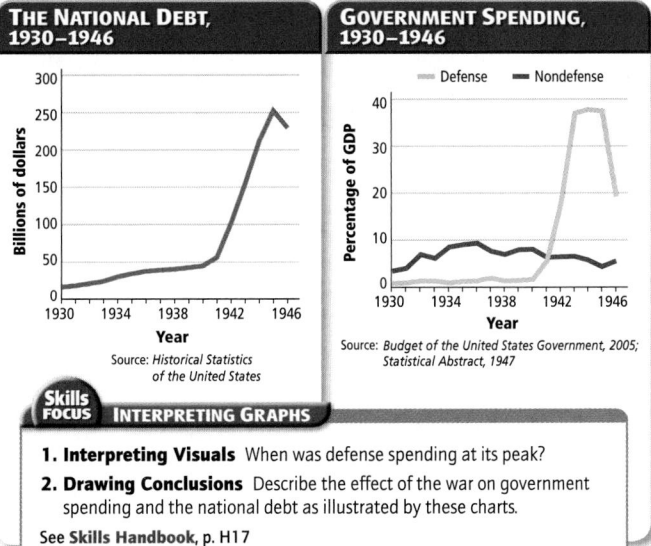

THE NATIONAL DEBT, 1930–1946

Source: *Historical Statistics of the United States*

GOVERNMENT SPENDING, 1930–1946

Source: *Budget of the United States Government, 2005; Statistical Abstract, 1947*

Skills FOCUS   INTERPRETING GRAPHS

1. **Interpreting Visuals** When was defense spending at its peak?
2. **Drawing Conclusions** Describe the effect of the war on government spending and the national debt as illustrated by these charts.

See **Skills Handbook**, p. H17

SECTION 4 ASSESSMENT

Online Quiz
Keyword: SD7 HP24

Reviewing Ideas, Terms, and People

1. **a. Recall** What were the purposes of **rationing** and scrap drives?
   b. Summarize What kinds of sacrifices were required of people on the home front?
   c. Predict What might have happened had people on the home front been unwilling to support the war?

2. **a. Describe** What did the Office of War Information seek to do?
   b. Draw Conclusions What can you conclude from the fact that the federal government had an organization in charge of propaganda?

3. **a. Recall** What concern led to the **internment** of Japanese Americans?
   b. Explain What factors made the experience of interned Japanese Americans so difficult?

4. **a. Identify** Name two actions the federal government took to support the war effort during World War II.

   b. Compare How did the changes in the federal government during the Great Depression compare to the changes during World War II?

Critical Thinking

5. **Identifying Supporting Details** Copy the chart below and use information from the section to find supporting details for the main idea given.

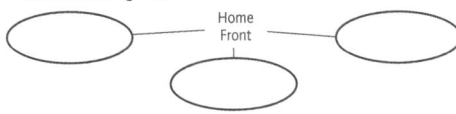
Home Front

FOCUS ON WRITING

6. **Narrative** Based on what you have read in this section, write a one-paragraph account about the internment of Japanese Americans on the West Coast in World War II.

THE UNITED STATES IN WORLD WAR II **799**

LANDMARK SUPREME COURT CASES

Constitutional Issue: Equal Protection

Korematsu v. United States

Word Help

curtail cut short, reduce
suspect doubtful, questionable
scrutiny close examination

Info to Know

The Equal Protection Clause Fred Korematsu's appeal was based on the equal protection clause in the Constitution. This is found in Section 1 of the Fourteenth Amendment (ratified in 1868), where all citizens are guaranteed equal protection of the laws:

". . . No State shall make or enforce any law which shall abridge the privileges or immunities of the citizens of the United States; nor shall any State deprive any person of life, liberty, or property, without due process of law; nor deny to any person within its jurisdiction the equal protection of the laws."

Answers

Critical Thinking 1. *The Virginia law made interracial marriages illegal. The Supreme Court ruled that the law violated both equal protection and due process clauses of the Fourteenth Amendment. The Court ruled that "...the freedom to marry or not marry a person of another race resides with the individual and cannot be infringed by the state." In this decision, the Court clearly held that classifications by race were suspect and only justifiable by compelling reasons.*
2. *possible answers—It is appropriate because the nation was attacked and we need ways of countering terrorism and fighting terrorists within our own country. It is a violation of rights because the United States is the world's best example of democracy, and we should work hard to protect the civil rights of all citizens and residents, regardless of national origin or race.*

800

Korematsu v. United States (1944)

Why It Matters In wartime, citizens are sometimes fearful of those who have common ancestry with the enemy. But the American population includes people from all over the world, and almost all people who live here are loyal to this country. In *Korematsu v. United States,* the U.S. Supreme Court tried to find the right balance between the rights of Japanese Americans and wartime needs.

Background of the Case

In February 1942 President Roosevelt signed an executive order that resulted in the relocation of 110,000 Japanese Americans to internment camps. Fred Korematsu refused the order and was arrested. Korematsu was in his 20s. He was of Japanese ancestry but had been born in Oakland, California, and was an American citizen. In court, Korematsu was found guilty of violating the executive order. He appealed his case to the Supreme Court.

The Decision

The Supreme Court ruled against Korematsu. Writing for the majority, Justice Hugo Black began by noting that "all legal restrictions which curtail [limit] the civil rights of a single racial group are immediately suspect" and must be given "rigid scrutiny." In this wartime situation, however, there was no easy way to separate loyal Americans of Japanese descent from those who might not support the country. The Court ruled that the relocation order was justified as a temporary wartime measure. Black rejected the argument that the relocation was racially motivated.

❝Korematsu was excluded because we are at war with the Japanese Empire ... [W]hen under conditions of modern warfare our shores are threatened by hostile forces, the power to protect must be commensurate [equal] with the threatened danger.❞

THE IMPACT TODAY Although Fred Korematsu lost his case, he continued to work for civil rights. He finally succeeded in having his conviction overturned in 1983, and in 1998 he received the Presidential Medal of Freedom from President Bill Clinton. Korematsu died in 2005.

go.hrw.com
Research Online
Keyword: SS Court

CRITICAL THINKING

1. **Analyze the Impact** *Korematsu* v. *the United States* established the idea that classifications based on race are "suspect" and have to be supported by a compelling government interest. Using the keyword above, read about *Loving* v. *Virginia,* a case in which the Supreme Court used "strict scrutiny" to decide whether a state law prohibiting interracial marriage was constitutional. What individual interests did the law violate?

2. **You Be the Judge** The USA Patriot Act, enacted shortly after the terrorist attacks of September 11, 2001, authorizes the Immigration and Naturalization Service to detain immigrants suspected of terrorism for lengthy, or even indefinite, periods. Is this a violation of civil rights or an appropriate use of military authority? Explain your answer in a short paragraph.

Skills Focus: Identifying Problem and Solution

At Level

Reading Skill
Korematsu v. United States

1. Have students read all of Section 1 of the Fourteenth Amendment of the Constitution. Point out that the Fourteenth Amendment was originally passed to define citizenship and to prevent the states from interfering in the rights of African Americans who were citizens of the United States. It was this section of the amendment, however, that was used in Korematsu's appeal.

2. Have students write an essay about this case. Students should explain how and why laws should protect the rights of individuals while helping to ensure the safety of society as a whole.

3. Have volunteers read their essays to the class.
   LS Logical-Mathematical

   Alternative Assessment Handbook, Rubric 37: Writing Assignments

World War II Ends

BEFORE YOU READ

MAIN IDEA

While the Allies completed the defeat of the Axis Powers on the battlefield, Allied leaders were making plans for the postwar world.

READING FOCUS

1. How did the Allies defeat Germany and win the war in Europe?
2. How did the Allies defeat Japan and win the war in the Pacific?
3. What challenges faced the United States after victory?

KEY TERMS AND PEOPLE

Yalta Conference
occupy
V-E Day
Harry S Truman
Enola Gay
V-J Day
United Nations
Potsdam Conference

TAKING NOTES As you read, take notes on how the war came to end and its aftermath. Write your notes in a graphic organizer like the one shown below.

Europe	Pacific	Post-war

THE INSIDE STORY

What happened when the Soviet and American forces met? By April 1945, American forces had crossed Germany's western border and were moving steadily eastward. At the same time, their Soviet allies were driving westward toward the German capital of Berlin. Each side knew that when they met, Hitler's fate would be sealed.

Sometime around noon on April 25, a group of American troops spotted a Soviet force on the other side of the Elbe River. The Americans identified themselves as friendly forces. Once they had made contact, the Americans headed across the Elbe. Some swam and others took boats to the other side. There they met a group of Soviet soldiers for the first time.

The soldiers shook hands, embraced, and offered toasts to the leaders of their countries. They danced and sang. All present promised that they would do everything they could to make sure that their nations would build a lasting peace.

News of the meeting on the Elbe River set off celebrations in the United States and in the Soviet Union. There were still several days of fighting ahead before Germany surrendered, but everyone was convinced that the linking of the two main Allied forces doomed the Germans.

In the days ahead, the scene from that first meeting at the Elbe was repeated many times, as American and Soviet units linked up, posed for pictures and enjoyed their success in the war. Yet these moments of friendship and joy would soon fade away. American forces still had fighting to do in the Pacific. At the same time, tension between the Soviet Union and the United States was growing.

A HISTORIC Meeting

◄ American (left) and Soviet brothers in arms reach out across the Elbe River.

THE UNITED STATES IN WORLD WAR II **801**

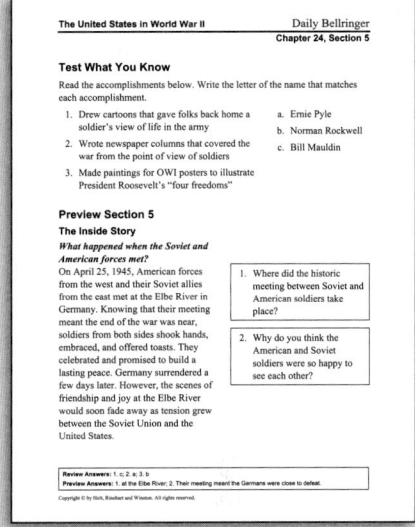

Teach the Main Idea

[At Level]

World War II Ends

1. **Teach** Ask students the Reading Focus questions to teach this section.

2. **Apply** Have students work in pairs to create charts that compare the way the war ended in Europe with the way it ended in the Pacific.

3. **Review** Review student comparisons as a class. Have students identify the most important similarities and differences in the way the war ended in the two regions.

4. **Practice/Homework** At one time, World War I was known as "the war to end all wars." Obviously, it did not end war. Have each student write a brief essay about whether that title rightfully belongs to World War II. Students should back their opinions with logical arguments. **LS Logical-Mathematical, Verbal-Linguistic**

📝 Alternative Assessment Handbook, Rubric 37: Writing Assignments

❶ How did the Allies defeat Germany and win the war in Europe? *Allied troops crossed the Rhine; Germans realized there was little reason to continue to fight; Soviet forces from the east met Allied forces from the west; Berlin fell; Germany surrendered*

Winning the War in Europe

Describe What plans were made at the Yalta Conference for Germany and Eastern Europe? *Germany, and its capital city of Berlin, were to be divided into four sectors to be occupied by the Americans, Soviets, British, and French. Elections were to be held following the war in the Eastern European nations that were occupied by the Soviets.*

Make Inferences How did Hitler's order to defend the Rhine turn out to be deadly? *The Allies were able to trap many German defenders. A quarter million were taken prisoner, and tens of thousands were killed.*

Predict Do you think that if Allied forces had reached Berlin before the Soviets, they could have prevented the division of the city? *possible answer—no, Allies would have held to the agreement to partition the city.*

Toward Victory in Europe

Describe Guide students in a discussion of the destruction of European cities during the war. Have students focus on the massive effort that would be needed to rebuild the infrastructure, homes, businesses, and industries.

Winning the War in Europe

In the first section of this chapter you read about the Battle of the Bulge. In those few desperate days of combat, over 80,000 Allied troops were killed, wounded, or captured. As bad as those figures were, the result for the German army was even worse. It had risked much in the attack and suffered a crushing defeat. Germany now had few soldiers left to defend the homeland from the 4 million Allied troops poised on its western border. To the east were millions of Soviet soldiers, who had been pushing the Germans westward since the heroic Soviet stand at Stalingrad. They stood waiting to launch a final assault.

ACADEMIC VOCABULARY
sector a part or division

The Yalta Conference In January 1945 Franklin D. Roosevelt took the presidential oath of office for the fourth time. He had run in 1944 believing that he needed to see the nation through to victory. A majority of the American voters had agreed.

Shortly after Roosevelt's inauguration, the president left for a conference of the Allied leaders. The meeting was held in the resort town of Yalta, in the Soviet Union. The so-called Big Three—Roosevelt, Winston Churchill, and Joseph Stalin—met to make plans for the end of the war and the peace that was to follow.

A key goal of the **Yalta Conference** was to reach an agreement on what to do with the soon-to-be-conquered Germany. The three leaders agreed to divide the country into four sectors. The Americans, Soviets, British, and French would each occupy one of these sectors. To **occupy** means to take control of a place by placing troops in it. The Soviet Union, which had the largest army, was given the largest zone. It covered most of the eastern half of

Toward Victory in Europe

By the spring of 1945, the Allies were closing in on Hitler. At left, U.S. army infantrymen blast their way through a German city. Below, an American soldier is lifted into the air by Russians celebrating their liberation from a German camp.

802

Collaborative Learning

At Level

Reliving the Yalta Conference

Research Required

1. Organize the class into three groups. One group will represent the United States, another will represent Great Britain, and the third will represent the Soviet Union.

2. Have each group research the positions its country took at the Yalta Conference. Have students use the following questions to guide their research: What were the postwar goals of each country? What compromises was each country ready to make to reach an agreement?

3. Have each group select one person to play the part of its member of the "big three"— Franklin Roosevelt, Winston Churchill, and Joseph Stalin.

4. Have students take turns presenting their group's position to the class. Then guide the class in a discussion of the goals and results of the Yalta Conference. **LS Interpersonal, Verbal-Linguistic**

📝 Alternative Assessment Handbook, Rubrics 14: Group Activity; and 30: Research

Germany. The American, British, and French zones covered the western half. The capital city of Berlin, which lay in the Soviet zone, was similarly divided into four sectors.

Another agreement at Yalta had to do with the fate of Poland and other Eastern European countries now occupied by the Soviets. Stalin agreed to hold elections in these countries following the war. As you will read, this was a promise Stalin would not keep.

Stalin also committed to a third major decision. He said that the Soviet Union would declare war on Japan three months after Germany was defeated.

Though all the participants at Yalta had been allies in the fight to defeat the Axis, the conference had been tense. Friction between the Soviet Union and the other Allies was growing. Nevertheless, Roosevelt cheerfully reported the success of the meeting to the Congress.

HISTORY'S VOICES

❝Of course we know that it was Hitler's hope... that we would not agree, that some slight crack might appear in the solid wall of Allied unity... But Hitler has failed. Never before have the major Allies been more closely united—not only in their war aims but also in their peace aims.❞

—Franklin D. Roosevelt, March 1, 1945

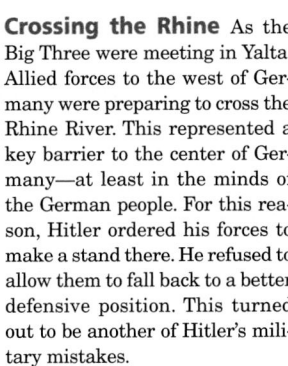

Crossing the Rhine As the Big Three were meeting in Yalta, Allied forces to the west of Germany were preparing to cross the Rhine River. This represented a key barrier to the center of Germany—at least in the minds of the German people. For this reason, Hitler ordered his forces to make a stand there. He refused to allow them to fall back to a better defensive position. This turned out to be another of Hitler's military mistakes.

German troops began blowing up bridges over the Rhine in order to slow the Allies. On March 7, 1945, however, American forces managed to capture a bridge at Remagen. They did this while the Germans were still moving their own forces to the eastern side. The Germans fought desperately to destroy the bridge and keep it out of American hands. They used every weapon in their arsenal against it, including the powerful V-2 rocket. Yet the bridge stood even under this vicious bombardment. Meanwhile, Allied troops and tanks rumbled steadily across.

Once the Allies crossed the Rhine, the foolishness of Hitler's order to defend the river became clear. The Allies were able to surround and capture a quarter million German soldiers. Tens of thousands more were killed.

The question of Berlin With the Rhine crossed, German resistance weakened. Allied planes roamed the skies freely, raining bombs down on German targets. Allied troops began moving speedily across Germany.

Now some Allied leaders, knowing that the Soviets would claim any German land they captured, hoped to claim the prize of Berlin before the Soviets did so. The possibility of beating the Soviets to Berlin had once seemed unlikely. Just days before, the western lines were 200 miles away from the German capital, while the Soviets rested just 30 miles outside the city. Since the Rhine crossing, however, the situation had changed. It was no sure thing the Soviets would get there first.

In spite of these facts, General Eisenhower decided not to make a drive toward Berlin itself. Although German defenses were crumbling, he believed the battle for the city would be a bloody one. He also knew that Allied leaders had already reached an agreement with the Soviets about how to divide Berlin. This meant that some of the territory American soldiers might fight and die for would be turned over to the Soviets anyway. In addition, Eisenhower knew that the war in the Pacific was still raging. He felt it was most important to preserve American forces and supplies and make it as easy as possible to send them to the Pacific when the fighting in Europe was done.

With the decision to leave Berlin to the Soviets made, Eisenhower's forces moved rapidly through Germany. They did receive a blow on April 12, 1945, when President Roosevelt died. Although the president had not been in good health, his death was unexpected. Many American soldiers had known no other president during their adult lives. Roosevelt's death saddened the troops. It did not, however, slow the drive to victory.

Info to Know

World War II Films Many films have been made about actual events that took place during World War II. One of them is *The Bridge of Remagen,* rated PG. Made in 1969, it is about the Allied attempts to capture the bridge over the Rhine toward the end of the war.

Teaching Tip

Remind students that films based on historic events may not necessarily be historically accurate. Usually, they take liberties with the facts in order to appeal to audiences.

Recent Scholarship

In *Berlin–The Downfall 1945*, British historian Antony Beevor examines the Soviets' rush to reach Berlin, a rush that led to the death of 70,000 Russian soldiers. Why were the Soviets in such a hurry to reach Berlin? The traditional explanation is that it was a combination of Soviet pride and mistrust of the West. Beevor recently made a startling discovery—a document showing that the Soviets were trying to reach the German nuclear research center in Berlin before the Americans got there. Soviet scientists were eager to find out what the Germans had been developing during the war. When the Soviets arrived at the German research center, they discovered three tons of uranium oxide. It was enough to allow them to start working on their first nuclear weapon.

Berlin-The Downfall 1945, by Antony Beevor. Viking, 2002

Skills Focus: Comparing and Contrasting   At Level

Reading Skill
The Question of Berlin

1. Organize students into groups of five students. Remind students that it was General Eisenhower's decision whether or not to push his troops to Berlin. Have each group study the issue and the options available to Eisenhower. Then have each group select one student to serve as its moderator, and split each group into two teams. Have one team support an attempt to capture Berlin before the Soviets; the other team will oppose the plan.

2. Have each group debate this issue. Students may use information from their textbooks, or they may conduct additional research to help support their arguments for or against a hurried drive to Berlin. When each group has finished its debate, have the moderators announce the winning position: for or against the drive to Berlin. **LS Verbal-Linguistic**

    📖 Alternative Assessment Handbook, Rubric 10: Debates

2 How did the Allies defeat Japan and win the war in the Pacific? *by using the atomic bomb against the cities of Hiroshima and Nagasaki*

Winning the War in the Pacific

Explain How did the Allies hope to force Japan to surrender? *by putting a blockade in place or by bombing Japan heavily*

Evaluate Do you believe that the U.S. was justified in dropping the atomic bomb on the city of Hiroshima? *possible answers—yes, Japan was warned; Truman believed that this action would, by ending the war, save lives; no, too many innocent civilians were killed in the bombings*

American Civil Liberty
Women and Minorities in the Military

Today a number of African Americans hold the rank of four-star general in the U.S. Army, and in 1989 Colin Powell became the first African American to serve as chairman of the Joint Chiefs of Staff. Over 200,000 women serve in the U.S. military, and almost 35,000 women serve as officers.

Answers

American Civil Liberty *African Americans had served with distinction in the war and deserved equal treatment and the same rights as other soldiers.*

Reading Check *The Germans saw the Rhine as a major barrier and their last chance to protect their country.*

804

Women and Minorities in the Military

At the beginning of World War II, only two African Americans had been line officers in the army. One was Benjamin O. Davis Sr., the first African American general. The other was his son, Benjamin O. Davis Jr., who commanded the famous Tuskegee Airmen, a squadron of African American fighter pilots who flew wartime missions in North Africa and Europe. Like his father, Davis Jr. was eventually promoted to general.

The Davises and other African Americans in World War II served in segregated units. In 1948 President Harry S Truman signed legislation that began racial integration in the military.

Members of women's military units also wanted fair treatment. In most branches of the armed services, women's units did not receive veterans' benefits. Leaders such as Oveta Culp Hobby and Mary Agnes Hallaren fought to change this.

In 1948 Truman signed the Women's Armed Services Integration Act. Still, American women continued to serve in separate units until 1978. Today women make up about 20 percent of the U.S. military.

Drawing Conclusions Why did events in World War II lead Truman to end segregation in the military?

Members of the U.S. Air Force in Iraq during Operation Iraqi Freedom

---

Hitler's death In the final weeks of April 1945 the steady destruction of the German resistance continued. One by one, units from the Soviet Union met up with other Allied forces. At the same time, Berlin was under heavy bombardment. On April 30 Hitler finally recognized that all hope was lost. He committed suicide in his Berlin bunker.

As news of Hitler's death spread, fighting came to a halt. Berlin surrendered on May 2. The German armies scattered elsewhere gave up the fight. Finally, Karl Dönitz, who had taken over as Germany's leader following Hitler's death, agreed to a surrender on May 7. The surrender was to take effect on May 8. In the United States, this was proclaimed **V-E Day**—Victory in Europe Day.

Celebrations erupted in the United States and throughout Europe. "I was alive! And I was going to stay alive," recalled one soldier of his joyful reaction to the German surrender. This fortunate young American could enjoy the Allied victory. Yet many others still had work to do. This was especially true for those still fighting for their lives in a place called Okinawa.

READING CHECK Identifying the Main Idea
What was the significance of crossing the Rhine in winning the war in Europe?

Winning the War in the Pacific

As you have read, the Allies did capture Okinawa—but at a terrible cost. The horrors of this combat were reflected in the high rates of battle-related psychological casualties. Thousands of Allied soldiers and sailors suffered from battle fatigue and other disorders. These conditions were serious enough to require medical treatment.

The experience of the Allies in fighting the Japanese made many of them dread the prospect of invading the major islands of Japan. Nevertheless, General MacArthur and Admiral Nimitz went forward with developing plans for a massive invasion. The costs would be enormous. Some officials believed that capturing Japan might produce as many as 1 million Allied casualties.

Japan continues fighting Other Allied military leaders hoped to force Japan to surrender by putting a blockade in place or by bombing Japan heavily. In fact, Allied bombs had already caused severe damage to Japanese cities. In March 1945 Major General Curtis LeMay had experimented with a bombing

---

Skills Focus: Analyzing Primary Sources

Reading Like a Historian Skill
Executive Order No. 9981

1. Write the following excerpt from President Truman's Executive Order No. 9981 for students to see:

   It is hereby declared to be the policy of the President that there shall be equality of treatment and opportunity for all persons in the armed services without regard to race, color, religion or national origin.

2. Guide students in a discussion of what this order meant.

3. Ask students why they think President Truman issued an executive order rather than asking Congress to pass a law that would have had the same effect.

4. Have students summarize the difference between an executive order and a law.

   LS Verbal-Linguistic

   Alternative Assessment Handbook, Rubric 11: Discussions

tactic that was designed to produce a tremendous firestorm in the bombed area. The first of LeMay's raids, on Tokyo, killed nearly 84,000 Japanese and destroyed nearly 270,000 buildings. One American compared the effect of the bombs to "a tornado started by fires." The flames were so intense that river water was heated to the boiling point.

The bombing of Tokyo stunned the people of Japan. The defeat at Okinawa was another blow. Still they vowed to fight on.

Some leaders within the Japanese government saw the need for peace. During June and July of 1945 these officials began to seek contact with the Soviet Union. They hoped that the Soviets could help arrange an agreement for peace with the other Allies. These talks went slowly. Meanwhile, American war plans moved steadily forward.

The atomic bomb You have already read about the U.S. program to build an atomic bomb. The Manhattan Project continued throughout the war. In late 1944 leaders of the project declared that the bomb would be ready by the summer of 1945.

Vice President **Harry S Truman** had become president after Roosevelt's death in April. The new president had known nothing about the bomb prior to assuming the presidency. Now he had to decide whether the United States should use this fearsome new weapon.

Truman formed a group to advise him about using the bomb. This group debated where the bomb should be used and whether the Japanese should be warned. After carefully considering all the options, Truman decided to drop the bomb on a Japanese city. There would be no warning.

Truman and the Allies did, however, give the Japanese one last chance to avoid the bomb. On July 26 they issued a demand for Japan's surrender. Failure to give up, the demand read, would lead to "prompt and utter destruction." The Japanese failed to respond. The plan to drop the atomic bomb went forward.

On August 6, 1945, an American B-29 named the *Enola Gay* flew over the city of Hiroshima (hee-roh-SHEE-mah) and dropped its atomic bomb. Seconds later, the bomb exploded.

HISTORY'S VOICES

"I witnessed a yellowish scarlet plume rising like a candle fire high in the sky surrounded by pitch black swirling smoke… At the same moment… houses levitated [rose] a little and then crushed down to the ground like domino pieces. It was just like a white wavehead coming toward me."

—Memoir of Takeharu Terao, Hiroshima survivor

Hiroshima

Nearly everything within a one-mile radius of the blast was destroyed when an atomic bomb hit Hiroshima. Heavy damage extended three miles out. Lighter damage reached as far as 12 miles out from the center of the blast.

805

Skills Focus: Identifying Problem and Solution

At Level

Reading Skill
Dropping the Atomic Bomb

Background: The decision to drop the atomic bomb was made while President Truman was in Germany for the Potsdam Conference.

1. Guide students in a brief discussion of the difficult decision facing President Truman and of the factors that led the United States to use atomic weapons against Japan. *the enormous costs of invading (capturing Japan might cost as many as a million Allied casualties) and continued Japanese refusal to surrender*

2. Have students write a speech in which Truman explains to the American people that the United States will use atomic weapons against Japan. In their speeches students should explain and justify the decision.

3. Have volunteers deliver the speeches they have written to the class. **LS** **Logical-Mathematical, Verbal-Linguistic**

Alternative Assessment Handbook, Rubric 37: Writing Assignments

❸ What challenges faced the United States after victory? *the spread of communism and Soviet influence; rebuilding Europe and Japan*

The Challenges of Victory

Recall What new concern faced the United States following the end of the war? *that communism and Soviet influence might spread in the postwar world*

Analyze Why do you think the task of rebuilding Europe created tension between wartime allies the United States and the Soviet Union? *Both wanted to play a major role in Europe, to ensure democratic traditions or to spread communism.*

📓 CRF: Biography: Leo Szilard

Counterpoints

Dropping the Atomic Bomb
Summarize Read the quotes from both Stimson and Szilard aloud to the class. Then have students read the viewpoints themselves. Ask students to paraphrase and summarize the quotes. Ask for volunteers to share their summaries. Guide students in a discussion of these two viewpoints.

Answers

Reading Like a Historian *that using an atomic bomb sets a precedent for future use of such devastating weapons*

Reading Check *using the atomic bomb against the cities of Hiroshima and Nagasaki*

806

Dropping the Atomic Bomb

It fell to Secretary of War Henry Stimson to advise President Truman on whether or not to drop the atomic bomb.

❝ The face of war is the face of death . . . The decision to use the atomic bomb was a decision that brought death to over a hundred thousand Japanese. No explanation can change that fact and I do not wish to gloss it over. But this deliberate, premeditated destruction was our least abhorrent choice. ❞

Henry Stimson, 1947

Physicist Leo Szilard's work on nuclear reactions was key to the development of the bomb, and he felt a moral responsibility to speak against its use.

❝ Using atomic bombs against Japan is one of the greatest blunders of history. Both from a practical point of view on a ten-year scale and from the point of view of our moral position. I went out of my way and very much so in order to prevent it. ❞

Leo Szilard, 1945

Skills FOCUS | **READING LIKE A HISTORIAN**

Identifying Points of View Henry Stimson focuses on the immediate need to end the war. What consideration does Leo Szilard emphasize?

See **Skills Handbook**, pp. H28–H29

In a single terrible blast, most of Hiroshima was reduced to rubble. Some 80,000 residents died immediately, and 35,000 were injured. Two-thirds of the city's 90,000 buildings were destroyed. Fires raged everywhere.

In spite of the horror of Hiroshima, Japan's leaders took no action to end the war. For three days, they debated their next step. On August 9 the United States dropped a second bomb on Nagasaki (nah-gah-SAH-kee). The death toll there was 40,000.

Amazingly, even this did not bring an end to the war. Japanese emperor Hirohito (hir-oh-HEE-toh) favored surrender, but military leaders resisted. Some even tried to overthrow the Japanese government and continue the war. They failed. Finally, on August 15—known from then on to the Allies as **V-J Day**—Hirohito announced the end of the war in a radio broadcast. It was the first time the Japanese people had ever heard the emperor's voice.

THE IMPACT TODAY

Government
The United States remains part of the United Nations, an organization it was instrumental in creating, and is a member of the UN Security Council.

READING CHECK **Summarizing** What finally brought victory for the Allies in the war against Japan?

The Challenges of Victory

Winning World War II had been a monumental effort for the United States and its allies. Peace would bring its own challenges.

You have read about the Yalta Conference, where the Allies began to discuss postwar plans for Europe. This planning continued throughout the spring and summer of 1945.

The creation of the United Nations In June 1945 representatives from 50 countries, including the United States, met in San Francisco, California, to establish a new organization—the **United Nations**. Like the League of Nations formed after World War I, the United Nations (UN) was meant to encourage cooperation among nations and to prevent future wars. You will read more about the UN in future chapters.

The Potsdam Conference The next month, leaders of the Allied nations met to carry on the work begun at Yalta. They met at

---

Skills Focus: Drawing Conclusions
Above Level

Reading Skill
World War II: The Final Costs

Research Required

1. Have students conduct research to determine the final costs of World War II in human life, cultural loss through the Holocaust, and economic terms. Create a class chart showing the results of the research.

2. Have each student write an essay in which they tell what, in their opinions, was the most devastating cost of World War II. In their essays, students should support their choices with facts and explain their reasoning.

3. Have volunteers read their essays to the class. As each student reads his or her choice, write it for the class to see.

4. Use the information in the student essays to make a class chart showing the final costs of the war. Then guide the class in a discussion of the findings. What did students cite as the most costly? **LS Logical-Mathematical**

📓 Alternative Assessment Handbook, Rubrics 30: Research; and 37: Writing Assignments

the German city of Potsdam. There was growing American concern that communism and Soviet influence might spread in the postwar world. Truman had hoped that if he met with Stalin, he could get the Soviet leader to live up to his promises from Yalta. In this regard, the **Potsdam Conference** was not a success.

Rebuilding Europe and Japan The United States also faced the difficult task of helping to rebuild Europe and Japan. In Japan, General Douglas MacArthur directed the effort to create a new, democratic government and rebuild the nation's economy. MacArthur skillfully walked a fine line between showing respect for Japanese traditions and insisting on democratic values. He helped the Japanese create a new constitution that reflected many American ideals, such as equality for women.

As with the Nazis in Europe, Japanese war crimes did not go unpunished. Seven key figures in wartime Japan, including leader Hideki Tojo, were tried and executed for their crimes.

The United States also faced a difficult task in rebuilding war-torn Europe. As you will read in the next chapter, this process resulted in increasing tensions with America's wartime ally, the Soviet Union. In the coming years, this relationship would only grow worse.

READING CHECK **Identifying Problems and Solutions** What was the UN meant to accomplish?

CAUSES AND EFFECTS OF WORLD WAR II
QUICK FACTS

CAUSES
- Isolationism had helped lead the United States not to resist German, Japanese, and Italian aggression in the 1930s.
- Germany invaded Poland, and Japan attacked the United States.

EFFECTS
- The Allies occupied Japan and parts of Europe.
- War led to renewed commitment to the idea of collective security and creation of the United Nations.
- Conflict began between the Soviet Union and the other Allies over the fate of conquered European areas.
- The United States emerged as the world's strongest military power.

SECTION 5 ASSESSMENT

go.hrw.com
Online Quiz
Keyword: SD7 HP24

Reviewing Ideas, Terms, and People

1. a. Identify What is the significance of the following terms: Yalta Conference, V-E Day
b. Explain What were the issues surrounding Eisenhower's decision not to push to Berlin?
c. Evaluate What do you think Eisenhower's greatest responsibility was as the war wound down in Europe? Did he fulfill this responsibility?

2. a. Define Write a brief definition of the following term: V-J Day
b. Make Inferences What can you infer about the atomic bomb from the fact that some people felt that it should not have been dropped without warning?
c. Predict How do you think the decision to drop the bomb will affect the United States in the future?

3. a. Identify What is the significance of the following terms: United Nations, Potsdam Conference

b. Elaborate Why do you think that rebuilding a war-torn country is so difficult?

Critical Thinking

4. Identifying Supporting Details Copy the chart below and use information from the section to find supporting details for the main idea given.

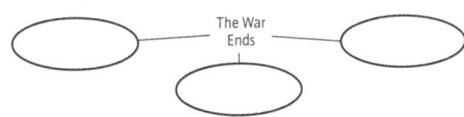

The War Ends

FOCUS ON WRITING

5. Descriptive Write a paragraph in which you describe the circumstances of the end of the war in either Europe or in the Pacific theater.

THE UNITED STATES IN WORLD WAR II **807**

Section 5 Assessment Answers

1. a. Yalta Conference—Allies agreed to divide Germany; V-E Day—Victory in Europe
b. bloody battles; Berlin was going to be divided among Allies; need to save American forces for the war in the Pacific
c. finish war; preserve American lives; yes

2. a. August 15, 1945, Victory in Japan Day
b. People understood the devastation and civilian deaths caused by the bomb.
c. possible answers—people might fear the U.S., believe U.S. was determined to win wars at any cost

3. a. United Nations—organization formed to prevent future wars; Potsdam Conference—meeting of Allies to carry on work begun at Yalta
b. infrastructure and economy have to be rebuilt

4. V-E Day; atomic bomb; V-J Day

5. Europe—devastation, tension between Allies; Pacific—Hiroshima and Nagasaki destroyed; U.S. directs new government

---

Direct Teach

Causes and Effects of World War II

Have students write a paragraph about what they consider to be the chief cause and longest-lasting effect of World War II. Students should give valid reasons for their choices.

Quick Facts Transparency: Causes and Effects of World War II

Review & Assess

Close

Ask students to explain how consideration of human costs by Allied leaders helped to shape their decisions in the final days of World War II.

Review

Online Quiz, Section 5

Daily Test Practice Transparency

Assess

SE Section 5 Assessment

Progress Assessment: Section 5 Quiz

Alternative Assessment Handbook

Reteach

Interactive Reader and Study Guide, Section 5

Interactive Skills Tutor CD-ROM

Answers

Reading Check *encourage cooperation among nations; prevent future wars*

807

History and Geography

Island-Hopping

Activity **The Route to Japan** Have students find or create their own maps of the Pacific Ocean that show the island groups. Have students locate the islands described in the feature, and then have them calculate the distance from one island to another. For example, how far did planes have to fly from Pearl Harbor in the Hawaiian Islands to reach the next island in the island-hopping strategy? How far is it from Saipan to Iwo Jima, from Iwo Jima to Okinawa, and from Okinawa to Tokyo?

LS Logical-Mathematical

Info to Know

Okinawa's History Okinawa is a large island with an area of about 870 square miles, about twice the size of the cities of Los Angeles or Phoenix. For centuries the island of Okinawa was independent, but in the 14th century the island came under Chinese sovereignty. In 1879 Okinawa was annexed by Japan. After World War II the island was under U.S. control, but in 1972 Okinawa was returned to Japan, although the United States maintained a military presence on the island.

*Interactive HISTORY & Geography

ISLAND HOPPING
The Route to Japan

In the early weeks of the war, Japan seized key islands in the Pacific to form a defensive barrier. To end the war, the United States planned to bomb and invade the Japanese mainland, but getting there proved enormously difficult and costly. It took nearly four years for the United States to push back the Japanese defenses, one island at a time. Each island captured served as a base to launch air raids or to protect American naval forces, who then moved on to attack the next island. The U.S. strategy was known as "island hopping." This map shows some of the islands that the U.S. forces captured on route to Japan.

HOKKAIDO

Tokyo

Sea of Japan

JAPAN

KYUSHU

CHINA

OKINAWA

TAIWAN

Moving into Range Aircraft carriers were crucial for fighting in the vast Pacific Ocean. U.S. carriers transported fighter planes, torpedo bombers, and dive-bombers, many of which had only a 200-mile range, to battle sites.

Okinawa, April–June, 1945
Okinawa was the southernmost of the Japanese home islands. After costly fighting, U.S. forces seized the island as a base for launching the final invasion of Japan.

808

Skills Focus: Analyzing Primary Sources

At Level

Reading Like a Historian Skill
Military Planes and Ships

Research Required

1. Have students conduct outside research on the airplanes, including the B-29, and aircraft carriers that were used during the war in the Pacific. Students should focus their research on how fast these airplanes flew, how much and what they carried, where they could land, and other relevant military questions.

2. Then have students compare these World War II military airplanes and carriers with

contemporary models. How have they changed over time?

3. Have students prepare illustrated reports about their findings. Students may wish to prepare multimedia reports or PowerPoint presentations with the information. **LS Verbal-Linguistic, Visual-Spatial**

📖 Alternative Assessment Handbook, Rubrics 9: Comparing and Contrasting; and 22: Multimedia Presentations

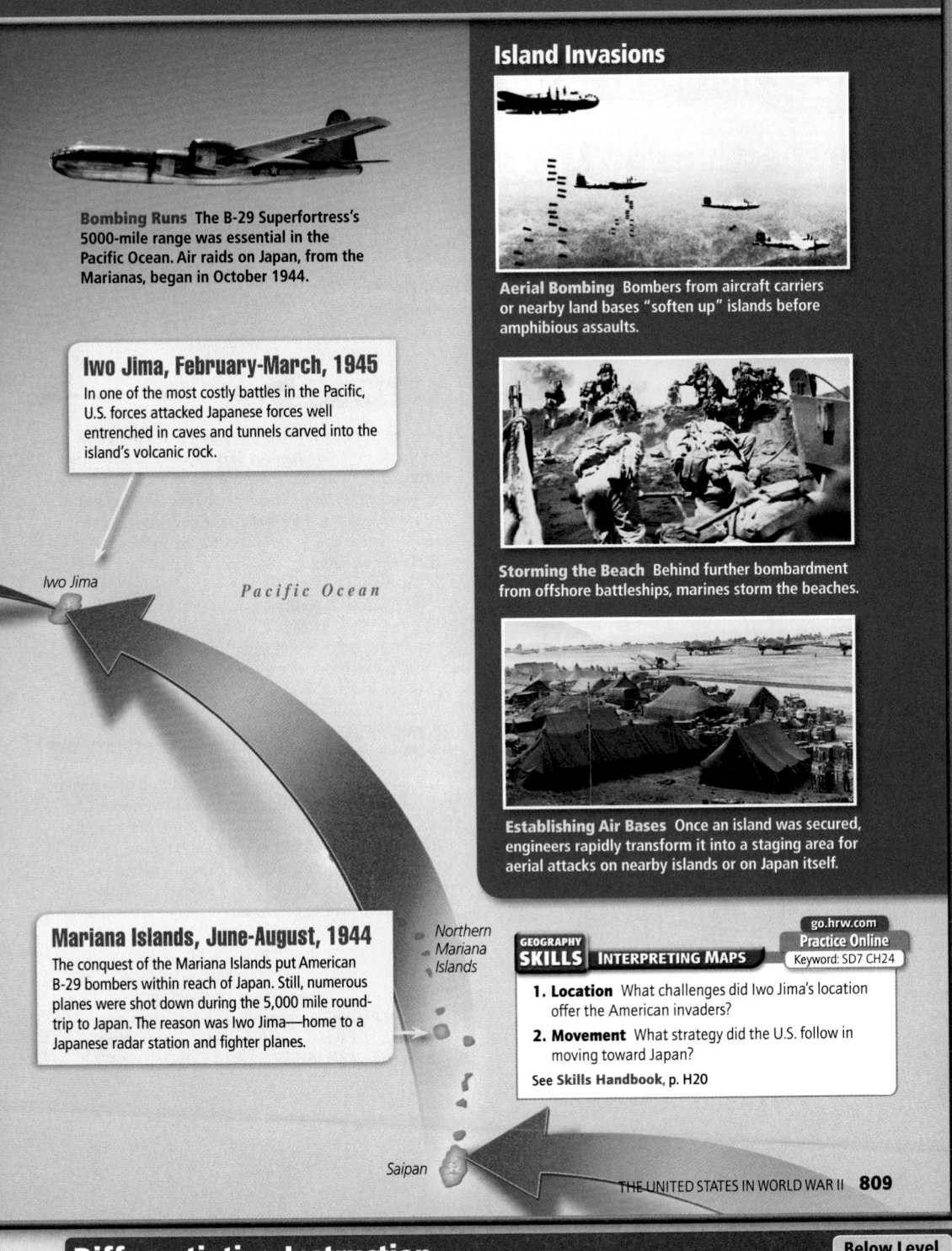

Island Invasions

Bombing Runs The B-29 Superfortress's 5000-mile range was essential in the Pacific Ocean. Air raids on Japan, from the Marianas, began in October 1944.

Aerial Bombing Bombers from aircraft carriers or nearby land bases "soften up" islands before amphibious assaults.

Storming the Beach Behind further bombardment from offshore battleships, marines storm the beaches.

Establishing Air Bases Once an island was secured, engineers rapidly transform it into a staging area for aerial attacks on nearby islands or on Japan itself.

Iwo Jima, February–March, 1945
In one of the most costly battles in the Pacific, U.S. forces attacked Japanese forces well entrenched in caves and tunnels carved into the island's volcanic rock.

Iwo Jima

Pacific Ocean

Mariana Islands, June–August, 1944
The conquest of the Mariana Islands put American B-29 bombers within reach of Japan. Still, numerous planes were shot down during the 5,000 mile round-trip to Japan. The reason was Iwo Jima—home to a Japanese radar station and fighter planes.

Northern Mariana Islands

Saipan

GEOGRAPHY SKILLS **INTERPRETING MAPS**

go.hrw.com
Practice Online
Keyword: SD7 CH24

1. **Location** What challenges did Iwo Jima's location offer the American invaders?
2. **Movement** What strategy did the U.S. follow in moving toward Japan?

See Skills Handbook, p. H20

THE UNITED STATES IN WORLD WAR II **809**

Perspectives on Life in Uniform

Word Help

swell terrific
era period of time
exulting rejoicing, celebrating

Interpreting Political Cartoons

Activity **World War II Cartoons**
Have students look carefully at the faces of the two men in the cartoon. Ask volunteers to describe the expressions on their faces. *sad, depressed* Have students follow the pattern of Mauldin's cartoon and create their own cartoon, showing the conditions under which soldiers lived and worked during the war. Have volunteers share their cartoons with the class, or make a classroom bulletin board with student work.

Info to Know

Military Nurses In 1941 the Army Nurse Corps had fewer than 1,000 nurses. By the end of the war, more than 50,000 American women had served as nurses. They were stationed at field hospitals in Europe, on hospital ships, and on islands in the Pacific.

Info to Know

German and Italian prisoners of war
A number of prisoner of war camps were built in the United States during World War II. Following the surrender of Rommel's Afrika Korps in 1943, 150,000 enemy prisoners were sent to the U.S. During the last few months of the war, about 60,000 prisoners of war arrived in the U.S. each month. At war's end, the United States had over 500 prisoner of war camps, and about 425,000 enemy prisoners.

Perspectives on Life in Uniform

Historical Context The documents below provide different information on the hardships and sacrifices of American military personnel during World War II.

Task Examine the documents and answer the questions that follow. Then write an essay about the hardships U.S. soldiers faced. Use facts from the documents and from this chapter to support the position you take in your thesis statement.

DOCUMENT 1

Cartoonist Bill Mauldin chronicled the sufferings of the everyday soldier in *Stars and Stripes*, a newspaper published by the U.S. Army. His gritty cartoons featured the characters Willie and Joe, who stood for all ordinary soldiers. Mauldin served during the entire war and was wounded in battle in Sicily.

"Joe, yestiddy ya saved my life an' I swore I'd pay ya back. Here's my last pair of dry socks."

DOCUMENT 2

Army nurses saw much of the worst suffering of the war up close. June Wandrey served as a combat nurse during some of the bloodiest battles in North Africa and western Europe. She helped save many lives and was awarded eight battle stars for her service under fire. She wrote this letter to her family in Wautoma, Wisconsin, in January 1944.

"We now have a mix of wounded, medical patients, and battle-fatigued soldiers . . . The wounded were happy to be missing only one arm or leg . . . I have a terrible earache but as usual I have to work. The patients need me."

DOCUMENT 3

For many Americans, the war was draining both physically and spiritually. Paul Curtis was from a small town in Tennessee. Fighting in the Italian campaign was unlike anything he had ever experienced. In this letter home from May 1944, he tried to explain his reactions to his brother. Curtis was killed in action shortly after writing this letter.

"Take a combination of fear, anger, hunger, thirst, exhaustion, disgust, loneliness, homesickness, and wrap that all up in one reaction and you might approach the feelings a fellow has. It makes you feel mighty small, helpless, and alone . . . Without faith, I don't see how anyone could stand this."

810 CHAPTER 24

Skills Focus: Analyzing Primary Sources

At Level

Reading Like a Historian Skill
World War II

1. Organize the class into five groups. Assign each group one of the five documents.

2. Have each group conduct research into the topic, person, or issues raised in the document. For example, one group might research the role of Army nurses during the war; another might research activities of the USO.

3. When each group has finished its research, have students prepare a presentation for the class about their research. Ask students to present their information in a medium other than an oral report or essay—a large poster, a storyboard, or perhaps a PowerPoint presentation.

4. Allow class time for each group to share its presentation.

DOCUMENT 4

Many African American soldiers faced an extra hardship during the war. In addition to the dangers and shortages experienced by all soldiers, African Americans also encountered racial discrimination. Corporal Rupert Trimmingham wrote the following letter to *Yank*, a weekly magazine published by the U.S. Army. In the letter, Trimmingham refers to "Old Man Jim Crow," a name for the discriminatory laws then in force across much of the United States.

"Myself and eight other Negro soldiers were on our way from Camp Claiborne, La., to the hospital here at Fort Huachuca, Arizona ... We could not purchase a cup of coffee at any of the lunchrooms around there ... As you know, Old Man Jim Crow rules. But that's not all; 11:30 A.M. about two dozen German prisoners of war, with two American guards, came to the station. They entered the lunchroom, sat at the tables, had their meals served, talked, smoked, in fact had quite a swell time. I stood on the outside looking on ... Are we not American soldiers, sworn to fight for and die if need be for this our country?"

DOCUMENT 5

Popular comedian Bob Hope never served in the armed forces, but he traveled throughout the war zones entertaining the troops for the United Service Organizations (USO). In 1944 he wrote *I Never Left Home*, a memoir of his experiences during the war. In the preface he told the public about the soldiers he encountered. President Lyndon Johnson awarded Hope the Presidential Medal of Freedom in 1969. Hope was still entertaining American troops far from home at the age of 90, when he took his act to the Persian Gulf on the eve of the first Persian Gulf War.

"I saw your sons and your husbands, your soldiers and your sweethearts. I saw how they worked, fought, and lived. I saw some of them die. I saw more courage, more good humor in the face of discomfort, more love in an era of hate, and more devotion to duty than could ever exist under tyranny.

I saw American minds, American skill, and American strength breaking the backbone of evil ... And I came back to find people exulting over the thousand plane raids over Germany... and saying how wonderful they are! Those people never watched the face of a pilot as he read a bulletin board and saw his buddy marked up missing...

Dying is sometimes easier than living through it ..."

Skills FOCUS — READING LIKE A HISTORIAN

1. **a. Identify** Refer to Document 1. What does the character of Willie offer to Joe in exchange for saving his life?
   b. Interpret What does this cartoon say about the living conditions and supplies for soldiers?

2. **a. Identify** Refer to Document 2. What was Wandrey's job?
   b. Analyze Why were the wounded soldiers happy to be missing only one arm or leg?

3. **a. Identify** Refer to Document 3. What is the overall impression that Curtis gives of his experience?
   b. Elaborate How do you think Curtis's faith helped him during the war?

4. **a. Identify** Refer to Document 4. Why could the African American soldiers not buy coffee at the southern bases?

   b. Analyze How might seeing the German soldiers being treated better than African American soldiers have affected Trimmingham's views of the war?

5. **a. Identify** Refer to Document 5. What was Bob Hope's role in the war?
   b. Explain What did Hope mean when he wrote, "Dying is sometimes easier than living through it"?

6. **Document-Based Essay Question** Consider the question below and form a thesis statement. Using examples from Documents 1, 2, 3, 4, and 5, create an outline and write a short essay supporting your position.
   What kinds of hardships and suffering did American soldiers face during World War II?
   See Skills Handbook, pp. H28–H29, H31

THE UNITED STATES IN WORLD WAR II **811**

Primary Source

"You know that being an American is more than a matter of where you or your parents came from. It is a belief that all men are created free and equal and that everyone deserves an even break. It is a respect for the dignity of men and women without regard to race, creed, or color. That is our creed."
— Harry S Truman

Speech, October 26, 1948

Critical Thinking How do you think Rupert Trimmingham would have responded to Truman's comments about the American creed? *possible answers—with applause, appreciation, and hope; with skepticism and recognition that many Americans did not agree with this view*

Answers

Reading Like a Historian 1. a. *dry socks;* **b.** *conditions were very difficult; basic necessities were in short supply;* **2. a.** *Army nurse;* **b.** *They were still alive.* **3. a.** *It is a horrible, wearing experience.* **b.** *His faith sustained him, gave him the strength to keep going.* **4. a.** *racial discrimination; African Americans were prevented by Jim Crow laws from entering some cafes, and some cafes and lunchrooms refused to serve African Americans.* **b.** *negatively; He is appalled and angry that prisoners of war were treated better than African American soldiers who were fighting for their country.* **5. a.** *He was a traveling entertainer.* **b.** *possible answers—those who were left mourned the death of their fellow soldiers; may have felt they should have been able to prevent the death; may have wondered why they had been singled out to live;* **6.** *possible answer—injuries, illness, fear, homesickness, discrimination*

811

Differentiating Instruction

Below Level

English-Language Learners

1. Organize the class into mixed-ability pairs. Have each pair read and review the documents to help ensure that all students understand the information.

2. Have students select three documents. Then have them create three drawings, one showing the scene portrayed in each document. Students should write a caption for each

drawing that conveys or summarizes the information in the document.

3. Have students share their work with the class.

4. Guide students in a discussion of the view of war presented in these documents.

Answers

Visual Summary

Review and Inquiry Review the graphic organizer with students. Then organize the class into mixed-ability pairs. Have each pair find and list at least one cause and effect for each item on the time line.

Quick Facts Transparency: The United States in World War II

Reviewing Key Terms and People

1. A **ghetto** was a neighborhood where Nazis confined Jewish people.

2. **Operation Overlord** was the planned Allied invasion of France.

3. American general **Dwight D. Eisenhower** was in charge of the Allied invasion of North Africa and the D-Day landing at Normandy.

4. Japanese Americans living on the West Coast faced **internment**, forced relocation and confinement.

5. **Final Solution** refers to the Nazi plan to murder all Jews who lived in Europe and Soviet Union.

6. More than 12,000 troops were killed in the **Battle of Okinawa**.

7. American general **Douglas MacArthur** led the defense of the Philippines and helped create a democratic government in Japan.

8. **Rationing**, limiting the supply of certain products, was imposed on American families during the war.

9. In the **Battle of Midway** Japan's navy suffered devastating losses.

10. The **Tuskegee Airmen** were African American pilots.

11. President **Harry S Truman** made the decision to drop atomic bombs on Japan.

12. Japanese **kamikaze** pilots flew planes into enemy ships.

Comprehension and Critical Thinking

13. a. Operation Torch—American troops in North Africa; Operation Overlord—D-Day invasion; U.S. leadership in war.
   b. 1941—Allies break German code, supply Allies with war mate-

Visual Summary: The United States in World War II

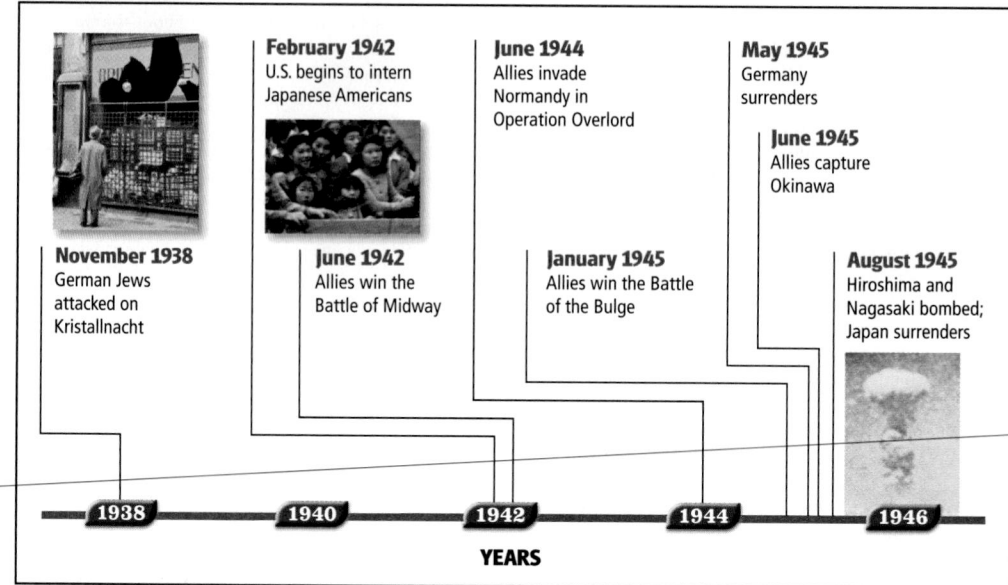

November 1938 German Jews attacked on Kristallnacht

February 1942 U.S. begins to intern Japanese Americans

June 1942 Allies win the Battle of Midway

June 1944 Allies invade Normandy in Operation Overlord

January 1945 Allies win the Battle of the Bulge

May 1945 Germany surrenders

June 1945 Allies capture Okinawa

August 1945 Hiroshima and Nagasaki bombed; Japan surrenders

1938   1940   1942   1944   1946

YEARS

Reviewing Key Terms and People

For each term or name below, write a sentence explaining its significance to World War II.

1. ghetto
2. Operation Overlord
3. Dwight D. Eisenhower
4. internment
5. Final Solution
6. Battle of Okinawa
7. Douglas MacArthur
8. rationing
9. Battle of Midway
10. Tuskegee Airmen
11. Harry S Truman
12. kamikaze

Comprehension and Critical Thinking

SECTION 1 *(pp. 770–777)*

13. a. **Recall** What were Operation Torch and Operation Overlord, and what was their significance?
   b. **Sequence** Create a brief time line of U.S. involvement in Europe between 1941 and 1944.
   c. **Elaborate** Explain how American success in the Battle of the Atlantic may have affected the outcome of Operation Overlord.

SECTION 2 *(pp. 778–783)*

14. a. **Describe** What was the Holocaust?
   b. **Compare** Did Hitler's attitudes toward Jews change over time? Explain.
   c. **Evaluate** What do you think of Roosevelt's decision to focus all his energy on defeating the Germans and Japanese rather than trying to rescue the Jews in Nazi camps?

rial; 1942—troops land in North Africa; 1943—German forces defeated in North Africa; Allied invasion of Italy; 1944—D-Day invasion
   c. Supply lines and troop movement through the Atlantic had been made secure.

14. a. mass murder of Jews
   b. No, but official policies changed.
   c. possible answers—Roosevelt had to focus attention on defeating Germany before Allied forces could rescue Jews; Allies could have done more to help save Jews.

15. a. American fleet destroyed at Pearl Harbor

   b. Japanese ships and planes destroyed; Japanese sea power greatly reduced
   c. country that controlled the seas could land troops, resupply, and establish air bases

16. a. rationing; women left home to work in factories
   b. ads for war bonds; propaganda films, posters, and newspaper articles
   c. Government regulations and boards grew; federal budget increased, income tax rates increased

17. a. V-E Day, marked German surrender; V-J Day, marked Japanese surrender

History's Impact video program
Review the video to answer the closing question: Why did the United States emerge as a global superpower after World War II?

Answers

SECTION 3 *(pp. 785–792)*

15. a. Recall Why did the Japanese have early success against the United States in the Pacific?

b. Explain Why was the Battle of Midway such an important victory for the United States?

c. Elaborate Why do you think air and sea power were so important in the Pacific?

SECTION 4 *(pp. 793–799)*

16. a. Recall What sacrifices did Americans on the home front have to make for the war effort?

b. Summarize How did the federal government try to encourage Americans to support the war effort?

c. Elaborate In what ways did World War II increase the power of the American government and its influence in everyday life?

SECTION 5 *(pp. 801–807)*

17. a. Identify Write a brief explanation of the significance of the following terms: V-E Day, V-J Day

b. Contrast How did the behavior of German soldiers compare to the behavior of Japanese soldiers in the final months before each side surrendered?

c. Evaluate How do you think the experience of World War I affected the decisions made at the end of World War II?

Using the Internet

go.hrw.com
Practice Online
Keyword: SD7 CH24

18. The Allied invasion of France, often called D-Day, began on June 6, 1944. Within a few weeks, the Allies had landed nearly a million soldiers on the beaches of Normandy, and Germany's forces were in serious trouble. Using the keyword above, do research to learn more about the events of D-Day. Then create a report that describes the invasion and its importance in ending the war in Europe.

Analyzing Primary Sources

Reading Like a Historian
This photograph was taken after the capture of Mount Suribachi on Iwo Jima. It was soon printed in newspapers all across the United States and became one of the most recognizable images of the war.

19. Describe What is the significance of the moment captured in this photograph?

20. Draw Conclusions Why do you think this image had such a powerful impact on the public?

Critical Reading

Read the passage in Section 4 under the heading "Winning American Support for the War." Then answer the questions that follow.

21. The government demonstrated its need to influence public opinion on the war by

A making Hollywood movies.

B establishing the Office of War Information.

C outlawing religious services.

D forbidding negative talk about the war effort.

22. In the *Barnette* ruling, the Supreme Court held that

A people could be forced to listen to patriotic speeches.

B it was illegal to make movies that did not support the war effort.

C religious groups had to support the war effort.

D people could not be forced to salute the flag.

WRITING FOR THE SAT

Think about the following issue.

Following the Japanese attack on Pearl Harbor, some military and government officials worried about a Japanese attack on the mainland of the United States. Though they had no evidence of any plot, they were especially concerned that such an attack would be aided by some of the many residents of Japanese ancestry then living in the western states.

23. Assignment Was the government right to single out residents of Japanese ancestry as a special threat to the United States? Write a short essay in which you develop your position on this issue. Support your point of view with reasoning and examples from your reading and studies.

THE UNITED STATES IN WORLD WAR II **813**

b. German armies gave up after Hitler's death; Japanese showed no sign of surrendering.

c. efforts must be made to stop world wars; UN had full U.S. support; U.S. was committed to establishing a democratic government in Japan and to rebuilding Europe

Using the Internet

18. Go to the HRW Web site and enter the keyword shown to access a rubric for this activity.

KEYWORD: SD7 CH24

Analyzing Primary Sources

19. marked victory in a hard-fought battle

20. symbolized American bravery and determination

Critical Reading

21. B

22. D

Writing for the SAT

23. possible answers—yes, civil liberties can be suspended to protect the nation; no, Japanese living on the West Coast were loyal American citizens.

A rubric for this activity is provided in the Chapter Resource File: Writing for the SAT.

History's Impact Video Program

much of Europe and Asia in ruins, while U.S. military and economy grew stronger

Review and Assessment Resources

Review and Reinforce

- CRF: Chapter Review Activity
- Quick Facts Transparencies: Causes and Effects of World War II, The United States in World War II
- Spanish Chapter Summaries Audio CD Program
- Online Chapter Summaries in Spanish
- OSP Holt PuzzlePro; Quiz Show for ExamView
- Quiz Game CD-ROM

Assess

- PASS: Chapter Test, Forms A and B
- Alternative Assessment Handbook
- OSP ExamView Test Generator, Chapter Test
- Differentiated Instruction Modified Worksheets and Tests CD-ROM: Chapter Test
- HOAP Holt Online Assessment Program (in the Premier Online Edition)

Reteach/Intervene

- Interactive Reader and Study Guide
- Differentiated Instruction Teacher Management System: Lesson Plans for Differentiated Instruction
- Differentiated Instruction Modified Worksheets and Tests CD-ROM: Chapter Test
- Interactive Skills Tutor CD-ROM

go.hrw.com
Online Resources
KEYWORD: SD7 CH24

The Cold War Begins

Chapter Overview	Reproducible Resources	Technology Resources
CHAPTER 25 pp. 814–845 **Overview: In this chapter, students will analyze the causes and effects of the Cold War.**	**Differentiated Instruction Teacher Management System:*** • Instructional Benchmarking Guides • Lesson Plans for Differentiated Instruction **Interactive Reader and Study Guide:** Chapter Summary* **Chapter Resource File:*** • Focus on Writing Activity: The Korean War • Social Studies Skills Activity: Drawing Conclusions • Chapter Review Activity **American History Outline Maps** **Pre-AP Activities Guide for American History***	Live Ink® Online Reading Help Student Edition on Audio CD Program Differentiated Instruction Modified Worksheets and Tests CD-ROM Interactive Skills Tutor CD-ROM United States History Primary Source Library CD-ROM Power Presentations with Video CD-ROM History's Impact: American History Video Program (VHS/DVD): The Cold War Begins Online Chapter Summaries in Spanish
Section 1: **The Iron Curtain Falls on Europe** **The Main Idea:** As World War II ended, tensions between the Soviet Union and the United States led to an era known as the Cold War.	**Differentiated Instruction Teacher Management System:** Section 1 Lesson Plan* **Interactive Reader and Study Guide:** Section 1 Summary* **Chapter Resource File:*** • Vocabulary Builder Activity, Section 1	**Daily Bellringer Transparency:** Section 1* **Map Transparency:** Divided Germany, 1949* **Daily Test Practice Transparency:** Section 1*
Section 2: **Healing the Wounds of War** **The Main Idea:** After World War II, the United States faced the challenge of returning to life during peacetime.	**Differentiated Instruction Teacher Management System:** Section 2 Lesson Plan* **Interactive Reader and Study Guide:** Section 2 Summary* **Chapter Resource File:*** • Vocabulary Builder Activity, Section 2	**Daily Bellringer Transparency:** Section 2* **Quick Facts Transparency:** Programs for a Safer World* **Daily Test Practice Transparency:** Section 2*
Section 3: **The Second Red Scare** **The Main Idea:** The start of the Cold War and events at home helped trigger a second Red Scare.	**Differentiated Instruction Teacher Management System:** Section 3 Lesson Plan* **Interactive Reader and Study Guide:** Section 3 Summary* **Chapter Resource File:*** • Vocabulary Builder Activity, Section 3	**Daily Bellringer Transparency:** Section 3* **Map Transparency:** Spread of Communism, 1945–1949* **Daily Test Practice Transparency:** Section 3*
Section 4: **The Korean War** **The Main Idea:** Cold War tensions finally erupted in a shooting war in 1950.	**Differentiated Instruction Teacher Management System:** Section 4 Lesson Plan* **Interactive Reader and Study Guide:** Section 4 Summary* **Chapter Resource File:*** • Vocabulary Builder Activity, Section 4	**Daily Bellringer Transparency:** Section 4* **Map Transparency:** Korea* **Daily Test Practice Transparency:** Section 4*

 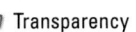
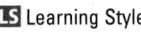 
HOLT
History's Impact
American History Video Program (VHS/DVD)
The Cold War Begins

Review, Assessment, Intervention

 Quick Facts Transparencies: Causes of the Cold War, Programs for a Safer World, Population, 1950, The Cold War Begins

 Spanish Chapter Summaries Audio CD Program

 **Progress Assessment Support System (PASS):** Chapter Test*

 **Differentiated Instruction Modified Worksheets and Tests CD-ROM:** Modified Chapter Test

OSP **One-Stop Planner CD-ROM:** ExamView Test Generator (English/Spanish)

HOAP **Holt Online Assessment Program (HOAP),** in the Holt Premier Online Student Edition

 PASS: Section 1 Quiz*

 Online Quiz: Section 1

 Alternative Assessment Handbook

 PASS: Section 2 Quiz*

 Online Quiz: Section 2

 Alternative Assessment Handbook

 PASS: Section 3 Quiz*

 Online Quiz: Section 3

 Alternative Assessment Handbook

 PASS: Section 4 Quiz*

 Online Quiz: Section 4

 Alternative Assessment Handbook

NC RESOURCES

The following resources were developed to help North Carolina educators teach the standards and objectives of North Carolina's eleventh grade standard course of study in United States history.

- United States history EOC Test Prep Workbook
- Teacher's Support System
- North Carolina One-Stop Planner

And be sure to direct your students to **go.hrw.com** for online access to the EOC Test Prep Workbook.

go.hrw.com
EOC Test Prep
KEYWORD: SE7 NC

Holt Online Learning

go.hrw.com
Teacher Resources
KEYWORD: SD7 TEACHER

go.hrw.com
Student Resources
KEYWORD: SD7 CH25

- Document-based Questions
- Interactive Multimedia Activities

- Current Events
- Chapter-based Internet Activities
- and more!

Holt Premier
Online Student Edition

Complete online support for interactivity, assessment, and reporting

- Interactive Maps and Notebook
- Standardized Test Prep
- Homework Practice and Research Activities Online

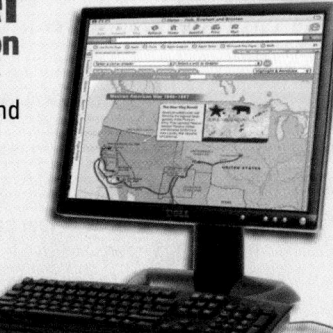

CHAPTER 25 PLANNING GUIDE

Before You Teach

The Big Picture
Robert D. Schulzinger

The Early Cold War America's World War II partnership with the Soviet Union ended abruptly as British and American leaders feared that the Soviet Union sought to dominate Europe. In 1947 the United States adopted the policy of containment, and the more than forty-year-long Cold War began. The Truman administration provided military and economic aid for countries the United States considered threatened by Communist subversion. In 1948 the United States broke a Soviet-imposed blockade on Berlin with an airlift of essential supplies, and it formed NATO, an anti-Soviet military alliance, in 1949.

Postwar Life at Home At home Americans concentrated on rebuilding their fortunes and families disrupted by the Depression and the war. An unprecedented economic expansion began as veterans bought new homes, cars, and appliances, and the birth rate soared. Opportunities expanded for racial minorities, and in 1948 President Truman ordered the desegregation of the armed forces. Americans also confronted new fears. The growing Cold War sparked a Red Scare, as several spy cases convinced many Americans of a deadly peril from domestic Communists. In response, Congress investigated Communists and passed anti-Communist laws. In 1950 Senator Joseph McCarthy started a series of reckless charges that Communists had infiltrated the highest levels of the federal government.

The Korean War The Cold War became a hot conflict in June 1950 when North Korean troops attacked South Korea across the 38th parallel. The Truman administration believed the North Korean attack was part of a coordinated international Communist strategy to begin World War III. The United States led a United Nations military coalition to force the North Koreans to withdraw. Three years of bloody fighting followed, until an armistice restored the border between North and South Korea roughly where it had been when the war erupted.

Recent Scholarship

Causes of the Cold War Who bears responsibility for the outbreak of the Cold War? In the 1950s historians wrote that the Soviet Union's unquenchable thirst for domination forced the United States to respond. Some later historians claimed that the Truman administration favored confrontation over diplomacy with the Soviet Union. Melvyn P. Leffler argues in *A Preponderance of Power: National Security, the Truman Administration, and the Cold War* (1992) that the Soviet Union represented a significant but limited threat, and the Truman administration consistently sought to expand the reach of American power in the early Cold War.

Differentiating Instruction

 Differentiated Instruction Teacher Management System
- Lesson Plans for Differentiated Instruction
- Differentiated Instructional Benchmarking Guides
- Interactive Reader and Study Guide

 Spanish Chapter Summaries Audio CD Program

 Online Chapter Summaries in Spanish

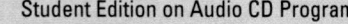 Student Edition on Audio CD Program

 Differentiated Instruction Modified Worksheets and Tests CD-ROM
- Vocabulary Flash Cards
- Modified Vocabulary Builder Activities
- Modified Chapter Review Activity
- Modified Chapter Test

OSP One-Stop Planner CD-ROM
- ExamView Test Generator (English and Spanish)
- PuzzlePro
- Quiz Show for ExamView
- Transparencies and Videos

TE Differentiated Activities in the Teacher's Edition
- Moving the Germans After the War, p. 818
- The 1948 Election, p. 826
- Bomb Shelter Supplies, p. 843

Reading Like a Historian
Sam Wineburg

The Optimism of the Counterfactual

Some 37,000 American soldiers lost their lives in the Korean War. A decade later, American forces were back in Southeast Asia, this time in Vietnam, where more than 58,000 Americans perished. In both conflicts, our adversaries received crucial support from the Chinese. Indeed, one might argue, without Chinese support these wars might have remained skirmishes rather than the all-out conflicts that they turned out to be.

What If?

But what if both Korea and Vietnam could have been avoided? What if, instead of emerging as an adversary at the end of World War II, the Chinese Communists had been brought into the American fold as a "soft" Communist state, similar to Yugoslavia under Tito?

This scenario is less far-fetched than it may seem. In 1945 Mao Zedong and Zhou Enlai tried to convey a secret telegram to President Roosevelt offering to come to the United States and present their cause. The meeting never materialized—but what if it had?

The Ground Rules

Such "what ifs" are known in history as "counterfactuals." Thinking counterfactually is an intellectual exercise that imagines a past that could have been, but turned out otherwise. Counterfactual reasoning abides by two ground rules: first, the counterfactual must stay as close to the historical record as possible, and second, it must obey the constraints of what historical actors knew and believed, rather than what we know today.

The Pulitzer-prize winning historian Barbara Tuchman asked in a 1972 *Foreign Affairs* essay what might have happened "If Mao Had Come to Washington." Relying on declassified documents, Tuchman published for the first time the telegram sent by American officials conveying Mao's desire to meet the president.

"Yenan government [the Communists] wants to dispatch to America an . . . unofficial group to interpret and explain to American civilians . . . the present situation and problems of China . . . Mao and Chou will be immediately available either singly or together for exploratory conference at Washington should President Roosevelt express desire to receive them."

What Really Happened

The Chinese request met a roadblock in the form of Ambassador Patrick J. Hurley, an inexperienced diplomat who had fallen under the spell of Chiang Kai-shek and his minions. But even if Mao's memo had reached Roosevelt immediately, it is doubtful it would have had much effect.

In January 1945 Roosevelt's plate was full. He was in the midst of preparations for the Yalta Conference to discuss the fate of a postwar Europe, not to mention a host of other concerns—making plans to set up the Allied military administrations in Japan, Germany, and Italy; the organization of a tribunal system to mete out justice to Axis criminals; rebuilding a war-torn Europe and creating a United Nations; and impending trouble in Greece and Turkey. The China situation would have been just one more card in a shuffle of thorny and pressing concerns. Roosevelt himself would be dead in four months.

Past and Present

Counterfactual thinking hones students' intellectual skills by imagining an alternative past. By engaging the counterfactual we also remind ourselves of history's most important lesson for the present:

Our actions—and in the case of this scenario, our inactions—matter. The notion that there could have been multiple pasts reminds us in our darkest moments that the way things now seem is not the way things must be. We have choices in a democracy. That is why the counterfactual is really about hope.

From essay "If Mao Had Come to Washington" by Barbara W. Tuchman from *Foreign Affairs*, Vol. 51, No. 1, October 1972.

• Chapter Preview •

Standards Focus

Social Studies Competency Goals

Goal 10 The learner will analyze United States involvement in World War II and the war's influence on international affairs in following decades.

10.04, 10.05

The Big Idea and Essential Questions

To foster student understanding of this chapter's big idea, design your lesson to address each section's essential question.

Big Idea After the end of World War II, the struggle between democracy and communism led to a long Cold War of ideas with occasional outbreaks of fighting.

Essential Questions

1. How did tensions between the Soviet Union and the United States develop into the Cold War?
2. What challenges did the U.S. population and military face when returning to peacetime life?
3. What triggered the Red Scare of the late 1940s and early 1950s?
4. How did Cold War tensions erupt into warfare in 1950?

CHAPTER 25

1945–1953

The COLD WAR Begins

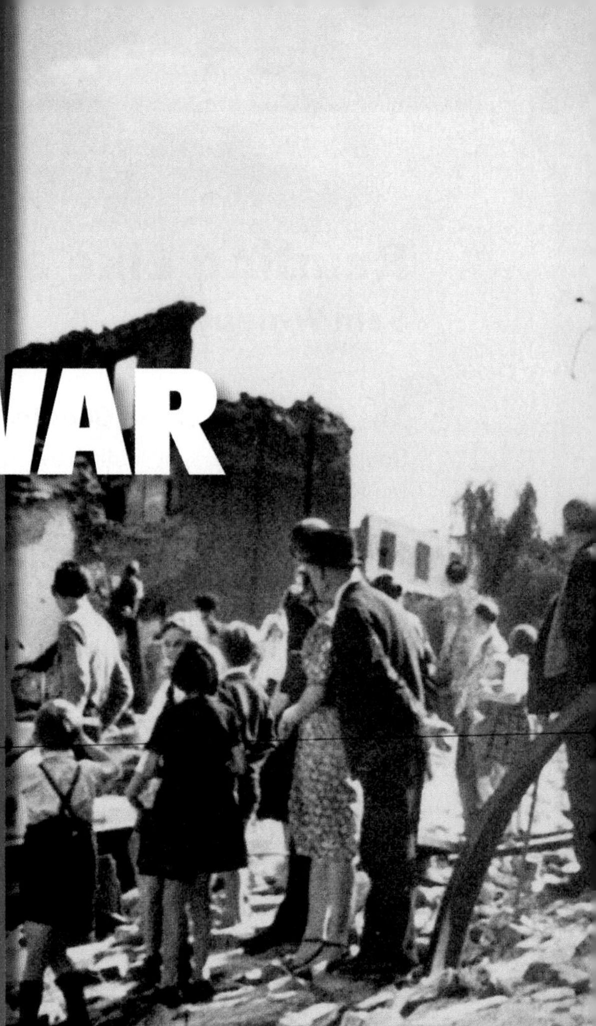

THE BIG PICTURE The Cold War was born in the uneasy World War II alliances between the Soviet Union and democratic nations. After the war, the struggle between democracy and communism led to a long war of ideas with occasional outbreaks of fighting.

North Carolina Standards

Social Studies Objectives

10.04 Elaborate on changes in the direction of foreign policy related to the beginnings of the Cold War.

10.05 Assess the role of organizations established to maintain peace and examine their continuing effectiveness.

Language Arts Objectives

2.01 Research and analyze ideas, events, and/or movements related to United States culture by:

- locating facts and details for purposeful elaboration.

Skills FOCUS READING LIKE A HISTORIAN

A group of Berliners gaze up at a U.S. military cargo plane bringing them supplies during the Soviet blockade of their city in 1948. The Berlin Airlift, as it was known, lasted until 1949.

Interpreting Visuals What do you think it was like, for Berliners and Americans, during the heightened tensions of this Cold War incident?

See **Skills Handbook**, p. H30

U.S.

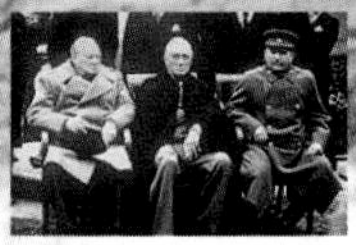

February 1945 President Roosevelt meets with Allied leaders at the Yalta Conference to discuss postwar issues.

1945

June 1945 Delegates from 50 nations meet in San Francisco to found the United Nations.

World

814

Key to Differentiating Instruction

Below Level

Basic-level activities designed for all students encountering new material

At Level

Intermediate-level activities designed for average students

Above Level

Challenging activities designed for honors and gifted-and-talented students

Standard English Mastery

Activities designed to improve standard English usage

Introduce the Chapter

At Level

The Cold War Begins

1. Review with students how World War II ended in Germany and in Japan.
2. Explain to students that while Americans were jubilant about the end of the war, they were also concerned about the rising threat of communism and the potential spread and use of weapons of mass destruction, like the atomic bomb. Guide students in a discussion of how Americans are still concerned about the potential spread and use of weapons of mass destruction.
3. Have students write a journal entry from the perspective of an American public school student in the 1950s. Students should explain how the threat of communism and the potential for a nuclear war have changed their daily lives. **LS Verbal-Linguistic**

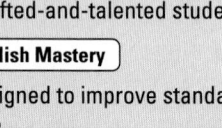

Alternative Assessment Handbook, Rubric 11: Discussions

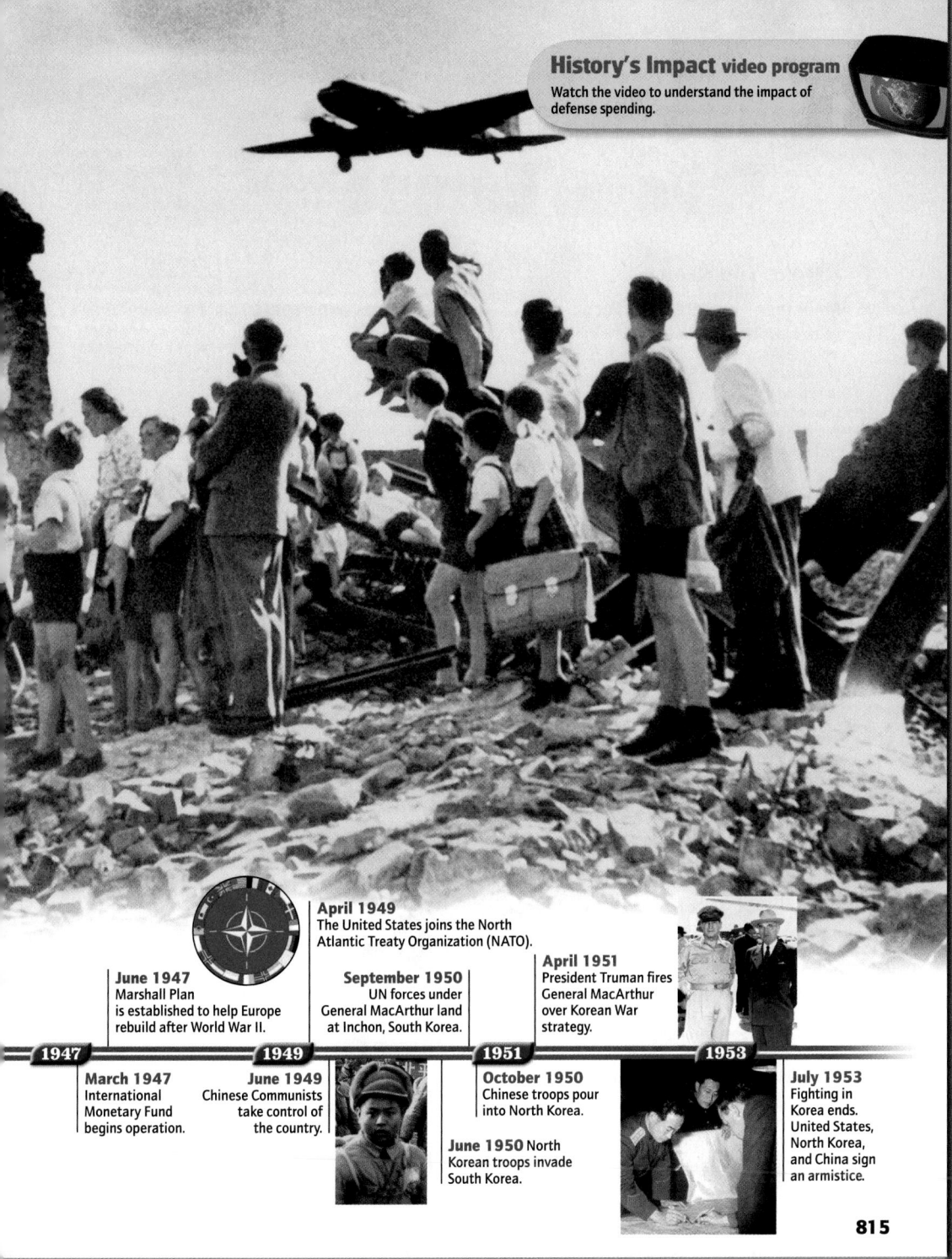

April 1949
The United States joins the North Atlantic Treaty Organization (NATO).

June 1947
Marshall Plan is established to help Europe rebuild after World War II.

September 1950
UN forces under General MacArthur land at Inchon, South Korea.

April 1951
President Truman fires General MacArthur over Korean War strategy.

1947

March 1947
International Monetary Fund begins operation.

1949

June 1949
Chinese Communists take control of the country.

1951

October 1950
Chinese troops pour into North Korea.

June 1950 North Korean troops invade South Korea.

1953

July 1953
Fighting in Korea ends. United States, North Korea, and China sign an armistice.

815

• **Chapter Preview** •

HOLT
History's Impact
► **Video Program: The Cold War Begins**
See the Video Teacher's Guide for strategies for using the video segment.

Reading Like a Historian
Berlin, 1948 Have students examine the photograph carefully. What are the people doing? What are they wearing? *looking up at an airplane; suits, dresses, children are wearing school uniforms* Remind students that entire cities were destroyed during World War II, and life was difficult throughout Europe.

go.hrw.com
Online Resources

Chapter Resources:
KEYWORD: SD7 CH25

Teacher Resources:
KEYWORD: SD7 TEACHER

Explore the Time Line

1. When did the Yalta conference take place? *February 1945*

2. How much time elapsed between General MacArthur's successful attack at Inchon and his firing? *7 months*

3. What events occurred in 1949? *U.S. joined NATO, Communists took control of China*

Info to Know

UN Troops in Korea The Korean War was a UN police action and involved troops from 21 nations around the world.

Draw Conclusions Why do you think so many nations contributed to the UN's Korean War effort? *possible answer—felt it was their duty to help, part of membership in UN*

Answers

Reading Like a Historian (p. 814)
possible answer—frightening, uncertain

815

The Iron Curtain Falls on Europe

Bellringer

The Inside Story. . . Use the **Daily Bellringer Transparency** to help students answer the question.

📄 Daily Bellringer Transparency, Section 1

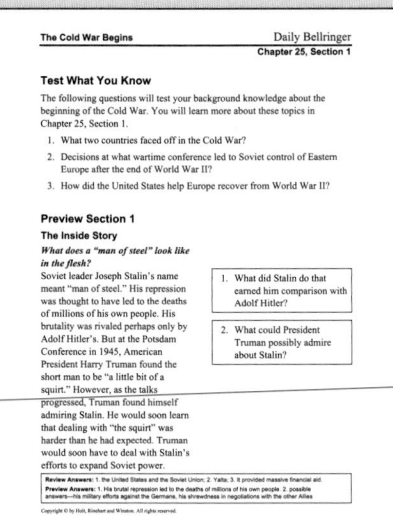

Academic Vocabulary

Review with students the high-use academic term in this section.

justified based on sound reasoning (p. 817)

📄 CRF: Vocabulary Builder Activity, Section 1

Taking Notes

United States feared spread of communism; disputes over military strategy in World War II; Soviets upset over secret development of atomic bomb; Soviet Union suppresses freedom in Eastern Europe; U.S. resists Soviet expansion

BEFORE YOU READ

MAIN IDEA

At the end of World War II, tensions between the Soviet Union and the United States deepened, leading to an era known as the Cold War.

READING FOCUS

1. What were the roots of the Cold War?

2. What was the Iron Curtain?

3. How did the United States respond to Soviet actions in Europe?

4. What was the crisis in Berlin in the late 1940s, and how was it resolved?

KEY TERMS AND PEOPLE

Cold War
Iron Curtain
containment
George F. Kennan
Truman Doctrine
Marshall Plan
Berlin Airlift
NATO

 **TAKING NOTES** As you read, take notes on the causes of the Cold War. Record your notes in a graphic organizer like the one shown here.

Causes ➡ The Cold War

 **THE INSIDE STORY**

What does a "man of steel" look like in the flesh? When the Potsdam Conference began in the summer of 1945, President Truman already knew the legend of Soviet leader Joseph Stalin, whose last name meant "man of steel." Stalin's brutal repression of his own people was thought to have led to millions of deaths. His brutality was rivaled perhaps only by Hitler's. Now, on July 17, 1945, this man of steel stood in the doorway across the room from Truman.

As Truman sized up Stalin, he began to realize why Franklin Roosevelt had referred to him as Uncle Joe. The five-foot, five-inch-tall leader was "a little bit of a squirt," Truman would later recall. As Stalin discussed the matters facing the Allied leaders in the days ahead—including the possibility of Soviet entry into the war with Japan and the future of Poland and the rest of Eastern Europe—Truman even found himself admiring the man.

Truman would soon learn that dealing with Stalin was more difficult than he first expected. As you will read, in the months after the Potsdam Conference, Truman would have to deal with Stalin's efforts to expand Soviet power. ■

President Truman Sizes Up STALIN

▲ President Truman (center) shoulder to shoulder with Stalin

Teach the Main Idea

At Level

The Iron Curtain Falls on Europe

1. **Teach** Ask students the Reading Focus questions to teach this section.

2. **Apply** Organize the class into small groups. Have each group discuss and define the term *Cold War*. Then have students use the information in their text to make a list of causes of the Cold War.

3. **Review** Have volunteers from each group read their definitions and lists to the class. Guide students in a discussion of the ways

in which the Cold War affected the foreign policy of the United States.

4. **Practice/Homework** Have students write a one-page newspaper article announcing the end of the Soviet blockade of Berlin on May 12, 1949. In their articles students should describe and summarize the Berlin Airlift. **LS Interpersonal, Verbal-Linguistic**

📄 Alternative Assessment Handbook, Rubrics 11: Discussions; and 37: Writing Assignments

The Roots of the Cold War

Following World War II, the United States and the Soviet Union entered an era of high tension and bitter rivalry known as the **Cold War**. The roots of the Cold War reached back many years. As far back as the 1920s and 1930s, the United States had viewed the Soviet Union as a potential enemy. Americans were hostile to the ideas of communism and had at times feared its spread in the United States.

World War II alliances Despite the American fear of communism, the United States and the Soviet Union joined as allies against Nazi Germany during World War II. The two countries were not truly friends, however. Indeed, after the Germans and Soviets signed their nonaggression pact in 1939, President Roosevelt had worried that the Germans and the Soviets might join forces. He feared the United States might one day be fighting against Stalin and his armies.

Nevertheless, when Hitler's forces invaded the Soviet Union in 1941, the Americans offered to help Stalin by providing military equipment. This was not an expression of support for the Soviet dictator. It was a practical move aimed at helping defeat Hitler, who was seen as a bigger threat. Over time, the Soviets received many tons of American shipments under the Lend-Lease program.

Yet even as the United States sent supplies to the Soviet Union, the two countries argued over military strategy. Early in World War II, Stalin urged the United States and Great Britain to launch an immediate invasion of Europe. This, Stalin believed, would force the Germans to remove some of their troops from the Soviet Union. Several times Roosevelt promised Stalin that the invasion was on its way. With each delay, Stalin fumed. The American and British inaction, he complained, "leaves the Soviet Army . . . to do the job alone." Hard feelings between the Soviets and the Americans and British grew.

The atomic bomb Another issue that created mistrust between the United States and the Soviet Union was the development of the atomic bomb by the United States. As you have read previously, the Manhattan Project was a tightly guarded secret. Nevertheless,

CAUSES OF THE COLD WAR

CAUSES

Philosophical Differences
- Soviet Union: communism, totalitarian dictatorship
- United States: free-enterprise capitalism, republic

World War II Conflicts
- Soviets wanted British and Americans to open a second European front earlier in war.
- United States secretly developed atomic bomb.

Postwar Conflicts
- Soviet Union refused to live up to wartime promises of elections in Eastern Europe.
- United States made efforts to resist Soviet expansion.

The Cold War
- An era of high tension between the United States and the Soviet Union.

Soviet spies had managed to steal the plans and Soviet scientists followed them closely. The Soviets saw the weapon as a threat and soon began to develop an atomic bomb of their own.

READING CHECK Identifying the Main Idea
What were the roots of the conflict between the United States and the Soviet Union?

The Iron Curtain Descends

After World War II, the United States and Britain were worried about what the Soviet Union might do. In particular, they were concerned that Stalin aimed to gain control of Eastern Europe. This was not a new concern. As you have read, in the Yalta and Potsdam conferences during World War II, American and British leaders pressed Stalin to hold free elections in Soviet-occupied lands, such as Poland.

The Americans and British had good reason to be concerned about Stalin's plans. He had no intention of giving up political and economic control over Eastern Europe. In Stalin's view, he was fully <u>justified</u> in wanting to control Eastern Europe. The Soviet Union had just

ACADEMIC VOCABULARY
justified based on sound reasoning

2 What was the Iron Curtain? *sharp political division between Communist Eastern Europe and democratic Western Europe*

The Iron Curtain Descends

Explain Why was the United States alarmed by the Soviet treatment of Germans living in Poland and other countries of Eastern Europe? *The Germans were supposed to be removed in an orderly and humane manner; they were relocated with great brutality.*

Summarize Why did Stalin want to hold onto Eastern Europe? *create a protective barrier between the Soviet Union and the West*

Make Judgments Do you think Stalin was justified in wanting to control Eastern Europe? Explain. *possible answers—Yes, the German invasion was part of a history of European attacks, and he wanted a line of Soviet-friendly nations as protection. No, after the war the Allies should have been able to trust each other.*

📖 Political Cartoons Activities for American History: Cartoon 49: Behind the Iron Curtain

The Iron Curtain in Europe
The Iron Curtain, 1948
Compare Have students refer to the atlas in their text and compare this map with a current map of Europe.

---

emerged from a terrible war in which as many as 30 million or more Soviets had died. To Stalin, the German invasion from the West had been part of a long history of attacks originating from Europe. Stalin believed that he could increase the security of his country by creating a line of Soviet-friendly nations between the Soviet Union and its historic enemies in Western Europe.

Communism spreads To achieve his goal in Eastern Europe, Stalin used whatever means necessary. In some cases, he outlawed political parties or newspapers that opposed the Communists. The Soviets also jailed or killed some political opponents and sometimes even rigged elections to ensure the success of Communist candidates. In these ways, the Soviets managed to install Communist governments throughout Eastern Europe during the postwar years.

Soon, every nation in Eastern Europe had a Soviet-friendly Communist government in place. Most of these governments were under the direct control of Stalin and the Soviet Union. The lone exception was the nation of Yugoslavia. There, Josip Broz Tito, who won fame fighting the Nazis during World War II, was firmly in control. Though he was a Communist, Tito refused to take orders from the Soviet Union. His wide popularity in Yugoslavia helped him remain in power.

The United States was also alarmed by the Soviet treatment of Germans living in Poland and the other countries of Eastern Europe. During the war, the Allies had agreed that Germans living in these areas should be removed in an "orderly and humane manner." After the war, however, the Soviets relocated the Germans with great brutality. Several hundred thousand Germans died, as millions were forced to relocate to the western section of Germany, which was occupied by the United States, Britain, and France.

The Iron Curtain American and British leaders were saddened to see Eastern Europeans, who had already suffered greatly during World War II, fall under the control of a dictator. They were also concerned that the Soviet Union would not stop at Eastern Europe.

In response, President Truman urged his secretary of state, James Byrnes, to get tough with the Soviets. "Unless Russia is faced with an iron fist and strong language," Truman wrote, "another war is in the making."

In 1946 former British prime minister Winston Churchill traveled to the United States.

The Iron Curtain in Europe

After World War II, Stalin helped install Communist governments throughout Eastern Europe. Here, a poster of Stalin (center) hangs above a doorway in newly Communist East Germany in 1946. The spread of communism concerned American and British leaders. In a famous speech, British Prime Minister Winston Churchill (far right) described a sharp division between Europe's Communist and non-Communist nations—a division that he famously termed "the Iron Curtain."

THE IRON CURTAIN, 1948

DENMARK
NETHERLANDS
UNITED KINGDOM
BELGIUM
LUX.
FRANCE
SWITZERLAND
POLAND
EAST GERMANY
WEST GERMANY
CZECHOSLOVAKIA
AUSTRIA
HUNGARY
ITALY
ROMANIA
YUGOSLAVIA
BULGARIA
ALBANIA
GREECE
SOVIET UNION

Differentiating Instruction

Above Level

Advanced Learners/GATE

Research Required

1. Organize the class into small groups. Have each group conduct outside research to learn more about the removal of Germans from other countries in Central and Eastern Europe following World War II. Have students make a list of facts about the removal, including reasons and results.

2. Have each student use information from the list of facts to write an editorial taking a position either for or against the forced removal of Germans from other countries after the war.

Positions should be backed by reasons and facts.

3. Have volunteers read their editorials to the class.

4. As an extension, guide students in a discussion of other instances in U.S. and world history where forced relocation has occurred and the consequences. *Trail of Tears, Cherokee removal, Japanese internment* **LS** **Interpersonal, Verbal-Linguistic**

📖 Alternative Assessment Handbook, Rubric 17: Letters to Editors

On March 5 he delivered a speech in Fulton, Missouri, in which he sharply attacked the Soviet Union for creating what he called an **Iron Curtain**. The term reflected Churchill's belief that communism had created a sharp division in Europe.

HISTORY'S VOICES

❝ A shadow has fallen upon the scenes so lately lighted by the Allied victory. Nobody knows what Soviet Russia and its Communist international organization intends to do in the immediate future, or what are the limits, if any, to their expansive . . . tendencies . . . It is my duty to place before you certain facts about the present position of Europe. From Stettin in the Baltic to Trieste in the Adriatic an iron curtain has descended across the Continent. ❞

—Winston Churchill, Speech at Westminster College

In the Soviet Union, Stalin's reaction to Churchill's speech was harsh. He used Churchill's words to help persuade his people that the United States and Great Britain were enemies of the Soviet Union. This became his excuse to rebuild the Soviet Union's military strength—which slowed the pace of rebuilding the shattered Soviet countryside.

READING CHECK **Making Inferences** Why did Churchill use the term *Iron Curtain*?

"An iron curtain has descended upon the Continent."

–Winston Churchill, March 1946

The United States Responds

The end of World War II and the start of the Cold War presented American leaders with a challenge. The United States was now one of the world's two most powerful nations. The other was an increasingly hostile Soviet Union.

American leaders felt they needed a new policy to deal with the situation. That is, the United States had to become the leader of all nations committed to democratic ideals and freedoms, even as the Soviet Union sought to expand its power and influence.

Containment and the Truman Doctrine

The policy that the United States adopted in the late 1940s was known as **containment**. The creator of the containment policy was an American diplomat and expert on the Soviet Union named **George F. Kennan**. Kennan believed the United States should resist Soviet attempts to expand its power and influence wherever those attempts occurred. To Kennan, containment was not limited to military force. It also involved providing economic aid to other countries in order to strengthen them against the Soviet Union.

Kennan's containment policy was put to the test in 1947. That year, President Truman informed Congress of an urgent need to provide emergency economic and military aid to Greece and Turkey. Both countries were facing Soviet pressure. In Greece, Soviet-supported Communists were trying to take advantage of postwar economic problems to gain power. In Turkey, the Soviet government was trying to gain more control.

President Truman argued that providing aid would help both the Greek and Turkish governments resist Soviet expansion. In the process, he issued what came to be called the **Truman Doctrine**:

HISTORY'S VOICES

❝ I believe it must be the policy of the United States to support free peoples who are resisting subjugation [forced control] by armed minorities or outside pressures . . .

I believe that our help should be primarily through economic and financial aid which is essential to economic stability and orderly political processes. ❞

—Harry S Truman, speech to joint session of Congress, March 12, 1947

THE IMPACT TODAY

Government
Kennan's containment policy guided U.S. foreign affairs for decades, including the decision to send troops to Vietnam in the 1960s.

THE COLD WAR BEGINS **819**

Reading Focus

The United States Responds

Identify Who was George Marshall? *former military leader and secretary of state; called for aid to rebuild Europe*

Analyze What is the connection between the Marshall Plan and Kennan's containment policy? *The Marshall Plan provided food and farm equipment, and rebuilt factories and homes in Western Europe, strengthening them against the Soviets—one of the goals of containment.*

Identify Cause and Effect What was the result of the Marshall Plan? *Recipient countries were soon feeding their people and providing jobs for workers, which built strong political and economic ties between the U.S. and Western Europe.*

Evaluate Why do you think the Soviet Union refused U.S. aid? *possible answers—wanted to develop own program of aid; would have seemed weak if it accepted U.S. aid*

📄 CRF: Primary Source Activity: Stuttgart, Germany: Before and After the Marshall Plan

Info to Know

Marshall Plan At an economic conference held in Paris soon after George C. Marshall's speech, Soviet foreign minister Vyacheslav Molotov put down the secretary of state's proposal as "nothing but a vicious American scheme for using dollars to buy its way" into European affairs. Ultimately, Soviet pressure prevented Czechoslovakia, Poland, Romania, and other Eastern European nations from taking part in the Marshall Plan.

Answers

Photo *Communism appealed to people who were suffering economically, so economic recovery would lessen the appeal of communism.*

820

The Marshall Plan

THE MARSHALL PLAN

Purpose: A U.S. financial aid program to rebuild the economies of European countries in order to create stable conditions for democratic governments.

Total amount of aid: $13.4 billion

Number of countries that received aid: 17

Countries that received the most aid: Great Britain, France, and Italy

Residents lined the streets as the millionth ton of Marshall-Plan goods were paraded through Athens, Greece, in December 1949. The Marshall Plan focused its efforts on struggling countries such as Greece, which was in the midst of a civil war against Communist rebels. The plan, originally called the European Recovery Program, is credited with boosting Western Europe's gross national product by 15 to 25 percent. In 1953 George Marshall received the Nobel Peace Prize for crafting the plan that, noted the prize presenter, "has become inseparably connected with his name." *How would economic recovery discourage communism?*

Following Truman's speech, a bipartisan Congress voted in favor of the United States providing hundreds of millions of dollars in aid to Greece and Turkey, to fight Communist influence. In both countries, the Soviets did not succeed in gaining control.

The Marshall Plan The war-related economic problems facing Greece were severe. They were not, however, unusual. Across Europe, World War II had devastated cities and ruined farms. Railroads, factories, and mines lay idle. Though the fighting was over, people were continuing to suffer, and hunger and poverty were widespread.

Many Americans felt moved to help the people of Europe, who had already suffered so much from the war. Americans also realized that, if conditions grew worse, more Europeans might turn to communism. Indeed, as the people of Europe became more desperate, the influence of Soviet communism grew. In several European nations, strong Communist movements were beginning to appear.

In June 1947, George C. Marshall, the former World War II military leader and now secretary of state, gave a speech at Harvard University. In it he called for a massive American program of aid to help Europe rebuild and get back on its economic feet.

HISTORY'S VOICES

❝ Our policy is directed not against any country or doctrine but against hunger, poverty, desperation, and chaos. Its purpose should be the revival of working economy in the world so as to permit the emergence of political and social conditions in which free institutions can exist.❞

—George C. Marshall, commencement address, Harvard University, June 5, 1947

The **Marshall Plan**, as this vision came to be known, was an enormous undertaking. Between 1948 and 1951, the U.S. government spent over 13 billion dollars in 17 different countries. This aid bought food and farm equipment. It also rebuilt factories and homes. Marshall's original plan even offered aid to the Soviet Union and its allies. But Stalin refused the aid.

With the help of the Marshall Plan, Western Europe was soon feeding its hungry and providing jobs for its workers. Western European countries were also able to buy products from American factories, which helped the

---

Social Studies Skill

The Marshall Plan

1. Guide the class in a discussion of Europe's economic problems after the war. Ask: why did the United States fear that economic problems would make European nations more vulnerable to communism? How was the Marshall Plan supposed to help contain the spread of communism? How much money did the U.S. give through the Marshall Plan? How much more might the U.S. have given if the Soviet Union or Eastern European countries had accepted the U.S. offer?

2. Have students write an essay about what they believe might have happened if Stalin had accepted the offer of aid. Have students address the potential costs and benefits.

LS Verbal-Linguistic, Logical-Mathematical

📄 Alternative Assessment Handbook, Rubric 42: Writing to Inform

postwar economy grow in the United States. Finally, the Marshall Plan helped the United States build strong political support in Western Europe. This support would be vital in the Cold War years to come.

READING CHECK **Identifying Cause and Effect** How did the United States respond to the growing tension with the Soviets in the late 1940s?

The Crisis in Berlin

After World War II, the Allies had divided Germany into four zones of occupation—British, French, and American in the western area and Soviet in the east. The capital of Berlin, which lay within the Soviet zone, was also divided into four zones.

With the start of the Cold War, the lines dividing Germany became sharper. It became clear that the Soviets planned to keep their zone under Communist control. The British and Americans, meanwhile, began to take steps to set up a free, democratic government within their zones. The French would later join this effort. The western zone eventually became known as the Federal Republic of Germany, or West Germany. The British and the Americans also took steps to set up a democratic government in West Berlin.

The Soviets block traffic The Soviets were not pleased by the idea of a Western-style government and economy in the middle of the Soviet zone of occupation. In June 1948 they decided to take drastic action. The Soviets announced that they would block any road, rail, or river traffic into West Berlin. Suddenly, West Berlin's 2.1 million residents had been cut off from sources of food, coal, and other basic necessities.

In fact, West Berlin was not completely cut off because there were airstrips in the city. The Western powers could try to supply West Berlin by air. It was a risky plan. Some officials did not believe it was even possible to supply all the needs of a major city by aircraft. Another danger was that the Soviets might try to stop the planes or shoot them down. This could lead to war.

In the end, the Western leaders decided that they had to take the risk. Their only hope for keeping West Berlin free was a massive airlift. The plan went forward.

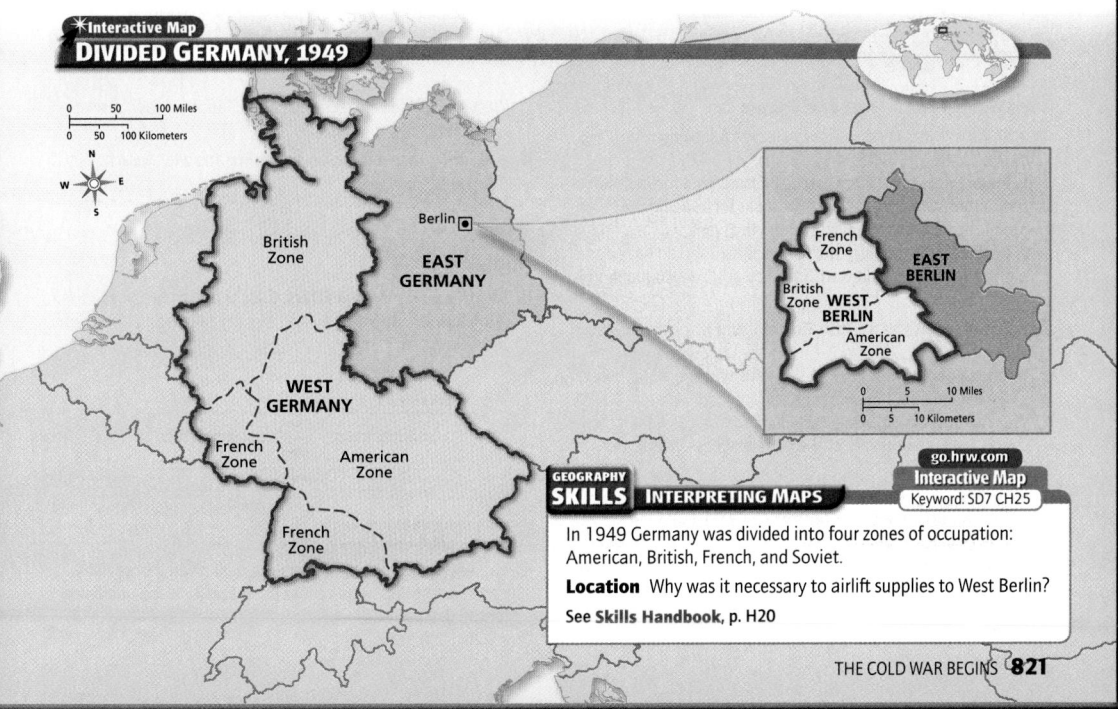

Interactive Map
DIVIDED GERMANY, 1949

British Zone
Berlin
EAST GERMANY
WEST GERMANY
French Zone
American Zone
French Zone

French Zone
British Zone
WEST BERLIN
American Zone
EAST BERLIN

0   5   10 Miles
0   5   10 Kilometers

0   50   100 Miles
0   50   100 Kilometers

GEOGRAPHY SKILLS **INTERPRETING MAPS**

go.hrw.com
Interactive Map
Keyword: SD7 CH25

In 1949 Germany was divided into four zones of occupation: American, British, French, and Soviet.

Location Why was it necessary to airlift supplies to West Berlin?
See Skills Handbook, p. H20

THE COLD WAR BEGINS **821**

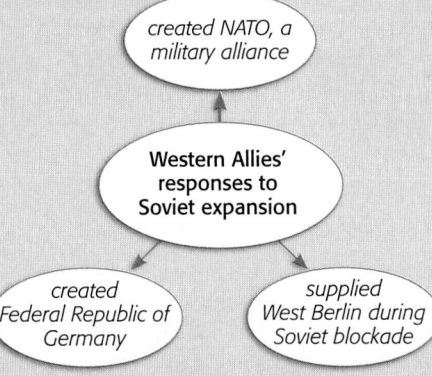

The Crisis in Berlin

Recall How long did the Berlin Airlift continue? *from June 1948 until May 1949, 11 months*

Summarize What is NATO and why was it formed? *alliance of European nations, Iceland, U.S., and Canada; to provide security against armed attack*

📋 CRF: History and Geography Activity: The Berlin Blockade and Airlift

📋 Political Cartoons Activities for American History: Cartoon 50: The Berlin Airlift

Remind students that Germany was not unified as a single country, the Federal Republic of Germany, until 1990.

Close

Guide the class in a discussion of the events that led to the Cold War.

Review

🖥 Online Quiz, Section 1

🖥 Daily Test Practice Transparency

Assess

SE Section 1 Assessment

📋 Progress Assessment: Section 1 Quiz

📋 Alternative Assessment Handbook

Reteach

📋 Interactive Reader and Study Guide, Section 1

💿 Interactive Skills Tutor CD-ROM

Answers

Reading Check *The Soviets announced they would block any ground traffic into West Berlin, which cut millions of people off from the basic necessities of life.*

822

The Berlin airlift begins Within days of the Soviet blockade, British and American airplanes began making deliveries to the people of West Berlin. Every day, the planes flew an average of 7,000 tons of supplies into West Berlin. Hundreds of flights landed, unloaded, and took off again.

To the amazement of the Soviet leaders, the **Berlin airlift** continued week after week, month after month. The airlift also got bigger. To allow more planes to land, the Allies built another airfield in the French sector of Berlin. In the month of April 1949, nearly 1,400 separate flights took place and nearly 400,000 tons of supplies were delivered.

There were tragedies, however. Some 70 American and British citizens died in airplane crashes. At least five German civilians on the ground were also killed.

In spite of these problems, the airlift continued. Finally, in the face of Allied determination, the Soviet Union lifted its blockade on May 12, 1949. By that time, American, British, and French planes had made nearly 280,000 flights into Berlin. American pilots flew two-thirds of them, leading the way.

NATO forms The widening conflict with the Soviet Union made many Western Europeans very uncomfortable. They realized that if war were to break out, they would be no match for the huge Soviet army. In order to provide a measure of security, Belgium, France, Luxembourg, the Netherlands, and the United Kingdom joined together in a system of common defense in 1948.

The crisis in Berlin helped make other Western nations aware of the wisdom of this action. In April 1949 the United States and six other nations joined the original five to create a new military alliance—the North Atlantic Treaty Organization, or **NATO**. (The other six nations were Canada, Denmark, Iceland, Italy, Norway, and Portugal.) According to the North Atlantic Treaty, an armed attack against one of the member nations would be considered an attack against all.

In the mid-1950s, Greece, Turkey, and the newly created West Germany joined NATO. Today 26 countries, including several former Communist nations, are NATO members.

READING CHECK **Summarizing** What was the crisis in Berlin?

SECTION 1 ASSESSMENT

go.hrw.com
Online Quiz
Keyword: SD7 HP25

Reviewing Ideas, Terms, and People

1. **a. Define** Write a brief definition for the following term: **Cold War**
   b. Make Inferences What can be inferred from the fact that the United States did not share its plans for building the atomic bomb with the Soviets during the war?
   c. Evaluate Do you think the United States should have done more to improve relations with the Soviet Union during World War II? Explain.

2. **a. Recall** What was the **Iron Curtain**, and why was that term chosen?
   b. Draw Conclusions Why do you think western leaders were so concerned about the Iron Curtain?
   c. Elaborate Do you think the United States was right to be concerned about the fate of the people of Eastern Europe? Explain.

3. **a. Define** Write a brief definition for each of the following terms: **containment, Truman Doctrine, Marshall Plan**
   b. Analyze What were two different ways that the Marshall Plan benefited the United States?
   c. Predict How do you think the Marshall Plan will affect relationships between the United States and the countries of

Western Europe who received the aid? Support your answer with details from the section.

4. **a. Recall** What was the **Berlin Airlift**, and why was it necessary?
   b. Explain What were the risks in attempting to supply West Berlin by air?

Critical Thinking

5. **Identifying Cause and Effect** Copy the chart below and use information from the section to identify causes and effects of the Cold War.

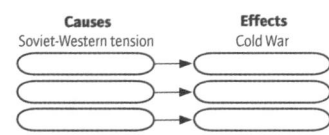

Causes		Effects
Soviet-Western tension	→	Cold War
	→	
	→	

FOCUS ON WRITING

6. **Expository** Write a paragraph explaining whether or not you think George F. Kennan's containment policy was a good idea for the United States.

822 CHAPTER 25

Section 1 Assessment Answers

1. **a.** rivalry between U.S. and Soviet Union
   b. U.S. did not trust Soviet Union
   c. no, could have jeopardized security

2. **a.** sharp division between Eastern and Western Europe created by communism
   b. feared Soviets would take over Europe
   c. yes, Stalin was a serious threat; no, home front needed help

3. **a.** prevent the spread of communism; provide aid to countries trying to resist communism; aid to rebuild Europe

   b. created strong economic ties and allies; spurred sales of U.S. goods abroad
   c. will strengthen ties to U.S.

4. **a.** supplies flown into West Berlin to avoid Soviet blockade
   b. plane crashes; difficult; Soviets might decide to fire on Allies

5. See chart in section.

6. good—built political support for U.S.; bad—angered Communists, costly

SECTION 2
Healing the Wounds of War

BEFORE YOU READ

MAIN IDEA
Following the end of World War II, U.S. military forces—and the rest of the country—faced the challenge of returning to life during peacetime.

READING FOCUS
1. What was life like in America after World War II?
2. What happened in politics in postwar America?
3. How did the United States and other countries try to build a better world after the war?

KEY TERMS AND PEOPLE
GI Bill
baby boom
Fair Deal
Universal Declaration of Human Rights
World Bank
International Monetary Fund
General Agreement on Tariffs and Trade

TAKING NOTES As you read, take notes on what life was like for different groups of Americans. Record your notes in a graphic organizer like the one shown here.

Group	Details
Returning GIs	
Baby Boomers	
Organized Labor	
Minorities	

Challenges for RETURNING SOLDIERS

▲ Returning soldiers fight for jobs at a coal-mining operation in 1946.

THE INSIDE STORY

What did the veterans of World War II have to worry about? In 1946 a popular song told the tale of a soldier returning home from World War II. "Not so long ago when the bullets screamed," went one of the verses, "many was the happy dream I dreamed." Indeed, millions of soldiers had survived the terror of combat by looking forward to their return to a bright future in the United States. Yet as the song continued, it told of a different sort of homecoming for the World War II veteran.

"Now the mighty war over there is won,
Troubles and trials have just begun
As I face that terrible enemy sign, 'No Vacancy.'"

This song tells of just one of the challenges facing veterans of the war, who returned to America by the millions within a few short months of V-J and V-E days. These men and women found shortages of housing—and, as the picture shows above, difficulty finding work. For these veterans who had given so much to their country, the bumpy transition back to life in the United States was a bitter one.

As you will read, however, this troubled transition period was remarkably brief. The federal government did much to help returning soldiers resume their lives and move the country forward beyond the war. American consumers did the rest. ■

THE COLD WAR BEGINS **823**

Preteach

Bellringer
The Inside Story. . . Use the **Daily Bellringer Transparency** to help students answer the question.
🖫 Daily Bellringer Transparency, Section 2

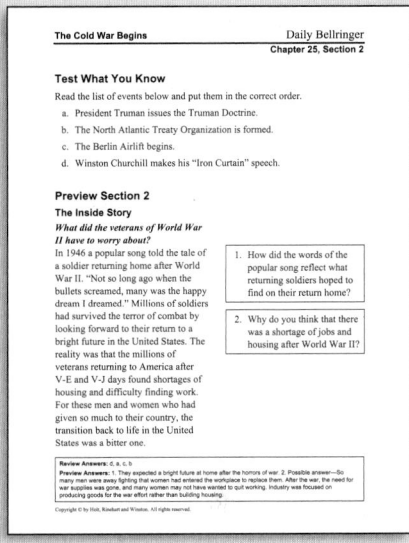

Taking Notes
Returning GIs—adjustment back to civilian life, find work, go to school, raise families; Baby Boomers—larger families stimulated economy; Organized Labor—power of labor unions restricted; Minorities—desegregation of military

Teach the Main Idea

At Level

Healing the Wounds of War

1. **Teach** Ask students the Reading Focus questions to teach this section.

2. **Apply** Have students create an outline of the section using the heads as main points. Have students identify at least two main ideas under each of the blue subheadings.

3. **Review** Review student outlines as a class. Guide students in a discussion of the 1946 and 1948 elections.

4. **Practice/Homework** Have students write a brief essay in which they analyze the relationship between President Truman's Executive Order 9981 and the UN Universal Declaration of Human Rights, which was produced under the leadership of Eleanor Roosevelt. **LS Verbal-Linguistic, Logical-Mathematical**

📝 Alternative Assessment Handbook, Rubrics 13: Graphic Organizers; and 42: Writing to Inform

1 What was life like in America after World War II? *demand for consumer goods and housing spurred the economy; dramatic rise in the birthrate; also a time of labor unrest*

Life in America After World War II

Recall What was the effect of Executive Order 9981? *It desegregated the military.*

Identify Cause and Effect Why did the U.S. economy boom after World War II? *millions returned to civilian life; people had delayed making purchases during the war; were eager to buy consumer goods; demand for housing was high; rising birthrate contributed to demand for goods*

Predict What effects will the GI Bill's educational benefits have on the American economy? *In the short run, it will reduce unemployment by helping veterans go to college or get advanced job training. In the long run, it will create a well-educated population.*

The Impact Today
GI Bill

While the GI Bill remains important, many military personnel receive educational benefits through National Guard and Reserve Tuition Assistance, which allows part-time soldiers to pursue their education while serving in the National Guard or Reserves.

Life in America after World War II

The end of World War II was a joyous occasion for Americans. Yet it was also a time of concern. During the war, the nation's factories had worked overtime to supply the Allied forces. Now the orders for tanks, planes, ships, and weapons dropped sharply. Some experts predicted serious economic trouble.

At the same time, nearly all of the 12 million men and women who had been serving in the armed forces at the end of the war were returning to civilian life. Many of these returning veterans would be looking for jobs. But often jobs simply were not available. In addition, some women workers were pressured to leave their jobs so a male veteran could take their places. In general, however, most veterans did eventually find jobs.

THE IMPACT TODAY

Government
The GI Bill remains in effect today. Since 1944, about 21 million Americans have received GI Bill tuition benefits, and about 17.5 million Americans have received GI Bill home loans.

The GI Bill This shift actually began before World War II ended. In June 1944, President Roosevelt signed the Servicemen's Readjustment Act of 1944. The act became known as the **GI Bill.** GI, which stood for "government issue," was a nickname for members of the armed forces.

The GI Bill included several features aimed at helping veterans make a smooth entry into civilian life. For example, it provided money for veterans to attend college or receive advanced job training. It helped arrange for loans for those wishing to buy a home, farm, or business. The GI Bill also provided help in finding work as well as a year's worth of unemployment benefits for those who could not find work. As you have read, the government had promised financial bonuses to World War I veterans but had not delivered. Now, after World War II, veterans were not receiving cash bonuses, but they were receiving immediate benefits.

Increasing demand The GI Bill helped millions of GIs make a successful return to civilian life. At the same time, civilians helped spur the postwar economy. During the war, the federal government took steps to control what products American industry could make. For example, car production stopped so that factories could turn out tanks and equipment.

After the war, demand for consumer goods rose sharply. People who had delayed purchases during the war now decided to buy. Returning veterans built houses, which increased the demand for furniture and appliances.

The GI Bill in Action

The GI Bill helped millions of World War II veterans earn college degrees. Many attended college while raising their families. Here, veterans celebrate after graduating from the University of Colorado. GI Bill benefits included
- money for college or job training
- loans for homes, farms, or businesses
- unemployment pay of $20 a week for up to a year
- assistance finding jobs

824 CHAPTER 25

Skills Focus: Analyzing Primary Sources

Reading Like a Historian Skill
The GI Bill

Materials butcher paper, colored markers

1. Organize the class into small groups. Have each group develop a series of questions to ask a World War II veteran about the GI Bill and its benefits. Questions should focus on how GI Bill benefits affected veterans and their families.

2. Have each student try to locate a World War II veteran to interview. Students should use their questions as a starting point for the

interview. If students are unable to locate veterans to interview, have them use primary sources to answer the questions.

3. When students have completed the interviews or their research, have them meet in their groups and discuss their results.
LS Interpersonal, Visual-Spatial

Alternative Assessment Handbook, Rubrics 1: Acquiring Information; and 28: Posters

Many more Americans also began having families. The two decades following World War II marked the beginning of the **baby boom**, a dramatic rise in the birthrate. Larger families created demand for larger cars. In this way, the postwar economy made an unexpectedly smooth shift from providing the tools of war to providing the products of peace.

Labor unions after the war During the war, the government had sought to prevent labor disputes that might affect wartime production. After the war, unions began seeking the increases in wages that had been limited during the war. Starting in 1946, the number of strikes rose sharply. In 1947 Congress passed the Taft-Hartley Act over President Truman's veto. This law greatly reduced the power of labor unions. For example, it empowered the president to stop strikes when the national interest was at stake.

Racial minorities after the war You have read about efforts early in the war to ensure equal opportunity for African Americans in wartime government and industry jobs. These efforts continued after the war. President Truman was committed to expanding opportunities for African Americans. After meeting strong opposition from members of Congress, he decided to take action on his own. In June 1948, Truman issued Executive Order 9981.

HISTORY'S VOICES

❝It is hereby declared to be the policy of the President that there shall be equality of treatment and opportunity for all persons in the armed services without regard to race, color, religion, or national origin.❞

—Harry S Truman, Executive Order 9981, July 26, 1948

Truman's order ended segregation in the U.S. armed forces. This was a major step forward for African Americans. It would also help pave the way for future gains.

Hispanic Americans were another group seeking opportunities after the war. Several hundred Hispanic veterans joined together in the American GI Forum. This group worked hard to win full access for Hispanic veterans to the benefits they had earned for their military service. In 1948 they won national attention for their efforts on behalf of Felix Longoria, a Mexican American soldier who had been killed

in the last days of World War II. When his body was returned to his Texas hometown, the local funeral home refused to provide services because of Longoria's Mexican background. The GI Forum and its Texas leader, Hector Garcia, accepted Senator Lyndon Johnson's offer that Longoria be buried at Arlington National Cemetery. The case helped highlight the contributions of Hispanic Americans.

READING CHECK **Summarizing** What challenges did the United States face after World War II?

Politics in Postwar America

When President Roosevelt died suddenly in April 1945, Harry S Truman had been vice president for less than three months. In fact, Truman barely knew Roosevelt and had little knowledge of the many issues and decisions the president had been dealing with. After he was sworn in as the new president, Truman told reporters:

HISTORY'S VOICES

❝[I]f you ever pray, pray for me now. I don't know if you fellas ever had a load of hay fall on you, but when they told me what happened yesterday, I felt like the moon, the stars, and all the planets had fallen on me.❞

—Harry S Truman to reporters, April 13, 1945

Politics in Postwar America

Explain What challenges did Harry Truman face upon becoming president? *had to lead Allies through the end of the war; guide the nation from war to peace; faced political criticism from all sides*

Identify What was the Fair Deal and what became of it? *Truman's domestic plan; Congress did not support it; few of the Fair Deal ideas became law*

Contrast How did the way people in Washington, D.C., perceive Truman differ from the way he was perceived elsewhere? *In Washington, he was the target of many jokes, but people responded well to him elsewhere.*

American Civil Liberty

Integration and the Military

The report issued by the President's Committee on Civil Rights was called "To Secure These Rights." It recommended ending segregation in the military. It also called for the creation of the Commission on Civil Rights and a permanent civil rights section in the Department of Justice.

Answers

Making Inferences *possible answer—stronger and more unified military*

American Civil Liberty

Integration and the Military

During World War II, about 1 million African Americans were drafted into the military. All of these soldiers, sailors, and marines served in segregated units.

In 1946 President Harry S Truman appointed the President's Committee on Civil Rights. The committee said that segregation made the armed forces less effective than they would be if they were integrated.

Backed by the committee's report, Truman decided to end racial segregation in the United States military. On July 26, 1948, he signed Executive Order 9981. This executive order required "equality of treatment and opportunity for all persons in the armed services without regard to race, color, religion, or national origin."

Although some military leaders resisted, by 1949 all branches had developed plans for integration. Today all positions in the military are open to people who are qualified, regardless of race or ethnicity.

Making Inferences What might Truman have hoped to gain by ending segregation in the military?

In October 1948, James Leroy Brown (center) became the first African American to receive his wings as a Navy pilot.

Truman faced huge challenges. He had to lead the Allies through the end of the war while guiding the nation through the shift from wartime to peace. He also had to deal with political criticism that came from all sides. Many Democrats compared him unfavorably to their hero, Roosevelt. Republicans saw in Truman someone they thought they could finally defeat.

The 1946 elections in Congress The attacks on Truman grew stronger as the 1946 elections in Congress approached. One key complaint was inflation, or a rise in prices. During the war, the government had acted to keep prices low. After the war, price controls were relaxed. Prices shot up as a result, and Truman took the blame.

The 1946 elections were a disaster for the Democrats. Republicans gained so many seats that they were now the majority in Congress for the first time since 1930. With this majority, Republicans fought against Truman with increased strength. Truman found it difficult to put in place his own programs. One exception was the Marshall Plan, which you read about in Section 1. His handling of the Berlin Crisis was another of his few accomplishments.

The 1948 presidential election As the presidential election of 1948 approached, Truman appeared to be in trouble. His popularity with voters was low. Even his fellow Democrats did not fully support him. Liberals broke off to back former vice president Henry Wallace, who ran under the banner of the Progressive Party. Many southern Democrats were angry at Truman's support for civil rights. They supported South Carolina governor Strom Thurmond, who ran as a Dixiecrat.

With his popularity low and his party divided, Truman seemed certain to lose the election. In a poll of 50 political writers published in a leading newsmagazine a few weeks before election day, every single one predicted a Republican victory. Newspapers made fun of him openly. "Mr. Truman is the most complete fumbler and blunderer this nation has seen in high office in a long time," wrote the *Los Angeles Times*. The Republican candidate, Governor Thomas Dewey of New York, was confident of victory.

Refusing to give up, Truman set off on a whirlwind campaign across the country. His tough-talking, plainspoken style had made him the target of many jokes in Washington, D.C. But elsewhere people responded well to Truman's style. He made a special point of criticizing Republicans in the House and Senate. When he complained about the "do-nothing Congress," crowds cheered in support.

In spite of Truman's efforts, most experts did not think he had a chance. Yet on election

---

Differentiating Instruction

Below Level

English-Language Learners

1. Guide students in discussing why so many Americans believed that Republican Thomas Dewey would win the presidential election in 1948.

2. To help students understand some of the issues that affected the election, copy the following graphic organizer for them to see. Omit the italicized answers. Have students copy the graphic organizer onto their own papers and complete it.

3. Have volunteers share their answers with the class. Complete the master graphic organizer for the students to see. Have students correct their work and retain the organizer as a study tool. **LS Visual-Spatial, Logical-Mathematical**

📝 Alternative Assessment Handbook, Rubric 13: Graphic Organizers

📦 Graphic Organizer Transparencies

The 1948 Election

President Truman's Record
• *Led nation through end of war*
• *Opposed the Taft-Hartley Act*
• *Supported civil rights*

↓

Splits in the Democratic Party
• *Liberal Democrats supported Wallace*
• *Southern Democrats supported Thurmond*

↓

Election and Results
• *Truman set off on a whirlwind campaign*
• *Truman complained about the Congress*
• *Truman won election*

day, the voters handed Truman a victory. It was one of the most surprising election outcomes in American history.

Having won the election, Truman finally felt strong enough to put forward his own plan for the country. It was called the **Fair Deal**. It included a number of programs in the tradition of the New Deal. This included a federal health insurance program and new funding for education. Congress, however, did not support Truman's program. Few of his Fair Deal ideas ever became law. Meanwhile, new problems in Korea came to dominate the president's attention. You will read about the Korean War in Section 4.

READING CHECK **Drawing Conclusions** Why do you think the Democrats faced problems in the politics of the postwar era?

Trying to Build a Better World

World War II helped give rise to the political tensions of the Cold War. It also gave rise to a strong desire to understand and prevent the causes of war. After two catastrophic conflicts, many people were anxious to find new ways to prevent a third.

One result was the establishment of the United Nations (UN). Its creation started in the final days of the war. Representatives of 50 nations met in June 1945 to create the UN Charter, the written agreement that outlines its aims and principles. The UN Charter was ratified in October 1945. The UN was officially born. Over the years, it would welcome many new members.

The UN Charter committed its members to "save succeeding generations from the scourge of war" and to "reaffirm faith in fundamental human rights." It called for members to respect treaties and agreements and to promote the progress and freedom of all people. Member nations agreed to live in peace and to unite to maintain security. Force would be used only to serve the common interests of the membership. The charter also called for the use of international organizations to promote economic and social advancement.

Human rights Soon after its formation, the United Nations established the Commission on Human Rights. The U.S. representative to this commission was the former first lady Eleanor Roosevelt. She became the chairperson of the commission, helping to soothe tensions between members from different countries. Different countries sometimes had very different ideas about what kinds of human rights all people ought to have and how to achieve them.

PROGRAMS FOR A SAFER WORLD

As World War II came to an end, the countries of the world began seeking ways to prevent the problems and conflicts that helped lead to war. Leaders in the United States and other countries paved the way in establishing the following:

World Bank (1944)	• Organization for providing loans and advice to countries for the purpose of reducing poverty
International Monetary Fund (1944)	• System for promoting orderly financial relationships between countries • Designed to prevent economic crises and to encourage trade and economic growth
United Nations (1945)	• Organization in which member nations agree to settle disputes by peaceful means • Replaced the League of Nations
General Agreement on Tariffs and Trade (1946)	• Agreement among member nations on rules and regulations for international trade • Focused on reducing tariffs and other trade barriers

THE COLD WAR BEGINS **827**

Skills Focus: Summarizing   At Level

Reading Skill
Building a Better World

1. Point out to students that the United States never joined the League of Nations. It took Senate approval for the U.S. to join the United Nations. Have each student write a speech that a member of Congress might have given to the voters back home explaining what the United Nations is, why it was founded, and how it intends to accomplish its goals.

2. Have volunteers deliver their speeches.

3. As an extension, have students create a PowerPoint or multimedia presentation supporting the information in their speeches.

4. Guide students in a discussion of the ways in which the following programs worked to create a better world: the United Nations, the World Bank, and the International Monetary Fund. **LS Verbal-Linguistic, Kinesthetic**

Alternative Assessment Handbook, Rubric 22: Multimedia Presentations

Direct Teach

Reading Focus

3 How did the United States and other countries try to build a better world after the war? *by working together to form the United Nations, World Bank, International Monetary Fund, and General Agreement on Tariffs and Trade*

Trying to Build a Better World

Recall In what instances is force permissible under the United Nations charter? *when it serves the common interests of its members*

Make Inferences Why do you think former first lady Eleanor Roosevelt was chosen to head the Commission on Human Rights? *possible answer—She supported civil rights during her husband's administration.*

CRF: Biography: Bernard Baruch

Programs for a Safer World

Make Inferences How would organizations like the World Bank and the International Monetary Fund help make the world safer? *possible answer—Reducing poverty and creating stable economies would lead to more stable governments and help reduce international tension.*

Quick Facts Transparency: Programs for a Safer World

Answers

Reading Check *some Americans disliked Truman's support for civil rights; blamed Democrats for postwar problems, especially the rise of inflation*

827

Primary Source

"We the Peoples of the United Nations Determined to save succeeding generations from the scourge of war, which twice in our lifetime has brought untold sorrow to mankind, and to reaffirm faith in fundamental human rights, in the dignity and worth of the human person, in the equal rights of men and women and of nations large and small . . . Have Resolved to Combine our Efforts to Accomplish these Aims."

Charter of the United Nations,
Preamble, June 1945

• Review & Assess •

Close

Have students summarize the challenges that faced the United States following World War II.

Review

- Online Quiz, Section 2
- Daily Test Practice Transparency

Assess

SE Section 2 Assessment
- Progress Assessment: Section 2 Quiz
- Alternative Assessment Handbook

Reteach

- Interactive Reader and Study Guide, Section 2
- Interactive Skills Tutor CD-ROM

Answers

Reading Check *UN, World Bank, IMF, GATT*

828

The democratic United States and Communist Soviet Union, for instance, had different ideas about how to secure basic economic rights.

In December 1948, the commission presented to the UN General Assembly the **Universal Declaration of Human Rights**. This document set high goals for all member nations of the UN. For example, it declared a belief that all human beings are born free and equal. It called for an end to slavery, torture, and inhumane punishment. It demanded a variety of civil rights, including the right to assembly and the right to access to courts. It also stated that elementary education should be free and available to all. The UN General Assembly adopted the declaration and directed member countries to publicize it.

Trade and economic development

World War II had raised a number of concerns about the financial relationships between countries. These problems had helped bring about the Great Depression. Now they threatened to limit trade and create conflict between nations. Many leaders hoped that solving these problems would lead to greater prosperity around the world. This, in turn, would promote peace.

Even before the war was over, representatives of many of the world's great powers met at a conference in Bretton Woods, New Hampshire. Out of this conference came an agreement to create two new organizations—the **World Bank** and the **International Monetary Fund** (IMF).

The World Bank aimed to help poor countries build their economies. It provided grants of money and loans to help with projects that could provide jobs and wealth.

Economic policy was the focus of the International Monetary Fund. Prior to the creation of the IMF, countries often followed economic policies that served their own interests, regardless of whether they hurt other countries. Such practices often had a harmful effect on world trade, which hurt everyone. The IMF was designed to encourage economic policies that promoted international trade. For example, the IMF helped build confidence in the values of different countries' currencies.

The **General Agreement on Tariffs and Trade** (GATT) was another international organization created to promote economic cooperation. The GATT, which took effect in 1948, was designed to reduce barriers to trade.

READING CHECK **Identifying Problems and Solutions** Name some international organizations that aimed to build a better world in the years after World War II.

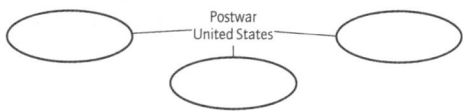

SECTION 2 ASSESSMENT

go.hrw.com
Online Quiz
Keyword: SD7 HP25

Reviewing Ideas, Terms, and People

1. a. Define Write a brief definition for each of the following terms: **GI Bill, baby boom**
   b. Explain Following World War II, how did the United States manage to avoid the severe economic problems that some people had expected?
   c. Predict How do you think Truman's decision to desegregate the U.S. armed forces will affect African Americans and their growing demands for civil rights?

2. a. Recall What was the outcome and significance of the elections of 1946?
   b. Make Inferences What can you infer about Truman's successful tactic of attacking the "do-nothing Congress"?
   c. Elaborate How do you explain the fact that so many political observers were wrong about Truman and the presidential election of 1948?

3. a. Identify What was the UN, and why was it created?
   b. Summarize By what means did the United States and other countries seek to make the world better during the postwar era?

c. Elaborate Based on what you have read here and in other chapters, how do you think efforts to improve countries' economies and international trade will help promote peace in the future?

Critical Thinking

4. Identifying the Main Idea Copy the chart below and use information from the section to identify details that support the main idea given.

Postwar
United States

FOCUS ON WRITING

5. Persuasive From the point of view of a member of the Commission of Human Rights, write and present a speech in favor of the Universal Declaration of Human Rights. Use details from the section in your speech.

828 CHAPTER 25

Section 2 Assessment Answers

1. a. GI Bill provided money to help returning veterans get jobs and education; baby boom was increase in birthrate
b. GI Bill helped returning veterans; demand for consumer goods fueled economy
c. empower them to seek equal rights

2. a. Republicans gained a majority in Congress and limited Truman's social reforms.
b. made voters believe that Truman would fight for ordinary Americans
c. out of touch with most voters

3. a. international organization dedicated to preventing war and working for human rights
b. rebuilding war-torn countries; establishing organizations to prevent future wars
c. make countries economically stronger, help settle disputes peacefully, cooperate to protect economic and political interests

4. GI Bill helps returning veterans; demand for consumer goods increase; birthrate rises

5. reinforced fundamental beliefs of freedom and equality; called for end to slavery, torture, inhumane punishment

SECTION 3

The Second Red Scare

BEFORE YOU READ

MAIN IDEA

The start of the Cold War and events at home helped trigger a second Red Scare in the late 1940s and early 1950s.

READING FOCUS

1. Why was the fear of communism growing in the late 1940s?
2. What methods and actions did the government use to fight the spread of communism at home?
3. Who was Senator Joseph McCarthy, and what was his role in the second Red Scare?

KEY TERMS AND PEOPLE

Chiang Kai-shek
Mao Zedong
House Un-American
   Activities Committee
Hollywood Ten
Alger Hiss
Joseph McCarthy
McCarthyism

TAKING NOTES As you read, take notes about the fears that led to the second Red Scare. Record your notes in a graphic organizer like the one shown here.

> Fears
>
> ↓
>
> The Red Scare

THE INSIDE STORY

How did the White House find out that the Soviets had the atomic bomb? Everyone realized the day would eventually come, though many did not expect it so soon. They even had a code name for describing the situation—Vermont. Still, the realization that the Soviet Union had likely exploded an atomic weapon came as a tremendous shock to most Americans.

For David Lilienthal, head of the Atomic Energy Commission, the news came in the form of a visit from an army general. Lilienthal was on vacation on the island of Martha's Vineyard off the coast of Massachusetts. As he was returning to his home on the evening of September 19, 1949, the general was waiting for him with a grave message: The Soviets had the atomic bomb and had conducted a test explosion.

The next morning, Lilienthal flew to Washington, D.C., to meet with President Truman and several of his advisers. The group debated how to handle the news. Should the public be told? How would they react?

Truman decided that the public must be informed. He presented the information himself several days later. As you will read, the news hit the nation hard. Soon, Americans were in the grips of another Red Scare. ◢

▲ The news that the Soviet Union had tested an atomic bomb sent shock waves of fear through the nation.

THE COLD WAR BEGINS **829**

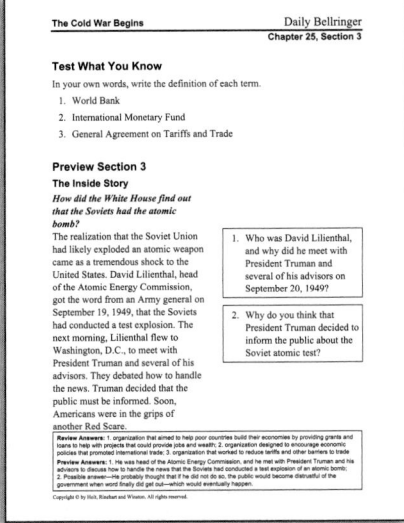

Teach the Main Idea

The Second Red Scare

1. **Teach** Ask students the Reading Focus questions to teach this section.

2. **Apply** Have students review the section and create a cause-and-effect chart for the second Red Scare.

3. **Review** Review student charts as a class. *Causes—concern over spread of communism in Europe; Soviet development of atomic weapons; Communist takeover of China; spy cases; McCarthyism; Effects— HUAC investigations; Truman's plan* to ensure loyalty of federal employees; McCarran Act; spy cases; McCarthyism. Have students explain why spy cases and McCarthyism were causes and effects.

4. **Practice/Homework** Have students write a brief editorial about the House Un-American Activities Committee. Do they support or oppose its actions? Why?
   LS Visual-Spatial, Verbal-Linguistic

📄 Alternative Assessment Handbook, Rubric 13: Graphic Organizers

1 Why was the fear of communism growing in the late 1940s? *Americans worried about spread of communism in Europe; crisis in Berlin; Soviet Union test of atomic weapons; Communist control of China*

Growing Fear of Communism

Identify What event caused President Truman to decide to strengthen the nation's military? *discovery that the Soviet Union had detonated an atomic bomb*

Recall Why did China's Nationalist leaders flee to Taiwan? *Communists gained control of most of mainland China.*

Summarize How did Mao Zedong's Communists end up taking control of China? *When Japan withdrew, Communists took advantage of the opportunity to seize power; drove out the Nationalists.*

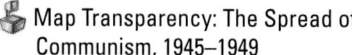 Map Transparency: The Spread of Communism, 1945–1949

Biography

Anne Revere (1903–1990) Best known as Elizabeth Taylor's mother in *National Velvet*, Anne Revere won critical acclaim throughout her acting career of 40 films. Nominated three times for Oscars, Revere won a Best Supporting Actress Oscar in 1945 for her work in *National Velvet*. In 1951, the House Un-American Activities Committee accused Revere of being a Communist. Revere pleaded the Fifth Amendment and was blacklisted, effectively ending her acting career for the decade. Eventually, Revere returned to Broadway and even won a Tony in 1960 for her role in *Toys in the Attic*.

Answers

Interpreting Maps *possible answer— size of the country and number of people meant that a large part of that area was now Communist*

830

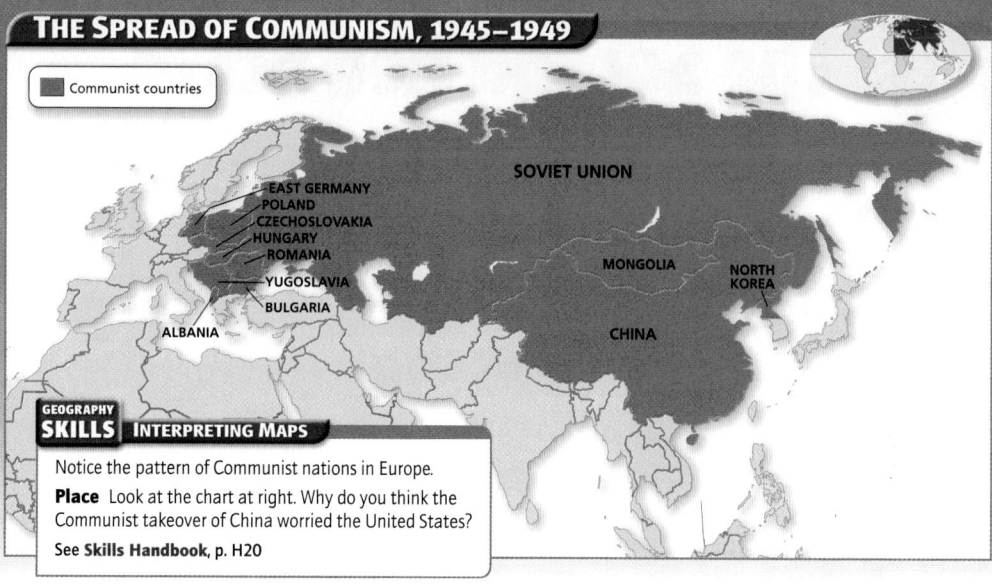

THE SPREAD OF COMMUNISM, 1945–1949

☐ Communist countries

EAST GERMANY
POLAND
CZECHOSLOVAKIA
HUNGARY
ROMANIA
YUGOSLAVIA
BULGARIA
ALBANIA
SOVIET UNION
MONGOLIA
NORTH KOREA
CHINA

GEOGRAPHY SKILLS | **INTERPRETING MAPS**

Notice the pattern of Communist nations in Europe.

Place Look at the chart at right. Why do you think the Communist takeover of China worried the United States?

See **Skills Handbook**, p. H20

Growing Fear of Communism

The postwar years were a tense time in the United States. American leaders worried about the spread of communism in Europe. In 1948 the crisis over Berlin drove the tension level even higher.

Then in 1949, two events added greatly to the nation's anxiety. First came the discovery that the Soviet Union possessed an atomic weapon. Then came the news that Communists had gained control of China, the most populous country in the world.

Soviet atomic weapons The first hint of trouble occurred in late August 1949. U.S. aircraft flying over the North Pacific Ocean picked up signs of unusual radioactivity in the atmosphere. American scientists quickly figured out what had happened. In September, President Truman issued a short, terse statement that confirmed the Soviet Union had **detonated** an atomic bomb.

Truman's announcement came as a great shock to the nation. No longer could the country rely on this terribly destructive weapon as the basis of its defense against the Soviets. Soon, Truman would seek to strengthen the nation's military against a possible Soviet threat.

ACADEMIC VOCABULARY
detonate to cause an explosion

The threat of Communist China Within days of the announcement that the Soviets had atomic weapons, the United States learned that Communists in China had gained nearly full control of the country. The so-called Nationalist government of **Chiang Kai-shek** had fled mainland China for the island of Taiwan. Chiang had been a loyal friend to the United States during World War II. He—and the United States—continued to claim that the Nationalist Party represented the one true government of all China. Now, outside of Taiwan, the Nationalists had no power. China was in the hands of the Communist Party. A new People's Republic of China had been born.

The Communist takeover of China had been many years in the making. At the end of World War II, the defeated Japanese had withdrawn from China. Led by **Mao Zedong**, Chinese Communists used this opportunity to gain control of large areas, especially in northern China.

In a civil war between Nationalists and Communists, the United States supported the Nationalists' effort to defeat communism. Chiang's Nationalist government, however, was riddled with corruption and poor leadership. As a result, Mao's Communists steadily gained power in China.

830 CHAPTER 25

Collaborative Learning

At Level

Mao Zedong and Chiang Kai-shek

Research Required

Materials: plain paper, colored markers

1. Organize the class into small groups. Have half of the groups research the life and politics of Mao Zedong and the other half research the life of Chiang Kai-shek and the politics of Nationalist China.

2. Have each group develop an encyclopedia article in which they discuss the history of the Communist takeover of mainland China and the establishment of a Nationalist government on Taiwan. Have students conclude their

articles with a brief summary of the political situation that exists today between China and Taiwan. Have students create visuals, maps, and a sequencing chart to illustrate their articles. Students should also include a bibliography with their articles.

3. Have volunteers from each group share their encyclopedia articles with the class.

LS Interpersonal, Verbal-Linguistic

Alternative Assessment Handbook, Rubric 3: Artwork; and 20: Map Creation

POPULATION, 1950

QUICK FACTS

NATO Members	Communist Nations
The United States and Canada 171,550,000	Soviet Union 180,980,000
Western Europe 173,882,000	Eastern Europe 106,055,000
	China 554,760,000
Total 345,432,000	**Total** 841,795,000

The Communist victory in China delivered another shock to the American people. Americans did not yet know if Chinese communism was equivalent to Soviet communism. Many worried that China would increase the Communist threat to the United States.

READING CHECK **Identifying Cause and Effect** What events helped increase the fear of communism for the American public in the late 1940s?

Fighting the Spread of Communism at Home

The events of 1949 fed an already strong anti-Communist feeling in the United States. Indeed, for several years, concern had been growing about possible Communist influence in American government. Efforts were already underway to root out disloyal people.

Investigating communism Since the 1930s, the House of Representatives had had a **House Un-American Activities Committee**, or HUAC. This committee's original purpose was to investigate the full range of radical groups in the United States, including Fascists and Communists. Over time, however, it came to

focus only on the possible threat of communism in the United States. This focus existed even before the start of the Cold War. It sharpened significantly as the Soviets emerged as the chief enemy of the United States.

The most famous HUAC investigation began in 1947. Its goal was to explore possible Communist influence in the American film industry. The committee collected the names of Hollywood writers and directors who were thought to hold radical political views. Ten of these people, when called before HUAC, refused to answer questions about their beliefs or those of their colleagues. As a result of this refusal, the **Hollywood Ten** were found guilty of contempt of Congress and were sentenced to a year in jail.

The case alarmed others in Hollywood. Many now agreed to provide names of possible Communists to HUAC. Others refused to provide names, and for this they were placed on a blacklist—a list from which all the major Hollywood employers refused to hire. The careers of several hundred writers, actors, directors, and producers were damaged.

In another case that attracted widespread attention, the Atomic Energy Commission accused atomic bomb scientist J. Robert Oppenheimer of Communist sympathies. The commission stripped him of his top-secret security clearance.

Truman and loyalty The public fear of communism also put pressure on American leaders. No leader wanted to appear weak when dealing with communism. This included the president. Truman felt he had to take action because Republicans in Congress were claiming that Communists were working in the federal government. To help address this charge, Truman created a new plan for ensuring the loyalty of government officials. Under the plan, all federal employees would be investigated. Those found to be disloyal to the United States could be barred from federal employment.

The investigations turned up little evidence of disloyalty. Over the next few years, 3 million people were investigated. A few thousand federal workers resigned, and about 200 were judged disloyal. The investigations troubled some Americans. They made it clear, however, that the Truman administration was serious about fighting communism.

ACADEMIC VOCABULARY
equivalent equal in importance

Reading Focus

❷ What methods and actions did the government use to fight the spread of communism at home? *The House Un-American Activities Committee investigated possible radicals; Truman created a plan to investigate all government officials' loyalty; Smith Act; McCarran Act*

Fighting the Spread of Communism at Home

Recall What was the original purpose of the House Un-American Activities Committee? *investigate radical groups in the U.S.*

Explain Why did Truman create a plan to investigate federal employees to determine their loyalty? *Republicans in Congress claimed that Communists were working in the federal government.*

Make Judgments Do you think that people should be fired, blacklisted, or otherwise punished for their political beliefs? Explain your answer. *possible answers—no, because the Constitution guarantees us freedom of speech and freedom of association; yes—employers should have the right to keep people with dangerous or threatening ideas out of jobs*

Activity Who Were the Hollywood Ten? Have students conduct outside research on the Hollywood Ten. Then have each student write a brief biography of one of the men, telling why he was targeted and how it affected his career.
LS Verbal-Linguistic

Quick Facts Transparency: Population, 1950

CRF: Biography: Herblock

Skills Focus: Identifying Problem and Solution   [At Level]

Reading Skill
A Question of Loyalty

1. Write the following scenario for students to see: The local school district has decided that any student who questions school policy is a negative or dangerous influence. School principals, working together, have decided to give detention to all students suspected of disagreeing with school policy.

2. Have students read the scenario, then write a one-page response to it.

3. Have volunteers read their responses.

4. Guide the class in a discussion of the scenario and their responses. Tell students that this is essentially what the United States government did to people whose loyalty was questioned, but that in some cases the consequences were much greater. **LS** Logical-Mathematical, Verbal-Linguistic

Alternative Assessment Handbook, Rubric 37: Writing Assignments

---

Answers

Reading Check *Soviets developed atomic weapons; China became a Communist country.*

831

Fighting the Spread of Communism at Home

Explain Why did Truman veto the McCarran Act? *He believed it would make a mockery of the Bill of Rights and American claims to stand up for freedom in the world, which would delight the Communists.*

Make Generalizations How did a series of spy cases fuel the fear of communism? *by convincing Americans that Communists were infiltrating the government and giving atomic secrets to the Soviets*

Info to Know

The Rosenbergs In 2001 Ethel Rosenberg's brother, David Greenglass, admitted that he had lied under oath, incriminating his sister and her husband to save himself. Because he cooperated with the investigation, he escaped with a 15-year sentence. The Rosenbergs might have saved themselves if they had confessed and turned in other Communist Party spies. However, they refused to do so and were executed.

Major Spy Cases

Alger Hiss, 1948

Accused of being a spy for the Soviets, Alger Hiss prepares to testify to HUAC in 1948. Although he denied the charges, evidence later showed Hiss had lied to HUAC. In 1950 he was convicted of perjury, or lying under oath, and sentenced to prison. Soviet documents decoded by American intelligence and declassified in the 1990s confirmed Hiss's guilt in the case.

Klaus Fuchs, 1950

Fuchs, a nuclear physicist, worked on the Manhattan Project. During his work on the development of the atomic bomb, he transmitted information to the Soviet Union, including detailed drawings of "Fat Man," the bomb the United States dropped on Nagasaki, Japan, in World War II. After serving nine years in prison, Fuchs settled in East Germany.

Ethel and Julius Rosenberg, 1951

The Rosenbergs were convicted of passing military secrets to the Soviets, including information from Ethel's brother, who was an employee on the Manhattan Project. They received the death sentence and were executed in 1953. The Rosenbergs were the first U.S. civilians to be executed for espionage.

The Smith Act In 1949 Truman made another show of his commitment to fight communism at home. The government charged several leaders of the Communist Party in the United States under the Smith Act. This 1940 law made it a crime to call for the overthrow of the U.S. government or belong to an organization that did so.

The Communist Party officials were convicted. These convictions, and the Smith Act itself, were upheld in the 1951 Supreme Court ruling in *Dennis* v. *United States*. The Court considered that the domestic danger posed by Communists was "grave and probable" and justified limits on their free speech. (Later, in *Yates* v. *United States*, the Court held that it was a crime only when a person called for specific actions to overthrow the government.)

The McCarran Act In 1950 Congress took further action to fight communism in the United States. The McCarran Internal Security Act required Communist organizations to register with the government and established a special board to investigate Communist involvement. The act also made it illegal to plan for a creation of a totalitarian dictatorship and prevented Communists or other radicals from entering the United States.

Truman vetoed the bill, stating that it "would delight the Communists, for it would make a mockery of the Bill of Rights and of our claims to stand for freedom in the world." But Congress easily overrode Truman's veto.

Spy cases Fear of communism was also fueled by a series of spy cases in the late 1940s. One case involved a former government official named **Alger Hiss**. In 1948 former Communist spy Whittaker Chambers accused Hiss of being part of a 1930s plot to place Communists inside the government. Hiss denied the charges. Then in a dramatic move, Chambers led investigators to his Maryland farm. There, hidden in a hollowed-out pumpkin, they found several rolls of top-secret government microfilm. Chambers said the stolen film had come from Hiss.

Hiss could not be charged with spying—many years had passed since his alleged crime. He was charged, however, with lying under oath. Hiss was eventually convicted and served some years in prison. Future president Richard Nixon played a key role in the investigation.

Skills Focus: Identifying Cause and Effect

Reading Skill

Fighting Communism in the United States

1. To help students understand the U.S. government's actions to fight communism in the United States and how these actions affected Americans' daily lives during the Cold War, have students create a graphic organizer showing the way in which the government took action to limit the spread of communism within the country.

2. Have volunteers share their organizers with the class.

3. Guide students in a discussion of the ways in which the loss of basic, constitutional rights might affect our everyday lives. Ask students if they believe the government should restrict individual rights in order to protect the general public. **LS** **Visual-Spatial**

   Alternative Assessment Handbook, Rubrics 11: Discussions; and 13: Graphic Organizers

Another famous case involved the theft of atomic secrets. Klaus Fuchs was a German-born scientist who had worked on the Manhattan Project during World War II. Investigators learned that he gave American atomic secrets to the Soviet Union, including detailed drawings. Fuchs was sentenced to 14 years in prison though he served just 9 years.

The Fuchs case raised fears about atomic spies operating inside the United States. Indeed, investigators soon found several Americans who admitted providing atomic secrets to the Soviets. One of them charged that his sister and brother-in-law—Ethel and Julius Rosenberg—were leaders of the spy ring.

At the trial, the Rosenbergs denied the charges. They also refused to answer questions about their political activities, which included past involvement with communism. They were convicted of conspiracy to commit espionage, or spying. The Rosenbergs received the death sentence and were executed in 1953.

READING CHECK **Identifying the Main Idea** Name some examples of efforts to fight communism in the United States in the late 1940s and early 1950s.

Senator Joseph McCarthy

On February 9, 1950, a U.S. senator named **Joseph McCarthy** visited Wheeling, West Virginia to deliver a speech before a Republican women's group. His topic was a familiar one to Americans of that day—the dangers of communism. In his speech, McCarthy claimed that there were 205 known Communists working for the U.S. Department of State. In a later speech, he went a step further. Waving a list before the crowd, he said it contained the names of 57 Communists in the State Department.

The rise of McCarthyism McCarthy's charges created a sensation. For many Americans, his claim was all too easy to believe. It helped explain recent events, such as the loss of China and the Soviet development of the atomic bomb. But McCarthy never produced the list of names he claimed to be holding in his speech. A Senate committee looked into his charges and found no evidence of Communists in the State Department.

By that time, however, many frightened Americans did not need any evidence. Even if he had been wrong with his first list, they

THE IMPACT TODAY

Recent Scholarship
In 1995 the National Security Agency released information on Soviet spy communications during the Cold War. These files provided further evidence that the Rosenbergs were guilty.

The McCarthy Hearings

COMMUNIST PARTY ORGANIZATION U.S.A—FEB. 9, 1950

Senator Joseph McCarthy presents a map of alleged Communist Party organization to Army counsel Joseph Welch as part of the Army-McCarthy hearing in 1954. *How does McCarthy's use of a map give support to his claims?*

833

Skills Focus: Identifying Main Idea and Details

At Level

Reading Skill
McCarthyism

Standard English Mastery

1. Have students write a newspaper editorial in which they denounce the tactics used by Joseph McCarthy. Editorials should describe ways in which McCarthy's activities led to violations of constitutional rights. Have volunteers read their editorials to the class.

2. Remind students that McCarthy sometimes used faked evidence to discredit people. One of these was Maryland Senator Millard Tydings who served in the Senate for four

terms. After Senator Tydings denounced McCarthy's charges of infiltration of the State and Defense Departments as "complete hogwash," Tydings lost his bid for re-election. Ask students what they think Tydings's response might have been to their editorials.

🔲 **Verbal-Linguistic**

📄 Alternative Assessment Handbook, Rubric 17: Letters to Editors

figured, he was clearly on the right track. In this way, just by making accusations, McCarthy had earned for himself a reputation as the nation's top Communist fighter.

With his newfound fame, McCarthy went on the attack. He made many new charges, but none were backed up with any evidence. When people complained about his methods, McCarthy suggested that maybe they had secrets to hide. Truman dismissed him as a "ballyhoo artist who has to cover up his shortcomings by wild charges." One critic, the political cartoonist Herblock, dubbed McCarthy's tactic of spreading fear and making baseless charges **McCarthyism**. The public, however, seemed willing to believe McCarthy.

Then in the 1950 elections, McCarthy made a special effort to bring about the defeat of Maryland senator Millard Tydings. Tydings was one of President Truman's strongest supporters. It was his committee that had investigated McCarthy's first claims and found them to be false. In the Tydings campaign, McCarthy produced faked photographs showing Tydings talking to the head of the American Communist Party. Tydings was defeated.

McCarthyism quickly spread beyond the Senate. In other branches of government, at universities, in labor unions, and in private businesses, the hunt for Communists geared up. The FBI and even private investigators produced names of people with questionable political views. People who refused to help with investigations were also named.

Officials and employers feared that failure to take action would open them to charges of being "soft on communism," in other words, weak in dealing with it. Across the United States, thousands of people were fired for political reasons.

McCarthy's fall Meanwhile, Senator McCarthy continued his campaign from the Senate. He became increasingly wild in his charges. After winning re-election in 1952, he began to go after fellow Republicans. In 1954 he attacked the U.S. Army, claiming that it was protecting Communists. His Senate hearings were televised, which spread his anti-Communist message widely. Still, the public increasingly came to view McCarthy's tactics as unfair. As you will read, the fear of communism in the United States would remain for some time. But the career of Senator Joseph McCarthy—and McCarthyism—would soon fade away.

READING CHECK **Making Generalizations** What did Joseph McCarthy aim to do?

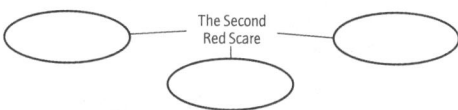

SECTION 3 ASSESSMENT

go.hrw.com
Online Quiz
Keyword: SD7 HP25

Reviewing Ideas, Terms, and People

1. **a. Recall** How did the Communist takeover of China and the Soviet explosion of an atomic bomb affect the United States?
   b. Draw Conclusions Do you think that it was reasonable to conclude from the advance of communism in the late 1940s that communism was "winning"?
   c. Predict How do you think the events of 1949 would affect the U.S. policy toward communism in the future?

2. **a. Identify** Who were the **Hollywood Ten**, and what was their significance in the late 1940s?
   b. Summarize What was the effect of the growing fear of communism at home?
   c. Elaborate Why do you think Julius and Ethel Rosenberg received the death sentence?

3. **a. Define** Write a brief definition of the following term: McCarthyism
   b. Explain Why was Senator McCarthy able to win recognition as a great fighter of communism without actually identifying any Communists?

   c. Elaborate Why do you think some people were unwilling to stand up to McCarthy and his hunt for Communists?

Critical Thinking

4. **Identifying the Main Idea** Copy the chart below and use information from the section to identify details that support the main idea given.

   The Second Red Scare

FOCUS ON WRITING

5. **Expository** Do you think Truman's investigation of federal employees was justified? Write a short essay in which you explain your position on this issue. Use details from the section to support your explanation.

SECTION 4: The Korean War

BEFORE YOU READ

MAIN IDEA

Cold War tensions finally erupted in a shooting war in 1950. The United States confronted a difficult challenge defending freedom halfway around the world.

READING FOCUS

1. What was the situation in Korea before the war began in 1950?
2. What were the circumstances that led to the start of the Korean War?
3. What were the key battles of the Korean War?
4. How did the fighting in the Korean War end?

KEY TERMS AND PEOPLE

38th parallel
Kim Il Sung
Syngman Rhee
police action
Inchon
Panmunjom

TAKING NOTES As you read, take notes on key events of the Korean War. Record your notes in a graphic organizer like the one shown here. You may need to add more rows.

Event	Date

▲ These soldiers became the first ground troops to enter into combat in Korea.

Crisis in Korea

THE INSIDE STORY

How did the Korean War begin for American troops? The soldiers of Task Force Smith—a group of some 400 soldiers shipped to Korea in 1950—never really had time to be afraid. Just days before, they had been a half-equipped and undertrained unit stationed in Japan. Few of their members had any combat experience—a fact that concerned no one since there was no combat for them to take part in.

That changed with the sudden, surprise invasion of South Korea by North Korean forces in late June 1950. As the North Koreans drove deep into South Korean territory, President Truman authorized the use of American ground forces to stop the advance. That meant Task Force Smith would be transferred from Japan to Korea.

General Douglas MacArthur referred to the soldiers as "that arrogant display of strength." Upon their arrival in South Korea, the troops were greeted with cheers. They drove out to meet the enemy, each soldier carrying two days worth of food and ammunition. They expected that the North Koreans would never dare to do battle with the mighty Americans.

Of course, the North Koreans were not impressed. As you will read, they quickly pushed aside the ill-prepared Task Force Smith. The bloody Korean War was on. ◼

THE COLD WAR BEGINS **835**

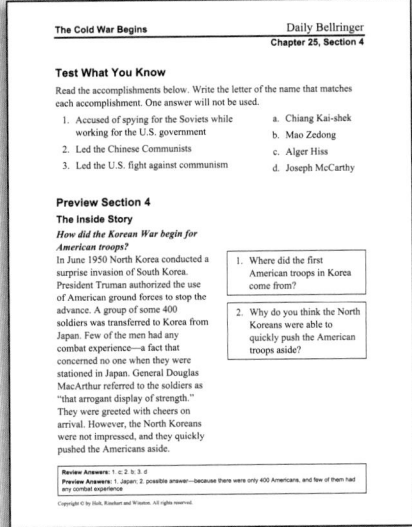

1 What was the situation in Korea before the war began in 1950? *Korea had been divided at the 38th parallel, Soviet Union controlled the north; Americans were in charge of the south.*

Korea Before the War

Recall Which neighboring nations have had a strong influence on Korea? *China, Japan, Russia*

Explain How did North Korea come under Soviet control? *After Japan's surrender, Soviets took control of North Korea.*

Evaluate How do you think the North and South Korean goals of reunifying the country differed? *possible answer—Each wanted its own system of government to prevail.*

🎲 Map Transparency: Korea

Answers

Interpreting Maps 1. *It splits the country in half.* **2.** *China, because China was a Communist country and could support Communist North Korea in fighting South Korea, the U.S., and the UN.*

Reading Check *Korea was occupied by Japan. To accept the Japanese surrender and provide security, the Allies agreed to temporarily divide Korea into halves.*

KOREA

CHINA

Yalu River

NORTH KOREA

40°N

Pyongyang •

Present-day border

Boundary set by Allies, 1945

38th Parallel

Panmunjom

Inchon •

Seoul •

Sea of Japan

Yellow Sea

SOUTH KOREA

0   100   200 Miles

0   100   200 Kilometers
Albers equal-area projection

• Pusan

35°N

125°E   130°E

GEOGRAPHY SKILLS   INTERPRETING MAPS

1. Location Why was the 38th parallel chosen as a dividing line?

2. Place What nation shares a border with North Korea, besides South Korea? Why is this significant?

See **Skills Handbook**, p. H20

THE IMPACT TODAY

Government

Today Kim Il Sung's son, Kim Jong Il, is the leader of North Korea. North Korea remains a Communist country, while South Korea has a democratic government.

Korea before the War

The 600-mile-long Korean Peninsula lies between China and Japan. The peninsula is also close to Russia, which in 1950 was part of the Soviet Union. China, Japan, and Russia have long held a strong influence over the Korean people. After 1905 Korea came under the control of the Japanese. Japan dominated and occupied the peninsula.

Then in 1945 the Allies defeated the Japanese in World War II. As you have read, the Allies had agreed to divide control of the conquered Germany among several Allied nations. A similar sort of agreement was reached regarding Japanese-occupied Korea. At the Yalta Conference in February 1945, the Allies agreed that Korea should be free following the war. For purposes of accepting the Japanese surrender and providing postwar security in

Korea, however, the Allies also agreed to temporarily divide Korea into northern and southern parts. The dividing line was to be the parallel at 38° north latitude. The Soviet Union would control Korea north of the **38th parallel**. South of it, the Americans would be in charge. In fact, the Soviets played virtually no role in the military defeat of Japan. Stalin did not declare war on Japan until after the dropping of the first atomic bomb at Hiroshima. Nevertheless, after the Japanese surrender, the Soviets took control of North Korea.

The presence of the Soviets and Americans in Korea was meant to be temporary. As in Germany, however, the start of the Cold War led to problems. In North Korea, the Soviet Union tried to establish a Communist system of government. The North called itself the Democratic People's Republic of Korea. Its first leader was **Kim Il Sung**, who sought to reunify North and South Korea under Communist control.

In South Korea, the United States promoted a democratic system. South Korea, known as the Republic of Korea, was led by president **Syngman Rhee**. Although an elected leader, Rhee held dictatorial control over South Korea. Like Kim Il Sung, he hoped the two halves of Korea would be reunified.

Both the North and the South held the goal of bringing together the two Korean halves into one whole, but they had different ideas of how best to reunify the country. Efforts toward unification continued in the late 1940s. In the end, however, these efforts led to war.

READING CHECK   **Summarizing** How did the status of Korea prior to June 1950 lead to its division into northern and southern halves?

The Start of the Korean War

In the dark, early hours of June 25, 1950, more than 100,000 North Korean troops crossed the 38th parallel and invaded South Korea. Kim Il Sung had ordered the invasion, hoping to reunify all of Korea under his rule.

The troops carried Soviet-made weapons and drove Soviet-made tanks. In the recent past, some border skirmishes had occurred between North and South Korean troops, but this was different. From the outset it was clear that this was a major attack. The future of South Korea was at stake.

Skills Focus: Sequencing

Reading Skill
The Korean War Starts

1. Draw the following sequence chart for students to see. Omit the italicized answers. Have students work in mixed-ability pairs to copy and complete the chart, filling in the events that led up to the commitment of U.S. troops and UN involvement in the Korean War.

2. Have volunteers share their answers with the class. Complete the master chart for students

to see. Have students correct their own work and retain the chart as a study tool.

LS Interpersonal, Visual-Spatial

📘 Alternative Assessment Handbook, Rubric 13: Graphic Organizers

🎲 Graphic Organizer Transparencies

Allies agree that Korea should be divided
↓
Communist government in North Korea; democratic system in South Korea
↓
North Korea builds up forces along the 38th parallel
↓
United States and Soviet Union withdraw their troops
↓
North Korea invades South Korea

The attack came as a surprise to most leaders in the United States. Tensions on the peninsula had been high, and some observers had noticed a buildup of North Korean forces along the 38th parallel. Still, nobody in the Truman administration had anticipated serious fighting there. In fact, American troops stationed in South Korea since the end of the war had recently completed their withdrawal from the country. This had been part of a large-scale decrease in the size of U.S. armed forces that had been taking place in recent years. Because of this, the United States was not well prepared to fight in Korea. Nevertheless, the decision to fight was made quickly.

The role of the United States In President Truman's mind, South Korea was where the United States had to take a stand against Communist aggression. South Korea was a small country, unable to defend itself against an enemy supported by the Soviet Union or Communist China. Failure to defend South Korea might send a signal to other nations that the United States would not help defend their freedom. It was even feared that a failure to act could lead to a wider war. In a message to Congress about the situation in Korea, Truman said:

HISTORY'S VOICES

❝For ourselves, we seek no territory or domination over others . . . We are concerned with advancing our prosperity and our well-being as a Nation, but we know that our future is inseparably joined with the future of other free peoples.❞

—Harry S Truman, July 1950

Truman's viewpoint was shared by many others, including World War II hero General Dwight D. Eisenhower. "We'll have a dozen Koreas soon," Eisenhower declared, "if we don't take a firm stand."

Meanwhile, on the battlefield, the situation was getting more serious by the hour. Within days of the invasion, the North Korean force had pushed back the South Korean defenses and captured the capital city of Seoul. Truman realized something had to be done, and it had to be done soon. He ordered American naval and air forces to support South Korean ground troops. Then he asked the United Nations to approve the use of force to stop the North Korean invasion.

The role of the UN The United Nations Security Council voted unanimously in favor of the use of force. Under the UN rules, five key countries held the power to veto UN Security Council decisions. That is, those five countries could single-handedly vote against a measure and defeat it.

One of the countries holding a veto was the Soviet Union. However, at the time of the UN vote on North Korea, the Soviet representative was absent, in protest over the UN's admission of Nationalist China. Therefore, the soviet representative was not there to veto the use of force against North Korea.

This twist, however, would not be enough to save the South Koreans. It soon became clear that American ground troops were needed. This was a step Truman had been reluctant to take. He feared that sending ground troops might trigger the start of another world war. It soon became clear, however, that there was no other way to stop the North Korean onslaught. On June 30 Truman ordered American ground troops into action.

The military force sent to Korea would be a United Nations force. Technically, the whole effort was referred to as a UN **police action**. The United States never declared war. Its commander was to be none other than General Douglas MacArthur. American soldiers made up the largest part of the force. Some 15 other nations contributed a total of 40,000 troops. This combined force then joined what was left of the South Korean military in a desperate fight to save the country.

READING CHECK **Sequencing** What events occurred at the beginning of the war in Korea?

Key Battles of the Korean War

American soldiers had entered the battle in South Korea. Unfortunately, North Korean troops greatly outnumbered and outgunned South Korea's defenders. Fighting conditions were miserable. Summer heat and heavy rains sapped what little strength the soldiers had after days of desperate combat.

Throughout the month of July, the news from Korea was discouraging. By the end of the month, the North Koreans had pushed UN

THE COLD WAR BEGINS **837**

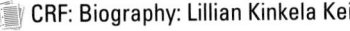
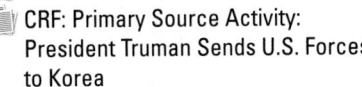

❸ What were the key battles of the Korean War? *Pusan; Inchon*

Key Battles of the Korean War

Recall Why was the Inchon landing important? *changed the course of the war; UN forces quickly recaptured Seoul*

Identify Cause and Effect What happened as a result of MacArthur's decision to try to take all of North Korea? *a huge force of 260,000 Chinese troops poured across the border, pushing the UN forces back south of Seoul*

Evaluate Why was it important to hold the port of Pusan? *possible answer—to keep a presence in South Korea; give UN forces a port*

Info to Know

Korea's Leaders Syngman Rhee was in his seventies when he became president of South Korea. A strong anti-Communist and advocate of Korean independence, Rhee had spent more than 30 years in the United States as a political exile. Kim Il Sung was in his mid-thirties when he became premier of Communist North Korea. As a guerrilla fighter in the 1930s, he had opposed the Japanese occupation of Korea. Kim had received training in the Soviet Union and was the leader of a special Korean unit of the Soviet army in World War II.

---

forces all the way to the southeastern tip of South Korea. Here the UN forces formed a line around the port city of Pusan. This 130-mile-long line, soldiers were told, needed to be held at all costs.

The Inchon landing In fact, UN forces held the port of Pusan. By early September, the Communist attack had stalled. Meanwhile, thousands of UN troops and tons of equipment were unloading at Pusan daily. Now MacArthur wanted to go on the offensive.

MacArthur's plan was daring and brilliant. It called for UN forces to make an amphibious landing behind North Korean lines at the port city of **Inchon**, on South Korea's western coast. Inchon was an unlikely place for such an assault. Its natural features made an attack by sea very risky. Chief among these features were the extremely high tides in Inchon's waters.

To MacArthur, the disadvantages of attacking at Inchon only meant that the North Koreans would not expect it. Surprise would be the key to his success. "We shall land at Inchon," he promised, "and I shall crush them."

MacArthur's plan worked beautifully. Within 24 hours of the September 15 invasion at Inchon, a 70,000-troop force had secured a solid landing and regained some ground. See the History Close-Up feature opposite to learn more about the Inchon landing.

North Korea on the run The Inchon landing helped bring about an amazing change in fortunes in South Korea. UN forces quickly moved out from Inchon to recapture Seoul. The North Koreans had stretched themselves too thin chasing the UN forces all the way south to Pusan. They were powerless to stop the force moving out of Inchon.

Meanwhile, the UN launched another offensive from Pusan. This attack broke through the North Korean line and started marching northward. Huge numbers of North Korean troops were destroyed or forced to surrender.

The turnaround was startling. The UN had been facing defeat in August. Only a few months later, by October 1, all of South Korea was back in UN hands.

American leaders now faced the question of whether to stop at the 38th parallel. North Korea's forces were in tatters. MacArthur favored taking all of North Korea. One concern

about this plan, however, was the possibility that the Chinese or Soviets might come to the defense of North Korea. A top Chinese official issued just such a warning. But the Americans decided the risk was worth taking. Truman also supported the plan.

Moving into North Korea continued to seem like a good idea through the days of October and November. UN forces made solid progress. There were some reports of Chinese troops filtering into North Korea and joining the battle. By the end of November, however, MacArthur was preparing for a major push. He said his new plan would end the Korean War. Then just as the general's plan was getting under way, it happened: A huge force of 260,000 Chinese troops poured across the Yalu River, which was North Korea's border with China. Again there had been an unexpected turnaround, but this time it favored the North Koreans.

UN forces retreat With the Chinese attack, MacArthur's promise of a quick victory disappeared. In fact, the UN forces suddenly faced defeat. According to MacArthur, the size of the Chinese force was simply too large. Just as in the early days of the war, UN forces were soon in full retreat.

In the case of the 8th Army, this retreat went all the way back south of Seoul. It was the longest such fallback in U.S. military history. To make matters worse, the brutal Korean winter had arrived. Temperatures in some areas dropped well below 0°F. In places such as the Chosin Reservoir, American soldiers suffered terribly under the wintry conditions.

MacArthur is fired As 1951 began, the situation in Korea once again seemed dire for the Americans and the UN. In MacArthur's view, the UN faced a choice between defeat by the Chinese or a major war with them. He called for expanding the war by bombing the Chinese mainland and bringing Nationalist Chinese forces into the fighting. He even called for the use of atomic weapons.

MacArthur, as it turned out, was wrong. In January 1951, a force led by Lieutenant General Matthew Ridgway not only stopped the Chinese onslaught but actually went on the offensive. By April 1951 Ridgway's men had pushed the Chinese back to the 38th parallel.

Collaborative Learning

At Level

Settling the North Korean Conflict

1. Organize students into small groups. Have students review the information in the text about MacArthur's plan for ending the war in Korea. Remind students that MacArthur was tremendously popular and well respected as a military leader.

2. Have each group consider the options available to the UN for ending the Korean conflict, including the use of atomic bombs. Have each group decide which option would be best for all concerned: the North and

South Koreans, the Chinese, the Soviets, and UN forces. Have students prepare a written defense of their choice.

3. Have volunteers from each group conduct a debate on this issue.

4. At the conclusion of the debate, have students explain which of the arguments presented might lead to peace in Asia. **LS Interpersonal**

📃 Alternative Assessment Handbook, Rubrics 10: Debates; and 11: Discussions

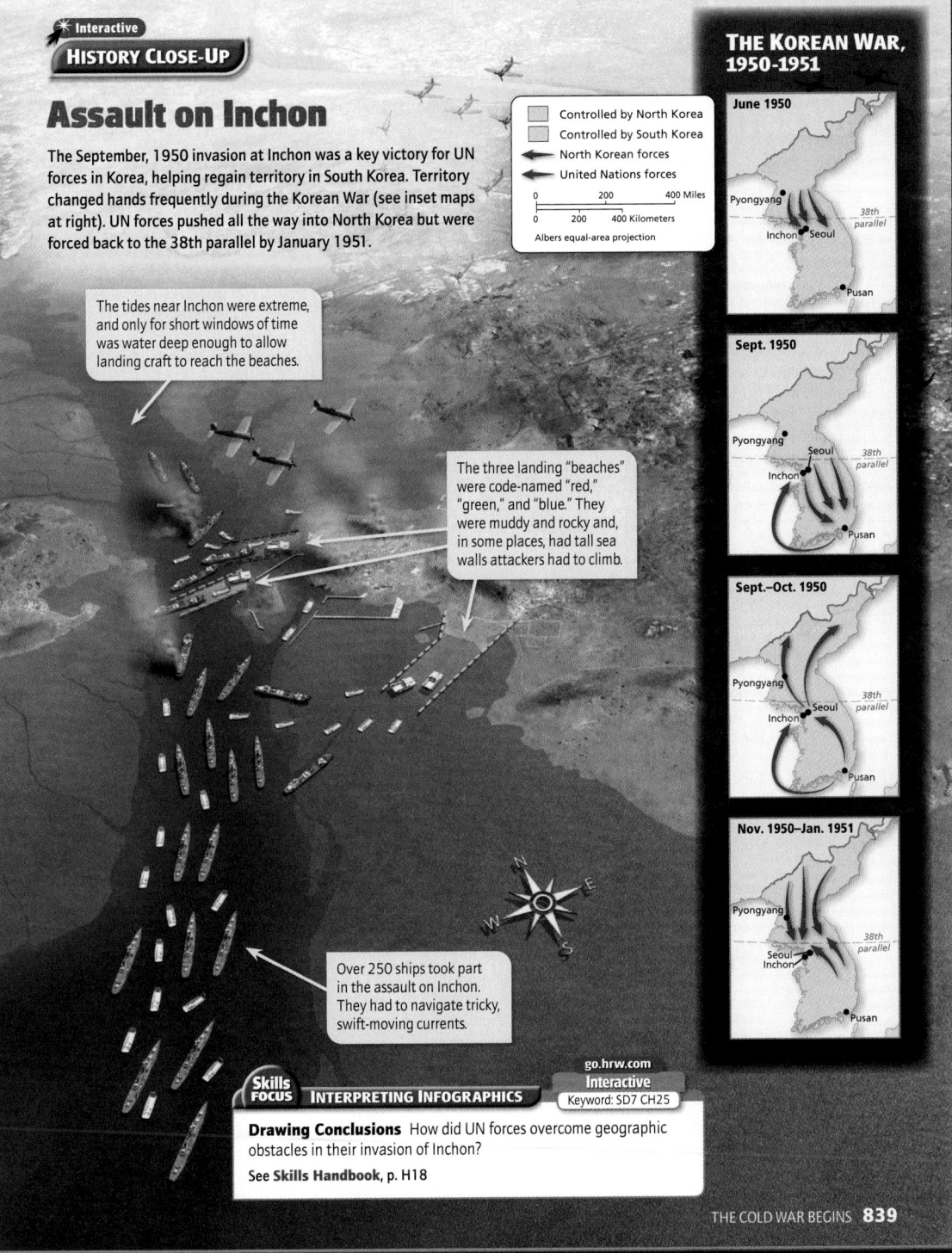

Assault on Inchon

The September, 1950 invasion at Inchon was a key victory for UN forces in Korea, helping regain territory in South Korea. Territory changed hands frequently during the Korean War (see inset maps at right). UN forces pushed all the way into North Korea but were forced back to the 38th parallel by January 1951.

The tides near Inchon were extreme, and only for short windows of time was water deep enough to allow landing craft to reach the beaches.

The three landing "beaches" were code-named "red," "green," and "blue." They were muddy and rocky and, in some places, had tall sea walls attackers had to climb.

Over 250 ships took part in the assault on Inchon. They had to navigate tricky, swift-moving currents.

THE KOREAN WAR, 1950-1951

Controlled by North Korea
Controlled by South Korea
North Korean forces
United Nations forces

0   200   400 Miles
0   200   400 Kilometers
Albers equal-area projection

June 1950

Pyongyang
Inchon Seoul
38th parallel
Pusan

Sept. 1950

Pyongyang
Seoul
38th parallel
Inchon
Pusan

Sept.–Oct. 1950

Pyongyang
Seoul
38th parallel
Inchon
Pusan

Nov. 1950–Jan. 1951

Pyongyang
38th parallel
Seoul
Inchon
Pusan

Skills FOCUS
INTERPRETING INFOGRAPHICS

go.hrw.com
Interactive
Keyword: SD7 CH25

Drawing Conclusions How did UN forces overcome geographic obstacles in their invasion of Inchon?

See Skills Handbook, p. H18

THE COLD WAR BEGINS **839**

Primary Source

"There is a right kind and a wrong kind of victory . . . The kind of victory (MacArthur) had in mind—victory by the bombing of Chinese cities, victory by . . . expanding the conflict to all of China—would have been the wrong kind of victory."

— Harry S Truman

Memoirs II, Years of Trial and Hope

Info to Know

The Korean War The Korean War is sometimes referred to as "the forgotten war." Although the war ended in 1953, the Korean War Veterans Memorial in Washington, D.C., was not dedicated until 1995.

✳ **Interactive History Close-Up:**
Korean Wars

Teaching Tip

Remind students that the U.S. Congress, not the president, has the power to declare war. The Korean War was not an official U.S. war; it was a UN police action. It was fought without a formal U.S. declaration of war.

Skills Focus: Interpreting Movement Maps

At Level

Social Studies Skill
Troop Movement

1. Use a map of the world to show students the location of Korean Peninsula in relation to the United States, China, and the former Soviet Union.

2. Have students examine the movement maps on this page. Direct their attention to the UN troop movement shown in the third map. Review reasons why troops retreated to Pusan, and then circled around to Inchon.

3. Have students calculate how far North Korean and Allied forces traveled during the war. Have students share their calculations. Then guide students in a review of the purpose of movement maps. Have students explain why it is helpful to be able to trace routes and troop movements as they study history.

LS **Visual-Spatial, Logical-Mathematical**

📖 Alternative Assessment Handbook, Rubric 21: Map Reading

Answers

Interpreting Infographics *they timed their assault for when the tide was highest; climbed tall sea walls*

839

Reading Focus

Key Battles of the Korean War

Describe What was the public reaction when President Truman fired General MacArthur? *outrage*

Evaluate Do you think President Truman made the right decision when he fired MacArthur? *possible answers—Yes, MacArthur left the president no choice. No, a reasonable solution could have been found that would have been less humiliating for the general and allowed both men to emerge as victors.*

Reading Focus

4 How did the fighting in the Korean War end? *negotiations led to armistice signed on July 27, 1953*

Fighting Ends in Korea

Summarize Why did negotiations for peace drag on for so long? *disputes over boundary lines; issue of prisoners of war; other continued unresolved arguments*

Evaluate What did the Korean War accomplish? *possible answers—South Koreans maintained their freedom; U.S. showed it would send troops when needed*

Answers

Faces of History *family history, education, experience in World War I*

Reading Check *North Korea invaded South Korea; North Korea captured Seoul; UN troops sent to South Korea; UN forces defeat North Korea at Inchon, recapture Seoul; Chinese troops aid North Korea, UN forces stop the Chinese and push North Koreans back to the 38th parallel*

840

FACES OF HISTORY

Douglas MACARTHUR
1880–1964

Born to a Civil War veteran who became a high-ranking army officer and raised on a series of military bases across the United States, Douglas MacArthur naturally chose a career in the military. He wrote in his memoirs, "My first memory was the sound of bugles." In 1903 he graduated first in his class at the U.S. military academy at West Point. During World War I he fought in France, where he was promoted to the rank of brigadier general. Known for his bravery and daring on the battlefield, he became the most decorated American soldier of World War I.

As supreme Allied commander in occupied Japan, MacArthur made one of his most important contributions to history—he helped Japan rebuild itself as a democratic nation. After President Truman removed him from command in the Korean War, MacArthur returned home. He died in 1964, still admired for his World War II victories and his leadership in occupied Japan.

Analyze What experiences prepared MacArthur for his leadership roles during World War II and after?

Ridgway's success called into question MacArthur's harsh warnings about the need to expand the war. It especially called into question MacArthur's recommendation to use atomic weapons. Truman began to believe that peace was possible without losing South Korea or triggering a larger war with China or even the Soviets.

MacArthur was dismayed by Truman's attitude. He wanted to see communism defeated in Asia even if meant expanding the <u>scope</u> of the war. Increasingly, he made public statements that challenged the authority of the president. He made threats against the Chinese government even as American officials were exploring ways to stop the fighting in Korea.

Truman faced a serious challenge. To many Americans, MacArthur was a major hero of World War II. They supported his goal of taking the war to the Chinese. Truman, though, wanted to avoid widening the war. Further, he could not allow a general to disobey the president and make his own policy. Truman decided he had to fire MacArthur.

The American public swiftly reacted to the MacArthur firing. While a few leaders supported the president's action, many Americans were outraged. "The American nation has never

ACADEMIC VOCABULARY
scope extent or size

840 CHAPTER 25

---

been in a greater danger," warned the *Chicago Tribune.* "It is led by a fool who is surrounded by knaves."

This anger only grew when MacArthur appeared before Congress for a dramatic farewell address. Some 30 million Americans watched his speech on television.

HISTORY'S VOICES

❝In war, there is no substitute for victory. There are some who for varying reasons would appease Red China. They are blind to history's clear lesson, for history teaches with unmistakable emphasis that appeasement but begets new and bloodier war.❞

—General Douglas MacArthur, April 19, 1951

MacArthur closed with the emotional words, "Old soldiers never die; they just fade away." Americans everywhere wept and cheered for their World War II hero.

READING CHECK **Sequencing** What was the sequence of the fighting in Korea from the start of the war through April 1951?

Fighting Ends in Korea

Before long, the uproar over the MacArthur firing died down. Congress investigated the matter. The nation's leading military officers testified that Truman had been right in firing MacArthur.

Meanwhile, in July 1951, the United States entered into peace talks to end the fighting. By this point, 80,000 Americans had been wounded and nearly 14,000 were dead. South Korea and other UN forces had also suffered greatly. So had the Chinese and North Koreans.

Unsuccessful negotiations for peace

One major obstacle during the peace talks was the location of the boundary between North Korea and South Korea. UN forces by that point had actually managed to fight a short distance north of the 38th parallel. The UN wanted the boundary to be there. But the Communists insisted on setting the boundary precisely at the 38th parallel. This dispute helped break off negotiations at the end of the summer.

Meanwhile, the two military forces strengthened their positions. Now and then one side or the other would launch an attack. The goal was not to gain territory but to improve position.

Skills Focus: Drawing Conclusions
At Level

Reading Skill
The Costs of the Korean War

1. Have each student make a list of the gains and losses for the participants in the Korean War. In their lists, have students include the human cost for all who were involved. Have students share their lists with the class.

2. Guide students in a discussion of the outcome of the war. Remind students that after the war, the border between North and South Korea remained at the 38th parallel. Ask: What did the war change, if anything?

3. Have each student write a one-page essay about the Korean War explaining whether or not they believe the gains of the war made it worth the losses. In their conclusions, have students suggest alternative actions that might have been taken to resolve the conflict.

4. Ask volunteers to read their essays to the class. **LS** **Verbal-Linguistic, Logical-Mathematical**

Alternative Assessment Handbook, Rubric 37: Writing Assignments

Examples of such actions were the battles of Bloody Ridge and Heartbreak Ridge. These were fought in the late summer and early fall of 1951. Both battles followed a similar pattern: The two forces took turns winning, then losing, key hilltops. Though little was gained, losses were heavy. In these and other battles during this time, the UN suffered 40,000 casualties.

Negotiations resumed in October but again hit a major snag. This time the issue was prisoners of war. Hoping that the UN would continue to fight for unification, Syngman Rhee refused to send North Korean or Chinese prisoners back to Communist countries. This hindered the peace negotiations. Few major moves were happening on the battlefield, but the steady shelling and sniping was a deadly threat.

All of 1952 passed in a similar way. Negotiators meeting in the town of **Panmunjom** (PAHN-MOOHN-JAWM) argued over details of a peace agreement. At the same time, small-scale fighting claimed thousands of casualties.

Events of 1953 Meanwhile, 1952 was a presidential election year in the United States. American voters elected the World War II hero Dwight D. Eisenhower. Eisenhower would be inaugurated in January 1953. You will read more about Eisenhower's presidency in the next chapter.

In his campaign, Eisenhower had promised to end the Korean War. Once in office, he set about achieving this goal. At the same time, the Communists also seemed to want the war to end. Negotiators at Panmunjom worked toward agreement.

Though the end of the conflict was coming, the fighting remained deadly. Indeed, the Communists seemed to step up the fighting in the hope of gaining a last-minute advantage. During the final two months, UN forces suffered 57,000 casualties. The Communists lost 100,000. Finally, however, the guns fell silent on July 27. On that day, negotiators reached an armistice agreement.

The Korean War had left the map of Korea looking much as it had in early 1950, before the war began. The North Koreans had lost only a small amount of territory. The human costs, however, were much more significant. Some 37,000 American soldiers had died. Almost 60,000 UN troops from other countries were killed. Communist forces suffered some 2 million casualties. Perhaps as many as 3 million North and South Korean civilians were killed or injured.

READING CHECK **Sequencing** What events helped bring about the end of the fighting in the Korean War?

SECTION 4 ASSESSMENT

go.hrw.com
Online Quiz
Keyword: SD7 HP25

Reviewing Ideas, Terms, and People

1. **a. Identify** Identify the significance of the following term: 38th parallel
   b. Explain Why were there two different views about the way in which Korea might be reunified?

2. **a. Describe** What were the events that started the Korean War?
   b. Draw Conclusions Why did Truman believe it was important to defend a small country such as South Korea?
   c. Elaborate Why do you think the fighting in Korea was referred to as a **police action**?

3. **a. Recall** What was the significance of **Inchon** in the war?
   b. Make Generalizations How would you describe the major pattern of fighting in the first year of the Korean War?
   c. Rate Consider the arguments of both MacArthur and Truman about the possibility of a wider war with China. Which argument do you think was stronger? Explain.

4. **a. Identify** What is the significance of **Panmunjom**?

   b. Make Generalizations What happened to the kind of fighting that took place in the final phase of the war?
   c. Evaluate Considering the cost of the war and what was gained, do you think the United States was right to fight in Korea? Explain.

Critical Thinking

5. **Sequencing** Copy the chart below and use information from the section to sequence the events following the information provided.

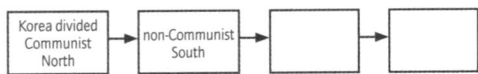

FOCUS ON WRITING

6. **Expository** Write a paragraph in which you explain the events that led to the beginning of the Korean War.

THE COLD WAR BEGINS **841**

Section 4 Assessment Answers

1. **a.** dividing line of Korea
   b. Soviets (Communists) controlled the north; U.S. (democracy) controlled the south.

2. **a.** North Korea invaded South Korea
   b. to take a stand against Communist aggression
   c. U.S. Congress did not issue declaration of war; was a UN action, not U.S.

3. **a.** key victory that allowed UN forces to control territory in South Korea
   b. back and forth with no clear winner
   c. possible answers—Truman's, he did not

   want to start a war; MacArthur's, his plan would have stopped the Chinese

4. **a.** Korean town where peace negotiations took place
   b. It became more deadly.
   c. possible answers—yes, the U.S. had to take a stand against communism; no, border remained the same, no one won

5. North invades South, UN becomes involved

6. possible answer—Korea divided, U.S. and Soviet forces leave, North invades South

---

Direct Teach

The Impact Today
North Korea
In January 2002, President George W. Bush described North Korea as "a regime arming with missiles and weapons of mass destruction, while starving its citizens." He said the nation was part of "an axis of evil, arming to threaten the peace of the world . . ."

Review & Assess

Close
Have students summarize the events of the Korean War and their relation to the Cold War.

Review
Online Quiz, Section 4
Daily Test Practice Transparency

Assess
SE Section 4 Assessment
Progress Assessment: Section 4 Quiz
Alternative Assessment Handbook

Reteach
Interactive Reader and Study Guide, Section 4
Interactive Skills Tutor CD-ROM

Answers

Reading Check *1951 peace talks begin; negotiations stall and fighting continues; Eisenhower elected; negotiations begin again; armistice signed in July 1953*

841

The Cold War at Home

Word Help

subversive revolutionary

Analyzing Primary Sources

Activity Document 1 is a cartoon by Herblock, as *Washington Post* cartoonist Herbert Block signed his work. Have students locate several of Herblock's cartoons on the Internet. Many Web sites display Herblock's cartoons and can easily be located by using the search terms "Herblock" and "political cartoons." Then conduct a discussion of the ways in which Herbert Block portrayed Cold War hysteria and the people who were responsible for fanning its flames, such as Joseph McCarthy and Richard Nixon.

Primary Source

In 1947, future president Ronald Reagan was called before the House Un-American Activities Committee. As president of the Screen Actors Guild, Reagan responded to accusations of Communist activities: "In opposing [Communists], the best thing to do is make democracy work . . . As a citizen, I would hesitate to see any political party outlawed on the basis of its political ideology . . . I do not believe the Communists have ever at any time been able to use the motion picture screen as a sounding board for their philosophy or ideology."

— Ronald Reagan

Testimony to House Un-American Activities Committee, October 23, 1947

The Cold War at Home

Historical Context The documents below provide different perspectives on the domestic impact of the Cold War.

Task Examine the documents and answer the questions that follow. Then you will be asked to write an essay about the domestic impact of the Cold War, using facts from the documents and from the chapter to support the position you take in your thesis statement.

DOCUMENT 1

In the aftermath of World War II, the House Un-American Activities Committee, or HUAC, investigated possible Communist subversion everywhere, from schools to labor unions to the entertainment industry. The political cartoon below was published in the *Washington Post* in 1947.

"IT'S OKAY—WE'RE HUNTING COMMUNISTS"
from *The Herblock Book* (Beacon Press, 1952)

DOCUMENT 2

In 1947 President Truman signed Executive Order 9835 in order to ban Communists and Fascists from federal employment. The order outlined procedures for investigating the background of federal employees. Although no actual espionage was discovered among government workers, many people were investigated in the years following Executive Order 9835. Below is an excerpt of the order.

"Part I
INVESTIGATION OF APPLICANTS
There shall be a loyalty investigation of every person entering the civilian employment of any department or agency of the executive branch of the Federal Government. . . .

Part V
STANDARDS [for Employment]
Activities and associations of an applicant or employee which may be considered in connection with the determination of disloyalty may include one or more of the following:
  Membership in, affiliation with or sympathetic association with any foreign or domestic organization, association, movement, group or combination of persons, designated by the Attorney General as totalitarian, fascist, communist, or subversive, or as having adopted a policy of advocating or approving the commission of acts of force or violence to deny other persons their rights under the Constitution of the United States, or as seeking to alter the form of government of the United States by unconstitutional means . . ."

Skills Focus: Analyzing Primary Sources   At Level

Reading Like a Historian Skill
First Amendment Rights

1. Remind students that the First Amendment to the United States Constitution guarantees freedom of speech and freedom of assembly. Guide the class in a discussion of this and other Constitutional rights that were sometimes trampled during the Cold War.

2. Have each student write a brief essay exploring the implications of Document 2, using the following questions as a guide: Does Executive Order 9835 appear to violate any Constitutional rights? Should the government be able to single out members of any particular group either for discrimination or special treatment? Do you agree with the terms of Executive Order 9835?

3. Have volunteers read their essays to the class.
   LS Logical-Mathematical

   Alternative Assessment Handbook, Rubric 37: Writing Assignments

DOCUMENT 3

This photograph shows a man building a bomb shelter in the backyard of a private home in 1951. These reinforced underground rooms were built for protection in the event of an atomic attack. During the 1950s and 1960s, bomb shelters became increasingly popular as Americans' fears of nuclear war grew.

Info to Know

Bomb Shelters In 1959, construction began on a bomb shelter that could house all 535 members of the U.S. Congress, along with their top aides, in the event of a nuclear attack. The project took two and a half years to finish at an estimated cost of $86 million. The West Virginia bunker contained dormitories, a medical clinic, a power plant, a water purification plant, and a television studio. Although the site was kept ready for decades, it was never used.

Primary Source

The 1951 short film *Duck and Cover* featured Bert the Turtle, who taught children what to do in case an atomic bomb fell—"duck and cover." The film can easily be located on the Internet by searching for "Bert the Turtle." Download the film and view it with the class.

Skills FOCUS READING LIKE A HISTORIAN

1. a. Describe Refer to Document 1. What does the car symbolize in this political cartoon?
b. Identify What is happening to the people who are in the car's path?
c. Analyze What point of view does this cartoon present about the House Un-American Activities Committee?

2. a. Identify Refer to Document 2. Name three activities that would exclude a person from working for the federal government in 1947.
b. Interpret Why might President Truman have considered this executive order necessary?

3. a. Identify Refer to Document 3. When finished, how would this structure protect people from a bomb?
b. Analyze What does this photograph suggest about the impact of the Cold War on American society?

4. Document-Based Essay Question Consider the question below and form a thesis statement. Using examples from Documents 1, 2, and 3, create an outline and write a short essay supporting your position.
How did the Cold War affect domestic policy and American society?

See *Skills Handbook,* pp. H28–H29, H30

THE COLD WAR BEGINS **843**

Differentiating Instruction

Below Level

Learners Having Difficulty

1. Divide the class into groups of four or five students. Tell students that in 1950, many Americans were concerned about safety in case of a war with the Soviet Union. Have each group draw plans for a bomb shelter that a family might have used in the 1950s.

2. Next, have each group make a list of supplies that would be needed in the bomb shelter. Remind students that they would need food, water, and medical supplies to last for at

least several days, and that they would not have electricity.

3. Have volunteers from each group share its plans and lists with the rest of the class.

4. Guide the class in a discussion of bomb shelters. Ask students if they believe bomb shelters are still necessary. Why or why not?
LS Interpersonal, Visual-Spatial

Answers

Reading Like a Historian 1. a. *the House Un-American Activities Committee* **b.** *They are being run over.* **c.** *that it recklessly disregards people's lives;* **2. a.** *possible answer—affiliation with the Communist Party; advocating violence against other Americans; advocating the violent overthrow of the U.S. government;* **b.** *because of fear that Communists and subversives were infiltrating the government;* **3. a.** *possible answer—might protect against falling debris;* **b.** *possible answer—made Americans terrified of prospect of atomic war;* **4.** *Answers will vary, but students' essays may include fear of communism; House Un-American Activities Committee; bomb shelters; McCarthyism; Smith Act; McCarran Act; and spy cases.*

Answers

Visual Summary

Review and Inquiry Organize the class into groups of three students. Have students prepare a one-minute radio announcement for each bulleted item. Have volunteers present their radio announcements.

🔲 Quick Facts Transparency: The Cold War Begins

Reviewing Key Terms and People

1. e.
2. k.
3. b.
4. h.
5. a.
6. c.
7. d.
8. f.
9. j.
10. g.
11. i.

Comprehension and Critical Thinking

12. a. Iron Curtain
   b. Americans hostile to communism and feared its spread; disputes over military strategy in World War II; Soviet Union felt threatened that the U.S. created atomic bomb
   c. possible answers—U.S. postwar economy grew; created strong ties and alliances between U.S. and Western Europe

13. a. Veterans returned from war and needed to find jobs and restart lives; minorities continued struggle for equal rights.
   b. no one wanted another war like World War II; great interest in helping countries improve economically and democratically
   c. economic stability at home and abroad

14. a. fear of communism within the United States
   b. hearings and investigations by House Un-American Activities

Visual Summary: The Cold War Begins

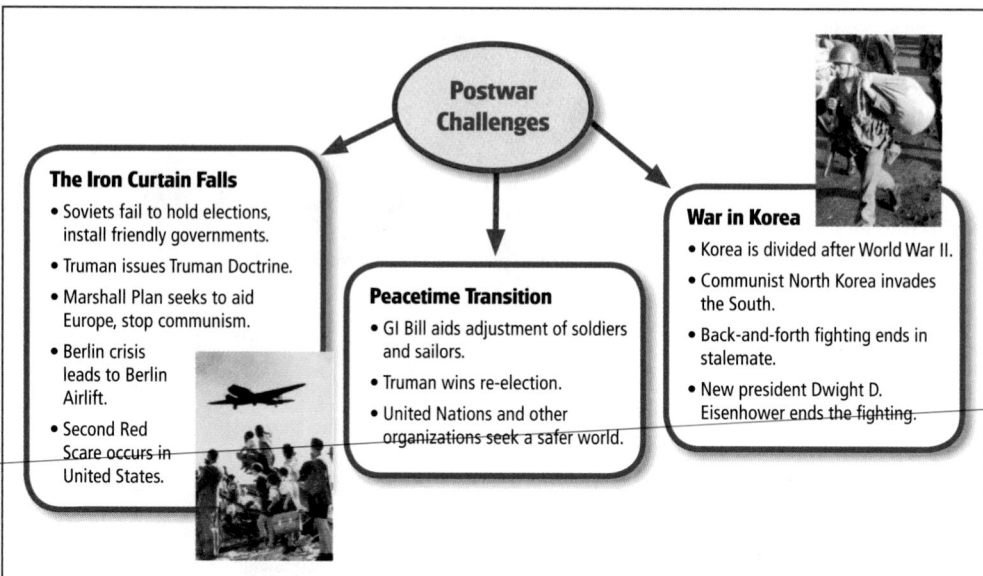

Postwar Challenges

The Iron Curtain Falls
- Soviets fail to hold elections, install friendly governments.
- Truman issues Truman Doctrine.
- Marshall Plan seeks to aid Europe, stop communism.
- Berlin crisis leads to Berlin Airlift.
- Second Red Scare occurs in United States.

Peacetime Transition
- GI Bill aids adjustment of soldiers and sailors.
- Truman wins re-election.
- United Nations and other organizations seek a safer world.

War in Korea
- Korea is divided after World War II.
- Communist North Korea invades the South.
- Back-and-forth fighting ends in stalemate.
- New president Dwight D. Eisenhower ends the fighting.

Reviewing Key Terms and People

Identify the correct term or person from the chapter that best fits each of the following descriptions.

1. Truman policy for limiting spread of communism
2. Alliance formed after World War II
3. Postwar rise in U.S. birthrate
4. Effort to help rebuild Europe after World War II
5. Helped many former soldiers get a college education, start a business, or buy a home
6. Term for method of making reckless attacks on people's reputations
7. A major turning point of the Korean War occurred here
8. Communist leader in China
9. Group blacklisted for refusing to help in effort to uncover Communists
10. Accused of spying against the United States
11. The period of high tension between the United States and Soviet Union

a. GI Bill
b. baby boom
c. McCarthyism
d. Inchon
e. containment
f. Mao Zedong
g. Alger Hiss
h. Marshall Plan
i. Cold War
j. Hollywood Ten
k. NATO

Committee, prosecution and conviction of Hollywood Ten, creation of blacklists in entertainment industry, Smith Act, McCarran Act, prosecution and conviction of Alger Hiss, conviction and execution of Rosenbergs, McCarthy Senate hearings
   c. similar—fear of spread of communism from Russia; different—first Red Scare died down with no lasting or serious effects while second one helped fuel the fight in Korea and McCarthyism in America

15. a. Cold War tension between U.S. and Soviet Union; North Korean invasion
   b. North Korea invaded South Korea; North Korea captured Seoul; UN troops sent to defend South Korea; UN forces defeated North Korea at Inchon, recaptured Seoul; Chinese troops aided North Korea; UN forces pushed the North Koreans back
   c. possible answers—yes, showed that Communist aggression would not be tolerated; no, communism still existed

History's Impact video program

Review the video to answer the closing question: How did the Cold War and the increase in American defense spending affect life during the 1950s?

Comprehension and Critical Thinking

SECTION 1 *(pp. 816–822)*

12. a. Identify What was the term that described the dividing line between Communist Eastern Europe and non-Communist Western Europe?

b. Sequence What were the events that led up to and marked the beginning phases of the Cold War?

c. Rate What do you think was the most important benefit of the Marshall Plan? Explain your answer.

SECTION 2 *(pp. 823–828)*

13. a. Describe What difficult adjustments faced the people of the United States after the war?

b. Draw Conclusions Why do you think there was so much interest after the war in creating organizations to improve conditions for people in the United States and around the world?

c. Elaborate What was the common idea behind the GI Bill and programs such as the International Monetary Fund and the World Bank established after World War II?

SECTION 3 *(pp. 829–834)*

14. a. Recall What was the second Red Scare?

b. Sequence Identify the sequence of events discussed in the section that contributed to the rising Red Scare.

c. Evaluate How was the second Red Scare similar to and different from the Red Scare of 1919?

SECTION 4 *(pp. 835–841)*

15. a. Describe What events led to the Korean War?

b. Sequence Describe the major events of the war in the order in which they occurred.

c. Rate Do you think the United States and the United Nations in Korea made an effective defense against the spread of communism?

Using the Internet

go.hrw.com
Practice Online
Keyword: SD7 CH25

16. During the twentieth century, the history of the city of Berlin was closely connected with the history of the Cold War. Using the keyword above, do research to learn about Berlin in the twentieth century, beginning after World War II and ending with the fall of the Berlin Wall. Then create a report that explains the significance of Berlin in the Cold War.

Analyzing Primary Sources

Reading Like a Historian
This photograph depicts a parade celebrating the millionth ton of Marshall-Plan goods delivered to Europe.

17. Identify Study the photograph. In what country was it taken?

18. Draw Conclusions Why do you think a parade was held to celebrate this shipment of goods?

Critical Reading

Read the passage in Section 3 that begins with the heading "Truman and loyalty." Then answer the questions that follow.

19. Based on this passage, it seems that

  A. Truman was deeply anti-Communist.

  B. Truman did not care about communism

  C. Truman took action against communism mainly to satisfy the public.

  D. communism was a serious threat.

20. Truman's loyalty investigations produced

  A. little evidence of Communist influence in government.

  B. thousands of Communists in government.

  C. complete support from the public.

  D. widespread anger among the public.

 FOCUS ON WRITING

Expository Writing *Expository writing gives information, explains why or how, or defines a process. To practice expository writing, complete the assignment below.*

Writing Topic **The Korean War**

21. Assignment Based on what you have read in this chapter, write a paragraph that explains why the United States became involved in the Korean War.

THE COLD WAR BEGINS **845**

Answers

Using the Internet

16. Go to the HRW Web site and enter the keyword shown to access a rubric for this activity.

KEYWORD: SD7 CH25

Analyzing Primary Sources

17. Greece

18. possible answer—was a milestone in the aid effort and showed how much help had been given to those in need

Critical Reading

19. C

20. A

Focus on Writing

21. U.S. involvement in Korean War: stop Communist aggression from North Korea; take a stand against communism; show world that U.S. stands up for smaller nations and helps allies; UN troops needed manpower; last ditch effort to save South Korea

A rubric for this activity is provided in Chapter Resource File: Focus on Writing Activity: The Korean War.

History's Impact
Video Program

Americans became terrified about the possibility of nuclear war with the Soviet Union and the spread of communism around the world.

Review and Assessment Resources

Review and Reinforce

- CRF: Chapter Review Activity
- Quick Facts Transparencies:
  Causes of the Cold War; Programs for a Safer World; Population, 1950; The Cold War Begins
- Spanish Chapter Summaries Audio CD Program
- Online Chapter Summaries in Spanish
- OSP Holt PuzzlePro; Quiz Show for ExamView
- Quiz Game CD-ROM

Assess

- PASS: Chapter Test, Forms A and B
- Alternative Assessment Handbook
- OSP ExamView Test Generator, Chapter Test
- Differentiated Instruction Modified Worksheets and Tests CD-ROM: Chapter Test
- HOAP Holt Online Assessment Program (in the Premier Online Edition)

Reteach/Intervene

- Interactive Reader and Study Guide
- Differentiated Instruction Teacher Management System: Lesson Plans for Differentiated Instruction
- Differentiated Instruction Modified Worksheets and Tests CD-ROM: Chapter Test
- Interactive Skills Tutor CD-ROM

go.hrw.com
Online Resources
KEYWORD: SD7 CH25

CHAPTER 26 PLANNING GUIDE

Chapter Overview	Reproducible Resources	Technology Resources
CHAPTER 26 pp. 846–871 **Overview: In this chapter,** students will analyze the economic growth and prosperity the nation experienced after World War II, as well as the Cold War arms race with the Soviet Union.	**Differentiated Instruction Teacher Management System:*** • Instructional Benchmarking Guides • Lesson Plans for Differentiated Instruction **Interactive Reader and Study Guide:** Chapter Summary* **Chapter Resource File:*** • Writing for the SAT Activity: Nuclear Weapons • Social Studies Skills Activity: Analyzing Alternative Interpretations of the Past • Chapter Review Activity **American History Outline Maps** **Pre-AP Activities Guide for American History***	Live Ink® Online Reading Help Student Edition on Audio CD Program Differentiated Instruction Modified Worksheets and Tests CD-ROM Interactive Skills Tutor CD-ROM United States History Primary Source Library CD-ROM Power Presentations with Video CD-ROM History's Impact: American History Video Program (VHS/DVD): Postwar America Online Chapter Summaries in Spanish
Section 1: **The Eisenhower Era** **The Main Idea:** The presidency of Dwight D. Eisenhower was shaped in large part by the Cold War and related conflicts.	**Differentiated Instruction Teacher Management System:** Section 1 Lesson Plan* **Interactive Reader and Study Guide:** Section 1 Summary* **Chapter Resource File:*** • Vocabulary Builder Activity, Section 1 • Biography Activity: Gary Powers	Daily Bellringer Transparency: Section 1* Map Transparency: Cold War Conflict Areas, 1950s* Daily Test Practice Transparency: Section 1* Internet Activity: The Creation of Israel
Section 2: **Atomic Anxiety** **The Main Idea:** The growing power of, and military reliance on, nuclear weapons helped create significant anxiety in the American public in the 1950s.	**Differentiated Instruction Teacher Management System:** Section 2 Lesson Plan* **Interactive Reader and Study Guide:** Section 2 Summary* **Chapter Resource File:*** • Vocabulary Builder Activity, Section 2 • Biography Activity: Admiral Rickover • Primary Source Activity: Basement Fallout Shelter	Daily Bellringer Transparency: Section 2* Daily Test Practice Transparency: Section 2* Internet Activity: Preparing for a Nuclear War
Section 3: **The Television Age** **The Main Idea:** Television was a major influence on American culture in the 1950s, mirroring larger changes in technology and culture.	**Differentiated Instruction Teacher Management System:** Section 3 Lesson Plan* **Interactive Reader and Study Guide:** Section 3 Summary* **Chapter Resource File:*** • Vocabulary Builder Activity, Section 3 • Biography Activity: Allen Ginsberg • Primary Source Activity: Federal-Aid Highway Act of 1956 • Literature Activity: *The Natural*	Daily Bellringer Transparency: Section 3* Daily Test Practice Transparency: Section 3* Internet Activity: Popular Culture of the 1950s

HOLT

History's Impact
American History Video Program (VHS/DVD)
Postwar America

Review, Assessment, Intervention

 Quick Facts Transparency: Postwar America

 Spanish Chapter Summaries Audio CD Program

 **Progress Assessment Support System (PASS):** Chapter Test*

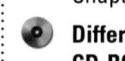 **Differentiated Instruction Modified Worksheets and Tests CD-ROM:** Modified Chapter Test

OSP **One-Stop Planner CD-ROM:** ExamView Test Generator (English/Spanish)

HOAP **Holt Online Assessment Program (HOAP),** in the Holt Premier Online Student Edition

 PASS: Section 1 Quiz*

 Online Quiz: Section 1

 Alternative Assessment Handbook

 PASS: Section 2 Quiz*

 Online Quiz: Section 2

 Alternative Assessment Handbook

 PASS: Section 3 Quiz*

 Online Quiz: Section 3

 Alternative Assessment Handbook

NC RESOURCES

The following resources were developed to help North Carolina educators teach the standards and objectives of North Carolina's eleventh grade standard course of study in United States history.

• United States history EOC Test Prep Workbook
• Teacher's Support System
• North Carolina One-Stop Planner

And be sure to direct your students to **go.hrw.com** for online access to the EOC Test Prep Workbook.

go.hrw.com
EOC Test Prep
KEYWORD: SE7 NC

Holt Online Learning

go.hrw.com
Teacher Resources
KEYWORD: SD7 TEACHER

go.hrw.com
Student Resources
KEYWORD: SD7 CH26

• Document-based Questions
• Interactive Multimedia Activities

• Current Events
• Chapter-based Internet Activities
• and more!

Holt Premier
Online Student Edition

Complete online support for interactivity, assessment, and reporting

• Interactive Maps and Notebook
• Standardized Test Prep
• Homework Practice and Research Activities Online

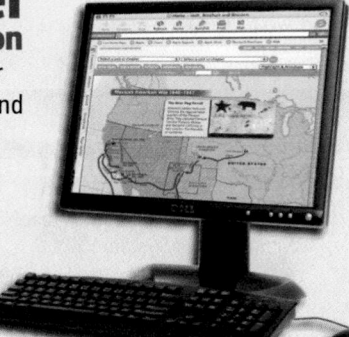

The Big Picture
Robert D. Schulzinger

Eisenhower: A Nonpartisan President In 1952 Americans elected General Dwight Eisenhower, a World War II hero, as the first Republican president in twenty years. Domestically he fostered a spirit of bipartisan cooperation and consensus. Despite having criticized the Truman administration for failing to roll back Communist territorial advances, he advocated containment. He quickly concluded an armistice agreement ending the unpopular Korean War, and after Stalin's death in 1953 sought better relations with the Soviet Union. These efforts bore some fruit, but the Cold War intensified in his second term as the United States and the Soviet Union engaged in an atomic arms race.

Atomic Anxiety Americans became alarmed at the terrifying destructive power of atomic weapons when the United States and the Soviet Union amassed arsenals of atomic and hydrogen bombs in the 1950s. In 1957 the Soviet Union launched Sputnik, the first artificial satellite, and soon both nations developed Intercontinental Ballistic Missiles, which took the arms race into outer space. The U.S. government created a large civil defense program to help Americans survive a potential Soviet attack, but the program itself added to Americans' fear of atomic war.

The Culture of the Fifties The United States became an increasingly suburban country in which new technologies changed the culture. Television quickly became a powerful force, but one which critics complained coarsened cultural life. Still, TV was hugely popular, and many enduring categories of programming, such as soap operas, crime dramas, and game shows, got their start in the early years of the medium. Other technological breakthroughs like the transistor, the integrated circuit, the computer, antibiotics, and the anti-polio vaccine greatly improved the quality of life. The reputation of scientists soared during the 1950s.

Recent Scholarship

Curing Polio Polio terrified Americans after World War II. In the summer of 1952, 57,000 people, many of them children, came down with the crippling disease. In *Polio: An American Story* (2005), David Oshinsky explains how ordinary Americans, scientists, the National Foundation for Infantile Paralysis, and the federal government joined the fight to eliminate the disease. Dr. Jonas Salk developed a vaccine which was tested on millions of children in 1954. The following year, on the tenth anniversary of Roosevelt's death, scientists announced that the vaccine was effective. Polio was virtually eradicated over the next few years.

Differentiating Instruction

Differentiated Instruction Teacher Management System
- Lesson Plans for Differentiated Instruction
- Differentiated Instructional Benchmarking Guides
- Interactive Reader and Study Guide

 Spanish Chapter Summaries Audio CD Program

 Online Chapter Summaries in Spanish

 Student Edition on Audio CD Program

 Differentiated Instruction Modified Worksheets and Tests CD-ROM
- Vocabulary Flash Cards
- Modified Vocabulary Builder Activities
- Modified Chapter Review Activity
- Modified Chapter Test

OSP One-Stop Planner CD-ROM
- ExamView Test Generator (English and Spanish)
- PuzzlePro
- Quiz Show for ExamView
- Transparencies and Videos

TE Differentiated Activities in the Teacher's Edition
- The Warsaw Pact, p. 851
- Civil Defense Posters, p. 859
- TV in the 1950s, p. 862

Reading Like a Historian
Sam Wineburg

The Checkered History of Checkers

It is hard to understand—at least from the excerpt our chapter presents on page 849—why Richard Nixon's "Checkers" speech was such a hit. How could a hokey story about a black and white cocker spaniel for six-year-old Tricia elicit a million telegrams, saving Nixon's place on the presidential ticket and in so doing change the course of history?

While Nixon's appearance before the country has gone down as the "Checker's Speech," Checkers actually comprises a miniscule part of the address. Transcribed, the speech runs over 4,700 words. The excerpt quoted in our chapter represents less than 3% of the entire speech.

The Rest of the Speech

The longest sections detailed Nixon's humble roots, how he and his four brothers toiled in his parents' grocery store, how he worked his way through college and later law school, served his country in the South Pacific in World War II, and entered public service after his discharge. Assailed by his critics for shady financial dealings, he opened up his checkbook to the American people—revealing that he and his wife Pat bought a house in Washington, D.C., for $41,000 (for which they still owed $20,000); that he owned a second home in Whittier, California, that cost $13,000; that he had a $4,000 life insurance policy on himself but nothing on his two girls; that in addition to mortgages on both the Washington and Whittier houses, he carried a $4,500 bank loan—at $4\frac{1}{2}$ percent interest. "That's about it," Nixon told the American people. "That's what we have. And that's what we owe. It isn't very much. But Pat and I have the satisfaction that every dime we've got is honestly ours."

From our Oprah-Dr. Phil-Maury Povich vantage point, it is difficult to understand just how unusual it was in 1952 for a public figure to come before the American people and bare his soul. Television was still a new medium (the '52 election was the first to feature paid political ads) and no one knew for sure how a political message, mixing sound and image and broadcast over a small screen, would fare.

The Common Man

Nixon's appeal to America as a common man with humble roots (compared to the Democratic candidate, Adlai Stevenson, who "inherited a fortune from his father" Nixon told his listeners) established television as the preeminent forum for swaying minds in American political contests.

Nixon's speech was a triumph. Americans perceived him as an ordinary guy, hardworking and dedicated to his family—just like them. No matter what his attackers said, Nixon was going to keep the cocker spaniel that made little Tricia happy. If it came down to being a heartbeat away from the presidency or a wagging tail away from his daughter and family, Nixon told the American people that he would choose the latter. It was a winning message, then as now.

We remember the Checkers excerpt because it seemed to be a spontaneous outpouring by a man under siege. However, as with most events in Nixon's political career, the reference to the cocker spaniel was anything but spontaneous. In a 1983 interview Nixon talked about his admiration for the rhetorical skills of Franklin Delano Roosevelt, and recalled how once, under fierce attack, FDR set his attackers off balance by invoking his beloved Scottish Terrier, Fala ("These Republican leaders have not been content with attacks on me, or my wife, or on my sons. No, not content with that, they now include my little dog Fala").

"So I remembered Checkers, and that's why I said what I did about Checkers," Nixon told historian Frank Gannon 31 years after his speech. But whether a spontaneous outpouring of emotion or a calculated move to tug at his audience's heartstrings, Nixon's speech was a masterful use of a medium in its infancy.

 **Standards Focus**

Social Studies Competency Goals
Goal 11 The learner will trace economic, political, and social developments and assess their significance for the lives of Americans during this time period.
11.01

The Big Idea and Essential Questions

To foster student understanding of this chapter's big idea, design your lesson to address each section's essential question.

Big Idea While the United States experienced a period of economic growth and prosperity, the Cold War cast a dark cloud over international relations.

Essential Questions

1. How did the Cold War shape the presidency of Dwight D. Eisenhower?

2. How did the American public react to the growing power of and military reliance on nuclear weapons?

3. How did television both shape and reflect American cultural life in the 1950s?

Key to Differentiating Instruction

Below Level

Basic-level activities designed for all students encountering new material

At Level

Intermediate-level activities designed for average students

Above Level

Challenging activities designed for honors and gifted-and-talented students

Standard English Mastery

Activities designed to improve standard English usage

846 CHAPTER 26

CHAPTER
26 1945–1960

Postwar America

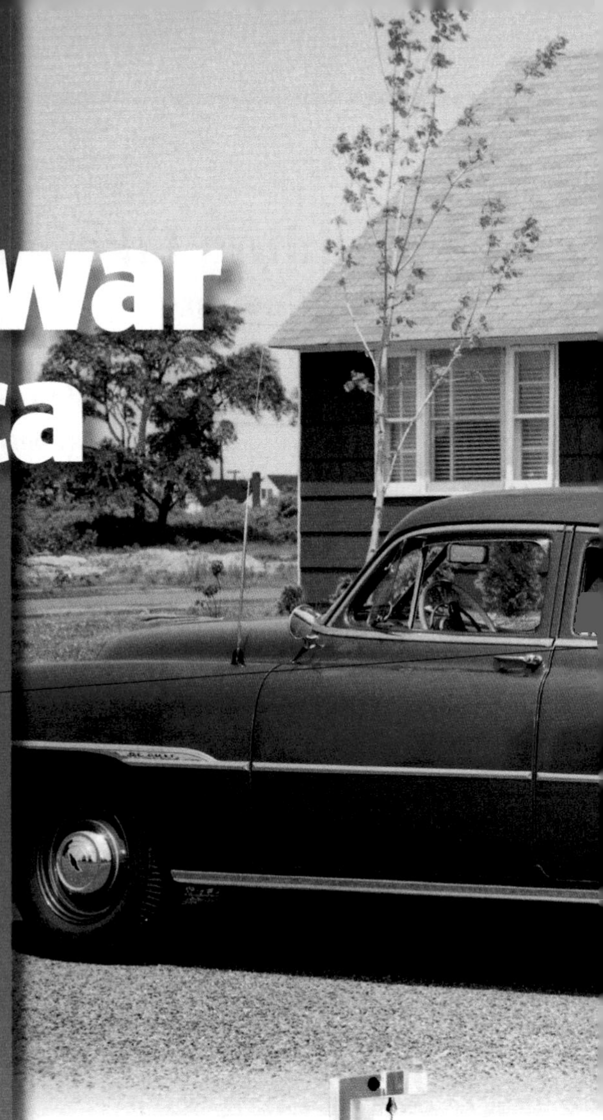

THE BIG PICTURE In the years following World War II, the nation experienced tremendous economic growth and prosperity, transforming the way middle-class people lived. The Cold War arms race with the Soviet Union, however, cast a dark cloud of anxiety over the Eisenhower years.

NC **North Carolina Standards**

Social Studies Objectives
11.01 Describe the effects of the Cold War on economic, political, and social life in America.
11.05 Examine the impact of technological innovations that have impacted American life.

Language Arts Objectives
1.03 Demonstrate the ability to read, listen to and view a variety of increasingly complex print and non-print informational texts appropriate to grade level and course literary focus, by:
- demonstrating comprehension of main ideas and supporting details.
2.01 Research and analyze ideas, events, and/or movements related to United States culture by:
- locating facts and details for purposeful elaboration.

Skills FOCUS **READING LIKE A HISTORIAN**

After the war, Americans eagerly bought products that were denied them during the war years. Many people also moved to newly created suburbs. A neat home with a white picket fence came to symbolize middle-class prosperity in the postwar years.
Interpreting Visuals What signs of prosperity can you identify for this family of five?
See **Skills Handbook**, p. H30

846

U.S.

World

1945

1945 Nuremberg trials of Nazi leaders begins.

1947 Bell Laboratories invents the transistor.

Introduce the Chapter [At Level]

Postwar America

1. World War II ended when the United States dropped atomic bombs on Hiroshima and Nagasaki completely destroying the cities. A few years later the United States was involved in the Korean War. In the 1950s Americans were concerned about the threat of communism and the potential use of weapons of mass destruction, like the atomic bomb.

2. Have students study the two time lines in the chapter and scan the information about potential nuclear attack.

3. Have each student write a series of journal entries from the perspective of a student in the 1950s. Students should explain whether or not they believe that school emergency "duck and cover" drills are necessary and how such drills affect their feelings about the possibility of nuclear war. **LS** **Verbal-Linguistic**

Alternative Assessment Handbook, Rubric 15: Journals

Reading Like a Historian

The Ideal Family Have students take a moment to examine the image on these pages. What does the appearance and position of the figures in the photo tell you about them? *possible answer— They seem to value cleanliness, neatness, and family togetherness.*

Interpreting Visuals A family, including the mother, father, and three children, load up their car for an exciting picnic at the beach.

June 1951
The first computer comes on the market.

October 1952
The United States tests a hydrogen bomb.

June 1956
Congress approves funds for the Interstate Highway System.

May 1960
Soviets shoot down an American U-2 spy plane.

1948 — 1951 — 1954 — 1957 — 1960

1948
The nation of Israel is founded.

March 1953
Soviet leader Joseph Stalin dies.

1956
Egypt takes control of the Suez Canal.

1957
Soviets launch *Sputnik*, the first artificial satellite.

847

Explore the Time Line

1. When was the first computer available to the American public? *1951*

2. When was the nation of Israel created? *1948*

3. When did the United States begin major highway building programs? *1956*

Info to Know

Military Bases Overseas military bases were an important part of U.S. strategy after World War II. The overseas bases served two purposes. First, U.S. military forces might be able to stop any attack before it reached the U.S. mainland. Second, the bases would allow the U.S. to respond quickly to crises in Europe or Asia.
Evaluate How might nations who agreed to have U.S. military bases on their soil benefit from the arrangement? *benefits—U.S. might protect them in case of attack*

Answers

Reading Like a Historian (p. 846)
nice clothing, new car, well-kept home

Preteach

Bellringer

The Inside Story. . . Use the **Daily Bellringer Transparency** to help students answer the question.

📇 Daily Bellringer Transparency, Section 1

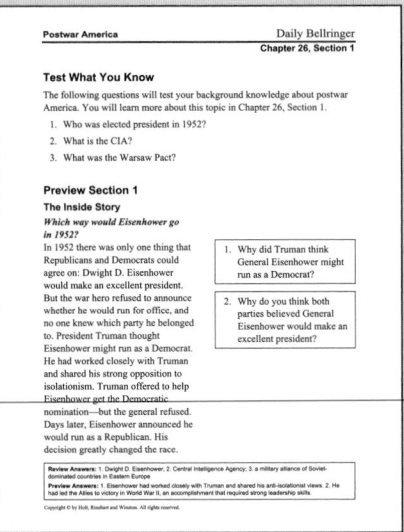

Academic Vocabulary

Review with students the high-use academic term in this section.

imply to express indirectly (p. 849)

📋 CRF: Vocabulary Builder Activity, Section 1

Taking Notes

brinkmanship—making threats to get results, but not following through on threats; massive retaliation—use of overwhelming force to settle serious conflicts; Eisenhower Doctrine—U.S. would respond to the request for help from any Middle Eastern nation resisting communism.

The Eisenhower Era

BEFORE YOU READ

MAIN IDEA

The presidency of Dwight D. Eisenhower was shaped in large part by the Cold War and related conflicts.

READING FOCUS

1. What were the circumstances of Eisenhower's election in 1952?
2. How did the continuing Cold War affect the Eisenhower administration?
3. What were the Cold War "hot spots" of the 1950s?

KEY TERMS AND PEOPLE

Richard M. Nixon
John Foster Dulles
brinkmanship
massive retaliation
CIA
Nikita Khrushchev
Warsaw Pact
summit
SEATO
Eisenhower Doctrine

TAKING NOTES As you read, take notes on Eisenhower's Cold War policies. Record your notes in a graphic organizer like the one shown here. You may need to add more rows.

Policy	How It Worked

THE INSIDE STORY

Which party would Eisenhower pick in 1952?
If there was one thing on which Republicans and Democrats could agree in 1952, it was that General Dwight D. Eisenhower would make an excellent president. The World War II hero had an outstanding reputation with voters on both sides of the political divide. Yet as the election year approached, Eisenhower refused to announce whether he would seek the White House. In fact, no one really knew for certain which political party he might belong to.

President Truman seemed to think that Eisenhower might run as a Democrat. After all, the general had worked closely with Truman and with Franklin Roosevelt before that. In 1948 Truman had reportedly even offered to run with Eisenhower—as the vice presidential candidate on a ticket headed by the general. What's more, Truman and Eisenhower shared a strong opposition to the isolationist views of the leading Republican figure of the day, Senator Robert Taft of Ohio. In late 1951 Truman questioned Eisenhower on his willingness to run. He reportedly offered his help in getting Eisenhower the Democratic nomination. Eisenhower replied that he was not interested in politics.

Days later, the nation received startling news. Eisenhower would in fact be seeking the presidency—as a Republican. The entry of the popular war hero into the 1952 presidential race greatly changed the campaign. As you will read, there would be more surprises to follow. ◾

▲ **"Likeable Ike" on the campaign trail in 1952**

Teach the Main Idea

At Level

The Eisenhower Era

1. **Teach** Ask students the Reading Focus questions to teach this section.

2. **Apply** Have students create an outline of the section using the red and blue heads as main points. Have students identify at least two main ideas under each of the blue subheadings.

3. **Review** Have students identify the foreign policy issues in their outlines that they feel might become the most problematic for the United States. Guide students in a discussion of the growing role of the United States in world affairs.

4. **Practice/Homework** In 1956 the United States withdrew financial support for Egypt's Aswan Dam project. Have each student write a letter to the editor of the local newspaper supporting or opposing this action. 🄻 **Verbal-Linguistic**

   📋 Alternative Assessment Handbook, Rubric 17: Letters to Editors

The Election of 1952

Truman's admiration for Eisenhower may have affected his decision not to seek re-election in 1952. The year before, the states had ratified the Twenty-second Amendment. This set a 10-year limit on the number of years a president could serve. Truman was specifically excluded from the amendment's limits. Still, he felt he had served long enough. "In my opinion," he declared, "eight years as president is long enough and sometimes too much for any man to serve in this capacity."

Stevenson vs. Eisenhower With the race wide open, Democrats nominated Illinois governor Adlai Stevenson. Republicans chose Eisenhower, known to the public as "Ike."

On the campaign trail, Eisenhower sharply criticized the Democrats for their handling of the Korean War. Peace talks had been dragging on for months, and soldiers were dying by the thousands. Eisenhower vowed that if elected he would go to Korea to end the war. In response, Democrats noted that if Eisenhower knew how to end the Korean war, he should have done so long ago.

American voters, however, seemed to trust and admire Eisenhower. As election day neared, polls showed him well in the lead.

Nixon and the Checkers speech The Eisenhower campaign did hit one major snag. It involved Ike's vice presidential running mate, **Richard M. Nixon**. Nixon was a senator from California who had made his name as a strong anti-Communist, having led the investigation of Alger Hiss.

During the 1952 campaign, reporters alleged that Nixon had an $18,000 fund made up of gifts from political supporters. At the time, such a fund was not illegal. Nixon's critics, however, implied that he was dishonest.

In a dramatic move, Nixon went on television to defend his conduct. His outstanding performance in the so-called Checkers speech saved his spot on the Republican ticket. With the issue behind them, the Eisenhower campaign moved on to a solid election-day victory.

READING CHECK Summarizing What were the key events of the presidential campaign of 1952?

PRIMARY SOURCES

Speech

In what became known as the Checkers speech, Richard M. Nixon admitted having a secret political fund but denied using it improperly. He detailed his personal finances—and admitted to having accepted one special gift in 1952. The speech was well received, and it saved his political career.

"We did get something, a gift, after the election. A man down in Texas heard [my wife] Pat on the radio mention the fact that our two youngsters would like to have a dog, and . . . the day before we left on this campaign trip we got a message from Union Station down in Baltimore, saying they had a package for us. We went down to get it. You know what it was? It was a little cocker spaniel dog, in a crate that he had sent all the way from Texas, black and white, spotted, and our little girl, Tricia, the six-year-old, named it Checkers. And, you know, the kids, like all kids, loved the dog, and I just want to say this, right now, that regardless of what they say about it, we're going to keep it."

Nixon used the image of his daughter and her puppy to build sympathy.

Skills Focus READING LIKE A HISTORIAN

1. **Analyzing Primary Sources** What was the gift that Nixon admitted to having received?
2. **Drawing Conclusions** Why do you think the speech was effective at ending the scandal?

See **Skills Handbook**, pp. H12, H28–H29

The Cold War Continues

True to his promise, Eisenhower traveled to Korea in December 1952. There he began the task of getting the stalled peace talks going. The effort proved difficult. A cease-fire was not achieved until July 1953. Even with the end of the fighting in Korea, the Cold War continued to rage throughout the 1950s and to dominate Eisenhower's presidency.

ACADEMIC VOCABULARY
imply to express indirectly

Eisenhower's Cold War policies At the center of Eisenhower's foreign policy team was Secretary of State **John Foster Dulles**. Dulles had played a role in the Truman administration.

Reading Focus

1 What were the circumstances of Eisenhower's election in 1952? *Eisenhower criticized Democrats' handling of the Korean War; Democrats pointed out that Eisenhower had been involved with American policy in the Korean conflict; voters seemed to trust and admire Eisenhower; criticism of Nixon's secret fund led Nixon to make his Checkers speech*

The Election of 1952

Recall Why did President Truman decide not to seek reelection in 1952? *He felt that eight years as president was enough.*

Make Judgments In Richard Nixon's Checkers speech, did he directly address the charges against him? Explain your answer. *possible answer—He just diverted the public's attention by focusing on a dog and his children, rather than on the secret fund.*

📋 CRF: History and Geography Activity: Presidential Election of 1952

📋 Political Cartoons Activities for American History: Cartoon 51: "I Like Ike"

Primary Sources

Speech
Activity The Checkers Speech
Have students write a brief analysis of the emotional appeal of this speech.

LS Verbal-Linguistic, Logical-Mathematical

Answers

Reading Like a Historian 1. *a dog;*
2. *diverted attention from scandal to his family and small children*

Reading Check *Truman decided not to run; Eisenhower and Stevenson chosen as candidates; Nixon's secret fund; the Checkers speech*

Collaborative Learning

At Level

The 1952 Election

Research Required

1. Organize the class into an even number of small groups. Assign one of the two presidential candidates, Dwight Eisenhower or Adlai Stevenson, to each group.

2. Have each group use both primary and secondary sources to conduct research on its candidate, focusing on why he was chosen to run for president and his positions on the issues in the election.

3. Have each group prepare a report based on its research and present it to the class.

4. Conduct a discussion of the two candidates based on student reports. Then ask students which candidate they would vote for if they had been able to vote in the 1952 election. Keep a tally. How would the class's election results have compared with those of the 1952 election? **LS** Interpersonal, Verbal Linguistic

📋 Alternative Assessment Handbook, Rubrics 30: Research; and 42: Writing to Inform

❷ How did the continuing Cold War affect the Eisenhower administration? *led to an escalation of the arms race; policies of brinkmanship and massive retaliation; use of CIA agents in secret actions against foreign Communist targets*

The Cold War Continues

Explain How did the Soviet Union strengthen its grip on Eastern Europe? *Warsaw Pact; using force to put down demonstrations and attempts to bring about reforms*

Analyze How did the concept of massive retaliation fit in with the policy of brinkmanship? *Brinkmanship was the threat of using force; massive retaliation backed up that threat with the pledge of overwhelming force, including nuclear weapons.*

Identify Cause and Effect How did the 1955 summit between Eisenhower and Khrushchev ultimately damage U.S.–Soviet relations? *The Soviets rejected an open skies treaty; U.S. sent U-2 aircraft into Soviet airspace to spy; in 1960, the Soviets shot down an American U-2 and captured the pilot, souring relations between the two countries.*

Time Line

Height of the Cold War Discuss the illustration of the teeter-totter. Use the following questions as a guide: Who are the two men shown? *Khrushchev and Eisenhower*; What is the object at the bottom of the picture? *a missile*; What message do you think the artist is trying to convey? *possible answer—the tension of the Cold War*

go.hrw.com
Online Resources
KEYWORD: SD7 CH26
TOPIC: THE CREATION OF ISRAEL

Like Eisenhower, he was sharply critical of the Democrats' foreign policy. In particular, Dulles wanted to revise the nation's approach to communism. Rather than merely containing it, as Truman had called for, Dulles spoke of rolling it back.

To stand against the Soviets, Dulles favored building more nuclear weapons. Only the threat of nuclear war, he believed, would stop the Soviets. Dulles's belief was a part of the policy known as **brinkmanship**, the diplomatic art of going to the brink of war without actually getting into war. The practice of brinkmanship involved making threats that were strong enough to bring results without having to follow through on the threats.

Related to this notion was Dulles's concept of **massive retaliation**. This was the pledge that the United States would use overwhelming force against the Soviet Union, including nuclear weapons, to settle a serious conflict.

While Dulles presented the public face of American foreign policy, there was also a secret side. The Central Intelligence Agency, or **CIA**, was formed in 1947 to collect information about—and spy on—foreign governments. The CIA was increasingly active in the 1950s. In addition to collecting information, CIA agents also took part in secret actions against hostile governments. For example, during Eisenhower's first term CIA agents helped overthrow governments in Guatemala and Iran.

Changes in the Soviet Union In March 1953 longtime Soviet leader Joseph Stalin died. His death brought an end to a terrible period in Soviet history. A ruthless dictator, he had been responsible for the deaths of millions of his own citizens. He had also led the Soviet Union in its domination of Eastern Europe and the start of the Cold War.

Stalin's death raised many questions in the United States. Observers were unsure what policies his successor would pursue. Eventually, **Nikita Khrushchev** emerged as the new leader. Many political prisoners jailed under Stalin were freed. Nevertheless, the Soviet Union remained a Communist dictatorship—and a bitter rival of the United States.

The Warsaw Pact forms In 1955 the Soviets established a new organization called the **Warsaw Pact**. This was a military alliance with the Soviet-dominated countries of Eastern Europe. It was roughly similar in purpose to NATO. The Warsaw Pact, however, was entirely under the control of the Soviet Union. Warsaw Pact nations stood ready to defend each other and the Soviet Union. At the same time, the pact was a tool that helped the Soviets solidify control in Eastern Europe.

Communist control was firm—and when necessary, ruthless. For example, in June 1956 soldiers violently put down an anti-Communist protest in Poland. Dozens were killed.

Several months later, a larger uprising occurred in Hungary. There, many citizens rose up to demand changes to their harsh, Soviet-style government. Some also sought the return of a former leader, Imre Nagy. Nagy was a Communist, but he favored a more democratic system of government.

Height of the Cold War

In the 1950s Cold War tensions reached new heights as the United States and the Soviet Union maneuvered for power and influence.

This cartoon of Khrushchev and Eisenhower appeared on the cover of *Newsweek* in 1959.

November 1952
Eisenhower is elected president, in part on the strength of his tough anti-Communist stance.

March 1953
Stalin dies; eventually Nikita Khrushchev emerges as the new Soviet leader.

July 1953
Fighting in Korea ends in a stalemate.

Skills Focus: Identifying Problem and Solution   At Level

Reading Skill
Cold War Policies of the 1950s

1. Tell the class that it was the responsibility of the State Department to advise President Eisenhower on the secretary's policies of rolling back communism, brinkmanship, and massive retaliation. Have each student write a memorandum to the president outlining the reasons behind the policies Secretary Dulles is recommending.

2. Guide students in a discussion of the policies of rollback, brinkmanship, and massive retaliation. Ask students to predict how these policies would affect relations with the Soviet Union and other Communist countries, how they would affect relations with the rest of the world, and what psychological effect they would have on the American people.

LS Verbal-Linguistic, Logical-Mathematical

Alternative Assessment Handbook, Rubrics 11: Discussions; and 40: Writing to Describe

In response to public demands, Nagy was named prime minister in late October. Once in office, he promised new reforms for Hungary. He also tried to force the withdrawal of Soviet troops from his country. When these efforts failed, he declared that Hungary would withdraw from the Warsaw Pact.

As demonstrations continued in the Hungarian capital of Budapest, the Soviets used the unrest as an excuse to send in military forces. Soviet tanks rolled through the streets, and planes bombed the city. The Hungarians fought back, but they could not resist the Soviets. The Soviets had sent a powerful message: They were in control in Eastern Europe.

U.S.-Soviet relations Although the 1950s were a time of Cold War tension, the Americans and Soviets did meet in the first postwar U.S.-Soviet summit in 1955. A **summit** is a meeting of the heads of government. The summit took place in Geneva, Switzerland.

Eisenhower proposed an "open skies" treaty. Under it, both the Soviets and the Americans could fly over each other's territory to learn more about the other's military abilities. Eisenhower believed this would help lower tensions because neither side would have to imagine the worst about the other's military strength. The Soviets, however, rejected the proposal.

This setback did not shake voters' faith in Eisenhower and his handling of international affairs. He easily won re-election in 1956, again defeating Adlai Stevenson.

The Soviet rejection of the open skies proposal did not prevent Eisenhower from seeking

information about the Soviet military. The United States sent U-2 aircraft into Soviet airspace to inspect their military facilities. The U-2s carried advanced spying equipment and flew at altitudes thought to be out of reach of Soviet defenses. In 1960, however, the Soviets shot down pilot Francis Gary Powers's U-2 spy plane and captured Powers. Powers was freed in 1962 in exchange for the U.S. release of a captured Soviet spy. The incident greatly damaged U.S.-Soviet relations.

READING CHECK **Identifying Cause and Effect** Identify several events that represent the continuation of the Cold War in the 1950s.

Cold War "Hot Spots"

The Cold War had led to armed conflict in Korea. Cold War tensions also flared in several other spots around the world in the 1950s.

Vietnam and the seeds of war In 1954 France lost a bloody struggle to keep control of its Southeast Asian colony in Vietnam. After a terrible defeat in the battle of Dien Bien Phu, the French sought peace with the Vietnamese rebels who had been fighting to oust them. Among these rebels were many Communists.

The peace talks between the French and Vietnamese reflected Cold War rivalries. The final agreement divided Vietnam in northern and southern halves. The north came under the control of Communist leader Ho Chi Minh. As in Korea, this division was supposed to be temporary. The peace agreement called for a

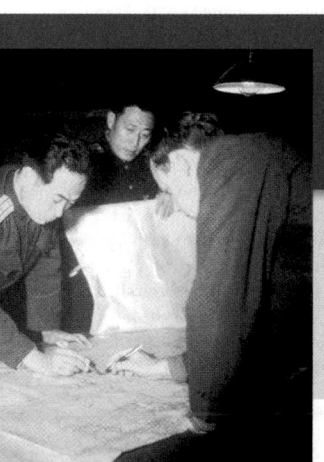

Peace talks in Panmunjom stall as the partition between the two Koreas is negotiated.

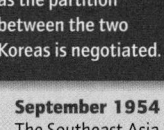

The military used high-altitude aircraft on spying missions.

© BERNARD CROCHET COLLECTION/PHOTOS12.COM

September 1954	**May 1955**	**1956**	**January 1957**
The Southeast Asia Treaty Organization is formed to stop communism in Southeast Asia.	The Warsaw Pact is formed between the Soviet Union and the countries it dominated in Eastern Europe.	Poland and Hungary rebel against Communist rule; Egypt seizes the Suez Canal, and Israel, Great Britain, and France attack.	The President issues the Eisenhower Doctrine, intended to resist communism in the Middle East; he later sends troops into Lebanon.

POSTWAR AMERICA **851**

Differentiating Instruction

Above Level

Advanced Learners/GATE

Research Required

1. Organize the class into small groups. Have each group use reliable Internet sites or traditional print sources to conduct research on the Warsaw Pact. Have students begin by reading the treaty that established the alliance, then conduct research on why the treaty was written and how its terms were actually carried out.

2. Have each group write a report comparing the treaty's stated goals with the ways in which

the treaty actually worked. In their analyses, have students look carefully at the way in which the treaty was worded.

3. Ask volunteers to read their reports to the class. **LS Interpersonal, Verbal-Linguistic**

Alternative Assessment Handbook, Rubrics 14: Group Activity; and 42: Writing to Inform

Direct Teach

Reading Focus

3 What were the Cold War "hot spots" of the 1950s? *Korea, Vietnam, and the Middle East*

Cold War "Hot Spots"

Explain Why was Vietnam divided in two? *Vietnamese defeated French; peace talks divided into Communist and non-Communist sections; elections would later determine government of united Vietnam*

Make Inferences Why might the division of Vietnam into Communist North Vietnam and non-Communist South Vietnam concern Americans? *possible answer—The U.S. had just finished fighting in Korea, which had been similarly divided, so U.S. worried about possible conflict in Vietnam.*

CRF: Biography: Gary Powers

Info to Know

The Geneva Summit The Geneva Summit of 1955 was the first meeting of the "Big Four" nations, the United States, the Soviet Union, Great Britain, and France, since the Potsdam Conference ten years before. The Soviet rejection of the open skies proposal came as no surprise—they already knew far more about American military facilities than the United States knew about theirs.

Answers

Reading Check *Warsaw Pact formed; CIA secret missions; Soviets put down rebellions; Soviet rejection of open skies treaty; U2 spy missions; capture of U2 pilot Gary Powers*

851

Cold War "Hot Spots"

Explain Why were Americans concerned about the outcome of the 1956 election for a new government in Vietnam? *They were afraid that it might lead to a Communist victory, which might lead to the spread of communism in the region—the "domino effect."*

Define What was the Eisenhower Doctrine? *a policy set forth by President Eisenhower in January 1957 that declared the right of the United States to help, on request, any nation in the Middle East trying to resist armed Communist aggression*

Cold War Conflict Areas, 1950s

Interpreting Maps Use a wall map of the world to help students locate the SEATO members. Ask students why they think that Britain, France, and the United States were involved in this treaty organization.

📦 Map Transparency: Cold War Conflict Areas, 1950s

Answers

Interpreting Maps 1. *Eastern Europe;* **2.** *Poland, Hungary*

COLD WAR CONFLICT AREAS, 1950s

Poland and Hungary Anti-Communist uprisings in 1956 led to violent Soviet responses, especially in Hungary.

Eastern Europe The Warsaw Pact, formed in 1955, was a Communist answer to NATO.

Vietnam The end of French colonial rule sparked U.S. fears of Communist expansion in Southeast Asia.

The Middle East Egypt's ties to the Soviets and seizure of the Suez Canal nearly led to U.S.-Soviet conflict in 1956.

Conflict area

0   250   500 Miles
0   250   500 Kilometers
Miller projection

GEOGRAPHY SKILLS INTERPRETING MAPS

1. Region Which part of Europe was under the domination of the Soviet Union?

2. Place Which countries tried to resist Soviet dominance?

See Skills Handbook, p. H20

1956 election. Vietnamese voters would then get to choose for themselves what kind of government they would have.

For Eisenhower, this agreement was unacceptable: An election might lead to a Communist victory. Communism in Vietnam could lead to the spread of communism in the region.

HISTORY'S VOICES

❝You have a row of dominoes set up, you knock over the first one, and what will happen to the last one is the certainty that it will go over very quickly . . .

But when we come to the possible sequence of events, the loss of [Vietnam], of Burma, of Thailand, of the Peninsula, and Indonesia following . . . the possible consequences of the loss are just incalculable to the free world.❞

—Dwight D. Eisenhower, press conference, April 7, 1954

To address this danger, the United States and its anti-Communist allies created a new organization. This was called the Southeast Asia Treaty Organization, or **SEATO**. Members included Australia, Great Britain, France, New Zealand, Pakistan, the Philippines, Thailand, and the United States. SEATO nations agreed to work together to resist Communist aggression.

SEATO and the United States supported the creation of a new anti-Communist nation in 1955: South Vietnam. In the coming years, the United States provided much military and economic support to this government. Unfortunately, its president, Ngo Dinh Diem, angered his own people with his harsh leadership.

Meanwhile, the North Vietnamese were growing impatient. They still wanted to unite all of Vietnam under their control. This set the stage for later armed conflict.

Skills Focus: Sequencing

At Level

Reading Skill
The U.S. and the Middle East

1. To help students understand the sequence of events in the Middle East during the mid-1950s, draw the graphic organizer for students to see.

2. Have each student copy and complete the organizer. Students should add more boxes as needed to include the following information: *U.S. withdraws financial support for Aswan Dam, Nasser seizes control of Suez Canal and blocks Israel's outlet to the Red Sea, Israel launches attack on Egypt, Britain and France join Israel against Egypt, Soviets threaten to enter fight on Egypt's side, Eisenhower insists all attackers leave Egypt, Egypt keeps Suez Canal*

LS Visual-Spatial

📓 Alternative Assessment Handbook, Rubric 13: Graphic Organizers

📦 Graphic Organizer Transparencies

Nasser seeks Soviet support to unite and strengthen the Arab nations

↓

↓

↓

President Eisenhower issues the Eisenhower Doctrine

Trouble in the Middle East The Middle East was another region troubled by Cold War tensions. These tensions were heightened by the conflict between Jews and Arabs. This conflict reached a crisis point in 1948, when Israel declared its independence. The creation of Israel followed a UN resolution dividing Palestine into a Jewish and an Arab state.

Israel's Arab neighbors—Egypt, Syria, Jordan, Lebanon, and Iraq—immediately attacked Israel. In the war that followed, Israel won. The land that had been set aside for the Palestinians came under the control of Israel and the nations of Jordan and Egypt.

In 1954 Gamal Abdel Nasser rose to power in Egypt. Nasser sought to unite and strengthen the Arab nations. Toward this goal, he was willing to seek the support of the Soviet Union.

U.S. leaders were unhappy with Nasser's growing relationship with the Soviet Union. In 1956 the United States withdrew its financial support for a major Egyptian building project, the Aswan High Dam.

In response, Nasser seized control of the Suez Canal, the vital waterway between the Mediterranean Sea and the Red Sea. A British-controlled company owned the canal, through which Europe received two-thirds of its petroleum. Britain and France wanted to continue to use the canal and to protect their oil supplies.

Egypt's action in the Suez also blocked Israel's only outlet to the Red Sea. In response, Israel launched a military attack on Egypt. The British and French quickly sent in their forces to take control of the canal. The Soviets then threatened to enter the fight on the side of Egypt. This, Eisenhower knew, might draw the United States into the conflict.

The Suez crisis ended when Eisenhower insisted that the invaders leave Egypt. A wider conflict was averted, although Egypt kept control of the canal. The incident also demonstrated the leadership of the United States over its European allies.

The Suez crisis had not resulted in a larger war over the Suez Canal. Eisenhower was worried, however, about the growing influence of the Soviets in the Middle East. In January 1957 he issued the **Eisenhower Doctrine**. This declared the right of the United States to help, on request, any nation in the Middle East trying to resist armed Communist aggression.

Using the doctrine, Eisenhower sent marines into Lebanon in 1958 to help put down a popular uprising against Lebanon's government. Though no Communists threatened Lebanon, Eisenhower wanted to prevent a wider crisis that might invite Soviet involvement.

READING CHECK Identifying the Main Idea What made the Cold War "hot spots" hot?

THE IMPACT TODAY

Economics
Some 25,000 ships pass through the Suez Canal annually, carrying about 14 percent of the world's shipping.

Primary Source

"If power-hungry Communists should either falsely or correctly estimate that the Middle East is inadequately defended, they might be tempted to use open measures of armed attack. If so, that would start a chain of circumstances which would almost surely involve the United States in military action. I am convinced that the best insurance against this dangerous contingency is to make clear now our readiness to cooperate fully and freely with our friends of the Middle East in ways consonant with the purposes and principles of the United Nations."

— Dwight D. Eisenhower

The Eisenhower Doctrine on the Middle East, A Message to Congress, January 5, 1957

Review & Assess

Close
Guide the class in a discussion of the Eisenhower administration's Cold War policies.

Review
📡 Online Quiz, Section 1
🎲 Daily Test Practice Transparency

Assess
SE Section 1 Assessment
📋 Progress Assessment: Section 1 Quiz
📋 Alternative Assessment Handbook

Reteach
📋 Interactive Reader and Study Guide, Section 1
📀 Interactive Skills Tutor CD-ROM

SECTION 1 ASSESSMENT

go.hrw.com
Online Quiz
Keyword: SD7 HP26

Reviewing Ideas, Terms, and People

1. **a. Recall** What were the key issues and individuals of the 1952 presidential campaign?
   b. Elaborate How did Nixon's Checkers speech help the Eisenhower campaign?

2. **a. Define** Write a brief definition of each of the following terms: **brinkmanship, massive retaliation, Warsaw Pact.**
   b. Compare How was the Warsaw Pact similar to and different from NATO?
   c. Evaluate What do you think were the strengths and weaknesses of Dulles's policy of brinkmanship and massive retaliation?

3. **a. Describe** How did Cold War tensions contribute to conflicts in Vietnam and in Egypt?
   b. Explain What did President Eisenhower mean when he compared Vietnam to a domino?

c. Elaborate Do you think Eisenhower was right to request that Great Britain, France, and Israel end their attack on Egypt during the Suez crisis? Explain.

Critical Thinking

4. **Identifying the Main Idea** Copy the chart below and use information from the section to record details that support the main idea of the section.

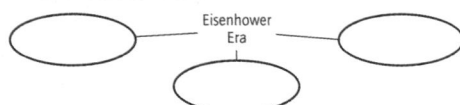

Eisenhower Era

FOCUS ON SPEAKING

5. **Persuasive** Assume the point of view of President Eisenhower. Make a speech to British, French, and Israeli leaders urging them to end their attack on Egypt.

POSTWAR AMERICA **853**

Section 1 Assessment Answers

1. **a.** Korea; Nixon's secret fund; Eisenhower, Stevenson
   b. put scandal behind other issues

2. **a.** going to the brink of war; use of overwhelming force; Eastern European military alliance
   b. nations agreed to help each other; Warsaw Pact controlled by Soviet Union
   c. possible answer—strengths, kept military strong; weakness, could have taken U.S. into war

3. **a.** showed increasing aggression over communism
   b. If Vietnam fell, other nations would follow.
   c. possible answer—yes, otherwise a world war might have broken out

4. brinkmanship, massive retaliation; Warsaw Pact; conflicts in Vietnam, Middle East

5. possible answer—attack could lead to destructive world war

Answers

Reading Check *tension between Communist and non-Communist nations*

853

Bellringer

The Inside Story. . . Use the **Daily Bellringer Transparency** to help students answer the question.

📖 Daily Bellringer Transparency, Section 2

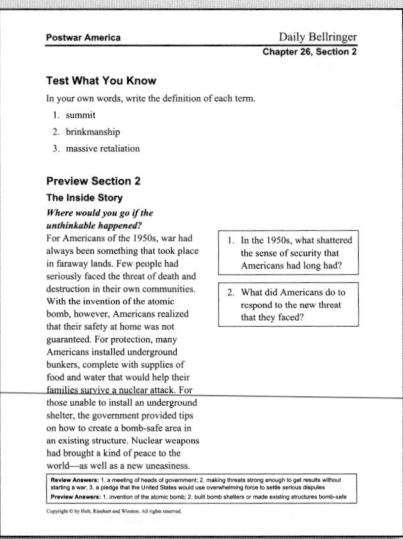

Academic Vocabulary

Review with students the high-use academic terms in this section.

equipped fitted with; possessing certain equipment (p. 856)

issued officially distributed (p. 859)

📖 CRF: Vocabulary Builder Activity, Section 2

Taking Notes

hydrogen bomb; nuclear fallout

SECTION 2 — Atomic Anxiety

BEFORE YOU READ

MAIN IDEA
The growing power of, and military reliance on, nuclear weapons helped create significant anxiety in the American public in the 1950s.

READING FOCUS
1. What was the hydrogen bomb, and when was it developed?
2. What was the arms race, and what were its effects in the United States?
3. How did Americans react to the growing threat of nuclear war?

KEY TERMS AND PEOPLE
hydrogen bomb
ICBM
Sputnik
satellite
NASA
nuclear fallout

TAKING NOTES As you read, take notes on Americans' fears about nuclear weapons and war. Record your notes in a graphic organizer like the one shown here.

> Growth of Nuclear Weapons
>
> Americans' Fears

THE INSIDE STORY

Where would you go if the unthinkable happened?
To Americans of the 1950s, war was something that took place in faraway lands. Few people had seriously faced the threat of death and destruction in their own communities. The atomic bomb, however, changed that comfortable feeling. With the bomb came the realization that devastation could come to them with no more warning than the wail of an air-raid siren.

How could Americans living in such a world protect their families? Some sought protection in backyard bomb shelters. Homeowners across the country were urged to install underground bunkers, complete with supplies of food and water that would help them and their loved ones survive a nuclear attack. There were a number of models available on the market. Popular magazines included helpful plans for do-it-yourselfers. For those unable to install an underground shelter, the government provided tips on how to create a bomb-safe area within an existing structure.

Nuclear weapons had brought a kind of peace to the world. They also brought uneasiness. As you will read, this tension colored much of American life in the 1950s. ◢

Three Rooms, Two Baths, One Bomb Shelter

▶ In theory, a family could survive up to five days in one of these underground backyard shelters.

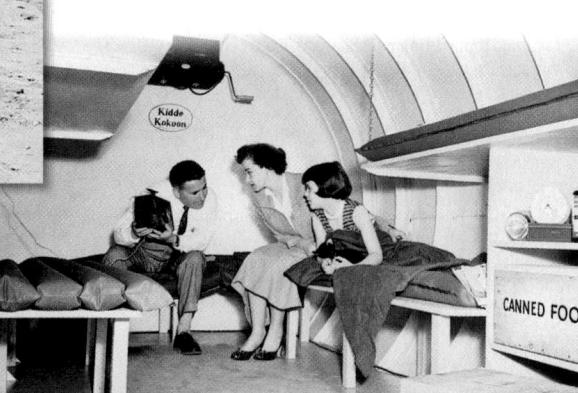

Teach the Main Idea
                At Level

Atomic Anxiety

1. **Teach** Ask students the Reading Focus questions to teach this section.

2. **Apply** Have students work in pairs to create graphic organizers showing how the United States and the Soviet Union "played leapfrog" with each other, each matching technological developments made by the other, during the 1950s.

3. **Review** Review student graphic organizers as a class. Have students identify any important turning points. *Students should*

mention the launching of Sputnik, *which put the Soviet Union ahead of the U.S. in the space race.*

4. **Practice/Homework** Have students identify one of the lasting effects of the rivalry between the United States and the Soviet Union and write a brief essay discussing it. **LS Visual-Spatial, Verbal-Linguistic**

📖 Alternative Assessment Handbook, Rubric 9: Comparing and Contrasting

The Hydrogen Bomb

The atomic bombs that the United States used at the end of World War II had changed the world. Their terrible power persuaded Japanese leaders to do what millions of Allied soldiers had been unable to get them to do: surrender. Military strategy would never be the same.

American leaders chose not to use nuclear weapons during the Korean War. Nevertheless, these weapons were clearly a key part of the nation's military future. Even as soldiers were dying in Korea, the United States was building up its atomic stockpile and testing new and improved weapons. Nuclear testing took place in a variety of locations, including New Mexico, Nevada, Colorado, Mississippi, and Alaska.

Among the weapons being studied during this time was a different kind of nuclear device: the **hydrogen bomb**. The atomic bombs that destroyed Hiroshima and Nagasaki used energy that came from splitting apart atoms. The new hydrogen bomb would get its power from the fusing together of hydrogen atoms. Fusion is the same process that creates the energy of the sun and stars. Harnessed into a weapon, fusion had the potential to create a blast hundreds of times more powerful than an atomic bomb. Indeed, the hydrogen bomb—also known as the H-bomb or super bomb—was so potentially devastating that some scientists argued against ever building it.

HISTORY'S VOICES

❝In determining not to proceed to develop the super bomb, we see a unique opportunity of providing by example some limitations on the totality of war and thus of limiting the fear and arousing the hopes of mankind.❞
—Report of the General Advisory Committee of the Atomic Energy Commission, October 1949

In spite of these concerns, development of the hydrogen bomb went forward in the late 1940s and early 1950s. President Truman had made the final decision. "It is part of my responsibility as commander-in-chief," he declared, "to see to it that our country is able to defend itself against any possible aggressor." Truman did not want to take the chance that the Soviet Union would develop its own hydrogen bomb. That would give the Soviet Union a significant military advantage over the United States.

The first hydrogen bomb, detonated in 1951, was code-named "Mike," for *megaton*.

THE FIRST HYDROGEN BOMB TEST

When detonated: November 1, 1952, Eniwetak Atoll, Marshall Islands

Amount of energy released: 10.4 megatons, equivalent to 10.4 million tons of TNT

Size of fireball: 3 miles in diameter

Height of mushroom cloud: more than 25 miles

By 1952 scientists had solved the difficult technical challenges of building a hydrogen bomb. On November 1 they tested it. The blast was beyond anything they had imagined. The island on which the bomb had been placed simply vanished. "I was stunned," recalled one observer of the explosion. "It looked as though it blotted out the whole horizon."

POSTWAR AMERICA **855**

❷ What was the arms race, and what were its effects in the United States? *competition between U.S. and Soviets to prevent the other country from gaining newer technology or weapons; U.S. began to build large stockpiles of weapons and look for new and better ways of delivering those weapons to their targets*

The Arms Race

Describe How did U.S. military strategy change during the Eisenhower administration? *It shifted away from traditional forces, such as soldiers and tanks, and relied more on nuclear weapons.*

Summarize Why was the first H-bomb impractical? *massive size; no way to deliver the million-pound bomb*

Evaluate What advantage did intercontinental ballistic missiles have over nuclear-armed bombers? *possible answers—They didn't require pilots and could probably be launched more quickly, and travel faster, than bombers.*

📄 CRF: Biography: Hyman George Rickover

The explosion of the H-bomb once again put the United States ahead of the Soviet Union in weapons technology. This lead, however, was short-lived. In August 1953 the Soviets successfully tested a hydrogen bomb of their own.

READING CHECK Drawing Conclusions
Why did President Truman decide to develop the hydrogen bomb?

The Arms Race

The United States and the Soviets again had roughly the same technology. Each side, however, remained concerned that the other would gain an advantage. To prevent this, both countries began to build stockpiles of weapons. They also sought new and better ways of delivering those weapons to potential targets.

Each improvement or technological advance by one country was met with some response by the other. Thus the United States and Soviet Union began an arms race—an international contest between countries seeking a military advantage over each other.

ACADEMIC VOCABULARY
equipped fitted with; possessing certain equipment

New military strategies The arrival and advance of nuclear weapons forced American leaders to reconsider the way the United States built its military defenses. When Eisenhower took office, he scaled back the nation's reliance on so-called conventional forces, such as soldiers and tanks. In their place, he increased reliance on nuclear weapons. This shift helped lead to the development of John Foster Dulles's policies of brinkmanship and massive retaliation. Instead of resisting its enemies with armies at the point of attack, the United States would seek to prevent its enemies from attacking in the first place by promising a devastating nuclear response.

Eisenhower and Dulles's strategies placed great importance on keeping the lead in the arms race. The American threat of massive retaliation would be more effective if its forces were superior to those of any adversary.

THE IMPACT TODAY
Science and Technology
In recent times, the United States and other nations have worked to prevent the spread of nuclear weapons to developing countries, including Iran and North Korea.

New bombs The first American hydrogen bomb was massive, not just in its destructive power but also in its size. It stood three stories tall and weighed a million pounds. It was so big, there would have been no way to actually use the weapon against an enemy.

Scientists therefore worked hard to reduce the size of the H-bomb. Before long, they had succeeded in making weapons that could be more easily delivered to enemy targets. The first such bomb was tested in 1954.

Early on, the United States focused on aircraft as the means of delivering nuclear weapons. As a result, the U.S. Air Force grew substantially in the 1950s. While Eisenhower was cutting budgets in many other parts of the military, he spent large amounts on new long-range bomber aircraft, such as the B-52. These bombers had the ability to deliver nuclear weapons anywhere in the world.

The U.S. fleet of bombers was spread across dozens of locations in Europe, Africa, and elsewhere. The American nuclear arsenal was constantly on the move. Bombers were always in the air, and those on the ground were ready to take off within 15 minutes. This helped ensure that no enemy would be able to destroy the American ability to launch an attack.

While the United States at first relied on aircraft to carry its nuclear weapons, scientists were hard at work developing missiles that could be equipped with these weapons. The effort involved reducing the size of the weapons themselves. It also involved developing missiles that could reach enemy targets accurately.

The development of missiles represented a major technological challenge. In the early 1950s, American rockets were capable of carrying a small nuclear weapon only a short distance. By the end of the 1950s, Americans had developed intercontinental ballistic missiles, or **ICBMs**. The ICBMs could travel thousands of miles and strike very close to their intended targets. They could also deliver powerful nuclear weapons.

Other new technologies While scientists were exploring the atom's destructive power, they were also learning to use it for other purposes. In 1954 the U.S. Navy launched the first nuclear-powered submarine. On this vessel, the USS *Nautilus*, nuclear fuel heated water to create steam. This steam powered the engine.

Unlike earlier submarines, the *Nautilus* could travel for months without needing to refuel. Thus, vessels such as the *Nautilus* could perform missions over greater distances. Nuclear-powered submarines were also capable of traveling at high speeds underwater.

856 CHAPTER 26

The Rise of the Defense Industry

1. Guide students in a discussion of the shift from traditional armed forces to an increased reliance on nuclear weapons under the Eisenhower administration.

2. Organize the class in small groups. Have each group conduct research on the rise of the defense industry during the Cold War and write a brief report on its findings, using the following questions as a guide: What were the effects of a permanent defense industry on the economy?

How was defense industry research funded? What new technologies developed by the defense industry later proved to have non-military uses?

3. Have volunteers from each group read their reports to the class. **LS** Interpersonal, Verbal-Linguistic

📄 Alternative Assessment Handbook, Rubrics 30: Research; and 37: Writing Assignments

Answers

Reading Check *to give U.S. significant military advantage; wanted to keep up with Soviets in case they were building H-bomb*

Several years after launching the *Nautilus*, the United States began fitting its nuclear-powered submarines with nuclear missiles. By sending some of its nuclear weapons underwater and out of reach of enemy attack, the United States had found another way to ensure that any enemy move could be met with a devastating nuclear response.

Nuclear power was put to use for peaceful purposes on land as well. Nuclear power plants in the United States began to produce electricity for homes and businesses in 1957.

Soviet advances in technology The Soviet Union was also improving and expanding its weapons. Throughout the 1950s, the Soviets built new and improved weapons and delivery systems. The Soviets did lag behind the United States in the number of weapons it possessed. Nevertheless, it was well understood that any nuclear attack would lead to terrible destruction for both sides.

Soviet technological skill was demonstrated in shocking fashion in 1957. On October 4 the

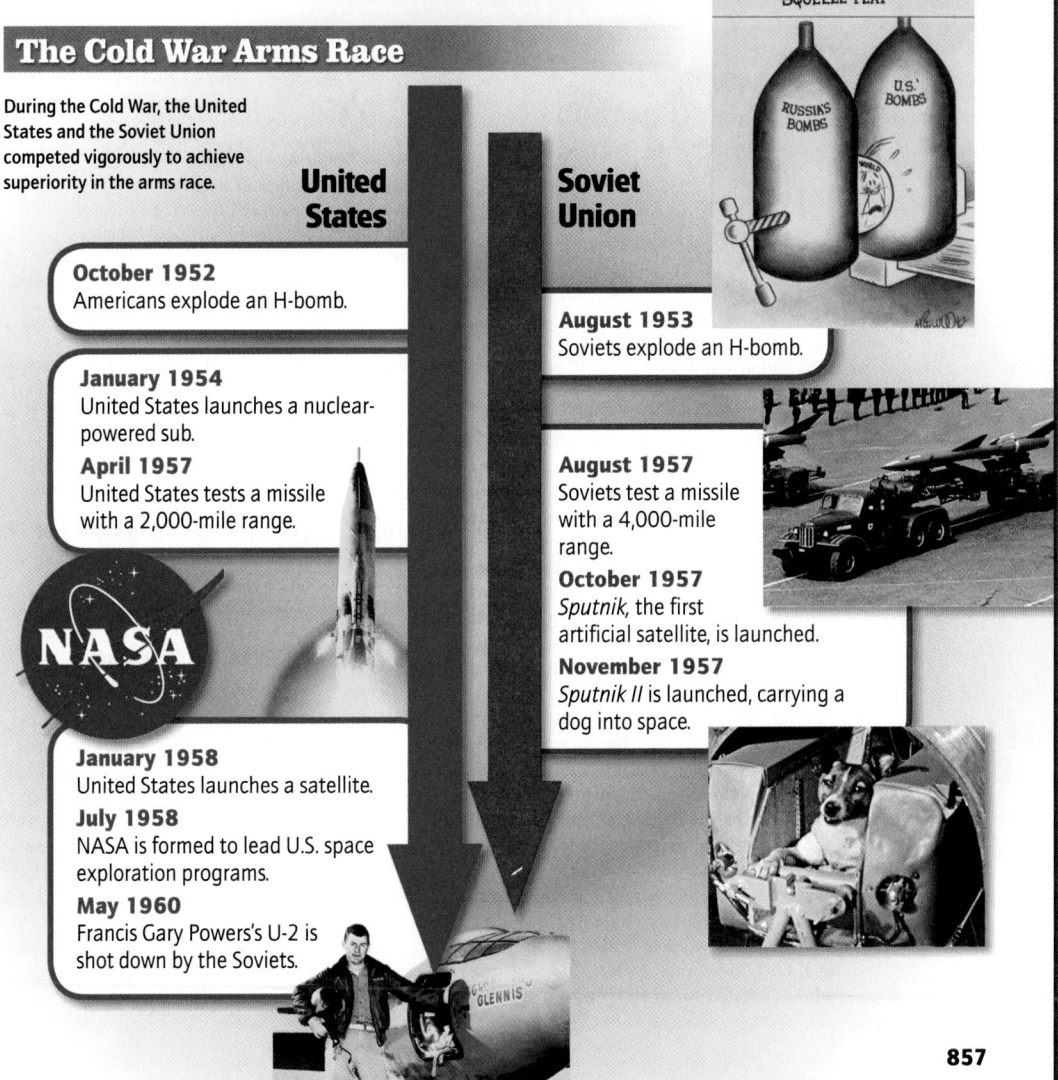

The Cold War Arms Race

During the Cold War, the United States and the Soviet Union competed vigorously to achieve superiority in the arms race.

United States

October 1952
Americans explode an H-bomb.

January 1954
United States launches a nuclear-powered sub.

April 1957
United States tests a missile with a 2,000-mile range.

January 1958
United States launches a satellite.

July 1958
NASA is formed to lead U.S. space exploration programs.

May 1960
Francis Gary Powers's U-2 is shot down by the Soviets.

Soviet Union

August 1953
Soviets explode an H-bomb.

August 1957
Soviets test a missile with a 4,000-mile range.

October 1957
Sputnik, the first artificial satellite, is launched.

November 1957
Sputnik II is launched, carrying a dog into space.

SQUEEZE PLAY

857

Direct Teach

Reading Focus

The Arms Race

Recall Identify a nondestructive use of nuclear energy. *providing electricity for homes and businesses*

Summarize Why did the United States keep B-52 bombers in the air at all times? *helped ensure that no enemy could destroy American ability to strike*

The Cold War Arms Race

Identify Which events in this time line involve nuclear energy? *Americans explode an H-bomb; Soviets explode an H-bomb; U.S. launches a nuclear-powered sub*

Info to Know

Radioactive Fallout One of the dangers of testing nuclear devices is the presence in the atmosphere of radioactive fallout. Over time, it can travel around the world and finally fall to earth with rain or other precipitation. These radioactive materials can then enter the food supply and cause serious health problems. For example, Strontium-90 falls on plants, which are eaten by cattle. It is then eaten by humans in the form of dairy products. In the body, it becomes part of the bone, and can cause leukemia and cancer.

Skills Focus: Analyzing Primary Sources

At Level

Reading Like a Historian Skill
Peaceful Uses of Nuclear Energy

Research Required

1. Tell students that in 1953 President Eisenhower gave a speech before the members of the United Nations. In this "Atoms for Peace" speech, Eisenhower advocated the use of nuclear energy for peaceful purposes.

2. Have each student conduct research on the peaceful uses of nuclear energy and write a brief, illustrated report about the different uses of nuclear energy.

3. Ask volunteers to share their reports with the class.

4. Guide the class in a discussion of peaceful uses of nuclear energy, looking at both the problems it solves and the potential problems it creates. **LS Verbal-Linguistic, Logical-Mathematical**

📰 Alternative Assessment Handbook, Rubrics 30: Research; and 42: Writing to Inform

❸ How did Americans react to the growing threat of nuclear war? *with fear that there would be an actual attack; some people built bomb shelters in their yards*

Americans React to the Threat of Nuclear War

Define What is nuclear fallout? *particles of radioactive material produced by nuclear explosions; falls through the atmosphere like rain to the ground*

Explain Why is nuclear fallout so hazardous? *exposure can cause burns and increase the risk of future health problems, such as cancer and birth defects; danger lasts for many years*

Info to Know

Sputnik **and the U.S.** When the Soviet Union beat the United States in the race to be first into space with the launch of *Sputnik* on October 4, 1957, it caused a furor in the United States. The public feared that the Soviets' ability to launch satellites into space meant that they also had the ability to launch missiles that could carry nuclear weapons to the United States. On January 31, 1958, the United States launched Explorer I, which was responsible for the discovery of the Van Allen radiation belts around the Earth.

Answers

Reading Like a Historian *possible answers—lawyers look at things in terms of defense and offense; scientists look at the ways science can improve life*

Reading Check *National Aeronautics and Space Administration; took charge of and consolidated nation's space exploration program in order to compete with Soviet space program*

COUNTERPOINTS

The Arms Race

When John Foster Dulles spoke of "retaliatory power," he was speaking of nuclear weapons.

The Russell-Einstein Manifesto took its name from Nobel Prize winners Bertrand Russell and Albert Einstein. Nine other scientists signed the document.

❝ [T]he principal deterrent to aggressive war is mobile retaliatory power. This retaliatory power must be vast in terms of its potential . . . The essential is that a would-be aggressor should realize that he cannot make armed aggression.❞

John Foster Dulles, 1957

❝ There lies before us, if we choose, continual progress in happiness, knowledge, and wisdom. Shall we, instead, choose death, because we cannot forget our quarrels?❞

Albert Einstein and others, 1955

Skills FOCUS **READING LIKE A HISTORIAN**

Identifying Points of View Dulles was a lawyer, and Einstein was a scientist. How might each man's point of view have been influenced by his profession?

See Skills Handbook, pp. H28–H29

Soviets launched the first-ever artificial satellite, named *Sputnik*. A **satellite** is an object that orbits around the Earth. *Sputnik* was small, only about the size of a basketball and weighed 200 pounds. The Soviets launched *Sputnik II* less than a month later. This satellite carried a dog, the first living creature to orbit Earth in space.

The *Sputnik* launches caused great concern in the United States. To many Americans, it signaled that the Soviets had surpassed American scientists in terms of technical skill and knowledge. Many worried this would translate into better, more accurate weaponry.

The United States was quick to respond to the *Sputnik* challenge. By January 1958, the United States was ready to launch a satellite of its own. In addition, in July of that year Congress established the National Aeronautics and Space Administration, or **NASA**. This new agency took charge of the nation's programs for exploring outer space. You will read more about NASA in future chapters.

The American people also took a hard look at their educational system. Many wondered whether a decline in the nation's schools had enabled the Soviet Union to surpass the United States in technological achievement. In response to this concern, Congress in 1958 passed the National Defense Education Act, which provided hundreds of millions of dollars for education in the United States.

READING CHECK **Identifying Cause and Effect** What was NASA, and how was its creation related to the arms race of the 1950s?

Americans React to the Threat of Nuclear War

After World War II, Americans had experience with the dangers of war. With the Japanese attack on Pearl Harbor, they had even experienced an attack by a foreign enemy. But the threat of nuclear attack was something new.

For the first time, Americans had to face the possibility that entire cities might be destroyed in the fireball of a nuclear explosion. Another fear was **nuclear fallout**, streams of radioactive particles produced by nuclear explosions. Such radiation drifts down through

---

Skills Focus: Evaluating Historical Interpretation
At Level

Reading Like a Historian Skill
The Human Side of the Cold War

1. Organize the class into small groups. Have each group develop a series of questions that they would like to ask someone who lived during the Cold War. Students should focus their questions on Cold War–related events that created specific memories.

2. Have each student locate a person who lived during the Cold War and conduct an interview based on their questions. If students cannot locate someone to interview, they may use primary sources.

3. Have volunteers read their interviews to the class. Then discuss the interviews and similarities and differences in the subjects' experiences. Have students evaluate reasons for the differences. **LS Interpersonal**

Alternative Assessment Handbook, Rubric 24: Oral Presentations

the atmosphere like rain to the ground. Exposure to nuclear fallout can cause burns and increase the risk of future health problems, such as cancer and birth defects. The environmental dangers from nuclear fallout can last for many years.

The American public was reminded of the terrible effects of nuclear fallout following the testing of a hydrogen bomb in the Marshall Islands in 1954. In that incident, bad weather spread a large cloud of nuclear fallout over a large area. The fallout harmed sailors on a Japanese fishing boat. One died as a result. In addition, many people living on the islands near the huge blast were forced to leave their homes—permanently. The levels of radioactivity left behind were too high for people to safely endure.

Strengthening civil defense American foreign policy was designed to prevent war. But there was no way to be sure that war would never come. As a result, American leaders also worked to prepare the nation for what to do in the event of a nuclear attack.

The Truman administration created the Federal Civil Defense Administration (FCDA) to help educate and prepare the public for nuclear emergencies. The FCDA stressed the key role of the average citizen in being ready to handle a crisis. In a nuclear war, the thinking went, the public might not be able to depend on the military to keep them safe.

In the words of FCDA leader Millard Caldwell, the "back yard may be the next front line." Indeed, during the Eisenhower administration, a strong civil defense program was seen as a good way to deter Soviet aggression.

To help educate the public, the FCDA issued materials, such as the booklet "How to Survive an Atomic Bomb." Educational films such as *Duck and Cover*, which featured a friendly turtle named Bert, taught schoolchildren techniques for protecting themselves from the deadly effects of a nuclear blast.

Air-raid sirens were installed in communities across the country. Tested on a regular basis, their haunting wail became a familiar sound to millions of Americans.

Women played a central role in the FCDA's civil defense program. They were seen as the keepers of the family and the guardians of the home. It became their job, according to the FCDA, to prepare the home for emergency—and to recognize the warning signals of attack.

The FCDA began staging tests of the nation's civil defense program in 1955. These tests, called Operation Alert, explored the

ACADEMIC VOCABULARY

issued officially distributed

Preparing for Attack

The government encouraged people to prepare for nuclear attack. At left, students practice the "duck and cover" drill, which was supposed to help protect them from injury in the event of a nuclear blast. *Why were Americans so fearful of attack?*

859

• **Direct Teach** •

Reading Focus

Americans React to the Threat of Nuclear War

Summarize What role did the Federal Civil Defense Administration expect women to play in the civil defense program? *Women were expected to prepare the home for emergency and recognize the warning signals of attack.*

Make Inferences Why might a strong civil defense program have helped deter Soviet aggression? *possible answer—by showing that the United States was prepared for the possibility of nuclear war*

📄 CRF: Primary Source Activity: Basement Fallout Shelter

Teaching Tip

"Duck and cover" drills were a standard part of the school year, much like fire drills or any other emergency-preparedness drills at school.

Preparing for Attack

Drawing Inferences Guide the class in a discussion of fallout shelters. Ask students whether they think that fallout shelters would have any real benefit in the case of nuclear war, or whether the chief benefit was psychological, in helping to dispel fears of nuclear war.

Differentiating Instruction

Below Level

English-Language Learners

Materials construction paper, colored pencils or markers

1. Guide students in a discussion of civil defense. Make sure students understand the concept of civil defense and the goals of the Federal Civil Defense Administration.

2. Pair students. Have each pair develop a theme and design a poster for the Federal Civil Defense Administration. The purpose of the posters should be to promote citizen preparedness in the event of a nuclear war.

3. Review poster themes with each pair and either approve their ideas or help the students come up with a suitable idea.

4. Have each pair create a poster illustrating its theme. Posters should have simple wording. Place posters on display for the rest of the class to see. **LS Interpersonal, Visual-Spatial**

📄 Alternative Assessment Handbook, Rubric 28: Posters

Answers

Photo *media coverage, government warnings, and school drills drew national attention to terrible destruction of nuclear warfare*

Americans React to the Threat of Nuclear War

Explain Why did Eisenhower warn Americans about the "military-industrial complex"? *saw establishment of permanent arms industry as threat to freedom*

Evaluate How did nuclear fears affect American culture in the 1950s? *movies and comic books had plots that centered on the dangers of radiation and life in a nuclear world*

● **Review & Assess** ●

Close

Guide students in a discussion of the ways in which the growing importance and power of nuclear weapons affected Americans' sense of well-being.

Review

- Online Quiz, Section 2
- Daily Test Practice Transparency

Assess

SE Section 2 Assessment

- Progress Assessment: Section 2 Quiz
- Alternative Assessment Handbook

Reteach

- Interactive Reader and Study Guide, Section 2
- Interactive Skills Tutor CD-ROM

Answers

Reading Check *government warnings; media coverage; air-raid siren testing*

---

possible effects of a nuclear attack on major American urban areas. They took into account the results of the 1954 hydrogen bomb test, in which significant nuclear fallout spread over an area of 7,000 square miles.

The results of the 1955 Operation Alert were deeply disturbing. According to the FCDA's evaluation in the densely populated New York City area, a nuclear attack could leave millions dead and millions more injured and homeless.

In other cities, participation in the tests was inconsistent. In Washington, D.C., for example, the U.S. Congress simply ignored the exercise and continued its work.

In case anyone had had any doubt, Operation Alert made it clear that a true nuclear attack on a major urban area would have terrible, long-lasting results.

HISTORY'S VOICES

❝This demonstration gives new emphasis to President Eisenhower's dictum [statement] that war no longer presented the possibility of victory or defeat, but only the alternative of varying degrees of destruction.❞

—*The New York Times,* June 16, 1955

Nuclear fears The government's efforts did raise preparedness. It also raised fears, leading many Americans to build bomb shelters in their yards. The public also began to express concern over the testing of nuclear weapons and

the effects of nuclear fallout. These concerns eventually helped lead to negotiations with the Soviet Union for a treaty limiting nuclear testing. The Limited Test-Ban Treaty was ratified in 1963.

Nuclear fears also affected the culture of the times. A number of 1950s movies had plots that centered on the dangers of radiation. Comic books for young readers featured heroes and villains doing battle in a nuclear world.

The military-industrial complex While the public learned to live with the fear of nuclear attack, President Eisenhower used part of his farewell address in 1961 to inform them of a new danger: the "military-industrial complex." In the past, Eisenhower said, the United States had no permanent arms industry. When war came, factories changed from making cars, for example, to making tanks. By the 1950s, however, that had changed.

"We have been compelled to create a permanent armaments industry of vast proportions," Eisenhower said. While necessary, he noted, it was still a threat to freedom. "The potential for the disastrous rise of misplaced power exists and will persist," Eisenhower warned. Thus, as the 1950s ended and a new decade began, Americans had a new challenge to face.

READING CHECK **Identifying Supporting Details** How were the American people regularly reminded of the threat of nuclear war?

SECTION 2 ASSESSMENT

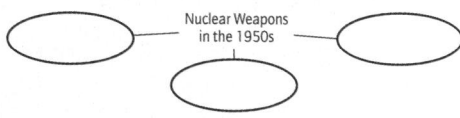
go.hrw.com
Online Quiz
Keyword: SD7 HP26

Reviewing Ideas, Terms, and People

1. a. Describe How did the **hydrogen bomb** differ from the atomic weapons used on Hiroshima and Nagasaki?
   b. Draw Conclusions How do you think a more powerful weapon such as the hydrogen bomb would fit within the policies of brinkmanship and massive retaliation?

2. a. Define Write a brief definition of each of the following terms: ICBM, *Sputnik*, NASA
   b. Summarize Why was the Soviet development of a satellite so significant to the people of the United States?
   c. Predict How do you think the race to find an edge in nuclear weapons will affect the nature of nuclear weapons in the decades to come?

3. a. Describe What was the job of the FCDA?
   b. Contrast How did the nuclear threat differ from the kinds of threats that had faced the American people in the past?

Critical Thinking

4. Identifying the Main Idea Copy the chart below and use information from the section to record details that support the main idea of the section. Refer to the main idea at the beginning of this section.

Nuclear Weapons
in the 1950s

FOCUS ON WRITING

5. Narrative Write a brief narrative paragraph that tells the story of the arms race of the 1950s. Include details from this section.

860 CHAPTER 26

Section 2 Assessment Answers

1. a. H-bomb was more powerful
   b. would serve as a strong deterrent

2. a. ICBM—ballistic missiles that could travel long distances; *Sputnik*—successful Soviet satellite; NASA—U.S. space agency
   b. many Americans worried that Soviets had more technical skills and knowledge than Americans; afraid Soviets would develop better, more accurate weapons
   c. possible answer—will become more and more powerful

3. a. help educate and prepare public for nuclear emergencies
   b. military might not be able to protect people; would have long-lasting effects

4. H-bomb; ICBMs; FCDA; bomb shelters

5. possible answer—U.S. and Soviets built new bombs and missiles; Soviets launched *Sputnik* I and II, gained space advantage; U.S. prepared for nuclear war at home and militarily

The Television Age

BEFORE YOU READ

MAIN IDEA

Television was a major influence on American culture in the 1950s, mirroring larger changes in technology and culture.

READING FOCUS

1. How did television change American life in the 1950s?
2. What other technological developments occurred during the 1950s?
3. How was American culture changing during the 1950s?

KEY TERMS AND PEOPLE

Lucille Ball
transistor
integrated circuit
Jonas Salk
vaccine
Levittown
Sunbelt
Interstate Highway System

TAKING NOTES As you read, take notes about Americans' lifestyles during the 1950s. Record your notes in a graphic organizer like the one shown here.

Entertainment and Culture	Housing	Transportation

THE INSIDE STORY

How did a redhead become a star in black-and-white? Television was still quite new in 1951 when the *I Love Lucy* show was first broadcast. The nation quickly fell in love with the zany antics of the show's characters: the redheaded Lucy Ricardo, played by Lucille Ball, and her bandleader husband Ricky, played by Desi Arnaz. At the peak of the show's success, two of three television sets in the country were tuned in for every episode.

The show helped shape the future of television itself. Prior to *I Love Lucy*, TV did not have its own style and distinctive art. Programs were little more than filmed versions of radio programs or vaudeville routines. But under the shrewd guidance of Ball and Arnaz, *I Love Lucy* pioneered new production techniques. For example, the show was filmed rather than broadcast live. This enabled the stars to perfect their comic routines—with hilarious results.

The program also broke ground with its casting. In 1951 Ball was a movie star in decline. Cuban-born Arnaz spoke with a thick Spanish accent. Neither fit the mold of the traditional star of the time. Yet their chemistry—the two were married in real life—was remarkable. Together they produced some of the most memorable moments in TV history. In the process, they helped television revolutionize American life.

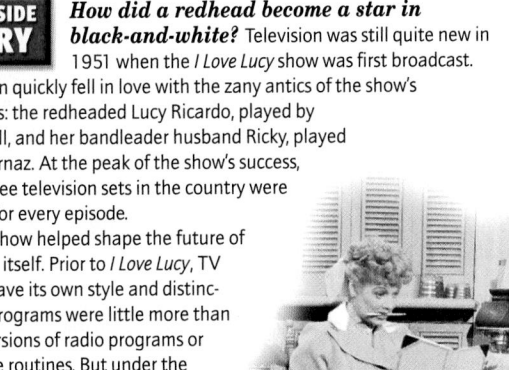

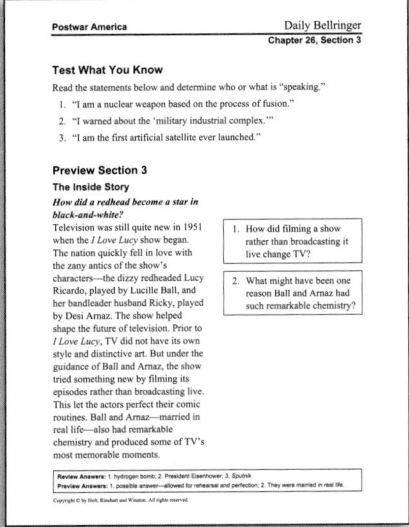

▲ Ball's new ideas changed how TV shows were made.

Teach the Main Idea

At Level

The Television Age

1. **Teach** Ask students the Reading Focus questions to teach this section.

2. **Apply** Have students list ways that life in the United States during the early 1950s was similar to and different from life today.

3. **Review** Ask volunteers to share their lists with the class. Then guide the class in a discussion of new developments of the 1950s that we take for granted today.

4. **Practice/Homework** Tell students that even in the 1950s, citizens were concerned about the effect of television on American society. Have each student write an editorial explaining what might be done to reduce television's impact on families and society.
   LS Logical-Mathematical, Verbal-Linguistic
   📝 Alternative Assessment Handbook, Rubric 17: Letters to Editors

---

Academic Vocabulary

Review with students the high-use academic term in this section.

categories groups or classes whose members share common features (p. 862)

revise change or modify (p. 865)

📄 CRF: Vocabulary Builder Activity, Section 3

Taking Notes

Entertainment and Culture—variety of television programs; boom times; Housing—suburban developments, relocation to Sunbelt; Transportation—Interstate Highway System

1 How did television change American life in the 1950s? *brought political candidates, news, advertisements, and entertainment into people's living rooms*

Television Changes American Life

Explain How did television change American politics? *political leaders quickly learned that TV had the power to change their relationships with voters; could both help and hurt their reputations by exposing their true behavior to the public*

Summarize How did advertising change as a result of television? *At first, a single advertiser sponsored a program, and advertising was integrated into the program. Advertisers shifted to one- or two-minute segments, and the modern TV commercial was born. By 1960 television had become the major method of advertising in the country.*

Evaluate How did television's influence begin to concern some people? *They began to question the effects of spending so many hours watching TV. They were especially concerned that it might have a negative impact on children.*

Television Changes American Life

Though broadcast television was still young when **Lucille Ball** captured the hearts of the nation, TV technology had existed for a number of years. Scientists had been working on it at least since the 1920s. By the end of World War II, television was ready for home use. Postwar consumers, eager to spend after years of wartime sacrifice, purchased the new devices. Between 1945 and 1950, some 5 million TV sets appeared in American homes.

That was just the beginning. During the 1950s, the number of Americans owning TVs continued to rise. By 1959 more than 40 million American homes had at least one set.

TV and politics One field in which television had an immediate impact was politics. America's leaders quickly learned that TV had great power to change their relationships with the voters. You have read how vice presidential candidate Richard Nixon used television in 1952 to appeal to the voting public. As you will read later, Nixon would also find that TV could do harm to a candidate's image.

Television also altered the career of Senator Joseph McCarthy, the Communist hunter. The televised 1954 Army-McCarthy hearings finally gave the public the chance to see his disgraceful, bullying behavior. The hearings left his once-lofty reputation ruined and his career in tatters.

Television advertising Advertisers were another group that quickly recognized the promise of television. TV's combination of picture and sound gave it more persuasive potential than radio. By 1960 television was the major method of advertising in the country.

Early TV advertising was patterned after radio advertising. A single advertiser sponsored the broadcast of an entire program. On programs such as the *Colgate Comedy Hour*, the line between program and advertisement was blurry. The product being sold was actually a part of the action.

As the cost of producing entire TV programs rose, advertisers shifted to buying just one- or two-minute segments during shows to sell their products. Ads were separated from programming, and the TV commercial was born.

ACADEMIC VOCABULARY

categories groups or classes with members that share common features

THE IMPACT TODAY

Science and Technology Today most televisions are built to include a device called the V-chip. This device allows concerned adults to block the display of certain programs, such as those that contain violent content.

Programming Of course, for most Americans, television was mainly about the programs. Each day and night, audiences tuned in to watch their favorites. The *I Love Lucy* show was only one example of many popular television programs.

Television's first big hit was the *Texaco Star Theater*, starring comedian Milton Berle, which later became the *Milton Berle Show*. Berle's great success earned him the nickname "Mr. Television." His hugely popular program of comedy and music is credited with helping television get established in its earliest days.

The hit show *American Bandstand* got its appeal from another cultural movement of the 1950s: rock and roll music. The show, which began in 1957, featured young people dancing to popular songs. *American Bandstand* remained on television until 1987.

The 1950s also saw the introduction of some of the many categories of programs popular today. Daytime dramas (known as soap operas), crime dramas, and game shows almost all got their start during this decade. To help people keep track of their favorite programs, a magazine called *TV Guide* began publishing.

Concerns about television As television's popularity ballooned, some people began to question its effects. Of special concern was TV's possible impact on children.

On several occasions in the 1950s, Congress looked into the effects of violent content on young viewers. To address this concern, the TV industry adopted its own voluntary standards. For example, the industry promised that law enforcement would always appear in a positive light and that criminals would always be presented as "bad guys." Satisfied, Congress took no formal action to limit television content during the 1950s. Still, Americans would continue to discuss the effect of television on children for years to come.

TV experienced a scandal in the late 1950s when the public learned that a popular game show had been rigged. Congress held hearings into the matter, and one of the contestants involved, Charles Van Doren, wound up leaving his job as a university professor.

READING CHECK **Identifying Cause and Effect** What were some of the effects of television on American life and culture in the 1950s?

Differentiating Instruction

Below Level

Special Education Students

Standard English Mastery

1. Review with students the information in the text about television in the 1950s. Pair students, and have each pair make a list of things they learned about television during that time period.

2. Have each pair write two sentences describing television in the 1950s.

3. Ask volunteers to share their sentences with the rest of the class. **LS Interpersonal, Verbal-Linguistic**

📝 Alternative Assessment Handbook, Rubric 37: Writing Assignments

Answers

Reading Check *gave people more insight into political leaders, entertained people with comedies and music programs, programs' content influenced by government*

Milestones in Television History

Television has made history, and it has recorded history. Along the way, many changes have taken place in television. In the 1950s three major networks—ABC, CBS, and NBC—dominated TV broadcasting with shows aimed at the same general audience. Today the major networks share the television market with hundreds of cable networks airing programs tailored to specific age groups and interests.

A 1950 TV set ▲

1950 9 percent of U.S. households have televisions.

1951 Coast-to-coast live television broadcasts begin.

1954 CBS and NBC begin regular color broadcasting, even though just 1 percent of U.S. households own a color TV set. The NBC "peacock" logo is shown above. ▲

TV Guide magazine is published for the first time.

1960 The first televised presidential debate takes place.

87 percent of U.S. households have televisions. Programming is aimed at a family audience. ▼

1963 ABC, CBS, and NBC broadcast four days of continuous live coverage of the assassination and funeral of President John F. Kennedy. Millions of people around the world watch the state funeral on TV.

1969 *Sesame Street* airs for the first time, breaking new ground in children's educational programming.

An estimated 720 million people watch the first moon landing on live television. ▼

1970 The sitcom *Julia* is the first to feature an African American actor in the title role, played by Diahann Caroll. ▶

1971 Under federal law, cigarette advertising is banned on television and radio.

1972 The first cable network, Home Box Office (HBO), begins broadcasting.

1980 Cable News Network (CNN) offers the first 24-hour news service. ▼

1986 The *Challenger* space shuttle explodes just over a minute after takeoff. Millions of Americans witness the disaster on live TV.

1999 V-chip technology is introduced, allowing parents to block violent or unsuitable television programming from their children.

Today 98 percent of U.S. households have televisions. 76 percent of TV households have more than one set. About 68 percent of TV households have cable TV.

SKILLS FOCUS **INTERPRETING INFOGRAPHICS**

Making Generalizations In what ways has television changed since the 1950s?
See Skills Handbook, p. H18

---

❷ What other technological developments occurred during the 1950s? *The transistor, integrated circuit, computer, and polio vaccine were developed.*

Other Technological Developments of the 1950s

Recall When were the first computers built? *in the 1940s*

Predict How would UNIVAC impact the future of American business? *possible answer—would make computers available to businesses; businesses able to expand by using computers to help with some tasks*

Evaluate Why was the development of a vaccine against polio so important? *A vaccine could prevent death or long-term physical effects of polio and allow children to live a normal life.*

Linking to Today

The Computer Today a single computer chip has greater processing capacity than the entire ENIAC computer, which occupied a large room.

Answers

Linking to Today *too large, difficult to use*

864

Other Technological Developments of the 1950s

Television was certainly the most popular technological innovation of the 1950s. A number of other breakthroughs, however, also helped to transform American life.

Transistors and computers Machines have been used to perform calculations for thousands of years. In the 1940s, however, researchers began to build the first of what we might recognize today as computers. These devices used electricity to perform complicated calculations. For example, in Great Britain, scientists used an early type of computer to help break communications codes during World War II.

To build the first computers, scientists used thousands of vacuum tubes. These were glass and metal devices that helped form the complicated electronic workings of the machines. Because computers used so many tubes, they took up hundreds of square feet of floor space. They also drew large amounts of electricity.

In 1947 scientists at Bell Laboratories developed a device called the **transistor**. These devices worked much like tubes but with several advantages. For one, they were smaller. They also did not break as often as tubes did.

The invention of transistors led to the improvement of all kinds of electronics, from radios to televisions. Transistors also made possible smaller and more efficient computers.

In 1951 the first computer available for commercial use hit the market. It was called the UNIVAC, short for universal automatic computer. The UNIVAC earned fame for predicting the outcome of the 1952 presidential election based on early returns.

Use of computers continued to expand in the 1950s. New computer makers, such as International Business Machines (IBM), entered the market. The computers were still large. (A complete UNIVAC system could weigh 30,000 pounds.) Even relatively inexpensive systems cost up to $50,000 or more. Nevertheless, large companies and government agencies purchased computers. By the end of the decade, for example, banks were using computers to help process checks.

Meanwhile, computer technology continued to improve. In 1958 scientists developed the **integrated circuit**, a single piece of material that includes a number of transistors and other electronic components. Also known as computer chips, integrated circuits made possible the dizzying advancement of computer technology in the years ahead.

The Computer Revolution

The first general-purpose electronic computer was developed in the 1940s. The Electronic Numerical Integrator and Computer (ENIAC) was about 80 feet long, 8 feet high, and 2 feet deep.

New developments allowed more people to use computers. By the 1980s, Apple Computer had popularized tools such as the mouse, and Compaq had developed a portable computer that weighed 28 pounds.

Today, laptop computers weigh just a few pounds and do not require wires. Powerful computing devices fit in the palm of your hand.

Drawing Conclusions Why was ENIAC not useful to most people?

Today, a computerized gadget that hangs on your keychain has more than a thousand times the data storage of the room-sized ENIAC.

Skills Focus: Comparing and Contrasting   `At Level`

Reading Skill
Miniaturization

Materials construction paper, colored markers, scissors, glue

1. Guide the class in a discussion of the ways in which the development of the transistor and the integrated circuit allowed products such as computers to be made smaller. What other products can they think of that have been affected in this way?

2. Pair students. Have each pair create a collage showing items that have been affected by

miniaturization. On the left side of their collages, students should include pictures of old-fashioned, full-sized items. On the right side, they should include pictures of modern miniaturized versions of those items. An arrow should be drawn showing the progression from full size to miniaturized. Display student collages for all to see. **LS Visual-Spatial**

📖 Alternative Assessment Handbook, Rubric 3: Artwork

The Salk vaccine Earlier in this book, you read about Franklin D. Roosevelt and his bout with polio. The disease left him without the use of his legs. Another common effect of polio, which often struck children, was an impaired ability to breathe. Many victims died.

Polio was a contagious disease. Outbreaks were all too common in the early 1900s. When polio hit, it spread quickly. For weeks at a time, parents would keep their children out of school or other public places.

The worst year on record for polio in the United States came in 1952. More than 57,000 people came down with the dreaded disease. That year, scientist **Jonas Salk** developed a new polio vaccine. A **vaccine** is a preparation that uses a killed or weakened form of a germ to help the body build defenses against that germ. Vaccines are often given by injection.

The public announcement of the discovery of the polio vaccine came in 1955, and Salk became a hero. Children began receiving the shot, and the number of polio cases plunged.

READING CHECK **Summarizing** What were two major technological developments of the 1950s?

Cultural Change in the 1950s

The 1950s in the United States is often viewed as a time of peace and prosperity. For some, this was true. At the same time, though, the richness and variety of American life formed a more complicated picture.

Boom times The threats of nuclear war and the spread of communism did cause unease for millions of Americans. At the same time, many people took comfort in the nation's stunning economic success. Indeed, in the 1950s the United States had clearly emerged as the world's greatest economic power. The American people made up just 6 percent of the world's population. Yet American workers and farmers produced about one-third of the world's goods and services.

As you have read, the years after World War II saw a sharp increase in birthrates—a baby boom. The baby boom continued throughout the 1950s. To house these growing families, builders such as Bill and Alfred Levitt created whole new communities of individual houses. (See the History Close-Up on the next page.)

Jonas Salk dedicated his career to fighting diseases that kill and maim people. After helping develop a vaccine for influenza for the Army during World War II, Salk turned his attention to fighting polio.

Salk worked for eight years to develop a polio vaccine. Confident of success, he tested his vaccine on himself, his wife, and their three sons in 1952. None of them became ill. After further testing, Salk's polio vaccine began to be used for mass vaccinations nationwide.

Salk refused to patent the vaccine. He did not want to profit from it. Rather, he wanted it made available to as many people as possible. Salk later served as a spokesperson for vaccinations. In 1995 he announced a new search—for an HIV vaccine.

Draw Conclusions In what ways was Salk's commitment to ending polio truly heroic?

New homes were filled with new stoves, refrigerators, and washing machines. New TVs ran ads urging people to want and buy even more.

Americans also purchased automobiles by the millions. To help fuel the desire of consumers, carmakers <u>revised</u> the styling of cars regularly. All this buying meant busy factories and high company profits. This, in turn, meant plentiful jobs. Employment was generally high in the 1950s. Wages rose steadily.

Indeed, a leading economist of the time, John Kenneth Galbraith, used the term "affluent society" to describe America in the postwar years. Yet Galbraith's view of the United States was not a positive one. In fact, he criticized an America overly focused on its own wealth.

HISTORY'S VOICES

❝The family which takes its . . . air-conditioned, power-steered, and power-braked automobile out for a tour passes through cities that are badly paved, made hideous by litter, blighted buildings, billboards, and posts for wires that should long since have been put underground.❞
—John Kenneth Galbraith, *The Affluent Society,* 1958

Another critic of the 1950s was Michael Harrington. His book *The Other America,* published in 1962, described the plight of the nation's poor. In his view, people living in poverty had been forgotten amid the economic success of the 1950s.

ACADEMIC VOCABULARY
revise changing or modifying

THE IMPACT TODAY

Daily Life
The postwar baby boom is having a huge effect on society today, as this large population is entering retirement. Health care costs are expected to rise as the "boomers" age and require more services.

Cultural Change in the 1950s

Identify What population trend began in the 1950s? *the shift to the Sunbelt, southern and western portions of U.S.*

Analyze How were Americans pushed toward "sameness" in the 1950s? *Business workers began to lose their individuality; suburban developments looked very similar.*

Make Inferences How do you think the development of the interstate highway system affected railroads? *possible answer—declined because easier for cars and trucks to travel throughout the U.S.*

📄 CRF: Biography: Allen Ginsberg

📄 CRF: Primary Source Activity: Federal-Aid Highway Act of 1956

Recent Scholarship

Just 50 years ago polio was a feared disease and a constant worry for children and parents. In *Splendid Solution: Jonas Salk and the Conquest of Polio*, Jeffrey Kluger describes the team effort and the resources that were mobilized to combat the disease.

Splendid Solution: Jonas Salk and the Conquest of Polio by Jeffrey Kluger. Putnam, 2005.

About the Illustration

This illustration is an artist's conception based on available sources. Historians, however, are uncertain exactly what this scene looked like.

Still another critic of the 1950s was William H. Whyte. In his book *The Organization Man,* he observed the push toward "sameness" and the increasing loss of individuality among the growing class of business workers.

New communities Many new homes built in the 1950s were parts of new suburban developments. The most famous of these was the enormous **Levittown**, New York, started in 1947 by Bill and Alfred Levitt.

The key to the success of Levittown and the many similar communities built in the postwar years was affordability: A family could purchase a single-family home at a reasonable price, often financed with the help of the government under the terms of the GI Bill.

Levittown was not a diverse community. Like many builders at the time, the Levitts at first refused to sell to African Americans.

The Levitts later built other communities in New Jersey and Pennsylvania. Overall, however, the U.S. population was beginning a shift in settlement toward the warmer southern and western portions of the United States, the so-called **Sunbelt**. In the 1950s the wide availability of home air conditioning helped make this move practical. This population shift has continued to the present.

California was (and still is) a major Sunbelt destination. At the start of the 1950s, just over 10.5 million people called California home. Over the next 10 years, more than 5 million people moved to the state.

Northern population centers such as New York and Illinois grew much more slowly. The shift from the North to the South and West was dramatized in the late 1950s when two New York baseball teams, the Brooklyn Dodgers and New York Giants, moved to California.

HISTORY CLOSE-UP

Building Levittown

Levittown, New York was a large community that eventually included more than 17,000 mass-produced homes. Levittown became a symbol for the many similar suburban towns that sprang up during the postwar years.

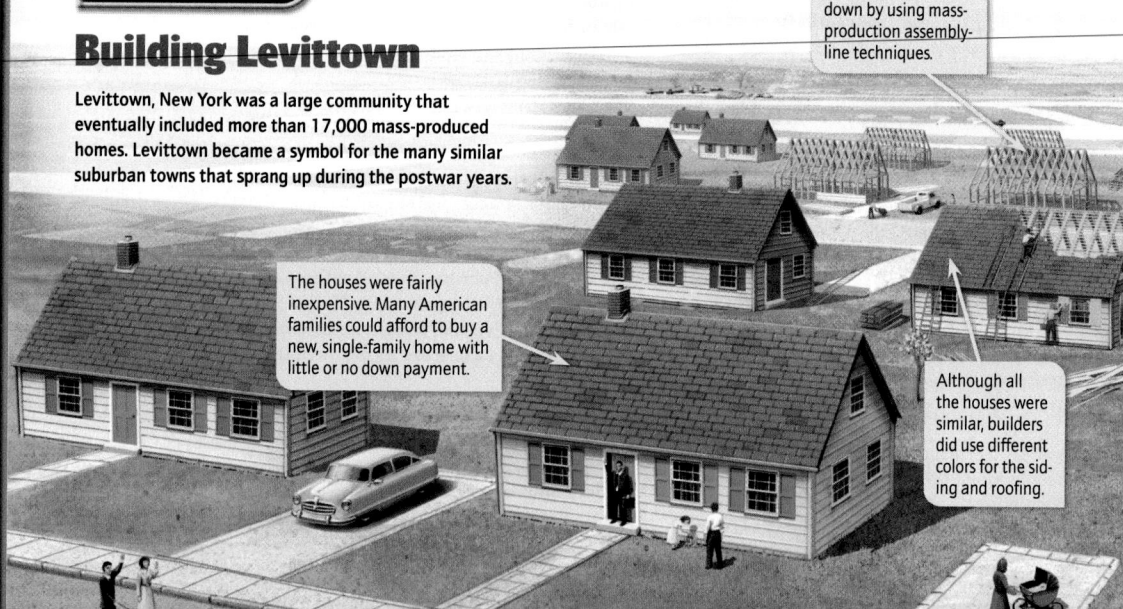

Developers kept costs down by using mass-production assembly-line techniques.

The houses were fairly inexpensive. Many American families could afford to buy a new, single-family home with little or no down payment.

Although all the houses were similar, builders did use different colors for the siding and roofing.

866

Skills Focus: Analyzing Costs and Benefits　　　　**At Level**

Social Studies Skill
Life in the 1950s

1. Guide students in a discussion of life during the 1950s. Discuss conformity, the rise of consumerism, the growth of suburbs, and migration to the Sunbelt.

2. Have students analyze the image in the Building Levittown feature. Remind students that communities like these were developed all across the United States, row upon row of houses that were similar in design.

3. Have students write an essay in which they analyze the costs and benefits of these types of homes and the resulting communities. Have students answer these questions: Why might it be cheaper and more efficient to build a development of very similar houses? Who was attracted to these communities?

4. Have volunteers read their essays to the class.
   LS Verbal-Linguistic, Logical-Mathematical

📄 Alternative Assessment Handbook, Rubric 37: Writing Assignments

New highways During the 1950s the United States launched an ambitious building project: the **Interstate Highway System**. This system was designed to be a network of high-speed roads for interstate travel, all built on the same design.

President Eisenhower had long favored such a system. In 1956 Congress finally approved funding for a planned 40,000-mile system. With its construction, the United States reinforced its commitment to cars and trucks as its main means of ground transportation.

The art of rebellion Interestingly, the arts of the 1950s often stressed rebellion against sameness and conformity. Film stars such as Marlon Brando and James Dean built images

as rebels who defied social norms. Jack Kerouac and other writers of the Beat generation also took the position of outsiders. They borrowed language from African American jazz music and rejected many social norms.

In popular music, rock and roll represented the rebellion of young people. Early stars such as Elvis Presley shocked many older Americans with his on-stage behavior. (Rock and roll was also influenced by African American musical forms, including jazz and rhythm and blues.)

If America seemed fascinated with the image of the rebel, it was mainly a male image. Women in film and literature tended to fill more traditional roles. It would be several years before women began to make their rebellion from the limits of American cultural norms.

READING CHECK **Summarizing** What were some key features of cultural change in the 1950s?

The Levittown planners created shopping areas, recreation centers, schools, and other attractive features for residents.

Skills FOCUS **INTERPRETING INFOGRAPHICS**

Scenes such as this were common in the 1950s. **Analyzing Information** What might make such communities attractive places to live?

See Skills Handbook, p. H18

SECTION 3 ASSESSMENT

go.hrw.com
Online Quiz
Keyword: SD7 HP26

Reviewing Ideas, Terms, and People

1. **a. Recall** What was the significance of **Lucille Ball** and Milton Berle in the 1950s?
   b. Draw Conclusions Why do you think Richard Nixon used television as a means of persuading the public that he had done no wrong in 1952?

2. **a. Define** Write a brief definition of each of the following terms: **transistor, integrated circuit, vaccine**
   b. Make Inferences Why do you think the development of the computer was so important in spite of the fact that only large companies could afford computers in the 1950s?

3. **a. Identify** What was the significance of **Levittown** and the **Sunbelt** in the 1950s?
   b. Contrast How did the concepts of the "affluent society" and the "other America" relate to the general prosperity of the 1950s?

Critical Thinking

4. **Identifying the Main Idea** Copy the chart below and use information from the section to record details that support the main idea of the section.

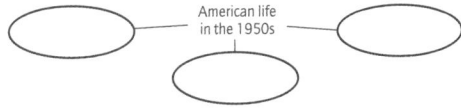

American life in the 1950s

FOCUS ON WRITING

5. **Descriptive** Assume the point of view of a citizen of the United States in the 1950s. Write a letter to a friend in another country describing the changing life and culture in your country.

POSTWAR AMERICA **867**

Section 3 Assessment Answers

1. **a.** helped establish television as a popular medium
   b. possible answer—more convincing if he was seen instead of just heard over the radio; gave him a much larger audience

2. **a.** transistor—led to improved electronic products; integrated circuit—single piece that contains transistors and other components; vaccine—helps body build its own immunity
   b. led to revolution in research and business

3. **a.** affordable, identical housing in suburbs; migration to the South and the West
   b. employment was high, wages rose, contributing to affluence; those living in poverty were generally ignored

4. television and popular culture; development of computers and advances in medicine; "sameness" and migration to Sunbelt

5. possible answer—baby boom; housing communities; highways; more consumer goods; advances in technology and medicine

Info to Know

Route 66 Also known as "The Mother Road" and "The Main Street of America," U.S. Highway 66 included close to 2,500 miles of road between Los Angeles and Chicago. Built in 1926, it was one of the first paved highways in the U.S. By connecting small towns and large cities, Route 66 enabled Americans to travel much farther in their cars. Beginning in the late 1950s, the interstate highway system began to replace the original road. Today, sections of the road are maintained and preserved as "Historic Route 66."

CHAPTER

26 DOCUMENT-BASED INVESTIGATION

Perspectives on Interstate Highways

Historical Context The documents below provide information on the impact of the Interstate Highway System.

Task Examine the documents and answer the questions that follow. Then you will be asked to write an essay about the impact of the Interstate Highway System, using facts from the documents and from the chapter to support the position you take in your thesis statement.

DOCUMENT 1

The Interstate Highway System was developed in response to public pressure to improve the nation's roads. In this excerpt from a speech given to Congress on February 22, 1955, President Eisenhower discusses the importance of U.S. highways.

"Our unity as a nation is sustained by free communication of thought and by easy transportation of people and goods. The ceaseless flow of information throughout the Republic is matched by individual and commercial movement over a vast system of inter-connected highways criss-crossing the Country and joining at our national borders with friendly neighbors to the north and south.

"Together, the uniting forces of our communication and transportation systems are dynamic elements in the very name we bear—United States. Without them, we would be a mere alliance of many separate parts.

"The Nation's highway system is a gigantic enterprise, one of our largest items of capital investment. Generations have gone into its building ... One in every seven Americans gains his livelihood and supports his family out of it. But, in large part, the network is inadequate for the nation's growing needs ...

"To correct these deficiencies is an obligation of Government at every level. The highway system is a public enterprise. As the owner and operator, the various levels of Government have a responsibility for management that promotes the economy of the nation and properly serves the individual user."

DOCUMENT 2

Within a few short years of the creation of the Interstate Highway System, trucks replaced railroads as the major means of freight transportation. These charts show how the amount of available railroad and highway transportation changed within 50 years.

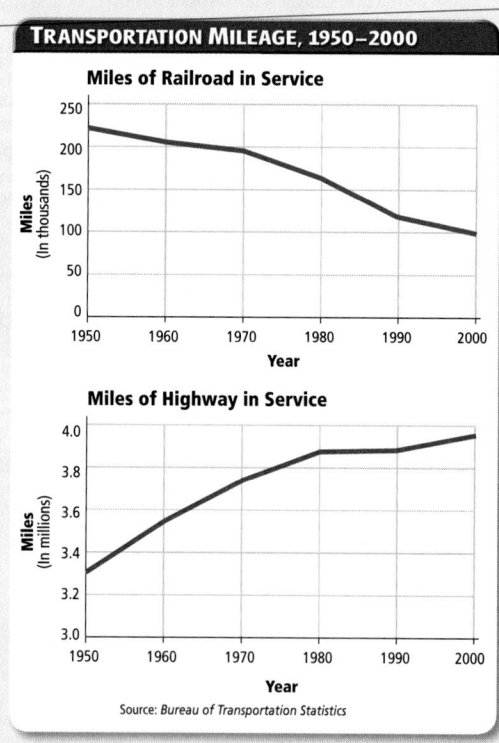

TRANSPORTATION MILEAGE, 1950–2000

Source: *Bureau of Transportation Statistics*

868 CHAPTER 26

Skills Focus: Identifying Problem and Solution   **At Level**

Reading Skill
Rising Gasoline Prices and Transportation

1. Tell students that gasoline prices are expected to increase as demand rises, especially as demand grows in developing countries such as China.

2. Guide the class in a discussion of the changes that will need to take place as a result of increasing gasoline prices.

3. Have each student write a plan for the future of transportation in the United States.

4. Ask volunteers to share their plans with the class.

5. Guide the class in a discussion of the plans that have been presented. Which plans would be the most effective? Why?

LS Logical-Mathematical, Verbal-Linguistic

📄 Alternative Assessment Handbook, Rubric 37: Writing Assignments

DOCUMENT 3

Even with the expansion of air travel, driving by car is still the preferred means of getting around today. People routinely drive to destinations hundreds of miles away. In the year 2000 alone, domestic travelers spent nearly $500 billion visiting other places in the United States. The maps below show how U.S. highways expanded between 1950 and 2000. The red lines indicate interstate highways. Green lines are other highways.

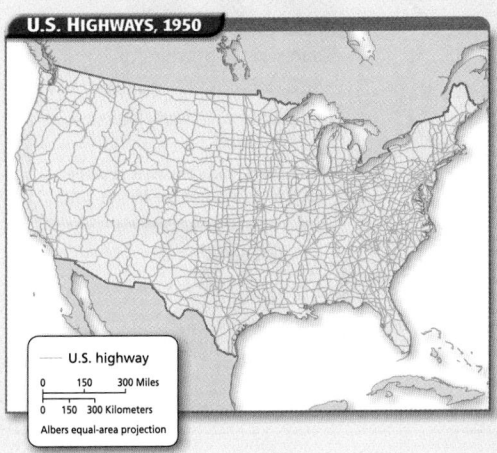

U.S. HIGHWAYS, 1950

— U.S. highway

0   150   300 Miles

0 150 300 Kilometers

Albers equal-area projection

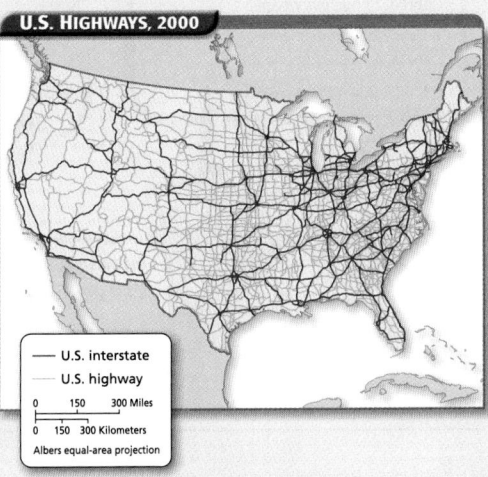

U.S. HIGHWAYS, 2000

— U.S. interstate

— U.S. highway

0   150   300 Miles

0 150 300 Kilometers

Albers equal-area projection

Skills FOCUS   READING LIKE A HISTORIAN

1. **a. Identify** Refer to Document 1. What is Eisenhower's view of the highway system?
   b. Elaborate Why do you think Eisenhower thought it was the government's obligation to improve the highway system?

2. **a. Describe** Refer to Document 2. What happened to railroad and highway mileage during this period?
   b. Analyze What do you think were some of the reasons that highways came to replace railroads?

3. **a. Describe** Refer to Document 3. Where were most

highways concentrated in 1950? in 2000?
   b. Elaborate What do you think a similar map of highways in 2050 will look like? Explain.

4. **Document-Based Essay Question** Consider the question below and form a thesis statement. Using examples from Documents 1, 2, and 3, create an outline and write a short essay supporting your position.
   How did the expansion of highways affect the United States?

See **Skills Handbook**, pp. H17, H20, H28–H29

Skills Focus: Comparing and Contrasting   [At Level]

Reading Skill
Highways vs. Other Roads

1. Pair students. Have each pair list the advantages and disadvantages of interstate highways over other roads. Have each pair also list things that travelers would miss by taking interstate highways instead of other roads.

2. Have volunteers share their lists with the rest of the class.

3. Guide the class in a discussion of the ways in which a community might be affected if more travelers went through it on local roads instead of interstate highways. Would the changes be good or bad? **LS Interpersonal, Logical-Mathematical**

869

Answers

Visual Summary

Review and Inquiry Have students examine the visual summary carefully. Then have students select items that continue to present challenges and problems for the United States today. Have volunteers identify the items they have selected and explain why they believe these are current, problematic issues for the country.

🖳 Quick Facts Transparency: Postwar America

Reviewing Key Terms and People

1. b.
2. a.
3. d.
4. b.
5. c.
6. a.

Comprehension and Critical Thinking

7. a. Hungary—uprising against harsh rule put down by Soviets; demonstrated Soviet control in Eastern Europe; Vietnam—divided into Communist and non-Communist halves; contention over what kind of government united Vietnam would have; Egypt—crisis over Suez Canal; demonstrated growing power and leadership of U.S.
b. vowed to end Korean War and roll back communism
c. possible answers—yes, he increased weapons research and development; sent aid to South Vietnam; Eisenhower Doctrine; no, Truman was equally concerned about spread of communism; Korean War

8. a. U.S. and Soviet military arms build-up; both built H-bombs and other weapons
b. Nuclear war would be total war with devastating effects on civilian population.
c. increased awareness and fears, some built bomb shelters; possible answer—people were trying to protect themselves

9. a. computers, transistors, integrated circuits, polio vaccine
b. those living in poverty were left behind or forgotten; Americans focused on wealth; some felt that individuality was lost as people and communities became very similar
c. possible answers—technologies that led to the computer revolution, which changed the ways Americans lived and conducted their business; medical advances, which protected health and well-being, prolonged life

Visual Summary: Postwar America

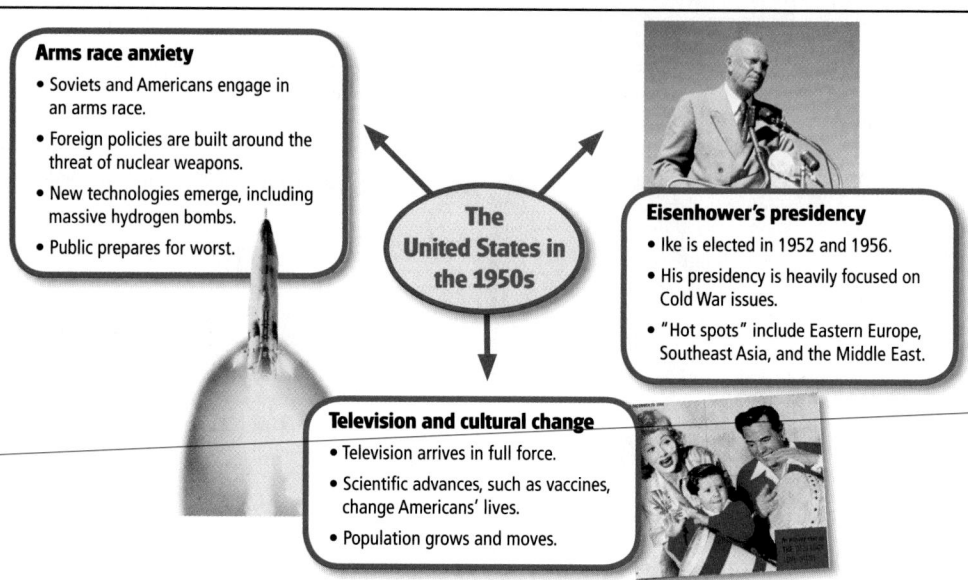

Arms race anxiety
- Soviets and Americans engage in an arms race.
- Foreign policies are built around the threat of nuclear weapons.
- New technologies emerge, including massive hydrogen bombs.
- Public prepares for worst.

The United States in the 1950s

Eisenhower's presidency
- Ike is elected in 1952 and 1956.
- His presidency is heavily focused on Cold War issues.
- "Hot spots" include Eastern Europe, Southeast Asia, and the Middle East.

Television and cultural change
- Television arrives in full force.
- Scientific advances, such as vaccines, change Americans' lives.
- Population grows and moves.

Reviewing Key Terms and People

For each of the following questions, choose the letter that corresponds to the best available answer.

1. Following the launch of *Sputnik*, the U.S. government established which of the following?
   a. SEATO   **c.** ICBM
   b. NASA   **d.** CIA

2. Brinkmanship and massive retaliation are both associated with which person?
   a. John Foster Dulles   **c.** Nikita Khrushchev
   b. Jonas Salk   **d.** Richard M. Nixon

3. This weapon raised the stakes in the conflict between the United States and the Soviet Union in the Cold War.
   a. integrated circuit   **c.** *Sputnik*
   b. transistor   **d.** H-bomb

4. Which of the following was under the influence of the Soviet Union?
   a. SEATO   **c.** CIA
   b. Warsaw Pact   **d.** Interstate Highway System

5. Which term represents the new suburban housing developments that appeared in the postwar years?
   a. Sunbelt   **c.** Levittown
   b. Interstate Highway System   **d.** integrated circuit

6. Jonas Salk is associated with which of these 1950s inventions?
   a. polio vaccine   **c.** transistor
   b. satellites   **d.** Sunbelt

Using the Internet

10. Go to the HRW Web site and enter the keyword shown to access a rubric for this activity.

KEYWORD: SD7 CH26

Analyzing Primary Sources

11. people who were concerned about nuclear war and radioactive fallout; more affluent who could afford to build a bomb shelter

12. possible answer—indefinitely, provided supplies lasted

History's Impact video program
Review the video to answer the closing question:
How did Americans' knowledge of other places
change after the introduction of the television?

Comprehension and Critical Thinking

SECTION 1 *(pp. 848–853)*

7. a. Identify What is the significance of each of the following to the events described in this section? Hungary, Vietnam, Egypt

b. Contrast How did Eisenhower claim to differ in his ideas about foreign policy compared with Truman?

c. Evaluate Do you think that Eisenhower actually was different from Truman in the way that he claimed? Explain your answer.

SECTION 2 *(pp. 854–860)*

8. a. Describe What was the arms race, and how did it evolve in the 1950s?

b. Summarize How did the arms race in the 1950s change the concept of victory and defeat in war?

c. Evaluate What were some effects of the government's efforts to educate people about how to respond to a nuclear attack? Why do you think people responded this way?

SECTION 3 *(pp. 861–867)*

9. a. Recall What were some of the major technological advancements of the 1950s?

b. Draw Conclusions How did the economic prosperity of the 1950s also present certain challenges to the country?

c. Rank In your opinion, which was the most significant technological change of the 1950s in terms of its long-term impact on the nation? Explain your reasoning.

Using the Internet

go.hrw.com
Practice Online
Keyword: SD7 CH26

10. *I Love Lucy* and other programs captivated the attention of American television audiences during the 1950s. Some of those TV programs are still broadcast on cable and satellite channels today. Using the keyword above, do research to learn more about popular television programs of the 1950s. Then create a report that explains the appeal of those programs in the 1950s and why some of those programs remain popular among some audiences today. Refer to specific examples from your research.

Analyzing Primary Sources

Reading Like a Historian The photograph shows an example of a bomb shelter from the 1950s.

11. Identify Who do you think might be interested and able to buy and install a bomb shelter?

12. Draw Conclusions How long do you think someone could survive in the type of shelter shown here?

Critical Reading

Read the passage from Section 1 under the heading "Cold War 'Hot Spots.'" Then answer the following question.

13. According to this passage, Eisenhower believed that

A it would be foolish to fight over communism in Vietnam.

B it was necessary to fight over communism in Vietnam.

C the French had failed to hold the line against Communist aggression.

D the United States would be better off waiting to see what happened in Vietnam and then reacting.

WRITING FOR THE SAT

Think about the following issue:

In Vietnam, following the departure of the French, it appeared that a truly free election might lead to the election of a Communist regime that was friendly with the Soviet Union.

14. Assignment Was the United States correct to support the creation of an anti-Communist South Vietnam? Write a short essay in which you develop your position on this issue. Support your point of view with reasoning and examples from your reading and studies.

POSTWAR AMERICA **871**

Answers

Critical Reading

13. B

Writing for the SAT

14. possible answers—yes, increased Communist control in Vietnam could lead to a "domino" effect in East Asia; no, as long as a fair election was held, U.S. should accept results

A rubric for this activity is provided in Chapter Resource File: Writing for the SAT: Nuclear Weapons.

History's Impact Video Program

were able to learn more about other places through news and other programs; places that were far away now seemed much closer and more real

---

Review and Assessment Resources

Review and Reinforce

- CRF: Chapter Review Activity
- Quick Facts Transparency: Postwar America
- Spanish Chapter Summaries Audio CD Program
- Online Chapter Summaries in Spanish
- OSP Holt PuzzlePro; Quiz Show for ExamView
- Quiz Game CD-ROM

Assess

- PASS: Chapter Test, Forms A and B
- Alternative Assessment Handbook
- OSP ExamView Test Generator, Chapter Test
- Differentiated Instruction Modified Worksheets and Tests CD-ROM: Chapter Test
- HOAP Holt Online Assessment Program (in the Premier Online Edition)

Reteach/Intervene

- Interactive Reader and Study Guide
- Differentiated Instruction Teacher Management System: Lesson Plans for Differentiated Instruction
- Differentiated Instruction Modified Worksheets and Tests CD-ROM: Chapter Test
- Interactive Skills Tutor CD-ROM

go.hrw.com
Online Resources
KEYWORD: SD7 CH26

Summarizing the Unit

During the period covered by this unit, the United States assumed the role of a world leader, economic powerhouse, and military giant. Guide students in a discussion of the following questions: *Is the role of the United States in the world becoming more dominant or less dominant. Why? In what fields? Is the changing role of our country positive or negative? How does it affect you?*

Connecting to Themes

Remind students that during the Cold War, many Americans worried about a nuclear attack by a Communist country. Ask students what kinds of threats the United States faces today from other countries and how these threats compare with the threat of nuclear attack during the Cold War.

UNIT 8 IN BRIEF — Below is a chapter-by-chapter summary of the main ideas covered in Unit 8.

CHAPTER 23 — World War II Erupts
1939–1941

MAIN IDEA After World War I, unsettled conditions in Europe and beyond led to the rise of ruthless dictators. One of these leaders, Germany's Adolf Hitler, led Europe into another great war in 1939. The United States was eventually drawn into World War II after being attacked by Germany's ally, Japan.

SECTION 1 The Treaty of Versailles helped create conditions for the rise of powerful dictators.

SECTION 2 Appeasement failed to stop Hitler's aggression. On September 1, 1939, Germany invaded Poland, starting World War II. Within a year, only Great Britain stood between Hitler and control of Europe.

SECTION 3 As tensions grew in Europe and Asia in the 1930s, President Roosevelt slowly overcame isolationist feeling in the United States. That feeling was shattered completely with Japan's attack on Pearl Harbor on December 7, 1941.

SECTION 4 The United States mobilized its military forces and its industries to fight World War II. The effort changed the nation and gave new opportunities to women and minority groups.

CHAPTER 24 — United States in World War II
1941–1945

MAIN IDEA World War II was fought in two theaters. Hard fighting by the Allies brought victory first in Europe and then in the Pacific.

SECTION 1 With the American entry into the war, the Allies focused first on Europe. As the Soviets fought desperately on their home soil, the rest of the Allies invaded North Africa and then, on D-Day, France.

SECTION 2 Adolf Hitler pursued first the persecution of Jews and then their systematic destruction. The resulting Holocaust claimed 6 million innocent lives.

SECTION 3 After early losses, the Allies won a key victory in the Battle of Midway. This was followed by a series of hard-fought victories, including battles at Iwo Jima and Okinawa.

SECTION 4 Americans at home worked hard to support the war. The attack on Pearl Harbor led the government to intern thousands of innocent Japanese Americans.

SECTION 5 By late 1944 the Germans were under pressure from both east and west by the Allies. They finally surrendered in May 1945. Meanwhile, the Japanese only surrendered after the Americans dropped two atomic weapons in early August 1945.

CHAPTER 25 — The Cold War Begins
1945–1953

MAIN IDEA After World War II, the United States took its place as a world leader and an adversary of the Soviet Union in the Cold War.

SECTION 1 Tensions between the United States and the Soviet Union that had simmered during the war rose to the surface in the postwar years, resulting in the start of the Cold War.

SECTION 2 The United States helped its own people adjust to the return of peacetime with the GI Bill. It also helped lead the rest of the world toward a more peaceful future through the creation of the United Nations.

SECTION 3 A Communist takeover of China and the Soviet acquisition of an atomic bomb led to a Second Red Scare, led by Senator Joseph McCarthy.

SECTION 4 Cold War tensions led to war in Korea, as the United States and its United Nations allies took a stand against Communist aggression.

CHAPTER 26 — Postwar America
1945–1960

MAIN IDEA In the 1950s Cold War conflict and a nuclear arms race worried many Americans, who nevertheless found diversion in television and other new ways of living.

SECTION 1 Dwight D. Eisenhower became president in 1952 and helped bring about a tough approach toward communism.

SECTION 2 The development of the hydrogen bomb and the growing arms race between the United States and the Soviet Union created great anxiety for many people.

SECTION 3 The introduction of the television and other new technologies led to significant changes in the way of life of many Americans.

Unit Resources

Review and Reinforce
- CRF: Chapter Review Activity
- Spanish Chapter Summaries Audio CD Program
- OSP Holt PuzzlePro; GameTool for ExamView
- Quiz Game CD-ROM

Assess
- PASS: Unit Test, Forms A and B
- Alternative Assessment Handbook
- OSP ExamView Test Generator
- Differentiated Instruction Modified Worksheets and Tests CD-ROM: Chapter Tests
- HOAP Holt Online Assessment Program (in the Premier Online Edition)

Reteach/Intervene
- Interactive Reader and Study Guide
- Differentiated Instruction Teacher Management System: Lesson Plans for Differentiated Instruction
- Differentiated Instruction Modified Worksheets and Tests CD-ROM: Chapter Tests
- Interactive Skills Tutor CD-ROM

go.hrw.com
Online Resources

KEYWORDS: SD7 CH23, SD7 CH24, SD7 CH25, SD7 CH26

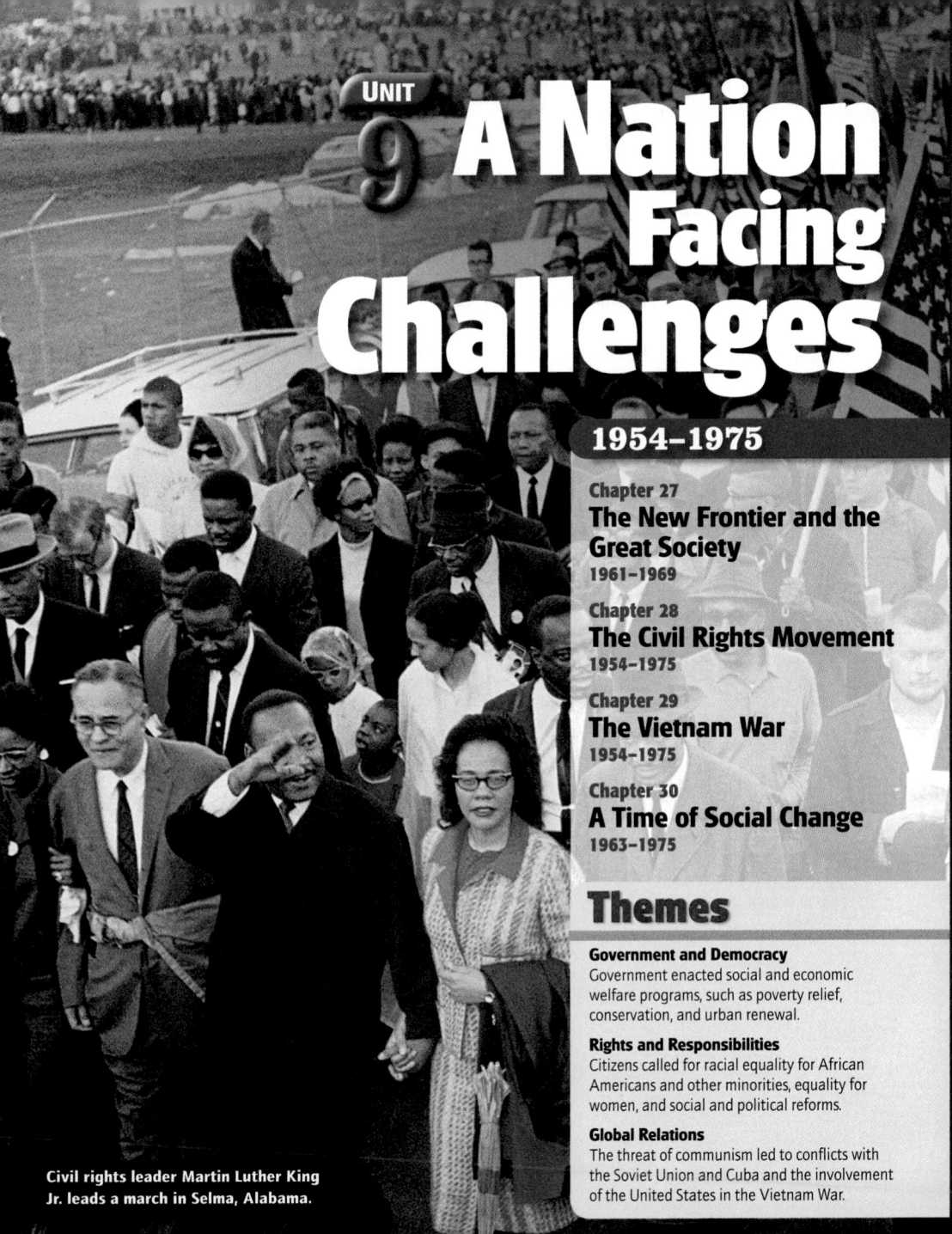

Themes

Government and Democracy
Government enacted social and economic welfare programs, such as poverty relief, conservation, and urban renewal.

Rights and Responsibilities
Citizens called for racial equality for African Americans and other minorities, equality for women, and social and political reforms.

Global Relations
The threat of communism led to conflicts with the Soviet Union and Cuba and the involvement of the United States in the Vietnam War.

Civil rights leader Martin Luther King Jr. leads a march in Selma, Alabama.

873

Introducing the Unit

Tell students that in this unit they will read about two presidential programs: John F. Kennedy's New Frontier and Lyndon Johnson's Great Society. Guide students in a discussion of the following questions: *What new frontiers should America explore today? What makes a society great?*

Connecting to Themes

Activity **Rights and Responsibilities** Divide students into mixed ability pairs. Have each pair list what they believe are the five most important rights of an American citizen and the five most important responsibilities of an American citizen. **LS Verbal-Linguistic**

Reading Like a Historian

Interpreting Visuals
The Selma Marches The image shown here is of the third Selma, Alabama march. The first was held to protest a murder during a voter registration drive. The second march was attacked by state troopers, and became known as Bloody Sunday. The third march featured Martin Luther King Jr., who disappointed some followers by turning back at a barricade of state troopers rather than risk violence.

Unit Resources

Planning

- Differentiated Instruction Teacher Management System: Unit Pacing Guide
- One-Stop Planner CD-ROM: Teacher Management System
- Power Presentations with Video CD-ROM

Differentiating Instruction

- Differentiated Instruction Teacher Management System: Lesson Plans for Differentiated Instruction
- Pre-AP Activities Guide for American History
- Differentiated Instruction Modified Worksheets and Tests CD-ROM

Enrichment

- Civic Participation Activities Guide
- CRF: Economics and History Activity
- CRF: Interdisciplinary Project
- American History Primary Source Library CD-ROM

Assessment

- PASS: Unit Test, Forms A & B
- Alternative Assessment Handbook
- OSP ExamView Test Generator
- HOAP Holt Online Assessment Program (in the Premier Online Edition)

The Differentiated Instruction Teacher Management System
provides a planning and instructional benchmarking guide for this unit.

Making Generalizations

Have volunteers suggest generalizations about current U.S. politics, economy, or foreign relations. Write several on the board. Then have students provide factual details that support or disprove the generalizations.

Word Help

consciously knowingly

Info to Know

The Youngest President John F. Kennedy was the youngest man ever elected to the presidency, at the age of 43. However, he was not the youngest man ever to hold the office. That distinction belongs to Theodore Roosevelt. Roosevelt was 42 years old when he assumed the presidency after William McKinley was assassinated in 1901. The oldest president was Ronald Reagan, who was 77 when he left office in 1989.

Teaching Tip

Divide students into partners. Have each pair choose a paragraph from a chapter in this unit and write a one-sentence generalization about the information in this paragraph. Then have students switch their sentences with another group and evaluate whether the details in the text support the generalization. Have volunteers share their generalizations with the class.

Skills Planner

To give students more opportunities to practice this skill, see the following activities in the teacher's edition: Kennedy's New Frontier, p. 888; Freedom Summer Volunteers, p. 927; Troop Morale, p. 959; Noncombatants in Vietnam, p. 961; The Counterculture, p. 1005.

Prepare to Read

Making Generalizations

Find practice for **Making Generalizations** in the **Skills Handbook,** p. H13

A generalization is a broad statement that tells how different examples are similar in some way. Experienced readers make generalizations that enable them to understand and remember what they are reading.

Before You Read
Read the headings to determine what the passage will be about. Then make a mental list of what you already know about the subject matter.

While You Read
List facts from the passage. How do they compare with your prior knowledge of the subject matter?

After You Read
Use your prior knowledge and facts from the reading to make a generalization about what the passage means to you.

Kennedy's Media Strategy

Presidents before and after Kennedy have been masters of the media. Franklin Delano Roosevelt used his radio "fireside chats" to inspire the nation during the Great Depression and World War II. Ronald Reagan, an experienced radio, television, and film actor, became known as the Great Communicator for his skill in conveying his messages directly to the voters. But Kennedy was the first president to consciously use access to the media as part of his strategy for governing the nation.

The passage mentions more than one president.

Image and reality Photographs of the president often showed him engaged in athletic activities like sailing, swimming, or playing touch football. Kennedy understood how such pictures would shape his image and boost his appeal. Like Roosevelt, he understood that images showing him in less-than-top physical shape might lessen the country's confidence in his abilities. In reality, Kennedy struggled with health problems most of his life. He suffered from Addison's disease, a sometimes fatal condition. A bad back kept him in nearly constant pain.

Kennedy and Roosevelt both tried to convey images of strength.

READING CHECK Making Generalizations
How is an effective use of the media important to presidents?

Test Prep Tip

Some tests may ask you to make generalizations from a given reading passage. Look for clue words such as *all, everyone, many, most, few, generally, never, often, always,* and *usually* that indicate generalizations. Then make sure that the facts in the passage support the entire generalization.

874 UNIT 9

Skills Focus: Making Generalizations At Level

Reading Skill
Assessing Knowledge Before and After Reading

1. Write the following statement on the board: *In the 1960s, young people rebelled against the establishment.* Remind students that this statement is a generalization, or a broad assertion based on analysis of details.

2. Have students make a list of ten generalizations they think are true about the 1960s. Have volunteers share their generalizations with the class. Encourage

students to provide evidence to support their generalizations.

3. Guide the class in a discussion of how generalizations can shape people's perspectives. Ask students if generalizations represent facts or opinions. **LS Verbal-Linguistic**

📖 Alternative Assessment Handbook, Rubric 12: Drawing Conclusions

Reading like a Historian

Evaluating Sources

Find practice for **Evaluating Sources** in the **Skills Handbook**, p. H34

Historians evaluate sources in many ways. They consider the author of a source. They think about where, when, and why a source was created. Most historians believe that the closer in time and place an author is to a given event, the more likely it is that the source is a reliable one.

Strategies historians use:

- What was the author's intent in creating the source? Is the source meant to persuade, inform, or entertain?
- What historical events were occurring at the time the source describes? What events does the source depict?
- How soon after the event was the source created? Did the author have firsthand knowledge of the event?

Photojournalism often combines text and a photograph. Its purpose is to inform and express a point of view. The word *savage* has a negative and violent connotation.

Civil rights activists used marches and other forms of nonviolent protest to spur change.

This photograph was taken and published at about the same time that the events were occurring. The photograph is a primary source.

Skills FOCUS READING LIKE A HISTORIAN

As You Read Try to determine the author of the source, the intended audience, and the author's purpose.
As You Study Use the time-and-place rule to evaluate the reliability of each historical source. Use reliable sources to help you understand historical context.

A NATION FACING CHALLENGES **875**

Evaluating Sources

Have volunteers suggest important events in America over the last 50 years. Then guide the class in a discussion of what primary sources could be located for each event. Ask students how they would determine which sources are reliable.

Primary Source

After being jailed for his part in a civil rights demonstration in Alabama in 1963, Martin Luther King Jr. wrote a letter to eight local religious leaders. The clergymen had criticized the demonstrations as unnecessary and counter-productive. They encouraged King and his followers to wait for the new Birmingham city government to act on his demands for justice. In his letter, King replied, "For years now I have heard the word 'Wait!' It rings in the ear of every Negro with piercing familiarity. This 'Wait' has almost always meant 'Never.'... We have waited for more than 340 years for our constitutional and God-given rights. The nations of Asia and Africa are moving with jetlike speed toward gaining political independence, but we still creep at horse-and-buggy pace toward gaining a cup of coffee at a lunch counter. Perhaps it is easy for those who have never felt the stinging darts of segregation to say, 'Wait.'"

— Martin Luther King Jr.
Letter from a Birmingham Jail, April 16, 1963

Skills Focus: Evaluating Sources
At Level

Reading Like a Historian Skill
Evaluating Photographs of Historical Events
Research Required

1. Have students use a reliable Internet site to find a photograph related to one of the historical events discussed in this unit. Students might locate a photo of a civil rights protest, combat in Vietnam, or an important figure of the period.

2. Have students research the photographer's background and connections to the event,

the purpose of the photograph, and any other relevant factors.

3. Have volunteers share their sources and evaluations with the class. Guide the class in a discussion about how to evaluate a photograph. **LS Visual-Spatial, Verbal-Linguistic**

Alternative Assessment Handbook, Rubric 16: Judging Information

Chapter Overview	Reproducible Resources	Technology Resources
CHAPTER 27 pp. 876–905 **Overview: In this chapter, students will analyze Kennedy's New Frontier and Johnson's Great Society.**	**Differentiated Instruction Teacher Management System:*** • Instructional Benchmarking Guides • Lesson Plans for Differentiated Instruction **Interactive Reader and Study Guide:** Chapter Summary* **Chapter Resource File:*** • Focus on Writing Activity: The New Frontier of John F. Kennedy • Social Studies Skills Activity: Making Generalizations • Chapter Review Activity **American History Outline Maps** **Pre-AP Activities Guide for United States History***	**Live Ink® Online Reading Help** **Student Edition on Audio CD Program** **Differentiated Instruction Modified Worksheets and Tests CD-ROM** **Interactive Skills Tutor CD-ROM** **United States History Primary Source Library CD-ROM** **Power Presentations with Video CD-ROM** **History's Impact: American History Video Program (VHS/DVD):** The New Frontier and the Great Society **Online Chapter Summaries in Spanish**
Section 1: **Kennedy and the Cold War** **The Main Idea:** President Kennedy continued the Cold War policy of resisting the spread of communism by offering help to other nations and threatening to use force if necessary.	**Differentiated Instruction Teacher Management System:** Section 1 Lesson Plan* **Interactive Reader and Study Guide:** Section 1 Summary* **Chapter Resource File:*** • Vocabulary Builder Activity, Section 1 • Biography Activity: Llewellyn Thompson • History and Geography Activity: The Bay of Pigs Invasion • Primary Source Activity: Executive Committee Discusses the Soviet Missiles in Cuba	**Daily Bellringer Transparency:** Section 1* **Daily Test Practice Transparency:** Section 1 **Internet Activity:** The Cuban Missile Crisis
Section 2: **Kennedy's Thousand Days** **The Main Idea:** John F. Kennedy brought energy, initiative, and important new ideas to the presidency.	**Differentiated Instruction Teacher Management System:** Section 2 Lesson Plan* **Interactive Reader and Study Guide:** Section 2 Summary* **Chapter Resource File:*** • Vocabulary Builder Activity, Section 2 • Biography Activity: Robert H. Lawrence, Jr.	**Daily Bellringer Transparency:** Section 2* **Daily Test Practice Transparency:** Section 2 **Internet Activity:** New Frontiers
Section 3: **The Great Society** **The Main Idea:** President Johnson used his political skills to push Kennedy's proposals through Congress and expanded them with his own vision of the Great Society.	**Differentiated Instruction Teacher Management System:** Section 3 Lesson Plan* **Interactive Reader and Study Guide:** Section 3 Summary* **Chapter Resource File:*** • Vocabulary Builder Activity, Section 3 • Biography Activity: Rachel Carson • Primary Source Activity: Johnson Promotes the Great Society • Literature: *One Flew Over the Cuckoo's Nest* by Ken Kesey	**Daily Bellringer Transparency:** Section 3* **Daily Test Practice Transparency:** Section 3 **Internet Activity:** The Great Society

go.hrw.com
Print Resource
Transparency

LS Learning Styles
Audio CD
CD-ROM

Video
SE Student Edition
TE Teacher's Edition

OSP One-Stop Planner CD-ROM

*also on One-Stop Planner CD-ROM

HOLT

History's Impact
American History Video Program (VHS/DVD)
The New Frontier and the Great Society

Review, Assessment, Intervention

Quick Facts Transparency: The New Frontier and the Great Society Visual Summary

Spanish Chapter Summaries Audio CD Program

Progress Assessment Support System (PASS): Chapter Test*

Differentiated Instruction Modified Worksheets and Tests CD-ROM: Modified Chapter Test

OSP One-Stop Planner CD-ROM: ExamView Test Generator (English/Spanish)

HOAP Holt Online Assessment Program (HOAP), in the Holt Premier Online Student Edition

PASS: Section 1 Quiz*

Online Quiz: Section 1

Alternative Assessment Handbook

PASS: Section 2 Quiz*

Online Quiz: Section 2

Alternative Assessment Handbook

PASS: Section 3 Quiz*

Online Quiz: Section 3

Alternative Assessment Handbook

NC RESOURCES

The following resources were developed to help North Carolina educators teach the standards and objectives of North Carolina's eleventh grade standard course of study in United States history.

- United States history EOC Test Prep Workbook
- Teacher's Support System
- North Carolina One-Stop Planner

And be sure to direct your students to **go.hrw.com** for online access to the EOC Test Prep Workbook.

go.hrw.com
EOC Test Prep
KEYWORD: SE7 NC

Holt Online Learning

go.hrw.com
Teacher Resources
KEYWORD: SD7 TEACHER

go.hrw.com
Student Resources
KEYWORD: SD7 CH27

- Document-based Questions
- Interactive Multimedia Activities

- Current Events
- Chapter-based Internet Activities
- and more!

Holt Premier
Online Student Edition
Complete online support for interactivity, assessment, and reporting

- Interactive Maps and Notebook
- Standardized Test Prep
- Homework Practice and Research Activities Online

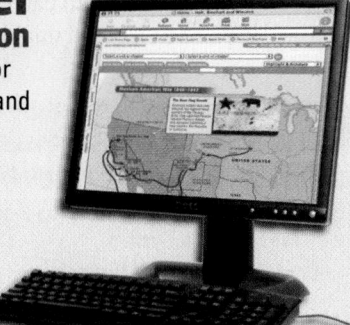

CHAPTER 27 PLANNING GUIDE

The Big Picture
Robert D. Schulzinger

The Crisis Years, 1960–1963 John F. Kennedy won the presidency in 1960 partly by promising to compete more vigorously with the Soviet Union. He used the 1961 crisis in Berlin to demonstrate America's resolve, and that same year the CIA helped anti-Castro exiles invade Cuba in a failed attempt to overthrow the Communist government. The Soviet Union installed nuclear-armed missiles in Cuba in 1962, and Kennedy imposed a naval blockade to force Nikita Khrushchev to remove the Soviet weapons. After the Cuban missile crisis, the two leaders cooperated more closely in an effort to avoid war. Kennedy also created the Peace Corps and the Alliance for Progress, two popular programs that used non-military means to promote American values abroad.

The New Frontier at Home The New Frontier projected hope and optimism, and Kennedy's attractive family contributed to a sense of glamour and youthful energy. Kennedy vowed to accelerate economic growth and address the neglected problems of the poor; he also invested heavily in a space program to surpass the Soviet program. His assassination shocked the nation and the world, and the murder left a bitter memory of unfulfilled hopes.

The Great Society Kennedy died with little of his agenda having been enacted into law, but the new president, Lyndon B. Johnson, persuaded Congress to pass the most ambitious series of social and economic reforms since the New Deal. The Civil Rights Act of 1964 and the Voting Rights Act of 1965 sought an end to racial segregation and discrimination. The War on Poverty provided job training and employment opportunities for the rural and urban poor. The Great Society created Medicare and Medicaid, provided aid to education and housing, and protected the environment, but a public backlash slowed the pace of reform.

Recent Scholarship

The Peace Corps and the American Spirit Elizabeth Cobbs Hoffman's *"All You Need is Love": The Peace Corps and the Spirit of the 1960s* (1998) shows how the Peace Corps married American idealism and practicality. From its start in 1961 through 2004 over 178,000 Americans served in more than 100 countries around the world. People in the host countries often marveled at the volunteers' enthusiasm and can-do spirit, and service abroad had an even greater effect on the volunteers themselves as they learned about the many cultures of the world. Many Peace Corps volunteers went on to careers in which they helped their fellow Americans gain better understanding of other peoples' ways of living and thinking.

Differentiating Instruction

Differentiated Instruction Teacher Management System
- Lesson Plans for Differentiated Instruction
- Differentiated Instructional Benchmarking Guides
- Interactive Reader and Study Guide

 Spanish Chapter Summaries Audio CD Program

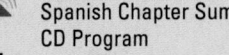 Online Chapter Summaries in Spanish

 Student Edition on Audio CD Program

 Differentiated Instruction Modified Worksheets and Tests CD-ROM
- Vocabulary Flash Cards
- Modified Vocabulary Builder Activities
- Modified Chapter Review Activity
- Modified Chapter Test

OSP One-Stop Planner CD-ROM
- ExamView Test Generator (English and Spanish)
- PuzzlePro
- Quiz Show for ExamView
- Transparencies and Videos

TE Differentiated Activities in the Teacher's Edition
- The Berlin Crisis, p. 882
- Life in a Divided City, p. 883
- Kennedy's Assassination, p. 891
- Miranda Warning, p. 901

Reading Like a Historian
Sam Wineburg

Corroboration: the "Great Corrective"

"We were eyeball to eyeball and I think the other fellow just blinked," is how Dean Rusk, secretary of state under John F. Kennedy, characterized the outcome of the Cuban missile crisis. Rusk and other members of JFK's Ex Comm held the world in their hands that Saturday night. Their actions would determine whether the world would go up in flames in World War III.

Rusk's phrase became the banner for Cold Warriors who advocated a continued arms buildup. The "other fellow blinked," they argued, only because of America's arms advantage. Fail to maintain that strength, they warned, and the Soviets would soon be camping at our doorsteps.

The Cuban Missile Crisis

On page 885, our chapter tells the story of this tense time by describing two letters sent by Nikita Khrushchev to President Kennedy, the first on Friday, October 26, and the second on Saturday, October 27. According to our chapter, the first letter demanded that the United States pledge never to invade Cuba in return for the removal of Soviet missiles in Cuba. The second letter, described as "tougher," demanded "that the United States remove its missiles from Turkey. The Ex Comm advised Kennedy to ignore the second letter and accept the offer in the first letter. The president did so."

Our textbook's account is supported by Robert F. Kennedy's *Thirteen Days*, the diary the president's brother kept during the crisis and published a year after his assassination. RFK described how after the Ex Comm met on Saturday, October 27, he phoned Soviet Ambassador Anatoly F. Dobrynin and asked to meet that night at the Department of Justice.

When RFK and Dobrynin broached the issue of missiles in Turkey, RFK stated that "there could be no quid pro quo or any arrangement made under this kind of threat or pressure and that in the last analysis this was a decision that would have to be made by NATO."

Making Comparisons

What happens when we compare RFK's account of the Dobrynin conversation with a description of the same conversation that appears in Khrushchev's *The Last Testament*, published posthumously in 1974?

Based on Dobrynin's cable to Moscow, Khrushchev wrote: "President Kennedy said that in exchange for withdrawal of our missiles, he would remove American missiles from Turkey and Italy." In other words, a flat out quid pro quo.

Who, then, do we believe?

The Search for Evidence

Here is where the historian searches for corroborating evidence—the act of comparing across accounts to arrive at our best approximation of what happened. In the words of historian and author Barbara Tuchman, corroboration is the "great corrective" without which historical practice would "slip easily into the invalid." Corroboration is one of the cornerstones of thinking historically.

The pursuit of corroborating evidence leads us to a 1989 conference on the Cuban missile crisis in which Ted Sorensen, presidential counsel and friend to both John and Robert Kennedy, dropped a bombshell. He announced that he wanted to make a "confession."

A Confession

"I was editor of Robert Kennedy's book," Sorensen told the rapt audience. "And the diary was very explicit that [the missile agreement] was part of the deal." But because the missile deal was still secret when *Thirteen Days* was published in 1969, Sorensen took it upon himself to act as censor and "edit that out of [RFK's] diaries."

So, back to our question. Who do we believe, Robert Kennedy, Nikita Khrushchev, or Ted Sorensen? In this fortunate case, corroboration allows us to believe all three.

Standards Focus

Social Studies Competency Goals
Goal 11 The learner will trace economic, political, and social developments and assess their significance for the lives of Americans during this time period.
 11.01

 The Big Idea and Essential Questions

To foster student understanding of this chapter's big idea, design your lesson to address each section's essential question.

Big Idea Presidential policies of the 1960s attempted to find solutions for a number of unsolved problems, from ignorance and prejudice to poverty and inequalities in education.

Essential Questions

1. What strategies did President John F. Kennedy use to resist the spread of communism?

2. How did President Kennedy change the presidency?

3. How did President Lyndon B. Johnson work to put his vision of American society into action?

Key to Differentiating Instruction

Below Level

Basic-level activities designed for all students encountering new material

At Level

Intermediate-level activities designed for average students

Above Level

Challenging activities designed for honors and gifted-and-talented students

Standard English Mastery

Activities designed to improve standard English usage

876 CHAPTER 27

CHAPTER 27 1961–1969

The New Frontier and the Great Society

THE BIG PICTURE John F. Kennedy said America's New Frontier lay in finding solutions for "unsolved problems of peace and war, unconquered pockets of ignorance and prejudice . . ." In Lyndon Johnson's Great Society, every citizen had the right to health care, education, housing, and equal opportunities.

NC **North Carolina Standards**

Social Studies Objectives
11.01 Describe the effects of the Cold War on economic, political, and social life in America.

Language Arts Objectives
2.01 Research and analyze ideas, events, and/or movements related to United States culture by:
• locating facts and details for purposeful elaboration.
3.01 Use language persuasively in addressing a particular issue by:
• establishing and defending a point of view.

Skills FOCUS **READING LIKE A HISTORIAN**

Astronaut John Glenn (right) shows President Kennedy the interior of space capsule *Friendship 7*, the vessel in which Glenn became the first American to orbit the Earth. Winning the race to conquer space was an important Cold War goal for President Kennedy.
Interpreting Visuals What is Kennedy's reaction to the space capsule?

See Skills Handbook, p. H30

U.S.
January 1961 President John F. Kennedy is inaugurated.

1961

World
April 1961 Soviets launch the first manned orbiting spacecraft.

August 1961 East Germany closes crossing points between East and West Berlin.

876

Introduce the Chapter | At Level

The New Frontier and the Great Society

1. Guide students in a discussion of how change affects their daily lives. There may be new policies or new buildings at school; favorite stores close; there may be changes in community athletics programs.

2. Have students list changes that have occurred within the past year that have affected them directly. Have students share their lists and discuss the effects of these changes.

3. Tell students that in the 1960s Americans were ready for a change, and the United States adopted many new policies and programs; it was a time of the space race, social change, and a time when the Supreme Court became actively involved in civil rights.

4. Tell students that in this chapter they will learn about the reforms that came from the visions of two presidents, John F. Kennedy, a young, vigorous idealist, and Lyndon B. Johnson, a seasoned senator and astute politician. **LS** **Verbal-Linguistic**

November 1963
President Kennedy is assassinated. Lyndon B. Johnson becomes president.

July 1964
Congress passes Civil Rights Act of 1964.

July 1965
Congress funds Medicaid and Medicare.

January 1968
U.S. Navy spy ship *Pueblo* is captured by North Korea.

1963

1965

1967

1969

October 1964
Khrushchev is forced to resign as Soviet leader.

January 1966
Indira Gandhi becomes India's first woman prime minister.

August 1968
Soviet army crushes revolt in Czechoslovakia.

877

• Chapter Preview •

HOLT

History's Impact
► **Video Program: The New Frontier and the Great Society**
See the Video Teacher's Guide for strategies for using the video segment.

Reading Like a Historian

The *Friendship 7* Have students take a moment to examine the image on these pages. Why are so many people crowded around the spacecraft? *possible answers—They are eager to look at this new technology; they may be accompanying President Kennedy.*

Interpreting Visuals President John F. Kennedy, surrounded by his advisers, peers into the *Friendship 7* capsule. The capsule, part of the first United States manned space program called the Mercury Program, was launched by an Atlas rocket and orbited the Earth three times on February 20, 1962. After staying aloft for 4 hours and 55 minutes, it splashed down in the Atlantic Ocean.

go.hrw.com
Online Resources
Chapter Resources:
KEYWORD: SD7 CH27
Teacher Resources:
KEYWORD: SD7 TEACHER

Explore the Time Line

1. How long was John F. Kennedy President of the United States? *nearly 3 years; January 1961 to November 1963*

2. What was significant about Indira Ghandi? *She became India's first woman prime minister in January 1966.*

3. When did Congress fund Medicaid and Medicare? *July 1965*

Info to Know

The Cuban Missile Crisis During a worldwide radio broadcast Khrushchev announced that the Soviet Union and the U.S. had come to an agreement. The Soviet Union would remove "offensive" weapons from Cuba if the U.S. agreed not to invade the island. Khrushchev called for UN inspectors to verify the missile removal. Fidel Castro was not involved in the agreement between the Soviet Union and the United States. Castro initially refused UN oversight, but eventually he agreed to observation of the missile removal.

Answers

Reading Like a Historian (p. 876)
curiosity; interest

Bellringer

The Inside Story. . . Use the **Daily Bellringer Transparency** to help students answer the question.

🖎 Daily Bellringer Transparency, Section 1

| The New Frontier and the Great Society | Daily Bellringer |
| | Chapter 27, Section 1 |

Test What You Know

The following questions will test your background knowledge about President John F. Kennedy and the Cold War. You will learn more about these topics in Chapter 27, Section 1.

1. What two candidates ran for president in the 1960 election?
2. Where did the Bay of Pigs invasion take place?
3. What two governments faced off during the Cuban missile crisis?

Preview Section 1

The Inside Story

How does television shape public opinion?

On September 26, 1960, 70 million Americans watched Vice President Nixon and Senator John Kennedy in the first televised presidential debate. Nixon, recently released from the hospital, looked pale, ill, and tired. Kennedy, just returning from a trip to California, appeared tan, fit, and well rested. Those who watched the debate on television believed Kennedy won, while radio listeners gave Nixon the edge. For days afterwards, crowds flocked to see the handsome Kennedy at campaign rallies, while Nixon's staff had to reassure supporters of his "excellent" health.

1. Why might radio listeners and television viewers have had different opinions of the candidates' performances in the debates?
2. How were the campaigns affected as a result of the televised debates?

Review Answers: 1. Richard Nixon and John F. Kennedy; 2. Cuba; 3. the United States and the Soviet Union
Preview Answers: 1. Television viewers were affected by the candidates' appearances, but radio listeners were not; 2. Huge crowds turned out for Kennedy, while supporters of Nixon had to be reassured of his health.

Copyright © by Holt, Rinehart and Winston. All rights reserved.

Academic Vocabulary

Review with students the high-use academic terms in this section.

authority firm self-assurance (p. 879)

interpreted understood within the context of the circumstances (p. 882)

entity something that has a separate and distinct existence (p. 886)

🖎 CRF: Vocabulary Builder Activity, Section 1

Taking Notes

invasion a disaster because Castro knew of attack, CIA greatly underestimated Castro's strength; Khrushchev erects wall to prevent East Berliners escaping to West Berlin; Soviet Union installs missiles in Cuba, escalating political moves between the U.S. and the Soviet Union increase threat of war

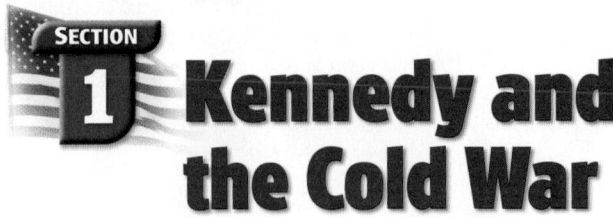

SECTION 1

Kennedy and the Cold War

BEFORE YOU READ

MAIN IDEA

President Kennedy continued the Cold War policy of resisting the spread of communism by offering help to other nations and threatening to use force if necessary.

READING FOCUS

1. In what ways did Kennedy's election as president suggest change?
2. Why did the Bay of Pigs invasion take place, and with what results?
3. Why did the Berlin crisis develop, and what was its outcome?
4. What caused the Cuban missile crisis, and how was war avoided?
5. How did Kennedy's foreign policy reflect his view of the world?

KEY TERMS AND PEOPLE

John F. Kennedy
Robert Kennedy
Fidel Castro
Bay of Pigs invasion
Lyndon B. Johnson
Cuban missile crisis
Peace Corps
Alliance for Progress
flexible response

TAKING NOTES As you read, take notes about Cold War crises that President Kennedy's administration faced. Record your notes in a graphic organizer like the one shown here.

Crisis	What Happened
Bay of Pigs invasion	
Berlin crisis	
Cuban missile crisis	

The Great Debates

THE INSIDE STORY

How does television shape public opinion? On September 26, 1960, some 70 million Americans watched Vice President Richard Nixon and Senator John Kennedy in the first televised presidential debate. Nixon was just two weeks out of the hospital. During that time he had covered 15,000 miles, campaigning in 25 states. He had lost so much weight that his shirt collar sagged around his neck. On the day of the debate, he pored over his notes until just before air time.

Kennedy had a leisurely dinner and took a nap before the debate. Still tan from several days of campaigning in sunny California, he refused the traditional TV makeup. Nixon refused makeup too. In his gray suit, Nixon looked pale, ill, and tired. Kennedy's dark suit and deep tan added to his rested and fit appearance.

The hour-long debate was broadcast on both radio and television. Radio listeners thought Nixon narrowly won, while those watching on television gave Kennedy the edge. For days afterward, huge crowds turned out at campaign rallies to see the handsome candidate in the flesh. In contrast, Nixon's staff reassured his supporters that "Mr. Nixon is in excellent health and looks good in person."

Three more debates took place. Although some reporters at the time called them the Great Debates, the Kennedy-Nixon debates probably did not change the outcome of the 1960 election. They did increase the average American's interest in politics, however. The debates also set the standard for modern election campaigns. Voters today expect candidates for office at practically every level to appear in televised debates. ◼

◀ Kennedy's appearance gave him great appeal to a television audience.

Teach the Main Idea

At Level

Kennedy and the Cold War

1. **Teach** Ask the students the Reading Focus questions to teach this section.

2. **Apply** Draw five computer monitors for students to see, and label the top of each with the main topics of this section. Have students identify the main ideas of each topic, and write them on the computer monitors. Have students copy the graphic organizer onto their own papers.

3. **Review** Have students identify the links

among the topics and explain the ways in which these topics relate to each other.

4. **Practice/Homework** Have students write the script for a telephone conversation that might have taken place between President Kennedy and his brother Robert as they discussed one of the problems or crises facing the nation during this time.

LS Visual-Spatial, Verbal-Linguistic

🖎 Alternative Assessment Handbook, Rubrics 11: Discussions; and 13: Graphic Organizers

Kennedy Becomes President

The personal contrasts between **John F. Kennedy** and Richard Nixon were far greater than their political differences in the 1960 presidential campaign. Kennedy was born into a wealthy and politically powerful Massachusetts family, while Nixon was a self-made "common man" from a small town in southern California.

Although the two men were about the same age, Kennedy's movie-star good looks made him appear much younger. During their four television debates, he spoke with ease and authority. To many Americans, the 43-year-old senator represented America's future. Nixon's ties to the 70-year-old Eisenhower made him seem a part of America's past.

The election of 1960 Kennedy emphasized this contrast by adopting the term "new frontier" for his campaign. "There are new frontiers for America to conquer," he declared, "not frontiers on a map, but frontiers of the mind, the will, and the spirit of man."

During the election campaign, Kennedy played on the nation's Cold War fears by claiming the United States had fallen behind the Soviet Union in the development of nuclear missiles. He also claimed that the prosperity of the 1950s was not reaching the poor. "Seventeen million Americans go to bed hungry at night," Kennedy charged. Vice President Nixon defended President Eisenhower's record, which made him appear opposed to new ideas.

Despite Kennedy's personal appeal, some Protestant voters were concerned because he was a Roman Catholic. They feared that Kennedy might put the views of the Catholic Church over those of the American public. The election of 1960 was one of the closest in American history. Fewer than 120,000 votes separated the two candidates out of nearly 69 million ballots cast.

Kennedy's victory by a 303–219 margin in the electoral college was more comfortable. He became the youngest person and the first Catholic elected president. Fifteen southern electors, however, cast their ballots for Virginia's Democratic senator Harry Byrd, who was not even a candidate. This weakness in Kennedy's southern support coupled with his narrow victory in the popular vote would later cause problems for his presidency.

One incident in October might have helped Kennedy's election campaign. Civil rights leader Martin Luther King Jr. was arrested in Georgia during a protest. Kennedy telephoned King's wife, Coretta, to express his concern. **Robert Kennedy**, the candidate's brother, persuaded the judge to release King on bail.

King's father told the press he had planned to vote for Nixon but that Kennedy's call to his daughter-in-law had changed his mind. The Kennedy campaign printed 2 million leaflets that told the story of this incident. The leaflets were passed out in African American churches the Sunday before election day.

Kennedy takes office Kennedy's inaugural address focused on his theme of change. It also took a strong anti-Communist tone.

ACADEMIC VOCABULARY
authority firm self-assurance

HISTORY'S VOICES

❝Let the word go forth from this time and place, to friend and foe alike, that the torch has been passed to a new generation of Americans—born in this century, tempered by war, disciplined by a hard and bitter peace . . . Let every nation know, whether it wishes us well or ill, that we shall pay any price, bear any burden, meet any hardship, support any friend, oppose any foe, in order to assure the survival and the success of liberty. ❞

—John F. Kennedy, Inaugural Address, January 20, 1961

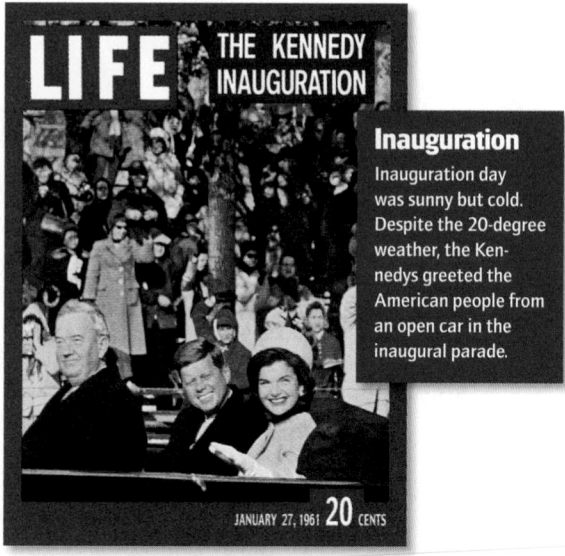

Inauguration
Inauguration day was sunny but cold. Despite the 20-degree weather, the Kennedys greeted the American people from an open car in the inaugural parade.

THE NEW FRONTIER AND THE GREAT SOCIETY **879**

Kennedy Becomes President

Explain How did President Kennedy's advisers differ from past presidential advisers? *They were young, very well educated experts in their fields.*

Draw Conclusions Why do you think Kennedy's cabinet was different from his advisory groups? *possible answers—experienced, well known, respected people in the cabinet; automatically had respect from government peers; advisory group was composed of friends outside government circles*

📖 CRF: History and Geography Activity: The Bay of Pigs Invasion

Tell students that the Spanish name for the Bay of Pigs is the Bahía de los Cochinos; on most maps, the Bay of Pigs is listed under its Spanish name. The bay is located on Cuba's southern coast, not too far from the town of Cienfuegos. Havana is on the other side of the island.

Answers

Photo *He established the first Communist government in the Western Hemisphere and made anti-U.S. speeches.*

Reading Check *possible answer— rarely held cabinet meetings; cabinet members and advisers were much younger than Eisenhower's*

880

In his inaugural address, Kennedy did not specify his policy goals at home because so much division existed over domestic issues. However, he made accomplishing domestic goals a top priority. "If we are to regain . . . leadership on our domestic problems, it must be presidential leadership," he maintained.

To advance his programs, Kennedy gathered a group of advisers that some people called "the best and the brightest." National Security Adviser McGeorge Bundy had been a dean at Harvard University. Special Assistant Arthur Schlesinger had taught history there. Another adviser was a professor at Massachusetts Institute of Technology (MIT).

Most of Kennedy's advisers were young like he was—some were still in their 30s. Ted Sorensen, who helped develop domestic policies and programs, was just 32 years old. Kennedy called Sorensen his "intellectual blood bank." But no one was closer to the president than his own brother, Robert ("Bobby") Kennedy. He included his 36-year-old brother in his cabinet by making him attorney general.

Except for Bobby, cabinet members had less influence on President Kennedy than did his White House advisers. In foreign affairs, for example, Kennedy relied more on National Security Adviser Bundy than on Secretary of State Dean Rusk or Secretary of Defense Robert McNamara. Kennedy also held cabinet meetings less often than Eisenhower did— only once a month unless Kennedy cancelled the meeting. At an average age of 47, President Kennedy's cabinet was relatively young. Its members averaged 10 years younger than President Eisenhower's.

READING CHECK **Contrasting** How did Kennedy differ from Eisenhower as president?

The Bay of Pigs Invasion

Kennedy would soon need Rusk and McNamara's advice as well as that of Bundy. During the 1960 campaign, Kennedy learned that the Central Intelligence Agency (CIA) was secretly training about 1,500 Cuban exiles in Central America in order to invade Cuba. Many of the trainees were Cuban Americans the CIA had recruited in south Florida. President Eisenhower had authorized the project in the hope of overthrowing Cuba's dictator **Fidel Castro**.

Background to the invasion Fidel Castro came to power in Cuba in 1959 after a two-year guerrilla war against Fulgencio Batista, the U.S.-backed dictator of Cuba. As Castro's followers increased in number, his tactics grew bolder. When his rebel force marched on Havana, Cuba's capital city, Batista fled the country. On January 8, 1959, Castro entered Havana and declared victory.

During his revolt, Castro gained the support of many Cubans by promising to restore people's rights and freedoms. Once in power, however, he

Communist Neighbor
Fidel Castro established the first Communist nation in the Western Hemisphere. He railed against the United States in speeches and forged ties between Cuba and the Soviet Union. *Why did the U.S. government find Castro's actions so alarming?*

Skills Focus: Identifying Cause and Effect

At Level

Reading Skill
The Bay of Pigs Invasion

1. Write the following questions for all students to see: What was the Bay of Pigs? Why did the Bay of Pigs invasion fail? What were some of the possible consequences of the failed invasion?

2. Have students copy the questions onto their own papers. Then have students work in mixed-ability pairs to answer the questions and list at least three reasons for the failure and three potential consequences.

3. Have students develop a list of five to ten questions that President Kennedy might have been asked about the Bay of Pigs invasion. Have students exchange papers and write a response to each question.

4. Have volunteers rehearse and present their questions and answers to the class.
   🆚 **Kinesthetic, Verbal-Linguistic**

📝 Alternative Assessment Handbook, Rubric 12: Drawing Conclusions

followed a more radical course. His government seized private businesses, including American companies on the island. In addition, Castro began making anti-American speeches. U.S.-Cuban relations were further strained when Castro signed a trade agreement with the Soviet Union in February 1960. Eisenhower responded by cutting off American economic and diplomatic ties with Cuba.

The invasion of Cuba The CIA believed an invasion of Cuba would inspire its people to rise up against Castro. Eisenhower doubted this prediction, but he let planning continue to keep all options open. Besides, he knew that the new president would have to make the decision whether to approve an invasion.

Kennedy asked his advisers about the plan to invade Cuba. Opinions were mixed. Schlesinger was openly and strongly opposed. "You would dissipate [lose] all the extraordinary good will . . . toward the new administration throughout the world," he warned.

The president was in a bind. He considered Castro's communism a threat to all of Latin America. In fact, Kennedy had attacked Eisenhower during the campaign for not taking stronger action against Castro. He felt that he could not back down now. When the CIA assured Kennedy that the invasion would succeed, he gave the go-ahead.

The **Bay of Pigs invasion** was a disaster. The *New York Times* reported the plan a week before the invasion began. Kennedy publicly denied the story. Then on April 15, 1961, an air strike by old, unmarked U.S. bombers flown from Nicaragua by Cuban exiles failed to destroy Cuba's air force. Even worse, a bomber damaged in the attack landed at Key West, Florida, instead of returning to Nicaragua. With the U.S. connection now exposed, Kennedy cancelled additional air strikes on Cuba that had been planned for April 16 and 17.

The land invasion on April 17 had little chance of success. Warned by the air attack, Castro was prepared. When the force of Cuban exiles came ashore at the Bay of Pigs, Castro's troops rushed to the scene. Pinned down at their landing site, the invaders fought for nearly three days.

Former vice president Nixon and others urged Kennedy to send U.S. troops to Cuba to rescue the invasion force and overthrow

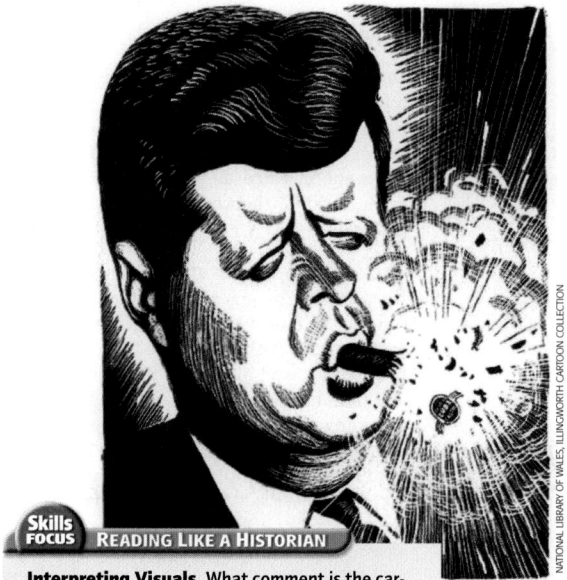

Skills FOCUS **READING LIKE A HISTORIAN**

Interpreting Visuals What comment is the cartoonist making on Kennedy's dealings with Cuba? What specific incident do you think the cartoon is referencing?

Castro. Concerned about how such a response might affect U.S.-Soviet relations, the president rejected this advice.

Poor planning and the lack of U.S. air cover had doomed the Bay of Pigs invasion to failure. Also, the CIA had greatly underestimated Castro's support. The expected anti-Castro uprising in Cuba never took place. The nearly 1,200 surviving invaders were captured and put in prison. In December 1962 Kennedy obtained their release in return for $52 million in food and medical aid to Cuba.

Instead of eliminating the threat of communism so close to the United States, the Bay of Pigs incident actually strengthened Castro's ties to the Soviet Union. Increasingly, he looked to the Soviets for protection from the United States. Soviet leader Nikita Khrushchev welcomed the closer relations. "We shall render [the] Cuban government all necessary assistance," he declared.

READING CHECK **Drawing Conclusions** Why did Kennedy decide to go ahead with the CIA's plan to invade Cuba?

Direct Teach

Reading Focus

❷ Why did the Bay of Pigs invasion take place, and with what results? *attempted invasion of Cuba and overthrow of Castro by CIA-trained exiles; invasion was a disaster*

The Bay of Pigs Invasion

Recall Who authorized the CIA to train Cuban exiles for the invasion? *President Eisenhower*

Recall Why did President Eisenhower allow the CIA to plan an invasion even though he doubted how effective it might be? *knew he would be out of office before invasion was ready; next president could decide whether to approve invasion*

Summarize Why did the Bay of Pigs invasion fail? *press leaks; well prepared Cuban troops; U.S. underestimated Castro's support*

Info to Know

The Bay of Pigs In March 2001 a Bay of Pigs Conference was held in Havana, Cuba. Cuban government and military representatives, and former officials in the Kennedy Administration attended. During the conference, many documents detailing efforts to establish friendly relations between Cuba and the U.S. were released. Documents included summaries of Castro's perceptions during the invasion and correspondence that documents the Kennedy Administration's subsequent efforts to mend relations with Cuba.

Skills Focus: Making Written Presentations

At Level

Reading Like a Historian Skill
The Bay of Pigs Invasion

1. Tell students that the failed Bay of Pigs invasion was widely reported in U.S. newspapers. Guide students in a discussion of the U.S. view of Cuba and communism. Was it, and is it, dangerous having a Communist dictatorship so close to the U.S.?

2. Have students write a letter to the editor of a newspaper. In their letters students should make the point that the United States should have taken a different approach to the

invasion so that it did not end in a disaster. Students should propose different ways that the U.S. could have prepared and then acted once the invasion began.

3. Have volunteers read their letters to the class. Then guide students in a discussion of the ideas expressed in the letters.

LS Verbal-Linguistic

Alternative Assessment Handbook, Rubric 17: Letters to Editors

Answers

Reading Like a Historian *that they will blow up in his face; the Bay of Pigs invasion*

Reading Check *had criticized Eisenhower for not taking stronger action against Castro; felt he had to follow CIA's plan*

The Berlin Crisis

One reason Kennedy rejected sending U.S. forces into Cuba was that he feared it would cause Khrushchev to retaliate in Europe. Khrushchev, however, interpreted Kennedy's failure to intervene in Cuba as a sign of weakness. It encouraged Khrushchev to press the United States in Berlin.

ACADEMIC VOCABULARY
interpreted understood within the context of the circumstances

The Vienna conference Kennedy invited Khrushchev to meet with him in Vienna, Austria, in June 1961. The president hoped to ease tensions with the Soviet Union. Instead, Khrushchev demanded that the United States and its allies recognize Communist East Germany as an independent nation. He also demanded that the United States withdraw from West Berlin.

Khrushchev said he would sign a treaty with East Germany in December if these demands were not met. He warned that East Germany could then decide for itself what to do about Berlin. Kennedy would not be bullied.

Berlin's significance Berlin had long been a problem for the Soviet Union. The western half of the city was an island of freedom surrounded by East Germany. In the first half of 1961 alone, about 200,000 East Germans escaped communism by slipping past guards to safety in West Berlin.

Some of Kennedy's advisers were concerned that East Germany might use force to gain control of West Berlin. All agreed that Khrushchev was using Berlin to test America's will in Europe and that any action East Germany took would have the approval and backing of the Soviet Union.

Determined to meet the Soviet test, Kennedy acted to show America's strength and resolve. He called reserve troops to active duty, launched a program to build shelters in the United States against nuclear attack, and began a troop buildup in West Germany. Khrushchev responded by threatening to mobilize troops. Realizing how dangerous the situation had become, Kennedy waited for the Soviet leader to make the next move.

The Berlin Wall Khrushchev's response came on August 13, 1961, when Communist forces closed the crossing points between East and West Berlin. Within hours, some 25,000 East German soldiers were in place to guard a hastily erected barbed wire barrier around West Berlin. The temporary fencing was soon replaced with a high concrete wall, to block further escapes to freedom.

Kennedy responded to the construction of the Berlin Wall by sending 1,500 troops from West Germany to West Berlin. Vice President **Lyndon B. Johnson** visited West Berlin to reassure its people that America would not abandon them. Kennedy, however, was relieved. He believed that Khrushchev would now not attempt to seize West Berlin. "A wall is a . . . lot better than a war," he concluded.

The Berlin Wall divided families, neighborhoods, streets, and even cemeteries. As time passed it was extended and fortified. The concrete sections eventually spanned most of the nearly 100 miles around West Berlin. Trenches were dug to keep vehicles from crashing though the wall. The East Germans later built a second wall parallel to the first one. The corridor between the two walls was patrolled by soldiers and attack dogs.

Nearly two years after the crisis was past, Kennedy went to West Berlin to renew his commitment to the city. At an outdoor rally near the Berlin Wall, he gave one of the greatest speeches of his presidency—his *"Ich bin ein Berliner"* ("I am a Berliner") speech. Speaking in English, he noted the wall's importance as a symbol of the failures of communism.

HISTORY'S VOICES

❝There are many people in the world who really don't understand . . . the great issue between the free world and the communist world. Let them come to Berlin. There are some who say that communism is the wave of the future. Let them come to Berlin. And there are some who say in Europe and elsewhere we can work with the communists. Let them come to Berlin.❞

—John F. Kennedy, June 26, 1963

As the huge crowd cheered wildly, Kennedy ended his speech by declaring, "All free men, wherever they may live, are citizens of Berlin, and, therefore, as a free man I take pride in the words 'Ich bin ein Berliner.'"

READING CHECK **Identifying Cause and Effect** Why was the Berlin Wall constructed?

The Berlin Wall

The Berlin Wall was built in 1961 to block East Germans from escaping to freedom in West Berlin. Part of the wall divided the city itself, separating its democratic and Communist sectors. This scene shows the wall in Berlin as it looked in 1963, the year President Kennedy visited the city.

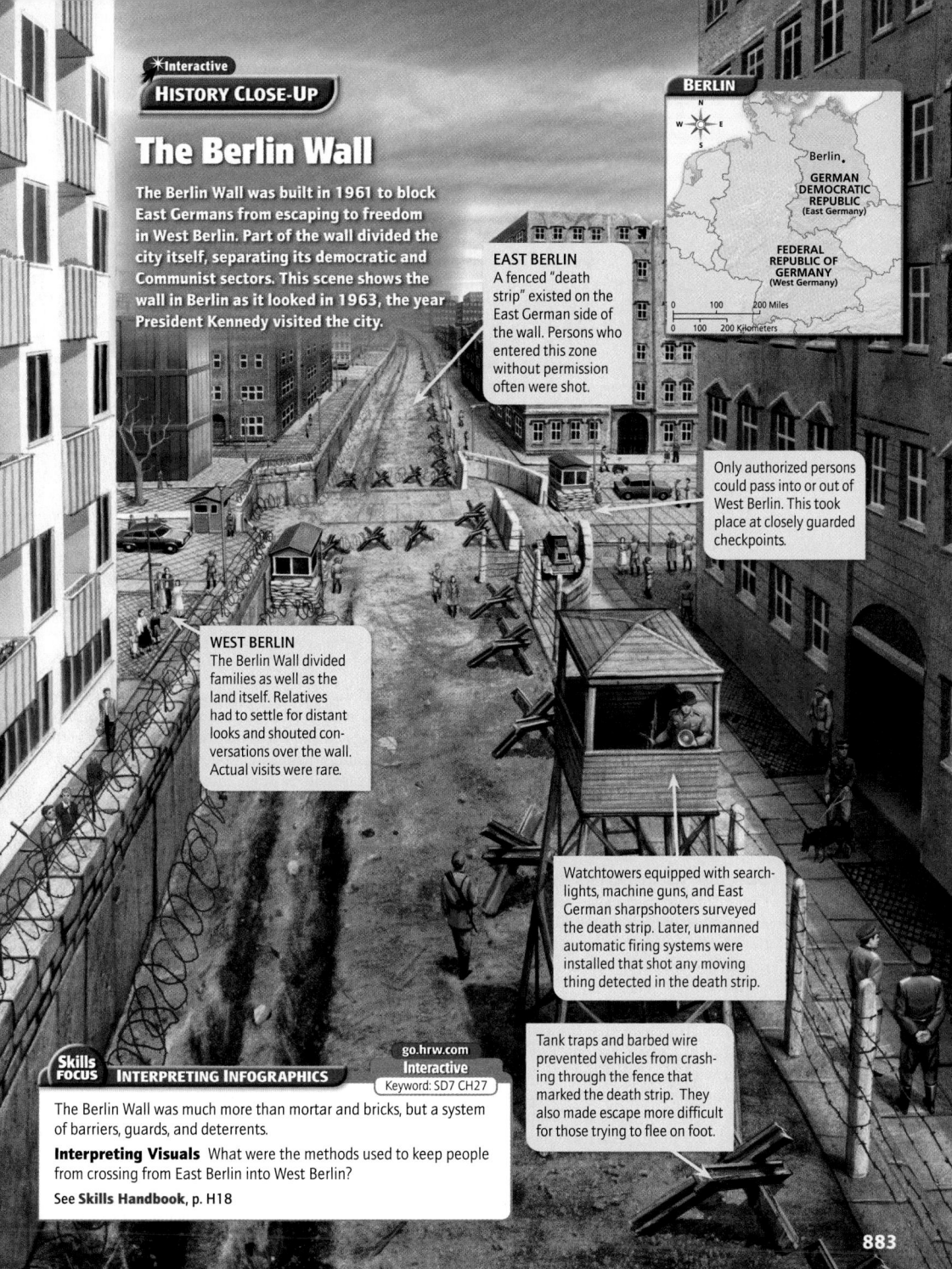

BERLIN

Berlin
GERMAN DEMOCRATIC REPUBLIC
(East Germany)

FEDERAL REPUBLIC OF GERMANY
(West Germany)

0   100   200 Miles
0 100   200 Kilometers

EAST BERLIN
A fenced "death strip" existed on the East German side of the wall. Persons who entered this zone without permission often were shot.

Only authorized persons could pass into or out of West Berlin. This took place at closely guarded checkpoints.

WEST BERLIN
The Berlin Wall divided families as well as the land itself. Relatives had to settle for distant looks and shouted conversations over the wall. Actual visits were rare.

Watchtowers equipped with searchlights, machine guns, and East German sharpshooters surveyed the death strip. Later, unmanned automatic firing systems were installed that shot any moving thing detected in the death strip.

Tank traps and barbed wire prevented vehicles from crashing through the fence that marked the death strip. They also made escape more difficult for those trying to flee on foot.

Skills FOCUS   INTERPRETING INFOGRAPHICS

go.hrw.com
Interactive
Keyword: SD7 CH27

The Berlin Wall was much more than mortar and bricks, but a system of barriers, guards, and deterrents.

Interpreting Visuals What were the methods used to keep people from crossing from East Berlin into West Berlin?

See **Skills Handbook, p. H18**

883

History Close-Up
Divided Berlin

Although construction of the Berlin Wall officially began on the night of August 12, 1961, work continued on it for many years. By the 1980s the wall extended 28 miles through Berlin and a further 75 miles around West Berlin, separating it from the rest of East Germany. During the wall's 28 year history, approximately 5,000 East Germans managed to cross the wall to safety in West Berlin, while another 5,000 were captured in the attempt. One hundred and ninety-one people were killed while crossing the wall. On November 9, 1989, the East German government opened the country's borders with West Germany, and the wall itself began to be torn down.

About the Illustration

This illustration is an artist's conception based on available sources. Historians, however, are uncertain exactly what this scene looked like.

✸ **Interactive History Close-Up:**
The Berlin Wall

Differentiating Instruction

Advanced Learners/GATE

1. Have students conduct research on the Internet and find reliable sources that contain primary source documents about the building of the Berlin Wall, stories from East Germans who successfully escaped, and how the wall affected families who had relatives on either side.

2. Have students use the information in the documents to write a short fictional account of life in partitioned Berlin. Have students incorporate quotes, illustrations, and other information from their research. In addition, have students provide a complete bibliography with an explanation of why they believe the Internet sources they used were reliable and valid.

3. Have students share their accounts with the entire class or within small groups.
   LS Verbal-Linguistic

   Alternative Assessment Handbook, Rubrics 30: Research; and 40: Writing to Describe

Answers

Interpreting Visuals *checkpoints, wall, barbed wire, tank traps, armed guards on foot and in watchtowers, attack dogs*

Reading Focus

4 What caused the Cuban missile crisis, and how was war avoided? *Cold War military build up; Soviet decision to put anti-aircraft missiles and nuclear missiles in Cuba; U.S. naval blockade; removal of missiles in exchange for U.S. promise not to invade Cuba*

The Cuban Missile Crisis

Describe What U.S. actions alarmed the Soviet Union? *U.S. placed nuclear missiles in Turkey; anti-Castro activities in U.S.*

Describe How did Khrushchev react to U.S. actions? *put SAMs and nuclear missiles in Cuba*

Draw Conclusions Do you think that President Kennedy believed Khrushchev when he denied placing missiles in Cuba? *possible answers— did not believe him but Kennedy needed proof before taking aggressive action; Kennedy may have believed him, but wanted concrete evidence*

🗺 Map Transparency: Nuclear Threat from Cuba

go.hrw.com
Online Resources
KEYWORD: SD7 CH27
TOPIC: THE CUBAN MISSILE CRISIS

Answers

Interpreting Maps 1. *about 125 miles;* **2.** *Florida, Cuba, Haiti, Dominican Republic, Jamaica, Puerto Rico, Bahamas, parts of Mexico, British Honduras, Honduras*

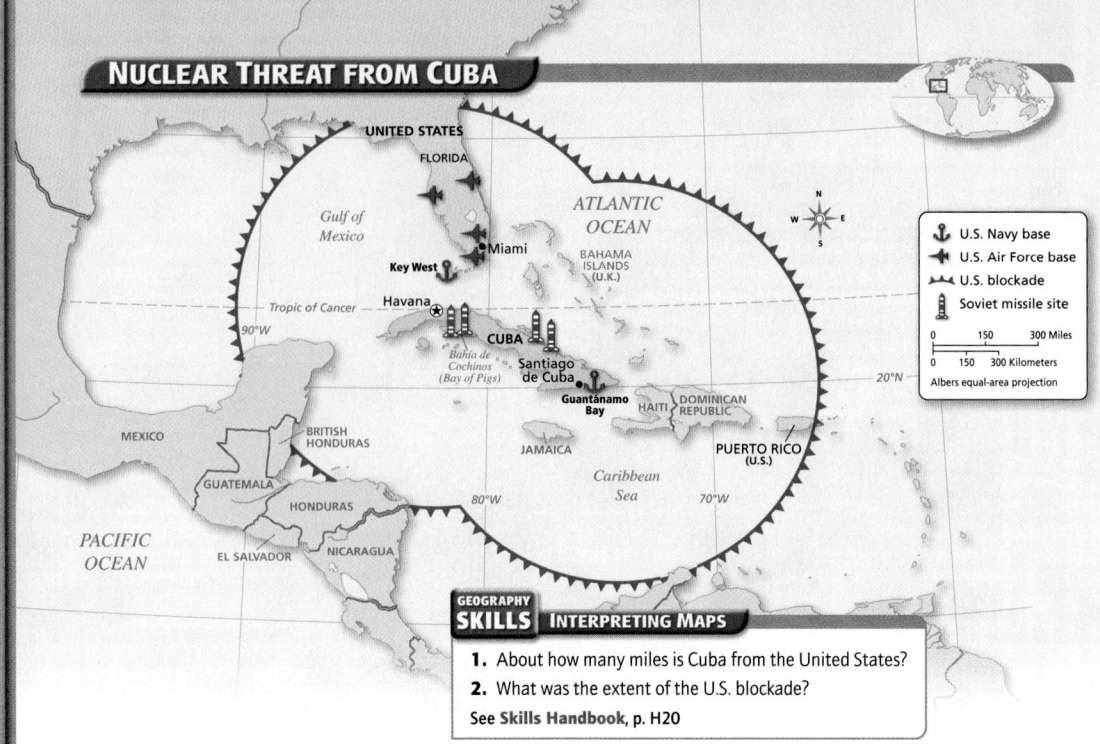

NUCLEAR THREAT FROM CUBA

- ⚓ U.S. Navy base
- ✈ U.S. Air Force base
- ⚔ U.S. blockade
- 🗼 Soviet missile site

0 — 150 — 300 Miles
0 — 150 — 300 Kilometers
Albers equal-area projection

GEOGRAPHY SKILLS INTERPRETING MAPS

1. About how many miles is Cuba from the United States?
2. What was the extent of the U.S. blockade?

See *Skills Handbook*, p. H20

The Cuban Missile Crisis

Khrushchev's continued testing of Kennedy's resolve led to the Cold War's most dangerous crisis. For several days in October 1962, the United States and the Soviet Union teetered on the brink of nuclear war as Kennedy sought a peaceful solution to the **Cuban missile crisis**.

Buildup to the crisis The origins of the Cuban missile crisis can be found in the policies and politics of both the United States and the Soviet Union. U.S. actions in the Bay of Pigs and Berlin crises encouraged hard-line leaders in the Soviet Union. They pushed Khrushchev to be more aggressive.

Some Americans continued to call for an invasion of Cuba after the Bay of Pigs. This concerned Khrushchev because he had pledged to defend Cuba. The Soviets were also concerned about nuclear missiles the United States had placed in Turkey. Khrushchev thought this threat on the Soviet Union's southwestern border justified putting similar missiles near the southern border of the United States.

Kennedy faced similar pressures. Some American politicians blamed him for the Bay of Pigs disaster and accused him of being "soft on communism." Republicans announced that Cuba would be their main issue in the 1962 congressional election campaign. Khrushchev decided to upgrade Cuba's defenses with antiaircraft weapons called surface-to-air missiles (SAMs). He also convinced Castro to allow the secret installation of offensive nuclear missiles that would be controlled by the Soviet Union.

The crisis begins Republicans' pressure on Kennedy increased as Khrushchev pumped aid into Cuba. Kennedy responded by ordering U-2 spy-plane flights over the island. On August 29, 1962, one of these flights detected the SAMs.

The Soviets pointed out that the SAMs were defensive missiles. They denied charges they were placing offensive missiles in Cuba. Kennedy reported the Soviets' denial to the nation, warning that if it proved untrue, "the gravest issues would arise." Moscow replied that a U.S. attack on Cuba would mean war.

884 CHAPTER 27

Skills Focus: Identifying Problem and Solution [At Level]

Reading Skill
The Cuban Missile Crisis

1. The United States did not like it, but the Soviet government believed that arming Cuba was an appropriate reaction to U.S. placing nuclear weapons in Turkey.

2. Have students write a brief essay from the viewpoint of a Soviet official regarding the missile crisis. Students should explain why arming Cuba was seen as a necessary protective measure for the Soviet Union. Have volunteers read their essays to the class.

Then have students write about the Cuban missile crisis from the viewpoint of a member of President Kennedy's advisory group.

3. Guide students in a discussion of the crisis and the actions and reactions of both the Soviet Union and the United States.

🔲 Verbal-Linguistic, Logical-Mathematical

📖 Alternative Assessment Handbook, Rubric 43: Writing to Persuade

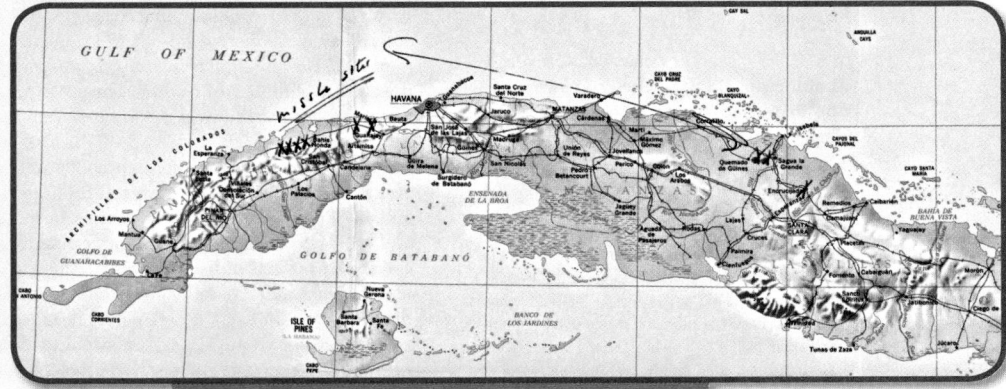

At a Cabinet briefing during the Cuban missile crisis, President Kennedy marked this map of Cuba with a series of X marks, the words *missile sites*, and a black arrow to show locations of Soviet activity as photographed by U-2 spy planes.

As administration officials continued to assure the American people, the spy flights continued. Then on October 14, photos taken from a U-2 plane provided the first solid evidence that the Soviets had lied.

Managing the crisis Kennedy assembled a group of advisers, known as the Ex Comm, to help him decide on a response. He usually did not attend the Ex Comm's daily meetings. He wanted to follow his normal schedule until he was ready to reveal what he knew to the Soviets and to the American people.

Ex Comm's military members favored an air strike against the missile sites, perhaps followed by an invasion of Cuba. Secretary of Defense McNamara and Robert Kennedy argued for a naval blockade instead. Like an air strike, the blockade would be an act of war, but it seemed less likely to provoke a missile launch from Cuba or the Soviet Union. A blockade would also give the Soviets the chance to avoid war by removing the missiles themselves. The president agreed with this reasoning.

On October 22, Kennedy went on television to tell Americans about the Soviet threat. He put U.S. forces on full alert. Some 550 bombers armed with nuclear weapons took to the air and 100,000 troops assembled in Georgia. He wanted to be prepared for war and to show Khrushchev the seriousness of the situation.

As the world nervously watched and waited, several Soviet ships carrying missile parts continued toward Cuba. Khrushchev warned that trying to stop them would mean war. Then on October 24, as they neared the U.S. blockade, they turned back.

Two days later, Kennedy received a letter from Khrushchev offering to remove the missiles if the United States pledged to never invade Cuba. The next day he received a tougher letter from Khrushchev demanding that the United States remove its missiles from Turkey. The Ex Comm advised Kennedy to ignore the second letter and accept the offer in the first letter. The president did so, and Khrushchev announced he would dismantle the missiles.

Effects of the crisis This incident is the closest the world has ever come to nuclear war. Kennedy and Khrushchev both took steps to ease tensions between their countries. In 1963 they set up a hotline to allow U.S. presidents and Soviet leaders to communicate directly in times of crisis. The United States, the Soviet Union, and Great Britain also signed the Limited Nuclear Test Ban Treaty to end the testing of nuclear weapons in the atmosphere and underwater.

THE IMPACT TODAY

Government
Kennedy's pledge that the United States would never invade Cuba caused many Cuban Americans to switch their support to the Republican Party. The Cuban American community remains strongly Republican today.

READING CHECK Drawing Inferences Why was the Cuban missile crisis such an important event?

THE NEW FRONTIER AND THE GREAT SOCIETY **885**

5 How did Kennedy's foreign policy reflect his view of the world? *believed that common links united all people; U.S. should work worldwide to help others*

Kennedy's Foreign Policy

Recall What was the purpose of the Peace Corps? *train and send educators, health care workers, agricultural advisers to help in Africa, Asia, Latin America*

Summarize Why wasn't the Alliance for Progress as successful as the Peace Corps? *provided aid to leaders who did not always have support of their people*

Close

Guide students in a discussion of President Kennedy's foreign and domestic policy successes and failures.

Review

Online Quiz, Section 1

Daily Test Practice Transparency

Assess

SE Section 1 Assessment

Progress Assessment: Section 1 Quiz

Alternative Assessment Handbook

Reteach

Interactive Reader and Study Guide, Section 1

Interactive Skills Tutor CD-ROM

Answers

Reading Check *sent educators, health care workers, agricultural advisers, and financial aid to poor countries*

886

Kennedy's Foreign Policy

In a 1963 speech at American University in Washington, D.C., Kennedy answered those who criticized his foreign policy. He summarized the values he thought should guide America's relations with other nations.

HISTORY'S VOICES

❝What kind of peace do we seek? Not a [peace] enforced on the world by American weapons of war . . . not merely peace for Americans but peace for all men and women . . . For, in the final analysis, our most basic common link is that we all inhabit this small planet. We all breathe the same air. We all cherish our children's future. And we are all mortal.❞

—John F. Kennedy, June 10, 1963

ACADEMIC VOCABULARY
entity something that has a separate and distinct existence

Kennedy also tried to express these principles in his foreign policy through programs to help poorer nations. The **Peace Corps** was the most successful. This entity trained and sent volunteers to Africa, Asia, and Latin America to serve for two years as educators, health care workers, and agricultural advisers, or in other jobs that aided the host country's development. The Peace Corps encouraged women and African Americans to volunteer.

Most volunteers were young college graduates. They were instructed not to argue the merits of U.S. foreign policy and to respect the culture of their host country. The program increased goodwill toward the United States throughout the world.

Another of Kennedy's foreign-policy programs was the **Alliance for Progress**. It offered billions of dollars in aid to build schools, hospitals, roads, low-cost housing, and power plants in Latin America. The program was intended to counter communism's influence in the region. It never lived up to its hopes, partly because aid often went to anti-Communist dictators who had little support among their people.

In other areas Kennedy followed the Cold War policies of his predecessors. He continued the nuclear arms buildup begun by Eisenhower as well as Truman's practice of containment. He also developed the strategy of **flexible response**. This involved strengthening conventional American forces so the nation would have other options than nuclear weapons in times of crisis.

READING CHECK **Summarizing** How did the Peace Corps and the Alliance for Progress help other nations?

---

go.hrw.com
Online Quiz
Keyword: SD7 HP27

Reviewing Ideas, Terms, and People

1. a. Define What did John F. Kennedy mean by the term "new frontier"?
b. Analyze In what ways did Kennedy represent change to the American people?
c. Elaborate How do you think Kennedy chose his advisers?

2. a. Describe Why were U.S.-Cuban relations strained when Kennedy took office?
b. Make Inferences Why would a strong Soviet alliance with a Latin American nation make the United States uneasy?
c. Predict Do you think the Bay of Pigs invasion could have been more successful? How?

3. a. Identify What demands did Khrushchev make at the conference in Vienna?
b. Draw Conclusions Why was Kennedy relieved when he heard about the Berlin Wall?

4. a. Recall What was the immediate set of events that resulted in the Cuban missile crisis?
b. Analyze Why did Kennedy choose a blockade over an air strike in dealing with Soviet missiles in Cuba?

c. Evaluate Do you think Kennedy handled the Cuban missile crisis well? Is there anything he should have done differently?

Critical Thinking

5. Identifying Cause and Effect Review your notes on Cold War crises faced by President Kennedy's administration. Then copy the graphic organizer below and use it to identify the causes and effects of those crises.

Causes	Crisis	Effects

FOCUS ON WRITING

6. Expository President Kennedy and many other Americans believed that the Peace Corps was a good way to aid other nations. Would you be interested in becoming a Peace Corps volunteer? Write a paragraph explaining why or why not.

Section 1 Assessment Answers

1. a. frontiers of the mind, the will, and spirit
b. wealth, good looks, youth, vigor
c. similar backgrounds, shared idealism

2. a. Castro's anti-American speeches; trade agreement with the Soviet Union
b. communism very close to U.S.
c. possible answer—yes, more troops or air cover could have been sent

3. a. U.S. and allies recognize East Germany and withdraw from West Berlin
b. believed that Khrushchev would not invade West Berlin

4. a. Cuba armed with Soviet weapons
b. seemed less likely to provoke war
c. possible answer—yes, allowed for a peaceful settlement

5. Castro, Bay of Pigs, strong Cuban/Soviet relations; Soviet demands, Berlin Crisis, Berlin Wall; Soviet weapons in Cuba, Cuban Missile Crisis, weapons removed, Limited Nuclear Test Ban Treaty

6. possible answers—yes, opportunity to help people in another country; no, help should be applied to Americans in U.S.

Kennedy's Thousand Days

BEFORE YOU READ

MAIN IDEA

John F. Kennedy brought energy, initiative, and important new ideas to the presidency.

READING FOCUS

1. What was Kennedy's New Frontier?
2. In what ways did the Warren Court change society in the early 1960s?
3. What impact did Kennedy's assassination have on the nation and the world?

KEY TERMS AND PEOPLE

Jacqueline Kennedy
New Frontier
mandate
Earl Warren
Warren Court
Lee Harvey Oswald
Warren Commission

TAKING NOTES As you read, take notes on new programs that John F. Kennedy proposed during his presidency. Record your notes in a graphic organizer like the one shown here. You may need to add more circles.

Kennedy's new ideas

THE INSIDE STORY

How did the Kennedys bring style and glamour to the White House?

John F. Kennedy brought something to the White House that had not been seen since the early 1900s—young children. The press carried pictures of the president's toddlers playing in the Oval Office and stories of their pony strolling through the White House gardens. The young family was shown sailing on the blue waters off Cape Cod, in Massachusetts. The image of youth and vitality was unmistakable. It was visual reinforcement of what Kennedy had promised at the start of his campaign—a "new generation of leadership."

In addition to youth, the Kennedy White House was a picture of style. The handsome young president was complemented by his glamorous first lady, Jacqueline. The pair dazzled observers with their movie-star appearance. But beyond the glittery exterior was a genuine appreciation of beauty. Jacqueline Kennedy made the White House a showplace for art, music, and theater. State dinners became cultural events. Many Americans responded with enthusiasm to her grace, charm, and sense of style.

Of course, Kennedy could not lead the nation on style alone. As you will read, the outward image of youth and vigor helped set a tone for politics and change that pushed the nation in new directions. ◼

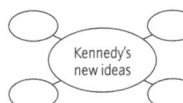

▲ **John and Jacqueline Kennedy brought youthful elegance to the White House.**

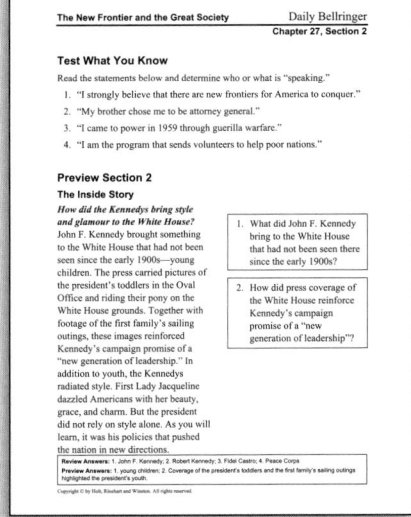

Teach the Main Idea

At Level

Kennedy's Thousand Days

1. **Teach** Ask the students the Reading Focus questions to teach this section.

2. **Apply** Have students draw one large triangle on their own papers and label each side of the triangle with one of the main topics of this section: Kennedy's New Frontier; The Warren Court; The Kennedy Assassination. Have students draw lines out from the sides of the triangle and list the main ideas of each topic on the lines.

3. **Review** Have volunteers share the main ideas they listed on their triangles.

4. **Practice/Homework** Have students write a newspaper editorial on the sequence of events and problems facing the United States during Kennedy's "thousand days."

   LS Visual-Spatial, Logical-Mathematical

   📝 Alternative Assessment Handbook, Rubric 17: Letters to Editors

Direct Teach

Reading Focus

❶ What was Kennedy's New Frontier?
name given to Kennedy's plan to change the nation

Kennedy's New Frontier

Recall Why was Jacqueline Kennedy so popular? *young, beautiful, refined, mother of two children, strong interest in the arts*

Analyze Why did Kennedy's domestic plans lack congressional support? *Many in Congress did not agree with Kennedy's plans for reform.*

Elaborate Why do some people believe that Kennedy used the media more effectively than other presidents? *used the media to make himself appear youthful, athletic, and devoted to his family and family values*

Tracing History
Exploration
Summarize Have students create their own visuals to illustrate this time line. Then have students work in pairs to write newspaper headlines and a brief summary of each event shown.

go.hrw.com
Online Resources

KEYWORD: SD7 CH27
TOPIC: NEW FRONTIERS

Kennedy's New Frontier

Many Americans were struck by the youth and vitality of the Kennedy White House. Few presidents have been more available to the media. Even fewer have used it as successfully to obtain the public image they desired.

Image and reality Photographs of the president often showed him engaged in physical activities like sailing and swimming. Kennedy understood how such pictures would shape his image and boost his appeal. In reality, he struggled with health problems most of his life. He suffered from Addison's disease, a fatiguing and sometimes painful condition. A bad back kept him in nearly constant pain.

First lady **Jacqueline Kennedy** and the couple's two young children contributed to the sense of glamour and energy that surrounded Kennedy's presidency. Caroline and John Jr. were the first young children to live in the White House since 1908. Although Jacqueline Kennedy tried to protect the children's privacy, the president encouraged the press to photograph and write about them. He knew that this information also would help to create a favorable public opinion of his presidency.

Just 31 years old when Kennedy became president, Jacqueline was, like her husband, very attractive and from a wealthy family. "Jackie" was the more refined of the two and had a great interest in the arts. She made the White House the nation's unofficial cultural center by hosting elaborate events featuring world-famous artists and musicians.

Kennedy and Congress Americans seemed to like the Kennedys more than they liked his **New Frontier**. Because the president had spoken so often of a new frontier during the election campaign, this was the name given to his plans for changing the nation. Most Americans in the early 1960s were not reform minded, however.

The makeup of Congress reflected the American public's mood. Conservative southern Democrats often joined with Republicans to block many of Kennedy's proposals. In addition, Kennedy's narrow victory in the 1960 election denied him the clear **mandate**, or authorization to act, he needed to convince Congress that the people agreed with his plans.

For example, Kennedy asked Congress to reduce taxes to fight rising unemployment. This action would give consumers more money to

TRACING HISTORY

Exploration

Early explorers travelled the Earth in search of new places and experiences. Today such curiosity takes people into space and to robotic exploration of the oceans. Study the time line to learn about how key events in American history have transformed the nature of exploration over time.

THE GRANGER COLLECTION, NEW YORK

1804–1806 Lewis and Clark explore the new territory acquired by the United States in the Louisiana Purchase of 1803. The expedition included Sacagawea, a Shoshone guide.

1927 Charles A. Lindbergh makes the first nonstop transatlantic solo flight from New York to Paris.

1800

1900

1932 Amelia Earhart becomes the first woman to make a solo flight across the Atlantic Ocean. In 1937 she vanishes while attempting to fly around the world.

888 CHAPTER 27

Skills Focus: Making Generalizations | At Level

Reading Skill
Kennedy's New Frontier

1. Guide the students in a discussion of President Kennedy's New Frontier, his vision, and plans for the nation.

2. Have students write a letter that an American teenager in 1960 might have written to a pen pal in Europe describing the new young president, his beautiful wife, and most importantly, how President Kennedy plans

to make the country better for all Americans. In their conclusions, students should explain why President Kennedy represents America's future.

3. Have volunteers read their letters to the class.
🅛🅢 **Verbal-Linguistic**

Alternative Assessment Handbook, Rubric 25: Personal Letters

spend, which would lead businesses to produce more goods and hire more workers. Despite his urgings, Congress failed to act. Congressional leaders also ignored Kennedy's proposals to provide federal aid to education and to create a health care plan for older Americans.

In some cases Kennedy's popularity and presidential powers allowed him to solve problems without depending on Congress. For example, the nation's major steel producers announced big price increases in 1962. Kennedy was concerned this would lead to inflation. When some steel-company executives refused to roll back the price increases, he cancelled government contracts to buy steel from those companies. He also began a vigorous campaign against them in the media. The steel companies soon gave in to the president's pressure and cancelled their price increases.

Although Kennedy was among the nation's wealthiest presidents, he sought ways to help poor Americans. He convinced Congress to pass the Area Redevelopment Act in 1961, which gave financial assistance to economically distressed regions. Congress also created a program to retrain workers in areas with high unemployment and raised the minimum wage from $1.00 to $1.25 per hour.

The space program Kennedy's foreign-policy crises helped to create the program that came to symbolize the New Frontier—the exploration of space. In April 1961 the Soviet Union launched the first human into space in a one-orbit flight. It was nearly a year before U.S astronaut John Glenn matched the Soviet accomplishment.

Khrushchev claimed the Soviet lead in space showed the superiority of communism. Coupled with the Cold War embarrassment of the Bay of Pigs, Americans were dismayed. "Is there any place where we can catch them [the Soviets]?" President Kennedy asked his advisers. In May 1961 Kennedy made a bold proposal to Congress to restore America's world prestige.

HISTORY'S VOICES

❝ This nation should commit itself to achieving the goal, before this decade is out, of landing a man on the moon and returning him safely to the earth. No single space project . . . will be more impressive to mankind, or more important for the long-range exploration of space . . . But in a very real sense, it will not be one man going to the moon . . . it will be an entire nation. **❞**

—John F. Kennedy, May 25, 1961

THE IMPACT TODAY

Science and Technology

In 2004, President George W. Bush announced that Americans would return to the moon by 2015 and establish a permanent U.S. base there by 2020.

1962 Astronaut John Glenn becomes the first American to orbit the Earth.

1983 Astronaut Sally Ride becomes the first American woman in space on the space shuttle *Challenger*.

2005 Space shuttle engineer John Phillips dazzles the world by repairing the *Discovery* in space.

2000

1947 USAF Major Chuck Yeager breaks the sound barrier by flying faster than the speed of sound.

1969 Astronaut Neil Armstrong becomes the first person to set foot on the moon.

1985 Robert Ballard discovers the wreck of RMS *Titanic* and revolutionizes undersea exploration by using remotely controlled submersible devices.

THE NEW FRONTIER AND THE GREAT SOCIETY **889**

Skills Focus: Identifying Cause and Effect

At Level

Reading Skill
Kennedy's New Frontier

1. Have students review the information in the text about the increases in steel prices and how the president forced steel producers to roll back their price increases. Discuss with students how President Kennedy waged a media war against the steel companies.

2. Have students create two political cartoons that cover the increase in steel prices, the president's reaction, his actions, or the capitulation of the steel companies.

3. Have students share their cartoons with the class.

4. Guide students in a discussion of Kennedy's success with the steel industry, as well as his political battles on other program goals, including tax reduction, federal aid to education, and health care for the elderly.

LS Logical-Mathematical, Verbal-Linguistic

Alternative Assessment Handbook, Rubric 27: Political Cartoons

• Direct Teach •

Reading Focus

Kennedy's New Frontier

Explain How did President Kennedy deal with steel companies who refused to roll back steep price increases? *cancelled their government contracts; started a media campaign against them*

Summarize How did the space race become part of the Cold War? *Soviets first to have humans in space; claimed it showed superiority of communism; U.S. needed to catch up; rivalry grew from military weapons into space race*

Rate Do you think President Kennedy's domestic goal was to make poor people richer, rich people poorer, or to make all Americans richer? Explain your answer. *possible answers—make all richer because in helping the least fortunate, all will benefit; rich will become poorer, because financial programs for disadvantaged took money from the rich; poor become richer with programs designed to help the poor*

CRF: Biography: Robert Henry Lawrence, Jr.

Primary Source

"For on this generation of Americans falls the full burden of proving to the world that we really mean it when we say all men are created equal and are equal before the law. All of us might wish at times that we lived in a more tranquil world, but we don't. And if our times are difficult and perplexing, so are they challenging and filled with opportunity."

— Robert F. Kennedy

Speech, University of Georgia Law School, May 6, 1961

Reading Focus

② In what ways did the Warren Court change society in the early 1960s? *major advances in civil rights; extended individual rights and freedoms*

The Warren Court

Recall What was the outcome of *Brown* v. *Board of Education*? *Racial segregation in public schools was banned.*

Recall In *Escobedo* v. *Illinois* what legal right was granted to individuals? *right to have lawyer present when being questioned by police*

Elaborate Why do you think that several Supreme Court decisions focused on voter rights? *possible answers—first attempts at securing civil rights for all; cases slowly making their way to the Supreme Court; Americans were starting to pursue fair voting and principle of one person, one vote through the court system*

Primary Source

"To separate [children] from others of similar age and qualifications solely because of their race generates a feeling of inferiority as to their status in the community that may affect their hearts and minds in a way unlikely ever to be undone."

— Earl Warren
Brown v. *Board of Education of Topeka,* 1954

Answers

Faces of History *brought youth, energy, style to the White House; known for her sense of fashion, grace, glamour*

Reading Check *to try to beat Soviets; counter claim of Communist superiority; raise the morale of American public*

890

FACES OF HISTORY

John and Jacqueline KENNEDY
1917–1963, 1929–1994

In November 1960 John F. Kennedy became the youngest elected U.S. president in history. John and his 31-year-old wife, Jacqueline, brought youth, energy, and style to the White House. Known for her sense of fashion, grace, and glamour as the first lady, Jacqueline promoted the arts and culture.

The first lady quickly rose to the top of the list of America's most admired women. Her popularity spread beyond U.S. borders and often exceeded that of the president. On a 1961 trip to Europe, President Kennedy introduced himself as "the man who accompanied Jacqueline Kennedy to Paris." When the Kennedys met Nikita Khrushchev, the Soviet leader said, "I'd like to shake her hand first."

The young couple also experienced tragedy during their years in the White House. In August 1963 the Kennedys' third child, Patrick, died just two days after his birth. Tragedy struck again with John Kennedy's assassination. The country mourned with Jacqueline and the two young Kennedy children.

Make Inferences For what reasons did Jacqueline Kennedy increase the president's appeal and prestige?

The president also asked Congress to fund the unmanned exploration of space. These proposals made the space race as much a part of the Cold War as the conflict over Cuba had been. This race, however, was one the United States would win.

READING CHECK **Identifying Cause and Effect** Why did Kennedy propose a mission to the moon and the unmanned exploration of space?

The Warren Court

During Kennedy's presidency, Supreme Court decisions were responsible for major changes in American society. Under the leadership of Chief Justice **Earl Warren**, controversial Court rulings greatly extended individual rights and freedoms. Many historians regard Warren as second only to John Marshall as the most important chief justice. The Supreme Court's influence on the nation incresed greatly during Warren's nearly 16 years as chief justice.

890 CHAPTER 27

Earl Warren did not have a positive record on civil rights when President Eisenhower appointed him chief justice in 1953. As California's attorney general, Warren had called for the internment of Japanese Americans during World War II. Later, as governor of California, he fought against an effort to make the state's Assembly more representative of the people.

Yet as chief justice, Warren led the Court in 1954 to one of the most significant civil rights advances in U.S. history. He persuaded the other justices in *Brown* v. *Board of Education* to ban racial segregation in the nation's schools. You will read more about this landmark case in the next chapter.

Then in the early 1960s, the **Warren Court** issued a series of decisions concerning other reforms. These decisions required some of the legislative reforms Warren had opposed when he had been governor of California.

Voting-rights reform One significant reform made important changes in the way that legislative representation was determined. In the mid-1900s it was standard practice for states not to redraw the boundaries of their legislative districts to reflect changes in the population.

As cities grew, however, their representation in state legislatures did not. In Tennessee, for example, the boundaries of legislative districts had not changed since 1901. By 1960 densely populated urban areas had the same number of state legislators as sparsely populated rural regions.

In *Baker* v. *Carr* (1962), the Court declared that this situation denied urban voters the equal protection of law required by the Fourteenth Amendment. The Court went further in *Westberry* v. *Sanders* (1964) and *Reynolds* v. *Sims* (1964) when it ruled that legislative districts must have equal populations. This reform guaranteed that each citizen's vote has equal weight, a principle known as "one person, one vote."

The rights of the accused The Warren Court also extended the Bill of Rights to the actions of state governments. In *Mapp* v. *Ohio* (1961), the Court established that the search warrants required by the Fourth Amendment apply to state and local police too, not just to

---

Collaborative Learning

At Level

The Warren Court

Research Required

Materials poster board, colored markers

1. Tell students that the Supreme Court cases discussed in this section had a huge impact on American society at the time and that these cases continue to protect the rights of American citizens.

2. Organize the class into small groups. Have students in each group select one of the Warren Court decisions discussed in the section. Have students research the case to learn more about the decision and

what changes the law made in the protection of individual rights.

3. When students have finished their research, have each group create a storyboard or an illustrated collage of the Warren Court decisions.

4. Display the storyboards and collages, and have volunteers from each group present and explain its work. **⑤ Visual-Spatial**

✎ Alternative Assessment Handbook, Rubrics 8: Collages; and 30: Research

searches conducted by federal agents. In *Gideon v. Wainwright* (1963), the Supreme Court ruled that states must provide free lawyers to poor persons being tried for crimes. In *Escobedo v. Illinois* (1964), the justices decided that a person has a right to a lawyer during police questioning. In 1966 the Court extended these rights again in the case of *Miranda* v. *Arizona*. You will read more about this case in Landmark Supreme Court Cases at the end of this chapter.

Religious freedom In other important cases, the Warren Court defined the religion guarantees of the First Amendment. In *Engel* v. *Vitale* (1962), for example, the justices banned formal prayers in public schools. A year later the Court prohibited daily Bible readings in school. The Supreme Court ruled that both activities violated the First Amendment's guarantee that government would not make any religion the nation's "official" religion.

READING CHECK **Summarizing** How did the Warren Court extend individual rights and freedoms?

The Kennedy Assassination

As 1964 approached, President Kennedy worked to build support for his re-election campaign. To help win the backing of southern Democrats, Kennedy flew to Texas in late 1963. On November 22, President Kennedy rode in an open car of a motorcade through the city of Dallas to the site where he was to deliver a speech. With the first lady by his side, the president waved to the cheering crowds that lined his route.

Then shots rang out from the sixth floor of a schoolbook depository building as the motorcade passed by. Kennedy slumped over, fatally wounded. Within hours, Vice President Johnson, who was with the Kennedys on the trip, was sworn in as president aboard Air Force One.

Kennedy's tragic death shocked the nation and the world. People today still remember what they were doing when they heard the terrible news. Donna Shalala, who later served in President Bill Clinton's cabinet, was working with the Peace Corps in Iran at the time.

Death of a President

Left, President and Mrs. Kennedy shortly before the assassin's bullets struck. Right, Kennedy's widow, Jacqueline, and their children, John and Caroline, wait for the president's funeral to begin. **Why do you think it was important for the nation to have a state funeral?**

891

891

Review & Assess

Close

Have students write a short eulogy that captures President Kennedy's achievements.

Review

- Online Quiz, Section 2
- Daily Test Practice Transparency

Assess

- **SE** Section 2 Assessment
- Progress Assessment: Section 2 Quiz
- Alternative Assessment Handbook

Reteach

- Interactive Reader and Study Guide, Section 2
- Interactive Skills Tutor CD-ROM

Answers

Reading Check *investigate the assassination of the president; no conspiracy found; Oswald and Ruby acted alone*

892

"I . . . recall a beggar walking up to me in the street and I said 'No, I don't have any money.' He said, 'I don't want any money. I just want to tell you how sorry I am that your young president died.'**"**

—Donna Shalala, quoted in *Ordinary Americans*

White House correspondent Helen Thomas later remarked, "The legacy of hope died with him. You never had that same sense again that we were moving forward."

The Warren Commission Within hours of the shooting, Dallas police arrested **Lee Harvey Oswald**, a troubled loner with connections to the Soviet Union and Cuba. Two days later, as police were transferring Oswald from the Dallas Police Department to the county jail, Oswald was shot to death by Jack Ruby, a Dallas nightclub owner with ties to organized crime. These strange circumstances caused some people to question whether Oswald had acted alone in killing the president.

President Johnson named a commission headed by Chief Justice Earl Warren to investigate the assassination. The **Warren Commission**, after a 10-month investigation, reported that there was no conspiracy and that Oswald and Ruby had each acted alone. Despite lingering suspicions, additional government investigations and many private ones have never found credible evidence of a conspiracy.

An end and a beginning The Kennedy assassination deeply affected all Americans. The Kennedy family and supporters made a great effort to shape the nation's memory of the fallen president. Jacqueline Kennedy arranged a funeral to rival that of President Lincoln's nearly a century before. Broadcast live on national television, it concluded with the president's burial at Arlington National Cemetery, on a hillside overlooking the capital, with a continuously burning flame at the site.

"In many ways the drama of [Kennedy's] presidency outweighed its achievements," wrote Clark Clifford, an adviser to several presidents. Yet Clifford acknowledged that "[Kennedy] offered a vast promise to a whole new generation of Americans." In world affairs, that promise was realized by improved relations with the Soviet Union following the Cuban missile crisis and the goodwill toward America that the Peace Corps produced.

At home, Kennedy's accomplishments were less impressive. Yet, even during his presidency, Kennedy had acknowledged that the nation's social, economic, and environmental problems would take many years to solve. It remained up to his successor, Lyndon B. Johnson, to carry on his work. As president, Johnson would achieve greater legislative success than Kennedy.

READING CHECK **Drawing Conclusions** What was the purpose and conclusion of the Warren Commission?

SECTION 2 ASSESSMENT

go.hrw.com
Online Quiz
Keyword: SD7 HP27

Reviewing Ideas, Terms, and People

1. **a. Describe** What public image did Kennedy project?
   b. Analyze How did Kennedy deal with the threat of increased steel prices?
   c. Evaluate Do you think the space race was an important part of the Cold War? Explain your answer.

2. **a. Define** What was the "one person, one vote" standard?
   b. Predict How do you think the Warren Court's decisions would expand people's rights in the future?

3. **a. Describe** What event made Lyndon Johnson president on November 22, 1963?
   b. Make Inferences Why did the fate of President Kennedy affect people so deeply?
   c. Evaluate Do you agree that "the drama of [Kennedy's] presidency outweighed its achievements"? Why or why not?

Critical Thinking

4. **Analyze Information** Review your notes on President Kennedy's proposed programs. Then copy the graphic organizer below and use it to show the results of those ideas.

Kennedy's Ideas	Results

FOCUS ON SPEAKING

5. **Expository** Explain to a classmate what you see as President Kennedy's legacy to the American people. Support your opinion with facts, arguments, and examples.

892 CHAPTER 27

Section 2 Assessment Answers

1. **a.** young, athletic, attractive
   b. cancelled government contracts with steel companies; media campaign against them
   c. possible answer—yes, to show that America could surpass Soviets

2. **a.** each citizen's vote has equal weight
   b. possible answer—allow personal freedom; protect legal rights of less fortunate

3. **a.** assassination of President Kennedy
   b. possible answer—His death shocked the nation and the world.

   c. possible answer—no, provided Americans with hope for the future

4. Ideas—space exploration, reduce taxes, provide aid to education, health care for older Americans, help the poor; Results—1962 American in space, Congress fails to act, ignores proposal, Congress passes the Area Redevelopment Act, raises minimum wage

5. possible answer—encouraged people to reach out, help, achieve great things

The Great Society

BEFORE YOU READ

MAIN IDEA

President Johnson used his political skills to push Kennedy's proposals through Congress and expanded them with his own vision of the Great Society.

READING FOCUS

1. Why was Lyndon Johnson's background good preparation for becoming president?

2. Why was Johnson more successful than Kennedy in getting Congress to enact Kennedy's agenda?

3. In what ways did Johnson's Great Society change the nation?

4. What foreign-policy issues were important in Johnson's presidency?

KEY TERMS AND PEOPLE

War on Poverty
Job Corps
VISTA
Great Society
Barry Goldwater
Medicaid
Medicare
Johnson Doctrine
Pueblo incident

TAKING NOTES As you read, take notes on programs enacted under President Johnson. Record your notes in a graphic organizer like the one shown here.

Continuing Kennedy's legacy	Johnson's new programs

THE INSIDE STORY

What made President Johnson an effective leader? Lyndon Johnson had an ability to get what he wanted that few others could match—or were able to resist. The skills that made Johnson a highly effective majority leader in the Senate helped him to quickly become a strong president following President Kennedy's death.

Knowledge was the basic element in Johnson's leadership style. To Lyndon Johnson, information was power. He made it a point to learn everything he could about his subject and about the people with whom he was dealing. He claimed to know the strengths and weaknesses of each senator—how far each could be pushed, in what direction, and by what means.

One of Johnson's most effective methods was what journalists called "The Treatment." One person who received The Treatment described it "as if a St. Bernard had licked your face for an hour [and] had pawed you all over."

First, Johnson closed in on his target, until his face was just a couple of inches away. Then words poured out of him in a torrent as his eyes widened and narrowed. If the target tried to say something, Johnson never allowed the chance. He countered objections before they could even be spoken. "He'd come on just like a tidal wave," one senator reported. "There was nothing delicate about him." Observers of The Treatment called it an almost hypnotic experience that rendered its targets stunned and helpless. ◼

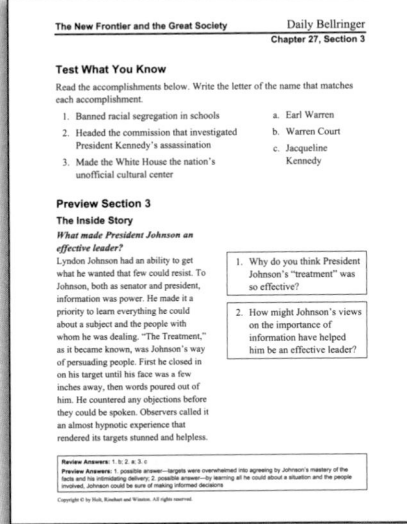

THE **Johnson** *"TREATMENT"*

▶ Johnson (right) overwhelmed friends and opponents alike.

---

❶ Why was Lyndon Johnson's background good preparation for becoming president? *had great political skills; good relationships in the Senate; strong support from the South*

Johnson Becomes President

Explain Why was Lyndon Johnson unhappy as vice president? *missed the power he had in the Senate*

Make Generalizations In addition to his political skills, what other strengths did Johnson bring to the presidency? *tenacity, determination, compassion; ability to persuade; genuine desire to help others*

Predict How might President Kennedy's legacy have been different if Johnson had remained Senate majority leader instead of becoming vice president? *possible answer— Johnson might have been able to help push through reform and civil rights legislation.*

Johnson Becomes President

As vice president, Lyndon B. Johnson had little opportunity to showcase his political talents. Those talents, however, were one reason John F. Kennedy wanted Johnson as his vice president. Another reason was that Kennedy needed a running mate in 1960 who would help the Democrats win the South. Kennedy might have been better served, however, had Johnson remained in the Senate, where his political skills might have helped to get Kennedy's programs enacted.

Kennedy and Johnson made an unlikely team. A large and intense man, Johnson shared none of Kennedy's good looks, polish, or charm. While Kennedy showed off his beautiful young children to reporters, Johnson was known to display the surgery scars on his abdomen. His often crude language reflected the macho ranching culture from which he came. Born and raised in the rural Hill Country of central Texas, he was hardworking and ambitious. In spite of his sometimes overbearing manner, he had a genuine desire to help others.

Johnson gave up school teaching for government work during the Great Depression. When President Franklin D. Roosevelt created the National Youth Administration (NYA) in 1935, a New Deal agency that found work for young people, Johnson sought the job

of state director for Texas. At age 26 he was the youngest NYA director in the nation. Two years later he ran for Congress, where he served his Hill Country district until 1948. Then Texans statewide elected him to the U.S. Senate.

After just one term as a senator, Johnson's Democratic colleagues made him majority leader in the Senate. He soon developed a close relationship with the Republican president Dwight D. Eisenhower. Johnson used his powerful Senate position and Eisenhower's popularity to force compromises in Congress and pass the first civil rights laws since Reconstruction. By 1960 he had more influence in Washington, D.C., than any other Democrat.

Although Johnson campaigned hard for Kennedy's election in 1960, he was unhappy as vice president. He missed the power he had exercised as Senate majority leader. Even more than Kennedy, Johnson promoted an expanded role for government in making Americans' lives better. He also had a greater concern for the poor and underprivileged. These differences were probably due to the two men's differing backgrounds, including Johnson's experience as part of the New Deal.

Despite his sometimes crude behavior, Johnson was a compassionate man. He was saddened by his inability to comfort Jacqueline Kennedy on the plane ride back from Dallas following her husband's death. When he told the nation in his first speech as president, "All I have I would have given gladly not to be standing here today," he truly meant his words.

READING CHECK **Summarizing** Why was Lyndon Johnson well qualified to be president?

FACES OF HISTORY

Lyndon B. JOHNSON
1908–1973

A former Texas high school teacher and long-time member of Congress, Lyndon Johnson ran for the Democratic Party presidential nomination in 1960. Unable to defeat Senator John F. Kennedy of Massachusetts for the nomination, Johnson accepted Kennedy's offer of the vice presidency in order to unite the party.

As president, Johnson carried out an ambitious set of social reforms. After winning the presidential election in 1964, he soon escalated U.S. involvement in Vietnam. Unwilling to let communism advance, he sent American troops into battle. As the Vietnam War dragged on without success, Johnson's popularity with voters decreased. In March 1968 he decided not to run for re-election.

Make Inferences How would Johnson's acceptance of the vice presidency have helped to unite the Democratic Party?

Enacting Kennedy's Agenda

Johnson's mastery of the political process, along with his years of experience in Washington, allowed him to manage the transition of the presidency with great skill and tact. He reassured the nation by promising no great changes from the previous administration. Johnson demonstrated that intent by asking Kennedy's cabinet and advisers to continue serving in the new administration. "I constantly had before me the picture that Kennedy had selected me," he later recalled. "It was my duty to carry on and this meant his people as well as his programs. They were part of his legacy."

Collaborative Learning

Enacting Kennedy's Agenda

1. Guide students in a discussion about President Johnson's first days in office.

2. Organize the class into small groups. Have each group make a list of the strengths that Lyndon Johnson brought to the presidency and the obstacles that he faced.

3. Have students use the information from their lists to write a personal letter to President Johnson encouraging him to use his strengths to overcome the obstacles facing him.

Students should urge the president to work with Congress to pass reform legislation improving civil rights and life for the poor. Have students format their letters using the proper form of address.

4. Have volunteers read their letters to the class.

LS Interpersonal, Visual-Spatial

📰 Alternative Assessment Handbook, Rubric 25: Personal Letters

📊 Graphic Organizer Transparencies

Answers

Faces of History *possible answer— southerner; united the party under one candidate*

Reading Check *experienced as a senator and as vice president; genuine desire to help others; exercised power as former Senate majority leader*

The Job Corps

Among the programs created during the War on Poverty was the Job Corps, a program for young people age 16 to 24 who have not graduated from high school. Today some 60,000 students live on more than 120 Job Corps campuses, where they complete their education and learn a vocation and job-hunting skills.

One of the best-known Job Corps participants is boxer George Foreman. After leaving high school, he joined the Job Corps and learned construction and forestry. A Job Corps counselor also taught Foreman to box, and he went on to win an Olympic gold medal and the heavyweight championship of the world.

Although Foreman's achievements are not typical, Job Corps participants are more successful than other high school dropouts. One study found that Job Corps participants earn about 11 percent more income than dropouts who do not become part of the Job Corps program.

A Job Corps recruiter shares information with high school students in Miami, Florida.

Drawing Conclusions How does the Job Corps represent the ideas of President Johnson's War on Poverty?

The new president also pledged to carry on the New Frontier. Speaking to a joint session of Congress, he called on its members to pass Kennedy's programs, which they had blocked for so long. "Let us here highly resolve that John Fitzgerald Kennedy did not live—or die—in vain," Johnson declared.

HISTORY'S VOICES

❝John F. Kennedy told his countrymen that our national work would not be finished 'in the . . . life of this administration, nor even perhaps in our lifetime . . . But,' he said, 'let us begin.' Today, in this moment of new resolve, I would say to all my fellow Americans, let us continue. This is our challenge—not to hesitate, not to pause, not to turn about and linger over this evil moment, but to continue on our course so that we may fulfill the destiny that history has set for us.❞

—Lyndon B. Johnson, speech to Congress, November 27, 1963

The War on Poverty After Congress passed the Area Redevelopment Act in 1961, Kennedy had told an adviser, "I want to go beyond the things that have already been accomplished." His interest in antipoverty programs was fueled in part by social activist Michael Harrington's influential book published in 1962.

Harrington's *The Other America* was a study of poverty in the United States that shattered the popular belief that all Americans had benefited from the postwar prosperity.

HISTORY'S VOICES

❝They [the poor] exist within the most powerful and rich society the world has ever known. Their misery has continued while the nation talked of itself as being 'affluent' [wealthy] . . . In this way tens of millions of human beings became invisible. They dropped out of sight and out of mind . . . How long shall we ignore this underdeveloped nation in our midst?❞

—Michael Harrington, *The Other America,* 1962

Kennedy's staff had begun work on a series of antipoverty programs he wanted to present as part of his 1964 re-election campaign. Johnson was told of Kennedy's planned antipoverty proposals on November 23, 1963, his first full day in office. "Go ahead," the new president ordered. "Give it the highest priority. Push ahead full tilt."

In his first State of the Union Address in January 1964, Johnson declared "unconditional war on poverty" in America. To launch the **War on Poverty** he asked Congress to pass the Economic Opportunity Act. Congress granted his request in August 1964.

Enacting Kennedy's Agenda

Recall What were the effects of the Tax Reduction Act? *economy grew; unemployment declined; tax revenue increased*

Contrast What was the difference between VISTA and the Peace Corps? *Peace Corps sent volunteers to work in foreign countries; VISTA volunteers worked in the United States.*

Biography

Faith Ringgold (1930–) As a child, Faith Ringgold loved to listen to her parents tell stories. Throughout her life, Ringgold sought a way to combine her passion for storytelling with her artistic talent. Beginning in the 1960s, Ringgold used her knowledge of African arts and history to experiment with new forms of art. In 1963, Ringgold created a collection of paintings known as the American People series, which conveyed the civil rights movement from a female point of view. However, Ringgold is best known for her "story quilts"—a unique invention that combined pieces of fabric, painted images, and handwritten narratives of African American history.

Answers

Reading Like a Historian *that the nation faces nuclear war and the possibility of losing innocent lives if President Johnson is not re-elected*

Reading Check *asked them to prove that Kennedy did not live or die in vain and to continue his plans for America*

The Economic Opportunity Act funded several new antipoverty programs. The **Job Corps** offered work-training programs for unemployed youth. Volunteers in Service to America, or **VISTA**, was a domestic version of the Peace Corps that provided help to poor communities in the United States. Other programs provided basic education for adults, work opportunities for unemployed fathers and mothers, and help to fight rural poverty and assist migrants. These programs were run directly out of the White House by the newly created Office of Economic Opportunity (OEO). Congress gave the OEO $1 billion to operate them.

Other initiatives passed Johnson also pushed for passage of Kennedy's tax-cut bill and civil rights legislation, both of which had been stalled in Congress. Senate conservatives demanded that the president promise to hold government spending to $100 billion if taxes were cut. Johnson knew the government would not need even that much money. He cleverly told the press, however, how difficult it was to write a budget that met this requirement. Believing it had won a victory, Congress passed the Tax Reduction Act in February 1964.

The law had the effect that Kennedy had hoped for. The nation's economy grew by more than 10 percent, and unemployment declined. As a result, tax <u>revenue</u> actually increased.

The Tax Reduction Act illustrated the difference in the way Kennedy and Johnson approached getting legislation passed.

ACADEMIC VOCABULARY
revenue income from a specific source

"Kennedy felt that the way to get the tax cut was to educate the Congress and . . . persuade them to go for it," an aide to both presidents later recalled. "Johnson used his incomparable technique to get the thing through."

"No memorial . . . could more eloquently honor President Kennedy's memory than the earliest possible passage of the civil rights bill for which he fought so long," Johnson told Congress. "We have talked long enough in this country about equal rights . . . It is time now to . . . write it in the books of law." In July, after more than a year of division and debate, Congress passed the landmark Civil Rights Act of 1964. (You will read more about the Civil Rights Act and the circumstances surrounding its passage in the next chapter.)

READING CHECK **Identifying the Main Idea** How did Johnson convince Congress to pass Kennedy's programs?

The Great Society

President Johnson wanted to do more than just follow in Kennedy's footsteps, however. He had ambitious plans of his own. "If you look at my record, you would know that I am a Roosevelt New Dealer," he told an adviser. "As a matter of fact, . . . John F. Kennedy was a little too conservative to suit my taste."

Johnson described his own plans for the nation in a commencement address at the University of Michigan in May 1964.

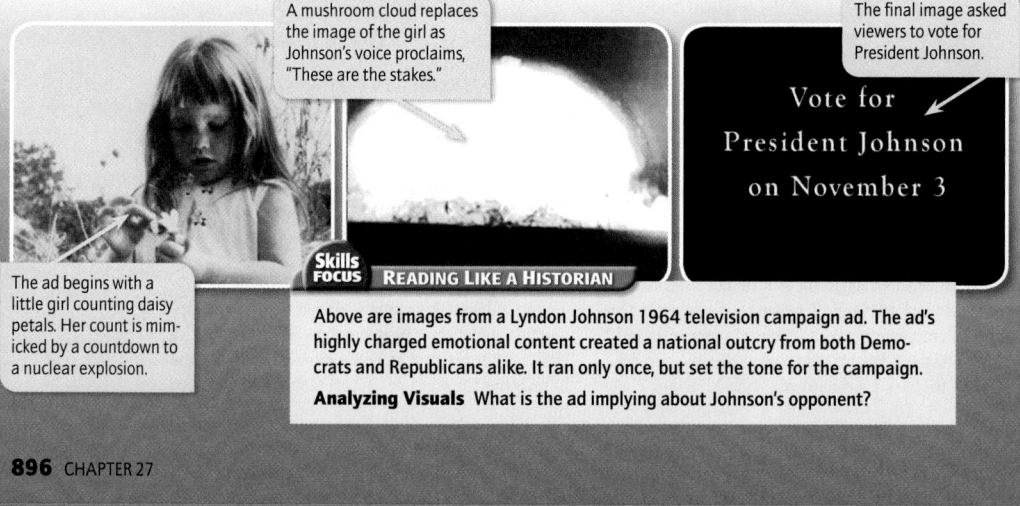

A mushroom cloud replaces the image of the girl as Johnson's voice proclaims, "These are the stakes."

The final image asked viewers to vote for President Johnson.

Vote for President Johnson on November 3

The ad begins with a little girl counting daisy petals. Her count is mimicked by a countdown to a nuclear explosion.

Skills Focus **READING LIKE A HISTORIAN**

Above are images from a Lyndon Johnson 1964 television campaign ad. The ad's highly charged emotional content created a national outcry from both Democrats and Republicans alike. It ran only once, but set the tone for the campaign.

Analyzing Visuals What is the ad implying about Johnson's opponent?

Skills Focus: Interpreting Visuals
At Level

Reading Like a Historian Skill
The 1964 Presidential Campaign

1. Have students carefully examine the images at the bottom of this page. Guide students in a discussion of the significance of the child with the daisy juxtaposed to the nuclear blast.

2. Have students explain how this campaign advertisement played into America's fears about nuclear war and worked to Johnson's advantage in the 1964 presidential election campaign.

3. Have students write a campaign speech that President Johnson could have delivered to U.S. citizens about keeping America strong and safe, while opposing Goldwater's suggestion to use nuclear weapons to end the war in Vietnam.

4. Have volunteers read their speeches to the class. **LS** **Visual-Spatial, Verbal-Linguistic**

Alternative Assessment Handbook, Rubric 24: Oral Presentations

Government's Role in Shaping Society

As senator and vice president, Hubert Humphrey acted on his belief that the government should play an active role in society.

❝ [W]e call upon all Americans to join us in making our country a land of opportunity for our young, a home of security and dignity for our elderly, and a place of . . . care for our afflicted . . . Let us take those giant steps forward . . . to build the great society. ❞

Hubert Humphrey, 1964

Senator Barry Goldwater opposed President Johnson's Great Society— which Hubert Humphrey had played a large part in creating.

❝ I've always stood for government that is limited and balanced and against the ever increasing concentrations of authority in Washington . . . I believe we must . . . not continue drifting endlessly down and down for a time when all of us, our lives, our property, our hopes, and even our prayers will become just cogs in a vast government machine. ❞

Barry Goldwater, 1964

Skills Focus READING LIKE A HISTORIAN

Analyzing Primary Sources In what ways do both speakers try to win support by playing on the emotions of their listeners?

See **Skills Handbook, pp. H28–H29**

HISTORY'S VOICES

❝ We have the opportunity to move not only toward the rich society and the powerful society, but upward to the Great Society. The Great Society rests on abundance and liberty for all. It demands an end to poverty and racial injustice . . . I want to talk to you today about three places where we begin to build the Great Society—in our cities, in our countryside, and in our classrooms. ❞

—Lyndon Johnson, May 22, 1964

The 1964 election The phrase Johnson used— **Great Society**—became the term for the domestic programs of his administration. To achieve his goals for the Great Society, Johnson worked hard to ensure his victory in the 1964 presidential election. He easily won the Democratic Party's nomination for president and chose Hubert Humphrey, a liberal senator from Minnesota, as his running mate. The Republicans selected Senator **Barry Goldwater**, a conservative from Arizona, as their nominee. The vast differences in the two candidates' views gave voters a clear choice.

Goldwater set the tone of the campaign in his acceptance speech at the Republican National Convention by declaring that "extremism in the defense of liberty is no vice." The Democrats portrayed him as a radical who would lead the country into a nuclear war and turn back the clock on the nation's social progress. When Goldwater suggested using nuclear weapons to end the growing war in Vietnam, he convinced many voters that he indeed was a dangerous extremist. (You will read about the Vietnam War in an upcoming chapter.)

Goldwater's attacks on the Great Society also seemed to prove the Democrats' claims about him. "We are all equal in the eyes of God," he proclaimed, "but we are equal *in no other respect*." He charged that government programs to help people were similar to communism and that they posed a threat to the nation's freedom.

In November, the voters provided Johnson with the mandate he sought. The president received 61 percent of the popular vote in the biggest election landslide of the century. His

THE NEW FRONTIER AND THE GREAT SOCIETY **897**

Skills Focus: Making Oral Presentations

At Level

Reading Like a Historian Skill

The 1964 Election

Research Required

1. Have students conduct outside research about the 1964 presidential campaign and the way in which Barry Goldwater conducted his campaign.

2. Organize students in small groups. Have each group use its research to prepare a campaign slogan, a campaign poster, and a speech that Goldwater might have given during the campaign. Have students incorporate quotes from Goldwater into their speeches.

3. Have one volunteer from each group present its campaign material, and have another volunteer from each group present their speeches to the class.

4. Guide students in a discussion of the reasons why some viewed Goldwater as a dangerous extremist. **LS** **Interpersonal, Visual-Spatial**

📝 Alternative Assessment Handbook, Rubrics 24: Oral Presentations; and 30: Research

Direct Teach

Reading Focus

❸ In what ways did Johnson's Great Society change the nation? *passed civil rights, education reform, and environmental laws; established Medicaid, Medicare, and other programs designed to improve life*

The Great Society

Recall How did President Johnson describe himself? *as a Roosevelt New Dealer*

Analyze What do you think Goldwater meant when he said that government programs to help people were similar to communism? *possible answer—government-sponsored social reforms controlled lives of citizens just as communism controlled lives of citizens; also limited individual freedoms*

📄 CRF: Primary Source Activity: Lyndon Johnson Promises the Great Society

📄 U.S. History Political Cartoon Activity: Cartoon 54: Johnson's Great Society

Counterpoints

Government's Role in Shaping Society

Interpret Have students work in mixed-ability pairs to write paraphrases of Humphrey's and Goldwater's remarks. Guide students in a discussion of the role of government. Have students address this question: Should the federal government take giant steps to end poverty and care for those in need as Humphrey argued, or should government programs be limited in scope and size, as Goldwater argued?

Answers

Reading Like a Historian *Humphrey connected patriotism with the care of the elderly; Goldwater warned that government would become big and dehumanizing*

The Great Society

Explain What was the Elementary and Secondary School Act? *first large-scale program of government aid to public schools*

Analyze Why did President Johnson focus on providing government aid to public schools? *had personal interest in providing education for the children of the poor*

Make Judgments Which program do you think was more significant, Medicare or Head Start? *possible answers—Medicare, because it provided health care, a life necessity; Head Start, because it gave children from poor families a better education*

🗔 Quick Facts Transparency: Major Great Society Programs

go.hrw.com
Online Resources
KEYWORD: SD7 CH27
TOPIC: THE GREAT SOCIETY

486–52 victory in the electoral college was even more one-sided. Democrats also strengthened their majorities in both houses of Congress.

Creating the Great Society Now that he had been elected president in his own right, Johnson pushed even harder for his plans. He told aides at an inaugural ball, "Don't stay up late. There's work to be done. We're on our way to the Great Society."

Johnson had a personal interest in providing education for the children of the poor. In 1965 Congress passed the Elementary and Secondary Education Act, the first large-scale program of government aid to public schools. The Higher Education Act created the first federal scholarships for needy college students. In February 1965 the OEO launched Head Start, an education program for the preschool children of low-income parents.

THE IMPACT TODAY

Economics
Today more than 12 percent of the U.S. population receives health care through Medicaid. Nearly half of those covered are children.

The president also persuaded Congress to pass the Omnibus Housing Act in 1965. To oversee this and other federal housing programs, Congress created the Department of Housing and Urban Development (HUD). Johnson appointed Robert Weaver to head this new department, making him the first African American to be part of a president's cabinet.

In July 1965 Congress authorized funds for states to set up **Medicaid**—a program that provides free health care for poor people. At the same time it created **Medicare**, a health care program for people over age 65. Johnson traveled to Independence, Missouri, to sign the bill into law in front of Harry Truman, the 81-year-old former president who had first proposed such a program. "No longer will older Americans be denied the healing miracle of modern medicine," Johnson declared. "No longer will illness crush and destroy . . . [their] savings."

MAJOR GREAT SOCIETY PROGRAMS

QUICK FACTS

Year Enacted	Legislation	Purpose and Provisions
1964	Economic Opportunity Act	Created the Job Corps, VISTA, and eight other programs to fight the "war on poverty"
1964	Tax Reduction Act	Cut income tax rates up to 30%, with the greatest cuts going to lower-income Americans
1964	Civil Rights Act	Outlawed discrimination in housing, employment, and public accommodations; authorized federal government to enforce desegregation
1964	Wilderness Preservation Act	Protected 9.1 million acres of national forest from development
1965	Elementary and Secondary Education Act	Provided aid to school systems based on number of students from low-income homes
1965	Social Security Amendments	Established Medicare and Medicaid
1965	Voting Rights Act	Ended the requirement that voters pass literacy tests and allowed federal supervision of voter registration
1965	Omnibus Housing Act	Provided housing for low-income Americans
1965	Water Quality Act	Required states to clean up rivers and lakes
1965	Clean Air Act Amendments	Established exhaust emission standards for new motor vehicles
1965	Higher Education Act	Provided scholarships and low-interest loans for college students
1966	National Traffic and Motor Vehicle Safety Act	Established safety standards for automobiles and tires
1967	Air Quality Act	Set guidelines on air pollution and increased the federal government's power to enforce clean-air standards

898 CHAPTER 27

Skills Focus: Interpreting Charts

Below Level

Social Studies Skill
The Great Society

Materials construction paper, colored markers

1. Review the chart showing the major Great Society programs with students.

2. Organize the class into small groups. Have each group create a series of four posters. Each poster should describe and promote one Great Society program: improving education, environment, civil rights, and public safety.

3. Ask volunteers to share their posters with the class. You might wish to create a class display of the posters and use them as a section review. **LS Kinesthetic, Visual-Spatial**

📝 Alternative Assessment Handbook, Rubric 28: Posters

Political Cartoon

President Johnson"s long-standing ties in the Senate and public sympathy after the assassination of President Kennedy helped win support for many issues that had been stalled for months or years. This cartoon, called "Maestro of the 88," reflects on Johnson's relationship with Congress.

Johnson's influence as a senator was so great that he has been called a Master of the Senate. A *maestro* is someone who is a master in the arts, especially music.

These "song lyrics" represent important legislation that Congress passed soon after Johnson became president.

The eighty-eighth Congress met from 1963 to 1965. A piano has 88 keys.

Skills Focus READING LIKE A HISTORIAN

Interpreting Political Cartoons What message is the artist trying to convey about Johnson's influence over Congress?

See Skills Handbook, p. H31

Many programs of the Great Society were intended to promote a better life for Americans regardless of their economic status. For example, improving the environment was a major emphasis of Johnson's presidency. He signed laws to improve the quality of the air and water as well as other important environmental measures.

Preserving the outdoors and the nation's natural beauty was especially important to Lady Bird Johnson, the first lady. She asked her husband to push the Highway Beautification Act through Congress in October 1965. This law limited advertising along main highways and provided federal funds for landscaping and roadside rest areas. It came to be called Lady Bird's bill.

The decline of the Great Society The peak years for the Great Society were 1965 and 1966. Congress passed 181 of the 200 major bills President Johnson requested during that period. However, some members of Congress expressed substantial concern over the rapid pace of reform called for by Johnson.

The outcome of the midterm elections of 1966 suggested that many Americans shared these concerns. The Democrats retained their majorities in both houses of Congress, but the Republicans gained 47 seats in the House of Representatives and 3 in the Senate. This shift enabled conservatives to slow down Johnson's legislative program.

The new Congress, however, did enact some Great Society proposals into law. One was the Public Broadcasting Act. This law, enacted in 1967, created the Corporation for Public Broadcasting (CPB) to provide public affairs, cultural, and educational programs. The CPB then created the Public Broadcasting System (PBS) for television and National Public Radio (NPR). The programming of PBS and NPR provide alternatives to the offerings of commercial television and radio.

The Truth-in-Lending Act, also passed in 1967, required lenders to inform consumers of actual costs of credit transactions. A 1968 law established the nation's wild and scenic rivers program. These and many other key Great Society reforms continue to provide benefits to Americans today.

READING CHECK **Identifying the Main Idea** What was the overall goal of the Great Society?

Skills Focus: Interpreting Political Cartoons   At Level

Reading Like a Historian Skill
Creating a New Political Cartoon

1. Have students study the political cartoon on this page. Then guide students in a discussion about the image of President Johnson depicted in the cartoon. Have students determine and explain whether the image of President Johnson is positive or negative.

2. Have students create two new cartoons featuring President Johnson and Great Society legislation. One of the cartoons should be a positive reflection of Great Society goals and one should focus on the great costs the government incurred when they began to implement these programs.

3. Have volunteers display and explain their cartoons to the class. **S Visual-Spatial**

   Alternative Assessment Handbook, Rubric 27: Political Cartoons

---

Reading Focus

The Great Society

Recall How was Congress able to slow down Johnson's legislative program? *Republicans gained congressional seats in 1966 elections.*

Evaluate Do you think that PBS and NPR serve as important alternatives to commercial television and radio in today's society? Explain your answer. *possible answers—no, PBS and NPR advertise; many of their programs are not that different from commercial TV and radio; yes, they provide valuable public information and educational programs that cannot be found on commercial stations*

CRF: Biography: Rachel Carson

Primary Sources
The Great Society

Apply Review the cartoon with students. Then have students write song lyrics for a Great Society song using legislation from the chart and a familiar tune. **S Auditory-Musical**

Answers

Reading Like a Historian *He knew how to get legislation through Congress.*

Reading Check *abundance and liberty for all, end poverty and racial injustice*

④ What foreign-policy issues were important in Johnson's presidency? *Vietnam War; preventing spread of communism; improving relations with Soviet Union; Pueblo incident*

Johnson's Foreign Policy

Recall Which war occupied the Johnson administration? *Vietnam War*

Describe What were the focal points of President Johnson's foreign policy? *fighting spread of communism; improving relations with Soviet Union*

📖 CRF: Literature Activity: *One Flew Over the Cuckoo's Nest* by Ken Kesey

Close

Guide students in a review of the Great Society programs.

Review

🖥 Online Quiz, Section 3

📠 Daily Test Practice Transparency

Assess

SE Section 3 Assessment

📄 Progress Assessment: Section 3 Quiz

📄 Alternative Assessment Handbook

Reteach

📄 Interactive Reader and Study Guide, Section 3

💿 Interactive Skills Tutor CD-ROM

Answers

Reading Check *to prevent a Communist dictatorship*

Johnson's Foreign Policy

Another factor in the decline of the Great Society was the increasing involvement of the United States in the Vietnam War. You will read more details about the Vietnam War in an upcoming chapter.

At the end of 1966 some 385,000 U.S. combat troops were in Vietnam. The U.S. government was spending about $2.5 billion each month on the war. Budgetary pressures mounted as the nation tried to afford both a major war and expensive social programs at home. As one member of Congress put it, "We cannot have guns and butter."

Johnson chose guns over butter because, like Kennedy, he was fully committed to stopping the spread of communism. Johnson sent 22,000 U.S. troops in 1965 to end a revolt in the Dominican Republic. He justified his actions by declaring that revolutions in Latin America were not just local concerns when "the object is the establishment of a Communist dictatorship." This guideline for intervention became known as the **Johnson Doctrine**.

As he fought the spread of communism, President Johnson also continued Kennedy's efforts to improve relations with the Soviet

Union. In March 1967 the first direct treaty between the two nations since 1917 took effect. The treaty protected each country's diplomats from harassment by authorities in the other country.

A month later, the United States and the Soviet Union joined 58 other nations to ban weapons in outer space. After war broke out between Israel and its Arab neighbors in June, Johnson met Soviet leader Aleksey Kosygin in New Jersey to discuss the situation.

A crisis developed in January 1968 when North Korean forces captured the *Pueblo*, a U.S. Navy spy ship, off the coast of Communist North Korea. U.S. officials claimed the *Pueblo* had been in international waters and demanded its return.

When the North Koreans refused, Johnson ordered the call-up of some 14,000 national guard, air force, and navy reserves. At the same time he sought a negotiated settlement to the ***Pueblo*** **incident**. The crisis was resolved in December when the North Koreans released the crew but kept the ship.

READING CHECK **Making Inferences** Why did Johnson involve the United States in the affairs of the Dominican Republic?

SECTION 3 ASSESSMENT

go.hrw.com
Online Quiz
Keyword: SD7 HP27

Reviewing Ideas, Terms, and People

1. **a. Identify** What were some of Johnson's political accomplishments before he became president?
   b. Compare and Contrast In what ways were Johnson and Kennedy alike and different?
   c. Predict How do you think Johnson's experiences would help him as president?

2. **a. Identify** What Kennedy programs did Johnson help pass?
   b. Analyze In what ways did the Economic Opportunity Act address poverty?
   c. Elaborate Which of the laws and programs Johnson enacted do you think is the most important? Why?

3. **a. Describe** What were Johnson's main goals for the **Great Society**?
   b. Make Inferences Why did some people find **Barry Goldwater's** views threatening?
   c. Evaluate How would you rate Johnson's domestic achievements? Explain your answer.

4. **a. Identify** What were Johnson's most significant foreign-policy concerns?

b. Analyze How did the Vietnam War affect the growth of Johnson's Great Society?
c. Evaluate Do you think Johnson's response to communism in the **Johnson Doctrine** was effective? Why or why not?

Critical Thinking

5. **Sequence** Review your notes on President Johnson's achievements. Then copy the graphic organizer below and use it to record those achievements in chronological order. You may need to add more boxes.

```
[    ] → [    ] → [    ] → [    ]
```

FOCUS ON WRITING ✏

6. **Persuasive** Suppose you live in the mid-1960s. Write a letter to your senator expressing support for the Great Society. Use the chart on page 898 to describe the solutions being offered to attack such problems as poverty, discrimination, and pollution.

Section 3 Assessment Answers

1. **a.** Senate majority leader, vice president
   b. desire to help others, concern for poor; age, social graces, political approach
   c. possible answer—politically astute, able to convince people to follow his ideas

2. **a.** Economic Opportunity Act, Tax Reduction Act, Civil Rights Act
   b. funded antipoverty programs, job training, community help, adult education
   c. possible answer—The Civil Rights Act; step toward equality

3. **a.** abundance and liberty for all; end to

poverty and racial injustice
   b. He might lead nation into nuclear war.
   c. great, civil rights reforms, Great Society

4. **a.** Vietnam, Dominican Republic, relations with Soviet Union, *Pueblo*
   b. unable to afford domestic programs
   c. possible answer—yes, allowed U.S. to stop spread of communism

5. See Major Great Society Programs chart.

6. Solutions may include more jobs, better housing, improved health care, expanded civil rights, and a cleaner environment.

Miranda v. Arizona (1966)

Why It Matters The Fifth Amendment protects a criminal defendant from being forced to be a witness against himself or herself. The Sixth Amendment gives the right to an attorney in criminal cases. If a suspect is unaware of these rights, the police cannot interrogate him or her without informing the suspect about his or her rights.

Background of the Case

In 1963 Mexican immigrant Ernesto Miranda was arrested in Arizona. Police questioned him for two hours. He confessed to a serious crime, was tried and convicted, and sentenced to jail. The Arizona Supreme Court upheld his conviction.

The U.S. Supreme Court had ruled in *Brown* v. *Mississippi* (1936) that confessions coerced, or forced, by state or local officials violated the due process clause of the Fourteenth Amendment. In *Gideon* v. *Wainwright* (1963), the Court held that a criminal defendant who cannot afford an attorney can have one appointed without charge. Miranda's lawyer argued that police must inform a suspect of these rights before questioning.

The Decision

The Supreme Court ruled that police must protect a suspect's right against self-incrimination before questioning him or her.

> ❝ [T]he person must be warned that he has a right to remain silent, that any statement he does make may be used as evidence against him, and that he has a right to the presence of an attorney, either retained or appointed. ❞

Police may then question the suspect if he waives these rights. But they must stop if the suspect says he or she wants a lawyer or no longer wants to talk to police. If police do not follow these procedures, any confession or admissions that the suspect makes cannot be used as evidence against him or her at trial in court.

THE IMPACT TODAY *Miranda* was one of the Warren Court's most controversial decisions. Those who disagreed with the ruling warned it could allow guilty people to go free just because of police officers' errors. Today police in the United States carry cards with the Miranda warnings printed on them and routinely "Mirandize" suspects by "reading them their rights" prior to questioning.

CRITICAL THINKING

go.hrw.com
Research Online
Keyword: SS Court

1. **Analyze the Impact** The year after *Miranda* was decided, the Court was faced with the question of whether an accused person is entitled to have counsel present when being shown to prosecution witnesses for identification at a line-up. How is this like the situation in *Miranda*? How is it different? How would you decide this question?

2. **You Be the Judge** Many states have laws requiring a person suspected of committing a crime to identify himself to police. Based on *Miranda*, are such laws constitutional, or does the person have the right to refuse to give police any information? Explain your reasoning in a short paragraph.

THE NEW FRONTIER AND THE GREAT SOCIETY **901**

Word Help

interrogate to question
waive voluntarily give up or let go

Fifth and Sixth Amendments

The Fifth and Sixth Amendment became linked together in *Miranda* v. *Arizona*. In this decision, the Court established "concrete constitutional guidelines" for state and local police when they conduct an interrogation. The Court ruled 5-4 that prosecutors could not use incriminating statements obtained during interrogation unless strict procedures had been followed. One week later the Court ruled that it would not apply the *Miranda* decision retroactively to convictions that had already been made.

Primary Source

Chief Justice Earl Warren defined interrogation by police as "questioning initiated by law enforcement officers after a person has been taken into custody or otherwise deprived of his freedom of action in any significant way."

— Earl Warren

Miranda v. *Arizona*

Differentiating Instruction

Below Level

Special Education Students

1. Have students copy the Miranda warning.
   1. You have the right to remain silent.
   2. Anything you say can and will be used against you in a court of law. **3.** You have the right to talk to a lawyer and to have a lawyer present with you while you are being questioned. **4.** If you cannot afford to hire a lawyer, one will be appointed to represent you before any questioning if you wish. **5.** You can decide at any time to exercise these rights and not answer any questions or make any

statements. **Waiver** Do you understand each of these rights that I have explained to you? Having these rights in mind, do you wish to talk to us now?

2. Guide students in a discussion of the questions in the waiver. Ask students why these questions are important in protecting *Miranda* rights. **LS Verbal-Linguistic**

   Alternative Assessment Handbook, Rubric 11: Discussions

Answers

Critical Thinking 1. *similar, deals with rights of person accused of crime; different, deals with right itself, not accused person's knowledge of rights;* **2.** *possible answer—These laws are unconstitutional; person has right to refuse because answers might be self-incriminating; based on* Miranda, *suspect can remain silent and request an attorney*

The New Frontier and Great Society

Historical Context The documents below provide information on President John F. Kennedy's New Frontier and President Lyndon Johnson's Great Society programs.

Task Examine the documents and answer the questions that follow. Then you will be asked to write an essay about Kennedy's New Frontier and Johnson's Great Society, using facts from the documents and from the chapter to support the position you take in your thesis statement.

Word Help

abolish put an end to
forebears ancestors
capacities capabilities

MISCONCEPTION ALERT

Although President John F. Kennedy implemented the Peace Corps, he was not the first to come up with the idea. Future vice president Hubert Humphrey and U.S. Congressman Henry S. Reuss actually proposed the idea while serving in the U.S. Senate in the late 1950s.

Info to Know

The Peace Corps Today Since 1961, over 170,000 volunteers have served in 138 countries. Today's Peace Corps workers help people around the world in areas ranging from HIV/AIDS education and prevention to the development of information technology and new businesses. But the organization's goal remains the same: to promote understanding between nations and help people to develop better lives for themselves, their children, and their communities.

DOCUMENT 1

President John F. Kennedy came into office with bold ideas and an agenda that came to be known as the New Frontier. He explained some of the goals of this program in his inaugural address.

"[M]an holds in his mortal hands the power to abolish all forms of human poverty and all forms of human life. And yet the same revolutionary beliefs for which our forebears fought are still at issue around the globe . . .

"We dare not forget today that we are the heirs of that first revolution. Let the word go forth from this time and place, to friend and foe alike, that the torch has been passed to a new generation of Americans . . .

"Let every nation know, whether it wishes us well or ill, that we shall pay any price, bear any burden, meet any hardship, support any friend, oppose any foe, to assure the survival and the success of liberty . . .

"To those people in the huts and villages of half the globe struggling to break the bonds of mass misery, we pledge our best efforts to help them help themselves . . . If a free society cannot help the many who are poor, it cannot save the few who are rich . . .

"In your hands, my fellow citizens, more than mine, will rest the final success or failure of our course . . .

"And so, my fellow Americans, ask not what your country can do for you; ask what you can do for your country."

DOCUMENT 2

One component of the New Frontier was the creation of the Peace Corps to help developing countries improve their economies, education, and infrastructure. Thousands of young volunteers heeded Kennedy's call and went to help the poor in foreign countries. Here a Peace Corps volunteer is helping to inoculate children in Bolivia.

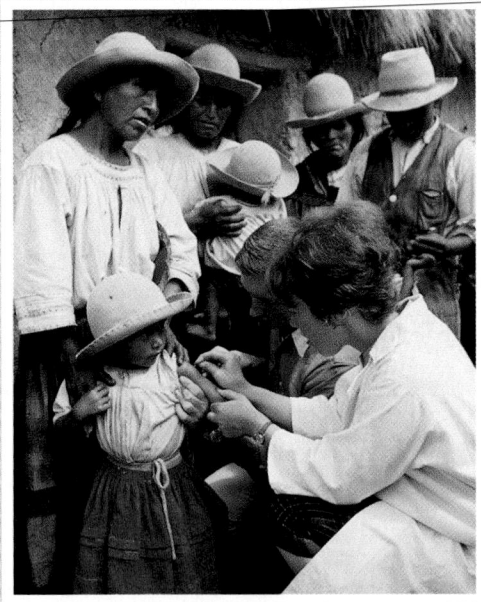

Skills Focus: Analyzing Primary Sources   At Level

Reading Like a Historian Skill   Research Required

The Peace Corps

1. Divide the class into groups of four or five students. Have each group come up with a series of questions that they would like to ask someone who has served in the Peace Corps. They should ask where the person served, and what his or her job was.

2. Have each student find and interview a person who has worked in the Peace Corps. Students may want to record the interviews for the sake of accuracy, but they should be written down and edited before being turned in. If students cannot locate a former Peace Corps volunteer, they can use memoirs or other primary sources.

3. Ask volunteers to read their interviews to the class. Then guide the class in a discussion of the similarities and differences in the subjects' experiences. **LS Interpersonal, Verbal-Linguistic**

    Alternative Assessment Handbook, Rubric 18: Listening

DOCUMENT 3

President Lyndon Johnson came into office with his own bold goals, namely the creation of the Great Society, in which problems such as poverty and racism would be wiped out. In the following speech, he explains his War on Poverty, a key element of creating the Great Society.

"We are citizens of the richest and most fortunate nation in the history of the world . . .

"The path has not been an easy one. But we have never lost sight of our goal—an America in which every citizen shares all the opportunities of his society, in which every man has a chance to advance his welfare to the limit of his capacities.

"We have come a long way toward this goal. We still have a long way to go. The distance which remains is the measure of the great unfinished work of our society. To finish that work I have called for a national war on poverty. Our objective: total victory . . .

"The war on poverty is not a struggle simply to support people, to make them dependent on the generosity of others. It is a struggle to give people a chance. It is an effort to allow them to develop and use their capacities, as we have been allowed to develop and use ours, so that they can share, as others share, in the promise of this nation.

"Because it is right, because it is wise, and because, for the first time in our history, it is possible to conquer poverty . . ."

DOCUMENT 4

Many conservatives opposed Lyndon Johnson's Great Society programs. His costly programs would increase the size of government, they argued. They feared a larger central government would rob people of their democratic freedoms. Actor Ronald Reagan was new to politics when he delivered the following speech in October 1964. He asked voters to support Republican Barry Goldwater in his campaign for the presidency. Goldwater lost the election to Johnson, but the speech made Reagan a rising star in politics. Reagan would one day become the 40th president of the United States.

In this vote-harvesting time, they use terms like the "Great Society," or as we were told a few days ago by the President, we must accept a greater government activity in the affairs of the people . . .

"This is the issue of this election: Whether we believe in our capacity for self-government or whether we abandon the American revolution and confess that [the government] can plan our lives for us better than we can plan them ourselves . . .

We have so many people who can't see a fat man standing beside a thin one without coming to the conclusion the fat man got that way by taking advantage of the thin one. So they're going to solve all the problems of human misery through government and government planning . . .

No government ever voluntarily reduces itself in size. So governments' programs, once launched, never disappear . . ."

Skills FOCUS READING LIKE A HISTORIAN

1. a. Identify Refer to Document 1. What goals of the New Frontier does Kennedy emphasize in this excerpt?
b. Elaborate How do you think the Cold War influenced the ideas Kennedy expresses here?

2. a. Describe Refer to Document 2. What is happening in this image?
b. Analyze How does this program help achieve Kennedy's goals?

3. a. Identify Refer to Document 3. What does Johnson hope to achieve?
b. Elaborate Do you think his goal was realistic?

4. a. Identify Refer to Document 4. Who do the "fat man" and the "thin one" represent?

b. Explain What did Reagan mean when he said "they're going to solve all the problems of human misery through government and government planning"?

5. Document-Based Essay Question Consider the question below and form a thesis statement. Using examples from Documents 1, 2, 3, and 4, create an outline and write a short essay supporting your position. How were some of the goal were President Kennedy's New Frontier and President Johnson's Great Society similar to and different from one another?

See **Skills Handbook**, p. H28, H30

THE NEW FRONTIER AND THE GREAT SOCIETY **903**

Info to Know

Antipoverty Spending Between 1962 and 1968, the federal government's spending on the poor rose from almost $12 billion to approximately $27 billion, more than doubling. According to government statistics, the percent of America living in poverty fell from 20 percent to 12 percent, as approximately 12 million Americans moved above the official poverty line.

Answers

Reading Like a Historian 1. a. *to stamp out poverty and carry democracy around the world;* **b.** *possible answer— By helping poor countries stamp out poverty, America could win the support of nations that might otherwise be tempted to side with the Soviet Union and move toward communism.* **2. a.** *A Peace Corps volunteer is vaccinating a child in Bolivia.* **b.** *by helping the poor in foreign countries;* **3. a.** *He hopes to wipe out poverty and provide equal opportunities to everyone.* **b.** *possible answers—no, because the only way to wipe out poverty would be to redistribute all wealth; yes, because America has the resources to help the poor;* **4. a.** *possible answer— wealth and poverty;* **b.** *those in government who support Great Society, expanding social programs;* **5.** *possible answer—both aimed at using resources of American people to improve society; New Frontier addressed international problems; Great Society addressed domestic problems*

Collaborative Learning

The War on Poverty

At Level

Research Required

1. Divide the class into groups of four or five students. Tell them that in 1968, it looked as though the United States could win the War on Poverty because the percentage of the population living in poverty had dropped from 20 percent in 1962 to 12 percent. While the poverty rate has changed from year to year, in 2004 the percentage of people living in poverty was close to 13 percent.

2. Have each group conduct research to find out what is being done today to combat poverty.

3. Have each group write a plan for wiping out poverty in the next 20 years.

4. Ask volunteers from each group to share their plans with the class.

5. Guide the class in a discussion of the plans. Do students think it is realistic to believe that poverty can be eliminated? **LS Interpersonal, Logical-Mathematical**

Alternative Assessment Handbook, Rubric 35: Solving Problems

Answers

Visual Summary

Review and Inquiry Have students write one sentence describing or explaining each event on the time line. Have volunteers share their sentences with the class.

Quick Facts Transparency: The New Frontier and the Great Society

Reviewing Key Terms and People

1. Fidel Castro
2. Bay of Pigs invasion
3. Cuban missile crisis
4. flexible response
5. Alliance for Progress
6. mandate
7. Earl Warren
8. Lee Harvey Oswald
9. Warren Commission
10. VISTA
11. Barry Goldwater
12. Medicare
13. *Pueblo* incident
14. Johnson Doctrine

Comprehension and Critical Thinking

15. **a.** U.S. trained Cuban exiles to invade Cuba; air strikes failed, land attacks were not a surprise; Castro was able to defeat invading troops
b. showed U.S. commitment to help people in need all over the world; volunteers instructed to not argue the merits of U.S. foreign policy and to respect the culture of their host country
c. possible answer—divide families, create unemployment, increase tensions between East and West

16. **a.** an antipoverty act
b. to disprove Khrushchev's claim of superiority; restore America's world prestige
c. greatly extended individual rights and freedoms

17. **a.** Johnson had exceptional political talents and would win southern votes necessary to win the election.

b. so that Kennedy would not have lived or died in vain; also believed in civil rights and helping disadvantaged
c. made public feel safer in the face of nuclear war; Goldwater's views were seen as extremist

Using the Internet

18. Go to the HRW Web site and enter the keyword shown to access a rubric for this activity.

KEYWORD: SD7 CH27

Visual Summary: The New Frontier and the Great Society

January 1961
Kennedy takes office as the youngest elected president.

March 1961
Kennedy announces Alliance for Progress program.

April 1961
Bay of Pigs invasion fails in Cuba.

August 1961
East German Communists build Berlin Wall.

October 1962
Cuban missile crisis threatens war with USSR.

August 1963
Limited Test Ban Treaty signed.

November 1963
Kennedy is assassinated; Johnson becomes president.

January 1964
Johnson announces War on Poverty.

July 1964
Congress passes Civil Rights Act.

August 1964
Congress passes Economic Opportunity Act.

November 1964
Johnson defeats Goldwater in landslide.

February 1965
Active U.S. involvement in Vietnam War begins.

April 1965
Johnson sends marines to Dominican Republic.

August 1965
Congress passes Voting Rights Act.

July 1965
Congress creates Medicare and Medicaid programs.

April 1967
Outer Space Treaty is signed.

January 1968
North Korea captures *Pueblo* and its crew.

1961 — 1962 — 1963 — 1964 — 1965 — 1966 — 1967 — 1968 — 1969

YEARS

Reviewing Key Terms and People

Complete each sentence by filling in the blank with the correct term or person.

1. The dictator _____ came to power in Cuba in 1959.
2. A disastrous attempt by the CIA to invade Cuba became known as the _____.
3. The _____ brought the United States and the Soviet Union to the brink of nuclear war.
4. Kennedy's strategy of _____ involved strengthening conventional U.S. forces to avoid using nuclear weapons in times of crisis.
5. The _____ offered economic aid to Latin American countries.
6. Because of his narrow victory in 1960, Kennedy never had a strong _____ for his plans.
7. The chief justice of the Supreme Court during Kennedy's presidency was _____.

8. Dallas police arrested _____ for the assassination of President Kennedy.
9. The _____ reported that there was no conspiracy in the assassination of President Kennedy.
10. A domestic version of the Peace Corps called _____ helped poor communities in the United States.
11. Johnson's Republican opponent in the 1964 election was _____.
12. Under the Great Society, a government health care program for people over 65 called _____ was begun.
13. The _____ was resolved when North Korea kept the ship but released its crew.
14. The _____ was the president's justification for U.S. intervention in Latin America when there was the threat of a Communist dictatorship.

Analyzing Primary Sources

19. Kennedy rejects a peace "enforced on the world by American weapons of war," and wants a peace for "all men and women."

20. We must live with each other on the same planet and must try to coexist peacefully.

Critical Reading

21. C

22. A

History's Impact video program
Review the video to answer the closing question:
How did advances in technology as a result of the space program change American life?

Comprehension and Critical Thinking

SECTION 1 *(pp. 878–886)*

15. a. Describe What happened at the Bay of Pigs invasion?

b. Draw Conclusions In what ways did the Peace Corps increase goodwill for the United States?

c. Evaluate How might the Berlin Wall affect the lives of people in East and West Berlin?

SECTION 2 *(pp. 887–892)*

16. a. Identify What was the Area Redevelopment Act of 1961?

b. Make Inferences Why was Congress willing to fund the space race?

c. Elaborate Why were the reforms of the Warren Court important to the nation?

SECTION 3 *(pp. 893–900)*

17. a. Recall Why did Kennedy choose Johnson as his vice president?

b. Analyze Why did Johnson decide to carry out Kennedy's initiatives?

c. Elaborate Why do you think Americans voted so overwhelmingly for Johnson in the presidential election of 1964?

Using the Internet

go.hrw.com
Practice Online
Keyword: SD7 CH27

18. The Berlin Wall remained in place from 1961 to 1989, when it was finally torn down. Using the keyword above, do research on the significance of the Berlin Wall. Then write a report about the ways the construction and destruction of this barrier changed the world.

Analyzing Primary Sources

Reading Like a Historian In response to criticism of how he handled the Cuban missile crisis, Kennedy made a speech. Read an excerpt from that speech in the History's Voices passage in Section 1 that begins, "What kind of peace do we seek?"

19. Identify What kind of peace does Kennedy reject? What kind of peace does he want?

20. Analyze Why is it important to remember our "common link"?

Critical Reading

Read the passage in Section 3 that begins with the heading "Creating the Great Society." Then answer the questions that follow.

21. According to the passage, one thing limited along major highways by the Highway Beautification Act was

A landscaping.

B rest areas.

C billboards.

D streetlights.

22. The appointment of Robert Weaver as secretary of the Department of Housing and Urban Development was significant because

A he was the first African American to be part of a president's cabinet.

B he was the youngest cabinet member ever.

C Congress had originally rejected his nomination.

D he was a conservative Republican who had previously opposed President Johnson.

FOCUS ON WRITING

Expository Writing *Expository writing gives information, explains why or how, or defines a process. To practice expository writing, complete the assignment below.*

Writing Topic The New Frontier of John F. Kennedy

23. Assignment Based on what you have read in this chapter, write a paragraph that explains what the New Frontier was and how it was presented to the American people.

Answers

Focus on Writing

23. possible answer—The New Frontier was part of Kennedy's campaign platform that encouraged Americans to find new ways to combat problems such as poverty, prejudice, and war. It played on the nation's Cold War fears and desire to get ahead of the Soviet Union after falling behind in the development of nuclear weapons.

A rubric for this activity is provided in the CRF: Focus on Writing Activity: The New Frontier of John F. Kennedy

History's Impact
Video Program

innovations that made it possible to travel to space are still in use today; experiments performed in space have had a major impact on science

Review and Assessment Resources

Review and Reinforce

- CRF: Chapter Review Activity
- Quick Facts Transparencies: Major Great Society Programs, The New Frontier and the Great Society
- Spanish Chapter Summaries Audio CD Program
- Online Chapter Summaries in Spanish
- OSP Holt PuzzlePro; Quiz Show for ExamView
- Quiz Game CD-ROM

Assess

- PASS: Chapter Test, Forms A and B
- Alternative Assessment Handbook
- OSP ExamView Test Generator, Chapter Test
- Differentiated Instruction Modified Worksheets and Tests CD-ROM: Chapter Test
- HOAP Holt Online Assessment Program (in the Premier Online Edition)

Reteach/Intervene

- Interactive Reader and Study Guide
- Differentiated Instruction Teacher Management System: Lesson Plans for Differentiated Instruction
- Differentiated Instruction Modified Worksheets and Tests CD-ROM: Chapter Test
- Interactive Skills Tutor CD-ROM

go.hrw.com
Online Resources
KEYWORD: SD7 CH27

Chapter 28 Planning Guide

The Civil Rights Movement

Chapter Overview	Reproducible Resources	Technology Resources
CHAPTER 28 pp. 906–945 **Overview:** In this chapter, students will analyze the struggles that African Americans faced fighting discrimination.	**Differentiated Instruction Teacher Management System:** • Instructional Benchmarking Guides • Lesson Plans for Differentiated Instruction **Interactive Reader and Study Guide** **Chapter Resource File*:** • Writing for the SAT Activity: Affirmative Action • Social Studies Skills Activity: Making Oral Presentations • Chapter Review Activity **American History Outline Maps** **Pre-AP Activities Guide for American History** **Reading Like a Historian Toolkit**	**Live Ink® Online Reading Help** **Student Edition on Audio CD Program** **Differentiated Instruction Modified Worksheets and Tests CD-ROM** **Interactive Skills Tutor CD-ROM** **United States History Primary Source Library CD-ROM** **Power Presentations with Video CD-ROM** **History's Impact: American History Video Program (VHS/DVD)** **Online Chapter Summaries in Spanish**
Section 1: **Fighting Segregation** **The Main Idea:** The civil rights movement made inroads into racial segregation.	**Differentiated Instruction Teacher Management System:** Section 1 Lesson Plan* **Interactive Reader and Study Guide*** **Chapter Resource File***	**Daily Bellringer Transparency:** Section 1* **Daily Test Practice Transparency:** Section 1*
Section 2: **Freedom Now!** **The Main Idea:** Civil rights became a nationwide movement during the 1960s.	**Differentiated Instruction Teacher Management System:** Section 2 Lesson Plan* **Interactive Reader and Study Guide*** **Chapter Resource File***	**Daily Bellringer Transparency:** Section 2* **Daily Test Practice Transparency:** Section 2*
Section 3: **Voting Rights** **The Main Idea:** African Americans gained voting rights in the South.	**Differentiated Instruction Teacher Management System:** Section 3 Lesson Plan* **Interactive Reader and Study Guide*** **Chapter Resource File***	**Daily Bellringer Transparency:** Section 3* **Daily Test Practice Transparency:** Section 3*
Section 4: **Changes and Challenges** **The Main Idea:** Continued inequalities caused many to lose faith in the civil rights movement.	**Differentiated Instruction Teacher Management System:** Section 4 Lesson Plan* **Interactive Reader and Study Guide*** **Chapter Resource File***	**Daily Bellringer Transparency:** Section 4* **Daily Test Practice Transparency:** Section 4*
Section 5: **The Movement Continues** **The Main Idea:** Although its accomplishments continued to benefit society, the civil rights movement declined by the 1970s.	**Differentiated Instruction Teacher Management System:** Section 5 Lesson Plan* **Interactive Reader and Study Guide*** **Chapter Resource File***	**Daily Bellringer Transparency:** Section 5* **Daily Test Practice Transparency:** Section 5*

 go.hrw.com   Print Resource   Transparency

LS Learning Styles   Audio CD   CD-ROM

Video   **SE** Student Edition   **TE** Teacher's Edition

OSP One-Stop Planner CD-ROM

*also on One-Stop Planner CD-ROM

HOLT

History's Impact
American History Video Program (VHS/DVD)

The Civil Rights Movement

Review, Assessment, Intervention

 Quick Facts Transparency: The Civil Rights Movement

 Spanish Chapter Summaries Audio CD Program

 Progress Assessment Support System (PASS): Chapter Test*

Differentiated Instruction Modified Worksheets and Tests CD-ROM: Modified Chapter Test

OSP **One-Stop Planner CD-ROM:** ExamView Test Generator (English/Spanish)

HOAP **Holt Online Assessment Program (HOAP),** in the Holt Premier Online Student Edition

 PASS: Section 1 Quiz*

 Online Quiz: Section 1

 Alternative Assessment Handbook

 PASS: Section 2 Quiz*

 Online Quiz: Section 2

 Alternative Assessment Handbook

 PASS: Section 3 Quiz*

 Online Quiz: Section 3

 Alternative Assessment Handbook

 PASS: Section 4 Quiz*

 Online Quiz: Section 4

 Alternative Assessment Handbook

 PASS: Section 5 Quiz*

Online Quiz: Section 5

Alternative Assessment Handbook

NC RESOURCES

The following resources were developed to help North Carolina educators teach the standards and objectives of North Carolina's eleventh grade standard course of study in United States history.

- United States history EOC Test Prep Workbook
- Teacher's Support System
- North Carolina One-Stop Planner

And be sure to direct your students to **go.hrw.com** for online access to the EOC Test Prep Workbook.

go.hrw.com
EOC Test Prep
KEYWORD: SE7 NC

Holt Online Learning

go.hrw.com
Teacher Resources
KEYWORD: SD7 TEACHER

go.hrw.com
Student Resources
KEYWORD: SD7 CH28

- Document-based Questions
- Interactive Multimedia Activities

- Current Events
- Chapter-based Internet Activities
- and more!

Holt Premier
Online Student Edition
Complete online support for interactivity, assessment, and reporting

- Interactive Maps and Notebook
- Standardized Test Prep
- Homework Practice and Research Activities Online

CHAPTER 28 PLANNING GUIDE

The Big Picture

Robert D. Schulzinger

The Growth of the Civil Rights Movement A nationwide multiracial movement struggled to end racial segregation and discrimination in the decades after World War II. In 1954 the Supreme Court declared segregation in public education unconstitutional in *Brown* v. *Board of Education of Topeka, Kansas*. Civil rights organizations led nonviolent boycotts, sit-ins, Freedom Rides, pickets, and mass rallies to heighten awareness of racial injustice. Brutality directed at civil rights workers by segregationists forced Presidents Eisenhower and Kennedy to send armed federal troops and U.S. marshals to protect the civil rights of African American students and civil rights demonstrators.

Civil Rights Legislation In August 1963 Martin Luther King Jr. electrified a large crowd gathered in front of the Lincoln Memorial by calling for the passage of a civil rights law. Hundreds of civil rights volunteers traveled to Mississippi during the Freedom Summer of 1964 to help register African Americans to vote. Segregationists confronted the volunteers with brutality, intimidation, and murder, but civil rights legislation went forward. Congress passed a Civil Rights Act banning discrimination in employment and public accommodation in 1964. A march by thousands of black and white voting rights advocates from Selma to Montgomery, Alabama, in 1965 helped pass the Voting Rights Act.

Challenges to the Civil Rights Movement Ending legal or de jure segregation in southern states proved easier than overcoming the harsh realities of de facto segregation in the rest of the country. African American frustration exploded into violence in numerous cities. The civil rights movement fractured as many urban, young African Americans abandoned nonviolent tactics and called for Black Power. In the 1970s African Americans and other racial minorities continued to advance as more schools became desegregated, housing discrimination diminished, and employment opportunities expanded.

Recent Scholarship

Evaluating the King Years Taylor Branch has published two massive volumes of his trilogy *America in the King Years*. *Parting the Waters* (1988) and *Pillar of Fire* (1998) take the story of the civil rights movement through 1965 and the final volume, *At Canaan's Edge* (2006), concludes with King's death in 1968. Branch paints on a vast canvas, and he brings an uncanny intimacy to protest marches, confrontations between police, Ku Klux Klansmen, and civil rights demonstrators, and the inner workings of government on all levels. He makes the reader feel what it was like to be a part of one of the most significant social movements in American history.

Differentiating Instruction

 Differentiated Instruction Teacher Management System
- Lesson Plans for Differentiated Instruction
- Differentiated Instructional Benchmarking Guides
- Interactive Reader and Study Guide

 Spanish Chapter Summaries Audio CD Program

 Online Chapter Summaries in Spanish

 Student Edition on Audio CD Program

 Differentiated Instruction Modified Worksheets and Tests CD-ROM
- Vocabulary Flash Cards
- Modified Vocabulary Builder Activities
- Modified Chapter Review Activity
- Modified Chapter Test

OSP One-Stop Planner CD-ROM
- ExamView Test Generator (English and Spanish)
- PuzzlePro
- Quiz Show for ExamView
- Transparencies and Videos

TE Differentiated Activities in the Teacher's Edition
- A Movement Begins in Montgomery, Alabama, p. 910
- The Civil Rights Act of 1964, p. 922
- *Letter from Birmingham Jail*, p. 924
- Voter Education Project Discussion, p. 926
- Civil Rights Groups, p. 934
- Fractures in the Movement, p. 935

Reading Like a Historian
Sam Wineburg

Movements and Individuals

Close your eyes and try to imagine Rosa Parks, the heroine of the monumental Montgomery bus boycott. Now try the same exercise, this time imagining the social movement that made this boycott a success.

Visualizing Abstractions

Difficult, isn't it? Social movements are comprised of many nameless, faceless individuals, who each perform a different role, some major, some minor, all of varying durations. A social movement is an abstraction. And abstractions, by definition, are notoriously difficult to visualize.

No one knew for sure whether the Montgomery bus boycott would succeed. African American riders constituted the majority of the ridership of Montgomery City Lines, but on the Monday morning of December 5, 1955, three days after Rosa Parks' arrest, not a single black person boarded a bus. Yet, somehow, thousands made it to their jobs, collected their children from school, got the groceries they needed for dinner, and made their way home. The key to understanding the power, magnitude, and effectiveness of a social movement—an undertaking that depends on, but rises above, the efforts of any single individual—is unlocking the word "somehow."

A Growing Movement

Tension had been building for years. In Montgomery alone there were 68 different organizations dedicated to advancing the rights of African American citizens. In 1955 the Women's Political Council (WPC), founded by Professor Mary Fair Burks of Alabama State University, had responded to over 30 complaints about the indignities faced by black riders on city buses. One of these was the case of Claudette Colvin. On March 2, 1955, nearly 8 months before Rosa Parks, 15-year-old Claudette, an "A" student at Booker T. Washington High School, refused to give up her seat to a white rider, and was forcibly removed from the bus. In doing so, she followed in the footsteps of other black women—Geneva Johnson, Viola White, Katie Wingfield, Espie Worthy—who were similarly ill-treated when they stood up to the power of Montgomery City Lines.

News Spreads Quickly

News of the arrest of Parks, on Thursday, December 1, spread quickly throughout Montgomery's black community. Jo Ann Robinson, a professor of English at Alabama State who followed Dr. Burks as head of the WPC, conferred that evening with Fred Grey, one of two black lawyers in Montgomery. When she suggested that a boycott was in order, he asked, "Are you ready?" Robinson answered yes, and by the middle of that night, she had typed up a leaflet announcing the action. Using Alabama State's mimeograph machine, she found 35 reams of paper to duplicate 17,500 sheets, which, cut into thirds, came to 52,500 leaflets—enough, and then some, for every member of Montgomery's 50,000-strong black community. By mid-Friday, Montgomery was abuzz with the planned boycott. Robinson and other members of the WPC spent the rest of the weekend charting assembly points for Monday pickups, arranging with black taxi drivers for subsidized rates of ten cents a passenger, and organizing 200 private cars and trucks for alternative transport.

What Students Know

If students know anything about the bus boycott they will know the names of Martin Luther King Jr. and Rosa Parks—but not Claudette Colvin, Mary Fair Burks, and Jo Ann Robinson. Fifty thousand black citizens of Montgomery refused to ride buses for 13 consecutive months, breaking the back of the Montgomery City Lines and dealing a devastating blow to Jim Crow.

Mass movements are notoriously difficult to visualize. But without them, it is doubtful that any significant social change would ever occur.

Social Studies Competency Goals
Goal 11 The learner will trace economic, political, and social developments and assess their significance for the lives of Americans during this time period.
11.02

The Big Idea and Essential Questions

To foster student understanding of this chapter's big idea, design your lesson to address each section's essential question.

Big Idea In the mid-1960s, many African Americans fought discrimination in a number of ways, resulting in meaningful government protection of basic rights.

Essential Questions

1. How did the civil rights movement begin to make progress in the mid-1900s?

2. How was segregation largely abolished in the 1960s?

3. What challenges did African Americans face in their struggle to achieve voting rights and political power in the South?

4. What led some young African Americans to lose faith in the civil rights movement and seek alternative solutions?

5. What was the lasting impact of the civil rights movement?

Key to Differentiating Instruction

Below Level

Basic-level activities designed for all students encountering new material

At Level

Intermediate-level activities designed for average students

Above Level

Challenging activities designed for honors and gifted-and-talented students

Standard English Mastery

Activities designed to improve standard English usage

906 CHAPTER 28

CHAPTER
28 1954–1975
The Civil Rights MOVEMENT

THE BIG PICTURE In the mid-1900s, many African Americans rose up against the treatment they had endured for decades. They fought discrimination through court cases and non-violent resistance. Their efforts resulted in meaningful government protections of basic civil rights.

North Carolina Standards

Social Studies Objectives
11.02 Trace major events of the Civil Rights Movement and evaluate its impact.

Language Arts Objectives
3.01 Use language persuasively in addressing a particular issue by:
- establishing and defending a point of view.
3.02 Select an issue or theme and take a stance on that issue by:
- reflecting the viewpoint(s) of Americans of different times and places.
- supporting the argument with specific reasons.

 Skills FOCUS READING LIKE A HISTORIAN

More than 200,000 civil rights demonstrators gathered peacefully at the Lincoln Memorial in Washington, D.C., in 1963. In his most famous speech, civil rights leader Martin Luther King Jr. told those gathered that "we have come here today to dramatize a shameful condition."
Interpreting Visuals How do you think this event affected public opinion? Explain.

See Skills Handbook, p. H30

906

U.S.

May 1954 Supreme Court rules that segregation in public schools is unconstitutional.

1954

World

1956 The Soviet army brutally crushes a revolt against Communist rule in Hungary.

Introduce the Chapter | At Level

The Civil Rights Movement

1. Guide students in a review of what they know about the civil rights movement. Tell students that in this chapter they will add to their knowledge about the movement.

2. Have students look through the chapter, and write down each of the section titles and the main red heads within each section. Have students retain this as a basic outline for the chapter that they can fill in as they read the chapter. In addition, have students list each of the Supreme Court cases discussed in the

chapter. Remind them that many civil rights changes came about as a result of legal action.

3. As students review each section of this chapter, have them complete their chapter outline.

4. As an extension, have students create an illustrated time line for this chapter.
LS Verbal-Linguistic

Alternative Assessment Handbook, Rubric 1: Acquiring Information

February 1960
Protesters in Greensboro, North Carolina, challenge racial segregation of public facilities.

August 1963
Civil rights protesters stage March on Washington.

July 1964
President Johnson signs the Civil Rights Act of 1964 into law.

April 1968
Civil rights leader Martin Luther King Jr. is killed.

April 1971
The Supreme Court upholds the use of busing to integrate schools.

1958

1962

1966

1970

1974

1960
Nazi war criminal Adolf Eichmann is captured in Argentina.

1967
South African surgeon Christian Barnard performs first successful human heart transplant.

1970
Rhodesian prime minister declares the country an independent and racially segregated republic.

1975
Khmer Rouge leader Pol Pot takes over in Cambodia.

907

Chapter Preview

Reading Like a Historian

The March on Washington Each person who spoke during the March on Washington was allowed seven minutes. Martin Luther King Jr. was the keynote speaker and he had prepared his speech the night before. During his address, however, he gave up on his prepared notes and gave his famous and inspirational "I Have a Dream" speech.

Interpreting Visuals More than 200,000 people thronged to Washington, D.C., to hear Martin Luther King Jr. and other civil rights leaders speak. What message do you think this large number of people who participated, both black and white, sent to Americans who were watching the event? *The civil rights movement was no longer small or regional, or just a movement by African Americans.*

Explore the Time Line

1. When did the Soviet army stop a revolt in Hungary? *1956*

2. When did the Supreme Court rule that busing was an acceptable means to ensure school integration? *1971*

3. How long did it take from the time the Supreme Court declared school segregation illegal until the Civil Rights Act of 1964 was signed? *10 years*

Info to Know

Nonviolent Protest Mohandas Gandhi, who led the struggle for India's independence from Great Britain, served as inspiration for the nonviolent protests of Martin Luther King Jr. Gandhi also inspired another African American minister, James Lawson, who visited Gandhi in India. When he returned to the United States, Lawson began to organize workshops on nonviolent methods of protest.

Evaluate Why do you think civil rights leaders eventually began to turn away from Gandhi's teachings and methods, which had proven to be successful?

Answers

Reading Like a Historian (p. 906)
possible answer—it energized public opinion; helped make lasting changes in civil rights

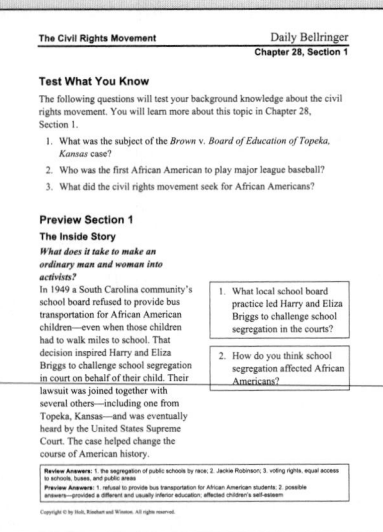

Fighting Segregation

BEFORE YOU READ

MAIN IDEA

In the mid-1900s, the civil rights movement began to make major progress in correcting the national problem of racial segregation.

READING FOCUS

1. What was the status of the civil rights movement prior to 1954?
2. What were the key issues in the Supreme Court's ruling in *Brown v. Board of Education of Topeka, Kansas,* and what was its impact?
3. How did events in Montgomery, Alabama, help launch the modern civil rights movement?

KEY TERMS AND PEOPLE

CORE
Jackie Robinson
Thurgood Marshall
Little Rock Nine
Rosa Parks
Montgomery bus boycott
Martin Luther King Jr.
SCLC

TAKING NOTES As you read, take notes on major events in the civil rights movement from the end of the 1940s through 1957. Record your notes in a graphic organizer like the one shown here. You may need to add more rows.

Event	Date

Civil Rights PIONEERS

▼ Harry and Eliza Briggs (middle row, at either side of their child Catherine) with plaintiffs and supporters of *Briggs v. Elliott.*

THE INSIDE STORY

What does it take to turn ordinary people into activists? For Harry and Eliza Briggs, it was bad enough that their child had to attend a segregated school in their South Carolina community. But when the school board refused a request for school bus transportation—in spite of the fact that some African American children had to walk as much as 10 miles to school—they had had enough. Harry and Eliza Briggs joined 18 other parents in a legal challenge aimed at ending segregation of the local schools. With the help of the NAACP, they filed *Briggs v.*

Elliott in 1950. Harry and Eliza Briggs paid dearly for their actions. Both of them lost their jobs. Harry had to leave the state to find work to support his family.

Yet their legal challenge went forward. Soon, it was joined together with four other cases, including a case from Topeka, Kansas, for argument before the Supreme Court of the United States. In 2004, Congressional Gold Medals of Honor were awarded posthumously to civil rights pioneers Harry and Eliza Briggs and two other South Carolina citizens, the Reverend Joseph S. DeLaine and Levi Pearson, who were part of their lawsuit. ◼

The Civil Rights Movement Prior to 1954

The Briggses played a key role in launching the modern civil rights movement in the United States. Yet this movement was not really new. You read in earlier chapters about the long struggle for African American rights. This fight had its start with the opposition to slavery in colonial days. It continued in the 1800s with the abolition movement and the Civil War. Slavery ended after the Civil War, and formerly enslaved people enjoyed some rights for a time during Reconstruction.

African American rights suffered setbacks after Reconstruction. In the late 1800s, legalized racism returned to the South. Supported by the Supreme Court's 1896 ruling in *Plessy v. Ferguson,* the segregation of African Americans and whites was the law of the land in much of the United States in the early 1900s.

In the late 1800s and early 1900s, a new group of champions joined the battle for civil rights. They included Booker T. Washington and W.E.B. Du Bois. You read about the role of Du Bois in the founding of the National Association for the Advancement of Colored People, or NAACP. This organization formed in 1909. In the decades ahead, it would be a powerful voice in the struggle to improve the legal rights of African Americans. The NAACP also fought to bring an end to racial violence.

The Great Depression of the 1930s presented new challenges to African Americans. Although the entire nation suffered, African Americans fared worse than others. President Roosevelt's New Deal helped win him the support of many African American voters. First Lady Eleanor Roosevelt was a staunch supporter of civil rights. Yet the president was unwilling to push too hard for greater rights for African Americans out of concern that it would anger his southern white supporters.

The 1940s: a decade of progress In earlier chapters, you read about some of the civil rights gains of the 1940s. For example, during World War II, A. Philip Randolph managed to force a federal ban against discrimination

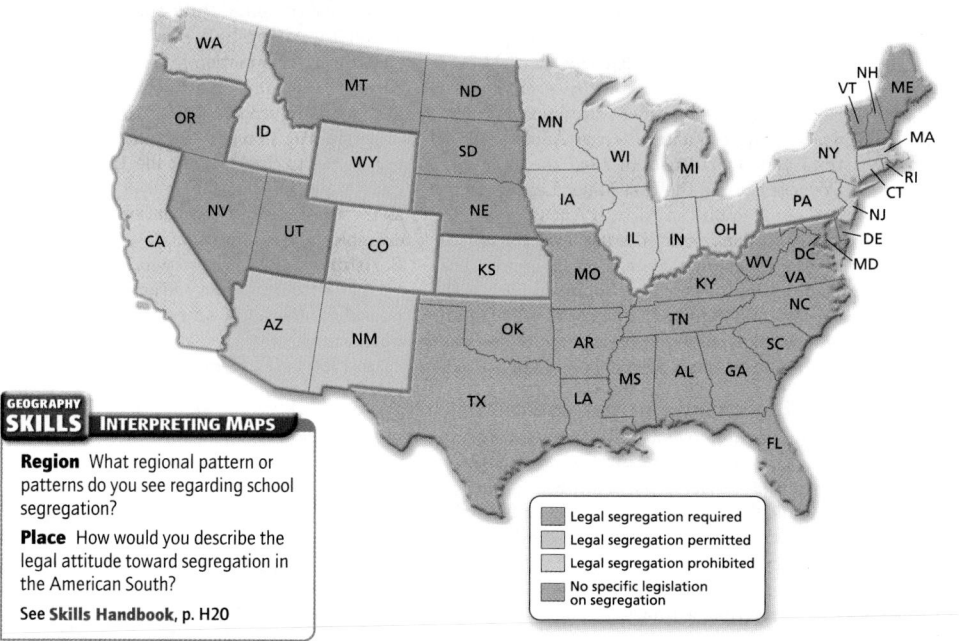

SCHOOL SEGREGATION, 1952

GEOGRAPHY SKILLS | **INTERPRETING MAPS**

Region What regional pattern or patterns do you see regarding school segregation?

Place How would you describe the legal attitude toward segregation in the American South?

See Skills Handbook, p. H20

Legend:
- Legal segregation required
- Legal segregation permitted
- Legal segregation prohibited
- No specific legislation on segregation

Reading Focus

❶ What was the status of the civil rights movement prior to 1954? *possible answer—after Reconstruction, African Americans suffered setbacks; segregation legalized; World War II ban against discrimination in defense-related work; desegregation of armed forces; NAACP set up Legal Defense Fund; cases arose that chipped away at the separate but equal ruling*

The Civil Rights Movement Prior to 1954

Recall Who established the NAACP? *W.E.B. DuBois and his colleagues*

Describe What was life like for African Americans after the Civil War and during the Reconstruction period? *former slaves enjoyed some rights during Reconstruction*

Make Inferences Why do you think that President Franklin D. Roosevelt did not push harder for civil rights? *did not want to lose political support for New Deal programs*

📦 Map Transparency: School Segregation, 1952

Collaborative Learning

At Level

African American Life

1. Guide students in a discussion about life for African Americans during the period after Reconstruction and through the Great Depression of the 1930s. Record student ideas for all to see.

2. Have students copy the information onto their papers.

3. Organize the class into small groups. Have students review and analyze the points on their lists. Then have each group create an illustrated time line showing the events prior to 1954 that led to the civil rights battle.

4. As an extension, have students write a paragraph summarizing the civil rights movement prior to 1954. **LS Interpersonal, Visual-Spatial**

📓 Alternative Assessment Handbook, Rubrics 36: Time Lines; and 37: Writing Assignments

---

Answers

Interpreting Maps *largely prohibited in the North; segregation required by law*

The Civil Rights Movement Prior to 1954

Explain What does the abbreviation CORE stand for and what was the focus of the organization? *Congress of Racial Equality; nonviolent protest to gain civil rights for African Americans*

Make Inferences Why do you think that the NAACP focused on attacking racism through the court system? *possible answer—believed real changes would come from laws ensuring fair and equal treatment for African Americans*

🔲 Quick Facts Transparency: Early Civil Rights Victories

📄 CRF: Biography: James Peck

Info to Know

Jackie Robinson As the first African American to play professionally in the major leagues, Jackie Robinson carried a heavy burden. In addition to working hard to be a great ballplayer, he had to endure the reactions of racist baseball fans and the hurtful actions of his fellow team members. Jackie Robinson's courage and determination were a frustration for some and an inspiration for others.

Answers

Reading Check *organizations dedicated to expanding civil rights; nonviolent protests; lawsuits; legal actions*

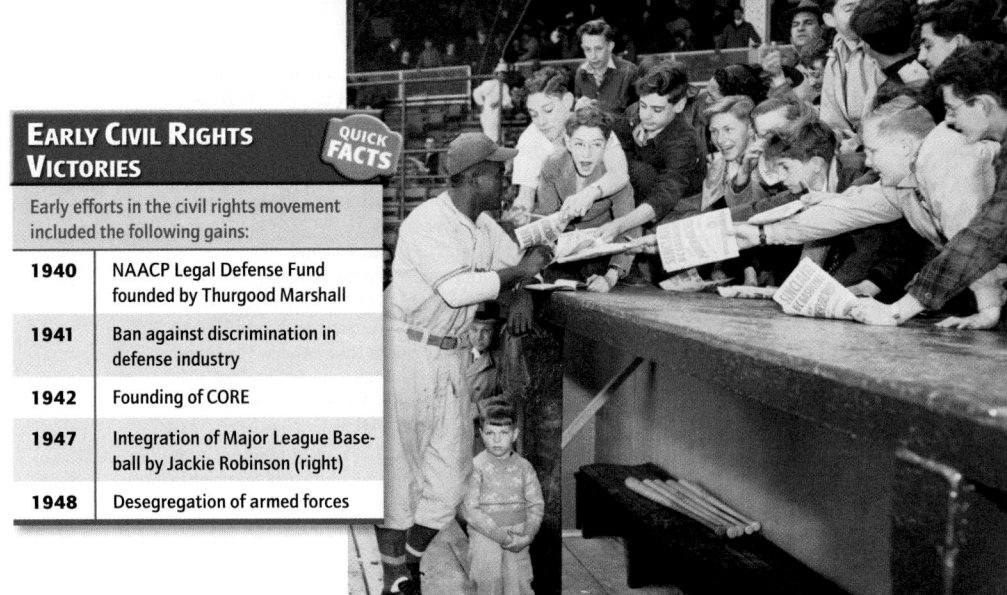

EARLY CIVIL RIGHTS VICTORIES

QUICK FACTS

Early efforts in the civil rights movement included the following gains:

1940	NAACP Legal Defense Fund founded by Thurgood Marshall
1941	Ban against discrimination in defense industry
1942	Founding of CORE
1947	Integration of Major League Baseball by Jackie Robinson (right)
1948	Desegregation of armed forces

in defense-related work. Another key development in the 1940s was the founding of the Congress of Racial Equality, or **CORE**. This organization was dedicated to nonviolent protest. Its methods would have a strong effect on civil rights activists in the years ahead.

The end of the 1940s saw several key changes in the march toward greater civil rights. One was President Truman's order to desegregate the armed forces. Another came from popular culture. In 1947 the Brooklyn Dodgers became the first Major League Baseball team to put an African American on its roster. Millions admired **Jackie Robinson** for his great skill as an athlete. Millions more were inspired by his courage. Robinson bore with bravery and dignity the pressure of being an individual so many people wanted to see succeed—and so many others expected to see fail.

Seeking change in the courts While Randolph, Robinson, and others worked to bring change to American society, the NAACP continued its strategy of attacking racism through the courts. This was a method the organization had used from its earliest days to combat such discriminatory practices as the use of grandfather clauses to keep African Americans from voting.

In the 1930s Charles Hamilton Houston began an NAACP campaign to attack the concept of "separate but equal." Houston chose to focus on segregation in education. One of his former students, **Thurgood Marshall**, soon joined him. Marshall knew firsthand the effects of discrimination in education. He was once denied admission to the University of Maryland law school because of his race.

Under Houston and Marshall, NAACP lawyers began to chip away at the 1896 Supreme Court ruling in *Plessy* v. *Ferguson*, which served as the legal basis of segregation. In 1938, for example, in *Missouri ex rel. Gaines* v. *Canada, Registrar of the University of Missouri,* the NAACP successfully argued against Missouri's refusal to offer a law school education to African Americans.

In 1950 the Supreme Court ruled in *Sweatt* v. *Painter* that the separate law school for African Americans at the University of Texas was inferior to the one for whites. The Court also held that just being separate from the white school was likely to harm the preparation of African American students for a career in law.

READING CHECK **Identifying Problems and Solutions** What were some of the methods by which civil rights were expanded in the years before 1954?

Differentiating Instruction

Below Level

English-Language Learners

1. Draw a basic, large sequencing diagram for students to see. Label the chart: Desegregation.

2. Have students copy the chart and complete it with the events that led up to the Montgomery bus boycott through the 1956 Supreme Court decision outlawing segregation on public buses.

3. Have volunteers complete the large class diagram for all to see. Have students correct their charts and retain them as a study tool.

4. Have students select the one event they believe was most important in the desegregation effort. Have students write a brief essay explaining the significance of their chosen event. 🔲 **Visual-Spatial, Verbal-Linguistic**

📄 Alternative Assessment Handbook, Rubrics 13: Graphic Organizers; and 42: Writing to Inform

Brown v. Board of Education

The NAACP's early success had focused on graduate schools, which affected only a small number of people around the country. In the 1950s Marshall began focusing on the nation's elementary and high schools. At the time, millions of students around the country attended segregated schools. For African Americans, these were almost always inferior schools.

To press its cause, the NAACP needed a case. As you read at the start of this section, it found one in South Carolina, with Harry and Eliza Briggs. NAACP lawyers found another one in the case of Linda Brown, in Topeka, Kansas. You will read about the details of the Kansas case in Landmark Supreme Court Cases later in this section.

The Supreme Court hears *Brown* In both the *Briggs* and *Brown* cases, the lower courts upheld the practice of segregation. Yet these defeats did not stop Marshall and the NAACP. In fact, they provided an opportunity to bring the issue of school segregation to the Supreme Court. The Court combined the cases and several others from around the country into a single case. It was known as *Brown* v. *Board of Education of Topeka, Kansas*.

The Supreme Court was aware of the case's great significance. It heard arguments over a two-year period. The Court also considered research about segregation's effects on African American children. In one study, black children were shown dolls that were identical except for skin color. The children had more positive feelings about the white-skinned dolls than about the dark-skinned dolls they resembled. This and other tests suggested that segregation had harmed the self-image of young students.

In 1954 Chief Justice Earl Warren issued the Supreme Court's decision. All nine justices agreed that separate schools for African Americans and whites violated the Constitution's guarantee of equal protection of the law.

HISTORY'S VOICES

❝Education is perhaps the most important function of state and local governments . . . It is doubtful that any child may reasonably be expected to succeed in life if he is denied the opportunity of an education. Such an opportunity . . . is a right that must be made available to all on equal terms . . . Does segregation of children in schools solely on the basis of race . . . deprive the children of the minority group of equal educational opportunities? We believe that it does.❞

—Chief Justice Earl Warren, *Brown v. Board of Education of Topeka, Kansas,* May 17, 1954

Ending Legal Segregation

For many decades following the 1896 Supreme Court ruling in *Plessy* v. *Ferguson,* the concept of "separate but equal" was used to deny African Americans equal protection of the law. Segregation denied African Americans the education—and the dignity—they needed in order to achieve true social equality.

When the NAACP and its lawyers decided to attack the policy of "separate but equal," they knew it would be a long process. They understood that even if they were able to quickly overturn *Plessy,* it would take longer to destroy the attitudes that supported segregation. Instead, they sought to chip away

at the *Plessy* ruling and slowly pave the way for true social change.

The strategy worked. By 1954 several cases had weakened the "separate but equal" policy and had in fact begun to break down the walls of segregation in education. The Supreme Court's forceful, unanimous decision in *Brown* v. *Board of Education of Topeka, Kansas,* showed clearly that legally enforced segregation could be challenged.

Identifying Problems and Solutions Why did the NAACP try to chip away at the *Plessy* ruling bit by bit?

Thurgood Marshall (center) and colleagues in front of the Supreme Court building after their victory

THE CIVIL RIGHTS MOVEMENT **911**

Skills Focus: Comparing and Contrasting

Reading Skill
Brown v. Board of Education

1. Write the following statement for students to see: *Separate is not equal.* Have students copy the statement onto their own papers.

2. Organize the class into mixed-ability pairs, and have each pair identify an example from their study of U.S. history that supports this statement. Have students write a brief explanation of how this example supports the statement.

3. Have volunteers share their examples with

the class, and create a class list for all to see. Guide students in a discussion of the events, how they are similar, and how they are different.

4. Have students copy the information and retain the list as a study tool. **LS Visual-Spatial, Logical-Mathematical**

📖 Alternative Assessment Handbook, Rubric 11: Discussions

Brown v. Board of Education

Analyze Do you think that those who organized massive resistance believed their tactics would stop integration? *possible answers— yes, because could stop integration in short-term; future rulings might overturn* Brown*; no, because could not continue resistance permanently*

Draw Conclusions Did *Brown* v. *Board of Education* immediately change the pattern of segregation in public schools? *no, not all complied (massive resistance); initial decision did not give specific date for public school segregation to end*

📄 CRF: Primary Source Activity: Integrating Central High School in Little Rock

Primary Source

From the Little Rock Nine:

"I tried to see a friendly face somewhere in the mob—someone who maybe would help. I looked into the face of an old woman and it seemed a kind face, but when I looked at her again, she spat on me . . . Just then a white man sat down beside me and patted my shoulder. He raised my chin and said 'Don't let them see you cry.'"

— Elizabeth Eckford

"I don't intend to quit. We'll try again. It's still my school, and I'm entitled to it."

— Ernest Green

Answers

Linking to Today *for her behavior and racist attitude*

Reading Check *segregation was widespread; many southerners supported policy; earlier court decisions approving segregation*

912

ACADEMIC VOCABULARY

integrate to combine two groups in such a way that one becomes fully part of the other

THE IMPACT TODAY

Government

In 1998 Central High School became a national historic site. It continues to educate students and is operated jointly by the Little Rock school district and the National Park Service.

The Little Rock crisis At the time of the *Brown* decision, 21 states had schools that were segregated by law. The Supreme Court's ruling declared segregation unconstitutional, but it offered no firm guidance about how or when desegregation should occur.

Some states quickly prepared to integrate their schools. In other states, however, there was strong opposition. Virginia Democratic senator Harry Byrd Jr. organized a movement known as massive resistance, under which officials at all levels pledged to block integration.

In Virginia, for example, the legislature passed laws forcing the closure of any school planning to integrate. Laws also assisted white students wishing to attend private schools. It was more than a year before the federal courts stopped this practice.

Little Rock, Arkansas, was another trouble spot. In 1957 Governor Orval Faubus violated a federal court order to integrate Little Rock's Central High School. Claiming that white extremists were threatening violence, he warned that "blood would run in the streets" if nine African Americans tried to attend the school. Just before the school year was to start, he ordered the Arkansas National Guard to keep them out.

On September 4, 1957, a crowd of angry whites harassed the black students as they arrived for the first day of school. When they reached the door, the soldiers turned them away. The Guard made no effort to protect them from the hostile crowd, who spat at them and tore their clothing.

For nearly three weeks the Guard prevented the African American students, now known as the **Little Rock Nine**, from entering the school. Meanwhile, President Eisenhower tried to persuade Faubus to back down. Finally, on September 24, Eisenhower went on national television to announce that he was sending federal troops to end the standoff. The next day, protected by U. S. soldiers with fixed bayonets, the Little Rock Nine entered Central High School.

For the rest of the school year, the African American students endured great abuse. Other students constantly shoved them in the halls. Their lives were threatened. The one senior among the Little Rock Nine had to be guarded at graduation. When his name was called at the ceremony, none of his classmates or their families clapped for him.

Meanwhile, Faubus continued to seek ways to stop school integration. In the end he failed. However, the events in Little Rock revealed to many Americans just how strong racism was in some parts of the nation.

READING CHECK **Identifying Problems and Solutions** What kinds of issues faced the Supreme Court in making its *Brown* decision?

Integrating Central High School

The famous photograph at right shows Elizabeth Eckford, one of the Little Rock Nine, walking to Little Rock's Central High School on September 4, 1957. The white girl shouting at Eckford is Hazel Massery. Massery later regretted what she had done. She decided that she did not want to be, as she put it, the "poster child of the hate generation, trapped in the image captured in the photograph." In 1963 Massery apologized to Eckford. The two women later became friends and have spoken publicly together about their experiences.

Identifying the Main Idea Why did Hazel Massery apologize to Elizabeth Eckford?

Eckford and Massery in 1957 (above) and later, after becoming friends (left)

912 CHAPTER 28

Skills Focus: Summarizing

Reading Skill

Brown and Massive Resistance

1. Have students review the information in the text about massive resistance, including the actions of Arkansas Governor Faubus and President Eisenhower.

2. Have students develop a newspaper report of the resistance movement in Little Rock, Arkansas. Students should describe the ways in which state and local officials tried to disregard the Supreme Court decision.

3. Have volunteers read their news reports to the class. Then, guide students in a discussion of the ideas expressed in the reports.

4. Have students create a political cartoon that illustrates the futility of massive resistance to the *Brown* v. *Board of Education* Supreme Court decision. Have volunteers share their cartoons with the class. **LS Verbal-Linguistic**

📄 Alternative Assessment Handbook, Rubrics 23: Newspapers; and 27: Political Cartoons

Brown v. Board of Education of Topeka, Kansas (1954)

Why It Matters By 1950 public schools in many parts of the United States were segregated. Under the Supreme Court's decision in *Plessy* v. *Ferguson,* separate schools for African American and white students were legally acceptable as long as the facilities were equal in quality. In practice, schools for African American children were generally far below the quality of schools for whites.

Background of the Case

Linda Brown, an African American third-grader in Topeka, Kansas, lived just blocks away from the nearest elementary school. However, that was a whites-only school, so she had to walk five blocks and then take a bus for two miles to reach the elementary school for blacks. The NAACP recruited Brown's parents and other Topeka residents to challenge segregation in the public schools. The Supreme Court recognized the harm segregation did to African American students. "The impact is greater when it has the sanction of law," it noted, "for the policy of separating the races is usually interpreted as denoting the inferiority of the Negro group."

The Decision

Chief Justice Earl Warren wrote an opinion for a unanimous Supreme Court that reversed the *Plessy* decision's "separate but equal" doctrine for public schools. Warren wrote that schools segregated by race were unconstitutional:

> ❝We conclude that in the field of public education the doctrine of 'separate but equal' has no place. Separate educational facilities are inherently [by their nature] unequal . . . Such segregation is a denial of the equal protection of the laws.❞

In 1955 the Supreme Court issued a follow-up decision, now called *Brown II,* ordering that desegregation proceed "with all deliberate speed."

THE IMPACT TODAY A decade after *Brown,* few schools had been integrated. In the early 1970s many communities turned to busing to integrate schools by force. But busing proved highly controversial, and many communities stopped busing by the late 1990s. Nevertheless, by the early 2000s, schools were much more integrated than they had been before *Brown.* Changing demographics were largely responsible for this trend.

CRITICAL THINKING

go.hrw.com
Research Online
Keyword: SS Court

1. **Analyze the Impact** Using the keyword above, read about the Supreme Court's 1971 decision in *Swann* v. *Charlotte-Mecklenburg Board of Education.* How was this case like *Brown*? In what way did the Court's decision in *Swann* move beyond the decision in *Brown*?

2. **You Be the Judge** *Brown* found that separate facilities were inherently unequal in education, but the case did not directly affect other types of legally imposed segregation. After *Brown,* how should a judge rule on a challenge to segregation in public transportation, restaurants, or hotels? Explain your answer in a short paragraph.

THE CIVIL RIGHTS MOVEMENT **913**

Brown v. Board of Education of Topeka, Kansas

Word Help

recruited enlisted the help of
sanction approval, consent

Info to Know

The Equal Protection Clause Like other cases students have studied, including *Korematsu* v. *United States,* the *Brown* case was based on the equal protection clause found in Section I of the Fourteenth Amendment, where all citizens are guaranteed equal protection of the laws. Remind students that when the Supreme Court ordered desegregation of public schools, the law applied equally to those states that had laws segregating public schools and those states that did not have segregation laws.

Primary Source

"Having proclaimed the equality of all men in the preamble to the Declaration of Independence, the nation's founders had then elected, out of deference to the slaveholding South, to omit that definition of equalitarian democracy from the Constitution. It took a terrible civil war to correct that omission . . . It was into this moral void that the Supreme Court under Earl Warren now stepped. Its opinion in *Brown v. Board of Education* . . . represented . . . a reconsecration of American ideals."

— Robert Kluger

Simple Justice, 1977

Skills Focus: Analyzing Secondary Sources   **At Level**

Reading Like a Historian Skill   **Research Required**
An Important Ruling

1. Remind students that much has been written about *Brown* v. *Board.*

2. Have students locate and read at least three secondary source documents about this case. Then have students compile a chart that shows details of the case and similarities and differences among the secondary sources.

3. Have students write an essay in which they provide a summary of the case and then compare and contrast the documents that

they used. Students should attach copies of the documents they used to their essays.

4. Guide students in a discussion of the differences between primary and secondary sources. Which are easier to find and read? Which provide the most accurate account?

LS Verbal-Linguistic

Alternative Assessment Handbook, Rubrics 9: Comparing and Contrasting; and 40: Writing to Describe

Answers

Critical Thinking 1. *Both rulings supported integration; in* Swann, *Court recommended specific methods for achieving integration, such as busing, racial balance ratios, and changing school districts.* **2.** *possible answer—* Brown *opened the door to eliminate segregation in all public facilities, so judges should rule against any form of segregation.*

913

❸ How did events in Montgomery, Alabama, help launch the modern civil rights movement? *African Americans were inspired; organized boycotts and protests throughout the South*

A Boycott Begins in Montgomery, Alabama

Recall What was the SCLC and what was the group's purpose? *Southern Christian Leadership Conference; to organize nonviolent protests against segregation*

Describe Who were the first members of the SCLC? *members of the Montgomery Improvement Association and other groups, ministers; open to all races and religions*

Draw Conclusions Why was it important that SCLC be all-inclusive, open to all races and religions? *possible answer—purpose of the organization was to protest discrimination, so the organization itself should not discriminate*

📄 CRF: Biography: Virginia Foster Durr

📄 CRF: Biography: Septima Poinsette Clark

📄 Political Cartoons Activities for American History: Cartoon 56: The Montgomery Boycott

A Boycott Begins in Montgomery, Alabama

The Supreme Court's *Brown* decision had an enormous impact on society. Yet it directly affected only schools. Elsewhere in the South, a great variety of other public places and facilities remained segregated.

The Montgomery bus boycott One example of these segregated public facilities was the bus system in Montgomery, Alabama. African American riders, who made up two-thirds of bus passengers, had to pay their fare at the front of the bus, leave the bus, then enter again through the rear doors. They were forbidden from sitting in the front rows, which were reserved for white passengers. If those front rows filled, all African Americans riding in the next row had to give up their seats. Sharing a row with a white passenger was not allowed.

African Americans in Montgomery had endured these conditions for years. Even before the *Brown* ruling, local groups had sought to end segregation on the buses. It was not until 1955 that decisive action was taken, however.

In that year, a local NAACP member named **Rosa Parks** boarded a Montgomery bus after a day of work. She sat in the section reserved for African Americans. The white section soon filled, however. Parks was ordered to give up her seat and make her row available to white riders. She refused and was arrested.

The NAACP recognized the opportunity Parks's arrest presented. With her cooperation, the organization called for a one-day boycott of the city bus system. Some 90 percent of African American riders stayed off the buses that day. This response convinced community leaders to continue the **Montgomery bus boycott**. To lead this effort, they formed the Montgomery Improvement Association. The group selected as its leader a young minister of a local Baptist church named **Martin Luther King Jr.**

The boycott created hardship for Montgomery's African Americans. Many depended on the buses to get to work and to do errands.

The boycott also hurt the bus system and other white businesses. As a result, many of the city's whites tried to weaken it. Police harassed African Americans who took part in the boycott. When the city's black churches set up car pools to help their members get around, insurers cancelled the auto insurance policies of the cars' owners. King and other African American leaders became targets of violent threats.

Montgomery Bus Boycott

Rosa Parks was arrested for not surrendering her bus seat to a white passenger, setting in motion the Montgomery bus boycott. Below, boycotters wait for rides at a carpool station. The success of the boycott helped make Martin Luther King Jr. a nationally known civil rights leader.

914 CHAPTER 28

Skills Focus: Identifying Problem and Solution
At Level

Reading Skill
Montgomery, Alabama

1. Have students review the information in the text about the 1956 Supreme Court decision that led to the desegregation of public buses. Have students develop their own Supreme Court decision, a paragraph explaining why bus segregation was unconstitutional.

2. Have volunteers read their decisions to the class.

3. Guide students in a discussion of the reactions of whites to the actions of African Americans during the bus boycott. Remind students that in many parts of the country segregation did not exist; in the South, however, it had been legalized for many years.

4. Have students explain why nonviolent protests, like the Montgomery bus boycott, can be a very effective way to correct social injustices. **LS Verbal-Linguistic**

📄 Alternative Assessment Handbook, Rubrics 11: Discussions; and 42: Writing to Inform

As the boycott continued, court challenges to segregation of city buses also moved forward. The Supreme Court finally ruled on the subject in late 1956. By then, the boycott was a year old. The Court held that segregation on buses was unconstitutional.

Integration of the buses moved forward. There were some tense moments, including threats of violence against buses and local African American leaders. The tension, however, eventually faded. Integrated buses became a fact of life in Montgomery and elsewhere.

Birth of the SCLC The success of the Montgomery bus boycott inspired African Americans elsewhere. In communities across the South, groups organized boycotts of their own.

In January 1957, representatives of the Montgomery Improvement Association and several other groups met in Atlanta, Georgia. The goal was to form a new group that would organize protest activities taking place all across the region. This group became known as the Southern Christian Leadership Conference, or **SCLC**. Martin Luther King Jr., the leader of the successful Montgomery boycott, was elected leader of the SCLC.

As its name suggests, the SCLC was heavily influenced by the Christian faith. Many of its members, such as King, were members of the clergy. However, the SCLC was open to people of all races and faiths. At its heart was a com-

FACES OF HISTORY

Rosa PARKS
1913–2005

When Rosa Parks refused to give up her seat on a bus in 1955, she already had a long history of community activism. In 1943 she became one of the first women to join the local NAACP chapter, where she served as its secretary. She also had experience protesting discrimination on the city's buses. In 1943 her protest of mistreatment on a bus resulted in the driver forcefully removing her from the bus.

In 1957 Parks and her family moved to Detroit. She joined the staff of Representative John Conyers Jr. in 1965, working there for 22 years. For her role in the civil rights movement, Parks received the Presidential Medal of Freedom in 1996 and the Congressional Gold Medal in 1999. After her death in 2005, she became the first woman to lie in honor in the U.S. Capitol rotunda, a tribute only given to the most significant national leaders.

Make Inferences Why was it significant that Rosa Parks had experience as an activist before her 1955 bus protest?

mitment to mass, nonviolent action. You will read more about nonviolent protest in the next section. You will also read about the spread of the campaign to end segregation from the bus stops of Montgomery to other public places throughout the South.

READING CHECK **Making Generalizations** What was the nature of the movement created by the successful Montgomery bus boycott?

SECTION 1 ASSESSMENT

go.hrw.com
Online Quiz
Keyword: SD7 HP28

Reviewing Ideas, Terms, and People

1. a. Describe How did Jackie Robinson bring change to American society?
b. Compare How were the NAACP and CORE similar?
c. Predict What do you think will be the final result of Charles Hamilton Houston and Thurgood Marshall's challenges to segregated education?

2. a. Identify What Supreme Court decision had been the legal basis for the segregation of public schools?
b. Make Inferences Why do you think African American students want to attend integrated schools, despite hardships?
c. Evaluate How successful was the *Brown* v. *Board of Education of Topeka, Kansas* decision in desegregating schools?

3. a. Describe What was the goal of the SCLC?
b. Analyze Why was Rosa Parks arrested?

c. Evaluate Did the Montgomery bus boycott achieve its goals? Explain why or why not.

Critical Thinking

4. Categorizing Review your notes on the major events of the early civil rights movement. Then copy the graphic organizer below and use it to list legal and social civil rights victories.

Legal Victories	Social Victories

FOCUS ON WRITING

5. Persuasive Write a flyer encouraging African Americans to join in the Montgomery bus boycott. Make sure your flyer explains why it is important for people to participate.

THE CIVIL RIGHTS MOVEMENT **915**

Direct Teach

Faces of History
Rosa Parks
"Mother of the Civil Rights Movement" Rosa Parks was listed as one of *Time* magazine's most influential people of the twentieth century. She was 42 years old when she refused to give up her seat on the Montgomery bus. Later she said, "I did not get on the bus to get arrested . . . I got on the bus to go home." When Rosa Parks died at the age of 92, she became the first woman to lie in honor at the Capitol Rotunda in Washington, D.C.

Review & Assess

Close
Guide students in a discussion of the ways in which the civil rights movement began to end segregation.

Review
Online Quiz, Section 1
Daily Test Practice Transparency

Assess
SE Section 1 Assessment
Progress Assessment: Section 1 Quiz
Alternative Assessment Handbook

Reteach
Interactive Reader and Study Guide, Section 1
Interactive Skills Tutor CD-ROM

Section 1 Assessment Answers

1. a. first African American to play on a major league baseball team
b. dedicated to the practice of nonviolent protest and ending racial discrimination
c. possible answer—schools will become integrated; desegregation will slowly come to an end

2. a. *Plessy* v. *Ferguson*
b. wanted a good education
c. limited success at first

3. a. to organize protest activities all across the South

b. for not giving up her seat on a bus to a white rider
c. possible answer—yes; buses became integrated

4. Legal—*Missouri ex rel. Gaines* v. *Canada, Registrar of the University of Missouri*, *Sweatt* v. *Painter, Brown* v. *Board of Education*; Social—integration of schools, Little Rock crisis, Montgomery bus boycott

5. possible answer—movement will be more effective if more people are involved

Answers

Faces of History *her experience as an activist provided her with knowledge about the larger civil rights community and a support system to assist her*

Reading Check *possible answer—nonviolent movement for change; led to the organization of other boycotts and the SCLC*

915

Bellringer

The Inside Story... Use the **Daily Bellringer Transparency** to help students answer the question.

📓 Daily Bellringer Transparency, Section 2

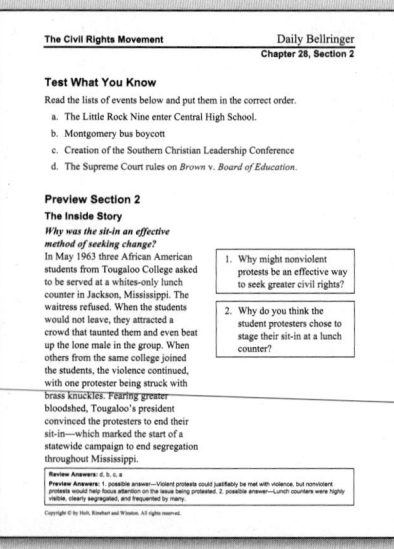

Academic Vocabulary

Review with students the high-use academic terms in this section.

enforce to require something to happen (p. 918)

restore to put something back into its former or original condition (p. 922)

📓 CRF: Vocabulary Builder Activity, Section 2

Taking Notes

boycotts, Freedom Rides, sit-ins, organized nonviolent protests, the Albany movement, Birmingham campaign, assassination of Medgar Evers

Freedom Now!

BEFORE YOU READ

MAIN IDEA

The quest for civil rights became a nationwide movement in the 1960s as African Americans won political and legal rights, and segregation was largely abolished.

READING FOCUS

1. What are sit-ins and Freedom Rides, and why were they important in the 1960s?

2. How was the integration of higher education achieved in the South?

3. What role did Albany, Georgia, and Birmingham, Alabama, play in the history of civil rights?

4. What concerns and events led to the passage of the Civil Rights Act of 1964?

KEY TERMS AND PEOPLE

Mohandas Gandhi
James Farmer
SNCC
Freedom Riders
James Meredith
Medgar Evers
Civil Rights Act of 1964

TAKING NOTES As you read, take notes on major activities that helped lead to the enactment of the Civil Rights Act of 1964. Record your notes in a graphic organizer like the one shown here.

Causes → Civil Rights Act of 1964

SITTING DOWN FOR CIVIL RIGHTS

▲ Student protesters hold their ground at a lunch counter sit-in.

THE INSIDE STORY *How can you win by being beaten?* On May 28, 1963, Anne Moody, Memphis Norman, and Pearlena Lewis, three students from Tougaloo College in Jackson, Mississippi, attempted to place an order at a whites-only lunch counter. The waitress told them to move to the back counter, which was for African Americans. "We would like to be served here," Moody replied. Instead, the waitress closed the counter. The three black students remained seated as a form of protest.

A hostile crowd gathered around the protesters. A man pulled Norman from his stool and beat him. Joan Trumpauer, one of Tougaloo's two white students, took his place. Lois Chaffee, a white faculty member, and John Salter, a Native American professor, soon joined the protesters.

The crowd dumped food on the protesters. Someone hit Salter with brass knuckles, and others poured table salt into his open wound. Still the protesters sat at the counter, refusing to leave or fight back. Finally, fearing greater violence, Tougaloo's president convinced the demonstrators to end their sit-in.

That night the protesters were honored at a huge rally for civil rights. Local NAACP leader Medgar Evers announced that the sit-in was the start of a campaign to end segregation not only in Jackson but throughout Mississippi. ∎

916 CHAPTER 28

Teach the Main Idea
At Level

Freedom Now!

1. **Teach** Ask students the Reading Focus questions to teach this section.

2. **Apply** Draw four large ovals for students to see. Label the top of each oval with one of the four main heads from this section. Guide students in a discussion of the four topics. Have students identify the main points of each topic and use the ovals as graphic organizers.

3. **Review** Use the completed graphic organizer as a review tool, and have students explain

how these topics relate to each other.

4. **Practice/Homework** Have students develop a list of ten questions they would like to have asked James Farmer or Martin Luther King Jr. about the importance of nonviolence and how it works in achieving social justice. Have students exchange papers and write answers to the questions.
LS Visual-Spatial, Verbal-Linguistic

📓 Alternative Assessment Handbook, Rubric 13: Graphic Organizers

Sit-ins and Freedom Rides

The events in Jackson, Mississippi, illustrate tactics that had become common in the civil rights movement in late 1950s and early 1960s. In addition to boycotts, such as the one in Montgomery you read about in Section 1, civil rights workers used other direct, nonviolent methods to confront discrimination and racism. These tactics frequently provoked a violent response from their opponents.

The strategy of nonviolence Many of the tactics used in the civil rights movement were based on those of **Mohandas Gandhi.** Gandhi, who died in 1948, had been a leader in India's struggle for independence from Great Britain. Gandhi organized actions in which protesters were willing to suffer harm instead of inflicting it. He taught that this nonviolent approach would expose injustice and force those in power to end it. Nonviolent resistance, he believed, was the best way to achieve change in a society in which others held most of the power.

American civil rights leaders such as **James Farmer** of CORE, Martin Luther King Jr. of SCLC, and others shared Gandhi's views. "There is more power in socially organized masses . . . than there is in guns in the hands of a few desperate men," King wrote. "We shall so appeal to your heart and conscience that we will win you in the process."

In the early 1950s, James Lawson, an African American minister, visited India and studied Gandhi's teachings. With King's encouragement, Lawson began conducting workshops on nonviolent methods in Nashville, Tennessee, and on the campuses of African American colleges across the South. He trained hundreds of students, including some whites who supported the civil rights movement. One participant described the weekly workshops.

HISTORY'S VOICES

❝We would practice such things as how to protect your head from a beating and how to protect each other. If one person was taking a severe beating, we would practice other people putting their bodies in between that person and the violence, so that the violence would be more distributed and hopefully no one would get seriously injured. We would practice not striking back if someone struck us.❞

—Diane Nash in *Voices of Freedom* (1990)

The sit-in movement Lawson was nearly ready to launch a sit-in campaign in Nashville when on February 1, 1960, four college students in Greensboro, North Carolina, began a sit-in of their own after ordering coffee at a lunch counter in a Woolworth's store. Denied service because of their race, the four young men stayed in their seats, expecting to be arrested. When they were not, they remained at the lunch counter until the store closed.

The next day, they returned with more students. By day three, protesters filled 63 of the lunch counter's 66 seats. The daily sit-ins soon attracted hundreds of supporters. The story of these dedicated and well-behaved students, who ended each day's protest with a prayer, quickly became national news. In mid-February, Lawson's Nashville sit-ins began.

The four students who began the sit-in at Greensboro had not attended Lawson's workshops. They had read about his methods, however. The Greensboro protest won important white support. "As long as those who seek a change . . . seek it in a peaceful manner, their power (and their haunting image on the white man's conscience) will not diminish," the *Greensboro Daily News* wrote in an editorial.

THE CIVIL RIGHTS MOVEMENT **917**

917

Reading Focus

Sit-ins and Freedom Rides

Contrast In what ways were sit-ins and Freedom Rides different? *Sit-ins were a series of protests confined to specific locations; Freedom Ride protesters traveled from city to city by bus protesting policies that were illegal.*

Explain The success of the Freedom Riders came with death and bloodshed. Why was SNCC more successful than CORE in conducting Freedom Rides? *CORE-sponsored Freedom Rides ended after members were beaten and refused tickets; SNCC members refused to give up; eventually received support of federal marshals*

Evaluate Do you think President Kennedy should have done more to enforce the Court's order regarding equal accommodations in bus stations? *possible answers—yes, he could have sent federal marshals immediately; no, he provided resources for the attorney general to deal with the problems*

📄 CRF: Primary Source Activity: A Freedom Rider Bus in Anniston, Alabama

📦 Map Transparency: Freedom Rides, 1961

Info to Know

Freedom Riders 40 Years Later In November 2001, Jackson, Mississippi, was the site of the 40th Reunion of the Freedom Riders and their families. Unlike their reception forty years ago, the Freedom Riders were welcomed and praised. The governor of Mississippi, Ronnie Musgrove, proclaimed the day as Freedom Riders Day and honored the Freedom Riders for continuing their 1961 mission in spite of the violence.

📑 American History Outline Maps: Desegregation

Answers

Interpreting Maps 1. *from Washington, D.C., south to New Orleans, Louisiana; they made it to Jackson, Mississippi;* **2.** *possible answer—jailing of 300 plus riders shows resistance of southerners*

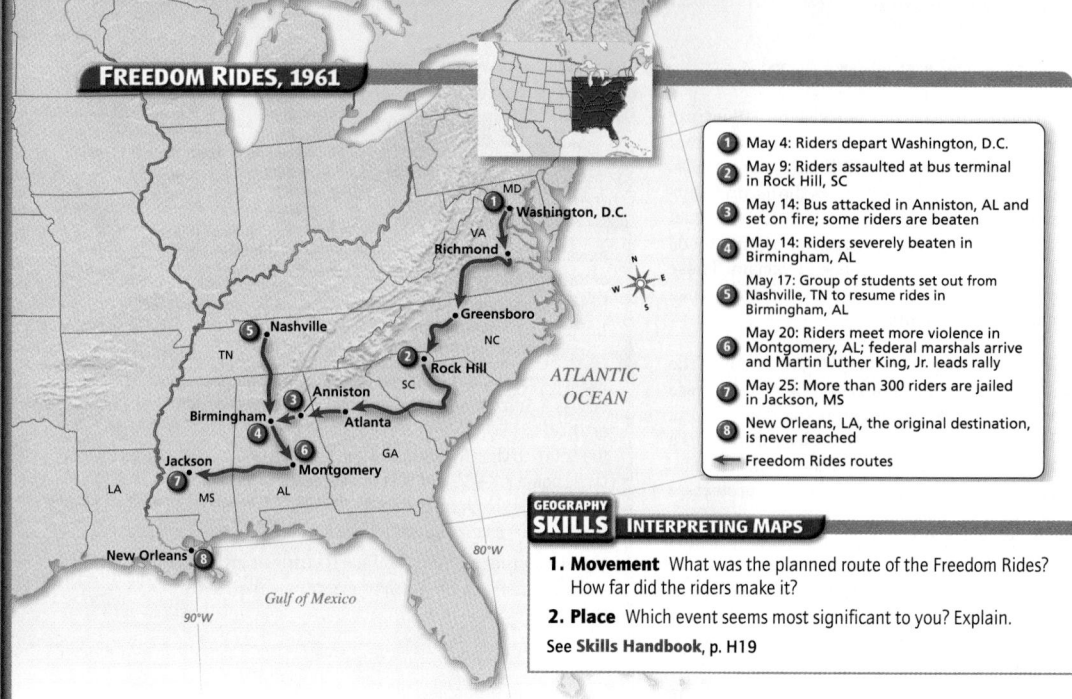

FREEDOM RIDES, 1961

1. May 4: Riders depart Washington, D.C.
2. May 9: Riders assaulted at bus terminal in Rock Hill, SC
3. May 14: Bus attacked in Anniston, AL and set on fire; some riders are beaten
4. May 14: Riders severely beaten in Birmingham, AL
5. May 17: Group of students set out from Nashville, TN to resume rides in Birmingham, AL
6. May 20: Riders meet more violence in Montgomery, AL; federal marshals arrive and Martin Luther King, Jr. leads rally
7. May 25: More than 300 riders are jailed in Jackson, MS
8. New Orleans, LA, the original destination, is never reached

← Freedom Rides routes

GEOGRAPHY SKILLS INTERPRETING MAPS

1. **Movement** What was the planned route of the Freedom Rides? How far did the riders make it?
2. **Place** Which event seems most significant to you? Explain.

See **Skills Handbook**, p. H19

ACADEMIC VOCABULARY

enforce to require something to happen

During the next two months, protesters in about 50 southern cities began to use the sit-in tactic. In many places, white onlookers attacked the participants with food and other objects. Demonstrators, some of whom were white, were sometimes beaten. By April some 2,000 protesters had been arrested. "We do not consider going to jail a sacrifice but a privilege," a jailed demonstrator proclaimed. "Sixty days is not long to spend in jail. We will do it again for a cause as great as this one."

Despite the arrests and violence—or perhaps because of them—sit-ins were generally successful at getting business owners to change their policies. In May several stores in Nashville ended segregation at their lunch counters. The Greensboro sit-ins ended in July with the integration of lunch counters there. In October, Woolworth's and three other national chains integrated lunch counters nationwide.

The sit-ins marked a shift in the civil rights movement. They showed young African Americans' growing impatience with the slow pace of change. Sit-in leaders formed the Student Nonviolent Coordinating Committee, or **SNCC**, to conduct other nonviolent protests.

The Freedom Rides The success of the student sit-ins inspired CORE to plan its own nonviolent action in 1961. In December 1960 the Supreme Court had ordered that facilities in bus stations serving interstate travelers be open to all passengers, regardless of race. The Court's order, however, was not being enforced. Newly elected president John F. Kennedy, though a supporter of civil rights, seemed unwilling to anger southern whites.

Members of CORE decided to draw attention to the situation by sending a group of **Freedom Riders** on a bus trip through the South. At each stop the African American riders would go into the whites-only waiting rooms and try to use facilities such as restrooms and lunch counters. "We felt we could count on the racists of the South to create a crisis so that the federal government would be compelled to enforce the law," James Farmer later explained.

On May 4, 1961, a group of 13 volunteers, including Farmer, left Washington, D.C., by bus, bound for New Orleans, Louisiana. They tried to use the facilities in bus stations in towns they passed through. At first they experienced only mild harassment. Then on May 14, one

918 CHAPTER 28

Skills Focus: Analyzing Bias in Historical Interpretation [Above Level]

Reading Like a Historian Skill
Sit-ins and Freedom Rides

Research Required

1. Have students conduct outside research to learn more about the Freedom Riders and the reaction they received while in the South. Have students find articles written at the time of the Freedom Rides.

2. Have students write an essay in which they analyze the bias in the articles they have found. Have students attach copies of the articles to their essays.

3. Have volunteers read their primary source documents to the class.

4. As an extension, visit the Freedom Riders Foundation Web site and obtain a copy of Mississippi Governor Musgrove's proclamation honoring the Freedom Riders. Read it to the class and guide students in a discussion of the ways viewpoints and attitudes change over time. **LS Verbal-Linguistic, Interpersonal**

📝 Alternative Assessment Handbook, Rubric 37: Writing Assignments

of the buses was swarmed by a mob outside of Anniston, Alabama. The mob firebombed the bus and beat the Freedom Riders as they escaped. Newspapers nationwide showed the incident on their front pages.

Another Freedom Ride bus reached Birmingham, Alabama, where it was attacked by a group armed with baseball bats and metal pipes. One Freedom Rider suffered permanent brain damage, and another required dozens of stitches to close the wounds to his head. No police arrived to stop the savage beatings. When the bus company refused to sell the Freedom Riders tickets to continue their journey, the CORE-sponsored Freedom Ride disbanded.

Federal intervention SNCC leader Diane Nash refused to give in to the violence, however. She gathered a group of SNCC members to continue the Freedom Rides from Nashville. Fearing death, several of them made out wills or wrote letters of farewell to loved ones before leaving for Birmingham.

Attorney General Robert Kennedy arranged with Alabama's governor to provide police protection for the SNCC volunteers. When their bus reached Montgomery, however, the police disappeared. The SNCC riders were attacked by yet another mob. An aide to President John Kennedy, at the scene as an observer, was among those beaten unconscious. Outraged at the governor's betrayal, the attorney general sent 600 federal marshals to Montgomery to protect the Freedom Riders.

On May 24 the SNCC riders reached Jackson, Mississippi. There they were arrested and jailed for using the bus station's whites-only facilities. The next day more volunteers arrived in Jackson, vowing to continue the rides. They were also arrested.

During the next four months, several hundred Freedom Riders rode buses through the lower South. The protest ended in September 1961, when the federal Interstate Commerce Commission finally issued tough new rules forcing integration of bus and train stations.

READING CHECK **Comparing** In what ways were the sit-ins and the Freedom Rides similar?

Integrating Higher Education

While SNCC and CORE attempted to achieve change using nonviolent protest, the NAACP pushed ahead with its legal campaign against school segregation. By 1960 it had expanded its efforts to include colleges and universities. White lawyers collaborated with the NAACP. In 1961 the organization obtained a court order requiring the University of Georgia to admit two African American students.

Charlayne Hunter and Hamilton Holmes were only in school a few days before they were suspended after white students rioted. A federal judge ordered their reinstatement. Robert Kennedy publicly praised the school for its respect for the law. He called the two students "freedom fighters" for returning to campus

Desegregating Colleges

James Meredith's entrance into the University of Mississippi made him a famous name in civil rights (right). Governor Wallace of Alabama (left) blocks African American students from entering a university. *How did the defiance of state governments affect efforts to desegregate higher education?*

MEREDITH OFF TO ENROLL; BARNETT ACTION BLOCKED

919

919

Integrating Higher Education

Identify Who was James Meredith? *first African American student to attend the University of Mississippi*

Summarize How did some people of Mississippi react to the integration of the university? *with mob violence and riots*

Evaluate Which do you think was most effective in dealing with the riots in Mississippi, President Kennedy's appeal or sending in federal troops? *possible answers—president's words helped people see that rioting was futile; sending in the troops was more effective because they did stop the riots and ensure integration of the university*

Faces of History

Martin Luther King Jr.

Nobel Peace Prize When Martin Luther King Jr. accepted his Nobel Peace Prize, he gave an inspiring talk about the ongoing struggle for human rights. In his speech, King said, "I accept this award on behalf of a civil rights movement which is moving with determination and a majestic scorn for risk and danger to establish a reign of freedom and a rule of justice . . . this award . . . is a profound recognition that nonviolence is the answer to the crucial political and moral question of our time."

Answers

Faces of History *became a powerful, inspirational speaker; role as minister brought him respect*

Reading Check *with court orders and federal troops*

Martin Luther KING Jr.

1929–1968

Martin Luther King Jr. entered Morehouse College in Atlanta, Georgia, at age 15 and graduated in 1948. He became an ordained minister while attending Morehouse. After religious training in Pennsylvania, King attended Boston University, where he completed a doctoral degree in religion in 1955. At all three schools, King studied the teachings on nonviolent protest of Indian leader Mohandas Gandhi.

The powerful speaking abilities for which King was known developed slowly. He received C's in his first public speaking courses in Pennsylvania. By his third year there, however, his professors were praising the impression he made in public speeches and discussions.

In 1953 King married Coretta Scott, an Alabamian he met in Boston. The next year they moved to Montgomery, Alabama, where King became pastor of a Baptist church. The Montgomery bus boycott boosted him to leadership in the civil rights movement. In 1964 King was awarded the Nobel Peace Prize for his work for civil rights.

Draw Conclusions How did King's education prepare him for his role in the civil rights movement?

---

amidst all the threats. Although Hunter especially suffered continuing hostility and taunts, both she and Holmes graduated in 1963.

Greater trouble erupted at the University of Mississippi when **James Meredith** attempted to enroll there in September 1962. A federal court ruled that the university had rejected Meredith's application "solely because he was a Negro," and ordered him to be admitted. On Sunday evening, September 30, Meredith arrived on campus. He was accompanied by 500 federal marshals that Robert Kennedy had ordered to protect him. A mob of 2,500 protesters, many of them nonstudents, met the group with violence.

As the riot worsened, President Kennedy went on national television to announce that he was sending in troops. "The eyes of the nation and the world are upon you," he told Mississippians. "The honor of your university and the state are in the balance." The troops arrived in the predawn hours of Monday morning and finally ended the protest. By then, however, hundreds of people had been injured and two killed. One of the dead was a journalist from France, sent to cover Meredith's enrollment.

In the months that followed, Meredith was frequently harassed by groups of white students. Yet a few students defied their peers and drank coffee with him or sat at his table at mealtimes. A small force of marshals remained at the university to protect Meredith until he graduated in the summer of 1963.

At the University of Alabama, Governor George Wallace in June 1963 physically blocked Vivian Malone and James Hood from enrolling. "This action is in violation of rights reserved to the state by the Constitution of the United States," Wallace proclaimed. However, after his speech and symbolic defiance of a court order to integrate the university, Wallace stepped aside.

READING CHECK **Making Generalizations** How were public universities in Georgia, Mississippi, and Alabama integrated?

Albany and Birmingham

In late 1961 Albany, Georgia, became a battleground in the civil rights movement. SNCC began a sit-in in Albany's bus station in November because local officials were ignoring the Interstate Commerce Commission's new integration rules. When demonstrators were arrested, SNCC notified the U.S. Justice Department. The federal government, however took no action.

The Albany Movement By mid-December more than 500 protesters had been jailed. Local civil rights leaders brought national attention to the situation by inviting Martin Luther King Jr. to lead more demonstrations. The campaign was called the Albany Movement. "We will wear them down with our capacity to suffer," King promised. He was soon arrested for leading a march on city hall. King refused to pay the fine. He vowed to remain in jail until the city agreed to desegregate. "I hope thousands [of others] will join me," he said.

Albany police chief Laurie Prichett had studied King's tactics, however. "His method was nonviolence . . . to fill the jails, same as Gandhi in India," Prichett said later. "And once they filled the jails, we'd have no capacity to arrest and then we'd have to give in to his demands." Prichett made arrangements with every jail in the surrounding area, so he was

---

Reading Skill
Integration at the University of Alabama

1. Organize students into pairs. Have each pair develop a telephone conversation in which one student is telling the other about the integration at the University of Alabama. The other student will ask questions about what happened when Vivian Malone and James Hood began attending the university.

2. Have volunteers read their phone conversations to the class.

3. Guide students in a discussion of the integration of the southern universities discussed in the section. Call the students' attention to George Wallace's quote and his actions after the speech. Have students explain why Governor Wallace made these comments and then stepped aside and allowed integration to continue.

LS Kinesthetic, Interpersonal

Alternative Assessment Handbook, Rubrics 11: Discussions; and 14: Group Activity

able to arrest all the protesters. In addition, when the national press arrived to cover King's sentencing, Pritchett had King's fine paid, so King was released instead.

Opponents of integration also took advantage of divisions in the Albany Movement. The local leaders who began it became upset when the SCLC took control. Sensing this, city officials refused to negotiate with anyone but local leaders and would not negotiate at all as long as King was in town. In August 1962, King called off his demonstrations and left Albany. City officials then refused to meet with the local leaders. The protests resumed without King but failed to accomplish their goals.

The nine-month Albany Movement was a major defeat for King. It proved to be an important experience, however. After Albany, King vowed that the SCLC would organize its own campaigns rather than aid campaigns begun by others. His new strategy soon proved successful in Birmingham.

The Birmingham campaign King next focused his efforts on Birmingham, Alabama. Birmingham was known for its strict enforcement of segregation. With help from entertainer Harry Belafonte, King raised several hundred thousand dollars to fund a campaign against Birmingham's segregation laws. Volunteers taught local African Americans the techniques of nonviolence in the city's African American churches.

King's effort began in April 1963 with sit-ins and marches. Authorities quickly arrested the protesters. King had counted on this response to motivate more people to join the protests and focus national attention on the city. At first his strategy worked. On April 12 King and hundreds more were arrested and jailed.

The next day a group of local white clergy took out a full-page ad in the city's newspaper. They attacked King's actions as unwise and untimely. In his jail cell, King rejected these charges with a letter written in the margins of the newspaper. His response gained fame as the "Letter from a Birmingham Jail."

When King was released a few days later, he found fewer adult African Americans willing to risk losing their jobs by going to jail. Another SCLC leader urged King to use children instead. On May 2 demonstrators between the ages six and eighteen sang and chanted as they marched to lines of police set up to stop them. More than 900 were arrested and jailed.

The next day, Birmingham police chief Eugene "Bull" Connor used police and firefighters to break up a group of about 2,500

Witness to Violence

Images of peaceful protesters in Birmingham being attacked by police dogs and swept away by high-pressure fire hoses shocked the nation. *How did President Kennedy react?*

921

Albany and Birmingham

Recall How did the chief of police in Albany, Georgia undermine Martin Luther King Jr.'s protest? *arranged to have jail space in surrounding towns so that he could arrest and jail all protesters*

Summarize What lesson did Martin Luther King Jr. learn from the Albany Movement? *never aid campaigns started by others; organize his own campaigns in the future*

4 What concerns and events led to the passage of the Civil Rights Act of 1964? *images of violence in Birmingham; assassination of Medgar Evers; March on Washington*

The Civil Rights Act of 1964

Explain What finally motivated President Kennedy to take action in the area of civil rights? *images of the violence in Birmingham as covered by the national media*

Analyze Why was Medgar Evers assassinated? *effective civil rights leader; head of NAACP in Mississippi; threat to white supremacists*

Elaborate Why do you think President Kennedy had resisted pushing strong civil rights legislation? *possible answer—did not want to alienate voters; lacked Congressional support*

🔲 Quick Facts Transparency: Major Civil Rights Reforms

Answers

Reading Check *alike—nonviolent protests, protesters were arrested; different—Albany was unsuccessful while Birmingham was successful; Birmingham police used extreme violence against protesters while Albany police did not*

922

African American students as they gathered for another march. As television cameras and press photographers recorded the scene, the authorities struck. They blasted the protesters with fire hoses. The force of the water knocked the protesters down, tore their clothes, and left some of them bloody on the ground.

Connor repeated these actions for the next several days, as the nation watched on television. Finally, after hundreds of demonstrators had been jailed, federal negotiators succeeded in getting city officials to agree to many of

ACADEMIC VOCABULARY
restore to put something back into its former or original condition

MAJOR CIVIL RIGHTS REFORMS

Brown v. Board of Education of Topeka, Kansas (1954)	• declared segregated public schools unconstitutional
Civil Rights Act of 1957	• established a federal Civil Rights Commission to investigate violations of civil rights • created a civil rights division within the Justice Department to enforce civil rights laws • authorized the federal government to prosecute anyone interfering with another person's right to vote
Executive Order 11063 (November 20, 1962)	• banned racial and religious discrimination in housing built or purchased with federal aid
Civil Rights Act of 1964	• banned discrimination in public accommodations • outlawed unequal voting requirements • barred discrimination in employment based on race, gender, religion, or national origin • established the Equal Employment Opportunity Commission • applied federal power to speed integration of schools and other public facilities
Voting Rights Act of 1965	• suspended literacy tests and other devices used to exclude black voters • authorized federal supervision of voter registration • allowed federal workers to register voters
Civil Rights Act of 1968 (Fair Housing Act)	• banned racial discrimination in the sale, rental, or financing of housing • made harming civil rights workers a federal crime

922 CHAPTER 28

King's demands. King called the agreement "the most magnificent victory for justice we've seen in the Deep South."

Some white people in Birmingham refused to accept the compromise. The motel where King was staying and the home of his brother were bombed. When some African Americans rioted, President Kennedy declared that he would not let extremists on either side destroy the agreement. He sent federal troops to Birmingham to restore order.

READING CHECK **Comparing and Contrasting** How were the Albany and Birmingham campaigns alike, and how did they differ?

The Civil Rights Act of 1964

You have read about Kennedy's approach on civil rights. He had believed that moving slowly was the best way to make progress. The events in Alabama, however, changed his mind.

HISTORY'S VOICES

❝The fires of frustration and discord are burning in every city, North and South . . . We face . . . a moral crisis as a country and as a people . . . We cannot say to 10 percent of the population that . . . the only way . . . to get their rights is to go into the streets and demonstrate. I think we owe them and we owe ourselves a better country than that.❞
—John Kennedy, June 11, 1963

Kennedy announced that he would ask for sweeping legislation designed to finally end segregation in public accommodations—hotels, restaurants, theaters, and other establishments that serve the public.

The assassination of Medgar Evers A murder just hours after Kennedy's speech helped put the president's concerns into sharp focus. The head of the NAACP in Mississippi, **Medgar Evers**, was shot dead in his front yard. Evers was one of the movement's most effective leaders. His slaying shocked many Americans.

Police quickly arrested a Ku Klux Klan member named Byron De La Beckwith. All-white juries failed to reach a verdict in two trials, and De La Beckwith went free. Some 30 years later, however, authorities tried him yet a third time. In 1994, at the age of 73, De La Beckwith was finally convicted and sentenced to life in prison.

Differentiating Instruction

Below Level

Special Education Students

1. Draw a large flowchart for all students to see. Label the flowchart: Major Civil Rights Legislation.

2. Have students copy the flowchart as shown, and complete it by listing the events that led to the Civil Rights Act of 1964. Students may have to add boxes. 🄻 **Visual-Spatial, Logical-Mathematical**

📓 Alternative Assessment Handbook, Rubric 13: Graphic Organizers

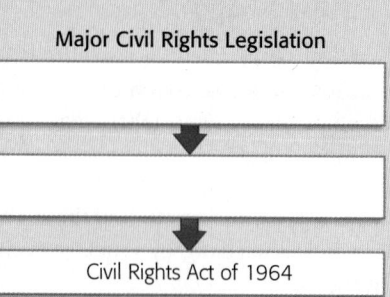

Major Civil Rights Legislation

↓

↓

Civil Rights Act of 1964

The March on Washington To build support for the civil rights movement, African American leaders planned a huge march on the nation's capital for August 1963. In June, when President Kennedy called for a civil rights law, African American leaders decided to include demands for its passage as one of the march's goals.

The March on Washington for Jobs and Freedom took place on August 28, 1963. It was the largest civil rights demonstration ever held in the United States. More than 200,000 people of all races covered the National Mall. Major civil rights figures addressed the crowd from the steps of the Lincoln Memorial. Gospel singer Mahalia Jackson, folk singer Joan Baez, and other popular entertainers of the day performed for the crowd.

Martin Luther King Jr. delivered the last speech at the day-long rally. He started by reviewing African Americans' long struggle throughout history for freedom. Then, urged on by Mahalia Jackson and other listeners nearby, King put aside his prepared remarks and began to speak from his heart. His speech became known as the "I Have a Dream" speech.

HISTORY'S VOICES

❝ I have a dream that one day this nation will rise up and live out the true meaning of its creed: 'We hold these truths to be self-evident; that all men are created equal.' . . . I have a dream that my four little children will one day live in a nation where they will not be judged by the color of their skin, but the content of their character. I have a dream today! ❞

—Martin Luther King Jr., August 28, 1963

Passing the Civil Rights Act The good feeling produced by the March on Washington was short-lived. The next month a bomb exploded in a Birmingham church, killing four young African American girls. Then in November, President Kennedy was assassinated. His vice president, Lyndon Johnson, took office.

President Johnson supported passage of a strong civil rights bill. Although some southerners in Congress fought hard to kill it, Johnson signed it into law on July 2, 1964. The **Civil Rights Act of 1964** banned discrimination in employment and in public accommodations.

 THE IMPACT TODAY

Government
The conviction in Evers's killing has encouraged the FBI to reopen other old cases from the civil rights movement. In 2002 a jury convicted a man long suspected in the Birmingham church bombing.

READING CHECK **Summarizing** Why did a strong civil rights bill finally become law in 1964?

---

go.hrw.com
Online Quiz
Keyword: SD7 HP28

SECTION 2 ASSESSMENT

Reviewing Ideas, Terms, and People

1. **a. Identify** What civil rights tactic was based on the ideas and actions of **Mohandas Gandhi**?
   b. Summarize What was the basic belief behind the tactic of nonviolence?
   c. Elaborate Why do you think the sit-ins were successful?

2. **a. Describe** How did the NAACP work for the integration of colleges and universities?
   b. Make Inferences Why did so many federal marshals accompany **James Meredith** to the University of Mississippi?
   c. Predict Do you think the rioting at the University of Mississippi affected people's opinions about segregation? Why or why not?

3. **a. Identify** What began the Albany Movement?
   b. Make Inferences Why did Martin Luther King Jr. decide to focus on Birmingham?
   c. Elaborate Why did federal negotiators want Birmingham officials to agree to many of King's demands?

4. **a. Define** What was the goal of the March on Washington?
   b. Analyze What inspired President Kennedy to begin focusing on civil rights?

c. Evaluate Do you think the **Civil Rights Act of 1964** went far enough? Explain why or why not. What substitute or additional provisions might the law have contained?

Critical Thinking

5. **Identify Cause and Effect** Review your notes on the Civil Rights Act of 1964. Then copy the graphic organizer below and use it to list the causes and effects of the law. You may need to add more circles.

FOCUS ON WRITING

6. **Persuasive** Write a letter to your representative in Congress, explaining why he or she should vote for the Civil Rights Act of 1964. Be sure to include in your letter persuasive arguments that support your position.

THE CIVIL RIGHTS MOVEMENT **923**

Section 2 Assessment Answers

1. **a.** nonviolent protest
   b. exposes injustice and forces those in power to end it
   c. possible answer—constant reminder of the issues; protesters did not give up

2. **a.** legal campaign
   b. to protect him
   c. possible answer—yes, white rioters caused violence, government determined to integrate public schools

3. **a.** ICC's rules regarding integration ignored
   b. its strict enforcement of segregation

   c. possible answer—to end the negative publicity the city was receiving

4. **a.** to build support for the civil rights movement
   b. images of Birmingham police violence
   c. possible answer—no, it could have offered more protection to African Americans

5. Causes—violent riots, March on Washington, Effects—ban on discrimination in employment and public accommodations

6. possible answer—will ban discrimination; necessary to protect civil rights of African Americans

923

Excerpt from *Letter from a Birmingham Jail* by Martin Luther King Jr.

Word Help

diligently actively, thoroughly

paradoxical puzzling, contradictory

advocate encourage, support

conversely the opposite of, on the other hand

relegating assigning

ordinances laws, regulations

Meet the Writer

Martin Luther King Jr. Baptist minister and civil rights leader Martin Luther King Jr. gained national prominence during the Montgomery bus boycott. His speaking abilities, inspiring voice, and dedication to nonviolent change provided leadership and strength to the civil rights movement. King understood the power of the media, especially of television, and he was able to gain national coverage of sit-ins and protest marches. King was key in helping to secure the passage of the 1964 Civil Rights Act and the 1965 Voting Rights Act. Decades after his death, King's thoughts, writings, and vision continue to influence civil rights.

Info to Know

Birmingham Clergy The ad in the Birmingham newspaper was placed by white clergymen, but not all the black clergy in Birmingham supported King and his tactics.

About the Reading While protesting segregation in Birmingham, Alabama, Martin Luther King Jr. was arrested and held in a Birmingham jail. The following is an excerpt from a letter that King wrote in response to a full-page ad in a local newspaper. The ad, taken out by eight members of the clergy, denounced the protests. King's letter clearly presents his philosophy on nonviolence.

AS YOU READ Consider the dangers that Martin Luther King Jr. as well as other social activists faced by standing up for the causes they believed in.

Excerpt from

Letter from a Birmingham Jail

by Martin Luther King Jr.

Men drinking from segregated water fountains in the South

You express a great deal of anxiety over our willingness to break laws. This is certainly a legitimate concern. Since we so diligently urge people to obey the Supreme Court's decision of 1954 outlawing segregation in the public schools, at first glance it may seem rather paradoxical for us consciously to break laws. One may well ask: "How can you advocate breaking some laws and obeying others?" The answer lies in the fact that there are two types of laws: just and unjust. I would be the first to advocate obeying just laws. One has not only a legal but a moral responsibility to obey just laws. Conversely, one has a moral responsibility to disobey unjust laws. I would agree with St. Augustine that "an unjust law is no law at all."

Now, what is the difference between the two? How does one determine whether a law is just or unjust? A just law is a man-made code that squares with the moral law or the law of God. An unjust law is a code that is out of harmony with the moral law. To put it in the terms of St. Thomas Aquinas: An unjust law is a human law that is not rooted in eternal law and natural law. Any law that uplifts human personality is just. Any law that degrades human personality is unjust.

All segregation statutes are unjust because segregation distorts the soul and damages the personality. It gives the segregator a false sense of superiority and the segregated a false sense of inferiority. Segregation, to use the terminology of the Jewish philosopher Martin Buber, substitutes an "I-it" relationship for an "I-thou" relationship and ends up relegating persons to the status of things. Hence segregation is not only politically, economically and sociologically unsound, it is morally wrong and sinful. Paul Tillich said that sin is separation. Is not segregation an existential expression of man's tragic separation, his awful estrangement, his terrible sinfulness? Thus it is that I can urge men to obey the 1954 decision of the Supreme Court, for it is morally right; and I can urge them to disobey segregation ordinances, for they are morally wrong.

Skills FOCUS READING LIKE A HISTORIAN

Literature as Historical Evidence How does King's letter show the importance of religious thought in the civil rights movement?

See Skills Handbook, p. H32

924 CHAPTER 28

Differentiating Instruction

Above Level

Advanced Learners/GATE

1. Guide students in a discussion of Martin Luther King Jr.'s protests in Birmingham in April 1963, and of the full-page ad in the Birmingham newspaper written by white clergymen. Remind students that this ad attacked King's actions as extreme and unjustified.

2. Have students write a new full-page newspaper ad responding to Martin Luther King Jr. and the points he makes in his letter

from the Birmingham jail. Tell students that the ad should have a banner headline and be signed by the student.

3. Have volunteers read their ads to the class. Then guide students in a discussion of the presentations. Did King persuade most groups to understand his viewpoint? Why or why not? **LS Interpersonal, Verbal-Linguistic**

   Alternative Assessment Handbook, Rubric 43: Writing to Persuade

Answers

Reading Like a Historian *reference to just laws, the laws of God, references to religious scholars Thomas Aquinas, Martin Buber, and Paul Tillich*

Voting Rights

BEFORE YOU READ

MAIN IDEA

In the 1960s, African Americans gained voting rights and political power in the South, but only after a bitter and hard-fought struggle.

READING FOCUS

1. What methods did civil rights workers use to gain voting rights for African Americans in the South?

2. How did African American political organizing become a national issue?

3. What events led to passage of the Voting Rights Act?

KEY TERMS AND PEOPLE

Voter Education Project
Twenty-fourth Amendment
Freedom Summer
Mississippi Freedom
   Democratic Party
Fannie Lou Hamer
Voting Rights Act of 1965

TAKING NOTES As you read, take notes on major 1960s struggles for voting rights for African Americans in the South. Record your notes in a graphic organizer like the one shown here.

Freedom Summer	MFDP	Selma Campaign

THE INSIDE STORY

What did the 2000 election in Selma symbolize? On March 7, 1965, about 600 people marching for voting rights were attacked and beaten by police as they crossed the Edmund Pettus Bridge in Selma, Alabama. The savage attack gained national attention and became one of the most notorious events of the civil rights movement.

Thirty-five years later, in 2000, Selma made national news again when James Perkins became the city's first African American mayor. Perkins was twelve years old when the march took place. He wanted to join, but his parents, fearing that violence might erupt, refused to let him go. However, like many other Selma residents, Perkins never forgot that fateful and bloody day.

The candidate Perkins defeated in 2000, Joe Smitherman, had been Selma's mayor in 1965. He did not take part

in the beatings at the bridge. But back then, Smitherman opposed voting rights for African Americans. He later apologized for his views. This helped him stay in office for ten terms, as the number of African American voters in his city increased from 150 in 1964 to 9,000—some 65 percent of Selma's voters—in 2000.

Perkins focused his campaign in 2000 on economic issues instead of race, but some Selma residents organized their own effort to defeat Smitherman. For months, demonstrators stood at the Edmund Pettus Bridge holding signs reading "Remember the Blood" and shouting to passing cars, "Joe gotta go!"

Within minutes of the announcement of James Perkins's victory, thousands of his supporters poured back and forth across the bridge in cars and on foot, honking and cheering. "This is the final step of the march over the bridge," said one supporter about the election's significance. "This is the dream that Dr. King wanted." ■

SELMA,
Now and Then

◀ Selma mayor James Perkins, with the Edmund Pettus Bridge in the background

THE CIVIL RIGHTS MOVEMENT **925**

Teach the Main Idea

At Level

Voting Rights

1. **Teach** Ask students the Reading Focus questions to teach this section.

2. **Apply** Draw three ladders for students to see. Label the top of each ladder with the main topics of the section: Gaining Voting Rights, Political Organizing, The Voting Rights Act. Have students copy the ladders and list the main ideas of each topic on the corresponding rungs.

3. **Review** As you review the section, have students name the events that led to the Voting Rights Act of 1965.

4. **Practice/Homework** Have students write a newspaper editorial supporting passage of the Voting Rights Act of 1965. **LS Visual-Spatial, Verbal-Linguistic**

   Alternative Assessment Handbook, Rubric 17: Letters to Editors

---

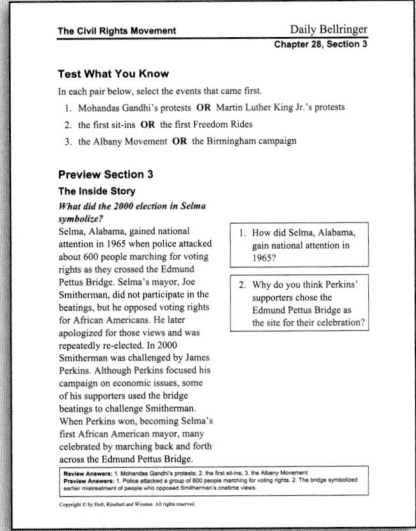

❶ What methods did civil rights workers use to gain voting rights for African Americans in the South? *voter education and registering voters*

Gaining Voting Rights

Recall What was the purpose of the Voter Education Project? *to register southern African Americans to vote*

Make Inferences Why had poll taxes been considered a legal means to prevent African Americans from voting? *The tax was not based on race or gender; it affected the many African Americans who could not afford to pay the tax.*

Elaborate In what ways did Mississippi present the greatest challenge to the VEP workers? *The VEP workers in Mississippi faced criminal acts of violence.*

Tell students that poll taxes were first used by the ancient Greeks and Romans; after conquering new territory, they taxed the conquered people in order to raise revenue. Poll taxes have also been used by England and Russia, along with the United States.

Gaining Voting Rights

James Perkins and the many other African Americans who hold elective offices across the nation today owe much to the civil rights struggles of the 1960s. Voting rights for African Americans, like other victories of the civil rights movement, were achieved at great human cost and sacrifice.

Registering voters The nonviolent methods of the civil rights movement troubled the Kennedy administration because of the violent reactions they provoked. After the brutal attacks on the Freedom Riders in 1961, Attorney General Robert Kennedy met with SNCC leaders. He urged them to focus on voter registration rather than on protests. The vote was the key to changing things in the South, Kennedy claimed. He said that civil rights workers could count on federal government protection if they took this approach.

In 1962 SNCC, CORE, and other groups founded the **Voter Education Project** (VEP) to register southern African Americans to vote. However, the groups soon discovered that opposition to African American suffrage was as great as opposition to ending segregation. Marches to register voters were attacked by mobs or broken up by the police. Project workers routinely were beaten or jailed.

Mississippi presented the greatest challenge. VEP workers there lived in daily fear for their safety. A local farmer helping one voter registration drive was killed. The state legislator who shot him was aquitted. The lone African American witness to the crime was later found shot to death.

In spite of such terror tactics, the Voter Education Project was a success. In 1962 fewer than 1.4 million of the South's 5 million African American adults were registered to vote. By 1964 the VEP had registered more than a half million more African American voters. Only in Mississippi were results discouraging. "We are powerless to register people in significant numbers anywhere in the state," SNCC organizer Robert Moses told the VEP in a report.

The Twenty-fourth Amendment Congress passed the **Twenty-fourth Amendment** to the Constitution in August 1962 and submitted it to the states for ratification. The amendment banned states from taxing citizens to vote. Many southern states required these poll taxes as a way to keep African Americans from voting. Because the tax was not based on gender or race, it was constitutional. But since more African Americans than whites were poor, it affected them most.

Although the Twenty-fourth Amendment's ban on poll taxes applied only to elections

TRACING HISTORY

Civil Rights

The Declaration of Independence says that all people are born with "unalienable rights," but it took nearly 200 years to see that promise extended to all Americans. Study the time line to learn about key events in the struggle for civil rights.

1700

1800

1865–1870 The Thirteenth, Fourteenth, and Fifteenth Amendments abolish slavery, grant citizenship to African Americans, and give the vote to African American men.

1791 The First Amendment in the Bill of Rights guarantees freedom of religious worship.

An Islamic prayer service

926

Differentiating Instruction

Advanced Learners/GATE

1. Guide students in a discussion about the successes and failures of the Voter Education Project. Have students take notes during the discussion.

2. Have students use their notes to write a short story describing the obstacles faced by project workers and the reasons for their eventual success.

3. Have volunteers read their short stories to the class.

4. As an extension, have students write a one-act play about the daily life of a voter education worker. **LS** **Interpersonal, Verbal-Linguistic**

📖 Alternative Assessment Handbook, Rubrics 11: Discussions; and 15: Journals

for president or Congress, it increased hopes that change was on the way. As the proposed amendment worked its way through the ratification process, voting rights leaders planned more projects, concentrating on Mississippi.

Freedom Summer The Twenty-fourth Amendment became part of the Constitution in January 1964. A call went out for college students willing to spend their summer in Mississippi, registering African Americans to vote.

When school let out, hundreds of volunteers gathered at an Ohio college to train for a project called **Freedom Summer**. Most of the trainers—mainly SNCC workers—were from poor southern African American families. The student volunteers were mainly white, northern, and upper middle class. One volunteer later recalled why he took part.

HISTORY'S VOICES

❝I grew up in New York City. I had been raised in a family where being Jewish was important in terms of identifying with the underdog, with people who were suffering repression and discrimination . . . It was tremendously impressive and exciting. For me, it was a tremendous privilege to be allowed to participate in this movement for racial justice. At eighteen years old, to be able to be involved in this kind of a struggle was very important to me.❞

—Peter Orris in *Voices of Freedom* (1990)

Volunteers were trained to register voters or to teach at summer school. Mississippi spent about $82 per year to educate each white student but less than $22 per black student. In addition, many black schools in Mississippi closed during the cotton harvest to provide cheap child labor. The project's Freedom Schools offered African American students much-needed help in reading and math as well as instruction in black history and the civil rights movement.

Besides educating children and registering voters, project workers hoped to start a freedom movement in Mississippi that would continue after the volunteers left. Project leader Robert Moses had another goal: Just getting everyone through the summer alive would be an accomplishment, he said.

Crisis in Mississippi The first 200 volunteers arrived in Mississippi on June 20, 1964. The very next day one of them went missing. Andrew Goodman, a college student from New York, had gone with two CORE workers, James Chaney and Michael Schwerner, to inspect an African American church that had recently been bombed. They were arrested for speeding in Philadelphia, Mississippi, and held in jail until evening. After paying a fine, the three men drove off into the night. They were never heard from again.

1964 The Civil Rights Act of 1964 guarantees voting rights and prohibits gender-based discrimination.

Intercollegiate women's basketball game

1972 Title IX of the Higher Education Act prohibits gender discrimination in all areas of higher education, including athletics.

1900

2000

1920 The Nineteenth Amendment guarantees women the right to vote.

Georgia Supreme Court Chief Justice Leah Ward Sears

2005 Leah Ward Sears becomes the chief justice of the Georgia Supreme Court, the first African American woman chief justice in the country.

927

Direct Teach

Reading Focus

❷ How did African American political organizing become a national issue? *Mississippi Freedom Democratic Party came to Democratic National Convention and asked to replace the white Mississippi delegation*

Political Organizing

Identify Who was Fannie Lou Hamer? *Mississippi Freedom Democratic Party leader; presented MFDP case at nationally televised Democratic Convention*

Summarize How was the matter of the Mississippi Freedom Democratic Party settled? *compromise offered: two MFDP delegates were designated as voting members; compromise rejected*

Draw Conclusions In what way was the MFDP successful and in what way was it unsuccessful? *successful— paved way for future political power of minorities and women; unsuccessful— widened the split within civil rights movement*

Answers

American Civil Liberty *outlawed poll tax in federal elections; removed economic barrier to voting for many African Americans*

Reading Check *Voter Education Project; passage of the Twenty-fourth Amendment; Freedom Summer*

928

American Civil Liberty

Twenty-fourth Amendment

In 1870 the Fifteenth Amendment granted African American men the right to vote in federal elections. Still, many states set requirements that made voting difficult for African Americans. One example was the poll tax. Many people could not afford this tax. Often, however, anyone whose father or grandfather had been eligible to vote did not have to pay it. In this way, many whites avoided the tax. Many African Americans could not.

One result of the civil rights movement of the 1950s and 1960s was a new amendment to the Constitution. The Twenty-fourth Amendment outlawed poll taxes in federal elections. This amendment was reinforced by a 1966 Supreme Court decision that poll taxes were illegal in state and local elections.

Identifying Cause and Effect In what ways would the Twenty-fourth Amendment increase the political power of African Americans?

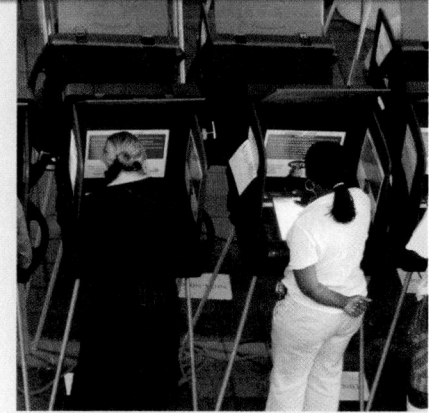

All Americans today cast their ballots free of the poll tax.

President Lyndon Johnson ordered a massive hunt for the three young men. In August their bodies were found in an earthen dam near Philadelphia, Mississippi. The incident cast gloom over Freedom Summer. Two-thirds of the volunteers went home. Many of those who remained suffered through shootings, beatings, bombings, and arrests.

THE IMPACT TODAY

Government
In 2005 another of the killers was convicted and sentenced to prison for the murders of Goodman, Chaney, and Schwerner.

In December the FBI arrested 21 suspects in the murders of Goodman, Chaney, and Schwerner. Most were members of the Ku Klux Klan. When the state dropped all charges, they were brought to trial in federal court for violating civil rights laws. Seven were convicted and received prison sentences ranging from 4 to 10 years. They were the first convictions ever in Mississippi for killing a civil rights worker.

In spite of the violence, organizers considered Mississippi's Freedom Summer project a success. The Freedom Schools taught 3,000 students, and more than 17,000 African Americans in Mississippi applied to vote. When state elections officials accepted only about 1,600 of these applications helped to show that a federal law was needed to secure voting rights for African Americans.

READING CHECK **Summarizing** What steps were taken to help African Americans register to vote?

Political Organizing

Freedom Summer was often overshadowed by the 1964 presidential election campaign. Most African American leaders wanted Johnson to defeat the Republican candidate Barry Goldwater, who had voted against the Civil Rights Act of 1964. You read about the election in the previous chapter. To help Johnson, Martin Luther King Jr. and other civil rights leaders agreed to suspend their protests until after election day.

SNCC, however, refused to agree. SNCC leaders wanted to protest segregation within the Democratic Party itself. "It is time for the Democratic Party to clean itself of racism," John Lewis, the head of SNCC, told the press.

As part of Freedom Summer, SNCC helped the **Mississippi Freedom Democratic Party** (MFDP) to organize. The MFDP elected sixty-eight delegates to the Democratic National Convention in August 1964. They arrived at the convention and asked to be seated instead of the all-white delegation sent by the state's Democratic Party.

The convention's credentials committee held a hearing to decide which delegates should represent Mississippi. **Fannie Lou Hamer**, an MFDP leader, presented her group's case. Her

928 CHAPTER 28

Skills Focus: Making Written Presentations [At Level]

Reading Like a Historian Skill
Political Organizing

1. Review the information in the text about the 1964 Democratic National Convention and the MFDP. Tell students that state delegates for national political conventions are usually elected, and remind students that the delegates sit as a state block on the convention floor.

2. Have each student write a television news report about the events at the 1964 convention, including the positions taken by the Student Nonviolent Coordinating Committee, the MFDP, the NAACP, and the Southern Christian Leadership Conference. You might wish to have English-Language Learners or Struggling Readers work in mixed-ability pairs to complete the assignment.

3. Have volunteers read their reports to the class.
   LS Verbal-Linguistic, Kinesthetic

   Alternative Assessment Handbook, Rubric 37: Writing Assignments

testimony was carried live on national television. Hamer, a poor sharecropper, told how on the day she registered to vote she was fired from the plantation where she had lived for 18 years. She described how she was beaten in jail after being arrested for attending a voter registration meeting. Hamer wept as she concluded her powerful statement.

HISTORY'S VOICES

❝All this on account of us wanting to register, to become first-class citizens, and if the Freedom Democratic Party is not seated now, I question America. Is this America, the land of the free and the home of the brave where we have to sleep with our telephones off the hooks because our lives be threatened daily because we want to live as decent human beings in America?❞

—Fannie Lou Hamer, August 22, 1964

While Hamer's powerful testimony was on the air, President Johnson was trying to control any political damage to the Democratic Party. In a quickly arranged news conference, he offered to compromise with the MFDP.

The compromise that party leaders proposed was to seat two members of the MFDP delegation and classify the rest as nonvoting "guests" of the convention. Although the NAACP and SCLC supported the compromise, SNCC and the MFDP opposed it. "We didn't come all this way for just two votes," Hamer declared. "We must stop playing the game of token recognition for real change," the MFDP said in a statement rejecting the compromise.

The MFDP's challenge failed in the end. It also helped widen a split that was developing in the civil rights movement. But it helped pave the way for future increases in the power of minorities and women in American politics.

READING CHECK Identifying Problems and Solutions How did the MFDP represent the drive for political organization among African Americans?

The Voting Rights Act

Following passage of the Civil Rights Act of 1964, the SCLC shifted its main focus to voting rights for African Americans. "The right to vote was the issue, replacing public accommodation as the mass concern of a people hungry for a place in the sun," Martin Luther King Jr. later wrote of the movement's new focus.

The Selma campaign In January 1965 King began a campaign to gain voting rights for African Americans by organizing marches in Selma, Alabama. "We will dramatize the situation to arouse the federal government by marching by the thousands to the places of registration," he declared.

By the end of January more than 2,000 marchers had been arrested. Police acted with restraint. They did not want to give King the confrontation he was seeking. King then repeated a tactic he had used earlier in Birmingham. He forced police to jail him along with several hundred other marchers, including many children.

King's arrest had the desired effect. The national media swarmed into Selma. The mass arrests and images of children being sent off to jail began appearing on the networks' evening news programs.

March from Selma

Above, police lay in wait for civil rights marchers as they cross the Edmund Pettus Bridge, March 7, 1965. Right, John Lewis, the SNCC leader who organized the first Selma march, is beaten by state troopers after crossing the bridge on what came to be known as Bloody Sunday.

THE CIVIL RIGHTS MOVEMENT **929**

Direct Teach

Reading Focus

Political Organizing

Recall How did Fannie Lou Hamer's speech affect President Johnson? *worried him; motivated him to make offer of compromise to MFDP*

Analyze What did Fannie Lou Hamer mean when she said that African Americans should stop playing the game of token recognition? *possible answers—civil rights groups should work toward significant changes, become a strong political voting block*

Info to Know

Fannie Lou Hamer "Sick and tired of being sick and tired . . . " Fannie Lou Hamer spoke the above words in an interview with *The Nation* in 1964. As a member of the Mississippi Freedom Democratic Party, her speech at the nationally televised Democratic National Convention in Atlantic City was both moving and shocking. Fannie Lou Hamer's speech was not viewed live, since it was pre-empted by the president's press conference. However, later that evening, the networks aired her complete speech for national viewers to see and hear. A year after Fannie Lou Hamer's speech, President Johnson signed the Voting Rights Act.

Answers

Reading Check *It showed African Americans' willingness and resolution to make permanent civil rights changes.*

929

③ What events led to passage of the Voting Rights Act? *Civil Rights Act of 1964; Selma march*

The Voting Rights Act

Recall What issue replaced the issue of public accommodations in the civil rights movement? *the right to vote*

Describe What was the purpose of the Selma campaign? *to get the attention of the federal government to voting rights problems*

Draw Conclusions Do you think the Selma campaign helped or hurt the civil rights movement? Explain your answer. *possible answers—helpful because it drew national media attention; hurtful because it resulted in more violence and death*

 CRF: History and Geography Activity: Selma-to-Montgomery March

Close

Have students list the events that led to the Voting Rights Act of 1965.

Review

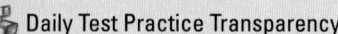 Online Quiz, Section 3

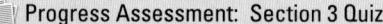 Daily Test Practice Transparency

Assess

SE Section 3 Assessment

Progress Assessment: Section 3 Quiz

Alternative Assessment Handbook

Reteach

Interactive Reader and Study Guide, Section 3

Interactive Skills Tutor CD-ROM

Answers

Reading Check *vast number of people involved; violence shocked many Americans; brought national attention to need for changes in federal law*

930

Tensions rose in mid-February, when police attacked a march in nearby Marion, Alabama. Two state troopers shot and killed a marcher. A few days later King announced a four-day march from Selma to Montgomery, the state capital, to protest police brutality. Governor George Wallace issued an order prohibiting the march. "[It] will not be tolerated," he warned.

The Selma march On Sunday, March 7, 1965, about 600 African Americans began the 54-mile march. Just across the Edmund Pettus Bridge, on the way out of Selma, city and state police blocked their way. After firing tear gas at the marchers, police attacked with clubs, chains, and electric cattle prods. TV networks showed film of the savage violence.

King was not present on the March 7 march. He announced that it would resume on March 9. In a controversial decision, he led the group only to the base of the bridge—not across it. The pause was only temporary, however. After receiving promises of federal protection, the marchers finally reached Montgomery on March 25.

The Voting Rights Act of 1965 A week later, President Johnson gave a nationally televised address to a joint session of Congress. "At times history and fate meet . . . to shape a turning point in man's unending search for freedom," he observed. "So it was last week in Selma, Alabama." The president asked for quick passage of a tough voting rights law. "It is wrong—deadly wrong—to deny any of your fellow Americans the right to vote," Johnson declared. "Outside this chamber is the outraged conscience of a nation."

The **Voting Rights Act of 1965** passed in Congress by large majorities. King, James Farmer, Rosa Parks, and other civil rights leaders attended the president's signing ceremony on August 6.

The law proved to be one of the most important pieces of civil rights legislation ever passed. It gave the federal government powerful tools with which to break down longstanding barriers to African American voting rights. The impact was felt quickly. Within three weeks more than 27,000 African Americans in Mississippi, Alabama, and Louisiana registered to vote. African American candidates were soon elected to state and local offices, helping to break the long-held political power of those who supported segregation.

READING CHECK **Identifying Cause and Effect** How did the Selma march help to secure passage of the Voting Rights Act of 1965?

SECTION 3 ASSESSMENT

go.hrw.com
Online Quiz
Keyword: SD7 HP28

Reviewing Ideas, Terms, and People

1. **a. Identify** What was the goal of the Voter Education Project?
   b. Compare How were the obstacles faced by the Voter Education Project and **Freedom Summer** workers similar?
   c. Elaborate Why do you think African American voter registration efforts faced such fierce resistance?

2. **a. Describe** Who was **Fannie Lou Hamer** and what was her goal?
   b. Analyze Why did some civil rights groups suspend their protests before the election of 1964?
   c. Evaluate Do you think the **Mississippi Freedom Democratic Party** was right to reject President Johnson's compromise? Explain your viewpoint.

3. **a. Define** What was the Selma campaign?
   b. Make Inferences How did the media help the marchers' cause in Selma?
   c. Elaborate Why do you think so many members of Congress supported the **Voting Rights Act of 1965**?

930 CHAPTER 28

Critical Thinking

4. **Analyze Information** Review your notes on African Americans' struggle for political equality. Then copy the graphic organizer below and use it to list the events in the struggle, what injustice each event targeted, and the effects of those actions.

Event	Injustice	Effects

FOCUS ON SPEAKING

5. **Expository** Make a short speech supporting either the Twenty-fourth Amendment or the Voting Rights Act of 1965. In your speech, explain the likely benefits of the new law.

Section 3 Assessment Answers

1. **a.** register southern African Americans to vote
   b. attacked by objectors, efforts broken up by police, workers were beaten and jailed
   c. possible answer—whites might be turned out of office if blacks voted

2. **a.** spoke at DNC; wanted rights and freedoms for African Americans
   b. to help Johnson win the election
   c. possible answer—no, they should have been happy to have some representation

3. **a.** effort to gain voting rights for African Americans in Selma, Alabama

   b. by showing the shocking and savage violence inflicted upon peaceful marchers
   c. possible answer—to stop the violence

4. Event—VEP; Twenty-fourth Amendment, Freedom Summer; Selma march; Injustice—voting rights denied; Effect—poll taxes outlawed, Voting Rights Act of 1965

5. possible answer—Twenty-fourth Amendment makes poll taxes illegal; will remove economic barriers to voting for African Americans

Reynolds v. Sims (1964)

Why It Matters *Reynolds* v. *Sims* provided the Court's philosophy behind the "one person, one vote" standard. Because of this ruling, all states had to change their methods for electing state legislators.

Background of the Case

By 1960 about three-fourths of Alabama voters lived in cities, but rural voters still controlled both houses of the legislature. A group of Birmingham citizens sued, claiming that their votes had substantially less impact than the votes of people from rural counties.

In earlier cases the Supreme Court ruled that federal courts could not tell state legislatures how to handle representation issues. But in 1960 the Court struck down an Alabama law designed to keep African American votes from deciding elections. This case opened the door to judicial review of apportionment decisions. However, the Birmingham plaintiffs still had to convince the Court that Alabama's legislative districts were so unfair as to be unconstitutional.

The Decision

Chief Justice Earl Warren wrote the opinion of the Court. He emphasized that the individual citizen is the key component of a democratic society:

> **❝**Legislators represent people, not trees or acres. Legislators are elected by voters, not farms or cities or economic interests . . . A citizen, a qualified voter, is no more nor no less so because he lives in the city or on the farm. This is the clear and strong command of our Constitution's Equal Protection Clause.**❞**

The Court held that seats in both branches of state legislatures had to be apportioned based on population. Each elected official in a particular state had to represent approximately the same number of voters. This "one person, one vote" standard has become a hallmark of democracy.

THE IMPACT TODAY Members of New York's state assembly wrap up a legislative session. Based on *Reynolds* v. *Sims*, seats in state legislatures must be apportioned based on population. The U.S. Census Bureau provides guidelines to assist states in gathering population data to redraw their district boundaries.

go.hrw.com
Research Online
Keyword: SS Court

CRITICAL THINKING

1. **Analyze the Impact** Using the keyword above, read about the decision in *Baker* v. *Carr*, decided two years before *Reynolds*. What was the issue in *Baker*? How did that decision pave the way for the plaintiffs in *Reynolds* to bring their case?

2. **You Be the Judge** The New York Education Law said that only the parents or guardians of public school children—or the owners or renters of property—could vote in school district elections. A man living in the Union School District No. 15 brought suit after he was not allowed to vote in a school district election. He was not a parent of a student and he neither rented nor owned property in the district. Does New York's law deny him equal protection? How should the court rule on his claim? Explain your reasoning in a paragraph.

THE CIVIL RIGHTS MOVEMENT **931**

Info to Know

Justice John Marshall Harlan Chief Justice Earl Warren has described the Supreme Court decision in this case as the most significant decision in his entire judicial career. The Court, however, was not unanimous in its decision; the vote was 8-1. Justice Harlan was the dissenter, and in his dissent Harlan argued that the decision supported " . . . a current mistaken view of the Constitution and the constitutional function of this Court. This view . . . is that every major social ill in this country can find its cure in some 'constitutional' principle . . . "

Info to Know

Reynolds v. *Sims* This Supreme Court decision was based on the Equal Protection Clause of the Fourteenth Amendment. The Court's decision in this case affected not only Alabama, but it also immediately affected apportionment in Colorado, Delaware, Maryland, New York, and Virginia.

Skills Focus: Analyzing Bias in Historical Interpretation   [At Level]

Reading Like a Historian Skill   **Research Required**
One Person, One Vote

1. Have students conduct outside research to find the decision written by Chief Justice Earl Warren and the dissent written by Justice Harlan. Have students also find commentary about the arguments both justices used in this case.

2. Have volunteers read the arguments written by the two justices to the class. Guide students in a discussion of the different views the two justices had about the role of Supreme Court in this case.

3. Have students use the arguments and their discussion notes to write an essay analyzing the ruling in *Reynolds* v. *Sims*. Then have students analyze bias they found in the legal commentaries about this landmark case.

LS Verbal-Linguistic

Alternative Assessment Handbook, Rubrics 1: Acquiring Information; and 18: Listening

Answers

Critical Thinking 1. *issue in* Baker *was that Tennessee's failure to redistrict had created electoral districts with significantly unequal population; issue in* Reynolds *was similar;* **2.** *possible answers—yes, as a voter and a citizen living in the district, he should be allowed equal protection and the right to vote; no, he has no abiding interest in the school district and its decisions do not affect him*

Changes and Challenges

BEFORE YOU READ

MAIN IDEA

Continued social and economic inequalities caused many young African Americans to lose faith in the civil rights movement and integration and seek alternative solutions.

READING FOCUS

1. Why did the civil rights movement expand to the North?
2. What fractures developed in the civil rights movement, and what was the result?
3. What events led to the death of Martin Luther King Jr., and how did the nation react?

KEY TERMS AND PEOPLE

de jure segregation
de facto segregation
Kerner Commission
Stokely Carmichael
Black Power
Black Panther Party
Malcolm X

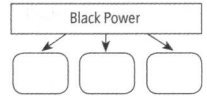

TAKING NOTES As you read, take notes on organizations that promoted Black Power during the 1960s. In each box of a diagram like the one below, fill in the name and details about one organization.

> Black Power

The March Against Fear

▼ King (left) and Carmichael (right) on the March Against Fear in Mississippi

932

THE INSIDE STORY

How did the March Against Fear widen a split in the civil rights movement? In June 1966 James Meredith, the University of Mississippi's first African American graduate, began a 27-day march from Memphis, Tennessee, to Jackson, Mississippi, to encourage African Americans to register to vote. On the second day of what he called his March Against Fear, Meredith was shot and wounded. About 150 SCLC and SNCC members gathered to finish his march. Among them were Martin Luther King Jr. of SCLC and SNCC's young new leader, Stokely Carmichael.

The march was a harrowing experience. Vehicles swerved at the marchers, forcing them off the highway. People threw bottles, rocks, and firecrackers. "What are we waiting for, till they kill some of us?" some marchers began to ask. "I'm not much for that nonviolence stuff any more," an angry marcher announced on the highway one day.

As they marched, demonstrators shouted the SCLC's familiar call-and-response chant: "What do we want?" "Freedom now!" Soon, however, SNCC marchers began offering a new response: "Black power!" Whenever the chant began, each side tried to drown out the other. Finally, King and Carmichael agreed to abandon the chant for the rest of the march. Journalists accompanying the march had already noticed the conflict, however. They reported this visible break in the unity of the civil rights movement. ▪

Preteach

Bellringer

The Inside Story. . . Use the **Daily Bellringer Transparency** to help students answer the question.

📗 Daily Bellringer Transparency, Section 4

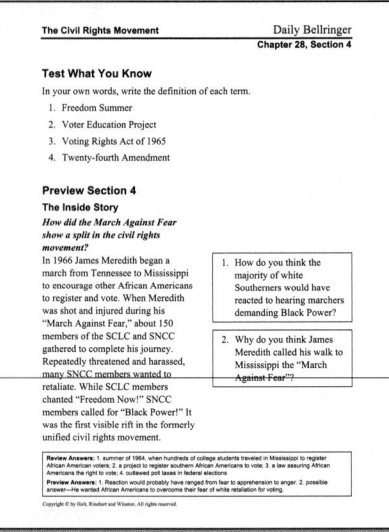

Taking Notes

Black Panthers: give African Americans control over their communities, used violence to attempt to do so; Black Muslims: preached messages of black nationalism, self-discipline and self-reliance; SNCC: new leader Stokely Carmichael focused on political and economic power

---

Teach the Main Idea

At Level

Changes and Challenges

1. **Teach** Ask students the Reading Focus questions to teach this section.

2. **Apply** Have students create an outline of the section using the red and blue headings as the main points.

3. **Review** Review the Reading Focus questions with the students. Have them use the information in their outlines to answer each of the questions.

4. **Practice/Homework** Have students create a sequencing diagram that lists and organizes the main changes and challenges of this period in chronological order. Have the students label their diagrams "Changes and Challenges." **LS Logical-Mathematical, Visual-Spatial**

📝 Alternative Assessment Handbook, Rubric 13: Graphic Organizers

De Facto Segregation

ECONOMIC CONDITIONS IN SELECTED CITIES, 1960

■ Minorities ■ Whites

Percentage of population earning less than $3,000 per year

(bar graph: y-axis Percentage 0–35; x-axis City — Chicago, Detroit, New York City)

Note: In 1960, the U.S. Census Bureau did not collect data by race at the metropolitan level. Instead, they collected data by white and non-white.

Source: *United States Census Bureau*

Skills FOCUS INTERPRETING GRAPHS

De facto segregation was reflected in the economic status of the population. How great was the difference in the incomes of whites and minorities in the cities shown in this graph?

See Skills Handbook, p. H16

About 350 demonstrators, guarded by police, march through an all-white Chicago neighborhood to protest housing discrimination in the Chicago real estate industry in 1966. Housing discrimination was a form of de facto segregation.

Expanding the Movement

The March Against Fear marked a turning point in the drive for civil rights. The movement had done much to bring an end to **de jure segregation**, or segregation by law, in the South. However, Meredith's shooting provided grim evidence that changes in laws had not altered attitudes. Especially outside the South, African Americans were challenging the movement's tactics. Many began to question whether nonviolent protest was the best means to genuine and permanent change.

Conditions outside the South African Americans in the South and outside the South faced similar but slightly different conditions. Most states did not deny African Americans voting rights. Nor did they require segregated public accommodations. Yet segregation was widespread in America. In most places it was **de facto segregation**—segregation that exists through custom and practice rather than by law. De jure segregation ends when the laws that create it are repealed. De facto segregation can be more difficult to overcome.

Most African Americans outside the South lived in cities. However, they often faced conditions like those faced by black southerners. For example, few real estate agents would take African Americans to homes for sale in white

neighborhoods. White homeowners willing to show their house to African American buyers incurred the anger of their neighbors. As a result, African Americans often had no choice but to live in all-black parts of town.

In addition, discrimination by banks made it hard to borrow money to buy or improve property in African American neighborhoods. This caused homeownership there to be low and many buildings to decay. Job discrimination against African Americans led to high unemployment and poverty in these neighborhoods, making the situation worse.

Urban unrest Frustration over these conditions exploded into violence. From 1964 to 1967, racial unrest erupted in most of the nation's large cities. Some of the worst violence took place in the poor, African American neighborhood of Watts in Los Angeles. In 1965, about 35,000 African Americans took part in a six-day riot that destroyed entire city blocks. Some 3,000 people were arrested and 34 were killed before police and troops restored order.

A week of violence in Detroit in July 1967 resulted in 43 deaths and thousands of injuries and arrests. After the riot, President Johnson

THE CIVIL RIGHTS MOVEMENT **933**

933

Expanding the Movement

Recall What reasons did the Kerner Commission give as the cause of urban rioting? *poverty and discrimination*

Explain Why did the SCLC campaign fail in Chicago? *African Americans were concerned about economic issues, not segregation issues.*

Info to Know

Discrimination Today—Hate Crimes
Hate crimes are a manifestation of discrimination. Like the discrimination in the South and the North, hate crimes are based on real or perceived differences among people. Hate crimes exist because of racial hatred, resentment of ethnic minorities, religious discrimination, and gender bias.

Teaching Tip

To help students understand the turmoil of the 1960s, remind them of these events that shocked the nation: John F. Kennedy assassinated, November 22, 1963; Malcolm X assassinated, February 21, 1965; Martin Luther King Jr. assassinated, April 4, 1968; Robert F. Kennedy assassinated, June 6, 1968.

Answers

Reading Check *expand civil rights progress to African Americans in northern cities, where the challenges were mainly economic*

934

Divisions within the Movement

Black Power

At the 1968 Summer Olympics, African American members of the U.S. track team Tommie Smith (left) and John Carlos (right) gave the Black Power salute as they received their medals. Many saw the Black Power movement as threatening because it abandoned the concept of non-violence.

Black Panther Party

The Black Panther Party formed in Oakland, California, in 1966 as a militant group that called for an armed revolution to achieve African American liberation.

Nation of Islam

Elijah Muhammad led the Nation of Islam from 1934 to 1975. Here he is speaking to a group of followers. The Nation of Islam promoted economic independence for African Americans as well as racial separation.

934

---

appointed the **Kerner Commission** to study the causes of urban rioting. Its report placed the blame on poverty and discrimination. "Our nation," the report warned, "is moving toward two societies, one black and one white—separate and unequal."

The movement moves north The riots convinced King that the movement's gains in the South had bypassed millions of African Americans. This awareness spurred him to focus his attention on Chicago in 1966.

The SCLC's Chicago campaign lasted eight months. It was one of King's biggest failures. Chicago's African Americans did not share his civil rights focus. They had the right to vote, and they did not consider themselves segregated. Their concerns were mainly economic.

Chicago authorities also failed to provide the confrontations that worked so well for King in the South. Chicago police had strict orders against using force. Without such brutality, King found it hard to attract the media attention on which he relied to sway public opinion.

In July, King took his marches into Chicago's white neighborhoods. This tactic worked. Residents showered marchers with rocks and bottles. Unlike in the South, however, police protected the marchers. In addition, King's new strategy weakened his northern white support. He found that some whites who had criticized racism in the South had no interest in seeing it exposed in the North. In August, King hollowly declared victory and left Chicago.

READING CHECK **Summarizing** What did King hope to accomplish by expanding the civil rights movement into Chicago?

Fractures in the Movement

Most white Americans viewed the civil rights movement as a unified effort. In fact, it was made up of diverse groups united by the goal of ending racial discrimination. By the mid-1960s, however, conflicts among these groups had developed.

The first signs of trouble arose from Freedom Summer in 1964. As harassment of SNCC and CORE workers in Mississippi increased, some of them rejected the philosophy of non-violence. As you have read, unity was further weakened when the NAACP, CORE, and the

---

Learners Having Difficulty

1. Tell students that in this chapter a number of civil rights groups are discussed, and many had abbreviations for their names.

2. Have students create a chart listing each of the civil rights groups discussed in the chapter, the abbreviation of the group's name, and the group's goals. Students should include the following in their charts: CORE, NAACP, SCLC, SNCC, VEP, MFDP.

3. Have volunteers share the information on their charts, and create a class chart for all to see. Have students correct their work and retain the charts as a study tool.

LS **Visual-Spatial, Intrapersonal**

📖 Alternative Assessment Handbook, Rubric 13: Graphic Organizers

🗄 Graphic Organizer Transparencies

Tactics of Change

Martin Luther King's commitment to nonviolence never wavered.

" [V]iolence . . . seeks to annihilate rather than convert . . . Nonviolence is a powerful and just weapon . . . which cuts without wounding and ennobles the man who wields it. "

Martin Luther King Jr., 1964

Malcolm X was blunt and uncompromising. He inspired hatred from some and respect from others.

" [N]ow you're facing a situation where the young Negro's coming up. They don't want to hear that 'turn-the-other-cheek' stuff, no. . . . There's new thinking coming in. There's new strategy coming in . . . It'll be ballots, or it'll be bullets. It'll be liberty, or it will be death. "

Malcolm X, 1964

Skills FOCUS READING LIKE A HISTORIAN

Identifying Points of View What does King mean when he says that nonviolence "cuts without wounding"? To what is Malcolm X referring when he speaks of "ballots" or "bullets"?

See Skills Handbook, pp. H28–H29

SCLC favored the compromise offered the Mississippi Freedom Democratic Party at the Democratic National Convention. SNCC members accused the other groups of betrayal.

Black Power Cracks in the movement widened in May 1966, when **Stokely Carmichael** replaced the moderate John Lewis as head of SNCC. Under Carmichael's leadership, SNCC abandoned the philosophy of nonviolence.

Carmichael's support of aggressive action became clear during the March Against Fear in June 1966. The SNCC leader was among those arrested when the marchers stopped in Greenwood, Mississippi. After being released, Carmichael addressed a rally of about 3,000 protesters. With his arm raised in a clenched-fist salute, he shouted his defiance.

HISTORY'S VOICES

" This is the twenty-seventh time I have been arrested—and I ain't going to jail no more. The only way we're going to stop them white men from whippin' us is to take over. We been saying freedom for six years—and we ain't got nothin'. What we gonna start now is 'Black Power!' "

—Stokely Carmichael, June 17, 1966

As onlookers cheered, Carmichael yelled, "What do you want?" "Black power!" the crowd roared back. The next day the slogan became newspaper headlines across the nation.

Many critics believed the Black Power movement to be a call to violent action. Carmichael rejected this interpretation. He explained **Black Power** as African Americans' dependence on themselves to solve problems. "Integration is irrelevant," he declared. "Political and economic power is what black people have to have." He called on African Americans to form their own separate political organizations.

Like SNCC, CORE also abandoned nonviolence and endorsed Black Power in 1966. In 1967 CORE gave up its commitment to being a multiracial organization.

The Black Panthers Black Power appealed to many young African Americans. It inspired two young community activists, Huey Newton and Bobby Seale, to found a group called the **Black Panther Party** in Oakland, California, in October 1966. The Panthers rejected nonviolence and called for violent revolution as a means of African American liberation.

THE CIVIL RIGHTS MOVEMENT **935**

Direct Teach

Reading Focus

❷ What fractures developed in the civil rights movement, and what was the result? *division among leaders about when to compromise and whether to use violent or nonviolent tactics*

Fractures in the Movement

Recall What was one of the first major signs of trouble in the civil rights movement? *when some members of CORE and SNCC members rejected the nonviolence philosophy*

Summarize What was Black Power? *movement encouraging African Americans to be self-reliant and form separate political organizations*

Draw Conclusions Why do you think that discontent developed in civil rights organizations in 1964? *possible answers—members had different expectations; tired of violent responses to their nonviolent tactics; differences in opinions among members; belief that different leaders would achieve different results, be more successful*

Counterpoints

Tactics of Change

Evaluate Ask students to identify the audiences they think Martin Luther King Jr. and Malcolm X appealed to. Why might some groups fear the philosophy of Malcolm X?

go.hrw.com
Online Resources
KEYWORD: SD7 CH28
TOPIC: BLACK POWER

Answers

Reading Like a Historian *King—nonviolence is as powerful as violence but leaves no physical marks; Malcolm X—grant African Americans the right to vote or violence will result*

Differentiating Instruction

Above Level

Advanced Learners/GATE

1. Write the following statement for the students to see: *The civil rights movement is broken beyond repair.* Have students copy the statement onto their own paper.

2. Have students review the information in the text and prepare reasoned arguments supported by facts that agree or disagree with the statement. Students may wish to conduct outside research on the issue and add that information to their arguments.

3. Organize a class debate on the issue. Have students use the arguments they prepared to support their position.

4. As an extension, have students write a summary of the arguments presented in the debate. **LS Kinesthetic, Logical-Mathematical**

📖 Alternative Assessment Handbook, Rubrics 10: Debates; and 37: Writing Assignments

935

Fractures in the Movement

Explain Who were the Black Muslims? *members of Nation of Islam; large, influential group that expressed ideas of Black Power*

Describe In what ways was Malcolm X different from Martin Luther King Jr.? *Malcolm X did not embrace philosophy of nonviolence; believed that it weakened African Americans and the civil rights movement*

Analyze Why do you think Malcolm X began to call for racial harmony? *possible answers—visit to Saudi Arabia instilled new ideas about peace and change; believed that civil rights leaders needed to work together to be most effective*

Biography

Alex Haley (1921–1992) Beginning in 1959, writer Alex Haley conducted a series of interviews with leading African Americans, including Elijah Muhammad, Miles Davis, and Muhammad Ali. Haley's interviews with Malcolm X resulted in *The Autobiography of Malcolm X*, an authoritative and widely respected biography of the Black Muslim leader. However, Haley is most well known for *Roots: The Saga of an American Family*. Published in 1976, this novel chronicles seven generations of the Haley family, from the enslavement of Haley's ancestors through Haley's own life. The book was adapted into a popular television miniseries and drew national attention to the history and modern issues of African Americans.

Answers

Reading Check *They rejected nonviolence as a means of protest.*

To achieve some of their goals, the Panthers carried guns and monitored African American neighborhoods to guard against police brutality. Confrontations between Black Panthers and the police in the late 1960s led to several shootouts resulting in deaths on both sides.

Black Muslims One of the largest and most influential groups expressing the ideas of Black Power was the Nation of Islam. Based on the Islamic religion, it was founded in 1930. Its members were called Black Muslims.

The group's leader, the Honorable Elijah Muhammad, preached a message of black nationalism, self-discipline, and self-reliance. Rules forbade smoking, gambling, and alcohol and stressed cleanliness and thrift. Men and women dressed conservatively. During the Great Depression, Black Muslims would not accept any government assistance.

By the 1960s the Nation of Islam had as many as 65,000 followers. Young African Americans, especially from the North's urban slums, were drawn to the Black Muslims' image and to a fiery minister known as **Malcolm X**. (Some Black Muslims took the surname "X" to represent the loss of their original, African identities.) Malcolm X offered a message of hope, defiance, and black pride. "Revolutions are never based upon . . . begging a corrupt society or a corrupt system to accept us into it," Malcolm X said. "Revolutions overturn systems."

At first, Malcolm X was also critical of King and nonviolence. "Any Negro who teaches other Negroes to turn the other cheek is disarming the Negro . . . [of] his natural right to defend himself," he charged. Many white Americans found his message frightening. King and other civil rights leaders thought him an extremist.

In 1964, however, Malcolm X broke with Elijah Muhammad and the Black Muslims. He visited Islam's holy sites in Saudi Arabia and returned a changed man. Although Malcolm X continued to preach Black Power, he began cooperating with other civil rights leaders and called for racial harmony. "If the white people realize what the alternative is," he noted, "perhaps they will be more willing to hear Dr. King." In February 1965, a few weeks after making this observation, Malcolm X was assassinated by Black Muslims who considered him a traitor to their cause.

READING CHECK **Identifying Supporting Details** How did Black Muslims reflect fractures in the civil rights movement?

The Death of Martin Luther King Jr.

Moments after Martin Luther King Jr. was shot, his aides frantically pointed to the source of the gunshots (left).

936

Skills Focus: Making Oral Presentations

At Level

Reading Like a Historian Skill
Eulogy for Martin Luther King Jr.

1. Review the information in the chapter about Martin Luther King Jr. Tell students that his assassination shocked the nation.

2. Have students work individually or in pairs to prepare a eulogy, a speech that is given at a funeral, to honor Martin Luther King Jr.

3. Have volunteers read their eulogies to the class. Then guide students in a review of the accomplishments of this civil rights leader.
Verbal-Linguistic, Interpersonal

Alternative Assessment Handbook, Rubric 24: Oral Presentations

The Assassination of King

King's disappointing Chicago campaign increased his awareness that economic issues must be part of the civil rights movement. With this in mind, he went to Memphis, Tennessee, in March 1968 to aid African American sanitation workers who were on strike against discrimination in the city's work and pay policies. King led a march to city hall on March 28 and then remained in Memphis to speak at a rally on April 3.

The next day James Earl Ray, a white sniper with a high-powered rifle, shot and killed King as he stood on the balcony of his motel. Within hours, rioting erupted in more than 120 cities as enraged African Americans across the nation responded to the assassination. Within three weeks, 46 people were dead, some 2,600 were injured, and more than 21,000 were arrested. Nearly 55,000 troops were required to restore order. One civil rights leader noted that King would have been outraged by the violent reaction to his death.

Robert Kennedy, who was running for president at the time, was about to give a campaign speech in an African American neighborhood of Indianapolis, Indiana, when he learned of

King's widow, Coretta Scott King, mourns at his funeral (left). Below, mules pull King's casket, symbolizing his work on behalf of the poor. Some 50,000 mourners joined the procession.

the shooting. After informing the audience of the tragedy, he recalled King's message while making an impassioned appeal for calm.

HISTORY'S VOICES

❝You can be filled with bitterness and with hatred and a desire for revenge. We can move in that direction as a country, in great polarization, black people amongst blacks and white people amongst whites, filled with hatred toward one another. Or we can make an effort, like Martin Luther King did, to understand and to comprehend, and replace that violence, that stain of bloodshed that has spread across the land, with . . . compassion and love.❞

—Robert Kennedy, April 4, 1968

READING CHECK **Summarizing** What were the circumstances of King's death?

SECTION 4 ASSESSMENT

go.hrw.com
Online Quiz
Keyword: SD7 HP28

Reviewing Ideas, Terms, and People

1. **a. Describe** What did the **Kerner Commission** conclude?
   b. Contrast What is the difference between **de jure segregation** and **de facto segregation**?
   c. Predict How do you think urban unrest could have been prevented or stopped?

2. **a. Identify** What was the **Black Panther Party**?
   b. Contrast How were the goals of supporters of the **Black Power** movement different from those of other civil rights groups?
   c. Elaborate Why do you think many African Americans were drawn to leaders such as **Stokely Carmichael** and **Malcolm X**?

3. **a. Describe** Why did Martin Luther King Jr. go to Memphis, Tennessee, in March 1968?
   b. Make Inferences Why would King have been upset about the public reaction to his death?
   c. Predict What long-term effect do you think King's death will have on the civil rights movement?

Critical Thinking

4. **Categorizing** Review your notes on the Black Power movement. Then copy the graphic organizer below and use it to list traditional and Black Power civil rights groups and leaders.

Traditional	Black Power

FOCUS ON WRITING

5. **Expository** Write a paragraph either for or against Black Power. Explain why you would or would not have supported its goals and methods.

THE CIVIL RIGHTS MOVEMENT **937**

SECTION 5 The Movement Continues

BEFORE YOU READ

MAIN IDEA

The civil rights movement was in decline by the 1970s, but its accomplishments continued to benefit American society.

READING FOCUS

1. How did the SCLC's goals change and with what results?
2. For what reasons did the Black Power movement decline?
3. What civil rights changes took place in the 1970s, and what were their results?

KEY TERMS AND PEOPLE

Poor People's Campaign
Ralph Abernathy
Civil Rights Act of 1968
affirmative action
John Lewis
Andrew Young
Jesse Jackson

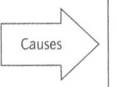 **TAKING NOTES** As you read, take notes on reasons why the civil rights movement declined during the 1970s. Record your notes in a graphic organizer like the one shown here.

Causes → Decline of Civil Rights Movement

THE INSIDE STORY *Would you endure miserable conditions to seek changes that you believed to be right?* A covered wagon pulled by mules would have attracted attention on the streets of Washington, D.C., even if not accompanied by tens of thousands of demonstrators protesting their poverty. Another strange sight was the community of tents and shacks that 2,500 of these protesters—African Americans, Native Americans, Hispanic Americans, and whites among them—occupied on the National Mall. They called their settlement Resurrection City.

Longtime SCLC leader Ralph Abernathy explained why the protesters were there. "The poor are no longer divided. We're not going to let the white man put us down any more," he declared. "It's not white power, and I'll give you some news, it's not black power, either. It's poor power and we're going to use it."

Unusually heavy spring rains quickly put Resurrection City ankle-deep in mud, making sanitation and trash collection difficult. Each day, however, determined groups of demonstrators organized marches from their miserable surroundings to federal agencies throughout the city. The marches were designed to demand that the government do more to combat poverty. "We have business on the road to freedom," Abernathy encouraged one group of protesters as they marched toward Capitol Hill: "We must prove to white America that you can kill the leader but you cannot kill the dream." ◼

▶ The Poor People's Campaign set off to combat economic inequality as the next phase of the civil rights movement.

The Poor People's Campaign

938 CHAPTER 28

Teach the Main Idea

At Level

The Movement Continues

1. **Teach** Ask students the Reading Focus questions to teach this section.

2. **Apply** Have students scan the chapter and make a list of the civil rights leaders that are discussed in the section. Then have students add information about each of these people and why they are important in the history of the civil rights movement.

3. **Review** As you review the section, guide students in a discussion of the sequence of events in the civil rights movement following the deaths of Malcolm X and Martin Luther King Jr.

4. **Practice/Homework** Have the students write a brief essay that summarizes the political advances made by African Americans in the 1960s and 1970s.
   LS Visual-Spatial, Verbal-Linguistic

📖 Alternative Assessment Handbook, Rubric 40: Writing to Describe

---

A Change in Goals

The **Poor People's Campaign** marked an important expansion of the civil rights movement. By 1967 changes in the law had achieved basic rights for African Americans. Martin Luther King Jr. believed, however, that most African Americans were still prevented from achieving equality because they were poor. He decided to alert the nation to the economic plight not only of African Americans, but of all poor people.

King's death prevented him from leading this effort. That task fell to his successor as the head of the SCLC, **Ralph Abernathy**. In May 1968, thousands of protesters came to the nation's capital to be part of the Poor People's Campaign. A Mississippi woman explained why she joined the protest.

HISTORY'S VOICES

❝I'm here because when I was a child, I got taken out of school and put to work on the farm helping my family . . . Then I got married and had kids, and my husband worked in the cotton fields . . . But he got sick and don't work much no more and there ain't hardly no cotton to get picked by hand anyway . . . So I came here with the Campaign to tell people that we got to be treated like human beings—that we have a right to live because we've earned that right but we've yet to be paid.❞

—Henrietta Franklin, quoted in the *Washington Post*, May 24, 1968

The Poor People's Campaign turned out to be a disaster. Besides bad weather, the SCLC experienced terrible media relations. Some Resurrection City residents harassed reporters. About 200 protesters turned out to be members of inner-city gangs. The campaign's organizers eventually sent them home. After six weeks of problems, police used tear gas to empty Resurrection City and then tore it down.

Without King's eloquence and leadership, the Poor People's Campaign also failed to express clearly the protesters' needs and demands. Some conservative members of Congress believed they saw elements of communism in the campaign's beliefs and goals. All these factors combined to cause the SCLC and its role in the civil rights movement to decline.

READING CHECK   Identifying the Main Idea
How did the Poor People's Campaign represent a change of goals for the civil rights movement?

The Decline of Black Power

The civil rights movement took place at the height of the Cold War, when the nation's fear of communism was at its height. FBI director J. Edgar Hoover was convinced that the major civil rights groups were led by Communists.

In 1956 Hoover created a secret program within the FBI to keep an eye on many types of groups that were involved in the unrest that was plaguing society. Spies and informers working for the FBI posed as supporters of these groups and reported the groups' plans and activities back to the government.

At first, King was Hoover's main target in the civil rights movement. As the Black Power movement grew, however, he instructed his agents to disrupt and otherwise interfere with the activities of other civil rights groups he considered a threat to American society.

For example, to disrupt SNCC—and at the same time weaken the Black Panthers—FBI spies in SNCC spread false rumors that the Panthers intended to kill SNCC leaders. The FBI also forged harmful posters, leaflets, and correspondence that appeared to come from the groups it had targeted.

Hoover was especially concerned about the Black Panthers. The FBI encouraged local authorities to combat the Panthers by any means possible. Police raided the Panthers'

THE CIVIL RIGHTS MOVEMENT **939**

The Congressional Black Caucus

Retired North Carolina Supreme Court Chief Justice Henry Frye swears in members of the Congressional Black Caucus of the 109th Congress. Founded in 1970 as an organization of African American members of the House of Representatives, the group's mission is to address legislative concerns of black and minority citizens.

AFRICAN AMERICAN GAINS IN THE CIVIL RIGHTS MOVEMENT

African American Elected Officials:
1,469 in 1970; 9,040 in 2000

African Americans Not Living in Poverty:
45% in 1960; 78% in 2000

African American College Graduates:
3.3% in 1960; 16.5% in 2000

headquarters in cities across the country. Since Black Panthers usually were armed, violent conflict sometimes resulted. Law enforcement authorities also sometimes shot Black Panther members whether they resisted or not. By the early 1970s, armed violence had led to the killing or arrest of many Black Panther leaders. Others had fled the United States in order to avoid arrest.

SNCC also collapsed with FBI help. In 1967, H. Rap Brown replaced Stokely Carmichael as head of SNCC. Urged on by his staff—many of whom were on the FBI's payroll—Brown took increasingly radical and shocking positions. As a result, SNCC's membership declined rapidly. The group disbanded in the early 1970s.

> **READING CHECK** Identifying Main Ideas
> How did federal action help lead to a decline of the Black Power movement?

New Changes and Gains

In spite of the challenges, the civil rights movement did make gains in the late 1960s. For example, just a week after Martin Luther King Jr.'s death, President Johnson signed the **Civil Rights Act of 1968**. Also called the Fair Housing Act, the law banned discrimination in the sale or rental of housing.

Busing and political change Despite the 1954 *Brown* decision, urban schools were still largely segregated in the late 1960s. This was a result of de facto segregation. Years of housing discrimination had contributed to segregated neighborhoods in many cities.

The Fair Housing Act was a step toward ending this situation. However, it would take years to overcome decades of discrimination and to achieve integrated neighborhoods. Meanwhile, many city schools would remain segregated.

To speed integration of city schools, courts began ordering that some students be bused from their neighborhoods to schools in other parts of the city. Busing met fierce opposition, especially in the North. Court-ordered busing in Boston in 1974, for example, led to two years of sometimes violent protests. Denver opponents of busing burned school buses.

Forced busing speeded the migration of whites from cities to suburbs. This development increased the political power of African Americans. By 1974 Cleveland, Detroit, Los Angeles, Washington, Atlanta, and several smaller cities had elected black mayors.

Affirmative action As you read in Section 2, the Civil Rights Act of 1964 banned discrimination in employment. By the late 1960s, the U.S. Justice Department was taking legal

940 CHAPTER 28

action against employers for violating this law. At the same time, the government helped businesses and colleges set up **affirmative action** programs that gave preference to minorities and women in hiring and admissions. These programs were designed to help make up for past discrimination against these groups.

Affirmative action and busing were divisive issues in the 1970s. It is difficult to assess clearly their contribution to the Republican Party's success in the late 1900s and early 2000s. However, backlash against these programs helped Republicans lure two important groups of voters away from the Democratic Party—white southerners and urban, working-class whites.

The new Black Power As African Americans in the South exercised their newly won voting rights—and were more politically active nationwide—it became clear that Black Power did not die in the 1970s. It merely took on a new form and meaning.

By 1970 the populations of more than 100 counties in the South were at least 50 percent African American. The African Americans who took over elected offices in these and other places governed as well as the white officials they replaced. In addition, many African Americans who played important roles in the civil rights movement later provided other services to the nation. For example, Thurgood Marshall,

the NAACP lawyer who argued the *Brown* case before the Supreme Court, later became the Court's first African American justice.

John Lewis took part in some of the first sit-ins in 1960. He was also a Freedom Rider in 1961 and participated in the Selma march in 1965. The head of SNCC in the early 1960s, Lewis was elected in 1986 to the first of many terms representing the people of Atlanta, Georgia, in Congress.

As a staff member of the SCLC and a close adviser to King, **Andrew Young** played a key role in the 1963 Birmingham campaign and in the Selma march. In 1972 he became Georgia's first African American member of Congress since Reconstruction. Young later served as U.S. ambassador to the United Nations and as mayor of Atlanta. You will read more about Young's career later in this book.

Jesse Jackson was another young activist who went on to leave his own mark on the nation. Jackson founded his own civil rights organization, Operation PUSH, and became an international figure for his work on behalf of poor and oppressed peoples around the world. His campaigns for the Democratic presidential nomination in the 1980s raised the real possibility that the nation might one day have an African American president.

READING CHECK **Summarizing** What political changes did busing, affirmative action, and Black Power bring to America in the 1970s?

ACADEMIC VOCABULARY

assess determine the importance of

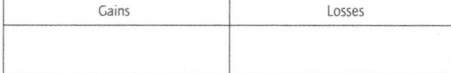

SECTION 5 ASSESSMENT

go.hrw.com
Online Quiz
Keyword: SD7 HP28

Reviewing Idea, Terms, and People

1. **a. Identify** Who succeeded Martin Luther King Jr. as head of the SCLC?
   b. Analyze Why did the Poor People's Campaign fail?
   c. Elaborate Why did Martin Luther King Jr. treat poverty as a civil rights issue?

2. **a. Describe** How did J. Edgar Hoover and the FBI weaken the Black Panthers?
   b. Make Inferences How did the Cold War influence Hoover and the FBI's attitude about the Black Power movement?

3. **a. Define** What was busing, and what was its purpose?
   b. Contrast How was the role of Black Power different during and after the 1970s than before the 1970s?
   c. Elaborate Why do you think many people have opposed affirmative action?

Critical Thinking

4. **Identifying Supporting Details** Review your notes on the decline of the civil rights movement. Then copy the graphic organizer below and use it to list gains and losses for African Americans that accompanied the movement's decline.

Gains	Losses

FOCUS ON WRITING

5. **Expository** Write a statement suggesting ways to prevent the civil rights movement from declining. Include an assessment of whether the civil rights movement is needed today.

THE CIVIL RIGHTS MOVEMENT **941**

• **Direct Teach** •

Reading Focus

New Changes and Gains

Recall What was the new Black Power? *the empowerment of African Americans, which enabled them to take on new leadership roles in their communities*

Describe How did John Lewis, Andrew Young, and Jesse Jackson become leaders of the new Black Power? *Lewis elected to Congress representing Georgia; Young became Georgia's first African American member of Congress since Reconstruction; Jesse Jackson founded the civil rights organization, Operation PUSH*

📄 CRF: Literature Activity: *A Raisin in the Sun* by Lorraine Hansberry

• **Review & Assess** •

Close

Guide students in a discussion of the decline of the civil rights movement and the impact of the movement on the lives of African Americans today.

Review

🔵 Online Quiz, Section 5

📦 Daily Test Practice Transparency

Assess

SE Section 5 Assessment

📄 Progress Assessment: Section 5 Quiz

📄 Alternative Assessment Handbook

Reteach

📄 Interactive Reader and Study Guide, Section 5

💿 Interactive Skills Tutor CD-ROM

Answers

Reading Check *new educational and employment opportunities for African Americans*

941

The Government and Equal Rights

Word Help

integration the bringing together of different racial or ethnic groups

domestic of one's home country

Info to Know

White Citizens Councils To some white southerners, May 17, 1954, was known as "Black Monday." That was the day that the U.S. Supreme Court handed down its decision in the case of *Brown* v. *Board of Education*, outlawing segregation in public schools. Many southerners saw the ruling as a threat to their way of life. In September 1954, opponents of desegregation in Mississippi organized White Citizens Councils. These groups held mass meetings, supported pro-segregation legislation, gave out pamphlets, and used economic pressure against both African Americans and whites who supported desegregation. By 1955, White Citizens Councils had 50,000 members and were active in several states.

The Government and Equal Rights

Historical Context The documents below provide information on views of government intervention for equal rights.

Task Examine the documents and answer the questions that follow. Then you will be asked to write an essay about the federal government's role in establishing equal rights for Americans, using facts from the documents and from the chapter to support the position you take in your thesis statement.

DOCUMENT 1

Many white southerners viewed integration as a social question that should not be answered by the federal government. Some argued that segregation would eventually end on its own. Federal intervention, they argued, would only create hostility and resentment. Robert Patterson was a white Mississippi native who opposed government-enforced integration. In the following interview, he explained his views on the integration of restaurants and motels.

> "That's not social integration, that's forced integration under the might of the federal government . . . To be subjected to integration is one thing, but to submit to it is something else entirely. We are being subjected to integration; we're not submitting to it. And you will find that white people do not frequent places where there are a whole lot of Negroes through choice. And I think gradually . . . things will resegregate themselves."

DOCUMENT 2

Some people who supported civil rights cautioned that the federal government risked a backlash if it moved too fast to change society. Clifford H. Baldowski was a white editorial cartoonist for the *Atlanta Journal-Constitution* who supported civil rights. The following cartoon, published in 1963, depicts Attorney General Robert F. Kennedy trying to ensure the success of needed federal civil rights legislation.

". . . Wait a minute . . . Somebody has gotta keep this thing on the track!"

Skills Focus: Recognizing Bias

Below Level

Reading Like a Historian Skill
Perspectives on Segregation

1. Guide the class in a discussion of Document 1. Ask students to look for examples of bias. How does Patterson try to make his arguments appear legitimate? Why does Patterson compare the relationship between southern whites and African Americans to the relationship between Jews and Arabs?

2. Divide the class into small groups. Have each group review Document 2, 3, or 4 and identify examples of bias. Encourage students to distinguish between facts and opinions in each document.

3. Have a volunteer from each group share their findings with the class. Guide the class in a discussion of whether or not any document can be free from bias. **LS Interpersonal, Logical-Mathematical**

DOCUMENT 3

Many African Americans did not believe that white officials in the South would protect equal rights unless the federal government forced them to do so. Fannie Lou Hamer called on the federal government to intervene in Mississippi, a state in which a majority black population was largely prevented from participating in local and state government. In the following interview, she recalled how Byron De La Beckwith, the assassin of civil rights leader Medgar Evers, was set free by two all-white juries.

"America that is divided against itself cannot stand, and we cannot say that we have all this unity they say we have when black people are being discriminated against in every city in America I have visited.

"I was in jail [for protesting] when Medgar Evers was murdered and nothing, I mean nothing has been done about that . . . We can no longer ignore the fact that America is NOT the 'land of the free and the home of the brave.'"

DOCUMENT 4

Some African American leaders warned the federal government that it needed to enforce equal rights not just because it was the right thing to do but in order to prevent violence. In the following speech from 1964, Malcolm X urged government leaders to enforce equal rights before people took matters into their own hands.

"America is the only country in history in a position to bring about a revolution without violence and bloodshed. But America is not morally equipped to do so.

Why is America in a position to bring about a bloodless revolution? Because the Negro in this country holds the balance of power and if the Negro in this country were given what the Constitution says he is supposed to have, the added power of the Negro in this country would sweep all of the racists and segregationists out of office. It would change the entire political structure of the country. It would wipe out the southern segregationism that now controls America's foreign policy, as well as America's domestic policy.

And the only way without bloodshed that this can be brought about is that the black man has to be given full use of the ballot in every one of the 50 states. But if the black man doesn't get the ballot, then you are going to be faced with another man who forgets the ballot and starts using the bullet."

Skills FOCUS — READING LIKE A HISTORIAN

1. **a. Identify** Refer to Document 1. To Patterson, what is the difference between "subjected" and "submitting"?
   b. Elaborate Do you think Patterson sees voluntary integration ever taking place without force? Explain.

2. **a. Describe** Refer to Document 2. Who is driving?
   b. Interpret What does this cartoon reflect about the role that Robert F. Kennedy played in civil rights legislation?

3. **a. Identify** Refer to Document 3. What is the main hypocrisy that Hamer sees?
   b. Analyze How does the example of Byron De La Beckwith support Hamer's call for federal intervention?

4. **a. Describe** Refer to Document 4. To Malcolm X, what was the most important right that the government needed to protect for African Americans?
   b. Elaborate Do you think Malcolm X's reasons for needing government intervention are valid? Explain.

5. **Document-Based Essay Question** Consider the question below and form a thesis statement. Using examples from Documents 1, 2, 3, and 4, create an outline and write a short essay supporting your position. What role should the government have in enforcing equal rights for Americans?

See **Skills Handbook**, pp. H28–H29, H30

THE CIVIL RIGHTS MOVEMENT **943**

Skills Focus: Comparing and Contrasting

At Level

Reading Skill
The Road to Equality

1. Remind students that Fannie Lou Hamer and Malcolm X both worked for the same cause: equal rights for African Americans.

2. Pair students. Have each pair create a list of similarities in the approaches Fannie Lou Hamer and Malcolm X took toward equal rights. Then have them list differences in the two leaders' approaches.

3. Have volunteers share their lists. Write the answers on the board to create a class list.

4. Guide the class in a discussion of the approaches the two leaders took in the struggle for equal rights. Ask students what other approaches might have been effective.

LS Interpersonal, Logical-Mathematical

Alternative Assessment Handbook, Rubric 9: Comparing and Contrasting

943

CHAPTER
28

Chapter Review

Visual Summary

Review and Inquiry Organize students into five groups. Assign each group one of the sections of the chapter and the information in the Visual Summary. Have students write a radio announcement with a two-sentence summary of the events in their section. Then have volunteers from each group make the radio announcement of the events.

Quick Facts Transparency: The Civil Rights Movement

Reviewing Key Terms and People

1. Civil Rights Act of 1964
2. John Lewis
3. de facto segregation
4. Freedom Riders
5. Freedom Summer
6. Jesse Jackson
7. Martin Luther King Jr.
8. Medgar Evers
9. Twenty-fourth Amendment

Comprehension and Critical Thinking

10. **a.** ban against discrimination in defense-related work, founding of CORE, 1948 desegregation of the armed forces, addition of Jackie Robinson to the Brooklyn Dodgers
    b. walked, shared cars, set up carpools to avoid using the bus system
    c. Their earlier cases gradually chipped away at the *Plessy* ruling; the Court ruled to integrate several law schools.

11. **a.** conduct nonviolent protests against segregation
    b. forced him to send in federal troops
    c. peaceful demonstrations; made reactions seem ugly and violent

Visual Summary: The Civil Rights Movement

Fighting Segregation	Freedom Now!	Voting Rights	Changes and Challenges	The Movement Continues
• Early civil rights groups included the NAACP and CORE. • In 1954 the Supreme Court ordered an end to racial segregation in public schools. • A bus boycott in Montgomery, Alabama, launched the SCLC and the modern civil rights movement.	• Sit-ins and Freedom Rides provoked violent reactions from some white southerners. • Violent response to marches in Birmingham, Alabama, shocked the nation. • The March on Washington helped lead to the Civil Rights Act of 1964.	• Some white southerners tried to block efforts of African Americans to vote. • African Americans in Mississippi organized to increase their political power. • A brutal attack on a protest in Selma, Alabama, helped win support for the Voting Rights Act of 1965.	• Civil rights leaders began attacking de facto segregation in the North in the mid-1960s. • Differences within the civil rights movement weakened it and led to the rise of Black Power. • The assassination of Martin Luther King Jr. caused urban unrest.	• King's death and the Poor People's Campaign helped lead to the decline of SCLC. • Internal divisions and an FBI campaign weakened some civil rights groups. • The civil rights movement resulted in important gains for African Americans.

Reviewing Key Terms and People

Identify the correct term or person from the chapter that best fits each of the following descriptions.

1. Law banning discrimination in employment and in public facilities
2. Leader of SNCC in the 1960s who many years later was elected to Congress from the state of Georgia
3. A type of discrimination that exists through custom and practice instead of by law
4. Groups of people who traveled through the South challenging segregation at bus stations
5. Project for college students to spend their summer vacation registering African Americans to vote in Mississippi
6. African American politician and civil rights leader who campaigned for the Democratic presidential nomination in the 1980s
7. Minister and civil rights leader who supported nonviolent resistance
8. NAACP leader who was murdered at his home by a member of the Ku Klux Klan
9. Part of the Constitution banning states from taxing citizens to vote in elections

Comprehension and Critical Thinking

SECTION 1 *(pp. 908–915)*

10. **a. Recall** What civil rights gains were made in the 1940s?
    b. Analyze How did the African American community support the Montgomery bus boycott?
    c. Elaborate How did Thurgood Marshall and the NAACP's earlier work contribute to the *Brown v. Board of Education of Topeka, Kansas,* decision?

12. **a.** registered southern African Americans to vote
    b. to prove that the movement could not be easily stopped or put down
    c. showed the Democratic Party that African Americans would take the actions necessary to gain a voice in the party

13. **a.** "Black Power!"
    b. economic hardships, discrimination, poverty
    c. King made an effort to replace violence with compassion and love to make a difference.

14. **a.** Lewis represented Georgia in Congress; Young served as Georgia's first African American member of Congress since Reconstruction, as the U.S. ambassador to the United Nations, and as the mayor of Atlanta.
    b. FBI intervention and a decline of membership
    c. possible answer—better media relations and a stronger, more positive voice for finding nonviolent solutions to poverty

History's Impact video program

Review the video to answer the closing question: How did civil rights activists push for equality during the 1950s and 1960s?

SECTION 2 *(pp. 916–923)*

11. a. Identify What were the goals of SNCC?

b. Draw Conclusions What effect did racial violence have on President Kennedy's approach to civil rights?

c. Evaluate What do you think made the strategy of nonviolence effective?

SECTION 3 *(pp. 925–930)*

12. a. Describe What did Freedom Summer accomplish?

b. Draw Conclusions Why did Martin Luther King Jr. resume the march from Selma to Montgomery, Alabama after it met with violence?

c. Predict How do you think the actions of the Mississippi Freedom Democratic Party affected the Democratic Party?

SECTION 4 *(pp. 932–937)*

13. a. Identify What slogan did Stokely Carmichael introduce at a SNCC rally?

b. Compare How were conditions similar for African Americans in the South and in the North?

c. Elaborate Why is the legacy of Martin Luther King Jr. so important?

SECTION 5 *(pp. 938–941)*

14. a. Describe How did civil rights leaders such as John Lewis and Andrew Young continue serving the nation after the 1960s?

b. Analyze Why did SNCC collapse?

c. Predict What could have made the Poor People's Campaign more successful?

Using the Internet

go.hrw.com
Practice Online
Keyword: SD7 CH28

15. The policy of affirmative action resulted from the civil rights movement, but it remains controversial today. Using the keyword above, do research to learn about court cases and controversies related to affirmative action. Then create a report that analyzes how these questions and decisions have shaped affirmative action policies today.

Analyzing Primary Sources

Reading Like a Historian Read the History's Voices passage in Section 2 from Diane Nash that begins: "We would practice such things …" Nash was training to take part in civil rights demonstrations.

16. Identify What were the civil rights workers practicing?

17. Draw Conclusions Why do you think civil rights workers needed this kind of training?

Critical Reading

Read the passage in Section 4 that begins with the heading "Fractures in the Movement." Then answer the question that follows.

18. The first major signs of trouble in the civil rights movement occurred when some workers

A rejected the philosophy of nonviolence.

B split off and formed their own groups.

C made speeches in favor of Black Power.

D disagreed at the 1964 Democratic National Convention.

WRITING FOR THE SAT

Think about the following issue.

Martin Luther King Jr. was an inspiring leader who was highly effective at communicating and motivating African Americans and whites. He was clearly the most important and influential leader of the civil rights movement in the mid-1950s through the late 1960s.

19. Assignment Did King's death bring an end to the civil rights movement? Write a short essay in which you develop your position on this issue. Support your point of view with reasoning and examples from your reading and studies.

Answers

Using the Internet

15. Go to the HRW Web site and enter the keyword shown to access a rubric for this activity.

KEYWORD: SD7 CH28

Analyzing Primary Sources

16. defending against violence and responding to such attacks

17. possible answer—often attacked violently even if peacefully protesting

Critical Reading

18. B

Writing for the SAT

19. possible answer—no, positive changes continued to occur

A rubric for this activity is provided in Chapter Resource File: Writing for the SAT Activity: Affirmative Action.

History's Impact Video Program

many civil rights groups used sit-ins, marches, speeches, and other forms of protest to fight for equality

Review and Assessment Resources

Review and Reinforce

📓 CRF: Chapter Review Activity

🖥 Quick Facts Transparencies: Early Civil Rights Victories, Major Civil Rights Reforms, The Civil Rights Movement

🔊 Spanish Chapter Summaries Audio CD Program

💻 Online Chapter Summaries in Spanish

OSP Holt PuzzlePro; Quiz Show for ExamView

💿 Quiz Game CD-ROM

Assess

📝 PASS: Chapter Test, Forms A and B

📝 Alternative Assessment Handbook

OSP ExamView Test Generator, Chapter Test

💿 Differentiated Instruction Modified Worksheets and Tests CD-ROM: Chapter Test

HOAP Holt Online Assessment Program (in the Premier Online Edition)

Reteach/Intervene

📓 Interactive Reader and Study Guide

🖥 Differentiated Instruction Teacher Management System: Lesson Plans for Differentiated Instruction

💿 Differentiated Instruction Modified Worksheets and Tests CD-ROM: Chapter Test

💿 Interactive Skills Tutor CD-ROM

go.hrw.com
Online Resources

KEYWORD: SD7 CH28

Chapter 29 Planning Guide

The Vietnam War

Chapter Overview	Reproducible Resources	Technology Resources
CHAPTER 29 pp. 946–983 **Overview:** In this chapter, students will analyze the causes and resolution of the Vietnam War.	**Differentiated Instruction Teacher Management System:*** • Instructional Benchmarking Guides • Lesson Plans for Differentiated Instruction **Interactive Reader and Study Guide:** Chapter Summary* **Chapter Resource File:*** • Focus on Writing Activity: The Response to the Protests at the 1968 Democratic Convention • Social Studies Skills Activity: Interpreting Cartograms • Chapter Review Activity **American History Outline Maps** **Pre-AP Activities Guide for American History***	**Live Ink® Online Reading Help** **Student Edition on Audio CD Program** **Differentiated Instruction Modified Worksheets and Tests CD-ROM** **Interactive Skills Tutor CD-ROM** **United States History Primary Source Library CD-ROM** **Power Presentations with Video CD-ROM** **History's Impact: American History Video Program (VHS/DVD):** The Vietnam War **Online Chapter Summaries in Spanish**
Section 1: **The War Develops** **The Main Idea:** Concern about the spread of communism led the United States to become increasingly involved in Vietnam.	**Differentiated Instruction Teacher Management System:** Section 1 Lesson Plan* **Interactive Reader and Study Guide:** Section 1 Summary* **Chapter Resource File:*** • Vocabulary Builder Activity, Section 1	**Daily Bellringer Transparency:** Section 1* **Map Transparency:** Indochina, 1950* **Internet Activity:** Growing Conflicts in Vietnam
Section 2: **U.S. Support of the War at Home and Abroad** **The Main Idea:** As the United States sent increasing numbers of troops to defend South Vietnam, some Americans began to question the war.	**Differentiated Instruction Teacher Management System:** Section 2 Lesson Plan* **Interactive Reader and Study Guide:** Section 2 Summary* **Chapter Resource File:*** • Vocabulary Builder Activity, Section 2	**Daily Bellringer Transparency:** Section 2* **Internet Activity:** Soldiers' Memories
Section 3: **1968: A Turning Point** **The Main Idea:** As the Vietnam War dragged on and increasingly appeared to be unwinnable, deep divisions developed in American society.	**Differentiated Instruction Teacher Management System:** Section 3 Lesson Plan* **Interactive Reader and Study Guide:** Section 3 Summary* **Chapter Resource File:*** • Vocabulary Builder Activity, Section 3	**Daily Bellringer Transparency:** Section 3* **Map Transparency:** The Vietnam Conflict, 1964–1975* **Internet Activity:** Conflicts at Home
Section 4: **The War Ends** **The Main Idea:** President Nixon eventually ended U.S. involvement in Vietnam, but the war had lasting effects.	**Differentiated Instruction Teacher Management System:** Section 4 Lesson Plan* **Interactive Reader and Study Guide:** Section 4 Summary* **Chapter Resource File*:** • Vocabulary Builder Activity, Section 4	**Daily Bellringer Transparency:** Section 4* **Internet Activity:** Last Phases of the Vietnam War

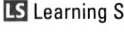 

HOLT

History's Impact
American History Video Program (VHS/DVD)

The Vietnam War

Review, Assessment, Intervention

 Quick Facts Transparencies: Causes of the Vietnam War, The Vietnam War

 Spanish Chapter Summaries Audio CD Program

 Progress Assessment Support System (PASS): Chapter Test*

Differentiated Instruction Modified Worksheets and Tests CD-ROM: Modified Chapter Test

OSP **One-Stop Planner CD-ROM:** ExamView Test Generator (English/Spanish)

HOAP **Holt Online Assessment Program (HOAP),** in the Holt Premier Online Student Edition

 PASS: Section 1 Quiz*
 Online Quiz: Section 1
 Alternative Assessment Handbook

PASS: Section 2 Quiz*
Online Quiz: Section 2
Alternative Assessment Handbook

 PASS: Section 3 Quiz*
 Online Quiz: Section 3
 Alternative Assessment Handbook

 PASS: Section 4 Quiz*
 Online Quiz: Section 4
 Alternative Assessment Handbook

 **RESOURCES**

The following resources were developed to help North Carolina educators teach the standards and objectives of North Carolina's eleventh grade standard course of study in United States history.

- United States history EOC Test Prep Workbook
- Teacher's Support System
- North Carolina One-Stop Planner

And be sure to direct your students to **go.hrw.com** for online access to the EOC Test Prep Workbook.

go.hrw.com
EOC Test Prep
KEYWORD: SE7 NC

Holt Online Learning

go.hrw.com
Teacher Resources
KEYWORD: SD7 TEACHER

go.hrw.com
Student Resources
KEYWORD: SD7 CH29

- Document-based Questions
- Interactive Multimedia Activities

- Current Events
- Chapter-based Internet Activities
- and more!

Holt Premier
Online Student Edition
Complete online support for interactivity, assessment, and reporting

- Interactive Maps and Notebook
- Standardized Test Prep
- Homework Practice and Research Activities Online

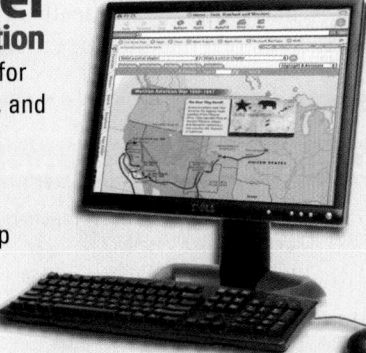

CHAPTER 29 PLANNING GUIDE

The Big Picture

Robert D. Schulzinger

Roots of a War Americans consistently considered Vietnam through the lens of global American interests, and they often ignored Vietnamese realities. The United States supported France in its war against Ho Chi Minh's Vietminh, but in 1954 declined to send American troops to fight alongside the French. After French forces surrendered, the United States backed the creation of South Vietnam, and in 1960 sent military advisers to help that republic suppress a Communist-led insurgency. John F. Kennedy sent more advisers after he became president, but the government of South Vietnam continued to lose popular support among its people. American leaders secretly helped South Vietnamese army officers plot to depose leader Ngo Dinh Diem, who was killed in November 1963.

The American War President Lyndon Johnson greatly expanded the American role in the war with massive air attacks and more than 500,000 ground troops. The Americans sought to prevent the infiltration of troops and supplies from North to South and to destroy Viet Cong and North Vietnamese forces in the South, but it was difficult for American commanders to show progress in a war without front lines. The American armed forces included many draftees who were younger, poorer, and less well-educated than troops in World War II or Korea. A large antiwar movement developed as the war continued and the events of 1968 shook American confidence.

The End of the War President Richard Nixon tried to end American military involvement in Vietnam while preserving the independence of South Vietnam. The United States steadily reduced its troop levels in Vietnam from 1969 to 1972 and negotiated peace with North Vietnam. The two countries agreed to a cease fire and the removal of all American forces in 1973, but the deadly war resumed between North and South Vietnam. The North and the Viet Cong defeated the government of South Vietnam in 1975 and unified the country under Communist rule.

Recent Scholarship

What Might Have Happened? What would John F. Kennedy have done in Vietnam had he not been assassinated in November 1963? President Lyndon Johnson insisted that he tried to follow Kennedy's policies in Vietnam, but many Americans later questioned whether the United States would have been so deeply involved in Vietnam had Kennedy lived. Fredrik Logevall argues in *Choosing War: The Lost Chance for Peace and the Escalation of War in Vietnam* (1999) that Johnson consistently favored more assertive policies toward the war than Kennedy wanted, and that Johnson ignored real opportunities to end the war in 1964.

Differentiating Instruction

 Differentiated Instruction Teacher Management System
- Lesson Plans for Differentiated Instruction
- Differentiated Instructional Benchmarking Guides
- Interactive Reader and Study Guide

Spanish Chapter Summaries Audio CD Program

 Online Chapter Summaries in Spanish

Student Edition on Audio CD Program

 Differentiated Instruction Modified Worksheets and Tests CD-ROM
- Vocabulary Flash Cards
- Modified Vocabulary Builder Activities
- Modified Chapter Review Activity
- Modified Chapter Test

OSP One-Stop Planner CD-ROM
- ExamView Test Generator (English and Spanish)
- PuzzlePro
- Quiz Show for ExamView
- Transparencies and Videos

TE Differentiated Activities in the Teacher's Edition
- Colonial Vietnam, p. 949
- The Air War, p. 957
- 1968 Presidential Election, p. 967
- Air Strikes in Cambodia, p. 973

Reading Like a Historian
Sam Wineburg

History and Our Right to Know

Near midnight on August 4, 1964, President Lyndon Johnson went on television to address the American people. He told them of "repeated acts of violence" committed by the North Vietnamese, who had attacked a U.S. patrol boat, the *Maddox*, two days before.

In describing these events, our chapter uses delicate language. "Later it was learned," we are told on page 955, "that President Johnson did not present a completely accurate picture of the incident in the Gulf of Tonkin."

Learning the Truth

Two questions arise. First, what does our chapter mean when it says that "Johnson had not presented a complete picture"? Second, how was the truth "later learned"?

Both questions require that we go back a few steps. Early in the day on August 4, 1964, President Johnson sent Secretary of Defense Robert McNamara to brief members of Congress about the situation in the Gulf of Tonkin. When McNamara suggested that the *Maddox* attack was unprovoked, he met fierce opposition from Senator Wayne Morse (D-OR).

Morse claimed that McNamara was withholding from Congress a crucial bit of information. Several days before the *Maddox* incident, South Vietnamese gunships had shelled Hon Me and Hon Ngu, two small islands close to the North Vietnamese coastline. "I think we are kidding the world," Morse told McNamara, "if you try to give the impression that when the South Vietnamese naval boats bombarded two islands . . . we were not implicated."

McNamara's Claim

McNamara bristled at the thought. With his trademark certainty, he responded: "Our Navy played absolutely no part in, was not associated with, and was not aware of, any South Vietnamese actions . . . I say this flatly, this is the fact."

When McNamara said this, he was deceiving Congress and lying to the American people.

The Facts

From documents that have since come to light, we now know of OPLAN 34A, a series of joint covert actions between the U.S. military, the CIA, and the South Vietnamese forces. As John Prados of George Washington University's National Security Archive wrote, "The 34-A missions were unilaterally controlled by the U.S., using boats procured and maintained by the U.S. Navy, attacking targets selected by the CIA, in an operation paid for by the United States."

Elsewhere, McNamara implicated himself in this ruse. When he called Johnson on the morning of August 4 to confer about his appearance before the Senate, he made a suggestion—ultimately rejected—of sharing information with Congress about OPLAN 34A. Fatefully, the phone conversation was tape-recorded.

How did historians get to the bottom of this?

The Evidence

In the case of Johnson's taped conversations, one week after his death, his personal assistant Mildred Stegall delivered eight boxes of audio recordings and transcripts to the director of the LBJ Library, Harry Middleton. Stegall told Middleton that it was the president's wish that these boxes remain sealed for 50 years. But fearing the rapid deterioration of these 1960s-era tapes, Middleton started the preservation process.

Our knowledge of OPLAN 34A, on the other hand, comes largely through a right that few Americans know they enjoy. In 1966 Congress passed the Freedom of Information Act, which was later strengthened with the Mandatory Declassification Review program. Using these laws, and a business letter describing what we want to know, you and I and any other citizen can petition our government to learn about events, meetings, and deliberations that had been previously classified "top secret."

While the government can reject requests for information, and certain categories of information are exempt, it is impossible to conceive of historical research without these safeguards. Simply put, the Freedom of Information Act guarantees Americans the "right to know."

From essay: "40th Anniversary of the Gulf of Tonkin Incident" by John Prados from *The National Security Archive*, August 4, 2004.

Social Studies Competency Goals
Goal 11 The learner will trace economic, political, and social developments and assess their significance for the lives of Americans during this time period.

 11.04

The Big Idea and Essential Questions

To foster student understanding of this chapter's big idea, design your lesson to address each section's essential question.

Big Idea The Vietnam War was the first televised war that brought its horrors into American living rooms. Seemingly unwinnable, the war bitterly divided the nation and brought down the president.

Essential Questions

1. How did the United States become involved in Vietnam?

2. Why did some Americans begin to question U.S. involvement in Vietnam?

3. How did the views of the American public develop as the war dragged on and began to appear unwinnable?

4. What was the lasting impact of the Vietnam War on the United States and Southeast Asia?

Key to Differentiating Instruction

Below Level

Basic-level activities designed for all students encountering new material

At Level

Intermediate-level activities designed for average students

Above Level

Challenging activities designed for honors and gifted-and-talented students

Standard English Mastery

Activities designed to improve standard English usage

946 CHAPTER 29

CHAPTER
29 1954–1975

The Vietnam War

 THE BIG PICTURE It was the first war to invade American homes via television. For years TV brought the Vietnam War into American living rooms. Seemingly unwinnable, the U.S. war effort brought down a president and bitterly divided the nation.

NC **North Carolina Standards**

Social Studies Objectives
11.04 Identify the causes of United States involvement in Vietnam and examine how this involvement affected society.

Language Arts Objectives
2.01 Research and analyze ideas, events, and/or movements related to United States culture by:
• locating facts and details for purposeful elaboration.
3.01 Use language persuasively in addressing a particular issue by:
• establishing and defending a point of view.
3.02 Select an issue or theme and take a stance on that issue by:
• reflecting the viewpoint(s) of Americans of different times and places.

Skills FOCUS **READING LIKE A HISTORIAN**

Members of the 1st Squadron, 9th Cavalry, burst out of their helicopter and into action in Chu Lai, South Vietnam, in 1967. U.S. involvement in the Vietnam War was reaching its peak at this time.
Interpreting Visuals What does this photo suggest about soldiers' commitment to the war?

See Skills Handbook, p. H30

946

U.S.

1953
United States aids France in Indochina War.

 **1954**

World

May 1954 French forces at Dien Bien Phu surrender to the Vietminh.

Introduce the Chapter

At Level

The Vietnam War

1. Guide students in a discussion about social and political problems that face the nation today. Then tell students that in this chapter they will learn about one of the most troubled periods in recent U.S. history, the Vietnam War era.

2. Have students scan the chapter and make a list of the reasons the United States was drawn into the war and public reaction to the number of troops involved. Have volunteers share their lists with the class, and create a class list for all to see.

3. Then guide students in a discussion of reasons that the U.S. has gone to war in recent years. How are the reasons similar? Different?

4. Have students write a brief essay in which they compare and contrast reasons that the U.S. fought the Vietnam War with reasons it has fought more recent wars. **LS Verbal-Linguistic**

Alternative Assessment Handbook, Rubric 9: Comparing and Contrasting

HOLT

History's Impact

▶ **Video Program: The Vietnam War**
See the Video Teacher's Guide for strategies for using the video segment.

Reading Like a Historian

Interpreting Visuals The focus of this image is soldiers jumping out of a helicopter to join a battle in progress. Helicopters were first used by the U.S. military in World War II in a limited capacity. During the Korean War helicopters were more numerous, but were used mainly for search and rescue and medical evacuations. The Vietnam War saw the first use of helicopters for troop movements and combat support.

1960
The United States starts supplying military assistance to South Vietnam.

August 1964
Congress passes the Tonkin Gulf Resolution, expanding U.S. involvement in Vietnam.

April 1965
Antiwar demonstration in Washington, D.C., draws more than 200,000 protesters.

END THE DRAFT

January 1973
The United States agrees to withdraw all troops from South Vietnam.

1958

1962

1966

1970

1974

January 1959
Communist guerillas, led by Fidel Castro, take control of Cuba.

January 1968
Communist forces launch the Tet Offensive.

April 30, 1975
South Vietnam surrenders to North Vietnam.

947

go.hrw.com
Online Resources

Chapter Resources:
KEYWORD: SD7 CH29

Teacher Resources:
KEYWORD: SD7 TEACHER

Explore the Time Line

1. When did the U.S. begin to supply military assistance to South Vietnam? *1960*

2. What was the Tonkin Gulf Resolution? *expanded U.S. involvement*

3. How many years after the Tet Offensive did the U.S. agree to withdraw all troops from South Vietnam? *five*

Info to Know

Guerrilla Warfare The United States and North Vietnam fought the war very differently. The U.S. used massive air power. The North Vietnamese used guerrilla warfare. In Spanish the term *guerrilla* means "little war," and the French term *guerre* means "war." Those involved in guerrilla warfare do not engage in traditional battles. Instead they use harassment techniques.

Answers

Reading Like a Historian
(p. 946) *the actions of the soldiers— rushing to aid their comrades—suggests strong commitment to the war*

Bellringer

The Inside Story. . . Use the **Daily Bellringer Transparency** to help students answer the question.

🖥 Daily Bellringer Transparency, Section 1

Academic Vocabulary

Review with students the high-use academic terms in this section.

intervene get involved in, get in the middle of (p. 953)

enable to give enough power, opportunity, or ability (p. 955)

📄 CRF: Vocabulary Builder Activity, Section 1

Taking Notes

Ho Chi Minh—born in central Vietnam; worked for Vietnam's independence, Communist, wanted to reunify North and South Vietnam; Ngo Dinh Diem—Roman Catholic, South Vietnamese leader, refused to participate in Communist government, supported by U.S. government; murdered by South Vietnamese

---

BEFORE YOU READ

MAIN IDEA
Concern about the spread of communism led the United States to become increasingly involved in Vietnam.

READING FOCUS
1. How did Southeast Asia's colonial history produce increased tensions in Vietnam?
2. What policies did Presidents Truman and Eisenhower pursue in Vietnam after World War II?
3. What events and conditions caused growing conflicts between North Vietnam and South Vietnam?
4. Why did Presidents Kennedy and Johnson increase U.S. involvement in Vietnam?

KEY TERMS AND PEOPLE
Ho Chi Minh
Vietminh
domino theory
Dien Bien Phu
Geneva Conference
Ngo Dinh Diem
Vietcong
Tonkin Gulf Resolution

TAKING NOTES As you read, take notes on the roles of Ho Chi Minh and Ngo Dinh Diem in Vietnamese history. Write your notes in a graphic organizer like this one.

Ho Chi Minh	Ngo Dinh Diem

THE INSIDE STORY

How did President Woodrow Wilson disappoint Ho Chi Minh? Paris in 1919 was an exciting place to be for 28-year-old Nguyen That Thanh (NY-uhn TAHT TAHN). He was one of some 50,000 Southeast Asians from the colony of French Indochina who were living in France at the end of World War I. Most of these Vietnamese worked in factories, aiding the French war effort.

Nguyen That Thanh, however, had come for a different reason: to convince the other Vietnamese in France to support Vietnam's independence. He was inspired by the Fourteen Points that U.S. president Woodrow Wilson had issued during World War I. Wilson's Fourteen Points called for self-determination for all people—that is, letting people decide how they want to be governed.

Wilson was among the leaders who met in Paris in 1919 to negotiate the peace treaty and plan the postwar world. Nguyen wrote to the president asking that his Fourteen Points be applied to the people of Southeast Asia. He hand-delivered his letter to American officials at the peace conference, but he was turned away.

There was little chance that Wilson could have convinced France to give up its control of Vietnam. Yet Nguyen was very disappointed that the president ignored his letter. He bitterly complained of being deceived by Wilson's "song of freedom." Nguyen left France in 1923. In 1941 he returned to Vietnam to lead its fight for independence. By then he was known by a new name: Ho Chi Minh. ◾

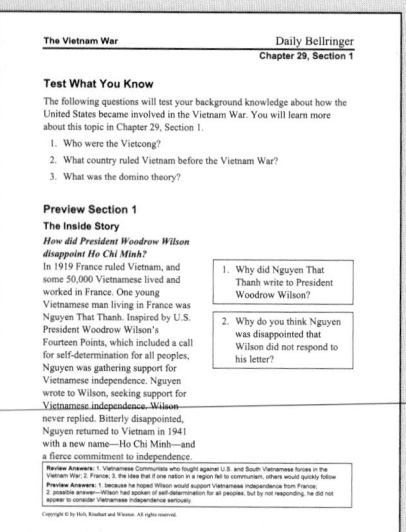

A Disappointed FAN

▲ As a young man in France, Nguyen That Thanh began working toward Vietnamese independence.

Teach the Main Idea

At Level

The War Develops

1. **Teach** Ask students the Reading Focus questions to teach this section.

2. **Apply** Organize students into pairs. Have each pair construct a time line of the following events: young Ho Chi Minh hopes to see Woodrow Wilson; Vietnam declares independence; war between Vietnamese and French troops begins; U.S. pays most of the costs of French army in Vietnam; French surrender; 3,000 American advisors in Vietnam; nearly 500 Americans have been killed; Tonkin Gulf Resolution

3. **Review** Discuss ways in which the fear of communism might have affected American foreign policy in the 20th century.

4. **Practice/Homework** Have students write a paragraph on lessons the U.S. could have learned from the French defeat.
LS Interpersonal, Visual-Spatial

📄 Alternative Assessment Handbook, Rubrics 36: Time Lines; and 37: Writing Assignments

The French Presidential Palace, located in the city of Hanoi, remains a powerful reminder of French colonial influence.

1 How did Southeast Asia's colonial history produce increased tensions in Vietnam? *Vietnamese had learned to hate occupiers; had gained some experience fighting them; after fighting Japanese in World War II, inspired to fight French occupation*

Colonial Vietnam

Recall By what name do we know Nguyen That Thanh? *Ho Chi Minh*

Analyze How did the experience of the Vietminh during World War II prepare it for war with France? *They learned to fight against a superior enemy with some success.*

Evaluate Why did Ho Chi Minh expect the United States to support Vietnam's bid for independence? *He saw similarities between Vietnam's struggle and the American Revolution.*

Primary Source

"Vietnam has the right to enjoy freedom and independence . . . the whole Vietnamese people is resolved to bring all its spirit and its power, its life, and its possessions to preserve this right of freedom and independence."

— Ho Chi Minh

Speech at Ba Dinh Square, Hanoi, September 2, 1945

Colonial Vietnam

The Southeast Asian nation of Vietnam is bordered by China to the north and by Laos and Cambodia to the west. Rich agricultural resources have long made the country ripe for foreign invasion. China invaded northern Vietnam's Red River Delta around 200 BC. The Vietnamese people struggled for independence for centuries, finally driving out Chinese rulers in the early 1400s.

Vietnam's independence again was threatened in the mid-1800s, as European powers competed to build colonial empires. Despite fierce resistance from the Vietnamese, France gained control of Vietnam by 1883. The French later combined Vietnam with Laos and Cambodia to form French Indochina.

A nationalist leader Many Vietnamese were driven into poverty under French rule. The French raised taxes and gave the Vietnamese no civil rights under French authority.

These conditions helped to fuel a growing nationalist movement in Vietnam. Nguyen That Thanh emerged as one of its leaders. He came to be known by a new name, **Ho Chi Minh**, meaning "He Who Enlightens."

Ho Chi Minh was born in a village in central Vietnam in 1890. He participated in several tax revolts against the French before leaving home and traveling around the world in the early 1900s. After President Wilson declined to meet him at the Paris Peace Conference, Ho Chi Minh joined the French Communist Party. "It was patriotism, not communism, that inspired me," he claimed.

While living in China and the Soviet Union in the 1920s and 1930s, Ho Chi Minh continued to work for Vietnam's independence and to study communism. He came to believe that a Communist revolution was a way Vietnam could gain freedom from foreign rulers.

Changing rulers Control of Vietnam again changed hands during World War II, when the Japanese army occupied Indochina. Ho Chi Minh returned to Vietnam in 1941 and organized a group to resist the Japanese occupation. The group was called the League for the Independence of Vietnam, or the **Vietminh** (vee-eht-MIN). The Vietminh was led by Communists, but the group was open to non-Communists who were committed to independence. During World War II, the Vietminh attacked Japanese forces and were able to liberate parts of northern Vietnam.

In 1945 Japan surrendered to the Allies and withdrew from Indochina. The Vietminh took the opportunity to declare Vietnam an independent country. Thousands of people gathered in Hanoi, Vietnam's capital, to hear Ho Chi Minh speak on September 2. Hoping to gain American support for Vietnam's independence, he quoted from the Declaration of Independence.

THE VIETNAM WAR **949**

FACES OF HISTORY

Ho Chi MINH
1890–1969

Ho Chi Minh was a rebel from a young age. The school he attended taught that France was trying to improve Vietnam. Ho Chi Minh told other students that France was actually an invader, a view he formed by reading banned books. He was soon kicked out of school.

When he was 21 he went to London, where he met Asian workers who he believed were overworked and underpaid. In France he became a Communist, but he criticized the French Communist Party for not opposing colonialism more strongly. He called for revolution in Southeast Asia and moved to south China to train Vietnamese exiles. He amassed an army of supporters who would eventually wage the twentieth century's longest and costliest battle against colonialism.

Draw Conclusions Why did Ho adopt Communist beliefs?

HISTORY'S VOICES

❝All men are created equal. They are endowed by their Creator with certain unalienable Rights; among these are Life, Liberty, and the pursuit of Happiness . . . The whole Vietnamese people, animated [driven to action] by a common purpose, are determined to fight to the bitter end against any attempt by the French colonialists to reconquer their country. We are convinced that the Allied nations, which . . . have acknowledged the principles of self-determination and equality of nations, will not refuse to acknowledge the independence of Vietnam.❞

—Ho Chi Minh, September 2, 1945

Ho Chi Minh believed that Vietnam's fight for independence from France was similar to the American colonies' struggle for independence from Great Britain. He expected that the United States would support the Vietnamese nationalist movement.

READING CHECK **Drawing Conclusions** Why did Ho Chi Minh work for Vietnam's independence from France?

Vietnam after World War II

As Ho Chi Minh feared, the French reclaimed Vietnam as a colony after World War II. In December 1946 the Vietnamese people again began battling French rule.

The first Indochina war President Harry Truman disappointed Ho Chi Minh after World War II, as Wilson had after World War I. Truman saw the situation in Indochina in terms of the struggle against communism. He decided to support France, a key ally in the effort to block Communist expansion in Europe. He was also unwilling to back the Vietminh because many of its members were Communists.

Events in Asia soon revealed the extent of Communist expansion. The Communist army of Mao Zedong seized China in 1949. The next year, Communist North Korea invaded South Korea. At the same time, several Communist-led nationalist revolts were raging in Indonesia, Malaya, and the Philippines. These events strengthened the U.S. commitment to contain communism in Southeast Asia.

The domino theory After Dwight D. Eisenhower became president of the United States in 1953, he warned that if Vietnam fell to communism, other Southeast Asian countries would quickly follow. The belief that communism would spread to neighboring countries was called the **domino theory.** "You have a row of dominoes set up," Eisenhower explained. "You knock over the first one, and what will happen to the last one is a certainty that it will go over very quickly."

The United States sent arms, ammunition, supplies, and money to the French forces in Vietnam. By 1954 the United States was paying more than 75 percent of the cost of France's war. Despite the massive U.S. aid, the French were losing, suffering defeat after defeat.

The Vietminh used guerrilla tactics effectively. They attacked French forces without warning and then disappeared into the jungle. Ho Chi Minh compared this type of warfare to a fight between a tiger and an elephant.

HISTORY'S VOICES

❝If the tiger ever stands still, the elephant will crush him with his mighty tusks. But the tiger does not stand still . . . He will leap upon the back of the elephant, tearing huge chunks from his hide, and then the tiger will leap back into the dark jungle. And slowly the elephant will bleed to death. That will be the war of Indochina.❞

—Ho Chi Minh, quoted in *America Inside Out* by David Schoenbrun. Copyright © 1994 by McGraw-Hill Companies, Inc. All rights reserved. Reprinted by permission of the publisher.

France is defeated The French soldiers made a last stand in a valley in northwestern Vietnam called **Dien Bien Phu** (DYEN BYEN FOO). About 40,000 Vietminh troops surrounded 15,000 French troops. The French commander clung to the hope of a U.S. rescue, telling his soldiers, "The 'free world' will not let us down."

Eisenhower, however, had no intention of sending U.S. soldiers into another war in Asia so soon after the Korean War. The French forces at Dien Bien Phu surrendered to the Vietminh on May 7, 1954.

In eight years of fighting, the two sides had lost nearly 300,000 soldiers. Surviving Vietnamese forces had gained valuable experience fighting a guerrilla war against an enemy with superior weapons and technology. This would prove to be an important factor in the years ahead.

The Geneva Conference After the French surrender, representatives from France, Vietnam, Cambodia, Great Britain, Laos, China, the Soviet Union, and the United States gathered in Geneva, Switzerland. The goal of the **Geneva Conference** was to work out a peace agreement and arrange for Indochina's future.

The Geneva Accords were signed in July 1954. A cease-fire was worked out, and Vietnam was temporarily divided at the 17th parallel. Vietminh forces would control the northern part of Vietnam, and the French would withdraw from the country. A demilitarized zone (DMZ) along the 17th parallel would act as a buffer zone to prevent fighting between the north and south.

According to the Geneva Accords, general elections were to be held in July 1956. These elections would reunify the country under one government. The United States, however, believed that Ho Chi Minh and the Communists would win a nationwide election. The United States therefore never fully supported the peace agreements.

China's Communist government had been aiding the Vietminh in the war and hoped to limit U.S. influence in the region. The United States, meanwhile, did not want to see all of Vietnam fall under Communist control.

READING CHECK **Identifying Cause and Effect** Why did the United States support France instead of Vietnam after World War II?

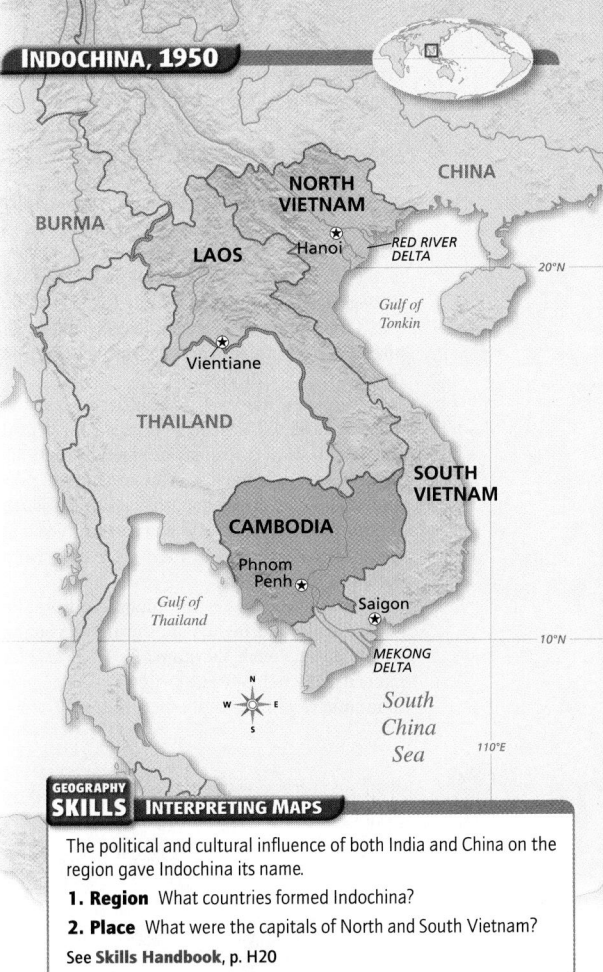

INDOCHINA, 1950

CHINA
NORTH VIETNAM
BURMA
LAOS · Hanoi — RED RIVER DELTA
20°N
Gulf of Tonkin
· Vientiane
THAILAND
SOUTH VIETNAM
CAMBODIA
Phnom Penh ·
Gulf of Thailand
· Saigon
MEKONG DELTA
10°N
South China Sea
110°E

GEOGRAPHY SKILLS **INTERPRETING MAPS**

The political and cultural influence of both India and China on the region gave Indochina its name.
1. **Region** What countries formed Indochina?
2. **Place** What were the capitals of North and South Vietnam?
See **Skills Handbook**, p. H20

Growing Conflict in Vietnam

With North Vietnam in the control of Ho Chi Minh and his Communist forces, President Eisenhower hoped to at least prevent communism from spreading to South Vietnam. He pinned his hopes on the South Vietnamese leader, **Ngo Dinh Diem** (NGOH DIN dee-EM).

Vietnam's leaders Diem, a Roman Catholic, had served as a high-ranking official in the colonial government under French rule. He was taken hostage by the Vietminh in 1945 and brought to see Ho Chi Minh. Ho asked

THE VIETNAM WAR **951**

Direct Teach

Reading Focus

Vietnam after World War II

Identify What happened at Dien Bien Phu? *The French army suffered its final defeat at the hands of the Vietminh.*

Make Inferences What useful experience did the Vietnamese take away from Dien Bien Phu? *They had learned how to fight a successful guerrilla war against a powerful foe.*

Evaluate Why did the United States not support the Geneva Accords? *The American government was worried that elections would result in the Communists coming to power.*

Reading Focus

❸ What events and conditions caused growing conflicts between North Vietnam and South Vietnam? *Ngo Dinh Diem, the American favorite in South Vietnam, was corrupt and refused to allow elections; Ho wanted to reunify the country and began to support rebels in the south.*

Growing Conflict in Vietnam

Identify Who was the South Vietnamese leader? *Ngo Dinh Diem*

Explain Why was Ngo Dinh Diem so popular with the American government? *Diem spent two years in the United States, where he came to know some leaders, who liked his anti-Communist position.*

Map Transparency: Indochina, 1950

Answers

Interpreting Maps 1. *Laos, Cambodia, North Vietnam, and South Vietnam;* **2.** *North Vietnam—Hanoi; South Vietnam—Saigon*

Reading Check *France was an ally against communism in Europe; Vietnamese leader Ho Chi Minh was a Communist*

951

Growing Conflict in Vietnam

Recall Why did Ngo Dinh Diem refuse to allow the 1956 elections? *He feared that Ho Chi Minh would win the elections.*

Analyze How did Diem's Catholicism affect the South Vietnamese? *Diem's favoritism toward Catholics upset the large Buddhist population and created substantial opposition to the government.*

Activity **Diem's Refusal** Have students write a letter from Ngo Dinh Diem to Ho Chi Minh in which Diem refuses Ho's offer to join the Communist government. Have volunteers share their letters with the class.

LS Verbal-Linguistic

Growing Divisions

Predict How might these images affect American support for Diem's government? *possible answer—decrease U.S. support because of international attention to ill treatment of Vietnamese*

Diem to become part of his Communist government, believing Diem would bring support from Catholics. Diem, whose brother had been murdered by the Vietminh, refused the offer. Despite Diem's refusal to cooperate, he was released.

Vietminh forces later tried unsuccessfully to assassinate Diem. He then fled Vietnam and traveled for several years. He spent two years in the United States, where he met American leaders. Diem impressed them with his strong anti-Communist views. He returned to Vietnam after France's defeat in 1954 and became the president of South Vietnam.

Very soon, however, U.S. officials became disappointed with Diem's corrupt and brutal leadership. In a presidential election in 1955, Diem claimed to have won more than 98 percent of the vote. In Saigon, the capital of South Vietnam, election results showed he received 200,000 more votes than there were registered voters in the city.

Diem's government was unpopular from the start. He showed favoritism toward Catholics, which upset South Vietnam's large Buddhist majority. He handed out top government jobs to members of his family. In addition, Diem's land policies favored wealthy landowners at the expense of the peasants. His security forces tortured and imprisoned his political opponents. American leaders were disturbed by these and other actions by Diem. Nevertheless, they preferred Diem's government to a Communist takeover.

In North Vietnam, Ho Chi Minh's leadership became increasingly totalitarian and repressive. Forsaking his earlier commitment to human rights, he struck with brutal force, breaking up the estates of large colonial landowners. He gave the land to the peasants, which made him immensely popular.

Fearing that Ho Chi Minh would win the 1956 election set by the Geneva Accords, Diem barred the election in South Vietnam. Like Germany and Korea, Vietnam continued to be divided into separate Communist and non-Communist countries. This was unacceptable to Ho Chi Minh, who wanted to unite Vietnam as a nation under one Communist government.

A civil war By the late 1950s, Diem's opponents in South Vietnam were in open revolt. In 1959 Communist leaders in North Vietnam began supplying weapons to Vietminh rebels

Growing Divisions in Vietnam

952

Skills Focus: Summarizing

Below Level

Reading Skill

Corruption in the Diem Regime

1. Review the information in the text about the corruption and brutality of the Diem regime.

2. Organize students into mixed-ability pairs. Have each pair develop a list of the problems within the Diem regime and then propose corrections that Diem could have made to improve his popularity and eliminate fraud and corruption in the government.

3. Have volunteers share their lists with the class and create a class list for all to see.

4. Have students use the information in their lists, or from the class list, to write a letter to the editor of a U.S. newspaper insisting that the Diem government eliminate corruption before receiving any further U.S. support.

LS Verbal-Linguistic

Alternative Assessment Handbook, Rubrics 13: Graphic Organizers; and 17: Letters to Editors

who had remained in the south after the defeat of the French.

The following year, the Vietminh in South Vietnam formed the National Liberation Front (NLF). The NLF's military forces were called **Vietcong**, meaning Vietnamese Communists. Not all members of the NLF were Communists, but they were united in the goal of overthrowing Diem's regime.

Some peasants joined the Vietcong because they opposed Diem's government, but others did so because they feared retaliation from the Vietcong if they did not. The Vietcong assassinated thousands of South Vietnamese government officials. Soon, much of the countryside was under Vietcong control.

In 1960 Ho Chi Minh expanded the effort to reunify North and South Vietnam. More supply routes leading to South Vietnam were established. North Vietnamese Army (NVA) forces also began coming into the country to fight alongside the Vietcong.

President Eisenhower decided to intervene in the conflict in 1955. The United States began supplying South Vietnam with money and weapons. Eisenhower began sending military advisers to train South Vietnam's army—the

Army of the Republic of Vietnam (ARVN)—to use American weaponry.

By the end of Eisenhower's presidency, there were about 900 U.S. military advisers in South Vietnam. Many of these advisers had become frustrated with the corruption and inefficiency present in the ARVN.

READING CHECK **Summarizing** Why was Ngo Dinh Diem's government unpopular?

Increasing U.S. Involvement

Elected in 1960, President John F. Kennedy was a firm believer in the domino theory. Kennedy was eager to display U.S. strength in Vietnam.

You read in an earlier chapter about the two Cold War disasters that began Kennedy's presidency, the Bay of Pigs invasion and the building of the Berlin Wall. In the aftermath of these incidents, Kennedy hoped that aiding South Vietnam would be a sign of continued U.S. resolve and strength. "Now we have a problem in making our power credible," he warned, "and Vietnam is the place [to do so]."

President Kennedy hesitated to send official combat forces into South Vietnam, however. Instead, he decided to increase the number of military advisers and army special forces, or Green Berets, in that country. In December 1961 there were about 3,000 U.S. advisers in South Vietnam. By 1963 that number had increased to about 16,000.

The advisers were not supposed to take part in combat, but many did. For example, helicopter pilots fired rockets and machine guns at Vietcong targets. Green Berets often accompanied the ARVN on dangerous ambush operations. As Vietcong attacks mounted, Kennedy authorized U.S. personnel to engage in direct combat. The number of Americans killed or wounded climbed steadily. In 1961 some 14 Americans were killed. In 1963 the number rose to nearly 500.

Diem's overthrow Meanwhile, Diem's government grew more and more unpopular. When Buddhist leaders opposed his rule, Diem struck back by arresting and killing Buddhist protesters. To bring attention to the situation, several Buddhist monks killed themselves by publicly setting themselves on fire. Gruesome photographs were printed in newspapers around

In mid-1963 Buddhists began protesting Diem's oppression of their religion. At left, Buddhist demonstrators clash with police. In a terrible protest that focused world attention on Diem, Buddhist monk Quang Duc set himself on fire at a busy Saigon intersection.

ACADEMIC VOCABULARY
intervene get involved in, get in the middle of

THE VIETNAM WAR **953**

Reading Focus

Increasing U.S. Involvement

Recall What happened to Ngo Dinh Diem? *He was murdered by South Vietnamese plotters; U.S. had supported his overthrow.*

Predict What would have happened to South Vietnam following Diem's death if the United States had not expanded its military role? *possible answer—South Vietnam would have been quickly conquered by stronger Vietcong forces.*

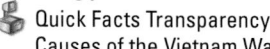 Quick Facts Transparency: Causes of the Vietnam War

Primary Source

"In the Vietnamese army, a majority of the soldiers were Buddhists. I am a Buddhist. I had a lot of trouble with my family, who reproached me for having attacked the pagodas. But it wasn't true . . . actually it was units loyal to Diem who attacked the pagodas . . . So then we had to do something to show Diem: either he had to change his policies, or we would have to change Mr. Diem."

— South Vietnamese General Tran Van Don

Vietnam: A Television History, America's Mandarin (1954–1963)

CAUSES OF THE VIETNAM WAR
QUICK FACTS

- **Vietnam's desire for freedom from colonial rule** France reclaimed Vietnam as a colony after World War II. The Communist-led Vietminh fought against French rule.

- **U.S. fears of the spread of communism (the domino theory)** Fearing that communism would spread throughout Southeast Asia if Communists took over Vietnam, the United States supported France. Despite U.S. aid, French rule of Vietnam ended in 1954.

- **South Vietnam's failure to comply with the Geneva Accords** After the French surrender, Vietnam was temporarily divided. North Vietnam was controlled by the Vietminh. Under the Geneva Accords, elections to unify the country under one government were set for 1956, but South Vietnam's leader refused to hold them.

- **Efforts by North Vietnam to reunite the nation under Communist rule** By 1959 North Vietnam began sending weapons to Vietminh in South Vietnam with the goal of unifying the country under a Communist government.

- **U.S. support for the anti-Communist government of South Vietnam** The United States supported South Vietnam with military advisers and later with troops.

Early in the war, U.S. personnel served primarily as military advisers and trainers. Here, South Vietnamese soldiers exit a helicopter under the watchful eye of an American officer.

---

the world. The images shocked Americans, and public opinion turned sharply against Diem.

American officials threatened to withdraw support unless Diem changed his policies. Yet he refused to alter his stand against Buddhists.

In response, U.S. leaders secretly began to support a plot within the South Vietnamese army to overthrow Diem. Henry Cabot Lodge Jr., the ambassador to South Vietnam, sent a cable to Washington describing the situation.

HISTORY'S VOICES

❝We are launched on a course from which there is no respectable turning back: the overthrow of the Diem government. There is no turning back because there is no possibility, in my view, that the war can be won under a Diem administration.❞

—Henry Cabot Lodge Jr., August 29, 1963

In November 1963 the South Vietnamese plotters murdered Diem. Although Kennedy and his top advisers supported Diem's overthrow, they did not seek his assassination. The removal of Diem from power, however, did nothing to ease President Kennedy's growing con-

cern over U.S. involvement in Vietnam. Shortly before Diem's murder, Kennedy had said of the South Vietnamese: "In the final analysis it is their war. They are the ones who have to win or lose it."

It cannot be known for sure whether Kennedy would have changed U.S. policy toward Vietnam. Just three weeks after Diem's death, President Kennedy himself was assassinated in Dallas, Texas.

The Tonkin Gulf Resolution When Vice President Lyndon B. Johnson took over as president, he inherited a rapidly deteriorating situation in South Vietnam. Although the ARVN had about 300,000 soldiers, the South Vietnamese government was on the brink of collapse. North Vietnamese forces were slipping into South Vietnam at an ever-increasing rate. By March 1964 the Vietcong controlled about 40 percent of South Vietnam.

President Johnson became convinced that only an expanded U.S. military involvement in South Vietnam could prevent a Communist victory. To increase the American military effort there, however, Johnson needed to obtain authority from the U.S. Congress. In 1964 an incident off the coast of North Vietnam gave him the opportunity to ask for this authority.

954 CHAPTER 29

Skills Focus: Identifying Problem and Solution
At Level

Reading Skill
President Johnson and the War

1. Guide students in a discussion about the overthrow of Diem and the increasing U.S. involvement in Vietnam. Ask students if they believe that the U.S. government should be involved in removing corrupt presidents from office.

2. Tell students that following the assassination of President Kennedy, responsibility for the Vietnam War fell to President Lyndon B. Johnson. President Johnson knew he needed

support of the nation and of Congress to increase U.S. involvement in the war.

3. Have students write a television news report about why President Johnson believes that this is the right course for the nation.

4. Have volunteers present their news reports to the class. **LS Verbal-Linguistic**

📋 Alternative Assessment Handbook, Rubric 23: Newspapers

Near midnight on August 4, 1964, President Johnson appeared on national television. He made the dramatic announcement that on August 2 the USS *Maddox*, a navy destroyer, had been attacked by North Vietnamese torpedo boats in the Gulf of Tonkin, off the North Vietnamese coast.

Johnson said that the attack on the *Maddox* "was repeated today by a number of hostile vessels attacking two U.S. destroyers [the *Maddox* and the *C. Turner Joy*] with torpedoes." He called for a swift military response.

HISTORY'S VOICES

❝Repeated acts of violence against the Armed Forces of the United States must be met not only with alert defense, but with positive reply. That reply is being given as I speak to you tonight. Air action is now in execution against gunboats and certain supporting facilities in North Vietnam which have been used in these hostile operations.❞
—Lyndon B. Johnson, speech on August 4, 1964

Later it was learned that President Johnson did not present a completely accurate picture of the incident in the Gulf of Tonkin. Johnson was in the middle of his 1964 presidential election campaign against Senator Barry Goldwater, a strong anti-Communist. Johnson wanted to avoid charges from Senator Goldwater and the Republicans that he was soft on communism.

The president claimed that the attack on the USS *Maddox* was unprovoked. In fact, the *Maddox* had been on a spying mission and had fired first.

As for the second attack, U.S. sailors may have mistaken interference on their radar and sonar for enemy boats and torpedoes. At the time, however, most members of Congress did not know the factual details surrounding the two incidents.

The **Tonkin Gulf Resolution** was approved by Congress on August 7. The resolution <u>enabled</u> the president to take "all necessary measures to repel any armed attack against forces of the United States." Johnson and his advisers now had authority to expand the war.

Senator Wayne Morse of Oregon was one of only two senators to oppose the Tonkin Gulf Resolution. "I believe that history will record we have made a great mistake," he predicted. "We are in effect giving the President war-making powers in the absence of a declaration of war."

READING CHECK **Identifying Cause and Effect** What circumstances led Congress to pass the Tonkin Gulf Resolution?

ACADEMIC VOCABULARY

enable to give enough power, opportunity, or ability

---

go.hrw.com
Online Quiz
Keyword: SD7 HP29

SECTION 1 ASSESSMENT

Reviewing Ideas, Terms, and People

1. **a. Define** What was French Indochina?
   b. Analyze How did French rule influence **Ho Chi Minh**'s decision to embrace communism?
   c. Elaborate Do you think Ho Chi Minh's comparison of Vietnam after World War II and colonial America was valid? Explain.

2. **a. Describe** According to the **domino theory**, what did American leaders think might happen if Vietnam became a Communist country?
   b. Make Inferences Do you think the Geneva Accords eased American concerns about a domino effect in Southeast Asia? Why or why not?

3. **a. Identify** Who were the **Vietcong**?
   b. Analyze Cause and Effect What was Eisenhower's response to the growing strength of the Vietcong?
   c. Evaluate Do you think the United States was justified in supporting **Ngo Dinh Diem**? Why or why not?

4. **a. Describe** What happened to the USS *Maddox* in the Gulf of Tonkin?

   b. Predict How might the **Tonkin Gulf Resolution** affect the power of the presidency?

Critical Thinking

5. **Draw Conclusions** Review your notes on the leaders of North Vietnam and South Vietnam. Then copy the graphic organizer below and use it to list the causes for the decline in popularity of Ngo Dinh Diem's government.

Cause	Effect
	The popularity of Ngo Dinh Diem's government declined.

FOCUS ON WRITING

6. **Expository** Suppose that you are the communications director in the Kennedy or Johnson White House. Write a press release that explains the president's decision to increase U.S. military involvement in Vietnam.

THE VIETNAM WAR **955**

Section 1 Assessment Answers

1. **a.** Vietnam, Laos, and Cambodia
   b. believed Communist revolution could free Vietnam from foreign rulers
   c. possible answer—valid, because both countries wanted the right to rule themselves

2. **a.** other Southeast Asian countries would fall to communism
   b. no; feared Ho Chi Minh and the Communists would win a nationwide election

3. **a.** Communists in South Vietnam
   b. sent South Vietnam money and weapons, trained their troops

   c. possible answers—yes, he was better than the Communist alternative; no, his regime was corrupt and brutal

4. **a.** attacked by North Vietnamese torpedoes
   b. possible answer—increase power by giving more control over the military

5. corruption; gave government jobs to family; favored Catholics and wealthy; imprisoned and tortured opponents

6. possible answer—Without U.S. military, South Vietnam will become Communist, other countries in Southeast Asia will follow.

Reading Focus

Increasing U.S. Involvement

Recall What was the Gulf of Tonkin incident? *The U.S. claimed that North Vietnamese ships had engaged in unprovoked attacks against the U.S. ship* Maddox.

Evaluate How did the Tonkin Gulf Resolution help Johnson's war plans? *He was given the power to expand the war without a formal declaration of war by Congress.*

● **Review & Assess** ●

Close

Ask students to explain how fear of communism affected American policy toward Vietnam.

Review

Online Quiz, Section 1

Daily Test Practice Transparency

Assess

SE Section 1 Assessment

Progress Assessment: Section 1 Quiz

Alternative Assessment Handbook

Reteach

Interactive Reader and Study Guide, Section 1

Interactive Skills Tutor CD-ROM

Answers

Reading Check USS Maddox *torpedoed*

955

U.S. Support of the War at Home and Abroad

BEFORE YOU READ

MAIN IDEA

As the United States sent increasing numbers of troops to defend South Vietnam, some Americans began to question the war.

READING FOCUS

1. Why did U.S. superiority in the air war fail to win quickly in Vietnam?
2. What made the ground war in Vietnam so difficult to fight?
3. How were U.S. forces mobilized for the war?
4. How and why did public opinion about the war gradually change?

KEY TERMS AND PEOPLE

Operation Rolling Thunder
Ho Chi Minh Trail
William Westmoreland
pacification
doves
hawks
J. William Fulbright

TAKING NOTES As you read, take notes on the characteristics and tactics of U.S. soldiers in the Vietnam War. Write your notes in a graphic organizer like this one.

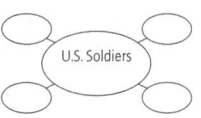

U.S. Soldiers

THE INSIDE STORY

Why do some people risk their lives to serve their country? The young men who volunteered to fight in Vietnam came mostly from rural America or from industrial neighborhoods in the nation's cities. Many recruits were the sons of American soldiers who had fought in World War II or the Korean War. For young men fresh out of high school, serving in Vietnam seemed to be an adventure as well as a patriotic duty.

Eighteen-year-old Rod Kane was just such a person. After graduating from high school in 1964, he went to see the recruiter. "I want to be in the infantry, like my Uncle Paul . . . Maybe I should do something like save people, like medics," Kane said.

"If you volunteer for three years, I can guarantee you medics school," the recruiter promised. "Remember what President Kennedy said," he urged. "'Ask not what your country can do for you. Ask what you can do for your country.'"

It sounded good to Kane. In 1965, army infantry member and medic Rod Kane arrived in Vietnam. ■

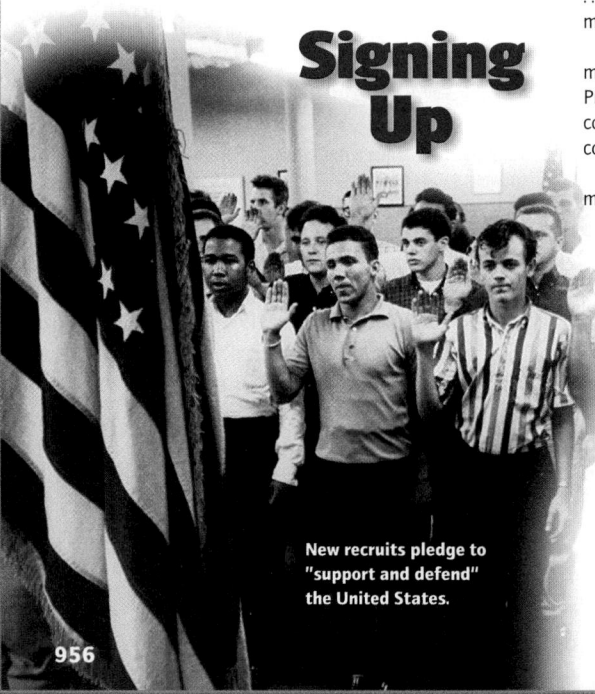

Signing Up

New recruits pledge to "support and defend" the United States.

956

The Air War

The first major direct U.S. military activity in Vietnam took place in the air. President Johnson ordered **Operation Rolling Thunder**, a bombing campaign over North Vietnam, in March 1965. He wanted to weaken the enemy's ability and will to fight. He also wanted to assure South Vietnam of his commitment to its independence.

U.S. pilots bombed military targets in North Vietnam, such as army bases and airfields. They also bombed anything North Vietnam would find useful in the war effort, including bridges, roads, railways, and power plants.

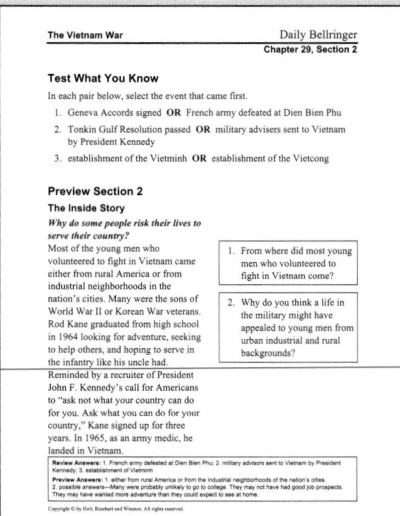

Teach the Main Idea

At Level

U.S. Support of the War at Home and Abroad

Materials construction paper, colored markers

1. **Teach** Ask students the Reading Focus questions to teach this section.

2. **Apply** Organize students into small groups. Have each group design two posters, one opposing the war in Vietnam and one supporting it. Groups should include important points about the war, and explain the reasons for their position.

3. **Review** Have groups display their posters

for the class. Then as you review the section, ask students to describe how perceptions of unfairness might have affected Americans' feelings about the war.

4. **Practice/Homework** Have students use the information in their group posters to write a song with lyrics that either support or oppose the Vietnam War. **LS Auditory-Musical, Visual-Spatial**

📝 Alternative Assessment Handbook, Rubrics 26: Poems and Songs; and 28: Posters

Rolling Thunder

U.S. Air Force pilots flying Vietnamese Skyraiders drop napalm on Vietcong targets. Operation Rolling Thunder aimed to weaken the enemy, disrupt the Ho Chi Minh Trail, and defoliate the countryside. *Why did U.S. involvement in Vietnam begin with air power instead of ground troops?*

One of the main targets of Operation Rolling Thunder was the **Ho Chi Minh Trail**. The trail was a network of paths that began in North Vietnam, snaked through Laos and Cambodia, and ended in South Vietnam. The North Vietnamese used the trail to send weapons, soldiers, food, and other supplies to the Vietcong and NVA forces in South Vietnam.

Much of the Ho Chi Minh Trail ran through thick jungle areas, making movement along it all but invisible from the air. American planes began spraying jungle areas with defoliants, or chemicals that destroy vegetation. The goal of this spraying was to expose enemy supply routes and hiding places. A chemical called Agent Orange was the most widely used type of defoliant.

American forces used several other types of weapons in the air war. Napalm, a jellied form of gasoline, was used to create firebombs that destroyed farms and forests. "Cluster bombs" sprayed sharp metal fragments when they exploded. Pilots also carried out attacks called carpet bombing, a strategy in which strings of bombs dropped from high altitudes destroy large areas of land with no specific target.

The bombing did not succeed in its goal of weakening the enemy's war effort, however.

Instead of cutting off aid to the Vietcong, the flow of troops and supplies from North Vietnam to the south actually increased. When roads or bridges on the Ho Chi Minh Trail were damaged, the Vietcong quickly repaired them or did without them. They also had underground bunkers that protected soldiers and supplies.

Another reason the Communist forces were able to withstand the bombing was that they received massive support from the Soviet Union and China. Both Communist powers provided North Vietnam with soldiers, economic aid, and high-tech weapons, including radar and antiaircraft guns.

Frustrated by the lack of progress, Johnson broadened the air war. By late 1968 more than 1 million tons of bombs had been dropped on North Vietnam. Targets in Laos, Cambodia, and parts of South Vietnam were also bombed.

One unintended effect of the American bombing campaign was that it led many South Vietnamese to join the Vietcong. Soon the forces opposing American troops included an increasing number of South Vietnamese.

READING CHECK **Identifying the Main Idea**
What did U.S. forces hope to accomplish by bombing the Ho Chi Minh Trail?

THE VIETNAM WAR **957**

Reading Focus

❶ Why did U.S. superiority in the air war fail to win quickly the Vietnam War? *aid to Vietcong increased; Vietcong quickly rebuilt damaged roads and bridges; underground bunkers protected Vietnamese soldiers and supplies*

The Air War

Recall What was Agent Orange? *a chemical defoliant that U.S. planes sprayed on Vietnamese jungle areas to destroy vegetation*

Analyze Why did the Ho Chi Minh Trail continue to be useful even with massive bombing? *It ran through jungle areas, was hard to see, and was easily repaired after bombings.*

Summarize How much international aid came to North Vietnam? *China and the Soviet Union sent soldiers, economic aid, and high tech weapons, like anti-aircraft guns and radar.*

📄 CRF: History and Geography Activity: The Ho Chi Minh Trail

Answers

Photo *Ho Chi Minh Trail very difficult to access except by air*

Reading Check *interrupt the flow of supplies and troops moving into South Vietnam from the North*

Differentiating Instruction

Below Level

English-Language Learners

1. Guide students in a discussion of America's air war against North Vietnam. Then copy the graphic organizer at right for all to see. Have students copy the organizer onto their own papers.

2. Organize students into mixed-ability pairs. Have each pair complete their graphic by listing the Vietcong and North Vietnamese responses to American air power on the right wing. *possible answers—rebuilt damaged*

roads and bridges; used underground bunkers to protect soldiers and supplies

3. Have volunteers share their completed graphic organizers with the class.
LS **Interpersonal, Visual-Spatial**
📄 Alternative Assessment Handbook, Rubric 13: Graphic Organizers
📦 Graphic Organizer Transparencies

American Power:
regular bombs
Agent Orange
napalm
cluster bombs
carpet bombing

VC and North
Vietnamese response:

957

Reading Focus

❷ What made the ground war in Vietnam so difficult to fight? *Vietnamese used guerrilla tactics; war fought in jungles, rice paddies, and rural villages; difficult to differentiate Vietcong from Vietnamese civilians; enemy was able to recruit more and more troops*

The Ground War

Identify Who was William Westmoreland? *American general who led the U.S. ground troops in South Vietnam*

Make Judgments Why was the U.S. pacification program unlikely to win support from the South Vietnamese? *Vietnamese civilians resented being forced from their homes and villages.*

📄 CRF: Biography: Lewis William Walt

History Close-Up

Vietcong Tunnels

Activity **Life in a Tunnel** Have students write two journal entries from the perspective of a Vietcong soldier hiding in an underground tunnel during combat. Have volunteers share their entries. Then guide the class in a discussion of how the use of underground tunnels helped or hurt the Vietcong forces.
LS Verbal-Linguistic

About the Illustration

This illustration is an artist's conception based on available sources. Historians, however, are uncertain exactly what this scene looked like.

The Ground War

THE IMPACT TODAY

Government
In part because of Vietnam, the question of U.S. involvement in a foreign war comes under intense scrutiny today. Recent presidents have been pressured to make the case for a compelling national interest before sending U.S. forces to hostile overseas situations.

As the war continued, Johnson called for an escalation, or buildup, of U.S. ground forces in Vietnam. The number of American troops in South Vietnam grew from 185,000 at the end of 1965 to 486,000 two years later.

U.S. strategy In response to the guerrilla tactics used by Communist forces, General **William Westmoreland**, the commander of U.S. ground troops in South Vietnam, ordered thousands of search-and-destroy missions to drive enemy forces out of their hideouts. Ground troops located Vietcong and NVA positions and then called in air strikes to bomb them. Once an area was "cleared" the ground patrols moved on to search for other enemy positions.

American troops on search-and-destroy missions often cut through the thick jungle, fighting foes they rarely saw. Other times, they waded through rice paddies or searched rural villages. One U.S. commander, Captain Myron Harrington, described what it was like to lead a company of 100 marines.

HISTORY'S VOICES

❝After a while, survival was the name of the game as you sat there in the semidarkness, with the firing going on constantly, like at a rifle range. And the horrible smell. You tasted it as you ate your rations, as if you were eating death . . . You went through the full range of emotions, seeing your buddies being hit, but you couldn't feel sorry for them because you had the others to think about.❞

—Captain Myron Harrington,
quoted in *Vietnam* by Stanley Karnow

After search-and-destroy patrols left an area, villages seldom remained clear for long. Returning Vietcong and NVA troops sometimes terrorized civilians they believed had aided the Americans.

ACADEMIC VOCABULARY

instituted established or started

To improve rural security, U.S. forces instituted a program of **pacification**. Its goal was to "win the hearts and minds" of the South Vietnamese people—to pacify, or calm, opposition—especially in the countryside.

Nonmilitary pacification involved construction projects to improve the country's infrastructure and economy. Militarily, pacification involved moving people out of their villages when Vietcong were concentrated

nearby. Villagers were relocated to safe camps and given food and housing. American troops then burned the village to prevent the Vietcong from using it.

U.S. planners hoped that driving out the Vietcong would help win the support of South Vietnamese civilians. Many civilians, however, resented being moved off their land and having their villages destroyed.

As armies fought from village to village, it was difficult for U.S. military leaders to show progress on a map. Instead, they measured success with body counts, or the number of enemy killed. It often was difficult for troops to make accurate counts in the midst of hectic jungle firefights. Also, high military officials sometimes inflated the body counts reported by units in the field.

Declining troop morale The first U.S. ground troops in Vietnam were convinced that they would succeed. Marine lieutenant Philip Caputo remembered his early confidence.

HISTORY'S VOICES

❝Our expectations were, we were going to stay there a month to 90 days, help the South Vietnamese recover, and then we would get out . . . We got this idea that the United States was invincible . . . that, being U.S. Marines, our mere presence in Vietnam was going to terrify the enemy into quitting.❞

—Lieutenant Philip Caputo, CNN interview, June 1996

In reality, American troops confronted many of the same challenges the French had faced. Aided by NVA troops, the Vietcong struck at U.S. patrols and government-held villages and then melted back into the jungle. Some Vietnamese peasants seemed peaceful by day but aided or even became the Vietcong at night. The Vietcong also had the major advantage of knowing the local geography.

U.S. combat soldiers faced constant danger. Each path could lead into an enemy ambush. Each step could trip a deadly mine or a booby trap such as Punji stakes, which were sharpened bamboo sticks concealed in a hole or mud. On patrol, American troops found it nearly impossible to tell the difference between a Vietcong fighter and a civilian.

Caputo later described the sense of uncertainty he and his fellow marines felt when interacting with Vietnamese civilians.

958 CHAPTER 29

Skills Focus: Analyzing Bias in Historical Interpretation   At Level

Reading Like a Historian Skill   **Research Required**
Military Tactics in Vietnam

1. Guide students in a review of General Westmoreland's search-and-destroy missions and the pacification program.

2. Have students find at least two primary source documents about either the search-and-destroy policy or the pacification program. Students should find one document that supports the military tactic and one document that opposes it.

3. Organize the class into small groups. Each group should identify biases that they find in

the documents.

4. Have students write an analysis of the two primary source documents they found. In their analyses students should explain the historical bias, if it exists, in the documents. Students should also analyze the differing opinions presented in the documents.
LS Verbal-Linguistic, Logical-Mathematical

📄 Alternative Assessment Handbook, Rubrics 9: Comparing and Contrasting; and 30: Research

Vietcong Tunnels

The Vietcong had a vast system of underground tunnels some of which had been built in the 1940s. The tunnels served as hiding places during combat. They also served as living quarters, places to store food and weapons, and locations to tend wounded soldiers. This illustration depicts a typical complex in one of the larger tunnel systems. By 1965 the tunnels stretched underground from Saigon to the Cambodian border, a distance of about 120 miles.

Firing Post

The Vietcong used tunnel meeting rooms to plan attacks on U.S. soldiers.

Air Vents

Bomb Shelter

Kitchen

Dormitory

Special doors were installed to protect against bomb blasts and poison-gas attacks.

Bicycle-powered generators provided electricity for tunnel rooms.

Some tunnels held traps that would injure invaders.

Hospital

Weapons Storage

Skills FOCUS: INTERPRETING INFOGRAPHICS

The Vietcong could not compete in firepower, but they used tunnels and other types of guerrilla warfare.

Drawing Conclusions How did the tunnel structure meet the military and personal needs of the Vietcong?

See Skills Handbook, p. 18

Wells were dug to provide fresh water inside the tunnel system.

959

Skills Focus: Making Generalizations

Reading Skill
Troop Morale

1. Guide students in a discussion about the declining U.S. troop morale in Vietnam. Have students work in pairs to make a list of the challenges and obstacles American soldiers faced as they fought in a humid jungle far from home.

2. Have students write a letter from a young American solider or nurse to his or her family at home in the United States talking about the conditions under which they lived and fought.

3. Have volunteers read their letters to the class.

4. As an extension, have students find actual letters written by soldiers serving in Vietnam, and compare their understanding of life in Vietnam with that expressed in the primary source documents. **LS Verbal-Linguistic**

Alternative Assessment Handbook, Rubrics 30: Research; and 37: Writing Assignments

---

Reading Focus

The Ground War

Recall Why were the body counts reported in the press often wrong? *U.S. military officials often inflated them, and included civilians as well as enemy troops.*

Explain Why were body counts used rather than traditional war progress through territory? *difficult to show geographic progress when fighting from village to village*

Make Inferences What made some American troops think they could succeed in Vietnam where French troops had failed? *They believed that the American forces were invincible and that the Vietnamese would be terrified of them.*

CRF: Biography: Dickey Chappelle

Info to Know

Punji Sticks Tips of punji sticks were often coated with filth so that an infection would develop in the wound. These sticks were not designed to kill the person who stepped on them, but they were designed to wound an enemy and slow the progress of a military unit.

CRF: Primary Source Activity: Search-and-Destroy Mission in Vietnam

CRF: Literature Activity: *The Things They Carried* by Tim O'Brien

Answers

Interpreting Infographics *It provided a concealed space for sleeping, eating, fighting, and medical care.*

③ How were U.S. forces mobilized for the war? *Forces drafted, college students got deferments. The war was largely fought by the poor and minorities.*

U.S. Forces Mobilize

Recall How many Americans served in the Vietnam War? *more than 2 million*

Make Inferences Why was the war mainly fought by the poor? *College students avoided the draft; poor less likely to go to college.*

Teaching Tip

Remind students that the Selective Service Act, which requires young men between the ages of 21 and 30, to register to be drafted in the armed forces, was passed into law by Congress in 1917 as the U.S. began to mobilize for World War I.

Info to Know

Conscientious Objectors During the Vietnam War, some young people became conscientious objectors and refused to serve in the military because of religious or philosophical views against war or killing. It is a federal felony to refuse to answer a draft call. However, when a person's religious beliefs are well-established and consistent, he can be excused from military service. Conscientious objectors conduct non-violent work, including driving an ambulance.

Answers

Reading Check *NVA struck U.S. patrols and then melted back into the jungle; Vietcong blended in with civilians, used land mines, booby traps, sniper attacks*

960

"You didn't and couldn't really trust them," he said. "You did develop this intense suspicion. You were constantly watching them, and that got to be kind of wearing after a while."

Despite these obstacles, U.S. troops inflicted enormous casualties on the Communist forces. This did not lead to victory, however. With the continued aid of China and the Soviet Union, North Vietnam was able to send a steady stream of supplies and soldiers to the South.

The Vietcong also refilled their ranks by recruiting civilians. Some South Vietnamese began to help the Communists or join the Vietcong. Destruction from American air strikes and the pacification policy turned many peasants into Vietcong fighters.

READING CHECK **Summarizing** What fighting strategies did the NVA and the Vietcong use?

U.S. Forces Mobilize

More than 2.5 million Americans served in the Vietnam War. On average, the soldiers who served in Vietnam were slightly younger than the U.S. troops who fought in Korea and World War II. Most Vietnam soldiers were not well educated. Some 80 percent of the American troops had a high school education or less.

The draft At the start of the war, most American troops were professional soldiers—volunteers who enlisted in the armed forces. As the American force in Vietnam steadily increased, however, the U.S. government depended more and more heavily on drafted soldiers.

About 25 percent of the young men who registered for the draft were excused from service for health reasons. Another 30 percent received deferments, or postponements of service. Men enrolled in college were able to get deferments. Enrollment at American colleges and universities skyrocketed as a result. Draft boards monitored student progress, however, and could cancel a deferment if a student's grades were too low.

Because college students could get draft deferments, young men from higher-income families were less likely to serve in Vietnam. Poor Americans served in numbers greater than their proportion of the general population. "I'm bitter," said one firefighter whose son died in the war. "The college types, the professors, they go to Washington and tell the government what to do . . . But their sons, they don't end up in the swamps over there, in Vietnam."

Large numbers of African Americans traditionally enlisted in the military. For this reason, a high percentage of soldiers in combat positions were African American during the war's early years, when much of the fighting was done by volunteers. Therefore, the casualty rates of black soldiers at first were very high. For example, African Americans accounted for at least one fifth of all U.S. battle deaths in 1965 even though they made up 11 percent of the American population.

As the war continued, however, the draft largely ended this inequity. In 1969 the government made an attempt to reform the makeup of the military by instituting a lottery system for the draft. This lottery system drafted men based on birth dates chosen at random.

By putting an end to many deferments, it made the draft fairer, because now income levels were less important in determining who had to serve. Finally, in 1973 the government ended the unpopular draft and returned to filling its ranks with volunteers.

About 3 percent of eligible young men escaped the draft altogether during the Vietnam War, either by refusing to register or by leaving the United States. Thousands of American men went to Canada to avoid being sent to Vietnam.

One young man who fled to Canada commented on his experience. "I ran into quite a few Americans on the run from the draft," he reported. "They were scared . . . Most had been cut off from their parents who branded them cowards and traitors."

Noncombat positions Most Americans who went to Vietnam served in non-combat positions, such as those in administration, communications, engineering, medical care, and transportation. Even in these noncombat roles, however, soldiers faced dangers from the fighting. Enemy rockets and mortars often struck seemingly safe positions.

About 10,000 American military women served in noncombat positions, mostly as nurses. Some 20,000 to 45,000 more women worked in civilian capacities, many as volunteers for the Red Cross or other humanitarian relief organizations.

Skills Focus: Comparing and Contrasting   At Level

Reading Skill
The Draft

1. Review the history of the mobilization for the Vietnam War. Have students compare this information with information in the text about how the United States mobilized for World War I and World War II and the soldiers who served in these wars.

2. Have students work in pairs to develop a list of reasons why the draft during the Vietnam War came to be seen by some as unfair to the poor and minorities. Have students refer to the information in their text to find factual information to add to their lists.

3. Have volunteers read their lists to the class, and create a class list for all to see. **LS** **Visual-Spatial, Verbal-Linguistic**

   Alternative Assessment Handbook, Rubrics 13: Graphic Organizers; and 43: Writing to Persuade

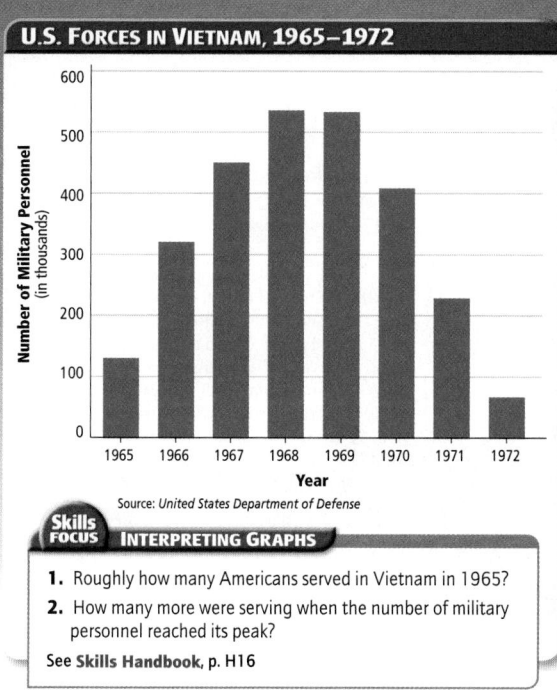

U.S. FORCES IN VIETNAM, 1965–1972

Number of Military Personnel (in thousands)

Source: United States Department of Defense

Skills FOCUS INTERPRETING GRAPHS

1. Roughly how many Americans served in Vietnam in 1965?
2. How many more were serving when the number of military personnel reached its peak?

See Skills Handbook, p. H16

U.S. military involvement in Vietnam peaked in 1968. Above, military nurses prepare wounded U.S. soldiers at a Saigon military base for their journey home in 1967.

Sylvia Lutz Holland was one of many nurses assigned to evacuation hospitals, where wounded troops were brought by helicopter. She had the heavy responsibility of deciding who to treat first.

"You'd look at the wounds, check the vital signs, and just make a decision—he's a go or he can wait," the nurse recalled. "We had to move fast."

Although nurses did not carry guns into battle, they were exposed to the horrors of combat on a daily basis.

HISTORY'S VOICES

❝ If the Army took a hill, we saw what was left over. I remember one boy who was brought in missing two legs and an arm, and his eyes were bandaged. A general came in later and pinned a Purple Heart on the boy's hospital gown, and the horror of it all was so amazing that it just took my breath away. ❞

—nurse Edie Meeks, *Newsweek* interview, March 8, 1999

READING CHECK Making Inferences How did the draft change the U.S. force in Vietnam?

Public Opinion Shifts

Most Americans supported U.S. involvement in the Vietnam War at first. By the end of 1968, however, more than 16,000 Americans had been killed in combat. A growing number of Americans began to question the wisdom of U.S. policy regarding involvement in Vietnam.

The media's impact News media coverage of the Vietnam War had a strong impact on American public opinion. During previous wars the military had imposed tight restrictions on the press. In Vietnam, however, reporters and television crews accompanied soldiers on patrol and interviewed people throughout South Vietnam.

Television coverage brought scenes of firefights and burning villages into Americans' living rooms. For this reason, the Vietnam War has been called the first "living room war."

The U.S. government allowed TV crews to cover the war, hoping television reports would show Americans that U.S. forces were making

THE VIETNAM WAR **961**

Public Opinion Shifts

Recall Who were the hawks and doves? *Hawks supported the goals of the war; doves opposed the war.*

Analyze What effect did the Vietnam War have on President Johnson's domestic agenda? *drained resources from domestic programs to support the war effort*

Evaluate Do you think the antiwar movement had a significant effect on American opinion toward the war? *possible answers—yes, highly visible protests drew attention to problems with the war; no, tactics used by the movement had the opposite effect, angering people and causing them to support the government*

📋 CRF: Primary Source Activity: Questioning the U.S. Involvement in Vietnam

Counterpoints

Views on the Vietnam War

Evaluate How does McGovern attempt to make the Vietnam War seem absurd? *He speaks of "saving the Vietnamese" even if that requires destroying the people and the country to do so.*

Answers

Reading Like a Historian *possible answer—His experience might have caused him to see the dark side of war, the loss of life and injuries, and the negative outcome of bombing villages and destroying homes.*

962

Views on the Vietnam War

National Security Adviser Walt W. Rostow believed that communism must be halted—by force if necessary.

Outspoken and plain-talking, Senator George McGovern opposed U.S. involvement in Vietnam.

❝ We are honoring a treaty which committed us to 'act to meet the common danger' in the face of 'aggression by means of armed attack' . . . And we are answering . . . the question: Are the word and commitment of the United States reliable? ❞

Walt W. Rostow, 1967

❝ We seem bent upon saving the Vietnamese from Ho Chi Minh, even if we have to kill them and demolish their country to do it . . . I do not intend to remain silent in the face of what I regard as a policy of madness which, sooner or later, will envelop my son and American youth by the millions for years to come. ❞

George McGovern, 1967

Skills Focus — READING LIKE A HISTORIAN

Recognizing Bias McGovern served as a bomber pilot during World War II. How might that experience have influenced his outlook on war?

See Skills Handbook, p. H33

ACADEMIC VOCABULARY

resource something that is made use of

progress in Vietnam. But to many Americans, the images they saw on television contradicted the optimistic government reports on the progress of the war. Some reporters questioned or criticized the government's reports as well. They reported on the ineffectiveness of South Vietnamese troops. In addition, they accused the U.S. government of inflating body counts to create the appearance of success.

Hawks and doves As the gap between official reports and media accounts widened, debate at home increased. Johnson was criticized by both **doves**—people who opposed the war—and **hawks**—people who supported the war's goals. Some hawks disapproved of the government's handling of the war. They believed more troops and heavier bombing were necessary to victory. Air force general Curtis LeMay expressed this view. "Here we are at the height of our power. The most powerful nation in the world. And yet we're afraid to use that power."

Doves had a variety of reasons for opposing the war. Diplomat George Kennan, for example, argued that Vietnam was not crucial to American national security. Pediatrician and author Dr. Benjamin Spock and others claimed that the United States was fighting against the wishes of a majority of Vietnamese. Martin Luther King Jr. expressed concern that the war was draining needed <u>resources</u> from Great Society programs.

HISTORY'S VOICES

❝ I watched the [antipoverty] program broken and eviscerated [gutted] as if it were some idle political plaything of a society gone mad on war, and I knew that America would never invest the necessary funds or energies in rehabilitation of its poor so long as Vietnam continued to draw men and skills and money like some demonic, destructive suction tube. ❞

—Martin Luther King Jr., sermon opposing the Vietnam War, 1967

Many other civil rights activists argued that it was unfair to expect African Americans to fight for democracy in a foreign land when discrimination continued at home. Polls showed that African Americans were much more likely than whites to believe that U.S. involvement in the war was a mistake.

Skills Focus: Analyzing Primary Sources

At Level

Reading Like a Historian Skill

Opposition and Support for the War

1. Guide students in a review of the opposition to and support for the war.

2. Have students work individually or in pairs to write paraphrases of the three quotes about the war on this page by Rostow, McGovern, and King. Have students share their paraphrases with the class.

3. Guide students in a discussion of the quotes, and then have students write a paragraph in which they explain which person they believe makes the strongest case for or against the war and why. **LS Verbal-Linguistic, Intrapersonal**

📋 Alternative Assessment Handbook, Rubric 37: Writing Assignments

Doves in Congress also became more vocal as the war continued. **J. William Fulbright** of Arkansas, head of the Senate Foreign Relations Committee, criticized Johnson's policies as too extreme. He held televised committee hearings in 1966 to give the war's critics a public voice.

The antiwar movement As opposition to the war grew, a large antiwar movement developed. The movement attracted a broad range of people, including students, civil rights workers, doctors, homemakers, retirees, and teachers.

Much of the antiwar activity took place on college campuses, where students held antiwar rallies and debates. Faculty members held teach-ins, where they sought to educate students about the war. Student opponents of the war also protested the draft and the presence of the Reserve Officers' Training Corps (ROTC) on campus.

One of the most vocal antiwar groups was Students for a Democratic Society (SDS). By the end of 1965, the SDS had members on 124 college campuses across the country. In April 1965, SDS members led the first national antiwar demonstration. More than 20,000 people marched to the Capitol in Washington, D.C., where they delivered a petition to Congress demanding that lawmakers "act immediately to end the war." The SDS and other antiwar groups also protested against universities that conducted research for the military. Some young men protested the draft by burning their draft cards, which the government sent to each man at the time he registered for the draft.

President Lyndon Johnson responded to the protests by insisting that the United States was protecting an ally against an aggressor. Secretary of State Dean Rusk put it this way: If the United States failed to support South Vietnam, what ally would ever trust the United States again?

While antiwar protesters were highly visible, they made up a small percentage of the U.S. population. Many Americans opposed the antiwar movement, especially the actions of the extreme groups. They were particularly angered by the burning of draft cards or American flags. Many veterans of previous wars spoke out against men who avoided the draft. Some opponents of the antiwar movement held rallies in support of the war, carrying signs with messages such as "America, Love It or Leave It" and "My Country, Right or Wrong."

READING CHECK **Identifying Cause and Effect** How and why did television affect public opinion about the Vietnam War?

SECTION 2 ASSESSMENT

go.hrw.com
Online Quiz
Keyword: SD7 HP29

Reviewing Ideas, Terms, and People

1. **a. Identify** What was **Operation Rolling Thunder**?
   b. Draw Conclusions Why do you think Operation Rolling Thunder failed to lead to a quick victory?

2. **a. Describe** What dangers did American soldiers face in Vietnam?
   b. Analyze Why did the U.S. program of **pacification** fail?
   c. Elaborate How do you think the pacification program might have been improved?

3. **a. Recall** Who was most likely to be drafted to serve in the Vietnam War?
   b. Draw Conclusions How do you think American soldiers fighting in Vietnam felt about the young men who tried to avoid being drafted?
   c. Elaborate What factors would a young man have weighed in deciding whether to flee the United States to avoid the draft?

4. **a. Describe** What were the views of the **doves** and the **hawks** during the Vietnam War?

b. Evaluate Do you think groups such as the SDS had much influence on public opinion about the Vietnam War? Why or why not?

Critical Thinking

5. **Contrast** Review your notes on the tactics of U.S. soldiers in the Vietnam War. Then copy the graphic organizer below and use it to contrast U.S. military strategies with those of the North Vietnamese Army and Vietcong.

U.S. Military	North Vietnamese Army, Vietcong

FOCUS ON WRITING

6. **Persuasive** Either as an antiwar or pro-government demonstrator, write a speech that you would give at a rally about the Vietnam War.

THE VIETNAM WAR **963**

Reading Focus

Public Opinion Shifts

Identify What was the SDS? *Students for a Democratic Society, an outspoken antiwar group*

Develop Why do you think most antiwar activities took place on college campuses? *possible answer—students were of the age most directly affected by the war (eligible for the draft)*

Review & Assess

Close

Guide students in a discussion of this question: How likely was it that the United States could have won the Vietnam War?

Review

Online Quiz, Section 2

Daily Test Practice Transparency

Assess

SE Section 2 Assessment

Progress Assessment: Section 2 Quiz

Alternative Assessment Handbook

Reteach

Interactive Reader and Study Guide, Section 2

Interactive Skills Tutor CD-ROM

Section 2 Assessment Answers

1. **a.** bombing over North Vietnam
   b. possible answers—jungle location; support from Soviet Union and China, quick repair of roads and bridges, protected by underground bunkers

2. **a.** jungle, land mines, booby traps, snipers, difficulty identifying the enemy
   b. Civilians resented leaving land.
   c. allow civilians to stay on land

3. **a.** poor; minorities; non-college-bound males
   b. possible answers—bitter, resentful, angry
   c. personal beliefs, family opinions

4. **a.** doves—opposed the war; hawks—supported the war's goals
   b. possible answer—yes; present on most college campuses, got media coverage

5. U.S.—massive air bombings; moved civilians from villages, search-and-destroy methods; NVA, Vietcong—guerrilla warfare, snipers, surprise attacks, land mines, booby traps

6. U.S. has obligation to defend Vietnam from Communists; Vietnam should fend for itself

Answers

Reading Check *brought the war into homes; showed brutality; contradicted military claims of progress*

963

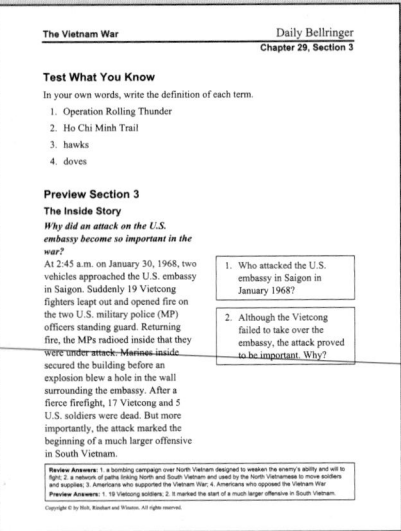

The Vietnam War   Daily Bellringer
                                    Chapter 29, Section 3

Test What You Know

In your own words, write the definition of each term.

1. Operation Rolling Thunder
2. Ho Chi Minh Trail
3. hawks
4. doves

Preview Section 3

The Inside Story

Why did an attack on the U.S. embassy become so important in the war?

At 2:45 a.m. on January 30, 1968, two vehicles approached the U.S. embassy in Saigon. Suddenly 19 Vietcong fighters leapt out and opened fire on the two U.S. military police (MP) officers standing guard. Returning fire, the MPs radioed inside that they were under attack. Marines inside secured the building before an explosion blew a hole in the wall surrounding the embassy. After a fierce firefight, 17 Vietcong and 5 U.S. soldiers were dead. But more importantly, the attack marked the beginning of a much larger offensive in South Vietnam.

1. Who attacked the U.S. embassy in Saigon in January 1968?

2. Although the Vietcong failed to take over the embassy, the attack proved to be important. Why?

Review Answers: 1. a bombing campaign over North Vietnam designed to weaken the enemy's ability and will to fight; 2. a network of paths linking North and South Vietnam and used by the North Vietnamese to move soldiers and supplies; 3. Americans who supported the Vietnam War; 4. Americans who opposed the Vietnam War
Preview Answers: 1. 19 Vietcong soldiers; 2. It marked the start of a much larger offensive in South Vietnam.

Copyright © by Holt, Rinehart and Winston. All rights reserved.

Taking Notes

Tet Offensive—massive Communist attack; U.S. begins to realize victory may not be possible; 1968 election—Vietnam is a major issue; Johnson decides not to run; Nixon is elected and promises to bring war to an end

go.hrw.com
Online Resources
KEYWORD: SD7 CH29
TOPIC: CONFLICTS AT HOME

BEFORE YOU READ

MAIN IDEA

As the Vietnam War dragged on and increasingly appeared to be unwinnable, deep divisions developed in American society.

READING FOCUS

1. What was the Tet Offensive?
2. What were the effects of the Tet Offensive?
3. How did President Johnson try to find a solution to the war?
4. How did the election of 1968 illustrate divisions in American society?

KEY TERMS AND PEOPLE

Tet Offensive
Robert S. McNamara
Eugene McCarthy
Hubert Humphrey
George Wallace

TAKING NOTES As you read, take notes on the main events of the Vietnam War in 1968 and their significance. Organize your notes in a graphic organizer like the one below.

Vietnam War, 1968

Event	Significance

THE INSIDE STORY

Why did an attack on the U.S. Embassy become so important in the war? At 2:45 a.m. on January 31, 1968, two vehicles approached the compound that housed the U.S. embassy in Saigon, South Vietnam's capital city. At the compound's entrance, 19 Vietcong fighters jumped out and opened fire with automatic weapons. The two American military police (MP) officers guarding the entrance returned fire as they backed through the heavy steel gate and locked it. Then they radioed Signal 300, the code for an enemy attack.

Suddenly, a huge explosion shook the neighborhood as the attackers blew a hole in the high concrete wall surrounding the compound. "They're coming in—help me!" one MP shouted into his radio. Then the radio went silent.

Both MPs were killed as the Vietcong poured through the hole in the wall. The MPs, however, had managed to delay the attackers long enough to allow the marines inside the compound to seal the main embassy building. Other U.S. troops rushed to the scene. A fierce firefight spread across the grounds of the compound.

By 9:15 a.m. the fighting was over. All but two of the Vietcong were dead, along with five American soldiers.

General William Westmoreland arrived a few minutes later. "It's a relatively small incident," he declared. His assessment proved to be wrong. The assault on the embassy was part of a much larger attack that ultimately changed the course of the Vietnam War. ◼

▼ Saigon erupted into a battle zone in the months following the attack on the U.S. Embassy.

Under Attack

964

Teach the Main Idea

At Level

1968: A Turning Point

1. **Teach** Ask students the Reading Focus questions to teach this section.

2. **Apply** Arrange students in two groups. Have students prepare for a debate in which one side argues that the Tet Offensive was a defeat for the NVA and Vietcong, and the other side holds that it was a defeat for the U.S. Have groups compile their arguments and then have volunteers from each side debate the issue for the class.

3. **Review** As you review the section,

have students assess which side was most committed to winning.

4. **Practice/Homework** Have students write a paragraph predicting what Americans might have thought if officials had stopped reporting that the U.S. was winning in Vietnam. **LS Interpersonal, Verbal-Linguistic**

 Alternative Assessment Handbook, Rubrics 9: Comparing and Contrasting; 11: Discussions; and 41: Writing to Express

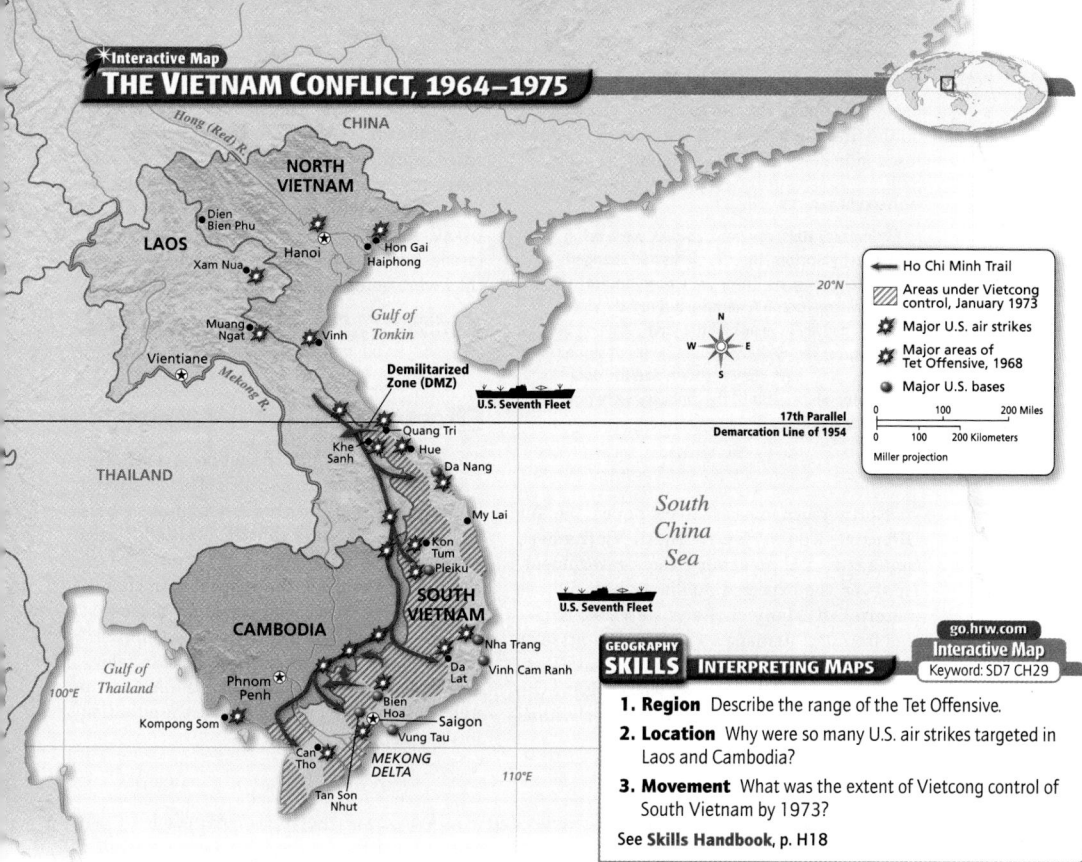

CHINA

Hong (Red) R.

NORTH VIETNAM

LAOS

Dien Bien Phu

Xam Nua

Hanoi
Hon Gai
Haiphong

Muang Ngat

Vientiane

Vinh

Gulf of Tonkin

Mekong R.

THAILAND

Demilitarized Zone (DMZ)

Quang Tri
Khe Sanh
Hue
Da Nang

My Lai

Kon Tum
Pleiku

CAMBODIA

SOUTH VIETNAM

Nha Trang
Da Lat
Vinh Cam Ranh

South China Sea

Phnom Penh

Kompong Som

Bien Hoa
Saigon
Vung Tau

Can Tho

MEKONG DELTA

Tan Son Nhut

Gulf of Thailand

100°E
110°E
20°N

U.S. Seventh Fleet

U.S. Seventh Fleet

17th Parallel
Demarcation Line of 1954

Legend:
- ← Ho Chi Minh Trail
- ▨ Areas under Vietcong control, January 1973
- ✷ Major U.S. air strikes
- ✷ Major areas of Tet Offensive, 1968
- ● Major U.S. bases

N W E S

0   100   200 Miles
0   100   200 Kilometers
Miller projection

GEOGRAPHY SKILLS INTERPRETING MAPS

go.hrw.com
Interactive Map
Keyword: SD7 CH29

1. **Region** Describe the range of the Tet Offensive.

2. **Location** Why were so many U.S. air strikes targeted in Laos and Cambodia?

3. **Movement** What was the extent of Vietcong control of South Vietnam by 1973?

See Skills Handbook, p. H18

The Tet Offensive

The Vietcong assault on the U.S. Embassy marked the start of the **Tet Offensive**, a series of massive coordinated attacks throughout South Vietnam. The Tet Offensive caused 1968 to become a critical year in the Vietnam War.

Khe Sanh In late 1967 U.S. military leaders began noticing increased traffic on the Ho Chi Minh Trail. They suspected a major assault was coming. In January 1968 thousands of NVA and Vietcong troops struck an isolated U.S. military base in Khe Sanh (KAY sahn), in northwestern South Vietnam. Communist troops surrounded the base and pounded it with artillery fire. News reporters compared the siege to the French battle at Dien Bien Phu in 1954. After the 77-day siege ended, however, the Americans still held Khe Sanh.

General Westmoreland concluded that preparations for the Khe Sanh assault explained the increased Ho Chi Minh Trail traffic. In fact, Khe Sanh and other rural attacks were diversions. Their purpose was to draw U.S. and ARVN forces away from urban areas, where the major strikes were planned.

The main attacks The main Communist offensive began on January 30, 1968. This was the start of Tet, the Vietnamese New Year. In previous years, the opposing sides had observed a cease-fire during the holiday, with many South Vietnamese soldiers actually going home to celebrate.

In 1968 the Vietcong and North Vietnamese troops took advantage of this moment to launch an offensive. During the crippling campaign, some 84,000 Communist soldiers attacked 12 U.S. military bases and more than

THE VIETNAM WAR **965**

965

The Tet Offensive

Recall What happened when the U.S. Embassy in Saigon was attacked at the beginning of the Tet Offensive? *many Americans and South Vietnamese civilians were killed; did not encourage South Vietnamese to join Communist cause as Vietcong had hoped*

Make Judgments Do you believe, as did General Westmoreland, that the Tet Offensive was a defeat for the Communists? *yes—Vietcong and NVA lost many soldiers and cities; no, Tet was a major psychological victory for North Vietnam and the Vietcong*

② What were the effects of the Tet Offensive? *showed that no part of South Vietnam was safe from attack; caused Americans to doubt the government's policies in the war; allowed other Democrats to challenge President Johnson's reelection*

Effects of the Tet Offensive

Recall Who was Walter Cronkite? *a highly trusted and respected news anchor, who came to doubt that the war could be won*

Explain How did the Tet Offensive cause many Americans to doubt that the U.S. would soon win the war? *demonstrated that no area in South Vietnam was safe from attack*

Answers

Linking to Today *immediate communication, media embedded with the troops*

Reading Check *They hoped the South Vietnamese would revolt against their government.*

966

---

100 cities across South Vietnam. The U.S. Embassy was one of several Saigon sites attacked on the first night. A South Vietnamese government official recalled the assault.

HISTORY'S VOICES

> ❝Embassy staff, covered in blood, were being treated by doctors. Humble clerks had changed their pens for guns. There were dead bodies everywhere—some American, but mostly Viet Cong. They lay in heaps on the lawn, staining the green grass red with blood . . . Chunks of stone and concrete were strewn about, and the once beautiful white walls of the embassy were now full of bullet holes.❞
>
> —Tran Van Huong, quoted in *Nam: The Vietnam Experience, 1965–75*

North Vietnamese leaders hoped the Tet Offensive would inspire South Vietnamese civilians to rise up against their government. However, the expected public support did not materialize. Many civilians were left homeless from the damage caused by the attacks. The Communists also slaughtered South Vietnamese people they believed were helping the Americans. This also turned many civilians against the Vietcong.

General Westmoreland described the Tet Offensive as a decisive defeat for the Communists. After more than a month of fighting, the cities captured by the Vietcong and NVA were retaken, and about 45,000 enemy soldiers were killed. About 1,100 American and 2,300 ARVN troops also died. Despite suffering such heavy losses, however, the Communists showed that they were determined to keep fighting.

READING CHECK **Identifying the Main Idea** Why did the Communists launch the Tet Offensive?

Effects of the Tet Offensive

The Tet Offensive showed that no part of South Vietnam was safe from attack. This shattered many people's belief that Communist forces were weakening and that the United States would soon win the war.

Walter Cronkite, the respected anchor of *CBS Evening News*, said privately, "I thought we were winning the war! What . . . is going on?" In February 1968 Cronkite broadcast a television report in which he offered the American public his personal assessment of the situation in Vietnam.

Linking TO Today

Battlefield Reporting

Photographs of Civil War battlefields and newsreels from World War II helped to inform civilians about those wars. Yet frequently this information was well out of date by the time it reached the American public.

As technology improved, the way people learned about wars changed. During the Vietnam War, relatively lightweight cameras and improved shipping service meant that stories could be filmed and flown back to the United States within 24 hours. The evening news brought dramatic and disturbing images of the war into American homes.

During the Iraq War in 2003, reporters relied on laptop computers and satellite videophones. News traveled around the world almost instantly, reaching the United States via the Internet as well as by television.

Working conditions also changed for reporters. In Vietnam, journalists often traveled with troops, but they were not officially connected to the military. During the Iraq War, reporters could choose to be "embedded" with a military unit. They received training and an honorary rank. Journalists gained greater access to troops. However, critics charged that the arrangement compromised the objectivity and scope of their reporting.

Drawing Conclusions What were the biggest changes in war coverage during the last 150 years?

A U.S. news photographer during the Iraq War uses a computer, generator, and satellite phone to send his images back to the office.

966 CHAPTER 29

Reading Skill
Guerrilla Warfare

1. Review the results of the Tet Offensive with students. Have students total the number of people who died during it. Guide students in a discussion of the number, and ask them how they think the American people might have reacted when they learned it.

2. Remind students that body counts were often used as a measure of success during the Vietnam War. Ask students if they believe body counts of dead enemy soldiers are a good measure of success in guerrilla warfare.

3. Organize students in small groups and have the groups discuss the use of body counts as a measure of military success. Then have students write a brief essay supporting or opposing this practice and explaining why.

LS Verbal-Linguistic, Logical-Mathematical

Alternative Assessment Handbook, Rubrics 11: Discussions; and 42: Writing to Inform

❝ We have been too often disappointed by the optimism of the American leaders . . . For it seems now more certain than ever that the bloody experience of Vietnam is to end in a stalemate. ❞

—Walter Cronkite on CBS television, February 27, 1968

Growing doubts The president despaired when he heard Cronkite's words. "If I've lost Cronkite I've lost middle America," Johnson said. Major national magazines such as *Time* and *Newsweek* also expressed doubts about the war and began to call for its end.

Public criticism of the government's policies grew louder and more intense. Johnson felt trapped as picketers surrounded the White House chanting, "Hey, hey, LBJ, how many kids did you kill today?"

Many leaders within the Johnson administration also became critical of his policies. As secretary of defense for both Presidents Kennedy and Johnson, **Robert S. McNamara** had played a key role in shaping U.S. strategy in Vietnam. By 1968, however, he had become discouraged by America's lack of success in the war. He began openly seeking ways to launch peace negotiations to end it.

Democratic challengers As Johnson sought re-election in 1968, roughly 3 out of 4 Americans opposed his policies in Vietnam. The president found himself facing challengers for his party's nomination. Minnesota senator **Eugene McCarthy**, a vocal critic of the war, finished a strong second to Johnson in the New Hampshire primary in March. Soon afterward, New York senator Robert Kennedy, the former U.S. attorney general, entered the race.

Shaken by the divisions in his party, an exhausted Johnson made a shocking announcement during a speech on national television.

HISTORY'S VOICES

❝ With America's sons in the fields far away, with America's future under challenge right here at home . . . I do not believe that I should devote an hour or a day of my time to any personal partisan causes . . . Accordingly, I shall not seek, and I will not accept, the nomination of my party for another term as president. ❞

—Lyndon Johnson, March 31, 1968

READING CHECK **Identifying Cause and Effect** How did the media react to the Tet Offensive?

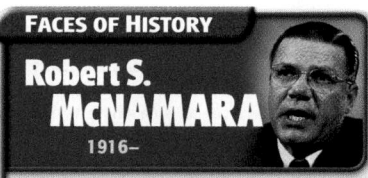

FACES OF HISTORY

Robert S. McNAMARA
1916–

After college, Robert McNamara attended Harvard University, earning a master's degree in business administration. He then taught for a few years until he joined the military during World War II. Following the war, McNamara took a job at Ford, helping to make the automobile company more profitable.

In 1961 McNamara joined President Kennedy's cabinet as head of the Defense Department. He introduced modern business practices to the military and strengthened its conventional fighting capability. As the conflict in Vietnam grew, McNamara became the leading spokesperson and chief prosecutor of what some called McNamara's war. By 1968, however, he had doubts about the war. He resigned as defense secretary and took a position as head of the World Bank.

Summarize What changes did McNamara make to the military?

Johnson Seeks a Solution

General Westmoreland argued that the Tet Offensive had been devastating to the enemy. He believed that if more ground troops were sent to Vietnam, he could deliver a crushing blow to the weakened Communists. In March 1968 he sent President Johnson a request for 206,000 more soldiers.

When the *New York Times* reported Westmoreland's request, many Americans were outraged. They wondered why more U.S. troops were needed if the war was being won, as the government had been insisting. In part because of the strong public outcry, the president denied Westmoreland's request.

Johnson knew he needed to reassess his entire war strategy, but his own advisers could not agree on the best course. Many U.S. military leaders believed that the administration was not doing all that could be done to win the war. In particular, some officers felt that Johnson's decision not to invade North Vietnam with ground troops unfairly limited them in fighting the war.

Even before the Tet Offensive, McNamara and some other government leaders had come to believe that Johnson's war policies were too extreme. McNamara suggested limiting the air strikes and reversing the escalation of the war.

THE VIETNAM WAR **967**

Johnson Seeks a Solution

Recall What alterations to President Johnson's policies in Vietnam did McNamara suggest? *limiting air strikes; stopping the policy of escalating the war*

Analyze Why did peace talks between the U.S. and North Vietnam stall so quickly? *Each side had demands that the other found unacceptable.*

4 How did the election of 1968 illustrate divisions in American society? *Democrats were divided after convention; many Americans despised tactics of the antiwar movement; generation gap as young adults found themselves at odds with their parents*

The Election of 1968

Identify Who was Hubert Humphrey? *Johnson's vice president; Democratic candidate for president in 1968*

Contrast How did the policies of McCarthy, Kennedy, and Humphrey differ? *McCarthy and Kennedy called for a rapid end to the war; Humphrey supported the Johnson administration's policies in Vietnam*

Answers

Reading Check *attempted to seek a peace agreement*

968

HISTORY'S VOICES

❝The picture of the world's greatest superpower killing or seriously injuring 1,000 non-combatants a week, while trying to pound a tiny backward nation into submission on an issue whose merits are hotly disputed is not a pretty one.❞

—Robert S. McNamara, letter to President Johnson, May 19, 1967

Johnson agreed it was time to try to negotiate with North Vietnam. In the same televised speech in which he stated he would not run for re-election, he announced that he would seek a peace agreement to end the war.

In May 1968 delegates from North Vietnam and the United States met in Paris. Immediately the talks stalled over two issues. The United States wanted all NVA troops out of South Vietnam, and North Vietnam would not accept a temporary South Vietnam government that included the U.S.-backed president, Nguyen Van Thieu. The two sides would not reach an agreement for several more years.

READING CHECK **Summarizing** How did President Johnson try to end the Vietnam War before the conclusion of his presidency?

The Election of 1968

After Johnson withdrew from the 1968 presidential campaign, his vice president, **Hubert Humphrey**, entered the race. The Vietnam War was a key issue among voters. Humphrey defended the administration's war policies. His Democratic rivals, Senators Eugene McCarthy and Robert Kennedy, called for a rapid end to the war. When Kennedy announced his candidacy, he explained his position on Vietnam.

HISTORY'S VOICES

❝The reality of recent events in Vietnam has been glossed over with illusions . . . I have tried in vain to alter our course in Vietnam before it further saps our spirit and our manpower, further raises the risks of wider war, and further destroys the country and the people it was meant to save. I cannot stand aside from the contest that will decide our nation's future and our children's future.❞

—Robert F. Kennedy, March 16, 1968

The Democratic primary fight Kennedy quickly gained ground in the race by winning primaries in Indiana and Nebraska. In June

A Year of Turmoil: 1968

❶ Johnson does not seek reelection

Wearied by events during the Vietnam War, Johnson declines to seek another term. His vice president, Hubert Humphrey, joins the race.

❷ Robert Kennedy enters the race for president

Kennedy, the Democratic frontrunner, celebrates his victory in the California primary with a speech at the Ambassador Hotel.

❸ Kennedy is assassinated

Moments later Kennedy is gunned down in the hotel kitchen. Restaurant worker Juan Romero comforts the fatally wounded senator.

968 CHAPTER 29

Collaborative Learning

At Level

Johnson Tries to Find a Solution

1. Organize students into small groups and have each group make a list of the problems President Johnson faced in Vietnam in early 1968. Have volunteers share their lists with the class, and create a large class list for all to see. Have all students copy the class list.

2. Have each group discuss possible solutions to each of the problems facing Johnson and add the proposed solutions to their list.

3. Have students use the information from their group list to write an advisory memorandum

to the president outlining steps that he might take to solve the problems or greatly improve the situation in Vietnam .

4. Have volunteers read their memoranda to the class. **LS Interpersonal, Verbal-Linguistic**

   Alternative Assessment Handbook, Rubrics 11: Discussions; 12: Drawing Conclusions; and 43: Writing to Persuade

he won the crucial California primary. This made him the favorite to win the Democratic presidential nomination.

As he finished his victory speech in a Los Angeles hotel, Kennedy flashed a victory sign to the audience and declared, "On to Chicago, and let's win there." Chicago was the location for the upcoming Democratic National Convention, where delegates would choose the party's presidential candidate.

After Senator Robert Kennedy walked off the stage, a gunman shot him three times. He died less than 24 hours later. The assassin, Sirhan Sirhan, was a Jordanian immigrant who was angry about Kennedy's support for the nation of Israel.

The Democratic Convention In August, the remaining candidates fought for the nomination at the Democratic National Convention. Inside the convention hall, the delegates debated between McCarthy and Humphrey. Some people thought McCarthy's position on the war showed personal weakness. Others disliked Humphrey because he was too close to Johnson's failed war policies.

Outside the hall, chaos erupted in the streets of Chicago. About 10,000 protesters from across the country had gathered to demand an immediate end to the war and to pressure the delegates to reject Johnson's Vietnam policies. They held rallies and chanted antiwar slogans calling for "Peace now!"

Chicago mayor Richard Daley dispatched thousands of police and national guard troops to maintain order. The situation soon exploded into violence, when a huge group of demonstrators attempted to march on the convention hall. Some protesters threw rocks and bottles at the police. Daley described them as "a lawless violent group of terrorists menacing the lives of millions of our people."

The police clubbed demonstrators with rifle butts and clubs and used tear gas to disperse the crowd. Scuffles even broke out inside the convention hall. Many people, including innocent bystanders, were injured as well.

Television reporters and camera crews recorded the violence. They showed that in some instances police officers reacted with excessive force. Viewers watching the live coverage on television were shocked at the brutality. The

❹ Protests at the Democratic Convention
Antiwar delegates inside the Chicago convention hall pressured candidates to support a quick end to the war.

❺ Chaos erupts outside the convention
In the streets of Chicago, emotional protests met with a brutal police response. Radical activists, the so-called Chicago Seven, were found guilty of conspiring to incite riots, but their convictions were later overturned.

969

Reading Focus

The Election of 1968

Identify Who was George Wallace? *former governor of Alabama; ran for president under the American Independent Party*

Analyze How did so many people across the country learn about the demonstrations, chaos, and violence in Chicago? *It was thoroughly covered by TV and print media.*

Interpret What did the chaos at the Democratic National Convention reveal about divisions in American society? *generation gap; young adults felt at odds with their parents*

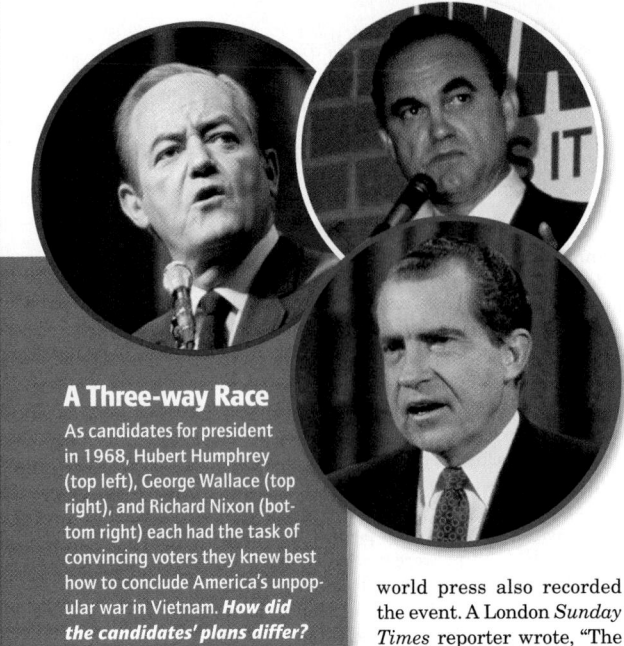

A Three-way Race
As candidates for president in 1968, Hubert Humphrey (top left), George Wallace (top right), and Richard Nixon (bottom right) each had the task of convincing voters they knew best how to conclude America's unpopular war in Vietnam. *How did the candidates' plans differ?*

world press also recorded the event. A London *Sunday Times* reporter wrote, "The kids screamed and were beaten to the ground . . . I saw one girl surrounded by cops, screaming, 'Please God, help me. Help me.'"

More than 600 Chicago protesters were arrested. Despite the disturbances, convention delegates reached a decision and nominated Hubert Humphrey. He chose Senator Edmund Muskie of Maine as his running mate.

The chaos at the Democratic National Convention was one symptom of a growing "generation gap" over government, politics, and the Vietnam War. Many teenagers and young adults of the 1960s found themselves at odds with their parents, who had experienced the Great Depression and World War II. Young people accused the previous generation of valuing material comfort over justice and equality. Younger Americans also increasingly distrusted their political leaders, while older Americans urged them to have confidence in their government.

Richard Nixon, Republican A divided Democratic Party improved the Republicans' chances of winning the presidency. Former vice president Richard Nixon swept the Republican primaries and easily won the nomination at the Republican National Convention in Miami

Beach, Florida. Nixon chose Governor Spiro Agnew of Maryland as his running mate. He made this choice, in part, to attract conservative southern voters.

Nixon appealed to the patriotism of many mainstream Americans. Even people who were sympathetic to the antiwar movement had been put off by the behavior of protesters at the Democratic National Convention in Chicago. In a time of chaos, many Americans appreciated Nixon's promise of "law and order."

Nixon told voters that the "war must be ended. It must be ended honorably." He claimed to have a secret plan to end the war. He refused to explain his plan, saying that doing so might interfere with Johnson's efforts to achieve a peace settlement. Many voters were skeptical of a plan they could learn nothing about.

George Wallace, independent Another serious candidate in the race was former Alabama governor **George Wallace**. Earlier in the 1960s Wallace had gained national attention for his staunch opposition to the civil rights movement and school desegregation. Wallace was nominated for president by the American Independent Party. In his speeches, he raged against war protesters.

Wallace's strongest supporters were Democrats who opposed liberal policies. Many of these voters were conservative Democratic white southerners and working-class whites from across the nation. Although Wallace was a Democrat, Republicans feared that Wallace might take votes from Nixon.

The election campaign Nixon led in the polls for most of the campaign. As election day neared, though, his lead narrowed. Humphrey made some gains in the polls in September, after a speech in which he finally separated himself from Johnson's Vietnam policies. Humphrey said that he believed the bombing of North Vietnam should be stopped. He also argued that more responsibility for the war should go to South Vietnamese forces.

In addition, progress was made in the peace talks in Paris. The North Vietnamese agreed to include South Vietnamese representatives in the discussions if the air strikes on North Vietnam were stopped. Just days before the vote, President Johnson announced an end to the bombing of North Vietnam.

Skills Focus: Analyzing Secondary Sources · At Level

Reading Like a Historian Skill
The 1968 Election · Research Required

1. Remind students that the media covered the 1968 conventions thoroughly, and people across the nation saw the dissension, the chaos, police actions, and the violence.

2. Have students conduct outside research using reliable Internet sites and traditional print sources to read more about the 1968 election.

3. Have students use the information from their research to create two political cartoons,

complete with titles and captions, about the candidates Richard Nixon and Hubert Humphrey.

4. Have volunteers share their cartoons, and then display them for the class to see.
LS Visual-Spatial, Verbal-Linguistic

📝 Alternative Assessment Handbook, Rubrics 27: Political Cartoons; and 30: Research

Answers

Photo *Humphrey defended Democratic administration's war policies; Wallace denounced war protesters; Nixon promised to win the war with honor*

The election results The results of the popular election in November were very close. Just 510,000 votes separated Nixon and Humphrey, out of 73 million cast. Nixon received 43.4 percent of the vote, while Humphrey received 42.7 percent. As expected, Wallace was an important factor in the race, as nearly 10 million people, or 13.5 percent of electorate, voted for him.

In the electoral college, Nixon's margin of victory was wider. He carried the heavily populated states of California, Illinois, Ohio, and Florida and won many more electoral votes than the other two candidates combined. Nixon received 301 electoral votes to Humphrey's 191. Wallace, who won five states, received 46 electoral votes. This and his percentage of the popular vote made him one of the most successful third-party candidates in U.S. history.

Nixon's comfortable victory in the electoral college provided him with a mandate that the popular vote denied him. This sense of approval gave Nixon the confidence to pursue new policies to achieve victory in Vietnam—policies that would raise divisions over the war to a level not yet seen.

READING CHECK **Drawing Conclusions** How did events at the 1968 Democratic National Convention illustrate the divisions that existed within the Democratic Party?

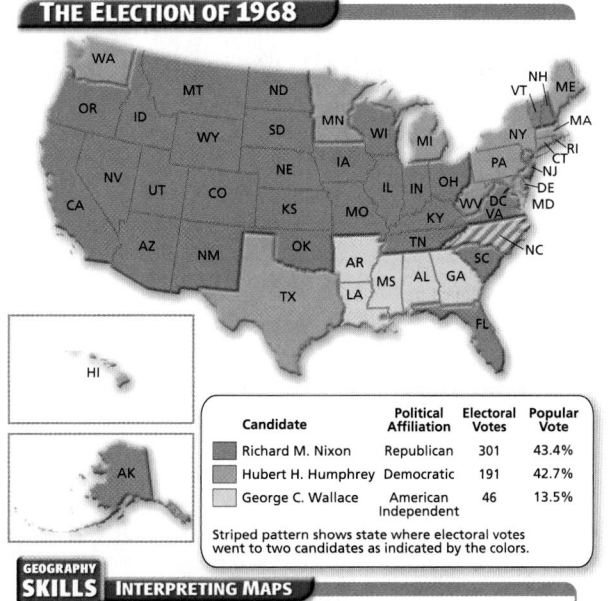

THE ELECTION OF 1968

Candidate	Political Affiliation	Electoral Votes	Popular Vote
Richard M. Nixon	Republican	301	43.4%
Hubert H. Humphrey	Democratic	191	42.7%
George C. Wallace	American Independent	46	13.5%

Striped pattern shows state where electoral votes went to two candidates as indicated by the colors.

GEOGRAPHY SKILLS | **INTERPRETING MAPS**

1. **Region** What effect did the presence of a third-party candidate have on the outcome of the race between the two major party candidates? Explain.

2. **Place** How did the electoral vote differ in North Carolina?

See Skills Handbook, p. H21

SECTION 3 ASSESSMENT

go.hrw.com
Online Quiz
Keyword: SD7 HP29

Reviewing Ideas, Terms, and People

1. a. Recall Why did NVA and Vietcong forces attack the U.S. military base at Khe Sanh?
b. Contrast How did the **Tet Offensive** differ from previous fighting in Vietnam?
c. Evaluate Do you think the Tet Offensive should be considered a turning point in the Vietnam War? Why or why not?

2. a. Identify What were **Walter Cronkite**'s views on the war after the Tet Offensive?
b. Analyze Why did President Johnson decide not to run for re-election in 1968?
c. Elaborate Why do you think **Robert S. McNamara** changed his mind about the Vietnam War?

3. a. Recall How did Americans view General William Westmoreland's March 1968 request for more troops?
b. Design What advice would you have given President Johnson about how to proceed with the war in 1968? Why?

4. a. Identify Who won the presidential election of 1968?

b. Analyze What was the goal of the protesters at the 1968 Democratic National Convention?
c. Predict How might the election of 1968 affect the course of the Vietnam War?

Critical Thinking

5. Sequence Review your notes on the main events of the Vietnam War in 1968. Then copy the graphic organizer below and use it to put the events in the correct sequence.

FOCUS ON SPEAKING

6. Descriptive As a television news journalist, deliver a report giving Americans an update on the events of either the Tet Offensive or the Democratic National Convention.

THE VIETNAM WAR **971**

Bellringer

The Inside Story. . . Use the **Daily Bellringer Transparency** to help students answer the question.

📦 Daily Bellringer Transparency, Section 4

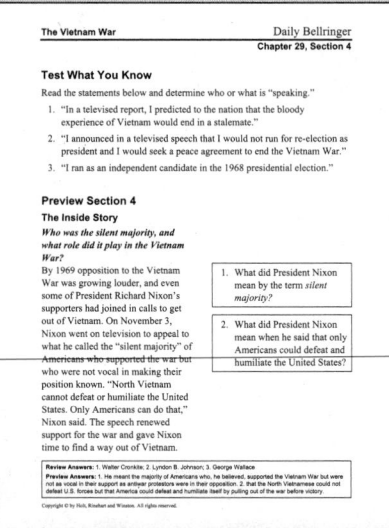

The Vietnam War   Daily Bellringer
                         Chapter 29, Section 4

Test What You Know

Read the statements below and determine who or what is "speaking."

1. "In a televised report, I predicted to the nation that the bloody experience of Vietnam would end in a stalemate."
2. "I announced in a televised speech that I would not run for re-election as president and I would seek a peace agreement to end the Vietnam War."
3. "I ran as an independent candidate in the 1968 presidential election."

Preview Section 4

The Inside Story

Who was the silent majority, and what role did it play in the Vietnam War?

By 1969 opposition to the Vietnam War was growing louder, and even some of President Richard Nixon's supporters had joined in calls to get out of Vietnam. On November 3, Nixon went on television to appeal to what he called the "silent majority" of Americans who supported the war but who were not vocal in making their position known. "North Vietnam cannot defeat or humiliate the United States. Only Americans can do that," Nixon said. The speech renewed support for the war and gave Nixon time to find a way out of Vietnam.

1. What did President Nixon mean by the term *silent majority*?
2. What did President Nixon mean when he said that only Americans could defeat and humiliate the United States?

Review Answers: 1. Walter Cronkite; 2. Lyndon B. Johnson; 3. George Wallace
Preview Answers: 1. He meant the majority of Americans who, he believed, supported the Vietnam War but were not as vocal in their support as antiwar protestors were in their opposition. 2. that the North Vietnamese could not defeat U.S. forces but that America could defeat and humiliate itself by pulling out of the war before victory.

Copyright © by Holt, Rinehart and Winston. All rights reserved.

Academic Vocabulary

Review with students the high-use academic term in this section.

analyze examine something carefully (p. 975)

📝 CRF: Vocabulary Builder Activity, Section 4

Taking Notes

devastated people and land of Southeast Asia; thousands of U.S. troops killed; thousands more wounded; veterans had trouble adjusting when they returned home; presidential war powers limited

go.hrw.com
Online Resources

KEYWORD: SD7 CH29
TOPIC: LAST PHASES OF
THE VIETNAM WAR

BEFORE YOU READ

MAIN IDEA

President Nixon eventually ended U.S. involvement in Vietnam, but the war had lasting effects on the United States and in Southeast Asia.

READING FOCUS

1. How did President Nixon's policies widen U.S. involvement in the war?
2. How and why did protests against the war increase?
3. How did Nixon achieve an end to U.S. involvement in Vietnam?
4. What was the war's legacy in the United States and in Vietnam?

KEY TERMS AND PEOPLE

Henry Kissinger
Vietnamization
silent majority
My Lai massacre
Pentagon Papers
George McGovern
Twenty-sixth Amendment
Khmer Rouge
War Powers Act

TAKING NOTES As you read, take notes on the effects of the Vietnam War. List the effects in a graphic organizer like the one below.

Effects of Vietnam War

Appealing to the Silent Majority

▼ Nixon greets a crowd of enthusiastic supporters in 1969.

972

THE INSIDE STORY

Who was the silent majority, and what role did it play in the Vietnam War?
In October 1969 thousands of protesters converged on Washington to voice their opposition to the Vietnam War. In Congress, demands increased that President Nixon withdraw American forces from Vietnam. Even some of the president's supporters joined the calls to end American involvement in the war.

Despite these events, Nixon remained convinced that most Americans still supported the war. He was confident that these hardworking, law-abiding citizens were simply too busy supporting their families and too intimidated by the radical antiwar protests to make their voices heard.

Nixon asked the television networks for airtime to deliver a major address. Contrary to the usual practice, no advance copies of his speech were released to the media. Speculation was immense. Was the president about to announce a U.S. troop withdrawal from Vietnam? Instead, on November 3, 1969, he went on television to denounce the antiwar protesters and appeal to the American people.

"To you, the great silent majority of my fellow Americans, I ask for your support," Nixon said. "Because, let us understand: North Vietnam cannot defeat or humiliate the United States. Only Americans can do that."

Nixon's speech renewed support for the war effort and dealt a setback to the antiwar movement. Although these effects proved only temporary, the "silent majority" speech bought Nixon time to find a way out of Vietnam.■

Teach the Main Idea

At Level

The War Ends

1. **Teach** Ask students the Reading Focus questions to teach this section.

2. **Apply** Organize students into small groups. Assign half the groups to represent the American government and the other half to represent North Vietnam during the steps and negotiations that led to U.S. withdrawal from Vietnam. Have each group develop a list of actions they will undertake, beginning with Nixon's first term in office, to end the war on favorable terms to itself.

3. **Review** Have volunteers from each group read their plans to the class. As you review the section, guide students in a discussion about reasonable steps or ways, if any, that the United States could have taken to achieve victory in Vietnam.

4. **Practice/Homework** Have students develop an outline based on their lists.
   LS Interpersonal, Verbal-Linguistic

   📝 Alternative Assessment Handbook, Rubric 11: Discussions

Widening the War

During his presidential campaign, Nixon had pledged that if elected he would end the war in Vietnam. Once in office, he and National Security Adviser **Henry Kissinger** devised plans to fulfill this promise. In 1969 Kissinger began secret peace negotiations in Paris with North Vietnamese revolutionary Le Duc Tho (LAY duhk TOH). "I don't look back on our meetings with any great joy," Kissinger later said of these tense talks. "Yet he was a person of substance and discipline who defended the position he represented with dedication."

Vietnamization Kissinger's secret negotiations were part of a larger U.S. strategy aimed at achieving what Nixon called "peace with honor." A part of this plan was a strategy called **Vietnamization**. This involved turning over more of the fighting in Vietnam to the South Vietnamese while gradually bringing U.S. ground troops home.

Nixon's hope was that Vietnamization would give South Vietnamese leaders enough time to create a stable anti-Communist government. If this could not be achieved, Nixon wanted to delay the collapse of the South Vietnamese government until after the U.S. troops were gone. This would at least help to avoid the appearance of an embarrassing U.S. defeat.

Nixon began slowly withdrawing American forces from South Vietnam. When he took office in 1969, there were some 540,000 U.S. troops in that country. By the end of 1972, the number had been reduced to just over 24,000.

Antiwar activists opposed Nixon's plan for Vietnamization because it did not immediately end the war. Yet Nixon was convinced that he had the firm backing of the **silent majority** of Americans who he believed disapproved of antiwar protesters and generally supported the government's goals in Vietnam.

Laos and Cambodia Although he withdrew U.S. troops from Vietnam, Nixon at the same time also secretly expanded the war. In early 1969 he ordered the bombing of Cambodia, with the goal of disrupting supply lines along the Ho Chi Minh Trail. Nixon also wanted to demonstrate to North Vietnam that he was willing to widen the war in order to gain more favorable terms at the negotiating table.

He concealed the air strikes from the American people—including members of Congress and even some key military leaders.

The war expanded further in 1970, when Nixon sent U.S. and ARVN troops into Cambodia, and into Laos the following year, to destroy North Vietnamese army bases. Nixon also renewed the bombing of North Vietnam, hoping to pressure the country's leaders into seeking peace. "I call it the Madman Theory," he told his chief of staff, H. R. Haldeman. "I want the North Vietnamese to believe that I've reached the point where I might do anything to stop the war."

As Johnson had done before him, Nixon underestimated the opposition's resolve, which survived even the death of Ho Chi Minh in 1969. North Vietnam staged a major invasion in March 1972, driving deep into South Vietnam.

READING CHECK   **Identifying the Main Idea**
Why did Nixon order the bombing of Cambodia?

Tough Negotiators
President Nixon's national security adviser, Henry Kissinger (left), and North Vietnamese leader Le Duc Tho (right) negotiated an end to the war in secret meetings in Paris. *What other strategies did Nixon plan to bring an end to the war?*

973

Reading Focus

❷ **How and why did protests against the war increase?** *After news of the invasion of Cambodia, campus protests increased sharply, with violence and deaths in some places.*

Increasing Protests

Recall What happened at Kent State? *After violent protests, National Guard troops fired on students, killing four.*

Summarize Why did students and faculty at a number of universities go on strike? *to protest the shootings of students and the war*

Develop Do you think President Nixon's comment about not letting the minority dictate his actions in Vietnam was valid? Explain your answer. *possible answers—yes, the president must take the course of action he believes is best for the nation, cannot set policy based on public opinion; no, it was no longer a minority of Americans that wanted out of Vietnam*

📖 Political Cartoons Activities for American History: Cartoon 57: Around in Circles

Primary Source

*Tin soldiers and Nixon's coming
We're finally on our own
This summer I hear the drumming
Four dead in Ohio!
Four dead in Ohio!*

From "Ohio" by Neil Young. Copyright © 1970 by Neil Young. Reproduced by permission of **Broken Arrow Music Corporation, a division of Cotillion Music Inc., BMI (Broadcast Music Inc.).**

Increasing Protests

On April 30, 1970, Nixon announced that he had ordered U.S. troops into Cambodia. Antiwar protests intensified around the country, especially on college campuses. "As much as we hated the war on April 29, we hated it more on April 30," said Tom Grace, a student at Kent State University in Ohio.

Campus violence On May 2, 1970, antiwar demonstrators at Kent State University set fire to the campus Reserve Officers' Training Corps (ROTC) building. The governor of Ohio sent National Guard troops to control further demonstrations. On May 4, students gathered in a grassy area on campus for an antiwar rally. The troops ordered the students to disperse. When some students threw rocks and shouted insults at the soldiers, several soldiers began firing into the crowd. Four students were killed, and nine others were injured. Some of those who were shot were not protesting but simply passing by on the way to class.

Nine days later, a similar incident occurred at Jackson State College in Mississippi. State police fired at protesters inside a dormitory, killing two students and wounding nine.

Americans were horrified by the images of young people shot dead on college campuses. Students and faculty members on campuses nationwide went on strike. These protests forced hundreds of colleges and universities to shut down temporarily.

The antiwar movement grows Nixon was convinced that the antiwar protesters represented only a minority of Americans. "I recognize that some of my fellow citizens disagree with the plan for peace that I have chosen," he said. "I would be untrue to my oath of office to be dictated by the minority." Nevertheless, by late 1969 polls showed that more than half of Americans opposed the war.

As public opinion turned increasingly against the war, the peace movement began to seem more mainstream and respectable to many middle-class Americans. It gradually became clear that the opponents of the war included more than just college students and other young Americans.

In 1969, for example, a coalition of antiwar groups consisting of clergy, trade unionists, and veterans established October 15 as a nationwide day of protest. Millions of people

Americans React to the War

Below, demonstrators show their support for the war. Right, an antiwar rally turns tragic at Kent State University in Ohio, leaving four students dead. At far right, war protesters take their cause to the nation's capital.

974 CHAPTER 29

Skills Focus: Summarizing

Below Level

Reading Skill
Kent State and Jackson State College

1. Review the information in the text about the shootings at Kent State University and Jackson State College with students.

2. Organize students in mixed-ability pairs and have each design a poster commemorating the deaths and injuries of the college students at these two colleges.

3. Have volunteers share their posters with the class, and then display posters in the classroom.

4. As an extension, have students write a poem or song lyrics about these two events, honoring the students who died. **LS Visual-Spatial, Auditory-Musical**

📖 Alternative Assessment Handbook, Rubrics 26: Poems and Songs; and 28: Posters

took part in peaceful demonstrations on what was called Moratorium Day, calling for a moratorium, or halt, to the war.

A month later more than 250,000 protesters gathered in Washington, D.C., for the largest antiwar demonstration in U.S. history. Police lined up buses in front of the White House to form a barrier between Nixon, who was inside, and the thousands of marchers in the streets.

In an especially emotional demonstration in April 1971, members of Vietnam Veterans Against the War gathered in front of the Capitol. Some 800 veterans threw down their war medals to protest the war. Never before had returning U.S. soldiers so strongly opposed a war that was still being fought.

Radical protests A small minority of protesters believed that demonstrations and marches did not go far enough to end the war. Some radical antiwar groups turned to violent measures. A group called the Weathermen set off more than 5,000 bombs in places such as the New York City police department, the Pentagon, and the Capitol.

In October 1969 the Weathermen carried out the Days of Rage, a failed attempt to shut down the city of Chicago. Group members

armed with clubs, lead pipes, chains, and gas masks clashed with police. Six Weathermen were shot, and many more were arrested. The negative reaction to the Days of Rage showed that most antiwar protesters did not support extremist groups or terrorist measures.

Troubling revelations In late 1969 Americans learned about a dark episode in the war's history. In March 1968 U.S. troops under the command of Lieutenant William Calley had entered the village of My Lai (mee LY) on a search-and-destroy mission to find Vietcong fighters. Although none were found, the soldiers killed at least 450 women, children, and elderly men.

The **My Lai massacre** was initially kept quiet by high-ranking military officials, but eventually former soldiers began talking about what they had witnessed. Calley was charged with murder in September 1969.

The My Lai atrocities further intensified the divisions between war supporters and opponents. Calley insisted that he had merely been doing his duty in the war on communism.

"We weren't in My Lai to kill human beings, really," he said. "We were there to kill ideology that is carried by—I don't know—pawns." Calley was convicted of murder and sentenced to life in prison. He was paroled in 1974.

In 1971 another news story boosted the momentum of the antiwar movement. The *New York Times* published a collection of secret government documents that traced the history of U.S. military involvement in Vietnam since the Truman years. Known as the **Pentagon Papers**, they revealed that government officials had been misleading the American people about the war for years. The leak angered and embarrassed President Nixon. Government lawyers failed to persuade the U.S. Supreme Court to suppress their publication.

Daniel Ellsberg, a former official at the Department of Defense, leaked the papers to the press. Ellsberg had originally been a supporter of the war. While spending time in Vietnam, however, he analyzed the effects of American policy and concluded that few South Vietnamese civilians supported the U.S.-backed government.

ACADEMIC VOCABULARY
analyze examine something carefully

READING CHECK **Contrasting** How did radical groups differ from other antiwar protesters?

THE VIETNAM WAR **975**

Reading Focus

❸ How did Nixon achieve an end to U.S. involvement in Vietnam? *After all attempts to bomb the North Vietnamese into concessions failed, Nixon agreed to remove all U.S. troops and help rebuild Vietnam.*

End of U.S. Involvement

Recall What was the Twenty-sixth Amendment? *lowered voting age from 21 to 18*

Analyze What was the effect of Kissinger's comment that peace with Vietnam was at hand? *ensured landslide victory for Nixon*

Evaluate What did the "Christmas bombing" accomplish? *nothing; North Vietnam did not yield*

Recent Scholarship

Why the North Won the Vietnam War is a collection of essays by nine scholars and diplomats who look back at Vietnam and examine how the United States, a world superpower, was defeated by a Third World country. In these essays editor Marc Gilbert provides new thinking about the war, and the essays provide interesting insights into U.S. strategy in Vietnam. The work takes an important look at the reasons why the United States failed to win the war.

Why the North Won the Vietnam War, edited by Marc Jason Gilbert, Palgrave Macmillan, 2002

Answers

Reading Check *U.S. forces would be withdrawn; U.S. would help rebuild Vietnam; both sides would release prisoners of war*

End of U.S. Involvement

In 1972 Nixon campaigned for re-election while continuing his efforts to achieve peace with honor in Vietnam. His Democratic challenger, Senator **George McGovern** of South Dakota, was well known for his outspoken criticism of the war.

The 1972 election McGovern insisted that the Vietnam War be brought to an immediate end. "We have heard many times that Vietnam will no longer be an issue by the time the fall election approaches," he said in July 1972. "For the sake of the thousands of Vietnamese peasants still dying from American bombing raids, the GIs still dying . . . the American POWs [prisoners of war] rotting in the jails of Hanoi, I sincerely hope it will not be an issue."

McGovern hoped the ratification of the **Twenty-sixth Amendment** would boost his election chances. Passed in 1971, the amendment lowered the voting age from 21 to 18. Many of McGovern's supporters were young people.

As he had done in 1968, Nixon stressed law and order at home and assured voters that he would bring a quick end to the war. Just weeks before the election, Henry Kissinger announced a breakthrough in the long negotiations in Paris. "Peace is at hand," he declared. This announcement helped Nixon win by a landslide, with 60.7 percent of the popular vote to McGovern's 37.5 percent. In the electoral college, McGovern carried only Massachusetts and the District of Columbia.

A peace agreement Despite Kissinger's prediction, the peace talks stalled. To force North Vietnam to make concessions, Nixon ordered around-the-clock bombings of the North Vietnamese cities of Hanoi and Haiphong in late December 1972. The intense two-week air campaign, the so-called Christmas bombing, failed to sway the North Vietnamese. Nixon called off the bombing, and the talks resumed.

Officials from North Vietnam, South Vietnam, and the United States finally reached a settlement in January 1973. The United States agreed to withdraw all of its troops from South Vietnam and to help rebuild Vietnam. Both sides agreed to release all prisoners of war. But the agreement did not settle the key issue behind the war from the start: the political future of South Vietnam.

READING CHECK **Identifying the Main Idea** What were the terms of the 1973 peace agreement?

The Legacy of Vietnam

Two years after U.S. troops were withdrawn, North Vietnamese troops invaded South Vietnam. In April 1975 they reached Saigon. The

A former prisoner of war in Vietnam has a joyful reunion with his family. American casualties from the war included:
• 600 American POWs
• 300,000 wounded
• 58,000 dead
• 2,500 missing

976 CHAPTER 29

Skills Focus: Sequencing

At Level

Reading Skill
End of U.S. Involvement

1. Guide students in a discussion of the events that led to the January 1973 peace agreement.

2. Have students use the information in this section to create a sequencing diagram or flow chart that shows the events discussed in this section, from Nixon's election in 1968 to the 1973 peace agreement.

3. Have students share their diagrams with the class. Create a class diagram for all to see. Have students correct their own work and

retain the diagram as a study tool.

4. As an extension, have students write an editorial about the 1973 peace agreement. In their editorials students should explain whether or not the agreement meant victory for the United States. **LS Visual-Spatial, Verbal-Linguistic**

📄 Alternative Assessment Handbook, Rubrics 13: Graphic Organizers; and 17: Letters to Editors

U.S. military rushed to evacuate Americans still working in the city. As North Vietnamese troops overran the American embassy, helicopters airlifted thousands of people to safety on U.S. warships offshore.

Many of the Vietnamese who had helped the Americans were also desperate to leave South Vietnam. They feared they would be jailed or killed by North Vietnamese officials as punishment for their actions. Some 130,000 Vietnamese were evacuated and flown to the United States. Many more were left behind.

On April 30, 1975, South Vietnam surrendered. The North Vietnamese then set up a Communist government in the south. After more than two decades of "temporary" division, Vietnam became a reunited country.

Violence consumes Cambodia The fall of Saigon did not end the fighting in Southeast Asia. In 1975 Communist forces called the **Khmer Rouge** (kuh-MER ROOZH) gained control of Cambodia. In a brutal campaign of slaughter, the Khmer Rouge killed 1.5 million people in an attempt to subdue the country. Following a border dispute, Vietnamese forces invaded Cambodia in 1979. They overthrew the Khmer Rouge and installed a puppet government. The Vietnamese occupation lasted until 1989, when UN peacekeeping forces were deployed to monitor the fragile peace.

Effects on Southeast Asia The Vietnam War was devastating to the people of Southeast Asia. About 185,000 South Vietnamese soldiers and 450,000 South Vietnamese civilians were killed in the war. The number of Vietcong and NVA war dead is estimated at about 1 million.

The war also caused severe environmental damage in Vietnam. U.S. planes dropped some 8 million tons of bombs in the region as well as defoliants that contaminated food and water.

More than 1.5 million South Vietnamese fled the country after the fall of Saigon. Many of these refugees braved the open sea in tiny, crowded boats. Other Southeast Asian refugees, such as the Hmong (MUHNG) from Laos, also escaped postwar conditions in Southeast Asia. About 700,000 Southeast Asian refugees eventually settled in the United States.

Le Ly Hayslip was one of the many Vietnamese refugees who started a new life in America. Born in a village near Da Nang in 1949,

Autobiography

In 1967 navy pilot and future Arizona senator John McCain was shot down over North Vietnam. He spent more than five years as a prisoner of war, much of it in solitary confinement. In his memoirs he recalled how he and the other prisoners developed a tapping system so that they could secretly send each other messages.

> "The punishment for communicating could be severe, and a few POWs, having been caught and beaten for their efforts, had their spirits broken as their bodies were battered. Terrified of a return trip to the punishment room, they would lie still in their cells when their comrades tried to tap them up on the wall. Very few would remain uncommunicative for long. To suffer all this alone was less tolerable than torture . . . Almost all would recover their strength in a few days and answer the summons to rejoin the living."
>
> —from *Faith of My Fathers: A Family Memoir,* by John McCain and Mark Salter

 READING LIKE A HISTORIAN

Analyzing Primary Sources How did McCain's captors try to stop soldiers from communicating?
See Skills Handbook, pp. H28–H29

she grew up amid constant warfare. In her book *When Heaven and Earth Changed Places,* Hayslip offered a message.

HISTORY'S VOICES

> ❝Do not feel sorry for me—I made it; I am okay. Right now, though, there are millions of other poor people around the world—girls, boys, men, and women—who live their lives the way I did in order to survive. Like me, they did not ask for the wars which swallowed them. They ask only for peace—the freedom to love and live a full life—and nothing more.❞
>
> —Le Ly Hayslip, *When Heaven and Earth Changed Places*

Effects on veterans About 58,000 Americans were killed in the Vietnam War. Around 600 others were held as POWs. Some POWs spent several years in North Vietnamese jails, where they often endured long periods of torture and solitary confinement.

Reading Focus

4 What was the war's legacy in the United States and in Vietnam?
U.S.—veterans experienced difficult and ongoing problems; economy was damaged; many people changed their view of the government; Vietnam—war spread to Cambodia; Communist government; region suffered economically and environmentally; tremendous loss of lives

The Legacy of Vietnam

Recall Who were the Khmer Rouge? *Communists who seized control of Cambodia; murdered about 1.5 million people*

Analyze How did the war change the makeup of the U.S. population? *More than 700,000 Southeast Asian refugees settled in the United States.*

Elaborate Why do you think many refugees were willing to travel across the sea on tiny, crowded boats in order to leave Vietnam? *possible answer—terrified of new Communist government; nation had been environmentally and economically damaged by warfare*

Primary Sources

Autobiography

Evaluate How do you think John McCain's experiences as a prisoner of war influenced his career as a political leader and U.S. senator? *possible answers—gave him more credibility in military matters; more cautious about entering into military conflict*

Skills Focus: Analyzing Primary Sources

Below Level

Reading Like a Historian Skill
Vietnamese Refugees

Standard English Mastery

1. Guide students in a review of the information under the heading "Effects on Southeast Asia."

2. Organize students into mixed-ability pairs. Have each pair write a paraphrase of Le Ly Hayslip's quote in History's Voices. Have students share their paraphrases in small groups of six to eight students.

3. Have each student use the information in the quote and their paraphrases to write a short

letter from Hayslip to family members left in Vietnam telling them that she is okay and ready to start a new life in the United States.

4. Have volunteers read their letters to the class.
LS Interpersonal, Verbal-Linguistic

📋 Alternative Assessment Handbook, Rubrics 14: Group Activity; and 37: Writing Assignments

Answers

Reading Like a Historian *through torture and beatings*

The Legacy of Vietnam

Recall How many U.S. soldiers died or were wounded in Vietnam? *about 58,000 killed; some 300,000 wounded*

Analyze Why did many veterans experience ongoing problems from their service in Vietnam? *Many had serious injuries; some had been exposed to dangerous chemicals like Agent Orange; some suffered from post traumatic stress disorder.*

Contrast How were Vietnam War veterans treated differently than veterans of previous wars? *not greeted with celebrations or praise; targets of anger and shame some Americans felt about the war*

📑 CRF: Biography: Max Cleland

Vietnam Veterans Memorial

The Vietnam Veterans Memorial includes the Wall (left) and the Three Servicemen Statue (below). The smooth, black-granite wall, nearly 500 feet long, lists the 58,249 names of the military men and women who died or were listed as missing in action.

The Wall was designed by a Yale architecture student, Maya Ying Lin (right).

About 2,500 American soldiers were reported missing in action in the war. Some 300,000 U.S. soldiers were wounded. Because of improving emergency medical services, many who would have died from serious wounds in previous wars were saved. As a result, a great number of paralyzed and otherwise severely disabled veterans returned home.

Some U.S. soldiers exposed to dangerous defoliants later developed cancer and other diseases. Their children born after the war have had high rates of birth defects. In 1984 the makers of Agent Orange were forced to create a fund to help veterans and their families.

Unlike the veterans of previous American wars, soldiers returning from Vietnam were not greeted with celebrations and ticker-tape parades. On the contrary, Vietnam War veterans often became targets for the anger or shame many of their fellow citizens felt about the war. Veterans told of being verbally abused and of people spitting on them. After having served their country in horrendous circumstances,

veterans were stunned by the negative reception. One Vietnam War veteran later described how painful it was to be made a scapegoat for an unpopular war.

HISTORY'S VOICES

❝I wondered if my country would ever welcome us back. Welcome all of us in body and spirit. Or would we always remain a flaw in America's vision of itself.❞

—Frederick Downs Jr.,
Aftermath: A Soldier's Return from Vietnam

Some veterans had trouble readjusting to civilian life. Many suffered from a condition called post-traumatic stress disorder. Memories of their horrible experiences caused nightmares, violent behavior, or flashbacks. The war's aftermath tore families apart.

"When I got back everything was changed," said one veteran. "I have flashbacks and people can't understand me sometimes. I sit by myself and I just think. You try to talk to somebody about it, they think you're out of your mind."

Skills Focus: Analyzing Primary Sources
At Level

Reading Like a Historian Skill
Effects of the War on Veterans
Research Required

1. Have students review the information in the text about Vietnam veterans' experiences after the war. Guide students in a discussion of how the experience of Vietnam veterans compared to the experience of World War II veterans.

2. Divide students into small groups. Have each group conduct outside research to locate several quotes from returning Vietnam veterans.

3. Have students write letters to members of Congress asking that the government provide

adequate care for veterans. In their letters students should cite information from these quotes and give reasons for their request.

4. Have volunteers read their letters to the class. Guide the class in a discussion of the challenges faced by Vietnam veterans and how the government might have addressed those challenges. **LS Interpersonal, Verbal-Linguistic**

📑 Alternative Assessment Handbook, Rubrics 5: Business Letters; and 14: Group Activity

The war's political impact In the end, the United States failed to prevent the Communists from taking over South Vietnam. The U.S. government spent more than $150 billion on the Vietnam War. The spending added greatly to the national debt and fueled inflation. It also diverted funds that might have gone to domestic programs, such as education.

The war changed how many Americans viewed government. Some were angry about officials misleading them. Some thought both Johnson and Nixon had exceeded their constitutional powers by waging an undeclared war.

Seeking to prevent another Vietnam, Congress passed the **War Powers Act** in 1973. This law reaffirms Congress's constitutional right to declare war. It sets a 60-day limit on the presidential commitment of U.S. troops to foreign conflicts without a specific authorization by Congress or a declaration of war.

Another legacy of the Vietnam War is the impact it has had on the way Americans think about foreign conflicts. Before committing troops to a foreign conflict, leaders and the public often debate whether or not the nation is getting into another Vietnam.

Healing from the war Coming to terms with the Vietnam conflict has been an ongoing process for Americans. An important step

was taken with the dedication of the Vietnam Veterans Memorial in Washington, D.C., in 1982. The memorial was designed by Maya Ying Lin, a Chinese American who was a 21-year-old architecture student at Yale University when her design was chosen.

The memorial is a long wall of polished black granite, inscribed with the names of the more than 58,000 Americans who died or went missing in Vietnam. Bruce Weigl explained why he and many other veterans were drawn to the memorial's dedication ceremony. "We came to find the names of those we lost in the war, as if by tracing the letters cut into the granite we could find what was left of ourselves."

Vietnam veterans in government were among the leaders of a subsequent effort to rebuild relations between the United States and Vietnam. The two countries resumed normal relations in 1995. In 1997 Douglas "Pete" Peterson, a former air force pilot who spent six years as a POW in North Vietnam, became the new U.S. ambassador to Vietnam. "It's a tragic history that we've shared as two peoples," he observed. "No one can change that, but there is a great deal we can all do about the future."

READING CHECK **Identifying Cause and Effect** What effects has the Vietnam War had on American veterans?

---

go.hrw.com
Online Quiz
Keyword: SD7 HP29

Reviewing Ideas, Terms, and People

1. a. Describe What was President Nixon's Madman Theory?
b. Analyze What role did **Henry Kissinger** have in the Vietnam War?
c. Rate How well do you think Nixon's **Vietnamization** strategy worked? Explain.

2. a. Identify What was the **silent majority**?
b. Make Generalizations How did Americans react to the My Lai massacre?
c. Elaborate Why do you think Daniel Ellsberg leaked the Pentagon Papers?

3. a. Recall What issues helped President Nixon win re-election in 1972?
b. Draw Conclusions Why do you think Nixon defeated George McGovern by so wide a margin in the 1972 election?
c. Evaluate Did Nixon's bombing of North Vietnam achieve its goal? Explain.

4. a. Identify What was the War Powers Act?
b. Make Inferences Why did so many people leave Vietnam after the fall of Saigon?

Critical Thinking

5. Categorize Review your notes on the effects of the Vietnam War. Then copy the graphic organizer below and use it to list the effects of the war on different groups of people.

Group	Effect
North Vietnamese	
South Vietnamese	
Americans	

FOCUS ON WRITING

6. Narrative Write a poem that honors the fallen American soldiers who served in the Vietnam War.

THE VIETNAM WAR **979**

Section 4 Assessment Answers

1. a. making North Vietnamese think Nixon would do anything to end the war
b. Nixon's National Security Adviser; held secret peace negotiations with NVA
c. possible answer—did not work; South Vietnamese forces unable to stop invasion

2. a. majority of Americans silently supporting war
b. horrified, unbelieving; fueled protests
c. possible answer—no longer supported U.S. policy in Vietnam

3. a. push for order at home; end to war
b. Kissinger's announcement that Vietnam

War was almost over
c. no, NVA determined to fight

4. a. reaffirmed Congress's right to declare war
b. homes destroyed, food and water contaminated; fear of NVA troops

5. North Vietnamese—1 million dead; South Vietnamese—about .5 million dead, Communist government; Americans— thousands dead, lack of trust in government.

6. Poems will vary.

• Direct Teach •

Reading Focus

The Legacy of Vietnam

Recall Who is Maya Ying Lin? *Chinese American architecture student who designed the Vietnam Veterans Memorial in Washington D.C.*

Explain How did the War Powers Act of 1973 limit presidential authority? *reaffirmed Congress' right to declare war; placed 60-day limit on president's ability to commit U.S. troops without a formal declaration of war by Congress*

Analyze Why do you think Vietnam veterans led the effort to establish normal relations with Vietnam? *understood better than most the shared history that the two nations experienced*

• Review & Assess •

Close

Ask students this question: How did the war affect the United States and Vietnam?

Review

Online Quiz, Section 4

Daily Test Practice Transparency

Assess

SE Section 4 Assessment

Progress Assessment: Section 4 Quiz

Alternative Assessment Handbook

Reteach

Interactive Reader and Study Guide, Section 4

Interactive Skills Tutor CD-ROM

Answers

Reading Check *many paralyzed or severely disabled; developed illnesses from exposure to chemicals; difficulty readjusting to civil life; experienced post traumatic stress disorder*

The Tet Offensive

Word Help

attrition wearing away
stalemate deadlock, tie
escalation increase

Primary Source

"Vietnam was the first war ever fought without any censorship. Without censorship, things can get terribly confused in the public mind."

— William Westmoreland

Time, April 5, 1982

The Tet Offensive

Historical Context The documents below provide a look at the Tet Offensive in 1968, one of the key turning points in the Vietnam War.

Task Examine the documents and answer the questions that follow. Then write an essay about the effects of the Tet Offensive on the Vietnam War. Use facts from the documents and from the chapter to support the position you take in your thesis statement.

DOCUMENT 1

The Tet Offensive was a surprise attack during the Vietnamese New Year. The North Vietnamese Army (NVA) and the Vietcong (VC) achieved tactical surprise but sustained high casualties. This table shows the casualties for each side.

TET OFFENSIVE CASUALTIES

Force	Killed in Action	Wounded in Action	Missing in Action	Captured in Action
U.S. Forces	1,536	7,764	11	unknown
ARVN	2,788	8,299	587	unknown
NVA/VC	45,000	unknown	unknown	6,691

Source: Combat Area Casualty File of 11/93, National Archives

DOCUMENT 2

General William Westmoreland commanded U.S. forces in Vietnam from 1964 to 1968. In 1976 he published his memoirs of the war in a book titled *A Soldier Reports*. In this excerpt he discusses a press conference he held at the U.S. Embassy following the defeat of the Tet Offensive.

"...I took the opportunity to try to put the Embassy raid and the countryside attacks into perspective. Contrary to rumor, I said, none of the Viet Cong had gotten inside the Chancery. Damage to the building was superficial. As for the big offensive throughout the country, the enemy, by coming out into the open, was exposing himself to tremendous casualties. Fully conscious of American and South Vietnamese strength and ability, I had no hesitation in saying that the enemy was inviting defeat.

"My efforts at perspective went for nought. The attack on the Embassy, Don Oberdorfer wrote later, 'seemed to give the lie to the rosy projections and victory claims that Westmoreland and others had been dishing out.' Oberdorfer said that the reporters could hardly believe their ears. 'Westmoreland was standing in the ruins and saying everything was great.'

"That attitude on the part of the American reporters undoubtedly contributed to the psychological victory the enemy achieved in the United States. What would they have had me say, that the walls were tumbling down when I knew they were not? That the enemy was winning when I knew he was on the verge of a disastrous military defeat?"

980 CHAPTER 29

Skills Focus: Making Oral Presentations   At Level

Reading Like a Historian Skill
Hawks versus Doves

1. Divide the class into two halves. Have one half represent supporters of the U.S. involvement in the Vietnam War in 1968. Have the other half represent opponents of the war.

2. Conduct a classroom debate on the following question: Should the U.S. do whatever is necessary to win the war, or should the U.S. seek an honorable withdrawal from Vietnam?

3. Have each student write a one-page paper telling which position he or she would personally take and why.

4. Have volunteers read their papers to the class. Guide the class in a discussion of alternatives. What terms might the U.S. have dictated as a condition of withdrawal? **LS Logical-Mathematical, Verbal-Linguistic**

   Alternative Assessment Handbook, Rubric 10: Debates

DOCUMENT 3

On February 24, 1968, the Department of Defense began the process of drafting 48,000 more soldiers for the Vietnam War. This cartoon by Hugh Haynie appeared in the Louisville, Kentucky *Courier-Journal* a few days later.

DOCUMENT 4

Walter Cronkite was the anchor for CBS News from 1962 to 1981. In February 1968 Cronkite traveled to Vietnam to see firsthand the conditions following the Tet Offensive. In his broadcast on February 27, 1968, he offered a personal assessment of the situation.

"Who won and who lost in the great Tet offensive against the cities? I'm not sure. The Vietcong did not win by a knockout, but neither did we. The referees of history may make it a draw . . .

"We have been too often disappointed by the optimism of the American leaders, both in Vietnam and Washington, to have faith any longer in the silver linings they find in the darkest clouds . . .

"To say that we are closer to victory today is to believe, in the face of the evidence, the optimists who have been wrong in the past. To suggest we are on the edge of defeat is to yield to unreasonable pessimism. To say that we are mired in stalemate seems the only realistic, yet unsatisfactory, conclusion. On the off chance that military and political analysts are right, in the next few months we must test the enemy's intentions in case this is indeed his last big gasp before negotiations. But it is increasingly clear to this reporter that the only rational way out then will be to negotiate, not as victors, but as an honorable people who lived up to their pledge to defend democracy, and did the best they could."

Skills Focus: READING LIKE A HISTORIAN

1. a. Identify Refer to Document 1. Which group experienced the largest number of battle-related deaths?

b. Analyze Based solely on the casualty statistics, which side was victorious?

2. a. Identify Refer to Document 2. What did General Westmoreland hope to achieve in the press conference?

b. Interpret What opinion does Westmoreland have of the press?

3. a. Identify Refer to Document 3. What is the Vietnam War compared with in this political cartoon?

b. Analyze Why might this cartoon be seen as a response to the increase in the draft?

4. a. Identify Refer to Document 4. What outcome does Cronkite predict for the war?

b. Elaborate What course of events does Cronkite suggest in order to achieve that outcome?

5. Document-Based Essay Question Consider the question below and form a thesis statement. Using examples from Documents 1, 2, 3, and 4, create an outline and write a short essay supporting your position.
How did the Tet Offensive affect Americans' perceptions of the situation in Vietnam?

See **Skills Handbook**, pp. H28–H29, H31

THE VIETNAM WAR **981**

Info to Know

Walter Cronkite During his 18 years as anchor of the *CBS Evening News*, Walter Cronkite earned the nickname "the most trusted man in America." Although Cronkite first gained national attention for his reporting as a war correspondent during World War II, he is perhaps best remembered for his reporting on the Vietnam War. Cronkite's personal motto had been "fast, accurate, and unbiased," but he made an exception when he voiced his strong opposition to the Tet Offensive and the Vietnam War. Because of his role in shaping television reporting, his name has become a synonym for "news anchor" in some countries; Dutch anchors are called *Cronkiters*, and Swedish anchors *Kronkiters*.

Answers

Reading Like a Historian
1. a. *the North Vietnamese Army and the Vietcong;* **b.** *U.S.;* **2. a.** *to put attacks into perspective;* **b.** *poor opinion; believed that they didn't understand the significance of the attacks;* **3. a.** *a spider web;* **b.** *possible answer—This cartoon emphasized how more and more resources were needed before the U.S. could withdraw.* **4. a.** *stalemate— neither side winning;* **b.** *to test the enemy over the next several months to see if the enemy was about to give up;* **5.** *possible answer—many Americans no longer felt confident U.S. would win the war; public increasingly critical of U.S. involvement in Vietnam*

Skills Focus: Drawing Conclusions

`At Level`

Reading Skill
The World in Your Living Room

`Research Required`

1. Tell students that the Vietnam War was the first major international conflict that unfolded before people's eyes on their television sets. Since then, every major war and most catastrophes have been broadcast as they happen.

2. Guide students in a discussion of the role television plays in our understanding of the world around us. Ask students to name major events that have been televised as they happen. Make a list for the class to see.

3. Have each student choose one of the events from the list and write an analysis of the television coverage of it. Tell students to indicate how television handled the coverage, and how people's perceptions of the event may have been shaped by television and by particular reporters. **LS Logical-Mathematical, Verbal-Linguistic**

Alternative Assessment Handbook, Rubric 12: Drawing Conclusions

Answers

Visual Summary

Review and Inquiry Review the time line with students. Then have them identify the events that they believe contributed most to antiwar protests and which events led directly to the end of the war.

🖝 Quick Facts Transparency: The Vietnam War

Reviewing Key Terms and People

1. Khmer Rouge
2. Hubert Humphrey
3. silent majority
4. Vietminh
5. Robert McNamara
6. Twenty-sixth Amendment
7. Dien Bien Phu
8. Operation Rolling Thunder
9. Richard Daley
10. William Westmoreland
11. domino theory
12. Geneva Conference
13. pacification

Comprehension and Critical Thinking

14. **a.** guerrilla warfare
b. cease fire; Vietnam temporarily divided along the 17th parallel; Vietminh forces would control the northern part; French forces would control the southern part; demilitarized zone between two zones; to reunify a country under one elected government
c. possible answer—to show that the United States would not tolerate spread of communism; would support anti-Communist movements

15. **a.** by bombing it through Operation Rolling Thunder
b. wanted to focus on domestic issues; the war drained funds from domestic programs; believed it was unfair for African Americans to fight for a country that discriminated against them
c. possible answers—yes, people at home would not have been so aware of the loss of life and bloody battles,

---

Visual Summary: The Vietnam War

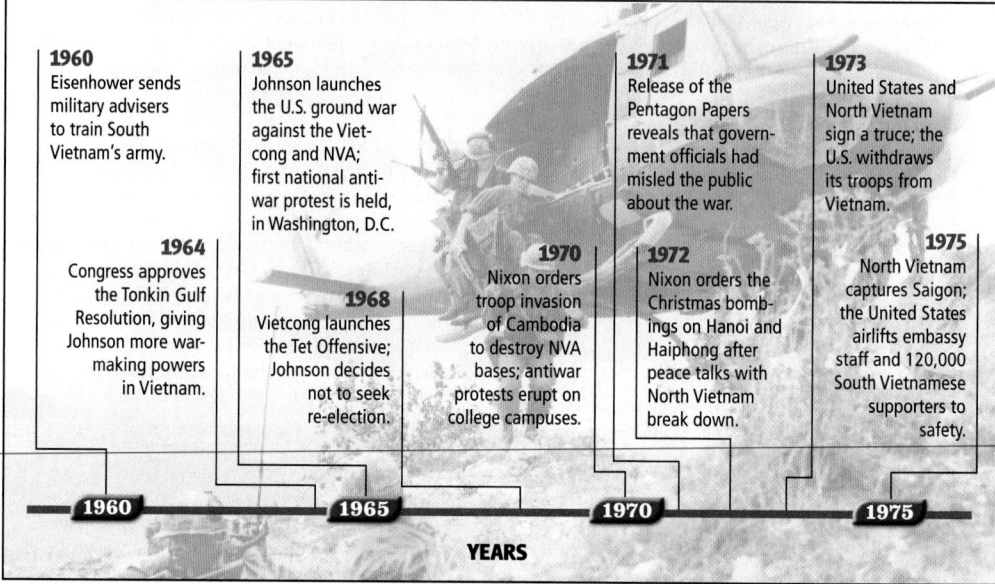

1960
Eisenhower sends military advisers to train South Vietnam's army.

1964
Congress approves the Tonkin Gulf Resolution, giving Johnson more war-making powers in Vietnam.

1965
Johnson launches the U.S. ground war against the Vietcong and NVA; first national antiwar protest is held, in Washington, D.C.

1968
Vietcong launches the Tet Offensive; Johnson decides not to seek re-election.

1970
Nixon orders troop invasion of Cambodia to destroy NVA bases; antiwar protests erupt on college campuses.

1971
Release of the Pentagon Papers reveals that government officials had misled the public about the war.

1972
Nixon orders the Christmas bombings on Hanoi and Haiphong after peace talks with North Vietnam break down.

1973
United States and North Vietnam sign a truce; the U.S. withdraws its troops from Vietnam.

1975
North Vietnam captures Saigon; the United States airlifts embassy staff and 120,000 South Vietnamese supporters to safety.

1960   1965   1970   1975

YEARS

Reviewing Key Terms and People

Complete each sentence by filling the blank with the correct term or person.

1. Communist forces called the _____ took over the Cambodian government and slaughtered about 1.5 million people.
2. _____ _____ was the Democratic presidential candidate in 1968.
3. Nixon called people who disapproved of antiwar protesters and generally supported the government's Vietnam goals the _____.
4. Ho Chi Minh originally founded the _____ to resist the Japanese occupation of Vietnam.
5. Secretary of Defense _____ _____ at first supported and carried out the war in Vietnam but later tried to find a way to end it.
6. The _____ lowered the voting age in the United States from 21 to 18.

7. The French army was defeated by the Vietminh at _____.
8. In a campaign called _____, U.S. pilots bombed and destroyed much of North Vietnam.
9. Chicago mayor _____ _____ ordered police and National Guard troops to keep order during the 1968 Democratic Convention.
10. General _____ _____ commanded U.S. ground troops in South Vietnam.
11. The _____ was the reason the United States wanted to defeat communism in Vietnam.
12. After the French were defeated in 1954, representatives from several nations met at the _____ to work out a peace agreement for Indochina.
13. The strategy of _____ was designed to keep Vietnamese civilians safe and win their support.

982 CHAPTER 29

---

that U.S. might not be winning as reported by government and military officials; no, print media could have used pictures and stories to convey same horror

16. **a.** people were arrested; police used tear gas and violence to break up the protests
b. because the U.S. wanted all NVA troops out of South Vietnam and North Vietnam did not want a temporary South Vietnamese government
c. possible answer—people began to see what was actually happening in Vietnam and that U.S. troops were not as effective as

the government had been telling the public

17. **a.** American policy of turning over fighting in Vietnam to South Vietnamese forces
b. police opened fire on unarmed students who were protesting the war
c. possible answers—no, cost thousands of innocent lives, expensive, a waste of government resources and did not put an end to communism like originally hoped for; yes, prevented spread of communism during course of the war

Comprehension and Critical Thinking

SECTION 1 *(pp. 948–955)*

14. a. Identify What kinds of tactics did the Vietminh use to fight the French?

b. Analyze What were the terms of the 1954 Geneva Accords? What was the purpose of the proposed 1956 election?

c. Elaborate Why do you think President Kennedy wanted to show U.S. resolve in Vietnam?

SECTION 2 *(pp. 956–963)*

15. a. Describe How did American troops try to disrupt the Ho Chi Minh Trail?

b. Analyze Why did many civil rights advocates oppose the Vietnam War?

c. Predict Do you think Americans' opinions about the Vietnam War would have been different had there been no television reporting? Explain your answer.

SECTION 3 *(pp. 964–971)*

16. a. Describe What happened to protesters during the Democratic National Convention in 1968?

b. Analyze Why did Johnson's negotiations with North Vietnam fail to result in a peace agreement?

c. Elaborate Why do you think the Tet Offensive had such a strong effect on public opinion in the United States?

SECTION 4 *(pp. 972–979)*

17. a. Identify What was Vietnamization?

b. Compare How were the incidents at Kent State University and Jackson State College similar?

c. Evaluate Was the Vietnam War a success for the United States? Why or why not?

Using the Internet

go.hrw.com
Practice Online
Keyword: SD7 CH29

18. During the Vietnam War, U.S. air strikes used dangerous chemicals such as napalm and Agent Orange. Using the keyword above, do research to find out what was known about them at the time and about the short- and long-term effects of these chemicals. Then create a report that analyzes the ways in which veterans, Vietnamese civilians, the U.S. military, and other groups have responded to these effects.

History's Impact video program

Review the video to answer the closing question: What role did American public opinion play during the Vietnam War?

Analyzing Primary Sources

Reading Like a Historian In Section 2, read the History's Voices passage from Myron Harrington that begins "After a while, survival was the name of the game." He described his experience in Vietnam.

19. Describe What was Harrington's experience in Vietnam like?

20. Draw Conclusions Based on details in the source, what was Harrington's role in the war?

Critical Reading

Read the passage near the end of Section 4 that begins with the heading "The war's political impact." Then answer the questions that follow.

21. According to the passage, the Vietnam War has made Americans today

  A open to accepting large numbers of refugees.

  B likely to suffer post-traumatic stress disorder.

  C debate whether they are getting into another Vietnam before committing troops to a conflict.

  D eager to fight communism in Southeast Asia.

22. Which of the following resulted from government spending on the Vietnam War?

  A inflation and a higher national debt

  B the fall of Saigon

  C the passage of the War Powers Act

  D the rise to power of the Khmer Rouge

FOCUS ON WRITING

Persuasive Writing *Persuasive writing takes a position for or against an issue, using facts and examples as supporting evidence. To practice persuasive writing, complete the assignment below.*

Writing Topic The response to the protests at the 1968 Democratic National Convention

23. Assignment Based on what you have read in this chapter, write a brief editorial to convince people that Chicago mayor Richard Daley's response to the protests was either necessary or too extreme.

THE VIETNAM WAR **983**

Answers

Using the Internet

18. Go to the HRW Web site and enter the keyword shown to access a rubric for this activity.

KEYWORD: SD7 CH29

Analyzing Primary Sources

19. possible answer—traumatic, frightening

20. leader of other soldiers; trying to help them survive

Critical Reading

21. C

22. A

Focus on Writing

23. possible answer—The government has an obligation to ensure the safety of all citizens and to use whatever force is necessary to restore peace and protect its citizens; beating and arresting young people who were protesting was a senseless act of police brutality and an overreaction to the situation.

A rubric for this activity is provided in the Chapter Resource File: Focus on Writing: The Response to the Protests at the 1968 Democratic Convention.

History's Impact Video Program

large antiwar movement; Nixon elected after promising to end war; increasing public protests eventually helped bring war to an end

Review and Assessment Resources

Review and Reinforce

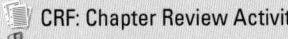

- CRF: Chapter Review Activity
- Quick Facts Transparencies: Causes of the Vietnam War, The Vietnam War
- Spanish Chapter Summaries Audio CD Program
- Online Chapter Summaries in Spanish
- OSP Holt PuzzlePro; Quiz Show for ExamView
- Quiz Game CD-ROM

Assess

- PASS: Chapter Test, Forms A and B
- Alternative Assessment Handbook
- OSP ExamView Test Generator, Chapter Test
- Differentiated Instruction Modified Worksheets and Tests CD-ROM: Chapter Test
- HOAP Holt Online Assessment Program (in the Premier Online Edition)

Reteach/Intervene

- Interactive Reader and Study Guide
- Differentiated Instruction Teacher Management System: Lesson Plans for Differentiated Instruction
- Differentiated Instruction Modified Worksheets and Tests CD-ROM: Chapter Test
- Interactive Skills Tutor CD-ROM

go.hrw.com
Online Resources

KEYWORD: SD7 CH29

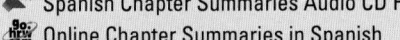

Chapter 30 Planning Guide

A Time of Social Change

Chapter Overview	Reproducible Resources	Technology Resources
CHAPTER 30 pp. 984–1011 **Overview:** In this chapter, students will analyze how the African American civil rights movement inspired women, Native Americans, and Latinos to fight against social, political, and economic inequality.	**Differentiated Instruction Teacher Management System:*** • Instructional Benchmarking Guides • Lesson Plans for Differentiated Instruction **Interactive Reader and Study Guide:** Chapter Summary* **Chapter Resource File:*** • Writing for the SAT: The Equal Rights Amendment • Social Studies Skills Activity: Making Written Presentations • Chapter Review Activity **American History Outline Maps** **Pre-AP Activities Guide for United States History***	Live Ink® Online Reading Help Student Edition on Audio CD Program Differentiated Instruction Modified Worksheets and Tests CD-ROM Interactive Skills Tutor CD-ROM United States History Primary Source Library CD-ROM Power Presentations with Video CD-ROM History's Impact: American History Video Program (VHS/DVD): A Time of Social Change Online Chapter Summaries in Spanish
Section 1: **Women and Native Americans Fight for Change** **The Main Idea:** In the 1960s women and Native Americans struggled to achieve social justice.	**Differentiated Instruction Teacher Management System:** Section 1 Lesson Plan* **Interactive Reader and Study Guide:** Section 1 Summary* **Chapter Resource File:*** • Vocabulary Builder Activity, Section 1 • Biography Activity: Phyllis Schlafly • Primary Source Activity: Gloria Steinem Testifies in Support of the ERA • Literature Activity: *The Feminine Mystique*	Daily Bellringer Transparency: Section 1* Daily Test Practice Transparency: Section 1* Internet Activity: The Women's Rights Movement
Section 2: **Latinos Fight for Rights** **The Main Idea:** In the 1960s Latinos struggled to achieve social justice.	**Differentiated Instruction Teacher Management System:** Section 2 Lesson Plan* **Interactive Reader and Study Guide:** Section 2 Summary* **Chapter Resource File:*** • Vocabulary Builder Activity, Section 2 • Biography Activity: Ruben Salazar	Daily Bellringer Transparency: Section 2* Daily Test Practice Transparency: Section 2* Internet Activity: The UFW and the Latino Rights Movement
Section 3: **Culture and Counterculture** **The Main Idea:** The counterculture that emerged in the 1960s and 1970s left a lasting impact on American life.	**Differentiated Instruction Teacher Management System:** Section 3 Lesson Plan* **Interactive Reader and Study Guide:** Section 3 Summary* **Chapter Resource File:*** • Vocabulary Builder Activity, Section 3 • Biography Activity: John Lennon • Primary Source Activity: Mario Savio at a Free Speech Movement Rally	Daily Bellringer Transparency: Section 3* Daily Test Practice Transparency: Section 3* Internet Activity: The Counterculture

HOLT
History's Impact
American History Video Program (VHS/DVD)
A Time of Social Change

Review, Assessment, Intervention

Quick Facts Transparencies: Major Native American Legislation, A Time of Social Change

Spanish Chapter Summaries Audio CD Program

Progress Assessment Support System (PASS): Chapter Test*

Differentiated Instruction Modified Worksheets and Tests CD-ROM: Modified Chapter Test

OSP   **One-Stop Planner CD-ROM:** ExamView Test Generator (English/Spanish)

HOAP   **Holt Online Assessment Program (HOAP),** in the Holt Premier Online Student Edition

---

PASS: Section 1 Quiz*

 Online Quiz: Section 1

Alternative Assessment Handbook

PASS: Section 2 Quiz*

 Online Quiz: Section 2

Alternative Assessment Handbook

PASS: Section 3 Quiz*

 Online Quiz: Section 3

Alternative Assessment Handbook

 **RESOURCES**

The following resources were developed to help North Carolina educators teach the standards and objectives of North Carolina's eleventh grade standard course of study in United States history.

- United States history EOC Test Prep Workbook
- Teacher's Support System
- North Carolina One-Stop Planner

And be sure to direct your students to **go.hrw.com** for online access to the EOC Test Prep Workbook.

go.hrw.com
EOC Test Prep
KEYWORD: SE7 NC

Holt ●nline Learning

go.hrw.com
Teacher Resources
KEYWORD: SD7 TEACHER

go.hrw.com
Student Resources
KEYWORD: SD7 CH30

- Document-based Questions
- Interactive Multimedia Activities

- Current Events
- Chapter-based Internet Activities
- and more!

Holt Premier
Online Student Edition
Complete online support for interactivity, assessment, and reporting

- Interactive Maps and Notebook
- Standardized Test Prep
- Homework Practice and Research Activities Online

CHAPTER 30 PLANNING GUIDE

Before You Teach

The Big Picture
Robert D. Schulzinger

Civil Rights for Women and Native Americans The movement for civil rights for African Americans and the opposition to the war in Vietnam encouraged other Americans to press for equality and change. A new feminist movement arose in the 1960s and 1970s demanding social, political, and economic equality for women. Although the Equal Rights Amendment was not ratified, women made significant advances in employment and political representation. Native Americans also organized demonstrations and court challenges, and pushed for legislation to reverse centuries of hardship and discrimination. Native Americans regained control of tribal lands, but they remained among the poorest people in the country.

The Rise of Hispanic Power Mexican Americans also sought to improve their poor economic, educational, and political standing in American society. In 1969 César Chávez led the National Farm Workers Association to victory in a five-year-long strike against grape growers that brought international attention to the harsh conditions for migrant farm workers. A Chicano movement which employed many of the militant tactics of Black Power arose in the southwest. By the 1980s Latinos throughout the United States expressed new confidence and pride in their heritage, and they made significant advances in employment and election to public office.

The Counterculture The large baby boom generation which reached late adolescence and early adulthood in the 1960s produced a counterculture that challenged some of the basic tenets of mainstream American society. The youth movement expressed outrage over racial discrimination, demanded an end to the Vietnam War, and defied the authority of leaders of higher education. The counterculture valued personal expression through rock music, experimentation with drugs, joining rural communes, or seeking enlightenment through alternative religious or spiritual practices. Many Americans rejected the counterculture as disrespectful and threatening to traditional values. While the movement faded, the counterculture left a legacy of greater informality and acceptance of different lifestyles.

Recent Scholarship

Reclaiming Ancestral Lands Charles Wilkinson's *Blood Struggle: The Rise of the Modern Indian Nations* (2005) recounts how more than 100 Native American tribes with different historical and cultural traditions gradually organized to reclaim control over their ancestral homes. They adapted the legal strategies of the civil rights movement to reverse the 1950s government policy of termination of Indian rights. From the 1970s onward, Native American tribes won a series of court battles and laws restoring their sovereign rights to water, timber, grazing, and petroleum and mineral extraction on millions of acres across the United States.

Differentiating Instruction

 Differentiated Instruction Teacher Management System
- Lesson Plans for Differentiated Instruction
- Differentiated Instructional Benchmarking Guides
- Interactive Reader and Study Guide

 Spanish Chapter Summaries Audio CD Program

 Online Chapter Summaries in Spanish

 Student Edition on Audio CD Program

 Differentiated Instruction Modified Worksheets and Tests CD-ROM
- Vocabulary Flash Cards
- Modified Vocabulary Builder Activities
- Modified Chapter Review Activity
- Modified Chapter Test

OSP One-Stop Planner CD-ROM
- ExamView Test Generator (English and Spanish)
- PuzzlePro
- Quiz Show for ExamView
- Transparencies and Videos

TE Differentiated Activities in the Teacher's Edition
- The Women's Liberation Movement, p. 989
- Federal Policy and Native Americans, p. 990
- The Lives of Native Americans, p. 991
- Movements for Latino Rights, p. 999
- Culture and Counterculture, p. 1004

Reading Like a Historian
Sam Wineburg

Remaking History

Americans first celebrated Earth Day in 1970 as an expression of the growing need to safeguard the environment from degradation. Soon thereafter, the environmental movement became forever linked to Native Americans when a public service television announcement aired that tugged at viewers' heart-strings. In the television spot, a Native American, bedecked in full headdress, canoes up a stream littered with floating bottles, wrappers, and other refuse. The camera zooms in to show a lone tear falling down the proud Indian's face. A celestial voice intones: "People start pollution. People can stop it."

During the 1970s, Americans' blatant disregard for the environment was often contrasted with Native Americans' reverence for the earth's holiness.

Using History for Modern Purposes

History was recruited in this effort. One of the most quoted documents came from Chief Sealth—for whom Seattle is named—from a speech originally delivered in 1854 and later sent as a letter to President Franklin Pierce. Some of the chief's most poignant lines included: "We are part of the earth and it is part of us"; "Contaminate your bed and you will . . . suffocate in your own waste"; "Man did not weave the web of life; he is merely a strand in it." Sealth lamented in his letter to President Pierce: "I have seen a thousand rotting buffaloes on the prairie, left by the white man who shot them from a passing train."

Over 100 years later, Chief Sealth's words moved a nation. They were quoted on the Senate floor by John H. Chafee (R-Rhode Island) and invoked by journalist Bill Moyers in his famous interview with scholar Joseph Campbell. Supreme Court Justice William O. Douglas quoted them in his autobiography. But more than anything, it was a children's book that sealed Chief Sealth's legacy. *Brother Eagle, Sister Sky*, by illustrator Susan Jeffers, climbed as high as No. 5 on the 1992 *New York Times* bestseller list, eventually selling a half million copies—nearly unheard of for an oversized picture book.

One Little Problem

There was only one problem with Sealth's canoni-zation as our nation's premier environmentalist. The whole thing is a fake—or, as a 1993 *Reader's Digest* article put it, a "Little Green Lie." The "letter" to President Pierce was the invention of screenwriter Ted Perry, for a 1971 film that was later broadcast on ABC. Perry's producer felt the message would have greater impact if the words were spoken by a wise Native American—not a contemporary filmmaker. The rest, we might say, is fake history.

In the desire to find a Native American icon, Americans not only alighted on Chief Sealth but remade him in their own environmentally-correct image. And he proved a good candidate for this remake. By many accounts, Sealth was a charismatic speaker. And he did, in fact, give a speech in 1854, but it was probably delivered (this is uncertain) in his native Salish language (Duwamish or Suquamish), translated into Chinook Jargon, and then into English. The speech would have been forgotten had it not been resurrected by Dr. Henry A. Smith, rendered in florid Victorian English, and reprinted some 33 years later in 1887 in the *Seattle Sunday Star*.

An Unlikely Speech

This, alone, should've raised questions about words that soar Jonathan Livingston Seagull-like above dozens of spiritual Internet sites. But even a sober reading of the text would set off alarms to anyone remotely interested in the truth. Spending his entire life in the Pacific Northwest, Sealth was as likely to have seen "rotting buffaloes on the prairie" as he was to have seen unicorns scaling the face of Mt. Rainier—not to mention the fact that the railroad didn't reach the Puget Sound until 29 years after Sealth gave the speech.

As historian Robert F. Berkhofer explains in *The White Man's Indian: Images of the American Indian from Columbus to the Present* (1978), reformers have long used romanticized—and historically inaccurate—notions of Native Americans as mouthpieces for social causes. In the process, the variety and complexity of Native Americans are homogenized into an undifferentiated blur.

Most galling in Chief Sealth's case are attempts to attribute his "environmental beliefs" to the spiritual traditions of Native Americans.

Chief Sealth was a baptized Roman Catholic.

Chapter Preview

Standards Focus

Social Studies Competency Goals

Goal 11 The learner will trace economic, political, and social developments and assess their significance for the lives of Americans during this time period.

11.03

The Big Idea and Essential Questions

To foster student understanding of this chapter's big idea, design your lesson to address each section's essential question.

Big Idea Inspired by the African American civil rights movement, women, Native Americans, and Latinos stood up for equality, while at the same time, a youthful counterculture sought a new way of life.

Essential Questions

1. How did women and Native Americans struggle to achieve social justice?
2. How did Latinos fight for equality in the 1960s?
3. What was the counterculture, and what was its lasting impact?

Key to Differentiating Instruction

Below Level

Basic-level activities designed for all students encountering new material

At Level

Intermediate-level activities designed for average students

Above Level

Challenging activities designed for honors and gifted-and-talented students

Standard English Mastery

Activities designed to improve standard English usage

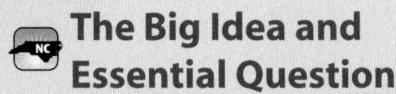

CHAPTER 30

1963–1975

A Time of Social Change

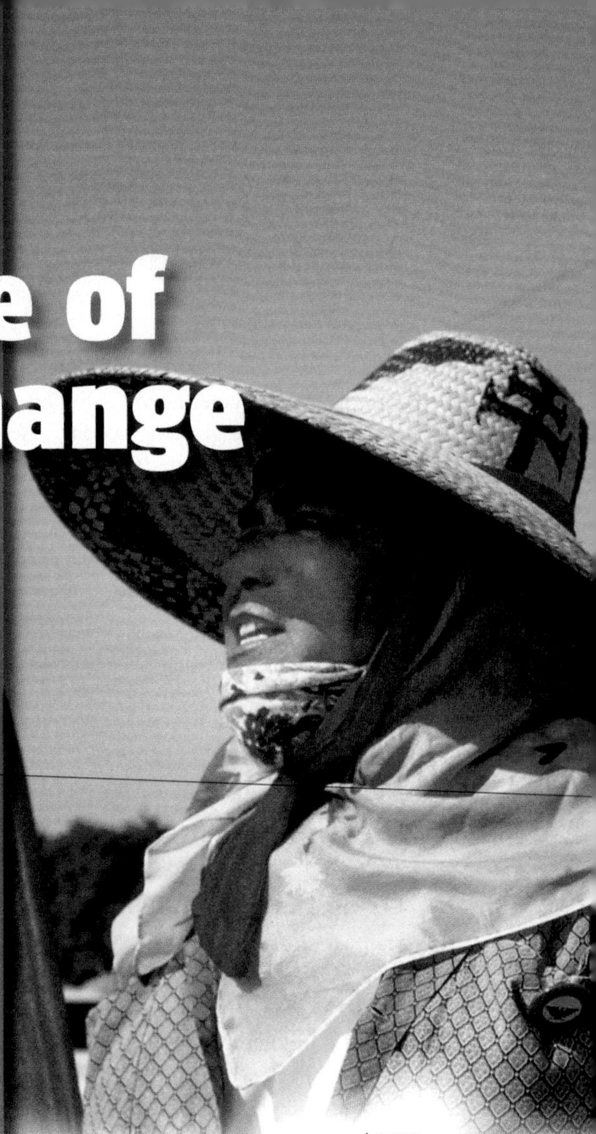

THE BIG PICTURE Inspired by the African American civil rights movement, women, Native Americans, and Latinos all stood up against social, political, and economic inequality in the 1960s. At the same time a youthful counterculture turned its back on mainstream society in search of a new way of life.

North Carolina Standards

Social Studies Objectives

11.03 Identify major social movements including, but not limited to, those involving women, young people, and the environment, and evaluate the impact of these movements on the United States' society.

Language Arts Objectives

2.01 Research and analyze ideas, events, and/or movements related to United States culture by:

- locating facts and details for purposeful elaboration.

3.02 Select an issue or theme and take a stance on that issue by:

- reflecting the viewpoint(s) of Americans of different times and places.

Skills Focus READING LIKE A HISTORIAN

These farmworkers call out from a picket line. Beginning in the 1960s, farmworkers began organizing, using strikes and initiating boycotts to fight for better working conditions and better wages.

Interpreting Visuals What does this photograph tell you about the workers' commitment and determination?

See **Skills Handbook**, p. H30

U.S.

1964 Title VII of the Civil Rights Act of 1964 outlaws gender discrimination in employment.

1963

World

1964 South African rebel leader Nelson Mandela is sentenced to life in prison.

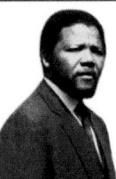

Introduce the Chapter

At Level

A Time of Social Change

1. Guide students in a discussion of how the civil rights movement changed American society. Ask students to predict how the civil rights efforts of African Americans affected others.
2. Tell students that in this chapter they will learn about women, Native Americans, and Latinos who stood up for their rights.
3. Have students work in pairs to scan the chapter and make a list of challenges each group faced. Have volunteers share information from their lists and create a class list for all to see. Then guide students in a discussion of these issues. Which are similar and which are different?
4. Have students write a brief summary of the problems that faced women, Native Americans, and Latinos during the 1960s and identify which issues are still problematic today. **LS Verbal-Linguistic**

Alternative Assessment Handbook, Rubric 11: Discussions

• Chapter Preview •

HOLT
History's Impact
► **Video Program: A Time of Social Change**
See the Video Teacher's Guide for strategies for using the video segment.

Reading Like a Historian
Interpreting Visuals Female farm workers hold picket signs and demand recognition of their complaints.

1965
Farmworkers begin a strike in Delano, California.

WOODSTOCK
3 DAYS OF PEACE AND MUSIC...AND LOVE

1969
400,000 attend the Woodstock Music and Art Fair in upstate New York.

1972
Congress approves the Equal Rights Amendment.

1973
Federal marshals and Indian activists face off at Wounded Knee, South Dakota.

1965 | 1967 | 1969 | 1971 | 1973 | 1975

1967
Israel defeats Egypt, Jordan, and Syria in the Six-Day War.

1971
The UN recognizes Communist China and expels Nationalist China (Taiwan).

1973
Egypt and Syria attack Israel, beginning the Yom Kippur War.

1975
Saigon, capital of South Vietnam, falls to North Vietnam, ending the Vietnam War.

985

go.hrw.com
Online Resources

Chapter Resources:
KEYWORD: SD7 CH30

Teacher Resources:
KEYWORD: SD7 TEACHER

Explore the Time Line

1. According to the time line, what events took place in 1973? *Face off at Wounded Knee; Yom Kippur War begins*

2. When did Congress approve the Equal Rights Amendment? *1972*

3. What provision outlawed gender discrimination in employment? *Title VII of the Civil Rights Act of 1964*

Info to Know

The Legal Right to Picket In 1776, Pennsylvania was the first state to include guarantees for peaceable assembly and petition of the government in its declarations of rights. Why? Probably in part because Pennsylvania's founder, William Penn, a Quaker, was arrested in 1670 in London for expressing his religious views.

Answers

Reading Like a Historian
(p. 984) *The expressions on the picketers' faces indicate strong commitment and determination*

Bellringer

The Inside Story. . . Use the **Daily Bellringer Transparency** to help students answer the question.

📖 Daily Bellringer Transparency, Section 1

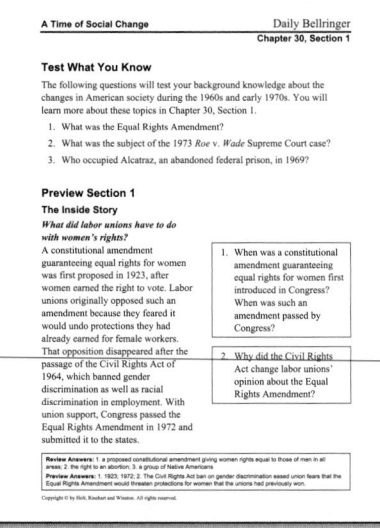

A Time of Social Change   Daily Bellringer
             Chapter 30, Section 1

Test What You Know

The following questions will test your background knowledge about the changes in American society during the 1960s and early 1970s. You will learn more about these topics in Chapter 30, Section 1.

1. What was the Equal Rights Amendment?
2. What was the subject of the 1973 *Roe v. Wade* Supreme Court case?
3. Who occupied Alcatraz, an abandoned federal prison, in 1969?

Preview Section 1

The Inside Story

What did labor unions have to do with women's rights?

A constitutional amendment guaranteeing equal rights for women was first proposed in 1923, after women earned the right to vote. Labor unions originally opposed such an amendment because they feared it would undo protections they had already earned for female workers. That opposition disappeared after the passage of the Civil Rights Act of 1964, which banned gender discrimination as well as racial discrimination in employment. With union support, Congress passed the Equal Rights Amendment in 1972 and submitted it to the states.

1. When was a constitutional amendment guaranteeing equal rights for women first introduced in Congress? When was such an amendment passed by Congress?

2. Why did the Civil Rights Act change labor unions' opinion about the Equal Rights Amendment?

Academic Vocabulary

Review with students the high-use academic terms in this section.

inquiry investigation, examination (p. 987)

allocate set aside for a specific purpose (p. 991)

📝 CRF: Vocabulary Builder Activity, Section 1

Taking Notes

1. *low wages and few promotions;* 2. *most jobs in low-paying service sector;* 3. *many jobs considered "men's jobs," not open to women*

---

go.hrw.com

Online Resources

KEYWORD: SD7 CH30
TOPIC: THE WOMEN'S
RIGHTS MOVEMENT

SECTION 1

Women and Native Americans Fight for Change

BEFORE YOU READ

MAIN IDEA

In the 1960s women and Native Americans struggled to achieve social justice.

READING FOCUS

1. What led to the revival of the women's movement?
2. Which issues were important to the women's liberation movement?
3. What were the lives of Native Americans like by the early 1960s?
4. How did Native Americans fight for fairness?

KEY TERMS AND PEOPLE

Betty Friedan
feminism
National Organization for Women
Equal Rights Amendment
Phyllis Schlafly
Roe v. Wade
American Indian Movement
Russell Means

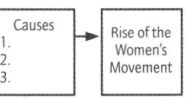 **TAKING NOTES** As you read, take notes on the causes of the rise of the women's movement. Write your notes in a graphic organizer like the one shown below.

Causes
1.
2.
3.
→ Rise of the Women's Movement

A Failed Amendment

THE INSIDE STORY

What did labor unions have to do with women's rights?

"Equality of rights under the law shall not be denied or abridged by the United States or by any state on account of sex." This was the wording of a constitutional amendment that Congress proposed in 1972.

▼ **Demonstrators show their support of the Equal Rights Amendment at a rally in Washington, D.C., in 1981.**

986

Many Americans regarded this Equal Rights Amendment (ERA) as long overdue. After all, Congress had been considering it for 49 years.

When the Nineteenth Amendment extended suffrage to women in 1920, an amendment guaranteeing equality with men in other areas had seemed a logical next step. The ERA was first introduced in Congress in 1923 and then introduced again in every subsequent session. The result was always the same—defeat. Powerful labor unions opposed the ERA because they feared it would undo protections they had won for women workers.

In the 1960s the civil rights movement changed everything. Hoping to weaken support for the proposed Civil Rights Act, which aimed to ban racial discrimination in employment, opponents added a ban on gender discrimination. To their dismay, the bill passed anyway.

Passage of the Civil Rights Act of 1964 pumped new life into the ERA. With special protections for women workers now outlawed by the Civil Rights Act, the unions no longer had a reason to oppose the ERA. In fact, they gradually reversed their position and backed it.

Representative Martha Griffiths of Michigan, a state where unions were strong, lobbied hard for the ERA. Congress finally passed it in 1972 and submitted it to the states for ratification. In the states, though, supporters of the ERA would fight a losing battle. ■

Teach the Main Idea
            At Level

Women and Native Americans

1. **Teach** Ask students the Reading Focus questions to teach this section.

2. **Apply** Draw four large rectangles for students to see. Label the top of each rectangle with one of the four topics of this section—Revival of the Women's Movement; The Women's Liberation Movement; The Lives of Native Americans; and Native Americans Fight for Fairness. Have students scan the section and make a list of the people discussed in each topic.

Write the names in each rectangle.

3. **Review** Guide students in a discussion of the ways these people changed the country.

4. **Practice/Homework** Have students write a one-page report for a European newspaper that summarizes and highlights the struggle of women and Native Americans to achieve social justice in the United States. **LS Visual-Spatial, Verbal-Linguistic**

📝 Alternative Assessment Handbook, Rubric 37: Writing Assignments

Revival of the Women's Movement

After the Nineteenth Amendment gave women the right to vote in 1920, the organized movement for women's rights declined. In the 1960s, some women began to question once more why they were still considered unequal—and what should be done about it.

Experiences at work To understand the revival of the women's movement, it is important to know what many women's lives were like in the 1950s and early 1960s. Throughout the 1950s more women began to join the workforce. By 1963, nearly one-third of American workers were women.

Yet on average, women in 1963 earned only 60 percent of what men earned. One reason for this difference was that most women worked in service jobs, such as retail sales, clerical work, and domestic service. These jobs typically paid poorly. Many of the better-paying jobs, such as those in manufacturing and construction, were considered men's domain. Even when women had the same jobs as men, however, they often received lower wages than men did.

In 1961 President John F. Kennedy ordered a formal <u>inquiry</u> into the position of women in American society. The Presidential Commission on the Status of Women reported that women did experience discrimination at work. Employers paid women less than men and promoted them less often. This report opened many people's eyes to the need for change.

Experiences at home Even though increasing numbers of women entered the workforce, many other women remained full-time homemakers. A popular idea in the 1950s was that women would be happiest as wives, mothers, and homemakers. Women tended to marry young; their average age at marriage was 20 years old. Many women who delayed marriage and built careers often left their jobs once they got married.

ACADEMIC VOCABULARY

inquiry investigation, examination

American Women: A Statistical Profile

During the latter half of the twentieth century, women began playing a greater role in public life, working at paid employment in greater numbers than ever before and attaining higher levels of education. *How do you think these experiences would lead women to seek social equality?*

WOMEN IN THE LABOR FORCE, 1950–2000

Source: United States Census Bureau

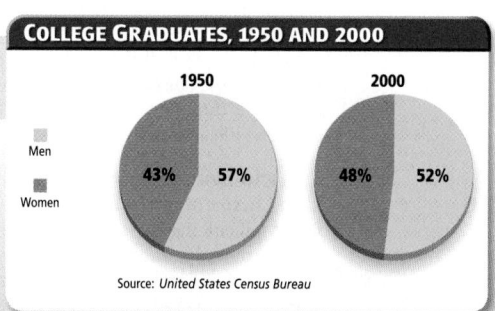

COLLEGE GRADUATES, 1950 AND 2000

1950 — Men 43%, Women 57%
2000 — Men 48%, Women 52%

Men
Women

Source: United States Census Bureau

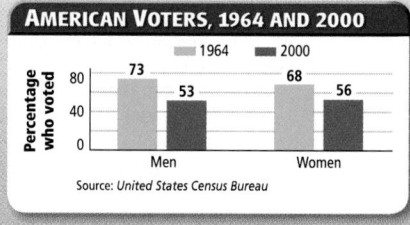

AMERICAN VOTERS, 1964 AND 2000

1964 / 2000

Men: 73 / 53
Women: 68 / 56

Source: United States Census Bureau

Skills FOCUS   INTERPRETING GRAPHS

Did a higher percentage of men or women vote in the year 2000?

See Skills Handbook, pp. H16, H17

A TIME OF SOCIAL CHANGE **987**

Skills Focus: Identifying Problem and Solution

At Level

Reading Skill
Commission on the Status of Women

Standard English Mastery

1. Guide students in a discussion about the revival of the women's movement in the United States. Ask students to identify specific issues that revived the women's movement.

2. Have students work in pairs to write a summary of the class discussion.

3. Have students work individually or in mixed-ability pairs to write an advisory memorandum to the president summarizing the findings of the Presidential Commission on the Status of Women. In their memos, have students include proposals on ways to remedy the "bad news" of the Commission's report.

4. Have volunteers read their memorandums to the class. **LS** **Interpersonal, Kinesthetic**

   Alternative Assessment Handbook, Rubrics 11: Discussions; and 37: Writing Assignments

---

● **Direct Teach** ●

Reading Focus

1 What led to the revival of the women's movement? *women questioned traditional roles; gender discrimination in workplace*

Revival of the Women's Movement

Describe What factors contributed to women's dissatisfaction in the workplace? *paid less than men; fewer promotions; often worked in service jobs; faced discrimination*

Contrast In what ways are career paths different for college-educated women today than in the 1960s? *today's women closer to receiving equal pay for equal work; more opportunities for promotion*

Elaborate What alternatives were available to women in the 1960s? *delay marriage and work in a job that paid poorly; marry and become full-time homemaker*

Teaching Tip

Remind students that today's labor laws protect women and provide leave for special health issues, including pregnancy and childbirth.

Primary Source

"The problem that has no name—which is simply the fact that American women are kept from growing to their full human capacities—is taking a far greater toll on the physical and mental health of our country than any known disease."
— Betty Friedan
The Feminine Mystique, p. 364

Answers

Caption *possible answer—greater involvement in public life led to increasing awareness that women were not treated equally*

Interpreting Graphs *women*

987

Revival of the Women's Movement

Describe What was the major conclusion of Betty Friedan's book *The Feminine Mystique*? *Women felt trapped in their domestic roles.*

Compare In what way was the civil rights movement similar to the women's rights movement? *struggle for equal rights; discrimination resulted from the notion of superiority of one group*

Make Inferences Why were women unaware of gender-based discrimination until they organized group discussions? *Women had considered their experiences as individual and confined to their own personal experience.*

📰 CRF: Literature Activity: *The Feminine Mystique* by Betty Friedan

📰 CRF: History and Geography Activity: The Equal Rights Amendment

Info to Know

Betty Friedan After the publication of her novel, *The Feminine Mystique*, in 1963, Betty Friedan continued to help shape both society's attitudes about women and women's views of themselves. As a result, in 1993, she was inducted into the National Women's Hall of Fame. She also served as co-chairperson of Women, Men and Media, an organization that conducts research on the media from a gender-based perspective.

Answers

Faces of History *unfair, unequal treatment led to fight for women's rights*

Reading Check *unequal wages and poor-paying jobs; Presidential Commission on the Status of Women; emphasis on women's role as homemakers; The Feminine Mystique*

988

FACES OF HISTORY

Betty FRIEDAN
1921–2006

After graduating from Smith College, Betty Friedan settled in New York and became a journalist. This was during World War II, when women were filling the jobs of men who had left to fight. Friedan discovered that women reporters were being paid less than men doing the same work. When Friedan requested maternity leave, her employer fired her.

Friedan became a pioneer of the women's movement with her best-selling book, *The Feminine Mystique*. She has remained a vocal feminist leader, calling for reforms to aid women and families, such as increased childcare, flexible work schedules, and equal pay.

Analyze A popular saying of the women's movement was "The personal is political." How did this fit Friedan's own life?

Life as a homemaker did not make all women happy, however. **Betty Friedan** (free-DAN) conducted a survey of college-educated women and found that many were dissatisfied with their lives. Nearly all of the survey respondents were full-time homemakers. In her 1963 book, *The Feminine Mystique*, Friedan concluded that many women felt trapped by domestic life, rather than fulfilled by it.

Consciousness raising By the late 1960s, *The Feminine Mystique* had sparked a national debate about the roles and rights of women. Some women organized small group discussions. In these consciousness-raising sessions, women discovered that the discrimination they experienced individually was part of a larger pattern of discrimination based on gender. More and more women came to feel like second-class citizens.

Ironically, even the civil rights movement—a movement aimed at eliminating discrimination—harbored discriminatory attitudes toward women. In 1964 two female volunteers for the Student Nonviolent Coordinating Committee (SNCC) noted that SNCC's "assumption of male superiority" was "as widespread and . . . as crippling to . . . women as the assumptions of white supremacy are to the Negro."

READING CHECK **Summarizing** What factors contributed to the revival of the women's movement?

The Women's Liberation Movement

In the late 1960s and 1970s, the movement for women's rights was known by several different names—the women's liberation movement, the feminist movement, and the equal rights movement. The core belief of the women's liberation movement was **feminism**, the conviction that women and men should be socially, politically, and economically equal.

Feminists cheered the passage of the Civil Rights Act of 1964. The act banned gender discrimination in employment and created the Equal Employment Opportunity Commission to enforce the law. Yet it soon became clear that many government officials gave low priority to fighting gender-based discrimination.

NOW In 1966 a group of feminists formed the **National Organization for Women** (NOW). This women's rights organization fought gender discrimination in the workplace, schools, and justice system. It also worked to end violence against women and to achieve abortion rights.

Members of NOW used many tactics to achieve their goals. They lobbied government officials to change the laws. They filed lawsuits to seek equality through the justice system. They also staged rallies, marches, and other nonviolent protests.

The first president of NOW was Betty Friedan. She and Pauli Murray—the first African American woman Episcopal priest and a co-founder of NOW—wrote NOW's original Statement of Purpose.

HISTORY'S VOICES

❝We believe that women will do most to create a new image of women by acting now, and by speaking out in behalf of their own equality, freedom, and human dignity . . . in an active, self-respecting partnership with men. By so doing, women will develop confidence in their own ability to determine actively, in partnership with men, the conditions of their life, their choices, their future and their society.❞

—NOW's Statement of Purpose, 1966

The Equal Rights Amendment NOW actively campaigned for passage of the **Equal Rights Amendment** (ERA). This proposed amendment to the Constitution promised

---

Skills Focus: Making Inferences

At Level

Reading Skill
The Women's Liberation Movement

1. Guide students in a discussion of the issues that resulted in the women's liberation movement. Have students work in small groups to answer this question: How have women today benefited from the women's liberation movement of the 1960s? Have students take notes during their small-group discussions.

2. Have students use their notes to create two political cartoons: one that represents the traditional roles of women in the past and one that represents women today.

3. Have volunteers share their political cartoons with the class. 🅛 **Visual-Spatial, Interpersonal**

📰 Alternative Assessment Handbook, Rubric 27: Political Cartoons

equal treatment for men and women in all spheres, not just employment. Before it could take effect, though, the ERA had to be ratified by at least 38 states.

At first ratification seemed certain. NOW organized a 1978 march in support of the ERA that drew more than 100,000 people to Washington, D.C. Some people, however, viewed the ERA as a threat to traditional family life. Critics warned that the ERA would cancel laws that distinguished between men and women. They argued that women would be drafted into the military and that men and women would have to share public restrooms.

Conservative groups launched a campaign to defeat the ERA. One of the most outspoken critics of the ERA was **Phyllis Schlafly**. She argued that it would take away legal protections that women already had without conferring any new benefits. By the 1982 deadline set by Congress, the ERA was three states short of ratification. It failed to become law.

Roe v. Wade Another significant issue for the women's movement was the campaign for abortion rights. The Supreme Court struck down state laws that banned abortion in the 1973 landmark case **Roe v. Wade**. The Court ruled that such laws violated a constitutional right to privacy.

The decision sparked a debate that continues to this day. Supporters argued that women could not achieve equality until they could control when or whether to have children. Supporters also believed that legal abortion was necessary to protect women's health. They argued that many women would otherwise resort to inept, "back-alley" practitioners who often botched the procedure.

Many people opposed the decision because of religious or moral beliefs that fetal life was sacred and should be protected. Other opponents of the ruling argued that the Court's assumption of a right to privacy strayed too far from the original intent of the Constitution.

THE IMPACT TODAY

Government
For more than 20 years after its failure to become law, the ERA continued to be reintroduced into every session of Congress, but failed to pass again.

COUNTERPOINTS

The ERA

Writer and editor Gloria Steinem was a leading feminist fighting for the Equal Rights Amendment.

❝ [E]qual pay for equal work, equal chance for advancement, and equal training or encouragement . . . When black people leave their 19th century roles, they are feared. When women dare to leave theirs, they are ridiculed. We understand this, and accept the burden of ridicule. It won't keep us quiet anymore. ❞

Gloria Steinem, 1970

Phyllis Schlafly believed that the ERA was "a fraud" and that women were most fulfilled by their roles as wives and mothers.

❝ There is no gain in ERA for women . . . There is no way ERA can add anything to the effect of the Equal Employment Opportunity Act of 1972, the education amendments of 1972, and the Equal Credit Opportunity Act of 1974. ❞

Phyllis Schlafly, 1975

 STOP ERA

Skills FOCUS READING LIKE A HISTORIAN

1. **Comparing** Steinem compares the plight of women to which group? Why?
2. **Identifying Points of View** What reasons does Schlafly give for opposing the ERA?

See Skills Handbook, pp. H10, H28–29

---

❸ What were the lives of Native Americans like by the early 1960s? *high unemployment rates; poverty; poor health conditions; high infant death rate*

The Lives of Native Americans

Explain What was the termination policy? *federal policy to grant Native Americans same rights as other Americans and end their status as wards of the government*

Draw Conclusions Why did the termination policy fail? *placed Native Americans in different environment without jobs or social services assistance; ended federal services that they depended on*

Evaluate Do you believe that the Declaration of Indian Purpose was successful? *possible answers—yes, served as inspiration, statement of intent, began fight for rights; no, unable to reverse termination policy*

Activity **The Lives of Native Americans** Have students write two journal entries from the perspective of a Native American in the early 1960s. Ask volunteers to share their entries with the class.

📝 Political Cartoons Activities for American History: Cartoon 59: Bella Abzug

---

Teaching Tip

Have students review the information about the Dawes Act in their text before you begin teaching the information in this section about Native Americans.

Answers

Reading Check *for—equal treatment for men and women in all spheres, not just employment; against—would take away existing legal protection for women but provide nothing in return*

990

Effects of the women's movement The women's movement had many notable successes in the 1970s. By the end of the decade, the number of women holding professional jobs had increased, although most women still held low-paying jobs. For example, in 1970 just 5 percent of the nation's lawyers were women. A decade later, 12 percent of American lawyers were women.

More women also began to move into senior positions in government. More female politicians were elected to Congress, although they still made up less than 5 percent of its members. Representatives Bella Abzug and Shirley Chisholm of New York received national attention. Abzug became an outspoken supporter of women's issues in Congress. In 1972 Shirley Chisholm—the first African American woman elected to Congress—became the first African American woman to run for president.

The pace of the feminist movement slowed in the late 1970s, however. There was a perception that its leaders and its beneficiaries were mainly wealthy white women. Many working-class and nonwhite women felt that the movement offered little to address the problems they faced.

READING CHECK **Summarizing** What were the arguments for and against the ERA?

THE IMPACT TODAY

Daily Life
By the early twenty-first century, nearly half the nation's law students and medical students were women, and a majority of workers in professional positions were women.

The Lives of Native Americans

Just as many women felt they were held back in mid-twentieth-century America, so did many Native Americans. Indian groups had suffered injustices since colonial times. During the 1950s, negative stereotypes of Indians still persisted, and hardships abounded.

Living conditions Native Americans did not share the prosperity many Americans experienced in the 1950s. As a group, they suffered some of the highest unemployment rates in the nation. The average income of Native American men was less than half that of white American men. Mary Crow Dog recalled growing up poor on a Sioux reservation in South Dakota: "We had no shoes and went barefoot most of the time. I never had a new dress."

The Native American population suffered disproportionately from poor health. Rates of alcoholism and tuberculosis were alarmingly high. Native Americans had lower life expectancy than other Americans, and their children were more likely to die in infancy.

Termination policy During the presidency of Dwight D. Eisenhower, the federal government began a policy called termination. The

---

TRACING HISTORY

Native American Policy and Activism

Native American peoples have struggled to retain their ways of life ever since European colonists first arrived in America. Study the time line to learn more about Native Americans and government policies.

990 CHAPTER 30

1838 Some 18,000 Cherokee embarked upon the Trail of Tears as they were forced to move from the Southeast to Oklahoma.

1800

1887 The Dawes Act split Native American land into individual plots and allowed surplus land to be sold to settlers.

Differentiating Instruction

Below Level

Special Education Students

Materials construction paper, scissors, glue, colored markers

1. Have students search the Internet or print sources to find and copy pictures and articles about federal government polices regarding Native Americans.

2. Have students paste the pictures and articles onto the construction paper. Have students

label each picture with the name of the corresponding federal policy.

3. Have students share their collages. Guide students in a discussion about the different government policies toward Native Americans. **LS** **Visual-Spatial, Kinesthetic**

📝 Alternative Assessment Handbook, Rubrics 8: Collages; and 30: Research

goal was to "end the status of Indians as wards of the government and grant them all the rights and prerogatives pertaining to American citizenship." The architects of the policy hoped to draw Native Americans out of their isolated reservations and into mainstream society. The method for doing this, however, was to stop federal services to reservations and relocate Native Americans to the cities.

Between 1952 and 1967, some 200,000 Native Americans were resettled in this way. However, the government failed to <u>allocate</u> resources to help them adjust to urban life. The results were disastrous. Most of the Native Americans affected by termination remained desperately poor.

A movement emerges Many Native Americans believed the time had come for an organized movement for Native American rights. In 1961 a group of about 700 Native Americans from 64 nations held a conference in Chicago to oppose the termination policy and create a political agenda for change.

At the conference a Chippewa-Cree activist named D'Arcy McNickle drafted the Declaration of Indian Purpose. This document condemned termination. It also boldly stated Native Americans' intention to take control over their own lives.

HISTORY'S VOICES

❝ Since our Indian culture is threatened by presumption of being absorbed by the American society, we believe we have the responsibility of preserving our precious heritage . . . What we ask of America is not charity . . . We ask only that the nature of our situation be recognized and made the basis of policy and action. ❞

—Declaration of Indian Purpose, June 1961

The declaration marked the beginning of what became known as the Red Power movement. A new sense of unity arose among Native Americans as different groups joined forces to confront common challenges.

ACADEMIC VOCABULARY
allocate set aside for a specific purpose

READING CHECK **Identifying the Main Idea** What factors led Native Americans to begin an organized fight for their rights?

Native Americans Fight for Fairness

In 1968 President Lyndon B. Johnson declared his support for Indian self-determination. He established the National Council on Indian Opportunity to get Native Americans more involved in setting policy regarding Indian affairs. Real change, though, came through the efforts of Native American political activists.

1953 Congress adopted the termination policy, moving many Native Americans to cities and cutting aid to reservations.

1969 Occupation of Alcatraz began, awakening the public to Native Americans' struggle for self-determination.

1900

2000

1934 The Indian Reorganization Act set up Tribal Business Councils and stopped the sale of tribal lands.

1972 The Indian Education Act established culturally appropriate educational programs for Native American students.

2005 Nearly 40 percent of federally recognized Indian nations earn money and create jobs by running gambling casinos.

A TIME OF SOCIAL CHANGE **991**

Differentiating Instruction

Above Level

Advanced Learners/GATE

Research Required

Materials butcher paper, colored markers

1. Have students conduct outside research using the Internet and traditional print sources to learn more about the lives of Native Americans from the beginning of the 20th century through the present day.

2. Have students make copies of the information and visuals. Then have students

create a PowerPoint presentation or mural showing the results of their research about Native American life.

3. Have students share their murals or presentations with the class. **LS** **Visual-Spatial, Intrapersonal**

📄 Alternative Assessment Handbook, Rubrics 22: Multimedia Presentations; and 30: Research

● **Direct Teach** ●

Reading Focus

❹ How did Native Americans fight for fairness? *increased involvement in decisions affecting them; occupied Alcatraz; founded AIM and National Indian Education Association*

Native Americans Fight for Fairness

Recall What was President Lyndon Johnson's policy goal for Native Americans? *to foster self-determination for Native Americans*

Analyze How did President Johnson view Native Americans? *as people with a unique culture who should be treated with dignity and respect*

Evaluate Why was the establishment of the National Council on Indian Opportunity a timely move by President Johnson? *activism by Native Americans showed the urgency of the situation*

Biography

Leslie Marmon Silko (1948–) Coming from a mixed Native American, white, and Mexican ancestry, Leslie Marmon Silko offers a unique perspective on the tension between Native American and white cultures. After growing up on the Laguna Pueblo reservation in New Mexico, Silko began to write poetry in order to find a connection between the stories she had heard as a child and the contemporary experiences of Native Americans. Silko's first novel, *Ceremony*, chronicled the efforts of a World War II veteran to reconnect with his Laguna heritage in order to heal from his wartime experiences.

Answers

Reading Check *poverty, poor living conditions; lack of respect for native cultures; policies such as termination*

991

Native Americans Fight for Fairness

Explain What was the connection between the 1868 Treaty of Fort Laramie and the occupation of Alcatraz? *treaty gave the Native Americans the right to claim surplus federal territory; Native Americans used right as the basis for occupation*

Summarize What significant changes resulted from the occupation of Alcatraz? *Congress passed laws to help self-determination, education, and health; Washington state returned Mount Adams to the Yakima; New Mexico returned 48,000 acres of Sacred Blue Lake lands to the Taos Pueblo*

Draw Conclusions What element of the Trail of Broken Treaties protest was most effective and why? *media coverage because government was embarrassed into meeting and negotiating with Native Americans*

Info to Know

Russell Means Before Russell Means led the American Indian Movement, he held a wide variety of jobs, ranging from a ballroom dance instructor to a rodeo rider. In the 1990s, Means portrayed Native Americans in movies such as *The Last of the Mohicans* and *Natural Born Killers*.

Answers

Faces of History *by being active in many social justice organizations, founding organization to combat stereotypes*

992

The occupation of Alcatraz In 1969 a group of Native Americans tried to reclaim Alcatraz Island, the site of an abandoned federal prison in San Francisco Bay. They claimed that the 1868 Treaty of Fort Laramie gave them the right to use any surplus federal territory.

The highly publicized occupation lasted nearly 18 months, until federal marshals removed the Indians by force. Although they did not succeed in gaining ownership of Alcatraz, the occupiers did draw attention to the plight of Native Americans. Partly as a result, New Mexico returned 48,000 acres of the Sacred Blue Lake lands to the Taos Pueblo in 1970. Indian nations in Washington State, Maine, and Connecticut also settled land claims.

John Trudell, a Santee Sioux, found the Alcatraz occupation to be a transforming experience. "Alcatraz put me back into my community and helped me remember who I am. It was a rekindling of the spirit. Alcatraz made it easier for us to remember who we are."

AIM The Alcatraz Island takeover helped invigorate the **American Indian Movement** (AIM), founded in Minnesota in 1968 by Dennis Banks, Clyde Bellecourt, and others. Originally focused on urban Native Americans, AIM became the major force behind the larger Red Power movement. AIM called for renewal of traditional cultures, economic independence, and better education for Indian children.

THE IMPACT TODAY

Culture
Alcatraz is now a popular tourist attraction in San Francisco. Visitors who tour the old prison can also study exhibits and watch a film about the Indian occupation of the island.

FACES OF HISTORY

Clyde BELLECOURT
1939–

It is little wonder that Clyde Bellecourt became a Native American activist. He developed a passion for social justice early on, listening to his mother tell stories about attending boarding school and being punished for speaking her native language.

Bellecourt has been influential in many Native American organizations, including AIM, the Indian School System, and the International Indian Treaty Council, which seeks to protect traditional cultures and sacred lands. More recently, he helped organize the National Coalition on Racism in Sports and the Media, which demonstrates against sports teams whose names perpetuate racial and cultural stereotypes. Bellecourt believes that things are destined to change for Native Americans, that there is "a spiritual rebirth going on."

Explain How has Bellecourt helped Native Americans?

Russell Means, one of AIM's best-known leaders, summarized the organization's importance to Native Americans in an interview in a 2002 PBS television documentary.

HISTORY'S VOICES

❝Before AIM, Indians were dispirited, defeated and culturally dissolving. People were ashamed to be Indian . . . We put Indians and Indian rights smack dab in the middle of the public consciousness for the first time since the so-called Indian Wars . . . [AIM] laid the groundwork for the next stage in regaining our sovereignty and self-determination as a nation.❞

—Russell Means, "Alcatraz Is Not an Island"

In an era when many civil rights groups used nonviolent strategies, AIM sometimes used more forceful tactics. In November 1972, for example, AIM and several other Native American rights groups staged a protest called the Trail of Broken Treaties. Protesters marched to the Bureau of Indian Affairs (BIA) in Washington, D.C., to demand changes in the relationship between Native Americans and the government. Angered by the government's lack of support, the protesters took over BIA headquarters. Officials were embarrassed by the media coverage and agreed to appoint a committee to study the demands. In return, the protesters ended the occupation.

In February 1973, AIM took its most dramatic action on the Pine Ridge Reservation in Wounded Knee, South Dakota. This was where U.S. soldiers had killed more than 300 Sioux in 1890. Now, some 80 years later, conflict unfolded again. The Oglala Sioux president, Richard Wilson, had banned all AIM activities on the reservation, calling AIM a "lawless" band of "social misfits." AIM believed that Wilson's tribal government was corrupt. About 200 AIM members occupied Wounded Knee in order to force the federal government to investigate the tribal government. They also wanted an investigation of alleged misconduct at the Bureau of Indian Affairs.

After AIM members seized Wounded Knee, federal agents arrived to drive them out. For 71 days AIM and U.S. marshals faced off. Finally, after two AIM activists had been killed and a federal marshal wounded, the government agreed to consider AIM's grievances. The siege ended, but the government did not follow through on its promise to AIM.

Skills Focus: Analyzing Primary Sources

Reading Like a Historian Skill

Native Americans Fight for Fairness

1. Divide students into small groups. Have each group conduct research on the Internet to locate quotes, interviews, or other primary sources from leaders in the movement for equal rights for Native Americans, such as Russell Means and D'Arcy McNickle.

2. Have students write letters to members of Congress asking that the government protect the rights of Native Americans. In their letters students should cite information

from their primary sources and give reasons for their request.

3. Have volunteers read their letters to the class. Guide the class in a discussion of the challenges faced by Native Americans and how the government might have addressed those challenges. **LS** **Verbal-Linguistic**

Alternative Assessment Handbook, Rubrics 5: Business Letters; and 30: Research

Other organizations AIM was not the only organization fighting for Native American rights at this time. Many other organizations focused on particular needs.

The National Indian Education Association, formed in 1969, fought to improve access to education for Native Americans. The Native American Rights Fund, founded in 1971, provided legal services to Native Americans. The Council on Energy Resource Tribes helped its member nations gain control over their natural resources and choose whether to protect or develop them.

These groups, and others like them, worked to protect Native Americans' rights, improve standards of living, and do it all in a manner consistent with Native Americans' cultures and traditions. Today reservations are home to many Indian-owned businesses, including oil and natural gas companies. Tourism is booming on Indian lands, and Native American arts and crafts have increased in value.

Assessing progress During the era of Red Power activism, Native Americans made important legislative gains. Congress passed a number of laws in the 1970s to enhance education, health care, voting rights, and religious freedom for Native Americans.

The Red Power movement also instilled greater pride in Native Americans and generated wider appreciation of Native American culture. N. Scott Momaday, a Kiowa author, won the prestigious Pulitzer Prize for Fiction in 1969. Fritz Scholder led the New American Indian Art movement, which depicted Native American life in a fresh way, free of clichés.

Despite their accomplishments, Native Americans continued to face many problems. Unemployment rates remained high in the 1970s, averaging 40 percent and reaching as high as 90 percent on some reservations. The high school dropout rate among Native Americans was the highest in the nation.

> **READING CHECK** **Identifying Cause and Effect** What were the results of the Indian occupation of Alcatraz Island?

MAJOR NATIVE AMERICAN LEGISLATION

 QUICK FACTS

Alaska Native Claims Settlement Act, 1971
This act turned over 44 million acres of land to Alaska Natives and provided $962.5 million to settle other land claims by Alaska Natives.

Indian Self-Determination and Education Assistance Act, 1975
This act allowed tribes to implement their own education, health, and housing programs with government funding.

Indian Child Welfare Act, 1978
This act set standards for adoptions of Native American children, giving preference to relatives, members of the tribe, and Native American foster parents over white families.

SECTION 1 ASSESSMENT

go.hrw.com
Online Quiz
Keyword: SD7 HP30

Reviewing Ideas, Terms, and People

1. a. Identify What was *The Feminine Mystique*?
b. Explain How did *The Feminine Mystique* inspire the women's movement?
c. Elaborate What expectations were placed on women at home and in the workplace during the 1950s?

2. a. Define What is feminism?
b. Draw Conclusions Why was *Roe v. Wade* controversial?
c. Evaluate Given the failure of the Equal Rights Amendment to be ratified, was the women's movement of the 1960s and 1970s a success or a failure? Explain.

3. a. Recall What was the Declaration of Indian Purpose?
b. Make Inferences How do you think Native Americans felt about the federal government's termination policy?

4 a. Describe What was the American Indian Movement?
b. Analyze How did the occupation of Alcatraz affect AIM?

c. Evaluate How successful was the Native American fight for fairness? Explain.

Critical Thinking

5. Organizing Information Copy the chart below and record key characteristics of the women's movement and the Red Power movement in the 1960s and 1970s.

Movement	Goals	Leaders	Key Issues

> **FOCUS ON WRITING**

6. Persuasive Suppose it is 1960. Write a letter to the editor opposing the U.S. government's policy of termination and suggesting reforms.

A TIME OF SOCIAL CHANGE **993**

Section 1 Assessment Answers

1. a. Betty Friedan's book, concluding that women felt trapped by domestic life
b. sparked debate about equal rights
c. be happy as wife and mother

2. a. equality for men and women
b. legalized abortion
c. possible answer—success, it drew attention to problems and led to reform

3. a. document condemning termination
b. abandoned and angry

4. a. movement to improve life for all Native Americans

b. inspired AIM to further protest movements
c. possible answers—Native Americans gained pride and prospered, but hardships still remain

5. women's—equality and opportunity; Betty Friedan, Gloria Steinem; less pay for same work, abortion rights; Red Power—create positive change, D'Arcy McNickle, Russell Means; oppose termination

6. possible answer—abandons Native Americans without housing or job training; protect their culture instead

---

Direct Teach

Reading Focus

Native Americans Fight for Fairness

Recall What problems do Native Americans still face today? *high unemployment, high rate of high-school dropouts*

Evaluate What was the significance of the Red Power movement? *drew attention to the concerns and living conditions of Native Americans; gave Native Americans renewed sense of pride in their culture and the need to preserve it*

🔖 Quick Facts Transparency: Major Native American Legislation

---

Review & Assess

Close
Guide students in a discussion of the struggle of Native Americans and women to achieve equality and social justice.

Review
Online Quiz, Section 1

🔖 Daily Test Practice Transparency

Assess

SE Section 1 Assessment
📑 Progress Assessment: Section 1 Quiz
📑 Alternative Assessment Handbook

Reteach

📑 Interactive Reader and Study Guide, Section 1
💿 Interactive Skills Tutor CD-ROM

Answers

Reading Check *drew attention to Native Americans' plight; some land claims settled; inspired action by Native Americans*

Bellringer

The Inside Story. . . Use the **Daily Bellringer Transparency** to help students answer the question.

🔖 Daily Bellringer Transparency, Section 2

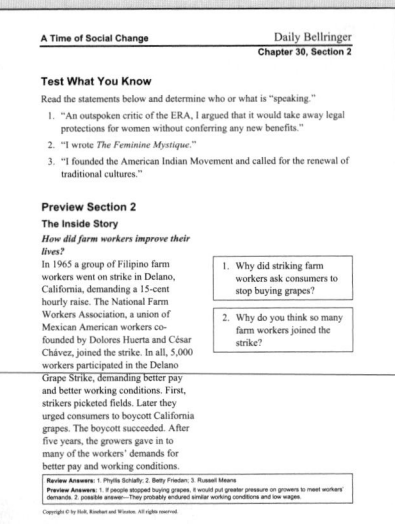

Academic Vocabulary

Review with students the high-use academic term in this section.

contemporary existing during the same period of time (p. 997)

📄 CRF: Vocabulary Builder Activity, Section 2

Taking Notes

Alianza: worked to regain lands in Southwest; Crusade for Justice: promoted Mexican nationalism; MAYO: educational opportunities, economic independence; La Raza Unida: education, improved public services; Brown Berets: protested police action in Los Angeles, supported other groups; boricua: Puerto Rican movement for economic opportunities, neighborhood improvement

go.hrw.com
Online Resources
KEYWORD: SD7 CH30
TOPIC: THE UFW AND THE LATINO RIGHTS MOVEMENT

Latinos Fight for Rights

BEFORE YOU READ

MAIN IDEA
In the 1960s Latinos struggled to achieve social justice.

READING FOCUS
1. What were the lives of Latinos like in the early 1960s?
2. What event launched Latinos' struggle for social justice?
3. What were the main goals of the movements for Latino rights?

KEY TERMS AND PEOPLE
social justice
César Chávez
Chicano
Rodolfo "Corky" Gonzales
José Angel Gutiérrez
La Raza Unida Party
boricua

TAKING NOTES As you read, take notes on the major organizations in the movement for Latino rights. Write your notes in a graphic organizer like the one shown below, adding as many rows as you need.

Organization	Key Facts

THE INSIDE STORY

How did farmworkers improve their lives? In 1965, Filipino workers began a strike against grape growers around Delano, California, in the state's agricultural San Joaquin Valley. Demanding a 15-cent increase in their hourly wages, they asked Mexican American farmworkers to join them. Dolores Huerta and César Chávez, co-founders of the National Farm Workers Association, a union of Mexican American farmworkers, agreed to help. Some 5,000 grape workers walked off their jobs.

The now-famous Delano Grape Strike lasted five years. It was bitter and hard-fought. Strikers picketed the fields to convince the nonstriking workers to join them. Growers sprayed the pick-eters with farm chemicals and drove tractors through the fields to choke them with dust.

To build support for the strike, Chávez led a 250-mile march to the state capital at Sacramento. As the march passed through towns along the way, many farmworkers joined it. By the time it reached Sacramento, the number of marchers had grown from just a few hundred to more than 5,000.

▲ **César Chávez (right) leads striking farmworkers.**

When picketing and marches did not win the strike, Huerta sent union activists around the nation to set up local boycott committees. Committee members stood outside supermarkets to tell customers about conditions for workers in the fields. They urged shoppers to support the strike by not buying California grapes.

The Great Grape Boycott proved successful. By 1969 it had even spread to Great Britain. As people in other European nations considered joining the boycott, the growers gave in and finally settled with the union. The Delano Grape Strike was the first major victory in a long, difficult struggle to improve the lives and working conditions of migrant farmworkers.

Teach the Main Idea

At Level

Latinos Fight for Rights

1. **Teach** Ask students the Reading Focus questions to teach this section.

2. **Apply** Draw a large triangle for students to see. Label each angle with the topics of the section: The Lives of Latinos, Launching the Struggle for Social Justice, and Movements for Latino Rights. Have students copy the triangle. Then have students work in pairs and write the main ideas of each topic on the sides of the triangle.

3. **Review** As you review the section, use the triangle as a graphic organizer, and have students identify the main ideas they have written on their triangles. Have students identify the links among the three topics.

4. **Practice/Homework** Have students create a sequencing diagram that shows the Latino struggle for civil rights.
   LS Visual-Spatial, Verbal-Linguistic

📄 Alternative Assessment Handbook, Rubric 13: Graphic Organizers

The Lives of Latinos

In 1960 more than 900,000 Latinos lived in the United States. A Latino is any person of Latin American descent. Latinos may also be called Hispanics, but *Hispanic* has a slightly different meaning. It encompasses all people of Spanish-speaking ancestry, including those whose families came from Spain.

The U.S. Latino population increased sharply during the 1960s. This was partly because the Immigration Act of 1965 gave preference to immigrants with relatives already in the country. Eligible Latinos, especially Mexicans, streamed in.

Latinos, however, often struggled in the United States. In 1960 one-third of Mexican American families lived below the poverty line. Twice as many Mexican Americans as white Americans were unemployed. About 80 percent of Mexican Americans worked in low-paying, unskilled jobs, such as farm labor, household service, construction, or factory work.

Latinos faced discrimination in education too. Their children often attended schools with less qualified teachers, fewer resources, and shabbier facilities than other American schools. Few of their teachers were Hispanic or able to speak Spanish. In this discouraging environment, about 75 percent of Latino students dropped out before finishing high school.

In politics Latinos had far less power than the size of their population would warrant. State legislatures drew the boundaries of election districts in ways that kept Latino voices scattered. The number of Latinos in political office was very small. In addition, Latinos were often excluded from serving on juries.

READING CHECK **Comparing and Contrasting** How did Latinos' living standards compare to those of other Americans in the early 1960s?

Launching the Struggle for Social Justice

As other groups began campaigning for their rights, Latinos also sought **social justice,** or the fair distribution of advantages and disadvantages in society. One of the earliest efforts was made in the farm fields of California. Migrant

THE IMPACT TODAY

Government
In 2003 the U.S. Census Bureau announced that Latinos had become the nation's largest minority group. The political power that comes with such numbers is apparent as major political parties now make serious efforts to attract Latino voters.

Hispanic Americans: A Statistical Profile

According to the U.S. census taken in 2000, more than half of all immigrants to the United States that year came from Latin America. Specifically, one fourth of all immigrants that year came from Mexico.

HISPANIC IMMIGRANTS TO THE UNITED STATES, 1960 AND 2000

Country / Region of Origin
Mexico ▪ Cuba ▪ South America ▪ Central America

1960
6%
11%
73%
10%

2000
15%
16%
64%
5%

Source: United States Census Bureau

HISPANIC AMERICAN POPULATION, 1950–2000

Source: Population Reference Bureau; United States Census Bureau

Skills FOCUS **INTERPRETING GRAPHS**

1. How has the place of origin of Hispanic immigrants changed since 1960?
2. How has the rate of Hispanic immigration changed over time?

See Skills Handbook, pp. H16, H17

A TIME OF SOCIAL CHANGE **995**

Direct Teach

Reading Focus

❶ What were the lives of Latinos like in the early 1960s? *1/3 of families below poverty level; high unemployment; limited education*

The Lives of Latinos

Recall In 1960, what percent of Mexican Americans were working in low-paying unskilled jobs? *80 percent*

Analyze What barriers did Latinos face in education? *schools had few teachers and were run-down; few teachers were Latino or spoke Spanish; high dropout rate*

Elaborate Discuss the political environment for Latinos. *sometimes excluded from serving on juries; voting power diluted; few held political office*

Activity **The Lives of Latinos** Have students work in small groups to list the ways that Latinos were prevented from achieving equality in the U.S. in the 1960s.
LS Interpersonal, Verbal-Linguistic

Info to Know

Dolores Huerta In April 2005, Dolores Huerta celebrated her 75th birthday. Selected Woman of the Year in 1998 by the United Farm Workers of America, Dolores Huerta has successfully balanced her role as activist, mother, and grandmother. Her most recent labor campaigns have been with the California strawberry industry, where workers lack decent housing and health benefits and work in hostile and unsafe environments.

Answers

Interpreting Graphs *1. more today from Central and South America; 2. it has increased*

Reading Check *many poor and unemployed; often worked low-paying jobs, faced discrimination*

Collaborative Learning

At Level

Latinos Fight for Rights

1. Guide students in a discussion about the lives of Latinos in the 1960s and the beginning of their struggle for social justice.

2. Organize students into small groups. Have each group create a written, face-to-face conversation between César Chávez and Dolores Huerta when they meet to discuss the need for an organized effort on behalf of the grape field workers. The conclusion of the conversation should be the proposal to help organize a strike against California grape growers. In their conversations students should include possible benefits and dangers of the strike for the workers.

3. Have volunteers from each group read their written conversation to the class.
LS Verbal-Linguistic, Interpersonal

Alternative Assessment Handbook, Rubrics 14: Group Activity; and 24: Oral Presentations

2 What event launched Latinos' struggle for social justice?
five-year Delano Grape Strike

Launching the Struggle for Social Justice

Recall What is social justice? *fair distribution of advantages and disadvantages in society*

Describe What was life like for the migrant workers in the farm fields of California? *workers received low wages for back-breaking work*

Make Inferences Why do you think farm worker reform began in California? *California crops need large number of workers; farm labor pay has traditionally been low*

Activity **The Delano Grape Strike** Have students work in mixed-ability pairs to list the sequence of events of the Delano Grape Strike. Create a class list and have students correct their own lists and retain them as a study tool.

LS Interpersonal, Verbal-Linguistic

Political Cartoons Activities for American History: Cartoon 60: César Chávez

---

FACES OF HISTORY

César CHÁVEZ
1927–1993

César Chávez spent his early years on his family's small farm in Arizona. When the farm failed during the Great Depression, his family moved to California and lived in migrant labor camps. Chávez left school in the eighth grade to work in the fields. After serving in the navy, he returned to California and to the life of a migrant worker.

In 1952 Chávez began a career as an activist, joining the Community Service Organization and registering Mexican Americans to vote. In 1962 he co-founded the National Farm Workers Association to help migrant farmworkers unionize. In the photo at right, Chávez (center) is talking with grape pickers. After his success in the grape strike, Chávez turned to organizing workers in California's lettuce fields and migrant fruit pickers in Florida's citrus groves.

Make Inferences Why was Chávez so successful in his efforts to organize migrant farmworkers?

---

agricultural workers, many of whom were Latinos, received low wages for backbreaking labor. In 1965 farmworkers went on strike in Delano, California. The National Farm Workers Association soon joined the strike, under the leadership of **César Chávez** and Dolores Huerta.

Chávez and Huerta knew that the strike needed publicity. Simply stopping work in the fields would not draw enough attention to their cause. So, as you read at the beginning of this section, union activists and sympathetic volunteers stood in front of grocery stores nationwide, urging Americans not to buy grapes.

HISTORY'S VOICES

“ Grapes must remain an unenjoyed luxury for all as long as the barest human needs and basic human rights are still luxuries for farm workers. The grapes grow sweet and heavy on the vines, but they will have to wait while we reach out first for our freedom. The time is ripe for our liberation. **”**

—Dolores Huerta, "Proclamation of the Delano Grape Workers for International Boycott Day," 1969

The success of the strike made César Chávez a national figure, respected for his tireless support of migrant workers and his commitment to nonviolent protest. Chávez's leadership inspired many Mexican Americans to fight discrimination in their lives. The union's symbol, a black Aztec eagle, came to represent the Mexican American civil rights movement that developed during the late 1960s.

READING CHECK **Identifying Main Idea and Details** How did farmworkers enlist the help of consumers to achieve better working conditions?

Movements for Latino Rights

César Chávez proved the effectiveness of mass action. While he fought for farmworkers, other Latino activists pursued different agendas.

Defining the Chicano movement In the late 1960s some Mexican Americans began to embrace a form of cultural nationalism similar to the Black Power movement supported by black nationalists. They called themselves **Chicanos**, a shortened form of *mexicanos*. The name conveyed their ethnic pride and commitment to political activism.

In earlier generations the term *Chicano* had carried a negative connotation. Now Chicanos adopted the name proudly. They used the term

---

Skills Focus: Recognizing Bias | Above Level

Reading Like a Historian Skill
Farm Owners and Farm Workers

1. Guide students in a discussion of the 1965 farm workers strike. Ask students to consider the actions and reactions of the growers as well as farm workers at the beginning of the strike.

2. Have students conduct outside research to find information from both sides involved in the Delano Grape Strike: the workers and the growers. Have students make copies of the documents.

3. Have students analyze the documents and underline passages that represent a particular bias.

4. Have students write a short editorial entitled *The Delano Grape Strike: A Look Back.* In their editorials, have students analyze the bias they found in their documents.

LS Intrapersonal, Verbal-Linguistic

Alternative Assessment Handbook, Rubrics 30: Research; and 42: Writing to Inform

---

Answers

Faces of History *understood the people and the problems they faced; had already helped register Mexican Americans to vote*

Reading Check *appealed to shoppers; went to grocery stores and urged them to boycott grapes*

Mexican American to describe someone who had assimilated—someone who held American views rather than Mexican ones.

Alianza One early Chicano leader was Reies López Tijerina. He formed the Alianza Federal de Mercedes (Federal Alliance of Land Grants) to focus on the enduring issue of land rights.

After winning the Mexican-American War in 1848, the United States had signed the Treaty of Guadalupe Hidalgo, promising to respect Mexicans' land claims in territories it annexed. Despite this promise, Mexican Americans had lost tens of thousands of acres over the years—often through fraud or deception. In Rio Arriba County, New Mexico, for example, some 60 percent of the land once belonging to Mexican Americans had been taken away—much of it by the federal government.

In 1967 Tijerina and his followers charged into the Rio Arriba County courthouse to demand justice. A gun battle broke out, and two police officers were wounded. The incident focused national attention on the unfair seizure of Mexican American lands. However, Tijerina was later arrested because of his activities, and Alianza eventually broke up.

The Crusade for Justice Another leading figure in the Chicano movement was **Rodolfo "Corky" Gonzales**. A former boxer, Gonzales became active in Democratic Party politics and antipoverty programs in Denver, Colorado, during the late 1950s and early 1960s. Over time, though, he grew to believe that mainstream politics did little to help Mexican Americans.

In 1966 Gonzales founded the Crusade for Justice, a group that promoted Mexican American nationalism. Operating out of an old church, the group provided legal aid, a theater for enhancing cultural awareness, a Spanish-language newspaper, and other community services. It also ran a school that offered children free bilingual classes and lessons in Chicano culture.

Gonzales credited the Crusade for Justice with igniting the "nationalism that now exists here in the Southwest. It has been a dream of the past, but we're now creating a reality out of it." He popularized the use of the nationalist term *Chicano*. Gonzales also composed a poem, "I Am Joaquín," which served as an anthem for the Chicano movement.

HISTORY'S VOICES

❝I have endured in the rugged mountains / Of our country / I have survived the toils and slavery of the fields. / I have existed / In the barrios [Latino neighborhoods] of the city / In the suburbs of bigotry / In the mines of social snobbery / In the prisons of dejection / In the muck of exploitation / And / In the fierce heat of racial hatred. / And now the trumpet sounds, / The music of the people stirs the / Revolution. / Like a sleeping giant it slowly / Rears its head / To the sound of / Tramping feet / Clamoring voices / Mariachi strains . . . / And in all the fertile farmlands, / the barren plains, / the mountain villages, / smoke-smeared cities, / we start to MOVE. / La raza! [The people!] / Méjicano! [Mexican!] / Español! [Spanish!] / Latino! / Chicano! / Or whatever I call myself, / I look the same / I feel the same / I cry / And / Sing the same. / I am the masses of my people and / I refuse to be absorbed.❞

—Rodolfo Gonzales, "I Am Joaquín"

In March 1969 Gonzales and the Crusade for Justice sponsored the National Chicano Liberation Youth Conference. Conference delegates produced *El Plan Espiritual de Aztlán*, or the Spiritual Plan of Aztlán. The plan called upon Chicanos to reclaim the lands of the Southwest. The ultimate goal was to build a unified Chicano community that was empowered to determine its own future.

MAYO Mexican Americans in Texas also turned to protest during the 1960s. In 1967 a group of college students in San Antonio formed the Mexican American Youth Organization (MAYO). The founders of MAYO, including **José Angel Gutiérrez**, wanted to achieve economic independence for Mexican Americans, to gain local control over the education of Hispanic children, and to achieve power for Latinos through the creation of a third political party.

Under Gutiérrez's leadership, MAYO organized school walkouts and mass demonstrations to protest discrimination against Mexican Americans. MAYO's aggressive tactics were a departure from the moderate approach of more established contemporary Latino organizations, such as the League of United Latin American Citizens.

"Most of our traditional organizations will sit there and pass resolutions and mouth off at conventions, but they'll never take on the gringo [white American]," Gutiérrez charged.

THE IMPACT TODAY

Culture
Spanish-language newspapers have become big business in the United States. In 2002 there were 35 dailies with a combined circulation of more than 1.7 million.

ACADEMIC VOCABULARY
contemporary
existing during the same period of time

Direct Teach

Reading Focus

3 What were the main goals of the movements for Latino rights? *economic independence; improvements in education; political power; end to job discrimination; control neighborhoods; regain lands*

Movements for Latino Rights

Identify Who was Rodolfo "Corky" Gonzales? *Chicano leader in late 1950s and early 1960s; founded Crusade for Justice; wanted to form unified Chicano community*

Explain How did the meaning of the term *Chicano* change during the 1960s? *previously had negative connotation; in 1960s, used to show pride of those who supported activism*

Contrast How were the goals of the Crusade for Justice and the Mexican American Youth Organization (MAYO) different? *Crusade for Justice—to promote Mexican American nationalism; MAYO—to achieve economic independence, to gain local control over education, and to gain political power through the creation of a new political party*

Activity **I am Joaquin** Have students read the poem on this page and write their own poem with the same message that Gonzales conveys.

LS Verbal-Linguistic

CRF: Biography: Ruben Salazar

Skills Focus: Summarizing

At Level   Standard English Mastery

Reading Skill
Movements for Latino Rights

1. Draw the chart shown here for students to see. Omit the answers. Have students copy it and use their text to complete it with details about the three organizations.

2. Have students use the information in their charts to write a brief essay in which they compare and contrast the organizations.

LS Visual-Spatial, Verbal-Linguistic

Alternative Assessment Handbook, Rubrics 13: Graphic Organizers; and 37: Writing Assignments

THREE MOVEMENTS FOR LATINO RIGHTS

Organization	Alianza	Crusade for Justice	MAYO
Leader	Reies López Tijerina	Rodolfo "Corky" Gonzales	José Angel Gutiérrez
Goals	Regain lands taken at end of 1848 Mexican American War	Meet educational needs; provide legal aid; promote Mexican American nationalism; empower Mexican Americans	Achieve economic independence for Mexican Americans; control education of Chicano children; achieve political power through creation of new political party
Outcomes	Bloodshed; Tijerina was arrested; group dissolved	Sponsored National Chicano Liberation Youth Conference; Called on Chicanos to build a unified community	Improved conditions in schools serving Latino children

Reading Focus

Movements for Latino Rights

Explain Why was MAYO not supported by all Latinos? *Some didn't support MAYO's aggressive tactics.*

Summarize What were the goals of MAYO? *economic independence for Mexican Americans, gain control of education of Latino children; political power for Latino community*

Draw Conclusions What new goals did La Raza Unida add to the Latino social movement and what goals were similar? *new goals— education for children of migrant workers, end job discrimination, improved public services; similar goals—bilingual education*

🖥 History Close-Up: The Chicano Movement

Recent Scholarship

From Out of the Shadows: Mexican Women in Twentieth-Century America is an examination of the roles Mexican American women have held in this country and the ways in which they have strengthened communities in the Southwest. Vicki Ruiz, a historian, provides a thorough view of Mexican American culture, and she discusses the struggles Mexican American women have faced and the political protests they have initiated.

From Out of the Shadows: Mexican Women in Twentieth-Century America by Vicki Ruiz. Oxford University Press, 1999

"They'll never stand up to him and say, 'Hey man, things have got to change . . . We've had it long enough!'"

Not all Latinos approved of MAYO's tactics. Henry B. Gonzalez, a member of Congress from San Antonio, was a vocal critic. "MAYO styles itself . . . [as all] good and the Anglo-American as . . . [all] evil. That is not merely ridiculous, it is drawing fire from the deepest wellsprings of hate," Gonzalez declared. "One cannot fan the flames of bigotry one moment and expect them to disappear the next."

MAYO did force changes, though, especially in education. In 1969 Gutiérrez helped organize a student protest in Crystal City, Texas, where about 80 percent of the population was Mexican American. Many local high school students fumed about discrimination. They wanted more Mexican American teachers and a bilingual education program. They also wanted their cheerleaders and homecoming queen to be elected by the students, not appointed by teachers.

The protest began when teachers appointed two Anglo students as cheerleaders. Chicano students' complaints to school officials had no effect. Gutiérrez helped the students organize a boycott of the school. The U.S. Justice Department intervened to resolve the crisis. The settlement required the school board to meet most of the students' demands, including bilingual and bicultural education.

The success at Crystal City inspired students in other Texas schools. MAYO supported numerous student walkouts to protest the crumbling conditions of schools, the lack of Latino teachers, and rules against speaking Spanish. After many of these boycotts, students gained the reforms they were seeking.

La Raza Unida After his success in Crystal City, Gutiérrez formed **La Raza Unida Party** (RUP). (The name means "the united people.") The party campaigned for bilingual education, improved public services, education for children of migrant workers, and an end to job discrimination. In 1970, RUP candidates were elected to offices in several Texas cities with large Chicano populations.

HISTORY CLOSE-UP

The Chicano Movement

During the 1960s and 1970s Mexican Americans forged political power by embracing their cultural identity.

Dolores Huerta

Dolores Huerta took an interest in social activism from a young age. In her early 20s she was active in a Mexican American self-help group called the Community Service Organization. It was there that she first met César Chávez. Together they founded the National Farm Workers Association. In the late 1960s she met feminist leader Gloria Steinem, whose influence led Huerta to incorporate feminist ideals into the Chicano movement.

La Raza Unida

José Angel Gutiérrez (above) founded La Raza Unida to spur political change in Crystal City, Texas. The party moved to the state level in 1972, backing Ramsey Muñiz for governor and supporting many Chicana candidates for other offices. Although Muñiz did not win his race, La Raza Unida successfully changed the landscape of Texas politics.

998

Skills Focus: Comparing and Contrasting | At Level

Reading Skill
Movements for Latino Rights

1. Guide students in a discussion of the social movements for Latino rights, highlighting the goals of the organizations discussed in the section.

2. Have students create a diagram that includes each group or movement discussed in the section.

3. Organize students into small groups, and have students in each group work together to complete the diagrams showing similarities and differences among the Latino groups and movements.

4. Have volunteers from each group present and review one of the movements or groups on their diagram with the class. **LS Visual-Spatial, Kinesthetic**

📝 Alternative Assessment Handbook, Rubrics 9: Comparing and Contrasting; and 13: Graphic Organizers

🖥 Graphic Organizer Transparencies

Rodolfo Gonzales also organized a Colorado branch of the RUP. The Colorado party did not have many election victories, but it drew attention to Chicano causes. The RUP expanded into other parts of the Southwest as well. In Arizona, New Mexico, and California, it registered some 10,000 new voters and ran candidates for several state offices.

In the late 1970s, disagreements among RUP leaders caused the party to fall apart. However, for the better part of a decade it symbolized growing Chicano power.

The Brown Berets In the late 1960s the Brown Berets emerged as one of the most militant organizations in the Chicano movement. Founded by working-class Chicano students in Los Angeles in 1967, the Brown Berets began their activism by protesting against police brutality in East Los Angeles.

Soon the group also began fighting for bilingual education, better school conditions, Chicano studies, and more Chicano teachers. In school walkouts in California, the Brown Berets protected striking students by standing

between them and the police. "When the cops moved in," one observer noted, "it was the Berets that were dragged behind bars."

The Brown Berets also supported the efforts of Chicanos in New Mexico to recover their historic lands. They lent their support to the United Farm Workers' campaigns, and they protested the high death rate of Chicano soldiers in the Vietnam War. They worked with African American civil rights groups as well, such as the Black Panther Party and the Southern Christian Leadership Conference.

The Brown Berets received much media attention because of their strong rhetoric and action-oriented protests. They also gained the notice of law enforcement officials, who tracked their activities and infiltrated the group. The publicity strengthened the Chicano movement in California and helped it spread farther. By 1970 there were 60 Brown Beret groups across the Southwest.

In the Brown Berets, as in many Chicano organizations, men held positions of leadership and women often struggled to have their voices heard. Women participated in marches and

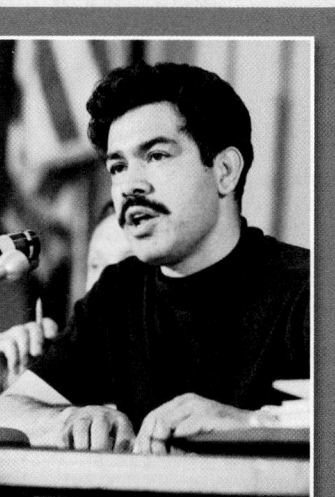

Corky Gonzales

Rodolfo "Corky" Gonzales, boxer turned activist, knew firsthand the plight of many poor Mexican Americans. Born to migrant farmworkers, Gonzales urged Mexican Americans to embrace their cultural heritage. He saw Chicano nationalism as a way for his people to gain economic independence and political power.

Student Activism

In 1969 some 700 Mexican American high school students in Crystal City, Texas, boycotted class. The strike began as a protest of the mainly Anglo cheerleading squad, but it grew to include broader educational issues. The students' action forced the school to abandon its discriminatory policies.

 Skills FOCUS **INTERPRETING INFOGRAPHICS**

Chicanos were among the many groups of Americans fighting for their rights in the 1960s and 1970s.

Drawing Conclusions Why do you think Chicanos wanted their own political party?

See Skills Handbook, p. H18

A TIME OF SOCIAL CHANGE **999**

Movements for Latino Rights

Explain What was the boricua movement? *movement by Puerto Ricans to achieve social justice*

Describe What led to the migration of Puerto Ricans to the United States? *slow economic growth in Puerto Rico after 1898 Spanish-American War; lack of opportunities in Puerto Rico; wanted to share in post–World War II economic boom in U.S.*

Elaborate How did the goals of the boricua movement change over time? *initially focused on independence of island of Puerto Rico; shifted to self-government for Puerto Rico and better conditions for all Puerto Ricans*

PRIMARY SOURCES

Mural

Some Chicano artists expressed their cultural pride by creating murals. This art form has a long history in Mexico, dating to Aztec times. Today hundreds of public buildings throughout the West contain murals celebrating Chicanos' heritage . This scene from a California mural shows the economic transformation of Mexican Americans.

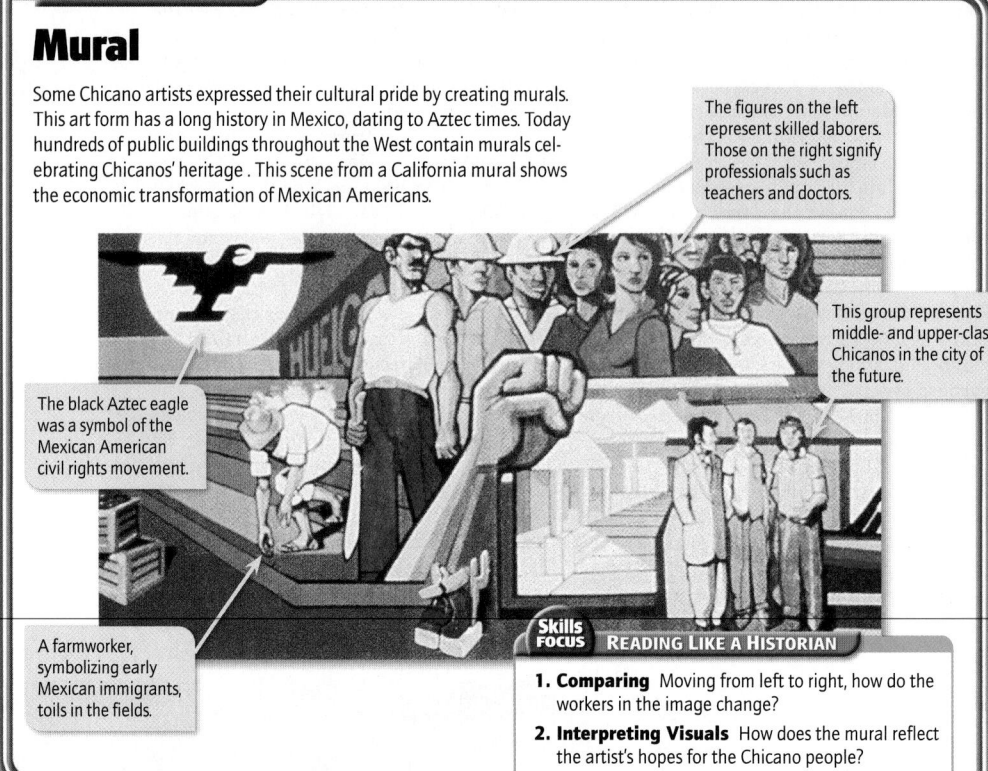

The figures on the left represent skilled laborers. Those on the right signify professionals such as teachers and doctors.

This group represents middle- and upper-class Chicanos in the city of the future.

The black Aztec eagle was a symbol of the Mexican American civil rights movement.

A farmworker, symbolizing early Mexican immigrants, toils in the fields.

Skills FOCUS READING LIKE A HISTORIAN

1. **Comparing** Moving from left to right, how do the workers in the image change?
2. **Interpreting Visuals** How does the mural reflect the artist's hopes for the Chicano people?

See Skills Handbook, p. H30

---

demonstrations, but those actions were always led by men. As one female member noted, "They [the men] wanted to make all the decisions and we always got the [unpleasant] jobs."

The Brown Berets disbanded in 1972 after a series of demonstrations turned violent. Public opinion within the Mexican American community began to turn against their activities. Although the Brown Berets were not successful in ending police brutality in East Los Angeles, the group succeeded in raising awareness of the struggles Chicanos often faced.

The boricua movement Boricua is the name by which many Puerto Ricans refer to themselves. Like the term *Chicano*, it expresses ethnic pride and support for political activism.

The island of Puerto Rico has been governed as a U.S. territory since the United States acquired the island from Spain after the Spanish-American War in 1898. Slow economic growth and lack of opportunity in Puerto Rico in the early 1900s prompted some Puerto Ricans to migrate to the mainland United States.

The pace of migration increased after World War II, as many Puerto Ricans hoped to share in the economic boom the United States experienced after the war. Some U.S. companies even recruited workers from Puerto Rico, viewing the island as a source of cheap labor. New York, Chicago, and several other U.S. cities developed large Puerto Rican communities. In New York, for example, Puerto Ricans made up more than 9 percent of the city's population by 1964.

1000 CHAPTER 30

Skills Focus: Interpreting Visuals

At Level

Reading Like a Historian Skill
Chicano Artwork

Research Required

1. Have students carefully examine the image at the top of this page. Guide students in a discussion of what message the image conveys.

2. Have students search reliable Internet sites or traditional print sources for pictures drawn by other Chicano artists.

3. Have students choose a picture that they would like to write about. Have students print out or copy their selected picture

and write an essay about how the artist conveys his or her message. Students should also explain why they chose this particular picture.

4. Have volunteers share their pictures and essays with the class. **LS Visual-Spatial, Logical-Mathematical**

Alternative Assessment Handbook, Rubrics 1: Acquiring Information; and 40: Writing to Describe

---

Answers

Reading Like a Historian 1. *jobs change from farm labor to prosperous middle-class, educated;* **2.** *that they will attain legal, political, and economic equality and opportunities*

Like other minority groups, Puerto Ricans in the United States experienced social and economic discrimination. Holding low-paying jobs, many had to live in run-down neighborhoods and send their children to overcrowded, substandard schools. In the 1950s and 1960s, they organized to seek change.

The boricua movement sprang from the calls of some Puerto Ricans, both in Puerto Rico and on the mainland, for the island's independence. When this demand failed to gain much support, even within the Puerto Rican community, the movement's goals gradually shifted to self-government for Puerto Rico and better conditions for all Puerto Ricans.

Among those pushing for social justice for Puerto Ricans were the Young Lords, a militant boricua organization inspired by the Black Panthers. In 1969 the New York City chapter of the Young Lords barricaded streets until the city promised more frequent trash pickups in Puerto Rican neighborhoods. The Young Lords also called for local control of Puerto Rican communities, as well as better health care, employment, and educational opportunities.

Other boricua groups shared some of the Young Lords' goals but not their methods. One group called Taller Boricua (meaning "Puerto Rican Workshop") was founded in 1970 as a community arts organization in New York. It provided art education programs as a means of encouraging cultural, social, and economic development in the Puerto Rican community. Similar groups now exist in many other American cities.

Cuban Americans After Fidel Castro seized power in Cuba in 1959, many well-to-do Cubans fled Castro's Communist government for the United States. After 78,000 Cubans left in 1962, Castro banned further emigration. The exodus continued nonetheless. About 50,000 people left on flights allowed by the Cuban government between 1965 and 1973. However, most refugees made dangerous, illegal voyages to the United States in small boats.

The majority of Cubans who arrived during this period were professionals and business people. Unlike most other Latinos, they had left their homeland for political reasons, not economic ones. Therefore, they did not generally suffer the economic disadvantages that prompted other Latino groups to demand social justice. Instead, most Cuban Americans who organized for change were seeking changes for Cuba—the overthrow of Castro and communism—and not for themselves.

READING CHECK **Making Generalizations** What issues were most important to the movements for Latino rights?

SECTION 2 ASSESSMENT

go.hrw.com
Online Quiz
Keyword: SD7 HP30

Reviewing Ideas, Terms, and People

1. **a. Recall** What is the difference between the terms *Hispanic* and *Latino*?
   b. Summarize What economic, educational, and political challenges did many Latinos face in the early 1960s?
   c. Elaborate Do you think that speaking Spanish was an asset or a drawback for Latinos in the 1960s? Explain.

2. **a. Identify** Who were **César Chávez** and Dolores Huerta?
   b. Explain How did farmworkers pressure grape growers to address their demands?
   c. Predict Do you think the grape boycott would have turned out differently if strikers had used violent tactics? Explain.

3. **a. Describe** What do the terms *Chicano* and *boricua* have in common?
   b. Sequence What experiences led **José Angel Gutiérrez** to form a new political party?
   c. Rank With which issue do you think the Latino rights movements had the most success? Explain.

Critical Thinking

4. **Comparing and Contrasting** Copy the chart below and record the similarities and differences between MAYO and **La Raza Unida Party**.

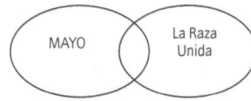

MAYO   La Raza Unida

FOCUS ON WRITING

5. **Expository** Reread the excerpt from **Rodolfo Gonzales's** poem, "I Am Joaquín." In your own words, analyze the excerpt. What past hardships does Gonzales describe? How have the conditions of his people changed, and why? What emotions are conveyed in his poem? Why would this poem be considered an anthem of the Chicano movement?

A TIME OF SOCIAL CHANGE **1001**

Direct Teach

Reading Focus

Movements for Latino Rights

Identify Who were the Young Lords? *militant boricua organization inspired by Black Panthers*

Develop How do you understand the term "militant" as used in the context of social movements in the United States? *willing to use violence to achieve goals; Brown Berets and Young Lords were very forceful in obtaining their objectives*

Review & Assess

Close

Guide students in a discussion of the struggle of Latinos to achieve social justice in the 1960s.

Review

Online Quiz, Section 2

Daily Test Practice Transparency

Assess

SE Section 2 Assessment

Progress Assessment: Section 2 Quiz

Alternative Assessment Handbook

Reteach

Interactive Reader and Study Guide, Section 2

Interactive Skills Tutor CD-ROM

Section 2 Assessment Answers

1. **a.** Hispanic—all Spanish-speaking people; Latino—people of Latin American descent
   b. lived in poverty; had poor educational opportunities; limited political power
   c. possible answer—drawback, few teachers spoke Spanish, hard to get by without English

2. **a.** founded National Farm Workers Association; organized grape strike
   b. urged shoppers to boycott grapes
   c. possible answer—yes, shoppers may not have joined boycott

3. **a.** express pride, empowerment, and certain political beliefs
   b. success in MAYO
   c. possible answer—improving education and economic opportunities; laws ensure equal rights, schools better educate Spanish-speaking children

4. wanted better educational and economic opportunities; La Raza Unida, political party, MAYO, college students

5. possible answer—Latinos have suffered, but advancing, retain cultural identity

Answers

Reading Check *education, job opportunities, economic advancement, political equality*

1001

Bellringer

The Inside Story. . . Use the **Daily Bellringer Transparency** to help students answer the question.

📑 Daily Bellringer Transparency, Section 3

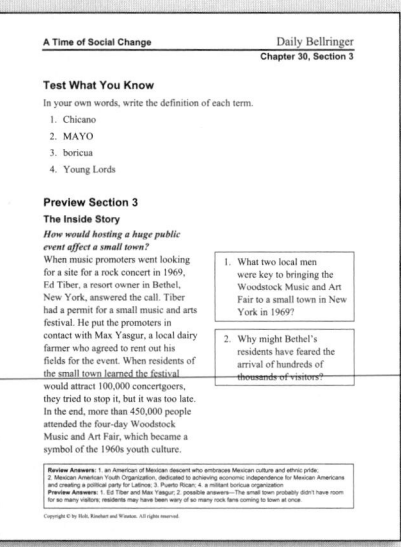

A Time of Social Change   Daily Bellringer
                                                Chapter 30, Section 3

Test What You Know

In your own words, write the definition of each term.

1. Chicano
2. MAYO
3. boricua
4. Young Lords

Preview Section 3
The Inside Story
How would hosting a huge public event affect a small town?

When music promoters went looking for a site for a rock concert in 1969, Ed Tiber, a resort owner in Bethel, New York, answered the call. Tiber had a permit for a small music and arts festival. He put the promoters in contact with Max Yasgur, a local dairy farmer who agreed to rent out his fields for the event. When residents of the small town learned the festival would attract 100,000 concertgoers, they tried to stop it, but it was too late. In the end, more than 450,000 people attended the four-day Woodstock Music and Art Fair, which became a symbol of the 1960s youth culture.

| 1. What two local men were key to bringing the Woodstock Music and Art Fair to a small town in New York in 1969? |
| 2. Why might Bethel's residents have feared the arrival of hundreds of thousands of visitors? |

Review Answers: 1. an American of Mexican descent who embraces Mexican culture and ethnic pride; 2. Mexican American Youth Organization, dedicated to achieving economic independence for Mexican Americans and creating a political party for Latinos; 3. Puerto Rican; 4. a militant boricua organization
Preview Answers: 1. Ed Tiber and Max Yasgur; 2. possible answers—The small town probably didn't have room for so many visitors; residents may have been wary of so many rock fans coming to town at once.

Copyright © by Holt, Rinehart and Winston. All rights reserved.

Academic Vocabulary

Review with students the high-use academic term in this section.

relevant having practical application or value for society (p. 1003)

📝 CRF: Vocabulary Builder Activity, Section 3

Taking Notes

Causes—large numbers of youth; blamed parents' generation for nation's problems; discontent among young, student activism; Effects—Free Speech Movement, hippie movement, changes in art and music

go.hrw.com
Online Resources

KEYWORD: SD7 CH30
TOPIC: COUNTERCULTURE

BEFORE YOU READ

MAIN IDEA

The counterculture that emerged in the 1960s and 1970s left a lasting impact on American life.

READING FOCUS

1. What led to the rise of the counter-culture?
2. What was life like in the counter-culture?
3. How did mainstream American society react to the counterculture?
4. What legacy did the counterculture leave behind?

KEY TERMS AND PEOPLE

counterculture
Establishment
Free Speech Movement
flower children
Summer of Love
pop art

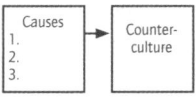

TAKING NOTES As you read, take notes on the causes and effects of the counterculture. Write your notes in a graphic organizer like the one shown below.

Causes		Counter-culture
1.		
2.	→	
3.		

THE INSIDE STORY

How would hosting a huge public event affect a small town?
The word was out. Some rich music promoters needed a place to hold a rock concert. In tiny Bethel, New York, resort owner Ed Tiber had a permit from town officials for a small music and arts festival to attract business to his resort hotel. He put the concert's organizers in touch with Max Yasgur, a nearby dairy farmer. They paid Yasgur $75,000 to hold their concert in one of his fields.

As workers prepared the site, Bethel's 3,900 residents became concerned that the expected 100,000 concert-goers might overwhelm their town. Signs went up: "Buy No Milk. Stop Max's Hippie Music Festival." There was no turning back, though. Too many tickets to the concert had already been sold—nearly 190,000!

Despite opposition, the Woodstock Music and Art Fair began on schedule, on August 15, 1969. By then it had snowballed into a four-day event attended by more than 400,000 people. Woodstock astounded Bethel and became a defining experience for a whole generation. ◢

Rock Concert in a Small Town

▼ The band Jefferson Airplane rocks for a crowd that stretches as far as the eye can see.

1002

Teach the Main Idea

At Level

Culture and Counterculture

1. **Teach** Ask students the Reading Focus questions to teach this section.

2. **Apply** Draw four large ladders for students to see. Label the top of each ladder with one of the four topics of this section. Have students copy the ladders, scan the section, and list the main events for each topic on the corresponding ladder rungs.

3. **Review** As you review the section, have students identify the main issues for each

topic. Have students explain the relationship among the topics.

4. **Practice/Homework** Have students prepare a script for a ten-minute television report on the rise, the reaction to, and the legacy of the counterculture era of the 1960s and 1970s. 🅛🅢 **Visual-Spatial, Verbal-Linguistic**

📝 Alternative Assessment Handbook, Rubric 37: Writing Assignments

Student protest leader Mario Savio makes a peace sign with his hand at a rally at the University of California, Berkeley. Students at Berkeley fought the school administration for free-speech rights and inspired campus protests nationwide.

Rise of the Counterculture

The **counterculture** of the 1960s was a rebellion of teens and young adults against mainstream American society. These young Americans, called hippies, believed that society's values were hollow and its priorities were misplaced. Turning their backs on the mainstream—which they called the **Establishment**—hippies wanted to create an alternative culture based on peace and love.

The youth culture Where did the counterculture come from? First of all, the number of teens and young adults in the United States rose dramatically in the 1960s. Between 1960 and 1970 the number of Americans aged 15 through 24 increased almost 50 percent.

Second, these young people were living in turbulent times. They blamed their parents' generation for the problems the nation faced—the threat of nuclear war, racial discrimination and segregation, the Vietnam War, and environmental pollution. They vowed to do things differently.

Rebellion against the dominant culture was not something new. The Beat generation of the 1950s also broke with mainstream America. Beatniks questioned traditional values, challenged authority, and experimented with nonconformist lifestyles. Although beatniks were few in number, the Beat generation would influence the hippie culture that arose later.

Rising student activism On college campuses in the 1960s, students enjoyed newfound independence. They began rebelling against school policies they considered restrictive, unjust, or not <u>relevant</u>. At the University of California at Berkeley, students had often used one of the entrances to the campus as a place for speech making and political organizing. In September 1964, university officials banned that activity at the campus entrance. Students protested loudly. They picketed and held sit-ins, nonviolent demonstrations in which they sat down and refused to move.

On October 1, 1964, a former student named Jack Weinberg set up a table in the banned area to collect donations for CORE, a civil rights group. Police arrived to arrest him for trespassing. Hundreds of students surrounded the police car so that it could not move. Student Mario Savio climbed on top of the car and urged more students to join the protest.

For 32 hours the students surrounded the car and prevented the police from taking Weinberg away. Other students protested at the main administration building. However, university officials refused to drop the charges against Weinberg. California governor Edmund Brown issued a statement: "This will not be tolerated. We must have—and will continue to have—law and order on our campuses." Some 500 police officers were called out as the crowd swelled to more than 7,000 demonstrators.

ACADEMIC VOCABULARY

relevant having practical application or value for society

A TIME OF SOCIAL CHANGE **1003**

Rise of the Counterculture

Summarize What was the significance of Arthur Goldberg's statement? *summed up the Free Speech Movement on campuses*

Predict What effect do you believe the actions of Governor Edmund Brown will have on his career? *possible answers—negative, public objected to the way that the students were treated; positive, voters want order on public campuses*

2 What was life like in the counterculture? *thousands of young people left school, jobs, traditional homes in search of new life; rejected traditional work ethic*

Life in the Counterculture

Identify What was Haight-Ashbury? *run-down neighborhood in San Francisco; center for counterculture*

Make Inferences If Haight-Ashbury is described as the center for the counterculture, how would you describe U. C. Berkeley's relationship to the counterculture during this period? *possible answer—launch pad for the counterculture movement*

Activity Life in the Counterculture Have students work in mixed-ability pairs to paraphrase the quote by Carol Brightman. Then guide students in a discussion of what Brightman meant by "You were on the edge there." **LS Verbal-Linguistic**

CRF: Interdisciplinary Project: Create a Pop Art Museum Display

Counterculture Life

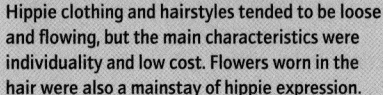

Hippie clothing and hairstyles tended to be loose and flowing, but the main characteristics were individuality and low cost. Flowers worn in the hair were also a mainstay of hippie expression.

Members of the Family of the Mystic Arts (above) lived in this Oregon commune for over a year. Communes had high ideals but were often short-lived.

The protest came to a nonviolent end when university officials agreed to consider students' grievances. A few weeks later, though, the university decided to discipline Savio and another organizer of the protest, Arthur Goldberg. In response, about a thousand students took over the campus administration building in a massive sit-in. On December 3, more than 600 police arrested nearly 800 students.

For the next few days, a student strike shut down the campus. As pressure mounted—from the faculty as well as the student body—administrators finally agreed to ease restrictions on students' political activities.

The events in Berkeley marked the beginning of the **Free Speech Movement**, which swept campuses across the nation. Arthur Goldberg summed up the goal this way: "We ask only the right to say what we feel when we feel like it. We'll continue to fight for this freedom, and we won't quit until we've won." Students used the tactics of civil disobedience to protest a variety of injustices. In the process, they shocked mainstream Americans, who expected young people not to question authority.

READING CHECK Summarizing What major influences led to the rise of the counterculture?

Life in the Counterculture

Throughout the 1960s, thousands of teens and young adults abandoned school, jobs, and traditional home life in search of a more freewheeling existence. Like the beatniks of the 1950s, hippies rejected the materialism and work ethic of older generations. Instead, they wanted to live simply and "do your own thing."

Some hippies formed communities in run-down urban neighborhoods, such as San Francisco's Haight-Ashbury district. Haight-Ashbury became the most famous center of the counterculture. Young people flocked there because of the cheap rents and flourishing hippie culture. Urban hippie communities in general attracted many newcomers because of the promise of a new lifestyle. Writer Carol Brightman spoke about the freedom of moving to Berkeley in 1970.

HISTORY'S VOICES

66 Coming to California and settling in the Bay Area, [I] was . . . looking for a cultural experience outside the mainstream . . . Berkeley was like a liberated zone, you know . . . You were on the edge there. 99

—Carol Brightman, interview with David Gans, 1999

1004 CHAPTER 30

Differentiating Instruction

Below Level

Learners Having Difficulty

1. Have students create a flowchart showing the events that led to the Summer of Love in 1967. Have students begin their charts with the September 1964 events at U.C. Berkeley.

2. Have students work in small groups to compare and share their charts. Have students correct their own work and retain the flowcharts as a study tool. **LS Visual-Spatial, Logical-Mathematical**

Alternative Assessment Handbook, Rubric 13: Graphic Organizers

Graphic Organizer Transparencies

Answers

Reading Check *discontent among young; student activism; Free Speech Movement*

This detail from a poster by the artist Peter Max (left) is an example of psychedelic art, or art that mimics a drug-induced state. Below is the psychedelic album cover to the Broadway musical *Hair*, which celebrated the counterculture and shocked the Establishment.

Other hippies "dropped out" of society by joining rural communes—collectively run communities—where they attempted to live in harmony with nature. Residents of communes often avoided modern conveniences. They grew their own food and shared all property. Their intention was to build communities based on peace and love.

Hippie culture Hippies sought new experiences in a variety of ways. Some looked for enlightenment through Eastern religions, such as Buddhism. Others searched for answers through astrology or the occult. Many others experimented with illegal drugs, such as marijuana and LSD, or "acid." Timothy Leary, a former Harvard University psychology instructor, promoted the use of LSD as a way to open and expand the mind. Leary urged others to "tune in, turn on, and drop out."

Hippies expressed their sense of freedom through a casual and colorful style of clothing. Bright, tie-dyed T-shirts were popular. Many African Americans adopted the dashiki, a pullover-style African shirt usually decorated with vivid colors. Some men wore beads as a rejection of the traditional necktie. Men also began wearing longer hair and beards. Some African Americans sported Afros, a hairstyle that came to symbolize racial pride. Other hippies wore flowers in their hair and called themselves **flower children**.

The counterculture's decline The height of the hippie movement was the summer of 1967. In San Francisco, this was known as the **Summer of Love**. A generation proclaimed the dawning of a blissful new age. Although the country was at war in Vietnam and wracked by racism and sexism, hippies professed peace, love, and harmony.

These ideals were difficult to achieve, however. The freedom that hippies sought often led to serious problems. Many young people struggled with drug addiction—or worse. Singer Janis Joplin and guitarist Jimi Hendrix died from overdoses of drugs, as did other less-famous members of the counterculture.

Hippies expected to find mellow living by moving to communes and places such as Haight-Ashbury. However, many hippies had no means of supporting themselves. The lack of rules often led to conflict. The counterculture also attracted sinister characters such as Charles Manson, who moved to Haight-Ashbury in 1967. Two years later Manson and a handful of his followers committed a mass murder in California that horrified the nation.

READING CHECK **Contrasting** How did the counterculture lifestyle differ from that of traditional, middle-class Americans?

Mainstream Society Reacts

Some observers of the counterculture were put off by the unkempt appearance of hippies. George Harrison, a member of the legendary British music group the Beatles, recalled his surprise when he visited Haight-Ashbury in 1967. "I expected them to all be nice and clean and friendly and happy." Instead, he saw them as "hideous, spotty little teenagers" who "were all terribly dirty and scruffy."

On a deeper level, many mainstream Americans objected to the unconventional values of the counterculture. They viewed hippies' attitudes and actions as disrespectful, uncivilized, and threatening. Some believed that American society as a whole was losing its sense of right and wrong.

THE IMPACT TODAY

Daily Life
Blue jeans were considered work clothing until hippies began wearing them. Today people of all ages and economic backgrounds wear jeans regularly.

A TIME OF SOCIAL CHANGE **1005**

Reading Focus

4 What legacy did the counterculture leave behind? *impact on attitudes, art, and music in American society*

The Counterculture's Legacy

Identify Cause and Effect In what way did the counterculture affect American attitudes? *the permissiveness of the counterculture resulted in casual fashions and a new open-mindedness about lifestyles and social behavior*

Evaluate What is the significance of Woodstock, other than being a music concert? *It was a celebration of an era and marked the peak of the counterculture movement.*

Info to Know

Movie Ratings The counterculture influenced the arts, including film, by relaxing the rules of censorship. The movie industry responded with a movie ratings system. This system became the means by which parents judged whether a specific film was appropriate for their children. The Motion Picture Association of America (MPAA) annually conducts a nationwide poll of parents. Overall, parents of children under the age of 13 feel that the movie rating system is useful in helping them to make informed decisions about movie choices for their children.

Answers

Reading Like a Historian *critically; language, dress, attitude are criticized*

Reading Check *believed the nation was losing sense of right and wrong; concerned by drug use and what they saw as threatening attitudes, loss of moral values*

To many in the Establishment, it appeared that society was unraveling. Unrest on college campuses particularly troubled FBI director J. Edgar Hoover.

HISTORY'S VOICES

❝It would be foolhardy for educators, public officials, and law enforcement officers to ignore or dismiss lightly the revolutionary terrorism invading college campuses. It is a serious threat to both the academic community and a lawful and orderly society.❞

—J. Edgar Hoover, in *The Review of the News*, September 11, 1968

A daring television comedy called *All in the Family* dramatized both the older generation's distrust of the counterculture and the younger generation's desire to change society. Premiering in 1971, the program featured a bigoted, working-class character named Archie Bunker. Archie bluntly criticized hippies, Vietnam War protesters, and anyone else who didn't fit his view of what Americans should be. Archie's son-in-law, Mike Stivic, was a college student fighting against the Establishment. The lack of understanding between Archie Bunker and Mike Stivic was symbolic of the divisions in American society at the time.

READING CHECK **Identifying the Main Idea** Why did many Americans find the counterculture to be so alarming?

The Counterculture's Legacy

The counterculture did not last long. However, it did make a lasting impact on American culture, particularly in attitudes, art, and music.

Attitudes The permissiveness of the counterculture affected the wider American society. Many Americans became more casual in the way they dressed and more open-minded about lifestyles and social behavior. Attitudes toward sexual behavior loosened. In movies, on television, and in books and magazines, people wanted to explore topics that had once been taboo, including sexual activity and violence.

PRIMARY SOURCES

Political Cartoon

The attitudes and lifestyles of the counterculture shocked many Americans. As this cartoon depicts, some Americans believed hippies were defiant youths with no respect for authority.

Many people felt that hippies were hypocrites for criticizing the older generation while relying on their parents' money to support them.

"Doubledome" was a slang term for an intellectual who supported silly ideas.

Skills FOCUS **READING LIKE A HISTORIAN**

Interpreting Political Cartoons Do you think the artist viewed hippies sympathetically or critically? Explain.

See **Skills Handbook**, p. H31

1006 CHAPTER 30

Skills Focus: Analyzing Primary Sources

At Level

Reading Like a Historian Skill
Perspectives on the Counterculture

1. Guide students in a review of the causes and effects of the counterculture of the 1960s.

2. Have students find at least two primary source documents about the counterculture. Students should find one document written by someone who participated in the counterculture and one document written by someone who witnessed the movement.

3. Organize the class into small groups and have students share their documents with the group.

4. Have students write an analysis of the two primary source documents they found.

5. Have volunteers read their analyses and share their documents with the class. **LS Verbal-Linguistic, Logical-Mathematical**

📖 Alternative Assessment Handbook, Rubrics 9: Comparing and Contrasting; and 30: Research

Art and film The counterculture's questioning of tradition and authority extended into the art world. Many artists of the 1960s argued that art had become a slave to elite tastes. They claimed that established artists created works only to please a few cultural critics.

In this period, a new style developed called **pop art.** Aiming to appeal to popular tastes, artists took inspiration from elements of the popular culture, including advertising, comic books, and movies. Andy Warhol led the pop art movement. He painted common, mass-produced objects such as Campbell Soup cans and Coke bottles. He also produced works featuring brightly colored likenesses of celebrities such as Marilyn Monroe and John F. Kennedy.

Film also underwent a broadening of subject matter as censorship rules relaxed. The film industry adopted a rating system ranging from G to X to inform audiences about the content of movies. The rating system was designed to gain favor with the viewing public, who wanted more information about what they would see on screen. Some people argued, however, that moral standards began to decline, because movies rated for mature audiences drew larger crowds than family-oriented films.

Music The counterculture had a tremendous influence on popular music. Rock and roll became an outlet for young people to express their discontent and their desire for change.

The Beatles, for example, moved from love songs like "I Want to Hold Your Hand" to more topical songs such as "Revolution." The group also brought new ideas and techniques to rock and roll music. Their performances electrified audiences and influenced countless other musicians.

Bob Dylan was another key figure on the music scene. Hailed as the spokesperson of his generation, Dylan found audiences wildly responsive to political songs like "The Times They Are A Changin'" and "Masters of War."

One of the most significant events of the period was the Woodstock Music and Art Fair, commonly known as Woodstock. In August 1969, some 400,000 people attended the music festival in rural upstate New York. Massive traffic jams led officials to close the roads leading to the area. Those who made it to Woodstock had to deal with driving rain, knee-deep mud, and shortages of food and water.

Despite the enormous crowds, the festival was peaceful. Over four days, many of the most popular musicians and bands performed, including Jimi Hendrix, Janis Joplin, Joan Baez, and the Grateful Dead. Woodstock was more than just a rock concert. It was the celebration of an era, and it marked the high point of the counterculture movement.

READING CHECK **Drawing Conclusions** How did the values of the counterculture influence art and music?

SECTION 3 ASSESSMENT

go.hrw.com
Online Quiz
Keyword: SD7 HP30

Reviewing Ideas, Terms, and People

1. **a. Identify** What factors contributed to the rise of the **counterculture** in the 1960s?
   b. Make Inferences Why did university officials at Berkeley want to shut down the **Free Speech Movement**?
   c. Evaluate Did university officials handle the conflict with students appropriately? Explain.

2. **a. Recall** Who were the **flower children**?
   b. Analyze What were members of the counterculture trying to achieve?
   c. Evaluate Was the decline of the counterculture avoidable? Why or why not?

3. **a. Identify** Who was Archie Bunker?
   b. Interpret Why would J. Edgar Hoover describe student activism as "revolutionary terrorism"?

4. **a. Describe** What was Woodstock?
   b. Summarize What effects did the counterculture have on the broader society?

Critical Thinking

5. **Identifying Cause and Effect** Copy the chart below and record the causes and effects of the counterculture.

The Counterculture

FOCUS ON SPEAKING

6. **Persuasive** What would you have said if you were addressing the crowd at the Berkeley student protests in 1964?

A TIME OF SOCIAL CHANGE **1007**

Section 3 Assessment Answers

1. **a.** large youth population; discontent with problems facing the country
   b. wanted to have law and order on campus
   c. possible answers—yes, university officials agreed to listen to students; no, students punished

2. **a.** participants in the counterculture
   b. live simply, live in harmony with nature, build communities based on peace and love
   c. possible answers—unavoidable, lacked resources; avoidable, needed more dedicated people

3. **a.** television character representing the Establishment
   b. thought they were a serious threat

4. **a.** large music festival
   b. outlet to express discontent

5. Causes—large numbers of youth; blamed parents' generation for nation's problems; Effects—Free Speech Movement, hippie movement, changes in art and music

6. possible answers—focus on improving society; create real change

---

Reading Focus

The Counterculture's Legacy

Recall What is pop art and how did it get its name? *art inspired by elements of popular culture: advertising, celebrities, comic books, and movies; got its name from its appeal to popular tastes*

Explain Why did some people oppose the new standards for movies? *believed they allowed box-office receipts, rather than artistic concerns, to decide content*

📖 CRF: Biography: John Lennon

● **Review & Assess** ●

Close
Guide students in a discussion of the counterculture that emerged during the 1960s and the 1970s.

Review
🖥 Online Quiz, Section 3
🖨 Daily Test Practice Transparency

Assess
SE Section 3 Assessment
📑 Progress Assessment: Section 3 Quiz
📑 Alternative Assessment Handbook

Reteach
📑 Interactive Reader and Study Guide, Section 3
💿 Interactive Skills Tutor CD-ROM

Answers
Reading Check *pop art appealed to popular tastes; rock 'n' roll developed new themes and techniques*

1007

The Women's Movement

Word Help

self-determination the power to make up one's own mind

self-enrichment the power to improve oneself

self-realization the full development of one's self, skills, and talents

impede prevent

Primary Source

"This is no simple reform. It really is a revolution. Sex and race because they are easy and visible differences have been the primary ways of organizing human beings into superior and inferior groups and into the cheap labour on which this system still depends. We are talking about a society in which there will be no roles other than those chosen or those earned. We are really talking about humanism."

— Gloria Steinem

Address to the Women of America, July 10, 1971, Washington, D.C.

The Women's Movement

Historical Context The documents below provide different information on the women's movement during the late 1960s and early 1970s.

Task Examine the documents and answer the questions that follow. Then write an essay about the women's movement. Use facts from the documents and from the chapter to support the position you take in your thesis statement.

DOCUMENT 1

In 1969 students protested at the University of Chicago after it refused to extend the appointment of Marlene Dixon, a professor known for her radical political views. The Chicago Women's Liberation Union issued this statement in support of the protests.

"What does women's freedom mean? It means freedom of self-determination, self-enrichment, the freedom to live one's own life, set one's own goals, the freedom to rejoice in one's own accomplishments. It means the freedom to be one's own person in an integrated life of world, love, play, motherhood: the freedoms, rights, and privileges of first class citizenship, of equality in relationships of love and work: the right to choose to make decisions or not to: the right to full self-realization and to full participation in the life of the world. That is the freedom we seek in women's liberation.

To achieve these rights we must struggle as all other oppressed groups must struggle: one only has the rights one fights for. We must come together, understand the common problems, despair, anger, the roots and processes of our oppression: and then together, win our rights to a creative and human life.

At the U of C we see the *first large action, the first important struggle of women's liberation*. This university—all universities—discriminate against women, impede their full intellectual development, deny them places on the faculty, exploit talented women and mistreat women students."

DOCUMENT 2

Bill Mauldin created drawings that commented on current events for the *St. Louis Post-Dispatch* and the *Chicago Sun-Times*. In this cartoon, he comments on the challenges facing the women's movement.

"WELL, GIRLS, AT LEAST THE ONLY WAY WE CAN GO IS UP."

Skills Focus: Analyzing Primary Sources

At Level

Reading Like a Historian Skill
The Fight for Equal Rights

Research Required

1. Divide the class into two halves. Remind students that Congress passed the Equal Rights Amendment (ERA) in 1972, but the states still needed to ratify it. Have one half represent supporters of the ERA and the other half represent opponents of the ERA.

2. Give students time to research the wording of the Equal Rights Amendment.

3. Conduct a classroom debate on whether your state should ratify the Equal Rights

Amendment. Encourage students to focus on the wording of the ERA and how it should be interpreted.

4. Have each student write a one-page paper explaining his or her own position in regard to the Equal Rights Amendment. Ask volunteers to read their papers to the class.
LS **Logical-Mathematical, Verbal-Linguistic**

Alternative Assessment Handbook, Rubric 10: Debates

DOCUMENT 3

Over the past several decades, women's lives have changed in many ways. This table presents statistics that indicate women's progress in education, employment, athletics, and government service.

EDUCATION AND EARNINGS	1970	2002
Number of female college students (approximate)	3,000,000	9,300,000
Percentage of college students who were women	40.5 percent	56.4 percent
Percentage of undergraduate and graduate degrees received by women	40.8 percent	57.8 percent
Percentage of doctoral degrees received by women	13.3 percent	45.5 percent
Women's earnings compared to every dollar earned by men	59.4 cents	76.6 cents
ATHLETICS	**1970**	**2002**
Number of female participants in high school athletics	294,000	2,856,350
Percentage of participants in high school athletics who were women	7.4 percent	41.7 percent
CORPORATE LEADERSHIP AND GOVERNMENT SERVICE	**1970**	**2002**
Number of female chief executive officers of Fortune 500 companies	0	6
Percentage of female federal civilian employees	30.3 percent	45 percent
Number of women elected to U.S. House of Representatives	10	59
Number of women elected to U.S. Senate	1	13

Sources: Statistical Abstract of the United States, 1976, 2004–2005; National Federation of State High School Associations Participation Figure History; National Committee on Pay Equity; femmx, Volume 10, issue 1, May 2002

Skills FOCUS READING LIKE A HISTORIAN

1. a. Recall Refer to Document 1. Why are the protests important, according to the Chicago Women's Liberation Union?
b. Interpret How does this statement encourage cooperation with other groups?

2. a. Describe Refer to Document 2. How does Mauldin portray equal rights for women?
b. Analyze Based on this cartoon, what is Mauldin's attitude toward the women's movement?

3. a. Identify Refer to Document 3. Which category shows the least change over time?

b. Make Inferences How might changes in educational achievement and changes in government employment be related?

4. Document-Based Essay Question Consider the question below and form a thesis statement. Using examples from Documents 1, 2, and 3, create an outline and write a short essay supporting your position.
How did the women's movement contribute to change in the United States?

See **Skills Handbook**, pp. H15, H28–H29, H31

A TIME OF SOCIAL CHANGE **1009**

Skills Focus: Analyzing Alternative Interpretations of the Past

Reading Like a Historian Skill
Chronicling the Women's Movement

At Level

1. Divide the class into groups of four or five students. Have each group come up with a series of questions that they would like to ask people about how their lives have changed as a result of the women's movement.

2. Have each student find a person who witnessed the women's liberation movement in the 1960s and 1970s. Have students conduct an interview based on their questions. Students may want to record the interviews

for the sake of accuracy, but they should be written down and edited before being turned in.

3. Ask volunteers to read their interviews to the class. Then guide the class in a discussion of similarities and differences in the subjects' experiences. **LS Interpersonal, Verbal-Linguistic**

📓 Alternative Assessment Handbook, Rubric 1: Acquiring Information

Info to Know

Title IX In 1972 President Richard Nixon signed the Federal Education Amendments into law. Title IX of these amendments outlawed discrimination on the basis of sex in federally funded educational programs. The law's effect on college athletics has been controversial. In 1974, 1975, and 1977, amendments were proposed to exclude from Title IX sports that generated an income; all three efforts failed. According to the Supreme Court's ruling on the matter, each college must have a ratio of male-to-female athletes that reflects its ratio of male-to-female students.

Answers

Reading Like a Historian
1. **a.** *because women need to achieve self-determination, self-enrichment, and self-realization; women need to be able to participate fully in the life of the world;* **b.** *It says that women must struggle as all other oppressed groups must struggle and come together, understand common problems and the roots and processes of their oppression, and act together to win their rights;* 2. **a.** *as existing atop a mountain, with many huge obstacles in the path;* **b.** *that it is an uphill climb;* 3. **a.** *number of chief executive officers of Fortune 500 companies who were women;* **b.** *possible answer—Women who have more education are more likely to qualify for and receive government employment;* 4. *possible answer—lobbied the government, filed lawsuits, and held mass actions in order to provide women with new opportunities in education and the workplace*

Visual Summary

Review and Inquiry Review the time line with students. Then have them write a two-sentence description of each event. Have students share their descriptions with the class or in small groups.

Quick Facts Transparency: A Time of Social Change

Reviewing Key Terms and People

1. c.
2. a.
3. f.
4. e.
5. b.
6. g.
7. d.
8. i.
9. h.

Comprehension and Critical Thinking

10. **a.** proposed amendment to ensure equal rights for men and women
b. Indian Education Act, American Indian Movement brought attention to their plight
c. many felt that gains they had already secured for their people would be lost

11. **a.** militant Chicano organization
b. shared—desire for job opportunities, educational opportunities, improved health care; Cuban Americans were usually more prosperous and well educated, left Cuba for political reasons, not economic reasons
c. possible answer—improved education could lead to better job opportunities, more financial stability, and more political power

12. **a.** live simply, live in harmony with peace and nature, find answers to problems, new enlightenment
b. saw as disrespectful and uncivilized; objected to unconventional values; believed hippies had lost their sense of right and wrong

c. possible answers—positive, new trends in art and music, new fashions, return to simpler lifestyle; negative, disrespect, loose morals, drug use, aimless, young people quit school

Using the Internet

13. Go to the HRW Web site and enter the keyword shown to access a rubric for this activity.

KEYWORD: SD7 CH30

Visual Summary: A Time of Social Change

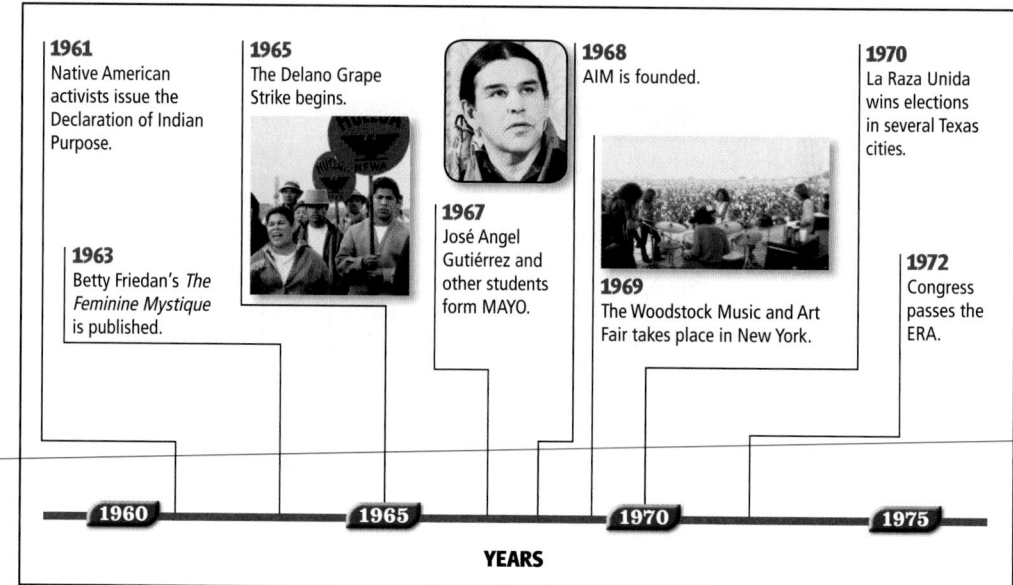

1961 Native American activists issue the Declaration of Indian Purpose.

1963 Betty Friedan's *The Feminine Mystique* is published.

1965 The Delano Grape Strike begins.

1967 José Angel Gutiérrez and other students form MAYO.

1968 AIM is founded.

1969 The Woodstock Music and Art Fair takes place in New York.

1970 La Raza Unida wins elections in several Texas cities.

1972 Congress passes the ERA.

1960   1965   1970   1975

YEARS

Reviewing Key Terms and People

Match each lettered definition with the correct numbered item at right.

a. Rebellion of teens and young adults against mainstream American society

b. Another popular name for hippies

c. Name by which many Puerto Ricans refer to themselves

d. A leader of the American Indian Movement

e. Conservative leader who opposed the ERA

f. Founder of MAYO who campaigned against anti-Latino discrimination in Texas schools

g. Chicano founder of the Crusade for Justice and author of the poem "I Am Joaquín"

h. Organization founded by José Angel Gutiérrez to strengthen Latinos' political power

i. Chicano labor leader who championed the rights of migrant farmworkers

1. boricua
2. counterculture
3. José Angel Gutiérrez
4. Phyllis Schlafly
5. flower children
6. Rodolfo "Corky" Gonzales
7. Russell Means
8. César Chávez
9. La Raza Unida Party

1010 CHAPTER 30

Analyzing Primary Sources

14. Answers should include references to hardship, hard work, exploitation, subject to racial hatred.

15. Gonzales expresses the determination to maintain sense of self-identify, culture, and the hope for a better future.

History's Impact video program
Review the video to answer the closing question:
How has the right of assembly allowed Americans
to have a voice in social and political change?

Comprehension and Critical Thinking

SECTION 1 *(pp. 986–993)*

10. a. Recall What was the ERA?

b. Summarize What gains did Native Americans make in the 1970s?

c. Elaborate Not all women supported NOW, nor did all Native Americans support AIM. Why was this the case?

SECTION 2 *(pp. 994–1001)*

11. a. Identify Who were the Brown Berets?

b. Compare and Contrast What did Chicano and Puerto Rican activists have in common, and how did they differ from Cuban Americans?

c. Develop Why do you think that the issue of fairness in education was so important to the Latino movements for equal rights?

SECTION 3 *(pp. 1002–1007)*

12. a. Describe What were the goals of the counterculture?

b. Analyze Why did some people find the counterculture threatening?

c. Evaluate Did the counterculture have more positive or negative effects on American culture and society? Explain.

Using the Internet

go.hrw.com
Practice Online
Keyword: SD7 CH30

13. President Bill Clinton awarded César Chávez the Presidential Medal of Honor in 1994. Using the keyword above, do research to learn about Chávez's activism after the Delano Grape Strike. Then write a short biography of Chávez, highlighting the important achievements of his leadership after the strike.

Analyzing Primary Sources

Reading Like a Historian The epic poem "I Am Joaquín" called on Chicano youths to find strength and pride in their culture and history. Reread the excerpt in Section 2.

14. Describe How does the poet describe the lives of Mexican Americans in the past?

15. Draw Conclusions What made this poem inspirational to a generation of Chicanos?

Critical Reading

Read the passages in Section 1 that discuss the occupation of Alcatraz and AIM. Then answer the questions that follow.

16. Why was the Indian occupation of Alcatraz Island significant?

A Congress gave Native Americans the right to use any surplus government property.

B It led to the founding of the American Indian Movement.

C It drew attention to injustices against Native Americans and encouraged AIM activists.

D The Bureau of Indian Affairs agreed to consider Native Americans' grievances.

17. Which of the following statements is true?

A The goals of AIM were to protect Native Americans' traditional ways of life, foster economic independence, and improve educational opportunities.

B The American Indian Movement was founded with the intention of helping Native Americans who lived on reservations.

C AIM activists seized Wounded Knee in retaliation for the killing of 300 Sioux in 1890.

D AIM's tactics were limited to nonviolent marches and demonstrations.

WRITING FOR THE SAT

Think about the following issue:

Throughout the 1960s, thousands of teens and young adults rebelled against mainstream American society. They abandoned school, jobs, and traditional home life in search of a more freewheeling existence. They wanted to live simply and "do your own thing."

18. Assignment Was the counterculture a bold experiment in nontraditional living or a self-indulgent escape from reality? Write a short essay in which you develop your position on this issue. Support your point of view with reasoning and examples from your reading and studies.

Answers

Critical Reading

16. C

17. A

Writing for the SAT

18. possible answers—bold experiment because hippies tried to establish communities that would be self-sufficient where people would live in peace and harmony; self-indulgent because did not have realistic methods for achieving goals and involved the disruption of mainstream American values;

A rubric for this activity is provided in the Chapter Resource File: Writing for the SAT: The Equal Rights Amendment.

History's Impact Video Program

Having the right to gather and demonstrate publicly has allowed groups to make their beliefs known and fight for changes.

Review and Assessment Resources

Review and Reinforce

- CRF: Chapter Review Activity
- Quick Facts Transparencies: Major Native American Legislation, A Time of Social Change
- Spanish Chapter Summaries Audio CD Program
- Online Chapter Summaries in Spanish
- OSP Holt PuzzlePro; Quiz Show for ExamView
- Quiz Game CD-ROM

Assess

- PASS: Chapter Test, Forms A and B
- Alternative Assessment Handbook
- OSP ExamView Test Generator, Chapter Test
- Differentiated Instruction Modified Worksheets and Tests CD-ROM: Chapter Test
- HOAP Holt Online Assessment Program (in the Premier Online Edition)

Reteach/Intervene

- Interactive Reader and Study Guide
- Differentiated Instruction Teacher Management System: Lesson Plans for Differentiated Instruction
- Differentiated Instruction Modified Worksheets and Tests CD-ROM: Chapter Test
- Interactive Skills Tutor CD-ROM

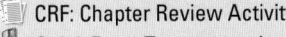

go.hrw.com
Online Resources

KEYWORD: SD7 CH30

Summarizing the Unit

Divide students into small groups. Have students review their lists of the rights and responsibilities of an American citizen from the unit opener activity. Then have each group revise and rewrite their previous lists based on what they learned in this unit. Have groups report on how their perceptions of American citizenship have changed.

Connecting to Themes

Guide students in a discussion of the following question: *Did the United States become a more democratic country between 1954 and 1975? Why or why not?* Remind students to support their opinions with specific details from the unit's four chapters and from their outside reading.

UNIT **9 IN BRIEF**

Below is a chapter-by-chapter summary of the main ideas covered in Unit 9.

CHAPTER 27 The New Frontier and the Great Society
1961–1969

MAIN IDEA Both Presidents Kennedy and Johnson pushed for major changes in American society while confronting the threat of communism overseas.

SECTION 1 President Kennedy fought communism by supporting West Berlin when the Communists erected the Berlin Wall. He turned back a Communist threat to the United States when he faced down the Soviet Union in the Cuban missile crisis.

SECTION 2 Kennedy was a youthful, popular president whose thousand days in office showed promise. His assassination in 1963 deeply shocked the nation and the world.

SECTION 3 President Johnson convinced Congress to pass several of Kennedy's programs after his death. Johnson built on these reforms with programs of his own in an effort to create a Great Society in America.

CHAPTER 28 The Civil Rights Movement
1954–1975

MAIN IDEA The civil rights movement won key victories in gaining racial equality for African Americans.

SECTION 1 The civil rights movement's early successes included efforts to end segregation in education, including the landmark *Brown* decision, and the Montgomery bus boycott.

SECTION 2 Nonviolent protests often met with violent responses. The March on Washington in August 1963 called for a federal law to end segregation. The Civil Rights Act of 1964 banned discrimination in employment and public accommodations.

SECTION 3 The Twenty-fourth Amendment inspired increased efforts to gain voting rights for southern African Americans. Violent responses to a voter registration drive in Mississippi and a peaceful march in Selma, Alabama, gained national attention, helping to secure passage of the Voting Rights Act of 1965.

SECTION 4 Divisions developed in the civil rights movement in the late 1960s over such issues as tactics and de facto segregation. The assassination of Martin Luther King Jr. further weakened the movement.

SECTION 5 Busing and affirmative action programs in the 1970s continued to combat segregation and discrimination.

CHAPTER 29 The Vietnam War
1954–1975

MAIN IDEA The Vietnam War began as an effort to resist the spread of communism. As it continued, divisions arose over U.S. involvement in the war.

SECTION 1 American involvement in Vietnam began as support for France against a Communist-led war for independence. When the French were defeated and Vietnam was divided, U.S. support shifted to the anti-Communist government of South Vietnam.

SECTION 2 In 1965 President Johnson sent the first U.S. fighting forces to South Vietnam. The war escalated as U.S. troop strength increased. Ground troops faced great challenges in fighting North Vietnamese and Viet Cong forces that used unconventional tactics.

SECTION 3 The Tet Offensive in 1968 led increasing numbers of Americans to question U.S. involvement in Vietnam. The issue provoked growing protest and shaped the presidential election of 1968.

SECTION 4 President Nixon negotiated an end to U.S. involvement in the war in 1973. Fighting continued, however, and South Vietnam surrendered to North Vietnam in 1975.

CHAPTER 30 A Time of Social Change
1963–1975

MAIN IDEA The 1960s and 1970s were a time of great social and political change for many groups in American society.

SECTION 1 Women and Native Americans formed new organizations to promote political, social, and economic equality in American society.

SECTION 2 Latinos sought equality through the peaceful, nonviolent tactics of César Chávez, as well as the more militant methods of groups like MAYO and the Brown Berets.

SECTION 3 The counterculture of the 1960s grew out of a youth movement rooted in the beliefs of peace and love.

1012 UNIT 9 IN BRIEF

Unit Resources

Review and Reinforce
- CRF: Chapter Review Activity
- Spanish Chapter Summaries Audio CD Program
- OSP Holt PuzzlePro; GameTool for ExamView
- Quiz Game CD-ROM

Assess
- PASS: Unit Test, Forms A and B
- Alternative Assessment Handbook
- OSP ExamView Test Generator
- Differentiated Instruction Modified Worksheets and Tests CD-ROM: Chapter Tests
- HOAP Holt Online Assessment Program (in the Premier Online Edition)

Reteach/Intervene
- Interactive Reader and Study Guide
- Differentiated Instruction Teacher Management System: Lesson Plans for Differentiated Instruction
- Differentiated Instruction Modified Worksheets and Tests CD-ROM: Chapter Tests
- Interactive Skills Tutor CD-ROM

go.hrw.com
Online Resources

KEYWORDS: SD7 CH27, SD7 CH28, SD7 CH29, SD7 CH30

10

Looking Toward the Future

1968–Present

Chapter 31
A Search for Order
1968–1980

Chapter 32
A Conservative Era
1980–1992

Chapter 33
Into the Twenty-first Century
1992–Present

Themes

Government and Democracy
Public trust in government was tested by political scandals, and Americans re-examined the role of government in the United States.

Global Relations
The end of the Cold War presented new challenges in foreign affairs, and the United States and other countries confronted international terrorism.

Science and Technology
Innovations such as the Internet affected nearly all areas of everyday life.

Fireworks light the sky above the Capitol at a Fourth of July celebration in Washington, D.C.

1013

Unit Preview

Introducing the Unit
Remind students that some periods in U.S. history have earned nicknames, such as the Era of Good Feelings, or the Roaring Twenties. Have students suggest a nickname for America today and justify their reasoning.

Connecting to Themes
Activity **Science and Technology** Have volunteers contribute to a class list of scientific and technological advances since 1990. Remind students to think of advances in such fields as medicine, communications, computers, transportation, industry, and agriculture. Then guide students in a discussion of the following questions: *Which technological or scientific advance will have the biggest influence on future generations? Why?* **LS Verbal-Linguistic**

Reading Like a Historian
Interpreting Visuals
Celebration Fireworks have long been a staple of Independence Day celebrations. Fireworks became especially popular in the United States in the mid 19th century. However, injuries associated with fireworks, and the fire danger they pose, eventually resulted in their regulation in many states.

Unit Resources

Planning
- Differentiated Instruction Teacher Management System: Unit Pacing Guide
- One-Stop Planner CD-ROM: Teacher Management System
- Power Presentations with Video CD-ROM

Differentiating Instruction
- Differentiated Instruction Teacher Management System: Lesson Plans for Differentiated Instruction
- Pre-AP Activities Guide for American History
- Differentiated Instruction Modified Worksheets and Tests CD-ROM

Enrichment
- Civic Participation Activities Guide
- CRF: Economics and History Activity
- CRF: Interdisciplinary Project
- American History Primary Source Library CD-ROM

Assessment
- PASS: Unit Test, Forms A & B
- Alternative Assessment Handbook
- OSP ExamView Test Generator
- HOAP Holt Online Assessment Program (in the Premier Online Edition)

The Differentiated Instruction Teacher Management System
provides a planning and instructional benchmarking guide for this unit.

Prepare to Read

Summarizing

Have each student select a short article from a magazine or newspaper about a current event. Have students write a summary of their articles. Have volunteers share their summaries with the class.

Info to Know

War in Afghanistan The Afghan guerrillas fighting against the Soviet occupation were known as the mujaheddin, or "holy warriors." The rebels received aid from the United States. Among the mujaheddin was a wealthy Saudi Arabian named Osama bin Laden. Following the Soviet withdrawal in 1989, civil war continued. In 1996, the government was taken over by a radical Islamic fundamentalist party called the Taliban.

Skills Planner

To give students more opportunities to practice this skill, see the following activities in the teacher's edition: Nixon's Foreign Policies, p. 1020; A Conservative Agenda, p. 1048; The Reagan Revolution, p. 1049; Protecting American Interests, p. 1056; The Berlin Wall Falls, p. 1061; Growing Diversity, p. 1100.

Summarizing

Find practice for **Summarizing** in the **Skills Handbook**, p. H6

Summarizing helps you understand and remember what you read. In a summary you use your own words to restate your reading. Summaries should use fewer words and highlight only the key points.

Before You Read
Skim headings and visuals to preview the text and form a general idea of its content.

While You Read
Pick out main ideas and key details that support the main ideas.

After You Read
Write a summary of the reading, restating in your own words the key ideas contained in the text and images.

This heading tells you the topic—problems that President Carter encountered.

Crises Overwhelm Carter

In his first years in office, Carter enjoyed some successes and suffered through some failures. In 1979, however, a series of events occurred that seemed to overwhelm his entire presidency.

Main Idea A series of events plagued Carter's presidency.

The Soviets invade Afghanistan

In 1978 the government of Afghanistan was toppled in a coup. Afghanistan's new Communist leaders were friendly to the Soviet Union. Yet this new pro-Soviet Afghan government was not stable. When it showed signs of crumbling, the Soviets acted. In December 1979, they invaded Afghanistan.

READING CHECK **Summarizing** How would you describe President Carter's final two years in office?

Detail A coup and instability in the Afghan government led the Soviets to invade Afghanistan in 1979.

Test Prep Tip

Tests often ask you to choose the best summary of a particular reading passage. Before reading the answer options, try summarizing the passage in your own words. Then read the choices and determine which one best fits your summary.

Skills Focus: Summarizing

Below Level

Reading Skill
Summarizing Historical Texts

1. Have students choose a subsection from one of the chapters in this unit. Then have students write a summary of the subsection, using the techniques on this page.

2. Have students exchange summaries with a partner and evaluate the summary. Students may use the following questions as a guide: Does the summary include all of the most important ideas? Does the summary leave out unimportant details? Does the summary use the writer's own words? Does the summary accurately reflect the text?

3. Have students provide each other with useful suggestions for writing better summaries.
   LS Verbal-Linguistic, Intrapersonal

   Alternative Assessment Handbook, Rubric 14: Group Activity

Reading like a Historian

Making Oral and Written Presentations

Find practice for **Making Oral and Written Presentations** in the
Skills Handbook, pp. H40–H41.

Presentations are written or verbal reports on a topic that you have researched. There are specific steps to follow for any kind of presentation, as well as some skills that apply to oral presentations and some that apply only to written presentations.

1. Identify a topic that you wish to learn more about for your presentation.
2. Formulate a hypothesis. This will be the main idea of your presentation.
3. Organize facts, data, and details to support your hypothesis.
4. Express your ideas and arguments clearly and persuasively.

Strategies historians use:

- Choose a central idea or theme on which to focus your presentation. This theme should be specific to help structure your research.
- Keep a bibliography of all of the sources you consult in your research. You should always know where you found your facts.
- Proofread your presentation, whether it is written or oral, to ensure that it is well organized and grammatically correct.

This is the topic of the presentation. All the facts should relate to the topic, "Reaganomics."

Oral Presentation Notes, American History

Reaganomics:

(1) **President Ronald Reagan, 1980-1988**

(2) **tax cuts and smaller federal government**

(3) **increased military spending,**

(4) **supply-side economics, "voodoo economics"**
  (George H. W. Bush)

(5) **1981-1982 – worst economic recession since the Great**
  Depressive Depression

Whenever you use a quote, be sure to label the its source.

Proofreading is important, even in oral presentation notes like these. Reading the wrong word can confuse both you and your audience.

Skills FOCUS READING LIKE A HISTORIAN

As You Read Make an index card for each fact or piece of data you find. Be sure to include the source information.
As You Study Write an outline that shows how your presentation will be organized. Make sure that all of your facts support your main idea in a meaningful way.

Making Oral and Written Presentations

Divide class into pairs. Have each pair select a topic from this unit they would like to research. Have students write a brief outline on how to prepare an oral presentation on their topic. Students should point out difficulties that might arise as well as possible sources, approaches to use, and treatments of the topic.

Word Help

hypothesis theory, explanation

Info to Know

Reaganomics Most historians and economists believe "Reaganomics" was based on the theory of supply-side economics. This theory, which became popular in the 1970s, states that lowering taxes will spur productivity gains, raise employment rates, and boost economic growth. The economic growth will, in turn, lead to more tax revenue for the government, even though taxes are collected at lower rates. George H. W. Bush called the theory "voodoo economics" during the 1980 Republican presidential primary season. After being chosen as Reagan's vice presidential running mate, he curbed his criticism.

Skills Planner

To give students more opportunities to practice this skill, see the following activity in the teacher's edition: Reagan and Gorbachev in Red Square, p. 1055.

Skills Focus: Making Oral and Written Presentations   [At Level]

Reading Like a Historian Skill   [Research Required]
Researching and Giving a Presentation

1. Have students select a topic from this unit to research. Review with students techniques for researching and organizing a presentation.

2. Have each student research and prepare an oral or written presentation.

3. Have students give their oral presentations or make their written presentations available for a class file. Allow time for questions and discussion of issues raised in the presentations. **LS Verbal-Linguistic**

 Alternative Assessment Handbook, Rubric 29: Presentations

Chapter 31 Planning Guide

A Search for Order

Chapter Overview	Reproducible Resources	Technology Resources
CHAPTER 31 pp. 1016–1043 **Overview:** In this chapter, students will analyze Nixon, Ford, and Carter and their respective successes and failures in office.	**Differentiated Instruction Teacher Management System:*** • Instructional Benchmarking Guides • Lesson Plans for Differentiated Instruction **Interactive Reader and Study Guide:** Chapter Summary* **Chapter Resource File:*** • Focus on Writing Activity: Ford's Pardon of Nixon • Social Studies Skills Activity: Analyzing Costs and Benefits • Chapter Review Activity **American History Outline Maps** **Pre-AP Activities Guide for American History***	Live Ink® Online Reading Help Student Edition on Audio CD Program Differentiated Instruction Modified Worksheets and Tests CD-ROM Interactive Skills Tutor CD-ROM United States History Primary Source Library CD-ROM Power Presentations with Video CD-ROM History's Impact: American History Video Program (VHS/DVD): A Search for Order Online Chapter Summaries in Spanish
Section 1: **The Nixon Years** **The Main Idea:** Beyond the ongoing turmoil of the Vietnam War, the Nixon administration did enjoy some notable success.	**Differentiated Instruction Teacher Management System:** Section 1 Lesson Plan* **Interactive Reader and Study Guide:** Section 1 Summary* **Chapter Resource File:*** • Vocabulary Builder Activity, Section 1 • Biography Activity: Harry Blackmun	Daily Bellringer Transparency: Section 1* Map Transparency: OPEC Members in the Mideast and Africa* Quick Facts Transparency: Causes and Effects of the Yom Kippur War* Daily Test Practice Transparency: Section 1* Internet Activity: Nixon's Policies
Section 2: **From Watergate to Ford** **The Main Idea:** The Nixon presidency became bogged down in scandal, leading to the first presidential resignation in American history and the administration of Gerald Ford.	**Differentiated Instruction Teacher Management System:** Section 2 Lesson Plan* **Interactive Reader and Study Guide:** Section 2 Summary* **Chapter Resource File:*** • Vocabulary Builder Activity, Section 2 • Biography Activity: Barbara Jordan • Primary Source Activity: Justice Department Memo Concerning the Indictment of Richard Nixon	Daily Bellringer Transparency: Section 2* Daily Test Practice Transparency: Section 2* Internet Activity: The Watergate Scandal
Section 3: **Carter's Presidency** **The Main Idea:** Jimmy Carter used his reputation for honesty to win the presidency in 1976, but he soon met challenges that required other qualities as well.	**Differentiated Instruction Teacher Management System:** Section 3 Lesson Plan* **Interactive Reader and Study Guide:** Section 3 Summary* **Chapter Resource File:*** • Vocabulary Builder Activity, Section 3 • Biography Activity: Lois Gibbs • Primary Source Activity: An American Hostage in Iran	Daily Bellringer Transparency: Section 3* Quick Facts Transparency: The Camp David Accords* Daily Test Practice Transparency: Section 3* Internet Activity: Jimmy Carter

Icon	Resource	Icon	Resource	Icon	Resource
go.hrw.com	go.hrw.com	Print Resource	Print Resource	Transparency	Transparency
LS	Learning Styles	Audio CD	Audio CD	CD-ROM	CD-ROM
Video	Video	SE	Student Edition	TE	Teacher's Edition
OSP	One-Stop Planner CD-ROM				

*also on One-Stop Planner CD-ROM

HOLT

History's Impact
American History Video Program (VHS/DVD)
A Search for Order

Review, Assessment, Intervention

Quick Facts Transparencies: Causes and Effects of the Yom Kippur War; The Camp David Accords; A Search for Order

Spanish Chapter Summaries Audio CD Program

Progress Assessment Support System (PASS): Chapter Test*

Differentiated Instruction Modified Worksheets and Tests CD-ROM: Modified Chapter Test

OSP **One-Stop Planner CD-ROM:** ExamView Test Generator (English/Spanish)

HOAP **Holt Online Assessment Program (HOAP),** in the Holt Premier Online Student Edition

---

PASS: Section 1 Quiz*

Online Quiz: Section 1

Alternative Assessment Handbook

PASS: Section 2 Quiz*

Online Quiz: Section 2

Alternative Assessment Handbook

PASS: Section 3 Quiz*

Online Quiz: Section 3

Alternative Assessment Handbook

NC RESOURCES

The following resources were developed to help North Carolina educators teach the standards and objectives of North Carolina's eleventh grade standard course of study in United States history.

• United States history EOC Test Prep Workbook
• Teacher's Support System
• North Carolina One-Stop Planner

And be sure to direct your students to **go.hrw.com** for online access to the EOC Test Prep Workbook.

go.hrw.com
EOC Test Prep
KEYWORD: SE7 NC

Holt Online Learning

go.hrw.com
Teacher Resources
KEYWORD: SD7 TEACHER

go.hrw.com
Student Resources
KEYWORD: SD7 CH31

• Document-based Questions
• Interactive Multimedia Activities

• Current Events
• Chapter-based Internet Activities
• and more!

Holt Premier
Online Student Edition
Complete online support for interactivity, assessment, and reporting

• Interactive Maps and Notebook
• Standardized Test Prep
• Homework Practice and Research Activities Online

Before You Teach

The Big Picture
Deborah Gray White

The Nixon Years Although a conservative, Nixon was a moderate on several issues. As a conservative he supported limited government, traditional values, and anti-communism. To solidify his southern base he adopted a strategy that opposed desegregation, busing, and voting rights for African Americans. He was tough on crime and drug use. As a liberal, he supported environmental protection, Social Security, help for the poor, and affirmative action. He took a realpolitik approach to foreign affairs. He entered into arms reduction agreements with the Soviet Union, opened relationships with China, and had Henry Kissinger negotiate peace agreements between Israel, Egypt, and Syria, which led to the end of the oil embargo imposed by OPEC. At home, though Americans celebrated the first lunar walk, rising prices and high unemployment plagued the economy.

From Watergate to Ford Nixon's second term was consumed by the Watergate scandal. Although Nixon never revealed what he knew about the break-in at the Democratic headquarters in the Watergate Hotel, he was eventually forced to resign. Gerald Ford, the man who had replaced Agnew as vice president when Agnew was forced to resign for taking bribes, had a difficult few years. His pardon of Nixon made him unpopular, inflation continued, and Congress tied his hands in foreign policy.

Carter's Presidency Carter's inaugural walk symbolized his common man appeal. His controversial pardon of Vietnam draft dodgers helped soothe the domestic tension over Vietnam. Carter's focus on human rights, the environment and energy, and his successful mediation of peace between Israel and Egypt were generally praised. However, two environmental disasters, his ineffective response to the Soviet Union's invasion of Afghanistan, and his inability to gain the release of hostages seized in Iran all made Carter appear weak. As gas prices rose, the public lost confidence in the nation's direction, and in Carter himself.

Recent Scholarship

An Important Decade The 1970s, like the 1920s or 1950s, is a twentieth century decade that is often dismissed as a "tweener," an in-between era of little consequence. Historian Bruce Schulman takes this interpretation to task in his insightful study *The Seventies: The Great Shift in American Culture, Politics, and Society* (2001). As Schulman surveys America's shift from liberal to conservative politics, the emergence of the Sunbelt, the impact of new immigrants on American society, and the various social movements from women's liberation to gay rights, he finds that the seventies was the time when America "reinvented" itself for the twenty-first century.

Differentiating Instruction

Differentiated Instruction Teacher Management System
- Lesson Plans for Differentiated Instruction
- Differentiated Instructional Benchmarking Guides
- Interactive Reader and Study Guide

 Spanish Chapter Summaries Audio CD Program

 Online Chapter Summaries in Spanish

 Student Edition on Audio CD Program

 Differentiated Instruction Modified Worksheets and Tests CD-ROM
- Vocabulary Flash Cards
- Modified Vocabulary Builder Activities
- Modified Chapter Review Activity
- Modified Chapter Test

OSP One-Stop Planner CD-ROM
- ExamView Test Generator (English and Spanish)
- PuzzlePro
- Quiz Show for ExamView
- Transparencies and Videos

TE Differentiated Activities in the Teacher's Edition
- Nixon's Foreign Policies, p. 1020
- Carter's Foreign Policy, p. 1036
- Iran and the United States, p. 1037

BEFORE YOU TEACH

Reading Like a Historian
Sam Wineburg

Memory and its Discontents

Sir Frederic C. Bartlett's *Remembering* (1932) is a classic in the annals of psychology. In a series of ingenious experiments, Bartlett showed memory to be a creative "effort after meaning" rather than a verbatim recall of prior events. We remember the gist of what happened. But with this gist come distortions, elaborations, and outright inventions.

An Impressive Memory?

Our ability to recall the past is the fulcrum of the entire judicial process, and this was nowhere more evident than in the 1973 congressional hearings on Watergate. John Dean, White House counsel, shined as the unparalleled star of this drama. As Dean dazzled his interlocutors by rattling off presidential conversations from months before, it became apparent that this was a man with no ordinary memory.

Dean completed his testimony in June 1973, but soon thereafter, the committee learned that a paranoid Nixon had surreptitiously taped all presidential conversations. With these tapes' transcription came an opportunity to compare Dean's recall with the actual words spoken in the Oval Office.

Comparing Memory and Reality

Ulric Neisser, a pioneer in the field of cognitive science, compared Dean's testimony to the actual transcript of conversations from months before.

On September 15, 1972, three months after the Watergate break-in and arrests, Dean met with the president and chief of staff H. R. Haldeman.

The meeting lasted nearly an hour. The president greeted Dean with these words: "Hi, how are you? You had quite a day today, didn't you? You got Watergate on the way, didn't you?"

For the rest of the discussion on Watergate, the president was mostly silent as Dean and Haldeman discussed the case. Before moving to the next agenda item, Nixon offered Dean this bone: "The way you have handled all this seems to me has been very skillful."

Subpoenaed to appear before Congress some nine months later, John Dean submitted a 245-page written statement. Describing the September 15 meeting, he wrote: "When I arrived at the Oval Office . . . The President asked me to sit down . . . The President then told me . . . I had done a good job and he appreciated how difficult a task it had been . . . I responded that I could not take credit because others had done much more difficult things than I had done . . . I also told him there was a long way to go before this matter would end."

Truth and Memory

"Hardly a word of Dean's account is true," wrote psychologist Neisser. The meeting does not begin with the president asking Dean to sit down; praise is not forthcoming. When it does come, Dean accepts it rather than appearing undeserving. At no time did the president talk about the difficulty of the task. At no time did Dean imply that there would be "a long way to go." If anything, the exchange conveyed the impression that things were under control.

How do we account for these discrepancies, particularly if we assume that Dean was trying to tell the truth? Overall, in fact, the transcripts corroborated Dean's testimony. But much of what Dean "remembered" from September 15 contained elements from other meetings or from conversations with others. Some of his distortions were things Dean wished had happened. In retrospect, if things don't turn out the way we want, our memories can improve them. Neisser analyzed other conversations in which Dean is better at capturing the gist. But even here, Dean messes up the details.

The lesson: We can't do without memory, but nor can we fully trust it.

From "John Dean's Memory: A Case Study" by Ulric Neisser from *Cognition*, No. 9. Published by Elsevier Sequois S.A., Lausanne, 1981.

Standards Focus

Social Studies Competency Goals
Goal 11 The learner will trace economic, political, and social developments and assess their significance for the lives of Americans during this time period.

Goal 12 The learner will identify and analyze trends in domestic and foreign affairs of the United States during this time period.

11.06, 12.01, 12.02, 12.04

The Big Idea and Essential Questions

To foster student understanding of this chapter's big idea, design your lesson to address each section's essential question.

Big Idea Both Presidents Nixon and Carter achieved great diplomatic successes in times of international turmoil—but also made decisions that ended their presidencies.

Essential Questions

1. What successes did the Nixon administration achieve?

2. What events led to the downfall of the Nixon presidency?

3. What challenges did President Jimmy Carter face?

Key to Differentiating Instruction

Below Level

Basic-level activities designed for all students encountering new material

At Level

Intermediate-level activities designed for average students

Above Level

Challenging activities designed for honors and gifted-and-talented students

Standard English Mastery

Activities designed to improve standard English usage

CHAPTER

31 1968–1980

A Search for ORDER

THE BIG PICTURE Following the Vietnam War, Americans searched for order but their political leaders stumbled badly. President Nixon, accused of covering up a crime, was forced to resign. President Carter was denied a second term for failing to provide strong leadership in relations with Iran and the Soviet Union.

North Carolina Standards

Social Studies Objectives
11.06 Identify political events and the actions and reactions of the government officials and citizens, and assess the social and political consequences.
12.01 Summarize significant events in foreign policy since the Vietnam War.
12.02 Evaluate the impact of recent constitutional amendments, court rulings, and federal legislation on United States citizens.
12.04 Identify and assess the impact of social, political, and cultural changes in the United States.

Language Arts Objectives
2.01 Research and analyze ideas, events, and/or movements related to United States culture by:
• locating facts and details for purposeful elaboration.

Skills FOCUS READING LIKE A HISTORIAN

New York City celebrates the return of astronauts Neil A. Armstrong, Michael Collins, and Edwin E. "Buzz" Aldrin (right to left) with a grand ticker-tape parade in the summer of 1969. The trio had recently completed a historic trip to the moon—a first for humans. **Making Inferences** How might great achievements affect a society searching for order?

See Skills Handbook, p. H7

July 20, 1969 Neil Armstrong becomes the first man to walk on the moon.

U.S. **1968** Richard Nixon is elected president.

1968

World

1969 The ruling council of the Palestine Liberation Organization elects Yasser Arafat to head the PLO.

1016

Introduce the Chapter

At Level

A Search for Order

1. Guide students in a discussion of the nature of change. Do they like change and challenges in their personal lives, or is it difficult to adjust to new ways of doing things?

2. Tell students that in this chapter they will learn about three presidents, Nixon, Ford, and Carter, and the challenges they faced both at home and abroad.

3. Have students work in pairs to scan the chapter and make a list of challenges each

president faced. Have volunteers share information from their lists and create a class list for all to see.

4. Have students write a brief summary of the problems that faced all three presidents and identify which issues are still problematic today. **LS Verbal-Linguistic**

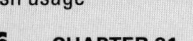 Alternative Assessment Handbook, Rubric 11: Discussions

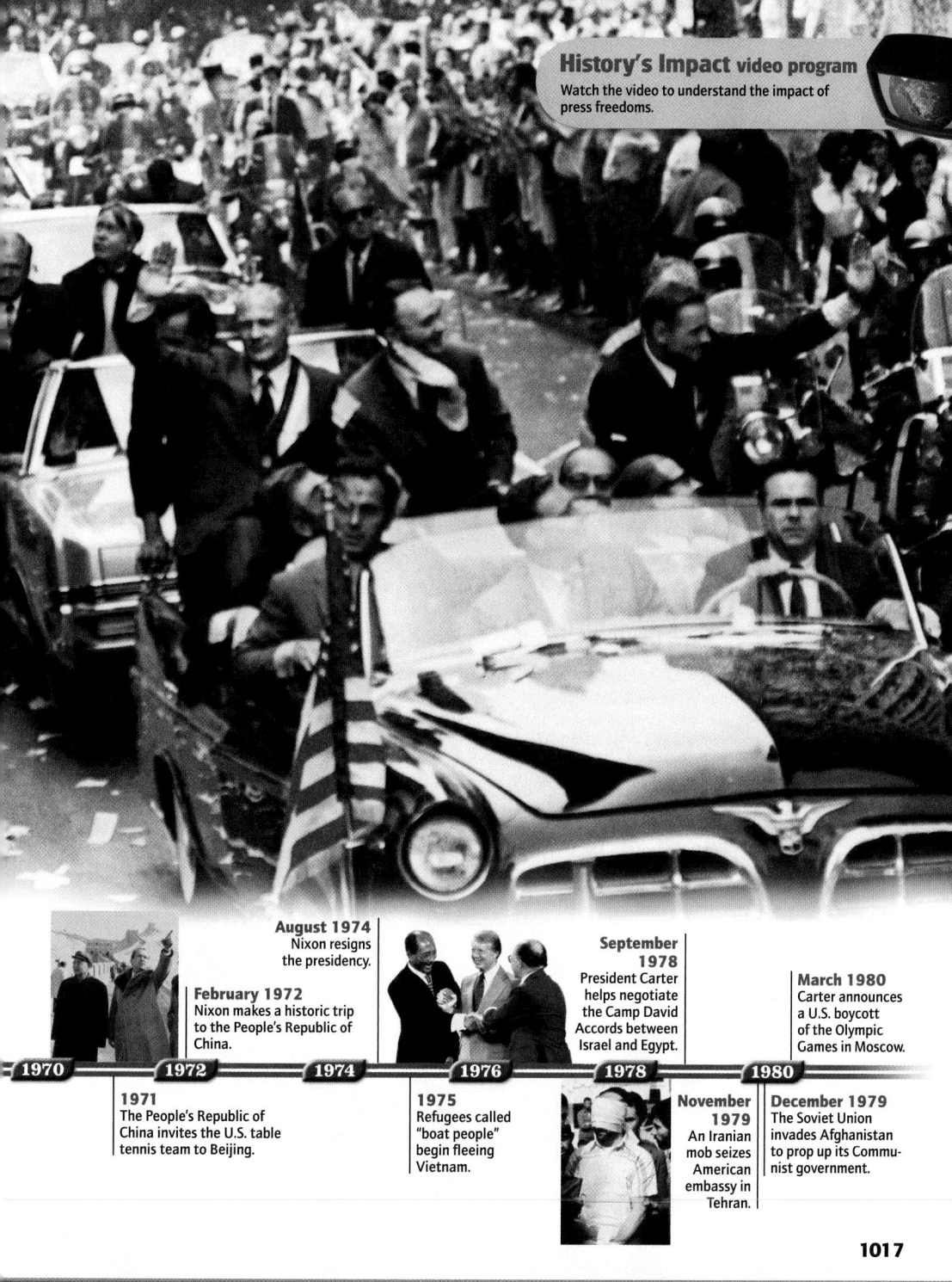

History's Impact video program
Watch the video to understand the impact of press freedoms.

February 1972
Nixon makes a historic trip to the People's Republic of China.

August 1974
Nixon resigns the presidency.

September 1978
President Carter helps negotiate the Camp David Accords between Israel and Egypt.

March 1980
Carter announces a U.S. boycott of the Olympic Games in Moscow.

1970 — 1972 — 1974 — 1976 — 1978 — 1980

1971
The People's Republic of China invites the U.S. table tennis team to Beijing.

1975
Refugees called "boat people" begin fleeing Vietnam.

November 1979
An Iranian mob seizes American embassy in Tehran.

December 1979
The Soviet Union invades Afghanistan to prop up its Communist government.

1017

• Chapter Preview •

HOLT

History's Impact

► **Video Program: A Search for Order**
See the Video Teacher's Guide for strategies for using the video segment.

Reading Like a Historian

Return to Earth Have students take a moment to examine the image on these pages. Do students think the nation is proud of the astronauts? Have students list details supporting their answers. *possible answer—yes, presence of motorcade, waving crowd, and American flags show that they are important and honored*

Interpreting Visuals On August 13, 1969, New Yorkers turned out by the thousands to honor the astronauts of the *Apollo 11* mission during their visit to the city. The parade, which ran along Broadway and Park Avenue, was the largest in the city's history.

go.hrw.com
Online Resources

Chapter Resources:
KEYWORD: SD7 CH31

Teacher Resources:
KEYWORD: SD7 TEACHER

Explore the Time Line

1. When did President Nixon visit China? *February 1972*

2. How long did Richard Nixon's presidency last? *About 5 years; from his inauguration in late 1968 to his resignation in August 1974*

3. What events on the time line involve Middle Eastern countries? *PLO election of Arafat, Camp David Accords, seizure of American embassy in Iran*

Info to Know

China During the 1950s the Soviet Union was China's major foreign trade partner, but by the mid-1960s Japan and Hong Kong had replaced the Soviet Union as major trading partners. Following normalization of relations, the U.S. became a major trade partner as well, both in imports and exports.

Analyze Why was it important to improve U.S. relations with the People's Republic of China? *possible answers—China is a giant nation, need to establish some kind of diplomatic and trade relationship*

Answers

**Reading Like a Historian
(p. 1016)** *possible answer—Pride in their accomplishments might bring people closer together.*

Bellringer

The Inside Story. . . Use the **Daily Bellringer Transparency** to help students answer the question.

📦 Daily Bellringer Transparency, Section 1

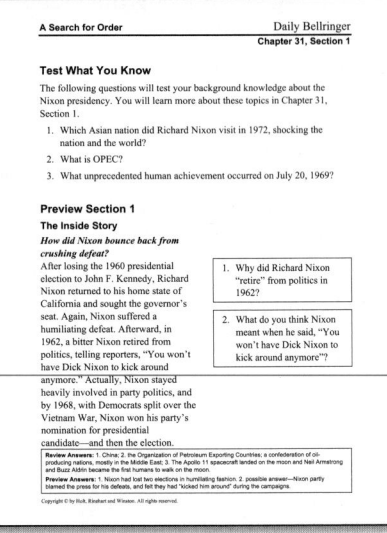

Academic Vocabulary

Review with students the high-use academic term in this section.

innovations new ideas or advances (p. 1020)

region an area of the world (p. 1022)

📄 CRF: Vocabulary Builder Activity, Section 1

Taking Notes

Foreign Policy—SALT, SALT I, opened relations with China, Kissinger's efforts to resolve conflict in the Middle East; Domestic Policy—New Federalism, a shift in power from federal to state governments and revenue sharing; Southern Strategy, expanded Nixon's support in the traditionally Democratic South, attempted to stop implementation of 1965 Voting Rights Act, slow forced integration, opposed busing of students; Fighting Crime, kept federal courts from preventing local police from fighting crime and appointed conservative judges to federal court openings

---

The Nixon Years

BEFORE YOU READ

MAIN IDEA

Beyond the ongoing turmoil of the Vietnam War, the Nixon administration did enjoy some notable success.

READING FOCUS

1. What were the key features of Nixon's politics and domestic policies?

2. How did Nixon carry out his foreign policies with regard to China and the Soviet Union?

3. How did trouble in the Middle East affect the Nixon administration?

4. What were some of the major social and cultural events at home in the Nixon years?

KEY TERMS AND PEOPLE

realpolitik
détente
SALT I
OPEC
shuttle diplomacy
Apollo 11
Neil Armstrong

TAKING NOTES As you read, take notes on the major events and accomplishments of the Nixon administration. Record your notes in a graphic organizer like the one shown here.

Foreign Policy	Domestic Policy

THE INSIDE STORY

How did Nixon bounce back from crushing defeat? By 1962 Richard Nixon seemed to be an utterly defeated man. Still recovering from having lost the presidential election of 1960 to John F. Kennedy, Nixon had sought the governor's office in his home state of California. Again, however, he suffered a humiliating defeat. In a surprising move, he announced his retirement from politics the day after the election. "You won't have Dick Nixon to kick around anymore," he angrily told reporters, whom he had blamed for his defeat. The man who had once been the second most powerful man in the world and who had come within a few thousand votes of being president was now a bitter man.

But Nixon was far from finished in politics. Out of office and out of the spotlight, he remained active in Republican politics in the 1960s. After wins in the 1968 presidential primaries, it became clear that he was an electable candidate. He won his party's nomination. Then, as the Democrats squabbled and divided over the Vietnam War and civil rights, he emerged as the winner in a close election.

Nixon had made a remarkable political comeback. Far from being through with politics, the most memorable years of his political career lay ahead of him. These included achievements in the 1970s for which he is favorably remembered. ▪

Nixon's Comeback to Success

▶ Richard Nixon gives the victory salute that would become his trademark gesture.

1018

Teach the Main Idea

At Level

The Nixon Years

1. **Teach** Ask students the Reading Focus questions to teach this section.

2. **Apply** Draw four large ovals. Label the top of each oval with one of the topics of this section: Nixon's Politics and Domestic Policies, Nixon's Foreign Policies, Trouble in the Middle East, and Major Events at Home. Discuss each topic, using the ovals to list the main events for each topic. **LS Visual-Spatial**

3. **Review** As you review the section, have students identify the issues in each topic that they believe to be the most serious or problematic.

4. **Practice/Homework** Have students write a one-page press release that describes the challenges and accomplishments of the Nixon presidency. **LS Verbal-Linguistic, Interpersonal**

📄 Alternative Assessment Handbook, Rubric 42: Writing to Inform

Nixon's Politics and Domestic Policies

Richard Nixon's 1968 political comeback high-lighted what had already been a long and successful career. Before his losses in 1960 and 1962, he had built a reputation as a strong opponent of communism and as a solid conservative. Recall that in American politics, conservatives tend to favor smaller, less active government. They also favor what are seen as more traditional values.

Nixon the conservative Indeed, Nixon entered the presidency promoting a number of conservative ideas. For example, he had campaigned on the belief that the federal government had grown too large.

HISTORY'S VOICES

❝[W]e have been deluged by government programs for the unemployed, programs for the cities, programs for the poor, and we have reaped from these programs an ugly harvest of frustrations, violence and failure across the land . . . I say it's time to quit pouring billions of dollars into programs that have failed in the United States of America.❞

—Richard Nixon, Acceptance Speech, August 8, 1968

"It's time," Nixon continued, "to have power go back from Washington to the states and to the cities of this country all over America." The solution he proposed came to be called the New Federalism. A key feature of this proposal was the concept of revenue sharing. This meant that money collected by the federal government would be shifted to states and cities. Local governments, Nixon believed, would do a better job of spending the taxpayers' money than the federal government would.

The southern strategy Early in his career, Nixon had supported civil rights for African Americans. As president, however, he crafted a "southern strategy" designed to appeal to former segregationists in the South. Nixon's goal was to ensure electoral success by expanding his support in the traditionally Democratic region. Based on this strategy, Nixon tried unsuccessfully to weaken the 1965 Voting Rights Act. He urged a slowdown in forced integration in the South. He also opposed the busing of students from their home neighborhoods to schools in another part of the city. This had been a court-

ordered way of integrating schools in places where neighborhoods were all-black or all-white. Nixon favored letting local governments take action rather than having the federal government force them to act.

As a result of action at the state level, many communities made real progress toward desegregation. Still, de facto segregation—that is, segregation in fact though not by law—continued in many places, including in many northern cities, for some time. Nixon, meanwhile, gained the favor of many white voters in the South.

Drugs and crime Nixon also took a firm stand against crime and drug use. "Time is running out for the merchants of crime and corruption in American society," he promised. He shared conservatives' concern about federal court rulings that put limits on the powers of the police. (Recall what you have read about rulings such as *Miranda* v. *Arizona*.) He therefore sought to name conservative judges for openings on the federal courts. Though the Senate rejected two of his Supreme Court nominees, Nixon was able to fill four openings on the court.

FACES OF HISTORY

Richard NIXON
1913–1994

Richard Nixon accomplished much in a political career that spanned nearly three decades. In addition to his accomplishments, he also won a reputation for tough political tactics.

Born and raised in California, Nixon excelled in college and law school. After serving in the navy in World War II, he pursued a political career. In 1946 he won election to Congress in part on the strength of a strong anti-Communist message. As a House member, he won national attention for his role in the trial of accused spy Alger Hiss. This political success was followed by a 1950 campaign for a Senate seat. He won this election after accusing his opponent of being soft on communism.

Now a national figure, Nixon served as vice president for two terms under Dwight D. Eisenhower. He only narrowly missed winning election to the presidency in 1960. Yet this and his 1962 loss in the race for governor of California left their mark on Nixon. His fear of another loss would lead him to campaign excesses in the future.

Explain How did Nixon's experiences in 1960 and 1962 affect the way he approached political campaigns?

Nixon's Politics and Domestic Policies

Identify What was the purpose of the Clean Air Act? *regulate levels of air pollution*

Summarize What programs or legislation did Nixon promote to help the poor and working-class Americans? *Food Stamps; Occupational Safety and Health Act; extended affirmative action programs*

Evaluate After reviewing legislation supported by President Nixon, do you think he was a true conservative? Explain your answer. *possible answers—yes, he was concerned with the federal budget and allied himself with conservative ideals; no, while he supported conservatives, he also helped pass legislation that was supported by liberals*

Info to Know

The "Southern Strategy" On July 14, 2005, the chairman of the Republican National Committee, Ken Mehlman, attended the national convention of the NAACP held in Milwaukee, Wisconsin. In his speech to NAACP delegates, Mehlman said that Nixon's "southern strategy" was wrong. In addition, on behalf of the Republican Party, Mehlman apologized for not reaching out to African Americans and for supporting political issues that resulted in the polarization of whites and blacks.

Answers

Reading Check *conservative about states' rights issues and spending, but willing to take liberal stances on affirmative action, environmental protection laws, and workplace safety*

1020

The other side of Richard Nixon While Nixon had a solid conservative record, he was sometimes willing to take more liberal stances. For example, he expanded the role of the federal government by increasing funding for programs such as food stamps, which helped people with low incomes buy groceries. He also increased payments for Social Security.

Nixon's environmentalism Nixon also took a special interest in the environment. Concern about pollution had been growing in the United States for several years. In 1962 author Rachel Carson had published *Silent Spring*, which warned of the harmful effects of chemicals on the natural world.

By 1970 widespread concern led to massive Earth Day demonstrations all across the country. Millions of Americans took part in these events, at which information and ideas about the environment were shared.

Nixon responded to this growing national issue. In 1970 he signed the Clean Air Act, which sought to regulate levels of air pollution created by factories and other sources. That same year, Nixon worked to establish the Environmental Protection Agency to help carry out the nation's environmental laws and policies.

THE IMPACT TODAY

Government
In its first three decades, OSHA helped reduce workplace fatalities by 60 percent—at the same time that the size of the American workforce more than doubled.

Other Nixon policies Late in 1970 Nixon signed the Occupational Safety and Health Act. This created a large new organization within the federal government. At its heart was the Occupational Health and Safety Administration, or OSHA, which worked to prevent work-related injury and illness. OSHA set and enforced safety standards in the workplace and provided safety training and education.

While Nixon pursued his southern strategy, he also took steps to advance affirmative action. As you have read, this refers to active measures taken by the government to overcome the effects of past discrimination against minority groups.

Early in his administration, Nixon encouraged the setting of specific hiring goals and timetables for overcoming discrimination in companies doing business with the government. He also extended affirmative action programs to the hiring of women.

ACADEMIC VOCABULARY
innovations new ideas or advances

READING CHECK **Summarizing** How did Nixon's basic political beliefs affect his domestic policies?

1020 CHAPTER 31

Nixon's Foreign Policies

When Nixon was running for office in 1968, the war in Vietnam was the major issue facing the voters. You have read about Nixon's troubled efforts to bring that crisis to a close. Yet Vietnam was only one of the foreign-policy issues facing Nixon during his presidency. In general, Nixon met these challenges with great success.

Henry Kissinger and realpolitik Henry Kissinger, who helped negotiate an end to the Vietnam War, was deeply involved in shaping much of Nixon's foreign policy. Nixon named Kissinger as his national security adviser in 1969. Kissinger later became secretary of state. In both roles, he was guided by the notion of realpolitik. **Realpolitik** means basing foreign policies on realistic views of national interest rather than on broad rules or principles.

Kissinger believed the United States should consider each foreign-policy conflict or question from the standpoint of what is best for America. The government should not, Kissinger believed, be bound by promises to fight communism or promote freedom wherever it is threatened. Henry Kissinger's realpolitik marked a significant change from earlier policies such as containment.

Détente Nixon had built his reputation as a tough opponent of communism. Voters knew they were electing a strong and forceful leader. However, as Nixon once remarked, "Sometimes those on the right can do things which those on the left can only talk about." Indeed, as president Nixon took steps to ease tensions with Cold War enemies. These efforts were referred to as **détente** (day-TAHNT).

The policy of détente was strongly influenced by Henry Kissinger's realpolitik. The goal was to build a more stable world in which the United States and its adversaries accepted one another's place.

In 1969 Nixon entered into discussions with the Soviets to slow the ongoing arms race. These were known as the Strategic Arms Limitation Talks (SALT). In addition to increasing numbers of weapons, the United States and the Soviet Union each had recently made innovations in weapons technology. For example, each had recently built antiballistic

---

Differentiating Instruction

Below Level

English-Language Learners

1. Draw a two-column table for students to see. Label the top of the table *Nixon's Foreign Policy*. Have students copy the table onto their own papers. On the left side of the diagram, have students write the words: *Key Elements*; on the right side, the word: *Explanation*.

2. Have students complete the table by listing the major elements of Nixon's foreign policy and explaining each element. If students have

difficulty completing the table, have them work in mixed-ability pairs.

3. Have volunteers share the information from their graphic organizers, and complete the class diagram for students to see. Have students correct their tables and retain the diagrams as a study tool. **LS Visual-Spatial**

📖 Alternative Assessment Handbook, Rubric 13: Graphic Organizers

📄 Graphic Organizer Transparencies

missile, or ABM, defense systems. Many people considered ABM systems to be a threat to peace. It was feared they would undermine the power balance that helped prevent nuclear war during the Cold War. If one side thought it could survive a nuclear attack, the thinking went, it might be more likely to launch one itself.

The SALT meetings dragged on for several years. Finally, in 1972 Nixon visited Moscow for a summit. At that meeting, Nixon and Soviet leader Leonid Brezhnev agreed to an ABM treaty that bound each country to strict limits in the building of missile systems.

Nixon and Brezhnev also agreed to a five-year slowdown in building new offensive weapons. Following the end of these talks—now called **SALT I**—negotiators began a second round of discussions on arms limitation. These became known as SALT II. You will read more about them later.

Nixon in China Shortly after taking office, President Nixon told his closest advisers about one of his key goals for his presidency: improving relations with the Communist People's Republic of China. At that time, the People's

Republic had little contact with the United States and most of the rest of the world.

Yet Nixon saw great opportunity in improving relations with the Communist giant. Such a step would put pressure on the Soviet Union. Both China and the Soviets practiced communism, but they had become bitter rivals in recent years. Nixon knew that by becoming friendlier with China, he could make the Soviets uncomfortable and pressure them into a more cooperative relationship with the United States.

Nixon had to move carefully. The United States did not formally recognize the People's Republic of China. It considered the Republic of China on Taiwan to be the true Chinese government. Thus, the effort to reach out to the People's Republic took place in secrecy.

Nevertheless, Nixon's plan went forward. In 1971 the People's Republic made a surprise invitation to an American table tennis team to play in a tournament. The team members became the first Americans to visit mainland China since 1949.

Later, Kissinger made a secret trip to the People's Republic to explore a possible

Nixon Visits China

- **January 1969** Nixon informs key staff of his desire to improve relations with the People's Republic of China.

- **May 1969** Using Pakistan as a go-between, U.S. officials begin talking with Communist Chinese representatives.

- **April 1971** A U.S. table tennis team visits the People's Republic of China.

- **July 1971** Kissinger makes a secret trip to the People's Republic of China to pave the way for Nixon's visit.

- **February 1972** Nixon travels to the People's Republic and meets with Communist leader Mao Zedong.

◄ Nixon tours the Great Wall of China in February 1972.

A SEARCH FOR ORDER **1021**

❸ How did trouble in the Middle East affect the Nixon administration? *1973 support of Israel created tensions with Soviets; oil embargo by Arab countries created oil shortages and increased costs*

Trouble in the Middle East

Identify What is OPEC and why is it important to the U.S.? *Organization of Petroleum Exporting Countries; able to control flow and prices of oil*

Identify Cause and Effect Why did some Arab nations refuse to send oil to the United States following the Yom Kippur War? *to punish U.S. for helping Israel*

Evaluate The oil embargo following the Yom Kippur War created severe problems in the U.S. economy. What do you think would happen to the U.S. economy today if Arab nations began an oil embargo? *possible answer—terrible toll; U.S. depends on foreign oil to fuel its industries and transportation systems*

📇 Quick Facts Transparency: Causes and Effects of the Yom Kippur War

Teaching Tip

Remind students of the differences between the Communist People's Republic of China, and the Republic of China, located on Taiwan. Have students find mainland China and Taiwan on the map in the atlas of their texts. Tell students that the two nations are important and that they will learn more about them in the chapter.

Answers

Reading Check *improve relations with these Communist countries*

---

presidential visit. The meeting went well. In July 1971, Nixon announced that he would go to the People's Republic in early 1972.

The news shocked some Americans and pleased others. Some were upset that Nixon seemed to be abandoning Nationalist China and embracing the Communists. Nixon assured these critics that that was not the case. Many Americans, however, supported the move.

In February Nixon's team took off for China. There he met with top Chinese leaders, including the aging Mao Zedong. The visit was a huge success for Nixon. He and Mao recognized the benefits of a closer relationship. Toward that end, they agreed to disagree about Taiwan.

The trip also seemed to have the hoped-for effect on the Soviets. Shortly after the China visit, Nixon and Brezhnev reached agreement in the SALT I meetings.

ACADEMIC VOCABULARY
region an area of the world

READING CHECK **Identifying the Main Idea** What was the primary goal of Richard Nixon's foreign policy with regard to the Soviet Union and China?

Trouble in the Middle East

The Middle East had been a point of conflict for many years. In 1967 Israel went to war against several of its Arab neighbors. As a result of the Six-Day War, Israel occupied territory that had belonged to or been controlled by the Arab nations of Egypt, Syria, and Jordan.

CAUSES AND EFFECTS OF THE YOM KIPPUR WAR
QUICK FACTS

CAUSES
- Israel occupied Arab-controlled land in the Six-Day War.
- The United Nations passed a resolution urging Israel to leave occupied lands and Arab nations to recognize Israel.
- Arabs and Israelis were unable to reach agreement on either point of the UN resolution.

EFFECTS
- Tension between United States and the Soviet Union grew.
- Arab oil-producing nations decided on an oil embargo.

Following the war's end, the United Nations passed a resolution that called for Israel to withdraw from these occupied lands and for Arab states to recognize Israel's right to exist. However, there was disagreement on exactly what the resolution required. Israel—with U.S. support—continued to dispute with its Arab neighbors for the next several years.

In 1973 this ongoing conflict finally erupted in war. On the Jewish holy day of Yom Kippur, Egypt and Syria attacked Israel.

The fighting affected the United States in a number of ways. One effect was the threat of Soviet involvement. In response to events on the battlefield, the Soviet Union offered supplies to the Egyptians and the Syrians.

The United States in turn sent supplies to the Israelis. The Soviets also threatened to send troops to aid the embattled Egyptians. Conflict in the region threatened to turn into a superpower confrontation.

Oil embargo Another effect of the war was the decision of several Arab nations to impose an oil embargo. An embargo is the refusal by a country to ship a product or products from its ports.

Shortly after the start of the Yom Kippur War, the Arab oil-producing countries of the Middle East jointly agreed not to ship any oil to the United States and certain other countries. This was a response to American support for Israel. The Arab countries were part of a group called the Organization of Petroleum Exporting Countries, or **OPEC**.

At the time of the embargo, the United States was dependent on OPEC oil for a significant amount of its large petroleum needs. That dependence was growing. In 1970 the United States had gotten just over a fifth of its oil from foreign sources. By 1973 that figure had risen to about a third.

The Arab oil embargo contributed to an energy crisis in the United States. As gasoline became scarce, drivers sometimes had to wait in long lines at gas stations to fill their tanks. When they got to the pump, they often found that prices for gasoline had risen sharply.

The oil embargo affected more than just people who drove cars. For example, it drove up the cost of operating machines in factories. It cost farmers more to harvest their crops. The embargo also increased the cost of

---

Skills Focus: Analyzing Bias in Historical Interpretation [Above Level]

Reading Like a Historian Skill
The Yom Kippur War

1. Have students list the events and problems that led up to and followed the Yom Kippur War.

2. Have students conduct outside research using reliable Internet sites and traditional print sources to read accounts of the war, and reasons for the war, from both Arab and Israeli viewpoints. Students may wish to work together to collect and share their documents.

3. Have students analyze the bias and the

viewpoints in the documents they have located. Then have students create an annotated bibliography explaining the bias they believe is in each of the documents. Students should justify their reasoning with factual information about the war. Students should attach copies of their documents to the bibliography. 🄻 **Intrapersonal, Verbal-Linguistic**

📓 Alternative Assessment Handbook, Rubric 30: Research

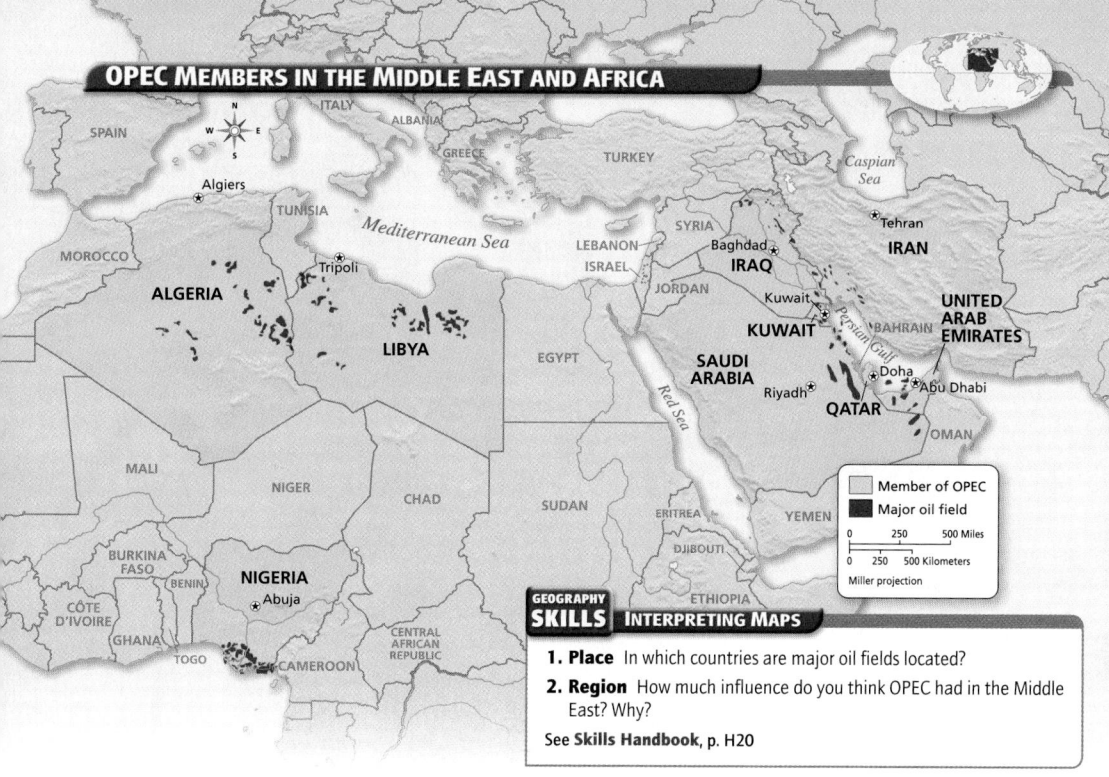

OPEC MEMBERS IN THE MIDDLE EAST AND AFRICA

GEOGRAPHY SKILLS | **INTERPRETING MAPS**

1. **Place** In which countries are major oil fields located?
2. **Region** How much influence do you think OPEC had in the Middle East? Why?

See **Skills Handbook, p. H20**

See **Skills Handbook, p. H20**

---

transporting products from farms and factories to stores. Prices for all kinds of products thus began to rise. As you will read, this rapid rise in prices would cause serious problems throughout the U.S. economy.

Kissinger and shuttle diplomacy

To help resolve the crisis in the Middle East, Henry Kissinger went to work. Unable to get all the parties involved to meet together to discuss possible solutions, he started what came to be called **shuttle diplomacy**. That is, he traveled—shuttled—from group to group, trying to work out separate agreements to end the fighting. For example, he negotiated peace between Israel and Egypt. Then he helped bring about a separate deal between Israel and Syria. In this way, the military conflict came to an end. Eventually, the oil embargo was also lifted.

READING CHECK **Identifying Cause and Effect** How did the trouble in the Middle East affect the United States in the early 1970s?

Major Events at Home

In an earlier chapter, you read about the American program to put astronauts on the moon. During the Nixon years, the United States finally achieved this history-making goal.

Throughout the mid-1960s, the American public followed the progress of the NASA astronauts with great interest. Every few months brought another launch and another step toward the goal of a lunar landing. These triumphs were also marred by tragedy. In 1967 three astronauts died in a terrible launchpad fire. In spite of this setback, the Apollo space program continued.

The climax came in July 1969. On the 16th of that month, a flight known as **Apollo 11** made a successful liftoff from Cape Kennedy, also known as the Kennedy Space Center, in Florida. On board were three modern-day pioneers—astronauts **Neil Armstrong**, Edwin "Buzz" Aldrin, and Michael Collins.

A SEARCH FOR ORDER **1023**

Skills Focus: Analyzing Primary Sources

At Level

Reading Like a Historian Skill
The First Moon Landing

1. Have students work individually or in pairs to find primary source documents about the first moon landing. Sources might include NASA documents, reports from the engineers who worked on the project, and memoirs of Aldrin, Armstrong, and Collins. Students might also find newspaper accounts of the event.

2. Have students write a summary of the information they find in the documents.

Then have students write a conclusion in which they answer these questions: Why was this a historic moment in U.S. and world history? How long do you think it will be before the U.S. once again sends astronauts to the moon? **LS** **Verbal-Linguistic, Logical-Mathematical**

Alternative Assessment Handbook, Rubrics 30: Research; and 40: Writing to Describe

---

1023

History Close-Up
The First Moon Landing

Describe Have students write a description of the *Apollo 11* lunar landing. *spacecraft split into two separate compartments; lunar module held two astronauts; Armstrong walked out on moon first; Armstrong and Aldrin planted American flag on moon surface* Then have students write a newspaper article in which they capture the excitement of the moment among U.S. citizens who have just witnessed this event. Tell students that watching the astronauts plant the American flag was a memorable, historic event, and that most people who were alive in 1969 remember watching the coverage on television.

Primary Source

"I knew I was alone in a way that no earthling has ever been before."
— Michael Collins
Time, December 11, 1972

"It [the moon] has a stark beauty all its own. It's like much of the high desert of the United States. It's different, but it's very pretty out here."
— Neil Armstrong
transcript, NASA Langley Research Center

" . . . Because of what you have done, the heavens have become part of man's world. And as you talk to us from the Sea of Tranquility, it inspires us to bring peace and tranquility to earth. For one priceless moment in the history of man, all the people on this earth are truly one."
— President Richard M. Nixon
to the astronauts
July 20, 1969

✴ **Interactive History Close-Up:**
Lunar Landing

Answers

Interpreting Infographics 1. *large amount of equipment had to be taken;* **2.** *low gravity and soft soil*

1024

✴Interactive
HISTORY CLOSE-UP

The First Moon Landing

The successful landing of human beings on the surface of the moon was a triumph of technology— and of the American will and spirit of exploration.

The lunar module was designed to withstand the low gravitational forces of the moon, which were one-sixth those of Earth.

The large amounts of equipment made the interior of the lunar module cramped and noisy.

The large footpads were designed to ensure the module did not sink into the soft lunar soil.

Skills FOCUS INTERPRETING INFOGRAPHICS

go.hrw.com
Interactive
Keyword: SD7 CH31

1. **Making Inferences** Why do you think conditions were so cramped in the lunar landing module?
2. **Drawing Conclusions** What factors made landing on the moon difficult?

See **Skills Handbook**, pp. H12, H18

1024 CHAPTER 31

Skills Focus: Analyzing Infographics

At Level

Social Studies Skill
Apollo 11

Materials poster board, colored markers

1. Review the infographic of the first moon landing with students. Tell students that due to media coverage of NASA, the astronauts were well known. Many Americans stayed home to watch television coverage of the *Apollo 11* flight.

2. Have students work in small groups to develop a storyboard for a news broadcast about this historic event.

3. Have volunteers share their storyboards with the class.

4. As an extension, guide students in a discussion of the political benefits of the Apollo flight to the Nixon administration.
   LS Interpersonal, Logical-Mathematical

📝 Alternative Assessment Handbook, Rubrics 3: Artwork; and 14: Group Activity

After a journey of several days, the crew of *Apollo 11* swung into orbit around the moon. As their spacecraft sailed miles above the moon's surface, a separate craft split off from the main part. One part was the control module *Columbia*, in which Collins remained. The other part was a lunar module called the *Eagle*, which carried Aldrin and Armstrong.

On July 20 the *Eagle* landed on the moon's surface. Back on Earth, millions of viewers watched the flawless landing on television. Several anxious hours later, Neil Armstrong made his way out of the module. Wearing a heavy space suit, he slowly backed down a ladder. "That's one small step for a man," crackled his voice over the radio as he stepped onto the moon, "one giant leap for mankind." The mission started years before by President John F. Kennedy had been achieved at last.

Soon Armstrong was joined by Aldrin. The pair set up a camera and carried out a variety of tasks. This included planting an American flag in the lunar soil.

HISTORY'S VOICES

❝ So many people have done so much to give us this opportunity to place this American flag on the surface. To me it was one of the prouder moments of my life, to be able to stand there and quickly salute the flag. ❞

—Edwin "Buzz" Aldrin, news conference, August 12, 1969

Inflation and price controls The success of the lunar landing gave the nation and Nixon a lift. However, Nixon knew that it was not enough to ensure his future in office. As the memory of *Apollo 11* faded and the election of 1972 approached, Nixon grew concerned.

A particular worry was the high rate of inflation, or the overall rise in prices. In the months leading up to the 1972 election, this stood at an unacceptable 5 percent, and it was rising. Unemployment was also at an uncomfortably high level.

Nixon had traditionally favored limited government involvement in the economy. Now, however, he believed action was needed. In August 1971 he announced a 90-day freeze of wages and prices. That is, businesses could not increase the prices they charged for their products or the wages they paid their workers. This, Nixon hoped, would act as a brake on inflation.

The immediate impact of Nixon's measures was positive. Inflation did appear to slow, at least for a while. Nixon seemed to have successfully addressed a major economic concern of the voters.

Unfortunately, Nixon had not solved the problem of inflation permanently. The oil crisis of 1973–1974 would soon send prices sharply higher again. The wage and price controls that had worked before failed to bring relief. Meanwhile, the second term Nixon had worked so hard to secure dissolved into scandal. You will read about this in the next section.

READING CHECK **Summarizing** What were two major events affecting the United States during Nixon's first term in office?

THE IMPACT TODAY

Science and Technology
NASA's moon explorations ended in the early 1970s. In early 2004 President George W. Bush announced a new goal for U.S. space exploration: a return to the moon and, eventually, human missions to the planet Mars.

SECTION 1 ASSESSMENT

go.hrw.com
Online Quiz
Keyword: SD7 HP31

Reviewing Ideas, Terms, and People

1. **a. Identify** What kind of political reputation did Nixon have when he was elected president in 1969?
   b. Draw Conclusions Why do you think Nixon sometimes favored conservative policies and sometimes took more liberal positions?

2. **a. Define** Write a brief definition of each of the following terms: realpolitik, détente
   b. Interpret What do you think Nixon meant when he said, "Sometimes those on the right can do things which those on the left can only talk about"?

3. **a. Describe** What were the key events in the Middle East that occurred in 1973?
   b. Sequence What was the sequence of events surrounding the Arab oil embargo?

4. **a. Identify** What is the significance of *Apollo 11*?
   b. Compare How did Nixon's handling of the inflation problem match his overall political philosophies?

Critical Thinking

5. **Identifying the Main Idea** Copy the chart below and use information from the section to record details that support the section's main idea.

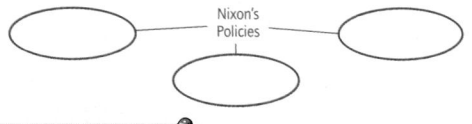

Nixon's Policies

FOCUS ON WRITING

6. **Descriptive** Based on the events described in this section, write a brief descriptive paragraph about Nixon's performance, including details of his major policies and accomplishments.

A SEARCH FOR ORDER **1025**

New York Times Co. v. United States

Word Help

disclosed made known, revealed
injunction a legal order
expedited accelerated, faster than usual

Info to Know

First Amendment Rights In this case both the *New York Times* and the *Washington Post* argued that the restraints imposed by the injunction were an infringement of their First Amendment rights. The Nixon administration argued that national security interests outweighed these rights. The Court decided 6-3 against the administration. Justices Potter and White thought that First Amendment rights could sometimes be abridged, but that this case did not warrant such action.

Primary Source

"But I cannot say that disclosure of any of them [the Pentagon Papers] will surely result in direct, immediate, and irreparable damage to our Nation or its people."

— Justice Potter Stewart
New York Times Co. v. United States

LANDMARK SUPREME COURT CASES
Constitutional Issue: Freedom of the Press

New York Times Co. v. United States (1971)

Why It Matters This case considered whether newspapers could be prevented from publishing information that the government did not want disclosed to the public on the grounds that it might harm national security.

Background of the Case

In 1971 the *New York Times* began publishing portions of a secret Defense Department study of the Vietnam War. The Pentagon Papers had been leaked by former Defense Department economist Daniel Ellsberg. The Nixon administration went to court to prevent publication of the information.

The Decision

In its ruling the Court noted the strong presumption that "prior restraint"—that is, prevention of speech or the publication of information—is unconstitutional. The government therefore had a "heavy burden" to show that blocking publication is justified. The government failed to do so, the Court held.

There were several separate concurring or dissenting opinions. Some justices argued that under the First Amendment the government can never restrict publication of news. Others argued that government sometimes has the right to keep certain matters secret in the interest of national security but that this was not such a case. One justice suggested that the publishers might be prosecuted but only after publication.

In the end, however, the ruling upheld the key role of the press in educating and informing the public:

❝ [T]he only effective restraint upon executive policy and power in the areas of national defense and international affairs may lie in an enlightened citizenry—in an informed and critical public opinion which alone can here protect the values of democratic government. **❞**

— Justice Potter Stewart

THE IMPACT TODAY The issue of prior restraint of news and the possible threat to national security in the release of certain information in newspapers and other news outlets remains a difficult one. Since the terrorist attacks of September 11, 2001, for example, the government and the press have differed over ways to manage the release of information about the nation's ongoing fight against terrorism.

go.hrw.com
Research Online
Keyword: SS Court

CRITICAL THINKING

1. **Analyze the Impact** Using the keyword above, read about *New York Times Co. v. Sullivan*, another important First Amendment case involving the same newspaper. What is the ruling of the case? Why did the Court allow the media greater flexibility in writing about public figures than in stories about private individuals?

2. **You Be the Judge** The events of September 11, 2001, and the ongoing war on terrorism have raised new concerns about the proper balance between governmental secrecy and open disclosure and discussion in the press. How might these contemporary concerns affect the decision in a case like *New York Times Co. v. United States* today? Explain your answer in a short paragraph.

Answers

Critical Thinking 1. *Court ruled in favor of the Times' right to publish because the newspaper did not publish with intent to libel or with malice; the public has a right to know what goes on with public figures;* **2.** *Proponents of First Amendment rights will continue to argue that to sustain democracy, Americans must have freedom of speech and the press must continue to exercise its rights and responsibilities. On the other hand, security of all citizens is also a paramount concern for government officials.*

Collaborative Learning

At Level

The Pentagon Papers

1. Organize students into small groups. Have students review the information in the text about the Pentagon Papers and Daniel Ellsberg's role in releasing them to the *New York Times*. Have students in each group prepare written arguments either in favor of releasing the information or against releasing this information. Students should consider the advantages and disadvantages of releasing the papers.

2. Have volunteers from each group conduct a class debate on the issue. At the conclusion of the debate, guide students in a discussion of the second question in the feature: Are there circumstances under which First Amendment rights should be abridged? If so, what are those circumstances? **LS** **Interpersonal**

📖 Alternative Assessment Handbook, Rubrics 10: Debates; and 14: Group Activity

SECTION 2 From Watergate to Ford

BEFORE YOU READ

MAIN IDEA

The Nixon presidency became bogged down in scandal, leading to the first presidential resignation in American history and the administration of Gerald Ford.

READING FOCUS

1. What were the main events of the presidential election of 1972?

2. How did the Watergate scandal unfold?

3. Who was Gerald Ford, and what were the highlights of his presidency?

KEY TERMS AND PEOPLE

Watergate scandal
executive privilege
Saturday night massacre
transcript
Gerald R. Ford

TAKING NOTES As you read, take notes about the Watergate scandal and its aftermath. Record your notes in a graphic organizer like the one shown here.

Watergate

Before	During	After

A Piece of Tape Brings Down a Presidency

THE INSIDE STORY *How did a little piece of tape trigger one of history's great scandals?* When security guard Frank Wills first noticed the piece of tape covering a door latch in the garage of the Watergate hotel-office complex on June 17, 1972, he was not alarmed. He figured that someone during the day had probably been making deliveries and had wanted to keep the door from locking. Wills removed the tape and continued to patrol the building.

Later, however, Wills returned to the door and checked it again. Someone had replaced the tape he had removed earlier. This time, Wills called the police.

When the police arrived, they began their search for the intruders they suspected were in the building. Eventually, they surprised a group of five men who had broken into the offices of the Democratic National Committee, which were housed in the Watergate. The group was in the process of installing or repairing advanced eavesdropping equipment. They also had cameras and appeared to be planning to photograph the contents of filing cabinets.

It was not clear at first exactly why the burglars had broken into the office. Nor was it known right away whether they had been working on behalf of some other people or group. In fact, many dismissed the incident as nothing more

than the bumbling handiwork of petty crooks. As you will read, however, the story caught the attention of reporters at the *Washington Post*. As a result of their efforts, Watergate would soon be a household word.

► Frank Wills made the discovery that led to the arrest of the Watergate burglars.

1027

Teach the Main Idea

At Level

From Watergate to Ford

1. **Teach** Ask students the Reading Focus questions to teach this section.

2. **Apply** Draw three ladders for students to see. Label the top of each ladder with one of the three topics of this section: The Election of 1972, The Scandal Unfolds, Gerald Ford's Presidency. Guide students in a discussion of each topic. As you discuss the topic use the ladders as a graphic organizer.

3. **Review** As you review the section, have the students identify the main issues under each topic.

4. **Practice/Homework** Have the students write a one-page broadcast report for the evening television news that outlines the events of the Watergate scandal. **LS Visual-Spatial, Verbal-Linguistic**

📝 Alternative Assessment Handbook, Rubrics 11: Discussions; and 42: Writing to Inform

---

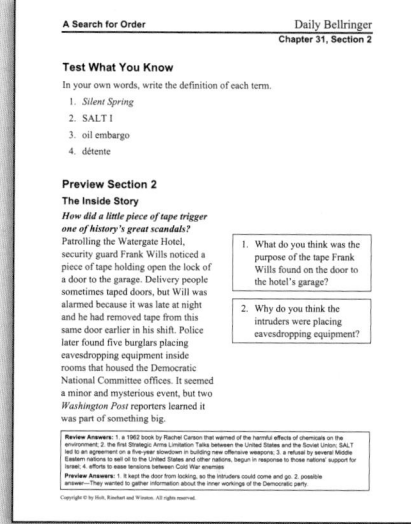
Academic Vocabulary

Review with students the high-use academic term in this section.

affect to change or influence something (p. 1029)

📝 CRF: Vocabulary Builder Activity, Section 2

Taking Notes

Before—Democratic National Committee headquarters break-in, Nixon reelected, Washington Post articles implicate Nixon campaign; During—Senate investigation, existence of White House tapes revealed, Nixon tries and fails to keep them private, Nixon resigns; After—Ford becomes president, pardons Nixon

---

❶ What were the main events of the presidential election of 1972? *Nixon wanted to ensure his election; used illegal tactics; Watergate break-in traced to members of Nixon's campaign team; Nixon defeated McGovern in a landslide*

The Election of 1972

Explain Why do you think Republican presidential advisers agreed to break into the Democratic National Committee headquarters? *wanted to take every measure to ensure that president was reelected*

Summarize How did the administration's role in the burglaries come to light? *discovery of check for $25,000 to one of burglars had been sent via presidential election campaign fund*

Make Inferences Why could the work of Bob Woodward and Carl Bernstein be considered brave and patriotic? *brave: Nixon despised the news media and often got even with those who crossed him; patriotic: Bernstein and Woodward were exposing Nixon's corruption, deception of the public*

📝 CRF: History and Geography Activity: Presidential Elections, 1968 and 1972

The Election of 1972

Richard Nixon's first term had been eventful. Though he had experienced his share of troubles, Nixon had also enjoyed many triumphs.

This was fortunate for Nixon, for he was deeply concerned about his political future. Indeed, many of his first-term actions had been aimed at shoring up support with the voters. Having both lost and won the presidency by tiny margins, he was leaving nothing to chance in 1972. In fact, he was prepared to support illegal actions to help ensure re-election.

Nixon had a well-earned reputation as a political scrapper from his days in Congress. At times Nixon's supporters used underhanded tactics during the first term of his presidency.

To do his political dirty work, Nixon advisers John Ehrlichman and H. R. Haldeman had created a group that came to be known as the "Plumbers." Their job was to respond to "leaks" of secret information—and to investigate Nixon's political enemies.

In 1971, for example, the Plumbers broke into the offices of Daniel Ellsberg's psychiatrist. Ellsberg was a former government official who had leaked key documents about the Vietnam War to the *New York Times*. These were the so-called Pentagon Papers. The Plumbers had hoped to find information they could use to embarrass Ellsberg and damage his reputation and credibility.

In 1972 Nixon and his team turned their attention to the upcoming presidential election. Nixon's chances for re-election seemed very good. Many of his recent moves, such as his trip to China, had been highly popular with the voters.

Still, Nixon's team did not rest easy. In early 1972, they hatched a plan to send a team of burglars to break into the offices of the Democratic National Committee at the Watergate hotel-office complex. The purpose of the burglary appeared to be to collect information about Democratic strategy that might be useful in the president's re-election campaign.

As you have read, the Watergate plot ended with the arrest of five burglars. The bungled break-in hardly made news when it occurred. It soon became clear that the men had connections to the president. National news organizations paid little attention to the incident.

The story did not die, however. Two young reporters on the staff of the *Washington Post*, Bob Woodward and Carl Bernstein, continued to investigate the break-in. They began to uncover troubling facts about the burglars' links to the White House. In August they reported that one of the Watergate burglars had received a $25,000 check that had been originally sent to the president's re-election campaign. By October the *Post* was reporting that the Watergate break-in was actually part of a widespread spying effort by members of the Nixon campaign.

TIME LINE

Watergate

June 17, 1972 Burglars were caught during a break-in at the Watergate (left).

June 18, 1972 Carl Bernstein and Bob Woodward helped report the first in a series of stories on the break-in (below).

November 7, 1972 Nixon won re-election in a landslide (above).

July 13, 1973 Alexander Butterfield revealed the existence of the White House taping system.

May 18, 1973 The Senate Watergate Committee began televised hearings into the scandal.

1028

Skills Focus: Drawing Conclusions   [At Level]

Reading Skill
The Watergate Break-In

1. Guide students in a discussion about the break-in at the Watergate Hotel. Remind students that someone had to be the person to tell the president that the break-in had not gone well, and in fact, a check given to one of the burglars had been traced to the president's election campaign fund.

2. Have students write a memo to President Nixon explaining the problems that occurred

during the break-in, the initial investigative reporting by Bernstein and Woodward, and the potential problems the president now faces as a result of the check.

3. Have volunteers present their memos to the class in the form of a presidential briefing. **LS** **Interpersonal, Kinesthetic**

📝 Alternative Assessment Handbook, Rubric 40: Writing to Describe

If the public noticed the *Post* stories at this time, it did not <u>affect</u> their voting. In November Nixon was handed one of the most overwhelming victories in U.S. history. His opponent, South Dakota senator and Vietnam War critic George McGovern, managed to carry only Massachusetts and the District of Columbia.

READING CHECK **Making Inferences** What can you infer about Nixon's level of confidence about the election of 1972 based on his actions?

The Scandal Unfolds

With his re-election, Nixon may have believed any trouble related to the Watergate break-in was behind him. He was wrong. Indeed, the scandal was just about to break.

By February 1973 seven men involved with the break-in had been convicted or had pleaded guilty to a variety of crimes. Among them were several officials who had worked in the White House and for Nixon's re-election campaign. During the burglars' trials questions emerged about what other White House officials may have been involved in illegal activities. People began to wonder whether Nixon had known about the wrongdoing taking place around him and helped to cover it up.

Meanwhile, the *Washington Post* continued to investigate the story. Now the public—and members of Congress—were paying attention to the stories.

In response to the growing controversy, Nixon ordered his staff to conduct a full investigation. In April 1973 Haldeman and Erlichman resigned from their White House jobs, as did Nixon's attorney general. In addition, Nixon fired John Dean, the lawyer he had appointed to investigate what was now called the **Watergate scandal**. The moves were meant to signal the president's tough action against wrongdoing. "There can be no whitewash at the White House," he declared.

These actions calmed many Republicans in Congress. For example, Representative Gerald Ford praised Nixon for "cleaning house." He declared, "I am absolutely positive he had nothing to do with this mess."

Democrats were not so sure. They demanded that the president appoint someone who was not part of his own administration to look into the scandal. This sort of independent investigator is now known as a special prosecutor. In May Nixon agreed to take this step. Nixon's attorney general Elliot Richardson appointed a Harvard Law School professor named Archibald Cox to the job.

Butterfield's bombshell Also in May, a Senate committee began its own investigation. The committee held televised hearings. Millions of viewers tuned in to get answers to the famous question of Tennessee Republican senator Howard Baker: "What did the president know, and when did he know it?"

ACADEMIC VOCABULARY
affect to change or influence something

THE IMPACT TODAY

Government
In May 2005 Americans learned the name of a key but secret figure in the Watergate story as reported by the *Washington Post*. Mark Felt, a former top FBI official, was revealed as the secret source for many *Washington Post* stories about the scandal.

April 30, 1974
The White House released edited transcripts of the tapes (left).

August 8, 1974
Richard Nixon announced his resignation from the presidency (right).

October 20, 1973
In the Saturday night massacre, Nixon fired the special prosecutor.

July 24, 1974
The Supreme Court ruled that the White House must turn over the tapes.

Skills FOCUS **INTERPRETING TIME LINES**
Which event suggests that the public was not immediately concerned by the events of June 1972?
See Skills Handbook, p. H14

A SEARCH FOR ORDER **1029**

1029

The Scandal Unfolds

Explain What is executive privilege? *presidential right to keep official conversations and meetings private; a presidential right to privacy*

Make Inferences What was so significant about the Saturday night massacre? *possible answer—President Nixon appeared to be challenging the constitutional system itself.*

Elaborate Why was the revelation of the White House tapes so significant? *Tapes would answer many questions about the president's involvement.*

📃 CRF: Biography: Harry A. Blackmun

📃 CRF: Biography: Barbara Jordan

📄 U.S. History Political Cartoon Activity: Cartoon 61: The Tape Tug-of-War

Primary Sources
Political Cartoon

Compare Have students examine the political cartoon and then create a cartoon of their own using the same caption but a different image. Have volunteers share their cartoons with the class.

PRIMARY SOURCES

Political Cartoon

At the height of the Watergate scandal in 1973, President Richard Nixon held a press conference to declare his innocence in the case. This political cartoon appeared shortly after that press conference.

President Nixon was famous for raising his arms and making the "V for Victory" sign with his fingers.

A sanctuary refers to a safe place for someone fleeing the law.

Speaking of sanctuaries . . .

Skills Focus **READING LIKE A HISTORIAN**

1. **Interpreting Political Cartoons** What is the "sanctuary" that Nixon is hiding behind?
2. **Identifying Points of View** What is the message that the artist is trying to send?

See *Skills Handbook*, pp. H28–H29, H31

The hearings produced plenty of drama. For example, early in June, John Dean told the committee that he had talked many times with Nixon about Watergate and its cover-up. These statements appeared to go against the president's own words. Then on July 16, 1973, a former presidential aide named Alexander Butterfield revealed that since 1971 Nixon had tape-recorded all conversations in his offices.

The Saturday night massacre News of the existence of White House tapes caused great excitement. Investigators realized that the recordings might answer many outstanding questions about the president's actions.

Nixon, however, did not want to give up the tapes. He argued that the constitutional separation of powers and the principle of executive privilege gave him the right to withhold them. **Executive privilege** holds that a president must be able to keep official conversations and meetings private. Such guarantees of privacy, the thinking goes, help ensure that the president gets open and honest advice.

Investigators rejected Nixon's claim of executive privilege. They argued that the tapes they were interested in hearing did not involve official presidential business. Rather, the investigators wanted to listen to Nixon's discussions of political matters—his re-election campaign—and possible illegal actions. Such conversations were not protected by executive privilege, investigators claimed.

Special Prosecutor Cox and the Senate Watergate committee continued to seek the tapes. They both issued subpoenas demanding Nixon hand them over. A subpoena is a legal order requiring the recipient to bring a certain item to court.

Nixon's response was harsh. In the so-called **Saturday night massacre**, he ordered attorney general Elliot Richardson to fire Special Prosecutor Cox. Richardson refused to do so and instead quit his job. Then Nixon ordered Richardson's assistant to fire Cox. He also refused and resigned. Nixon finally persuaded the third-ranking official in the Justice Department to fire Cox.

Many people were stunned by Nixon's actions. Not only did his innocence seem in doubt, it appeared that the president was challenging the constitutional system itself.

Skills Focus: Making Generalizations
At Level

Reading Skill
Watergate Journals

1. Review the information in the text about the Watergate scandal and the resignation of President Nixon. Tell students that the nation was shocked, but Americans were also saddened that their president felt it necessary to publicly declare, "I'm not a crook."

2. Have students create a series of diary or journal entries that might have been written by a political observer of the time. Have students entitle their journals "Innocence Lost." Have students include the observer's feelings as he or she learns the truth about the president's cover-up.

3. Have volunteers read their diary entries to the class. **LS Verbal-Linguistic, Logical-Mathematical**

📃 Alternative Assessment Handbook, Rubric 15: Journals

Answers

Reading Like a Historian 1. *the presidency, represented by the presidential seal;* **2.** *Nixon is lying about his role in the Watergate scandal and trying to use the power of the presidency to protect himself.*

❝ Whether ours shall continue to be a government of laws and not of men is now for Congress and ultimately the American people to decide. **❞**

—Archibald Cox, October 20, 1973

The crisis continues Public confidence in the president was very low. Yet a determined Nixon continued to deny his involvement in either the break-in or the cover-up. "People have got to know whether or not their president is a crook," he said. "Well, I'm not a crook." Meanwhile, he continued to delay release of the tapes. The White House also revealed that a critical, 18-minute portion of the tapes had been unexplainably erased.

Nixon's presidency was now in serious trouble. There were calls for impeachment and for Nixon to resign as president. As the pressure mounted in the spring of 1974, Nixon released some transcripts of the tapes. A **transcript** is a written record of a spoken event. Though Nixon denied it, the pages seemed to contain many suggestions that he had known about and covered up illegal activity. At the same time, the release of the transcripts did not satisfy investigators. They continued legal action aimed at gaining access to the tapes themselves.

Nixon resigns The Supreme Court of the United States finally settled the question of the White House tapes. In late July the Court ruled that Nixon had to obey the subpoenas and produce the tapes. Without waiting for the president to comply, the House Judiciary Committee voted to recommend impeachment of the president. The reasons included Nixon's alleged obstruction of justice and his failure to obey subpoenas.

Nixon could see that his support in Congress was thin. He must also have known that the tapes would reveal clear evidence of his own wrongdoing. On August 8, 1974, he spoke to the American people. For the first time in American history, a president resigned the office. "By taking this action," he said, "I hope that I will have hastened the start of the process of healing . . ."

READING CHECK **Sequencing** What was the key sequence of events as the Watergate scandal unfolded?

Gerald Ford's Presidency

Watergate was only one of the problems facing Richard Nixon. In early 1973, just as the Watergate scandal was about to explode, investigators began exploring the activities of Vice President Spiro T. Agnew, former governor of Maryland. Agnew was eventually accused of taking payments in return for political favors and cheating on his taxes. After pleading no contest to the tax charge, he resigned in disgrace. Agnew became only the second U.S. vice president to resign.

To replace Agnew, Nixon chose the Republican leader in the House of Representatives, **Gerald R. Ford**. With Nixon's resignation, Ford became president. He was the first person ever to become president without having been elected either president or vice president.

At his swearing in on August 9, 1974, Ford said he understood the unusual situation he was in. "I am acutely aware you have not elected me as your President," he noted. Still, he urged the nation and the government to move forward.

HISTORY'S VOICES

❝ My fellow Americans, our long national nightmare is over.

Our Constitution works; our great Republic is a government of laws and not of men. Here the people rule. **❞**

—Gerald R. Ford, August 9, 1974

Ford pardons Nixon Less than a month after taking office, President Ford granted a full pardon to Richard Nixon for any crime he may have committed. A pardon is a formal, legal forgiveness for a crime. Ford's action ensured that Nixon could not be tried in court or punished for any of his actions involving the Watergate affair. Many Americans reacted to the pardon with outrage. Some even wondered

Ford said he pardoned Nixon to shift attention "from the pursuit of a fallen President to the pursuit of the urgent needs of a rising nation." **Why did many people question this decision?**

Skills Focus: Making Generalizations

At Level

Reading Skill
President Ford Takes Office

1. Have students create two cartoons depicting Ford's presidency. One should reflect Ford's success as president; the other should reflect his failure.

2. Have volunteers share and explain their cartoons to the class.

3. Organize the students into small groups. Have each group work together to create a campaign slogan for President Ford's

re-election campaign. The slogan should focus on the president's accomplishments during his short time in office.

4. Have volunteers from each group share its slogan with the class. **LS Visual-Spatial, Verbal-Linguistic**

📇 Alternative Assessment Handbook, Rubrics 27: Political Cartoons; and 34: Slogans and Banners

---

Reading Focus

❸ Who was Gerald Ford, and what were the highlights of his presidency? *president after Nixon; pardoned Nixon; faced inflation; limited ability to act in foreign affairs; worked with Soviet Union on space project*

Gerald Ford's Presidency

Recall Why did Vice President Agnew resign? *tax fraud; took payments in return for political favors*

Identify Cause and Effect What was the effect of the presidential pardon granted to Nixon? *ensured that he would not go to trial or be punished in any way for Watergate*

Activity **Presidential Pardon** Have students write a press release announcing that President Ford has issued a complete pardon to President Nixon for his involvement in Watergate. **LS Verbal-Linguistic**

MISCONCEPTION
///ALERT

Remind students that Richard Nixon was not impeached. He resigned before impeachment proceedings and the trial in the Senate that would have taken place.

Info to Know

President Ford and Small Government President Ford believed that the influence of the federal government should be small. This political belief is best captured in the following quote: "A government big enough to give us everything we want is a government big enough to take from us everything we have."

Answers

Photo *possible answer—had lost faith in politicians after Watergate*

Reading Check *break-in, Washington Post exposure, Senate hearings, subpoena of White House tapes, resignation*

Reading Focus

Gerald Ford's Presidency

Identify Who served as secretary of state during the Ford administration? *Henry Kissinger*

Summarize What difficulties did President Ford face? *negative reaction to his pardon of President Nixon; Democrats controlled Congress; inflation*

• Review & Assess •

Close

Guide students in a discussion of the Watergate scandal and the events that led to President Nixon's resignation.

Review

- Online Quiz, Section 2
- Daily Test Practice Transparency

Assess

- **SE** Section 2 Assessment
- Progress Assessment: Section 2 Quiz
- Alternative Assessment Handbook

Reteach

- Interactive Reader and Study Guide, Section 2
- Interactive Skills Tutor CD-ROM

Answers

Reading Check *criticized for pardoning Nixon; some suspected he had made a deal with Nixon*

1032

---

openly whether Ford had promised to pardon Nixon prior to his resignation.

There was no evidence of such a deal, and Ford denied it flatly. He also took the unusual step of testifying about the pardon before a congressional committee.

Ford as president Ford, a Republican, found that his job as president was made more difficult by the fact that the Democrats controlled Congress. For example, he believed that inflation was a serious problem for the economy. To help fight it, he proposed cutting the amount of money that the U.S. government spent—spending that he felt drove prices even higher.

Congress, however, passed many spending bills against his wishes. Ford used his power to veto these spending bills on dozens of occasions. In spite of these efforts, inflation continued at a high rate.

In foreign affairs, President Ford had to overcome problems of the past. The experience of the Vietnam War had caused Congress to place limits on the powers of the president. In 1975 South Vietnam was about to fall to North Vietnam. Ford tried to send aid to the South Vietnamese, but Congress blocked this effort. The president did, however, help nearly 250,000 people flee South Vietnam before the arrival of the Communists.

Congress also refused to allow Ford to aid forces fighting Cuban-backed Communists in the African country of Angola. Ford complained about the loss of presidential power, but he seemed powerless in the matter.

Ford was able to take action when a Cambodian naval ship seized the American cargo ship *Mayaguez* and its 39-man crew. A military raid did recover the ship and crew, though 41 Americans died in the operation.

One of Ford's first acts as president had been to announce that Henry Kissinger would remain as his secretary of state. Ford also worked to maintain the Nixon policy of détente. He and Soviet leader Leonid Brezhnev agreed to new and larger limits on nuclear weapons.

Also during Ford's presidency, the United States and the Soviet Union worked jointly on a space project. The highlight was a meeting in space between U.S. and Soviet astronauts.

An election challenge In spite of his successes, Ford faced serious political problems. In the 1976 election, he faced opposition even from within his own party. In the primary elections to determine the Republican nominee, former California governor Ronald Reagan did well.

Ford won the nomination, but only after a close struggle. Clearly, the contest for the White House, in which he would face Governor Jimmy Carter of Georgia, would be difficult.

READING CHECK **Evaluating** How did the Watergate scandal affect Gerald Ford's presidency?

SECTION 2 ASSESSMENT

go.hrw.com
Online Quiz
Keyword: SD7 HP31

Reviewing Ideas, Terms, and People

1. **a. Describe** What were the circumstances of the break-in at the Watergate?
   b. Draw Conclusions Why might members of one political campaign want to spy on or steal information from another campaign?

2. **a. Define** Write a brief definition of each of the following terms: special prosecutor, **executive privilege**, subpoena
   b. Make Generalizations Why do you think the **Saturday night massacre** troubled many Americans?
   c. Elaborate Why do you think many people accused Nixon of acting as if he were above the law?

3. **a. Recall** How did the decision to **pardon** Nixon affect Ford?
   b. Make Inferences What can you infer from the fact that Ford issued so many vetoes?

Critical Thinking

4. **Identifying Cause and Effect** Copy the chart below and use information from the section to give effects of the causes given.

Cause	Effect
Watergate burglars arrested	
Butterfield reveals existence of tapes	
Nixon ordered to hand over tapes	
Ford pardons Nixon	

FOCUS ON SPEAKING

5. **Persuasive** Deliver a speech in which you argue either for or against President Ford's decision to pardon former President Nixon. Be sure to use information from the section in making your argument.

1032 CHAPTER 31

Section 2 Assessment Answers

1. **a.** Democratic Committee offices broken into, paid for by Nixon campaign
   b. gain access to plans and strategy

2. **a.** independent investigator; presidential right to keep official conversations and meetings private; requires recipient to bring a certain item to court
   b. possible answer—seemed the president challenging constitutional system
   c. possible answer—tried to bend rules

3. **a.** hurt him; public was outraged
   b. possible answers—Ford strongly

disagreed with congressional goals and means.

4. burglars—investigation into presidential connection, *Washington Post* articles; Butterfield—Senate subpoena; Nixon—attempts to erase parts of tapes; pardon—public assumed Ford made deal with Nixon

5. possible answers—for: public needs to know what happened; against: public needs to move past scandal

Carter's Presidency

BEFORE YOU READ

MAIN IDEA

Jimmy Carter used his reputation for honesty to win the presidency in 1976, but he soon met challenges that required other qualities as well.

READING FOCUS

1. What were some of the difficult domestic challenges facing Carter and the nation in the late 1970s?

2. What were Carter's greatest foreign-policy triumphs and challenges?

3. How did international crises affect Carter's presidency?

KEY TERMS AND PEOPLE

James Earl "Jimmy" Carter
SALT II
Camp David Accords
Ayatollah Ruhollah Khomeini

TAKING NOTES As you read, take notes about the successes and challenges Jimmy Carter faced in office. Record your notes in a graphic organizer like the one shown here.

Carter's Presidency

Domestic Issues	Foreign Policy

THE INSIDE STORY *How can the world's most powerful man show a common touch?* In American politics, an inaugural parade is typically a moment of great pomp and circumstance. But for **James Earl "Jimmy" Carter**, it was another opportunity to remind the American people that he would be a different kind of leader from the ones they had been used to in their recent, difficult past. It was a message Carter had stressed throughout his successful 1976 presidential campaign against President Gerald Ford.

Following his swearing in—at which the new president had asked to use the nickname Jimmy rather than his more formal, full name—Carter set off on the ceremonial trip down Pennsylvania Avenue from the Capitol to the White House. Jimmy Carter, however, would not make this trip in the traditional way. Rather than riding in a limousine, separated from the people by a layer of steel and bulletproof glass, he would walk. Surprising all observers, Carter, new first lady Rosalynn Carter, and their young daughter, Amy, left their limousine behind and strode among the crowd. All the while, the new leader of the most powerful nation on earth waved to the people and flashed his warm smile.

Carter's inaugural walk was without precedent in modern American political history. It was clear that he aimed to be a different type of president—one who did not consider himself above the people. Later, Carter would reinforce this message by refusing to allow the traditional playing of the song "Hail to the Chief" to announce his arrival at important events.

Jimmy Carter succeeded at creating the image of a down-to-earth, honest man. But he would soon learn that a reputation for trustworthiness was not enough to lead the nation through difficult times. ◼

WALKING
to the
White House

▼ The Carters charmed the nation by walking to the White House on inauguration day.

Teach the Main Idea

At Level

Carter's Presidency

1. **Teach** Ask students the Reading Focus questions to teach this section.

2. **Apply** Draw three large ovals for students to see. Label the top of each oval with one of the three topics of this section: Challenges Facing the Nation, Carter's Foreign Policy, International Crises. Have students scan the section and find at least three points for each topic. Have volunteers share their points with the class and write them in the ovals.

3. **Review** As you review the section, have students explain how the images in this section relate to each of the main topics.

4. **Practice/Homework** Have students write a one-page essay that summarizes the problems that plagued the Carter's presidency. **LS Visual-Spatial, Verbal-Linguistic**

Alternative Assessment Handbook, Rubrics 11: Discussions; and 40: Writing to Describe

---

1 What were some of the difficult domestic challenges facing President Carter and the nation in the late 1970s? *inflation, unemployment; energy crisis, environmental problems*

Challenges Facing the Nation

Recall What did America know of President Carter when he came to office? *honest, religious; former peanut farmer and governor of Georgia*

Summarize What steps did President Carter take to solve the energy problem? *established Department of Energy to help achieve goals of conservation and development of new energy supplies*

Make Inferences What was the significance of President Carter's promise to never lie to Americans? *rebuilt confidence in presidential office in aftermath of Watergate*

🗒 CRF: Literature Activity: *The Bluest Eye* by Toni Morrison

Linking to Today

Oil Consumption

Identify Guide students in a discussion of U.S. energy policy today. Which countries supply most of the U.S. oil imports? Does the nation still rely heavily on imported oil for its energy needs? What other sources of energy are being developed in their state?

Answers

Linking to Today *possible answers—gas prices would skyrocket, people would be unable to buy gas, unable to get to work, school and other places people need to go, force the government to create more widely used public transportation*

1034

Linking TO Today

Oil Consumption

In 1973 an oil embargo by Arab nations and higher prices led to long lines at American gas stations. Then in 1979 another energy crisis began.

A revolution in Iran stopped oil exports from that country. Exports later resumed but at a lower level than before. Other countries raised the price of their oil exports too, and prices skyrocketed in the United States. In response, President Carter urged Americans to consume less oil.

Although many people have worked during the last few decades to limit their use of oil, consumption has continued

to increase. Today the United States has less than 5 percent of the world's population but uses a quarter of its oil. Many people fear that the nation depends too heavily on foreign oil.

Most nations use oil primarily for heat and power. In the United States, however, transportation accounts for about two-thirds of oil use. During the Iraq War and following Hurricanes Katrina and Rita in 2005, rising gasoline costs troubled many consumers.

Making Inferences How might an oil embargo affect the United States today?

Cars streaming through their daily rush-hour commute in New York City

Challenges Facing the Nation

As he strode along the parade route on inauguration day, Jimmy Carter seemed in many ways to be the right man at the right time for the United States. The former peanut farmer and Georgia governor came across as an honest man of deep religious faith. He had never worked in Washington, D.C. His simple promise—"I'll never lie to you"—was just what the weary American public wanted to hear.

Carter wasted no time trying to help the nation heal some of the wounds from the past. A day after being sworn in as president, he issued a pardon to thousands of American men who had avoided the draft during the Vietnam War. The pardon enabled many men who had fled the country to return home without fear of being charged with a crime. Not everyone supported this action. Yet with it, Carter fulfilled one of his campaign promises.

The economy and energy Carter also tried to tackle problems in two other areas that had troubled earlier administrations. One was the economy. Inflation and unemployment stood at unacceptably high levels. Carter tried to address both concerns. During his time in office, the economy added many new jobs. Yet, as you will read, Carter was unable to bring

down inflation. Indeed, the problem only seemed to get worse.

Carter had more success in addressing the nation's energy problems. Recalling the oil crisis of 1973–1974 and fearing another one, he made the development of a national energy policy a top priority.

HISTORY'S VOICES

❝I know some of you may doubt that we face real energy shortages. The 1973 gasoline lines are gone, and our homes are warm again. But our energy problem is worse tonight than it was in 1973 or a few weeks ago in the dead of winter. It is worse because more waste has occurred, and more time has passed by without our planning for the future.❞

—Jimmy Carter, April 18, 1977

Carter's goals included easing dependence on foreign oil through energy conservation, developing new energy supplies, and loosening government regulation of the American oil industry. To help develop and carry out his new policies, he pushed for the establishment of a new cabinet-level Department of Energy.

Carter also sought to change the habits and attitudes of the American people. He urged Americans to conserve fuel. Citizens were asked to turn down their heat and air conditioning and drive fewer miles. Car buyers

---

Skills Focus: Drawing Conclusions   At Level

Reading Skill
Nixon's Domestic Policies

1. Organize students into small groups. Have half of the groups use the information in Section 1 to analyze Nixon's response to inflation, unemployment, and the oil crisis. Have the other half of the groups use the information in Section 3 to analyze Carter's response to inflation, unemployment, and energy problems.

2. Ask each group to share its responses with the class. Guide the class in a discussion

comparing the domestic policies of Nixon and Carter.

3. Have students make a list of Carter's strengths and weaknesses as president. Have students write a paragraph describing how these strengths and weaknesses influenced Carter's response to problems during his presidency.

LS Interpersonal, Verbal-Linguistic

🗒 Alternative Assessment Handbook, Rubrics 35: Solving Problems; and 43: Writing to Persuade

were urged to buy models that offered greater fuel efficiency. U.S. automakers were offered incentives to build cars that met new, tougher fuel-efficiency standards.

Carter promoted the development of alternative energy sources, such as solar and wind power. He promoted laws by which Americans were able to lower their taxes by installing energy-saving equipment in their homes.

These and other Carter energy policies were successful at helping reduce American dependence on foreign oil. American production of energy also increased under Carter.

Environmental concerns Carter was concerned not only about energy but also about the environment. He believed that conserving fuel was a key way to avoid "mounting pressure to plunder the environment." In order to prevent this from happening, the president led a years-long battle to win passage of the Alaska National Interest Lands Conservation Act. This law helped protect more than 100 million acres of land and doubled the size of the nation's park and wildlife refuge system.

But the Carter years were also marred by environmental questions and crises. In 1979 a mishap at a nuclear power plant located at Three Mile Island in Pennsylvania terrified the nation. For a time, officials seemed unsure how to correct problems that threatened a massive release of radiation into the environment. Some people in the immediate area of the plant were evacuated. In the end, very little radiation was released, and no one suffered any ill effects. However, public concern about the safety of nuclear power continued to grow.

Another environmental disaster was uncovered at Love Canal in New York. There, long-buried chemicals left behind by a chemical company began seeping up through the ground. Exposure to the chemicals was linked to the high rates of birth defects in the community. To solve the problem, the state of New York bought the homes of some 200 residents. The government then began the costly task of cleaning up the mess. Experts warned that there were likely many more toxic waste sites like Love Canal around the country.

READING CHECK Identifying Supporting Details Find two examples of how energy created major challenges for Carter and the nation.

Carter's Foreign Policy

Jimmy Carter came to office with no real foreign-policy experience and no background in federal government. He brought his own ideas to the field of foreign affairs with mixed results.

Carter also brought some new faces. Among them was Andrew Young. An African American with a background in the civil rights movement, Young served as American ambassador to the United Nations. His appointment helped highlight Carter's strong civil rights background. Indeed, Carter made dozens of top-level appointments of African Americans, women, and Hispanic Americans.

A focus on human rights During the presidential campaign, Carter had promised that the concept of human rights would be at the forefront of his foreign policy. This promise was repeated in his inaugural address when he declared, "Our commitment to human rights must be absolute." By human rights Carter meant the basic ideas of human freedom as outlined in the United Nations Declaration of Human Rights. For Carter, friends and enemies alike would be expected to uphold the highest standards in the treatment of their citizens.

ACADEMIC VOCABULARY
efficiency the ability to produce a desired result with little waste

THE IMPACT TODAY

Science and Technology
The Three Mile Island incident helped dampen interest in nuclear energy. Throughout the 1980s, 1990s, and early 2000s, the United States planned or built hardly any new nuclear power facilities.

Andrew Young at the UN

Andrew Young first rose to prominence during the civil rights movement in the 1950s and 1960s. *Why do you think Young's background helped prepare him to represent Carter's foreign policy?*

1035

● **Direct Teach** ●

Reading Focus

Challenges Facing the Nation

Recall What two environmental disasters occurred during the Carter administration? *Three Mile Island; Love Canal*

Make Inferences What was the significance of the discovery of the chemical seepage at Love Canal? *raised awareness of other toxic waste sites around the country, linked to high rates of birth defects in community*

🗐 CRF: Biography: Lois Gibbs

Reading Focus

❷ What were Carter's greatest foreign-policy triumphs and challenges? *improved relations with Soviet Union; SALT II; recognized China; Camp David Accords; Panama Canal Treaty; took human rights seriously*

Carter's Foreign Policy

Identify What was SALT II? *agreement between U.S. and Soviet Union limiting certain types of nuclear weapons*

Make Inferences What was the significance of Carter's appointment of Andrew Young as U.S. ambassador? *demonstrated Carter's commitment to civil and human rights*

Evaluate In what ways did President Carter's commitment to human rights help and hurt him? *possible answers— help: upheld high standards in treatment of citizens; hurt: may have placed human rights ahead of other issues; very difficult to change social issues in other countries*

Skills Focus: Drawing Conclusions
At Level

Reading Skill
Carter's Foreign Policy

Draw a two-column table for students to see. Label the top of the table *President Carter's Report Card*. Label the left column *Challenge* and the right column *Grade*. Have students copy the table onto their own paper and complete it. Have volunteers share their completed report cards with the class. **LS Visual-Spatial, Logical-Mathematical**

🗐 Alternative Assessment Handbook, Rubric 13: Graphic Organizers

🗐 Graphic Organizer Transparencies

President Carter's Report Card

Challenge	Grade
Inflation	
Unemployment	
Energy Crisis	
Human Rights	
Soviet Foreign Policy	
Foreign Policy with Egypt and Israel	
Foreign Policy with Afghanistan	
Foreign Policy with Iran	

Answers

Photo *possible answer—he was probably skilled at difficult negotiations*

Reading Check *economic issues, potential oil crisis, environmental concerns*

1035

Carter's Foreign Policy

Describe What were the key features of the Camp David Accords? *Egypt, Israel, and Jordan will work to resolve key questions about the future of Palestinians; Israel and Egypt will work to negotiate peace treaty; Egypt and Israel will grant each other full recognition*

Summarize What was the general American reaction to the Panama Canal treaty? *disapproval; giving up the canal represented decline in America's power*

Develop What does it mean when one country refuses to recognize another? *no diplomatic relationships, no economic ties, it is as if the other country does not exist*

 U.S. History Political Cartoon Activity: Cartoon 62: Who is Jimmy Kissinger?

QUICK FACTS **The Camp David Accords**

Describe Have students write a newspaper headline and brief article announcing that Egypt and Israel had reached an agreement to negotiate a peace treaty, and the two bitter enemies had shaken hands publicly.

Quick Facts Transparency: The Camp David Accords

go.hrw.com
Online Resources

KEYWORD: SD7 CH31
TOPIC: JIMMY CARTER

THE CAMP DAVID ACCORDS

The Camp David Accords were a major breakthrough in relations between Egypt and Israel, two countries that had fought several costly, bloody wars. Anwar el-Sadat, Jimmy Carter, and Menachem Begin (left to right) shake hands at the successful conclusion of their meeting at Camp David. Key parts of the accords declared that:

- Egypt and Israel, along with Jordan and Palestinian representatives, would agree to work to resolve questions about the Palestinians' future.

- Israel and Egypt would agree to work to negotiate a peace treaty.

- Egypt and Israel would agree to grant each other full recognition.

Soviet relations The Soviet Union was one target of President Carter's criticism about human rights violations. In a letter written to Soviet leader Leonid Brezhnev just days after taking office, Carter mentioned his concerns. Brezhnev's response politely but firmly declared that each side should stay out of the other's internal affairs.

In spite of disagreements over human rights, American and Soviet negotiators did conclude a treaty in 1979 known as **SALT II**. Talks on this treaty had begun at the end of SALT I, which you read about in Section 1. SALT II called for limits on certain kinds of nuclear weapons.

The Panama Canal treaties Another early Carter foreign-policy effort involved the Panama Canal. American control of the canal had been the source of conflict between the United States and Panama for some time. In 1977 Carter and Panama's leader reached an agreement by which Panama would take control of the canal by the end of 1999. The Senate narrowly approved the treaties Carter had negotiated. For many Americans, however, the loss of control of the canal represented a decline in American power.

Recognizing China In 1979 Carter took the final step in a process that had begun during the Nixon administration. He formally recognized the government of the Communist People's Republic of China. This move required the United States to formally end its official recognition of the Republic of China on Taiwan, which claimed to be the true Chinese government. Under Carter's action, however, the United States would officially recognize only one China—the Communist People's Republic.

The Camp David Accords Carter's greatest foreign-policy achievement centered on the long-standing conflict between Israel and Egypt. The two nations had fought frequently in recent decades. Fighting had occurred in 1967 and in the Yom Kippur War. In the aftermath of the 1973 war, Israel still occupied Egyptian territory on the Sinai Peninsula. Egypt still did not recognize Israel's right to exist. These were just some of the issues dividing the nations.

In 1978 Carter invited Egyptian president Anwar el-Sadat (AHN-wahr el-suh-DAHT) and Israeli prime minister Menachem Begin (men-AH-kem BAY-gin) to explore solutions to their bitter divisions. The meeting took place at Camp David, a presidential retreat located in Maryland. At the meeting, Carter painstakingly guided Sadat and Begin to a historic agreement. This came to be known as the **Camp David Accords**. For their efforts, Begin and Sadat were awarded the Nobel Peace Prize in 1979.

READING CHECK **Summarizing** What were the main highlights of Carter's foreign policy?

1036 CHAPTER 31

Differentiating Instruction

Below Level

Learners Having Difficulty

1. Discuss Carter's foreign policy accomplishments with the class. Have students work in pairs to create a time line of these accomplishments.

2. Have volunteers create a class time line for all to see. Have students correct their own work and retain the time line as a study tool.

3. Have students illustrate their time lines and have volunteers share their illustrations with the class. **LS Visual-Spatial, Kinesthetic**

Alternative Assessment Handbook, Rubric 36: Time Lines

Graphic Organizer Transparencies

Answers

Reading Check *human rights; Soviet relations, SALT II, Panama Canal treaties, recognized China, Camp David Accords*

International Crises

In his first years in office, Carter enjoyed some success and suffered through some difficulties. In 1979, however, a series of events occurred that seemed to overwhelm his presidency.

Soviets invade Afghanistan In 1978 the government of Afghanistan was toppled in a coup. The Communist leaders who took power were friendly to the Soviet Union. Yet this new pro-Soviet Afghan government was not stable. When it showed signs of crumbling in late 1979, the Soviets invaded. Their goal was to ensure continued Communist rule in Afghanistan.

The Soviet invasion of Afghanistan caused great anxiety within the United States. The attack not only threatened the U.S.– Soviet relationship. It also called into question Carter's ability to respond effectively to Soviet aggression. Carter's national security adviser summarized the problem in a memo to the president days after the invasion: "Soviet 'deci-

siveness'," he wrote, "will be contrasted with our restraint, which will no longer be labeled as prudent but increasingly as timid."

Several days after the invasion, Carter detailed the American response. It included the decision to block shipment of grain to the Soviet Union. In addition, Carter announced that the United States would not take part in the Olympics, set to take place in the Soviet Union in the summer of 1980.

Both the Olympic boycott and the grain embargo were unpopular with the public. To some they appeared to hurt the United States at least as much as they hurt the Soviet Union. As a result, Carter and the United States appeared weak.

Iranian hostage crisis While the Afghanistan crisis upset many Americans, it was not the major news story of the day. That story came from the country of Iran.

Early in 1979, a revolution in Iran had led to the overthrow of that country's long-time

Resolving the Hostage Crisis

National security adviser Zbigniew Brzezinski (ZBIG-nyoo bruzh-IN-skee) focused on U.S. interests.

Negotiation and compromise were well-known trademarks of Secretary of State Cyrus Vance.

" [I]t is important that we get our people back. But [our] greater responsibility is to protect the honor and dignity of our country and its foreign policy interests. At some point that greater responsibility could become more important than the safety of our diplomats. I hope we never have to choose between the hostages and our nation's honor in the world, but... [we] must be prepared for that occurrence. "

Zbigniew Brzezinski, 1979

" The President and this nation will ultimately be judged by our restraint in the face of provocation, and on the safe return of our hostages. We have to keep looking for ways to reach Khomeini and peacefully resolve this. "

Cyrus Vance, 1979

Skills FOCUS   READING LIKE A HISTORIAN

Identifying Points of View When the Carter administration launched a military mission to rescue the hostages, Vance resigned his post. How do the quotes help you to understand this fact?

See Skills Handbook, pp. H28–H29

A SEARCH FOR ORDER **1037**

Differentiating Instruction

Above Level

Advanced Learners/GATE

Research Required

1. Have students conduct outside research to learn more about the Iranian hostage crisis and the relationship between Iran and the United States today.

2. Have students create maps, visuals, charts and graphs to show the results of their research, including both historical and current trends, problems, and achievements.

3. Have students incorporate this information into a multimedia presentation about

the relationship between Iran and the United States.

4. Have volunteers share their multimedia presentations with the class. Then guide students in a discussion about the historical and current relationship between the two countries. **LS Visual-Spatial, Intrapersonal**

📓 Alternative Assessment Handbook, Rubrics 22: Multimedia Presentations; and 30: Research

Biography

Toni Morrison (1931–) Known for her celebration of the African American community, Toni Morrison combines compassion and acute observation in her novels on the experiences of African American women. In Morrison's first novel, *The Bluest Eye*, a teenage African American girl longs to conform to white standards of beauty. In 1987, Morrison published her most critically acclaimed work, *Beloved*, which chronicles the experiences of a slave and her daughter. In all of her works, Morrison uses mythic elements to depict the struggle of African Americans to find their individual and cultural identity.

Answers

Reading Like a Historian *Vance says he wanted to solve the conflict peacefully, not militarily.*

1037

Close

Guide students in a discussion of the challenges, successes, and shortcomings of the Carter administration.

Review

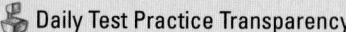 Online Quiz, Section 3

Daily Test Practice Transparency

Assess

SE Section 3 Assessment

Progress Assessment: Section 3 Quiz

Alternative Assessment Handbook

Reteach

Interactive Reader and Study Guide, Section 3

Interactive Skills Tutor CD-ROM

ruler, known as the shah. The shah had long enjoyed American support, but among his people he had built a reputation for brutal repression. After his overthrow, Iran came under the control of an Islamic religious leader known as the **Ayatollah Ruhollah Khomeini** (eye-uh-TOHL-uh roo-HAHL-uh koh-MAYN-ee). Khomeini preached a strongly anti-American message.

In October 1979 the American government allowed the shah to enter the United States to receive treatment for cancer. This action enraged many Iranians. On November 4 a mob attacked the American embassy in Tehran, Iran's capital. They captured several dozen American employees. It soon became clear that Iran's leaders supported this attack.

In the United States, the hostage-taking was greeted with outrage. Newscasts fueled American anger by showing nightly scenes of Iranian protesters burning American flags.

President Carter appeared powerless to end the Iranian hostage crisis. His efforts to negotiate the safe return of the hostages went nowhere. He then approved a military mission to rescue the hostages. This failed tragically when mechanical problems led to a helicopter crash that killed eight soldiers. The scenes of smoldering American wreckage in the Iranian desert hurt Carter's chances for re-election.

A crisis of confidence The hostage crisis dragged on throughout the presidential election year of 1980. To make matters worse for Carter, the events in Iran had disrupted the production of oil there. As a result, gasoline prices shot up in 1979. This helped drive up prices for many goods in the United States. Inflation soared. The economy struggled badly.

Carter was in serious trouble politically. Even he seemed to recognize the threat as he described the downcast mood of the country in a major speech.

HISTORY'S VOICES

❝It is a crisis of confidence.

It is a crisis that strikes at the very heart and soul and spirit of our national will. We can see this crisis in the growing doubt about the meaning of our own lives and in the loss of a unity and purpose for our nation.❞

—Jimmy Carter, July 15, 1979

Carter's view of the mind-set of the nation was not incorrect. What he did not realize was that many voters held him responsible for this crisis of confidence.

READING CHECK **Making Inferences** Why did the events of 1979 and 1980 seem to overwhelm Carter's presidency?

SECTION 3 ASSESSMENT

go.hrw.com
Online Quiz
Keyword: SD7 HP31

Reviewing Ideas, Terms, and People

1. **a. Identify** What were the key domestic issues facing the Carter administration?
   b. Explain Explain how energy was at the center of so many of the challenges facing the United States in the late 1970s.
   c. Predict How successful do you think President Carter would be in his call for the American people to change their energy habits?

2. **a. Recall** What was the guiding principle behind Jimmy Carter's foreign policy?
   b. Draw Conclusions Why do you think the **Camp David Accords** are considered Carter's greatest foreign-policy success?
   c. Elaborate How did Carter's focus on human rights in foreign policy differ from the policy of realpolitik stressed by Nixon and Ford?

3. **a. Identify** Who was **Ayatollah Ruhollah Khomeini**?
   b. Make Generalizations How did the American people interpret Carter's responses to the crises of 1979–1980?

Critical Thinking

4. **Identifying the Main Idea** Copy the chart below and use information from the section to record details that support the main idea of the section.

Domestic Issues — The Carter Presidency — Crises of 1979–1980 — Foreign Policy

FOCUS ON WRITING

5. **Descriptive** Using information from the section, write a brief description of what you think Jimmy Carter was like as a president. Include information about how you think his style and personality helped and hurt him.

1038 CHAPTER 31

Section 3 Assessment Answers

Answers

Reading Check *the public blamed him for the problems; he did not know how to fix them and still gain the approval of the public*

1038

1. **a.** economy, energy, environment
   b. U.S. dependent on foreign oil; lack of conservation; oil embargo
   c. possible answer—not successful, energy needed for heating and automobiles

2. **a.** human rights
   b. ended a long-standing conflict
   c. based on ideals, not realistic views of national interest

3. **a.** Islamic leader who took over Iran
   b. blamed him; saw him as weak

4. Domestic Issues—struggling economy, energy problems, environmental concerns; Foreign Policy—human rights, Soviet relations, Panama Canal treaties, recognized China, Camp David Accords; Crises of 1979–1980—hostage crisis, Soviet invasion of Afghanistan

5. possible answers—compassion and honesty helped earn trust of public; unwillingness to use military created difficulties in foreign policy

Regents of the University of California v. *Bakke* (1978)

Why It Matters Affirmative action programs have helped create opportunities for many minorities. However, favoring a minority applicant for a job or for a spot in graduate school may also mean that a qualified majority applicant will be turned down. *Bakke* was the first Supreme Court case to consider the constitutionality of what is called "reverse discrimination."

Background of the Case

A white male named Alan Bakke applied to the medical school of the University of California at Davis and was not accepted. The school had a special program that set aside a certain number of spots for minority applicants. Under this program, some minority students with lower qualifications than Bakke were admitted to the school. Bakke sued, and the Supreme Court of California agreed that it was unconstitutional to discriminate in favor of the minority applicants. The university appealed to the Supreme Court.

The Decision

In a 5–4 ruling, the Court found that the University's "set-aside" program was unconstitutional because it totally excluded white applicants from consideration for certain spots. The Court ordered Bakke admitted to the university. The Court also held that the school could consider race as one factor in future admissions decisions.

Bakke did not resolve the question of just what role affirmative action could play in university admissions. This means that the *Bakke* decision did not offer clear guidance on how affirmative action could properly be used. However, the opinion did help focus national attention on this difficult question.

THE IMPACT TODAY Affirmative action programs such as those that led to the *Bakke* case have played a part in increasing diversity in many graduate school programs, including the law school at the University of Michigan. (The photo above is from a class at that university.) The question of just where the line lies between reasonable affirmative action and improper reverse discrimination continues to stir controversy in the United States.

CRITICAL THINKING

go.hrw.com
Research Online
Keyword: SS Court

1. **Analyze the Impact** Using the keyword above, read about the Supreme Court's decision in *Sweatt v. Painter* (1950). How did the issues in *Sweatt* differ from the issues in *Bakke*? What changes had taken place in the country between the decisions?

2. **You Be the Judge** After *Bakke*, the University of Michigan Law School began giving extra consideration in the admissions process to African Americans, Hispanic Americans, and Native Americans. These applicants therefore had a greater chance of admission than students with similar qualifications from other groups. Is this policy constitutional? Write a short paragraph explaining your answer.

A SEARCH FOR ORDER **1039**

Regents of the University of California v. *Bakke*

Word Help

majority larger percentage or number

Info to Know

Medical Program at U.C. Davis When Allan Bakke applied to medical school at U.C. Davis, 16 of the 100 openings were reserved for members of minority groups. Minority students could compete for any of the 100 openings, but white students had only 84 openings.

Legal Grounds The Fourteenth Amendment provides that no state shall deny any person equal protection of the law. Title VI of the 1964 Civil Rights Act says, "No person in the United States shall, on the ground of race, color, or national origin be excluded from participation in, be denied the benefits of, or be subjected to discrimination under any program or activity receiving federal financial assistance." These were the legal grounds for the *Bakke* case.

Skills Focus: Analyzing Primary Sources

At Level

Reading Like a Historian Skill
The *Bakke* Case

Research Required

1. Have students work in small groups to learn more about the justices' opinions in this case. Have students obtain copies of the actual opinions written by the justices and compare the opinions in their groups.

2. Have students in each group prepare a summary of the major points in each decision. Have volunteers from each group share their summaries with the class.

3. Select nine students and have them represent the justices. Have these students present each justice's view on the *Bakke* case to the class.
LS Interpersonal, Kinesthetic

📖 Alternative Assessment Handbook, Rubrics 24: Oral Presentations; and 30: Research

Answers

Critical Thinking 1. *in* Sweatt *case, separate facilities existed for black and white students; schools had been desegregated, quotas and affirmative action programs had been established*
2. *possible answers—no, because white applicants should not be penalized; yes, because race can be one of several factors in admissions decisions*

The Watergate Crisis

Word Help

subpoena a written legal order

grist grain that is to be ground in a mill (often used figuratively)

Primary Source

In a 1999 interview, Herbert Block reflected on the legacy of President Nixon: "Richard Nixon, even though he is no longer with us, keeps reminding us of what he was like through the tapes that keep being released. In that respect, you might say that he is still his own worst enemy although there might be lots of competition for that title."

— Herbert Block

1999

The Watergate Crisis

Historical Context The documents below provide information about taped conversations in the White House, which became an important part of the Watergate investigation.

Task Examine the documents and answer the questions that follow. Then write an essay on the proposed topic. Use facts from the documents and from the chapter to support the position you take in your thesis statement.

DOCUMENT 1

The Gallup Organization is a polling group. One of the statistics they regularly track is a president's job-approval rating—the percentage of people who agree with the president's actions and decisions. This graph shows changes in job-approval ratings for President Nixon during the Watergate crisis.

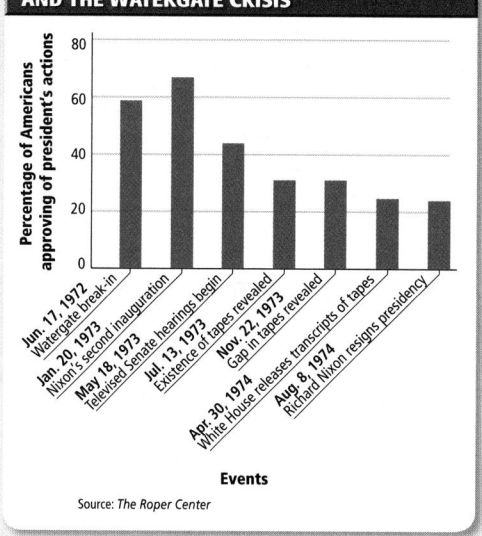

PRESIDENTIAL APPROVAL RATINGS AND THE WATERGATE CRISIS

Percentage of Americans approving of president's actions

Events

Jun. 17, 1972 Watergate break-in
Jan. 20, 1973 Nixon's second inauguration
May 18, 1973 Televised Senate hearings begin
Jul. 13, 1973 Existence of tapes revealed
Nov. 22, 1973 Gap in tapes revealed
Apr. 30, 1974 White House releases transcripts of tapes
Aug. 8, 1974 Richard Nixon resigns presidency

Source: *The Roper Center*

DOCUMENT 2

On April 29, 1974, President Nixon addressed the nation. He talked about the subpoena demanding additional transcripts for tape recordings made in the White House and his decision to obey the subpoena.

"Ever since the existence of the White House taping system was first made known last summer, I have tried vigorously to guard the privacy of the tapes. I have been well aware that my effort to protect the confidentiality of Presidential conversations has heightened the sense of mystery about Watergate and, in fact, has caused increased suspicions of the President. Many people assume that the tapes must incriminate the President, or that otherwise, he would not insist on their privacy.

"But the problem I confronted was this: Unless a President can protect the privacy of the advice he gets, he cannot get the advice he needs . . .

I want there to be no question remaining about the fact that the President has nothing to hide in this matter . . . "

I realize that these transcripts will provide grist for many sensational stories in the press. Parts will seem to be contradictory with one another, and parts will be in conflict with some of the testimony given in the Senate Watergate committee hearings . . .

In giving you these records—blemishes and all—I am placing my trust in the basic fairness of the American people."

Skills Focus: Analyzing Secondary Sources

At Level

Reading Like a Historian Skill

Research Required

The Question of Character

1. Tell students that in his later years, Richard M. Nixon tried to rehabilitate his reputation through his books, hoping to go down in history as a great statesman rather than as the only U.S. president ever forced to resign.

2. Divide students into groups of four or five students. Have each group conduct research on Nixon's accomplishments, the various charges that were made against him, and his attempts to deflect them, such as his "Checkers" speech. (Students may want to look at Herblock's other cartoons depicting Nixon.)

3. Have students write a brief essay in which they explain their impression of Nixon's true character based on the research they conducted.

4. Ask volunteers to read their character sketches to the rest of the class.

LS Interpersonal, Verbal-Linguistic

DOCUMENT 3

Cartoonist Herbert Block, known as Herblock, created many cartoons commenting on Nixon's presidency and the Watergate crisis. This cartoon ran in newspapers on May 24, 1974.

From *Herblock: A Cartoonist's Life* (TIMES BOOKS, 1998)

DOCUMENT 4

In this transcript of one of the White House tapes, President Richard Nixon talks with White House Chief of Staff H. R. Haldeman. The two men discuss the FBI investigation, specifically mentioning acting FBI director L. Patrick Gray and assistant director Mark Felt. This exchange, which took place on June 23, 1972, is known as the Smoking Gun conversation.

Haldeman: Okay—that's fine. Now, on the investigation, you know, the Democratic break-in thing, we're back to the—in the, the problem area because the FBI is not under control . . . and . . . their investigation is now leading into some productive areas . . . And, and it goes in some directions we don't want it to go. . . [T]he way to handle this now is for us to have [Deputy Director of the CIA Vernon A.] Walters call Pat Gray and just say, "Stay . . . out of this . . . this is ah, business here we don't want you to go any further on it." That's not an unusual development . . .
President: Um huh.
Haldeman: . . . and, uh, that would take care of it.
President: What about Pat Gray . . . ?
Haldeman: He'll call Mark Felt in . . . and say, "We've got a signal from across the river to, to put the hold on this." And that will fit rather well because the FBI agents who are working the case, at this point, feel that's what it is. This is CIA.

SKILLS FOCUS · READING LIKE A HISTORIAN

1. **a. Identify** Refer to Document 1. What event corresponds to Nixon's lowest job-approval rating?
   b. Interpret How did developments in Watergate affect public opinion regarding President Nixon?

2. **a. Identify** Refer to Document 2. Why does the president say he is releasing the transcripts?
   b. Evaluate Why do you think the president may have decided to make this speech to the American people?

3. **a. Identify** Refer to Document 3. What is shown in the cartoon?
   b. Elaborate What is the cartoonist's opinion of Nixon?

4. **a. Identify** Refer to Document 4. Why does Haldeman refer to the break-in as a "problem area"?

   b. Explain How does the president respond to Haldeman's suggestion to end the FBI investigation?
   c. Analyze Why was this called the Smoking Gun conversation?

5. **Document-Based Essay** Consider the question below and form a thesis statement. Using examples from Documents 1, 2, 3, and 4, create an outline and write a short essay supporting your position.
   What role did the White House tapes play in the Watergate crisis?

   See **Skills Handbook, pp. H17, H28–H29, H31**

Collaborative Learning

At Level

The White House Tapes

1. Guide the class in a discussion of Nixon's April 29, 1974 address and the revelations that were made in the "Smoking Gun" conversation. How did Nixon continue to try to manipulate the way people thought of him? How well do students think he succeeded?

2. Pair students. Have each pair draw a political cartoon related to the Watergate crisis. They

   may want to illustrate either Document 2 or Document 4.

3. Have each pair share its cartoon with the rest of the class. **LS Interpersonal, Visual-Spatial**

   📄 Alternative Assessment Handbook, Rubric 27: Political Cartoons

Document-Based Investigation

Info to Know

The 18 ½ Minute Gap Rose Mary Woods, Nixon's personal secretary, gained instant fame when she was called before Judge John Sirica's court. Woods was asked to explain an 18 ½ minute gap in the tape of a conversation between Nixon and H. R. Haldeman three days after the Watergate break-in. Woods said that she must have accidentally caused the gap. Her attempts to demonstrate to the court how she might have accidentally erased that portion of the tape during a telephone conversation came to be known as "the Rose Mary Woods stretch."

Answers

Reading Like a Historian 1. a. *resignation;* **b.** *with each development, approval rating declined;* **2. a.** *to try to end the public's suspicion of him and his motives;* **b.** *possible answer—to limit the damage the transcripts might cause; to justify what the public would read in the transcripts;* **3. a.** *Nixon apparently trying to add in the word "NOT" between the words "I AM" and "A CROOK."* **b.** *He appears to think that Nixon is a crook and a liar.* **4. a.** *The FBI is tracing the break-in to those associated with Nixon.* **b.** *He agrees with it.* **c.** *because it proves Nixon knew about the Watergate break-in and encouraged attempts to end the investigation;* **5.** *possible answer— demonstrated Nixon's willingness to tamper with evidence; illustrated Nixon knew about the break-in and attempts to cover it up*

1041

Chapter Review

Answers

Visual Summary

Review and Inquiry Review the information in the visual summary with students. Then divide students into six groups. Have three groups provide an oral summary of the achievements of one of the presidents discussed in the chapter: Nixon, Ford, and Carter. Then have the other three groups provide an oral summary of the problems that faced each of these presidents.

📽 Quick Facts Transparency: A Search for Order

Reviewing Key Terms and People

1. transcript
2. realpolitik
3. Camp David Accords
4. *Apollo 11*
5. Saturday night massacre
6. OPEC
7. Executive privilege
8. Ayatollah Ruhollah Khomeini
9. SALT I
10. détente

Comprehension and Critical Thinking

11. a. opened talks with Communist China, which put Russia on the defensive since Russia and China were rivals
b. took liberal actions when necessary even though he was largely conservative in philosophy and viewpoint
c. possible answers—it was the best for the country; he wanted to make a significant change in the government; politically good moves

12. a. to gain access to information and Democratic strategies that could help Nixon win the election
b. possible answer—tense, a constant struggle between the powers in the federal government
c. possible answer—maybe; sometimes honesty is the best policy; lying and cover-ups lead to serious problems

Visual Summary: A Search for Order

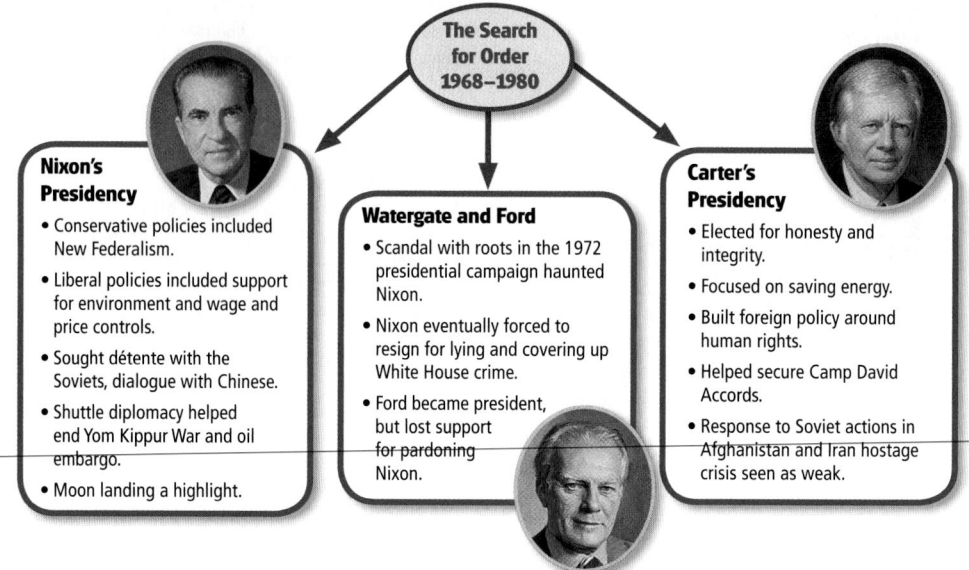

The Search for Order 1968–1980

Nixon's Presidency
- Conservative policies included New Federalism.
- Liberal policies included support for environment and wage and price controls.
- Sought détente with the Soviets, dialogue with Chinese.
- Shuttle diplomacy helped end Yom Kippur War and oil embargo.
- Moon landing a highlight.

Watergate and Ford
- Scandal with roots in the 1972 presidential campaign haunted Nixon.
- Nixon eventually forced to resign for lying and covering up White House crime.
- Ford became president, but lost support for pardoning Nixon.

Carter's Presidency
- Elected for honesty and integrity.
- Focused on saving energy.
- Built foreign policy around human rights.
- Helped secure Camp David Accords.
- Response to Soviet actions in Afghanistan and Iran hostage crisis seen as weak.

Reviewing Key Terms and People

Complete each sentence by filling the blank with the correct term or person.

1. Nixon at first refused to hand over the Watergate tapes, but he did offer to provide a _____.
2. Henry Kissinger practiced something called _____ rather than following broad rules for the conduct of foreign policy.
3. Carter helped bring about the _____ between Israel and Egypt.
4. The nation watched in wonder as _____ fulfilled its mission to the moon.
5. During the _____ Nixon ordered the firing of the special prosecutor.
6. The organization called _____ organized an oil embargo against the United States.
7. _____ holds that a president must be able to keep official conversations and meetings private.

8. Following the overthrow of the shah, _____ became the leader of Iran.
9. During Nixon's administration, the United States and the Soviets reached an agreement limiting nuclear weapons known as _____.
10. The improvement in relations between the United States and the Soviet Union in the early 1970s was known as _____.

Comprehension and Critical Thinking

SECTION 1 *(pp. 1018–1025)*

11. a. Describe What was the significance of President Nixon's trip to the People's Republic of China in 1972?
b. Contrast In what ways did Nixon's policies while president differ from some of his previously stated positions?

13. a. came across as an honest man of deep religious faith, appeared to be someone the public could trust, made a simple promise "I'll never lie to you"
b. possible answer—as a well-meaning, but ineffective president who had trouble managing crises
c. possible answer—try to blame him for America's struggles and show that a new president will provide a solution

Using the Internet

14. Go to the HRW Web site and enter the keyword shown to access a rubric for this activity.

KEYWORD: SD7 CH31

History's Impact video program

Review the video to answer the closing question: Why is freedom of the press a crucial part of a democratic society?

c. Elaborate What do you think were the reasons for Nixon's willingness to pursue goals and programs that varied greatly from his past conservative beliefs?

SECTION 2 *(pp. 1027–1032)*

12. a. Recall What was the purpose of the break-in at the Watergate Hotel?

b. Summarize How would you summarize the conflict between Nixon and those investigating the Watergate scandal?

c. Predict Do you think Nixon could have survived had he admitted early in the scandal that his office had been involved in the Watergate break-in? Explain.

SECTION 3 *(pp. 1033–1038)*

13. a. Describe What qualities did Jimmy Carter use to win public support in the election of 1976?

b. Make Generalizations How did Carter come to be regarded by the public by the end of his term?

c. Predict How do you think Carter's opponents will attack his record in the election of 1980?

Using the Internet

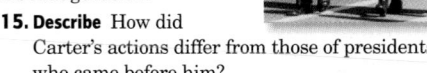

go.hrw.com
Practice Online
Keyword: SD7 CH31

14. The Iran hostage crisis that began in 1979 caused public outrage—and deep concern about the waning prestige of the United States. Using the keyword above, do research to learn more about the hostage crisis. Then create a time line and brief report on its effects on the presidential election of 1980.

Analyzing Primary Sources

Reading Like a Historian This picture shows Jimmy Carter, his wife Rosalynn, and daughter Amy walking to the White House on the day of his inauguration.

15. Describe How did Carter's actions differ from those of presidents who came before him?

16. Make Inferences What kind of message do you think Carter tried to send through his decision to walk?

Critical Reading

Read the passage in Section 2 that begins with the heading "The Saturday night massacre." Then answer the questions that follow.

17. Nixon sought to have the special prosecutor fired because

A. he revealed information about the Watergate tapes.

B. he sought to obtain the tapes in spite of Nixon's refusal to hand them over.

C. he was not doing enough to get to the bottom of the Watergate scandal.

D. he was thought to be part of the cover-up.

18. Which of the following most closely represents Nixon's argument against handing over the tapes?

A. The tapes included no relevant information.

B. He was afraid the tapes would prove his guilt.

C. He believed it was his legal right as president to keep official conversations private.

D. He did not believe that the Constitution permitted the creation of a special prosecutor.

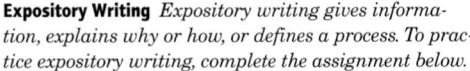

FOCUS ON WRITING

Expository Writing *Expository writing gives information, explains why or how, or defines a process. To practice expository writing, complete the assignment below.*

Writing Topic Ford's Pardon of Nixon

19. Assignment Based on what you have read in this chapter, write a paragraph that describes the public's reaction to President Ford's pardon of Richard Nixon. If you have acess to a computer, use a word processing program to create and format your paragraph.

Answers

Analyzing Primary Sources

15. Previous presidents drove past the public in cars or rode on horses rather than walking.

16. possible answer—wanted to appear as humble servant of the people and as a regular citizen

Critical Reading

17. B

18. C

Focus on Writing

19. possible answer—Public was concerned that President Ford had made a secret deal with Nixon— the presidency for a full pardon. Like all citizens, Nixon should not be above the law and deserved a trial to determine his innocence or guilt.

A rubric for this activity is provided in Chapter Resource File: Focus on Writing: Ford's Pardon of Nixon.

History's Impact Video Program

a free press informs the public and provides a check on government power

---

Review and Assessment Resources

Review and Reinforce

- CRF: Chapter Review Activity
- Quick Facts Transparencies: Causes and Effects of the Yom Kippur War, The Camp David Accords, A Search for Order
- Spanish Chapter Summaries Audio CD Program
- Online Chapter Summaries in Spanish
- OSP Holt PuzzlePro; Quiz Show for ExamView
- Quiz Game CD-ROM

Assess

- PASS: Chapter Test, Forms A and B
- Alternative Assessment Handbook
- OSP ExamView Test Generator, Chapter Test
- Differentiated Instruction Modified Worksheets and Tests CD-ROM: Chapter Test
- HOAP Holt Online Assessment Program (in the Premier Online Edition)

Reteach/Intervene

- Interactive Reader and Study Guide
- Differentiated Instruction Teacher Management System: Lesson Plans for Differentiated Instruction
- Differentiated Instruction Modified Worksheets and Tests CD-ROM: Chapter Test
- Interactive Skills Tutor CD-ROM

go.hrw.com
Online Resources
KEYWORD: SD7 CH31

Chapter 32 Planning Guide

A Conservative Era

Chapter Overview	Reproducible Resources	Technology Resources
CHAPTER 32 pp. 1044–1075 **Overview: In this chapter, students will analyze the changes, events, and ideas that arose during the Reagan and Bush years.**	**Differentiated Instruction Teacher Management System:*** • Instructional Benchmarking Guides • Lesson Plans for Differentiated Instruction **Interactive Reader and Study Guide:** Chapter Summary* **Chapter Resource File:*** • Writing for the SAT: The Space Shield • Social Studies Skills Activity: Sequencing • Chapter Review Activity **American History Outline Maps** **Pre-AP Activities Guide for American History***	**Live Ink® Online Reading Help** **Student Edition on Audio CD Program** **Differentiated Instruction Modified Worksheets and Tests CD-ROM** **Interactive Skills Tutor CD-ROM** **United States History Primary Source Library CD-ROM** **Power Presentations with Video CD-ROM** **History's Impact: American History Video Program (VHS/DVD):** A Conservative Era **Online Chapter Summaries in Spanish**
Section 1: **Reagan's First Term** **The Main Idea:** In 1980 a conservative government took control with Ronald Reagan's election.	**Differentiated Instruction Teacher Management System:** Section 1 Lesson Plan* **Interactive Reader and Study Guide*** **Chapter Resource File:*** • Vocabulary Builder Activity, Section 1	**Daily Bellringer Transparency:** Section 1* **Daily Test Practice Transparency:** Section 1*
Section 2: **Reagan's Foreign Policy** **The Main Idea:** President Reagan took a hard line against communism around the world.	**Differentiated Instruction Teacher Management System:** Section 2 Lesson Plan* **Interactive Reader and Study Guide*** **Chapter Resource File:*** • Vocabulary Builder Activity, Section 2	**Daily Bellringer Transparency:** Section 2* **Daily Test Practice Transparency:** Section 2*
Section 3: **A New World Order** **The Main Idea:** In 1988 Reagan's vice president, George H.W. Bush, won election.	**Differentiated Instruction Teacher Management System:** Section 3 Lesson Plan* **Interactive Reader and Study Guide*** **Chapter Resource File:*** • Vocabulary Builder Activity, Section 3	**Daily Bellringer Transparency:** Section 3* **Map Transparency:** The Persian Gulf War, 1991* **Daily Test Practice Transparency:** Section 3*
Section 4: **Life in the 1980s** **The Main Idea:** The 1980s and early 1990s saw major technological, economic, and social changes.	**Differentiated Instruction Teacher Management System:** Section 4 Lesson Plan* **Interactive Reader and Study Guide*** **Chapter Resource File:*** • Vocabulary Builder Activity, Section 4	**Daily Bellringer Transparency:** Section 4* **Daily Test Practice Transparency:** Section 4*

Review, Assessment, Intervention

 Quick Facts Transparencies: Reagan's Foreign Policy, A Conservative Era

 Spanish Chapter Summaries Audio CD Program

 Progress Assessment Support System (PASS): Chapter Test*

Differentiated Instruction Modified Worksheets and Tests CD-ROM: Modified Chapter Test

OSP One-Stop Planner CD-ROM: ExamView Test Generator (English/Spanish)

HOAP Holt Online Assessment Program (HOAP), in the Holt Premier Online Student Edition

 PASS: Section 1 Quiz*

 Online Quiz: Section 1

 Alternative Assessment Handbook

 PASS: Section 2 Quiz*

 Online Quiz: Section 2

Alternative Assessment Handbook

 PASS: Section 3 Quiz*

Online Quiz: Section 3

Alternative Assessment Handbook

 PASS: Section 4 Quiz*

 Online Quiz: Section 4

 Alternative Assessment Handbook

NC RESOURCES

The following resources were developed to help North Carolina educators teach the standards and objectives of North Carolina's eleventh grade standard course of study in United States history.

- United States history EOC Test Prep Workbook
- Teacher's Support System
- North Carolina One-Stop Planner

And be sure to direct your students to **go.hrw.com** for online access to the EOC Test Prep Workbook.

go.hrw.com
EOC Test Prep
KEYWORD: SE7 NC

Holt Online Learning

go.hrw.com
Teacher Resources
KEYWORD: SD7 TEACHER

go.hrw.com
Student Resources
KEYWORD: SD7 CH32

- Document-based Questions
- Interactive Multimedia Activities

- Current Events
- Chapter-based Internet Activities
- and more!

Holt Premier
Online Student Edition
Complete online support for interactivity, assessment, and reporting

- Interactive Maps and Notebook
- Standardized Test Prep
- Homework Practice and Research Activities Online

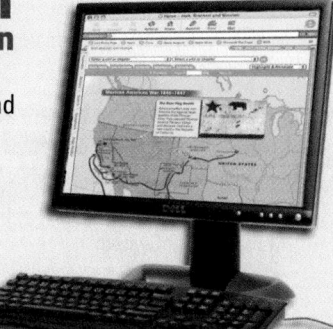

The Big Picture
Deborah Gray White

Reagan's First Term A political sea change took place with the election of Ronald Reagan. A proponent of military preparedness, smaller government, tax cuts, and conservative social policies, Reagan headed a newly reorganized Republican party that brought together grassroots Christians, disenchanted Democrats, and traditional Republicans. Their effective use of think tanks, media, grassroots organizing, and corporate funding made them formidable. To stimulate the economy Reagan reduced taxes and cut social programs, but events did not go according to his plan.

Reagan's Foreign Policy A fierce anti-Communist, Reagan committed billions of American dollars to defense spending. Openly confronting Soviet policies in Eastern Europe, his demands for more democracy coincided with the Soviet Union's economic collapse, a worker revolt in Poland, and the ascendancy of Mikhail Gorbachev, which together led to a thawing of the Cold War. Elsewhere, Reagan supported anti-Communist regimes in El Salvador, Nicaragua, and Grenada. Despite the loss of American troops in Lebanon, the illegal sale of arms for hostages in Iran and support of the Nicaraguan contras, Reagan remained popular.

A New World Order During George H. W. Bush's presidency the Soviet Union dissolved and Eastern Europe experienced a wave of peaceful and violent revolutions. While reform was crushed in China, apartheid came to an end in South Africa. The U.S. military brought down a dictator in Panama and halted the aggression of Saddam Hussein in Iraq.

Life in the 1980s While computer technology changed the way people lived, and the space shuttle was put to new military and commercial uses, the deficit soared, the savings and loan industry failed, and many were plunged into poverty. As the culture wars fueled clashes over Supreme Court nominations and the Court's decisions in turn fueled the culture wars, a terrible disease named AIDS spread to millions around the world.

Recent Scholarship

Much has been made of the political mobilization of the Christian fundamentalist movement for conservative causes. In *Not By Politics Alone: The Enduring Influence of the Christian Right* (1998), Sara Diamond argues that the Christian Right exists first and foremost as a culture rather than as a political movement. As Diamond deconstructs the ways and means by which a variety of Christian groups fulfill the emotional and social needs of their flocks, she reveals how and why the movement came to be such a critical and effective base for the Republican party.

Differentiating Instruction

Differentiated Instruction Teacher Management System
- Lesson Plans for Differentiated Instruction
- Differentiated Instructional Benchmarking Guides
- Interactive Reader and Study Guide

 Spanish Chapter Summaries Audio CD Program

 Online Chapter Summaries in Spanish

 Student Edition on Audio CD Program

 Differentiated Instruction Modified Worksheets and Tests CD-ROM
- Vocabulary Flash Cards
- Modified Vocabulary Builder Activities
- Modified Chapter Review Activity
- Modified Chapter Test

OSP One-Stop Planner CD-ROM
- ExamView Test Generator (English and Spanish)
- PuzzlePro
- Quiz Show for ExamView
- Transparencies and Videos

TE Differentiated Activities in the Teacher's Edition
- Reagan's Economic Plan, p. 1050
- School Rules, p. 1052
- Other Bush-Era Conflicts, p. 1063
- Women Justices on the Supreme Court, p. 1069
- Important People Posters, p. 1070

Reading Like a Historian

Sam Wineburg

The Fiction of Historical Fiction

Thirteen years in the making, Edmund Morris's *Dutch: A Memoir of Ronald Reagan* appeared in print in 1999 amidst a maelstrom of controversy. Morris had received an unheard of advance of three million dollars for this authorized presidential biography. While this payout caused a stir, it was nothing compared to the brouhaha that erupted once critics got their hands on the book.

Morris adopted the unconventional strategy of inserting himself into his biography—not as his real self, the son of a British pilot, born in Kenya on May 27, 1940—but a made-up self, born in 1912, who pops in and out of Ronald Reagan's life at key moments. Morris's invented self is saved from drowning by young Reagan the lifeguard, attends Reagan's football games at Eureka College, and observes the actor's rise as Hollywood star. The massive biography comes jammed with 168 pages of footnotes, some that refer to verifiable historical events, but others that reference fabricated incidents pulled from thin air. Nowhere in the volume does Morris lay out the secrets of his narrative strategy. It is impossible to discern when Morris's narrative is based on real events and when it is based on dreamy reverie.

The Reviews Come In

The reception of Morris's book by historians was not pretty. UCLA's Lynn Hunt called it a "cheap trick." Reviewing *Dutch* in the *American Historical Review*, Berkeley's Michael Rogin called it a "harlequin historical romance," labeling its narrative strategy a "counterfeit scholarly apparatus." The harshest criticism was reserved for Morris's bogus footnotes.

Reviewing the book in *Perspectives: Newsletter of the American Historical Association*, Kate Masur issued this summary verdict: "Fake notes cheapen the real work of writing history."

The controversy over *Dutch* touches the heart of teaching history: How to help young people learn the difference between true stories and those that are "truth-like." If adults are taken in by well-crafted pieces of historical fiction, how much more difficult must it be for students, just learning to distinguish fact from fiction?

The Strengths of Historical Fiction

Many teachers turn to historical fiction for precisely the reason these books appear on best-seller lists: they are good reads with strong storylines, powerful narrative arcs, and happy endings. The best examples of this genre are so compelling that we say to ourselves, "This has to be true, how can it *not* be?" Good historical fiction can create interest where it never was before.

At the same time, the casual use of historical fiction—without clearly and explicitly demarcating for students what makes history history and what makes fiction fiction—can undermine a key rationale for history's place in the curriculum: its ability to help young people understand the relationship between claim and evidence, its ability to teach students to differentiate between a story well-told and a story well-supported.

History can be only a "little bit" fictional in the same way that a woman can be only a "little bit" pregnant. In able hands, historical fiction can be a powerful teaching tool, but it should always come packaged with a warning label: "Use With Extreme Caution."

Standards Focus

Social Studies Competency Goals
Goal 12 The learner will identify and analyze trends in domestic and foreign affairs of the United States during this time period.
12.01, 12.02, 12.03, 12.04

 The Big Idea and Essential Questions

To foster student understanding of this chapter's big idea, design your lesson to address each section's essential question.

Big Idea The election of Ronald Reagan ushered in a new conservative era, during which the Cold War ended and huge changes were made in economic and social policy.

Essential Questions

1. Why did Ronald Reagan's conservative agenda appeal to the American public in 1980?

2. How did President Reagan respond to communism around the world?

3. What challenges did President George H.W. Bush face during his term in office?

4. What was the impact of the major technological, economic, and social changes that occurred in the 1980s and early 1990s?

Key to Differentiating Instruction

Below Level

Basic-level activities designed for all students encountering new material

At Level

Intermediate-level activities designed for average students

Above Level

Challenging activities designed for honors and gifted-and-talented students

Standard English Mastery

Activities designed to improve standard English usage

CHAPTER 32
1980–1992

A Conservative ERA

THE BIG PICTURE Ronald Reagan won the presidency in 1980 by appealing to a discontented electorate with the promise to return to a simpler time and conservative values. Reagan and his successor, George H. W. Bush, presided over the end of the Cold War and huge changes in economic and social policy.

North Carolina Standards

Social Studies Objectives

12.01 Summarize significant events in foreign policy since the Vietnam War.

12.02 Evaluate the impact of recent constitutional amendments, court rulings, and federal legislation on United States citizens.

12.03 Identify and assess the impact of economic, technological, and environmental changes in the United States.

12.04 Identify and assess the impact of social, political, and cultural changes in the United States.

Language Arts Objectives

2.01 Research and analyze ideas, events, and/or movements related to United States culture by:
  • locating facts and details for purposeful elaboration.

Skills Focus **READING LIKE A HISTORIAN**

Reagan loved a crowd, and the crowds loved him. His vitality, gentle humor, and dynamic speaking style charmed even his opponents. **Interpreting Visuals** What can you infer about Reagan's personality from this photograph?

See Skills Handbook, p. H30

1044

U.S.

September 1981 Sandra Day O'Connor becomes first female U.S. Supreme Court Justice.

1980

World

1980 Lech Walesa's Solidarity trade union leads protests in Poland.

Introduce the Chapter
At Level

A Conservative Era

1. Tell students that in this chapter they will learn about major shifts in world power and the emergence of the United States as the world's remaining military and economic superpower.

2. Have students scan the chapter and make a list of foreign policy challenges and changes in the world that occurred during the 1980s.

3. Have students use the information from their lists to create a chart that can show events and consequences. Then as students read the chapter, have them complete the chart listing the consequence of each foreign policy event.
LS Visual-Spatial
Alternative Assessment Handbook, Rubric 7: Charts

History's Impact video program
Watch the video to understand the impact of the collapse of the Berlin Wall.

HOLT
History's Impact
▶ Video Program: A Conservative Era
See the Video Teacher's Guide for strategies for using the video segment.

Reading Like a Historian
Analyzing a Photograph Ronald Reagan was a popular president who kept in touch with ordinary citizens. Even though he was shot by a would-be assassin in 1981, Reagan continued to appear in public throughout his presidency.

1982
Deepest U.S. recession since the Great Depression begins.

November 1985
Reagan and Gorbachev meet in the first of their arms reduction summits.

January 1989
George H. W. Bush becomes president.

February 1991
In First Gulf War, U.S.-led coalition ousts Iraq from Kuwait.

1982   1984   1986   1988   1990   1992

October 1983
Suicide bombers attack U.S. peacekeepers in Lebanon, killing 241.

March 1985
Mikhail Gorbachev becomes leader of the Soviet Union.

June 1989
China crushes pro-democracy protests in Tiananmen Square.

November 1989
Berlin Wall falls as protests bring down Communist regimes in Eastern Europe.

1045

go.hrw.com
Online Resources
Chapter Resources:
KEYWORD: SD7 CH32
Teacher Resources:
KEYWORD: SD7 TEACHER

Explore the Time Line

1. Who was the first female Supreme Court justice, and when was she appointed? *Sandra Day O'Connor; September 1981*

2. When did Mikhail Gorbachev become leader of the Soviet Union? *March 1985*

3. When did the Berlin Wall fall? *November 1989*

Info to Know

Sandra Day O'Connor After serving on the Supreme Court for over 24 years, Associate Justice Sandra Day O'Connor officially resigned from the Court in 2006. Appointed by President Reagan, she was unanimously confirmed by the Senate. O'Connor established herself as a moderate conservative voice on the Court and was the swing vote on a number of high-profile cases that came before the Court, including the 2000 presidential election case, several abortion-related cases, and several affirmative action cases.

Answers
Reading Like a Historian (p. 1044)
warm, personable, enjoyed people

1045

Bellringer

The Inside Story. . . Use the **Daily Bellringer Transparency** to help students answer the question.

📁 Daily Bellringer Transparency, Section 1

Academic Vocabulary

Review with students the high-use academic terms in this section.

welfare public assistance to the needy (p. 1047)

advocate support, endorse (p. 1049)

📁 CRF: Vocabulary Builder Activity, Section 1

Taking Notes

greater military strength, suppression of communism, cutting size of government, deregulation of certain industries, cutting taxes, appoint conservatives to the judiciary

---

BEFORE YOU READ

MAIN IDEA

In 1980 Americans voted for a new approach to governing by electing Ronald Reagan, who powerfully promoted a conservative agenda.

READING FOCUS

1. As the 1980 presidential election approached, why was America a nation ready for change?
2. What was the Reagan revolution, and who supported it?
3. What were the key ideas of Reagan's economic plan, and what were its effects?

KEY TERMS AND PEOPLE

Ronald Reagan
New Right
Jerry Falwell
Nancy Reagan
David A. Stockman
supply-side economics
budget deficit

TAKING NOTES As you read, take notes on Reagan's goals for government and the economy. Record your notes in a graphic organizer like the one shown here.

President Reagan's Goals

"A City UPON A HILL"

▼ Reagan's ease in front of an audience and gifted speaking style gave him wide appeal.

THE INSIDE STORY

What event marked the rise of the Reagan revolution?
As California governor **Ronald Reagan** faced an audience in Washington, D.C., on January 25, 1974, he was witnessing something new. It was the first-ever Conservative Political Action Conference. Reagan was among friends.

Modern conservative politics had been born in defeat. Senator Barry Goldwater of Arizona, whom Reagan had supported, lost the 1964 presidential race in spectacular fashion. Richard Nixon had brought some conservative credentials into office when he was elected president in 1968, but his administration had been wracked with scandals. By 1974 conservatives were looking for someone to lead them.

Ronald Wilson Reagan was the man they were looking for. As he spoke to the crowd, Reagan laid out themes that would become familiar to the nation in the years ahead. He spoke of the need for greater military strength. He criticized the size and inefficiency of government. He praised the accomplishments of American business and the wonder of the free enterprise system.

Drawing on his gift at using stories to illustrate his points, Reagan reached back into American history to a sermon given in 1630 by John Winthrop, the first governor of Massachusetts Bay Colony. He reminded his listeners that Winthrop had compared the colony to "a city upon a hill" with "the eyes of all people upon us." Driven by hope and a love of freedom, America was Reagan's vision of that "city upon a hill."

Reagan's day in the national spotlight was still years away. Yet on that January day in 1974, it was possible to see it coming. ◾

1046 CHAPTER 32

Teach the Main Idea

At Level

Reagan's First Term

1. **Teach** Ask students the Reading Focus questions to teach this section.

2. **Apply** Draw three large ovals for students to see. Label the top of each oval with one of the three topics of this chapter—A Nation Ready for Change; The Reagan Revolution; and Reagan's Economic Plan. Guide students in a discussion of each topic. As you discuss the topics, use the ovals as a graphic organizer.

3. **Review** As you review the section, have students identify the main issues within each topic.

4. **Practice/Homework** Have students write a one-page television news report that outlines the highlights and problems of Reagan's administration. Have volunteers read their TV reports to the class. **LS Visual-Spatial, Verbal-Linguistic**

📝 Alternative Assessment Handbook, Rubrics 11: Discussions; and 40: Writing to Describe

On the strength of the speech, California Republicans recruited him to run for governor in 1966. Reagan easily defeated the incumbent Democrat, Edmund "Pat" Brown.

As governor, Reagan had trouble meeting his goals for cutting the size of government. He expressed frustration with the job of controlling a large bureaucracy. After serving two terms, Reagan set his sights on a bigger job. "I feel I'm better qualified to be president than governor," he told a supporter.

Reagan would have to wait. He lost the Republican presidential nomination twice, to Richard Nixon in 1968 and to Gerald Ford in 1976. By 1980, however, Reagan had a strong and growing base of support.

Reagan's conservative support Ronald Reagan's journey from New Deal Democrat to conservative Republican made him a hero of a growing movement called the **New Right**. This was a coalition of conservative media commentators, think tanks, and grassroots Christian groups. Many of the groups had been formed to oppose specific liberal causes, such as the abortion rights gained under *Roe* v. *Wade*.

The New Right <u>advocated</u> major reversals in liberal government, economic, and social policies. The movement endorsed school prayer, deregulation, lower taxes, a smaller government, a stronger military, and the teaching of a Bible-based account of human creation. It opposed gun control, abortion, homosexual rights, school busing to achieve desegregation, the Equal Rights Amendment, affirmative action, and nuclear disarmament.

The New Right grew in influence with the rise of televangelism, or TV ministries led by evangelical Christians. One televangelist leader of the New Right, the Rev. **Jerry Falwell**, founded a political activist organization called Moral Majority in 1979. The name came from the group's belief that a majority of Americans agreed with conservative moral values.

Reagan gave the New Right an eloquent and persuasive voice. He drew many Americans to his side, including a large number of Democrats. These so-called Reagan Democrats shifted their allegiance from the Democratic Party in the elections of 1980 and 1984. They voted for Reagan to express their frustration with the Democratic Party's stands on social and racial issues and on national security.

A powerful personality The stage presence Reagan developed as an actor served him well in politics. On the campaign trail he became known as the Great Communicator. As president he gained the nickname the Great Persuader. To gain support for his programs, he threw his energies and charm into winning over conservative southern and western Democrats in Congress. If that didn't work, he spoke directly to voters through skillful television addresses. The newsmagazine *Time* referred to him as "the velvet steamroller."

Perhaps Reagan's greatest ally was his wife, **Nancy Reagan**, a former actor. She played a major role in running of the White House. She advised her husband on policy issues and fiercely protected his interests. As First Lady, she headed a "Just Say No" antidrug campaign.

Reagan's presidential agenda Reagan's chief goals were largely those of the New Right. He pledged to reduce the federal bureaucracy, deregulate certain industries, cut taxes, increase the defense budget, take a hard line with the Soviet Union, and appoint conservative judges to the federal judiciary.

In his first few months, the president got much of what he wanted. Congress passed a tax cut, eliminated some social programs, reduced the budgets of many federal agencies, and passed the largest-ever peacetime increase in

ACADEMIC VOCABULARY
advocate support, endorse

Reading Focus

❸ What were the key ideas of Reagan's economic plan, and what were its effects? *key ideas—reduce taxes, cut federal budget, strengthen nation's defenses; effects—worst recession since Great Depression, unemployment, inflation*

Reagan's Economic Plan

Recall What were the two goals of Reaganomics? *reduce taxes, cut federal budget*

Identify Cause and Effect What was the cause of the recession of 1981 and 1982? *The execution of Reaganomics resulted in less money to offset the increased spending; interest rates increased, and the unemployment rate increased.*

Activity **Reaganomics** Have students write a brief essay either supporting or opposing Reagan's economic policies and explaining their position. Guide the class in a discussion of whether Reaganomics was a success or a failure.
LS **Verbal-Linguistic**

📄 CRF: Economics Activity: The Federal Budget Deficit

📄 CRF: Literature Activity: *The Bonfire of the Vanities* by Tom Wolfe

go.hrw.com
Online Resources
KEYWORD: SD7 CH32
TOPIC: SANDRA DAY O'CONNOR

Answers

Reading Check *make government smaller; deregulate certain industries; cut taxes; increase defense spending*

---

the defense budget. As head of the executive branch, Reagan could carry out some of his reforms without going to Congress. For example, he instructed federal agencies to roll back regulations on many industries. With each step toward achieving his agenda, Reagan seemed to be answering those who had felt the nation could no longer be governed effectively.

Reagan's image only grew stronger when he survived an assassination attempt in 1981. With a bullet in his left lung, the 70-year-old president kept his sense of humor. "Honey," he told the First Lady, "I forgot to duck." Reagan's positive outlook in the face of adversity created goodwill that helped him achieve his agenda.

Reagan's easygoing manner did not prevent him from taking decisive action. In August 1981 Reagan faced a strike by the nation's air traffic controllers. As federal employees, the 13,000 members of the Professional Air Traffic Controllers' Organization (PATCO) were forbidden to strike. Reagan warned them—and then he fired them all. Despite the resulting confusion at airports, the public generally approved of the president's uncompromising actions.

READING CHECK **Summarizing** How did Reagan want to change the federal government?

Reaganomics
- Reaganomics: Reagan's plan for tax and spending cuts
- supply-side economics: theory that breaks for businesses will increase supply of goods and services, aiding the economy

Below, Reagan meets with budget director David A. Stockman.

1050

Reagan's Economic Plan

Reagan's blueprint for remaking government required a new economic plan. It was nicknamed Reaganomics. The plan had two goals: 1) reduce taxes to stimulate economic growth, and 2) cut the federal budget. Reagan appointed a controversial young budget director, **David A. Stockman**, to sell his plan to a skeptical Congress. Stockman's job was to get Congress to put the Reagan plan into effect in 40 days.

Supply-side economics Reaganomics was based on an economic theory known as **supply-side economics**. According to that theory, tax cuts and business incentives stimulate investment. Investment encourages economic growth. A growing economy, in turn, results in an increased supply of goods and services. Supply-side theory appealed to conservatives, who supported free enterprise and minimal government regulation.

Stockman pressed Congress for tax cuts for upper-income Americans and for businesses. Supply-side supporters believed that the tax relief would produce a series of benefits. Individuals would invest their tax savings. Businesses would use investment funds to expand and hire more workers. Expanding businesses would generate more tax revenue, allowing the government to eliminate any budget deficit. A **budget deficit** is the amount by which government spending for a year exceeds government income.

Stockman succeeded in getting Congress to pass numerous major components of Reaganomics. During Reagan's first six years as president, tax rates on the wealthiest Americans dropped from 70 percent of their income to 28 percent. Critics claimed that the tax breaks simply made the rich richer. They predicted that little of the new wealth would "trickle down" to the working class, as Reaganomics predicted. Critics also warned that tax cuts, combined with increases in military spending, would drive the federal deficit higher, increasing the national debt.

Reagan's own vice president, George H. W. Bush, had questioned the plan to cut taxes and boost military spending at the same time. Back in 1980, when Bush was competing with Reagan for the Republican nomination, he had labeled Reagan's plan "voodoo economics."

Differentiating Instruction

Below Level

Special Education Students

Materials construction paper, scissors, glue, colored markers

1. Organize the class into small groups. Have students in each group work together to find photographs of President Reagan in old newspapers and magazines. Have students look for pictures that show different expressions, situations, and moods.

2. Have students make copies of the pictures and paste them onto construction paper.

Have students label each picture as sad, happy, deep in thought, tired, or angry.

3. Have groups identify events that happened during President Reagan's first term that match each one of the pictures, and then write the event under the picture. Have volunteers share their posters with the class. **LS** **Visual-Spatial, Interpersonal**

📄 Alternative Assessment Handbook, Rubrics 3: Artwork; and 14: Group Activity

Recession and recovery Events did not go quite according to Reagan's plan. In 1981 and 1982, the nation suffered the worst recession since the Great Depression. Unemployment rose, and government revenues plunged. Meanwhile, federal spending soared, largely because of huge defense increases. With less tax money to pay for the increased government spending, the federal budget deficit skyrocketed. Stockman told a magazine that "None of us really understands what's going on with all these numbers." He left the administration and later wrote a critique of Reaganomics.

The actions of the Federal Reserve Board contributed to the recession. The Federal Reserve had steadily raised interest rates from 1979 to 1982 in an effort to reduce inflation. Higher interest rates made it more expensive for businesses to borrow money to expand.

By 1983, with inflation at a low 4 percent, the Federal Reserve had reduced interest rates. The collapse of OPEC's ability to set high oil prices also helped lower inflation. The economy began to grow at a brisk pace. Economic growth was uneven, however, and largely favored the wealthy. Unemployment eased. Nevertheless, federal revenues lagged far behind spending. Faced with a severe budget crisis, Congress put the brakes on federal spending. In 1985 it passed the Balanced Budget and Emergency

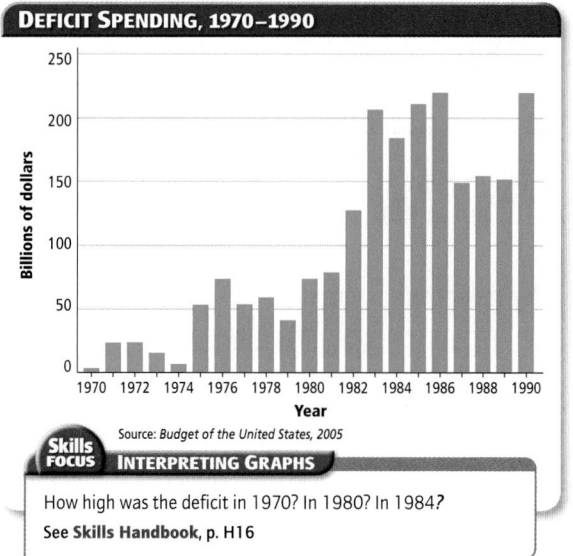

DEFICIT SPENDING, 1970–1990

Billions of dollars (y-axis: 0, 50, 100, 150, 200, 250)

Year (x-axis: 1970, 1972, 1974, 1976, 1978, 1980, 1982, 1984, 1986, 1988, 1990)

Source: Budget of the United States, 2005

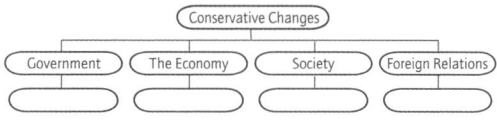

Skills Focus   INTERPRETING GRAPHS

How high was the deficit in 1970? In 1980? In 1984?

See Skills Handbook, p. H16

Deficit Control Act, or the Gramm-Rudman-Hollings Act. The measure required mandatory budget cuts to curb the deficit.

READING CHECK   Summarizing What were the key elements of Reaganomics?

SECTION 1 ASSESSMENT

go.hrw.com
Online Quiz
Keyword: SD7 HP32

Reviewing Ideas, Terms, and People

1. **a. Recall** Why was America said to be in a state of malaise in the late 1970s?
   b. Make Inferences What do you think Carter was trying to accomplish in his malaise speech, and why did it backfire?
   c. Rate What made Reagan's message so effective among voters?

2. **a. Recall** What types of groups and individuals supported Reagan's rise to the presidency?
   b. Analyze What skills earned Reagan his nicknames the Great Communicator, the Great Persuader, and the Velvet Steamroller?
   c. Evaluate How did conservative ideas represent a change from the recent past?

3. **a. Define** Write a brief definition for each of the following terms: **Reaganomics, supply-side economics**
   b. Contrast How did the assumptions of Reaganomics differ from the outcomes?

c. Predict What effect would the Gramm-Rudman-Hollings bill have on funding of federal programs?

Critical Thinking

4. **Identifying the Main Idea** Copy the web diagram below and use information from the section to show what types of changes conservatives wanted to make.

Conservative Changes
- Government
- The Economy
- Society
- Foreign Relations

FOCUS ON SPEAKING

5. **Expository** President Reagan communicated strong ideas to the American public. Choose one of his ideas and write a brief speech explaining it, using facts to support your account.

A CONSERVATIVE ERA **1051**

Section 1 Assessment Answers

1. **a.** concern over President Carter's leadership, gas crisis, and Iran hostage crisis
   b. asked Americans to help solve problems through their own actions; seemed to blame Americans
   c. optimistic, energetic, conservative

2. **a.** conservatives; Democrats frustrated with party's stand on social and racial issues, and national defense
   b. used plain language, at ease with people, wit, charm; determined

   c. different stand on issues like gun control, abortion, school busing, affirmative action

3. **a.** reduce taxes, cut federal budget; tax cuts and incentives to stimulate economy
   b. nation suffered a terrible recession
   c. programs might not receive same funding

4. smaller government; cut taxes and federal budget; conservative social agenda; hard line on communism

5. Students should use facts to defend the idea chosen.

Landmark Supreme Court Cases

New Jersey v. T.L.O.

Word Help

delinquency illegal actions

Info to Know

Fourth Amendment and Public School Students It was not until the 1980s that the Supreme Court used the Fourth Amendment in cases involving public school students. Justice Byron White wrote for the Court in this case and stated that school officials could indeed search a student as long as "there are reasonable grounds for suspecting that the search will turn up evidence that the student has violated or is violating either the law or the rules of the school."

LANDMARK SUPREME COURT CASES

Constitutional Issue: Search and Seizure

New Jersey v. T.L.O. (1985)

Why It Matters Under the Fourth Amendment, police must have probable cause before they can conduct a search. In this case, the Supreme Court ruled that school officials may search a student without violating the Fourth Amendment if there is reasonable suspicion that the student has broken the law or a specific school rule.

Background of the Case

In 1980 a New Jersey high school student whose initials were T.L.O. was accused of smoking in the school bathroom. When T.L.O. claimed that she did not smoke, the assistant principal looked in her purse and found cigarettes. Then he noticed a package of rolling papers. Searching further he found marijuana and letters indicating that T.L.O. was selling drugs. T.L.O. later admitted to selling marijuana, and the State of New Jersey brought delinquency charges against her. She was sentenced to one year of probation. T.L.O. appealed her conviction, arguing that there was no probable cause to search her purse. She asked for a new trial at which the evidence from her purse could not be used against her.

THE IMPACT TODAY Based on the Fourth Amendment arguments used in the *T.L.O.* case, the Supreme Court has issued rulings permitting school officials to conduct random screenings for weapons using metal detectors (above) and to conduct random drug testings of students wishing to participate in extracurricular sports and clubs. Many school boards are developing guidelines for how to interpret and carry out the Court's rulings on these controversial topics.

The Decision

The Supreme Court ruled that the Fourth Amendment's prohibition on unreasonable searches and seizures does apply to searches conducted by public school officials. In addition, schoolchildren do have legitimate expectations of privacy, and their belongings may not be searched unreasonably. However, school officials are not required to follow the same standards as police. School officials need only reasonable grounds for *suspecting* that the search will turn up evidence that the student has violated school rules. The search must be conducted in ways that are reasonably related to the goal of the search. Judged by this standard, the search of T.L.O.'s purse was reasonable and did not violate the Constitution.

CRITICAL THINKING

go.hrw.com
Research Online
Keyword: SS Court

1. **Analyze the Impact** Using the keyword above, read about the 1961 decision in *Mapp* v. *Ohio*. In what ways was the reasoning in *Mapp* important to the decision in *New Jersey* v. *T.L.O.*?

2. **You Be the Judge** Based on *New Jersey* v. *T.L.O.*, should a school be allowed to require student athletes to submit to random drug testing, or does that policy violate the reasonable search provision of the Fourth Amendment? Explain your answer in a short paragraph.

Differentiating Instruction

Below Level

English-Language Learners

Standard English Mastery

1. Review the case with students to help ensure that all students understand the background of the court ruling.

2. Have students write a brief essay summarizing the case outcome and explaining the justification for the ruling.

3. Then have students revise the school rules in accordance with the ruling in *New Jersey* v. *T.L.O.* **LS Verbal-Linguistic**

📖 Alternative Assessment Handbook, Rubric 42: Writing to Inform

Answers

Critical Thinking 1. *In* Mapp *the Court ruled that evidence obtained in violation of the Fourth Amendment protection against unreasonable search and seizure must be excluded. In this case, the Court ruled that if students are suspected of violating the law, a search is acceptable.* **2.** *possible answers—no, drug testing is an unacceptable interpretation; it is a search of one's body, not possessions; yes, possession of drugs is illegal and it is reasonable to check for drug use*

SECTION 2 Reagan's Foreign Policy

BEFORE YOU READ

MAIN IDEA
President Reagan took a hard line against communism around the world.

READING FOCUS
1. How did President Reagan help to bring about the end of the Cold War?
2. What foreign trouble spots persisted during Reagan's presidency?
3. How did the Iran-Contra Affair undermine the president?

KEY TERMS AND PEOPLE
Strategic Defense Initiative
Lech Walesa
Solidarity
Mikhail Gorbachev
INF Treaty
apartheid
Iran-Contra affair
Oliver North

TAKING NOTES As you read, take notes on key foreign policy challenges that faced President Reagan. Record your notes in a graphic organizer like the one shown here. You may need to add more circles.

Foreign-Policy Challenges

THE INSIDE STORY

Can simple words knock down a cement wall? For the United States and its allies in the West, the Berlin Wall had long been a symbol of the harsh reality of life in the Soviet empire. The massive wall dividing Communist East Berlin from the free West told a stark tale of two systems. On one side, citizens freely approached the wall and turned its entire length into an exuberant canvas of colorfully painted designs and slogans. On the other, armed guards and barriers kept citizens away for fear that they might escape to freedom in the West.

In 1987, some 25 years after the Berlin Wall was constructed, Ronald Reagan gave a speech at a famous Berlin Wall landmark known as the Brandenburg Gate. Reagan's speech went out not only to the people of West Berlin, whom he addressed directly, but also to the people in East Berlin. Loudspeakers carried his words into the air and over the wall.

President Reagan's message was clear and simple. He called out the name of the Soviet leader.

"Mr. Gorbachev, open this gate. Mr. Gorbachev—Mr. Gorbachev, tear down this wall!"

The message of defiance and confrontation would characterize Reagan's hard-line Cold War stance throughout his first term. Gorbachev, for his part, did not respond immediately to Reagan's demand in Berlin. But in time, the Soviet leader indeed would have to answer. ◼

▶ **In West Berlin, citizens exercised freedom of expression on their side of the Berlin Wall.**

"Mr. Gorbachev, Tear Down This Wall!"

A CONSERVATIVE ERA **1053**

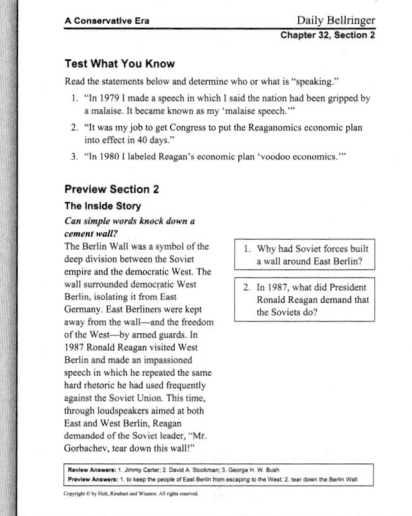
Academic Vocabulary

Review with students the high-use academic terms in this section.

initiate begin, launch, take the first step (p. 1054)
regime government, administration (p. 1056)
📋 CRF: Vocabulary Builder Activity, Section 2

Taking Notes
relations with Soviet Union, INF, El Salvador, Nicaragua, Lebanon, South Africa, Iran-Contra affair

---

Teach the Main Idea
At Level

Reagan's Foreign Policy

1. **Teach** Ask students the Reading Focus questions to teach this section.

2. **Apply** Draw a large triangle for students to see. Label each angle with one of the three topics of this section: Reagan and the Cold War, Trouble Spots Abroad, and The Iran-Contra Affair. Have students scan each section and make a list of the main ideas under each topic on the triangle. Have students copy the triangle onto their own papers and retain it as a study tool.

3. **Review** As you review the section, have students identify the successes and failures of President Reagan's foreign policy.

4. **Practice/Homework** Have students write a one-page advisory memorandum to the president to summarize one foreign policy crisis and give the president advice on the best way to resolve the problem.
LS Visual-Spatial, Logical-Mathematical

📋 Alternative Assessment Handbook, Rubrics 13: Graphic Organizers; and 37: Writing Assignments

Reading Focus

❶ How did President Reagan help to bring about the end of the Cold War? *strong language against Soviet Union; increased military budget; developed relationship with Gorbachev; INF treaty*

Reagan and the Cold War

Recall What was the Strategic Defense Initiative (SDI)? *potential weapon that would act as a shield to protect the U.S. against Soviet missiles*

Analyze Why was the Soviet Union opposed to the SDI concept? *believed that it would enable U.S. to launch first strike against Soviet Union*

Elaborate Do you think President Reagan's assessment of the Soviet Union as the "focus of evil" was a correct assessment? *possible answers—yes, it was spreading revolt and was a threat to U.S. way of life; no, the U.S. was much stronger militarily and economically, it was not helpful to relations between the two countries*

Activity **Gorbachev and Reagan** Divide students into small groups. Have each group write a script for one of the meetings between Reagan and Gorbachev. Have two volunteers from each group read their script to the class.
LS Verbal-Linguistic, Kinesthetic

📝 Political Cartoons Activities for American History: Cartoon 63: Strategic Defense Initiative

Primary Source

"We must look for ways to improve the international situation and build a new world—and we must do it together."
— Mikhail Gorbachev
Speech to the United Nations, 1988

Answers

Interpreting Graphs *Defense spending had doubled.*

1054

Reagan and the Cold War

Staunch opposition to communism was a bedrock principle that shaped Ronald Reagan's political life. Yet as president, Reagan joined in a complex relationship with a new Soviet leader to help end the 40-year Cold War.

The "Evil Empire" President Reagan rejected the policies of containment and détente pursued by previous presidents. He did not want to accommodate communism. He wanted to destroy it. He used thundering language to condemn the Soviet Union as "the focus of evil in the modern world."

HISTORY'S VOICES

❝I urge you to beware the temptation … to ignore the facts of history and the aggressive impulses of an evil empire, to simply call the arms race a giant misunderstanding and thereby remove yourself from the struggle between right and wrong and good and evil.❞
—President Ronald Reagan, "Evil Empire" speech, March 8, 1983

> **ACADEMIC VOCABULARY**
> **initiate** begin, launch, take the first step

Reagan's strong position worsened relations with the Soviets during his first term. But it also won considerable praise. He forged bonds with like-minded foreign leaders, including conservative British prime minister Margaret Thatcher and Polish-born Pope John Paul II. Still, critics viewed Reagan's approach as reckless. At a time when the two superpowers had their fingers on the nuclear trigger, some people feared he would set off World War III.

Military spending soars Urging "peace with strength," Reagan obtained massive increases in defense spending. Between 1981 and 1985 the Pentagon budget grew from about $150 billion to some $250 billion.

Much of the new spending went to nuclear weapons. In 1981 the president unveiled a plan to add thousands of new nuclear warheads. Two years later, the U.S. military installed new nuclear missiles in Europe. The presence of new weapons aimed at Soviet cities angered the USSR. It ended arms control talks and boycotted the 1984 Olympic Games in Los Angeles.

In 1983 Reagan initiated the creation of a new defensive weapon: a shield in space to protect the United States against incoming Soviet missiles. Reagan put all his persuasive skills to work to promote the concept, named the **Strategic Defense Initiative** (SDI).

Opponents, including many scientists, scoffed at SDI, saying it would be too expensive and would not work. They nicknamed it Star Wars, after the popular science-fiction

Reagan's Defense Buildup

This cartoon, like many critics, charged that Reagan's massive military spending came at the expense of other valuable programs.

DEFENSE SPENDING, 1980–1988

[Bar graph showing Billions of dollars on y-axis (0 to 300) and Year on x-axis (1980, 1982, 1984, 1986, 1988), with bars rising from about 130 in 1980 to nearly 300 in 1988]

Source: *Budget of the United States Government, 2005*

Skills FOCUS **INTERPRETING GRAPHS**

Compare defense spending in 1980, shortly before Reagan took office, with that near the end of his presidency in 1988.

See Skills Handbook, pp. H16

1054 CHAPTER 32

Skills Focus: Interpreting Political Cartoons   [At Level]

Reading Like a Historian Skill
President Reagan and the Soviet Union

1. Guide students in a discussion of the increase in military spending during the Reagan administration and the steps that led to the end of the Cold War.

2. Review the cartoon on this page to ensure that all students understand it. Have students work in pairs to analyze the cartoon. Have students answer this question: Is the cartoon fair, accurate, and unbiased? Have students

explain their reasoning. Make a list of the student responses for all to see.

3. Have each student create a political cartoon showing the same point as the one in the feature.

4. Have volunteers share their cartoons with the class. **LS** Interpersonal, Visual-Spatial

📝 Alternative Assessment Handbook, Rubric 27: Political Cartoons

movie. The Soviets viewed SDI as an offensive weapon rather than a defensive one, saying it would allow the United States to launch a first strike without fear of retaliation.

Reagan hoped SDI would ease the growing pressures for disarmament. Across the United States and Europe, hundreds of thousands of supporters of a nuclear freeze—a halt in production of all atomic weapons—marched in massive demonstrations.

"I would agree to freeze if only we could freeze the Soviets' global desires," Reagan said. Yet increasingly, the Soviet Communists were less concerned with global conquest than with their own political survival.

A weakened Soviet Union The long rule of Leonid Brezhnev, from 1964 to 1982, saw the USSR rise to the height of its power and then begin to decline. By the late 1970s, the Soviet economy was shrinking. Industrial and farm production, population growth, education, medical care, and other indicators of prosperity fell sharply. A country rich in farmland became an importer of food. Government corruption was rampant.

Soviet weakness became strikingly clear in 1980 when the USSR failed to contain a dramatic series of events in Poland. Under the leadership of an electrician named **Lech Walesa**, some 17,000 workers in the city of Gdansk locked themselves in a factory to protest steep rises in food prices. The daring move riveted the world. The strikes spread, finally forcing the Soviet-backed government to legalize independent trade unions. Walesa was elected to lead a new, independent union called **Solidarity**. More than a union, Solidarity was a freedom movement.

U.S.-Soviet relations warm The death of Leonid Brezhnev and two other Soviet leaders in quick succession brought a visionary new leader to power in 1985. **Mikhail Gorbachev** believed that the only way to salvage the Soviet economy was to strike a deal with America.

The emergence of Gorbachev gave Reagan an opportunity. In the 1984 election, the Reagan-Bush ticket had beaten former Vice President Walter Mondale and his running mate, Representative Geraldine Ferraro of New York. As he began his second term, Reagan was ready to negotiate with the Soviets.

PRIMARY SOURCES

Speech

On June 6, 1984, Ronald Reagan spoke in France to observe the fortieth anniversary of the Normandy invasion on D-Day. This passage from his "Boys of Pointe du Hoc" speech reflects Reagan's speaking style and foreign-policy views.

"The men of Normandy had faith that what they were doing was right, faith that they fought for all humanity, faith that a just God would grant them mercy on this beachhead or on the next … [T]here is a profound moral difference between the use of force for liberation and the use of force for conquest. You [U.S. veterans of D-Day] were here to liberate, not to conquer, and so you and those others did not doubt your cause. And you were right not to doubt.

You all knew that some things are worth dying for. One's country is worth dying for, and democracy is worth dying for, because it's the most deeply honorable form of government ever devised by man. All of you loved liberty. All of you were willing to fight tyranny, and you knew the people of your countries were behind you."

Skills FOCUS **READING LIKE A HISTORIAN**

1. **Identifying Points of View** According to Reagan, what proved that the Normandy invasion was the right action?
2. **Analyzing Primary Sources** What does this speech reflect about Reagan's political views?

See **Skills Handbook**, p. H28–29

In four meetings from 1985 through 1988, Reagan and Gorbachev changed the superpower relationship. Their talks produced the Intermediate-Range Nuclear Forces (INF) Treaty, the first agreement to actually reduce nuclear arms instead of simply halting production. The **INF Treaty**, ratified in 1988, ordered the destruction of a whole class of weapons—more than 2,500 missiles, many of which faced each other in Europe.

In 1988 Reagan stood in Moscow's Red Square and embraced the leader of the once "evil empire." The Cold War was almost over.

READING CHECK **Summarizing** What actions did Reagan take to help end the Cold War?

• **Direct Teach** •

Reading Focus

Reagan and the Cold War

Describe How did the Soviet economy fare under Leonid Brezhnev? *negative growth, prosperity declined, suffered from government corruption, poor planning, bad management*

Summarize Why was Lech Walesa so successful? *Soviet Union was weak; Walesa quickly gained support of many workers*

Make Inferences What can you infer from the fact that President Reagan and Mikhail Gorbachev met four times between 1985 and 1988? *INF treaty difficult to achieve; took time to build trust and cooperation*

📄 CRF: Primary Source Activity: Tearing Down the Berlin Wall

📄 CRF: Biography: Aleksandr Solzhenitsyn

Primary Sources

Speech

Summarize Have students work in pairs to write a paraphrase of Reagan's speech. Then have students write a television commentary about the speech and present it to the class.

Teaching Tip

Have students locate the regions and countries discussed in this section on a map of the world. You might wish to distribute world maps and have students color code them as you study this chapter.

📄 American History Outline Maps: The World

Answers

Reading Like a Historian 1. *soldiers were liberating, not conquering, France;* **2.** *believed in using force to protect democracy and liberty*

Reading Check *met four times with Gorbachev; signed INF treaty*

1055

Skills Focus: Making Oral Presentations

At Level

Reading Like a Historian Skill
Reagan and Gorbachev in Red Square

1. Guide students in a discussion of the Cold War and the events that led to the creation of the INF treaty by President Reagan and Soviet leader Mikhail Gorbachev.

2. Organize students into small groups. Have each group work together to create a television broadcast about the 1988 meeting between the two leaders and their embrace in Red Square. Possible topics for students

to cover in their broadcast include the evil empire speech, the SDI initiative, and the historic nature of this meeting. Have students prepare a script for their broadcast.

3. Have volunteers present the newscast to the class. **LS Auditory-Musical, Interpersonal**

📄 Alternative Assessment Handbook, Rubric 24: Oral Presentations

Nicaragua

Lebanon

② What foreign trouble spots persisted during Reagan's presidency? *El Salvador, Nicaragua, Lebanon, Grenada, South Africa*

Trouble Spots Abroad

Identify Who was José Napoleón Duarte? *moderate leader elected in El Salvador in 1984*

Explain Why did President Reagan cut off aid to the Sandinistas in Nicaragua? *believed they were supported by the Soviet Union*

Develop Do you think U.S. presidents should be able to circumvent congressional rulings if they believe it is in the best interests of the U.S. to do so? *possible answers—yes, the president is elected to serve and should have some freedom to act; no, it upsets the constitutional balance of power*

Activity **Foreign Conflicts** Have students work in small groups to list similarities and differences in the ways that Reagan handled foreign conflicts during his presidency. Create a class list on the board and have students copy it into their notes and retain it as a study tool.
LS **Visual-Spatial**

Info to Know

Sandinistas The Sandinistas took their name from César Augusto Sandino, a guerrilla leader who had fought U.S. intervention in Nicaragua between 1927 and 1933. During the Nicaraguan civil war of 1926–1927, Sandino refused to accept an end to the war until all U.S. forces were removed from the country. Although this extended the fighting, U.S. troops were finally withdrawn in 1933. While negotiating a peace agreement with President Juan Bautista Sacasa, Sandino was murdered by the National Guard, under the direction of future dictator Anastasio Somoza.

Trouble Spots Abroad

Regional conflicts often force presidents to choose where to become involved militarily. Reagan's choices reflected his view of American interests in the world in the 1980s.

Upheaval in Latin America Nowhere was the fight against communism more urgent to Reagan than Latin America. The United States supported several anti-Communist governments and rebel groups in the region during the Reagan years. Some of these regimes were repressive, but Reagan believed U.S. support was necessary to prevent the spread of communism in those countries. U.S. actions focused on two Central American nations, El Salvador and Nicaragua.

In tiny El Salvador, peasants were caught in a violent civil war between Marxist guerrillas and government troops supported by armed extremist groups. The Reagan administration gave its support to a relatively moderate leader who won election in 1984, José Napoleón Duarte. The civil war dragged on until peace was reached in 1992.

Meanwhile, a civil war in neighboring Nicaragua drew the president's staff into what would become the most serious crisis to affect the Reagan White House. The United States

ACADEMIC VOCABULARY
regime government, administration

had at one time supported Nicaraguan dictator Anastasio Somoza Debayle. In 1979 a Marxist-leaning group known as the Sandinistas, with aid from Cuba's Communist government, ousted Somoza. At first the Sandinista governed as part of a coalition of political groups, but soon Sandinista dominance became clear.

When Reagan took office, he cut off aid to Nicaragua, saying that the Sandinistas were supported by the USSR. In 1981 Reagan approved $20 million for the Central Intelligence Agency (CIA) to equip and train a Sandinista opposition group, the Contras. The effort stalled when the CIA conducted sabotage operations in Nicaragua, including laying mines in two Nicaraguan ports, without informing Congress. As the secret activities came to light, Congress cut off funds to the Contras and banned all direct or indirect U.S. military support for them.

Reagan remained determined to help the Contras. He told his national security adviser, Robert McFarlane, "I want you to do whatever you have to do to help these people [the Contras] keep body and soul together." His staff took this as a signal to find a way around Congress's restrictions. Americans would soon learn that the White House continued to fund the Contras despite the congressional ban.

1056 CHAPTER 32

Skills Focus: Summarizing

At Level

Reading Skill
Protecting American Interests

1. Draw a blank table for students to see, and have them copy it onto their own papers. Label each row with a foreign trouble spot: El Salvador, Nicaragua, Lebanon, Grenada, and South Africa.

2. Have students complete the table by listing the events that led to trouble in these countries.

3. Have volunteers complete the class table and explain each event they have added to it.
LS **Visual-Spatial, Logical-Mathematical**

Alternative Assessment Handbook, Rubric 13: Graphic Organizers

Graphic Organizer Transparencies

At far left, a Contra rebel wears a baseball cap that shows U.S. support of his struggle against the Sandinista government in Nicaragua. At near left, the U.S. embassy in Beirut, Lebanon, is damaged following a suicide attack on April 18, 1983, in which 63 people were killed. *What other conflicts was the United States involved in during the Reagan administration?*

Tragedy in Lebanon President Reagan believed that American interests required stability in the Middle East. For years the Mediterranean coastal country of Lebanon had been ripped apart by civil war. Muslim and Christian factions battled for control of the country. Various groups, including the Palestine Liberation Organization (PLO), used Lebanon as a base for attacks against Israel to the south. In 1982 Israel invaded and occupied southern Lebanon to expel the PLO and try to form a new, reliably friendly government. The invasion threatened to turn Lebanon's civil war into a general Middle East war.

In 1983 an international peacekeeping force, including some 800 U.S. Marines, arrived in Lebanon's capital, Beirut. On October 23, a suicide bomber drove a truck full of explosives into the marine barracks in Beirut. The blast leveled the building, killing 241 sleeping soldiers inside. This tragedy and the bombing of the U.S. embassy a few months earlier were the first suicide terrorist attacks against the United States.

The incidents ignited an intense debate in America about the role of the military in violent, unstable regions. Reagan decided to withdraw the troops from Lebanon. Anti-American groups claimed victory.

Victory in Grenada A few days before the bombing in Lebanon, a violent Communist coup took place in the tiny Caribbean country of Grenada (gruh-NAY-duh). Cuban troops were helping build an airstrip on the island, raising fears that it could become a Communist outpost. Reagan also worried about the fate of some 800 U.S. students in medical school there.

Two days after the Lebanon bombing, with the nation still in shock, Reagan sent 5,000 marines to invade Grenada. They took the island in two days, with a loss of 19 soldiers. The victory aided Reagan in the 1984 election.

Apartheid in South Africa Reagan took a less activist position in confronting the South African government. For decades, the official policy of **apartheid** ("apartness") had enforced legalized racial segregation throughout South African society. Under apartheid the minority white population enjoyed great privileges. Meanwhile, the government forcibly relocated millions of people categorized as nonwhite to desolate frontier lands. Nonwhites were banned from decent jobs, schools, and housing and were prohibited from owning land, voting, or traveling freely.

American companies and investments in the resource-rich land helped keep the white regime in power. Starting in the 1970s, anti-apartheid groups urged nations to divest, or withdraw investments, from South Africa.

Reagan preferred a policy of "constructive engagement"—that is, maintaining business ties while offering incentives for reform and engaging in diplomacy with the government. Critics charged that the policy enriched a corrupt, white minority regime. In 1986 Congress overrode a Reagan veto to pass the Comprehensive Anti-Apartheid Act, which imposed trade limits and other sanctions.

READING CHECK **Summarizing** How did the Reagan administration respond to crises in Lebanon, Grenada, and South Africa?

The Iran-Contra Affair

Despite the congressional ban on U.S. funds for the Contras' war against the Nicaraguan government, Reagan's national security staff sought to continue the funding. The United States was then facing terrorism in the Middle

THE IMPACT TODAY

Government
Terrorists have used suicide bombings to strike in Israel and in Iraq. The terrorist attacks against the United States on September 11, 2001, also were suicide attacks.

❸ How did the Iran-Contra affair undermine the president? *cast suspicion on the president about his involvement in the affair*

The Iran-Contra Affair

Explain What was the Iran-Contra affair? *selling weapons to Iran to obtain release of hostages in Lebanon; money from the sale was diverted to support the Contras*

Analyze Why was the Iran-Contra affair illegal? *violated U.S. weapons embargo on Iran*

⬚ Quick Facts Transparency: Reagan's Foreign Policy

⬚ CRF: Biography: Oliver North

Close

Guide students in a discussion of the position that President Ronald Reagan took against communism.

Review

⬚ Online Quiz, Section 2

⬚ Daily Test Practice Transparency

Assess

SE Section 2 Assessment

⬚ Progress Assessment: Section 2 Quiz

⬚ Alternative Assessment Handbook

Reteach

⬚ Interactive Reader and Study Guide, Section 2

⬚ Interactive Skills Tutor CD-ROM

Answers

Reading Check *Congress began investigation; top members of administration denied knowledge of fund diversion; criminal charges filed against North; North convicted of destroying government documents and perjury*

REAGAN'S FOREIGN POLICY

Latin America	• U.S. backs moderate Duarte in El Salvador civil war. • Reagan backs anti-Communist Contras in Nicaragua. • White House defies Congress ban on Contra funding.
Lebanon	• Following civil war, U.S. sends 800 peacekeepers. • October 1983: Suicide bomber hits marine barracks. • 241 Americans killed; U.S. withdraws from Lebanon.
Grenada	• 1983 Communist coup strands 800 U.S. students. • Cuba's role and students' safety concern Reagan. • U.S. launches two-day invasion, restores democracy.
South Africa	• Reagan prefers "constructive engagement" with white minority government to combat apartheid. • 1986: Congress imposes sanctions over Reagan veto.

East, where American civilians in Lebanon were being kidnapped by pro-Iranian groups.

In 1985 the situations in Nicaragua and the Middle East became linked. National Security Adviser Robert McFarlane persuaded Reagan to approve sales of weapons to Iran, hoping that Iran would help obtain the release of U.S. hostages in Lebanon. This violated a U.S. arms embargo as well as Reagan's own principle of refusing to negotiate with terrorists.

The **Iran-Contra affair** unfolded when members of the National Security Council staff secretly diverted money from the illegal Iran arms sales to the Contras in Nicaragua. Vice Admiral John Poindexter and Lieutenant Colonel **Oliver North** carried out the plan.

When the scheme was revealed in 1986, Congress wanted to know if anyone higher up was involved. It launched an investigation modeled after the Watergate probe of Nixon.

Reagan admitted authorizing the Iran arms sales but denied knowledge of the diversion of funds to the Contras. Vice President Bush, Defense Secretary Caspar Weinberger, and other staff made similar statements.

The full details of the affair are not known because members of the administration engaged in a cover-up of their actions. North admitted destroying key documents. High-level Reagan staff were found to have lied in testimony to Congress and withheld evidence. North was convicted of destroying government documents and perjury. The conviction later was overturned on technicalities.

READING CHECK **Sequencing** Trace the significant events that led to prosecutions in the Iran-Contra affair.

SECTION 2 ASSESSMENT

go.hrw.com
Online Quiz
Keyword: SD7 HP32

Reviewing Ideas, Terms, and People

1. a. Identify Explain how each of these terms and people relates to the ending of the Cold War: **Strategic Defense Initiative, Lech Walesa, Solidarity, Mikhail Gorbachev**
b. Make Inferences What influence do you think SDI and U.S. defense spending had on Soviet leaders' thinking about the Cold War?
c. Evaluate To what extent do you think Reagan and Gorbachev shaped the events of the Cold War, and to what extent did they encounter changes already in progress?

2. a. Define Write a brief definition for this term: **apartheid**
b. Contrast Contrast the reasons for U.S. involvement in Lebanon, Grenada, and South Africa.
c. Evaluate What do you think were the advantages and disadvantages of Reagan's "constructive engagement" policy in South Africa?

3. a. Recall What was Oliver North's role in the **Iran-Contra** affair?
b. Make Inferences What can you infer about Reagan's relationship with Congress from the Iran-Contra Affair?

c. Rate Do you think North's actions were justifiable given (a) circumstances in Nicaragua or (b) pressure from the president to help the Contras?

Critical Thinking

4. Making Decisions Copy the chart below and use information from the section to identify the choices Reagan had to make in various conflicts.

Reagan Foreign-Policy Choices

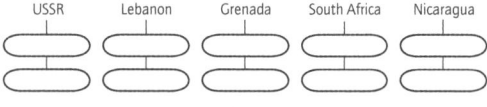

| USSR | Lebanon | Grenada | South Africa | Nicaragua |

FOCUS ON WRITING

5. Descriptive As a reporter covering the appearance of Reagan and Gorbachev in Red Square in 1988, describe the historic meeting of former enemies.

Section 2 Assessment Answers

1. a. U.S. determination to protect itself; led Polish freedom movement; Polish freedom movement; signed INF
b. created concern, alarm
c. possible answer—not much, in office at the right time

2. a. legalized racial segregation
b. peacekeeping operation; prevent Communists from building airstrip; end apartheid
c. keep doors open; no reason for change

3. a. diverted money from arms sales to Contras
b. strained; different views on Contras
c. possible answers—no, following illegal orders is illegal; yes, he was a loyal soldier

4. USSR—continue to arm; sign INF; Lebanon—keep peacekeepers in; withdraw troops; Grenada—allow airstrip; invade; South Africa—support apartheid; impose sanctions; Nicaragua—allow Sandinista government; support Contras

5. former enemies publicly embracing

SECTION 3 — A New World Order

BEFORE YOU READ

MAIN IDEA
In 1988 Reagan's vice president, George H. W. Bush, won election to a term that saw dramatic changes in the world.

READING FOCUS
1. What factors influenced the election of 1988?
2. How did Soviet society become more open?
3. What chain of events led to the collapse of the Soviet empire?
4. What other global conflicts emerged near the end of the Cold War?

KEY TERMS AND PEOPLE
George H. W. Bush
glasnost
perestroika
velvet revolution
Boris Yeltsin
Tiananmen Square massacre
Saddam Hussein
Operation Desert Storm
Nelson Mandela

TAKING NOTES As you read, take notes identifying the steps on the way to the breakup of the Soviet Union. Record your notes in a graphic organizer like the one shown here.

↓
| |
↓
| Breakup of the Soviet Union |

THE INSIDE STORY

How do you make the transition from vice president to commander in chief? On December 7, 1988, Vice President **George H. W. Bush** was basking in the glory of his victory in the 1988 presidential election. Yet he was still second in command to a very powerful and popular Ronald Reagan.

Thus the summit taking place that day on Governor's Island in New York Harbor had clear symbolic meaning. The Americans were there to meet with Soviet leader Mikhail Gorbachev. Ronald Reagan was still president, and he would conduct the discussions with his Soviet counterpart. Bush, however, was a living symbol of a change soon to take place: the orderly, democratic transfer of power in the U.S. government.

Before the formal talks began, the three men informally answered questions from reporters. Reagan gave his positive reaction to the recently announced decision by Gorbachev to reduce the number of troops in Europe. Bush was then asked for his reaction. His first response was similar to one he had given for the previous eight years: He supported whatever the president said. But then, with a reference to his upcoming January 20 inauguration, Bush extended an invitation to the assembled reporters: "Give me a ring on the 21st."

Indeed, the Reagan era would soon be over. The presidency of George H. W. Bush was about to begin. ■

Passing the Torch

▼ Gorbachev, Reagan, and Bush meet under the watchful eye of Lady Liberty.

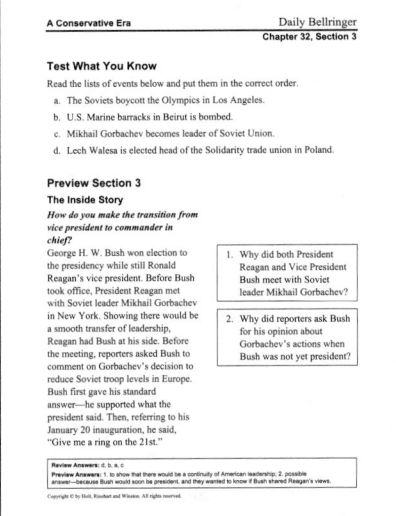

Teach the Main Idea

At Level

A New World Order

1. **Teach** Ask students the Reading Focus questions to teach this section.

2. **Apply** Have students scan the section and make a list of the red and blue heads and the names of the people who are discussed in the section. Then have students work in pairs to develop a brief paragraph explaining why this section is entitled *A New World Order*.

3. **Review** As you review the section, have volunteers read their paragraphs and have students identify the events that contributed to this new world order.

4. **Practice/Homework** Have students write a one-page newspaper article summarizing and analyzing George H.W. Bush's shift from vice president to president. **LS Visual-Spatial, Logical-Mathematical**

🗒 Alternative Assessment Handbook, Rubric 23: Newspapers

❶ What factors influenced the election of 1988? *lack of public interest; negative campaigns; low voter turnout*

The Election of 1988

Explain Why was Jesse Jackson considered a strong contender for the Democratic Party nomination? *won most votes on "Super Tuesday"; drew support from whites and African Americans*

Analyze What was the major problem facing George Bush in the election of 1988? *shaky economy*

❷ How did Soviet society become more open? *glasnost, or opening, lifting of media censorship; perestroika, restructuring government bureaucracy*

The Opening of the USSR

Explain How did glasnost affect Soviet society? *media censorship lifted; citizens could criticize government and government policies*

Elaborate How did Gorbachev restructure the economy? *dismantled central planning system; gave local officials more authority; pushed through many social and political reforms*

The Election of 1988

George Herbert Walker Bush came from a wealthy and powerful family. In World War II he had served with distinction as a navy pilot. Following careers in banking and oil, Bush entered politics in 1967 as a member of Congress from Texas. He served under presidents Nixon, Ford, and Reagan—as U.S. ambassador to the United Nations, as head of the Central Intelligence Agency, and as vice president.

In 1988 the Republican Party nominated George H.W. Bush as its presidential candidate and Indiana senator Dan Quayle as his running mate. They joined a presidential race that was notable for its lack of public attention. Excitement peaked early in the election year when an African American candidate, the Reverend Jesse Jackson, ran for the Democratic Party's nomination.

Jackson, a major civil rights leader and a liberal candidate, had run in 1984 with little success. This time, however, he achieved an upset, winning the most votes on Super Tuesday, the day when most states hold primary elections. Jackson's candidacy earned significant support from both white and black voters. In the end, however, Governor Michael Dukakis of Massachusetts won the most delegates and became the Democratic Party's nominee.

Many people attribute the low 50.1 percent voter turnout in the general election to the negativity of the campaign. The Democratic ticket of Michael Dukakis and his running mate, Texas senator Lloyd Bentsen, challenged Bush on the weak economy. The Bush campaign shot back with a series of advertisements that portrayed Dukakis as soft on crime. The tough ads contrasted with Bush's stump speech calling for a "kinder, gentler" America.

Despite a shaky economy, Bush earned support with his promise to continue the Reagan economic plan: "Read my lips: No new taxes." The Bush-Quayle ticket beat Dukakis and Bentsen by 426 electoral votes to 111.

When George Bush suceeded Ronald Reagan as president, the world stood on the verge of a democratic awakening. In four short years President Bush would take part in intense dramas around the globe.

READING CHECK **Summarizing** What events triggered the most interest in the 1988 election?

THE IMPACT TODAY

Science and Technology
A 2005 Chernobyl Forum report on the 20-year impact of the disaster revealed that only about 50 deaths could be directly linked to the accident, rather than thousands as previously estimated. Still, the report predicted that as many as 4,000 people could eventually die from radiation exposure, and some 5 million live in contaminated areas.

1060 CHAPTER 32

The Opening of the USSR

For nearly 70 years, citizens in the closed Soviet society risked great danger in speaking out or acting against the government. Dissidents—those who protested Soviet rule—were imprisoned and exiled. Basic freedoms of speech, religion, and association were nearly nonexistent. Mikhail Gorbachev sought to change Soviet society, opening it not only to the West but also to internal dissent.

Glasnost and perestroika As part of his plan to reform the failing Soviet system, Gorbachev announced a new era of **glasnost**, or "opening." He lifted media censorship, allowing public criticism of the government. Gorbachev held press interviews, a stunning contrast to the secrecy in which the Kremlin had operated.

Soviet citizens, cautious at first, began to speak openly. They complained about the price of food, of empty store shelves, and of their sons dying in the Soviet occupation of Afghanistan.

Gorbachev also undertook the huge process of **perestroika**, the "restructuring" of the corrupt government bureaucracy. The program was launched with much excitement and hope.

To restructure the shattered economy, Gorbachev dismantled the Soviet central planning system, giving local officials more authority over farm and factory production. He fired about 40 percent of regional officials and pushed through a flurry of reforms:

- 1986: Soviet scientist and dissident Andrey Sakharov was released from exile.
- 1989: Free elections took place for the first time since 1917.
- 1989: The Soviet Union withdrew from Afghanistan.
- 1989: Gorbachev visited China, easing tensions along the Soviet-Chinese border.

One glaring exception to glasnost occurred in 1986, when the Soviets attempted to cover up the world's worst nuclear accident. The meltdown of the Chernobyl nuclear plant near Kiev, the capital of Ukraine, was detected when deadly radiation drifted across Europe. The lead caused deaths and widespread illness. About 350,000 people had to be relocated from the region. The site remains uninhabitable.

READING CHECK **Identifying Cause and Effect** What effects did glasnost and perestroika have on the Soviet economy, government, and society?

Skills Focus: Recognizing Bias

Above Level

Reading Like a Historian Skill
Perestroika and Glasnost

Research Required

1. Have students conduct outside research on the changes that occurred within the Soviet Union in the late 1980s and how *perestroika* and *glasnost* affected ordinary citizens. Tell students to look for primary and secondary sources from Europe and the Soviet Union, as well as from the United States.

2. Have students write an essay explaining the changes that occurred within the Soviet Union. In their essays students should

compare and discuss the various points of view presented in the sources. In the conclusions, students should explain what might account for the differing points of view.

3. Organize the class into small groups. Have students read their essays and share their sources with their group members.

LS **Interpersonal, Verbal-Linguistic**

📖 Alternative Assessment Handbook, Rubrics 9: Comparing and Contrasting; and 30: Research

Answers

Reading Check (left) *Jesse Jackson's run for Democratic nomination; Bush's pledge about no new taxes;* **(right)** *opened Soviet society; allowed economic and political reforms to begin*

Soviet Shortages

The Soviet Union experienced healthy economic growth after World War II, but it did not last. Soviet leaders focused on expanding heavy industry instead of creating adequate supplies of consumer goods. Store shelves were often empty, creating a thriving black market in food and other goods.

The Soviet Empire Collapses

The call for *glasnost* and *perestroika* awakened hopes for freedom throughout the Soviet empire. A spirit of nationalism, long repressed and feared by Soviet authorities, rose in the subject nations of Eastern Europe.

Eastern Europe crumbles Gorbachev knew the USSR could no longer afford to support the ailing Eastern European economies. He ordered a large troop pullback from the region and warned local leaders to adopt reforms.

Dissidents and ordinary citizens didn't wait for reforms. They created their own paths to freedom. All across Eastern Europe, dreams of a better life inspired revolutions in the late 1980s. The Polish trade union Solidarity forced the government to hold elections, and in December 1990 Lech Walesa became president. Hungarian officials opened their country's border with Austria in August 1989, and people streamed to the West. In Czechoslovakia, a nonviolent **velvet revolution**—so called because it was peaceful—swept the Communists from power in November 1989. Dissident playwright Vaclav Havel became president.

In Romania, revolution turned violent. Demonstrations brought down the government of one of the Soviet bloc's cruelest dictators, Nicolae Ceausescu, in December 1989. Ceausescu and his wife, Elena, were executed.

The fall of the Berlin Wall Gorbachev's call for openness made him very popular in Europe, especially in East and West Germany. Protesters at a fortieth anniversary celebration of the East German state in October 1989 chanted "Gorby, help us!"

But still the Berlin Wall remained, the repressive symbol of Soviet communism. With so many barriers falling, could the Berlin Wall continue to divide the German people?

Hoping to calm rising protests, the East German government flung open the gates of the Berlin Wall on November 9, 1989. Thousands of East Berliners poured through to freedom. As border guards looked on helplessly, jubilant Berliners scaled the wall from both sides. They pulled down the razor wire, climbed atop the wall, and danced on it. With axes and sledgehammers and their bare hands, they spontaneously began ripping down the wall.

Writing on the tenth anniversary of the fall of the Berlin Wall, one reporter looked back on the spectacular sights and sounds of history being made.

HISTORY'S VOICES

❝And then I hear the noise. Pick, pick, pick. Chuck, chuck, chuck. Growing louder and louder as hundreds of hammers and chisels attack the wall, taking it down chip by chip. I laugh and laugh—and cry at the same time.❞

—BBC reporter Tim Weber, November 9, 1989

Skills Focus: Summarizing

At Level

Reading Skill
The Berlin Wall Falls

1. Have students work in small groups to talk about the events surrounding the fall of the Berlin Wall. Have them reread the account in the text.

2. Have each student use the information from their group discussions to write an "eyewitness" account of the fall of the Berlin Wall. Tell students to try to capture the emotion of the people on both sides of the wall in their accounts.

3. Have students illustrate their accounts. Have volunteers share their accounts and illustrations with the class.

4. As an extension, have students write a poem commemorating the fall of the Berlin Wall and the triumph of democracy.
LS Visual-Spatial, Auditory-Musical

📋 Alternative Assessment Handbook, Rubric 26: Poems and Songs

The Soviet Empire Collapses

Summarize Explain the events that led to the seizure and release of Gorbachev. *seized by Communists in a coup; Boris Yeltsin led revolt against the Communists; when soldiers and tanks came to arrest Yeltsin, unarmed citizens came to help; soldiers backed down; Gorbachev released*

Draw Conclusions Do you believe Gorbachev was a positive or negative force in the history of the Soviet Union? *possible answers— positive because his actions led to freedom and reform; negative because he was unable to stabilize Russia*

Evaluate How do you think that history will view Gorbachev? *possible answers—as a hero who aided in the end of the nuclear arms race, helped bring down Berlin Wall, helped Soviet Union move toward reform; as someone who did not understand the consequences of his actions*

Activity **Mr. Gorbachev's place in history** Have students write a paraphrase of the quote in History's Voices. Then have students write a paragraph expressing their opinion about the quote. Do they agree or disagree with it? Have students share their paraphrases and paragraphs with the class.

LS Verbal-Linguistic

📄 American History Outline Maps: The Breakup of the Soviet Union

An Empire Falls

Pressured by U.S. threats and the dead weight of his ailing Soviet empire, Gorbachev cracked open a door to democracy—and millions of oppressed people rushed through.

① Poland

Electrician Lech Walesa leads a strike and starts a revolution.
- In 1989, Solidarity forces the government to hold elections.
- Walesa is elected president in 1989; the Communists fall.

② Romania

One of the cruelest Communist regimes falls the hardest.
- In December 1989 violent protests sweep the country.
- Dictator Ceausescu and his wife are executed.

People around the world watched in awe as TV cameras recorded the triumph of democracy. Less than a year later, on October 3, 1990, East Germany and West Germany were reunified as one nation.

The end of the Soviet Union With the Soviet empire crumbling, Communist Party officials in the USSR stood to lose power, prestige, and wealth. The world waited anxiously to see how far they would allow Gorbachev to go. With Gorbachev preparing to sign a treaty granting partial freedoms to the Soviet republics in 1991, hard-line Communist Party leaders had had enough. They seized Gorbachev in a coup d'état.

Help for the captive president came from **Boris Yeltsin**, leader of the Russian Republic. Yeltsin had quit the Communist Party and was actually a liberal opponent of Gorbachev. Now, however, he led a popular revolt against the Communist coup. As soldiers and tanks rolled into Red Square to arrest Yeltsin, a mass of unarmed Russians flooded the plaza, surrounding them. What would happen? At a tense moment, Yeltsin climbed atop a tank and addressed the cheering crowd. Soldiers looked the other way. Some even joined the protest.

The balance of power tipped, and the army backed down. Gorbachev was released and restored to power in the Kremlin. But, he would not stay long. The forces that Gorbachev had unleashed quickly overwhelmed him. Beginning in 1990, Soviet republics had begun declaring their independence. In late 1991 most of the former Soviet republics, including Russia, formed a loose federation called the Commonwealth of Independent States (CIS).

Gorbachev resigned as president, and no one was named to replace him. The Soviet Union dissolved. Yeltsin now led a severely weakened superpower. A journalist later assessed Gorbachev's place in history:

HISTORY'S VOICES

❝One can argue about what degree of direct credit Mr. Gorbachev deserves for ending the nuclear arms race or for bringing down the Berlin wall. It can credibly be suggested that Russia itself, pinned mercilessly beneath the staggering burdens of Bolshevism, could not have moved in any other direction and that Mr. Gorbachev just happened to be there when the society began to collapse. But he was there, and it is hard to imagine that history won't reward him handsomely for his role.❞

—"A Visionary Who Put an Era Out of Its Misery," *The New York Times*, January 7, 1997

1062 CHAPTER 32

Skills Focus: Sequencing

Below Level

Reading Skill
The Soviet Empire Collapses

1. To help students understand the sequence of events that led to the end of the Soviet Union, have them work in pairs to create a sequencing diagram of the events that led to the end of the Soviet Union and the formation of the CIS.

2. Have students begin their diagrams with the fall of Communist governments in Poland, Czechoslovakia, and Romania and end with the CIS.

3. Create a large class diagram for all to see. As you discuss the events, have students correct their own work and retain their diagrams as a study tool. **LS Visual-Spatial**

📄 Alternative Assessment Handbook, Rubric 13: Graphic Organizers

📄 Graphic Organizer Transparencies

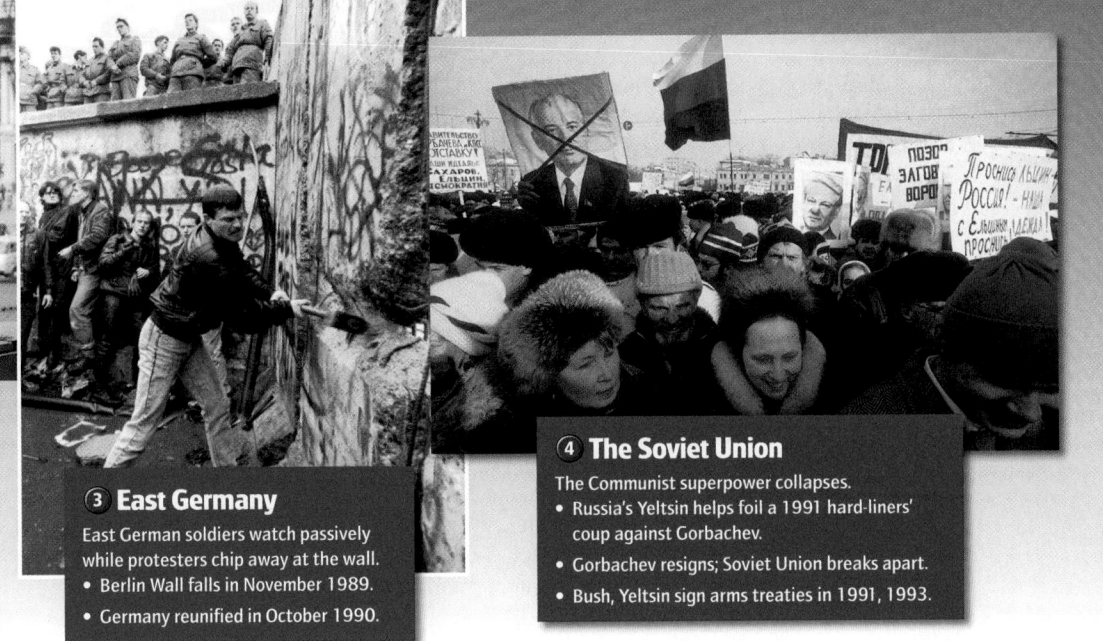

③ East Germany

East German soldiers watch passively while protesters chip away at the wall.
- Berlin Wall falls in November 1989.
- Germany reunified in October 1990.

④ The Soviet Union

The Communist superpower collapses.
- Russia's Yeltsin helps foil a 1991 hard-liners' coup against Gorbachev.
- Gorbachev resigns; Soviet Union breaks apart.
- Bush, Yeltsin sign arms treaties in 1991, 1993.

Reading Focus

④ What other global conflicts emerged near the end of the Cold War? *U.S. invasion of Panama; freedom in South Africa; democracy crushed in China; First Persian Gulf War*

Other Bush-Era Conflicts

Explain What was the Tiananmen Square massacre? *Chinese troops fired on unarmed civilian protesters.*

Make Inferences What was the significance of the image of one man facing Chinese tanks? *showed courage and the brutality of Chinese army*

Activity **Foreign Conflicts**
Have students work in small groups to create a chart comparing and contrasting the foreign policy challenges of Bush's administration. Then guide students in a discussion of similarities and differences in the ways Bush handled each of these conflicts. **LS Visual-Spatial**

Political Cartoons Activities for American History: Cartoon 64: Muscle Power

---

It was fitting that George Bush, former head of America's Cold War spy agency, the CIA, was the president who would preside over the ending of the Cold War. Less than one month after the fall of the Berlin Wall, Bush and Gorbachev met to discuss arms reduction. In 1991 they agreed on a Strategic Arms Reduction Treaty (START) to cut stockpiles of long-range nuclear weapons.

Two months after the collapse of the USSR, Bush and Yeltsin met at Camp David. They issued a joint statement declaring that the United States and Russia no longer regarded each other as "potential adversaries." The leaders signed a START II agreement in 1993. Bush said START II offered "a future free from fear." Yeltsin called it "a treaty of hope."

READING CHECK **Making Generalizations**
How did Gorbachev's call for *glasnost* and *perestroika* help bring down the Soviet Union?

Other Bush-Era Conflicts

President Bush guided the nation through other foreign-policy challenges. By 1991 he spoke hopefully of creating a "new world order," free of the Cold War rivalries.

China: democracy crushed Inspired in part by events in the Soviet Union, a generation of Chinese students called on their Communist leaders to embrace reforms. In April 1989 they led huge pro-democracy demonstrations that filled Tiananmen Square in the Chinese capital of Beijing. For two hope-filled months, Chinese officials tolerated the protests. Change seemed possible. Then hard-line officials ran out of patience.

On June 4 a line of tanks rolled toward Tiananmen Square. As cameras recorded the scene, a man ran into the street and stood in front of the tanks. For half an hour, he halted their progress. The image of the lone rebel defying Chinese authority sent a powerful message around the world. Then the man melted back into the crowd. The tanks surrounded the protesters and opened fire. Hundreds of unarmed people, including children, were gunned down in the **Tiananmen Square massacre**.

President Bush announced an arms embargo but said America had to stay "engaged" with China. Democratic reform would take much longer in China than in the rest of the Communist world. But the protests showed a desire for freedom that was heard by China's leaders.

THE IMPACT TODAY

Government
In 2002 President George W. Bush and Russian President Vladimir Putin replaced START II with the SORT, Strategic Offensive Reduction Treaty, which calls for cuts to overall arsenals rather than to specific weapon types.

Primary Source

"Under this agreement our Governments would agree that upon entry into force of the Treaty, the United States of America and the Russian Federation shall deactivate, by December 31, 2003, all strategic nuclear delivery vehicles which will be eliminated under the Treaty, by removing their nuclear reentry vehicles or taking other jointly agreed steps."
— Madeleine K. Albright

September 26, 1997
Joint Agreed Statement, START II

Answers

Reading Check *allowed citizens freedom to express discontent with government, restructure corrupt government bureaucracy*

Differentiating Instruction

Below Level

English-Language Learners

Research Required

Materials construction paper, scissors, glue, colored markers

1. Have students search the Internet or traditional print sources to find pictures of the people and events discussed in this section including Manuel Noriega, W. F. de Klerk, Nelson Mandela, Tiananmen Square, Saddam Hussein, and Operation Desert Storm.

2. Have students paste the pictures onto the construction paper, and label each

picture with the name or the event.

3. Have students share their posters and discuss the importance of the people and the events discussed in the section.

4. As an extension, have students write a dialogue between the president and secretary of defense in which the problems are discussed and solutions are proposed.
LS Visual-Spatial, Interpersonal

Alternative Assessment Handbook, Rubrics 3: Artwork; and 8: Collages

Other Bush-Era Conflicts

Explain Why did the United States forces arrest Manuel Noriega? *charged with racketeering and drug trafficking; convicted on numerous charges*

Identify Who is Nelson Mandela? *black South African leader released from prison in 1990; won Nobel Peace Prize*

Explain Why was it appropriate that de Klerk and Mandela shared the Nobel Peace Prize in 1993? *They worked together to eliminate apartheid.*

Map Transparency: The Persian Gulf War, 1991

Interactive Map: The Persian Gulf War, 1991

Info to Know

President Bush's Job Approval Rating During the Persian Gulf War President Bush's approval rating reached nearly 90 percent. Political analysts note, however, that presidents have often received high approval ratings during times of national crisis, and that such ratings often prove to be short-lived.

Panama: a dictator falls During the 1980s, Colonel Manuel Noriega basically ran the country of Panama. As head of the armed forces, he brutally suppressed opposition. Evidence that he was involved in smuggling drugs to the United States led a U.S. court to indict him in 1988. In 1989 Noriega seized direct control of Panama and declared a state of war with the United States. At stake was the security of the Panama Canal, which was scheduled to be turned over to Panamanian control in 1999.

When Noriega's soldiers shot and killed a U.S. marine in December 1989, President Bush ordered an invasion of Panama. U.S. troops arrested Noriega and moved him to Florida. He was later convicted of drug trafficking and other charges.

The Persian Gulf War In August 1990 the ruthless dictator of Iraq, **Saddam Hussein**, invaded the neighboring country of Kuwait.

The attack on the tiny, oil-rich kingdom shocked the United States and other Western countries—which depended on petroleum supplies from Kuwait—as well as the Arab nations in the region. Concerns rose further when reports surfaced of atrocities by Iraqi troops against Kuwaiti civilians. President Bush vowed that Saddam's "aggression would not stand."

The UN imposed sanctions on Iraq and set a deadline of January 15, 1991, for the withdrawal of Iraqi troops. Meanwhile, President Bush used his diplomatic skills to assemble a strong multinational military coalition.

Saddam remained defiant. The deadline passed. On January 16, 1991, the U.S.-led force attacked, starting with heavy bombing raids on targets in Kuwait and Iraq. On the Iraq–Saudi Arabia border and on warships in the Persian Gulf, a force of some 690,000 troops from the United States, Britain, France, and a number of Arab nations prepared to strike.

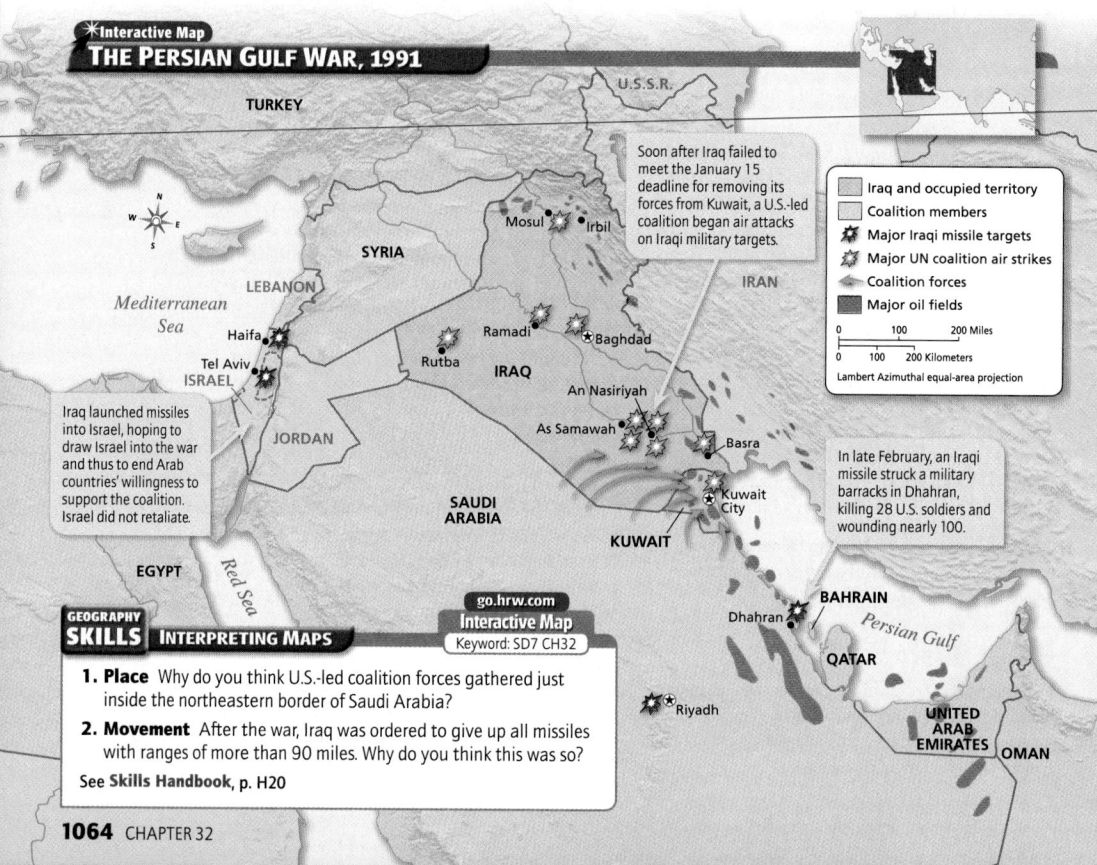

Interactive Map
THE PERSIAN GULF WAR, 1991

Soon after Iraq failed to meet the January 15 deadline for removing its forces from Kuwait, a U.S.-led coalition began air attacks on Iraqi military targets.

Iraq launched missiles into Israel, hoping to draw Israel into the war and thus to end Arab countries' willingness to support the coalition. Israel did not retaliate.

In late February, an Iraqi missile struck a military barracks in Dhahran, killing 28 U.S. soldiers and wounding nearly 100.

	Iraq and occupied territory
	Coalition members
	Major Iraqi missile targets
	Major UN coalition air strikes
	Coalition forces
	Major oil fields

0   100   200 Miles
0   100   200 Kilometers
Lambert Azimuthal equal-area projection

GEOGRAPHY SKILLS   INTERPRETING MAPS

go.hrw.com
Interactive Map
Keyword: SD7 CH32

1. **Place** Why do you think U.S.-led coalition forces gathered just inside the northeastern border of Saudi Arabia?

2. **Movement** After the war, Iraq was ordered to give up all missiles with ranges of more than 90 miles. Why do you think this was so?

See **Skills Handbook**, p. H20

1064 CHAPTER 32

Skills Focus: Interpreting Movement Maps   At Level

Social Studies Skill
The Persian Gulf War

1. Review the map of the Persian Gulf War with students. Then distribute outline maps of the Middle East. Have students label Syria, Jordan, Saudi Arabia, Iraq, Iran, Kuwait, Egypt, Israel, Lebanon, the Persian Gulf, Red Sea, and the Mediterranean Sea on their maps.

2. Have students trace the military operations in Iraq and Kuwait during the Persian Gulf War on their own maps.

3. Have students write a summary of the problems the United States, Britain, and France might have encountered as they supplied their troops for the war. **LS Visual-Spatial, Logical –Mathematical**

Alternative Assessment Handbook, Rubrics 20: Map Creation; and 21: Map Reading

Answers

Interpreting Maps 1. *location was close to both Kuwait and Iraq;* **2.** *so that Israel and other allies would not be attacked*

The ground war, launched on February 23, was short and swift. Iraqi troops retreated and scattered. Coalition forces returned Kuwait's royal family to power within a few days.

The campaign, **Operation Desert Storm**, was a conventional (non-nuclear) war. But it was unlike any war before it. The harsh desert terrain and long distances between targets made high technology airpower the most effective military tool. Nearly radar-proof Stealth bombers launched laser-guided bombs from afar. And long-range cruise missiles soared hundreds of miles from ships in the Gulf to hit targets in downtown Baghdad, the Iraqi capital.

Because so much of the campaign took place from the air, little of the violence appeared on the world's television sets, despite widespread coverage. The coalition tallied fewer than 500 casualties, including 148 Americans. An estimated 20,000 Iraqi soldiers and some 2,400 Iraqi civilians died.

The Persian Gulf War would not be the last conflict to involve the United States and Iraq. As you will read in the next chapter, U.S. involvement in Iraq would continue.

South Africa: new freedom While Eastern Europe was throwing off its chains, a similar miracle was occurring in South Africa. In 1989 the white government elected F. W. de Klerk as president. Like Gorbachev, de Klerk triggered a chain of events that resulted in a new system of government.

De Klerk sought a gradual, orderly lifting of apartheid. He released political prisoners including **Nelson Mandela**, a former guerrilla fighter imprisoned in 1964. Despite threats of civil war by white opposition, de Klerk and Mandela worked to end apartheid. A new constitution followed, and in 1994 the nation's first all-race elections were held. Mandela and his African National Congress party won.

Sharing the Nobel Peace Prize with de Klerk in 1993, Mandela praised the work of Dr. Martin Luther King Jr., whose call to nonviolent protest had inspired the antiapartheid movement. In language echoing the American Declaration of Independence, he saw a better day:

HISTORY'S VOICES

❝Thus shall we live, because we will have created a society which recognizes that all people are born equal, with each entitled in equal measure to life, liberty, prosperity, human rights and good governance.❞

—Nelson Mandela, Nobel lecture, December 10, 1993

READING CHECK **Identifying Main Ideas** What victories and setbacks for democracy occurred near the end of the Cold War?

---

go.hrw.com
Online Quiz
Keyword: SD7 HP32

SECTION 3 ASSESSMENT

Reviewing Ideas, Terms, and People

1. **a. Identify** Who were the main candidates in the 1988 presidential election?
   b. Make Inferences What can be inferred from the low voter turnout in the 1988 election?
   c. Develop Why did Jesse Jackson's big victory in the primaries generate so much excitement?

2. **a. Define** Write a brief definition for each of the following terms: *glasnost, perestroika*
   b. Analyze Why did Mikhail Gorbachev believe that *glasnost* and *perestroika* were necessary?
   c. Predict Why was it dangerous for Gorbachev to launch such big social and economic changes in the USSR?

3. **a. Identify** How did **Boris Yeltsin** come to power?
   b. Compare and Contrast How did Czechoslovakia's **velvet revolution** compare with the other Soviet-bloc uprisings?
   c. Rate What year do you think was the biggest turning point in ending the Cold War?

4. **a. Describe** What roles did Manuel Noriega, **Nelson Mandela**, and **Saddam Hussein** have in Bush-era conflicts?
   b. Rank Which Bush-era conflicts turned out to be the best and worst for the spread of democracy? Explain your choices.

Critical Thinking

5. **Identifying Cause and Effect** Copy the chart below and use information from the section to identify the causes of the fall of the Soviet empire.

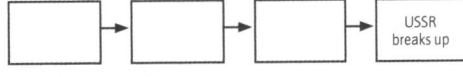

FOCUS ON WRITING

6. **Descriptive** Suppose you were one of the young people who climbed atop the Berlin Wall in triumph. Write a letter to an American friend describing the experience.

A CONSERVATIVE ERA **1065**

Primary Source

"During my lifetime I have dedicated myself to this struggle of the African people. I have fought against white domination, and I have fought against black domination. I have cherished the ideal of a democratic and free society in which all persons will live together in harmony and with equal opportunities. It is an ideal which I hope to live for and achieve. But, if needs be, it is an ideal for which I am prepared to die."
— Nelson Mandela

April 20, 1964

Review & Assess

Close

Discuss changes that took place around the world during George H. W. Bush's presidency.

Review

Online Quiz, Section 3

Daily Test Practice Transparency

Assess

SE Section 3 Assessment

Progress Assessment: Section 3 Quiz

Alternative Assessment Handbook

Reteach

Interactive Reader and Study Guide, Section 3

Interactive Skills Tutor CD-ROM

Section 3 Assessment Answers

1. **a.** George Bush, Jesse Jackson, Michael Dukakis
   b. lack of interest, negative campaign
   c. African American candidate; had support from black and white communities

2. **a.** *glasnost*—opening of Soviet society; *perestroika*—government restructuring
   b. time to change poor economy
   c. might not be able to control changes

3. **a.** Gorbachev captured by Communists; Yeltsin led popular revolt against Communists
   b. transition to democratic government

   was peaceful; other uprisings were violent
   c. possible answer—1989, fall of Berlin Wall

4. **a.** Noriega—Panamanian dictator arrested by U.S.; Mandela—helped end apartheid in South Africa; Hussein—Iraqi dictator, invaded Kuwait, Persian Gulf War
   b. possible answer—end of apartheid; massacre in China

5. *glasnost* and *perestroika*; revolutions in Eastern Europe; fall of Berlin Wall

6. possible answer—incredibly exciting day in history; cheering crowds

Answers

Reading Check *Panama—victory in 1989 when dictator removed from power; Persian Gulf—victory in 1991 as UN military coalition forced Iraqi troops out of Kuwait; South Africa—victory in 1994 as new constitution and election dismantled apartheid; China—setback in 1989 as tanks gunned down protesters*

1065

1066 CHAPTER 32

Bellringer

The Inside Story. . . Use the **Daily Bellringer Transparency** to help students answer the question.

Daily Bellringer Transparency, Section 4

A Conservative Era	Daily Bellringer
	Chapter 32, Section 4

Test What You Know

In your own words, write the definition of each term.

1. *glasnost*
2. *perestroika*
3. velvet revolution
4. Tiananmen Square massacre

Preview Section 4

The Inside Story

How did two guys in a garage change the world?

The 1980s saw changes in technology that transformed the way people live. One of the first dramatic moments in the revolution came in 1977, when a college dropout named Steve Jobs and his friend Steve Wozniak developed a computer small enough to fit on a desk. Called the Apple II, the machine brought computers into people's homes for the first time. At about the same time, another college dropout, Bill Gates, developed a new system to operate computers. His software, and his company, Microsoft, changed the world of computers, and would change the world itself.

1. What technology that you use frequently was invented after 1980?
2. Why did the Apple II represent a dramatic change in computers?

Review Answers: 1. a policy of openness begun by Mikhail Gorbachev; 2. restructuring of the Soviet government under Gorbachev; 3. a peaceful revolution that ended Communist rule in Czechoslovakia in 1989; 4. Chinese tanks gunning down unarmed people who were taking part in pro-democracy demonstrations in Beijing
Preview Answers: 1. possible answers—cell phones, DVD players, CD players, instant messaging, digital cameras, GPS systems; 2. It was small enough to fit on a desk, and it could be used by people in their homes.

Copyright © by Holt, Rinehart and Winston. All rights reserved.

Taking Notes

tax increases, increased unemployment, and higher poverty rates

---

BEFORE YOU READ

MAIN IDEA

The 1980s and early 1990s saw major technological, economic, and social changes that produced both progress and intense conflicts.

READING FOCUS

1. How did new technologies such as the space shuttle affect society?
2. How did changes in the economy of the 1980s affect various groups of Americans?
3. What other changes and challenges did U.S. society face in the 1980s?

KEY TERMS AND PEOPLE

Steve Jobs
Bill Gates
space shuttle
Alan Greenspan
savings and loan crisis
Sandra Day O'Connor
Clarence Thomas

 **TAKING NOTES** As you read, take notes identifying the effects of the rising national debt during the 1980s and early 1990s. Record your notes in a graphic organizer like the one shown here.

Rising National Debt → Effects

Dawn of the Digital Age

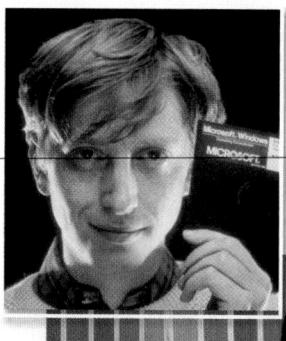

The innovations of Bill Gates (left) and Steve Jobs (below) changed the way Americans live, work, and play.

THE INSIDE STORY

How did two guys in a garage change the world? Try to envision the technology—or lack of it—in the year 1980. There were no home computers, CDs, DVDs, or plasma-screen TVs; no cell phones or e-mail. Microwaves and VCRs were still quite new. In 1980 people rushed to buy a new game played right on the television: Pac Man.

All that would change in the 1980s. New inventions brought immense changes in the way people lived—changes as significant, perhaps, as the invention of the printing press and the automobile.

While some revolutions start on a battlefield or in a laboratory, the personal computer revolution started in a garage in Cupertino, California. That's where **Steve Jobs**, a restless college dropout, and a friend, Steve Wozniak, started a small business called Apple Computer. The Apple II home computer was introduced in 1977. More a toy than a tool at first, Apple computers soon transformed the way Americans lived and worked.

Computers existed already, but Apple made them smaller—small enough to be usable at home on a desktop. Jobs's genius was in recognizing that computers could have appeal far beyond the community of scientists, military engineers, and other academics already using them.

Like Steve Jobs, **Bill Gates** was born in 1955 and dropped out of college to form a company. His Seattle-based company, Microsoft, invented a new type of computer-operating software. The time was ripe for his innovation. When Gates leased the software to the largest computer manufacturer, IBM (International Business Machines), a business giant was born. Microsoft soon became the world leader in computer software.

1066 CHAPTER 32

Teach the Main Idea

At Level

Life in the 1980s

1. **Teach** Ask students the Reading Focus questions to teach this section.

2. **Apply** Draw three large ladders for students to see. Label the top of each ladder with one of the three topics of this section: The Space Shuttle Blasts Off, The Economy of the 1980s, and Changes and Challenges in American Society. As you discuss each topic, list the main events on the appropriate rungs of each ladder.

3. **Review** As you review the section, guide students in a discussion of the relationships among the three topics, and have students copy the completed graphic organizer.

4. **Practice/Homework** Have students write a one-page summary of the challenges and problems facing the United States during the 1980s. **LS Visual-Spatial, Verbal-Linguistic**

Alternative Assessment Handbook, Rubrics 11: Discussions; and 13: Graphic Organizers

The Space Shuttle Blasts Off

Besides the computer, one of the more stunning technological developments of the 1980s was a new type of spacecraft. Unlike previous spacecraft, the new **space shuttle** could be reused after each flight. It lifted off like a rocket but returned to Earth like an airplane. Engineers at the National Aeronautics and Space Administration (NASA) had been developing a reusable spacecraft since the 1970s. They saw the space shuttle as a workhorse, carrying satellites and scientific experiments into space on a routine basis.

On April 12, 1981, millions of television viewers around the world watched the triumphant liftoff of the first shuttle, *Columbia*, from Cape Kennedy, Florida. At Air Force Plant 42 in Palmdale, California, where *Columbia* was built, "There was not a dry eye in the whole place," former plant commander Joe Davies recalled.

On January 28, 1986, tragedy struck the shuttle program when *Challenger* exploded after liftoff. All seven astronauts on board died, including the first private passenger, schoolteacher Christa McAuliffe. President Reagan led the nation in mourning.

Under President Reagan, NASA explored military and commercial uses for the space shuttle. This shift in priorities, along with proposals for the Star Wars (SDI) missile defense program, raised concerns about the militarization of space. The first military satellite was launched by the space shuttle in 1985.

Beyond space exploration, the shuttle program also benefited society more directly. Technologies developed or discovered by scientists on the program led to the development of such products as infrared cameras for detecting fires and a treatment for brain tumors.

READING CHECK **Summarizing** What hopes and disappointments did the space shuttle create?

The *Challenger* Space Shuttle Tragedy

The large picture shows the *Challenger* space shuttle launch on January 28, 1986. Just 73 seconds after liftoff, the *Challenger* exploded, killing the crew. Spectators reacted with horror as they watched the explosion. The *Challenger* crew included the space program's first civilian passenger, New Hampshire schoolteacher Christa McAuliffe (back row, second from left).

1067

❷ How did changes in the economy of the 1980s affect various groups of Americans? *farmers suffered; many industry workers lost jobs; some Americans lost jobs in corporate "downsizing"; wealthiest Americans profited from Reagan's tax cuts and growing economy*

The Economy of the 1980s

Explain How did tax cuts and increased military spending increase the deficit? *More money went out than came in.*

Identify Cause and Effect How did business and securities deregulation cause economic trouble? *corporate raiders bought stock of declining companies at low prices; merged or sold off the companies, causing corporate downsizing and massive layoffs*

Evaluate How would you rate President George H. W. Bush on his handling of the economy? *possible answer—poor, because raised taxes, deficit continued to grow, poverty and unemployment rose*

Activity **The American Economy in the 1980s** Divide the class into two groups. Have one group represent Americans who support Reagan's economic policies and the other group represent those who oppose Reagan's economic policies. Have the two groups debate the success of Reagan's economic policies.

The Economy of the 1980s

Like most periods in American history, the 1980s witnessed both good and bad economic trends. Some were not apparent until the late 1980s and the early 1990s.

Uneven economic growth The 1980s marked the longest period of U.S. peacetime economic growth up to that time. The gross domestic product (GDP), the total value of goods and services produced by the nation, grew at an average annual rate of 3.5 percent from 1982 to 1989. The stock market, too, rose to then historic highs, slowed only temporarily by a crash in 1987.

The strong growth was achieved without the high inflation that had troubled the country throughout the 1970s. The deep recession of 1982 helped to slash inflation, though at the cost of high unemployment. Moves by the Federal Reserve Board also helped. Under chairperson Paul Volcker and his successor, **Alan Greenspan**, "the Fed," as it is known, actively raised and lowered interest rates to help avoid either recession or inflation.

Following the recovery, inflation stayed under 5 percent during the rest of the 1980s and early 1990s. Unemployment slowly dropped as well. Some people credit Reaganomics for many of the positive economic trends of the 1980s. Others point to the Federal Reserve Board.

But the strong economic growth of the 1980s was unevenly distributed. Many farmers, for example, did poorly during the decade. In 1986 and 1988 droughts struck the Midwest, turning cropland into wasteland. The droughts were followed by destructive floods. Meanwhile, crop and farmland prices declined. Farmers became mired in debt.

The recession of 1982–83 had struck older U.S. industries, such as steel and automobile production, particularly hard. Many factories closed, throwing tens of thousands out of work. Bankruptcies rose 50 percent in one year. Homelessness increased sharply in many cities. Yet the relief provided by the Reagan tax cuts mainly benefited wealthier Americans.

Rising deficits Reagan's tax cuts, coupled with increased military spending, threatened to undermine the success in combating inflation. With expenditures far outstripping tax revenue, the government's annual budget deficit nearly tripled, from $74 billion in 1980 to $221 billion in 1986. The national debt grew from about $1.2 trillion to $5.7 trillion. The interest alone on the debt increased 61 percent between 1980 and 1986. The huge government borrowing needed to fund the deficit raised fears of renewed inflation.

Another troubling economic sign was the rising U.S. trade deficit, the difference between the value of American exports and imports. The trade deficit grew throughout the 1980s as Asian economies roared to life, producing high quality goods such as automobiles by using cheaper labor and new, efficient processes.

Financial deregulation The deregulation of financial services under Reagan led to innovative business practices that changed the face of American business. Led by business tycoons such as Ivan Boesky, corporate raiders bought declining companies at a low price. They restructured them by merging them, selling off pieces of them, or dissolving them. They then sold the new entities at high prices. This corporate downsizing resulted in huge employee layoffs. Not all firms wanted to be purchased, so corporate raiders engaged in hostile takeovers. Supporters maintained that corporate raiders weeded out weak companies and improved productivity.

Savings and loan crisis The deregulation of the savings and loan (S&L) industry showed some of the risks of deregulation. S&Ls traditionally had used the money deposited to make home mortgage loans. Deregulation allowed S&Ls to offer other services, such as credit cards and investment management.

During a 1980s housing boom, deregulated S&Ls loaned out too much of their wealth. When the boom went bust, borrowers defaulted on their loans. S&Ls went bankrupt on a massive scale. The **savings and loan crisis** forced the federal government to step in and guarantee the deposits. The bailout cost taxpayers an estimated $152 billion.

Bush and the economy The S&L crisis and a recession that began in late 1990 forced President Bush to break his campaign pledge of "no new taxes." The tax hike did not prevent the deficit from climbing to $271 billion in 1992.

THE IMPACT TODAY

Government In 2005 Ben S. Bernanke became chair of the Federal Reserve Board. Bernanke succeeded Alan Greenspan, who retired after heading the Federal Reserve Board for 18 years.

Skills Focus: Drawing Conclusions
At Level

Reading Skill
The Economy of the 1980s

1. Draw a two-column table for students to see. Label the table as shown. Omit the italicized answers. Have students copy and complete the table by listing the economic problems and grading the president based on the way in which he handled each challenge.
   S Visual-Spatial

   📋 Alternative Assessment Handbook, Rubric 13: Graphic Organizers

   🖨 Graphic Organizer Transparencies

PRESIDENT BUSH'S ECONOMIC REPORT CARD

Challenge	Grade
Save Social Security	
Slow Unemployment	
Slow Inflation	
Strengthen Military	
Reduce Deficit	

The Savings and Loan Crisis

Some members of Congress had grave concerns about the specific costs and methods of the S&L bailout.

Many lawmakers believed the government had to bail out savings and loans and restore depositors' money, despite the cost.

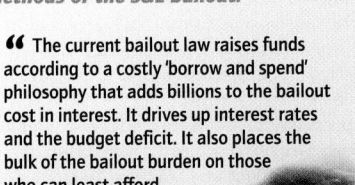

❝ The current bailout law raises funds according to a costly 'borrow and spend' philosophy that adds billions to the bailout cost in interest. It drives up interest rates and the budget deficit. It also places the bulk of the bailout burden on those who can least afford to bear it: America's working and poor families. ❞

Rep. Joseph P. Kennedy II

(D., MA), 1990

❝ The deposit insurance grew out of the hard-learned lesson of the banking crisis that helped trigger the Great Depression. A failure to stand behind federally insured deposits would condemn us to repeat the mistakes of the past. People would lose their money and their faith in their Government, and there would be a bank panic rivaling the runs on deposits 60 years ago. ❞

Rep. James McDermott

(D., WA), 1989

> **Skills FOCUS   READING LIKE A HISTORIAN**
>
> **Identifying Points of View** How did the two legislators differ? Were they necessarily in complete opposition to one another? Explain.
>
> **See Skills Handbook, pp. H28–H29**

Unemployment and poverty rose significantly during his term. Despite his foreign-policy successes, economic troubles at home proved to be Bush's political downfall.

> **READING CHECK   Identifying Supporting Details** List major economic trends of the 1980s.

Changes and Challenges in American Society

Social issues proved increasingly divisive in the 12 years of the Reagan and Bush administrations. Political controversies opened new cultural battle lines in America.

Milestones During the elections of the 1980s, pollsters identified a gender gap in voting patterns. Women were voting in greater proportions than men, and they voted more Democratic. Politicians began to pay more attention to women voters and their interests.

Several women in politics achieved notable milestones. In 1981 President Reagan chose an Arizona judge, **Sandra Day O'Connor**, to be the first woman on the U.S. Supreme Court. Reagan also appointed a woman, Jeane Kirkpatrick, to serve as ambassador to the United Nations. In 1984 Democratic presidential candidate Walter Mondale named the first woman, New York Congresswoman Geraldine Ferraro, to run on a major party ticket.

Another milestone of the era was the passage of the Americans with Disabilities Act. The law, signed by President Bush in 1990, represented the culmination of years of work by activists for disabled Americans. It outlawed discrimination on the basis of physical impairment and required employers to make "reasonable accomodations" for people with disabilities.

Changes in immigration law New waves of refugees from Southeast Asia and from poverty and upheaval in Cuba, Haiti, and other parts of Latin America triggered revisions

A CONSERVATIVE ERA **1069**

---

3 What other changes and challenges did U.S. society face in the 1980s? *politicians took more interest in women voters and their issues, women appointed to high public office; changes in immigration policy; conservative judges appointed to Supreme Court; court battles over controversial social issues, including abortion; outbreak of AIDS*

Changes and Challenges in American Society

Identify Who was Geraldine Ferraro? *vice presidential candidate, first woman to run on a major party ticket*

Explain Why was the appointment of Justice Sandra Day O'Connor a landmark event? *first woman ever to serve on the Supreme Court*

Make Judgments Why do you think it took so long for politicians to see women as an important voting bloc? *Historically, women had voted as their husbands did; women's issues had not come to the forefront until the 1960s and after; women began to seek change through the political process.*

> **Activity** **New Challenges for Americans** Have students write a brief essay predicting how new progress for women, changes in immigration law, and the discovery of AIDS will affect the future of American society.
> **LS Verbal-Linguistic**

Differentiating Instruction

Above Level

Advanced Learners/GATE

Research Required

1. Remind students that Sandra Day O'Connor was the first woman justice appointed to the Supreme Court. Have students make a list of women justices and then use secondary sources to write a brief background of each.

2. Have students locate primary and secondary sources that examine and suggest how the Supreme Court may have changed or been affected by the women justices. Have students write a summary of their findings.

3. Have students identify and read one Supreme

Court case in which one of the women justices wrote either the majority opinion or a significant dissenting opinion. Have students write a brief summary of the case and an analysis of the position taken by the justice. In their analyses students should examine the decision in detail and try to explain the reasoning behind the decision.
LS Verbal-Linguistic

📄 Alternative Assessment Handbook, Rubrics 30: Research; and 42: Writing to Inform

Answers

Reading Like a Historian *McDermott supported government bailout in order to prevent a bank panic; Kennedy opposed government bailout because concerned about cost for poor Americans; possible answer—no, both concerned about effect on ordinary Americans*

Reading Check *GDP grew; inflation and unemployment slowed; rising deficit, fluctuating interest rates; corporate downsizing; savings and loan crisis; farm problems*

Changes and Challenges in American Society

Explain What part did Robert Bork play in the Reagan administration? *nominated by President Reagan to fill Supreme Court vacancy, but was rejected by Senate*

Describe What is the Equal Access Act? *requires that schools receiving federal funding must give equal access to the facilities to those who seek to express "religious, political, philosophical or other content"*

Make Judgments Would you describe President Bush as a politician with conservative values or a conservative with political aspirations? *either or both can be defended; students should explain choice*

Activity Justice Clarence Thomas Have students write a paragraph explaining why Supreme Court nominee Clarence Thomas should have been accepted or rejected during the Senate confirmation hearing.

CRF: Biography: Richard John Neuhaus

Info to Know

Robert Bork President Reagan nominated Robert Bork to the Supreme Court, but he did not receive Senate confirmation. Prior to his nomination, however, Bork worked for President Nixon during the Watergate-era Saturday Night Massacre. It was Bork who fired special prosecutor Archibald Cox after Attorney General Elliot Richardson and Deputy Attorney General William Ruckelshaus each refused to do so and resigned.

Answers

American Religious Liberty
the extent to which religious beliefs should be a part of political leadership and institutions

---

in U.S. immigration policy during the 1980s. Laws passed in 1980 and 1986 increased legal immigration limits and granted legal status to nearly 3 million undocumented immigrants living in the United States. It also toughened penalties on employers who knowingly hired undocumented workers. Despite these measures, illegal immigration continued to grow.

Court battles over social issues During the Reagan and Bush administrations, the Supreme Court ruled on several sensitive landmark cases. The rulings in these cases are still being felt today.

In the 1985 case *New Jersey* v. *T.L.O.*, the Court ruled that schools have the right to search students' belongings without being in violation of the Fourth Amendment's prohibition of unreasonable searches. You can read more about this case in the Landmark Supreme Court Cases in Section 1 of this chapter.

In *Westside Community School District* v. *Mergens*, the Supreme Court in 1990 ruled that a high school in Omaha, Nebraska, had to allow students to form an after-school Christian group that could meet on school grounds. Upholding the Equal Access Act, the ruling required schools that receive federal funding to provide equal access to student groups seeking to express "religious, political, philosophical, or other content."

Following the 1973 *Roe* v. *Wade* decision legalizing abortion, the Court issued rulings that further defined the scope of *Roe*. In the 1992 case *Planned Parenthood of Southeastern PA* v. *Casey*, the Court ruled that a state could require a woman seeking an abortion to give informed consent, to wait 24 hours, and in the case of a minor, to obtain parental consent.

In another sensitive case, the Court set a precedent in cases involving the removal of life-support equipment from a critically ill patient. Nancy Cruzan sustained severe brain damage in a car accident and was said to be in a "persistent vegetative state," kept alive by a feeding tube and other medical means. The 1990 ruling in *Cruzan* v. *Director, Missouri Dept. of Health* recognized an adult's right to refuse medical treatment. But it ruled that the state could require "clear and convincing evidence" that the patient would have wanted to have life support removed under the circumstances.

Battles over Supreme Court nominees President Reagan had the rare opportunity to fill three seats on the Supreme Court. He also

American Religious Liberty

Churches and Politics

In recent decades, Christian conservatives have been a powerful political force. Christian fundamentalism and evangelism became popular in the 1920s and gained new power when Reagan came to office. Fundamentalists and evangelicals believe in a strict interpretation of the Bible as a source of clear direction and values in society.

One leading Baptist fundamentalist minister, Jerry Falwell, called for conservative Christians to become more active in politics. He believed that the country was facing problems because its political leaders had turned away from the Christian values upon which, he said, the United States was founded. Falwell and other conservative Christians, including the Reverend Pat Robertson and Eagle Forum founder Phyllis Schlafly, maintained that they were promoting their right to practice religion. Some opponents felt that the increased influence of religion in politics threatened the separation of church and state. The nation continues to seek ways to balance the rights of religious groups with the rights of those who have other opinions and beliefs.

Identifying the Main Idea What is the basic disagreement between some fundamentalists and their critics?

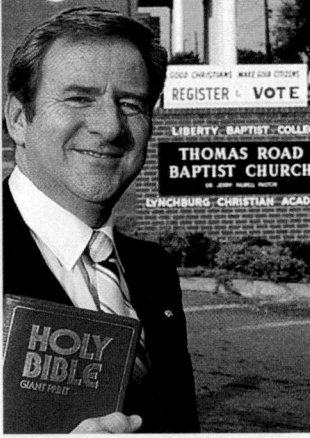

Falwell began his career at the Thomas Road Baptist Church.

Differentiating Instruction

Below Level

English-Language Learners

Research Required

Materials construction paper, colored markers

1. Have students work in pairs to search the Internet or use traditional print sources to find old pictures and articles about the people discussed in this section: Geraldine Ferraro, Sandra Day O'Connor, Robert Bork, Clarence Thomas, Anita Hill, Nancy Cruzan.

2. Have students copy and paste the pictures and articles onto construction paper.

3. Under each picture, have students write a sentence summarizing the importance of the person and the name of the president, either Reagan or Bush, who is most closely associated with that person.

4. Have volunteers share their completed posters with the class. **LS Visual-Spatial, Interpersonal**

Alternative Assessment Handbook, Rubric 28: Posters

appealed about half the judges in the federal court system. Both Reagan and Bush sought to appoint conservative judges, at times setting off furious confirmation clashes in the Senate.

In 1987 Reagan nominated Robert Bork, a law professor and appeals court judge. Bork advocated a strict interpretation of the Constitution. Many senators and liberal groups feared he would roll back *Roe* v. *Wade* and civil rights laws. After angry hearings, the Senate rejected Bork. It later confirmed Reagan's next nominee, Anthony Kennedy.

Another battle took place over a Bush nominee to the Supreme Court in 1991. This nominee was **Clarence Thomas**, a conservative African American judge and former head of the federal Equal Opportunity Employment Commission (EEOC). In televised hearings, the Judiciary Committee investigated charges by law professor Anita Hill that Thomas had sexually harassed her when she worked for him at the EEOC. Hill underwent aggressive questioning by Republican senators defending Thomas, which offended many women. Thomas narrowly won confirmation.

A deadly disease In 1981 scientists identified what has since become one of the worst outbreaks of infectious disease in human history: acquired immunodeficiency syndrome, or AIDS. The deadly disease is caused by the human

Clarence Thomas's confirmation hearings were dominated by the accusation of sexual harassment. Critics were also concerned over his level of experience and his reluctance to reveal his stance on controversial issues.

immunodeficiency virus (HIV). AIDS first appeared among homosexual men and intravenous drug users, and the means of contracting it was not known. As a result, people with AIDS suffered discrimination. Scientists eventually determined that the disease is spread through transmission of bodily fluids, including sexual contact. AIDS has since spread to millions of men and women around the world.

READING CHECK **Summarizing** What major social changes occurred in the 1980s and early 1990s?

SECTION 4 ASSESSMENT

go.hrw.com
Online Quiz
Keyword: SD7 HP32

Reviewing Ideas, Terms, and People

1. a. Identify What pioneering roles did **Steve Jobs** and **Bill Gates** have in American society?
b. Make Inferences How do you think people reacted to the rapid technological changes brought about by the invention of personal computers?
c. Evaluate Do you think Reagan's emphasis on using the **space shuttle** for military and commercial purposes was wise, or should it have been reserved for scientific use only?

2. a. Recall What role did **Alan Greenspan** have in the changing U.S. economy?
b. Analyze Explain the connection between deregulation and trends such as hostile takeovers and the **savings and loan crisis**.
c. Evaluate How would you characterize the overall impact of Reaganomics?

3. a. Identify What firsts did Geraldine Ferraro and **Sandra Day O'Connor** achieve?
b. Predict What would be the long-term effects of Reagan's decision to nominate conservative justices to the Supreme Court?

Critical Thinking

4. Identifying Cause and Effect Copy the chart below, and complete it with the causes and effects.

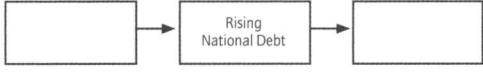

Rising National Debt

FOCUS ON WRITING

5. Persuasive Make the case for or against "trickle down" economic policies, using facts from the section.

A CONSERVATIVE ERA **1071**

Wealth in the 1980s

Word Help

indulge gratify a wish
fiscal financial

Primary Source

Ivan Boesky, a financier, was one of the inspirations for the character of Gordon Gekko. In 1986, Boesky spoke about greed at the commencement address for the University of California, Berkeley: "Greed is all right, by the way . . . I think greed is healthy. You can be greedy and still feel good about yourself."

Info to Know

Invasion of the Body Snatchers

Released in 1956, *Invasion of the Body Snatchers* was a science-fiction film that told the story of aliens who took over a small California town. The aliens replaced the residents of the town with beings that appeared identical, but lacked individuality and feelings. As the aliens replaced the humans while they were asleep, no one was aware of the change. This film has been interpreted in many ways. Some critics believed the aliens represent communism, which terrified many Americans in the 1950s. Other critics claimed that the aliens depicted McCarthyism. According to director Don Siegel, the film conveyed the fact that most humans are simply not motivated enough to resist a destructive movement.

CHAPTER 32 DOCUMENT-BASED INVESTIGATION

Wealth in the 1980s

Historical Context The documents below provide different information about wealth in the 1980s: getting it, losing it, and being fascinated by it.

Task Examine the documents and answer the questions that follow. Then you will be asked to write an essay about how Americans viewed wealth in the 1980s, using facts from the documents and from the chapter to support the position you take in your thesis statement.

DOCUMENT 1

The rising stock market created enormous wealth for American stockholders. Some corporate managers became more concerned with companies' stock prices and profits than with their products. In the 1987 movie *Wall Street*, corporate raider Gordon Gekko, based on real-life characters such as Ivan Boesky, tells stockholders that his takeover of their company will benefit them because he will hire managers who will maximize profits for investors.

> "Well, ladies and gentlemen, we're not here to indulge in fantasy, but in political and economic reality. America—America has become a second-rate power. Its trade deficit and its fiscal deficit are at nightmare proportions. Now, in the days of the free market, when our country was a top industrial power, there was accountability to the stockholder. The Carnegies, the Mellons, the men that built this great industrial empire, made sure of it because it was their money at stake. Today, management has no stake in the company! . . .
>
> "The new law of evolution in corporate America seems to be survival of the unfittest. Well, in my book you either do it right or you get eliminated. . . .
>
> "I am not a destroyer of companies. I am a liberator of them! The point is, ladies and gentleman, is that greed—for lack of a better word—is good. Greed is right. Greed works. Greed clarifies, cuts through, and captures the essence of the evolutionary spirit. Greed, in all of its forms—greed for life, for money, for love, knowledge—has marked the upward surge of mankind. And greed—you mark my words—will not only save Teldar Paper, but that other malfunctioning corporation called the USA."

1072 CHAPTER 32

DOCUMENT 2

Corporate raiders bought vulnerable companies in order to reorganize and sell them or to break them up and sell off their valuable parts. Other tactics that produced great wealth on Wall Street included investments in junk bonds as well as greenmail—a tactic of tricking other investors into buying stock at a high price. The 1985 cartoon below comments on these tactics. It is titled "Invasion of the Corporate Body Snatchers," a spoof on a popular movie about aliens who take over the world.

"INVASION OF THE CORPORATE BODY SNATCHERS" FROM *HERBLOCK AT LARGE* (PANTHEON BOOKS, 1987)

Skills Focus: Making Written Presentations

At Level

Reading Like a Historian Skill

Research Required

Wall Street Greed

1. Guide the class in a discussion of the tactics used in the 1980s to gain wealth from the stock market.

2. Divide the class into small groups. Have each group research one of the tactics they have read about, such as greenmail, junk bonds, leveraged buyouts, or corporate raiders. Have each group write a brief report on how the tactic works and provide at least one example of its use during the 1980s.

3. Have volunteers read their reports to the class.
   LS Interpersonal, Verbal-Linguistic

   Alternative Assessment Handbook, Rubric 29: Presentations

DOCUMENT 3

The economic boom of the 1980s saw an increase in incomes for many families without the high inflation that had wiped out most income increases in the 1970s. Some of the biggest beneficiaries of the 1980s boom were richer families, who saw their incomes increase, largely from successful investments. The chart below shows the changes in wealth for families in the lowest, middle, and highest income brackets.

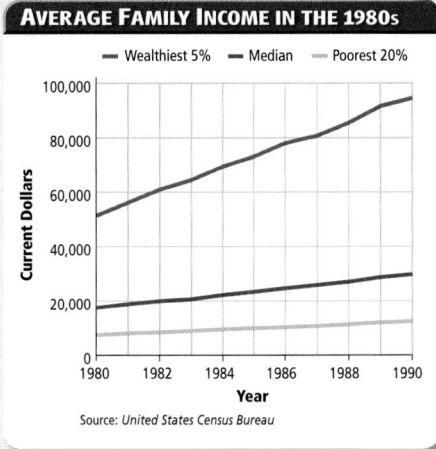

AVERAGE FAMILY INCOME IN THE 1980s

— Wealthiest 5% — Median Poorest 20%

Source: United States Census Bureau

DOCUMENT 4

Americans were fascinated by the wealthy in the 1980s. Young people throughout the country copied the preppy look, imitating fashions associated with wealthy families of the East Coast. The most popular television shows were nighttime soap operas like *Dallas* and *Dynasty* that portrayed glamorous, if troubled, lives of rich families. In *Dynasty*, the large, oil-rich Carrington family lived an opulent lifestyle, yet they personified the saying that wealth doesn't bring happiness. Millions of viewers tuned in each week to watch the Carrington spouses, parents, and children viciously fight and plot against one another.

Primary Source

In 1984, pop singer Madonna had a hit with the song "Material Girl," which summed up American interest in and attitude toward wealth:

... the boy with the cold hard cash
Is always Mr. Right
'Cause we are living in a material
*   world*
And I am a material girl
You know that we are living in a mate-
*   rial world*
And I am a material girl.

From "Material Girl" by Peter Brown and Robert Rans. Copyright © 1984 by Peter Brown and Robert Rans. Reproduced by permission of **Candy Castle Music, BMI (Broadcast Music Inc.).**

Skills FOCUS — READING LIKE A HISTORIAN

1. a. Summarize Refer to Document 1. What does Gekko say about greed?
b. Interpret What point is Gekko trying to make about the American economy?

2. a. Describe Refer to Document 2. How does the cartoonist portray corporate tactics?
b. Analyze What message is the cartoonist trying to send about the effects of such tactics on businesses?

3. a. Make Generalizations Refer to Document 3. What trends in income took place during this time period?
b. Elaborate How did the income gap between the richest and poorest families change from 1980 to 1990?

4. a. Contrast Refer to Document 4. How does the picture convey the image of wealth?
b. Elaborate How do you think the public's fascination with wealthy families on television reflected their views of wealth in the real world?

5. Document-Based Essay Question Consider the question below and form a thesis statement. Using examples from Documents 1, 2, 3, and 4, create an outline and write a short essay supporting your position.
How did American culture reflect fascination with and concerns about wealth during the 1980s?

See Skills Handbook, pp. H28–29, H31, H16

A CONSERVATIVE ERA **1073**

Collaborative Learning

At Level

Obsessed with Wealth

Materials construction paper, colored markers

1. Guide the class in a discussion of the American obsession with wealth, or the illusion of it, during the 1980s.

2. Divide the class into small groups. Have each group brainstorm to come up with ideas about goods or services that would have appealed to Americans during the 1980s. Have volunteers share their ideas with the class.

3. Have each group choose one of the goods or services and create a full-page magazine advertisement for it. Display student advertisements for the class to see.
LS Interpersonal, Visual-Spatial
Alternative Assessment Handbook, Rubric 2: Advertisements

Visual Summary

Review and Inquiry Organize the class into ten small groups, and assign each group one of the bulleted items in the Visual Summary. Have each group prepare a cause-and-effect statement for the bulleted item and explain why and what happened as a result of the bulleted statement. Have a volunteer from each group present its explanation to the class.

Quick Facts Transparency: A Conservative Era

Reviewing Key Terms and People

1. **Sandra Day O'Connor** was the first woman to serve on the U.S. Supreme Court.

2. During the **velvet revolution** in Czechoslovakia, Communist leaders were swept from power.

3. **Bill Gates** founded Microsoft.

4. The **space shuttle** could fly repeated missions and land on the ground.

5. During the **Tiananmen Square massacre** Chinese troops fired on unarmed protesters.

6. The **New Right** was a coalition of conservative media commentators, think tanks, and grassroots Christian groups.

7. **Lech Walesa** led the Polish Solidarity union and freedom movement.

8. **Clarence Thomas** was appointed to the Supreme Court in 1991.

9. The **Strategic Defense Initiative** was a space-based defensive weapon.

10. In the **Iran-Contra affair**, weapons were sold to Iran to obtain release of hostages in Lebanon; money was diverted to fund Contras in Nicaragua.

11. **David A. Stockman** was Reagan's economic adviser.

12. **Ronald Reagan** held conservative views.

Visual Summary: A Conservative Era

Reagan's First Term
- Under President Reagan, people have renewed confidence in America.
- Conservative policies begin, such as smaller government and increased defense spending
- Supply-side economics, lower taxes, and big deficits occur.

Reagan's Foreign Policy
- The Soviet Union becomes a partner in arms control.
- Staunch anti-communism leads to the invasion of Grenada and the Iran-Contra scandal.

The Reagan and Bush Administrations

The New World Order
- George H. W. Bush becomes president.
- Soviet empire collapses, although China remains Communist.
- "New world order" proves dangerous, as United States goes to war with Iraq.

Life in the 1980s
- Good economic times, although not for all.
- Social issues divide society and lead to Supreme Court battles.

Reviewing Key Terms and People

For each term or name below, write a sentence explaining its significance.

1. Sandra Day O'Connor
2. velvet revolution
3. Bill Gates
4. space shuttle
5. Tiananmen Square massacre
6. New Right
7. Lech Walesa
8. Clarence Thomas
9. Strategic Defense Initiative
10. Iran-Contra affair
11. David A. Stockman
12. Ronald Reagan

Comprehension and Critical Thinking

SECTION 1 *(pp. 1046–1051)*

13. **a. Identify** Write a brief explanation of the following terms: supply-side economics, Reaganomics.

b. Analyze How did Ronald Reagan represent the conservative response to the liberalism of the 1960s?

c. Rank How important were social changes to conservatives? How important were economic and governmental changes?

SECTION 2 *(pp. 1053–1058)*

14. **a. Recall** What was Solidarity? How did it rise to power?

b. Draw Conclusions How was the success of Solidarity an early indicator of troubles for the Soviet Union?

c. Evaluate Was Ronald Reagan successful in increasing pressure on the Soviet Union for change? Explain.

Comprehension and Critical Thinking

13. **a.** supply-side economics—tax cuts and business incentives will stimulate the economy; Reaganomics—reduce taxes, cut federal budget
b. wanted to reduce the federal bureaucracy, deregulate certain industries, cut taxes, increase the defense budget, take a stronger stance against the Soviet Union, and appoint conservative judges
c. possible answer—economic changes and reducing the size of the government more important

14. **a.** Polish labor union; emerged after a strike by electrical workers protesting increases in food prices; became a freedom movement
b. Soviet-backed government legalized labor unions
c. possible answer—yes, made Berlin Wall an issue; met with Gorbachev to discuss cuts in military spending

15. **a.** plan to reform Soviet system, restructure economy and government.
b. Soviet Union dissolved; START I and START II, Panamanian dictator removed from power; end of apartheid in South Africa; First Gulf War; China

History's Impact video program

Review the video to answer the closing question:
What did the collapse of the Berlin Wall signify for
both the United States and the rest of the world?

SECTION 3 (pp. 1059–1065)

15. a. Describe How did *glasnost* and *perestroika*
come about in the Soviet Union? What were they
meant to accomplish?

b. Sequence What major foreign-policy challenges
occurred during the administration of President
George H. W. Bush?

c. Elaborate Why did the START talks represent
such a major change in U.S.–Soviet relations?

SECTION 4 (pp. 1066–1071)

16. a. Identify Explain the significance of the following: Alan Greenspan, savings and loan crisis.

b. Generalize What major trends occurred in the
American economy during the 1980s?

c. Evaluate In 1980 Ronald Reagan asked the
country, "Are you better off than you were four
years ago?" How do you think most Americans
would have answered that question at the end of
his presidency?

Using the Internet

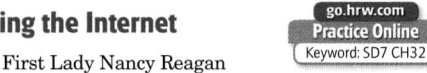

go.hrw.com
Practice Online
Keyword: SD7 CH32

17. First Lady Nancy Reagan
was a complicated figure in American politics and
history. She was criticized for the way she ran the
White House and influenced her husband. She
also was greatly admired by many Americans.
Using the keyword above, research and write a
short biography of Nancy Reagan that emphasizes
her impact on the country and on her husband's
administration.

Analyzing Primary Sources

Reading Like a Historian Reread the quotation from
President Reagan's "evil empire" speech in Section 2.
Then answer the following questions.

18. How did Reagan distinguish his view of the Soviet
Union from others' views?

19. What words does Reagan use to emphasize his
opinion of the Soviet Union and its goals?

Critical Reading

*Read the American Civil Liberty feature in Section 1
titled "Smaller Government." Then answer the
questions that follow.*

20. Ronald Reagan opposed big government because
he believed that

A taxes on poor people were too high.

B government did not control industries such as
petroleum and airlines.

C government did not provide enough services.

D government spent too much and regulated too
much.

21. Reagan wanted to change government by

A increasing the budget deficit.

B deregulating industries and cutting taxes.

C placing restrictions on key industries.

D increasing spending on social programs.

WRITING FOR THE SAT

Think about the following issue.

**To battle apartheid in South Africa, the Reagan
administration preferred a policy of "constructive engagement." Critics wanted to cut off relations with the white government and withdraw
U.S. investments in the South African economy.
Reagan disagreed, saying that if the United
States withdrew, it would have no bargaining
power with which to influence government
policy. Congress opposed Reagan and placed a
boycott on some South African products.**

22. Assignment When a government such as South
Africa pursues repressive policies against its
people, should the United States punish it harshly
by boycotting its products and severing government relations? Or, should it allow U.S. businesses
to continue to operate in the country, using the
threat of withdrawal to force the government to
change its ways? Support your answer with reasoning and facts.

A CONSERVATIVE ERA **1075**

c. significant arms reduction; no
longer adversaries

16. a. chairman, Federal Reserve
Board; risky loans, bankruptcies
b. economic growth; threat of
inflation; increase in trade deficit;
savings and loan crisis; recession
c. possible answer—better because
of economic growth

Using the Internet

17. Go to the HRW Web site and
enter the keyword shown to
access a rubric for this activity.

KEYWORD: SD7 CH32

Analyzing Primary Sources

18. does not see arms race as giant
misunderstanding

19. "aggressive impulses"; "right and
wrong and good and evil"

Critical Reading

20. D

21. B

Writing for the SAT

22. possible answer—boycotts, severing
relations are most effective

A rubric for this activity is provided
in the Chapter Resource File: Writing
for the SAT: The Strategic Defense
Initiative.

History's Impact
Video Program

that Soviet-Style communism was
collapsing

Review and Assessment Resources

Review and Reinforce

- CRF: Chapter Review Activity
- Quick Facts Transparencies:
  Reagan's Foreign Policy; A Conservative Era
- Spanish Chapter Summaries Audio CD Program
- Online Chapter Summaries in Spanish
- OSP Holt PuzzlePro; Quiz Show for ExamView
- Quiz Game CD-ROM

Assess

- PASS: Chapter Test, Forms A and B
- Alternative Assessment Handbook
- OSP ExamView Test Generator, Chapter Test
- Differentiated Instruction Modified
  Worksheets and Tests CD-ROM: Chapter Test
- HOAP Holt Online Assessment Program
  (in the Premier Online Edition)

Reteach/Intervene

- Interactive Reader and Study Guide
- Differentiated Instruction Teacher
  Management System: Lesson Plans
  for Differentiated Instruction
- Differentiated Instruction Modified
  Worksheets and Tests CD-ROM: Chapter Test
- Interactive Skills Tutor CD-ROM

go.hrw.com
Online Resources
KEYWORD: SD7 CH32

Into the Twenty-First Century

Chapter Overview	Reproducible Resources	Technology Resources
CHAPTER 33 pp. 1076–1111 **Overview:** In this chapter, students will analyze the presidencies of Clinton and Bush as they faced challenges at home and abroad.	**Differentiated Instruction Teacher Management System:*** • Instructional Benchmarking Guides • Lesson Plans for Differentiated Instruction **Interactive Reader and Study Guide:** Chapter Summary* **Chapter Resource File:*** • Focus on Writing Activity: The Future of America • Social Studies Skills Activity: Recognizing Bias • Chapter Review Activity **American History Outline Maps** **Pre-AP Activities Guide for American History***	Live Ink® Online Reading Help Student Edition on Audio CD Program Differentiated Instruction Modified Worksheets and Tests CD-ROM Interactive Skills Tutor CD-ROM United States History Primary Source Library CD-ROM Power Presentations with Video CD-ROM History's Impact: American History Video Program (VHS/DVD) Online Chapter Summaries in Spanish Graphic Organizer Transparencies
Section 1: **The Clinton Years** **The Main Idea:** Bill Clinton's presidential administration faced both challenges and scandals.	**Differentiated Instruction Teacher Management System:** Section 1 Lesson Plan* **Interactive Reader and Study Guide:** Section 1 Summary* **Chapter Resource File***	Daily Bellringer Transparency: Section 1* Daily Test Practice Transparency: Section 1*
Section 2: **George W. Bush's Presidency** **The Main Idea:** Following a troubled election, Republican George W. Bush won the White House and strongly promoted his agenda.	**Differentiated Instruction Teacher Management System:** Section 2 Lesson Plan* **Interactive Reader and Study Guide:** Section 2 Summary* **Chapter Resource File***	Daily Bellringer Transparency: Section 2* Daily Test Practice Transparency: Section 2*
Section 3: **How September 11, 2001, Changed America** **The Main Idea:** Terrorist attacks on September 11, 2001 changed America's view of the world.	**Differentiated Instruction Teacher Management System:** Section 3 Lesson Plan* **Interactive Reader and Study Guide:** Section 3 Summary* **Chapter Resource File***	Daily Bellringer Transparency: Section 3* Daily Test Practice Transparency: Section 3*
Section 4: **Looking Ahead** **The Main Idea:** A new century found the U.S. facing an era of opportunity and challenge.	**Differentiated Instruction Teacher Management System:** Section 4 Lesson Plan* **Interactive Reader and Study Guide:** Section 4 Summary* **Chapter Resource File***	Daily Bellringer Transparency: Section 4* Daily Test Practice Transparency: Section 4*

History's Impact
American History Video Program (VHS/DVD)
Into the Twenty-First Century

Review, Assessment, Intervention

Quick Facts Transparencies: Foreign Policy Team, Into the Twenty-First Century

Spanish Chapter Summaries Audio CD Program

Progress Assessment Support System (PASS): Chapter Test*

Differentiated Instruction Modified Worksheets and Tests CD-ROM: Modified Chapter Test

OSP **One-Stop Planner CD-ROM:** ExamView Test Generator (English/Spanish)

HOAP **Holt Online Assessment Program (HOAP),** in the Holt Premier Online Student Edition

PASS: Section 1 Quiz*
Online Quiz: Section 1
Alternative Assessment Handbook

PASS: Section 2 Quiz*
Online Quiz: Section 2
Alternative Assessment Handbook

PASS: Section 3 Quiz*
Online Quiz: Section 3
Alternative Assessment Handbook

PASS: Section 4 Quiz*
Online Quiz: Section 4
Alternative Assessment Handbook

NC RESOURCES

The following resources were developed to help North Carolina educators teach the standards and objectives of North Carolina's eleventh grade standard course of study in United States history.

• United States history EOC Test Prep Workbook
• Teacher's Support System
• North Carolina One-Stop Planner

And be sure to direct your students to **go.hrw.com** for online access to the EOC Test Prep Workbook.

go.hrw.com
EOC Test Prep
KEYWORD: SE7 NC

Holt Online Learning

go.hrw.com
Teacher Resources
KEYWORD: SD7 TEACHER

go.hrw.com
Student Resources
KEYWORD: SD7 CH33

• Document-based Questions
• Interactive Multimedia Activities

• Current Events
• Chapter-based Internet Activities
• and more!

Holt Premier
Online Student Edition
Complete online support for interactivity, assessment, and reporting
• Interactive Maps and Notebook
• Standardized Test Prep
• Homework Practice and Research Activities Online

CHAPTER 33 PLANNING GUIDE

Before You Teach

The Big Picture
Deborah Gray White

The Clinton Years The presidency of Bill Clinton, a centrist, was marked by economic prosperity and a budget surplus, although initial public enthusiasm waned after Clinton raised taxes and presented his health care program. Republicans responded with their Contract With America and took control of Congress in 1994. Still, Clinton pushed through a welfare reform bill and helped the nation cope with the domestic terrorist attack in Oklahoma. In foreign policy, Clinton supported free trade agreements, and American soldiers joined UN troops in Somalia and Haiti, and NATO troops in the region of the former Yugoslavia. In 1998, Clinton was impeached for lying about an improper relationship with a White House intern. After a highly contested election George W. Bush was elected president in 2000.

George W. Bush's Presidency The early years of Bush's first term were marked by tax cuts, faith-based initiatives, and the No Child Left Behind Act, but Bush's presidency was defined by the September 11, 2001, terrorist attacks on the United States. In retaliation, American forces attacked the Taliban government of Afghanistan that harbored apparent 9/11 planner Osama bin Laden. At home a Department of Homeland Security was created and the controversial USA PATRIOT Act was passed. Over the objections of many of its allies, American forces led an invasion of Iraq in search of weapons of mass destruction, which Bush feared might be used against the United States.

A New Century: Looking Ahead By 2050 white Americans may well comprise less than half of the nation's inhabitants. Life expectancy will increase, America's population will age, and the Sun Belt will grow. The nation must face the challenge of meeting the medical and energy needs of its citizens while protecting them from terrorist attacks and natural disasters.

Recent Scholarship

Immigration and the Future It has been predicted that by the year 2050 America's minority groups will make up 50 percent of the nation's population. But will they all get along? And in the face of large scale immigration from Asia and Latin America, what will happen to African Americans, historically the nation's largest minority? In *Collision Course: The Strange Convergence of Affirmative Action and Immigration Policy in America* (2002), the late historian and political scientist Hugh Davis Graham puts recent immigration and civil rights policy into historical perspective and explains the conflicting nature of the two policy issues.

Differentiating Instruction

Differentiated Instruction Teacher Management System
- Lesson Plans for Differentiated Instruction
- Differentiated Instructional Benchmarking Guides
- Interactive Reader and Study Guide

 Spanish Chapter Summaries Audio CD Program

 Online Chapter Summaries in Spanish

 Student Edition on Audio CD Program

 Differentiated Instruction Modified Worksheets and Tests CD-ROM
- Vocabulary Flash Cards
- Modified Vocabulary Builder Activities
- Modified Chapter Review Activity
- Modified Chapter Test

OSP One-Stop Planner CD-ROM
- ExamView Test Generator (English and Spanish)
- PuzzlePro
- Quiz Show for ExamView
- Transparencies and Videos

TE Differentiated Activities in the Teacher's Edition
- Ethnic Unrest in the Former Yugoslavia, p. 1082
- The 2000 Presidential Election, p. 1086
- The USA PATRIOT Act, p. 1097
- Images of Chinatown, p. 1105
- Letter From a New Neighborhood, p. 1105
- Creating a Quiz, p. 1106

Reading Like a Historian
Sam Wineburg

Fact and Opinion

Young people have a notoriously difficult time distinguishing fact from opinion. What can snare them is a "just the facts" rhetorical style shorn of the qualifiers ("may," "might," "must have," "seemed") that signal contestable claims. A case in point is the question of Osama bin Laden's goals for the 9/11 attacks.

Motivation

In the chapter, we are told that during the 1980s, bin Laden "adopted the goal of promoting a worldwide Islamic revolution" and that achieving it "required the destruction of the United States." This is what motivated bin Laden's attacks.

Certainly it is easy to find statements from radical Islamic groups that call for America's destruction. But is it the case that bin Laden thought that three planes would deal the United States a fatal blow?

Not according to Mark Danner, a political reporter who has journeyed to Iraq, Algeria, and Morocco to study Islamic extremism. Danner's views appeared in a cover article of the *New York Times Magazine* on the fourth anniversary of the 9/11 attacks.

Bin Laden's Goal

Commanding no state, no field army, and no permanent base, bin Laden was under no illusion that he could defeat the United States. To do so he would need a nuclear arsenal beyond his wildest dreams, and even more improbable, a launching pad for it.

But that, Danner argues, was not bin Laden's goal. Rather, in planning the attacks, bin Laden sought to puncture the myth of American invincibility.

A Worldwide Revolution

Which brings us to our chapter's second claim—that bin Laden's ultimate goal was a "worldwide Islamic revolution," to convert the globe to the faith of Muhammad. Danner and others argue that bin Laden's goal was not so much the spread of an Islamic revolution to the United States, South America, and other non-Muslim nations, but to bring an Islamic revolution to Jordan, Egypt, Saudi Arabia, and the Gulf States.

Here is where students will be completely confused because a scan of the CIA World Factbook (http://www.cia.gov/cia/publications/factbook/index.html) shows that in all of these countries the major religion is Islam. Why on earth would bin Laden want to spread Islam to countries that are already Muslim?

And this is the point when we must explain to students the nature of Islamic fundamentalism that claims that only its brand of Islam is authentic. Under intolerance's banner, adherents of these groups murder fellow Muslims in Egypt, Iraq, Saudi Arabia, Turkey, and elsewhere.

The Difficulty of Interpretation

That 9/11 happened, that radical Islam took responsibility for it: these are facts. But the precise motivation for the attack—no matter how forcefully stated in our chapter, by Mark Danner, or by me in the words you are now reading—remains murky, at least for the time being. Such is the nature of interpretations, which are by definition contestable and subject to questions about the adequacy of argument and the warrant for assertions.

Teaching students to analyze rather than memorize is what distinguishes the teaching of history in a democracy from its counterpart in a theocracy. That is why historical analysis is no mere intellectual game.

It is democracy's life force.

Standards Focus

Social Studies Competency Goals
Goal 12 The learner will identify and analyze trends in domestic and foreign affairs of the United States during this time period.
12.01, 12.02, 12.03, 12.05, 12.06

 The Big Idea and Essential Questions

To foster student understanding of this chapter's big idea, design your lesson to address each section's essential question.

Big Idea Americans faced the twenty-first century with hope, determination, and a readiness to embrace challenges at home and abroad.

Essential Questions

1. What challenges did President Bill Clinton face during his terms in office?

2. What were the achievements of the presidency of George W. Bush?

3. How did the events of September 11, 2001, change the United States and its views of the world?

4. What opportunities and challenges does the United States face as it heads into the future?

CHAPTER

33 1992–Present

Into the Twenty-First Century

THE BIG PICTURE Americans faced the twenty-first century with hope, determination, and a readiness to embrace all challenges.

North Carolina Standards

Social Studies Objectives

12.01 Summarize significant events in foreign policy since the Vietnam War.

12.02 Evaluate the impact of recent constitutional amendments, court rulings, and federal legislation on United States citizens.

12.03 Identify and assess the impact of economic, technological, and environmental changes in the United States.

12.05 Assess the impact of growing racial and ethnic diversity in American society.

12.06 Assess the impact of twenty-first century terrorist activity on American society.

Language Arts Objectives

3.02 Select an issue or theme and take a stance on that issue by:
  • reflecting the viewpoint(s) of Americans of different times and places.

Skills FOCUS **READING LIKE A HISTORIAN**

Tens of thousands of runners race across the Verrazano-Narrows Bridge during the annual New York City Marathon. About 260 million people watch the event on television. **Interpreting Visuals** How do you think the terrorist attacks of September 11, 2001, affected interest in this event?

See Skills Handbook, p. H30

U.S.
January 1993 Bill Clinton becomes president.

1992

World
1993 Israel and the PLO sign the Oslo Accords.

1994 UN forces land in Haiti to restore democracy.

1076

Key to Differentiating Instruction

Below Level
Basic-level activities designed for all students encountering new material

At Level
Intermediate-level activities designed for average students

Above Level
Challenging activities designed for honors and gifted-and-talented students

Standard English Mastery
Activities designed to improve standard English usage

Introduce the Chapter   **At Level**

Into the Twenty-First Century

1. Guide students in a discussion of some of the environmental problems, social problems, and health-related issues the nation is currently facing.

2. Tell students that in this chapter they will learn about two recent presidents: Bill Clinton and George W. Bush. During their administrations, the nation faced new challenges, one of which was terrorism.

3. Have students work in pairs to make a list of the issues each president faced, and the

issues the nation faced in the early 2000s. Have volunteers share information from their lists and create a class list for all to see. Then guide students in a discussion of these issues.

4. Have students write a brief summary of the problems that faced these two presidents and identify which still exist today. **LS Verbal-Linguistic**

  Alternative Assessment Handbook, Rubrics 9: Comparing and Contrasting; and 35: Solving Problems

● **Chapter Preview** ●

HOLT

History's Impact

▶ **Video Program: Into the Twenty-First Century**
See the Video Teacher's Guide for strategies for using the video segment.

Reading Like a Historian

Interpreting Visuals

The New York City Marathon began in 1970 when just over 100 runners participated. By the late 1970s, over 9,000 people participated, and in 2005, 85,000 people from around the world applied to run the 26.2 mile course that finishes in Central Park.

April 1995
A terrorist bomb destroys the Federal Building in Oklahoma City, killing 168 people.

December 1998
The U.S. House of Representatives votes to impeach President Clinton.

September 11, 2001
Foreign terrorists attack the World Trade Center and the Pentagon.

March 2003
President George W. Bush orders invasion of Iraq to remove Saddam Hussein from power.

November 2004
President George W. Bush wins re-election.

`1995`   `1998`   `2001`   `2004`

1998
Serbian leader Slobodan Milosevic sends troops into Kosovo to drive ethnic Albanians from the region.

January 1999
The United States and NATO stop "ethnic cleansing" of Kosovo.

October 2005
Iraqis approve a new constitution.

1077

go.hrw.com
Online Resources

Chapter Resources:
KEYWORD: SD7 CH33

Teacher Resources:
KEYWORD: SD7 TEACHER

Explore the Time Line

1. According to the time line, who was Slobodan Milosevic? What did he do? *Serbian leader; sent troops into Kosovo to try to drive Albanians from the region*

2. How many years elapsed between the Oklahoma City bombing and the attacks on the World Trade Center and Pentagon? *6 years*

3. When did the United States send troops into Iraq? *2003*

Info to Know

North Korea In 2004 six nations, the two Koreas, China, Russia, Japan, and the United States, began talks and negotiations to end North Korea's nuclear weapons program. In 2005 North Korea pledged to end its nuclear weapons program in exchange for energy aid, economic cooperation, and security assurances.
Analyze Why was ending North Korea's nuclear weapon development particularly important to South Korea, China, Russia, and Japan? *Their geographic location put them in imminent danger.*

Answers

Reading Like a Historian (p. 1076)
possible answer—More people than usual probably attended in order to show support for the city and victims of the terrorist attacks.

Bellringer

The Inside Story. . . Use the **Daily Bellringer Transparency** to help students answer the question.

📖 Daily Bellringer Transparency, Section 1

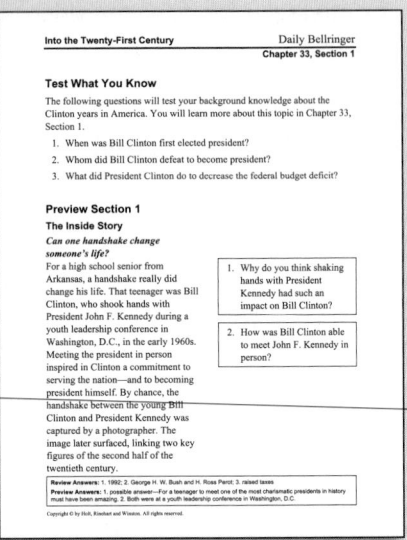

Into the Twenty-First Century   Daily Bellringer
                                                  Chapter 33, Section 1

Test What You Know

The following questions will test your background knowledge about the Clinton years in America. You will learn more about this topic in Chapter 33, Section 1.

1. When was Bill Clinton first elected president?
2. Whom did Bill Clinton defeat to become president?
3. What did President Clinton do to decrease the federal budget deficit?

Preview Section 1

The Inside Story

Can one handshake change someone's life?

For a high school senior from Arkansas, a handshake really did change his life. That teenager was Bill Clinton, who shook hands with President John F. Kennedy during a youth leadership conference in Washington, D.C., in the early 1960s. Meeting the president in person inspired in Clinton a commitment to serving the nation—and to becoming president himself. By chance, the handshake between the young Bill Clinton and President Kennedy was captured by a photographer. The image later surfaced, linking two key figures of the second half of the twentieth century.

1. Why do you think shaking hands with President Kennedy had such an impact on Bill Clinton?

2. How was Bill Clinton able to meet John F. Kennedy in person?

Academic Vocabulary

Review with students the high-use academic term in this section.

administration the carrying out or management of government (p. 1079)

📝 CRF: Vocabulary Builder Activity, Section 1

Taking Notes

Domestic—federal budget deficit reduction, unsuccessful health-care reform, welfare reform, Oklahoma City bombing, impeachment; Foreign—Palestine and Israel, Somalia and Rwanda, Haiti, Bosnia, Serbia, passage of NAFTA; Scandal—Whitewater, sexual impropriety charges, impeachment

---

BEFORE YOU READ

MAIN IDEA

Bill Clinton was a new type of Democrat, and his administration faced challenges for a new millennium—and scandals as old as politics.

READING FOCUS

1. What were the key events in the political rise of Bill Clinton?
2. What were some major domestic-policy questions facing Clinton?
3. What were some major foreign-policy challenges facing Clinton?
4. What events led to scandal and impeachment proceedings during the Clinton presidency?

KEY TERMS AND PEOPLE

Bill Clinton
Hillary Rodham Clinton
Al Gore
Contract with America
terrorism
NAFTA

TAKING NOTES As you read, take notes on the major events of the Clinton presidency. Record your notes in a graphic organizer like the one shown here.

Clinton Presidency

Domestic	Foreign	Scandal

Shaking History by the Hand

▼ Sixteen-year-old Bill Clinton, a future president, shakes hands with President Kennedy.

1078

THE INSIDE STORY

Can one handshake change someone's life? Yes, it can, according to **Bill Clinton**. Clinton was a high school senior in Arkansas when he had the opportunity to travel to Washington, D.C., for a youth leadership conference. A highlight of the trip was a visit to the White House, where participants lined up to meet President John F. Kennedy. Among the first to shake the president's hand was Bill Clinton. Nobody at the time knew it, but the handshake, captured by photographers, linked two men who would one day be viewed as key figures in the second half of the twentieth century.

The young Clinton realized it was a central moment in his life. That handshake, he later recalled, changed him. He had long been interested in leadership and politics. But meeting John F. Kennedy in person instilled in him a new commitment: to serve the nation by leading it as president.

Clinton wasted little time in reaching for his dream. After working his way through college and law school, he began a career of public service. ◢

Bill Clinton's Political Rise

Bill Clinton did become a successful politician, rising to the highest positions in state government as a very young man. When he was just 30 years old, he became attorney general of Arkansas. Two years later, at the age of 32, he became the nation's youngest governor. Politically, Clinton represented a new kind of Democrat. He was not as conservative as many Republicans but not as liberal as many other Democrats. In other words, he was a centrist.

Clinton's reputation grew steadily. In the late 1980s, he chaired the National Governors Association. There he focused on issues such as improving public education and reforming the welfare system. He also chaired the Democratic Leadership Council, an organization of centrists. Clearly, Clinton was a Democrat on the rise.

Teach the Main Idea

At Level

The Clinton Years

1. **Teach** Ask students the Reading Focus questions to teach this section.

2. **Apply** Have students create an outline of the section using the heads as main points. Have students identify at least two main ideas under each of the blue subheadings.

3. **Review** Review student outlines as a class. Have students identify the points in their outlines that they feel are most important or most interesting. Guide students in a

discussion of the leadership role the United States began to take in the post-Cold War world.

4. **Practice/Homework** Have students write an assessment of the Clinton administration's successes and failures and how the administration might be viewed 100 years from now. 🔳 **Visual-Spatial, Verbal-Linguistic**

📋 Alternative Assessment Handbook, Rubrics 13: Graphic Organizers; and 42: Writing to Inform

Clinton the candidate It was no surprise, then, when Clinton sought the Democratic nomination for the presidency in 1992. During his campaign, he stressed the need for a national health-care system and middle-class tax cuts. He also skillfully deflected questions about his past. These included charges that he had evaded the draft during the Vietnam War.

Clinton's campaign also featured a major role for his wife, **Hillary Rodham Clinton**. She was regarded as one of the country's top lawyers. Clinton made it clear that his <u>administration</u> would rely on her skill and guidance.

The 1992 election Clinton won the Democratic nomination and ran against President George H.W. Bush. Clinton named a fellow southerner, Senator **Al Gore** of Tennessee, as his running mate. The race also featured independent candidate H. Ross Perot.

In the campaign, Clinton presented himself as the protector of the middle class. His message helped produce a solid victory. He won 370 electoral votes to Bush's 168, although Clinton received less than 50 percent of the popular vote. Although Perot received 19 percent of the popular vote, he carried no state.

> **READING CHECK** **Identifying Cause and Effect** What were some of the key factors in Clinton's rise to the presidency?

Domestic Policy Issues

During his campaign, Bill Clinton made a number of promises about domestic matters. His record in fulfilling those promises was mixed.

Deficit reduction As you have read, Clinton proposed cutting taxes for middle class Americans during the 1992 campaign. Soon after taking office, however, he changed his plan. Citing budget deficits, which continued to rise sharply, he pushed through a major increase in taxes.

Clinton's move was criticized by some Republicans. They predicted the tax increase would hurt the economy. "The deficit four years from now will be higher than it is today, not lower," claimed Senator Phil Gramm of Texas.

This prediction turned out to be false. In fact, the United States in 1993 was entering a time of prosperity. As the decade continued, the nation experienced a long period of low unemployment and interest rates. Other features of the booming 1990s economy are shown in the graphs on the next page.

Health-care reform Reform of the nation's health-care system was another major 1992 campaign issue for Clinton. In 1992 health-care costs were rising sharply. Meanwhile, Clinton observed, tens of millions of Americans

ACADEMIC VOCABULARY
administration officials and staff of the government, especially the executive branch

The Clinton Style

Bill Clinton's warmth and charm made him an effective candidate. He won both the 1992 and 1996 presidential elections. In his State of the Union address at the start of his second term (inset), Clinton stated that the country had recovered not only its economic strength but also its optimism.

1079

Skills Focus: Analyzing Costs and Benefits

At Level

Social Studies Skill

Research Required

Clinton's Health-Care Reform Plan

1. Organize the class into small groups. Have half of the groups represent supporters of Clinton's health-care reform plan and the other half represent opponents of the Clinton plan. Have students conduct outside research to learn more about the attempts to reform health-care. Then have each group prepare arguments for a classroom debate.

2. Have each group select one student to present its views, and then conduct the debate on the desirability of adopting Clinton's health-care reform plan.

3. At the conclusion of the debate, have each student write a one-page essay telling which position he or she would personally take and why.

4. Have volunteers read their essays to the class.
   LS **Logical-Mathematical, Verbal-Linguistic**
   Alternative Assessment Handbook, Rubrics 10: Debates; and 43: Writing to Persuade

Direct Teach

Reading Focus

1 What were the key events in the political rise of Bill Clinton? *attorney general of Arkansas, nation's youngest governor; chaired the National Governors Association and Democratic Leadership Council*

Bill Clinton's Political Rise

Recall What issues did Bill Clinton focus on in his campaign for the presidency? *need for a national health-care system; tax cuts for the middle class*

Contrast How did Bill Clinton differ politically from other politicians? *centrist, not as liberal as many Democrats, not as conservative as many Republicans*

Explain How did Bill Clinton win the election without winning a majority of the popular vote? *won solid victory in electoral votes*

Reading Focus

2 What were some major domestic policy questions facing Clinton? *how to reduce the budget deficit, how to reform health-care and welfare*

Domestic Policy Issues

Explain Why did President Clinton change his mind about cutting taxes? *wanted to deal with the rising budget deficit*

Evaluate How did Clinton's actions to cut the budget deficits end up surprising his critics? *They ushered in a time of amazing prosperity.*

Answers

Reading Check *successful, young politician; centrist*

Domestic Policy Issues

Recall How did Clinton bounce back following the major Republican victory in the 1994 midterm elections? *addressed issues raised by Republicans, such as welfare reform*

Evaluate Why did Clinton's attempt to offer health-care coverage to all Americans fail to win support? *Many people were unwilling to risk major changes to the health-care system.*

Activity Domestic Successes and Failures Create a chart on the board with a column for successes and a column for failures. Have volunteers fill in domestic policy issues from Clinton's presidency and explain their reasoning.
LS Visual-Spatial, Verbal-Linguistic

The Economy in the 1990s

The Dow Jones Industrial Average consists of 30 stocks and is a leading indicator for the New York Stock Exchange. NASDAQ is an electronic stock market where trades are made through computer and telecommunications networks. You might wish to bring in the stock market pages from a newspaper to help students understand that stock prices rise and fall and are monitored daily.

Info to Know

Health Care The increasing financial burden of health care became a major issue for federal and state governments in the early 1990s. In 1960 spending on health care had accounted for 5.3 percent of the nation's gross national product (GNP), and the total bill for health care in the United States came to $27.1 billion. By 1990 health care represented 12.2 percent of GNP, and total costs that year came to $666.2 billion.

Answers

Interpreting Graphs 1. *almost $300 billion; became a surplus;* **2.** *slow growth in the 1980s, spectacular growth in the 1990s*

1080

---

had little or no health insurance. The public, it seemed, was anxious for change.

To explore solutions to these problems, Clinton named a special task force headed by First Lady Hillary Clinton. After months of study, the group proposed a government-sponsored program of health care. Response to the proposal was mixed. The plan offered coverage to all Americans, but many people were unwilling to risk major changes to the health-care system. The plan was defeated after months of debate.

The 1994 elections The defeat of Clinton's health-care plan reflected a discontent with Clinton's leadership. The new president had failed to deliver on several campaign promises. The tax hike of 1993 was also unpopular.

The discontent helped contribute to a major Republican victory in the 1994 midterm elections. Many Republicans, led by Representative Newt Gingrich of Georgia, campaigned with a document they called the **Contract with America**. The Contract included plans to balance the budget, fight crime, and provide tax cuts for many Americans. The Contract with America appealed to many

voters. Republicans gained 54 seats in the House and 8 seats in the Senate. They took control of both houses of Congress for the first time in 40 years.

Welfare reform In spite of this defeat, Clinton bounced back. He did this by addressing several issues the Republicans had raised, including reform of the welfare system. Since the Great Depression, welfare programs had paid cash to poor families. Many people, however, had come to believe that this system was often misused. The Contract with America included plans for welfare reform. Democrats, including Clinton, opposed the plan proposed by the Contract with America.

In 1996, however, Clinton proposed his own welfare-reform plan. It limited the time people could receive benefits and required most recipients to find work within two years of getting benefits. Congress approved this plan.

Other challenges During the 1990s, the Internet emerged as a major means of communication and commerce. It also presented challenges, however. For example, many adults were concerned that children would be exposed

---

The Economy in the 1990s

Left, shoppers enjoy the benefits of a strong economy at a mall. Disposable income— that is, income available for spending or saving—grew during the 1990s. Americans' rate of savings fell drastically in the 1990s.

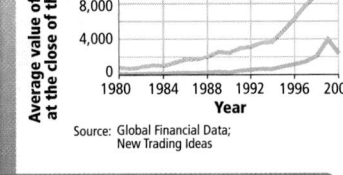

FEDERAL DEFICITS AND SURPLUSES, 1980–2000

Billions of dollars

200
0
-200
-400

1980 1984 1988 1992 1996 2000
Year

Source: *Budget of the United States Government, 2005*

STOCK MARKET, 1980–2000

— NASDAQ — Dow Jones

Average value of shares at the close of the year

12,000
8,000
4,000
0

1980 1984 1988 1992 1996 2000
Year

Source: Global Financial Data; New Trading Ideas

Skills FOCUS INTERPRETING GRAPHS

1. How high were the federal deficits before Clinton took office? How did the federal deficit change in the late 1990s?

2. Compare the rate of growth in the stock market in the 1980s and the 1990s.

See Skills Handbook, pp. H16, H17

Skills Focus: Interpreting Line Graphs

At Level

Social Studies Skill
The Stock Market

Prep Required   **Research Required**

1. Review with students what the stock market is and how it works. Then tell students how to interpret a line graph and explain that a line graph may be used to measure changes in the value of a particular stock.

2. Bring in a copy of a daily newspaper for students to look at. Have each student select one stock from the listing in the newspaper. Have students monitor their stocks over the course of a week by using online or print

resources. Students should record any changes in price over the course of the week and use this information to create a line graph.

3. Have volunteers share their line graphs with the class. Guide the class in a discussion of the potential risks and benefits of using the stock market. **LS Logical-Mathematical, Visual-Spatial**

Alternative Assessment Handbook, Rubric 7: Charts

to inappropriate material on the Internet. The White House helped push a 1996 law to limit the use of the Internet for transmitting certain sexually explicit material. In *Reno* v. *ACLU*, however, the Supreme Court struck down this law as a violation of the freedom of speech.

Clinton also faced the task of helping the nation cope with tragedy. In 1995 terrorists exploded a bomb in the Murrah Federal Building in Oklahoma City, Oklahoma. **Terrorism** is the use of violence by individuals or groups to advance political goals.

The Oklahoma City blast killed 168 people, including many children. More than 500 people were injured. Two Americans, Timothy McVeigh and Terry Nichols, were convicted for their roles in the crime. (McVeigh was executed in 2001. Nichols was sentenced to life in prison.)

Another challenge facing Clinton was re-election. In 1996 he defeated Republican senator Bob Dole of Kansas. H. Ross Perot again ran, this time on the Reform Party ticket.

READING CHECK Summarizing In what sense was Clinton's success in domestic policy "mixed"?

Foreign Policy Challenges

When Bill Clinton came into office, the United States was still struggling to understand the post–Cold War world. With the threat of communism gone, Clinton had to determine where American interests lay and how to protect them. The new environment would present its share of challenges to the new president.

Early success in the Middle East In September 1993, Clinton hosted a ceremony for the signing of a major peace agreement between Israel and the Palestinians. The agreement was known as the Oslo Accords. Israeli prime minister Yitzhak Rabin and Palestinian chairman Yasser Arafat agreed to self-rule for the Palestinians in certain areas. The Palestinians agreed to recognize Israel's right to exist. The agreement also set the stage for ongoing negotiations in the Middle East.

Much of the promise of the Oslo Accords was never realized. Yitzhak Rabin died at the hands of an assassin in 1995. Still, the signing was a historic high point in President Clinton's first term.

Born in the small town of Hope, Arkansas, Bill Clinton excelled in school despite a troubled home life. He graduated from Georgetown University and Yale Law School. From the time he was in high school, Clinton dreamed of entering politics. In 1976 he won a race for Arkansas Attorney General. In 1978 at the age of 32, Clinton won the governorship. He won the seat again in 1982.

Clinton went on to win the presidency in 1992. As president, he achieved the first balanced budget since the 1960s. Winning re-election in 1996, he became the first Democrat since Franklin D. Roosevelt to win a second term.

Summarize What were some of President Clinton's major achievements?

Somalia Early in his term, Clinton faced a difficult challenge in the African country of Somalia. Before Clinton took office, President Bush had sent American forces there to help a UN program distribute food to starving Somali victims of a civil war within their country.

By 1993 the UN's mission had grown. Now UN forces were working to end the fighting itself. A number of American forces died in the violence. The worst incident occurred in October 1993. In a bloody battle in the Somali capital of Mogadishu, 18 Americans were killed and 84 were wounded. Many Somalis also died. Clinton chose to withdraw American forces. The bitter experience helped discourage Clinton from sending forces to the African country of Rwanda in 1994 to stop a terrible genocide that claimed hundreds of thousands of lives.

Haiti In 1994 the UN acted to settle a violent dispute in the Caribbean nation of Haiti. The goal was to remove a military dictator who had taken over Haiti's government by force. Clinton pledged the use of American troops to lead the UN effort. In September, the force landed in Haiti. Their presence helped bring about a generally peaceful change in government.

The former Yugoslavia Yugoslavia was a country that had formed after World War I. Within its borders lived several ethnic groups that were historical enemies and that had dreams of their own independence. During the

THE IMPACT TODAY

Government
One topic left for future negotiation under the Oslo Accords was the presence of Israeli settlements in the occupied territories. In 2005, Israel removed the settlements, which had long caused conflict with the Palestinians.

INTO THE TWENTY-FIRST CENTURY **1081**

3 What were some major foreign policy challenges facing Clinton? *Middle East peace agreement, war in Somalia, political turmoil in Haiti, war in the former Yugoslavia, promoting international trade*

Foreign Policy Challenges

Recall What were the main provisions of the Oslo Accords? *The Palestinians would get self-rule in certain areas and recognize Israel's right to exist.*

Draw Conclusions Why did the United States struggle to understand the post-Cold War world? *The world was no longer divided into two major opposing camps, but composed of many different factions.*

Make Judgments Do you think the United States should have sent military troops to Rwanda? *possible answers—yes, U.S. troops should have been sent in to stop the genocide; no, the U.S. cannot stop determined people from committing brutalities*

📄 CRF: Biography: Madeleine Albright

Answers

Faces of History *balanced the budget, won re-election*

Reading Check *reducing the federal deficit successful; health-care reform unsuccessful*

Skills Focus: Identifying Main Idea and Details

Reading Skill
Peacekeeping after the Cold War

1. To help students assess the success of the United States in helping promote and maintain world peace after the Cold War, copy the graphic organizer at far right for students to see. Omit the italicized answers. Have each student copy the graphic organizer and complete it.

2. Have volunteers complete the class chart, and have students correct their own work.
LS Visual-Spatial, Logical-Mathematical
📄 Alternative Assessment Handbook, Rubric 13: Graphic Organizers
📄 Graphic Organizer Transparencies

Oslo Accords, major peace agreement between Israel and the Palestinians (September 1993)

U.S. forces join UN effort to end violence in Haiti (September 1994)

U.S. forces join UN peacemaking forces in Somalia

U.S. Peacemaking Efforts, 1993–2000

Dayton Accords to end fighting in Bosnia Herzegovina (1995)

U.S. urges NATO to act to stop action against ethnic Albanians and force Serb troops to leave Kosovo (1999)

1081

Foreign Policy Challenges

Explain What is the purpose of NAFTA? *remove most tariffs and trade barriers among the U.S., Mexico, and Canada; increase trade*

Summarize Why did Yugoslavia dissolve into violence? *country formed after World War I with several ethnic groups that had been enemies; had been held together by its leader until his death; by the 1990s, Yugoslavia no longer existed; violence raged within and between the countries that replaced it*

Counterpoints

Views on Free Trade

Make Judgments Which of the two points of view expressed here do you think is closer to reality? Why? *possible answers—Perot's; many companies have relocated to Mexico because of lower production costs and the fact that they can import their products into the U.S. without paying a tariff; Clinton's; the U.S. has not suffered the immense job loss that was feared*

go.hrw.com
Online Resources

KEYWORD: SD7 CH33
TOPIC: NAFTA

Answers

Reading Like a Historian
Clinton—lower tariffs mean more exports and more domestic jobs; Perot—American companies will relocate to Mexico, where their costs are lower

---

Views on Free Trade

In the early days of his administration, President Clinton worked hard to persuade Congress and the American people to support the North American Free Trade Agreement (NAFTA).

Business leader H. Ross Perot opposed NAFTA and free trade during his independent campaign for the presidency in 1992.

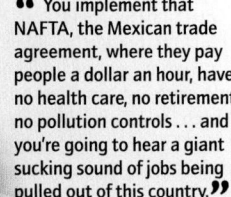

❝ [U]nder NAFTA more jobs will stay home here in America and more American exports will head to Mexico . . . If you want to create more American jobs, if you want to lower the differences in cost of production in America and Mexico, if you want to take down barriers in Mexico to exports, then you should want NAFTA. ❞

President Clinton, 1993

❝ You implement that NAFTA, the Mexican trade agreement, where they pay people a dollar an hour, have no health care, no retirement, no pollution controls . . . and you're going to hear a giant sucking sound of jobs being pulled out of this country. ❞

H. Ross Perot, 1992

Skills FOCUS READING LIKE A HISTORIAN

Analyzing Primary Sources Why does Clinton think NAFTA will create American jobs? Why does Perot expect the opposite?

See Skills Handbook, p. H28–H29

Cold War, the country was held together by its leader, Josip Broz Tito. Soon after Tito's death in 1980, however, the country began to unravel. By the 1990s Yugoslavia no longer existed. In its place were several smaller countries. Within and between these countries, violence raged.

Clinton was deeply involved in efforts to end the bloodshed. In 1995 he helped bring about the Dayton Accords, an agreement aimed at ending fighting in the new country of Bosnia and Herzegovina. In 1999 he urged NATO to act against Serbia, another country formed from the former Yugoslavia. His goal was to stop the Serb army's attempt to force ethnic Albanians from the Serbian region of Kosovo. NATO forces conducted a bombing campaign that forced Serb troops to leave Kosovo.

Promoting international trade Another issue awaiting Bill Clinton when he took office was the North American Free Trade Agreement, or **NAFTA**. Under this agreement, the

United States, Mexico, and Canada became one large free-trade zone. This meant that most products could be sold across the borders of these countries without tariffs or trade barriers. President Bush had completed negotiations on the agreement before he left office. It became Clinton's job to win congressional approval. Facing stiff opposition, Clinton fought for and won passage of NAFTA in the fall of 1993.

Some critics believed NAFTA would cost American jobs. They argued that because Mexican factories paid lower wages, they could make and sell goods at a lower cost than American-made goods. Without tariffs to make Mexican goods more expensive, many feared American factories would go out of business.

Clinton and supporters of NAFTA believed the agreement would increase trade, which would help the economy. Indeed, increasing trade was a major Clinton goal. During his presidency, the United States took part in the creation of the World Trade Organization (WTO).

THE IMPACT TODAY

Economics
In August 2005, President George W. Bush signed the Central American-Dominican Republic Free Trade Agreement, or CAFTA-DR. The agreement is designed to break down trade barriers between the United States and several Latin American neighbors.

Differentiating Instruction

Below Level

English-Language Learners

1. Have students review the passage about the former Yugoslavia and then name the two ethnic groups involved in the Kosovo crisis. *Serbs and Albanians*

2. Guide students in a discussion of the reasons that NATO launched air strikes against Serbia in 1999.

3. Have each student use the information from the class discussion to write headlines for

two newspaper articles related to the unrest in Kosovo and the NATO response to it.

4. Have volunteers read their headlines to the class. **LS** **Logical-Mathematical, Verbal-Linguistic**

📄 Alternative Assessment Handbook, Rubric 37: Writing Assignments

The WTO replaced the General Agreement on Tariffs and Trade (GATT). It was meant as a means of settling trade disputes and forming rules for global trade. Clinton pushed for other trade agreements as well. For example, he fought for permanent normal trade status for China, the world's most populous country.

READING CHECK **Identifying Supporting Details** How did the end of the Cold War affect Clinton's foreign policy?

Scandal and Impeachment

Clinton had won the presidency in spite of questions about his past. His election, however, did not end the controversy. Soon came even more scandal.

Throughout his first term, Clinton faced investigation about an investment he and his wife had made in a failed real estate project in the 1970s. The project was known as Whitewater. Among several legal questions related to Whitewater, observers wondered whether the Clintons and their business partners had acted improperly in getting and using loans.

Special prosecutor Kenneth Starr led the Whitewater investigation. Though he never filed any Whitewater-related charges against Clinton, three former Clinton business associates were found guilty of various crimes.

Clinton also faced charges that while he was governor of Arkansas, he had sexually harassed a female state employee. That woman, named Paula Jones, brought a lawsuit against the president. In the course of this case, information emerged suggesting that the president had conducted an improper relationship with a 21-year-old White House intern named Monica Lewinsky. Starr then extended the scope of his investigation to include Clinton's relationship with Lewinsky.

Eventually, Clinton was accused of lying under oath about his relationship with Lewinsky. He was also accused of trying to influence Lewinsky's testimony. Clinton later admitted he had conducted an improper relationship, but he said he did not lie under oath.

The House of Representatives responded by approving two articles of impeachment against Clinton in November 1998. Clinton was the first president to face a Senate impeachment trial since Andrew Johnson in 1868.

In order to remove a president from office, a two-thirds majority in the Senate must vote to convict. In early 1999 the Senate voted 55–45 against conviction on the first article of impeachment and voted 50–50 on the second article. Clinton remained in office to complete his term.

READING CHECK **Sequencing** What role did scandal play in Bill Clinton's presidency?

---

go.hrw.com
Online Quiz
Keyword: SD7 HP33

SECTION 1 ASSESSMENT

Reviewing Ideas, Terms, and People

1. a. Recall Who were the key figures in the election of 1992?
b. Make Inferences What can you infer from the performance of H. Ross Perot in the 1992 election?

2. a. Define Write a brief definition of the following term: Contract with America
b. Summarize What do you think were Clinton's greatest successes and his greatest failures during his time in office?

3. a. Identify What were the major foreign-policy issues facing the Clinton administration?
b. Make Generalizations Toward what goals did the United States use military force during Clinton's time in office?

4. a. Identify Identify and briefly describe the significance of the Whitewater scandal.
b. Explain On what grounds did the House of Representatives approve articles of impeachment against Clinton?

Critical Thinking

5. Identifying the Main Idea Copy the chart below and use information from the section to record details that support the main idea of the section.

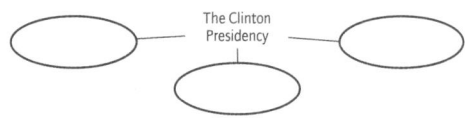

The Clinton Presidency

FOCUS ON WRITING

6. Narrative President Clinton was known for overcoming setbacks to achieve political success. Write a brief paragraph telling of some of the setbacks and recoveries of the Clinton administration.

INTO THE TWENTY-FIRST CENTURY **1083**

LANDMARK SUPREME COURT CASES
Constitutional Issue: Search and Seizure

Landmark Supreme Court Cases

Vernonia School District v. Acton

Word Help

random unplanned, without a definite aim or purpose

intrusions interferences without permission or invitation

The Fourth Amendment

"The right of the people to be secure in their persons, houses, papers, and effects, against unreasonable searches and seizures, shall not be violated, and no Warrants shall issue, but upon probable cause, supported by Oath or affirmation, and particularly describing the place to be searched, and the persons or things to be seized."

The Dissenting Opinion

Justice Sandra Day O'Connor wrote the dissenting opinion in the case of *Vernonia School District* v. *Acton*. In it, she found that the search was in fact unreasonable, and therefore violated the Fourth Amendment. Following are the opening and closing statements of her opinion:

"By the reasoning of today's decision, the millions of these students who participate in interscholastic sports, an overwhelming majority of whom have given school officials no reason whatsoever to suspect they use drugs at school, are open to an intrusive bodily search . . .

"Having reviewed the record here, I cannot avoid the conclusion that the District's suspicionless policy of testing all student-athletes sweeps too broadly, and too imprecisely, to be reasonable under the Fourth Amendment."

Vernonia School District v. Acton (1995)

Why It Matters The Fourth Amendment prevents the government from making unreasonable searches. In this case, the Supreme Court found it reasonable to "search" student athletes by making them submit to drug testing.

Background of the Case

Officials in the Vernonia School District in Oregon were concerned about the extent of drug use by students. The school district adopted a rule requiring student athletes to submit to random drug testing. When James Acton signed up to play seventh-grade football, he and his parents refused to sign the consent form for drug testing. The school did not let him play, so Acton sued, arguing that the drug testing violated the search and seizure clause of the Fourth Amendment. The trial court ruled that he had no valid constitutional claim and dismissed his case, but the court of appeals reinstated the case. The school district then appealed to the Supreme Court.

The Decision

The Supreme Court ruled that random drug testing of student athletes is not a violation of the Fourth Amendment's search and seizure clause. First, the Court held that drug testing is a "search" under the Fourth Amendment. The question was whether the search was reasonable. The Court decided that the school district had a legitimate concern about student drug use and that the testing program was designed to have a minimal impact on students' privacy. Finally, the Court held that students were not required to go out for sports, and those who did should expect some intrusions on their privacy. The manner and extent of the search were reasonable, the Court held, so the drug testing was lawful under the Constitution.

THE IMPACT TODAY Public high schools can now require student athletes to submit to drug testing as a condition of playing sports. The Supreme Court's decision gives schools more power to detect and discourage drug abuse by student athletes.

CRITICAL THINKING

go.hrw.com
Research Online
Keyword: SS Court

1. **Analyze the Impact** Using the keyword above, find and read the text of the Fourth Amendment. Could the Supreme Court have found that the school drug testing was not a search within the meaning of the Constitution?

2. **You Be the Judge** Based on the *Vernonia School District* decision, should a school be allowed to require drug testing for students who participate in nonsports activities, such as the yearbook or chess club? Explain your answer in a short paragraph.

Skills Focus: Analyzing Alternative Interpretations of the Past

Reading Like a Historian Skill
Vernonia School District v. Acton

At Level | Research Required

1. Have students locate at least three secondary source documents about *Vernonia School District* v. *Acton*. Then have students compile a chart that shows details of the case and similarities and differences among the sources.

2. Have students write an essay in which they provide a summary of the case and then compare and contrast the documents that they used. Students should attach copies of the documents they found.

3. Guide students in a discussion of the different ways that the sources interpreted the *Vernonia School District* v. *Acton* ruling. Which provide the most accurate account? Which might contain the most bias? Have students explain their reasoning. **LS Verbal-Linguistic**

   Alternative Assessment Handbook, Rubrics 9: Comparing and Contrasting; and 40: Writing to Describe

Answers

Critical Thinking 1. *possible answer—yes, see Sandra Day O'Connor's dissenting opinion;*
2. *possible answers—Use of illegal drugs is illegal, therefore, schools have the right to insist that students involved in any activity can be tested for drug use; schools have no right to perform random drug testing on any student.*

George W. Bush's Presidency

BEFORE YOU READ

MAIN IDEA

Following a troubled election, Republican George W. Bush won the White House and strongly promoted his agenda.

READING FOCUS

1. What were the unusual circumstances of the election of 2000?

2. What were key components of George W. Bush's domestic policy?

3. What were the key components and figures in Bush's foreign policy?

KEY TERMS AND PEOPLE

George W. Bush
budget surplus
Bush v. *Gore*
dot-com
dividend
Condoleezza Rice
Donald Rumsfeld

TAKING NOTES As you read, take notes about the events surrounding the election of George W. Bush and his policies once in office. Record your notes in a graphic organizer like the one shown here.

Bush Takes Office

2000 Election	Domestic Policy	Foreign Policy

THE INSIDE STORY

What happened on the night of the 2000 presidential election?
For **George W. Bush**, it had been a night of great tension. At the end of a hard-fought campaign for president, the Republican candidate sat down with his family to watch the election returns on TV.

First came news that Democratic candidate Al Gore had apparently won the popular vote in Florida—a state that was key to the outcome of the election. Two hours later, the news organizations that had made this report took an extraordinary step— they retracted their announcement and declared the winner in Florida uncertain. Then at around 2 a.m., these same news organizations announced that Bush had won Florida—and with it the presidency. Gore, following the election-night custom, called Bush to acknowledge Bush's victory and congratulate the new president-elect.

But the drama was not yet over. An hour after Gore's telephone call, the news organizations switched their call again! Florida was once more considered too close to call. Gore called his opponent once again—this time taking back his admission of defeat. The election in Florida was over, but who had won the presidency? It would take more than a month to determine the answer. ◾

An Election Night to Remember

▼ George W. Bush (center) awaits results with his father, former president George H. W. Bush, and brother Jeb.

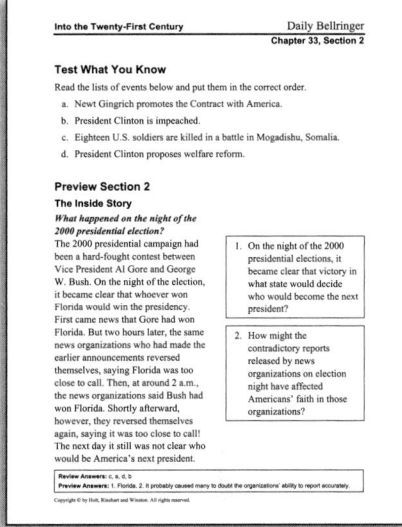
Taking Notes

2000 election—lack of majority of popular vote; uncertainty about election winner; Domestic Policy—tax cuts, No Child Left Behind, faith-based initiatives; Foreign Policy—cancelled Anti-Ballistic Missile Treaty, promoted Middle East road map to peace, response to September 11, 2001, attacks

Teach the Main Idea

At Level

George W. Bush's Presidency

1. **Teach** Ask students the Reading Focus questions to teach this section.

2. **Apply** Have students create an outline of the section using the heads as main points. Have students identify at least two main ideas under each of the blue subheadings.

3. **Review** Have students explain how George W. Bush came to be president following the election of 2000. Guide students in a discussion of the ways in which this might have affected Bush's

relationship with Congress.

4. **Practice/Homework** Tell students that the creation of the White House Office of Faith-Based Initiatives sparked controversy because it used federal money to fund religious organizations that provide community service. Have each student write an editorial giving his or her views on the subject. **LS Visual-Spatial, Verbal-Linguistic**

📝 Alternative Assessment Handbook, Rubric 17: Letters to Editors

1085

1 What were the unusual circumstances of the election of 2000? *extremely tight race, outcome came down to the results in Florida, outcome challenged in the courts, George W. Bush won, but had fewer popular votes than Al Gore*

The Election of 2000

Explain Why did the state of Florida become so important in the presidential election? *close popular and electoral vote, became clear that the race would be decided by Florida's results*

Make Judgments Do you think having a single system for casting votes in all U.S. elections would have prevented the legal battles that followed the 2000 presidential election? Why or why not? *possible answer— Yes, there were several types of ballots in use in Florida alone, which could cause confusion. Having a single voting method could have prevented any question of political manipulation.*

🗳 Map Transparency: The Election of 2000

✳ Interactive Map: The Election of 2000

Bring in a photo of a punch-card ballot for students to see. Explain to them how the machine punches out the hole, and describe what a "hanging chad" is. Ask students if they believe that a fully punched ballot is the only one that should be counted, and if not, what determination should be used to count, or not count, a ballot.

Answers

Interpreting Maps *Bush—lower Midwest and South; Gore—Northeast, upper Midwest, Pacific Coast*

1086

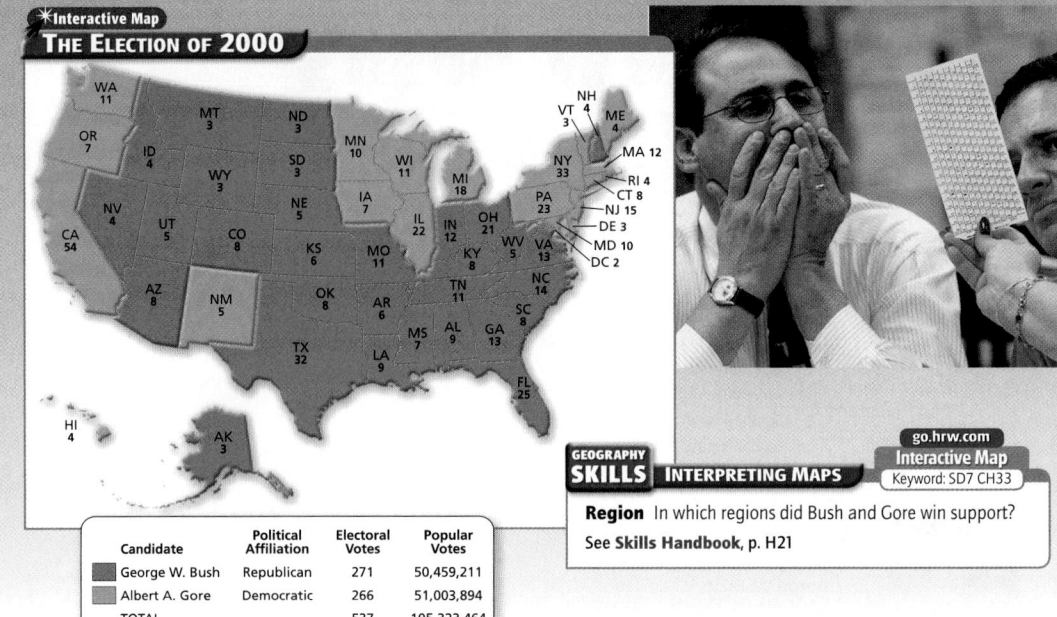

✳ Interactive Map
THE ELECTION OF 2000

GEOGRAPHY SKILLS INTERPRETING MAPS

go.hrw.com
Interactive Map
Keyword: SD7 CH33

Region In which regions did Bush and Gore win support?
See **Skills Handbook**, p. H21

Candidate	Political Affiliation	Electoral Votes	Popular Votes
George W. Bush	Republican	271	50,459,211
Albert A. Gore	Democratic	266	51,003,894
TOTAL		537	105,323,464

The Election of 2000

With President Clinton finishing his second term, both parties knew the 2000 race was wide open. It turned out to be one of the closest, most controversial elections in U.S. history.

The nominees During Clinton's presidency, the American economy prospered. The federal government had a **budget surplus**, which meant that its income exceeded its spending. Although the country's future looked bright, some Democrats were uncomfortable with Clinton's image.

Nobody understood the situation better than Clinton's vice president, Al Gore. As the Democratic nominee in the 2000 presidential race, Gore wanted to claim credit for the success of the past. He also needed to set himself apart from Clinton. "We're entering a new time," he declared as he accepted his party's nomination. "We're electing a new president. And I stand here tonight as my own man." For his running mate, Gore made a historic choice: Connecticut senator Joe Lieberman, who became the first Jewish American to seek that high office.

The Republicans chose George W. Bush as their candidate. The son of former president George H.W. Bush, he had served six years as governor of Texas. Bush's running mate was Dick Cheney of Wyoming. Cheney had a long record that included service in Congress and in several previous administrations.

The 2000 election also featured the third-party candidacy of Ralph Nader. A longtime advocate for American consumers, Nader ran as the leader of the Green Party, a liberal party that supported environmental causes.

A troubled election As election day 2000 approached, polls indicated a tight race. The polls were correct. Election-night returns showed a close popular and electoral vote. It soon became clear that the race hinged on the outcome in a single state—Florida. Whoever won there would win the election.

As you have read, election returns in Florida were amazingly close. The result was confusion, with news organizations changing their reports several times about who had won the state. The matter remained unresolved through the night and into the next morning.

1086 CHAPTER 33

Differentiating Instruction

Below Level

Learners Having Difficulty

1. Have students name the things that made the 2000 presidential candidates and the election unusual. As students name reasons the election was unusual, write them for the class to see. *Gore's desire to distance himself from Clinton; Bush was the son of a previous president; the third-party candidacy of Ralph Nader; the length of time it took to determine a winner; the fact that the winner did not have a majority of the popular votes*

2. Have each student create a cartoon depicting one of the unusual aspects of the 2000 presidential campaign.

3. Have volunteers share their cartoons with the class, explaining what they are trying to show.
LS Verbal-Linguistic, Visual-Spatial

Alternative Assessment Handbook, Rubric 27: Political Cartoons

A pair of reporters examine an incorrectly punched ballot during a manual election recount in Fort Lauderdale, Florida, in early December 2000. Controversy over incorrectly punched ballots and so-called butterfly ballots stalled election results. *How was the outcome finally decided?*

Critics argued that the butterfly ballot used in Palm Beach County, Florida, confused many voters.

Recounts and legal wrangling Florida election officials quickly performed a recount of the ballots. As with the original vote count, this was performed by machine. The recount gave Bush a lead of just over 300 votes out of a total of nearly 6 million Florida ballots cast.

Meanwhile, Democrats were raising questions about the Florida balloting. One concern was that thousands of ballots had gone uncounted by vote-counting machines. Many ballots had been rejected because voters had made mistakes in marking them. For example, some ballots required voters to make their choices by punching a hole in the ballot. In some cases, the hole was not clean or complete enough for the counting machine to read. Democrats argued that in many cases, the choice of the voters was obvious even though the ballot-counting equipment did not count the ballot. Because the race was so close, they said, it made sense to recount all ballots by hand. They hoped that among the uncounted ballots they would gain enough votes to win the state.

Another type of punch-card ballot used in Florida was the butterfly ballot shown above.

Some observers argued that the butterfly ballot's design led some voters to mistakenly select someone other than their intended choice.

Republicans were generally opposed to hand recounts of ballots. One reason was that hand counting introduced the role of human error and individual judgment. They also objected to Democratic plans to recount only in areas that were thought to be heavily Democratic.

Over the next few days, Democrats and Republicans took turns filing lawsuits aimed at forcing or preventing recounts. In some counties, recounts were completed. Absentee ballots were also tallied, some of which were challenged by Democrats.

Bush v. Gore On December 8, Gore won what seemed like a key legal victory. The Florida Supreme Court ordered that hand recounts had to take place in certain Florida counties.

The Bush campaign appealed the ruling to the U.S. Supreme Court. The Court issued its decision in **Bush v. Gore** on December 12, 2000. The ruling held that the Florida Supreme Court's recount order was unconstitutional because it failed to provide clear standards by which the ballots were to be counted. Further, the Court held, there was no time to create standards for use statewide.

The day after the decision, Gore publicly accepted his defeat in the race. That evening, George W. Bush addressed the nation on television as the president-elect. He urged Americans to unite for the future.

HISTORY'S VOICES

❝I was not elected to serve one party, but to serve one nation.

The president of the United States is the president of every single American, of every race and every background.

Whether you voted for me or not, I will do my best to serve your interests and I will work to earn your respect.❞

—George W. Bush, December 13, 2000

On January 20, 2001, Bush was sworn in as president. He became only the fourth person in American history to have won the presidency in spite of having received fewer popular votes than his opponent.

READING CHECK Sequencing What was the sequence of key events in the election of 2000?

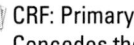
THE IMPACT TODAY

Government
In 2002 President Bush signed into law the Help America Vote Act, which provided funds to help states replace punch-card voting machines with electronic voting systems. The law required states to have the new voting systems in place by 2006.

● **Direct Teach** ●

Reading Focus

The Election of 2000

Explain Why did Democrats want ballots recounted by hand? *believed ballot-counting machines were not accurate*

Summarize Why did the U.S. Supreme Court overrule the Florida Supreme Court? *ruling failed to provide clear standards for ballot recounts*

Activity **The 2000 Election**
Divide students into pairs. Have each pair create one campaign poster supporting the election of Gore and another campaign poster supporting the election of Bush. Have volunteers share their posters with the class.
LS Kinesthetic, Visual-Spatial

CRF: Primary Source Activity: Al Gore Concedes the 2000 Election

Info to Know

Electoral College In the 2000 presidential election Al Gore won the popular vote but lost the election to George W. Bush, winner of the electoral vote. In most states, the electoral college votes are awarded in a "winner-take-all" fashion, meaning that even though Bush won Florida by fewer than 600 votes, he won all 25 electoral votes. The number of electoral votes in the states won, and not the overall popular vote count, decides the outcome of the election.

Skills Focus: Identifying Problem and Solution   At Level

Reading Skill
Improving the Election Process

1. Guide the class in a discussion of the aftermath of the 2000 presidential election using the following questions as a guide: Why was the outcome of the Florida election so important? Why did votes need to be recounted in Florida? What kinds of irregularities were found? What solutions were tried? What court challenges took place? How was the problem finally resolved? When

was the election finally decided?

2. Have each student write a brief essay telling what could be done to prevent similar problems in future presidential elections.

3. Have volunteers read their essays to the class.
LS Logical-Mathematical, Verbal-Linguistic

Alternative Assessment Handbook, Rubrics 11: Discussions; and 40: Writing to Describe

Answers

Photo *by the Supreme Court*
Reading Check *close race; Florida winner would win the election; lawsuits about ballot recounts in Florida; Florida Supreme Court ruling for hand recounts; Bush's appeal to the Supreme Court; Supreme Court ruling that Florida's Supreme Court ruling was unconstitutional*

Direct Teach

Reading Focus

❷ What were key components of George W. Bush's domestic policy? *tax cuts, the No Child Left Behind Act, creation of the White House Office of Faith-Based Initiatives, Medicare prescription benefit, Social Security reform*

Bush's Domestic Policy

Recall How did the U.S. economy respond to the tax cuts? *instead of improving went into a recession*

Explain What is the purpose of the No Child Left Behind Act? *to improve education by requiring that states develop academic standards and test students annually to ensure that those standards are met*

Summarize What caused the stock market to fall in the early 2000s? *Many Internet companies failed to perform as expected, and several large corporations were hit by scandals involving dishonest accounting methods.*

CRF: History and Geography Activity: 2004 Presidential Election

Recent Scholarship

The Votes That Counted: How the Court Decided the 2000 Presidential Election by political scientist Howard Gillman is an analysis of the court actions and decisions in the 2000 presidential election. Gillman argues that the Florida Supreme Court ruled consistently in its three unanimous decisions, but he also contends that the majority decision of the U.S. Supreme Court was arbitrary and partisan. The book gives the reader a good understanding of the key legal issues involved in this historic case.

The Votes that Counted. How the Court Decided the 2000 Presidential Election, by Howard Gillman. University of Chicago Press, 2001.

Bush's Domestic Policy

The 1990s had been a prosperous time. By the time Bush took office, however, the picture was beginning to change. For example, even before the election, the once booming stock market had begun to fall. This was due in large part to the collapse in the price of many Internet-related stocks.

THE IMPACT TODAY

Daily Life

States also create initiatives to improve public education. For example, California issued a new Master Plan for Education in 2002. The purpose of the Master Plan is to provide all students with access to "the educational components that are essential to a high quality education system and that foster the attainment of the educational expectations set by the State."

In the 1990s the Internet represented a whole new way of doing business. Many investors had hoped to make big money buying shares of Internet pioneers. These companies were known as **dot-coms**, after the .com that appears in many Internet addresses. Investors gambled billions on dot-coms. They paid high prices for the stock of companies that had never earned a profit. They expected the companies to make money one day. When the profits failed to appear, however, investors began to sell their stocks. As a result, prices dropped.

Stock prices were also hurt by a series of scandals that hit several large corporations in the early 2000s. The scandals involved dishonest accounting methods designed to make the companies more attractive to investors.

In addition to the drop in the stock market, the overall economy began to slow. Shortly after Bush took office, the United States was officially entering a recession. Though Bush was not responsible for this development, it did affect his domestic policies.

Tax cuts During the campaign, Bush had promised to cut taxes. At that time, the country enjoyed a budget surplus. When he took office, he quickly urged Congress to take action.

HISTORY'S VOICES

> **"You see, the growing surplus exists because taxes are too high and government is charging more than it needs. The people of America have been overcharged and on their behalf, I'm here asking for a refund."**
>
> —George W. Bush, February 27, 2001

Bush also argued that cutting taxes would help spur the now slumping economy. By lowering taxes and letting Americans keep more of their income to spend, Bush reasoned, business would improve. He believed this would provide more jobs and higher incomes.

By June, the Republican-controlled Congress had delivered on Bush's request. In addition to cutting tax rates, the new law addressed some long-standing complaints about the tax code. For example, it helped reduce the so-called marriage penalty. This is a part of the tax code that causes many married people to pay higher taxes than they would if they were single. The new law also lowered the estate tax, a tax on property inherited after a person's death.

Despite Bush's tax cuts, however, the economy did not improve. Instead, it went into recession. This recession was made worse by the terrorist attacks of September 11, 2001, which you will read about in the next section.

By 2003 Bush was again looking to cut taxes in hopes of promoting economic growth. Congress again passed a tax cut, which included the elimination of taxes on **dividends**. A dividend is a portion of a company's profits paid to its shareholders.

Education, health care, and more Shortly after taking office, Bush announced a major plan for improving education. The plan became the basis for a 2001 law, the No Child Left Behind (NCLB) Act. A key part of NCLB was a requirement that states develop academic standards and test students annually to ensure that those standards are met.

Another early Bush program was the White House Office of Faith-Based Initiatives. This office helps religious community-service organizations of all faiths develop greater access to federal funding. Bush viewed religious groups as effective tools for delivering services to needy groups such as the homeless, troubled youth, and former prison inmates. Critics, however, worried that the program might cross the constitutional line separating church and state.

In 2003 Bush signed into law a major update to the Medicare program. Included in this update was a new benefit to help Medicare recipients pay for prescription medicines.

Bush's second term In 2004 Bush ran for a second term in office. The Democrats nominated Senator John Kerry of Massachusetts. In addition to attacking Bush's foreign policy, Kerry criticized Bush's handling of the economy. He noted that the government was again running large deficits—that is, spending more than it takes in. In spite of these attacks, Bush won re-election in another close contest.

Skills Focus: Identifying Cause and Effect

At Level

Research Required

Reading Skill

The Dot-Com Bubble

1. Organize the class into small groups. Have each group conduct research on the dot-com phenomenon that fueled the growth in the stock market during much of the 1990s.
2. Have each group prepare a multimedia presentation about the dot-com phenomenon. Have students explain what dot-coms are, what happened to many of these companies, why it happened, and how their failures and subsequent negative impact on the stock market could have been prevented. Students should also mention several dot-com companies that survived and explain why they were able to survive.
3. Have volunteers share their analyses and presentations with the class. **LS Interpersonal, Logical-Mathematical**

Alternative Assessment Handbook, Rubrics 14: Group Activity; and 22: Multimedia Presentations

No Child Left Behind

In 2001 Congress passed an amendment to the Elementary and Secondary Education Act of 1965. Known as No Child Left Behind (NCLB), the law is intended to improve education across the United States.

No Child Left Behind says that all students should reach at least minimal proficiency on state academic achievement standards and state academic tests. Under the law, students will take standardized tests every year to show what they have learned. The results will be used to decide whether students are getting the education they need.

Many states already had testing programs in place before NCLB was put into effect. Remaining states had until

the 2005–2006 school year to make sure that their tests addressed their state's academic standards.

Not everyone agrees that NCLB is the solution to improving education. In 2003 the National Education Association, a teachers' union, filed a lawsuit arguing that the federal government was not providing enough money to support the required changes. A lawsuit filed by the state of Connecticut in 2005 also opposed the idea that states should pay for federal education goals.

Making Inferences Why might leaders feel that standardized testing is a useful tool for measuring what students have learned?

High school students take a standardized test.

Bush soon announced a top priority for his second term: reform of Social Security. Recall that this system uses money collected from taxpayers to help fund payments to retired Americans. Bush noted that in the future, taxpayers would be unable to pay all the benefits due to retirees. He proposed reforms that would allow taxpayers to create private accounts to fund their retirement. The plan, however, faced considerable public opposition. By late 2005 Congress had not acted on it.

Bush also faced decisions over Supreme Court vacancies. In 2005, Justice Sandra Day O'Connor announced her retirement and Chief Justice William Rehnquist died. To replace Rehnquist as Chief Justice, Bush nominated John Roberts, who won Senate confirmation in September 2005. To replace O'Connor, Bush nominated conservative judge Samuel Alito. On January 31, 2006, Alito won Senate confirmation in a 58-42 vote, one of the tightest margins in recent history.

READING CHECK **Identifying Problems and Solutions** What were some of the problems Bush hoped to address with his domestic policies?

Bush's Foreign Policy

Even before taking office in 2001, Bush assembled his foreign-policy staff. He chose Colin Powell as secretary of state. Powell had been a general in the army and chair of the Joint Chiefs of Staff during the Persian Gulf War of 1991. Bush named **Condoleezza Rice** as his national security adviser. Rice had been on the faculty of Stanford University and had served in the administration of George H. W. Bush.

Soon after the 2004 election, Powell resigned and Rice became secretary of state. For secretary of defense, Bush selected **Donald Rumsfeld**, who had earlier held this post and other key government posts.

During the 2000 election campaign, Bush had promised to limit the use of American troops for what he termed "nation building." For example, he criticized Clinton's use of troops in Somalia and Haiti. "I think our troops ought to be used to fight and win war," he said.

With this in mind, Bush called for a review of the nation's armed forces early in his presidency. He wanted to ensure that the military was prepared to fight the kinds of conflicts the United States might face in the future.

Reading Focus

Bush's Foreign Policy

Analyze How did the nuclear threat to the U.S. change between the early 1970s and the early 2000s? *In the early 1970s, it had come from the Soviet Union during the Cold War. By the early 2000s, it was not Russia that posed the threat but terrorist states.*

Identify Cause and Effect What was the result of Bush's decision to cancel the Anti-Ballistic Missile Treaty? *some friction with Russia and China*

🏷 Quick Facts Transparency: Foreign Policy Team

Review & Assess

Close

Have students summarize the major events that took place during the presidency of George W. Bush.

Review

🌐 Online Quiz, Section 2

🏷 Daily Test Practice Transparency

Assess

SE Section 2 Assessment

📖 Progress Assessment: Section 2 Quiz

📖 Alternative Assessment Handbook

Reteach

📖 Interactive Reader and Study Guide, Section 2

💿 Interactive Skills Tutor CD-ROM

Answers

Reading Check *Bush criticized use of troops by Clinton, called for review of armed forces; Russia no longer nuclear threat*

Bush's Foreign Policy Team — QUICK FACTS

Colin Powell

Colin Powell, a retired four-star general, served as secretary of state during George W. Bush's first term. Powell was the first African American to hold this position.

Donald Rumsfeld

As Bush's secretary of defense, Rumsfeld's main challenge was to direct response to the terrorist attacks of September 11, 2001.

Condoleezza Rice

Rice served as Bush's national security adviser during his first term. She replaced Colin Powell as secretary of state during Bush's second term.

Bush also decided to cancel the 1972 Anti-Ballistic Missile (ABM) Treaty. This agreement had been forged with the Soviet Union during the Cold War. Bush argued that the nation no longer faced a nuclear threat from Russia. Instead, he believed the danger was from some terrorist state. Therefore, Bush planned to move forward with development of a missile defense system. At the same time, Bush planned steep cuts in the nation's nuclear arsenal. This, he said, signaled his own commitment to reducing the threat to other nations.

The decision on the ABM treaty caused some friction with Russia and China. In general, however, Bush worked to build better relations with both countries. For example, he relied heavily on China's cooperation in putting pressure on North Korea to end its program for building nuclear weapons.

Bush also helped promote the so-called Middle East road map to peace. This historic document established a two-state vision—that is, an independent Palestinian state as well as the Jewish state of Israel.

By far, however, the most important foreign-policy event of the Bush administration occurred on September 11, 2001. This event set in motion a series of events that continue to affect the United States today. You will be reading about September 11 in the next section.

READING CHECK **Contrasting** How did Bush's foreign policy differ from Clinton's?

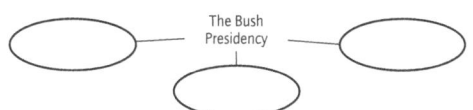

SECTION 2 ASSESSMENT

go.hrw.com
Online Quiz
Keyword: SD7 HP33

Reviewing Ideas, Terms, and People

1. a. Describe What factors made the 2000 election unusual?
b. Contrast How did the positions of the Democrats and Republicans differ in the 2000 election with regard to hand recounting of ballots?

2. a. Define Write a brief definition of each of the following terms: **budget surplus, dot-com, dividend**
b. Analyze How did the change in the economic situation in the United States affect George W. Bush's presidency?

3. a. Identify Besides the terrorist attacks of September 11, 2001, what were the major foreign-policy issues facing the Bush administration?
b. Make Generalizations How did Bush's foreign policy reflect the realities of a post-Cold War world?

Critical Thinking

4. Identifying the Main Idea Copy the chart below and use information from the section to record details that support the main idea of the section.

The Bush Presidency

FOCUS ON SPEAKING

5. Narrative Write and deliver a news story about the key events of the 2000 presidential election. The account should tell what made the election so unusual in American politics.

Section 2 Assessment Answers

1. a. close election, Supreme Court involvement
b. Democrats wanted hand recounts, Republicans objected

2. a. budget surplus—federal government revenues higher than expenses; dot-com—Internet-based company; dividend—portion of company profits paid to shareholders
b. Bush urged tax cuts and changes to tax codes to spur struggling economy; recession followed; growing budget deficits

3. a. cancellation of the 1972 ABM Treaty; Middle East road map to peace

b. threat more likely from terrorists, not Russia; pressured North Korea to end nuclear-weapons building program

4. elected without popular majority; tax cuts, reforms in education, health care, and Social Security; worked on Middle East relations, missile defense system, reduced U.S. nuclear arsenal, cancelled ABM Treaty

5. possible answer—very tight race, came down to Florida, Supreme Court ruled against hand recount, Bush did not win popular vote

How September 11, 2001, Changed America

BEFORE YOU READ

MAIN IDEA

A horrific attack on September 11, 2001, awakened the nation to the threat of terrorism and changed America's view of the world.

READING FOCUS

1. What happened on September 11, 2001?
2. What was the background to the September 11 attacks?
3. How did the United States respond to the attacks?
4. How did the 9/11 attacks eventually lead to war with Iraq?

KEY TERMS AND PEOPLE

9/11
Rudolph Giuliani
Osama bin Laden
al Qaeda
Taliban
Department of Homeland Security
USA PATRIOT Act

 TAKING NOTES As you read, take notes about the terrorist attacks of September 11, 2001, and their aftermath. Record your notes in a graphic organizer like the one shown here.

September 11 Attacks → Immediate Effects

Attack on the World Trade Center

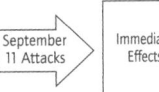 **THE INSIDE STORY**

What would you do if terrorists struck your neighborhood? On September 11, 2001, students at Stuyvesant High School in New York City were not at all prepared for terror to strike their community. Yet that morning, just as school was getting started, an aircraft slammed into one of the Twin Towers of the World Trade Center, about five blocks away. A short while later, a second airplane struck the second tower.

The students fled the school in search of safety. Among them was Ethan Moses, the photographer for the Stuyvesant High School newspaper, *The Spectator*. When he left the school, he took his camera along. As a student journalist, he felt driven to record what was taking place in his neighborhood—even though he was terrified by the tragedy unfolding before him. Before turning to run for his own safety, he snapped the image you see here of one of the Twin Towers collapsing.

Moses knew that he must preserve the images of what took place that day. Like Americans throughout the country, he overcame his horror and faced the September 11 attacks with courage and resolve. ◼

◀ **The horror of September 11, 2001, changed the way Americans looked at themselves and the world.**

INTO THE TWENTY-FIRST CENTURY **1091**

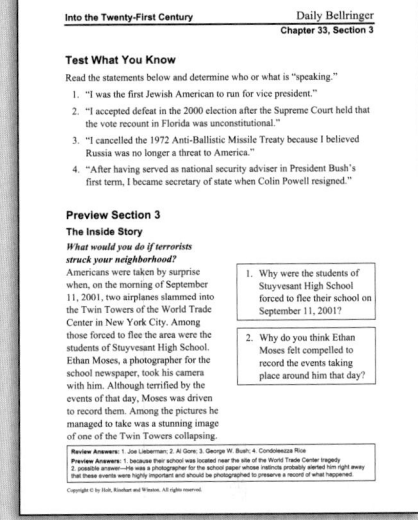

Reading Focus

1 What happened on September 11, 2001? *terrorists hijacked four passenger planes, two were used to destroy World Trade Center in New York City, one crashed into the Pentagon; fourth plane crashed in a field in the Pennsylvania countryside*

September 11, 2001

Recall When did it become apparent that the crash of an airliner into one of the towers of the World Trade Center was deliberate and not accidental? *less than 20 minutes later, when a second aircraft flew into the second tower*

Identify Cause and Effect Why did the towers of the World Trade Center collapse after being struck? *Fires caused by the planes' nearly full fuel tanks caused the buildings' structures to become fatally weakened.*

Activity **9/11** Have students write a brief paragraph describing the events of September 11, 2001. Then guide students in a discussion of the significance of these events for Americans.
LS Verbal-Linguistic

Answers

Interpreting Infographics
1. *patriotism;* **2.** *attack had been on symbols of U.S. might*

September 11, 2001

Shortly after 8:45 A.M. on September 11, 2001, people around the country began to hear startling reports of a terrible crash in New York City. An airliner had slammed into one of the 110-story-tall Twin Towers of the World Trade Center. This complex housed thousands of offices and businesses.

A deliberate attack Just 17 minutes after the first jet crashed, a second aircraft flew into the second of the Twin Towers. It became clear that the crashes were part of a deliberate attack. President Bush appeared before reporters to issue a brief statement. "Today we've had a national tragedy," he declared. He then assured the public that he had ordered the "full resources of the federal government" to respond to the disaster.

In fact, the attack—and its devastating effects—had just begun. In New York, firefighters and police officers rushed to the World Trade Center to help get people out of the burning towers. Military officials launched fighter aircraft to guard against any further attack. The Federal Aviation Administration (FAA) frantically gathered information about other possible hijackings. Hijacking is a terrorist act in which a plane is forced to go somewhere other than its intended destination. To prevent terrorists from getting control of more planes, the FAA also halted all commercial flights.

Unfortunately, there was nothing the FAA could do to stop the deadly flight of planes already in the air. Less than an hour after the first plane hit in New York, another slammed into the Pentagon, the mammoth headquarters of the Department of Defense located just outside Washington, D.C.

The Twin Towers collapse By now, millions of people were watching events unfold on television or listening to the news on the

HISTORY CLOSE-UP

The Attacks of September 11, 2001

Firefighters in New York City grapple with the devastation of the terrorist attacks on September 11 (center). That same day a trio of firefighters raise an American flag at the site of the World Trade Center (far right). On September 12, firefighters and rescue workers hang a huge flag on the damaged Pentagon (bottom).

Two flights out of Boston—American Airlines Flight 11 and United Airlines Flight 175—hit the World Trade Center.

United Airlines Flight 93, which originated in Newark, NJ, crashed in southwestern Pennsylvania.

American Airlines Flight 77, bound from Virginia to Los Angeles, flew into the Pentagon in Arlington, VA.

Attack site

0 50 100 Miles
0 50 100 Kilometers
Albers equal-area projection

CANADA · ME · VT · NH · MA · Boston · CT · RI · Lake Erie · New York · Newark · PA · NJ · Somerset County · ATLANTIC OCEAN · MD · DE · Washington, D.C. · WV · Arlington · VA

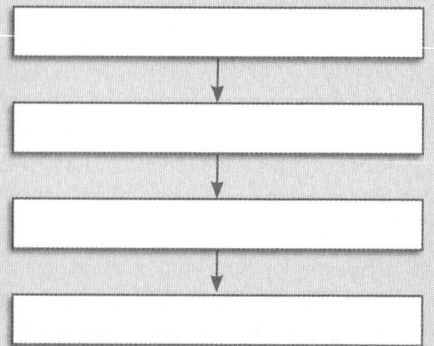

Skills FOCUS **INTERPRETING INFOGRAPHICS**

1. **Making Inferences** Based on these pictures, what was a common emotional reaction to the 9/11 attacks?
2. **Drawing Conclusions** How do you explain this reaction?
See **Skills Handbook**, p. H18

1092

Skills Focus: Sequencing

At Level

Reading Skill
September 11, 2001

1. To help students understand the sequence of events on September 11, 2001, draw a graphic organizer similar to the one shown here. Have students copy the organizer and complete it. Students will need to add boxes.

2. Review the graphic organizers as a class. Students should have these answers. *First airliner slams into one tower of World Trade Center; second aircraft flies into other tower of World Trade Center. Rescue workers arrive. FAA halts all commercial flights. Third airliner crashes into the Pentagon. South Tower collapses. Fourth airliner crashes in Pennsylvania field. North Tower collapses. Another damaged building collapses when the Twin Towers come down.* **LS** Visual-Spatial

Alternative Assessment Handbook, Rubric 13: Graphic Organizers

Graphic Organizer Transparencies

radio. But the worst was yet to come. Ten minutes after the Pentagon crash came the shocking collapse of the World Trade Center's South Tower. Fires caused by the plane's nearly full fuel tanks had caused a fatal weakening of the building's structure. The horrifying event was captured by TV cameras for viewers everywhere to see. Shortly after that came news of a fourth plane crash, this one in a field in the Pennsylvania countryside. Then at about 10:30 A.M., the North Tower collapsed in a massive cloud of dust and debris.

The stunned nation did not know it yet, but the worst was over. Later in the day, another building that had been damaged when the Twin Towers came down collapsed. But there were no more hijackings or plane crashes.

The death toll The nation next turned to face the horrible reality of what had taken place. To begin with, the four planes had carried 265 people, including passengers and crew. All were dead. In addition, at the Pentagon, 125 people were killed by the plane's impact and

the fires that followed. The number of victims at the World Trade Center was not known, but the estimates were in the thousands. (After several years of investigation, the New York death toll stood at 2,749.) It was clear that the attacks of **9/11** would surpass Pearl Harbor and other great disasters of American history in terms of lives lost.

The nation reacts The nation was overcome by a wave of grief and anger. At the same time, recognition of the bravery of those who responded to the disaster gave people comfort and strength. Americans were awestruck by the heroism of New York's rescue workers. Several hundred firefighters and police officers had run willingly into the burning towers, only to perish when they collapsed. Many also admired the steady leadership of New York's mayor, **Rudolph Giuliani**.

There were also reports that the plane that crashed in Pennsylvania may have been forced down by the heroic actions of its passengers. Telephone calls from passengers aboard the

● **Direct Teach** ●

History Close-Up

The Attacks of September 11, 2001

World Trade Center Towers Each a little more than 1,360 feet high and consisting of 110 floors, the Twin Towers of the World Trade Center were designed to withstand significant structural damage. Completed in the early 1970s, the towers were built from 200,000 tons of steel and 425,000 cubic yards of concrete. Each building's construction featured two sets of steel columns. The outer perimeter was composed of closely spaced steel columns in the form of a rectangle, which formed a load-bearing exterior wall. The inner core of steel columns connected to concrete floors over ceiling trusses. On September 11, 2001, the buildings collapsed from the heat of burning jet fuel, which weakened the steel columns, resulting in the collapse of both towers.

📖 Interdisciplinary Project: Write a Poem About September 11

Skills Focus: Identifying Main Idea and Details

At Level

Reading Skill
Responding to Tragedy

1. Guide the class in a discussion of the events that took place on 9/11 and in the days that followed. How did Americans respond to the attacks on that day and in the following days?

2. Have each student write a newspaper article about some aspect of 9/11 that particularly interests them. (Students may wish to conduct

additional research to help them write their articles.)

3. Have volunteers read their articles to the class. 🔊 **Verbal-Linguistic**

📖 Alternative Assessment Handbook, Rubric 23: Newspapers

September 11, 2001

Explain How do we know what happened on board the airplane that crashed in Pennsylvania on September 11? *Telephone calls from passengers indicated that they knew about the other attacks and decided to try to stop the terrorists.*

Define What is "Ground Zero"? *the site where the Twin Towers once stood*

2 What was the background to the September 11 attacks? *Osama bin Laden led terrorist network called al Qaeda in plot against the U.S.; members of al Qaeda entered U.S., learned to fly planes, and hijacked planes on 9/11*

Background to the Attacks

Recall Why did Osama bin Laden go to Afghanistan? *to help fight Soviet invaders*

Explain Why did the 9/11 hijackers choose long, cross-country routes rather than shorter ones? *so that the planes would be fully loaded with fuel*

Sequence What other anti-American terrorist activities were linked to Osama bin Laden? *the 1993 bombing of the World Trade Center; training attackers who killed American soldiers in Mogadishu, Somalia; bombings of the U.S. embassies in Kenya and Tanzania; bombing of the USS Cole*

📝 CRF: Primary Source Activity: George W. Bush Responds to the September 11, 2001, Attacks

Answers

Reading Check *planes hijacked, flew into World Trade Towers and Pentagon, one plane crashed in a field*

A Nation Pulls Together

A Michigan rally bursts into cheers after the playing of "God Bless America" (right). Below, New Yorkers memorialize the victims of the attack with a candlelight vigil.

SEPTEMBER 11, 2001

ACADEMIC VOCABULARY
rational based on reason

plane indicated they knew about the other attacks and had decided to stop the terrorists on board from hitting their next target.

Inspired by these stories, Americans reached out to the victims of 9/11. Blood collection centers received two-and-a-half times the normal donations in the days after 9/11. Millions of dollars poured into charities. Rescue workers from around the country traveled to New York to help with the recovery efforts at Ground Zero, the site where the Twin Towers had stood.

HISTORY'S VOICES

❝The camaraderie among the workers in the zone reminds me of the stories we've heard about the World War, where men and women are thrown together by a common cause, share tragedies and victories, and are forever bound to one another by their effort. ❞

—Joel Meyerowitz, artist's statement to the exhibit "Images from Ground Zero"

Americans also strengthened their resolve to face the challenge ahead. Patriotic feelings soared, and millions of people displayed American flags. It was clear that the United States was now engaged in a new kind of war: a war on terrorism.

READING CHECK **Sequencing** What were the key events of September 11, 2001?

1094 CHAPTER 33

THE IMPACT TODAY
Daily Life
Al Qaeda also targeted U.S. allies, including Great Britain. In July 2005, a bombing in London's subway and bus system killed 52 people. The bombing was linked to al Qaeda.

Background to the Attacks

Investigators, meanwhile, were trying to determine who was responsible for the attacks. One rational theory focused on **Osama bin Laden**. A member of a wealthy Saudi Arabian family, bin Laden had gone to Afghanistan in the 1980s to help fight Soviet invaders. During this time, he adopted the goal of promoting a worldwide Islamic revolution. Islam is one of the world's major religions, and it is based on the teachings of the prophet Muhammad, who lived about AD 570–632. Achieving an Islamic revolution, bin Laden claimed, required the destruction of the United States. Bin Laden had also been angered by the presence of American military forces in Saudi Arabia during the Persian Gulf War. This he saw as an insult to Islam.

To carry out his campaign against his enemies, bin Laden developed a terrorist network. This was known as **al Qaeda**, or "the base."

By 2001 bin Laden and al Qaeda were well known to American officials. During the 1990s, these terrorists had made a number of threats against the United States and announced the goal of killing Americans. Bin Laden had links to a 1993 bombing at the World Trade Center that killed six people. He was also accused of helping to train some of the attackers who killed 18 American soldiers in Mogadishu, Somalia, in 1993. In August 1998 bombings at the U.S. embassies in the African countries of Kenya and Tanzania killed 224. After establishing a link between the bombings and bin

Reading Skill
Fighting Terrorism

Research Required

1. Have students write two or three paragraphs outlining what steps they might have taken to find those responsible for the September 11, 2001, attacks.

2. Have students conduct research to determine the steps U.S. leaders took to find those responsible and bring them to justice, and summarize their research in two or three paragraphs.

3. Have students write one more paragraph comparing the steps they would have taken with the steps the U.S. government took.

4. Have volunteers read their final paragraphs to the class. **LS Logical-Mathematical, Verbal-Linguistic**

📝 Alternative Assessment Handbook, Rubric 37: Writing Assignments

Laden's network, President Clinton launched a missile attack into a suspected al Qaeda training camp in Afghanistan. Bin Laden and his organization survived. In 2000 they carried out a bomb attack on an American naval vessel, the USS *Cole*, which was visiting a port in the Middle Eastern country of Yemen. Seventeen Americans died in the blast.

Meanwhile, investigators later learned, al Qaeda was busy planning the 9/11 attacks. As part of this plan, terrorists began entering the United States in early 2000. They enrolled in American flight schools, where they learned the basics of flying airliners.

By September 11 they were ready to act. In the morning hours, they boarded flights at several East Coast airports. They chose long, cross-country routes so that the planes would be fully loaded with fuel. Once in the air, the hijackers—19 in total—seized control of the aircrafts. To do so, they used ordinary box cutters as weapons. It was a complicated plan that used simple methods. Tragically, it worked just as they had planned.

READING CHECK **Identifying the Main Idea**
What is Osama bin Laden's background and his reasons for using terrorism?

The United States Responds

Fires were still burning in New York and at the Pentagon when President Bush issued a clear warning to the world. "We will make no distinction between the terrorists who committed these acts and those who harbor them," he declared. With suspicion quickly focusing on Osama bin Laden and his al Qaeda network, Bush's warning seemed especially directed toward the nation of Afghanistan.

War in Afghanistan Afghanistan had endured terrible suffering in the late 1900s. The 1979 invasion by the Soviet Union had been followed by years of bloody fighting and civil war. Out of this chaos, a group known as the **Taliban** had gained control over most of the country. The Taliban governed according to a strict application of Islamic law. For example, women were required to wear clothing that covered nearly every inch of their bodies. They were forbidden from attending school or leaving home without a male relative. Punishment for offenses was swift and harsh.

The Taliban also enjoyed a close relationship with Osama bin Laden. Recall that bin Laden operated al Qaeda training camps in

Responding to the Attacks

President Bush meets with his National Security Council on September 12, 2001, to plan America's response to the terrorist attacks on the nation. Attention focused on Afghanistan (see map below), a landlocked country in south-central Asia with a mountainous terrain and extreme climate.

AFGHANISTAN

TURKMENISTAN · UZBEKISTAN · TAJIKISTAN

Herat · Jalalabad · Kabul · Tora Bora

AFGHANISTAN

Kandahar · PAKISTAN · IRAN

0   100   200 Miles
0   100 200 Kilometers

1095

The United States Responds

Describe How was the Department of Homeland Security created? *Bush and Congress combined 22 government agencies and 180,000 employees into a cabinet-level organization.*

Recall How did lawmakers try to satisfy critics of the USA PATRIOT Act? *by agreeing to let some provisions of the law expire after a certain period of time*

Predict How might history have been different if the Taliban had handed Osama bin Laden over to the United States? *The U.S. and allies might not have attacked Afghanistan; Taliban might still be in power. The U.S. might not have invaded Iraq, Osama bin Laden would have been tried for his crimes.*

Primary Source

"Whether we bring our enemies to justice, or bring justice to our enemies, justice will be done."

— George W. Bush

Address to joint session of Congress,
September 20, 2001

U.S. soldiers in the Khakeran Valley of Afghanistan search a house for weapons in June 2005 in a continuing effort to root out Taliban presence in the region.

THE IMPACT TODAY

Government
The creation of the Department of Homeland Security marked one of the most far-reaching government reorganizations in American history. It was followed by a planned overhaul of the nation's entire intelligence structure.

Afghanistan. This was done with the cooperation of the Taliban. For his part, bin Laden provided support to the Taliban in its struggle to control Afghanistan.

When it became clear that bin Laden and al Qaeda were likely responsible for the 9/11 attacks, Bush put pressure on the Taliban. He insisted that Taliban leaders seize bin Laden and hand him over to the United States.

In spite of this pressure, the Taliban remained defiant. By the end of September, it was clear they would not give in to American demands. So, on October 7, 2001, the United States, along with ally Great Britain, launched a military attack on Taliban strongholds throughout Afghanistan.

HISTORY'S VOICES

❝ We're a peaceful nation. Yet, as we have learned, so suddenly and so tragically, there can be no peace in a world of sudden terror. In the face of today's new threat, the only way to pursue peace is to pursue those who threaten it. ❞

—George W. Bush, October 7, 2001

In fighting the Taliban, the United States relied heavily on fighters of Afghanistan's Northern Alliance. This armed group opposed the Taliban and controlled a small part of Afghanistan. Within weeks, anti-Taliban forces captured the capital of Kabul. By early December, the Taliban was defeated.

Less successful was the hunt for Osama bin Laden. American and Northern Alliance forces at one point thought they had him trapped in the mountainous Tora Bora region of Afghanistan. The site was bombed heavily. Bin Laden, however, managed to avoid capture.

In spite of this setback, the American operation in Afghanistan was considered a success. At the end of December, representatives of several major groups in Afghanistan met to select a new interim leader for the country. They made plans to create a new constitution and government. Presidential elections took place in 2004, and parliamentary elections went forward in 2005. Afghanistan would continue to face serious problems. These included continued fighting by surviving members of the Taliban. However, the country's role as a terrorist base was greatly reduced.

Fighting terrorism at home While American troops were fighting in Afghanistan, President Bush and Congress were working to fight terrorism at home. To coordinate these efforts, Bush and Congress began work on what would become the **Department of Homeland Security**. This cabinet-level organization combined 22 government agencies and 180,000 employees. Its functions included maintaining a color-coded warning system for terrorist threats.

Also in the days after 9/11, the nation experienced a frightening introduction to another kind of terrorist threat: biological agents. In several locations in the eastern United States, 18 people came down with a rare but deadly infection caused by the anthrax bacteria. Five people died. The anthrax had apparently been sent through the mail in a deliberate attempt to infect people. For several anxious weeks, Americans wondered how widespread the anthrax attacks had been. It soon became clear that the crisis was limited to a handful of specific locations. For a nation still recovering from 9/11, however, the incident was alarming.

In Congress, lawmakers took up the question of how to prevent future terrorist attacks. One solution proposed by the White House was to strengthen the powers of law-enforcement to

Skills Focus: Analyzing Costs and Benefits

At Level

Social Studies Skill

Research Required

Homeland Security

1. Remind students of the history of the Department of Homeland Security. Its creation required a massive reorganization of the federal government and its agencies. Organize the class into small groups. Have each group conduct research on the organization, the purposes, and the costs and benefits of creating a new government agency, the Department of Homeland Security.

2. Have each group write an illustrated report on

the Department of Homeland Security. What key agencies make up the department? How do they work together in times of national emergency? Students should include charts and graphs summarizing the results of their research.

3. Have volunteers share their reports with the class. **LS Interpersonal, Verbal-Linguistic**

📖 Alternative Assessment Handbook, Rubrics 24: Oral Presentations; and 30: Research

investigate possible terrorists. These proposals became the basis of the **USA PATRIOT Act**. This law made it easier for law enforcement to secretly collect information about suspected terrorists. Indeed, some critics complained that the USA PATRIOT Act gave law enforcement too much power and posed a threat to basic freedoms. To address these concerns, Congress agreed to let some provisions of the law expire after a certain period of time.

READING CHECK **Identifying Problems and Solutions** How did the U.S. government respond to the threat of terrorism after 9/11?

War in Iraq

Following the success in Afghanistan, President Bush delivered his State of the Union address in January 2002. "What we have found in Afghanistan," he said, "confirms that, far from ending there, our war against terror is only beginning." Further, he identified Iraq as a possible future foe.

Following the Persian Gulf War in 1991, Iraq had agreed to destroy its weapons of mass destruction. To ensure that Iraq's leader, Saddam Hussein, was living up to this agreement, the UN placed weapons inspectors inside the country. With each passing year, however, the Iraqi leader grew more and more uncooperative with these inspection efforts. In response, the UN removed its inspectors entirely in 1998.

Since that time, observers believed the Iraqis had been busy building banned weapons. Given the events of 9/11, this greatly concerned President Bush. "The United States will not permit the world's most dangerous regimes to threaten us with the world's most destructive weapons," he declared.

Throughout the fall of 2002 and the winter of 2003, Bush sought to build support for forceful action against Saddam Hussein. Under this pressure, Iraq allowed a new round of UN weapons inspections. This turned up no weapons of mass destruction. Bush, however, insisted that Iraq had failed to account for weapons it was known to have possessed after

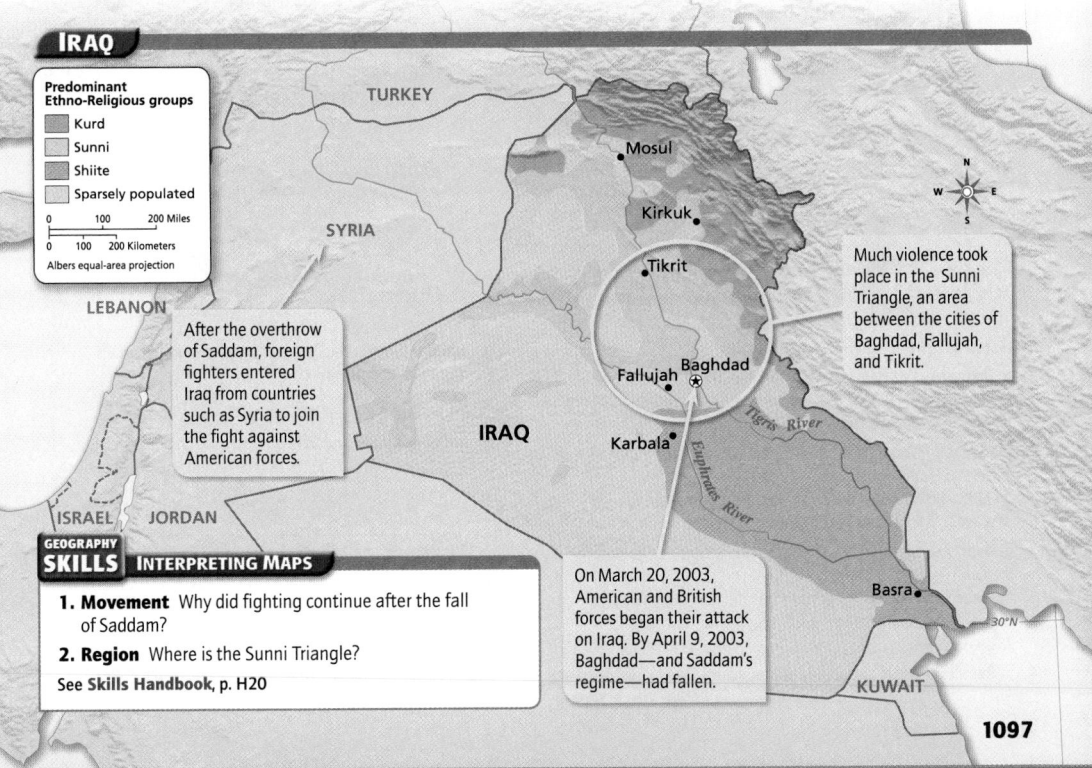

IRAQ

Predominant Ethno-Religious groups
- Kurd
- Sunni
- Shiite
- Sparsely populated

0   100   200 Miles
0   100   200 Kilometers
Albers equal-area projection

TURKEY

SYRIA

LEBANON

ISRAEL   JORDAN

Mosul

Kirkuk

Tikrit

Fallujah   Baghdad

IRAQ   Karbala

Tigris River

Euphrates River

Basra

30°N

KUWAIT

Much violence took place in the Sunni Triangle, an area between the cities of Baghdad, Fallujah, and Tikrit.

After the overthrow of Saddam, foreign fighters entered Iraq from countries such as Syria to join the fight against American forces.

On March 20, 2003, American and British forces began their attack on Iraq. By April 9, 2003, Baghdad—and Saddam's regime—had fallen.

GEOGRAPHY SKILLS **INTERPRETING MAPS**

1. **Movement** Why did fighting continue after the fall of Saddam?
2. **Region** Where is the Sunni Triangle?

See Skills Handbook, p. H20

1097

Differentiating Instruction

Above Level

Advanced Learners/GATE

Research Required

1. Have students research the USA PATRIOT Act and outline its major points. Review student outlines with the class.

2. Guide the class in a discussion of the act. Ask students if they agree with all of its points. If not, have students identify those points with which they do not agree and have them explain their reasoning.

3. Have students consider whether they would support or oppose the USA PATRIOT Act if they were in Congress. Have students write a brief essay explaining their position.

4. Have volunteers read their essays to the class.
LS **Logical-Mathematical, Verbal-Linguistic**

Alternative Assessment Handbook, Rubrics 30: Research; and 42: Writing to Inform

Direct Teach

Reading Focus

4 How did the 9/11 attacks eventually lead to war with Iraq? *After success in Afghanistan, Bush said that the war against terror was just beginning, and identified Iraq as a possible future foe.*

War in Iraq

Recall What did Iraq agree to do following the Persian Gulf War? *destroy its weapons of mass destruction*

Explain Why did the UN place inspectors inside Iraq? *to ensure that Iraq would destroy its weapons of mass destruction*

Activity **A Second War** Have students review the information in the text about the first Persian Gulf War. Create a class list comparing and contrasting the first war with the later war in Iraq. **LS** **Verbal-Linguistic**

Map Transparency: Iraq

Info to Know

The Fertile Crescent Iraq is the location of the Fertile Crescent, the land along the Tigris and Euphrates rivers where the first civilizations of the Middle East and Mediterranean emerged. In ancient times, Iraq was known as Mesopotamia, the "land between two rivers." Because of its riches, it was a prized conquest of the Persian, Greek, Roman, and Ottoman empires. In the 7th century it became an important part of the Islamic world. Following the breakup of the Ottoman Empire after World War I, Iraq became a British protectorate, achieving official independence in 1932.

Answers

Interpreting Maps 1. *Foreign fighters entered the country to fight American forces.* **2.** *between cities of Baghdad, Fallujah, and Tikrit*

Reading Check *invaded Afghanistan to attack the Taliban; created Department of Homeland Security; passed the USA PATRIOT Act*

1097

Reading Focus

War in Iraq

Identify Cause and Effect What reasons did President Bush give for attacking Iraq? *Iraq had failed to account for weapons it was known to have possessed; government claimed to have information about new Iraqi weapons systems.*

Elaborate Why do you think the UN removed its weapons inspectors from Iraq when Saddam Hussein became uncooperative? *lacked power to make him cooperate; pointless to keep weapons inspectors in country*

📄 CRF: Biography: Kanan Makiya

• **Review & Assess** •

Close

Guide the class in a discussion of the events of September 11, 2001, and how they changed America's view of the world.

Review

🖥 Online Quiz, Section 3

📦 Daily Test Practice Transparency

Assess

SE Section 3 Assessment

📝 Progress Assessment: Section 3 Quiz

📝 Alternative Assessment Handbook

Reteach

📝 Interactive Reader and Study Guide, Section 3

💿 Interactive Skills Tutor CD-ROM

Answers

Faces of History *focus changed to protecting against further terrorist attacks*

Reading Check *Iraq agreed to destroy weapons of mass destruction after Persian Gulf War, didn't cooperate with UN inspectors, U.S. concerned about Iraq creating weapons of mass destruction*

FACES OF HISTORY

George W. BUSH
1946–

George W. Bush did not initially seek a life in politics. Though his father, George H. W. Bush, had served as a member of Congress and in other government posts, Bush decided to pursue a business career. A failed bid for Congress in 1978 did nothing to change his mind. Then following his father's term as president, Bush won the race for governor of Texas and was re-elected in 1998. His campaign for the presidency followed two years later. Bush was re-elected to a second term in 2004. After 9/11, Bush's primary focus as president became protecting the nation against the threat of terrorism. His administration will forever be defined by his leadership in the wake of the 9/11 attacks.

Explain How did the 9/11 attacks change Bush's presidency?

the Persian Gulf War. Members of his administration also claimed to have information about new Iraqi weapons systems. Many of America's longtime allies argued against going to war. Still, Bush insisted the Iraqi threat must be countered. With the support of Great Britain and several other countries, American forces stormed into Iraq in March 2003.

The United States and its allies made quick work of Iraq's military. By early April, Saddam Hussein's regime had fallen. Saddam was captured in late 2003.

The United States then moved to establish a new Iraqi government. In June 2004 American officials handed control over to an interim Iraqi government. American forces remained to help keep order and train a new Iraqi security force.

Elections in early 2005 began the process by which Iraqis would create a new constitution. Conflict between rival religious and ethnic groups complicated the process. In October 2005, voters approved a new constitution.

Iraq, however, continued to experience serious problems. Terrorists, who included former Saddam loyalists and religious extremists, continued to take a terrible toll on American soldiers and on Iraqi civilians and those who joined the new police and security forces.

The ongoing violence created political problems for Bush. He also faced criticism when it became clear that Saddam Hussein had apparently not possessed weapons of mass destruction at the start of the war.

The president overcame these questions to win re-election in 2004. He reminded voters that Saddam had been a brutal dictator and that his removal from power made the world a safer place. He assured Americans that progress was being made toward a more peaceful, democratic Iraq. He also made clear that U.S. forces would remain in Iraq for as long as necessary to ensure peace and order there.

READING CHECK **Sequencing** Describe the events leading up to and following the war in Iraq.

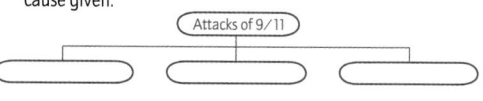

SECTION 3 ASSESSMENT

go.hrw.com
Online Quiz
Keyword: SD7 HP33

Reviewing Ideas, Terms, and People

1. **a. Describe** What is the significance of 9/11?
   b. Summarize How would you summarize the reaction of the American people to the attacks of 9/11?

2. **a. Identify** Who or what are the following: **Osama bin Laden, al Qaeda**
   b. Make Inferences Why do you think Osama bin Laden decided to try to destroy the United States?

3. **a. Describe** Why did the United States attack Afghanistan in 2001?
   b. Make Inferences What can you infer from the fact that the United States received wide support for its attack on Afghanistan?

4. **a. Recall** Why did the United States attack Iraq in 2003?

1098 CHAPTER 33

b. Explain Why did Bush think that removing Saddam Hussein was important?

Critical Thinking

5. **Identifying Cause and Effect** Copy the chart below and use information from the section to record the effects of the cause given.

Attacks of 9/11

FOCUS ON WRITING

6. **Narrative** Write a brief narrative that recounts the major events of September 11, 2001, and its aftermath.

Section 3 Assessment Answers

1. **a.** major terrorist attack on U.S.
   b. grief, anger, recognition of bravery and heroism of rescue workers

2. **a.** Osama—Saudi promoting Islamic revolution; al Qaeda—terrorist network
   b. possible answer—U.S. military in Saudi Arabia seen as insult to Islam

3. **a.** refused to turn Osama over to U.S.
   b. possible answer—many sympathetic to U.S. and concerned about future terrorism

4. **a.** concern about weapons of mass destruction; to remove dictator Saddam Hussein
   b. Saddam thought to have dangerous weapons; might seek to attack U.S.

5. creation of Dept. of Homeland Security; war in Afghanistan, removal of Taliban; war in Iraq, removal of Saddam Hussein

6. hijackers use airplanes to destroy World Trade Towers, attack Pentagon; Dept. of Homeland Security created; attempt to find Osama bin Laden leads to invasion of Afghanistan and removal of Taliban government; war in Iraq

BEFORE YOU READ

MAIN IDEA

The dawn of a new century found the United States facing a new era of opportunity and challenge.

READING FOCUS

1. How is the face of the American population changing?

2. What promise does new technology hold for the United States?

3. What challenges confront the United States in the future?

KEY TERMS AND PEOPLE

Antonio Villaraigosa
IT
genetic engineering

TAKING NOTES As you read, take notes on the major questions and concerns facing the United States in the coming decades. Record your notes in a graphic organizer like the one shown here.

Looking Ahead

Population	
Technological	
Challenges	

THE INSIDE STORY

What can a mayoral election tell us about the future of America? The last time Los Angeles had a Hispanic American mayor, the "city" was actually a small frontier community of 6,000 people. The year was 1872.

Since that time, Los Angeles has grown into the second-largest city in the United States. A significant part of that growth was the result of immigration from Mexico and other countries of Central and South America. The growing number of Latino residents—and voters—in Los Angeles formed an increasingly powerful voice in local politics. Yet before 2005 and the election of **Antonio Villaraigosa** (vee-uh-ry-GOH-suh), Hispanics in Los Angeles had never been able to muster the political strength necessary to elect one of their own to the mayor's office. In the 2005 election, Villaraigosa drew support from voters of many backgrounds. His victory, however, was especially significant to the city's 1.7 million Latinos, who make up slightly less than half the city's population.

Villaraigosa's election was a landmark to people all across the country. As you will read, the forces that made California's population so diverse are also at work throughout the rest of the country. The minority groups of yesterday and today are growing, and they will play a leading role in the nation's future. ◢

A Latino Mayor for Los Angeles

► Antonio Villaraigosa takes the oath of office as the mayor of Los Angeles.

1099

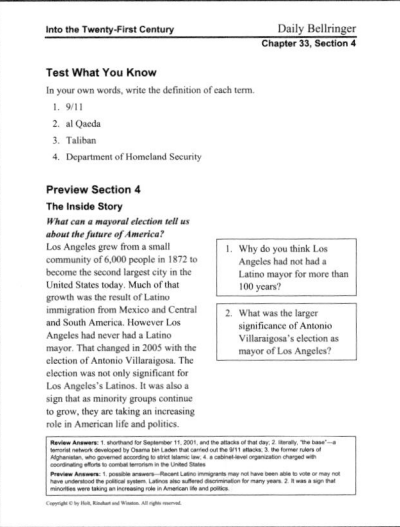
Teach the Main Idea   At Level

Looking Ahead

1. **Teach** Ask students the Reading Focus questions to teach this section.

2. **Apply** Organize the class into small groups. Have each group discuss the ways in which the United States is changing in the 21st century. Have students scan the section and make a list of trends in population and technological advances.

3. **Review** Review student lists of changes as a class. Have students name challenges that the United States faces as a result of

these changes.

4. **Practice/Homework** Have each student write an essay on the best way to balance the need for energy and economic growth with the need to minimize the costs of obtaining them—both monetary and environmental. **LS Interpersonal, Verbal-Linguistic**

Alternative Assessment Handbook, Rubrics 1: Acquiring Information; and 42: Writing to Inform

1099

Reading Focus

❶ How is the face of the American population changing? *minority groups growing; population aging*

America's Changing Face

Explain Why is the American population aging? *The post-World War II baby boomers are growing older. The next generation is much smaller due to lower birthrates.*

Identify Cause and Effect What are the reasons for the population growth in the South and West? *Warmer climates attract people and businesses. Lower labor costs draw business, which attracts more residents.*

📄 CRF: Literature Activity: *The Tortilla Curtain* by T. Coraghessan Boyle

Biography

August Wilson (1945–2005) After his own experiences with poverty and racism, playwright August Wilson chronicled the challenges facing African Americans throughout the 20th century. Mostly self-educated, Wilson participated in the civil rights movement in the 1960s before he began to write plays in the 1980s. Wilson won his first Pulitzer Prize in 1987 for *Fences*, which dealt with a father and son's struggle to confront racism in athletics. In 1990, Wilson won another Pulitzer Prize for *The Piano Lesson*. In this play, a brother and sister debate what to do with a piano that was once traded for their enslaved grandparents. Throughout his many plays, Wilson uses lyrical language to depict the difficulty of balancing mainstream American values with African culture.

Answers

Interpreting Graphs *increases in people of Hispanic origin*

America's Changing Face

Throughout American history, migration, immigration, and even slavery brought new groups to America. Such changes have sometimes led to conflict between different groups. In general, however, history shows that the nation has grown richer and stronger as it has grown more <u>diverse</u>.

ACADEMIC VOCABULARY
diverse including great variety

Tomorrow's population The makeup of America's population is continually changing. The U.S. census measures these changes. The most recent census was held in 2000. By looking back just 20 years, you can see significant population trends. (See the graphs below.)

Census officials also look into the future. Minority groups today, including African Americans, Hispanic Americans, and Asian Americans, make up about 30 percent of the population. By 2050 they will make up about 50 percent of the population. The Asian American population is expected to more than triple. The Hispanic American population is predicted to grow by nearly 190 percent and make up nearly one-fourth of the population.

The changing population has already caused a reaction in the United States. You have read about growing resistance, mainly among white Americans, to affirmative action programs. Such programs were designed to help minority groups overcome discrimination. In California voters approved Proposition 209 in 1996. This amendment to the state constitution outlawed the use of racial preferences in decisions such as university admissions. Under Proposition 209, public institutions in California can no longer consider a job or school applicant's race, gender, or ethnic background.

Regional changes Many Americans will also be changing where they live. The warmer regions of the South and the West are expected to grow at a faster rate than the colder Northeast and Midwest. The warmer climate attracts people and businesses, in part because of lower energy costs. Labor costs have tended to be lower in the South and West, another factor that attracts businesses to the area.

Census projections predict that between 2000 and 2030, the populations of the South and West will rise about 45 percent, compared to a 30 percent growth of the total U.S. population. Nevada and Arizona may double their populations. Texas, Florida, and California could each gain 9 million residents. Meanwhile, the Northeast will gain a mere 7.6 percent in population. The Midwest will gain only 10 percent. West Virginia and North Dakota may actually see their populations decrease.

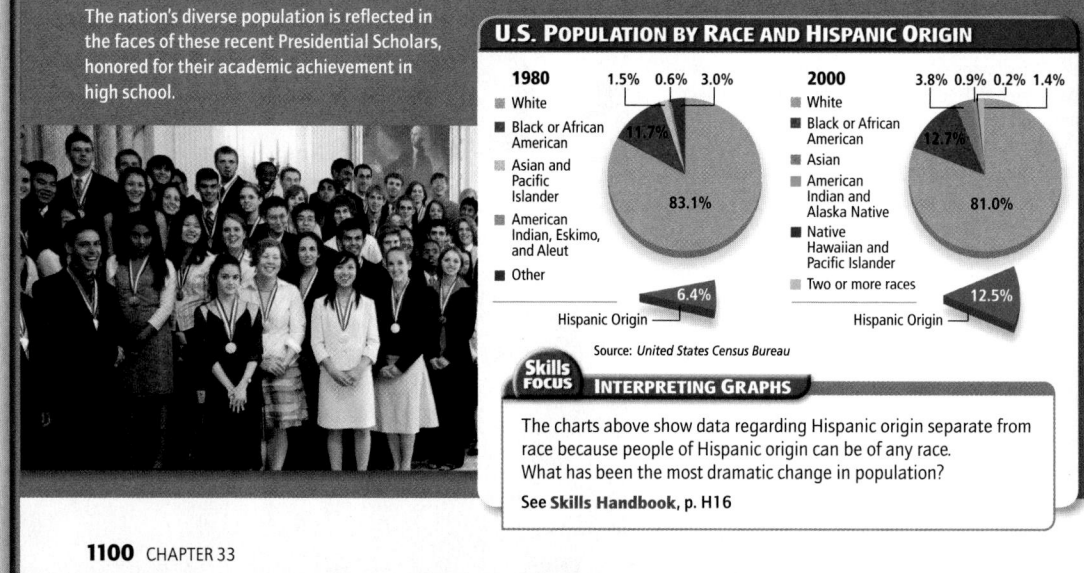

The nation's diverse population is reflected in the faces of these recent Presidential Scholars, honored for their academic achievement in high school.

U.S. POPULATION BY RACE AND HISPANIC ORIGIN

1980   1.5% 0.6% 3.0%
- White
- Black or African American — 11.7%
- Asian and Pacific Islander
- American Indian, Eskimo, and Aleut
- Other
83.1%

Hispanic Origin — 6.4%

2000   3.8% 0.9% 0.2% 1.4%
- White
- Black or African American — 12.7%
- Asian
- American Indian and Alaska Native
- Native Hawaiian and Pacific Islander
- Two or more races
81.0%

Hispanic Origin — 12.5%

Source: *United States Census Bureau*

Skills Focus **INTERPRETING GRAPHS**

The charts above show data regarding Hispanic origin separate from race because people of Hispanic origin can be of any race. What has been the most dramatic change in population?

See Skills Handbook, p. H16

1100 CHAPTER 33

Skills Focus: Summarizing
At Level

Reading Skill
Research Required
Growing Diversity

1. Organize the class into small groups. Have each group conduct research into changes in diversity in your community or state since 1990. Use the following questions as a guide: What ethnic groups are represented? Approximately what percentage of the population is made up of different ethnic groups? Approximately what percentage of the population was born in another country? How have these data changed since 1990?

2. Have each group write a report, complete with graphs and charts.

3. Have volunteers from each group share their reports with the class.

4. Guide the class in a discussion of their findings. What trends do they notice? How do they think the population will change in the next 20 years?

LS **Interpersonal, Logical-Mathematical**

📄 Alternative Assessment Handbook, Rubrics 13: Graphic Organizers; and 42: Writing to Inform

Immigration and Religion

Immigrants coming to the United States have always brought their cultures, languages, and traditions with them. They also bring their religious beliefs. Most settlers in the original English colonies were Protestants. Later immigration increased the numbers of Catholics, Jews, and other groups. Recently, new immigrants have brought even greater religious diversity. As more immigrants come from Asia, Africa, and Latin America, new cultures and religions have been introduced to the United States.

Today about 80 percent of people in the United States identify themselves as Christians. Among organized religions, the next largest is Judaism, with almost 2 percent of the population. Religions such as Islam, Buddhism, and Hinduism are growing, although members of each faith still make up less than 1 percent of the total population.

The First Amendment of the Constitution guarantees the "free exercise" of religion, which means that anyone may practice his or her beliefs. By guaranteeing freedom of religion, the Constitution has allowed the United States to become increasingly diverse in terms of religion.

Drawing Conclusions How is the Constitution connected to growing religious diversity?

The Constitution guarantees this convention attendee the right to openly practice his Sikh religion.

A graying population Americans are also getting older. People over age 64 are the country's fastest-growing age group. Between 2000 and 2050, the overall U.S. population is expected to increase some 50 percent. The number of people ages 65 to 84, however, could double. Meanwhile, the 20 to 40 age group may grow by just 25 percent.

Who are these soon-to-be older Americans? Many are baby boomers born between 1946 and 1964. The baby boom was followed by a sharp drop in birthrates in the mid-1960s and 1970s. This "baby bust" helps explain why younger age groups are growing at a slower rate today.

The growing proportion of retirees to working people will affect programs such as Social Security. Benefits paid to retirees come from the taxes on the wages of working people. Experts predict that in the future, payouts from the system will exceed taxes collected. As you read in Section 2, President Bush sought to address this problem in 2005 by proposing changes to Social Security. The debate over Social Security will likely continue for some time.

READING CHECK **Summarizing** How would you describe the changing face of America?

The Promise of Technology

As it has throughout history, technological change will help shape the nation's future. New ideas and new ways of working will keep the nation strong, prosperous, healthy, and secure.

Computers Computer use continues to expand rapidly. In 1980 less than 1 percent of the American population owned a computer. Today the figure is over 60 percent. Most computers are also connected to the Internet. The infrastructure that supports these connections has now covered nearly the entire country. Many people who do not have access to the Internet at home may access it at libraries or schools. In addition, computer technology is working its way into our lives in countless ways. Cars, household appliances, and many other objects contain tiny computers.

ACADEMIC VOCABULARY
infrastructure
the basic facilities of a community for transportation, communication, and more

HISTORY'S VOICES

❝This is the decade where computing technology will go from being an add-on, overlaid on our normal activities, to becoming part of the fabric of our everyday lives . . . This technology is moving forward faster today than ever before . . .❞

—Bill Gates, speech, June 25, 2003

Skills Focus: Comparing and Contrasting

Reading Skill

Charting Change

1. Organize the class into small groups. Have each group conduct research into population growth in their community or state since 1990. Use the following questions as a guide: What was the population in 1990? What was it in 2000? What is the estimated population today? What percentage of the population fell into each of the following age groups: under 19, 19–34, 35–64, 65–84, 85 and up in 1990? In 2000? Today?

2. Have each group create a series of graphs that show these trends.

3. Guide the class in a discussion of their findings. What trends do they notice? How do they think the population will change in the next 20 years? **LS** **Interpersonal, Visual-Spatial**

Alternative Assessment Handbook, Rubric 13: Graphic Organizers

Graphic Organizer Transparencies

The Promise of Technology

Compare How does the number of wireless telephones compare with the number of land line phones? *As of 2005, wireless telephones outnumber land line phones.*

Explain Why do some people object to genetically modified crops? *They worry about possible health effects and that altered genes may get into wild plants, such as weeds, making them hard to control.*

Make Judgments Do you think the United States should try to build a station on the moon and send humans to Mars? Why or why not? *possible answer—Yes. Americans have always been interested in exploring new frontiers, and the continued exploration of space could bring many benefits besides the knowledge we will gain.*

One example of the melding of computers with everyday devices is the telephone. Computerized wireless phone use is growing rapidly in the United States. In fact, the number of wireless phone lines had surpassed the number of landline phones by 2005.

Computerized information technology, or **IT**, is also bringing change to American business. IT is a way of allowing businesses to organize and examine information in more productive ways. For example, an IT system can make it possible for a company's sales, manufacturing, and shipping departments to share the exact same information on their computer screens. Customers can use their own computers to check on the status of orders or to shop online. These capabilities help make a business more efficient. Being more efficient helps reduce the costs of doing business and increases profits.

Agriculture Technology continues to bring changes to agriculture. One leading example is **genetic engineering**. By carefully altering the genes of a species of plant, scientists have been able to produce varieties with certain desirable features. For example, scientists can genetically engineer corn so that the plant is more resistant to herbicides farmers use to control weeds. As a result, farmers can control weeds

more effectively while doing less harm to their crop. Scientists have also engineered crops to resist pests. This means more crops and less use of pesticides. There are many other possible uses for genetic engineering as well.

Like many other technological changes, genetic engineering has created controversy. Some people worry about possible health effects of genetically modified crops. Another concern is that altered genes will get into wild plants. For example, the gene that makes corn resistant to herbicide could make its way into weeds. This would make the weeds harder to control and more damaging to crops.

Exploration The American people continue to demonstrate a spirit of discovery. President Bush in early 2004 laid out the next goal in the ongoing journey into unexplored places: building a space station on the moon and eventually sending human beings to Mars. This plan is in its early stages. There are huge technical challenges to be overcome. However, it would be unwise to doubt the ability of the American people to solve these problems.

READING CHECK **Identifying Supporting Details** How do you think developments in technology will affect the United States in the future?

A Determined Nation

Advances in Medicine
A researcher at a California laboratory adds DNA samples to a gel in an effort to unlock the mysteries of cancer on the genetic level. Genetic research has become the core of medical science.

Exploring Space
Mission team members delight as the first images from *Opportunity*, an unmanned six-wheeled rover exploring the surface of Mars, flood the video screens at a NASA control room in Pasadena, California, January 2004.

1102 CHAPTER 33

Answers

Reading Check *possible answer— They will continue to improve Americans' health and working conditions.*

Challenges for the Future

The people of the United States have been blessed with great plenty—and with the skill and spirit to create a better future for themselves. Throughout American history, they have used these qualities to overcome the many challenges they have faced. The future will also hold challenges—and opportunity.

Health and health care The average American born in 1900 could expect to live 47 years. Today life expectancy is over 77 years on average. By 2025 experts project that that number will be around 80. By 2050 life expectancy may reach into the mid-80s.

There are many reasons for this projected rise in life expectancy. Medical researchers are learning more each day about the causes of and cures for diseases. They are developing powerful new medicines to help combat a variety of once deadly conditions.

While health care offers great promise for the future, it also presents some of the greatest challenges. One of these is cost. You read in Section 1 about the rising cost of medical care and insurance, including publicly funded programs such as Medicare and Medicaid. Complicating the issue of cost is the rising age of the American population. Older people typically require

more medical care than younger people. At the same time, many elderly do not have enough resources with which to pay for it.

You also read about the large number of Americans who lack sufficient health-care coverage. It seems likely that the availability of health care, how to pay for it, and what role the government should play in providing it will be major concerns in American public life for years to come.

The ongoing ravages of diseases such as HIV infection and AIDS are another major health-care challenge. HIV/AIDS continues to spread widely in this country and in the rest of the world. It is estimated that tens of millions of people worldwide will die from HIV/AIDS in coming decades. In Africa in particular, HIV threatens to devastate entire countries. America will be at the forefront of the global fight against this terrible disease.

Energy and the environment The American economy is the largest in the world. To keep this economy growing requires energy. In fact, the United States is by far the world's largest energy consumer.

One challenge with regard to energy is supply. The gap between what the United States uses and what it produces has been widening. To fill this gap, the United States has imported

Hurricane Relief and Recovery
Much of New Orleans, Louisiana, was under water following Hurricane Katrina, August 2005 (below). This make-shift shop in Waveland, Mississippi (right), helps storm survivors begin to piece their lives back together.

INTO THE TWENTY-FIRST CENTURY **1103**

Direct Teach

Reading Focus

❸ **What challenges confront the United States in the future?** *finding the resources to provide health-care to those who need it, fighting HIV/AIDS, and balancing the need for energy and economic growth with the need to minimize the costs of obtaining it (including environmental costs)*

Challenges for the Future

Make Inferences What are the implications of an aging population for the cost of health-care? *Older people typically need more medical care than younger people, but tend to have fewer resources to pay for it. This helps drive up the expense of publicly funded programs such as Medicare. As the population continues to age, these costs will climb exponentially.*

Identify Cause and Effect How does health-care present us with both promises and challenges for the future? *It is extending average life expectancy, which results in an aging population that will have trouble paying for the increased medical care.*

Activity **Confronting Problems** Make a class list of problems America will face in the future. Then have each student write a brief paragraph suggesting a solution for one of these problems. **LS Verbal-Linguistic**

go.hrw.com
Online Resources
KEYWORD: SD7 CH33
TOPIC: CHALLENGES FROM NATURE

Skills Focus: Identify Problem and Solution   **At Level**

Reading Skill
Meeting Our Energy Needs   **Research Required**

Materials poster paper and colored markers

1. Organize the class into small groups. Have each group conduct research into "alternative" sources of energy—that is, sources other than fossil fuels (coal, petroleum products, and natural gas).

2. Have each group make a table listing the alternative energy sources, and indicating the advantages and disadvantages of each.

3. Have volunteers share their lists with the

class. Create a master table for students to see, and fill in each of the alternative energy sources as they are mentioned, along with the advantages and disadvantages.

4. Have each group make a poster promoting the use of the alternative energy source of its choice and display the posters.
LS Interpersonal, Visual-Spatial

📖 Alternative Assessment Handbook, Rubric 28: Posters

Close

Guide the class in a discussion of the changes and challenges facing the United States in the new century.

Review

📺 Online Quiz, Section 4

📦 Daily Test Practice Transparency

Assess

SE Section 4 Assessment

📑 Progress Assessment: Section 4 Quiz

📑 Alternative Assessment Handbook

Reteach

📑 Interactive Reader and Study Guide, Section 4

💿 Interactive Skills Tutor CD-ROM

---

energy from other countries. By 2005 the country was importing just under a third of its energy. Americans remained heavily dependent on foreign oil. More than half of U.S. supplies came from foreign sources. That number is expected to rise to 70 percent by 2025.

Americans will continue to debate the best way to balance the need for energy and economic growth and the need to minimize the costs of obtaining it. These costs include the risk of pollution and environmental harm in drilling for and using fossil fuels such as petroleum. Another possible cost is the danger of dependence on foreign energy supplies. You have read, for example, about economic problems in the United States resulting from interruptions in Middle Eastern energy supplies.

Meanwhile, the search continues for energy sources that are cleaner and easier to obtain. One promising technology is hydrogen fuel cells. These use plentiful hydrogen to generate power—without producing pollution. Fuel cell technology exists today. In fact, NASA has used fuel cells in its spacecraft for decades. Much work remains in order to make them useful and affordable for ordinary consumers.

Rebuilding after Hurricane Katrina In late August 2005 the United States received a harsh reminder of the vulnerability of its people and economy to natural disaster. Hurricane Katrina devastated a large area along the coast of the Gulf of Mexico, including parts of Alabama, Mississippi, and Louisiana. The city of New Orleans, much of which lies below sea level, was flooded when levees holding back surrounding waters failed.

The human suffering caused by the storm was immense. More than 1,000 people died. Hundreds of thousands lost their homes and their source of livelihood. Weeks later, a second hurricane—Hurricane Rita—struck the region, adding to the misery.

The economic impact of Katrina and Rita reached far beyond the Gulf Coast. Interruption of oil production and refining immediately sent fuel prices soaring. In addition, the nation experienced disruption in the supply of many products that enter the country through the busy port of New Orleans. Experts predicted that the cost of the storm would be measured in the hundreds of billions of dollars.

While Katrina and Rita delivered a cruel blow, few Americans doubted that the region and the country would recover. As you have read, the story of the United States is the story of a people who have risen to every challenge. The obstacles before the nation have changed with time. But the spirit of the American people has remained always steady.

READING CHECK **Comparing** How are the challenges facing the United States today similar to—and different from—challenges of the past?

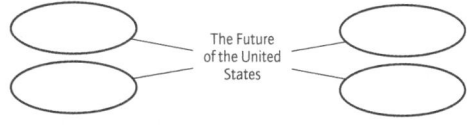

SECTION 4 ASSESSMENT

go.hrw.com
Online Quiz
Keyword: SD7 HP33

Reviewing Ideas, Terms, and People

1. a. Identify What are two major trends in the makeup of the American population?
b. Explain Why do you think that changes in the makeup of the population create challenges for a nation and society?

2. a. Identify What are some of the fields and areas in which technology is likely to change American life in the future?
b. Analyze Why do you think the United States continues to seek to explore unknown places, such as Mars?

3. a. Recall What is the general trend in the overall health of the nation as measured by life expectancy?
b. Explain In what ways do the successes of medicine also contribute to the greatest challenges facing the health-care system?
c. Evaluate On what basis is it safe to predict that the United States will meet the challenges it faces in the future?

Critical Thinking

4. Identifying the Main Idea Copy the chart below and use information from the section to record details that support the main idea of the section.

The Future of the United States

FOCUS ON WRITING

5. Persuasive Write a letter to an elected leader in which you try to persuade him or her to support or oppose one of the technological innovations discussed in this section.

1104 CHAPTER 33

Section 4 Assessment Answers

1. a. growing minority populations; aging population
b. possible answer—different needs that must be addressed and met

2. a. technology-based businesses; agriculture; space exploration
b. possible answer—explore limits of human potential; excitement of visiting new places

3. a. Increasing life expectancy demonstrates better health and health care.
b. increased life expectancy creates need for more health-care for aging population;

role of government debated
c. has met many challenges and solved difficult problems in the past

4. meeting needs of changing population; improving technology; satisfying growing health-care needs; finding new supplies of energy and protecting the environment

5. possible answers—Genetic engineering of foods can help increase crop production. Genetically modified crops might have serious environmental and health consequences.

Answers

Reading Check *similar—energy needs, environmental concerns, disaster management; different—aging population and uninsured strain health-care system*

American *Literature*

AMY TAN (1952–)

About the Reading Amy Tan drew on the experiences of family members in her 1989 novel, *The Joy Luck Club*, which tells the stories of four Chinese women and their Chinese American daughters. In the following excerpt Lindo Jong, one of the main characters, recalls her first days after arriving in the United States in the1940s.

AS YOU READ Consider the difficulties involved with moving to a new place.

Excerpt from

The Joy Luck Club

by Amy Tan

When I arrived, nobody asked me questions. The authorities looked at my papers and stamped me in. I decided to go first to a San Francisco address given to me by this girl in Peking. The bus put me down on a wide street with cable cars. This was California Street. I walked up this hill and then I saw a tall building. This was Old St. Mary's. Under the church sign, in handwritten Chinese characters, someone had added: "A Chinese Ceremony to Save Ghosts from Spiritual Unrest 7 a.m. and 8:30 a.m." I memorized this information in case the authorities asked me where I worshipped my religion. And then I saw another sign across the street. It was painted on the outside of a short building: "Save Today for Tomorrow, at Bank of America." And I thought to myself, This is where American people worship. See, even then I was not so dumb! Today that church is the same size, but where that bank used to be, now there is a tall building, fifty stories high, where you and your husband-to-be work and look down on everybody.

My daughter laughed when I said this. Her mother can make a good joke.

Chinatown in San Francisco during a Chinese New Year festival

So I kept walking up this hill. I saw two pagodas, one on each side of the street, as though they were the entrance to a great Buddha temple. But when I looked carefully, I saw the pagoda was really just a building topped with stacks of tile roofs, no walls, nothing else under its head. I was surprised how they tried to make everything look like an old imperial city or an emperor's tomb. But if you looked on either side of these pretend-pagodas, you could see the streets became narrow and crowded, dark, and dirty. I thought to myself, Why did they choose only the worst Chinese parts for the inside? Why didn't they build gardens and ponds instead? Oh, here and there was the look of a famous ancient cave or a Chinese opera. But inside it was always the same cheap stuff.

So by the time I found the address the girl in Peking gave me, I knew not to expect too much.

 Skills FOCUS | **READING LIKE A HISTORIAN**

1. **Summarizing** How would you characterize Lindo Jong's first reactions to Chinatown in San Francisco?

2. **Literature as Historical Evidence** How does this excerpt describe the struggle of immigrants to adapt to a new culture?

See Skills Handbook, p. H32

INTO THE TWENTY-FIRST CENTURY **1105**

Differentiating Instruction

Learners Having Difficulty
Below Level

Tell students that Amy Tan provides a vivid picture of San Francisco's Chinatown from the point of view of a newly arrived Chinese woman. Have students look for pictures of Chinatown that could be used to illustrate this passage. Have volunteers share their pictures with the class. **LS Interpersonal, Visual-Spatial**

📓 Alternative Assessment Handbook, Rubric 3: Artwork

Advanced Learners/GATE
Above Level
Research Required

Have students create a summary of the impression their own neighborhood would make on a newly arrived immigrant from a different culture. Have students write letters describing their neighborhood to a person living in a foreign country. **LS Logical-Mathematical, Verbal-Linguistic**

📓 Alternative Assessment Handbook, Rubric 25: Personal Letters

American Literature

The Joy Luck Club

Word Help

characters symbols or letters of an alphabet

pagodas an East Asian or Indian temple in the form of a tower

Buddha the religious philosopher and teacher who founded Buddhism

imperial of an empire

Meet the Writer

Amy Tan Amy Tan was born in 1952 in Oakland, California. Her parents were Chinese immigrants. After her father and brother both died of brain tumors within a year of each other, Tan fell into a pattern of conflict with and defiance of her mother. After college, Tan pursued a successful career as a business writer. Eventually, she found that her work had become a compulsive habit. She took up jazz piano and began to write fiction. After receiving a $50,000 advance from a publisher for *The Joy Luck Club*, Tan quit business writing and finished the book in a little more than four months.

The Origins of *The Joy Luck Club*

Just as Amy Tan was beginning to achieve success as a fiction writer, her mother fell ill. Tan vowed that if her mother recovered, she would take her back to China. There her mother would be able to see the daughter she had been forced to leave behind when she fled the Communists in 1949. In 1987 Tan and her mother left for China. The trip gave her a new perspective on her troubled relationship with her mother and inspired her to write *The Joy Luck Club*.

Answers

Reading Like a Historian
1. *impersonal, uncaring, unsympathetic;*
2. *difficult to find help; insufficient resources and sometimes lack of welcome*

Hispanic Growth and Influence

Activity **The Influence of Hispanics** Have students work with a partner to list ten ways Hispanics have influenced life in your community or state. Encourage students to think about such areas as popular culture, work patterns, food, recreation, schools, churches, government, language, and retail establishments. Have students share and discuss their lists.

LS Verbal-Linguistic

MISCONCEPTION ALERT

Remind students that Hispanics include people of many different national origins. While the U.S. Census Bureau estimates that about 64 percent of Hispanics in the United States are of Mexican origin, another 10 percent are Puerto Rican. Cubans, Salvadorans, and Dominicans make up about 3 percent each. The remainder are from various Central American, South American, and other countries.

HISTORY & Geography

Hispanic Growth and Influence

Hispanics, with a population of 40.4 million at the end of 2004, make up 14 percent of the total U.S. population. They are the country's largest and fastest growing minority group. By 2020 Hispanics will total an estimated 60.4 million and account for half of the growth of the U.S. labor force. With their rising numbers have come newfound political and economic powers. Many people point to the Hispanic vote as a key factor in recent presidential elections.

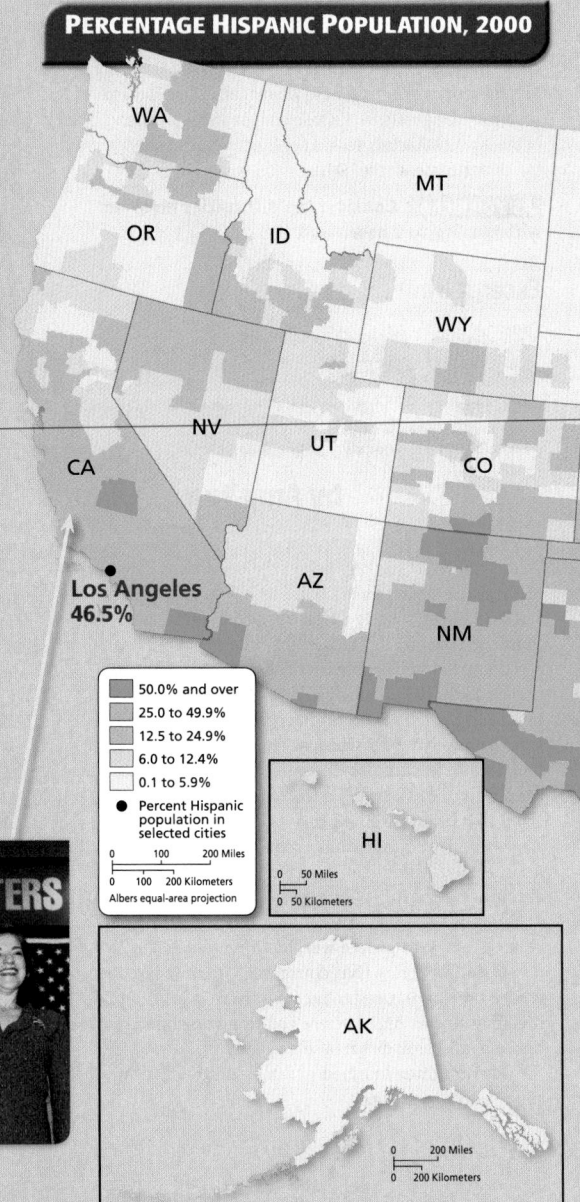

PERCENTAGE HISPANIC POPULATION, 2000

HISPANIC POPULATION GROWTH, 1960 - 2000

- - - Total population
- —— Hispanic population

Source: Population Reference Bureau; United States Census Bureau

Los Angeles 46.5%

- 50.0% and over
- 25.0 to 49.9%
- 12.5 to 24.9%
- 6.0 to 12.4%
- 0.1 to 5.9%
- ● Percent Hispanic population in selected cities

0   100   200 Miles
0   100   200 Kilometers
Albers equal-area projection

0   50 Miles
0   50 Kilometers

0   200 Miles
0   200 Kilometers

Winning Elections

Californians Loretta and Linda Sanchez are the first sisters to serve together in the U.S. Congress. They joined 22 other Hispanic Americans serving in the House of Representatives and over 6,000 Hispanic Americans holding elected office.

1106

Differentiating Instruction

Below Level

Learners Having Difficulty

1. Have students use the information available at the Web site of the U.S. Census Bureau to make a 10-question multiple choice quiz about Hispanics in the United States.

2. Have students print out their quizzes, providing a separate answer key. Have students assemble in small groups and exchange quizzes.

3. Guide students in a discussion of what they found surprising about the quiz answers.

   LS Verbal-Linguistic, Intrapersonal

   Alternative Assessment Handbook, Rubric 41: Writing to Express

Spending Power

Illinois's Hispanic population grew by 650,000 from 1990 to 2000, with most settling in Chicago. Overall Hispanic spending power has grown, too. To attract a larger piece of the Hispanic market, Chicago's Tribune Company turned its Spanish-language weekly, *¡Exito!*, into the daily *Hoy*.

College Bound

As the number of U.S.-educated Hispanics has risen, so has the proportion of those who attend college. To better serve the area's Dominican population, which is larger than the population of the Dominican Republic, the City University of New York offers a degree in Dominican Studies.

MISCONCEPTION ALERT

Because of increasing rates of intermarriage, many Americans now consider themselves as belonging to more than one racial group. Since 1980, approximately one-fourth of all Hispanic couples have been interracial, meaning that an individual of Hispanic origin married someone of another race or ethnicity.

Info to Know

Distribution in America Hispanics of different national origin are not equally distributed around the country. Miami-Dade County, Florida, is home to approximately half the population of Cuban Americans; New York City is home to approximately half the population of Dominican Americans. Nearly 50 percent of Hispanics in the United States live in either Texas or California.

Chicago 26.0%

New York 27.0%

San Antonio 58.7%

Houston 37.4%

Swing Voters

Mel Martinez immigrated to Florida from Cuba at age 15. In 2004 he became the first Cuban American elected to the U. S. Senate. In 2000 President Bush took Florida by 537 votes, but he won 80 percent of the Cuban vote.

Immigration

After California, Texas has the largest Hispanic population, mostly of Mexican origin. Unlike with earlier European immigrants, Mexican immigration has not come in a single wave, but rather in a continuous flow for over a century.

GEOGRAPHY SKILLS — INTERPRETING MAPS

1. **Location** Look at some of the major areas of Hispanic American concentration. Why might these areas have been attractive? Why might other areas be unattractive?

2. **Movement** Why might Mexican immigration be occurring in a continuous flow instead of a single wave?

See **Skills Handbook**, p. H20

Skills Focus: Analyzing Infographics

Below Level

Social Studies Skill
Analyzing Information to Make Generalizations

1. Remind students that generalizations are made by analyzing details to see what broader statements they can support. You may want to give students an example and show how it can be supported by the data on the map. *possible answer—Except along the nation's southern border, big cities tend to have larger Hispanic populations than rural areas; places like New York, Chicago, and Washington, D.C., are shown as having high percentages of Hispanics.*

2. Have students work with a partner to make generalizations about the feature map showing centers of Hispanic population.

3. Have pairs of students share their generalizations with the class and support them with data from the infographic.

LS Verbal-Linguistic, Visual-Spatial

Alternative Assessment Handbook, Rubric 12: Drawing Conclusions

Answers

Interpreting Maps 1. *possible answers—presence of other Hispanics; nearness to Hispanic homelands; availability of jobs; less discrimination than in other areas;* **2.** *possible answers—no single event like a potato famine to encourage immigration; nearness of Mexico; lack of barriers to movement*

The Global Economy and Society

Historical Context The documents below provide different information on the effects of globalization on economics and society.

Task Examine the documents and answer the questions that follow. Then write an essay about globalization. Use facts from the documents and from the chapter to support the position you take in your thesis statement.

Word Help

globalization the process of giving things a worldwide outlook

hybridization creation of something by combining elements that have mixed origins

synthetic artificial; made by combining parts

protectionist having to do with the protection of local things or ideas from outside influences

cultural imperialism domination of other cultures by one culture and its products

Primary Source

"We are living through a transformation that will rearrange the politics and economics of the coming century. There will be no *national* products or technologies, no national corporations, no national industries. There will no longer be national economies."

— Robert Reich

From *The Work of Nations: Preparing Ourselves for 21st-Century Capitalism* by Robert B. Reich. Copyright © 1991 by Robert B. Reich. Reproduced by permission of **Alfred A. Knopf, a division of Random House, Inc., www.randomhouse.com.**

DOCUMENT 1

This cartoon comments on the increase in outsourcing—sending local jobs overseas in order to take advantage of lower labor costs in other countries.

"The last step says to dismantle the whole thing and ship all the jobs overseas."

DOCUMENT 2

In 2003 the editor in chief of *Reason* magazine interviewed author Tyler Cowen about his book *Creative Destruction: How Globalization Is Changing the World's Cultures.* Cowen's book suggests that globalization benefits most people around the world.

"*Reason*: Give an example that characterizes the sort of cultural exchange . . . you discuss . . .

"Tyler Cowen: The first point to make is that all examples characterize it. The only question is, how much of it do we already see? Look at a book and ask yourself, where does paper come from, where does printing come from, where do the ideas in the book come from? What's the religious background of the author? You're already talking about the Middle East, China, Europe, the United States. Just about anything you can find

reflects a synthetic [not natural; made by humans] culture based on trade . . .

"*Reason*: One of the problems with arguments about cultural loss is that they are often advanced for protectionist reasons. So, for instance, we have the French decrying [complaining about] U.S. cultural imperialism and insisting on domestic-content rules and the like. What are the effects of trying to hold back cultural creative destruction?

"Tyler Cowen: The good news is that it cannot easily be held back . . . Look at the French. For all the noise they make, Paris is remarkably open to African and Middle Eastern cultures—and to Hollywood movies, for that matter. . . As a whole, the world has been moving toward freer trade for quite a while."

Skills Focus: Drawing Conclusions

At Level | **Standard English Mastery**

Reading Skill
Outsourcing

1. Guide the class in a discussion of outsourcing. Ask students what kinds of jobs they are aware of that have been outsourced.

2. Have each student write an editorial either supporting or opposing outsourcing. Students should explain the reasoning for their position and support it with evidence. If students oppose outsourcing, they may suggest

possible alternatives.

3. Have volunteers read their editorials to the class. Then guide the class in a discussion of how outsourcing might help or harm local, national, and global economies and communities. **LS Verbal-Linguistic**

Alternative Assessment Handbook, Rubric 17: Letters to Editors

DOCUMENT 3

Economic changes have affected people all over the world. This *Newsweek* article, published in 2001, examines the effects of globalization on women in different countries.

"For European women, globalization's fallen trade barriers, blurred national boundaries and new technology have brought the best of times—and the worst. The European Union's freedom of movement created more career opportunities, but increased competition, and with it, stress . . . Creeping Americanization has shaken up antique boardroom attitudes—but also ushered in a 24/7 work schedule. Leaner company structures make it easier to negotiate part-time work, but harder to get paid maternity leave or a pension. A boom economy means women have little trouble finding jobs, but with cuts in education and health, they may have trouble getting trained for good ones—or finding child care while they're at them."

DOCUMENT 4

Mark Rice-Oxley is a reporter for *The Christian Science Monitor*. In this article, published in 2004, he discusses how the spread of American culture affects societies around the world.

"Stick a pin in a map and there you'll find an example of U.S. influence. Hollywood rules the global movie market, with up to 90 percent of audiences in some European countries. Even in Africa, 2 of 3 films shown are American. Few countries have yet to be touched by McDonald's and Coca-Cola . . .

"America's preeminence is hardly surprising. Superpowers throughout the ages sought to perpetuate their way of life: from the philosophy and mythology of the ancient Greeks to the law and language of the Romans; from the art and architecture of the Tang dynasty and Renaissance Italy to the sports and systems of government of the British . . .

"So how much good does American culture bring to the world? And how long will it last? Ian Ralston cautions against sweeping dismissals of U.S. pop culture. British television may be saturated with American sitcoms and movies, but while some are poor, others are quite good, he says . . . Others note that it is not all one-way traffic. America may feast largely on a diet of homegrown culture, but it imports modestly as well: soccer, international cuisine, Italian fashion, and, increasingly, British television."

Skills FOCUS — READING LIKE A HISTORIAN

1. a. Identify Refer to Document 1. What are the boys in the cartoon building?
b. Interpret How does this cartoon illustrate changes in employment patterns?
2. a. Identify Refer to Document 2. What example does Cowen use to support his point that globalization creates synthetic cultures?
b. Interpret Based on this excerpt, what is Cowen's opinion about the effects of free trade on culture?
3. a. Identify Refer to Document 3. How has the spread of technology affected work habits in foreign countries?
b. Analyze Do you think the article would conclude that globalization has benefited or harmed European women?

4. a. Identify Refer to Document 4. How, according to the article, is the spread of American culture similar to that of past empires?
b. Elaborate How does this article suggest that the spread of culture affects people in the United States and other countries?
5. Document-Based Essay Question Consider the question below and form a thesis statement. Using examples from Documents 1, 2, 3, and 4, create an outline and write a short essay supporting your position. How does the global economy affect cultures and societies around the world?

See **Skills Handbook,** pp. H28–H29, H30

Collaborative Learning

At Level

Globalization

1. Tell students that the United States has been accused of cultural imperialism, or forcing its products and way of life on other countries.

2. Pair students. Have each pair make a list of foreign ideas and products that have been imported into the United States. Have students try to identify the countries of origin for each product or idea.

3. Have volunteers share their lists with the rest of the class. Create a class list on the board.

4. Guide the class in a discussion of the effects of globalization. Ask students how other cultures have influenced American culture.
LS Interpersonal, Logical-Mathematical
Alternative Assessment Handbook, Rubric 12: Drawing Conclusions

Document-Based Investigation

Info to Know

Americanization While perspectives on Americanization may differ, there is little disagreement about the increasing globalization of American culture. Today McDonald's has stores in more than 100 countries and Starbucks has stores in 37 countries. The Coca-Cola Company has close to 400 brands in over 200 countries. According to Charles Krauthammer in an article for *Time* magazine, Americanization is a positive development: "America is in a position to re-shape norms, alter expectations and create new realities." For others, such as American journalist Thomas Friedman, the spread of American culture is dangerous, has created hatred of Americans, and led to threats against the United States. As early as 1998, in an article for *The New York Times*, Friedman argued that Americanization may lead to terrorist activities against the United States.

Answers

Reading Like a Historian 1. a. *a factory model;* **b.** *The U.S. has lost many manufacturing jobs because businesses have relocated factories overseas.*
2. a. *a book;* **b.** *that free trade benefits most people by increasing cultural diversity and promoting economic growth;* **3. a.** *it has created a 24/7 work schedule, part-time work easier to find, maternity leave or a pension harder;* **b.** *possible answers—benefited because opened up new career opportunities; harmed because limited opportunities for education and health care;* **4. a.** *Like the U.S., empires have always tried to perpetuate their way of life.* **b.** *people in other countries are increasingly exposed to American movies and restaurants; Americans perceived as perpetuating their way of life;* **5.** *possible answers—increases cultural diversity and economic prosperity; provides more career opportunities for workers*

Visual Summary

Review and Inquiry Organize the class into groups of four. Have each student in the group prepare a detailed summary of a different topic in the visual summary. Have students share their summaries with their group members.

Quick Facts Transparency: Into the Twenty-first Century

Reviewing Key Terms and People

1. USA PATRIOT Act
2. NAFTA
3. Antonio Villaraigosa
4. Osama bin Laden
5. dot-com
6. Contract with America
7. Department of Homeland Security
8. dividends
9. genetic engineering
10. IT
11. *Bush* v. *Gore*

Comprehension and Critical Thinking

12. **a.** centrist; stressed need for national health-care system and tax cuts for the middle class
    b. possible answer—able to deflect criticism; Americans generally supported his policies despite the scandals
    c. possible answer—strength, addressed Americans' concerns, left Republicans with little to attack

13. **a.** tax cuts, education and health-care reform, changes to Social Security
    b. stimulate the economy, Americans would spend more, businesses would improve
    c. possible answer—did not have popular majority, made it difficult to claim mandate for legislation

14. **a.** terrorists attacked the United States
    b. grief, anger, outpouring of support for victims and rescuers

Visual Summary: Into the Twenty-first Century

The Clinton Administration
- Welfare reform was achieved, but health-care reform was not.
- The nation became drawn into conflicts in Somalia, Haiti, and the former Yugoslavia.
- Despite impeachment, President Clinton completed his two terms.

The Bush Administration
- President Bush won a controversial election in 2000 and re-election in 2004.
- His domestic policy focused on tax cuts, education, and Medicare reform.
- His foreign policy was dominated by response to the terrorist attacks of September 11, 2001.

The 1990s and Beyond

Terrorism and War
- The attacks of September 11, 2001, shifted national focus to terrorism.
- In the war on terror, the United States attacked Afghanistan and Iraq.
- The United States created the Department of Homeland Security and passed new laws to fight terrorism.

Looking Ahead
The twenty-first century should bring:
- demographic changes—greater diversity and an aging population.
- technological changes in communication, medicine, agriculture, and space exploration.
- challenges in health care, energy, and the environment.

Reviewing Key Terms and People

Identify the correct term or person from the chapter that best fits each of the following descriptions.

1. Law passed in the aftermath of 9/11 aimed at enhancing investigative powers
2. Trade agreement involving Mexico and Canada
3. Elected mayor of Los Angeles in 2005
4. Terrorist believed responsible for 9/11
5. Nickname for the type of Internet company that appeared in the 1990s
6. Republican package of proposals and legislation from 1994
7. New cabinet-level organization created in the aftermath of 9/11
8. Payments made by corporations to stockholders
9. A technology designed to improve agriculture by altering the genetic material of plants
10. Use of computer technology to efficiently use information
11. Supreme Court case that finally settled the presidential election of 2000

Comprehension and Critical Thinking

SECTION 1 *(pp. 1078–1083)*

12. **a. Describe** How would you describe the basic political beliefs of Bill Clinton?
    b. Make Inferences What can you infer from the fact that Clinton was able to survive so many political scandals?
    c. Evaluate Do you think Clinton's willingness to adopt policies of his political opponents was a strength or a weakness?

c. possible answers—effective, many people killed, financially expensive, demonstrated vulnerability of the U.S.; not very effective, Americans came together to fight terrorism, increased patriotism

15. **a.** growing minority populations; population is getting older
    b. causes—better heath care, nutrition, baby boomers aging; effects—health-care expenses expected to rise

c. possible answers—more significant, because global problems, advanced technology complicates problems; less significant, because of strong economy, position of international power

History's Impact video program

Review the video to answer the closing question: How have the events of September 11, 2001, changed life in the United States?

SECTION 2 *(pp. 1085–1090)*

13. a. Recall What were President George W. Bush's major goals for domestic policy?

b. Summarize What reasons did President Bush give for wanting to cut taxes?

c. Elaborate How do you think the circumstances of Bush's election in 2000 affected his ability to govern? Explain your answer.

SECTION 3 *(pp. 1091–1098)*

14. a. Recall What is the significance of the date September 11, 2001?

b. Make Generalizations Describe the emotional reactions of the American people to the catastrophe of September 11th.

c. Evaluate How effective do you think the terrorist attacks were in damaging the United States? Explain your answer.

SECTION 4 *(pp. 1099–1104)*

15. a. Recall How is the American population expected to change in the decades ahead?

b. Summarize What are some of the causes and effects of the increase in the population of older Americans?

c. Rank Do you think the challenges facing the United States today are more or less significant than the challenges this country has faced in previous eras? Explain your answer.

Using the Internet

go.hrw.com
Practice Online
Keyword: SD7 CH33

16. Choose of one of the following topics: communication, medicine, agriculture, transportation, or industry. Using the keyword above, do research to learn how technology has affected the topic of your choice. Then write a brief report that summarizes your findings. In your report, include at least three ways that technology has an impact on the topic you chose.

Analyzing Primary Sources

Reading Like a Historian After the 2000 presidential election, officials in many Florida communities struggled to read ballots that had been rejected by the automatic vote-counting machines.

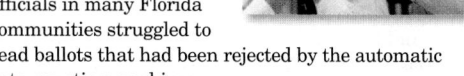

17. Describe What do you think these election officials are trying to figure out by looking at this ballot?

18. Explain Why do you think the hand counting of ballots as shown here was a controversial process?

Critical Reading

Read the passage in Section 3 that begins with the heading "The United States Responds." Then answer the question that follows.

19. Why did the United States invade Afghanistan?

A. to take revenge on the people of Afghanistan

B. to remove the Taliban regime that had harbored Osama bin Laden

C. to use Afghanistan as a military base for the war on terrorism

D. to help distract the American public from their problems at home

FOCUS ON WRITING

Descriptive Writing *Descriptive writing uses concrete details to help a reader visualize a person, place, or thing. To practice descriptive writing, complete the assignment below.*

Writing Topic The Future of the United States

20. Assignment Based on what you have read in this chapter, write a paragraph that describes the United States 20 years from now. If you have access to a computer, use a word processing program to create and format your paragraph.

Answers

Using the Internet

16. Go to the HRW Web site and enter the keyword shown to access a rubric for this activity.

KEYWORD: SD7 CH33

Analyzing Primary Sources

17. who the voter intended to vote for

18. somewhat subjective and dependent upon human interpretation

Critical Reading

19. B

Focus on Writing

20. possible answer—The population will consist of many minorities, and the population will have many older people. Telecommunications and advanced computers will be commonplace in homes and businesses, and technology will be in use in almost every facet of life.

A rubric for this activity is provided in Chapter Resource File: Focus on Writing Activity: The Future of America.

History's Impact Video Program

increased concerns about terrorism and security in United States; USA PATRIOT Act enacted and Department of Homeland Security established

---

Review and Assessment Resources

Review and Reinforce

- CRF: Chapter Review Activity
- Quick Facts Transparencies: Foreign Policy Team, Into the Twenty-first Century
- Spanish Chapter Summaries Audio CD Program
- Online Chapter Summaries in Spanish
- OSP Holt PuzzlePro; Quiz Show for ExamView
- Quiz Game CD-ROM

Assess

- PASS: Chapter Test, Forms A and B
- Alternative Assessment Handbook
- OSP ExamView Test Generator, Chapter Test
- Differentiated Instruction Modified Worksheets and Tests CD-ROM: Chapter Test
- HOAP Holt Online Assessment Program (in the Premier Online Edition)

Reteach/Intervene

- Interactive Reader and Study Guide
- Differentiated Instruction Teacher Management System: Lesson Plans for Differentiated Instruction
- Differentiated Instruction Modified Worksheets and Tests CD-ROM: Chapter Test
- Interactive Skills Tutor CD-ROM

go.hrw.com
Online Resources

KEYWORD: SD7 CH33

UNIT **10** IN BRIEF

Below is a chapter-by-chapter summary of the main ideas covered in Unit 10.

CHAPTER 31 — A Search for Order
1968–1980

MAIN IDEA Richard Nixon achieved notable successes during his time in office, such as improving relations with the People's Republic of China. His involvement in the Watergate scandal, however, led to his resignation. His successors, Presidents Gerald Ford and Jimmy Carter, sought to help the nation recover from Watergate and face ongoing economic and foreign-policy challenges, which included high inflation and the continuing Cold War.

SECTION 1 Early in his presidency, Richard Nixon was able to promote improved relations with Communist China and the Soviet Union. He also had some success in pursuing domestic policies, including his stance on civil rights, the environment, and the economy.

SECTION 2 In his second term, Nixon's presidency unraveled in the Watergate scandal, as the nation slowly learned of his role in a criminal conspiracy to spy on his political opponents—and to cover it up. His successor, Gerald Ford, struggled to escape the scandal's undertow.

SECTION 3 Jimmy Carter came to office hoping to help the nation move beyond its troubled past. However, his presidency foundered on familiar problems, including economic trouble and foreign-policy crises with Iran and the Soviet Union.

CHAPTER 32 — A Conservative Era
1980–1992

MAIN IDEA Ronald Reagan and his successor George H. W. Bush dominated the 1980s with their conservative message of smaller government and a tougher stance against communism. During this time, the Cold War came to an end and the United States faced a new set of economic and foreign-policy challenges.

SECTION 1 Ronald Reagan came to office on the strength of his personality and a strong conservative message. He led a national reconsideration of many of the basic questions about the relationship between government and its people.

SECTION 2 A staunch anti-Communist, Reagan increased defense spending and spoke strongly against the Soviet Union. Foreign difficulties in Grenada, South Africa, Lebanon, and Iran characterized his time in office as well.

SECTION 3 George H. W. Bush presided over the end of the Cold War. He was also the first president to face the challenges of the post–Cold War world, when he led the nation—and numerous allies—into war against Iraq in the Persian Gulf War of 1990.

SECTION 4 The 1980s were a time of economic ups and downs, technological advances, and controversial cases in the Supreme Court.

CHAPTER 33 — Into the Twenty-first Century
1992–Present

MAIN IDEA Americans faced the twenty-first century with hope, determination, and a readiness to confront challenges at home and abroad.

SECTION 1 Bill Clinton used his political skills and voter dissatisfaction with George H. W. Bush's handling of the economy to reach the White House. Clinton's presidency was a time of economic growth, complex foreign-policy challenges—and political scandal.

SECTION 2 George W. Bush won a controversial election in 2000. He faced an economic downturn, which he countered with tax cuts and his own domestic-policy agenda. Following his re-election in 2004, Bush launched an initiative to reform the Social Security system.

SECTION 3 On September 11, 2001, the United States became the target of international terrorists. The attacks refocused the nation on a new enemy and led to war overseas and significant governmental changes at home.

SECTION 4 American society is changing as a result of a more diverse population and new advances in technology. The nation continues to face its challenges with a spirit of determination.

1112 UNIT 10 IN BRIEF

REFERENCE SECTION

Key Events in American History

The World Almanac Key Events in American History is a brief summary of important turning points in the history of the nation. It provides a capsule description of an event or movement along with brief accounts of its significance. Use this section to review the content in *American Anthem*.

12,000 B.C.E. Migrations to America

The first people arrived in North America at least 14,000 years ago, during the last Ice Age. With much of Earth's water frozen in ice sheets, sea levels dropped and a land bridge connected Asia and North America. Hunters from Siberia migrated over the land bridge to North America.

Significance The migration brought the first people to the Western Hemisphere. Archaeologists think that by about 11,000 years ago Native Americans were living in both North and South America.

1492–1502 Columbus's Voyages

In 1492 Italian-born explorer Christopher Columbus sailed west from Europe with the goal of finding a sea route to Asia. His ships landed on the Caribbean island of Hispaniola. Believing he had reached the Indies, Columbus called the people he met "Indians." Columbus made three more journeys to the Americas, exploring Caribbean islands and making stops in Central and South America.

Significance Columbus' voyages opened the Western Hemisphere to exploration and conquest by Spain and other European powers. They also led to the Columbian Exchange—an exchange of plants, animals, and diseases between the Western Hemisphere and Europe and Africa.

1607 Settlement of Jamestown

Founded in Virginia in 1607, Jamestown was the first permanent English colony in North America. Plagued by an unhealthy location, the colony barely managed to survive. Captain John Smith provided critical leadership. John Rolfe planted tobacco in Jamestown, giving the colony a cash crop that was in high demand in England. A small group of enslaved Africans arrived in Jamestown in 1619. That same year, colonists held a ceremony of thanksgiving to mark their safe arrival in Virginia.

Significance After Jamestown, the English established other colonies along the east coast of North America. Successful tobacco farming in Jamestown led to the growth of plantation agriculture and slave labor. The Virginia House of Burgesses, established in 1619, was America's first elected legislature.

1620 Pilgrims arrive at Plymouth

The Pilgrims were religious dissenters from the Church of England who sought the freedom to worship according to their beliefs. In 1620 they traveled to North America on the *Mayflower*. The Pilgrims founded a colony at Plymouth, Massachusetts, which survived with the aid of friendly Wampanoag Indians. The colony marked its first harvest with a feast which forms the basis for the Thanksgiving holiday.

Significance The Pilgrims were the first colonists motivated to found a colony by a desire to freely practice their own religion. This became an important motivation for several other groups of colonists, and eventually the free practice of religion became a fundamental principle of the U.S. Constitution.

1651–1673 Navigation Acts

The Navigation Acts were a series of trade laws passed by the English government between 1651 and 1673. The laws sought to control trade with England's colonies to the benefit of the mother country. Among other things, the laws required that colonial goods be shipped only on English ships.

Significance England got what it wanted from the Navigation Acts—raw materials and tax revenues from the colonies. Colonists, on the other hand, were angered by the laws and often avoided paying taxes by smuggling goods into and out of the colonies.

1730s–1740s The Great Awakening

The Great Awakening was a religious revival in the English colonies that began in the 1730s. One of its leading voices was the colonial Puritan clergyman Jonathan Edwards, who appealed to his listeners' fears and emotions. Another was the English Methodist minister George Whitefield, who moved large audiences to cry and confess their sins.

Significance The Great Awakening countered the spread of Enlightenment ideas in the colonies, which were causing some people to question long-accepted religious beliefs. It led to the growth of new Protestant denominations in America, including the Methodist, Baptist, and Presbyterian churches.

1754–1763 French and Indian War

The Seven Years' War was the fourth and decisive war fought between Britain and France for control of land in North America. It's European phase is known as the Seven Years' War, but colonists called this conflict the French and Indian War because France and its Indian allies battled Britain and the colonists. After several early setbacks, the British won the crucial Battle of Quebec in 1759. France surrendered the following year.

Significance The French and Indian War marked the end of French power in North America. Britain gained all of France's lands east of the Mississippi River, helping to establish the basis for a mighty British empire. British leaders tried to recover some of cost of the war by taxing colonists, a policy which led to growing tensions between Britain and its colonies in America.

1765 Stamp Act

Passed by Parliament in 1765, the Stamp Act was a tax designed to raise money from colonists to help pay the cost of protecting the colonies. Resentful colonists called this "taxation without representation" because they had no voice in Parliament. In October 1765, delegates from nine colonies met at the Stamp Act Congress to protest the tax. Parliament repealed the Stamp Act in 1766.

Significance The Stamp Act was the first time Parliament had directly taxed the colonists. Colonial leaders from different regions, who were not used to working together, united to protest the tax. The united action of leaders from different colonies would become a model for future action.

1770 Boston Massacre

Tensions between British soldiers and the people of Boston were growing in early 1770. This anger exploded on March 5, 1770, when a group of British soldiers opened fire on a colonial mob that was taunting and threatening them. Local colonial leaders called the event the Boston Massacre, describing it as a deliberate attack on innocent civilians.

Significance The Boston Massacre served the cause of radicals like Samuel Adams who were eager to paint the British as cruel oppressors. The Massacre became a rallying cry for proponents of independence from Britain.

1775–1783 American Revolution

The American colonies' fight for independence from Britain began in April 1775 with the Battles of Lexington and Concord. Over the next six years, George Washington led the often undermanned and poorly equipped Continental Army. The American victory at the Battle of Saratoga in 1777 was a pivotal turning point; it convinced the French to join the war on the American side. The last significant battle was Washington's defeat of Lord Cornwallis' army at Yorktown, Virginia, in 1781.

Significance The Treaty of Paris, which ended the war in 1783, acknowledged the independence of the United States. The American Revolution was the first successful democratic revolution against a colonial ruler. A direct result was the establishment of the United States of America as a independent democratic republic.

1776 Declaration of Independence

Written largely by Thomas Jefferson in June 1776, the Declaration of Independence explained the reasons colonial leaders decided to break free from Britain and declared the United States to be an independent country. It was presented to Congress on July 2, 1776, and members voted to declare independence on that day. Two days later, on July 4, Congress approved the Declaration of Independence.

Significance The Declaration marked a point of no return for Americans—people were now forced to take sides in the struggle between Patriots and Loyalists. In addition, the Declaration boldly stated the principles of government that form the basis for American democracy, and it has been an inspiration to other freedom movements ever since.

1786 Shays's Rebellion

High taxes forced many Massachusetts farmers into heavy debt in the 1780s. When a court ordered their farms and homes be sold to pay the debts, Daniel Shays, a Revolutionary War veteran, led a rebellion. After some success delaying court proceedings, the rebellion was quickly put down by state militia.

Significance Shays's Rebellion frightened many Americans and helped convince them that the central government under the Articles of Confederation was not strong enough to deal with the country's problems. This fueled the movement to form a stronger federal government, which led to the Constitutional Convention.

1787 Northwest Ordinance

Congress passed the Northwest Ordinance to encourage orderly settlement and the formation of new states on the land north and west of the Ohio River. The law promised settlers religious freedom and barred slavery. It also set up a system for the eventual admission of new states.

Significance The Northwest Ordinance created a pattern for settlement in western territory, leading to a rapid expansion of the population of these lands. It also barred slavery from the Northwest Territory, which later became the states of Ohio, Indiana, Illinois, Michigan, Wisconsin, and part of Minnesota.

1787 Constitutional Convention

Delegates came to the convention in Philadelphia to discuss ways to strengthen the Articles of Confederation. Instead they drafted an entirely new plan of government, the United States Constitution.

Significance Ratified in 1788, the Constitution defined a plan of government—with checks and balances between three branches of government—that has endured for well over 200 years. The Bill of Rights, ten amendments protecting the freedoms of individual Americans, was ratified in 1791.

1803 *Marbury* v. *Madison*

The case of *Marbury* v. *Madison* was brought by William Marbury, who was appointed to a judgeship in 1801 by outgoing President John Adams. When incoming President Thomas Jefferson refused to give Marbury his commission, Marbury sued to get it. The Supreme Court ruled that it did not have the power to force Jefferson to deliver the commission. The Justices also declared that the law that had given the Court that power—the Judiciary Act of 1789—was unconstitutional.

Significance *Marbury* v. *Madison* established the Supreme Court's right to declare that a law violates the Constitution. This power, known as judicial review, greatly expanded the influence of the Supreme Court.

1803 Louisiana Purchase

President Jefferson sent James Monroe to France to try to attempt to buy New Orleans, a port of critical importance to western farmers. Much to Monroe's surprise, the French offered to sell all of Louisiana, stretching from the Mississippi River to the Rocky Mountains. The final price of the Louisiana Purchase was about $15 million.

Significance The Louisiana Purchase almost doubled the size of the United States, opening up huge new tracts of land to future American settlement. It also removed an important foreign power as an obstacle for American expansion in North America.

1812 The War of 1812

The War of 1812 between Great Britain and the United States actually lasted three years, from 1812-1815. It arose from a dispute over American rights to trade with France, Britain's enemy in the Napoleonic Wars. Native American efforts, aided by the British, to resist United States expansion also played a role in triggering conflict. The war ended with no clear winner.

Significance The war's conclusion reaffirmed American independence and spurred a period of intense patriotic feeling. Two of its military heroes, William Henry Harrison and Andrew Jackson, later went on to become presidents. Francis Scott Key wrote "Star-Spangled Banner," the national anthem, to celebrate American resistance to British bombardment of Fort McHenry in Baltimore harbor.

1820s–1830s Second Great Awakening

The Second Great Awakening was a national religious movement that was especially strong in the North. Americans attended revivals, embraced religious teachings, and joined churches in record numbers. New religious denominations, including the Mormon Church, were formed at this time.

Significance By 1850 the majority of Americans considered themselves to be Protestant. The Second Great Awakening helped launch the Reform Era, which lasted from about 1830 to 1860. Inspired by religious ideals, Americans attempted to reshape society by promoting temperance, improved education, and other reforms.

1820 Missouri Compromise

Missouri's desire to join the Union as a slave state sparked a crisis, because the Union was then balanced between slave states and free states. In 1820 Congress reached a compromise: Missouri was admitted to the union as a slave state, while Maine entered the Union as a free state. In addition, the Missouri Compromise banned slavery in the Louisiana Territory north of a line stretching west from the southern border of Missouri.

Significance The Missouri Compromise temporarily defused the tension between free and slave states, but it did not end the debate over slavery in western lands. The crisis illustrated the intense feelings of sectionalism that would eventually split the nation in two.

1823 Monroe Doctrine

After the former Spanish colonies in Latin America won their independence, U.S. leaders were concerned that Britain and other European nations might try to expand their influence in the Western Hemisphere. In 1823 President James Monroe issued the Monroe Doctrine, declaring that the Western Hemisphere was no longer open to colonization by European countries. Any attempt to do so, Monroe declared, would be viewed as a hostile act directed against the United States.

Significance The Monroe Doctrine was a bold statement for the young United States to make. European powers did not welcome the policy, but for the most part they did not challenge it. In the decades after the Monroe Doctrine, the United States continued to expand its influence in Latin America.

1825 Completion of the Erie Canal

The 363-mile long Erie Canal ran across New York State, connecting the Great Lakes with the Hudson River. The canal provided a quick and economical way to ship manufactured goods to the west and farm products to the east.

Significance Trade generated by the Erie Canal helped make New York City into a great trading and financial center. The success of the canal set off a "canal craze" in the United States. Within 15 years a network of canals crisscrossed the northeast. These transportation improvements contributed to rapid economic growth.

1830 Indian Removal Act

In 1830 President Andrew Jackson signed the Indian Removal Act, which called for the relocation of five Indian tribes from the Southeast to an area west of the Mississippi River. Though the Supreme Court declared the forced relocation unconstitutional, Jackson refused to follow the Court's decision.

Significance The Indian Removal Act demonstrated that Native Americans had little protection under the law in the United States. U.S. Army troops supervised the removal of the tribes to Indian Territory. The forced removal of the Cherokee became known as the Trail of Tears, as thousands died on the miserable journey west.

1835–1836 Texas Revolution

In the 1820s a small group of Americans moved to Texas at the invitation of the Mexican government. The new residents clashed with Mexican authorities, who banned slavery and wanted all residents to follow Roman Catholicism. When the Texans moved to armed resistance, Antonio López de Santa Anna, the dictator of Mexico, marched an army into Texas to crush the revolt. The Texans defeated Santa Anna, and declared their independence.

Significance Texas became an independent country known as the Republic of Texas. The United States annexed Texas in 1845, angering Mexican leaders. This set in motion a chain of events that led to the Mexican-American War.

1846–1848 Mexican-American War

A dispute over the southern boundary of Texas led to the outbreak of the Mexican-American War in 1846. American forces drove through Mexican defenses and captured Mexico City. Under the terms of the Treaty of Guadalupe Hidalgo, which ended the war in 1848, Mexico was forced to cede more than half a million square miles of land to the United States. This land included areas that became the states of Arizona, New Mexico, and California.

Significance The Mexican Cession vastly increased the size of the United States and helped fulfill the claims of manifest destiny. California became part of the United States just as gold was discovered there. The war also contributed to poor relations with Mexico for many years to come.

1848 Seneca Falls Convention

Held in July 1848 in Seneca Falls, New York, the Seneca Falls Convention was the country's first women's rights convention. It was organized by Lucretia Mott and Elizabeth Cady Stanton. Stanton wrote the Seneca Falls Declaration, which stated that "all men and women are created equal."

Significance The Seneca Falls Convention marked the beginning of an ongoing national campaign for women's rights. One of the main goals was women's suffrage, which was achieved in 1920 with the passage of the Nineteenth Amendment.

1849 California Gold Rush

In 1848 a carpenter discovered gold in the American River in northern California. People as far away as Asia, South America, and Europe heard the news and headed to California, dreaming of striking it rich. The mass migration to California of miners—and business people who made money off the miners—is known as the Gold Rush. By 1854 300,000 people had migrated to California.

Significance The Gold Rush resulted in the rapid growth of California, which became a state in 1850. It also contributed to the wealth of a nation and helped fuel the dream of instant riches that has become part of American culture.

1854 The Birth of the Republican Party

The Republican Party began when former members of the Whig, Free Soil, and Democratic parties came together in opposition to the Kansas Nebraska Act. The main issue uniting Republicans was opposition to the expansion of slavery in the West.

Significance By 1860 and the election of Abraham Lincoln as president, the Republican Party had become what it remains today, one of the two major political parties in the United States.

1857 The *Dred Scott* Decision

Dred Scott was an enslaved person owned by Dr. John Emerson, an army surgeon from Missouri. In the 1830s, Emerson brought Scott to Illinois and other free areas of the North. After returning to Missouri, Scott sued for his freedom, arguing that by living where slavery was illegal, he had become free. The Supreme Court ruled against Scott in 1858. Chief Justice Roger Taney noted that the Fifth Amendment to the Constitution protected the property rights of slaveholders. In addition, the Court ruled that since the Constitution forbade Congress from making laws depriving people of their property, the Missouri Compromise was unconstitutional.

Significance The Dred Scott decision added to the explosive tension between the North and South over slavery. Most white Southerners saw the ruling as a great victory. Many Northerners were outraged, fearing the government now lacked the authority to bar slavery in any territory.

1860–1861 Secession of the South

On December 20, 1860, soon after Abraham Lincoln's election as president, South Carolina became the first state to secede. Mississippi, Florida, Alabama, Georgia, Louisiana, Texas followed quickly. In response to the fall of Fort Sumter in April 1861, Lincoln called on the remaining states to supply soldiers to put down the southern rebellion. Rather than comply, Virginia, North Carolina, Tennessee, and Arkansas seceded and joined the Confederacy.

Significance The secession of the southern states, along with Lincoln's determination to hold the Union together, resulted in the Civil War.

1861–1865 The Civil War

The Civil War began in April 1861 with the Confederate attack on Fort Sumter. The South won key early battles, largely thanks to the superior military skill of its generals. Northern victories at Vicksburg and Gettysburg in 1863 helped turn the tide of the war. The fighting ended in April 1865, when Confederate commander General Robert E. Lee surrendered to Union commander General Ulysses S. Grant at Appomattox Court House, Virginia.

Significance More than 600,000 Americans died in the Civil War, making it the costliest war in U.S. history. Fighting left the South's farms, factories, and transportation system in ruins. The Northern victory ensured the preservation of the Union and led to the end of slavery everywhere in the United States.

1862 Homestead Act

The Homestead Act allowed any head of a household over the age of 21 to claim 160 acres of public land. Each homesteader had to build a home on the land, make improvements, and farm the land for five years before gaining full ownership of the land. In the 124 years the Act was in force, nearly two million people tried to claim land under its provisions.

Significance The Homestead Act led to rapid settlement of the Great Plains, which had previously been considered a "Great American Desert." Settlers turned this into one of the most productive farming regions in the world. Many of the settlers were immigrants from northern Europe, whose descendants still populate the Great Plains today.

1862 Emancipation Proclamation

Announced in September 1862, Lincoln's Emancipation Proclamation declared that as of January 1, 1863, all slaves in areas of the South in rebellion against the Union would be free. Its immediate impact was limited, since unconquered areas of the South were not effected. It also did not free slaves in the Border States, which were still in the Union.

Significance The Emancipation Proclamation widened the goals of the war to include the end of slavery. It also helped assure the neutrality of Great Britain, which had been expected to enter the war on the side of the Confederacy. Strong anti-slavery sentiment in Great Britain made any plans to aid the Confederacy unfeasible.

1865 Assassination of Lincoln

Lincoln was assassinated on April 14, 1865, five days after Lee's surrender. He was attending a play at Ford's Theater when John Wilkes Booth, a well known actor and a bitter Confederate sympathizer, entered Lincoln's box and shot him in the head. Booth escaped from the scene, but was hunted down and died in a shoot out with Union troops.

Significance Lincoln's death produced a national outpouring of grief. As a successful wartime leader, Lincoln might have been able to push his relatively lenient Reconstruction plan through Congress. Vice President Andrew Johnson, a southerner, had far less influence with Republican congressional leaders. A fierce battle between Johnson and Congress over the direction of Reconstruction soon began.

1865–1877 Reconstruction

Reconstruction was the process of readmitting the Southern states into the Union after the Civil War. After Southern leaders passed Black Codes to limit the rights of African Americans, the Republican controlled Congress passed the Reconstruction Acts. These acts divided the South into five military districts under the control of the U.S. Army and required southern states to ratify the Fourteenth Amendment and write new state constitutions guaranteeing freedmen the right to vote. A major political struggle over Reconstruction policy between President Andrew Johnson and Congress led to Johnson's impeachment and near conviction.

Significance Reconstruction included three Constitutional amendments that initially helped African Americans. But enforcement of these reforms was dependent on the presence of the Union Army in the South. When the army withdrew in 1877, reconstruction collapsed and African Americans were denied their civil rights. Reconstruction also contributed to the lasting bitterness between North and South.

1865-1870 Reconstruction Amendments

The Thirteenth Amendment abolished slavery in the United States. The Fourteenth Amendment conferred citizenship on all persons born in the United States, thus extending citizenship to all freed African Americans. It also said that people could not be deprived of life, liberty or property without due process of law. The Fifteenth Amendment made it unconstitutional to deprive a citizen of the the right to vote because of "race, color, or previous condition of servitude."

Significance The three amendments helped make full citizens of freed African Americans during Reconstruction. With the collapse of Reconstruction, however, African Americans lost most of their rights until the Civil Rights Movement of the mid-1900s.

1869 Completion of the Transcontinental Railroad

In 1862 Congress provided land for the building of a transcontinental railroad to connect the East and West coasts of the United States. Workers for the Union Pacific Railroad laid tracks west from Nebraska while Central Pacific Railroad built tracks east from California. The workforce was made up largely of immigrants from China, Ireland, and Germany, as well as African Americans and Native Americans. On May 10, 1869, the two rail lines met at Promontory Summit in Utah Territory.

Significance The rail line helped speed up the settlement of the West by making it easier to move people, goods, and resources across the country. It helped unite the country, both physically and economically. Other transcontinental railroads were soon built, and regional railroads expanded.

1876 Invention of the Telephone

In 1876 Scottish-born Alexander Graham Bell patented his design for a "talking telegraph," or, as it came to be known, telephone. Companies quickly found it to be an essential business tool, and people wanted them in their homes.

Significance Along with inventions such as the telegraph and typewriter, the telephone was part of a communication revolution in the 1800s. By 1900 more than a million telephones had been installed in offices and homes across the nation.

1880s–1910s New Wave of Immigrants

Prior to 1880 most immigrants had come to the United States from northern and western Europe. Beginning in the 1880s, waves of immigrants came from southern and eastern Europe. Millions came every decade until 1920. Thousands of immigrants came from Asia as well.

Significance Between 1880 and 1910, nearly 18 million newcomers came to the United States. The new immigrants helped power America's growing industries. The wave of immigration also changed the makeup of the American population. By 1910 nearly one out of every seven Americans was foreign-born.

1883 Pendleton Civil Service Act

The Pendleton Civil Service Act was designed to end the spoils system, a long-standing practice of filling government jobs with supporters of the winning political party. The law required that federal appointments be based on merit, not on political connections. It also guaranteed the rights of people to compete for jobs regardless of race, religion or national origin.

Significance The new law initially applied to only 10 percent of federal jobs, but was still an important first step in reducing corruption in the federal government. By 1980 the law applied to more than 90 percent of all federal positions.

1886 Formation of the AFL

Samuel Gompers formed the American Federation of Labor (AFL) in 1886. The AFL was a coalition of skilled workers in trade and craft unions. Unlike more radical unions, the AFL was more concerned with better wages and working conditions than with pushing larger political reforms.

Significance The AFL became the most powerful union of its time. Gompers used collective bargaining and strikes to gain higher wages and shortened work hours for union workers.

1887 Dawes Act

The Dawes Act divided up Native American reservation lands, allotting small individual plots to families. The goal of the law was to encourage Native Americans to value private property and live more like typical American farmers. The land many Native Americans received included desert or near-desert lands unsuitable for farming. Many who did want to farm could not afford the tools, animals, seed, and other supplies necessary to get started.

Significance Under the Dawes Act, land not allotted to Native Americans was sold, thus decreasing the amount of land under Indian control. Native American traditional life was weakened, and poverty on reservations became more widespread.

1890 Formation of the National American Woman Suffrage Association

The National American Woman Suffrage Association was the largest suffrage group in the United States. NAWSA activists worked to persuade state legislatures to grant women the vote.

Significance NAWSA's membership grew to nearly 2 million under the leadership of Carrie Chapman Catt. Working at both the state and federal levels, the organization played a key role in pressuring Congress to pass the Nineteenth Amendment, granting women full voting rights. A successor organization, the League of Women's Voters, exists today.

1890 Sherman Anti-Trust Act

Though the United States had a tradition of laissez-faire capitalism, in the late 1800s the federal government became concerned about the power of expanding corporations. The Sherman Antitrust Act made it illegal for corporations to form trusts that interfered with free trade.

Significance The Sherman Anti-Trust Act was the first federal action taken against trusts. The act was vaguely written, however, and corporations were easily able to avoid prosecution. The government soon stopped trying to enforce the Sherman Act. Consolidation of corporations continued. Congress later toughened the regulation of trusts by passing the Clayton Antitrust Act in 1914.

1896 *Plessy* v. *Ferguson*

Plessy v. *Ferguson* provided the legal justification for segregation in the South. The Supreme Court ruled that "separate but equal" facilities for blacks and whites did not violate the equal protection clause of the Fourteenth Amendment.

Significance *Plessy* v. *Ferguson* gave the force of federal law to the segregation practices that had been initiated in the South after the end of Reconstruction. The ruling was overturned in 1954 by the Supreme Court's decision in the *Brown* v. *Board of Education of Topeka, Kansas* case.

1898 Spanish-American War

The Spanish-American War was a four-month conflict in which American forces defeated Spain in Cuba and the Philippines. In the treaty ending the war, the United States gained control of Cuba, Puerto Rico, Guam, and the Philippines. Cuba was quickly granted independence, but remained under American influence.

Significance The Spanish-American War marked the establishment of the United States as a major international power. The capture of colonies set off a broad debate in the United States between expansionists and anti-imperialists. In the Philippines, Filipino nationalists rebelled against American rule. United States forces eventually crushed the rebellion in a war that lasted 15 years and claimed the lives of hundreds of thousands of Filipinos and over 4,000 U.S. soldiers.

1899 Open Door Policy

In the late 1890s Japan and European powers carved out spheres of influence in China. Fearing the United States would be shut out of trade with China, U.S. Secretary of State John Hay proposed the Open Door Policy. This policy would give all nations equal trading rights in China.

Significance The Open Door Policy was neither accepted nor rejected right away by other imperialist powers. The Boxer Rebellion, however, convinced Western nations that competing among themselves threatened their ability to exploit China. This led to increased support for the Open Door Policy.

1903 Invention of the Airplane

Orville and Wilbur Wright, two bicycle mechanics from Dayton, Ohio, built the first successful airplane. On December 17, 1903, at Kitty Hawk, North Carolina, Orville Wright became the first man ever to fly an airplane.

Significance Orville Wright's first flight lasted just 12 seconds, but it was the first true airplane flight in history. The Wright brothers and others began manufacturing airplanes. Air travel quickly changed transportation, increased demand for oil, and affected warfare.

1908 Henry Ford Begins selling Model T Automobiles

Henry Ford's goal was to build a car that most working Americans could afford. He achieved this in 1908 with the introduction of his Model T. Ford used the assembly line to produce cars quickly and cheaply, lowering the Model T's price to less than $500.

Significance By 1929 there were almost 30 million cars in the country. The auto industry created huge spin-off industries, such as road construction, oil refining, and gasoline retailing. The invention of the assembly line changed the way goods were produced. The wide availability of cars made it easier for more people to live some distance from their jobs, which led to the rise of suburbs.

1909 Founding of NAACP

A multiracial group of activists, including Ida Wells-Barnett, W.E.B. Du Bois, and Jane Addams, formed the National Association for the Advancement of Colored People (NAACP), to fight for the rights of African Americans. Early actions included defending African Americans falsely accused of crimes and protesting segregation in the federal government.

Significance The NAACP was the first national civil rights organization. In 1954 NAACP lawyers won the case of *Brown* v. *Board of Education of Topeka, Kansas*, in which the Supreme Court declared segregation in public schools to be unconstitutional.

1913 Passage of Sixteenth Amendment

The Sixteenth Amendment gave Congress the power to levy taxes based on personal income. The Treasury Department set up the Internal Revenue Service to collect income taxes.

Significance Under the first income tax laws, less than one percent of the population paid income taxes. This percentage, along with income tax rates, rose as government grew and the nation faced challenges such as World Wars I and II.

1914 Opening of the Panama Canal

Work on the Panama Canal began in May 1904 and lasted until 1914. The 50-mile canal across the Isthmus of Panama connected the Atlantic and Pacific Oceans, greatly shortening maritime travel times.

Significance The Panama Canal helped make the United States a great naval power by allowing the U.S. fleet to move more quickly from the Atlantic to the Pacific. It also greatly facilitated world trade. Protecting the canal and other economic interests became a central element of U.S. foreign policy in Latin America.

1914–1918 World War I

Increasingly intense rivalries in Europe, along with growing feelings of nationalism and a system of military alliances, led to the start of World War I. The primary opponents were the Central Powers (Germany, Austria-Hungary and Italy) and the Allied Powers (Great Britain, France and Russia). New technology such as machine guns and poison gas made this the deadliest war the world had seen to that point. The United States entered the war in 1917, helping the Allies gain eventual victory.

Significance World War I caused levels of casualties far higher than any previous war—combat, disease, and starvation killed more than 14 million people. Another 7 million men were left permanently disabled. The war led to the overthrow of monarchies in Russia, Austria-Hungary, Germany, and Turkey, and contributed to the rise of the Communists to power in Russia. The Treaty of Versailles, which ended the war, imposed harsh penalties on Germany, causing bitterness that later contributed to the outbreak of World War II.

1910s–1920s The Great Migration

In the early 1900s most African Americans lived in the South, where strict segregation laws kept them in a separate but unequal world. The Great Migration was a massive movement of African Americans from the South to the North, where they hoped to find economic opportunity and greater personal freedom. This movement accelerated with the outbreak of World War I, as northern factories needed workers to meet the demand for war supplies.

Significance The Great Migration was the largest internal migration in American history. Hundreds of thousands of African Americans streamed into northern cities such as New York, Chicago, and Detroit. This led to a mixing of cultures, and transformed race from a regional to a national issue.

1919 Treaty of Versailles

The Treaty of Versailles ended World War I. Against the advice of President Woodrow Wilson, Germany was forced to make large reparations payments to the Allies. The treaty also created nine new nations and established the League of Nations, an international organization designed to settle disputes, protect democracy, and prevent future wars.

Significance It is widely believed that the harsh terms of the Treaty of Versailles contributed to the rise of the Nazis in Germany and, therefore, the start of World War II. In the United States, Wilson's unwillingness to compromise with the Senate led to rejection of the treaty by the United States.

1920–1933 Prohibition

Prohibition was a period lasting from 1920 to 1933 during which the manufacture, transportation, and sale of alcohol was outlawed by the 18th Amendment. Prohibition proved unenforceable and was repealed by the 21st Amendment in 1933.

Significance Prohibition led to the creation of organized criminal groups who defied the law. It also led to strengthening of the Bureau of Investigation, forerunner to today's FBI, to combat crime. Its failure widely discredited efforts to legislate what many considered an area of private morality.

1919 The Palmer Raids

During the Red Scare that followed World War I, fear of Communists and radicals grew to an intense level in the United States. The Palmer Raids, led by U.S. Attorney General Mitchell Palmer, were a series of government raids on suspected radicals. Thousands of suspects were arrested, in some cases without proper legal authority.

Significance Far from criticizing the Palmer raids, many Americans cheered, or demanded even tougher action. This demonstrated the level of fear that existed in American society. The Red Scare gradually died out as it became clear that radicals had little power or support in the United States.

1920s Harlem Renaissance

The Harlem Renaissance was a creative movement of African American writers, musicians and artists that took place in the New York City neighborhood of Harlem in the 1920s. Important writers of the movement included James Weldon Johnson, Zora Neale Hurston, and Langston Hughes. Jacob Lawrence and William Johnson were two artists who won fame, as did such musicians as Paul Robeson, Louis Armstrong, and Duke Ellington.

Significance The Harlem Renaissance enriched American culture. Writers and artists made important contributions to American culture. Jazz swept the nation, contributing to a major cultural movement in the 1920s.

1930s The Dust Bowl

In the 1930s, drought and poor farming practices led to massive dust storms that turned portions of the Great Plains into what became known as the Dust Bowl. It was one of the worst ecological disasters in American history.

Significance The Dust Bowl contributed to a mass migration west among displaced farmers. The refugees from Dust Bowl states such as Oklahoma, sometimes called "Okies," came to represent the difficulties of the 1930s. The Dust Bowl led to improved efforts at soil conservation.

1929 Stock Market Crash

Despite underlying weakness in the economy, the stock market continued to rise in 1929. In September, prices began to weaken. The great crash came on "Black Tuesday," October 29, 1929, when stock prices collapsed.

Significance Both individual investors and businesses were devastated by the stock market crash. The crash marked the beginning of large decline in the economy that became known as the Great Depression. The crash also led to reforms of the stock market, including the creation of the Securities and Exchange Commission.

1930 Smoot-Hawley Tariff

The Smoot-Hawley Tariff was intended to ease the plight of American farmers by raising tariffs on imported farm products. This tariff also raised tariff rates on many kinds of manufactured goods. The tariff rates under Smoot-Hawley were higher than at any point in American history.

Significance European nations responded to the American tariff with high tariffs of their own. International trade dropped 66 percent from its 1929 levels, causing economies everywhere to suffer. In this way, the tariff can be said to have deepened the Great Depression worldwide.

1932 Franklin D. Roosevelt elected President

As the 1932 presidential election approached, many Americans blamed President Herbert Hoover for causing the Great Depression, or at least for failing to provide relief from the crisis. Democratic nominee Franklin D. Roosevelt promised swift government action to improve the economy. Roosevelt won the election in a landslide.

Significance In addition to winning the White House, the Democratic Party gained firm control of both houses of Congress. This gave President Roosevelt the ability to push though his New Deal legislation, which changed the role of government in American life.

1933–1945 The Holocaust

Soon after gaining power in Germany in 1933, Adolf Hitler began using the power of the government to persecute German Jews. German conquests early in World War II brought nearly all of Europe's 9 million

Jews under Nazi control. The Nazis attempted to exterminate the entire Jewish population of Europe. This became known as the Holocaust.

Significance The Nazis murdered 6 million Jews in the Holocaust, decimating the Jewish population of Europe. Nazis also killed about 5 million others, including prisoners of war, disabled people, and Gypsies. After the war, many of the Nazi leaders were convicted of war crimes by an international court. These trials were meant to demonstrate the commitment of people around the world to prevent a repetition of the Holocaust.

1935 Passage of the Social Security Act

Signed into law by President Roosevelt on August 14, 1935, the Social Security Act created a program that provided pensions for many Americans age 65 and older. These pensions were paid for by a new tax on workers and employers.

Significance The Social Security Act marked a significant expansion of the role of government in the lives of Americans. Its passage showed that government intended to take a greater share of responsibility for the well-being of citizens.

1935 Passage of the Wagner Act

Named for its sponsor, Senator Robert F. Wagner, the Wagner Act outlawed many of the anti-labor strategies in wide use among business leaders in the 1930s. The act created the National Labor Relations Board (NLRB), which had the power to investigate unfair labor practices and assure employees the right to collective bargaining.

Significance The Wagner Act was a major victory for organized labor. In the four years after the act's passage, union membership jumped from under 3.8 million members to over 6.5 million members.

1939-1945 Manhattan Project

The Manhattan Project was a top-secret government program to develop an atomic bomb during World War II. It was motivated by the danger that Germany might be the first to develop atomic weapons. Manhattan Project scientists worked in Los Alamos, New Mexico. They successfully tested the first atomic bomb near Alamogordo, New Mexico, on July 16, 1945.

Significance The Manhattan Project initiated the age of nuclear weapons. In August 1945, U.S. planes dropped atomic bombs on the Japanese cities of Hiroshima and Nagasaki, forcing Japan's surrender in World War II. During the Cold War that followed World War II, the United States and Soviet Union competed in a nuclear arms race.

1941 Lend-Lease Act

Passed by Congress during World War II, the Lend-Lease Act gave the U.S. government authority to make weapons available to Great Britain without regard for its ability to pay. Lend-lease aid was extended to the Soviet Union after the Nazis invaded Soviet territory in March 1941.

Significance At the time the Lend-Lease Act was passed, Britain was standing alone against Germany in World War II and desperately needed the assistance. Lend-Lease aid helped both Britain and the Soviet Union resist German attacks. It also moved the United States one step closer to full participation in World War II.

1941 Attack on Pearl Harbor

On Sunday morning, December 7, 1941, Japanese forces launched a surprise attack on the American naval base at Pearl Harbor, Hawaii. Catching American forces completely unprepared, Japanese planes inflicted devastating damage on U.S. aircraft and ships at Pearl Harbor. Some 2,400 Americans were killed in the attack.

Significance The Pearl Harbor attack shocked and outraged Americans, erasing isolationist feeling in the United States. The United States immediately declared war on Japan. Japan's ally, Germany, declared war on the United States. United States forces played a major role in winning World War II, the largest and deadliest war in world history.

1942 Japanese American Internment

Fearing that Japanese Americans living along the West Coast might aid an attack by Japan, in March 1942 the federal government forcibly removed some 110,000 people of Japanese ancestry—most of them American citizens—to desolate inland internment camps. Most evacuees remained confined until the internment order was lifted in December 1944.

Significance Many of the internees lost their homes and belongings—some $400 million in property—as well as their jobs. In 1988 President Ronald Reagan signed a bill authorizing the payment of $20,000 to each surviving Japanese American evacuees and apologized for the violation of their civil liberties.

1942 Battle of Midway

Fought in the Pacific Ocean between June 3 and 6, 1942, the Battle of Midway was a major World War II naval battle between U.S. and Japanese forces. Using intelligence gained from intercepted and decoded Japanese messages, U.S. aircraft carrier-based planes surprised and sank four Japanese aircraft carriers with a loss of only one carrier.

Significance The Battle of Midway was a major turning point in the war in the Pacific. Japanese naval power, which had been a key to its early success, was greatly reduced. American forces were able to begin gaining back territory from Japan.

1944 D-Day

June 6, 1944, was D-Day—the day the Allies invaded Nazi-held Western Europe. In the largest combined air and sea invasion in history, more than 150,000 soldiers stormed the beaches at Normandy, France. Facing fierce German resistance, the Allies gained a beachhead from which to begin their massive invasion of Europe.

Significance D-Day was a major turning point of the war in Europe. The United States and Britain drove toward Germany from the west, while the Soviet Army attacked from the east. Germany was forced to surrender in May 1945.

1948-1949 Berlin Airlift

In June 1948, the Soviets suddenly blocked road, rail, and river traffic into West Berlin, cutting off the city's people from sources of food and fuel. In the Berlin Airlift, American and British pilots flew around the clock, bringing necessities into West Berlin by air. They sustained the effort until May 1949, when the Soviets lifted their blockade.

Significance The Berlin Airlift demonstrated how deeply committed the United States was to opposing the expansion of communism and Soviet power. This commitment became the central theme of U.S. foreign policy throughout the Cold War.

1947-1951 Marshall Plan

Named for its architect, U.S. Secretary of State George C. Marshall, the Marshall Plan was a U.S. program to help the nations of Western Europe recover World War II. The United States government spent over 13 billion to buy food and farm equipment and to rebuild factories and homes.

Significance The Marshall Plan was very successful in helping Western European economies recover from the devastation of World War II. The program also strengthened political and economic ties between the United States and Western Europe.

1950-1953 Korean War

The Korean War began in 1950 when communist North Korea invaded South Korea. A United Nations force, made up mostly of American troops, entered the war to block the North Korean invasion. Chinese troops fought alongside the North Koreans. After several major back and forth battles, the war ended in 1953 with North and South Korea divided along almost the same border as before the war.

Significance The Korean War was the first "shooting war" in the Cold War between Communists and U.S. forces. The United States defended South Korea to show it would protect nations from Communist attack. U.S. troops are still stationed in South Korea, more than fifty years after the fighting ended.

1954 *Brown* v. *Board of Education of Topeka, Kansas* Decision

The "Brown" in this landmark Supreme Court case was an African American third-grader named Linda Brown, who was forced to travel a long distance to a segregated school in Topeka, Kansas. NAACP lawyers sued, demanding that Brown be allowed to enroll in an all-white school that was much closer to her home. In 1954 The Supreme Court ruled unanimously that separate schools for African American and white students were by their nature unequal, and thus unconstitutional.

Significance By declaring that segregation in public schools was a violation of the Constitution's guarantee of equal protection of the law, the Court reversed *Plessy* v. *Ferguson* (1896), which had established the constitutionality of segregated facilities. This victory was just the beginning of the civil rights movement that changed the nation in the 1950s and 1960s.

1955–1956 Montgomery Bus Boycott

In December 1955 Rosa Parks, an African American woman, was arrested in Montgomery, Alabama, for refusing to move to the back of a segregated city bus. African Americans, led by Martin Luther King Jr., organized the Montgomery Bus Boycott to protest Parks' arrest and segregation on city buses. After more than a year, the boycott achieved its goal when the Supreme Court ruled the segregation policy unconstitutional.

Significance Beyond achieving local goals in Montgomery, the bus boycott made a national impact by inspiring similar boycotts in other southern cities. Martin Luther King Jr. gained nationwide attention and became a powerful leader of the growing civil rights movement.

1958 Formation of NASA

In 1957 the Soviet Union shocked the United States by launching Sputnik, the first-ever artificial satellite, into space. The United States responded in 1958 with the creation of the National Aeronautics and Space Administration (NASA), a government agency dedicated to the exploration of space.

Significance NASA led the United States past the Soviet Union in the space race, moving quickly from single satellites to manned flights orbiting the Earth to the Apollo program that successfully landed men on the moon. NASA exhibited the success of American technology and boosted American pride and confidence during the Cold War.

1950s Television changes American life

Television ownership exploded in the 1950s, and by the end of the decade over 40 million American homes had at least one television set. Watching television became a favorite national pastime, as families across the country tuned in to the same comedies, game shows, and music programs.

Significance Television, like radio and movies, provided Americans with common cultural experiences. By 1960 TV had become the major means of advertising in the country. Politicians quickly learned that TV had an enormous power to impact their relationship with voters.

1954–1973 Vietnam War

In the Vietnam War the United States fought to try to prevent Communist forces from taking over all of Vietnam. U.S. troops supported non-Communist South Vietnam against Communist North Vietnam and guerilla forces known as the Vietcong. Though U.S. troop levels in Vietnam topped 500,000 in 1968, victory seemed nowhere in sight. With the American public turning against the war, the government began gradually withdrawing troops from Vietnam. The last soldiers left in 1973. In 1975 North Vietnam succeeded in taking over all of Vietnam.

Significance More than 58,000 Americans died in Vietnam, and more than 2 million Vietnamese soldiers and civilians were killed. The war caused bitter divisions in American society, as some protested the fighting, while others backed the government. Misleading statements by military and government leaders about the progress of the war caused many Americans to lose some faith in their government.

1962 Cuban Missile Crisis

In April 1961 Cuban exiles, backed by the United States, tried to invade Cuba and overthrow its dictator, Fidel Castro. The invasion of the Bay of Pigs failed. In October 1962 U.S. spy planes discovered that the Soviet Union was installing nuclear missiles in Cuba. The missiles would be able to strike almost any location in the United States. President John F. Kennedy demanded that the missiles be removed and announced that U.S. warships would enforce a naval blockade of Cuba. For several days the world watched and waited for the Soviet response. The crisis finally lifted when Khrushchev agreed to dismantle the Soviet missiles in Cuba in return for a U.S. promise not to invade the island.

Significance The Cuban missile crisis marked the closest the world has ever come to the outbreak of nuclear war. Sobered by the experience, Kennedy and Khrushchev took steps to ease Cold War tensions. They set up a hot line that would allow American and Soviet leaders to communicate directly during times of crisis, and signed the Limited Nuclear Test Ban Treaty, banning the testing of nuclear weapons in the atmosphere and underwater.

1963 March on Washington

In the aftermath of police violence against civil rights protests, on August 28 about 250,000 people from across the country, about a quarter of them white, took part in the March on Washington for Jobs and Freedom. The march brought together several major civil rights organizations to demand school desegregation, jobs programs, a minimum wage, and various civil rights laws.

Significance Part protest and part celebration, the demonstration was the largest ever in Washington and the first to be covered on television. It is remembered for the peacefulness of the event and for the stirring "I Have a Dream" speech by Martin Luther King Jr., one of the most famous in U.S. history.

Civil Rights Act of 1964

Following the assassination of President Kennedy, the new president, Lyndon Johnson, secured passage of a landmark civil rights bill first proposed by President Kennedy. The Civil Rights Act of 1964 banned segregation in public places and discrimination in employment. It set up the Equal opportunity Commission to end job discrimination—another provision allowed the government to withhold federal funds from school districts that violated integration orders.

Significance The Civil Rights Act of 1964 has been called the most significant civil right law since the Reconstruction amendments. The Civil Rights Act, along with the Voting Right Act of 1965, were major victories for the civil rights movement. These new laws gave the federal government the power to prevent racial discrimination.

1965 Passage of Medicare & Medicaid

Established in 1965, Medicaid and Medicare were parts of President Lyndon B. Johnson's ambitious program of domestic reform known as the Great Society. Medicaid is a government program that provides free or low-cost health care for poor people. Medicare is a government funded health care program for people over age 65.

Significance Medicare and Medicaid have helped provide health services for millions of Americans. Like New Deal programs of the 1930s, Johnson's Great Society programs expanded the role of the federal government in American society.

1965–1970 United Farm Workers Grape Boycott

In 1965 farm workers in California went on strike when their employer cut their pay during the grape harvest. César Chávez and Dolores Huerta, cofounders of the National Farm Workers Association (NFWA), helped lead a nationwide grape boycott to support striking farm workers. Millions of Americans refused to buy grapes.

Significance The pressure on the grape growers eventually forced them to negotiate a settlement. The success of the grape boycott brought César Chávez to national prominence as a leader in the fight for civil rights for Hispanic Americans.

1966 Formation of National Organization for Women (NOW)

The National Organization for Women (NOW) is a women's rights organization founded by women's rights leaders in 1966. NOW actively campaigned for passage of the Equal Rights Amendment (ERA). Though the ERA eventually failed, NOW helped women make important gains in the 1970s.

Significance The organization continues to be an influential voice in American politics. NOW's goals include fighting discrimination in the workplace, schools, and the justice system. It also works to end violence against women and to protect women's reproductive rights.

1969 Apollo 11 Moon Landing

The goal of NASA's Apollo program was to land American astronauts on the moon. The program achieved this goal with the Apollo 11 mission. On July 20, 1969, Neil Armstrong and Buzz Aldrin became the first humans to walk on the moon. Millions of amazed viewers around the world watched the moon landing on television.

Significance The Apollo 11 mission fulfilled a bold promise made by President Kennedy at the start of the 1960s to place a man on the moon in that decade. It was a triumph for American technology and was a source of wonder and pride to Americans, as well as people all over the world.

1970 Creation of the Environmental Protection Agency

In 1970 Congress established the Environmental Protection Agency (EPA) to research, monitor, and set and enforce standards on air and water quality and noise and radiation pollution. The EPA administers the "Superfund" toxic waste cleanup act, established in 1980.

Significance The creation of the EPA was one of Richard M. Nixon's presidential legacies. The agency has overseen the restoration of polluted waterways, the creation of antipollution standards for industries, and the cleanup of toxic waste sites throughout the country.

1972 Nixon Goes to China

As part of his "realpolitik" approach to foreign policy, President Richard Nixon made a historic visit to communist China in 1972. Nixon hoped that improved U.S.-China relations would spur the Soviets also to seek better relations with the United States.

Significance The visit was a huge success for Nixon. Not only did U.S.-China relations improve, but the trip also had the hoped-for effect on the Soviets: shortly after the China visit, Nixon and Soviet leaders reached a nuclear arms control agreement. This opened a period of détente, a time of easing Cold War tensions.

1965 Immigration Act of 1965

This act repealed the national-origin immigration quotas in effect since 1924 and set hemisphere-based quotas instead. Priority was given to those applicants with relatives already in the United States and possessing desired job skills. The effect was to open up immigration to people from countries that had previously been denied entry to the United States.

Significance The act triggered a new wave of immigration to the United States that continues today. Asian and Latin American nations replaced European nations as the main sources of immigrants, altering the cultural mix in the United States.

1979 Iran Hostage Crisis

On November 4, 1979, a student-led Islamic revolutionary group opposed to American support of the pro-Western Iranian government seized the U.S. Embassy in Iranian capital, Tehran. The rebels held 52 Americans hostage for 444 days. President Jimmy Carter imposed economic penalties, conducted diplomatic negotiations, and ordered a rescue attempt, which failed. The hostages were released on the day of Ronald Reagan's inauguration, January 20, 1981.

Significance The crisis, and the poorly executed military rescue attempt, traumatized the country and strongly contributed to Carter's election defeat in 1980. It marked a sharp decline in relations between the United States and the Muslim world.

1982 Strategic Arms Reduction Talks

After more than a decade of work to limit increases in the superpowers' nuclear forces, President Ronald Reagan and Soviet leader Mikhail Gorbachev began negotiations aimed at reducing the huge stockpiles of atomic weapons. The talks resulted in the Strategic Arms Reduction Treaty (START), signed by Gorbachev and President George H. W. Bush in 1991.

Significance START took place during the collapse of the Soviet empire and the end of the Cold War. START II, signed by Bush and Russian President Boris Yeltsin in 1993, was never ratified by the United States, but the two countries have far exceeded the nuclear reduction goals of START I and II.

1991 Collapse of the Soviet Union

In the 1980s economic and political reforms by Soviet leader Mikhail Gorbachev led to calls for greater freedom in the Soviet Union and Eastern Europe. Under this pressure, communist governments in Eastern Europe began collapsing in 1989. In 1991 the Soviet government itself collapsed as former Soviet republics declared their independence.

Significance The fall of the Soviet Union marked the end of the Cold War. Millions of people in Eastern Europe and the former Soviet Union gained freedom from communist dictatorships. The United States was left as the world's only superpower.

1991 Operation Desert Storm

In August 1990 Iraqi dictator Saddam Hussein invaded and conquered the neighboring oil-rich nation of Kuwait. President George H.W. Bush built an international coalition of allies to oppose the Iraqi action. In Operation Desert Storm, a U.S.-led coalition drove Hussein's troops out of Kuwait.

Significance The U.S.-led forces succeeded in freeing Kuwait from Iraqi control, demonstrating the effectiveness of international cooperation. Saddam Hussein, however, remained in power in Iraq. Just over 12 years later, the United States would be at war with Hussein again.

1993 Passage of NAFTA

Passed in 1993, the North American Free Trade Agreement (NAFTA) eliminated trade barriers between the United States, Mexico, and Canada. This allowed most products to be sold across borders without tariffs. The agreement caused controversy, with critics arguing it would cost American jobs, and supporters insisting it would increase trade.

Significance The debate over NAFTA was part of a larger debate about international trade and globalization. This will continue to be a major issue for Americans as the world's economies become more interconnected.

2001 Terrorist Attacks of 9/11

On September 11, 2001, terrorists hijacked four planes, crashing two of them into the towers of the World Trade Center in New York City and a third into the Pentagon near Washington, D.C. A fourth plane crashed in Pennsylvania after passengers attempted to take back the plane from the terrorists. It is believed the target for that plane was either the Capitol or the White House. A total of about 3,000 people were killed in these attacks—making these attacks even deadlier than the attack on Pearl Harbor in 1941.

Significance President George W. Bush declared a war on terror. U.S. officials identified the hijackers as members of al Qaeda, an extremist Islamic terrorist group led by Osama bin Laden and based in Afghanistan. In October 2001, U.S. forces invaded Afghanistan, driving out the Taliban government, which had supported bin Laden. The ongoing war against terror has been the main focus of U.S. foreign policy since the September 11 attacks.

2003 Iraq War

Following the success in Afghanistan, President Bush focused on the concern that Iraqi leader Saddam Hussein was building weapons of mass destruction. These weapons, Bush argued, could be used against the United States or given to a terrorist. Working in 2002 and 2003, UN weapons inspections turned up no evidence of weapons of mass destruction. Saddam, however, refused to fully cooperate with these inspections. Though many of America's allies argued against going to war, Bush insisted the Iraqi threat must be countered. With the support of Great Britain and several other allies, American forces invaded and quickly conquered Iraq in 2003. Saddam was captured in late 2003.

Significance In June 2004, American officials handed control over to an Iraqi government. Iraqis began electing their own leaders in 2005. The violence continued, however, as insurgents thought to include Saddam loyalists and Islamic extremists carried out deadly attacks against American troops and Iraqis. To date, American and international teams have found no weapons of mass destruction.

Presidents

1 **GEORGE WASHINGTON**
Born: 1732 Died: 1799
Years in Office: 1789–97
Political Party: None
Home State: Virginia
Vice President:

2 **JOHN ADAMS**
Born: 1735 Died: 1826
Years in Office: 1797–1801
Political Party: Federalist
Home State: Massachusetts
Vice President: Thomas Jefferson

3 **THOMAS JEFFERSON**
Born: 1743 Died: 1826
Years in Office: 1801–09
Political Party: Republican*
Home State: Virginia
Vice Presidents: Aaron Burr,
George Clinton

4 **JAMES MADISON**
Born: 1751 Died: 1836
Years in Office: 1809–17
Political Party: Republican
Home State: Virginia
Vice Presidents: George Clinton,
Elbridge Gerry

5 **JAMES MONROE**
Born: 1758 Died: 1831
Years in Office: 1817–25
Political Party: Republican
Home State: Virginia
Vice President: Daniel D. Tompkins

6 **JOHN QUINCY ADAMS**
Born: 1767 Died: 1848
Years in Office: 1825–29
Political Party: Republican
Home State: Massachusetts
Vice President: John C. Calhoun

7 **ANDREW JACKSON**
Born: 1767 Died: 1845
Years in Office: 1829–37
Political Party: Democratic
Home State: Tennessee
Vice Presidents: John C. Calhoun,
Martin Van Buren

8 **MARTIN VAN BUREN**
Born: 1782 Died: 1862
Years in Office: 1837–41
Political Party: Democratic
Home State: New York
Vice President: Richard M. Johnson

* The Republican Party of the third through sixth presidents is not the party of Abraham Lincoln, which was founded in 1854.

9 WILLIAM HENRY HARRISON
Born: 1773 **Died:** 1841
Years in Office: 1841
Political Party: Whig
Home State: Ohio
Vice President: John Tyler

10 JOHN TYLER
Born: 1790 **Died:** 1862
Years in Office: 1841–45
Political Party: Whig
Home State: Virginia
Vice President: None

11 JAMES K. POLK
Born: 1795 **Died:** 1849
Years in Office: 1845–49
Political Party: Democratic
Home State: Tennessee
Vice President: George M. Dallas

12 ZACHARY TAYLOR
Born: 1784 **Died:** 1850
Years in Office: 1849–50
Political Party: Whig
Home State: Louisiana
Vice President: Millard Fillmore

13 MILLARD FILLMORE
Born: 1800 **Died:** 1874
Years in Office: 1850–53
Political Party: Whig
Home State: New York
Vice President: None

14 FRANKLIN PIERCE
Born: 1804 **Died:** 1869
Years in Office: 1853–57
Political Party: Democratic
Home State: New Hampshire
Vice President: William R. King

15 JAMES BUCHANAN
Born: 1791 **Died:** 1868
Years in Office: 1857–61
Political Party: Democratic
Home State: Pennsylvania
Vice President: John C. Breckinridge

16 ABRAHAM LINCOLN
Born: 1809 **Died:** 1865
Years in Office: 1861–65
Political Party: Republican
Home State: Illinois
Vice Presidents: Hannibal Hamlin,
Andrew Johnson

17 ANDREW JOHNSON
Born: 1808 **Died:** 1875
Years in Office: 1865–69
Political Party: Republican
Home State: Tennessee
Vice President: None

18 ULYSSES S. GRANT
Born: 1822 **Died:** 1885
Years in Office: 1869–77
Political Party: Republican
Home State: Illinois
Vice Presidents: Schuyler Colfax, Henry Wilson

19 RUTHERFORD B. HAYES
Born: 1822 **Died:** 1893
Years in Office: 1877–81
Political Party: Republican
Home State: Ohio
Vice President: William A. Wheeler

20 JAMES A. GARFIELD
Born: 1831 **Died:** 1881
Years in Office: 1881
Political Party: Republican
Home State: Ohio
Vice President: Chester A. Arthur

21 CHESTER A. ARTHUR
Born: 1829 **Died:** 1886
Years in Office: 1881–85
Political Party: Republican
Home State: New York
Vice President: None

22 GROVER CLEVELAND
Born: 1837 **Died:** 1908
Years in Office: 1885–89
Political Party: Democratic
Home State: New York
Vice President: Thomas A. Hendricks

23 BENJAMIN HARRISON
Born: 1833 **Died:** 1901
Years in Office: 1889–93
Political Party: Republican
Home State: Indiana
Vice President: Levi P. Morton

24 GROVER CLEVELAND
Born: 1837 **Died:** 1908
Years in Office: 1893–97
Political Party: Democratic
Home State: New York
Vice President: Adlai E. Stevenson

25 WILLIAM McKINLEY
Born: 1843 **Died:** 1901
Years in Office: 1897–1901
Political Party: Republican
Home State: Ohio
Vice Presidents: Garret A. Hobart, Theodore Roosevelt

26 THEODORE ROOSEVELT
Born: 1858 **Died:** 1919
Years in Office: 1901–09
Political Party: Republican
Home State: New York
Vice President: Charles W. Fairbanks

27 WILLIAM HOWARD TAFT
Born: 1857   **Died:** 1930
Years in Office: 1909–13
Political Party: Republican
Home State: Ohio
Vice President: James S. Sherman

28 WOODROW WILSON
Born: 1856   **Died:** 1924
Years in Office: 1913–21
Political Party: Democratic
Home State: New Jersey
Vice President: Thomas R. Marshall

29 WARREN G. HARDING
Born: 1865   **Died:** 1923
Years in Office: 1921–23
Political Party: Republican
Home State: Ohio
Vice President: Calvin Coolidge

30 CALVIN COOLIDGE
Born: 1872   **Died:** 1933
Years in Office: 1923–29
Political Party: Republican
Home State: Massachusetts
Vice President: Charles G. Dawes

31 HERBERT HOOVER
Born: 1874   **Died:** 1964
Years in Office: 1929–33
Political Party: Republican
Home State: California
Vice President: Charles Curtis

32 FRANKLIN D. ROOSEVELT
Born: 1882   **Died:** 1945
Years in Office: 1933–45
Political Party: Democratic
Home State: New York
Vice Presidents: John Nance Garner, Henry Wallace, Harry S Truman

33 HARRY S TRUMAN
Born: 1884   **Died:** 1972
Years in Office: 1945–53
Political Party: Democratic
Home State: Missouri
Vice President: Alben W. Barkley

34 DWIGHT D. EISENHOWER
Born: 1890   **Died:** 1969
Years in Office: 1953–61
Political Party: Republican
Home State: Kansas
Vice President: Richard M. Nixon

35 JOHN F. KENNEDY
Born: 1917   **Died:** 1963
Years in Office: 1961–63
Political Party: Democratic
Home State: Massachusetts
Vice President: Lyndon B. Johnson

36 Lyndon B. Johnson
Born: 1908   **Died:** 1973
Years in Office: 1963–69
Political Party: Democratic
Home State: Texas
Vice President: Hubert H. Humphrey

37 Richard M. Nixon
Born: 1913   **Died:** 1994
Years in Office: 1969–74
Political Party: Republican
Home State: California
Vice Presidents: Spiro T. Agnew,
Gerald R. Ford

38 Gerald R. Ford
Born: 1913   **Died:** 2006
Years in Office: 1974–77
Political Party: Republican
Home State: Michigan
Vice President: Nelson A. Rockefeller

39 Jimmy Carter
Born: 1924
Years in Office: 1977–81
Political Party: Democratic
Home State: Georgia
Vice President: Walter F. Mondale

40 Ronald Reagan
Born: 1911   **Died:** 2004
Years in Office: 1981–89
Political Party: Republican
Home State: California
Vice President: George Bush

41 George Bush
Born: 1924
Years in Office: 1989–93
Political Party: Republican
Home State: Texas
Vice President: J. Danforth Quayle

42 Bill Clinton
Born: 1946
Years in Office: 1993–2001
Political Party: Democratic
Home State: Arkansas
Vice President: Albert Gore Jr.

43 George W. Bush
Born: 1946
Years in Office: 2001–
Political Party: Republican
Home State: Texas
Vice President: Richard B. Cheney

Supreme Court Decisions

Gibbons v. Ogden (1824)

Significance: The first case to deal with the commerce clause of the Constitution, *Gibbons v. Ogden* reaffirmed Congress's exclusive power to regulate interstate and foreign commerce.

Background: Aaron Ogden held a monopoly license issued by New York state to operate a steamboat ferry service between New Jersey and New York. Thomas Gibbons had a federal license to travel along the coast and began operating a competing ferry between New York and New Jersey. Ogden sued to protect his monopoly and won. Gibbons appealed the decision to the Supreme Court.

Decision: By a vote of 6–0, the Court ruled in favor of Gibbons. Chief Justice John Marshall wrote the opinion. The Court determined that the states could regulate transportation within their own borders but not between states. The power to regulate commerce between states belonged only to Congress, so Gibbons's federal license was valid. The ruling broadly defined commerce to include more than simply the exchange of goods, but also the transportation of people and the use of new inventions such as the steamboat.

Worcester v. Georgia (1832)

Significance: This case showed the limits of the Court's power to enforce one of its decisions if it chose not to use further legal action to compel cooperation. As a result, Georgia and other states continued to force American Indian tribes off lands protected by treaties with the federal government.

Background: The state of Georgia wanted to remove Cherokee Indians from lands the Indians held by federal treaty. Samuel Worcester, a mis-

sionary who worked with the Cherokee Nation, was arrested and convicted for refusing to leave the lands. Worcester appealed, charging that Georgia had no legal authority on Cherokee lands.

Decision: This case was decided in favor of Worcester by a 5–1 vote. Chief Justice John Marshall spoke for the majority, which ruled that the Cherokee Nation was "a distinct community occupying its own territory." Under the Constitution and the treaties between the United States and the Cherokees, only the federal government, and not the state of Georgia, had the power to control dealings with the Cherokee people. Georgia defied the decision, and President Andrew Jackson refused to act to uphold the Supreme Court's decision.

Civil Rights Cases (1883)

Significance: This decision limited Congress's ability to outlaw "whites only" facilities. As a result, blacks in many areas continued to be subject to inferior treatment. This situation continued until the Civil Rights Movement of the 1950s and 1960s led to new civil rights laws based on the commerce clause rather than on the Fourteenth Amendment.

Background: After the Civil War, many facilities of public accommodation like hotels, theaters, restaurants, and buses were restricted to whites only, or had separate (and often inferior) sections for blacks. In the Civil Rights Act of 1875, Congress attempted to outlaw this race-based discrimination. The U.S. government and blacks who had been denied admission to these facilities brought a series of cases seeking to enforce the Act. The cases were appealed to the U.S. Supreme Court and were combined for decision.

Justice Scalia

Justice Ginsberg

Justice Souter

Justice Roberts

Justice Alito

Decision: In an opinion by Justice Joseph P. Bradley, the Court ruled that although the Fourteenth Amendment prohibited racial discrimination by the state and federal governments, it did not give Congress the power to outlaw discrimination by private individuals or businesses. Because the law went beyond Congress's authority, it was ruled unconstitutional.

Justice John Harlan wrote a strong dissent, arguing that many states were refusing to protect the basic rights of black people and that Congress should have the power under the Fourteenth Amendment to make all citizens equal.

Wabash, St. Louis & Pacific R.R. v. Illinois (1886)

Significance: The ruling marked the end of railroad regulation by the individual states and led to the passage of the federal Interstate Commerce Act the following year. In preventing individual states from interfering with national commerce, the case helped develop a more unified national economy.

Background: In *Munn* v. *Illinois* (1877) the Supreme Court had allowed states to regulate areas of interstate commerce where Congress had not acted. Following the logic of that ruling, Illinois passed a law allowing it to control railroad rates by regulating the shipping contracts of railroads passing through Illinois. The state sued the Wabash, St. Louis & Pacific Railroad for not following the law. The railroad responded that the law did not apply to shipments going from Illinois to another state.

Decision: In a 6–3 decision written by Justice Samuel F. Miller, the Court drew back from *Munn v. Illinois* and overruled Illinois's railroad law. The commerce clause, the Court ruled, prevents states from imposing direct burdens on interstate commerce. This meant that states could not enact laws that interfered with the free flow of goods across the country.

United States v. E.C. Knight Co. (1895)

Significance: The ruling was a major setback for federal antitrust regulation. Freed by this case from the fear of federal prosecution, manufacturers began a period of significant merger and consolidation. Manufacturing monopolies continued largely unrestricted until President Theodore Roosevelt tackled "trust busting" in the early 1900s.

Background: In the early 1890s, the American Sugar Refining Company bought out its major competitors. The purchases gave American Sugar Refining, owned by E.C. Knight Co., almost total control over the manufacturing of refined sugar in the United States. The U.S. government sued, claiming the company had violated the Sherman Antitrust Act. This act, passed in 1890, outlawed monopolies and prohibited "restraint of trade" in interstate commerce.

Decision: The Supreme Court ruled 8–1 in favor of Knight. Chief Justice Melville Fuller wrote the majority opinion, taking a very narrow view of commerce that distinguished the manufacture of goods from their sale. Under this analysis, Congress could regulate sales under the commerce clause, but it did not have the power to regulate manufacturing.

In Re Debs (1895)

Significance: This case confirmed the federal government's power to get an injunction (court order) to end unlawful strikes and force striking workers to return to work. The government used injunctions to stop major strikes for the next 30 years.

Background: In 1894 workers making railroad cars at the Pullman Company rebelled against poor working conditions. After the company hired armed guards to subdue the protesters, the American Railroad Union refused to handle trains with Pullman cars. The strike disrupted rail service nationwide,

Justice Stevens

Justice Breyer

Justice Thomas

Justice Kennedy

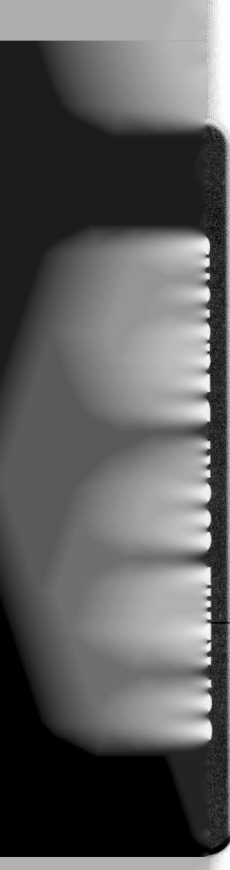

and railroad managers sought federal intervention. The government claimed the strike was impeding interstate trade and interfering with delivery of the U.S. mail—a federal offense. When the union ignored a court order to stop the strike, the union's leader, Eugene V. Debs was jailed for contempt of court. He petitioned for release on the grounds that the order was unconstitutional.

Decision: The Supreme Court ruled unanimously against Debs. Justice David Brewer wrote that the federal government has control over interstate commerce and the delivery of the mails and therefore had the right to ask a judge to stop the strike. The strike created a public nuisance by interfering with the mail, so the judge acted correctly in ordering it stopped and in jailing Debs for contempt when he refused to obey the order.

Northern Securities Co. v. United States (1904)

Significance: This ruling revived the federal government's power to prohibit monopolies, a power that had been undercut by *United States* v. *E.C. Knight Co.* (1895). The government's victory in this case resulted in the dissolution of the Northern Securities Company and paved the way for stricter regulation of large corporations.

Background: In 1901 three competing railroads that ran from the Pacific Northwest to the Great Lakes agreed to merge by turning over their stock to a new holding company, the Northern Securities Company. The U.S. government sued under the Sherman Antitrust Act. It claimed that the holding company was created to reduce competition in the railroad business and therefore violated the Sherman Act's prohibition on restraint of commerce. The Northern Securities Company argued that it merely owned the railways' stock and did not itself engage in commerce. It was a state-chartered corporation, and federal interference would violate state powers protected by the Tenth Amendment.

Decision: In a 5–4 decision, the Supreme Court sided with the government. The states can charter corporations, but corporations are still subject to federal law, and the Sherman Antitrust Act did apply in this case. The Court interpreted the act broadly, ruling that a business combination was illegal if it restrained commerce in any way, even if it didn't directly engage in commerce.

Lochner v. New York (1905)

Significance: This decision limited the states' ability to regulate labor and industry. For more than 30 years, *Lochner* was used as a precedent to strike down state laws such as minimum-wage laws, child labor laws, and regulations on the banking and transportation industries.

Background: In 1895 the state of New York passed a labor law limiting bakers to working no more than 10 hours per day or 60 hours per week. The purpose of the law was to protect the health of bakers, who worked in hot, damp conditions and breathed in large quantities of flour dust. In 1902 Joseph Lochner, the owner of a small bakery in New York, claimed that the state law violated his Fourteenth Amendment due process rights by depriving him of the freedom to make contracts with employees.

Decision: The case was decided in Lochner's favor by a 5–4 vote. The Supreme Court ruled that the right to sell and buy labor was implicit in the Fourteenth Amendment's concept of personal liberty. Thus any state law restricting that right was unconstitutional. The Court rejected the argument that limited work hours were necessary to prevent worker exploitation.

Muller v. Oregon (1908)

Significance: This was the first case in which the Supreme Court recognized social conditions (in this case, women's health) as a factor in judging the constitutionality of state laws. The decision marked the beginning of the Court's gradual retreat from the strict doctrine of *Lochner* v. *New York* (1905), which had appeared to prohibit state regulation of the workplace.

Background: In 1903 Oregon passed a law limiting workdays to 10 hours for women workers in laundries and factories. In 1905 Curt Muller's Grand Laundry was found guilty of breaking this law. Muller appealed, arguing (as Lochner successfully had) that the state law violated his freedom of contract. When the matter came to the Supreme Court, lawyer Louis D. Brandeis presented Oregon's case in a novel and compelling way. He supplied not only legal arguments, but also medical, social, and economic data on the impact of long working hours on women's health.

Decision: In 1908 a unanimous Supreme Court upheld the Oregon law. The Court agreed that the government had a legitimate interest in women's well-being and concluded that the 10-hour law was a valid way of protecting that interest. Although the Court did not overrule *Lochner*, it did show a willingness to accept some workplace regulation as justifiable.

Watkins v. United States (1957)

Significance: This decision recognized limits on congressional investigations. Congress may not expose the private affairs of citizens unless they pertain to a legitimate legislative inquiry.

Background: In 1954 the House Un-American Activities Committee was investigating communists. The committee subpoenaed John Watkins, a labor organizer, to testify. Watkins was willing to answer questions about his affiliation with the Communist Party and also to identify current party members. He refused, however, to name people who had left the party. Watkins was convicted for contempt of Congress, a federal offense.

Decision: Chief Justice Earl Warren wrote the Court's 6–1 decision holding that Watkins's conviction violated the due process clause of the Fifth Amendment. Watkins did not have to answer questions unrelated to the official inquiry of the committee. The Court ruled that the committee failed to clearly define the scope of its inquiry and to establish the relevance of questions about former members of the Communist Party.

Mapp v. Ohio (1961)

Significance: This decision created the legal rule that states cannot use evidence obtained from an illegal search in state criminal proceedings.

Background: In 1957 the police forced their way into Dollree Mapp's house without a search warrant. They were looking for a suspected bomber, but instead they found obscene pictures. Mapp was arrested and convicted for possession of pornography—a crime in Ohio. Mapp appealed to the Supreme Court, which had ruled in 1914 that evidence illegally obtained by the police could not be used in a federal criminal prosecution. The purpose of this "exclusionary rule" was to encourage the police to respect individuals' Fourth Amendment rights. However, until the *Mapp* case, states could decide for themselves whether to follow the exclusionary rule.

Decision: The Supreme Court ruled in Mapp's favor, 6–3. The majority held that the due process clause of the Fourteenth Amendment makes the protections of the Fourth Amendment apply to the states. Thus the exclusionary rule applies in state criminal cases as well as in federal court.

Baker v. Carr (1962)

Significance: This decision held that federal courts could review apportionment, or the distribution of seats, in state legislatures. The case led to the widespread redrawing of legislative districts to equalize representation and ensure "one person, one vote." As a result, political power shifted from rural to urban areas in most states.

Background: Many states had kept the same legislative district lines for decades, despite dramatic population shifts as people moved from the country to the cities. In Tennessee rural voters made up a minority of the population, but they had far more representatives in government than urban voters. Charles Baker and others brought suit against Joseph Carr, the Tennessee secretary of state, claiming that as urban dwellers, their votes were so diluted that they were denied equal protection under the law. The case reached the Supreme Court after being dismissed by the federal district court, which considered apportionment a political question to be decided by the legislature.

Decision: The Supreme Court did not rule on the legality of Tennessee's voting districts. However, it affirmed that the courts can indeed consider such cases. Justice William Brennan wrote that a state's failure to apportion its legislative districts equally would violate the equal protection clause of the Fourteenth Amendment. Thus Baker's constitutional rights were at stake, and the case went back to the federal district court for trial.

Engel v. Vitale (1962)

Significance: This was a landmark case on the subject of religious freedom. In a ruling that remains highly controversial, the Supreme Court held that state-sponsored prayer in public schools is unconstitutional. Attempts have since been made to amend the Constitution to permit prayer, but none have succeeded.

Background: The New York Board of Regents wrote a short, nondenominational prayer for students to say at the beginning of the school day. A group of parents sued, arguing that the prayer violated the establishment clause of the First Amendment—the clause banning the establishment of religion. Although students could remain silent during the prayer, the parents claimed they would always feel pressure to join in the recitation.

Decision: By a 7–1 margin, the Court agreed with the parents and invalidated the school prayer. Justice Hugo Black wrote for the majority. He pointed out that prayer is clearly a religious activity and that under the First Amendment, promoting prayer "is no part of the business of government." The lone dissenter, Justice Potter Stewart, argued that the establishment clause forbids only the creation of an official state religion; it should not be interpreted to deny schoolchildren the opportunity to pray voluntarily.

Gideon v. Wainwright (1963)

Significance: This case established the right of all criminal defendants to be given a lawyer if they cannot afford one. The ruling reflected a growing concern to ensure equal justice for the poor.

Background: Clarence Earl Gideon was accused of robbery in Florida. Gideon could not afford a lawyer for his trial, and the judge refused to supply him with one for free. Gideon tried to defend himself and was found guilty. He eventually appealed to the U.S. Supreme Court, claiming that the lower court's denial of a court-appointed lawyer violated his Sixth and Fourteenth Amendment rights.

Decision: The Supreme Court ruled unanimously in Gideon's favor in 1963. The Court agreed that the Sixth Amendment's right to counsel requires the government to provide a lawyer if the defendant cannot afford one. The Court also agreed that the due process clause of the Fourteenth Amendment makes the Sixth Amendment's right to counsel binding on the states as well as on the federal government.

Heart of Atlanta Motel v. United States (1964)

Significance: This decision upheld the Civil Rights Act of 1964, which banned racial discrimination in places of public accommodation.

Background: The owner of the Heart of Atlanta Motel, a whites-only facility that served many interstate travelers, sued to overturn the Civil Rights Act of 1964. His primary argument was that the law went beyond Congress's authority to regulate interstate commerce under the commerce clause. A trial court ruled against the motel, and the owner appealed to the Supreme Court.

Decision: The Supreme Court found that Congress had carefully limited Title II of the Civil Rights Act to facilities that had a direct and substantial relation to the interstate flow of goods and people. Testimony before Congress had shown that Americans were increasingly mobile and that black travelers in particular often faced difficulty finding accommodations. Writing for a unanimous court, Justice Tom C. Clark concluded that Title II was therefore a valid exercise of congressional power under the commerce clause.

Tinker v. Des Moines Independent Community School District (1969)

Significance: This case established the right of public school students to express political opinions at school.

Background: Some high school and junior high school students in Des Moines, Iowa, planned to wear black armbands to school to show their opposition to the Vietnam War. Two days before they were going to start this protest, the school board created a new policy forbidding armbands at school. Three students, including Mary Beth Tinker and John Tinker, wore the armbands and were suspended. They sued the school district, claiming that the armband rule violated their First Amendment right of free speech.

The Decision: By a 7–2 margin, the Court agreed with the students. Justice Abe Fortas wrote that students do not "shed their constitutional rights to freedom of speech . . . at the schoolhouse gate." Protected speech includes not only spoken words but also "symbolic speech," or acts that express an opinion. Although school officials have the right to set rules, these rules must respect the First Amendment. Here the students had not been disruptive and their armbands did not interfere with anyone else's rights. Also, students were allowed to wear other political symbols, such as campaign buttons. School officials could not constitutionally pick which opinions students could express and which would be prohibited.

Reed v. Reed (1971)

Significance: This was the first case to hold that gender discrimination violates the Fourteenth Amendment equal protection clause. *Reed* v. *Reed* case was later used to strike down other statutes that discriminated against women.

Background: Cecil and Sally Reed were separated when their son Richard died. Each parent asked to be appointed administrator of Richard's modest estate. According to Idaho law at that time, when picking between two equally qualified administrators, "males must be preferred to females." When the judge appointed Cecil as the law required, Sally sued, challenging the gender preference in the law.

Decision: Chief Justice Warren Burger wrote the unanimous Supreme Court decision. Although some distinctions based on gender are permissible, the distinction must be reasonable rather than arbitrary. Because there is no reason to assume that men will be better administrators than women, the law did not have any rational basis. The Court therefore ruled that the law was unconstitutional. This did not mean that Sally would automatically get appointed, but it did require the probate judge to assess her qualifications and make a considered choice between her and Cecil.

Roe v. Wade (1973)

Significance: This case established a woman's right to an abortion as part of the constitutional right of privacy. The decision led to an ongoing battle in American politics between "pro-life" and "pro-choice" voters.

Background: In 1970 an unmarried, pregnant Texas woman filed suit to overturn the state's anti-abortion law. Texas, like many other states, had made it a crime for anyone to perform an abortion except to save the life of the mother. The case was argued before the Supreme Court in 1971 and then reargued at the Court's request in 1972. The plaintiff was called by a fictitious name, Jane Roe, to protect her privacy.

Decision: The Court voted 7–2 to invalidate the Texas law. Writing for the majority, Justice Harry Blackmun concluded that a woman's rights to privacy and control over her own body needed to be balanced against the state's interest in protecting maternal health and preserving the potentiality of human life. During the first trimester (three-month period) of pregnancy, abortion would be at the discretion of the woman and her physician. During the second trimester the state could impose restrictions related to the woman's health. In the final trimester the state could prohibit abortions entirely except where medically necessary to protect the life or health of the mother. Blackmun also concluded that the fetus did not have rights under the Fourteenth Amendment because the original intent of the Constitution and of that amendment was not to consider an unborn child as a "person." Justice Byron White wrote a strong dissent saying that nothing in the Constitution guaranteed the right to abortion.

United States v. Nixon (1974)

Significance: This decision led to the resignation of President Richard Nixon. The case confirmed that the president is not above the law and that the Supreme Court makes the final decision on constitutional questions.

Background: In 1972 senior Nixon administration officials helped plan, and then cover up, a break-in at the Democratic Party's campaign headquarters in the Watergate building in Washington. After the break-in came to light, a special prosecutor began a criminal investigation. He subpoenaed President Nixon to turn over secret tape recordings of conversations with his aides, but Nixon refused. He claimed "executive privilege," a right that past presidents had asserted to withhold information from other branches of government in order to protect confidentiality or the public good.

Decision: In a unanimous opinion written by Chief Justice Warren Burger, the Supreme Court ordered President Nixon to deliver his secret Oval Office tapes to the special prosecutor. The Court insisted that the president is not immune from the judicial process. Executive privilege may be invoked under certain circumstances, but in this case, President Nixon did not claim that military, diplomatic, or sensitive national security matters were at stake. Moreover, under the constitutional separation of powers, the legitimate needs of the courts in criminal proceedings may outweigh the President's need for confidentiality.

Texas v. Johnson (1989)

Significance: This case decided whether the First Amendment allows the burning of the U.S. flag as a form of symbolic speech. The decision has been controversial because it involves the flag, one of our national symbols. Since this case was decided, several amendments banning flag burning have been proposed in Congress but have not been adopted.

Background: Gregory Lee Johnson burned an American flag as part of a political demonstration during the 1984 Republican National Convention in Dallas, Texas. Johnson was convicted of violating a Texas law that made it a crime to desecrate, or treat disrespectfully, the national flag. He was sentenced to one year in prison and fined $2,000. The Texas Court of Criminal Appeals reversed Johnson's conviction, reasoning that burning the flag was a form of symbolic speech protected by the First Amendment. Texas then appealed to the U.S. Supreme Court.

Decision: The Court ruled for Johnson, 5–4, in an opinion written by Justice William Brennan. Brennan accepted the argument that flag burning is constitutionally protected as a form of symbolic speech—like the students wearing armbands in *Tinker* v. *Des Moines Independent Community School District* (1969). Brennan recognized that many people might be deeply upset by Johnson's actions, but he wrote that "government may not prohibit the expression of an idea [because it is] offensive." Chief Justice William Rehnquist dissented, writing that "for more than 200 years, the

American flag has occupied a unique position as the symbol of our Nation, a uniqueness that justifies a governmental prohibition against flag burning in the way respondent Johnson did here."

Cruzan v. Director, Missouri Department of Health (1990)

Significance: This was the first "end of life" medical treatment case to reach the Supreme Court. In its ruling, the Court recognized that even unconscious patients have the right to refuse medical care (through their parents or guardians). At the same time, the Court allowed the states flexibility in setting standards for deciding whether to approve the termination of treatment.

Background: Nancy Cruzan was seriously injured in an auto accident. Because she was unable to swallow, her doctors put in a feeding tube to give her food and liquids. She remained unconscious in a persistent vegetative state for years afterwards. Eventually, when it became clear that she had virtually no chance of improvement, her parents asked the Missouri Supreme Court to instruct the doctors to stop administering food and liquids artificially. This action would have ended Cruzan's life. The state court denied the parents' request because they had not presented "clear and convincing" evidence of what their daughter would have wanted, as required by Missouri law. The parents then asked the U.S. Supreme Court to hear the case.

Decision: Chief Justice William Rehnquist wrote for the majority in a 5–4 decision. He stated that Missouri could constitutionally decline to grant the parents' request where they had not presented "clear and convincing" evidence that Cruzan herself would have wanted feeding and hydration discontinued. Although the Court upheld the state's right to set standards for deciding when medical treatment can be terminated, it also was willing to assume that people have a constitutional right to refuse life-sustaining medical treatment such as feeding by a tube. The decision left open the possibility that the parents could return to the trial court with more conclusive evidence of their daughter's wishes, which they eventually did. The trial court ultimately authorized removal of the feeding tube, and Cruzan died soon afterwards.

Planned Parenthood of Southeastern Pennsylvania v. Casey (1992)

Significance: This case upheld the basic premise of *Roe* v. *Wade,* even though the Supreme Court had become more conservative with the appointment of several new justices. The decision introduced a more flexible legal approach that gave state legislatures more leeway in imposing restrictions on abortions.

Background: Pennsylvania's 1982 Abortion Control Act outlined three conditions that had to be met before an abortion could be performed. First, under an "informed consent" rule, doctors were required to tell women the health risks and possible complications of having an abortion. This information had to be provided at least 24 hours in advance of the procedure. Second, a "spousal notification" rule required married women to notify their husbands. Third, a "parental notification" rule required minors to notify their parents. Five abortion clinics and one physician brought suit to challenge the constitutionality of these requirements.

Decision: The Supreme Court issued a plurality decision, meaning that no single opinion had the support of a majority of the justices. Justices Sandra Day O'Connor, Anthony Kennedy, and David Souter wrote the plurality opinion and other justices joined in various parts. The decision created a new "undue burden" standard for abortion cases, saying that abortion laws must not have "the purpose or effect of placing a substantial obstacle in the path of a woman seeking an abortion of a nonviable fetus." Using this standard, the Court invalidated the spousal notification requirement because it gave husbands too much control over their wives' medical decisions and would be dangerous in cases of spousal abuse. However, the Court accepted the 24-hour waiting period and the informed consent and parental notification requirements, finding that none of these imposed an undue burden on abortion seekers.

Vernonia School District v. Acton (1995)

Significance: This decision allowed schools to administer drug tests to all students who wanted to play sports. The case paved the way for *Board of Education* v. *Earls* (2002), which allowed drug testing for students in all extracurricular activities.

Background: In an effort to reduce drug use, particularly among student athletes, the Vernonia (Oregon) School District started a program for random urinalysis drug testing of students participating in sports. Jason Acton signed up for seventh grade football, but he and his parents refused to sign the consent form for drug testing. When he was not allowed to play, he sued the school district. In his view, the drug testing constituted an unreasonable search of his body, in violation of the Fourth Amendment. The trial court dismissed the

case but an appellate court reinstated it. Eventually the case went to the Supreme Court.

Decision: In a 6–3 decision, the Supreme Court upheld the school district's drug testing policy. Justice Antonin Scalia wrote that the district's collection and testing of urine amounted to a reasonable search. Vernonia students could choose whether or not to go out for sports, and those who did could expect some restrictions and intrusions on their privacy. The urine samples were collected in ways that minimized the violation of students' privacy. Moreover, given the government's interest in reducing student drug use, the extent of the search was reasonable and permissible. In dissent, Justice Sandra Day O'Connor argued that the blanket testing of student athletes was more intrusive and less reasonable than a suspicion-based testing of students who actually appeared to be using drugs.

Bush v. *Gore* (2000)

Significance: As a practical matter, this case decided the 2000 presidential election, confirming George W. Bush as the winner. The question before the Court was whether ballots that could not be read by voting machines should be recounted by hand. The broader issue was whether the Supreme Court would overrule the Florida Supreme Court on its interpretation of Florida state law.

Background: The 2000 presidential election between Democrat Al Gore and Republican George W. Bush was extremely close. As the votes were counted, it became clear that the winner of Florida's electoral votes would win the election. According to the first count, Bush won the state of Florida by a few hundred votes, and Florida's Election Commission declared Bush the victor. However, about 60,000 ballots were not counted because of problems reading them mechanically. Gore challenged the outcome, and the Florida Supreme Court ordered counties to recount all those votes by hand. Bush appealed to the U.S. Supreme Court, which ordered a halt to the recounts while it considered the case.

The Decision: On December 12, 2000, the Supreme Court voted 5–4 to end the hand recount of votes. The majority said that the Florida Supreme Court had ordered the recount without clarifying what was a valid vote. The contested ballots were not always clearly marked, and different vote counters might use different standards to tally them. The Court said that this inconsistency meant that votes were treated arbitrarily, based on a counter's choice rather than on fixed standards. This arbitrariness violated the due process and equal protection clauses of the Constitution. Furthermore, because the deadline for counting the votes under Florida law had expired, there was no time for the state to create new rules for the recount.

Hamdi v. *Rumsfeld* and *Rasul* v. *Bush* (2004)

Significance: These cases considered whether the Constitution's promise of due process applies to Americans or foreigners accused of fighting against the United States in its war on terror. The prisoners in both cases sought access to lawyers and the right to have their incarceration reviewed by an American court.

Background **Detaining American Citizens:** Yaser Hamdi, an American citizen, was captured in Afghanistan in 2001 and accused of fighting for the Taliban against the United States. The U.S. military declared Hamdi an "enemy combatant" and claimed the right to hold him indefinitely without trial and without access to an attorney.

Detaining Foreigners at Guantanamo Bay: Shafiq Rasul and two other foreign nationals were captured abroad and confined for over two years at Guantanamo Bay Naval Base in Cuba. They tried to challenge the legality of their detention in the U.S. courts. Cuba leases the base to the United States. In a World War II era case, the Court had ruled that "if an alien is outside the country's sovereign territory, then . . . the alien is not permitted access to the courts of the United States to enforce the Constitution."

Decisions: Although there was no majority opinion in *Hamdi,* the Court ruled 6–3 that Hamdi had a right to a limited hearing at which he could contest the government's determination that he was an enemy combatant. Justice Sandra Day O'Connor wrote that "a state of war is not a blank check for the president when it comes to the rights of the nation's citizens." Hamdi was ultimately released to Saudi Arabia in October, 2004, after agreeing to give up his U.S. citizenship.

In *Rasul,* a six-justice majority concluded that the prisoners had the right to go to the federal courts for review of their claims that they were unlawfully held in indefinite detention. The government eventually released two of the prisoners in *Rasul* and announced its intention to try the third before a military tribunal. Other cases have been filed challenging the constitutionality of the military tribunals.

Facts About the States

State	Year of Statehood	2005 Population	Area (Sq. Mi.)	Population Density (Sq Mi.)	Capital
Alabama	1819	4,527,166	50,744	89.2	Montgomery
Alaska	1959	661,110	571,951	1.2	Juneau
Arizona	1912	5,868,004	113,635	51.6	Phoenix
Arkansas	1836	2,777,007	52,068	53.3	Little Rock
California	1850	36,038,859	155,959	231.1	Sacramento
Colorado	1876	4,617,962	103,718	44.5	Denver
Connecticut	1788	3,503,185	4,845	723.1	Hartford
Delaware	1787	836,687	1,954	428.2	Dover
District of Columbia*	—	551,136	61	9,035.0	—
Florida	1845	17,509,827	53,927	324.7	Tallahassee
Georgia	1788	8,925,796	57,906	154.1	Atlanta
Hawaii	1959	1,276,552	6,423	198.7	Honolulu
Idaho	1890	1,407,060	82,747	17.0	Boise
Illinois	1818	12,699,336	55,584	228.5	Springfield
Indiana	1816	6,249,617	35,867	174.2	Indianapolis
Iowa	1846	2,973,700	55,869	53.2	Des Moines
Kansas	1861	2,751,509	81,815	33.6	Topeka
Kentucky	1792	4,163,360	39,728	104.8	Frankfort
Louisiana	1812	4,534,310	43,562	104.1	Baton Rouge
Maine	1820	1,318,557	30,862	42.7	Augusta
Maryland	1788	5,600,563	9,774	573.0	Annapolis
Massachusetts	1788	6,518,868	7,840	831.5	Boston
Michigan	1837	10,207,421	56,804	179.7	Lansing
Minnesota	1858	5,174,743	79,610	65.0	St. Paul

*Note: The District of Columbia is a Federal District; it is not a state.

State	Year of Statehood	2005 Population	Area (Sq. Mi.)	Population Density (Sq Mi.)	Capital
Mississippi	1817	2,915,696	46,907	62.2	Jackson
Missouri	1821	5,765,166	68,886	83.7	Jefferson City
Montana	1889	933,005	145,552	6.4	Helena
Nebraska	1867	1,744,370	76,872	22.7	Lincoln
Nevada	1864	2,352,086	109,826	21.4	Carson City
New Hampshire	1788	1,314,821	8,968	146.6	Concord
New Jersey	1787	8,745,279	7,417	1,179.1	Trenton
New Mexico	1912	1,902,057	121,356	15.7	Santa Fe
New York	1788	19,258,082	47,214	407.9	Albany
North Carolina	1789	8,702,410	48,711	178.7	Raleigh
North Dakota	1889	635,468	68,976	9.2	Bismarck
Ohio	1803	11,477,557	40,948	280.3	Columbus
Oklahoma	1907	3,521,379	68,667	51.3	Oklahoma City
Oregon	1859	3,596,083	95,997	37.5	Salem
Pennsylvania	1787	12,426,603	44,817	277.3	Harrisburg
Rhode Island	1790	1,086,575	1,045	1,039.8	Providence
South Carolina	1788	4,239,310	30,109	140.8	Columbia
South Dakota	1889	771,803	75,885	10.2	Pierre
Tennessee	1796	5,965,317	41,217	144.7	Nashville
Texas	1845	22,775,044	261,797	87.0	Austin
Utah	1896	2,417,998	82,144	29.4	Salt Lake City
Vermont	1791	630,979	9,250	68.2	Montpelier
Virginia	1788	7,552,581	39,594	190.8	Richmond
Washington	1889	6,204,632	66,544	93.2	Olympia
West Virginia	1863	1,818,887	24,078	75.5	Charleston
Wisconsin	1848	5,554,343	54,310	102.3	Madison
Wyoming	1890	507,268	97,100	5.2	Cheyenne

American Flag

The American flag is a symbol of the nation. It is recognized instantly, whether as a big banner waving in the wind or a tiny emblem worn on a lapel. The flag is so important that it is a major theme of the national anthem, "The Star-Spangled Banner." One of the most popular names for the flag is the Stars and Stripes. It is also known as Old Glory.

THE MEANING OF THE FLAG

The American flag has 13 stripes—7 red and 6 white. In the upper-left corner of the flag is the union—50 white five-pointed stars against a blue background.

The 13 stripes stand for the original 13 American states, and the 50 stars represent the states of the nation today. According to the U.S. Department of State, the colors of the flag also are symbolic:

Red stands for courage.

White symbolizes purity.

Blue is the color of vigilance, perseverance, and justice.

DISPLAYING THE FLAG

It is customary not to display the American flag in bad weather. It is also customary for the flag to be displayed outdoors only from sunrise to sunset, except on certain occasions. In a few special places, however, the flag is always flown day and night. When flown at night, the flag should be illuminated.

Near a speaker's platform, the flag should occupy the place of honor at the speaker's right. When carried in a parade with other flags, the American flag should be on the marching right or in front at the center. When flying with the flags of the 50 states, the national flag must be at the center and the highest point. In a group of national flags, all should be of equal size and all should be flown from staffs, or flagpoles, of equal height.

The flag should never touch the ground or the floor. It should not be marked with any insignia, pictures, or words. Nor should it be used in any disrespectful way—as an advertising decoration, for instance. The flag should never be dipped to honor any person or thing.

SALUTING THE FLAG

The United States, like other countries, has a flag code, or rules for displaying and honoring the flag. For example, all those present should stand at attention facing the flag and salute it when it is being raised or lowered or when it is carried past them in a parade or procession. A man wearing a hat should take it off and hold it with his right hand over his heart. All women and hatless men should stand with their right hands over their hearts to show their respect for the flag. The flag should also receive these honors during the playing of the national anthem and the reciting of the Pledge of Allegiance.

THE PLEDGE OF ALLEGIANCE

The Pledge of Allegiance was written in 1892 by Massachusetts magazine (*Youth's Companion*) editor Francis Bellamy. (Congress added the words "under God" in 1954.)

I pledge allegiance to the flag of the United States of America and to the republic for which it stands, one nation under God, indivisible, with liberty and justice for all.

Civilians should say the Pledge of Allegiance with their right hands placed over their hearts. People in the armed forces give the military salute. By saying the Pledge of Allegiance, we promise loyalty ("pledge allegiance") to the United States and its ideals.

Biographical Dictionary

 A

Abernathy, Ralph (1926–1990) Martin Luther King Jr.'s successor as head of the Southern Christian Leadership Conference; he led the Poor People's Campaign after King's death. (p. 939)

Adams, Abigail (1744–1818) Wife of President John Adams, mother of President John Quincy Adams, writer, and American feminist, she was also the first First Lady to live in what was later known as the White House. (p. 120)

Adams, John (1735–1826) American statesman; he was a delegate to the Continental Congress, a member of the committee that drafted the Declaration of Independence, vice president to George Washington and second president of the United States. (p. 115)

Adams, John Quincy (1767–1848) Son of President John Adams and secretary of state to James Monroe; he largely formulated the Monroe Doctrine. He was the sixth president of the United States and later became a representative in Congress. (p. 241)

Adams, Samuel (1722–1803) American revolutionary who led the agitation that led to the Boston Tea Party; he signed the Declaration of Independence. (p. 107)

Addams, Jane (1860–1935) American social worker and activist; she was the co-founder of Hull House, an organization that focused on the needs of immigrants. She won the Nobel Peace Prize in 1931. (p. 498)

Aguinaldo, Emilio (1869–1964) Self-proclaimed President of the new Philippine Republic in 1899; he fought for Filipino independence from the United States. (p. 561)

Anderson, Marian (1897–1993) Singer who fought discrimination in the 1930s; Eleanor Roosevelt arranged for her to perform on the steps of the Lincoln Memorial in 1939. (p.723)

Anderson, Robert (1805–1871) Union commander in charge of Fort Sumter when it was attacked by the Confederacy. (p. 357)

Anthony, Susan B. (1820–1906) American social reformer; she was active in the temperance, abolitionist, and women's suffrage movements and was co-organizer and president of the National Woman Suffrage Association. (p. 532)

Armstrong, Louis (1901–1971) Leading African American jazz musician during the Harlem Renaissance; he was a talented trumpeter whose style influenced many later musicians. (p. 659)

Armstrong, Neil (1930–) American astronaut; he was the first man to set foot on the moon. (p. 1023)

Arthur, Chester A. (1829–1886) Vice president of the United States in 1880; he became the twenty-first president of the United States upon the death of James Garfield (p. 502)

Austin, Moses (1767–1828) American banker who requested land in Texas from the Mexican government on which to build a colony; he died before he received the land and his son, Stephen Austin, later founded a colony there. (p. 303)

Austin, Stephen F. (1793–1836) American colonizer in Texas; after helping Texas win independence from Mexico, he became secretary of state for the Texas Republic. (p. 303)

 B

Ball, Lucille (1911–1989) Actress and star of the television comedy series *I Love Lucy*, one of the most popular programs of the 1950s. (p. 862)

Baltimore, Lord (1580?–1632) (also known as George Calvert) English and the first Lord Baltimore; he requested land to establish a colony for Catholics in America, but died before it was granted. His son, the second Lord Baltimore later established a settlement in Maryland in 1632. (p. 65)

Barton, Clara (1821–1912) Founder of the American Red Cross; she administered care to the Union soldiers during the American Civil War. (p. 378)

Baruch, Bernard (1870–1965) American business leader and head of the War Industries Board during World War I; he later advised many American political leaders. (p. 599)

Beecher, Catharine (1800–1878) American educator and the daughter of Lyman Beecher; she promoted education for women in such writings as *An Essay on the Education of Female Teachers*. She founded the first all-female academy. (p. 282)

Bell, Alexander Graham (1847–1922) American inventor and educator; his interest in electrical and mechanical devices to aid the hearing-impaired led to the development and patent of the telephone. (p. 479)

Bell, John (1797–1869) American politician; he was nominated for president in 1860 by the Constitutional Union Party because of his moderate pro-slavery and pro-Union views. (p. 342)

Bethune, Mary McLeod (1875–1955) African American leader and advocate; she served as Director of Negro Affairs in the National Youth Administration and led the Black Cabinet of unofficial African American advisors to Franklin D. Roosevelt. (p. 718)

bin Laden, Osama (1957–) Founder of al Qaeda, the terrorist network responsible for the attacks of September 11, 2001 and other attacks. (p. 1094)

Booth, John Wilkes (1838–1865) Actor and Confederate supporter who assassinated Abraham Lincoln. (p. 407)

Bradford, William (1590–1657) Leader of the Pilgrims who came to New England aboard the Mayflower and established a colony at Plymouth; he served as the governor of Plymouth from 1621 to 1656. (p. 52)

Bradley, Omar (1893–1981) American general who led the Allied troops in Operation Overlord during World War II. (p. 775)

Breckinridge, John C. (1821–1875) American politician; he served as vice president under President James Buchanan and ran for president as a Southern Democrat in 1860. (p. 342)

Brown, John (1800–1859) American abolitionist; he started the Pottawatomie Massacre in Kansas to revenge killings of abolitionists. He later seized the federal arsenal at Harpers Ferry, Virginia, to encourage a slave revolt. He was tried and executed. (p. 331)

Brutus Name used by Robert Yates (1738–1801), an American lawyer and leader of the Antifederalists, when writing letters to the Constitutional Convention in opposition of the Constitution. (p. 159)

Bryan, William Jennings (1860–1925) American lawyer and Populist politician, he favored the free coinage of silver, an economic policy expected to help farmers. He was a Democratic candidate for president in 1896 and was defeated by William McKinley. He later led the prosecution in the Scopes Trial. (p. 651)

Buchanan, James (1791–1868) American politician and fifteenth president of the United States; he was chosen as the Democratic nominee for president in 1854 for being politically experienced and not offensive to slave states. (p. 332)

Burr, Aaron (1756–1836) American soldier, lawyer, senator, and vice president of the U.S. (1801–1805); he shot and killed Alexander Hamilton in a duel in 1804, was arrested for treason against the U.S. in 1807 and later acquitted. His trial ended his political career. (p. 215)

Bush, George H. W. (1924–) American politician and the forty-first president of the United States; he was president at the end of the Cold War and during Operation Desert Storm. (p. 1059)

Bush, George W. (1946–) American politician and the forty-third president of the United States; the son of former president George H.W. Bush. (p. 1085)

Calhoun, John C. (1782–1850) American politician and supporter of slavery and states' rights; he served as vice president to Andrew Jackson and was instrumental in the South Carolina nullification crisis. (p. 249)

Carmichael, Stokely (1941–1998) Civil rights activist in the United States; he was an important leader of the black nationalism movement in the 1960s. (p. 935)

Carnegie, Andrew (1835–1919) American industrialist and humanitarian; he focused his attention on steelmaking and made a fortune through his vertical integration method. (p. 469)

Carter, James Earl "Jimmy" (1924–) Thirty-ninth president of the United States; he negotiated a peace agreement between Israel and Egypt. He was awarded the Nobel Prize for Peace in 2002 for his work in international diplomacy. (p. 1033)

Castro, Fidel (1926–) Communist political leader of Cuba; he helped overthrow the Cuban government in 1959 and seized control of the country, exercising total control of the government and economy. (p. 880)

Chamberlain, Neville (1869–1940) British prime minister; he supported the policy of appeasement, allowing Hitler to gain land and power in the 1930s. (p. 745)

Chaplin, Charlie (1889–1977) British comedian and movie star; he became famous for playing the character of the "Little Tramp" in silent movies in the 1920s. (p. 662)

Chávez, César (1927–1993) American activist; he co-founded the National Farm Workers Association as part of his commitment to improving the working conditions of migrant workers on American farms. (p. 996)

Chiang Kai-shek (1887–1975) Leader of the Chinese Nationalist government and a strong U.S. ally; his government was defeated by the Communists in 1949. (p. 830)

Chief Joseph (c.1840–1904) Chief of the Nez Percé tribe; he led resistance against white settlement in the Northwest. He eventually surrendered, but his eloquent surrender speech earned him a place in American history. (p. 442)

Churchill, Winston (1874–1965) British prime minister; he opposed the policy of appeasement and led Great Britain through World War II. (p. 747)

Clark, George Rogers (1752–1818) American Revolutionary soldier and frontier leader; he captured the British trading village of Kaskaskia during the Revolution and encouraged Indian leaders to remain neutral. (p. 133)

Clark, William (1770–1838) American soldier and friend of Meriwether Lewis; he was invited to explore the Louisiana Purchase and joined what became known as the Lewis and Clark expedition. (p. 219)

Clemenceau, Georges (1841–1929) French Premier during World War I; he was a member of the Big Four at the Paris Peace Conference after World War I. (p. 607)

Cleveland, Grover (1837–1908) Twenty-second and twenty-fourth president of the United States; he promoted civil service reform and a merit system of advancement for government jobs. (p. 476)

Clinton, Hillary Rodham (1947–) American politician and lawyer; she was a particularly influential First Lady during her husband Bill Clinton's presidency. She was elected to the U.S. Senate in 2000. (p. 1079)

Clinton, William Jefferson "Bill" (1946–) Forty-second president of the United States; he became the second U.S. president to be impeached. (p. 1078)

Columbus, Christopher (1451–1506) Italian explorer who reached the Americas in 1492 while searching for a western sea route from Europe to Asia. (p. 30)

Coolidge, Calvin (1872–1933) Thirtieth president of the United States; he became president upon the death of President Warren G. Harding. He was known for his honesty and his pro-business policies. (p. 636)

Cornwallis, Charles (1738–1805) (Also known as Lord Cornwallis) British general and commander of the British army at the battle of Yorktown in 1781. After the defeat of the British army he was forced to surrender to the Americans, ending the American Revolution. (p. 134)

Coronado, Francisco Vázquez de (1510?–1554) Spanish explorer who explored parts of the southwestern United States in search of the legendary Seven Cities of Gold. (p. 42)

Cortés, Hernán (1485–1547) Spanish conquistador; he conquered Mexico and brought about the fall of the Aztec Empire. (p. 41)

Coughlin, Father Charles (1891–1979) Catholic priest and popular radio broadcaster; his broadcasts praised Hitler and criticized Franklin D. Roosevelt's New Deal policies. (p. 704)

Creel, George (1876–1953) Newspaper reporter and political reformer; he was appointed by President Woodrow Wilson to head the Committee on Public Information. (p. 603)

Custer, George Armstrong (1839–1876) American army officer in the Civil War; he became a Native American fighter in the West and was killed with his troops in the Battle of the Little Bighorn. (p. 441)

Darrow, Clarence (1857–1938) Famous American criminal lawyer; he defended John Scopes's right to teach evolution in the Scopes Trial. (p. 651)

Davis, Jefferson (1808–1889) First and only president of the Confederate States of America after the election of President Abraham Lincoln in 1860 led to the secession of many southern states. (p. 347)

Debs, Eugene V. (1855–1926) Leader of the American Railway Union and supporter of the Pullman strike; he was the Socialist Party candidate for president five times. (p. 476)

Dewey, George (1937–1917) Commander of the U.S. Navy's Asiatic Squadron; he led the attack in the Pacific during the Spanish-American War. (p. 560)

Díaz, Porfirio (1830-1915) Mexican general and politician; he was president and dictator of Mexico for a total of 30 years. He ruled the people of Mexico harshly but encouraged foreign investment. (p. 573)

Dix, Dorothea (1802–1887) American philanthropist and social reformer; she helped change the prison system nationwide by advocating the development of state hospitals to treat the mentally ill instead of imprisonment. (p. 269)

Dole, Sanford B. (1844–1926) American sugar tycoon; he helped overthrow Queen Liliuokalani and later served as president and governor of Hawaii. (p. 555)

Doolittle, James (1896–1993) U.S. Army officer; he won a promotion for leading a bombing raid on Tokyo and other Japanese cities during World War II. (p. 787)

Douglas, Stephen A. (1813–1861) American politician and pro-slavery nominee for president; he debated Abraham Lincoln about slavery during the Illinois senatorial race. He proposed the unpopular Kansas-Nebraska Act, and he established the Freeport Doctrine, upholding the idea of popular sovereignty. (p. 325)

Douglass, Frederick (1817–1895) American abolitionist and writer, he escaped slavery and became a leading African American spokesman and writer. He published an autobiography, *The Narrative of the Life of Frederick Douglass*, and founded the abolitionist newspaper, the *North Star*. (p. 288)

Drake, Edwin L. (1819–1880) He drilled the first commercial oil well in the United States, drawing oil prospectors to the West. (p. 461)

Drake, Sir Francis (c.1540–1596) English naval captain; he circumnavigated the globe in 1577, plundering Spanish ships and towns as he sailed. (p. 45)

Du Bois, W. E. B. (1868–1963) African American educator, editor, and writer; he led the Niagara Movement, calling for economic and educational equality for African Americans. He helped found the National Association for the Advancement of Colored People (NAACP). (p. 509)

Dulles, John Foster (1888–1959) Secretary of State under President Dwight D. Eisenhower; he favored building up the American nuclear arsenal as part of an effort to decrease Soviet influence around the world. (p. 849)

Earhart, Amelia (1897–1937?) American pilot; she was the first woman to fly across the Atlantic Ocean and set many speed and distance records. She disappeared over the Pacific Ocean in 1937. (p. 663)

Edison, Thomas Alva (1847–1931) American inventor of over 1,000 patents; he invented the light bulb and established a power plant that supplied electricity to parts of New York City. (p. 480)

Edwards, Jonathan (1703–1758) Important and influential revivalist leader in the Great Awakening religious movement; he delivered dramatic sermons on the choice between salvation and damnation. (p. 86)

Eisenhower, Dwight D. (1890–1969) Thirty-fourth president of the United States; he led the Allied invasion of North Africa and the D-Day invasion of France and commanded the Allied forces in Europe during World War II. He faced many Cold War challenges as president. (p. 773)

Emerson, Ralph Waldo (1803–1882) American essayist and poet; he was a supporter of the transcendentalist philosophy of self-reliance. (p. 269)

Equiano, Olaudah (c.1750–1797) African American abolitionist; he was an enslaved African who was eventually freed, became a leader of the abolitionist movement, and wrote *The Interesting Narrative of the Life of Olaudah Equiano*. (p. 82)

Eriksson, Leif (c.980–?) Viking seaman who was the first European to land on the continent of North America (p. 30)

Evers, Medgar (1925–1963) Head of the NAACP in Mississippi, he was shot and killed in front of his home in 1963 by a member of the Ku Klux Klan. (p. 922)

Falwell, Jerry (1933–2007) American evangelist; he founded an organization called the Moral Majority that is known for its conservative views. (p. 1049)

Farmer, James (1920–1999) American civil rights leader and founder of the Congress of Racial Equality (CORE); he believed in the practice of nonviolence as a means of achieving his organization's goals. (p. 917)

Fillmore, Millard (1800–1874) Thirteenth president of the United States; he oversaw the passage of the Compromise of 1850. (p. 325)

Finney, Charles Grandison (1792–1875) American clergyman and educator; he became influential in the Second Great Awakening after a dramatic religious experience and conversion. (p. 267)

Fitzgerald, F. Scott (1896–1940) American writer famous for his novels and stories, such as *The Great Gatsby*, capturing the mood of the 1920s. He gave the decade the nickname the "Jazz Age." (p. 664)

Ford, Gerald R. (1913–2006) Thirty-eighth president of the United States; he became President after the resignation of Richard Nixon. (p. 1031)

Ford, Henry (1863–1947) American business leader; he revolutionized factory production through use of the assembly line and popularized the affordable automobile. (p. 629)

Franco, Francisco (1892–1975) Fascist dictator of Spain; he led the nationalists to victory in the Spanish Civil War in the 1930s and controlled the Spanish government for nearly 40 years. (p. 742)

Franklin, Benjamin (1706–1790) American statesman; he was a philosopher, scientist, inventor, writer, publisher, first U.S. postmaster, and member of the committee to draft the Constitution. (p. 84)

Franz Ferdinand, Archduke (1863–1914) Heir to the throne of Austria-Hungary whose assassination by a Serb nationalist started World War I. (p. 582)

Frémont, John (1813–1890) American explorer, army officer, and politician; he was chosen as the first Republican candidate for president. Against the spread of slavery, he was rejected by all but the free states as a "single issue" candidate in the election of 1856. (p. 332)

Friedan, Betty (1921–2006) American feminist and writer; her book, *The Feminine Mystique*, explored the frustrations of women with their domestic lives in the 1950s and 1960s. (p. 988)

Fulbright, J. William (1905–1995) American politician, he was a U.S. senator from Arkansas who was chairman of the Senate Foreign Relations Committee from 1959 to 1974 and strongly advocated peace talks in the Vietnam War. (p. 963)

Fulton, Robert (1765–1815) American engineer and inventor; he built the first commercially successful full-sized steamboat, the *Clermont*, which led to the development of commercial steamboat ferry services for goods and people. (p. 255)

Gálvez, Bernardo de (1746–1786) Governor of Spanish Louisiana; he captured key cities from the British, greatly aiding the American Patriot movement and enabling the Spanish acquisition of Florida. (p. 134)

Gandhi, Mohandas (1869–1948) Leader of India's struggle for independence from Great Britain; he taught nonviolent resistance, which was later practiced by many civil rights leaders in the 1950s and 1960s. (p. 917)

Garfield, James A. (1831–1881) Twentieth president of the United States; he was elected in 1880 but was assassinated only months after inauguration. (p. 502)

Garrison, William Lloyd (1805–1879) American journalist and reformer; he published the famous antislavery newspaper, the *Liberator*, and helped found the American Anti-Slavery Society, promoting immediate emancipation and racial equality. (p. 288)

Garvey, Marcus (1887–1940) African American leader who promoted self-reliance for African Americans; he started the Universal Negro Improvement Society (UNIA), which urged African Americans to take pride in their heritage. (p. 656)

Gates, Bill (1955–) American computer programmer and entrepreneur; he co-founded Microsoft Corporation, the world's largest computer software company. (p. 1066)

Gaulle, Charles de (1890–1970) French military and political leader; he led the Free French government and army in World War II. He remained an important figure in France's postwar government. (748)

George, David Lloyd (1863–1945) British prime minister during World War I; he was a member of the Big Four at the Paris Peace Conference in 1919. (p. 607)

Geronimo (1829–1909) Chiricahua Apache leader; he evaded capture for years and led an opposition struggle against white settlements in the American Southwest until his eventual surrender. (p. 442)

Gershwin, George (1898–1937) Composer whose famous piece "Rhapsody in Blue" showed the impact of jazz music on the 1920s. (p. 665)

Giuliani, Rudolph (1944 –) American lawyer and politician; he was the mayor of New York City from 1993 to 2002 and was praised for his leadership after the terrorist attacks of September 11, 2001. (p. 1093)

Glidden, Joseph (1813–1906) Farmer who received a patent for barbed wire in 1874. (p. 448)

Göering, Hermann (1893–1946) German Nazi leader and one of Hitler's top assistants; he played a key role in persecuting Jews and in making Germany a totalitarian Nazi state before and during World War II. (p. 783)

Goldwater, Barry (1909–1998) American politician; he was a U.S. senator from Arizona and the Republican Party's presidential candidate in 1964. He was known for his extreme conservatism. (p. 897)

Gompers, Samuel (1850–1924) American labor leader; he helped found the American Federation of Labor to campaign for workers' rights. (p. 475)

Gonzales, Rodolfo "Corky" (1928–2005) Politician and activist; he founded an urban civil rights group called the Crusade for Justice and was a leader in the Chicano movement in the 1960s. (p. 997)

Gorbachev, Mikhail (1931–) Russian politician; he was the last president of the Soviet Union before the country's collapse in 1991. (p. 1055)

Gore, Al (1948–) American politician; he was vice president under President Clinton and the Democratic presidential candidate in the 2000 election. (p. 1079)

Grant, Ulysses S. (1822–1885) Eighteenth president of the United States; he received a field promotion to lieutenant general in charge of all Union forces. He accepted General Robert E. Lee's surrender at Appomattox Courthouse, ending the Civil War. (p. 366)

Greene, Nathaniel (1742–1786) American general during the Revolution and commander of the Army of the South; he is credited with having saved the Southern colonies from the British army. (p. 134)

Greenspan, Alan (1926–) American economist; he became Federal Reserve Board Chairman in 1987. (p. 1068)

Grenville, George (1712–1770) English politician whose policy of taxing the American colonists contributed to the start of the American Revolution. (p. 94)

Griffith, D.W. (1875–1948) Filmmaker who produced *Birth of a Nation* during World War I, which introduced many advanced filmmaking techniques. (p. 662)

Guthrie, Woody (1912–1967) American singer and songwriter; he wrote and performed songs about the experiences of common people during the Great Depression. He wrote the song "This Land Is Your Land." (p. 685)

Guitierrez, Jose Angel (1944–) American activist; he was among a group of students to found the Mexican American Youth Organization (MAYO) to work for Mexican American rights. (p. 997)

H

Hamer, Fannie Lou (1917–1977) American civil rights activist; she was a prominent leader of the Mississippi Freedom Democratic Party. (p. 928)

Hamilton, Alexander (1755–1804) American statesman and member of the Continental Congress and the Constitutional Convention; he was an author of the *Federalist Papers*, which supported ratification of the Constitution. He was the first secretary of treasury under George Washington and developed the Bank of the United States. (p. 158)

Harding, Warren G. (1865–1923) Twenty-ninth president of the United States; his policies favored business, but his administration was known for scandals. (p. 635)

Harrison, William Henry (1773–1841) American politician; he served as the governor of Indian Territory and fought Tecumseh in the Battle of Tippecanoe. He was the ninth president of the United States. (p. 225)

Hayes, Rutherford B. (1822–1893) Nineteenth president of the United States; he was a Civil War general and hero and, in the disputed presidential election of 1876, he was chosen president by a special electoral committee. (p. 426)

BIOGRAPHICAL DICTIONARY

Hearst, William Randolph (1863–1951) American journalist; he was famous for sensational news stories, known as yellow journalism, that stirred feelings of nationalism and formed public opinion for the Spanish-American War. (p. 559)

Hiss, Alger (1904–1996) Former U.S. government official who was accused in 1948 of participating in a Communist spy ring. He denied the charges, but was convicted of lying under oath in 1950. (p. 832)

Hitler, Adolf (1889–1945) Totalitarian dictator of Germany; his invasion of European countries led to World War II. He believed in the supremacy of the German Aryan race and was responsible for the mass murder of millions of Jews and others in the Holocaust. (p. 741)

Ho Chi Minh (1890–1969) Vietnamese revolutionary leader and president of the Democratic Republic of Vietnam from 1945 to 1969; he wanted to bring communism to South Vietnam. (p. 949)

Hobby, Oveta Culp (1874–1964) Director of the Women's Army Corps during World War II; she held the rank of colonel. She later became the second woman cabinet member by serving as secretary of health, education, and welfare. (p. 760)

Hoover, Herbert (1874–1964) Thirty-first president of the United States; he helped save Europe from starvation after World War I but as president failed to deal effectively with the Great Depression. (p. 674)

Houston, Sam (1793–1863) American lawyer, politician, and soldier; he led U.S. settlers in a fight to secure Texas against Mexico and was instrumental in Texas' admission to the United States in 1845. (p. 306)

Huerta, Victoriano (1854–1916) Mexican general and politician; he overthrew Madero as Mexican president and faced revolts with many revolutionary leaders. His government was not recognized by the United States. (p. 573)

Hughes, Charles Evans (1862–1948) American politician who served as secretary of state and participated in the Washington Naval Conference. He served on the Supreme Court and helped the court deal with controversial New Deal laws. (p. 639)

Hughes, Langston (1902–1967) African American poet who described the rich culture of African American life using rhythms influenced by jazz music. He wrote of African American hope and defiance, as well as the culture of Harlem and had a major impact on the Harlem Renaissance (p. 657)

Humphrey, Hubert (1911–1978) American politician, he was vice president under President Johnson, and presidential candidate of the Democratic Party in 1968 after Johnson decided not to seek re-election. (p. 968)

Hurston, Zora Neale (1891–1960) African American writer and folklore scholar who played a key role in the Harlem Renaissance. (p. 654)

Hussein, Saddam (1937–2006) President of Iraq from 1979–2003; he began wars with Iran and Kuwait, and established a brutal dictatorship in Iraq. He was captured and removed from power in 2003 by American-led forces. (p. 1064)

Hutchinson, Anne (1591–1643) Puritan leader who angered other Puritans by claiming that people's relationship to God did not need guidance from ministers; she was tried and convicted of undermining church authorities and was banished from Massachusetts colony; she later established the colony of Portsmouth in present-day Rhode Island. (p. 54)

Isabella, Queen (1451–1504) Queen of Spain who, together with her husband, King Ferdinand II, believed in uniting Spain under Catholicism; she funded Columbus' expedition in search of the New World. (p. 26)

Jackson, Andrew (1767–1845) Nicknamed Old Hickory, he was an American hero in the Battle of New Orleans. He defeated the Creek Indians, securing 23 million acres of land and his election as the seventh president of the United States marked an era of democracy called Jacksonian Democracy. (p. 227)

Jackson, Jesse (1941–) American civil rights leader, minister, and politician; he was an adviser to Martin Luther King Jr. He became famous for his work on behalf of underprivileged peoples around the world, and mounted campaigns for the Democratic presidential nomination in the 1980s. (p. 941)

Jackson, Thomas "Stonewall" (1824–1863) American Confederate general; he led the Shenandoah Valley campaign and fought with Lee in the Seven Days' Battles and the First and Second Battles of Bull Run. (p. 364)

Jay, John (1745–1829) American statesman and member of the Continental Congress; he authored some of the Federalist Papers and negotiated Jay's Treaty with Great Britain to settle outstanding disputes. (p. 160)

Jefferson, Thomas (1743–1826) American statesman; he was member of two Continental Congresses, chairman of the committee to draft the Declaration of Independence, the Declaration's main author and one of its signers, and the third president of the United States. (p. 115)

Jobs, Steve (1955–) American entrepreneur; he founded Apple Computer in 1977, a company that helped popularize personal computers. (p. 1066)

Johnson, Andrew (1808–1875) American politician who became the seventeenth president of the United States upon the assassination of Lincoln. He was impeached for his unpopular ideas about Reconstruction and held onto the office by a one-vote margin. (p. 407)

Johnson, Hiram W. (1866–1945) Governor of California and U.S. senator; he helped form the Progressive Party, or Bull Moose Party, and ran as its vice presidential candidate with Theodore Roosevelt in 1912. (p. 543)

Johnson, James Weldon (1871–1938) NAACP leader and writer; he wrote poetry and, with his brother, the song "Lift Every Voice and Sing." He was a key figure in the Harlem Renaissance. (p. 657)

Johnson, Lyndon B. (1908–1973) Thirty-sixth president of the United States; he took office after the assassination of John F. Kennedy. (p. 882)

Kearney, Denis (1847-1907) Irish immigrant leader of the Workingmen's Party; he opposed Chinese immigration in California in the late 1870s. (p. 494)

Kearny, Stephen (1794–1848) American general who fought in the Mexican-American War, leading forces that captured New Mexico and helping in the capture of California from Mexico. (p. 310)

Kennan, George F. (1904–) American diplomat and expert on the Soviet Union; he developed the U.S. policy of containment to counter Soviet expansion after World War II. (p. 819)

Kennedy, Jacqueline (1929–1994) American First Lady; she was the wife of President Kennedy and was known for her style and social grace. (p. 888)

Kennedy, John F. (1917–1963) Thirty-fifth president of the United States; he was the youngest person and the first Roman Catholic elected president. He was assassinated in Dallas, Texas in 1963. (p. 879)

Kennedy, Robert (1925–1968) American politician; he was Attorney General during his brother President Kennedy's presidency, and was assassinated during his bid for the 1968 Democratic presidential nomination. (p. 879)

Keynes, John Maynard (1883–1946) British economist; his revolutionary economic theory provided the basis for some of Franklin D. Roosevelt's successful policies. (p. 716)

Khomeini, Ayatollah Ruhollah (1900?–1989) Islamic leader who led a revolution to overthrow Iran's government in 1979; he ruled the country for the next ten years on a strongly anti-American platform. (p. 1038)

Khrushchev, Nikita (1894–1971) Leader of the Soviet Union during the building of the Berlin Wall and the Cuban Missile Crisis. He and President Kennedy signed the Limited Nuclear Test Ban Treaty in 1963, temporarily easing Cold War tensions. (p. 850)

Kim Il Sung (1912–1994) Communist leader of North Korea; his attack on South Korea in 1950 started the Korean War. He remained in power until 1994. (p. 836)

King, Martin Luther Jr. (1929–1968) American civil rights leader; he was a celebrated and charismatic advocate of civil rights for African Americans in the 1950s and 1960s. He was assassinated in 1968. (p. 914)

Kissinger, Henry (1923–) German-born political scientist; he was an important foreign policy advisor during the 1960s and 1970s. He won the Nobel Prize for Peace for negotiating the cease-fire agreement that ended the Vietnam War. (p. 973)

La Follette, Robert M. (1855–1925) Progressive American politician; he was active in local Wisconsin issues and challenged party bosses. As governor, he began the reform program called the Wisconsin Idea to make state government more professional. (p. 527)

Lafayette, Marquis de (1757–1834) French statesman and officer who viewed the American Revolution as important to the world; he helped finance the Revolution and served as major general. (p. 130)

Lange, Dorothea (1895–1965) American photographer who recorded the Great Depression by taking pictures of the unemployed and rural poor. (p. 719)

Lee, Robert E. (1807–1870) American general; he refused Lincoln's offer to head the Union Army and agreed to lead Confederate forces. He successfully led several major battles until his defeat at Gettysburg, and he surrendered to the Union's Commander General Grant at Appomattox Courthouse. (p. 335)

Lewis, John L. (1880–1969) American labor leader, president of the United Mine Workers, and founder of the Congress of Industrial Organizations (CIO); he helped win labor victories through strategies such as the sit-down strike. (p. 712)

Lewis, John (1940–) American politician and civil rights activist; he took part in major protest and sit-ins in the 1960s and became the head of the Student Nonviolent Coordination Committee (SNCC). He was elected to Congress in 1986. (p. 941)

Lewis, Meriwether (1774–1809) Former army captain selected by President Jefferson to explore the Louisiana Purchase; he lead the expedition that became known as the Lewis and Clark expedition. (p. 219)

Liliuokalani (1838–1917) Queen of the Hawaiian Islands; she opposed annexation by the United States but lost power in a U.S.-supported revolt, which led to the installation of a new government in Hawaii. (p. 555)

Lincoln, Abraham (1809–1865) Sixteenth president of the United States; he promoted equal rights for African Americans in the famous Lincoln-Douglas debates. He issued the Emancipation Proclamation and set in motion the Civil War, determined to preserve the Union. He was assassinated in 1865. (p. 338)

Lindbergh, Charles A. (1902–1974) American pilot; he became the first person to fly alone across the Atlantic Ocean nonstop in 1927. He was a hero to millions of Americans. (p. 662)

Little Turtle (1752–1812) Chief of the tribe of Miami and Shawnee Native Americans; he won the greatest victory Native Americans had ever achieved over white armies in 1791. (p. 211)

Lodge, Henry Cabot (1850–1924) U.S. senator and head of the Committee of Foreign Relations; he led the reservationists in opposition to the League of Nations. (p. 609)

Long, Huey P. (1893–1935) Louisiana politician and senator; he criticized the New Deal and set up the Share Our Wealth Society. He wanted to tax wealthy Americans and give more money to poor Americans. (p. 704)

Longstreet, James (1809–1865) Confederate general who commanded Pickett's Charge at the Battle of Gettysburg. (p. 384)

Lowell, Francis (1775–1817) American industrialist who developed the Lowell system. He hired young women to live and work in his mill. (p. 253)

Lucas, Eliza (1722–1793) Plantation manager in the Carolinas; she was the first person to successfully grow Indigo in the colonies. (p. 81)

Luther, Martin (1483–1546) German monk who protested against the Catholic Church in 1517; which led to calls for reform and the movement known as the Reformation. (p. 25)

MacArthur, Douglas (1880–1964) American general, he commanded U.S. troops in the Southwest Pacific during World War II and administered Japan after the war ended. He later commanded UN forces at the beginning of the Korean War until he was removed by President Truman. (p. 787)

Madero, Francisco (1873–1913) President of Mexico after Porfirio Díaz fled the country; he tried to establish a democratic government in Mexico. (p. 573)

Madison, James (1751–1836) American statesman; he was a delegate to the Constitutional Convention, the fourth president of the United States, and the author of some of the *Federalist Papers*. He is called the "father of the Constitution" for his proposals at the Constitutional Convention. (p. 151)

Malcolm X (1925–1965) Well-known supporter of the Nation of Islam and black leader; he spoke in support of black separatism, black pride, and the use of violence for self-protection. (p. 936)

Mandela, Nelson (1918–) Former guerrilla fighter who helped end apartheid; he became the first black president of South Africa. (p. 1064)

Mann, Horace (1796–1859) American educator; he is considered the father of American public education. (p. 268)

Mansa Musa (died 1332) Leader of Mali who held power from 1307 to 1332. (p. 19)

Mao Zedong (1893–1976) Leader of the Chinese Communists, he led a successful revolution and established a Communist government in China in 1949. (p. 830)

Marshall, George C. (1880–1959) American general and politician; he led U.S. mobilization for World War II and helped plan the nation's war strategy. He also developed the postwar European Recovery Program called the Marshall Plan. (p. 759)

Marshall, Thurgood (1908–1993) American jurist; he was the first African American to serve on the Supreme Court. (p. 910)

Martí, José (1853–1895) Cuban writer and independence fighter; he was killed in battle but became a symbol of Cuba's fight for freedom. (p. 559)

Mauldin, Bill (1921–2003) American cartoonist whose World War II cartoons gave people at home a soldier's point of view on life in the army. (p. 795)

McCarthy, Eugene (1916–) American politician, he was a U.S. senator who vied for the 1968 Democratic presidential nomination against President Johnson. (p. 967)

McCarthy, Joseph (1908–1957) U.S. senator from Wisconsin who gained national fame in the late 1940s and early 1950s by aggressively charging that communists were working in the U.S. government. He lost support in 1954, after making baseless attacks on U.S. Army officials. (p. 833)

McClellan, George (1826–1885) American army general put in charge of Union troops and later removed by Lincoln for failure to press Lee's Confederate troops in Richmond. (p. 364)

McGovern, George (1922–) American politician; he was the Democratic candidate for the presidency in 1972 losing to Richard Nixon. (p. 976)

McKinley, William (1843–1901) Twenty-fifth president of the United States; he enacted protective tariffs in the McKinley Tariff Act of 1890 and acquired Cuba, Puerto Rico, Guam, and the Philippines during his administration. He was later assassinated. (p. 505)

McNamara, Robert S. (1916–) American businessman and public official; he was the U.S. secretary of defense from 1961–1968. (p. 967)

McNickle, D'Arcy (1904–1977) Native American activist; he drafted the Declaration of Indian Purpose, a document that asserted the rights of Native Americans in the United States. (p. 991)

McPherson, Aimee Semple (1890–1944) American fundamentalist preacher who was well-known for her glamorous presentation. (p. 650)

Meade, George (1815–1872) American army officer; he served as a Union general at major Civil War battles. He forced back General Lee's Confederate army at Gettysburg but failed to obtain a decisive victory. (p. 384)

Means, Russell (1939–) One leader of the American Indian Movement. (p. 992)

Meredith, James (1933–) Civil rights activist who entered the University of Mississippi after being denied admission because of his race. His entrance led to violent riots on the school's campus. (p. 920)

Mitchell, Billy (1879–1936) American general who supported the development of air power in the military. (p. 639)

Monroe, James (1758–1831) Leading Revolutionary figure, negotiator of the Louisiana Purchase, and the fifth president of the United States. He put forth the Monroe Doctrine establishing the U.S. sphere of influence in the Western Hemisphere that became the foundation of U.S. foreign policy. (p. 241)

Morse, Samuel F.B. (1791–1872) American artist and inventor; he applied scientists' discoveries of electricity and magnetism to develop the telegraph. (p. 255)

Mott, Lucretia (1793–1880) American reformer; she planned the Seneca Falls Convention with Elizabeth Cady Stanton, the first organized meeting for women's rights in the United States. (p. 283)

Muhammad, Askia (?–1538) Ruler of the West African kingdom of Songhai from 1493–1528; he was known for encouraging a revival of Muslim learning during his rule. (p. 20)

Muir, John (1838–1914) Naturalist who believed the wilderness should be preserved in its natural state. He was largely responsible for the creation of Yosemite National Park in California. (p. 539)

Mussolini, Benito (1883–1945) Italian Fascist leader; he ruled as Italy's dictator for more than 20 years beginning in 1922 and made Italy a totalitarian state. His alliance with Adolf Hitler brought Italy into World War II. (p. 740)

Nation, Carry (1846–1911) Temperance advocate; she took extreme measures to further her cause by entering saloons in her native state of Kansas and smashing bottles of alcohol with a hatchet. (p. 531)

Nast, Thomas (1840–1902) American political cartoonist; he helped turn public attention to the corruption of Tammany Hall and Boss Tweed. (p. 501)

Ngo Dinh Diem (1901–1963) Vietnamese political leader; he became president of South Vietnam in 1955. He was assassinated in 1963. (p. 951)

Nimitz, Chester (1885–1966) American admiral; he won major victories in the Battle of the Coral Sea and the Battle of Midway, stopping the Japanese advance during World War II. (p. 788)

Nixon, Richard M. (1913–1994) Thirty-seventh president of the United States and vice-president under President Eisenhower; he resigned from his second term because of the Watergate scandal. (p. 849)

North, Oliver (1943–) Officer in the U.S Marines, he is known for his role in the Iran-Contra affair. (p. 1058)

O'Connor, Sandra Day (1930–) First woman on the Supreme Court; she was appointed by President Reagan in 1981 and announced her resignation in 2005. (p. 1069)

Oglethorpe, James (1696–1785) English soldier and humanitarian; he founded the colony of Georgia as a haven where debtors from England could come and begin new lives. (p. 63)

Oliver, James (1823–1908) American plow maker who developed a new plow with a sharper edge that helped farmers plow their fields with much less effort. (p. 453)

Olmsted, Frederick Law (1822–1903) American landscape architect; he designed New York City's Central Park, Boston's "Emerald Necklace" network of parks, and other urban parks. (p. 496)

Oppenheimer, J. Robert (1904–1967) American physicist; he led the Manhattan Project laboratory in Los Alamos, which developed the first nuclear bomb. (p. 762)

Oswald, Lee Harvey (1939–1963) The accused assassin of President Kennedy. (p. 892)

Otis, Elisha (1811–1861) American mechanic and inventor, he invented the mechanized safety elevator. (p. 496)

Paine, Thomas (1737–1809) American political philosopher and author; he urged an immediate declaration of independence from England in his anonymously and simply written pamphlet, *Common Sense*. (p. 117)

Palmer, A. Mitchell (1872–1936) U.S. attorney general and opponent of communism; he ordered the Palmer raids against radicals and aliens during the Red Scare of 1919 and 1920. (p. 624)

Parks, Rosa (1913–2005) American civil rights activist; she was arrested in 1955 after refusing to give her seat on a public bus to a white man. Her arrest led to a widespread bus boycott that was an important chapter in the civil rights movement. (p. 914)

Patton, George S. (1885–1945) American general; he was involved in North Africa, Italy, and the Battle of the Bulge during World War II. (p. 776)

Paul, Alice (1885–1977) American social reformer, suffragist, and activist; she was the founder of the National Woman's Party (NWP) that worked to obtain women's suffrage. (p. 544)

Penn, William (1644–1718) Quaker leader who founded a colony in Pennsylvania; the colony provided an important example of representative self-government and became a model of freedom and tolerance. (p. 60)

Perkins, Frances (1882–1965) First American woman to head an executive or cabinet department; she served as secretary of labor in Franklin D. Roosevelt's administration. She played an important role in shaping New Deal jobs programs and labor policy. (p. 718)

Pershing, John J. (1860–1948) American army commander; he commanded the expeditionary force sent into Mexico to find Pancho Villa. He was the major general and commander in chief of the American Expeditionary Forces in World War I. (p. 575)

Pierce, Franklin (1804–1869) Fourteenth president of the United States; he condemned Kansas's free-soil government as rebels, which led to the Sack of Lawrence in 1856. (p. 331)

Pike, Zebulon M. (1779–1813) Army officer sent on a mission to explore the West, he was ordered to find the headwaters of the Red River. He attempted to climb what is now known as Pikes Peak in Colorado. (p. 219)

Pinchot, Gifford (1865–1946) Conservationist who was chief of the Forest Service. Under his leadership millions of acres of land were added to the national forests under his leadership. (p. 540)

Pocahontas (c.1595–1617) Algonquian princess; she saved the life of John Smith when he was captured and sentenced to death by the Powhatan. She was later taken prisoner by the English, converted to Christianity, and married colonist John Rolfe. (p. 47)

Polk, James (1795–1849) Eleventh president of the United States; he negotiated the establishment of the Oregon Territory for the U.S. and acquired much land as a result of the Mexican-American War. (p. 299)

Pitt, William (1708–1778) English leader in Parliament who opposed taxing American colonists, but also opposed their requests for independence. (p. 93)

Ponce de León, Juan (1460–1521) Spanish explorer who explored Puerto Rico and became its governor in 1509. In 1513 he discovered landed off the east coast of Florida while looking for a fabled "fountain of youth" and claimed the region for Spain. (p. 41)

Pontiac (c.1720–1769) Ottawa chief who united the Great Lakes' Indians to try to halt the advance of European settlements. He attacked British forts in a battle known as Pontiac's Rebellion and eventually surrendered in 1766. (p. 94)

Popé Indian shaman who led a revolt of Pueblo Indiana in 1680 against the Spanish in present-day New Mexico, driving out the Spanish and restoring the Pueblo way of life. The Spanish retook the area upon his death in 1692, but the Pueblo culture remained a part of this region. (p. 44)

Powderly, Terence V. (1849–1924) American labor leader for the Knights of Labor; he removed the secrecy originally surrounding the organization, leading to its becoming the first truly national American labor union. (p. 474)

Powhatan (1550?–1618) Algonquin Indian chief who was the head of the Powhatan Confederacy of Algonquin Peoples; he was also the father of Pocahontas. (p. 47)

Publius (1811–1861) The author name used by James Madison, Alexander Hamilton, and John Jay when writing the *Federalist Papers*. (p. 160)

Pulitzer, Joseph (1847–1911) American journalist and newspaper publisher; he established the Pulitzer Prize for public service and advancement of education. (p. 559)

Pyle, Ernie (1900–1945) American journalist and war correspondent; he reported on World War II from the point of view of an ordinary soldier. (p. 795)

Randolph, A. Philip (1889–1979) African American union and civil rights leader; his protests during World War II led President Roosevelt to ban discrimination in government and defense jobs. (p. 763)

Reagan, Nancy (1921–) Wife of President Ronald Reagan; she headed a campaign against drugs. (p. 1049)

Reagan, Ronald (1911–2004) American politician and the fortieth president of the United States; his presidency focused on arms control, economics, and the end of the Cold War. (p. 1046)

Revels, Hiram (1822–1901) American clergyman, educator, and politician; he became the first African American in the U.S. Senate. (p. 418)

Rice, Condoleezza (1954–) American educator and politician; she was national security adviser (2001–2005) and secretary of state (2005–) under President George W. Bush. (p. 1089)

Riis, Jacob (1849–1914) Newspaper reporter, reformer, and photographer; his book, *How the Other Half Lives*, shocked Americans with its descriptions of slum conditions and led to tenement housing legislation in New York. (p. 522)

Robeson, Paul (1898–1976) African American actor and singer who promoted African American rights and left-wing causes. (p. 659)

Robinson, Jackie (1919–1972) American baseball player; he was the first black player in the major leagues. (p. 910)

Rochambeau, Count de (1725–1807) French general who led troops against the British Army during the Revolutionary War. (p. 134)

Rockefeller, John D. (1839–1937) American industrialist and philanthropist; he made a fortune in the oil business and used vertical and horizontal integration to establish a monopoly on the steel business. (p. 468)

Rolfe, John (1585–1622) English colonist who was the first tobacco grower in Virginia, he helped make tobacco a profitable export to England; he married the Algonquian princess Pocahontas. (p. 48)

Rommel, Erwin (1891–1944) German general during World War II; he commanded the Afrika Korps and was nicknamed the Desert Fox for his leadership. (p. 772)

Roosevelt, Eleanor (1884–1962) Wife of President Franklin D. Roosevelt, social reformer, writer, and diplomat; she supported equal rights for women and African Americans. She served as the first U.S. ambassador to the United Nations. (p. 700)

Roosevelt, Franklin Delano (1882–1945) Thirty-second president of the United States; he was elected president four times. He led the United States during the major crises of the Great Depression and World War II. (p. 699)

Roosevelt, Theodore (1858–1919) Twenty-sixth president of the United States; he focused his efforts on trust busting, environmental conservation, and strong foreign policy. (p. 535)

Rumsfeld, Donald (1932–) American public official; he has held various government positions including secretary of defense (1975–77; 2001–) (p. 1089)

Sacagawea (1786?–1812) Shoshone woman who, along with French fur trapper husband, accompanied and aided Lewis and Clark on their expedition. (p. 219)

Salk, Jonas (1914–1995) Scientist who developed the polio vaccine in 1952. (p. 865)

Santa Anna, Antonio López de (1794–1876) Mexican general, president and dicatator; he fought in the Texas Revolution and seized the Alamo but was defeated and captured by Sam Houston at San Jacinto. (p. 305)

Schlafly, Phyllis (1924–) American conservative columnist; she is known for speaking out for conservative causes, such as her opposition to the Equal Rights Amendment (ERA). (p. 989)

Scott, Winfield (1786–1866) American army general who fought in the War of 1812, the Mexican-American War, and the Civil War; he also ran for president in 1852 but lost the election. (p. 311)

Selassie, Haile (1892–1975) Emperor of Ethiopia; he resisted the Italian invasion of Ethiopia during World War II and later helped modernize Ethiopia. (p. 743)

Sherman, William Tecumseh (1820–1891) Union army officer; his famous March to the Sea captured Atlanta, Georgia, an important turning point in the war. (p. 391)

Sinclair, Upton (1878–1968) Novelist whose 1906 book, *The Jungle*, depicted the unsanitary conditions at a meatpacking plant. Public outcry from the book led to consumer-protection laws. (p. 538)

Singleton, Benjamin "Pap" (1809–1892) African American leader, community builder, and former slave; he encouraged African Americans to build their own communities in the West. He later supported Black Nationalism and encouraged African Americans to move to Africa. (p. 452)

Sitting Bull (c.1831–1890) Native American leader who became head chief of the entire Sioux nation. He encouraged other Sioux leaders to resist government demands to buy lands on the Black Hills reservations. (p. 441)

Slater, Samuel (1768–1835) English industrialist who brought a design for a textile mill to America; known as the founder of the American cotton industry. (p. 251)

Smith, Bessie (1898?–1937) African American blues singer who played an important part in the Harlem Renaissance. (p. 659)

Smith, John (c.1580–1631) English colonist to the Americas who helped found Jamestown Colony. (p. 47)

Stalin, Joseph (1879–1953) Totalitarian dictator of the Soviet Union; he led the Soviet Union through World War II and created a powerful Soviet sphere of influence in Eastern Europe after the war. (p. 742)

Stanton, Elizabeth Cady (1815–1902) American suffrage leader; she organized the Seneca Falls Convention with Lucretia Mott. The convention was the first organized meeting for women's rights in the United States. (p. 283)

Steffens, Lincoln (1866–1936) Muckraker and managing editor of *McClure's* magazine; he exposed government corruption in his 1904 book, *The Shame of the Cities*. (p. 523)

Stevens, Thaddeus (1792–1868) American lawyer and politician; he was the leader of the Radical Republicans in the Reconstruction effort and was an opponent and critic of Andrew Johnson's policies. (p. 406)

Stockman, David A. (1946–) American politician; he was appointed by President Reagan to help put his economics plan into action. (p. 1050)

Stowe, Harriet Beecher (1811–1896) American author and daughter of Lyman Beecher; she was an abolitionist and author of the famous antislavery novel, *Uncle Tom's Cabin*. (p. 325)

Sunday, Billy (c.1862–1935) American fundamentalist minister; used colorful language and powerful sermons to drive home the message of salvation through Jesus and to oppose radical and progressive groups. (p. 650)

Syngman Rhee (1875–1965) Korean leader who became president of South Korea after World War II and led South Korea during the Korean War. (p. 836)

T

Taft, William Howard (1857–1930) Twenty-seventh president of the United States; he angered progressives by moving cautiously toward reforms and by supporting the Payne-Aldrich Tariff. He lost Roosevelt's support and was defeated for a second term. (p. 541)

Tarbell, Ida (1857–1944) Investigative journalist; she wrote a report condemning the corrupt business practices of John D. Rockefeller in *McClure's* magazine. These articles became the basis for her book, *The History of the Standard Oil Company*. (p. 523)

Taylor, Zachary (1874–1850) American general and twelfth president of the United States, he led American troops during the Mexican-American War. He was the first president elected after the Mexican-American War, but died only 16 months after taking office. (p. 310)

Tecumseh (1768–1813) Shawnee chief who attempted to form an Indian confederation to resist white settlement in the Northwest Territory. (p. 225)

Thomas, Clarence (1948–) Associate justice on the Supreme Court; he was appointed in 1991 and was the second African American to serve on the court. (p. 1071)

Thoreau, Henry David (1817–1862) American writer and transcendentalist philosopher; he studied nature and published a magazine article, "Civil Disobedience," as well as his famous book, *Walden Pond*. (p. 270)

Tocqueville, Alexis de (1805–1859) French philosopher, politician and author; his work, *Democracy in America*, encouraged Americans to form their own culture rather than mimicking that of Europeans. (p. 239)

Tojo, Hideki (1884–1948) Japanese nationalist and general; he took control of Japan during World War II. He was later tried and executed for war crimes. (p. 750)

Townsend, Dr. Francis (1867–1960) New Deal critic who focused on the needs of older Americans; his ideas for a pension plan for retirees contributed to the formation of Social Security. (p. 705)

Travis, William (1809–1836) American lawyer and commander of Texas forces at the Alamo. (p. 306)

Truman, Harry (1884–1972) Thirty-third president of the United States; he became president upon the death of President Franklin D. Roosevelt. He led the United States through the end of World War II and the beginning of the Cold War. (p. 805)

Tubman, Harriet (c.1820–1913) American abolitionist who escaped slavery and assisted other enslaved Africans to escape. She is the most famous Underground Railroad conductor. (p. 286)

Turner, Frederick Jackson (1861–1932) American historian; he developed the idea that the existence of the frontier made the United States distinctive. (p. 451)

Turner, Nat (1800–1831) American slave leader; he claimed that divine inspiration had led him to end the slavery system. He led the most violent slave revolt in U.S. history; he was tried, convicted, and executed. (p. 286)

Tweed, William Marcy (1823–1878) American politician, he gained control of New York City's Tammany Hall became known as Boss Tweed. He was convicted of stealing from the New York City treasury. (p. 501)

Tyler, John (1790–1862) Tenth president of the United States; he favored annexation of Texas and signed the joint resolution of Congress into law three days before his term ended in 1845. (p. 309)

V

Van Buren, Martin (1782–1862) Eighth president of the United States; he extended the 10-hour work day plan, initiated by Jackson, to include other groups in 1840. (p. 277)

Vanderbilt, Cornelius (1794–1877) American business leader who controlled the New York Central Railroad and up to 4,500 miles of railroad track; he later donated $1 million to a Tennessee university. (p. 470)

Villa, Francisco "Pancho" (1878–1923) Mexican bandit and revolutionary leader; he led revolts against Carranza and Huerta. He was pursued by the United States but evaded General Pershing. (p. 573)

Villaraigosa, Antonio (1953–) Latino mayor of Los Angeles, elected to office in 2005. (p. 1099)

Walesa, Lech (1943–) Polish labor leader and electrician, he was president of Poland from 1990–1995. (p. 1055)

Wald, Lillian (1867–1940) Founder of the Henry Street Settlement house in New York City. (p. 498)

Wallace, George (1919–1998) American politician; he was a four-time governor of Alabama who fought against segregation in the South in the 1960s. (p. 970)

Warren, Earl (1891–1974) American jurist and politician, he was Chief Justice of the Supreme Court from 1953 to 1969. Under his leadership the court made many decisions that extended individual rights. (p. 890)

Washington, Booker T. (1856–1915) African American educator and civil rights leader; he was born into slavery and later became head of the Tuskegee Institute for career training for African Americans. (p. 509)

Washington, George (1732–1799) First president of the United States; he served as a representative to the Continental Congresses and commanded the Continental Army during the Revolutionary War. (p. 90)

Watie, Stand (1806–1871) Cherokee leader and Confederate general; he was the only Native American on either side to hold such rank in the war. (p. 382)

Webster, Noah (1758–1843) American author who published works on American grammar and language, his most famous work was *An American Dictionary of the English Language*, published in 1828, which included thousands of words that had not been previously defined in other dictionaries. (p. 240)

Westmoreland, William (1914–) American general in the U.S. Army; he was the commander of U.S. ground troops in South Vietnam during the Vietnam War. (p. 958)

Whitefield, George (1714–1770) British minister who held religious open-air meetings throughout the American colonies during the Great Awakening. (p. 86)

Whitney, Eli (1765–1825) American inventor whose cotton gin changed cotton harvesting procedures and enabled large increases in cotton production; he introduced the technology of mass production through the development of interchangeable parts in gun-making. (p. 256)

Wilhelm II, Kaiser (1859–1941) German emperor and king of Prussia; his militarism helped cause and prolong World War I. (p. 583)

Wilkie, Wendell (1892–1944) Franklins Roosevelt's opponent in the 1940 Presidential election. (p. 755)

Willard, Frances (1839–1898) Temperance and women's suffrage advocate, she was a leader in the Women's Christian Temperance Union (WCTU) and the Prohibition Party. (p. 531)

William and Mary King William III (1650–1702) and Queen Mary II (1662–1694); Rulers of Great Britain who replaced King James II as a result of the Glorious Revolution. (p. 74)

Williams, Roger (1603–1683) Puritan Separatist who was banished from the Massachusetts Bay Colony in 1635 for preaching that government and religion should be separate, and that settlers should compensate Native Americans for their land, rather than taking it. He later established a colony in Providence, Rhode Island in 1636 where all religions were welcome. (p. 54)

Wilson, Woodrow (1856–1924) Twenty-eighth president of the United States; he proposed the League of Nations after World War I. His reform legislation included direct election of senators, prohibition, and women's suffrage. He also created the Federal Reserve System and the Federal Trade Commission, and he enacted child labor laws. (p. 543)

Winthrop, John (1588–1649) Leader of the Massachusetts Bay Colony who led Puritan colonists to Massachusetts to establish an ideal Christian community; he later became the colony's first governor. (p. 53)

Wright, Orville (1871–1948) and **Wilbur** (1867–1912) American pioneers of aviation; they went from experiments with kites and gliders to piloting the first successful gas-powered airplane flight and later founded the American Wright Company to manufacture airplanes. (p. 479)

Young, Andrew (1932–) American politician with a background in the civil rights movement; he served as American ambassador to the United Nations under President Carter. (p. 941)

Yeltsin, Boris (1931–2007) Russian politician and president of Russia in the 1990s; he was the first popularly elected leader of the country. (p. 1062)

Zapata, Emiliano (1879–1919) Mexican revolutionary, he led the revolt against Porfirio Díaz in the south of Mexico during the Mexican Revolution. (p. 573)

The United States of America: Political

CANADA

WASHINGTON
Seattle
Tacoma
Olympia ★
Spokane
Portland
Salem ★
Eugene

OREGON

Cape Mendocino

Goose Lake

Shasta Lake

Sacramento River

Berkeley
Oakland
San Francisco
San Francisco Bay
San Jose
Monterey Bay

San Joaquin River

Reno
★ Carson City

NEVADA

Fresno

CALIFORNIA

Santa Barbara
Ventura
Los Angeles
Long Beach
Anaheim
Santa Ana
San Diego
Channel Islands
Riverside
Palm Springs

PACIFIC OCEAN

Las Vegas

Lake Mead

Colorado River

IDAHO
★ Boise
Sun Valley

Snake River

Pocatello

MONTANA
Great Falls
Helena ★
Billings

Yellowstone Lake

WYOMING

Cheyenne ★

Ogden
★ Salt Lake City
Provo

UTAH

ARIZONA
Flagstaff

Phoenix ★

Casa Grande
Tucson

Gila River

Salton Sea

NORTH DAKOTA
★ Bismarck

SOUTH DAKOTA
Pierre ★
Rapid City

NEBRASKA

Boulder
Vail
★ Denver
Aspen
Colorado Springs

COLORADO
Pueblo

Arkansas River

KANSAS

Taos
Santa Fe ★
Albuquerque

NEW MEXICO

Las Cruces
El Paso

OKLAHOMA
Oklahoma City
Lawton

Amarillo

Lubbock

Abilene
Fort Worth

Midland
Odessa

TEXAS

Austin
San Antonio

Corpus Christi
Laredo
Padre Island

MEXICO

To understand the relative locations of Alaska and Hawaii, as well as the vast distances separating them from the rest of the United States, see the world map.

HAWAII
Kauai
Niihau
Oahu
Honolulu ★
Molokai
Lanai
Maui
Kahoolawe
Hilo
Hawaii

PACIFIC OCEAN

0   75   150 Miles
0   75   150 Kilometers
Projection: Mercator

RUSSIA

Bering Strait

ARCTIC OCEAN

Nome
Yukon River
Fairbanks

ALASKA

Anchorage
Valdez
Skagway
Juneau

Gulf of Alaska
Kodiak Island
Alexander Archipelago

CANADA

Bering Sea
St. Lawrence Island
St. Matthew Island
Nunivak Island
Attu Island

0   250   500 Miles
0   250   500 Kilometers
Projection: Albers Equal Area

PACIFIC OCEAN

Gulf of California

ATLAS

CANADA

Grand Forks
Fargo
MINNESOTA
Duluth
Superior
Marquette
Sault Ste. Marie
MICHIGAN
Lake Superior

MAINE
Augusta
Burlington
Montpelier
Portland
Lake Champlain
VT
NH
Concord
Manchester
St. Lawrence River
Hudson R.

WISCONSIN
Minneapolis
St. Paul
Green Bay
Madison
Milwaukee
Lake Michigan
Lake Huron
Grand Rapids
Saginaw
Lansing
Detroit
Ann Arbor

Sioux Falls
Sioux City
IOWA
Cedar Rapids
Davenport
Des Moines
Rockford
Chicago
Gary
South Bend
Fort Wayne
Toledo
Cleveland
Youngstown
Akron
Lake Erie
Erie

Lake Ontario
Rochester
Syracuse
Buffalo
NEW YORK
Albany
Springfield
MA
Boston
Worcester
Providence
Cape Cod
Hartford
CT
RI
New Haven
Bridgeport
Long Island Sound
Yonkers
Long Island
Jersey City
Newark
New York City
Trenton

Omaha
Lincoln
MISSOURI
Kansas City
Kansas City
Topeka
Peoria
INDIANA
Springfield
Indianapolis
ILLINOIS
St. Louis
East St. Louis
Dayton
Cincinnati
OHIO
Columbus
PENNSYLVANIA
Allentown
Harrisburg
Pittsburgh
Philadelphia
Camden
Atlantic City
NJ
DE
Baltimore
MD
Dover
Washington, D.C.
Annapolis
Delaware Bay
Susquehanna River

ATLANTIC OCEAN

Wichita
Jefferson City
Lake of the Ozarks
Louisville
Evansville
Frankfort
Lexington
KENTUCKY
Ohio River
WEST VIRGINIA
Charleston
VIRGINIA
Richmond
Newport News
Norfolk
Virginia Beach
Chesapeake
70°W
35°N
Cape Hatteras

Keystone Lake
Tulsa
Fayetteville
Springfield
Lake Barkley
Kentucky Lake
Nashville
TENNESSEE
Chattanooga
Knoxville
Asheville
Charlotte
NORTH CAROLINA
Winston-Salem
Greensboro
Durham
Raleigh

Eufaula Lake
Lake Texoma
ARKANSAS
Little Rock
Pine Bluff
Memphis
Huntsville
Greenville
SOUTH CAROLINA
Columbia

National capital
State capitals
Other cities
0 100 200 Miles
0 100 200 Kilometers
Projection: Albers Equal Area

Dallas
Shreveport
MISSISSIPPI
Vicksburg
Meridian
Jackson
ALABAMA
Birmingham
Montgomery
Atlanta
GEORGIA
Macon
Columbus
Savannah
Savannah River
Charleston
Sea Islands
30°N

Waco
LOUISIANA
Beaumont
Houston
Baton Rouge
Biloxi
New Orleans
Chandeleur Islands
Mobile
Pensacola
Tallahassee
Jacksonville
Gainesville
FLORIDA
Cape Canaveral

Galveston
Gulf of Mexico
N
W E
S
St. Petersburg
Orlando
Tampa
Lake Okeechobee
Fort Myers
Fort Lauderdale
Miami
Cape Sable
Florida Keys
THE BAHAMAS
25°N
Straits of Florida
80°W
75°W

Minnesota River
Red River
Missouri River
Mississippi River
Red River
95°W
90°W
85°W
25°N

The United States of America: Physical

CANADA

MEXICO

COAST RANGES

CASCADE RANGE

ROCKY

MOUNTAINS

GREAT INTERIOR PLAINS

SIERRA NEVADA

GREAT BASIN

COLORADO PLATEAU

Coast Ranges

Mount Rainier
14,410 ft.
(4,392 m)

Puget Sound

Franklin D. Roosevelt Lake

Pend Oreille

Flathead River

Flathead Lake

Milk River

Missouri River

Fort Peck Lake

Lake Sakakawea

Columbia River

Bitterroot Range

Salmon River Mts.

Salmon River

CONTINENTAL

Lewis Range

Clark Fork

Yellowstone River

Bighorn Mts.

Powder River

Lake Oahe

Sawtooth Mts.

Grand Tetons

Yellowstone Lake

Bighorn River

Black Hills

Cheyenne River

White River

James River

Klamath River

Goose Lake

Snake River

Columbia Plateau

Gannett Peak
13,804 ft.
(4,207 m)

Wind River Range

Cape Mendocino

Shasta Lake

Pyramid Lake

Great Salt Lake

Wasatch Range

Uinta Mts.

DIVIDE

Front Range

North Platte River

South Platte River

Republican River

San Francisco Bay

Sacramento River

Lake Tahoe

Utah Lake

Green River

Mount Elbert
14,433 ft.
(4,400 m)

Pikes Peak
14,110 ft.
(4,301 m)

Smoky Hill River

Central Valley

COLORADO

Monterey Bay

San Joaquin River

Mount Whitney
14,494 ft.
(4,419 m)

Death Valley

Colorado River

Lake Powell

San Juan River

San Luis Valley

Sangre De Cristo Mts.

Mojave Desert

Lake Mead

Grand Canyon

Painted Desert

DIVIDE

PACIFIC

OCEAN

Channel Islands

Salton Sea

Imperial Valley

Sonoran Desert

Gila River

Rio Grande

CONTINENTAL

Canadian River

Pecos River

Colorado River

Amistad Reservoir

Rio Grande

Nueces River

Padre Island

Gulf of California

To understand the relative locations of Alaska and Hawaii, as well as the vast distances separating them from the rest of the United States, see the world map.

45°N
40°N
35°N
30°N
125°W
120°W

HAWAII

Kauai
Niihau
Oahu
Molokai
Lanai
Maui
Kahoolawe
Hawaii

PACIFIC OCEAN

Mauna Kea
13,796 ft.
(4,206 m)

22°N
19°N
160°W
155°W

| 0 | 75 | 150 Miles |
| 0 | 75 | 150 Kilometers |

Projection: Mercator

RUSSIA

ARCTIC OCEAN

BROOKS RANGE

Bering Strait

Arctic Circle

Yukon River

Tanana River

CANADA

St. Lawrence Island

St. Matthew Island

Nunivak Island

Kuskokwim River

ALASKA RANGE

Mount McKinley
20,320 ft.
(6,194 m)

Bering Sea

Attu Island

Kodiak Island

Gulf of Alaska

Alexander Archipelago

PACIFIC OCEAN

55°N
50°N
40°N
170°E
180°
150°W
55°N

| 0 | 250 | 500 Miles |
| 0 | 250 | 500 Kilometers |

Projection: Albers Equal Area

CANADA

Red River

Mesabi Range

Isle Royale

Lake Superior

Minnesota River

Mississippi River

Wisconsin River

Lake Michigan

Lake Huron

St. Lawrence River

St. Lawrence Seaway

St. John River

Longfellow Mts.

Penobscot River

Lake Champlain

Green Mts.

White Mts.

Connecticut River

Adirondack Mts.

Lake Ontario

Cape Cod

Hudson River

Long Island Sound

Long Island

Des Moines River

Missouri River

Kansas R.

Illinois River

Wabash River

Scioto River

PLATEAU

Allegheny R.

Susquehanna River

ALLEGHENY

APPALACHIAN

MOUNTAINS

Delaware River

Monongahela R.

Kanawha River

Potomac River

Delaware Bay

Chesapeake Bay

ATLANTIC OCEAN

40

70°W

OR

PLAINS

Ohio River

James River

Lake of the Ozarks

OZARK PLATEAU

Keystone Lake

Lake Barkley

Cumberland River

Cumberland Plateau

BLUE RIDGE MOUNTAINS

Roanoke River

Pamlico Sound

Cape Hatteras

35°N

White River

Kentucky Lake

Great Smoky Mts.

Eufaula Lake

Arkansas River

Tennessee River

PIEDMONT

Lake Texoma

Ouachita Mts.

Coosa River

Oconee River

Savannah River

Trinity River

Sabine River

Red River

Mississippi River

Tombigbee River

Pearl River

Alabama R.

Chattahoochee River

Altamaha River

Sea Islands

Brazos River

Toledo Bend Reservoir

GULF

COASTAL

PLAIN

Chandeleur Islands

Mississippi Delta

Okefenokee Swamp

FLORIDA PENINSULA

Cape Canaveral

80°W

N
W   E
S

GULF

Gulf of Mexico

85°W

90°W

25°N

95°W

Lake Okeechobee

The Everglades

Cape Sable

Florida Keys

Straits of Florida

THE BAHAMAS

25°N

75°W

ELEVATION

Feet		Meters
13,120		4,000
6,560		2,000
1,640		500
656		200
(Sea level) 0		0 (Sea level)
Below sea level		Below sea level

0   100   200 Miles

0   100   200 Kilometers

Projection: Albers Equal Area

World: Political

ATLAS

ARCTIC OCEAN

Greenland (DENMARK)

ALASKA (U.S.)

Godthåb

ICELAND

Arctic

60°N

CANADA

Aleutian Islands

Winnipeg

Vancouver

Ottawa   Montreal

NORTH AMERICA

Chicago   Toronto

UNITED STATES

New York City

40°N

Washington, D.C.

ATLANTIC OCEAN

Rabat

Los Angeles

Casablanca

MOROCCO

Houston

Bermuda (U.K.)

WESTERN SAHARA (Sovereignty Disputed)

MEXICO

Tropic of Cancer

20°N

Mexico City

MAURITANIA   MA

Nouakchott

HAWAII (U.S.)

CAPE VERDE

SENEGAL

Dakar

Bamako   BURKIN

GAMBIA

GUINEA-BISSAU   GUINEA   FAS

Caracas

SIERRA   GHA

VENEZUELA   GUYANA

LEONE   CÔTE

SURINAME

D'IVOIRE

Bogotá   Georgetown

Paramaribo   FRENCH GUIANA (FRANCE)

LIBERIA

COLOMBIA

PACIFIC OCEAN

Quito

0°   Equator

Galápagos Islands (ECUADOR)   ECUADOR

KIRIBATI

PERU

SOUTH AMERICA

Lima

BRAZIL

SAMOA   American Samoa

BOLIVIA   Brasília

La Paz

Sucre

20°S

TONGA

Tropic of Capricorn

PARAGUAY   Rio de Janeiro

São Paulo

CHILE   Asunción

ATLANTIC OCEAN

URUGUAY

Santiago   Buenos Aires   Montevideo

ARGENTINA

Falkland Islands (U.K.)

South Georgia (U.K.)

South Sandwich Islands

Legend:

Boundaries

⊛ National capitals

• Other cities

0   500   1,000 Miles

0   500   1,000 Kilometers

Projection: Mollweide

60°S

160°W   140°W   120°W   100°W   80°W   60°W   40°W   20°W

Antarctic Circle

Caribbean inset:

0   200   400 Miles

0   200   400 Kilometers

Projection: Mercator

90°W   80°W

FLORIDA (U.S.)

70°W

Nassau

Tropic of Cancer

BAHAMAS

60°W

Havana

ATLANTIC OCEAN

CUBA

Turks and Caicos Is. (U.K.)

20°N

GULF OF MEXICO

Cayman Is. (U.K.)

HAITI   DOMINICAN REPUBLIC

Virgin Islands (U.S. and U.K.)

Port-au-Prince

1

MEXICO   BELIZE

JAMAICA   Kingston

Santo Domingo

Guadeloupe (FRANCE)

Belmopan

Puerto Rico (U.S.)   2

GUATEMALA   HONDURAS

CARIBBEAN SEA

3   Martinique (FRANCE)

Guatemala City   Tegucigalpa

Netherlands Antilles (NETHERLANDS)

4   5   6

San Salvador   NICARAGUA

Aruba (NETHERLANDS)

EL SALVADOR   Managua

Port-of-Spain   7

COSTA RICA   Panama City

TRINIDAD AND TOBAGO

San José

10°N

PANAMA   VENEZUELA

PACIFIC OCEAN

COLOMBIA   GUYANA

90°W

COUNTRY	CAPITAL
1 Antigua and Barbuda	St. Johns
2 St. Kitts and Nevis	Basseterre
3 Dominica	Roseau
4 St. Lucia	Castries
5 St. Vincent and the Grenadines	Kingstown
6 Barbados	Bridgetown
7 Grenada	St. George's

ARCTIC OCEAN

RUSSIA

EUROPE

Moscow

KAZAKHSTAN Astana Ulaanbaatar MONGOLIA Harbin

ASIA

Almaty KYRGYZSTAN Beijing NORTH KOREA JAPAN
Istanbul GEORGIA Baku UZBEKISTAN Tashkent P'yŏngyang Seoul Tokyo
Ankara ARMENIA TURKMENISTAN TAJIKISTAN Tianjin SOUTH KOREA Nagoya Yokohama
TURKEY AZERBAIJAN Ashgabat CHINA Osaka
Tunis Nicosia SYRIA Tehran Kabul Islamabad Wuhan
Algiers CYPRUS Beirut Damascus IRAN AFGHANISTAN PAKISTAN Delhi NEPAL Chongqing Shanghai
TUNISIA LEBANON Baghdad Kathmandu BHUTAN
Tripoli Jerusalem JORDAN IRAQ KUWAIT New Delhi BANGLADESH Guangzhou Taipei
ALGERIA ISRAEL Amman BAHRAIN QATAR OMAN Muscat Calcutta Dhaka Hong Kong TAIWAN
LIBYA Cairo SAUDI ARABIA UNITED ARAB INDIA MYANMAR LAOS Hanoi
EGYPT Riyadh EMIRATES Mumbai (Bombay) (BURMA) Northern Mariana (U.S.)

AFRICA NIGER CHAD OMAN YEMEN Chennai (Madras) Yangon (Rangoon) THAILAND VIETNAM Manila PACIFIC OCEAN
Niamey N'Djamena ERITREA Sanaa SRI LANKA CAMBODIA Bangkok PHILIPPINES Guam (U.S.) MARSHALL ISLANDS
NIGERIA Khartoum Asmara DJIBOUTI Colombo Phnom Penh Ho Chi Minh City
BENIN Abuja SUDAN Addis Ababa ETHIOPIA MALDIVES Kuala Lumpur BRUNEI PALAU FEDERATED STATES OF MICRONESIA
TOGO Lagos CENTRAL AFRICAN REPUBLIC MALAYSIA
EQUATORIAL GUINEA CAMEROON UGANDA SOMALIA Singapore SINGAPORE NAURU KIRIBATI
SÃO TOMÉ AND PRÍNCIPE GABON REP. OF THE CONGO KENYA INDONESIA Equator 0°
CABINDA (ANGOLA) DEMOCRATIC REPUBLIC OF THE CONGO RWANDA Nairobi PAPUA NEW GUINEA TUVALU
Kinshasa BURUNDI Jakarta Surabaya Port Moresby SOLOMON ISLANDS
Luanda TANZANIA Dodoma SEYCHELLES EAST TIMOR
ANGOLA MALAWI Dar es Salaam VANUATU
ZAMBIA COMOROS INDIAN OCEAN New Caledonia (FRANCE) FIJI
Lusaka MOZAMBIQUE MADAGASCAR Antananarivo
NAMIBIA ZIMBABWE Harare MAURITIUS Réunion (FRANCE) AUSTRALIA
Windhoek BOTSWANA Maputo Tropic of Capricorn
Gaborone Pretoria SWAZILAND
Johannesburg Bloemfontein LESOTHO Sydney
SOUTH AFRICA Canberra NEW ZEALAND
Cape Town Melbourne Wellington

ANTARCTICA Tasmania

COUNTRY	CAPITAL
1 Czech Republic	Prague
2 Slovakia	Bratislava
3 Slovenia	Ljubljana
4 Croatia	Zagreb
5 Bosnia and Herzegovina	Sarajevo
6 Macedonia	Skopje
7 Serbia	Belgrade
8 Montenegro	Podgorica
9 Lithuania	Vilnius
10 Latvia	Riga
11 Estonia	Tallinn

0 250 500 Miles
0 250 500 Kilometers
Projection: Mollweide

ICELAND Reykjavik Arctic Circle SWEDEN FINLAND Helsinki RUSSIA
NORWAY Oslo St. Petersburg
UNITED KINGDOM North Sea Stockholm 11 10
Dublin DENMARK Copenhagen 9 Minsk
IRELAND NETHERLANDS Berlin Warsaw BELARUS Moscow
London Amsterdam The Hague GERMANY POLAND
BELGIUM Brussels 1 Kiev UKRAINE
ATLANTIC OCEAN Paris LUXEMBOURG Vienna 2 Budapest MOLDOVA Chișinău
SWITZERLAND Bern AUSTRIA HUNGARY ROMANIA
FRANCE MONACO LIECHTENSTEIN 3 Bucharest
ITALY 4 BULGARIA
Corsica (FRANCE) SAN MARINO 5 7 Sofia Black Sea
ANDORRA VATICAN CITY Rome 8 Tirane ALBANIA
PORTUGAL Madrid Balearic Is. (SPAIN) Sardinia (ITALY) 6 GREECE
Lisbon SPAIN Mediterranean Sea Athens
Gibraltar (U.K.) Sicily MALTA Crete

North America: Political

ARCTIC OCEAN

ASIA

EUROPE

North Pole

ICELAND

Point Barrow

Queen Elizabeth Islands

Ellesmere Island

Greenland (DENMARK)

ALASKA (U.S.)

Beaufort Sea

Banks Island

Baffin Bay

Cape Farewell

Anchorage

Victoria Island

Baffin Island

Denmark Strait

Yukon River

Great Bear Lake

Juneau

Alexander Archipelago

Great Slave Lake

Southampton Island

Hudson Strait

Labrador Sea

Queen Charlotte Islands

Coats Island

Mansel Island

Vancouver Island

Peace River

Hudson Bay

Anticosti Island

Newfoundland

Edmonton

CANADA

St. Pierre and Miquelon (FRANCE)

Vancouver

Calgary

Lake Winnipeg

Prince Edward Island

Cape Breton Island

Seattle

Winnipeg

Lake Superior

Quebec

Portland

Columbia River

Lake Huron

Montreal

PACIFIC OCEAN

Missouri River

Minneapolis

Lake Michigan

Ottawa

Toronto

Lake Ontario

Lake Erie

Boston

Cape Cod

Cape Mendocino

Snake River

Milwaukee

Detroit

Cleveland

New York City

Philadelphia

ATLANTIC OCEAN

Great Salt Lake

Salt Lake City

Platte River

Chicago

Columbus

Baltimore

Washington, D.C.

San Francisco

San Jose

Denver

Kansas City

St. Louis

Ohio R.

Norfolk

Colorado River

Indianapolis

UNITED STATES

Los Angeles

San Diego

Tijuana

Phoenix

Red River

Memphis

Atlanta

Birmingham

Cape Hatteras

Bermuda (U.K.)

Rio Grande

Dallas

Austin

San Antonio

Houston

New Orleans

Mississippi River

Jacksonville

Cape Canaveral

Tropic of Cancer

THE BAHAMAS

Gulf of California

Gulf of Mexico

Florida Keys

Miami

Nassau

Turks and Caicos Islands (U.K.)

DOMINICAN REPUBLIC

Puerto Rico (U.S.)

ST. KITTS & NEVIS

Monterrey

Havana

CUBA

San Juan

ANTIGUA & BARBUDA

MEXICO

Mérida

Cayman Is. (U.K.)

Kingston

Port-au-Prince

HAITI

Santo Domingo

Virgin Is. (U.S., U.K.)

Guadeloupe (FRANCE)

DOMINICA

BARBADOS

Guadalajara

Mexico City

JAMAICA

Martinique (FRANCE)

ST. LUCIA

ST. VINCENT AND THE GRENADINES

Puebla

Balsas R.

Caribbean Sea

Netherlands Antilles (NETHERLANDS)

GRENADA

Belmopan

BELIZE

Aruba (NETHERLANDS)

GUATEMALA

HONDURAS

Tegucigalpa

TRINIDAD AND TOBAGO

Guatemala City

NICARAGUA

San Salvador

Managua

Panama Canal

EL SALVADOR

San José

Panama City

COSTA RICA

PANAMA

SOUTH AMERICA

Legend

- Boundaries
- ⊛ National capitals
- • Other cities

0   300   600 Miles
0   300   600 Kilometers
Projection: Azimuthal Equal Area

South America: Political

CENTRAL
AMERICA

Caribbean Sea

Barranquilla
Cartagena

Caracas

VENEZUELA

Georgetown
Paramaribo

ATLANTIC
OCEAN

Medellín

Bogotá

GUYANA

Cayenne

COLOMBIA

SURINAME

FRENCH
GUIANA
(FRANCE)

*Malpelo
Island*
(COLOMBIA)

Cali

Río Negro

Amazon River

Equator 0°

Quito

Amazon River

Belém

ECUADOR

Guayaquil

*Galápagos
Islands*
(ECUADOR)

0° Equator

PERU

BRAZIL

Recife

Trujillo

Marañón River

Ucayali River

Callao

Lima

Arequipa

*Lake
Titicaca*

La Paz

*Lake
Poopó*

BOLIVIA

Sucre

Brasília

São Francisco River

Salvador

**PACIFIC
OCEAN**

Belo Horizonte

Paraguay River

Campinas

PARAGUAY

São Paulo

Rio de Janeiro

Asunción

Curitiba

Tropic of Capricorn

Tropic of
Capricorn

San Félix Island
(CHILE)

*San Ambrosio
Island*
(CHILE)

Pôrto Alegre

CHILE

Uruguay River

Córdoba

*Juan Fernández
Islands*
(CHILE)

Valparaíso
Santiago

Rosario

URUGUAY

Buenos Aires

Montevideo

Río de la Plata

**ATLANTIC
OCEAN**

ARGENTINA

Boundaries

National capitals

Other cities

0	250	500 Miles
0	250	500 Kilometers

Projection: Azimuthal Equal Area

*Strait of
Magellan*

*Falkland
Islands* (U.K.)

*South Georgia
Island*
(U.K.)

*Tierra del
Fuego*

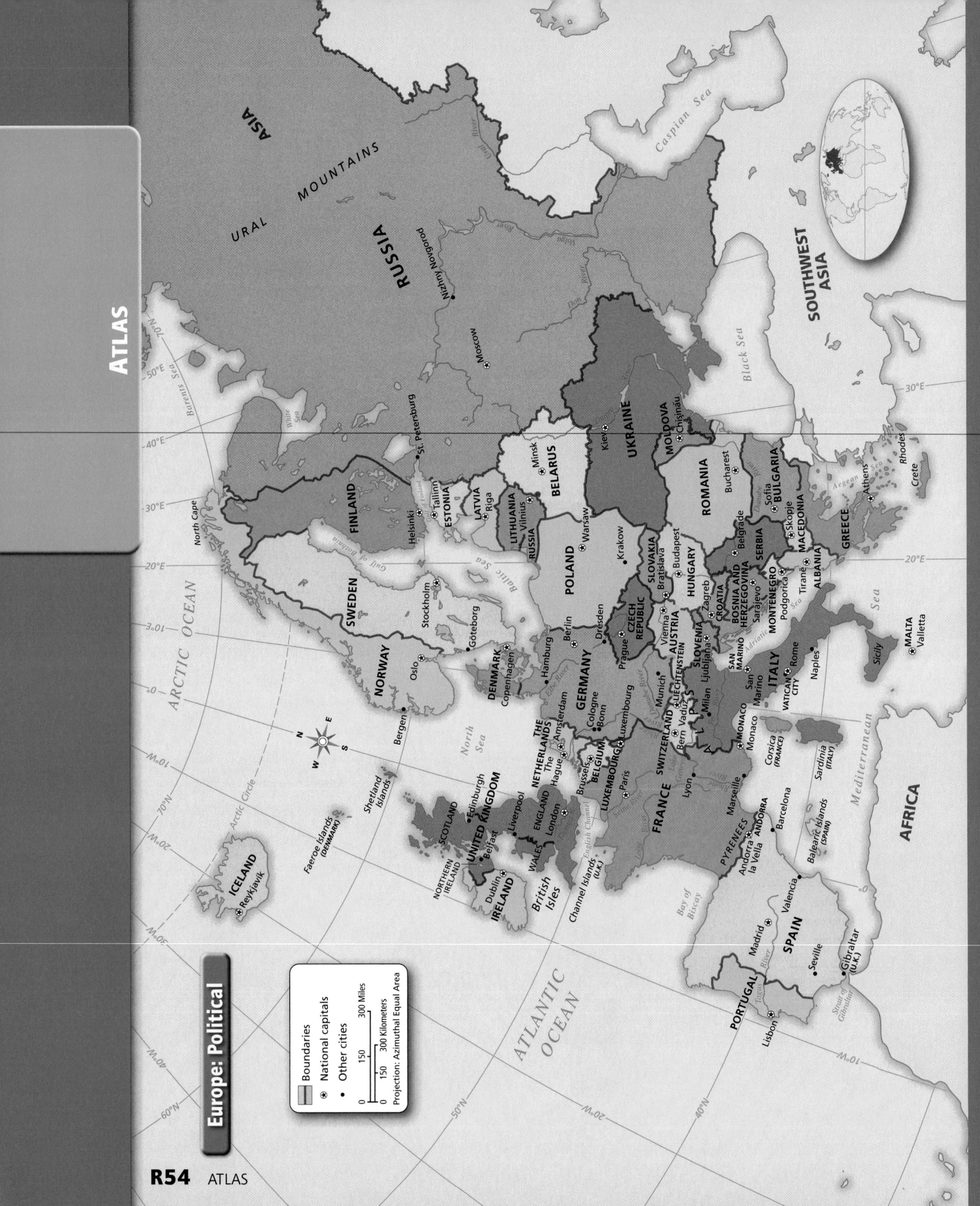

Europe: Political

Boundaries
⊛ National capitals
• Other cities

0   150   300 Miles
0   150   300 Kilometers
Projection: Azimuthal Equal Area

ASIA

URAL MOUNTAINS

RUSSIA

Nizhny Novgorod

Moscow

Ural River

Volga River

Don River

Caspian Sea

Black Sea

SOUTHWEST ASIA

Barents Sea

White Sea

North Cape

St. Petersburg

FINLAND

Helsinki

ESTONIA
Tallinn

LATVIA
Riga

LITHUANIA
Vilnius

RUSSIA

Minsk

BELARUS

Kiev

UKRAINE

MOLDOVA
Chişinău

ROMANIA
Bucharest

BULGARIA
Sofia

SERBIA
Belgrade

MACEDONIA
Skopje

Danube River

Gulf of Finland

Warsaw

POLAND

Krakow

SLOVAKIA
Bratislava

HUNGARY
Budapest

Vienna
AUSTRIA

Zagreb
CROATIA

SLOVENIA
Ljubljana

BOSNIA AND
HERZEGOVINA
Sarajevo

MONTENEGRO
Podgorica

ALBANIA
Tiranë

GREECE

Athens

Aegean Sea

Rhodes

Crete

SWEDEN

Stockholm

Göteborg

Baltic Sea

Gulf of Bothnia

ARCTIC OCEAN

Arctic Circle

Shetland Islands

Faeroe Islands
(DENMARK)

NORWAY

Oslo

Bergen

DENMARK
Copenhagen

Hamburg

Berlin

GERMANY

Dresden

Prague
CZECH REPUBLIC

Munich

LIECHTENSTEIN
Vaduz

Milan

SAN
MARINO
San Marino

ITALY
Rome

VATICAN CITY

Naples

Sicily

MALTA
Valletta

North Sea

Cologne
Bonn

Amsterdam
THE
NETHERLANDS
The Hague

Elbe River

Rhine River

Brussels
BELGIUM

LUXEMBOURG
Luxembourg

Paris

FRANCE

SWITZERLAND
Bern

Lake Geneva

Lyon

Marseille

MONACO
Monaco

Corsica
(FRANCE)

Sardinia
(ITALY)

Mediterranean Sea

Adriatic Sea

ICELAND
Reykjavik

SCOTLAND
Edinburgh

NORTHERN
IRELAND
Belfast

IRELAND
Dublin

Liverpool

ENGLAND
London

WALES

UNITED KINGDOM

British Isles

English Channel

Channel Islands
(U.K.)

Bay of Biscay

ANDORRA
Andorra la Vella

PYRENEES

Barcelona

Balearic Islands
(SPAIN)

SPAIN
Madrid

Valencia

Seville

Gibraltar
(U.K.)

Strait of Gibraltar

PORTUGAL
Lisbon

Tagus River

AFRICA

ATLANTIC OCEAN

AFRICA

N
W   E
S

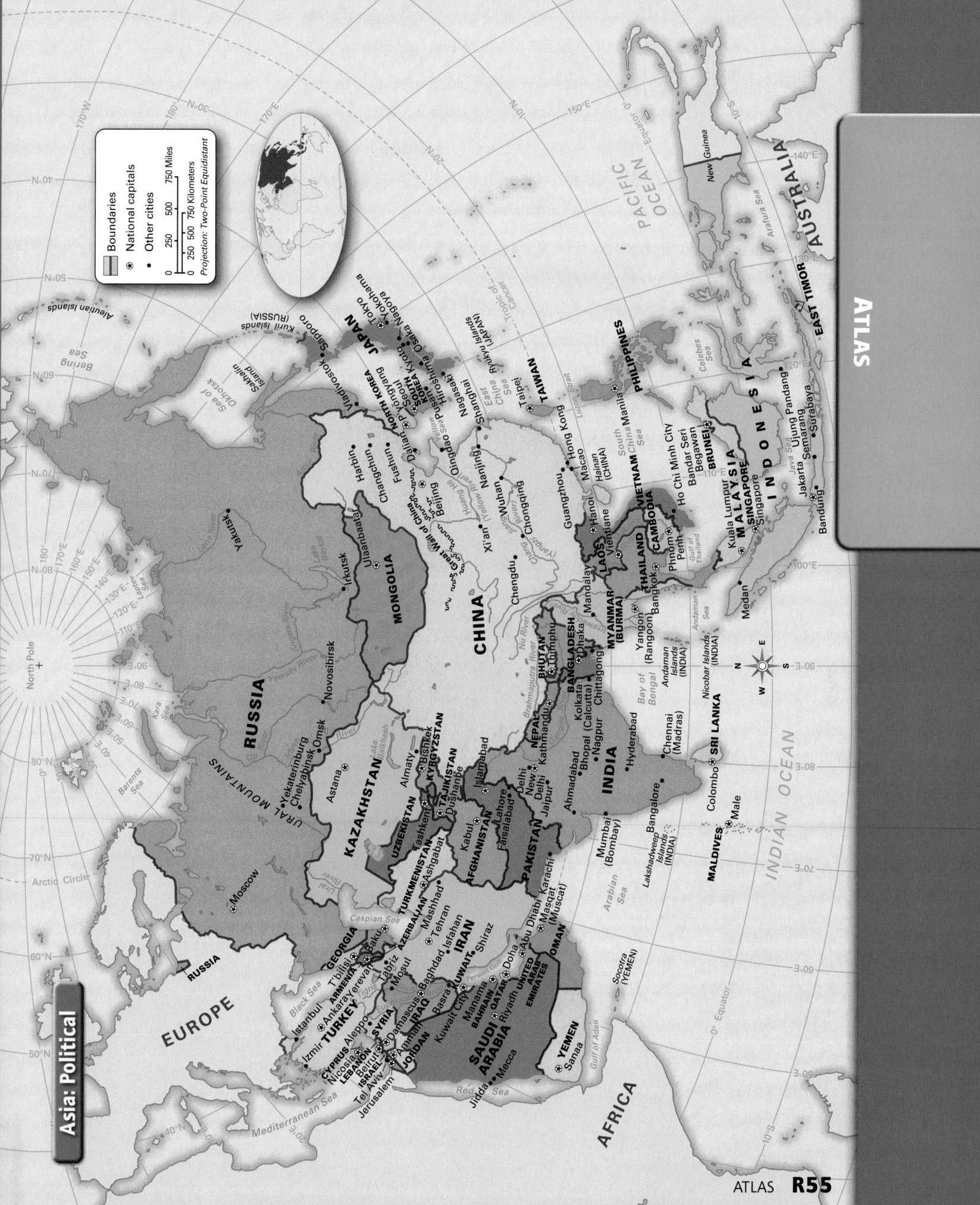

Asia: Political

Boundaries
⊛ National capitals
• Other cities

0 250 500 750 Miles
0 250 500 750 Kilometers
Projection: Two-Point Equidistant

EUROPE

RUSSIA

Moscow

Yekaterinburg
Chelyabinsk
Omsk
Novosibirsk

Astana

KAZAKHSTAN

Almaty
Bishkek
KYRGYZSTAN
Tashkent
UZBEKISTAN
TAJIKISTAN
Dushanbe
TURKMENISTAN
Ashgabat
Mashhad

Kabul
AFGHANISTAN

Lake Balkhash

Irkutsk

MONGOLIA
Ulaanbaatar

Lake Baikal

Yakutsk

CHINA

Great Wall of China

Beijing
Xi'an
Chengdu
Chongqing
Wuhan
Nanjing
Shanghai

Harbin
Changchun
Fushun
Dalian

NORTH KOREA
P'yongyang
SOUTH KOREA
Seoul
Pusan
Osaka
Kyoto
Nagoya
Tokyo
Yokohama
Sapporo

JAPAN

Hiroshima
Nagasaki

Vladivostok

Sea of Okhotsk
Sakhalin Island
Kuril Islands (RUSSIA)

Aleutian Islands

Bering Sea

Qingdao
Yellow Sea

Taipei
TAIWAN

Hong Kong
Macao
Hainan (CHINA)

Guangzhou

East China Sea
Ryukyu Islands (JAPAN)

PACIFIC OCEAN

New Guinea

AUSTRALIA

EAST TIMOR

INDONESIA

Arafura Sea

Celebes Sea

PHILIPPINES
Manila

South China Sea

Luzon Strait

Hanoi
VIETNAM
Vientiane
LAOS
THAILAND
Bangkok
CAMBODIA
Phnom Penh
Ho Chi Minh City
Bandar Seri Begawan
BRUNEI
MALAYSIA
Kuala Lumpur
SINGAPORE
Singapore

Gulf of Thailand

MYANMAR (BURMA)
Mandalay
Yangon (Rangoon)

BANGLADESH
Dhaka
Chittagong

BHUTAN
Thimphu
NEPAL
Kathmandu

INDIA

Kolkata (Calcutta)
Bhopal
Nagpur
Hyderabad
Chennai (Madras)
Bangalore
SRI LANKA
Colombo
Male
MALDIVES

Mumbai (Bombay)

Ahmadabad
New Delhi
Delhi
Jaipur
Lahore
Faisalabad
PAKISTAN
Islamabad
Karachi

Bay of Bengal

Andaman Islands (INDIA)
Nicobar Islands (INDIA)

Andaman Sea

Lakshadweep Islands (INDIA)

Arabian Sea

INDIAN OCEAN

RUSSIA

GEORGIA
T'bilisi
ARMENIA
Yerevan
AZERBAIJAN
Baku
Tabriz
Mosul
IRAN
Tehran
Isfahan
Shiraz
Mashhad

Caspian Sea

Black Sea

Istanbul
Ankara
TURKEY
Izmir
Aleppo
CYPRUS
Nicosia
LEBANON
Beirut
ISRAEL
Tel Aviv
Jerusalem
SYRIA
Damascus
JORDAN
Amman

IRAQ
Baghdad
Basra
KUWAIT
Kuwait City
BAHRAIN
Manama
QATAR
Doha
Riyadh
SAUDI ARABIA
Mecca
Jidda

UNITED ARAB EMIRATES
Abu Dhabi
Masqat (Muscat)
OMAN

YEMEN
Sanaa

Socotra (YEMEN)

Gulf of Aden

Red Sea

Mediterranean Sea

AFRICA

North Pole

Arctic Circle

URAL MOUNTAINS

Barents Sea
Kara Sea

Tigris River
Euphrates
Persian Gulf
Gulf of Oman

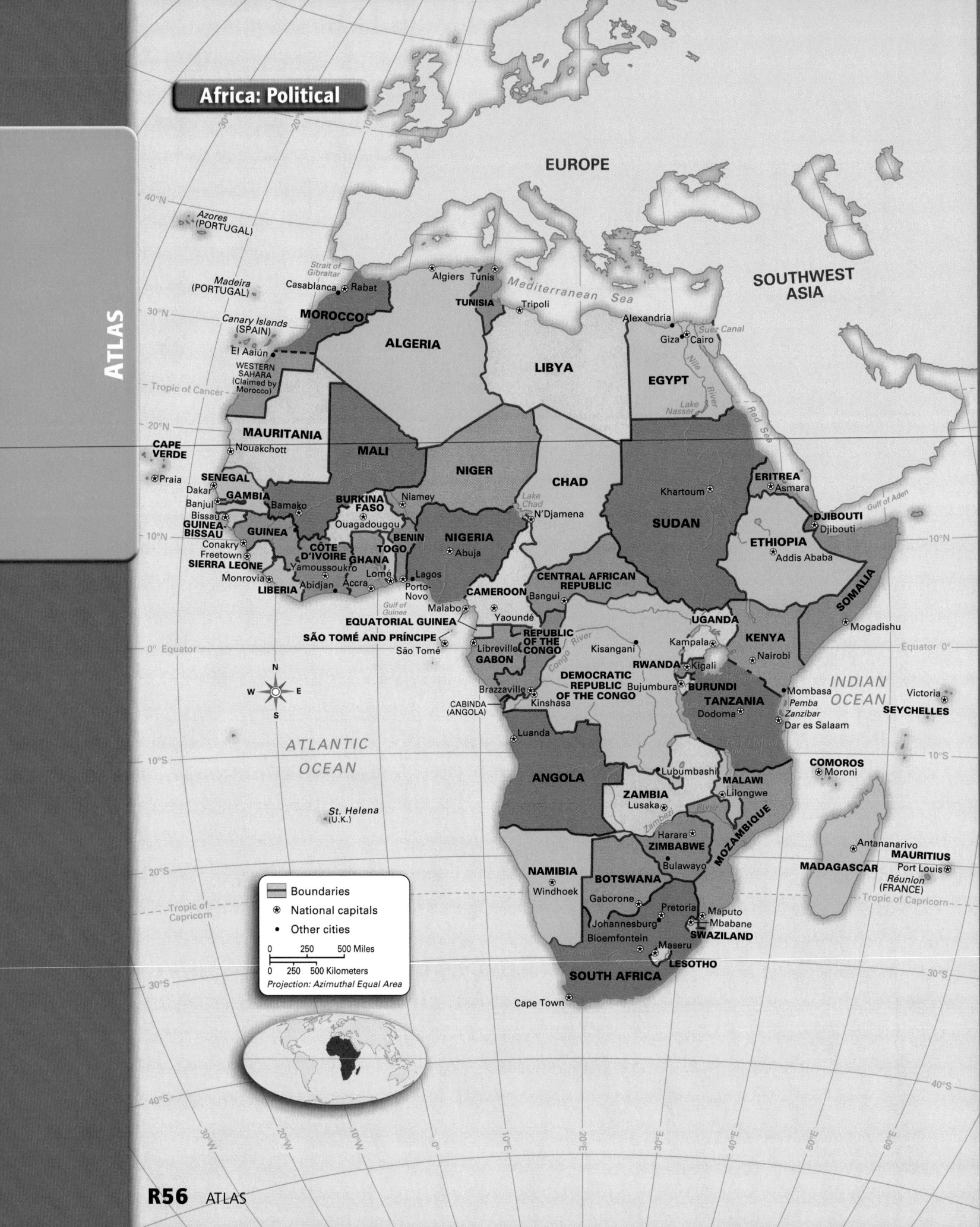

Africa: Political

EUROPE

SOUTHWEST ASIA

Mediterranean Sea

Legend:
- Boundaries
- ⊛ National capitals
- • Other cities

0   250   500 Miles
0   250   500 Kilometers
Projection: Azimuthal Equal Area

ATLAS

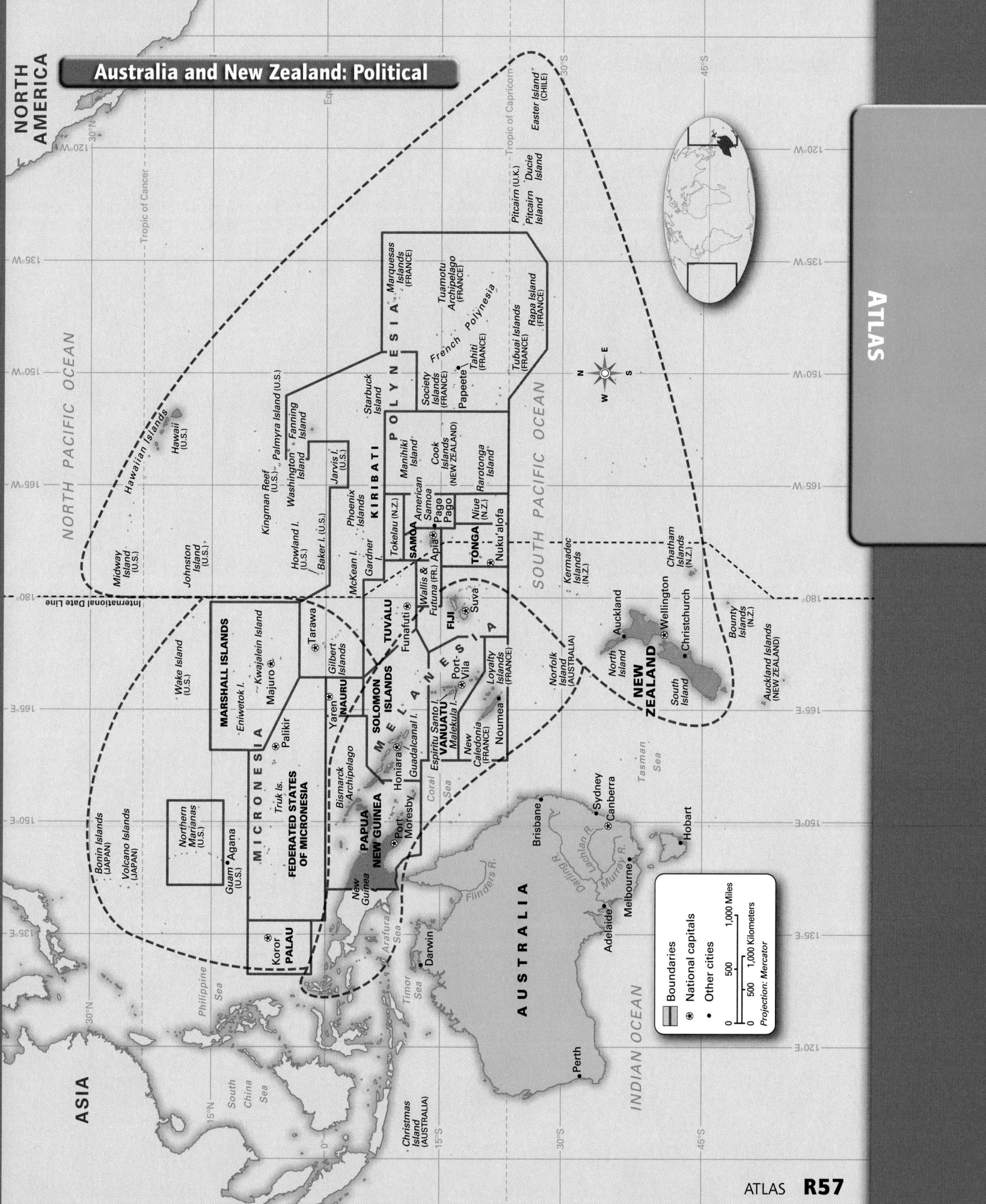

Australia and New Zealand: Political

NORTH AMERICA

ATLAS

ASIA

NORTH PACIFIC OCEAN

SOUTH PACIFIC OCEAN

INDIAN OCEAN

POLYNESIA

MICRONESIA

MELANESIA

KIRIBATI

MARSHALL ISLANDS

FEDERATED STATES OF MICRONESIA

PALAU

PAPUA NEW GUINEA

SOLOMON ISLANDS

NAURU

TUVALU

VANUATU

FIJI

SAMOA

TONGA

NEW ZEALAND

AUSTRALIA

Marquesas Islands (FRANCE)
Tuamotu Archipelago (FRANCE)
French Polynesia
Rapa Island (FRANCE)
Society Islands (FRANCE)
Tahiti (FRANCE)
Papeete
Tubuai Islands (FRANCE)
Starbuck Island
Manihiki Island
Cook Islands (NEW ZEALAND)
Rarotonga Island
Pitcairn (U.K.)
Ducie Island
Easter Island (CHILE)
Pitcairn Island

Hawaiian Islands
Hawaii (U.S.)
Palmyra Island (U.S.)
Fanning Island
Washington Island
Kingman Reef (U.S.)
Phoenix Islands
Jarvis I. (U.S.)
Howland I. (U.S.)
Baker I. (U.S.)
McKean I.
Gardner
Tokelau (N.Z.)
American Samoa
Pago Pago
Niue (N.Z.)
Apia
Nuku'alofa

Midway Island (U.S.)
Johnston Island (U.S.)
Wake Island (U.S.)
Kwajalein Island
Eniwetok I.
Majuro
Palikir
Tarawa
Gilbert Islands
Yaren
Funafuti
Wallis & Futuna (FR.)
Suva
Port-Vila
Espiritu Santo I.
Malekula I.
Loyalty Islands (FRANCE)
New Caledonia (FRANCE)
Noumea
Norfolk Island (AUSTRALIA)
Kermadec Islands (N.Z.)
Auckland
North Island
Wellington
Christchurch
South Island
Chatham Islands (N.Z.)
Bounty Islands (N.Z.)
Auckland Islands (NEW ZEALAND)

Bonin Islands (JAPAN)
Volcano Islands (JAPAN)
Northern Marianas (U.S.)
Guam (U.S.)
Agana
Truk Is.
Bismarck Archipelago
Honiara
Guadalcanal I.
Port Moresby
New Guinea
Koror

Christmas Island (AUSTRALIA)

Philippine Sea
South China Sea
Timor Sea
Arafura Sea
Coral Sea
Tasman Sea

Darwin
Brisbane
Sydney
Canberra
Melbourne
Hobart
Adelaide
Perth

Flinders R.
Darling R.
Lachlan R.
Murray R.

Tropic of Cancer
Equator
Tropic of Capricorn
International Date Line

NORTH
N E
W S

Boundaries
⊛ National capitals
• Other cities

500   1,000 Miles
0   500   1,000 Kilometers
Projection: Mercator

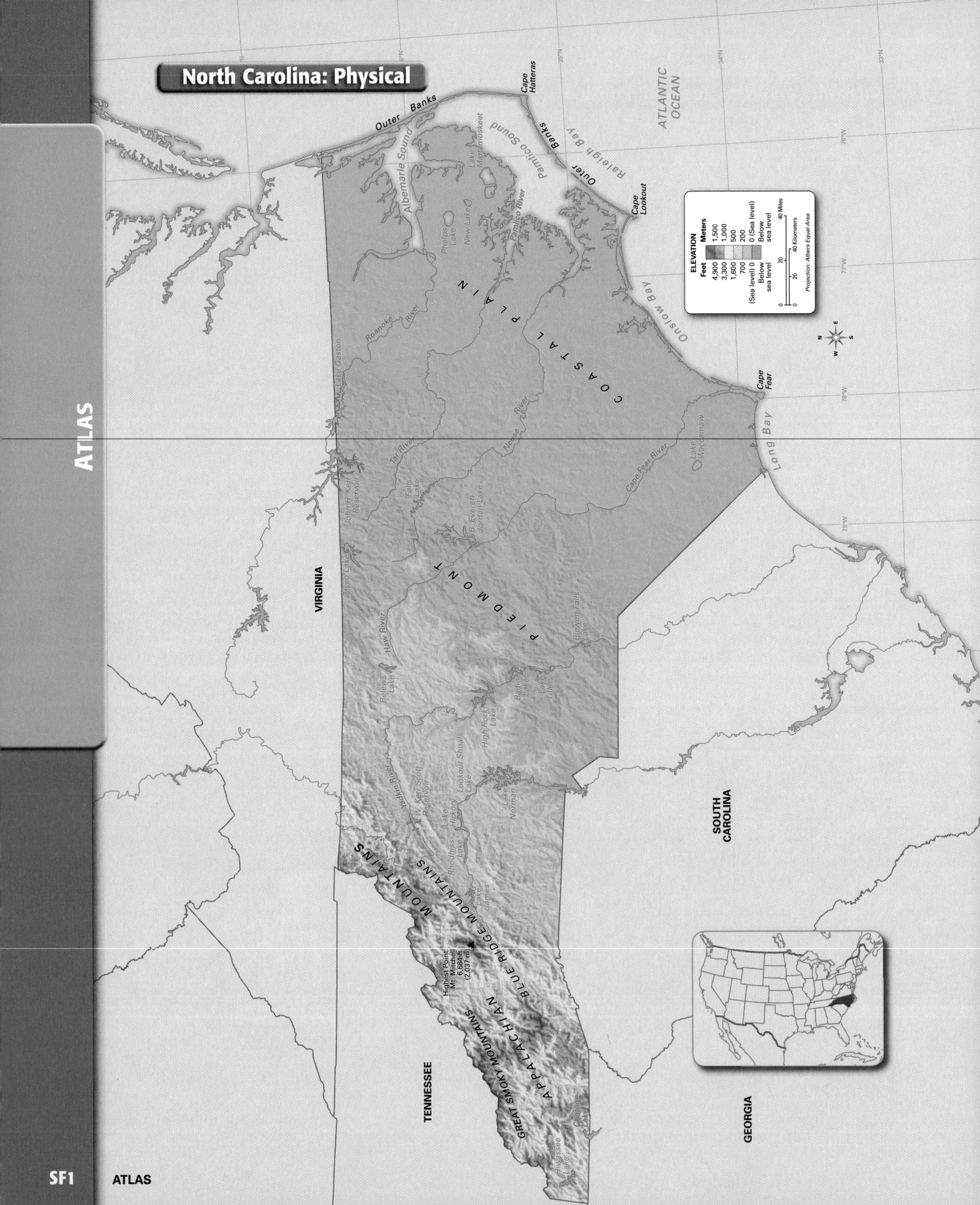

North Carolina: Physical

ATLANTIC OCEAN

Cape Hatteras

Outer Banks

Outer Banks

Albemarle Sound

Pamlico Sound

Lake Mattamuskeet

Pamlico River

Raleigh Bay

Cape Lookout

Phelps Lake

New Lake

Onslow Bay

COASTAL PLAIN

Roanoke River

Lake Gaston

Neuse River

Cape Fear

Tar River

Falls Lake

B. Everett Jordan Lake

Cape Fear River

Long Bay

Lake Waccamaw

PIEDMONT

Kerr Reservoir

John H. Kerr Reservoir

VIRGINIA

Haw River

Belews Lake

Badin Lake

Lake Tillery

Blewett Falls Lake

High Rock Lake

Lake Norman

Yadkin River

W. Kerr Scott Reservoir

Lookout Shoals Lake

Lake Hickory

Rhodhiss Lake

SOUTH CAROLINA

MOUNTAINS

Lake James

Highest Point: Mt. Mitchell 6,684 ft (2,037 m)

TENNESSEE

GREAT SMOKY MOUNTAINS

APPALACHIAN

BLUE RIDGE MOUNTAINS

Tuckasegee River

GEORGIA

ELEVATION

Feet	Meters
4,900	1,500
3,300	1,000
1,600	500
700	200
0 (Sea level)	0 (Sea level)
Below sea level	Below sea level

Projection: Albers Equal-Area

40 Miles

40 Kilometers

N
W   E
S

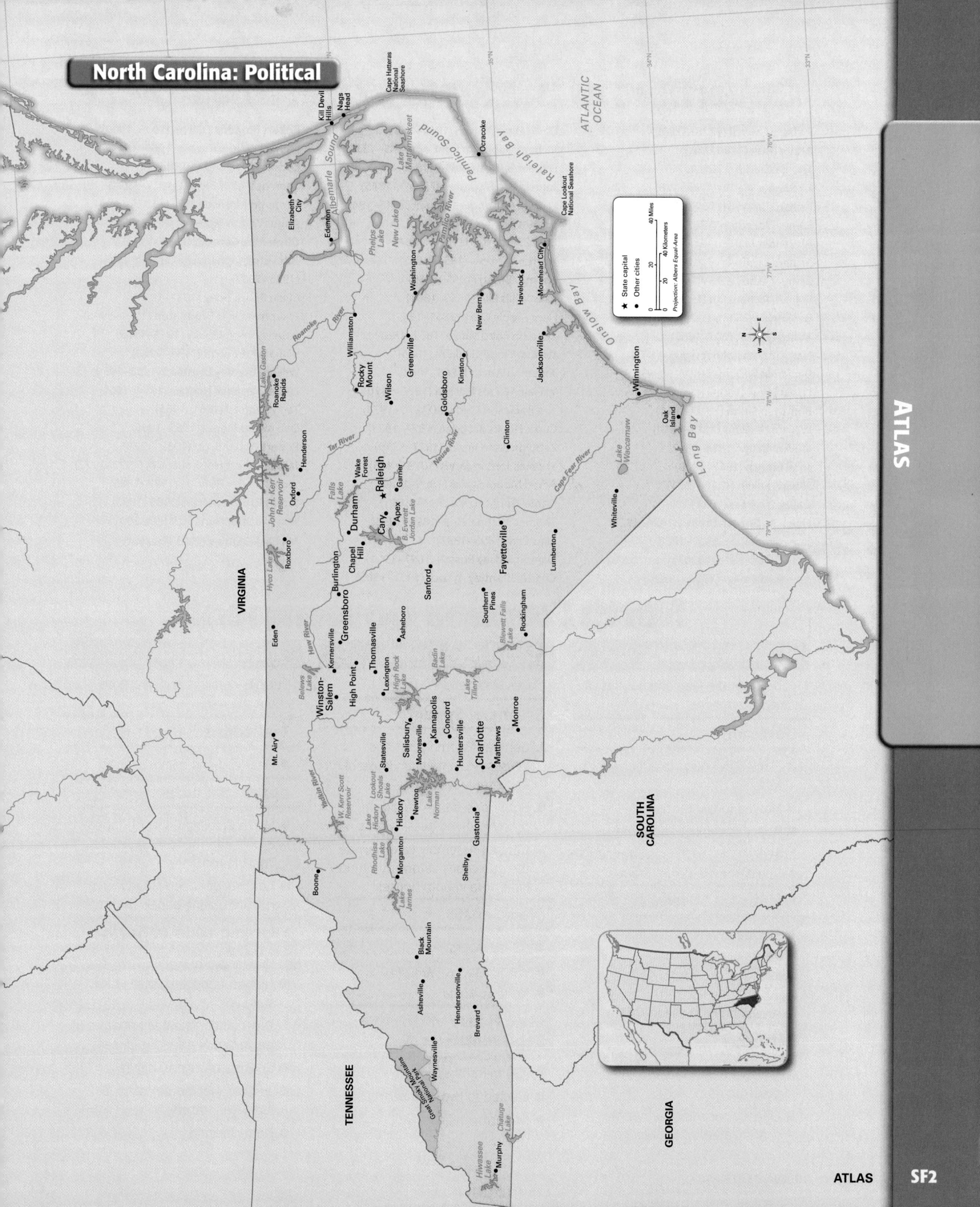

North Carolina: Political

ATLANTIC OCEAN

Cape Hatteras National Seashore

Kill Devil Hills
Nags Head

Ocracoke

Cape Lookout National Seashore

Albemarle Sound

Pamlico Sound

Raleigh Bay

Elizabeth City

Edenton

Phelps Lake

New Lake

Lake Mattamuskeet

Roanoke River

Williamston

Washington

Pamlico River

Greenville

Morehead City

Havelock

New Bern

Onslow Bay

Roanoke Rapids

Rocky Mount

Wilson

Goldsboro

Kinston

Jacksonville

Wilmington

Lake Gaston

Henderson

Tar River

Clinton

Neuse River

Oak Island

Lake Waccamaw

Long Bay

Oxford

John H. Kerr Reservoir

Wake Forest

Raleigh

Garner

Falls Lake

Durham

Cary

Apex

B. Everett Jordan Lake

Fayetteville

Whiteville

Cape Fear River

Roxboro

VIRGINIA

Hyco Lake

Chapel Hill

Burlington

Sanford

Lumberton

Eden

Greensboro

Kernersville

Haw River

Southern Pines

Rockingham

Biscoe Falls Lake

Thomasville

Asheboro

Mt. Airy

Belews Lake

Winston-Salem

High Point

Lexington

High Rock Lake

Badin Lake

Lake Tillery

Monroe

Yadkin River

Statesville

Salisbury

Kannapolis

Concord

Charlotte

Matthews

Huntersville

Mooresville

W. Kerr Scott Reservoir

Lookout Shoals Lake

Newton

Hickory

Lake Hickory

Lake Norman

Gastonia

Rhodhiss Lake

Morganton

Shelby

Boone

Lake James

Black Mountain

Asheville

Hendersonville

Brevard

TENNESSEE

Great Smoky Mountains National Park

Waynesville

Hiwassee Lake

Chatuge Lake

Murphy

SOUTH CAROLINA

GEORGIA

Legend

★ State capital
● Other cities

40 Miles
40 Kilometers

Projection: Albers Equal-Area

N E W S

Governors of the State of North Carolina

Richard Caswell (1776–1780)
Abner Nash (1780–1781)
Thomas Burke (1781–1782)
Alexander Martin (1782–1785)
Richard Caswell (1784–1787)
Samuel Johnston (1787–1789)
Alexander Martin (1789–1792)
Richard Dobbs Spaight, Sr. (1792–1795)
Samuel Ashe (1795–1798)
William Richardson Davie (1798–1799)
Benjamin Williams (1799–1802)
James Turner (1802–1805)
Nathaniel Alexander (1805–1807)
Benjamin Williams (1807–1808)
David Stone (1808–1810)
Benjamin Smith (1810–1811)
William Hawkins (1811–1814)
William Miller (1814–1817)
John Branch (1817–1820)
Jesse Franklin (1820–1821)
Gabriel Holmes (1821–1824)
Hutchins Gordon Burton (1824–1827)
James Iredell, Jr. (1827–1828)
John Owen (1828–1830)
Montford Stokes (1830–1832)

David Lowry Swain (1832–1835)
Richard Dobbs Spaight, Jr. (1835–1836)
Edward Bishop Dudley (1836–1841)
John Motley Morehead (1841–1845)
William Alexander Graham (1845–1849)
Charles Manly (1849–1850)
David Settle Reid (1851–1854)
Warren Winslow (1854–1855)
Thomas Bragg (1855–1859)
John Willis Ellis (1859–1861)
Henry Toole Clark (1861–1862)
Zebulon Baird Vance (1862–1865)
William Woods Holden (1865)
Jonathan Worth (1865–1868)
William Woods Holden (1868–1870)
Tod Robinson Caldwell (1870–1874)
Curtis Hooks Brogden (1874–1877)
Zebulon Baird Vance (1877–1879)
Thomas Jordan Jarvis (1879–1885)
Alfred Moore Scales (1885–1889)
Daniel Gould Fowle (1889–1891)
Thomas Michael Holt (1891–1893)
Elias Carr (1893–1897)
Daniel Lindsay Russell (1897–1901)
Charles Brantley Aycock (1901–1905)

Robert Broadnax Glenn (1905–1909)
William Walton Kitchin (1909–1913)
Locke Craig (1913–1917)
Thomas Walter Bickett (1917–1921)
Cameron Morrison (1921–1925)
Angus Wilton McLean (1925–1929)
Oliver Max Gardner (1929–1933)
John Christoph Blucher Ehringhaus (1933–1937)
Clyde Roark Hoey (1937–1941)
Joseph Melville Broughton (1941–1945)
Robert Gregg Cherry (1945–1949)
William Kerr Scott (1949–1953)
William Bradley Umstead (1953–1954)
Luther Hartwell Hodges (1954–1961)
Terry Sanford (1961–1965)
Dan Killian Moore (1965–1969)
Robert Walter Scott (1969–1973)
James Eubert Holshouser, Jr. (1973–1977)
James Baxter Hunt, Jr. (1977–1985)
James Grubbs Martin (1985–1993)
James Baxter Hunt, Jr. (1993–2001)
Michael F. Easley (2001–Present)

North Carolina Government

Executive Branch

Carries out the laws and policies of state government

Governor

- Elected by voters to a four-year term
- Limited to two terms
- Appoints cabinet and some judges
- Chairs the Council of State

Lieutenant Governor

- Elected by voters to a four-year term
- Holds various responsibilities, including replacing the governor should he or she leave office

Cabinet

- Consists of officials appointed by governor
- Offers advice to governor on specific areas of knowledge

Legislative Branch

Makes state laws

Bicameral System

- General Assembly has two houses—Senate and House of Representatives
- Both houses take part in presenting and passing laws
- General Assembly can override the governor's veto with a three-fifths vote in both houses

State Senate

- 50 members
- Elected to two-year terms
- No term limits

State House of Representatives

- 120 members
- Elected to two-year terms
- No term limits

Judicial Branch

Decides conflicts and questions about the law

Trial Courts

- Hear civil and criminal cases

Appellate Courts

- North Carolina Court of Appeals is only intermediate appellate court in the state
- Consists of fifteen judges who rule in rotating panels of three

Supreme Court of North Carolina

- Highest appellate court in the state
- Determines statewide principles of law in deciding specific lawsuits
- Consists of seven justices
- Justices elected by voters to eight-year terms
- No term limits

North Carolina Facts

State tree	Pine
State bird	Cardinal
State reptile	Eastern box turtle
State mammal	Gray squirrel
State fish	Channel bass
State shell	Scotch bonnet
State flower	Dogwood
State vegetable	Sweet potato
Capital	Raleigh
Year of Statehood	1789 (12th state)
Nickname	The Old North State, Tar Heel State
Motto	Esse Quam Videri (To be rather than to seem)
Song	"The Old North State"
Highest Elevation	Mt. Mitchell, 6,684 feet above sea level
Lowest Elevation	Sea level
Total area	53,819 square miles
National rank in total area	28
Total Coastline	301 miles
Largest city	Charlotte
Largest lake	Mattamuskeet
Number of counties	100
Population	8,683,242 (as of 2005)
National rank in population	11
Length (North to South)	190 miles
Width (East to West)	505 miles

The cardinal is the North Carolina state bird.

The coast of North Carolina

Mapping the Earth
Using Latitude and Longitude

A **globe** is a scale model of the earth. It is useful for showing the entire earth or studying large areas of the earth's surface.

A pattern of lines circles the globe in east-west and north-south directions. It is called a **grid.** The intersection of these imaginary lines helps us find places on the earth.

The east-west lines in the grid are lines of **latitude.** Lines of latitude are called **parallels** because they are always parallel to each other. These imaginary lines measure distance north and south of the **equator.** The equator is an imaginary line that circles the globe halfway between the North and South Poles. Parallels measure distance from the equator in **degrees.** The symbol for degrees is °. Degrees are further divided into **minutes.** The symbol for minutes is ´. There are 60 minutes in a degree. Parallels north of the equator are labeled with an N. Those south of the equator are labeled with an S.

The north-south lines are lines of **longitude.** Lines of longitude are called **meridians.** These imaginary lines pass through the Poles. They measure distance east and west of the **prime meridian.** The prime meridian is an imaginary line that runs through Greenwich, England. It represents 0° longitude.

Lines of latitude range from 0°, for locations on the equator, to 90°N or 90°S, for locations at the Poles. Lines of longitude range from 0° on the prime meridian to 180° on a meridian in the mid-Pacific Ocean. Meridians west of the prime meridian to 180° are labeled with a W. Those east of the prime meridian to 180° are labeled with an E.

Lines of Latitude

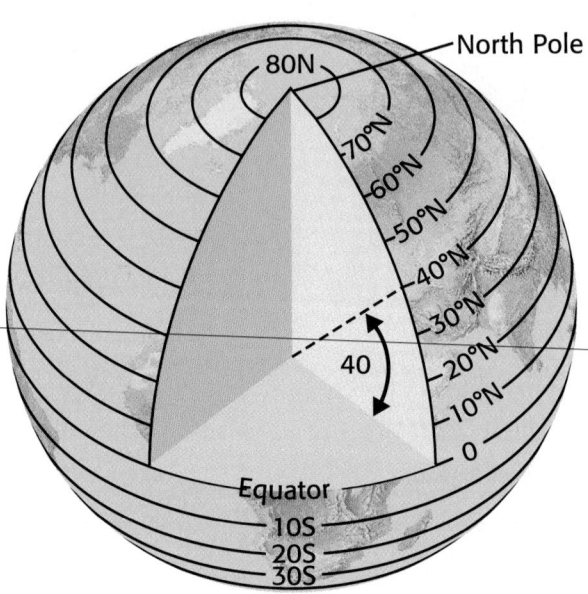

Lines of Longitude

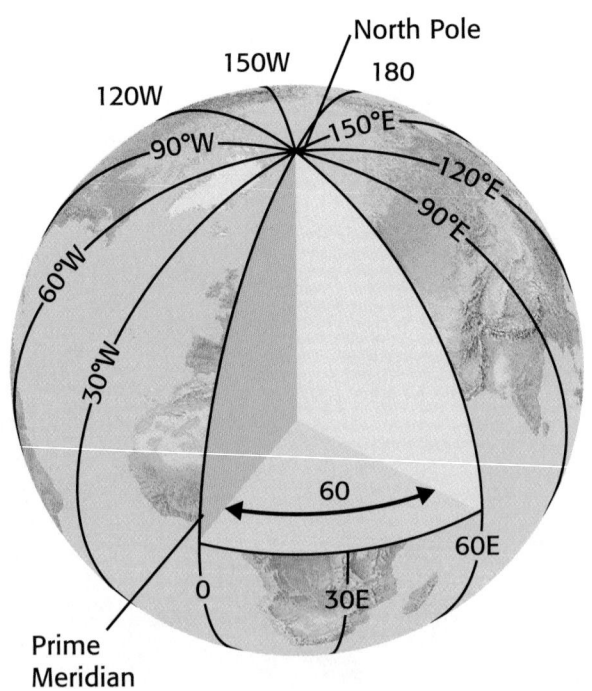

The equator divides the globe into two halves, called **hemispheres**. The half north of the equator is the Northern Hemisphere. The southern half is the Southern Hemisphere. The prime meridian and the 180° meridian divide the world into the Eastern Hemisphere and the Western Hemisphere. However, the prime meridian runs right through Europe and Africa. To avoid dividing these continents between two hemispheres, some mapmakers divide the Eastern and Western hemispheres at 20°W. This places all of Europe and Africa in the Eastern Hemisphere.

Our planet's land surface is divided into seven large landmasses, called **continents**. They are identified in the maps on this page. Landmasses smaller than continents and completely surrounded by water are called **islands**.

Geographers also organize Earth's water surface into parts. The largest is the world ocean. Geographers divide the world ocean into the Pacific Ocean, the Atlantic Ocean, the Indian Ocean, and the Arctic Ocean. Lakes and seas are smaller bodies of water.

Northern Hemisphere

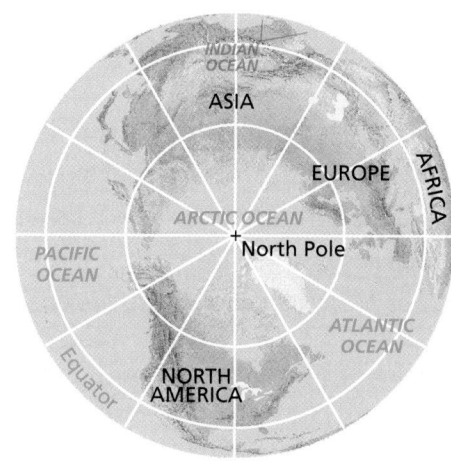

Southern Hemisphere

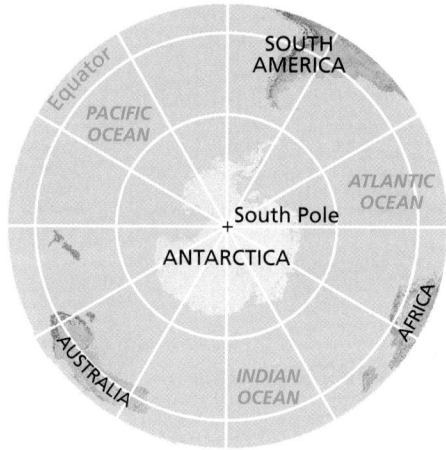

Western Hemisphere

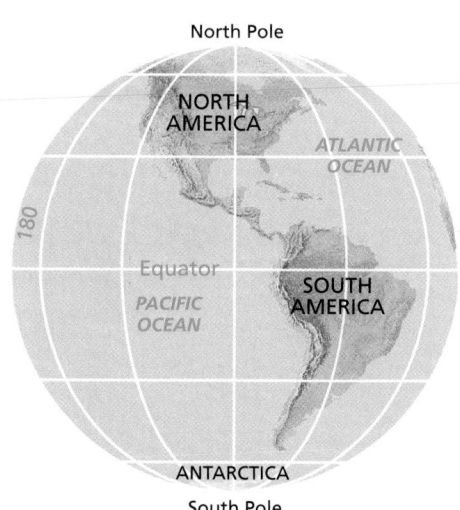

Eastern Hemisphere

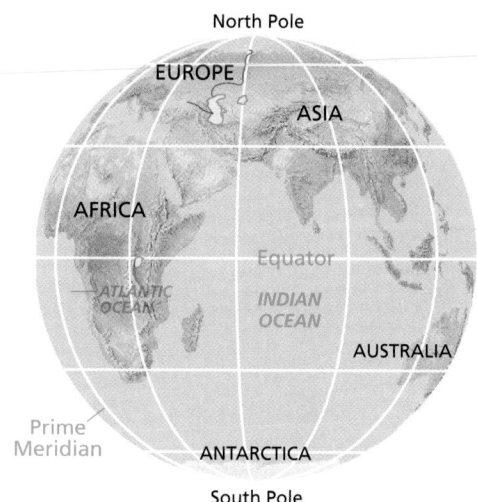

Mapmaking
Understanding Map Projections

A **map** is a flat diagram of all or part of the earth's surface. Mapmakers have created different ways of showing our round planet on flat maps. These different ways are called **map projections**. Because the earth is round, there is no way to show it accurately in a flat map. All flat maps are distorted in some way. Mapmakers must choose the type of map projection that is best for their purposes. Many map projections are one of three kinds: cylindrical, conic, or flat-plane.

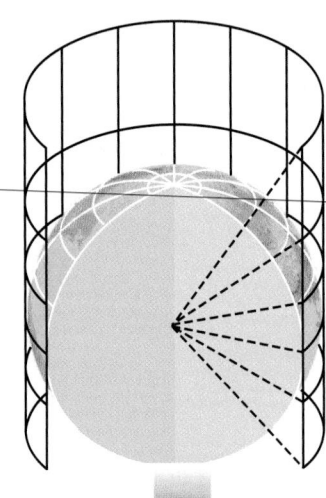

Paper cylinder

Cylindrical Projections

Cylindrical projections are based on a cylinder wrapped around the globe. The cylinder touches the globe only at the equator. The meridians are pulled apart and run parallel to each other instead of meeting at the Poles. This causes landmasses near the Poles to appear larger than they really are. The map below is a Mercator projection, one type of cylindrical projection. Navigators use the Mercator projection because it shows true direction and shape. However, it distorts the size of land areas near the Poles.

Mercator projection

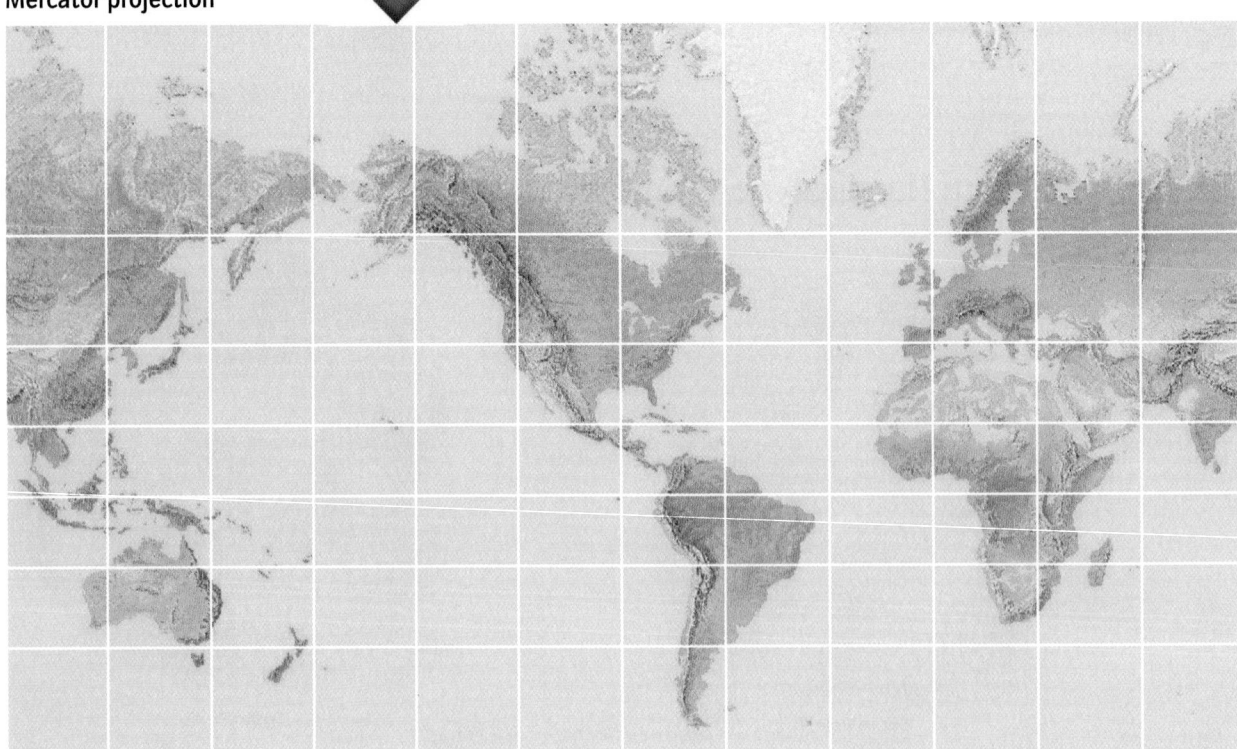

Conic Projections

Conic projections are based on a cone placed over the globe. A conic projection is most accurate along the lines of latitude where it touches the globe. It retains almost true shape and size. Conic projections are most useful for showing areas that have long east-west dimensions, such as the United States.

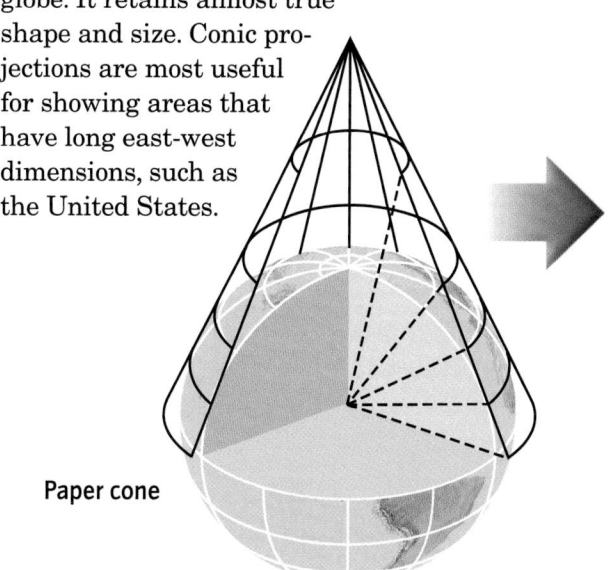

Paper cone

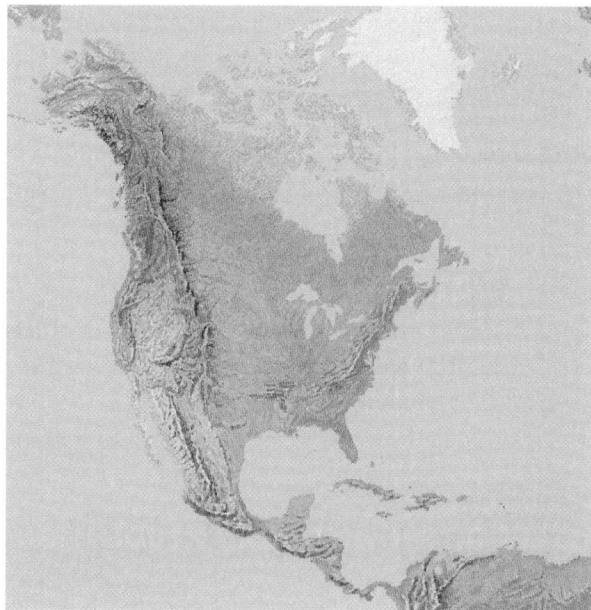

Conic projection

Flat-plane Projections

Flat-plane projections are based on a plane touching the globe at one point, such as at the North Pole or South Pole. A flat-plane projection is useful for showing true direction for airplane pilots and ship navigators. It also shows true area. However, it distorts the true shapes of landmasses.

Flat plane

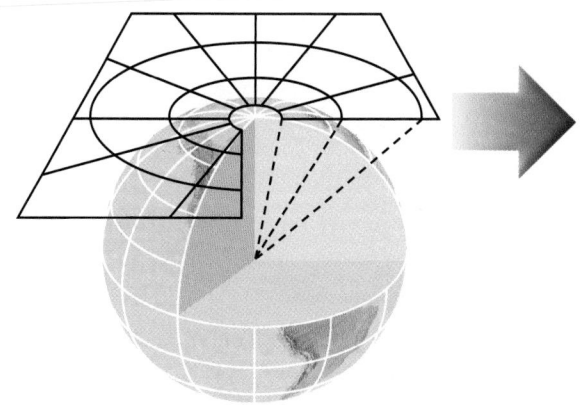

Flat-plane projection

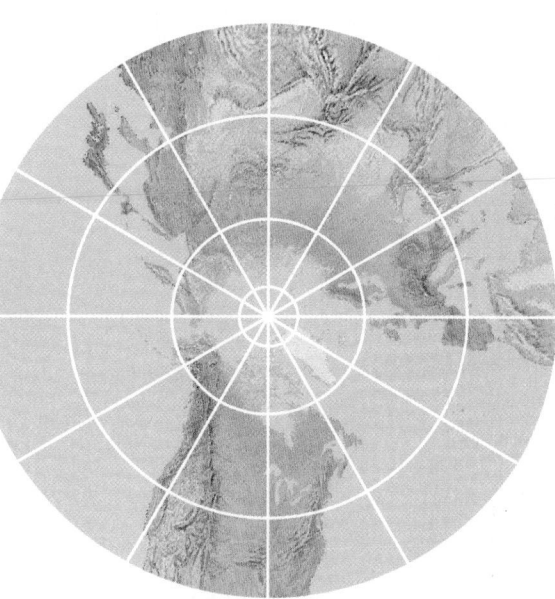

Map Essentials
How to Read a Map

Maps are like messages sent out in code. Mapmakers provide certain elements that help us translate these codes. These elements help us understand the message they are presenting about a particular part of the world. Of these elements, almost all maps have titles, directional indicators, scales, and legends. The map below has all four of these elements, plus two more—a locator map and an interactive keyword.

1 Title

A map's **title** shows what the subject of the map is. The map title is usually the first thing you should look at when studying a map, because it tells you what the map is trying to show.

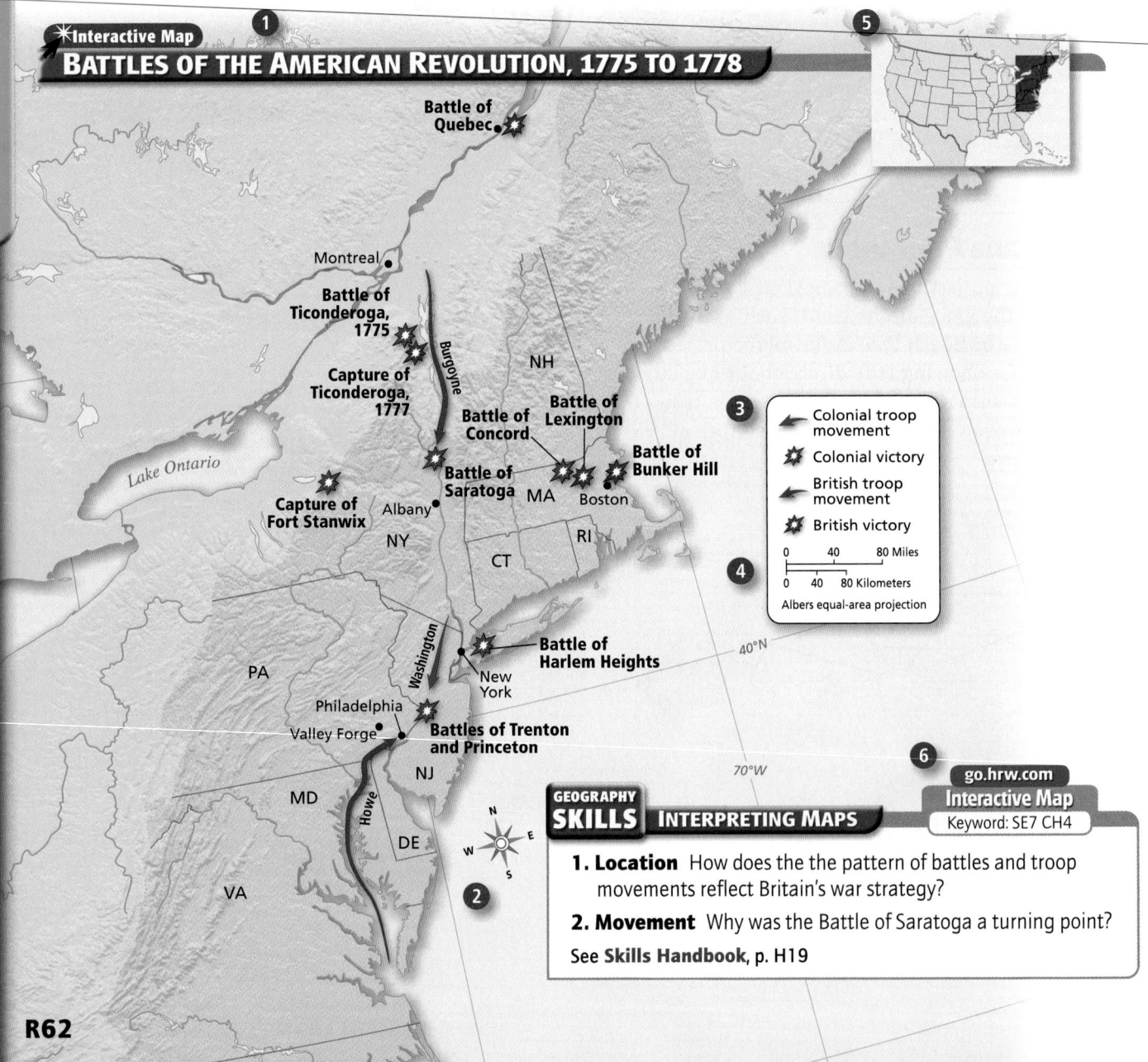

Interactive Map

BATTLES OF THE AMERICAN REVOLUTION, 1775 TO 1778

Battle of Quebec

Montreal

Battle of Ticonderoga, 1775

Capture of Ticonderoga, 1777

Burgoyne

NH

Battle of Concord

Battle of Lexington

Battle of Bunker Hill

Lake Ontario

Capture of Fort Stanwix

Battle of Saratoga

Albany

MA

Boston

NY

RI

CT

3
- Colonial troop movement
- Colonial victory
- British troop movement
- British victory

0   40   80 Miles
0   40   80 Kilometers

4 Albers equal-area projection

40°N

Battle of Harlem Heights

Washington

PA

New York

Philadelphia

Battles of Trenton and Princeton

Valley Forge

70°W

NJ

MD

Howe

DE

VA

2 (compass rose: N, S, E, W)

5 (locator map)

6

go.hrw.com
Interactive Map
Keyword: SE7 CH4

GEOGRAPHY SKILLS | **INTERPRETING MAPS**

1. Location How does the the pattern of battles and troop movements reflect Britain's war strategy?

2. Movement Why was the Battle of Saratoga a turning point?

See **Skills Handbook**, p. H19

❷ Compass Rose

A directional indicator shows which way north, south, east, and west lie on the map. Some mapmakers use a "north arrow," which points toward the North Pole. Remember, "north" is not always at the top of a map. The way a map is drawn and the location of directions on that map depend on the perspective of the mapmaker. Most maps in this textbook indicate direction by using a compass rose. A **compass rose** has arrows that point to all four principal directions, as shown.

❸ Legend

The **legend**, or key, explains what the symbols on the map represent. Point symbols are used to specify the location of things, such as cities, that do not take up much space on the map. Some legends show colors that represent elevations. Other maps might have legends with symbols or colors that represent things such as roads, the movement of military forces and battles. Legends can also show political divisions, economic resources, land use, population density, and climate.

❹ Scale

Mapmakers use scales to represent the distances between points on a map. Scales may appear on maps in several different forms. The maps in this textbook provide a bar **scale**. Scales give distances in miles and kilometers. The scale is often found in the legend. In this textbook, the type of projection used to make the map is shown below the scale bar.

To find the distance between two points on the map, place a piece of paper so that the edge connects the two points. Mark the location of each point on the paper with a line or dot. Then compare the distance between the two dots with the map's bar scale. Because distances on a scale are given in large intervals, you may have to approximate the actual distance.

❺ Locator Map

A **locator** map shows where in the world the area on the map is located. The area shown on the main map is shown in red on the locator map. The locator map also shows surrounding areas so the map reader can see how the information on the map relates to neighboring lands.

❻ Interactive Keyword

Some maps in this textbook are interactive. If you go online to the Holt website and type in the map's keyword, you can learn more about the places and events shown on the map.

go.hrw.com
Interactive Map
Keyword: SE7 CH4

Working with Maps
Using Different Kinds of Maps

The Atlas in this textbook includes both physical and political maps. **Physical maps** show the major physical features in a region. These features include things like mountain ranges, rivers, oceans, islands, deserts, and plains. **Political maps** show the major political features of a region, such as countries and their borders, capitals, and other important cities.

Historical Map

In this textbook most of the maps you will study are historical maps. Historical maps, such as the one below, show information about the past. This information might be which lands a country controlled, where a certain group of people lived, what large cities were located in a region, or how a place changed over time. Often colors are used to indicate the different things on the map. Be sure to look at the map title and map legend first to see what the map is showing. What does this map show?

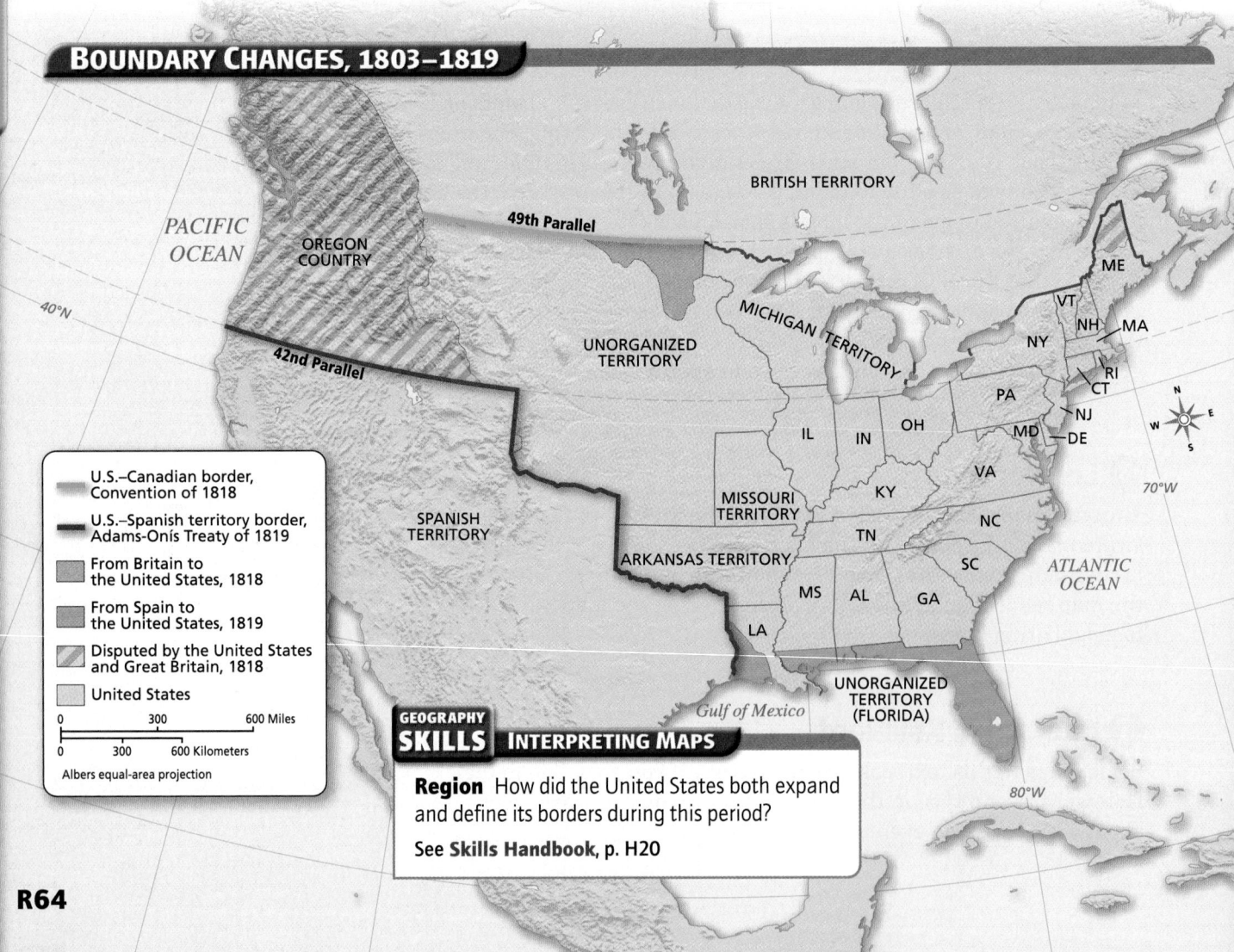

BOUNDARY CHANGES, 1803–1819

U.S.–Canadian border, Convention of 1818

U.S.–Spanish territory border, Adams-Onís Treaty of 1819

From Britain to the United States, 1818

From Spain to the United States, 1819

Disputed by the United States and Great Britain, 1818

United States

0   300   600 Miles

0   300   600 Kilometers

Albers equal-area projection

GEOGRAPHY SKILLS **INTERPRETING MAPS**

Region How did the United States both expand and define its borders during this period?

See **Skills Handbook**, p. H20

THE LOUISIANA PURCHASE AND WESTERN EXPEDITIONS

PACIFIC OCEAN

BRITISH TERRITORY

Disputed by United States and Britain

Columbia R.

OREGON COUNTRY

LOUISIANA PURCHASE

ROCKY MOUNTAINS

North Platte R.

Missouri R.

Mississippi R.

SPANISH TERRITORY

GREAT PLAINS

St. Charles

MICHIGAN TERRITORY (1805)

INDIANA TERRITORY

OH

Ohio R.

VT
NH
NY
MA
CT
RI

MAINE DISTRICT (MA)

PA

NJ
MD
DE

VA

KY

TN

NC

SC

ATLANTIC OCEAN

MISSISSIPPI TERRITORY

GA

New Orleans

SPANISH TERRITORY

Gulf of Mexico

CONTINENTAL DIVIDE

40°

30°

70°

90°W

80°W

Legend:
- U.S. states and territories in 1804
- Louisiana Purchase (acquired 1803)
- Lewis and Clark's expedition, 1804–1806

0   200   400 Miles
0   200   400 Kilometers
Albers equal-area projection

GEOGRAPHY SKILLS INTERPRETING MAPS

go.hrw.com
Practice Online
Keyword: SE7 CH6

1. Movement About how long was Lewis and Clark's route?

2. Region What new problems do you think the Louisiana Purchase might present for the United States and for Native Americans?

See **Skills Handbook,** p. H19

Route Map

One special type of historical map is called a route map. A route map, like the one above, shows the route, or path, that someone or something followed. Route maps can show things like trade routes, invasion routes, or the journeys and travels of people. The routes on the map are usually shown with an arrow. If more than one route is shown, several arrows of different colors may be used. What does this route map show?

The maps in this textbook will help you study and understand history. By working with these maps, you will see where important events happened, where empires rose and fell, and where people moved. In studying these maps, you will learn how geography has influenced history.

Geographic Dictionary

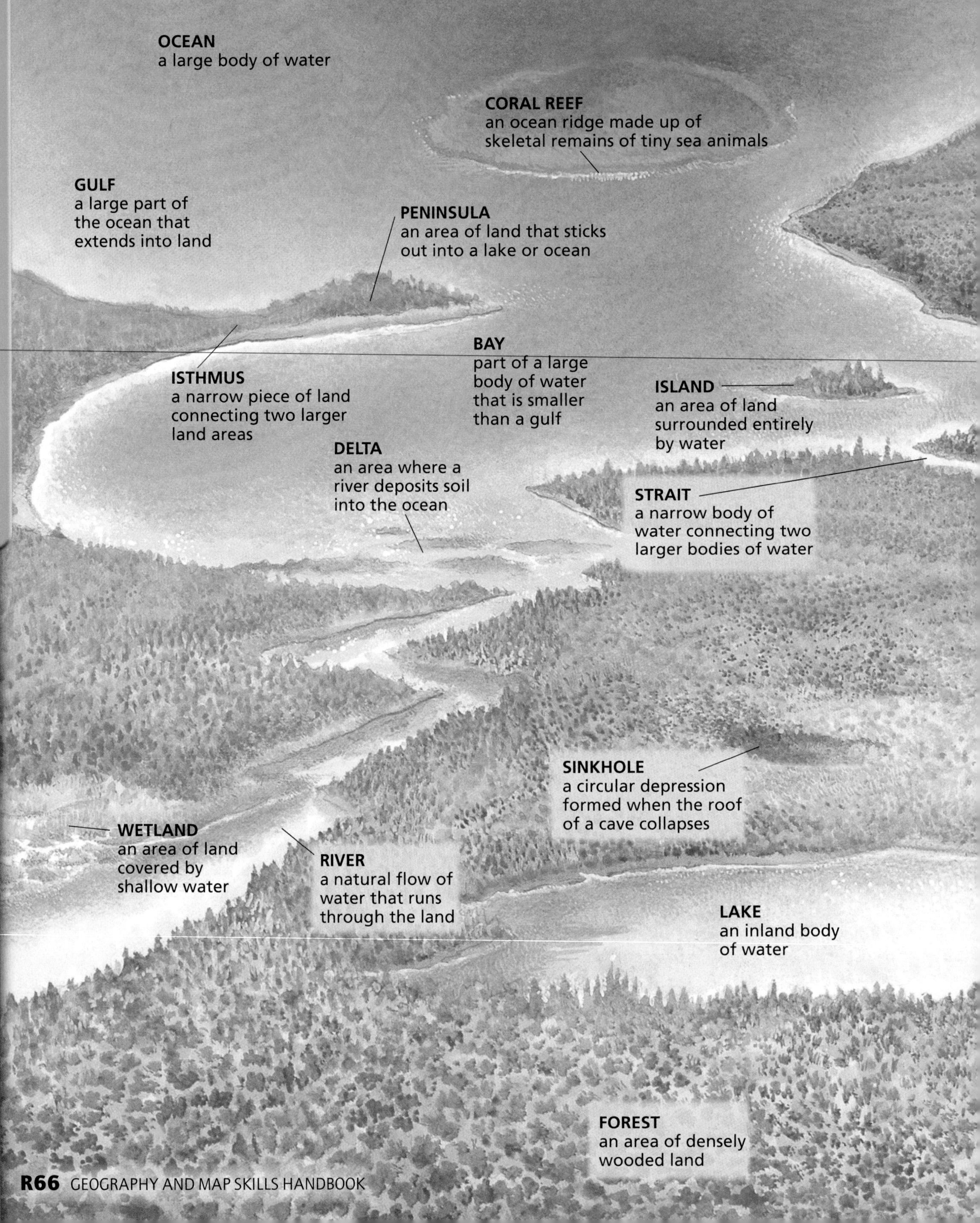

OCEAN
a large body of water

CORAL REEF
an ocean ridge made up of
skeletal remains of tiny sea animals

GULF
a large part of
the ocean that
extends into land

PENINSULA
an area of land that sticks
out into a lake or ocean

BAY
part of a large
body of water
that is smaller
than a gulf

ISLAND
an area of land
surrounded entirely
by water

ISTHMUS
a narrow piece of land
connecting two larger
land areas

DELTA
an area where a
river deposits soil
into the ocean

STRAIT
a narrow body of
water connecting two
larger bodies of water

SINKHOLE
a circular depression
formed when the roof
of a cave collapses

WETLAND
an area of land
covered by
shallow water

RIVER
a natural flow of
water that runs
through the land

LAKE
an inland body
of water

FOREST
an area of densely
wooded land

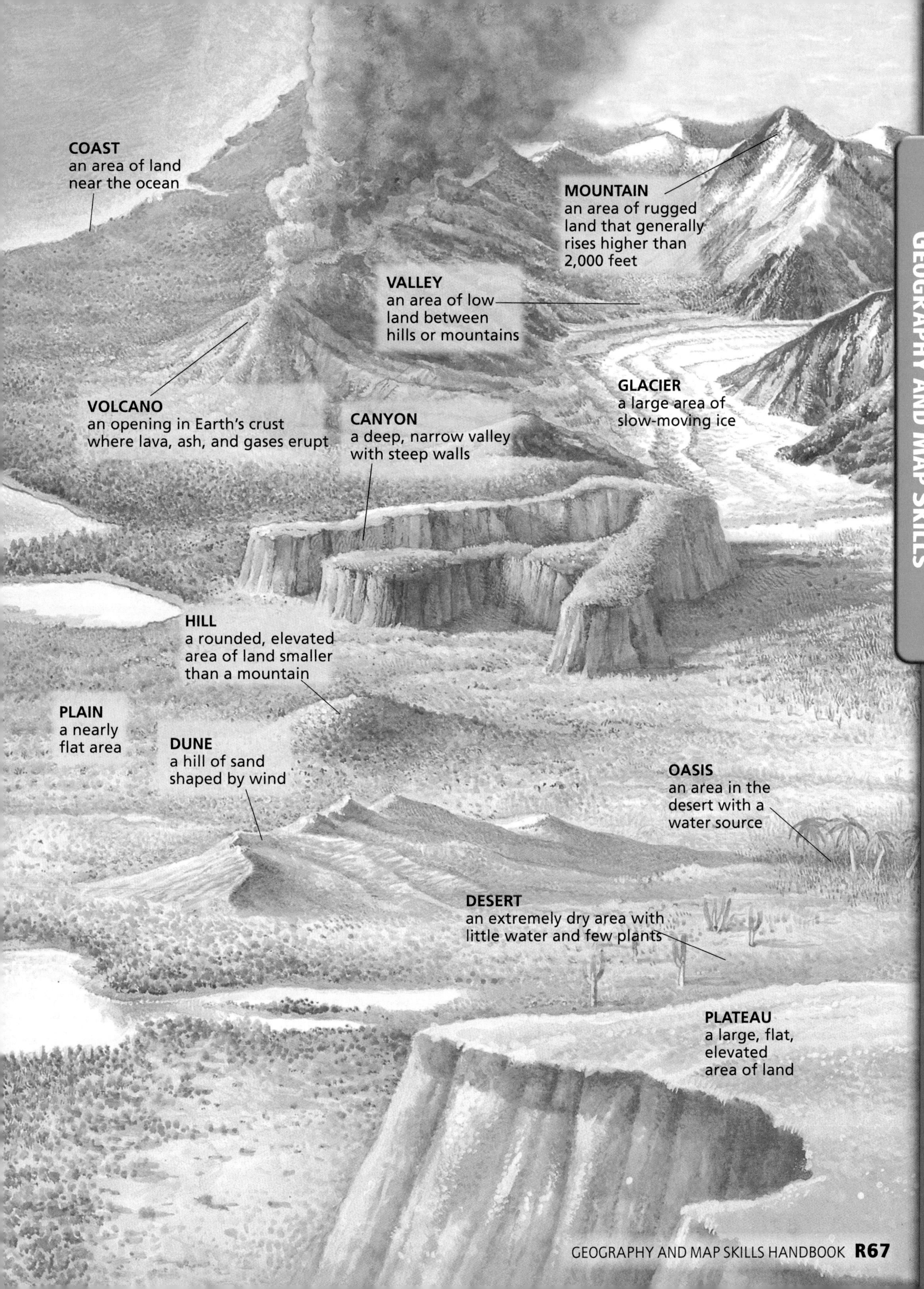

COAST
an area of land
near the ocean

MOUNTAIN
an area of rugged
land that generally
rises higher than
2,000 feet

VALLEY
an area of low
land between
hills or mountains

GLACIER
a large area of
slow-moving ice

VOLCANO
an opening in Earth's crust
where lava, ash, and gases erupt

CANYON
a deep, narrow valley
with steep walls

HILL
a rounded, elevated
area of land smaller
than a mountain

PLAIN
a nearly
flat area

DUNE
a hill of sand
shaped by wind

OASIS
an area in the
desert with a
water source

DESERT
an extremely dry area with
little water and few plants

PLATEAU
a large, flat,
elevated
area of land

Themes and Essential Elements of Geography

by Dr. Christopher L. Salter

To study the world, geographers have identified 5 key themes, 6 essential elements, and 18 geography standards.

"How should we teach and learn about geography?" Professional geographers have worked hard over the years to answer this important question.

In 1984 a group of geographers identified the 5 Themes of Geography. These themes did a wonderful job of laying the groundwork for good classroom geography instruction. Teachers used the 5 Themes in classrooms, and geographers taught workshops on how to apply the 5 Themes in everyday life.

By the early 1990s, however, some geographers felt the 5 Themes were too broad. They created the 18 Geography Standards and the 6 Essential Elements. The 18 Geography Standards include more detailed information about what geography is, and the 6 Essential Elements are like a bridge between the 5 Themes and 18 Standards.

Look at the chart to the right. It shows how each of the 5 Themes connects to the 6 Essential Elements and 18 Geography Standards. For example, the theme of Location is related to The World in Spatial Terms and, through it, to the first three Standards. Study the chart carefully to see how the other Themes, Elements, and Standards are related.

The last Essential Element and the last two Standards cover The Uses of Geography. These key parts of geography were not covered by the 5 Themes. They emphasize how geographical knowledge can be applied to the study of history and current events and also be used to plan for the future.

5 Themes of Geography

Location The theme of location describes where something is.

Place Place describes the features that make a site unique.

Regions Regions are areas that share common characteristics.

Movement This theme looks at how and why people and things move.

Human-Environment Interaction People interact with their environment in many ways.

6 Essential Elements

18 Geography Standards

I. The World in Spatial Terms

1. How to use maps and other tools
2. How to use mental maps to organize information
3. How to analyze the spatial organization of people, places, and environments

II. Places and Regions

4. The physical and human characteristics of places
5. How people create regions to interpret Earth
6. How culture and experience influence people's perceptions of places and regions

III. Physical Systems

7. The physical processes that shape Earth's surface
8. The distribution of ecosystems on Earth

IV. Human Systems

9. The characteristics, distribution, and migration of human populations
10. The complexity of Earth's cultural mosaics
11. The patterns and networks of economic interdependence on Earth
12. The patterns of human settlement
13. The forces of cooperation and conflict

V. Environment and Society

14. How human actions modify the physical environment
15. How physical systems affect human systems
16. The distribution and meaning of resources

VI. The Uses of Geography

17. How to apply geography to interpret the past
18. How to apply geography to interpret the present and plan for the future

MAGNA CARTA, 1215

VOCABULARY

relief a payment made by the heir of a deceased tenant to a lord for the privilege of succeeding to the tenant's estate.

barony land held by a baron

fief land given to a noble in return for a pledge of loyalty and military service in Feudalism

ward a child who is not ready to inherit the title and responsibilities due him

rancour bad feeling

laity people who are not clergy

In the early 1200s King John of England angered the nobility when he imposed high taxes. The nobles joined forces with the Archbishop of Canterbury and in 1215 forced the king to sign the Magna Carta (Latin for "Great Charter"). The main point established by the Magna Carta was that the king, like all other people in England, was subject to the rule of law. The document also established the due process of law and the right to a fair and speedy trial as basic rights enjoyed by all people in England. These principles endured as part of English law and became part of American law in the Bill of Rights.

1. In the first place have granted to God, and by this our present charter confirmed for us and our heirs for ever that the English church shall be free, and shall have its rights undiminished and its liberties unimpaired ... We have also granted to all free men of our kingdom, for ourselves and our heirs for ever, all the liberties written below, to be had and held by them and their heirs of us and our heirs.

2. If any of our earls or barons or others holding of us in chief by knight service dies, and at his death his heir be of full age and owe relief he shall have his inheritance on payment of the old relief, namely the heir or heirs of an earl 100 for a whole earl's barony, the heir or heirs of a baron 100 for a whole barony, the heir or heirs of a knight 100s, at most, for a whole knight's fee; and he who owes less shall give less according to the ancient usage of fiefs.

3. If, however, the heir of any such be under age and a ward, he shall have his inheritance when he comes of age without paying relief and without making fine.

40. To no one will we sell, to no one will we refuse or delay right or justice.

41. All merchants shall be able to go out of and come into England safely and securely and stay and travel throughout England, as well by land as by water, for buying and selling by the ancient and right customs free from all evil tolls, except in time of war and if they are of the land that is at war with us ...

42. It shall be lawful in future for anyone, without prejudicing the allegiance due to us, to leave our kingdom and return safely and securely by land and water, save, in the public interest, for a short period in time of war—except for those imprisoned or outlawed in accordance with the law of the kingdom and natives of a land that is at war with us and merchants (who shall be treated as aforesaid).

62. And we have fully remitted and pardoned to everyone all the ill-will, indignation and rancour that have arisen between us and our men, clergy and laity, from the time of the quarrel. Furthermore, we have fully remitted to all, clergy and laity, and as far as pertains to us have completely forgiven, all trespasses occasioned by the same quarrel between Easter in the sixteenth year of our reign and the restoration of peace. And, besides, we have caused to be made for them letters testimonial patent of the lord Stephen archbishop of Canterbury, of the lord Henry archbishop of Dublin and of the aforementioned bishops and of master Pandulf about this security and the aforementioned concessions.

63. An oath, moreover, has been taken, as well on our part as on the part of the barons, that all these things aforesaid shall be observed in good faith and without evil disposition. Witness the above-mentioned and many others. Given by our hand in the meadow which is called Runnymede between Windsor and Staines on the fifteenth day of June, in the seventeenth year of our reign.

Source: "English Bill of Rights." Britannica Online. Vers. 99.1. Encyclopedia Britannica. 1994–1999. Encyclopedia Britannica, Inc.

THE MAYFLOWER COMPACT, 1620

In 1620 the Pilgrims left England bound for Virginia. A storm blew the Mayflower off course, and the Pilgrims made landfall in present-day Massachusetts. In Virginia the Pilgrims would have come under the laws governing that colony. In Massachusetts there were no laws, so the Pilgrims drew up a framework for self-government.

We whose names are underwritten, the loyal subjects of our dread Sovereign Lord King James, by the Grace of God of Great Britain, France and Ireland, King, Defender of the Faith, etc.

Having undertaken, for the Glory of God and advancement of the Christian Faith and Honour of our King and Country, a Voyage to plant the First Colony in the Northern Parts of Virginia, do by these presents sol-emnly and mutually in the presence of God and one of another, Covenant and Combine ourselves together into a Civil Body Politic, for our better ordering and preservation and furtherance of the ends aforesaid; and by virtue hereof to enact, constitute and frame such just and equal Laws, Ordinances, Acts, Constitutions and Offices, from time to time, as shall be thought most meet and convenient for the general good of the Colony, unto which we promise all due submission and obedience. In witness whereof we have hereunder sub-scribed our names at Cape Cod, the 11th of November, in the year of the reign of our Sov-ereign Lord King James, of England, France and Ireland the eighteenth, and of Scotland the fifty-fourth. Anno Domini 1620.

Source: *Of Plymouth Plantation.* William Bradford, 1630–1654. Samuel Eliot Morison, Ed., 1952. Pp. 75–76

VOCABULARY
covenant enter into a binding agreement

ENGLISH BILL OF RIGHTS, 1689

In 1689, after the change of government known as the Glorious Revolution, Parliament passed the English Bill of Rights. This act ensured that Parliament would have power over the monarchy. The bill also protected the rights of English citizens. This part of the document contains a list of royal wrongdoings that would no longer be permitted.

By assuming and exercising a power of dis-pensing with and suspending of laws and the execution of laws without consent of Parlia-ment; . . .

By levying money for and to the use of the Crown by pretence of prerogative for other time and in other manner than the same was granted by Parliament;

By raising and keeping a standing army within this kingdom in time of peace without consent of Parliament, and quarter-ing soldiers contrary to law; . . .

And excessive bail hath been required of persons committed in criminal cases to elude the benefit of the laws made for the liberty of the subjects;

And excessive fines have been imposed;

And illegal and cruel punishments inflicted;

And several grants and promises made of fines and forfeitures before any conviction or judgment against the persons upon whom the same were to be levied;

All which are utterly and directly con-trary to the known laws and statutes and freedom of this realm . . .

Source: "English Bill of Rights." Britannica Online. Vers. 99.1. Encyclopedia Britannica. 1994–1999. Encyclopedia Britan-nica, Inc.

VOCABULARY
prerogative privi-lege
quartering to provide lodging or living places for people
elude avoid
forfeitures the compulsory surrender of property or money as a penalty

VIRGINIA STATUTE FOR RELIGIOUS FREEDOM, 1786

VOCABULARY

propagation spread

proscribing forbidding or prohibiting

emolument payment for performing a duty or holding an office

The Virginia Statute for Religious Freedom, written by Thomas Jefferson and passed by Virginia's legislature in 1786, was an early statement of the rights of citizens to worship freely without experiencing coercion from government. The act was an inspiration to writers of the Bill of Rights.

. . . to compel a man to furnish contributions of money for the propagation of opinions which he disbelieves, is sinful and tyrannical; that even the forcing him to support this or that teacher of his own religious persuasion, is depriving him of the comfortable liberty of giving his contributions to the particular pastor . . . that our civil rights have no dependence on our religious opinions, any more than our opinions in physics or geometry; that therefore the proscribing any citizen as unworthy the public confidence by laying upon him an incapacity of being called to Offices of trust and emolument, unless he profess or renounce this or that religious opinion, is depriving him injuriously of those privileges and advantages to which in common with his fellow-citizens he has a natural right . . .

Be it enacted by the General Assembly, That no man shall be compelled to frequent or support any religious worship, place, or ministry whatsoever, nor shall be enforced, restrained, molested, or burthened in his body or goods, nor shall otherwise suffer on account of his religious opinions or belief; but that all men shall be free to profess, and by argument to maintain, their opinion in matters of religion, and that the same shall in no wise diminish enlarge, or affect their civil capacities.

. . . yet we are free to declare, and do declare, that the rights hereby asserted are of the natural rights of mankind, and that if any act shall be hereafter passed to repeal the present, or to narrow its operation, such act shall be an infringement of natural right.

Source: *Statutes at Large of Virginia.* W.W. Hening, Ed., Vol. 12. 1823. Pp. 84–86.

FEDERALIST PAPER No. 10, 1787

VOCABULARY

latent hidden

animosity dislike

vex anger

discern understand or recognize

convened brought together

The Federalist Papers were a series of essays written in favor of ratifying the United States Constitution. The Papers were written by James Madison, Alexander Hamilton and John Jay. In Federalist Paper No. 10, *James Madison addressed critics who said that the United States was too large to be governed by a strong central government. Critics claimed there were too many interest groups, or "factions," to be ruled by a democratically elected government. Madison acknowledged the presence and problem of factions. He argued however, that the republican form of government under the Constitution was best able to deal with the problem by helping different factions negotiate solutions.*

By a faction, I understand a number of citizens, whether amounting to a majority or a minority of the whole, who are united and actuated by some common impulse of passion, or of interest, adversed to the rights of other citizens . . .

The latent causes of faction are thus sown in the nature of man; and we see them everywhere brought into different degrees of activity, according to the different circumstances of civil society. A zeal for different opinions concerning religion, concerning government, and many other points, as well of speculation as of practice; an attachment to different leaders ambitiously contending for pre-eminence and power; or to persons of other descriptions whose fortunes have been interesting to the human passions, have, in turn, divided mankind into parties, inflamed them with mutual animosity, and rendered them much more disposed to vex and oppress each other than to co-operate for their common good . . .

The inference to which we are brought is, that the CAUSES of faction cannot be removed, and that relief is only to be sought in the means of controlling its EFFECTS . . . A republic, by which I mean a government in which the scheme of representation takes place, opens a different prospect, and promises the cure for which we are seeking.

The two great points of difference between a democracy and a republic are: first, the delegation of the government, in the latter, to a small number of citizens elected by the rest; secondly, the greater number of citizens, and greater sphere of country, over which the latter may be extended . . .

The effect of the first difference is, on the one hand, to refine and enlarge the public views, by passing them through the medium of a chosen body of citizens, whose wisdom may best <u>discern</u> the true interest of their country, and whose patriotism and love of justice will be least likely to sacrifice it to temporary or partial considerations . . . [I]t may well happen that the public voice, pronounced by the representatives of the people, will be more consonant to the public good than if pronounced by the people themselves, <u>convened</u> for the purpose.

. . . [I]t clearly appears, that the same advantage which a republic has over a democracy, in controlling the effects of faction, is enjoyed by a large over a small republic, is enjoyed by the Union over the States composing it.

Source: *The Federalist or The New Constitution.* Papers by Alexander Hamilton, James Madison, and John Jay. New York Heritage Press. Introduction by Carl Van Doren. 1945.

OBJECTIONS TO THIS CONSTITUTION OF GOVERNMENT, 1787

George Mason played a behind-the-scenes role in the Revolutionary War and wrote Virginia's Declaration of Rights. He attended the Constitutional Convention in 1787. Mason criticized the proposed Constitution for allowing slavery, creating a strong central government, and lacking a bill of rights. As a result, he refused to sign the Constitution. In the following excerpt, Mason explains why he would not sign the Constitution.

There is no Declaration of Rights, and the laws of the general government being <u>paramount</u> to the laws and constitution of the several States, the Declarations of Rights in the separate States are no security. Nor are the people secured even in the enjoyment of the benefit of the common law.

In the House of Representatives there is not the substance but the shadow only of representation . . .

The Senate have the power of altering all money bills, and of originating <u>appropriations</u> of money, and the salaries of the Officers of their own appointment, in conjunction with the president of the United States, although they are not the representatives of the people or <u>amenable</u> to them . . .

The Judiciary of the United States is so constructed and extended, as to absorb and destroy the judiciaries of the several States; thereby rendering law as tedious, intricate and expensive, and justice as unattainable, by a great part of the community, as in England, and enabling the rich to oppress and ruin the poor.

The President of the United States has no Constitutional Council, a thing unknown in any safe and regular government. He will therefore be unsupported by proper information and advice, and will generally be directed by <u>minions</u> and favorites; or he will become a tool to the Senate . . .

The President of the United States has the unrestrained power of granting pardons for treason, which may be sometimes exercised to screen from punishment those whom he had secretly instigated to commit the crime, and thereby prevent a discovery of his own guilt . . .

Source: Gunston Hall Plantation

VOCABULARY

paramount most imporant

appropriations money designated by the government to be spent

amenable friendly towards or responsible towards

minions people who are overly servile or submissive to their leader

WASHINGTON'S FAREWELL ADDRESS, 1796

VOCABULARY
infractions violations

In 1796, at the end of his second term as president, George Washington wrote his farewell address with the help of Alexander Hamilton and James Madison. In it he spoke of the dangers facing the young nation. He warned against the dangers of political parties and sectionalism, and he advised the nation against permanent alliances with other nations.

In contemplating the causes, which may disturb our Union, it occurs as matter of serious concern, that any ground should have been furnished for characterizing parties by geographical discriminations—Northern and Southern—Atlantic and Western . . .

To the efficacy and permanency of your Union, a government for the whole is indispensible. No alliances, however strict, between the parts can be an adequate substitute; they must inevitably experience the infractions and interruptions which all alliances in all times have experienced . . .

The great rule of conduct for us, in regard to foreign nations, is, in extending our commercial relations, to have with them as little political connexion [connection] as possible. So far as we have already formed engagements, let them be fulfilled with perfect good faith. Here let us stop . . .

Source: *Annals of Congress,* 4th Congress, pp. 2869–2880. American Memory Library of Congress. 1999.

JEFFERSON'S FIRST INAUGURAL ADDRESS, 1801

VOCABULARY
presentiments feeling about something that will happen in the future
transcendent uplifting
auspices protection, support
reposed placed trust in
preeminent finest, the best

In 1800 Thomas Jefferson, representing the Democratic-Republican Party, defeated the Federalist candidate, President John Adams. Jefferson used his inaugural address of March 1801 to try to bridge the gap between the new political parties and to reach out to the Federalists.

Friends and Fellow-Citizens:

Called upon to undertake the duties of the first executive Office of our country, I avail myself of the presence of that portion of my fellow-citizens which is here assembled to express my grateful thanks for the favor with which they have been pleased to look toward me, to declare a sincere consciousness that the task is above my talents, and that I approach it with those anxious and awful presentiments which the greatness of the charge and the weakness of my powers so justly inspire. A rising nation, spread over a wide and fruitful land, traversing all the seas with the rich productions of their industry, engaged in commerce with nations who feel power and forget right, advancing rapidly to destinies beyond the reach of mortal eye when I

contemplate these transcendent objects, and see the honor, the happiness, and the hopes of this beloved country committed to the issue, and the auspices of this day, I shrink from the contemplation, and humble myself before the magnitude of the undertaking . . .

I repair, then, fellow-citizens, to the post you have assigned me. With experience enough in subordinate Offices to have seen the difficulties of this the greatest of all, I have learnt to expect that it will rarely fall to the lot of imperfect man to retire from this station with the reputation and the favor which bring him into it. Without pretensions to that high confidence you reposed in our first and greatest revolutionary character, whose preeminent services had entitled him to the first place in his country's love and destined for him the fairest page in the volume of faithful history, I ask so much confidence only as may give firmness and effect to the legal administration of your affairs.

Source: Inaugural Addresses of the Presidents of the United States. 1989. Bartleby Library.

DENMARK VESEY DOCUMENT, 1822

Some enslaved African Americans tried to strike back against the slave system in the South. Denmark Vesey, a free African American living in Charleston, South Carolina, was accused of planning a massive and violent revolt in 1822. Vesey and others were caught and executed. Today some scholars have questioned if the conspiracy was real, arguing that Vesey was framed. Included below is an excerpt from an observer of the time.

At the head of this conspiracy stood Denmark Vesey, a free negro; with him the idea undoubtedly originated. For several years before he disclosed his intentions to any one, he appears to have been constantly and assiduously engaged in endeavoring to embitter the minds of the colored population against the white. He rendered himself perfectly familiar with all those parts of the Scriptures, which he thought he could pervert to his purpose; and would readily quote them, to prove that slavery was contrary to the laws of God; that slaves were bound to attempt their emancipation, however shocking and bloody might be the consequences, and that such efforts would not only be pleasing to the Almighty, but were absolutely enjoined, and their success predicted in the Scriptures . . .

In the selection of his leaders, Vesey showed great penetration and sound judgment. Rolla was plausible, and possessed uncommon self-possession; bold and ardent, he was not to be deterred from his purpose by danger. Ned's appearance indicated that he was a man of firm nerves, and desperate courage. Peter was intrepid and resolute, true to his engagements, and cautious in observing secrecy where it was necessary; he was not to be daunted nor impeded by difficulties, and though confident of success, was careful in providing against any obstacles or casualties which might arise, and intent upon discovering every means which might be in their power if thought of before hand. Gullah Jack was regarded as a Sorcerer, and as such feared by the natives of Africa, who believe in witchcraft.

He was not only considered invulnerable, but that he could make others so by his charms; and that he could and certainly would provide all his followers with arms. He was artful, cruel, bloody; his disposition in short was diabolical. His influence amongst the Africans was inconceivable. Monday was firm, resolute, discreet and intelligent . . .

As Vesey, from whom all orders emanated, and perhaps to whom only all important information was conveyed, died without confessing any thing, any opinion formed as to the numbers actually engaged in the plot, must be altogether conjectural; but enough has been disclosed to satisfy every reasonable mind, that considerable numbers were concerned. Indeed the plan of attack, which embraced so many points to be assailed at the same instant, affords sufficient evidence of the fact.

Source: *A NARRATIVE OF THE Conspiracy and Intended Insurrection, AMONGST A PORTION OF THE Negroes in the State of South-Carolina, In the Year 1822.*

VOCABULARY

assiduously diligently, with persistence

enjoined commanded

emanated coming from a source

PRIMARY SOURCE LIBRARY

MONROE DOCTRINE, 1823

VOCABULARY

interposition placing in the middle

manifestation a sign or appearance

disposition attitude

de facto actual

In 1823 President James Monroe proclaimed the Monroe Doctrine. Designed to end European influence in the Western Hemisphere, it became a cornerstone of United States. foreign policy.

With the existing colonies or dependencies of any European power we have not interfered and shall not interfere. But with the governments who have declared their independence and maintained it, and whose independence we have, on great consideration and on just principles, acknowledged, we could not view any interposition for the purpose of oppressing them, or controlling in any other manner their destiny, by any European power in any other light than as the manifestation of an unfriendly disposition toward the United States . . .

Our policy in regard to Europe, which was adopted at an early stage of the wars which have so long agitated that quarter of the globe, nevertheless remains the same, which is not to interfere in the internal concerns of any of its powers; to consider the government de facto as the legitimate government for us; to cultivate friendly relations with it, and to preserve those relations by a frank, firm, and manly policy, meeting in all instances the just claims of every power, submitting to injuries from none.

Source: "The Monroe Doctrine" by James Monroe reprinted in *The Annals of America: Volume 5, 1821–1832.* Encyclopedia Britannica. 1976.

SENECA FALLS DECLARATION OF SENTIMENTS, 1848

VOCABULARY

hitherto previously

deriving receiving from a source

One of the first documents to express the desire for equal rights for women was the Declaration of Sentiments, issued in 1848 at the Seneca Falls Convention in Seneca Falls, New York. Led by Elizabeth Cady Stanton and Lucretia Mott, the delegates adopted a set of resolutions modeled on the Declaration of Independence.

When, in the course of human events, it becomes necessary for one portion of the family of man to assume among the people of the earth a position different from that which they have hitherto occupied, but one to which the laws of nature and of nature's God entitle them, a decent respect to the opinions of mankind requires that they should declare the causes that impel them to such a course.

We hold these truths to be self-evident: that all men and women are created equal; that they are endowed by their Creator with certain inalienable rights; that among these are life, liberty, and the pursuit of happiness; that to secure these rights governments are instituted, deriving their just powers from the consent of the governed. Whenever any form of government becomes destructive of these ends, it is the right of those who suffer from it to refuse allegiance to it, and to insist upon the institution of a new government, laying its foundation on such principles, and organizing its powers in such form, as to them shall seem most likely to effect their safety and happiness.

Source: "Seneca Falls Declaration on Women's Rights" reprinted in *The Annals of America: Volume 7, 1841–1849.* by Encyclopedia Britannica. 1976.

CALHOUN AND WEBSTER ON THE COMPROMISE OF 1850

In March 1850 the Senate debated the admission of California into the Union as a free state. The debate eventually led to the Compromise of 1850, brokered by Senator Henry Clay of Kentucky, known as the "Great Compromiser." Senator John C. Calhoun of South Carolina, opposed the Compromise. Too ill to speak or even walk, he was carried into the Senate, where another senator read his speech. It was Calhoun's last appearance in the Senate. A few weeks later, he died. On March 7, Senator Daniel Webster of Massachusetts replied to Calhoun. Excerpts from both speeches are given below.

From the speech of John C. Calhoun:

The question then recurs: What is the cause of this discontent? It will be found in the belief of the people of the Southern States, as prevalent as the discontent itself, that they can not remain, as things now are, consistently with honor and safety, in the Union. The next question to be considered is: What has caused this belief?

One of the causes is, undoubtedly, to be traced to the long-continued agitation of the slave question on the part of the North, and the many aggressions which they have made on the rights of the South during the time. I will not enumerate them at present, as it will be done hereafter in its proper place.

There is another lying back of it—with which this is intimately connected—that may be regarded as the great and primary cause. This is to be found in the fact that the equilibrium between the two sections in the government as it stood when the Constitution was ratified and the government put in action has been destroyed. At that time there was nearly a perfect equilibrium between the two, which afforded ample means to each to protect itself against the aggression of the other; but, as it now stands, one section has the exclusive

power of controlling the government, which leaves the other without any adequate means of protecting itself against its encroachment and oppression.

The result of the whole is to give the Northern section a predominance in every department of the government, and thereby concentrate in it the two elements which constitute the federal government: a majority of States, and a majority of their population, estimated in federal numbers. Whatever section concentrates the two in itself possesses the control of the entire government . . .

It is a great mistake to suppose that disunion can be effected by a single blow. The cords which bind these States together in one common Union are far too numerous and powerful for that. Disunion must be the work of time. It is only through a long process, and successively, that the cords can be snapped until the whole fabric falls asunder. Already the agitation of the slavery question has snapped some of the most important, and has greatly weakened all the others.

If the agitation goes on, the same force, acting with increased intensity, as has been shown, will finally snap every cord, when nothing will be left to hold the States together except force. But surely that can with no propriety of language be called a Union when the only means by which the weaker is held connected with the stronger portion is force. It may, indeed, keep them connected; but the connection will partake much more of the character of subjugation on the part of the weaker to the stronger than the union of free, independent, and sovereign States in one confederation, as they stood in the early stages of the government, and which only is worthy of the sacred name of Union.

Source: National Center for Public Policy Research

VOCABULARY
equilibirium balance
subjugation conquest

PRIMARY SOURCE LIBRARY

From the speech of Daniel Webster:

Mr. President [of the Senate], I wish to speak to-day, not as a Massachusetts man, nor as a Northern man, but as an American, and a member of the Senate of the United States . . . I speak to-day for the preservation of the Union . . .

Mr. President, I should much prefer to have heard from every member on this floor declarations of opinion that this Union could never be dissolved, than the declaration of opinion by any body, that, in any case, under the pressure of any circumstances, such a dissolution was possible. I hear with distress and anguish the word "secession," especially when it falls from the lips of those who are patriotic, and known to the country, and known all over the world, for their political services. Secession! Peaceable secession! Sir, your eyes and mine are never destined to see that miracle. The dismemberment of this vast country without convulsion! The breaking up of the fountains of the great deep without ruffing the surface! Who is so foolish, I beg every body's pardon, as to expect to see any such thing? . . .

There can be no such thing as peaceable secession. Peaceable secession is an utter impossibility. Is the great Constitution under which we live, covering this whole country, is it to be thawed and melted away by secession, as the snows on the mountain melt under the influence of a vernal sun, disappear almost unobserved, and run off? No, Sir! No, Sir! I will not state what might produce the disruption of the Union; but, Sir, I see as plainly as I see the sun in heaven what that disruption itself must produce; I see that it must produce war, and such a war as I will not describe, in its twofold character.

Peaceable secession! Peaceable secession! The concurrent agreement of all the members of this great republic to separate! A voluntary separation, with alimony on one side and on the other. Why, what would be the result?

Where is the line to be drawn? What States are to seceded? What is to remain American? What am I to be? An American no longer? Am I to become a sectional man, a local man, a separatist, with no country in common with the gentlemen who sit around me here, or who fill the other house of Congress? Heaven forbid! Where is the flag of the republic to remain? Where is the eagle still to tower? or is he to cower, and shrink, and fall to the ground? Why, Sir, our ancestors, our fathers and our grandfathers, those of them that are yet living amongst us with prolonged lives, would rebuke and reproach us; and our children and our grandchildren would cry out shame upon us, if we of this generation should dishonor these ensigns of the power of the government and the harmony of that Union which is every day felt among us with so much joy and gratitude . . .

And now, Mr. President, instead of speaking of the possibility or utility of secession, instead of dwelling in those caverns of darkness, instead of groping with those ideas so full of all that is horrid and horrible, let us come out into the light of day; let us enjoy the fresh air of Liberty and Union; let us cherish those hopes which belong to us; let us devote ourselves to those great objects that are fit for our consideration and action; let us raise our conceptions to the magnitude and the importance of the duties that devolve upon us; let our comprehension be as broad as the country for which we act, our aspirations as high as its certain destiny; let us not be pigmies in a case that calls for men. Never did there devolve on any generation of men higher trusts than now devolve upon us, for the preservation of this Constitution and the harmony and peace of all who are destined to live under it.

Source: Dartmouth College

FREDERICK DOUGLASS'S "THE SIGNIFICANCE OF EMANCIPATION IN THE WEST INDIES," 1857

On August 3, 1857, Frederick Douglass gave a speech in Canadaigua, New York in which he discussed freedom for slaves in the West Indies. In this speech Douglass described what he called his "philosophy of reform," which was that successful struggles for liberty always require tremendous effort and sacrifice.

Let me give you a word of the philosophy of reform. The whole history of the progress of human liberty shows that all concessions yet made to her august claims, have been born of earnest struggle. The conflict has been exciting, agitating, all-absorbing, and for the time being, putting all other tumults to silence. It must do this or it does nothing. If there is no struggle there is no progress. Those who profess to favor freedom and yet depreciate agitation, are men who want crops without plowing up the ground, they want rain without thunder and lightening. They want the ocean without the awful roar of its many waters.

This struggle may be a moral one, or it may be a physical one, and it may be both moral and physical, but it must be a struggle.

Power concedes nothing without a demand. It never did and it never will. Find out just what any people will quietly submit to and you have found out the exact measure of injustice and wrong which will be imposed upon them, and these will continue till they are resisted with either words or blows, or with both. The limits of tyrants are prescribed by the endurance of those whom they oppress. In the light of these ideas, Negroes will be hunted at the North, and held and flogged at the South so long as they submit to those devilish outrages, and make no resistance, either moral or physical. Men may not get all they pay for in this world; but they must certainly pay for all they get. If we ever get free from the oppressions and wrongs heaped upon us, we must pay for their removal. We must do this by labor, by suffering, by sacrifice, and if needs be, by our lives and the lives of others."

Source: *The Frederick Douglass Papers. Series One: Speeches, Debates, and Interviews. Volume 3: 1855–63.* Edited by John W. Blassingame. New Haven: Yale University Press, p. 204.

VOCABULARY

august impressive, majestic

tumults noises, disturbances

depreciate put down, dismiss

LINCOLN'S FIRST INAUGURAL ADDRESS, 1861

Abraham Lincoln knew that his victory in the 1860 presidential election threatened to tear the country apart. In his inaugural address on March 4, 1861, Lincoln pledged that there would be no war unless the South chose to begin one. In the excerpt below, he explains his reasons for believing secession to be unconstitutional and urges the South not to destroy the Union.

Fellow-Citizens of the United States:

In compliance with a custom as old as the Government itself, I appear before you to address you briefly and to take in your presence the oath prescribed by the Constitution of the United States to be taken by the President "before he enters on the execution of this Office . . .

I have no purpose, directly or indirectly, to interfere with the institution of slavery in the States where it exists. I believe I have no lawful right to do so, and I have no inclination to do so. Those who nominated and elected me did so with full knowledge that I had made this and many similar declarations and had never recanted them; and more than this, they placed in the platform for my acceptance, and as a law to themselves and to me, the clear and emphatic resolution which I now read:

. . . In any law upon this subject ought not all the safeguards of liberty known in civilized and humane jurisprudence to be introduced, so that a free man be not in any case surrendered as a slave? And might it not be well at the same time to provide by

VOCABULARY

recanted publicly withdrew or repudiated a statement

emphatic forceful or insistent

jurisprudence a system or body of law

law for the enforcement of that clause in the Constitution which guarantees that "the citizens of each State shall be entitled to all privileges and immunities of citizens in the several States? . . .

It follows from these views that no State upon its own mere motion can lawfully get out of the Union; that resolves and ordinances to that effect are legally void, and that acts of violence within any State or States against the authority of the United States are insurrectionary or revolutionary, according to circumstances.

I therefore consider that in view of the Constitution and the laws the Union is unbroken, and to the extent of my ability, I shall take care, as the Constitution itself expressly enjoins upon me, that the laws of the Union be faithfully executed in all the States . . .

One section of our country believes slavery is right and ought to be extended, while the other believes it is wrong and ought not to be extended. This is the only substantial dispute.

Physically speaking, we can not separate. We can not remove our respective sections from each other nor build an impassable wall between them. A husband and wife may be divorced and go out of the presence and

beyond the reach of each other, but the different parts of our country can not do this.

This country, with its institutions, belongs to the people who inhabit it. Whenever they shall grow weary of the existing Government, they can exercise their constitutional right of amending it or their revolutionary right to dismember or overthrow it . . .

In your hands, my dissatisfied fellow-countrymen, and not in mine, is the momentous issue of civil war. The Government will not assail you. You can have no conflict without being yourselves the aggressors. You have no oath registered in heaven to destroy the Government, while I shall have the most solemn one to "preserve, protect, and defend it."

I am loath to close. We are not enemies, but friends. We must not be enemies. Though passion may have strained it must not break our bonds of affection. The mystic chords of memory, stretching from every battlefield and patriot grave to every living heart and hearthstone all over this broad land, will yet swell the chorus of the Union, when again touched, as surely they will be, by the better angels of our nature.

Source: Inaugural Addresses of the Presidents of the United States. 1989. Bartleby Library.

THE EMANCIPATION PROCLAMATION

After the Union army victory at the Battle of Antietam, President Abraham Lincoln decided to issue the Emancipation Proclamation, which freed all enslaved people in states under Confederate control. The proclamation, which went into effect on January 1, 1863, was a step toward the Thirteenth Amendment (1865), which ended slavery in all of the United States.

That on the 1st day of January, in the year of our Lord 1863, all persons held as slaves within any state or designated part of a state, the people whereof shall then be in rebellion against the United States, shall be then, thenceforward, and forever free; and the executive government of the United States, including the military and naval authority thereof, will recognize and maintain the

freedom of such persons and will do no act or acts to repress such persons, or any of them, in any efforts they may make for their actual freedom . . .

And I further declare and make known that such persons of suitable condition will be received into the armed service of the United States to garrison forts, positions, stations, and other places, and to man vessels of all sorts in said service. And upon this act, sincerely believed to be an act of justice, warranted by the Constitution upon military necessity, I invoke the considerate judgment of mankind and the gracious favor of Almighty God.

Source: "Emancipation Proclamation" by Abraham Lincoln. *Reprinted in The Annals of America: Volume 9, 1858–1865.* Encyclopedia Britannica, Inc. 1976.

LINCOLN'S GETTYSBURG ADDRESS, 1863

On November 19, 1863, Abraham Lincoln addressed a crowd gathered to dedicate a cemetery at the Gettysburg battlefield. His short speech, which is excerpted below, reminded Americans of the ideals on which the Republic was founded.

Four score and seven years ago our fathers brought forth on this continent a new nation, conceived in liberty and dedicated to the proposition that all men are created equal.

Now we are engaged in a great civil war, testing whether that nation or any nation so conceived and so dedicated can long endure. We are met on a great battlefield of that war. We have come to dedicate a portion of that field as a final resting-place for those who here gave their lives that that nation might live. It is altogether fitting and proper that we should do this.

But in a larger sense, we cannot dedicate—we cannot consecrate—we cannot hallow—this ground. The brave men, living and dead, who struggled here have consecrated it far above our poor power to add or detract. The world will little note nor long remember what we say here, but it can never forget what they did here. It is for us, the living, rather, to be dedicated here to the unfinished work which they who fought here have thus far so nobly advanced.

It is rather for us to be here dedicated to the great task remaining before us—that from these honored dead we take increased devotion to that cause for which they gave the last full measure of devotion; that we here highly resolve that these dead shall not have died in vain; that this nation, under God, shall have a new birth of freedom; and that government of the people, by the people, for the people shall not perish from the earth.

Source: "The Gettysburg Address" by Abraham Lincoln. *Reprinted in The Annals of America: Volume 9, 1858–1865.* Encyclopedia Britannica, Inc. 1976

VOCABULARY
score twenty years
consecrated made holy

LINCOLN'S SECOND INAUGURAL ADDRESS, 1865

On March 4, 1865, President Lincoln laid out his approach to Reconstruction in his second inaugural address. As the excerpt below shows, Lincoln hoped to peacefully reunite the nation and its people.

At this second appearing to take the oath of the Presidential Office there is less occasion for an extended address than there was at the first. Then a statement somewhat in detail of a course to be pursued seemed fitting and proper. Now, at the expiration of four years, during which public declarations have been constantly called forth on every point and phase of the great contest which still absorbs the attention and engrosses the energies of the nation, little that is new could be presented. The progress of our arms, upon which all else chiefly depends, is as well known to the public as to myself, and it is, I trust, reasonably satisfactory and encouraging to all. With high hope for the future, no prediction in regard to it is ventured.

On the occasion corresponding to this four years ago all thoughts were anxiously directed to an impending civil war. All dreaded it, all sought to avert it. While the inaugural address was being delivered from this place, devoted altogether to saving the Union without war, urgent agents were in the city seeking to destroy it without war—seeking to dissolve the Union and divide effects by negotiation. Both parties deprecated war, but one of them would make war rather than let the nation survive, and the other would accept war rather than let it perish, and the war came . . .

With malice toward none, with charity for all, with firmness in the right as God gives us to see the right, let us strive on to finish the work we are in, to bind up the nation's wounds, to care for him who shall have borne the battle and for his widow and his orphan, to do all which may achieve and cherish a just and lasting peace among ourselves and with all nations.

Source: Inaugural Addresses of the Presidents of the United States. 1989. Bartleby Library.

VOCABULARY
deprecated made little of
malice desire to cause injury; hatred

DECLARATION OF RIGHTS FOR WOMEN

VOCABULARY

buoyant cheerful, capable of floating

jubilee a special anniversary

benedictions blessings

usurpations takings by force and without right

Included below are excerpts from a speech made by Susan B. Anthony on July 4, 1876. Anthony used the occasion—the 100th anniversary of the approval of the Declaration of Independence—to speak out in support of rights for women.

Susan B. Anthony, July 4, 1876

While the nation is buoyant with patriotism, and all hearts are attuned to praise, it is with sorrow we come to strike the one discordant note, on this one-hundredth anniversary of our country's birth. When subjects of kings, emperors, and czars from the old world join in our national jubilee, shall the women of the republic refuse to lay their hands with benedictions on the nation's head? . . . Yet we cannot forget, even in this glad hour, that while all men of every race, and clime, and condition, have been invested with the full rights of citizenship under our hospitable flag, all women still suffer the degradation of disfranchisement.

The history of our country the past one hundred years has been a series of assumptions and usurpations of power over woman, in direct opposition to the principles of just government, acknowledged by the United States as its foundations, which are:

First–the natural rights of each individual

Second–the equality of these rights

Third–that rights not delegated are retained by the individual

Fourth–that no person can exercise the rights of others without delegated authority

Fifth–that the non-use of rights does not destroy them

And for the violation of these fundamental principles of our government, we arraign our rulers on this Fourth day of July, 1876 . . .

These articles of impeachment against our rulers we now submit to the impartial judgment of the people. To all these wrongs and oppressions woman has not submitted in silence and resignation. From the beginning of the century, when Abigail Adams, the wife of one president and the mother of another, said, "We will not hold ourselves bound to obey laws in which we have no voice or representation," until now, woman's discontent has been steadily increasing, culminating nearly thirty years ago in a simultaneous movement among the women of the nation, demanding the right of suffrage . . .

And now, at the close of a hundred years, as the hour hand of the great clock that marks the centuries points to 1876, we declare our faith in the principles of self-government; our full equality with man in natural rights . . . We ask of our rulers, at this hour, no special favors, no special privileges, no special legislation. We ask justice, we ask equality, we ask that all the civil and political rights that belong to citizens of the United States, be guaranteed to us and our daughters forever.

Source: *History of Women's Suffrage,* Elizabeth C. Stanton et al., eds., Vol.III, 1887.

THE FOURTEEN POINTS, 1918

On January 8, 1918, nearly a year before the end of World War I, Woodrow Wilson presented his plan for a postwar peace to the U.S. Congress. Wilson came to the Paris Peace Conference in 1919 with these same 14 points.

1. Open covenants of peace, openly arrived at, after which there shall be no private international understandings of any kind but diplomacy shall proceed always frankly and in the public view.
2. Absolute freedom of navigation upon the seas, outside territorial waters, alike in peace and in war . . .
3. The removal, so far as possible, of all economic barriers and the establishment of an equality of trade conditions . . .
4. Adequate guarantees given and taken that national armaments will be reduced to the lowest point consistent with domestic safety.
5. A free, open-minded, and absolutely impartial adjustment of all colonial claims, based upon a strict observance of the principle that in determining all such questions of sovereignty the interests of the populations concerned must have equal weight with the equitable claims of the government whose title is to be determined.
6. The evacuation of all Russian territory . . .
7. Belgium . . . must be evacuated and restored, without any attempt to limit . . . sovereignty . . .
8. All French territory should be freed and the invaded portions restored, and the wrong done to France by Prussia in 1871 in the matter of Alsace-Lorraine, which has unsettled the peace of the world for nearly fifty years, should be righted, in order that peace may once more be made secure in the interest of all.
9. A readjustment of the frontiers of Italy should be effected along clearly recognizable lines of nationality.
10. The peoples of Austria-Hungary . . . should be accorded the freest opportunity of autonomous development.
11. Rumania, Serbia, and Montenegro should be evacuated . . .
12. The Turkish portions of the present Ottoman Empire should be assured a secure sovereignty, but the other nationalities which are now under Turkish rule should be assured an undoubted security of life and an absolutely unmolested opportunity of an autonomous development,
13. An independent Polish state should be erected which should include the territories inhabited by indisputably Polish populations
14. A general association of nations must be formed under specific covenants for the purpose of affording mutual guarantees of political independence and territorial integrity to great and small states alike.

Source: Avalon Project of Yale University Law School

VOCABULARY
sovereignty supremacy of authority, the independence of a nation
autonomous independent

FOUR FREEDOMS SPEECH, 1941

In January 1941, while World War II raged in Europe and Asia, many Americans hoped the United States would stay out of the war. President Franklin D. Roosevelt understood this public feeling, but believed it was important that the United States help Great Britain resist Nazi Germany. Roosevelt gave this speech on January 6, 1941 to win greater support for his policy of providing aid to the enemies of Germany and Japan.

I have called for personal sacrifice. I am assured of the willingness of almost all Americans to respond to that call.

A part of the sacrifice means the payment of more money in taxes. In my Budget Message I shall recommend that a greater portion of this great defense program be paid for from taxation than we are paying today. No person should try, or be allowed, to get rich out of this program; and the principle of tax payments in accordance with ability to pay should be constantly before our eyes to guide our legislation.

If the Congress maintains these principles, the voters, putting patriotism ahead of pocketbooks, will give you their applause.

In the future days, which we seek to make secure, we look forward to a world founded upon four essential human freedoms.

The first is freedom of speech and expression—everywhere in the world.

The second is freedom of every person to worship God in his own way—everywhere in the world.

The third is freedom from want—which, translated into world terms, means economic understandings which will secure to every nation a healthy peacetime life for its inhabitants—everywhere in the world.

The fourth is freedom from fear—which, translated into world terms, means a world-wide reduction of armaments to such a point and in such a thorough fashion that no nation will be in a position to commit an act of physical aggression against any neighbor—anywhere in the world.

That is no vision of a distant millennium. It is a definite basis for a kind of world attainable in our own time and generation. That kind of world is the very <u>antithesis</u> of the so-called new order of tyranny which the dictators seek to create with the crash of a bomb.

Source: Franklin D. Roosevelt Presidential Library and Museum

VOCABULARY
antithesis exact opposite

JOHN F. KENNEDY INAUGURAL ADDRESS, 1961

VOCABULARY
forebears ancestors

President John F. Kennedy took office on January 20, 1961, at the height of the Cold War. In his inaugural address, Kennedy spoke of the immense responsibility entrusted to his generation of Americans.

The world is very different now. For man holds in his mortal hands the power to abolish all forms of human poverty and all forms of human life. And yet the same revolutionary beliefs for which our <u>forebears</u> fought are still at issue around the globe—the belief that the rights of man come not from the generosity of the state, but from the hand of God.

We dare not forget today that we are the heirs of that first revolution. Let the word go forth from this time and place, to friend and foe alike, that the torch has been passed to a new generation of Americans—born in this century, tempered by war, disciplined by a hard and bitter peace, proud of our ancient heritage—and unwilling to witness or permit the slow undoing of those human rights to which this Nation has always been committed, and to which we are committed today at home and around the world.

Let every nation know, whether it wishes us well or ill, that we shall pay any price, bear any burden, meet any hardship, support any friend, oppose any foe, in order to assure the survival and the success of liberty . . .

In the long history of the world, only a few generations have been granted the role of defending freedom in its hour of maximum danger. I do not shrink from this responsibility—I welcome it. I do not believe that any of us would exchange places with any other people or any other generation. The energy, the faith, the devotion which we bring to this endeavor will light our country and all who serve it—and the glow from that fire can truly light the world.

And so, my fellow Americans: ask not what your country can do for you—ask what you can do for your country.

My fellow citizens of the world: ask not what America will do for you, but what together we can do for the freedom of man.

Source: Avalon Project of Yale University Law School

MARTIN LUTHER KING JR.'S SPEECH IN MEMPHIS, 1968

In 1968 Martin Luther King, Jr. went to Memphis to march in support of striking sanitation workers. The strikers were mostly African American. On April 3, 1968, King gave the following speech. He makes reference to an earlier incident in which he was stabbed by a deranged woman. The wound was so close to King's heart, doctors announced, that that if he had sneezed, he would have died. The day after delivering this speech, King was assassinated.

April 3, 1968, Memphis, Tennessee

And I want to say tonight, I want to say that I am happy that I didn't sneeze. Because if I had sneezed, I wouldn't have been around here in 1960, when students all over the South started sitting-in at lunch counters. And I knew that as they were sitting in, they were really standing up for the best in the American dream. And taking the whole nation back to those great wells of democracy which were dug deep by the Founding Fathers in the Declaration of Independence and the Constitution. If I had sneezed, I wouldn't have been around in 1962, when Negroes in Albany, Georgia, decided to straighten their backs up. And whenever men and women straighten their backs up, they are going somewhere, because a man can't ride your back unless it is bent. If I had sneezed, I wouldn't have been here in 1963, when the black people of Birmingham, Alabama, aroused the conscience of this nation, and brought into being the Civil Rights Bill. If I had sneezed, I wouldn't have had a chance later that year, in August, to try to tell America about a dream that I had had. If I had sneezed, I wouldn't have been down in Selma, Alabama, been in Memphis to see the community rally around those brothers and sisters who are suffering. I'm so happy that I didn't sneeze . . .

Well, I don't know what will happen now. We've got some difficult days ahead. But it doesn't matter with me now. Because I've been to the mountaintop. And I don't mind. Like anybody, I would like to live a long life. Longevity has its place. But I'm not concerned about that now. I just want to do God's will. And He's allowed me to go up to the mountain. And I've looked over. And I've seen the promised land. I may not get there with you. But I want you to know tonight, that we, as a people, will get to the promised land. And I'm happy, tonight. I'm not worried about anything. I'm not fearing any man. Mine eyes have seen the glory of the coming of the Lord.

Source: American Federation of State, County and Municipal Employees

CÉSAR CHÁVEZ SPEECH, 1984

VOCABULARY
implements tools
chattel personal
property a slave

In 1962 César Chávez formed the United Farm Workers, a labor union for migrant farm workers. In the 1984 speech excerpted below, Chávez described the goals that motivated his life's work and spoke of the contribution the farm workers movement had made to improving lives for Hispanic Americans everywhere.

All my life, I have been driven by one dream, one goal, one vision: To overthrow a farm labor system in this nation which treats farm workers as if they were not important human beings. Farm workers are not agricultural implements. They are not beasts of burden to be used and discarded . . .

I'm not very different from anyone else who has ever tried to accomplish something with his life. My motivation comes from my personal life—from watching what my mother and father went through when I was growing up; from what we experienced as migrant farm workers in California.

That dream, that vision, grew from my own experience with racism, with hope, with the desire to be treated fairly and to see my people treated as human beings and not as chattel. It grew from anger and rage—emotions I felt 40 years ago when people of my color were denied the right to see a movie or eat at a restaurant in many parts of California. It grew from the frustration and humiliation I felt as a boy who couldn't understand how the growers could abuse and exploit farm workers when there were so many of us and so few of them . . .

I began to realize what other minority people had discovered: That the only answer—the only hope—was in organizing. More of us had to become citizens. We had to register to vote. And people like me had to develop the skills it would take to organize, to educate, to help empower the Chicano people . . .

All Hispanics—urban and rural, young and old—are connected to the farm workers' experience. We had all lived through the fields—or our parents had. We shared that common humiliation. How could we progress as a people, even if we lived in the cities, while the farm workers—men and women of our color—were condemned to a life without pride? How could we progress as a people

while the farm workers—who symbolized our history in this land—ere denied self-respect? . . .

The UFW was the beginning! We attacked that historical source of shame and infamy that our people in this country lived with. We attacked that injustice, not by complaining; not by seeking handouts; not by becoming soldiers in the War on Poverty.

Farm workers acknowledged we had allowed ourselves to become victims in a democratic society—a society where majority rule and collective bargaining are supposed to be more than academic theories or political rhetoric. And by addressing this historical problem, we created confidence and pride and hope in an entire people's ability to create the future . . .

The union's survival—its very existence—sent out a signal to all Hispanics that we were fighting for our dignity, that we were challenging and overcoming injustice, that we were empowering the least educated among us—the poorest among us . . . I didn't really appreciate it at the time, but the coming of our union signaled the start of great changes among Hispanics that are only now beginning to be seen.

I've traveled to every part of this nation. I have met and spoken with thousands of Hispanics from every walk of life—from every social and economic class. One thing I hear most often from Hispanics, regardless of age or position—and from many non-Hispanics as well—is that the farm workers gave them hope that they could succeed and the inspiration to work for change . . . And Hispanics across California and the nation who don't work in agriculture are better off today because of what the farm workers taught people about organization, about pride and strength, about seizing control over their own lives.

Terrorists attacked the United States on the morning of September 11, 2001, crashing planes into the World Trade Center in New York City and the Pentagon building near Washington, D.C. At 8:30 on the evening of September 11, President George W. Bush addressed the nation from the White House.

Good evening. Today, our fellow citizens, our way of life, our very freedom came under attack in a series of deliberate and deadly terrorist acts. The victims were in airplanes, or in their offices; secretaries, businessmen and women, military and federal workers; moms and dads, friends and neighbors. Thousands of lives were suddenly ended by evil, despicable acts of terror.

The pictures of airplanes flying into buildings, fires burning, huge structures collapsing, have filled us with disbelief, terrible sadness, and a quiet, unyielding anger. These acts of mass murder were intended to frighten our nation into chaos and retreat. But they have failed; our country is strong.

A great people has been moved to defend a great nation. Terrorist attacks can shake the foundations of our biggest buildings, but they cannot touch the foundation of America. These acts shattered steel, but they cannot dent the steel of American resolve. America was targeted for attack because we're the brightest beacon for freedom and opportunity in the world. And no one will keep that light from shining.

Today, our nation saw evil, the very worst of human nature. And we responded with the best of America—with the daring of our rescue workers, with the caring for strangers and neighbors who came to give blood and help in any way they could.

Immediately following the first attack, I implemented our government's emergency response plans. Our military is powerful, and it's prepared. Our emergency teams are working in New York City and Washington, D.C. to help with local rescue efforts.

Our first priority is to get help to those who have been injured, and to take every precaution to protect our citizens at home and around the world from further attacks.

The functions of our government continue without interruption. Federal agencies in Washington which had to be evacuated today are reopening for essential personnel tonight, and will be open for business tomorrow. Our financial institutions remain strong, and the American economy will be open for business, as well.

The search is underway for those who are behind these evil acts. I've directed the full resources of our intelligence and law enforcement communities to find those responsible and to bring them to justice. We will make no distinction between the terrorists who committed these acts and those who harbor them.

I appreciate so very much the members of Congress who have joined me in strongly condemning these attacks. And on behalf of the American people, I thank the many world leaders who have called to offer their condolences and assistance.

America and our friends and allies join with all those who want peace and security in the world, and we stand together to win the war against terrorism. Tonight, I ask for your prayers for all those who grieve, for the children whose worlds have been shattered, for all whose sense of safety and security has been threatened. And I pray they will be comforted by a power greater than any of us, spoken through the ages in Psalm 23: "Even though I walk through the valley of the shadow of death, I fear no evil, for You are with me."

This is a day when all Americans from every walk of life unite in our resolve for justice and peace. America has stood down enemies before, and we will do so this time. None of us will ever forget this day. Yet, we go forward to defend freedom and all that is good and just in our world.

Thank you. Good night, and God bless America.

Source: The White House

English and Spanish Glossary

MARK	AS IN	RESPELLING	EXAMPLE
a	alphabet	a	*AL-fuh-bet
ā	Asia	ay	AY-zhuh
ä	cart, top	ah	KAHRT, TAHP
e	let, ten	e	LET, TEN
ē	even, leaf	ee	EE-vuhn, LEEF
i	it, tip, British	i	IT, TIP, BRIT-ish
ī	site, buy, Ohio	y	SYT, BY, oh-HY-oh
	iris	eye	EYE-ris
k	card	k	KAHRD
ō	over, rainbow	oh	OH-vuhr, RAYN-boh
ů	book, wood	ooh	BOOHK, WOOHD
ó	all, orchid	aw	AWL, AWR-kid
ói	foil, coin	oy	FOYL, KOYN
aů	out	ow	OWT
ə	cup, butter	uh	KUHP, BUHT-uhr
ü	rule, food	oo	ROOL, FOOD
yü	few	yoo	FYOO
zh	vision	zh	VIZH-uhn

*A syllable printed in small capital letters receives heavier emphasis than the other syllable(s) in a word.

Phonetic Respelling and Pronunciation Guide

Many of the key terms in this textbook have been respelled to help you pronounce them. The letter combinations used in the respelling throughout the narrative are explained in the following phonetic respelling and pronunciation guide. The guide is adapted from *Merriam-Webster's Collegiate Dictionary, Eleventh Edition; Merriam-Webster's Biographical Dictionary;* and *Merriam-Webster's Geographical Dictionary.*

A

abolition movement movement to end slavery in the United States (p. 288)
movimiento abolicionista movimiento para poner fin a la esclavitud en Estados Unidos

Adams-Onís Treaty (1819) an agreement in which Spain gave East Florida to the United States (p. 241)
tratado de Adams y Onís (1819) acuerdo en el que España cedió el territorio del este de la Florida a Estados Unidos

affirmative action programs that gave preference to minorities and women in hiring and admissions (p. 941)
acción afirmativa programas que les daban preferencia a los grupos minoritarios y a las mujeres en cuestión de empleos y de ingreso en la universidad (pág. 941)

agricultural revolution a change in way of life that occurred about 7,000 years ago, when hunter-gatherer societies began to stay in one place and grow their own food (p. 7)
revolución agrícola un cambio en el estilo de vida que ocurrió hace unos 7,000 años atrás, cuando las sociedades de cazadores y recolectores comenzaron a establecerse en un solo sitio y a cultivar sus alimentos

Al Qaeda Osama bin Laden's terrorist network (p. 1094)
Al Qaeda red terrorista de Osama bin Laden

Alamo Spanish mission in San Antonio, Texas; the site of a famous battle of the Texas Revolution in 1836 (p. 306)

El Álamo misión española en San Antonio, Texas; escenario de una famosa batalla durante la Revolución Texana de 1836

Albany Plan of Union (1754) first plan for uniting the colonies; proposed by Ben Franklin (p. 92)
Plan de Unión de Albany (1754) primer plan para unir a las colonias propuesto por Ben Franklin.

alien citizen of another country living in the United States (p. 624)
extranjero ciudadano de otro país que reside en Estados Unidos

Alien and Sedition Acts (1798) laws passed by Congress that allowed the government to deport foreigners and jail critics (p. 213)
Leyes de Extranjeros y Sedición (1798) leyes aprobadas por un Congreso que permitían al gobierno deportar a los extranjeros y encarcelar a las personas que lo criticaban

Alliance for Progress President Kennedy's program to provide economic aid to Latin America (p. 886)
Alianza para el Progreso programa iniciado por el presidente Kennedy mediante el cual se le brindó ayuda económica a América Latina

Allied Powers alliance between Britain, France, and Russia; later joined by the United States in World War I (p. 584)
potencias aliadas alianza formada durante la Primera Guerra Mundial entre Inglaterra, Francia y Rusia, a la que luego se unió Estados Unidos

the Allies the alliance of Britain, France, and Russia in World War II (p. 748)

Aliados alianza entre Inglaterra, Francia y Rusia durante la Segunda Guerra Mundial

American Federation of Labor (AFL) labor organization that united skilled workers into national unions for specific industries (p. 475)
Federación Estadounidense del Trabajo (AFL, por sus siglas en inglés) organización que unió a los obreros especializados en sindicatos nacionales para industrias específicas

American Indian Movement (AIM) organization founded in 1968 by Native American leaders calling for a renewal of Native American culture and recognition of Native Americans' rights (p. 992)
Movimiento Indígena Norteamericano (AIM, por sus siglas en inglés) organización fundada en 1968 por líderes de los indígenas norteamericanos que formentó la renovación de la cultura indígena norteamericana y el reconocimiento de los derechos de los indígenas

Americanization process in which Native Americans were forced to abandon their traditional cultures and adopt the culture of white America (p. 442)
americanización proceso mediante el cual se obligó a los indígenas norteamericanos a abandonar su cultura tradicional y a adoptar la cultura de los estadounidenses blancos

Anaconda Plan name given to the Civil War plan devised by Union General Winfield Scott to seal the South off from the rest of the world (p. 360)
Anaconda Plan nombre que se le dio al plan de guerra concebido por el general norteño Winfield Scott para aislar al Sur del resto del mundo

anarchist radicals who believe in the destruction of government (p. 627)
anarquista radical que cree en la destrucción del gobierno

Angel Island an island in the San Francisco bay that was an entry point for many Asian immigrants to the United States beginning in 1910 (p. 492)
isla Angel isla en la bahía de San Francisco que fue el punto de ingreso para muchos inmigrantes asiáticos a partir de 1910

Antifederalists people who opposed ratification of the Constitution (p. 158)
antifederalistas personas que se oponían a la ratificación de la Constitución

anti-Semitism anti-Jewish beliefs (p. 779)
antisemitismo creencias en contra de los judíos

apartheid the South African government's official policy of legalized racial segregation throughout society (p. 1057)
apartheid politica oficial del gobierno sudafricano de segregación racial legalizada en toda la sociedad

Apollo 11 U.S. space mission, which, in 1969, landed the first person, Neil Armstrong, on the moon (p. 1023)
Apollo 11 misión espacial estadounidense que en el año 1969 llevó a la primera persona, Neil Armstrong, a la Luna

appeasement giving in to the demands of uncompromising powers to avoid war (p. 747)
apaciguamiento aceptar a las exigencias de las potencias que no quieren ceder, con el fin de evitar la guerra

arms race competition between nations to gain an advantage in weapons (p. 638)

carrera armamentista competencia entre varios países para obtener una ventaja en las armas

Articles of Confederation (1777) the document that created the first central government for the United States; it was replaced by the Constitution in 1789 (p. 146)
Artículos de la Confederación (1777) documento que creó el primer gobierno central en Estados Unidos; fue reemplazado por la Constitución en 1789

artillery large, mounted guns (p. 357)
artillería grandes armas colocadas en una base

assembly line a mass-production process in which a product moved forward through many work stations (p. 629)
cadena de montaje proceso de producción masiva en el que el producto avanza de puesto en puesto

associative state the term for President Hoover's vision of voluntary partnership between business associations and the government (p. 688)
estado asociativo término que usó el presidente Hoover para referirse al vínculo voluntario entre las asociaciones empresariales y el gobierno

Atlantic Charter (1941) a statement of American and British goals for the defeat of the Nazis and their vision for the postwar world (p. 755)
Carta del Atlántico (1941) declaración de las metas estadounidenses y británicas para derrotar a los nazis, y de su visión para el mundo después de la guerra

atomic bomb a bomb which uses energy released by splitting atoms to create an enormous explosion (p. 762)
bomba atómica artefacto explosivo que usa energía liberada por la división de los átomos, creando así una explosión enorme

Axis Powers the alliance of Germany, Italy and Japan in World War II (p. 750)
potencias del Eje la alianza formada entre Alemania, Italia y Japón durante la Segunda Guerra Mundial

Aztec a Mesoamerican society that lived in the central valley of present-day Mexico from about the 14th through 16th centuries (p. 9)
azteca sociedad mesoamericana que vivió en el valle central de lo que hoy es México entre los siglos XIV y XVI, aproximadamente

baby boom a dramatic rise in the birthrate following World War II (p. 825)
baby boom aumento marcado en la tasa de natalidad después de la Segunda Guerra Mundial

Bacon's Rebellion (1676) an atttack led by Nathaniel Bacon against American Indians and the colonial government in Virginia (p. 50)
Rebelión de Bacon (1676) ataque encabezado por Nathaniel Bacon contra los indígenas norteamericanos y el gobierno colonial en Virginia

balance of power a system in which each nation or alliance has equal strength (p. 584)
equilibrio del poder sistema en el que cada país o alianza tiene igual poderío

balance of trade the relationship between a country's imports and exports (p. 73)

balanza comercial relación entre lo que el país importa y exporta

Bank of the United States a national bank chartered by Congress in 1791 to provide security for the U.S. economy (p. 207)

Banco de Estados Unidos banco nacional formado por el Congreso en 1791 para dar estabilidad a la economía de Estados Unidos

barter an exchange of goods without using money (p. 16)

trueque intercambio de bienes sin dinero

Bataan Death March (1942) forced march of American and Filipino prisoners of war captured by the Japanese in the Philippines during World War II (p. 787)

Marcha de la Muerte de Bataan (1942) marcha forzada de prisioneros de guerra estadounidenses y filipinos capturados por los japoneses en las Islas Filipinas durante la Segunda Guerra Mundial

Battle of Antietam (1862) a Union victory in the Civil War that marked the bloodiest single-day battle in U.S. military history (p. 370)

batalla de Antietam (1862) victoria del ejército de la Unión durante la Guerra Civil que fue la batalla de un solo día más sangrienta de la historia militar de Estados Unidos

Battle of Atlanta (1864) Civil War battle which led to the Union army's siege and capture of Atlanta and the final phase of the war (p. 391)

batalla de Atlanta (1864) batalla de la Guerra Civil tras la que el ejército de la Unión sitió y capturó la ciudad de Atlanta al final de la guerra

Battle of the Bulge (1944) World War II battle between Germany and the Allied forces; the German advance created a "bulge" in the Allied battle lines, though the Allies eventually prevailed (p. 776)

batalla del Bulge (de Árdenas) (1944) batalla de la Segunda Guerra Mundial entre Alemania y las fuerzas aliadas; la ofensiva alemana creó una especie de "acumalción" o "bulge"en las líneas aliadas, aunque los aliados salieron victoriosos al final

Battle of Bunker Hill (1775) a Revolutionary War battle in Boston that showed the colonists could fight well against the British army (p. 116)

batalla de Bunker Hill (1775) batalla de la Guerra de Independencia estadounidense en Boston que demostró que los colonos podían luchar bien contra el ejército británico

Battle of Chancellorsville (1863) Civil War battle that was one of the Confederate army's major victories (p. 384)

batalla de Chancellorsville (1863) batalla de la Guerra Civil que fue una las mayores victorias del Ejército Confederado

Battle of Chickamauga (1863) Confederate victory during the Civil War; one of the bloodiest battles as a result of a Union campaign to capture Chattanooga (p. 387)

batalla de Chickamauga (1863) victoria de la Confederación durante la Guerra Civil que también fue una de las batallas más sangientas, resultado de una campaña de la Unon para apoderarse de Chattanooga

Battle of Cold Harbor (1864) Civil War battle which caused nearly 7,000 Union army casualties (p. 391)

batalla de Cold Harbor (1864) batalla de la Guerra Civil en la cual murieron casi 7,000 soldados del ejército de la Unión

Battle of Fallen Timbers (1794) battle between U.S. troops and an American Indian confederation that ended Indian efforts to halt white settlement in the Northwest Territory (p. 212)

batalla de Fallen Timbers (1794) batalla entre las tropas estadounidenses y una confederación de indígenas norteamericanos que puso fin a los intentos de los indígenas por detener el establecimiento de los blancos en el Territorio del Noroeste

Battle of Gettysburg (1863) a Union Civil War victory that turned the tide against the Confederates at Gettysburg, Pennsylvania (p. 384)

batalla de Gettysburg (1863) victoria del ejército de la Unión durante la Guerra Civil que cambió el curso de la guerra en contra de los confederados en Gettysburg, Pensilvania

Battle of Glorieta Pass (1862) Civil War battle in which Union troops and volunteers stopped a Confederate invasion in northern New Mexico (p. 382)

batalla de Glorieta Pass (1862) batalla de la Guerra Civil, en la Unión y voluntarios detuvieron la invasión de la Confederación en la parte norte de Nuevo México

Battle of Iwo Jima (1945) a World War II battle between Japanese forces and invading U.S. troops (p. 792)

batalla de Iwo Jima (1945) batalla de la Segunda Guerra Mundial entre las fuerzas japonesas y las fuerzas estadounidenses invasoras

Battle of the Little Bighorn (1876) Battle in which Sioux forces led by Chief Sitting Bull defeated a U.S. Army troop led by Lieutenant Colonel George Armstrong Custer (p. 441)

batalla de Little Bighorn (1876) batalla en la que guerreros de la tribu sioux comandados por el jefe Sitting Bull derrotaron a las tropas del ejército estadounidense comandadas por el teniente coronel George Armstrong Custer

Battle of Midway (1942) a key naval and air battle between Japan and the United States in World War II (p. 788)

batalla de Midway (1942) batalla naval y aérea clave entre Japón y Estados Unidos durante la Segunda Guerra Mundial

Battle of New Orleans (1815) the greatest U.S. victory in the War of 1812; actually took place two weeks after a peace treaty had been signed ending the war (p. 227)

batalla de Nueva Orleáns (1815) la mayor victoria estadounidense en la Guerra de 1812; tuvo lugar dos semanas después de que se firmara el tratado de paz en el que se declaraba el final de la guerra

Battle of Okinawa (1945) World War II battle between Japanese forces and invading U.S. troops (p. 792)

batalla de Okinawa (1945) batalla de la Segunda Guerra Mundial entre las fuerzas japonesas y las tropas estadounidenses invasoras

Battle of Pea Ridge (1862) the Civil War's biggest battle west of the Mississippi River, in Arkansas (p. 382)

batalla de Pea Ridge (1862) la batalla más importante de la Guerra Civil al oeste del río Mississippi, en Arkansas

Battle of San Juan Hill (1898) battle in the Spanish-American War in which 8,000 U.S. soldiers fought to seize control over San Juan Hill (p. 562)

batalla de San Juan Hill (1898) batalla de la Guerra Hispanoamericana en la cual 8,000 soldados estadounidenses lucharon para apoderarse de la loma de San Juan

Battle of Saratoga (1777) a Revolutionary War battle in New York that resulted in a major defeat of British troops (p. 128)
batalla de Saratoga (1777) batalla de la Guerra de Independencia estadounidense que tuvo lugar en Nueva York y en la que las fuerzas británicas sufrieron una de sus peores derrotas

Battle of Shiloh (1862) a Civil War battle in Tennessee in which the Union army gained greater control over the Mississippi River valley (p. 366)
batalla de Shiloh (1862) batalla de la Guerra Civil en Tennessee en la que el ejército de la Unión adquirió mayor control sobre el valle del río Mississippi

Battle of Spotsylvania (1864) an 11-day series of clashes in the Civil War (p. 391)
batalla de Spotsylvania (1864) serie de combates durante 11 días en la Guerra Civil

Battle of Veracruz (1914) major conflict in the Mexican Revolution (p. 574)
Battle of Veracruz (1914) importante conflicto en la Revolución Mexicana

Battle of the Wilderness (1864) Civil War battle that was so fierce, the woods where it was fought caught fire and burned, killing many wounded soldiers (p. 391)
batalla de Wilderness (1864) batalla de la Guerra Civil que fue tan feroz que el bosque en la cual se peleó se incendió hasta no quedar nada, causando la muerte de muchos soldados heridos

Battle of Yorktown (1781) a three-week-long siege by the Americans and French that trapped most of the British Army at Yorktown, Virginia (p. 135)
batalla de Yorktown (1781) asedio de tres semanas en el que los estadounidenses y los franceses atraparon a la mayor parte del ejército británico en Yorktown, Virginia

Bay of Pigs invasion (1961) the failed attempt of Cuban exiles backed by the U.S. to overthrow the Cuban socialist government of Fidel Castro (p. 881)
invasión de la Bahía de Cochinos (1961) intento fallido de exiliados cubanos respaldados por Estados Unidos de derrocar al gobierno socialista cubano de Fidel Castro

bayonet constitution (1887) a constitution the king of Hawaii was forced to sign which severely restricted his power and deprived most Hawaiians of the vote (p. 555)
constitución de las bayonetas (1887) constitución que el rey de Hawai se vio obligado a firmar restringiendo gravemente su poder y privando a la mayoría de los hawaianos del voto

Bear Flag Revolt (1846) a revolt against Mexico by American settlers in California who declared the territory an independent republic (p. 311)
Rebelión de Bear Flag (1846) rebelión en contra de México iniciada por colonos estadounidenses que declararon al territorio de California una república independiente

benevolent society an aid organization set up by residents of a community to help its immigrants (p. 493)
sociedad benéfica organización de ayuda organizada por residentes de una comunidad para ayudar a sus inmigrantes

Berlin Airlift a program in which the United States and Britain shipped supplies by air to West Berlin during a Soviet blockade of all routes to the city; lasted from 1948–1949 (p. 822)
Puente Aéreo de Berlín programa mediante el cual Estados Unidos e Inglaterra enviaban suministros a Berlín Occidental durante un bloqueo soviético de todas las rutas hacia la ciudad; duró de 1948 a 1949

Bessemer process a process developed in the 1850s that led to faster, cheaper steel production (p. 461)
proceso Bessemer proceso de producción de acero más económico y rápido, desarrollado en la década de 1850

Big Four name given to the leaders of the Allied Powers who dominated the Paris Peace Conference following the Allied victory in World War I (p. 607)
Cuatro Grandes nombre que se les dio a los líderes de las potencias aliadas que dominaron la Conferencia de Paz en París tras la victoria de los Aliados en la Primera Guerra Mundial

Bill of Rights the first 10 amendments to the United States Constitution; ratified in 1791 (p. 159)
Declaración de Derechos primeras 10 enmiendas hechas a la Constitución de Estados Unidos.; aprobada en 1791

Black Cabinet group of African Americans Franklin D. Roosevelt appointed to key government positions; they served as unofficial advisors to the president (p. 718)
Gabinete Negro un grupo de afroamericanos que Franklin D. Roosevelt designó para que ocuparan cargos importantes en el gobierno; fueron asesores extraoficiales del presidente

Black Codes laws passed in the southern states during Reconstruction that greatly limited the freedom and rights of African Americans (p. 411)
Códigos Negros leyes aprobadas en los estados sureños en la época de la Reconstrucción que limitaron en gran medida la libertad y los derechos de los afroamericanos

Black Panther Party a group formed in 1966, inspired by the idea of Black Power, that provided aid to black neighborhoods; often thought of as radical or violent (p. 935)
Partido Black Panther grupo formado en 1966, inspirado en la noción del poder negro, que prestó ayuda en barrios predominantemente negros; a menudo fue considerado un grupo radical o violento

Black Power an African American social movement in the late 1960s that advocated unity and self-reliance to address injustice (p. 935)
poder negro movimiento social afroamericano que surgió a fines de la década de 1960; partidario de la unidad e interdependencia para enfrentar la injusticia

Black Tuesday Tuesday, October 29, 1929, the day that the stock market crashed (p. 677)
martes negro martes 29 de octubre de 1929, día en que se desplomó el mercado de valores

blacklist a list or register of people who are being denied a particular freedom or privilege (p. 475)
lista negra lista de personas a quienes se les niega una libertad o privilegio particular

Bleeding Kansas (1856) nickname given to Kansas after violence erupted between anti-slavery and pro-slavery groups (p. 330)
Kansas sangriento (1856) sobrenombre dado al estado de Kansas luego de que estalló la violencia entre grupos a favor y en contra de la esclavitud

blitzkrieg a German word meaning "lightning war" (p. 748)
blitzkrieg palabra en alemán que significa "guerra relámpago"

Bolsheviks a group of Russian radicals, led by Vladimir I. Lenin, who played a major role in the 1917 revolution in Russia (p. 623)
bolcheviques grupo de radicales rusos, dirigidos por Vladimir I. Lenin, que tuvo un rol muy importante en la Revolución Rusa de 1917

bonanza farm large-scale farm with expensive machinery, professional managers, and hired laborers working at specialized tasks (p. 453)
granja de bonanza granja de gran escala con maquinaria costosa, administradores profesionales y obreros contratados para hacer tareas especializadas

bootlegger people who smuggled liquor during Prohibition (p. 652)
contrabandista persona que comerciaba clandestinamente con licores durante la época de la Prohibición

border states Delaware, Kentucky, Maryland, and Missouri; slave states in between the North and the South that did not join the Confederacy during the Civil War (p. 358)
estados fronterizos Delaware, Kentucky, Maryland y Missouri; estados esclavistas entre el Norte y el Sur y que no se unieron a la Confederación durante la Guerra Civil

boricua the name by which many Puerto Ricans refer to themselves; it expresses pride, empowerment, and certain political beliefs (p. 1000)
boricua nombre con el que se refieren muchos puertorriqueños a ellos mismos; expresa orgullo, poderío y ciertas creencias políticas

Boston Massacre (1770) an incident where British soldiers fired into a crowd of colonists, killing five people (p. 109)
Masacre de Boston (1770) incidente en el que los soldados británicos dispararon contra una multitud de colonos, matando a cinco personas

Boxer Rebellion (1900) a siege of a foreign settlement in Beijing by Chinese nationalists who were angry at foreign involvement in China (p. 556)
Rebelión de los Boxers (1900) asentamiento extranjero en Beijing por parte de un grupo de nacionalistas chinos que estaban en desacuerdo con la participación extranjera en China

Bracero program (1942) program that allowed poor Mexican workers to work temporarily in the U.S. (p. 763)
programa de braceros (1942) programa que les dio a los trabajadores mexicanos pobres la oportunidad de trabajar temporalmente en Estados Unidos

brinkmanship a strategy that involves countries getting to the verge of war without actually going to war (p. 850)
política arriesgada estrategia que implica que los países llegan al borde de la guerra sin entrar en batalla

Brownsville incident (1906) the accusation of twelve members of the African American 25th Infantry of a shooting spree in Brownsville, Texas (p. 545)
incidente de Brownsville (1906) acusación de doce soldados del batallón 25 de Infantería, compuesto de afroamericanos de una matanza en Brownsville, Texas

budget deficit the amount by which government spending for a year exceeds government income (p. 1050)

déficit presupuestario cantidad en la cual los gastos del gobierno superan sus ingresos en un año determinado

budget surplus when a government's income exceeds its spending (p. 1086)
excedente presupuestario cuando los ingresos de un gobierno son mayores que sus gastos

bully pulpit a platform used to publicize and seek support for important issues (p. 536)
tribuna plataforma usada para promocionar y solicitar apoyo para temas de importancia

Bureau of Indian Affairs (BIA) the federal agency that managed the Native American reservations (p. 442)
Oficina de Asuntos Indígenas (BIA, por sus siglas en inglés) agencia federal que administraba las reservas de indígenas norteamericanos

Bush v. Gore Supreme Court case that ruled the Florida Supreme Court's recount in the 2000 presidential election was unconstitutional (p. 1087)
Bush contra Gore caso en el que la Corte Suprema decidió que el recuento efectuado por la Corte Suprema de Florida en la elección presidencial de 2000 fue inconstitucional

Butterfield Trail a 2,800 mile long trail that carried mail and passengers between St. Louis and San Francisco (p. 301)
camino de Butterfield camino de 2,800 millas por el que se transportaban correo y pasajeros entre St. Louis y San Francisco (pág. 301)

buying on margin buying stocks with loans from brokers (p. 675)
comprar a crédito comprar acciones con dinero prestado por los corredores

C

cabinet group of advisors that heads the executive branch of government (p. 203)
gabinete grupo de asesores que encabeza la rama ejecutiva del gobierno

California Trail an overland trail that led migrants to California during the Gold Rush (p. 299)
camino de California camino por tierra que llevó a los emigrantes a California durante la fiebre del oro

Camp David Accords (1978) peace agreement mediated by President Carter between Egyptian President Anwar Sadat and Israeli Prime Minister Menachem Begin (p. 1036)
Acuerdos de Camp David (1978) acuerdos de paz entre el presidente egipcio Anwar Sadat y el primer ministro israelí Menachem Begin en los que el presidente Carter actuó como mediador

capitalism economic system in which most businesses are privately owned (p. 467)
capitalismo sistema económico en el que la mayoría de las empresas son de propiedad privada

caravel a sailing vessel that uses square and triangular sails to help it sail against the wind (p. 27)
carabela barco con velas cuadras y triangulares que sirven para navegar contra el viento

carpetbagger derogatory nickname given by Southern critics to northern Republicans who came south during Reconstruction (p. 417)

carpetbagger apodo despectivo que les dieron los críticos sureños a los republicanos norteños que vinieron al Sur durante Reconstrucción

cash-and-carry (1939) law aimed at aiding the Allies during World War II, allowed countries at war to purchase American goods as long as they paid cash and picked up their orders in American ports (p. 754)

pague y lleve (1939) ley cuyo objetivo era ayudar a los Aliados durante la Segunda Guerra Mundial; permitía que los países en guerra compraran productos estadounidenses siempre y cuando pagaran en efectivo y recogieran sus pedidos en puertos estadounidenses

cash crops agricultural products grown to be sold (p. 80)

cultivos comerciales productos agrícolas que se cultivan para venderlos

casualties military term for those killed, wounded, or missing in action (p. 364)

bajas término militar que se refiere a los muertos, heridos o desaparecidos en acción

cavalry soldiers who fight on horseback (p. 365)

caballería soldados que luchan montados a caballo

Central Powers alliance between Germany, Austria-Hungary and the Ottoman Empire (p. 584)

poderes centrales alianza entre Alemania, Austria-Hungría y el Imperio otomano

checks and balances the Constitutional system that prevents any branch of government from becoming too powerful (p. 155)

equilibrio de poderes sistema establecido por la Constitución para evitar que ninguna rama del gobierno adquiera demasiada autoridad en relación con las demás

Chicano name adopted by Mexican Americans in the late 1960s to refer to a person of Mexican descent living in the U.S. (p. 996)

Chicano nombre adoptado por los mexicano-americanos a fines de la década de 1960 para referirse a una persona de ascendencia mexicana que reside en Estados Unidos

Chinese Exclusion Act law that banned Chinese immigration for 10 years declaring that no Chinese people already in the United States could become citizens (p. 494)

Ley de Exclusión de los Chinos ley que prohibió la inmigración china durante 10 años y declaró que ningún chino que ya residiera en Estados Unidos podía obtener la ciudadanía estadounidense

Chisholm Trail a trail that ran from San Antonio, Texas, to Abilene, Kansas, established by Jesse Chisholm in the late 1860s for cattle drives (p. 448)

camino de Chisholm camino desde San Antonio, Texas hasta Abilene, Kansas, creado por Jesse Chisholm a finales de la década de 1860 para arrear ganado

CIA Central Intelligence Agency; collects intelligence information and takes part in secret actions against foreign targets (p. 850)

CIA Agencia Central de Inteligencia; recoge información y participa en acciones secretas contra objetivos en el exterior del país

CIO a group that broke away from the AFL to form the Committee for Industrial Organization (p. 712)

CIO grupo que se separó de la AFL para formar la Comisión para la Organización Industrial

Civil Rights Act (1866) law that gave African Americans legal rights equal to those of white Americans (p. 413)

Ley de Derechos Civiles (1866) ley que les dio a los afroamericanos derechos legales igualés a los de los estadounidenses blancos

Civil Rights Act of 1964 act signed it into law on July 2, 1964 that banned discrimination in employment and in public accommodations (p. 923)

Ley de Derechos Civiles de 1964 ley firmada el 2 de julio de 1964 que prohibió la discriminación en el empleo y en los establecimientos públicos

Civil Rights Act of 1968 law that banned discrimination in the sale or rental of housing (p. 940)

Ley de Derechos Civiles de 1968 ley que prohibió la discriminación en la venta y alquiler de viviendas

clan a group of people related by blood (p. 10)

clan grupo de personas emparentadas entre sí por la misma sangre

Clayton Antitrust Act (1914) law that made illegal certain monopolistic business practices; it also legalized strikes, boycotts, and peaceful picketing (p. 543)

Ley Clayton Antimonopolios (1914) ley que prohibió ciertas práticas comerciales monopolísticas y legalizó las huelgas, los boicots y los piquetes pacíficos

code talkers Navajos who served as radio operators in the Marines during World War II translating important military messages into the Navajo language (p. 791)

codificadores navajos que durante la Segunda Guerra Mundial prestaron servicios en la marina estadounidense como operadores de radio, traduciendo importantes mensajes militares al idioma navajo

Cold War an era of high tension and bitter rivalry known between the United States and the Soviet Union following the end of World War II (p. 817)

Guerra Fría era de grandes tensiones y gran rivalidad entre Estados Unidos y la Unión Soviética después de concluida la Segunda Guerra Mundial

colonization the establishing of colonies, regions governed by a foreign power (p. 31)

colonización establecimiento de colonias, regiones gobernadas por potencias extranjeras

Columbian Exchange the transfer of plants, animals, and diseases between the Americas and Europe, Asia, and Africa (p. 33)

intercambio colombino intercambio de plantas, animales y enfermedades entre las Américas y Europa, Asia y África

Committee on Public Information created by President Wilson, this committee's objective was to maximize national loyalty and support for World War I (p. 603)

Comité de Información Pública creado por el presidente Wilson; su objetivo era aprovechar al máximo la lealtad y el apoyo de la nación durante la Primera Guerra Mundial

committees of correspondence committees created by the Massachusetts House of Representatives in the 1760s to help towns and colonies share information about resisting British laws (p. 109)

comités de correspondencia comités creados por la Cámara de Representantes de Massachusetts en la década de 1760 para que los pueblos y las colonias compartieran información que los ayudara a resistirse a las leyes británicas

Common Sense (1776) a pamphlet written by Thomas Paine that criticized monarchies and convinced many American colonists of the need to break away from Britain (p. 117)
Sentido común (1776) folleto escrito por Thomas Paine en el que criticaba a las monarquías con el fin de convencer a los colonos estadounidenses de la necesidad de independizarse de Gran Bretaña

communism economic and political system in which governments own the means of production and control economic planning (p. 623)
comunismo sistema económico y político en el que los gobiernos poseen los medios de producción y controlan la planificación económica

Communists people who seek the equal distribution of wealth and the end of all private property (p. 594)
comunistas personas que buscan una distribución igualitaria de la riqueza y el fin de todo tipo de propiedad privada

Compromise of 1850 Henry Clay's proposed agreement that allowed California to enter the Union as a free state and divided the rest of the Mexican Cession into two territories where slavery would be decided by popular sovereignty
Compromiso de 1850 acuerdo redactado por Henry Clay en que se permitía a California entrar en la Unión como estado libre y se proponía la división de la Cesión Mexicana en dos partes donde la esclavitud sería reglamentada por soberanía popular

Compromise of 1877 an agreement to settle the disputed presidential election of 1876; Democrats agreed to accept Republican Rutherford B. Hayes as president in return for the removal of federal troops from the South (p. 427)
Compromiso de 1877 acuerdo en el que se resolvió la disputa de las elecciones presidenciales de 1876; los demócratas aceptaron al republicano Rutherford B. Hayes como presidente a cambio del retiro de las tropas federales del Sur

Comstock Lode Nevada gold and silver mine discovered by Henry Comstock in 1859 (p. 445)
veta de Comstock mina de oro y plata descubierta en Nevada por Henry Comstock en 1859

concentration camp a detention site created for military or political purposes to confine, terrorize, and, in some cases, kill civilians (p. 779)
campo de concentración lugar de detención creado con fines militares o políticos para recluir, atemorizar y, en algunos casos, asesinar a civiles

Confederate States of America the nation formed by the southern states when they seceded from the Union (p. 347)
Estados Confederados de América nación formada por los estados del Sur cuando se separaron de la Unión

confederation a group in which each member keeps control of internal affairs but all members cooperate on certain issues, such as defense (p. 75)
confederación grupo en el que cada miembro retiene el control de sus asuntos internos pero todos juntos colaboran en ciertos asuntos, como la defensa

conquistadors Spanish soldiers and explorers who led military expeditions in the Americas and captured land for Spain (p. 41)
conquistadores soldados y exploradores español que encabezó expediciones militares en América y capturó territorios en nombre de España

conscription required service in the military (p. 376)
conscripción servicio militar obligatorio

Constitutional Convention (1787) a meeting held in Philadelphia at which delegates from the states wrote the Constitution (p. 151)
Convención Constitucional (1787) encuentro en Filadelfia en el que los delegados de los estados redactaron la Constitución

containment U.S. policy adopted in the late 1940s to stop the spread of Communism by providing economic and military aid to countries opposing the Soviets (p. 819)
contención política adoptada por Estados Unidos a fines de la década de 1940 para detener la diseminación del comunismo proporcionando ayuda económica y militar a los países que se oponían a los soviéticos

Continental Army the army created by the Second Continental Congress in 1775 to defend the American colonies from Britain (p. 115)
Ejército Continental ejército creado por el Segundo Congreso Continental en 1775 para defender las colonias estadounidenses de Gran Bretaña

convoy system a military technique of transport in which ships were surrounded by destroyers or cruisers for protection (p. 594)
sistema de convoy grupo de varios barcos o vehículos, incluso naves de combate armadas, que por ser numeroso ofrece seguridad

cooperative an organization that is owned and controlled by its members (p. 689)
cooperativa organización que pertenece y es controlada por sus miembros

Copperheads a group of northern Democrats who opposed abolition and sympathized with the South during the Civil War (p. 377)
copperheads grupo de demócratas del Norte que se oponían a la abolición de la esclavitud y simpatizaban con los sureños durante la Guerra Civil

CORE Committee of Racial Equality; an organization dedicated to the practice of nonviolent protest (p. 910)
CORE Comité por la Igualdad Racial; organización dedicada a la práctica de protestas no violentas

Cotton Belt a region stretching from South Carolina to east Texas where most U.S. cotton was produced during the mid-1800s (p. 257)
cinturón algodonero zona que se extiende desde Carolina del Sur hasta el este de Texas, en la que se producía la mayor parte del algodón cosechado en Estados Unidos a mediados del siglo XIX

cotton diplomacy the South's use of cotton as a tool of foreign policy during the Civil War (p. 362)
diplomacia del algodón el uso del algodón por parte del Sur como recurso de política exterior durante la Guerra Civil

cotton gin a machine invented by Eli Whitney in 1793 to remove seeds from short-staple cotton (p. 257)

desmotadora de algodón máquina inventada por Eli Whitney en 1793 para separar las semillas del algodón de fibra corta

counterculture a rebellion of teens and young adults against mainstream American society in the 1960s (p. 1003)
cultura alternativa rebelión de adolescentes y jóvenes adultos contra la corriente dominante de la sociedad estadounidense durante la década de 1960

credit system of borrowing money from banks to make purchases, then paying it back later with interest (p. 632)
crédito sistema de tomar prestado dinero de un banco para hacer compras y luego pagarlo con intereses

Crittenden Compromise (1860) plan created by Senator John Crittenden which proposed amending the Constitution to ban slavery north of the old Missouri Compromise line and to guarantee that it would not be interfered with south of that line (p. 348)
Compromiso de Crittenden (1860) plan creado por el senador John Crittenden en el que se proponía enmendar la Constitución prohibiendo la esclavitud al norte de la antigua línea del Compromiso de Missouri garantizando que no se interferiría al sur de esa línea

Crusades (1091–1295) a series of holy wars led by Christian kings to regain parts of the Middle East from the Muslim Turks (p. 24)
cruzadas (1091–1295) serie de guerras santas dirigidas por los reyes cristianos con el fin de recuperar de los musulmanes turcos partes del Oriente conocidas como Tierra Santa

Cuban missile crisis (1962) confrontation between the United States and the Soviet Union over Soviet missiles in Cuba (p. 884)
crisis de los misiles de Cuba (1962) enfrentemiento entre Estados Unidos y la Unión Soviética provocado por la instalación de misiles soviéticos en Cuba

cult of domesticity a movement that arose during the Industrial Revolution urging women to remain in the home environment (p. 281)
culto de la domesticidad movimiento que surgió durante la Revolución Industrial que fomentaba que las mujeres permanecieran en el hogar

Dawes Act (1887) legislation passed by Congress that split up Indian reservation lands among individual Indians and promised them citizenship (p. 443)
Ley de Adjudicación General de Dawes (1887) ley aprobada por el Congreso que dividía el terreno de las reservas indígenas entre sus habitantes y les prometía la ciudadanía

D-day (1944) June 6, 1944, the first day of the Allied invasion of Normandy in World War II (p. 775)
Día D (1944) 6 de junio de 1944, primer día de la invasión de Normandía por parte de los Aliados en la Segunda Guerra Mundial

de facto segregation segregation that exists through custom and practice rather than by law (p. 933)
segregación de facto segregación que existe por costumbre y práctica y no por ley

de jure segregation segregation by law (p. 933)
segregación de jure segregación establecida por ley

de Lôme letter (1898) letter written by Spain's minister to the United States ridiculing President McKinley that was published in a major newspaper (p. 560)
carta de Lôme (1898) carta escrita por el ministro español en los Estados Unidos ridiculizando al presidente McKinley, publicada en los periódicos más importantes

debt peonage system where workers are tied to their jobs until they can pay off debts they owe their employer (p. 510)
peonaje por deudas sistema mediante el cual los trabajadores no pueden abandonar su empleo sino hasta que terminen de pagar las deudas que le deben a su empleador

deficit when a government spends more money than it takes in (p. 716)
déficit cuando el gobierno gasta más dinero del que recauda

delegated powers powers given to each branch of the national government by the Constitution (p. 163)
poderes delegados poderes que la Constitución le otorga a cada rama del gobierno nacional

Democratic Party a political party formed by supporters of Andrew Jackson after the presidential election of 1824 (p. 246)
Partido Demócrata partido político formado por partidarios de Andrew Jackson después de las elecciones presidenciales de 1824

Democratic-Republicans a political party founded in the 1790s by Thomas Jefferson, James Madison, and other leaders who wanted to preserve the power of the state governments and promote agriculture (p. 208)
demócratas-republicanos un partido político fundado en la década de 1790 por Thomas Jefferson, James Madison y otros líderes que deseaban conservar el poder de los gobiernos estatales y promover la agricultura

Department of Homeland Security U.S. government department created by the Bush administration after the attacks of September 11, 2001, to protect the United States (p.1096)
Departmento de Seguridad Nacional departamento del gobierno estadounidense creado por el gobierno de Bush luego de los ataques del 11 de septiembre de 2001 para proteger al país

deportation being sent back to one's country of origin (p. 624)
deportación ser devuelto al país de origen

détente efforts President Nixon took in the late 1960s and early 1970s to lower Cold War tensions (p. 1020)
distensión campaña del presidente Nixon para reducir las tensiones de la Guerra Fría a finales de los años 60 y principios de los años 70

dictatorship government by a leader or group that holds unchallenged power and authority (p. 741)
dictadura forma de gobierno en la que el poder y la autoridad ilimitados se se concentran en una persona o grupo

Dien Bien Phu site of a battle between the French and the Vietminh in 1954; the French lost the battle and control of Vietnam (p. 951)

Dien Bien Phu aldea en Vietnam donde los franceses y el Vietminh lucharon una batalla en 1954; los franceses perdieron la batalla y el control de Vietnam

dividend a payment made by a company to its shareholders (p. 1088)
dividendo cantidad que una compañía paga a sus accionistas

division of labor when certain people do certain kinds of work (p. 16)
división del trabajo cuando ciertas personas hacen ciertos tipos de trabajos

dollar diplomacy President Taft's policy of influencing Latin America through economic intervention (p. 569)
diplomacia del dólar política creada por el presidente Taft para influir en América Latina mediante la intervención económica

domino theory a belief that if Vietnam fell to Communists, other countries of Southeast Asia would follow (p. 950)
teoría de los dominós creencia de que si Vietnam caía en manos comunistas, también caerían otros países del sureste asiático

dot-coms companies whose products or services are marketed on the Internet (1088)
punto coms empresas cuyos productos o servicios se comercializan en Internet

doves people opposed to a war (p. 962)
palomas personas que se oponen a la guerra

***Dred Scott* decision** (1857) a U.S. Supreme Court ruling that African Americans were not U.S. citizens, that the Missouri Compromise's restriction on slavery was unconstitutional, and that Congress did not have the right to ban slavery in any federal territory (p. 333)
decisión *Dred Scott* (1857) decisión de la Corte Suprema dictaminando que los afroamericanos no eran ciudadanos estadounidenses, que las restricciones sobre la esclavitud del Compromiso de Missouri eran inconstitucionales y que el Congreso no tenía el derecho de prohibir la esclavitud en ningún territorio federal

drought a period of very dry weather (p. 684)
sequía período de tiempo muy seco

dugout shelter dug out of the sides of hills (p. 453)
refugio lugar excavado de la ladera de una colina

Dust Bowl a nickname for the Great Plains regions hit by drought and dust storms in the early 1930s (p. 684)
Tazón de Polvo apodo dado a las regiones de las Grandes Planicies azotadas por la sequía y las tormentas de polvo a principios de la década de 1930

Eighteenth Amendment (1919) a constitutional amendment that outlawed the production and sale of alcoholic beverages in the United States; repealed in 1933 (p. 532)
Decimoctava enmienda (1919) enmienda constitucional que prohibió la producción y venta de bebidas alcohólicas en Estados Unidos; revocada en 1933

Eisenhower Doctrine (1957) declared the right of the United States to help, on request, any nation in the Middle East trying to resist armed Communist aggression (p. 853)

Doctrina Eisenhower (1957) declaró el derecho de Estados Unidos de ayudar, cuando se lo solicitaran, a cualquier país del Medio Oriente en su resistencia contra la agresión armada de los comunistas

Elkins Act (1903) law passed by Congress which prohibited railroads from accepting rebates from their best customers (p. 538)
Ley de Elkins (1903) ley aprobada por el Congreso para prohibirles a los ferrocarriles recibir a devoluciones de dinero de sus mejores clientes

Ellis Island an island in New York harbor that was an entry point for immigrants coming to the United States between 1892 and 1954 (p. 491)
isla Ellis isla en el puerto de Nueva York que fue el punto de ingreso de inmigrantes a Estados Unidos entre 1892 y 1954

emancipation freeing of the slaves (p. 372)
emancipación liberación de los esclavos

Emancipation Proclamation (1862) an order issued by President Abraham Lincoln freeing the slaves in areas rebelling against the Union (p. 372)
Proclamación de Emancipación (1862) decreto emitido por el presidente Abraham Lincoln para liberar a los esclavos en las regiones rebeladas contra la Unión

embargo the banning of trade with a country (p. 362)
embargo prohibición del comercio con un país

Embargo Act (1807) a law that prohibited American merchants from trading with other countries (p. 225)
Ley de Embargo (1807) ley que prohibía a los comerciantes estadounidenses comerciar con otros países

empresarios contractors who recruited settlers and established colonies for the Mexican government (p. 304)
empresarios contratistas que reclutaban colonos y establecían colonias para el gobierno mexicano

Enforcement Acts group of laws passed by Congress in 1870 and 1871 that banned the activities of groups like the Ku Klux Klan; empowered the army and courts to capture and punish KKK members (p. 425)
Leyes de Acatamiento grupo de leyes aprobadas por el Congreso en 1870 y 1871 que prohibieron las actividades de grupos como el Ku Klux Klan; autorizó al ejército y las cortes federales a capturar y castigar a los miembros del Ku Klux Klan

English Bill of Rights document drafted by Parliament to set limits on the monarch's powers (p. 74)
Declaración de Derechos inglesa documento redactado por el Parlamento para establecer límites a los poderes de los monarcas

Enlightenment movement that began in Europe in the late 1600s as people began examining the natural world, society, and government; also called the Age of Reason (p. 85)
Ilustración movimiento que comenzó en Europa a fines del siglo XVII cuando la gente empezó a estudiar el mundo natural, la sociedad y el gobierno; también se conoce como la Edad de la Razón

Enola Gay the nickname of the American plane that dropped the atomic bomb on the Japanese city of Hiroshima in World War II (p. 805)
Enola Gay nombre del avión desde el cual se lanzó la bomba atómica sobre la ciudad japonesa de Hiroshima durante la Segunda Guerra Mundial

entrepreneur risk taker who starts new ventures within the economic system of capitalism (p. 297, 467)
empresario persona que toma riesgos y emprende nuevas operaciones dentro del sistema económico del capitalismo

Equal Rights Amendment (ERA) a proposed constitutional amendment barring discrimination on the basis of sex (p. 988)
Enmienda de Igualdad de Derechos (ERA, por sus siglas en inglés) enmienda constitucional propuesta que prohibía la discriminación basada en el sexo

Erie Canal canal running from Albany to Buffalo, New York; completed in 1825 (p. 254)
canal de Erie canal que va desde Albany a Búfalo, en el estado de Nueva York; se terminó de construir en 1825

Establishment the social, economic, and political leaders of a nation who hold power and influence (p. 1003)
clase dirigente líderes sociales, económicos y políticos de un país que tienen poder e influencia

evolution theory which holds that inherited characteristics of a population change over generations and that as a result of these changes, new species sometimes arise (p. 650)
evolución teoría que explica que la características heredadas de una población cambian de una generación a otra y que, como consecuencia de esos cambios, a veces surgen nuevas especies

executive branch the division of the federal government that includes the president and the administrative departments (p. 145)
poder ejecutivo división del gobierno federal que incluye al presidente y a los departamentos administrativos

executive privilege policy that a president must be free to keep his or her official conversations and meetings private (p. 1030)
privilegio ejecutivo política que afirma que un presidente debe contar con la libertad de mantener la confidencialidad de sus conversaciones y reuniones oficiales

Exodusters African Americans who settled western lands in the late 1800s (p. 452)
Exodusters afroamericanos que se establecieron en el oeste a finales del siglo XIX

Fair Deal plan proposed by President Truman that included a number of programs in the tradition of the New Deal (p. 827)
Trato Justo plan propuesto por el presidente Truman que incluyó una serie de programas en la tradición del New Deal

fascism a system of government that focuses on the good of the state rather than on the individual citizens (p. 740)
fascismo sistema de gobierno que se concentra en el bienestar del estado en lugar del bienestar de los ciudadanos

The Federalist collection of essays on the principles of government written in defense of the Constitution in 1787 (p. 160)

El federalista colección de ensayos sobre los principios de gobierno escritos en defensa de la Constitución en 1787

Federalists people who supported ratification of the Constitution (p. 158)
federalistas personas que apoyaban la ratificación de la Constitución

Federal Reserve System the nation's central bank (p. 676)
Sistema Reserva Federal banco central de la nación

Federal Reserve Act (1913) law that created a central fund from which banks could borrow to prevent collapse during a financial panic (p. 543)
Ley de la Reserva Federal (1913) ley que creó un fondo central del cual los bancos tomarían prestados fondos para evitar el colapso durante un pánico económico

feminism the principle that women and men should have equal social, political, and economic rights (p. 988)
feminismo principio según el cual las mujeres y los hombres deben gozar de igualdad de derechos sociales, políticos y económicos

Fifteenth Amendment (1870) gave African American men the right to vote (p. 415)
Decimoquinta enmienda (1870) otorgó a los hombres afroamericanos el derecho al voto

Final Solution the Nazi Party's plan to murder the entire Jewish population of Europe and the Soviet Union (p. 780)
Solución Final plan del partido nazi de asesinar a toda la población judía de Europa y la Unión Soviética

fireside chat conversational radio addresses given by President Franklin D. Roosevelt (p. 700)
charlas informales discursos radiales a modo de conversación que daba Franklin D. Roosevelt

First Battle of Bull Run (1861) the first major battle of the Civil War, resulting in a Confederate victory (p. 364)
primera batalla de Bull Run (1861) un gran batalla de la Guerra Civil, que resultó en una victoria de la Confederación

First Continental Congress (1774) a meeting of colonial delegates in Philadelphia to decide how to respond to the abuses of authority by the British government (p. 110)
Primer Congreso Continental (1774) reunión de delegados de las colonias en Filadelfia para decidir cómo responderían a los abusos de la autoridad del gobierno británico

flapper a young woman in the 1920s who wore her hair bobbed, wore makeup, dressed in flashy, skimpy clothes, and lived a life of independence and freedom (p. 648)
flapper jovencita que en la década de 1920 lucía el pelo a la moda, usaba maquillaje, se ponía ropa elegante y escasa, y vivía una vida de independencia y libertad

flexible response a response strategy to nuclear tensions that involved strengthening conventional U.S. forces so the nation would have options other than nuclear weapons in times of crisis (p. 886)
respuesta flexible estrategia de repuesta a las tensiones nucleares que implicó fortalecer las fuerzas convencionales de Estados Unidos para que el país contara con otras opciones además de las armas nucleares en cualquier época de crisis

flower children a slang term for hippies (p. 1005)
niños de las flores expresión popular para los hippies

Foraker Act (1900) established that the United States would appoint the upper house of Puerto Rico's legislature, as well as its governor (p. 567)
Ley de Foraker (1900) estableció que Estados Unidos designaría a los miembros de la cámara alta de la legislatura de Puerto Rico así como su gobernador

foreclosure when a lender takes over ownership of a property from an owner who has failed to make loan payments (p. 682)
ejecución hipotecaria cuando el prestamista se apodera de una propiedad porque el propietario no ha pagado las cuotas del préstamo

Fourteen Points President Woodrow Wilson's plan for organizing post-World War I Europe and for avoiding future wars (p. 607)
Catorce Puntos plan del presidente Woodrow Wilson para organizar Europa después de la Primera Guerra Mundial y para evitar futuras guerras

Fourteenth Amendment (1866) gave full rights of citizenship to all people born or naturalized in the United States, except for American Indians (p. 414)
Decimocuarta enmienda (1866) otorga derechos totales de ciudadanía a todas las personas nacidas en Estados Unidos o naturalizadas estadounidenses, con excepción de los indígenas norteamericanos

free blacks African Americans who were not slaves (p. 286)
negros libres afroamericanos que no eran esclavos

Free Speech Movement counterculture movement during the 1960s (p. 1004)
Movimiento por la Libertad de Expresión movimiento en contra de la cultura dominante que tuvo lugar en la década de 1960

freedmen a term for emancipated slaves (p. 373)
libertos término para referirse a los esclavos emancipados

Freedmen's Bureau an agency established by Congress in 1865 to help poor people throughout the South (p. 404)
Oficina de Esclavos Libertos agencia creada por el Congreso en 1865 para ayudar a los pobres en el Sur

Freedom Riders activists who challenged segregation in bus terminals in the South in 1961 (p. 918)
Pasajeros de la Libertas activistas que en 1961 desafiaron la segregación en las terminales de autobuses del sur

Freedom Summer a volunteer project in which college students spent their summer vacation in Mississippi, registering African Americans to vote (p. 927)
Verano de la libertad proyecto voluntario en el que un grupo de estudiantes universitarios pasaron sus vacaciones de verano en el estado de Mississippi, inscribiendo a afroamericanos para votar

Freeport Doctrine (1858) a statement made by Stephen Douglas during the Lincoln-Douglas debates stating how people could use popular sovereignty to determine if their state or territory should permit slavery (p. 341)
Doctrina de Freeport (1858) declaración hecha por Stephen Douglas durante los debates Lincoln-Douglas que señalaba que el pueblo podía usar la soberanía popular para decidir si su estado o territorio debía permitir la esclavitud

free-soilers members of a political party called the Free-Soil Party; it was formed in 1848 by antislavery northerners (p. 327)

free-soilers integrantes de un partido político llamado Free-Soil Party (partido de las tierras libre); formado en 1848 por norteños opuestos a la esclavitud

Fugitive Slave Act (1850) a law that made it a crime to help runaway slaves (p. 325)
Ley de Esclavos Fugitivos (1850) ley que hacía que ayudar a un esclavo a escapar de su amo fuera un delito

fundamentalism a belief in the literal interpretation of a particular religion's doctrine or holy books (p. 650)
fundamentalismo creencia en la interpretación literal de la doctrina o de los libros sagrados de una religión

G

General Agreement on Tariffs and Trade (GATT) international organization that works to reduce tariffs and other barriers to trade (p. 828)
Acuerdo General sobre Aranceles y Comercio (GATT, por sus siglas en inglés) organización internacional que trabaja para reducir los aranceles y otras barreras para el comercio

genetic engineering artificial modification of genes or genetic material (p. 1102)
ingeniería genética modificación artificial de los genes o del material genético

Geneva Conference (1954) international meeting in Geneva, Switzerland to restore peace in Indochina (p. 951)
Convención de Ginebra (1954) cumbre internacional celebrada en Ginebra, Suiza, para restablecer la paz en Indochina

genocide the killing of an entire people (p. 780)
genocidio exterminio de un pueblo entero

Gentlemen's Agreement pact made between the United States and Japan in which Japan agreed to limit immigration to the U.S., and in exchange President Roosevelt agreed to put pressure on the city of San Francisco to rescind an order that forced children of Japanese parents to attend segregated schools (p. 494)
Acuerdo entre Caballeros pacto alcanzado entre Estados Unidos y Japón por el que Japón se comprometió a limitar la inmigración a Estados Unidos y a cambio el presidente Roosevelt se comprometió a presionar a la ciudad de San Francisco para que revocara una orden que obligaba a los hijos de padres japoneses a acudir a escuelas segregadas

ghetto an area where people from a specific ethnic background live as a group (p. 780)
gueto lugar en el que vive una comunidad de personas de un origen étnico particular

GI Bill (1944) act that helped veterans make a smooth entry into civilian life by providing money for attending college or for advanced job training (p. 824)
Ley de Veteranos (1944) ley que facilitó la reintegración de los veteranos a la vida civil con ayudas económicas que les permitieron ir a la universidad u obtener formación profesional avanzada

glasnost Russian word for "opening;" refers to a new era of media freedom on the Soviet Union under Mikhail Gorbachev (p. 1060)
glasnost palabra rusa que significa "apertura;" se refiere a una nueva era de libertad en los medios que se vivió en la Unión Soviética bajo Mikhail Gorbachev

Glorious Revolution (1688) a nonviolent revolution in which leaders of Britain's Parliament invited Mary, daughter of King James II, and her husband, the Dutch ruler William of Orange, to replace King James II (p. 74)
Revolución Gloriosa (1688) revolución pacífica por la que los líderes del Parlamento británico invitaron a María, hija del rey James II y a su esposo, el gobernante holandés Guillermo de Orange, a reemplazar al rey James II

gold rush (1849) the mass migration of people to California after gold was discovered there (p. 299)
fiebre del oro (1849) la migración masiva de personas a California tras el descubrimiento de oro allí

grandfather clause a law added to the Constitution of many Southern states, stating that a man could vote if he, his father, or his grandfather had been eligible to vote before January 1, 1867 (p. 508)
cláusula de los abuelos ley agregada a la Constitución de muchos estados del Sur que establecía que un hombre podía votar si él, su padre o su abuelo habían tenido derecho al voto antes del 1º de enero de 1867

Great Awakening a religious movement in the American colonies in the 1730s and 1740s (p. 86)
Gran Despertar movimiento religioso que tuvo gran popularidad en las colonias estadounidenses en las décadas de 1730 y 1740

Great Compromise (1787) an agreement worked out at the Constitutional Convention establishing that a state's population would determine representation in the lower house of the legislature, while each state would have equal representation in the upper house (p. 154)
Gran Compromiso (1787) acuerdo redactado durante la Convención Constitucional en el que se establece que la población de un estado debe determinar su representación en la cámara baja de la asamblea legislativa y que cada estado debe tener igual representación en la cámara alta

Great Depression (1929– 1930s) the most severe economic downturn in the history of the United States (p. 681)
Gran Depresión (de 1929 a la década de 1930) la crisis económica más grave de la historia de Estados Unidos

Great Irish Famine period in Ireland during the mid-1880s, when a blight on the potato crop caused about 1 million people to die of starvation (p. 273)
Gran Hamburna Irlandesa período de la historia de Irlanda a mediados de la década de 1880 durante el cual una plaga en la cosecha de papas (patatas) hizo morir de hambre a aproximadamente 1 millón de personas

Great Migration the movement of nearly 16,000 Europeans from Europe to New England from 1620 to 1643 (p. 53); the major relocation of African Americans from 1910 into the 1920s to northern cities (p. 655)
Gran Migración traslado de casi 16,000 europeos de Europa a Nueva Inglaterra entre 1620 y 1643; gran traslado de afroamericanos a las ciudades del Norte desde 1910 hasta la década de 1920

Great Society the term for the domestic programs of the Johnson administration (p. 897)
Gran Sociedad término que se refiere a los programas de política doméstica del gobierno del presidente Johnson

gross national product (GNP) the total value of all goods and services produced in the nation (p. 673)

producto interior bruto (GNP, por sus siglas en inglés) el valor total de todos los bienes y servicios producidos en el país

guerrilla war fighting marked by sabotage, ambushes, and other surprise attacks (p. 332)
guerra de guerrillas enfrentamientos marcados por el sabotaje, las emboscadas y otros ataques por sorpresa

habeas corpus the constitutional protection against unlawful imprisonment (p. 377)
hábeas corpus protección constitucional contra el encarcelamiento ilegal

hard-rock mining mining that requires cutting deep shafts in solid rock to extract the ore (p. 446)
minería de roca dura explotación minera en la que es necesario hacer huecos profundos en la roca sólida para extraer el mineral

Harlem Renaissance a blossoming of African American art and literature that began in the 1920s (p. 656)
Renacimiento de Harlem florecimiento del arte y la literatura afroamericanas que comenzó en la década de 1920

hawks people who are supportive of a war's goals (p. 962)
halcones personas que apoyan los objetivos de una guerra

headrights 50-acre grants of land offered by the Virginia Company beginning in 1618 in order to attract settlers to the New World (p. 49)
concesiones áreas de tierra de 50 acres ofrecidas por Virginia Company a partir de 1618 para atraer pobladores al Nuevo Mundo

Hepburn Act (1906) law that authorized the Interstate Commerce Commission to set maximum railroad rates and gave it the power to regulate other companies engaged in interstate commerce (p. 538)
Ley Hepburn (1906) ley que autorizó que la Comisión Interestatal de Comercio fijara precios máximos para el ferrocarril y le dio el poder para regular otras empresas que participaban en el comercio interestatal

hobo a homeless person, typically one who is traveling in search of work (p. 680)
vagabundo persona sin hogar que por lo general viaja de un sitio a otro en busca de trabajo

Ho Chi Minh Trail a network of paths from North Vietnam to South Vietnam (p. 957)
Ruta de Ho Chi Minh red de senderos que comunica Vietnam del Norte con Vietnam del Sur

Hollywood Ten Hollywood writers and directors who were thought to be radicals and called before HUAC; they refused to cooperate and were sentenced to short prison terms (p. 931)
los diez de Hollywood escritores y directores de Hollywood considerados radicales y convocados por el HUAC; se negaron a cooperar y fueron condenados a corto tiempo en prisión

Holocaust the killing of millions of Jews and others by Nazis during World War II (p. 783)

ENGLISH AND SPANISH GLOSSARY

Holocausto asesinato de millones de judíos y de otras personas por parte de los nazis durante la Segunda Guerra Mundial

Homestead Act (1862) a law passed by Congress to encourage settlement in the West by giving government-owned land to small farmers (p. 450)
Ley de Heredad (1862) ley aprobada por el Congreso para fomentar la colonización del oeste del país mediante la cesión de tierras del gobierno a pequeños agricultores

Hoover Dam a dam built in the 1930s with funding from the federal government to control the Colorado River (p. 688)
Presa Hoover presa construida en la década de 1930 con financiamiento del gobierno federal para controlar el río Colorado

Hooverville makeshift shantytowns that sprung up during the Great Depression (p. 683)
Hooverville barriadas improvisadas que surgieron durante la Gran Depresión

horizontal integration owning all the businesses in a certain field (p. 468)
integración horizontal ser dueño de todas las empresas de un campo específico

House of Burgesses America's first law-making body, formed in July 1619 by representatives from the different communities in Virginia (p. 49)
Cámara de Burgueses la primera cámara legislativa de Estados Unidos; formada en julio de 1619 por representantes de las distintas comunidades de Virginia

House Un-American Activities Committee (HUAC) committee formed in the House of Representatives in the 1930s to investigate radical groups in the United States; it later came to focus on the threat of communism in the United States during World War II and the Cold War (p. 834)
Comité de Actividades Antiestadounidenses (HUAC, por sus siglas en inglés) comité formado en la Cámara de Representantes en la década de 1930 para investigar a los grupos radicales en Estados Unidos; más tarde se enfocó en la amenaza comunista en Estados Unidos durante la Segunda Guerra Mundial y la Guerra Fría

Hundred Days (1933) the first hundred days of Franklin Roosevelt's term as president (p. 702)
Cien Días (1933) primeros cien días del gobierno de Franklin Roosevelt como presidente

hunter-gatherers people who hunt animals and gather wild plants to provide for their needs (p. 7)
cazadores y recolectores personas que satisfacen sus necesidades cazando animales y recolectando plantas silvestres

hydraulic mining method of mining that uses water under high pressure to blast away gravel and dirt to expose the minerals underneath (p. 446)
minería hidráulica método de explotación minera que utiliza agua con alta presión para hacer volar la grava y la tierra, y así exponer el mineral que se oculta debajo.

hydrogen bomb a nuclear weapon that gets its power from the fusing together of hydrogen atoms (p. 855)
bomba de hidrógeno arma nuclear que obtiene su energía de la fusión de átomos de hidrógeno

ICBM intercontinental ballistic missiles; guided missiles that could travel thousands of miles and strike targets accurately (p. 856)
MBIC misiles balísticos intercontinentales; misiles guiados que podían recorrer miles de millas y alcanzar objetivos con precisión

impeachment the process used by a legislative body to bring charges of wrongdoing against a public official (p. 415)
acusación proceso utilizado por un grupo legislativo para presentar cargos en contra de un funcionario público

imperialism the practice of extending a nation's power by gaining territories for a colonial empire (p. 553)
imperialismo práctica de ampliar el poder de una nación mediante la anexión de otros territorios para formar un imperio colonial

impressment the practice of forcing people to serve in the army or navy (p. 225)
leva práctica que obligaba a las personas a servir en el ejército o la marina

Inca American Indian society that lived in the Andes Mountains of South America from about the 12th century, until Spanish conquest in the mid-16th century (p. 9)
incas sociedad indígena americana que vivió en la cordillera de los Andes, en América del Sur, aproximadamente desde el siglo XII hasta la conquista española a mediados del siglo XVI

Inchon a port city in western South Korea on the Yellow Sea; site of major battle in the Korean War (p. 839)
Inchon ciudad portuaria en el oeste de Corea del Sur a orillas del mar Amarillo; fue el lugar de una importante batalla de la Guerra de Corea

incumbent the person who currently holds a public office (p. 727)
titular la persona que ocupa un puesto oficial actualmente

indentured servants people whose employers pay for passage to the country they wish to emigrate to, food, and shelter; in return the indentured servants agree to work for the employer for a certain number of years (p. 49)
sirvientes por contrato personas a los que sus empleadores les pagaban el pasaje al país al que deseaban emigrar, la comida y el alojamiento; a cambio, los sirvientes por contrato se comprometían a trabajar para el empleador durante un determinado número de años

Indian Removal Act (1830) a congressional act that authorized the removal of Native Americans who lived east of the Mississippi River (p. 247)
Ley de Expulsión de Indígenas (1830) ley redactada por el Congreso que autorizaba la expulsión de los indígenas norteamericanos que vivían al este del río Mississippi

Industrial Revolution a period of rapid growth in the use of machines in manufacturing and production that began in the mid-1700s (p. 252)
Revolución Industrial período de rápido desarrollo debido al uso de maquinaria en la fabricación y producción que comenzó a mediados del siglo XVIII

infantry foot soldiers (p. 364)
infantería soldados de a pie

inflation increased prices for goods and services combined with the reduced value of money (pp. 129, 739)
inflación alza en los precios de los bienes y servicos al mismo tiempo que se produce una reducción en el valor del dinero

initiative a method of allowing voters to propose a new law on the ballot for public approval (p. 527)
iniciativa método que permite a los votantes proponer una ley en la boleta electoral para la aprobación del público

installment buying paying for an item over a period of time with a series of small payments (p. 632)
compra a plazos pagar por un artículo a lo largo de un período de tiempo mediante una serie de pequeños pagos

integrated circuit a computer chip that includes a number of transistors and other electronic components (p. 864)
circuito integrado chip de computadora que contiene un número de transistores y de otros componentes electrónicos

Intermediate-range Nuclear Forces (INF) Treaty a treaty between the United States and the Soviet Union that ordered the destruction of thousands of missiles (p. 1055)
Tratado de Fuerzas Nucleares de Alcance Intermedio (FNAI) tratado entre Estados Unidos y la Unión Soviética que ordenó la destrucción de miles de misiles

International Monetary Fund organization designed to encourage economic policies that promote international trade (p. 828)
Fondo Monetario Internacional organización diseñada para fomentar políticas económicas que promueven el comercio internacional

internment the forced relocation and confinement of Japanese-Americans to concentration camps (p. 797)
internamiento el traslado forzoso y el confinamiento de los japoneses-americanos en campos de concentración

Interstate Highway System a network of high-speed roads built to make interstate travel faster and easier (p. 867)
sistema de autopistas interestatales red de carreteras de alta velocidad construidas para facilitar y agilizar los viajes interestatales

Intolerable Acts (1774) laws passed by Parliament to punish the colonists for the Boston Tea Party and to tighten government control of the colonies (p. 110)
Leyes Intolerables (1774) leyes apropadas por el Parlamento inglés para castigar a los colonos que participaron en el Motín del Té de Boston y para aumentar su control sobre las colonias

Iran-Contra affair secret U.S. sales of weapons to Iran in an attempt to secure the release of U.S. hostages held in Lebanon in 1986 (p. 1058)
asunto Irán-Contra venta secreta de armas de Estados Unidos a Irán para lograr la liberación de los rehenes estadounidenses detenidos en el Líbano en 1986

Iron Curtain term coined by Winston Churchill in 1946 to describe an imaginary line dividing Communist countries in the Soviet bloc from countries in Western Europe during the Cold War (p. 819)
cortina de hierro término creado por Winston Churchill en 1946 para describir la línea imaginaria que dividía a los países comunistas del bloque soviético de los países de Europa occidental durante la Guerra Fría

ironclads armored gunboats covered with iron plates up to three inches thick (p. 366)
acorazados barcos armados y cubiertos con placas de hierro de hasta tres pulgadas de espesor

Iroquois Native American group of the Northeast (p. 14)
iroqueses grupo indígena norteamericano del Norest

Iroquois League an alliance of Native Americans (p. 92)
Liga de los Iroqueses alianza de indígenas norteamericanos

Islam the Muslim religion (p. 19)
Islam religión de los musulmanes

isolationism a policy in which a nation avoids entanglement in foreign wars (p. 591)
aislacionismo política por la que una nación evita participar en guerras ajenas

IT computerized information technology (p. 1102)
TI tecnología de información computarizada

Jacksonian Democracy an expansion of voting rights during the Andrew Jackson administration (p. 246)
democracia jacksoniana ampliación del derecho al voto durante el gobierno del presidente Andrew Jackson

Jay's Treaty (1794) an agreement negotiated by John Jay to work out problems between Britain and the United States over northwestern lands, British seizure of U.S. ships, and U.S. debts owed to the British (p. 211)
Tratado de Jay (1794) acuerdo negociado por John Jay para resolver los problemas entre Gran Bretaña y Estados Unidos por los territorios del noroeste, por la incautación británica de barcos estadounidenses y por las deudas estadounidenses con los ingleses

jazz type of American music that blends several different musical forms from the Deep South (p. 659)
jazz typo de musical estadounidense que mezcla varias formas musicales del Sur y sureste del país

Jim Crow laws laws that enforced segregation in the southern states (p. 508)
leyes de Jim Crow leyes que impusieron la segregación racial en los estados sureños

Job Corps program under President Johnson that offered work-training programs for unemployed youth (p. 896)
Job Corps programa del presidente Johnson que ofrecía programas de formación laboral a los jóvenes desempleados

Johnson Doctrine President Johnson's philosophy that revolutions in Latin America were not just local concerns when "the object is the establishment of a Communist dictatorship" (p. 900)
Doctrina Johnson filosofía del presidente Johnson según la cual las revoluciones en América Latina dejaban de ser un asunto de interés local cuando "el objetivo es el establecimiento de una dictadura comunista."

joint-stock companies businesses formed by groups of people who jointly make an investment and share in the profits and losses (p. 47)
sociedades por acciones empresas formadas por grupos de personas que invierten conjuntamente y comparten las ganancias y las pérdidas

judicial branch the division of the federal government that is made up of the national courts (p. 145)
poder judicial división del gobierno federal formada por las cortes nacionales

judicial review the Supreme Court's power to declare acts of Congress unconstitutional (p. 220)
recurso de inconstitucionalidad poder de la Corte Suprema para declarar inconstitucionales las acciones del Congreso

Judiciary Act of 1789 legislation passed by Congress that created the federal court system (p. 204)
Ley de Judicatura de 1789 ley aprobada por el Congreso para crear el sistema federal de tribunales

Judiciary Act of 1801 act passed by Congress that created new positions in the judicial branch (p. 220)
Ley de Judicatura de 1801 ley aprobada por el Congreso para crear nuevos puestos en el poder judicial

K

kamikaze in World War II, a pilot who agreed to load his aircraft with bombs and crash it on an enemy ship (p. 791)
kamikaze en la Segunda Guerra Mundial, piloto que accedía a cargar su avión con bombas para estrellarlo contra un barco enemigo

Kansas-Nebraska Act (1854) a law that allowed voters in Kansas and Nebraska to choose whether or not to allow slavery (p. 326)
Ley de Kansas y Nebraska (1854) ley que permitió a los votantes de Kansas y Nebraska decidir si permitirían o abolición de la esclavitud

Kellogg-Briand Pact treaty signed in 1928 that rejected war as a way of solving problems between countries (p. 639)
Pacto de Kellogg-Briand tratado firmado en 1928 que rechazó la guerra como un medio para solucionar los problemas entre países

Kerner Commission committee appointed to study the causes of urban rioting after violence in Detroit in July 1967 (p. 934)
Comisión Kerner comité nombrado para estudiar las causas de los disturbios urbanos ocurridos después de actos de violencia en Detroit en julio de 1967

Khmer Rouge Communists who took over Cambodia in 1975 (p. 977)
Khmer Rouge comunistas que arrebataron el poder en Camboya en 1975

King Cotton name given by Southerners to indicate the economic and political importance of cotton production in the southern states (p. 258)
Rey Algodón nombre utilizado por los habitantes del Sur para indicar la importancia económica y política de la producción de algodón en los estados sureños

King Philip's War (1675) war fought between the Wampanoag and English settlers in southern New England, led by a Wampanoag leader named Metacomet, known to the English as "King Philip" (p. 56)
Guerra del Rey Felipe (1675) guerra entre los indios wampanoag y los pobladores ingleses del sur de Nueve Inglaterra liderados por el jefe wampanoag llamado Metacomet, conocido por los ingleses como "Rey Felipe"

kinship family relationship (p. 15)
parentesco relación de familia

Knights of Labor secret society that became the first truly national labor union in the United States (p. 474)
Knights of Labor sociedad secreta que se convirtió en el primer sindicato verdaderamente nacional en Estados Unidos

Know-Nothings a mid-1800s secret anti-immigration fraternal organization; this group later became a political party called the American Party (p. 275)
Know-Nothings hermandad secreta antiinmigrantes de mediados del siglo XIX; más tarde, el grupo se convirtió en un partido político llamado Partido Americano

Kristallnacht (1938) a German word for broken glass; an event that occurred on the nights of November 9 and 10 in which Hitler's Nazis encouraged Germans to riot against Jews, and nearly 100 Jews died (p. 779)
Kristallnacht (1938) palabra en alemán que significa vidrios de los cristales rotos; acontecimiento que tuvo lugar las noches del 9 y 10 de noviembre en que los nazis de Hitler animaron a los alemanes a participar en disturbios callejeros contra los judíos y murieron cerca de cien judíos

Ku Klux Klan a secret society that used terror and violence to keep African Americans from obtaining their civil rights (p. 412)
Ku Klux Klan sociedad secreta que usaba el terror y la violencia para impedir que los afroamericanos obtuvieran sus derechos civiles

Kwakiutl Native American group of the Pacific Northwest (p. 12)
kwakiutl grupo de indígenas norteamericanos de la costa noroeste del Pacífico

L

La Raza Unida Party organization formed in the 1960s aimed at helping Mexican Americans (p. 998)
Partido La Raza Unida organización formada en la década de 1960 con el motivo de ayudar a los mexicano americanos

labor movement reform movement working to secure higher wages, shorter hours, and safer working conditions (p. 276)
movimiento obrero movimiento reformista que buscaba obtener salarios más altos, jornadas más cortas y condiciones laborales más seguras

laissez-faire in French, meaning "allow to do;" a business system where companies are allowed to conduct business without interference by the government (p. 467)
laissez-faire "dejar hacer" en francés en el mundo de los negocios un sistema en el que las compañías llevan a cabo sus actividades comerciales sin interferencia del gobierno

Land Ordinance of 1785 legislation passed by Congress authorizing surveys and the division of public lands in the western region of the country (p. 149)
Ordenanza de Territorios de 1785 ley aprobada por el Congreso en el que se autorizaron las mediciones de terreno y la división de territorios públicos en el oeste del país

League of Nations international body of nations formed in 1919 to prevent wars (p. 607)
Liga de las Naciones organización internacional de naciones formada en 1919 con el fin de prevenir las guerras

Lecompton Constitution a pro-slavery state constitution written by delegates to the constitutional convention in the Kansas territory in 1857 (p. 334)
Constitución de Lecompton constitución estatal a favor de la exclavitud redactada por delegados de la convención constitucional en el territorio de Kansas en 1857

legislative branch the division of the federal government that proposes bills and passes them into laws (p. 145)
poder legislativo división del gobierno federal que propone proyectos de ley y los aprueba para convertirlos en leyes

Lend-Lease Act (1940) program that gave the government power to make weapons available to Great Britain without regard for its ability to pay (p. 755)
Ley de Préstamo y Arriendo (1940) programa que le dio al gobierno la autoridad para poner armas a disposición de Gran Bretaña sin importar si podía pagarlas

Levittown a New York town of mass-produced homes, which became a symbol for many similar suburban towns built during the post-World War II years (p. 866)
Levittown pueblo de Nueva York formado por viviendas fabricadas en serie que se convirtió en el símbolo de muchos pueblos suburbanos similares que se construyeron tras la Segunda Guerra Mundial

Lewis and Clark Expedition an expedition led by Meriwether Lewis and William Clark that began in 1804 to explore the Louisiana Purchase (p. 219)
expedición de Lewis y Clark expedición encabezada por Meriwether Lewis y William Clark que partió en 1804 para explorar el territorio adquirido en la Compra de Luisiana

Liberal Republicans group of Republicans that broke with the Republican party over the Enforcement Acts scandals of the Grant administration (p. 425)
republicanos liberales grupo de republicanos que se separaron del partido republicano a raíz de los escándalos de las Leyes de Acatamiento del gobierno del presidente Grant

Liberty bonds bonds that American citizens bought to help pay for the costs of World War I (p. 598)
bonos Liberty bonos que compraron los ciudadanos de Estados Unidos para ayudar a pagar los costos de la Primera Guerra Mundial (pag. 598)

Lincoln-Douglas debates a series of debates between Republican Abraham Lincoln and Democrat Stephen Douglas during the 1858 U.S. Senate campaign in Illinois (p. 341)
debates Lincoln-Douglas serie de debates entre el republicano Abraham Lincoln y el demócrata Stephen Douglas durante la campaña de 1858 para el Senado estadounidense en Illinois

lineage ancestry (p. 20)
linaje ascendencia

literacy test a test that determines a person's ability to read (p. 494)
prueba de alfabetización prueba que determina la capacidad de leer de una persona (p. 494)

Little Rock Nine nine African American students who first integrated Central High School in Little Rock, Arkansas, in 1957 (p. 912)
los nueve de Little Rock primeros nueve estudiantes de raza negra en integrar Central High School en Little Rock, Arkansas, en el año 1957

longhouse a large wooden building built by the Iroquois (p. 14)
longhouse edificio grande de madera construido por los iroquois

loose construction a way of interpreting the Constitution that agrees with the federal government taking actions that the Constitution does not specifically forbid (p. 206)
interpretación flexible interpretación de la Constitución que permite al gobierno federal tomar acciones que la Constitución no prohíbe de manera específica

Louisiana Purchase (1803) the purchase of land between the Mississippi River and the Rocky Mountains that doubled the size of the United States (p. 218)
Compra de Luisiana (1803) compra del territorio localizado entre el río Mississippi y las montañas Rocosas que duplicó el tamaño de Estados Unidos

Lowell girls name given to women who worked in Lowell textile mills (p. 253)
Lowell girls nombre dado a las mujeres que trabajaban en las fábricas textiles de Lowell

Loyalist a colonist who sided with Britain in the American Revolution (p. 116)
leal colono que se puso de parte de Gran Bretaña durante la Guerra de Independencia estadounidense

Luftwaffe the German air force (p. 749)
Luftwaffe fuerza aérea alemana

Lusitania British ship sunk by a German U-Boat in 1915 (p. 590)
Lusitania banco británico hundido por un submarino alemán U-Boat en 1915

lynching the murder of an individual by a group or mob (p. 509)
linchamiento el asesinato de una persona por un grupo o una muchedembre

Magna Carta (1215) a charter of liberties agreed to by King John of England, it made the king obey the same laws as citizens (p. 24)
Carta Magna (1215) carta de libertades firmada por el rey Juan de Inglaterra que estableció que el rey debía obedecer las mismas leyes que los ciudadanos

mandate authorization to act (p. 888)
mandato autorización para actuar

Manhattan Project the top-secret program to build an atomic bomb during World War II (p. 762)
Proyecto Manhattan programa secreto para construir una bomba atómica durante la Segunda Guerra Mundial

manifest destiny a belief shared by many Americans in the mid-1800s that the United States should expand across the continent to the Pacific Ocean (p. 297)

destino manifiesto creencia de muchos estadounidenses a mediados del siglo XIX de que Estados Unidos debía expandirse por todo el continente hasta llegar al océano Pacífico

Marshall Plan (1947) plan for the reconstruction of Europe after World War II; announced by the U.S. Secretary of State George C. Marshall (p. 820)
Plan Marshall (1947) plan para la reconstrucción de Europa después de la Segunda Guerra Mundial; anunciado por el secretario de estado estadounidense George C. Marshall

martial law type of rule in which military commanders are in control and citizens' rights and freedoms are suspended (p. 358)
ley marcial tipo de gobierno en el que las fuerzas militares toman el control y se suspenden los derechos y libertades de los ciudadanos

mass transit public transportation systems that carry large numbers of people (p. 478)
transporte público sistemas de transporte colectivo que llevan a grandes cantidades de personas

massive retaliation the United States' willingness to use nuclear force to settle disputes (p. 850)
represalia masiva disposición de Estados Unidos a usar armas nucleares para resolver disputas

matrilineal tracing ancestry through the mother (p. 15)
matrilineal establecimiento de los antepasados a través de la madre

Maya Mesoamerican society that lived in present-day Mexico from about the 3rd century through the 14th century (p. 8)
mayas sociedad mesoamericana que vivió en lo que hoy es México desde el siglo III hasta el siglo XIV aproximadamente

Mayflower Compact (1620) a document written by the Pilgrims establishing themselves as a political society and setting guidelines for self-government (p. 51)
Pacto del Mayflower (1620) documento redactado por los peregrinos en el que formaban una sociedad política y establecían los principios para gobernarse a sí mismos

McCarthyism the name critics gave to Joseph McCarthy's tactic of spreading fear and making baseless charges (p. 834)
macarthismo nombre que los críticos dieron a la táctica empleada por Joseph McCarthy para infundir miedo y hacer acusaciones sin fundamento

McCulloch v. Maryland (1819) Supreme Court case that declared the Second Bank of the United States was constitutional (p. 240)
McCulloch contra Maryland (1819) caso de la Corte Suprema que declaró que el banco Segundo Banco de Estados Unidos era constitucional

Meat Inspection Act (1906) law that required government inspection of meat shipped across state lines (p. 538)
Ley de Inspección de la Carne (1906) ley que exigió que el gobierno inspeccionara la carne que se enviaba de un estado a otro (pág. 538)

Medicaid a government program that provides free health care for poor people (p. 898)
Medicaid programa del gobierno que brinda atención médica gratuita a los pobres

Medicare a health care program for people over age 65 (p. 898)
Medicare programa de atención médica para personas mayores de 65 años

mercantilism economic system used from about the 1500s to the 1700s; held that a nation's power was directly related to its wealth (p. 73)
mercantilismo sistema económico usado entre los siglos XVI y XVIII aproximadamente; sostenía que el poder de una nación estaba directamente relacionado con su riqueza

Mexican Cession more than 500,000 square miles of land turned over to the United States by Mexico after the Mexican-American War (p. 311)
Cesión Mexicana más de 500,000 millas cuadradas de territorio cedido a Estados Unidos por México después de la Guerra contra México

Mexican Revolution a revolution led by Francisco Madero in 1910 that eventually forced the Mexican dictator Porfirio Díaz to resign (p. 573)
Revolución Mexicana revolución encabezada por Francisco Madero en 1910 que al final obligó a renunciar al dictador mexicano Porfirio Díaz

Mexican-American War (1846–1848) war fought between the United States and Mexico in which the U.S. gained more than 500,000 square miles of land in the United States (p. 310)
Guerra contra México (1846–1848) guerra librada entre Estados Unidos y México en la que los primeros conquistaron más de 500,000 millas cuadradas de territorio para Estados Unidos

Middle Ages period of European history, from the fall of the Roman Empire to the Renaissance (p. 24)
Edad Media período de la historia europea desde la caída del Imperio romano hasta el Renacimiento

Middle Passage a voyage that brought enslaved Africans across the Atlantic Ocean to North America and the West Indies (p. 79)
Paso Central viaje a través del océano Atlántico que trajo a los africanos esclavizados a América del Norte y a las Antillas

militarism the expansion of arms and the policy of military preparedness (p. 583)
militarismo aumento de la cantidad de armas y política de preparación militar para la guerra

minimum wage the lowest wage an employer can legally pay a worker (p. 726)
salario mínimo salario más bajo que un patrón puede pagar legalmente a un trabajador

minutemen American colonial militia members ready to fight at a minute's notice (p. 110)
milicianos del minuto miembros de la milicia norteamericana en la época colonial preparados para combatir con aviso de un minuto

missionary people sent by their church to teach and convert others to their religion (p. 42)
misionero personas enviadas por su iglesia a enseñar y convertir a otras a su religión

mission system a way of living used by the Spanish in the Americas, in which settlements were designed to convert local Indians to Catholicism and make them into loyal Spanish subjects (p. 303)

sistema de las misiones forma de vida usada por los españoles en las Américas, bajo la cual los asentamientos se diseñaban con el propósito de convertir a los indígenas locales al catolicismo y obligarlos a ser fieles servidores de España

Mississippi Freedom Democratic Party a political party created in 1964 with the purpose of winning seats at the 1964 Democratic National Convention (p. 928)
Partido Demócrata por la Libertad de Mississippi partido político creado en 1964 con el fin de obtener puestos en la Convención Nacional Demócrata de 1964

Missouri Compromise (1820) an agreement that allowed Missouri to enter the Union as a slave state and Maine to enter as a free state and outlawed slavery in any territories or states north of 36°30′ N. latitude (p. 243)
Compromiso de Missouri (1820) acuerdo redactado en el que se aceptaba a Missouri en la Unión como estado esclavista y a Maine como estado libre y prohibía la esclavitud en los territorios o estados ubicados al norte del paralelo 36°30′ N

monopoly having complete control in the marketplace, without any outside competition (p. 468)
monopolio control absoluto del mercado, sin competencia externa

Monroe Doctrine (1823) President James Monroe's statement forbidding further colonization in the Americas and declaring that any attempt by a foreign country to colonize would be considered an act of hostility (p. 242)
Doctrina Monroe (1823) declaración hecha por el presidente James Monroe en la que se prohibía la colonización adicional del continente americano a partir de entonces y en que se declaró que cualquier intento de colonización por parte de otro país se consideraría un acto hostil

Montgomery bus boycott (1955) a boycott of the Montgomery, Alabama bus system in response to the racial segregation of city buses (p. 914)
boicot de los autobuses en Montgomery (1955) boicot del sistema de autobuses de Montgomery, Alabama, como reacción a la segregación racial en los autobuses de la ciudad

Mormon Trail 1,300-mile-long route used by Mormons to travel west to Utah (p. 299)
Ruta de los Mormones ruta de 1,300 millas que usaron los mormones para viajar hacia el oeste a Utah

Morrill Act (1862) a federal law passed by Congress that gave land to western states to encourage them to build colleges (p. 450)
Ley Morrill (1862) ley federal aprobada por el Congreso para otorgar tierras a los estados del oeste con el fin de fomentar la construcción de universidades

muckrakers a term coined for journalists who "raked up" and exposed corruption and problems of society (p. 523)
muckrakers término creado para llamar a los periodistas que se dedicaban a investigar y exponer la corrupción y los problemas de la sociedad

Muslims followers of Islam (p. 19)
musulmanes seguidores del Islam

My Lai Massacre (1968) a massacre of hundreds of unarmed Vietnamese civilians by American soldiers during the Vietnam War (p. 975)
Masacre de My Lai (1968) matanza de cientos de civiles vietnamitas desarmados a manos de soldados estadounidenses durante la Guerra de Vietnam

NASA National Aeronautics and Space Administration; agency in charge of the United States' programs for exploring outer space (p. 858)
NASA (por sus siglas en inglés) Administración Nacional de Aeronáutica y el Espacio; agencia encargada de los programas estadounidenses de exploración del espacio exterior

National American Woman Suffrage Association (NAWSA) an organization founded by Elizabeth Cady Stanton and Susan B. Anthony in 1890 to obtain women's suffrage (p. 534)
Asociación Nacional Estadounidense para el Sufragio Femenino (NAWSA, por sus siglas en inglés) organización fundada en 1890 por Elizabeth Cady Stanton y Susan B. Anthony para obtener el derecho al voto de las mujeres

National Association for the Advancement of Colored People (NAACP) an organization founded in 1909 by W. E. B. Du Bois and other reformers to bring attention to racial inequality (p. 509)
Asociación Nacional para el Progreso de la Gente de Color (NAACP, por sus siglas en inglés) organización fundada en 1909 por W. E. B. Du Bois y otros reformadores para dirigir la atención hacia la desigualdad racial

National Association of Colored Women an organization founded in 1896 that worked to fight poverty, segregation, lynchings, and the persistence of Jim Crow laws (p. 532)
Asociación Nacional de Mujeres de Color organización fundada en 1896 para combatir la pobreza, la segregación, los linchamientos y las leyes de Jim Crow

National Grange a social and educational organization for farmers (p. 503)
Granja Nacional organización social y educativa para los agricultores

nationalism sense of pride and devotion to a nation (p. 240)
nacionalismo sentimiento de orgullo y lealtad a una nación

National Organization for Women (NOW) a women's rights group formed in 1966 (p. 988)
Organización Nacional en pro de la Mujeres (NOW, por sus siglas en inglés) grupo defensor de los derechos de la mujer creado en 1966

National Road also called the Cumberland Road, when it was completed in 1841 it stretched from Cumberland, Maryland 800 miles west to Vandalia, Illinois (p. 253)
Camino Nacional también llamado Camino de Cumberland cuando se terminó en 1841, cubría 800 millas al oeste, desde Cumberland, Maryland, hasta Vandalia, Illinois

National War Labor Board (1918) this board mediated disputes between workers and management (p. 601)
Junta Nacional del Trabajo en Tiempos de Guerra (1918) esta junta mediaba en los conflictos entre trabajadores y patronos

nativism an opposition to immigration by the citizens living in a country (p. 274); distrust of foreigners (p. 626)

nativismo oposición a la inmigración por parte de los ciudadanos que viven en un país; desconfianza hacia los extranjeros

NATO North Atlantic Treaty Organization; an international defense alliance formed in 1949 (p. 822)
OTAN Organización del Tratado del Atlántico Norte; alianza internacional de defensa formada en 1949

Navigation Acts series of laws passed between 1651 and 1663 by Parliament stating that all goods coming from Europe or Africa to the colonies had to travel on British ships manned with a British crew (p. 73)
Leyes de Navegación serie de leyes aprobadas entre 1651 y 1663 por el Parlamento; las leyes afirmaban que todos los bienes provenientes de Europa o África con destino a las colonias tenían que viajar en barcos británicos comandados por una tripulación británica

neutral in a war, not aiding either side (p. 753)
neutral en una guerra, que no ayuda a ningún bando

Neutrality Act (1935) a United States act aimed at helping prevent the nation from being drawn into a war (p. 752)
Ley de Neutralidad (1935) ley estadounidense creada para ayudar a impedir que la nación se viera involucrada en una guerra

Neutrality Proclamation (1793) a statement made by President George Washington that the United States would not side with any of the nations at war in Europe following the French Revolution (p. 210)
Proclamación de Neutralidad (1793) declaración en la que el presidente George Washington anunció que Estados Unidos no sería aliado de ninguna de las naciones europeas en guerra después de la Revolución Francesa

New Deal a plan by President Franklin Roosevelt intended to bring economic relief, recovery, and reforms to the country after the Great Depression (p. 702)
Nuevo Trato plan del presidente Franklin Roosevelt para traer ayuda, recuperación y reformas económicas al país después de la Gran Depresión

New Freedom Woodrow Wilson's plan of reform which called for tariff reductions, banking reform, and stronger antitrust legislation (p. 543)
Nueva Libertad plan de reformas de Woodrow Wilson que abogaba por reducciones arancelarias de los aranceles, reformas bancarias y leyes antimonopolio más estrictas

New Frontier the nickname given to President Kennedy's plans for changing the nation (p. 888)
Nueva Frontera apodo dado a los planes del presidente Kennedy para transformar a la nación

New Jersey Plan a proposal to create a unicameral legislature with equal representation of states rather than representation by population (p. 153)
Plan de Nueva Jersey propuesta para la creación de un gobierno de una sola cámara que contara con la misma representación por parte de cada estado, sin basarse en el número de habitantes

New Right a coalition of conservative media commentators, think tanks, and grassroots Christian groups (p. 1049)
Nueva Derecha coalición de analistas conservadores de los medios de asesoría estretégica, grupos de estudiosos y organizaciones cristianas de base popular

New South name used by some Southerners to describe the South after Reconstruction (p. 427)

Nuevo Sur nombre usado por algunos sureños para describir el Sur después de la Reconstrucción (pág. 427)

Newlands Reclamation Act (1902) law that allowed the federal government to build irrigation projects to make marginal lands productive (p. 539)
Ley de Reclamación de Nuevas Tierras (1902) ley que permitía al gobierno federal llevar a cabo proyectos de irrigación para hacer productivas las tierras de poco rendimiento

9/11 terrorist attacks on the World Trade Center in New York City and the Pentagon in Washington, D.C., that took place on September 11, 2001 (p. 1093)
11-S ataques terroristas contra el World Trade Center en la ciudad de Nueva York y el Pentágono en Washington, D.C., que tuvieron lugar el 11 de septiembre de 2001

Nineteenth Amendment (1920) gave women the right to vote (p. 544)
Decimonovena enmienda (1920) otorgó a la mujer el derecho al voto

nomads people who move from place to place (p. 7)
nómadas personas que se trasladan de un lugar a otro

North American Free Trade Agreement (NAFTA) (1993) an agreement in which the United States, Mexico, and Canada became one large free-trade zone (p. 1082)
Tratado de Libre Comercio de América del Norte (TLCAN) (1993) acuerdo según el cual Estados Unidos, México y Canadá se convirtieron en una gran zona de libre comercio

Northwest Ordinance (1787) legislation passed by Congress to establish a political structure for the Northwest Territory and create a system for the admission of new states (p. 149)
Ordenanza del Noroeste (1787) ley aprobada por el Congreso para establecer una estructura política en el Territorio del Noroeste y crear un proceso para la incorporación de nuevos estados

nuclear fallout harmful particles of radioactive material produced by nuclear explosions (p. 858)
lluvia radiactiva partículas dañinas de material radiactivo producido por explosiones nucleares

nullification the act of declaring something void (p. 214)
anulación acto de declarar que algo es inválido

nullification crisis a dispute led by John C. Calhoun that said that states could ignore federal laws if they believed those laws violated the Constitution (p. 250)
crisis de anulación controversia liderada por John C. Calhoun que argumentaba que los estados no tenían que obedecer las leyes federales si consideraban que esas leyes desobedecían la Constitución

O

occupy to take control of a place by placing troops in it (p. 802)
ocupar tomar el control de un lugar colocando tropas allí

Okie nickname for a farmer who left the Dust Bowl in search of work (p. 685)
Okie apodo dado a los granjeros que se fueron de Tazón de Polvo en busca de trabajo

Olmec one of the first major American Indian societies in Mesoamerica (p. 8)

olemcas una de las primeras sociedades indígenas norteamericanas de importancia en Mesoamérica

OPEC Organization of Petroleum Exporting Countries; organization that coordinates petroleum policies of major producing countries (p. 1022)

OPEP Organización de Países Exportadores de Petróleo; organización que coordina las políticas petroleras de los principales países productores

Open Door policy a policy established by the United States in 1899 to promote equal access for all nations to trade in China (p. 556)

política de puertas abiertas política establecida por Estados Unidos en 1899 para promover el acceso igualitario por igual a todas las naciones al comercio con China

Operation Desert Storm U.S.-led war to end Iraq's occupation of Kuwait in 1990–1991 (p. 1065)

Operación Tormenta del Desierto guerra dirigida por Estados Unidos para ponerle fin a la ocupación de Kuwait por parte de Irak entre 1990 y 1991

Operation Overlord (1944) the code name for the Allied invasion of mainland Europe in World War II, starting with the D-Day landings (p. 775)

Operación Overlord (1944) nombre en clave de la invasión de Europa continental por parte de los Aliados en la Segunda Guerra Mundial; empezó con los desembarcos del Día D

Operation Rolling Thunder a U.S. bombing campaign in North Vietnam in March 1965 (p. 956)

Operación Trueno Galopante ofensiva de bombardeos estadounidenses en Vietnam del Norte en marzo de 1965

Operation Torch (1942) the code name for the Allied invasion of North Africa during World War II (p. 773)

Operación Antorcha (1942) nombre en clave de la invasión del norte de África por parte de los Aliados durante la Segunda Guerra Mundial

oral tradition unwritten history passed down through stories and legends (p. 19)

tradición oral historia no escrita transmitida a través de relatos y leyendas

Oregon Trail a 2,000-mile trail through the Great Plains from western Missouri to the Oregon Territory (p. 298)

Camino de Oregón ruta de 2,000 millas que cruzaba las Grandes Planicies desde el oeste de Missouri hasta el Territorio de Oregón

Pacific Railway Act (1862) congressional measure which gave land to railroad companies to help facilitate the construction of a railroad and telegraph line from the Missouri River to the Pacific Ocean (p. 450)

Ley del Ferrocarril del Pacífico (1862) medida del Congreso por la que se entregaban terrenos a las compañías de ferrocarriles para facilitar la construcción de un ferrocarril y de una línea de telégrafo desde el río Missouri hasta el océano Pacífico

pacification a program in the Vietnam War in which U.S. troops would move South Vietnamese from their villages and burn the villages down (p. 958)

pacificación programa durante la Guerra de Vietnam en el que las tropas de Estados Unidos sacaban a los vietnamitas del Sur de sus aldeas y las incendiaban

pacifist a person who does not believe in the use of military force (p. 752)

pacifista persona que no cree en el uso de la fuerza militar

Palmer raids (1918) a series of government attacks on suspected radicals in the United States led by the U.S. Attorney General, A. Mitchell Palmer (p. 624)

redadas de Palmer (1918) serie de ataques del gobierno sobre supuestos radicales de Estados Unidos dirigidos por el secretario de justicia, A. Mitchell Palmer

Panmunjom town in the demilitarized zone between North and South Korea where peace talks took place following the Korean War (p. 841)

Panmunjom pueblo ubicado en la zona desmilitarizada entre Corea del Norte y Corea del Sur, donde se llevaron a cabo las negociaciones para firmar un tratado de paz después de la Guerra de Corea

Peace Convention (1861) a meeting called by Virginia leaders after the defeat of the Crittendon Compromise to deal with the issue of slavery in the United States

Convención de Paz (1861) reunión convocada por los líderes de Virginia para tratar el asunto de la esclavitud en Estados Unidos después del rechazo del Compromiso de Crittenden

Peace Corps a program that trains and sends volunteers to poor nations to serve as educators, health care workers, agricultural advisers, and in other jobs (p. 886)

Cuerpo de Paz programa que entrena y envía voluntarios a países pobres de todo el mundo para trabajar como educadores, trabajadores de salud, consejeros agrícolas y en otros trabajos

Pentagon Papers papers that revealed that government officials had been misleading the American people about the progress of the Vietnam War for many years (p. 975)

Papeles del Pentágono documentos que revelaron que los funcionarios del gobierno engañaron al pueblo durante muchos años con respecto al progreso de la guerra de Vietnam

Pequot War (1637) war between the Pequot Indians and the Dutch settlers and their Naragansett and Mohegan Indian allies (p. 56)

Guerra Pequot (1637) guerra entre los indígenas pequot y los pobladores holandeses y sus aliados, los indígenas naragansett y mohegan

perestroika Russian word for "restructuring;" refers to the restructuring of the corrupt government bureaucracy in the Soviet Union under Mikhail Gorbachev (p. 1060)

perestroika palabra rusa que significa "reestructuración," se refiere a la reestructuración bajo Mikhail Gorbachev de la burocracia gubernamental corrupta de la Unión Soviética

Pickett's Charge (1863) a failed Confederate attack during the Civil War led by General George Pickett at the Battle of Gettysburg (p. 386)

ataque de Pickett (1863) ataque fallido del ejército confederado, al mando del general George Pickett, en la batalla de Gettysburg de la Guerra Civil

Pinckney's Treaty (1795) an agreement between the United States and Spain that changed Florida's border and made it easier for American ships to use the port of New Orleans (p. 211)
Tratado de Pinckney (1795) acuerdo entre Estados Unidos y España que modificó los límites de la Florida y facilitó a los barcos estadounidenses el uso del puerto de Nueva Orleáns

placer mining searching for gold by using pans or other devices to wash gold nuggets out of loose rock (p. 446)
minería con bandeja manera de buscar el oro con bandejas u otros utensilios que con la ayuda del agua separan las pepitas de oro de las piedras sueltas

plantation a large farm that usually specialized in growing one kind of crop for profit (p. 21)
plantación granja de gran tamaño que por lo general se especializa en un cultivo específico con el fin de obtener ganancias

platform a declaration of the principles for which a group stands (p. 342)
plataforma declaración de los principios en los que cree un grupo

Platt Amendment a part of the Cuban constitution that limited Cuba's right to make treaties, gave the United States the right to intervene in Cuban affairs, and required Cuba to sell or lease land to the U.S. (p. 566)
Enmienda Platt parte de la constitución cubana redactada bajo la supervisión de Estados Unidos que limitaba el derecho de Cuba a firmar tratados, otorgaba a Estados Unidos el derecho a intervenir en los asuntos cubanos y exigía a Cuba vender o arrendar tierras a Estados Unidos

Plessy v. Ferguson (1896) U.S. Supreme Court case that established the separate-but-equal doctrine for public facilities (p. 508)
Plessy* contra *Ferguson (1896) caso en el que la Corte Suprema estableció la doctrina de "separados pero iguales" en los lugares públicos

pocket veto a presidential power to prevent a bill passed in the last 10 days of a legislative session from becoming law by simply ignoring it (p. 406)
veto de bolsillo poder del presidente que le permite impedir la aprobación de un proyecto de ley aprobado en los 10 días anteriores de una sesión legislativa al no hacerle caso

police action phrase to describe the U.S. intervention in Korea in 1950 (p. 837)
acción policial frase usada para describir la intervención de Estados Unidos en Corea en 1950

poll tax a special tax that a person had to pay in order to vote (p. 508)
impuesto electoral impuesto especial que debía pagar una persona para poder votar

Pony Express a system of messengers that carried mail between relay stations on a route 2,000 miles long in 1860 and 1861 (p. 301)
Pony Express sistema de mensajeros que transportaban el correo entre estaciones de relevo a lo largo de una ruta de 2,000 millas entre 1860 y 1861

Poor People's Campaign an expansion of the civil rights movement that tried to raise awareness about poverty among people of all races (p. 939)

Campaña por los Pobres ampliación del movimiento de los derechos civiles que intentaba crear una mayor conciencia sobre la pobreza entre las personas de todas las razas

pop art a style of art in the 1950s and 1960s intended to appeal to popular tastes (p. 1007)
arte pop estilo artístico de las décadas de 1950 y 1960 que pretendía atraer a los gustos populares

popular sovereignty the idea that political authority belongs to the people (p. 326)
soberanía popular idea de que la autoridad política pertenece al pueblo

Populist Party a political party formed in 1892 that supported free coinage of silver, work reforms, immigration restrictions, and government ownership of railroads and telegraph and telephone systems (p. 505)
Partido Populista partido político formado en 1892 que apoyaba la libre producción de monedas de plata, reformas laborales y restricciones de la inmigración, además de apoyar que el gobierno fuera dueño de los sistemas ferroviario, telegráfico y telefónico

Potsdam Conference (1945) meeting among leaders of the Allies near the end of World War II (p. 807)
Conferencia de Potsdam (1945) encuentro de los líderes aliados celebrado poco antes del final de la Segunda Guerra Mundial

Pottawatomie Massacre (1856) an incident in which abolitionist John Brown and seven other men murdered pro-slavery Kansans (p. 332)
Mascare de Pottawatomie (1856) incidente en el que el abolicionista John Brown y siete hombres más asesinaron a varios habitantes pro esclavistas de Kansas

Proclamation of 1763 law created by British officials that prohibited colonists from settling in areas west of the Appalachian Mountains (p. 95)
Proclamación de 1763 ley creada por los funcionarios británicos que prohibía a los colonos asentarse al oeste de los montes Apalaches

productivity the amount of product made by a worker or a machine (p. 631)
productividad cantidad de un producto fabricada por un trabajador o una máquina

progressivism group of reform movements of the late 1800s that focused on urban problems, the plight of workers, and corrupt political machines (p. 523)
progresivismo grupo de movimientos reformistas de finales del siglo XIX que se concentraba en los problemas urbanos, como las dificultades de los trabajadores y las maquinarias políticas corruptas

prohibition a ban on alcohol that became law in 1920; the ban was lifted in 1933 (p. 531)
prohibición suspensión de la venta de bebidas alcohólicas que se convirtió en ley en 1920; se elimnó en 1933

propaganda information designed to influence public opinion (p. 603)
propaganda información diseñada para influir en la opinión pública

proprietary colonies grants of land given by the King to his loyal friends (p. 61)
colonias en propiedad concesiones de tierra otorgadas por el rey a sus amigos leales

protectorate a country that is controlled by an outside government (p. 566)
　protectorado país controlado por un gobierno externo

Protestants reformers who protested certain practices of the Catholic Church (p. 26)
　protestantes reformistas que protestaban por ciertas prácticas de la Iglesia católica

provisional temporary (p. 347)
　provisional temporal

public works government-funded building projects (p. 699)
　obras públicas proyectos de construcción financiados por el gobierno

pueblo a word meaning "town" in Spanish (p. 9)
　pueblo palabra en español que significa "ciudad"

Pueblo Native American group of the Southwest (p. 12)
　pueblo grupo indígena norteamericano del Suroeste

***Pueblo* incident** North Korean capture of the *Pueblo*, a Navy spy ship, off the coast of Communist North Korea (p. 900)
　incidente del *Pueblo* captura por parte de Corea del Norte del *Pueblo*, un barco espía de la armada, cerca de la costa de Corea del Norte, un país comunista

Pure Food and Drug Act (1906) law that forbade the manufacture, sale, or transportation of food and patent medicine containing harmful ingredients, and required that containers of food and medicines carry ingredient labels (p. 538)
　Ley de Alimentos y los Medicamentos Puros (1906) ley que prohibió la fabricación, venta o transporte de alimentos y de medicamentos patentados con ingredientes dañinos y que requirió que los envases de los alimentos y los medicamentos llevaran etiquetas con los ingredientes

Puritans a group of English Protestants who wanted to "purify" the Church of England through reforms (p. 52)
　puritanos grupo de protestantes ingleses que querían "purificar" la Iglesia de Inglaterra con reformas

push-pull model of immigration example of immigration where factors that cause people to leave their homeland are "pushes," and factors that encourage people to travel to another country are called "pulls" (p. 273)
　modelo de inmigración de expulsión y atracción ejemplo de inmigración en el que los factores que explican la salida de la gente de sus países de origen se llaman factores "de expulsión" y los que animan a la gente a trasladarse a otro país se llaman factores "de atracción"

Quaker member of a Protestant sect founded in the 1640s in England (p. 60)
　cuáquero miembro de una secta protestante fundada en la década de 1640 en Inglaterra

Quarantine Speech (1937) Franklin D. Roosevelt's speech following the Japanese attack on China in which he called on America to take clear sides in the current world conflicts (p. 754)
　Discurso de la Cuarentena (1937) discurso pronunciado por Franklin D. Roosevelt después del ataque japonés a China en el instó a los estadounidenses a tomar una posición clara en los conflictos mundiales del momento

racial etiquette strict rules of behavior that governed the social and business interactions of white and black Americans (p. 509)
　etiqueta racial reglas estrictas de conducta que regían la interacción social y comercial entre estadounidenses blancos y negros

radical a person with extreme views (p. 325)
　radical persona con puntos de vista extremos

Radical Republicans members of Congress who felt that southern states needed to make great social changes before they could be readmitted to the Union (p. 412)
　republicanos radicales miembros del Congreso convencidos de que los estados del Sur necesitaban realizar grandes cambios sociales antes de poder a ser readmitidos en la Unión

rationing limiting the amount of a certain product each individual can get (p. 794)
　racionamiento limitación de la cantidad de cierto producto que puede obtener cada persona

realpolitik basing foreign policies on realistic views of national interest rather than on broad rules or principles (p. 1020)
　realpolitik basar la política exterior en perspectivas realistas de los intereses nacionales en lugar de basarla en reglas o principios generales amplios

recall a vote to remove an official from office (p. 527)
　destitución votación para retirar a un funcionario de su cargo

Reconstruction Acts (1867-68) the laws that put the southern states under U.S. military control and required them to draft new constitutions (p. 414)
　Leyes de Reconstrucción (1867-68) leyes que pusieron a los estados del Sur bajo el control militar estadounidense y los obligaron a reformar sus constituciones

Reconstruction Finance Corporation a program that provided aid to struggling banks and other institutions during the Great Depression (p. 690)
　Corporación Financiera de la Reconstrucción programa que proporcionó ayuda a los bancos y demás instituciones que se encontraban en dificultades durante la Gran Depresión

Redcoats British soldiers who fought against the colonists in the Revolutionary War (p. 126)
　casacas rojas soldados británicos que lucharon contra los colonos en la Guerra de Independencia estadounidense

Redeemers name taken in the late 1870s by democrats who now controlled southern states (p. 425)
　redentores nombre adoptado a finales de la década de 1870 por los demócratas que entonces controlaban los estados del Sur

Red Scare widespread fear of communism (p. 624)
　terror rojo temor generalizado al comunismo

referendum a procedure that allows voters to approve or reject a law already proposed or passed by government (p. 527)
　referéndum medida que permite a los ciudadanos votar para aprobar o rechazar una ley previamente propuesta o aprobada por el gobierno

Reform Era (1830–1860) period during which thousands of Americans sought to reshape American life (p. 267)
Era de la Reforma (1830–1860) período durante el cual miles de estadounidenses quisieron cambiar la forma de vida en Estados Unidos

reform societies groups that were organized to promote social reforms (p. 281)
sociedades reformistas grupos que se formaban para promover reformas sociales

Reformation a religious movement within the Catholic Church in the 1500s; led to the establishment of the Protestant Church (p. 26)
Reforma movimiento religiosa dentro de la Iglesia católica en el siglo XVI; condujo al establecimiento de la Iglesia protestante

Renaissance an era of learning and creativity that began in Italy in the 1300s and spread throughout Europe (p. 25)
Renacimiento era de aprendizaje y creatividad que empezó en Italia en el siglo XIV y se extendió por el resto de Europa

reparations payments designed to make up for the damage of something (pp. 608, 638)
indemnizaciones pagos designados para compensar el daño causado por algo

republic a political system in which the citizens of a region elect representatives to run the government (p. 145)
república sistema político en el que los ciudadanos de una región eligen representantes para dirigir el gobierno

Republic of California name taken by California after American settlers declared it independent from Mexico in 1846 (p. 310)
República de California nombre adoptado por California después de que los pobladores estadounidenses declararon el territorio independiente de México en 1846

Republic of Texas name taken by Texas after it won its independence from Mexico in 1836 (p. 307)
República de Texas nombre adoptado por Texas después de lograr independizarse de México en 1836

Republican Party a political party formed in the 1850s to stop the spread of slavery in the West (p. 328)
Partido Republicano partido político formado en la década de 1850 para detener la expansión de la esclavitud hacia el Oeste

reserved powers powers in the Constitution not specifically given to the federal government but instead left to the states (p. 163)
poderes reservados poderes establecidos en la Constitución y no otorgados específicamente al gobierno federal, sino a los estados

Restoration (1660–1685) name given to the period of reign of the English King Charles II; the monarchy was restored in England with his ascension to the throne (p. 61)
Restauración (1660–1685) nombre dado al período del reinado de Carlos II de Inglaterra porque al subir él al trono, se restauró la monarquía en Inglaterra

Roe v. Wade (1973) Supreme Court decision that made abortion legal in the United States (p. 989)
Roe contra Wade (1973) decisión de la Corte Suprema que legalizó aborto en Estados Unidos

Roosevelt Corollary a change to the Monroe Doctrine, saying that the United States could intervene in the internal affairs of Latin American nations (p. 569)
Corolario de Roosevelt cambio en la Doctrina Monroe en la que se declaraba que Estados Unidos podía intervenir en los asuntos internos de los países latinoamericanos

Rosie the Riveter a popular symbol for working women of World War II (p. 761)
Rosie la remachadora símbolo popular de las mujeres trabajadoras durante la Segunda Guerra Mundial

Rough Riders a cavalry regiment organized by Theodore Roosevelt (p. 562)
Jinetes Rudos regimiento de caballería organizado por Theodore Roosevelt

royal colony a colony under direct control of the king (p. 55)
colonia real colonia bajo el control directo del rey

Russo-Japanese War (1904–1905) war between Russia and Japan over Manchuria (p. 557)
Guerra Ruso-Japonesa (1904–1905) guerra por Manchuria entre Rusia y Japón

SALT I discussions between the United States and the Soviets to slow the ongoing arms race in the late 1960s and early 1970s (p. 1021)
SALT I conversaciones entre Estados Unidos y la Unión Soviética para frenar la carrera armamentista a finales de la década de 1960 y comienzos de la década de 1970

SALT II continuing discussions in 1979 between the United States; SALT II set limits on certain kinds of nuclear weapons (p. 1036)
SALT II conversaciones entre Estados Unidos y la Unión Soviética en 1979; SALT II fijó límites sobre ciertos tipos de armas nucleares

salutary neglect idea that the colonies benefited by being left alone, without too much British interference (p. 76)
abandono saludable ideea que sostenía que las colonias se beneficiaban si se les daba más libertad, sin demasiada interferencia británica

Sand Creek Massacre (1864) U.S. Army's killing of about 150 Cheyenne elderly, women, and children at Sand Creek Reservation in Colorado Territory (p. 440)
Masacre de Sand Creek (1864) matanza por parte del ejército de Estados Unidos de unos 150 ancianos, mujeres y niños cheyenes en la reserva de Sand Creek en el territorio de Colorado

Santa Fe Trail an important trail west from Independence, Missouri to Santa Fe, New Mexico (p. 297)
Camino de Santa Fe importante ruta que va hacia el oeste desde Independence, Missouri, hasta Santa Fe, Nuevo México

satellite an object that orbits around a planet (p. 858)
satélite objeto que gira alrededor de un planeta

Saturday night massacre part of the Watergate Scandal in which Nixon ordered his attorney general to fire special prosecutor Archibald Cox (p. 1030)
masacre del sábado en la noche parte del escándalo Watergate en la que Nixon ordenó a su secretario de justicia que despidiera al fiscal especial Archibald Cox

ENGLISH AND SPANISH GLOSSARY

savings and loan crisis a financial disaster in which the federal government had to step in and pay back loans for many S & L institutions (p. 1068)
crisis de ahorro y préstamo catástrofe financiera en la que el gobierno federal se vio obligado a intervenir y pagar los préstamos de muchas instituciones de ahorro y préstamo

scalawag name given by former Confederates to southerners who supported the shift in power to Congress and the army in the South during Reconstruction (p. 416)
scalawag nombre dado por los antiguos confederados a aquellos habitantes del Sur que apoyaron el cambio del poder al Congreso y al ejército en el Sur durante la Reconstrucción

Schenck v. *United States* (1917) court case that explained the limits of the First Amendment (p. 604)
Schenck contra *Estados Unidos* (1917) juicio en el que se explicaron los límites de la Primera enmienda

SCLC Southern Christian Leadership Conference; a group formed in Georgia in 1957 to organize civil rights protest activities (p. 915)
SCLC Conferencia del Liderazgo Cristiano del Sur; grupo formado en Georgia en 1957 para organizar las actividades de protesta en favor de los derechos civiles

SEATO Southeast Asia Treaty Organization; group of nations that agreed to work together to resist Communist aggression (p. 852)
SEATO Organización del Tratado del Sureste Asiático; grupo de naciones que se comprometieron a trabajar juntas para resistir la agresión comunista

secede break away from (p. 250)
secesión separación

Second Bank of the United States a national bank created by Congress in 1816 and overseen by the federal government, its purpose was to regulate state banks (p. 248)
Segundo Banco de Estados Unidos banco nacional creado por el Congreso en 1816 y supervisado por el gobierno federal con la función de reglamentar los bancos estatales

Second Continental Congress (1775) a meeting of colonial delegates in Philadelphia to decide how to react to fighting at Lexington and Concord (p. 115)
Segundo Congreso Continental (1775) reunión de delegados coloniales en Filadelfia para tomar decisiones acerca de los enfrentamientos en Lexington y Concord

Second Great Awakening a period of religious evangelism that began in the 1790s and became widespread in the United States by the 1830s (p. 267)
Segundo Gran Despertar período de evangelización religiosa iniciado en la década de 1790 que se extendió por Estados Unidos para la década de 1830

Second New Deal (1935) a new set of programs in the spring of 1935 including additional banking reforms, new tax laws, new relief programs (p. 710)
Segundo Nuevo Trato (1935) nuevo conjunto de programas de la primavera de 1935 que incluyó reformas bancarias, nuevas leyes sobre impuestos y nuevos programas de ayuda social

sectionalism devotion to the interests of one geographic region over the interests of the entire country (pp. 213, 240)

regionalismo dedicación a los intereses de una región geográfica y no a los del país

Selective Service Act (1921) act which required men between the ages of 21 and 30 to register to be drafted into the armed forces (p. 593)
Ley del Servicio Militar Selectivo (1921) ley que exigía que los hombres entre los 21 y los 30 años se inscribieran para ser reclutados por las fuerzas armadas

self-determination the right of people to decide their own political status (p. 607)
autodeterminación derecho de las peronas a decidir su propia situación política

Seneca Falls Convention (1848) the first national women's rights convention at which the Declaration of Sentiments was written (p. 282)
Convención de Seneca Falls (1848) primera convención nacional a favor de los derechos de la mujer, en la cual se redactó la Declaración de Sentimientos

settlement house neighborhood center staffed by professionals and volunteers for education, recreation, and social activities in poor areas (p. 498)
organización de servico a la comunidad centro social en el que trabajan profesionales y voluntarios que promueven la educación, la recreación y las actividades sociales en las zonas pobres

Seventeenth Amendment (1913) allowed American voters to directly elect U.S. senators (p. 527)
Decimoséptima enmienda (1913) permite a los votantes estadounidenses elegir directamente a los senadores de Estados Unidos

sharecropping a system used on southern farms after the Civil War in which farmers worked land owned by someone else in return for a small portion of the crops (p. 421)
cultivo de aparceros sistema usado en las granjas del sur después de la Guerra Civil en el cual los agricultores labraban las tierras de otra persona a cambio de una pequeña porción de la cosecha

Sherman Antitrust Act (1890) a law that made it illegal to create monopolies or trusts that restrained free trade (p. 473)
Ley Antimonopolio Sherman (1890) ley que prohibió la creación de monopolios o consorcios que restringieran el libre comercio

shuttle diplomacy negotiation style in which a mediator shuttles between groups, trying to work out agreements to end a disagreement (p. 1023)
diplomacia de ir y venir estilo de negociación en la que el mediador va y viene entre distintos grupos para intentar alcanzar acuerdos que pongan fin a un desacuerdo

silent majority phrase used by President Nixon to describe people who supported the government's Vietnam policies but did not express their opinions publicly (p. 973)
mayoría silenciosa frase utilizada por el presidente Nixon para describir a las personas que apoyaban la política del gobierno en Vietnam pero no expresaban su opinión en público

sit-down strike a strike in which workers refuse to work or leave the workplace until a settlement is reached (p. 713)
huelga de brazos caídos huelga en la que los trabajadores se niegan a trabajar o a abandonar el lugar de trabajo hasta que se alcance un convenio laboral

Sixteenth Amendment (1913) law that allowed Congress to levy taxes based on an individual's income (p. 542)
Decimosexta enmienda (1913) ley que permitió al Congreso recaudar impuestos en base a los ingresos de una persona

Smoot-Hawley Tariff Act (1930) extremely high tariff on farm products and manufactured goods (p. 690)
Ley Arancel Smoot-Hawley (1930) arancel muy alto sobre los productos agrícolas y los bienes fabricados

SNCC Student Nonviolent Coordinating Committee; student civil rights organization in the 1960s (p. 918)
SNCC Comité Coordinador No Violento de Estudiantes; organización estudiantil de derechos civiles de la década de 1960

social contract an agreement between a people and their government or ruler, stating that if a government (or ruler) did not protect citizens and their rights, they were justified in overthrowing it (p. 85)
contrato social acuerdo entre un pueblo y su gobierno o gobernante que establece que si el gobierno (o el gobernante) no protege a sus ciudadanos y sus derechos, el pueblo tiene justificación para derrocarlo

social Darwinism a view of society based on Charles Darwin's scientific theory of natural selection (p. 467)
darwinismo social visión de la sociedad basada en la teoría científica de la selección natural de Charles Darwin

Social Gospel the idea that religious faith should be expressed through good works (p. 498)
evangelio social idea según la cual la fe religiosa se debe expresar por medio de buenas obras

social justice the fair distribution of advantages and disadvantages in a society (p. 995)
justicia social distribución justa de las ventajas y desventajas en una sociedad

Social Security a system for providing pensions for many Americans age 65 and older (p. 711)
Seguro Social sistema para proporcionar pensiones a la mayoría de estadounidenses mayores de 65 años

sod house home built from squares of turf and soil of the prairie, stacked up like bricks (p. 449)
casa de tepe casa construida con cuadrados de césped y tierra de las praderas, apilados como ladrillos

Solidarity an independent labor union founded in Soviet-controlled Poland in 1980 (p. 1055)
Solidaridad sindicato obrero independiente fundado en Polonia en 1980, cuando el país todavía estaba controlado por la Unión Soviética

Solid South name given to the South after Reconstruction, because it was so heavily Democratic (p. 427)
Sólido Sur nombre dado al Sur después de la Reconstrucción debido a que los demócratas representaban una mayoría aplastante

Southern Homestead Act (1866) law that set aside 45 million acres of government-owned land in southern states to provide free farms for African Americans (p. 420)
Ley de Heredad del Sur (1866) ley que reservó 45 millones de acres de terrenos controlados por el gobierno en los estados del sur para entregar granjas gratuitas a los afroamericanos

space shuttle a reusable spacecraft able to land on the ground like an airplane, and that could be used to transport people and supplies into space (p. 1067)
transbordador espacial nave espacial reutilizable capaz de aterrizar en la tierra igual que un avión y que se puede utilizar para transportar personas y suministros al espacio

speakeasy illegal bars where alcohol was served during Prohibition (p. 653)
bar clandestino bar ilegal donde se servían bebidas alcohólicas durante la época de la Prohibición

sphere of influence an area where foreign countries control the trade or natural resources of another nation or area (p. 556)
esfera de influencia zona de un país cuyos recursos naturales y comercio son controlados por otro país o zona

spoils system a politicians' practice of giving government jobs to his or her supporters (p. 246)
tráfico de influencias práctica de los políticos de dar empleos en el gobierno a las personas que los apoyan

Sputnik (1957) the first artificial satellite; launched by the Soviets (p. 858)
Sputnik (1957) primer satélite artificial; lanzado por la Unión Soviética

Square Deal Theodore Roosevelt's 1904 campaign slogan; expressed his belief that the needs of workers, business, and consumers should be balanced (p. 536)
Square Deal lema de la campaña de Theodore Roosevelt de 1904; expresaba su creencia en el equilibrio entre las necesidades de los trabajadores, los empresarios y los consumidores

Stamp Act (1765) a law passed by Parliament that raised tax money by requiring colonists to pay for an official stamp whenever they bought paper items (p. 107)
Ley del Sello ley aprobada por el Parlamento para recaudar impuestos en la que se obligaba a los colonos a pagar un sello oficial cada vez que compraran artículos de papel

states' rights belief that the power of the states should be greater than the power of the federal government (p. 249)
derechos estatales creencia de que el poder de los estados debe ser mayor que el del gobierno federal

Stono Rebellion (1739) rebellion by about 100 enslaved African Americans in South Carolina against Southern planters (p. 83)
Rebelión de Stono (1739) rebelión de unos 100 esclavos negros en Carolina del Sur contra hacendados sureños

Strategic Defense Initiative President Reagan's proposed defensive space shield that would knock out incoming Soviet missiles (p. 1054)
Iniciativa de Defensa Estratégica escudo protector espacial propuesto por el presidente Reagan con la idea que pudiera bloquear los misiles soviéticos que se acercaran

strict construction a way of interpreting the Constitution that allows the federal government to take only those actions the Constitution specifically says it can (p. 206)
interpretación estricta interpretación de la Constitución que sólo permite al gobierno federal realizar las acciones permitidas de manera específica en ella

subsidy a government payment that is aimed at achieving some public benefit (p. 702)
subsidio pago del gobierno destinado a lograr un beneficio parar el público

suburb smaller towns that are located outside a larger urban area (p. 631)
suburbio pueblos más pequeños ubicados en las afueras de una ciudad

Summer of Love the height of the hippie movement during the Summer of 1967 in San Francisco (p. 1005)
Verano del Amor punto máximo del movimiento hippie que tuvo lugar durante el verano de 1967 en San Francisco

summit a meeting of the heads of government (p. 851)
cumbre encuentro de jefes de estado

Sunbelt the southern and western portions of the United States (p. 866)
Sunbelt (cinturón del sol) estados del sur y el oeste de Estados Unidos

supply-side economics the economic theory that tax cuts and business incentives will stimulate the economy (p. 1050)
economía de la oferta teoría económica según la cual los recortes de impuestos y los incentivos para las compañías estimularán la economía

***Sussex* pledge** a pledge Germany issued which included a promise not to sink merchant vessels "without warning and without saving human lives" (p. 591)
promesa de *Sussex* compromiso de Alemania que incluía la promesa de que no hundirían los barcos mercantes "sin avisar ni sin salvar las vidas humanas"

sweatshop small workshop set up in a tenement rather than in centralized factories (p. 473)
fábrica explotadora pequeño taller montado en una casa de vecindad en lugar de en fábricas centralizadas

swing a type of jazz music popular in the 1930s (p. 722)
swing tipo de música de jazz popular en la década de 1930

Taino Arawakan Indian group living on the islands of the present-day Greater Antilles when Christopher Columbus arrived there in 1492 (p. 31)
taínos grupo indígena arahuaco que vivía en las islas que hoy son las Antillas Mayores cuando Cristóbal Colón llegó en 1492

Taliban group that took control over most of Afghanistan following the Soviet occupation in 1979 (p. 1095)
Talibán grupo que tomó el control de la mayor parte de Afganistán tras la ocupación soviética de 1979

Tampico incident (1914) confrontation between the U.S. and Mexico at Tampico Bay, Mexico, involving the arrest of American sailors by the Mexican government (p. 574)
incidente de Tampico (1914) enfrentamiento entre Estados Unidos y México en la bahía de Tampico, México, durante lel cual el gobierno mexicano arrestó a unos marineros estadounidenses

Teapot Dome a federally owned piece of land in Wyoming that was the site of a government scandal in 1921 when President Harding's secretary of the interior accepted bribes in return for allowing oil companies to drill for oil there (p. 636)

Teapot Dome nombre de un terreno federal en Wyoming que fue el centro de un escándalo gubernamental en 1921; el secretario del interior del presidente Harding aceptó sobornos para permitir que las empresas petroleras excavaran pozos allí

Tejanos Texans of Mexican heritage (p. 304)
tejanos texanos con ascendencia mexicana

telegraph a machine perfected by Samuel F. B. Morse in 1832 that uses pulses of electric current to send messages across long distances through wires (p. 255)
telégrafo máquina perfeccionada por Samuel F. B. Morse en 1832 que emplea impulsos eléctricos transmitidos por cables para enviar mensajes a grandes distancias

temperance movement a social reform effort begun in the mid-1800s to encourage people to drink less alcohol (p. 267)
movimiento de abstinencia movimiento de reforma social iniciado a mediados del siglo XIX para fomentar la disminución en el consumo de bebidas alcohólicas

tenant farming system of farming where farmers rented their land from the landowner and were allowed to grow whatever crop they chose (421)
agricultura de arriendo sistema de agricultura en el que los agricultores arriendan la tierra del propietario y pueden cultivar lo que quieran

tenement poorly built, overcrowded housing where many immigrants lived (p. 276)
casa de vecinos casas mal construidas donde vivían amontonados una gran cantidad de inmigrantes

Ten-Percent Plan President Abraham Lincoln's plan for Reconstruction (p. 405)
Plan del Diez por Ciento plan de Reconstrucción del presidente Abraham Lincoln

terrorism the use of violence by individuals and groups to advance political goals (p. 1081)
terrorismo uso de la violencia por parte de individuos y grupos con el fin de alcanzar metas políticas

Tet Offensive a series of major attacks launched by Communist forces in South Vietnam in 1968 (p. 955)
ofensiva del Tet serie de ataques importantes realizado por fuerzas comunistas en Vietnam del Sur en 1868

Texas Revolution (1835–1836) war of independence fought by Texans to gain independence from Mexico (p. 306)
Revolución Texana (1835–1836) guerra de independencia luchada por los texanos para independizarse de México

Thirteenth Amendment (1865) outlawed slavery (p. 391)
Decimotercera enmienda (1865) abolió la esclavitud

38th parallel line of latitude that divides North and South Korea (p. 836)
paralelo 38 línea de latitud que divide a Corea del Norte de Corea del Sur

Three-Fifths Compromise (1787) an agreement stating that enslaved people would be counted as three-fifths of a person when determining a state's population for representation in the lower house of Congress (p. 154)
Compromiso de los Tres Quintos (1787) acuerdo en el que se estableció que las personas exclavizadas contarían como tres quintas partes de una persona para determinar la representación de ese estado en la cámara baja del Congreso

Tiananmen Square massacre (1989) a large pro-democracy protest in China that resulted in the government using military force, killing hundreds (p. 1063)
Masacre de la Plaza de Tiananmen (1989) gran manifestación de protesta a favor de la democracia en China, en la que el gobierno usó fuerzas militares y dio muerte a cientos de personas

Toleration Act (1649) a Maryland law that made restricting the religious rights of Christians a crime (p. 65)
Ley de Tolerancia (1649) ley de Maryland que hizo ilegal la restricción de los derechos religiosos de los cristianos

Toltec people who dominated central Mexico around AD 900; known for their skills as warriors, artisans, and builders (p. 8)
toltecas grupo que dominó la zona central de México alrededor del año 900 d. de C.; eran reconocidos por sus destrezas como guerreros, artesanos y constructores

Tonkin Gulf Resolution (1964) congressional resolution that authorized military action in Southeast Asia (p. 955)
Resolución del Golfo de Tonkin (1964) resolución del Congreso que autorizó las acciones militares en el sureste de Asia

totalitarian form of government in which the person or party in charge has absolute control over all aspects of life (p. 741)
totalitario forma de gobierno en la que la persona o el partido que está a cargo tiene control absoluto sobre todos los aspectos de la vida

Trail of Tears (1838-39) an 800-mile forced march made by the Cherokee from their homeland in Georgia to Indian Territory (p. 248)
Ruta de las Lágrimas (1838-39) marcha forzada de 800 millas que realizó la tribu cherokee desde su territorio natal en Georgia hasta el Territorio Indígena

transatlantic crossing the Atlantic Ocean (p. 662)
transatlántico que atraviesa el océano Atlántico

transcendentalist movement movement whose members believed that knowledge is not found only by observation of the world, but also through reason, intuition, and personal spiritual experiences (p. 269)
movimiento trascendentalista movimiento cuyos miembros creían en la convicción de que el conocimiento no se obtiene sólo observando el mundo, sino mediante la razón, la intuición y las experiencias espirituales personales

transcontinental railroad a railroad system that crossed the continental United States (p. 463)
ferrocarril transcontinental sistema de trenes que cruzaba la parte continental de Estados Unidos de un extremo a otro

transcript a written record of a spoken event (p. 1031)
transcripción registro escrito de un suceso oral

transistor small electrical devices that can be found in computers and other machines (p. 864)
transistores pequeños dispositivos eléctricos de las computadoras y otras máquinas

Treaty of Ghent (1814) a treaty signed by the United States and Britain ending the War of 1812 (p. 227)
Tratado de Gante (1814) tratado firmado por Estados Unidos y Gran Bretaña para dar fin a la Guerra de 1812

Treaty of Greenville (1795) an agreement between Native American confederation leaders and the U.S. government that gave the United States Indian lands in the Northwest Territory (p. 212)
Tratado de Greenville (1795) acuerdo entre los líderes de la confederación de indígenas norteamericanos y el gobierno estadounidense que otorgó a Estados Unidos parte del Territorio del Noroeste

Treaty of Guadalupe Hidalgo (1848) a treaty that ended the Mexican-American War and gave the United States much of Mexico's northern territory (p. 311)
Tratado de Guadalupe Hidalgo (1848) tratado que daba por terminada la Guerra mexicano-estadounidense y daba posesión a Estados Unidos de gran parte del norte del territorio mexicano

Treaty of Paris (1763) agreement that ended the Seven Years' War in Europe and divided up the land in North America between Britain, France, and Spain (p. 93)
Tratado de París (1763) convenio que puso fin a la Guerra de los Siete Años en Europa y que repartió las tierras de América del Norte entre Gran Bretaña, Francia y España

Treaty of Paris (1783) agreement that officially ended the Revolutionary War and established British recognition of the independence of the United States (p. 136)
Tratado de París (1783) acuerdo de paz que oficialmente daba por terminada la Guerra de Independencia estadounidense y en el que Gran Bretaña reconocía la independencia de Estados Unidos

Treaty of Tordesillas (1494) agreement between Spain and Portugal that created an imaginary north-south line which divided the territory of the Americas (p. 40)
Tratado de Tordesillas (1494) acuerdo entre España y Portugal mediante el cual se creó una línea imaginaria que atravesaba de norte a sur y dividía el territorio de las Américas

Treaty of Versailles (1919) treaty ending World War I that required Germany to pay huge war reparations and established the League of Nations (p. 609)
Tratado de Versailles tratado que puso fin a la Primera Guerra Mundial, que le impuso a Alemania el pago de indemnizaciones económicas y que establecío la Liga de las Naciones

trench warfare a form of combat in which soldiers dug trenches, or deep ditches, to seek protection from enemy fire and to defend their positions (p. 588)
guerra de trincheras forma de combate en la que la que los soldados excavan trincheras o zanjas profundas para protegerse del fuego enemigo y defender sus posiciones

Trent affair (1861) incident in which two Confederate leaders secretly boarded a British ship named the *Trent* en route to Britain, and were then captured by Union forces and brought back to the United States (p. 381)
asunto del *Trent* (1861) incidente en el que dos líderes confederados abordaron clandestinamente el *Trent*, un barco británico que llevaba el correo hacia Gran Bretaña; las fuerzas de la Unión los capturaron y los devolvieron a los Estados Unidos

triangular trade trading networks in which goods and slaves moved among England, the American colonies, and Africa (p. 79)

comercio triangular redes de intercambio de esclavos y bienes entre Inglaterra, las colonias americanas y África

Triple Alliance a military alliance between Germany, Austria-Hungary and Italy (p. 583)
Triple Alianza alianza militar entre Alemania, Austria-Hungría e Italia

Triple Entente a military alliance between Great Britain, France, and Russia (p. 584)
Triple Entente alianza militar entre Gran Bretaña, Francia y Rusia

Truman Doctrine (1947) President Truman's pledge to provide economic and military aid to countries threatened by communism (p. 819)
Doctrina Truman (1947) promesa del presidente Truman de dar ayuda económica y militar a los países amenazados por el comunismo

Tuskegee Airmen unit of African American pilots that fought in World War II (p. 774)
Aviadores de Tuskegee unidad de pilotos afroamericanos que combatió en la Segunda Guerra Mundial

Twelfth Amendment stated that electors must cast separate ballots for president and vice president (p. 216)
Decimosegunda enmienda dice que los electores deben votar de forma separada para los cargos de presidente y vicepresidente

Twenty-fourth Amendment (1964) banned states from taxing citizens to vote in elections (p. 926)
Vigésimocuarta enmienda (1964) prohibió a los estados cobrarles impuestos a los ciudadanos por votar en las elecciones

Twenty-sixth Amendment (1971) lowered the legal voting age from 21 to 18 (p. 976)
Vigésimosexta enmienda (1971) redujo la edad legal para votar de 21 a 18 años

two-party system a system of government in which there are two groups with differing political opinions (p. 208)
sistema bipartidista sistema de gobierno en el que hay dos grupos con diferentes opiniones políticas

U-boats small submarines named after the German word *unterserboot*, which means "undersea boat" (p. 591)
U-boat pequeño submarino cuyo nombre proviene de la palabra alemana *unterserboot*, que significa "bote submarino"

Uncle Tom's Cabin (1852) an antislavery novel written by Harriet Beecher Stowe (p. 325)
La cabaña del tío Tom (1852) novela abolicionista escrita por Harriet Beecher Stowe

Underground Railroad a network of people who helped enslave people escape to the North (p. 286)
Tren Clandestino red de personas que ayudó a los esclavos a escapar hacia el Norte

United Nations an international organization that encourages cooperation among nations (p. 806)
Naciones Unidas (ONU) organización internacional que fomenta la cooperación entre países

Universal Declaration of Human Rights (1948) document that stated all human beings are created free and equal; tried to set standards for human rights (p. 828)
Declaración Universal de los Derechos Humanos (1948) documento que afirma que todos los seres humanos nacen libres e iguales e intentó establecer normas para los derechos humanos

urban working class social class made up of poor and uneducated workers (p. 276)
clase trabajadora urbana clase social compuesta por trabajadores pobres y con pocos estudios

USA PATRIOT Act (2001) law passed by Congress making it easier for the FBI and other law enforcement agencies to collect information about suspected terrorists (p. 1097)
Ley Patriota Estadounidense (2001) ley aprobada por el Congreso que facilita al FBI y a otros agentes de la ley recoger en secreto información acerca de presuntos terroristas

utopian movement movement during the late 1700s and into the mid-1899s whose members worked to establish a perfect society through utopian communities (p. 270)
movimiento utópico movimiento cuyos miembros se esforzaron por establecer una sociedad perfecta mediante comunidades utópicas que tuvieron popularidad Estados Unidos a fines del siglo XVIII y a comienzos y mediados del siglo XIX

vaccine a preparation that uses a killed or weakened form of a germ to help the body build its own defenses against that germ (p. 865)
vacuna preparación que utiliza una forma muerta o debilitada de un germen para ayudar al cuerpo a desarrollar sus propias defensas contra dicho germen

Valley Forge location in Pennsylvania where the Continental Army spent the winter of 1777–1778 under extremely harsh conditions (p. 129)
Valley Forge lugar en Pensilvania donde el Ejército Continental pasó el invierno de 1777 a 1778 bajo condiciones extremadamente rigurosas

values the key ideas and beliefs a person holds (p. 649)
valores ideas y creencias claves de una persona

V-E day (1945) May 8, 1945; the date when the Allies celebrated victory in Europe World War II (p. 804)
Día del Armisticio (1945) 8 de mayo de 1945, fecha en que los Aliados celebraron la victoria en Europa de la Segunda Guerra Mundial

velvet revolution a quick, peaceful revolution that swept the Communists from power in Czechoslovakia in 1989 (p. 1061)
revolución de terciopelo revolución breve y pacífica que en 1989 sacó del poder a los comunistas en Checoslovaquia

vertical integration the business practice of owning all of the businesses involved in each step of a manufacturing process (p. 468)
integración vertical práctica empresarial de poseer todas las empresas implicadas en cada paso de un proceso de fabricación

Vichy France French government set up with the Germans that ruled the southern half of France during World War II (p. 748)
  Francia Vichy gobierno establecido en Francia en cooperación con Alemania, que gobernó la mitad sur de Francia durante la Segunda Guerra Mundial

Vietcong the military forces of the National Liberation Front, a group that wanted to overthrow the government in Vietnam (p. 953)
  Vietcong fuerzas militares del Frente de Liberación Nacional, un grupo Grupo que quería derrocar el gobierno de Vietnam

Vietminh a group that resisted the Japanese occupation in Vietnam (p. 949)
  Vietminh grupo que se resistió a la ocupación japonesa de Vietnam

Vietnamization a plan to end the Vietnam war that involved turning over the fighting to the South Vietnamese while U.S. troops gradually pulled out (p. 973)
  vietnamización plan para dar fin a la guerra de Vietnam que conllevaba el traspaso de la lucha a los vietnamitas del sur mientras las tropas de Estados Unidos se retiraban gradualmente

Vikings sea raiders from Scandinavia (p. 30)
  vikingos piratas escandinavos

Virginia and Kentucky Resolutions resolutions drafted by Jefferson and Madison arguing that the Alien and Sedition Acts were unconstitutional (p. 214)
  Resoluciones de Virginia y Kentucky resoluciones redacradas por Jefferson y Madison que sostenían que las Leyes de Extranjeros y Sedición eran inconstitucionales

Virginia Declaration of Rights (1776) a declaration of citizens' rights issued by the Virginia Convention (p. 118)
  Declaración de Derechos de Virginia (1776) declaración de derechos civiles proclamada por la Convención de Virginia

Virginia Plan (1787) the plan for government in which the national government would have supreme power and a legislative branch would have two houses with representation determined by state population (p. 152)
  Plan de Virginia (1787) plan de gobierno según el cual el gobierno nacional tendría poder supremo y habría un poder legislativo con dos cámaras en las que la representación de cada estado sería determinada por el número de habitantes

VISTA a domestic version of the Peace Corps that provided help to poor communities in the U.S. in the 1960s (p. 896)
  VISTA versión nacional e interna del Cuerpo de Paz que ayudó a las comunidades pobres de Estados Unidos durante la década de 1960

V-J Day (1945) August 15, 1945; the date when the Allies declared victory over Japan in World War II (p. 806)
  Día V-J (1945) 15 de agosto de 1945; fecha en que los Aliados declararon la victoria sobre Japón durante la Segunda Guerra Mundial

Voter Education Project group founded in 1962 to register southern African Americans to vote (p. 926)
  Proyecto para la Educación de Votantes grupo fundado en 1962 para inscribir como votantes a los afroamericanos del sur

Voting Rights Act of 1965 civil rights law that banned literacy tests and other practices that discouraged blacks from voting (p. 930)
  Ley del Derecho al Voto de 1965 ley de derechos civiles que prohibió las pruebas de lectura y escritura y otras prácticas que trataban de impedir que los afroamericanos votaran

Wade-Davis Bill (1864) a reconstruction plan that required a majority of a southern state's white male citizens to pledge loyalty to the United States before elections could be held (p. 406)
  Ley Wade-Davis (1864) plan de reconstrucción que requería que una mayoría de los ciudadanos varones blancos de un estado sureño prometieran lealtad a Estados Unidos antes de que se pudieran celebrar elecciones

wage earner person who is paid a set amount by a business owner instead of making income from his or her own enterprise (p. 276)
  asalariado persona que recibe una cantidad de dinero fija del propietario de una empresa en vez de obtener sus ingresos a través de una empresa propia

War Hawks American politicians who called for war in response to the incident with the *Chesapeake* and the *Leopard* (p. 226)
  Halcones de Guerra políticos estadounidenses que ejercieron presión para que se declarara la guerra como respuesta al incidente con el *Chesapeake* y el *Leopard*

War on Poverty set of programs introduced by President Johnson to fight poverty (p. 895)
  Guerra contra la Pobreza conjunto de programas introducidos por el presidente Johnson para combatir la pobreza

War Powers Act (1973) law that set a 60-day limit on the presidential commitment of U.S. troops to foreign conflicts (p. 979)
  Ley de Poderes de Guerra (1973) ley que limita a 60 días el plazo de envío de tropas estadounidenses a conflictos internacionales por parte del presidente

War Refugee Board a group established by President Franklin D. Roosevelt that helped 20,000 Jews who might otherwise have fallen into the hands of the Nazis (p. 782)
  Junta de Refugiados de Guerra grupo establecido por el Presidente Franklin D. Roosevelt que ayudó a 20,000 judíos que de otra manera podrían haber caído en manos de los nazis

Warren Commission a commission headed by Chief Justice Earl Warren to investigate the assassination of President Kennedy (p. 892)
  Comisión Warren comisión presidida por el presidente de la Corte Suprema Earl Warren para investigar el asesinato del presidente Kennedy

Warren Court a term that refers to the years when Earl Warren served as Chief Justice of the Supreme Court (p. 890)
  Coret de Warren término que hace referencia a los años en que Earl Warren ocupó el cargo de juez presidente de la Corte Suprema

ENGLISH AND SPANISH GLOSSARY

Warsaw Pact a military alliance established in 1955 of the Soviet-dominated countries of Eastern Europe (p. 850)
Pacto de Varsovia alianza militar establecida en 1955 por los países de Europa oriental controlados por la Unión Soviética

Watergate scandal a political scandal that resulted in President Nixon's resignation in 1974 (p. 1029)
escándalo Watergate escándalo político que produjo la renuncia del presidente Nixon en 1974

welfare capitalism system in which companies provided fringe benefits to employees in an effort to promote worker satisfaction and loyalty (p. 631)
capitalismo del bienestar sistema por el que las empresas proporcionan prestaciones a sus empleados para promover la satisfacción y lealtad de los trabajadores

Whiskey Rebellion (1794) a protest of small farmers in Pennsylvania against new taxes on whiskey (p. 208)
Rebelión del Whisky (1794) protesta de pequeños agricultores de Pensilvania contra los nuevos impuestos sobre el whisky

wildcatters name given to oil prospectors who came to Pennsylvania in the mid and late 1800s (p. 461)
cazadores de pozos nombre dado a los prospectores de petróleo que llegaron a Pensilvania a mediados y a finales del siglo XIX

wolf pack a submarine tactic in which submarines hunt as a group and attack at night (p. 771)
manada de lobos táctica de los submarinos por la que éstos buscan al enemigo en grupo y atacan de noche

Women's Christian Temperance Movement reform organization that led the fight against alcohol in the late 1800s (p. 531)
Movimiento Cristiano Femenino por la Abstinencia oranización reformista que lideró la lucha en contra del consumo de alcohol a fines del siglo XIX

Worcester v. Georgia (1832) the Supreme Court ruling that stated that the Cherokee nation was a distinct territory over which only the federal government had authority (p. 248)
Worcester contra Georgia (1832) decisión de la Corte Suprema que estableció que la nación cherokee era un territorio distinto sobre el que sólo el gobierno federal tenía autoridad

World Bank helps poor countries build their economies by providing grants and loans to help with projects that could provide jobs and wealth (p. 828)
Banco Mundial ayuda a los países pobres a desrrollar sus economías mediante subsidios y préstamos para invertir en proyectos que pueden generar empleos y riqueza

Wounded Knee Massacre (1890) the U.S. Army's killing of approximately 300 Sioux at Wounded Knee Creek in South Dakota (p. 441)
Masacre de Wounded Knee (1890) matanza de aproximadamente 300 indios sioux en Wounded Knee Creek, Dakota del Sur.

writs of assistance (1767) law that gave British customs officers the right to search colonists' homes for smuggled goods without a search warrant (p. 108)
orden judicial de asistencia (1767) ley que dio a los funcionarios de aduanas británicos el derecho a registrar las casas de los colonos en busca de bienes de contrabando sin una orden de registro

xenophobia fear of foreigners (p. 475)
xenofobia miedo a los extranjeros

XYZ Affair (1797) an incident in which French agents attempted to get a bribe and loans from U.S. diplomats in exchange for an agreement that French privateers would no longer attack American ships (p. 213)
asunto XYZ (1797) incidente en el que funcionarios franceses intentaron obtener sobornos y préstamos de diplomáticos estadounidenses a cambio de un acuerdo por el cual los barcos corsarios franceses no atacarían más a los barcos estadounidenses

Yalta Conference (1945) meeting between Franklin Roosevelt, Winston Churchill, and Joseph Stalin to reach agreement on what to do with Germany after World War II (p. 802)
Conferencia de Yalta (1945) cumbre celebrada entre Franklin Roosevelt, Winston Churchill y Joseph Stalin para llegar a un acuerdo acerca de lo que harían con Alemania después de la Segunda Guerra Mundial

yellow journalism the reporting of exaggerated stories in newspapers to increase sales (p. 559)
prensa amarillista reporraje de artículos exagerados en la prensa para aumentar las ventas

yeoman in the colonies, farmers living on small farms rather than on large plantations (p. 81)
campesino en las colonias, los granjeros que vivían en pequeñas granjas en lugar de en grandes plantaciones

Zimmermann note a telegram sent to a German official in Mexico before World War I; it proposed an alliance between Germany and Mexico (p. 592)
nota de Zimmermann telegrama enviado a un funcionario alemán en México antes del inicio de la Primera Guerra Mundial; proponía una alianza entre Alemania y México

zoot suit riot a series of riots in Los Angeles, California during World War II, between soldiers stationed in the city and Mexican American youths because of the zoot suits they wore (p. 763)
disturbios de zoot suit serie de ataques contra mexicanoamericanos por parte de marineros estadounidenses en Los Angeles

PHOTOGRAPH © 2005 MUSEUM OF FINE ARTS, BOSTON

Index

KEY TO INDEX

c = chart	g = graph	m = map
q = quotation	p = picture	

INDEX

INDEX

INDEX

Credits and Acknowledgments

For permission to reproduce copyrighted material, grateful acknowledgment is made to the following sources:

Bantam Books, a division of Random House, Inc.: Quote by Diane Nash from *Voices of Freedom* by Henry Hampton and Steve Fayer. Copyright © 1990 by Blackside, Inc.

Barnes & Nobles Books: Quotes by William Calley, Tran Van Duong, Robert S. McNamara, and David Vandivier from *NAM: Vietnam 1965–75.* Copyright © 1995 by Barnes & Nobles Books.

CBS, a division of Viacom Inc.: Broadcast "We Are Mired in Stalemate" by Walter Cronkite from *CBS Evening News with Walter Cronkite,* Feb. 27, 1968. Copyright © 1968 by CBS Broadcasting Inc.

CNN: From interview with Phillip Caputo from "On landing in Vietnam with the U.S. Marines in 1965" from "Episode 11: Vietnam" from *CNN.* Copyright © 1998 by Cable News Network.

Christian Science Monitor: From "In 2,000 Years, Will the World Remember Disney or Plato?" by Mark Rice-Oxley from *Christian Science Monitor,* January 15, 2004. Copyright © 2004 by Christian Science Publishing Society.

Donadio & Olson: Quote by Kitty McCulloch from *Hard Times* by Studs Terkel. Copyright © 1970 by Studs Terkel. Published by Pantheon Books, a division of Random House, Inc.

Doubleday, a division of Random House, Inc., www.randomhouse.com.: From *When Heaven and Earth Changed Places: A Vietnamese Woman's Journey from War to Peace* by Le Ly Hayslip. Copyright © 1989 by Le Ly Hayslip. From *A Soldier Reports* by General William C. Westmoreland. Copyright © 1976 by William C. Westmoreland.

Encyclopaedia Britannica: From "Marshall, Thurgood" from *Encyclopaedia Britannica Online,* available at http://search.eb.com/eb/article-9051119, on October 21, 2005. Copyright © 2005 by Encyclopaedia Britannica. From "World War I" from *Encyclopaedia Britannica Online,* available at http://80-search.eb.com.ezproxy.libraries.wright.edu:2048/3b/article-9110198, on October 25, 2005. Copyright © 2005 by Encyclopaedia Britannica.

Geraldine Gonzales: From *I am Joaquín / Yo soy Joaquín: An Epic Poem* by Rodolfo Gonzales. Copyright © 1967 by Rodolfo Gonzales.

GRM Associates, Inc., Agents for the Estate of Ida M. Cullen: "Yet Do I Marvel" from *Color* by Countee Cullen. Copyright © 1925 by Harper & Brothers: copyright renewed 1953 by Ida M. Cullen.

HarperCollins, Inc.: From *Tituba of Salem Village* by Ann Petry. Copyright © 1964 by Ann Petry.

Hill and Wang, a division of Farrar, Straus & Giroux, LLC; electronic format by permission of Georges Borchardt, Inc.: From *Night* by Elie Wiesel, translated by Stella Rodway. Copyright © 1958 by Les Editions de Minuit; English translation copyright © 1960 by MacGibbon & Kee, renewed © 1988 by The Collins Publishing Group. All rights reserved.

The History Channel, a division of A & E Television Network: From "Letter from Stull Holt, Sept. 1, 1917" from "Dear Home: Letters from WWI" from *The History Channel,* available on http://www.historychanel.com/letters/stull_holt.html, August 9, 2005. Copyright © 1996-2005 by A&E Television Networks.

The Heirs to the Estate of Martin Luther King, Jr., c/o Writers House, Inc. as agent for the proprietor: "I Have a Dream" by Martin Luther King, Jr. Copyright © 1963 by Martin Luther King, Jr.; copyright renewed © 1991 by Coretta Scott King. From "Letter from Birmingham Jail" from *Why We Can't Wait* by Martin Luther King, Jr. Copyright © 1963 by Martin Luther King, Jr., copyright renewed © 1991 by Coretta Scott King.

Ron Kovic: From *Born on the Fourth of July* by Ron Kovic. Copyright © 1976 by Ron Kovic.

Louisiana State University Press: Quotes by Bouchereau, DeLucca, Reid Draffen, Warren Moses, Solomon Radasky, James Spillman, Major General Kenneth William Dobson Strong, Frank Walk, and Martin Wasserman from *War Stories: Remembering World War II* by Elizabeth Mullener, with a foreword by Stephen E. Ambrose. Copyright © 2002 by Louisiana State University Press.

Merle's Girls Music: From "Sing Your Heart Out, Country Boy" by Merle Travis from Capitol Single #258, May 1946, available at http://www.fortunecity.com/tinpan/parton/2/novacanc.html, July 7, 2005. Copyright © 1946, 1975 by Hill and Range Songs.

The Nation Company, L.P.: From "Mr. Roosevelt's Magic" from *The Nation,* vol. 142, no. 3680, January 15, 1936. Copyright 1936 by The Nation.

The New York Times Company: From "A Visionary Who Put an Era Out of Its Misery" a review of *Memoirs* by Mikhail Gorbachev from *The New York Times,* January 7, 1997. Copyright © 1997 by Michael Specter.

Newsweek, Inc.: From "Nursing the Dying" by Edie Meeks from *Newsweek,* March 8, 1999, p. 61. Copyright © 1999 by Newsweek, Inc. All rights reserved. From "Women of the New Century" by Carla Power, Toula Vlahou, Stefan Theil, Barbie Nadeau, and Emma Daly from *Newsweek International,* January 8, 2001 p. 14. Copyright © 2001 by Newsweek, Inc. All rights reserved. From "The Hard Truth of Immigration" by Robert J. Samuelson from *Newsweek,* June 13, 2005. Copyright © 2005 by Newsweek. All rights reserved.

W. W. Norton & Company, Inc.: From "The Shadow of Death" and "Coda" from *In the Presence of Mine Enemies: War in the Heart of America, 1859–1863* by Edward L. Ayers. Copyright © 2003 by Edward L. Ayers.

PBS Online, a division of WGBH Educational Foundation: From "War Letters" by Paul Curtis, available on http://www.pbs.org/wgbh/amex/warletters/letters/warletter_06.html, July 14, 2005. Copyright © 2005 PBS Online/WGBH. From "War Letters" by Rupert Trimmingham, available on http://www.pbs.org/wgbh/amex/warletters/letters/warletter_06.html, July 14, 2005. Copyright © 2005 PBS Online/WGBH. From letter by June Wandrey from "War Letters" available at http://www.pbs.org/wgbh/amex/warletters/letters/warletter_09.html, on July 14, 2005. Copyright © 1999-2001 by PBS Online/WGBH.

G. P. Putnam's Sons, a division of Penguin Group (USA) Inc.; electronic format by Sandra Dijkstra Literary Agency; audio format by New Millennium: From "Queen Mother of the Western Skies" from *The Joy Luck Club* by Amy Tan. Copyright © 1989 by Amy Tan.

Random House, Inc., www.randomhouse.com: Statement by Chicago Women's Liberation; February 1969 from *Sisterhood is Powerful: An Anthology of Writing's from the Women's Liberation Movement,* edited by Ron Morgan. Copyright © 1970 by Robin Morgan.

reasononline: From "Really Creative Destruction: Economist Tyler Cowen argues for the cultural benefits of globalization" from *reasononline,* August–September 2003, available at http://www.reason.com/0308/cr.ng.really.shtm, October 28, 2005. Copyright © 2003 by reasononline.

Estate of Erich Maria Remarque: From *All Quiet on the Western Front* by Erich Maria Remarque. Copyright 1929, 1930 by Little, Brown and Company; copyright renewed © 1957, 1958 by Erich Maria Remarque. All rights reserved. "Im Westen Nichts Neues" copyright 1928 by Ullstein A. G.; copyright renewed © 1956 by Erich Maria Remarque.

The Richmond Organization (TRO): From "Pastures of Plenty" words and music by Woody Guthrie. Copyright © 1960, 1963 by TRO-Ludlow Music, Inc.

Scribner, an imprint of Simon & Schuster Adult Publishing Group: From *The Great Gatsby* by F. Scott Fitzgerald. Copyright 1925 by Charles Scribner's Sons. Copyright renewed 1953 by Frances Scott Fitzgerald Lanahan.

Scribner, a division of Simon & Schuster, Inc.: From *A Farewell to Arms* by Ernest Hemingway. Copyright 1929 by Charles Scribner's Sons; copyright renewed © 1957 by Ernest Hemingway.

Simon & Schuster: From *I Never Left Home* by Bob Hope. Copyright 1944 by Bob Hope.

State of Michigan: From "Eye-witness accounts" from *Pearl Harbor Remembered . . . ,* available at http://www.michiganhistorymagazine.com/extra/pearl_harbor/stories.html, on July 14, 2005. Copyright © 2005 by The State of Michigan.

Texas A & M University Press: From "The Death of Davy Crockett" from *With Santa Anna in Texas: A Personal Narrative of the Revolution / José Enrique de la Peña* by Carmen Perry. Copyright © 1997 by Perry Carmen.

United States Holocaust Memorial Museum: From "Gerda Weissmann Klein: Born 1924: Bielsko, Poland" from "Personal Histories: Liberation," as available at http://www.ushmm.org/museum/exhibit/online/phistories, on July 14, 2005. Copyright © United States Holocaust Memorial Museum, Washington, D.C.

The University of Georgia Press: Quote by Nell Blackshear from *Living Atlanta: An Oral History of the City 1914–1948* by Clifford Kuhn, Harlon Joye, and E. Bernard West. Copyright © 1990 by the University of Georgia Press Athens, Georgia 30602.

University of Washington Press: From "Poem # 32" by Anonymous from *Island: Poetry and History of Chinese Immigrants on Angel Island, 1910–1940* by Him Mark Lai, Genny Lim, and Judy Yung. Copyright © 1991 by University of Washington Press.

Viking Penguin, a division of Penguin Group (USA): From *The Grapes of Wrath* by John Steinbeck. Copyright 1939 and renewed © 1967 by John Steinbeck

Warner Bros. Publications U.S. Inc., Miami, FL., 33014: From "Brother, Can You Spare a Dime," lyrics by Yip Harburg, music by Jay Gorney. Copyright 1931 by Warner Brs., Inc., E.Y. Harburg, and J. Gorney. All rights reserved.

Washington Post Company: From "A Tip of That Hat" by Tom Vinciguerra from "Remembering Franklin Delano Roosevelt" from *The Washington Post Online,* available http://www.washingtonpost.com/wp-srv/local/longterm/tours/fdr/, 7/14/05. Copyright © 1997 by The Washington Post Company.

Sources Cited:

From "Roger Tuttrup" from *The Good War: An Oral History of World War Two* by Studs Terkel. Published by Ballantine Books, New York, 1985.

From *Anxious Decades: America in Prosperity and Depression 1920–1941* by Michael E. Parrish. Published by W. W. Norton & Company, New York, 1992.

Quotes by Myron Harrington and Do from *Vietnam: A History* by Stanley Karnow. Published by Penguin Books, New York, 1983.

From "Puttin' On Ole Massa" from *Narrative of William Wells Brown: A Fugitive Slave written by himself.* Published by Prentice-Hall, Inc., Englewood Cliffs, NJ, 1963.

Quotes by Zbig Brzezinski and Cyrus Vance from *Crisis: The Last Year of the Carter Presidency* by Hamilton Jordan. Published by G. P. Putnam's Sons, New York, NY, 1982.

From "A Black GI" (retitled "An African American GI in Vietnam (1969-1970)" from *Everything We Had: An Oral History of the Vietnam War* by Al Santoli. Published by Random House, Inc., New York, 1981.

From *Patriots: The Vietnam War Remembered from All Sides* by Christian G. Appy. Published by Viking Penguin, New York, NY 2003.

From "Honor and Humiliation" by Ben Isaacs from *Hard Times: An Oral History of the Great Depression* by Studs Terkel. Published by Washington Square Press, New York, NY, 1970.

From "Pete Peterson—Assignment Hanoi" from web site accessed at http://www.pbs.org/hanoi/home.htm., on June 30, 2005. Published by WGBH Educational Foundation, Boston, MA, 1999.

From the June 1993 Gateway Greens' Compost-Dispatch Speech at the May Day rally against NAFTA, read by Rainbow Coalition member Gene Bruskin for Reverend Jesse Jackson.

From "Artist's Statement" by Joel Meyerowitz from *After September 11 Images from Ground Zero* at http://www.911exhibit.state.gov/artist_statement.cfm, July 19, 2005.

"A Personal Record of Hiroshima A-bomb Survival (No. 1) re-post: Takeharu Terao 91/03/03 13:32" from http://www.coara.or.jp/~ryoji/abomb/a-bomb1.html, July 8, 2005.

Photo Credits

Cover: Joseph Sohm/PictureQuest.

Front Matter: Page ii, (Schulzinger) Bill Salaz/HRW Photo; ii, (Ayers) Ian Bradshaw/HRW Photo; ii, (de la Teja) Sam Dudgeon/HRW; ii, (Gray-White) Michael Denora/ HRW Photo; ii, (Wineburg) HRW Photo/Gary Benson Photography; v, The Granger Collection, New York;vi, ©Superstock/SuperStock; vii (t), Private Collection/PRC Archive; vii (t), Thomas Cole, *A View of the Mountain Pass Called the Notch of the White Mountains*, Andrew w. Mellon Fund, Photograph © 2005 Board of Trustees, National Gallery of Art, Washington, DC; (b) Gallery of the Republic; viii, The Art Archive/ Culver Pictures;ix (t), Smithsonian American Art Museum, Washington, DC/Art Resource, NY; ix (b), Library of Congress, Detroit Publishing Company Collection, LC-USZC4-1584; x (tl), Janice L. and David J. Frent Collection of Political Americana; x (tr), Janice L. and David J. Frent Collection of Political Americana; x (c), Janice L. and David J. Frent Collection of Political Americana; x (b), Courtesy The Delaware Military Heritage and Education Foundation, Inc.; xi (Robeson) ©Photo by Sasha/Getty Images; (Smith) ©Bettmann/ CORBIS; (Armstrong) © Reuters/STR/Getty Images; xi (b), Culver Pictures, Inc.; xii (t), © US Air Force/Collection of David Ethell; xii (b), © Photo by Walter Sanders/Time Life Pictures/Getty Images; xiii, © Matt Herron/Take Stock; xiv (t), © Arthur Schatz/Time Life Pictures/Getty Images; xiv (b), © Pete Saloutos/CORBIS; xv, © CORBIS; xvi, Library of Congress; xix, © CORBIS; xxi, Retrofile.com/Getty Images; xxii, Gladys City Museum, Beaumont, Texas; xxvi (t), HRW Photo/Gary Benson Photography; xxvi, (b) National Portrait Gallery, Smithsonian Institution, Washington, DC/Art Resource, NY; xxxii, (c) Brand X Pictures, (all others) Image Club Graphics; H1, Smithsonian American Art Museum, Washington, DC/Art Resource, NY; H16 (bc), Harvey Schwartz/ Index Stock Imagery; H16 (b), © Tom Nebbia/CORBIS; H16 (c), © London Aerial Photo Library/ CORBIS; H16 (t), Earth Satellite Corporation/Science Photo Library/Photo Researchers, Inc.; H16 (tc), © Frans Lemmens/The Image Bank/Getty Images; H24 (l), © Robert W. Kelley/Time Life Pictures/Getty Images; H24 (c), © Bettmann/CORBIS; H24 (r), Photo by Hugo Jaeger/Timepix/Time Life Pictures/Getty Images; H25 (tr), The Museum of American Political Life, University of Hartford, West Hartford, CT; H25 (br), © Mike Segar/REUTERS/CORBIS; H25 (tl), Picture Research Consultants & Archives; H26 (tl), © Michael Ventura/Folio, Inc.; H26 (b), © Bettmann/CORBIS; H26 (tr), Ric Francis/AP/Wide World Photos; H27 (tl), Zuma Press Photos; H27 (bl), © Bettmann/

CREDITS AND ACKNOWLEDGMENTS

CORBIS; H27 (tr), © CORBIS; H27 (br), © Justin Sullivan/ Getty Images; H29, Collection of the American Numismatic Society, New York; H30, © Woburn Abbey Collection, Bedford Estate; H31, The Granger Collection, New York; T6, The Granger Collection, New York; T7, The Granger Collection, New York; T23, Library of Congress; T24 (l), © Bettmann/CORBIS; T24 (r), Picture Research Consultants & Archives. **Unit One**: Page 1, The Granger Collection, New York. **Chapter 1**: Pages 4 - 5 (t), © Steve Vidler/SuperStock; 5 (cl), © Richard A. Cooke /CORBIS; 5 (cr), Cahokia Mounds Historic Site; 5 (b), © Royalty-Free/CORBIS; 06 (l), Dr. George Frison, Hell Gap Prehistoric Site, University of Wyoming; 6 (r), Arizona State Museum, University of Arizona; 8 (t), © Kevin Schafer/CORBIS; 8 (c), © David Muench/CORBIS; 8 (b), © Richard A. Cooke /CORBIS; 09 (tl), Cahokia Mounds Historic Site; 9 (tr), BMI/Michael Zabe; 9 (b), © Stuart Westmoreland/CORBIS; 11, © John Griffin/ Florida Museum of Natural History; 14 (t), © Royalty-Free/ CORBIS; 14 (b), © Marilyn "Angel" Wynn/Nativestock Pictures; 15, National Museum of the American Indian, Smithsonian Institution, Washington, DC. Photo #092104PRWL047; 17 (l), © John Bigelow Taylor. Franck H. McClung Museum, the University of Tennessee; 17 (r), The Field Museum of Natural History, [neg. A29TC], Chicago; 18, National Geographic Image Collection; 20, Giraudon/Art Resource, NY; 21, © MARCEL MOCHET/AFP/Getty Images; 23, North Wind Picture Archives; 24, National Archives; 25, HIP /Art Resource, NY; 29, Wolverhampton Art Gallery, West Midlands, UK/ Bridgeman Art Library; 30, SuperStock; 32, Architect of the Capitol. **Chapter 2**: Pages 34-35, © Burstein Collection/CORBIS; 34 (t), © Dan Heller Photography; 34 (b), Jacka Photography; 36, Library of Congress/ PRC Archive; 38 (c), The Granger Collection, New York; 38 (b), Michel Zabe; 39 (b), Private Collection; 40, The Art Archive / Marine Museum Lisbon / Dagli Orti; 41, The Granger Collection, New York; 44, © Woburn Abbey Collection, Bedford Estate; 46, The Granger Collection, New York; 48, Private Collection; 49, Library of Congress; 51, Private Collection; 54 (l), © Bettmann/CORBIS; 54 (r), American Antiquarian Society; 55, Art Ref: PRC Archive; 57 (t), Yale Collection of American Literature, Beinecke Rare Book and Manuscript Library. Photo by Carl Van Vechten, published by permission of the Carl Van Vechten Trust; 57 (b), © Peabody Essex Museum, Salem, MA/ Bridgeman Art Library; 58, © Kevin Fleming/ CORBIS; 59, © Raymond Gehman/CORBIS; 60 (l), Historical Society of Pennsylvania; 60 (r), Historical Society of Pennsylvania; 61 (l), Museum of London, Great Britain, HIP/ Art Resource, NY; 61 (r), Victoria & Albert Museum, London/ Art Resource, NY; 61 (b), Cheltenham Art Gallery & Museums, Gloucestershire, UK/Bridgeman Art Library; 64, © Stapleton Collection/CORBIS; 65, State Capitol, Commonwealth of Virginia, Courtesy Library of Virginia, image altered.; 66 (l), National Portrait Gallery, Smithsonian Institution, Washington, DC/Art Resource, NY; 66 (r), New York State Office of General Services, Executive Mansion, Albany, New York; 67, © Buena Vista Pictures/Courtesy Everett Collection ; 68 (r), The Granger Collection, New York; 68 (l), Private Collection. **Chapter 3**: Pages 70 - 71, "View of Boston Common" (detail) about 1750. Object Place: Boston, Massachusetts, United States. Hannah Otis, 1732–1801. Wool, silk, metallic threads, and beads on linen ground; predominately tent stitch; original frame and glass. 61.59 x 133.98 cm (24 1/4 x 52 3/4 in.). Museum of Fine Arts, Boston. Gift of a Friend of the Department of American Decorative Arts and Sculpture, a Supporter of the Department of American Decorative Arts and Sculpture, Barbara L. and Theodore B. Alfond, and Samuel A. Otis; and William Francis Warden Fund, Harriet Otis Cruft Fund, Otis Norcross Fund, Susan Cornelia Warren Fund, Arthur Tracy Cabot Fund, Seth K. Sweetser Fund, Edwin E. Jack Fund, Helen B. Sweeney Fund, William E. Nickerson Fund, Arthur Mason Knapp Fund, Samuel Putnam Avery Fund, Benjamin Pierce Cheney Fund, and Mary L. Smith Fund. 1996.26; 70 (b), Peter Newark's American Pictures; 71 (c), National Portrait Library, London/Bridgeman Art Library; 71 (b), Private Collection/ The Bridgeman Art Library; 72, PHOTOGRAPH COURTESY PEABODY ESSEX MUSEUM [detail neg. #17530]; 73, PHOTOGRAPH COURTESY PEABODY ESSEX MUSEUM] [neg. #M11588]; 74, Massachusetts State Archives ; 75, HIP/Art Resource, NY; 77, The Granger Collection, New York; 82, Royal Albert Memorial Museum, Exeter, Devon, UK/The Bridgeman Art Library; 84, Picture Research Consultants & Archives; 86, The Granger Collection, New York; 88, A Bicentennial Gift to America from a Grateful Armenian-American People, 1978. #1978.15.12, Photograph © The Metropolitan Museum of Art; 90-91, The Union League of Philadelphia; 92, American Antiquarian Society; 95, The Granger Collection, New York; 96 (l), © British Museum, London; 96 (r), Smithsonian Institution, Washington, DC, photo #93-2845; 97, Abby Aldrich Rockefeller Folk Art Collection, Colonial Williamsburg Foundation; 98, Picture Research Consultants & Archives. **Unit Two**: Page 101, ©Superstock/SuperStock. **Chapter 4**: Pages 104-105 (t), Sinclair Hamilton Collection, Department of Rare Books and Special Collections/ Princeton University Libraries; 104 (b), The Granger Collection, New York; 105 (cl), © Bettmann/ CORBIS; 105 (cr), © Superstock/SuperStock; 105 (b), Private Collection/ Bridgeman Art Library; 106, Picture Research Consultants & Archives; 107, Library of Congress/PRC Archive; 109, © Bettmann/ CORBIS; 111, Library of Congress/PRC Archive; 114, Colonial Williamsburg Foundation; 116, *Attack on Bunker's Hill, with The Burning of Charlestown*. Gift of Edgar William and Bernice Chrysler Garbisch, Photograph by Richard Carafelli, Image © 2005 Board of Trustees, National Gallery of Art, Washington, DC; 119 (l), Private Collection; 119 (r), © New-York Historical Society, New York, USA/ Bridgeman Art Library; 120, Courtesy of the Massachusetts Historical Society; 121-124 (border), © Richard Cummins/CORBIS; 125, Rhode Island Historical Society; 126 (l), © Kathy McLaughlin/The Image Works; 126 (r), © Kelley-Mooney Photography/CORBIS; 127, Reunion de Musees Nationaux/Art Resource, NY; 130, Chicago Historical Society, #138885; 131 (t), © Bettmann/CORBIS; 131 (b), North Wind Picture Archives; 132, (detail) Art Gallery, Williams Center, Lafayette College, Easton, PA. Gift of Mrs. John Hubbard; 137 (both), National Archives/PRC Archive; 138 (l), Courtesy of the John Carter Brown Library at Brown University; 138 (r), Trustees of the Boston Public Library; 139, Library of Congress/PRC Archive; 140, Sinclair Hamilton Collection, Department of Rare Books and Special Collections/Princeton University Libraries. **Chapter 5**: Pages 142-143, ©Superstock/SuperStock; 142 (c), National Archives/PRC Archive; 142 (b), Culver Pictures, Inc.; 143 (c), © Dennis Degnan/CORBIS; 143 (b), Reunion de Musees Nationaux/Art Resource, NY; 144 (t), Eric P. Newman/ Numismatic Education Society; 144 (bl), Picture Research Consultants & Archives; 144 (r), Collection of the American Numismatic Society, New York; 145, Private Collection/PRC Archive; 147 (l), © MPI/Getty Images; 147 (r), Painting by Gregory Stapko, Collection of the Supreme Court of the United States; 150, The Granger Collection, New York; 151, Library of Congress/PRC Archive; 152-153, Hall of Representatives, Washington, DC/ Bridgeman Art Library; 155 (l), © Royalty Free/CORBIS; 155 (c), Image Copyright © 2007 PhotoDisc, Inc.; 155 (r), © Royalty Free/CORBIS; 157 (b), Independence National Historical Park . Detail, "Rising Sun" chair; 157 (inset), Hall of Representatives, Washington, DC/ Bridgeman Art Library; 159, American Antiquarian Society; 160 (l), Charles Willson Peale, *James Madison*, 1792, oil on canvas, 0126.1006, From the Collection of Gilcrease Museum, Tulsa; 160 (r), Colonial Williamsburg Foundation; 162, Jill Brady/Maine Sunday Telegram; 166 (l), National Archives/ PRC Archive; 166 (r), Hall of Representatives, Washington, DC/ Bridgeman Art Library. **Constitution**: Pages 168-169, © Paul Conklin/PhotoEdit; 170-197 (border), © Richard Cummins/ CORBIS; 174 (l), Dennis Cook/AP/Wide World Photos; 174-75 (bc), © Mark Wilson/Getty Images; 175 (r), © Brooks Kraft/CORBIS; 176, © Royalty-Free/CORBIS; 186 (l), © Yang Liu/CORBIS; 186 (r), Norm Detlaff, Las Cruces Sun-News/AP/Wide World Photos; 187 (l), © Bettmann/CORBIS; 187 (c), © David Young-Wolff/ PhotoEdit; 187 (r), © Bettmann/CORBIS; 191, Library of Congress/PRC Archive; 193, Library of Congress; 195 (l), © Bettmann/CORBIS; 195 (r), © Oscar White/CORBIS; 196 (tl), Dr. Hector P. Garcia Papers, Special Collections & Archives, Texas A&M University-Corpus Christi, Bell Library; 196 (bl), Texas State Library & Archives Commission; 196 (r), © 1978 Matt Herron/TakeStock; 199, Texas State Library & Archives Commission. **Chapter 6**: Pages 200-201 (t), Virginia Historical Society; 200 (b), Giraudon/Art Resource, NY; 201 (bl), © New-York Historical Society/Reuters/Corbis; 201 (br), The Granger Collection, New York; 202, National Portrait Gallery, Smithsonian Institution, Washington, DC/ Art Resource, NY; 203, 205, 206 (both), The Granger Collection, New York; 207, Lauros/Giraudon/ Bridgeman Art Library; 209, Reunion de Musees Nationaux/Art Resource, NY; 210, HRW Photo Research Library; 211, Courtesy Ohio Historical Society; 213, The Granger Collection, New York; 215 (l), © Bettmann/CORBIS; 215 (r), The Art Archive/ Chateau de Blernacourt/Dagli Orti; 218 (t), The Granger Collection, New York; 218 (b), (detail) *Mission San Carlos Del Rio Carmelo* by Oriana Day, oil on canvas 20 x 30 (50.8 x 76.2 cm), Gift of Mrs. Eleanor Martin. Fine Arts Museum of San Francisco; 219 (tl), ©SUPERSTOCK/SuperStock; 219 (tr), Lake County (IL) Museum / Curt Teich Postcard Archive; 219 (b), Oregon Historical Society, #OrHi 1645; 218-219 (bkgd), Used by permission, Utah State Historical Society, all rights reserved; 220, [#1867.306] Collection of The New-York Historical Society; 221 (t), Getty Images; 221 (b), William J. Hennessy Jr.; 222 (tl), © Connie Ricca/ CORBIS; 222 (b), © Bob Rowan/Progressive Image/CORBIS; 223 (t), © Tom Bean/CORBIS; 223 (b), North Wind Picture Archives; 224 (l), The Granger Collection, New York; 224 (r), © Bettmann/CORBIS; 225, The Field Museum of Natural History, [neg. #A993851], Chicago; 229, The Granger Collection, New York; 230 (both), The Granger Collection, New York. **Unit Three**: Page 233, ©SuperStock, Inc./ SuperStock; 235, William Gladstone Collection. **Chapter 7**: Pages 236-237, Historical Society of Pennsylvania, Fourth of July Celebration in Center Square by John Lewis Krimmel (Bc 882 K897); 236 (b), Bildarchive Preussischer Kulturbesitz/Art Resource, NY; 237 (bl), United Nations; 237 (br), © Stapleton Collection/CORBIS; 238, Private Collection/ PRC Archive; 239, Thomas Cole, *A View of the Mountain Pass Called the Notch of the White Mountains*, Andrew w. Mellon Fund, Photograph © 2005 Board of Trustees, National Gallery of Art, Washington, DC; 240 (tl), New York State Office of Parks, Recreation and Historic Preservation, Clermont State Historic Site, Taconic Region; 240 (tr), National Portrait Gallery, Smithsonian Institution, Washington, DC/Art Resource, NY; 240 (cl), Private Collection; 240 (cr), ©Superstock/Superstock; 240 (b), Chicago Historical Society, #P&S 1995.008; 244 (t), Getty Images; 244 (b), © Lief Skoogfors/CORBIS; 245, Library of Congress/PRC Archive; 246, Memphis Brooks Museum of Art; 248, Sinclair Hamilton Collection, Department of Rare Books and Special Collections, Princeton University Library; 249, [neg. 46519] Collection of The New-York Historical Society; 251, Picture Research Consultants & Archives; 252 (t), National Museum of American History, Smithsonian Institution, Washington, DC, neg. no 73-11287; 252 (l), Division of History and Technology/National Museum of American History, Smithsonian Institution, Washington, DC. Photo # 86-9625 by Eric Long; 252 (r), National Museum of American History, Smithsonian Institution, Washington, DC. Photo # 2005-10045; 253 (tl), The Granger Collection, New York; 253 (r), Charles Phillips; 253 (b), Jack Naylor Collection/Picture Research Consultants & Archives; 254, [#34684] Collection of The New-York Historical Society; 256, © Bettmann/CORBIS; 258, (detail) *Hauling the Whole Week's Pickings* by William Henry Brown. The Historic New Orleans Collection; 260, North Wind Picture Archives; 261, The Granger Collection, New York; 263, Private Collection/ PRC Archive. **Chapter 8**: Pages 264-265 (t), [neg. #44227] Collection of The New-York Historical Society; 265 (cr), Private Collection; 265 (b), *Coffin Ships-Below Decks* by Rodney Charman. Albert F. Egan Jr. & Dorothy Egan Foundation, Inc. Nantucket, Mass.; 266 (cl), Trenton Psychiatric Hospita/Photo by Josh Nefsky; 266 (c), Onondaga Historical Association, #19981.21.171B; 266 (revival), Library of Congress/PRC Archive; 267 (all), Oberlin College Archives, Oberlin, Ohio; 268, Picture Research Consultants & Archives; 269, Trenton Psychiatric Hospital/Photo by Josh Nefsky; 271 (t), Courtesy of Concord Free Public Library; 271 (b), © Royalty-Free/CORBIS; 272, Lester S. Levy Collection, Milton S. Eisenhower Library, Johns Hopkins University; 273, *Coffin Ships-Below Decks* by Rodney Charman. Albert F. Egan Jr. & Dorothy Egan Foundation, Inc. Nantucket, Mass.; 274 (l), Jane White Johnson, her husband, Thomas Johnson and baby, Jenna c. 1850, #93.49.1, Museum of the City of New York; 274 (r), [#41082] Collection of The New-York Historical Society; 276, Zuma Press Photos; 277, © Bettmann/CORBIS; 278, Library of Congress; 279 (t), Courtesy of the Bostonian Society/Old State House 279 (bl), *Irish immigrants on board the Odessa, ship's cook* by Rodney Charman. Albert F. Egan Jr. & Dorothy Egan Foundation, Inc. Nantucket, Mass.; 280, Coline Jenkins/Elizabeth Cady Stanton Trust; 283, The Granger Collection, New York; 284–285, William Gladstone Collection; 287, Library of Congress/PRC Archive; 288, Onondaga Historical Association, #19981.21.171B; 289, Courtesy of the Massachusetts Historical Society; 291 (l), Library of Congress; 291 (r), Library of Congress ; 293, [neg. #44227] Collection of The New-York Historical Society. **Chapter 9**: Pages 294-295 (t), Albert Bierstadt, "The Oregon Trail", oil on canvas. Butler Institute of American Art; 295 (cl), Gallery of the Republic; 295 (cr), © George F. Mobley/ Getty Images; 295 (b), Library of Congress/PRC Archive; 296, Colorado Historical Society (10025774/F20280) All Rights Reserved; 299, Seaver Center for Western History Research, Natural History Museum of Los Angeles County; 300, Smithsonian American Art Museum, Washington, DC/ Art Resource, NY; 302, #di_01943, The Center for American History, The University of Texas at Austin; 303, Texas State Library and Archives Commission; 304, The Granger Collection, New York; 308, © Bettmann/CORBIS; 310, Society of California Pioneers; 313 (l), Courtesy Everett Collection ; 313 (r), © Touchstone Pictures/Everett Collection ; 314 (t), Colorado Historical Society; 314 (b), Society of California Pioneers. **Unit Four**: Page 317, The Art Archive/ Culver Pictures; Chicago Historical Society, #P&S 1955.0398. **Chapter 10**: Pages 320-321 (t), © Bettmann/CORBIS; 320 (b), © CORBIS; 321 (c), Chicago Historical Society, #i22204; 321 (b), India Office Library & Records, The British Library; 322 (t), © Hulton-Deutsch Collection/CORBIS; 322 (b), Library of Congress; 325 (t), Chicago Historical Society, #i22204; 325 (b), Picture Research Consultants & Archives; 328, © Benjamin Lowy/CORBIS; 329, Kansas State Historical Society; 333, The Granger Collection, New York; 334, Missouri Historical Society; 335, Boston Athenaeum; 336 (t), Getty Images; 336 (b), Dennis Cook/AP/Wide World Photos; 337, The Granger Collection, New York; 338 (l), Abraham Lincoln Birthplace National Historic Site; 338 (c), Library of Congress; 338 (r), Courtesy The Lilly Library, Indiana University, Bloomington, Indiana; 340 (l), Library of Congress; 340 (r), Library of Congress/PRC Archive; 342, Sally Andersen-Bruce, Museum of American Political Life; 344 (t), © Bettmann/CORBIS; 344 (b), Kansas Museum of History; 346, Library of Congress/PRC Archive; 347, Chicago Historical Society, #1920.175; 351, Library of Congress, LC-USZ62-1959. ; 352,
© Bettmann/CORBIS. **Chapter 11**: Pages 354-355 (t), State Museum of Pennsylvania, Pennsylvania Historical and Museum Collection; 354 (c), © CORBIS; 354 (b), The Granger Collection, New York; 355 (cl), ©SuperStock; 355 (cr), National Geographic Image Collection; 355 (b), Courtesy of the International Red Cross; 356, The Museum of the Confederacy Richmond, Virginia. Photography by Katherine Wetzel; 357, Anne S.K. Brown Military Collection, Brown University Library; 358, Courtesy of The Lincoln Museum, Fort Wayne, IN (#0-42); 361, Library of Congress/PRC Archive; 363, Library of Congress; 364 (l), Picture Research Consultants & Archives; 364 (c), © Bettmann/CORBIS; 364 (r), Naval Historical Center; 365 (l), The Museum of the Confederacy Richmond, Virginia. Photography by Katherine Wetzel; 365 (r), Ron Rubles Enterprises; 367, Chicago Historical Society, #1932.27; 368, National Park Service; 371, U.S. Capitol Historical Society; 372 (b), Library of Congress, Brady Civil War Collection; 372 (br), Courtesy of the Massachusetts Historical Society; 373, © Larry Kolvoord/The Image Works; 374, Rochester Museum & Science Center, Rochester, NY; 375, Anne S.K. Brown Military Collection, Brown University Library; 376, National Archives (NARA); 377, Gettysburg National Military Park; 378, © Bettmann/ CORBIS; 379 (t), Used by permission of Orchard House/ Louisa May Alcott Memorial Association; 379 (b), National Archives/PRC Archive; 380, © SuperStock; 381, Library of Congress; 389 (r), Naval Historical Center; 390, National Archives (NARA); 391 (l), National Archives (NARA); 391 (r), Library of Congress; 392, Yale University Art Gallery, New

R144 CREDITS AND ACKNOWLEDGMENTS

Haven, CT/Bridgeman Art Library; 395, National Geographic Image Collection; 396 (l), Library of Congress, #LC-B8184-10037; 396 (r), Collection of Kean E. Wilcox; 398 (l), Anne S.K. Brown Military Collection, Brown University Library; 398 (c), National Park Service; 398 (r), National Geographic Image Collection. **Chapter 12**: Pages 400-401, Courtesy of the Charleston Renaissance Gallery, Robert M. Hicklin Jr., Inc. Charleston, SC; 400 (b), The Granger Collection, New York; 401 (c), Herbert F. Johnson Museum of Art, Cornell University; 401 (bl), © Michael Maslan Historic Photographs/CORBIS; 401 (br), © Hulton-Deutsch Collection/CORBIS; 402, Chicago Historical Society, #P&S 1955.0398; 403, Library of Congress; 405, The Western Reserve Historical Society, Cleveland, Ohio; 406, Library of Congress; 407, Anne S.K. Brown Military Collection, Brown University Library; 409 (t), Getty Images; 409 (b), © Sketch by Art Lein/Pool/Reuters/CORBIS; 410, Library of Congress/PRC Archive; 412, Cook Collection, The Valentine Museum; 413, The Granger Collection, New York; 415, The Granger Collection, New York; 416, Chickamauga and Chattanooga National Military Park; 417, Library of Congress/PRC Archive; 418, Herbert F. Johnson Museum of Art, Cornell University; 419 (tr), The Valentine Museum; 419 (cr), © Bettmann/CORBIS; 419 (cl), Cook Collection, The Valentine Museum; 419 (b), © CORBIS; 421, Brown Brothers; 422, Brown Brothers; 423, The Granger Collection, New York; 424, Library of Congress/PRC Archive; 426 (t), © CORBIS; 426 (b), © Bettmann/CORBIS; 429 (l), [neg. 50473] Collection of The New-York Historical Society; 429 (r), Collection of Thomas H. Gandy and Joan W. Gandy; 430, Courtesy of the Charleston Renaissance Gallery, Robert M. Hicklin Jr., Inc. Charleston, SC. **Unit Five**: Page 433, The Granger Collection, New York.; **Chapter 13**: Pages 436-437 (t), National Archives (NARA); 437 (cl), © Bettmann/CORBIS; (cr), © Bettmann/CORBIS; 437 (b), © Hulton-Deutsch Collection/CORBIS; 438, National Anthropological Archives, Smithsonian Institution, Washington, D.C., neg. #81-9626; 439, Smithsonian American Art Museum, Washington, DC/Art Resource, NY; 442, National Anthropological Archives, Smithsonian Institution, Washington DC, neg. 43201-B; 443 (both), National Anthropological Archives, Smithsonian Institution, Washington DC; 444, University of Washington Libraries, UW 4770; 446, Colorado Historical Society (F2276) All Rights Reserved; 447, Courtesy of Texas Department of Transportation; 449, © Topham/The Image Works; 450 (l), Archives & Manuscript Division of the Oklahoma Historical Society; 450-451, Archives & Manuscript Division of the Oklahoma Historical Society;; 451 (r), Archives & Manuscripts Division of the Oklahoma Historical Society; 452, Kansas State Historical Society; 453, History of Technology Division, National Museum of American History, Smithsonian Institution, Washington, DC. Photo # 76-9598. 454, Chicago Historical Society, neg #i21030; 455, Library of Congress, # Portfolio 134, folder 13, ephemera; 456 (both), Archives & Manuscript Division of the Oklahoma Historical Society; 457, (detail) University of Washington Libraries, UW 4770. **Chapter 14**: Pages 458-459 (t), © Bettmann/CORBIS; 458 (b), © Hulton Archive/ Getty Images; 459 (c), © Bettmann/CORBIS; (b), © Archivo Iconografico, S.A./CORBIS; 460, National Archives; 461, Gladys City Museum, Beaumont, Texas; 465 (t), © Bettmann/CORBIS; 466, Photo © Richard Cheek for Preservation Society of Newport County; 467 (l), The Granger Collection, New York; (r), Library of Congress; 469, Collection of The New-York Historical Society; 470, © Bettmann/CORBIS; 471, (t) Sears Modern Home mail order catalogue, 1918 (b) © Steve Warble; 472-473, Library of Congress; 474 (t), Courtesy Gore Place; (b), George Meany Memorial Archives; 475 (l), © Roger Ressmeyer/CORBIS; (r), Brian Kersey/UPI Photo/NewsCom; 474-475 (bkgd) Library of Congress, Bain Collection; 477, National Air & Space Museum, Smithsonian Institution, Washington, D.C., #A26767B-2; 478 (t), Los Angeles Public Library; (b), Reed Saxon/AP/Wide World Photos; 480, Ford Archives, Henry Ford Museum; 481, 483 Picture Research Consultants & Archives; 485, Library of Congress, #LC-DIG-NCLC-01581. **Chapter 15**: Pages 486-87 (t), Library of Congress, Detroit Publishing Company Collection ; 486 (b), National Museum of American History, Cultural History Division, Smithsonian Institution, Washington, DC. Cat # 31979.0131.01; 486 © National Archives; 487 (b), © Bettmann/CORBIS; 488, Keystone-Mast Collection/University of California at Riverside/California Museum of Photography, #X97322; 490 (l), © Charles E. Rotkin/CORBIS; (r), Trustees of the Watts Gallery, Compton, Surrey, UK The Bridgeman Art Library; 491 (t), National Archives (NARA); (b), © Spencer Grant/PhotoEdit; 490-491 (bkgd), © Bill Ross/CORBIS; 493, Copyright The New York Public Library / Art Resource, NY; 495, © Kindra Clineff Photography; 498, University of Illinois at Chicago, The University Library, Jane Addams Memorial Collection, JAMC neg. 109; 499, Library of Congress/PRC Archive; 500, Picture Research Consultants & Archives; 502, Chicago Historical Society, #DN0000739; 503, Library of Congress; 504, Nebraska Historical Society; 505, Kansas State Historical Society, Topeka; 506, Picture Research Consultants & Archives; 507, Brown Brothers; 508, Tusekegee University Library; 509 (l), Brown Brothers; (r), The Schomburg Center for Research in Black Culture, New York Public Library, Astor, Lenox and Tilden Foundations; 510, Texas State Library & Archives Commission; 511 (t), Getty Images; (b), © Jeff Greenberg/PhotoEdit; 513, San Francisco History Center, San Francisco Public Library; 514 (tl), Trustees of the Watts Gallery, Compton, Surrey, UK/ Bridgeman Art Library; (tr), Picture Research Consultants & Archives; (bl), Copyright The New York Public Library / Art Resource, NY; (br), Chicago Historical Society, #DN0000739; 515, Keystone-Mast Collection/ University of California at Riverside/California Museum of Photography, #X97322. **Unit Six**: Page 517, Museum of the City of New York, USA / Bridgeman Art Library. **Chapter 16**: Pages 520-521 (t), Library of Congress; 520 (c), Keystone-Mast Collection/California Museum of Photography /University of California at Riverside/; (b), © Bettmann/CORBIS; 521 (c), Brown Brothers; (b), © Bettmann/CORBIS; 522, *How the Other Half Lives: an old rear tenement in Roosevelt Street, 1890*, Jacob Riis, Museum of the City of New York; 525 (inset), © Underwood & Underwood/CORBIS; 526, Brown Brothers; 528 (t), © Hulton-Deutsch Collection/ CORBIS; 528 (b), Library of Congress; 529, Sophia Smith Collection, Smith College; 530 (l), New York State Historical Association, Cooperstown; (r), Picture Research Consultants & Archives; 531 (t), Brown Brothers; (bl), Picture Research Consultants & Archives; (r), © Jeff Greenberg/PhotoEdit; 530-531, (bkgd), © Bettmann/CORBIS; 532, Kansas State Historical Society, Topeka; 533, Library of Congress; 535, Theodore Roosevelt Collection/Harvard Library; 537 (l), Keystone-Mast Collection/California Museum of Photography /University of California at Riverside; (r), The Granger Collection, New York; 538, Library of Congress; 539, © Joseph Sohm/Chromosohm, Inc./CORBIS; 541, The Granger Collection, New York; 542 (all), Janice L. and David J. Frent Collection of Political Americana; 544 (l), Library of Congress; (r), Library of Congress/ PRC Archive; 546, North Wind Picture Archives; 548, Library of Congress; 549, The Granger Collection, New York. **Chapter 17**: Pages 550-551 (t), National Guard Bureau.; Pages 550 (b), Picture Research Consultants & Archives; 551 (cl), © Underwood & Underwood/CORBIS; (cr), © Hulton-Deutsch Collection/CORBIS; (b), Brown Brothers; 552, Library of Congress; 554, Lake County (IL) Museum / Curt Teich Postcard Archives; 555, © Douglas Peebles/CORBIS; 556, Snark/Art Resource, NY; 558, © Bettmann/CORBIS; 559, © CORBIS; 562, Chicago Historical Society; 563 (both), Library of Congress; 565, 566, The Granger Collection, New York; 567, © Underwood & Underwood/CORBIS; 572, Brown Brothers; 573 (tl, tr), © Bettmann/CORBIS; (bl), © CORBIS; (br), © Underwood & Underwood/CORBIS; 574, © Hulton-Deutsch Collection/CORBIS; 577, C. J. Taylor, artist. Courtesy The Bishop Museum; 578 (bkgd), National Guard Bureau; 579, Lake County (IL) Museum/Curt Teich Postcard Archives. **Chapter 18**: Pages 580-581 (t), Courtesy The Delaware Military Heritage and Education Foundation, Inc.; 580 (b), Picture Research Consultants & Archives; 581 (cl), ©SuperStock; (cr), Library of Congress; (b), The Art Archive/Imperial War Museum; 582, © CORBIS; 588, Retrofile.com/Getty Images; 590, ©SuperStock; 591, © CORBIS; 592 (l), © Trustees of the Imperial War Museum, London, #Q53033; (r), © CORBIS; 593 (l), © Bettmann/CORBIS; (r), © Trustees of the Imperial War Museum, London; 594 (both), National Archives; 596, Brown Brothers; 597 (t), Charles Scribner's Sons/AP/Wide World Photos; (b), National Archives, War & Conflict #615; 598 (t), Library of Congress; 598-599, Brown Brothers; 599 (r), © Bettmann/CORBIS; 600, Brown Brothers; 601, Picture Research Consultants & Archives; 602 (l), Culver Pictures, Inc.; (r), © CDC/PHIL/CORBIS; 603, National Archives/PRC Archive; 605 (t), Getty Images; (b), AP/Wide World Photos; 606, © Bettmann/CORBIS; 609 (l), Picture Research Consultants & Archives; (r), Photo by Keystone/Getty Images; 613, AP/Wide World Photos; 614 (l), Retrofile.com/Getty Images; (c), National Archives/PRC Archive; (r), © Bettmann/CORBIS; 615, Library of Congress. **Unit Seven**: Page 617, © New-York Historical Society/Bridgeman Art Library. **Chapter 19**: Pages 620-621 (t), Caulfield & Shook Collection #CS71790, Photographic Archives, University of Louisville; 620 (b), National Museum of Health & Medicine, Armed Forces Institute of Pathology; 621 (bl), © Culver Pictures/SuperStock; (c), © Bettmann/CORBIS; (br), © Photo by Wolf Suschitsky/ Pix Inc./Time Life Pictures/Getty Images; 622, National Museum of Health & Medicine, Armed Forces Institute of Pathology; 623, David Longstreath/ AP/Wide World Photos; 624, The Granger Collection, New York; 625, © Bettmann/CORBIS; 627, Digital Image © the Museum of Modern Art/Licensed by SCALA/Art Resource, NY. © Estate of Ben Shahn/Licensed by VAGA, New York, NY ; 628, Macy's Federated Department Stores; 629, © CORBIS; 630 (tl), General Motors Corp. Used with permission, GM Media Archives; (bl), Akron University Archives/Goodyear Photo Collection; (c), National Museum of American History, Smithsonian Institution, Washington, DC, Behring Center. Neg. # 71-181; (tr), © Bettmann/CORBIS; 630-631, Curt Teich Postcard Archives, Lake County Museum, Illinois; 632 (l), Library of Congress/ PRC Archive; (r), Picture Research Consultants & Archives; 634, © Bettmann/CORBIS; 635, The Granger Collection, New York; 636 (l), White House Historical Association (White House Collection); (r), White House Historical Association (White House Collection)/ Photo by National Geographic Society; 637, © CORBIS; 638, Library of Congress; 642 (l), © Bettmann/CORBIS; (r), National Museum of American History, Smithsonian Institution, Washington, DC, Behring Center. Neg. # 71-181; 642 (b), White House Historical Association (White House Collection); 643, Picture Research Consultants & Archives. **Chapter 20**: Pages 644-645, Brown Brothers.; 644 (b), Picture Research Consultants & Archives.; 645 (cl), Library of Congress; (cr), Picture Research Consultants & Archives; (b), ©SuperStock; 646, © Bettmann/CORBIS; 647 (l), Lewis Wickes Hine/George Eastman House; (r), HRW Photo Research Library; 648, Lake County (IL) Museum /Curt Teich Postcard Archives; 650 (l), The Granger Collection, New York; (r), AP/Wide World Photos; 651, University of Tennessee Library Special Collections, Robinson and Hicks Collections; 652 (l), Kansas State Historical Society, Topeka; (r), © Bettmann/CORBIS; 653, © Bettmann/CORBIS; 654, Photo by Carl Van Vechten, courtesy Carl Van Vechten Trust. With the permission of the Zora Neale Hurston Trust. The Beinecke Rare Book and Manuscript Library, Yale University Library; 656 (t), Crisis Publishing Co., Inc.; (b), The publisher wishes to thank The Crisis Publishing Co., Inc., the publisher of the magazine of the National Association for the Advancement of Colored People for the use of this work that was first published in the April 1923 issue of "The Crisis Magazine." General Research and Reference Division; Schomburg Center for Research in Black Culture; The New York Public Library; Astor, Lenox and Tilden Foundations; 657, Yale Collection of American Literature, The Beinecke Rare Book and Manuscript Library, Yale University; 658 (l), © Photo by Sasha/Getty Images; (cl), © Reuters/STR/Getty Images; (tc), The Beinecke Rare Book and Manuscript Library, Yale University Library; (bl), © Bettmann/CORBIS; (tr), Private Collection; 658 (br), Aaron Douglas, *Into Bondage*, 1936. Oil on canvas, 60 3/8 x 60 1/2 in. Corcoran Gallery of Art, Washington, D.C. Museum Purchase and Partial Gift of Thurlow Evans Tibbs, Jr., The Evans-Tibbs Collection 1996.9; 660, © Bettmann/ CORBIS; 661 (t), Picture Research Consultants & Archives; (b), © Bettmann/CORBIS; 662, Collection of Hershenson-Allen Archives; 663 (t), Picture Research Consultants & Archives; (b), (Art Reference) © Bettmann/CORBIS; 664 (t), © Bettmann/CORBIS; (cl), © Bettmann/CORBIS; (cr), © Bettmann/CORBIS; (b), Picture Research Consultants & Archives; 667, Picture Research Consultants & Archives; 668 (l), HRW Photo Resarch Library; (c), © Bettmann/CORBIS; (r), © Reuters/STR/Getty Images; 669, © Bettmann/CORBIS. **Chapter 21**: Pages 670-671, Courtesy The Chicago Defender; 670 (c), American Stock Photos/Getty Images; (b), American Stock/Getty Images; 671 (cl), © CORBIS; (cr), AP/Wide World Photos; (bl), © Bettmann/CORBIS; (br), © Bettmann/CORBIS; 672, © Bettmann/CORBIS; 673, © CORBIS; 676-677, © Bettmann/CORBIS; 678, The Granger Collection, New York; 680, Library of Congress/PRC Archive; 682-683, *West Houston and Mercer Streets. October 25, 1935*, by Berenice Abbott/Museum of the City of New York 686 (t), © Bettmann/CORBIS; © CORBIS ; 686 (t), © Bettmann/CORBIS; (b), Library of Congress; 687, AP/Wide World Photos; 688, Hoover Dam National Historic Landmark; 689, Franklin D. Roosevelt Library; 690, © Bettmann/CORBIS; 691, AP/Wide World Photos/ National Archives (NARA); 692, Library of Congress; 693, Library of Congress, #LC-USZ62-131700; 694 (l), Library of Congress; (r), American Stock Photos/Getty Images; 695, The Granger Collection, New York. **Chapter 22**: Pages 696-697 (t), Courtesy of Roosevelt Arts Project, Photo by Josh Nefsky; 696 (c), Janice L. and David J. Frent Collection of Political Americana; (b), Photo by Hugo Jaeger/ Timepix/ Time Life Pictures/Getty Images; 697 (b), © Hulton Archive/Getty Images; (cl), (art reference) Picture Research Consultants & Archives; (cr), Library of Congress, FSA Collection; 698, Brigham Young University Museum of Art; 700, © Bettmann/CORBIS; 701 (l), Franklin D. Roosevelt Library; (r), © Bettmann/CORBIS; 702 (t), © Bettmann/CORBIS; (r), Culver Pictures, Inc.; 703, © Bettmann/CORBIS; 704, © 1934 by the Chicago Tribune, cartoon by Carey Orr/ Franklin D. Roosevelt Library; 707, Library of Congress/PRC Archive; 708 (t), Getty Images 708 (b), Alex Wong/Getty Images/NewsCom; 709, Photo by New York Times Co./Getty Images; 710-711, Smithsonian American Art Museum, Washington, DC/Art Resource, NY 713, Library of Congress/PRC Archive; 714, © Bettmann/CORBIS; 715, © 1999 J.N. "Ding" Darling Foundation; 717, © Bettmann/CORBIS; 718, Bethune Museum and Archives; 719 (bl), © The Dorothea Lange Collection, Oakland Museum of California, City of Oakland. Gift of Paul S. Taylor; 719 (t), Library of Congress ; (cr), © Gordon Parks; (br), Library of Congress; 720, © Bettmann/CORBIS; 721 (l), © 1933 Universal Studios. All Rights Reserved. The Granger Collection, New York.; (c), Photofest; (r), Photo courtesy of the Theatre Historical Society of Elmhurst, Illinois; 723, Photo by Hulton Archive/Getty Images; 725 (l), © CORBIS; (r), Cornell University, Uris Library, Daniel Reed Papers; 726 (t), © CORBIS; (b), Library of Congress; 729 (l), Library of Congress/PRC Archive; (r), © The New Yorker Collection, 1935, Peter Arno. From Cartoonbank.com. All rights reserved.; 730 (l), © Bettmann/CORBIS; (c), © 1999 J.N. "Ding" Darling Foundation; (r), (art reference) Picture Research Consultants & Archives; 731, © Bettmann/CORBIS.; **Unit Seven**: Page 733, U.S. Naval Institute Photo Archives. **Chapter 23**: Pages 736-737, Photo by Hugo Jaeger/Timepix/ Time Life Pictures/Getty Images ; 736 (b), © CORBIS; 737 (cl), © Bettmann/CORBIS; (cr), National Archives (NARA); (bl), © Photo by Keystone/Getty Images; (br), © Bettmann/CORBIS; 738, © Bettmann/CORBIS; 739, AKG-Images, London; 740, Photo by Hugo Jaeger/ Timepix/ Time Life Pictures/Getty Images; 741, AP/Wide World Photos; 742, © Victor Korotayev/ Reuters/CORBIS; 743, Cartoon by Willard Combes, The Cleveland Press, 1939/Library of Congress; 744 (l), © Photo by Central Press/Getty Images; (r), © Photo by Keystone/Getty Images; 751, © Thomas McAvoy/ Time Life PIctures/Getty Images; 752 (t), Library of Congress/ PRC Archive; (b), The Granger Collection, New York; 752 (bkgd) © Bettmann/CORBIS; 753 (t), © Bettmann/CORBIS; (b), © Ron Sachs/CORBIS; 754, The Granger Collection, New York; 756, National Archives (NARA); 758, © CORBIS; 759, © Swim Ink/CORBIS; 760, National Archives/ Collection of David Ethell; 761, Lockheed-California Company; 762, The Schomburg Center for Research in Black Culture, New York Public Library, Astor, Lenox and Tilden Foundations/ Art Resource, NY; 764, National Archives/Jeffrey Ethell Collection; 765, © Myron Davis/ Time Life Pictures/Getty Images; 766 (l), Photo by Hugo Jaeger/Time Life Pictures/Getty Images; (cl), AP/Wide World Photos; (cr), National Archives (NARA); (r), © CORBIS; 767, National Archives/Collection of David Ethell;

768-69 (t), © CORBIS; 769 (cr), U.S. Naval Institute Photo Archives; (cl), © CORBIS; (b), © Bettmann/CORBIS; 770, U.S. Naval Institute Photo Archive; 774 (l), © U.S. Air Force/ Collection of David Ethell; (r), © Bettmann/CORBIS; 775, © Bettmann/CORBIS; 778, Bundesarchiv Koblenz; 779, © BPK; 781, © Bettmann/CORBIS; 784 (t), © JEFF CHRISTENSEN/ Reuters/CORBIS; (b), © H. Miller/Hulton Archive/Getty Images; 785, Joe Rosenthal/ AP/Wide World Photos; 786, © CORBIS; 787, © Bettmann/CORBIS; 789 (l), © Bettmann/ CORBIS; (r), © Bettmann/CORBIS; 791, Eriko Sugita/ Reuters Photo Archive/NewsCom; 793 (t), © Minnesota Historical Society/CORBIS; (b), AP/Wide World Photos; 794 (l), Jeffrey Ethell Collection; (r), Picture Research Consultants & Archives; 796, Private Collection; 798, © Bettmann/CORBIS; 800 (t), Getty Images; (b), Dennis Cook/ AP/Wide World Photos; 801, © Bettmann/CORBIS; 802 (l), U.S. Naval Institute Photo Archives; (r), Photo by Fred Ramage/Keystone/Getty Images; 804, Defense Visual Information Center; 805 (b), National Archives/PRC Archive; (inset), U.S. Naval Institute Photo Archives; 806 (l), © Thomas D. McAvoy/Time Life Pictures/Getty Images; (r), © Bettmann/CORBIS; 808, © CORBIS; 809 (tl), © CORBIS; (tr), © Museum of Flight/CORBIS; 809 (c), © Bettmann/ CORBIS; (b), © CORBIS; 810, From UP FRONT by Bill Mauldin, © 1945 The World Publishing Company. Courtesy the Estate of Bill Mauldin; 812 (l), © BPK; (c), © Bettmann/ CORBIS; (r), U.S. Naval Institute Photo Archives; 813, Joe Rosenthal/AP/Wide World Photos. **Chapter 25**: Pages 814-815 (t), © Photo by Walter Sanders/Time Life Pictures/Getty Images; 814 (b), © Bettmann/CORBIS; 815 (cl), Courtesy of NATO; (cr), © CORBIS; (bl), © Baldwin H. Ward and Kathryn C. Ward/CORBIS; (br), © Photos12.com-Oasis; 816, Courtesy Harry S. Truman Library; 818, © Hulton-Deutsch Collection/CORBIS; 819, Photo by George Skadding/Time Life Pictures/Getty Images; 820, AP/Wide World Photos; 823, AP/Wide World Photos; 824, Courtesy Floyd Walters; 825, © Bettmann/CORBIS; 826, Library of Congress, NAACP Collection; 829, Republished with permission of Globe Newspaper Company, Inc.; 832 (t), © Bettmann/CORBIS; (c), © Hulton-Deutsch Collection/CORBIS; (b), AP/Wide World Photos; 833, © Bettmann/CORBIS; 835, AP/Wide World Photos; 840, © Photo by Carl Mydans/Time Life Pictures/ Getty Images; 842, "IT'S OKAY-WE'RE HUNTING COMMUNISTS" from *The Herblock Book* (Beacon Press, 1952) /Library of Congress, #LC-USZ62-127327; 843, Photo by Loomis Dean/ Time & Life Pictures/Getty Images; 844 (l), © Photo by Walter Sanders/Time Life Pictures/Getty Images; 844 (r), AP/Wide World Photos; 845, AP/Wide World Photos. **Chapter 26**: Pages 846-847 (t), © Ewing Galloway/Index Stock Imagery, Inc.; 846 (b), The Henry Samueli School of Engineering, University of California at Irvine; 847 (cl), © CORBIS; (cr), © Bernard Crochet Collection/Photos12.com; (bl), The Art Archive/National Archives, Washington, DC; (br), Sovfoto/ Eastfoto; 848, © Bettmann/CORBIS; 850, © 1959 by Newsweek, Inc. All rights reserved. Reprinted by permission.; 851 (l), © Photos12.com-Oasis; (r), © Bernard Crochet Collection/Photos12.com; 854 (both), © Bettmann/ CORBIS; 855, © CORBIS; 857 (l), /AP/Wide World Photos; (cl), © Bettmann/CORBIS; (bl), © Bettmann/CORBIS; (tr), Library of Congress, LC-USZ62-37409. 1950 cartoon by Art Wood; (cr), © CORBIS; (br), Sovfoto/Eastfoto; 858 (l), Schutz/ AP/Wide World Photos; 858 (r), © AFP/Getty Images; 859, Paul F. Kutta, courtesy Reminisce magazine; 861 (t), Photofest; (b), Look Magazine Collection, Library of Congress/PRC Archive; 863 (tl), CPIO Partners Image Collection; (l), Courtesy NBC; (bl), H. Armstrong Roberts/ Retrofile.com; (c), NASA; (tr), TM & Copyright © 20th Century Fox Film Corp. All Rights Reserved/Everett Collection; (br), © Wally McNamee/CORBIS; 864 (l), © Bettmann/CORBIS; (r), Courtesy James Foster; 865, © CORBIS; 870 (l), © Bettmann/CORBIS; (tr), © Bettmann/ CORBIS; (br), Look Magazine Collection, Library of Congress/PRC Archive; 871, © Bettmann/CORBIS; **Unit Nine**: 873, © Matt Herron/Take Stock.; **Chapter 27**: Pages 876-77, © John Dominis/Time Life Pictures/Getty Images; 876 (c), Photo by Leonard McComb/Life Magazine © Time, Inc./Time Life Pictures/Getty Images; (b), © Peter Turnley/ CORBIS; 877 (cl), AP/Wide World Photos; (cr), LBJ Library Collection; (b), AP/Wide World Photos; 878, National Archives/Time Life Pictures/Getty Images; 879, Photo by Leonard McComb/Life Magazine © Time, Inc./Time Life Pictures/Getty Images; 880, © Bettmann/CORBIS; 881, National Library of Wales, Illingworth Cartoon Collection; 885 (l), The John F. Kennedy Library; (r), Defense Department/AP/Wide World Photos; 887, John F. Kennedy Library; 888 (t), The Granger Collection, New York; (b), © Underwood Photo Archives/ SuperStock; 889 (tl), NASA; (r), NASA; 888-889 (bkgd), NASA; 890 (l), © Bettmann/ CORBIS; (r), © Stanley Tretick/Sygma/CORBIS; 891 (l), © Bettmann/CORBIS; (r), Black Star/Stockphoto.com; 893, Yoichi Okamoto/LBJ Library Collection; 894, © Bettmann/ CORBIS; 895, © Jeff Greenberg/PhotoEdit; 896, Lyndon B. Johnson Presidential Library/ Lightstream/ Picture Research Consultants & Archives; 897 (l), © Bettmann/ CORBIS; (r), Art Rickerby/Time Life Pictures/Getty Images; 898, Mark Antman/The Image Works; 899, LBJ Library Collection. © Estate of Karl Hubenthal; 901 (t), Getty Images; (b), © Michael Newman/PhotoEdit; 902, © David S. Boyer/National Geographic Image Collection. **Chapter 28**: Pages 906-907, © Robert W. Kelley/Time & Life Pictures/ Getty Images; 907, © Bettmann/CORBIS; 908, Courtesy of Nathaniel Briggs; 910, © Bettmann/CORBIS; 911, © Bettmann/CORBIS; 912 (both) Photo by Will Counts from *A Life is More Than a Moment*. Indiana University, courtesy Vivian Counts; 913 (t), Getty Images; (b), © Spencer Grant/ PhotoEdit; 914 (l), AP/Wide World Photos; 914 (tr), © Photo by William H. Alden/Evening Standard/Getty Images; 914 (br), Dan Weiner, courtesy Sandra Weiner; 915, Photo by Don Cravens/Time & Life Pictures/Getty Images); 916, State Historical Society of Wisconsin; 917, © Bettmann/ CORBIS; 919 (l), © Bettmann/CORBIS; (r), Photo by Warren Leffler, US News & World Report Magazine Collection, Library of Congress; 920, AP/Wide World Photos; 921 (l), Charles Moore/Black Star/stockphoto.com; (r), Charles Moore/Black Star/stockphoto.com; 924 (t), © Bettmann/ CORBIS; (b), © Bettmann/CORBIS; 925, 925, AP/Wide World Photos; 926-927, (bkgd) © Robert W. Kelley/Time & Life Pictures/Getty Images; 927 (t), © Michelle Bridwell/ PhotoEdit; (br), Ric Feld/AP/Wide World Photos; 928, © Jeff Greenberg/PhotoEdit; 929 (t), Photo by Charles Moore/Black Star/stockphoto.com. Cover © Time Life Collection/Getty Images; (b), © Bettmann/CORBIS; 931 (t), Getty Images; (b), Tim Roske/AP/Wide World Photos; 932 (t), © David J. Frent/ CORBIS; (b), © Flip Schulke/CORBIS; 933, AP/Wide World Photos; 934 (l), © Bettmann/CORBIS; (t), AP/Wide World Photos; (c), © Bettmann/CORBIS; 935 (l), © Bettmann/ CORBIS; (r), Robert Parent/Time Life Pictures/Getty Images; 936 (l), © Joseph Louw/Time & Life Pictures/Getty Images; (r), © Flip Schulke/CORBIS; 937, AP/Wide World Photos; 938-939, © James L. Amos/CORBIS; 940, © Alex Wong/Getty Images; 942, "Wait a Minute-- Somebody has gotta keep this thing on track!" Cartoon by Baldy, [Atlanta Constitution, ca. 1963]. From the Clifford H. Baldowski Editorial Cartoon Collection, Richard B. Russell Library for Political Research and Studies, The University of Georgia Libraries. **Chapter 29**: Pages 946-947, Sgt. Howard Breedlove, U.S. Army; 946, © Bettmann/CORBIS; 947 (c), Shelly Rusten/Black Star/stockphoto.com; (b), © Bettmann/ CORBIS; 948, Photo12.com-Oasis; 949, © R. Ian Lloyd/ Masterfile; 950, © Hulton Archive/Getty Images; 952, Horst Faas/AP/Wide World Photos; 953, Malcolm Browne/AP/Wide World Photos; 954, Photograph by Larry Burrows; 956, © Photo by Art Rickerby/Time Life Pictures/Getty Images; 957, Photo by Larry Burrows/ Time Magazine/Time & Life Pictures/Getty Images; 961, © Bettmann/CORBIS; 962 (l), © Bettmann/CORBIS; (r), Photo by Francis Miller/Time Life Pictures/Getty Images; 964, © Bettmann/CORBIS; 966, Photo by Jose Genoa via Getty Images; 967, © James Atherton/CORBIS; 968 (l), Bob Daugherty/AP/Wide World Photos; (br), © Photo by Bill Eppridge/Time & Life Pictures/ Getty Images; 969 (l), © Bettmann/CORBIS; (tr), © Bettmann/CORBIS; (r), © Jeffrey Blankfort/Jeroboam; 970 (l), © Wally McNamee/CORBIS; (tr), © Bettmann/CORBIS; (br), © Bettmann/CORBIS; 972, © Wally McNamee/CORBIS; 973, © Bettmann/CORBIS; 974 (l), Paul Fusco/Magnum Photos; (r), John Filo; 975, © Wally McNamee/CORBIS; 976, © Bettmann/CORBIS; 978 (tl), © Catherine Karnow/ CORBIS ; (bl), Charles Tasnadi/AP/Wide World Photos; (c), © Wally McNamee/CORBIS; (br), © William Manning/ CORBIS; 981, Collection of Judge and Mrs. Hugh Haynie Smith; 982 (bkgd), Sgt. Howard Breedlove, U.S. Army. **Chapter 30**: Pages 984-985 (t), © Bob Fitch/Take Stock; 984 (b), © MARY BENSON/CORBIS SYGMA; 985 (c), Library of Congress/PRC Archive; (bl), AP/Wide World Photos; (r), Picture Research Consultants & Archives; 986, © Bettmann/ CORBIS; 988, AP/Wide World Photos; 989 (r), © Bettmann/ CORBIS; (l), Mary Ellen Mark; 990 (t), Troy Anderson; (b), Rare Book Room, Library of Congress; 991 (t), Photo by Ralph Crane/ Time Life Pictures/Getty Images; (b), Courtesy of the Haskell Cultural Center and Museum, Haskell Indian Nations University, Lawrence, Kansas; 990-991 (bkgd), © CORBIS; 992, AP/Wide World Photos; 994, Paul Fusco/ Magnum Photos; 996 (l), © 1970 Matt Herron/Take Stock; (r), © Arthur Schatz/Time Life Pictures/Getty Images; 998 (l), Arthur Schatz/ Time Life Pictures/Getty Images; (r), AP/ Wide World Photos; 999 (l), © 1966 Maria Varela/Take Stock; (r), The UT Institute of Texan Cultures, No. E-0018-205#4, Express News Collection, courtesy Hearst Corporation; 1000, Courtesy of the Neally Library, Santa Ana College, Santa Ana, California; 1002, © Henry Diltz/CORBIS; 1003, AP/ Wide World Photos; 1004 (l), Pictorial Press; (r), Photo by John Olson/ Time Life Pictures/Getty Images; 1005 (l), "Life is So Beautiful" Vintage Poster, 16" x 10.75", 1968 © Peter Max 2005.The American Cancer Society; 1006, Jack Knox Cartoon Collection; 1008, © The Estate of Bill Mauldin, 1974. Courtesy, Library of Congress; 1010 (l), Paul Fusco/Magnum Photos; (c), AP/Wide World Photos; (r), © Henry Diltz/ CORBIS. **Unit Ten**: Page 1013, © Pete Saloutos/CORBIS. **Chapter 31**: Pages 1016-17, Photo by NASA/Newsmakers/ Getty Images; 1016 (c), NASA; (b), AP/Wide World Photos; 1017 (cl), © CORBIS; (rc), Jimmy Carter Presidential Library; (b), Alain Mingam/Gamma Press Images; 1018, © Photo by Vernon Merritt III/Time Life Pictures/Getty Images; 1019, AP/Wide World Photos; 1021, © CORBIS; 1024, NASA; 1026 (t), Getty Images; (b), © Lee Snider/The Image Works; 1027, © Dennis Brack; 1028 (l), © Joseph Sohm; Chromosohm, Inc./CORBIS; (t), © Bettmann/CORBIS; (bc), AP/Wide World Photos; 1029 (l), Wally McNamee/ CORBIS; (r), © Owen Franken/CORBIS; 1030, Cartoon by Paul Conrad. Copyright, Los Angeles Times Syndicate. Reprinted with permission.; 1031, Photo by Time Inc./ Time Life Pictures/Getty Images; 1033, Jimmy Carter Presidential Library; 1034, © Sonda Dawes/The Image Works; 1035, Dennis Brack/Black Star; 1036, Jimmy Carter Presidential Library; 1037, Alain Mingam/Gamma Press Images; 1039 (t), Getty Images; (b), Philip Dattilo/University of Michigan Law School; 1041, From *Herblock: A Cartoonist's Life* (Times Books, 1998).; 1042 (l), White House Historical Association (White House Collection); (r), White House Historical Association (White House Collection); 1042 (b), White House Historical Association (White House Collection); 1043, Jimmy Carter Presidential Library.; **Chapter 32**: Pages 1044-45 © CORBIS; 1044 (c), Photo by Robert Oakes, National Geographic Society. Courtesy, Supreme Court of the United States, The Supreme Court Historical Society; (b), © 1998 Chris Niedenthal/Black Star/Stockphoto.com; 1045 (cl), © CORBIS; (cr), Bill Gentile/SIPA Press; (br), © Reuters/CORBIS; 1046, © Bettmann/CORBIS; 1047, © CORBIS; 1048, "LEAVE THE FACADES- IT'LL BE JUST LIKE HOLLYWOOD." © 1981 Herblock in the Washington Post. Courtesy The Herblock Foundation, Library of Congress; 1049, Photo by Hulton Archive/Getty Images; 1050, Courtesy Ronald Reagan Presidential Library; 1052 (t), Getty Images; (b), © Michael Newman/PhotoEdit; 1053, © Reuters/CORBIS; 1054, © Tribune Media Services, Inc. All Rights Reserved. Reprinted with permission.; 1056 (l), © Bill Gentile/CORBIS; (r), AP/Wide World Photos; 1059, Ronald Reagan Presidential Library; 1061, © Peter Turnley/ CORBIS; 1062 (l), © 1998 Chris Niedenthal/Black Star/ stockphoto.com; (r), © Peter Turnley/CORBIS; 1063 (l), © Reuters/CORBIS; (r), © Alain Nogues/CORBIS SYGMA; 1066, (Jobs) © Diana Walker/Time & Life Pictures/Getty Images; 1066, (Gates) © Deborah Feingold/Getty Images; 1067 (tl), NASA; (r), © CORBIS; (bc), © Bettmann/CORBIS; 1069 (l), Photo by Diana Walker/Time Life Pictures/Getty Images; (r) Betty Udesen/Seattle Times; 1070, Wally McNamee/Woodfin Camp & Associates; 1071, © Reuters/ CORBIS; 1072, INVASION OF THE CORPORATE BODY SNATCHERS from *Herblock At Large* (Pantheon, Books, 1987). Library of Congress, LC-USZ62-126883; 1073 (r), © ABC/Photofest; 1074 (bkgd) © CORBIS.; **Chapter 33**: 1076, (b) Ira Wyman Pages 1076-77 (t), © Reuters/CORBIS; 1077 (c), © Eric Draper/White House Photos/CORBIS; (b), © ATEF HASSAN/Reuters/CORBIS; 1078, © Arnie Sachs/CORBIS; 1079 (l) Ira Wyman (r), © Wally McNamee/CORBIS; 1080, © Nick Gunderson/CORBIS; 1081, Courtesy the White House; 1082 (l), © Wally McNamee/CORBIS; (r), Ron Heflin/AP/ Wide World Photos; 1084 (t), Getty Images; (b), Bob Daemmrich Photo, Inc.; 1085, © Rick Wilking/Reuters/ CORBIS; 1086, Marta Lavandier/AP/Wide World Photos; 1087, © DUYOS ROBERT CORBIS SYGMA; 1089, © Gary Conner/PhotoEdit; 1090 (t), AP/Wide World Photos; (c), © Reuters/CORBIS; (b), Doug Mills/AP/Wide World Photos; 1091, Ethan Moses; 1092-1093, © Peter Morgan/REUTERS/ CORBIS; 1093 (tr), © Thomas E. Franklin/The Bergen Record/Getty Images; (br), © Larry Downing/REUTERS/ CORBIS; 1094 (l), Joe Raedle/Getty Images/Newscom; (r), © Bill Pugliano/Getty Images; 1095, © Mai/Mai/Time Life Pictures/Getty Images; 1096, Tomas Munita/AP/Wide World Photos; 1098, © Eric Draper/White House Photos/CORBIS; 1099, © Ted Soqui/CORBIS; 1100, Eric Draper/AP/Wide World Photos; 1101, © Jeff Greenberg/The Image Works; 1102 (l), AP/Wide World Photos; (r), © Justin Sullivan/Getty Images; 1103 (l), Vincent Laforet/AP/Wide World Photos; (r), © Marianne Todd/Getty Images; 1105 (t), Photo by Frank Capri/Hulton Archive/Getty Images; (b), © David R. Frazier/ The Image Works; 1106, © Reuters/CORBIS; 1107 (tl), HOY newspaper, Chicago edition, 13 July 2005. © 2005 Chicago Tribune Company. All Rights Reserved. Used with permission.; (tr), AP/Wide World Photos/ THE DAILY PROGRESS; (bl), © Dinodia/SuperStock; 1108, © Carol Simpson Productions; 1110 (bkgd), © Reuters/CORBIS; Marta Lavandier/AP/Wide World Photos. **Back Mattter**: Presidents: Pages R17-R21, White House Historical Association (White House Collection); R21 (last) The White House, photo by Eric Draper. Supreme Court: R22 (l, c, cl) © Jason Reed/Reuters/CORBIS; (cr) AP/Wide World Photos/ SUPREME COURT; (r) PABLO MARTINEZ MONSIVAIS/ AFP/Getty Images; R23 (all) © Jason Reed/Reuters/CORBIS; R32, © PhotoDisc/Getty Images. Bio Dictionary: Pages R33 (r), Look Magazine Collection, Library of Congress/ PRC Archive; R33 (l), © Reuters/STR/Getty Images; R34, National Anthropological Archives, Smithsonian Institution, Washington DC, neg. 43201-B; R35 (l), Trenton Psychiatric Hospita/Photo by Josh Nefsky; (r), Picture Research Consultants & Archives; R36, AP/Wide World Photos; R39 (l), © Bettmann/CORBIS; (tr), AP/Wide World Photos; (br), Library of Congress; R40, Robert Parent/Time Life Pictures/ Getty Images; R41, The Granger Collection, New York; R42 (l), Photo by Don Cravens/Time & Life Pictures/Getty Images) ; (r), Photo by Hulton Archive/Getty Images; (t), Franklin D. Roosevelt Library; (c), Library of Congress; (b), The Granger Collection, New York; R44, Library of Congress/ PRC Archive; R45, Reunion de Musees Nationaux/Art Resource, NY, R117, *View of Boston Common* (detail) about 1750. Object Place: Boston, Massachusetts, United States Hannah Otis, 1732–1801. Wool, silk, metallic threads, and beads on linen ground; predominately tent stitch; original frame and glass. 61.59 x 133.98 cm (24 1/4 x 52 3/4 in.). Museum of Fine Arts, Boston. Gift of a Friend of the Department of American Decorative Arts and Sculpture, a Supporter of the Department of American Decorative Arts and Sculpture, Barbara L. and Theodore B. Alfond, and Samuel A. Otis; and William Francis Warden Fund, Harriet Otis Cruft Fund, Otis Norcross Fund, Susan Cornelia Warren Fund, Arthur Tracy Cabot Fund, Seth K. Sweetser Fund, Edwin E. Jack Fund, Helen B. Sweeney Fund, William E. Nickerson Fund, Arthur Mason Knapp Fund, Samuel Putnam Avery Fund, Benjamin Pierce Cheney Fund, and Mary L. Smith Fund. 1996.26.

Staff Credits

Karen Arneson, Tim Barnhart, Kristina Bigelow, Paul Blankman, Jeremy Brady, Gillian Brody, Henry Clark, Grant Davidson, Nina Degollado, Lydia Doty, Sergio Durante, Chase Edmond, Bob Fullilove, Janet Harrington, Wendy Hodge, Cathy Jenevein, Liz Kline, Kadonna Knape, Cathy Kuhles, Bob McClellan, Joe Melomo, Richard Metzger, Jennifer Nonenmacher, Nathan O'Neal, Elizabeth Parker, Jay Pearmon, Beth Prevelige, Michael Rinella, Nancy Rogier, Allison Rudmann, Beth Sample, Annette Saunders, Paul Selfa, Kay Selke, Chris Smith, Dakota Smith, Christine Stanford, Jeannie Taylor, Diana Holman Walker, Tracy C. Wilson, Sara Zettner